# Baseball

# Prospectus

# 2012

# Baseball Prospectus 2012

THE ESSENTIAL GUIDE TO THE 2012 BASEBALL SEASON

EDITED BY KING KAUFMAN AND CECILIA M. TAN

R.J. Anderson • Bradley Ankrom • Tommy Bennett

Craig Brown • Derek Carty • Jason Collette • Cliff Corcoran

Jeff Euston • Ken Funck • Rebecca Glass • Steven Goldman

Kevin Goldstein • Gary Huckaby • Jay Jaffe • Christina Kahrl

King Kaufman • Ben Lindbergh • Sam Miller • Rob McQuown

Marc Normandin • Jason Parks • Cecilia M. Tan • Colin Wyers

Geoff Young

WILEY

John Wiley & Sons, Inc.

For general information about our other products and services, please contact our
Customer Care Department within the United States at (800) 762-2974,
outside the United States at (317) 572-3993 or fax (317) 572-4002.

Wiley also publishes its books in a variety of electronic formats and by print-on-demand. Some
content that appears in standard print versions of this book may not be available in other formats.
For more information about Wiley products, visit us at www.wiley.com.

ISBN 978-0-470-62207-0 (paper); ISBN 978-1-118-19768-4 (ebk)
ISBN 978-1-118-19769-1 (ebk); ISBN 978-1-118-19770-7 (ebk)

Printed in the United States of America

10 9 8 7 6 5 4 3 2 1

# CONTENTS

# Foreword

*Ken Tremendous*

**Welcome Address**

Society for Aphorism and Conjecture Research, Education Division (SACRED)

*March 14, 2022*

azy Journalists, Conventional Wisdom Spouters, Augurers,

instincts, to tell us who was good at baseball and who was bad. We took the perfectly reasonable stance that people should accept the things that they were told when they were children and never doubt their validity. Questioning dogma was pointless and rude, we thought, and had no place in baseball journalism.

On the other side were a bunch of twerps who "proved" that we were "wrong" by using so-called "numbers" that they "wrote down" and "casually pointed at" while "explaining what they meant."

And somehow, back in 2012, those twerps were *winning*. Batting average was being replaced by "OPS." Poetic musings on Derek Jeter's calm eyes and intangible leadership were being drowned out by ad hominem claims about his complete lack of lateral mobility. Everyone stopped watching *Around the Horn*. Things were spiraling out of control.

But today, just a decade later, the world is a very different place. Those geeks have gone scuttling back to their caves, and SACRED stands victorious. Our membership has swelled into the millions. Our influence is felt across all media platforms and in every major-league front office. Today, thanks to our hard work, America is free from the tyranny of "science" and "analysis" and "information." And, most importantly, we are finally free from "nerds."

*[Hold for applause.]*

Just to recap some of our most recent accomplishments:

*By Federal law, "wins" is now the only criterion by which the Hall of Fame election committee may judge pitchers—and all current members are up for review. Out: Bert Blyleven. In: Jack Morris. (And yes, we know Blyleven had more wins than Morris, but Morris had one that counted.)*

*Likewise, batters can only be judged by Batting Average, RBIs, Amount of Hustling, Postseason Success, and Overall Leadership Abilities. Let's all say a special welcome to the Hall of Fame Class of 2021: Tommy Herr, Mark Lemke, and Juan*

*There must be, by Commissioner Decree, a life-size statue of David Eckstein outside every major league baseball stadium. You twerps never appreciated him enough when he was playing. Now you have to.*

*As per the wishes of SACRED founding member John Kruk, "not hot-dogging" is now an official criterion for Hall of Fame consideration.*

*Teams are now awarded between one and three extra runs per game based on how dirty their uniforms are. And all sacrifice bunts are worth three Tradition Points.*

*Dusty Baker is the president of the United States.*

*[Hold for applause. Wave to President Dusty.]*

The man who popularized "clogging up the basepaths" as a way to describe average-speed hitters successfully getting on base, ladies and gentlemen. Sir, it's an honor to have you here.

This is truly a golden age for our movement. No longer do we have to suffer the indignity of having our beliefs and discussions dissected and attacked by the whiny blogger class. Those blogger types are all gone. Do you know where they are? I have a guess. I bet you anything they're in—

*[Everyone in unison, probably]*

—their mothers' basements!

So: How did we get here?

How did we reclaim the soul of baseball from those Ivy League twits who cared more about numbers and stats than the taste of a good hot dog . . . who would rather do research than sit in the bleachers at Wrigley and drink a cold one with their dad, who is teaching them wisdom . . . who cared more about learning things and understanding them than they did about autographs and stickball and bringing your mitt to the game and SmartBall and hustling?

It all began back in the spring of 2012, with the eradication of the Baseball Prospectus annual.

Baseball Prospectus—even the name is nerdy—was a collective of horrifying egghead twits who actively hated baseball. They sought nothing less than the complete destruction of our way of life and the game we love; they wanted to reduce it to column after column of cold, heartless numbers.

Every year, more and more people became aware of, and were brainwashed by, their mathematics-based fandom. Just as one example: In 2007 their so-called PECOTA model predicted that the White Sox, who'd won 90 games in 2006, would fall all the way to 72 wins—and many people believed them! I guess they forgot about a little thing called "heart." (That the White Sox won exactly 72 games in 2007 is irrelevant. The point is, it was a ridiculous prediction.)

A few years later, we witnessed the absurd crowning of Felix Hernandez as the 2010 AL Cy Young Award Winner despite the fact that he only had 13 wins, (an indignity that has since been reversed, as the award was retroactively stripped from Hernandez and properly given to 21 game-winner C.C. Sabathia).

Reeling from these absurd indignities, a group of likeminded heroes formed SACRED, an organization whose sole purpose was to protect baseball from absurd, Godless, and un-American activities. SACRED launched a full-on assault against the insidious creep of statistics-based analysis, which had continued to insinuate itself into mainstream baseball, unabated. Specifically, we targeted the tip of the nerd spear: Baseball Prospectus itself.

Late one night, several SACRED agents raided a warehouse and destroyed every extant copy of the *Baseball Prospectus 2012* annual—a yearly rallying point for their cause. By destroying it, we denied their loyal soldiers their most dangerous weapon: analyzed data. And their reign of terror began to wane.

The dominoes fell quickly. Stat-minded GMs were run out of town and replaced with heartier, more traditionally minded folk. *Baseball Tonight* was replaced by *Thinkin' With M'Gut, With Ozzie Guillen*. Billy Beane's self-serving autobiography, *Moneyball*, was banned from public libraries. Fantasy Baseball was declared illegal and replaced by the far more enjoyable Fantasy Who Will Sing *God Bless America* During the Seventh Inning Stretch?™ Joe Morgan and Bill Plaschke recorded an album of jazz standards that remains number 1 on the Billboard charts to this day. Rob Neyer and Joe Posnanski were locked in a bamboo cage dangling above Citi Field. And baseball began to be fun again.

This year, as we celebrate our accomplishments, let us be mindful of those dark days. Let us always remember how close we came to a horrifying Age of Enlightenment. And let us be ever vigilant—for someday, and I suspect it will be soon, Baseball Prospectus will rise again.

# Preface

The end of the 2011 baseball season was as magical as they come. A final day for the ages gave way to an exciting postseason, with four of the seven series going the distance and no sweeps. Then the whole thing climaxed with one of the greatest World Series games in history, one that

from his family home in Venezuela by gunmen, then rescued, unhurt, in a daring raid two days later. Ryan Braun, the National League MVP, failed a drug test, a result he was disputing at press time.

On the other hand, it was an offseason during which baseball patted itself on the back for continued labor peace, signing a new collective bargaining agreement with very little fanfare or media attention. That new CBA will do little to affect the game in the season just ahead, but it may cause significant changes in the way teams draft and recruit players in the future. How teams adapt to the new financial ecology remains to be seen. While first the NFL and then the NBA were locked out and protesters who were fighting for economic fairness pitched tents near Wall Street and in dozens of other cities, baseball's stakeholders decided that they have it pretty good and that it was in their best interest to keep it that way. The talks and their outcome were characterized by various involved parties as "win-win," though there was grumbling among fans of low-revenue teams that the new restrictions on spending in the draft and international free agency would close one of the few avenues their favorite teams have for keeping pace with the big, rich teams.

Two more notable changes won't be felt right away. The Houston Astros will move from the NL Central to the AL West in 2013, meaning that the two leagues will have the same number of teams, something that's only been the case for five of the last 35 years. And since both leagues will have an odd number of teams—something that's never happened—the Astros move also means that starting in 2013, there will be year-long interleague play. The other big change will be a second wild-card team, which will be added no later than 2013.

The most dramatic baseball move of the offseason happened at the Winter Meetings, when the game's greatest player, Albert Pujols, shocked the baseball world by agreeing to a 10-year, $254 million contract with the Los Angeles Angels. So the Astros will have that to look forward to in the

Ramirez to the Brewers. Trades had an unusual number of prominent young pitchers on the move, including Mat Latos, Trevor Cahill, Edinson Volquez, Gio Gonzalez, Travis Wood, and Sean Marshall.

As we put the 17th edition of Baseball Prospectus's annual to bed, there are still two months of offseason to go, and the Hot Stove continues to steam. One old chestnut so often roasted on that stove is "every team is in first place on Opening Day." If you're reading *Baseball Prospectus 2012*, however, you might not quite share that sentiment. Most trades are not "win-win." Who are the winners and losers this winter? Our writers are never hesitant to praise the winning moves, nor to call out the delusions of the GMs who hope they've built a winner, or at least that no one notices for a while if they haven't.

We notice. We're not always right, but we're usually looking in the right place. *Baseball Prospectus 2012*, like its predecessors, is an attempt to make sense of the chaos, not just the sometimes tragic chaos of these cold months, but also the wonderful bedlam that makes up any baseball season, any summer, and more importantly, what it means for the coming season and beyond.

The 2011 season certainly had its share of pandemonium, or have you forgotten the last night of the regular season, or Game 6 of the World Series? An entire book could be devoted to either of those nights, and the odds are that it won't be long until more than one will be. But this is not one of those books, because any baseball season is more than even all of its dramatic moments put together.

Perhaps the offseason seemed more chaotic than usual to us, though, because we did make one major change in the way *Baseball Prospectus 2012* is done. In the past, each player was listed with the team he played for in the previous year. This year, we have moved players to the team they will be playing for come Opening Day . . . at least, for as many players as we could bring up to date before we went to press. We can see from the number of unsigned free agents still hanging, and the needs of certain teams, that more moves will be made between when we had to stop tinkering and when you received your copy of the book. At press time, Prince Fielder, Roy Oswalt, and Japanese import Yu Darvish remained unsigned, with Darvish in negotiations with the Rangers, who won the bidding for the right to talk to him. But we've made our best attempt to match as many players as possible with their 2012 organizations.

Speaking of Darvish, since he didn't have a team yet, we couldn't put him into a chapter. So here is a little scouting report on him: Breathless optimists may perhaps be forgiven for gushing that he will be the best thing since Roger Clemens/sushi/sliced bread, but some scouts have a tendency to over-exoticize his stuff. (Remember all the hoopla over Daisuke Matsuzaka's "gyroball"?) Yes, he's half-Iranian/half-Japanese, but the ball is still round, and he still throws it much like other human beings who are 6-foot-5, 220 pounds. Darvish's stuff isn't exotic, but it is by all accounts varied. He is a "drop and drive" guy, with six pitches: He will be all of 25 years old and has a lifetime ERA under 2.00. But he will be facing better hitters, more varied weather, and longer travel, and he'll be learning new ballparks.

Another potentially exciting import is Yoenis Cespedes. Scouts have been drooling at the prospect of the 26-year-old outfielder escaping his native Cuba for years, but it was a series of highly entertaining promotional videos put out by his representative, Edgar Mercedes, that made him a household name. The good news is he's the real deal, an ultra-athletic tool shed with plus-plus power, above-average speed and a cannon for an arm. Whenever he's able to get his paperwork in order to come to the U.S. from the Dominican Republic, he'll likely command a deal larger than what the Reds gave Aroldis Chapman in 2010. He'll need a few months in Triple-A to get acclimated, but his floor is Mike Cameron, and his ceiling is through the roof.

What else will 2012 bring? Will someone go worst to first like the Arizona Diamondbacks did last year? Will there be an epic stumble out of the gate like those of the Boston Red Sox and Tampa Bay Rays, a mind-boggling end-of-season collapse like those of the very same Red Sox and Atlanta Braves, or a comeback for the ages like those of the very same Rays and the eventual World Series champion St. Louis Cardinals?

No, not just like. It's never the same twice. There probably won't be a 19-inning game decided on a blown call at home plate this year. We won't see another star player suffer through 496 misery-filled plate appearances exactly like Adam Dunn, but an epic slump will probably happen to someone. Ryan Vogelsong can't surprise us again the way he did last year, and Matt Kemp and Curtis Granderson can't blow away their pasts in quite the same way, but someone will surprise us. Someone will have a monster year.

Who will it be? How it will it go? We're happy to say we don't know. That's why it's so exciting. But the talented team of writers, editors, statistical analysts, and all-around baseball savants who wrote this book have some educated thoughts on the matter. Thousands of them, in fact.

They say there's a difference between the team on the field and the team on paper. One has to watch the games all season long to see the team on the field, but this book is where one finds the most definitive paper. Within these pages you'll read about the outlook for all 30 teams, this year and beyond. You'll find an opinion, guided by both statistical analysis and scouting observation, about every single player likely to have even the slightest impact in the major leagues in 2012 and many whose presence won't be felt until future years.

We were handed stewardship of *Baseball Prospectus 2012* by the annual's longtime editor, Steven Goldman, who has guided us in his continuing role as BP's Editor-in-Chief. In last year's preface, Steve wrote, "This book serves multiple purposes. It can be a fantasy guide or a season preview, but to us, more than anything else, it is a snapshot of state-of-the-art thought on the art of building a winning baseball team."

What he said. We hope you enjoy *Baseball Prospectus 2012*, and that you indeed find it "The essential guide to the 2012 baseball season."

*King Kaufman, San Francisco*
*Cecilia Tan, Boston*
*December 23, 2011*

# Statistical Introduction

*Colin Wyers*

They will tell you "you had to be there." They *lie*.

I remember being a young boy, and being in awe of all the greats: Ruth, Mays, Gehrig, Williams, Cobb, Aaron, Musial, DiMaggio. I didn't see them. I wasn't there. But I *knew*. Flipping through stacks of cardboard (packaged with

a telescope not quite in focus. Every year we turn the knob a little to the left or the right and things get a little clearer. (Of course, sometimes the game is a little—or a lot—out of focus for *them* as well. Their picture never gets any clearer, though.)

So we continue to turn that knob, little by little, and each year we see a little more. Last year we made a rather large twist of the knob; this year we move the knob much more subtly. We hope you find that we keep moving it in the right direction.

## Offense

At the core of everything we do to measure offense is True Average, which attempts to measure everything a player does at the plate—hitting for power, taking walks, striking out, and even making "productive" outs—on the familiar scale of batting average. A player with a TAv of .260 is average, .300 is exceptional, .200 is rather awful.

True Average also accounts for the context a player performs in—the baseline for average is not what the typical player has done, but what we expect the typical player would have done given similar opportunities. That means we adjust based on the mix of parks a player plays in. Rather than use a blanket park adjustment for every player on a team, a player who plays a disproportionate number of his games at home will see that reflected in his stats, for instance. We also adjust based upon league quality; the average player in the AL is better than the average player in the NL, and True Average accounts for this.

Because hitting runs isn't the entirety of scoring runs, we

also look at a player's Baserunning Runs. BRR accounts for the value of a player's ability to steal bases, of course, but it also accounts for his ability to go first to third on a single or advance on a fly ball.

and comparing those plays made to his peers at that position (with an adjustment for the tendencies of pitchers—handedness and ground ball rate primarily among them).

The general move in the sabermetric community has been toward stats based on zone data—where human stringers record the type of batted ball (grounder, liner, fly ball) and its presumed landing location, and that data is used to compile expected outs to compare a fielder's performance to. Many people abandoned metrics based on adjusted range factor for other metrics that incorporated this zone-based data.

The trouble is that this zone data—unlike the sorts of data that we use in the calculation of the statistics you see in this book—was never made publicly available; the data was recorded by commercial data providers who kept the raw data privately, only disclosing it to a select few who paid large sums for it.

But as we've seen the field of zone-based defensive analysis open up—more data and more metrics based upon that data coming to light—what we've seen is that the conclusions of zone-based defensive metrics don't hold up especially well to outside scrutiny. Different data providers can come to very different conclusions about the same events—based upon their recording practices and their observational vantage point. And two metrics based upon the same data set can come to radically different conclusions based upon their starting assumptions—assumptions that haven't been tested, using methods that can't be duplicated or verified by outside analysts.

And we've seen that the quality of the fielder can bias the data. Zone-based fielding metrics will tend to attribute more expected outs to good fielders than bad fielders, irrespective of the distribution of batted balls. Scorers who work in parks with high press boxes will tend to score more line drives than scorers who work in parks with low press boxes.

Because of the secrecy surrounding the underlying data, we've barely begun to scratch the surface of quantifying these problems and their effects. But because of this, we have abandoned our efforts to produce our own zone-based metric for inclusion in this book. Simply put, there is no evidence to show that the inclusion of zone-based data improves defensive metrics over the short run, and much evidence that incorporating the data causes severe distortions over the long run.

Instead, we've revised FRAA to incorporate play-by-play data, allowing us to study the issue of defense at a much more granular level, but without resorting to the sorts of subjective data used in some other fielding metrics. We count how many plays a player made, as well as expected plays for the average player at that position based upon a pitcher's estimated groundball tendencies and the handedness of the batter. There are also adjustments for park and the base-out situations; depending on whether there are runners on base, as well as the number of outs, the shortstop may position himself differently, and we account for that in the average baselines.

Still, measuring individual fielding is a much less precise endeavor than measuring a player's hitting. So you'll often see player comments discussing a fielder's ability or performance in ways that directly contradict the stat block printed above. This seems to stick in the craws of many readers. To which I can only respond: If everything about a player could be captured by the stat block, we wouldn't need the comments at all. And until we've advanced to a far greater point of certainty in fielding analysis than where we are now, I (as a reader myself, as well as the man behind the figures in the book) would rather have comments that told me information that the metrics don't capture than information the metrics do capture. Sometimes those additional comments will be wrong and the metric right, and sometimes it'll be the other way around, but until we're sure which is which I find it's much more useful to have both than to behave as though we have much more certainty than we really do.

## Pitching

Of course, new findings about fielding influence how we measure pitching as well.

Probably the most radical finding about either was made by Voros McCracken, who stated, "There is little if any difference among major-league pitchers in their ability to prevent hits on balls hit in the field of play."

This was an extremely controversial finding when first published, but later research has by-and-large validated it (if softened the impact of it a bit). McCracken (and others) went forth from that finding to come up with a variety of defense-independent pitching measures.

The trouble is that many efforts to separate pitching from fielding have ended up also in some respects separating pitching from pitching—looking at only a handful of variables (typically walks, strikeouts, and home runs—the "three true outcomes") in isolation from the situation in which they occurred.

What we've done with our new pitching statistic (the name, "Fair RA," may seem familiar, but it's an entirely new metric) is to take a pitcher's actual results—not just what happened, but when it happened as well—and adjust them for the quality of his defensive support, as measured by FRAA.

Now, applying FRAA to pitchers in this sense is easier than applying it to fielders. We don't have to worry about figuring out which fielder is responsible for making an out, only identifying the likelihood of an out being made. So there is far less uncertainty here than there is in fielding analysis.

That's not the same as no uncertainty, of course. And again, we're right at the beginning of a renewed effort to study the impact of batted-ball distribution on fielding, and in turn how pitchers can affect batted-ball distribution. What we are finding is that "little if any difference" does not, in fact, mean no difference, and that there may be pitchers who have the ability to prevent hits on balls in play. What we are struggling to do now is improve our ability to figure out who those pitchers were in short time spans—a single season, or even several seasons.

The way I like to look at it is: any effort to put a single number to a player's contributions is a good place to start a discussion, but a poor place to finish it. Sabermetrics provides us with a framework for talking about baseball, not a way to silence debate.

Also, Fair RA means exactly that, a number scaled to a pitcher's runs allowed per game, not his earned runs allowed per game. The concept of an "earned" run seems less and less expressive as we come to terms with how little errors tell us about a player's fielding abilities. And looking only at earned runs tends over time to overrate three kinds of pitchers:

1. Pitchers who play in parks where scorers tend to hand out more errors. Looking at differences in error rates between parks tells us that scorers can in fact differ significantly in how likely they are to score any given play as an error (as opposed to an infield hit);
2. Groundball pitchers. A substantial proportion of errors occur on groundballs, ERA will tend to overrate groundball pitchers compared to fly-ball pitchers of equal ability; and

3. Pitchers who aren't very good. Good pitchers tend to allow fewer unearned runs than bad pitchers, for the simple fact that good pitchers have more ways to get out of jams than bad pitchers. They're more likely to get a strikeout to end the inning, and less likely to give up a home run.

In short, looking at ERA (or metrics scaled to ERA) provides a distorted picture of what a pitcher actually accomplished. This is something we've long preached at Baseball Prospectus—and by starting to move away from ERA and toward RA in our advanced pitching metrics, we hope to encourage more people to move in this direction.

outs, and home runs allowed. FIP is attempting to answer a different question than Fair RA; instead of saying how well a pitcher performed, it tells us how much of a pitcher's performance we think is due to things the pitcher has direct control over. Over time, there are pitchers who consistently over and underperform their FIPs through some skill that isn't picked up by the rather limited components; FIP may be useful in identifying pitchers who were "lucky" and "unlucky" but some caution must be exercised, lest we throw the baby out with the bathwater.

## Projection

Of course, many of you aren't turning to this book just for a look at what a player has done, but a look at what a player is going to do—the "deadly accurate" PECOTA projections mentioned in bold type on the cover.

PECOTA, initially developed by Nate Silver (who has moved on to greater fame as a political analyst), consists of three parts:

1. Major-league equivalencies, to allow us to use minor-league stats to project how a player will perform in the majors;
2. Baseline forecasts, which use weighted averages and regression to the mean to produce an estimate of a player's true talent level;
3. A career-path adjustment, which incorporates information on how comparable players' stats changed over time.

That basic approach is still retained. We've made a series of refinements, though, to improve upon the process. PECOTA may again someday declare the end of Ichiro, for instance, but it won't be this year—he's projected for another season of more than 200 hits.

Now that we've gone over how the book has changed from previous years, let's go over what's inside the book.

## The Team Prospectus

The bulk of this book comprises team chapters, with one for each of the 30 major-league franchises. On the first page of

oped by David Smyth and Brandon Heipp.

### DIAMONDBACKS PROSPECTUS
**2011 W-L: 94-68, 1st in NL West**

| | | | |
|---|---|---|---|
| **Pythag** | .546 | 8th | **Ballpark:** Chase Field (3-yr. PF: 106). Forcing pitchers to learn desert survival skills since 1998 |
| **RS/G** | 4.51 | 9th | |
| **RA/G** | 4.09 | 11th | |
| **TAv** | .256 | 18th | **2011:** A balanced young team with a mediocre pen (at last!) climbs from worst to first |
| **TAv-P** | .254 | 10th | |
| **FIP** | 3.99 | 16th | |
| **DER** | .714 | 11th | **2012:** If Upton gets some hitting help and the young pitchers come through, a repeat |
| **DL** | 571 | 6th | |
| **B-Age** | 28.2 | 8th | **Action Items:** Lock up Hudson and Kennedy, give younglings a shot, pray Goldschmidt hits 30 dingers |
| **P-Age** | 27.0 | 5th | |
| **Salary** | $55.9 | 25th | |
| **M$/MW** | $.945 | 2nd | |

A team's run-scoring ability is represented by True Average. Then we have several metrics for a team's pitching and defense. TAv-P is opponent's TAv against, FIP presents team Fielding Independent Pitching, and DER rates the team's defensive efficiency Ratio, essentially 1-BABIP.

We've also incorporated several new statistics into this year's team summaries. DL refers to how many days a team's players logged on the disabled list over the course of a season. B-Age and P-Age tell us the average age of a team's hitters and pitchers, respectively.

Salary, of course, refers to a team's total payroll, in millions of dollars. But we've supplemented that with a team's marginal dollars per marginal wins, a metric created by Doug Pappas to show how efficiently a team is spending its money.

## Position Players

After an opening essay, each chapter moves on to the player comments. Position players are listed first, in alphabetical order, and each player is listed with the major-league team with which he was employed as of January 1, 2012, meaning that free agents who eventually change teams will be listed under their previous employer.

The player-specific sections (see Joey Bats' listing below) begin with biographical information before moving onto the column headers and actual data. Other than cups of coffee at the various levels—trimmed out in the interest of space and in accordance with small-sample-size theory—all relevant seasons and partial seasons will be listed. The column headers begin with more standard information like year, team, level (majors or minors, and which level of the minors), and the raw, untranslated tallies found on the back of a baseball card: PA (Plate Appearances), R (Runs), 2B (doubles), 3B (triples), HR (home runs), RBI (runs batted in), BB (walks), SO (strikeouts), SB (stolen bases), and CS (caught stealing).

Following those are the untranslated triple-slash-rate statistics: batting average (BA), on-base percentage (OBP), and slugging percentage (SLG). Their "slash" nickname is derived from the occasional presentation of slash-delimitation, such as noting that Joey Votto hit .309/.416/.531. Each of the three statistics is flawed on its own, but put together they describe the "shape" of a hitter's production—whether he's a slap-hitting "punch and judy" type, or an all-or-nothing power hitter, or simply an all-around amazing hitter like Albert Pujols. It's followed up by True Average, which rolls all those things and more into one easy-to-digest number.

BABIP stands for Batting Average on Balls in Play, and is meant to show how well a hitter did when he put the ball in play. An especially low or high BABIP may mean a hitter was especially lucky or unlucky—but it may not. Line-drive hitters will tend to have especially high BABIPs from season to season; so will speedy runners who beat out more grounders for base hits.

Next is Baserunning Runs (BRR), which as mentioned earlier covers all sorts of baserunning accomplishments, not just stolen bases.

The last column is WARP, Wins Above Replacement Player, which means we've left out VORP altogether. That doesn't mean we've discarded the underpinnings of VORP— we simply determined it wasn't necessary to have two ways of measuring the same player's contributions relative to replacement. For anyone who misses the VORP scale, it's simple enough to convert; a player with a WARP of 2.0 would have a VORP roughly equal to 20.

WARP combines a player's batting runs above average (derived from a player's True Average), BRR, FRAA, an adjustment based upon position played, and a credit for plate appearances based upon the difference between the "replacement level" (derived from looking at the quality of players added to a team's roster after the start of the season) and the league average.

Why the replacement-level adjustment? Why not leave everything relative to average? The answer is playing time— if you have two players who are totally average (in terms of hitting, fielding, position, and baserunning) but one plays in a dozen games and one plays in 120 games, the latter of the two is clearly more valuable to his team. At the same time, it is easy to envision a player who plays so poorly he is less valuable the more he plays: a first baseman who bats .200 with walks and power to match is easily hurting his team the more he plays. Replacement level gives us a way to see how a player's playing time is helping—or hurting—his team.

## Pitchers

Now let's look at how pitchers are presented, looking at last year's AL Cy Young and MVP winner Justin Verlander.

The first line and the YEAR, TM, LVL, and AGE columns are the same as in the hitter's example above. The next set of columns—W (Wins), L (Losses), SV (Saves), G (Games pitched), GS (Games Started), IP (Innings Pitched), H (Hits), HR, BB, SO, BB9, SO9—are the actual, unadjusted cumulative stats compiled by the pitcher during each season.

**Jose Bautista**  RF

Born: **10/19/1980** Age: **31**
Bats: **R** Throws: **R** Height: **6' 1"** Weight: **195**
Breakout: **1%** Improve: **42%** Collapse: **2%**
Attrition: **5%** MLB: **95%**

**Comparables:**
Reggie Smith, Frank Robinson, Roger Maris

| YEAR | TEAM | LVL | AGE | PA | R | 2B | 3B | HR | RBI | BB | SO | SB | CS | AVG_OBP_SLG | TAv | BABIP | BRR | FRAA | WARP |
|---|---|---|---|---|---|---|---|---|---|---|---|---|---|---|---|---|---|---|---|
| 2009 | TOR | MLB | 28 | 404 | 54 | 13 | 3 | 13 | 40 | 56 | 85 | 4 | 0 | .235/.349/.408 | .268 | .275 | 3.9 | -2.9 | 1.4 |
| 2010 | TOR | MLB | 29 | 683 | 109 | 35 | 3 | 54 | 124 | 100 | 116 | 9 | 2 | .260/.378/.617 | .341 | .233 | -1.6 | -12.4 | 6.5 |
| 2011 | TOR | MLB | 30 | 655 | 105 | 24 | 2 | 43 | 103 | 132 | 111 | 9 | 5 | .302/.447/.608 | .370 | .309 | 1.4 | 10.3 | 10.3 |
| 2012 | TOR | MLB | 31 | 621 | 87 | 28 | 2 | 31 | 89 | 87 | 118 | 7 | 3 | .259/.370/.501 | .304 | .275 | -0.2 | RF -2, 3B 2 | 4.2 |

Next is GB%, which is the percentage of all batted balls that were hit on the ground including both outs and hits. The average GB% for a major-league pitcher in 2007 was about 45 percent; a pitcher with a GB% anywhere north of 50 percent can be considered a good groundball pitcher. As mentioned above, this is based upon the observation of human stringers and can be skewed based upon a number of factors. We've included the number as a guide, but please approach it skeptically.

BABIP is the same statistic as for batters, but often tells you more, since most pitchers have very little control over their batting average on balls in play. A high BABIP is more

any way.

Fair RA has been covered in some depth above, and is the basis of WARP for pitchers. Significantly, incorporating play-by-play data allows us to set different replacement levels for starting pitchers and relievers. Relief pitchers have several advantages over starters—they can give their best effort on every pitch, and hitters have fewer chances to pick up on what they're doing. That means that it's significantly easier to find decent replacements for relief pitchers than it is for starting pitchers, and that's reflected in the replacement level for each.

We also credit starters for pitching deeper into games and "saving the pen." A starting pitcher who's able to go deep into a game (while pitching effectively) allows a manager to keep his worst relievers in the pen and bring his best relievers out to preserve a lead.

All of this means that WARP values for relief pitchers (especially closers) will seem lower than what we've seen in the past—and may conflict with how we feel about relief aces coming in and "saving" the game. But the save, while a model of how we feel about a pitcher's performance—a successful save means a win, while a failed save typically means a loss—does not describe how teams win games. In other words, saves give extra credit to the closer for what his

teammates did to put him in a save spot to begin with; WARP is incapable of feeling excitement over a successful save, and judges them dispassionately.

## PECOTA

Both pitchers and hitters have PECOTA projections for next season, as well as a set of biographical details that describe the performance of that player's comparable players according to PECOTA.

The 2012 line is the PECOTA projection for the player in

comparable players:

- Breakout Rate is the percent chance that a player's production will improve by at least 20 percent relative to the weighted average of his performance over his most recent seasons.
- Improve Rate is the percent chance that a player's production will improve at all relative to his baseline performance. A player who is expected to perform just the same as he has in the recent past will have an Improve Rate of 50 percent.
- Collapse Rate is the percent chance that a position player's equivalent runs produced per PA will decline by at least 25 percent relative to his baseline performance over his past three seasons.
- Attrition Rate operates on playing time rather than performance. Specifically, it measures the likelihood that a player's playing time will decrease by at least 50 percent relative to his established level.

Breakout Rate and Collapse Rate can sometimes be counterintuitive for players who have already experienced a radical change in their performance levels. It's also worth noting that the projected decline in a given player's rate performances might not be indicative of an expected decline in

**Justin Verlander**
Born: 2/20/1983 Age: **29**
Bats: **R** Throws: **R** Height: **6' 6''** Weight: **200**
Breakout: **11%** Improve: **35%** Collapse: **37%**
Attrition: **6%** MLB: **97%**
Comparables:
Chris Young, Jon Rauch, Jake Peavy

| YEAR | TEAM | LVL | AGE | W | L | SV | G | GS | IP | H | HR | BB | SO | EqBB9 | EqSO9 | GB% | BABIP | WHIP | ERA | FIP | FRA | WARP |
|------|------|-----|-----|---|---|----|---|----|-----|-----|----|----|-----|-------|-------|-----|-------|------|------|------|------|------|
| 2009 | DET | MLB | 26 | 19 | 9 | 0 | 35 | 35 | 240 | 219 | 20 | 63 | 269 | 3.3 | 2.4 | 38% | .323 | 1.17 | 3.45 | 2.85 | 3.29 | 6.1 |
| 2010 | DET | MLB | 27 | 18 | 9 | 0 | 33 | 33 | 224¹ | 190 | 14 | 71 | 219 | 3.3 | 2.8 | 42% | .289 | 1.16 | 3.37 | 2.94 | 3.33 | 5.2 |
| 2011 | DET | MLB | 28 | 24 | 5 | 0 | 34 | 34 | 251 | 174 | 24 | 57 | 250 | 3.2 | 2.0 | 42% | .237 | 0.92 | 2.40 | 3.03 | 3.18 | 5.8 |
| 2012 | DET | MLB | 29 | 15 | 7 | 0 | 29 | 29 | 202¹ | 181 | 18 | 56 | 191 | 2.5 | 8.5 | 41% | .292 | 1.17 | 3.05 | 3.30 | 3.31 | 4.2 |

underlying ability or skill, but rather something of an anticipated correction following a breakout season.

The final piece of information, listed just to the right of the player's Attrition Rate, are his three highest scoring comparable players as determined by PECOTA, and a similarity score from 0–100 describing how similar a player's comps are to him. Occasionally, a player's top comparables will not be representative of the larger sample that PECOTA uses. It's also important to note that established major leaguers are compared to other major leaguers only, while minor-league players may be compared to major-league or minor-league players, with PECOTA strongly preferring the latter. All comparables represent a snapshot of how the listed player was performing at the same age as the current player, so if a 23-year-old hitter is compared to Sammy Sosa, he's actually being compared to a 23-year-old Sammy Sosa, not the decrepit Orioles version of Sosa, nor to Sosa's career as a whole.

## The Managers' Statistics

Each team chapter ends with a manager's comment and data breaking down his tactical tendencies. Though it is often difficult to isolate a manager's contributions to a team, comparing specific data modeled after well-documented plays and styles to the league average helps determine what a manager likes to do, even if we are still precluded from translating that information into actual wins and losses.

Following the year, team, and actual record, Pythag +/- lets us know by how many games the team under- or over-performed its Pythagenpat record. Mike Scioscia's Angels exceeded their projected record by four games, and exceeded it in the previous two seasons as well. That isn't necessarily an endorsement of Scioscia—keep in mind that Pythag +/- is a mathematical expression of team performance, not an interpretation of the manager's work, even though it has become commonplace to attribute Actual/Pythag discrepancies to the skipper.

Pitching staff usage follows, first with Avg PC reporting the average pitch count of his starting pitchers with the subsequent 100+P and 120+P offering the number of games in which the starters exceeded certain pitch thresholds. QS is the total number of quality starts—a start of at least six innings and with no more than three runs allowed—a

manager received from his starting pitchers. BQS is Blown Quality Starts, a Baseball Prospectus stat that measures games in which the starter delivered a quality start through six innings before losing it in the seventh inning or later by allowing runs to give him four or more. That said, a Blown Quality Start is not necessarily an indictment of the manager's abilities or tactics. A number of factors ranging from excellent offensive support to extremely poor bullpen support can lead a manager to leave his starter in a game after he's thrown six quality innings. Conversely, the decision by a manager to "bank" quality starts by restricting his starters to only six innings can have downsides as well as it increases his bullpen's workload and the opportunity for the pen to blow a game in which a starter was cruising.

Speaking of bullpen support, the next stats in the manager table tally how many pitching changes a manager made over the course of the season (REL) and how many times the reliever called upon didn't allow any runners, his own or inherited, to score (REL w Zero R). Bequeathed runners also count against REL w Zero R, meaning that relievers who exit with runners on that subsequently score prevent a manager from "padding" his tally here. Concluding the pitching section, IBB is quite simply the number of intentional walks the manager ordered during the given season, which can definitely be a mark of managerial strategy so long as outliers like Albert Pujols are accounted for.

Managers do more than manage pitchers, however; their usage of a bench can lead to added or lost performance. Subs lets us know the number of defensive replacements he employed throughout the regular season, while PH, PH Avg, and PH HR report the offensive statistics of pinch-hitters called upon. We then turn to the so-called "small ball" tactics, starting with the running game. The manager's aggressiveness on the bases is broken down by successful steals of second and third base (SB2, SB3) and times caught (CS2, CS3). We also provide the number of sacrifices a team attempted (SAC Att) and their success rate (SAC %). Be sure to keep in mind the differences between leagues as National League sacrifice attempts are greatly inflated by the fact that the pitchers hit. To correct for this, we list the number of times a manager got a successful sacrifice from a position player (POS SAC), which allows for comparisons between the two leagues. We finish up with Squeeze, which counts the number of successful squeeze plays the team executed over the

## MANAGER: MIKE SCIOSCIA

| YEAR | TEAM | W-L | Pythag +/- | Avg PC | 100+ P | 120+ P | QS | BQS | REL | REL w Zero R | IBB | Subs | PH | PH Avg | PH HR | SB2 | CS2 | SB3 | CS3 | SAC Att | SAC % | POS SAC | Squeeze | Swing | In Play |
|---|---|---|---|---|---|---|---|---|---|---|---|---|---|---|---|---|---|---|---|---|---|---|---|---|---|
| 2009 | ANA | 97-65 | 1 | 97.1 | 83 | 1 | 70 | 9 | 434 | 269 | 35 | 48 | 79 | .308 | 2 | 22 | 5 | 2 | 1 | 64 | 67.2% | 41 | 4 | 180 | 134 |
| 2010 | ANA | 80-82 | 0 | 204.3 | 162 | 160 | 108 | 6 | 410 | 325 | 66 | — | 172 | .174 | 0 | 14 | 10 | 0 | 3 | 140 | 72.9% | 100 | 6 | 400 | 125 |
| 2011 | ANA | 86-76 | 1 | 101.0 | 98 | 11 | 98 | 8 | 386 | 313 | 34 | — | 75 | .154 | 2 | 18 | 4 | 1 | 1 | 78 | 80.8% | 59 | 7 | 417 | 144 |

season. Finally, we have a couple of statistics that attempt to measure the manager's hit-and-run tactics. Swing is the number of times a hitter swung at a pitch while the runners were in motion, while In Play reflects how many times a manager's hitters swung and made contact while those runners were off to the races. Granted, swings on steal attempts do not always translate to hit-and-run attempts, but managers who greatly deviate from the average can be assumed to be staunch proponents or opponents of the strategy.

# Arizona Diamondbacks

When Kevin Towers assumed the position of Diamondbacks general manager in the final days of the 2010 season, the job seemed to promise a fair share of impending punishment. Towers mentioned two goals: cutting down on the team's his-

managed to follow a last-place finish with a first-place finish in the following season during the six-division era that dawned in 1994 could have been counted on Antonio Alfonseca's six-fingered hand; a standard complement of fingers could have accommodated them if you excluded the 2006 D-Backs, who tied for last in the West before their 2007 turnaround, and Mordecai Brown could have handled the trio that hadn't finished last in four-team divisions. Only three additional teams pulled off the single-season turnaround during the four-division period of 1969-93, and none of those completed the feat before 1991. Not surprisingly, in light of the rarity of such reversals, the Diamondbacks weren't a popular preseason pick to unseat the reigning World Series champion Giants and claim the NL West title.

With such lofty ambitions likely buried deep in the back of his mind, Towers set about improving the weaknesses he'd targeted after taking over. The 2010 club he'd inherited had struck out more frequently than any team had before, going down swinging or looking in just under a quarter of its plate appearances. To some extent, the situation resolved itself. Chris Snyder had already been shipped to Pittsburgh at the trading deadline, and Towers allowed Adam LaRoche to leave as a free agent, which subtracted two strikeout-prone bats from the roster. He toyed with selling low on Justin Upton

but refrained when he couldn't secure a suitable package; the right fielder would go on to cut his strikeout rate significantly in a resurgent 2011 campaign. But Towers did send main offender Mark Reynolds to Baltimore in December.

As a result of those changes

| | | |
|---|---|---|
| TAv | .256 | 18th |
| TAv-P | .254 | 10th |
| FIP | 3.99 | 16th |
| DER | .714 | 11th |
| DL | 571 | 6th |
| B-Age | 28.2 | 8th |
| P-Age | 27.0 | 5th |
| Salary | $55.9 | 25th |
| M$/MW | $.945 | 2nd |

**2011:** A balanced young team with a mediocre pen (at last!) climbs from worst to first

**2012:** If Upton gets some hitting help and the young pitchers come through, a repeat

**Action Items:** Lock up Hudson and Kennedy, give younglings a shot, pray Goldschmidt hits 30 dingers

power, so one shouldn't read too much into the fact that the two teams with the fewest whiffs went to the World Series last season. Still, as we observed in our Arizona essay in *BP2011*, stacking a lineup with strikeout-prone bats has historically been an unsuccessful strategy, producing a compounding effect that contributes to volatile runscoring. By no means were the Diamondbacks adept at making contact in Towers's first full season at the helm—they still struck out at the fourth-highest rate in the NL—but their tendency toward strikeouts was no longer a serious handicap.

## Table 1. Extreme Makeover, Baseball Edition: Single-Season Worst-to-First Team Turnarounds

| Team | Year 1 | Year 1 Finish | Year 2 | Year 2 Finish |
|---|---|---|---|---|
| Braves | 1990 | 6 | 1991 | 1 |
| Twins | 1990 | 7 | 1991 | 1 |
| Phillies | 1992 | 6 | 1993 | 1 |
| Giants | 1996 | 4 | 1997 | 1 |
| Padres | 1997 | 4 | 1998 | 1 |
| Diamondbacks | 1998 | 5 | 1999 | 1 |
| Diamondbacks | 2006 | 4 | 2007 | 1 |
| Cubs | 2006 | 6 | 2007 | 1 |
| Rays | 2007 | 5 | 2008 | 1 |
| Diamondbacks | 2010 | 5 | 2011 | 1 |

That left one liability lingering on Towers's offseason to-do list. The Diamondbacks bullpen posted an abysmal 5.99 FRA in 2010, by far the worst in baseball and .79 runs higher than the next-worst NL unit. Towers, who showed a knack for assembling some of baseball's best and most cost-efficient bullpens while in San Diego, seemed like the perfect man to reengineer Arizona's relief corps. The Reynolds trade helped to kill two team weaknesses with one transaction, since the D-Backs' bounty was hard-throwing right-hander David Hernandez, who became a consistent setup man for the Snakes, earning the second-highest Leverage Index among Arizona relievers. (Fellow righty reliever Kam Mickolio, who also came over in the deal, was less successful, though he struck out nearly 10 batters per nine innings at Triple-A Reno.)

In a slight departure from his usual pattern of low-cost acquisitions, Towers gambled on often-injured free-agent reliever J.J. Putz, whose health mostly held up in his first season as the club's closer. Towers also successfully filled the pen's lefty specialist slot with Rule 5 find Joe Paterson and made another trade to reinforce his relief corps at the deadline, sending extraneous pieces Brandon Allen and Jordan Norberto to Oakland for Brad Ziegler, one of the most dependable bullpen arms in baseball (albeit one somewhat limited by his susceptibility to southpaws). The net result of Towers's tinkering was an improvement in bullpen FRA of nearly a run and a half, giving the D-Backs a 4.69 mark that ranked 17th in baseball. The team's starters were similarly solid-but-unspectacular, ranking 17th overall at 4.41. Since Towers's bullpen investments paid off, he went back to the well over the winter, adding another off-brand former closer with injury issues in Takashi Saito and trading for another consistent Oakland reliever in Craig Breslow.

Still, despite Reynolds' aversion to contact and the bullpen help he brought back, there was a downside to running him out of town. In the process of striking out, walking, or homering in nearly half of his plate appearances for the Orioles, Reynolds recorded a .286 True Average, which would have been the best mark among non-Upton Diamondbacks with at least 150 PA. The Snakes scored the fourth-most runs in the NL, but the hitter-friendly confines of Chase Field helped camouflage some of their offensive inadequacies. Their .256 TAv revealed a slightly below-average offense that ranked in the middle of the NL pack. Reynolds' departure left the hot corner in the hands of Ryan Roberts, whose bat mostly went south after an excellent April, as well as a host of offensive zeroes like Melvin Mora, Sean Burroughs, Geoff Blum, and Cody Ransom. In addition, while retaining LaRoche would not have represented a solution, his departure nonetheless left a void at first base that the Diamondbacks spent most of the season trying to fill with subpar bats. Paul Goldschmidt's promotion in August brought some stability to the cold

corner, though it's not clear whether his ceiling is high enough to admit him to the upper echelons of the position.

Miguel Montero and Gerardo Parra are coming off excellent seasons, and Chris Young and Stephen Drew can be counted on to contribute if healthy, but aside from Upton, the lineup features very little star power, and significant uncertainty remains on the infield corners and at second base, where the Diamondbacks are desperately hoping to get more of the good Aaron Hill they saw at the end of last season. Instead of shoring up one of their weaker positions, the Diamondbacks shot themselves in the foot in December by signing free-agent Jason Kubel to a two-year deal, which relegated the younger, cheaper, and more productive Parra to a fourth-outfielder role. Aside from the erstwhile left fielder, little assistance can be expected from the bench—it's fair to wonder whether any team really needs Blum, John McDonald, or Willie Bloomquist, let alone all three of them, but the Diamondbacks acted quickly to corner the market on offensively inept utility men.

In short, the Diamondbacks had a mediocre offense and a run-of-the-mill rotation and relief corps, and unlike the 2008 Rays, the last team to leapfrog their divisional opponents in a single season, their defense also placed in the middle of the pack, ranking 11th with a 0.714 defensive efficiency. The lone standout aspect of their attack, the third-best baserunning performance in the NL, was worth less than a win. So what made them so good? The uncomfortable truth for Arizona fans is that despite their 94 wins, the Diamondbacks *weren't* particularly good—surprisingly successful, certainly, especially in light of their shedding a quarter of their payroll and spending less than all but two other NL teams, but still something well short of the dominant performers that their record suggests they were.

Arizona's improbable playoff appearance was in part the product of a weak division and a large helping of luck. The Diamondbacks outplayed their third-order winning percentage—a metric based on underlying statistics and adjusted for quality of opponents—by 10 1/2 games, the biggest margin in baseball. The D-Backs finished with an eight-game cushion in the NL West, and that's the only performance that counts in determining which teams get tickets to October. But in the third-order standings, they beat out the Giants by only one game and actually finished behind the Dodgers, which should temper our expectations for this season.

The Diamondbacks went 28-16 in one-run games, giving them the best winning percentage of any team in those contests, which often hinge as heavily on luck as they do on skill, though an improved bullpen didn't hurt. They also benefited from another factor largely determined by chance: good health. The Diamondbacks suffered the fewest injuries and days lost to injury of any NL team. According to BP injury guru Corey Dawkins, they surrendered only an estimated

2.0 WARP to the DL and day-to-day ailments—half as much as any other team in their division—with Drew's ankle fracture accounting for the majority of the damage. Even if the Diamondbacks medical staff deserves much of the credit, the Snakes can expect more aches and pains to plague them in 2012.

Of course, none of that means there isn't plenty of hope on Arizona's horizon, as the team's formerly fallow farm system has been rebuilt by a combination of fruitful trades orchestrated by former interim GM Jerry DiPoto, astute drafting by former scouting director Tom Allison, who was let go after Towers came to town, and—at least in 2011—the

who finished fifth in the Rookie of the Year voting but might not have the stuff to sustain his success, the team possesses unparalleled pitching riches in the minor leagues.

Even with former first-rounder Jarrod Parker shipped off to Oakland—in exchange for Trevor Cahill, a more established pitcher only six months his senior—it's easy to make the case that the D-Backs have five or six minor-league arms more promising than their best position player prospect. Trevor Bauer, the third-overall pick in last year's amateur draft, could contend for a rotation spot as soon as this spring. Tyler Skaggs, whom the Diamondbacks acquired in the 2010 Dan Haren trade, might be in the big leagues by September. Archie Bradley, yet another 2011 first-rounder, is behind those two but possesses the same top-of-the-rotation talent. And a few other arms of varying abilities figure to make strong cases for the middle or end of the rotation in the next few seasons. Given that profusion of young pitching, it's not difficult to envision the Snakes' best starter last season being their fourth- or fifth-best by 2013, although as always the TNSTAAPP principle applies.

It is important to note that the Diamondbacks feature a fly-ball staff; 30.1 percent of their batted balls allowed were hit in the air last season, the highest rate in baseball. Although Cahill keeps the ball on the ground and Wade Miley might do the same, none of Arizona's up-and-coming arms is a budding Brad Ziegler in the grounder department,

so that percentage might not see a substantial change. In one sense, that tendency works against the Snakes, since fly balls travel farther in Arizona's dry air; Chase Field's home run factor ranks sixth-highest among major-league parks. But the danger is diminished somewhat by an outfield that in 2011 featured three players capable of playing center field in Young, Parra, and Upton. Thanks to that trio's efforts in tracking down balls that might have found gaps or corners on teams with less rangy players in the pastures, the Diamondbacks allowed the third-lowest park-adjusted slugging percentage on balls in play in the NL last season, though they'll have trouble repeating that performance with

already in place, Matt Williams and Jay Bell, winning 100 games and pulling off their first worst-to-first reversal. That all-out veteran effort culminated in a 2001 World Series victory and gave the D-Backs the distinction of being the quickest team to a title, but that aging club soon ran out of steam, sending Arizona back to the cellar (and nearly halving the '99 team's win total) by 2004. The 2007 team arose from the ashes with a new core, but that core has had a bumpy ride, alternating between first- and last-place finishes of its own.

The signings of Towers and skipper Kirk Gibson to respective three-year extensions with two club options give the team one sort of stability. Still, the Diamondbacks are in an unusual spot in that they have few gaping holes in which to plug in players for easy improvements, but even fewer players capable of producing more than three or four wins above replacement, a state of affairs that hampers both their upside and their flexibility. The organization's current crop of pitching prospects should produce more stars, but impact position players will be harder to come by for the foreseeable future. Although experience suggests that a team can never have too much pitching, a rotation can hold only so many arms; once the Diamondbacks determine which ones they think will pan out, they'll have to be proactive in selling off the surplus in exchange for offensive talent from other teams, lest an imbalanced roster limit their capacity to keep surprising us with success.

# HITTERS

## Henry Blanco    C

Born: 8/29/1971 Age: 40
Bats: R Throws: R Height: 6' 0" Weight: 170
Breakout: 3% Improve: 16% Collapse: 8%
Attrition: 23% MLB: 48%

Comparables:
Carlton Fisk, Greg Myers, Birdie Tebbetts

| YEAR | TEAM | LVL | AGE | PA | R | 2B | 3B | HR | RBI | BB | SO | SB | CS | AVG_OBP_SLG | TAv | BABIP | BRR | FRAA | WARP |
|------|------|-----|-----|-----|----|----|----|----|-----|----|----|----|----|--------------|------|-------|------|-------|------|
| 2009 | SDN | MLB | 37 | 232 | 21 | 12 | 0 | 6 | 16 | 26 | 50 | 0 | 0 | .235/.320/.382 | .251 | .282 | -1.1 | -1.3 | 0.7 |
| 2010 | NYN | MLB | 38 | 144 | 10 | 5 | 0 | 2 | 8 | 11 | 26 | 1 | 0 | .215/.271/.300 | .217 | .248 | -1.1 | 0.1 | 0.1 |
| 2011 | ARI | MLB | 39 | 112 | 12 | 3 | 1 | 8 | 12 | 12 | 21 | 0 | 1 | .250/.330/.540 | .290 | .239 | -0.1 | -0.6 | 0.9 |
| 2012 | ARI | MLB | 40 | 250 | 26 | 10 | 1 | 6 | 25 | 19 | 53 | 1 | 0 | .229/.290/.359 | .232 | .268 | 0 | C -2 | 0.8 |

Blanco hit so well last year that he was almost forced to resign in disgrace from the International Brotherhood of Backup Catchers, but ultimately the first-time offender was forgiven his delusions of grandeur and allowed to keep his membership card on the basis of his unimpeachable record of poor hitting. Chase Field may have had something to do with his erupting for a home run every 12.5 at-bats after hitting one every 41.1 at-bats over his first 13 seasons. He hit .313/.400/.792 with six of his homers at home, while on the road he hit like his old self. The D-Backs brought him back for an encore. Even if—okay, better make that when—his bat returns to its old ways, Arizona can count on his strong arm: he threw out 11 of 24 attempted basestealers (45.8 percent) last season.

## Willie Bloomquist    SS

Born: 11/27/1977 Age: 34
Bats: R Throws: R Height: 6' 0" Weight: 185
Breakout: 2% Improve: 23% Collapse: 11%
Attrition: 30% MLB: 81%

Comparables:
Adam Everett, Alvin Dark, Edgar Renteria

| YEAR | TEAM | LVL | AGE | PA | R | 2B | 3B | HR | RBI | BB | SO | SB | CS | AVG_OBP_SLG | TAv | BABIP | BRR | FRAA | WARP |
|------|------|-----|-----|-----|----|----|----|----|-----|----|----|----|----|--------------|------|-------|------|-----------|------|
| 2009 | KCA | MLB | 31 | 468 | 52 | 11 | 8 | 4 | 29 | 27 | 73 | 25 | 6 | .265/.308/.355 | .236 | .309 | 2.5 | 0.4 | 0.4 |
| 2010 | CIN | MLB | 32 | 18 | 0 | 0 | 0 | 0 | 0 | 1 | 3 | 0 | 0 | .294/.333/.294 | .221 | .357 | -0.2 | -0.1 | -0.1 |
| 2010 | KCA | MLB | 32 | 181 | 31 | 10 | 1 | 3 | 17 | 8 | 25 | 8 | 5 | .265/.296/.388 | .240 | .294 | -0.3 | -0.9 | 0.1 |
| 2011 | ARI | MLB | 33 | 381 | 44 | 10 | 2 | 4 | 26 | 23 | 51 | 20 | 10 | .266/.317/.340 | .234 | .300 | 0.3 | -3.3 | -0.1 |
| 2012 | ARI | MLB | 34 | 322 | 34 | 10 | 3 | 3 | 28 | 20 | 54 | 17 | 7 | .261/.310/.345 | .235 | .304 | -0.8 | SS -2, LF 0 | 0.2 |

Sabermetrician Tom Tango has proposed "Wins Above Willie" as a fitting name for a total-value statistic, and Bloomquist once again showed why last season. His embodiment of a concept that critics say isn't real makes him more valuable as a teaching tool than a player—after a decade in the majors, he's accumulated just 1.0 WARP, and as he heads into his age-34 season, there is plenty of time for his decline phase to erase even that modest sum. Bloomquist endeared himself to Arizona fans with a scrappy .306 average in April but hit just .257/.315/.323 after returning from a hamstring strain suffered late that month. Aside from his forgettable performance, Bloomquist's calling card is his flexibility in the field (which boils down to an ability to be bad at a multitude of positions), but Stephen Drew's injury limited Bloomquist to just three positions in 2011, including a mere one game at second base, since his dubious services were often required at shortstop. One thing Bloomquist has always been able to do is steal at a high rate of success, but even that skill deserted him last season. Nonetheless, he re-signed for two seasons, which he'll spend battling John McDonald for backup at-bats.

## Geoff Blum    3B

Born: 4/26/1973 Age: 39
Bats: B Throws: R Height: 6' 4" Weight: 193
Breakout: 0% Improve: 19% Collapse: 12%
Attrition: 25% MLB: 53%

Comparables:
Todd Zeile, Melvin Mora, Cal Ripken Jr.

| YEAR | TEAM | LVL | AGE | PA | R | 2B | 3B | HR | RBI | BB | SO | SB | CS | AVG_OBP_SLG | TAv | BABIP | BRR | FRAA | WARP |
|------|------|-----|-----|-----|----|----|----|----|-----|----|----|----|----|--------------|------|-------|------|----------|------|
| 2009 | HOU | MLB | 36 | 427 | 34 | 14 | 1 | 10 | 49 | 33 | 61 | 0 | 1 | .247/.314/.367 | .241 | .266 | -1.1 | -9.3 | -0.8 |
| 2010 | HOU | MLB | 37 | 218 | 22 | 10 | 1 | 2 | 22 | 15 | 33 | 0 | 0 | .267/.321/.356 | .243 | .311 | 2.1 | 0.1 | 0.2 |
| 2011 | ARI | MLB | 38 | 55 | 8 | 3 | 0 | 2 | 10 | 5 | 9 | 0 | 0 | .224/.309/.408 | .226 | .237 | 0.3 | 0.3 | 0.0 |
| 2012 | ARI | MLB | 39 | 250 | 26 | 11 | 1 | 5 | 24 | 17 | 41 | 0 | 0 | .236/.293/.356 | .232 | .265 | -0.1 | 3B 1, SS -1 | 0.4 |

Blum and Melvin Mora spent the season vying to be Arizona's least productive 38-year-old third baseman. Mora edged out Blum, -0.6 to 0.0 WARP, but it wasn't a fair fight: Even though Mora was released in late June, he had more opportunities to make his case. Blum did the team a favor by hurting his knee in spring training, which allowed Ryan Roberts to claim the starting job. The knee eventually required surgery that delayed Blum's debut until mid-July, and seven games later, he broke his right pinkie while fielding a ground ball and disappeared till September. Blum might have done his best work for the Diamondbacks while he was on the DL, but he got the last laugh: Unlike Mora, he'll be back for another season of replacement-level play.

## Bobby Borchering    3B

Born: 10/25/1990 Age: 21
Bats: B Throws: R Height: 6' 4" Weight: 200
Breakout: 0% Improve: 6% Collapse: 5%
Attrition: 12% MLB: 19%

Comparables:
Chris Marrero, Tony Horton, Alberto Odreman

| YEAR | TEAM | LVL | AGE | PA | R | 2B | 3B | HR | RBI | BB | SO | SB | CS | AVG_OBP_SLG | TAv | BABIP | BRR | FRAA | WARP |
|------|------|-----|-----|-----|----|----|----|----|-----|----|----|----|----|--------------|------|-------|------|----------|------|
| 2009 | MSO | RK | 18 | 93 | 10 | 8 | 1 | 2 | 11 | 5 | 27 | 0 | 0 | .241/.290/.425 | .301 | .328 | -0.8 | -6 | 0.1 |
| 2010 | SBN | A | 19 | 588 | 74 | 31 | 2 | 15 | 74 | 54 | 128 | 1 | 1 | .270/.343/.423 | .278 | .331 | -3.6 | -16 | 0.6 |
| 2011 | VIS | A+ | 20 | 590 | 80 | 29 | 3 | 24 | 92 | 49 | 162 | 4 | 1 | .267/.332/.469 | .284 | .337 | -0.2 | -6.3 | 2.3 |
| 2012 | ARI | MLB | 21 | 250 | 24 | 10 | 1 | 7 | 26 | 12 | 76 | 0 | 0 | .213/.253/.352 | .215 | .277 | 0 | 3B -7, 1B -2 | -0.7 |

Borchering is still young for his league, but he's old enough to know the truth: Prospects at his position don't often post batting averages in the mid-.200s in the minors and live to tell the tale. Last season, the 2009 first-rounder went from being a third baseman who was often referred to as a "future first base type" to a player who actually saw more time at first than at third. That ratio is likely to grow even more lopsided in favor of first in the coming seasons, since Borchering lacks the quickness and strong arm that come in handy at the hot corner. The switch-hitter has a sweet swing and plenty of power, but unless he can make more contact or start walking twice as often, he won't unseat Paul Goldschmidt or distinguish himself from the legion of other corner infielders en route to Phoenix.

**Sean Burroughs** 3B
Born: **9/12/1980** Age: **31**
Bats: **L** Throws: **R** Height: **6' 3"** Weight: **200**
Breakout: **2%** Improve: **20%** Collapse: **11%**
Attrition: **21%** MLB: **69%**

| YEAR | TEAM | LVL | AGE | PA | R | 2B | 3B | HR | RBI | BB | SO | SB | CS | AVG/OBP/SLG | TAv | BABIP | BRR | FRAA | WARP |
|------|------|-----|-----|-----|----|----|----|----|-----|----|----|----|----|-------------|------|-------|------|------|------|
| 2011 | RNO | AAA | 30 | 110 | 19 | 11 | 2 | 2 | 25 | 7 | 8 | 0 | 2 | .412/.450/.618 | .329 | .435 | -1 | 0.5 | 1.0 |
| 2011 | ARI | MLB | 30 | 115 | 8 | 4 | 0 | 1 | 8 | 3 | 15 | 1 | 0 | .273/.289/.336 | .205 | .305 | -0.4 | 0 | -0.3 |
| 2012 | MIN | MLB | 31 | 250 | 28 | 13 | 2 | 3 | 26 | 12 | 34 | 2 | 1 | .276/.313/.388 | .250 | .307 | -0.2 | 3B 0 | 1.3 |

**Matt Davidson** 3B
Born: **3/26/1991** Age: **21**
Bats: **R** Throws: **R** Height: **6' 4"** Weight: **210**
Breakout: **0%** Improve: **3%** Collapse: **3%**
Attrition: **7%** MLB: **11%**

**Comparables:**
Thomas Neal, Jonathan Waltenbury, Jaime Ortiz

| YEAR | TEAM | LVL | AGE | PA | R | 2B | 3B | HR | RBI | BB | SO | SB | CS | AVG/OBP/SLG | TAv | BABIP | BRR | FRAA | WARP |
|------|------|-----|-----|-----|----|----|----|----|-----|----|-----|----|----|-------------|------|-------|------|------------|------|
| 2009 | YAK | A- | 18 | 299 | 29 | 15 | 0 | 2 | 28 | 21 | 75 | 0 | 2 | .241/.311/.319 | .227 | .325 | 0.4 | 8.1 | 0.6 |
| 2010 | SBN | A | 19 | 475 | 58 | 35 | 3 | 16 | 79 | 43 | 109 | 0 | 2 | .289/.374/.504 | .304 | .359 | -2.4 | 0.4 | 2.8 |
| 2010 | VIS | A+ | 19 | 84 | 6 | 1 | 0 | 2 | 11 | 12 | 25 | 0 | 0 | .169/.298/.268 | .204 | .227 | -1.2 | 0.6 | -0.4 |
| 2011 | VIS | A+ | 20 | 606 | 93 | 39 | 1 | 20 | 106 | 52 | 147 | 0 | 1 | .277/.348/.465 | .291 | .340 | -1.7 | -3.5 | 3.0 |
| 2012 | ARI | MLB | 21 | 250 | 23 | 11 | 0 | 5 | 23 | 14 | 74 | 0 | 0 | .206/.261/.329 | .211 | .274 | 0 | 3B 1, 1B -1 | -1.0 |

Davidson, a slightly better, slightly younger version of Bobby Borchering (who was selected 19 picks before him in the 2009 draft), experienced similar—albeit less severe—struggles to make contact at High-A last season. After spending 2010 trading off at the hot corner in South Bend, both played 135 games for Visalia split between the infield corners and DH. Since they appeared at the same positions for the same team, scouts had ample opportunity to make an informed comparison between the two, and most came away liking Davidson better, both for his bat and for his better chance of sticking at third thanks to a superior fielding percentage and a stronger arm. How they do at Double-A could be the real decider.

**Stephen Drew** SS
Born: **3/16/1983** Age: **29**
Bats: **L** Throws: **R** Height: **6' 2"** Weight: **185**
Breakout: **3%** Improve: **29%** Collapse: **7%**
Attrition: **19%** MLB: **94%**

**Comparables:**
Jimmy Rollins, Brendan Harris, John Valentin

| YEAR | TEAM | LVL | AGE | PA | R | 2B | 3B | HR | RBI | BB | SO | SB | CS | AVG/OBP/SLG | TAv | BABIP | BRR | FRAA | WARP |
|------|------|-----|-----|-----|----|----|----|----|-----|----|-----|----|----|-------------|------|-------|------|------|------|
| 2009 | ARI | MLB | 26 | 595 | 71 | 29 | 12 | 12 | 65 | 49 | 87 | 5 | 1 | .261/.320/.428 | .257 | .288 | 1.2 | 5.1 | 2.6 |
| 2010 | ARI | MLB | 27 | 633 | 83 | 33 | 12 | 15 | 61 | 62 | 108 | 10 | 5 | .278/.352/.458 | .288 | .321 | 2.5 | -2.2 | 4.4 |
| 2011 | ARI | MLB | 28 | 354 | 44 | 21 | 5 | 5 | 45 | 30 | 74 | 4 | 4 | .252/.317/.396 | .258 | .313 | 1.4 | -2.6 | 1.2 |
| 2012 | ARI | MLB | 29 | 388 | 48 | 21 | 6 | 9 | 49 | 31 | 67 | 4 | 2 | .265/.327/.440 | .270 | .301 | -0.3 | SS -3 | 2.4 |

Drew left the D-Backs in the lurch when he broke his ankle sliding into home plate on July 20 (to add insult to injury, he was out), but his season was already well on the way to disappointment after an age-27 career year. It's time to accept that Drew will never put together the monster season forecasted for him by scouts and statheads alike, but even reduced expectations leave room for a passable defender and an above-average hitter for whom roughly 10 other NL teams would gladly swap their shortstops. It would be a shame if Drew's early promise relegated him to the same land of the perpetually underappreciated where his big brother J.D. has been for the better part of a decade. October surgery for a sports hernia complicated his rehab from the ankle fracture and could put his status for Opening Day in doubt.

### Adam Eaton — CF

Born: 12/6/1988 Age: 23
Bats: L Throws: L Height: 5' 10'' Weight: 180
Breakout: 2% Improve: 40% Collapse: 9%
Attrition: 22% MLB: 72%

Comparables:
Ron Fairly, Oscar Gamble, Scott Lusader

| YEAR | TEAM | LVL | AGE | PA | R | 2B | 3B | HR | RBI | BB | SO | SB | CS | AVG/OBP/SLG | TAv | BABIP | BRR | FRAA | WARP |
|---|---|---|---|---|---|---|---|---|---|---|---|---|---|---|---|---|---|---|---|
| 2010 | MSO | RK | 21 | 282 | 48 | 14 | 4 | 7 | 37 | 35 | 44 | 20 | 8 | .385/.504/.575 | .386 | .457 | 0.9 | 6.2 | 4.8 |
| 2011 | VIS | A+ | 22 | 301 | 54 | 15 | 3 | 6 | 39 | 42 | 41 | 24 | 8 | .332/.455/.492 | .350 | .379 | 4.4 | 2.8 | 4.8 |
| 2011 | MOB | AA | 22 | 255 | 31 | 7 | 4 | 4 | 28 | 30 | 35 | 10 | 6 | .302/.409/.429 | .312 | .345 | -3.5 | 3 | 2.3 |
| 2012 | ARI | MLB | 23 | 250 | 28 | 9 | 2 | 4 | 23 | 22 | 50 | 9 | 4 | .250/.332/.362 | .252 | .302 | -0.3 | CF -1, RF 2 | 0.7 |

Eaton—not to be confused with the journeyman starter who went to his major-league grave a few years ago—has climbed quite a few prospect lists over the past two seasons by virtue of a .340/.456/.500 start to his pro career. As that line and his 5'9 frame suggest, he doesn't possess a lot of power, but he has an excellent eye and enough pop to keep pitchers honest. He walked more than he struck out at High-A last year, and after going Mobile at midseason, he continued to hit for a high average in the Arizona Fall League. With A.J. Pollock entrenched in center, Eaton switched to right in the Southern League. Since his glove profiles better in a corner, he has the makings of an excellent fourth outfielder or a scrappy second-division starter; a strong Triple-A season could vault him out of tweener territory to stay. Not bad for a 19th-round pick.

### Paul Goldschmidt — 1B

Born: 9/10/1987 Age: 24
Bats: R Throws: R Height: 6' 4'' Weight: 245
Breakout: 3% Improve: 25% Collapse: 26%
Attrition: 38% MLB: 83%

Comparables:
Carlos Pena, Hee-Seop Choi, Chris Carter

| YEAR | TEAM | LVL | AGE | PA | R | 2B | 3B | HR | RBI | BB | SO | SB | CS | AVG/OBP/SLG | TAv | BABIP | BRR | FRAA | WARP |
|---|---|---|---|---|---|---|---|---|---|---|---|---|---|---|---|---|---|---|---|
| 2009 | MSO | RK | 21 | 331 | 51 | 27 | 3 | 18 | 62 | 36 | 74 | 4 | 3 | .334/.414/.638 | .355 | .400 | -1 | 2.8 | 3.7 |
| 2010 | VIS | A+ | 22 | 599 | 102 | 42 | 3 | 35 | 108 | 57 | 161 | 5 | 1 | .314/.390/.606 | .336 | .395 | -2.5 | -5.4 | 5.0 |
| 2011 | MOB | AA | 23 | 457 | 84 | 21 | 3 | 30 | 94 | 82 | 92 | 9 | 3 | .306/.435/.626 | .361 | .331 | 4.6 | 4 | 6.3 |
| 2011 | ARI | MLB | 23 | 177 | 28 | 9 | 1 | 8 | 26 | 20 | 53 | 4 | 0 | .250/.333/.474 | .281 | .323 | 1.4 | -2.4 | 0.6 |
| 2012 | ARI | MLB | 24 | 268 | 34 | 12 | 1 | 13 | 37 | 27 | 78 | 2 | 1 | .244/.323/.470 | .277 | .300 | 0 | 1B -12, CF 0 | 1.4 |

The Snakes didn't quite strike gold as the calendar turned to August, but they did strike Goldschmidt, which was almost as good given that Chase Field held more Latino voters in favor of SB 1070 than first basemen who could hit last season. At the time of his promotion, Goldschmidt led the minors with 30 homers and ranked second with 82 walks. Not only was he on the verge of matching the power numbers he put up in a full 2010 season, but his plate discipline had made a marked improvement, as evidenced by a K:BB ratio that had improved to 1.12 after two years over 2.00. That performance helped him repeat as the organization's Player of the Year and likely would have given way to further fireworks had he not bypassed Triple-A, but it didn't fully translate to the major-league level, where Goldschmidt proved highly susceptible to strikeouts. That wasn't enough to keep him from being the best of a bad first-base bunch, but it didn't ease concerns about his long swing. However, roughly half of his strikeouts came in the first third of his plate appearances, so he may already have made some adjustments.

### Aaron Hill — 2B

Born: 3/21/1982 Age: 30
Bats: R Throws: R Height: 6' 0'' Weight: 195
Breakout: 1% Improve: 51% Collapse: 5%
Attrition: 9% MLB: 87%

Comparables:
Felix Mantilla, Orlando Hudson, Brandon Phillips

| YEAR | TEAM | LVL | AGE | PA | R | 2B | 3B | HR | RBI | BB | SO | SB | CS | AVG/OBP/SLG | TAv | BABIP | BRR | FRAA | WARP |
|---|---|---|---|---|---|---|---|---|---|---|---|---|---|---|---|---|---|---|---|
| 2009 | TOR | MLB | 27 | 734 | 103 | 37 | 0 | 36 | 108 | 42 | 98 | 6 | 2 | .286/.330/.499 | .288 | .288 | 1.5 | 9.1 | 5.1 |
| 2010 | TOR | MLB | 28 | 580 | 70 | 22 | 0 | 26 | 68 | 41 | 85 | 2 | 2 | .205/.271/.394 | .241 | .196 | -0.2 | 4.2 | 0.9 |
| 2011 | TOR | MLB | 29 | 429 | 38 | 15 | 1 | 6 | 45 | 23 | 53 | 16 | 3 | .225/.270/.313 | .217 | .242 | -1.4 | -5 | -1.5 |
| 2011 | ARI | MLB | 29 | 142 | 23 | 12 | 2 | 2 | 16 | 12 | 19 | 5 | 4 | .315/.386/.492 | .298 | .356 | 1.5 | 2.2 | 1.3 |
| 2012 | ARI | MLB | 30 | 539 | 63 | 29 | 2 | 18 | 67 | 34 | 83 | 15 | 6 | .255/.307/.427 | .260 | .271 | -0.4 | 2B 1 | 1.7 |

Hill has become something of a cipher after spending 2007-10 alternating seasons of roughly five wins with seasons in which he played near replacement level. That hot-and-cold pattern persisted into 2011, with a big improvement in 33 games after his August trade from Toronto. In this case, the classic "change of scenery" trade seemed to pay dividends, but the improvement was built upon an unsustainable BABIP. After Kevin Towers declined the infielder's $8 million options for 2012 and 2013, he explained, "I don't want to get too crazy about six weeks. There's a reason [the Blue Jays] moved him." However, the upside proved too tantalizing to ignore, and Towers eventually inked him to a two-year deal for $11 million. Judging by Hill's track record, it might not be long before his scenery changes again.

### Jason Kubel — RF

Born: 5/25/1982 Age: 30
Bats: L Throws: R Height: 6' 0'' Weight: 190
Breakout: 3% Improve: 37% Collapse: 3%
Attrition: 15% MLB: 90%

Comparables:
Terrmel Sledge, Johnny Callison, Matt Stairs

| YEAR | TEAM | LVL | AGE | PA | R | 2B | 3B | HR | RBI | BB | SO | SB | CS | AVG/OBP/SLG | TAv | BABIP | BRR | FRAA | WARP |
|---|---|---|---|---|---|---|---|---|---|---|---|---|---|---|---|---|---|---|---|
| 2009 | MIN | MLB | 27 | 578 | 73 | 35 | 2 | 28 | 103 | 56 | 106 | 1 | 1 | .300/.369/.539 | .311 | .327 | -0.6 | 1.3 | 3.9 |
| 2010 | MIN | MLB | 28 | 582 | 68 | 23 | 3 | 21 | 92 | 56 | 116 | 0 | 1 | .249/.323/.427 | .263 | .280 | -2.9 | -1.8 | 0.4 |
| 2011 | MIN | MLB | 29 | 401 | 37 | 21 | 1 | 12 | 58 | 32 | 86 | 1 | 1 | .273/.332/.434 | .273 | .326 | -2 | -2.2 | 0.8 |
| 2012 | ARI | MLB | 30 | 417 | 52 | 21 | 2 | 15 | 54 | 37 | 83 | 1 | 1 | .265/.332/.453 | .277 | .302 | -0.1 | RF -0, LF -0 | 1.5 |

After an off 2010, Kubel got off to a great start—.310/.355/.465 through the end of May—that seemed like the opening act of another season like his stellar 2009. Unfortunately, a sprained left foot cost him all of June and most of July; he hit just .229/.304/.398 the rest of the way and missed the season's final two weeks after re-aggravating the injury. Kubel wound up with essentially the same rate stats as in 2010, albeit with a higher batting average due to a 46-point spike in BABIP and a slight dip in his walk rate. You'd think the combination of his down season and his limitations in the field, on the bases, and against lefties (.239/.313/.365 career, compared to .282/.342/.490 against righties) would have conspired to keep his price down, but the Diamondbacks gave him a guaranteed $16 million over the next two seasons to replace a superior player—Gerardo Parra—in left.

**John McDonald** SS

Born: 9/24/1974 Age: 37
Bats: R Throws: R Height: 6' 0" Weight: 175
Breakout: 0% Improve: 25% Collapse: 5%
Attrition: 30% MLB: 62%

| YEAR | TEAM | LVL | AGE | PA | R | 2B | 3B | HR | RBI | BB | SO | SB | CS | AVG_OBP_SLG | TAv | BABIP | BRR | FRAA | WARP |
|---|---|---|---|---|---|---|---|---|---|---|---|---|---|---|---|---|---|---|---|
| 2009 | TOR | MLB | 34 | 156 | 18 | 7 | 0 | 4 | 13 | 1 | 18 | 0 | 2 | .258/.271/.384 | .236 | .269 | -1.4 | 0.4 | -0.1 |
| 2010 | TOR | MLB | 35 | 163 | 27 | 9 | 2 | 6 | 23 | 6 | 26 | 2 | 1 | .250/.273/.454 | .256 | .260 | 1.9 | -0.4 | 0.7 |
| 2011 | TOR | MLB | 36 | 182 | 19 | 8 | 1 | 2 | 20 | 8 | 18 | 2 | 4 | .250/.285/.345 | .236 | .267 | 0.8 | 4.6 | 0.8 |

not be enough to make up for his absent offense.

**Miguel Montero** C

Born: 7/9/1983 Age: 28
Bats: L Throws: R Height: 6' 0" Weight: 197
Breakout: 4% Improve: 22% Collapse: 8%
Attrition: 34% MLB: 91%

Comparables:
Dave Sax, Charlie O'Brien, Ryan Doumit

| YEAR | TEAM | LVL | AGE | PA | R | 2B | 3B | HR | RBI | BB | SO | SB | CS | AVG_OBP_SLG | TAv | BABIP | BRR | FRAA | WARP |
|---|---|---|---|---|---|---|---|---|---|---|---|---|---|---|---|---|---|---|---|
| 2009 | ARI | MLB | 25 | 470 | 61 | 30 | 0 | 16 | 59 | 38 | 78 | 1 | 2 | .294/.355/.478 | .283 | .327 | -0.4 | -2 | 2.8 |
| 2010 | ARI | MLB | 26 | 331 | 36 | 20 | 2 | 9 | 43 | 29 | 71 | 0 | 1 | .266/.332/.438 | .256 | .318 | -2.8 | 0.6 | 1.2 |
| 2011 | ARI | MLB | 27 | 553 | 65 | 36 | 1 | 18 | 86 | 47 | 97 | 1 | 1 | .282/.351/.469 | .279 | .317 | -2 | 2 | 3.8 |
| 2012 | ARI | MLB | 28 | 477 | 60 | 28 | 2 | 16 | 62 | 39 | 89 | 1 | 1 | .269/.335/.455 | .278 | .303 | -0.1 | C 1 | 3.1 |

The D-Backs made Montero their catcher of the future when they traded Chris Snyder to the Pirates in 2010. They might not have gotten the best possible return—D.J. Carrasco, Ryan Church, and Bobby Crosby are all either out of the game already or rapidly approaching retirement—but in light of Snyder's injury issues last season, it looks like they backed the right backstop. According to WARP, Montero was a top-five catcher in 2011, his first All-Star campaign, and that's without giving him full credit for his defense. Arizona's catcher cupboard is bare behind Montero, who won't turn 29 until July. It's time to start talking extension.

**Xavier Nady** 1B

Born: 11/14/1978 Age: 33
Bats: R Throws: R Height: 6' 6" Weight: 220
Breakout: 1% Improve: 22% Collapse: 5%
Attrition: 19% MLB: 64%

Comparables:
Jorge Toca, Dmitri Young, Ben Broussard

| YEAR | TEAM | LVL | AGE | PA | R | 2B | 3B | HR | RBI | BB | SO | SB | CS | AVG_OBP_SLG | TAv | BABIP | BRR | FRAA | WARP |
|---|---|---|---|---|---|---|---|---|---|---|---|---|---|---|---|---|---|---|---|
| 2009 | NYA | MLB | 30 | 29 | 4 | 4 | 0 | 0 | 2 | 1 | 6 | 0 | 0 | .286/.310/.429 | .229 | .364 | 0.6 | -0.1 | 0.0 |
| 2010 | CHN | MLB | 31 | 347 | 33 | 13 | 0 | 6 | 33 | 17 | 85 | 0 | 0 | .256/.306/.353 | .230 | .326 | 1.9 | -2.7 | -0.9 |
| 2011 | ARI | MLB | 32 | 223 | 26 | 11 | 0 | 4 | 35 | 10 | 46 | 2 | 0 | .248/.287/.359 | .239 | .294 | -0.3 | -1.7 | -0.4 |
| 2012 | ARI | MLB | 33 | 250 | 29 | 13 | 0 | 8 | 30 | 13 | 53 | 1 | 0 | .266/.315/.424 | .262 | .313 | 0 | 1B -2, RF -1 | 0.9 |

Diamondbacks first basemen combined for a .264 TAv last season, the 26th-best mark in the majors. A number of subpar first-sackers bore some blame, but none more than Nady, who brought up the rear at -2.7 VORP. As has been the case throughout his career, Nady was at his worst against righties, but in 2011, his worst (.248/.282/.307) was even worse than usual. His season came to an end on August 12, when the Mets' Dillon Gee—who throws just hard enough to hurt someone—broke his left hand with a fastball. Nady had already begun to give way to Paul Goldschmidt, so the fateful pitch really just put him out of his misery. As a below-average batter with a below-average glove, Nady's already had a surprisingly long major-league leash.

### Lyle Overbay — 1B

Born: 1/28/1977 Age: 35
Bats: L Throws: L Height: 6' 3" Weight: 215
Breakout: 2% Improve: 20% Collapse: 4%
Attrition: 29% MLB: 75%

**Comparables:**
Richie Hebner, Erubiel Durazo, Kevin Millar

| YEAR | TEAM | LVL | AGE | PA | R | 2B | 3B | HR | RBI | BB | SO | SB | CS | AVG_OBP_SLG | TAv | BABIP | BRR | FRAA | WARP |
|------|------|-----|-----|-----|----|----|----|----|-----|----|-----|----|----|-------------|------|-------|------|------|------|
| 2009 | TOR | MLB | 32 | 500 | 57 | 35 | 1 | 16 | 64 | 74 | 95 | 0 | 0 | .265/.372/.466 | .290 | .305 | -1.1 | 4.3 | 2.1 |
| 2010 | TOR | MLB | 33 | 607 | 75 | 37 | 2 | 20 | 67 | 67 | 131 | 1 | 0 | .243/.329/.433 | .273 | .285 | -2.1 | -0.9 | 1.0 |
| 2011 | ARI | MLB | 34 | 49 | 3 | 4 | 0 | 1 | 10 | 6 | 11 | 1 | 0 | .286/.388/.452 | .284 | .367 | 0.1 | 0.8 | 0.2 |
| 2011 | PIT | MLB | 34 | 391 | 40 | 17 | 1 | 8 | 37 | 36 | 77 | 1 | 1 | .227/.300/.349 | .232 | .269 | -1.5 | -3 | -0.9 |
| 2012 | ARI | MLB | 35 | 447 | 52 | 25 | 2 | 12 | 48 | 48 | 94 | 1 | 0 | .239/.323/.398 | .259 | .283 | -0.1 | 1B 0 | 0.6 |

Arizona signed Overbay in mid-August to be a lefty caddy for Goldschmidt. That was eight days after Overbay had been released by the Pirates to clear roster room for Derrek Lee. In Pittsburgh, Overbay's $5 million salary and poor performance had earned him the moniker "Lyle Overpay." Generally, if you can't hit enough to hold on to your job with a perennial loser on the fringes of the playoff race, you won't be of much use to a frontrunner, but Overbay served the Snakes well enough in his brief time with the team to convince Towers to bring him back for more in 2012. You know how people say you really have to mash to be considered a first-base prospect? Overbay hit .342/.411/.531 in five minor-league seasons, and he's barely made the grade.

### Chris Owings — SS

Born: 8/12/1991 Age: 20
Bats: R Throws: R Height: 5' 10" Weight: 175
Breakout: 0% Improve: 4% Collapse: 1%
Attrition: 5% MLB: 9%

**Comparables:**
Garabez Rosa, Daniel Santana, Hector Gomez

| YEAR | TEAM | LVL | AGE | PA | R | 2B | 3B | HR | RBI | BB | SO | SB | CS | AVG_OBP_SLG | TAv | BABIP | BRR | FRAA | WARP |
|------|------|-----|-----|-----|----|----|----|----|-----|----|-----|----|----|-------------|------|-------|------|---------|------|
| 2009 | MSO | RK | 17 | 111 | 20 | 5 | 1 | 2 | 10 | 3 | 25 | 3 | 0 | .306/.324/.426 | .300 | .383 | 1.8 | 0.1 | 1.3 |
| 2010 | SBN | A | 18 | 271 | 39 | 19 | 2 | 5 | 28 | 9 | 50 | 1 | 3 | .298/.325/.447 | .272 | .351 | -0.2 | 2.7 | 1.8 |
| 2011 | VIS | A+ | 19 | 555 | 67 | 29 | 6 | 11 | 50 | 15 | 130 | 10 | 4 | .246/.274/.388 | .239 | .305 | -1.2 | 12.6 | 2.0 |
| 2012 | ARI | MLB | 20 | 250 | 21 | 11 | 1 | 3 | 23 | 2 | 68 | 2 | 1 | .213/.222/.310 | .186 | .275 | -0.1 | SS 11, LF -0 | -1.6 |

Owings probably wasn't the best hitter with that surname in the Arizona organization last season—and the other Owings was a pitcher. Chris struck out in 23.4 percent of his plate appearances for Visalia—more often than any shortstop in the majors—and his 8.7 K:BB ratio was easily the worst among players with at least 500 PA in High-A (or Double-A or Triple-A, for that matter). In an even more disturbing development for a player whose future depends on his glove, Owings committed the most errors in the California League. He's still young for his level, but his struggles in the field could make him a second baseman down the road. Unfortunately for him, there are few roads for second basemen with sub-.300 OBPs that don't end in early retirement.

### Gerardo Parra — LF

Born: 5/6/1987 Age: 25
Bats: L Throws: L Height: 6' 0" Weight: 197
Breakout: 5% Improve: 36% Collapse: 2%
Attrition: 15% MLB: 69%

**Comparables:**
Andre Ethier, Keith Smith, Chris Pettit

| YEAR | TEAM | LVL | AGE | PA | R | 2B | 3B | HR | RBI | BB | SO | SB | CS | AVG_OBP_SLG | TAv | BABIP | BRR | FRAA | WARP |
|------|------|-----|-----|-----|----|----|----|----|-----|----|-----|----|----|-------------|------|-------|------|---------|------|
| 2009 | MOB | AA | 22 | 130 | 23 | 3 | 1 | 3 | 12 | 22 | 13 | 7 | 4 | .361/.469/.491 | .340 | .391 | 0 | 0.2 | 1.3 |
| 2009 | ARI | MLB | 22 | 491 | 59 | 21 | 8 | 5 | 60 | 25 | 89 | 5 | 7 | .290/.324/.404 | .242 | .346 | 1.7 | -3.6 | -0.2 |
| 2010 | ARI | MLB | 23 | 393 | 31 | 19 | 6 | 3 | 30 | 23 | 76 | 1 | 0 | .261/.308/.371 | .234 | .322 | 1.1 | 8 | 0.9 |
| 2011 | ARI | MLB | 24 | 493 | 55 | 20 | 8 | 8 | 46 | 43 | 82 | 15 | 1 | .292/.357/.427 | .275 | .342 | 0.8 | 14.9 | 3.5 |
| 2012 | ARI | MLB | 25 | 448 | 54 | 21 | 7 | 7 | 52 | 30 | 81 | 8 | 3 | .282/.334/.421 | .265 | .332 | -0.1 | LF 7, RF 0 | 1.3 |

Just as it seemed that Parra's top-prospect past would come to fourth-outfielder fruition, he put it all together. While he might be stretched in center field, both advanced metrics and Gold Glove voters agree that he's a standout in left. Parra's not all about range, though: He showed a strong arm as well. His offensive skills improved to the point that he's not solely reliant upon his defense to make him an everyday player, as improved plate discipline translated into gains in his walk rate and isolated power that put his overall performance at the plate slightly above the level of the average NL left fielder's. As if determined to demonstrate that there were no weak points to his game, he also stole 15 bases in 16 attempts. As he enters his age-25 season, he still has room to grow, but he's already one of the NL's most underappreciated players—even by his own team, which platooned him with Collin Cowgill down the stretch despite his contributions beyond the batter's box and reverse splits in the past two seasons, then signed Jason Kubel to replace him in December.

### A.J. Pollock — CF

Born: 12/5/1987 Age: 24
Bats: R Throws: R Height: 6' 2" Weight: 205
Breakout: 6% Improve: 33% Collapse: 8%
Attrition: 28% MLB: 65%

**Comparables:**
Dave Sappelt, Clay Timpner, Brandon Guyer

| YEAR | TEAM | LVL | AGE | PA | R | 2B | 3B | HR | RBI | BB | SO | SB | CS | AVG_OBP_SLG | TAv | BABIP | BRR | FRAA | WARP |
|------|------|-----|-----|-----|-----|----|----|----|-----|----|----|----|----|-------------|------|-------|------|---------|------|
| 2009 | SBN | A | 21 | 277 | 36 | 12 | 3 | 3 | 22 | 16 | 36 | 10 | 4 | .271/.320/.376 | .273 | .304 | 2.1 | 10.3 | 2.6 |
| 2011 | MOB | AA | 23 | 608 | 103 | 41 | 5 | 8 | 73 | 44 | 86 | 36 | 7 | .307/.357/.444 | .289 | .346 | 1 | -1.5 | 2.9 |
| 2012 | ARI | MLB | 24 | 250 | 26 | 12 | 1 | 3 | 25 | 11 | 47 | 9 | 2 | .251/.287/.358 | .230 | .297 | 0.2 | CF -6, RF 0 | 0.0 |

Look up "tweener" in the dictionary, and—well, okay, you probably won't find a picture of Pollock peering out at you, unless the editor had a large art budget and a keen awareness of Double-A prospects. Still, "tweener" is the term most often associated with Pollock, whose defense in center is still seen as fringy and whose bat isn't quite big enough for a corner. He proved that he wouldn't be hampered by any lingering effects of the elbow fracture that cost him all of 2010, upping his average from its 2009 level and stealing bases at an 84 percent clip. However, unless the D-Backs think he projects to replace Chris Young in center, he might be of more value to them as trade bait.

**Ryan Roberts**     **3B**

Born: **9/19/1980** Age: **31**
Bats: **R** Throws: **R** Height: **6' 0"** Weight: **190**
Breakout: **1%** Improve: **45%** Collapse: **8%**
Attrition: **10%** MLB: **83%**

Comparables:
Rance Mulliniks, Graig Nettles, Robin Ventura

| YEAR | TEAM | LVL | AGE | PA | R | 2B | 3B | HR | RBI | BB | SO | SB | CS | AVG_OBP_SLG | TAv | BABIP | BRR | FRAA | WARP |
|------|------|-----|-----|-----|----|----|----|----|-----|----|----|----|----|-------------|-----|-------|------|----------|------|
| 2009 | ARI | MLB | 28 | 351 | 41 | 17 | 2 | 7 | 25 | 40 | 55 | 7 | 3 | .279/.367/.416 | .269 | .320 | 0.6 | -3 | 0.8 |
| 2010 | RNO | AAA | 29 | 412 | 62 | 25 | 2 | 11 | 55 | 56 | 73 | 16 | 6 | .265/.369/.444 | .272 | .307 | 1.3 | 5.1 | 1.9 |
| 2010 | ARI | MLB | 29 | 71 | 8 | 4 | 0 | 2 | 9 | 3 | 17 | 0 | 0 | .197/.229/.348 | .206 | .229 | -0.3 | -0.3 | -0.3 |
| 2011 | ARI | MLB | 30 | 555 | 86 | 25 | 2 | 19 | 65 | 66 | 98 | 18 | 9 | .249/.341/.427 | .277 | .275 | 2.6 | 1.9 | 3.1 |
| 2012 | ARI | MLB | 31 | 474 | 56 | 22 | 3 | 12 | 51 | 52 | 92 | 13 | 5 | .249/.335/.404 | .264 | .289 | -0.4 | 3B -0, 2B 1 | 2.0 |

A mid-March injury to Geoff Blum gave Roberts a starting gig, and his April ensured that he'd

**Justin Upton**     **RF**

Born: **8/25/1987** Age: **24**
Bats: **R** Throws: **R** Height: **6' 4"** Weight: **205**
Breakout: **0%** Improve: **25%** Collapse: **3%**
Attrition: **31%** MLB: **87%**

Comparables:
Gene Hiser, Carlos Quintana, Jayson Werth

| YEAR | TEAM | LVL | AGE | PA | R | 2B | 3B | HR | RBI | BB | SO | SB | CS | AVG_OBP_SLG | TAv | BABIP | BRR | FRAA | WARP |
|------|------|-----|-----|-----|-----|----|----|----|-----|----|-----|----|----|-------------|-----|-------|------|------|------|
| 2009 | ARI | MLB | 21 | 588 | 84 | 30 | 7 | 26 | 86 | 55 | 137 | 20 | 5 | .300/.366/.532 | .297 | .360 | -1.3 | 10.3 | 4.5 |
| 2010 | ARI | MLB | 22 | 571 | 73 | 27 | 3 | 17 | 69 | 64 | 152 | 18 | 8 | .273/.356/.442 | .275 | .354 | -0.8 | 2.6 | 1.8 |
| 2011 | ARI | MLB | 23 | 674 | 105 | 39 | 5 | 31 | 88 | 59 | 126 | 21 | 9 | .289/.369/.529 | .311 | .319 | 2.3 | 4.3 | 5.2 |
| 2012 | ARI | MLB | 24 | 613 | 83 | 31 | 7 | 24 | 88 | 58 | 147 | 17 | 7 | .276/.353/.493 | .296 | .333 | -0.7 | RF 3 | 3.4 |

After racking up 4.5 WARP at age 21 in 2009, Upton, whose scouting reports and draft position supported the stats, seemed assured of a smooth, Griffey-like rise to stardom. But he hit an unexpected speed bump in 2010, as his strikeout rate rose and his isolated power fell by over 25 percent, prompting the D-Backs to shop him around over the winter. Another season like that and Upton might have been viewed as a partial disappointment like his brother B.J. Instead, he bounced back and then some, hitting more homers while cutting down on his Ks—two trends that rarely occur in tandem. Not only that, but his play in the field earned him his first Fielding Bible Award. At age 24 and with a nearly five-win season under his belt, it's safe to assume he's off the market.

**Chris Young**     **CF**

Born: **9/5/1983** Age: **28**
Bats: **R** Throws: **R** Height: **6' 3"** Weight: **180**
Breakout: **0%** Improve: **41%** Collapse: **1%**
Attrition: **7%** MLB: **93%**

Comparables:
Carlos Beltran, Merv Rettenmund, Curtis Granderson

| YEAR | TEAM | LVL | AGE | PA | R | 2B | 3B | HR | RBI | BB | SO | SB | CS | AVG_OBP_SLG | TAv | BABIP | BRR | FRAA | WARP |
|------|------|-----|-----|-----|----|----|----|----|-----|----|-----|----|----|-------------|-----|-------|------|------|------|
| 2009 | RNO | AAA | 25 | 63 | 17 | 5 | 1 | 3 | 9 | 9 | 13 | 2 | 2 | .370/.460/.667 | .350 | .447 | -0.3 | -1.8 | 0.6 |
| 2009 | ARI | MLB | 25 | 501 | 54 | 28 | 4 | 15 | 42 | 59 | 133 | 11 | 4 | .212/.311/.400 | .243 | .268 | 2.8 | -5.5 | 0.2 |
| 2010 | ARI | MLB | 26 | 664 | 94 | 33 | 0 | 27 | 91 | 74 | 145 | 28 | 7 | .257/.341/.452 | .279 | .296 | 2.7 | 4.7 | 4.1 |
| 2011 | ARI | MLB | 27 | 659 | 89 | 38 | 3 | 20 | 71 | 80 | 139 | 22 | 9 | .236/.331/.420 | .273 | .275 | 5.3 | -5.9 | 2.6 |
| 2012 | ARI | MLB | 28 | 620 | 76 | 33 | 4 | 23 | 80 | 62 | 145 | 19 | 7 | .243/.322/.445 | .270 | .285 | -0.3 | CF -1 | 2.6 |

Is Young a good center fielder, a poor one, or one who fluctuates from year to year? His FRAA has alternated between positive and negative numbers in each of his six major-league seasons, but he was a Gold Glove finalist last season and routinely makes spectacular plays in center. He's also settled in as a comfortably above-average hitter, cutting down on his strikeouts in three straight seasons. Young hits for low averages, but it's not because of his Ks: Despite his speed, he's a low-BABIP hitter because of his tendency to get under the ball. The right-handed hitter has popped up 16.9 percent of his batted balls since 2009, by far the highest rate among players with at least 1500 plate appearances over that span. Young's speed makes him good at many things, but beating out infield flies isn't one of them.

## PITCHERS

### Craig Breslow

Born: 8/8/1980 Age: 31
Bats: L Throws: L Height: 6' 2" Weight: 180
Breakout: 8% Improve: 47% Collapse: 30%
Attrition: 10% MLB: 92%

Comparables:
Dave Righetti, Sid Fernandez, Ken Dayley

| YEAR | TEAM | LVL | AGE | W | L | SV | G | GS | IP | H | HR | BB | SO | EqBB9 | EqSO9 | GB% | BABIP | WHIP | ERA | FIP | FRA | WARP |
|------|------|-----|-----|---|---|----|----|----|------|-----|----|----|----|-------|-------|-----|-------|------|------|------|------|------|
| 2009 | MIN | MLB | 28 | 1 | 2 | 0 | 17 | 0 | 14¹ | 11 | 3 | 11 | 11 | 6.9 | 6.9 | 34% | .222 | 1.53 | 6.28 | 6.84 | 7.31 | -0.2 |
| 2009 | OAK | MLB | 28 | 7 | 5 | 0 | 60 | 0 | 55¹ | 37 | 5 | 18 | 44 | 2.9 | 7.2 | 33% | .219 | 0.99 | 2.60 | 3.81 | 4.60 | 0.5 |
| 2010 | OAK | MLB | 29 | 4 | 4 | 5 | 75 | 0 | 74² | 53 | 9 | 29 | 71 | 3.5 | 8.6 | 31% | .228 | 1.10 | 3.01 | 3.88 | 4.06 | 0.6 |
| 2011 | OAK | MLB | 30 | 0 | 2 | 0 | 67 | 0 | 59¹ | 69 | 4 | 21 | 44 | 3.2 | 6.7 | 40% | .348 | 1.52 | 3.79 | 3.62 | 4.48 | 0.3 |
| 2012 | ARI | MLB | 31 | 3 | 1 | 1 | 62 | 0 | 58² | 50 | 6 | 21 | 48 | 3.2 | 7.3 | 40% | .287 | 1.22 | 3.68 | 3.97 | 4.00 | 0.8 |

Breslow, an independent league discovery during Towers' tenure in San Diego, has described himself as a "right-handed left-hander", by which he means that he's more effective against opposite-handed hitters, a contention borne out by his platoon splits. Last year the split was particularly extreme, as he held righties to a .263 TAv while allowing a lofty .348 figure to southpaws, but in most seasons it's freed his managers to use him against multiple batters. After 279 innings, his career FIP is over three quarters of a run higher than his 3.06 career ERA. What he'll be worth to the Diamondbacks, who acquired him in the Trevor Cahill deal, depends on whether he can continue to be a low-BABIP guy. One thing the cerebral Yale biochem major probably can't do is keep his home-run rate as low as it was last season: Even after curbing his fly-ball tendencies to some extent, he owns the 20th-highest fly-ball percentage among pitchers with at least 250 IP since 2008, which won't play as well in Chase Field as it did in the Coliseum.

### Charles Brewer

Born: 4/7/1988 Age: 24
Bats: R Throws: R Height: 6' 5" Weight: 205
Breakout: 34% Improve: 61% Collapse: 17%
Attrition: 18% MLB: 89%

Comparables:
Fernando Hernandez, Vicente Padilla, Homer Bailey

| YEAR | TEAM | LVL | AGE | W | L | SV | G | GS | IP | H | HR | BB | SO | EqBB9 | EqSO9 | GB% | BABIP | WHIP | ERA | FIP | FRA | WARP |
|------|------|-----|-----|---|---|----|----|----|------|-----|----|----|----|-------|-------|-----|-------|------|------|------|------|------|
| 2009 | MSO | RK | 21 | 7 | 4 | 0 | 17 | 7 | 54² | 55 | 5 | 18 | 71 | 2.5 | 10.0 | 51% | .299 | 1.06 | 2.47 | 3.78 | 4.58 | 2.2 |
| 2010 | SBN | A | 22 | 4 | 5 | 0 | 13 | 13 | 69 | 50 | 3 | 19 | 66 | 2.6 | 10.2 | 47% | .288 | 1.09 | 1.83 | 3.32 | 3.55 | 1.3 |
| 2010 | VIS | A+ | 22 | 7 | 3 | 0 | 14 | 14 | 81² | 71 | 5 | 13 | 73 | 1.7 | 8.3 | 50% | .306 | 1.09 | 2.97 | 3.45 | 4.29 | 0.9 |
| 2011 | MOB | AA | 23 | 1 | 1 | 0 | 11 | 11 | 52¹ | 51 | 2 | 22 | 53 | 3.3 | 8.3 | 45% | .316 | 1.28 | 2.58 | 3.15 | 3.90 | 1.0 |
| 2012 | ARI | MLB | 24 | 1 | 2 | 0 | 5 | 5 | 25² | 25 | 3 | 10 | 17 | 3.6 | 6.1 | 45% | .304 | 1.39 | 4.81 | 4.57 | 5.22 | 0.0 |

The right-handed starter's stat line survived the dreaded Double-A jump intact, but his body didn't, as his season was interrupted first by a concussion and then by a line drive that broke his hand in June. Brewer made up some of those lost innings and worked on a cutter in the Arizona Fall League, and he could contend for a rotation spot at some point next season, but all the work ethic in the world might not help him overtake the better pitching prospects ahead of him on the organizational depth chart.

### Trevor Cahill

Born: 3/1/1988 Age: 24
Bats: R Throws: R Height: 6' 4" Weight: 210
Breakout: 27% Improve: 52% Collapse: 20%
Attrition: 11% MLB: 92%

Comparables:
Steve Hargan, Storm Davis, Milt Pappas

| YEAR | TEAM | LVL | AGE | W | L | SV | G | GS | IP | H | HR | BB | SO | EqBB9 | EqSO9 | GB% | BABIP | WHIP | ERA | FIP | FRA | WARP |
|------|------|-----|-----|----|----|----|----|----|------|-----|----|----|-----|-------|-------|-----|-------|------|------|------|------|------|
| 2009 | OAK | MLB | 21 | 10 | 13 | 0 | 32 | 32 | 178² | 185 | 27 | 72 | 90 | 3.6 | 4.5 | 49% | .274 | 1.44 | 4.63 | 5.38 | 6.19 | -0.5 |
| 2010 | OAK | MLB | 22 | 18 | 8 | 0 | 30 | 30 | 196² | 155 | 19 | 63 | 118 | 2.9 | 5.4 | 57% | .237 | 1.11 | 2.97 | 4.16 | 4.52 | 2.1 |
| 2011 | OAK | MLB | 23 | 12 | 14 | 0 | 34 | 34 | 207² | 214 | 19 | 82 | 147 | 3.6 | 6.4 | 57% | .306 | 1.43 | 4.16 | 4.14 | 4.79 | 0.5 |
| 2012 | ARI | MLB | 24 | 12 | 10 | 0 | 31 | 31 | 194 | 172 | 19 | 68 | 124 | 3.2 | 5.7 | 55% | .281 | 1.24 | 3.88 | 4.25 | 4.22 | 2.3 |

What a difference a BABIP makes. Cahill posted FIPs just .02 runs apart in 2010 and 2011, but his ERA rose well over a run last season—to match his 2010 FIP perfectly—thanks to the most predictable BABIP correction in baseball. When he's not enjoying unusually good fortune on balls in play, Cahill is no better than a league-average innings muncher, but he's just embarking on his age-24 season and won't become overly expensive till 2015. Although he misses more bats than some pitch-to-contact types, he recorded the majors' sixth-highest groundball rate last season, which should help him survive the transition to a less forgiving park after joining the D-Backs' predominantly fly-ball-oriented staff in a December swap that sent Jarrod Parker to Oakland.

### Josh Collmenter

Born: 2/7/1986 Age: 26
Bats: R Throws: R Height: 6' 3" Weight: 235
Breakout: 22% Improve: 60% Collapse: 20%
Attrition: 9% MLB: 88%

Comparables:
Pat Jarvis, Joel Pineiro, Joe Blanton

| YEAR | TEAM | LVL | AGE | W | L | SV | G | GS | IP | H | HR | BB | SO | EqBB9 | EqSO9 | GB% | BABIP | WHIP | ERA | FIP | FRA | WARP |
|------|------|-----|-----|----|----|----|----|----|------|-----|----|----|-----|-------|-------|-----|-------|------|------|------|------|------|
| 2011 | ARI | MLB | 25 | 10 | 10 | 0 | 31 | 24 | 154¹ | 137 | 17 | 28 | 100 | 1.6 | 5.8 | 35% | .260 | 1.07 | 3.38 | 3.77 | 3.63 | 2.5 |
| 2012 | ARI | MLB | 26 | 7 | 7 | 0 | 19 | 19 | 113² | 110 | 13 | 37 | 69 | 2.9 | 5.5 | 40% | .288 | 1.29 | 4.25 | 4.45 | 4.62 | 0.8 |

First, the good news: A year after posting a near-6.00 ERA in the PCL, Collmenter spent all but one start of his season in the majors, finishing with a better-than-average ERA and the third-highest WARP among rookie pitchers. That—plus the successful showing in the Arizona Fall League that preceded it—would've qualified as a successful debut for any player, let alone one who wasn't well-regarded by prospect hounds, didn't make the Opening Day roster, and started out in the bullpen once he did get called up. The bad news is that Collmenter is essentially the same pitcher who struggled in Triple-A, which means he's not the safest bet to repeat his first-season heroics. Collmenter has a quirky delivery with an unorthodox release point, the sort of skill that beats hitters like gangbusters the first time they see it but lacks the staying power of, say, a 90-mph fastball (his barely averaged 87). Only Roy Halladay and Cliff Lee had better walk rates among NL pitchers with at least 150 innings, but that stinginess with free passes was out of character for Collmenter, and he'll be in trouble if his control regresses. A mustache can take you only so far.

### Patrick Corbin
Born: 7/19/1989 Age: 22
Bats: L Throws: L Height: 6' 4" Weight: 165
Breakout: 26% Improve: 39% Collapse: 12%
Attrition: 8% MLB: 85%

| YEAR | TEAM | LVL | AGE | W | L | SV | G | GS | IP | H | HR | BB | SO | EqBB9 | EqSO9 | GB% | BABIP | WHIP | ERA | FIP | FRA | WARP |
|------|------|-----|-----|---|---|----|----|----|-----|----|----|----|----|-------|-------|-----|-------|------|------|------|------|------|
| 2009 | ORM | RK | 19 | 4 | 2 | 0 | 13 | 12 | 46¹ | 63 | 6 | 13 | 49 | 2.1 | 8.9 | 50% | .341 | 1.51 | 5.05 | 4.33 | 5.81 | 0.5 |
| 2010 | CDR | A | 20 | 8 | 0 | 0 | 9 | 9 | 58¹ | 46 | 2 | 8 | 41 | 1.5 | 6.5 | 52% | .291 | 1.06 | 3.86 | 3.40 | 4.45 | 0.5 |
| 2010 | VIS | A+ | 20 | 0 | 1 | 0 | 8 | 8 | 26 | 17 | 1 | 9 | 29 | 3.1 | 10.4 | 50% | .291 | 1.00 | 1.38 | 3.13 | 2.69 | 0.8 |

part from the pitch-to-contact philosophy he preached, but his walk rate improved enough to keep him out of trouble. Corbin could still add some speed to a sinking fastball that sits around 90 and gets groundballs, and his slider is already effective enough to have helped him strike out a third of the southpaws he faced last season.

### Sam Demel
Born: 10/23/1985 Age: 26
Bats: R Throws: R Height: 6' 1" Weight: 215
Breakout: 14% Improve: 50% Collapse: 18%
Attrition: 27% MLB: 91%

Comparables:
Boone Logan, Yhency Brazoban, Roberto Novoa

| YEAR | TEAM | LVL | AGE | W | L | SV | G | GS | IP | H | HR | BB | SO | EqBB9 | EqSO9 | GB% | BABIP | WHIP | ERA | FIP | FRA | WARP |
|------|------|-----|-----|---|---|----|----|----|-----|----|----|----|----|-------|-------|-----|-------|------|------|------|------|------|
| 2009 | MID | AA | 23 | 0 | 2 | 11 | 27 | 0 | 29¹ | 23 | 1 | 9 | 26 | 2.8 | 8.0 | 57% | .265 | 1.09 | 0.61 | 2.83 | 3.95 | 0.5 |
| 2009 | SAC | AAA | 23 | 2 | 3 | 3 | 28 | 0 | 32¹ | 30 | 1 | 21 | 37 | 5.9 | 9.2 | 49% | .309 | 1.49 | 3.62 | 3.61 | 2.32 | 1.3 |
| 2010 | SAC | AAA | 24 | 2 | 0 | 6 | 22 | 0 | 28² | 16 | 1 | 6 | 18 | 2.8 | 8.8 | 53% | .268 | 1.08 | 1.25 | 3.88 | 4.04 | 0.3 |
| 2010 | ARI | MLB | 24 | 2 | 1 | 2 | 37 | 0 | 37 | 42 | 5 | 12 | 33 | 2.9 | 8.0 | 53% | .325 | 1.46 | 5.35 | 4.13 | 5.69 | -0.2 |
| 2011 | ARI | MLB | 25 | 2 | 2 | 0 | 34 | 0 | 25² | 31 | 4 | 13 | 15 | 4.6 | 5.3 | 59% | .329 | 1.71 | 4.21 | 5.60 | 6.91 | -0.6 |
| *2012* | *ARI* | *MLB* | *26* | *1* | *1* | *0* | *29* | *0* | *28²* | *27* | *3* | *12* | *23* | *3.8* | *7.1* | *53%* | *.308* | *1.38* | *4.69* | *4.22* | *5.10* | *0.0* |

Demel's 2011 season was a step back from his 2010 in more ways than one. Since his 2010 wasn't impressive to begin with, that step took him back to Triple-A. In 25 2/3 innings interspersed with a stint on the DL for shoulder tendinitis, a rehab assignment in Reno, and a subsequent demotion, Demel's K:BB ratio was less than half of what it had been the season before, lefties tattooed him to the tune of a .379/.500/.552 line, and his fastball was 3 mph slower. Another step in the same direction might take him off the 40-man roster.

### Zach Duke
Born: 4/19/1983 Age: 29
Bats: L Throws: L Height: 6' 3" Weight: 210
Breakout: 22% Improve: 61% Collapse: 18%
Attrition: 16% MLB: 78%

Comparables:
Mike Maroth, Carlos Perez, Butch Henry

| YEAR | TEAM | LVL | AGE | W | L | SV | G | GS | IP | H | HR | BB | SO | EqBB9 | EqSO9 | GB% | BABIP | WHIP | ERA | FIP | FRA | WARP |
|------|------|-----|-----|----|----|----|----|----|-----|-----|----|----|-----|-------|-------|-----|-------|------|------|------|------|------|
| 2009 | PIT | MLB | 26 | 11 | 16 | 0 | 32 | 32 | 213 | 231 | 23 | 49 | 106 | 2.1 | 4.5 | 50% | .301 | 1.31 | 4.06 | 4.20 | 5.03 | 1.4 |
| 2010 | PIT | MLB | 27 | 8 | 15 | 0 | 29 | 29 | 159 | 212 | 25 | 51 | 96 | 2.9 | 5.4 | 49% | .343 | 1.65 | 5.72 | 4.98 | 5.28 | -0.1 |
| 2011 | ARI | MLB | 28 | 3 | 4 | 1 | 21 | 9 | 76² | 101 | 6 | 19 | 32 | 2.2 | 3.8 | 50% | .343 | 1.57 | 4.93 | 3.96 | 4.54 | 0.7 |
| *2012* | *ARI* | *MLB* | *29* | *4* | *6* | *0* | *18* | *14* | *83* | *100* | *10* | *18* | *33* | *2.0* | *3.5* | *50%* | *.325* | *1.43* | *5.47* | *4.63* | *5.95* | *-0.5* |

First impressions are powerful. Duke is the equivalent of the guy who wears a snappy suit to an interview and lands a job, only to spend the next several years taking two-hour lunch breaks, using his phone for personal calls, and stealing paper from the printer. It's hard to say how much Duke's fluky 14-start debut in 2005 has to do with the chances he's gotten since then—he is a lefty, after all—but among hurlers with at least 900 innings pitched over the intervening six seasons, only Aaron Cook has had a lower strikeout rate than Duke's 4.5 per nine. A line drive fractured Duke's hand in mid-March, keeping him out until late May, but once he did return, both his fastball velocity (86.5) and strikeout rate (3.8 per nine) plummeted, leaving him too dependent on his decent control and moderate groundball ability to get him out of trouble. In mid-July, he became a reliever, posting an improved ERA but an even sorrier strikeout rate. If he doesn't stick in the bullpen, he won't like what comes next.

### Barry Enright

Born: 3/30/1986 Age: 26
Bats: R Throws: R Height: 6' 4" Weight: 220
Breakout: 24% Improve: 55% Collapse: 16%
Attrition: 27% MLB: 83%

Comparables:
Rich Bordi, Larry Christenson, Jackson Todd

| YEAR | TEAM | LVL | AGE | W | L | SV | G | GS | IP | H | HR | BB | SO | EqBB9 | EqSO9 | GB% | BABIP | WHIP | ERA | FIP | FRA | WARP |
|---|---|---|---|---|---|---|---|---|---|---|---|---|---|---|---|---|---|---|---|---|---|---|
| 2009 | MOB | AA | 23 | 10 | 9 | 0 | 27 | 27 | 156 | 171 | 16 | 37 | 103 | 2.1 | 5.9 | 44% | .316 | 1.33 | 3.98 | 3.90 | 4.46 | 2.9 |
| 2010 | MOB | AA | 24 | 4 | 1 | 0 | 14 | 14 | 93² | 46 | 6 | 12 | 50 | 1.4 | 8.0 | 41% | .253 | 1.02 | 2.88 | 3.86 | 3.77 | 2.1 |
| 2010 | ARI | MLB | 24 | 6 | 7 | 0 | 17 | 17 | 99 | 97 | 20 | 29 | 49 | 2.6 | 4.5 | 37% | .254 | 1.27 | 3.91 | 5.65 | 5.09 | 0.8 |
| 2011 | RNO | AAA | 25 | 9 | 5 | 0 | 21 | 21 | 122² | 133 | 21 | 43 | 89 | 3.1 | 6.3 | 36% | .291 | 1.38 | 5.21 | 5.68 | 5.43 | 1.7 |
| 2011 | ARI | MLB | 25 | 1 | 4 | 0 | 7 | 7 | 37² | 50 | 11 | 15 | 21 | 3.6 | 5.0 | 40% | .315 | 1.73 | 7.41 | 6.95 | 6.90 | -0.5 |
| 2012 | ARI | MLB | 26 | 4 | 6 | 0 | 14 | 14 | 82 | 89 | 14 | 24 | 43 | 2.6 | 4.8 | 40% | .299 | 1.38 | 5.38 | 5.25 | 5.84 | -0.5 |

The honeymoon period lasted six starts. After that, Enright's lousy 2011 took precedence over his superficially successful 2010, and he found himself in Reno to stay, save for a lone shellacking in a mid-July spot start. The fly-baller suffered from the same gopher-itis that afflicted him in 2010, allowing 1.7 home runs per nine innings across two levels, and this time he didn't have the BABIP luck to survive the barrage. He did successfully live-tweet Daniel Hudson's wedding in early November, complete with video and pictures, so he could make a smooth transition into a second career as a wedding photographer if his uneven performance in the Venezuelan Winter League carries over into 2012.

### Armando Galarraga

Born: 1/15/1982 Age: 30
Bats: R Throws: R Height: 6' 5" Weight: 180
Breakout: 35% Improve: 47% Collapse: 29%
Attrition: 9% MLB: 86%

Comparables:
Dave Mlicki, Greg Harris, Ernie Johnson

| YEAR | TEAM | LVL | AGE | W | L | SV | G | GS | IP | H | HR | BB | SO | EqBB9 | EqSO9 | GB% | BABIP | WHIP | ERA | FIP | FRA | WARP |
|---|---|---|---|---|---|---|---|---|---|---|---|---|---|---|---|---|---|---|---|---|---|---|
| 2009 | DET | MLB | 27 | 6 | 10 | 0 | 29 | 25 | 143² | 158 | 24 | 67 | 95 | 4.2 | 6.0 | 41% | .298 | 1.57 | 5.64 | 5.52 | 6.35 | -0.9 |
| 2010 | DET | MLB | 28 | 4 | 9 | 0 | 25 | 24 | 144¹ | 143 | 21 | 51 | 74 | 3.2 | 4.6 | 39% | .262 | 1.34 | 4.49 | 5.06 | 4.91 | 0.7 |
| 2011 | ARI | MLB | 29 | 3 | 4 | 0 | 8 | 8 | 42² | 47 | 13 | 22 | 28 | 4.6 | 5.9 | 43% | .260 | 1.62 | 5.91 | 7.26 | 6.97 | -1.0 |
| 2012 | ARI | MLB | 30 | 4 | 4 | 0 | 11 | 11 | 63¹ | 61 | 10 | 23 | 39 | 3.3 | 5.5 | 43% | .281 | 1.33 | 4.90 | 5.11 | 5.32 | 0.0 |

Galarraga was much further away from perfection last season than a blown call by Jim Joyce. After Arizona traded for him in late January, he showed why fly-ball pitchers aren't a good fit for Chase Field, coughing up 13 round-trippers in his eight starts, seven of them in just 17 innings at home. Galarraga appeared gracious in the wake of his 2010 almost-perfecto, but he was anything but after being sent to Reno in May, admitting that he'd complied with the team's wishes only so he could collect on his $2.3 million and that he didn't think he had anything to work on. He ran up an ERA over 9.00 with more walks than strikeouts before an arm injury ended his season in mid-July, suggesting either that sulking impacts performance or that he had even more to work on than the D-Backs thought.

### David Hernandez

Born: 5/13/1985 Age: 27
Bats: R Throws: R Height: 6' 4" Weight: 215
Breakout: 24% Improve: 60% Collapse: 21%
Attrition: 23% MLB: 81%

Comparables:
Luis Tiant, Matt Turner, Robb Nen

| YEAR | TEAM | LVL | AGE | W | L | SV | G | GS | IP | H | HR | BB | SO | EqBB9 | EqSO9 | GB% | BABIP | WHIP | ERA | FIP | FRA | WARP |
|---|---|---|---|---|---|---|---|---|---|---|---|---|---|---|---|---|---|---|---|---|---|---|
| 2009 | BAL | MLB | 24 | 4 | 10 | 0 | 20 | 19 | 101¹ | 118 | 27 | 46 | 68 | 4.1 | 6.0 | 31% | .286 | 1.62 | 5.42 | 6.66 | 6.90 | -0.8 |
| 2010 | BAL | MLB | 25 | 8 | 8 | 2 | 41 | 8 | 79¹ | 72 | 9 | 42 | 72 | 4.8 | 8.2 | 29% | .286 | 1.44 | 4.31 | 4.45 | 4.97 | 0.2 |
| 2011 | ARI | MLB | 26 | 5 | 3 | 11 | 74 | 0 | 69¹ | 49 | 4 | 30 | 77 | 3.9 | 10.0 | 34% | .257 | 1.14 | 3.38 | 2.91 | 3.70 | 0.9 |
| 2012 | ARI | MLB | 27 | 3 | 2 | 3 | 50 | 3 | 64¹ | 57 | 9 | 26 | 57 | 3.6 | 7.9 | 35% | .294 | 1.29 | 4.36 | 4.46 | 4.74 | 0.3 |

After converting to relief in late May 2010, Hernandez picked up a mile per hour on his fastball and nearly doubled his K rate to 10.9 per nine. Both upticks proved sustainable in his first big-league season spent entirely in the bullpen after Kevin Towers took a liking to what he saw of the new Hernandez and acquired him in the Mark Reynolds deal. Hernandez rewarded Towers' faith with a strong setup season, earning the highest-leverage outings of any Arizona pitcher other than J.J. Putz. He did limit opposing batters to a .253 BABIP and only four home runs despite the second-highest fly ball percentage among Diamondbacks who pitched at least 50 innings, so there could be some regression coming.

### David Holmberg

Born: 7/19/1991 Age: 20
Bats: R Throws: L Height: 6' 5" Weight: 219
Breakout: 53% Improve: 73% Collapse: 12%
Attrition: 2% MLB: 33%

Comparables:
Don Drysdale, Milt Pappas, Dick Brodowski

| YEAR | TEAM | LVL | AGE | W | L | SV | G | GS | IP | H | HR | BB | SO | EqBB9 | EqSO9 | GB% | BABIP | WHIP | ERA | FIP | FRA | WARP |
|---|---|---|---|---|---|---|---|---|---|---|---|---|---|---|---|---|---|---|---|---|---|---|
| 2009 | BRI | RK | 17 | 2 | 2 | 0 | 14 | 7 | 40 | 40 | 5 | 18 | 37 | 4.1 | 8.3 | 50% | .307 | 1.45 | 4.72 | 4.96 | 6.25 | -0.3 |
| 2010 | MSO | RK | 18 | 1 | 4 | 0 | 7 | 7 | 37¹ | 47 | 2 | 7 | 47 | 1.7 | 11.3 | 56% | .398 | 1.45 | 3.86 | 2.97 | 5.60 | -0.1 |
| 2010 | GRF | RK | 18 | 1 | 1 | 0 | 8 | 8 | 40¹ | 31 | 2 | 6 | 17 | 2.0 | 6.5 | 56% | .349 | 1.51 | 4.47 | 4.48 | 5.71 | -0.7 |
| 2011 | SBN | A | 19 | 8 | 3 | 0 | 14 | 14 | 83 | 57 | 3 | 12 | 77 | 1.4 | 8.8 | 52% | .265 | 0.94 | 2.39 | 2.62 | 3.59 | 1.6 |
| 2011 | VIS | A+ | 19 | 3 | 3 | 0 | 13 | 13 | 71¹ | 73 | 5 | 35 | 76 | 4.4 | 9.6 | 45% | .342 | 1.51 | 4.67 | 4.31 | 4.40 | 0.9 |
| 2012 | ARI | MLB | 20 | 2 | 3 | 0 | 8 | 8 | 43 | 45 | 5 | 20 | 26 | 4.2 | 5.5 | 48% | .312 | 1.53 | 5.58 | 4.90 | 6.06 | -0.3 |

If Holmberg never throws a pitch at the major-league level, the Snakes still will have come out ahead in the Edwin Jackson trade, courtesy of Daniel Hudson's contributions. However, Holmberg seems determined to tip the trade further in their favor. The 19-year-old southpaw mastered the Midwest League, finishing with a flourish at that level by making five consecutive scoreless starts with 31 strikeouts and one walk in 34 frames. After a promotion to High-A at midseason, his walk rate suffered but his strikeout rate ticked up. Holmberg's 6'4 frame finally yielded the velocity that was expected of it, turning an 88-90-mph fastball into one that ranged from 90-94, and he already possessed solid secondary stuff and control. The scary thing is that all of that might make him only the organization's fourth- or fifth-best lefty pitching prospect.

**Daniel Hudson**
Born: 3/9/1987 Age: 25
Bats: R Throws: R Height: 6' 5" Weight: 220
Breakout: 12% Improve: 35% Collapse: 25%
Attrition: 8% MLB: 97%

Comparables:
Adam Wainwright, Jered Weaver, Kevin Millwood

| YEAR | TEAM | LVL | AGE | W | L | SV | G | GS | IP | H | HR | BB | SO | EqBB9 | EqSO9 | GB% | BABIP | WHIP | ERA | FIP | FRA | WARP |
|---|---|---|---|---|---|---|---|---|---|---|---|---|---|---|---|---|---|---|---|---|---|---|
| 2009 | WNS | A+ | 22 | 4 | 3 | 0 | 8 | 8 | 45 | 31 | 3 | 13 | 49 | 2.6 | 9.8 | 53% | .257 | 0.98 | 3.40 | 3.04 | 3.70 | 1.1 |
| 2009 | BIR | AA | 22 | 7 | 0 | 0 | 9 | 9 | 56¹ | 37 | 1 | 10 | 63 | 1.6 | 10.1 | 39% | .269 | 0.83 | 1.60 | 1.79 | 2.21 | 1.8 |
| 2009 | CHA | MLB | 22 | 1 | 1 | 0 | 6 | 2 | 18² | 16 | 3 | 9 | 14 | 4.3 | 6.8 | 34% | .236 | 1.34 | 3.38 | 5.34 | 5.97 | 0.0 |
| 2010 | CHR | AAA | 23 | 11 | 4 | 0 | 17 | 17 | 93¹ | 52 | 7 | 19 | 71 | 3.0 | 10.4 | 44% | .273 | 1.20 | 3.47 | 3.72 | 3.92 | 1.9 |
| 2010 | CHA | MLB | 23 | 1 | 1 | 0 | 3 | 3 | 15² | 17 | 1 | 11 | 14 | 6.3 | 8.0 | 30% | .364 | 1.79 | 6.32 | 4.20 | 4.59 | 0.0 |
| 2010 | ARI | MLB | 23 | 7 | 1 | 0 | 11 | 11 | 79² | 51 | 7 | 16 | 70 | 1.8 | 7.9 | 40% | .217 | 0.84 | 1.69 | 3.24 | 3.10 | 1.9 |

**Chris Jakubauskas**
Born: 12/22/1978 Age: 33
Bats: L Throws: R Height: 6' 3" Weight: 215
Breakout: 12% Improve: 29% Collapse: 26%
Attrition: 21% MLB: 86%

Comparables:
Craig Lefferts, Charles Nagy, Frank Tanana

| YEAR | TEAM | LVL | AGE | W | L | SV | G | GS | IP | H | HR | BB | SO | EqBB9 | EqSO9 | GB% | BABIP | WHIP | ERA | FIP | FRA | WARP |
|---|---|---|---|---|---|---|---|---|---|---|---|---|---|---|---|---|---|---|---|---|---|---|
| 2009 | SEA | MLB | 30 | 6 | 7 | 0 | 35 | 8 | 93 | 91 | 15 | 27 | 47 | 2.6 | 4.5 | 46% | .254 | 1.27 | 5.32 | 5.17 | 5.91 | -0.3 |
| 2010 | PIT | MLB | 31 | 0 | 1 | 0 | 1 | 1 | 0² | 2 | 0 | 0 | 0 | 0.0 | 0.0 | % | .500 | 3.00 | 27.00 | 3.11 | 4.22 | 0.0 |
| 2011 | BAL | MLB | 32 | 2 | 2 | 0 | 33 | 6 | 72¹ | 93 | 11 | 29 | 52 | 3.6 | 6.5 | 46% | .349 | 1.69 | 5.72 | 4.93 | 5.57 | 0.0 |
| 2012 | ARI | MLB | 33 | 3 | 3 | 0 | 25 | 9 | 65² | 69 | 8 | 20 | 38 | 2.8 | 5.2 | 46% | .305 | 1.36 | 4.88 | 4.54 | 5.30 | 0.1 |

Jakubauskas has spent his entire MLB career as a swing man, splitting time in the rotation and bullpen as far back as 2007 in Double-A after the Mariners plucked him from the independent leagues. In the majors, he's been less successful as a starter (4.7 K/9, 3.4 BB/9) then as a reliever (5.8 K/9, 2.9 BB/9), when he can keep his fastball consistently at 91-92 mph as opposed to 89. Having only a looping curve to play off his relatively straight heater also suits him better for work out of the pen. Jakubauskas spent the second half of last season in the bullpen for the Orioles, occasionally being asked to pitch two or three innings at a time, and that seems to be the role he's best suited for. He'll try to win a spot in Arizona's bullpen.

**Ian Kennedy**
Born: 12/19/1984 Age: 27
Bats: R Throws: R Height: 6' 1" Weight: 190
Breakout: 13% Improve: 56% Collapse: 29%
Attrition: 11% MLB: 90%

Comparables:
Jensen Lewis, Ramon Ramirez, Justin Verlander

| YEAR | TEAM | LVL | AGE | W | L | SV | G | GS | IP | H | HR | BB | SO | EqBB9 | EqSO9 | GB% | BABIP | WHIP | ERA | FIP | FRA | WARP |
|---|---|---|---|---|---|---|---|---|---|---|---|---|---|---|---|---|---|---|---|---|---|---|
| 2009 | NYA | MLB | 24 | 0 | 0 | 0 | 1 | 0 | 1 | 0 | 0 | 2 | 1 | 18.0 | 9.0 | % | .000 | 2.00 | 0.00 | 10.14 | 9.12 | 0.0 |
| 2010 | ARI | MLB | 25 | 9 | 10 | 0 | 32 | 32 | 194 | 163 | 26 | 70 | 168 | 3.2 | 7.8 | 39% | .261 | 1.20 | 3.80 | 4.35 | 4.44 | 2.6 |
| 2011 | ARI | MLB | 26 | 21 | 4 | 0 | 33 | 33 | 222 | 186 | 19 | 55 | 198 | 2.2 | 8.0 | 40% | .274 | 1.09 | 2.88 | 3.19 | 3.76 | 3.1 |
| 2012 | ARI | MLB | 27 | 12 | 9 | 0 | 28 | 28 | 181² | 154 | 19 | 57 | 151 | 2.8 | 7.5 | 39% | .284 | 1.16 | 3.63 | 3.84 | 3.94 | 2.7 |

With so many valuable pieces changing hands, it's tough to say who got the best of the three-team swap that brought Kennedy to the D-Backs in late 2009, but it's hard to be upset when your haul includes a Cy Young contender. Despite his league-leading win total and winning percentage, Kennedy wasn't the NL's best pitcher—he ranked 11th in WARP—but his record wasn't just a product of the 11th-highest run support among qualifying NL starters, either. Although he sports the sixth-lowest BABIP among pitchers with at least 400 innings over the last two seasons, a big correction might not be coming: like other perennial low-BABIP arms like Matt Cain and Jered Weaver, he's adept at inducing pop-ups, which don't often fall in for hits.

### Wade Miley

Born: 11/13/1986 Age: 25
Bats: L Throws: L Height: 6' 2'' Weight: 220
Breakout: 21% Improve: 57% Collapse: 14%
Attrition: 11% MLB: 88%

Comparables:
Matt Chico,Chuck Stobbs,Zach Jackson

| YEAR | TEAM | LVL | AGE | W | L | SV | G | GS | IP | H | HR | BB | SO | EqBB9 | EqSO9 | GB% | BABIP | WHIP | ERA | FIP | FRA | WARP |
|---|---|---|---|---|---|---|---|---|---|---|---|---|---|---|---|---|---|---|---|---|---|---|
| 2009 | SBN | A | 22 | 5 | 9 | 0 | 21 | 21 | 113$^2$ | 127 | 8 | 29 | 91 | 2.3 | 7.2 | 58% | .343 | 1.37 | 4.12 | 3.80 | 5.41 | 0.0 |
| 2010 | VIS | A+ | 23 | 4 | 5 | 0 | 14 | 14 | 80$^1$ | 76 | 1 | 34 | 45 | 4.1 | 5.6 | 68% | .326 | 1.47 | 3.25 | 4.17 | 5.24 | -0.1 |
| 2010 | MOB | AA | 23 | 5 | 3 | 0 | 13 | 13 | 72$^2$ | 43 | 2 | 20 | 47 | 3.5 | 7.8 | 61% | .301 | 1.21 | 1.98 | 3.48 | 4.09 | 0.9 |
| 2011 | MOB | AA | 24 | 0 | 2 | 0 | 14 | 14 | 75$^1$ | 71 | 6 | 27 | 45 | 3.3 | 5.5 | 57% | .283 | 1.35 | 4.78 | 4.34 | 5.22 | 0.0 |
| 2011 | RNO | AAA | 24 | 4 | 1 | 0 | 8 | 8 | 54$^1$ | 53 | 4 | 16 | 55 | 2.7 | 9.3 | 51% | .331 | 1.27 | 3.64 | 3.55 | 3.99 | 1.2 |
| 2011 | ARI | MLB | 24 | 4 | 2 | 0 | 8 | 7 | 40 | 48 | 6 | 18 | 25 | 4.1 | 5.6 | 49% | .328 | 1.65 | 4.50 | 5.04 | 5.64 | -0.2 |
| 2012 | ARI | MLB | 25 | 4 | 5 | 0 | 12 | 12 | 71$^1$ | 78 | 9 | 29 | 38 | 3.6 | 4.8 | 53% | .313 | 1.49 | 5.29 | 5.00 | 5.75 | -0.3 |

Three starts by Jason Marquis cost the Diamondbacks $2.5 million and a marginal prospect. Seven starts down the stretch by Miley, Marquis's replacement, cost them a ticket to Phoenix and the pro-rated major-league minimum. That's why it's so nice to have the surplus of young, major-league-ready arms that the Diamondbacks do. Miley's stuff and stats made great strides in 2010, and he took another step forward last season. Strangely, he had his most success in Reno, one of the worst environments for pitchers in all of organized baseball; the lefty was the only arm on the Aces to pitch over 25 innings with an ERA below 4.25. His strikeout rate ticked up there, too, though he didn't miss as many bats in the majors. Southpaws who can touch the mid-90s and get groundballs without walking the ballpark are scarce, and Miley could do a credible job in the back of the D-Backs' rotation right now.

### Micah Owings

Born: 9/28/1982 Age: 29
Bats: R Throws: R Height: 6' 6'' Weight: 225
Breakout: 39% Improve: 55% Collapse: 21%
Attrition: 12% MLB: 84%

Comparables:
Tommy Greene,Ken Forsch,Paul Wilson

| YEAR | TEAM | LVL | AGE | W | L | SV | G | GS | IP | H | HR | BB | SO | EqBB9 | EqSO9 | GB% | BABIP | WHIP | ERA | FIP | FRA | WARP |
|---|---|---|---|---|---|---|---|---|---|---|---|---|---|---|---|---|---|---|---|---|---|---|
| 2009 | CIN | MLB | 26 | 7 | 12 | 1 | 26 | 19 | 119$^2$ | 126 | 18 | 64 | 68 | 4.8 | 5.1 | 38% | .282 | 1.59 | 5.34 | 5.63 | 5.44 | 0.9 |
| 2010 | LOU | AAA | 27 | 0 | 1 | 0 | 8 | 5 | 20$^1$ | 16 | 2 | 8 | 11 | 4.4 | 5.8 | 39% | .264 | 1.48 | 2.22 | 5.65 | 4.91 | 0.2 |
| 2010 | CIN | MLB | 27 | 3 | 2 | 0 | 22 | 0 | 33$^1$ | 28 | 3 | 25 | 35 | 6.8 | 9.4 | 32% | .294 | 1.59 | 5.40 | 4.70 | 5.51 | 0.1 |
| 2011 | RNO | AAA | 28 | 3 | 1 | 0 | 7 | 7 | 39 | 41 | 5 | 9 | 27 | 2.1 | 6.2 | 45% | .295 | 1.28 | 4.85 | 4.86 | 6.18 | 0.5 |
| 2011 | ARI | MLB | 28 | 8 | 0 | 0 | 33 | 4 | 63 | 56 | 8 | 23 | 44 | 3.3 | 6.3 | 39% | .264 | 1.25 | 3.57 | 4.44 | 5.21 | 0.0 |
| 2012 | ARI | MLB | 29 | 3 | 2 | 0 | 27 | 6 | 58$^2$ | 56 | 8 | 22 | 39 | 3.4 | 6.0 | 38% | .289 | 1.32 | 4.71 | 4.77 | 5.12 | 0.1 |

Okay, so maybe there's still *something* to the notion of Owings as a pitcher, albeit not a starting one. After struggling a bit in the rotation at Triple-A Reno, he returned to relief at the major-league level, making a few starts between low-leverage outings in the middle innings. His second extended stint in a big-league bullpen wasn't plagued by the same control problems that stymied him in 2010, giving him superficial statistics good enough to earn a spot on the postseason roster. Between that and his pedestrian performance at the plate (4-for-19 without an extra-base hit), the idea of his reinventing himself as a position player seems a lot less exciting than it did a year ago, though a disturbing drop in velocity of nearly three mph and a forthcoming BABIP correction suggest that his future on the mound isn't so hot, either.

### Joe Paterson

Born: 5/19/1986 Age: 26
Bats: R Throws: L Height: 6' 2'' Weight: 210
Breakout: 30% Improve: 60% Collapse: 18%
Attrition: 12% MLB: 91%

Comparables:
Chad Billingsley,Kevin Jepsen,Greg Harris

| YEAR | TEAM | LVL | AGE | W | L | SV | G | GS | IP | H | HR | BB | SO | EqBB9 | EqSO9 | GB% | BABIP | WHIP | ERA | FIP | FRA | WARP |
|---|---|---|---|---|---|---|---|---|---|---|---|---|---|---|---|---|---|---|---|---|---|---|
| 2009 | NRW | AA | 23 | 5 | 6 | 10 | 55 | 0 | 69 | 53 | 3 | 25 | 73 | 3.1 | 9.0 | 50% | .262 | 1.03 | 1.96 | 2.85 | 3.52 | 1.4 |
| 2010 | FRE | AAA | 24 | 4 | 3 | 2 | 46 | 0 | 54$^1$ | 33 | 1 | 13 | 34 | 4.0 | 8.1 | 51% | .305 | 1.45 | 3.48 | 3.82 | 5.14 | 0.1 |
| 2011 | ARI | MLB | 25 | 0 | 3 | 1 | 62 | 0 | 34 | 28 | 1 | 15 | 28 | 4.0 | 7.4 | 55% | .276 | 1.26 | 2.91 | 3.41 | 5.44 | -0.1 |
| 2012 | ARI | MLB | 26 | 2 | 1 | 0 | 36 | 0 | 30$^2$ | 28 | 3 | 12 | 24 | 3.5 | 7.0 | 50% | .299 | 1.30 | 4.16 | 4.08 | 4.52 | 0.2 |

Paterson's 34 frames last season were the fourth-least ever thrown by a pitcher with at least 60 appearances, behind only Tony Fossas, Arizona predecessor Mike Myers, and the ageless Jesse Orosco, whom Paterson probably had a poster of in his childhood bedroom. Like those previous practitioners of the situational lefty trade, Paterson can expect his yearly ERAs to fluctuate wildly without much of a change in his underlying performance, since BABIP variations over the small samples that constitute his seasons will largely determine how his stat lines look at first glance. Fortunately, 2011 was a low-BABIP year, but Paterson's peripherals suggest that he can survive—maybe for decades—even when fewer balls bounce his way and more than 5 percent of his flies leave the park.

### J.J. Putz

Born: 2/22/1977 Age: 35
Bats: R Throws: R Height: 6' 6'' Weight: 220
Breakout: 14% Improve: 39% Collapse: 31%
Attrition: 20% MLB: 83%

Comparables:
Rafael Betancourt,Rich Gossage,Pedro Martinez

| YEAR | TEAM | LVL | AGE | W | L | SV | G | GS | IP | H | HR | BB | SO | EqBB9 | EqSO9 | GB% | BABIP | WHIP | ERA | FIP | FRA | WARP |
|---|---|---|---|---|---|---|---|---|---|---|---|---|---|---|---|---|---|---|---|---|---|---|
| 2009 | NYN | MLB | 32 | 1 | 4 | 2 | 29 | 0 | 29$^1$ | 29 | 1 | 19 | 19 | 5.8 | 5.8 | 46% | .295 | 1.64 | 5.22 | 4.15 | 4.65 | 0.1 |
| 2010 | CHA | MLB | 33 | 7 | 5 | 3 | 60 | 0 | 54 | 41 | 4 | 15 | 65 | 2.5 | 10.8 | 49% | .278 | 1.04 | 2.83 | 2.49 | 3.98 | 0.9 |
| 2011 | ARI | MLB | 34 | 2 | 2 | 45 | 60 | 0 | 58 | 41 | 4 | 12 | 61 | 1.9 | 9.5 | 44% | .250 | 0.91 | 2.17 | 2.51 | 3.33 | 1.0 |
| 2012 | ARI | MLB | 35 | 3 | 1 | 19 | 56 | 0 | 52$^1$ | 41 | 5 | 16 | 53 | 2.7 | 9.1 | 45% | .291 | 1.08 | 2.94 | 3.34 | 3.20 | 1.2 |

On the first leg of Putz's two-year, $10 million deal, the oft-injured reliever pitched as well as he had since his heyday in Seattle and succeeded in high-leverage spots and appearances on short or no rest, both of which gave him trouble with the White Sox. He did seem poised to fall apart when he missed roughly a month at midseason with elbow inflammation after allowing runs in two consecutive appearances, but he showed no ill effects following his return in late July, pitching to a 0.77 second-half ERA. Any delivery could be his last, but unless his elbow finally gives up the ghost in 2012, his contract will continue to look reasonable compared to those of some of his late-inning counterparts.

**Takashi Saito**

Born: 2/14/1970 Age: 42
Bats: L Throws: R Height: 6' 2" Weight: 202
Breakout: 13% Improve: 34% Collapse: 27%
Attrition: 19% MLB: 72%

**Comparables:**

| YEAR | TEAM | LVL | AGE | W | L | SV | G | GS | IP | H | HR | BB | SO | EqBB9 | EqSO9 | GB% | BABIP | WHIP | ERA | FIP | FRA | WARP |
|------|------|-----|-----|---|---|----|---|----|-----|----|----|----|----|-------|-------|-----|-------|------|------|------|------|------|
| 2009 | BOS | MLB | 39 | 3 | 3 | 2 | 56 | 0 | 55² | 50 | 6 | 25 | 52 | 4.0 | 8.4 | 35% | .291 | 1.35 | 2.43 | 4.29 | 4.50 | 0.7 |
| 2010 | ATL | MLB | 40 | 2 | 3 | 1 | 56 | 0 | 54 | 41 | 4 | 17 | 69 | 2.8 | 11.5 | 44% | .287 | 1.07 | 2.83 | 2.46 | 2.82 | 1.3 |
| 2011 | MIL | MLB | 41 | 4 | 2 | 0 | 30 | 0 | 26² | 21 | 2 | 9 | 23 | 3.0 | 7.8 | 45% | .264 | 1.12 | 2.03 | 3.37 | 3.73 | 0.4 |
| 2012 | ARI | MLB | 42 | 2 | 1 | 0 | 33 | 0 | 30² | 24 | 3 | 9 | 31 | 2.7 | 9.2 | 45% | .292 | 1.07 | 2.87 | 3.33 | 3.12 | 0.7 |

**Joe Saunders**

Born: 6/16/1981 Age: 31
Bats: L Throws: L Height: 6' 4" Weight: 210
Breakout: 17% Improve: 37% Collapse: 25%
Attrition: 14% MLB: 70%

**Comparables:**
Chris Jakubauskas, Jarrod Washburn, Brian Gordon

| YEAR | TEAM | LVL | AGE | W | L | SV | G | GS | IP | H | HR | BB | SO | EqBB9 | EqSO9 | GB% | BABIP | WHIP | ERA | FIP | FRA | WARP |
|------|------|-----|-----|----|----|----|----|----|------|-----|----|----|-----|-------|-------|-----|-------|------|------|------|------|------|
| 2009 | ANA | MLB | 28 | 16 | 7 | 0 | 31 | 31 | 186 | 202 | 29 | 64 | 101 | 3.1 | 4.9 | 48% | .289 | 1.43 | 4.60 | 5.21 | 5.72 | 0.1 |
| 2010 | ARI | MLB | 29 | 3 | 7 | 0 | 13 | 13 | 82² | 97 | 11 | 19 | 50 | 2.1 | 5.4 | 46% | .315 | 1.40 | 4.25 | 4.46 | 4.80 | 0.5 |
| 2010 | ANA | MLB | 29 | 6 | 10 | 0 | 20 | 20 | 120² | 135 | 14 | 45 | 64 | 3.4 | 4.8 | 44% | .308 | 1.49 | 4.62 | 4.64 | 4.74 | 0.9 |
| 2011 | ARI | MLB | 30 | 12 | 13 | 0 | 33 | 33 | 212 | 210 | 29 | 67 | 108 | 2.8 | 4.6 | 46% | .275 | 1.31 | 3.69 | 4.74 | 4.66 | 0.8 |
| 2012 | ARI | MLB | 31 | 10 | 11 | 0 | 28 | 28 | 178¹ | 184 | 23 | 48 | 93 | 2.4 | 4.7 | 46% | .299 | 1.30 | 4.64 | 4.65 | 5.04 | 0.4 |

Saunders didn't make D-Backs fans forget Dan Haren—if anyone Arizona obtained in the 2010 trade does that, it will be Tyler Skaggs—but if you didn't watch the games and looked at his stat line only long enough to see his ERA and innings pitched total, it was like Haren never left. At the time of the trade, then-interim GM Jerry DiPoto summoned the scorn of the bloggerati by repeatedly citing Saunders' .628 career winning percentage in an effort to make the salary dump easier to swallow. Ironically, the righty has run a 15-20 record since then while improving upon his career Angels ERA by almost half a run. However, that apparent improvement rests on the shakiest of foundations, since Saunders' 4.6 K/9 was the lowest among qualified NL pitchers in 2011. As Bill James once said, "There is simply no such thing as a starter who has a long career with a low strikeout rate." The D-Backs have been reading their *Baseball Abstracts*: They non-tendered Saunders in December.

**Bryan Shaw**

Born: 11/8/1987 Age: 24
Bats: B Throws: R Height: 6' 2" Weight: 210
Breakout: 29% Improve: 58% Collapse: 20%
Attrition: 18% MLB: 88%

**Comparables:**
Mike Pelfrey, Mike Witt, Nelson Briles

| YEAR | TEAM | LVL | AGE | W | L | SV | G | GS | IP | H | HR | BB | SO | EqBB9 | EqSO9 | GB% | BABIP | WHIP | ERA | FIP | FRA | WARP |
|------|------|-----|-----|---|---|----|----|----|------|----|----|----|----|-------|-------|-----|-------|------|------|------|------|------|
| 2009 | VIS | A+ | 21 | 3 | 7 | 0 | 30 | 19 | 107¹ | 96 | 7 | 40 | 95 | 3.4 | 8.0 | 59% | .291 | 1.27 | 4.70 | 4.26 | 6.23 | -0.7 |
| 2010 | MOB | AA | 22 | 5 | 9 | 2 | 33 | 13 | 101¹ | 58 | 1 | 25 | 51 | 3.8 | 6.7 | 60% | .295 | 1.43 | 4.26 | 3.59 | 5.05 | -0.2 |
| 2011 | MOB | AA | 23 | 1 | 1 | 7 | 15 | 0 | 20² | 14 | 1 | 8 | 15 | 3.5 | 6.5 | 51% | .236 | 1.11 | 0.87 | 3.64 | 4.90 | 0.1 |
| 2011 | ARI | MLB | 23 | 1 | 0 | 0 | 33 | 0 | 28¹ | 30 | 2 | 8 | 24 | 2.5 | 7.6 | 60% | .333 | 1.34 | 2.54 | 3.49 | 4.16 | 0.1 |
| 2012 | ARI | MLB | 24 | 2 | 1 | 0 | 22 | 3 | 37² | 37 | 4 | 15 | 23 | 3.6 | 5.5 | 53% | .297 | 1.38 | 4.80 | 4.56 | 5.22 | 0.0 |

Shaw's first full season in the bullpen since his 2008 professional debut resulted in his making the majors. Shaw racked up 16 saves between Mobile and Reno, took well to the NL West, and has a power sinker that averages 93 and tops out at 95, but he doesn't miss as many bats as the typical closer candidate, which could restrict him to setup duty. What the '08 second-rounder does do is keep the ball out of the air, which should serve him well in Chase Field.

## Tyler Skaggs

Born: 7/13/1991 Age: 20
Bats: L Throws: L Height: 6' 5" Weight: 195
Breakout: 49% Improve: 63% Collapse: 20%
Attrition: 16% MLB: 94%

**Comparables:**
Mike McQueen, Chris Zachary, Terry Forster

| YEAR | TEAM | LVL | AGE | W | L | SV | G | GS | IP | H | HR | BB | SO | EqBB9 | EqSO9 | GB% | BABIP | WHIP | ERA | FIP | FRA | WARP |
|------|------|-----|-----|---|---|----|---|----|------|----|----|----|-----|-------|-------|-----|-------|------|------|------|------|------|
| 2010 | CDR | A | 18 | 8 | 4 | 0 | 19 | 14 | 82$^1$ | 58 | 5 | 14 | 66 | 2.3 | 9.0 | 50% | .303 | 1.20 | 3.61 | 3.64 | 4.46 | 1.0 |
| 2011 | VIS | A+ | 19 | 1 | 3 | 0 | 17 | 17 | 100$^2$ | 81 | 6 | 34 | 125 | 3.0 | 11.2 | 53% | .310 | 1.14 | 3.22 | 3.39 | 3.57 | 2.2 |
| 2011 | MOB | AA | 19 | 1 | 0 | 0 | 10 | 10 | 57$^2$ | 56 | 4 | 18 | 89 | 2.3 | 11.4 | 45% | .317 | 1.04 | 2.50 | 2.16 | 3.29 | 1.6 |
| 2012 | ARI | MLB | 20 | 3 | 3 | 0 | 9 | 9 | 49$^2$ | 45 | 5 | 18 | 44 | 3.2 | 7.9 | 47% | .305 | 1.26 | 4.06 | 3.83 | 4.41 | 0.5 |

In *BP2011*, we wrote, "We're two years away from knowing if Skaggs is a star or back-of-the-rotation starter." With one year remaining on that timeline, "star" looks like the more likely outcome for the 2009 supplemental first rounder. Previously a one-level-per-year prospect, Skaggs mastered High-A and moved on to Double-A in 2011, boosting his strikeout rate above 11 batters per nine at both levels without a corresponding increase in walks. For that performance, he earned the organization's Pitcher of the Year honors, following in the footsteps of such Diamondbacks luminaries as Bret Prinz, Brian Bruney, and Enrique Gonzalez. From here, his path will diverge from theirs; after bumping his velocity into the 92-93 range and further refining a changeup to accompany a plus curve, the lefty's stuff has made up much of the difference between projection and reality. The 20-year-old could use another full season in the minors, but he should be ready to form a young and talented righty-lefty tandem with Bauer at the top of the 2013 rotation. Dan Haren who?

## Brad Ziegler

Born: 10/10/1979 Age: 32
Bats: R Throws: R Height: 6' 5" Weight: 200
Breakout: 8% Improve: 45% Collapse: 36%
Attrition: 16% MLB: 97%

**Comparables:**
Braden Looper, Tim Hudson, Orel Hershiser

| YEAR | TEAM | LVL | AGE | W | L | SV | G | GS | IP | H | HR | BB | SO | EqBB9 | EqSO9 | GB% | BABIP | WHIP | ERA | FIP | FRA | WARP |
|------|------|-----|-----|---|---|----|---|----|------|----|----|----|----|-------|-------|-----|-------|------|------|------|------|------|
| 2009 | OAK | MLB | 29 | 2 | 4 | 7 | 69 | 0 | 73$^1$ | 82 | 2 | 28 | 54 | 3.4 | 6.6 | 62% | .352 | 1.50 | 3.07 | 3.21 | 4.39 | 0.7 |
| 2010 | OAK | MLB | 30 | 3 | 7 | 0 | 64 | 0 | 60$^2$ | 54 | 4 | 28 | 41 | 4.2 | 6.1 | 56% | .278 | 1.35 | 3.26 | 4.09 | 4.74 | 0.1 |
| 2011 | OAK | MLB | 31 | 3 | 2 | 1 | 43 | 0 | 37$^2$ | 38 | 0 | 13 | 29 | 3.1 | 6.9 | 73% | .328 | 1.35 | 2.39 | 2.64 | 4.55 | 0.1 |
| 2011 | ARI | MLB | 31 | 0 | 0 | 0 | 23 | 0 | 20$^2$ | 15 | 0 | 6 | 15 | 2.6 | 6.5 | 66% | .259 | 1.02 | 1.74 | 2.41 | 4.49 | 0.0 |
| 2012 | ARI | MLB | 32 | 3 | 1 | 1 | 59 | 0 | 53$^2$ | 49 | 3 | 18 | 35 | 2.9 | 5.9 | 61% | .304 | 1.24 | 3.69 | 3.63 | 4.01 | 0.7 |

Ziegler has been an inveterate worm-killer since his 2008 debut, but he took his ground-balling to even greater heights (so to speak) last season, keeping 70.3 percent of his balls in play allowed on the ground, the highest rate of any hurler with a minimum of 50 innings pitched save for Jonny Venters. Thanks to that aversion to air balls and a corresponding uptick in strikeout rate, Ziegler is actually a better pitcher now than he was in '08, despite a slightly less awe-inspiring ERA. The righty's 2.16 mark was matched by a 2.56 FIP, so don't let that first number scare you—Ziegler is one of the most dependable arms in the bullpen business, not another low-BABIP mirage about to blow up in a slightly larger sample. The sidearmer does have to be used judiciously to get the most out of his talents, since he's terrible against left-handed hitters.

# LINEOUTS

## HITTERS

| PLAYER | TEAM | LVL | AGE | PA | R | 2B | 3B | HR | RBI | BB | SO | SB-CS | AVG/OBP/SLG | TAv | BABIP | BRR | FRAA | WARP |
|--------|------|-----|-----|----|---|----|----|----|-----|----|----|-------|-------------|-----|-------|-----|------|------|
| RF C. Gillespie | RNO | AAA | 27 | 582 | 100 | 19 | 16 | 12 | 79 | 81 | 91 | 24-5 | .300/.405/.479 | .292 | .343 | 6.2 | 8.3 | 4.4 |
| | ARI | MLB | 27 | 7 | 2 | 0 | 0 | 1 | 4 | 1 | 1 | 0-0 | .333/.429/.833 | .404 | .250 | 0 | 0 | 0.1 |
| C R. Hammock | RNO | AAA | 34 | 120 | 18 | 7 | 1 | 5 | 21 | 15 | 17 | 0-0 | .257/.353/.495 | .281 | .259 | 1 | -0.2 | 0.9 |
| RF M. Krauss | MOB | AA | 23 | 504 | 69 | 25 | 6 | 16 | 65 | 64 | 123 | 3-3 | .242/.340/.439 | .272 | .299 | 1.7 | -0.8 | 1.5 |
| CF R. Langerhans | RNO | AAA | 31 | 171 | 23 | 10 | 2 | 6 | 23 | 39 | 31 | 8-1 | .308/.468/.554 | .338 | .362 | 1 | -3.2 | 1.8 |
| | TAC | AAA | 31 | 255 | 46 | 10 | 0 | 16 | 37 | 37 | 63 | 3-6 | .313/.416/.584 | .349 | .372 | -1.9 | 1.5 | 2.8 |
| | SEA | MLB | 31 | 64 | 6 | 0 | 0 | 3 | 6 | 11 | 22 | 0-1 | .173/.317/.346 | .267 | .222 | -0.4 | -1.1 | 0.0 |
| 3B M. Mora | ARI | MLB | 39 | 135 | 5 | 6 | 0 | 0 | 16 | 2 | 24 | 0-1 | .228/.244/.276 | .193 | .271 | -1.4 | 0.7 | -0.5 |
| SS C. Ransom | RNO | AAA | 35 | 432 | 86 | 29 | 3 | 27 | 92 | 55 | 94 | 10-3 | .317/.405/.629 | .316 | .358 | 3.1 | 3.1 | 4.7 |
| | ARI | MLB | 35 | 37 | 3 | 2 | 0 | 1 | 4 | 3 | 9 | 1-0 | .152/.243/.303 | .186 | .174 | 0.5 | 0.6 | -0.1 |
| C K. Schmidt | RNO | AAA | 26 | 374 | 47 | 24 | 3 | 9 | 45 | 21 | 66 | 1-3 | .280/.330/.445 | .252 | .324 | 0.1 | -0.7 | 1.3 |
| 3B R. Wheeler | MOB | AA | 22 | 531 | 69 | 30 | 2 | 16 | 89 | 45 | 102 | 3-4 | .294/.358/.465 | .280 | .343 | -5 | -1.4 | 1.9 |
| LF D. Winfree | RNO | AAA | 25 | 157 | 27 | 5 | 1 | 9 | 37 | 15 | 22 | 8-1 | .321/.389/.575 | .316 | .315 | 1.4 | -2.5 | 1.2 |

Right-handed-hitting outfielder **Cole Gillespie** is essentially Collin Cowgill, only almost two years older, with less center field experience, and with one fewer "l." ⊘ You'd think **Robby Hammock**'s last name would have inspired him to try retirement by now, but the utility man seems to be a believer in the philosophy that where there's a PA, there a way. Last season, he got two in the bigs. ⊘ Like the player he's often been compared to, Adam Dunn, doughy Double-A outfielder **Marc Krauss** had a disappointing season, failing to repeat the home run power he showed in 2010. ⊘ **Ryan Langerhans** hit .311/.437/.573 at Triple-A and appeared in 61 games in center, but he's amply demonstrated that he has neither the bat nor the glove to replicate that performance where it counts. ⊘ The bloom is off late-blooming **Melvin Mora**, who went homerless before earning his release in late June. We've likely seen the last of the 40-year-old. ⊘ There's nothing wrong with raking in Reno, as **Cody Ransom** did, but to paraphrase Jeff Foxworthy, if that's how you spend your age-35 season, you might be a marginal major leaguer. ⊘ **Konrad Schmidt** is a Henry Blanco injury away from being a marginal major leaguer for life. He lacks Blanco's arm and receiving skills, but he has the body type down, and a better bat. ⊘ Unlike Bobby Borchering, **Ryan Wheeler** stands a good chance at sticking at third. His first Double-A season was a success, but his bat probably won't break the Ryan Roberts mold. ⊘ Last season, Triple-A journeyman **David Winfree** finally found out that the key to cracking a 40-man was starting

| | | | | | | | | | | | | | | | | | | | | |
|---|---|---|---|---|---|---|---|---|---|---|---|---|---|---|---|---|---|---|---|---|
| Z. Kroenke | RNO | AAA | 27 | 10 | 3 | 0 | 128¹ | 179 | 14 | 52 | 78 | 3.5 | 5.1 | 49% | .354 | 1.74 | 5.89 | 5.27 | 6.19 | 0.8 |
| | ARI | MLB | 27 | 0 | 1 | 0 | 4 | 6 | 1 | 1 | 3 | 2.2 | 6.8 | 67% | .357 | 1.75 | 9.00 | 5.49 | 6.54 | -0.1 |
| J. Lewis | COH | AAA | 27 | 3 | 2 | 2 | 28 | 37 | 4 | 13 | 20 | 4.8 | 7.1 | 21% | .375 | 1.96 | 5.14 | 5.06 | 6.10 | 0.1 |
| K. Mickolio | RNO | AAA | 27 | 3 | 4 | 6 | 58 | 62 | 4 | 26 | 67 | 3.9 | 9.8 | 45% | .335 | 1.43 | 4.97 | 3.67 | 4.88 | 0.9 |
| | ARI | MLB | 27 | 0 | 0 | 0 | 6² | 10 | 0 | 3 | 7 | 4.1 | 9.4 | 23% | .455 | 1.95 | 6.75 | 2.24 | 4.44 | 0.1 |
| Y. Ortega | VIS | A+ | 24 | 1 | 0 | 9 | 39¹ | 37 | 3 | 21 | 58 | 4.8 | 13.3 | 47% | .374 | 1.47 | 4.81 | 3.73 | 5.13 | 0.1 |
| M. Zagurski | LEH | AAA | 28 | 4 | 0 | 11 | 54¹ | 47 | 3 | 28 | 65 | 4.5 | 10.4 | 51% | .328 | 1.29 | 2.65 | 3.28 | 4.48 | 0.7 |
| | PHI | MLB | 28 | 0 | 0 | 0 | 3¹ | 4 | 1 | 3 | 4 | 8.1 | 10.8 | 50% | .333 | 2.10 | 5.40 | 7.19 | 6.38 | -0.1 |

**Yhency Brazoban** resurfaced after a season lost to injury and one bouncing around the minors, striking out 42 batters in 36 1/3 Triple-A frames. The Diamondbacks gave him a look after he requested his release from the Rangers, then kicked off the next leg of his world tour by selling him to the Fukuoka SoftBank Hawks in late July. ⊘ After struggling in relief at Triple-A in 2010, former lefty specialist **Zach Kroenke**'s first full season in a minor-league rotation went poorly—shocking, we know. ⊘ Once a closer candidate for the Indians, **Jensen Lewis** struggled in Columbus last season and was released in June, but he's only 27 and was useful as recently as 2010. The Diamondbacks signed him in November, dashing our dreams that he'd become a paid spokesman for the Manhattan furniture company that bears his name. ⊘ The lesser reliever acquired in the Mark Reynolds trade, 6'9 righty **Kameron Mickolio** had high-BABIP issues for the second straight Triple-A season. Sooner or later, the strikeouts will shine through. ⊘ Six-foot-one Dominican right-hander **Yonata Ortega**'s fastball touches 98, but his scale hasn't touched 198 in ages. A few extra pounds might not be a problem, but it's not a great sign when you miss bats and still outweigh your strikeout-to-walk ratio. ⊘ The D-Backs acquired **Mike Zagurski** from the Phillies in late September and will give him a shot this season, which means Arizona's strength and conditioning coordinator has his work cut out for him.

## MANAGER: KIRK GIBSON

| YEAR | TEAM | W-L | +/- | Pythag PC | Avg 100+ P | 120+ P | QS | BQS | REL | REL w Zero R | IBB | Subs | PH | PH Avg | PH HR | SB2 | CS2 | SB3 | CS3 | SAC Att | SAC % | POS SAC | Squeeze | Swing | In Play |
|---|---|---|---|---|---|---|---|---|---|---|---|---|---|---|---|---|---|---|---|---|---|---|---|---|---|
| 2010 | ARI | 34-49 | 0 | 188.7 | 83 | 83 | 56 | 3 | 247 | 181 | 38 | — | 302 | .235 | 0 | 3 | 1 | 0 | 1 | 64 | 84.4% | 24 | 0 | 153 | 31 |
| 2011 | ARI | 94-68 | 1 | 96.9 | 80 | 0 | 90 | 6 | 463 | 375 | 16 | — | 248 | .206 | 5 | 16 | 2 | 0 | 0 | 96 | 61.5% | 26 | 3 | 306 | 79 |

In steering the low-payroll Diamondbacks from worst place to first place in the span of a single season, Gibson added another "I don't believe what I just saw"-worthy accomplishment to his career record, though this one was a team effort that took even longer to complete than his painful trudge around the bases in the 1988 World Series. As is always the case when a skipper presides over a remarkable reversal in a team's fortunes, even one driven by Pythagorean overperformance, it's hard to say how much credit Gibson deserves (though the BBWAA voters didn't hesitate to make him Manager of the Year); after all, he didn't work any immediate miracles with the losing club he inherited from A.J. Hinch in 2010. Perhaps the highest compliment that can be paid to Gibson is that he got out of the way and let his team play. The Diamondbacks recorded the fewest sacrifice hits and handed out the fewest intentional walks in the senior circuit; Gibson called for free passes just over 20 percent as often as Atlanta's IBB-happy Fredi Gonzalez. However, Gibson wasn't the perfect sabermetric manager. It's possible to find fault with Gibson's batting orders: Willie Bloomquist was the team's most frequent leadoff man, while Gerardo Parra, one of the team's best hitters, usually languished in the eighth slot (when he wasn't being pointlessly platooned with Collin Cowgill). Gibson earned plenty of praise for improving Arizona's preparation, motivation, and clubhouse culture, the sort of intangible effects that some take on faith and others cynically dismiss as byproducts of winning instead of its cause. Now that he's righted the ship, he'll have plenty of time to make sure it stays afloat: Not long after his team's exit from the NLDS, Gibson received an extension that will keep him in Arizona through at least 2014.

# Atlanta Braves

The good times were back. Atlanta entered August 25 leading the wild card by 9 1/2 games with 30 to play. Teams with leads that great and finish lines that close tend to be postseason locks. Atlanta was no different. The Braves had every reason to begin designing, printing, and distribut-

director Roy Clark were the brain trust. The games were on TBS. These are not those Braves—not in their winning ways, not in personnel. The Braves have not won a postseason series since 2001, and they've reached the postseason just once in the past six years.

| | | |
|---|---|---|
| RA/G | | |
| TAv | .247 | 26th |
| TAv-P | .240 | 3rd |
| FIP | 3.46 | 3rd |
| DER | .712 | 14th |
| DL | 662 | 10th |
| B-Age | 28.9 | 18th |
| P-Age | 28.7 | 22nd |
| Salary | $92.2 | 15th |
| M$/MW | $1.96 | 12th |

**2011:** What's more amazing, blowing a 9 1/2-game wild-card lead, or holding it in the first place?

**2012:** A deep rotation, a solid core, and talented prospects. Watch out, Philly

**Action Items:** More offense, especially from short and the outfield

play another game or not. Win and Atlanta would play at least once more; lose and no such guarantees existed. Because fate is cruel, the Braves would do battle with the Phillies, while the Cardinals—now tied with the Braves in the wild card—would face the Astros. St. Louis scored five runs in the first inning and cruised to an eight-run victory. While they were doing that, Atlanta took a two-run lead into the seventh inning and a one-run lead into the ninth.

ing director. Between Fredi Gonzalez, Frank Wren, and Tony DeMacio, the trio has fewer than 10 years of combined experience with the Braves in their current positions. Most organizations are doing well to keep a piece or two of the triumvirate intact for more than a decade. The Braves have had two managers and two general managers since 1991, and three scouting directors since 1981. Change is not something the Braves are accustomed to, but some-

Play the game a thousand times and the Braves walk away with a victory almost 90 percent of the time. Baseball is beloved for its unpredictability for good reason, and the Braves would blow the lead in the ninth. Bitter division rivals headed to extra innings knowing that the Braves would have to win to avoid elimination. The 10th saw no scoring, nor the 11th. The 12th came and went with the Braves stranding the winning run on third. The 13th saw the eventual winning run score after Hunter Pence hit a broken-bat single that never left the infield. The Cardinals were in, the Phillies were in. The Braves were out.

During the Braves' run of the 1990s and 2000s, they were teases. Regular-season giants, postseason dwarves. Atlanta produced a 15-year stretch honeycombed with 14 division titles and a lone World Series victory. Who can forget: Manager Bobby Cox, GM John Schuerholz, and scouting

thing that has popped up in succession in recent years.

Atlanta's organizational culture shock carries off the field and beyond the front offices into the previously sacrosanct draft war room. Clark and predecessor/mentor Paul Snyder had a simple philosophy: take the most athletic baseball player they could find. Often, that player would hail from some backwoods town in Georgia, where he'd grown up rooting for the Braves. The organization would use this as a negotiating ploy, and the player would sign on the dotted line to join his favorite team. Atlanta, meanwhile, reaped the benefits of having high-ceiling players with whom they were intimately familiar. Seeing two, three, four Georgians in the Braves top five, six, seven picks was once a common sight, but no more. Under DeMacio, the Braves have shifted to a more conservative philosophy in risk and cost. The team now targets collegiate players with lower ceilings and higher likelihood of becoming major leaguers, thus eschewing the old way—or, as many called it, the Braves way.

Some things have remained constant, such as the Braves' allegiance to signing and developing international, and especially Latin American, talent. The glory days of yore included products of the system such as Andruw Jones, Javy Lopez, and Rafael Furcal. The glory days of the future could include a number of international players, too, particularly if the top prospects work out. With a strong developmental team still in place, the Braves have as good a chance as any team to turn these unpolished stones into gems.

Turning question marks into exclamation points is an art Wren has mastered at the major-league level. Contending teams sometimes lose sight of a fundamental reality when building their lineups to compete against All-Star teams. That reality is that the bench matters, too. Playing baseball is not an easy task. It takes a toll mentally, physically, and spiritually on the everyday players. All those games, all that travel, all those late nights spent partying to get away from the game for a while, they add up. Players need a day off every now and again, and having a good bench allows a team to be more accommodating. Otherwise, an All-Star lineup will win games, but a minor league bench can lose them.

Wren tipped his hand on benches when he acquired a number of depth pieces at the trade deadline—an unsexy quartet of Matt Diaz, Jack Wilson, Wes Helms, and Wil Nieves. The purpose was not to push the Braves over the top but to buttress an already impressive roster in case of injury. The moves proved prescient, if fruitless, as Diaz and Wilson started games over the final week. Praising Wren and leaving it at that is one way to go about business, but curious minds want to know: Just how good is Wren at building a bench? Alternatively, is this a case where the anecdotes get ahead of reality?

A problem in evaluating benches is trying to define a bench player. Since American League teams often carry four bench players, and National League teams—not burdened by the designated hitter—carry five, that means you would expect the number of bench players per team to be a touch more than 4.5, given that there are more NL teams. Sure enough, the parameters we came up with returned a tally of 4.7 bench players per team. The playing time constrictions used to come up with that rate called for no more than 3.3 plate appearances per game played, but at least 40 games played. From there, Wins Above Replacement Player can be added to easily evaluate the merit of a team's bench.

As the above table suggests, the Braves have shown a proficiency in building talented benches. Just as impressive is the money Atlanta has paid for such superlative production from its reserves. Despite leading the league in WARP, the Braves rank only 10th in bench-player salary. It should be noted that a team's tally can be skewed by having a

high-priced player in a bench capacity, but then again, why should that team be treated any differently? Any argument centered around the Braves spending too much on their bench while neglecting the other areas of the team seems baseless.

## Top benches 2008-11

| NL Team | WARP | AL Team | WARP |
|---|---|---|---|
| Atlanta | 9.6 | Tampa Bay | 4.1 |
| Milwaukee | 8.7 | Detroit | 3.9 |
| Cincinnati | 8.0 | New York | 3.7 |
| Chicago | 7.5 | Seattle | 3.4 |
| Colorado | 5.1 | Minnesota | 3.4 |

How the Braves were able to generate production without writing massive checks becomes obvious once you examine the acquisitions of their key contributors. Atlanta signed Martin Prado as an international free agent from Venezuela as a teenager. Omar Infante came over in a trade for Jose Ascanio that also netted Atlanta Will Ohman. The Braves signed David Ross after he spent time in five other organizations. Brooks Conrad and Jose Constanza were minor-league free agents. Even Matt Diaz, the first time Atlanta acquired him, came over as a journeyman without major-league success in exchange for Ricardo Rodriguez, a pitcher who would exit organized baseball a season later. And so on. The only honest-to-goodness major leaguer with a bunch of pre-Braves success to star in a bench role was Eric Hinske.

## Top Braves individual bench seasons 2008-11

| Season | Player | PA | WARP |
|---|---|---|---|
| 2008 | Martin Prado | 254 | 1.5 |
| 2009 | David Ross | 151 | 1.4 |
| 2010 | Brooks Conrad | 177 | 1.1 |
| 2010 | David Ross | 145 | 1.1 |
| 2009 | Omar Infante | 229 | 0.9 |

You get the feeling that if the Braves were only more open about their use of sabermetrics, they would become community darlings. Instead, Atlanta's stubbornness when it comes to perceived loafers like Yunel Escobar casts them as unenlightened, ossified in their prehistoric ways. The Braves will be just fine, though, as their methodology seems to find undervalued players by the handful.

Atlanta's methodology seems to work when it comes to finding any type of player. The offseason consisted of trolling the market for potential trades. After shipping Derek Lowe's contract to Cleveland, the Braves spent the early portion of the offseason shopping starting pitcher Jair Jurrjens and left fielder Martin Prado. Atlanta annually seems to be a corner outfielder and some health away from being a threat in the postseason, and on paper, the 2012 season looks no different. With a scary amount of rotation depth, young high-upside prospects in the minors, and a solid core, the Braves are in a good position to rival the Phillies as the division's powerhouse for the next few seasons. They might not be TBS's Braves, but they could bring the good times back.

# HITTERS

### Christian Bethancourt  C

Born: 9/2/1991 Age: 20
Bats: R Throws: R Height: 6' 3" Weight: 175
Breakout: 1% Improve: 2% Collapse: 0%
Attrition: 1% MLB: 4%

| YEAR | TEAM | LVL | AGE | PA | R | 2B | 3B | HR | RBI | BB | SO | SB | CS | AVG_OBP_SLG | TAv | BABIP | BRR | FRAA | WARP |
|------|------|-----|-----|----|----|----|----|----|-----|----|----|----|----|-------------|-----|-------|-----|------|------|
| 2009 | BRA | RK | 17 | 131 | 22 | 9 | 1 | 2 | 19 | 11 | 22 | 7 | 0 | .284/.352/.431 | .275 | .337 | 1.2 | -0.2 | 0.6 |
| 2009 | DNV | RK | 17 | 56 | 10 | 5 | 0 | 2 | 8 | 6 | 16 | 1 | 1 | .260/.339/.480 | .318 | .344 | 0 | -0.4 | 0.6 |
| 2010 | ROM | A | 18 | 420 | 31 | 19 | 2 | 3 | 34 | 14 | 62 | 11 | 3 | .251/.280/.331 | .236 | .290 | -1.4 | -0.2 | 0.3 |
| 2011 | ROM | A | 19 | 235 | 25 | 10 | 3 | 4 | 33 | 8 | 27 | 6 | 3 | .303/.323/.430 | .276 | .323 | 1.5 | 0.9 | 1.6 |

treats the strike zone like a theory, and his susceptibility to secondary pitches make him a candidate to post the worst walk-to-strikeout ratio on the team.

### Michael Bourn  CF

Born: 12/27/1982 Age: 29
Bats: L Throws: R Height: 6' 0" Weight: 180
Breakout: 1% Improve: 36% Collapse: 15%
Attrition: 26% MLB: 84%

Comparables:
Todd Donovan, Lew Ford, Chris Duffy

| YEAR | TEAM | LVL | AGE | PA | R | 2B | 3B | HR | RBI | BB | SO | SB | CS | AVG_OBP_SLG | TAv | BABIP | BRR | FRAA | WARP |
|------|------|-----|-----|----|----|----|----|----|-----|----|----|----|----|-------------|-----|-------|-----|------|------|
| 2009 | HOU | MLB | 26 | 678 | 97 | 27 | 12 | 3 | 35 | 63 | 140 | 61 | 12 | .285/.354/.384 | .261 | .366 | 10.9 | 3.4 | 3.2 |
| 2010 | HOU | MLB | 27 | 605 | 84 | 25 | 6 | 2 | 38 | 59 | 109 | 52 | 12 | .265/.341/.346 | .251 | .329 | 10.4 | 6.9 | 3.3 |
| 2011 | HOU | MLB | 28 | 473 | 64 | 26 | 7 | 1 | 32 | 38 | 90 | 39 | 7 | .303/.363/.403 | .277 | .381 | 4.4 | -1.8 | 2.4 |
| 2011 | ATL | MLB | 28 | 249 | 30 | 8 | 3 | 1 | 18 | 15 | 50 | 22 | 7 | .278/.321/.352 | .250 | .346 | 2.2 | -5.3 | 0.3 |
| 2012 | ATL | MLB | 29 | 655 | 73 | 24 | 7 | 5 | 57 | 55 | 129 | 55 | 12 | .269/.333/.356 | .249 | .331 | 1.7 | CF 1 | 1.5 |

After the Braves came up short on acquiring Hunter Pence, they found a match on Houston's *other* outfielder without sacrificing a top-tier arm. On paper, acquiring Bourn to replace Jordan Schafer at leadoff and in center field made sense. At the time of the trade, Bourn looked like a player who would eclipse multiple career highs by season's end. That momentum for a statistical slaughter ended once Bourn put on the Braves' colors, and he limped to a meager finish by striking out more often, walking less often, and hitting for less power than he had earlier in the season with Houston. Even Bourn's stolen base success rate dipped once he joined Atlanta. Bourn will receive an opportunity to validate the trade, but PECOTA is bearish.

### Brooks Conrad  3B

Born: 1/16/1980 Age: 32
Bats: B Throws: R Height: 6' 0" Weight: 190
Breakout: 8% Improve: 26% Collapse: 9%
Attrition: 25% MLB: 77%

Comparables:
Rico Petrocelli, Cody Ransom, Phil Nevin

| YEAR | TEAM | LVL | AGE | PA | R | 2B | 3B | HR | RBI | BB | SO | SB | CS | AVG_OBP_SLG | TAv | BABIP | BRR | FRAA | WARP |
|------|------|-----|-----|----|----|----|----|----|-----|----|----|----|----|-------------|-----|-------|-----|------|------|
| 2009 | GWN | AAA | 29 | 469 | 66 | 25 | 0 | 12 | 64 | 53 | 108 | 13 | 1 | .269/.363/.422 | .276 | .339 | 5 | 0.5 | 2.2 |
| 2009 | ATL | MLB | 29 | 58 | 7 | 1 | 2 | 2 | 8 | 3 | 14 | 0 | 0 | .204/.259/.407 | .210 | .237 | 0.6 | 0.1 | -0.1 |
| 2010 | ATL | MLB | 30 | 177 | 31 | 11 | 1 | 8 | 33 | 16 | 45 | 5 | 1 | .250/.324/.487 | .279 | .301 | 2 | -0.4 | 1.1 |
| 2011 | ATL | MLB | 31 | 122 | 11 | 5 | 0 | 4 | 13 | 15 | 41 | 2 | 0 | .223/.325/.388 | .260 | .322 | 0.5 | -0.1 | 0.3 |
| 2012 | MIL | MLB | 32 | 250 | 28 | 11 | 1 | 9 | 29 | 23 | 72 | 4 | 1 | .223/.299/.404 | .246 | .279 | 0.2 | 3B -1, 2B -1 | 1.0 |

Conrad has an excuse if he is dizzy, because the last 24 months have resembled a bad elevator ride. He started 2010 as a minor-league lifer, recorded some big hits that made him a regular-season hero, flubbed a few defensive chances that turned him into a postseason goat, and then spent 2011 nestled into a bench role. Reserve life is one that fits Conrad well. His defensive position is whichever spot needs filling, and his offensive output is limited by a long swing. Being flexible in the field and at the plate (he switch-hits) makes him a useful pinch-hitter or defensive sub, but not a starting-caliber player. Credit Fredi Gonzalez for recognizing this.

### Jose Constanza — CF

Born: 9/1/1983 Age: 28
Bats: L Throws: L Height: 5' 10" Weight: 150
Breakout: 6% Improve: 37% Collapse: 7%
Attrition: 23% MLB: 81%

Comparables:
Freddy Guzman, Nyjer Morgan, Norris Hopper

| YEAR | TEAM | LVL | AGE | PA | R | 2B | 3B | HR | RBI | BB | SO | SB | CS | AVG_OBP_SLG | TAv | BABIP | BRR | FRAA | WARP |
|------|------|-----|-----|-----|----|----|----|----|-----|----|----|----|----|-------------|------|-------|------|---------|------|
| 2009 | AKR | AA | 25 | 575 | 98 | 15 | 7 | 0 | 46 | 75 | 65 | 49 | 14 | .282/.372/.342 | .276 | .317 | 9.2 | 2.2 | 3.8 |
| 2010 | COH | AAA | 26 | 448 | 69 | 11 | 8 | 1 | 32 | 35 | 54 | 34 | 6 | .319/.367/.394 | .253 | .359 | 2.7 | -6.2 | 0.4 |
| 2011 | GWN | AAA | 27 | 363 | 47 | 2 | 4 | 1 | 25 | 25 | 41 | 23 | 8 | .312/.361/.351 | .246 | .353 | 2.8 | 1.3 | 0.7 |
| 2011 | ATL | MLB | 27 | 119 | 21 | 1 | 1 | 2 | 10 | 6 | 14 | 7 | 4 | .303/.339/.385 | .285 | .333 | 1.8 | 2.3 | 0.8 |
| 2012 | ATL | MLB | 28 | 250 | 28 | 6 | 2 | 2 | 20 | 20 | 34 | 14 | 5 | .280/.338/.345 | .249 | .317 | -0.2 | CF -4, LF 2 | 0.6 |

Anyone who predicted Constanza would start in Jason Heyward's place prior to last season deserves a straitjacket as a prize. Blinding speed and defensive aptitude make Constanza a functional bench player, perfect for pinch-running and defensive substitution assignments—as does a bat that belongs to the slash family tree, even if he did hit as many home runs in the majors as he did over his last two seasons in Triple-A. The Braves would be wise to install Constanza as the fifth outfielder and leverage his skills properly. They would also be wise never to play him over Heyward for any stretch of time again.

### Matt Diaz — LF

Born: 3/3/1978 Age: 34
Bats: R Throws: R Height: 6' 2" Weight: 200
Breakout: 1% Improve: 15% Collapse: 12%
Attrition: 27% MLB: 85%

Comparables:
Carl Furillo, Lee Lacy, Hank Bauer

| YEAR | TEAM | LVL | AGE | PA | R | 2B | 3B | HR | RBI | BB | SO | SB | CS | AVG_OBP_SLG | TAv | BABIP | BRR | FRAA | WARP |
|------|------|-----|-----|-----|----|----|----|----|-----|----|----|----|----|-------------|------|-------|------|---------|------|
| 2009 | ATL | MLB | 31 | 425 | 56 | 18 | 4 | 13 | 58 | 35 | 90 | 12 | 5 | .313/.390/.488 | .301 | .383 | -4 | -5.9 | 1.6 |
| 2010 | ATL | MLB | 32 | 244 | 27 | 17 | 2 | 7 | 31 | 13 | 44 | 3 | 1 | .250/.302/.438 | .264 | .282 | 0.7 | 2.3 | 0.7 |
| 2011 | PIT | MLB | 33 | 231 | 14 | 12 | 1 | 0 | 19 | 11 | 44 | 4 | 2 | .259/.303/.324 | .228 | .324 | -0.8 | -4.6 | -1.0 |
| 2011 | ATL | MLB | 33 | 37 | 2 | 1 | 0 | 0 | 1 | 1 | 8 | 1 | 0 | .286/.297/.314 | .205 | .357 | -0.3 | 0.1 | -0.2 |
| 2012 | ATL | MLB | 34 | 250 | 29 | 11 | 1 | 5 | 27 | 14 | 49 | 5 | 2 | .276/.325/.399 | .261 | .326 | -0.2 | LF 0, RF -5 | 1.0 |

Lassoed from Pittsburgh late in the season to serve in reserve, Diaz's uncharacteristic trouble with southpaws worsened upon re-arrival in Atlanta. Fredi Gonzalez used Diaz better than Clint Hurdle had by maximizing his exposure to lefties—78 percent of his plate appearances, as opposed to 49 percent in Pittsburgh. Diaz managed to hit for average vs. lefties, so the culprit was a ghostly slugging percentage. A return to hitting lefties will make him the haute piece of bench decoration he served as during his first tour in Atlanta.

### Brandon Drury — 3B

Born: 8/21/1992 Age: 19
Bats: R Throws: R Height: 6' 3" Weight: 190
Breakout: 0% Improve: 0% Collapse: 1%
Attrition: 2% MLB: 2%

Comparables:
Josh Vitters, Yunior Figueroa, Mario Martinez

| YEAR | TEAM | LVL | AGE | PA | R | 2B | 3B | HR | RBI | BB | SO | SB | CS | AVG_OBP_SLG | TAv | BABIP | BRR | FRAA | WARP |
|------|------|-----|-----|-----|----|----|----|----|-----|----|----|----|----|-------------|------|-------|------|---------|------|
| 2010 | BRA | RK | 17 | 207 | 20 | 7 | 1 | 3 | 17 | 9 | 50 | 2 | 2 | .198/.248/.292 | .186 | .250 | 0.7 | -2.7 | -1.0 |
| 2011 | DNV | RK | 18 | 278 | 40 | 23 | 0 | 8 | 54 | 6 | 35 | 3 | 0 | .347/.367/.525 | .312 | .373 | 0 | -2 | 2.4 |
| 2012 | ATL | MLB | 19 | 250 | 19 | 9 | 0 | 2 | 19 | 5 | 61 | 0 | 0 | .198/.219/.269 | .174 | .252 | 0 | 3B 3, 2B 0 | -2.4 |

The Braves converted Drury, their 13th-round pick from Oregon, from shortstop to third base and watched as he struggled in his first exposure to professional ball, striking out in more than a quarter of his at-bats. He took a step forward in 2011 and almost won the Appalachian League batting title. Above-average bat speed combined with a quick swing on a big frame can lead to some damaging blows, and Drury has the potential to turn into a nice power hitter. In the interim, he still needs to work on his approach, and there is every reason to believe he will, given his high marks in makeup.

### Luis Durango — CF

Born: 4/23/1986 Age: 26
Bats: B Throws: R Height: 5' 10" Weight: 160
Breakout: 1% Improve: 44% Collapse: 6%
Attrition: 19% MLB: 68%

Comparables:
Alex Cole, Brad Coon, Joey Gathright

| YEAR | TEAM | LVL | AGE | PA | R | 2B | 3B | HR | RBI | BB | SO | SB | CS | AVG_OBP_SLG | TAv | BABIP | BRR | FRAA | WARP |
|------|------|-----|-----|-----|----|----|----|----|-----|----|----|----|----|-------------|------|-------|------|---------|------|
| 2009 | SAN | AA | 23 | 560 | 78 | 9 | 2 | 0 | 25 | 81 | 70 | 44 | 17 | .281/.378/.309 | .274 | .316 | 3.2 | -0.3 | 2.2 |
| 2009 | SDN | MLB | 23 | 14 | 3 | 0 | 0 | 0 | 0 | 2 | 2 | 2 | 1 | .545/.615/.545 | .414 | .667 | 1.1 | -0.1 | 0.4 |
| 2010 | POR | AAA | 24 | 423 | 42 | 5 | 2 | 0 | 24 | 45 | 59 | 35 | 16 | .300/.367/.325 | .271 | .344 | -0.1 | 5.1 | 2.0 |
| 2010 | SDN | MLB | 24 | 53 | 8 | 0 | 0 | 0 | 4 | 4 | 7 | 5 | 0 | .250/.308/.250 | .196 | .293 | 1.2 | -0.7 | 0.0 |
| 2011 | OKL | AAA | 25 | 180 | 33 | 2 | 1 | 0 | 9 | 22 | 23 | 18 | 9 | .273/.362/.299 | .237 | .318 | 1.3 | -0.2 | 0.1 |
| 2011 | HOU | MLB | 25 | 7 | 0 | 0 | 0 | 0 | 1 | 1 | 1 | 0 | 0 | .167/.286/.167 | .186 | .200 | -0.1 | -0.2 | -0.1 |
| 2012 | ATL | MLB | 26 | 250 | 25 | 6 | 1 | 1 | 16 | 25 | 44 | 13 | 5 | .244/.324/.296 | .227 | .292 | -0.4 | CF -1, LF -3 | -0.3 |

Durango is a switch-hitting waterbug who spent 2011 traveling the country. He started in San Diego's camp, was claimed off waivers by Houston, then signed with the Braves as a minor-league free agent. A spacious park seems to best fit Durango's bunt-heavy approach, which leaves fielders playing as far in as when children bat at a picnic softball game. However, Atlanta has found use for similar players like Jose Constanza, and Durango's .373 on-base percentage over the last three seasons suggests he could stick as a fifth outfielder somewhere. At least until he loses a step.

**Freddie Freeman**    **1B**

Born: **9/12/1989** Age: **22**
Bats: **L** Throws: **R** Height: **6' 6"** Weight: **225**
Breakout: **2%** Improve: **33%** Collapse: **4%**
Attrition: **17%** MLB: **68%**

**Comparables:**
Mike Ivie, Jason Thompson, Billy Butler

| YEAR | TEAM | LVL | AGE | PA | R | 2B | 3B | HR | RBI | BB | SO | SB | CS | AVG_OBP_SLG | TAv | BABIP | BRR | FRAA | WARP |
|---|---|---|---|---|---|---|---|---|---|---|---|---|---|---|---|---|---|---|---|
| 2009 | MYR | A+ | 19 | 297 | 43 | 19 | 0 | 6 | 34 | 26 | 41 | 1 | 4 | .302/.397/.447 | .293 | .341 | -2.3 | 0.3 | 1.0 |
| 2009 | MIS | AA | 19 | 169 | 15 | 8 | 0 | 2 | 24 | 11 | 19 | 0 | 0 | .248/.317/.342 | .242 | .273 | -0.5 | 0.6 | -0.4 |
| 2010 | GWN | AAA | 20 | 519 | 73 | 35 | 2 | 18 | 87 | 43 | 84 | 6 | 2 | .319/.384/.521 | .297 | .359 | -0.5 | -0.6 | 2.5 |
| 2010 | ATL | MLB | 20 | 24 | 3 | 1 | 0 | 1 | 1 | 0 | 8 | 0 | 0 | .167/.167/.333 | .193 | .200 | -0.1 | 0.1 | -0.1 |
| 2011 | ATL | MLB | 21 | 635 | 67 | 32 | 0 | 21 | 76 | 53 | 142 | 4 | 4 | .282/.346/.448 | .280 | .339 | -2.1 | -5.1 | 0.8 |
| 2012 | ATL | MLB | 22 | 535 | 65 | 25 | 1 | 16 | 63 | 39 | 108 | 3 | 2 | .271/.332/.426 | .271 | .315 | -0.4 | 1B -13 | 1.3 |

Finding a harmony between the scouting reports and defensive metrics about Freeman is impossible. Folks who watched Freeman know about his picking-and-scooping abilities as well as his strong arm, characteristics that fan the flames of contention. Freeman's offensive output is less controversial. He became the youngest first baseman in club history to belt 20-plus home runs during the regular season, and produced at rates better than league-average. The downsides to Freeman's season at the plate were his strikeouts (more than expected), issues against left-handed pitching, and wayward plate discipline. Still,

Attrition: **16%** MLB: **83%**

**Comparables:**
Keith Mitchell, Gary Carter, Curt Blefary

| YEAR | TEAM | LVL | AGE | PA | R | 2B | 3B | HR | RBI | BB | SO | SB | CS | AVG_OBP_SLG | TAv | BABIP | BRR | FRAA | WARP |
|---|---|---|---|---|---|---|---|---|---|---|---|---|---|---|---|---|---|---|---|
| 2011 | ATL | MLB | 21 | 454 | 50 | 18 | 2 | 14 | 42 | 51 | 93 | 9 | 2 | .227/.319/.389 | .254 | .260 | -0.6 | 3 | 0.5 |
| 2012 | ATL | MLB | 22 | 461 | 59 | 20 | 3 | 15 | 54 | 56 | 88 | 8 | 3 | .267/.363/.439 | .291 | .308 | -0.1 | RF 4, CF -0 | 2.4 |

Less than two years ago, Braves fans were touting Heyward as the next hometown hero. After a disappointing 2011, some of those same fans were lamenting having Heyward instead of Mike Stanton. Heyward started April looking right and killing everything—smashing seven home runs and owning an OPS near 900. Unfortunately for Heyward, the season extended into late September, but his offensive production did not. He wound up on the disabled list due to shoulder inflammation, and Chipper Jones took the time to add insult to injury by questioning his toughness. When Heyward returned, Fredi Gonzalez then sprinkled some salt into the wound by opting to bench Heyward for Matt Diaz and Jose Constanza. The J-Hey Kid still profiles as one of baseball's next great stars, but he needs to duplicate and exceed his freshman campaign. For now, give Heyward the benefit of the doubt that he will do just that in 2012.

**Brandon Hicks**    **SS**

Born: **9/14/1985** Age: **26**
Bats: **R** Throws: **R** Height: **6' 3"** Weight: **200**
Breakout: **1%** Improve: **45%** Collapse: **6%**
Attrition: **21%** MLB: **79%**

**Comparables:**
Grant Psomas, Felipe Lopez, Jose Valentin

| YEAR | TEAM | LVL | AGE | PA | R | 2B | 3B | HR | RBI | BB | SO | SB | CS | AVG_OBP_SLG | TAv | BABIP | BRR | FRAA | WARP |
|---|---|---|---|---|---|---|---|---|---|---|---|---|---|---|---|---|---|---|---|
| 2009 | MIS | AA | 23 | 534 | 63 | 25 | 4 | 10 | 48 | 53 | 131 | 17 | 1 | .237/.317/.373 | .258 | .302 | 1.6 | 1.8 | 2.4 |
| 2010 | GWN | AAA | 24 | 287 | 27 | 9 | 1 | 7 | 22 | 20 | 74 | 10 | 6 | .211/.279/.333 | .199 | .265 | 1.3 | 3.8 | -0.1 |
| 2010 | ATL | MLB | 24 | 6 | 7 | 0 | 0 | 0 | 0 | 1 | 2 | 0 | 0 | .000/.167/.000 | .096 | .000 | 0.7 | 0.1 | 0.0 |
| 2011 | GWN | AAA | 25 | 407 | 52 | 14 | 1 | 18 | 50 | 41 | 137 | 8 | 3 | .252/.333/.446 | .255 | .354 | 0.5 | -0.1 | 1.4 |
| 2011 | ATL | MLB | 25 | 22 | 1 | 0 | 0 | 0 | 1 | 1 | 9 | 0 | 0 | .048/.091/.048 | .061 | .083 | -0.6 | -0.1 | -0.5 |
| 2012 | ATL | MLB | 26 | 250 | 25 | 8 | 1 | 6 | 23 | 20 | 76 | 5 | 2 | .216/.283/.345 | .226 | .290 | -0.1 | SS -0, 3B 0 | 0.2 |

Last year we wrote that the fact that Hicks got a grand total of six plate appearances in his 16 games tells you everything about his bat. If you did not believe us then, maybe you will be more inclined to now. Hicks combines a hitch in his swing with an uppercut, a combination not conductive to contact or major league success. Given his ability to play each infield position and his occasional pop, Hicks could become a reserve. More likely is a career as a fringe player.

**Eric Hinske**    **LF**

Born: **8/5/1977** Age: **34**
Bats: **L** Throws: **R** Height: **6' 3"** Weight: **225**
Breakout: **1%** Improve: **27%** Collapse: **6%**
Attrition: **32%** MLB: **86%**

**Comparables:**
Chris Richard, Cliff Floyd, Charlie Maxwell

| YEAR | TEAM | LVL | AGE | PA | R | 2B | 3B | HR | RBI | BB | SO | SB | CS | AVG_OBP_SLG | TAv | BABIP | BRR | FRAA | WARP |
|---|---|---|---|---|---|---|---|---|---|---|---|---|---|---|---|---|---|---|---|
| 2009 | NYA | MLB | 31 | 98 | 13 | 3 | 0 | 7 | 14 | 10 | 25 | 1 | 0 | .226/.316/.512 | .287 | .222 | 0.3 | -1.7 | 0.3 |
| 2009 | PIT | MLB | 31 | 126 | 18 | 9 | 0 | 1 | 11 | 17 | 27 | 0 | 0 | .255/.373/.368 | .263 | .333 | -0.4 | 0.7 | 0.2 |
| 2010 | ATL | MLB | 32 | 320 | 38 | 21 | 1 | 11 | 51 | 33 | 75 | 0 | 0 | .256/.338/.456 | .275 | .308 | -0.6 | -0.4 | 0.7 |
| 2011 | ATL | MLB | 33 | 264 | 24 | 10 | 0 | 10 | 28 | 26 | 71 | 0 | 1 | .233/.311/.403 | .248 | .288 | 0.2 | 0.4 | 0.3 |
| 2012 | ATL | MLB | 34 | 259 | 30 | 11 | 1 | 9 | 30 | 27 | 62 | 2 | 1 | .235/.322/.413 | .263 | .280 | -0.1 | LF -1, 1B 1 | 1.1 |

Hinske owns a World Series ring, a Rookie of the Year award, and an equally redoubtable back tattoo. Despite never improving on 2002, he has become a fixture on a contender's bench and has appeared in the postseason in four of the last five seasons. Hinske excels vs. righties, struggles vs. lefties, and can fill in at each of the four corner positions. Such a skill set is a luxury to have on the bench. Factor in the great clubhouse reviews he receives and the Braves' decision to exercise his option is no surprise.

**Chipper Jones**    **3B**

Born: 4/24/1972 Age: 40
Bats: B Throws: R Height: 6' 4" Weight: 185
Breakout: 1% Improve: 18% Collapse: 9%
Attrition: 17% MLB: 69%

Comparables:
Mike Schmidt, Rafael Palmeiro, Stan Musial

| YEAR | TEAM | LVL | AGE | PA | R | 2B | 3B | HR | RBI | BB | SO | SB | CS | AVG_OBP_SLG | TAv | BABIP | BRR | FRAA | WARP |
|------|------|-----|-----|-----|----|----|----|----|-----|----|-----|----|----|---------------|------|-------|------|--------|------|
| 2009 | ATL | MLB | 37 | 596 | 80 | 23 | 2 | 18 | 71 | 101 | 89 | 4 | 1 | .264/.388/.430 | .285 | .287 | -0.5 | -9.9 | 2.0 |
| 2010 | ATL | MLB | 38 | 381 | 47 | 21 | 0 | 10 | 46 | 61 | 47 | 5 | 0 | .265/.381/.426 | .286 | .281 | -0.3 | 1.9 | 2.4 |
| 2011 | ATL | MLB | 39 | 512 | 56 | 33 | 1 | 18 | 70 | 51 | 80 | 2 | 2 | .275/.344/.470 | .288 | .295 | -4.9 | -12.6 | 0.8 |
| 2012 | ATL | MLB | 40 | 456 | 61 | 21 | 1 | 14 | 54 | 62 | 66 | 3 | 1 | .282/.379/.449 | .297 | .307 | 0 | 3B -6 | 3.6 |

The legend goes like this: Bobby Cox, unsold on Jones's leadership ability, signed off on drafting the switch-hitting third baseman after finding out that Jones punched an opponent who yakked at his pitcher. Jones fittingly broke his hand in the act, because hitting and breaking are his two dependable qualities. When hearty and hale, Jones is a top-10 offensive third baseman who makes up for declining power output and an ill-stricken glove with healthy strikeout and walk rates. Jones has not played in more than 150 games since 2003, missing at least three weeks in every season since 2004. There will be retirement talk with 2012 being Jones's last contractually guaranteed season, but his option for 2013 vests with a reachable 123 games played.

**Mycal Jones**    **SS**

Born: 5/30/1987 Age: 25
Bats: R Throws: R Height: 5' 11" Weight: 165
Breakout: 4% Improve: 35% Collapse: 5%
Attrition: 24% MLB: 60%

Comparables:
Shane Mack, Rich Becker, Steve Garrabrants

| YEAR | TEAM | LVL | AGE | PA | R | 2B | 3B | HR | RBI | BB | SO | SB | CS | AVG_OBP_SLG | TAv | BABIP | BRR | FRAA | WARP |
|------|------|-----|-----|-----|----|----|----|----|-----|----|----|----|----|---------------|------|-------|------|-----------|------|
| 2009 | DNV | RK | 22 | 282 | 50 | 18 | 6 | 4 | 27 | 26 | 55 | 19 | 4 | .258/.338/.430 | .289 | .314 | 3.6 | 0 | 2.3 |
| 2010 | ROM | A | 23 | 219 | 27 | 12 | 0 | 6 | 34 | 11 | 48 | 6 | 3 | .261/.302/.412 | .266 | .311 | 1.7 | -2.8 | 1.0 |
| 2010 | MYR | A+ | 23 | 318 | 51 | 19 | 1 | 7 | 22 | 31 | 66 | 15 | 4 | .269/.356/.422 | .288 | .328 | 4.2 | -8.4 | 1.9 |
| 2011 | MIS | AA | 24 | 449 | 63 | 25 | 1 | 7 | 36 | 56 | 90 | 17 | 6 | .252/.359/.381 | .273 | .314 | 0.7 | 3.4 | 2.3 |
| 2012 | ATL | MLB | 25 | 250 | 24 | 10 | 1 | 4 | 20 | 18 | 62 | 7 | 2 | .212/.276/.314 | .213 | .267 | -0.1 | SS -2, CF 0 | -0.5 |

Jones is an athletic marvel with tools that are still waiting to progress beyond the ornamental phase. Atlanta drafted him from a Florida junior college and moved him from shortstop to center field last season. Leadoff is the most logical landing spot for Jones's skill set since he steals bases (a career 77 percent success rate) and takes walks to overcome a contact deficiency. Soon to be 25, Jones is more raw than the age or assignment to Triple-A suggests, though he could still work his way into the majors before long.

**Matt Lipka**    **SS**

Born: 4/15/1992 Age: 20
Bats: R Throws: R Height: 6' 2" Weight: 188
Breakout: 0% Improve: 6% Collapse: 1%
Attrition: 4% MLB: 10%

Comparables:
Freddy Galvis, Drew Cumberland, Hak-Ju Lee

| YEAR | TEAM | LVL | AGE | PA | R | 2B | 3B | HR | RBI | BB | SO | SB | CS | AVG_OBP_SLG | TAv | BABIP | BRR | FRAA | WARP |
|------|------|-----|-----|-----|----|----|----|----|-----|----|----|----|----|---------------|------|-------|------|-----------|------|
| 2010 | BRA | RK | 18 | 210 | 33 | 8 | 4 | 1 | 24 | 14 | 22 | 20 | 3 | .302/.359/.401 | .307 | .337 | 3.8 | -1.1 | 2.1 |
| 2011 | ROM | A | 19 | 585 | 78 | 21 | 3 | 1 | 37 | 42 | 83 | 28 | 14 | .247/.305/.304 | .237 | .288 | 4.5 | 3.7 | 1.4 |
| 2012 | ATL | MLB | 20 | 250 | 21 | 8 | 1 | 1 | 17 | 10 | 50 | 6 | 3 | .216/.248/.270 | .189 | .265 | -0.5 | SS 3, 2B 1 | -1.7 |

Selected with the supplemental pick received for losing Mike Gonzalez, Lipka forewent a football scholarship at the University of Alabama to sign with the Braves. His introduction to Low-A ball went poorly—save a strong September—and proved that he still remains more projection than results. Blessed with tremendous bat and foot speed along with an above-average arm, Lipka could turn into something special if he hits on all cylinders. That seems unlikely, however, as he is still unrefined at the plate and in the field in part because of his previous dual-sport commitments. He's a hard worker, though. The Braves may elect to push him, and had him play center field during instructs—possibly a prelude to a position change.

**Brian McCann**    **C**

Born: 2/20/1984 Age: 28
Bats: L Throws: R Height: 6' 4" Weight: 210
Breakout: 2% Improve: 35% Collapse: 5%
Attrition: 20% MLB: 95%

Comparables:
Charlie O'Brien, Dave Sax, Yogi Berra

| YEAR | TEAM | LVL | AGE | PA | R | 2B | 3B | HR | RBI | BB | SO | SB | CS | AVG_OBP_SLG | TAv | BABIP | BRR | FRAA | WARP |
|------|------|-----|-----|-----|----|----|----|----|-----|----|----|----|----|---------------|------|-------|------|------|------|
| 2009 | ATL | MLB | 25 | 551 | 63 | 35 | 1 | 21 | 94 | 49 | 83 | 4 | 1 | .281/.349/.486 | .288 | .297 | -1.9 | 1.5 | 4.1 |
| 2010 | ATL | MLB | 26 | 566 | 63 | 25 | 0 | 21 | 77 | 74 | 98 | 5 | 2 | .269/.375/.453 | .292 | .297 | -3.4 | 1.5 | 4.3 |
| 2011 | ATL | MLB | 27 | 527 | 51 | 19 | 0 | 24 | 71 | 57 | 89 | 3 | 2 | .270/.351/.466 | .284 | .287 | -2.6 | 3.6 | 3.5 |
| 2012 | ATL | MLB | 28 | 504 | 66 | 26 | 0 | 19 | 66 | 50 | 73 | 3 | 1 | .278/.354/.468 | .292 | .293 | -0.1 | C 2 | 4.0 |

McCann is the best-hitting catcher in the National League and anyone who suggests otherwise is committing an act of impertinence. His career low in home runs over a full season is 18, his career-worst on-base percentage is .320 (the only time he finished at less than .349), and his slugging percentage has always ended at more than .450. Offensive production like that has earned McCann six straight All-Star appearances while making up for defensive deficiencies—namely that he does not throw out many baserunners. McCann has two seasons left on his current contract, assuming the Braves pick up a 2013 club option. Look for that to become a regular talking point sooner rather than later if the Joe Mauer hoopla was any indication.

**Tyler Pastornicky** SS
Born: **12/13/1989** Age: **22**
Bats: **R** Throws: **R** Height: **6' 0''** Weight: **170**
Breakout: **2%** Improve: **18%** Collapse: **10%**
Attrition: **20%** MLB: **54%**
**Comparables:**
Lenny Faedo, Andres Blanco, Drew Cumberland

| YEAR | TEAM | LVL | AGE | PA | R | 2B | 3B | HR | RBI | BB | SO | SB | CS | AVG_OBP_SLG | TAv | BABIP | BRR | FRAA | WARP |
|------|------|-----|-----|-----|----|----|----|----|-----|----|----|----|----|-------------|------|-------|------|------|------|
| 2009 | LNS | A | 19 | 459 | 63 | 11 | 9 | 1 | 31 | 39 | 50 | 51 | 15 | .269/.334/.346 | .253 | .301 | 2.9 | -1.2 | 1.6 |
| 2009 | DUN | A+ | 19 | 66 | 9 | 3 | 0 | 0 | 3 | 3 | 7 | 6 | 3 | .270/.303/.317 | .235 | .304 | -0.6 | 2.4 | 0.4 |
| 2010 | DUN | A+ | 20 | 331 | 50 | 16 | 0 | 6 | 35 | 39 | 49 | 24 | 7 | .258/.345/.376 | .264 | .289 | 4.8 | -2.1 | 1.7 |
| 2010 | MIS | AA | 20 | 160 | 22 | 5 | 2 | 2 | 15 | 16 | 22 | 11 | 2 | .254/.323/.366 | .274 | .274 | -0.1 | -3 | 0.7 |
| 2011 | MIS | AA | 21 | 395 | 50 | 13 | 5 | 6 | 36 | 24 | 34 | 20 | 8 | .299/.345/.414 | .272 | .315 | -0.1 | -9.9 | 1.3 |

could be the Opening Day shortstop.

**Martin Prado** LF
Born: **10/27/1983** Age: **28**
Bats: **R** Throws: **R** Height: **6' 2''** Weight: **170**
Breakout: **1%** Improve: **30%** Collapse: **9%**
Attrition: **26%** MLB: **75%**
**Comparables:**
Frank Catalanotto, Juan Rivera, Lou Skizas

| YEAR | TEAM | LVL | AGE | PA | R | 2B | 3B | HR | RBI | BB | SO | SB | CS | AVG_OBP_SLG | TAv | BABIP | BRR | FRAA | WARP |
|------|------|-----|-----|-----|-----|----|----|----|-----|----|----|----|----|-------------|------|-------|------|-----------|------|
| 2009 | ATL | MLB | 25 | 503 | 64 | 38 | 0 | 11 | 49 | 36 | 59 | 1 | 3 | .307/.358/.464 | .281 | .331 | -1 | -4 | 1.7 |
| 2010 | ATL | MLB | 26 | 651 | 100 | 40 | 3 | 15 | 66 | 40 | 86 | 5 | 3 | .307/.350/.459 | .283 | .335 | 5.6 | -0.5 | 4.0 |
| 2011 | ATL | MLB | 27 | 590 | 66 | 26 | 2 | 13 | 57 | 34 | 52 | 4 | 8 | .260/.302/.385 | .245 | .266 | -1 | 2.6 | 0.8 |
| *2012* | *ATL* | *MLB* | *28* | *571* | *70* | *31* | *2* | *12* | *66* | *38* | *63* | *4* | *4* | *.293/.341/.427* | *.275* | *.310* | *-1* | *LF -1, 2B -1* | *2.4* |

There were questions about how Prado's bat would play in an outfield corner, but this was not what people had in mind. Prado's batting average cratered without enough walks or power to buoy his offensive value. He entered 2011 as a career .307 hitter through 1,500 plate appearances and ended the year as a career .293 hitter. You would expect most second and third basemen to translate to the outfield well defensively, and Prado did. There are no red flags suggesting Prado is heading for a permanent downfall, as he managed to strike out less often in 2011—suggesting this is about making good contact rather than any contact—and PECOTA thinks he will be just fine in 2012. The real mystery is whether the Braves enter the season with Prado as their starting left fielder.

**David Ross** C
Born: **3/19/1977** Age: **35**
Bats: **R** Throws: **R** Height: **6' 3''** Weight: **205**
Breakout: **1%** Improve: **34%** Collapse: **12%**
Attrition: **34%** MLB: **83%**
**Comparables:**
Roy Campanella, Jorge Posada, Jason Varitek

| YEAR | TEAM | LVL | AGE | PA | R | 2B | 3B | HR | RBI | BB | SO | SB | CS | AVG_OBP_SLG | TAv | BABIP | BRR | FRAA | WARP |
|------|------|-----|-----|-----|----|----|----|----|-----|----|----|----|----|-------------|------|-------|------|------|------|
| 2009 | ATL | MLB | 32 | 151 | 18 | 9 | 0 | 7 | 20 | 21 | 39 | 0 | 0 | .273/.380/.508 | .298 | .341 | -1.4 | 1.9 | 1.4 |
| 2010 | ATL | MLB | 33 | 145 | 15 | 13 | 2 | 2 | 28 | 20 | 28 | 0 | 1 | .289/.392/.479 | .293 | .359 | -1.9 | 0.7 | 1.1 |
| 2011 | ATL | MLB | 34 | 170 | 14 | 7 | 0 | 6 | 23 | 16 | 51 | 0 | 1 | .263/.333/.428 | .272 | .358 | -3.2 | 0.9 | 0.9 |
| *2012* | *ATL* | *MLB* | *35* | *250* | *29* | *10* | *1* | *8* | *27* | *28* | *64* | *1* | *1* | *.235/.323/.397* | *.257* | *.287* | *-0.1* | *C 3* | *1.9* |

Anointing Ross as the new Practically Perfect Backup Catcher now that Gregg Zaun is busy with his new career in television seems just. Ross makes up for not switch-hitting by offering pop and walks aplenty, thus separating him from the typically feckless-with-the-bat reserve backstops. Even with the offensive chops, Ross still brings it on defense—figuring as a plus receiver and avid hunter of bases-talers (a career 38 percent kill rate)—and reportedly embraces his role. Expect teams to line up around the block to make him a starter once he hits free agency at season's end.

**Edward Salcedo** 3B

Born: 7/30/1991 Age: 20
Bats: R Throws: R Height: 6' 4" Weight: 195
Breakout: 2% Improve: 4% Collapse: 0%
Attrition: 3% MLB: 7%

Comparables:
Bobby Borchering, Francisco Martinez, Jefry Marte

| YEAR | TEAM | LVL | AGE | PA | R | 2B | 3B | HR | RBI | BB | SO | SB | CS | AVG_OBP_SLG | TAv | BABIP | BRR | FRAA | WARP |
|------|------|-----|-----|-----|----|----|----|----|-----|----|-----|----|----|-------------|------|-------|-----|------|------|
| 2010 | ROM | A | 18 | 209 | 23 | 5 | 4 | 2 | 16 | 11 | 56 | 6 | 5 | .197/.236/.295 | .206 | .259 | 0.9 | 7.3 | 0.4 |
| 2011 | ROM | A | 19 | 566 | 83 | 27 | 6 | 12 | 68 | 41 | 105 | 23 | 10 | .248/.315/.396 | .273 | .289 | 5.9 | 4.5 | 3.6 |
| 2012 | ATL | MLB | 20 | 250 | 22 | 9 | 2 | 3 | 21 | 10 | 61 | 6 | 3 | .210/.245/.302 | .199 | .263 | -0.5 | 3B 1, SS 6 | -1.0 |

Atlanta spent $1.6 million to spring Salcedo from the Dominican Republic, and for good reason. Just 20, Salcedo has a chance to become a power-boasting cleanup hitter thanks to a 6-foot-3 frame with room to add weight. The Braves moved him from shortstop to the hot corner preemptively, thus alleviating concerns about range and foot speed while keeping his strong arm in play. The numbers from Salcedo's repeat stint at Rome do not scream portent. But he possesses above-average bat speed and his raw power potential is notable. As you would suspect, his pitch selection also needs some work. Superstardom is still a possibility, if not the likely destination.

**Andrelton Simmons** SS

Born: 9/4/1989 Age: 22
Bats: R Throws: R Height: 6' 3" Weight: 170
Breakout: 3% Improve: 15% Collapse: 9%
Attrition: 17% MLB: 38%

Comparables:
Jose Castro, Erick Aybar, Joaquin Arias

| YEAR | TEAM | LVL | AGE | PA | R | 2B | 3B | HR | RBI | BB | SO | SB | CS | AVG_OBP_SLG | TAv | BABIP | BRR | FRAA | WARP |
|------|------|-----|-----|-----|----|----|----|----|-----|----|-----|----|----|-------------|------|-------|-----|------|------|
| 2010 | DNV | RK | 20 | 269 | 36 | 11 | 1 | 2 | 26 | 16 | 14 | 18 | 4 | .276/.343/.356 | .295 | .286 | 0.5 | 14.3 | 4.1 |
| 2011 | LYN | A+ | 21 | 570 | 69 | 35 | 6 | 1 | 52 | 29 | 43 | 26 | 18 | .311/.351/.408 | .275 | .334 | 0.6 | 16.5 | 5.8 |
| 2012 | ATL | MLB | 22 | 250 | 24 | 11 | 1 | 1 | 21 | 8 | 33 | 8 | 5 | .253/.277/.319 | .215 | .283 | -0.9 | SS 18 | -0.3 |

*What's cooler than being cool? Ice cold!* And what's cooler than being ice cold? Simmons's bat prior to 2011. Equipped with a top-notch arm and more than enough range to play shortstop, Simmons's future relies upon how his bat develops. His results improved in his first full season despite a declining walk rate and increasing strikeout rate. Simmons is listed at a lithe 6-foot-2, 170 pounds, keeping any power aspirations in check. Should Simmons fail to develop at the plate, he could always take the route blazed by a similar former Braves shortstop—Tony Pena Jr.—and give the mound a go.

**Joe Terdoslavich** 1B

Born: 9/9/1988 Age: 23
Bats: B Throws: R Height: 6' 2" Weight: 200
Breakout: 5% Improve: 15% Collapse: 5%
Attrition: 13% MLB: 30%

Comparables:
Mark Hamilton, Carmelo Martinez, Micah Schnurstein

| YEAR | TEAM | LVL | AGE | PA | R | 2B | 3B | HR | RBI | BB | SO | SB | CS | AVG_OBP_SLG | TAv | BABIP | BRR | FRAA | WARP |
|------|------|-----|-----|-----|----|----|----|----|-----|----|-----|----|----|-------------|------|-------|-----|------|------|
| 2010 | ROM | A | 21 | 85 | 7 | 9 | 0 | 0 | 10 | 5 | 18 | 0 | 0 | .316/.365/.430 | .288 | .410 | -1.6 | -2.4 | 0.0 |
| 2010 | DNV | RK | 21 | 205 | 27 | 10 | 2 | 2 | 24 | 15 | 27 | 3 | 3 | .296/.351/.402 | .293 | .338 | -0.9 | -2.3 | 0.8 |
| 2011 | LYN | A+ | 22 | 536 | 72 | 52 | 2 | 20 | 82 | 41 | 107 | 2 | 0 | .286/.341/.526 | .295 | .324 | -1.3 | 2.7 | 3.1 |
| 2012 | ATL | MLB | 23 | 250 | 26 | 13 | 1 | 7 | 28 | 13 | 58 | 0 | 0 | .234/.273/.382 | .231 | .279 | 0 | 1B -7, 3B -0 | -0.6 |

Following a 20-home run regular season, Terdoslavich kept momentum rolling with a strong showing in the Arizona Fall League. An optimist might view the Braves deciding to try him out at the hot corner as a sign they believe in his athleticism. A pessimist would point out that it could mean they do not buy his bat. A realist would smack both upside the head, then point out that Freeman is younger than Terdoslavich. The odds are long that Terdoslavich becomes more than a bench player, barring a change in skill set.

**Dan Uggla** 2B

Born: 3/11/1980 Age: 32
Bats: R Throws: R Height: 6' 0" Weight: 200
Breakout: 2% Improve: 22% Collapse: 7%
Attrition: 13% MLB: 84%

Comparables:
Woodie Held, Ryne Sandberg, Tom Runnells

| YEAR | TEAM | LVL | AGE | PA | R | 2B | 3B | HR | RBI | BB | SO | SB | CS | AVG_OBP_SLG | TAv | BABIP | BRR | FRAA | WARP |
|------|------|-----|-----|-----|-----|----|----|----|-----|----|-----|----|----|-------------|------|-------|-----|------|------|
| 2009 | FLO | MLB | 29 | 668 | 84 | 27 | 1 | 31 | 90 | 92 | 150 | 2 | 1 | .243/.354/.459 | .275 | .274 | -0.5 | -2.2 | 2.5 |
| 2010 | FLO | MLB | 30 | 674 | 100 | 31 | 0 | 33 | 105 | 78 | 149 | 4 | 1 | .287/.369/.508 | .306 | .330 | 0.6 | -6.1 | 4.8 |
| 2011 | ATL | MLB | 31 | 672 | 88 | 22 | 1 | 36 | 82 | 62 | 156 | 1 | 3 | .233/.311/.453 | .270 | .253 | 1.9 | -3.9 | 2.4 |
| 2012 | ATL | MLB | 32 | 632 | 81 | 28 | 1 | 29 | 83 | 70 | 154 | 3 | 2 | .249/.338/.461 | .285 | .291 | -0.4 | 2B -6 | 3.6 |

Just when we were this close to calling Uggla a reliable commodity, he went and regained his wild card reputation. There are instances when numbers do not do a story justice. Uggla's 2011 season is one such case. He finished with a career high in home runs, coinciding with a career-low in doubles, remarkable since on Independence Day he had a .173/.241/.327 line. On the next day, Uggla embarked on the most unlikely 33-game hitting streak in recent memory, boosting his seasonal slash line stats to .231/.297/.450 by the streak's end. Uggla continued to hit and his True Average compared to his numbers posted in 2006, 2007, and 2009. Uggla is still a poor fielder, so his bat has to come true for him to make good on the four years and $53 million remaining on his contract. He amassed the totals in 2011, the Braves just hope he starts quicker in 2012.

**Jack Wilson** SS

Born: 12/29/1977 Age: 34
Bats: R Throws: R Height: 6' 1" Weight: 175
Breakout: 2% Improve: 26% Collapse: 8%
Attrition: 40% MLB: 81%

Comparables:
Aaron Miles, Keith Lockhart, Frank Bolling

| YEAR | TEAM | LVL | AGE | PA | R | 2B | 3B | HR | RBI | BB | SO | SB | CS | AVG_OBP_SLG | TAv | BABIP | BRR | FRAA | WARP |
|---|---|---|---|---|---|---|---|---|---|---|---|---|---|---|---|---|---|---|---|
| 2009 | PIT | MLB | 31 | 286 | 26 | 18 | 1 | 4 | 31 | 15 | 31 | 2 | 1 | .267/.304/.387 | .241 | .288 | -0.1 | 3.8 | 1.3 |
| 2009 | SEA | MLB | 31 | 116 | 11 | 5 | 0 | 1 | 8 | 6 | 17 | 1 | 0 | .224/.263/.299 | .207 | .256 | -0.6 | -1 | -0.5 |
| 2010 | SEA | MLB | 32 | 211 | 17 | 11 | 1 | 0 | 14 | 7 | 35 | 1 | 2 | .249/.282/.316 | .243 | .298 | -1.5 | 5 | 0.9 |
| 2011 | SEA | MLB | 33 | 187 | 22 | 8 | 0 | 0 | 11 | 9 | 27 | 5 | 2 | .249/.283/.295 | .253 | .291 | 0.9 | 0.5 | 0.7 |
| 2011 | ATL | MLB | 33 | 45 | 3 | 1 | 0 | 0 | 0 | 1 | 12 | 0 | 0 | .220/.238/.244 | .201 | .310 | 0.3 | -0.6 | -0.1 |
| 2012 | ATL | MLB | 34 | 250 | 26 | 12 | 1 | 2 | 22 | 12 | 31 | 5 | 2 | .264/.305/.346 | .234 | .289 | -0.4 | SS 4, 2B -0 | 0.5 |

Another player Frank Wren excavated from a non-contender's bench late in the season to act as a security blanket, Wilson did just that by starting five of the Braves' final seven games. Wilson is no longer a defensive wizard, and the only magic left in his bat turns it invisible. A litany of injuries—everything from a right foot contusion to hamstring strains and hand surgery—have robbed Wilson of the dependability factor that tends to give players of his caliber value. Now a free agent, Wilson is unlikely to net a starter's job, so the bench could become his second home.

| YEAR | TEAM | LVL | AGE | PA | R | 2B | 3B | HR | RBI | BB | SO | SB | CS | AVG_OBP_SLG | TAv | BABIP | BRR | FRAA | WARP |
|---|---|---|---|---|---|---|---|---|---|---|---|---|---|---|---|---|---|---|---|
| 2010 | SEA | MLB | 29 | 388 | 22 | 14 | 2 | 2 | 25 | 14 | 74 | 5 | 0 | .227/.278/.294 | .224 | .280 | -2.1 | 12.2 | 1.1 |
| 2011 | RNO | AAA | 30 | 64 | 11 | 5 | 2 | 1 | 12 | 4 | 7 | 2 | 0 | .351/.406/.561 | .289 | .380 | -0.4 | 0.5 | 0.5 |
| 2011 | MIL | MLB | 30 | 82 | 10 | 4 | 0 | 2 | 4 | 4 | 21 | 1 | 0 | .227/.266/.360 | .243 | .288 | 0.4 | -0.7 | 0.1 |
| 2011 | ARI | MLB | 30 | 10 | 3 | 1 | 0 | 0 | 1 | 0 | 1 | 0 | 0 | .200/.200/.300 | .194 | .222 | 0.2 | 0.1 | 0.0 |
| 2012 | ATL | MLB | 31 | 250 | 24 | 11 | 1 | 3 | 21 | 13 | 50 | 3 | 1 | .234/.285/.327 | .221 | .283 | -0.1 | SS 1, 2B -0 | 0.0 |

Wilson is surprisingly sixth on the list of shortstops by Fielding Runs Above Average-per-inning over the past three seasons combined (minimum 500 innings), with 21.5 FRAA in 1350 1/3 innings, behind usual suspects such as Brendan Ryan and Rafael Furcal. With his replacement-level bat and lack of a great defensive reputation, he is likely to start the season in Gwinnett, but could spend time as the Braves' backup shortstop before season's end.

**Matt Young** LF

Born: 10/3/1982 Age: 29
Bats: L Throws: R Height: 5' 9" Weight: 175
Breakout: 1% Improve: 50% Collapse: 4%
Attrition: 25% MLB: 87%

Comparables:
Lenny Green, Reggie Willits, Sam Fuld

| YEAR | TEAM | LVL | AGE | PA | R | 2B | 3B | HR | RBI | BB | SO | SB | CS | AVG_OBP_SLG | TAv | BABIP | BRR | FRAA | WARP |
|---|---|---|---|---|---|---|---|---|---|---|---|---|---|---|---|---|---|---|---|
| 2009 | MIS | AA | 26 | 571 | 81 | 22 | 10 | 4 | 33 | 94 | 59 | 42 | 16 | .289/.420/.407 | .303 | .322 | 5.7 | -5.9 | 4.0 |
| 2010 | GWN | AAA | 27 | 555 | 88 | 33 | 5 | 3 | 35 | 57 | 53 | 39 | 7 | .300/.380/.407 | .266 | .330 | 8.4 | 4.6 | 3.1 |
| 2011 | GWN | AAA | 28 | 428 | 64 | 16 | 4 | 1 | 24 | 57 | 59 | 17 | 7 | .273/.372/.347 | .252 | .321 | 4.6 | 1.5 | 1.4 |
| 2011 | ATL | MLB | 28 | 52 | 4 | 1 | 0 | 0 | 1 | 4 | 6 | 0 | 1 | .208/.269/.229 | .189 | .238 | 0 | -0.7 | -0.4 |
| 2012 | ATL | MLB | 29 | 250 | 27 | 10 | 2 | 1 | 18 | 29 | 35 | 12 | 4 | .254/.345/.331 | .251 | .293 | -0.1 | LF 2, CF -3 | 0.8 |

Young made his major league debut in April after spending more than 500 games in the upper minors with an on-base percentage of more than .380. The 5-foot-8 lefty swings a wet newspaper at the plate, but he majored in Strike Zone Philosophy, can steal bases, and plays defense—the Braves have even cross-trained him between the outfield and second base—all boosting his stock as a potential reserve. The lone positive from his major league stint is that the Braves thought well enough of him to give him a shot in the first place.

# PITCHERS

**Jairo Asencio**
Born: 5/5/1984 Age: 28
Bats: R Throws: R Height: 6' 3" Weight: 205
Breakout: 30% Improve: 51% Collapse: 25%
Attrition: 14% MLB: 86%
**Comparables:**
Bob James, Scott Sanders, Kevin Gregg

| YEAR | TEAM | LVL | AGE | W | L | SV | G | GS | IP | H | HR | BB | SO | EqBB9 | EqSO9 | GB% | BABIP | WHIP | ERA | FIP | FRA | WARP |
|---|---|---|---|---|---|---|---|---|---|---|---|---|---|---|---|---|---|---|---|---|---|---|
| 2009 | GWN | AAA | 25 | 5 | 4 | 27 | 58 | 0 | 71¹ | 66 | 4 | 19 | 77 | 2.4 | 9.5 | 49% | .297 | 1.19 | 3.28 | 2.52 | 3.46 | 1.5 |
| 2009 | ATL | MLB | 25 | 0 | 1 | 0 | 3 | 0 | 2² | 3 | 0 | 2 | 0 | 6.8 | 0.0 | 45% | .273 | 1.88 | 3.38 | 5.31 | 5.31 | 0.0 |
| 2011 | GWN | AAA | 27 | 3 | 2 | 26 | 47 | 0 | 54² | 39 | 3 | 22 | 70 | 3.6 | 11.5 | 47% | .283 | 1.12 | 1.81 | 2.60 | 3.76 | 1.1 |
| 2011 | ATL | MLB | 27 | 0 | 0 | 0 | 6 | 0 | 10¹ | 16 | 1 | 5 | 8 | 4.4 | 7.0 | 44% | .395 | 2.03 | 6.97 | 4.16 | 6.22 | -0.3 |
| 2012 | ATL | MLB | 28 | 1 | 0 | 1 | 19 | 0 | 23 | 22 | 2 | 9 | 19 | 3.5 | 7.4 | 46% | .314 | 1.33 | 4.23 | 3.86 | 4.60 | 0.1 |

After missing the 2010 season due to visa issues, the Sabana Grande del Palenque native returned to professional baseball in 2011 with a new name. Previously known as Luis Valdez, Asencio continued to throw a fastball that topped out in the mid-90s along with a slider and changeup. Look for Asencio to spend time in the majors in 2012 after a strong Triple-A campaign.

**Luis Avilan**
Born: 7/19/1989 Age: 22
Bats: L Throws: L Height: 6' 3" Weight: 165
Breakout: 25% Improve: 48% Collapse: 12%
Attrition: 7% MLB: 76%
**Comparables:**
Steve Carlton, Jerry Reuss, Cesar Jimenez

| YEAR | TEAM | LVL | AGE | W | L | SV | G | GS | IP | H | HR | BB | SO | EqBB9 | EqSO9 | GB% | BABIP | WHIP | ERA | FIP | FRA | WARP |
|---|---|---|---|---|---|---|---|---|---|---|---|---|---|---|---|---|---|---|---|---|---|---|
| 2009 | DNV | RK | 19 | 0 | 2 | 2 | 14 | 3 | 38¹ | 25 | 1 | 17 | 34 | 4.0 | 8.0 | 56% | .240 | 1.10 | 3.05 | 3.90 | 5.21 | -0.3 |
| 2010 | ROM | A | 20 | 2 | 1 | 0 | 10 | 0 | 20² | 14 | 1 | 9 | 18 | 3.9 | 9.1 | 56% | .250 | 1.16 | 2.61 | 3.85 | 4.14 | 0.2 |
| 2010 | MYR | A+ | 20 | 4 | 3 | 9 | 31 | 0 | 48 | 38 | 5 | 16 | 34 | 3.4 | 6.9 | 48% | .284 | 1.25 | 3.94 | 4.58 | 5.61 | -0.3 |
| 2011 | MIS | AA | 21 | 4 | 8 | 1 | 36 | 13 | 106¹ | 113 | 10 | 36 | 78 | 3.0 | 6.6 | 45% | .304 | 1.40 | 4.57 | 4.30 | 4.97 | 0.1 |
| 2012 | ATL | MLB | 22 | 1 | 1 | 0 | 14 | 2 | 32² | 34 | 4 | 15 | 17 | 4.1 | 4.6 | 43% | .301 | 1.51 | 5.43 | 5.13 | 5.90 | -0.2 |

The Braves left Avilan exposed in the 2010 Rule 5 draft, but felt strong enough about his 2011 to add him to the 40-man roster in November. What changed? Avilan showed his stuff can work against Double-A hitters and spent the final two months toiling away in the rotation. Another Venezuelan product, Avilan continued to start in winter ball and should figure into the Braves' Triple-A rotation plans at some point in 2012.

**Brandon Beachy**
Born: 9/3/1986 Age: 25
Bats: R Throws: R Height: 6' 4" Weight: 215
Breakout: 13% Improve: 42% Collapse: 19%
Attrition: 16% MLB: 93%
**Comparables:**
Yovani Gallardo, Al Hrabosky, Joba Chamberlain

| YEAR | TEAM | LVL | AGE | W | L | SV | G | GS | IP | H | HR | BB | SO | EqBB9 | EqSO9 | GB% | BABIP | WHIP | ERA | FIP | FRA | WARP |
|---|---|---|---|---|---|---|---|---|---|---|---|---|---|---|---|---|---|---|---|---|---|---|
| 2009 | MYR | A+ | 22 | 4 | 3 | 1 | 22 | 8 | 58 | 59 | 2 | 15 | 47 | 2.3 | 7.3 | 50% | .328 | 1.28 | 3.41 | 3.36 | 4.08 | 0.7 |
| 2010 | MIS | AA | 23 | 3 | 1 | 1 | 27 | 6 | 73² | 38 | 2 | 18 | 67 | 2.7 | 12.2 | 42% | .295 | 1.02 | 1.47 | 2.90 | 3.04 | 1.8 |
| 2010 | GWN | AAA | 23 | 2 | 0 | 1 | 8 | 7 | 45² | 30 | 1 | 5 | 33 | 1.2 | 9.5 | 44% | .302 | 1.01 | 2.17 | 2.83 | 3.50 | 1.1 |
| 2010 | ATL | MLB | 23 | 0 | 2 | 0 | 3 | 3 | 15 | 16 | 0 | 7 | 15 | 4.2 | 9.0 | 33% | .356 | 1.53 | 3.00 | 2.51 | 3.24 | 0.4 |
| 2011 | ATL | MLB | 24 | 7 | 3 | 0 | 25 | 25 | 141² | 125 | 16 | 46 | 169 | 2.9 | 10.7 | 36% | .312 | 1.21 | 3.68 | 3.16 | 3.64 | 2.1 |
| 2012 | ATL | MLB | 25 | 6 | 5 | 0 | 25 | 17 | 111 | 98 | 10 | 34 | 104 | 2.7 | 8.4 | 39% | .311 | 1.18 | 3.56 | 3.42 | 3.87 | 1.8 |

Beachy lacked an out pitch entering the season, but he seemed to manage just fine. By being able to locate his fastball, slider, and changeup for strikes, Beachy kept batters off balance and shrugged off hints of predictability, thereby managing to fan 169 batters in 141 2/3 innings pitched during his freshman campaign. PECOTA expects Beachy to concede to his prospect day expectations rather than repeat his star-like performance, but who can be sure? After all, nobody saw the Kokomo Kid getting this far.

**Billy Bullock**
Born: 2/27/1988 Age: 24
Bats: R Throws: R Height: 6' 7" Weight: 225
Breakout: 35% Improve: 55% Collapse: 16%
Attrition: 9% MLB: 94%
**Comparables:**
Jack Meyer, Henry Rodriguez, Mark Clear

| YEAR | TEAM | LVL | AGE | W | L | SV | G | GS | IP | H | HR | BB | SO | EqBB9 | EqSO9 | GB% | BABIP | WHIP | ERA | FIP | FRA | WARP |
|---|---|---|---|---|---|---|---|---|---|---|---|---|---|---|---|---|---|---|---|---|---|---|
| 2009 | BLT | A | 21 | 3 | 0 | 8 | 26 | 0 | 26¹ | 25 | 0 | 12 | 35 | 4.1 | 12.0 | 33% | .385 | 1.41 | 2.74 | 3.12 | 1.78 | 1.1 |
| 2010 | FTM | A+ | 22 | 0 | 4 | 14 | 28 | 0 | 37¹ | 29 | 2 | 16 | 37 | 4.6 | 10.9 | 45% | .403 | 1.55 | 3.62 | 3.69 | 4.76 | 0.2 |
| 2010 | NBR | AA | 22 | 2 | 4 | 13 | 30 | 0 | 36² | 24 | 3 | 20 | 39 | 5.9 | 14.7 | 46% | .404 | 1.58 | 3.43 | 4.41 | 4.54 | 0.2 |
| 2011 | MIS | AA | 23 | 3 | 1 | 11 | 50 | 0 | 49² | 32 | 2 | 32 | 65 | 6.2 | 11.8 | 55% | .275 | 1.39 | 4.53 | 3.68 | 4.91 | 0.1 |
| 2012 | ATL | MLB | 24 | 1 | 0 | 1 | 17 | 0 | 19² | 17 | 2 | 10 | 20 | 4.7 | 9.1 | 44% | .312 | 1.37 | 4.27 | 4.02 | 4.64 | 0.1 |

Tracing Bullock's Braves origins provides another excuse to credit the organization's ability to identify and develop undervalued talent, in this case: amateur free agents. They signed Scott Diamond back in 2007, left him unprotected in the 2010 Rule 5 draft, then traded Diamond's rights to the Twins for Bullock. Diamond had no chance to crack this year's Braves rotation or any in the next few seasons, but Bullock could find himself in the bullpen sooner rather than later. He is a big righty with a mean fastball (clocked in the upper-90s before) and no idea where the ball is headed once it leaves his grip.

## Jaye Chapman

Born: 5/22/1987 Age: 25
Bats: R Throws: R Height: 6' 1" Weight: 180
Breakout: 34% Improve: 60% Collapse: 12%
Attrition: 12% MLB: 89%
Comparables:
David Aardsma, Billy Koch, Cecilio Guante

| YEAR | TEAM | LVL | AGE | W | L | SV | G | GS | IP | H | HR | BB | SO | EqBB9 | EqSO9 | GB% | BABIP | WHIP | ERA | FIP | FRA | WARP |
|---|---|---|---|---|---|---|---|---|---|---|---|---|---|---|---|---|---|---|---|---|---|---|
| 2009 | ROM | A | 22 | 1 | 0 | 0 | 13 | 0 | 22² | 9 | 0 | 4 | 29 | 1.6 | 11.5 | 59% | .176 | 0.57 | 0.40 | 1.57 | 1.82 | 0.8 |
| 2009 | MYR | A+ | 22 | 1 | 2 | 0 | 27 | 0 | 35¹ | 35 | 3 | 20 | 37 | 5.1 | 9.4 | 52% | .330 | 1.56 | 4.33 | 4.06 | 5.10 | 0.0 |
| 2010 | MIS | AA | 23 | 1 | 4 | 0 | 36 | 1 | 50¹ | 43 | 0 | 14 | 38 | 4.5 | 9.5 | 45% | .398 | 1.69 | 5.19 | 3.06 | 4.82 | 0.0 |
| 2011 | GWN | AAA | 24 | 2 | 3 | 2 | 43 | 1 | 54¹ | 40 | 5 | 26 | 61 | 4.3 | 10.1 | 51% | .273 | 1.21 | 2.98 | 3.63 | 4.70 | 0.7 |
| 2012 | ATL | MLB | 25 | 1 | 0 | 0 | 13 | 0 | 16² | 16 | 2 | 8 | 12 | 4.5 | 6.7 | 40% | .304 | 1.45 | 4.84 | 4.76 | 5.26 | -0.0 |

Taken in the 16th round of the 2005 draft, Chapman's control issues made him an afterthought until 2011. In 52 games between Double-A and Triple-A, Chapman showed improved control. He is a short righty with a fastball that can sneak into the mid-90s and a plus changeup. Should Chapman keep throwing strikes, he will find his way into the majors before the 2012 season ends.

## Randall Delgado

| YEAR | TEAM | LVL | AGE | W | L | SV | G | GS | IP | H | HR | BB | SO | EqBB9 | EqSO9 | GB% | BABIP | WHIP | ERA | FIP | FRA | WARP |
|---|---|---|---|---|---|---|---|---|---|---|---|---|---|---|---|---|---|---|---|---|---|---|

pose Delgado, and that is a positive sign. Smooth arm action gives way to a fastball that can touch the mid-90s, and Delgado shows versatility with his plus-curveball by throwing the breaker for strikes or plunging it into the dirt. Delgado's changeup is more mundane, and he can overthrow the pitch at times, although he could develop it into a third above-average offering. Delgado may become a good team's number two starter or a lesser team's ace. More likely is that he takes his place as a number three starter.

## Cory Gearrin

Born: 4/14/1986 Age: 26
Bats: R Throws: R Height: 6' 4" Weight: 200
Breakout: 25% Improve: 57% Collapse: 19%
Attrition: 13% MLB: 91%
Comparables:
Mark Wohlers, Brandon Medders, Rich Gossage

| YEAR | TEAM | LVL | AGE | W | L | SV | G | GS | IP | H | HR | BB | SO | EqBB9 | EqSO9 | GB% | BABIP | WHIP | ERA | FIP | FRA | WARP |
|---|---|---|---|---|---|---|---|---|---|---|---|---|---|---|---|---|---|---|---|---|---|---|
| 2009 | MYR | A+ | 23 | 0 | 2 | 17 | 27 | 0 | 29¹ | 22 | 2 | 3 | 32 | 0.9 | 9.8 | 63% | .260 | 0.85 | 1.84 | 2.46 | 3.97 | 0.5 |
| 2009 | MIS | AA | 23 | 1 | 2 | 2 | 20 | 0 | 25¹ | 19 | 2 | 8 | 20 | 2.8 | 7.1 | 42% | .254 | 1.07 | 2.85 | 3.85 | 4.78 | 0.0 |
| 2010 | GWN | AAA | 24 | 3 | 5 | 0 | 52 | 0 | 80¹ | 42 | 4 | 21 | 42 | 3.6 | 7.4 | 67% | .252 | 1.30 | 3.36 | 4.14 | 4.89 | 0.8 |
| 2011 | GWN | AAA | 25 | 4 | 1 | 4 | 35 | 0 | 50 | 42 | 0 | 20 | 60 | 3.6 | 10.8 | 62% | .331 | 1.24 | 1.80 | 2.22 | 3.81 | 1.2 |
| 2011 | ATL | MLB | 25 | 1 | 1 | 0 | 18 | 0 | 18¹ | 17 | 0 | 12 | 25 | 5.9 | 12.3 | 61% | .370 | 1.58 | 7.85 | 2.56 | 3.56 | 0.3 |
| 2012 | ATL | MLB | 26 | 1 | 0 | 0 | 24 | 0 | 33² | 30 | 3 | 15 | 29 | 4.1 | 7.8 | 53% | .304 | 1.33 | 4.18 | 3.98 | 4.55 | 0.2 |

Gearrin is the logical successor to Peter Moylan. From arm slot (side) to prominent strengths (generates groundballs, annoys righties) and velocity (maxes out in the low-90s), Gearrin is like a Moylan facsimile. During his time in the majors he faced 50 right-handed batters, retiring 18 by strikeout and allowing 13 to reach base. Less impressive was Gearrin's performance against lefties, although four of his six walks issued were intentional in nature. A future righty specialist.

## Tommy Hanson

Born: 8/28/1986 Age: 25
Bats: R Throws: R Height: 6' 7" Weight: 220
Breakout: 14% Improve: 39% Collapse: 17%
Attrition: 9% MLB: 96%
Comparables:
Chad Billingsley, Chad Cordero, Adam Wainwright

| YEAR | TEAM | LVL | AGE | W | L | SV | G | GS | IP | H | HR | BB | SO | EqBB9 | EqSO9 | GB% | BABIP | WHIP | ERA | FIP | FRA | WARP |
|---|---|---|---|---|---|---|---|---|---|---|---|---|---|---|---|---|---|---|---|---|---|---|
| 2009 | GWN | AAA | 22 | 3 | 3 | 0 | 11 | 11 | 66¹ | 40 | 5 | 17 | 90 | 2.3 | 12.2 | 38% | .248 | 0.86 | 1.49 | 2.36 | 2.74 | 1.8 |
| 2009 | ATL | MLB | 22 | 11 | 4 | 0 | 21 | 21 | 127² | 105 | 10 | 46 | 116 | 3.2 | 8.2 | 41% | .279 | 1.18 | 2.89 | 3.46 | 4.01 | 2.1 |
| 2010 | ATL | MLB | 23 | 10 | 11 | 0 | 34 | 34 | 202² | 182 | 14 | 56 | 173 | 2.5 | 7.7 | 43% | .290 | 1.17 | 3.33 | 3.33 | 3.71 | 3.8 |
| 2011 | ATL | MLB | 24 | 11 | 7 | 0 | 22 | 22 | 130 | 106 | 17 | 46 | 142 | 3.2 | 9.8 | 41% | .271 | 1.17 | 3.60 | 3.64 | 3.89 | 1.2 |
| 2012 | ATL | MLB | 25 | 8 | 7 | 0 | 21 | 21 | 123¹ | 102 | 12 | 39 | 106 | 2.9 | 7.7 | 40% | .285 | 1.14 | 3.40 | 3.70 | 3.70 | 2.2 |

Tendinitis in Hanson's right shoulder limited him to 22 starts in his third major league season. When he did pitch, he showed a juiced up strikeout rate (from 7.7 batters per nine innings to 9.8) and allowed more gopherballs than during his first 55 starts in the majors. Hanson averaged a career-low innings pitched per start, and yet still found a way to throw more than 100 pitches in almost as many games in 2011 as he did in 2010 despite making 12 fewer starts. Everyone is waiting for Hanson's perception to shift from good starter to great starter, and it could come in 2012 if he can stay on the mound and out of the trainer's room.

## J.J. Hoover

Born: 8/13/1987 Age: 24
Bats: R Throws: R Height: 6' 4" Weight: 215
Breakout: 36% Improve: 60% Collapse: 20%
Attrition: 17% MLB: 91%

**Comparables:**
John Verhoeven, Jake Peavy, Frankie De La Cruz

| YEAR | TEAM | LVL | AGE | W | L | SV | G | GS | IP | H | HR | BB | SO | EqBB9 | EqSO9 | GB% | BABIP | WHIP | ERA | FIP | FRA | WARP |
|------|------|-----|-----|---|---|----|---|----|----|---|----|----|----|-------|-------|-----|-------|------|-----|-----|-----|------|
| 2009 | ROM | A | 21 | 7 | 6 | 1 | 25 | 18 | 134¹ | 135 | 9 | 25 | 148 | 1.7 | 9.9 | 47% | .341 | 1.19 | 3.35 | 2.85 | 3.46 | 2.3 |
| 2010 | MYR | A+ | 22 | 11 | 6 | 0 | 24 | 24 | 132² | 111 | 5 | 30 | 96 | 2.4 | 8.0 | 43% | .309 | 1.21 | 3.26 | 3.27 | 3.73 | 2.2 |
| 2011 | MIS | AA | 23 | 2 | 5 | 1 | 31 | 12 | 87 | 64 | 5 | 29 | 85 | 2.9 | 8.9 | 34% | .265 | 1.07 | 2.48 | 3.23 | 3.85 | 1.0 |
| 2012 | ATL | MLB | 24 | 2 | 2 | 0 | 10 | 6 | 38 | 37 | 4 | 15 | 28 | 3.6 | 6.5 | 39% | .309 | 1.37 | 4.64 | 4.28 | 5.04 | 0.1 |

Having tremendous starting pitching depth is not a victimless crime. Most organizations would view Hoover as a number four or five starter. Not Atlanta. By season's end Hoover pitched from the bullpen in Gwinnet, and that could be his major league home if he stays with the Braves. Hoover keeps a quick tempo and comes after batters with a low-90s fastball. He throws every secondary pitch under the sun, with a curveball being the best of the bunch and a changeup being the worst. Having a breadth of options is nice and helps to shake batters on his trail, but he lacks an out pitch. Another flaw in Hoover's game is his shaky command. Throwing strikes is one thing, throwing quality strikes is another.

## Tim Hudson

Born: 7/14/1975 Age: 36
Bats: R Throws: R Height: 6' 1" Weight: 160
Breakout: 21% Improve: 49% Collapse: 26%
Attrition: 8% MLB: 90%

**Comparables:**
Hiroki Kuroda, Chris Carpenter, Tom Candiotti

| YEAR | TEAM | LVL | AGE | W | L | SV | G | GS | IP | H | HR | BB | SO | EqBB9 | EqSO9 | GB% | BABIP | WHIP | ERA | FIP | FRA | WARP |
|------|------|-----|-----|---|---|----|---|----|----|---|----|----|----|-------|-------|-----|-------|------|-----|-----|-----|------|
| 2009 | ATL | MLB | 33 | 2 | 1 | 0 | 7 | 7 | 42¹ | 49 | 4 | 13 | 30 | 2.8 | 6.4 | 61% | .341 | 1.46 | 3.61 | 3.79 | 4.40 | 0.9 |
| 2010 | ATL | MLB | 34 | 17 | 9 | 0 | 34 | 34 | 228² | 189 | 20 | 74 | 139 | 2.9 | 5.5 | 65% | .253 | 1.15 | 2.83 | 4.12 | 4.61 | 2.8 |
| 2011 | ATL | MLB | 35 | 16 | 10 | 0 | 33 | 33 | 215 | 189 | 14 | 56 | 158 | 2.3 | 6.6 | 58% | .276 | 1.14 | 3.22 | 3.36 | 4.12 | 2.5 |
| 2012 | ATL | MLB | 36 | 12 | 10 | 0 | 28 | 28 | 187² | 173 | 15 | 49 | 99 | 2.4 | 4.8 | 60% | .288 | 1.18 | 3.56 | 3.97 | 3.87 | 2.8 |

Believe it or not, Hudson has now tallied more innings with the Braves than the Athletics. That Hudson has pitched back-to-back 200-plus inning seasons after recovering from August 2008 Tommy John surgery is a testament to the advances of modern medicine. A testament to the advances of Hudson is that he has made 10 or more starts in 12 big league seasons and recorded quality starts in 70 percent or higher in seven of those campaigns. With Derek Lowe exiled to Cleveland, Hudson becomes the only graybeard on an increasingly cherub-faced staff, and Atlanta will depend on him for leadership, stability, and everything else that lonely old pitchers provide to young rotations on contending teams.

## Jair Jurrjens

Born: 1/29/1986 Age: 26
Bats: R Throws: R Height: 6' 2" Weight: 160
Breakout: 17% Improve: 44% Collapse: 19%
Attrition: 5% MLB: 93%

**Comparables:**
Clay Hensley, Bob Sadowski, Pat Jarvis

| YEAR | TEAM | LVL | AGE | W | L | SV | G | GS | IP | H | HR | BB | SO | EqBB9 | EqSO9 | GB% | BABIP | WHIP | ERA | FIP | FRA | WARP |
|------|------|-----|-----|---|---|----|---|----|----|---|----|----|----|-------|-------|-----|-------|------|-----|-----|-----|------|
| 2009 | ATL | MLB | 23 | 14 | 10 | 0 | 34 | 34 | 215 | 186 | 15 | 75 | 152 | 3.1 | 6.4 | 45% | .274 | 1.21 | 2.60 | 3.64 | 4.13 | 3.6 |
| 2010 | ATL | MLB | 24 | 7 | 6 | 0 | 20 | 20 | 116¹ | 120 | 13 | 42 | 86 | 3.2 | 6.7 | 43% | .306 | 1.39 | 4.64 | 4.22 | 4.59 | 1.2 |
| 2011 | ATL | MLB | 25 | 13 | 6 | 0 | 23 | 23 | 152 | 142 | 14 | 44 | 90 | 2.6 | 5.3 | 44% | .273 | 1.22 | 2.96 | 3.95 | 4.25 | 1.2 |
| 2012 | ATL | MLB | 26 | 7 | 7 | 0 | 20 | 20 | 123 | 117 | 11 | 39 | 74 | 2.8 | 5.4 | 47% | .295 | 1.27 | 4.03 | 4.11 | 4.38 | 1.2 |

Jurrjens's 2011 presents a conundrum for the Braves. He posted a sub-3 earned run average for the second time in three seasons, but still provided reason for worry. A decline in velocity has left Jurrjens sitting in the upper-80s and topping out in the 93-94 mph range, as opposed to when he used to sit around 91 and touch 95-96. It would be unfair to implicate the velocity drop as the only party responsible for a career-low strikeout rate; however, it would be irresponsible to ignore it as a contributing factor. To Jurrjens's credit, he did shave a little off his walk rate, although his strikeout-to-walk ratio remained between 2.03 and 2.05 for the third consecutive season. Jurrjens is not as good as he showed last season, and the Braves would be smart to move him before he gets expensive or his elbow pops.

## Craig Kimbrel

Born: 5/28/1988 Age: 24
Bats: R Throws: R Height: 6' 0" Weight: 205
Breakout: 32% Improve: 51% Collapse: 17%
Attrition: 6% MLB: 96%

**Comparables:**
Chris Perez, Jonathan Broxton, Francisco Rodriguez

| YEAR | TEAM | LVL | AGE | W | L | SV | G | GS | IP | H | HR | BB | SO | EqBB9 | EqSO9 | GB% | BABIP | WHIP | ERA | FIP | FRA | WARP |
|------|------|-----|-----|---|---|----|---|----|----|---|----|----|----|-------|-------|-----|-------|------|-----|-----|-----|------|
| 2009 | MYR | A+ | 21 | 0 | 2 | 2 | 19 | 0 | 26¹ | 18 | 2 | 28 | 45 | 9.6 | 15.4 | 61% | .356 | 1.75 | 5.48 | 4.22 | 5.74 | -0.1 |
| 2010 | GWN | AAA | 22 | 3 | 2 | 23 | 48 | 0 | 55² | 20 | 2 | 29 | 56 | 5.7 | 13.4 | 59% | .240 | 1.13 | 1.62 | 3.76 | 3.71 | 1.0 |
| 2010 | ATL | MLB | 22 | 4 | 0 | 1 | 21 | 0 | 20² | 9 | 0 | 16 | 40 | 7.0 | 17.4 | 28% | .281 | 1.21 | 0.44 | 1.56 | 2.49 | 0.6 |
| 2011 | ATL | MLB | 23 | 4 | 3 | 46 | 79 | 0 | 77 | 48 | 3 | 32 | 127 | 3.7 | 14.8 | 45% | .317 | 1.04 | 2.10 | 1.49 | 2.39 | 2.2 |
| 2012 | ATL | MLB | 24 | 3 | 2 | 27 | 62 | 0 | 64² | 39 | 4 | 33 | 90 | 4.6 | 12.6 | 48% | .300 | 1.12 | 2.45 | 2.76 | 2.66 | 1.8 |

Few rookie seasons have impressed like Kimbrel's. Fredi Gonzalez used Kimbrel early and often, and Kimbrel ended the season with the second-most appearances in the majors, trailing teammate Jonny Venters. The best statistical nugget from Kimbrel's efforts were his 38 appearances in a row without allowing a run, the longest such streak since the most recent round of expansion. Kimbrel passed the eye test, too. If you trust PITCHf/x data, then no fastball Kimbrel threw went slower than 92 mph. Believable, given that Kimbrel's heater is a true plus-plus pitch that combines breakneck velocity with fine movement. The other plus-plus offering in Kimbrel's package, a slider, serves as a good put-away pitch. Should Kimbrel falter, expect to hear about usage to the point of abuse, but it takes a strong man to avoid using an arm like this as much as he can.

### Scott Linebrink

Born: **8/4/1976** Age: **35**
Bats: **R** Throws: **R** Height: **6' 4"** Weight: **185**
Breakout: **35%** Improve: **50%** Collapse: **21%**
Attrition: **6%** MLB: **90%**

**Comparables:**
Jack Morris, Joel Peralta, Jim Bunning

| YEAR | TEAM | LVL | AGE | W | L | SV | G | GS | IP | H | HR | BB | SO | EqBB9 | EqSO9 | GB% | BABIP | WHIP | ERA | FIP | FRA | WARP |
|------|------|-----|-----|---|---|----|---|----|-----|----|----|----|----|-------|-------|-----|-------|------|------|------|------|------|
| 2009 | CHA | MLB | 32 | 3 | 7 | 2 | 57 | 0 | 56 | 70 | 9 | 23 | 55 | 3.7 | 8.8 | 39% | .361 | 1.66 | 4.66 | 4.66 | 5.38 | 0.3 |
| 2010 | CHA | MLB | 33 | 3 | 2 | 0 | 52 | 0 | 57¹ | 59 | 11 | 17 | 52 | 2.7 | 8.2 | 34% | .296 | 1.33 | 4.40 | 4.77 | 5.31 | 0.0 |
| 2011 | ATL | MLB | 34 | 4 | 4 | 1 | 64 | 0 | 54¹ | 58 | 6 | 21 | 42 | 3.5 | 7.0 | 41% | .321 | 1.45 | 3.64 | 4.26 | 4.97 | -0.1 |
| *2012* | *ATL* | *MLB* | *35* | *3* | *1* | *0* | *53* | *0* | *51¹* | *50* | *7* | *16* | *39* | *2.8* | *6.8* | *41%* | *.304* | *1.28* | *4.39* | *4.39* | *4.77* | *0.2* |

Once upon a time, Linebrink's name belonged among the game's elite relievers. Nowadays, Linebrink keeps modest company, and his name is synonymous with humdrum veteran reliever. He does not excel at any one aspect—not even in retiring batters of a certain hand—but did everything just well enough

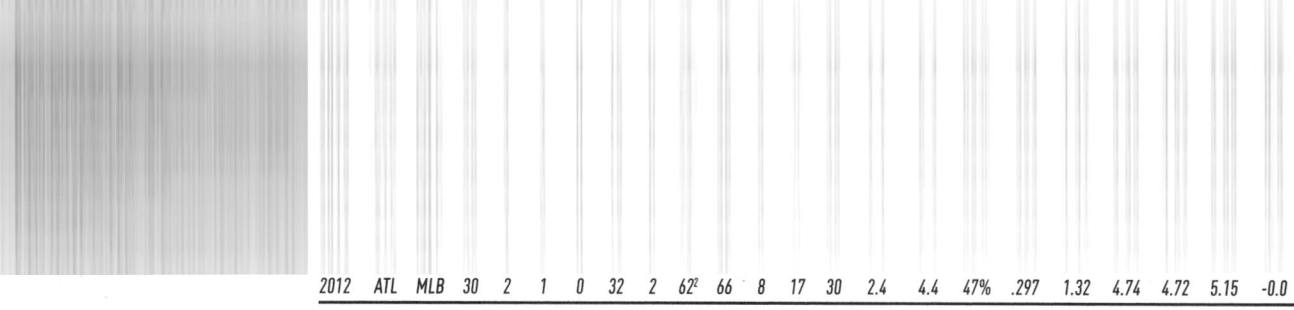

| 2012 | ATL | MLB | 30 | 2 | 1 | 0 | 32 | 2 | 62² | 66 | 8 | 17 | 30 | 2.4 | 4.4 | 47% | .297 | 1.32 | 4.74 | 4.72 | 5.15 | -0.0 |

The rubber-armed Martinez went multiple innings in 31 of his 46 appearances while admirably mopping up messes. Despite low walk rates and respectable groundball rates, Martinez may never become much more than a suitable long reliever thanks to pedestrian stuff. His fastball tops out in the low-90s and outside of his changeup, the rest of his arsenal fails to inspire confidence. If any team has the bullpen depth to avoid falling victim to the Peter Principle, Atlanta is it, so expect Martinez to return to his janitorial post in 2012.

### Kris Medlen

Born: **10/7/1985** Age: **26**
Bats: **B** Throws: **R** Height: **5' 11"** Weight: **190**
Breakout: **20%** Improve: **52%** Collapse: **23%**
Attrition: **5%** MLB: **98%**

**Comparables:**
Roy Oswalt, Zack Greinke, Erik Hanson

| YEAR | TEAM | LVL | AGE | W | L | SV | G | GS | IP | H | HR | BB | SO | EqBB9 | EqSO9 | GB% | BABIP | WHIP | ERA | FIP | FRA | WARP |
|------|------|-----|-----|---|---|----|---|----|-----|-----|----|----|----|-------|-------|-----|-------|------|------|------|------|------|
| 2009 | GWN | AAA | 23 | 5 | 0 | 0 | 8 | 6 | 37² | 20 | 0 | 10 | 44 | 2.4 | 10.5 | 45% | .241 | 0.80 | 1.19 | 1.61 | 2.44 | 1.3 |
| 2009 | ATL | MLB | 23 | 3 | 5 | 0 | 37 | 4 | 67² | 65 | 5 | 30 | 72 | 4.0 | 9.6 | 42% | .335 | 1.40 | 4.26 | 3.31 | 3.70 | 1.2 |
| 2010 | ATL | MLB | 24 | 6 | 2 | 0 | 31 | 14 | 107² | 108 | 13 | 21 | 83 | 1.8 | 6.9 | 44% | .305 | 1.20 | 3.68 | 3.80 | 4.27 | 1.4 |
| 2011 | ATL | MLB | 25 | 0 | 0 | 0 | 2 | 0 | 2¹ | 1 | 0 | 0 | 2 | 0.0 | 7.7 | 33% | .167 | 0.43 | 0.00 | 1.28 | 2.71 | 0.0 |
| *2012* | *ATL* | *MLB* | *26* | *1* | *1* | *0* | *5* | *2* | *18* | *17* | *2* | *5* | *15* | *2.4* | *7.3* | *44%* | *.311* | *1.19* | *3.67* | *3.82* | *3.99* | *0.3* |

Unearthed as a collegiate shortstop, Medlen makes the most of being 5-foot-10 by throwing in the low-to-mid-90s and tossing a great changeup. Medlen's first two big-league seasons consisted of splitting time between the bullpen and rotation, but his UCL popped in 2010, costing him most of 2011. A return to the bullpen makes sense given the Braves' rotation depth, and Medlen's reverse splits could provide a neat wrinkle for the team to exploit.

### Mike Minor

Born: **12/26/1987** Age: **24**
Bats: **R** Throws: **L** Height: **6' 4"** Weight: **210**
Breakout: **32%** Improve: **62%** Collapse: **19%**
Attrition: **12%** MLB: **95%**

**Comparables:**
Scott Sanderson, Jeremy Hellickson, Willie Adams

| YEAR | TEAM | LVL | AGE | W | L | SV | G | GS | IP | H | HR | BB | SO | EqBB9 | EqSO9 | GB% | BABIP | WHIP | ERA | FIP | FRA | WARP |
|------|------|-----|-----|---|---|----|----|----|------|----|----|----|----|-------|-------|-----|-------|------|------|------|------|------|
| 2010 | MIS | AA | 22 | 2 | 6 | 0 | 15 | 15 | 87 | 48 | 4 | 26 | 77 | 3.5 | 11.3 | 48% | .310 | 1.24 | 4.03 | 3.28 | 3.91 | 1.3 |
| 2010 | GWN | AAA | 22 | 4 | 1 | 0 | 6 | 6 | 33¹ | 13 | 1 | 8 | 23 | 3.2 | 10.0 | 50% | .267 | 0.93 | 1.89 | 3.26 | 2.94 | 1.0 |
| 2010 | ATL | MLB | 22 | 3 | 2 | 0 | 9 | 8 | 40² | 53 | 6 | 11 | 43 | 2.4 | 9.5 | 38% | .382 | 1.57 | 5.98 | 3.79 | 5.17 | 0.0 |
| 2011 | GWN | AAA | 23 | 4 | 5 | 0 | 16 | 16 | 100² | 93 | 12 | 27 | 99 | 2.4 | 8.9 | 45% | .299 | 1.19 | 3.13 | 3.69 | 4.59 | 1.5 |
| 2011 | ATL | MLB | 23 | 5 | 3 | 0 | 15 | 15 | 82² | 93 | 7 | 30 | 77 | 3.3 | 8.4 | 39% | .354 | 1.49 | 4.14 | 3.36 | 4.14 | 1.1 |
| *2012* | *ATL* | *MLB* | *24* | *6* | *6* | *0* | *18* | *18* | *101* | *98* | *10* | *32* | *85* | *2.8* | *7.6* | *43%* | *.322* | *1.28* | *4.13* | *3.76* | *4.49* | *0.9* |

Atlanta took body blows from the community after drafting Minor in 2009. The seventh overall pick is not one usually associated with risk aversion, but the gambit paid off. Minor increased his velocity and stock, shooting through the minors thanks to an already healthy arsenal that featured a plus changeup and improving breaking ball. Despite losing the fifth starter's job to Beachy in camp, Minor still made 15 starts and opened the season in the rotation due to a Jurrjens injury. Although he allowed a below league-average number of runs, the component measures suggest he pitched well. Expect Minor to open 2012 in the big-league rotation.

**Peter Moylan**
Born: 12/2/1978 Age: 33
Bats: R Throws: R Height: 6′ 3″ Weight: 200
Breakout: 21% Improve: 37% Collapse: 37%
Attrition: 11% MLB: 95%

Comparables:
Jim Mecir, Hoyt Wilhelm, Jose Mesa

| YEAR | TEAM | LVL | AGE | W | L | SV | G | GS | IP | H | HR | BB | SO | EqBB9 | EqSO9 | GB% | BABIP | WHIP | ERA | FIP | FRA | WARP |
|------|------|-----|-----|---|---|----|---|----|------|----|----|----|----|-------|-------|-----|-------|------|------|------|------|------|
| 2009 | ATL | MLB | 30 | 6 | 2 | 0 | 87 | 0 | 87 | 73 | 65 | 0 | 35 | 61 | 4.3 | 7.5 | 64% | .314 | 1.37 | 2.84 | 2.91 | 3.89 | 1.2 |
| 2010 | ATL | MLB | 31 | 6 | 2 | 1 | 85 | 0 | 63² | 53 | 5 | 37 | 52 | 5.2 | 7.4 | 69% | .282 | 1.41 | 2.97 | 4.33 | 5.88 | -0.5 |
| 2011 | ATL | MLB | 32 | 2 | 1 | 0 | 13 | 0 | 8¹ | 12 | 0 | 3 | 10 | 3.2 | 10.8 | 84% | .480 | 1.80 | 3.24 | 1.67 | 3.70 | 0.1 |
| 2012 | ATL | MLB | 33 | 1 | 1 | 0 | 26 | 0 | 19² | 17 | 1 | 8 | 14 | 3.5 | 6.6 | 62% | .296 | 1.26 | 3.66 | 3.66 | 3.98 | 0.3 |

Years after washing out of the Twins' system, Moylan pitched in the 2006 World Baseball Classic. Little known then, Moylan has become a mainstay in the Braves bullpen more than 250 innings later. Ol' faithful missed most of 2011 while recovering from two surgeries—one to fix a bulging disc, the other to repair a torn labrum and rotator cuff. Moylan's side-arm throwing, groundball-getting ways are a luxury in the bullpen, but the Braves have Cory Gearrin hanging around at a lower cost. A free agent at season's end, Moylan may continue his great story in another city.

**Eric O'Flaherty**
Born: 2/5/1985 Age: 27
Bats: L Throws: L Height: 6′ 3″ Weight: 195
Breakout: 26% Improve: 47% Collapse: 16%
Attrition: 12% MLB: 95%

Comparables:
Johnny Antonelli, Billy Pierce, Fernando Valenzuela

| YEAR | TEAM | LVL | AGE | W | L | SV | G | GS | IP | H | HR | BB | SO | EqBB9 | EqSO9 | GB% | BABIP | WHIP | ERA | FIP | FRA | WARP |
|------|------|-----|-----|---|---|----|---|----|------|----|----|----|----|-------|-------|-----|-------|------|------|------|------|------|
| 2009 | ATL | MLB | 24 | 2 | 1 | 0 | 78 | 0 | 56¹ | 52 | 2 | 18 | 39 | 2.9 | 6.2 | 55% | .294 | 1.24 | 3.04 | 3.41 | 3.83 | 0.8 |
| 2010 | ATL | MLB | 25 | 3 | 2 | 0 | 56 | 0 | 44 | 37 | 2 | 18 | 36 | 3.7 | 7.4 | 58% | .285 | 1.25 | 2.45 | 3.36 | 4.44 | 0.3 |
| 2011 | ATL | MLB | 26 | 2 | 4 | 0 | 78 | 0 | 73² | 59 | 2 | 21 | 67 | 2.6 | 8.2 | 57% | .285 | 1.09 | 0.98 | 2.51 | 3.46 | 1.1 |
| 2012 | ATL | MLB | 27 | 4 | 2 | 1 | 68 | 0 | 60² | 54 | 4 | 19 | 45 | 2.8 | 6.7 | 51% | .300 | 1.21 | 3.44 | 3.52 | 3.74 | 1.0 |

O'Flaherty showed symptoms of specialism while in Seattle. Since moving to Atlanta via waiver claim, O'Flaherty has become a full-fledged lefty terminator. Lefties have not posted an on-base percentage of more than .280 or a slugging percentage of more than .330 against him. He led the league in ERA in 2011 and is living proof that useful relievers are all over. You just have to give them a chance.

**Carlos Perez**
Born: 11/20/1991 Age: 20
Bats: L Throws: L Height: 6′ 3″ Weight: 195
Breakout: 30% Improve: 51% Collapse: 28%
Attrition: 17% MLB: 92%

Comparables:
David Clyde, Ray Sadecki, Bruce Robbins

| YEAR | TEAM | LVL | AGE | W | L | SV | G | GS | IP | H | HR | BB | SO | EqBB9 | EqSO9 | GB% | BABIP | WHIP | ERA | FIP | FRA | WARP |
|------|------|-----|-----|---|---|----|----|----|------|-----|----|----|-----|-------|-------|-----|-------|------|------|------|------|------|
| 2009 | BRA | RK | 17 | 1 | 2 | 0 | 10 | 5 | 30² | 35 | 2 | 13 | 23 | 3.8 | 6.7 | 54% | .344 | 1.56 | 5.28 | 4.53 | 5.91 | 0.2 |
| 2010 | DNV | RK | 18 | 2 | 0 | 0 | 6 | 6 | 32 | 18 | 0 | 10 | 26 | 3.9 | 7.6 | 60% | .257 | 1.06 | 1.12 | 3.10 | 4.26 | 1.1 |
| 2011 | ROM | A | 19 | 3 | 8 | 1 | 28 | 23 | 125 | 134 | 7 | 65 | 104 | 4.8 | 7.8 | 47% | .335 | 1.63 | 4.82 | 4.25 | 5.52 | -0.2 |
| 2012 | ATL | MLB | 20 | 1 | 3 | 0 | 7 | 7 | 34¹ | 40 | 4 | 21 | 15 | 5.4 | 3.9 | 47% | .317 | 1.75 | 6.61 | 5.68 | 7.19 | -0.6 |

Those dissuaded by Perez's underwhelming results were never true believers to begin with. Perez operates a long and lean body that smells of projection. His arm moves as if it has a hot date and his fastball can touch the mid-90s—with a power curve serving as its best friend. For Perez to reach his top-of-the-world upside, he has to hone his changeup and control. Until that happens, he will not merit a mention with the Braves' trio of Latin American pitching studs.

**Todd Redmond**
Born: 5/17/1985 Age: 27
Bats: R Throws: R Height: 6′ 4″ Weight: 215
Breakout: 41% Improve: 63% Collapse: 9%
Attrition: 19% MLB: 86%

Comparables:
Virgil Vasquez, Dustin Moseley, Jeremy Hernandez

| YEAR | TEAM | LVL | AGE | W | L | SV | G | GS | IP | H | HR | BB | SO | EqBB9 | EqSO9 | GB% | BABIP | WHIP | ERA | FIP | FRA | WARP |
|------|------|-----|-----|----|----|----|----|----|------|-----|----|----|-----|-------|-------|-----|-------|------|------|------|------|------|
| 2009 | GWN | AAA | 24 | 9 | 6 | 0 | 27 | 24 | 145 | 152 | 21 | 47 | 106 | 2.9 | 6.6 | 33% | .292 | 1.37 | 4.41 | 4.69 | 5.02 | 0.8 |
| 2010 | GWN | AAA | 25 | 9 | 10 | 0 | 28 | 28 | 162² | 108 | 12 | 31 | 97 | 2.4 | 7.9 | 36% | .298 | 1.23 | 4.26 | 3.87 | 4.63 | 2.3 |
| 2011 | GWN | AAA | 26 | 10 | 8 | 0 | 28 | 27 | 169² | 152 | 18 | 47 | 142 | 2.5 | 7.5 | 37% | .282 | 1.17 | 2.92 | 3.92 | 4.67 | 2.6 |
| 2012 | ATL | MLB | 27 | 3 | 4 | 0 | 9 | 9 | 55 | 58 | 8 | 16 | 32 | 2.6 | 5.2 | 36% | .304 | 1.34 | 4.95 | 4.80 | 5.38 | -0.1 |

The Braves acquired Redmond in exchange for Tyler Yates in 2008. After two pedestrian seasons in Triple-A, Redmond pitched well enough in 2011 to earn a 40-man roster spot. Despite being a physical presence (6-foot-3, 215 pounds), Redmond is all about pitchability. His fastball has average velocity and he throws a changeup and curveball to keep batters guessing. He relies on throwing strikes and avoiding walks. In another organization, he might sneak into the rotation as a number five starter.

## Zeke Spruill

Born: 9/11/1989 Age: 22
Bats: B Throws: R Height: 6' 5" Weight: 184
Breakout: 31% Improve: 57% Collapse: 23%
Attrition: 24% MLB: 83%

Comparables:
Fred Newman, Wilbur Wood, John Mitchell

| YEAR | TEAM | LVL | AGE | W | L | SV | G | GS | IP | H | HR | BB | SO | EqBB9 | EqSO9 | GB% | BABIP | WHIP | ERA | FIP | FRA | WARP |
|------|------|-----|-----|---|---|----|----|----|------|-----|----|----|----|-------|-------|-----|-------|------|------|------|------|------|
| 2009 | ROM | A | 19 | 8 | 6 | 1 | 20 | 19 | 116 | 120 | 9 | 24 | 95 | 1.9 | 7.4 | 59% | .310 | 1.24 | 3.03 | 3.64 | 5.54 | -0.7 |
| 2010 | MYR | A+ | 20 | 3 | 5 | 0 | 14 | 13 | 65 | 73 | 4 | 9 | 28 | 1.8 | 5.7 | 54% | .347 | 1.48 | 5.54 | 4.00 | 5.21 | 0.0 |
| 2011 | LYN | A+ | 21 | 6 | 6 | 0 | 20 | 20 | 129² | 108 | 7 | 23 | 92 | 1.6 | 6.4 | 56% | .264 | 1.01 | 3.19 | 3.21 | 4.42 | 1.8 |
| 2011 | MIS | AA | 21 | 3 | 2 | 0 | 7 | 7 | 45 | 45 | 3 | 17 | 16 | 3.4 | 3.2 | 37% | .275 | 1.38 | 3.20 | 4.92 | 5.09 | -0.1 |
| 2012 | ATL | MLB | 22 | 2 | 4 | 0 | 8 | 8 | 48² | 56 | 6 | 17 | 17 | 3.2 | 3.2 | 49% | .310 | 1.51 | 5.78 | 5.16 | 6.28 | -0.5 |

Another Georgia native drafted by the Braves, Spruill recovered from a rough 2010 season by passing a repeat trial in High-A. The gangly righty throws a low-90s sinker that he pounds the bottom of the zone with, and a worthwhile changeup. He is still developing a slider, but has a chance to vindicate the Braves' second-round selection after all. Look for him to open in Mississippi.

## Julio Teheran

| YEAR | TEAM | LVL | AGE | W | L | SV | G | GS | IP | H | HR | BB | SO | EqBB9 | EqSO9 | GB% | BABIP | WHIP | ERA | FIP | FRA | WARP |
|------|------|-----|-----|---|---|----|----|----|------|-----|----|----|----|-------|-------|-----|-------|------|------|------|------|------|

In a system loaded with talented young arms, Teheran rises to the top. Teheran made his major league debut at age 20 and could become a major league regular before turning 22. He has all the right weaponry you look for in a frontline starter: fastball velocity (he averaged 93 miles per hour in the majors), a plus secondary offering (his changeup), a third offering (a curveball that has plus potential), and good arm action. Add in that Teheran hides the ball well throughout his delivery, and that he receives rave reviews for his mound presence, and he could be the future staff ace.

## Anthony Varvaro

Born: 10/31/1984 Age: 27
Bats: R Throws: R Height: 6' 1" Weight: 195
Breakout: 25% Improve: 64% Collapse: 12%
Attrition: 8% MLB: 86%

Comparables:
Tim Scott, Randy Johnson, Jeff Parrett

| YEAR | TEAM | LVL | AGE | W | L | SV | G | GS | IP | H | HR | BB | SO | EqBB9 | EqSO9 | GB% | BABIP | WHIP | ERA | FIP | FRA | WARP |
|------|------|-----|-----|---|---|----|----|----|------|-----|----|----|----|-------|-------|-----|-------|------|------|------|------|------|
| 2009 | WTN | AA | 24 | 4 | 3 | 8 | 36 | 0 | 54¹ | 30 | 1 | 44 | 63 | 7.3 | 10.4 | 41% | .234 | 1.36 | 2.82 | 3.78 | 3.76 | 0.8 |
| 2010 | WTN | AA | 25 | 1 | 3 | 9 | 31 | 0 | 39¹ | 21 | 2 | 17 | 34 | 4.8 | 10.5 | 48% | .322 | 1.22 | 3.21 | 3.78 | 4.83 | 0.2 |
| 2010 | TAC | AAA | 25 | 0 | 0 | 0 | 19 | 0 | 25² | 16 | 1 | 11 | 16 | 4.9 | 9.1 | 47% | .259 | 1.48 | 5.25 | 4.95 | 4.55 | 0.3 |
| 2010 | SEA | MLB | 25 | 0 | 1 | 0 | 4 | 0 | 4 | 6 | 2 | 6 | 5 | 13.5 | 11.2 | 46% | .364 | 3.00 | 11.25 | 11.55 | 11.02 | -0.3 |
| 2011 | GWN | AAA | 26 | 2 | 8 | 1 | 38 | 0 | 59 | 37 | 3 | 33 | 69 | 5.3 | 10.5 | 47% | .276 | 1.22 | 2.90 | 3.34 | 4.48 | 0.7 |
| 2011 | ATL | MLB | 26 | 0 | 2 | 0 | 18 | 0 | 24 | 15 | 3 | 11 | 23 | 4.1 | 8.6 | 35% | .211 | 1.08 | 2.62 | 4.08 | 4.23 | 0.2 |
| 2012 | ATL | MLB | 27 | 1 | 0 | 0 | 22 | 0 | 30² | 29 | 4 | 19 | 24 | 5.7 | 7.0 | 42% | .305 | 1.59 | 5.60 | 5.19 | 6.09 | -0.3 |

The last time Atlanta rescued a reliever from Seattle, he led the major leagues in earned run average three seasons later. As unlikely as Varvaro is to assume Eric O'Flaherty's success, he does have perceived upside. With a fastball that can touch the mid-90s and two secondary offerings—a curveball and changeup, vestiges from his days as a starter—Varvaro is armed to wage war with any batter, although his time in the majors has shown a favoritism toward righties. Varvaro should split time between Gwinnet and Atlanta.

## Jonny Venters

Born: 3/20/1985 Age: 27
Bats: L Throws: L Height: 6' 4" Weight: 195
Breakout: 23% Improve: 38% Collapse: 11%
Attrition: 36% MLB: 93%

Comparables:
Royce Ring, Fernando Valenzuela, Courtney Duncan

| YEAR | TEAM | LVL | AGE | W | L | SV | G | GS | IP | H | HR | BB | SO | EqBB9 | EqSO9 | GB% | BABIP | WHIP | ERA | FIP | FRA | WARP |
|------|------|-----|-----|---|---|----|----|----|------|-----|----|----|----|-------|-------|-----|-------|------|------|------|------|------|
| 2009 | MIS | AA | 24 | 4 | 4 | 0 | 12 | 12 | 65¹ | 60 | 2 | 35 | 40 | 4.8 | 5.5 | 58% | .293 | 1.45 | 2.76 | 4.02 | 5.39 | 0.1 |
| 2009 | GWN | AAA | 24 | 4 | 8 | 0 | 17 | 17 | 91¹ | 111 | 7 | 44 | 60 | 4.1 | 5.7 | 51% | .333 | 1.59 | 5.62 | 4.37 | 5.89 | -0.3 |
| 2010 | ATL | MLB | 25 | 4 | 4 | 1 | 79 | 0 | 83 | 61 | 1 | 39 | 93 | 4.2 | 10.1 | 69% | .291 | 1.20 | 1.95 | 2.72 | 3.98 | 1.2 |
| 2011 | ATL | MLB | 26 | 6 | 2 | 5 | 85 | 0 | 88 | 53 | 2 | 43 | 96 | 4.4 | 9.8 | 74% | .250 | 1.09 | 1.84 | 2.74 | 3.72 | 0.9 |
| 2012 | ATL | MLB | 27 | 4 | 1 | 2 | 73 | 0 | 76² | 67 | 6 | 35 | 59 | 4.1 | 6.9 | 59% | .299 | 1.32 | 3.97 | 4.05 | 4.31 | 0.7 |

The 2011 league leader in relief appearances, Venters has more innings pitched than every reliever except Tyler Clippard over the past two seasons. Groundballs are good, and strikeouts are even better. When a pitcher can get bundles of both, you know superlatives are on the way. Venters does just that with his bowling ball sinker and much-improved breaker, sporting a strikeout rate exceeding one batter per inning pitched and a career groundball rate over 70 percent. The only blemish on an otherwise pristine picture is a high walk rate created by messy and complicated mechanics. Venters is 78 games from passing John Smoltz for 10th all-time in Braves relief appearances, and given how aggressive Fredi Gonzalez was in using him in 2011, Venters could reach that milestone in 2012.

**Arodys Vizcaino**
Born: **11/13/1990** Age: **21**
Bats: **R** Throws: **R** Height: **6' 1"** Weight: **190**
Breakout: **21%** Improve: **57%** Collapse: **10%**
Attrition: **2%** MLB: **89%**
**Comparables:**
Dennys Reyes, Alex Fernandez, Larry Dierker

| YEAR | TEAM | LVL | AGE | W | L | SV | G | GS | IP | H | HR | BB | SO | EqBB9 | EqSO9 | GB% | BABIP | WHIP | ERA | FIP | FRA | WARP |
|------|------|-----|-----|---|---|----|----|----|----|---|----|----|----|-------|-------|-----|-------|------|-----|-----|-----|------|
| 2009 | STA | A- | 18 | 2 | 4 | 0 | 10 | 10 | 42¹ | 34 | 2 | 15 | 52 | 3.2 | 11.1 | 52% | .296 | 1.16 | 2.13 | 2.61 | 3.39 | 0.8 |
| 2010 | ROM | A | 19 | 9 | 4 | 0 | 14 | 14 | 71² | 56 | 1 | 9 | 63 | 1.1 | 8.5 | 44% | .284 | 1.00 | 2.38 | 2.59 | 3.37 | 1.6 |
| 2011 | LYN | A+ | 20 | 2 | 2 | 0 | 9 | 9 | 40¹ | 31 | 3 | 10 | 37 | 2.2 | 8.3 | 43% | .252 | 1.02 | 2.45 | 3.09 | 3.71 | 1.0 |
| 2011 | MIS | AA | 20 | 2 | 3 | 0 | 11 | 8 | 49² | 44 | 3 | 18 | 55 | 3.3 | 10.0 | 49% | .315 | 1.25 | 3.81 | 3.14 | 4.07 | 0.6 |
| 2011 | ATL | MLB | 20 | 1 | 1 | 0 | 17 | 0 | 17¹ | 16 | 1 | 9 | 17 | 4.7 | 8.8 | 34% | .306 | 1.44 | 4.67 | 3.51 | 4.11 | 0.1 |
| 2012 | ATL | MLB | 21 | 2 | 3 | 0 | 13 | 7 | 43² | 43 | 5 | 17 | 31 | 3.5 | 6.3 | 41% | .305 | 1.37 | 4.59 | 4.44 | 4.98 | 0.2 |

Vizcaino is undersized, has an unorthodox delivery and an injury history, and lacks a tertiary pitch. He shot through the system in 2011—starting in Lynchburg and ending in Atlanta. In the interim, Vizcaino transitioned to the bullpen, which many scouts believe is his long-term destination, and overpowered major league hitters at times. Vizcaino commands a low-to-mid-90s fastball well while throwing his power curveball for strikes and burying it when necessary. The Braves have good reason to keep Vizcaino in the rotation for as long as possible, since his ultimate upside is a top-of-the-rotation starter, but with their rotation depth and other factors working against him, they may elect to add another elite reliever to their corps before the end of 2012.

## LINEOUTS

### HITTERS

| PLAYER | TEAM | LVL | AGE | PA | R | 2B | 3B | HR | RBI | BB | SO | SB-CS | AVG/OBP/SLG | TAv | BABIP | BRR | FRAA | WARP |
|--------|------|-----|-----|----|---|----|----|----|-----|----|----|-------|-------------|-----|-------|-----|------|------|
| SS N. Ahmed | DNV | RK | 21 | 284 | 46 | 13 | 2 | 4 | 24 | 30 | 46 | 18-6 | .262/.346/.379 | .273 | .305 | 2.5 | 16.3 | 3.5 |
| CF T. Cunningham | LYN | A+ | 22 | 386 | 59 | 12 | 4 | 4 | 20 | 33 | 47 | 14-6 | .257/.348/.353 | .263 | .289 | 5.5 | -4.5 | 1.2 |
| DH I. Gac | WNS | A+ | 25 | 587 | 91 | 31 | 1 | 33 | 96 | 58 | 144 | 0-1 | .279/.358/.535 | .296 | .323 | -1.3 | 0.6 | 2.7 |
| 1B M. Gomez | GWN | AAA | 26 | 557 | 76 | 34 | 2 | 24 | 90 | 38 | 131 | 6-2 | .304/.356/.522 | .287 | .364 | 2.8 | -1.4 | 2.4 |
| 3B D. Hernandez | GWN | AAA | 27 | 289 | 19 | 12 | 1 | 5 | 26 | 7 | 46 | 2-2 | .201/.229/.308 | .177 | .224 | 0.4 | -1.9 | -1.9 |
|  | ATL | MLB | 27 | 35 | 4 | 1 | 0 | 1 | 4 | 0 | 5 | 0-0 | .212/.212/.333 | .212 | .222 | -0.4 | -0.5 | -0.2 |
| 3B K. Kubitza | DNV | RK | 20 | 190 | 36 | 16 | 3 | 1 | 34 | 24 | 38 | 9-3 | .321/.407/.475 | .313 | .408 | 3.5 | -3.9 | 1.8 |
| 2B T. La Stella | ROM | A | 22 | 270 | 46 | 13 | 5 | 9 | 40 | 26 | 28 | 2-2 | .328/.401/.543 | .337 | .337 | 0.1 | -4.6 | 2.6 |
| RF A. Milligan | LYN | A+ | 23 | 258 | 35 | 19 | 4 | 12 | 40 | 16 | 76 | 1-0 | .291/.345/.557 | .296 | .380 | 1.5 | 0.2 | 1.5 |
| RF J. Parraz | SWB | AAA | 26 | 495 | 66 | 28 | 6 | 9 | 52 | 42 | 91 | 5-4 | .289/.362/.440 | .270 | .346 | 0.9 | -1.8 | 1.8 |
| LF A. Richardson | MIS | AA | 27 | 353 | 64 | 9 | 0 | 1 | 21 | 60 | 66 | 17-5 | .283/.430/.327 | .287 | .369 | 5.2 | 6.7 | 3.1 |
| 2B D. Sutton | PAW | AAA | 28 | 192 | 24 | 13 | 1 | 5 | 27 | 21 | 38 | 0-2 | .295/.382/.476 | .292 | .355 | -3.4 | -1.6 | 0.8 |
|  | BOS | MLB | 28 | 60 | 11 | 7 | 0 | 0 | 7 | 3 | 13 | 0-0 | .315/.362/.444 | .279 | .415 | 0.4 | 0.3 | 0.4 |

Atlanta popped UConn shortstop **Nick Ahmed** in the second round. Ahmed has gap power, good speed, and more than enough arm and passion to play the position, but his range and fluidity are limited, and there are questions about how his swing will translate to wooden bats. ⊘ The other compensatory pick acquired from Mike Gonzalez's departure turned into **Todd Cunningham**. A JuCo product, Cunningham's power has not translated to wood yet despite profiling as his best tool. ⊘ Carolina League MVP **Ian Gac** posted eye-popping numbers last year, but that's what a 25-year-old should do; to paraphrase Rick Blaine, he'll always have Gwinnett, but if you came here for a prospect, you were misinformed. ⊘ **Mauro Gomez** is a chubby first baseman who keeps hitting well enough to stay on the radar, just not well enough to be considered anything more than organizational depth. ⊘ Outrighted to the minors by Atlanta in August, **Diory Hernandez** had shown offensive life in the minors before, but flatlined in 2011. The Astros provide one of the best environments for him to sneak onto a roster as a utility infielder. ⊘ Atlanta's third-round pick, **Kyle Kubitza** comes with pop, discipline, and the ability to play third base. ⊘ **Tommy La Stella** is a buggy infielder from Coastal Carolina drafted in the eighth round. The book on La Stella is that he can hit, but he has to find a place on the diamond to play. True to form, La Stella hit .328/.401/.543 in his first exposure to professional ball. ⚾ The Braves liked outfielder **Adam Milligan** so much they drafted him three times. The injury bug thinks Milligan is a charming young lad too, and refuses to leave him alone. As such, Milligan's power potential—and keep in mind, he has 29 career home runs in 637 plate appearances—risks going to waste. ⚾ **Jordan Parraz** changes organizations more often than some odd people change underwear. Atlanta will be Parraz's fifth organization since the beginning of 2008. He has tools and could still prove useful as a bench player, but time is no longer on his side. ⚾ Yet another product of Atlanta's minor league free agency harvest, **Antoan Richardson** signed with the club after the 2009 season and reached the majors in 2011. He is a tiny outfielder who relies on drawing walks and stealing bases for his limited offensive value. ⚾ Remember the Hit Mechanic who worked with Ben Zobrist? He taught **Drew Sutton** the voodoo, too. Sutton's offense has not translated to the majors, but he can play multiple positions and his legal name—Stephen Drew Sutton—can inspire a misleading autograph.

## PITCHERS

| | | | | | | | | | | | | | | | | | | | | |
|---|---|---|---|---|---|---|---|---|---|---|---|---|---|---|---|---|---|---|---|---|
| C. Jones | KIN | A+ | 22 | 3 | 1 | 0 | 72$^1$ | 67 | 6 | 32 | 69 | 3.7 | 8.2 | 54% | .276 | 1.31 | 3.36 | 3.79 | 5.06 | 0.2 |
| B. Pruneda | MIS | AA | 22 | 2 | 7 | 11 | 64$^1$ | 55 | 3 | 40 | 71 | 5.6 | 9.9 | 51% | .321 | 1.48 | 3.50 | 3.80 | 5.30 | 0.0 |
| J. Rice | PAW | AAA | 25 | 2 | 3 | 4 | 85$^1$ | 77 | 6 | 42 | 89 | 4.4 | 9.4 | 34% | .307 | 1.39 | 3.69 | 3.68 | 4.50 | 1.0 |
| D. Richardson | GWN | AAA | 27 | 1 | 0 | 0 | 30 | 30 | 4 | 22 | 29 | 6.6 | 8.7 | 46% | .302 | 1.73 | 6.00 | 5.34 | 5.69 | 0.0 |
| | NWO | AAA | 27 | 3 | 1 | 2 | 32 | 31 | 2 | 20 | 35 | 5.6 | 9.8 | 48% | .341 | 1.59 | 3.66 | 4.33 | 5.04 | 0.0 |
| A. Russell | TBA | MLB | 28 | 1 | 2 | 0 | 32$^2$ | 31 | 2 | 20 | 13 | 5.5 | 3.6 | 55% | .271 | 1.56 | 3.03 | 5.17 | 6.59 | -0.7 |

**Erik Cordier** is a big and blocky right-hander with a zipper and control issues. His future is in the bullpen, since his stuff is no longer good enough to overcome those issues. ⚾ **David Filak** entered the 2010 draft with as much helium as a pitcher from SUNY Oneonta can, but disappointed in his first exposure to A-ball. The upside is there, as Filak is a big righty with a power arsenal (including a fastball that can touch the mid-90s), and is still green to pitching after catching in high school. ⚾ The Braves drafted **J.R. Graham** in the fourth round out of Santa Clara University. Still raw, he throws a fastball that operates in the mid- to upper-90s. He could turn into a late-inning reliever if he finds a secondary pitch. ⚾ **Dusty Hughes** and his high-80s fastball continue to bounce around the league. Hughes has faced more than 150 major-league lefties, and put 36.1 percent of them on base one way or another. Add in his struggles against righties, and Hughes seems unlikely to get another shot at 50-plus big-league innings any time soon. ⚾ The Braves acquired **Chris Jones** for Derek Lowe and salary relief in late October. Jones gets strikeouts not by the merit of his stuff, but with an assist from a funky delivery and low release point. He could develop into a useful specialist. ⚾ Wild, hard-throwing reliever **Benino Pruneda**'s ascent to the majors petered thanks to a decline in velocity and strikeouts. ⚾ Quite the bizarre year for **Jason Rice**, who was a part of four different organizations but pitched for just one. With quality stuff, he has a future as a middleman. ⚾ A 2006 fifth-round pick by the Red Sox, **Dustin Richardson** switched organizations twice in a year's time—first to the Marlins for Andrew Miller, then to the Braves off waivers seven months later. Richardson's struggles with walks and home runs make him a non-entity barring a gene-swapping incident with Tom Glavine in the near future. ⚾ **Adam Russell** is a giant right-hander with mid-90s velocity and respectable groundball rates. Previously successful with the Padres, Russell had his strikeout rates plummet with Tampa Bay, and he looked none the better in the minors. At his best, Russell has the potential to become a set-up man.

# MANAGER: FREDI GONZALEZ

| YEAR | TEAM | W-L | Pythag +/- | Avg PC | 100+ P | 120+ P | QS | BQS | REL | REL w Zero R | IBB | Subs | PH | PH Avg | PH HR | SB2 | CS2 | SB3 | CS3 | SAC Att | SAC % | POS SAC | Squeeze | Swing | In Play |
|---|---|---|---|---|---|---|---|---|---|---|---|---|---|---|---|---|---|---|---|---|---|---|---|---|---|
| 2009 | MIA | 87-75 | 1 | 92.6 | 44 | 1 | 72 | 4 | 529 | 346 | 60 | 74 | 278 | .280 | 8 | 9 | 6 | 0 | 1 | 106 | 66.0% | 26 | 3 | 127 | 92 |
| 2010 | MIA | 34-36 | 1 | 191.5 | 70 | 69 | 52 | 1 | 193 | 141 | 36 | — | 202 | .211 | 2 | 3 | 1 | 1 | 1 | 68 | 76.5% | 14 | 2 | 148 | 45 |
| 2011 | ATL | 89-73 | 1 | 95.9 | 56 | 0 | 86 | 3 | 510 | 435 | 73 | — | 257 | .175 | 8 | 6 | 1 | 0 | 3 | 115 | 70.4% | .39 | 2 | 289 | 86 |

They say good things come to those who wait. For Gonzalez, that meant a comfy new managerial gig away from Jeffrey Loria's interference. The Marlins fired Gonzalez after a 34-36 start to the 2010 season, but he landed on his feet within the division. For an organization that values continuity, Gonzalez's Braves history seemed too good to pass up, so Atlanta tabbed him to replace the retiring Bobby Cox. Gonzalez quickly joined a select fraternity by leading the league in intentional walks issued. Prior to 2011, Cox and another former Braves manager, Joe Torre, had ruled the league in free passes for the better part of the past half-decade. Gonzalez took an aggressive approach to the handling of his bullpen. Whenever he got the itch, he went to Eric O'Flaherty, Jonny Venters, or Craig Kimbrel. Relief arms like that are rare, and other managers would no doubt have done the same, but Gonzalez continued to use those three even after promising to reduce their workload. Whether that usage led to erratic September performances from the bullpen will be a barstool topic for years to come, as will Gonzalez's decision to bench Jason Heyward so the hot streak-riding Jose Constanza could stick in the lineup. Benching potential franchise corner-stones for career minor leaguers is not a good way to earn respect in the community, even if Gonzalez did it just to appease his clubhouse and motivate Heyward. Gonzalez also earned ire by attempting the second-most sacrifice bunts, although calling him a small-ball manager ignores that the Braves rarely ran, succeeding in 65 percent of their chances when they did.

# Baltimore Orioles

If there's one word that best describes the Orioles' offseason front office situation, it's debacle. No, maybe spectacle. Catastrophe? Or maybe a simple "disaster" tag best applies. Any way you slice it, you'd think the Orioles were trying to give away a case of chlamydia as opposed to their

To recap: Jerry Dipoto chose the Angels over the Orioles, Tony LaCava turned down Baltimore's offer, and DeJon Watson pulled his name out of the hat, but at least they were willing to be interviewed in the first place, unlike Andrew Friedman, Rick Hahn, and Allard Baird. The Twins wouldn't grant permission for the O's to interview Mike Radcliff either, but word is that Radcliff wasn't interested and the Twins were being nice. The Yankees' Damon Oppenheimer did receive permission, but he never interviewed and is said to have had similarly low interest. Finally, after being caught with their pants down more times than I'm sure they care to count, the O's settled on Dan Duquette as their new general manager, a man who's been out of major league baseball since 2002.

It's not hard to see why so many found the Orioles gig repugnant. We're talking about a team that hasn't cracked a .500 record in 14 years, just once finishing higher than fourth in the division. You see, the Orioles play in the AL East, which boasted four teams that finished at least .500 last season; just one other division in baseball had more than two. Between the cash-loaded Yankees and Red Sox, the player development machine that is the Rays, and the rising Jays, it will be quite the uphill battle for the O's to regain relevance in the division, much less compete.

Without a major overhaul both on and off the field, attempting to take down these powerhouses would be like storming Mount Olympus armed with a butter knife. You can't out-spend the Yankees or the Red Sox, and even if money weren't an issue, it'd be a challenge just to bring in enough brainpower to rival their front offices. The cash-strapped Rays have managed to succeed in this environment thanks to

be almost as difficult to out-Ray the Rays with S&D (scouting and development).

Exacerbating the problem is that, divisional landscape aside, the Baltimore gig was plenty unappealing on its own merits. It's been said that LaCava would have wanted to give the organization an overhaul, but owner Peter Angelos denied him permission to fire several long-standing employees. For a club that has been a loser for so long, accountability is key, and preventing the team's new GM from holding personnel accountable is not a winning strategy. When you look at the team's track record with drafting and player development, you can get a glimpse of why LaCava thought change was in order. From 1998 to 2008, the Orioles selected 26 players within the first 50 picks of the amateur draft, and just seven went on to play more than a full season in the majors—good for a mere 27 percent success rate (quite a bit below the major league average of 38 percent). And just two (Matt Wieters and Brian Roberts) developed into All-Stars. All of this is made even more remarkable when you realize that the O's have had seven picks in the top 10 and 12 in the top 20 over that period.

Aside from his own reputation for having this sort of heavy hand in the team's affairs, Angelos allows manager Buck Showalter a great deal of pull in the front office as well. No GM candidate would want so many voices whispering in his ear; when there are too many hands in the cookie jar, no one gets a cookie. As such, it's easy to see why someone like

| | | |
|---|---|---|
| TAv | .205 | 15th |
| TAv-P | .289 | 30th |
| FIP | 4.71 | 30th |
| DER | .698 | 28th |
| DL | 648 | 9th |
| B-Age | 28.3 | 10th |
| P-Age | 28.0 | 15th |
| Salary | $87.0 | 16th |
| M$/MW | $3.63 | 22nd |

experiment to field exactly replacement-level pitching staff

**2012:** The less said about the odds of an even worse rotation this year, the better

**Action Items:** A starter who can strike out 140 batters or post an xFIP under 4.00

LaCava didn't want the job: only partial autonomy but all of the blame when such a poor dynamic leads to (likely) continued failure.

Surely all of the candidates who turned Baltimore down have aspirations to be a general manager someday, but trying to do so in Baltimore would be an incredibly difficult entry point. They'd last a few years, and after failing to dethrone the AL East aristocracy, they'd be fired and have a difficult time ever finding another GM job again. Duquette being the one to ultimately accept the job makes a lot of sense since, having been out of the game so long, he wasn't likely to find another one anyway.

Still, if the Orioles weren't able to get their first option (or their second, or their third, or their eighth), they did manage to get someone who could wind up being a good fit for the job. Duquette has a loaded resume with plenty of experience as a major league general manager, holding that role with the Expos in 1992 and 1993 and with the Red Sox from 1994 to 2002. He has a strong background in S&D—previously holding the post of scouting director for the Brewers and director of player development for the Expos—which is going to be crucial for his tenure in Baltimore. If the Orioles can start stocking their farm better and developing those players better, their financial advantage over the Rays and Jays could put them back in contention.

Theoretically, the Orioles could be playoff contenders in the AL East, especially with the new collective bargaining agreement calling for a second wild-card team. After all, they have a higher payroll than both the Jays and Rays (they more than doubled the Rays' payroll in 2011), and there's no financial barrier to developing a quality farm system—quite the opposite, in fact, since more money enables the acquisition of higher quality S&D personnel. While Duquette has the background for this, his being out of the game for so long could prove problematic if he's not familiar enough with today's pool of talent in this regard. While LaCava had specific people in mind whom he wanted to bring to Baltimore, it's unclear if Duquette has that same certainty of vision.

Still, Duquette does bring skills to the table that should prove useful for Baltimore. In the BP book *Mind Game*, Duquette is described as a "failed Theo Epstein prototype." Another way of spinning that would be to say that Epstein is Dan Duquette 2.0. If Duquette has learned from the mistakes he made as Red Sox GM, O's fans would love to have an Epstein type of GM running their club. *Mind Game* discusses how Duquette's biggest failure wasn't an inability to assemble cost-effective talent but rather his "GMitis"—his inclination to tinker too much with his roster and not let the pieces he acquired prove their worth—along with a failure to maintain goodwill with his players, fans, and media. If your GM is going to have a hamartia—a tragic flaw—this isn't a bad one to have, since it may be correctable.

Duquette was described in *Mind Game* as having a knack for "buttressing his core talent with low-cost acquisitions, whether through trades, waiver claims, or inventive signings." This is going to prove crucial to Baltimore's ultimate ability to make it back to the playoffs. Once the O's manage to create a pipeline of young talent through their minor league system to the major league club, they will need to find the right pieces to surround this hypothetical young core with, and Duquette's apparent talent-identification ability combined with the O's sufficient payroll should allow the team to bring in quality complementary pieces.

### Table 1. What a Mess

| Name | GS | IP | ERA |
| --- | --- | --- | --- |
| Jeremy Guthrie | 32 | 203.2 | 4.37 |
| Zach Britton | 28 | 154.1 | 4.61 |
| Jake Arrieta | 22 | 119.1 | 5.05 |
| Alfredo Simon | 16 | 94.1 | 4.96 |
| Tommy Hunter | 11 | 68.1 | 5.00 |
| Brad Bergesen | 12 | 62.1 | 5.78 |
| Chris Tillman | 13 | 62 | 5.52 |
| Brian Matusz | 12 | 49.2 | 10.69 |
| Chris Jakubauskas | 6 | 27.1 | 6.91 |
| Jo-Jo Reyes | 5 | 23.2 | 6.85 |
| Mitch Atkins | 3 | 10.2 | 8.44 |
| Rick VandenHurk | 2 | 5.1 | 11.81 |

Task number one for Duquette will be rebuilding one of the most out-of-sorts rotations in the majors. In 2011, the Orioles posted the worst starter ERA in baseball at 5.39—more than a half-run worse than the next-worst rotation at 4.82 and a hypothetical replacement level pitcher's ERA of 4.68. Employing the strategy of throwing enough crap at the wall that something is bound to stick, the O's used the second-most starters in baseball (behind the Rockies, who had three starters log significant DL time and either traded or acquired another four midseason), but by the end of the year, the O's still had a very empty wall. In fact, just three of their starters managed an ERA better than 5.00, and just two were better than replacement level.

### Table 2. Kevin Goldstein's Prospect Ratings of Baltimore's Young Starters

| Pitcher | Current Age | Goldstein Rating | Rating Year |
| --- | --- | --- | --- |
| Jake Arrieta | 26 | 70 | 2010 |
| Zach Britton | 24 | 17 | 2011 |
| Dylan Bundy | 19 | 8 | 2012 |
| Brian Matusz | 25 | 18 | 2010 |
| Chris Tillman | 24 | 16 | 2009 |

The good news is that the O's rotation is young and potential-laden, with several young starters who could help them contend in a few years. Their 2011 first-round pick, Dylan Bundy, is mature beyond his age and will move through the system quickly, giving them a potential number-one starter by 2014. Zach Britton and Jake Arrieta both showed flashes of dominance last season and could form a potent 1-2-3 with Bundy. Throw in two lottery ticket, former five-star prospects in Brian Matusz and Chris Tillman, and the O's have a solid core for Duquette to start with.

On the offensive side of the ball, Duquette has a bit less to work with. At the major league level, he has two young, star-level players at premium defensive positions in Matt Wieters and Adam Jones, and a complementary but aging piece in Nick Markakis, who's is locked up through 2014. Aside from that, however, he has little in the way of players who will still be around when Baltimore hopes to contend, excluding lottery ticket third basemen Josh Bell and Chris Davis. In the minors, Manny Machado is a future star at yet another premium position (if his glove sticks at shortstop), but after him, Jonathan Schoop is the only other prospect who grades out at even four stars. A core of Wieters, Jones, and Machado would be great, but the lack of minor league depth empha-

### Table 3. Baltimore's Offensive Core

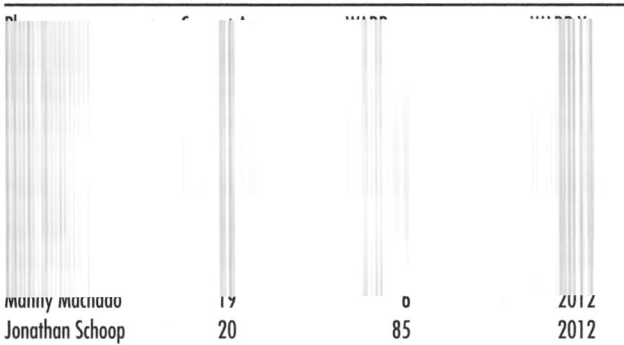

| | | | |
|---|---|---|---|
| Manny Machado | 19 | 0 | 2012 |
| Jonathan Schoop | 20 | 85 | 2012 |

manager who likes to have a say in player acquisition and an owner who is protecting the jobs of potential front office liabilities. If Duquette manages to pull this one off, he'll be deserving of all the praise you could possibly heap upon him.

## HITTERS

| Ryan Adams 2B |
|---|
| Born: 4/21/1987 Age: 25 |
| Bats: R Throws: R Height: 6' 0" Weight: 185 |
| Breakout: 1% Improve: 20% Collapse: 14% |
| Attrition: 46% MLB: 79% |
| **Comparables:** |
| Elliot Johnson, Reid Brignac, Jason Hardtke |

| YEAR | TEAM | LVL | AGE | PA | R | 2B | 3B | HR | RBI | BB | SO | SB | CS | AVG_OBP_SLG | TAv | BABIP | BRR | FRAA | WARP |
|---|---|---|---|---|---|---|---|---|---|---|---|---|---|---|---|---|---|---|---|
| 2009 | FRD | A+ | 22 | 235 | 27 | 14 | 0 | 2 | 25 | 19 | 41 | 2 | 4 | .288/.349/.381 | .266 | .349 | 0.3 | -2.6 | 0.2 |
| 2010 | BOW | AA | 23 | 594 | 81 | 43 | 0 | 15 | 68 | 47 | 121 | 2 | 3 | .298/.368/.464 | .278 | .363 | -1.1 | 7.2 | 3.4 |
| 2011 | NOR | AAA | 24 | 415 | 46 | 28 | 3 | 10 | 37 | 30 | 103 | 5 | 2 | .284/.341/.454 | .269 | .363 | -0.2 | -7.3 | 0.6 |
| 2011 | BAL | MLB | 24 | 96 | 9 | 4 | 0 | 0 | 7 | 6 | 25 | 0 | 0 | .281/.333/.326 | .213 | .391 | -1.3 | -1.6 | -0.5 |
| 2012 | BAL | MLB | 25 | 250 | 27 | 14 | 1 | 4 | 26 | 14 | 60 | 1 | 1 | .252/.302/.375 | .243 | .318 | -0.1 | 2B -0, 3B -0 | 0.6 |

Injuries in the Baltimore infield meant a windfall of starts for Adams, but he needs more development if he is to stick as a major league regular. He's unathletic, has poor range at second, and doesn't quite have the power to play at a corner, so if he does stick, it will be as a bat-first infielder. Bundles of doubles have kept his isolated power above .150 as he has risen through the minors, but those doubles haven't turned to home runs yet. His overall line has benefited from a perpetually high BABIP, which scouts equate to potential in his bat. Realistically, that BABIP will dip some in the majors, and he'll likely need to cut down on strikeouts to maintain those .280 batting averages.

| Robert Andino 2B |
|---|
| Born: 4/25/1984 Age: 28 |
| Bats: R Throws: R Height: 6' 1" Weight: 170 |
| Breakout: 2% Improve: 32% Collapse: 8% |
| Attrition: 24% MLB: 77% |
| **Comparables:** |
| Orlando Hudson, Luis Gonzalez, Bob Johnson |

| YEAR | TEAM | LVL | AGE | PA | R | 2B | 3B | HR | RBI | BB | SO | SB | CS | AVG_OBP_SLG | TAv | BABIP | BRR | FRAA | WARP |
|---|---|---|---|---|---|---|---|---|---|---|---|---|---|---|---|---|---|---|---|
| 2009 | BAL | MLB | 25 | 215 | 31 | 7 | 0 | 2 | 10 | 15 | 47 | 3 | 3 | .222/.274/.288 | .217 | .278 | -0.1 | 2 | 0.1 |
| 2010 | NOR | AAA | 26 | 588 | 72 | 30 | 4 | 13 | 76 | 29 | 110 | 16 | 3 | .264/.305/.405 | .248 | .308 | -1 | 8.4 | 2.1 |
| 2010 | BAL | MLB | 26 | 66 | 6 | 4 | 0 | 2 | 6 | 3 | 13 | 1 | 1 | .295/.333/.459 | .260 | .340 | -0.3 | -0.9 | 0.0 |
| 2011 | BAL | MLB | 27 | 511 | 63 | 22 | 0 | 5 | 36 | 41 | 83 | 13 | 3 | .263/.327/.344 | .245 | .311 | 1.9 | 0.8 | 1.1 |
| 2012 | BAL | MLB | 28 | 461 | 49 | 21 | 3 | 8 | 46 | 28 | 91 | 10 | 4 | .253/.300/.367 | .242 | .301 | -0.2 | 2B -3, SS 3 | 0.9 |

Andino earned the trophy for Best Cesar Izturis Impression this season, starting the year as a reserve infielder but accumulating over 500 plate appearances of barely above-replacement-level performance. Filling in at shortstop (for J.J. Hardy), second (for Brian Roberts), and third (post-Derrek Lee trade), Andino provided serviceable defense around the diamond and even played a little left field. He drove the nail into the Red Sox' coffin on the season's final day, but that's about all he did, posting a .249 True Average, in line with the rest of his career. At 28, there isn't much more to project in Andino's bat, with little power to speak of and poor on-base skills. He has some speed and won't kill the O's with his average, but those are the nicest things one could say about Andino's offense.

| Matt Angle | CF | YEAR | TEAM | LVL | AGE | PA | R | 2B | 3B | HR | RBI | BB | SO | SB | CS | AVG_OBP_SLG | TAv | BABIP | BRR | FRAA | WARP |
|---|---|---|---|---|---|---|---|---|---|---|---|---|---|---|---|---|---|---|---|---|---|
| | | 2009 | FRD | A+ | 23 | 553 | 78 | 17 | 4 | 1 | 32 | 59 | 72 | 40 | 12 | .289/.365/.347 | .275 | .330 | 3.8 | 3.9 | 3.5 |
| | | 2010 | BOW | AA | 24 | 70 | 11 | 2 | 0 | 1 | 9 | 6 | 5 | 5 | 2 | .383/.420/.467 | .318 | .386 | -0.5 | 1.1 | 0.9 |
| | | 2010 | NOR | AAA | 24 | 399 | 55 | 4 | 4 | 0 | 24 | 41 | 54 | 24 | 4 | .260/.335/.303 | .247 | .300 | 4.1 | 1.5 | 1.1 |
| | | 2011 | NOR | AAA | 25 | 489 | 67 | 13 | 3 | 4 | 33 | 47 | 88 | 27 | 3 | .271/.347/.344 | .254 | .329 | 6.1 | 5.5 | 2.6 |
| | | 2011 | BAL | MLB | 25 | 95 | 12 | 4 | 0 | 1 | 7 | 12 | 13 | 11 | 1 | .177/.293/.266 | .245 | .200 | 1.3 | 1 | 0.3 |
| | | 2012 | BAL | MLB | 26 | 250 | 26 | 8 | 1 | 1 | 19 | 22 | 41 | 13 | 3 | .253/.321/.320 | .238 | .298 | 0.5 | CF -1, LF 1 | 0.4 |

Born: 9/10/1985 Age: 26
Bats: L Throws: R Height: 5' 11" Weight: 175
Breakout: 1% Improve: 45% Collapse: 5%
Attrition: 18% MLB: 68%

Comparables:
Alex Cole, Brad Coon, Kenny Lofton

Angle's best tool is his speed, which he put on full display in his first taste of the big leagues: despite a mere .293 OBP, Angle stole 11 bases in 95 plate appearances thanks to an absurd 55 percent attempt rate and a 92 percent success rate. Widely considered the best defensive outfielder in the system, his bat is suspect. He has no power to speak of and struck out 18 percent of the time at Triple-A, unacceptable for a guy without pop and without Ichiro's BABIP. Still, he takes some walks, and if he can manage to stretch his tools, his best case scenario is becoming a toned-down version of Michael Bourn.

| Matt Antonelli | 3B | YEAR | TEAM | LVL | AGE | PA | R | 2B | 3B | HR | RBI | BB | SO | SB | CS | AVG_OBP_SLG | TAv | BABIP | BRR | FRAA | WARP |
|---|---|---|---|---|---|---|---|---|---|---|---|---|---|---|---|---|---|---|---|---|---|
| | | 2009 | POR | AAA | 24 | 219 | 25 | 11 | 2 | 4 | 22 | 26 | 30 | 1 | 1 | .196/.297/.339 | .240 | .210 | 0.6 | 0.2 | 0.0 |
| | | 2011 | SYR | AAA | 26 | 359 | 44 | 19 | 3 | 8 | 30 | 47 | 59 | 6 | 6 | .297/.393/.460 | .291 | .342 | -4 | 5.3 | 2.5 |
| | | 2012 | BAL | MLB | 27 | 250 | 26 | 10 | 1 | 4 | 20 | 28 | 45 | 3 | 2 | .220/.316/.331 | .240 | .257 | -0.4 | 3B 2, 2B -2 | 0.8 |

Born: 4/8/1985 Age: 27
Bats: R Throws: R Height: 6' 1" Weight: 200
Breakout: 1% Improve: 29% Collapse: 9%
Attrition: 22% MLB: 71%

Comparables:
Andy LaRoche, Paul Schaal, Steve Ontiveros

The former San Diego Padres second baseman of the future is now joining his second organization since the Pads gave up on him, but he once held a lot of promise and is still just 27 years old. The O's liked him enough to hand him a major league deal in the hopes that he'll impress in spring training and make the team as a utility infielder. After two miserable seasons at Triple-A for San Diego, Antonelli played well there for the Nationals in 2011, displaying his usually excellent patience to go with a power resurgence and contact hitting adeptness. He definitely has a chance to contribute in Baltimore and certainly can't be any worse than the Cesar Izturis/Blake Davis types the Orioles have been using in the backup infielder role.

| Xavier Avery | CF | YEAR | TEAM | LVL | AGE | PA | R | 2B | 3B | HR | RBI | BB | SO | SB | CS | AVG_OBP_SLG | TAv | BABIP | BRR | FRAA | WARP |
|---|---|---|---|---|---|---|---|---|---|---|---|---|---|---|---|---|---|---|---|---|---|
| | | 2009 | DEL | A | 19 | 509 | 55 | 15 | 8 | 2 | 36 | 27 | 111 | 30 | 10 | .262/.306/.340 | .251 | .336 | 1.5 | -5.8 | 0.5 |
| | | 2010 | FRD | A+ | 20 | 498 | 73 | 25 | 6 | 4 | 48 | 42 | 96 | 28 | 14 | .280/.348/.389 | .261 | .347 | 4.4 | -9.4 | 0.9 |
| | | 2010 | BOW | AA | 20 | 120 | 10 | 6 | 0 | 3 | 18 | 7 | 34 | 10 | 0 | .234/.288/.374 | .246 | .306 | 1.1 | 1.7 | 0.4 |
| | | 2011 | BOW | AA | 21 | 626 | 72 | 31 | 2 | 4 | 26 | 49 | 156 | 36 | 14 | .259/.324/.343 | .240 | .352 | 2.2 | -14.7 | -0.9 |
| | | 2012 | BAL | MLB | 22 | 250 | 22 | 10 | 1 | 2 | 19 | 12 | 66 | 10 | 4 | .218/.259/.296 | .201 | .289 | -0.2 | CF -13, LF -2 | -1.4 |

Born: 1/1/1990 Age: 22
Bats: L Throws: L Height: 6' 0" Weight: 180
Breakout: 3% Improve: 13% Collapse: 1%
Attrition: 10% MLB: 26%

Comparables:
Dave Martinez, David Paisano, Christopher White

Avery is the type of prospect scouts love to dream about: a multi-sport star in high school, the best athlete in Baltimore's system, loaded with potential. He passed up a football scholarship for pro ball, and was scouted out of the same rural Georgia baseball program that produced Nick Markakis and (Avery's workout partner) Jason Heyward. He is still quite raw, and his stats reflect it, but Avery has begun to spin his tools into on-field production, raising his walk rate and lowering his strikeout rate last season. He doesn't have much power projection, but he hits the ball hard, projects as an excellent defender, and, on the 20-80 scouting scale, he has 70 speed. While few project Avery as a superstar, most feel he'll be an everyday center fielder and leadoff man.

| Josh Bell | 3B | YEAR | TEAM | LVL | AGE | PA | R | 2B | 3B | HR | RBI | BB | SO | SB | CS | AVG_OBP_SLG | TAv | BABIP | BRR | FRAA | WARP |
|---|---|---|---|---|---|---|---|---|---|---|---|---|---|---|---|---|---|---|---|---|---|
| | | 2009 | BOW | AA | 22 | 127 | 18 | 5 | 0 | 9 | 24 | 11 | 28 | 0 | 0 | .289/.352/.570 | .326 | .312 | -0.6 | -2.5 | 0.8 |
| | | 2009 | CHT | AA | 22 | 391 | 47 | 30 | 2 | 11 | 52 | 50 | 70 | 3 | 5 | .296/.391/.497 | .302 | .348 | -2.8 | 0.2 | 2.8 |
| | | 2010 | NOR | AAA | 23 | 344 | 43 | 25 | 0 | 13 | 50 | 23 | 78 | 2 | 4 | .278/.331/.481 | .276 | .333 | -1.4 | -1.7 | 1.3 |
| | | 2010 | BAL | MLB | 23 | 161 | 15 | 5 | 0 | 3 | 12 | 2 | 53 | 0 | 1 | .214/.224/.302 | .204 | .301 | -0.6 | 1.5 | -0.5 |
| | | 2011 | NOR | AAA | 24 | 438 | 62 | 12 | 2 | 19 | 57 | 40 | 118 | 4 | 0 | .253/.320/.438 | .256 | .310 | 1.6 | 3.8 | 1.6 |
| | | 2011 | BAL | MLB | 24 | 65 | 6 | 0 | 0 | 0 | 6 | 4 | 25 | 0 | 0 | .164/.215/.164 | .158 | .278 | 1.2 | -1.6 | -0.6 |
| | | 2012 | BAL | MLB | 25 | 250 | 27 | 10 | 1 | 8 | 29 | 17 | 68 | 2 | 1 | .241/.292/.397 | .248 | .303 | -0.2 | 3B -3, RF -0 | 1.1 |

Born: 11/13/1986 Age: 25
Bats: B Throws: R Height: 6' 4" Weight: 220
Breakout: 12% Improve: 32% Collapse: 5%
Attrition: 39% MLB: 73%

Comparables:
Greg Norton, Russ Canzler, Dave Hollins

Once a promising Dodgers prospect, Bell has fallen from grace in his time with the Orioles. His two partial seasons with the big league club have been abysmal; he batted just .200 with a strikeout every three plate appearances. Unlike teammate Mark Reynolds, who has prodigious power, Bell can't get away with those kind of whiffs. Of course, neither of Bell's chances with Baltimore lasted long, and he's still had relative success at Triple-A Norfolk, with a more acceptable 25 percent strikeout rate and above-average power. If you want a straw to grasp at, how about the fact that he did raise his major league walk rate from 6.7 percent in 2010 to 9.1 in 2011 in a limited stint? He's now blocked by Chris Davis at third, but is anybody ever really blocked by Chris Davis at third?

**Endy Chavez** CF
Born: 2/7/1978 Age: 34
Bats: L Throws: L Height: 6' 1" Weight: 165
Breakout: 2% Improve: 24% Collapse: 8%
Attrition: 21% MLB: 76%

| YEAR | TEAM | LVL | AGE | PA | R | 2B | 3B | HR | RBI | BB | SO | SB | CS | AVG_OBP_SLG | TAv | BABIP | BRR | FRAA | WARP |
|------|------|-----|-----|----|----|----|----|----|-----|----|----|----|----|-------------|-----|-------|-----|------|------|
| 2009 | SEA | MLB | 31 | 182 | 17 | 3 | 1 | 2 | 13 | 14 | 22 | 9 | 1 | .273/.328/.342 | .245 | .302 | 0.5 | 3 | 0.5 |
| 2011 | ROU | AAA | 33 | 142 | 16 | 8 | 2 | 2 | 17 | 10 | 6 | 6 | 0 | .305/.353/.445 | .257 | .306 | -1.1 | -1.4 | 0.0 |
| 2011 | TEX | MLB | 33 | 274 | 37 | 11 | 3 | 5 | 27 | 10 | 30 | 10 | 5 | .301/.323/.426 | .273 | .321 | 1.6 | -3.9 | 0.9 |
| *2012* | *BAL* | *MLB* | *34* | *250* | *27* | *10* | *2* | *2* | *22* | *12* | *27* | *9* | *3* | *.274/.307/.354* | *.234* | *.294* | *0.1* | *CF 2, LF 0* | *0.9* |

**Blake Davis** RI
Born: 12/22/1983 Age: 28
Bats: L Throws: R Height: 6' 0" Weight: 170
Breakout: 3% Improve: 23% Collapse: 14%
Attrition: 32% MLB: 60%

**Comparables:**
Jon Weber, Rowland Office, Jose Cardenal

| YEAR | TEAM | LVL | AGE | PA | R | 2B | 3B | HR | RBI | BB | SO | SB | CS | AVG_OBP_SLG | TAv | BABIP | BRR | FRAA | WARP |
|------|------|-----|-----|----|----|----|----|----|-----|----|----|----|----|-------------|-----|-------|-----|------|------|
| 2009 | ABE | A- | 25 | 56 | 6 | 2 | 0 | 1 | 5 | 4 | 7 | 0 | 0 | .320/.370/.420 | .283 | .357 | 0.2 | -0.7 | 0.2 |
| 2009 | NOR | AAA | 25 | 197 | 21 | 4 | 2 | 1 | 14 | 14 | 40 | 3 | 2 | .211/.270/.272 | .208 | .264 | -0.7 | -0.8 | -0.6 |
| 2010 | NOR | AAA | 26 | 268 | 32 | 14 | 2 | 4 | 23 | 17 | 43 | 3 | 4 | .246/.288/.369 | .232 | .276 | -0.3 | 2.8 | 0.3 |
| 2011 | NOR | AAA | 27 | 252 | 28 | 3 | 3 | 5 | 27 | 15 | 46 | 6 | 5 | .280/.323/.384 | .249 | .326 | -0.1 | 0.2 | 0.3 |
| 2011 | BAL | MLB | 27 | 65 | 6 | 3 | 1 | 1 | 6 | 6 | 13 | 1 | 1 | .254/.323/.390 | .261 | .311 | -0.9 | -1.3 | 0.0 |
| *2012* | *BAL* | *MLB* | *28* | *250* | *25* | *9* | *2* | *4* | *23* | *16* | *51* | *4* | *3* | *.240/.290/.342* | *.230* | *.289* | *-0.5* | *RF 0, SS 1* | *-0.1* |

Blake Davis spent two months with the Orioles during his rookie season, but he only managed to step to the plate 65 times. Not a big part of the team's future plans, he was designated for assignment in September but cleared waivers and will stick around as organizational depth. If he is to make an impact, it will be as a utility man whose most valuable contribution is defensive versatility; he logged time at second, third, short, and all three outfield positions last year at Norfolk. Yes, he's a veritable Swiss Army Knife on defense, but on offense? Well, a .298 OBP across parts of three seasons at Triple-A doesn't bode well.

**Chris Davis** 1B
Born: 3/17/1986 Age: 26
Bats: L Throws: R Height: 6' 5" Weight: 235
Breakout: 3% Improve: 18% Collapse: 4%
Attrition: 32% MLB: 78%

**Comparables:**
Josh Fields, Pedro Castellano, Dallas McPherson

| YEAR | TEAM | LVL | AGE | PA | R | 2B | 3B | HR | RBI | BB | SO | SB | CS | AVG_OBP_SLG | TAv | BABIP | BRR | FRAA | WARP |
|------|------|-----|-----|----|----|----|----|----|-----|----|----|----|----|-------------|-----|-------|-----|------|------|
| 2009 | OKL | AAA | 23 | 194 | 27 | 12 | 1 | 6 | 30 | 25 | 39 | 0 | 1 | .327/.422/.521 | .327 | .400 | -2.6 | -4.7 | 1.1 |
| 2009 | TEX | MLB | 23 | 419 | 48 | 15 | 1 | 21 | 59 | 24 | 150 | 0 | 0 | .238/.284/.442 | .243 | .324 | 1.1 | -5.7 | -0.9 |
| 2010 | OKL | AAA | 24 | 444 | 67 | 31 | 2 | 14 | 80 | 37 | 105 | 3 | 2 | .327/.388/.520 | .305 | .416 | -1.5 | -5.7 | 2.5 |
| 2010 | TEX | MLB | 24 | 136 | 7 | 9 | 0 | 1 | 4 | 15 | 40 | 3 | 0 | .192/.279/.292 | .202 | .275 | -0.3 | 1 | -0.6 |
| 2011 | ROU | AAA | 25 | 210 | 39 | 14 | 1 | 24 | 66 | 11 | 58 | 1 | 0 | .368/.405/.824 | .382 | .412 | -0.6 | 0.1 | 3.4 |
| 2011 | TEX | MLB | 25 | 81 | 9 | 3 | 0 | 3 | 6 | 5 | 24 | 0 | 0 | .250/.296/.408 | .257 | .327 | -1.4 | -0.7 | -0.2 |
| 2011 | BAL | MLB | 25 | 129 | 16 | 9 | 0 | 2 | 13 | 6 | 39 | 1 | 0 | .276/.310/.398 | .268 | .390 | -0.9 | -1.8 | 0.1 |
| *2012* | *BAL* | *MLB* | *26* | *250* | *31* | *13* | *1* | *12* | *36* | *16* | *74* | *1* | *0* | *.261/.312/.478* | *.278* | *.330* | *0* | *1B -3, 3B -5* | *1.9* |

The centerpiece of the Koji Uehara deal, Chris Davis may finally be given a full season of at-bats in 2012, assuming he can stay healthy. His health is no given: he played through a partially torn labrum late in the year and suffered a sports hernia. If he can avoid injury setbacks, he's a good candidate for a Carlos Peña-style breakout. If he can't, he'll be remembered as strictly 4A. After years of riding the bus back and forth between Triple-A Round Rock and Arlington, Davis has proven all he can in the minors. He has the raw power of Thor, and that will be the tool to carry him.

### Ryan Flaherty — 2B

Born: 7/27/1986 Age: 25
Bats: L Throws: R Height: 6' 4" Weight: 220
Breakout: 0% Improve: 25% Collapse: 15%
Attrition: 34% MLB: 76%

Comparables: Tony Batista, Reid Brignac, Neil Walker

| YEAR | TEAM | LVL | AGE | PA | R | 2B | 3B | HR | RBI | BB | SO | SB | CS | AVG_OBP_SLG | TAv | BABIP | BRR | FRAA | WARP |
|---|---|---|---|---|---|---|---|---|---|---|---|---|---|---|---|---|---|---|---|
| 2009 | PEO | A | 22 | 543 | 81 | 24 | 5 | 20 | 81 | 50 | 98 | 7 | 6 | .276/.345/.470 | .296 | .309 | -4 | 6 | 3.8 |
| 2010 | DAY | A+ | 23 | 475 | 65 | 34 | 3 | 9 | 63 | 41 | 74 | 6 | 3 | .286/.354/.445 | .295 | .328 | 0.9 | 3.9 | 3.5 |
| 2010 | TEN | AA | 23 | 84 | 10 | 2 | 0 | 1 | 9 | 10 | 12 | 1 | 0 | .183/.293/.254 | .204 | .207 | -0.6 | -2 | -0.6 |
| 2011 | TEN | AA | 24 | 344 | 52 | 20 | 2 | 14 | 66 | 40 | 55 | 4 | 6 | .305/.384/.523 | .290 | .332 | -0.3 | -0.5 | 1.8 |
| 2011 | IOW | AAA | 24 | 186 | 22 | 11 | 1 | 5 | 22 | 10 | 44 | 1 | 0 | .237/.277/.399 | .223 | .288 | -0.7 | -0.6 | -0.3 |
| 2012 | BAL | MLB | 25 | 250 | 27 | 12 | 1 | 7 | 28 | 16 | 53 | 1 | 1 | .237/.287/.387 | .241 | .274 | -0.2 | 2B -1, 3B 1 | 0.6 |

Flaherty blasted Double-A pitching last season, but the wheels came off upon his promotion to Triple-A. That doesn't bode well for the Rule 5 pick, as he must spend the entire 2012 season in Baltimore or else be returned to the Cubs. If he sticks, Flaherty will likely fill a super-utilityman role, as the former first-rounder played six positions last season. He fits best in the infield, and he would project for above-average power if could find a way to stick at second base. He has good patience and a solid approach at the plate, which should make him a serviceable enough contact hitter, and his good instincts and a high baseball IQ will help as he attempts to make the jump to the majors.

### Vladimir Guerrero — RF

Born: 2/9/1975 Age: 37
Bats: R Throws: R Height: 6' 4" Weight: 235
Breakout: 0% Improve: 21% Collapse: 11%
Attrition: 19% MLB: 68%

Comparables: Hideki Matsui, Al Oliver, Mike Lowell

| YEAR | TEAM | LVL | AGE | PA | R | 2B | 3B | HR | RBI | BB | SO | SB | CS | AVG_OBP_SLG | TAv | BABIP | BRR | FRAA | WARP |
|---|---|---|---|---|---|---|---|---|---|---|---|---|---|---|---|---|---|---|---|
| 2009 | ANA | MLB | 34 | 407 | 59 | 16 | 1 | 15 | 50 | 19 | 56 | 2 | 1 | .295/.334/.460 | .273 | .313 | -1.2 | 0 | 0.8 |
| 2010 | TEX | MLB | 35 | 643 | 83 | 27 | 1 | 29 | 115 | 35 | 60 | 4 | 5 | .300/.345/.496 | .289 | .292 | -5.7 | 0 | 1.9 |
| 2011 | BAL | MLB | 36 | 590 | 60 | 30 | 1 | 13 | 63 | 17 | 56 | 2 | 2 | .290/.317/.416 | .256 | .302 | -1.8 | 0 | 0.1 |
| 2012 | BAL | MLB | 37 | 565 | 72 | 28 | 1 | 20 | 74 | 33 | 67 | 3 | 2 | .287/.335/.457 | .282 | .298 | -0.5 | RF -0, LF 0 | 1.9 |

In 2011, Vlad experienced his second big decline in three years. While he bounced back from the first, with a strong 2010 season in Texas, it's unlikely he'll repeat the feat. Three separate injuries marred his 2009 decline year, but his raw power remained intact. Last year, however, Vlad's age caught up with him and his raw power worsened: even when he did go deep, 54 percent of his homers barely cleared the fences. He remains a contact hitter, but Vlad's days of 20 home run seasons have likely gone the way of every sports show Comedy Central has ever tried. That's bad news for a guy who can no longer play the field adequately, or even inadequately.

### J.J. Hardy — SS

Born: 8/19/1982 Age: 29
Bats: R Throws: R Height: 6' 3" Weight: 181
Breakout: 2% Improve: 32% Collapse: 6%
Attrition: 16% MLB: 96%

Comparables: Jimmy Rollins, Nomar Garciaparra, Robin Yount

| YEAR | TEAM | LVL | AGE | PA | R | 2B | 3B | HR | RBI | BB | SO | SB | CS | AVG_OBP_SLG | TAv | BABIP | BRR | FRAA | WARP |
|---|---|---|---|---|---|---|---|---|---|---|---|---|---|---|---|---|---|---|---|
| 2009 | NAS | AAA | 26 | 74 | 7 | 2 | 0 | 4 | 12 | 3 | 9 | 0 | 0 | .254/.284/.451 | .247 | .241 | -0.2 | -1 | 0.0 |
| 2009 | MIL | MLB | 26 | 465 | 53 | 16 | 2 | 11 | 47 | 43 | 85 | 0 | 1 | .229/.302/.357 | .229 | .260 | 0.4 | 3.7 | 0.8 |
| 2010 | MIN | MLB | 27 | 375 | 44 | 19 | 3 | 6 | 38 | 28 | 54 | 1 | 1 | .268/.320/.394 | .261 | .299 | -0.3 | 1.8 | 1.8 |
| 2011 | BAL | MLB | 28 | 567 | 76 | 27 | 0 | 30 | 80 | 31 | 92 | 0 | 0 | .269/.310/.491 | .276 | .273 | 1.5 | 8.1 | 4.2 |
| 2012 | BAL | MLB | 29 | 498 | 60 | 23 | 2 | 18 | 64 | 35 | 76 | 1 | 1 | .264/.317/.444 | .270 | .279 | -0.1 | SS 3 | 2.6 |

After playing just as poorly in Minnesota as he had in Milwaukee, Hardy was acquired by the O's last winter for a pair of non-prospects, and the results were tremendous. Hardy took advantage of Camden's cozy left field, posting a career high 30 round-trippers to go with a return of his fielding prowess, resulting in a 4.2 WARP, almost identical to his 2008 season (4.0). Despite his success, PECOTA is doubtful . . . and wrong. In 2009, Hardy had some mechanical problems that caused his swing to get too long and hampered his ability to pull the ball. The result was too many balls to straightaway center—the deepest part of most ballparks. In 2010, he made adjustments but experienced several power-sapping wrist injuries and saw his fly-ball rate plummet. Health, reformed mechanics, a career-high fly-ball percentage, and Baltimore's friendly dimensions mean Hardy's power should repeat.

### Kyle Hudson — LF

Born: 1/7/1987 Age: 25
Bats: L Throws: L Height: 6' 0" Weight: 175
Breakout: 3% Improve: 21% Collapse: 2%
Attrition: 38% MLB: 64%

Comparables: Boomer Whiting, Fernando Valenzuela Jr., Chico Walker

| YEAR | TEAM | LVL | AGE | PA | R | 2B | 3B | HR | RBI | BB | SO | SB | CS | AVG_OBP_SLG | TAv | BABIP | BRR | FRAA | WARP |
|---|---|---|---|---|---|---|---|---|---|---|---|---|---|---|---|---|---|---|---|
| 2009 | DEL | A | 22 | 456 | 61 | 8 | 2 | 0 | 21 | 49 | 85 | 31 | 16 | .284/.360/.314 | .282 | .353 | 4 | -6.8 | 1.8 |
| 2010 | FRD | A+ | 23 | 598 | 83 | 17 | 3 | 0 | 28 | 62 | 129 | 40 | 15 | .260/.342/.304 | .250 | .337 | 6 | -4.4 | 0.9 |
| 2011 | FRD | A+ | 24 | 98 | 12 | 3 | 0 | 0 | 2 | 10 | 16 | 8 | 6 | .279/.354/.314 | .248 | .343 | 1.1 | -1.6 | 0.1 |
| 2011 | BOW | AA | 24 | 103 | 9 | 3 | 1 | 0 | 10 | 10 | 24 | 7 | 2 | .308/.376/.363 | .267 | .418 | -1.1 | 2.8 | 0.3 |
| 2011 | NOR | AAA | 24 | 284 | 39 | 7 | 1 | 0 | 11 | 33 | 55 | 26 | 8 | .297/.382/.333 | .260 | .382 | 1.7 | 3.7 | 1.4 |
| 2011 | BAL | MLB | 24 | 29 | 3 | 0 | 0 | 0 | 2 | 0 | 6 | 2 | 0 | .143/.143/.143 | .096 | .182 | 0.8 | -0.3 | -0.4 |
| 2012 | BAL | MLB | 25 | 250 | 23 | 7 | 1 | 1 | 16 | 20 | 59 | 12 | 5 | .234/.299/.281 | .216 | .307 | -0.5 | LF -3, CF -6 | -0.9 |

A former wide receiver in college, Hudson is a toolsy outfielder with a similar skill set to fellow prospect Matt Angle. He's as fast as whatever the opposite of molasses is—hot chili oil, maybe?—and he covers a lot of ground in the outfield. Partially as a result of his speed, he has posted high BABIPs at every level, but he also strikes out a lot and has absolutely no power. None. Hudson has a grand total of zero home runs in his professional career. He knows how to handle the strike zone, so if he hits in the majors, Hudson profiles as an everyday outfielder and potential leadoff man.

### Adam Jones — CF

Born: 8/1/1985 Age: 26
Bats: R Throws: R Height: 6' 3" Weight: 200
Breakout: 7% Improve: 41% Collapse: 4%
Attrition: 19% MLB: 91%

Comparables: Matt Kemp, Rocco Baldelli, Ellis Burks

| YEAR | TEAM | LVL | AGE | PA | R | 2B | 3B | HR | RBI | BB | SO | SB | CS | AVG_OBP_SLG | TAv | BABIP | BRR | FRAA | WARP |
|------|------|-----|-----|-----|----|----|----|----|-----|----|-----|----|----|-------------|------|-------|------|------|------|
| 2009 | BAL | MLB | 23 | 519 | 83 | 22 | 3 | 19 | 70 | 36 | 93 | 10 | 4 | .277/.335/.457 | .269 | .308 | 0.1 | 14.3 | 4.0 |
| 2010 | BAL | MLB | 24 | 621 | 76 | 25 | 5 | 19 | 69 | 23 | 119 | 7 | 7 | .284/.325/.442 | .268 | .328 | 2.4 | 5.9 | 3.7 |
| 2011 | BAL | MLB | 25 | 618 | 68 | 26 | 2 | 25 | 83 | 29 | 113 | 12 | 4 | .280/.319/.466 | .282 | .304 | 2.7 | -1.6 | 4.0 |
| 2012 | BAL | MLB | 26 | 581 | 71 | 26 | 4 | 20 | 77 | 28 | 115 | 9 | 5 | .276/.320/.451 | .274 | .314 | -0.7 | CF 5 | 2.7 |

Jones makes his living not on a single exemplary tool—like teammates Mark Reynolds with

Breakout: 0% Improve: 4% Collapse: 1%
Attrition: 5% MLB: 9%

Comparables: Jonathan Galvez, Jiovanni Mier, Tony La Russa

| YEAR | TEAM | LVL | AGE | PA | R | 2B | 3B | HR | RBI | BB | SO | SB | CS | AVG_OBP_SLG | TAv | BABIP | BRR | FRAA | WARP |
|------|------|-----|-----|-----|----|----|----|----|-----|----|-----|----|----|-------------|------|-------|------|------|------|
| 2012 | BAL | MLB | 19 | 250 | 25 | 10 | 1 | 5 | 24 | 17 | 56 | 3 | 1 | .224/.276/.346 | .226 | .269 | -0.2 | SS 4 | 0.2 |

While Machado is unlikely to reach Baltimore for at least another year and a half, he is Baltimore's top prospect and one of the top 10 prospects in baseball. The Orioles grabbed him as a 17-year-old in the first round of the 2010 draft with the third overall pick. All five of Machado's tools rate as above average, with contact hitting ranking as his best, thanks to excellent bat speed. His quick wrists and broad shoulders point to potential growth in the power department down the line. Throw in good defense at a premium position, and if everything goes according to plan, the Orioles will have a superstar to build around for years to come.

### Nick Markakis — RF

Born: 11/17/1983 Age: 28
Bats: L Throws: L Height: 6' 3" Weight: 195
Breakout: 0% Improve: 48% Collapse: 5%
Attrition: 15% MLB: 85%

Comparables: Magglio Ordonez, Andre Ethier, Al Kaline

| YEAR | TEAM | LVL | AGE | PA | R | 2B | 3B | HR | RBI | BB | SO | SB | CS | AVG_OBP_SLG | TAv | BABIP | BRR | FRAA | WARP |
|------|------|-----|-----|-----|----|----|----|----|-----|----|-----|----|----|-------------|------|-------|------|-----------|------|
| 2009 | BAL | MLB | 25 | 711 | 94 | 45 | 2 | 18 | 101 | 56 | 98 | 6 | 2 | .293/.347/.453 | .281 | .317 | 3.2 | -17 | 1.0 |
| 2010 | BAL | MLB | 26 | 709 | 79 | 45 | 3 | 12 | 60 | 73 | 93 | 7 | 2 | .297/.370/.436 | .280 | .331 | -0.8 | -2.4 | 2.5 |
| 2011 | BAL | MLB | 27 | 716 | 72 | 31 | 1 | 15 | 73 | 62 | 75 | 12 | 3 | .284/.351/.406 | .269 | .300 | 0.3 | -3 | 1.7 |
| 2012 | BAL | MLB | 28 | 671 | 87 | 40 | 2 | 18 | 82 | 64 | 93 | 9 | 3 | .290/.360/.451 | .290 | .317 | -0.2 | RF -5, 1B 0 | 3.4 |

Every year, PECOTA projects better for Markakis than he delivers, and at 29, his chances of delivering on his one-time superstar potential are dwindling. Coveted as both a hitter and a pitcher in the first round of the 2003 amateur draft, he has certainly been worth his selection as an outfielder, but he grades out as a merely above average player; just once has he posted a WARP above 3.0 (2008). Like teammate Adam Jones, Markakis has all five tools, but not to the extent Jones does. He had compensated for his four-year home run decline by cracking over 45 doubles each year from 2008–10, but he managed just 31 last season without much of an increase in big flies. Markakis isn't the star player the O's once hoped to build around. Sad face.

### Nolan Reimold — LF

Born: 10/12/1983 Age: 28
Bats: R Throws: R Height: 6' 5" Weight: 205
Breakout: 0% Improve: 33% Collapse: 5%
Attrition: 16% MLB: 86%

Comparables: Fred Lewis, Tom Tresh, Josh Willingham

| YEAR | TEAM | LVL | AGE | PA | R | 2B | 3B | HR | RBI | BB | SO | SB | CS | AVG_OBP_SLG | TAv | BABIP | BRR | FRAA | WARP |
|------|------|-----|-----|-----|----|----|----|----|-----|----|----|----|----|-------------|------|-------|------|------------|------|
| 2009 | NOR | AAA | 25 | 130 | 21 | 11 | 0 | 9 | 27 | 18 | 25 | 6 | 1 | .394/.488/.743 | .415 | .453 | -0.4 | -1.3 | 2.1 |
| 2009 | BAL | MLB | 25 | 411 | 49 | 18 | 2 | 15 | 45 | 47 | 77 | 8 | 2 | .279/.365/.466 | .287 | .316 | -0.5 | 0.2 | 2.1 |
| 2010 | NOR | AAA | 26 | 401 | 52 | 12 | 0 | 10 | 37 | 54 | 61 | 9 | 2 | .249/.366/.374 | .259 | .278 | -1.2 | -0.4 | 0.2 |
| 2010 | BAL | MLB | 26 | 131 | 9 | 5 | 0 | 3 | 14 | 12 | 26 | 0 | 0 | .207/.282/.328 | .214 | .236 | -0.9 | 0.1 | -0.4 |
| 2011 | NOR | AAA | 27 | 161 | 16 | 6 | 0 | 6 | 22 | 18 | 43 | 2 | 1 | .237/.329/.410 | .263 | .293 | 0 | 2.7 | 0.6 |
| 2011 | BAL | MLB | 27 | 305 | 40 | 10 | 3 | 13 | 45 | 28 | 57 | 7 | 2 | .247/.328/.453 | .282 | .264 | 0.3 | 2.2 | 1.7 |
| 2012 | BAL | MLB | 28 | 275 | 35 | 12 | 1 | 11 | 35 | 27 | 55 | 5 | 2 | .263/.342/.452 | .284 | .296 | 0 | LF 0, 1B -1 | 2.1 |

A stud in college, Reimold was a second round pick in 2006, climbing the ladder quickly and establishing himself as one of the Orioles' top prospects. After just 130 plate appearances at Triple-A, Reimold was promoted to the bigs in 2009, and he didn't disappoint, triple-slashing .279/.365/.466. A guy with good (and projectable) power, also capable of hitting for average, taking a walk, and swiping a few bags, Reimold had people excited for his sophomore season. Unfortunately, after offseason ankle surgery, Reimold proved ineffective to start 2010, was sent down, and wasn't heard from again until September call-ups. He remained an afterthought until Luke Scott was injured in July 2011, leaving left field open for Reimold to get another shot. Taking advantage, a healthy Reimold posted numbers almost identical to what he did in 2009. He seems poised to establish himself as a serviceable major league regular in 2012 if given a starting job. Word is he might platoon with Endy Chavez, though, which would limit his at-bats as the righty half of the platoon.

**Mark Reynolds    3B**

Born: 8/3/1983 Age: 28
Bats: R Throws: R Height: 6' 2" Weight: 200
Breakout: 2% Improve: 22% Collapse: 0%
Attrition: 24% MLB: 76%

Comparables:
Dallas McPherson, Marlan Coughtry, Mike Schmidt

| YEAR | TEAM | LVL | AGE | PA | R | 2B | 3B | HR | RBI | BB | SO | SB | CS | AVG_OBP_SLG | TAv | BABIP | BRR | FRAA | WARP |
|---|---|---|---|---|---|---|---|---|---|---|---|---|---|---|---|---|---|---|---|
| 2009 | ARI | MLB | 25 | 662 | 98 | 30 | 1 | 44 | 102 | 76 | 223 | 24 | 9 | .260/.349/.543 | .295 | .338 | -1.4 | 2.5 | 3.9 |
| 2010 | ARI | MLB | 26 | 596 | 79 | 17 | 2 | 32 | 85 | 83 | 211 | 7 | 4 | .198/.320/.433 | .263 | .257 | 1.5 | -0.5 | 1.6 |
| 2011 | BAL | MLB | 27 | 620 | 84 | 27 | 1 | 37 | 86 | 75 | 196 | 6 | 4 | .221/.323/.483 | .282 | .266 | -2.3 | -15.3 | 1.2 |
| 2012 | BAL | MLB | 28 | 578 | 74 | 24 | 2 | 31 | 82 | 64 | 189 | 9 | 4 | .236/.327/.477 | .284 | .305 | -0.5 | 3B -5, 1B -1 | 3.5 |

A third baseman for most of his major league career, Reynolds shifted to first on the arrival of Chris Davis and—mercifully, for all involved—will remain there this year. After an abysmal first six weeks, Reynolds proved to be a very savvy acquisition. The nearly 20 percent swing in home run park factors between Chase Field and Camden Yards for right-handed batters helped Reynolds and the O's, with Reynolds averaging a dinger every 12 at-bats from May 14 on. Even with his below replacement level April, he still posted the highest rate of homers on contacted balls in the majors. Of course, he strikes out, and he'll never hit for a high average. But his history of much higher BABIPs suggests he'll improve somewhat on the paltry .221 overall batting average he posted last year. His raw power is among the best in the majors, and his home park suits him.

**Brian Roberts    2B**

Born: 10/9/1977 Age: 34
Bats: B Throws: R Height: 5' 10" Weight: 170
Breakout: 0% Improve: 39% Collapse: 8%
Attrition: 20% MLB: 91%

Comparables:
Mark DeRosa, Lou Whitaker, Ray Durham

| YEAR | TEAM | LVL | AGE | PA | R | 2B | 3B | HR | RBI | BB | SO | SB | CS | AVG_OBP_SLG | TAv | BABIP | BRR | FRAA | WARP |
|---|---|---|---|---|---|---|---|---|---|---|---|---|---|---|---|---|---|---|---|
| 2009 | BAL | MLB | 31 | 717 | 110 | 56 | 1 | 16 | 79 | 74 | 112 | 30 | 7 | .283/.356/.451 | .280 | .318 | 2.3 | -11.9 | 2.4 |
| 2010 | BAL | MLB | 32 | 261 | 28 | 14 | 0 | 4 | 15 | 26 | 40 | 12 | 2 | .278/.354/.391 | .267 | .319 | 0.7 | -4.3 | 0.4 |
| 2011 | BAL | MLB | 33 | 178 | 18 | 7 | 1 | 3 | 19 | 12 | 21 | 6 | 1 | .221/.273/.331 | .215 | .236 | 2.2 | -0.5 | -0.1 |
| 2012 | BAL | MLB | 34 | 250 | 30 | 15 | 1 | 4 | 27 | 26 | 39 | 12 | 3 | .271/.346/.408 | .271 | .307 | 0.4 | 2B -6 | 2.0 |

Another year, another 100+ day DL stint. What else is new for Brian Roberts? In 2010 it was an abdominal strain that kept him sidelined; in 2011 it was a concussion. Talent isn't a question with Roberts; his ability to stay on the field is. The problem now, however, is that he's 34 years old and hasn't played a full season since 2009. Even if he can stay healthy in 2012, it's hard to know what to expect. His primary asset has always been his speed, but he's lost quite a bit of it over the past two seasons and is unlikely to ever steal 30 bases again. He could probably still pop a dozen or so homers in a full season and get on base at a clip of .350, though, which would be plenty of value for the O's. The team will be much happier if we're right about Roberts's PECOTA-projected .262 TAv than if he has another year at .215.

**Luke Scott    LF**

Born: 6/25/1978 Age: 34
Bats: L Throws: R Height: 6' 1" Weight: 210
Breakout: 0% Improve: 27% Collapse: 5%
Attrition: 25% MLB: 91%

Comparables:
Jerry Lynch, Charlie Maxwell, David Dellucci

| YEAR | TEAM | LVL | AGE | PA | R | 2B | 3B | HR | RBI | BB | SO | SB | CS | AVG_OBP_SLG | TAv | BABIP | BRR | FRAA | WARP |
|---|---|---|---|---|---|---|---|---|---|---|---|---|---|---|---|---|---|---|---|
| 2009 | BAL | MLB | 31 | 506 | 61 | 26 | 1 | 25 | 77 | 55 | 104 | 0 | 0 | .258/.340/.488 | .286 | .283 | -1.8 | 0.6 | 1.9 |
| 2010 | BAL | MLB | 32 | 517 | 70 | 29 | 1 | 27 | 72 | 59 | 98 | 2 | 0 | .284/.368/.535 | .315 | .304 | -6.1 | 0.2 | 2.8 |
| 2011 | BAL | MLB | 33 | 236 | 24 | 11 | 0 | 9 | 22 | 24 | 54 | 1 | 1 | .220/.301/.402 | .256 | .250 | -1.1 | 0.7 | 0.2 |
| 2012 | TBA | MLB | 34 | 281 | 35 | 13 | 1 | 12 | 37 | 29 | 61 | 1 | 0 | .243/.324/.450 | .285 | .272 | 0 | LF 1, 1B -0 | 1.8 |

Scott may have his weaknesses (age, lack of speed, and average-at-best defense), but his strengths entering 2011 were health and power. He had spent just 34 career days on the DL coming into the season and had bashed 75 homers from 2008–10 in less than full-time play. Unfortunately for Scott, a torn labrum robbed him of both playing time and performance in 2011. Non-tendered by the Orioles, he's not to be forgotten, especially if off-season LASIK and shoulder surgery prove successful in returning his productivity at the plate. Take his power and throw in good plate discipline, and you have a player perfectly suited for a DH role, especially if he finds a good park and lineup for his lefty bat. While he'll certainly carry risk, Scott could wind up as one of the best values on the free agent market this winter.

**Brandon Snyder**  1B

Born: 11/23/1986 Age: 25
Bats: R Throws: R Height: 6' 3" Weight: 215
Breakout: 5% Improve: 28% Collapse: 0%
Attrition: 16% MLB: 48%

Comparables:
Randy Bush,Tino Martinez,Johan Limonta

| YEAR | TEAM | LVL | AGE | PA | R | 2B | 3B | HR | RBI | BB | SO | SB | CS | AVG_OBP_SLG | TAv | BABIP | BRR | FRAA | WARP |
|------|------|-----|-----|-----|----|----|----|----|-----|----|-----|----|----|-------------|------|-------|------|-----------|------|
| 2009 | BOW | AA | 22 | 233 | 24 | 19 | 1 | 10 | 45 | 27 | 45 | 0 | 1 | .343/.426/.597 | .350 | .404 | -1.8 | -0.4 | 2.2 |
| 2009 | NOR | AAA | 22 | 297 | 36 | 18 | 2 | 2 | 43 | 24 | 64 | 3 | 1 | .248/.323/.355 | .245 | .321 | -0.3 | -1.3 | -0.3 |
| 2010 | NOR | AAA | 23 | 376 | 36 | 22 | 1 | 9 | 43 | 28 | 101 | 4 | 1 | .257/.326/.407 | .256 | .341 | 2.8 | 0 | 0.3 |
| 2010 | BAL | MLB | 23 | 20 | 1 | 2 | 0 | 0 | 3 | 0 | 3 | 0 | 1 | .300/.300/.400 | .244 | .353 | -0.8 | 0.6 | 0.0 |
| 2011 | NOR | AAA | 24 | 494 | 55 | 21 | 1 | 14 | 71 | 32 | 91 | 1 | 2 | .261/.312/.406 | .248 | .293 | -3.3 | 4.4 | 0.2 |
| 2011 | BAL | MLB | 24 | 17 | 2 | 1 | 0 | 0 | 1 | 3 | 4 | 0 | 0 | .231/.412/.308 | .273 | .333 | 0.2 | -0.5 | 0.0 |
| 2012 | TEX | MLB | 25 | 250 | 28 | 12 | 1 | 6 | 28 | 17 | 56 | 1 | 1 | .250/.310/.398 | .245 | .301 | -0.1 | 1B -9, 3B -0 | 0.0 |

Baltimore's first round pick in 2005, Snyder hasn't panned out as expected. The Orioles drafted him as a catcher, but multiple injuries forced the O's to try him at third base before he finally settled in at first. While he has adapted enough to play average defense, he doesn't have the power or patience needed for a first baseman. Snyder looks like a major league backup at best.

…Teagarden has the defensive skill-set behind the plate to offer some value at the major league level; he's a cerebral game-caller with a strong arm and good fundamentals. But as is often the case, when his bat starts to stink with the rot of a below-average hitter, his prowess behind the plate suffers as a result. If his bat can show signs of life—he did show power potential in his days as a legitimate prospect—Teagarden could be a cheap backup option behind the plate for the O's and an upgrade over Craig Tatum.

**Matt Wieters**  C

Born: 5/21/1986 Age: 26
Bats: B Throws: R Height: 6' 6" Weight: 230
Breakout: 1% Improve: 26% Collapse: 5%
Attrition: 22% MLB: 73%

Comparables:
A.J. Ellis,Keith Moreland,Hardy Peterson

| YEAR | TEAM | LVL | AGE | PA | R | 2B | 3B | HR | RBI | BB | SO | SB | CS | AVG_OBP_SLG | TAv | BABIP | BRR | FRAA | WARP |
|------|------|-----|-----|-----|----|----|----|----|-----|----|----|----|----|-------------|------|-------|------|----------|------|
| 2009 | NOR | AAA | 23 | 163 | 25 | 9 | 2 | 5 | 30 | 20 | 30 | 0 | 0 | .305/.391/.504 | .309 | .358 | -0.1 | -0.3 | 1.3 |
| 2009 | BAL | MLB | 23 | 385 | 35 | 15 | 1 | 9 | 43 | 28 | 86 | 0 | 0 | .288/.340/.412 | .255 | .356 | -4.3 | -0.1 | 0.6 |
| 2010 | BAL | MLB | 24 | 502 | 37 | 22 | 1 | 11 | 55 | 47 | 94 | 0 | 1 | .249/.319/.377 | .251 | .287 | -0.8 | -0.9 | 1.7 |
| 2011 | BAL | MLB | 25 | 551 | 72 | 28 | 0 | 22 | 68 | 48 | 84 | 1 | 0 | .262/.328/.450 | .266 | .276 | -2.2 | 3.2 | 3.4 |
| 2012 | BAL | MLB | 26 | 508 | 61 | 25 | 1 | 15 | 60 | 42 | 93 | 1 | 0 | .265/.327/.423 | .268 | .299 | 0 | C 0, 1B -0 | 2.7 |

While Wieters didn't catapult himself into the upper echelon of catchers as everyone once expected (and many still do), he did have a breakout 2011 campaign. As he continues adjusting to big league pitching, he cut down on strikeouts for the third straight season and finally had the power surge everyone has been waiting for. Doubling his home run output from 2010 and increasing his ISO by 60 points, Wieters displayed good power to all fields and could easily take another step forward in his age 26 season. The only drawback was a career-low BABIP, but there's plenty of reason to expect that to be higher in 2012. If Wieters can maintain the gains he made last year, he could settle in as a .285, 25-home-run type with a league average walk rate. Throw in his good defense, and Wieters is well on his way to becoming the star catcher the Orioles were hoping for.

# PITCHERS

**Jeremy Accardo**

Born: 12/18/1981 Age: 30
Bats: R Throws: R Height: 6' 3" Weight: 190
Breakout: 29% Improve: 52% Collapse: 18%
Attrition: 11% MLB: 88%

Comparables:
Ben McDonald,Bob Rush,Guillermo Mota

| YEAR | TEAM | LVL | AGE | W | L | SV | G | GS | IP | H | HR | BB | SO | EqBB9 | EqSO9 | GB% | BABIP | WHIP | ERA | FIP | FRA | WARP |
|------|------|-----|-----|---|---|----|----|----|-----|----|----|----|----|-------|-------|-----|-------|------|------|------|------|------|
| 2009 | LVG | AAA | 27 | 2 | 1 | 13 | 27 | 0 | 30 | 32 | 1 | 8 | 27 | 2.4 | 8.1 | 57% | .337 | 1.33 | 3.00 | 2.98 | 3.25 | 0.7 |
| 2009 | TOR | MLB | 27 | 0 | 0 | 1 | 26 | 0 | 24² | 23 | 2 | 17 | 18 | 6.2 | 6.6 | 47% | .309 | 1.62 | 2.55 | 5.05 | 4.52 | 0.3 |
| 2010 | LVG | AAA | 28 | 3 | 2 | 24 | 42 | 0 | 44 | 41 | 0 | 10 | 19 | 3.1 | 5.3 | 50% | .406 | 1.52 | 3.48 | 3.94 | 5.32 | 0.2 |
| 2010 | TOR | MLB | 28 | 0 | 1 | 0 | 5 | 0 | 6² | 12 | 0 | 3 | 3 | 4.1 | 4.1 | 44% | .444 | 2.25 | 8.10 | 3.95 | 6.77 | -0.2 |
| 2011 | NOR | AAA | 29 | 1 | 1 | 2 | 26 | 0 | 33¹ | 26 | 1 | 11 | 27 | 3.0 | 7.3 | 49% | .281 | 1.11 | 2.16 | 3.09 | 4.77 | 0.3 |
| 2011 | BAL | MLB | 29 | 3 | 3 | 0 | 31 | 0 | 37² | 43 | 5 | 18 | 23 | 4.3 | 5.5 | 39% | .322 | 1.62 | 5.73 | 5.08 | 4.95 | 0.0 |
| 2012 | BAL | MLB | 30 | 2 | 1 | 0 | 34 | 0 | 39² | 41 | 4 | 15 | 27 | 3.4 | 6.0 | 48% | .302 | 1.42 | 4.26 | 4.29 | 4.63 | 0.2 |

Accardo's days as a high-leverage reliever are gone. After saving 30 games for the Blue Jays in 2007, he completely fell apart the following season and has since been passed between seven different major and minor league teams. His velocity has fallen from over 94 mph in 2007 to under 92 mph in 2011, and all of his pitches come in on the same plane, never forcing a batter to change his eye-line. Unable to control any of his pitches particularly well, Accardo simply doesn't do anything well enough to stick in the majors anymore.

### Jake Arrieta

Born: 3/6/1986 Age: 26
Bats: R Throws: R Height: 6' 5" Weight: 225
Breakout: 23% Improve: 63% Collapse: 18%
Attrition: 25% MLB: 89%

Comparables:
Dan Meyer, Ricky Romero, A.J. Murray

| YEAR | TEAM | LVL | AGE | W | L | SV | G | GS | IP | H | HR | BB | SO | EqBB9 | EqSO9 | GB% | BABIP | WHIP | ERA | FIP | FRA | WARP |
|---|---|---|---|---|---|---|---|---|---|---|---|---|---|---|---|---|---|---|---|---|---|---|
| 2009 | BOW | AA | 23 | 6 | 3 | 0 | 11 | 11 | 59 | 45 | 4 | 23 | 70 | 3.5 | 10.7 | 38% | .287 | 1.15 | 2.59 | 3.02 | 3.28 | 1.3 |
| 2009 | NOR | AAA | 23 | 5 | 8 | 0 | 17 | 17 | 91² | 97 | 9 | 33 | 78 | 3.2 | 7.7 | 43% | .331 | 1.42 | 3.93 | 4.10 | 3.97 | 1.4 |
| 2010 | NOR | AAA | 24 | 6 | 2 | 0 | 12 | 11 | 73 | 43 | 3 | 26 | 45 | 4.2 | 7.9 | 50% | .255 | 1.12 | 1.85 | 3.94 | 4.32 | 1.0 |
| 2010 | BAL | MLB | 24 | 6 | 6 | 0 | 18 | 18 | 100¹ | 106 | 9 | 48 | 52 | 4.3 | 4.7 | 44% | .292 | 1.53 | 4.66 | 4.73 | 4.82 | 0.7 |
| 2011 | BAL | MLB | 25 | 10 | 8 | 0 | 22 | 22 | 119¹ | 115 | 21 | 59 | 93 | 4.4 | 7.0 | 48% | .274 | 1.46 | 5.05 | 5.37 | 5.88 | -0.4 |
| *2012* | *BAL* | *MLB* | *26* | *6* | *7* | *0* | *18* | *18* | *100¹* | *102* | *13* | *45* | *74* | *4.0* | *6.7* | *45%* | *.292* | *1.46* | *4.65* | *4.76* | *5.05* | *0.1* |

While Brian Matusz and Chris Tillman got the most hype of Baltimore's pitching prospect trio while they were coming up, Arrieta has enjoyed the most major league success of the three. He started the home opener for the O's in 2011, and pitched well before an August surgery to remove bone chips from his pitching elbow. Arrieta has two fastballs, a sinker to get ground-balls and a 92-mph four-seamer. The four-seamer sets up his two above average breaking balls—a slider and a curve—plus a show-me change. He has the stuff to generate strikeouts and induce grounders. Whether he steps up to become a second or third starter depends on how his control develops and his rehab post-surgery.

### Brad Bergesen

Born: 9/25/1985 Age: 26
Bats: L Throws: R Height: 6' 3" Weight: 215
Breakout: 22% Improve: 59% Collapse: 20%
Attrition: 16% MLB: 76%

Comparables:
Geno Espineli, Bobby Livingston, Mark Buehrle

| YEAR | TEAM | LVL | AGE | W | L | SV | G | GS | IP | H | HR | BB | SO | EqBB9 | EqSO9 | GB% | BABIP | WHIP | ERA | FIP | FRA | WARP |
|---|---|---|---|---|---|---|---|---|---|---|---|---|---|---|---|---|---|---|---|---|---|---|
| 2009 | BAL | MLB | 23 | 7 | 5 | 0 | 19 | 19 | 123¹ | 126 | 11 | 32 | 65 | 2.3 | 4.7 | 51% | .285 | 1.28 | 3.43 | 4.15 | 5.08 | 1.4 |
| 2010 | BAL | MLB | 24 | 8 | 12 | 0 | 30 | 28 | 170 | 193 | 26 | 51 | 81 | 2.7 | 4.3 | 50% | .290 | 1.44 | 4.98 | 5.11 | 5.48 | 0.1 |
| 2011 | BAL | MLB | 25 | 2 | 7 | 0 | 34 | 12 | 101 | 119 | 16 | 32 | 61 | 2.9 | 5.4 | 41% | .304 | 1.50 | 5.70 | 4.95 | 5.18 | 0.0 |
| *2012* | *BAL* | *MLB* | *26* | *6* | *6* | *0* | *25* | *16* | *108¹* | *120* | *14* | *28* | *53* | *2.3* | *4.4* | *51%* | *.290* | *1.37* | *4.67* | *4.68* | *5.07* | *0.0* |

Bergesen was one of the first pitchers to be thrown out of the revolving door that was Baltimore's rotation last season. He was demoted after nine starts, then returned in a bullpen role, making just three more starts the rest of the year. A pitch-to-contact guy who relies on groundball outs, those grounders were fewer and further between this season, dropping from his usual 50 percent to 41 percent. Part of the reason for that was an increased reliance on his four-seamer over his sinker and slider. If he can work down in the zone, he'll induce more grounders, but he's a back-end starter for a bad team at best, and the O's have plenty of those.

### Jason Berken

Born: 11/27/1983 Age: 28
Bats: R Throws: R Height: 6' 1" Weight: 175
Breakout: 31% Improve: 79% Collapse: 8%
Attrition: 7% MLB: 86%

Comparables:
Frank Castillo, Nate Robertson, Dave Heaverlo

| YEAR | TEAM | LVL | AGE | W | L | SV | G | GS | IP | H | HR | BB | SO | EqBB9 | EqSO9 | GB% | BABIP | WHIP | ERA | FIP | FRA | WARP |
|---|---|---|---|---|---|---|---|---|---|---|---|---|---|---|---|---|---|---|---|---|---|---|
| 2009 | BAL | MLB | 25 | 6 | 12 | 0 | 24 | 24 | 119² | 164 | 19 | 44 | 66 | 3.3 | 5.0 | 41% | .344 | 1.74 | 6.54 | 5.36 | 5.71 | 0.4 |
| 2010 | BAL | MLB | 26 | 3 | 3 | 0 | 41 | 0 | 62¹ | 64 | 5 | 19 | 45 | 2.7 | 6.5 | 49% | .314 | 1.33 | 3.03 | 3.56 | 4.72 | 0.3 |
| 2011 | BAL | MLB | 27 | 1 | 2 | 0 | 40 | 0 | 47 | 63 | 10 | 21 | 41 | 4.0 | 7.9 | 42% | .356 | 1.79 | 5.36 | 5.49 | 6.09 | -0.4 |
| *2012* | *BAL* | *MLB* | *28* | *2* | *1* | *1* | *34* | *2* | *50* | *59* | *7* | *17* | *32* | *3.0* | *5.7* | *46%* | *.318* | *1.51* | *5.13* | *4.76* | *5.57* | *-0.3* |

Giving up on Berken as a starter, the O's moved him to the bullpen at the start of 2010 with great success, watching him post a 3.59 FIP and using him in high leverage situations before he was diagnosed with a frayed rotator cuff and a slightly torn labrum in August. Returning for 2011, Berken posted solid peripherals, but his ERA was skewed by a seven-run, two-homer game in July. The story emerged later that Berken had been experiencing forearm issues, which soon rose to his elbow, leading to an eventual DL stint. If Berken can come back and remain healthy, he'd be a serviceable middle reliever or long man, but having undergone Tommy John surgery in 2005 and now dealing with shoulder and elbow troubles the past two years, that's far from a given.

### Zach Britton

Born: 12/22/1987 Age: 24
Bats: L Throws: L Height: 6' 4" Weight: 195
Breakout: 37% Improve: 64% Collapse: 18%
Attrition: 4% MLB: 97%

Comparables:
Steve Trout, Aaron Laffey, Jim Abbott

| YEAR | TEAM | LVL | AGE | W | L | SV | G | GS | IP | H | HR | BB | SO | EqBB9 | EqSO9 | GB% | BABIP | WHIP | ERA | FIP | FRA | WARP |
|---|---|---|---|---|---|---|---|---|---|---|---|---|---|---|---|---|---|---|---|---|---|---|
| 2009 | FRD | A+ | 21 | 9 | 6 | 0 | 25 | 24 | 140 | 123 | 6 | 55 | 131 | 3.5 | 8.4 | 68% | .296 | 1.27 | 2.70 | 3.40 | 5.17 | 0.6 |
| 2010 | BOW | AA | 22 | 7 | 3 | 0 | 15 | 14 | 87 | 49 | 2 | 11 | 43 | 2.9 | 7.0 | 66% | .296 | 1.20 | 2.48 | 3.29 | 4.30 | 0.9 |
| 2010 | NOR | AAA | 22 | 3 | 4 | 0 | 12 | 12 | 66¹ | 50 | 2 | 18 | 38 | 3.1 | 7.6 | 66% | .333 | 1.30 | 2.99 | 3.59 | 4.82 | 0.6 |
| 2011 | BAL | MLB | 23 | 11 | 11 | 0 | 28 | 28 | 154¹ | 162 | 12 | 62 | 97 | 3.6 | 5.7 | 55% | .309 | 1.45 | 4.61 | 4.04 | 4.91 | 1.0 |
| *2012* | *BAL* | *MLB* | *24* | *7* | *8* | *0* | *22* | *22* | *122¹* | *130* | *13* | *50* | *74* | *3.7* | *5.4* | *59%* | *.298* | *1.47* | *4.58* | *4.60* | *4.98* | *0.3* |

Britton started his rookie year strong, posting a 2.93 ERA through the end of May. Things derailed soon after, however, and he eventually landed on the DL with a shoulder strain. Britton has the potential to be an extreme groundball pitcher: his sinker, slider, and change are all serious weapons. But successful lefty sinkerballers—at least as starters—are rare, because of the pitch's extreme platoon split. He has a four-seamer and changeup to work in against right-handers, but he's performed considerably worse against them since Double-A and threw over 40 percent sinkers to them with Baltimore. He has also struggled with runners on base throughout his career, so while Britton has number-three starter potential, there are still question marks.

**Dana Eveland**
Born: **10/29/1983** Age: **28**
Bats: **L** Throws: **L** Height: **6′ 2″** Weight: **219**
Breakout: **22%** Improve: **46%** Collapse: **27%**
Attrition: **19%** MLB: **88%**

Comparables:

| YEAR | TEAM | LVL | AGE | W | L | SV | G | GS | IP | H | HR | BB | SO | EqBB9 | EqSO9 | GB% | BABIP | WHIP | ERA | FIP | FRA | WARP |
|---|---|---|---|---|---|---|---|---|---|---|---|---|---|---|---|---|---|---|---|---|---|---|
| 2009 | SAC | AAA | 25 | 8 | 6 | 0 | 21 | 21 | 124 | 133 | 12 | 51 | 92 | 3.7 | 6.7 | 56% | .315 | 1.48 | 4.94 | 4.58 | 5.15 | -0.3 |
| 2009 | OAK | MLB | 25 | 2 | 4 | 0 | 13 | 9 | 44 | 70 | 4 | 26 | 22 | 5.3 | 4.5 | 61% | .393 | 2.18 | 7.16 | 5.10 | 5.73 | 0.0 |
| 2010 | IND | AAA | 26 | 0 | 2 | 0 | 11 | 5 | 26 | 25 | 3 | 4 | 14 | 2.1 | 9.0 | 43% | .407 | 1.81 | 7.96 | 4.42 | 6.23 | 0.1 |
| 2010 | PIT | MLB | 26 | 0 | 1 | 0 | 3 | 1 | 9² | 15 | 0 | 5 | 3 | 4.7 | 2.8 | 39% | .385 | 2.07 | 8.38 | 4.66 | 6.59 | -0.1 |
| 2010 | TOR | MLB | 26 | 2 | 4 | 0 | 9 | 9 | 44² | 57 | 4 | 27 | 21 | 5.4 | 4.3 | 53% | .222 | 1.99 | 4.65 | 5.23 | 5.49 | 0.1 |

weakest teams in terms of True Average—roughed him up after he'd stifled them the first time around. Aside from throwing less of his 88 mph fastball and more offspeed stuff, he is essentially the same pitcher who has failed to stick in so many other teams' rotations. Traded to Baltimore in December, he seems to be the perfect fit for a team like the O's, who trotted out plenty of Eveland clones in 2011.

**Willie Eyre**
Born: **7/21/1978** Age: **33**
Bats: **R** Throws: **R** Height: **6′ 3″** Weight: **205**
Breakout: **20%** Improve: **53%** Collapse: **27%**
Attrition: **9%** MLB: **91%**

Comparables:
Tom Candiotti, Steve Rogers, Bob Welch

| YEAR | TEAM | LVL | AGE | W | L | SV | G | GS | IP | H | HR | BB | SO | EqBB9 | EqSO9 | GB% | BABIP | WHIP | ERA | FIP | FRA | WARP |
|---|---|---|---|---|---|---|---|---|---|---|---|---|---|---|---|---|---|---|---|---|---|---|
| 2009 | OKL | AAA | 30 | 0 | 0 | 2 | 19 | 2 | 34¹ | 24 | 1 | 12 | 25 | 3.1 | 6.6 | 50% | .247 | 1.05 | 2.10 | 3.51 | 3.70 | 0.5 |
| 2009 | TEX | MLB | 30 | 0 | 0 | 0 | 17 | 0 | 18 | 18 | 0 | 6 | 8 | 3.0 | 4.0 | 38% | .321 | 1.33 | 4.50 | 3.25 | 4.42 | 0.2 |
| 2010 | OKL | AAA | 31 | 5 | 4 | 2 | 49 | 0 | 72 | 45 | 1 | 20 | 30 | 3.1 | 7.4 | 46% | .306 | 1.38 | 3.50 | 4.24 | 4.32 | 0.9 |
| 2011 | SAC | AAA | 32 | 4 | 5 | 9 | 39 | 2 | 62 | 62 | 5 | 27 | 42 | 4.1 | 6.5 | 53% | .313 | 1.47 | 3.48 | 4.78 | 5.15 | 0.1 |
| 2011 | BAL | MLB | 32 | 2 | 2 | 0 | 19 | 0 | 18¹ | 12 | 2 | 5 | 10 | 2.5 | 4.9 | 51% | .185 | 0.93 | 3.44 | 4.21 | 4.80 | 0.0 |
| 2012 | BAL | MLB | 33 | 1 | 0 | 0 | 24 | 0 | 33² | 34 | 3 | 13 | 21 | 3.4 | 5.6 | 47% | .293 | 1.41 | 4.20 | 4.27 | 4.57 | 0.2 |

After inking a minor league deal with the A's in the offseason and posting a 3.53 ERA at Triple-A, Eyre opted out of his deal to sign with Baltimore in August. The Orioles recalled him after just 3 1/3 innings with their own Triple-A affiliate. He throws a 92-mph fastball that he can cut, and a breaking ball somewhere between a curve and a slider. The 32-year-old Eyre proved marginally effective with a 4.17 FIP, but there's really nothing special about him.

**Kevin Gregg**
Born: **6/20/1978** Age: **34**
Bats: **R** Throws: **R** Height: **6′ 7″** Weight: **200**
Breakout: **10%** Improve: **25%** Collapse: **49%**
Attrition: **6%** MLB: **97%**

Comparables:
Jay Witasick, Troy Percival, Armando Benitez

| YEAR | TEAM | LVL | AGE | W | L | SV | G | GS | IP | H | HR | BB | SO | EqBB9 | EqSO9 | GB% | BABIP | WHIP | ERA | FIP | FRA | WARP |
|---|---|---|---|---|---|---|---|---|---|---|---|---|---|---|---|---|---|---|---|---|---|---|
| 2009 | CHN | MLB | 31 | 5 | 6 | 23 | 72 | 0 | 68² | 60 | 13 | 30 | 71 | 3.9 | 9.3 | 39% | .260 | 1.31 | 4.72 | 4.89 | 5.07 | 0.4 |
| 2010 | TOR | MLB | 32 | 2 | 6 | 37 | 63 | 0 | 59 | 52 | 4 | 30 | 58 | 4.6 | 8.8 | 43% | .300 | 1.39 | 3.51 | 3.54 | 4.16 | 0.7 |
| 2011 | BAL | MLB | 33 | 0 | 3 | 22 | 63 | 0 | 59² | 58 | 7 | 40 | 53 | 6.0 | 8.0 | 44% | .302 | 1.64 | 4.37 | 4.92 | 5.44 | -0.2 |
| 2012 | BAL | MLB | 34 | 3 | 1 | 26 | 58 | 0 | 55 | 48 | 6 | 26 | 52 | 4.3 | 8.5 | 40% | .286 | 1.36 | 3.85 | 4.15 | 4.18 | 0.5 |

After a shaky outing last summer, Gregg told a reporter, "You obviously haven't acquired my taste in pitching yet." Who has, exactly? Gregg has always teetered at the edge of the cliff where passable falls into tragedy, and he finally fell in 2011. Signed to pitch the ninth inning for the O's because of his veteran closing experience, the kind of failure he experienced couldn't have come as a shock to very many BP readers. While he managed to post a 3.41 ERA before the All-Star break, things went south quickly in the second half for Gregg. His ERA ballooned to 5.68 and eventually he was pulled from the closer's role. Gregg is signed for $5.8 million, but it seems highly unlikely the Orioles will give him the ninth inning again.

## Jeremy Guthrie

Born: 4/8/1979 Age: 33
Bats: R Throws: R Height: 6' 2" Weight: 200
Breakout: 22% Improve: 43% Collapse: 37%
Attrition: 27% MLB: 86%

**Comparables:**
Bronson Arroyo, John Thomson, Steve Gromek

| YEAR | TEAM | LVL | AGE | W | L | SV | G | GS | IP | H | HR | BB | SO | EqBB9 | EqSO9 | GB% | BABIP | WHIP | ERA | FIP | FRA | WARP |
|------|------|-----|-----|---|---|----|---|----|----|---|----|----|----|-------|-------|-----|-------|------|-----|-----|-----|------|
| 2009 | BAL | MLB | 30 | 10 | 17 | 0 | 33 | 33 | 200 | 224 | 35 | 60 | 110 | 2.7 | 4.9 | 37% | .287 | 1.42 | 5.04 | 5.35 | 5.93 | 0.1 |
| 2010 | BAL | MLB | 31 | 11 | 14 | 0 | 32 | 32 | 209¹ | 193 | 25 | 50 | 119 | 2.1 | 5.1 | 43% | .255 | 1.16 | 3.83 | 4.41 | 4.39 | 2.3 |
| 2011 | BAL | MLB | 32 | 9 | 17 | 0 | 34 | 32 | 208 | 213 | 26 | 66 | 130 | 2.9 | 5.6 | 41% | .287 | 1.34 | 4.33 | 4.52 | 4.75 | 1.6 |
| 2012 | BAL | MLB | 33 | 10 | 11 | 0 | 28 | 28 | 182 | 187 | 26 | 47 | 105 | 2.3 | 5.2 | 42% | .279 | 1.29 | 4.26 | 4.68 | 4.63 | 0.9 |

Despite being below average at generating both strikeouts and groundballs, Guthrie has managed to be successful by boasting great control and a career .273 BABIP that, after over 1000 innings, PECOTA suggests is sustainable. Entering his third year of arbitration, Guthrie is getting expensive for a guy who relies so much on his defense and whose strikeout rate is barely passable. He may be worth it for another year or two, but the O's might want to start looking into trades for a guy whose balancing act rivals Cirque du Soleil. Inducing weak contact is the lynchpin of the whole act. There's a steep age curve for those tight-rope walkers, and at 33 years old, Guthrie is just one misstep away from plummeting.

## Tommy Hunter

Born: 7/3/1986 Age: 25
Bats: R Throws: R Height: 6' 4" Weight: 255
Breakout: 19% Improve: 49% Collapse: 18%
Attrition: 15% MLB: 96%

**Comparables:**
Casey Janssen, Scott McGregor, Jesse Litsch

| YEAR | TEAM | LVL | AGE | W | L | SV | G | GS | IP | H | HR | BB | SO | EqBB9 | EqSO9 | GB% | BABIP | WHIP | ERA | FIP | FRA | WARP |
|------|------|-----|-----|---|---|----|---|----|----|---|----|----|----|-------|-------|-----|-------|------|-----|-----|-----|------|
| 2009 | OKL | AAA | 23 | 3 | 2 | 0 | 8 | 8 | 49¹ | 53 | 5 | 16 | 35 | 2.9 | 6.4 | 41% | .322 | 1.40 | 3.83 | 4.44 | 4.82 | 0.2 |
| 2009 | TEX | MLB | 23 | 9 | 6 | 0 | 19 | 19 | 112 | 113 | 13 | 33 | 64 | 2.7 | 5.1 | 39% | .277 | 1.30 | 4.10 | 4.45 | 4.90 | 0.9 |
| 2010 | OKL | AAA | 24 | 1 | 2 | 0 | 6 | 6 | 26² | 18 | 1 | 7 | 8 | 3.7 | 4.7 | 54% | .270 | 1.46 | 4.04 | 4.73 | 5.15 | 0.0 |
| 2010 | TEX | MLB | 24 | 13 | 4 | 0 | 23 | 22 | 128 | 126 | 21 | 33 | 68 | 2.3 | 4.8 | 42% | .257 | 1.24 | 3.73 | 4.96 | 4.72 | 1.1 |
| 2011 | ROU | AAA | 25 | 2 | 2 | 1 | 8 | 5 | 26² | 37 | 2 | 3 | 16 | 1.0 | 5.4 | 54% | .361 | 1.50 | 5.06 | 3.96 | 4.61 | 0.4 |
| 2011 | TEX | MLB | 25 | 1 | 1 | 0 | 8 | 0 | 15¹ | 12 | 1 | 5 | 10 | 2.9 | 5.9 | 57% | .244 | 1.11 | 2.93 | 3.58 | 4.54 | 0.2 |
| 2011 | BAL | MLB | 25 | 3 | 3 | 0 | 12 | 11 | 69¹ | 88 | 11 | 10 | 35 | 1.3 | 4.5 | 41% | .316 | 1.41 | 5.06 | 4.72 | 4.62 | 0.4 |
| 2012 | BAL | MLB | 25 | 5 | 5 | 0 | 20 | 15 | 91¹ | 101 | 13 | 22 | 49 | 2.2 | 4.8 | 45% | .291 | 1.34 | 4.46 | 4.70 | 4.85 | 0.3 |

Acquired in the Koji Uehara deal, Hunter profiles as a back-of-rotation innings eater. Physical differences aside (Hunter looks like he could eat Guthrie for breakfast), Hunter has the potential to become the new Jeremy Guthrie for the O's—a guy who can throw 92-mph but, lacking a true swing-and-miss pitch, struggles to be even average at generating strikeouts. Like Guthrie, his ability to survive will hinge upon good control and treating his fielders to lots of steak dinners. He has a career .281 BABIP, but in just over 300 innings, that number's legitimacy is far from assured. Aside from his fastball, the uncanny resemblance to Guthrie continues as Hunter boasts an almost identical repertoire: an 11-to-5 curve, a two-seamer, a change, and a cutter that behaves a bit like Guthrie's slider.

## Jim Johnson

Born: 6/27/1983 Age: 29
Bats: R Throws: R Height: 6' 6" Weight: 224
Breakout: 31% Improve: 58% Collapse: 19%
Attrition: 7% MLB: 96%

**Comparables:**
Dave Schmidt, Alejandro Pena, Brad Ziegler

| YEAR | TEAM | LVL | AGE | W | L | SV | G | GS | IP | H | HR | BB | SO | EqBB9 | EqSO9 | GB% | BABIP | WHIP | ERA | FIP | FRA | WARP |
|------|------|-----|-----|---|---|----|---|----|----|---|----|----|----|-------|-------|-----|-------|------|-----|-----|-----|------|
| 2009 | BAL | MLB | 26 | 4 | 6 | 10 | 64 | 0 | 70 | 73 | 8 | 23 | 49 | 3.0 | 6.3 | 54% | .302 | 1.37 | 4.11 | 4.34 | 5.53 | 0.1 |
| 2010 | BAL | MLB | 27 | 1 | 1 | 1 | 26 | 0 | 26¹ | 32 | 2 | 5 | 22 | 1.7 | 7.5 | 51% | .357 | 1.41 | 3.42 | 3.05 | 4.72 | 0.1 |
| 2011 | BAL | MLB | 28 | 6 | 5 | 9 | 69 | 0 | 91 | 80 | 5 | 21 | 58 | 2.1 | 5.7 | 63% | .273 | 1.11 | 2.67 | 3.26 | 4.85 | 0.3 |
| 2012 | BAL | MLB | 29 | 3 | 1 | 4 | 54 | 0 | 66² | 68 | 7 | 19 | 42 | 2.6 | 5.7 | 52% | .293 | 1.31 | 3.87 | 4.16 | 4.21 | 0.6 |

The Orioles will be faced with an interesting decision to make about Johnson this offseason. Initially, there was talk that they wanted to move him into the rotation, but given Kevin Gregg's collapse and Johnson's own excellence in the pen, making him their full-time closer is now a legitimate option. While he's had two very good seasons in a row and despite throwing 95 mph, Johnson has never had a penchant for the strikeout, and it seems unlikely that would change as a starter. Despite his high velocity, he'd probably end up as a Nick Blackburn, a fourth-starter type with a below-average K rate, getting by on serviceable control and a lot of groundballs.

## Brian Matusz

Born: 2/11/1987 Age: 25
Bats: L Throws: L Height: 6' 6" Weight: 200
Breakout: 18% Improve: 48% Collapse: 18%
Attrition: 16% MLB: 94%

**Comparables:**
Mike Stanton, John Danks, Scott Olsen

| YEAR | TEAM | LVL | AGE | W | L | SV | G | GS | IP | H | HR | BB | SO | EqBB9 | EqSO9 | GB% | BABIP | WHIP | ERA | FIP | FRA | WARP |
|------|------|-----|-----|---|---|----|---|----|----|---|----|----|----|-------|-------|-----|-------|------|-----|-----|-----|------|
| 2009 | FRD | A+ | 22 | 4 | 2 | 0 | 11 | 11 | 66² | 56 | 5 | 21 | 75 | 2.8 | 10.1 | 52% | .300 | 1.15 | 2.16 | 3.06 | 3.75 | 1.2 |
| 2009 | BOW | AA | 22 | 7 | 0 | 0 | 8 | 8 | 46¹ | 31 | 2 | 11 | 46 | 2.1 | 8.9 | 47% | .250 | 0.91 | 1.56 | 2.49 | 3.36 | 0.9 |
| 2009 | BAL | MLB | 22 | 5 | 2 | 0 | 8 | 8 | 44² | 52 | 6 | 14 | 38 | 2.8 | 7.7 | 31% | .338 | 1.48 | 4.63 | 4.13 | 4.27 | 0.9 |
| 2010 | BAL | MLB | 23 | 10 | 12 | 0 | 32 | 32 | 175² | 173 | 19 | 63 | 143 | 3.2 | 7.3 | 37% | .295 | 1.34 | 4.30 | 4.02 | 4.67 | 1.7 |
| 2011 | NOR | AAA | 24 | 1 | 2 | 0 | 9 | 9 | 54² | 51 | 4 | 19 | 41 | 3.1 | 6.8 | 46% | .299 | 1.28 | 3.46 | 3.84 | 4.24 | 1.0 |
| 2011 | BAL | MLB | 24 | 1 | 9 | 0 | 12 | 12 | 49² | 81 | 18 | 23 | 38 | 4.3 | 6.9 | 28% | .384 | 2.11 | 10.69 | 7.63 | 7.68 | -1.3 |
| 2012 | BAL | MLB | 25 | 5 | 6 | 0 | 16 | 16 | 83² | 89 | 12 | 28 | 66 | 3.0 | 7.0 | 40% | .305 | 1.39 | 4.48 | 4.50 | 4.87 | 0.3 |

With big things expected of him in 2011, former top prospect Matusz fell flat on his face, compiling a big league ERA over 10.00. His two stints with the club sandwiched a demotion and he was exiled to the bench. Mere bad luck can't explain this one, but it is hard to pinpoint what caused his downfall as scouts don't believe there's an injury or mechanical issue to blame. He stopped throwing his two-seamer—which led to a drop in groundballs from 37 percent to 28 percent—his change-up appeared to be straighter with less tumbling action, and he lost three miles per hour off his fastball before his demotion; the velocity returned to the majors with Matusz, but he still allowed over five runs in all six of his starts. There are whispers that there's an issue with his work ethic, but does it say more about Matusz or the Orioles that a pitcher could log one of the worst seasons in history?

**Darren O'Day**
Born: 10/22/1982 Age: 29
Bats: R Throws: R Height: 6' 5" Weight: 225
Breakout: 14% Improve: 35% Collapse: 34%
Attrition: 12% MLB: 98%

| YEAR | TEAM | LVL | AGE | W | L | SV | G | GS | IP | H | HR | BB | SO | EqBB9 | EqSO9 | GB% | BABIP | WHIP | ERA | FIP | FRA | WARP |
|---|---|---|---|---|---|---|---|---|---|---|---|---|---|---|---|---|---|---|---|---|---|---|
| 2009 | NYN | MLB | 26 | 0 | 0 | 0 | 4 | 0 | 3 | 5 | 0 | 1 | 2 | 3.0 | 6.0 | 39% | .385 | 2.00 | 0.00 | 3.72 | 5.04 | 0.0 |
| 2009 | TEX | MLB | 26 | 2 | 1 | 2 | 64 | 0 | 55² | 36 | 3 | 17 | 54 | 2.7 | 8.7 | 43% | .241 | 0.95 | 1.94 | 3.04 | 3.44 | 1.2 |
| 2010 | TEX | MLB | 27 | 6 | 2 | 0 | 72 | 0 | 62 | 43 | 5 | 12 | 45 | 1.7 | 6.5 | 39% | .221 | 0.89 | 2.03 | 3.47 | 4.06 | 0.8 |

should have plenty of success in Baltimore.

**Troy Patton**
Born: 9/3/1985 Age: 26
Bats: B Throws: L Height: 6' 2" Weight: 185
Breakout: 23% Improve: 56% Collapse: 27%
Attrition: 17% MLB: 90%
Comparables:
Enrique Gonzalez, Stan Bahnsen, Nelson Briles

| YEAR | TEAM | LVL | AGE | W | L | SV | G | GS | IP | H | HR | BB | SO | EqBB9 | EqSO9 | GB% | BABIP | WHIP | ERA | FIP | FRA | WARP |
|---|---|---|---|---|---|---|---|---|---|---|---|---|---|---|---|---|---|---|---|---|---|---|
| 2009 | BOW | AA | 23 | 6 | 2 | 0 | 11 | 11 | 63¹ | 50 | 4 | 18 | 47 | 2.6 | 6.7 | 43% | .246 | 1.07 | 1.99 | 3.47 | 3.98 | 0.8 |
| 2009 | NOR | AAA | 23 | 1 | 3 | 0 | 9 | 9 | 44² | 62 | 12 | 14 | 26 | 2.8 | 5.2 | 32% | .336 | 1.70 | 6.44 | 6.75 | 7.63 | -0.8 |
| 2010 | NOR | AAA | 24 | 8 | 11 | 0 | 25 | 25 | 136 | 97 | 10 | 24 | 62 | 2.8 | 5.9 | 41% | .282 | 1.38 | 4.43 | 4.26 | 5.04 | 0.9 |
| 2010 | BAL | MLB | 24 | 0 | 0 | 0 | 1 | 0 | 0² | 1 | 0 | 1 | 1 | 13.5 | 13.5 | 50% | .500 | 3.00 | 0.00 | 4.55 | 1.59 | 0.0 |
| 2011 | NOR | AAA | 25 | 4 | 1 | 0 | 17 | 2 | 44¹ | 44 | 0 | 12 | 30 | 2.4 | 6.1 | 43% | .310 | 1.26 | 1.83 | 2.83 | 3.59 | 0.9 |
| 2011 | BAL | MLB | 25 | 2 | 1 | 0 | 20 | 0 | 30 | 25 | 2 | 5 | 22 | 1.5 | 6.6 | 40% | .258 | 1.00 | 3.00 | 2.96 | 3.52 | 0.5 |
| 2012 | BAL | MLB | 26 | 1 | 2 | 0 | 9 | 4 | 31 | 33 | 4 | 10 | 17 | 2.8 | 4.8 | 40% | .288 | 1.39 | 4.53 | 4.75 | 4.92 | 0.1 |

This season, Patton posted his first truly noteworthy campaign since undergoing major shoulder surgery in 2008. Prior to surgery, Patton had made most top 100 prospects lists for three years running and was a piece of the haul the team received for Miguel Tejada. Once expected to be a rotation mainstay, the 25-year-old Patton's destiny now looks to be a good setup man. Throwing a grounder-inducing two-seamer with a lot of arm-side run, a sweeping slider, some four-seamers, and a change-up, Patton could be a key piece of an Oriole bullpen that needs to be restocked following the trades of Koji Uehara and Mike Gonzalez and the potential move of Jim Johnson to the rotation.

**Zach Phillips**
Born: 9/21/1986 Age: 25
Bats: L Throws: L Height: 6' 2" Weight: 200
Breakout: 19% Improve: 49% Collapse: 20%
Attrition: 7% MLB: 92%
Comparables:
Billy Pierce, Bob Knepper, Chris Nabholz

| YEAR | TEAM | LVL | AGE | W | L | SV | G | GS | IP | H | HR | BB | SO | EqBB9 | EqSO9 | GB% | BABIP | WHIP | ERA | FIP | FRA | WARP |
|---|---|---|---|---|---|---|---|---|---|---|---|---|---|---|---|---|---|---|---|---|---|---|
| 2009 | BAK | A+ | 22 | 2 | 3 | 2 | 16 | 3 | 44 | 19 | 1 | 11 | 46 | 2.2 | 9.4 | 57% | .165 | 0.68 | 1.23 | 2.71 | 3.07 | 0.9 |
| 2009 | FRI | AA | 22 | 0 | 0 | 2 | 20 | 0 | 33² | 27 | 1 | 19 | 29 | 5.1 | 7.7 | 54% | .263 | 1.36 | 1.60 | 3.68 | 4.33 | 0.3 |
| 2010 | OKL | AAA | 23 | 3 | 2 | 1 | 33 | 1 | 50¹ | 36 | 1 | 14 | 24 | 5.2 | 7.2 | 55% | .343 | 1.57 | 3.22 | 4.26 | 5.56 | 0.0 |
| 2011 | ROU | AAA | 24 | 1 | 3 | 3 | 33 | 0 | 44² | 50 | 3 | 21 | 36 | 4.2 | 7.7 | 55% | .346 | 1.59 | 4.43 | 4.47 | 5.03 | 0.4 |
| 2011 | BAL | MLB | 24 | 0 | 0 | 0 | 10 | 0 | 8 | 6 | 1 | 2 | 8 | 2.2 | 9.0 | 39% | .227 | 1.00 | 1.12 | 3.44 | 4.90 | 0.0 |
| 2012 | BAL | MLB | 25 | 1 | 0 | 0 | 19 | 0 | 25 | 27 | 3 | 12 | 17 | 4.4 | 6.0 | 49% | .301 | 1.55 | 4.77 | 4.84 | 5.18 | -0.1 |

Coming from the Rangers at midseason (surprisingly, in neither the Koji Uehara nor the Mike Gonzalez deal), Phillips received his first taste of the big leagues at the end of August and pitched well for the Orioles down the stretch. The most likely scenario paints Phillips as a mere middle reliever, but there is a bit of upside here. His 90-mph fastball is his worst pitch. He throws an above average change-up and a grounder-inducing curveball that bears a striking resemblance to the one J.P. Howell found success with for several years. He'll notch enough Ks and groundballs to stick in the bigs if he can improve his control.

### Clay Rapada

Born: 3/9/1981 Age: 31
Bats: R Throws: L Height: 6' 6'' Weight: 200
Breakout: 24% Improve: 55% Collapse: 26%
Attrition: 23% MLB: 90%

**Comparables:**
Brendan Donnelly, Josh Kinney, Tyler Yates

| YEAR | TEAM | LVL | AGE | W | L | SV | G | GS | IP | H | HR | BB | SO | EqBB9 | EqSO9 | GB% | BABIP | WHIP | ERA | FIP | FRA | WARP |
|------|------|-----|-----|---|---|----|----|----|-----|----|----|----|----|-------|-------|-----|-------|------|------|------|------|------|
| 2009 | TOL | AAA | 28 | 3 | 2 | 5 | 42 | 0 | 45² | 50 | 1 | 18 | 47 | 3.3 | 9.3 | 41% | .377 | 1.47 | 2.76 | 2.56 | 3.70 | 1.0 |
| 2009 | DET | MLB | 28 | 0 | 0 | 0 | 3 | 0 | 3¹ | 4 | 1 | 2 | 2 | 5.4 | 5.4 | 50% | .273 | 1.80 | 5.40 | 7.64 | 5.50 | 0.0 |
| 2010 | OKL | AAA | 29 | 1 | 2 | 2 | 50 | 0 | 59¹ | 22 | 0 | 10 | 42 | 3.2 | 9.3 | 50% | .218 | 0.89 | 1.82 | 3.35 | 4.00 | 0.9 |
| 2010 | TEX | MLB | 29 | 0 | 0 | 0 | 13 | 0 | 9 | 6 | 2 | 7 | 5 | 7.0 | 5.0 | 33% | .160 | 1.44 | 4.00 | 7.16 | 6.27 | -0.1 |
| 2011 | NOR | AAA | 30 | 0 | 1 | 1 | 26 | 0 | 20² | 23 | 1 | 3 | 18 | 1.7 | 8.7 | 49% | .373 | 1.35 | 3.92 | 2.85 | 4.65 | 0.2 |
| 2011 | BAL | MLB | 30 | 2 | 0 | 0 | 32 | 0 | 16¹ | 14 | 3 | 8 | 18 | 3.9 | 9.9 | 36% | .268 | 1.29 | 6.06 | 4.71 | 4.22 | 0.2 |
| 2012 | BAL | MLB | 31 | 1 | 0 | 0 | 25 | 0 | 21² | 21 | 2 | 10 | 19 | 4.0 | 8.0 | 45% | .300 | 1.40 | 4.03 | 4.04 | 4.38 | 0.2 |

Throwing from what he calls a "submarine and sidearm mix," Rapada has bounced back and forth between the majors and minors for years, spending two stints each with Baltimore and Norfolk last season. He seems capable of being an effective lefty specialist with his arm angle, excellent two-seamer, and good slider, all pitches well-suited to get out opposite-handed batters. He has posted good peripherals in his years at Triple-A and simply needs to be given a shot.

### Jo-Jo Reyes

Born: 11/20/1984 Age: 27
Bats: L Throws: L Height: 6' 3'' Weight: 230
Breakout: 32% Improve: 57% Collapse: 23%
Attrition: 16% MLB: 76%

**Comparables:**
Al Jackson, Bud Daley, Sterling Hitchcock

| YEAR | TEAM | LVL | AGE | W | L | SV | G | GS | IP | H | HR | BB | SO | EqBB9 | EqSO9 | GB% | BABIP | WHIP | ERA | FIP | FRA | WARP |
|------|------|-----|-----|---|---|----|----|----|------|-----|----|----|----|-------|-------|-----|-------|------|-------|-------|-------|------|
| 2009 | GWN | AAA | 24 | 4 | 3 | 0 | 15 | 14 | 66 | 74 | 6 | 25 | 35 | 3.3 | 4.4 | 46% | .285 | 1.39 | 2.86 | 4.45 | 5.26 | 0.3 |
| 2009 | ATL | MLB | 24 | 0 | 2 | 0 | 6 | 5 | 27 | 27 | 4 | 13 | 21 | 4.3 | 7.0 | 52% | .291 | 1.48 | 7.00 | 4.98 | 6.10 | -0.1 |
| 2010 | GWN | AAA | 25 | 1 | 5 | 0 | 12 | 10 | 47¹ | 38 | 6 | 8 | 19 | 2.9 | 9.5 | 50% | .381 | 1.52 | 5.71 | 4.88 | 5.66 | 0.4 |
| 2010 | ATL | MLB | 25 | 0 | 0 | 0 | 1 | 0 | 3¹ | 10 | 2 | 3 | 2 | 8.1 | 5.4 | 33% | .500 | 3.90 | 24.30 | 12.41 | 11.70 | -0.3 |
| 2011 | BAL | MLB | 26 | 2 | 3 | 0 | 9 | 5 | 30² | 36 | 7 | 13 | 23 | 3.8 | 6.8 | 44% | .312 | 1.60 | 6.16 | 5.90 | 6.01 | -0.2 |
| 2011 | TOR | MLB | 26 | 5 | 8 | 0 | 20 | 20 | 110 | 140 | 14 | 35 | 64 | 2.9 | 5.2 | 42% | .330 | 1.59 | 5.40 | 4.67 | 5.17 | 0.2 |
| 2012 | PIT | MLB | 27 | 6 | 8 | 0 | 22 | 22 | 113² | 125 | 15 | 43 | 62 | 3.4 | 4.9 | 47% | .315 | 1.48 | 5.50 | 4.96 | 5.97 | -0.8 |

Reyes spent most of the season starting for the Blue Jays before he was designated for assignment in July and picked up by the O's, joining their carousel of starters. The thing is, after posting a 6.98 ERA before being shifted to the bullpen, he's the horse on the carousel that you would only ride if he was the only one left and, in the case of the Orioles, not broken (see Matusz, Arrieta, et al). He's only 25 and has good enough stuff—as far as guys who throw under 90 mph go—but he's never translated that stuff to much big league success.

### Alfredo Simon

Born: 5/8/1981 Age: 31
Bats: R Throws: R Height: 6' 5'' Weight: 230
Breakout: 36% Improve: 57% Collapse: 16%
Attrition: 20% MLB: 84%

**Comparables:**
Pascual Perez, Dave Bush, Claudio Vargas

| YEAR | TEAM | LVL | AGE | W | L | SV | G | GS | IP | H | HR | BB | SO | EqBB9 | EqSO9 | GB% | BABIP | WHIP | ERA | FIP | FRA | WARP |
|------|------|-----|-----|---|---|----|----|----|------|-----|----|----|----|-------|-------|-----|-------|------|------|------|------|------|
| 2009 | BAL | MLB | 28 | 0 | 1 | 0 | 2 | 2 | 6¹ | 8 | 5 | 2 | 3 | 2.8 | 4.3 | 22% | .167 | 1.58 | 9.95 | 13.41 | 13.71 | -0.3 |
| 2010 | BAL | MLB | 29 | 4 | 2 | 17 | 49 | 0 | 49¹ | 54 | 10 | 22 | 37 | 4.0 | 6.8 | 48% | .293 | 1.54 | 4.93 | 5.64 | 6.15 | -0.4 |
| 2011 | BAL | MLB | 30 | 4 | 9 | 0 | 23 | 16 | 115² | 128 | 15 | 40 | 83 | 3.1 | 6.5 | 43% | .317 | 1.45 | 4.90 | 4.45 | 4.57 | 0.7 |
| 2012 | BAL | MLB | 31 | 4 | 5 | 5 | 38 | 11 | 94¹ | 106 | 15 | 33 | 60 | 3.1 | 5.8 | 44% | .303 | 1.47 | 5.16 | 5.05 | 5.61 | -0.5 |

Yet another Oriole whose G and GS numbers are unequal, Simon began the year in the bullpen and was moved into the rotation when his teammates started going down in July. While the move didn't work out as well as the team hoped—he posted a 4.96 ERA in the rotation—at least it wasn't a total disaster. He has a varied arsenal, including a 94-95 mph heater, a plus splitter and cutter, and a two-seamer and slurve that he can get batters to drive into the ground, but he's never turned that arsenal into shut-down stuff consistently. He did have some dominating performances and could wind up as a quality arm if he can do that on a more regular basis.

### Pedro Strop

Born: 6/13/1985 Age: 27
Bats: R Throws: R Height: 6' 1'' Weight: 160
Breakout: 27% Improve: 44% Collapse: 38%
Attrition: 17% MLB: 87%

**Comparables:**
Jim Miller, Jeff Stevens, Edinson Volquez

| YEAR | TEAM | LVL | AGE | W | L | SV | G | GS | IP | H | HR | BB | SO | EqBB9 | EqSO9 | GB% | BABIP | WHIP | ERA | FIP | FRA | WARP |
|------|------|-----|-----|---|---|----|----|----|------|----|----|----|----|-------|-------|-----|-------|------|-------|------|------|------|
| 2009 | FRI | AA | 24 | 5 | 5 | 4 | 36 | 0 | 51¹ | 48 | 1 | 29 | 48 | 5.1 | 8.4 | 53% | .315 | 1.50 | 4.39 | 3.43 | 3.72 | 0.9 |
| 2009 | TEX | MLB | 24 | 0 | 0 | 0 | 7 | 0 | 7 | 6 | 0 | 4 | 9 | 5.1 | 11.6 | 35% | .353 | 1.43 | 7.71 | 2.29 | 3.37 | 0.2 |
| 2010 | OKL | AAA | 25 | 1 | 2 | 13 | 39 | 0 | 42¹ | 22 | 1 | 7 | 37 | 3.0 | 12.1 | 54% | .304 | 1.09 | 1.91 | 3.11 | 3.25 | 1.0 |
| 2010 | TEX | MLB | 25 | 0 | 0 | 0 | 15 | 0 | 10² | 17 | 2 | 11 | 11 | 9.3 | 9.3 | 35% | .441 | 2.62 | 10.12 | 6.80 | 8.02 | -0.4 |
| 2011 | ROU | AAA | 26 | 4 | 4 | 11 | 39 | 0 | 47² | 53 | 2 | 24 | 55 | 4.5 | 10.4 | 57% | .386 | 1.62 | 3.59 | 3.55 | 4.76 | 0.5 |
| 2011 | TEX | MLB | 26 | 0 | 1 | 0 | 11 | 0 | 9² | 7 | 0 | 7 | 9 | 6.5 | 8.4 | 52% | .269 | 1.45 | 3.72 | 3.68 | 4.39 | 0.1 |
| 2011 | BAL | MLB | 26 | 2 | 0 | 0 | 12 | 0 | 12¹ | 8 | 0 | 3 | 12 | 2.2 | 8.8 | 68% | .267 | 0.89 | 0.73 | 1.85 | 3.43 | 0.2 |
| 2012 | BAL | MLB | 27 | 1 | 1 | 1 | 28 | 0 | 29² | 28 | 3 | 15 | 28 | 4.5 | 8.5 | 47% | .312 | 1.46 | 4.23 | 4.15 | 4.60 | 0.1 |

Acquired from the Rangers in the Mike Gonzalez deal, Strop is an interesting darkhorse candidate to close for the O's if they have indeed seen enough of Kevin Gregg in the ninth and Jim Johnson moves to the rotation. He has an electric fastball—which managers love to see in a closer—that he pairs with a plus splitter and a developing slider. As is the case with many high velocity youngsters, control will be his biggest obstacle, but it's not such a sore spot that it renders him ineffective.

**Chris Tillman**
Born: 4/15/1988 Age: 24
Bats: R Throws: R Height: 6' 6'' Weight: 195
Breakout: 26% Improve: 61% Collapse: 18%
Attrition: 14% MLB: 84%

Comparables:
Felipe Paulino, Billy Loes, Luke Hochevar

| YEAR | TEAM | LVL | AGE | W | L | SV | G | GS | IP | H | HR | BB | SO | EqBB9 | EqSO9 | GB% | BABIP | WHIP | ERA | FIP | FRA | WARP |
|---|---|---|---|---|---|---|---|---|---|---|---|---|---|---|---|---|---|---|---|---|---|---|
| 2009 | NOR | AAA | 21 | 8 | 6 | 0 | 18 | 18 | 96² | 85 | 5 | 26 | 99 | 2.4 | 9.2 | 41% | .304 | 1.15 | 2.70 | 2.70 | 3.80 | 1.6 |
| 2009 | BAL | MLB | 21 | 2 | 5 | 0 | 12 | 12 | 65 | 77 | 15 | 24 | 39 | 3.3 | 5.4 | 39% | .302 | 1.55 | 5.40 | 6.14 | 6.61 | -0.5 |
| 2010 | NOR | AAA | 22 | 11 | 7 | 0 | 21 | 21 | 121¹ | 91 | 6 | 25 | 67 | 2.2 | 7.0 | 40% | .324 | 1.24 | 3.34 | 3.74 | 4.32 | 1.6 |
| 2010 | BAL | MLB | 22 | 2 | 5 | 0 | 11 | 11 | 53² | 51 | 9 | 31 | 31 | 5.2 | 5.2 | 42% | .258 | 1.53 | 5.87 | 5.86 | 5.84 | 0.1 |
| 2011 | NOR | AAA | 23 | 2 | 4 | 0 | 15 | 15 | 76¹ | 77 | 17 | 38 | 54 | 4.5 | 6.4 | 41% | .264 | 1.51 | 5.19 | 6.29 | 6.79 | -0.3 |
| 2011 | BAL | MLB | 23 | 3 | 5 | 0 | 13 | 13 | 62 | 77 | 5 | 25 | 46 | 3.6 | 6.7 | 41% | .350 | 1.65 | 5.52 | 4.03 | 4.92 | 0.3 |
| 2012 | BAL | MLB | 24 | 5 | 6 | 0 | 16 | 16 | 83¹ | 88 | 12 | 34 | 60 | 3.7 | 6.4 | 39% | .300 | 1.47 | 4.77 | 4.86 | 5.19 | 0.0 |

Tillman is one of the trickiest pitchers in baseball to figure out. He'll look great one start and terrible the next, and in three

Breakout: 25% Improve: 66% Collapse: 20%
Attrition: 13% MLB: 86%

Comparables:
Eric Gagne, Joe Coleman, Carl Erskine

| 2010 | BAL | MLB | 25 | 0 | 1 | 0 | 7 | 1 | 16¹ | 13 | 2 | 7 | 17 | 3.9 | 9.4 | 33% | .282 | 1.22 | 4.96 | 4.21 | 5.64 | 0.0 |
|---|---|---|---|---|---|---|---|---|---|---|---|---|---|---|---|---|---|---|---|---|---|---|
| 2011 | NOR | AAA | 26 | 4 | 7 | 0 | 26 | 26 | 154¹ | 136 | 23 | 38 | 107 | 2.3 | 6.3 | 39% | .252 | 1.17 | 4.43 | 4.78 | 5.54 | 0.4 |
| 2011 | BAL | MLB | 26 | 0 | 0 | 0 | 4 | 2 | 9 | 12 | 4 | 8 | 7 | 8.0 | 7.0 | 23% | .308 | 2.22 | 8.00 | 10.28 | 8.51 | -0.2 |
| 2012 | BAL | MLB | 27 | 3 | 3 | 0 | 9 | 9 | 48¹ | 48 | 7 | 19 | 40 | 3.5 | 7.4 | 36% | .290 | 1.39 | 4.62 | 4.61 | 5.02 | 0.1 |

The last pitcher through Baltimore's revolving door of a rotation, VandenHurk received two starts at the end of September after spending the year in Norfolk. An upside gamble they acquired from the Marlins in 2010, VandenHurk throws a 93-mph heater with good rise, a slider that has some bite, and a lesser-used slow curve and change. The 6-foot-5 Dutchman has yet to match his hoped for potential at age 27; his extreme fly ball tendencies put a limit on it. The O's have a lot of rotation candidates, but he'll get some starts in 2012, especially if he can put it all together at Triple-A.

**Pedro Viola**
Born: 6/29/1983 Age: 29
Bats: R Throws: L Height: 6' 2'' Weight: 185
Breakout: 33% Improve: 49% Collapse: 18%
Attrition: 25% MLB: 69%

Comparables:
Scott Dunn, Jeff Bajenaru, Agustin Montero

| YEAR | TEAM | LVL | AGE | W | L | SV | G | GS | IP | H | HR | BB | SO | EqBB9 | EqSO9 | GB% | BABIP | WHIP | ERA | FIP | FRA | WARP |
|---|---|---|---|---|---|---|---|---|---|---|---|---|---|---|---|---|---|---|---|---|---|---|
| 2009 | LOU | AAA | 26 | 2 | 2 | 8 | 54 | 0 | 49¹ | 48 | 7 | 33 | 57 | 6.0 | 10.4 | 43% | .320 | 1.64 | 5.48 | 4.69 | 6.57 | -0.3 |
| 2009 | CIN | MLB | 26 | 0 | 0 | 0 | 9 | 0 | 7 | 7 | 2 | 3 | 5 | 3.9 | 6.4 | 41% | .263 | 1.43 | 5.14 | 6.63 | 7.43 | -0.1 |
| 2010 | BOW | AA | 27 | 3 | 2 | 0 | 23 | 10 | 62² | 34 | 1 | 6 | 50 | 2.7 | 9.2 | 40% | .282 | 1.28 | 3.59 | 2.59 | 3.86 | 1.1 |
| 2010 | BAL | MLB | 27 | 0 | 0 | 0 | 2 | 0 | 1¹ | 1 | 1 | 1 | 3 | 6.8 | 20.2 | % | .000 | 1.50 | 13.50 | 10.55 | 18.02 | -0.1 |
| 2011 | BOW | AA | 28 | 2 | 1 | 4 | 40 | 0 | 39² | 26 | 2 | 13 | 40 | 2.9 | 9.1 | 37% | .250 | 0.98 | 2.04 | 3.11 | 3.48 | 0.6 |
| 2011 | BAL | MLB | 28 | 0 | 0 | 0 | 4 | 0 | 3² | 6 | 3 | 2 | 4 | 4.9 | 9.8 | 29% | .273 | 2.18 | 9.82 | 13.15 | 8.89 | -0.1 |
| 2012 | BAL | MLB | 29 | 1 | 1 | 0 | 12 | 1 | 17¹ | 18 | 2 | 8 | 15 | 4.3 | 7.6 | 42% | .308 | 1.52 | 4.83 | 4.36 | 5.24 | -0.0 |

While spending almost his entire season at Double-A Bowie for the second year in a row (this time exclusively in relief), Viola had two very short stints with the big boys in 2011. While he's old enough to be a non-prospect, Viola has put up good numbers at Double-A and is worth watching to see if his 93-mph fastball and average slider will play at the upper levels. His command is a bit lacking, but it's not inconceivable that he finds some success in low leverage innings.

**Mark Worrell**
Born: 3/8/1983 Age: 29
Bats: R Throws: R Height: 6' 2'' Weight: 215
Breakout: 26% Improve: 45% Collapse: 28%
Attrition: 12% MLB: 86%

Comparables:
T.J. Mathews, John Smoltz, Manny Delcarmen

| YEAR | TEAM | LVL | AGE | W | L | SV | G | GS | IP | H | HR | BB | SO | EqBB9 | EqSO9 | GB% | BABIP | WHIP | ERA | FIP | FRA | WARP |
|---|---|---|---|---|---|---|---|---|---|---|---|---|---|---|---|---|---|---|---|---|---|---|
| 2010 | POR | AAA | 27 | 1 | 4 | 0 | 25 | 0 | 33 | 18 | 4 | 10 | 29 | 3.0 | 9.3 | 40% | .219 | 1.36 | 5.45 | 4.79 | 5.28 | -0.2 |
| 2011 | NOR | AAA | 28 | 0 | 2 | 21 | 52 | 0 | 52² | 42 | 3 | 22 | 35 | 3.8 | 6.2 | 47% | .264 | 1.25 | 3.42 | 4.13 | 5.36 | 0.2 |
| 2011 | BAL | MLB | 28 | 0 | 0 | 0 | 4 | 0 | 2 | 6 | 2 | 2 | 3 | 9.0 | 13.5 | 22% | .571 | 4.00 | 36.00 | 16.06 | 17.94 | -0.3 |
| 2012 | BAL | MLB | 29 | 1 | 0 | 0 | 17 | 0 | 18 | 17 | 2 | 8 | 15 | 3.9 | 7.3 | 41% | .293 | 1.40 | 4.19 | 4.32 | 4.55 | 0.1 |

Once upon a time, Worrell was the closer of the future for the St. Louis Cardinals. In 2011, he had to settle for being the closer for the Norfolk Tides with a brief cup of coffee with the O's.

Relying on a deceptive delivery that's nearly side-arm, he throws his fastball just 88 mph now after it once sat in the low-to-mid 90s. Now three years past Tommy John surgery, Worrell may well end up a big league reliever, but it's more likely he's Triple-A fodder, giving this story a not-so-happy ending.

# LINEOUTS

## HITTERS

| PLAYER | TEAM | LVL | AGE | PA | R | 2B | 3B | HR | RBI | BB | SO | SB-CS | AVG/OBP/SLG | TAv | BABIP | BRR | FRAA | WARP |
|---|---|---|---|---|---|---|---|---|---|---|---|---|---|---|---|---|---|---|
| CF G. Davis | ABE | A- | 19 | 286 | 34 | 14 | 0 | 1 | 14 | 25 | 53 | 23-9 | .271/.337/.337 | .255 | .337 | 0.7 | 0.5 | 1.1 |
| SS B. Harris | NOR | AAA | 30 | 565 | 50 | 21 | 2 | 10 | 50 | 37 | 87 | 2-2 | .225/.282/.331 | .221 | .251 | 4.4 | -4.8 | -0.7 |
| 2B L. Hoes | FRD | A+ | 21 | 173 | 23 | 7 | 0 | 3 | 17 | 10 | 25 | 4-2 | .241/.297/.342 | .224 | .267 | 0.3 | -2.9 | -0.5 |
| | BOW | AA | 21 | 393 | 47 | 17 | 1 | 6 | 54 | 43 | 56 | 16-7 | .305/.379/.413 | .282 | .347 | -0.1 | 0.9 | 2.2 |
| DH R. Hughes | NOR | AAA | 27 | 383 | 54 | 25 | 2 | 15 | 59 | 36 | 111 | 3-3 | .249/.321/.465 | .263 | .320 | 1.3 | -0.8 | 0.7 |
| 1B J. Mahoney | BOW | AA | 24 | 355 | 43 | 24 | 5 | 11 | 67 | 25 | 84 | 7-2 | .289/.344/.502 | .294 | .349 | 0.6 | -0.6 | 1.9 |
| SS J. Schoop | DEL | A | 19 | 238 | 45 | 12 | 3 | 8 | 34 | 20 | 32 | 6-4 | .316/.376/.514 | .321 | .337 | 0.5 | 2.7 | 3.1 |
| | FRD | A+ | 19 | 329 | 37 | 12 | 2 | 5 | 37 | 22 | 44 | 6-3 | .271/.329/.375 | .256 | .304 | 2.3 | 5.5 | 1.6 |
| 1B M. Sweeney | MNT | AA | 23 | 305 | 25 | 11 | 1 | 7 | 29 | 35 | 92 | 1-0 | .154/.262/.282 | .202 | .204 | -1.0 | -1.9 | -1.8 |
| 3B B. Waring | BOW | AA | 25 | 449 | 60 | 21 | 3 | 21 | 59 | 33 | 127 | 0-0 | .222/.288/.443 | .250 | .264 | 1.8 | 6.0 | 1.3 |

A true 80 runner on the 20-80 scouting scale, **Glynn Davis** will be fun to watch if nothing else, but the Orioles should be excited because his bat and defense have some projectability too. ⊘ Gone are the days of playing every day for **Brendan Harris**, who didn't even merit a call-up when Brian Roberts went down, despite the likes of Cesar Izturis and Robert Andino taking starts. ⊘ A bat-first second baseman who can take a walk, **LJ Hoes** could be a solid big league regular if his glove doesn't push him off second, though if it does, there are few other positions his bat might handle. ⊘ Testing positive for an amphetamine, **Rhyne Hughes** will serve a 50-day suspension starting in 2012. Now 27 and with a questionable bat before this episode, the first baseman's future looks bleak. ⊘ Making big strides two years in a row has cemented **Joe Mahoney** in prospect conversations, but the massive, 6-foot-7 first bagger has still been old for each level, so he'll need to move quickly and keep hitting. ⊘ With a strong first year in full-season ball, **Jonathan Schoop** may now be Baltimore's top prospect aside from Machado. He has a ways to go, but a strong arm, a good bat, and projectable power could make him part of a very strong middle infield come 2014. ⊘ Selected in the Double-A portion of the Rule 5 draft over the winter, **Matthew Sweeney** has good raw power, but has had trouble staying healthy enough to use it. ⊘ Possessor of great power, **Brandon Waring** has spent two full seasons at Double-A working on his plate discipline and defense, but striking out 30 percent of the time still isn't good enough to have big league impact.

## PITCHERS

| PLAYER | TEAM | LVL | AGE | W | L | SV | IP | H | HR | BB | SO | EqBB9 | EqSO9 | GB% | BABIP | WHIP | ERA | FIP | FRA | WARP |
|---|---|---|---|---|---|---|---|---|---|---|---|---|---|---|---|---|---|---|---|---|
| M. Atkins | NOR | AAA | 25 | 2 | 5 | 0 | 94¹ | 95 | 10 | 37 | 74 | 3.5 | 7.1 | 36% | .304 | 1.40 | 5.44 | 4.64 | 5.70 | 0.3 |
| | BAL | MLB | 25 | 0 | 0 | 0 | 10² | 21 | 5 | 3 | 7 | 2.5 | 5.9 | 33% | .400 | 2.25 | 8.44 | 8.97 | 7.69 | -0.1 |
| R. Bundy | FRD | A+ | 21 | 8 | 4 | 0 | 121 | 102 | 8 | 31 | 100 | 2.3 | 7.4 | 50% | .278 | 1.10 | 2.75 | 3.44 | 4.04 | 1.6 |
| R. Drese | NOR | AAA | 35 | 1 | 1 | 0 | 44 | 57 | 3 | 14 | 8 | 2.9 | 2.2 | 51% | .370 | 1.77 | 6.55 | 4.92 | 6.37 | -0.2 |
| M. Hendrickson | NOR | AAA | 37 | 2 | 2 | 0 | 59² | 48 | 8 | 16 | 29 | 2.4 | 4.4 | 41% | .225 | 1.14 | 2.87 | 4.81 | 5.82 | 0.0 |
| | BAL | MLB | 37 | 1 | 0 | 0 | 11 | 15 | 1 | 6 | 5 | 4.9 | 4.1 | 68% | .368 | 1.91 | 5.73 | 4.97 | 5.89 | -0.1 |
| A. Loomis | CLR | A+ | 25 | 1 | 0 | 3 | 31² | 27 | 0 | 10 | 39 | 2.8 | 11.1 | 49% | .346 | 1.17 | 1.14 | 1.97 | 4.00 | 0.5 |
| W. Pelzer | BOW | AA | 25 | 5 | 6 | 1 | 76 | 75 | 6 | 43 | 64 | 5.3 | 7.7 | 49% | .322 | 1.59 | 4.14 | 4.73 | 5.95 | -0.4 |
| J. Rupe | NOR | AAA | 28 | 2 | 2 | 0 | 42 | 50 | 5 | 21 | 29 | 4.5 | 6.2 | 49% | .338 | 1.69 | 7.07 | 4.98 | 6.92 | -0.5 |
| | BAL | MLB | 28 | 0 | 0 | 0 | 14¹ | 16 | 5 | 6 | 7 | 3.8 | 4.4 | 63% | .239 | 1.53 | 5.65 | 8.29 | 9.19 | -0.5 |

Apparently, it *is* possible to induce fewer groundballs than Rick VandenHurk; **Mitch Atkins** beat him out at Triple-A this year 35 percent to 37 percent. That's not a good thing. ⊘ The older brother of O's 2011 first-rounder Dylan, **Robert Bundy** has good stuff and began to put it all together at High-A Frederick this year, dominating hitters and improving his control. ⊘ No longer a 14-game winner throwing over 95, **Ryan Drese** hadn't pitched since 2008 and hadn't made a major league appearance since 2006. With a terrible 2011 at Norfolk, it's unlikely he'll ever make it back. ⊘ The O's snagged **Andy Loomis** in the Triple-A portion of the Rule 5 draft in December, but having pitched just four innings above Single-A in his career, he might struggle to remain in Norfolk the entire year. ⊘ **Wynn Pelzer** has a plus fastball, a near-plus slider, and a change-up that needs work, but there are concerns his control will never be good enough to allow him to succeed, even as a middle reliever. ⊘ Released by the Orioles in August, **Josh Rupe** will seek out his fourth team in four years this winter. He gets groundballs, but he has poor control and can't strike out enough batters.

Buck Showalter received more press this offseason than usual, thanks to the shake-up in the Orioles front office. With team president Andy MacPhail stepping down, there were rumors that Showalter could move upstairs to take the reins. He'll ultimately stay on as field general, but it appears he will have input in personnel decisions. Showalter has been around the game a long time and doesn't have a reputation as a progressive thinker, more fitting the baseball man mold. Old-school attitudes fly well enough in the dugout, but the GM chair needs to be filled by someone who is open to varied approaches and is well-versed in the statistical side. Showalter is known as a strict leader who expects a lot of his players; a team stocked with youngsters will benefit from his presence in the clubhouse. On the field his tactics were a mixed bag in 2011. He employed the second fewest sacrifices in baseball but intentionally walked more batters than average. He wasn't afraid to plug new faces into the rotation when things weren't working, but there's only so much a manager can do when just three of the 12 starters he used posted ERAs under 5.00. While Showalter provides a net positive as skipper, the O's should be careful about giving him too much say in the front office, particularly in terms of major league acquisitions.

# Boston Red Sox

A team is never as good as it looks at its best, and never as bad as it appears at its worst. This isn't a new adage: it's been passed on enough that we can't pretend to know who said it first or that we made it up. The Red Sox nearly pulled off defying that first bit last summer, thanks to an offensive onslaught that rivaled any team you have seen in your lifetime—they looked like world-beaters. But, in the end, they played to a level far worse than the collective talent summed to.

Starting at the beginning: the 2010 Red Sox were a massively talented team, but one forced to deal with injury after injury to stars, bit pieces, and everyone in between. Following a first-round exit in 2009, this stuttering season became a disappointment to the Fenway Faithful, despite the 89-win finish. Even with lengthy and season-ending injuries to the likes of Dustin Pedroia, Kevin Youkilis, Jacoby Ellsbury, and Mike Cameron, the Red Sox led the American League in True Average in 2010. For 2011, they would get all of those players back and the offensive attack would be more potent than before. Just to be sure, though, Theo Epstein and Company added the most valuable trade asset on the market in Adrian Gonzalez, as well as one of the top free agents in Carl Crawford.

Not only were the bats of both a fit for the powerful lineup, but they were also defensive stalwarts at their respective positions. The Red Sox had a habit of collecting players like this, who could play both sides of the ball fabulously, and the addition of this pair caused that easy wave of December euphoria, in which winning the winter meetings was akin to winning the World Series.

Neither player came free, of course. Gonzalez cost the Red Sox in prospects, as they sent first baseman Anthony Rizzo, starting pitcher Casey Kelly, and low minors center fielder Reymond Fuentes to the Padres for one year of his services. Boston also signed Gonzalez to an extension that keeps him in town through 2018. Crawford also got paid, inking a seven-year, $142 million deal that will pay him $21 million for his age-35 season.

Gonzalez, fresh off of shoulder surgery and in a park that wasn't actively trying to hinder his production, raked for most of the year, quickly becoming a favorite of Sox fans. Crawford had a tougher time of it; from the outset he was trying too hard to earn his entire contract with each swing. A 431 OPS in April was easily the worst of a season that eventually got better, but it was a poor first impression.

That was about all there was to complain about in the lineup, though. Jarrod Saltalamacchia, quietly acquired at the 2010 trade deadline, stepped in as the starter after Victor Martinez signed with Detroit. Salty slugged .450 and played quality defense whenever he wasn't catching a knuckler. J.D. Drew struggled while playing with a shoulder injury, but rookie Josh Reddick stepped in and produced with a .290 TAv and defensive value, too. The 2010 holdovers—Pedroia, Youkilis, Scutaro, Ortiz, etc.—did what was expected of them, or more. There is a reason the Red Sox threatened the 1976 Cincinnati Reds and the 1982 Brewers for the greatest single-season offense of the last 50 years up until mid-August, and it's because the lineup, one through nine, was cartoonishly talented.

It was a good thing, too, as the pitching didn't have nearly as much luck. The bullpen was no longer an issue, thanks to late-winter pickups like Alfredo Aceves and Matt Albers, two pitchers who were non-tendered but combined to give the Red Sox much-needed relief innings. The pen ended up overworked as a unit, though, thanks to injuries.

Jon Lester missed a bit of time with a latissimus dorsi issue, and Josh Beckett had to skip starts due to a

## RED SOX PROSPECTUS
### 2011 W-L: 90-72, 3rd in AL East

| | | | |
|---|---|---|---|
| Pythag | .582 | 4th | **Ballpark:** Fenway Park (3-yr. PF: 99). The 100-year-old park is playing conservative as it ages |
| RS/G | 5.40 | 1st | |
| RA/G | 4.55 | 21st | |
| TAv | .291 | 1st | **2011:** Ellsbury, Pedroia, and Gonzalez are worth 21 extra wins, but Sox win only seven games in September |
| TAv-P | .264 | 18th | |
| FIP | 4.09 | 21st | |
| DER | .715 | 8th | **2012:** They'll be competitive, but everyone will worry the magic left town with you-know-who |
| DL | 821 | 23rd | |
| B-Age | 30.1 | 27th | |
| P-Age | 30.6 | 29th | **Action Items:** A tolerable performance from Lackey, Crawford, Buchholz, or Matsuzaka |
| Salary | $165.3 | 3rd | |
| M$/MW | $3.68 | 23rd | |

stomach illness—these were the least problematic of the issues. Daisuke Matsuzaka was far more horrific than anyone could have predicted, and it turned out it was because he needed Tommy John surgery. Clay Buchholz rarely looked right on the mound, and while he was still very much Clay Buchholz, it turned out he had a stress fracture in his spine that caused him to miss the second half of the season.

John Lackey required a cortisone shot in his elbow early on in the year, and by season's end, needed Tommy John surgery. He continued to pitch long enough to post the worst ERA and adjusted-ERA numbers ever for a Red Sox starter with 150 frames. Why? Because there was no one else to turn to. This wasn't for a lack of depth, either. The Red Sox

where he left off in 2010, and was intermittently useful and intolerable. Doubront showed up to camp out of shape, and spent the year recovering from minor injuries instead of filling in as the first man out of Pawtucket. Miller was terrible, and Weiland, who should have been relieving during September call-ups, instead took his lumps as a starter. Millwood opted out and headed to Colorado, almost immediately before the Red Sox would have thrown him against the wall, too.

The offense kept them afloat despite the pitching issues, but then injuries took their toll on the lineup, too. Youkilis attempted to play through pain, and, unlike in 2010 when he hid his thumb injury from everyone by continuing to mash, it was obvious he was hurting. Reddick sustained a ligament injury in his hand, and was no help or not around at all when needed in September. Saltalamacchia and Jason Varitek both appeared gassed—and then injured—during September. Mike Aviles, acquired at the deadline for bench depth, ended up being leaned on as one of the team's top offensive contributors down the stretch.

With the lineup in a less-than-optimal state, there was no saving the Wakefields, Millers, or Weilands anymore. Beckett and Lester weren't at their best, either, both starters having their worst month at the wrong time. Whereas mid-August was this team's zenith, when a playoff spot seemed all but a given and talk of just how fantastic the lineup was in an all-time sense mattered more than the next series, September was the Red Sox at their nadir. While it seemed that even a team limping as much as they were could make it through a month in which they were well over 90 percent assured of a playoff berth, it wasn't to be. Injuries took their toll, healthy players faltered, and the Rays, who at one point had odds of

roughly 1 percent to surpass the Sox, ended up in October after game 162.

Red Sox fans were stunned, and quickly searched for something to point to and blame. An article in the *Boston Globe* cited a laundry list of reasons, most of them pertaining to clubhouse attitude, even going so far as to accuse manager Terry Francona of dependence on pain medication. Lester, Beckett, and Lackey's late-season meltdowns were attributed to their consumption of beer, fried chicken, and video games on off days, rather than shoulder trouble, regression, and a need for Tommy John surgery. It's not that these things didn't contribute to the downfall at all: it's that they were being used as *the reason*, and as an excuse to bring

The 37-year-old Cherington was the assistant general manager the last two seasons, and part of the co-general managership from the 2005–06 offseason, when Epstein left town in a gorilla suit, leaving Jed Hoyer and Cherington to watch over the roster.

Cherington is part of the new generation of general managers. Not necessarily your stats-oriented leaders, but the kind that know how to marry a scouting background with an appreciation and understanding of analytical thinking and data. It's the same vision that Epstein—who was perceived as a pure stathead, but was no such thing—helped bring to the organization when he first took over in 2003, a vision he helped to build with Cherington. Cherington is only new to the job in the sense that his title changed.

In a way, he is the general manager version of his first manager hire, Bobby Valentine. Valentine has been in the game since the 1960s, when he was drafted by the Dodgers, and has been managing since the 1980s. He knows the old school—he lived it!—but also understands the value of gaining an advantage, of building an edge over his opponents. He was talking the *Moneyball* talk before Michael Lewis submitted his first draft to his publisher, and he has done more with it than just talk.

Valentine is the guy who can actually get away with wearing a T-shirt that states, "I'm Big In Japan," as he brought the Chiba Lotte Marines of the NPB more success than they ever had before. Valentine has been known to rankle his employers on more than one occasion, but for now, while this marriage is still a happy one, the Cherington/Valentine partnership could produce high-quality baseball at Fenway.

The Cherington era has started out quietly enough, but it's easy to see the big picture even in tiny moves. He let

Jonathan Papelbon sign with the Phillies without so much as a whimper, preferring instead to rebuild his pen without spending huge money on one arm. David Ortiz was told during negotiations that he could accept arbitration and receive a hefty one-year payout, or sign a multi-year deal for roughly the same amount of money total—the first was a favor out of loyalty in a down market for designated hitters, while the latter offer was a reminder that this is a business. The underachieving Jed Lowrie, who had no real place on a roster that also has Marco Scutaro and Mike Aviles, was sent to the Astros along with Weiland for five years of Mark Melancon, whom the Sox can use as a setup man or closer. Nick Punto was picked up to replace Lowrie, and while he won't provide Lowrie's offense, his glove is exponentially better, and one of the best among bench infielders.

The margins are where Cherington started, reemphasizing his repeated statements that the Red Sox have an incredibly talented team already in place. Cherington moved slowly this past winter because the market rewards those with patience. As they were not looking for any star-caliber players—that is what the 2010–11 offseason was for—they were free to wait out the demands of mid-level free agents, and let the closer market sort itself out. In the end, they worked a deal for Andrew Bailey, the A's closer and former Rookie of the Year.

With Lackey and Matsuzaka both out recovering from Tommy John surgery, the Red Sox need two starting pitchers.

The pitching market is thin, so it looks like Daniel Bard is likely to take on the role, despite a career in relief. He was a starter in college, but switched to relief after a horrid first professional campaign. The thing is, while starting he was using mechanics the Red Sox switched him to that killed his command and velocity. A return to the mechanics and approach he was drafted with brought back both heat and command.

As of press time, the Red Sox have not finished filling out their roster. But their plan is clear. Cherington has been looking everywhere for the best-fit options in both the bullpen and rotation, and is looking to add pieces without compromising the future of the team either financially or from a talent perspective. Melancon and his one year of service time is an example of this; others will surely follow before you get a chance to read this.

Cherington is thorough. This is a good thing, even if it might make fans wonder what the team is thinking. Exploring every avenue, when the front office is talented enough to figure out what should be effective, is a positive. This is why Bard will get a look as a starter, the team hasn't completely given up on Miller yet, and someone like Melancon could get an opportunity to close or set up in the toughest division in the game despite a relative lack of experience. After September, it might be hard to feel this way, but the Red Sox are still in good hands.

# HITTERS

**Lars Anderson**    1B

Born: 9/25/1987 Age: 24
Bats: L Throws: L Height: 6' 5" Weight: 215
Breakout: 4% Improve: 34% Collapse: 1%
Attrition: 17% MLB: 51%

**Comparables:**
Jeff Bagwell, Brock Peterson, Keith Hernandez

| YEAR | TEAM | LVL | AGE | PA | R | 2B | 3B | HR | RBI | BB | SO | SB | CS | AVG_OBP_SLG | TAv | BABIP | BRR | FRAA | WARP |
|------|------|-----|-----|----|----|----|----|----|-----|----|----|----|----|-------------|-----|-------|-----|------|------|
| 2009 | PME | AA | 21 | 512 | 50 | 23 | 0 | 9 | 51 | 63 | 114 | 2 | 0 | .233/.329/.345 | .242 | .293 | 0.1 | -1 | -0.8 |
| 2010 | PME | AA | 22 | 71 | 13 | 5 | 0 | 5 | 16 | 7 | 16 | 1 | 1 | .355/.420/.677 | .377 | .415 | -0.7 | -1.8 | 0.7 |
| 2010 | PAW | AAA | 22 | 462 | 49 | 32 | 3 | 10 | 53 | 44 | 109 | 2 | 2 | .262/.342/.428 | .261 | .334 | -6.5 | -3.9 | -0.7 |
| 2010 | BOS | MLB | 22 | 43 | 4 | 1 | 0 | 0 | 4 | 7 | 8 | 0 | 0 | .200/.326/.229 | .219 | .250 | 0.5 | -0.2 | -0.1 |
| 2011 | PAW | AAA | 23 | 577 | 65 | 31 | 2 | 14 | 78 | 80 | 120 | 5 | 0 | .265/.369/.422 | .278 | .322 | -4.1 | 3.1 | 1.6 |
| 2012 | BOS | MLB | 24 | 250 | 28 | 13 | 1 | 5 | 25 | 27 | 61 | 1 | 0 | .240/.325/.376 | .248 | .304 | 0 | 1B -12 | 0.1 |

Anderson has always been passive at the plate, to the point that even Gandhi wants to know what his deal is. That passivity and his long swing hurt him in 2010 and in the first half of 2011. While his bat sped up a little thanks to a less mechanical-looking approach, he remains as laid back as ever at the dish: he isn't swinging on pitches he should mash, the ones that would give him the power numbers needed from a first baseman. If not for the aborted Rich Harden deal, the Red Sox would have their 40-man spot back, and Anderson would have an opportunity with another team—something he is unlikely to see in Boston, given Adrian Gonzalez.

**Mike Aviles**    **2B**
Born: **3/13/1981** Age: **31**
Bats: **R** Throws: **R** Height: **5' 10''** Weight: **195**
Breakout: **2%** Improve: **35%** Collapse: **8%**
Attrition: **12%** MLB: **82%**

Comparables:
Michael Young, Rich Aurilia, Alvin Dark

| YEAR | TEAM | LVL | AGE | PA | R | 2B | 3B | HR | RBI | BB | SO | SB | CS | AVG_OBP_SLG | TAv | BABIP | BRR | FRAA | WARP |
|------|------|-----|-----|-----|-----|-----|-----|-----|-----|-----|-----|-----|-----|-------------|-----|-------|-----|------|------|
| 2009 | KCA | MLB | 28 | 127 | 10 | 3 | 1 | 1 | 8 | 4 | 26 | 1 | 0 | .183/.208/.250 | .168 | .223 | -0.3 | 2.1 | -0.5 |
| 2010 | OMA | AAA | 29 | 75 | 8 | 3 | 1 | 1 | 8 | 4 | 10 | 0 | 0 | .271/.320/.386 | .242 | .305 | 0.1 | -0.1 | 0.2 |
| 2010 | KCA | MLB | 29 | 448 | 63 | 16 | 3 | 8 | 32 | 20 | 49 | 14 | 5 | .304/.335/.413 | .261 | .327 | 1.5 | 3.5 | 1.8 |
| 2011 | OMA | AAA | 30 | 150 | 21 | 8 | 2 | 9 | 25 | 6 | 17 | 6 | 4 | .307/.329/.586 | .286 | .291 | -0.8 | 5.2 | 1.8 |
| 2011 | BOS | MLB | 30 | 107 | 17 | 6 | 0 | 2 | 8 | 4 | 17 | 4 | 2 | .317/.340/.436 | .276 | .361 | -0.2 | 1.2 | 0.6 |
| 2011 | KCA | MLB | 30 | 202 | 14 | 11 | 3 | 5 | 31 | 9 | 27 | 10 | 2 | .222/.261/.395 | .231 | .231 | -1.7 | 0.2 | -0.1 |
| *2012* | *BOS* | *MLB* | *31* | *349* | *41* | *18* | *3* | *7* | *42* | *15* | *50* | *10* | *4* | *.282/.314/.420* | *.255* | *.312* | *-0.3* | *2B 0, SS 3* | *1.4* |

Aviles appeared in just 53 games for the Royals before he was dealt to the Red Sox on July 30, and he played in 38 of their remaining 57 contests. Aviles had struggled as a bench player in Kansas City, but the plane ride to Boston did the trick, as he hit .317/.340/.436 the rest of the way, more like the Aviles we had come to expect from his two full seasons. He primarily filled in for the injured Kevin Youkilis at third, and, unlike Yamaico Navarro, who was dealt to the Royals to acquire Aviles, he is capable

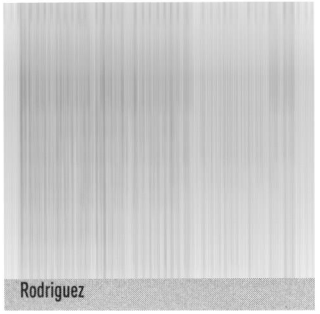

Rodriguez

importantly, Bogaerts is 18 years old and had a mere 280 pro plate appearances heading into this year. He is a long way off, of course, and his ceiling and floor are further apart than the two sides at a typical NBA labor meeting. Power potential doesn't necessarily mean success—ask Lars Anderson about that one—but he is, for now, a name to remember.

**Bryce Brentz**    **RF**
Born: **12/30/1988** Age: **23**
Bats: **R** Throws: **R** Height: **6' 2''** Weight: **180**
Breakout: **2%** Improve: **42%** Collapse: **1%**
Attrition: **6%** MLB: **79%**

Comparables:
Manny Ramirez, Brian Downing, Larry Walker

| YEAR | TEAM | LVL | AGE | PA | R | 2B | 3B | HR | RBI | BB | SO | SB | CS | AVG_OBP_SLG | TAv | BABIP | BRR | FRAA | WARP |
|------|------|-----|-----|-----|-----|-----|-----|-----|-----|-----|-----|-----|-----|-------------|-----|-------|-----|------|------|
| 2010 | LOW | A- | 21 | 286 | 28 | 14 | 4 | 5 | 39 | 21 | 76 | 5 | 4 | .198/.261/.340 | .229 | .260 | -1.2 | 2.3 | -0.1 |
| 2011 | GRN | A | 22 | 186 | 43 | 10 | 3 | 11 | 36 | 14 | 35 | 2 | 2 | .359/.414/.647 | .359 | .403 | -1.2 | 0.5 | 2.1 |
| 2011 | SLM | A+ | 22 | 321 | 48 | 15 | 1 | 19 | 58 | 26 | 80 | 1 | 1 | .274/.336/.531 | .281 | .311 | 1.2 | 0.6 | 1.4 |
| *2012* | *BOS* | *MLB* | *23* | *250* | *30* | *10* | *1* | *12* | *35* | *13* | *67* | *0* | *0* | *.249/.291/.456* | *.256* | *.294* | *0* | *RF -2, CF -0* | *0.7* |

Brentz was a major power threat in college, but his first taste of the pros left him wishing the bats were still made of aluminum. His first full season in the minors changed that, though, as Brentz decimated the Sally League before continuing his rampage at High-A Salem. Brentz doesn't walk much, but he did cut his strikeout rate despite moving up two levels. In that sense, Brentz might remind Red Sox fans of Josh Reddick, as Reddick never saw a pitch he didn't like until this year. Eventually, Brentz will be challenged by pitchers and forced to change his approach, but if he can adjust to those inevitable troubles, the 2011 season has given us an idea of his power potential.

**Carl Crawford**    **LF**
Born: **8/5/1981** Age: **30**
Bats: **L** Throws: **L** Height: **6' 3''** Weight: **203**
Breakout: **2%** Improve: **32%** Collapse: **6%**
Attrition: **21%** MLB: **82%**

Comparables:
Robin Yount, Matt Diaz, Rob Butler

| YEAR | TEAM | LVL | AGE | PA | R | 2B | 3B | HR | RBI | BB | SO | SB | CS | AVG_OBP_SLG | TAv | BABIP | BRR | FRAA | WARP |
|------|------|-----|-----|-----|-----|-----|-----|-----|-----|-----|-----|-----|-----|-------------|-----|-------|-----|------|------|
| 2009 | TBA | MLB | 27 | 672 | 96 | 28 | 8 | 15 | 68 | 51 | 99 | 60 | 16 | .305/.364/.452 | .290 | .342 | 1.5 | 11.2 | 4.8 |
| 2010 | TBA | MLB | 28 | 657 | 110 | 30 | 13 | 19 | 90 | 46 | 104 | 47 | 10 | .307/.356/.495 | .311 | .342 | 4.9 | 10.4 | 6.5 |
| 2011 | BOS | MLB | 29 | 538 | 65 | 29 | 7 | 11 | 56 | 23 | 104 | 18 | 6 | .255/.289/.405 | .251 | .299 | 3 | 2.5 | 1.3 |
| *2012* | *BOS* | *MLB* | *30* | *530* | *67* | *26* | *8* | *11* | *66* | *34* | *90* | *32* | *8* | *.291/.339/.445* | *.274* | *.335* | *0.6* | *LF 6* | *2.1* |

We predicted Crawford to lose *some* hits and walks from the move into Boston's stronger lineup and away from turf, but 2011 was disastrous. Between a .155/.204/.227 April and a month of games missed due to a hamstring injury, Crawford's line never recovered. He looked uncomfortable at the plate, and his swing was at its most ugly when he needed to protect the plate with two strikes. The result? The same number of whiffs as in 2010 in 119 fewer chances. Crawford isn't just in Boston for his bat, though, as he is a superior defender and baserunner, too. He also at least *started* to recover when he returned from his leg injury (.272/.303/.462 in last 209 PA). Crawford used to claim his legs would be stronger if he got off turf, but PECOTA sees those wheels fading.

**J.D. Drew**　　RF

Born: 11/20/1975 Age: **36**
Bats: **L** Throws: **R** Height: **6' 2"** Weight: **190**
Breakout: **0%** Improve: **35%** Collapse: **8%**
Attrition: **16%** MLB: **87%**

**Comparables:**
Frank Robinson, Bobby Abreu, Al Kaline

| YEAR | TEAM | LVL | AGE | PA | R | 2B | 3B | HR | RBI | BB | SO | SB | CS | AVG_OBP_SLG | TAv | BABIP | BRR | FRAA | WARP |
|------|------|-----|-----|-----|----|----|----|----|-----|----|-----|----|----|-------------|------|-------|------|------|------|
| 2009 | BOS | MLB | 33 | 539 | 84 | 30 | 4 | 24 | 68 | 82 | 109 | 2 | 6 | .279/.392/.522 | .308 | .319 | -0.1 | 2.7 | 3.8 |
| 2010 | BOS | MLB | 34 | 546 | 69 | 24 | 2 | 22 | 68 | 60 | 105 | 3 | 1 | .255/.341/.452 | .278 | .282 | 1 | 3.6 | 2.2 |
| 2011 | BOS | MLB | 35 | 286 | 23 | 6 | 1 | 4 | 22 | 33 | 58 | 0 | 1 | .222/.315/.302 | .239 | .270 | 0.3 | 6.4 | 0.6 |
| 2012 | BOS | MLB | 36 | 322 | 41 | 16 | 2 | 10 | 37 | 44 | 66 | 2 | 1 | .260/.364/.437 | .283 | .307 | -0.3 | RF 4 | 1.9 |

Isn't it odd that the last season of Drew's five-year deal was the campaign where he caught the least amount of flak from the pulpits? Maybe playing with a busted shoulder stirred sympathy. Or maybe everyone finally understood just how good he was from 2007-2010, when he had a combined TAv of .295 and played quality defense in a very difficult right-field corner. For all the complaints about Drew, he performed as well as Mike Lowell did over his own five years in Boston (for similar money), but for some reason Lowell is a hero, while Drew is a representation of all that was "wrong" with Theo Epstein's regime.

**Jacoby Ellsbury**　　CF

Born: 9/11/1983 Age: **28**
Bats: **L** Throws: **L** Height: **6' 2"** Weight: **185**
Breakout: **4%** Improve: **45%** Collapse: **4%**
Attrition: **12%** MLB: **92%**

**Comparables:**
Chris Denorfia, Amos Otis, Shane Victorino

| YEAR | TEAM | LVL | AGE | PA | R | 2B | 3B | HR | RBI | BB | SO | SB | CS | AVG_OBP_SLG | TAv | BABIP | BRR | FRAA | WARP |
|------|------|-----|-----|-----|-----|----|----|----|-----|----|----|----|----|-------------|------|-------|------|------|------|
| 2009 | BOS | MLB | 25 | 691 | 94 | 27 | 10 | 8 | 60 | 49 | 74 | 70 | 12 | .301/.355/.415 | .270 | .328 | 7.5 | -7.3 | 2.6 |
| 2010 | BOS | MLB | 26 | 83 | 10 | 4 | 0 | 0 | 5 | 4 | 9 | 7 | 1 | .192/.241/.244 | .186 | .217 | 1.1 | 0.7 | -0.3 |
| 2011 | BOS | MLB | 27 | 729 | 119 | 46 | 5 | 32 | 105 | 52 | 98 | 39 | 15 | .321/.376/.552 | .325 | .336 | 3.2 | 11.6 | 8.6 |
| 2012 | BOS | MLB | 28 | 556 | 74 | 31 | 6 | 12 | 71 | 40 | 72 | 40 | 10 | .308/.363/.462 | .287 | .336 | 0.8 | CF 5, LF 0 | 3.4 |

Ellsbury put together an MVP-caliber campaign, setting career-highs in everything except for triples and stolen bases, blowing away even the Johnny Damon-power comparisons that have dogged him since he was drafted in 2005. The difference? Ellsbury learned how to hit the low-inside fastball with authority, rather than whiffing on it as he had in the past. While his power is for real, the future will likely hold fewer opportunities to mash to this extreme degree: Ellsbury was in the top 10 in percentage of fastballs seen among qualifiers, alongside slugging behemoths like Emilio Bonifacio, Brett Gardner, Juan Pierre, and Elvis Andrus. Expect Ellsbury to see more breaking balls and secondary pitches in the future, once the league collectively realizes fastballs don't work like they used to.

**Adrian Gonzalez**　　1B

Born: 5/8/1982 Age: **30**
Bats: **L** Throws: **L** Height: **6' 3"** Weight: **190**
Breakout: **4%** Improve: **34%** Collapse: **6%**
Attrition: **14%** MLB: **95%**

**Comparables:**
Jeff Bagwell, Norm Cash, Eddie Murray

| YEAR | TEAM | LVL | AGE | PA | R | 2B | 3B | HR | RBI | BB | SO | SB | CS | AVG_OBP_SLG | TAv | BABIP | BRR | FRAA | WARP |
|------|------|-----|-----|-----|-----|----|----|----|-----|-----|-----|----|----|-------------|------|-------|------|------|------|
| 2009 | SDN | MLB | 27 | 681 | 90 | 27 | 2 | 40 | 99 | 119 | 109 | 1 | 1 | .277/.407/.551 | .328 | .278 | -2 | 9.9 | 6.6 |
| 2010 | SDN | MLB | 28 | 692 | 87 | 33 | 0 | 31 | 101 | 93 | 114 | 0 | 0 | .298/.393/.511 | .326 | .322 | -5 | 9.4 | 6.2 |
| 2011 | BOS | MLB | 29 | 715 | 108 | 45 | 3 | 27 | 117 | 74 | 119 | 1 | 0 | .338/.410/.548 | .324 | .380 | -8.1 | 8.8 | 5.6 |
| 2012 | BOS | MLB | 30 | 667 | 94 | 34 | 2 | 29 | 94 | 82 | 125 | 1 | 0 | .286/.377/.500 | .302 | .319 | 0 | 1B 7, RF -0 | 3.8 |

In his first full season free of Petco Park, Gonzalez nearly won a batting title, collected 75 extra-base hits, and hit .313/.455/.523 during Boston's September collapse despite playing with a sore shoulder and leg. Surgically repairing that shoulder during the 2010–11 offseason did more for his opposite-field doubles power and his defense than it did for his home run totals, but Fenway is not a kind mistress for lefty pull power. That said, Gonzo is well-acquainted with the Monster: a good thing considering the extension that keeps him in town through 2018. It's fair to worry about his .380 BABIP, but don't be surprised if he comes close to repeating the feat with his approach and this park, a la Manny Ramirez.

**Jose Iglesias**　　SS

Born: 1/5/1990 Age: **22**
Bats: **R** Throws: **R** Height: **6' 0"** Weight: **175**
Breakout: **2%** Improve: **16%** Collapse: **8%**
Attrition: **20%** MLB: **44%**

**Comparables:**
Jonathan Herrera, Gustavo Nunez, Lenny Faedo

| YEAR | TEAM | LVL | AGE | PA | R | 2B | 3B | HR | RBI | BB | SO | SB | CS | AVG_OBP_SLG | TAv | BABIP | BRR | FRAA | WARP |
|------|------|-----|-----|-----|----|----|----|----|-----|----|----|----|----|-------------|------|-------|------|------|------|
| 2010 | PME | AA | 20 | 236 | 29 | 10 | 3 | 0 | 13 | 8 | 49 | 5 | 2 | .285/.318/.357 | .238 | .364 | 4.2 | -7.5 | 0.2 |
| 2011 | PAW | AAA | 21 | 387 | 35 | 9 | 0 | 1 | 31 | 21 | 58 | 12 | 4 | .235/.285/.269 | .204 | .279 | -0.8 | 12.4 | 0.2 |
| 2011 | BOS | MLB | 21 | 6 | 3 | 0 | 0 | 0 | 0 | 0 | 2 | 0 | 0 | .333/.333/.333 | .236 | .500 | -0.6 | -0.2 | 0.0 |
| 2012 | BOS | MLB | 22 | 250 | 24 | 11 | 1 | 1 | 20 | 10 | 49 | 5 | 2 | .246/.282/.315 | .214 | .301 | -0.1 | SS 2 | -0.4 |

Iglesias had a better second half than first, but it would have been nearly impossible not to improve on a .227/.275/.245 line. To be fair, the Cuban-born Iglesias is only 21 years old, and was force-fed into Triple-A with just one year of pro ball under his belt—and before he mastered Double-A. At his best, we're talking about a bottom-of-the-order hitter who does just well enough to not be embarrassed, but with a glove so smooth, people should flock to his fielding drills like they do for Albert Pujols's batting practice. He'll spend 2011 in Triple-A in his attempt to become a passable hitter during the last year of Marco Scutaro's deal.

**Conor Jackson**   **LF**

Born: **5/7/1982** Age: **30**
Bats: **R** Throws: **R** Height: **6' 3"** Weight: **225**
Breakout: **3%** Improve: **33%** Collapse: **3%**
Attrition: **18%** MLB: **85%**

Comparables:
John Olerud, Mark Grace, Gail Hopkins

| YEAR | TEAM | LVL | AGE | PA | R | 2B | 3B | HR | RBI | BB | SO | SB | CS | AVG/OBP/SLG | TAv | BABIP | BRR | FRAA | WARP |
|---|---|---|---|---|---|---|---|---|---|---|---|---|---|---|---|---|---|---|---|
| 2009 | ARI | MLB | 27 | 110 | 8 | 4 | 0 | 1 | 14 | 11 | 16 | 5 | 0 | .182/.264/.253 | .198 | .207 | 0.2 | -1.7 | -0.7 |
| 2010 | ARI | MLB | 28 | 172 | 19 | 11 | 0 | 1 | 11 | 20 | 18 | 4 | 1 | .238/.326/.331 | .251 | .263 | 1.9 | 0.5 | 0.4 |
| 2010 | OAK | MLB | 28 | 69 | 6 | 2 | 0 | 1 | 5 | 11 | 9 | 2 | 0 | .228/.362/.316 | .246 | .255 | -0.1 | 0.1 | 0.0 |
| 2011 | OAK | MLB | 29 | 368 | 30 | 17 | 1 | 4 | 38 | 30 | 50 | 3 | 1 | .249/.315/.342 | .255 | .281 | -3 | -0.9 | -0.3 |
| 2011 | BOS | MLB | 29 | 22 | 2 | 0 | 0 | 1 | 5 | 2 | 3 | 0 | 0 | .158/.227/.316 | .198 | .125 | 0.2 | -0.2 | -0.1 |
| *2012* | *BOS* | *MLB* | *30* | *340* | *41* | *18* | *2* | *6* | *35* | *34* | *41* | *6* | *2* | *.272/.350/.402* | *.268* | *.296* | *0.2* | *LF -1, 1B -2* | *1.3* |

Jackson was acquired to give the team someone who could hit lefties and play the outfield, as Mike Aviles—originally acquired to do just that—was needed at third base. While at first this trade with Oakland made it seem as if there were no hard feelings about the aborted Rich Harden swap, Jackson's play in Boston should make it obvious these two teams are not BFFs. In fact, Billy Beane hates the Red Sox. Jackson played exactly as meh as he has for years, and made people pine for Darnell McDonald, something that seemed impossible just one month prior.

always toolsy and athletic, but this is the first time he had a chance to show it off, as his previous campaigns in Rookie ball and in the New York-Penn league were full of disappointment. While his .381 BABIP means the 20-year-old has more work to do than his line suggests, he has the power/speed potential to make him an intriguing prospect.

**Ryan Kalish**   **CF**

Born: **3/28/1988** Age: **24**
Bats: **L** Throws: **L** Height: **6' 2"** Weight: **205**
Breakout: **3%** Improve: **45%** Collapse: **1%**
Attrition: **22%** MLB: **93%**

Comparables:
J.D. Drew, Reggie Smith, Jim Eisenreich

| YEAR | TEAM | LVL | AGE | PA | R | 2B | 3B | HR | RBI | BB | SO | SB | CS | AVG/OBP/SLG | TAv | BABIP | BRR | FRAA | WARP |
|---|---|---|---|---|---|---|---|---|---|---|---|---|---|---|---|---|---|---|---|
| 2009 | SLM | A+ | 21 | 143 | 21 | 5 | 2 | 5 | 21 | 26 | 20 | 7 | 3 | .304/.437/.513 | .331 | .333 | 0.4 | 3.2 | 1.8 |
| 2009 | PME | AA | 21 | 437 | 63 | 19 | 4 | 13 | 56 | 42 | 87 | 14 | 3 | .271/.343/.440 | .271 | .320 | 3.5 | 9.1 | 2.9 |
| 2010 | PME | AA | 22 | 183 | 35 | 9 | 1 | 8 | 29 | 28 | 21 | 13 | 1 | .293/.411/.527 | .323 | .298 | 0.9 | 0.3 | 1.6 |
| 2010 | PAW | AAA | 22 | 160 | 22 | 9 | 1 | 5 | 18 | 14 | 32 | 12 | 2 | .294/.361/.476 | .288 | .349 | 3 | 5.1 | 1.6 |
| 2010 | BOS | MLB | 22 | 179 | 26 | 11 | 1 | 4 | 24 | 12 | 38 | 10 | 1 | .252/.305/.405 | .256 | .303 | 2 | 2.1 | 0.9 |
| 2011 | PAW | AAA | 23 | 96 | 9 | 6 | 0 | 0 | 9 | 8 | 20 | 4 | 3 | .209/.271/.279 | .191 | .265 | -1 | 3.9 | -0.2 |
| *2012* | *BOS* | *MLB* | *24* | *250* | *30* | *12* | *1* | *7* | *29* | *23* | *53* | *10* | *2* | *.259/.328/.416* | *.261* | *.307* | *0.3* | *CF 6, LF 2* | *1.2* |

Kalish came into 2011 as Boston's top outfield prospect, but a left-shoulder labrum tear in April set the tone for his year. When Kalish returned, the team discovered he was playing with a bulging disc in his neck that he had suffered while recovering from the labrum injury. He underwent neck surgery in September that isn't expected to impact his 2012, but while Kalish was healing, Josh Reddick burst upon the majors, leaving the matter open of just which above-average defender with questions about his bat is now at the top of the depth chart.

**Ryan Lavarnway**   **C**

Born: **8/7/1987** Age: **24**
Bats: **R** Throws: **R** Height: **6' 5"** Weight: **225**
Breakout: **1%** Improve: **17%** Collapse: **4%**
Attrition: **37%** MLB: **82%**

Comparables:
Chris Snyder, Rick Dempsey, Ramon Castro

| YEAR | TEAM | LVL | AGE | PA | R | 2B | 3B | HR | RBI | BB | SO | SB | CS | AVG/OBP/SLG | TAv | BABIP | BRR | FRAA | WARP |
|---|---|---|---|---|---|---|---|---|---|---|---|---|---|---|---|---|---|---|---|
| 2009 | GRN | A | 21 | 466 | 60 | 36 | 2 | 21 | 87 | 50 | 113 | 1 | 2 | .285/.372/.540 | .321 | .348 | -2.7 | -0.8 | 4.1 |
| 2010 | SLM | A+ | 22 | 360 | 66 | 18 | 0 | 14 | 63 | 44 | 62 | 1 | 0 | .289/.395/.487 | .309 | .325 | -0.7 | -0.1 | 3.0 |
| 2010 | PME | AA | 22 | 190 | 25 | 9 | 0 | 8 | 39 | 26 | 42 | 0 | 0 | .285/.399/.494 | .295 | .343 | 0 | -0.3 | 1.1 |
| 2011 | PME | AA | 23 | 239 | 35 | 5 | 0 | 14 | 38 | 25 | 47 | 0 | 0 | .284/.360/.510 | .295 | .298 | -1.8 | 0 | 1.4 |
| 2011 | PAW | AAA | 23 | 264 | 40 | 18 | 0 | 18 | 55 | 32 | 60 | 1 | 1 | .295/.390/.612 | .343 | .327 | -2.6 | -0.3 | 3.4 |
| 2011 | BOS | MLB | 23 | 43 | 5 | 2 | 0 | 2 | 8 | 4 | 10 | 0 | 0 | .231/.302/.436 | .285 | .259 | -0.4 | 0.1 | 0.1 |
| *2012* | *BOS* | *MLB* | *24* | *250* | *32* | *12* | *0* | *12* | *34* | *24* | *61* | *0* | *0* | *.257/.335/.471* | *.281* | *.299* | *0* | *C -1* | *2.3* |

Lavarnway led the Red Sox organization in home runs in 2011, giving him 77 over the last three seasons, and his first campaign with over 30. Given his lowest TAv since 2009 is .291, we knew he could mash: more importantly, Lavarnway's defense started to come around. He threw out 37 percent of runners between Double- and Triple-A, and gunned down the one runner who went on him in the majors, thanks to a better-than-average pop time and a strong arm. He also drew positive reviews from farm director Mike Hazen for his improved athleticism behind the plate, which resulted in more blocked pitches than in the past. His defense isn't quite there yet, but if 2011 is any indication, it is coming.

### Che-Hsuan Lin     CF

Born: 9/21/1988 Age: 23
Bats: R Throws: R Height: 6' 1" Weight: 180
Breakout: 1% Improve: 24% Collapse: 3%
Attrition: 11% MLB: 57%

**Comparables:**
J.B. Shuck, Len Dykstra, Michael Brantley

| YEAR | TEAM | LVL | AGE | PA | R | 2B | 3B | HR | RBI | BB | SO | SB | CS | AVG_OBP_SLG | TAv | BABIP | BRR | FRAA | WARP |
|------|------|-----|-----|-----|----|----|----|----|-----|----|----|----|----|-------------|------|-------|------|-----------|------|
| 2009 | SLM | A+ | 20 | 562 | 75 | 23 | 2 | 7 | 54 | 66 | 75 | 26 | 11 | .265/.357/.365 | .267 | .299 | -0.2 | 1.6 | 2.5 |
| 2010 | PME | AA | 21 | 543 | 88 | 17 | 4 | 2 | 34 | 72 | 63 | 26 | 12 | .275/.386/.343 | .269 | .315 | 2.7 | 16 | 4.6 |
| 2011 | PME | AA | 22 | 161 | 23 | 5 | 2 | 0 | 11 | 20 | 14 | 12 | 3 | .268/.373/.333 | .260 | .298 | -1.7 | 2 | 0.6 |
| 2011 | PAW | AAA | 22 | 378 | 49 | 11 | 1 | 2 | 25 | 38 | 51 | 16 | 4 | .235/.325/.293 | .231 | .271 | -1.1 | 5.5 | 0.5 |
| 2012 | BOS | MLB | 23 | 250 | 26 | 10 | 1 | 1 | 18 | 24 | 38 | 9 | 3 | .248/.328/.322 | .237 | .289 | -0.2 | CF 2, RF 0 | 0.3 |

Lin conquered two levels in his own little way in 2011. He continued to show no power at Double-A Portland, but made up for it by being phenomenal defensively. While his average and what little power he had vanished in his first taste of Pawtucket, Lin continued to walk, and stole bases when he did get on. Whether with Boston or elsewhere, Lin's future is as a bench outfielder who will out-defend anyone else on the roster, pinch-run, and maybe draw a walk if forced to bat, too. The ceiling isn't as high as Boston hoped back when they bid on his services, but he does have a major-league career ahead of him.

### Darnell McDonald     RF

Born: 11/17/1978 Age: 33
Bats: R Throws: R Height: 6' 0" Weight: 208
Breakout: 1% Improve: 26% Collapse: 7%
Attrition: 20% MLB: 88%

**Comparables:**
Casey Blake, Geronimo Berroa, Hank Bauer

| YEAR | TEAM | LVL | AGE | PA | R | 2B | 3B | HR | RBI | BB | SO | SB | CS | AVG_OBP_SLG | TAv | BABIP | BRR | FRAA | WARP |
|------|------|-----|-----|-----|----|----|----|----|-----|----|----|----|----|-------------|------|-------|------|-----------|------|
| 2009 | LOU | AAA | 30 | 304 | 42 | 22 | 7 | 9 | 40 | 16 | 56 | 8 | 3 | .314/.350/.539 | .308 | .362 | -1 | 5.4 | 2.4 |
| 2009 | CIN | MLB | 30 | 111 | 12 | 6 | 1 | 2 | 10 | 5 | 31 | 1 | 0 | .267/.306/.400 | .225 | .361 | -0.9 | 0.8 | -0.4 |
| 2010 | BOS | MLB | 31 | 363 | 40 | 18 | 3 | 9 | 34 | 30 | 85 | 9 | 1 | .270/.336/.429 | .270 | .342 | -3.4 | -2.2 | 0.7 |
| 2011 | BOS | MLB | 32 | 175 | 26 | 6 | 1 | 6 | 24 | 14 | 33 | 2 | 3 | .236/.303/.401 | .258 | .258 | 0 | 0.2 | 0.2 |
| 2012 | BOS | MLB | 33 | 250 | 30 | 13 | 2 | 6 | 29 | 18 | 56 | 6 | 2 | .267/.325/.419 | .259 | .326 | -0.2 | RF 1, CF 1 | 1.1 |

When forced to stretch his ability and assume the role of starting outfielder for the Red Sox in 2010, McDonald rose to the challenge and replicated Jacoby Ellsbury's pre-2011 value well over 117 games. Back on the bench where he belongs in 2011, though, McDonald struggled to ever get going. He did his job hitting lefties (.260/.333/.471) in an outfield full of left-handed hitters, but each at-bat against righties was like a slow death for everyone involved, except the opposition. Now 33, without much defensive ability to his credit, and with the occasional hit off lefties his only source of quality, McDonald will likely be buried on the 2012 Red Sox as a fifth outfielder, if he sticks there at all.

### Will Middlebrooks     3B

Born: 9/9/1988 Age: 23
Bats: R Throws: R Height: 6' 5" Weight: 200
Breakout: 6% Improve: 30% Collapse: 3%
Attrition: 25% MLB: 68%

**Comparables:**
Josh Bell, Edwin Encarnacion, Jose Moreno

| YEAR | TEAM | LVL | AGE | PA | R | 2B | 3B | HR | RBI | BB | SO | SB | CS | AVG_OBP_SLG | TAv | BABIP | BRR | FRAA | WARP |
|------|------|-----|-----|-----|----|----|----|----|-----|----|-----|----|----|-------------|------|-------|------|------|------|
| 2009 | GRN | A | 20 | 427 | 53 | 25 | 3 | 7 | 57 | 48 | 123 | 7 | 4 | .265/.351/.404 | .282 | .377 | 0.1 | -7 | 1.6 |
| 2010 | SLM | A+ | 21 | 481 | 69 | 31 | 2 | 12 | 70 | 35 | 121 | 5 | 3 | .276/.335/.439 | .279 | .358 | 1.1 | 12.6 | 3.5 |
| 2011 | PME | AA | 22 | 397 | 54 | 25 | 1 | 18 | 80 | 21 | 95 | 6 | 0 | .302/.345/.520 | .288 | .363 | -0.3 | -0.9 | 2.0 |
| 2011 | PAW | AAA | 22 | 60 | 4 | 0 | 0 | 2 | 8 | 3 | 18 | 3 | 1 | .161/.200/.268 | .164 | .189 | 0.9 | -0.2 | -0.5 |
| 2012 | BOS | MLB | 23 | 250 | 27 | 13 | 0 | 7 | 28 | 14 | 72 | 2 | 1 | .241/.286/.389 | .236 | .314 | 0 | 3B 4 | 0.6 |

Middlebrooks has improved in small spurts in each of his seasons as a professional, but 2011 was the first legitimate breakout campaign for the 22-year-old. One year after setting a career-high in two-baggers, the 2007 fifth-round pick just missed doubling his previous high for homers. Middlebrooks' strikeout rate once again dropped slightly, though that progress was more significant before Triple-A happened. While his walk rate didn't climb, it didn't fall significantly, either, a good sign given the levels involved. Middlebrooks is never going to walk much, but his impressive plate coverage should help his bat plenty in the majors as soon as 2013, combining with his plus glove to give the Sox their third baseman of the future.

### David Ortiz     1B

Born: 11/18/1975 Age: 36
Bats: L Throws: L Height: 6' 5" Weight: 230
Breakout: 2% Improve: 26% Collapse: 11%
Attrition: 16% MLB: 88%

**Comparables:**
Harmon Killebrew, Jeff Bagwell, Carlos Delgado

| YEAR | TEAM | LVL | AGE | PA | R | 2B | 3B | HR | RBI | BB | SO | SB | CS | AVG_OBP_SLG | TAv | BABIP | BRR | FRAA | WARP |
|------|------|-----|-----|-----|----|----|----|----|-----|----|-----|----|----|-------------|------|-------|------|------|------|
| 2009 | BOS | MLB | 33 | 627 | 77 | 35 | 1 | 28 | 99 | 74 | 134 | 0 | 2 | .238/.332/.462 | .273 | .262 | -3.9 | 0.4 | 1.0 |
| 2010 | BOS | MLB | 34 | 606 | 86 | 36 | 1 | 32 | 102 | 82 | 145 | 0 | 1 | .270/.370/.529 | .306 | .313 | -4.1 | -0.1 | 3.1 |
| 2011 | BOS | MLB | 35 | 605 | 84 | 40 | 1 | 29 | 96 | 78 | 83 | 1 | 1 | .309/.398/.554 | .318 | .321 | -5.1 | -0.1 | 3.8 |
| 2012 | BOS | MLB | 36 | 569 | 81 | 37 | 1 | 25 | 83 | 77 | 111 | 1 | 1 | .277/.376/.512 | .306 | .309 | -0.2 | 1B -0 | 3.5 |

Ortiz once again saw his performance dip in April, but this time around, he wasn't an easy out at the plate. He hit .267/.373/.395 with strikeouts in under 11 percent of his plate appearances, a massive shift from April 2010, when he whiffed nearly 40 percent of the time. That low punchout trend continued throughout the year, and Ortiz finished with his most productive season since 2007. While his power was still heavily pull-oriented, Ortiz went the other way more often, borrowing a modified version of the approach used by new teammate Adrian Gonzalez. This shift means Ortiz is more likely to continue producing for the next few years, whereas prior to 2011, no one would have been shocked if the purpose of this comment was to eulogize his career. Except for David Ortiz, of course.

### Dustin Pedroia — 2B

Born: 8/17/1983 Age: 28
Bats: R Throws: R Height: 5' 10" Weight: 180
Breakout: 2% Improve: 47% Collapse: 3%
Attrition: 6% MLB: 93%

Comparables:
Edgardo Alfonzo, Ian Kinsler, Bill Madlock

| YEAR | TEAM | LVL | AGE | PA | R | 2B | 3B | HR | RBI | BB | SO | SB | CS | AVG_OBP_SLG | TAv | BABIP | BRR | FRAA | WARP |
|---|---|---|---|---|---|---|---|---|---|---|---|---|---|---|---|---|---|---|---|
| 2009 | BOS | MLB | 25 | 714 | 115 | 48 | 1 | 15 | 72 | 74 | 45 | 20 | 8 | .296/.371/.447 | .287 | .297 | 2.9 | -3.3 | 4.1 |
| 2010 | BOS | MLB | 26 | 351 | 53 | 24 | 1 | 12 | 41 | 37 | 38 | 9 | 1 | .288/.367/.493 | .297 | .291 | 1.3 | -7.2 | 1.6 |
| 2011 | BOS | MLB | 27 | 731 | 102 | 37 | 3 | 21 | 91 | 86 | 85 | 26 | 8 | .307/.387/.474 | .304 | .325 | 1.4 | 2 | 5.7 |
| 2012 | BOS | MLB | 28 | 612 | 85 | 44 | 1 | 14 | 80 | 59 | 56 | 18 | 5 | .315/.385/.482 | .302 | .327 | 0.2 | 2B -4 | 4.7 |

Pedroia returned from his injury-shortened 2010 campaign and surgery that inserted a screw

Born: 11/8/1977 Age: 34
Bats: B Throws: R Height: 5' 10" Weight: 170
Breakout: 4% Improve: 21% Collapse: 9%
Attrition: 33% MLB: 80%

Comparables:
Jamey Carroll, Nelson Liriano, Tom Herr

| YEAR | TEAM | LVL | AGE | PA | R | 2B | 3B | HR | RBI | BB | SO | SB | CS | AVG_OBP_SLG | TAv | BABIP | BRR | FRAA | WARP |
|---|---|---|---|---|---|---|---|---|---|---|---|---|---|---|---|---|---|---|---|
| 2010 | MIN | MLB | 32 | 288 | 24 | 11 | 1 | 1 | 20 | 28 | 50 | 6 | 2 | .238/.313/.302 | .238 | .289 | -1.3 | 3.9 | 0.9 |
| 2011 | SLN | MLB | 33 | 166 | 21 | 8 | 4 | 1 | 20 | 25 | 21 | 1 | 1 | .278/.387/.421 | .293 | .319 | 1.8 | 2.3 | 1.6 |
| 2012 | BOS | MLB | 34 | 250 | 26 | 10 | 2 | 1 | 18 | 27 | 43 | 6 | 2 | .242/.324/.319 | .229 | .288 | 0 | 2B 1, SS -1 | 0.3 |

The Twins cut Punto loose after the 2010 season, choosing to pay a $500,000 buyout rather than pick up their $5 million option on his contract. The Cardinals swooped in and signed him to a one-year deal for just $750,000. After a solid start filling in at second, short, and third, Punto missed a total of almost three months with strains to his oblique and his right forearm. His .308/.424/.500 September helped the Cards during their stretch run, though, in which they made the playoffs only after game 162. The Red Sox signed him to an inexpensive two-year deal, giving them a Jed Lowrie replacement minus the bat, but plus a glove.

### Jarrod Saltalamacchia — C

Born: 5/2/1985 Age: 27
Bats: B Throws: R Height: 6' 5" Weight: 195
Breakout: 1% Improve: 17% Collapse: 3%
Attrition: 38% MLB: 71%

Comparables:
George Williams, Joe Hietpas, Johnny Blanchard

| YEAR | TEAM | LVL | AGE | PA | R | 2B | 3B | HR | RBI | BB | SO | SB | CS | AVG_OBP_SLG | TAv | BABIP | BRR | FRAA | WARP |
|---|---|---|---|---|---|---|---|---|---|---|---|---|---|---|---|---|---|---|---|
| 2009 | TEX | MLB | 24 | 310 | 34 | 12 | 0 | 9 | 34 | 22 | 97 | 0 | 2 | .233/.290/.371 | .223 | .320 | -1.9 | -0.7 | -0.1 |
| 2010 | OKL | AAA | 25 | 270 | 37 | 11 | 2 | 11 | 33 | 25 | 60 | 1 | 0 | .244/.328/.445 | .261 | .281 | -1.6 | -0.1 | 0.7 |
| 2010 | BOS | MLB | 25 | 25 | 2 | 3 | 0 | 0 | 1 | 6 | 4 | 0 | 0 | .158/.360/.316 | .256 | .200 | 0.3 | 0 | 0.1 |
| 2011 | BOS | MLB | 26 | 386 | 52 | 23 | 3 | 16 | 56 | 24 | 119 | 1 | 0 | .235/.288/.450 | .255 | .304 | -1.2 | -2.1 | 0.9 |
| 2012 | BOS | MLB | 27 | 292 | 34 | 15 | 1 | 9 | 34 | 24 | 83 | 1 | 1 | .247/.313/.415 | .254 | .322 | -0.1 | C -2, 1B -0 | 1.8 |

Now-departed GM Theo Epstein acquired Saltalamacchia at the trade deadline in 2010 as insurance against Victor Martinez leaving as a free agent. Salty did just what was needed out of him in that role, throwing out a career-high 31 percent of runners, playing in over 100 games for the first time, and posting a .215 Isolated Power. He wasn't perfect by any means—his April (547 OPS) and September (542) were horrific bookends on an otherwise quality year, and while it's mostly Tim Wakefield and his knuckler's fault (okay, almost entirely Wakefield's fault), he led the league in passed balls. Saltalamacchia was the primary starter in 2011, but that role might shift as soon as the middle of 2012, as top prospect Ryan Lavarnway will get a chance to win a regular gig this spring, and his bat looms large.

### Marco Scutaro — SS

Born: 10/30/1975 Age: 36
Bats: R Throws: R Height: 5' 11" Weight: 170
Breakout: 1% Improve: 19% Collapse: 13%
Attrition: 23% MLB: 78%

Comparables:
Barry Larkin, Alan Trammell, Mark Loretta

| YEAR | TEAM | LVL | AGE | PA | R | 2B | 3B | HR | RBI | BB | SO | SB | CS | AVG_OBP_SLG | TAv | BABIP | BRR | FRAA | WARP |
|---|---|---|---|---|---|---|---|---|---|---|---|---|---|---|---|---|---|---|---|
| 2009 | TOR | MLB | 33 | 680 | 100 | 35 | 1 | 12 | 60 | 90 | 75 | 14 | 5 | .282/.379/.409 | .283 | .304 | 0.7 | -1.3 | 4.3 |
| 2010 | BOS | MLB | 34 | 695 | 92 | 38 | 0 | 11 | 56 | 53 | 71 | 5 | 4 | .275/.333/.388 | .260 | .295 | 0.5 | 1 | 3.0 |
| 2011 | BOS | MLB | 35 | 445 | 59 | 26 | 1 | 7 | 54 | 38 | 36 | 4 | 2 | .299/.358/.423 | .274 | .312 | 2 | -0.7 | 2.5 |
| 2012 | BOS | MLB | 36 | 470 | 55 | 24 | 1 | 6 | 44 | 45 | 56 | 5 | 2 | .271/.344/.376 | .255 | .296 | -0.3 | SS -0, 2B 0 | 1.7 |

Scutaro just wrapped up the most productive two-year stretch at short for the Red Sox since the days of Nomar Garciaparra: the nearly six wins Scutaro produced in 2010–11 outnumber the total value of Sox shortstops from post-Nomar 2004 through 2009. Orlando Cabrera, Edgar Renteria, Julio Lugo, Alex Gonzalez, and Nick Green (yes, that Nick Green) combined for 5.5 WARP over 2,897 plate appearances before Scutaro came to town on a two-year, $12.5 million deal. With his 2012 option picked up, he has one more chance to add to that total.

### Kelly Shoppach    C

Born: 4/29/1980 Age: 32
Bats: R Throws: R Height: 6' 0'' Weight: 210
Breakout: 2% Improve: 25% Collapse: 15%
Attrition: 26% MLB: 86%

Comparables:
Mickey Tettleton, Johnny Bench, Todd Hundley

| YEAR | TEAM | LVL | AGE | PA | R | 2B | 3B | HR | RBI | BB | SO | SB | CS | AVG_OBP_SLG | TAv | BABIP | BRR | FRAA | WARP |
|------|------|-----|-----|-----|----|----|----|----|-----|----|----|----|----|----------------|------|-------|------|------|------|
| 2009 | CLE | MLB | 29 | 327 | 33 | 14 | 0 | 12 | 40 | 33 | 98 | 0 | 0 | .214/.335/.399 | .264 | .280 | -0.7 | -2 | 1.2 |
| 2010 | TBA | MLB | 30 | 187 | 17 | 8 | 0 | 5 | 17 | 20 | 71 | 0 | 0 | .196/.308/.342 | .250 | .313 | -1.2 | -1.1 | 0.2 |
| 2011 | TBA | MLB | 31 | 253 | 23 | 3 | 0 | 11 | 22 | 19 | 79 | 0 | 0 | .176/.268/.339 | .221 | .212 | -0.6 | -0.9 | 0.0 |
| 2012 | BOS | MLB | 32 | 250 | 29 | 11 | 0 | 9 | 28 | 22 | 83 | 0 | 0 | .221/.313/.402 | .252 | .302 | 0 | C -2 | 1.7 |

Defense didn't used to be Shoppach's strong suit back when he was originally with the Red Sox, but it has improved over the years, to the point where he gunned down over 40 percent of runners in 2011 with the Rays. Part of that was due to being the personal catcher of the man who led the league in pickoffs and who is notoriously good at holding runners (James Shields), but Shoppach's arm helped, too. While his TAv has dropped from .297 to .223 over the past four seasons, the Red Sox signed him specifically to face lefties, against whom he has hit .274/.373/.536 in his career. This leaves right-handed hurlers to the natural left-handed swing of switch-hitter Jarrod Saltalamacchia, giving the Red Sox a strong backstop platoon while Ryan Lavarnway works on his defense.

### Ryan Sweeney    RF

Born: 2/20/1985 Age: 27
Bats: L Throws: L Height: 6' 5'' Weight: 200
Breakout: 4% Improve: 35% Collapse: 6%
Attrition: 22% MLB: 76%

Comparables:
Mark Kotsay, Johnny Grubb, Johnny Groth

| YEAR | TEAM | LVL | AGE | PA | R | 2B | 3B | HR | RBI | BB | SO | SB | CS | AVG_OBP_SLG | TAv | BABIP | BRR | FRAA | WARP |
|------|------|-----|-----|-----|----|----|----|----|-----|----|----|----|----|----------------|------|-------|------|--------|------|
| 2009 | OAK | MLB | 24 | 534 | 68 | 31 | 3 | 6 | 53 | 40 | 67 | 6 | 5 | .293/.348/.407 | .276 | .327 | 4.1 | 8.9 | 3.5 |
| 2010 | OAK | MLB | 25 | 331 | 41 | 20 | 2 | 1 | 36 | 24 | 41 | 1 | 1 | .294/.342/.383 | .263 | .333 | 0.5 | -0.6 | 0.6 |
| 2011 | OAK | MLB | 26 | 299 | 34 | 11 | 3 | 1 | 25 | 33 | 48 | 1 | 1 | .265/.346/.341 | .260 | .319 | -3.2 | 0.8 | 0.7 |
| 2012 | BOS | MLB | 27 | 287 | 34 | 15 | 2 | 3 | 28 | 25 | 42 | 3 | 1 | .281/.345/.387 | .260 | .322 | -0.2 | RF 4, CF 0 | 1.0 |

A versatile defensive outfielder with on-base ability should be considered a valuable resource for a team to have cost-control over. Not that he lacks value, but as an everyday player, Sweeney falls flat. In the field, the former second round pick does have the aforementioned versatility, but he's not a 162 game center fielder. He's more of a hole-plugger, taking reps at a position that needs a warm body. At the plate, the 6-foot-4, 225-lb. athlete hits like a shortstop from the 1980s, making decent contact but managing a slugging percentage of only .341. Not to throw salt on the wound, but Cliff Pennington outslugged Sweeney, and Cliff Pennington isn't known for his slugging prowess.

### Jason Varitek    C

Born: 4/11/1972 Age: 40
Bats: B Throws: R Height: 6' 3'' Weight: 210
Breakout: 2% Improve: 16% Collapse: 9%
Attrition: 21% MLB: 52%

Comparables:
Harmon Killebrew, Todd Pratt, Greg Myers

| YEAR | TEAM | LVL | AGE | PA | R | 2B | 3B | HR | RBI | BB | SO | SB | CS | AVG_OBP_SLG | TAv | BABIP | BRR | FRAA | WARP |
|------|------|-----|-----|-----|----|----|----|----|-----|----|----|----|----|----------------|------|-------|------|------|------|
| 2009 | BOS | MLB | 37 | 425 | 41 | 24 | 0 | 14 | 51 | 54 | 90 | 0 | 0 | .209/.313/.390 | .250 | .235 | -2.4 | -1.3 | 0.8 |
| 2010 | BOS | MLB | 38 | 123 | 18 | 6 | 0 | 7 | 16 | 10 | 35 | 0 | 0 | .232/.293/.473 | .256 | .268 | -1.4 | -0.8 | 0.2 |
| 2011 | BOS | MLB | 39 | 250 | 32 | 10 | 1 | 11 | 36 | 21 | 67 | 0 | 0 | .221/.300/.423 | .257 | .264 | -2.3 | 0.4 | 0.8 |
| 2012 | BOS | MLB | 40 | 250 | 28 | 11 | 1 | 7 | 25 | 27 | 64 | 0 | 0 | .224/.315/.380 | .246 | .281 | 0 | C -1 | 1.5 |

At this point, Varitek's greatest strength is his ability to handle a pitching staff. He split playing time with Jarrod Saltalamacchia about 60/40 this year, but with far less success overall, as he was nearly an automatic out against right-handed pitchers. He also threw out just 14 percent of runners, allowing 73 of 88 baserunners to steal—and Varitek wasn't the one catching Tim Wakefield's slow floater, either. It has been a good run for Varitek, a career .256/.341/.435 catcher with a highly-regarded defensive past despite some of the present problems, but it might be the end for this 40-year-old.

### Kolbrin Vitek    3B

Born: 4/1/1989 Age: 23
Bats: R Throws: R Height: 6' 3'' Weight: 195
Breakout: 5% Improve: 17% Collapse: 1%
Attrition: 7% MLB: 37%

Comparables:
Tucker Ashford, Damion Easley, Dave Hilton

| YEAR | TEAM | LVL | AGE | PA | R | 2B | 3B | HR | RBI | BB | SO | SB | CS | AVG_OBP_SLG | TAv | BABIP | BRR | FRAA | WARP |
|------|------|-----|-----|-----|----|----|----|----|-----|----|----|----|----|----------------|------|-------|------|------|------|
| 2010 | LOW | A- | 21 | 239 | 30 | 13 | 3 | 4 | 30 | 26 | 61 | 13 | 2 | .270/.366/.422 | .276 | .367 | 0.4 | -2.4 | 0.6 |
| 2011 | SLM | A+ | 22 | 529 | 78 | 22 | 6 | 3 | 43 | 45 | 102 | 12 | 3 | .281/.350/.372 | .264 | .349 | 5.6 | 0.4 | 2.1 |
| 2012 | BOS | MLB | 23 | 250 | 24 | 11 | 1 | 1 | 19 | 15 | 58 | 3 | 1 | .233/.283/.305 | .211 | .302 | 0 | 3B 1 | -0.7 |

The question surrounding Vitek is just what is he supposed to be. He doesn't have a real defensive home, and his bat hasn't shown enough yet to make us not worry about that. Of course, he is just 22, and has all of 815 plate professional plate appearances to his credit. Dropping his punchout rate by 5 percent despite a promotion is a start, but a sub-.100 ISO for a third baseman without a glove is worrisome, especially one whose approach was supposedly as advanced as Vitek's. He's a prospect because he still projects to have better power as he fills out. He's going to need it, because given his defensive play at the hot corner, left field is calling.

**Kevin Youkilis    3B**

Born: **3/15/1979** Age: **33**
Bats: **R** Throws: **R** Height: **6' 2"** Weight: **220**
Breakout: **1%** Improve: **23%** Collapse: **2%**
Attrition: **9%** MLB: **82%**

**Comparables:**
Ron Santo, Troy Glaus, Frank Bolick

| YEAR | TEAM | LVL | AGE | PA | R | 2B | 3B | HR | RBI | BB | SO | SB | CS | AVG_OBP_SLG | TAv | BABIP | BRR | FRAA | WARP |
|------|------|-----|-----|-----|----|----|----|----|-----|----|-----|----|----|-------------|------|-------|-----|------|------|
| 2009 | BOS | MLB | 30 | 588 | 99 | 36 | 1 | 27 | 94 | 77 | 125 | 7 | 2 | .305/.413/.548 | .331 | .359 | 3.3 | 2.8 | 5.9 |
| 2010 | BOS | MLB | 31 | 435 | 77 | 26 | 5 | 19 | 62 | 58 | 67 | 4 | 1 | .307/.411/.564 | .347 | .327 | 1.7 | -1.8 | 4.4 |
| 2011 | BOS | MLB | 32 | 517 | 68 | 32 | 2 | 17 | 80 | 68 | 100 | 3 | 0 | .258/.373/.459 | .297 | .296 | 0.5 | -1.3 | 3.1 |
| 2012 | BOS | MLB | 33 | 471 | 68 | 30 | 2 | 17 | 65 | 57 | 91 | 4 | 1 | .291/.391/.503 | .313 | .337 | -0.1 | 3B 2, 1B 0 | 4.1 |

Youkilis was having a far better season than his final line indicates before a sports hernia and bursitis in his hip took him down. He played in just 22 of the team's games over the final two months of the year, hitting .190/.304/.342 in that stretch after posting a .273/.388/.486 line and .308 TAv prior to that. He

**Alfredo Aceves**

Born: **12/8/1982** Age: **29**
Bats: **R** Throws: **R** Height: **6' 4"** Weight: **220**
Breakout: **11%** Improve: **34%** Collapse: **31%**
Attrition: **9%** MLB: **96%**

**Comparables:**
Mel Rojas, Tim Belcher, Vida Blue

| YEAR | TEAM | LVL | AGE | W | L | SV | G | GS | IP | H | HR | BB | SO | EqBB9 | EqSO9 | GB% | BABIP | WHIP | ERA | FIP | FRA | WARP |
|------|------|-----|-----|----|----|----|----|----|-----|----|----|----|----|-------|-------|-----|-------|------|------|------|------|------|
| 2009 | NYA | MLB | 26 | 10 | 1 | 1 | 43 | 1 | 84 | 69 | 10 | 16 | 69 | 1.7 | 7.4 | 36% | .250 | 1.01 | 3.54 | 3.80 | 4.37 | 1.1 |
| 2010 | NYA | MLB | 27 | 3 | 0 | 1 | 10 | 0 | 12 | 10 | 1 | 4 | 2 | 3.0 | 1.5 | 50% | .200 | 1.17 | 3.00 | 5.05 | 5.76 | 0.0 |
| 2011 | BOS | MLB | 28 | 10 | 2 | 2 | 55 | 4 | 114 | 84 | 8 | 42 | 80 | 3.3 | 6.3 | 41% | .233 | 1.11 | 2.61 | 4.07 | 4.65 | 0.7 |
| 2012 | BOS | MLB | 29 | 4 | 2 | 1 | 43 | 6 | 83² | 81 | 9 | 26 | 59 | 2.7 | 6.3 | 44% | .283 | 1.27 | 3.87 | 4.12 | 4.21 | 1.1 |

It was unclear what the Red Sox would get out of the oft-injured Aceves and his balky back, but 2011 was the best-case scenario for all involved. Aceves remained healthy, and made four starts in the summer when holes opened in the rotation. His other 51 appearances came out of the bullpen, where he posted an ERA of 2.03, a K/BB of 2.3, and 93 of his 114 frames. He was useful as a long man soaking up innings after a short start—he was something of a tandem starter with Tim Wakefield for much of the year—or in high-leverage situations, where he held opponents to a 516 OPS. Master pitching strategist David Ortiz wanted Aceves to start in September, but his absence from the bullpen would have created a new set of problems.

**Matt Albers**

Born: **1/20/1983** Age: **29**
Bats: **L** Throws: **R** Height: **6' 1"** Weight: **205**
Breakout: **23%** Improve: **51%** Collapse: **29%**
Attrition: **19%** MLB: **80%**

**Comparables:**
Jon Switzer, Scott Radinsky, Justin Hampson

| YEAR | TEAM | LVL | AGE | W | L | SV | G | GS | IP | H | HR | BB | SO | EqBB9 | EqSO9 | GB% | BABIP | WHIP | ERA | FIP | FRA | WARP |
|------|------|-----|-----|----|----|----|----|----|-----|----|----|----|----|-------|-------|-----|-------|------|------|------|------|------|
| 2009 | BAL | MLB | 26 | 3 | 6 | 0 | 56 | 0 | 67 | 80 | 3 | 36 | 49 | 4.8 | 6.6 | 51% | .360 | 1.73 | 5.51 | 3.96 | 4.51 | 0.8 |
| 2010 | BAL | MLB | 27 | 5 | 3 | 0 | 62 | 0 | 75² | 78 | 6 | 34 | 49 | 4.0 | 5.8 | 58% | .306 | 1.48 | 4.52 | 4.21 | 6.21 | -0.8 |
| 2011 | BOS | MLB | 28 | 4 | 4 | 0 | 56 | 0 | 64² | 62 | 7 | 32 | 68 | 4.3 | 9.5 | 48% | .316 | 1.44 | 4.73 | 4.08 | 4.98 | 0.4 |
| 2012 | BOS | MLB | 29 | 2 | 1 | 0 | 48 | 0 | 57² | 65 | 7 | 26 | 41 | 4.1 | 6.4 | 51% | .316 | 1.57 | 5.07 | 4.71 | 5.51 | -0.2 |

Was 2011 a success or failure for the Albers experiment in Boston? The Sox signed a reliever cut loose before his second year of arbitration, one who had below-average strikeout and walk numbers, but an ability to induce grounders, and stuff that suggested strikeouts were possible. He punched out 9.5 per nine with the Red Sox, posting his first K/BB over two, but also imploded in the second half, allowing six of his seven homers over his last 29-1/3 innings. There is a lot to like about Albers despite his warts, and he remains inexpensive, under team control for one more year. In a bullpen now sans Papelbon, there is no reason for Boston to not give this arm another go.

### Scott Atchison

Born: 3/29/1976 Age: 36
Bats: R Throws: R Height: 6' 3'' Weight: 180
Breakout: 19% Improve: 40% Collapse: 42%
Attrition: 23% MLB: 84%

**Comparables:**
Bobby Shantz, Esteban Loaiza, Mark Langston

| YEAR | TEAM | LVL | AGE | W | L | SV | G | GS | IP | H | HR | BB | SO | EqBB9 | EqSO9 | GB% | BABIP | WHIP | ERA | FIP | FRA | WARP |
|---|---|---|---|---|---|---|---|---|---|---|---|---|---|---|---|---|---|---|---|---|---|---|
| 2009 | HNS | NPB | 33 | 5 | 3 | 0 | 75 | 0 | 90 | 60 | 3 | 20 | 81 | 2.0 | 8.1 | — | .247 | 0.89 | 1.70 | 2.05 | — | 0.0 |
| 2010 | BOS | MLB | 34 | 2 | 3 | 0 | 43 | 1 | 60 | 58 | 9 | 19 | 41 | 2.8 | 6.2 | 48% | .269 | 1.28 | 4.50 | 4.63 | 5.44 | -0.1 |
| 2011 | PAW | AAA | 35 | 4 | 1 | 5 | 36 | 1 | 61¹ | 47 | 5 | 9 | 64 | 1.3 | 10.6 | 49% | .298 | 0.96 | 2.64 | 2.85 | 4.40 | 0.7 |
| 2011 | BOS | MLB | 35 | 1 | 0 | 1 | 17 | 0 | 30¹ | 31 | 0 | 6 | 17 | 1.8 | 5.0 | 46% | .323 | 1.22 | 3.26 | 2.73 | 3.73 | 0.5 |
| 2012 | BOS | MLB | 36 | 1 | 1 | 0 | 30 | 0 | 44² | 46 | 5 | 13 | 35 | 2.7 | 7.1 | 44% | .310 | 1.34 | 4.16 | 3.97 | 4.53 | 0.4 |

Atchison was out of place in the 2010 bullpen. He is best suited to a mop-up role or as a long man who can soak up innings, but instead was considered the team's top middle reliever simply because everyone else failed. This past year was more his speed, as he split time between Pawtucket and Boston, throwing strike after strike resulting in lots of contact outs and few walks. In 2010, that meant tons of homers, but he got away souvenir-free this time. The Red Sox declined his option but kept him on the 40-man in order to house him in Triple-A to begin the year. Atchison has his uses, just bear in mind his limitations.

### Andrew Bailey

Born: 5/31/1984 Age: 28
Bats: R Throws: R Height: 6' 4'' Weight: 235
Breakout: 22% Improve: 49% Collapse: 28%
Attrition: 9% MLB: 94%

**Comparables:**
Juan Rincon, Manny Delcarmen, Derrick Turnbow

| YEAR | TEAM | LVL | AGE | W | L | SV | G | GS | IP | H | HR | BB | SO | EqBB9 | EqSO9 | GB% | BABIP | WHIP | ERA | FIP | FRA | WARP |
|---|---|---|---|---|---|---|---|---|---|---|---|---|---|---|---|---|---|---|---|---|---|---|
| 2009 | OAK | MLB | 25 | 6 | 3 | 26 | 68 | 0 | 83¹ | 49 | 5 | 24 | 91 | 2.6 | 9.8 | 42% | .220 | 0.88 | 1.84 | 2.60 | 2.95 | 2.2 |
| 2010 | OAK | MLB | 26 | 1 | 3 | 25 | 47 | 0 | 49 | 34 | 3 | 13 | 42 | 2.4 | 7.7 | 39% | .240 | 0.96 | 1.47 | 2.92 | 3.20 | 0.8 |
| 2011 | OAK | MLB | 27 | 0 | 4 | 24 | 42 | 0 | 41² | 34 | 3 | 12 | 41 | 2.6 | 8.9 | 38% | .274 | 1.10 | 3.24 | 2.89 | 3.07 | 1.0 |
| 2012 | BOS | MLB | 28 | 2 | 1 | 18 | 36 | 0 | 37 | 33 | 4 | 14 | 35 | 3.5 | 8.6 | 42% | .290 | 1.27 | 3.50 | 3.85 | 3.80 | 0.6 |

One of the hottest relief commodities on the market, Bailey was secured by the Red Sox after Papelbon's departure. The big righty closer has fought to stay healthy during his career, but when on the mound, the 27-year-old will solidify any bullpen. Armed with a husky frame, a husky plus fastball, a darting cutter, and a show curve, Bailey has the stuff to miss bats and the command profile to not only throw strikes, but to throw quality strikes with all three offerings. Next question: will the Boston media pressure cooker suit him or steam him? We'll find out.

### Daniel Bard

Born: 6/25/1985 Age: 27
Bats: R Throws: R Height: 6' 5'' Weight: 200
Breakout: 26% Improve: 54% Collapse: 25%
Attrition: 13% MLB: 96%

**Comparables:**
Billy Sadler, Bryan Harvey, Rich Gossage

| YEAR | TEAM | LVL | AGE | W | L | SV | G | GS | IP | H | HR | BB | SO | EqBB9 | EqSO9 | GB% | BABIP | WHIP | ERA | FIP | FRA | WARP |
|---|---|---|---|---|---|---|---|---|---|---|---|---|---|---|---|---|---|---|---|---|---|---|
| 2009 | BOS | MLB | 24 | 2 | 2 | 1 | 49 | 0 | 49¹ | 41 | 5 | 22 | 63 | 4.0 | 11.5 | 48% | .313 | 1.28 | 3.65 | 3.43 | 3.01 | 1.5 |
| 2010 | BOS | MLB | 25 | 1 | 2 | 3 | 73 | 0 | 74² | 45 | 6 | 30 | 76 | 3.6 | 9.2 | 47% | .218 | 1.00 | 1.93 | 3.34 | 3.90 | 1.0 |
| 2011 | BOS | MLB | 26 | 2 | 9 | 1 | 70 | 0 | 73 | 46 | 5 | 24 | 74 | 3.0 | 9.1 | 54% | .230 | 0.96 | 3.33 | 2.99 | 3.88 | 1.1 |
| 2012 | BOS | MLB | 27 | 3 | 1 | 2 | 57 | 0 | 59 | 50 | 6 | 28 | 63 | 4.3 | 9.5 | 49% | .290 | 1.32 | 3.60 | 3.81 | 3.91 | 0.9 |

Before Bard's rough September, in which he allowed 13 runs over 11 innings thanks to iffy mechanics that affected his fastball command, he went 25 appearances and 26 1/3 innings without allowing a run, posting a 25/6 K/BB. The former stretch seems to be the only one anyone remembers, especially while discussing Bard as a Jonathan Papelbon replacement. Gauging relievers based on a season's worth of work is difficult—if it weren't, building a good bullpen wouldn't be such an issue for most teams—so predicting Bard's success or failure as a closer on a few bad frames isn't wise. There is much more of that dominant mid-season streak on his resume than horrific struggles, and so long as his mechanics are in check, the great Bard is what we will be seeing more of. That's just one more reason the Red Sox plan to try Bard out as a starter this spring, rather than investing in the lightweight free agent market.

### Josh Beckett

Born: 5/15/1980 Age: 32
Bats: R Throws: R Height: 6' 5'' Weight: 190
Breakout: 18% Improve: 34% Collapse: 36%
Attrition: 6% MLB: 92%

**Comparables:**
Rafael Betancourt, Curt Schilling, Rick Aguilera

| YEAR | TEAM | LVL | AGE | W | L | SV | G | GS | IP | H | HR | BB | SO | EqBB9 | EqSO9 | GB% | BABIP | WHIP | ERA | FIP | FRA | WARP |
|---|---|---|---|---|---|---|---|---|---|---|---|---|---|---|---|---|---|---|---|---|---|---|
| 2009 | BOS | MLB | 29 | 17 | 6 | 0 | 32 | 32 | 212¹ | 198 | 25 | 55 | 199 | 2.3 | 8.4 | 48% | .292 | 1.19 | 3.86 | 3.68 | 4.27 | 3.5 |
| 2010 | BOS | MLB | 30 | 6 | 6 | 0 | 21 | 21 | 127² | 151 | 20 | 45 | 116 | 3.2 | 8.2 | 47% | .341 | 1.54 | 5.78 | 4.51 | 5.05 | 0.5 |
| 2011 | BOS | MLB | 31 | 13 | 7 | 0 | 30 | 30 | 193 | 146 | 21 | 52 | 175 | 2.4 | 8.2 | 42% | .249 | 1.03 | 2.89 | 3.61 | 3.83 | 3.1 |
| 2012 | BOS | MLB | 32 | 12 | 6 | 0 | 24 | 24 | 152 | 152 | 17 | 38 | 143 | 2.3 | 8.5 | 45% | .313 | 1.25 | 3.81 | 3.53 | 4.14 | 2.1 |

Beckett's seasons all come down to how he is feeling. When he was younger, blisters were what held him back. As he has aged, his back has become the source of his problems. In 2010, back pain kept him from commanding his curveball, forcing him to rely on his fastball. His back felt fine this past year, though, and Beckett—excepting September, when it was physically impossible for any Red Sox starter to pitch well—was the Beckett of old. Won't we all feel silly for getting on our soap boxes when it turns out the key ingredient in the Colonel's recipe has restorative back-healing properties?

## Michael Bowden

Born: 9/9/1986 Age: 25
Bats: R Throws: R Height: 6' 4" Weight: 215
Breakout: 14% Improve: 64% Collapse: 11%
Attrition: 11% MLB: 88%

**Comparables:**
Osiris Matos, Jesse Chavez, Brandon McCarthy

| YEAR | TEAM | LVL | AGE | W | L | SV | G | GS | IP | H | HR | BB | SO | EqBB9 | EqSO9 | GB% | BABIP | WHIP | ERA | FIP | FRA | WARP |
|---|---|---|---|---|---|---|---|---|---|---|---|---|---|---|---|---|---|---|---|---|---|---|
| 2009 | PAW | AAA | 22 | 4 | 6 | 0 | 24 | 24 | 126¹ | 106 | 11 | 47 | 88 | 3.3 | 6.3 | 32% | .259 | 1.21 | 3.14 | 4.03 | 4.88 | 0.6 |
| 2009 | BOS | MLB | 22 | 1 | 1 | 0 | 8 | 1 | 16 | 23 | 3 | 6 | 12 | 3.4 | 6.8 | 42% | .370 | 1.81 | 9.56 | 5.21 | 6.95 | -0.1 |
| 2010 | PAW | AAA | 23 | 6 | 4 | 1 | 31 | 16 | 105² | 58 | 9 | 26 | 56 | 3.2 | 6.6 | 23% | .240 | 1.14 | 3.66 | 4.34 | 4.64 | 0.9 |
| 2010 | BOS | MLB | 23 | 0 | 1 | 0 | 14 | 0 | 15¹ | 20 | 2 | 4 | 13 | 2.3 | 7.6 | 27% | .383 | 1.57 | 4.70 | 3.83 | 5.80 | -0.1 |
| 2011 | PAW | AAA | 24 | 2 | 2 | 16 | 41 | 0 | 52² | 43 | 5 | 18 | 61 | 3.1 | 10.4 | 39% | .297 | 1.16 | 2.73 | 3.24 | 4.49 | 0.7 |
| 2011 | BOS | MLB | 24 | 0 | 0 | 0 | 14 | 0 | 20 | 19 | 3 | 11 | 17 | 4.9 | 7.7 | 29% | .271 | 1.50 | 4.05 | 4.96 | 4.82 | 0.1 |
| *2012* | *BOS* | *MLB* | *25* | *2* | *1* | *0* | *15* | *2* | *29²* | *32* | *4* | *11* | *22* | *3.4* | *6.8* | *36%* | *.309* | *1.45* | *4.64* | *4.59* | *5.04* | *0.1* |

Bowden scrapped the curveball that once made him a top prospect, but which had grown flat and easy to mash. He replaced it with a cutter, and knowing he would be relieving exclusively in 2011, dominated Triple-A in his new full-time bullpen gig. As many have learned before him, though, Triple-A is not the majors, and though he kept the hits per nine under double-digits for the first time, he also allowed too many homers and walks. Bowden might still turn into a bullpen piece and have a career,

control cropped up again in 2011. In the first half, Britton couldn't find the plate, walking as many as he struck out. In the second half, Britton found the strike zone, but opponents hit .323 against him. Britton was one of Boston's top pitching prospects, but like fellow command-less hurler Stolmy Pimentel, no one knows quite what to make of him right now.

## Clay Buchholz

Born: 8/14/1984 Age: 27
Bats: L Throws: R Height: 6' 4" Weight: 190
Breakout: 27% Improve: 53% Collapse: 19%
Attrition: 11% MLB: 94%

**Comparables:**
Phil Coke, Billy Pierce, Jon Lester

| YEAR | TEAM | LVL | AGE | W | L | SV | G | GS | IP | H | HR | BB | SO | EqBB9 | EqSO9 | GB% | BABIP | WHIP | ERA | FIP | FRA | WARP |
|---|---|---|---|---|---|---|---|---|---|---|---|---|---|---|---|---|---|---|---|---|---|---|
| 2009 | PAW | AAA | 24 | 7 | 2 | 0 | 17 | 16 | 99 | 67 | 7 | 30 | 89 | 2.7 | 8.1 | 54% | .231 | 0.98 | 2.36 | 3.18 | 4.23 | 1.0 |
| 2009 | BOS | MLB | 24 | 7 | 4 | 0 | 16 | 16 | 92 | 91 | 13 | 36 | 68 | 3.5 | 6.7 | 54% | .281 | 1.38 | 4.21 | 4.74 | 5.27 | 1.0 |
| 2010 | BOS | MLB | 25 | 17 | 7 | 0 | 28 | 28 | 173² | 142 | 9 | 67 | 120 | 3.5 | 6.2 | 52% | .263 | 1.20 | 2.33 | 3.58 | 4.18 | 2.1 |
| 2011 | BOS | MLB | 26 | 6 | 3 | 0 | 14 | 14 | 82² | 76 | 10 | 31 | 60 | 3.4 | 6.5 | 51% | .265 | 1.29 | 3.48 | 4.38 | 4.33 | 1.0 |
| *2012* | *BOS* | *MLB* | *27* | *7* | *3* | *0* | *14* | *14* | *85¹* | *82* | *9* | *33* | *73* | *3.5* | *7.7* | *48%* | *.298* | *1.35* | *3.92* | *4.02* | *4.26* | *1.1* |

Buchholz allowed more homers in his 82 innings than he did in all of 2010, but a huge percentage of that damage came in his first start of the season against the Rangers, when he gave up four of his 10 bombs. Otherwise, he was the Buchholz we got used to seeing the year before, inducing grounders and weak contact with his fastball/cutter combo, and missing bats with his finest pitch, his change. Even though he was successful, he never seemed as comfortable on the mound, showing occasionally diminished velocity and iffy command. Was a stress fracture in his spine that was thought to be nothing actually more serious? Post-trade deadline tests said yes. Buchholz was ready to pitch again by the time the year ended, meaning he will be ready to go in the battle against FIP once more in 2012.

## Felix Doubront

Born: 10/23/1987 Age: 24
Bats: L Throws: L Height: 6' 3" Weight: 165
Breakout: 28% Improve: 51% Collapse: 27%
Attrition: 17% MLB: 87%

**Comparables:**
Juan Nieves, Jake Woods, Jeff Francis

| YEAR | TEAM | LVL | AGE | W | L | SV | G | GS | IP | H | HR | BB | SO | EqBB9 | EqSO9 | GB% | BABIP | WHIP | ERA | FIP | FRA | WARP |
|---|---|---|---|---|---|---|---|---|---|---|---|---|---|---|---|---|---|---|---|---|---|---|
| 2009 | PME | AA | 21 | 8 | 6 | 0 | 26 | 26 | 121 | 119 | 8 | 52 | 101 | 3.9 | 7.5 | 47% | .305 | 1.41 | 3.35 | 3.84 | 4.94 | 0.7 |
| 2010 | PME | AA | 22 | 4 | 0 | 0 | 8 | 8 | 43 | 24 | 0 | 9 | 22 | 3.6 | 8.0 | 45% | .316 | 1.30 | 2.51 | 3.34 | 4.03 | 0.7 |
| 2010 | PAW | AAA | 22 | 4 | 3 | 0 | 9 | 8 | 37 | 18 | 0 | 8 | 21 | 3.9 | 8.3 | 53% | .281 | 1.41 | 3.16 | 3.29 | 4.47 | 0.5 |
| 2010 | BOS | MLB | 22 | 2 | 2 | 2 | 12 | 3 | 25 | 27 | 3 | 10 | 23 | 3.6 | 8.3 | 46% | .320 | 1.48 | 4.32 | 4.09 | 4.17 | 0.3 |
| 2011 | PAW | AAA | 23 | 2 | 4 | 0 | 18 | 16 | 70¹ | 65 | 10 | 26 | 61 | 3.3 | 7.8 | 48% | .276 | 1.29 | 4.22 | 4.55 | 5.08 | 0.7 |
| 2011 | BOS | MLB | 23 | 0 | 0 | 1 | 11 | 0 | 10¹ | 12 | 1 | 8 | 6 | 7.0 | 5.2 | 45% | .344 | 1.94 | 6.10 | 5.48 | 7.16 | -0.2 |
| *2012* | *BOS* | *MLB* | *24* | *2* | *2* | *0* | *9* | *6* | *29²* | *35* | *4* | *14* | *20* | *4.2* | *6.1* | *44%* | *.324* | *1.65* | *5.78* | *5.02* | *6.28* | *-0.2* |

It is unfair, but if you're looking for one particular person to blame for the lack of pitching depth in September, Doubront is a place to start. Doubront was supposed to be ready to go as a starter when the Red Sox needed him—not Andrew Miller, not Kyle Weiland—but he came to camp out of shape, and it came back to bite him. Forearm inflammation, a groin strain, and a hamstring strain all caused him to miss time. Now, out of options and with 2011 something of a wasted year, he'll try to make things work out of Boston's bullpen.

### Rich Hill

Born: 3/11/1980 Age: 32
Bats: L Throws: L Height: 6' 6'' Weight: 205
Breakout: 23% Improve: 60% Collapse: 22%
Attrition: 11% MLB: 91%

Comparables:
Micah Bowie, Jack Taschner, Randy Myers

| YEAR | TEAM | LVL | AGE | W | L | SV | G | GS | IP | H | HR | BB | SO | EqBB9 | EqSO9 | GB% | BABIP | WHIP | ERA | FIP | FRA | WARP |
|------|------|-----|-----|---|---|----|----|----|-----|-----|----|----|----|-------|-------|-----|-------|------|------|------|------|------|
| 2009 | BAL | MLB | 29 | 3 | 3 | 0 | 14 | 13 | 57² | 68 | 7 | 40 | 46 | 6.2 | 7.2 | 35% | .341 | 1.87 | 7.80 | 5.26 | 6.12 | 0.0 |
| 2010 | PAW | AAA | 30 | 3 | 1 | 0 | 19 | 6 | 53 | 33 | 2 | 21 | 40 | 4.9 | 9.3 | 51% | .320 | 1.40 | 3.74 | 4.10 | 4.92 | 0.2 |
| 2010 | MEM | AAA | 30 | 4 | 3 | 0 | 23 | 4 | 46 | 26 | 4 | 21 | 35 | 5.9 | 9.2 | 39% | .306 | 1.41 | 4.30 | 5.36 | 5.83 | -0.2 |
| 2010 | BOS | MLB | 30 | 1 | 0 | 0 | 6 | 0 | 4 | 5 | 0 | 1 | 3 | 2.2 | 6.8 | 57% | .357 | 1.50 | 0.00 | 2.30 | 5.27 | 0.0 |
| 2011 | BOS | MLB | 31 | 0 | 0 | 0 | 9 | 0 | 8 | 3 | 0 | 3 | 12 | 3.4 | 13.5 | 36% | .214 | 0.75 | 0.00 | 1.56 | 3.44 | 0.2 |
| 2012 | BOS | MLB | 32 | 1 | 0 | 0 | 8 | 1 | 15 | 15 | 2 | 8 | 13 | 4.7 | 8.0 | 41% | .300 | 1.49 | 4.69 | 4.80 | 5.10 | 0.0 |

Fueled entirely by our suggestion in *Baseball Prospectus 2011* that Rich Hill be freed, the Red Sox gave him an opportunity to be their lefty out of the pen. Eight innings, 12 strikeouts and one walk later, everyone involved looked brilliant . . . but then came Tommy John surgery, ending Hill's season, and forcing Boston to look elsewhere for a southpaw savior. Too many lefties in the pen—and without any options remaining among them—meant Hill wasn't tendered a contract, but the Red Sox hope to stash him in the minors if no one else bites on his recovery time availability first.

### Bobby Jenks

Born: 3/14/1981 Age: 31
Bats: R Throws: R Height: 6' 4'' Weight: 270
Breakout: 12% Improve: 40% Collapse: 34%
Attrition: 2% MLB: 93%

Comparables:
Chad Qualls, Roger Clemens, Greg McMichael

| YEAR | TEAM | LVL | AGE | W | L | SV | G | GS | IP | H | HR | BB | SO | EqBB9 | EqSO9 | GB% | BABIP | WHIP | ERA | FIP | FRA | WARP |
|------|------|-----|-----|---|---|----|----|----|-----|----|----|----|----|-------|-------|-----|-------|------|------|------|------|------|
| 2009 | CHA | MLB | 28 | 3 | 4 | 29 | 52 | 0 | 53¹ | 52 | 9 | 16 | 49 | 2.7 | 8.3 | 48% | .283 | 1.27 | 3.71 | 4.51 | 4.69 | 0.5 |
| 2010 | CHA | MLB | 29 | 1 | 3 | 27 | 55 | 0 | 52² | 54 | 3 | 18 | 61 | 3.1 | 10.4 | 60% | .354 | 1.37 | 4.44 | 2.55 | 3.85 | 0.9 |
| 2011 | BOS | MLB | 30 | 2 | 2 | 0 | 19 | 0 | 15² | 22 | 1 | 12 | 17 | 7.5 | 9.8 | 40% | .429 | 2.23 | 6.32 | 4.02 | 5.26 | 0.0 |
| 2012 | BOS | MLB | 31 | 1 | 1 | 7 | 25 | 0 | 23 | 22 | 2 | 7 | 20 | 2.8 | 8.0 | 54% | .305 | 1.28 | 3.58 | 3.51 | 3.90 | 0.4 |

Jenks's disappointing biceps strain doesn't sound so bad when you consider what he has been through since the season ended. He underwent offseason surgery to repair a calcified ligament causing nerve damage in his spine. The ligament was discovered while treating Jenks for colitis, but surgery could not be performed immediately thanks to a pulmonary embolism in Jenks's lungs. Thankfully, Jenks is expected to be healthy and ready to go in the spring. Assuming he is indeed the Jenks of old, with the way the closer market exploded this past winter, his two-year, $12 million contract all of a sudden looks fantastic even with the lost season in mind.

### John Lackey

Born: 10/23/1978 Age: 33
Bats: R Throws: R Height: 6' 7'' Weight: 200
Breakout: 34% Improve: 42% Collapse: 32%
Attrition: 24% MLB: 85%

Comparables:
Bobby Tiefenauer, Bartolo Colon, Dan Giese

| YEAR | TEAM | LVL | AGE | W | L | SV | G | GS | IP | H | HR | BB | SO | EqBB9 | EqSO9 | GB% | BABIP | WHIP | ERA | FIP | FRA | WARP |
|------|------|-----|-----|----|----|----|----|----|------|-----|----|----|-----|-------|-------|-----|-------|------|------|------|------|------|
| 2009 | ANA | MLB | 30 | 11 | 8 | 0 | 27 | 27 | 176¹ | 177 | 17 | 47 | 139 | 2.4 | 7.1 | 47% | .304 | 1.27 | 3.83 | 3.77 | 4.26 | 2.2 |
| 2010 | BOS | MLB | 31 | 14 | 11 | 0 | 33 | 33 | 215 | 233 | 18 | 72 | 156 | 3.0 | 6.5 | 46% | .320 | 1.42 | 4.40 | 3.81 | 4.50 | 2.0 |
| 2011 | BOS | MLB | 32 | 12 | 12 | 0 | 28 | 28 | 160 | 203 | 20 | 56 | 108 | 3.2 | 6.1 | 42% | .340 | 1.62 | 6.41 | 4.74 | 5.20 | 0.5 |
| 2012 | BOS | MLB | 33 | 12 | 7 | 0 | 26 | 26 | 157¹ | 175 | 17 | 44 | 118 | 2.5 | 6.8 | 45% | .324 | 1.39 | 4.59 | 3.95 | 4.99 | 0.7 |

"Everything sucks in my life right now," he told the press in May. How do you snark at that? Lackey's 2011 was the worst ever for a Red Sox starting pitcher with as many innings pitched, but there are two causes to point to. On the side of things we can't measure, Lackey's wife had a miscarriage, underwent treatment for cancer, and the two filed for divorce late in the season. Then there was Lackey's elbow, which required a cortisone shot early in the year, deteriorated as the season dragged on, and finally gave out. Ignore the projection: he elected Tommy John surgery, setting him up for a 2013 return. His contract was written with this possibility in mind, so while the Red Sox will pay him to do nothing in 2012, Lackey will pitch in exchange for next-to-nothing (the league minimum) in 2015, after his initial five-year deal ends.

### Jon Lester

Born: 1/7/1984 Age: 28
Bats: L Throws: L Height: 6' 3'' Weight: 190
Breakout: 18% Improve: 43% Collapse: 31%
Attrition: 7% MLB: 93%

Comparables:
Jeff Calhoun, Craig Breslow, Rob Murphy

| YEAR | TEAM | LVL | AGE | W | L | SV | G | GS | IP | H | HR | BB | SO | EqBB9 | EqSO9 | GB% | BABIP | WHIP | ERA | FIP | FRA | WARP |
|------|------|-----|-----|----|---|----|----|----|------|-----|----|----|-----|-------|-------|-----|-------|------|------|------|------|------|
| 2009 | BOS | MLB | 25 | 15 | 8 | 0 | 32 | 32 | 203¹ | 186 | 20 | 64 | 225 | 2.8 | 10.0 | 49% | .314 | 1.23 | 3.41 | 3.20 | 3.73 | 4.6 |
| 2010 | BOS | MLB | 26 | 19 | 9 | 0 | 32 | 32 | 208 | 167 | 14 | 83 | 225 | 3.6 | 9.7 | 54% | .291 | 1.20 | 3.25 | 3.10 | 4.33 | 2.9 |
| 2011 | BOS | MLB | 27 | 15 | 9 | 0 | 31 | 31 | 191² | 166 | 20 | 75 | 182 | 3.5 | 8.5 | 51% | .287 | 1.26 | 3.47 | 3.86 | 4.43 | 2.0 |
| 2012 | BOS | MLB | 28 | 13 | 6 | 0 | 26 | 26 | 166¹ | 157 | 16 | 60 | 160 | 3.3 | 8.7 | 48% | .311 | 1.31 | 3.69 | 3.61 | 4.01 | 2.5 |

A poor finish to the year marred what was otherwise a fine campaign by Lester. It wasn't just September, either, when the Red Sox went 1-5 in his six starts and his season ERA climbed half-a-run, but August, too, when his trouble with command started. Lester, who has walked 3.3 per nine over the last three years, walked 4.5 per over the last two months, driving up his pitch count and shortening his starts at a time when the last thing the bullpen needed was to pitch more. A pitcher as good as Lester is allowed to struggle; even Roy Halladay has his bad days. Further removed from the latissimus dorsi strain that sidelined him in July, it's possible PECOTA's crush on him will be justified.

### Daisuke Matsuzaka
Born: 9/13/1980 Age: 31
Bats: R Throws: R Height: 6' 1'' Weight: 190
Breakout: 16% Improve: 45% Collapse: 23%
Attrition: 12% MLB: 93%

**Comparables:**
Mel Rojas, Don Elston, Aurelio Lopez

| YEAR | TEAM | LVL | AGE | W | L | SV | G | GS | IP | H | HR | BB | SO | EqBB9 | EqSO9 | GB% | BABIP | WHIP | ERA | FIP | FRA | WARP |
|------|------|-----|-----|---|---|----|----|----|-----|-----|----|----|-----|-------|-------|-----|-------|------|------|------|------|------|
| 2009 | BOS | MLB | 28 | 4 | 6 | 0 | 12 | 12 | 59¹ | 81 | 10 | 30 | 54 | 4.6 | 8.2 | 35% | .382 | 1.87 | 5.76 | 5.13 | 4.76 | 1.0 |
| 2010 | BOS | MLB | 29 | 9 | 6 | 0 | 25 | 25 | 153² | 137 | 13 | 74 | 133 | 4.3 | 7.8 | 35% | .286 | 1.37 | 4.69 | 4.02 | 4.87 | 1.0 |
| 2011 | BOS | MLB | 30 | 3 | 3 | 0 | 8 | 7 | 37¹ | 32 | 4 | 23 | 26 | 5.5 | 6.3 | 32% | .248 | 1.47 | 5.30 | 4.99 | 5.48 | 0.1 |
| *2012* | *BOS* | *MLB* | *31* | *4* | *2* | *0* | *9* | *9* | *51²* | *51* | *6* | *25* | *47* | *4.3* | *8.3* | *39%* | *.307* | *1.46* | *4.44* | *4.35* | *4.83* | *0.3* |

Matsuzaka frustrates Red Sox fans to no end thanks to his nibbling approach. That said, had he been healthy in 2011, rather than undergoing Tommy John surgery, it's likely the team's September performance would have been a footnote as they coasted, rather than a collapse. For all the aggravation surrounding Dice-K, he tends to be average, and that is something the Red Sox sorely lacked while relying on Tim Wakefield, Kyle Weiland, and Andrew Miller to fill in. Matsuzaka could be back by the end of 2012, but he has a history of healing as slowly as he works on the mound, meaning his final appearance in a Boston uniform might have already occurred.

It's amazing what adding a pitch can do. Melancon always had a lively fastball and an unhittable yakker, and he tended to be as successful as his control of the curve was in any given game. But throw in a cutter, and voilà, instant closer! He was ruthless against right-handed batters while allowing a .344 on-base percentage to lefties, but his overall effectiveness in 2011 was quite closer-worthy. The Red Sox swapped Jed Lowrie and Kyle Weiland for him, hoping that Melancon can take on high leverage situations, allowing for the trial run of Daniel Bard: Starting Pitcher during spring training.

### Andrew Miller
Born: 5/21/1985 Age: 27
Bats: L Throws: L Height: 6' 7'' Weight: 210
Breakout: 17% Improve: 61% Collapse: 18%
Attrition: 14% MLB: 87%

**Comparables:**
Felix Heredia, Steve Foucault, Bill Simas

| YEAR | TEAM | LVL | AGE | W | L | SV | G | GS | IP | H | HR | BB | SO | EqBB9 | EqSO9 | GB% | BABIP | WHIP | ERA | FIP | FRA | WARP |
|------|------|-----|-----|---|---|----|----|----|-----|-----|----|----|-----|-------|-------|-----|-------|------|------|------|------|------|
| 2009 | FLO | MLB | 24 | 3 | 5 | 0 | 20 | 14 | 80 | 85 | 7 | 43 | 59 | 4.8 | 6.6 | 50% | .313 | 1.60 | 4.84 | 4.41 | 4.93 | 0.5 |
| 2010 | JAX | AA | 25 | 1 | 8 | 0 | 18 | 18 | 85¹ | 72 | 4 | 47 | 49 | 6.4 | 7.0 | 51% | .374 | 1.86 | 6.01 | 4.81 | 6.05 | -1.0 |
| 2010 | FLO | MLB | 25 | 1 | 5 | 0 | 9 | 7 | 32² | 51 | 6 | 26 | 28 | 7.2 | 7.7 | 42% | .429 | 2.36 | 8.54 | 6.26 | 6.81 | -0.6 |
| 2011 | PAW | AAA | 26 | 1 | 3 | 0 | 13 | 12 | 65² | 42 | 2 | 35 | 61 | 4.8 | 8.4 | 51% | .237 | 1.17 | 2.47 | 3.51 | 3.68 | 1.5 |
| 2011 | BOS | MLB | 26 | 6 | 3 | 0 | 17 | 12 | 65 | 77 | 8 | 41 | 50 | 5.7 | 6.9 | 49% | .342 | 1.82 | 5.54 | 5.15 | 5.75 | 0.0 |
| *2012* | *BOS* | *MLB* | *27* | *5* | *5* | *0* | *16* | *16* | *74²* | *85* | *8* | *43* | *58* | *5.2* | *7.0* | *52%* | *.333* | *1.72* | *5.67* | *4.77* | *6.16* | *-0.4* |

Miller didn't damage the Red Sox in the way you would think, despite stats that suggest the opposite. Yes, he had an ERA of 5.54 that wouldn't have looked good even 10 years ago when offenses dominated, but the Red Sox went 9-3 in his starts, thanks to over *eight runs of support* per game. In a word, both the Sox and Miller were lucky. Despite a stretch in the minors and his first few appearances in the majors that suggested, hey, Miller *does* know where the strike zone is, he eventually turned back into a 6-foot-7, Andrew Miller-shaped pumpkin.

### Franklin Morales
Born: 1/24/1986 Age: 26
Bats: L Throws: L Height: 6' 1'' Weight: 170
Breakout: 27% Improve: 59% Collapse: 21%
Attrition: 10% MLB: 96%

**Comparables:**
Bob Cain, Felix Heredia, Pete Richert

| YEAR | TEAM | LVL | AGE | W | L | SV | G | GS | IP | H | HR | BB | SO | EqBB9 | EqSO9 | GB% | BABIP | WHIP | ERA | FIP | FRA | WARP |
|------|------|-----|-----|---|---|----|----|----|-----|-----|----|----|-----|-------|-------|-----|-------|------|------|------|------|------|
| 2009 | CSP | AAA | 23 | 2 | 2 | 0 | 8 | 8 | 41¹ | 39 | 4 | 19 | 37 | 4.1 | 8.1 | 45% | .310 | 1.40 | 3.49 | 4.52 | 5.28 | 0.4 |
| 2009 | COL | MLB | 23 | 3 | 2 | 7 | 40 | 2 | 40 | 38 | 4 | 23 | 41 | 5.2 | 9.2 | 31% | .318 | 1.52 | 4.50 | 4.11 | 4.41 | 0.7 |
| 2010 | CSP | AAA | 24 | 3 | 0 | 1 | 24 | 0 | 30¹ | 15 | 2 | 12 | 22 | 5.6 | 10.1 | 41% | .289 | 1.29 | 2.67 | 4.75 | 5.30 | 0.1 |
| 2010 | COL | MLB | 24 | 0 | 4 | 3 | 35 | 0 | 28² | 28 | 5 | 24 | 27 | 7.5 | 8.5 | 40% | .287 | 1.81 | 6.28 | 6.32 | 6.22 | -0.3 |
| 2011 | COL | MLB | 25 | 0 | 1 | 0 | 14 | 0 | 14 | 10 | 2 | 8 | 11 | 5.1 | 7.1 | 33% | .216 | 1.29 | 3.86 | 4.99 | 5.25 | 0.0 |
| 2011 | BOS | MLB | 25 | 1 | 1 | 0 | 36 | 0 | 32¹ | 30 | 4 | 11 | 31 | 3.1 | 8.6 | 31% | .306 | 1.27 | 3.62 | 3.96 | 4.72 | 0.2 |
| *2012* | *BOS* | *MLB* | *26* | *2* | *1* | *1* | *39* | *0* | *37²* | *40* | *5* | *22* | *30* | *5.2* | *7.0* | *44%* | *.309* | *1.63* | *5.27* | *5.09* | *5.73* | *-0.2* |

Freed from Coors Field, where his stuff was held back by the lack of air to interact with, Morales finally started to pitch well. He wasn't at the level he was expected to be years ago, when he was considered one of the top prospects in the game, but his 32 innings in Boston featured his best-ever K/BB, as well as curves and fastballs with movement. Morales and the man he replaced, Rich Hill, should be reminders—especially for the Red Sox, who perpetually struggle to build a quality bullpen—that nifty relief pieces don't always have to cost millions of dollars. Especially if you can take them from Colorado and into air density levels that don't guarantee failure.

### Anthony Ranaudo

Born: 9/9/1989 Age: 22
Bats: R Throws: R Height: 6' 8" Weight: 231
Breakout: 19% Improve: 50% Collapse: 25%
Attrition: 12% MLB: 75%

Comparables:
Kyle Davies, Jon Warden, Ryan Tucker

| YEAR | TEAM | LVL | AGE | W | L | SV | G | GS | IP | H | HR | BB | SO | EqBB9 | EqSO9 | GB% | BABIP | WHIP | ERA | FIP | FRA | WARP |
|------|------|-----|-----|---|---|----|----|----|------|----|----|----|----|-------|-------|-----|-------|------|------|------|------|------|
| 2011 | GRN | A | 21 | 4 | 1 | 0 | 10 | 10 | 46 | 35 | 4 | 16 | 50 | 3.1 | 9.8 | 41% | .274 | 1.11 | 3.33 | 3.79 | 3.55 | 1.2 |
| 2011 | SLM | A+ | 21 | 5 | 5 | 0 | 16 | 16 | 81 | 80 | 6 | 30 | 67 | 3.3 | 7.4 | 45% | .315 | 1.36 | 4.33 | 3.97 | 4.31 | 1.2 |
| 2012 | BOS | MLB | 22 | 2 | 2 | 0 | 6 | 6 | 30² | 35 | 4 | 15 | 20 | 4.5 | 5.9 | 43% | .317 | 1.65 | 5.64 | 5.06 | 6.14 | -0.2 |

Ranaudo was Boston's top pitching prospect heading into 2011, but his performance at two levels might have tempered expectations for him. Single-A was no issue, but the 21-year-old Ranaudo struggled to impress at High-A Salem, losing more than two strikeouts per nine, dropping expectations for him to a two or a three in the majors, at best. He will need consistent mechanics if he ever wants to reach that point, and must improve his changeup, a pitch that as of right now is not quite average and unable to complement his bender or fastball.

### Junichi Tazawa

Born: 6/6/1986 Age: 26
Bats: R Throws: R Height: 6' 0" Weight: 180
Breakout: 33% Improve: 55% Collapse: 18%
Attrition: 20% MLB: 92%

Comparables:
Fernando Nieve, Ross Ohlendorf, Catfish Hunter

| YEAR | TEAM | LVL | AGE | W | L | SV | G | GS | IP | H | HR | BB | SO | EqBB9 | EqSO9 | GB% | BABIP | WHIP | ERA | FIP | FRA | WARP |
|------|------|-----|-----|---|---|----|----|----|------|----|----|----|----|-------|-------|-----|-------|------|------|------|------|------|
| 2009 | PME | AA | 23 | 9 | 5 | 0 | 18 | 18 | 98 | 80 | 8 | 26 | 88 | 2.4 | 8.1 | 45% | .270 | 1.08 | 2.57 | 3.29 | 3.84 | 1.8 |
| 2009 | BOS | MLB | 23 | 2 | 3 | 0 | 6 | 4 | 25¹ | 43 | 4 | 9 | 13 | 3.2 | 4.6 | 23% | .386 | 2.05 | 7.46 | 5.59 | 5.75 | 0.1 |
| 2011 | PME | AA | 25 | 3 | 2 | 0 | 8 | 2 | 23 | 20 | 3 | 7 | 27 | 2.7 | 10.6 | 33% | .288 | 1.17 | 4.70 | 3.94 | 3.75 | 0.6 |
| 2011 | BOS | MLB | 25 | 0 | 0 | 0 | 3 | 0 | 3 | 3 | 1 | 1 | 4 | 3.0 | 12.0 | 12% | .286 | 1.33 | 6.00 | 5.73 | 4.32 | 0.0 |
| 2012 | BOS | MLB | 26 | 1 | 1 | 0 | 7 | 2 | 16² | 19 | 2 | 6 | 12 | 3.2 | 6.6 | 40% | .319 | 1.49 | 5.07 | 4.40 | 5.51 | 0.0 |

Tazawa underwent Tommy John in early 2010 and spent this past season working his way back to the majors. There were bumps in the road, as expected, but he pitched better as he moved through the minors, picking up strikeouts and cutting his walks until he was part of September's expanded roster in Boston. Like seemingly everyone else at Triple-A, Tazawa is likely destined to relieve, though his low-90s fastball and mid-70s curveball make him a quality fit in the pen. He does have the potential in his other secondary offerings to make a worthwhile attempt at starting again. It's not as if the Red Sox are overflowing with starting pitching depth at Triple-A that would get in his way.

### Tim Wakefield

Born: 8/2/1966 Age: 45
Bats: R Throws: R Height: 6' 3" Weight: 195
Breakout: 33% Improve: 64% Collapse: 14%
Attrition: 0% MLB: 52%

Comparables:
Satchel Paige, Gaylord Perry, Dutch Leonard

| YEAR | TEAM | LVL | AGE | W | L | SV | G | GS | IP | H | HR | BB | SO | EqBB9 | EqSO9 | GB% | BABIP | WHIP | ERA | FIP | FRA | WARP |
|------|------|-----|-----|----|----|----|----|----|------|-----|----|----|----|-------|-------|-----|-------|------|------|------|------|------|
| 2009 | BOS | MLB | 42 | 11 | 5 | 0 | 21 | 21 | 129² | 137 | 12 | 50 | 72 | 3.5 | 5.0 | 38% | .295 | 1.44 | 4.58 | 4.62 | 4.45 | 1.9 |
| 2010 | BOS | MLB | 43 | 4 | 10 | 0 | 32 | 19 | 140 | 153 | 19 | 36 | 84 | 2.3 | 5.4 | 39% | .289 | 1.35 | 5.34 | 4.49 | 4.93 | 0.7 |
| 2011 | BOS | MLB | 44 | 7 | 8 | 0 | 33 | 23 | 154² | 163 | 25 | 47 | 93 | 2.7 | 5.4 | 41% | .276 | 1.36 | 5.12 | 5.03 | 5.35 | 0.1 |
| 2012 | BOS | MLB | 45 | 8 | 6 | 0 | 28 | 18 | 128² | 147 | 18 | 44 | 78 | 3.1 | 5.4 | 39% | .304 | 1.49 | 5.21 | 4.84 | 5.66 | -0.4 |

Wakefield achieved three milestones in 2011. On July 24, he became one of 24 pitchers *ever* to record 2,000 strikeouts or more with the same team. He recorded career win 199 in the same game, but it took him a record-setting eight attempts to notch win 200, two more than fellow knuckler Charlie Hough, and one more than Steve Carlton. Some of them were hard-luck losses, but Wakefield, who has slowed down significantly the last two seasons, was also to blame. He gave up eight runs in win 199, and six in 200, but the Red Sox scored a combined 30 runs to nail down both W's. While Wakefield is on the record saying the fans deserve a chance to see him set the franchise record for wins—he is seven away from passing both Roger Clemens and Cy Young—the wait for 200 might have dampened the enthusiasm of everyone else.

### Dan Wheeler

Born: 12/10/1977 Age: 34
Bats: R Throws: R Height: 6' 4" Weight: 215
Breakout: 16% Improve: 38% Collapse: 35%
Attrition: 5% MLB: 89%

Comparables:
Keith Foulke, Jerry Koosman, Javier Vazquez

| YEAR | TEAM | LVL | AGE | W | L | SV | G | GS | IP | H | HR | BB | SO | EqBB9 | EqSO9 | GB% | BABIP | WHIP | ERA | FIP | FRA | WARP |
|------|------|-----|-----|---|---|----|----|----|------|----|----|----|----|-------|-------|-----|-------|------|------|------|------|------|
| 2009 | TBA | MLB | 31 | 4 | 5 | 2 | 69 | 0 | 57² | 41 | 11 | 9 | 45 | 1.4 | 7.0 | 33% | .199 | 0.87 | 3.28 | 4.53 | 4.84 | 0.5 |
| 2010 | TBA | MLB | 32 | 2 | 4 | 3 | 64 | 0 | 48¹ | 36 | 7 | 16 | 46 | 3.0 | 8.6 | 36% | .234 | 1.08 | 3.35 | 4.08 | 3.93 | 0.5 |
| 2011 | BOS | MLB | 33 | 2 | 2 | 0 | 47 | 0 | 49¹ | 47 | 7 | 8 | 39 | 1.5 | 7.1 | 33% | .274 | 1.11 | 4.38 | 3.81 | 4.67 | 0.4 |
| 2012 | BOS | MLB | 34 | 2 | 1 | 1 | 48 | 0 | 43¹ | 41 | 6 | 12 | 39 | 2.5 | 8.1 | 35% | .286 | 1.21 | 3.71 | 4.04 | 4.03 | 0.6 |

Wheeler started the year poorly, posting an ERA of 11.32 with four homers allowed through May 4, but following a stint on the DL for a calf strain, he was the Wheeler the Sox thought they were getting when they signed him for $3 million. In his final 39 frames, Wheeler posted a K/BB of 4.4 and an ERA of 2.54. The problem was that manager Terry Francona didn't seem to notice, utilizing Wheeler almost exclusively in situations considered to be low-leverage, even when the rest of the pen struggled. This also caused Wheeler to face lefties far more often than a ROOGY should: nearly 40 percent of his batters faced were left-handers, despite a career record that says that is a terrible, horrible, no good, very bad idea.

| **Alex Wilson** | | YEAR | TEAM | LVL | AGE | W | L | SV | G | GS | IP | H | HR | BB | SO | EqBB9 | EqSO9 | GB% | BABIP | WHIP | ERA | FIP | FRA | WARP |
|---|---|---|---|---|---|---|---|---|---|---|---|---|---|---|---|---|---|---|---|---|---|---|---|---|
| Born: 11/3/1986 Age: 25 | | 2009 | LOW | A- | 22 | 0 | 1 | 0 | 13 | 13 | 36 | 13 | 0 | 7 | 40 | 1.8 | 8.2 | 49% | .144 | 0.47 | 0.50 | 1.68 | 2.81 | 1.1 |
| Bats: R Throws: R Height: 6' 1" Weight: 215 | | 2010 | SLM | A+ | 23 | 2 | 1 | 0 | 11 | 11 | 55² | 29 | 3 | 11 | 44 | 2.4 | 8.1 | 51% | .236 | 1.04 | 3.39 | 3.28 | 3.79 | 1.0 |
| Breakout: 34% Improve: 62% Collapse: 9% | | 2010 | PME | AA | 23 | 4 | 5 | 0 | 16 | 16 | 78¹ | 62 | 8 | 20 | 38 | 3.9 | 6.4 | 41% | .323 | 1.65 | 6.67 | 4.76 | 5.91 | 0.0 |
| Attrition: 17% MLB: 89% | | 2011 | PME | AA | 24 | 9 | 4 | 0 | 21 | 21 | 112 | 97 | 7 | 37 | 96 | 3.0 | 8.0 | 47% | .302 | 1.25 | 3.05 | 3.53 | 4.01 | 2.3 |
| **Comparables:** John Lackey,Brad Clontz,Clay Carroll | | 2012 | BOS | MLB | 25 | 3 | 2 | 0 | 8 | 8 | 41² | 46 | 6 | 18 | 28 | 3.9 | 6.2 | 44% | .309 | 1.55 | 5.19 | 5.03 | 5.64 | -0.1 |

Wilson's stint at Portland was the first time the 24-year-old crossed the 100 inning mark at any

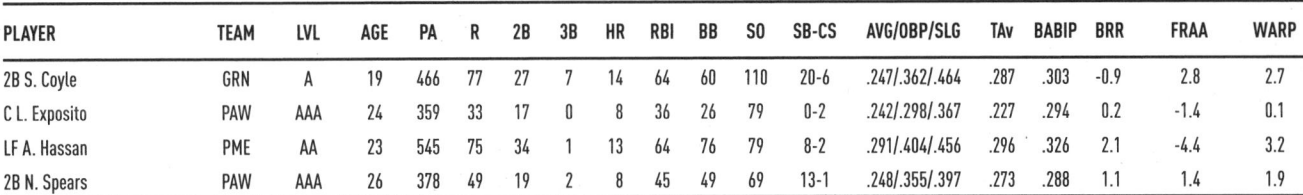

## HITTERS

| PLAYER | TEAM | LVL | AGE | PA | R | 2B | 3B | HR | RBI | BB | SO | SB-CS | AVG/OBP/SLG | TAv | BABIP | BRR | FRAA | WARP |
|---|---|---|---|---|---|---|---|---|---|---|---|---|---|---|---|---|---|---|
| 2B S. Coyle | GRN | A | 19 | 466 | 77 | 27 | 7 | 14 | 64 | 60 | 110 | 20-6 | .247/.362/.464 | .287 | .303 | -0.9 | 2.8 | 2.7 |
| C L. Exposito | PAW | AAA | 24 | 359 | 33 | 17 | 0 | 8 | 36 | 26 | 79 | 0-2 | .242/.298/.367 | .227 | .294 | 0.2 | -1.4 | 0.1 |
| LF A. Hassan | PME | AA | 23 | 545 | 75 | 34 | 1 | 13 | 64 | 76 | 79 | 8-2 | .291/.404/.456 | .296 | .326 | 2.1 | -4.4 | 3.2 |
| 2B N. Spears | PAW | AAA | 26 | 378 | 49 | 19 | 2 | 8 | 45 | 49 | 69 | 13-1 | .248/.355/.397 | .273 | .288 | 1.1 | 1.4 | 1.9 |

Second baseman **Sean Coyle** is sure to hear the Dustin Pedroia comparisons, as he is 5-foot-8 and well under 200 lbs. with plus batspeed, but that isn't fair to anyone, even if that anyone posted a .217 Isolated Power in Single-A as a 19-year-old. ⊘ 24-year-old backup catcher **Luis Exposito** made it to the majors for the first time, but didn't get into a game, so the poor guy doesn't have the player page to prove it. ⊘ Plate discipline is **Alex Hassan's** defining trait, but this walk machine has some potential pop as well if only he'll stop relying on his arms to do all the work; when his legs get involved, the ball goes very far. ⊘ **Nate Spears** is a fun player, mostly because not only does he have six positions with at least 13 games played, he has pitched two innings, too.

## PITCHERS

| PLAYER | TEAM | LVL | AGE | W | L | SV | IP | H | HR | BB | SO | EqBB9 | EqSO9 | GB% | BABIP | WHIP | ERA | FIP | FRA | WARP |
|---|---|---|---|---|---|---|---|---|---|---|---|---|---|---|---|---|---|---|---|---|
| C. Balcom-Miller | SLM | A+ | 22 | 3 | 1 | 0 | 34² | 24 | 2 | 11 | 37 | 2.9 | 9.6 | 74% | .275 | 1.01 | 2.34 | 3.04 | 3.92 | 0.6 |
| | PME | AA | 22 | 3 | 6 | 0 | 82¹ | 103 | 4 | 32 | 75 | 3.5 | 8.2 | 56% | .391 | 1.64 | 4.81 | 3.72 | 4.80 | 1.0 |
| T. Miller | BOS | MLB | 38 | 0 | 0 | 0 | 2 | 0 | 0 | 0 | 1 | 0.0 | 4.5 | 40% | .000 | 0.00 | 0.00 | 2.06 | 4.60 | 0.0 |
| | TOR | MLB | 38 | 0 | 0 | 0 | 3² | 6 | 1 | 2 | 2 | 4.9 | 4.9 | 43% | .385 | 2.18 | 4.91 | 7.15 | 5.30 | 0.0 |
| | SLN | MLB | 38 | 0 | 1 | 1 | 15² | 19 | 1 | 10 | 9 | 5.7 | 5.2 | 41% | .333 | 1.85 | 4.02 | 4.97 | 6.02 | -0.3 |
| H. Okajima | PAW | AAA | 35 | 8 | 0 | 0 | 51 | 39 | 3 | 9 | 49 | 1.6 | 8.5 | 38% | .263 | 0.94 | 2.29 | 2.61 | 3.48 | 1.1 |
| | BOS | MLB | 35 | 1 | 0 | 0 | 8¹ | 7 | 0 | 5 | 6 | 5.4 | 6.5 | 56% | .292 | 1.44 | 4.32 | 3.42 | 4.60 | 0.1 |
| S. Pimentel | SLM | A+ | 21 | 6 | 4 | 0 | 51² | 50 | 8 | 16 | 35 | 2.8 | 6.1 | 48% | .276 | 1.28 | 4.53 | 5.26 | 5.48 | 0.3 |
| | PME | AA | 21 | 0 | 9 | 0 | 50¹ | 75 | 8 | 23 | 30 | 4.1 | 5.4 | 34% | .372 | 1.95 | 9.12 | 6.14 | 6.22 | 0.2 |
| D. Reyes | BOS | MLB | 34 | 0 | 0 | 0 | 1² | 2 | 0 | 2 | 1 | 10.8 | 5.4 | 60% | .400 | 2.40 | 16.20 | 9.06 | 8.93 | -0.1 |
| R. Williams | PAW | AAA | 35 | 0 | 1 | 8 | 32 | 25 | 2 | 15 | 37 | 3.7 | 10.1 | 49% | .291 | 1.12 | 1.41 | 3.52 | 4.76 | 0.3 |
| | BOS | MLB | 35 | 0 | 1 | 0 | 8¹ | 10 | 0 | 5 | 6 | 5.4 | 6.5 | 48% | .357 | 1.80 | 6.48 | 3.42 | 5.31 | 0.0 |
| B. Workman | GRN | A | 22 | 6 | 7 | 0 | 131 | 128 | 10 | 33 | 115 | 2.3 | 7.9 | 43% | .317 | 1.23 | 3.71 | 3.63 | 4.04 | 2.3 |

**Chris Balcom-Miller**, the groundball strikeout machine known as "Baconator," was essentially stolen from the Colorado Rockies in exchange for Manny Delcarmen last year and his first half with High-A Salem reinforced that impression. ⊘ **Trever Miller** pitched for three teams in 2011, making 48 appearances but logging just 21-1/3 innings, but being left-handed has its perks: don't be surprised if he finds work again, despite recent events. ⊘ Lefty **Hideki Okajima** was only re-signed by Boston as insurance after they failed to get Scott Downs and only pitched in Boston because Dennys Reyes was a bust. Designated for assignment in June, Okajima demanded a trade, didn't go anywhere, and now the 35-year-old is a free agent. ⊘ One step forward, two steps back for **Stolmy Pimentel**, who allowed more than a run per inning, handed out walks and easy-to-destroy pitches left-and-right, and saw his strikeout rate drop upon being promoted to Double-A, resulting in a demotion back to High-A. ⊘ **Dennys Reyes** pitched fewer than two innings for Boston, as their Plan A for left-handed relief was sent packing before the first week of April had run its course. As the Red Sox lost all four April contests Reyes pitched in, the entire September collapse is his fault, in a sense. "Logical fallacy" you say? Whatever does that mean? We solved the mystery of the collapse; you should be thankful! ⊘ Terry Francona was a successful manager for many reasons, but his bullpen usage was not one of them. Case in point: **Randy Williams**, he of the career K/BB of 1.3 and a 5.82 ERA over five seasons, had 11 batters faced in situations considered high leverage in his eight-plus innings in Boston. ⊘ **Brandon Workman** was selected in the second round of the 2010 draft, and his first pro season at age 22 went well enough in the Sally League thanks to his high-80s cutter.

## MANAGER: BOBBY VALENTINE

Valentine has a background as a stats-oriented manager, and from an era when Sox fans still felt cursed, even. Valentine is always willing to try out new things if the result could be more winning baseball; when those nuggets of learning are presented by a front office as statistically inclined as Boston's, it's easy to see why his introductory press conference caused a collective swoon for even Red Sox Nation's toughest critics. Valentine might one day outstay his welcome—as every manager does—but for now, the Red Sox likely found the best man for the job.

# Chicago Cubs

Theo Epstein's career as general manager in Boston was given a running start when he took over a very good Red Sox club following Dan Duquette's dismissal in 2002. After exorcising the Curse of the Bambino in 2004 and adding a second World Series title in the final weeks of the season, during which the Red Sox dropped 20 of their final 27 games and squandered a nine-game wild-card lead, served as the catalyst for a multi-franchise game of executive musical chairs. In October, it was announced that San Diego GM Jed Hoyer and assistant GM Jason McLeod, both of whom had been hired by the Padres less than a year earlier, had resigned to take the same jobs in Chicago under Epstein, who had been named the Cubs' new team president. Padres senior vice president and former Diamondbacks GM Josh Byrnes was promoted to take Hoyer's place in San Diego and longtime assistant GM Ben Cherington was promoted to replace Epstein in Boston.

Curses and billy goats and Bartmans aside, it would be difficult to come up with more favorable conditions than what Epstein inherits in Chicago.

The Cubs have the pleasure of competing in the weakest division in baseball. Since

| CUBS PROSPECTUS | | |
|---|---|---|
| TAv-P | .262 | 16th |
| FIP | 4.08 | 20th |
| DER | .699 | 26th |
| DL | 585 | 7th |
| B-Age | 29.4 | 24th |
| P-Age | 29.7 | 26th |
| Salary | $134.3 | 6th |
| M$/MW | $5.42 | 28th |

another Zambrano blow up, management changes, and a finish below the Pirates

**2012:** Winning is off the table, but Theo's in town, and things should start to improve

**Action Items:** Infield, outfield, starting pitching, some sucker to take overpaid stars in trade

percentage for the NL Central division winner is .568, only slightly better than the league-worst .562 winning percentage posted by NL West champions.

Win or lose, the Cubs have drawn more than 3 million fans to Wrigley Field each year since 2004, and a 2011 Forbes estimate valued the franchise at $773 million. Cubs games reach fans from coast to coast thanks to a broadcast agreement with superstation WGN, and they have a clear mindshare advantage in Chicago over the crosstown White Sox.

Of course, if everything in Wrigleyville were going well, Jim Hendry would still be at the helm.

Unlike the 2002 Red Sox, which included Johnny Damon, Nomar Garciaparra, Pedro Martinez, and Manny Ramirez all between the ages of 28 and 30 and at or near their peaks, the Cubs roster that Epstein and Hoyer inherit is noticeably thin on young impact talent.

The Cubs rolled out the 12th-youngest collection of hitters in the NL last year, and their lineup frequently featured five hitters between the ages of 33 and 35. Carlos Peña, Reed Johnson, and Aramis Ramirez were the only thirtysomethings to post an OPS higher than 759. Peña and Reed departed as free agents after the season while Johnson re-upped. Right fielder Kosuke Fukudome was traded to Cleveland in a deadline deal last July. Those departures leave Alfonso Soriano, Marlon Byrd, and Jeff Baker as the only returning regulars or

### Table 1. Source of Top Performers, Boston Red Sox, 2003–11

| Player | WARP | Source | GM |
|---|---|---|---|
| David Ortiz | 35.9 | Free Agent | Epstein |
| Manny Ramirez | 34.1 | Free Agent | Duquette |
| Kevin Youkilis | 28.7 | Draft | Duquette |
| Jason Varitek | 22.0 | Trade | Duquette |
| Dustin Pedroia | 19.6 | Draft | Epstein |
| Johnny Damon | 16.7 | Free Agent | Duquette |
| Jacoby Ellsbury | 15.6 | Draft | Epstein |
| Josh Beckett | 15.5 | Trade | Epstein |
| Jonathan Papelbon | 13.6 | Draft | Epstein |
| Jon Lester | 13.2 | Draft | Duquette |

semi-regulars over the age of 30 on the 2012 roster. The new regime's first significant free-agent acquisition, however, was 32-year-old David DeJesus, signed for two years and $10 million to patrol right field.

Among the Gen Y crowd, shortstop Starlin Castro built upon his successful rookie season with improvements in nearly every offensive category as the youngest every-day player in the National League. Matt Garza, acquired in January from Tampa Bay, established himself as a legitimate number-two starter in his first season in Chicago, placing seventh in strikeouts per nine innings and tied for sixth in fewest home runs allowed among NL starters. The ebb and flow of BABIP contributed to catcher Geovany Soto slipping back into a funk at the plate after a 2010 bounce-back had inspired hope that the 2008 NL Rookie of the Year had returned to form.

On the farm, years of poor drafting have led to a dearth of blue-chip talent. The system's top prospect, 2009 first-rounder Brett Jackson, reached Triple-A in 2011 and could find at-bats in Chicago at some point in 2012. If history has taught us anything, however, Cubs fans would be wise to temper their expectations for Jackson. Over the last 20 years, Doug Glanville (8.9 career WARP) is the most productive first-round position player the Cubs have developed. Corey Patterson (1.1) and Brooks Kieschnick (1.4) round out the top three. It doesn't get a whole lot better in rounds two through five, either, as Ryan Theriot (5.3) and Kevin Orie (2.8) represent the cream of two decades' collective crops.

### Table 2. Position players drafted in Round 1

| Player Drafted | Career | WARP |
| --- | --- | --- |
| Terry Hughes | 1967 | -0.5 |
| Ralph Rickey | 1968 | – |
| Roger Metzger | 1969 | 6.7 |
| Gene Hiser | 1970 | -0.8 |
| Jerry Tabb | 1973 | -0.5 |
| Scot Thompson | 1974 | -2.2 |
| Brian Rosinski | 1975 | – |
| Bill Hayes | 1978 | 0.0 |
| Joe Carter | 1981 | 25.7 |
| Tony Woods | 1982 | – |
| Shawon Dunston | 1982 | 18.9 |
| Rafael Palmeiro | 1985 | 58.9 |
| Derrick May | 1986 | 1.0 |
| Ty Griffin | 1988 | – |
| Earl Cunningham | 1989 | – |
| Doug Glanville | 1991 | 8.9 |
| Brooks Kieschnick | 1993 | 1.4 |
| Corey Patterson | 1998 | 1.1 |
| Lou Montanez | 2000 | -1.4 |
| Ryan Harvey | 2003 | – |
| Tyler Colvin | 2006 | 0.6 |
| Josh Vitters | 2007 | – |
| Brett Jackson | 2009 | – |

Things have gone better when the Cubs have opted for an arm instead of a bat in the first round, though their hits—Kerry Wood, Jon Garland, and Mark Prior—would be a bit more impressive if Dusty Baker hadn't Dusty Bakered Wood and Prior (how thankful is Garland for the 1998 trade that shipped him to the South Side?).

Compare that to Epstein's record in Boston, where since 2003 the top five rounds have netted All-Stars Jonathan Papelbon, Dustin Pedroia, Jacoby Ellsbury, and Clay Buchholz, as well as the requisite chips to acquire Adrian Gonzalez and Victor Martinez via trade.

Only two of the top 10 players in Kevin Goldstein's ranking of Cubs prospects are pitchers. Dillon Maples instantly became the organization's top pitching prospect when he signed for $2.5 million out of a North Carolina high school in the 14th round of last year's draft, but he's yet to throw his first professional pitch and is at least four years away. The top arm in the upper levels, right-hander Trey McNutt, struggled at Double-A and could wind up in the bullpen.

In 2008-10, Chicago ranked 25th in total draft spending at $14.3 million, a figure that Epstein's Red Sox nearly doubled at $28.3 million during the same period. Surprisingly, after shelling out a combined $8.7 in 2009-10, the Cubs were one of the most aggressive teams in the 2011 draft, spending nearly $12 million and outpacing all but Pittsburgh, Washington, and Kansas City.

If there's anything Epstein and Hendry have in common it's a history of poor contract decisions. Despite overseeing the Cubs' first back-to-back winning seasons in more than 30 years in 2003-04, Hendry's tenure as Cubs GM will most likely be remembered for the mammoth mistakes he made with Alfonso Soriano and Carlos Zambrano. Soriano has never lived up to his eight-year, $136 million contract, delivering just one season out of five better than 2.7 WARP, and Zambrano has been suspended or placed on the restricted list four times since signing his five-year, $91.5 million deal in 2008.

Smaller sums were paid to Fukudome (4 years/$48 million) and Milton Bradley (3 years/$30 million), but the latter's behavior forced Hendry to ship him out of town after just one year. Fukudome, like the overwhelming majority of Japanese players to come to the U.S., underwhelmed in three-plus years as a Cub.

Much of the dead weight from Hendry's poor signings will slide off of the books when the contracts of Zambrano, Byrd, and Ryan Dempster expire after 2012. Soriano's deal still has three years and about $60 million remaining through 2014.

Epstein, too, has had his share of regrettable contracts, most notably the five years and $82.5 million paid to John Lackey, who has been a shell of his former Angelic self since coming to Boston in 2010. Carl Crawford's first season in Boston after signing a seven-year, $142 million contract was an unmitigated disaster, but he's still young enough, and presumably healthy enough, to bounce back in years two through seven. Several lesser free-agent deals (Julio Lugo for 4/$36 million, Matt Clement for 3/$25 million, arguably J.D. Drew for 5/$75 million) also backfired in Boston, but Epstein rarely gets credit for the right decisions he's made when locking up his own players to relatively affordable contract extensions (Table 3).

## Table 3. Contract Extensions Signed by Red Sox Players (Non-Free Agents), 2003-11

| Player | Amount | Years | AAV |
|---|---|---|---|

Clay Buchholz $29.945 million   2012-15 $7.486 million

After he cut ties with incumbent skipper Mike Quade, Epstein's managerial search led him to a familiar face in Dale Sveum, who served as Boston's third-base coach in 2003-04. After the 2004 championship, Sveum left Boston to become Ned Yost's bench coach in Milwaukee. In six years, he filled a variety of roles for the Brewers, including hitting coach, third-base coach, and interim manager after Yost was fired in 2008. Prior to going to Boston, Sveum had been named the top managerial prospect in the Eastern League by Baseball America after compiling a .502 winning percentage in three seasons.

If Sveum finishes anywhere near .500 in his first season in Chicago, there's a fair chance the Vatican will recognize it as a miracle.

A patently average offense took a hit over the winter when first baseman Peña and third baseman Ramirez were lost as free agents. Chicago was expected to be a major player for free agents Albert Pujols and Prince Fielder, but aside from occasional whispers that they could be one of Scott Boras's infamous "mystery teams," the Cubs were never firmly linked to either, though Fielder remained unsigned at press time.

Nine-year minor-league veteran Bryan LaHair enters

ing Ian Stewart does not qualify) sent reliever Sean Marshall to Cincinnati for middling young starter Travis Wood and change in December. Marshall could assume the closer's job in Cincinnati if free agent Francisco Cordero doesn't return, while Wood is likely to find a place near the back of the Cubs' 2012 rotation.

Because there are so few stars (or even potential stars) already in place, Cubs fans expecting Epstein to repeat the quick success he had in Boston are likely to be disappointed. Fortunately, patience is a virtue that North Siders have had plenty of time to hone.

# HITTERS

**Jeff Baker** 2B
Born: 6/21/1981 Age: 31
Bats: R Throws: R Height: 6' 3" Weight: 210
Breakout: 3% Improve: 37% Collapse: 10%
Attrition: 24% MLB: 69%
Comparables:
Luis Lopez, Ben Broussard, Razor Shines

| YEAR | TEAM | LVL | AGE | PA | R | 2B | 3B | HR | RBI | BB | SO | SB | CS | AVG_OBP_SLG | TAv | BABIP | BRR | FRAA | WARP |
|---|---|---|---|---|---|---|---|---|---|---|---|---|---|---|---|---|---|---|---|
| 2009 | CHN | MLB | 28 | 224 | 27 | 15 | 1 | 4 | 21 | 17 | 46 | 0 | 0 | .305/.362/.448 | .280 | .374 | -1.8 | 3.3 | 1.2 |
| 2009 | COL | MLB | 28 | 24 | 0 | 0 | 1 | 0 | 3 | 1 | 7 | 1 | 0 | .130/.167/.217 | .091 | .188 | 0 | 0 | -0.4 |
| 2010 | CHN | MLB | 29 | 224 | 29 | 13 | 2 | 4 | 21 | 16 | 50 | 1 | 0 | .272/.326/.413 | .250 | .340 | -0.6 | 1.6 | 0.4 |
| 2011 | CHN | MLB | 30 | 212 | 20 | 12 | 1 | 3 | 23 | 10 | 46 | 0 | 0 | .269/.302/.383 | .248 | .333 | 2.5 | -1.5 | 0.1 |
| 2012 | CHN | MLB | 31 | 250 | 29 | 13 | 2 | 6 | 28 | 18 | 58 | 1 | 0 | .266/.320/.410 | .260 | .331 | 0 | 2B -0, 3B 1 | | 1.4 |

One of the ex-GM's last moves was to make a splash about how Baker was not available in trade at the July deadline. Baker was hitting .304/.324/.422 at the time, but the teams rumored to have shown interest in him realized Baker's limitations (mainly the career .239/.292/.364 batting line against right-handed pitchers) and weren't going to dangle top prospects. With a lame-duck GM and Aramis Ramirez's 2012 status undecided, keeping Baker might have been a smart move, but the fact that he hit just .197/.260/.303 after Hendry's proclamation provided another punch line for those who found the Cubs to be a bad joke in 2011.

### Darwin Barney  2B

Born: 11/8/1985 Age: 26
Bats: R Throws: R Height: 5' 11" Weight: 180
Breakout: 2% Improve: 18% Collapse: 6%
Attrition: 15% MLB: 51%

**Comparables:**
Chip Hale, William Bergolla, Brent Butler

| YEAR | TEAM | LVL | AGE | PA | R | 2B | 3B | HR | RBI | BB | SO | SB | CS | AVG_OBP_SLG | TAv | BABIP | BRR | FRAA | WARP |
|------|------|-----|-----|-----|----|----|----|----|-----|----|----|----|----|----------------|------|-------|------|----------|------|
| 2009 | TEN | AA | 23 | 284 | 30 | 12 | 0 | 3 | 32 | 23 | 33 | 5 | 1 | .317/.369/.401 | .272 | .350 | -1.2 | 1.1 | 1.4 |
| 2009 | IOW | AAA | 23 | 229 | 25 | 12 | 1 | 0 | 17 | 13 | 32 | 4 | 1 | .264/.304/.330 | .237 | .308 | 1 | 2.3 | 0.6 |
| 2010 | IOW | AAA | 24 | 510 | 72 | 24 | 4 | 2 | 49 | 23 | 52 | 11 | 3 | .299/.333/.378 | .254 | .330 | -3.2 | 0.2 | 1.7 |
| 2010 | CHN | MLB | 24 | 85 | 12 | 4 | 0 | 0 | 2 | 6 | 12 | 0 | 0 | .241/.294/.291 | .218 | .284 | 2.7 | 0.7 | 0.4 |
| 2011 | CHN | MLB | 25 | 570 | 66 | 23 | 6 | 2 | 43 | 22 | 67 | 9 | 2 | .276/.313/.353 | .239 | .310 | 3.1 | 7.8 | 1.4 |
| 2012 | CHN | MLB | 26 | 502 | 54 | 22 | 3 | 3 | 46 | 22 | 68 | 7 | 2 | .274/.311/.355 | .239 | .310 | 0.1 | 2B 2, SS 1 | 0.8 |

Barney embodies all the traits that are often ridiculed by the sabermetric community. He's gritty, great on fundamentals, hustles all the time, has a selfless attitude, and is a good teammate. A natural shortstop, he has above-average range and a plus arm for the right side of the infield. His combination of attitude and fielding skill will support his marginal bat through a long career, though if he doesn't miraculously add some walks or power to his offensive game, he profiles more as a utility player than a regular.

### Jeff Bianchi  SS

Born: 10/5/1986 Age: 25
Bats: R Throws: R Height: 5' 11" Weight: 190
Breakout: 2% Improve: 20% Collapse: 8%
Attrition: 43% MLB: 76%

**Comparables:**
Pat Kelly, Matt Lawson, Jason Hardtke

| YEAR | TEAM | LVL | AGE | PA | R | 2B | 3B | HR | RBI | BB | SO | SB | CS | AVG_OBP_SLG | TAv | BABIP | BRR | FRAA | WARP |
|------|------|-----|-----|-----|----|----|----|----|-----|----|----|----|----|----------------|------|-------|------|----------|------|
| 2009 | WIL | A+ | 22 | 245 | 32 | 12 | 2 | 4 | 28 | 20 | 47 | 12 | 2 | .300/.357/.427 | .294 | .360 | 0.3 | 4 | 2.2 |
| 2009 | NWA | AA | 22 | 297 | 42 | 17 | 1 | 5 | 42 | 19 | 58 | 10 | 4 | .315/.360/.441 | .283 | .383 | -2.2 | 2.7 | 2.1 |
| 2011 | NWA | AA | 24 | 499 | 63 | 23 | 2 | 2 | 48 | 39 | 85 | 20 | 5 | .259/.320/.333 | .237 | .313 | 1.2 | 8.4 | 1.3 |
| 2012 | MIL | MLB | 25 | 250 | 25 | 11 | 1 | 3 | 23 | 15 | 57 | 7 | 2 | .244/.290/.346 | .226 | .304 | 0.1 | SS 3, 2B 1 | -0.1 |

"The former second-round draft pick has missed significant time due to injuries since signing in 2005. One year removed from Tommy John, he appeared in over 105 games last summer for only the second time in his career. He lost plate selectivity as he advanced through the Kansas City system and the injuries make playing defense a chore. Once thought of as a key prospect in the early stages of the Royals' rebuilding process, Bianchi was available on waivers to the Cubs, who are hoping that good health will allow his highly regarded talent to emerge.\

### Marlon Byrd  CF

Born: 8/30/1977 Age: 34
Bats: R Throws: R Height: 6' 1" Weight: 225
Breakout: 0% Improve: 25% Collapse: 4%
Attrition: 16% MLB: 92%

**Comparables:**
Kirby Puckett, Torii Hunter, Felipe Alou

| YEAR | TEAM | LVL | AGE | PA | R | 2B | 3B | HR | RBI | BB | SO | SB | CS | AVG_OBP_SLG | TAv | BABIP | BRR | FRAA | WARP |
|------|------|-----|-----|-----|----|----|----|----|-----|----|----|----|----|----------------|------|-------|------|----------|------|
| 2009 | TEX | MLB | 31 | 599 | 66 | 43 | 2 | 20 | 89 | 32 | 98 | 8 | 4 | .283/.329/.479 | .283 | .308 | -4.6 | -9.7 | 1.3 |
| 2010 | CHN | MLB | 32 | 630 | 84 | 39 | 2 | 12 | 66 | 31 | 98 | 5 | 1 | .293/.346/.429 | .279 | .335 | -3 | 6.2 | 4.0 |
| 2011 | CHN | MLB | 33 | 482 | 51 | 22 | 2 | 9 | 35 | 25 | 78 | 3 | 2 | .276/.324/.395 | .258 | .316 | -1.6 | 0.6 | 1.3 |
| 2012 | CHN | MLB | 34 | 484 | 60 | 26 | 3 | 11 | 57 | 29 | 83 | 5 | 2 | .285/.340/.429 | .276 | .328 | -0.2 | CF 0, LF 0 | 2.3 |

At three years and $15 million, Byrd looked like an economical and effective signing. When he was hitting .321/.374/.488 on July 17, 2010, and the Cubs were 10 games out, he had some nice trade value. The Cubs didn't sell high then, partly because they needed someone to play center field. But Byrd was hit in the face with a pitch on May 21, 2011, and hit just .255/.311/.380 after returning. When Byrd's healthy and confident at the plate, he contributes against both left-handed and right-handed pitching while covering enough ground to be an asset in center (the smallish territory in Wrigley Field helps). But the backloaded contract makes his price tag $6.5 million in 2012, and if the Cubs are doing the deep rebuild many expect, he'll likely be traded for prospects—far lesser ones, however, than if he'd been dealt in 2010.

### Tony Campana  CF

Born: 5/30/1986 Age: 26
Bats: L Throws: L Height: 5' 9" Weight: 165
Breakout: 1% Improve: 29% Collapse: 5%
Attrition: 29% MLB: 71%

**Comparables:**
Billy Baldwin, Emilio Bonifacio, Willy Taveras

| YEAR | TEAM | LVL | AGE | PA | R | 2B | 3B | HR | RBI | BB | SO | SB | CS | AVG_OBP_SLG | TAv | BABIP | BRR | FRAA | WARP |
|------|------|-----|-----|-----|----|----|----|----|-----|----|----|----|----|----------------|------|-------|------|----------|------|
| 2009 | PEO | A | 23 | 58 | 14 | 1 | 1 | 0 | 5 | 5 | 6 | 11 | 2 | .283/.345/.340 | .278 | .319 | 3.1 | -1 | 0.5 |
| 2009 | DAY | A+ | 23 | 473 | 56 | 8 | 2 | 0 | 25 | 34 | 78 | 55 | 16 | .284/.331/.312 | .246 | .340 | 0.9 | 0.3 | 0.7 |
| 2010 | TEN | AA | 24 | 550 | 76 | 22 | 5 | 0 | 39 | 44 | 82 | 48 | 20 | .319/.375/.384 | .272 | .376 | 1.2 | 1.6 | 2.9 |
| 2011 | IOW | AAA | 25 | 129 | 27 | 8 | 2 | 0 | 9 | 6 | 23 | 8 | 1 | .342/.383/.442 | .279 | .423 | 3.2 | -1.6 | 0.7 |
| 2011 | CHN | MLB | 25 | 155 | 24 | 3 | 0 | 1 | 6 | 8 | 30 | 24 | 2 | .259/.303/.301 | .218 | .321 | 4.2 | 0.3 | 0.3 |
| 2012 | CHN | MLB | 26 | 250 | 26 | 9 | 1 | 1 | 21 | 13 | 48 | 20 | 5 | .271/.313/.334 | .231 | .330 | 0.3 | CF -5, LF 0 | 0.0 |

Only seven qualifying batters registered a higher speed score than Campana's 7.5 in 2011, and it's no statistical illusion—he has the sort of wheels that cause even inveterate critics of the running game to gawk. His small stature makes him a longshot to develop into a starting position player, but he did go through the minors almost as quickly as he goes around the bases, with just 156 plate appearances below the High-A level, where he played most of 2009. With new

GM Theo Epstein's affinity for fast players who play good defense, Campana should manage to stay on the roster and even see playing time, but an upside of fourth outfielder seems more likely than a starting job.

| **Welington Castillo** C | YEAR | TEAM | LVL | AGE | PA | R | 2B | 3B | HR | RBI | BB | SO | SB | CS | AVG_OBP_SLG | TAv | BABIP | BRR | FRAA | WARP |
|---|---|---|---|---|---|---|---|---|---|---|---|---|---|---|---|---|---|---|---|---|
| Born: 4/24/1987 Age: 25 | 2009 | TEN | AA | 22 | 339 | 27 | 16 | 0 | 11 | 39 | 15 | 71 | 1 | 0 | .232/.274/.386 | .226 | .265 | -2.4 | 1.5 | 0.2 |
| Bats: R Throws: R Height: 5' 11'' Weight: 200 | 2010 | IOW | AAA | 23 | 272 | 35 | 17 | 1 | 13 | 59 | 19 | 58 | 0 | 2 | .255/.325/.498 | .265 | .284 | -1.2 | -1.4 | 1.1 |
| Breakout: 4% Improve: 20% Collapse: 7% | 2010 | CHN | MLB | 23 | 21 | 3 | 4 | 0 | 1 | 5 | 1 | 7 | 0 | 0 | .300/.333/.650 | .335 | .417 | -0.2 | 0.1 | 0.3 |
| Attrition: 36% MLB: 63% | 2011 | IOW | AAA | 24 | 251 | 38 | 9 | 0 | 15 | 35 | 20 | 57 | 0 | 0 | .286/.351/.524 | .301 | .321 | -0.8 | -0.7 | 1.9 |
| **Comparables:** | 2011 | CHN | MLB | 24 | 13 | 0 | 0 | 0 | 0 | 0 | 0 | 4 | 0 | 0 | .154/.154/.154 | .130 | .222 | -0.2 | -0.1 | -0.1 |
| Doug Camilli, Tom Pagnozzi, Denny Nino | 2012 | CHN | MLB | 25 | 250 | 27 | 11 | 1 | 9 | 30 | 12 | 65 | 0 | 0 | .240/.282/.405 | .241 | .289 | 0 | C -1 | 1.1 |

Castillo is following in the Cubs catching prospect tradition begun by Geovany Soto, playing badly (hitting bottom in 2009) before improving his aggressiveness—and with it his power—with an assist from minor-league hitting instructor Von Joshua.

| Wil Cordero, Jimmy Rollins, Lenny Faedo | 2011 | CHN | MLB | 21 | 715 | 91 | 36 | 9 | 10 | 66 | 35 | 96 | 22 | 9 | .307/.341/.432 | .269 | .344 | 0.3 | 2.6 | 4.0 |
|---|---|---|---|---|---|---|---|---|---|---|---|---|---|---|---|---|---|---|---|---|
| | 2012 | CHN | MLB | 22 | 644 | 79 | 34 | 7 | 8 | 74 | 31 | 89 | 19 | 9 | .304/.341/.424 | .272 | .341 | -1.5 | SS 5 | 3.4 |

Castro's critics say he doesn't walk enough, he doesn't have enough power, his defense is terrible, and he'll need to move to second base. But he shows good range and a strong arm, and his rate of errors per 162 games started has dropped. The thought of a move away from shortstop at this point in his career is pure folly. He became the youngest player to lead the National League in base hits, his "hitting" tool (to use scout-speak) is off the charts, and he's big enough to add homers to his nascent extra-base power. Some of the defensive weaknesses that have been reported do exist, but guys like Derek Jeter and Troy Tulowitzki were making more errors per game in the minors at age 21 than Starlin was in the majors. It would take a long memory indeed to recall the last time the Cubs had a position player show anywhere near this level of promise for future greatness.

| **Steve Clevenger** C | YEAR | TEAM | LVL | AGE | PA | R | 2B | 3B | HR | RBI | BB | SO | SB | CS | AVG_OBP_SLG | TAv | BABIP | BRR | FRAA | WARP |
|---|---|---|---|---|---|---|---|---|---|---|---|---|---|---|---|---|---|---|---|---|
| Born: 4/5/1986 Age: 26 | 2009 | TEN | AA | 23 | 89 | 12 | 4 | 3 | 1 | 10 | 10 | 8 | 0 | 0 | .364/.438/.532 | .333 | .391 | -1 | -0.5 | 1.0 |
| Bats: L Throws: R Height: 6' 1'' Weight: 195 | 2009 | IOW | AAA | 23 | 251 | 21 | 12 | 1 | 0 | 26 | 15 | 31 | 4 | 3 | .265/.310/.326 | .233 | .303 | -1.3 | -1.5 | -0.2 |
| Breakout: 2% Improve: 24% Collapse: 10% | 2010 | TEN | AA | 24 | 294 | 37 | 24 | 0 | 5 | 47 | 20 | 28 | 0 | 6 | .317/.369/.461 | .272 | .340 | -2.3 | -1.3 | 1.3 |
| Attrition: 46% MLB: 90% | 2011 | TEN | AA | 25 | 351 | 42 | 27 | 3 | 5 | 39 | 35 | 39 | 1 | 0 | .295/.363/.449 | .262 | .321 | -1.8 | 1 | 1.6 |
| **Comparables:** | 2011 | IOW | AAA | 25 | 97 | 9 | 3 | 1 | 3 | 15 | 9 | 7 | 1 | 0 | .407/.454/.570 | .346 | .410 | -0.7 | 0.5 | 1.4 |
| Clint Courtney, Marv Foley, Milt May | 2012 | CHN | MLB | 26 | 250 | 28 | 13 | 1 | 3 | 25 | 16 | 35 | 1 | 1 | .269/.317/.381 | .246 | .300 | -0.2 | C -1, 1B -1 | 1.3 |

While Clevenger put up okay numbers at Double-A, he was repeating the level and didn't show any progress from 2010. He draws enough walks and has good contact skills and extra-base power, so he isn't likely to be completely overwhelmed in the majors. But with rough defense and a marginal bat, the primary thing that makes him interesting as a potential backup catcher is that he bats left-handed, while the guys ahead of him on the depth chart—Geovany Soto and Welington Castillo— bat right-handed.

| **David DeJesus** RF | YEAR | TEAM | LVL | AGE | PA | R | 2B | 3B | HR | RBI | BB | SO | SB | CS | AVG_OBP_SLG | TAv | BABIP | BRR | FRAA | WARP |
|---|---|---|---|---|---|---|---|---|---|---|---|---|---|---|---|---|---|---|---|---|
| Born: 12/20/1979 Age: 32 | 2009 | KCA | MLB | 29 | 627 | 74 | 28 | 9 | 13 | 71 | 51 | 87 | 4 | 9 | .281/.347/.434 | .271 | .311 | 0.1 | 13.3 | 3.7 |
| Bats: L Throws: L Height: 6' 1'' Weight: 170 | 2010 | KCA | MLB | 30 | 394 | 46 | 23 | 3 | 5 | 37 | 34 | 47 | 3 | 3 | .318/.384/.443 | .287 | .355 | -1.6 | -1 | 1.5 |
| Breakout: 0% Improve: 29% Collapse: 6% | 2011 | OAK | MLB | 31 | 506 | 60 | 20 | 5 | 10 | 46 | 45 | 86 | 4 | 3 | .240/.323/.376 | .265 | .274 | 1.5 | 6.3 | 2.0 |
| Attrition: 22% MLB: 83% | 2012 | CHN | MLB | 32 | 453 | 54 | 20 | 5 | 6 | 46 | 38 | 65 | 5 | 4 | .275/.347/.396 | .265 | .310 | -1 | RF 3, LF 2 | 1.1 |
| **Comparables:** Spider Jorgensen, Jim King, Jorge Orta | | | | | | | | | | | | | | | | | | | | |

DeJesus somehow manages to sport a great reputation among Saber-aware fans—and front offices—for a corner outfielder with career numbers including a .421 slugging percentage and a walk rate of just 8.3 percent. Cubs fans can expect comparable defensive contributions to the high level Kosuke Fukudome had provided, accompanied by an offensive game with more base hits and fewer walks. The reasonable contract he signed means that he should be able to live up to expectations (or at least avoid being scapegoated), and the fact that he's been troubled with injuries throughout his career suggests that a fully healthy season still contains some upside, even though he's past his prime. Entering the season, DeJesus claims to be "100 percent" after his surgically repaired right hand bothered him throughout 2011.

**Blake DeWitt**    **2B**

Born: 8/20/1985 Age: 26
Bats: L Throws: R Height: 6' 0" Weight: 175
Breakout: 1% Improve: 37% Collapse: 4%
Attrition: 24% MLB: 76%

**Comparables:**
Bernard Gilkey,Chris Coghlan,Milt Thompson

| YEAR | TEAM | LVL | AGE | PA | R | 2B | 3B | HR | RBI | BB | SO | SB | CS | AVG_OBP_SLG | TAv | BABIP | BRR | FRAA | WARP |
|---|---|---|---|---|---|---|---|---|---|---|---|---|---|---|---|---|---|---|---|
| 2009 | ABQ | AAA | 23 | 407 | 64 | 21 | 9 | 7 | 47 | 48 | 44 | 2 | 2 | .256/.351/.426 | .250 | .276 | 2.6 | -7.7 | 0.2 |
| 2009 | LAN | MLB | 23 | 53 | 4 | 3 | 0 | 2 | 4 | 3 | 7 | 0 | 0 | .204/.245/.388 | .222 | .195 | -0.1 | -0.1 | -0.1 |
| 2010 | CHN | MLB | 24 | 204 | 18 | 9 | 1 | 4 | 22 | 17 | 37 | 1 | 0 | .250/.314/.375 | .244 | .290 | 0.1 | -0.1 | 0.2 |
| 2010 | LAN | MLB | 24 | 292 | 29 | 15 | 4 | 1 | 30 | 30 | 49 | 2 | 2 | .270/.352/.371 | .268 | .329 | -1.2 | -1.4 | 0.8 |
| 2011 | CHN | MLB | 25 | 243 | 21 | 11 | 4 | 5 | 26 | 12 | 31 | 1 | 0 | .265/.305/.413 | .250 | .289 | -1.4 | -0.1 | 0.2 |
| 2012 | CHN | MLB | 26 | 279 | 33 | 12 | 3 | 5 | 29 | 25 | 43 | 1 | 1 | .263/.332/.395 | .259 | .298 | -0.1 | 2B -4, 3B 1 | 1.5 |

DeWitt's walk rate plummeted when he joined the Cubs, but he was never as patient as his numbers with the Dodgers would suggest. He hit low in the lineup in Los Angeles and got intentional and semi-intentional walks he wouldn't get with the Cubs. He also stopped hitting right-handed pitching in 2011, but that's almost certainly a statistical fluctuation given his near-textbook approach at the plate. DeWitt remains a valuable utility player, and unless the Cubs start leaning far more to the left with the influx of Bostonians to the front office, the fact that DeWitt doesn't bat right-handed makes him a valuable commodity.

**Koyie Hill**    **C**

Born: 3/9/1979 Age: 33
Bats: B Throws: R Height: 6' 1" Weight: 190
Breakout: 3% Improve: 35% Collapse: 9%
Attrition: 44% MLB: 67%

**Comparables:**
Josh Paul,Hank Foiles,Chad Moeller

| YEAR | TEAM | LVL | AGE | PA | R | 2B | 3B | HR | RBI | BB | SO | SB | CS | AVG_OBP_SLG | TAv | BABIP | BRR | FRAA | WARP |
|---|---|---|---|---|---|---|---|---|---|---|---|---|---|---|---|---|---|---|---|
| 2009 | CHN | MLB | 30 | 284 | 26 | 12 | 2 | 2 | 24 | 27 | 78 | 0 | 0 | .237/.312/.324 | .222 | .333 | 0.3 | -0.8 | 0.0 |
| 2010 | CHN | MLB | 31 | 231 | 18 | 13 | 1 | 1 | 17 | 12 | 61 | 1 | 0 | .214/.254/.298 | .209 | .292 | 2.8 | 1 | -0.1 |
| 2011 | CHN | MLB | 32 | 153 | 15 | 3 | 1 | 2 | 9 | 14 | 40 | 1 | 0 | .194/.268/.276 | .195 | .258 | 0.1 | -0.9 | -0.5 |
| 2012 | CHN | MLB | 33 | 250 | 25 | 11 | 1 | 3 | 22 | 19 | 63 | 1 | 0 | .226/.287/.329 | .221 | .291 | 0 | C -1, 3B -0 | 0.3 |

In last year's edition, Hill was reported as having the sixth-worst season in the Retrosheet-era database among those with 200 PA in a season. This is significant only because he was actually worse in 2011 (by TAv), though with Geovany Soto not missing as much time, he didn't get 200 PA. He has a good reputation as a defender and play-caller, but the metrics haven't backed that up: He's thrown out just 21 percent over the past two seasons while allowing 38 wild pitches plus passed balls in just 894 1/3 innings of work.

**Brett Jackson**    **CF**

Born: 8/2/1988 Age: 23
Bats: L Throws: R Height: 6' 3" Weight: 210
Breakout: 1% Improve: 36% Collapse: 2%
Attrition: 14% MLB: 77%

**Comparables:**
Mike Jorgensen,B.J. Upton,Joe Benson

| YEAR | TEAM | LVL | AGE | PA | R | 2B | 3B | HR | RBI | BB | SO | SB | CS | AVG_OBP_SLG | TAv | BABIP | BRR | FRAA | WARP |
|---|---|---|---|---|---|---|---|---|---|---|---|---|---|---|---|---|---|---|---|
| 2009 | PEO | A | 20 | 128 | 30 | 5 | 1 | 7 | 17 | 11 | 32 | 11 | 1 | .295/.383/.545 | .325 | .356 | 0.9 | 2.3 | 1.7 |
| 2009 | BOI | A- | 20 | 106 | 14 | 1 | 1 | 1 | 15 | 17 | 20 | 2 | 1 | .330/.443/.398 | .314 | .418 | 0.1 | -4.1 | 0.5 |
| 2010 | DAY | A+ | 21 | 312 | 56 | 19 | 8 | 6 | 38 | 43 | 63 | 12 | 7 | .316/.421/.517 | .332 | .397 | 4.1 | 4 | 4.1 |
| 2010 | TEN | AA | 21 | 268 | 47 | 13 | 6 | 6 | 28 | 30 | 63 | 18 | 4 | .276/.366/.465 | .282 | .352 | 2 | -3.7 | 1.1 |
| 2011 | TEN | AA | 22 | 297 | 45 | 10 | 3 | 10 | 32 | 45 | 74 | 15 | 6 | .256/.373/.443 | .284 | .323 | 2.4 | -1.9 | 1.6 |
| 2011 | IOW | AAA | 22 | 215 | 39 | 13 | 2 | 10 | 26 | 28 | 64 | 6 | 1 | .297/.388/.551 | .320 | .402 | 2.5 | 4.8 | 2.7 |
| 2012 | CHN | MLB | 23 | 250 | 29 | 10 | 2 | 7 | 28 | 25 | 70 | 8 | 3 | .241/.323/.403 | .258 | .315 | -0.1 | CF -1, RF -1 | 1.2 |

In the early 2000s, the Tigers had a young left-handed outfielder who was considered to have no outstanding strength and who struck out too much. Fast forward to 2011, and Curtis Granderson led his league in runs scored and RBI. One anecdote won't change Brett Jackson's stars, but—like Granderson before him—Jackson is a high-energy player who carries the reputation of not having a standout skill. Yet, other than making contact, he's above average in all aspects of the game, and he compensates for his whiffs by taking enough pitches to rack up the walks. How much playing time Jackson sees for the 2012 Cubs will depend on a variety of factors, such as offseason acquisitions, service time manipulation, how he does in spring training, how well Byrd rebounds, and how Jackson's Triple-A season begins. But anything less than half a season would be a disappointment.

**Reed Johnson** RF

Born: 12/8/1976 Age: 35
Bats: R Throws: R Height: 5' 11" Weight: 180
Breakout: 1% Improve: 28% Collapse: 8%
Attrition: 28% MLB: 71%

Comparables:
Emil Brown, Hank Bauer, Brian Jordan

| YEAR | TEAM | LVL | AGE | PA | R | 2B | 3B | HR | RBI | BB | SO | SB | CS | AVG_OBP_SLG | TAv | BABIP | BRR | FRAA | WARP |
|------|------|-----|-----|-----|----|----|----|----|-----|----|----|----|----|-------------|------|-------|------|-----------|------|
| 2009 | CHN | MLB | 32 | 186 | 23 | 10 | 2 | 4 | 22 | 13 | 27 | 2 | 1 | .255/.330/.412 | .258 | .281 | 0.2 | -1.9 | 0.3 |
| 2010 | LAN | MLB | 33 | 215 | 24 | 11 | 2 | 2 | 15 | 5 | 50 | 2 | 2 | .262/.291/.366 | .243 | .336 | 1.5 | 3.2 | 0.5 |
| 2011 | CHN | MLB | 34 | 266 | 33 | 22 | 1 | 5 | 28 | 5 | 63 | 2 | 1 | .309/.348/.467 | .285 | .394 | 0.4 | -0.8 | 1.1 |
| 2012 | CHN | MLB | 35 | 250 | 28 | 13 | 1 | 3 | 25 | 11 | 52 | 3 | 2 | .266/.318/.376 | .248 | .324 | -0.3 | RF 1, CF -2 | 0.5 |

Johnson has been the backup quarterback in Chicago three of the past four years, unduly loved by fans. In 2011, he enhanced his legend, actually hitting right-handed pitching for a change (.312/.361/.468). That he did this on the strength of a .394 overall BABIP (.410 vs. RHP) won't escape the notice of the new regime in Chicago, and there's a good chance Johnson won't return. Regardless of his low earned-to-received love quotient from the fans, Johnson has been a very useful player—he has hit left-handed pitching with authority (.311/.369/.464 for his career), and when his back isn't acting up, he's been a good corner outfielder who can cover center field in a pinch.

...ter who never got an opportunity," spoke Theo when the input ..... tion when evaluating this statement, which is obviously false on its surface. Clearly, there have been plenty of hitters whose statistics show they aren't good major-league hitters, despite tearing up Triple-A. As team president, Epstein's is primarily a leadership position, and while mechanics of swing planes, quickness of swing, pitch recognition, and other hitting-instructor terms do have an impact on how well a batter hits, so does confidence. Sending a clear message that his work has been noticed to "an asset" (as Theo later referred to LaHair) can't do any harm.

**Carlos Peña** 1B

Born: 5/17/1978 Age: 34
Bats: L Throws: L Height: 6' 3" Weight: 210
Breakout: 0% Improve: 24% Collapse: 9%
Attrition: 13% MLB: 92%

Comparables:
Jack Clark, Carlos Delgado, Ken Phelps

| YEAR | TEAM | LVL | AGE | PA | R | 2B | 3B | HR | RBI | BB | SO | SB | CS | AVG_OBP_SLG | TAv | BABIP | BRR | FRAA | WARP |
|------|------|-----|-----|-----|----|----|----|----|-----|----|-----|----|----|-------------|------|-------|------|-------|------|
| 2009 | TBA | MLB | 31 | 570 | 91 | 25 | 2 | 39 | 100 | 87 | 163 | 3 | 3 | .227/.356/.537 | .309 | .250 | -0.7 | -8 | 2.4 |
| 2010 | TBA | MLB | 32 | 582 | 64 | 18 | 0 | 28 | 84 | 87 | 158 | 5 | 1 | .196/.325/.407 | .278 | .222 | 0.5 | -6.8 | 0.9 |
| 2011 | CHN | MLB | 33 | 606 | 72 | 27 | 3 | 28 | 80 | 101 | 161 | 2 | 2 | .225/.357/.462 | .288 | .267 | 0.1 | 0.2 | 2.2 |
| 2012 | CHN | MLB | 34 | 565 | 76 | 21 | 2 | 30 | 77 | 87 | 156 | 3 | 1 | .233/.360/.480 | .296 | .276 | -0.2 | 1B -2 | 2.8 |

Peña was exactly what the Cubs expected, though he took a while to get warmed up. He ended up posting rate stats just below his career marks, playing his standard good defense, and, well, disappearing at the plate against left-handed hurlers. The big swing gives him some of the best power in the game, though it comes at the price of maddeningly long slumps chock full of strikeouts. Peña provided a great clubhouse presence. Whether he'll again be able to find eight digits on his tax return remains to be seen, but he could get multi-year security from a team that doesn't want to pay the market rate for Albert Pujols or Prince Fielder.

**Dave Sappelt** CF

Born: 1/2/1987 Age: 25
Bats: R Throws: R Height: 5' 10" Weight: 193
Breakout: 6% Improve: 52% Collapse: 5%
Attrition: 21% MLB: 87%

Comparables:
Ken Landreaux, Paul Molitor, Angel Mangual

| YEAR | TEAM | LVL | AGE | PA | R | 2B | 3B | HR | RBI | BB | SO | SB | CS | AVG_OBP_SLG | TAv | BABIP | BRR | FRAA | WARP |
|------|------|-----|-----|-----|----|----|----|----|-----|----|----|----|----|-------------|------|-------|------|----------|------|
| 2009 | DYT | A | 22 | 331 | 44 | 14 | 7 | 3 | 25 | 23 | 46 | 26 | 11 | .269/.323/.392 | .277 | .307 | 1.2 | 10 | 2.7 |
| 2009 | SAR | A+ | 22 | 271 | 27 | 10 | 3 | 4 | 21 | 13 | 29 | 21 | 11 | .295/.330/.406 | .281 | .315 | 0.2 | 6.6 | 2.3 |
| 2010 | LYN | A+ | 23 | 77 | 7 | 5 | 0 | 0 | 4 | 5 | 15 | 6 | 4 | .282/.338/.352 | .261 | .357 | -0.4 | -0.4 | 0.2 |
| 2010 | CAR | AA | 23 | 372 | 53 | 19 | 8 | 9 | 62 | 31 | 46 | 15 | 13 | .361/.416/.548 | .344 | .394 | -3.7 | 4.4 | 4.6 |
| 2010 | LOU | AAA | 23 | 115 | 12 | 8 | 3 | 1 | 8 | 6 | 13 | 4 | 1 | .324/.365/.481 | .262 | .362 | -1.9 | 1.7 | 0.4 |
| 2011 | LOU | AAA | 24 | 336 | 40 | 16 | 3 | 7 | 29 | 30 | 39 | 4 | 4 | .313/.377/.458 | .283 | .339 | -2.5 | 0.7 | 1.4 |
| 2011 | CIN | MLB | 24 | 118 | 14 | 8 | 0 | 0 | 5 | 7 | 17 | 1 | 1 | .243/.289/.318 | .225 | .289 | 0.5 | 1.6 | 0.0 |
| 2012 | CHN | MLB | 25 | 250 | 29 | 12 | 2 | 4 | 27 | 13 | 40 | 8 | 5 | .276/.317/.397 | .254 | .314 | -0.9 | CF -0, LF 1 | 0.9 |

There's an easy temptation to pigeonhole Sappelt as a fourth outfielder. He's not the picture image of a center fielder: He's built more like a fire hydrant but motors around like a speedster. He has some power and some range and he helps some on offense, without having any one signature skill beyond out-of-fashion contact hitting. He's become a more patient hitter, and the glove will play. He shrugged off a month missed to a strained oblique to bounce back and earn an August promotion from the Reds. With Tony Campana, the Cubs are well-stocked with capable outfield reserves, or even a productive stopgap platoon solution for center field if Marlon Byrd is traded before Brett Jackson is deemed ready. Such a platoon could redefine the term "short-center fielder" from its meaning to most Chicagoans, where 16-inch softball is ever-popular.

| Alfonso Soriano | LF | YEAR | TEAM | LVL | AGE | PA | R | 2B | 3B | HR | RBI | BB | SO | SB | CS | AVG_OBP_SLG | TAv | BABIP | BRR | FRAA | WARP |
|---|---|---|---|---|---|---|---|---|---|---|---|---|---|---|---|---|---|---|---|---|---|
| Born: 1/7/1976 Age: 36 | | 2009 | CHN | MLB | 33 | 522 | 64 | 25 | 1 | 20 | 55 | 40 | 118 | 9 | 2 | .241/.303/.423 | .247 | .279 | -0.2 | -0.2 | 0.2 |
| Bats: R Throws: R Height: 6' 2" Weight: 160 | | 2010 | CHN | MLB | 34 | 548 | 67 | 40 | 3 | 24 | 79 | 45 | 123 | 5 | 1 | .258/.322/.496 | .284 | .295 | 2 | -6.4 | 1.8 |
| Breakout: 3% Improve: 24% Collapse: 12% | | 2011 | CHN | MLB | 35 | 508 | 50 | 27 | 1 | 26 | 88 | 27 | 113 | 2 | 1 | .244/.289/.469 | .257 | .266 | 0.8 | -7.9 | 0.3 |
| Attrition: 22% MLB: 73% | | 2012 | CHN | MLB | 36 | 487 | 60 | 26 | 2 | 22 | 69 | 32 | 111 | 7 | 2 | .259/.311/.469 | .273 | .296 | 0.1 | LF -4 | 1.8 |
| Comparables: | | | | | | | | | | | | | | | | | | | | | |
| Bob Nieman, David Dellucci, Bob Cerv | | | | | | | | | | | | | | | | | | | | | |

Most everyone who's seen Soriano play thinks he's a terrible fielder. And FRAA is starting to agree with this view now that he's no longer throwing out 19 baserunners in a year, as he did in 2007. But another advanced fielding metric, ultimate zone rating, says he's been 55 runs better than the average left fielder during his time with the Cubs. Considering that Soriano has amassed less than 10 WARP in his time in Chicago, 55 runs (approximately 5.5 WARP) would dramatically impact his value, percentage-wise. Of course, the elephant in the room is that he's been paid $82 million for this, so it's not as if he's been worth his salary either way. And the really painful part of the contract is still to come, as he's due $54 million more through 2014.

| Geovany Soto | C | YEAR | TEAM | LVL | AGE | PA | R | 2B | 3B | HR | RBI | BB | SO | SB | CS | AVG_OBP_SLG | TAv | BABIP | BRR | FRAA | WARP |
|---|---|---|---|---|---|---|---|---|---|---|---|---|---|---|---|---|---|---|---|---|---|
| Born: 1/20/1983 Age: 29 | | 2009 | CHN | MLB | 26 | 389 | 27 | 19 | 1 | 11 | 47 | 50 | 77 | 1 | 0 | .218/.321/.381 | .233 | .246 | -0.8 | 0.6 | 0.7 |
| Bats: R Throws: R Height: 6' 2" Weight: 230 | | 2010 | CHN | MLB | 27 | 387 | 47 | 19 | 0 | 17 | 53 | 62 | 83 | 0 | 1 | .280/.393/.497 | .309 | .324 | -2.9 | -1.7 | 3.1 |
| Breakout: 3% Improve: 31% Collapse: 4% | | 2011 | CHN | MLB | 28 | 474 | 46 | 26 | 0 | 17 | 54 | 45 | 124 | 0 | 0 | .228/.310/.411 | .251 | .280 | -2.3 | 3.3 | 1.8 |
| Attrition: 18% MLB: 86% | | 2012 | CHN | MLB | 29 | 429 | 56 | 22 | 1 | 17 | 56 | 50 | 97 | 0 | 0 | .266/.354/.467 | .291 | .314 | 0 | C 0 | 3.6 |
| Comparables: | | | | | | | | | | | | | | | | | | | | | |
| Chris Hoiles, Miguel Ojeda, Johnny Bench | | | | | | | | | | | | | | | | | | | | | |

With only one trip to the 15-day DL, 2011 was one of Soto's least injury-riddled seasons. Yet something was clearly wrong. He didn't seem to be reacting to pitches nearly as well, resulting in many more strikeouts, fewer walks, and more weakly hit balls. Or the answer may be more straightforward—Soto's two best seasons by rate stats, 2008 and 2010, followed episodes of dramatic weight loss, and Soto clearly wasn't as svelte in 2011 as he'd been the year before. Whether his mediocre 2011 season will serve as another sufficient bottom to help him shed some of his own bottom remains to be seen, but Soto's shown himself to be among the top hitting catchers in the game when properly motivated.

| Ian Stewart | 3B | YEAR | TEAM | LVL | AGE | PA | R | 2B | 3B | HR | RBI | BB | SO | SB | CS | AVG_OBP_SLG | TAv | BABIP | BRR | FRAA | WARP |
|---|---|---|---|---|---|---|---|---|---|---|---|---|---|---|---|---|---|---|---|---|---|
| Born: 4/5/1985 Age: 27 | | 2009 | COL | MLB | 24 | 491 | 74 | 19 | 3 | 25 | 70 | 56 | 138 | 7 | 4 | .228/.322/.464 | .257 | .270 | 0 | -5.6 | 0.6 |
| Bats: L Throws: R Height: 6' 4" Weight: 205 | | 2010 | COL | MLB | 25 | 441 | 54 | 14 | 2 | 18 | 61 | 45 | 110 | 5 | 2 | .256/.338/.443 | .270 | .308 | 1.4 | 3 | 2.7 |
| Breakout: 1% Improve: 37% Collapse: 4% | | 2011 | CSP | AAA | 26 | 195 | 29 | 10 | 1 | 14 | 42 | 22 | 51 | 1 | 0 | .275/.359/.591 | .271 | .308 | 0.7 | -2.9 | 0.7 |
| Attrition: 19% MLB: 91% | | 2011 | COL | MLB | 26 | 136 | 14 | 6 | 1 | 0 | 6 | 14 | 37 | 3 | 2 | .156/.243/.221 | .169 | .224 | -0.4 | -0.8 | -0.9 |
| Comparables: | | 2012 | CHN | MLB | 27 | 250 | 31 | 11 | 2 | 10 | 33 | 25 | 66 | 3 | 1 | .252/.333/.454 | .277 | .309 | -0.1 | 3B -0, 2B -0 | 2.6 |
| Josh Fields, Troy Glaus, Marty Brown | | | | | | | | | | | | | | | | | | | | | |

In Googling "Ian Stewart," up comes a book titled, "Professor Stewart's cabinet of mathematical curiosities." While there's not a chapter in there about the new Cubs third baseman going homerless for the Rockies in 2011, there could be. The outage certainly qualifies as "curious" for someone whose power was described as "jaw-dropping" in his prospect days. The Cubs are hoping that the combination of statistical fluctuation, a new home, and a new hitting coach will get Stewart back on track and crashing homers onto Sheffield Avenue. But while there's been a dearth of production from the left side for generations on the North Side, it would be foolhardy to expect too much out of Stewart—even in homer-happy Coors Field, he averaged just .246/.334/.454 in his three "good" seasons leading up to his "curious" 2011.

| Matthew Szczur | CF | YEAR | TEAM | LVL | AGE | PA | R | 2B | 3B | HR | RBI | BB | SO | SB | CS | AVG_OBP_SLG | TAv | BABIP | BRR | FRAA | WARP |
|---|---|---|---|---|---|---|---|---|---|---|---|---|---|---|---|---|---|---|---|---|---|
| Born: 7/20/1989 Age: 22 | | 2010 | BOI | A- | 20 | 82 | 17 | 9 | 0 | 0 | 8 | 6 | 11 | 1 | 0 | .397/.450/.521 | .321 | .468 | -1.9 | -0.2 | 0.5 |
| Bats: R Throws: R Height: 6' 2" Weight: 195 | | 2011 | PEO | A | 21 | 298 | 55 | 15 | 1 | 5 | 27 | 21 | 28 | 17 | 5 | .314/.366/.431 | .294 | .335 | 2.5 | 1.8 | 2.5 |
| Breakout: 6% Improve: 28% Collapse: 5% | | 2011 | DAY | A+ | 21 | 182 | 20 | 7 | 2 | 5 | 19 | 5 | 20 | 7 | 0 | .260/.283/.410 | .258 | .268 | -0.9 | 0.9 | 0.5 |
| Attrition: 22% MLB: 53% | | 2012 | CHN | MLB | 22 | 250 | 25 | 11 | 1 | 5 | 26 | 9 | 44 | 6 | 2 | .251/.277/.361 | .225 | .285 | 0.1 | CF 0, RF -1 | -0.3 |
| Comparables: | | | | | | | | | | | | | | | | | | | | | |
| Gorkys Hernandez, Jarvis Tatum, Thad Bosley | | | | | | | | | | | | | | | | | | | | | |

Szczur ("Caesar") is one of those prospects who elicits ratings all over the scale—even within BP, there's a szczism about him, with Kevin Goldstein omitting him entirely from his Cubs prospect list while Jason Parks had him in the team's top five. Two things are certain: He has blinding speed and great hand-eye coordination. To date, he hasn't translated his wheels (rated by some as an 80 skill) into either impact baserunning or impact fielding in center field. He's not expected to hit for power or to improve his throwing arm much, and he doesn't draw many walks. But he'd also been splitting his efforts between baseball and football until recently, he went to a cold-weather college, and he's still young, so there's time for him to tip the scales in his favor.

**Josh Vitters**    3B
Born: 8/27/1989 Age: 22
Bats: R Throws: R Height: 6' 3" Weight: 200
Breakout: 6% Improve: 29% Collapse: 4%
Attrition: 15% MLB: 54%

| YEAR | TEAM | LVL | AGE | PA | R | 2B | 3B | HR | RBI | BB | SO | SB | CS | AVG/OBP/SLG | TAv | BABIP | BRR | FRAA | WARP |
|------|------|-----|-----|-----|----|----|----|----|-----|----|----|----|----|-------------|-----|-------|------|------|------|
| 2009 | PEO | A | 19 | 288 | 42 | 12 | 1 | 15 | 46 | 7 | 42 | 4 | 0 | .316/.354/.535 | .317 | .330 | -1.4 | -4.2 | 1.7 |
| 2009 | DAY | A+ | 19 | 196 | 21 | 7 | 2 | 3 | 22 | 5 | 23 | 2 | 1 | .238/.262/.344 | .229 | .258 | 0.5 | -0.3 | 0.0 |
| 2010 | DAY | A+ | 20 | 120 | 16 | 8 | 0 | 3 | 13 | 8 | 22 | 4 | 1 | .291/.350/.445 | .309 | .341 | 0.4 | -3 | 0.5 |
| 2010 | TEN | AA | 20 | 228 | 28 | 12 | 0 | 7 | 26 | 13 | 41 | 2 | 0 | .223/.280/.393 | .231 | .244 | 0.4 | 2.4 | 0.7 |

while afield.

# PITCHERS

**Justin Berg**
Born: 6/7/1984 Age: 28
Bats: R Throws: R Height: 6' 4" Weight: 230
Breakout: 31% Improve: 55% Collapse: 31%
Attrition: 7% MLB: 83%

Comparables:
Ron Klimkowski, Scott Munter, Mike Perez

| YEAR | TEAM | LVL | AGE | W | L | SV | G | GS | IP | H | HR | BB | SO | EqBB9 | EqSO9 | GB% | BABIP | WHIP | ERA | FIP | FRA | WARP |
|------|------|-----|-----|---|---|----|----|----|-----|----|----|----|----|-------|-------|-----|-------|------|------|------|------|------|
| 2009 | IOW | AAA | 25 | 6 | 2 | 0 | 37 | 0 | 55² | 41 | 2 | 29 | 35 | 4.7 | 5.7 | 63% | .239 | 1.26 | 2.42 | 4.55 | 4.96 | 0.0 |
| 2009 | CHN | MLB | 25 | 0 | 0 | 0 | 11 | 0 | 12 | 10 | 0 | 1 | 7 | 0.8 | 5.2 | 55% | .270 | 0.92 | 0.75 | 2.14 | 2.51 | 0.4 |
| 2010 | IOW | AAA | 26 | 4 | 1 | 0 | 21 | 0 | 29² | 16 | 2 | 6 | 10 | 3.6 | 4.8 | 74% | .250 | 1.21 | 3.64 | 4.97 | 6.13 | -0.4 |
| 2010 | CHN | MLB | 26 | 0 | 1 | 0 | 41 | 0 | 40 | 45 | 3 | 20 | 14 | 4.5 | 3.2 | 54% | .288 | 1.62 | 5.18 | 5.11 | 7.00 | -0.7 |
| 2011 | IOW | AAA | 27 | 1 | 0 | 3 | 27 | 0 | 29² | 29 | 4 | 17 | 17 | 5.2 | 5.2 | 67% | .287 | 1.55 | 5.16 | 6.57 | 7.81 | -0.6 |
| 2011 | CHN | MLB | 27 | 0 | 0 | 0 | 8 | 0 | 12 | 11 | 1 | 6 | 6 | 4.5 | 4.5 | 53% | .270 | 1.42 | 3.75 | 5.08 | 6.71 | -0.2 |
| 2012 | CHN | MLB | 28 | 1 | 0 | 0 | 20 | 0 | 22² | 24 | 2 | 10 | 8 | 4.2 | 3.1 | 60% | .298 | 1.55 | 5.66 | 4.97 | 6.15 | -0.2 |

Berg's sinker works just fine, thank you. He's allowed a .265 batting average and a .361 slugging percentage for his career—not great, but with the groundball-induced double plays, it's good enough to hold a roster spot. Except that the other pitches don't work, and he frequently misses the strike zone for fear of getting them clobbered, leading to an an unacceptable .346 career on-base percentage allowed and a likely return to Triple-A.

**Chris Carpenter**
Born: 12/26/1985 Age: 26
Bats: R Throws: R Height: 6' 5" Weight: 220
Breakout: 24% Improve: 53% Collapse: 34%
Attrition: 24% MLB: 93%

Comparables:
Kevin Olsen, Butch Metzger, Shawn Hillegas

| YEAR | TEAM | LVL | AGE | W | L | SV | G | GS | IP | H | HR | BB | SO | EqBB9 | EqSO9 | GB% | BABIP | WHIP | ERA | FIP | FRA | WARP |
|------|------|-----|-----|---|---|----|----|----|-----|----|----|----|----|-------|-------|-----|-------|------|------|------|------|------|
| 2011 | IOW | AAA | 25 | 1 | 1 | 1 | 22 | 0 | 30¹ | 32 | 3 | 23 | 28 | 6.8 | 8.3 | 55% | .345 | 1.81 | 6.53 | 5.75 | 6.16 | -0.1 |
| 2011 | CHN | MLB | 25 | 0 | 0 | 0 | 10 | 0 | 9² | 12 | 1 | 7 | 8 | 6.5 | 7.4 | 47% | .355 | 1.97 | 2.79 | 4.86 | 5.43 | 0.0 |
| 2012 | CHN | MLB | 26 | 1 | 1 | 0 | 7 | 3 | 19 | 20 | 2 | 10 | 11 | 4.9 | 5.4 | 52% | .312 | 1.59 | 5.69 | 4.99 | 6.19 | -0.1 |

Only 10 pitchers had a pitch clocked faster than Carpenter did in 2011, and he topped 100 mph four times. He also landed on the disabled list with a strained oblique in August, and his terrible control all season long is a strong indicator that the arm was bothering him long before he acknowledged it. He's had frequent injuries dating back to college, suppressing his prospect value far below his talent level. So the Cubs have for the time being scrapped the idea of using him in the rotation, and he made no starts in 2011. The organization became cautiously optimistic that Carpenter is all the way back after he began blowing away hitters in the Arizona Fall League. If being limited to fastballs and sliders out of the pen keeps him healthy, Carpenter's pure stuff gives him the potential to continue his AFL success in the major leagues in 2012.

**Andrew Cashner**
Born: 9/11/1986 Age: 25
Bats: R Throws: R Height: 6' 7'' Weight: 210
Breakout: 24% Improve: 60% Collapse: 18%
Attrition: 13% MLB: 94%

Comparables:
Chad Gaudin, Anibal Sanchez, Pat Zachry

| YEAR | TEAM | LVL | AGE | W | L | SV | G | GS | IP | H | HR | BB | SO | EqBB9 | EqSO9 | GB% | BABIP | WHIP | ERA | FIP | FRA | WARP |
|---|---|---|---|---|---|---|---|---|---|---|---|---|---|---|---|---|---|---|---|---|---|---|
| 2009 | DAY | A+ | 22 | 0 | 0 | 0 | 12 | 12 | 42 | 31 | 1 | 15 | 34 | 3.2 | 7.3 | 50% | .250 | 1.10 | 1.50 | 3.18 | 3.67 | 0.9 |
| 2009 | TEN | AA | 22 | 3 | 5 | 0 | 12 | 12 | 58¹ | 53 | 1 | 31 | 43 | 4.2 | 6.3 | 49% | .256 | 1.23 | 3.40 | 3.55 | 4.73 | 0.9 |
| 2010 | TEN | AA | 23 | 3 | 1 | 0 | 6 | 6 | 36 | 14 | 0 | 11 | 27 | 3.2 | 10.5 | 49% | .269 | 0.97 | 2.75 | 2.97 | 3.21 | 1.0 |
| 2010 | CHN | MLB | 23 | 2 | 6 | 0 | 53 | 0 | 54¹ | 55 | 8 | 30 | 50 | 5.0 | 8.3 | 52% | .313 | 1.56 | 4.80 | 5.06 | 5.48 | 0.0 |
| 2011 | CHN | MLB | 24 | 0 | 0 | 0 | 7 | 1 | 10² | 3 | 1 | 4 | 8 | 3.4 | 6.8 | 56% | .077 | 0.66 | 1.69 | 3.84 | 2.98 | 0.2 |
| 2012 | SDN | MLB | 25 | 1 | 1 | 0 | 12 | 2 | 20¹ | 18 | 2 | 9 | 14 | 4.0 | 6.4 | 48% | .281 | 1.31 | 4.02 | 4.43 | 4.37 | 0.1 |

Every effort has been made to convert Cashner the TCU closer, considered to have the best stuff among college pitchers in the 2008 draft, into Cashner the Cubs front-line starter. As with Carpenter, Cashner has great fastball velocity—approaching 100 mph out of the bullpen—a nasty slider, and an injury history that makes everyone nervous. Unlike Carpenter, his changeup is good enough to continue efforts to keep him in the rotation, despite the fact that he works at a somewhat lesser velocity there. While his walk numbers suggest control issues, arm health is considered to be both more important and the underlying cause. If he can stay healthy for a full season, his control should be more than adequate to support his great stuff.

**Casey Coleman**
Born: 7/3/1987 Age: 24
Bats: L Throws: R Height: 6' 1'' Weight: 180
Breakout: 26% Improve: 55% Collapse: 26%
Attrition: 6% MLB: 96%

Comparables:
John Lannan, Larry Jaster, Neal Heaton

| YEAR | TEAM | LVL | AGE | W | L | SV | G | GS | IP | H | HR | BB | SO | EqBB9 | EqSO9 | GB% | BABIP | WHIP | ERA | FIP | FRA | WARP |
|---|---|---|---|---|---|---|---|---|---|---|---|---|---|---|---|---|---|---|---|---|---|---|
| 2009 | TEN | AA | 22 | 15 | 6 | 0 | 27 | 27 | 149 | 151 | 9 | 61 | 89 | 3.5 | 5.1 | 51% | .282 | 1.34 | 3.68 | 4.02 | 5.73 | -0.4 |
| 2010 | IOW | AAA | 23 | 10 | 7 | 0 | 20 | 20 | 117¹ | 74 | 5 | 15 | 38 | 2.7 | 4.5 | 57% | .271 | 1.20 | 4.07 | 4.40 | 4.90 | 1.4 |
| 2010 | CHN | MLB | 23 | 4 | 2 | 0 | 12 | 8 | 57 | 56 | 3 | 25 | 27 | 3.9 | 4.3 | 48% | .280 | 1.42 | 4.11 | 4.26 | 4.40 | 0.9 |
| 2011 | IOW | AAA | 24 | 2 | 1 | 0 | 12 | 12 | 74 | 69 | 11 | 22 | 54 | 2.7 | 6.6 | 49% | .280 | 1.23 | 3.65 | 5.10 | 4.90 | 1.0 |
| 2011 | CHN | MLB | 24 | 3 | 9 | 0 | 19 | 17 | 84¹ | 102 | 10 | 46 | 75 | 4.9 | 8.0 | 45% | .358 | 1.75 | 6.40 | 4.54 | 5.35 | 0.2 |
| 2012 | CHN | MLB | 24 | 5 | 7 | 0 | 17 | 17 | 97 | 102 | 11 | 38 | 51 | 3.5 | 4.7 | 50% | .304 | 1.43 | 5.06 | 4.80 | 5.50 | -0.1 |

Coleman knows how to pitch. In fact, he got tabbed "Mini-Maddux" after Ryne Sandberg compared him to Greg Maddux in 2009. But even though one frisky radar gun recorded him topping 94 mph in 2011, Casey's four-seam fastball is more likely to arrive at or below 90, and as he learns even more about how to pitch, he'll avoid tossing that four-seamer anywhere near the strike zone. His two-seamer, curve (against righties) and change (against lefties) are somewhat more effective, but Coleman's upside more closely resembles the career of Mike Maddux than that of Mike's little brother.

**Ryan Dempster**
Born: 5/3/1977 Age: 35
Bats: R Throws: R Height: 6' 3'' Weight: 195
Breakout: 26% Improve: 47% Collapse: 28%
Attrition: 10% MLB: 88%

Comparables:
Justin Speier, Joe Borowski, Kyle Farnsworth

| YEAR | TEAM | LVL | AGE | W | L | SV | G | GS | IP | H | HR | BB | SO | EqBB9 | EqSO9 | GB% | BABIP | WHIP | ERA | FIP | FRA | WARP |
|---|---|---|---|---|---|---|---|---|---|---|---|---|---|---|---|---|---|---|---|---|---|---|
| 2009 | CHN | MLB | 32 | 11 | 9 | 0 | 31 | 31 | 200 | 196 | 22 | 65 | 172 | 2.9 | 7.7 | 49% | .307 | 1.30 | 3.64 | 3.83 | 4.64 | 2.4 |
| 2010 | CHN | MLB | 33 | 15 | 12 | 0 | 34 | 34 | 215¹ | 198 | 25 | 86 | 208 | 3.6 | 8.7 | 50% | .298 | 1.32 | 3.85 | 4.02 | 4.29 | 2.7 |
| 2011 | CHN | MLB | 34 | 10 | 14 | 0 | 34 | 34 | 202¹ | 211 | 23 | 82 | 191 | 3.6 | 8.5 | 46% | .331 | 1.45 | 4.80 | 3.87 | 4.48 | 2.2 |
| 2012 | CHN | MLB | 35 | 10 | 11 | 0 | 29 | 29 | 176² | 169 | 19 | 63 | 145 | 3.2 | 7.4 | 48% | .316 | 1.31 | 4.36 | 4.03 | 4.74 | 1.2 |

With a winsome personality and a sense of humor, Dempster has managed to remain above most of the blame-tossing in Chicago despite results short of his paychecks, spats with his manager, and a self-inflicted injury in 2009 that cost him playing time. His velocity was down a tick in 2011, but the big jump in ERA wasn't really his fault—as shown by both his FIP and FRA—and the Cubs wasted no time picking up his $14 million option for 2012. Though he walks too many to front a rotation, Dempster's committed to his craft, mixing pitches and pitch sequences to support his two fastballs and nasty slider. All indications are that he'll be good enough and durable enough to rack up 200 innings again.

**Matt Garza**
Born: 11/11/1983 Age: 28
Bats: R Throws: R Height: 6' 5'' Weight: 185
Breakout: 25% Improve: 51% Collapse: 23%
Attrition: 5% MLB: 93%

Comparables:
Don Sutton, Heath Bell, Bill Singer

| YEAR | TEAM | LVL | AGE | W | L | SV | G | GS | IP | H | HR | BB | SO | EqBB9 | EqSO9 | GB% | BABIP | WHIP | ERA | FIP | FRA | WARP |
|---|---|---|---|---|---|---|---|---|---|---|---|---|---|---|---|---|---|---|---|---|---|---|
| 2009 | TBA | MLB | 25 | 8 | 12 | 0 | 32 | 32 | 203 | 177 | 25 | 79 | 189 | 3.5 | 8.4 | 40% | .274 | 1.26 | 3.95 | 4.21 | 4.58 | 2.1 |
| 2010 | TBA | MLB | 26 | 15 | 10 | 1 | 33 | 32 | 204² | 193 | 28 | 63 | 150 | 2.8 | 6.6 | 37% | .273 | 1.25 | 3.91 | 4.39 | 4.51 | 1.4 |
| 2011 | CHN | MLB | 27 | 10 | 10 | 0 | 31 | 31 | 198 | 186 | 14 | 63 | 197 | 2.9 | 9.0 | 48% | .312 | 1.26 | 3.32 | 2.92 | 3.70 | 2.7 |
| 2012 | CHN | MLB | 28 | 10 | 10 | 0 | 27 | 27 | 173² | 159 | 18 | 53 | 139 | 2.7 | 7.2 | 43% | .301 | 1.22 | 3.90 | 3.87 | 4.23 | 2.1 |

Garza pitched like a true ace in 2011, posting the eighth-best FIP among qualifying pitchers. His home run rate was completely out of character with his past and can't be expected to be repeated, but he has a broad repertoire, and the strikeouts aren't an illusion. He's averaged just 3.0 walks per nine innings over the past four seasons and should be a big help to the Cubs effort to turn things around, even though his fly-ball rate (and resultant homers) will likely keep him from the ranks of the elite.

## John Gaub

Born: 4/28/1985 Age: 27
Bats: R Throws: L Height: 6' 3" Weight: 210
Breakout: 36% Improve: 52% Collapse: 28%
Attrition: 25% MLB: 96%

**Comparables:**
Scott Williamson, John Rocker, Anthony Slama

| YEAR | TEAM | LVL | AGE | W | L | SV | G | GS | IP | H | HR | BB | SO | EqBB9 | EqSO9 | GB% | BABIP | WHIP | ERA | FIP | FRA | WARP |
|------|------|-----|-----|---|---|----|----|----|-----|----|----|----|----|-------|-------|-----|-------|------|------|------|------|------|
| 2009 | TEN | AA | 24 | 3 | 1 | 4 | 26 | 0 | 28² | 19 | 3 | 17 | 40 | 5.3 | 12.5 | 41% | .267 | 1.25 | 2.82 | 3.55 | 4.22 | 0.4 |
| 2009 | IOW | AAA | 24 | 1 | 1 | 1 | 26 | 0 | 31¹ | 17 | 1 | 15 | 40 | 4.6 | 11.5 | 43% | .235 | 1.05 | 1.73 | 2.75 | 2.50 | 0.9 |
| 2010 | IOW | AAA | 25 | 3 | 4 | 3 | 30 | 0 | 29 | 16 | 0 | 18 | 19 | 7.8 | 11.8 | 41% | .372 | 1.79 | 6.52 | 4.71 | 4.05 | 0.3 |
| 2011 | IOW | AAA | 26 | 0 | 2 | 7 | 50 | 0 | 55¹ | 41 | 5 | 39 | 72 | 6.5 | 12.2 | 50% | .298 | 1.48 | 3.42 | 4.48 | 4.61 | 0.5 |
| 2011 | CHN | MLB | 26 | 0 | 0 | 0 | 4 | 0 | 2² | 2 | 0 | 2 | 3 | 6.8 | 10.1 | 57% | .286 | 1.50 | 6.75 | 2.99 | 3.06 | 0.1 |
| 2012 | CHN | MLB | 27 | 1 | 0 | 0 | 19 | 0 | 19² | 16 | 2 | 11 | 21 | 5.1 | 9.8 | 40% | .306 | 1.36 | 4.00 | 4.07 | 4.35 | 0.2 |

There are concerns that Gaub won't wow major-league hitters as he's done to their minor-league counterparts so far, based mostly on the fact that he rarely tops 94 mph and that major-league hitters are too good to be deceived by his delivery. When winding up, Gaub has a lot of excess movement, which can be confusing, and he keeps the ball hidden a bit longer than most. The more likely culprit if Gaub isn't able to translate his fastball-slider combo into relief success would be his questionable control, a natural byproduct of his unconventional delivery. If he can lower his walk rate,

Entering the 2010 season, Grabow looked like a pitcher who was worthy of nothing more than an invitation to camp by some team, having posted pedestrian career numbers, lacking noteworthy stuff, and not even showing a lopsided platoon split to make him an effective LOOGY. Instead, the Cubs gave him a mind-numbing $7.5 million contract for two years. It took a front-office decapitation, but the sensation has returned, the contract has expired, and any expectation of similar remuneration is nothing but a pipe dream for Grabow.

## Jay Jackson

Born: 10/27/1987 Age: 24
Bats: R Throws: R Height: 6' 2" Weight: 195
Breakout: 31% Improve: 55% Collapse: 19%
Attrition: 14% MLB: 88%

**Comparables:**
Justin Verlander, Junichi Tazawa, Don Gullett

| YEAR | TEAM | LVL | AGE | W | L | SV | G | GS | IP | H | HR | BB | SO | EqBB9 | EqSO9 | GB% | BABIP | WHIP | ERA | FIP | FRA | WARP |
|------|------|-----|-----|----|---|----|----|----|------|-----|----|----|----|-------|-------|-----|-------|------|------|------|------|------|
| 2009 | DAY | A+ | 21 | 2 | 2 | 0 | 7 | 7 | 38¹ | 31 | 3 | 4 | 46 | 0.9 | 10.8 | 50% | .301 | 0.91 | 1.64 | 2.29 | 2.93 | 1.1 |
| 2009 | TEN | AA | 21 | 5 | 4 | 0 | 16 | 16 | 82² | 66 | 6 | 37 | 73 | 4.2 | 8.4 | 40% | .279 | 1.35 | 3.70 | 3.66 | 4.28 | 1.4 |
| 2010 | IOW | AAA | 22 | 11 | 8 | 0 | 32 | 25 | 157¹ | 103 | 11 | 35 | 77 | 2.7 | 6.8 | 38% | .294 | 1.28 | 4.63 | 4.81 | 4.70 | 1.3 |
| 2011 | IOW | AAA | 23 | 3 | 6 | 0 | 26 | 26 | 146² | 180 | 10 | 46 | 97 | 2.8 | 6.0 | 43% | .349 | 1.54 | 5.34 | 4.32 | 4.84 | 2.1 |
| 2012 | CHN | MLB | 24 | 3 | 3 | 0 | 9 | 9 | 50² | 50 | 6 | 16 | 34 | 2.9 | 6.1 | 40% | .305 | 1.32 | 4.59 | 4.35 | 4.99 | 0.2 |

Jackson will be an interesting data point in how the new Cubs front office interprets statistics. For years, the 8-14, 5.34 season at Iowa would have led a pitcher's team to pull the plug on his starting career based on his "failure" as a starting pitcher. For Jackson, it's a move that has been hinted at for years and should result in more consistent mid-90s heat. But it would also waste some of his assets, as he's a good hitter and fielder, and his other three pitches—slider, curve, and changeup—give him more variety than the typical two-pitch bullpen arm. Seen through a different statistical filter, his 2011 FIP was actually better than his 2010 as the luck pendulum swung the other direction for balls in play, and the fact that he's more often working down in the zone has helped temper his home run propensity. Even ignoring the poor "standard" stats, he profiles as no better than a back-of-rotation starter, but that would help a team a lot more than another generic middle relief pitcher.

## Rodrigo Lopez

Born: 12/14/1975 Age: 36
Bats: R Throws: R Height: 6' 2" Weight: 180
Breakout: 25% Improve: 45% Collapse: 38%
Attrition: 39% MLB: 72%

**Comparables:**
Turk Farrell, Don Robinson, Rick Wise

| YEAR | TEAM | LVL | AGE | W | L | SV | G | GS | IP | H | HR | BB | SO | EqBB9 | EqSO9 | GB% | BABIP | WHIP | ERA | FIP | FRA | WARP |
|------|------|-----|-----|---|----|----|----|----|------|-----|----|----|-----|-------|-------|-----|-------|------|------|------|------|------|
| 2009 | LEH | AAA | 33 | 7 | 5 | 0 | 18 | 18 | 100¹ | 122 | 9 | 14 | 71 | 1.3 | 6.4 | 46% | .345 | 1.36 | 4.31 | 3.38 | 4.46 | 1.1 |
| 2009 | PHI | MLB | 33 | 3 | 1 | 0 | 7 | 5 | 30 | 42 | 3 | 11 | 19 | 3.3 | 5.7 | 37% | .375 | 1.77 | 5.70 | 4.19 | 4.41 | 0.3 |
| 2010 | ARI | MLB | 34 | 7 | 16 | 0 | 33 | 33 | 200 | 227 | 37 | 56 | 116 | 2.5 | 5.2 | 40% | .293 | 1.41 | 4.99 | 5.24 | 5.42 | -0.6 |
| 2011 | GWN | AAA | 35 | 6 | 1 | 0 | 9 | 9 | 59 | 59 | 2 | 14 | 44 | 2.1 | 6.7 | 48% | .310 | 1.24 | 2.59 | 3.00 | 3.88 | 1.2 |
| 2011 | CHN | MLB | 35 | 6 | 6 | 0 | 26 | 16 | 97² | 116 | 18 | 30 | 54 | 2.7 | 5.0 | 43% | .308 | 1.48 | 4.42 | 5.36 | 5.06 | -0.2 |
| 2012 | CHN | MLB | 36 | 5 | 9 | 0 | 19 | 19 | 114² | 135 | 18 | 31 | 58 | 2.5 | 4.5 | 44% | .323 | 1.45 | 5.75 | 5.04 | 6.25 | -1.0 |

A surprise 200-inning starter in Arizona in 2010, Lopez was only able to find a job in Gwinnett to start the 2011 season. After a trade to Chicago, he joined a rotation that may well have been weaker than the Braves' Triple-A squad and helped pick up some of the pieces left by injuries to Andrew Cashner and Randy Wells. Earning 1.0 WARP every 172 innings in his career, Lopez has actually translated his slop (sub-90 mph fastball, slider, and changeup, for the most part) into a useful career, and his lack of acknowledged success means that he should be available for a near-minimum salary. He's a good example of how a team can fairly easily find a player to produce more than notional "replacement level" if they are willing to forego the chance for future upside.

**Scott Maine**
Born: 2/2/1985 Age: 27
Bats: L Throws: L Height: 6' 4'' Weight: 210
Breakout: 18% Improve: 51% Collapse: 28%
Attrition: 18% MLB: 89%

Comparables:
David Purcey, C.J. Wilson, David Cone

| YEAR | TEAM | LVL | AGE | W | L | SV | G | GS | IP | H | HR | BB | SO | EqBB9 | EqSO9 | GB% | BABIP | WHIP | ERA | FIP | FRA | WARP |
|------|------|-----|-----|---|---|----|---|----|----|---|----|----|----|-------|-------|-----|-------|------|-----|-----|-----|------|
| 2009 | MOB | AA | 24 | 3 | 3 | 5 | 36 | 0 | 47$^1$ | 56 | 2 | 15 | 46 | 2.9 | 8.8 | 44% | .386 | 1.50 | 2.66 | 2.78 | 3.41 | 1.2 |
| 2010 | IOW | AAA | 25 | 3 | 1 | 5 | 33 | 0 | 41 | 19 | 3 | 8 | 27 | 4.6 | 10.3 | 49% | .258 | 1.32 | 3.51 | 4.42 | 4.90 | 0.1 |
| 2010 | CHN | MLB | 25 | 0 | 0 | 0 | 13 | 0 | 13 | 9 | 1 | 5 | 11 | 3.5 | 7.6 | 55% | .216 | 1.08 | 2.08 | 3.57 | 3.52 | 0.2 |
| 2011 | IOW | AAA | 26 | 2 | 0 | 12 | 38 | 0 | 51$^1$ | 37 | 3 | 25 | 71 | 4.4 | 12.6 | 53% | .312 | 1.23 | 3.68 | 3.48 | 5.47 | 0.4 |
| 2011 | CHN | MLB | 26 | 0 | 0 | 0 | 7 | 0 | 7 | 11 | 4 | 5 | 5 | 6.4 | 6.4 | 44% | .304 | 2.29 | 10.29 | 11.14 | 11.19 | -0.4 |
| 2012 | CHN | MLB | 27 | 1 | 0 | 0 | 21 | 0 | 25$^2$ | 24 | 3 | 11 | 22 | 3.9 | 7.8 | 47% | .312 | 1.35 | 4.49 | 4.30 | 4.88 | 0.1 |

The primary piece in the 2009 Aaron Heilman trade, Maine works his fastball and either changeup or slider to get out both right-handed and left-handed batters. Since joining the Cubs organization, he's shown great peripherals in the minors, notably the lofty strikeout rate. He should be ready for a major-league bullpen job in 2012, and even though minor-league relief stats don't translate very well to the majors, he has enough velocity and movement that he could quickly become another two-way lefty to hold down the occasional seventh inning.

**Carlos Marmol**
Born: 10/14/1982 Age: 29
Bats: R Throws: R Height: 6' 3'' Weight: 180
Breakout: 19% Improve: 44% Collapse: 32%
Attrition: 14% MLB: 96%

Comparables:
Bryan Harvey, Michael Gonzalez, Nolan Ryan

| YEAR | TEAM | LVL | AGE | W | L | SV | G | GS | IP | H | HR | BB | SO | EqBB9 | EqSO9 | GB% | BABIP | WHIP | ERA | FIP | FRA | WARP |
|------|------|-----|-----|---|---|----|---|----|----|---|----|----|----|-------|-------|-----|-------|------|-----|-----|-----|------|
| 2009 | CHN | MLB | 26 | 2 | 4 | 15 | 79 | 0 | 74 | 43 | 2 | 65 | 93 | 7.9 | 11.3 | 41% | .258 | 1.46 | 3.41 | 4.02 | 4.27 | 1.0 |
| 2010 | CHN | MLB | 27 | 2 | 3 | 38 | 77 | 0 | 77$^2$ | 40 | 1 | 52 | 138 | 6.0 | 16.0 | 33% | .293 | 1.18 | 2.55 | 2.04 | 3.07 | 1.8 |
| 2011 | CHN | MLB | 28 | 2 | 6 | 34 | 75 | 0 | 74 | 54 | 5 | 48 | 99 | 5.8 | 12.0 | 41% | .302 | 1.38 | 4.01 | 3.51 | 4.66 | 0.4 |
| 2012 | CHN | MLB | 29 | 4 | 2 | 34 | 72 | 0 | 71$^2$ | 44 | 5 | 39 | 93 | 4.9 | 11.7 | 36% | .281 | 1.16 | 2.81 | 3.15 | 3.06 | 1.8 |

Marmol held opposing hitters to just a .205 batting average in 2011 while striking out 12 batters per nine innings. That these rates were disappointing is due to various factors. First, his 2010 season was one for the ages, with 16 K/9 and .147 batting average allowed. Signing a new three-year contract after that great season set expectations high. Then there's the fact that Marmol led the league (and tied for the MLB lead) in blown saves, with 10. Of more concern to the Cubs front office is the precipitous drop in velocity he demonstrated. In 2009 and 2010, his fastball averaged over 94 mph, but he rarely even topped 95 mph in 2011, and sat under 92. While his slider—his weapon of choice against most foes—is still a wipe-out pitch against hitters from either side of the plate, losing the edge on his fastball gives them a bit more time, and they now occasionally make solid contact, an all-but-unheard-of occurrence before 2011. Since Marmol pitches with a crazymaking lack of control, he needs to be nearly perfect when he does throw strikes to regain closer-worthy effectiveness.

**Marcos Mateo**
Born: 4/18/1984 Age: 28
Bats: R Throws: R Height: 6' 2'' Weight: 160
Breakout: 35% Improve: 62% Collapse: 17%
Attrition: 19% MLB: 75%

Comparables:
Gene Nelson, Jim Mecir, Ramon A. Ramirez

| YEAR | TEAM | LVL | AGE | W | L | SV | G | GS | IP | H | HR | BB | SO | EqBB9 | EqSO9 | GB% | BABIP | WHIP | ERA | FIP | FRA | WARP |
|------|------|-----|-----|---|---|----|---|----|----|----|----|----|----|-------|-------|-----|-------|------|-----|-----|-----|------|
| 2009 | TEN | AA | 25 | 5 | 7 | 0 | 34 | 14 | 97$^1$ | 101 | 10 | 45 | 77 | 4.0 | 6.5 | 45% | .290 | 1.44 | 4.07 | 4.58 | 4.47 | 0.9 |
| 2010 | TEN | AA | 26 | 0 | 0 | 4 | 17 | 1 | 20$^2$ | 15 | 1 | 1 | 14 | 1.3 | 12.6 | 58% | .378 | 1.26 | 2.17 | 2.97 | 4.00 | 0.4 |
| 2010 | CHN | MLB | 26 | 0 | 1 | 0 | 21 | 0 | 21$^2$ | 20 | 6 | 9 | 26 | 3.7 | 10.8 | 39% | .275 | 1.34 | 5.82 | 5.69 | 5.91 | -0.2 |
| 2011 | CHN | MLB | 27 | 1 | 2 | 0 | 23 | 0 | 23 | 24 | 2 | 10 | 25 | 3.9 | 9.8 | 36% | .367 | 1.48 | 4.30 | 3.25 | 4.60 | 0.1 |
| 2012 | CHN | MLB | 28 | 1 | 0 | 0 | 22 | 0 | 24$^2$ | 26 | 3 | 11 | 17 | 4.0 | 6.0 | 44% | .312 | 1.48 | 5.38 | 4.74 | 5.84 | -0.2 |

Mateo comes straight at hitters, blowing them away with his mid-90s heat and wicked slider, having shed his other offerings since being converted to short reliever in 2009. He again posted a great strikeout rate in 2011, but again missed a big chunk of the season with an injury, the latest edition being a forearm strain that ended his season in July. He has enough control that his arsenal will succeed in a late-inning role, assuming he can stay on the field.

**Trey McNutt**

Born: 8/2/1989 Age: 22
Bats: R Throws: R Height: 6' 5" Weight: 220
Breakout: 20% Improve: 49% Collapse: 21%
Attrition: 15% MLB: 78%

Comparables:
Mike Fornieles, Jim Ollom, Jon Warden

| YEAR | TEAM | LVL | AGE | W | L | SV | G | GS | IP | H | HR | BB | SO | EqBB9 | EqSO9 | GB% | BABIP | WHIP | ERA | FIP | FRA | WARP |
|------|------|-----|-----|---|---|----|----|----|-----|-----|----|----|----|-------|-------|-----|-------|------|------|------|------|------|
| 2009 | BOI | A- | 19 | 3 | 0 | 0 | 7 | 2 | 20¹ | 9 | 1 | 12 | 21 | 5.3 | 9.3 | 51% | .174 | 1.03 | 1.33 | 4.58 | 4.68 | 0.1 |
| 2010 | PEO | A | 20 | 6 | 0 | 0 | 13 | 13 | 59² | 37 | 0 | 23 | 67 | 3.6 | 10.6 | 46% | .291 | 1.12 | 1.51 | 2.81 | 3.49 | 1.3 |
| 2010 | DAY | A+ | 20 | 4 | 0 | 0 | 9 | 9 | 41 | 22 | 2 | 8 | 40 | 2.0 | 10.8 | 41% | .256 | 0.93 | 2.63 | 2.94 | 3.32 | 1.1 |
| 2011 | TEN | AA | 21 | 3 | 4 | 0 | 23 | 22 | 95 | 129 | 7 | 44 | 71 | 3.7 | 6.2 | 47% | .362 | 1.67 | 4.55 | 4.31 | 5.31 | 0.8 |
| 2012 | CHN | MLB | 22 | 2 | 3 | 0 | 8 | 8 | 35² | 38 | 4 | 16 | 22 | 4.0 | 5.5 | 44% | .318 | 1.52 | 5.44 | 4.77 | 5.92 | -0.1 |

To quote Kevin Goldstein, "McNutt fell apart mechanically." Making the jump to Double-A is often difficult, and McNutt has been working to find a third pitch to mix with his easy mid-90s heat and good slider, but he appeared to become his own worst enemy at times in 2011. He was trying to overthrow instead of trusting the stuff that made him a four-star prospect entering the season. If all of Theo's men can put Humpty Dumpty back together again, he's already advanced enough to join a rotation or the back end of a bullpen. And if the work on his curve and changeup pay dividends, the sky's still the limit. But that tiny word "if" makes the variance on his projections as extreme as they can be.

Russell uses his blistering 88-mph fastball and nuclear 80-mph slider to incinerate any hope lefty batters might have. Or at least he's held them to a .265 on-base percentage in his career, though nine home runs in 207 PA adds excitement to even his appearances in a LOOGY role. As a starter, he's a catastrophe waiting to happen; right-handed hitters have little trouble picking up his pitches and driving them. With a bit more experience, and used in roles where he can succeed, he should hang around for a few years.

**Jeff Samardzija**

Born: 1/23/1985 Age: 27
Bats: R Throws: R Height: 6' 6" Weight: 220
Breakout: 17% Improve: 42% Collapse: 30%
Attrition: 28% MLB: 85%

Comparables:
J.D. Durbin, David Palmer, Fred Green

| YEAR | TEAM | LVL | AGE | W | L | SV | G | GS | IP | H | HR | BB | SO | EqBB9 | EqSO9 | GB% | BABIP | WHIP | ERA | FIP | FRA | WARP |
|------|------|-----|-----|---|---|----|----|----|-----|-----|----|----|----|-------|-------|-----|-------|------|------|------|------|------|
| 2009 | CHN | MLB | 24 | 1 | 3 | 0 | 20 | 2 | 34² | 46 | 7 | 15 | 21 | 3.9 | 5.5 | 44% | .345 | 1.76 | 7.53 | 5.85 | 6.56 | -0.2 |
| 2010 | CHN | MLB | 25 | 2 | 2 | 0 | 7 | 3 | 19¹ | 21 | 4 | 20 | 9 | 9.3 | 4.2 | 30% | .262 | 2.12 | 8.38 | 8.28 | 7.40 | -0.3 |
| 2011 | CHN | MLB | 26 | 8 | 4 | 0 | 75 | 0 | 88 | 64 | 5 | 50 | 87 | 5.1 | 8.9 | 43% | .257 | 1.30 | 2.97 | 3.63 | 4.49 | 0.4 |
| 2012 | CHN | MLB | 27 | 3 | 3 | 0 | 39 | 6 | 73² | 75 | 9 | 36 | 47 | 4.4 | 5.7 | 43% | .305 | 1.50 | 5.26 | 4.98 | 5.72 | -0.3 |

"Shark" Samardzija is one of the more high-profile cases of a failed starting pitcher turning into an effective reliever, with his struggles constantly invoking questions about whether the former Notre Dame wide receiver chose the right sport. As a reliever, he was able to add a couple mph to his fastball and he continued using all four of his pitches en route to racking up a high innings total. As with Marmol, he walked far too many batters, but the .200 batting average allowed and sub-.300 slugging percentage allowed made him highly effective anyway. A bit of luck on balls in play indicates that Samardzija wasn't pitching as well as his stats, and the Cubs declined a relatively light $3 million option, with the expectation of signing him for less per year and more years.

**Hayden Simpson**

Born: 5/20/1989 Age: 23
Bats: R Throws: R Height: 6' 1" Weight: 170
Breakout: 41% Improve: 63% Collapse: 15%
Attrition: 24% MLB: 74%

Comparables:
Miguel Asencio, Phil Huffman, Nate Cornejo

| YEAR | TEAM | LVL | AGE | W | L | SV | G | GS | IP | H | HR | BB | SO | EqBB9 | EqSO9 | GB% | BABIP | WHIP | ERA | FIP | FRA | WARP |
|------|------|-----|-----|---|---|----|----|----|-----|-----|----|----|----|-------|-------|-----|-------|------|------|------|------|------|
| 2011 | PEO | A | 22 | 1 | 1 | 0 | 16 | 16 | 61¹ | 73 | 8 | 26 | 39 | 4.0 | 6.8 | 52% | .340 | 1.68 | 5.72 | 5.10 | 5.66 | -0.2 |
| 2012 | CHN | MLB | 23 | 1 | 3 | 0 | 7 | 7 | 20¹ | 26 | 3 | 11 | 6 | 5.0 | 2.8 | 47% | .325 | 1.82 | 7.29 | 6.16 | 7.93 | -0.4 |

Simpson could be the poster boy for why teams shun small pitchers, especially righties, on draft day. He wasn't exactly Juan Marichal, but he used his exaggerated leg kick to get clocked as fast as 98 mph for 2010 draft evaluators. At number 16, he was considered an overdraft by most, but none saw the precipitous drop in his velocity coming, as Simpson was having trouble sitting above 90 mph in 2011. As harsh as it sounds for the player in question, the best possible outcome for the Cubs now is that an injury will be revealed, and Simpson will have surgery and begin the long process of rehab. Otherwise he's just an undersized pitching prospect without good velocity, great control, or standout secondary pitches.

## Andy Sonnanstine

Born: 3/18/1983 Age: 29
Bats: L Throws: R Height: 6' 4" Weight: 185
Breakout: 22% Improve: 70% Collapse: 12%
Attrition: 7% MLB: 88%

Comparables:
Frank Tanana, John Smiley, Jack Kralick

| YEAR | TEAM | LVL | AGE | W | L | SV | G | GS | IP | H | HR | BB | SO | EqBB9 | EqSO9 | GB% | BABIP | WHIP | ERA | FIP | FRA | WARP |
|------|------|-----|-----|---|---|----|----|----|-----|-----|----|----|----|-------|-------|-----|-------|------|------|------|------|------|
| 2009 | TBA | MLB | 26 | 6 | 9 | 0 | 22 | 18 | 99² | 131 | 19 | 34 | 60 | 3.1 | 5.4 | 43% | .326 | 1.66 | 6.77 | 5.50 | 6.65 | -0.6 |
| 2010 | TBA | MLB | 27 | 3 | 1 | 1 | 41 | 4 | 81 | 83 | 11 | 27 | 50 | 3.0 | 5.6 | 45% | .277 | 1.36 | 4.44 | 4.84 | 5.91 | -0.7 |
| 2011 | DUR | AAA | 28 | 3 | 6 | 0 | 10 | 9 | 56 | 64 | 4 | 15 | 35 | 2.4 | 5.6 | 45% | .316 | 1.41 | 4.82 | 3.77 | 5.20 | 0.4 |
| 2011 | TBA | MLB | 28 | 0 | 2 | 0 | 15 | 4 | 35² | 40 | 10 | 12 | 12 | 3.0 | 3.0 | 47% | .259 | 1.46 | 5.55 | 7.13 | 6.39 | -0.4 |
| 2012 | CHN | MLB | 29 | 2 | 2 | 0 | 22 | 6 | 56¹ | 61 | 7 | 13 | 33 | 2.1 | 5.3 | 43% | .312 | 1.31 | 4.82 | 4.34 | 5.24 | 0.1 |

At one point last season, Sonnanstine was pitching so infrequently for the Rays it was possible to forget he was in the bullpen. Apparently Andrew Friedman did, because the club let Cory Wade exercise an out clause in his contract from Triple-A despite pitching well, while keeping Sonnanstine on the active roster. Sonnanstine was used in the lowest-leverage situations and still stank. He has always wanted a chance to be a starting pitcher again. He'll pursue that dream with the Cubs after signing a split contract.

## Nicholas Struck

Born: 10/7/1989 Age: 22
Bats: R Throws: R Height: 6' 0" Weight: 185
Breakout: 35% Improve: 64% Collapse: 18%
Attrition: 22% MLB: 82%

Comparables:
Johnny Kucks, Dave McNally, Alex Sanabia

| YEAR | TEAM | LVL | AGE | W | L | SV | G | GS | IP | H | HR | BB | SO | EqBB9 | EqSO9 | GB% | BABIP | WHIP | ERA | FIP | FRA | WARP |
|------|------|-----|-----|---|---|----|----|----|------|----|----|----|----|-------|-------|-----|-------|------|------|------|------|------|
| 2010 | PEO | A | 20 | 8 | 8 | 0 | 25 | 18 | 114² | 61 | 5 | 27 | 46 | 3.1 | 6.6 | 41% | .265 | 1.16 | 3.22 | 4.35 | 4.77 | 0.8 |
| 2011 | DAY | A+ | 21 | 6 | 2 | 0 | 10 | 10 | 50 | 55 | 2 | 16 | 47 | 2.9 | 8.5 | 51% | .361 | 1.42 | 3.42 | 3.17 | 4.76 | 0.6 |
| 2011 | TEN | AA | 21 | 1 | 1 | 0 | 6 | 6 | 35 | 42 | 0 | 6 | 26 | 1.5 | 6.7 | 46% | .362 | 1.37 | 2.31 | 2.41 | 3.97 | 0.9 |
| 2011 | IOW | AAA | 21 | 2 | 2 | 0 | 12 | 11 | 62¹ | 76 | 2 | 22 | 38 | 3.2 | 5.5 | 38% | .357 | 1.57 | 5.20 | 4.14 | 4.82 | 0.5 |
| 2012 | CHN | MLB | 22 | 2 | 3 | 0 | 9 | 8 | 45 | 50 | 5 | 17 | 21 | 3.5 | 4.3 | 42% | .317 | 1.50 | 5.47 | 4.85 | 5.95 | -0.2 |

Struck was a 39th-round pick and may be a long shot to ever hold down a major-league rotation spot, but he did negotiate a $125,000 signing bonus, more than about half the 10th-round picks, indicating that much of his slide in the draft was due to his scholarship offer from the University of Hawaii. And while he's undersized and doesn't throw in the mid-90s, he does work above 90 mph and has four pitches that all have promise. He also has a hard-nosed mentality, is very coachable, and earned two promotions in 2011 despite posting a BABIP over .350 at every stop (though his FIPs were quite good). He's yet to show that he can handle Triple-A hitters, but a good first half there in 2012 could get his bullpen/spot-start career going as soon as the second half.

## Casey Weathers

Born: 6/10/1985 Age: 27
Bats: R Throws: R Height: 6' 2" Weight: 205
Breakout: 34% Improve: 59% Collapse: 18%
Attrition: 7% MLB: 87%

Comparables:
John Axford, Joselo Diaz, Charlie Hough

| YEAR | TEAM | LVL | AGE | W | L | SV | G | GS | IP | H | HR | BB | SO | EqBB9 | EqSO9 | GB% | BABIP | WHIP | ERA | FIP | FRA | WARP |
|------|------|-----|-----|---|---|----|----|----|-----|----|----|----|----|-------|-------|-----|-------|------|------|------|------|------|
| 2011 | TUL | AA | 26 | 0 | 1 | 0 | 44 | 0 | 45² | 30 | 3 | 48 | 47 | 9.5 | 9.5 | 41% | .248 | 1.75 | 5.32 | 5.79 | 6.42 | -0.5 |
| 2012 | CHN | MLB | 27 | 1 | 0 | 1 | 14 | 0 | 14² | 13 | 1 | 10 | 13 | 6.0 | 8.1 | 46% | .305 | 1.54 | 5.09 | 4.36 | 5.53 | -0.0 |

You can never predict Weathers. The scorching heat this converted outfielder showed in his one full year on the mound at Vandy led the Rox to overdraft him with the eighth pick in 2007. Since then, scouts and meteorologists alike have been in a fog, as first his control dissipated, then he had Tommy John surgery in 2009, the effects of which linger still. The Cubs didn't give up much to get him, and his fastball still strikes like lightning, leading to huge strikeout rates. He's a risk, but if the control issues have all been part of a slower-than-usual injury recovery, there's a chance they will clear up suddenly and quickly, allowing his talent to shine. But it's best to have an umbrella—or another reliever option—close by, just in case.

## Randy Wells

Born: 8/28/1982 Age: 29
Bats: R Throws: R Height: 6' 6" Weight: 235
Breakout: 31% Improve: 61% Collapse: 23%
Attrition: 18% MLB: 86%

Comparables:
Casey Janssen, Tony Pena, Sergio Mitre

| YEAR | TEAM | LVL | AGE | W | L | SV | G | GS | IP | H | HR | BB | SO | EqBB9 | EqSO9 | GB% | BABIP | WHIP | ERA | FIP | FRA | WARP |
|------|------|-----|-----|----|----|----|----|----|------|-----|----|----|-----|-----|-----|-----|-------|------|------|------|------|------|
| 2009 | CHN | MLB | 26 | 12 | 10 | 0 | 27 | 27 | 165¹ | 165 | 14 | 46 | 104 | 2.5 | 5.7 | 49% | .292 | 1.28 | 3.05 | 3.84 | 4.53 | 2.3 |
| 2010 | CHN | MLB | 27 | 8 | 14 | 0 | 32 | 32 | 194¹ | 209 | 19 | 63 | 144 | 2.9 | 6.7 | 49% | .315 | 1.40 | 4.26 | 3.96 | 4.66 | 1.6 |
| 2011 | CHN | MLB | 28 | 7 | 6 | 0 | 23 | 23 | 135¹ | 141 | 23 | 46 | 82 | 3.1 | 5.5 | 44% | .277 | 1.39 | 4.99 | 5.06 | 5.44 | -0.6 |
| 2012 | CHN | MLB | 29 | 7 | 8 | 0 | 21 | 21 | 127 | 133 | 15 | 39 | 76 | 2.8 | 5.4 | 47% | .309 | 1.35 | 4.71 | 4.46 | 5.12 | 0.4 |

Wells is rumored to have taken his profession a bit less professionally than some, and results would support that something was definitely amiss early in the season. The converted catcher was starting to look like a success story before 2011, as any starting pitcher worthy of a rotation spot is worth significant money, even if his upside is only that of a mid-rotation guy. Before 2011, he mixed his four pitches well enough to confuse hitters, but last year his velocity was down, and he wasn't fooling much of anyone. The more benign explanation for Wells' struggles is that he tried to return too quickly from an early-season arm strain, as he held opposing hitters to a futile .218/.276/.347 batting line from August 24 through the end of the year. Assuming he hits the offseason workouts more diligently than his reputation would indicate, and entering 2012 with a healthy arm, he becomes a prime bounceback candidate, though the extent of such a bounce is limited.

### Kerry Wood

Born: 6/16/1977 Age: 35
Bats: R Throws: R Height: 6' 6" Weight: 225
Breakout: 12% Improve: 36% Collapse: 31%
Attrition: 16% MLB: 84%

**Comparables:**
Tom Gordon, Joe Nelson, Francisco Cordero

| YEAR | TEAM | LVL | AGE | W | L | SV | G | GS | IP | H | HR | BB | SO | EqBB9 | EqSO9 | GB% | BABIP | WHIP | ERA | FIP | FRA | WARP |
|---|---|---|---|---|---|---|---|---|---|---|---|---|---|---|---|---|---|---|---|---|---|---|
| 2009 | CLE | MLB | 32 | 3 | 3 | 20 | 58 | 0 | 55 | 48 | 7 | 28 | 63 | 4.6 | 10.3 | 41% | .295 | 1.38 | 4.25 | 4.20 | 4.22 | 0.8 |
| 2010 | CLE | MLB | 33 | 1 | 4 | 8 | 23 | 0 | 20 | 21 | 3 | 11 | 18 | 4.9 | 8.1 | 43% | .305 | 1.60 | 6.30 | 5.15 | 4.98 | 0.0 |
| 2010 | NYA | MLB | 33 | 2 | 0 | 0 | 24 | 0 | 26 | 14 | 1 | 18 | 31 | 6.2 | 10.7 | 36% | .236 | 1.23 | 0.69 | 3.35 | 2.89 | 0.6 |
| 2011 | CHN | MLB | 34 | 3 | 5 | 1 | 55 | 0 | 51 | 45 | 5 | 21 | 57 | 3.7 | 10.1 | 38% | .303 | 1.29 | 3.35 | 3.56 | 4.37 | 0.3 |
| 2012 | CHN | MLB | 35 | 3 | 1 | 4 | 50 | 0 | 47¹ | 39 | 4 | 19 | 49 | 3.7 | 9.2 | 41% | .308 | 1.24 | 3.68 | 3.44 | 4.00 | 0.7 |

Wood is the author of one of the best-pitched games in history, though its date, May 6, 1998, may as well qualify it as 19th century literature as far as Cubs fans are concerned. But Wood is still writing. He's the active leader in strikeouts per nine innings (1,000 IP minimum). His fastball averaged over 94 mph in 2011 and his slider over 90

Attrition: 16% MLB: 90%

**Comparables:**
Osiris Matos, Carlos Rosa, Don Gullett

| YEAR | TEAM | LVL | AGE | W | L | SV | G | GS | IP | H | HR | BB | SO | EqBB9 | EqSO9 | GB% | BABIP | WHIP | ERA | FIP | FRA | WARP |
|---|---|---|---|---|---|---|---|---|---|---|---|---|---|---|---|---|---|---|---|---|---|---|
| 2010 | CIN | MLB | 23 | 5 | 4 | 0 | 17 | 17 | 102² | 85 | 9 | 26 | 86 | 2.3 | 7.5 | 32% | .261 | 1.08 | 3.51 | 3.45 | 3.39 | 2.6 |
| 2011 | LOU | AAA | 24 | 1 | 2 | 0 | 10 | 10 | 52¹ | 64 | 6 | 17 | 47 | 2.9 | 8.1 | 43% | .365 | 1.55 | 5.33 | 4.02 | 4.95 | 0.3 |
| 2011 | CIN | MLB | 24 | 6 | 6 | 0 | 22 | 18 | 106 | 118 | 10 | 40 | 76 | 3.4 | 6.5 | 36% | .333 | 1.49 | 4.84 | 4.03 | 4.62 | 0.4 |
| 2012 | CHN | MLB | 25 | 6 | 7 | 0 | 19 | 19 | 112¹ | 110 | 12 | 39 | 77 | 3.1 | 6.2 | 39% | .305 | 1.33 | 4.50 | 4.26 | 4.89 | 0.6 |

In 2010, Wood posted WHIPs of 1.1 at both the Triple-A and major-league levels, and while his gas wasn't wowing people, his control of his sinker was excellent, and batters weren't thinking about how short he is or how short his fastball might be. Though he may not pop radar guns like Billy Wagner, he touches 94 MPH on occasion, and no less of an authority than Logan Morrison was quoted before the 2010 season as saying that Wood had the nastiest stuff he'd seen in the minors. But, alas, a little control and a little luck goes a long way, and Wood walked more people in 2011 and also saw his BABIP balloon. These reversals led to him losing first his rotation spot (to Homer Bailey), then his roster spot (optioned back and forth from Triple-A starting in June), then his spot on the Reds (traded to the Cubs after the season). The buy-low Cubs are hoping for growth such as fellow short southpaw Wandy Rodriguez showed, but would be content with their side of the trade if Wood merely continues posting his 3.74 career FIP for the next four seasons. After all, that was good enough for 44th out of 93 qualifying pitchers in 2011, and an above-average starter has value.

### Carlos Zambrano

Born: 6/1/1981 Age: 31
Bats: B Throws: R Height: 6' 5" Weight: 250
Breakout: 27% Improve: 63% Collapse: 23%
Attrition: 13% MLB: 95%

**Comparables:**
Jim Mecir, Bill Singer, Hoyt Wilhelm

| YEAR | TEAM | LVL | AGE | W | L | SV | G | GS | IP | H | HR | BB | SO | EqBB9 | EqSO9 | GB% | BABIP | WHIP | ERA | FIP | FRA | WARP |
|---|---|---|---|---|---|---|---|---|---|---|---|---|---|---|---|---|---|---|---|---|---|---|
| 2009 | CHN | MLB | 28 | 9 | 7 | 0 | 28 | 28 | 169¹ | 155 | 10 | 78 | 152 | 4.1 | 8.1 | 46% | .306 | 1.38 | 3.77 | 3.57 | 4.05 | 3.8 |
| 2010 | CHN | MLB | 29 | 11 | 6 | 0 | 36 | 20 | 129² | 119 | 7 | 69 | 117 | 4.8 | 8.1 | 45% | .309 | 1.45 | 3.33 | 3.74 | 4.82 | 1.4 |
| 2011 | CHN | MLB | 30 | 9 | 7 | 0 | 24 | 24 | 145² | 154 | 19 | 56 | 101 | 3.5 | 6.2 | 46% | .307 | 1.44 | 4.82 | 4.56 | 5.25 | 0.5 |
| 2012 | FLO | MLB | 31 | 8 | 7 | 0 | 21 | 21 | 125¹ | 115 | 11 | 53 | 94 | 3.8 | 6.8 | 47% | .303 | 1.34 | 4.30 | 4.11 | 4.68 | 0.7 |

There really isn't anything offensive Zambrano has done that hasn't been done by numerous ballplayers throughout the history of the game. But he's alienated enough of the wrong people that incidents as harmless as showing the wrong body language when being pulled from a game get interpreted as more evidence of what a "whack job" he is. Teammates, media, and fans tolerated his antics much more readily when he was making hitters look stupid with his heavy two-seam fastballs that sat around 93 mph supported by four-seamers reaching the upper 90s. Influenced by Carlos Silva during the junkballer's brief time on the Cubs, Zambrano has begun throwing all varieties of slop on occasion to compensate for the fact that his fastball is lucky to touch 95 mph once on a good day out of the bullpen. Hoping for him to avoid alienating anyone else, and also accepting a role as a back-of-rotation starter, seems like sheer optimism at this point.

# LINEOUTS

## HITTERS

| PLAYER | TEAM | LVL | AGE | PA | R | 2B | 3B | HR | RBI | BB | SO | SB-CS | AVG/OBP/SLG | TAv | BABIP | BRR | FRAA | WARP |
|--------|------|-----|-----|-----|-----|-----|-----|-----|-----|-----|-----|-------|-------------|-----|-------|-----|------|------|
| CF P. Chen | BOI | A- | 19 | 263 | 34 | 14 | 4 | 2 | 30 | 25 | 44 | 20-6 | .301/.363/.424 | .291 | .356 | 2.3 | -3.9 | 1.4 |
| RF R. Golden | BOI | A- | 19 | 265 | 36 | 10 | 5 | 7 | 39 | 28 | 68 | 5-2 | .242/.332/.420 | .282 | .310 | 0.0 | 3.2 | 1.6 |
| 2B J. Mota | TEN | AA | 24 | 81 | 5 | 4 | 0 | 2 | 8 | 2 | 14 | 0-1 | .221/.250/.351 | .208 | .246 | -0.1 | 2.1 | 0.0 |
|  | IOW | AAA | 24 | 220 | 24 | 15 | 1 | 5 | 30 | 9 | 32 | 1-1 | .289/.321/.446 | .265 | .318 | 2.1 | 3.3 | 1.6 |
| 3B M. Smith | IOW | AAA | 26 | 292 | 45 | 18 | 2 | 7 | 36 | 23 | 61 | 0-1 | .278/.344/.444 | .265 | .333 | 0.1 | -5.4 | 0.5 |

**Pin-Chieh Chen** has converted from second base to the outfield, has good all-around tools, and is on track to succeed at full-season ball in 2012. ⊘ **Reggie Golden** showed unexpected patience at the plate, and is still a five-tool player, though his speed hasn't often materialized in game situations, either at the plate or in the field. ⊘ More of an organizational soldier than a prospect, despite his relative youth, **Jonathan Mota** is willing to play any position. He's even pitched, though the 2010 experiment with catching didn't take. ⊘ Assuming Chicago gets more lefties into the starting lineup, **Marquez Smith** might have some use as a righty bat off the bench who can play multiple positions.

## PITCHERS

| PLAYER | TEAM | LVL | AGE | W | L | SV | IP | H | HR | BB | SO | EqBB9 | EqSO9 | GB% | BABIP | WHIP | ERA | FIP | FRA | WARP |
|--------|------|-----|-----|-----|-----|-----|-----|-----|-----|-----|-----|-------|-------|-----|-------|------|-----|-----|-----|------|
| J. Beliveau | TEN | AA | 24 | 4 | 0 | 3 | 57 | 38 | 7 | 14 | 76 | 2.1 | 10.9 | 33% | .226 | 0.88 | 1.89 | 3.07 | 3.41 | 1.4 |
| A. Cabrera | TEN | AA | 22 | 2 | 1 | 0 | 48² | 60 | 4 | 21 | 34 | 3.9 | 6.3 | 48% | .350 | 1.66 | 5.36 | 4.39 | 5.27 | 0.3 |
|  | IOW | AAA | 22 | 2 | 4 | 0 | 88² | 118 | 11 | 53 | 67 | 5.4 | 6.8 | 48% | .377 | 1.93 | 6.60 | 5.73 | 5.97 | -0.2 |
| E. Caridad | IOW | AAA | 27 | 1 | 0 | 4 | 37 | 45 | 4 | 27 | 27 | 6.6 | 7.3 | 34% | .363 | 2.11 | 8.27 | 6.03 | 7.58 | -0.5 |
| M. Carrillo | TEN | AA | 24 | 2 | 3 | 3 | 76¹ | 65 | 7 | 34 | 64 | 3.8 | 7.3 | 34% | .257 | 1.22 | 2.36 | 4.31 | 4.63 | 0.8 |
|  | IOW | AAA | 24 | 0 | 1 | 0 | 31 | 38 | 6 | 6 | 25 | 1.7 | 7.3 | 42% | .337 | 1.42 | 6.10 | 5.32 | 5.93 | 0.1 |
| R. Dolis | TEN | AA | 23 | 3 | 2 | 17 | 72² | 68 | 2 | 37 | 51 | 4.3 | 5.9 | 60% | .280 | 1.32 | 3.22 | 3.95 | 4.94 | 0.9 |
|  | CHN | MLB | 23 | 0 | 0 | 0 | 1¹ | 0 | 0 | 1 | 1 | 6.8 | 6.8 | 1.% | .000 | 0.75 | 0.00 | 3.74 | 4.12 | 0.0 |
| R. Lopez | PEO | A | 20 | 1 | 1 | 1 | 69 | 78 | 8 | 30 | 35 | 3.9 | 4.6 | 49% | .307 | 1.57 | 5.35 | 5.37 | 6.23 | -0.7 |
| R. Ortiz | IOW | AAA | 38 | 3 | 0 | 0 | 99¹ | 115 | 12 | 20 | 81 | 1.8 | 7.3 | 52% | .337 | 1.36 | 4.26 | 4.37 | 4.83 | 1.0 |
|  | CHN | MLB | 38 | 1 | 2 | 0 | 33¹ | 31 | 6 | 11 | 25 | 3.0 | 6.8 | 43% | .255 | 1.26 | 4.86 | 4.82 | 5.78 | -0.2 |
| B. Parker | TEN | AA | 26 | 0 | 2 | 3 | 24 | 19 | 1 | 12 | 18 | 4.9 | 7.5 | 47% | .281 | 1.38 | 4.12 | 3.97 | 4.52 | 0.3 |
|  | IOW | AAA | 26 | 1 | 0 | 4 | 51¹ | 37 | 5 | 27 | 60 | 4.7 | 10.5 | 40% | .269 | 1.25 | 2.81 | 4.36 | 4.34 | 0.7 |
| C. Rusin | TEN | AA | 24 | 1 | 0 | 0 | 76 | 76 | 5 | 15 | 45 | 1.9 | 5.8 | 54% | .307 | 1.26 | 3.91 | 3.76 | 4.43 | 1.5 |
|  | IOW | AAA | 24 | 2 | 1 | 0 | 62² | 70 | 8 | 14 | 46 | 2.0 | 6.6 | 55% | .335 | 1.34 | 4.02 | 4.65 | 5.05 | 0.2 |
| J. Stevens | TEN | AA | 27 | 1 | 0 | 2 | 41² | 38 | 1 | 18 | 59 | 3.5 | 11.2 | 46% | .339 | 1.20 | 2.59 | 2.15 | 3.48 | 1.1 |
|  | IOW | AAA | 27 | 0 | 0 | 0 | 23¹ | 40 | 5 | 12 | 15 | 4.6 | 5.8 | 38% | .398 | 2.23 | 10.03 | 6.91 | 7.53 | -0.3 |
|  | CHN | MLB | 27 | 0 | 0 | 0 | 7 | 4 | 1 | 7 | 4 | 9.0 | 5.1 | 42% | .167 | 1.57 | 5.14 | 7.14 | 9.23 | -0.2 |
| B. Wallach | PEO | A | 22 | 0 | 1 | 0 | 26¹ | 29 | 0 | 23 | 25 | 7.9 | 8.5 | 39% | .349 | 1.97 | 6.49 | 4.31 | 6.40 | -0.4 |
|  | DAY | A+ | 22 | 3 | 5 | 0 | 91 | 106 | 6 | 34 | 71 | 3.4 | 7.0 | 48% | .344 | 1.54 | 5.74 | 4.04 | 4.46 | 1.2 |

**Jeff Beliveau** has 18th-round stuff, but the lefty is crafty enough to befuddle minor-leaguers, and he'll get a chance soon to try it in the bigs. ⊘ **Alberto Cabrera** can reach 97 mph and may end up being another bullpen conversion if he can't iron out his secondary offerings and throw strikes more consistently. ⊘ Never to be confused with a future closer, **Esmailin Caridad** nonetheless looked very good in a few innings at the end of 2010, but a litany of injuries has set him back since. With health, he has the potential to help a pen in need. ⊘ **Marco Carrillo** doesn't throw hard or come with a prospect's pedigree, and his effectiveness hasn't improved when used out of the bullpen, but he's shown enough the past two seasons that he could be used in an emergency. ⊘ Given a very brief look in September, **Rafael Dolis** was clocked as high as 97 mph with one of his 40 pitches in 2011, but he'll need better command of either his curve or slider if he wants to get outs at the higher levels. ⊘ **Robinson Lopez**, as a starting prospect, made the Cubs Top 11 list entering the season, but wasn't throwing with the same velocity or movement in 2011, and a move to the pen didn't help. ⊘ There are only three pitchers who have amassed 1,000 or more innings pitched in their career and have allowed a higher TAv against than **Ramon Ortiz**. That he was better than several other Cubs pitchers summarizes Chicago's 2011 staff in a nutshell. ⊘ It hasn't quite been the Sergio Santos success story, but fireballing ex-catcher **Blake Parker** did enough at Iowa that he should get attention from other teams after being left off the Cubs' 40-man roster. ⊘ **Chris Rusin** doesn't throw overly hard and has a sloppy delivery, but he still manages to find the strike zone with uncanny regularity, and though his upside isn't much, he should at least carve out a career as a LOOGY. ⊘ When **Jeff Stevens** appears in a team's major-league pitching stats at the end of the season, it's a clear indicator that things didn't work out as hoped. ⊘ **Brett Wallach**, son of Tim, made scouts salivate back in 2009, but part of the Pavlovian response was based on projection that hasn't happened yet.

## MANAGER: DALE SVEUM

stint as hitting coach. He's shown leadership skills in his various coaching positions, and is expected to be a hard worker and open to some introduction of advanced concepts into the managerial routine. In choosing a rookie manager, the new front office has hopes that Sveum can turn into the face of the franchise. He has emphasized his belief that being body-language neutral is important, citing Joe Torre, Tony La Russa, and Jim Leyland as his biggest influences. That is likely to go a long way toward keeping things on track in Wrigley Field's tiny, archaic clubhouse and helping the team deal with the massive changes that appear to be on the horizon. It won't, however, win the hearts of the casual fans, who often confuse a steady mien with "not trying." He'll just have to win games to convince them.

# Chicago White Sox

Of the many dubious strategies guaranteed to help gamblers win their fortune the easy way, few are as simple, as subtly alluring, or as ultimately damaging as the martingale system. The concept is simple: you make a small initial wager on an even-money proposition, and if that first bet loses you continue to double the wager size until one finally wins. At that point you're ahead the amount of the initial wager, pocket that amount as profit, and make another small bet. Lather, rinse, repeat, all the while squirreling away a small profit each time a bet is won. Simple, right? Best of all, it's guaranteed to work . . . at least for a while.

The problem is that any bettor who dares give the martingale a spin will eventually run into a string of bad luck and lose a large number of bets in a row. When the size of the bet needed to recoup your last loss grows larger than your bankroll, you're stuck. Attempting the martingale at the blackjack table or the pass line or any other casino wager is even more perilous, as you can quickly reach the table's bet size limit regardless of the size of your stake. The martingale can provide small profits in the short term, but in the long run is virtually guaranteed to end in a crippling loss, wiping out any earlier gains.

Which brings us to White Sox GM Kenny Williams, a Stanford man who is certainly well aware of the martingale's pitfalls. As we've frequently noted in these pages, Williams is a born gambler and a smart one at that, known for taking risks on other teams' failed prospects and toxic assets, rehabilitating them, and frequently reaping a substantial reward. The Sox have done well on his watch, riding his aggressive, win-now attitude and his gambler's nerve, an approach epitomized by the organization's 2011 marketing slogan: "All In."

During the 11 seasons Williams has been at the helm, the Sox have posted only three losing seasons, collected two division titles, and won a World Series. However, each of those losing seasons have come in the six years since the Sox won their 2005 title, a period that has seen Williams make increasingly aggressive bets on veteran players to push his team over the hump, to no avail. Last season the Sox posted another losing record despite a payroll that ranked among the top five in baseball, a remarkable turn of events for a club that fancies itself a mid-market organization in a big-market town. With little help forthcoming from a farm system many consider the most barren in baseball, and with no money available to double down, Williams will have to walk away from the table and search for a new system to try. What that will be we can't be sure, but if history is any guide, it will be interesting to watch.

For organizations like the Sox not blessed with Amazon-sized revenue streams, the key to success is getting as much production as possible from young, cost-controlled players. Usually this is achieved through the slow, steady development of players within the organization's own farm system, but Williams has often chosen another path. The Sox have excelled at procuring talented young underachievers at a low cost from other organizations, relying on their excellent big league staff to turn them into assets. John Danks, Gavin Floyd, Matt Thornton, and Carlos Quentin all came to Chicago in that manner, and all have been significant contributors to whatever measure of success the Sox have realized over the past few seasons. At the same time, Williams seemingly decided it was not worthwhile to wait for the slow blossoming of players already in the organization, but instead used the farm system as a change purse to buy veterans like Nick Swisher and Javier Vazquez off the rack, with diminishing returns.

Those trades, along with a series of stingy and unproductive drafts, left the club competitive but unable to improve

## WHITE SOX PROSPECTUS
### 2011 W-L: 79-83, 3rd in AL Central

| | | |
|---|---|---|
| Pythag | .465 | 22nd |
| RS/G | 4.04 | 18th |
| RA/G | 4.36 | 17th |
| TAv | .260 | 15th |
| TAv-P | .259 | 15th |
| FIP | 3.69 | 6th |
| DER | .697 | 29th |
| DL | 344 | 2nd |
| B-Age | 30.0 | 26th |
| P-Age | 28.5 | 20th |
| Salary | $127.8 | 7th |
| M$/MW | $3.78 | 24th |

**Ballpark:** U.S. Cellular Field (3-yr. PF: 100). Now sporting a bronze statue of the Big Hurt

**2011:** Dunn's struggles mirror the team's, as a bad April digs a hole they never climb out of

**2012:** The AL's best pitching staff mostly returns, but so does one of the AL's worst offenses

**Action Items:** Adam Dunn and Alex Rios must play up to their big contracts

from within, leading in the late summer of 2009 to the series of jaw-dropping bets that have defined the Sox ever since. At the trade deadline Williams acquired ace starter Jake Peavy from the Padres for a collection of middling prospects and, more importantly, the willingness to assume the three years and $52 million remaining on his contract. Shortly thereafter the Sox struck again, placing a successful waiver claim on disappointing outfielder Alex Rios and the nearly $60 million he would be owed through 2014.

These moves affirmed that the Sox were willing to hunt for big game, but as The Stranger made clear in *The Big Lebowski*: "Sometimes you eat the bear, and sometimes . . .

ing. The Sox received solid production from him in 2010 but the enigmatic outfielder spent last season as a millstone, looking lost and uninterested at the plate and in the field, giving credence to the rumors of apathy that have long dogged him.

Last season Williams pressed his bets even further, signing leather-allergic slugger Adam Dunn to a four-year, $56 million deal and re-upping team captain Paul Konerko for three years and $37.5 million. Setting aside the fact that the Sox wouldn't have needed to fill a hole at DH had they not previously sacrificed Jim Thome to appease former manager Ozzie Guillen's misguided demand for improved baserunning, most analysts felt the Dunn signing was a solid one. Even the smartest bets can sometimes go wrong, however, and instead of providing the lefty thump the Sox needed last season, Dunn struggled through a historically inept year at the plate that left many wondering if he could ever recover. Konerko's late-career renaissance continued but wasn't enough to redeem the rest of the club's high-priced talent, combining with Peavy, Rios, and Dunn to post 1.3 WARP last season, at the cost of $52 million—fully two-thirds the payroll of the 2005 championship squad (see Table 1).

### Table 1: Smells Like Team Dispirit

| Name | 2011 Salary ($M) | 2011 WARP | 2012 Salary ($M) |
|------|------------------|-----------|------------------|
| Jake Peavy | $16 | 1.7 | $21* |
| Alex Rios | $12 | -0.6 | $12 |
| Adam Dunn | $12 | -2.5 | $14 |
| Paul Konerko | $12 | 2.7 | $12 |
| Total | $52 | 1.3 | $59 |

*includes $4 million buyout of $22 million club option in 2013

That foursome is due to earn another $59 million this year, and each enters the season with a giant question mark sewn on his jersey. Peavy's injury is unprecedented for a pitcher, and after spending last season struggling to regain his form is no sure bet to be healthy and effective. Dunn retains a solid batting eye but provides no value outside his bat, and if his power remains AWOL he may be on the Jack Cust career path. Konerko has been marvelously productive but will be 36 years old on Opening Day; at some point, Father Time will have his say. Rios has talent but rarely seems willing or able to apply it; his greatest future value to the Sox may be to function as the baseball equivalent of Bernie Lootz's shat-

the offseason with a free agent shopping list, but weren't able to competitively bid on popular staff anchor Mark Buehrle, whose move to Miami punched a hole in the rotation and unleashed a wave of fan discontent. The organization hopes promising lefty Chris Sale, one of their few successful top draft picks, can move from the pen to take Buehrle's spot, but his departure won't be the last shoe to drop. Danks has been signed to a five-year extension to stabilize the rotation, but Floyd and Thornton are frequently mentioned as trade possibilities. While Williams has yet to find an offer for them he finds attractive, the need to reduce payroll has already forced the trade of closer Sergio Santos and his modest contract to Toronto, and Quentin to the Padres for second-tier pitching prospects Simon Castro and Pedro Hernandez.

The Sox find themselves in offseason limbo, with an obvious need to re-tool for the future, but enough talent on hand to put them on the edge of contention should everything break the club's way. Punting on a season seems foreign to Williams's nature, so there's a chance most of his veterans will still be on hand for Opening Day, but even if that happens, their ability to compete now and in the near future depends on a long list of hopes. They'll hope that Peavy is healthy, Dunn is cured, Rios is focused, and Konerko is ageless. They'll hope Sale is a future ace, former phenom Gordon Beckham bounces back, and minor league veteran Alejandro De Aza can be an improvement on Juan Pierre—a reasonable bet, that. They'll hope third baseman Brent Morel will build on his productive September, outfielder Dayan Viciedo can keep his improved plate approach, Tyler Flowers can finally become a force behind the plate, and rookie Addison Reed can provide enough late-inning value to make up for the loss of Santos. That's a lot of wishes, and they're not likely to all come true, meaning things are likely to get worse before they get better.

Hope is not a plan, but in the long run the Sox have more going for them than just hope. Williams has shown himself to be a bold leader, and while his latest gambles have not paid off, his hands-on aggressiveness makes him as likely as any GM in the game to find the proper levers to shift his club back into contention. The trade of Santos for minor league starter Nestor Molina gave a glimpse of Williams at work: reducing payroll by dealing from a position of bullpen strength to address the complete lack of young rotation options in the system, while trusting his own evaluation of Molina to the exclusion of those who doubt. Molina may be a future star

or a future bust, but Williams didn't blink when the chance came to make a small bet on his future. Such decisiveness will serve the Sox well going forward.

Williams may have wagered his way into this predicament, but he isn't about to throw up his hands and quietly accept it, and his history shows he deserves a chance to work his way out of it. We long ago gave up guessing what he will do next, but unlike some GMs, we're certain he'll try something. Ozzie may be gone, and his mismatched buddy-cop routine with Williams may have run out of steam after seven sequels, but that doesn't mean things won't remain entertaining on the South Side.

# HITTERS

**Gordon Beckham**    **2B**
Born: 9/16/1986 Age: 25
Bats: R Throws: R Height: 6' 1" Weight: 190
Breakout: 0% Improve: 25% Collapse: 21%
Attrition: 43% MLB: 85%
**Comparables:**
Jim Lefebvre, Ron Dunn, Scott Sizemore

| YEAR | TEAM | LVL | AGE | PA | R | 2B | 3B | HR | RBI | BB | SO | SB | CS | AVG_OBP_SLG | TAv | BABIP | BRR | FRAA | WARP |
|------|------|-----|-----|-----|----|----|----|----|-----|----|-----|----|----|-------------|-----|-------|-----|------|------|
| 2009 | BIR | AA | 22 | 166 | 23 | 17 | 0 | 4 | 22 | 14 | 24 | 1 | 0 | .299/.364/.497 | .293 | .331 | 0.6 | 2 | 1.6 |
| 2009 | CHA | MLB | 22 | 430 | 58 | 28 | 1 | 14 | 63 | 41 | 65 | 7 | 4 | .270/.347/.460 | .279 | .290 | 2.5 | 0.9 | 2.6 |
| 2010 | CHA | MLB | 23 | 498 | 58 | 25 | 2 | 9 | 49 | 37 | 92 | 4 | 6 | .252/.317/.378 | .253 | .297 | -0.2 | -1.2 | 1.3 |
| 2011 | CHA | MLB | 24 | 557 | 60 | 23 | 0 | 10 | 44 | 35 | 111 | 5 | 3 | .230/.296/.337 | .242 | .276 | 0.3 | 6.8 | 0.9 |
| 2012 | CHA | MLB | 25 | 512 | 59 | 26 | 1 | 13 | 55 | 41 | 92 | 6 | 3 | .254/.324/.399 | .262 | .286 | -0.7 | 2B 1, 3B 1 | 1.7 |

For the second straight year, Beckham started the season batting in the two-hole but hacked his way to the bottom of the order, tortured by hurlers who learned he can't lay off high fastballs or sliders away. Once considered the future face of the franchise, Beckham's struggles sparked a clubhouse confrontation between Kenny Williams and former hitting coach Greg Walker after Williams hinted that Walker's tinkering had ruined the former *wunderkind*'s swing. True or not, Beckham's current approach clearly isn't working, and he'll need to adjust if he wants to make good on his immense talent. To his credit, he didn't take his offensive struggles with him to the field, having worked hard to become a plus defender at the keystone with a strong arm and good footwork on the pivot. A calmer clubhouse and reduced expectations may be just the elixir to help Beckham rediscover his stroke, and if he does there are still All-Star Games in his future.

**Ramon Castro**    **C**
Born: 3/1/1976 Age: 36
Bats: R Throws: R Height: 6' 4" Weight: 225
Breakout: 0% Improve: 16% Collapse: 11%
Attrition: 22% MLB: 68%
**Comparables:**
Roy Campanella, Jason Varitek, Barry Lyons

| YEAR | TEAM | LVL | AGE | PA | R | 2B | 3B | HR | RBI | BB | SO | SB | CS | AVG_OBP_SLG | TAv | BABIP | BRR | FRAA | WARP |
|------|------|-----|-----|-----|----|----|----|----|-----|----|----|----|----|-------------|-----|-------|-----|------|------|
| 2009 | CHA | MLB | 33 | 84 | 8 | 3 | 0 | 4 | 12 | 8 | 23 | 0 | 0 | .184/.262/.382 | .229 | .204 | -0.5 | -0.8 | -0.1 |
| 2009 | NYN | MLB | 33 | 87 | 5 | 5 | 0 | 3 | 13 | 8 | 16 | 0 | 0 | .253/.322/.430 | .243 | .283 | 0.1 | -0.6 | 0.2 |
| 2010 | CHA | MLB | 34 | 128 | 18 | 2 | 0 | 8 | 21 | 9 | 26 | 1 | 0 | .278/.328/.504 | .284 | .293 | 0.1 | 0.2 | 1.0 |
| 2011 | CHA | MLB | 35 | 75 | 6 | 3 | 0 | 4 | 10 | 7 | 23 | 0 | 0 | .235/.307/.456 | .267 | .293 | -0.9 | -0.7 | 0.2 |
| 2012 | CHA | MLB | 36 | 250 | 30 | 9 | 0 | 12 | 33 | 21 | 60 | 1 | 0 | .242/.308/.442 | .264 | .272 | 0 | C -3 | 2.3 |

Castro's season was cut short in July when his throwing hand got in the way of a Mark Buehrle fastball, proving yet again that the term "soft-tosser" is a relative one. The catching injury resulted in a broken finger that required four pins to heal. Despite that, Castro continues to demonstrate skills perfectly suited to the short side of a catching platoon: solid defense, an affable demeanor, and a talent for punishing left-handed pitching (.261/.336/.552 over the last three seasons). His absence allowed Tyler Flowers to plant his flag on the White Sox backup catcher job, meaning Castro will need to find a new set of teammates to paint an arrow and the words "Catch Ball Here" on his mitt.

**Jordan Danks**    **CF**
Born: 8/7/1986 Age: 25
Bats: L Throws: R Height: 6' 5" Weight: 210
Breakout: 3% Improve: 33% Collapse: 7%
Attrition: 25% MLB: 78%
**Comparables:**
Marcus Davis, Mike Cameron, Rick Miller

| YEAR | TEAM | LVL | AGE | PA | R | 2B | 3B | HR | RBI | BB | SO | SB | CS | AVG_OBP_SLG | TAv | BABIP | BRR | FRAA | WARP |
|------|------|-----|-----|-----|----|----|----|----|-----|----|-----|----|----|-------------|-----|-------|-----|------|------|
| 2009 | WNS | A+ | 22 | 138 | 25 | 11 | 2 | 3 | 21 | 18 | 32 | 5 | 1 | .322/.409/.525 | .318 | .417 | -1.1 | -2.4 | 1.0 |
| 2009 | BIR | AA | 22 | 330 | 50 | 12 | 1 | 6 | 20 | 37 | 73 | 7 | 3 | .243/.334/.356 | .249 | .301 | 2 | 1 | 0.9 |
| 2010 | CHR | AAA | 23 | 502 | 62 | 27 | 3 | 8 | 42 | 41 | 151 | 15 | 6 | .245/.309/.373 | .237 | .342 | 3.7 | -7.5 | -0.5 |
| 2011 | CHR | AAA | 24 | 535 | 65 | 24 | 6 | 14 | 69 | 57 | 155 | 18 | 4 | .257/.344/.425 | .259 | .356 | 1.6 | 3 | 1.9 |
| 2012 | CHA | MLB | 25 | 250 | 26 | 10 | 1 | 5 | 23 | 22 | 74 | 6 | 2 | .222/.296/.351 | .232 | .300 | -0.1 | CF -3, LF 0 | 0.1 |

After two disastrous campaigns in the upper minors, Danks has finally started showing signs of converting his considerable tools into some semblance of production. A 24-year-old slugging .425 in Triple-A doesn't exactly call for a *céilidh*, but it does provide fuel for optimists to think that the former Longhorn star is finally tapping into the power his size and swing have long foretold. His strikeout rate is still alarming and guarantees he'll never earn a full-time job, but his speed, athleticism, and glove—he won the 2011 Gold Glove as the best defensive center fielder in the whole minor leagues—might just earn him a fourth outfielder's job.

**Alejandro De Aza** LF

Born: 4/11/1984 Age: 28
Bats: L Throws: L Height: 6' 1" Weight: 174
Breakout: 1% Improve: 33% Collapse: 7%
Attrition: 30% MLB: 89%

Comparables:
David Murphy, Tito Francona, Ben Francisco

| YEAR | TEAM | LVL | AGE | PA | R | 2B | 3B | HR | RBI | BB | SO | SB | CS | AVG_OBP_SLG | TAv | BABIP | BRR | FRAA | WARP |
|---|---|---|---|---|---|---|---|---|---|---|---|---|---|---|---|---|---|---|---|
| 2009 | NWO | AAA | 25 | 307 | 45 | 21 | 5 | 8 | 34 | 27 | 53 | 11 | 5 | .300/.364/.506 | .305 | .338 | 0.7 | -4 | 1.8 |
| 2009 | FLO | MLB | 25 | 27 | 6 | 1 | 0 | 0 | 3 | 5 | 5 | 0 | 0 | .250/.385/.300 | .284 | .312 | 1 | 0.8 | 0.4 |
| 2010 | CHR | AAA | 26 | 358 | 53 | 21 | 4 | 5 | 49 | 29 | 60 | 16 | 3 | .302/.366/.440 | .280 | .355 | 4.4 | -0.1 | 1.8 |
| 2010 | CHA | MLB | 26 | 32 | 7 | 3 | 0 | 0 | 2 | 1 | 4 | 2 | 1 | .300/.323/.400 | .250 | .346 | 0.1 | -0.6 | -0.1 |
| 2011 | CHR | AAA | 27 | 435 | 64 | 29 | 5 | 9 | 37 | 33 | 72 | 22 | 11 | .322/.378/.494 | .288 | .373 | 1.9 | -1.4 | 2.5 |

lows the White Sox to exile Rios to a corner. Combine all that with the solid on-base skills he's shown in Triple-A, and De Aza can provide average production on the cheap—something the Sox can certainly use. Doling out starting gigs to minor league veterans is often a fool's errand, but with so little downside, there's reason to believe this is a gamble worth taking.

**Adam Dunn** 1B

Born: 11/9/1979 Age: 32
Bats: L Throws: R Height: 6' 7" Weight: 240
Breakout: 0% Improve: 36% Collapse: 3%
Attrition: 6% MLB: 94%

Comparables:
Carlos Pena, Ken Phelps, Mark McGwire

| YEAR | TEAM | LVL | AGE | PA | R | 2B | 3B | HR | RBI | BB | SO | SB | CS | AVG_OBP_SLG | TAv | BABIP | BRR | FRAA | WARP |
|---|---|---|---|---|---|---|---|---|---|---|---|---|---|---|---|---|---|---|---|
| 2009 | WAS | MLB | 29 | 668 | 81 | 29 | 0 | 38 | 105 | 116 | 177 | 0 | 1 | .267/.398/.529 | .310 | .324 | -2.9 | -11.2 | 2.5 |
| 2010 | WAS | MLB | 30 | 648 | 85 | 36 | 2 | 38 | 103 | 77 | 199 | 0 | 1 | .260/.356/.536 | .306 | .329 | -5.4 | -5.9 | 2.1 |
| 2011 | CHA | MLB | 31 | 496 | 36 | 16 | 0 | 11 | 42 | 75 | 177 | 0 | 1 | .159/.292/.277 | .218 | .240 | -6.5 | -2.4 | -2.7 |
| 2012 | CHA | MLB | 32 | 496 | 66 | 18 | 1 | 26 | 65 | 77 | 143 | 1 | 1 | .232/.358/.469 | .292 | .284 | -0.2 | 1B -5, LF -1 | 2.4 |

Having erred in not re-signing Jim Thome for the 2010 season, the Sox paid top dollar last year for Dunn to fill their DH void, only to watch his slugger's license expire. How historic was Dunn's power outage? There have been 2,300 qualifying player-seasons where a batter slugged over .500, and last year Dunn became the first to follow up such a year by slugging below .300. Whether due to age, changing leagues, adapting to the DH spot, or some random Ozzieball curse, Dunn spent the season at sea, unable to catch up to the fastballs he has traditionally crushed and posting a stomach-churning .064/.235/.074 line against lefties. The good news is Dunn's superior batting eye remains intact, and a newfound commitment to offseason cage work may perk up his reflexes and remind him how to put bat on ball with authority. None of that will stop him from being a Canyonero-sized millstone in the field and on the basepaths. While he's certain to improve at the plate, his days as one of baseball's most feared one-trick ponies might be over, unless the three years and $44 million left on his contract say otherwise.

**Eduardo Escobar** SS

Born: 1/5/1989 Age: 23
Bats: B Throws: R Height: 5' 11" Weight: 165
Breakout: 10% Improve: 35% Collapse: 9%
Attrition: 29% MLB: 65%

Comparables:
Cristian Guzman, Zoilo Versalles, Luis Aparicio

| YEAR | TEAM | LVL | AGE | PA | R | 2B | 3B | HR | RBI | BB | SO | SB | CS | AVG_OBP_SLG | TAv | BABIP | BRR | FRAA | WARP |
|---|---|---|---|---|---|---|---|---|---|---|---|---|---|---|---|---|---|---|---|
| 2009 | KAN | A | 20 | 514 | 64 | 10 | 7 | 3 | 41 | 29 | 91 | 20 | 6 | .256/.292/.328 | .250 | .300 | 2.3 | 3 | 2.3 |
| 2010 | WNS | A+ | 21 | 408 | 57 | 18 | 8 | 3 | 39 | 23 | 76 | 8 | 5 | .285/.322/.402 | .259 | .340 | -0.9 | 4.9 | 2.1 |
| 2010 | BIR | AA | 21 | 216 | 22 | 8 | 3 | 3 | 22 | 9 | 35 | 3 | 0 | .262/.287/.376 | .254 | .296 | -0.2 | 3.6 | 1.2 |
| 2011 | CHR | AAA | 22 | 536 | 55 | 23 | 4 | 4 | 49 | 27 | 104 | 13 | 8 | .266/.303/.354 | .229 | .327 | -4.9 | 0.5 | -0.4 |
| 2011 | CHA | MLB | 22 | 7 | 0 | 0 | 0 | 0 | 0 | 0 | 1 | 0 | 0 | .286/.286/.286 | .194 | .333 | 0 | 0.1 | 0.0 |
| 2012 | CHA | MLB | 23 | 250 | 24 | 9 | 2 | 2 | 21 | 11 | 54 | 5 | 2 | .237/.271/.320 | .212 | .289 | -0.3 | SS 4, 2B -0 | -0.4 |

Now that Ozzie has left the building, Escobar has become the most notable walk-averse Venezuelan shortstop in the White Sox' employ. The organization had hoped to see incremental improvement at the plate, but last year Triple-A pitchers exploited his impatient approach and sent his walk, strikeout, and power numbers spiraling into the danger zone from which prospects rarely recover. He is a plus defender, however, with a cannon arm and soft hands that should guarantee him a career as a reserve middle infielder, and keep him ahead of Osvaldo Martinez on the organizational depth chart. In baseball's worst farm system, that's more than enough to keep the development staff interested.

**Tyler Flowers**    C

Born: 1/24/1986 Age: 26
Bats: R Throws: R Height: 6' 5" Weight: 245
Breakout: 7% Improve: 28% Collapse: 7%
Attrition: 26% MLB: 84%

Comparables:
Eric Wedge, Tom Haller, Mike Napoli

| YEAR | TEAM | LVL | AGE | PA | R | 2B | 3B | HR | RBI | BB | SO | SB | CS | AVG_OBP_SLG | TAv | BABIP | BRR | FRAA | WARP |
|---|---|---|---|---|---|---|---|---|---|---|---|---|---|---|---|---|---|---|---|
| 2009 | BIR | AA | 23 | 317 | 54 | 18 | 2 | 13 | 43 | 57 | 76 | 3 | 0 | .302/.449/.548 | .356 | .390 | 0.8 | -0.3 | 4.8 |
| 2009 | CHR | AAA | 23 | 119 | 13 | 10 | 0 | 2 | 13 | 10 | 32 | 0 | 0 | .286/.361/.438 | .268 | .389 | 0.5 | 0.1 | 0.6 |
| 2009 | CHA | MLB | 23 | 20 | 3 | 1 | 0 | 0 | 0 | 3 | 8 | 0 | 0 | .188/.350/.250 | .223 | .375 | -0.2 | 0 | 0.0 |
| 2010 | CHR | AAA | 24 | 412 | 43 | 22 | 2 | 16 | 53 | 55 | 121 | 2 | 1 | .220/.335/.434 | .264 | .284 | -2.3 | -0.2 | 1.9 |
| 2010 | CHA | MLB | 24 | 15 | 2 | 0 | 0 | 0 | 0 | 4 | 5 | 0 | 0 | .091/.333/.091 | .198 | .167 | 0.4 | 0 | 0.0 |
| 2011 | CHR | AAA | 25 | 270 | 36 | 8 | 0 | 15 | 32 | 39 | 84 | 2 | 0 | .261/.390/.500 | .299 | .350 | -0.6 | -1.5 | 2.0 |
| 2011 | CHA | MLB | 25 | 129 | 13 | 5 | 1 | 5 | 16 | 14 | 38 | 0 | 1 | .209/.310/.409 | .260 | .261 | 0.2 | -0.2 | 0.6 |
| 2012 | CHA | MLB | 26 | 250 | 30 | 9 | 1 | 10 | 28 | 32 | 75 | 1 | 0 | .228/.343/.415 | .272 | .300 | 0 | C -1, 1B -0 | 2.6 |

Flowers has been the White Sox catcher-in-waiting since his arrival from Atlanta in 2008, and the backstop-sized backstop is finally ready to prove he's been worth the wait. An offense-first catcher with prodigious raw power and a patient approach—think Mike Napoli on Miracle-Gro—Flowers has worked hard to upgrade his receiving skills from disastrous to adequate, and last spring re-tooled his swing to overcome a fleeting case of lumber anemia and once again lay the wood to Triple-A hurlers. Ramon Castro's fractured finger gave Flowers his big break, and the organization came away convinced he can be a big league catcher. He'll start the season in a reserve role, but will likely end it as Chicago's TTO catcher-in-residence.

**Paul Konerko**    1B

Born: 3/5/1976 Age: 36
Bats: R Throws: R Height: 6' 4" Weight: 205
Breakout: 0% Improve: 36% Collapse: 9%
Attrition: 18% MLB: 87%

Comparables:
Kevin Mitchell, Rafael Palmeiro, Stan Musial

| YEAR | TEAM | LVL | AGE | PA | R | 2B | 3B | HR | RBI | BB | SO | SB | CS | AVG_OBP_SLG | TAv | BABIP | BRR | FRAA | WARP |
|---|---|---|---|---|---|---|---|---|---|---|---|---|---|---|---|---|---|---|---|
| 2009 | CHA | MLB | 33 | 621 | 75 | 30 | 1 | 28 | 88 | 58 | 89 | 1 | 0 | .277/.353/.489 | .289 | .282 | -2.1 | 2.9 | 2.3 |
| 2010 | CHA | MLB | 34 | 631 | 89 | 30 | 1 | 39 | 111 | 72 | 110 | 0 | 1 | .312/.393/.584 | .338 | .326 | -3.3 | -5.8 | 5.1 |
| 2011 | CHA | MLB | 35 | 639 | 69 | 25 | 0 | 31 | 105 | 77 | 89 | 1 | 1 | .300/.388/.517 | .315 | .304 | -6 | -9 | 2.9 |
| 2012 | CHA | MLB | 36 | 599 | 80 | 23 | 1 | 29 | 82 | 69 | 99 | 1 | 0 | .264/.356/.480 | .297 | .274 | -0.1 | 1B -5 | 3.1 |

Impressive as the numbers above may be—and his late-career surge has indeed been something to behold—they go only partway to describing Konerko's value to the White Sox. Paulie is the face of the franchise, a fan favorite and long-time team captain, a Marvin Miller Man of the Year finalist, and a voice of clubhouse sanity during an era of reality-show histrionics. His leadership skills and baseball wisdom had Kenny Williams at least momentarily considering a promotion to player/manager, an idea scotched not by concerns that he wasn't ready to run a ballclub, but fear that the added responsibility might erode Konerko's focus on remaining a run-producing force. Given all that, the $25.5 million he's set to earn through 2013 (some of it deferred) will be well-earned, never mind his declining glove, ponderous baserunning, and whatever offensive value Father Time sees fit to steal away in the interim.

**Brent Lillibridge**    SS

Born: 9/18/1983 Age: 28
Bats: R Throws: R Height: 6' 0" Weight: 190
Breakout: 1% Improve: 32% Collapse: 9%
Attrition: 33% MLB: 79%

Comparables:
Will Venable, Willie Crawford, Joe Lefebvre

| YEAR | TEAM | LVL | AGE | PA | R | 2B | 3B | HR | RBI | BB | SO | SB | CS | AVG_OBP_SLG | TAv | BABIP | BRR | FRAA | WARP |
|---|---|---|---|---|---|---|---|---|---|---|---|---|---|---|---|---|---|---|---|
| 2009 | CHR | AAA | 25 | 283 | 34 | 9 | 4 | 3 | 24 | 29 | 57 | 17 | 1 | .252/.337/.358 | .251 | .312 | 2.5 | 0.5 | 1.0 |
| 2009 | CHA | MLB | 25 | 112 | 9 | 2 | 0 | 0 | 3 | 14 | 26 | 6 | 3 | .158/.273/.179 | .177 | .217 | 1.3 | -1.7 | -0.8 |
| 2010 | CHR | AAA | 26 | 206 | 26 | 8 | 0 | 4 | 16 | 17 | 46 | 19 | 3 | .270/.335/.378 | .257 | .341 | 2.5 | 1.5 | 0.9 |
| 2010 | CHA | MLB | 26 | 101 | 19 | 5 | 2 | 2 | 16 | 3 | 36 | 5 | 3 | .224/.248/.378 | .212 | .333 | 0.1 | 0.2 | -0.3 |
| 2011 | CHA | MLB | 27 | 216 | 38 | 5 | 1 | 13 | 29 | 17 | 62 | 10 | 6 | .258/.340/.505 | .297 | .310 | 1.8 | 2.5 | 1.6 |
| 2012 | CHA | MLB | 28 | 250 | 27 | 8 | 2 | 7 | 26 | 21 | 67 | 12 | 4 | .225/.302/.375 | .242 | .283 | -0.3 | SS -1, 2B 0 | 0.4 |

Lillibridge is a likeable player and was a rare bright spot in an otherwise gloomy season at the Cell, shining defensively all over the diamond and delivering unexpected home run thump. It was exactly the sort of small-sample performance that prompts sports-radio chuckleheads to call up The Score and demand that some fleetingly productive grinder be permanently installed at the top of the order, despite years of evidence that their hero's true talent level is that of a utility player. Luckily, the White Sox know the difference, and will continue to get good value from Lillibridge by spotting him appropriately. He'll likely never hit this well again, and if he gets 400 at-bats this year, you'll know things have gone badly for the Sox.

**Osvaldo Martinez    SS**

Born: 5/7/1988 Age: 24
Bats: R Throws: R Height: 5' 11" Weight: 190
Breakout: 2% Improve: 18% Collapse: 11%
Attrition: 33% MLB: 72%

Comparables:
Edgar Renteria, Bucky Dent, Greg Smith

| YEAR | TEAM | LVL | AGE | PA | R | 2B | 3B | HR | RBI | BB | SO | SB | CS | AVG_OBP_SLG | TAv | BABIP | BRR | FRAA | WARP |
|------|------|-----|-----|-----|----|----|----|----|-----|----|----|----|----|-------------|-----|-------|-----|------|------|
| 2009 | JUP | A+ | 21 | 485 | 54 | 16 | 5 | 1 | 45 | 41 | 51 | 16 | 4 | .254/.321/.321 | .242 | .282 | 4.3 | 6.7 | 2.2 |
| 2010 | JAX | AA | 22 | 587 | 90 | 28 | 4 | 5 | 54 | 49 | 64 | 13 | 9 | .302/.366/.401 | .279 | .330 | 2.6 | -2.4 | 4.1 |
| 2010 | FLO | MLB | 22 | 48 | 8 | 4 | 1 | 0 | 2 | 4 | 6 | 1 | 0 | .326/.383/.465 | .295 | .378 | 1.1 | -0.4 | 0.4 |
| 2011 | NWO | AAA | 23 | 371 | 43 | 15 | 1 | 3 | 26 | 21 | 57 | 11 | 4 | .245/.296/.322 | .214 | .284 | -1.8 | -5.3 | -1.1 |
| 2011 | FLO | MLB | 23 | 23 | 0 | 0 | 0 | 0 | 0 | 1 | 9 | 0 | 0 | .130/.130/.130 | .086 | .214 | 0.5 | -0.1 | -0.3 |
| 2012 | CHA | MLB | 24 | 250 | 24 | 9 | 1 | 2 | 20 | 15 | 41 | 5 | 2 | .233/.283/.310 | .217 | .270 | -0.2 | SS 0, 2B -0 | -0.2 |

Half of the organization's haul for saying adios to Ozzie, Martinez saw his prospect flame dim significantly last year while hacking away like a futility-infielder-in-waiting for the Marlins. With average speed, little power, and questionable range at short, he'll need to rediscover the patience he demonstrated in 2010 to have any chance of moving past the more leather-capable Eduardo Escobar and into a big-league utility role.

dous speed and power potential but has yet to translate those tools into actual performance, and never will if he continues to whiff in over a third of his plate appearances. The Sox are willing to chalk last year up to rust and the burden of high expectations, but if Mitchell—already 23 and still inexperienced—can't get this battleship turned around quickly his career will be sunk before it gets started.

**Brent Morel    3B**

Born: 4/21/1987 Age: 25
Bats: R Throws: R Height: 6' 3" Weight: 220
Breakout: 8% Improve: 32% Collapse: 10%
Attrition: 29% MLB: 72%

Comparables:
Adrian Beltre, Jesus Guzman, Stan Royer

| YEAR | TEAM | LVL | AGE | PA | R | 2B | 3B | HR | RBI | BB | SO | SB | CS | AVG_OBP_SLG | TAv | BABIP | BRR | FRAA | WARP |
|------|------|-----|-----|-----|----|----|----|----|-----|----|----|----|----|-------------|-----|-------|-----|------|------|
| 2009 | WNS | A+ | 22 | 526 | 82 | 33 | 1 | 16 | 79 | 38 | 66 | 25 | 9 | .281/.337/.453 | .278 | .298 | 2.9 | 5.6 | 4.0 |
| 2010 | BIR | AA | 23 | 203 | 25 | 13 | 1 | 2 | 30 | 14 | 36 | 5 | 5 | .326/.378/.440 | .302 | .395 | -0.7 | 0.4 | 1.5 |
| 2010 | CHR | AAA | 23 | 324 | 40 | 24 | 4 | 8 | 34 | 13 | 50 | 3 | 0 | .320/.343/.503 | .295 | .356 | 0.9 | 1.2 | 2.9 |
| 2010 | CHA | MLB | 23 | 70 | 9 | 3 | 0 | 3 | 7 | 4 | 17 | 2 | 0 | .231/.271/.415 | .231 | .261 | 0.8 | -0.7 | 0.0 |
| 2011 | CHA | MLB | 24 | 444 | 44 | 18 | 1 | 10 | 41 | 22 | 57 | 5 | 4 | .245/.287/.366 | .245 | .262 | -0.9 | -1.3 | 0.5 |
| 2012 | CHA | MLB | 25 | 405 | 46 | 19 | 1 | 11 | 47 | 21 | 66 | 7 | 3 | .264/.305/.407 | .257 | .291 | -0.4 | 3B 1, SS -0 | 1.6 |

Morel has a plus glove but has long suffered from Josh Vitters Disease, wherein a young third baseman with excellent plate coverage puts the first pitch he can reach in play rather than waiting for something he can drive. His symptoms were greatly in evidence throughout his rookie season, as Morel didn't draw a walk until May 30, and had only 11 free passes, two home runs, and a punchless .247/.271/.333 line through the end of August. When Morel started to embrace the selectivity his coaches were preaching, however, the results were eye-popping, featuring a .224/.340/.553 September line with 15 walks and 8 home runs. There's always risk in reading too much into late-seasons results, but if Morel can carry his newfound patience forward he'll continue to unleash the power in his swing and will blow past that PECOTA projection.

**Juan Pierre    LF**

Born: 8/14/1977 Age: 34
Bats: L Throws: L Height: 6' 1" Weight: 170
Breakout: 4% Improve: 24% Collapse: 11%
Attrition: 29% MLB: 80%

Comparables:
Fernando Vina, Chuck Knoblauch, Steve Sax

| YEAR | TEAM | LVL | AGE | PA | R | 2B | 3B | HR | RBI | BB | SO | SB | CS | AVG_OBP_SLG | TAv | BABIP | BRR | FRAA | WARP |
|------|------|-----|-----|-----|----|----|----|----|-----|----|----|----|----|-------------|-----|-------|-----|------|------|
| 2009 | LAN | MLB | 31 | 425 | 57 | 16 | 8 | 0 | 31 | 27 | 27 | 30 | 12 | .308/.365/.392 | .267 | .331 | 1.6 | 1.7 | 1.3 |
| 2010 | CHA | MLB | 32 | 734 | 96 | 18 | 3 | 1 | 47 | 45 | 47 | 68 | 18 | .275/.341/.316 | .242 | .294 | 8.6 | 5.5 | 1.4 |
| 2011 | CHA | MLB | 33 | 711 | 80 | 17 | 4 | 2 | 50 | 43 | 41 | 27 | 17 | .279/.329/.327 | .242 | .294 | 10 | -1.2 | -0.2 |
| 2012 | CHA | MLB | 34 | 673 | 71 | 17 | 4 | 2 | 51 | 40 | 49 | 44 | 16 | .274/.328/.328 | .237 | .285 | -1.1 | LF -3, CF -0 | -0.2 |

Ozzie's decision last year to keep the powerless Pierre atop his lineup and starting in left field wasn't surprising, but it did fly in the face of several hard truths: speed is not defense, bunting and making contact is not on-base ability, and Juan Pierre isn't a lead-off man—he just plays one on TV. Anyone who fields a corner outfield position poorly, doesn't draw walks, is routinely thrown out trying to steal, and has less power than a Utah Democrat doesn't deserve 700 precious plate appearances, no matter how hard he works or how good he was a decade ago.

It's not Pierre's fault that clubs continue to pay him to do things he's no longer capable of, but any GM that signs him for more than a pinch-running role will have a lot of 'splainin' to do.

**A.J. Pierzynski**    C
Born: 12/30/1976 Age: 35
Bats: L Throws: R Height: 6' 4" Weight: 218
Breakout: 0% Improve: 22% Collapse: 12%
Attrition: 33% MLB: 75%

**Comparables:**
Darrin Fletcher, Bengie Molina, Toby Hall

| YEAR | TEAM | LVL | AGE | PA | R | 2B | 3B | HR | RBI | BB | SO | SB | CS | AVG_OBP_SLG | TAv | BABIP | BRR | FRAA | WARP |
|------|------|-----|-----|-----|----|----|----|----|-----|----|----|----|----|--------------|------|-------|------|------|------|
| 2009 | CHA | MLB | 32 | 535 | 57 | 22 | 1 | 13 | 49 | 24 | 52 | 1 | 1 | .300/.331/.425 | .259 | .312 | -3.4 | -2.8 | 1.2 |
| 2010 | CHA | MLB | 33 | 503 | 43 | 29 | 0 | 9 | 56 | 15 | 39 | 3 | 4 | .270/.300/.388 | .230 | .278 | -0.8 | -1.7 | 0.5 |
| 2011 | CHA | MLB | 34 | 500 | 38 | 29 | 1 | 8 | 48 | 23 | 33 | 0 | 0 | .287/.323/.405 | .250 | .291 | -2.7 | -0.9 | 0.7 |
| 2012 | CHA | MLB | 35 | 472 | 52 | 21 | 1 | 11 | 51 | 21 | 53 | 1 | 1 | .264/.303/.388 | .245 | .276 | -0.2 | C -2 | 1.4 |

It was déjà vu all over again last year at the Cell, as the White Sox signed A.J. for the fourth time and were rewarded with the same mix of singles, doubles, double-play grounders and opponent steals he always provides. If you sing ".280/.320/.420" into a smartphone, Shazam will identify it as a classic Pierzynski track. Such consistent mediocrity, paired with A.J.'s legendary durability, provides value, as it allows the organization to build the rest of the lineup knowing their catcher will neither carry nor sink it. With Pierzynski's latest deal expiring at the end of this season, the Sox plan to shift more work onto Tyler Flowers, but if the young slugger again fails to launch don't be surprised if A.J. re-ups for a fifth time.

**Alexei Ramirez**    SS
Born: 9/22/1981 Age: 30
Bats: R Throws: R Height: 6' 4" Weight: 185
Breakout: 4% Improve: 39% Collapse: 3%
Attrition: 9% MLB: 88%

**Comparables:**
Barry Larkin, Edgar Renteria, Jason Bartlett

| YEAR | TEAM | LVL | AGE | PA | R | 2B | 3B | HR | RBI | BB | SO | SB | CS | AVG_OBP_SLG | TAv | BABIP | BRR | FRAA | WARP |
|------|------|-----|-----|-----|----|----|----|----|-----|----|----|----|----|--------------|------|-------|------|------|------|
| 2009 | CHA | MLB | 27 | 606 | 71 | 14 | 1 | 15 | 68 | 49 | 66 | 14 | 5 | .277/.333/.389 | .257 | .288 | -0.1 | -6.9 | 1.5 |
| 2010 | CHA | MLB | 28 | 626 | 83 | 29 | 2 | 18 | 70 | 27 | 82 | 13 | 8 | .282/.313/.431 | .265 | .300 | 6.2 | 20.9 | 5.8 |
| 2011 | CHA | MLB | 29 | 684 | 81 | 31 | 2 | 15 | 70 | 51 | 84 | 7 | 5 | .269/.328/.399 | .254 | .288 | 1.4 | 7.5 | 3.2 |
| 2012 | CHA | MLB | 30 | 631 | 75 | 23 | 2 | 19 | 74 | 42 | 81 | 11 | 6 | .272/.324/.418 | .265 | .284 | -1.1 | SS 7 | 2.9 |

If Ramirez were a bit younger his 2011 campaign might have been called a consolidation season, that moment when a burgeoning star confirms a level of steady production before growing into his full potential. Now that he's on the wrong side of 30, however, it's far more likely Ramirez has reached his peak having never quite taken that great leap forward at the plate. Nonetheless, his defense remains superlative, showing great range, a cannon arm, and a flair for the dramatic, while oozing an athleticism that should help him retain his value in the field for years to come. Ramirez will never walk enough to be an asset at the top of the order or slug enough to be an outstanding run producer, but more importantly, he's not about to become a lineup void. Most teams would love to get that from their shortstop.

**Alex Rios**    CF
Born: 2/18/1981 Age: 31
Bats: R Throws: R Height: 6' 6" Weight: 180
Breakout: 1% Improve: 51% Collapse: 2%
Attrition: 11% MLB: 90%

**Comparables:**
Amos Otis, Vernon Wells, Eric Byrnes

| YEAR | TEAM | LVL | AGE | PA | R | 2B | 3B | HR | RBI | BB | SO | SB | CS | AVG_OBP_SLG | TAv | BABIP | BRR | FRAA | WARP |
|------|------|-----|-----|-----|----|----|----|----|-----|----|----|----|----|--------------|------|-------|------|-------|------|
| 2009 | CHA | MLB | 28 | 154 | 11 | 6 | 0 | 3 | 9 | 6 | 29 | 5 | 2 | .199/.229/.301 | .186 | .226 | -1 | -0.2 | -1.0 |
| 2009 | TOR | MLB | 28 | 479 | 52 | 25 | 2 | 14 | 62 | 31 | 78 | 19 | 3 | .264/.317/.427 | .264 | .289 | -0.2 | 5.7 | 1.9 |
| 2010 | CHA | MLB | 29 | 617 | 89 | 29 | 3 | 21 | 88 | 38 | 93 | 34 | 14 | .284/.334/.457 | .270 | .306 | 0 | 4.1 | 3.1 |
| 2011 | CHA | MLB | 30 | 570 | 64 | 22 | 2 | 13 | 44 | 27 | 68 | 11 | 6 | .227/.265/.348 | .216 | .237 | 2.1 | -1.2 | -0.7 |
| 2012 | CHA | MLB | 31 | 545 | 63 | 26 | 3 | 16 | 65 | 36 | 88 | 20 | 7 | .259/.312/.418 | .261 | .284 | -0.4 | CF 3, RF 1 | 1.7 |

The third leg in last year's Stool of Southside Lineup Disaster, Rios's season was in some ways the most discouraging. Whereas Adam Dunn's struggles at the plate were unprecedented, Rios has been here before, with his 2010 adequacy looking more and more like an outlier. While Gordon Beckham refused to let his sickly bat infect his glove, Rios often shambled around the outfield like a Sleestak with mono. His batting average dropped 60 points despite a huge drop in his strikeout rate, and sabermetric orthodoxy insists that his .237 BABIP will improve—but sabermetric orthodoxy hasn't watched Rios repeatedly make weak contact on pitches out of the zone. On the wrong side of 30 and owed $37 million over the next three years, Rios still has the skills to play a solid center field if he wants to and has nowhere to go but up at the plate, but no amount of squinting will make him the two-way star his contract demands.

**Tyler Saladino**    SS
Born: 7/20/1989 Age: 22
Bats: R Throws: R Height: 6' 0" Weight: 180
Breakout: 5% Improve: 24% Collapse: 7%
Attrition: 36% MLB: 79%

**Comparables:**
Jose Offerman, Angel Berroa, Bobby Grich

| YEAR | TEAM | LVL | AGE | PA | R | 2B | 3B | HR | RBI | BB | SO | SB | CS | AVG_OBP_SLG | TAv | BABIP | BRR | FRAA | WARP |
|------|------|-----|-----|-----|----|----|----|----|----|-----|----|----|----|----|--------------|------|-------|------|------|------|
| 2010 | KAN | A | 20 | 198 | 40 | 14 | 1 | 2 | 18 | 22 | 44 | 4 | 2 | .309/.395/.442 | .291 | .398 | 2.2 | -1.9 | 1.3 |
| 2010 | BRI | RK | 20 | 56 | 7 | 3 | 0 | 1 | 6 | 5 | 12 | 1 | 2 | .292/.364/.417 | .307 | .361 | -0.9 | -0.4 | 0.4 |
| 2011 | WNS | A+ | 21 | 464 | 75 | 26 | 9 | 16 | 55 | 51 | 90 | 7 | 7 | .270/.363/.501 | .292 | .310 | 2 | 11.4 | 5.4 |
| 2012 | CHA | MLB | 22 | 250 | 28 | 10 | 2 | 8 | 28 | 20 | 59 | 3 | 2 | .233/.302/.397 | .249 | .276 | -0.4 | SS 9 | 1.4 |

Saladino's impressive 2010 debut placed him on numerous prospect sleeper lists, and last year the former seventh round pick broke out in a big way. After missing a month with a broken hand, Saladino broke out the boom stick on Carolina League pitchers, maintaining a solid walk rate and showing unexpected home run pop. In the field he's more steady than spectacular, though most scouts feel he has the arm and instincts to remain at shortstop. Long on production but short on pedigree, Saladino will need to prove himself all over again at Double-A. If his power and patience carries forward into the high minors he'll profile more and more as a big league starter.

**Brandon Short** CF
Born: 9/9/1988 Age: 23
Bats: R Throws: R Height: 6' 2" Weight: 190
Breakout: 4% Improve: 21% Collapse: 6%
Attrition: 17% MLB: 55%
Comparables:

| YEAR | TEAM | LVL | AGE | PA | R | 2B | 3B | HR | RBI | BB | SO | SB | CS | AVG_OBP_SLG | TAv | BABIP | BRR | FRAA | WARP |
|---|---|---|---|---|---|---|---|---|---|---|---|---|---|---|---|---|---|---|---|
| 2009 | KAN | A | 20 | 390 | 56 | 19 | 3 | 7 | 55 | 27 | 78 | 12 | 1 | .284/.336/.417 | .270 | .337 | 2.4 | -2.7 | 1.5 |
| 2010 | WNS | A+ | 21 | 544 | 77 | 31 | 5 | 15 | 79 | 28 | 107 | 7 | 10 | .316/.367/.491 | .289 | .375 | 2.5 | -7 | 2.8 |
| 2011 | BIR | AA | 22 | 581 | 75 | 29 | 5 | 13 | 60 | 36 | 125 | 21 | 9 | .262/.318/.411 | .255 | .317 | 6.6 | -2.1 | 1.9 |
| 2012 | CHA | MLB | 23 | 250 | 25 | 10 | 1 | 5 | 25 | 10 | 61 | 4 | 2 | .229/.270/.348 | .220 | .283 | -0.3 | CF -6, RF -1 | -0.7 |

Born: 3/15/1991 Age: 21
Bats: R Throws: R Height: 6' 4" Weight: 195
Breakout: 0% Improve: 15% Collapse: 2%
Attrition: 13% MLB: 27%
Comparables:
Mike Anderson, Juan Gonzalez, Jason Place

| YEAR | TEAM | LVL | AGE | PA | R | 2B | 3B | HR | RBI | BB | SO | SB | CS | AVG_OBP_SLG | TAv | BABIP | BRR | FRAA | WARP |
|---|---|---|---|---|---|---|---|---|---|---|---|---|---|---|---|---|---|---|---|
| 2010 | KAN | A | 19 | 235 | 28 | 13 | 3 | 8 | 31 | 21 | 69 | 6 | 4 | .229/.305/.433 | .267 | .301 | 1 | 2.6 | 1.0 |
| 2011 | KAN | A | 20 | 597 | 95 | 36 | 2 | 24 | 87 | 60 | 172 | 8 | 4 | .241/.329/.457 | .268 | .309 | -1.9 | 3.6 | 2.6 |
| 2012 | CHA | MLB | 21 | 250 | 23 | 9 | 1 | 7 | 24 | 16 | 85 | 2 | 1 | .189/.246/.329 | .205 | .257 | -0.1 | CF -6, RF -0 | -1.2 |

Flash! Thunder! No tool in the Sox system generates as much excitement as Thompson's light-tower power, and no player would benefit more from learning to recognize friendly pitches. His second spin through the Sally League was hit-and-miss, as Thompson unleashed a long stroke that generated both moonshots and strikeouts with great frequency, and showed a welcome willingness to take a walk. The son of former NBA center Mychal Thompson, he's already 6-foot-3 at age 20 and most scouts expect him to outgrow center field, though his bat has the potential to play in a corner. The Sox can afford to take their time with him, and if Thompson can learn to make more contact and leverage his plus speed, he'll be the only prospect in the system with All-Star potential.

**Dayan Viciedo** RF
Born: 3/10/1989 Age: 23
Bats: R Throws: R Height: 6' 0" Weight: 240
Breakout: 4% Improve: 61% Collapse: 3%
Attrition: 10% MLB: 79%
Comparables:
Ruben Sierra, Ellis Valentine, Raul Mondesi

| YEAR | TEAM | LVL | AGE | PA | R | 2B | 3B | HR | RBI | BB | SO | SB | CS | AVG_OBP_SLG | TAv | BABIP | BRR | FRAA | WARP |
|---|---|---|---|---|---|---|---|---|---|---|---|---|---|---|---|---|---|---|---|
| 2009 | BIR | AA | 20 | 540 | 72 | 20 | 0 | 12 | 78 | 23 | 89 | 5 | 2 | .280/.320/.391 | .258 | .320 | 1.2 | -2.2 | 1.5 |
| 2010 | CHR | AAA | 21 | 363 | 42 | 15 | 0 | 20 | 47 | 11 | 78 | 1 | 1 | .274/.306/.493 | .251 | .298 | -1 | 0.9 | 0.3 |
| 2010 | CHA | MLB | 21 | 106 | 17 | 7 | 0 | 5 | 13 | 2 | 25 | 1 | 0 | .308/.321/.519 | .296 | .365 | -0.5 | -1.8 | 0.3 |
| 2011 | CHR | AAA | 22 | 505 | 60 | 28 | 0 | 20 | 78 | 45 | 83 | 2 | 1 | .296/.364/.491 | .285 | .324 | 3 | -7.9 | 1.9 |
| 2011 | CHA | MLB | 22 | 113 | 11 | 3 | 0 | 1 | 6 | 9 | 23 | 1 | 0 | .255/.327/.314 | .236 | .321 | 0.1 | -2.3 | -0.1 |
| 2012 | CHA | MLB | 23 | 250 | 29 | 10 | 0 | 9 | 31 | 12 | 52 | 1 | 0 | .264/.306/.427 | .259 | .301 | 0 | RF -5, 3B -1 | 0.9 |

One glance at Viciedo in a baseball uniform is enough to discern his main purpose in life: hitting a baseball very, very hard, and ideally going into a slow trot after doing so. The young Cuban has always shown outstanding raw power to all fields and an ability to hit for average, but last year he developed a more selective approach that resulted in a quadrupled walk rate and a significant raising of his offensive ceiling. He remains a defensive liability, however; the organization's latest scheme involves hiding him in the outfield, where he possesses an adequate arm but reads fly balls at a Kittle-garden level. With Carlos Quentin moving to San Diego, Viciedo will break camp as the everyday right fielder, and if his new approach sticks he has a chance to provide solid production at a fraction of the cost.

# PITCHERS

### Dylan Axelrod

Born: 7/30/1985 Age: 26
Bats: R Throws: R Height: 6' 1" Weight: 195
Breakout: 22% Improve: 49% Collapse: 24%
Attrition: 11% MLB: 87%

**Comparables:**
Pat Jarvis, Alfredo Aceves, Gary Nolan

| YEAR | TEAM | LVL | AGE | W | L | SV | G | GS | IP | H | HR | BB | SO | EqBB9 | EqSO9 | GB% | BABIP | WHIP | ERA | FIP | FRA | WARP |
|------|------|-----|-----|---|---|----|----|----|------|----|----|----|----|-------|-------|-----|-------|------|------|------|------|------|
| 2010 | WNS | A+ | 24 | 9 | 3 | 0 | 23 | 13 | 99¹ | 90 | 3 | 14 | 87 | 1.1 | 7.6 | 45% | .304 | 1.08 | 1.99 | 2.58 | 3.42 | 2.6 |
| 2011 | BIR | AA | 25 | 0 | 1 | 0 | 11 | 9 | 59¹ | 50 | 1 | 13 | 49 | 2.1 | 8.6 | 39% | .322 | 1.11 | 3.34 | 2.68 | 3.20 | 1.1 |
| 2011 | CHR | AAA | 25 | 2 | 1 | 0 | 15 | 15 | 91¹ | 74 | 2 | 21 | 75 | 2.1 | 7.4 | 47% | .273 | 1.04 | 2.27 | 2.70 | 3.40 | 2.4 |
| 2011 | CHA | MLB | 25 | 1 | 0 | 0 | 4 | 3 | 18² | 18 | 1 | 9 | 19 | 4.3 | 9.2 | 43% | .327 | 1.45 | 2.89 | 3.33 | 4.17 | 0.2 |
| 2012 | CHA | MLB | 26 | 3 | 3 | 0 | 11 | 8 | 56² | 60 | 6 | 20 | 37 | 3.2 | 5.9 | 43% | .303 | 1.42 | 4.38 | 4.33 | 4.76 | 0.2 |

Since signing him away from the Windy City ThunderBolts in 2009, the Sox have watched Axelrod charge his way through the system, ending last season with a successful September call-up. An undersized right-hander, command and control are his stock in trade. Axelrod needs to carefully spot his lackluster fastball before uncorking a nasty, late-breaking slider that creates a surprising number of punchouts. Axelrod's ceiling is that of a fifth starter, a role he'll nominally compete for this spring, though he profiles best as a swingman or slider-slinging ROOGY. While low-velo control artists run the constant risk of the league catching on to their tricks, if Axelrod can keep familiarity and contempt from getting too friendly he can have a career.

### Anthony Carter

Born: 4/4/1986 Age: 26
Bats: L Throws: R Height: 6' 4" Weight: 210
Breakout: 36% Improve: 71% Collapse: 14%
Attrition: 19% MLB: 91%

**Comparables:**
Allen Watson, Gabe White, Todd Stottlemyre

| YEAR | TEAM | LVL | AGE | W | L | SV | G | GS | IP | H | HR | BB | SO | EqBB9 | EqSO9 | GB% | BABIP | WHIP | ERA | FIP | FRA | WARP |
|------|------|-----|-----|---|---|----|----|----|------|-----|----|----|-----|-------|-------|-----|-------|------|------|------|------|------|
| 2009 | WNS | A+ | 23 | 11 | 7 | 0 | 27 | 27 | 154² | 156 | 23 | 43 | 123 | 2.5 | 6.9 | 41% | .286 | 1.24 | 4.36 | 4.70 | 6.11 | -0.2 |
| 2010 | BIR | AA | 24 | 1 | 4 | 22 | 46 | 2 | 57¹ | 33 | 4 | 15 | 37 | 3.5 | 9.1 | 33% | .293 | 1.20 | 3.93 | 4.01 | 5.09 | 0.0 |
| 2011 | CHR | AAA | 25 | 0 | 2 | 3 | 35 | 0 | 47¹ | 60 | 6 | 26 | 46 | 4.9 | 9.1 | 39% | .391 | 1.82 | 7.23 | 4.91 | 6.05 | -0.1 |
| 2012 | CHA | MLB | 26 | 1 | 0 | 0 | 13 | 0 | 16 | 19 | 3 | 8 | 8 | 4.3 | 4.7 | 40% | .306 | 1.68 | 6.10 | 6.14 | 6.63 | -0.3 |

In most organizations a 25-year-old reliever who suffered a mid-season demotion to Double-A isn't really a prospect, but this isn't most organizations. Carter commands attention with his upper-90s fastball, but last year he couldn't command the strike zone, issuing almost five free passes per nine and getting kicked around the yard like a gym ball at recess. If he can cut down on the walks while keeping his strikeout rate high he could someday have Mike MacDougal's career, for what that's worth. But let's be honest here—that almost never happens.

### Simon Castro

Born: 4/9/1988 Age: 24
Bats: R Throws: R Height: 6' 6" Weight: 210
Breakout: 19% Improve: 67% Collapse: 16%
Attrition: 15% MLB: 90%

**Comparables:**
Chris Resop, Bob Lacey, Chris Carpenter

| YEAR | TEAM | LVL | AGE | W | L | SV | G | GS | IP | H | HR | BB | SO | EqBB9 | EqSO9 | GB% | BABIP | WHIP | ERA | FIP | FRA | WARP |
|------|------|-----|-----|---|---|----|----|----|------|-----|----|----|-----|-------|-------|-----|-------|------|------|------|------|------|
| 2009 | FTW | A | 21 | 11 | 6 | 0 | 28 | 27 | 140¹ | 122 | 9 | 41 | 170 | 2.4 | 10.1 | 43% | .294 | 1.10 | 3.34 | 3.16 | 3.71 | 2.8 |
| 2010 | SAN | AA | 22 | 7 | 6 | 0 | 24 | 23 | 129² | 81 | 7 | 25 | 80 | 2.5 | 7.4 | 50% | .260 | 1.10 | 2.91 | 3.49 | 4.12 | 1.1 |
| 2011 | SAN | AA | 23 | 3 | 6 | 0 | 16 | 16 | 89¹ | 109 | 10 | 16 | 88 | 1.6 | 7.4 | 40% | .327 | 1.24 | 4.33 | 3.64 | 4.00 | 1.4 |
| 2012 | CHA | MLB | 24 | 2 | 3 | 0 | 8 | 8 | 41 | 43 | 5 | 18 | 28 | 4.0 | 6.2 | 43% | .297 | 1.49 | 4.89 | 4.74 | 5.32 | -0.0 |

The key ingredient coming to Chicago in the Carlos Quentin trade, Castro endured a disastrous season that saw him spend time in extended spring training after losing all sense of the strike zone at Triple-A Tucson, before picking up a few of the pieces in Double-A. He's armed with a mid-90s fastball, a solid slider, and a dodgy changeup, so many scouts see his future in the bullpen, but the Sox believe they can work out the mechanical kinks that led to his loss of command and see the big righty as their new Jose Contreras. If they're right he'll be a steal; if not, he's just another bullpen arm.

### Jesse Crain

Born: 7/5/1981 Age: 30
Bats: R Throws: R Height: 6' 2" Weight: 200
Breakout: 22% Improve: 59% Collapse: 24%
Attrition: 11% MLB: 93%

**Comparables:**
Matt Wise, Jeff Montgomery, Kevin Gregg

| YEAR | TEAM | LVL | AGE | W | L | SV | G | GS | IP | H | HR | BB | SO | EqBB9 | EqSO9 | GB% | BABIP | WHIP | ERA | FIP | FRA | WARP |
|------|------|-----|-----|---|---|----|----|----|------|----|----|----|----|-------|-------|-----|-------|------|------|------|------|------|
| 2009 | MIN | MLB | 28 | 7 | 4 | 0 | 56 | 0 | 51² | 48 | 3 | 27 | 43 | 4.7 | 7.5 | 46% | .302 | 1.45 | 4.70 | 4.09 | 4.55 | 0.6 |
| 2010 | MIN | MLB | 29 | 1 | 1 | 1 | 71 | 0 | 68 | 53 | 5 | 27 | 62 | 3.6 | 8.2 | 41% | .267 | 1.18 | 3.04 | 3.41 | 4.48 | 0.6 |
| 2011 | CHA | MLB | 30 | 8 | 3 | 1 | 67 | 0 | 65¹ | 50 | 7 | 31 | 70 | 4.3 | 9.6 | 36% | .270 | 1.24 | 2.62 | 3.73 | 4.33 | 0.6 |
| 2012 | CHA | MLB | 30 | 3 | 1 | 1 | 57 | 0 | 55¹ | 50 | 6 | 23 | 50 | 3.8 | 8.1 | 42% | .289 | 1.33 | 3.73 | 4.05 | 4.05 | 0.6 |

Crain spent his first year on the South Side making good on his new three-year, $13 million salary, or at least as much as he could working in relief, where the line between formidable and fungible can be wafer-thin. Once considered strictly a fireballer, Crain can still unleash a mid-90s fastball but now throws his slider almost half the time, more than any right-hander not named Marmol, and last year found a new changeup grip that helped him hold lefty bats to a .184/.311/.195 line. He seemed to tire down the stretch, but if manager Robin Ventura can ease back a bit on the throttle to keep him fresh, Crain's newly-expanded repertoire makes him a late-innings weapon against hitters of all stripes. Good thing too, since that's exactly what the Sox are paying him for—and with Sergio Santos now closing in Toronto, Crain may yet earn his salary in the ninth.

**John Danks**
Born: 4/15/1985 Age: 27
Bats: L Throws: L Height: 6' 2" Weight: 200
Breakout: 29% Improve: 61% Collapse: 27%
Attrition: 8% MLB: 91%

Comparables:
Harvey Haddix, Phil Coke, Fu-Te Ni

| YEAR | TEAM | LVL | AGE | W | L | SV | G | GS | IP | H | HR | BB | SO | EqBB9 | EqSO9 | GB% | BABIP | WHIP | ERA | FIP | FRA | WARP |
|------|------|-----|-----|---|---|----|----|----|------|-----|----|----|-----|-------|-------|-----|-------|------|------|------|------|------|
| 2009 | CHA | MLB | 24 | 13 | 11 | 0 | 32 | 32 | 200¹ | 184 | 28 | 73 | 149 | 3.3 | 6.7 | 46% | .269 | 1.28 | 3.77 | 4.64 | 5.12 | 1.5 |
| 2010 | CHA | MLB | 25 | 15 | 11 | 0 | 32 | 32 | 213 | 189 | 18 | 70 | 162 | 3.0 | 6.8 | 46% | .276 | 1.22 | 3.72 | 3.67 | 4.08 | 3.3 |
| 2011 | CHA | MLB | 26 | 8 | 12 | 0 | 27 | 27 | 170¹ | 182 | 19 | 46 | 135 | 2.4 | 7.1 | 46% | .315 | 1.34 | 4.33 | 3.86 | 4.13 | 2.2 |
| 2012 | CHA | MLB | 27 | 9 | 9 | 0 | 25 | 25 | 158² | 153 | 20 | 51 | 124 | 2.9 | 7.0 | 43% | .288 | 1.29 | 3.90 | 4.24 | 4.24 | 1.6 |

Last year Danks didn't take that big step forward some expected, stumbling out of the gate and losing his first eight decisions before regaining some traction en route to an 8-12 record. Win-

**Gavin Floyd**
Born: 1/27/1983 Age: 29
Bats: R Throws: R Height: 6' 6" Weight: 210
Breakout: 18% Improve: 43% Collapse: 28%
Attrition: 8% MLB: 92%

Comparables:
Gaylord Perry, Ed Halicki, Curt Schilling

| YEAR | TEAM | LVL | AGE | W | L | SV | G | GS | IP | H | HR | BB | SO | EqBB9 | EqSO9 | GB% | BABIP | WHIP | ERA | FIP | FRA | WARP |
|------|------|-----|-----|---|---|----|----|----|------|-----|----|----|-----|-------|-------|-----|-------|------|------|------|------|------|
| 2009 | CHA | MLB | 26 | 11 | 11 | 0 | 30 | 30 | 193 | 178 | 21 | 59 | 163 | 2.8 | 7.6 | 46% | .285 | 1.23 | 4.06 | 3.82 | 4.59 | 2.3 |
| 2010 | CHA | MLB | 27 | 10 | 13 | 0 | 31 | 31 | 187¹ | 199 | 14 | 58 | 151 | 2.8 | 7.3 | 50% | .327 | 1.37 | 4.08 | 3.43 | 4.07 | 3.2 |
| 2011 | CHA | MLB | 28 | 12 | 13 | 0 | 31 | 30 | 193² | 180 | 22 | 45 | 151 | 2.1 | 7.0 | 46% | .280 | 1.16 | 4.37 | 3.85 | 4.19 | 2.2 |
| 2012 | CHA | MLB | 29 | 9 | 10 | 0 | 26 | 26 | 166 | 161 | 22 | 50 | 127 | 2.7 | 6.9 | 44% | .288 | 1.27 | 3.90 | 4.30 | 4.24 | 1.7 |

Blessed with the best stuff on the White Sox starting staff, Floyd continues to show maddening inconsistency, producing masterpieces and disasterpieces with equal frequency. When he's on, Floyd gets ahead of hitters with well-located fastballs and puts them away with his curveball or an odd slider/cutter hybrid, drawing awkward swings and weak contact. When he's not, his breaking stuff flattens out, his fastball floats up in the zone, and last week's pop-flies become this week's bleacher souvenirs. Even Floyd's defense is inconsistent, as he was once again one of the easiest starters in baseball to run on. With talent like his, the chance of a breakout often seems imminent, but at this point even Vladimir and Estragon would stop waiting, and Floyd's willingness to sign a club-friendly extension through his arbitration years didn't seem like a pitcher confident in his own upside. There's value in being a mid-rotation starter, and Floyd may well be worth his $9.5 million club option in 2013, but Sox fans should stop thinking that he is going to be anything more.

**Philip Humber**
Born: 12/21/1982 Age: 29
Bats: R Throws: R Height: 6' 5" Weight: 210
Breakout: 24% Improve: 60% Collapse: 21%
Attrition: 17% MLB: 88%

Comparables:
Rawly Eastwick, Bob Welch, Nate Robertson

| YEAR | TEAM | LVL | AGE | W | L | SV | G | GS | IP | H | HR | BB | SO | EqBB9 | EqSO9 | GB% | BABIP | WHIP | ERA | FIP | FRA | WARP |
|------|------|-----|-----|---|---|----|----|----|------|-----|----|----|-----|-------|-------|-----|-------|------|------|------|------|------|
| 2009 | ROC | AAA | 26 | 7 | 9 | 0 | 23 | 22 | 119² | 135 | 15 | 45 | 87 | 3.4 | 6.5 | 39% | .312 | 1.50 | 5.34 | 4.65 | 5.22 | 0.5 |
| 2009 | MIN | MLB | 26 | 0 | 0 | 0 | 8 | 0 | 9 | 17 | 1 | 9 | 9 | 9.0 | 9.0 | 50% | .516 | 2.89 | 8.00 | 5.59 | 5.21 | 0.1 |
| 2010 | OMA | AAA | 27 | 5 | 6 | 0 | 21 | 20 | 118² | 72 | 7 | 13 | 45 | 1.5 | 6.1 | 51% | .269 | 1.27 | 4.47 | 4.45 | 5.70 | -0.3 |
| 2010 | KCA | MLB | 27 | 2 | 1 | 0 | 8 | 1 | 21² | 22 | 1 | 7 | 16 | 2.9 | 6.6 | 44% | .304 | 1.34 | 4.15 | 3.28 | 4.14 | 0.3 |
| 2011 | CHA | MLB | 28 | 9 | 9 | 0 | 28 | 26 | 163 | 151 | 14 | 41 | 116 | 2.3 | 6.4 | 48% | .276 | 1.18 | 3.75 | 3.62 | 3.65 | 2.6 |
| 2012 | CHA | MLB | 29 | 6 | 8 | 0 | 19 | 19 | 115 | 120 | 16 | 41 | 77 | 3.2 | 6.0 | 42% | .292 | 1.40 | 4.49 | 4.74 | 4.88 | 0.4 |

Ever notice how starters who throw a variety of off-speed pitches are "junkballers" when they fail, but have a "deep repertoire" when they succeed? Case in point, Philip Humber, a former top prospect who had been branded a Triple-A junkballer by the Twins, Royals, and Athletics before the White Sox grabbed him off the scrap heap last year and plugged him in as a temporary rotation patch. Humber responded by unleashing his deep repertoire—fastball, changeup, slider, and a knee-buckling curve he can throw for strikes—on an unprepared American League, with hitters posting a .218/.275/.321 line against him through the All-Star break. He regressed significantly in the second half once the book on him came out, but not so badly that there isn't hope he can have a career at the back end of the rotation. He won't be better than that, though.

### Gregory Infante

Born: 7/10/1987 Age: 24
Bats: R Throws: R Height: 6' 3" Weight: 185
Breakout: 51% Improve: 73% Collapse: 13%
Attrition: 10% MLB: 85%

Comparables:
Al McBean, Mudcat Grant, Jack Morris

| YEAR | TEAM | LVL | AGE | W | L | SV | G | GS | IP | H | HR | BB | SO | EqBB9 | EqSO9 | GB% | BABIP | WHIP | ERA | FIP | FRA | WARP |
|---|---|---|---|---|---|---|---|---|---|---|---|---|---|---|---|---|---|---|---|---|---|---|
| 2009 | KAN | A | 21 | 3 | 5 | 0 | 15 | 15 | 88¹ | 76 | 4 | 37 | 75 | 3.8 | 7.6 | 52% | .298 | 1.28 | 3.26 | 3.92 | 4.82 | 0.4 |
| 2009 | WNS | A+ | 21 | 1 | 2 | 0 | 6 | 5 | 20² | 18 | 3 | 23 | 10 | 10.0 | 4.3 | 44% | .242 | 1.98 | 7.83 | 8.32 | 9.31 | -0.5 |
| 2010 | WNS | A+ | 22 | 1 | 2 | 9 | 31 | 0 | 33² | 25 | 0 | 10 | 30 | 4.0 | 9.3 | 58% | .338 | 1.39 | 3.47 | 2.74 | 4.24 | 0.4 |
| 2010 | BIR | AA | 22 | 2 | 2 | 3 | 24 | 0 | 26¹ | 16 | 0 | 4 | 18 | 4.1 | 11.6 | 49% | .364 | 1.33 | 3.42 | 2.75 | 3.78 | 0.3 |
| 2010 | CHA | MLB | 22 | 0 | 0 | 0 | 5 | 0 | 4² | 2 | 0 | 4 | 5 | 7.7 | 9.6 | 40% | .200 | 1.29 | 0.00 | 3.48 | 4.65 | 0.0 |
| 2011 | CHR | AAA | 23 | 1 | 3 | 4 | 34 | 0 | 48¹ | 50 | 5 | 21 | 40 | 3.9 | 7.4 | 52% | .308 | 1.47 | 3.35 | 4.36 | 5.18 | 0.3 |
| 2012 | CHA | MLB | 24 | 1 | 0 | 0 | 13 | 0 | 15¹ | 17 | 2 | 10 | 8 | 5.9 | 4.8 | 47% | .294 | 1.76 | 5.98 | 5.81 | 6.50 | -0.3 |

Infante spent the year dealing gas from the Charlotte pen, a phrase the baseball-disinclined may take to mean he was selling nitrous oxide to fellow prisoners, but which you, Gentle Reader, understand to mean he used his mid-90s fastball in relief. Infante's already-shaky control took a small step backwards last year, he didn't miss as many bats as he had in the low minors, his mechanics are still a fright, and his secondary pitches are works-in-progress. On the plus side he clearly has enough stuff to retire major league hitters. With few other options in the system, he may get his shot this year.

### Nathan Jones

Born: 1/28/1986 Age: 26
Bats: R Throws: R Height: 6' 6" Weight: 185
Breakout: 26% Improve: 50% Collapse: 17%
Attrition: 10% MLB: 82%

Comparables:
Vladimir Nunez, Pete Filson, Ryan Drese

| YEAR | TEAM | LVL | AGE | W | L | SV | G | GS | IP | H | HR | BB | SO | EqBB9 | EqSO9 | GB% | BABIP | WHIP | ERA | FIP | FRA | WARP |
|---|---|---|---|---|---|---|---|---|---|---|---|---|---|---|---|---|---|---|---|---|---|---|
| 2009 | WNS | A+ | 23 | 2 | 1 | 0 | 32 | 0 | 49¹ | 48 | 4 | 15 | 44 | 2.4 | 7.8 | 46% | .312 | 1.16 | 3.65 | 3.59 | 4.63 | 0.5 |
| 2010 | WNS | A+ | 24 | 11 | 7 | 0 | 28 | 28 | 152¹ | 161 | 9 | 58 | 100 | 3.3 | 6.4 | 48% | .349 | 1.52 | 4.08 | 4.27 | 5.01 | 1.0 |
| 2011 | BIR | AA | 25 | 0 | 3 | 12 | 42 | 0 | 63¹ | 59 | 3 | 27 | 69 | 3.8 | 9.5 | 54% | .320 | 1.34 | 3.27 | 3.16 | 4.32 | 0.5 |
| 2012 | CHA | MLB | 26 | 1 | 2 | 0 | 9 | 4 | 26² | 31 | 4 | 16 | 17 | 5.3 | 5.7 | 43% | .316 | 1.75 | 5.97 | 5.68 | 6.49 | -0.4 |

After an abortive attempt by the team to make him a starter, Mr. Jones put a wiggle in the development staff's collective stride by thriving in a relief role last year. The towering right-hander used his high-90s fastball to greater effect in shorter stints, amping up his strikeout rate while keeping his walks in check. Not everything was ventilated slacks, however, as Jones still needs to better locate his power curve, and the only benefit to being 25 in the Southern League is cheaper car insurance than your teammates. Still, if Jones can consolidate his gains this year he may soon be able to fill a role at the back of the Sox bullpen.

### Jhan Marinez

Born: 8/12/1988 Age: 23
Bats: R Throws: R Height: 6' 2" Weight: 165
Breakout: 26% Improve: 56% Collapse: 23%
Attrition: 20% MLB: 93%

Comparables:
Dave Boswell, Gio Gonzalez, Billy McCool

| YEAR | TEAM | LVL | AGE | W | L | SV | G | GS | IP | H | HR | BB | SO | EqBB9 | EqSO9 | GB% | BABIP | WHIP | ERA | FIP | FRA | WARP |
|---|---|---|---|---|---|---|---|---|---|---|---|---|---|---|---|---|---|---|---|---|---|---|
| 2009 | JUP | A+ | 20 | 1 | 1 | 1 | 29 | 0 | 43 | 28 | 4 | 20 | 42 | 4.2 | 8.8 | 40% | .222 | 1.12 | 3.14 | 4.13 | 5.20 | -0.1 |
| 2010 | JUP | A+ | 21 | 0 | 1 | 4 | 21 | 1 | 25¹ | 9 | 0 | 7 | 33 | 5.0 | 15.7 | 26% | .409 | 1.03 | 1.42 | 1.87 | 3.48 | 0.4 |
| 2010 | FLO | MLB | 21 | 1 | 1 | 0 | 4 | 0 | 2² | 3 | 1 | 3 | 3 | 10.1 | 10.1 | 38% | .286 | 2.25 | 6.75 | 9.11 | 17.90 | -0.4 |
| 2011 | JAX | AA | 22 | 1 | 4 | 3 | 56 | 0 | 58 | 47 | 7 | 43 | 73 | 6.5 | 11.5 | 46% | .310 | 1.53 | 3.57 | 4.63 | 4.69 | 0.2 |
| 2012 | CHA | MLB | 23 | 1 | 0 | 2 | 16 | 0 | 17² | 16 | 2 | 11 | 18 | 5.6 | 9.2 | 42% | .299 | 1.53 | 4.57 | 4.51 | 4.97 | 0.0 |

A wispy reliever who nevertheless can dial his fastball up near triple digits, Marinez was the key return from the Ozzie trade and instantly became the best power arm in the system not named Addison Reed. After a brief taste of big-league meal money in 2010, Marinez spent last season in Double-A, where he stacked strikeout victims like cordwood but handed out free passes at an alarming rate. If he can learn to throw strikes and develop a better feel for his slider, it is easy to picture big outs in his future—though admittedly, you can say the same thing about virtually every hard-throwing young reliever in the game.

### Nestor Molina

Born: 1/9/1989 Age: 23
Bats: R Throws: R Height: 6' 2" Weight: 179
Breakout: 24% Improve: 66% Collapse: 17%
Attrition: 5% MLB: 94%

Comparables:
Don Drysdale, Scott Bankhead, Bob Welch

| YEAR | TEAM | LVL | AGE | W | L | SV | G | GS | IP | H | HR | BB | SO | EqBB9 | EqSO9 | GB% | BABIP | WHIP | ERA | FIP | FRA | WARP |
|---|---|---|---|---|---|---|---|---|---|---|---|---|---|---|---|---|---|---|---|---|---|---|
| 2009 | BLJ | RK | 20 | 3 | 0 | 1 | 15 | 2 | 37¹ | 26 | 0 | 2 | 24 | 1.0 | 7.7 | 63% | .321 | 0.94 | 1.69 | 2.20 | 4.02 | 1.0 |
| 2010 | LNS | A | 21 | 8 | 2 | 4 | 37 | 2 | 76² | 47 | 3 | 13 | 42 | 2.3 | 7.2 | 65% | .282 | 1.10 | 3.17 | 3.72 | 5.21 | 0.1 |
| 2011 | DUN | A+ | 22 | 5 | 1 | 0 | 21 | 18 | 108¹ | 102 | 8 | 14 | 115 | 1.2 | 9.6 | 50% | .325 | 1.07 | 2.58 | 2.64 | 3.90 | 2.4 |
| 2012 | CHA | MLB | 23 | 1 | 2 | 0 | 10 | 4 | 33¹ | 34 | 4 | 11 | 28 | 3.1 | 7.6 | 51% | .309 | 1.37 | 4.32 | 4.07 | 4.70 | 0.2 |

Molina was traded to the Sox last winter for closer Sergio Santos, as the organization attempted to bolster their system by dealing from a position of bullpen strength. Whether Molina was worth the cost is an open question, as his production has been stellar but his stuff may limit his ceiling. Armed with a low-90s fastball, a slider, a curveball, and an excellent changeup, Molina displayed terrific command as he racked up strikeouts in the low minors, avoided free passes, and succeeded in his first taste of Double-A. Some scouts question whether he can conjure up the same success against more advanced hitters, but clearly the Sox are believers, and whether Molina's ceiling is that of a fourth starter or something more, he's now the best starting pitcher prospect in the organization.

### Will Ohman

Born: 8/13/1977 Age: 34
Bats: L Throws: L Height: 6' 3" Weight: 195
Breakout: 33% Improve: 62% Collapse: 21%
Attrition: 10% MLB: 83%

**Comparables:**
John Bale, Brandon Knight, Mike Stanton

| YEAR | TEAM | LVL | AGE | W | L | SV | G | GS | IP | H | HR | BB | SO | EqBB9 | EqSO9 | GB% | BABIP | WHIP | ERA | FIP | FRA | WARP |
|------|------|-----|-----|---|---|----|----|----|-----|---|----|----|----|-------|-------|-----|-------|------|-----|-----|-----|------|
| 2009 | LAN | MLB | 31 | 1 | 0 | 1 | 21 | 0 | 12¹ | 12 | 4 | 8 | 7 | 5.8 | 5.1 | 26% | .229 | 1.62 | 5.84 | 8.08 | 6.29 | -0.1 |
| 2010 | FLO | MLB | 32 | 0 | 2 | 0 | 17 | 0 | 12 | 10 | 1 | 5 | 14 | 3.8 | 10.5 | 34% | .290 | 1.25 | 3.00 | 3.11 | 3.96 | 0.1 |
| 2010 | BAL | MLB | 32 | 0 | 0 | 0 | 51 | 0 | 30 | 30 | 3 | 18 | 29 | 5.4 | 8.7 | 53% | .329 | 1.60 | 3.30 | 4.31 | 4.82 | 0.1 |
| 2011 | CHA | MLB | 33 | 1 | 3 | 0 | 59 | 0 | 53¹ | 53 | 8 | 17 | 54 | 2.9 | 9.1 | 42% | .306 | 1.31 | 4.22 | 4.17 | 5.16 | 0.0 |
| 2012 | CHA | MLB | 34 | 3 | 1 | 1 | 60 | 0 | 45 | 44 | 5 | 19 | 41 | 3.7 | 8.1 | 41% | .300 | 1.37 | 4.02 | 4.09 | 4.37 | 0.3 |

The Sox went into last season with the dynamic lefty duo of Matt Thornton and Chris Sale al-

### Jake Peavy

Born: 5/31/1981 Age: 31
Bats: R Throws: R Height: 6' 2" Weight: 180
Breakout: 15% Improve: 43% Collapse: 23%
Attrition: 2% MLB: 96%

**Comparables:**
John Smoltz, Ted Higuera, Scott Linebrink

| YEAR | TEAM | LVL | AGE | W | L | SV | G | GS | IP | H | HR | BB | SO | EqBB9 | EqSO9 | GB% | BABIP | WHIP | ERA | FIP | FRA | WARP |
|------|------|-----|-----|---|---|----|----|----|------|-----|----|----|----|-------|-------|-----|-------|------|-----|-----|-----|------|
| 2009 | CHA | MLB | 28 | 3 | 0 | 0 | 3 | 3 | 20 | 11 | 1 | 6 | 18 | 2.7 | 8.1 | 51% | .204 | 0.85 | 1.35 | 2.89 | 3.24 | 0.5 |
| 2009 | SDN | MLB | 28 | 6 | 6 | 0 | 13 | 13 | 81² | 69 | 7 | 28 | 92 | 3.1 | 10.1 | 44% | .302 | 1.19 | 3.97 | 2.98 | 3.80 | 1.2 |
| 2010 | CHA | MLB | 29 | 7 | 6 | 0 | 17 | 17 | 107 | 98 | 13 | 34 | 93 | 2.9 | 7.8 | 43% | .280 | 1.23 | 4.63 | 3.98 | 4.16 | 1.5 |
| 2011 | CHA | MLB | 30 | 7 | 7 | 0 | 19 | 18 | 111² | 117 | 10 | 24 | 95 | 1.9 | 7.7 | 40% | .318 | 1.26 | 4.92 | 3.25 | 3.94 | 1.6 |
| 2012 | CHA | MLB | 31 | 6 | 6 | 0 | 18 | 18 | 105 | 95 | 11 | 32 | 98 | 2.8 | 8.4 | 43% | .293 | 1.21 | 3.23 | 3.61 | 3.51 | 2.0 |

Peavy's well-known competitiveness may be getting in the way of his obvious desire to get healthy and make good on his sizable contract, as the right-hander worked hard to return from shoulder surgery well ahead of schedule only to see his season devolve into a strange odyssey less notable for the mixing of pitches than the mixing of messages. Encouraging spring training results were cut short by shoulder tendinitis that Peavy described as a "minor blip on the radar," but wound up costing him a month of the season, followed by another DL trip for a groin strain. Soon after came the odd four-inning relief outing for which he volunteered between two late June starts. Peavy said he enjoyed "taking his tank to empty" during the appearance, but as ineffective starts began to pile up later in the summer, Peavy admitted the outing had set his season back and contributed to the fatigue and ineffectiveness that eventually shut him down in early September. There were fleeting glimpses of dominance but no sustained success, leaving Peavy and the Sox hoping that their efforts to wring out a few months of modest production last year didn't jeopardize a full year of ace-level production now.

### Jake Petricka

Born: 6/5/1988 Age: 24
Bats: R Throws: R Height: 6' 6" Weight: 170
Breakout: 21% Improve: 41% Collapse: 39%
Attrition: 30% MLB: 88%

**Comparables:**
Denny Bautista, Marty Bystrom, Bob Mahoney

| YEAR | TEAM | LVL | AGE | W | L | SV | G | GS | IP | H | HR | BB | SO | EqBB9 | EqSO9 | GB% | BABIP | WHIP | ERA | FIP | FRA | WARP |
|------|------|-----|-----|---|---|----|----|----|-----|----|----|----|----|-------|-------|-----|-------|------|-----|-----|-----|------|
| 2010 | BRI | RK | 22 | 2 | 4 | 0 | 8 | 8 | 34² | 23 | 1 | 6 | 31 | 1.8 | 9.9 | 61% | .297 | 0.92 | 2.85 | 2.90 | 4.59 | 0.6 |
| 2011 | KAN | A | 23 | 3 | 1 | 0 | 8 | 8 | 41² | 39 | 0 | 13 | 48 | 2.8 | 10.4 | 53% | .361 | 1.25 | 2.81 | 2.16 | 3.69 | 0.7 |
| 2011 | WNS | A+ | 23 | 4 | 7 | 0 | 13 | 13 | 67² | 71 | 3 | 26 | 46 | 3.5 | 6.1 | 59% | .309 | 1.43 | 4.39 | 3.72 | 5.21 | 0.5 |
| 2012 | CHA | MLB | 24 | 1 | 3 | 0 | 6 | 6 | 29¹ | 34 | 4 | 15 | 17 | 4.6 | 5.2 | 52% | .310 | 1.66 | 5.56 | 5.35 | 6.04 | -0.2 |

Petricka's first full pro season was a mixed bag, as the former second round pick showed off a heavy mid-90s fastball that hitters continually pounded into the dirt and he never contracted a case of the walksies, but he made little progress with his slider or changeup. Despite his college pedigree, Petricka will likely move through the system one rung at a time, and the club will give him every opportunity to remain a starter, though his stuff may play better in relief.

### Addison Reed

Born: **12/27/1988** Age: **23**
Bats: **L** Throws: **R** Height: **6' 5''** Weight: **215**
Breakout: **18%** Improve: **40%** Collapse: **44%**
Attrition: **9%** MLB: **86%**

**Comparables:**
Cole Hamels, Francisco Liriano, Clay Buchholz

| YEAR | TEAM | LVL | AGE | W | L | SV | G | GS | IP | H | HR | BB | SO | EqBB9 | EqSO9 | GB% | BABIP | WHIP | ERA | FIP | FRA | WARP |
|---|---|---|---|---|---|---|---|---|---|---|---|---|---|---|---|---|---|---|---|---|---|---|
| 2010 | GRF | RK | 21 | 1 | 0 | 1 | 13 | 2 | 30 | 8 | 1 | 4 | 41 | 1.8 | 13.2 | 44% | .179 | 0.77 | 1.80 | 2.33 | 3.59 | 1.9 |
| 2011 | WNS | A+ | 22 | 2 | 0 | 1 | 15 | 0 | 28¹ | 21 | 1 | 4 | 39 | 1.3 | 12.4 | 43% | .299 | 0.88 | 1.59 | 1.55 | 2.99 | 0.9 |
| 2011 | BIR | AA | 22 | 0 | 1 | 2 | 13 | 0 | 20² | 10 | 0 | 6 | 33 | 2.6 | 14.4 | 27% | .270 | 0.77 | 0.87 | 1.12 | 2.12 | 0.7 |
| 2011 | CHR | AAA | 22 | 0 | 0 | 2 | 11 | 0 | 21¹ | 8 | 2 | 3 | 28 | 1.3 | 11.8 | 41% | .150 | 0.52 | 1.27 | 2.25 | 2.60 | 0.6 |
| 2011 | CHA | MLB | 22 | 0 | 0 | 0 | 6 | 0 | 7¹ | 10 | 1 | 1 | 12 | 1.2 | 14.7 | 20% | .474 | 1.50 | 3.68 | 1.97 | 4.22 | 0.1 |
| 2012 | CHA | MLB | 23 | 1 | 0 | 0 | 15 | 0 | 26¹ | 22 | 3 | 9 | 30 | 3.2 | 10.4 | 41% | .300 | 1.19 | 3.10 | 3.43 | 3.36 | 0.5 |

Despite a name more reminiscent of Bob Seger's sax player than a bullpen bully, Reed began his first full pro season in the Sally League but ended it striking out Matt La Porta at Progressive Field, leaving a trail of over-matched hitters and hyperventilating prospect mavens in his wake. A former third-round pick from San Diego State, Reed has terrific command of his upper-90s fastball (note the ridiculous walk and strikeout rates), along with a slider and changeup that can be plus pitches. Reed has more than enough swing-and-miss stuff to someday get paid for three outs and a hug, and his development allowed the Sox to deal Sergio Santos knowing they've already identified their closer-in-waiting. For now the Sox will plant him in a setup role and watch his career take root, but few would be surprised to see him pitching the ninth before the season is out.

### Andre Rienzo

Born: **7/5/1988** Age: **23**
Bats: **R** Throws: **R** Height: **6' 4''** Weight: **160**
Breakout: **14%** Improve: **59%** Collapse: **18%**
Attrition: **21%** MLB: **87%**

**Comparables:**
Gus Keriazakos, Edwin Jackson, Ike Delock

| YEAR | TEAM | LVL | AGE | W | L | SV | G | GS | IP | H | HR | BB | SO | EqBB9 | EqSO9 | GB% | BABIP | WHIP | ERA | FIP | FRA | WARP |
|---|---|---|---|---|---|---|---|---|---|---|---|---|---|---|---|---|---|---|---|---|---|---|
| 2009 | BRI | RK | 21 | 2 | 6 | 0 | 13 | 9 | 54¹ | 55 | 4 | 13 | 49 | 2.2 | 8.1 | 50% | .325 | 1.25 | 4.14 | 3.56 | 5.30 | 0.6 |
| 2010 | KAN | A | 22 | 8 | 4 | 0 | 20 | 18 | 101 | 53 | 3 | 14 | 43 | 2.9 | 11.1 | 50% | .439 | 1.26 | 3.65 | 3.67 | 4.01 | 2.0 |
| 2011 | WNS | A+ | 23 | 6 | 5 | 0 | 25 | 22 | 116 | 108 | 4 | 66 | 118 | 5.1 | 9.2 | 46% | .326 | 1.50 | 3.41 | 3.41 | 4.38 | 2.2 |
| 2012 | CHA | MLB | 23 | 1 | 3 | 0 | 6 | 6 | 31 | 36 | 4 | 20 | 21 | 5.7 | 5.9 | 45% | .320 | 1.80 | 5.99 | 5.46 | 6.51 | -0.4 |

A lanky Brazilian import, Rienzo continues to climb the organizational ladder while striking out more than a man per inning, though his prospect status will wax if he can get his walk rate to wane. Rienzo's stuff is considerably less unusual than his background, as plenty of minor league starters can boast a mid-90s fastball and inconsistent secondary offerings, but few others can sing the *Hino Nacional Brasileiro* in Portuguese. A starter as of this moment, his most likely destination is the bullpen.

### Chris Sale

Born: **3/30/1989** Age: **23**
Bats: **L** Throws: **L** Height: **6' 6''** Weight: **170**
Breakout: **19%** Improve: **42%** Collapse: **40%**
Attrition: **11%** MLB: **75%**

**Comparables:**
Dave Righetti, Clay Buchholz, Francisco Liriano

| YEAR | TEAM | LVL | AGE | W | L | SV | G | GS | IP | H | HR | BB | SO | EqBB9 | EqSO9 | GB% | BABIP | WHIP | ERA | FIP | FRA | WARP |
|---|---|---|---|---|---|---|---|---|---|---|---|---|---|---|---|---|---|---|---|---|---|---|
| 2010 | CHA | MLB | 21 | 2 | 1 | 4 | 21 | 0 | 23¹ | 15 | 2 | 10 | 32 | 3.9 | 12.3 | 52% | .277 | 1.07 | 1.93 | 2.70 | 3.60 | 0.5 |
| 2011 | CHA | MLB | 22 | 2 | 2 | 8 | 58 | 0 | 71 | 52 | 6 | 27 | 79 | 3.4 | 10.0 | 52% | .269 | 1.11 | 2.79 | 3.16 | 3.78 | 1.1 |
| 2012 | CHA | MLB | 23 | 3 | 1 | 4 | 47 | 0 | 54¹ | 42 | 5 | 21 | 64 | 3.5 | 10.5 | 48% | .288 | 1.17 | 2.85 | 3.20 | 3.10 | 1.2 |

Sale spent his first full season in the bigs working out of the pen, moving his way up the bullpen pecking order and leaving White Sox fans hoping for great things. The lanky lefty has terrific velocity, unleashing mid-90s heat from a low three-quarters slot while mixing in a plus changeup, but it was the in-season development of a new slider grip that helped Sale baffle hitters to the tune of .154/.233/.265 in the second half. The Sox will move him to the rotation this year, and if Sale can continue to hold hitters to a .220 TAv—better than Jered Weaver—he'll be a Cy Young candidate. But extrapolating those numbers to a full starter workload is just the sort of voodoo sabermetrics you should learn to ignore during an election year. Nevertheless, Sale has the stuff to front Chicago's rotation for a long time, and his future is now.

### Hector Santiago

Born: **12/16/1987** Age: **24**
Bats: **R** Throws: **L** Height: **6' 1''** Weight: **210**
Breakout: **43%** Improve: **66%** Collapse: **11%**
Attrition: **9%** MLB: **87%**

**Comparables:**
Tyler Clippard, Erv Palica, Ubaldo Jimenez

| YEAR | TEAM | LVL | AGE | W | L | SV | G | GS | IP | H | HR | BB | SO | EqBB9 | EqSO9 | GB% | BABIP | WHIP | ERA | FIP | FRA | WARP |
|---|---|---|---|---|---|---|---|---|---|---|---|---|---|---|---|---|---|---|---|---|---|---|
| 2009 | WNS | A+ | 21 | 4 | 5 | 1 | 38 | 0 | 58 | 59 | 6 | 26 | 70 | 3.9 | 10.2 | 39% | .340 | 1.36 | 3.88 | 3.83 | 4.26 | 1.0 |
| 2010 | WNS | A+ | 22 | 5 | 5 | 2 | 37 | 1 | 60² | 60 | 3 | 17 | 54 | 2.8 | 9.0 | 38% | .341 | 1.35 | 4.15 | 3.26 | 4.44 | 0.8 |
| 2011 | WNS | A+ | 23 | 2 | 3 | 0 | 8 | 8 | 44 | 38 | 7 | 14 | 43 | 2.9 | 8.8 | 49% | .277 | 1.18 | 3.68 | 4.49 | 4.40 | 0.7 |
| 2011 | BIR | AA | 23 | 3 | 4 | 0 | 15 | 15 | 83¹ | 78 | 4 | 43 | 79 | 4.2 | 8.0 | 47% | .311 | 1.32 | 3.56 | 3.72 | 4.60 | 0.5 |
| 2011 | CHA | MLB | 23 | 0 | 0 | 0 | 2 | 0 | 5¹ | 1 | 0 | 1 | 2 | 1.7 | 3.4 | 60% | .067 | 0.38 | 0.00 | 2.87 | 2.00 | 0.2 |
| 2012 | CHA | MLB | 24 | 2 | 2 | 0 | 13 | 5 | 39¹ | 41 | 5 | 22 | 30 | 5.0 | 6.9 | 42% | .303 | 1.59 | 5.01 | 5.01 | 5.45 | -0.1 |

Santiago was taught the mysteries of the screwball by ex-Brewer Angel Miranda during winter ball prior to last season, and the pitch helped his rapid rise from minor league relief suspect to genuine prospect. While it's the screwgie that attracts curiosity seekers, it's Santiago's mid-90s portside gas that's helped him strike out more than a man per inning in his minor league career and earned him a brief call-up last July. He made a solid transition to the starting rotation last year, but his big league future lies in the pen, and with Chris Sale slated to move to the rotation Santiago, could go north as the pen's vestigial third lefty—the need for which you may question, but Hector certainly won't.

**Zach Stewart**
Born: **9/28/1986** Age: **25**
Bats: **R** Throws: **R** Height: **6' 3''** Weight: **205**
Breakout: **26%** Improve: **62%** Collapse: **10%**
Attrition: **9%** MLB: **93%**

**Comparables:**
Taylor Buchholz, Charles Hudson, Rollie Fingers

| YEAR | TEAM | LVL | AGE | W | L | SV | G | GS | IP | H | HR | BB | SO | EqBB9 | EqSO9 | GB% | BABIP | WHIP | ERA | FIP | FRA | WARP |
|------|------|-----|-----|---|---|----|---|----|----|----|----|----|----|-------|-------|-----|-------|------|-----|-----|-----|------|
| 2009 | SAR | A+ | 22 | 1 | 1 | 0 | 7 | 7 | 42¹ | 47 | 1 | 8 | 32 | 1.7 | 6.8 | 59% | .343 | 1.30 | 2.13 | 2.63 | 3.25 | 0.9 |
| 2009 | CAR | AA | 22 | 3 | 0 | 0 | 7 | 7 | 37 | 29 | 1 | 10 | 31 | 2.4 | 7.5 | 54% | .277 | 1.05 | 1.46 | 2.67 | 3.15 | 1.0 |
| 2010 | NHP | AA | 23 | 8 | 3 | 0 | 26 | 26 | 136¹ | 84 | 9 | 28 | 79 | 3.6 | 7.0 | 49% | .275 | 1.36 | 3.63 | 3.96 | 4.59 | 1.4 |
| 2011 | NHP | AA | 24 | 5 | 5 | 0 | 16 | 16 | 94¹ | 99 | 6 | 24 | 72 | 2.6 | 7.1 | 46% | .342 | 1.41 | 4.20 | 3.48 | 4.40 | 1.1 |
| 2011 | TOR | MLB | 24 | 0 | 1 | 0 | 3 | 3 | 16² | 26 | 2 | 5 | 10 | 2.7 | 5.4 | 47% | .421 | 1.86 | 4.86 | 4.50 | 4.89 | 0.0 |
| 2011 | CHA | MLB | 24 | 2 | 5 | 0 | 10 | 8 | 50² | 64 | 9 | 13 | 35 | 2.3 | 6.2 | 52% | .342 | 1.52 | 6.22 | 4.82 | 5.08 | 0.2 |
| *2012* | *CHA* | *MLB* | *25* | *4* | *6* | *0* | *15* | *15* | *81¹* | *92* | *10* | *32* | *55* | *3.5* | *6.1* | *48%* | *.317* | *1.52* | *4.93* | *4.63* | *5.35* | *-0.1* |

Born: **7/18/1976** Age: **35**
Bats: **L** Throws: **L** Height: **6' 7''** Weight: **220**
Breakout: **12%** Improve: **39%** Collapse: **38%**
Attrition: **10%** MLB: **94%**

**Comparables:**
Brian Fuentes, Jim Brewer, Billy Wagner

| YEAR | TEAM | LVL | AGE | W | L | SV | G | GS | IP | H | HR | BB | SO | EqBB9 | EqSO9 | GB% | BABIP | WHIP | ERA | FIP | FRA | WARP |
|------|------|-----|-----|---|---|----|---|----|----|----|----|----|----|-------|-------|-----|-------|------|-----|-----|-----|------|
| 2010 | CHA | MLB | 33 | 5 | 4 | 8 | 61 | 0 | 60² | 41 | 3 | 20 | 81 | 3.0 | 12.0 | 41% | .286 | 1.01 | 2.67 | 2.11 | 3.13 | 1.4 |
| 2011 | CHA | MLB | 34 | 2 | 5 | 3 | 62 | 0 | 59² | 60 | 3 | 21 | 63 | 3.2 | 9.5 | 49% | .331 | 1.36 | 3.32 | 2.66 | 3.67 | 1.0 |
| *2012* | *CHA* | *MLB* | *35* | *3* | *1* | *3* | *56* | *0* | *54¹* | *46* | *5* | *19* | *60* | *3.1* | *9.9* | *47%* | *.301* | *1.20* | *2.99* | *3.24* | *3.25* | *1.1* |

Sometimes it's not so much what you do, it's when you do it. If Thornton had set his alarm clock to start the season on April 24, he would have held batters to a .235/.291/.289 line for the year, numbers that are perfectly consistent with his recent dominance. However, since Thornton struggled out of the gate, Sergio Santos was handed the key to the executive washroom and the title of Vice President for Ninth Inning Operations. That's not to say there wasn't some wobble in Thornton's game, as his swinging strike rate dropped, but he still has more than enough stuff to work in high-leverage situations. With Santos now out of the picture, Thornton may get another chance to close, though handing him set-up duties would allow the Sox to plug in his heater whenever an emergency crops up.

# LINEOUTS

## HITTERS

| PLAYER | TEAM | LVL | AGE | PA | R | 2B | 3B | HR | RBI | BB | SO | SB-CS | AVG/OBP/SLG | TAv | BABIP | BRR | FRAA | WARP |
|---|---|---|---|---|---|---|---|---|---|---|---|---|---|---|---|---|---|---|
| C M. Blanke | KAN | A | 22 | 184 | 22 | 13 | 1 | 2 | 18 | 11 | 28 | 0-0 | .259/.311/.382 | .255 | .300 | 0.6 | -0.2 | 0.6 |
| | WNS | A+ | 22 | 266 | 25 | 9 | 0 | 7 | 25 | 22 | 43 | 0-0 | .236/.303/.363 | .236 | .258 | -0.1 | -1.4 | 0.3 |
| 2B T. Kuhn | BIR | AA | 24 | 470 | 61 | 28 | 10 | 1 | 55 | 39 | 64 | 16-5 | .341/.401/.464 | .298 | .395 | 0.3 | -0.1 | 3.8 |
| | CHR | AAA | 24 | 98 | 9 | 4 | 1 | 0 | 4 | 5 | 13 | 0-2 | .297/.327/.363 | .243 | .338 | 0.6 | -0.1 | 0.3 |
| C D. Lucy | CHR | AAA | 28 | 147 | 11 | 1 | 0 | 4 | 9 | 10 | 35 | 0-0 | .158/.233/.256 | .180 | .181 | 0 | 0.5 | -0.4 |
| | CHA | MLB | 28 | 11 | 1 | 1 | 0 | 0 | 1 | 1 | 5 | 0-0 | .200/.273/.300 | .214 | .400 | 0 | 0 | 0.0 |
| 1B C. Marrero | BIR | AA | 24 | 494 | 70 | 25 | 8 | 12 | 59 | 61 | 69 | 10-4 | .293/.385/.476 | .297 | .323 | 1.1 | -3.2 | 2.6 |
| RF J. Martinez | WNS | A+ | 22 | 333 | 45 | 13 | 3 | 5 | 29 | 13 | 44 | 2-3 | .314/.344/.422 | .249 | .352 | 0.7 | 3 | 0.7 |
| | BIR | AA | 22 | 220 | 19 | 13 | 1 | 1 | 16 | 15 | 25 | 5-2 | .295/.344/.385 | .248 | .330 | -3.8 | 0.6 | 0.0 |
| 3B D. McPherson | CHR | AAA | 30 | 426 | 54 | 27 | 0 | 20 | 69 | 31 | 126 | 1-2 | .283/.334/.505 | .270 | .367 | -1.8 | -3.8 | 0.9 |
| | CHA | MLB | 30 | 15 | 1 | 0 | 0 | 0 | 0 | 0 | 7 | 0-0 | .133/.133/.133 | .147 | .250 | -0.3 | 0.2 | -0.2 |
| C J. Phegley | BIR | AA | 23 | 394 | 43 | 21 | 2 | 7 | 50 | 23 | 61 | 1-2 | .242/.292/.368 | .232 | .271 | -3 | -0.3 | 0.4 |
| | CHR | AAA | 23 | 90 | 9 | 4 | 0 | 2 | 6 | 8 | 18 | 0-0 | .241/.326/.367 | .243 | .288 | -0.1 | -0.2 | 0.1 |
| LF B. Shoemaker | KAN | A | 24 | 431 | 68 | 28 | 2 | 11 | 65 | 43 | 78 | 7-3 | .319/.399/.493 | .313 | .375 | -0.8 | 4.2 | 3.4 |
| | WNS | A+ | 24 | 77 | 9 | 3 | 0 | 0 | 12 | 9 | 16 | 0-1 | .273/.351/.318 | .238 | .346 | -0.4 | -1.5 | -0.2 |
| C K. Smith | BRI | RK | 23 | 112 | 24 | 10 | 1 | 7 | 32 | 14 | 14 | 1-2 | .396/.482/.740 | .428 | .413 | -1.8 | -0.7 | 2.3 |
| | GRF | RK | 23 | 127 | 22 | 12 | 2 | 2 | 16 | 14 | 16 | 1-0 | .318/.417/.523 | .322 | .356 | 0.5 | -2.9 | 1.5 |
| 3B O. Vizquel | CHA | MLB | 44 | 182 | 18 | 7 | 1 | 0 | 8 | 9 | 18 | 1-2 | .251/.287/.305 | .225 | .278 | 0.1 | -2.5 | -0.4 |
| RF K. Walker | KAN | A | 20 | 180 | 25 | 1 | 2 | 0 | 15 | 14 | 64 | 10-4 | .228/.296/.259 | .223 | .374 | 1.5 | 1.5 | 0.0 |
| | GRF | RK | 20 | 72 | 16 | 7 | 1 | 0 | 9 | 7 | 17 | 11-5 | .333/.431/.483 | .328 | .455 | -1.3 | -9.5 | -0.2 |

Strong-armed catcher **Michael Blanke** impressed by throwing out baserunners at a 37 percent clip and continued to improve behind the dish, but if he can't awaken his slumbering bat the organization will stop giving a blank. ⊘ Former shortstop **Tyler Kuhn** spent his summer spraying line drives all over the upper minors, and with a lefty bat and the ability to play five positions at a near-adequate level, he may grow up to be an offense-first utility reserve. ⊘ Backstop **Donny Lucy** spent six weeks as a major leaguer due to the convergence of an A.J. Pierzynski injury and September roster expansion; those will likely be the only six weeks to see the convergence of Donny Lucy and a big league roster. ⊘ In his third season at Birmingham, **Christian Marrero** showed continued patience and improved power, but he's a liability in the outfield, and "third season at Birmingham" speaks volumes about his bat's suitability for first base. ⊘ Former top prospect **Jose Martinez** managed a full slate of games, hit for average, and worked his way up to Double-A, but he's no longer a center fielder and his bat has yet to produce enough thunder for a corner. ⊘ Quad-A slugger **Dallas McPherson** could probably launch 20 minor league bombs while wearing a blindfold, but his big league prospect status has long since been offered a cigarette and asked for final words. ⊘ Catcher **Josh Phegley** had surgery to remove his spleen before putting in a full season behind the dish; he has a strong arm, power potential, and there's no questioning his toughness, but he still struggles mightily to fulfill his Prime Directive: keep the ball from hitting the backstop. ⊘ The Kearney Zzywicz of the Sally League, corner outfielder **Brady Shoemaker** has spent the last two years beating up pitchers several years his junior; while that's certainly preferable to *not* beating them up, he'll need to provide age-appropriate entertainment in the high minors before he's cast as anything more than a bit player. ⊘ A former Pitt quarterback recruit, **Kevan Smith** was old for the rookie leagues but cut a wide swath, showing patience, power, and great athleticism; he's raw behind the plate, but any backstop who treats his bat as more than a fashion accessory is worth paying attention to. ⊘ Now that the Sox have wrung out his last few drops of value years after most analysts thought he had anything left to provide, **Omar Vizquel** can hold his head high as he totes his magic glove to the Hall of the Very Good. ⊘ Top pick **Keenyn Walker** is a switch-hitting center fielder with speed to burn and power potential; there are a lot of rough edges to smooth away, but he possesses tools you can dream on.

## PITCHERS

| PLAYER | TEAM | LVL | AGE | W | L | SV | IP | H | HR | BB | SO | EqBB9 | EqSO9 | GB% | BABIP | WHIP | ERA | FIP | FRA | WARP |
|---|---|---|---|---|---|---|---|---|---|---|---|---|---|---|---|---|---|---|---|---|
| B. Bruney | CHR | AAA | 29 | 1 | 0 | 7 | 20² | 12 | 0 | 7 | 28 | 3.9 | 13.1 | 60% | .279 | 1.02 | 1.31 | 1.69 | 2.80 | 0.6 |
| | CHA | MLB | 29 | 1 | 0 | 0 | 19² | 26 | 4 | 12 | 16 | 5.5 | 7.3 | 43% | .379 | 1.93 | 6.86 | 5.91 | 5.97 | -0.1 |
| R. Buch | KAN | A | 23 | 4 | 3 | 0 | 44¹ | 35 | 2 | 17 | 45 | 3.5 | 9.1 | 46% | .273 | 1.17 | 3.65 | 3.44 | 4.06 | 0.6 |
| | WNS | A+ | 23 | 4 | 4 | 0 | 56² | 52 | 10 | 23 | 48 | 3.7 | 7.6 | 41% | .273 | 1.32 | 4.92 | 5.30 | 6.40 | 0.0 |
| D. Davis | CHR | AAA | 35 | 2 | 2 | 0 | 52 | 51 | 2 | 12 | 46 | 2.1 | 8.0 | 47% | .325 | 1.21 | 2.60 | 2.72 | 3.62 | 1.2 |
| | CHN | MLB | 35 | 1 | 7 | 0 | 45² | 59 | 2 | 26 | 36 | 5.1 | 7.1 | 46% | .373 | 1.86 | 6.50 | 3.83 | 5.21 | -0.1 |
| D. Heath | CHR | AAA | 25 | 2 | 4 | 1 | 102² | 98 | 12 | 62 | 117 | 5.4 | 10.3 | 41% | .320 | 1.56 | 4.73 | 4.41 | 4.92 | 1.3 |
| P. Hernandez | LEL | A+ | 22 | 5 | 0 | 0 | 56² | 52 | 3 | 6 | 44 | 1.0 | 7.0 | 40% | .285 | 1.02 | 2.70 | 3.39 | 3.60 | 1.2 |
| | SAN | AA | 22 | 0 | 1 | 0 | 41¹ | 45 | 6 | 13 | 58 | 2.2 | 9.4 | 45% | .305 | 1.19 | 3.48 | 3.41 | 3.91 | 1.1 |
| C. Leesman | BIR | AA | 24 | 5 | 5 | 0 | 152 | 153 | 4 | 83 | 122 | 4.9 | 6.7 | 62% | .312 | 1.53 | 4.03 | 3.93 | 5.20 | 0.0 |

He still throws hard, but since those halcyon days as a Yankees bullpen cog, **Brian Bruney** has been cluttering his stat sheet with more stops than a Greyhound timetable; if he doesn't stop posting Boeing ERAs, it'll be time to go home. ⚾ Curveball stylist **Ryan Buch** had a productive season in the low minors, but will need to develop a stronger distaste for ball four; his eventual destination is the bullpen, where his stuff might just play up. ⚾ Rasputin-grade survivor **Doug Davis** couldn't stop the bleeding during nine starts with the Cubs, but fooled the kids in Triple-A after the Sox picked him up; still ticking despite a decade of substandard stuff and health, he'll likely bring his slow-and-slower routine to someone's spring training complex, unless a coterie of tsarist aristocrats take him for a long walk along the Neva first. ⚾ Fireballer **Deunte Heath** has swing-and-miss stuff but absolutely no control; if he can cut his walk rate in half this year, then cut it in half again next year, we'd be in a position to say he could become a bullpen asset if he'd cut his walk rate a little more. ⚾ With a low-90s fastball, a solid changeup, and a developing curve, lefty strike-thrower **Pedro Hernandez** posted terrific numbers in Double-A last year despite yawns from the scouting community; the Sox hope he can continue to fool most of the people most of the time and earn an eventual spot at the back of the rotation. ⚾ Hulking lefty **Charles Leesman** surrendered far too many walks in his second stroll through Double-A, and doesn't have the stuff or pedigree to make the organization overlook such generosity. ⚾ Veteran middle-man **Tony Pena** underwent elbow reconstruction in August after 20 non-descript innings, was released, and may not pitch in 2012. ⚾ He doesn't light up radar guns, but indy-league find **Dan Remenowsky** makes the most of his deceptive motion, solid breaking stuff, and excellent control to post ridiculous strikeout-to-walk ratios; since he conquered Double-A, the organization is taking his bullpen future seriously. ⚾ Lefties that can light up a gun like **Leyson Septimo** tend to get the glass-half-full treatment, thus the former Arizona farmhand will get yet another chance to prove he has any clue at all where his pitches are going. ⚾ Veteran lefty **Eric Stults** returned from Japan to deal a few relief innings in Colorado, then signed a minor league deal with the Sox; his fringy stuff and fly-ball tendencies make him a bad choice to administer a shot of adrenaline to the big club's heart.

# MANAGER: ROBIN VENTURA

After the organization's often-tempestuous eight-year relationship with Ozzie Guillen, it would be easy to characterize the hiring of Ventura as a typical "rebound date" choice. The popular conception is that they are polar opposites: Where Guillen was hyperkinetic, unconventional, and confrontational, Ventura is viewed as easygoing, traditional, and an organization man, more likely to work smoothly with Kenny Williams and certain to keep whatever differences they may have behind closed doors. However, missing in that analysis is the new skipper's reputation as a quietly demanding leader during his playing days—any player expecting a classic-rock cruise down the Ventura Highway will likely be in for a surprise. With Ventura having never run a clubhouse at any level, it's impossible to guess what sort of managerial tics or personnel fetishes he might display, but if he can build on his predecessor's legacy of solid pitching-staff management, the Sox will be in good hands.

# Cincinnati Reds

One year after the Reds won the NL Central, they reverted back to the below-.500 irrelevance from which they'd arisen. They couldn't even claim to have been a real disappointment. Setting aside questions such as how disappointing a team counting

their runs scored and allowed in terms of strength of schedule, you get 79 wins.

The easy assumption is that this was just another classic example of the Jamesian plexiglass principle in play, a team that overachieved in 2010 and regressed to its essential mediocrity. It may not be what you thought you'd get when figures associated—however fairly—with as much success as Walt Jocketty and Dusty Baker have been came aboard to guide the Reds' return to relevance. But the comedown made the ambitions of 2010—indeed, the entire design fueled by the pennant-winning track records of Jocketty and Baker—seem fruitless and pointless.

Put in that situation, a team can choose to interpret its immediate possibilities in all sorts of ways. It can decide that sliding back toward mediocrity was a matter of unhappy accident and essentially let it ride, they can decide they're really not contenders, or they can get serious. This winter, the Reds stuck with the ambitions fueled by what they'd achieved in 2010, and they got serious.

Credit them with not settling for the patsy role. Maybe it's a matter of playing in a division that has already produced two world champion Cardinals teams in the last six years, or two Brewers playoff teams in the last four, but in today's National League, unless you're a real basket-case franchise like the Astros or an also-ran that has already shot its bolt like

the Cubs or Mets, even the most modest ambitions can be rewarded, even before you add a fifth playoff team to the mix.

That's not to say everyone in the Fourth Estate gets around to seeing things this way. Perhaps the most exasperating element of the aftermath of the Reds' 2011 disappointment

more lucrative markets. This wasn't rooted in any particular truth so much as it was basic neomercantilist covetousness—Votto's really good, so why leave him in Cincinnati? He's only under contract for two more seasons, and his paydays accelerate to $9.5 million in 2012 and $17 million in 2013.

It's as if there's an automatic assumption that the Reds couldn't possibly harbor any ambitions for themselves, let alone pay a player that kind of money. Imagine the nerve, daring to contend in flyover country. That sort of parochial obsessiveness, the notion that all the great players simply *must* wind up in Boston or New York or Philadelphia, speaks volumes about the people convinced that this sort of stratification has to be.

However, it operates in ignorance of how very much the Reds can and do take their shot seriously, and ought to. The NL Central's balance of power for the immediate future has already been fundamentally altered with this winter's departures of Albert Pujols and Prince Fielder. Why should the Reds punt now? Just because the Padres did with Adrian Gonzalez after 2010? Just because the Reds *might* get a return as remarkable as the now-infamous Braves-Rangers Mark Teixeira trade of 2007?

To suggest as much misses the fact that a supply of prospects isn't the Reds' problem. If anything, the Reds' problem

| | | |
|---|---|---|
| TAv | .259 | 16th |
| TAv-P | .257 | 13th |
| FIP | 4.34 | 29th |
| DER | .718 | 3rd |
| DL | 666 | 11th |
| B-Age | 28.6 | 16th |
| P-Age | 27.4 | 9th |
| Salary | $80.8 | 19th |
| M$/MW | $2.23 | 15th |

**2011:** A losing record follows a division title, but all is not lost

**2012:** Reds hold onto Votto while the Cards and Brewers lose their big bats

**Action Items:** Three-win seasons from Latos, Cueto, and Bailey to cover for so-so offense

has been choosing from among the crowd of prospects they already have, and coming up with opportunities for them.

Consider the 2011 rotation. Even with a spring decision to bump Aroldis Chapman to the bullpen, the Reds had five reasonable options to choose from for the four slots after Arroyo: Johnny Cueto, Homer Bailey, Travis Wood, Edinson Volquez, and Mike Leake. Working around injuries and ineffectiveness, they tried everybody and failed to really commit to anybody other than Cueto.

They could keep hoping everyone got better, but that would have been hopelessly optimistic *for a team that thinks it can win now*. Remember, the Reds are operating in a competitive environment where the Brewers, Cardinals, Diamondbacks, and Phillies have proven more than willing to deal for top starters to enhance already accomplished rotations. The Giants still boast an exceptional crew of starting pitchers. These are the strongest contenders, in the past and going forward. The Reds could hold still and hope, again, that guys like Bailey and Arroyo would propel them to October (achieving little more than another quick October exit, as with 2010's three-and-out LDS experience). Or they could start making hard choices.

To Jocketty's credit, he did what you're supposed to do when your objective is to win now. He wanted to trade up in the rotation, and he had depth to deal from. You can argue about the execution, naturally: Trading Yasmani Grandal, Yonder Alonso, Brad Boxberger, and Edinson Volquez would be a lot to give up in any single deal, and whether Mat Latos was the right target is a huge question mark. But in the case of each of the four players dealt, the Reds could afford the exchange, winding up with Latos instead of Volquez in the rotation, still having Votto at first (with Neftali Soto in the wings) after dealing Alonso, and with Devin Mesoraco taking over behind the plate instead of waiting for Grandal.

The real question is whether Latos is going to be the ace they gave up so much to get. As with any high-strikeout pitcher, the ready reaction in the sabermetric community is to say of course he is: Metrics like FIP are wild for big strikeout rates. You can fidget a bit over his being a fly-ball pitcher moving from Petco to the Great American Ball Park, but he's a 24-year-old ace in the making with nearly identical FIP marks home and away (3.25 in San Diego, 3.30 everywhere else). Like Cueto, Latos is exactly the kind of starter the Reds can build contending teams around for the next four years, as well as giving them a tandem to use against the best teams in the league and have a fighting chance in one-, five-, or seven-game series. And because Latos will be under club control at below-market pricing, he's exactly the kind of front-end starter a budget-conscious club should covet to keep a multi-year window as a contender wide open.

Even if the Latos deal works out as well as you might expect, there's still the Reds' other major problem: Votto's loneliness in the lineup as their only impact bat. For the time being, Votto is Arthur without Lancelot, Gilgamesh without Enkidu, Achilles without Patroclus. Even Pujols had his Matt Holliday, Fielder his Ryan Braun.

Consider, who does Joey Votto usually get for sidekicks? An amiable collection of low-OBP guys who play good or great defense, hit homers in the Gap, and flail, bail, and fail on the road. Scott Rolen was supposed to be the difference-making "other" star, but with Rolen's fragility and advancing age, that's an increasingly brittle proposition spun with sugar and cemented with cortisone.

In short, this is the Chicago Cubs problem of old, a lineup that looks like a better offensive team than it is because its park makes everyone look like a slugger, perverting evaluations of the value of all of the non-Vottos. The lassitude this inspires is easy to understand; it isn't that Drew Stubbs or Brandon Phillips or Chris Heisey are bad exactly, it's that they're all about the same in terms of what they do for a team, particularly their walk rates. Adding Zack Cozart to the mix as the everyday shortstop in 2012 will just give the Reds another hack-happy chip off that particular block.

The hitter who might change all this is Jay Bruce as he heads into his peak seasons; if the Reds are smart and avoid the mistake they made with Paul O'Neill two decades ago, they could reap the benefits. Relative to his position, Mesoraco should be an asset, but whether he produces serious sock in the Gap remains to be seen.

The current collection of talent is young enough to provide a platform to win from, both in the next two seasons *and* beyond Votto's "last year" in 2013, whether he stays or goes. The core talents beyond Votto are just reaching that 25–29 sweet spot that generally defines most players' peak seasons, starting with Bruce but also thanks to a rotation featuring Cueto, Latos, and Bailey under team control through 2014.

In the long term, even after the exodus of ready-now stuff lost in the Latos trade, the Reds have made significant strides on the player-development front, so they're becoming even better equipped to sustain multi-year bids for contention. They've become increasingly active in the Latin American market. Signing Chapman, the Cuban Missile, was the high-profile move, but their scouting of and investments in Venezuela and the Dominican Republic in the last four years have been increasingly productive. The Reds are also among the industry's leaders in scouting and acquiring European talent; that may not have borne out results yet, but it's a new field that might eventually yield significant returns on their modest investments. They've also been considerably more aggressive yet unpredictable in the draft, proving willing to pay over slot (under the old CBA) while selecting a blend of ready-now and high-upside talent.

Look at all that and it's a compelling argument to win now and not cash in Votto, certainly not before they've sorted out how 2012 is going to go. Take in the Brewers' climbdown now that the Fielder window is shut, and the Reds' multi-year picture with Pujols in California, and there may be no better proposition for contention than the one you'll find in Cincinnati for the next four years. If Walt Jocketty figured that out while mainline commentators did not, that's to his credit.

# HITTERS

## Jay Bruce    RF

Born: 4/3/1987 Age: 25
Bats: L Throws: L Height: 6' 4" Weight: 205
Breakout: 2% Improve: 32% Collapse: 3%
Attrition: 35% MLB: 92%

| YEAR | TEAM | LVL | AGE | PA | R | 2B | 3B | HR | RBI | BB | SO | SB | CS | AVG_OBP_SLG | TAv | BABIP | BRR | FRAA | WARP |
|------|------|-----|-----|-----|----|----|----|----|-----|----|-----|----|----|--------------|------|-------|------|------|------|
| 2009 | CIN | MLB | 22 | 387 | 47 | 15 | 2 | 22 | 58 | 38 | 75 | 3 | 3 | .223/.303/.470 | .258 | .221 | -0.1 | 4.1 | 1.2 |
| 2010 | CIN | MLB | 23 | 573 | 80 | 23 | 5 | 25 | 70 | 58 | 136 | 5 | 4 | .281/.353/.493 | .289 | .334 | -0.7 | 23.4 | 5.0 |
| 2011 | CIN | MLB | 24 | 664 | 84 | 27 | 2 | 32 | 97 | 71 | 158 | 8 | 7 | .256/.341/.474 | .278 | .297 | 3.6 | -2.5 | 2.5 |
| 2012 | CIN | MLB | 25 | 606 | 80 | 24 | 3 | 32 | 89 | 56 | 138 | 7 | 5 | .264/.335/.495 | .288 | .296 | -.1 | 25.9 | 2.8 |

## Miguel Cairo    3B

Born: 5/4/1974 Age: 38
Bats: R Throws: R Height: 6' 1" Weight: 160
Breakout: 1% Improve: 24% Collapse: 16%
Attrition: 23% MLB: 68%

Comparables:
Cal Ripken Jr., Tony Fernandez, Melvin Mora

| YEAR | TEAM | LVL | AGE | PA | R | 2B | 3B | HR | RBI | BB | SO | SB | CS | AVG_OBP_SLG | TAv | BABIP | BRR | FRAA | WARP |
|------|------|-----|-----|-----|----|----|----|----|-----|----|-----|----|----|--------------|------|-------|------|------|------|
| 2009 | LEH | AAA | 35 | 315 | 44 | 12 | 2 | 5 | 33 | 15 | 40 | 8 | 1 | .287/.325/.392 | .250 | .317 | -0.8 | -5.5 | 0.2 |
| 2009 | PHI | MLB | 35 | 47 | 6 | 2 | 1 | 1 | 2 | 0 | 4 | 0 | 0 | .267/.283/.422 | .242 | .275 | 0.5 | -0.4 | 0.1 |
| 2010 | CIN | MLB | 36 | 226 | 30 | 12 | 0 | 4 | 28 | 17 | 30 | 4 | 0 | .290/.353/.410 | .277 | .320 | 0.2 | -5 | 0.5 |
| 2011 | CIN | MLB | 37 | 276 | 33 | 8 | 2 | 8 | 33 | 18 | 36 | 3 | 4 | .265/.330/.412 | .266 | .279 | 0.1 | 3.5 | 1.5 |
| 2012 | CIN | MLB | 38 | 250 | 27 | 10 | 1 | 4 | 25 | 15 | 37 | 5 | 2 | .256/.311/.371 | .242 | .283 | -0.1 | 3B -1, 2B 1 | 0.9 |

As a pinch-hitter, Cairo's useful as a guy with good zone coverage, but leave a fastball over the plate and he can lay some pretty mighty humiliation on a hurler in the Gap: He's belted all 12 of his homers as a Red at home. After last year's eight-bomb outbreak, the Reds gave Cairo the first multi-year contract of his career, $2 million for two years. How many guys do that after their 37th birthday? Not everyone can make the adjustment to bench player, and not everyone can handle pinch-hitting assignments. Being good enough may not be the same thing as being good, but Cairo's more useful as a 200 at-bats bit part than he ever was as a full-time player.

## Zack Cozart    SS

Born: 8/12/1985 Age: 26
Bats: R Throws: R Height: 6' 1" Weight: 195
Breakout: 2% Improve: 33% Collapse: 5%
Attrition: 30% MLB: 77%

Comparables:
Denny Hocking, Ramon Castro, Joe Millette

| YEAR | TEAM | LVL | AGE | PA | R | 2B | 3B | HR | RBI | BB | SO | SB | CS | AVG_OBP_SLG | TAv | BABIP | BRR | FRAA | WARP |
|------|------|-----|-----|-----|----|----|----|----|-----|----|-----|----|----|--------------|------|-------|------|------|------|
| 2009 | CAR | AA | 23 | 541 | 72 | 29 | 2 | 10 | 59 | 63 | 87 | 10 | 2 | .262/.361/.398 | .269 | .302 | 2.1 | 2.1 | 3.3 |
| 2010 | LOU | AAA | 24 | 610 | 91 | 30 | 4 | 17 | 67 | 40 | 107 | 30 | 4 | .255/.309/.416 | .245 | .285 | 3.9 | 6 | 2.6 |
| 2011 | LOU | AAA | 25 | 350 | 57 | 26 | 2 | 7 | 32 | 23 | 51 | 9 | 2 | .310/.357/.467 | .270 | .348 | 4.1 | 0.6 | 2.2 |
| 2011 | CIN | MLB | 25 | 38 | 6 | 0 | 0 | 2 | 3 | 0 | 6 | 0 | 0 | .324/.324/.486 | .254 | .345 | -0.3 | 1.6 | 0.3 |
| 2012 | CIN | MLB | 26 | 250 | 28 | 12 | 1 | 6 | 28 | 16 | 47 | 6 | 1 | .251/.305/.395 | .246 | .286 | 0.2 | SS 1 | 1.3 |

You might see Cozart as the last Reds shortstop left standing after the stickless Paul Janish didn't hit and the gloveless Edgar Renteria couldn't field, but he essentially won the 2012 job from his hospital bed: Two weeks after taking over at short in July he hyper-extended his left elbow and finished the year on the DL. He had Tommy John surgery on the elbow in August, then, once he could support himself on crutches, another surgery to clean out his right ankle. Cozart still deserves the shot on the strength of his résumé. An above-average defender with good power for a shortstop, he'll be an asset in a park that rewards anyone who can put a charge in the ball. Eventually, he'll be challenged by whichever one of the kids in the system demonstrates he can play short, but in the meantime Cozart's an effective right-now solution for a team that ought to be in win-now mode.

## Juan Duran — LF

Born: 9/2/1991 Age: 20
Bats: R Throws: R Height: 6' 8" Weight: 205
Breakout: 3% Improve: 6% Collapse: 1%
Attrition: 6% MLB: 10%

Comparables:
Telvin Nash, Cristian Santana, Denny Almonte

| YEAR | TEAM | LVL | AGE | PA | R | 2B | 3B | HR | RBI | BB | SO | SB | CS | AVG_OBP_SLG | TAv | BABIP | BRR | FRAA | WARP |
|---|---|---|---|---|---|---|---|---|---|---|---|---|---|---|---|---|---|---|---|
| 2009 | RDS | RK | 17 | 174 | 15 | 7 | 4 | 0 | 17 | 8 | 52 | 0 | 0 | .177/.220/.268 | .190 | .259 | -0.8 | 2.1 | -1.1 |
| 2010 | BIL | RK | 18 | 221 | 23 | 10 | 1 | 6 | 25 | 19 | 71 | 2 | 3 | .244/.308/.393 | .264 | .344 | -1.1 | -5.6 | -0.2 |
| 2011 | DYT | A | 19 | 404 | 48 | 21 | 2 | 16 | 71 | 34 | 152 | 1 | 4 | .264/.329/.463 | .289 | .405 | -2.6 | -2.4 | 1.6 |
| 2012 | CIN | MLB | 20 | 250 | 21 | 8 | 1 | 6 | 23 | 10 | 99 | 0 | 0 | .188/.222/.311 | .187 | .284 | 0 | LF -7, RF -4 | -2.5 |

Duran comes equipped with the Glenn Braggs suite of goodies, capable of eye-popping feats of strength in batting practice or while showing off his arm. The toolsy Dominican made his full-season debut stateside, delivering a mixed bag: He hit for power and shook off a slow start after being hampered with a bad hammy, but is getting your strikeout rate *almost* down to 30 percent in the second half really what we call progress? Just 20, Duran's still filling out, having already grown four inches and packed on at least 20 pounds since the Reds signed him to a $2 million bonus in 2007. His problems making contact and playing the field to some extent can be explained by his getting used to his changing body, but there's no getting around poor pitch recognition and bad instincts producing worse routes. Because of the talent he's still a wild card with upside, but he's far from a sure thing.

## Juan Francisco — 3B

Born: 6/24/1987 Age: 25
Bats: L Throws: R Height: 6' 3" Weight: 180
Breakout: 5% Improve: 29% Collapse: 9%
Attrition: 31% MLB: 76%

Comparables:
Dave Hollins, Brandon Wood, Brian Buscher

| YEAR | TEAM | LVL | AGE | PA | R | 2B | 3B | HR | RBI | BB | SO | SB | CS | AVG_OBP_SLG | TAv | BABIP | BRR | FRAA | WARP |
|---|---|---|---|---|---|---|---|---|---|---|---|---|---|---|---|---|---|---|---|
| 2009 | CAR | AA | 22 | 464 | 64 | 26 | 2 | 22 | 74 | 20 | 91 | 6 | 2 | .281/.319/.501 | .279 | .312 | -2.3 | -3.2 | 1.9 |
| 2009 | LOU | AAA | 22 | 99 | 17 | 5 | 1 | 5 | 19 | 4 | 24 | 0 | 0 | .359/.392/.598 | .336 | .444 | -2.4 | 2.3 | 1.2 |
| 2009 | CIN | MLB | 22 | 25 | 4 | 1 | 0 | 1 | 7 | 3 | 7 | 0 | 0 | .429/.520/.619 | .385 | .615 | 0.2 | 0.2 | 0.4 |
| 2010 | LOU | AAA | 23 | 329 | 46 | 24 | 4 | 18 | 59 | 16 | 81 | 1 | 0 | .286/.327/.565 | .294 | .335 | -1.1 | -6 | 1.8 |
| 2010 | CIN | MLB | 23 | 59 | 3 | 3 | 0 | 1 | 7 | 4 | 20 | 0 | 1 | .273/.322/.382 | .234 | .412 | -0.4 | -0.9 | -0.1 |
| 2011 | LOU | AAA | 24 | 314 | 46 | 23 | 1 | 15 | 50 | 10 | 65 | 0 | 0 | .307/.334/.540 | .285 | .348 | -1.3 | 0.6 | 1.8 |
| 2011 | CIN | MLB | 24 | 97 | 10 | 7 | 1 | 3 | 15 | 4 | 24 | 1 | 0 | .258/.289/.452 | .253 | .318 | 0.8 | -1.9 | 0.2 |
| 2012 | CIN | MLB | 25 | 250 | 31 | 13 | 1 | 11 | 37 | 9 | 60 | 1 | 0 | .272/.302/.478 | .268 | .316 | 0 | 3B -4, LF 0 | 2.1 |

It might seem as if Francisco has been around forever, but he's still just shy of 25. Giving him an extended look after Scott Rolen broke down around midseason last year would have made sense, but Destiny's not always some broad on a charger who arrives with trumpets; sometimes she's a loan shark with bills to pay and your IOU. Rolen may have been down, but Francisco was out, on the shelf with a knee injury at the time. If Francisco ever got to be an everyday player in the Gap, he'd hit 30 homers; he'd also struggle to draw more than 20 walks, and lefties pwn him. Awful range and a strong arm make him a 30-30 guy at the hot corner, able to start that many DPs and make just as many errors. Bobby Bonilla could do that and still help a team, but will Dusty trust Francisco, or just get frustrated with the boots and whiffs?

## Todd Frazier — 3B

Born: 2/12/1986 Age: 26
Bats: R Throws: R Height: 6' 4" Weight: 220
Breakout: 0% Improve: 41% Collapse: 4%
Attrition: 23% MLB: 90%

Comparables:
Dave Hollins, Tim Wallach, Hank Blalock

| YEAR | TEAM | LVL | AGE | PA | R | 2B | 3B | HR | RBI | BB | SO | SB | CS | AVG_OBP_SLG | TAv | BABIP | BRR | FRAA | WARP |
|---|---|---|---|---|---|---|---|---|---|---|---|---|---|---|---|---|---|---|---|
| 2009 | CAR | AA | 23 | 500 | 59 | 40 | 2 | 14 | 68 | 42 | 67 | 7 | 8 | .290/.354/.481 | .291 | .316 | -0.6 | 0.2 | 3.1 |
| 2009 | LOU | AAA | 23 | 69 | 9 | 5 | 0 | 2 | 9 | 6 | 12 | 2 | 0 | .302/.362/.476 | .282 | .347 | -0.1 | 1.1 | 0.4 |
| 2010 | LOU | AAA | 24 | 538 | 71 | 32 | 4 | 17 | 66 | 45 | 127 | 14 | 4 | .258/.334/.448 | .265 | .318 | 2.6 | 6.7 | 2.2 |
| 2011 | LOU | AAA | 25 | 359 | 47 | 18 | 1 | 15 | 46 | 34 | 82 | 17 | 4 | .260/.340/.467 | .275 | .302 | 1.4 | 2.6 | 1.8 |
| 2011 | CIN | MLB | 25 | 121 | 17 | 5 | 0 | 6 | 15 | 7 | 27 | 1 | 0 | .232/.289/.438 | .270 | .253 | 1.3 | -1 | 0.7 |
| 2012 | CIN | MLB | 26 | 250 | 30 | 13 | 0 | 10 | 33 | 18 | 51 | 6 | 2 | .259/.316/.447 | .268 | .292 | -0.2 | 3B 0, LF -0 | 1.8 |

You get the sense the Reds are not really any closer to knowing what Todd Frazier is than they were when they drafted him with the 34th overall pick in 2007. They've achieved some sense of what he isn't—a middle infielder—but if he's just bumping around the corners, opportunities are going to be harder to come by. Guys have managed to put together careers despite this sort of positional ambiguity: Scott Brosius went through it in the '90s and Michael Cuddyer more recently wandered from shortstop to second to third and the outfield corners. He's ready right now to help a winning team at all four corners.

## Brodie Greene — 2B

Born: 9/25/1987 Age: 24
Bats: R Throws: R Height: 6' 2" Weight: 195
Breakout: 0% Improve: 9% Collapse: 6%
Attrition: 15% MLB: 32%

Comparables:
Luis Rivas, Davey Johnson, Dickie Thon

| YEAR | TEAM | LVL | AGE | PA | R | 2B | 3B | HR | RBI | BB | SO | SB | CS | AVG_OBP_SLG | TAv | BABIP | BRR | FRAA | WARP |
|---|---|---|---|---|---|---|---|---|---|---|---|---|---|---|---|---|---|---|---|
| 2010 | LYN | A+ | 22 | 297 | 38 | 11 | 1 | 1 | 20 | 22 | 50 | 8 | 3 | .269/.329/.330 | .256 | .324 | 0.9 | -1.3 | 1.2 |
| 2011 | BAK | A+ | 23 | 556 | 79 | 21 | 6 | 14 | 79 | 41 | 75 | 36 | 9 | .287/.344/.436 | .268 | .312 | 5.1 | -4.3 | 2.8 |
| 2012 | CIN | MLB | 24 | 250 | 24 | 9 | 1 | 4 | 22 | 11 | 47 | 9 | 2 | .230/.267/.326 | .209 | .267 | 0.1 | 2B -0, SS -2 | -0.6 |

While the Reds might seem to have more defensively indeterminate floaters than your average organization, that's not a bad thing; after all, it affords the brass considerable flexibility in deciding what to do with a guy. Eventually. And assuming they actually come to a decision. After starring at Texas A&M, Greene's blend started out with the up-the-middle positions, but 16 quick errors in Bakersfield and he's already seen as stretched at short, moving across the keystone once Didi Gregorius was healthy, then staying at second even after the Dutchman's promotion. Greene was supposed to hit on the strength of his college career; if that power in the hitter-friendly Cal League translates to Double-A, he's officially interesting.

**Didi Gregorius    SS**
Born: 2/18/1990 Age: 22
Bats: L Throws: R Height: 6' 2" Weight: 160
Breakout: 1% Improve: 6% Collapse: 4%
Attrition: 7% MLB: 19%
Comparables:

| YEAR | TEAM | LVL | AGE | PA | R | 2B | 3B | HR | RBI | BB | SO | SB | CS | AVG_OBP_SLG | TAv | BABIP | BRR | FRAA | WARP |
|------|------|-----|-----|-----|-----|-----|-----|-----|-----|-----|-----|-----|-----|-------------|-----|-------|-----|------|------|
| 2009 | SAR | A+ | 19 | 74 | 8 | 4 | 0 | 0 | 2 | 1 | 9 | 0 | 0 | .254/.270/.310 | .213 | .286 | 0.5 | 0.6 | 0.1 |
| 2009 | BIL | RK | 19 | 225 | 28 | 10 | 1 | 1 | 16 | 12 | 27 | 8 | 6 | .314/.363/.387 | .298 | .354 | 2.1 | -11.8 | 0.6 |
| 2010 | DYT | A | 20 | 548 | 65 | 16 | 11 | 5 | 41 | 33 | 62 | 16 | 7 | .273/.324/.379 | .258 | .300 | 3.1 | -2.5 | 2.3 |
| 2011 | BAK | A+ | 21 | 203 | 30 | 12 | 1 | 5 | 28 | 10 | 25 | 8 | 8 | .303/.333/.457 | .277 | .323 | 0.1 | 1.6 | 1.4 |

**Billy Hamilton    SS**
Born: 9/9/1990 Age: 21
Bats: R Throws: R Height: 6' 2" Weight: 160
Breakout: 2% Improve: 15% Collapse: 0%
Attrition: 10% MLB: 25%
Comparables: Shawn O'Malley, Eduardo Escobar, Silvio Pena

| YEAR | TEAM | LVL | AGE | PA | R | 2B | 3B | HR | RBI | BB | SO | SB | CS | AVG_OBP_SLG | TAv | BABIP | BRR | FRAA | WARP |
|------|------|-----|-----|-----|-----|-----|-----|-----|-----|-----|-----|-----|-----|-------------|-----|-------|-----|------|------|
| 2009 | RDS | RK | 18 | 180 | 19 | 6 | 3 | 0 | 11 | 11 | 47 | 14 | 3 | .205/.251/.277 | .211 | .281 | 1.9 | 5.3 | 0.2 |
| 2010 | BIL | RK | 19 | 316 | 61 | 13 | 10 | 2 | 24 | 28 | 56 | 48 | 9 | .318/.385/.456 | .335 | .391 | 10.4 | 12.8 | 5.8 |
| 2011 | DYT | A | 20 | 610 | 99 | 18 | 9 | 3 | 50 | 52 | 133 | 103 | 20 | .278/.340/.360 | .277 | .360 | 16.4 | 4.1 | 5.9 |
| 2012 | CIN | MLB | 21 | 250 | 21 | 7 | 2 | 2 | 19 | 12 | 70 | 22 | 5 | .213/.251/.283 | .192 | .290 | 0.6 | SS 6, 2B 3 | -1.4 |

Even without 19th century Hall of Famer "Sliding Billy" to refer to, the basepaths aggression of this Billy Hamilton would earn the sobriquet. Five of the eight times in modern-era big-league baseball in which somebody's stolen 100 or more bases in the majors he has also wound up with more steals than runs scored; Hamilton's "achievement" on that score in the Cal League is cute and rare but also emblematic of the more basic challenge that for all the shenanigans nothing beats just simply getting on base. Hamilton walks well for a player of his youth but less than 10 percent of the time. The Reds gave him a full year at shortstop to see if he'd erase concerns about a weak arm for the position. He responded with a 39-error season.

**Ryan Hanigan    C**
Born: 8/16/1980 Age: 31
Bats: R Throws: R Height: 6' 1" Weight: 195
Breakout: 1% Improve: 35% Collapse: 11%
Attrition: 26% MLB: 88%
Comparables: Paul Lo Duca, Tim McCarver, Carlos Ruiz

| YEAR | TEAM | LVL | AGE | PA | R | 2B | 3B | HR | RBI | BB | SO | SB | CS | AVG_OBP_SLG | TAv | BABIP | BRR | FRAA | WARP |
|------|------|-----|-----|-----|-----|-----|-----|-----|-----|-----|-----|-----|-----|-------------|-----|-------|-----|------|------|
| 2009 | CIN | MLB | 28 | 293 | 22 | 6 | 1 | 3 | 11 | 37 | 31 | 0 | 0 | .263/.361/.331 | .246 | .289 | -0.8 | 2.5 | 1.3 |
| 2010 | LOU | AAA | 29 | 52 | 6 | 3 | 0 | 0 | 2 | 4 | 6 | 0 | 0 | .239/.327/.304 | .219 | .275 | 0.4 | -0.1 | 0.0 |
| 2010 | CIN | MLB | 29 | 243 | 25 | 11 | 0 | 5 | 40 | 33 | 21 | 0 | 0 | .300/.405/.429 | .296 | .313 | -1.4 | -0.8 | 1.7 |
| 2011 | CIN | MLB | 30 | 304 | 27 | 6 | 0 | 6 | 31 | 35 | 32 | 0 | 0 | .267/.356/.357 | .270 | .285 | 0.9 | -2 | 1.5 |
| 2012 | CIN | MLB | 31 | 279 | 34 | 10 | 0 | 6 | 27 | 31 | 33 | 0 | 0 | .274/.362/.390 | .270 | .293 | 0 | C -1 | 2.6 |

There's a natural temptation to want to multiply a guy's production into full-time play, especially when it's a hitter who can help you as much as Hanigan does with his OBP, not to mention a career 36 percent rate of gunning down stolen-base attempts. But historically, Hanigan has run out steam in the second half (losing almost 100 points in OPS in the majors), and he's never caught 100 games. That isn't to say he can't, but you can understand why he might be better off just wearing the uneasy crown of "Baseball's Best Backup Catcher" and being done with it.

### Chris Heisey — LF

Born: 12/14/1984 Age: 27
Bats: R Throws: R Height: 6' 1" Weight: 215
Breakout: 3% Improve: 26% Collapse: 4%
Attrition: 19% MLB: 80%

Comparables:
Wes Covington, Andy Barkett, Johnny Weekly

| YEAR | TEAM | LVL | AGE | PA | R | 2B | 3B | HR | RBI | BB | SO | SB | CS | AVG/OBP/SLG | TAv | BABIP | BRR | FRAA | WARP |
|---|---|---|---|---|---|---|---|---|---|---|---|---|---|---|---|---|---|---|---|
| 2009 | CAR | AA | 24 | 314 | 54 | 18 | 2 | 13 | 40 | 34 | 34 | 13 | 1 | .347/.426/.572 | .348 | .358 | 3.1 | -2.6 | 4.2 |
| 2009 | LOU | AAA | 24 | 271 | 37 | 17 | 1 | 9 | 37 | 14 | 43 | 8 | 2 | .278/.327/.465 | .274 | .303 | -0.3 | 0.2 | 1.2 |
| 2010 | LOU | AAA | 25 | 89 | 6 | 3 | 0 | 4 | 13 | 7 | 23 | 2 | 0 | .241/.307/.430 | .247 | .283 | 0.1 | -1.3 | 0.1 |
| 2010 | CIN | MLB | 25 | 226 | 33 | 10 | 1 | 8 | 21 | 16 | 57 | 1 | 2 | .254/.324/.433 | .268 | .312 | 2.2 | 0.4 | 1.1 |
| 2011 | CIN | MLB | 26 | 308 | 44 | 9 | 1 | 18 | 50 | 19 | 78 | 6 | 1 | .254/.309/.487 | .291 | .283 | 0.5 | 0.5 | 1.6 |
| 2012 | CIN | MLB | 27 | 285 | 37 | 12 | 1 | 14 | 41 | 20 | 64 | 5 | 1 | .266/.326/.479 | .281 | .298 | 0.1 | LF -0, CF -1 | 2.2 |

If anyone is the perfect Red, it might be Heisey. In essentially one season's worth of big-league stats (534 PAs), Heisey has hit 26 homers while cranking out a .254/.316/.465 line. That's swell, and he's certainly capable of a 30-homer season as an everyday player. But if you think he's really about to blow up, keep in mind that he's already 27 years old. He isn't building up to anything. This is exactly how good he is and exactly as good as he's going to be. He could pick up some ground by hitting lefties better than he has, but he's essentially another athletic, good-glove regular who bats righty, except that he's the one playing an outfield corner. If you've got genuinely great players at up-the-middle positions, that isn't a problem, but the Reds don't have a Morgan at second, Griffey in center, or Larkin at short; instead, they have guys who hit like Heisey, or a little worse.

### Paul Janish — SS

Born: 10/12/1982 Age: 29
Bats: R Throws: R Height: 6' 3" Weight: 190
Breakout: 8% Improve: 38% Collapse: 10%
Attrition: 25% MLB: 85%

Comparables:
Edgar Renteria, Tony Fernandez, Roberto Pena

| YEAR | TEAM | LVL | AGE | PA | R | 2B | 3B | HR | RBI | BB | SO | SB | CS | AVG/OBP/SLG | TAv | BABIP | BRR | FRAA | WARP |
|---|---|---|---|---|---|---|---|---|---|---|---|---|---|---|---|---|---|---|---|
| 2009 | CIN | MLB | 26 | 292 | 36 | 21 | 0 | 1 | 16 | 26 | 40 | 2 | 0 | .211/.296/.305 | .208 | .247 | 1.6 | 8 | 0.4 |
| 2010 | CIN | MLB | 27 | 228 | 23 | 10 | 0 | 5 | 25 | 22 | 30 | 1 | 3 | .260/.338/.385 | .258 | .283 | -1.3 | -2.9 | 0.4 |
| 2011 | LOU | AAA | 28 | 53 | 9 | 2 | 0 | 1 | 3 | 7 | 4 | 1 | 0 | .256/.377/.372 | .264 | .256 | 0.7 | 0.2 | 0.3 |
| 2011 | CIN | MLB | 28 | 366 | 27 | 14 | 1 | 0 | 23 | 18 | 46 | 3 | 2 | .214/.259/.262 | .205 | .244 | -0.2 | 4.7 | -0.1 |
| 2012 | CIN | MLB | 29 | 324 | 34 | 15 | 0 | 6 | 30 | 24 | 49 | 2 | 1 | .236/.303/.350 | .233 | .260 | -0.2 | SS 3, 3B -0 | 0.6 |

Among shortstops with a meaningful amount of playing time in the majors last season, Janish ranked among the top five afield via BIS Plus/Minus and Total Zone, rating with the likes of Brendan Ryan, Alex Gonzalez, Clint Barmes and Troy Tulowitzki. But while they've all got guaranteed money and jobs in 2012, as the worst hitter in the lot Janish is stuck trying to live down losing in the one shot he's gotten at an everyday job in the big leagues. At the plate, Janish is easily overpowered and pitchers have learned that they don't need to be cute with him, however patient he might want to be.

### Fred Lewis — LF

Born: 12/9/1980 Age: 31
Bats: L Throws: R Height: 6' 3" Weight: 190
Breakout: 1% Improve: 31% Collapse: 9%
Attrition: 25% MLB: 86%

Comparables:
Phil Bradley, Lloyd McClendon, John Rodriguez

| YEAR | TEAM | LVL | AGE | PA | R | 2B | 3B | HR | RBI | BB | SO | SB | CS | AVG/OBP/SLG | TAv | BABIP | BRR | FRAA | WARP |
|---|---|---|---|---|---|---|---|---|---|---|---|---|---|---|---|---|---|---|---|
| 2009 | SFN | MLB | 28 | 336 | 49 | 21 | 3 | 4 | 20 | 36 | 84 | 8 | 4 | .258/.348/.390 | .267 | .348 | 1.8 | 2.3 | 1.2 |
| 2010 | TOR | MLB | 29 | 480 | 70 | 31 | 5 | 8 | 36 | 38 | 104 | 17 | 6 | .262/.332/.414 | .264 | .325 | -0.2 | -0.7 | 0.9 |
| 2011 | CIN | MLB | 30 | 210 | 20 | 7 | 0 | 3 | 19 | 22 | 38 | 2 | 5 | .230/.321/.317 | .240 | .273 | -0.5 | 1.6 | -0.1 |
| 2012 | CIN | MLB | 31 | 263 | 31 | 12 | 3 | 5 | 28 | 25 | 60 | 8 | 3 | .257/.335/.403 | .263 | .321 | -0.5 | LF -1, RF 0 | 1.1 |

Expectations that Lewis might have made the perfect partner for Jonny Gomes in left were derailed early by a strained oblique that cost him the first month of the season. By the time he came back in May, he struggled to get on track, and he's not so good that he deserves many chances to overcome these setbacks. On a practical level, if you want to define replacement level in terms of who's freely available to man an outfield slot from one year to the next, it's somebody like Lewis, which is where he's at as we go to press—31 years old, unsigned, and merely moderately useful.

### Devin Lohman — SS

Born: 4/14/1989 Age: 23
Bats: R Throws: R Height: 6' 2" Weight: 185
Breakout: 5% Improve: 13% Collapse: 2%
Attrition: 10% MLB: 27%

Comparables:
Bobby Meacham, Brodie Greene, Michael Fisher

| YEAR | TEAM | LVL | AGE | PA | R | 2B | 3B | HR | RBI | BB | SO | SB | CS | AVG/OBP/SLG | TAv | BABIP | BRR | FRAA | WARP |
|---|---|---|---|---|---|---|---|---|---|---|---|---|---|---|---|---|---|---|---|
| 2010 | BIL | RK | 21 | 270 | 33 | 12 | 2 | 1 | 31 | 24 | 47 | 2 | 5 | .239/.317/.322 | .273 | .284 | -1.4 | -3.1 | 1.1 |
| 2011 | DYT | A | 22 | 235 | 14 | 5 | 1 | 1 | 31 | 17 | 47 | 9 | 2 | .208/.269/.256 | .219 | .261 | -0.4 | 0.2 | -0.3 |
| 2011 | BAK | A+ | 22 | 147 | 25 | 10 | 2 | 5 | 17 | 13 | 23 | 4 | 2 | .331/.400/.554 | .316 | .373 | -0.9 | -9.6 | 0.5 |
| 2011 | BIL | RK | 22 | 138 | 23 | 4 | 0 | 4 | 11 | 16 | 22 | 6 | 2 | .322/.420/.461 | .333 | .363 | -0.2 | -18.3 | 0.0 |
| 2012 | CIN | MLB | 23 | 250 | 21 | 8 | 1 | 3 | 19 | 14 | 60 | 3 | 1 | .202/.252/.287 | .192 | .252 | -0.1 | SS -9, 2B 1 | -1.5 |

A third-rounder out of Long Beach State in 2010, Lohman bounced all over the organization. He started slowly while playing second base, a position he had trouble adjusting to, in Dayton. That earned him a month-long demotion to the Pioneer League to pick up playing shortstop again, and that was followed by a bump back up the ladder to the High-A Cal League, about where a top-program player should have been at the end of his first full season. Unfortunately, the concerns that Lohman couldn't stick at short were borne out by error-prone fielding and poor range. He made progress at the plate, but he's another toolsy Reds prospect in search of a defensive home who might not have the bat to carry a slide down the defensive spectrum.

**Devin Mesoraco** C
Born: 6/19/1988 Age: 24
Bats: R Throws: R Height: 6' 2" Weight: 220
Breakout: 3% Improve: 18% Collapse: 4%
Attrition: 42% MLB: 83%

Comparables:
Matt Wieters, Ramon Castro, Rick Dempsey

| YEAR | TEAM | LVL | AGE | PA | R | 2B | 3B | HR | RBI | BB | SO | SB | CS | AVG/OBP/SLG | TAv | BABIP | BRR | FRAA | WARP |
|------|------|-----|-----|-----|----|----|----|----|-----|----|----|----|----|----|-----|-------|-----|------|------|
| 2009 | SAR | A+ | 21 | 357 | 32 | 22 | 1 | 8 | 37 | 35 | 76 | 0 | 1 | .228/.311/.381 | .250 | .273 | 0.4 | -2 | 0.6 |
| 2010 | LYN | A+ | 22 | 181 | 24 | 11 | 2 | 10 | 31 | 19 | 29 | 2 | 2 | .335/.417/.620 | .351 | .361 | -0.5 | 0.6 | 2.4 |
| 2010 | CAR | AA | 22 | 212 | 42 | 11 | 3 | 13 | 31 | 18 | 37 | 1 | 0 | .294/.368/.594 | .332 | .307 | 0.6 | 0.2 | 2.9 |
| 2010 | LOU | AAA | 22 | 58 | 5 | 3 | 0 | 3 | 13 | 6 | 14 | 0 | 1 | .231/.310/.462 | .298 | .257 | -0.4 | 0.3 | 0.6 |
| 2011 | LOU | AAA | 23 | 499 | 60 | 36 | 2 | 15 | 71 | 52 | 83 | 1 | 1 | .289/.371/.484 | .276 | .325 | -1.8 | 2.4 | 2.5 |
| 2011 | CIN | MLB | 23 | 53 | 5 | 3 | 0 | 2 | 6 | 3 | 10 | 0 | 0 | .180/.226/.360 | .210 | .184 | -0.4 | -0.1 | -0.1 |
| *2012* | *CIN* | *MLB* | *24* | *250* | *30* | *13* | *1* | *9* | *32* | *20* | *52* | *0* | *0* | *.251/.316/.443* | *.265* | *.284* | *0* | *C -0* | *2.1* |

**Brandon Phillips** 2B
Born: 6/28/1981 Age: 31
Bats: R Throws: R Height: 6' 0" Weight: 185
Breakout: 1% Improve: 31% Collapse: 2%
Attrition: 15% MLB: 89%

Comparables:
Don Money, Rod Booker, Orlando Hudson

| YEAR | TEAM | LVL | AGE | PA | R | 2B | 3B | HR | RBI | BB | SO | SB | CS | AVG/OBP/SLG | TAv | BABIP | BRR | FRAA | WARP |
|------|------|-----|-----|-----|-----|----|----|----|-----|----|----|----|----|----|-----|-------|-----|------|------|
| 2009 | CIN | MLB | 28 | 644 | 78 | 30 | 5 | 20 | 98 | 44 | 75 | 25 | 9 | .276/.329/.447 | .259 | .284 | 4.3 | -4.1 | 1.6 |
| 2010 | CIN | MLB | 29 | 687 | 100 | 33 | 5 | 18 | 59 | 46 | 83 | 16 | 12 | .275/.332/.430 | .266 | .293 | 4.9 | 5.8 | 3.3 |
| 2011 | CIN | MLB | 30 | 674 | 94 | 38 | 2 | 18 | 82 | 44 | 85 | 14 | 9 | .300/.353/.457 | .283 | .322 | 6.4 | -6.7 | 3.3 |
| *2012* | *CIN* | *MLB* | *31* | *636* | *80* | *28* | *3* | *24* | *85* | *39* | *89* | *18* | *9* | *.277/.328/.458* | *.275* | *.289* | *-1.4* | *2B -4* | *2.9* |

Phillips balances on the edge between park-inflated star and merely good ballplayer. In a typical year, he might slug a hundred points better in the Gap than on the road, but he still does enough away from his home park to help an offense. More troubling, however, is that, no matter how often he shows up on highlight reels, the various defensive metrics aren't unanimous about his value in the field. Can he help a team win? Absolutely, but the real problem is that he's getting paid as much as a sixth of the Reds' payroll, and he's simply not that critical a component to this or any team's success. No dummy, Phillips appears determined to stick around and work out an extension beyond his 2012 compensation of $12 million.

**Denis Phipps** CF
Born: 7/22/1985 Age: 26
Bats: R Throws: R Height: 6' 3" Weight: 177
Breakout: 4% Improve: 50% Collapse: 5%
Attrition: 24% MLB: 89%

Comparables:
Derek Bell, Devon White, Roberto Kelly

| YEAR | TEAM | LVL | AGE | PA | R | 2B | 3B | HR | RBI | BB | SO | SB | CS | AVG/OBP/SLG | TAv | BABIP | BRR | FRAA | WARP |
|------|------|-----|-----|-----|----|----|----|----|-----|----|-----|----|----|----|-----|-------|-----|------|------|
| 2009 | SAR | A+ | 23 | 540 | 51 | 32 | 5 | 10 | 55 | 31 | 108 | 18 | 8 | .239/.288/.385 | .251 | .284 | 1.3 | 8 | 2.1 |
| 2010 | LYN | A+ | 24 | 103 | 23 | 10 | 1 | 8 | 21 | 10 | 19 | 9 | 1 | .333/.398/.720 | .374 | .348 | 0.1 | 1.3 | 1.8 |
| 2010 | CAR | AA | 24 | 411 | 44 | 22 | 3 | 4 | 35 | 32 | 86 | 8 | 9 | .228/.296/.336 | .228 | .286 | -3.2 | -4.1 | -1.3 |
| 2011 | CAR | AA | 25 | 338 | 53 | 22 | 5 | 7 | 38 | 27 | 83 | 10 | 6 | .328/.382/.502 | .308 | .425 | 3.5 | 2.1 | 3.4 |
| 2011 | LOU | AAA | 25 | 173 | 30 | 12 | 2 | 5 | 26 | 13 | 41 | 4 | 1 | .380/.428/.576 | .325 | .487 | 2.3 | 0.1 | 2.3 |
| *2012* | *CIN* | *MLB* | *26* | *250* | *27* | *12* | *1* | *6* | *28* | *12* | *65* | *5* | *2* | *.248/.288/.391* | *.238* | *.313* | *-0.3* | *CF -1, RF -1* | *0.1* |

Phipps is the rare Dominican who signed years after his 16th or 17th birthday, but that was because he didn't start playing baseball until his late teens. Last season, he hit well for the first time in six years. If you're a BABIP-minded skeptic, you'll understandably sign up for a fresh mug of regression, but the upside is that you'll wind up with a Timo Perez kind of guy, an aggressive hacker with some value as a fourth outfielder.

**Cody Puckett** 2B
Born: 4/3/1987 Age: 25
Bats: R Throws: R Height: 5' 11" Weight: 175
Breakout: 3% Improve: 20% Collapse: 9%
Attrition: 44% MLB: 79%

Comparables:
Jason Hardtke, Bret Boone, Jorge Velandia

| YEAR | TEAM | LVL | AGE | PA | R | 2B | 3B | HR | RBI | BB | SO | SB | CS | AVG/OBP/SLG | TAv | BABIP | BRR | FRAA | WARP |
|------|------|-----|-----|-----|----|----|----|----|-----|----|-----|----|----|----|-----|-------|-----|------|------|
| 2009 | DYT | A | 22 | 538 | 76 | 35 | 1 | 19 | 67 | 39 | 138 | 19 | 1 | .263/.325/.459 | .275 | .327 | -0.3 | -13 | 0.8 |
| 2010 | LYN | A+ | 23 | 542 | 72 | 40 | 4 | 18 | 54 | 45 | 124 | 17 | 4 | .277/.348/.493 | .292 | .333 | 3.6 | 1.7 | 3.9 |
| 2011 | CAR | AA | 24 | 380 | 51 | 29 | 0 | 15 | 68 | 28 | 80 | 10 | 3 | .248/.313/.466 | .264 | .276 | 3.7 | -1.3 | 1.3 |
| *2012* | *CIN* | *MLB* | *25* | *250* | *26* | *13* | *0* | *9* | *30* | *12* | *70* | *5* | *1* | *.223/.268/.399* | *.231* | *.272* | *0.2* | *2B -4, LF -0* | *0.1* |

You might see that Puckett played a lot of second base and hit those 15 homers and think there's something to get excited about, but buyer beware: Puckett's a former college shortstop struggling to stick at up-the-middle positions, having already spent much of the second half in the outfield. He drew an assignment to the AFL, where he flopped thanks to a poor approach and merely sporadic awareness of the strike zone. Eight of the regular-season homers came off lefties, and he slugged only .429 against right-handers—does that sound like a starting corner outfielder? It shouldn't surprise you that he slipped through the Rule 5 draft unpicked, although he could prove to be a useful utilityman.

### Edgar Renteria    SS

Born: 8/7/1976 Age: 35
Bats: R Throws: R Height: 6' 2'' Weight: 172
Breakout: 0% Improve: 28% Collapse: 7%
Attrition: 19% MLB: 81%

**Comparables:**
Alvin Dark, Jerry Hairston, John Valentin

| YEAR | TEAM | LVL | AGE | PA | R | 2B | 3B | HR | RBI | BB | SO | SB | CS | AVG_OBP_SLG | TAv | BABIP | BRR | FRAA | WARP |
|------|------|-----|-----|-----|----|----|----|----|-----|----|----|----|----|-------------|------|-------|------|-----------|------|
| 2009 | SFN | MLB | 32 | 510 | 50 | 19 | 1 | 5 | 48 | 39 | 69 | 7 | 2 | .250/.307/.328 | .219 | .281 | 2.9 | -1.8 | -0.1 |
| 2010 | SFN | MLB | 33 | 267 | 26 | 11 | 2 | 3 | 22 | 21 | 43 | 3 | 0 | .276/.332/.374 | .245 | .323 | -0.8 | -2.1 | 0.4 |
| 2011 | CIN | MLB | 34 | 333 | 34 | 14 | 0 | 5 | 36 | 24 | 65 | 4 | 2 | .251/.306/.348 | .242 | .302 | -0.3 | 0.7 | 0.5 |
| 2012 | CIN | MLB | 35 | 300 | 34 | 12 | 1 | 5 | 29 | 22 | 47 | 4 | 1 | .268/.322/.375 | .248 | .303 | 0 | SS -2, 2B 0 | 1.4 |

Signing Renteria to balance Janish's leather with some pop at the plate might have sounded nice in the abstract, but he proved to be just another component from the 2010 Giants ready to turn into a pumpkin. It's possible he might cling to a career Omar Vizquel-style, but it just as easily could be the end; to move into the O-zone you have to have elder statesman cred and an automatic saving throw on charisma. In another time and place, Renteria would have been a Hall of Famer, if he'd had Frankie Frisch for a teammate; instead, he'll have to settle for two rings and a brief heyday as the best shortstop in the NL at the height of the steroid era. If there's anything to feel genuinely badly about, it's Renteria's finishing second to Todd Hollandsworth in Rookie of the Year voting in '96, an utter travesty at the time, even setting aside that expected future value is not a criterion.

### Henry Rodriguez    2B

Born: 2/9/1990 Age: 22
Bats: B Throws: R Height: 5' 11'' Weight: 150
Breakout: 5% Improve: 19% Collapse: 4%
Attrition: 16% MLB: 60%

**Comparables:**
Cesar Izturis, Bill Mazeroski, Rennie Stennett

| YEAR | TEAM | LVL | AGE | PA | R | 2B | 3B | HR | RBI | BB | SO | SB | CS | AVG_OBP_SLG | TAv | BABIP | BRR | FRAA | WARP |
|------|------|-----|-----|-----|----|----|----|----|-----|----|----|----|----|-------------|------|-------|------|-----------|------|
| 2009 | RDS | RK | 19 | 161 | 24 | 10 | 1 | 1 | 19 | 7 | 18 | 9 | 0 | .322/.356/.421 | .291 | .361 | 1.9 | -0.7 | 0.9 |
| 2010 | DYT | A | 20 | 547 | 76 | 37 | 3 | 14 | 78 | 22 | 70 | 33 | 13 | .307/.340/.473 | .298 | .334 | -0.1 | -5.9 | 3.0 |
| 2011 | BAK | A+ | 21 | 254 | 37 | 17 | 0 | 8 | 44 | 14 | 35 | 12 | 7 | .340/.378/.513 | .305 | .372 | 1.3 | -2.7 | 1.8 |
| 2011 | CAR | AA | 21 | 312 | 39 | 19 | 1 | 5 | 37 | 25 | 43 | 18 | 3 | .302/.367/.432 | .272 | .342 | 2.2 | -3 | 1.1 |
| 2012 | CIN | MLB | 22 | 250 | 26 | 12 | 0 | 5 | 27 | 7 | 45 | 11 | 4 | .250/.274/.370 | .223 | .284 | -0.2 | 2B -5, SS -1 | -0.2 |

Amid the throng of middle-infield maybes, Rodriguez offers some relief with his bat. Fifty extra-base hits, 30 steals, and a successful jump to Double-A? Everyone likes that. In 2011, Rodriguez added improved patience to his combination of excellent plate coverage, quick hands, line-drive power, and speed. Like a lot of switch-hitters, Rodriguez's real thunder comes from the right side of the plate, but he's no mere platoon player. Unfortunately, there's cause to keep the parade off Main Street: As young as he is, he remains a rough-edged thing in the field. His arm might have kept him at second, but poor range and mental errors have contributed to keeping him from finding a defensive home; he played third base in Venezuela this winter.

### Yorman Rodriguez    CF

Born: 8/15/1992 Age: 19
Bats: R Throws: R Height: 6' 3'' Weight: 184
Breakout: 0% Improve: 3% Collapse: 0%
Attrition: 2% MLB: 5%

**Comparables:**
Cesar Puello, Jose Martinez, Jonathan Garcia

| YEAR | TEAM | LVL | AGE | PA | R | 2B | 3B | HR | RBI | BB | SO | SB | CS | AVG_OBP_SLG | TAv | BABIP | BRR | FRAA | WARP |
|------|------|-----|-----|-----|----|----|----|----|-----|----|----|----|----|-------------|------|-------|------|-----------|------|
| 2009 | BIL | RK | 16 | 193 | 21 | 10 | 2 | 3 | 17 | 9 | 61 | 5 | 2 | .219/.259/.344 | .235 | .311 | 1 | -0.4 | -0.3 |
| 2009 | RDS | RK | 16 | 95 | 9 | 2 | 1 | 0 | 2 | 10 | 23 | 5 | 0 | .274/.351/.321 | .249 | .377 | -0.9 | 0.6 | 0.2 |
| 2010 | BIL | RK | 17 | 184 | 25 | 8 | 3 | 2 | 39 | 8 | 30 | 12 | 2 | .339/.367/.456 | .334 | .400 | 1.7 | -1.4 | 2.0 |
| 2011 | DYT | A | 18 | 310 | 38 | 10 | 4 | 7 | 40 | 25 | 84 | 20 | 8 | .254/.318/.393 | .259 | .337 | -2.7 | -3.9 | 0.2 |
| 2012 | CIN | MLB | 19 | 250 | 20 | 8 | 1 | 3 | 20 | 10 | 81 | 8 | 3 | .196/.227/.282 | .180 | .275 | -0.2 | CF -7, RF -6 | -2.6 |

Among the Reds' collection of Caribbean candy snapped up by a sharp squad of scouts, Rodriguez represents the biggest bet they've made on any one position player, as they paid the Venezuelan a then-record $2.5 million signing bonus. His full-season debut as a teen was rough, and his early-season effort in the field drew some criticism. Just as he seemed to get comfortable at the plate, he injured his shoulder on a dive that effectively ended his season a month early. He was also just 18 years old, so it's no surprise that he remains what he was before the year, a five-tool talent who has a lot of work ahead of him to translate those tools into production. If he improves his approach at the plate, he can reach the sky-high ceiling set for him when he signed; even if he doesn't, he was still a lottery ticket worth buying, because that's the nature of investing in foreign talent.

| **Scott Rolen** | **3B** | YEAR | TEAM | LVL | AGE | PA | R | 2B | 3B | HR | RBI | BB | SO | SB | CS | AVG_OBP_SLG | TAv | BABIP | BRR | FRAA | WARP |
|---|---|---|---|---|---|---|---|---|---|---|---|---|---|---|---|---|---|---|---|---|---|
| | | 2009 | CIN | MLB | 34 | 162 | 24 | 7 | 1 | 3 | 24 | 19 | 20 | 1 | 2 | .270/.364/.401 | .268 | .291 | 1.3 | -0.7 | 0.6 |
| | | 2009 | TOR | MLB | 34 | 373 | 52 | 29 | 0 | 8 | 43 | 26 | 42 | 4 | 2 | .320/.370/.476 | .301 | .341 | 1.3 | -1.6 | 3.0 |
| | | 2010 | CIN | MLB | 35 | 537 | 66 | 34 | 3 | 20 | 83 | 50 | 82 | 1 | 2 | .285/.358/.497 | .292 | .302 | -2.3 | 11.6 | 3.9 |
| | | 2011 | CIN | MLB | 36 | 269 | 31 | 20 | 2 | 5 | 36 | 10 | 36 | 1 | 0 | .242/.279/.397 | .246 | .262 | 0.1 | 1.4 | 0.7 |
| | | 2012 | CIN | MLB | 37 | 306 | 36 | 17 | 1 | 8 | 35 | 24 | 46 | 3 | 1 | .260/.327/.417 | .264 | .285 | -0.3 | 3B 5 | 2.0 |

Born: 4/4/1975 Age: 37
Bats: R Throws: R Height: 6' 5" Weight: 210
Breakout: 0% Improve: 16% Collapse: 17%
Attrition: 27% MLB: 72%
Comparables:
Joe Randa, Ken Boyer, Richie Hebner

Rolen's managed just two full-ish seasons in the last seven, and last year's problems with injuries to both shoulders hampered him before shutting him down altogether for surgery shortly after an All-Star selection he hadn't earned. We'll see if there's a usage pattern that can keep him healthy enough to contribute all year; regular rest (and playing time for Francisco or Frazier) might do the trick, but Rolen might not like it, and it remains to be seen if Dusty's willing to do it.

should silence concerns over his prospect status as a first baseman, even as he approaches the one stumbling block he can't hulk-smash out of existence: Joey Votto. A strong arm has led to experiments behind the plate; he'd be a bit chunky for an outfield corner, but if the Reds were willing to try to make Yonder Alonso an outfielder, you can't rule out they might try it with Soto. He's already on the 40-man, and if he keeps crushing pitches at this pace in Triple-A, it's going to be hard not to want to take a peek at some point.

| **Drew Stubbs** | **CF** | YEAR | TEAM | LVL | AGE | PA | R | 2B | 3B | HR | RBI | BB | SO | SB | CS | AVG_OBP_SLG | TAv | BABIP | BRR | FRAA | WARP |
|---|---|---|---|---|---|---|---|---|---|---|---|---|---|---|---|---|---|---|---|---|---|
| | | 2009 | LOU | AAA | 24 | 472 | 57 | 25 | 2 | 3 | 39 | 51 | 104 | 46 | 8 | .268/.351/.360 | .262 | .347 | 3.3 | 12 | 3.1 |
| | | 2009 | CIN | MLB | 24 | 196 | 27 | 5 | 1 | 8 | 17 | 15 | 49 | 10 | 4 | .267/.323/.439 | .269 | .325 | 0.7 | 0.3 | 0.8 |
| | | 2010 | CIN | MLB | 25 | 583 | 91 | 19 | 6 | 22 | 77 | 55 | 168 | 30 | 6 | .255/.329/.444 | .270 | .330 | 9.2 | 6.2 | 4.0 |
| | | 2011 | CIN | MLB | 26 | 681 | 92 | 22 | 3 | 15 | 44 | 63 | 205 | 40 | 10 | .243/.321/.364 | .250 | .343 | 4.9 | -3.2 | 1.5 |
| | | 2012 | CIN | MLB | 27 | 620 | 73 | 22 | 3 | 20 | 71 | 57 | 173 | 36 | 9 | .252/.326/.414 | .262 | .325 | 1 | CF 2, LF -0 | 2.3 |

Born: 10/4/1984 Age: 27
Bats: R Throws: R Height: 6' 5" Weight: 205
Breakout: 3% Improve: 37% Collapse: 4%
Attrition: 16% MLB: 74%
Comparables:
Chris Dickerson, Keith Miller, Adolfo Phillips

Stubbs is simultaneously one of the most entertaining players to watch and yet one of the most overrated everyday players in baseball. Graceful and acrobatic in center, he's a defender whose gifts are reflected, not amplified by, highlight reel regularity, and he's one of the best baserunners and basestealers around. But his career OPS on the road is 645; he's delivered a .112 ISO on the road compared to .198 at home. That doesn't make him a bad player by any means—because of his gifts, he's been able to exploit his environment quite handily, and not everybody would do as well given the same opportunity. But it limits his value to anyone besides the Reds, especially after he reaches arbitration next winter.

| **Chris Valaika** | **2B** | YEAR | TEAM | LVL | AGE | PA | R | 2B | 3B | HR | RBI | BB | SO | SB | CS | AVG_OBP_SLG | TAv | BABIP | BRR | FRAA | WARP |
|---|---|---|---|---|---|---|---|---|---|---|---|---|---|---|---|---|---|---|---|---|---|
| | | 2009 | LOU | AAA | 23 | 392 | 32 | 20 | 1 | 6 | 36 | 16 | 76 | 1 | 0 | .235/.274/.344 | .216 | .281 | 2.3 | 0.8 | -0.2 |
| | | 2010 | LOU | AAA | 24 | 459 | 49 | 28 | 2 | 4 | 53 | 19 | 72 | 3 | 3 | .304/.334/.408 | .250 | .355 | -4.7 | -3.1 | 0.3 |
| | | 2010 | CIN | MLB | 24 | 40 | 3 | 1 | 0 | 1 | 2 | 1 | 9 | 0 | 0 | .263/.282/.368 | .202 | .321 | -1.6 | 0 | -0.3 |
| | | 2011 | LOU | AAA | 25 | 453 | 39 | 18 | 0 | 7 | 37 | 21 | 65 | 1 | 0 | .261/.302/.355 | .228 | .291 | -2.6 | 8.5 | 0.3 |
| | | 2011 | CIN | MLB | 25 | 27 | 3 | 1 | 1 | 0 | 0 | 2 | 3 | 0 | 0 | .280/.333/.400 | .257 | .318 | 0.4 | 0.4 | 0.2 |
| | | 2012 | CIN | MLB | 26 | 250 | 25 | 11 | 1 | 5 | 25 | 11 | 47 | 0 | 0 | .242/.280/.358 | .223 | .280 | 0 | 2B -0, SS 0 | -0.1 |

Born: 8/14/1985 Age: 26
Bats: R Throws: R Height: 6' 1" Weight: 215
Breakout: 4% Improve: 18% Collapse: 5%
Attrition: 24% MLB: 48%
Comparables:
Jose Castillo, Josh Barfield, Jon Shave

The latest inheritor to the mantle of futility infielder's doom that once hung from the shoulders of the unremarkable, unlamentable Freddy Benavides, Valaika is a working-class utility infielder looking for his Steinbeck and having to settle for the febrile cruelties of our keyboards instead. Oh, the songs that might be sung about his intangibles, if only we had the voices to shout Valaika's name in praise or scorn to the skies above. Oh, the torrents of ink already spilled to grimly observe that he might accost the roster of some team you care for, and worse yet, get serious playing time. Lo, I see a word count worthy of a full-length player comment approaching . . . and there it is—Chris Valaika, everyone! Thank you so much for playing.

### Joey Votto — 1B

**Born:** 9/10/1983 **Age:** 28
**Bats:** L **Throws:** R **Height:** 6' 4'' **Weight:** 220
**Breakout:** 2% **Improve:** 48% **Collapse:** 1%
**Attrition:** 13% **MLB:** 95%

**Comparables:**
Norm Cash, Miguel Cabrera, Mark Teixeira

| YEAR | TEAM | LVL | AGE | PA | R | 2B | 3B | HR | RBI | BB | SO | SB | CS | AVG_OBP_SLG | TAv | BABIP | BRR | FRAA | WARP |
|------|------|-----|-----|-----|-----|----|----|----|-----|-----|-----|----|----|-------------|-----|-------|------|------|------|
| 2009 | CIN | MLB | 25 | 544 | 82 | 38 | 1 | 25 | 84 | 70 | 106 | 4 | 1 | .322/.414/.567 | .326 | .372 | -2 | 2.5 | 4.3 |
| 2010 | CIN | MLB | 26 | 648 | 106 | 36 | 2 | 37 | 113 | 91 | 125 | 16 | 5 | .324/.424/.600 | .348 | .361 | -1.2 | 2.3 | 6.7 |
| 2011 | CIN | MLB | 27 | 719 | 101 | 40 | 3 | 29 | 103 | 110 | 129 | 8 | 6 | .309/.416/.531 | .325 | .349 | -3.9 | 14.2 | 7.2 |
| 2012 | CIN | MLB | 28 | 661 | 100 | 35 | 1 | 33 | 103 | 82 | 124 | 10 | 4 | .305/.394/.546 | .326 | .337 | -0.6 | 1B 7 | 5.4 |

To belabor the obvious, there's an impressive consistency at work here. There isn't a fastball he can't hurt one way or another—up and in or low and away, he'll hammer it when he offers, and it's very rare to get him to chase after a breaking pitch outside. Most hitters' numbers drop when they face relievers for the first time. The reasons for that are pretty straightforward: pure stuff, securing the platoon advantage, unfamiliarity. Votto beats all of that: his 946 OPS is nifty enough, but it goes up against relievers, to 988 in a first at-bat against them. Some of that's a measure of the inevitable intentional walks, but his power numbers go up as well. You can call that consistency, self-awareness of what he can do and who he can do it to, or you can even call it clutch, since so many of those plate appearances happen late in games. So yeah, he's good.

## PITCHERS

### Jose Arredondo

**Born:** 3/30/1984 **Age:** 28
**Bats:** R **Throws:** R **Height:** 6' 1'' **Weight:** 175
**Breakout:** 28% **Improve:** 53% **Collapse:** 21%
**Attrition:** 9% **MLB:** 81%

**Comparables:**
Matt Lindstrom, Manny Delcarmen, Josh Kinney

| YEAR | TEAM | LVL | AGE | W | L | SV | G | GS | IP | H | HR | BB | SO | EqBB9 | EqSO9 | GB% | BABIP | WHIP | ERA | FIP | FRA | WARP |
|------|------|-----|-----|---|---|----|----|----|-----|----|----|----|----|-------|-------|-----|-------|------|------|------|------|------|
| 2009 | ANA | MLB | 25 | 2 | 3 | 0 | 43 | 0 | 45 | 47 | 6 | 23 | 47 | 4.6 | 9.4 | 45% | .333 | 1.56 | 6.00 | 4.32 | 5.13 | 0.2 |
| 2011 | CIN | MLB | 27 | 4 | 4 | 0 | 53 | 0 | 53 | 43 | 5 | 31 | 48 | 5.3 | 8.2 | 44% | .277 | 1.40 | 3.23 | 4.28 | 4.40 | 0.2 |
| 2012 | CIN | MLB | 28 | 2 | 1 | 0 | 40 | 0 | 42² | 37 | 5 | 18 | 37 | 3.7 | 7.7 | 47% | .296 | 1.28 | 4.06 | 4.26 | 4.41 | 0.4 |

The world may always need ditch-diggers, but it also needs its garbage men, and that's effectively all Arredondo was for the Reds in his comeback campaign from Tommy John surgery. Dusty trusted him just five times all year with leads of three runs or less. His biggest virtue is an assortment that doesn't limit him to situational roles, as he alternates splitters and sliders with a fairly standard low-90s fastball. The greatest threat to his job security is probably his just-acquired arbitration eligibility, because beyond basic competence there's not much to recommend the former shortstop for more than a staff-filler role.

### Bronson Arroyo

**Born:** 2/24/1977 **Age:** 35
**Bats:** R **Throws:** R **Height:** 6' 6'' **Weight:** 180
**Breakout:** 16% **Improve:** 48% **Collapse:** 15%
**Attrition:** 5% **MLB:** 82%

**Comparables:**
Doyle Alexander, Steve Gromek, Rick Wise

| YEAR | TEAM | LVL | AGE | W | L | SV | G | GS | IP | H | HR | BB | SO | EqBB9 | EqSO9 | GB% | BABIP | WHIP | ERA | FIP | FRA | WARP |
|------|------|-----|-----|----|----|----|----|----|------|-----|----|----|-----|-------|-------|-----|-------|------|------|------|------|------|
| 2009 | CIN | MLB | 32 | 15 | 13 | 0 | 33 | 33 | 220¹ | 214 | 31 | 65 | 127 | 2.7 | 5.2 | 46% | .268 | 1.27 | 3.84 | 4.74 | 5.33 | 0.4 |
| 2010 | CIN | MLB | 33 | 17 | 10 | 0 | 33 | 33 | 215² | 188 | 29 | 59 | 121 | 2.5 | 5.0 | 44% | .241 | 1.15 | 3.88 | 4.64 | 4.77 | 1.8 |
| 2011 | CIN | MLB | 34 | 9 | 12 | 0 | 32 | 32 | 199 | 227 | 46 | 45 | 108 | 2.0 | 4.9 | 40% | .281 | 1.37 | 5.07 | 5.68 | 5.48 | -0.2 |
| 2012 | CIN | MLB | 35 | 9 | 12 | 0 | 27 | 27 | 172 | 177 | 31 | 45 | 94 | 2.4 | 4.9 | 42% | .287 | 1.29 | 4.95 | 5.24 | 5.38 | -0.0 |

On the list of mistakes you can't afford, throwing down eight mil for an innings-eating junk-baller is one of those legacy misjudgments, the sort of decision that might have flown during the naughty Aughties, but ends up being a crippling budget-buster nowadays. But giving Arroyo a three-year, $35 million deal in December 2010, when he was already under option for 2011, will rank among the decade's worst deals, even if the Reds softened the blow by deferring payments out to 2021. Arroyo responded to his security by taking a tilt at the single-season homers-allowed records of Jose Lima (48, 2000 NL) and Bert Blyleven (50, 1986 AL). For Arroyo, this wasn't that remarkable a feat; he's a fly-ball pitcher and the Gap's no friend to anyone on the mound. But to make matters worse, his strikeout rate's on a three-year slide as overall strikeout rates climb to historic highs year after year. Arroyo's rate was tied for third-worst among NL ERA title qualifiers. Given that he's already throwing everything including the kitchen sink at people, hoping that he'll find a magic bullet amid all the slop might be hard to expect.

### Homer Bailey

Born: **5/3/1986** Age: **26**
Bats: **R** Throws: **R** Height: **6' 5"** Weight: **205**
Breakout: **27%** Improve: **52%** Collapse: **19%**
Attrition: **19%** MLB: **90%**

Comparables:
Andy Benes, Joe Hesketh, Fernando Nieve

| YEAR | TEAM | LVL | AGE | W | L | SV | G | GS | IP | H | HR | BB | SO | EqBB9 | EqSO9 | GB% | BABIP | WHIP | ERA | FIP | FRA | WARP |
|---|---|---|---|---|---|---|---|---|---|---|---|---|---|---|---|---|---|---|---|---|---|---|
| 2009 | LOU | AAA | 23 | 8 | 5 | 0 | 14 | 14 | 89² | 87 | 10 | 27 | 82 | 2.7 | 8.2 | 46% | .304 | 1.27 | 2.71 | 3.81 | 4.45 | 1.6 |
| 2009 | CIN | MLB | 23 | 8 | 5 | 0 | 20 | 20 | 113¹ | 115 | 12 | 52 | 86 | 4.1 | 6.8 | 43% | .304 | 1.47 | 4.53 | 4.37 | 5.01 | 0.6 |
| 2010 | CIN | MLB | 24 | 4 | 3 | 0 | 19 | 19 | 109 | 109 | 11 | 40 | 100 | 3.3 | 8.3 | 44% | .317 | 1.37 | 4.46 | 3.77 | 4.06 | 1.6 |
| 2011 | LOU | AAA | 25 | 2 | 1 | 0 | 6 | 6 | 30 | 34 | 1 | 6 | 22 | 1.8 | 6.6 | 37% | .333 | 1.33 | 3.00 | 2.81 | 3.97 | 0.5 |
| 2011 | CIN | MLB | 25 | 9 | 7 | 0 | 22 | 22 | 132 | 136 | 18 | 33 | 106 | 2.2 | 7.2 | 41% | .299 | 1.28 | 4.43 | 4.02 | 4.82 | 0.7 |
| 2012 | CIN | MLB | 26 | 6 | 8 | 0 | 20 | 20 | 117¹ | 118 | 16 | 41 | 84 | 3.2 | 6.5 | 44% | .309 | 1.36 | 4.74 | 4.59 | 5.15 | 0.4 |

The annual grumble of the Bailey involved injuries again, as he hurt his throwing shoulder twice (once while hitting). He did make progress, though, getting his strikeout rate back up near 20 percent in the second half. He also walked fewer, used his slider and change more effectively as chase pitches, and had 13 quality starts (four against the Astros) in 22 turns. If he can stay healthy enough to "just" become a fourth-slot rotation mediocrity he has Arroyo's example for the kind of payoffs that can bring.

in the second half. He's not really a LOOGY, since he has a good three-pitch assortment (holding righties to a 659 OPS), and he's not really getting to just let it rip, as he was Baker's fireman within innings, coming in with runners on base as often as not. In Baker's heavily scripted bullpen-usage patterns, Bray may not get a shot at being the next Matt Thornton, and his extensive injury history might argue against it, but the talent's there for him to convert a few save opportunities.

### Aroldis Chapman

Born: **2/28/1988** Age: **24**
Bats: **L** Throws: **L** Height: **6' 5"** Weight: **185**
Breakout: **46%** Improve: **67%** Collapse: **16%**
Attrition: **30%** MLB: **98%**

Comparables:
Dave Righetti, Sam McDowell, Herb Score

| YEAR | TEAM | LVL | AGE | W | L | SV | G | GS | IP | H | HR | BB | SO | EqBB9 | EqSO9 | GB% | BABIP | WHIP | ERA | FIP | FRA | WARP |
|---|---|---|---|---|---|---|---|---|---|---|---|---|---|---|---|---|---|---|---|---|---|---|
| 2010 | LOU | AAA | 22 | 9 | 6 | 8 | 39 | 13 | 95² | 56 | 2 | 36 | 90 | 4.9 | 11.8 | 49% | .344 | 1.35 | 3.57 | 3.18 | 4.10 | 1.9 |
| 2010 | CIN | MLB | 22 | 2 | 2 | 0 | 15 | 0 | 13¹ | 9 | 0 | 5 | 19 | 3.4 | 12.8 | 70% | .333 | 1.05 | 2.03 | 1.38 | 2.99 | 0.3 |
| 2011 | CIN | MLB | 23 | 4 | 1 | 1 | 54 | 0 | 50 | 24 | 2 | 41 | 71 | 7.4 | 12.8 | 54% | .244 | 1.30 | 3.60 | 3.25 | 4.36 | 0.4 |
| 2012 | CIN | MLB | 24 | 2 | 2 | 0 | 29 | 4 | 43¹ | 29 | 3 | 23 | 55 | 4.8 | 11.5 | 49% | .297 | 1.21 | 3.11 | 3.16 | 3.38 | 1.0 |

Like so many overhyped Cuban talents before him, Chapman disappointed lofty expectations, but you're still left with the talent: scary-good triple-digit velocity that he used to strike out almost 40 percent of the batters he faced after he came back up in June. The Reds wanted to look at moving him back into the rotation this winter, but the sore shoulder he came down with in the AFL kept him on the shelf. The trades for Mat Latos and Sean Marshall makes his role a bit ambiguous going into 2012. Although the Rangers' example with Neftali Feliz is there to guide the Reds, it wouldn't be surprising if Chapman succeeds as both a closer and a starting pitcher before he completes the last three seasons of his initial five-year contract.

### Daniel Corcino

Born: **8/26/1990** Age: **21**
Bats: **R** Throws: **R** Height: **6' 0"** Weight: **165**
Breakout: **23%** Improve: **54%** Collapse: **28%**
Attrition: **4%** MLB: **88%**

Comparables:
Camilo Pascual, Lindy McDaniel, Hayden Penn

| YEAR | TEAM | LVL | AGE | W | L | SV | G | GS | IP | H | HR | BB | SO | EqBB9 | EqSO9 | GB% | BABIP | WHIP | ERA | FIP | FRA | WARP |
|---|---|---|---|---|---|---|---|---|---|---|---|---|---|---|---|---|---|---|---|---|---|---|
| 2009 | BIL | RK | 18 | 1 | 4 | 3 | 20 | 0 | 25² | 23 | 2 | 15 | 30 | 5.3 | 10.5 | 44% | .339 | 1.48 | 4.90 | 4.35 | 5.57 | 0.1 |
| 2010 | DYT | A | 19 | 1 | 1 | 0 | 6 | 6 | 31¹ | 31 | 1 | 15 | 29 | 4.3 | 8.3 | — | .335 | 1.47 | 4.31 | 4.09 | 4.91 | 0.1 |
| 2010 | BIL | RK | 19 | 1 | 3 | 0 | 9 | 9 | 39² | 23 | 1 | 10 | 24 | 3.9 | 7.0 | 47% | .293 | 1.39 | 3.40 | 4.10 | 5.26 | -0.6 |
| 2011 | DYT | A | 20 | 11 | 7 | 0 | 26 | 26 | 139¹ | 134 | 10 | 36 | 162 | 2.2 | 10.1 | 41% | .319 | 1.16 | 3.42 | 2.93 | 3.74 | 3.0 |
| 2012 | CIN | MLB | 21 | 2 | 3 | 0 | 8 | 8 | 39 | 41 | 5 | 18 | 26 | 4.2 | 6.1 | 42% | .314 | 1.52 | 5.58 | 4.92 | 6.07 | -0.2 |

Any preconceived notions that right-handers under 6 feet tall might not stick as starters get chucked when they come attached to someone with heat that touches the mid-90s and an effective slider and change with tremendous separation. With those kinds of gifts, this young Dominican's getting taken seriously as a starter, and he rewarded that confidence with a solid full-season debut. He's a long way from ready, and he'll have to dispel concerns over durability year after year, but for the time being he's worth noting as another worthwhile product of the Reds' Caribbean scouting effort.

### Francisco Cordero

Born: 5/11/1975 Age: 37
Bats: R Throws: R Height: 6' 3" Weight: 200
Breakout: 18% Improve: 40% Collapse: 38%
Attrition: 10% MLB: 89%

Comparables:
Hoyt Wilhelm, Roger Clemens, Jay Howell

| YEAR | TEAM | LVL | AGE | W | L | SV | G | GS | IP | H | HR | BB | SO | EqBB9 | EqSO9 | GB% | BABIP | WHIP | ERA | FIP | FRA | WARP |
|---|---|---|---|---|---|---|---|---|---|---|---|---|---|---|---|---|---|---|---|---|---|---|
| 2009 | CIN | MLB | 34 | 2 | 6 | 39 | 68 | 0 | 66² | 58 | 2 | 30 | 58 | 4.1 | 7.8 | 42% | .306 | 1.32 | 2.16 | 3.06 | 3.55 | 1.2 |
| 2010 | CIN | MLB | 35 | 6 | 5 | 40 | 75 | 0 | 72² | 68 | 5 | 36 | 59 | 4.5 | 7.3 | 44% | .296 | 1.43 | 3.84 | 3.95 | 4.44 | 0.8 |
| 2011 | CIN | MLB | 36 | 5 | 3 | 37 | 68 | 0 | 69² | 49 | 6 | 22 | 42 | 2.8 | 5.4 | 50% | .215 | 1.02 | 2.45 | 3.98 | 3.80 | 0.7 |
| 2012 | CIN | MLB | 37 | 3 | 1 | 34 | 62 | 0 | 62 | 52 | 6 | 24 | 54 | 3.4 | 7.8 | 44% | .292 | 1.22 | 3.61 | 3.88 | 3.93 | 0.9 |

To paraphrase Pierre Trudeau, the essential ingredient of free agency is timing; Cordero had it once, getting a four-year, $45 million deal after 2007. Unfortunately, that set him up for serial spurning during this winter's stopperpocalypse, when it seemed like half the closers in baseball were free agents and all of them were getting deals before Cordero did. That's in part because he's no longer the same pitcher, relying heavily on his slider and change to make up for flagging velocity, mirrored in a strikeout rate that has plummeted to 15 percent, less than half what it was in his salad days in Milwaukee. If ever simple save totals were supposed to represent quality you'd put a price on, Cordero would have gotten serious money for his 327 career saves; as we go to press, he hasn't, reflecting the smarter industry he's struggling to survive in.

### Johnny Cueto

Born: 2/15/1986 Age: 26
Bats: R Throws: R Height: 5' 11" Weight: 185
Breakout: 25% Improve: 56% Collapse: 15%
Attrition: 16% MLB: 93%

Comparables:
Bob Welch, Steve Busby, Juan Oviedo

| YEAR | TEAM | LVL | AGE | W | L | SV | G | GS | IP | H | HR | BB | SO | EqBB9 | EqSO9 | GB% | BABIP | WHIP | ERA | FIP | FRA | WARP |
|---|---|---|---|---|---|---|---|---|---|---|---|---|---|---|---|---|---|---|---|---|---|---|
| 2009 | CIN | MLB | 23 | 11 | 11 | 0 | 30 | 30 | 171¹ | 172 | 24 | 61 | 132 | 3.2 | 6.9 | 43% | .294 | 1.36 | 4.41 | 4.65 | 5.24 | 0.4 |
| 2010 | CIN | MLB | 24 | 12 | 7 | 0 | 31 | 31 | 185² | 181 | 19 | 56 | 138 | 2.7 | 6.7 | 44% | .295 | 1.28 | 3.64 | 4.00 | 4.19 | 2.6 |
| 2011 | CIN | MLB | 25 | 9 | 5 | 0 | 24 | 24 | 156 | 123 | 8 | 47 | 104 | 2.7 | 6.0 | 55% | .254 | 1.09 | 2.31 | 3.42 | 3.98 | 1.4 |
| 2012 | CIN | MLB | 26 | 8 | 9 | 0 | 23 | 23 | 137² | 128 | 18 | 41 | 98 | 2.7 | 6.4 | 43% | .289 | 1.23 | 4.35 | 4.37 | 4.73 | 1.0 |

Shoulder trouble early and late kept Cueto from completing his bid for the ERA title, but in two-thirds of a season he did more than that to provide evidence of incipient acedom. He threw quality starts in 18 of 24 turns. His strikeout rate might have dropped, but it was part of an effort to induce more groundball outs, a sensible enough idea while pitching in the Gap. That paid off with more DPs (helped by a great move to first that keeps runners close), shorter at-bats, and being able to pitch deeper into games. As with any pitcher who has health and durability issues, you're going to worry. Add Dusty Baker to the mix and you'd be right to steer clear. But those things were true of Cueto before last year, and this sort of development is worth getting excited about.

### Carlos Fisher

Born: 2/22/1983 Age: 29
Bats: R Throws: R Height: 6' 5" Weight: 225
Breakout: 38% Improve: 52% Collapse: 20%
Attrition: 18% MLB: 76%

Comparables:
Jim Mecir, Dustin Nippert, Edwin Moreno

| YEAR | TEAM | LVL | AGE | W | L | SV | G | GS | IP | H | HR | BB | SO | EqBB9 | EqSO9 | GB% | BABIP | WHIP | ERA | FIP | FRA | WARP |
|---|---|---|---|---|---|---|---|---|---|---|---|---|---|---|---|---|---|---|---|---|---|---|
| 2009 | CIN | MLB | 26 | 1 | 1 | 0 | 39 | 0 | 52¹ | 50 | 4 | 31 | 48 | 5.3 | 8.3 | 45% | .329 | 1.55 | 4.47 | 4.05 | 4.13 | 0.6 |
| 2010 | LOU | AAA | 27 | 1 | 1 | 4 | 30 | 0 | 36¹ | 14 | 3 | 6 | 23 | 2.0 | 9.4 | 38% | .234 | 0.85 | 2.23 | 3.92 | 3.55 | 0.7 |
| 2010 | CIN | MLB | 27 | 1 | 1 | 0 | 18 | 0 | 22¹ | 22 | 1 | 13 | 21 | 5.2 | 8.5 | 43% | .328 | 1.57 | 5.64 | 3.69 | 4.26 | 0.3 |
| 2011 | LOU | AAA | 28 | 2 | 1 | 6 | 32 | 0 | 40¹ | 30 | 4 | 18 | 40 | 4.0 | 8.9 | 43% | .263 | 1.21 | 3.35 | 3.96 | 4.52 | 0.5 |
| 2011 | CIN | MLB | 28 | 0 | 3 | 0 | 17 | 0 | 24 | 25 | 3 | 11 | 17 | 4.1 | 6.4 | 47% | .289 | 1.50 | 4.50 | 4.70 | 4.83 | 0.0 |
| 2012 | CIN | MLB | 29 | 1 | 0 | 0 | 25 | 0 | 32² | 32 | 4 | 14 | 24 | 3.8 | 6.6 | 51% | .313 | 1.42 | 4.90 | 4.64 | 5.33 | -0.0 |

As a claim to fame, Fisher may have to settle for being the loser of the Reds' 19-inning loss to the Phillies on May 25, pitching into a sixth inning out of the pen. As a guy already boxed out by Arredondo for spare warm-body duties, being on the wrong side of glory is becoming something he's familiar with.

### Josh Judy

Born: 2/9/1986 Age: 26
Bats: R Throws: R Height: 6' 5" Weight: 200
Breakout: 28% Improve: 49% Collapse: 22%
Attrition: 25% MLB: 93%

Comparables:
Rich Thompson, Bud Norris, Ramon A. Ramirez

| YEAR | TEAM | LVL | AGE | W | L | SV | G | GS | IP | H | HR | BB | SO | EqBB9 | EqSO9 | GB% | BABIP | WHIP | ERA | FIP | FRA | WARP |
|---|---|---|---|---|---|---|---|---|---|---|---|---|---|---|---|---|---|---|---|---|---|---|
| 2009 | AKR | AA | 23 | 4 | 3 | 11 | 36 | 1 | 49¹ | 41 | 2 | 18 | 67 | 3.3 | 11.5 | 50% | .315 | 1.08 | 3.10 | 2.23 | 3.31 | 1.2 |
| 2010 | COH | AAA | 24 | 3 | 1 | 2 | 38 | 0 | 47 | 31 | 5 | 13 | 38 | 2.7 | 10.5 | 34% | .292 | 1.32 | 2.68 | 4.13 | 4.19 | 0.9 |
| 2011 | COH | AAA | 25 | 6 | 2 | 23 | 50 | 0 | 52 | 44 | 5 | 24 | 57 | 4.3 | 10.4 | 38% | .305 | 1.33 | 3.12 | 3.74 | 4.67 | 0.8 |
| 2011 | CLE | MLB | 25 | 0 | 0 | 0 | 12 | 0 | 14 | 18 | 4 | 4 | 10 | 2.6 | 6.4 | 23% | .326 | 1.57 | 7.07 | 7.06 | 8.62 | -0.5 |
| 2012 | CIN | MLB | 26 | 1 | 0 | 0 | 26 | 0 | 29¹ | 28 | 4 | 11 | 25 | 3.5 | 7.5 | 42% | .310 | 1.34 | 4.65 | 4.40 | 5.05 | 0.1 |

Just a 34th-round pick in 2007, Judy established himself as a quality relief prospect for the Indians after posting big strikeout numbers the past three years. A tall, aggressive reliever with good stuff, Judy boasts a four-seamer that sits in the low 90s and touches 96, while his slider has developed into a plus pitch that can generate whiffs. This two-pitch repertoire can make Judy an extreme fly-ball pitcher, and his struggle to keep the ball down in the zone embittered his cup of coffee in 2011. He has the stuff to succeed as a middle-innings reliever, but he may still need more seasoning.

## Mat Latos

Born: 12/9/1987 Age: 24
Bats: R Throws: R Height: 6' 7" Weight: 225
Breakout: 35% Improve: 61% Collapse: 20%
Attrition: 6% MLB: 99%

Comparables:
Tommy Hanson, Felix Hernandez, Tom Niedenfuer

| YEAR | TEAM | LVL | AGE | W | L | SV | G | GS | IP | H | HR | BB | SO | EqBB9 | EqSO9 | GB% | BABIP | WHIP | ERA | FIP | FRA | WARP |
|---|---|---|---|---|---|---|---|---|---|---|---|---|---|---|---|---|---|---|---|---|---|---|
| 2009 | SAN | AA | 21 | 5 | 1 | 0 | 9 | 9 | 47 | 32 | 0 | 9 | 46 | 1.7 | 8.8 | 41% | .256 | 0.87 | 1.91 | 1.92 | 3.02 | 1.1 |
| 2009 | SDN | MLB | 21 | 4 | 5 | 0 | 10 | 10 | 50² | 43 | 7 | 23 | 39 | 4.1 | 6.9 | 39% | .257 | 1.30 | 4.62 | 4.67 | 5.04 | -0.2 |
| 2010 | SDN | MLB | 22 | 14 | 10 | 0 | 31 | 31 | 184² | 150 | 16 | 50 | 189 | 2.4 | 9.2 | 46% | .275 | 1.08 | 2.92 | 3.03 | 3.20 | 4.0 |
| 2011 | SDN | MLB | 23 | 9 | 14 | 0 | 31 | 31 | 194¹ | 168 | 16 | 62 | 185 | 2.9 | 8.6 | 45% | .288 | 1.18 | 3.47 | 3.13 | 3.65 | 2.3 |
| 2012 | CIN | MLB | 24 | 10 | 9 | 0 | 27 | 27 | 165 | 137 | 16 | 50 | 141 | 2.7 | 7.7 | 44% | .284 | 1.13 | 3.20 | 3.66 | 3.48 | 3.7 |

Latos began last year on the disabled list due to bursitis in his throwing shoulder, and he struggled with his command upon returning. His fastball velocity was down slightly and he had trouble locating his curveball. There were concerns that perhaps the previous season's heavy workload had caught up with him. Then the second half came and Latos looked like his previous self again, with a 2.87 ERA, 8.8 K/9, and 3.8 K/BB in 14 starts. If Latos stays healthy and maintains focus—neither is a given with him—he could develop into one of the game's elite pitchers. That possibility is why the Reds paid so heavily in talent to acquire him to front their rotation, but moving from Petco

Comparables:
Frank Pastore, Juan Oviedo, Don Robinson

balanced against the big-time maybes of Latos, Cueto, and Bailey, Leake may be the closest thing to Don Sutton-style dull consistency in the rotation after he delivered 18 quality starts in 26 turns. He's not an out-and-out soft-tosser as much as a finesse right-hander, moving around the zone with cutters, sinkers, sliders, and changeups. Heading into his age-24 season, he's picking up durability through conditioning while working with the kind of pitch efficiency that might dispel even Dusty-inspired visions of a flameout.

## Sam LeCure

Born: 5/4/1984 Age: 28
Bats: R Throws: R Height: 6' 2" Weight: 205
Breakout: 20% Improve: 57% Collapse: 16%
Attrition: 37% MLB: 77%

Comparables:
Mark Huismann, Colby Lewis, Geraldo Guzman

| YEAR | TEAM | LVL | AGE | W | L | SV | G | GS | IP | H | HR | BB | SO | EqBB9 | EqSO9 | GB% | BABIP | WHIP | ERA | FIP | FRA | WARP |
|---|---|---|---|---|---|---|---|---|---|---|---|---|---|---|---|---|---|---|---|---|---|---|
| 2009 | LOU | AAA | 25 | 10 | 9 | 0 | 25 | 25 | 143¹ | 149 | 17 | 47 | 127 | 2.8 | 7.9 | 40% | .309 | 1.30 | 4.46 | 4.05 | 4.89 | 1.5 |
| 2010 | LOU | AAA | 26 | 8 | 3 | 0 | 15 | 15 | 98 | 63 | 5 | 18 | 68 | 2.1 | 8.0 | 55% | .315 | 1.23 | 3.67 | 3.54 | 4.93 | 0.9 |
| 2010 | CIN | MLB | 26 | 2 | 5 | 0 | 15 | 6 | 48 | 50 | 6 | 25 | 37 | 4.7 | 6.9 | 46% | .308 | 1.56 | 4.50 | 5.06 | 5.06 | 0.1 |
| 2011 | CIN | MLB | 27 | 2 | 1 | 0 | 43 | 4 | 77² | 57 | 10 | 21 | 73 | 2.4 | 8.5 | 48% | .241 | 1.00 | 3.71 | 3.75 | 4.22 | 0.9 |
| 2012 | CIN | MLB | 28 | 3 | 3 | 0 | 20 | 6 | 59² | 60 | 9 | 22 | 42 | 3.3 | 6.4 | 42% | .301 | 1.36 | 4.92 | 4.86 | 5.34 | 0.0 |

On a team with as many week-to-week crises in the rotation as the Reds had to deal with, LeCure was an indispensable man for the five months he was healthy enough to contribute. Calling him a low-velo guy would be a mistake; he's a utility pitcher who can occasionally dial up a 94-mph fastball, but he's also a five-pitch hurler who can hit the corners. He can be spotted in the rotation or handle multi-inning relief chores. If there were ever an "11th man Olympics" LeCure would be on the short list of favorites to medal, and as long as you don't insist he graduate from the role, you're in great shape.

## Kyle Lotzkar

Born: 10/24/1989 Age: 22
Bats: L Throws: R Height: 6' 5" Weight: 200
Breakout: 33% Improve: 64% Collapse: 15%
Attrition: 9% MLB: 73%

Comparables:
Juan Pizarro, Rick Ankiel, Mike Chris

| YEAR | TEAM | LVL | AGE | W | L | SV | G | GS | IP | H | HR | BB | SO | EqBB9 | EqSO9 | GB% | BABIP | WHIP | ERA | FIP | FRA | WARP |
|---|---|---|---|---|---|---|---|---|---|---|---|---|---|---|---|---|---|---|---|---|---|---|
| 2010 | RED | RK | 20 | 1 | 1 | 0 | 8 | 6 | 24¹ | 20 | 1 | 12 | 27 | 4.4 | 10.0 | — | .313 | 1.32 | 3.33 | 4.99 | — | 0.0 |
| 2011 | DYT | A | 21 | 3 | 2 | 0 | 14 | 14 | 66² | 56 | 9 | 30 | 78 | 3.4 | 9.7 | 40% | .272 | 1.14 | 4.32 | 4.80 | 4.96 | 0.6 |
| 2012 | CIN | MLB | 22 | 1 | 1 | 0 | 5 | 3 | 19² | 19 | 3 | 11 | 16 | 4.9 | 7.2 | 39% | .307 | 1.51 | 5.41 | 5.24 | 5.88 | -0.1 |

Five years after he was a supplemental first-rounder in the 2007 draft, the big, fragile Canadian managed a career-high in starts last season; that's now 43 in 4 1/2 seasons. Lotzkar also beaned 15 batters in those 14 turns, but you can understand how he might be working out some latent frustration over his elbow problems. He's still a live-armed prospect despite his many setbacks, but because of the delays the Reds had no choice but to add him to the 40-man roster this winter, another addition who handicaps their roster flexibility next season.

### Sean Marshall

Born: 8/30/1982 Age: 29
Bats: L Throws: L Height: 6' 8" Weight: 205
Breakout: 15% Improve: 47% Collapse: 26%
Attrition: 13% MLB: 95%

**Comparables:**
Rafael Perez, Don Mossi, Billy Pierce

| YEAR | TEAM | LVL | AGE | W | L | SV | G | GS | IP | H | HR | BB | SO | EqBB9 | EqSO9 | GB% | BABIP | WHIP | ERA | FIP | FRA | WARP |
|------|------|-----|-----|---|---|----|---|----|-----|----|----|----|----|-------|-------|-----|-------|------|------|------|------|------|
| 2009 | CHN | MLB | 26 | 3 | 7 | 0 | 55 | 9 | 85¹ | 91 | 10 | 32 | 68 | 3.4 | 7.2 | 52% | .318 | 1.44 | 4.32 | 4.15 | 4.68 | 1.2 |
| 2010 | CHN | MLB | 27 | 7 | 5 | 1 | 80 | 0 | 74² | 58 | 3 | 25 | 90 | 3.0 | 10.8 | 53% | .297 | 1.11 | 2.65 | 2.30 | 3.32 | 1.5 |
| 2011 | CHN | MLB | 28 | 6 | 6 | 5 | 78 | 0 | 75² | 66 | 1 | 17 | 79 | 2.0 | 9.4 | 60% | .322 | 1.10 | 2.26 | 1.83 | 3.16 | 1.5 |
| 2012 | CIN | MLB | 29 | 4 | 1 | 2 | 71 | 0 | 67² | 62 | 7 | 19 | 54 | 2.6 | 7.2 | 50% | .300 | 1.20 | 3.76 | 3.80 | 4.08 | 0.9 |

Marshall retains the vicious curve that's been his trademark up through the levels, and he now mixes in his fastball, which occasionally tops 93 mph, and slider to devastating effect. But although he has a starter's mix, the Cubs adopted an "if it ain't broke" attitude, rather than risk losing an exceptional set-up man. Marshall is a demonstrable asset as a reliever, and with his deal to the Reds he's sure to stay in the pen. He may even be in the saves mix, which could be the best thing for his incipient free agency after 2012, but the Reds have said they're interested in signing him beyond the one year he's under their contractual control.

### Nick Masset

Born: 5/17/1982 Age: 30
Bats: R Throws: R Height: 6' 5" Weight: 190
Breakout: 22% Improve: 65% Collapse: 21%
Attrition: 13% MLB: 90%

**Comparables:**
Matt Wise, Hoyt Wilhelm, Santiago Casilla

| YEAR | TEAM | LVL | AGE | W | L | SV | G | GS | IP | H | HR | BB | SO | EqBB9 | EqSO9 | GB% | BABIP | WHIP | ERA | FIP | FRA | WARP |
|------|------|-----|-----|---|---|----|---|----|-----|----|----|----|----|-------|-------|-----|-------|------|------|------|------|------|
| 2009 | CIN | MLB | 27 | 5 | 1 | 0 | 74 | 0 | 76 | 54 | 6 | 24 | 70 | 2.8 | 8.3 | 55% | .251 | 1.03 | 2.37 | 3.19 | 3.97 | 1.1 |
| 2010 | CIN | MLB | 28 | 4 | 4 | 2 | 82 | 0 | 76² | 64 | 7 | 33 | 85 | 3.9 | 10.0 | 47% | .295 | 1.27 | 3.40 | 3.41 | 4.01 | 1.1 |
| 2011 | CIN | MLB | 29 | 3 | 6 | 1 | 75 | 0 | 70¹ | 76 | 5 | 31 | 62 | 4.0 | 7.9 | 52% | .335 | 1.52 | 3.71 | 3.52 | 4.87 | 0.1 |
| 2012 | CIN | MLB | 30 | 4 | 1 | 2 | 73 | 0 | 68 | 64 | 8 | 25 | 54 | 3.3 | 7.2 | 49% | .307 | 1.30 | 4.21 | 4.25 | 4.57 | 0.5 |

Masset was a nifty deadline pickup for Ken Griffey Jr. in 2008, and since then he's given the Reds three years of durable high-leverage relief as Dusty's designated eighth-inning tight-game guy. Unfortunately, cracks started to show late last summer, as Masset generated fewer swings and misses in the second half, getting hammered for an 898 OPS against and a .412 BABIP. There was no injury that's come to light, so you can try to figure out if it was the workload wearing him down, the league finally catching up to him, or just one of those slippery problems with location and execution that you hope pitching coach Bryan Price can iron out.

### Logan Ondrusek

Born: 2/13/1985 Age: 27
Bats: R Throws: R Height: 6' 9" Weight: 225
Breakout: 18% Improve: 57% Collapse: 12%
Attrition: 12% MLB: 86%

**Comparables:**
Dave Stewart, Cal Eldred, Dock Ellis

| YEAR | TEAM | LVL | AGE | W | L | SV | G | GS | IP | H | HR | BB | SO | EqBB9 | EqSO9 | GB% | BABIP | WHIP | ERA | FIP | FRA | WARP |
|------|------|-----|-----|---|---|----|---|----|-----|----|----|----|----|-------|-------|-----|-------|------|------|------|------|------|
| 2009 | CAR | AA | 24 | 2 | 1 | 7 | 24 | 0 | 32² | 21 | 0 | 12 | 24 | 3.3 | 6.6 | 53% | .233 | 1.01 | 1.65 | 2.73 | 2.89 | 0.8 |
| 2009 | LOU | AAA | 24 | 0 | 0 | 12 | 19 | 0 | 20² | 16 | 1 | 2 | 15 | 0.9 | 4.8 | 59% | .217 | 0.87 | 1.74 | 2.76 | 3.87 | 0.3 |
| 2010 | CIN | MLB | 25 | 5 | 0 | 0 | 60 | 0 | 58² | 49 | 7 | 20 | 39 | 3.1 | 6.0 | 50% | .243 | 1.18 | 3.68 | 4.35 | 4.43 | 0.4 |
| 2011 | CIN | MLB | 26 | 5 | 5 | 0 | 66 | 0 | 61¹ | 55 | 6 | 28 | 41 | 4.1 | 6.0 | 51% | .261 | 1.35 | 3.23 | 4.40 | 5.50 | -0.4 |
| 2012 | CIN | MLB | 27 | 3 | 1 | 0 | 54 | 0 | 54¹ | 54 | 7 | 21 | 30 | 3.5 | 5.0 | 47% | .292 | 1.39 | 4.89 | 4.93 | 5.32 | -0.0 |

Baker likes using this hulking righty in tandem with Bray in the seventh and eighth innings, but, as with the southpaw, it isn't strictly situational. He used both every other day last year until August, when Ondrusek landed on the DL with a strained forearm after appearing in 56 of the Reds' first 114 games; he wasn't as effective after he was reactivated at the end of the month. As with Masset's second-half breakdown, you can wonder how much of it was a product of asking too much, because what doesn't get reflected in a simple appearances count is the number of times a guy warms up and sits back down, used or unused. If he's healthy, he should be able to build on last year's four-month run of effectiveness.

### Jordan Smith

Born: 2/4/1986 Age: 26
Bats: R Throws: R Height: 6' 5" Weight: 220
Breakout: 42% Improve: 67% Collapse: 15%
Attrition: 25% MLB: 74%

**Comparables:**
Dick Drago, Chris Mears, Curt Barclay

| YEAR | TEAM | LVL | AGE | W | L | SV | G | GS | IP | H | HR | BB | SO | EqBB9 | EqSO9 | GB% | BABIP | WHIP | ERA | FIP | FRA | WARP |
|------|------|-----|-----|---|---|----|---|----|-----|----|----|----|----|-------|-------|-----|-------|------|------|------|------|------|
| 2009 | CAR | AA | 23 | 5 | 3 | 0 | 13 | 13 | 73¹ | 77 | 4 | 21 | 39 | 2.6 | 4.8 | 52% | .305 | 1.34 | 3.44 | 3.69 | 4.41 | 0.5 |
| 2010 | CAR | AA | 24 | 1 | 3 | 9 | 27 | 0 | 28¹ | 29 | 3 | 6 | 11 | 2.5 | 4.5 | 54% | .356 | 1.63 | 5.09 | 4.79 | 5.98 | -0.2 |
| 2010 | CIN | MLB | 24 | 3 | 2 | 1 | 37 | 0 | 42 | 45 | 7 | 11 | 26 | 2.4 | 5.6 | 51% | .288 | 1.33 | 3.86 | 4.96 | 5.98 | -0.5 |
| 2011 | LOU | AAA | 25 | 0 | 4 | 7 | 24 | 0 | 26¹ | 25 | 2 | 9 | 13 | 3.1 | 4.4 | 49% | .277 | 1.29 | 3.08 | 4.38 | 5.53 | 0.0 |
| 2011 | CIN | MLB | 25 | 0 | 0 | 0 | 17 | 0 | 20 | 32 | 5 | 8 | 13 | 3.6 | 5.8 | 44% | .420 | 2.00 | 7.20 | 4.99 | 5.86 | -0.3 |
| 2012 | CIN | MLB | 26 | 1 | 0 | 0 | 29 | 0 | 32¹ | 38 | 5 | 11 | 13 | 3.0 | 3.7 | 51% | .310 | 1.50 | 5.92 | 5.43 | 6.44 | -0.4 |

Smith's brief run as a situational sinkerballer may have already shot its bolt. He was out of a big-league job little more than a month into the season, and he later lost time to a sore shoulder. Given the crush of prospects nowhere close to ready on the 40-man, bubble guys like Smith are in particular danger of being squeezed out. There isn't a ton of cause to want Smith in the first place, but the Reds have insisted on carrying him on the 40-man as we go to press.

**J.C. Sulbaran**

Born: 11/9/1989 Age: 22
Bats: R Throws: R Height: 6' 3" Weight: 220
Breakout: 13% Improve: 41% Collapse: 38%
Attrition: 14% MLB: 75%

**Comparables:**
Dick Drott, Gil Patterson, Rich Hand

| YEAR | TEAM | LVL | AGE | W | L | SV | G | GS | IP | H | HR | BB | SO | EqBB9 | EqSO9 | GB% | BABIP | WHIP | ERA | FIP | FRA | WARP |
|---|---|---|---|---|---|---|---|---|---|---|---|---|---|---|---|---|---|---|---|---|---|---|
| 2009 | DYT | A | 19 | 5 | 5 | 0 | 21 | 21 | $92^2$ | 94 | 19 | 51 | 100 | 5.0 | 9.7 | 34% | .314 | 1.56 | 5.24 | 6.29 | 6.98 | -0.9 |
| 2010 | DYT | A | 20 | 4 | 6 | 0 | 16 | 15 | $79^1$ | 65 | 6 | 42 | 68 | 5.6 | 9.4 | 44% | .303 | 1.60 | 4.99 | 4.96 | 5.03 | 0.0 |
| 2011 | BAK | A+ | 21 | 7 | 3 | 0 | 26 | 26 | 137 | 140 | 10 | 50 | 155 | 3.3 | 10.2 | 44% | .352 | 1.39 | 4.60 | 4.02 | 4.29 | 2.1 |
| 2012 | CIN | MLB | 22 | 2 | 4 | 0 | 8 | 8 | 42 | 43 | 6 | 22 | 31 | 4.8 | 6.6 | 39% | .309 | 1.55 | 5.86 | 5.16 | 6.37 | -0.3 |

It wasn't a pretty season in the aggregate, but the former pitcher from the Dutch Olympic and WBC team delivered his best all-around effort yet. The Cal League is no easy place to pitch, and Sulbaran's in-season improvements included better groundball and walk rates in the second half, not to mention just four hit batsmen after pelting 10 in his first 13 starts. There's still a question over his effort, and his ultimate upside isn't great, but if he harnesses an occasionally plus curve and change to complement a fastball that sits around 90, he could pitch his way into back-end rotation opportunities.

| | TEAM | LVL | AGE | PA | R | 2B | 3B | HR | RBI | BB | SO | SB-CS | AVG/OBP/SLG | TAv | BABIP | BRR | FRAA | WARP |
|---|---|---|---|---|---|---|---|---|---|---|---|---|---|---|---|---|---|---|
| C T. Barnhart | DYT | A | 20 | 372 | 47 | 24 | 2 | 3 | 45 | 37 | 87 | 2-1 | .273/.344/.367 | .267 | .320 | 0.0 | -0.0 | 2.7 |
| DH S. Buckley | BIL | RK | 21 | 258 | 38 | 11 | 3 | 14 | 41 | 23 | 73 | 6-4 | .289/.372/.551 | .329 | .364 | -1.4 | -22.8 | 0.2 |
| 1B D. Dorn | LOU | AAA | 26 | 494 | 52 | 30 | 1 | 18 | 74 | 36 | 133 | 2-0 | .248/.310/.440 | .249 | .309 | 0.9 | 1.9 | 0.3 |
| CF R. LaMarre | BAK | A+ | 22 | 503 | 78 | 17 | 3 | 6 | 47 | 42 | 97 | 52-14 | .279/.347/.371 | .259 | .339 | 2.2 | 7 | 2.7 |
| 1B D. Lutz | DYT | A | 22 | 506 | 85 | 23 | 3 | 20 | 75 | 34 | 125 | 5-4 | .301/.358/.492 | .307 | .375 | 0.0 | -0.9 | 3.1 |
| SS K. Negron | LOU | AAA | 25 | 465 | 54 | 16 | 4 | 9 | 45 | 22 | 102 | 11-1 | .216/.269/.338 | .209 | .260 | 5.3 | -4.9 | -1.0 |
| RF B. Rhinehart | CAR | AA | 26 | 137 | 21 | 5 | 0 | 7 | 29 | 17 | 30 | 1-1 | .287/.380/.513 | .302 | .321 | 0.0 | -0.8 | 0.8 |
| | HAR | AA | 26 | 323 | 55 | 17 | 2 | 21 | 59 | 39 | 59 | 1-1 | .283/.376/.587 | .329 | .286 | -0.2 | -2.8 | 2.4 |
| 3B D. Vidal | DYT | A | 21 | 514 | 85 | 37 | 1 | 20 | 85 | 44 | 111 | 3-2 | .280/.350/.498 | .315 | .325 | -2.9 | -7.1 | 4.2 |
| RF K. Waldrop | BIL | RK | 19 | 293 | 38 | 22 | 9 | 5 | 29 | 10 | 65 | 4-4 | .273/.305/.471 | .284 | .340 | -0.5 | -0.1 | 0.7 |

The Reds may have dealt catching in the Latos deal, but there's potentially more on tap in the form of **Tucker Barnhart**, a small catcher with a great arm (nabbing thieves at a 48 percent clip) and patience at the plate who passed his full-season debut with flying colors. ⊘ Far from just being a nepotista, **Sean Buckley,** son of the Reds scouting director, showed excellent power after getting taken in the sixth round of the 2011 draft. ⊘ **Danny Dorn**'s simply in the wrong organization to break through. He's not not much of an outfielder, and loses at least 200 points of OPS when a lefty pitches. ⊘ **Ryan LaMarre** played a better center than expected in his full-season debut; the longer he does that, the better his chances of beating a tweener's rap. ⊘ **Donald Lutz** may well be the best prospect out of Germany, but he has to pick up the finer points of first-base play, he struggles against lefties, and he's years away from being ready. ⊘ After a terrible 2011, **Kris Negron** might best serve as a warning to the Reds' horde of shortstops who don't play short that well and don't hit enough to get looks anywhere else. ⊘ Part of the package received for Jonny Gomes, "Kaiser" **Bill Rhinehart**'s big combined numbers in Double-A might gull you into seeing a prospect but he's spent most of the last four years in the Eastern League last year was his first genuinely good season and he's already 27. ⊘ **David Vidal** made progress at the hot corner while stepping up his power production in-season. Expect a Cal League breakout. ⊘ The other **Kyle Waldrop** is a toolsy two-sport star who might never create more confusion with the Twins pitcher, but his power potential deserves notice, so don't say we didn't warn you.

## PITCHERS

| PLAYER | TEAM | LVL | AGE | W | L | SV | IP | H | HR | BB | SO | EqBB9 | EqSO9 | GB% | BABIP | WHIP | ERA | FIP | FRA | WARP |
|---|---|---|---|---|---|---|---|---|---|---|---|---|---|---|---|---|---|---|---|---|
| T. Cingrani | BIL | RK | 22 | 2 | 2 | 0 | 51$^1$ | 35 | 1 | 6 | 80 | 1.1 | 14.0 | 49% | .330 | 0.80 | 1.75 | 1.80 | 2.03 | 2.2 |
| T. Crabbe | DYT | A | 23 | 2 | 2 | 1 | 24$^2$ | 21 | 2 | 7 | 20 | 2.6 | 9.1 | 53% | .288 | 1.18 | 3.65 | 3.89 | 4.79 | 0.2 |
|  | BAK | A+ | 23 | 1 | 3 | 0 | 111 | 97 | 9 | 46 | 123 | 3.7 | 10.0 | 49% | .312 | 1.29 | 3.41 | 4.15 | 4.22 | 1.7 |
| I. Guillon | BIL | RK | 19 | 3 | 3 | 0 | 63 | 78 | 11 | 46 | 61 | 6.6 | 8.7 | 42% | .362 | 1.97 | 6.57 | 6.97 | 6.85 | -0.5 |
| D. Hayes | DYT | A | 23 | 2 | 2 | 22 | 60 | 31 | 3 | 27 | 92 | 4.1 | 13.4 | 45% | .241 | 0.93 | 1.35 | 2.39 | 3.34 | 1.3 |
| J. Horst | LOU | AAA | 25 | 1 | 2 | 0 | 51$^1$ | 41 | 2 | 14 | 42 | 2.5 | 7.4 | 46% | .267 | 1.07 | 2.81 | 3.04 | 4.44 | 0.8 |
|  | CIN | MLB | 25 | 0 | 0 | 0 | 15$^1$ | 18 | 2 | 6 | 9 | 3.5 | 5.3 | 39% | .308 | 1.57 | 2.93 | 4.69 | 5.95 | -0.1 |
| D. Joseph | CAR | AA | 23 | 1 | 3 | 8 | 58$^1$ | 62 | 7 | 30 | 64 | 4.6 | 10.2 | 48% | .353 | 1.66 | 6.94 | 4.47 | 5.03 | 0.4 |
| C. Manno | HAG | A | 22 | 1 | 2 | 12 | 43$^1$ | 20 | 1 | 15 | 69 | 3.1 | 14.3 | 39% | .244 | 0.81 | 1.04 | 2.10 | 2.71 | 1.2 |
| C. Reineke | LOU | AAA | 29 | 6 | 5 | 1 | 126$^2$ | 143 | 13 | 39 | 77 | 2.8 | 5.5 | 39% | .312 | 1.44 | 3.84 | 4.38 | 5.11 | 0.7 |
|  | CIN | MLB | 29 | 0 | 1 | 0 | 6$^2$ | 5 | 2 | 6 | 3 | 8.1 | 4.1 | 40% | .167 | 1.65 | 6.75 | 9.14 | 7.58 | -0.2 |
| D. Renken | DYT | A | 22 | 6 | 8 | 0 | 113$^1$ | 99 | 10 | 39 | 141 | 3.1 | 11.2 | 49% | .326 | 1.22 | 3.18 | 3.21 | 4.00 | 1.9 |
|  | BAK | A+ | 22 | 1 | 0 | 0 | 30 | 36 | 4 | 13 | 24 | 3.9 | 7.2 | 35% | .333 | 1.63 | 4.80 | 5.77 | 5.60 | 0.1 |
| K. Texeira | KCA | MLB | 25 | 0 | 0 | 0 | 6$^1$ | 13 | 0 | 3 | 0 | 4.3 | 0.0 | 53% | .406 | 2.53 | 2.84 | 4.48 | 5.30 | 0.0 |

With their third-round pick of the 2011 draft, the Reds selected **Tony Cingrani**, a hard-throwing lefty out of Rice; having gotten his debut out the way, he could move up the ladder quickly. ⊘ While **Tim Crabbe** might be easy to overlook in a system stocked with bigger names, he's an athletic righty whose heat touches the mid-90s, and he complements it with a sharp slider. ⊘ Venezuelan tyro **Ismael Guillon** struggled badly with his low-90s/changeup mix at Billings. ⊘ As a college pitcher out of Vanderbilt picked in the 11th round of the 2010 draft, **Drew Hayes** was supposed to dominate in the Midwest League and did, but his heat touches the mid-90s, and that's more interesting than his save total. ⊘ Being left-handed and throwing a tick harder than most southpaws got **Jeremy Horst** a regular seat on the Louisville shuttle, but his struggle to acquire any mastery over his fellow lefties made him an easy choice to outright off the 40-man. ⊘ Whatever hopes there were that **Donnie Joseph** would be in his element as a power lefty prospect out of the pen got scragged by Southern League hitters. ⊘ The *objet de désir* received from the Nats in the Gomes dump, **Chris Manno** is a power lefty arm out of Duke who mowed down less-advanced kids in the Sally League. ⊘ Two years in the Reds organization might have brought native Ohioan **Chad Reineke** closer to pitching in front of friends and family, but as a sixth-starter wannabe, he's just roster flotsam searching for some suitably desperate team to give him a shot. ⊘ Not much was expected from 2010 25th-rounder **Daniel Renken**, but the Cal State-Fullerton product carved his way through the Midwest League with sharp command. ⊘ **Kanekoa Texeira** has an occasionally nice breaking pitch that isn't quite good enough to separate him from two-dozen other candidates for 12th man on a staff.

# MANAGER: DUSTY BAKER

| YEAR | TEAM | W-L | Pythag +/– | Avg PC | 100+ P | 120+ P | QS | BQS | REL | REL w Zero R | IBB | Subs | PH | PH Avg | PH HR | SB2 | CS2 | SB3 | CS3 | SAC Att | SAC % | POS SAC | Squeeze | Swing | In Play |
|------|------|-----|------------|--------|--------|--------|----|-----|-----|--------------|-----|------|-----|--------|-------|-----|-----|-----|-----|---------|-------|---------|---------|-------|---------|
| 2009 | CIN | 78-84 | 0 | 98.7 | 89 | 2 | 77 | 4 | 477 | 320 | 36 | 43 | 251 | .227 | 4 | 15 | 4 | 1 | 1 | 137 | 73.0% | 47 | 4 | 122 | 98 |
| 2010 | CIN | 91-71 | 1 | 195.5 | 158 | 157 | 111 | 5 | 501 | 408 | 64 | — | 512 | .236 | 20 | 14 | 5 | 0 | 2 | 200 | 75.0% | 68 | 6 | 322 | 99 |
| 2011 | CIN | 79-83 | 1 | 95.5 | 67 | 2 | 90 | 7 | 502 | 398 | 47 | — | 240 | .286 | 8 | 12 | 6 | 0 | 1 | 110 | 78.2% | 39 | 2 | 377 | 131 |

Dusty might get a "good fundamentals" rep but he's a fairly passive tactician on offense—not especially bunt-crazy or prone to setting his baserunners loose on the league to do much more than eliminate the double play. He struggled to find a reliable top-of-the-order combination to bat in front of Joey Votto, but he didn't have any obvious choices to make, and if the job-sharing arrangements at shortstop and left field flopped, he got good mileage out of his catching combo. On the pitching side

# Cleveland Indians

Rebuilding a major league baseball team is a precarious undertaking. Even if the process could be guaranteed to result in a contending team, intentionally reducing the quality of any major league roster risks alienating fans. The Indians began their current rebuild by trading CC Sabathia just nine months after blowing a three-games-to-one lead in the American League Championship Series, creating a radical change in the team's short-term outlook. It's no surprise that the organization wants to emerge from their rebuild just as quickly, but it is not clear that the team is as ready to contend as the front office would like to believe.

The Indians were the most surprising team in the majors in the first half of the 2011 season. Expected to linger near the bottom of the standings while graduating their top prospects and sorting out the players received in the 16 major-leaguers-for-prospects trades they had made over the previous three seasons, the Indians shot to the top of the American League Central in the season's opening week and spent just six days out of first place prior to July 21. Sensing an opportunity, Cleveland took advantage of a down year for the Rockies (10 games out in the National League West on July 21) and nabbed ace Ubaldo Jimenez for two top pitching prospects and two other minor leaguers.

The bold move brought in a tremendously talented young pitcher with a team-friendly contract, but it was too bold. Yes, the Indians were still in first place on July 21, and were just a game and a half back when Jimenez arrived in Cleveland. But they were also just 53-51 on the season at that point and had gone 33-43 dating back to May 4. The Indians were contenders for most of the summer of 2011 in part because they had a fluky 20-8 start to their season. That opening run included 11 wins against the Royals, Mariners, and Orioles, three more against a Red Sox team that couldn't get out of its

own way to start the season (or, as it turned out, to end it), and a pair of one-run wins against the Tigers.

The other reason they were still in contention was a lack of competition. The Twins were a disaster from Opening Day. The Royals were never expected to contend, and didn't. The White Sox were unable to get over the hump, not once getting above .500 between April 16 and August 14, and the eventual division champion Tigers started out in a 12-17 hole. They seemed ready to pass the Indians in mid-June, but then played .500 ball for a month and a half before finally hitting hyperdrive after the trading deadline.

The Indians, meanwhile, went 60-74 (.448) after that hot 28-game start and were outscored 660-554 over those final 134 games. After April, the only months during which they weren't significantly below .500 were May and August. In the former, they were outscored and went 12-12 after their 28th game of the season, while in the latter they went 15-13, but only outscored their opponents by one run, 125-124. The Indians' contention wasn't so much a fluke as it was an illusion.

It's hard to criticize any team for adding a pitcher as talented as Jimenez, who finished third in the NL Cy Young voting in 2010 and whose stuff rivals Justin Verlander's even if his command of it doesn't. Jimenez just turned 28 and will receive a paltry $4.2 million for the coming season. Even his options for the 2013 and 2014 seasons are team-friendly; the latter tops out at $9 million even if he reaches the innings and/or award requirements that increase the amount. However, having been traded, Jimenez now has the option to void that 2014 option, which means the Indians may have traded six years each of Drew Pomeranz, the 6-foot-5 lefty who was the fifth overall pick in the 2010 draft, and righty Alex White, the 15th overall pick in 2009, for only two years

| INDIANS PROSPECTUS | | | |
|---|---|---|---|
| 2011 W-L: 80-82, 2nd in AL Central | | | |
| Pythag | .464 | 23rd | **Ballpark:** Progressive Field (3-yr. PF: 96). Getting progressively more pitcher friendly |
| RS/G | 4.35 | 16th | |
| RA/G | 4.69 | 24th | |
| TAv | .265 | 10th | **2011:** Early-season success is a mirage, but higher-upside players acquired as the year goes on |
| TAv-P | .274 | 26th | |
| FIP | 4.10 | 22nd | |
| DER | .707 | 19th | **2012:** A solid young core plus Masterson and Jimenez could contend if the breaks go their way |
| DL | 742 | 15th | |
| B-Age | 27.8 | 5th | |
| P-Age | 26.4 | 1st | **Action Items:** Better fielding, a first baseman, pitching depth, the old Ubaldo Jimenez |
| Salary | $49.4 | 26th | |
| M$/MW | $1.16 | 3rd | |

of Jimenez. Even if Jimenez is inexpensive in dollars, he cost a lot in terms of talent. His acquisition was a win-now move for a team that doesn't appear ready to win now.

The Indians' dirty little secret is that their rebuild hasn't really gone particularly well. Cleveland traded the previous-year's AL Cy Young award winner in consecutive seasons, Sabathia in 2008, Cliff Lee in 2009. While those two helped deliver their new teams three pennants, the Indians and their fans found solace in the potential of the players acquired in those trades. Unfortunately, that potential is quickly eroding. The key player acquired in the Sabathia trade, first baseman Matt LaPorta, was supposed to be a masher in the heart of the lineup. He's now 27 and a career .238/.304/.397 hit-

knife himself: Tommy John surgery in September. He'll be 26 before he appears in another major league game.

In the Baseball Prospectus annual last year, we ran a list of the 29 players the Indians acquired in the 16 trades mentioned above. Scanning it now, there is very little to get excited about. Stealing Carlos Santana from the Dodgers for Casey Blake was a masterstroke, as Santana is quickly emerging as one of the best young catchers in the game. After Santana, Justin Masterson, a third starter, and Chris Perez, a closer with a rapidly declining strikeout rate, are the other two solid performers out of that entire list of 29 men.

Of course, there's more to the Indians than those 29, but optimism for the coming season is limited. Top prospects Jason Kipnis and Lonnie Chisenhall arrived last season to take over second and third base, but they combined for just 373 major league plate appearances and an aggregate .304 on-base percentage. Both likely need a few seasons of development and adjustment at the big league level before they fulfill their potential—if ever. Left fielder Nick Weglarz was supposed to emerge alongside those two and provide another middle-of-the-order bat, but injuries scuttled his season and may be a chronic concern for the 24-year-old. The Indians could expect a bounceback season from 29-year-old right fielder Shin-Soo Choo, whose run as the most underrated player in baseball was interrupted last year by a drunk driving arrest and a pair of injuries. That added production could be undermined by a regression from shortstop Asdrubal Cabrera, who more than doubled his career total with 25 home runs last year, many of which barely cleared the outfield wall. Travis Hafner has settled in at a reduced but still valuable level of production, buoyed as

much by his on-base skills as his power, but an ugly platoon split and nagging injuries prevent him from being a full-time solution at designated hitter.

One particularly telling transaction was the decision to bring back Grady Sizemore. After declining his $9 million option, the team devised an incentive-laden one-year deal with a base salary of $5 million and a promise of much center field playing time. The new deal could be worth $9.5 million if he makes 650 plate appearances and wins the Comeback Player of the Year award. Sizemore is now 29 years old, played in just 104 games over the last two seasons while hitting .220/.280/.379, and hasn't stolen a base and hit a home run in the same season since 2009. It's unclear if the actual

the World Series, they traded minor league lefty reliever Chris Jones to the Braves for the final year of Derek Lowe's contract and two-thirds of Lowe's salary. If the Jimenez deal was hard to criticize because of the quality of the pitcher the Indians received, the Lowe trade was hard to criticize because of how little it cost them. Jones is a non-prospect who has yet to pitch above A-ball, and Lowe will cost the Indians just $5 million, giving them a veteran top two in their rotation of Jimenez and Lowe for a combined $9.2 million. Add Masterson, control ninja Josh Tomlin, and whatever they can get out of Fausto Carmona, and the Indians' rotation looks to be a strength, but it might be better on paper than in reality. Consider that the 38-year-old Lowe has posted an 86 ERA+ since leaving the Dodgers after the 2008 season. Jimenez, meanwhile, lost a couple of miles per hour off his fastball last year, has seen his groundball rate erode over the last three seasons, and posted a 5.10 ERA in his first 11 starts in the DH league.

Still, one can see the upside on the Indians roster. Jimenez should be an ace. Lowe could be a solid number two. Masterson could be a strong three. Their high-leverage relief could be an asset with sophomore Vinnie Pestano in the primary set-up role behind Chris Perez, and rookie Zach Putnam ready to join in alongside righty Joe Smith and lefty Rafael Perez. Choo could have a big comeback season, as could Sizemore. Kipnis and Chisenhall could find their feet more quickly than expected. Santana could have a major breakout season. Asdrubal Cabrera, who is entering his age-26 season, could retain more of his seemingly fluky power than expected. Heck, even LaPorta could find himself in his age-27 season.

That could all happen, but it's not very likely. The cold, hard facts are that their rebuild hasn't been terribly fruitful. Without LaPorta or Weglarz fulfilling expectations, and with Hafner and Sizemore diminished, the lineup looks underpowered, and there are no significant reinforcements on the way. The Royals look to be the team of the near future in the AL Central. But with the Twins out of the way, the White Sox foundering, and the Tigers still vulnerable—particularly with Verlander likely to regress some from his MVP season—now may well be the time for the Indians to strike. Their chances aren't great, and it will be painful if Jimenez leaves for a big free agent payday after failing to turn Cleveland into a winner, but that's rebuilding. Sometimes things go awry and you have to deviate from the plan. The Indians have accelerated their timeframe, and in doing so, have raised the stakes considerably. If this team doesn't turn into a legitimate contender by 2013, it could be back to square one.

# HITTERS

### Michael Brantley    CF

Born: 5/15/1987 Age: 25
Bats: L Throws: L Height: 6' 3" Weight: 200
Breakout: 4% Improve: 31% Collapse: 1%
Attrition: 36% MLB: 79%

**Comparables:**
Joe Keough, Tom Poquette, Manny Jimenez

| YEAR | TEAM | LVL | AGE | PA | R | 2B | 3B | HR | RBI | BB | SO | SB | CS | AVG_OBP_SLG | TAv | BABIP | BRR | FRAA | WARP |
|---|---|---|---|---|---|---|---|---|---|---|---|---|---|---|---|---|---|---|---|
| 2009 | COH | AAA | 22 | 528 | 80 | 21 | 2 | 6 | 37 | 59 | 48 | 46 | 5 | .267/.347/.361 | .253 | .282 | 2.8 | -0.3 | 1.4 |
| 2009 | CLE | MLB | 22 | 121 | 10 | 4 | 0 | 0 | 11 | 8 | 19 | 4 | 4 | .312/.358/.348 | .252 | .376 | 0.2 | -1.3 | 0.1 |
| 2010 | COH | AAA | 23 | 316 | 54 | 13 | 2 | 4 | 29 | 34 | 28 | 13 | 5 | .319/.392/.425 | .277 | .337 | 4.3 | 5.6 | 2.4 |
| 2010 | CLE | MLB | 23 | 325 | 38 | 9 | 3 | 3 | 22 | 22 | 38 | 10 | 2 | .246/.296/.327 | .229 | .271 | 3.5 | -2.5 | -0.1 |
| 2011 | CLE | MLB | 24 | 496 | 63 | 24 | 4 | 7 | 46 | 34 | 76 | 13 | 5 | .266/.318/.384 | .254 | .303 | 0.5 | -4.3 | 0.6 |
| 2012 | CLE | MLB | 25 | 469 | 53 | 20 | 3 | 6 | 44 | 38 | 64 | 18 | 5 | .268/.329/.368 | .253 | .298 | 0.2 | CF -0, LF -2 | 1.0 |

Capable of stealing bases and scoring runs as the Indians' leadoff hitter, Brantley is a great example of a player who is more valuable in fantasy baseball than real baseball. He hasn't become the everyday outfielder the team hoped for, though he did have to play every day, thanks to injuries to his teammates. Lacking the elite strikeout and walk rates he posted as a minor leaguer, Brantley has very little power and isn't a very good defender in spite of his speed. If he could get on base more, the team might be able to hide his below-average arm in left field, but that is his only route to a future as something more than a fourth outfielder. If he returns from late season hamate bone surgery to a regular role in 2012, it will only be because the Indians lack better options.

### Asdrubal Cabrera    SS

Born: 11/13/1985 Age: 26
Bats: B Throws: R Height: 6' 1" Weight: 170
Breakout: 4% Improve: 33% Collapse: 8%
Attrition: 24% MLB: 92%

**Comparables:**
J.J. Hardy, John Valentin, Josh Wilson

| YEAR | TEAM | LVL | AGE | PA | R | 2B | 3B | HR | RBI | BB | SO | SB | CS | AVG_OBP_SLG | TAv | BABIP | BRR | FRAA | WARP |
|---|---|---|---|---|---|---|---|---|---|---|---|---|---|---|---|---|---|---|---|
| 2009 | CLE | MLB | 23 | 581 | 81 | 42 | 4 | 6 | 68 | 44 | 89 | 17 | 4 | .308/.361/.438 | .287 | .360 | 2.6 | -4.3 | 3.3 |
| 2010 | CLE | MLB | 24 | 425 | 39 | 16 | 1 | 3 | 29 | 25 | 60 | 6 | 4 | .276/.326/.346 | .247 | .318 | 0.7 | -2.8 | 1.0 |
| 2011 | CLE | MLB | 25 | 667 | 87 | 32 | 3 | 25 | 92 | 44 | 119 | 17 | 5 | .273/.332/.460 | .287 | .302 | 2.4 | -19.1 | 2.7 |
| 2012 | CLE | MLB | 26 | 580 | 69 | 31 | 2 | 10 | 61 | 44 | 97 | 13 | 5 | .274/.337/.401 | .266 | .313 | -0.2 | SS -10, 2B 0 | 2.8 |

So simply copying last year's "his value is diminished by a lack of power and walks" comment for Asdrubal is out of the question, huh? Cabrera is still below average in terms of walks (though he improved this year and talent evaluators believe he has more growing to do), but an unexpected power outburst rocked the baseball world as Droobs more than tripled his 90th percentile PECOTA home run projection. That he powered to a 13.3 percent HR/FB rate (compared to a career HR/FB of 3.3 percent entering 2011) makes us skeptical he can repeat his prodigious power output. Cabrera can hit for a decent average but below-average defense limits his value.

### Ezequiel Carrera    CF

Born: 6/11/1987 Age: 25
Bats: L Throws: L Height: 5' 11" Weight: 185
Breakout: 2% Improve: 33% Collapse: 8%
Attrition: 28% MLB: 80%

**Comparables:**
Del Unser, Richie Ashburn, Jim Eisenreich

| YEAR | TEAM | LVL | AGE | PA | R | 2B | 3B | HR | RBI | BB | SO | SB | CS | AVG_OBP_SLG | TAv | BABIP | BRR | FRAA | WARP |
|---|---|---|---|---|---|---|---|---|---|---|---|---|---|---|---|---|---|---|---|
| 2009 | WTN | AA | 22 | 405 | 68 | 12 | 4 | 2 | 38 | 59 | 62 | 27 | 13 | .337/.433/.416 | .314 | .396 | 6.5 | 0.1 | 4.1 |
| 2010 | COH | AAA | 23 | 183 | 19 | 7 | 3 | 1 | 16 | 12 | 34 | 11 | 3 | .286/.324/.385 | .251 | .336 | -2.4 | 7.8 | 1.1 |
| 2010 | TAC | AAA | 23 | 243 | 24 | 6 | 2 | 0 | 18 | 20 | 32 | 9 | 5 | .268/.329/.315 | .234 | .303 | -0.8 | 0.8 | 0.1 |
| 2011 | COH | AAA | 24 | 377 | 63 | 8 | 3 | 2 | 25 | 39 | 53 | 35 | 4 | .287/.371/.348 | .246 | .337 | 2.7 | 7.4 | 1.4 |
| 2011 | CLE | MLB | 24 | 226 | 27 | 8 | 3 | 0 | 14 | 16 | 35 | 10 | 5 | .243/.301/.312 | .224 | .293 | 0.1 | -4.4 | -0.6 |
| 2012 | CLE | MLB | 25 | 277 | 30 | 10 | 2 | 1 | 22 | 24 | 48 | 18 | 6 | .259/.329/.335 | .243 | .308 | -0.2 | CF 2, LF -1 | 0.5 |

Carrera has a skill set typical of many toolsy minor leaguers, most of whom wind up as bench players or Triple-A filler: plus speed, plus defense, no power, and a bat that will determine how much value he has to a major league team. Despite hip and hamstring injuries in 2010, Carrera's speed and defense were still very good this past season, during which he made his debut and filled in for various injured Indians outfielders. He could be a second-team starter in left or center if he can maintain the patience he showed in Triple-A this year and slap enough singles around.

**Lonnie Chisenhall 3B**
Born: 10/4/1988 Age: 23
Bats: L Throws: R Height: 6' 2'' Weight: 200
Breakout: 3% Improve: 32% Collapse: 3%
Attrition: 22% MLB: 71%
**Comparables:**
Eric Chavez, Eric Campbell, Andy Carey

| YEAR | TEAM | LVL | AGE | PA | R | 2B | 3B | HR | RBI | BB | SO | SB | CS | AVG_OBP_SLG | TAv | BABIP | BRR | FRAA | WARP |
|------|------|-----|-----|----|----|----|----|----|-----|----|----|----|----|-------------|-----|-------|-----|------|------|
| 2009 | KIN | A+ | 20 | 432 | 59 | 26 | 2 | 18 | 79 | 37 | 80 | 2 | 1 | .276/.346/.492 | .294 | .306 | 0.5 | -3.5 | 2.3 |
| 2009 | AKR | AA | 20 | 101 | 13 | 5 | 1 | 4 | 13 | 7 | 16 | 1 | 0 | .183/.240/.387 | .282 | .178 | 0.3 | -0.8 | 0.5 |
| 2010 | AKR | AA | 21 | 524 | 81 | 22 | 3 | 17 | 84 | 46 | 77 | 3 | 0 | .278/.357/.450 | .286 | .303 | -0.8 | -3.5 | 2.3 |
| 2011 | COH | AAA | 22 | 292 | 45 | 15 | 3 | 7 | 45 | 28 | 47 | 0 | 1 | .267/.353/.431 | .254 | .300 | -0.6 | 1.3 | 0.6 |
| 2011 | CLE | MLB | 22 | 223 | 27 | 13 | 0 | 7 | 22 | 8 | 49 | 1 | 0 | .255/.284/.415 | .254 | .299 | -0.3 | 4.3 | 1.0 |
| 2012 | CLE | MLB | 23 | 268 | 30 | 13 | 1 | 8 | 31 | 17 | 54 | 0 | 0 | .251/.306/.407 | .257 | .287 | 0 | 3B 0 | 1.6 |

Chisenhall was the subject of many a Cleveland bar fight last March over whether he was the team's top prospect. Brawlers fell into two camps: Team Lonnie and Team Jason. While Jason Kipnis had a tremendous rookie debut with the Tribe, Chisenhall

Breakout: 4% Improve: 49% Collapse: 2%
Attrition: 7% MLB: 92%
**Comparables:**
Oscar Gamble, J.D. Drew, Jack Clark

| YEAR | TEAM | LVL | AGE | PA | R | 2B | 3B | HR | RBI | BB | SO | SB | CS | AVG_OBP_SLG | TAv | BABIP | BRR | FRAA | WARP |
|------|------|-----|-----|----|----|----|----|----|-----|----|----|----|----|-------------|-----|-------|-----|------|------|
| 2011 | CLE | MLB | 28 | 358 | 37 | 11 | 3 | 8 | 36 | 36 | 78 | 12 | 5 | .259/.344/.390 | .272 | .317 | 1.2 | 3.7 | 1.6 |
| 2012 | CLE | MLB | 29 | 396 | 51 | 20 | 2 | 11 | 46 | 45 | 85 | 12 | 4 | .274/.368/.438 | .290 | .334 | -0.1 | RF 1, LF -0 | 2.3 |

If there's one thing we learned about Choo last year, it's that he can really hold his liquor; he registered a .20 on the breathalyzer during a DUI arrest. That's some way to show you're thankful for being let out of Korean military duty to continue playing baseball. In terms of on-field issues, Choo suffered through a power and BABIP drop-off, but much of that could be attributed to three separate DL stints, two for an oblique strain. Normally a pull hitter, Choo saw his spray pattern shift toward center, where the ball would die. Presumably the oblique strain limited his range of motion, especially if he was playing through discomfort before he hit the DL. With an offseason to heal up and get his mind straight, Choo should return to star-level production in 2012.

**Trevor Crowe CF**
Born: 11/17/1983 Age: 28
Bats: B Throws: R Height: 6' 1'' Weight: 190
Breakout: 7% Improve: 33% Collapse: 9%
Attrition: 43% MLB: 66%
**Comparables:**
Tyrell Godwin, Keith Smith, Tim Hummel

| YEAR | TEAM | LVL | AGE | PA | R | 2B | 3B | HR | RBI | BB | SO | SB | CS | AVG_OBP_SLG | TAv | BABIP | BRR | FRAA | WARP |
|------|------|-----|-----|----|----|----|----|----|-----|----|----|----|----|-------------|-----|-------|-----|------|------|
| 2009 | COH | AAA | 25 | 219 | 27 | 11 | 1 | 2 | 20 | 30 | 31 | 14 | 7 | .297/.397/.400 | .275 | .344 | 0.4 | 2 | 0.9 |
| 2009 | CLE | MLB | 25 | 202 | 22 | 9 | 3 | 1 | 17 | 11 | 39 | 6 | 0 | .235/.278/.333 | .228 | .288 | -0.6 | 0.8 | -0.1 |
| 2010 | COH | AAA | 26 | 128 | 21 | 4 | 1 | 1 | 13 | 7 | 19 | 6 | 1 | .244/.286/.319 | .217 | .283 | -0.6 | 2.3 | -0.1 |
| 2010 | CLE | MLB | 26 | 479 | 48 | 24 | 3 | 2 | 36 | 29 | 73 | 20 | 7 | .251/.302/.333 | .229 | .297 | -0.1 | 3.9 | 0.1 |
| 2011 | CLE | MLB | 27 | 32 | 6 | 1 | 0 | 0 | 2 | 4 | 9 | 3 | 0 | .214/.312/.250 | .190 | .316 | -0.8 | -0.8 | -0.3 |
| 2012 | CLE | MLB | 28 | 250 | 26 | 12 | 1 | 2 | 21 | 19 | 44 | 11 | 4 | .246/.307/.338 | .237 | .292 | -0.1 | CF 3, LF 1 | 0.1 |

Trevor Crowe, aka Ezequiel Carrera Sr., spent much of 2011 in Triple-A after he received his big opportunity in 2010 and failed to impress. Speed and defense are Crowe's calling cards, though neither is quite as good as Carrera's, and Crowe is three years older. With a career .268/.346/.394 triple-slash at Triple-A, Crowe's bat is less questionable than it is simply insufficient. With few years left before his speed goes into decline, Crowe looks like a Triple-A lifer or a defensive replacement/pinch runner on a bad team.

**Aaron Cunningham RF**
Born: 4/24/1986 Age: 26
Bats: R Throws: R Height: 6' 0'' Weight: 195
Breakout: 3% Improve: 41% Collapse: 7%
Attrition: 22% MLB: 84%
**Comparables:**
Franklin Gutierrez, Joe Hague, Chris Heisey

| YEAR | TEAM | LVL | AGE | PA | R | 2B | 3B | HR | RBI | BB | SO | SB | CS | AVG_OBP_SLG | TAv | BABIP | BRR | FRAA | WARP |
|------|------|-----|-----|----|----|----|----|----|-----|----|----|----|----|-------------|-----|-------|-----|------|------|
| 2009 | SAC | AAA | 23 | 375 | 62 | 24 | 1 | 11 | 48 | 33 | 74 | 11 | 4 | .302/.373/.479 | .304 | .360 | 0.7 | -6.1 | 2.0 |
| 2009 | OAK | MLB | 23 | 57 | 6 | 2 | 0 | 1 | 6 | 3 | 16 | 0 | 0 | .151/.211/.245 | .182 | .194 | -0.4 | -1.7 | -0.6 |
| 2010 | POR | AAA | 24 | 308 | 30 | 17 | 3 | 7 | 45 | 28 | 68 | 2 | 7 | .251/.332/.413 | .253 | .308 | -3.7 | -9.5 | -1.1 |
| 2010 | SDN | MLB | 24 | 147 | 17 | 12 | 1 | 1 | 15 | 7 | 28 | 1 | 3 | .288/.331/.417 | .263 | .349 | -1.3 | -0.4 | 0.1 |
| 2011 | SDN | MLB | 25 | 101 | 12 | 6 | 1 | 3 | 9 | 9 | 17 | 1 | 0 | .178/.257/.367 | .232 | .183 | 0.4 | 0.3 | 0.0 |
| 2012 | CLE | MLB | 26 | 250 | 28 | 14 | 1 | 5 | 27 | 19 | 57 | 4 | 2 | .250/.316/.391 | .256 | .309 | -0.5 | RF -5, LF -3 | 0.7 |

Cunningham hits the ball hard to all fields, runs well, and can play all three outfield spots. The downside is that he doesn't have much home-run power, isn't a good base stealer, and isn't blessed with a strong throwing arm. As he did in each of the three previous seasons, Cunningham split time between Triple-A and the big leagues, never getting an extended look at the higher level. This cycle ultimately led to Cunningham getting traded for the second time in two years, this time from the Padres to the Indians, and he'll now try to latch on as a fourth outfielder for Cleveland.

**Jason Donald** SS
Born: **9/4/1984** Age: **27**
Bats: **R** Throws: **R** Height: **6' 2"** Weight: **195**
Breakout: **2%** Improve: **35%** Collapse: **10%**
Attrition: **27%** MLB: **82%**

**Comparables:**
Jim Fregosi, Derek Jeter, Wayne Krenchicki

| YEAR | TEAM | LVL | AGE | PA | R | 2B | 3B | HR | RBI | BB | SO | SB | CS | AVG/OBP/SLG | TAv | BABIP | BRR | FRAA | WARP |
|------|------|-----|-----|----|---|----|----|----|-----|----|----|----|----|-------------|-----|-------|-----|------|------|
| 2009 | LEH | AAA | 24 | 230 | 26 | 15 | 1 | 1 | 16 | 14 | 53 | 6 | 0 | .236/.298/.332 | .228 | .310 | 0.5 | 4.2 | 0.5 |
| 2010 | COH | AAA | 25 | 165 | 27 | 10 | 2 | 2 | 17 | 21 | 33 | 10 | 2 | .277/.394/.423 | .260 | .350 | 2.5 | 1.5 | 0.8 |
| 2010 | CLE | MLB | 25 | 325 | 39 | 19 | 3 | 4 | 24 | 22 | 70 | 5 | 1 | .253/.312/.378 | .256 | .320 | 3.2 | -1 | 1.1 |
| 2011 | COH | AAA | 26 | 201 | 32 | 12 | 0 | 4 | 15 | 19 | 33 | 7 | 3 | .310/.397/.448 | .274 | .365 | 0.7 | -1.9 | 0.7 |
| 2011 | CLE | MLB | 26 | 143 | 13 | 6 | 1 | 1 | 8 | 7 | 35 | 3 | 2 | .318/.364/.402 | .290 | .423 | 0.2 | -2.8 | 0.8 |
| 2012 | CLE | MLB | 27 | 250 | 27 | 13 | 1 | 3 | 23 | 17 | 57 | 5 | 2 | .254/.315/.361 | .247 | .322 | -0.1 | SS -2, 2B -2 | 1.0 |

Donald's career has been something of a Greek tragedy, with injuries hampering him and relegating him to a bench role. While he hit well down the stretch trying to prove himself, he'll find himself in a utility role again as the Indians play the newer, shinier models. That's probably where he belongs, as he hasn't turned his once-promising tools—good contact hitting, projectable power for a middle infielder—into consistent production at the upper levels. His athleticism will give him value as a reserve who can play average defense backing up second, third, and short.

**Shelley Duncan** LF
Born: **9/29/1979** Age: **32**
Bats: **R** Throws: **R** Height: **6' 6"** Weight: **215**
Breakout: **1%** Improve: **20%** Collapse: **7%**
Attrition: **15%** MLB: **76%**

**Comparables:**
Kevin Barker, Carlton Fisk, Luke Scott

| YEAR | TEAM | LVL | AGE | PA | R | 2B | 3B | HR | RBI | BB | SO | SB | CS | AVG/OBP/SLG | TAv | BABIP | BRR | FRAA | WARP |
|------|------|-----|-----|----|---|----|----|----|-----|----|----|----|----|-------------|-----|-------|-----|------|------|
| 2009 | SWB | AAA | 29 | 527 | 85 | 30 | 1 | 30 | 99 | 64 | 94 | 2 | 0 | .277/.374/.546 | .327 | .290 | -1.7 | -7 | 3.6 |
| 2009 | NYA | MLB | 29 | 15 | 1 | 0 | 0 | 0 | 1 | 0 | 5 | 0 | 0 | .200/.200/.200 | .113 | .300 | -0.3 | 0 | -0.3 |
| 2010 | COH | AAA | 30 | 166 | 21 | 11 | 0 | 6 | 34 | 17 | 28 | 0 | 0 | .301/.382/.500 | .284 | .339 | 1.3 | -1.7 | 0.6 |
| 2010 | CLE | MLB | 30 | 259 | 29 | 10 | 0 | 11 | 36 | 26 | 76 | 1 | 0 | .231/.317/.419 | .269 | .294 | -1.4 | -2.3 | 0.9 |
| 2011 | COH | AAA | 31 | 137 | 20 | 3 | 0 | 5 | 19 | 24 | 24 | 1 | 0 | .202/.350/.367 | .231 | .207 | 0.1 | 2 | 0.1 |
| 2011 | CLE | MLB | 31 | 247 | 29 | 17 | 0 | 11 | 47 | 19 | 56 | 0 | 1 | .260/.324/.484 | .287 | .297 | 1.4 | -0.5 | 1.3 |
| 2012 | CLE | MLB | 32 | 274 | 34 | 12 | 0 | 12 | 35 | 29 | 66 | 1 | 0 | .239/.326/.443 | .275 | .275 | 0 | LF -2, RF -1 | 1.5 |

A former fan favorite in New York, Duncan surely made some new fans in Cleveland with his seven home run September, especially among those fantasy players he won championships for. With Sizemore, Choo, and Brantley chained to the table in the trainer's room, Duncan started in left field and certainly earned himself a roster spot for 2012. But it seems unlikely Duncan will enjoy long-term success as a starter. He's a mammoth of a man with good power and a home run stroke, but he has little in the way of contact or defensive skills and merely average patience.

**Kosuke Fukudome** RF
Born: **4/26/1977** Age: **35**
Bats: **L** Throws: **R** Height: **6' 1"** Weight: **190**
Breakout: **1%** Improve: **21%** Collapse: **10%**
Attrition: **24%** MLB: **68%**

**Comparables:**
Jeff DaVanon, Jim King, Wally Moon

| YEAR | TEAM | LVL | AGE | PA | R | 2B | 3B | HR | RBI | BB | SO | SB | CS | AVG/OBP/SLG | TAv | BABIP | BRR | FRAA | WARP |
|------|------|-----|-----|----|---|----|----|----|-----|----|----|----|----|-------------|-----|-------|-----|------|------|
| 2009 | CHN | MLB | 32 | 603 | 79 | 38 | 5 | 11 | 54 | 93 | 112 | 6 | 10 | .259/.375/.421 | .273 | .310 | -0.5 | -2.1 | 2.1 |
| 2010 | CHN | MLB | 33 | 429 | 45 | 20 | 2 | 13 | 44 | 64 | 67 | 7 | 8 | .263/.371/.439 | .280 | .287 | -0.4 | 1.3 | 1.7 |
| 2011 | CHN | MLB | 34 | 345 | 33 | 15 | 2 | 3 | 13 | 46 | 57 | 2 | 2 | .273/.374/.369 | .269 | .330 | -1.4 | 2.6 | 1.0 |
| 2011 | CLE | MLB | 34 | 258 | 26 | 12 | 1 | 5 | 22 | 15 | 53 | 2 | 4 | .249/.300/.371 | .235 | .298 | -0.8 | 4.7 | 0.1 |
| 2012 | CLE | MLB | 35 | 532 | 62 | 25 | 2 | 9 | 49 | 69 | 99 | 8 | 8 | .252/.351/.376 | .267 | .299 | -2.2 | RF 7, CF -2 | 1.3 |

Fukudome hasn't lived up to the hype he was billed with coming to the States, but he's still an above-average fielder capable of getting on base. Better against righties than lefties, Fukudome's numbers as an Indian took a hit as he started against every lefty save one. He was much more aggressive at the plate, to a fault. He has value as a great platoon player if he can return to his old, more patient approach.

**Travis Hafner** DH
Born: **6/3/1977** Age: **35**
Bats: **L** Throws: **R** Height: **6' 4"** Weight: **240**
Breakout: **3%** Improve: **26%** Collapse: **7%**
Attrition: **30%** MLB: **81%**

**Comparables:**
Frank Thomas, Erubiel Durazo, Andre Thornton

| YEAR | TEAM | LVL | AGE | PA | R | 2B | 3B | HR | RBI | BB | SO | SB | CS | AVG/OBP/SLG | TAv | BABIP | BRR | FRAA | WARP |
|------|------|-----|-----|----|---|----|----|----|-----|----|----|----|----|-------------|-----|-------|-----|------|------|
| 2009 | CLE | MLB | 32 | 383 | 46 | 19 | 0 | 16 | 49 | 41 | 67 | 0 | 0 | .272/.355/.470 | .292 | .297 | -2.7 | 0 | 1.4 |
| 2010 | CLE | MLB | 33 | 462 | 46 | 29 | 0 | 13 | 50 | 51 | 94 | 2 | 1 | .278/.374/.449 | .303 | .332 | -2.1 | 0 | 2.3 |
| 2011 | CLE | MLB | 34 | 368 | 41 | 16 | 0 | 13 | 57 | 36 | 78 | 0 | 0 | .280/.361/.449 | .294 | .332 | -1.2 | 0 | 1.6 |
| 2012 | CLE | MLB | 35 | 366 | 45 | 17 | 0 | 11 | 39 | 43 | 76 | 1 | 0 | .252/.350/.407 | .275 | .299 | 0 | — | 1.3 |

While Hafner was 34 years old this past season, his numbers have not yet begun to show much age-related decline. The injuries are nothing new for him, and he's unlikely to ever play a full season again, having avoided a DL-worthy injury just once since 2004. Still, his power has remained intact to go with good on-base skills. Cleveland will be happy to write Pronk's name on the DH line of the lineup card whenever he's capable of playing—at least against righties, as he's lacked both patience and power versus lefties for several years. He's expensive for what he is, but he's under contract for just one more season.

**Jack Hannahan** 3B
Born: 3/4/1980 Age: 32
Bats: L Throws: R Height: 6' 3" Weight: 205
Breakout: 6% Improve: 34% Collapse: 6%
Attrition: 19% MLB: 79%

Comparables:
Fernando Tatis, Dave Hansen, Roy Smalley

| YEAR | TEAM | LVL | AGE | PA | R | 2B | 3B | HR | RBI | BB | SO | SB | CS | AVG_OBP_SLG | TAv | BABIP | BRR | FRAA | WARP |
|------|------|-----|-----|-----|----|----|----|----|-----|----|----|----|----|-------------|-----|-------|------|------|------|
| 2009 | SAC | AAA | 29 | 88 | 8 | 7 | 0 | 2 | 11 | 7 | 27 | 0 | 1 | .222/.284/.383 | .253 | .308 | 0.1 | 1.1 | 0.2 |
| 2009 | OAK | MLB | 29 | 134 | 12 | 6 | 2 | 1 | 8 | 13 | 36 | 0 | 0 | .193/.278/.303 | .221 | .268 | -0.6 | 4 | 0.2 |
| 2009 | SEA | MLB | 29 | 167 | 15 | 8 | 0 | 3 | 11 | 17 | 35 | 1 | 1 | .230/.311/.345 | .250 | .279 | -0.9 | 0.2 | 0.2 |
| 2010 | TAC | AAA | 30 | 264 | 32 | 9 | 1 | 5 | 33 | 34 | 55 | 1 | 0 | .228/.333/.344 | .246 | .279 | -1.2 | 6 | 0.8 |
| 2010 | PAW | AAA | 30 | 128 | 15 | 8 | 0 | 4 | 12 | 17 | 27 | 2 | 0 | .255/.359/.436 | .272 | .304 | 0.5 | 8.8 | 1.4 |
| 2011 | CLE | MLB | 31 | 366 | 38 | 16 | 2 | 8 | 40 | 38 | 80 | 2 | 1 | .250/.331/.387 | .266 | .308 | -0.8 | 16.8 | 3.1 |

**Jason Kipnis** 2B
Born: 4/3/1987 Age: 25
Bats: L Throws: R Height: 6' 0" Weight: 185
Breakout: 1% Improve: 26% Collapse: 19%
Attrition: 43% MLB: 89%

Comparables:
Danny Richar, Jason Bates, Johnny Ray

| YEAR | TEAM | LVL | AGE | PA | R | 2B | 3B | HR | RBI | BB | SO | SB | CS | AVG_OBP_SLG | TAv | BABIP | BRR | FRAA | WARP |
|------|------|-----|-----|-----|----|----|----|----|-----|----|----|----|----|-------------|-----|-------|------|------|------|
| 2009 | MHV | A- | 22 | 129 | 19 | 8 | 3 | 1 | 19 | 15 | 18 | 3 | 3 | .306/.394/.459 | .328 | .359 | -1.7 | 4.5 | 1.7 |
| 2010 | KIN | A+ | 23 | 237 | 33 | 12 | 3 | 6 | 31 | 24 | 46 | 2 | 3 | .300/.387/.478 | .298 | .359 | 0.9 | -2.3 | 1.4 |
| 2010 | AKR | AA | 23 | 355 | 63 | 20 | 5 | 10 | 43 | 31 | 61 | 7 | 1 | .311/.383/.502 | .303 | .358 | 1 | 3.7 | 3.1 |
| 2011 | COH | AAA | 24 | 400 | 65 | 16 | 9 | 12 | 55 | 44 | 72 | 12 | 1 | .280/.362/.484 | .271 | .318 | 2.1 | 7.1 | 2.2 |
| 2011 | CLE | MLB | 24 | 150 | 24 | 9 | 1 | 7 | 19 | 11 | 34 | 5 | 0 | .272/.333/.507 | .299 | .312 | 0 | -1.5 | 0.9 |
| 2012 | CLE | MLB | 25 | 250 | 30 | 11 | 2 | 7 | 30 | 20 | 53 | 4 | 1 | .257/.325/.426 | .269 | .302 | 0 | 2B 2, LF 0 | 1.8 |

Kipnis burst onto the major league scene like gangbusters in late July. While minor oblique and hamstring injuries put him on the shelf for part of August, by the end of the season Kipnis had left little question as to why he's considered the top prospect in the Indians' system. While his seven home runs were a surprise—powered by a 20.2 percent HR/FB rate—he'll play every day at the keystone in 2012 . His quick, compact swing projects modest 15-20 home run power to go with a good batting average. Moved to second in 2010 to hide his below-average arm, Kipnis will manage to be an average defender while projecting as one of the top offensive weapons at the position.

**Matt LaPorta** 1B
Born: 1/8/1985 Age: 27
Bats: R Throws: R Height: 6' 3" Weight: 210
Breakout: 1% Improve: 35% Collapse: 1%
Attrition: 15% MLB: 68%

Comparables:
Justin Huber, Steve Pearce, Ryan Garko

| YEAR | TEAM | LVL | AGE | PA | R | 2B | 3B | HR | RBI | BB | SO | SB | CS | AVG_OBP_SLG | TAv | BABIP | BRR | FRAA | WARP |
|------|------|-----|-----|-----|----|----|----|----|-----|----|----|----|----|-------------|-----|-------|------|------|------|
| 2009 | COH | AAA | 24 | 393 | 63 | 23 | 2 | 17 | 60 | 42 | 56 | 1 | 3 | .299/.390/.530 | .297 | .316 | -2.2 | -5.9 | 1.1 |
| 2009 | CLE | MLB | 24 | 198 | 29 | 13 | 0 | 7 | 21 | 12 | 37 | 2 | 0 | .254/.308/.442 | .263 | .281 | 1 | 0.2 | 0.5 |
| 2010 | COH | AAA | 25 | 81 | 7 | 4 | 0 | 5 | 16 | 12 | 10 | 0 | 1 | .362/.457/.638 | .334 | .370 | -1 | -0.9 | 0.6 |
| 2010 | CLE | MLB | 25 | 425 | 41 | 15 | 1 | 12 | 41 | 46 | 82 | 0 | 0 | .221/.306/.362 | .241 | .250 | -2.7 | -14 | -2.1 |
| 2011 | CLE | MLB | 26 | 385 | 34 | 23 | 1 | 11 | 53 | 23 | 87 | 1 | 0 | .247/.299/.412 | .269 | .293 | -5.6 | -5.4 | -0.6 |
| 2012 | CLE | MLB | 27 | 381 | 45 | 19 | 1 | 12 | 45 | 33 | 76 | 1 | 1 | .251/.323/.419 | .268 | .287 | -0.1 | 1B -10, LF -1 | 1.1 |

Matt LaPorta's game is right out of a Joe Esposito song, the best arou—wait, that's not right. We thought we were talking about Albert Pujols for a second. While LaPorta once held that kind of potential, the centerpiece of the CC Sabathia deal has done nothing but disappoint in his time in the majors. While he has displayed average power, his plate discipline has been suspect, swinging at more out-of-zone pitches each year he's been at the show. While his .313/.400/.553 line across three Triple-A seasons is excellent, his inability to handle major league breaking pitches has been his downfall.

**Jose Lopez** 3B
Born: 11/24/1983 Age: 28
Bats: R Throws: R Height: 6'3" Weight: 170
Breakout: 1% Improve: 42% Collapse: 3%
Attrition: 14% MLB: 75%
Comparables:
Buddy Bell, Angel Chavez, Frank Malzone

| YEAR | TEAM | LVL | AGE | PA | R | 2B | 3B | HR | RBI | BB | SO | SB | CS | AVG_OBP_SLG | TAv | BABIP | BRR | FRAA | WARP |
|---|---|---|---|---|---|---|---|---|---|---|---|---|---|---|---|---|---|---|---|
| 2009 | SEA | MLB | 25 | 653 | 69 | 42 | 0 | 25 | 96 | 24 | 69 | 3 | 3 | .272/.303/.463 | .268 | .270 | -1.5 | -5.3 | 1.3 |
| 2010 | SEA | MLB | 26 | 622 | 49 | 29 | 0 | 10 | 58 | 23 | 66 | 3 | 2 | .239/.270/.339 | .219 | .254 | -3.5 | 20.2 | 1.6 |
| 2011 | NWO | AAA | 27 | 135 | 24 | 9 | 0 | 9 | 30 | 6 | 12 | 2 | 0 | .400/.430/.688 | .354 | .387 | 0.1 | -0.5 | 1.6 |
| 2011 | COL | MLB | 27 | 129 | 10 | 4 | 0 | 2 | 8 | 3 | 15 | 2 | 0 | .208/.233/.288 | .192 | .222 | -0.6 | -0.4 | -0.9 |
| 2011 | FLO | MLB | 27 | 113 | 13 | 8 | 0 | 6 | 13 | 4 | 13 | 0 | 0 | .226/.259/.472 | .263 | .205 | 1 | -0.9 | 0.1 |
| 2012 | CLE | MLB | 28 | 323 | 35 | 17 | 0 | 8 | 36 | 12 | 38 | 2 | 1 | .257/.289/.392 | .246 | .268 | -0.1 | 3B 6, 2B 0 | 1.0 |

Lopez joined his third organization in six months when the Marlins claimed him off waivers from Colorado in June, but a 3-for-29 start earned him a trip to Triple-A New Orleans a month later. He hit well upon his recall in mid-August, batting .365/.382/.788 through his first 56 plate appearances, but was squeezed out of regular at-bats once September call-ups arrived and as a result his own production cratered again. After spending the majority of his early career as a second baseman, he has split time between second and third base in recent years. Any value that defensive versatility may carry, however, is negated by his inability to play either of those positions competently any longer. Inking a minor league deal with the Indians this winter, Lopez will hope to contribute but could instead find himself taking Luis Valbuena's seat on the bus back and forth from Triple-A.

**Lou Marson** C
Born: 6/26/1986 Age: 26
Bats: R Throws: R Height: 6'2" Weight: 200
Breakout: 1% Improve: 27% Collapse: 13%
Attrition: 33% MLB: 66%
Comparables:
A.J. Ellis, Jorge Posada, Robinson Chirinos

| YEAR | TEAM | LVL | AGE | PA | R | 2B | 3B | HR | RBI | BB | SO | SB | CS | AVG_OBP_SLG | TAv | BABIP | BRR | FRAA | WARP |
|---|---|---|---|---|---|---|---|---|---|---|---|---|---|---|---|---|---|---|---|---|
| 2009 | COH | AAA | 23 | 116 | 10 | 5 | 1 | 1 | 9 | 10 | 19 | 1 | 0 | .243/.322/.340 | .216 | .289 | -0.4 | 0 | 0.0 |
| 2009 | LEH | AAA | 23 | 241 | 32 | 13 | 0 | 1 | 24 | 30 | 40 | 3 | 1 | .294/.382/.370 | .265 | .359 | -1.8 | -0.2 | 1.1 |
| 2009 | CLE | MLB | 23 | 52 | 6 | 6 | 0 | 0 | 4 | 7 | 14 | 0 | 0 | .250/.346/.386 | .248 | .355 | -0.2 | 0.1 | 0.2 |
| 2009 | PHI | MLB | 23 | 20 | 3 | 1 | 0 | 0 | 0 | 3 | 7 | 0 | 0 | .235/.350/.294 | .215 | .400 | 0.4 | 0.2 | 0.1 |
| 2010 | COH | AAA | 24 | 147 | 19 | 7 | 1 | 4 | 14 | 22 | 24 | 5 | 0 | .202/.327/.371 | .245 | .219 | 1.1 | 0.1 | 0.5 |
| 2010 | CLE | MLB | 24 | 294 | 29 | 15 | 0 | 3 | 22 | 26 | 55 | 8 | 1 | .195/.274/.286 | .217 | .234 | 0.8 | -0.9 | 0.5 |
| 2011 | CLE | MLB | 25 | 272 | 26 | 9 | 2 | 1 | 19 | 24 | 68 | 4 | 2 | .230/.300/.296 | .220 | .312 | 0.1 | 0.1 | 0.4 |
| 2012 | CLE | MLB | 26 | 260 | 28 | 12 | 1 | 3 | 21 | 27 | 57 | 3 | 1 | .239/.323/.333 | .244 | .303 | -0.1 | C -1 | 1.4 |

Another former Philly prospect from the Cliff Lee deal who hasn't panned out as expected. Marson has still managed to become a legit big leaguer due to his great defensive skills, particularly in terms of blocking pitches and throwing out runners, but with his career .218/.295/.305 triple-slash line, he might as well be swinging a Wiffle bat at the plate. His elite minor league walk rates haven't translated to success at the plate. A great defensive receiver will always have a spot as a backup catcher, even with numbers as anemic as these, but with starting catcher Carlos Santana spending time at first base and DH to stay fresh, Marson was overexposed. Marson drew 46 percent of the starts at catcher in 2011—much too high for a guy without a bat.

**Cord Phelps** 2B
Born: 1/23/1987 Age: 25
Bats: B Throws: R Height: 6'3" Weight: 200
Breakout: 0% Improve: 26% Collapse: 20%
Attrition: 43% MLB: 83%
Comparables:
Jim Lefebvre, Ron Dunn, Scott Sizemore

| YEAR | TEAM | LVL | AGE | PA | R | 2B | 3B | HR | RBI | BB | SO | SB | CS | AVG_OBP_SLG | TAv | BABIP | BRR | FRAA | WARP |
|---|---|---|---|---|---|---|---|---|---|---|---|---|---|---|---|---|---|---|---|---|
| 2009 | KIN | A+ | 22 | 582 | 72 | 27 | 5 | 4 | 53 | 93 | 97 | 17 | 14 | .261/.386/.363 | .279 | .318 | -1.2 | 1 | 2.5 |
| 2010 | AKR | AA | 23 | 218 | 25 | 8 | 3 | 2 | 23 | 15 | 29 | 1 | 4 | .296/.347/.397 | .270 | .337 | -1.1 | -4.9 | 0.1 |
| 2010 | COH | AAA | 23 | 273 | 41 | 20 | 4 | 6 | 31 | 24 | 39 | 3 | 2 | .317/.386/.506 | .300 | .357 | -3 | -2.8 | 1.5 |
| 2011 | COH | AAA | 24 | 434 | 51 | 25 | 4 | 14 | 63 | 51 | 89 | 3 | 6 | .294/.376/.492 | .270 | .348 | -3.2 | -2.2 | 1.1 |
| 2011 | CLE | MLB | 24 | 80 | 10 | 2 | 1 | 1 | 6 | 8 | 17 | 1 | 0 | .155/.241/.254 | .191 | .189 | 0.7 | -2.3 | -0.5 |
| 2012 | CLE | MLB | 25 | 250 | 28 | 11 | 2 | 4 | 24 | 26 | 49 | 3 | 2 | .252/.332/.377 | .260 | .303 | -0.6 | 2B -5, SS 0 | 1.4 |

While Phelps was the first to the majors among Cleveland's infield prospect trio (alongside Kipnis and Chisenhall) last season, he's definitely the runt of the litter, projecting as a fringe starter who gets by on hard work, hustle, and instincts rather than outstanding tools. He struggled in his time with the big boys and has poor speed for an infielder, but he does project to hit for a solid average with more gap than home run power. He'll play at least average defense at either second or third.

**Felix Pie** LF
Born: 2/8/1985 Age: 27
Bats: L Throws: L Height: 6'3" Weight: 170
Breakout: 6% Improve: 45% Collapse: 9%
Attrition: 32% MLB: 86%
Comparables:
Cleon Jones, Omar Infante, Trent Oeltjen

| YEAR | TEAM | LVL | AGE | PA | R | 2B | 3B | HR | RBI | BB | SO | SB | CS | AVG_OBP_SLG | TAv | BABIP | BRR | FRAA | WARP |
|---|---|---|---|---|---|---|---|---|---|---|---|---|---|---|---|---|---|---|---|---|
| 2009 | BAL | MLB | 24 | 281 | 38 | 10 | 3 | 9 | 29 | 24 | 58 | 1 | 3 | .266/.326/.437 | .257 | .309 | 0 | 8 | 1.5 |
| 2010 | BAL | MLB | 25 | 308 | 39 | 15 | 5 | 5 | 31 | 13 | 52 | 5 | 2 | .274/.305/.413 | .250 | .316 | 3.6 | 4.2 | 1.5 |
| 2011 | BAL | MLB | 26 | 175 | 15 | 8 | 1 | 0 | 7 | 10 | 32 | 3 | 2 | .220/.264/.280 | .205 | .273 | 0.1 | 2.3 | -0.5 |
| 2012 | CLE | MLB | 27 | 250 | 28 | 11 | 3 | 5 | 27 | 16 | 49 | 5 | 2 | .256/.306/.387 | .248 | .303 | -0.3 | LF 7, CF 0 | 0.5 |

Once considered one of the top prospects in the game, Pie is now considered little more than organizational depth. He received some playing time in left field for the O's in 2011 when Luke Scott was injured, but failed again, triple-slashing .220/.264/.280. Designated for assignment at the end of August to give younger September call-ups a look, Pie inked a minor league deal with the Tribe this winter with an opt-out clause if he doesn't break camp with the team. To his credit, he has always managed to hit at Triple-A (.299/.353/.477 across parts of four seasons), and his speed is still a plus tool (his best). He'll be just 27 this year, so all hope is not lost, but Pie is running out of time to adjust to major league pitching.

### Carlos Santana — C

Born: 4/8/1986 Age: 26
Bats: B Throws: R Height: 6' 0" Weight: 190
Breakout: 5% Improve: 34% Collapse: 2%
Attrition: 20% MLB: 93%

Comparables: Hobie Landrith, Tom Tischinski, Chris

| YEAR | TEAM | LVL | AGE | PA | R | 2B | 3B | HR | RBI | BB | SO | SB | CS | AVG_OBP_SLG | TAv | BABIP | BRR | FRAA | WARP |
|------|------|-----|-----|-----|----|----|----|----|-----|----|-----|----|----|-------------|------|-------|------|-----------|------|
| 2009 | AKR | AA | 23 | 535 | 91 | 30 | 2 | 23 | 97 | 90 | 83 | 2 | 2 | .290/.421/.530 | .332 | .314 | 2.8 | 1.6 | 6.9 |
| 2010 | COH | AAA | 24 | 246 | 39 | 14 | 1 | 13 | 51 | 45 | 39 | 6 | 0 | .316/.451/.597 | .331 | .340 | 1.7 | 0.7 | 3.1 |
| 2010 | CLE | MLB | 24 | 192 | 23 | 13 | 0 | 6 | 22 | 37 | 29 | 3 | 0 | .260/.401/.467 | .316 | .277 | -0.1 | 0.7 | 2.1 |
| 2011 | CLE | MLB | 25 | 658 | 84 | 35 | 2 | 27 | 79 | 97 | 133 | 5 | 3 | .239/.351/.457 | .290 | .263 | -1.8 | -0.6 | 3.6 |
| 2012 | CLE | MLB | 26 | 554 | 74 | 28 | 1 | 22 | 69 | 85 | 106 | 4 | 1 | .252/.371/.462 | .298 | .279 | -0.1 | C-0, 1B 1 | 4.1 |

### Grady Sizemore — CF

Born: 8/2/1982 Age: 29
Bats: L Throws: L Height: 6' 3" Weight: 200
Breakout: 3% Improve: 47% Collapse: 4%
Attrition: 9% MLB: 92%

Comparables: Chet Lemon, Ken Henderson, Brian Giles

| YEAR | TEAM | LVL | AGE | PA | R | 2B | 3B | HR | RBI | BB | SO | SB | CS | AVG_OBP_SLG | TAv | BABIP | BRR | FRAA | WARP |
|------|------|-----|-----|-----|----|----|----|----|-----|----|----|----|----|-------------|------|-------|------|------|------|
| 2009 | CLE | MLB | 26 | 503 | 73 | 20 | 6 | 18 | 64 | 60 | 92 | 13 | 8 | .248/.343/.445 | .284 | .275 | -1 | 3.7 | 2.8 |
| 2010 | CLE | MLB | 27 | 140 | 15 | 6 | 2 | 0 | 13 | 9 | 35 | 4 | 2 | .211/.271/.289 | .205 | .287 | 1.7 | -4 | -0.7 |
| 2011 | CLE | MLB | 28 | 295 | 34 | 21 | 1 | 10 | 32 | 18 | 85 | 0 | 2 | .224/.285/.422 | .252 | .284 | -0.7 | -3.9 | 0.1 |
| 2012 | CLE | MLB | 29 | 251 | 31 | 12 | 1 | 8 | 30 | 29 | 53 | 7 | 3 | .250/.348/.434 | .281 | .293 | -0.2 | CF -3 | 2.3 |

Once one of the most promising young players in baseball, Sizemore hasn't played a full season since 2008, barely accumulating 400 plate appearances over the past two seasons. His list of ailments reads like the worst Christmas wish list in the world—left knee microfracture surgery, right knee contusion, arthroscopic elbow surgery, and two sports hernias. Don't bet on Sizemore ever being healthy enough to be an everyday player again. When he is healthy, he still has some power, but the knee issues have sapped his speed and defense, and his plate discipline has dissipated over the past two seasons. Swinging at outside pitches nearly twice as much as he did earlier in his career, Sizemore may be pressing to make something happen. If Sizemore is to be successful in whatever time he manages to be on the field, he'll need to be more selective and stop trying to hit the five-run homer. The Tribe declined an $8.5 million option on him for 2012 that was once thought to be an enormous bargain. Signed to a one year, $5 million deal, he can make up the difference in bonuses tied to plate appearances.

### LeVon Washington — CF

Born: 7/26/1991 Age: 20
Bats: L Throws: R Height: 6' 0" Weight: 170
Breakout: 1% Improve: 1% Collapse: 2%
Attrition: 12% MLB: 14%

Comparables: Aaron Hicks, Cutter Dykstra, Juan Gonzalez

| YEAR | TEAM | LVL | AGE | PA | R | 2B | 3B | HR | RBI | BB | SO | SB | CS | AVG_OBP_SLG | TAv | BABIP | BRR | FRAA | WARP |
|------|------|-----|-----|-----|----|----|----|----|----|-----|----|----|----|----|-------------|------|-------|------|-------------|------|
| 2011 | LKC | A | 19 | 351 | 35 | 9 | 4 | 4 | 20 | 49 | 89 | 15 | 6 | .218/.331/.315 | .253 | .296 | 2.7 | -1.4 | -0.1 |
| 2012 | CLE | MLB | 20 | 250 | 22 | 8 | 1 | 3 | 17 | 22 | 74 | 5 | 2 | .193/.264/.276 | .203 | .267 | -0.2 | CF -16, LF -0 | -1.3 |

After all the prospect turnover in C-Town, Washington now ranks among the team's top minor leaguers. About as raw as they come, Wash is still young and has time to make good on all of his tools. An athletic player with plus-plus speed, Washington has the ceiling of an everyday center fielder, though at the moment, even his defense is still mooing. While he strikes out a lot, his strike zone judgment is developing and he knows how to draw a walk. Scouts are split on his power potential, but his destiny lies as a leadoff hitter whether he develops moderate power or not. A prospect to dream on, Washington is at least a couple of years from the majors.

# PITCHERS

### Fausto Carmona

Born: 12/7/1983 Age: 28
Bats: R Throws: R Height: 6' 5" Weight: 190
Breakout: 14% Improve: 44% Collapse: 32%
Attrition: 17% MLB: 86%

Comparables:
Steve Ontiveros, Scot Shields, Gary Majewski

| YEAR | TEAM | LVL | AGE | W | L | SV | G | GS | IP | H | HR | BB | SO | EqBB9 | EqSO9 | GB% | BABIP | WHIP | ERA | FIP | FRA | WARP |
|------|------|-----|-----|---|---|----|----|----|-----|-----|----|----|-----|-------|-------|-----|-------|------|------|------|------|------|
| 2009 | CLE | MLB | 25 | 5 | 12 | 0 | 24 | 24 | 125¹ | 151 | 16 | 70 | 79 | 5.0 | 5.7 | 56% | .322 | 1.76 | 6.32 | 5.41 | 6.57 | -1.0 |
| 2010 | CLE | MLB | 26 | 13 | 14 | 0 | 33 | 33 | 210¹ | 203 | 17 | 72 | 124 | 3.1 | 5.3 | 56% | .284 | 1.31 | 3.77 | 4.07 | 4.73 | 1.2 |
| 2011 | CLE | MLB | 27 | 7 | 15 | 0 | 32 | 32 | 188² | 205 | 22 | 60 | 109 | 2.9 | 5.2 | 56% | .296 | 1.40 | 5.25 | 4.60 | 5.32 | -0.4 |
| 2012 | CLE | MLB | 28 | 10 | 9 | 0 | 28 | 28 | 169² | 173 | 16 | 62 | 104 | 3.3 | 5.5 | 60% | .295 | 1.38 | 4.22 | 4.30 | 4.59 | 0.8 |

Despite a high ERA, Carmona posted a very similar year peripherally to his 2010—the first time he's managed to maintain good peripherals in back-to-back seasons. Unfortunately, that didn't translate to the same results as in 2010, as Carmona struggled mightily with runners on base, a problem that has plagued him for much of his career. With runners on, Carmona's strikeout rate plummets, and the runners are bound to score when so many balls are put into play. Pitching coach Tim Belcher thought he picked up what was causing the problem in June, but Carmona continued to struggle through the end of the season. While he has rediscovered the command that allowed him to be successful in 2007, and his sinker will always generate grounders, he'll need to find a way to strike batters out from the stretch. Without a real put-away pitch to begin with and having just once in his career posted a K/9 above 5.0 with runners on, that's far from assured.

### Carlos Carrasco

Born: 3/21/1987 Age: 25
Bats: R Throws: R Height: 6' 4" Weight: 215
Breakout: 37% Improve: 72% Collapse: 7%
Attrition: 15% MLB: 95%

Comparables:
James Baldwin, Billy Loes, Jae Kuk Ryu

| YEAR | TEAM | LVL | AGE | W | L | SV | G | GS | IP | H | HR | BB | SO | EqBB9 | EqSO9 | GB% | BABIP | WHIP | ERA | FIP | FRA | WARP |
|------|------|-----|-----|---|---|----|----|----|-----|-----|----|----|-----|-------|-------|-----|-------|------|------|------|------|------|
| 2009 | COH | AAA | 22 | 5 | 1 | 0 | 6 | 6 | 42¹ | 31 | 3 | 7 | 36 | 1.5 | 7.7 | 40% | .233 | 0.90 | 3.19 | 2.86 | 4.21 | 0.6 |
| 2009 | LEH | AAA | 22 | 6 | 9 | 0 | 20 | 20 | 114² | 118 | 14 | 38 | 112 | 3.0 | 8.8 | 43% | .319 | 1.36 | 5.18 | 3.96 | 5.03 | 0.4 |
| 2009 | CLE | MLB | 22 | 0 | 4 | 0 | 5 | 5 | 22¹ | 40 | 6 | 11 | 11 | 4.4 | 4.4 | 48% | .405 | 2.28 | 8.87 | 7.13 | 7.03 | -0.3 |
| 2010 | COH | AAA | 23 | 10 | 6 | 0 | 25 | 25 | 150¹ | 90 | 11 | 32 | 99 | 2.8 | 8.0 | 49% | .290 | 1.23 | 3.65 | 3.90 | 4.98 | 1.9 |
| 2010 | CLE | MLB | 23 | 2 | 2 | 0 | 7 | 7 | 44² | 47 | 6 | 14 | 38 | 2.8 | 7.7 | 57% | .323 | 1.37 | 3.83 | 4.10 | 4.54 | 0.2 |
| 2011 | CLE | MLB | 24 | 8 | 9 | 0 | 21 | 21 | 124² | 130 | 15 | 40 | 85 | 2.9 | 6.1 | 51% | .296 | 1.36 | 4.62 | 4.32 | 4.77 | 0.4 |
| 2012 | CLE | MLB | 25 | 5 | 6 | 0 | 16 | 16 | 94¹ | 100 | 13 | 36 | 70 | 3.5 | 6.7 | 45% | .303 | 1.45 | 4.80 | 4.66 | 5.22 | -0.2 |

Carrasco underwent Tommy John surgery in September, so this projection is most likely for 2013. Despite what looks on the surface like a poor 2011, Carrasco had an impressive year peripherally and seemed poised to become the best of the quartet of prospects that the Indians received for Cliff Lee. Of course, when Jason Donald and Lou Marson are in a group with you, that's kind of like having the best beard when your cohorts haven't started shaving yet. Armed with a 93-mph fastball, a plus change, and a solid breaking ball, Carrasco certainly has the stuff to be a number two starter if he can translate that stuff into a few more strikeouts.

### Chad Durbin

Born: 12/3/1977 Age: 34
Bats: R Throws: R Height: 6' 2" Weight: 175
Breakout: 16% Improve: 29% Collapse: 51%
Attrition: 19% MLB: 66%

Comparables:
Kane Davis, Jack Morris, Andy Messersmith

| YEAR | TEAM | LVL | AGE | W | L | SV | G | GS | IP | H | HR | BB | SO | EqBB9 | EqSO9 | GB% | BABIP | WHIP | ERA | FIP | FRA | WARP |
|------|------|-----|-----|---|---|----|----|----|-----|----|----|----|----|-------|-------|-----|-------|------|------|------|------|------|
| 2009 | PHI | MLB | 31 | 2 | 2 | 2 | 59 | 0 | 69² | 56 | 8 | 47 | 62 | 6.1 | 8.0 | 40% | .257 | 1.48 | 4.39 | 5.09 | 5.03 | 0.1 |
| 2010 | PHI | MLB | 32 | 4 | 1 | 0 | 64 | 0 | 68² | 63 | 7 | 27 | 63 | 3.5 | 8.3 | 45% | .298 | 1.31 | 3.80 | 3.99 | 4.57 | 0.5 |
| 2011 | CLE | MLB | 33 | 2 | 2 | 0 | 56 | 0 | 68¹ | 86 | 12 | 26 | 59 | 3.4 | 7.8 | 41% | .341 | 1.64 | 5.53 | 4.89 | 5.28 | -0.1 |
| 2012 | CLE | MLB | 34 | 3 | 1 | 0 | 54 | 0 | 62 | 63 | 8 | 26 | 46 | 3.7 | 6.6 | 45% | .295 | 1.44 | 4.50 | 4.66 | 4.89 | 0.0 |

While he was a bit unlucky on balls in play, this 12-year veteran was only relied upon in low leverage situations for Cleveland in 2011. Since scrapping his slider after the 2008 season and developing his cut fastball, he has become a more-than-capable mop-up man. Despite a fastball that sits at a mere 90 mph, he's capable of generating strikeouts thanks to an above-average curve and that cutter. He also mixes in a change to give hitters a different look.

### Jeanmar Gomez

Born: 2/10/1988 Age: 24
Bats: R Throws: R Height: 6' 4" Weight: 170
Breakout: 20% Improve: 39% Collapse: 38%
Attrition: 23% MLB: 92%

Comparables:
Julio Valera, Anthony Swarzak, George Susce

| YEAR | TEAM | LVL | AGE | W | L | SV | G | GS | IP | H | HR | BB | SO | EqBB9 | EqSO9 | GB% | BABIP | WHIP | ERA | FIP | FRA | WARP |
|------|------|-----|-----|---|---|----|----|----|-----|-----|----|----|-----|-------|-------|-----|-------|------|------|------|------|------|
| 2009 | AKR | AA | 21 | 11 | 4 | 0 | 22 | 22 | 123¹ | 129 | 12 | 44 | 117 | 2.9 | 8.0 | 48% | .301 | 1.27 | 3.43 | 3.65 | 4.18 | 1.6 |
| 2010 | COH | AAA | 22 | 8 | 8 | 0 | 20 | 20 | 116 | 88 | 10 | 28 | 47 | 3.3 | 6.1 | 47% | .300 | 1.47 | 5.20 | 4.59 | 5.78 | 0.6 |
| 2010 | CLE | MLB | 22 | 4 | 5 | 0 | 11 | 11 | 57² | 73 | 7 | 22 | 34 | 3.4 | 5.3 | 47% | .330 | 1.65 | 4.68 | 4.69 | 5.07 | 0.1 |
| 2011 | COH | AAA | 23 | 10 | 7 | 0 | 21 | 21 | 137² | 116 | 8 | 47 | 103 | 3.2 | 7.0 | 51% | .286 | 1.25 | 2.55 | 3.63 | 4.68 | 1.9 |
| 2011 | CLE | MLB | 23 | 5 | 3 | 0 | 11 | 10 | 58¹ | 73 | 6 | 15 | 31 | 2.3 | 4.8 | 53% | .325 | 1.51 | 4.47 | 4.16 | 4.53 | 0.5 |
| 2012 | CLE | MLB | 24 | 5 | 5 | 0 | 14 | 14 | 83² | 96 | 11 | 32 | 48 | 3.4 | 5.2 | 46% | .307 | 1.53 | 5.11 | 4.91 | 5.55 | -0.4 |

Gomez doesn't have the kind of stuff to overpower hitters, but he does have the kind of stuff that could one day make him an effective fifth starter. He might have competed for such a position in spring training had the Derek Lowe trade not made it likely he'll return for his third engagement at Triple-A. His fastball is a 90-mph sinker that can generate grounders, which he complements with a change-up and a slider. His biggest problem is that his control has been merely above average for Triple-A, and that could cause problems at the major league level. If he manages to miss enough bats and hit his spots a bit better, he could be of use to the Indians after a bit more seasoning.

**Nick Hagadone**
Born: **1/1/1986** Age: **26**
Bats: **L** Throws: **L** Height: **6' 6"** Weight: **230**
Breakout: **37%** Improve: **63%** Collapse: **20%**
Attrition: **10%** MLB: **90%**
Comparables:
Craig Breslow, Jim Maloney, David Cone

| YEAR | TEAM | LVL | AGE | W | L | SV | G | GS | IP | H | HR | BB | SO | EqBB9 | EqSO9 | GB% | BABIP | WHIP | ERA | FIP | FRA | WARP |
|---|---|---|---|---|---|---|---|---|---|---|---|---|---|---|---|---|---|---|---|---|---|---|
| 2009 | GRN | A | 23 | 0 | 2 | 0 | 10 | 10 | 25 | 13 | 0 | 14 | 32 | 5.0 | 11.5 | 69% | .236 | 1.08 | 2.52 | 3.06 | 3.31 | 0.8 |
| 2010 | KIN | A+ | 24 | 1 | 3 | 0 | 10 | 10 | 37² | 21 | 2 | 25 | 35 | 6.9 | 10.7 | 46% | .264 | 1.51 | 2.39 | 4.28 | 4.47 | 0.4 |
| 2010 | AKR | AA | 24 | 2 | 2 | 1 | 19 | 7 | 48 | 31 | 4 | 28 | 25 | 6.4 | 8.2 | 45% | .284 | 1.62 | 4.50 | 5.39 | 5.64 | 0.0 |
| 2011 | AKR | AA | 25 | 2 | 0 | 0 | 12 | 0 | 22² | 14 | 0 | 7 | 22 | 2.8 | 9.5 | 40% | .269 | 0.93 | 1.59 | 2.40 | 3.81 | 0.3 |
| 2011 | COH | AAA | 25 | 4 | 3 | 4 | 34 | 0 | 48¹ | 43 | 5 | 15 | 53 | 2.9 | 9.9 | 43% | .307 | 1.19 | 3.35 | 3.38 | 4.95 | 0.3 |

find himself pitching in Cleveland for the better part of 2012.

**Frank Herrmann**
Born: **5/30/1984** Age: **28**
Bats: **L** Throws: **R** Height: **6' 5"** Weight: **220**
Breakout: **9%** Improve: **53%** Collapse: **14%**
Attrition: **22%** MLB: **84%**
Comparables:
Donovan Osborne, Graeme Lloyd, Randy Tomlin

| YEAR | TEAM | LVL | AGE | W | L | SV | G | GS | IP | H | HR | BB | SO | EqBB9 | EqSO9 | GB% | BABIP | WHIP | ERA | FIP | FRA | WARP |
|---|---|---|---|---|---|---|---|---|---|---|---|---|---|---|---|---|---|---|---|---|---|---|
| 2009 | COH | AAA | 25 | 2 | 3 | 2 | 44 | 0 | 76 | 83 | 3 | 13 | 50 | 1.5 | 5.9 | 37% | .324 | 1.26 | 2.96 | 2.94 | 3.85 | 1.4 |
| 2010 | COH | AAA | 26 | 3 | 0 | 2 | 19 | 0 | 28² | 14 | 0 | 5 | 19 | 2.5 | 6.9 | 45% | .255 | 0.80 | 0.31 | 2.73 | 3.56 | 0.6 |
| 2010 | CLE | MLB | 26 | 0 | 1 | 1 | 40 | 0 | 44² | 48 | 6 | 9 | 24 | 1.8 | 4.8 | 37% | .288 | 1.28 | 4.03 | 4.46 | 5.62 | -0.2 |
| 2011 | CLE | MLB | 27 | 4 | 0 | 0 | 40 | 0 | 56¹ | 71 | 7 | 16 | 34 | 2.6 | 5.4 | 33% | .330 | 1.54 | 5.11 | 4.32 | 4.91 | 0.0 |
| 2012 | CLE | MLB | 28 | 2 | 1 | 0 | 39 | 0 | 50² | 60 | 7 | 14 | 26 | 2.5 | 4.6 | 39% | .308 | 1.46 | 4.89 | 4.80 | 5.31 | -0.2 |

The first Harvard man to make the majors since the 1980s, Herrmann has spent most of the past two seasons in Cleveland. Despite solid command, his lack of put-away stuff typecasts him as a seventh reliever type. He doesn't strike anybody out, and throwing his fastball three-quarters of the time, he allows far too many fly balls to function as more than organizational depth. With many of Cleveland's young relief prospects ready to make a major league impact, Herrman will likely see his MLB/Triple-A split reversed in 2012.

**David Huff**
Born: **8/22/1984** Age: **27**
Bats: **B** Throws: **L** Height: **6' 3"** Weight: **190**
Breakout: **35%** Improve: **56%** Collapse: **12%**
Attrition: **8%** MLB: **85%**
Comparables:
Pat Misch, Bob Moose, Edgar Gonzalez

| YEAR | TEAM | LVL | AGE | W | L | SV | G | GS | IP | H | HR | BB | SO | EqBB9 | EqSO9 | GB% | BABIP | WHIP | ERA | FIP | FRA | WARP |
|---|---|---|---|---|---|---|---|---|---|---|---|---|---|---|---|---|---|---|---|---|---|---|
| 2009 | COH | AAA | 24 | 5 | 1 | 0 | 7 | 7 | 39¹ | 35 | 5 | 16 | 32 | 3.7 | 7.3 | 34% | .275 | 1.30 | 4.35 | 4.39 | 5.06 | 0.3 |
| 2009 | CLE | MLB | 24 | 11 | 8 | 0 | 23 | 23 | 128¹ | 159 | 16 | 41 | 65 | 2.9 | 4.6 | 39% | .318 | 1.56 | 5.61 | 4.73 | 4.75 | 1.1 |
| 2010 | COH | AAA | 25 | 9 | 2 | 0 | 12 | 12 | 74¹ | 67 | 6 | 17 | 51 | 2.5 | 6.3 | 43% | .330 | 1.41 | 4.36 | 3.93 | 4.72 | 1.5 |
| 2010 | CLE | MLB | 25 | 2 | 11 | 0 | 15 | 15 | 79² | 101 | 14 | 34 | 37 | 3.8 | 4.2 | 38% | .313 | 1.69 | 6.21 | 5.80 | 5.29 | -0.2 |
| 2011 | COH | AAA | 26 | 9 | 3 | 0 | 18 | 18 | 107 | 108 | 10 | 27 | 64 | 2.5 | 5.6 | 35% | .299 | 1.32 | 3.87 | 4.07 | 4.83 | 1.2 |
| 2011 | CLE | MLB | 26 | 2 | 6 | 0 | 11 | 10 | 50² | 55 | 6 | 17 | 36 | 3.0 | 6.4 | 35% | .292 | 1.42 | 4.09 | 4.19 | 4.49 | 0.7 |
| 2012 | CLE | MLB | 27 | 4 | 5 | 0 | 13 | 13 | 76 | 84 | 10 | 24 | 46 | 2.9 | 5.4 | 42% | .300 | 1.43 | 4.74 | 4.65 | 5.15 | -0.1 |

While Huff's numbers were impressive in his first go-round at Triple-A in 2008, his strikeouts have decreased every year since; he hasn't even been average since 2009. More of a soft-tosser who never really had the stuff to be a strikeout guy, Huff throws a plus change, a 12-to-6 curve, and a slider to go with his 90-mph fastball. At the end of the 2010 season, Manny Acta said that Huff needs to command his fastball in order to be successful, which is spot on. If you're a fly-ball pitcher with limited strike-outs, your only path to a big league job is as a passable fifth starter with good command.

### Ubaldo Jimenez

Born: 1/22/1984 Age: 28
Bats: R Throws: R Height: 6' 5" Weight: 200
Breakout: 18% Improve: 60% Collapse: 18%
Attrition: 9% MLB: 89%

**Comparables:**
Jared Burton, Aaron Heilman, Ray Narleski

| YEAR | TEAM | LVL | AGE | W | L | SV | G | GS | IP | H | HR | BB | SO | EqBB9 | EqSO9 | GB% | BABIP | WHIP | ERA | FIP | FRA | WARP |
|------|------|-----|-----|---|---|----|---|----|----|---|----|----|----|-------|-------|-----|-------|------|-----|-----|-----|------|
| 2009 | COL | MLB | 25 | 15 | 12 | 0 | 33 | 33 | 218 | 183 | 13 | 85 | 198 | 3.5 | 8.2 | 55% | .287 | 1.23 | 3.47 | 3.32 | 4.11 | 4.6 |
| 2010 | COL | MLB | 26 | 19 | 8 | 0 | 33 | 33 | 221² | 164 | 10 | 92 | 214 | 3.7 | 8.7 | 50% | .274 | 1.15 | 2.88 | 3.13 | 3.63 | 4.5 |
| 2011 | CLE | MLB | 27 | 4 | 4 | 0 | 11 | 11 | 65¹ | 68 | 7 | 27 | 62 | 3.7 | 8.5 | 48% | .318 | 1.45 | 5.10 | 3.89 | 4.59 | 0.5 |
| 2011 | COL | MLB | 27 | 6 | 9 | 0 | 21 | 21 | 123 | 118 | 10 | 51 | 118 | 3.7 | 8.6 | 48% | .314 | 1.37 | 4.46 | 3.55 | 4.30 | 1.8 |
| 2012 | CLE | MLB | 28 | 10 | 8 | 0 | 25 | 25 | 160² | 150 | 13 | 69 | 142 | 3.9 | 7.9 | 51% | .300 | 1.36 | 3.86 | 3.78 | 4.19 | 1.5 |

Despite wildly different ERAs over the past three seasons, Jimenez has been remarkably consistent in terms of his peripherals, posting xFIPs (Expected Fielding Independent Pitching) of 3.59, 3.60, and 3.71. Despite a down 2011 (the only ERA over 4.00 in our trio), everyone knows Ubaldo is an ace and that a bounceback 2012 is on the horizon. Jimenez ran into a spot of bad luck last summer with a 65 percent strand rate, but losing 3 mph off his average fastball from 2010 can't be chalked up to misfortune. With his mid-90s heat and quality secondary offerings, his reputation as one of the game's best under-30 starters rivals Lindsay Lohan's reputation as one of the world's most annoying under-30 human beings. The Indians gave up quite the handsome sum to acquire him (Drew Pomeranz and Alex White), but they'll be happy that they have him locked up so cheaply with affordable options through 2014.

### Corey Kluber

Born: 4/10/1986 Age: 26
Bats: R Throws: R Height: 6' 5" Weight: 215
Breakout: 23% Improve: 66% Collapse: 15%
Attrition: 10% MLB: 76%

**Comparables:**
Mike Moore, Melido Perez, Dave Shipanoff

| YEAR | TEAM | LVL | AGE | W | L | SV | G | GS | IP | H | HR | BB | SO | EqBB9 | EqSO9 | GB% | BABIP | WHIP | ERA | FIP | FRA | WARP |
|------|------|-----|-----|---|---|----|---|----|----|---|----|----|----|-------|-------|-----|-------|------|-----|-----|-----|------|
| 2009 | LEL | A+ | 23 | 7 | 9 | 0 | 19 | 19 | 109 | 110 | 9 | 36 | 124 | 3.0 | 10.2 | 49% | .349 | 1.34 | 4.54 | 3.71 | 4.43 | 1.1 |
| 2009 | SAN | AA | 23 | 2 | 5 | 0 | 9 | 9 | 45 | 52 | 6 | 36 | 40 | 6.8 | 7.0 | 34% | .322 | 1.76 | 4.60 | 5.73 | 6.18 | -0.4 |
| 2010 | SAN | AA | 24 | 6 | 6 | 0 | 22 | 21 | 122² | 87 | 5 | 30 | 103 | 2.9 | 10.0 | 44% | .340 | 1.31 | 3.45 | 3.01 | 3.62 | 2.0 |
| 2011 | COH | AAA | 25 | 7 | 11 | 0 | 27 | 27 | 150² | 153 | 19 | 70 | 143 | 4.2 | 8.5 | 38% | .318 | 1.48 | 5.56 | 4.53 | 5.26 | 1.9 |
| 2011 | CLE | MLB | 25 | 0 | 0 | 0 | 3 | 0 | 4¹ | 6 | 0 | 3 | 5 | 6.2 | 10.4 | 40% | .400 | 2.08 | 8.31 | 4.22 | 4.82 | 0.0 |
| 2012 | CLE | MLB | 26 | 3 | 4 | 0 | 9 | 9 | 52² | 58 | 7 | 26 | 42 | 4.4 | 7.1 | 40% | .317 | 1.60 | 5.33 | 4.82 | 5.80 | -0.4 |

Acquired in the three-way trade that sent Jake Westbrook out of town in 2010, Kluber could eventually wind up as a major league contributor but is more likely to dwell in Triple-A. He's a fly-ball pitcher with below-average control and command, so he needs to rely on his stuff to succeed. The problem is that his stuff is mediocre. Kluber's average-grade fastball sits around 92 mph, and he complements it with a change-up and slider, but neither is a true plus pitch. Kluber will reside in the deep end of the Indians pitching talent pool, and if he gets more than a handful of starts it will be an indication Cleveland may be sinking in the Central.

### Chen Lee

Born: 10/21/1986 Age: 25
Bats: R Throws: R Height: 6' 0" Weight: 175
Breakout: 16% Improve: 47% Collapse: 28%
Attrition: 24% MLB: 74%

**Comparables:**
Joba Chamberlain, Sammy Gervacio, Karl Spooner

| YEAR | TEAM | LVL | AGE | W | L | SV | G | GS | IP | H | HR | BB | SO | EqBB9 | EqSO9 | GB% | BABIP | WHIP | ERA | FIP | FRA | WARP |
|------|------|-----|-----|---|---|----|---|----|----|---|----|----|----|-------|-------|-----|-------|------|-----|-----|-----|------|
| 2009 | KIN | A+ | 22 | 4 | 6 | 2 | 45 | 0 | 83¹ | 67 | 5 | 28 | 97 | 3.0 | 10.5 | 49% | .300 | 1.14 | 3.35 | 3.13 | 4.17 | 1.1 |
| 2010 | AKR | AA | 23 | 5 | 4 | 0 | 44 | 0 | 72² | 39 | 3 | 18 | 54 | 2.7 | 10.2 | 49% | .286 | 1.11 | 3.22 | 3.51 | 3.84 | 1.0 |
| 2011 | AKR | AA | 24 | 2 | 1 | 0 | 23 | 0 | 39² | 27 | 1 | 11 | 56 | 2.5 | 12.7 | 58% | .310 | 0.96 | 2.50 | 2.20 | 3.72 | 0.6 |
| 2011 | COH | AAA | 24 | 4 | 0 | 1 | 21 | 0 | 31² | 27 | 2 | 14 | 48 | 3.4 | 12.2 | 57% | .309 | 1.20 | 2.27 | 2.45 | 3.85 | 0.9 |
| 2012 | CLE | MLB | 25 | 1 | 0 | 1 | 15 | 0 | 23² | 21 | 2 | 10 | 24 | 3.7 | 9.2 | 48% | .300 | 1.30 | 3.66 | 3.54 | 3.98 | 0.3 |

A former Taiwanese Olympian with a fastball that touches 96 mph, Lee has dominated every level and deserves a shot with the Tribe soon. The velocity is a bit surprising coming from a pitcher with such a small frame, but Lee is the real deal, consistently hitting the 92-93 mph range. His go-to off-speed pitch is a plus slider with tilt, and Lee's good command and pitchability demonstrate that he's ready for the Show.

### Derek Lowe

Born: 6/1/1973 Age: 39
Bats: R Throws: R Height: 6' 7" Weight: 170
Breakout: 27% Improve: 50% Collapse: 14%
Attrition: 9% MLB: 74%

**Comparables:**
Dennis Martinez, Elmer Dessens, Gene Garber

| YEAR | TEAM | LVL | AGE | W | L | SV | G | GS | IP | H | HR | BB | SO | EqBB9 | EqSO9 | GB% | BABIP | WHIP | ERA | FIP | FRA | WARP |
|------|------|-----|-----|---|---|----|---|----|----|---|----|----|----|-------|-------|-----|-------|------|-----|-----|-----|------|
| 2009 | ATL | MLB | 36 | 15 | 10 | 0 | 34 | 34 | 194² | 232 | 16 | 63 | 111 | 2.9 | 5.1 | 57% | .333 | 1.52 | 4.67 | 4.02 | 5.22 | 0.9 |
| 2010 | ATL | MLB | 37 | 16 | 12 | 0 | 33 | 33 | 193² | 204 | 18 | 61 | 136 | 2.8 | 6.3 | 59% | .313 | 1.37 | 4.00 | 3.92 | 4.86 | 1.5 |
| 2011 | ATL | MLB | 38 | 9 | 17 | 0 | 34 | 34 | 187 | 212 | 14 | 70 | 137 | 3.4 | 6.6 | 60% | .332 | 1.51 | 5.05 | 3.67 | 4.46 | 1.6 |
| 2012 | CLE | MLB | 39 | 9 | 9 | 0 | 27 | 27 | 154¹ | 173 | 14 | 49 | 91 | 2.9 | 5.3 | 60% | .315 | 1.44 | 4.43 | 4.16 | 4.82 | 0.5 |

A reemerging slider led to some optimism about Lowe exiting 2010. The hype train kept chugging along in the new season after he yielded five runs in his first 24 2/3 innings pitched. Lowe then hit a bump by allowing five runs in his next start, and the train went into a tunnel and never came out down the stretch. Over Lowe's final 11 starts—stretching from August onward—he recorded just four quality starts when the Braves needed his experience and composure the most. Dealt for peanuts to the Indians this winter, Lowe will join Cleveland's vast collection of groundballing starters, but the league change figures to be quite unfriendly, and Lowe might just be hoping to avoid the indignity of an ERA higher than his strikeout per nine innings pitched rate.

**Justin Masterson**
Born: 3/22/1985 Age: 27
Bats: R Throws: R Height: 6' 7" Weight: 250
Breakout: 19% Improve: 50% Collapse: 27%
Attrition: 6% MLB: 95%

Comparables:
Mike Henneman, Jesse Crain, Ramon Troncoso

| YEAR | TEAM | LVL | AGE | W | L | SV | G | GS | IP | H | HR | BB | SO | EqBB9 | EqSO9 | GB% | BABIP | WHIP | ERA | FIP | FRA | WARP |
|------|------|-----|-----|---|---|----|----|----|-----|-----|----|----|-----|-------|-------|------|-------|------|------|------|------|------|
| 2009 | CLE | MLB | 24 | 1 | 7 | 0 | 11 | 10 | 57¹ | 56 | 5 | 35 | 52 | 5.5 | 8.2 | 59% | .317 | 1.59 | 4.55 | 4.40 | 5.18 | 0.3 |
| 2009 | BOS | MLB | 24 | 3 | 3 | 0 | 31 | 6 | 72 | 72 | 7 | 25 | 67 | 3.1 | 8.4 | 53% | .328 | 1.35 | 4.50 | 3.84 | 5.25 | 0.5 |
| 2010 | CLE | MLB | 25 | 6 | 13 | 0 | 34 | 29 | 180 | 197 | 14 | 73 | 140 | 3.7 | 7.0 | 60% | .327 | 1.50 | 4.70 | 3.90 | 4.74 | 1.1 |
| 2011 | CLE | MLB | 26 | 12 | 10 | 0 | 34 | 33 | 216 | 211 | 11 | 65 | 158 | 2.7 | 6.6 | 56% | .304 | 1.28 | 3.21 | 3.32 | 3.79 | 3.3 |
| *2012* | *CLE* | *MLB* | *27* | *11* | *9* | *0* | *29* | *29* | *179* | *179* | *15* | *65* | *140* | *3.3* | *7.0* | *57%* | *.307* | *1.36* | *3.94* | *3.82* | *4.29* | *1.5* |

After a 2010 season that saw Masterson post much better peripherals than his ERA indicated, he proved in 2011 that his 2010 was merely bad luck. That put to rest the notion that his unorthodox pitching style made him a DIPS theory outlier (a pitcher who over- or under-performs his peripherals due to a skill,

Bats: R Throws: R Height: 6' 7" Weight: 240
Breakout: 21% Improve: 53% Collapse: 32%
Attrition: 18% MLB: 94%

Comparables:
Randy Jones, Scott Baker, Tommy Hunter

| YEAR | TEAM | LVL | AGE | W | L | SV | G | GS | IP | H | HR | BB | SO | EqBB9 | EqSO9 | GB% | BABIP | WHIP | ERA | FIP | FRA | WARP |
|------|------|-----|-----|---|---|----|----|----|-----|-----|----|----|-----|-------|-------|------|-------|------|------|------|------|------|
| 2011 | CLE | MLB | 23 | 0 | 1 | 0 | 4 | 4 | 17² | 26 | 1 | 7 | 14 | 3.6 | 7.1 | 43% | .403 | 1.87 | 6.11 | 3.40 | 4.88 | 0.1 |
| *2012* | *CLE* | *MLB* | *24* | *4* | *4* | *0* | *12* | *12* | *67¹* | *76* | *8* | *21* | *41* | *2.8* | *5.4* | *45%* | *.308* | *1.44* | *4.69* | *4.47* | *5.09* | *-0.0* |

An underdog for the fifth starter job before the Derek Lowe deal, McAllister will surely begin the year in the minors now. He had a very good year at Triple-A in 2011, working on and improving his command, a key for a guy who gets by on control and guile. McAllister features several pitches, but none profile as true plus offerings yet. He throws a 90-mph fastball that can get some sink, a change-up, cutter, slider, and curve. If he's to be successful, it will be as a poor man's Josh Tomlin, commanding and mixing his pitches to keep hitters off balance. Unlike Tomlin, however, McAllister also profiles to get some groundballs if he can work down in the zone.

**Chris Perez**
Born: 7/1/1985 Age: 26
Bats: R Throws: R Height: 6' 5" Weight: 225
Breakout: 30% Improve: 58% Collapse: 20%
Attrition: 8% MLB: 90%

Comparables:
Byung-Hyun Kim, Daniel Bard, Joel Zumaya

| YEAR | TEAM | LVL | AGE | W | L | SV | G | GS | IP | H | HR | BB | SO | EqBB9 | EqSO9 | GB% | BABIP | WHIP | ERA | FIP | FRA | WARP |
|------|------|-----|-----|---|---|----|----|----|-----|-----|----|----|-----|-------|-------|------|-------|------|------|------|------|------|
| 2009 | SLN | MLB | 24 | 1 | 1 | 1 | 29 | 0 | 23² | 17 | 3 | 15 | 30 | 5.7 | 11.4 | 37% | .255 | 1.35 | 4.18 | 4.45 | 4.61 | 0.2 |
| 2009 | CLE | MLB | 24 | 0 | 1 | 1 | 32 | 0 | 33¹ | 24 | 5 | 12 | 38 | 3.2 | 10.3 | 35% | .253 | 1.08 | 4.32 | 4.16 | 6.20 | 0.0 |
| 2010 | CLE | MLB | 25 | 2 | 2 | 23 | 63 | 0 | 63 | 40 | 4 | 28 | 61 | 4.0 | 8.7 | 36% | .231 | 1.08 | 1.71 | 3.51 | 4.44 | 0.4 |
| 2011 | CLE | MLB | 26 | 4 | 7 | 36 | 64 | 0 | 59² | 46 | 5 | 26 | 39 | 3.9 | 5.9 | 31% | .240 | 1.21 | 3.32 | 4.30 | 5.14 | 0.0 |
| *2012* | *CLE* | *MLB* | *26* | *3* | *1* | *21* | *54* | *0* | *51²* | *40* | *5* | *24* | *53* | *4.2* | *9.3* | *38%* | *.271* | *1.25* | *3.35* | *3.80* | *3.64* | *0.8* |

Chris Perez is a bit of an enigma. With such a drastic three-year drop-off in his strikeout rate, thanks to a fastball that is now 2-mph slower with less rise, you'd think Perez's struggles would be many. But despite a 5.01 xFIP, Perez actually had a great 2011 season. You see, Perez has never allowed a BABIP higher than .271, and that was in his rookie year with the Cardinals. A fly-ball pitcher with below-average control, Perez is going to need every ounce of hit-preventing mojo he can muster if he can't find a way to regain his whiffs. There are some pitchers capable of consistently excellent BABIPs, especially among relievers, but identifying the contenders from the pretenders is a difficult task. If Perez is to remain a viable closer, he'll either need to prove himself a contender or start blowing the doors off hitters again. The Indians would be well served to have Plan B ready to go.

**Rafael Perez**
Born: 5/15/1982 Age: 30
Bats: L Throws: L Height: 6' 4" Weight: 185
Breakout: 27% Improve: 62% Collapse: 9%
Attrition: 5% MLB: 92%

Comparables:
Charles Nagy, John Grabow, Sparky Lyle

| YEAR | TEAM | LVL | AGE | W | L | SV | G | GS | IP | H | HR | BB | SO | EqBB9 | EqSO9 | GB% | BABIP | WHIP | ERA | FIP | FRA | WARP |
|------|------|-----|-----|---|---|----|----|----|-----|-----|----|----|-----|-------|-------|------|-------|------|------|------|------|------|
| 2009 | COH | AAA | 27 | 1 | 0 | 3 | 16 | 0 | 21² | 23 | 0 | 5 | 23 | 2.1 | 9.5 | 56% | .371 | 1.29 | 0.83 | 1.86 | 2.83 | 0.7 |
| 2009 | CLE | MLB | 27 | 4 | 3 | 0 | 54 | 0 | 48 | 66 | 5 | 25 | 32 | 4.7 | 6.0 | 51% | .377 | 1.90 | 7.31 | 4.85 | 5.32 | 0.2 |
| 2010 | CLE | MLB | 28 | 6 | 1 | 0 | 70 | 0 | 61 | 72 | 3 | 25 | 36 | 3.7 | 5.3 | 59% | .342 | 1.59 | 3.25 | 3.74 | 4.89 | 0.0 |
| 2011 | CLE | MLB | 29 | 5 | 2 | 0 | 71 | 0 | 63 | 59 | 2 | 19 | 33 | 2.7 | 4.7 | 59% | .285 | 1.24 | 3.00 | 3.33 | 4.66 | 0.2 |
| *2012* | *CLE* | *MLB* | *30* | *3* | *1* | *1* | *61* | *0* | *53¹* | *54* | *5* | *18* | *42* | *3.0* | *7.0* | *54%* | *.311* | *1.34* | *3.87* | *3.86* | *4.20* | *0.5* |

Coming off two seasons in which he teetered between inconsistent and ineffective, due in large part to a drop-off in his strike-out rate, Rafael Perez needed to find a way to get by when he could no longer get batters to swing through his stuff. Primarily a two-pitch pitcher, losing the bite on his slider following 2009 was devastating for the once-elite setup man. While the slider isn't what it once was, Perez had himself a consistently good 2011 season by sacrificing a bit of velocity for command. He lost a few more strikeouts in the process, but his walks fell dramatically, and when you're a pitcher who gets as many groundballs as Perez does, you can survive with good control and middling strikeout numbers. He's not the 3.00 ERA pitcher that we saw last year, but he's still a very capable seventh inning reliever.

### Vinnie Pestano

Born: 2/20/1985 Age: 27
Bats: R Throws: R Height: 6' 2'' Weight: 205
Breakout: 24% Improve: 53% Collapse: 26%
Attrition: 11% MLB: 95%

**Comparables:**
Mark Wohlers, Bryan Harvey, Rafael Soriano

| YEAR | TEAM | LVL | AGE | W | L | SV | G | GS | IP | H | HR | BB | SO | EqBB9 | EqSO9 | GB% | BABIP | WHIP | ERA | FIP | FRA | WARP |
|------|------|-----|-----|---|---|----|----|----|-----|----|----|----|----|-------|-------|-----|-------|------|------|------|------|------|
| 2009 | AKR | AA | 24 | 2 | 3 | 24 | 34 | 0 | 34² | 30 | 2 | 13 | 31 | 3.4 | 8.0 | 51% | .295 | 1.24 | 2.85 | 3.40 | 3.69 | 0.6 |
| 2010 | COH | AAA | 25 | 1 | 2 | 14 | 43 | 0 | 46¹ | 23 | 2 | 13 | 44 | 2.7 | 11.5 | 56% | .269 | 1.06 | 1.56 | 3.10 | 3.68 | 1.2 |
| 2010 | CLE | MLB | 25 | 0 | 0 | 1 | 5 | 0 | 5 | 4 | 0 | 5 | 8 | 9.0 | 14.4 | 30% | .400 | 1.80 | 3.60 | 2.85 | 3.39 | 0.1 |
| 2011 | CLE | MLB | 26 | 1 | 2 | 2 | 67 | 0 | 62 | 41 | 5 | 24 | 84 | 3.5 | 12.2 | 40% | .269 | 1.05 | 2.32 | 2.71 | 3.54 | 1.0 |
| 2012 | CLE | MLB | 27 | 3 | 1 | 1 | 48 | 0 | 47¹ | 41 | 5 | 20 | 51 | 3.7 | 9.7 | 48% | .300 | 1.28 | 3.39 | 3.69 | 3.69 | 0.7 |

It's rare to see a pitcher with such an unconventional side-arm delivery rack up so many strike-outs—these types usually get by on their deception and groundballs. Pestano used to be that type of pitcher when his arm slot was lower, but when he raised it and added a four-seamer in 2010, his stuff improved and the results were tremendous. Now throwing a 93-mph fastball that's even more effective given his still-deceptive delivery, the 2011 breakout can also cut the pitch and mix in a terrific sinker and a hard, slurvy breaking ball. Pestano will be a high-leverage reliever for years to come, but don't expect him to transition into closing since his arm slot and repertoire limit his effectiveness against lefties.

### Zach Putnam

Born: 7/3/1987 Age: 24
Bats: R Throws: R Height: 6' 3'' Weight: 225
Breakout: 38% Improve: 67% Collapse: 16%
Attrition: 12% MLB: 92%

**Comparables:**
Kevin Millwood, Jason Windsor, Bob Moose

| YEAR | TEAM | LVL | AGE | W | L | SV | G | GS | IP | H | HR | BB | SO | EqBB9 | EqSO9 | GB% | BABIP | WHIP | ERA | FIP | FRA | WARP |
|------|------|-----|-----|---|---|----|----|----|-----|----|----|----|----|-------|-------|-----|-------|------|------|------|------|------|
| 2009 | AKR | AA | 22 | 5 | 2 | 2 | 33 | 0 | 56² | 61 | 2 | 18 | 60 | 2.9 | 9.0 | 57% | .331 | 1.36 | 4.13 | 2.49 | 3.51 | 1.2 |
| 2010 | AKR | AA | 23 | 3 | 1 | 3 | 20 | 7 | 51¹ | 42 | 2 | 7 | 24 | 1.6 | 7.2 | 44% | .339 | 1.31 | 3.86 | 3.58 | 4.18 | 0.6 |
| 2010 | COH | AAA | 23 | 1 | 1 | 0 | 17 | 0 | 24¹ | 14 | 2 | 6 | 22 | 2.6 | 8.9 | 47% | .235 | 1.11 | 3.33 | 3.53 | 3.87 | 0.6 |
| 2011 | COH | AAA | 24 | 6 | 3 | 9 | 44 | 0 | 69 | 61 | 6 | 23 | 70 | 3.0 | 8.9 | 51% | .291 | 1.22 | 3.65 | 3.38 | 4.65 | 1.0 |
| 2011 | CLE | MLB | 24 | 1 | 1 | 0 | 8 | 0 | 7¹ | 10 | 1 | 0 | 9 | 0.0 | 11.0 | 35% | .409 | 1.36 | 6.14 | 3.20 | 3.67 | 0.1 |
| 2012 | CLE | MLB | 24 | 1 | 1 | 1 | 17 | 1 | 29 | 30 | 3 | 10 | 23 | 3.0 | 7.1 | 48% | .310 | 1.38 | 4.18 | 4.00 | 4.54 | 0.2 |

Taking a big step forward in his first full season at Triple-A, Putnam will compete for a spot in Cleveland's bullpen this spring and should be a mainstay for years to come. Already possessing a true knockout pitch in a brutal splitter that drops off the table, Putnam changed the grip on his slider this season to give him a second big-league-quality off-speed pitch. That slider complements a 92-93 mph fastball that touches 96. Putnam also improved his fastball command last season and has little left to learn in the minors. An athletic player who could have been drafted as a hitter, Putnam bounced between the rotation and bullpen before finally settling into a relief role in 2011. Shoulder issues hampered his effectiveness in the middle of the season, but he bounced back well and should be fine.

### Tony Sipp

Born: 7/12/1983 Age: 28
Bats: L Throws: L Height: 6' 1'' Weight: 190
Breakout: 22% Improve: 44% Collapse: 27%
Attrition: 12% MLB: 91%

**Comparables:**
John Henry Johnson, Bob Johnson, Sid Fernandez

| YEAR | TEAM | LVL | AGE | W | L | SV | G | GS | IP | H | HR | BB | SO | EqBB9 | EqSO9 | GB% | BABIP | WHIP | ERA | FIP | FRA | WARP |
|------|------|-----|-----|---|---|----|----|----|-----|----|----|----|----|-------|-------|-----|-------|------|------|------|------|------|
| 2009 | CLE | MLB | 25 | 2 | 0 | 0 | 46 | 0 | 40 | 27 | 5 | 25 | 48 | 5.6 | 10.8 | 38% | .253 | 1.30 | 2.92 | 4.24 | 3.75 | 0.9 |
| 2010 | CLE | MLB | 26 | 2 | 2 | 1 | 70 | 0 | 63 | 48 | 12 | 39 | 69 | 5.6 | 9.9 | 33% | .255 | 1.38 | 4.14 | 5.29 | 5.56 | -0.3 |
| 2011 | CLE | MLB | 27 | 6 | 3 | 0 | 69 | 0 | 62¹ | 45 | 10 | 24 | 57 | 3.5 | 8.2 | 28% | .220 | 1.11 | 3.03 | 4.47 | 4.94 | 0.2 |
| 2012 | CLE | MLB | 28 | 3 | 1 | 0 | 58 | 0 | 52¹ | 44 | 7 | 25 | 57 | 4.3 | 9.8 | 37% | .284 | 1.31 | 3.65 | 4.20 | 3.97 | 0.6 |

In his third season with the club, Sipp was promoted to high-leverage duties in 2011 and was appointed temporary closer in July when Chris Perez was placed on the bereavement list. His role and ERA, however, lend him more credit than he deserves. A .220 BABIP is unsustainable any way you cut it and will come back to bite him in 2012. Given his extreme fly-ball tendencies, those extra runners will be even more costly when paired with inevitable home runs. In 2011, there was just one pitcher in all of baseball who posted a higher HR/9 and a lower ERA than Sipp (Koji Uehara). He needs to keep pounding the zone—50 percent of pitches in 2011; 43 percent in 2010—in order to maintain the strides he made with his walk rate this season. If he can't, more hits *and* more walks will spell disaster.

### Joe Smith

Born: 3/22/1984 Age: 28
Bats: R Throws: R Height: 6' 3'' Weight: 205
Breakout: 12% Improve: 39% Collapse: 33%
Attrition: 20% MLB: 95%

**Comparables:**
Dean Chance, Geraldo Guzman, Andy Messersmith

| YEAR | TEAM | LVL | AGE | W | L | SV | G | GS | IP | H | HR | BB | SO | EqBB9 | EqSO9 | GB% | BABIP | WHIP | ERA | FIP | FRA | WARP |
|------|------|-----|-----|---|---|----|---|----|----|---|----|----|----|-------|-------|-----|-------|------|-----|-----|-----|------|
| 2009 | CLE | MLB | 25 | 0 | 0 | 0 | 37 | 0 | 34 | 30 | 4 | 13 | 30 | 3.4 | 7.9 | 56% | .277 | 1.26 | 3.44 | 4.06 | 4.44 | 0.4 |
| 2010 | COH | AAA | 26 | 2 | 1 | 2 | 20 | 0 | 23 | 15 | 0 | 9 | 12 | 3.9 | 7.4 | 67% | .326 | 1.17 | 1.96 | 3.66 | 4.92 | 0.2 |
| 2010 | CLE | MLB | 26 | 2 | 2 | 0 | 53 | 0 | 40 | 30 | 4 | 24 | 32 | 5.4 | 7.2 | 56% | .241 | 1.35 | 3.83 | 4.62 | 5.05 | 0.0 |
| 2011 | CLE | MLB | 27 | 3 | 3 | 0 | 71 | 0 | 67 | 52 | 1 | 21 | 45 | 2.8 | 6.0 | 58% | .260 | 1.09 | 2.01 | 2.94 | 3.91 | 0.8 |
| 2012 | CLE | MLB | 28 | 3 | 1 | 1 | 59 | 0 | 53¹ | 48 | 4 | 22 | 44 | 3.7 | 7.5 | 58% | .288 | 1.31 | 3.48 | 3.77 | 3.79 | 0.7 |

On the surface, Smith may look like a mere middle-relief specialist, but what he represents is so much more: the savviness the Cleveland front office can show at times. Part of the three-team deal that sent the Mets J.J. Putz, Smith was brushed off by the New York media as irrelevant because the Mets received a "similar" pitcher in Sean Green. Three years later Smith has posted a 2.87 ERA compared to Green's 4.57 in 50 percent more innings. Throwing somewhere between sidearm and submarine with a great sinker, Smith collects groundballs as easily as Brad Pitt collects fan mail. Finding the zone more frequently last season—52 percent of pitches compared to 47 percent in 2010—Smith

Crabtree

When the Indians acquired Talbot from the Rays before the 2010 season, GM Chris Antonetti said, "He's a guy we've had interest in for quite a while," and it was easy to see why. Talbot has the arsenal to be a groundballing fourth or fifth starter with his good sinker, plus change, above-average cutter, and a breaking ball that's between a hard curve and a slurvy slider. But while he pitched well in Columbus, he had lukewarm success in Cleveland at best, and he'll look for a new club in 2012. He made just 11 messy starts before getting demoted until September, with his calling card groundball rate falling well below league average. Talbot still has the potential to be a solid contributor if and only if he can pitch down in the zone. He doesn't possess swing-and-miss stuff aside from his changeup, and his command is unremarkable, so he'll need to become an ant-killer if he's to stick in the bigs.

### Josh Tomlin

Born: 10/19/1984 Age: 27
Bats: R Throws: R Height: 6' 2'' Weight: 195
Breakout: 33% Improve: 59% Collapse: 16%
Attrition: 13% MLB: 89%

**Comparables:**
Rusty Meacham, Brad Radke, Kevin Tapani

| YEAR | TEAM | LVL | AGE | W | L | SV | G | GS | IP | H | HR | BB | SO | EqBB9 | EqSO9 | GB% | BABIP | WHIP | ERA | FIP | FRA | WARP |
|------|------|-----|-----|---|---|----|---|----|----|---|----|----|----|-------|-------|-----|-------|------|-----|-----|-----|------|
| 2009 | AKR | AA | 24 | 16 | 9 | 0 | 26 | 25 | 145 | 157 | 22 | 27 | 140 | 1.7 | 7.8 | 38% | .299 | 1.21 | 4.16 | 3.88 | 4.26 | 2.1 |
| 2010 | COH | AAA | 25 | 8 | 4 | 0 | 20 | 17 | 107¹ | 55 | 7 | 29 | 58 | 2.8 | 6.7 | 39% | .244 | 1.08 | 2.68 | 4.14 | 4.56 | 1.6 |
| 2010 | CLE | MLB | 25 | 6 | 4 | 0 | 12 | 12 | 73 | 72 | 10 | 19 | 43 | 2.3 | 5.3 | 32% | .278 | 1.25 | 4.56 | 4.55 | 4.87 | 0.2 |
| 2011 | CLE | MLB | 26 | 12 | 7 | 0 | 26 | 26 | 165¹ | 157 | 24 | 21 | 89 | 1.1 | 4.8 | 40% | .254 | 1.08 | 4.25 | 4.31 | 4.15 | 2.1 |
| 2012 | CLE | MLB | 27 | 8 | 7 | 0 | 20 | 20 | 123¹ | 128 | 18 | 28 | 78 | 2.0 | 5.7 | 39% | .285 | 1.26 | 4.17 | 4.52 | 4.53 | 0.7 |

Josh Tomlin is a freak. Not in the Tim Lincecum sense, but rather in that he can do whatever he wants with a baseball. Put a grid over the strike zone and ask him to throw to the (x,y) coordinate (2,3); he'll ask you to provide coordinates with decimals out to the hundredth place. That's the kind of command he has. He doesn't strike many batters out, but he does throw five pitches for strikes. His fastball only averages 88 mph, but he throws both a four- and two-seamer, a plus cutter, a slow, loopy curve, and a lesser-used change. One of baseball's premier control artists—he led the majors in walk rate in 2011—Tomlin should be painting masterpieces as the Tribe's third or fourth starter for many years.

# LINEOUTS

## HITTERS

| PLAYER | TEAM | LVL | AGE | PA | R | 2B | 3B | HR | RBI | BB | SO | SB-CS | AVG/OBP/SLG | TAv | BABIP | BRR | FRAA | WARP |
|--------|------|-----|-----|-----|----|----|----|----|-----|----|----|-------|-------------|-----|-------|-----|------|------|
| C C. Chen | AKR | AA | 22 | 467 | 58 | 24 | 3 | 16 | 70 | 43 | 122 | 2-1 | .262/.330/.451 | .279 | .326 | -5 | -0.6 | 2.2 |
| 3B J. Goedert | COH | AAA | 26 | 322 | 39 | 18 | 0 | 15 | 39 | 33 | 60 | 0-0 | .271/.346/.493 | .259 | .292 | -1.7 | 8.5 | 1.4 |
| 1B N. Johnson | COH | AAA | 32 | 216 | 20 | 6 | 0 | 6 | 13 | 26 | 52 | 0-1 | .201/.316/.332 | .229 | .246 | -2 | 2.4 | -0.5 |
| LF A. Kearns | CLE | MLB | 31 | 174 | 18 | 5 | 1 | 2 | 7 | 18 | 48 | 0-4 | .200/.302/.287 | .225 | .280 | 0.8 | 1.9 | 0.1 |
| 2B A. LaRoche | SAC | AAA | 27 | 224 | 24 | 12 | 0 | 4 | 27 | 19 | 24 | 3-2 | .254/.335/.376 | .237 | .269 | 1.1 | -0.7 | 0.0 |
| | OAK | MLB | 27 | 104 | 10 | 6 | 1 | 0 | 5 | 8 | 19 | 0-0 | .247/.320/.333 | .219 | .311 | -1.8 | -0.8 | -0.5 |
| 1B B. Mills | AKR | AA | 24 | 258 | 37 | 16 | 1 | 11 | 49 | 22 | 37 | 0-0 | .300/.358/.522 | .298 | .312 | -3.1 | -2.6 | 0.7 |
| | COH | AAA | 24 | 133 | 13 | 6 | 0 | 7 | 18 | 10 | 22 | 0-0 | .269/.326/.496 | .271 | .272 | -2.1 | 1.5 | 0.3 |
| LF T. Neal | FRE | AAA | 23 | 239 | 35 | 13 | 3 | 2 | 25 | 13 | 50 | 7-6 | .295/.351/.409 | .242 | .375 | 0.1 | -2.3 | -0.2 |
| C M. Pagnozzi | CSP | AAA | 28 | 198 | 26 | 13 | 2 | 3 | 29 | 16 | 40 | 0-2 | .275/.337/.421 | .248 | .338 | -0.4 | 0.6 | 0.6 |
| | COL | MLB | 28 | 25 | 2 | 0 | 0 | 0 | 2 | 1 | 8 | 0-0 | .286/.348/.286 | .229 | .462 | -0.3 | 0.1 | 0.0 |
| | PIT | MLB | 28 | 9 | 0 | 0 | 0 | 0 | 1 | 0 | 2 | 0-0 | .250/.250/.250 | .160 | .333 | 0 | 0 | -0.1 |
| CF L. Rodriguez | LKC | A | 18 | 148 | 10 | 4 | 2 | 0 | 5 | 14 | 36 | 6-5 | .250/.320/.311 | .232 | .340 | 1.7 | -1 | -0.2 |
| | LKC | A | 19 | 394 | 41 | 28 | 7 | 11 | 42 | 13 | 83 | 10-7 | .246/.274/.449 | .266 | .286 | -1.2 | 2.1 | 2.1 |
| | IND | RK | 18 | 103 | 18 | 6 | 2 | 3 | 14 | 5 | 19 | 12-5 | .379/.408/.579 | .319 | .440 | 1.2 | 5.8 | 0.8 |
| LF N. Weglarz | AKR | AA | 23 | 172 | 25 | 8 | 0 | 3 | 12 | 36 | 43 | 0-1 | .179/.360/.306 | .247 | .239 | -2 | -3.4 | -0.5 |
| SS T. Wolters | MHV | A- | 19 | 313 | 50 | 10 | 3 | 1 | 20 | 30 | 49 | 19-4 | .292/.385/.363 | .296 | .353 | -0.1 | -0.6 | 2.3 |

With average-at-best defense, **Chun-Hsiu Chen**'s biggest challenge will be proving he can remain behind the plate now that his bat has carried him this far. If he sticks, he could eventually be a great replacement for Lou Marson. ⊘ Never considered much of a prospect, **Jared Goedert** may blaze his own trail to the majors by 2013 thanks to the good power he's showing, despite injuries and the lack of a real position. ⊘ After his second straight season with wrist issues, the perennially unhealthy **Nick Johnson** may decide to hang up his spikes for good. Once a prospect lauded for his patience and bat, Johnson's days as a big leaguer may be over. ⊘ After drawing 44 starts in place of Cleveland's infirmary-ridden outfielders, by August **Austin Kearns** had worn out his welcome with the Indians and he and his eroded skills were released. ⊘ Years before veteran good-glove, no-hit infielder **Andy LaRoche** was born, his father Dave was Cleveland's closer; the younger LaRoche will hope to get there after signing a minor league deal with the organization. ⊘ Former first-rounder, former top prospect, and current son of Houston manager Brad Mills, **Beau Mills** had fallen from grace before a 2011 resurgence. He'll need to prove himself more at Triple-A, but perhaps he won't have to settle for a coaching job like his old man—at least not right away. ⊘ A great return for Orlando Cabrera, **Thomas Neal** is a bit injury-prone but was a top prospect just two years ago. A fringe five-tool-type, Neal does lots well but nothing great. ⊘ After the Rockies waived **Matt Pagnozzi**, the Pirates jumped on. That marriage didn't last long, and with lackluster ability and no room for him in Cleveland, his apparent plan of 1) play poorly, 2) get cut, 3) latch onto another minor league squad, could continue to perpetuate itself. ⊘ **Luigi Rodriguez**, a converted second baseman with plus-plus speed, has taken to the outfield well and shows a good approach at the plate with a bit of pop. ⊘ While **Nick Weglarz** holds a lot of potential with his incredible patience, good approach, and power upside (given his size and strength), he suffered through injuries for the third season in a row. His only chance to get back on track with his development is to get healthy. ⊘ A good fundamental player, **Tony Wolters** may eventually be pushed to second base by Lindor, but his good approach, line drive stroke, and plus defense profile as a potential everyday player.

**PITCHERS**

| PLAYER | TEAM | LVL | AGE | W | L | SV | IP | H | HR | BB | SO | EqBB9 | EqSO9 | GB% | BABIP | WHIP | ERA | FIP | FRA | WARP |
|---|---|---|---|---|---|---|---|---|---|---|---|---|---|---|---|---|---|---|---|---|
| S. Barnes | COH | AAA | 23 | 7 | 4 | 0 | 88 | 80 | 12 | 34 | 90 | 3.5 | 9.2 | 43% | .293 | 1.30 | 3.68 | 4.23 | 4.46 | 1.6 |
| K. De La Cruz | AKR | AA | 22 | 4 | 2 | 2 | 86 | 69 | 3 | 53 | 88 | 6.0 | 9.9 | 32% | .319 | 1.48 | 4.19 | 3.77 | 4.56 | 0.9 |
| J. Germano | COH | AAA | 28 | 1 | 2 | 3 | 49 | 50 | 5 | 4 | 39 | 0.7 | 7.2 | 50% | .319 | 1.10 | 4.22 | 3.40 | 4.42 | 0.9 |
|  | CLE | MLB | 28 | 0 | 1 | 0 | 12² | 15 | 1 | 5 | 5 | 3.6 | 3.6 | 38% | .304 | 1.58 | 5.68 | 4.96 | 5.24 | -0.1 |
| F. Sterling | LKC | A | 18 | 2 | 3 | 0 | 41¹ | 31 | 4 | 25 | 35 | 5.4 | 7.6 | 40% | .265 | 1.35 | 4.14 | 4.88 | 5.58 | 0.1 |
|  | IND | RK | 18 | 2 | 3 | 0 | 26¹ | 26 | 3 | 8 | 31 | 2.7 | 10.6 | 41% | .343 | 1.29 | 4.10 | 4.62 | 4.33 | 0.4 |

In his first season at Triple-A, **Scott Barnes**, a lefty with a bit of deception in his delivery, pitched quite well. With an above-average fastball, a tight slider, and a change, Barnes could have a future as a back-end starter. ⌀ **Kelvin De La Cruz** has always been a tall, projectable lefty arm, and while he's begun to make good on his projectability in certain areas—like his

# MANAGER: MANNY ACTA

| YEAR | TEAM | W-L | Pythag +/- | Avg PC | 100+ P | 120+ P | QS | BQS | REL | REL w Zero R | IBB | Subs | PH | PH Avg | PH HR | SB2 | CS2 | SB3 | CS3 | SAC Att | SAC % | POS SAC | Squeeze | Swing | In Play |
|---|---|---|---|---|---|---|---|---|---|---|---|---|---|---|---|---|---|---|---|---|---|---|---|---|---|
| 2009 | WAS | 26-61 | 0 | 93.3 | 21 | 0 | 32 | 3 | 280 | 152 | 26 | 29 | 145 | .215 | 2 | 5 | 2 | 0 | 1 | 48 | 64.6% | 10 | 0 | 78 | 65 |
| 2010 | CLE | 69-93 | 0 | 193.3 | 158 | 155 | 105 | 3 | 470 | 382 | 72 | — | 136 | .169 | 2 | 11 | 4 | 0 | 0 | 98 | 87.8% | 82 | 6 | 319 | 108 |
| 2011 | CLE | 80-82 | 0 | 95.6 | 65 | 0 | 85 | 10 | 482 | 388 | 34 | — | 65 | .211 | 1 | 9 | 6 | 0 | 1 | 43 | 86.0% | 32 | 1 | 313 | 96 |

Manny Acta finished fourth in the Manager of the Year voting last year (behind three managers who helmed playoff teams), but it shouldn't be long before he's taking home the real hardware. Voters love a winning manager more than kids love cake, and if the youth-infused Indians make the transition into playoff contenders, Acta will look as fine as angel food. Praised for his ability to inspire players and make the most of the talent he is given, Acta is also a very sound tactician and a manager who is extremely open to taking suggestions from advanced analytics. The most widespread crime among major league managers is overmanaging, whereas one of Acta's greatest strengths as a tactician is what he *doesn't* do: he doesn't overwork his pitching staff, he doesn't attempt many sacrifices, and he doesn't offer many free passes.

# Colorado Rockies

No team spent more than the Rockies during the 2010–11 offseason. In a six-week span, they committed more than a quarter of a billion dollars to three players, extending the contracts of Troy Tulowitzki (10 years, $157.75 million), Carlos Gonzalez (seven years, $80 million), and Jorge De La Rosa (two years, $21.5 million).

With lofty deals came lofty expectations. Hilton Sports Book set the over-under at 86 wins, with multiple players expressing skepticism at such a low total. After winning 92 games in 2009 and a "disappointing" 83 in 2010, Colorado expected to contend in a weak NL West.

Optimism was so rampant that players even seemed to believe that a move to the team's new and cumbersomely named Salt River Fields at Talking Stick spring-training facility would help propel them to greater heights in 2011. In the waning days of camp, Tulowitzki compared the squad to the 2007 version that shocked everyone by capturing the NL pennant.

This wasn't just organizational propaganda, either. Our writers didn't offer a win total but picked the Rockies to finish second in the division. SI.com's Jon Heyman predicted that they would beat the Rangers in the World Series (he got half the equation right) behind Ubaldo Jimenez's Cy Young Award.

Such optimism appeared to be well-founded through April, when the Rockies went 17-8 despite getting almost nothing from Gonzalez and Jimenez. Unfortunately, they played at a .409 clip the rest of the way (better than only Houston, Minnesota, and Seattle), knocking them 13 victories shy of the preseason line and hopelessly out of contention.

The Rockies went 28-44 against NL West rivals and owned the division's worst run differential. Only Baltimore, which played in a much stronger division, lost more games against

opponents with a .500 record or better. By the time June arrived, fans were calling for Jim Tracy's head, or at least his job.

What went wrong? In a nutshell, everything.

Jimenez and third baseman Ian Stewart got hurt in spring training and never completely recovered. De La Rosa blew out his elbow 10 starts into the new deal. Former rotation mainstay Aaron Cook, hoping for a return to form, experienced shoulder soreness during spring training, then broke his right ring finger by slamming it in a door (not the favored method of rehabilitation from shoulder issues).

Tulowitzki (hip) and Gonzalez (wrist) had injuries of their own at various points. And what would a Rockies season be without pain in Todd Helton's back?

Still, injuries don't tell the whole story. According to Corey Dawkins and Ben Lindbergh, our resident injury experts, Colorado players spent 863 days on the disabled list, costing the team 4.5 WARP. In the NL West, only Arizona had fewer days on the DL, while San Francisco and Los Angeles lost more in terms of WARP.

Second base was a perpetual black hole. The Rockies had no adequate contingency plan for Stewart's unexpected suckitude at third. Ryan Spilborghs forgot how to hit. And so on.

The Rockies replaced hitting coach Don Baylor after 2010 with Carney Lansford, who sought to improve the team's production on the road and with two strikes. The results were less than stellar.

Lansford, who drew praise for his intensity, had Stewart move a full foot off the plate so he would be less susceptible to the inside strike. Stewart expressed confidence in his new coach at the time, saying, "Personally, for me, I think Carney's probably going to have a big impact."

## ROCKIES PROSPECTUS
### 2011 W-L: 73-89, 4th in NL West

| | | | |
|---|---|---|---|
| Pythag | .475 | 21st | **Ballpark:** Coors Field (3-yr. PF: 113). Notice no one's talking about the humidor anymore |
| RS/G | 4.54 | 8th | |
| RA/G | 4.78 | 27th | |
| TAv | .252 | 20th | **2011:** Too many holes in too many important spots despite a strong up-the-middle core |
| TAv-P | .256 | 12th | |
| FIP | 4.21 | 24th | |
| DER | .702 | 22nd | **2012:** Still a lot of holes, and they need to remember how to win at home |
| DL | 766 | 18th | |
| B-Age | 28.5 | 14th | |
| P-Age | 27.4 | 10th | **Action Items:** Starting pitching, third base, starting pitching, second base, starting pitching |
| Salary | $82.3 | 18th | |
| M$/MW | $2.84 | 19th | |

If only Stewart hadn't been so correct. The man who hit 43 home runs over the previous two seasons sustained a sprained right MCL during spring training, started out slowly during Colorado's hot April, and then got shipped to Triple-A two weeks into the season despite a lack of reasonable alternatives (Jose Lopez? Ty Wigginton?), finishing the big-league portion of his season homerless.

As for Lansford's other goals, the team's road offense improved under his watch, but not by much. The Rockies scored five more runs in 81 games away from Coors Field last year than they had under Baylor in 2010, going from .226/.303/.351 on the road to .242/.309/.373. The downside is that they scored 40 fewer runs and dropped 70 points of

the fact.

Offense isn't limited to hitting, though, and another of manager Tracy's goals was to have his club be more aggressive on the bases. To that end, Tracy put his runners in motion more often than any other big-league manager. The upside is that the Rockies stole 118 bases at a 73.8 percent clip in 2011, up from 99 at a 70.7 percent clip in 2010. The downside is that the rest of their running game stunk, as they fell from first in the majors in EqBRR in 2010 (14.0) to 18th in 2011 (-2.3). Their aggressiveness cost them runs. (Other metrics, such as those published by Baseball Info Solutions, were more forgiving but still showed the Rockies slipping last year.)

Between poor hitting, poor baserunning, and a pitching staff decimated by injuries, the Rockies found themselves in an unexpected position come July. And so, out of contention at the non-waiver trade deadline, they did the unthinkable: They traded Jimenez, arguably the best starting pitcher in franchise history, to Cleveland for prospects.

Thought to be part of the foundation (along with Tulowitzki and Gonzalez), Jimenez slipped considerably from his breakout 2010 campaign but started to show signs of being his old self before the trade. Over a 10-game stretch from the beginning of June to mid-July, he sported a 2.58 ERA and 4.2 K/BB in 66 1/3 innings.

It seemed a curious time for the Rockies to move their ace. In February, *Forbes*, on the basis of his salary and VORP, had cited Jimenez as baseball's best pitching bargain. There was talk of extending him after the 2011 season so that he could continue, along with Tulowitzki and Gonzalez, to lead the franchise toward a return to the postseason.

The trade to Cleveland highlighted a strange season for Jimenez. An infected cuticle on his right thumb in March eventually landed him on the DL after his first regular-season start. His fastball velocity dropped a couple of ticks upon his return, but this was attributed to mechanical issues. There were vague concerns about Jimenez being an injury risk due to his delivery. He was more hittable outside the strike zone than he had been in 2010.

Rockies GM Dan O'Dowd realized that he had a valuable trading chip and that his team needed to make plans for the future, even if that meant doing so without its ace. Two weeks before the trade, Troy Renck of the *Denver Post* dismissed the notion that Jimenez was on the table but noted that O'Dowd

primary returns were Alex White and Drew Pomeranz, both of whom saw action with the big club. White served up an alarming number of home runs in his brief stint, while questions abound regarding Pomeranz's control and ability to change speeds. He could be Al Leiter, or he could be Oliver Perez.

The usual risks notwithstanding, both prospects have talent. They could help the club as much as, or perhaps more than, Jimenez would have done going forward. O'Dowd achieved his stated goal of acquiring controllable starting pitchers. (He added another after the season, shipping catcher Chris Iannetta to the Angels for 23-year-old right-hander Tyler Chatwood, who had struggled with command as a rookie.)

Beyond the questions of White, Pomeranz, and Chatwood, additional uncertainties loom. Will Tulowitzki and Gonzalez justify their contracts, or will the Rockies come to regret those the way they have come to regret Helton's? What happens behind the plate with Iannetta gone? Can Dexter Fowler make it through a season without a Triple-A stint to figure out some aspect of his game, and can he learn to use his speed? How good is Jhoulys Chacin? What's on second?

The biggest move was signing Tulowitzki, on whom the Rockies have pinned their hopes and dreams. Colorado has gone off the proverbial deep end before with contracts, most notably the Mike Hampton debacle and more recently Helton's albatross.

Hampton's deal, you may recall, was so bad that the Rockies ended up paying Atlanta more money than most baseball players will make in a lifetime to take him off their hands. But then, he was a pitcher trying to earn a living in a place that eats pitchers for lunch.

Helton's nine-year, $141.5 million contract came with risk but made a certain amount of sense when he signed it prior to the 2003 season. He provided solid value (19.7 WARP) for the first three years before stumbling (9.8 WARP) over the final six. And although Helton is an institution in Colorado who rebounded at age 37, the difficult reality is that the Rockies paid him $104.45 million in 2006-11 to be Maicer Izturis (10.0 WARP over the same stretch).

Tulowitzki is a different animal. He plays shortstop and is two years younger than Helton was when the latter signed his extension. Still, the Rockies will owe Tulowitzki $20 million in each of his age 30-35 seasons, and few shortstops remain productive at those ages. Tulowitzki could follow the paths of Barry Larkin, Derek Jeter, or Miguel Tejada and excel well into his 30s. Then again, he could go the way of Nomar Garciaparra.

Tulowitzki is a great player, but even the great ones get hurt, grow old, and eventually become a drag on their teams' resources. The fact that he has missed an average of 33 games per season over the last four years isn't proof of anything, but neither can it make those who are paying him handsomely to help their franchise win games (and hopefully championships) feel good.

Gonzalez, meanwhile, started slowly but ended up with numbers similar to those from 2009. The key with him, as with Tulowitzki, is staying healthy.

As for the catching situation, O'Dowd signed 36-year-old Ramon Hernandez to a two-year, $6.4 million deal the same day Iannetta left town. Hernandez hasn't played in as many as 100 games since 2008, so youngster Wilin Rosario could see his window of opportunity open sooner rather than later.

Fowler finished strong . . . again. But only after a demotion to Triple-A . . . again. Chacin pitched like an ace in the season's first half. After the All-Star break, his command disappeared. If he can string two good halves together, the Rockies might have something special on their hands, although the same could have been said of Jimenez just a few years ago.

As for second base, the situation is dire enough that the Rockies seriously considered re-signing midseason acquisition Mark Ellis, who turns 35 in June and who can't be expected to provide much offense (Ned Colletti and the Dodgers rescued them from that potential mistake in November). Before Jamey Carroll signed with Minnesota, the Rockies were reportedly interested in bringing the 38-year-old Mayor of Scrappleton, who played for the club in 2006-07, back to Denver.

Beyond finding a solution to their keystone problem, the Rockies must remember how to win at home in 2012. Coors Field may not play like it did when steroids were prevalent and the humidor wasn't, but it remains the most extreme offensive environment in baseball. In the past, the Rockies have used this to great advantage, bludgeoning unsuspecting opponents in their arena. Colorado won more than 50 games at home in three of the four seasons prior to 2011. Even that brought no postseason guarantees (the Rockies won 52 at home in 2010, but lost 50 on the road).

Last year, they displayed uncharacteristic vulnerability at Coors Field, going 38-43 there. This marked their first losing record at home since they went 40-41 in 2005 and tied for their worst showing since moving to their current digs a decade earlier.

The Rockies need to figure out how to win on the road (not likely) or return to their home domination. Baylor had his team hitting at Coors Field. He and Lansford played together for the Angels and A's. Maybe they can sit down and brainstorm over macchiatos at Yellow Feather.

# HITTERS

**Nolan Arenado**     **3B**

Born: 4/16/1991 Age: 21
Bats: R Throws: R Height: 6' 2" Weight: 205
Breakout: 4% Improve: 17% Collapse: 3%
Attrition: 9% MLB: 29%

**Comparables:**
Derrell Griffith, Tony Cruz, Carlos Perdomo

| YEAR | TEAM | LVL | AGE | PA | R | 2B | 3B | HR | RBI | BB | SO | SB | CS | AVG_OBP_SLG | TAv | BABIP | BRR | FRAA | WARP |
|------|------|-----|-----|-----|-----|-----|-----|-----|-----|-----|-----|-----|-----|-------------|-----|-------|-----|------|------|
| 2009 | CAS | RK | 18 | 225 | 28 | 15 | 0 | 2 | 22 | 16 | 18 | 5 | 2 | .300/.357/.404 | .274 | .322 | 0.5 | -7.7 | 0.3 |
| 2010 | ASH | A | 19 | 400 | 45 | 41 | 1 | 12 | 65 | 19 | 52 | 1 | 3 | .308/.344/.520 | .286 | .333 | -3.3 | -6.5 | 1.5 |
| 2011 | MOD | A+ | 20 | 583 | 82 | 32 | 3 | 20 | 122 | 47 | 53 | 2 | 1 | .298/.349/.487 | .293 | .293 | 1.7 | -9.5 | 3.7 |
| 2012 | COL | MLB | 21 | 250 | 25 | 13 | 1 | 4 | 25 | 12 | 34 | 0 | 0 | .242/.278/.360 | .215 | .263 | 0 | 3B -4 | -0.3 |

Scouts have liked Arenado's power potential since he played shortstop in high school, and that potential finally started to bear fruit in the second half of 2011. Taken in the second round of the 2009 draft, he now plays third base, where his lack of range is less problematic. Arenado improved his walk rate from 4.8 percent in 2010 to 8.1 percent last year while reducing his strikeout rate from 13.0 percent to 9.1 percent. He will need to keep hitting at every level, as his glove is nothing special (although he has made strides in that area) and he has no speed.

| Charlie Blackmon CF | YEAR | TEAM | LVL | AGE | PA | R | 2B | 3B | HR | RBI | BB | SO | SB | CS | AVG_OBP_SLG | TAv | BABIP | BRR | FRAA | WARP |
|---|---|---|---|---|---|---|---|---|---|---|---|---|---|---|---|---|---|---|---|---|
| Born: 7/1/1986 Age: 25 | 2009 | MOD | A+ | 23 | 616 | 87 | 34 | 7 | 7 | 69 | 39 | 83 | 30 | 13 | .307/.372/.433 | .293 | .350 | -0.7 | -4.5 | 2.9 |
| Bats: L Throws: L Height: 6' 4" Weight: 200 | 2010 | TUL | AA | 24 | 381 | 53 | 22 | 4 | 11 | 55 | 32 | 43 | 19 | 7 | .297/.362/.484 | .306 | .311 | 1.8 | -4.9 | 2.4 |
| Breakout: 6% Improve: 39% Collapse: 7% | 2011 | CSP | AAA | 25 | 272 | 49 | 19 | 4 | 10 | 49 | 19 | 34 | 12 | 5 | .337/.393/.572 | .316 | .356 | 2.2 | 0.8 | 2.5 |
| Attrition: 30% MLB: 79% | 2011 | COL | MLB | 25 | 102 | 9 | 1 | 0 | 1 | 8 | 3 | 8 | 5 | 1 | .255/.277/.296 | .194 | .270 | -0.5 | -1.3 | -0.7 |
| Comparables: Shane Costa, Alex Ochoa, Tim Corcoran | 2012 | COL | MLB | 25 | 250 | 29 | 12 | 2 | 5 | 28 | 12 | 35 | 9 | 3 | .275/.317/.406 | .246 | .303 | -0.3 | CF -5, RF 0 | 0.5 |

A former second-round pick, Blackmon posted gaudy numbers at Triple-A Colorado Springs before being promoted to the big club in June. He spent most of his first three professional seasons in center field, but shifted to the corner in 2011. Although Blackmon doesn't possess the home-run power often associated with a corner spot, he does enough things well to enjoy a career as a fourth outfielder, possibly more.

**Andrew Brown RF**

| YEAR | TEAM | LVL | AGE | PA | R | 2B | 3B | HR | RBI | BB | SO | SB | CS | AVG_OBP_SLG | TAv | BABIP | BRR | FRAA | WARP |
|---|---|---|---|---|---|---|---|---|---|---|---|---|---|---|---|---|---|---|---|

...by the Rockies in October. Brown also has experience at third base and both corner outfield spots, although he is not an accomplished defender anywhere. He didn't do much in a brief trial with the Cardinals, but he has hit at every stop in the minors. If he catches a break or three, Brown could be this year's Jesus Guzman.

| Jorge Cantu 3B | YEAR | TEAM | LVL | AGE | PA | R | 2B | 3B | HR | RBI | BB | SO | SB | CS | AVG_OBP_SLG | TAv | BABIP | BRR | FRAA | WARP |
|---|---|---|---|---|---|---|---|---|---|---|---|---|---|---|---|---|---|---|---|---|
| Born: 1/30/1982 Age: 30 | 2009 | FLO | MLB | 27 | 643 | 67 | 42 | 0 | 16 | 100 | 47 | 81 | 3 | 1 | .289/.345/.443 | .272 | .310 | -1.2 | -4.3 | 1.2 |
| Bats: R Throws: R Height: 6' 4" Weight: 200 | 2010 | TEX | MLB | 28 | 105 | 9 | 4 | 1 | 1 | 2 | 6 | 19 | 0 | 0 | .235/.279/.327 | .219 | .282 | 0.9 | -0.9 | -0.4 |
| Breakout: 1% Improve: 27% Collapse: 6% | 2010 | FLO | MLB | 28 | 410 | 41 | 25 | 0 | 10 | 54 | 23 | 76 | 0 | 0 | .262/.310/.409 | .254 | .298 | -0.3 | -2.3 | -0.1 |
| Attrition: 17% MLB: 71% | 2011 | CSP | AAA | 29 | 125 | 16 | 6 | 0 | 5 | 18 | 6 | 16 | 0 | 0 | .280/.320/.458 | .230 | .289 | 0.9 | -1.6 | -0.2 |
| Comparables: Ross Gload, Jay Gibbons, Brad Fullmer | 2011 | SDN | MLB | 29 | 155 | 8 | 4 | 0 | 3 | 16 | 7 | 28 | 0 | 0 | .194/.232/.285 | .185 | .216 | 0.4 | -0.3 | -1.1 |
| | 2012 | COL | MLB | 30 | 250 | 30 | 14 | 1 | 7 | 31 | 16 | 41 | 1 | 0 | .273/.326/.437 | .261 | .302 | 0 | 3B -4, 1B 0 | 1.4 |

The Padres signed the veteran right-handed hitter to help buy time for prospect Anthony Rizzo at first base, but it didn't work. Cantu did as much for them as Jose Lopez did for the Rockies. Cantu signed with Colorado at the end of July and didn't hit at Triple-A. PECOTA likes his chances to rebound, but he might be one of those Carlos Baerga types whose career effectively ends in his twenties.

| Tyler Colvin RF | YEAR | TEAM | LVL | AGE | PA | R | 2B | 3B | HR | RBI | BB | SO | SB | CS | AVG_OBP_SLG | TAv | BABIP | BRR | FRAA | WARP |
|---|---|---|---|---|---|---|---|---|---|---|---|---|---|---|---|---|---|---|---|---|
| Born: 9/5/1985 Age: 26 | 2009 | DAY | A+ | 23 | 129 | 18 | 5 | 2 | 1 | 10 | 13 | 27 | 3 | 1 | .250/.333/.357 | .244 | .321 | 1.9 | 0 | 0.1 |
| Bats: L Throws: L Height: 6' 4" Weight: 190 | 2009 | TEN | AA | 23 | 330 | 51 | 13 | 7 | 14 | 50 | 16 | 57 | 5 | 5 | .300/.332/.524 | .284 | .325 | 2.2 | -3.2 | 1.3 |
| Breakout: 3% Improve: 30% Collapse: 8% | 2009 | CHN | MLB | 23 | 20 | 1 | 0 | 0 | 0 | 2 | 2 | 5 | 0 | 0 | .176/.250/.176 | .186 | .231 | 0.2 | 0.6 | 0.0 |
| Attrition: 23% MLB: 74% | 2010 | CHN | MLB | 24 | 394 | 60 | 18 | 5 | 20 | 56 | 30 | 100 | 6 | 1 | .254/.316/.500 | .275 | .296 | 1.2 | -0.5 | 1.4 |
| Comparables: Dan Ford, Eric Valent, Cory Keylor | 2011 | IOW | AAA | 25 | 212 | 32 | 12 | 6 | 7 | 32 | 5 | 55 | 1 | 1 | .256/.270/.478 | .244 | .312 | -0.5 | 0.1 | 0.2 |
| | 2011 | CHN | MLB | 25 | 222 | 17 | 8 | 3 | 6 | 20 | 14 | 58 | 0 | 0 | .150/.204/.306 | .183 | .175 | 1.2 | 1.8 | -0.8 |
| | 2012 | COL | MLB | 26 | 274 | 32 | 11 | 4 | 11 | 37 | 16 | 66 | 2 | 1 | .243/.290/.447 | .246 | .282 | 0 | RF -0, LF -1 | 0.4 |

Colvin's isolated power in 2010 was higher than all but 11 of the qualifying batters in the major leagues. He lost a lot of that tremendous power in 2011, but the problem was deeper—he lost some of the gains he'd made in plate discipline, and he wasn't centering up the ball at all, leading to a lot of weakly hit balls and thus easy outs. Colvin didn't even regroup as hoped in Triple-A. Still, a fly-ball hitter who plays half his games at Coors Field always has a chance. He'll be in the mix for at-bats at all three outfield spots as well as first base.

### Michael Cuddyer    RF

Born: 3/27/1979 Age: 33
Bats: R Throws: R Height: 6' 3" Weight: 202
Breakout: 0% Improve: 27% Collapse: 9%
Attrition: 17% MLB: 90%

Comparables:
Magglio Ordonez, Roger Maris, Andy Pafko

| YEAR | TEAM | LVL | AGE | PA | R | 2B | 3B | HR | RBI | BB | SO | SB | CS | AVG_OBP_SLG | TAv | BABIP | BRR | FRAA | WARP |
|---|---|---|---|---|---|---|---|---|---|---|---|---|---|---|---|---|---|---|---|
| 2009 | MIN | MLB | 30 | 650 | 93 | 34 | 7 | 32 | 94 | 54 | 118 | 6 | 1 | .276/.342/.520 | .291 | .295 | -1.2 | -16.8 | 1.3 |
| 2010 | MIN | MLB | 31 | 675 | 93 | 37 | 5 | 14 | 81 | 58 | 93 | 7 | 3 | .271/.336/.417 | .263 | .298 | 1.9 | -9.5 | 0.3 |
| 2011 | MIN | MLB | 32 | 584 | 70 | 29 | 2 | 20 | 70 | 48 | 95 | 11 | 1 | .284/.346/.459 | .293 | .312 | 0.1 | -3.1 | 2.5 |
| 2012 | COL | MLB | 33 | 566 | 72 | 28 | 5 | 17 | 72 | 49 | 93 | 7 | 2 | .277/.344/.452 | .274 | .310 | 0.2 | RF -5, 1B -3 | 1.8 |

Cuddyer rebounded from a subpar 2010 and again showed off his versatility, serving an extended stint at first base and spotting at second in addition to playing right field. But his season was uneven; he hit a searing .330/.410/.571 with 11 homers in June and July, a lukewarm .255/.303/.390 in the other four months. The flareup of a herniated disc in his neck—an ongoing problem since 2004—may have contributed to his late-season woes. Such was the state of the 2011 Twins that he wound up with the team's highest WARP. Cuddyer's widening platoon split over the past three years (.267/.320/.424 vs. righties, .300/.389/.569 vs. lefties) suggests he'd be better served by playing for a team that doesn't need to call on him for 600+ plate appearances a year. Failing that, a move to Coors Field should help.

### Dexter Fowler    CF

Born: 3/22/1986 Age: 26
Bats: B Throws: R Height: 6' 5" Weight: 175
Breakout: 1% Improve: 47% Collapse: 6%
Attrition: 15% MLB: 87%

Comparables:
Dusty Baker, Bobby Murcer, Chet Lemon

| YEAR | TEAM | LVL | AGE | PA | R | 2B | 3B | HR | RBI | BB | SO | SB | CS | AVG_OBP_SLG | TAv | BABIP | BRR | FRAA | WARP |
|---|---|---|---|---|---|---|---|---|---|---|---|---|---|---|---|---|---|---|---|
| 2009 | COL | MLB | 23 | 518 | 73 | 29 | 10 | 4 | 34 | 67 | 116 | 27 | 10 | .266/.363/.406 | .259 | .351 | 6.9 | -2.7 | 1.6 |
| 2010 | CSP | AAA | 24 | 124 | 23 | 10 | 4 | 2 | 13 | 17 | 27 | 1 | 0 | .340/.435/.566 | .295 | .442 | 0.7 | 1.3 | 1.0 |
| 2010 | COL | MLB | 24 | 505 | 73 | 20 | 14 | 6 | 36 | 57 | 104 | 13 | 7 | .260/.347/.410 | .257 | .328 | 3.1 | -1 | 1.2 |
| 2011 | CSP | AAA | 25 | 114 | 17 | 6 | 1 | 2 | 9 | 15 | 24 | 2 | 1 | .237/.345/.381 | .229 | .296 | 0.4 | 0.1 | -0.1 |
| 2011 | COL | MLB | 25 | 563 | 84 | 35 | 15 | 5 | 45 | 68 | 130 | 12 | 9 | .266/.363/.432 | .280 | .354 | 7.1 | 10 | 4.8 |
| 2012 | COL | MLB | 26 | 534 | 70 | 28 | 12 | 9 | 64 | 62 | 110 | 16 | 8 | .276/.366/.446 | .276 | .337 | -1.2 | CF 3 | 2.5 |

Fowler's skill set is baffling. He runs well but is a poor base-stealer. He isn't a power hitter but he struggles to make contact. For the second straight season, he spent a month at Triple-A trying to work out various issues. As was the case in 2010, Fowler seemed to wake up after returning from his demotion, hitting .288/.381/.498 and even swiping 10 bags in 13 attempts. His defense in center also improved. Fowler still has youth on his side, but at some point, the Rockies need to know that they can count on him for an entire season without having to ship him off to Colorado Springs for motivation.

### Cole Garner    LF

Born: 12/15/1984 Age: 27
Bats: R Throws: R Height: 6' 3" Weight: 210
Breakout: 6% Improve: 35% Collapse: 4%
Attrition: 10% MLB: 78%

Comparables:
Elston Howard, George Hendrick, Leonard Davis

| YEAR | TEAM | LVL | AGE | PA | R | 2B | 3B | HR | RBI | BB | SO | SB | CS | AVG_OBP_SLG | TAv | BABIP | BRR | FRAA | WARP |
|---|---|---|---|---|---|---|---|---|---|---|---|---|---|---|---|---|---|---|---|
| 2009 | TUL | AA | 24 | 440 | 65 | 25 | 4 | 16 | 64 | 23 | 78 | 13 | 5 | .288/.343/.492 | .292 | .320 | -0.4 | -4.3 | 1.7 |
| 2010 | CSP | AAA | 25 | 469 | 81 | 31 | 10 | 13 | 61 | 39 | 89 | 8 | 5 | .304/.370/.520 | .290 | .354 | 3 | 1.2 | 3.2 |
| 2011 | CSP | AAA | 26 | 203 | 38 | 8 | 5 | 8 | 35 | 10 | 47 | 4 | 2 | .330/.366/.557 | .288 | .396 | 0 | -2.3 | 0.8 |
| 2011 | COL | MLB | 26 | 10 | 1 | 0 | 0 | 0 | 3 | 1 | 6 | 0 | 0 | .222/.300/.222 | .188 | .667 | 0.2 | 0.2 | 0.0 |
| 2012 | NYA | MLB | 27 | 250 | 29 | 11 | 2 | 9 | 32 | 11 | 64 | 5 | 2 | .249/.292/.428 | .250 | .301 | -0.2 | LF -3, CF -2 | 0.6 |

Garner, who attended high school with former Rockies teammate Ian Stewart and Arizona right-hander Ian Kennedy, made it up to the big club for a handful of games in July. He spent most of 2011 at Triple-A for a second straight season and hit well when healthy, which wasn't often. Garner hasn't played in as many as 120 games since 2006. He isn't young and lacks overwhelming skills. If there is a window of opportunity for Garner, it is perilously close to shutting.

### Jason Giambi    1B

Born: 1/8/1971 Age: 41
Bats: L Throws: R Height: 6' 3" Weight: 200
Breakout: 0% Improve: 9% Collapse: 3%
Attrition: 14% MLB: 57%

Comparables:
Frank Robinson, Frank Thomas, Edgar Martinez

| YEAR | TEAM | LVL | AGE | PA | R | 2B | 3B | HR | RBI | BB | SO | SB | CS | AVG_OBP_SLG | TAv | BABIP | BRR | FRAA | WARP |
|---|---|---|---|---|---|---|---|---|---|---|---|---|---|---|---|---|---|---|---|
| 2009 | OAK | MLB | 38 | 328 | 39 | 13 | 0 | 11 | 40 | 50 | 72 | 0 | 0 | .193/.332/.364 | .271 | .218 | 0.5 | -2.5 | 0.3 |
| 2009 | COL | MLB | 38 | 31 | 4 | 1 | 0 | 2 | 11 | 7 | 8 | 0 | 0 | .292/.452/.583 | .332 | .357 | -0.2 | 0.1 | 0.3 |
| 2010 | COL | MLB | 39 | 222 | 17 | 9 | 0 | 6 | 35 | 35 | 47 | 2 | 0 | .244/.378/.398 | .270 | .289 | -0.3 | -0.8 | 0.3 |
| 2011 | COL | MLB | 40 | 152 | 20 | 6 | 0 | 13 | 32 | 17 | 45 | 0 | 0 | .260/.355/.603 | .322 | .284 | 0.1 | 0.2 | 1.2 |
| 2012 | COL | MLB | 41 | 250 | 32 | 9 | 1 | 12 | 31 | 34 | 56 | 1 | 0 | .239/.358/.451 | .280 | .268 | 0 | 1B -4 | 1.7 |

Giambi has made a remarkable late-career transition into lefty-swinging masher off the bench, a la Matt Stairs. Coors Field wasn't as much of a factor as you might think, as seven of Giambi's 13 homers in 2011 came on the road. Always a three-true-outcomes hitter, he pushed that approach to the extreme last year, with 49.3 percent of his plate appearances resulting in a home run, walk, or strikeout. Giambi probably could turn on a big-league fastball into his fifties. The only questions now are how long his body holds up and how long he wants to keep playing.

### Hector Gomez SS

Born: 3/5/1988 Age: 24
Bats: R Throws: R Height: 6' 3" Weight: 180
Breakout: 4% Improve: 25% Collapse: 5%
Attrition: 23% MLB: 70%

**Comparables:**
Cristian Guzman, Bill Almon, Angel Chavez

| YEAR | TEAM | LVL | AGE | PA | R | 2B | 3B | HR | RBI | BB | SO | SB | CS | AVG_OBP_SLG | TAv | BABIP | BRR | FRAA | WARP |
|------|------|-----|-----|-----|----|----|----|----|-----|----|----|----|----|-------------|------|-------|------|------|------|
| 2009 | MOD | A+ | 21 | 368 | 39 | 21 | 4 | 7 | 46 | 15 | 68 | 10 | 4 | .275/.312/.423 | .267 | .322 | -0.2 | -2.4 | 1.2 |
| 2010 | TRI | A- | 22 | 75 | 8 | 2 | 1 | 2 | 7 | 5 | 15 | 0 | 3 | .246/.297/.391 | .314 | .288 | -1.6 | 1.6 | 0.6 |
| 2011 | TUL | AA | 23 | 453 | 46 | 23 | 6 | 14 | 50 | 19 | 94 | 16 | 4 | .235/.272/.416 | .242 | .270 | 2.1 | 7.5 | 2.1 |
| 2011 | COL | MLB | 23 | 7 | 1 | 0 | 0 | 0 | 0 | 1 | 2 | 0 | 0 | .333/.429/.333 | .249 | .500 | 0.5 | 0 | 0.2 |
| 2012 | COL | MLB | 24 | 250 | 25 | 12 | 2 | 5 | 27 | 7 | 56 | 6 | 2 | .232/.255/.364 | .208 | .277 | 0 | SS 5 | -0.6 |

Gomez was highly regarded a few years ago but lost significant development time from 2008 to 2010 due to various injuries (Tommy John surgery being the most severe among them). Although he has decent pop for a shortstop, it comes at a steep price. In six minor-league seasons, Gomez has struck out more than four times as often as he has walked. If he can develop any plate discipline and learn to play a few more positions, he might make it someday as a utility player.

Coors Field to maximum advantage. Gonzalez has followed in Bichette's footsteps, knocking 42 of his 60 home runs in Denver over the past two seasons. During that same period, his OPS is more than 300 points higher at home than on the road, where he hits like teammate Ty Wigginton. Gonzalez slipped from his breakout 2010 campaign, mainly due to a slow start and slow finish that saw his season cut short by a nagging right wrist injury. From May to August, he was up to his old tricks, hitting .320/.395/.597 in 92 games. The extreme home/road splits will temper perceptions of his ability, but as long as he gets to play half his games at Coors Field, Gonzalez will put up silly numbers.

### Todd Helton 1B

Born: 8/20/1973 Age: 38
Bats: L Throws: L Height: 6' 3" Weight: 195
Breakout: 0% Improve: 17% Collapse: 12%
Attrition: 13% MLB: 74%

**Comparables:**
Rusty Staub, George Brett, Ron Fairly

| YEAR | TEAM | LVL | AGE | PA | R | 2B | 3B | HR | RBI | BB | SO | SB | CS | AVG_OBP_SLG | TAv | BABIP | BRR | FRAA | WARP |
|------|------|-----|-----|-----|----|----|----|----|-----|----|----|----|----|-------------|------|-------|------|------|------|
| 2009 | COL | MLB | 35 | 645 | 79 | 38 | 3 | 15 | 86 | 89 | 73 | 0 | 1 | .325/.416/.489 | .300 | .348 | -4 | -8.8 | 1.5 |
| 2010 | COL | MLB | 36 | 473 | 48 | 18 | 1 | 8 | 37 | 67 | 90 | 0 | 0 | .256/.362/.367 | .255 | .307 | -3.8 | -2.2 | -0.4 |
| 2011 | COL | MLB | 37 | 491 | 59 | 27 | 0 | 14 | 69 | 59 | 71 | 0 | 1 | .302/.385/.466 | .288 | .328 | -2.5 | 12.3 | 3.1 |
| 2012 | COL | MLB | 38 | 459 | 63 | 23 | 2 | 11 | 53 | 64 | 62 | 0 | 0 | .295/.394/.451 | .292 | .324 | -0.1 | 1B 2 | 2.2 |

Helton hasn't hit 20 homers in a season since 2005. He hasn't hit 40 doubles since 2007. Still, he enjoyed a nice rebound from 2010, when he appeared to be crawling along the Brian Giles path to retirement. Helton didn't return to 2009 levels but he put up respectable numbers for an old guy with a bad back that has largely robbed him of his once prodigious power. He hit .321/.400/.494 in the first half before fading down the stretch and missing most of September. Helton's body has taken a pounding over the years, and it's hard to imagine he's got much baseball left in him. As he showed in 2011, he can still hit over short stretches. If Helton is willing to accept a reduced role, perhaps he can continue to delay the inevitable a little longer.

### Ramon Hernandez C

Born: 5/20/1976 Age: 36
Bats: R Throws: R Height: 6' 1" Weight: 203
Breakout: 0% Improve: 27% Collapse: 5%
Attrition: 25% MLB: 72%

**Comparables:**
Ron Hassey, Yogi Berra, Mike Lieberthal

| YEAR | TEAM | LVL | AGE | PA | R | 2B | 3B | HR | RBI | BB | SO | SB | CS | AVG_OBP_SLG | TAv | BABIP | BRR | FRAA | WARP |
|------|------|-----|-----|-----|----|----|----|----|-----|----|----|----|----|-------------|------|-------|------|------|------|
| 2009 | CIN | MLB | 33 | 331 | 25 | 13 | 1 | 5 | 37 | 33 | 34 | 1 | 0 | .258/.336/.362 | .241 | .274 | -0.7 | 1.9 | 0.5 |
| 2010 | CIN | MLB | 34 | 352 | 30 | 18 | 1 | 7 | 48 | 29 | 49 | 0 | 0 | .297/.364/.428 | .275 | .332 | -1.5 | 3.6 | 2.5 |
| 2011 | CIN | MLB | 35 | 328 | 28 | 13 | 0 | 12 | 36 | 23 | 41 | 0 | 0 | .282/.341/.446 | .268 | .291 | -3.4 | 1 | 1.8 |
| 2012 | COL | MLB | 36 | 313 | 38 | 13 | 1 | 9 | 36 | 24 | 41 | 0 | 0 | .272/.336/.420 | .259 | .289 | 0 | C 2, 1B 0 | 1.9 |

In 2003-06, Hernandez ranked among the best catchers in baseball. As expected from a man in his mid-30s who squats for a living, production has fallen off since then, although he continues to be useful in a John Buck kind of way. Hernandez isn't as good or as young as the departed Chris Iannetta, who wore out his welcome in Denver by repeatedly failing to hit .240 but whose on-base skills made him valuable nonetheless. Hernandez hasn't played as many as 100 games since 2008, but when he's in the lineup, he'll help the young pitchers, provide occasional pop, and buy time for Wilin Rosario. If $6.4 million for two years seems a steep price to pay for that, just be grateful it isn't coming out of your pocket.

**Jonathan Herrera    2B**

Born: 11/3/1984 Age: 27
Bats: B Throws: R Height: 5' 10" Weight: 150
Breakout: 8% Improve: 36% Collapse: 7%
Attrition: 21% MLB: 82%
Comparables:
Chuck Knoblauch, Chris Getz, Dave Cash

| YEAR | TEAM | LVL | AGE | PA | R | 2B | 3B | HR | RBI | BB | SO | SB | CS | AVG_OBP_SLG | TAv | BABIP | BRR | FRAA | WARP |
|------|------|-----|-----|-----|----|----|----|----|-----|----|----|----|----|-------------|------|-------|------|----------|------|
| 2009 | CSP | AAA | 24 | 450 | 63 | 11 | 5 | 2 | 33 | 49 | 51 | 16 | 5 | .268/.345/.339 | .248 | .292 | 5.7 | 0.8 | 1.6 |
| 2010 | CSP | AAA | 25 | 260 | 30 | 6 | 1 | 2 | 17 | 27 | 29 | 3 | 3 | .261/.335/.324 | .234 | .283 | -0.6 | 7.2 | 0.9 |
| 2010 | COL | MLB | 25 | 257 | 34 | 6 | 2 | 1 | 21 | 25 | 36 | 2 | 2 | .284/.352/.342 | .246 | .330 | 0.4 | 4.7 | 0.7 |
| 2011 | COL | MLB | 26 | 320 | 28 | 5 | 1 | 3 | 14 | 28 | 40 | 4 | 4 | .242/.313/.299 | .229 | .273 | -0.7 | -0.4 | -0.3 |
| 2012 | COL | MLB | 27 | 288 | 34 | 9 | 2 | 4 | 27 | 26 | 36 | 6 | 3 | .281/.348/.378 | .253 | .307 | -0.3 | 2B 1, SS 1 | 1.3 |

Herrera won the starting second base job in spring training and provided a spark at the top of the order for about five weeks, hitting .303/.415/.404 through May 7. Then pitchers figured him out and he hit .214/.260/.250 the rest of the way. After losing his job to veteran import Mark Ellis, Herrera ended the season on the disabled list due to a broken right index finger. Herrera, who hit a remarkable .183/.258/.242 at Coors Field in 2011, broke his finger while shutting a door, which is both unfortunate and an apt metaphor for his career.

**Kevin Kouzmanoff    3B**

Born: 7/25/1981 Age: 30
Bats: R Throws: R Height: 6' 2" Weight: 210
Breakout: 2% Improve: 27% Collapse: 6%
Attrition: 33% MLB: 85%
Comparables:
Frank Thomas, Scott Brosius, Greg Dobbs

| YEAR | TEAM | LVL | AGE | PA | R | 2B | 3B | HR | RBI | BB | SO | SB | CS | AVG_OBP_SLG | TAv | BABIP | BRR | FRAA | WARP |
|------|------|-----|-----|-----|----|----|----|----|-----|----|-----|----|----|-------------|------|-------|------|------|------|
| 2009 | SDN | MLB | 27 | 573 | 50 | 31 | 1 | 18 | 88 | 27 | 106 | 1 | 0 | .255/.302/.420 | .248 | .285 | -2.3 | -6.5 | -0.2 |
| 2010 | OAK | MLB | 28 | 586 | 59 | 32 | 1 | 16 | 71 | 24 | 96 | 2 | 1 | .247/.283/.396 | .247 | .270 | -2.3 | -0.8 | 0.6 |
| 2011 | SAC | AAA | 29 | 279 | 41 | 24 | 1 | 13 | 58 | 11 | 36 | 1 | 1 | .302/.341/.550 | .289 | .308 | 0.7 | -3.4 | 1.5 |
| 2011 | OAK | MLB | 29 | 149 | 13 | 6 | 0 | 4 | 17 | 8 | 27 | 2 | 0 | .221/.262/.353 | .243 | .239 | 0.2 | -1.5 | 0.1 |
| 2011 | COL | MLB | 29 | 108 | 11 | 5 | 0 | 3 | 16 | 4 | 19 | 0 | 0 | .255/.315/.398 | .264 | .286 | -1.4 | -0.9 | 0.1 |
| 2012 | COL | MLB | 30 | 349 | 40 | 17 | 2 | 11 | 43 | 16 | 65 | 1 | 0 | .253/.299/.418 | .244 | .283 | 0 | 3B -4 | 1.1 |

Kouzmanoff came to Colorado from the A's toward the end of August to help plug the Rockies' season-wide hole at third base. He did what he always does, which is hit like Russ Davis and make plays that don't require him to move a whole lot. Kouzmanoff's ISO has slipped in each of his six big-league seasons. Last year's .137 is right there with the career marks of David DeJesus and Geoff Blum, which for a hitter devoid of on-base skills is unacceptable. Kouzmanoff, who opted for free agency after the season, has probably seen his last days as a starter at the hot corner.

**DJ LeMahieu    2B**

Born: 7/13/1988 Age: 23
Bats: R Throws: R Height: 6' 5" Weight: 205
Breakout: 8% Improve: 26% Collapse: 1%
Attrition: 16% MLB: 51%
Comparables:
Mitch Hilligoss, Josh Harrison, Barry Evans

| YEAR | TEAM | LVL | AGE | PA | R | 2B | 3B | HR | RBI | BB | SO | SB | CS | AVG_OBP_SLG | TAv | BABIP | BRR | FRAA | WARP |
|------|------|-----|-----|-----|----|----|----|----|-----|----|----|----|----|-------------|------|-------|------|------------|------|
| 2009 | PEO | A | 20 | 168 | 19 | 4 | 2 | 0 | 30 | 12 | 22 | 2 | 2 | .316/.371/.368 | .264 | .366 | -0.1 | 0 | 0.5 |
| 2010 | DAY | A+ | 21 | 600 | 63 | 24 | 5 | 2 | 73 | 29 | 61 | 15 | 7 | .314/.343/.386 | .265 | .343 | 0.1 | 4.7 | 2.7 |
| 2011 | TEN | AA | 22 | 202 | 32 | 15 | 2 | 2 | 27 | 11 | 22 | 4 | 3 | .358/.386/.492 | .306 | .389 | 0.1 | 2.9 | 1.8 |
| 2011 | IOW | AAA | 22 | 247 | 23 | 7 | 1 | 3 | 23 | 14 | 27 | 5 | 5 | .286/.328/.366 | .255 | .308 | -0.8 | 3.6 | 1.0 |
| 2011 | CHN | MLB | 22 | 62 | 3 | 2 | 0 | 0 | 4 | 1 | 12 | 0 | 0 | .250/.262/.283 | .196 | .312 | -0.7 | -0.7 | -0.2 |
| 2012 | COL | MLB | 23 | 250 | 27 | 10 | 2 | 2 | 24 | 9 | 37 | 3 | 2 | .277/.303/.364 | .230 | .314 | -0.4 | 2B 1, 3B 4 | 0.2 |

Another Cubs draft disappointment, LeMahieu lacks the power of a starting third baseman or the range of a middle infielder. His hitting tool is as good as advertised, and his inside-out swing kept his contact rate in the excellent range as he shot up through the levels in the Chicago system. The glass half full outlook is that he's big enough and young enough to grow into some power while retaining his contact rate, and he has decent athletic ability, even if he's not a burner on the basepaths or a particularly mobile fielder. In moving to Colorado, LeMahieu gains the advantages of playing half his games at Coors Field and replacing a slew of third baseman who hit like Jose Molina, the most prominent being the now-departed Ty Wigginton, who covers as much ground as the middle Molina brother.

**Chris Nelson    SS**

Born: 9/3/1985 Age: 26
Bats: R Throws: R Height: 6' 0" Weight: 175
Breakout: 7% Improve: 37% Collapse: 4%
Attrition: 37% MLB: 83%
Comparables:
Howard Kendrick, Danny Richar, Kevin Jordan

| YEAR | TEAM | LVL | AGE | PA | R | 2B | 3B | HR | RBI | BB | SO | SB | CS | AVG_OBP_SLG | TAv | BABIP | BRR | FRAA | WARP |
|------|------|-----|-----|-----|----|----|----|----|-----|----|----|----|----|-------------|------|-------|------|-----------|------|
| 2009 | TUL | AA | 23 | 122 | 21 | 5 | 2 | 4 | 17 | 12 | 21 | 5 | 2 | .280/.355/.477 | .331 | .313 | 1.3 | -2 | 1.4 |
| 2010 | CSP | AAA | 24 | 356 | 60 | 15 | 3 | 12 | 55 | 29 | 53 | 7 | 3 | .313/.376/.492 | .279 | .344 | -1.1 | -4.9 | 1.6 |
| 2010 | COL | MLB | 24 | 27 | 7 | 1 | 0 | 0 | 0 | 1 | 4 | 1 | 0 | .280/.308/.320 | .198 | .333 | 1.7 | -0.1 | 0.1 |
| 2011 | CSP | AAA | 25 | 315 | 52 | 20 | 5 | 11 | 65 | 17 | 48 | 3 | 3 | .329/.366/.547 | .270 | .357 | -1.1 | 0 | 1.5 |
| 2011 | COL | MLB | 25 | 189 | 20 | 10 | 1 | 4 | 16 | 7 | 35 | 3 | 1 | .250/.280/.383 | .220 | .289 | 0.7 | -1.7 | -0.4 |
| 2012 | COL | MLB | 26 | 250 | 31 | 12 | 3 | 8 | 34 | 14 | 44 | 4 | 2 | .284/.326/.459 | .266 | .317 | -0.2 | SS -2, 2B -4 | 1.9 |

Nelson, taken as a shortstop in the first round of the 2004 draft, now plays second and third base, and is a mediocre defender at both positions. At the plate, he has shown occasional power in the minors but struggles to differentiate between balls and strikes. If Nelson tightens up his zone and improves his defense, he could stick for a while as part of a big-league bench.

**Jordan Pacheco    C**
Born: 1/30/1986 Age: 26
Bats: R Throws: R Height: 6' 2" Weight: 190
Breakout: 1% Improve: 20% Collapse: 9%
Attrition: 44% MLB: 88%
Comparables:
Bob Boone, Kurt Suzuki, Dioner Navarro

| YEAR | TEAM | LVL | AGE | PA | R | 2B | 3B | HR | RBI | BB | SO | SB | CS | AVG_OBP_SLG | TAv | BABIP | BRR | FRAA | WARP |
|------|------|-----|-----|----|----|----|----|----|-----|----|----|----|----|-------------|-----|-------|-----|------|------|
| 2009 | ASH | A | 23 | 507 | 67 | 30 | 4 | 13 | 79 | 38 | 44 | 12 | 2 | .322/.382/.492 | .293 | .332 | 1.4 | -1.4 | 2.8 |
| 2010 | MOD | A+ | 24 | 460 | 59 | 27 | 3 | 5 | 70 | 54 | 36 | 5 | 6 | .321/.413/.444 | .313 | .343 | 1.4 | -0.6 | 4.3 |
| 2010 | TUL | AA | 24 | 91 | 11 | 5 | 0 | 1 | 19 | 6 | 6 | 1 | 1 | .333/.409/.436 | .297 | .352 | 0.5 | 0.4 | 0.8 |
| 2011 | CSP | AAA | 25 | 411 | 57 | 21 | 3 | 3 | 50 | 30 | 48 | 2 | 2 | .278/.343/.377 | .233 | .308 | 3.4 | 0.3 | 0.6 |
| 2011 | COL | MLB | 25 | 88 | 5 | 1 | 0 | 2 | 14 | 3 | 9 | 0 | 0 | .286/.318/.369 | .239 | .301 | -0.6 | -0.5 | -0.2 |
| 2012 | COL | MLB | 26 | 250 | 29 | 13 | 1 | 4 | 26 | 16 | 31 | 1 | 1 | .274/.327/.391 | .247 | .299 | -0.1 | C -1, 1B -0 | 1.0 |

Most of Pacheco's professional experience has come behind the plate, although he saw more action at first and third base after

Comparables:
Johermyn Chavez, Michael Burgess, Eric Anthony

..., Colorado's later round pick out of Clemson in 2010, showed plenty of power in his pro debut at Low-A Asheville. Part of this is due to his home park, which is conducive to home runs and which is where he hit 16 of his 21 bombs, but he is not a creation of his environment. The former college quarterback drives the ball to all fields and has decent on-base skills, although he could stand to make contact a bit more often. If he does that, Parker could put up scary numbers at Coors Field as early as 2013.

**Wilin Rosario    C**
Born: 2/23/1989 Age: 23
Bats: R Throws: R Height: 6' 0" Weight: 200
Breakout: 3% Improve: 18% Collapse: 7%
Attrition: 20% MLB: 55%
Comparables:
Jerry Moses, Kelly Mann, Al Pardo

| YEAR | TEAM | LVL | AGE | PA | R | 2B | 3B | HR | RBI | BB | SO | SB | CS | AVG_OBP_SLG | TAv | BABIP | BRR | FRAA | WARP |
|------|------|-----|-----|----|----|----|----|----|-----|----|----|----|----|-------------|-----|-------|-----|------|------|
| 2009 | MOD | A+ | 20 | 222 | 17 | 12 | 2 | 4 | 33 | 10 | 55 | 2 | 1 | .266/.300/.404 | .259 | .340 | -0.5 | -0.6 | 0.8 |
| 2010 | TUL | AA | 21 | 297 | 42 | 13 | 1 | 19 | 52 | 21 | 57 | 1 | 0 | .285/.341/.552 | .300 | .296 | -1 | -1.2 | 2.6 |
| 2011 | TUL | AA | 22 | 426 | 52 | 15 | 3 | 21 | 48 | 19 | 91 | 1 | 2 | .249/.284/.457 | .247 | .272 | 0.1 | -1.1 | 1.4 |
| 2011 | COL | MLB | 22 | 57 | 6 | 3 | 1 | 3 | 8 | 2 | 20 | 0 | 0 | .204/.228/.463 | .231 | .250 | -1 | -0.1 | 0.1 |
| 2012 | COL | MLB | 23 | 250 | 28 | 10 | 2 | 11 | 35 | 9 | 61 | 0 | 0 | .246/.273/.447 | .241 | .279 | 0 | C -2, 1B -0 | 1.1 |

Rosario is slow and doesn't have the greatest plate discipline, but he does everything else well. He has power (.182 ISO in nearly 1,600 minor-league plate appearances) and a strong arm (career 41 percent CS). Rosario's numbers at Double-A Tulsa were down in 2011 from the previous year at the same level, but he began the season still recovering from August 2010 surgery to repair a torn ACL in his right knee. If he stays healthy and learns to draw a few more walks, Rosario could do damage in Denver sooner rather than later.

**Seth Smith    RF**
Born: 9/30/1982 Age: 29
Bats: L Throws: L Height: 6' 4" Weight: 215
Breakout: 3% Improve: 40% Collapse: 2%
Attrition: 8% MLB: 93%
Comparables:
Bobby Bonilla, Billy Williams, Andre Ethier

| YEAR | TEAM | LVL | AGE | PA | R | 2B | 3B | HR | RBI | BB | SO | SB | CS | AVG_OBP_SLG | TAv | BABIP | BRR | FRAA | WARP |
|------|------|-----|-----|----|----|----|----|----|-----|----|----|----|----|-------------|-----|-------|-----|------|------|
| 2009 | COL | MLB | 26 | 387 | 61 | 20 | 4 | 15 | 55 | 46 | 67 | 4 | 1 | .293/.378/.510 | .282 | .324 | 2.4 | 6 | 2.4 |
| 2010 | COL | MLB | 27 | 398 | 55 | 19 | 5 | 17 | 52 | 35 | 67 | 2 | 1 | .246/.314/.469 | .264 | .256 | -0.5 | 5.3 | 1.3 |
| 2011 | COL | MLB | 28 | 533 | 67 | 32 | 9 | 15 | 59 | 46 | 93 | 10 | 2 | .284/.347/.483 | .281 | .320 | 2 | -0.1 | 1.8 |
| 2012 | COL | MLB | 29 | 474 | 66 | 26 | 6 | 18 | 70 | 46 | 77 | 6 | 2 | .288/.361/.507 | .293 | .313 | 0.2 | RF -0, LF 2 | 2.7 |

Smith is similar in some ways to his predecessor in right field, Brad Hawpe. Both are left-handed, listed at 6'3, 210 pounds, and attended colleges in the Southeastern Conference. Smith lacks Hawpe's home run power but a .210 career ISO is more than respectable. Smith makes better contact and is a superior defender in right which is praise and an insult all in one. Smith doesn't hit lefties (.217/.272/.304 in 2011 and .202/.269/.319 for his career) but as long as his managers continue to deploy him the way Earl Weaver deployed John Lowenstein back in the day, Smith should be useful enough.

### Ryan Spilborghs — RF

Born: 9/5/1979 Age: 32
Bats: R Throws: R Height: 6' 2" Weight: 190
Breakout: 1% Improve: 22% Collapse: 8%
Attrition: 15% MLB: 84%

Comparables:
Jay Johnstone, Al Zarilla, Roger Maris

| YEAR | TEAM | LVL | AGE | PA | R | 2B | 3B | HR | RBI | BB | SO | SB | CS | AVG_OBP_SLG | TAv | BABIP | BRR | FRAA | WARP |
|------|------|-----|-----|-----|----|----|----|----|-----|----|----|----|----|-------------|------|-------|------|------------|------|
| 2009 | COL | MLB | 29 | 393 | 55 | 24 | 3 | 8 | 48 | 34 | 79 | 9 | 5 | .241/.310/.395 | .236 | .288 | 2.3 | -0.3 | -0.1 |
| 2010 | COL | MLB | 30 | 388 | 41 | 20 | 2 | 10 | 39 | 39 | 83 | 4 | 5 | .279/.360/.437 | .269 | .341 | 0.9 | -2.8 | 0.8 |
| 2011 | COL | MLB | 31 | 223 | 22 | 8 | 1 | 3 | 22 | 19 | 49 | 2 | 2 | .210/.283/.305 | .202 | .260 | -2 | -2.3 | -1.4 |
| 2012 | COL | MLB | 32 | 250 | 32 | 12 | 2 | 7 | 31 | 25 | 45 | 4 | 3 | .280/.354/.447 | .275 | .321 | -0.6 | RF -1, LF -4 | 1.7 |

Spilborghs, who played Gary Roenicke to Seth Smith's John Lowenstein in 2010, turned into Kiko Garcia this past season. Awkward comparisons to old Orioles players aside, Spilborghs' entire game collapsed in 2011. He had no appreciable platoon splits, making him a less-than-sexy choice against left-handers. His power disappeared, ISO plummeting from .158 to .095. He hit .129/.182/.198 away from Coors Field, and while anything is possible in a small enough sample, hitting like a less powerful version of A.J. Burnett in any situation is never a good sign. Spilborghs missed almost all of the season's final two months due to plantar fasciitis in his right foot, which may help explain his struggles. Still, he isn't young and isn't a brilliant defender. If he can't hit, he has no game.

### Troy Tulowitzki — SS

Born: 10/10/1984 Age: 27
Bats: R Throws: R Height: 6' 4" Weight: 205
Breakout: 2% Improve: 39% Collapse: 5%
Attrition: 15% MLB: 88%

Comparables:
Joe Millette, Craig Gerber, Hanley Ramirez

| YEAR | TEAM | LVL | AGE | PA | R | 2B | 3B | HR | RBI | BB | SO | SB | CS | AVG_OBP_SLG | TAv | BABIP | BRR | FRAA | WARP |
|------|------|-----|-----|-----|-----|----|----|----|-----|----|-----|----|----|-------------|------|-------|------|------|------|
| 2009 | COL | MLB | 24 | 628 | 101 | 25 | 9 | 32 | 92 | 73 | 112 | 20 | 11 | .297/.377/.552 | .296 | .316 | -0.5 | -0.7 | 4.3 |
| 2010 | COL | MLB | 25 | 529 | 89 | 32 | 3 | 27 | 95 | 48 | 78 | 11 | 2 | .315/.381/.568 | .309 | .327 | 0.3 | 5.1 | 5.6 |
| 2011 | COL | MLB | 26 | 606 | 81 | 36 | 2 | 30 | 105 | 59 | 79 | 9 | 3 | .302/.372/.544 | .306 | .305 | -1.8 | -2.8 | 4.6 |
| 2012 | COL | MLB | 27 | 554 | 82 | 30 | 5 | 26 | 90 | 53 | 80 | 10 | 5 | .310/.380/.552 | .314 | .323 | -0.6 | SS 1 | 5.4 |

There was a stretch, from April 18 to May 31, when Tulowitzki forgot how to hit. After a torrid start, he batted .208/.253/.349 in those 38 games, during which the Rockies went 13-25 and effectively eliminated themselves from contention. Tulowitzki then returned to the business of destroying pitchers, hitting .333/.401/.583 the rest of the way. Like every other Rockies hitter, he posts better numbers at home, although in 2011 the difference was less pronounced than in some previous seasons. There will always be room for a good defensive shortstop who hits .274/.346/.462 away from Coors Field (as he has for his career), which is made evident by the number of general managers checking their watches to see if it is 2021 yet.

### Tim Wheeler — CF

Born: 1/21/1988 Age: 24
Bats: L Throws: R Height: 6' 5" Weight: 205
Breakout: 9% Improve: 46% Collapse: 2%
Attrition: 21% MLB: 76%

Comparables:
Rod Myers, Ray Lankford, Xavier Paul

| YEAR | TEAM | LVL | AGE | PA | R | 2B | 3B | HR | RBI | BB | SO | SB | CS | AVG_OBP_SLG | TAv | BABIP | BRR | FRAA | WARP |
|------|------|-----|-----|-----|-----|----|----|----|-----|----|-----|----|----|-------------|------|-------|------|------------|------|
| 2009 | TRI | A- | 21 | 309 | 44 | 13 | 3 | 5 | 35 | 29 | 60 | 10 | 4 | .256/.332/.381 | .276 | .310 | -0.4 | 5.2 | 1.9 |
| 2010 | MOD | A+ | 22 | 592 | 88 | 21 | 6 | 12 | 63 | 60 | 114 | 22 | 8 | .249/.340/.384 | .259 | .296 | 2.8 | 3 | 1.8 |
| 2011 | TUL | AA | 23 | 637 | 105 | 28 | 6 | 33 | 86 | 59 | 142 | 21 | 12 | .287/.365/.535 | .306 | .329 | -1.8 | -9.9 | 4.0 |
| 2012 | COL | MLB | 24 | 250 | 27 | 9 | 2 | 7 | 27 | 18 | 60 | 6 | 2 | .229/.291/.384 | .229 | .274 | -0.3 | CF -7, RF -0 | 0.0 |

A first-round pick in 2009, Wheeler saw his stock soar in 2011 thanks to an unexpected power outburst. After two disappointing seasons, he dominated the Texas League for much of the year before fading toward the end. Wheeler's plate discipline is lacking (and actually was worse in his breakout season than in 2010) and there is talk that he may not stick in center field. He remains more intriguing than promising, but the gap has closed since last year.

### Eric Young — 2B

Born: 5/25/1985 Age: 27
Bats: B Throws: R Height: 5' 11" Weight: 180
Breakout: 3% Improve: 33% Collapse: 6%
Attrition: 19% MLB: 73%

Comparables:
Brett Gardner, Bip Roberts, Bob Taylor

| YEAR | TEAM | LVL | AGE | PA | R | 2B | 3B | HR | RBI | BB | SO | SB | CS | AVG_OBP_SLG | TAv | BABIP | BRR | FRAA | WARP |
|------|------|-----|-----|-----|-----|----|----|----|-----|----|----|----|----|-------------|------|-------|------|-----------|------|
| 2009 | CSP | AAA | 24 | 552 | 118 | 21 | 10 | 7 | 43 | 56 | 79 | 58 | 14 | .299/.379/.430 | .279 | .337 | 11 | 19.3 | 5.3 |
| 2009 | COL | MLB | 24 | 61 | 7 | 1 | 0 | 1 | 1 | 4 | 12 | 4 | 4 | .246/.295/.316 | .208 | .295 | 0.8 | -0.9 | -0.2 |
| 2010 | COL | MLB | 25 | 189 | 26 | 5 | 1 | 0 | 8 | 17 | 32 | 17 | 6 | .244/.312/.285 | .222 | .300 | 2.4 | 4.1 | 0.2 |
| 2010 | CSP | AAA | 25 | 142 | 20 | 5 | 1 | 1 | 9 | 15 | 32 | 10 | 0 | .252/.340/.333 | .235 | .330 | 2 | 0.3 | 0.3 |
| 2011 | CSP | AAA | 26 | 275 | 61 | 18 | 9 | 2 | 28 | 39 | 36 | 17 | 1 | .363/.454/.552 | .311 | .416 | 4.7 | -3.4 | 2.0 |
| 2011 | COL | MLB | 26 | 229 | 34 | 4 | 3 | 0 | 10 | 26 | 38 | 27 | 4 | .247/.342/.298 | .230 | .304 | 4 | -2.4 | -0.1 |
| 2012 | COL | MLB | 27 | 265 | 32 | 10 | 4 | 3 | 26 | 27 | 44 | 21 | 5 | .280/.359/.396 | .263 | .328 | 0.7 | 2B 2, LF -2 | 1.7 |

Son of the original Colorado Rockie bearing the same name, Eric Jr. does everything his father did, only not as well. Young doesn't field well enough to play second base or hit well enough to play left field. He has decent on-base skills (at home, anyway) but zero power. His career .181/.270/.207 line away from Coors Field is problematic. Young is fast and uses his speed well, but he needs to add 40 points to his batting average to be useful in a poor-man's Luis Castillo kind of way. The name helps open the door, but as Bobby Bonds Jr. will attest, at some point you've got to do something.

# PITCHERS

### Matt Belisle

Born: 6/6/1980 Age: 32
Bats: R Throws: R Height: 6' 4" Weight: 190
Breakout: 13% Improve: 38% Collapse: 25%
Attrition: 16% MLB: 87%

**Comparables:**
Craig Swan, Larry Jansen, Ben Sheets

| YEAR | TEAM | LVL | AGE | W | L | SV | G | GS | IP | H | HR | BB | SO | EqBB9 | EqSO9 | GB% | BABIP | WHIP | ERA | FIP | FRA | WARP |
|------|------|-----|-----|---|---|----|----|----|------|----|----|----|----|-------|-------|-----|-------|------|------|------|------|------|
| 2009 | CSP | AAA | 29 | 1 | 1 | 9 | 33 | 4 | 58¹ | 57 | 2 | 15 | 45 | 2.3 | 7.3 | 56% | .322 | 1.25 | 3.09 | 3.13 | 4.11 | 1.1 |
| 2009 | COL | MLB | 29 | 3 | 1 | 0 | 24 | 0 | 31 | 35 | 6 | 5 | 22 | 1.5 | 6.4 | 42% | .293 | 1.29 | 5.52 | 4.73 | 5.67 | -0.1 |
| 2010 | COL | MLB | 30 | 7 | 5 | 1 | 76 | 0 | 92 | 84 | 7 | 16 | 91 | 1.6 | 8.9 | 49% | .314 | 1.09 | 2.93 | 2.70 | 3.99 | 1.6 |
| 2011 | COL | MLB | 31 | 10 | 4 | 0 | 74 | 0 | 72 | 77 | 5 | 14 | 58 | 1.8 | 7.2 | 55% | .333 | 1.26 | 3.25 | 3.04 | 4.63 | 0.5 |
| 2012 | COL | MLB | 32 | 3 | 1 | 1 | 60 | 0 | 65² | 73 | 8 | 14 | 42 | 1.9 | 5.7 | 49% | .328 | 1.33 | 4.93 | 4.15 | 5.36 | 0.2 |

Belisle has made a mid-career transition from eminently hittable starter to somewhat-less-hittable reliever. He possesses a resilient arm that has allowed him to soak up innings out of the Rockies bullpen each of the past two seasons. There is nothing fancy about Belisle's game, but he throws strikes and keeps the ball in the park, an excellent combination for a pitcher who calls Coors Field home. He has negligible home/road splits since coming to Colorado in 2009

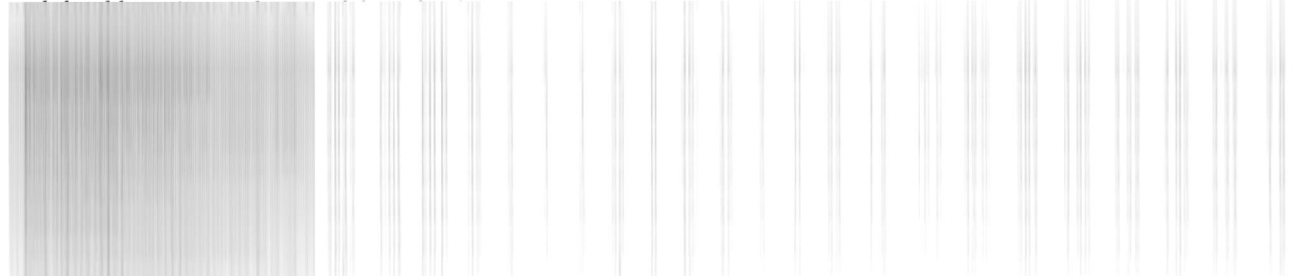

For someone who didn't reach the big leagues until age 28, Betancourt has had an excellent career. An extreme control pitcher, Betancourt owns a ridiculous 9.1 K/BB since coming to Colorado in July 2009. He is one of two pitchers in MLB history with at least 500 innings pitched and a K/BB higher than 4.5. (Kevin Slowey is the other.) Thanks to the addition of a changeup, Betancourt finally solved left-handed hitters in 2011. He was downright abusive at Coors Field, where he held opponents to a .191/.208/.261 line and allowed just one of his seven home runs despite being an extreme fly-ball pitcher. He could close games if given the opportunity, which is a distinct possibility.

### Chad Bettis

Born: 4/26/1989 Age: 23
Bats: R Throws: R Height: 6' 2" Weight: 193
Breakout: 22% Improve: 58% Collapse: 17%
Attrition: 13% MLB: 94%

**Comparables:**
Larry Dierker, Juan Marichal, Ray Crone

| YEAR | TEAM | LVL | AGE | W | L | SV | G | GS | IP | H | HR | BB | SO | EqBB9 | EqSO9 | GB% | BABIP | WHIP | ERA | FIP | FRA | WARP |
|------|------|-----|-----|---|---|----|----|----|------|-----|----|----|-----|-------|-------|-----|-------|------|------|------|------|------|
| 2010 | TRI | A- | 21 | 4 | 1 | 0 | 10 | 9 | 48¹ | 44 | 0 | 10 | 39 | 1.9 | 7.3 | — | .311 | 1.12 | 1.12 | 2.49 | 4.49 | 0.1 |
| 2011 | MOD | A+ | 22 | 8 | 1 | 0 | 27 | 27 | 169² | 148 | 10 | 48 | 193 | 2.4 | 9.8 | 47% | .303 | 1.10 | 3.34 | 3.43 | 3.82 | 3.1 |
| 2012 | COL | MLB | 23 | 3 | 2 | 0 | 8 | 8 | 45² | 45 | 5 | 17 | 33 | 3.4 | 6.5 | 45% | .310 | 1.36 | 4.61 | 4.30 | 5.01 | 0.4 |

Bettis works with a low- to mid-90s fastball but is inconsistent with his secondary pitches, leading some to believe that his future may lie in the bullpen. He threw strikes, missed bats, and kept the ball in the park in his full-season debut. The California League features a couple of extreme hitters ballparks, and while Bettis scuffled in his two starts at High Desert, his best outing of the year (7 IP, 3 H, 0 R, 2 BB, 11 K) came at Lancaster. His 2011 performance is promising, but Bettis will need to repeat that at higher levels to quell doubts about his repertoire and solidify his status as a future back-end rotation option.

### Rex Brothers

Born: 12/18/1987 Age: 24
Bats: L Throws: L Height: 6' 1" Weight: 205
Breakout: 34% Improve: 64% Collapse: 23%
Attrition: 19% MLB: 98%

**Comparables:**
Taylor Tankersley, Scott Kazmir, Scott Elbert

| YEAR | TEAM | LVL | AGE | W | L | SV | G | GS | IP | H | HR | BB | SO | EqBB9 | EqSO9 | GB% | BABIP | WHIP | ERA | FIP | FRA | WARP |
|------|------|-----|-----|---|---|----|----|----|------|----|----|----|----|-------|-------|-----|-------|------|------|------|------|------|
| 2010 | MOD | A+ | 22 | 0 | 2 | 3 | 33 | 0 | 37 | 16 | 0 | 14 | 36 | 4.6 | 10.5 | 56% | .232 | 1.05 | 2.68 | 3.01 | 4.20 | 0.3 |
| 2010 | TUL | AA | 22 | 2 | 1 | 4 | 24 | 0 | 23 | 12 | 2 | 11 | 22 | 7.0 | 10.6 | 53% | .238 | 1.39 | 3.91 | 4.11 | 5.79 | -0.1 |
| 2011 | CSP | AAA | 23 | 0 | 1 | 0 | 25 | 0 | 28 | 28 | 2 | 14 | 43 | 4.8 | 14.5 | 55% | .441 | 1.57 | 2.89 | 3.09 | 3.89 | 0.7 |
| 2011 | COL | MLB | 23 | 1 | 2 | 1 | 48 | 0 | 40² | 33 | 4 | 20 | 59 | 4.4 | 13.1 | 46% | .326 | 1.30 | 2.88 | 2.85 | 3.59 | 0.6 |
| 2012 | COL | MLB | 24 | 2 | 1 | 1 | 42 | 0 | 42 | 35 | 4 | 20 | 46 | 4.3 | 9.8 | 49% | .313 | 1.30 | 3.93 | 3.68 | 4.27 | 0.6 |

Brothers throws hard and with spotty command, which is a terrifying combination. Instilling fear in hitters is not a bad thing, although he does need to limit the free passes. Brothers struck out 31 percent of batters he faced in 99 career minor-league appearances. That number jumped to 34 percent in his debut with the Rockies. Opponents hit an unfathomable .118/.259/.191 against Brothers with men on base. If he improves his control just enough to keep batters from waiting him out, Brothers will be a dominant late-inning option now and into the future.

## Jhoulys Chacin

Born: 1/7/1988 Age: 24
Bats: R Throws: R Height: 6' 4" Weight: 200
Breakout: 30% Improve: 50% Collapse: 26%
Attrition: 15% MLB: 94%

Comparables:
Travis Wood, Gene Conley, Ervin Santana

| YEAR | TEAM | LVL | AGE | W | L | SV | G | GS | IP | H | HR | BB | SO | EqBB9 | EqSO9 | GB% | BABIP | WHIP | ERA | FIP | FRA | WARP |
|------|------|-----|-----|---|---|----|---|----|----|---|----|----|----|-------|-------|-----|-------|------|-----|-----|-----|------|
| 2009 | TUL | AA | 21 | 8 | 5 | 0 | 18 | 18 | 103¹ | 79 | 9 | 32 | 78 | 3.0 | 7.5 | 57% | .252 | 1.18 | 3.14 | 3.99 | 4.76 | 0.9 |
| 2009 | COL | MLB | 21 | 0 | 1 | 0 | 9 | 1 | 11 | 6 | 1 | 11 | 13 | 9.0 | 10.6 | 50% | .227 | 1.55 | 4.91 | 4.87 | 4.85 | 0.1 |
| 2010 | CSP | AAA | 22 | 3 | 2 | 0 | 7 | 7 | 35² | 15 | 0 | 12 | 23 | 4.3 | 8.6 | 72% | .254 | 1.23 | 1.51 | 3.86 | 3.73 | 0.9 |
| 2010 | COL | MLB | 22 | 9 | 11 | 0 | 28 | 21 | 137¹ | 114 | 10 | 61 | 138 | 4.0 | 9.0 | 47% | .290 | 1.27 | 3.28 | 3.57 | 4.63 | 1.3 |
| 2011 | COL | MLB | 23 | 11 | 14 | 0 | 31 | 31 | 194 | 168 | 20 | 87 | 150 | 4.0 | 7.0 | 57% | .264 | 1.31 | 3.62 | 4.20 | 4.55 | 2.6 |
| 2012 | COL | MLB | 24 | 11 | 8 | 0 | 26 | 26 | 156² | 148 | 18 | 67 | 108 | 3.9 | 6.2 | 55% | .298 | 1.37 | 4.78 | 4.60 | 5.19 | 0.9 |

In his first full season as a member of the Rockies starting rotation, Chacin established himself as the staff ace. He pitched as well at Coors Field as away from it. He worked a lot of innings and faded in the second half, with both his dominance (7.8 K/9 before the All-Star break, 5.7 after) and command (2.0 K/BB vs. 1.3) suffering. Still, he puts the ball past hitters and last year saw his already solid ground-ball rate rise dramatically. Even PECOTA's apparent skepticism is only around his ability to make 30 starts and keep his BABIP below average. Assuming there are no lingering effects from last year's heavy workload, he should deliver more of the same in 2012 and beyond.

## Tyler Chatwood

Born: 12/16/1989 Age: 22
Bats: R Throws: R Height: 6' 1" Weight: 185
Breakout: 22% Improve: 51% Collapse: 21%
Attrition: 11% MLB: 81%

Comparables:
Joe Bonikowski, Bruce Kison, Mark Gubicza

| YEAR | TEAM | LVL | AGE | W | L | SV | G | GS | IP | H | HR | BB | SO | EqBB9 | EqSO9 | GB% | BABIP | WHIP | ERA | FIP | FRA | WARP |
|------|------|-----|-----|---|---|----|---|----|----|---|----|----|----|-------|-------|-----|-------|------|-----|-----|-----|------|
| 2009 | CDR | A | 19 | 8 | 7 | 0 | 24 | 24 | 116¹ | 112 | 3 | 69 | 108 | 5.1 | 8.2 | 50% | .322 | 1.42 | 4.02 | 3.95 | 5.09 | 0.1 |
| 2010 | RCU | A+ | 20 | 8 | 3 | 0 | 14 | 13 | 81¹ | 61 | 6 | 27 | 61 | 4.0 | 7.7 | 64% | .302 | 1.32 | 1.77 | 4.31 | 4.68 | 0.4 |
| 2010 | ARK | AA | 20 | 4 | 6 | 0 | 12 | 12 | 68¹ | 55 | 3 | 26 | 27 | 3.6 | 4.7 | 52% | .319 | 1.45 | 3.82 | 4.34 | 4.78 | 0.0 |
| 2011 | ANA | MLB | 21 | 6 | 11 | 0 | 27 | 25 | 142 | 166 | 14 | 71 | 74 | 4.5 | 4.7 | 48% | .329 | 1.67 | 4.75 | 4.93 | 5.37 | -0.7 |
| 2012 | COL | MLB | 22 | 7 | 8 | 0 | 22 | 22 | 120 | 133 | 13 | 62 | 60 | 4.7 | 4.5 | 49% | .319 | 1.62 | 5.88 | 5.16 | 6.39 | -0.6 |

Chatwood's 2010 breakout in High-A made him a pretty good prospect for the Angels, but expecting him to thrive as the youngest player in the American League in 2011 was too optimistic. He did manage to survive lousy strikeout and walk rates through June, with the most double plays induced in baseball and an ERA in the mid-threes. His manager and pitching coach touted his guts and makeup, which are good for pitchers but even better for haunted houses—Chatwood's second half was downright horrifying. Don't judge his future by his peripherals; with a broad repertoire, two fastballs in the mid-90s, and the ability to get grounders when he needs them, Chatwood should improve across the board, though not necessarily enough to survive in Coors Field.

## Aaron Cook

Born: 2/8/1979 Age: 33
Bats: R Throws: R Height: 6' 4" Weight: 175
Breakout: 15% Improve: 61% Collapse: 14%
Attrition: 13% MLB: 78%

Comparables:
Ron Taylor, Ned Garver, Bob Purkey

| YEAR | TEAM | LVL | AGE | W | L | SV | G | GS | IP | H | HR | BB | SO | EqBB9 | EqSO9 | GB% | BABIP | WHIP | ERA | FIP | FRA | WARP |
|------|------|-----|-----|---|---|----|---|----|----|---|----|----|----|-------|-------|-----|-------|------|-----|-----|-----|------|
| 2009 | COL | MLB | 30 | 11 | 6 | 0 | 27 | 27 | 158 | 175 | 19 | 47 | 78 | 2.7 | 4.4 | 58% | .297 | 1.41 | 4.16 | 4.56 | 5.73 | 1.2 |
| 2010 | COL | MLB | 31 | 6 | 8 | 0 | 23 | 23 | 127² | 147 | 11 | 52 | 62 | 3.7 | 4.4 | 59% | .309 | 1.56 | 5.08 | 4.57 | 5.65 | 0.1 |
| 2011 | COL | MLB | 32 | 3 | 10 | 0 | 18 | 17 | 97 | 127 | 9 | 37 | 48 | 3.4 | 4.5 | 56% | .346 | 1.69 | 6.03 | 4.51 | 4.92 | 0.8 |
| 2012 | COL | MLB | 33 | 6 | 6 | 0 | 17 | 17 | 97² | 118 | 12 | 28 | 31 | 2.6 | 2.9 | 57% | .323 | 1.49 | 5.70 | 5.03 | 6.20 | -0.4 |

When healthy, Cook has succeeded in the Colorado rotation for the better part of a decade despite poor strikeout rates. He is a big guy whose finesse approach would make him an innings eater except for the fact that injuries have kept him from eating innings. Cook has topped the 170 mark just twice in his career, and shoulder and finger issues delayed his 2011 debut to June 8. He didn't fool anyone last year, posting the worst ERA of his career. Cook is the most strikeout-averse pitcher in the big leagues, filling the void created when Kirk Rueter retired in 2005. Cook's main challenges now are the same as they've always been: stay healthy enough to make it through an entire season and keep thriving despite allowing an extraordinary number of balls in play while pitching in baseball's most favorable offensive environment. The odds are against him, but that has been true for a long time.

## Jorge De La Rosa

Born: 4/5/1981 Age: 31
Bats: L Throws: L Height: 6' 2" Weight: 190
Breakout: 14% Improve: 54% Collapse: 24%
Attrition: 16% MLB: 91%

Comparables:
Rob Murphy, Joe Beckwith, Steve Carlton

| YEAR | TEAM | LVL | AGE | W | L | SV | G | GS | IP | H | HR | BB | SO | EqBB9 | EqSO9 | GB% | BABIP | WHIP | ERA | FIP | FRA | WARP |
|------|------|-----|-----|---|---|----|---|----|----|---|----|----|----|-------|-------|-----|-------|------|-----|-----|-----|------|
| 2009 | COL | MLB | 28 | 16 | 9 | 0 | 33 | 32 | 185 | 172 | 20 | 83 | 193 | 4.0 | 9.4 | 46% | .315 | 1.38 | 4.38 | 3.87 | 4.56 | 2.9 |
| 2010 | COL | MLB | 29 | 8 | 7 | 0 | 20 | 20 | 121² | 105 | 15 | 55 | 113 | 4.1 | 8.4 | 53% | .280 | 1.32 | 4.22 | 4.33 | 4.90 | 1.0 |
| 2011 | COL | MLB | 30 | 5 | 2 | 0 | 10 | 10 | 59 | 48 | 4 | 22 | 52 | 3.4 | 7.9 | 46% | .273 | 1.19 | 3.51 | 3.33 | 4.05 | 0.8 |
| 2012 | COL | MLB | 31 | 4 | 3 | 0 | 10 | 10 | 58² | 59 | 8 | 24 | 46 | 3.7 | 7.0 | 46% | .320 | 1.42 | 5.16 | 4.64 | 5.61 | 0.1 |

De La Rosa's season lasted 50 pitches into his 10th start, at which point he blew out his left elbow. De La Rosa, who has worked more than 130 innings just once over parts of eight seasons, isn't expected back until June at the earliest. It has become trendy in recent years to believe that Tommy John surgery is a miracle cure for ailing pitchers, but no procedure is without risk. Even if it works, command (never De La Rosa's strong suit) is often the last thing to return. Still, the odds are on his side, although that's easier to say when you aren't the one doing the rehab.

### Christian Friedrich

Born: **7/8/1987** Age: **24**
Bats: **R** Throws: **L** Height: **6' 5"** Weight: **215**
Breakout: **13%** Improve: **32%** Collapse: **46%**
Attrition: **8%** MLB: **93%**

**Comparables:**
Carlos Carrasco, Jason Hammel, Jae Kuk Ryu

| YEAR | TEAM | LVL | AGE | W | L | SV | G | GS | IP | H | HR | BB | SO | EqBB9 | EqSO9 | GB% | BABIP | WHIP | ERA | FIP | FRA | WARP |
|------|------|-----|-----|---|---|----|----|----|-----|-----|----|----|-----|-------|-------|-----|-------|------|------|------|------|------|
| 2011 | TUL | AA | 23 | 4 | 7 | 0 | 25 | 25 | 133¹ | 156 | 20 | 43 | 103 | 2.9 | 7.0 | 46% | .320 | 1.49 | 4.99 | 4.82 | 5.39 | -0.1 |
| 2012 | COL | MLB | 24 | 3 | 3 | 0 | 8 | 8 | 42 | 46 | 6 | 17 | 28 | 3.7 | 6.1 | 44% | .322 | 1.51 | 5.70 | 4.94 | 6.19 | -0.1 |

Elbow problems have plagued the former first-round pick over the past two seasons, making Friedrich's 2009 breakout campaign a distant memory. His velocity isn't what it once was, and neither are his numbers. Strikeouts? Declining. Hits and home runs? Increasing. The best that can be said of Friedrich's 2011 is that he managed to set career highs in starts and innings pitched. This is a good thing, and his pedigree will get him a few extra looks, but the trends are

K/BB dropped from 3.0 in 2010 to 1.4 last year in roughly the same number of innings. Likewise, his K/9 dropped from 7.1 to 5.0. This is a dangerous tradeoff that leaves Hammel with little margin for error. Some guys (Carl Pavano, Livan Hernandez, Mike Pelfrey) can survive with a K/9 of 5 or lower, but most cannot. Lacking the extreme ground-ball tendencies of teammate Aaron Cook, Hammel would be better suited to any other ballpark in baseball. Even then, unless the command returns, his future prospects are marginal.

### Matt Lindstrom

Born: **2/11/1980** Age: **32**
Bats: **R** Throws: **R** Height: **6' 5"** Weight: **210**
Breakout: **8%** Improve: **28%** Collapse: **54%**
Attrition: **33%** MLB: **95%**

**Comparables:**
LaTroy Hawkins, Matt Wise, Andy Messersmith

| YEAR | TEAM | LVL | AGE | W | L | SV | G | GS | IP | H | HR | BB | SO | EqBB9 | EqSO9 | GB% | BABIP | WHIP | ERA | FIP | FRA | WARP |
|------|------|-----|-----|---|---|----|----|----|-----|----|----|----|----|-------|-------|-----|-------|------|------|------|------|------|
| 2009 | FLO | MLB | 29 | 2 | 1 | 15 | 54 | 0 | 47¹ | 54 | 5 | 24 | 39 | 4.6 | 7.4 | 46% | .331 | 1.65 | 5.89 | 4.43 | 5.23 | 0.3 |
| 2010 | HOU | MLB | 30 | 2 | 5 | 23 | 58 | 0 | 53¹ | 68 | 5 | 20 | 43 | 3.4 | 7.3 | 50% | .362 | 1.65 | 4.39 | 3.84 | 4.93 | 0.1 |
| 2011 | COL | MLB | 31 | 2 | 2 | 2 | 63 | 0 | 54 | 52 | 3 | 14 | 36 | 2.3 | 6.0 | 50% | .293 | 1.22 | 3.00 | 3.27 | 4.65 | 0.2 |
| 2012 | COL | MLB | 32 | 3 | 1 | 7 | 55 | 0 | 49¹ | 50 | 5 | 17 | 36 | 3.0 | 6.5 | 47% | .322 | 1.36 | 4.48 | 4.10 | 4.87 | 0.4 |

Lindstrom quietly assembled a solid season working the seventh and eighth innings for the Rockies. His lack of dominance is puzzling for a pitcher with a fastball as good as his. The problem is that it tends to straighten out at times. Also, he often fails to command his slider, which allows hitters to put that pitch out of their minds and wait for the heater. Lindstrom struggled as a closer in Florida and Houston but seemed more comfortable setting up for the Rockies. Lindstrom has good stuff, but for most of his career, the results haven't matched. Unless he figures out what to do with the slider or learns some other pitch in its place, they probably never will.

### Tyler Matzek

Born: **10/19/1990** Age: **21**
Bats: **L** Throws: **L** Height: **6' 4"** Weight: **210**
Breakout: **28%** Improve: **60%** Collapse: **10%**
Attrition: **5%** MLB: **83%**

**Comparables:**
Sam McDowell, Mark Davis, Oliver Perez

| YEAR | TEAM | LVL | AGE | W | L | SV | G | GS | IP | H | HR | BB | SO | EqBB9 | EqSO9 | GB% | BABIP | WHIP | ERA | FIP | FRA | WARP |
|------|------|-----|-----|---|---|----|----|----|-----|----|----|----|----|-------|-------|-----|-------|------|------|------|------|------|
| 2010 | ASH | A | 19 | 5 | 1 | 0 | 18 | 18 | 89¹ | 30 | 4 | 26 | 49 | 6.2 | 8.9 | 38% | .241 | 1.39 | 2.92 | 4.05 | 5.65 | 0.3 |
| 2011 | ASH | A | 20 | 3 | 3 | 0 | 12 | 12 | 64 | 45 | 3 | 50 | 74 | 7.0 | 10.4 | 45% | .282 | 1.48 | 4.36 | 4.26 | 5.35 | 0.7 |
| 2011 | MOD | A+ | 20 | 0 | 2 | 0 | 10 | 10 | 33 | 34 | 5 | 46 | 37 | 12.5 | 10.1 | 38% | .333 | 2.42 | 9.82 | 8.02 | 8.40 | -0.7 |
| 2012 | COL | MLB | 21 | 2 | 2 | 0 | 6 | 6 | 29² | 30 | 4 | 23 | 22 | 7.1 | 6.7 | 40% | .313 | 1.78 | 6.46 | 5.80 | 7.02 | -0.3 |

After struggling to throw strikes in his professional debut, Matzek was pushed to High-A and saw his already high BB/9 double to a Robbie Beckettesque 12.5. After 10 disastrous starts at Modesto, the 2009 first-round pick returned to Asheville. There, after being allowed to leave the team briefly to work with his high school pitching coach, he got that number down to only 7.0. Matzek still throws hard (although his velocity sometimes wanders) and if there's a silver lining to his season it's that he pitched well over his final six starts (41 IP, 23 H, 14 R, 10 ER, 19 BB, 44 K). If he can build on that late success and find a way to harness his stuff, Matzek could end up at the front of a big-league rotation. Then again the same sentiment once applied to Beckett.

### Kevin Millwood

Born: 12/24/1974 Age: 37
Bats: R Throws: R Height: 6' 5" Weight: 205
Breakout: 17% Improve: 55% Collapse: 27%
Attrition: 16% MLB: 79%

Comparables:
Lindy McDaniel, Elmer Dessens, Joe Hoerner

| YEAR | TEAM | LVL | AGE | W | L | SV | G | GS | IP | H | HR | BB | SO | EqBB9 | EqSO9 | GB% | BABIP | WHIP | ERA | FIP | FRA | WARP |
|------|------|-----|-----|---|---|----|----|----|-----|-----|----|----|-----|-------|-------|-----|-------|------|------|------|------|------|
| 2009 | TEX | MLB | 34 | 13 | 10 | 0 | 31 | 31 | 198² | 195 | 26 | 71 | 123 | 3.2 | 5.6 | 44% | .275 | 1.34 | 3.67 | 4.84 | 5.09 | 1.7 |
| 2010 | BAL | MLB | 35 | 4 | 16 | 0 | 31 | 31 | 190² | 223 | 30 | 65 | 132 | 3.1 | 6.2 | 39% | .320 | 1.51 | 5.10 | 4.83 | 5.29 | -0.2 |
| 2011 | PAW | AAA | 36 | 2 | 1 | 0 | 13 | 13 | 73² | 79 | 7 | 25 | 66 | 3.1 | 8.1 | 46% | .340 | 1.41 | 4.28 | 3.74 | 4.43 | 1.0 |
| 2011 | COL | MLB | 36 | 4 | 3 | 0 | 9 | 9 | 54¹ | 58 | 9 | 8 | 36 | 1.3 | 6.0 | 46% | .293 | 1.21 | 3.98 | 4.26 | 4.53 | 0.8 |
| 2012 | COL | MLB | 37 | 6 | 5 | 0 | 15 | 15 | 90² | 103 | 13 | 29 | 54 | 2.9 | 5.4 | 44% | .328 | 1.46 | 5.55 | 4.84 | 6.03 | -0.2 |

After a miserable 2010 campaign with the Orioles, Millwood found himself without many job opportunities. He signed a minor-league deal with the Yankees, made three starts, then opted out of his contract. He then made 13 starts in the Boston organization before the Red Sox released him in August. Millwood latched on with the Rockies and pitched well for a Colorado team headed nowhere, which was not only surprising but also annoying to teams making a push for the postseason that could have used the extra arm . . . like, say, the Red Sox.

### Juan Nicasio

Born: 8/31/1986 Age: 25
Bats: R Throws: R Height: 6' 4" Weight: 200
Breakout: 17% Improve: 56% Collapse: 11%
Attrition: 10% MLB: 95%

Comparables:
Scott Sanderson, Zack Greinke, Edward Mujica

| YEAR | TEAM | LVL | AGE | W | L | SV | G | GS | IP | H | HR | BB | SO | EqBB9 | EqSO9 | GB% | BABIP | WHIP | ERA | FIP | FRA | WARP |
|------|------|-----|-----|---|---|----|----|----|-----|-----|----|----|-----|-------|-------|-----|-------|------|------|------|------|------|
| 2009 | ASH | A | 22 | 9 | 3 | 0 | 18 | 18 | 112 | 116 | 6 | 25 | 119 | 1.8 | 9.2 | 54% | .327 | 1.19 | 2.41 | 2.81 | — | 0.0 |
| 2011 | TUL | AA | 24 | 2 | 1 | 0 | 9 | 9 | 56² | 42 | 2 | 10 | 56 | 1.6 | 10.0 | 43% | .312 | 1.02 | 2.22 | 2.39 | 2.72 | 1.5 |
| 2011 | COL | MLB | 24 | 4 | 4 | 0 | 13 | 13 | 71² | 73 | 8 | 18 | 58 | 2.3 | 7.3 | 47% | .305 | 1.27 | 4.14 | 3.62 | 3.78 | 1.4 |
| 2012 | COL | MLB | 25 | 5 | 4 | 0 | 12 | 12 | 75¹ | 79 | 9 | 21 | 52 | 2.5 | 6.2 | 45% | .318 | 1.32 | 4.67 | 4.21 | 5.07 | 0.5 |

Nicasio's rookie season came to an abrupt and violent end on August 5 when he was struck in the right temple by a line drive off the bat of Washington's Ian Desmond. Nicasio suffered a fractured C1 vertebra, an injury most commonly sustained while diving into a shallow pool or in an automobile accident. Nicasio is alive, can walk, and vows to pitch again. He was in a neck brace for six weeks but had begun riding a stationary bike and running in a pool by season's end. Nicasio is in uncharted territory as far as baseball injuries are concerned, and where his career goes from here is anyone's guess.

### Drew Pomeranz

Born: 11/22/1988 Age: 23
Bats: R Throws: L Height: 6' 6" Weight: 230
Breakout: 29% Improve: 57% Collapse: 23%
Attrition: 11% MLB: 95%

Comparables:
Kelvim Escobar, Phil Hughes, Ray Crone

| YEAR | TEAM | LVL | AGE | W | L | SV | G | GS | IP | H | HR | BB | SO | EqBB9 | EqSO9 | GB% | BABIP | WHIP | ERA | FIP | FRA | WARP |
|------|------|-----|-----|---|---|----|----|----|-----|----|----|----|----|-------|-------|-----|-------|------|------|------|------|------|
| 2011 | KIN | A+ | 22 | 3 | 2 | 0 | 15 | 15 | 77 | 54 | 2 | 32 | 86 | 3.7 | 11.1 | 52% | .302 | 1.14 | 1.87 | 2.60 | 3.53 | 1.5 |
| 2011 | COL | MLB | 22 | 2 | 1 | 0 | 4 | 4 | 18¹ | 19 | 0 | 5 | 13 | 2.5 | 6.4 | 50% | .333 | 1.31 | 5.40 | 2.56 | 2.76 | 0.6 |
| 2012 | COL | MLB | 23 | 3 | 2 | 0 | 7 | 7 | 37 | 35 | 4 | 15 | 29 | 3.8 | 7.1 | 45% | .309 | 1.37 | 4.46 | 4.26 | 4.84 | 0.4 |

Part of the return from Cleveland for Ubaldo Jimenez, Pomeranz features a mid-90s fastball and backs it up with a good curve. His mechanics have been a concern at times in the past, but he's young enough that any issues should be correctable. Pomeranz reached the big leagues after just 20 games in the minors and held his own in four starts for the Rockies. Assuming he doesn't go Full Nuclear Poreda with the walks, Pomeranz should be a fixture at the top of Colorado's rotation for years to come.

### Matt Reynolds

Born: 10/2/1984 Age: 27
Bats: L Throws: L Height: 6' 6" Weight: 240
Breakout: 23% Improve: 55% Collapse: 29%
Attrition: 13% MLB: 90%

Comparables:
Mike Flanagan, Harvey Haddix, Tom Gorman

| YEAR | TEAM | LVL | AGE | W | L | SV | G | GS | IP | H | HR | BB | SO | EqBB9 | EqSO9 | GB% | BABIP | WHIP | ERA | FIP | FRA | WARP |
|------|------|-----|-----|---|---|----|----|----|-----|----|----|----|----|-------|-------|-----|-------|------|------|------|------|------|
| 2009 | MOD | A+ | 24 | 5 | 3 | 3 | 39 | 0 | 49 | 32 | 2 | 8 | 58 | 1.5 | 10.7 | 51% | .278 | 0.82 | 1.29 | 2.41 | 3.51 | 0.8 |
| 2009 | TUL | AA | 24 | 1 | 2 | 1 | 21 | 0 | 25² | 23 | 3 | 9 | 29 | 3.2 | 10.2 | 42% | .308 | 1.25 | 4.20 | 3.66 | 3.38 | 0.6 |
| 2010 | CSP | AAA | 25 | 1 | 3 | 7 | 50 | 0 | 55 | 30 | 1 | 12 | 48 | 2.6 | 11.0 | 47% | .337 | 1.18 | 2.62 | 3.26 | 3.98 | 1.1 |
| 2010 | COL | MLB | 25 | 1 | 0 | 0 | 21 | 0 | 18 | 10 | 2 | 5 | 17 | 2.5 | 8.5 | 43% | .186 | 0.83 | 2.00 | 3.83 | 5.60 | 0.1 |
| 2011 | COL | MLB | 26 | 1 | 2 | 0 | 73 | 0 | 50² | 48 | 10 | 18 | 50 | 3.2 | 8.9 | 39% | .288 | 1.30 | 4.09 | 4.65 | 4.57 | 0.4 |
| 2012 | COL | MLB | 27 | 2 | 1 | 0 | 50 | 0 | 43 | 42 | 6 | 15 | 34 | 3.0 | 7.0 | 46% | .310 | 1.32 | 4.63 | 4.48 | 5.03 | 0.3 |

After his June 6 appearance against San Diego, Reynolds had a 2.20 ERA in 27 appearances and was holding opponents to a .143/.200/.232 line. From that point forward, his ERA ballooned to 4.98, and opponents hit him to the tune of .303/.360/.621 in 46 games. Deployed as a LOOGY, Reynolds struggled against left-handed hitters in 2011. They batted .292/.324/.552 against him and hit six of the 10 homers he allowed. The league also caught up to him two months into the season. Beyond the four-month slump, if Reynolds can't get lefties out, it's hard to envision him having much of a career.

**Esmil Rogers**

Born: 8/14/1985 Age: **26**
Bats: R Throws: **R** Height: **6' 2"** Weight: **150**
Breakout: **25%** Improve: **54%** Collapse: **14%**
Attrition: **16%** MLB: **80%**

**Comparables:**
Ike Delock, Bryan Eversgerd, Bobby Shantz

| YEAR | TEAM | LVL | AGE | W | L | SV | G | GS | IP | H | HR | BB | SO | EqBB9 | EqSO9 | GB% | BABIP | WHIP | ERA | FIP | FRA | WARP |
|---|---|---|---|---|---|---|---|---|---|---|---|---|---|---|---|---|---|---|---|---|---|---|
| 2009 | TUL | AA | 23 | 8 | 2 | 0 | 15 | 15 | 94¹ | 87 | 2 | 19 | 83 | 1.8 | 7.9 | 46% | .310 | 1.12 | 2.48 | 2.55 | 3.02 | 2.6 |
| 2009 | CSP | AAA | 23 | 3 | 5 | 0 | 12 | 11 | 60² | 77 | 9 | 35 | 46 | 5.2 | 6.8 | 48% | .354 | 1.85 | 7.41 | 5.74 | 6.40 | 0.2 |
| 2009 | COL | MLB | 23 | 0 | 0 | 0 | 1 | 1 | 4 | 3 | 0 | 2 | 3 | 4.5 | 6.8 | 55% | .273 | 1.25 | 4.50 | 3.06 | 4.08 | 0.0 |
| 2010 | CSP | AAA | 24 | 3 | 3 | 0 | 12 | 11 | 61 | 39 | 2 | 11 | 38 | 2.8 | 7.8 | 54% | .314 | 1.33 | 5.75 | 3.93 | 4.68 | 1.2 |
| 2010 | COL | MLB | 24 | 2 | 3 | 0 | 28 | 8 | 72 | 94 | 5 | 26 | 66 | 3.2 | 8.2 | 51% | .390 | 1.67 | 6.12 | 3.47 | 4.37 | 1.1 |
| 2011 | COL | MLB | 25 | 6 | 6 | 0 | 18 | 13 | 83 | 110 | 14 | 47 | 63 | 5.1 | 6.8 | 43% | .357 | 1.89 | 7.05 | 5.58 | 6.08 | -0.3 |
| 2012 | COL | MLB | 26 | 4 | 5 | 0 | 22 | 13 | 84 | 101 | 11 | 34 | 49 | 3.6 | 5.2 | 44% | .341 | 1.61 | 6.28 | 4.95 | 6.82 | -0.8 |

Rogers was ineffective working mostly out of the bullpen in 2010, so the Rockies moved him to the rotation, where he added can't throw strikes or keep the ball in the park to his repertoire. The organization has stressed the importance of developing pitchers from within so that they don't have to adjust when moving from wherever they were to a less forgiving environment. It is a nice theory, but one that doesn't apply to Rogers, against whom opponents have hit .356/.418/.572 at Coors Field. Rogers

Slowey's gopher and durability woes put him on the rotation bubble with the Twins shortly after pitchers and catchers reported. Pushed into an unfamiliar relief role, he landed on the DL with bursitis and biceps tendinitis after appearing in three of the team's first four regular season games. A month later he returned, his rehab prolonged by the Twins stretching him out lest he be needed to fill a rotation spot. He made three appearances after returning; when the Twins tried to demote him, both to keep him stretched out and—as was widely reported—to punish him for a bad attitude, he was diagnosed with an abdominal strain that sidelined him for two more months. Despite some interest from other teams, the Twins failed to unload him at the deadline. They recalled him on August 19 and he posted a 7.25 ERA in eight starts, all losses. Slowey allowed eight homers over that stretch, and batters owned a .224 ISO against him—think Dan Uggla or Matt Holliday—which doesn't figure to improve with a move to Coors Field.

**Alex White**

Born: 8/29/1988 Age: **23**
Bats: R Throws: **R** Height: **6' 4"** Weight: **215**
Breakout: **33%** Improve: **68%** Collapse: **11%**
Attrition: **11%** MLB: **86%**

**Comparables:**
Frank Castillo, Mike Leake, Justin Germano

| YEAR | TEAM | LVL | AGE | W | L | SV | G | GS | IP | H | HR | BB | SO | EqBB9 | EqSO9 | GB% | BABIP | WHIP | ERA | FIP | FRA | WARP |
|---|---|---|---|---|---|---|---|---|---|---|---|---|---|---|---|---|---|---|---|---|---|---|
| 2010 | KIN | A+ | 21 | 2 | 3 | 0 | 8 | 8 | 44 | 26 | 4 | 15 | 27 | 3.9 | 8.4 | 55% | .232 | 1.16 | 2.86 | 4.43 | 4.78 | 0.2 |
| 2010 | AKR | AA | 21 | 7 | 7 | 0 | 18 | 17 | 106² | 57 | 5 | 15 | 44 | 2.3 | 6.4 | 56% | .260 | 1.11 | 2.28 | 3.83 | 3.96 | 1.7 |
| 2011 | CLE | MLB | 22 | 1 | 0 | 0 | 3 | 3 | 15 | 14 | 3 | 9 | 13 | 5.4 | 7.8 | 57% | .275 | 1.53 | 3.60 | 5.73 | 5.77 | -0.2 |
| 2011 | COL | MLB | 22 | 2 | 4 | 0 | 7 | 7 | 36¹ | 48 | 12 | 16 | 24 | 4.0 | 5.9 | 45% | .316 | 1.76 | 8.42 | 7.62 | 7.13 | -0.8 |
| 2012 | COL | MLB | 23 | 4 | 4 | 0 | 11 | 11 | 59 | 61 | 9 | 22 | 35 | 3.4 | 5.4 | 49% | .301 | 1.41 | 5.29 | 5.12 | 5.75 | 0.1 |

White came over in the Ubaldo Jimenez trade and got torched in his first trip through the National League. Cleveland's 2009 first-round pick served up home runs at a rate that would make Ken Dixon blush, finishing fourth on the Rockies in homers allowed despite not making his debut until August 23. The five he surrendered in a September 10 contest against the Reds tied for the most allowed in a game by any MLB pitcher in 2011. White never had gopheritis in the minors, so this could be nothing more than an adjustment period. Assuming he and the Rockies can work through those initial struggles, White should develop into a solid mid-rotation starter.

# LINEOUTS

## HITTERS

| PLAYER | TEAM | LVL | AGE | PA | R | 2B | 3B | HR | RBI | BB | SO | SB-CS | AVG/OBP/SLG | TAv | BABIP | BRR | FRAA | WARP |
|---|---|---|---|---|---|---|---|---|---|---|---|---|---|---|---|---|---|---|
| SS C. Adames | ASH | A | 19 | 459 | 63 | 17 | 2 | 8 | 44 | 42 | 74 | 2-0 | .273/.350/.386 | .253 | .315 | 2.8 | 7.8 | 2.7 |
| C E. Alfonzo | CSP | AAA | 32 | 101 | 21 | 7 | 0 | 12 | 37 | 2 | 16 | 2-1 | .319/.347/.777 | .330 | .265 | 0.5 | -0.2 | 1.3 |
| | COL | MLB | 32 | 79 | 2 | 1 | 0 | 1 | 9 | 3 | 13 | 0-0 | .267/.304/.320 | .224 | .311 | -0.8 | -0.2 | 0.0 |
| LF C. Dickerson | ASH | A | 22 | 435 | 78 | 27 | 5 | 32 | 87 | 39 | 99 | 9-6 | .282/.356/.629 | .303 | .296 | 0.8 | -0.7 | 2.7 |
| 2B B. Emaus | CSP | AAA | 25 | 186 | 37 | 10 | 2 | 9 | 28 | 20 | 24 | 3-3 | .313/.389/.564 | .289 | .321 | 1.4 | 0.2 | 1.5 |
| | NYN | MLB | 25 | 42 | 2 | 0 | 0 | 0 | 1 | 4 | 9 | 0-0 | .162/.262/.162 | .141 | .214 | 0.3 | 1.7 | -0.2 |
| 2B T. Field | TUL | AA | 24 | 544 | 77 | 22 | 3 | 17 | 61 | 53 | 108 | 9-4 | .271/.357/.439 | .281 | .316 | -0.4 | 0.9 | 2.7 |
| | COL | MLB | 24 | 51 | 4 | 0 | 0 | 0 | 3 | 3 | 14 | 0-0 | .271/.314/.271 | .211 | .382 | 0.7 | 1.1 | 0.1 |
| SS R. Herrera | CAS | RK | 18 | 275 | 38 | 6 | 8 | 6 | 34 | 27 | 62 | 5-4 | .284/.361/.449 | .273 | .358 | -1.7 | -14.1 | 0.0 |
| CF J. Hoffmann | ABQ | AAA | 26 | 533 | 91 | 23 | 3 | 22 | 84 | 44 | 102 | 14-4 | .297/.356/.497 | .271 | .331 | 1.3 | -16.5 | 0.5 |
| 1B J. Mather | GWN | AAA | 28 | 70 | 13 | 5 | 0 | 1 | 4 | 8 | 14 | 2-1 | .258/.343/.387 | .254 | .319 | 0.2 | -0.2 | 0.1 |
| | CSP | AAA | 28 | 234 | 36 | 14 | 1 | 6 | 31 | 18 | 39 | 3-0 | .321/.363/.483 | .264 | .357 | 3.3 | 1.6 | 1.0 |
| | ATL | MLB | 28 | 83 | 4 | 4 | 0 | 1 | 9 | 6 | 23 | 0-1 | .213/.272/.307 | .213 | .294 | -0.7 | -0.8 | -0.4 |
| CF R. Ortega | ASH | A | 20 | 519 | 77 | 26 | 8 | 9 | 66 | 28 | 90 | 32-19 | .294/.335/.438 | .267 | .344 | -0.1 | -1.8 | 2.7 |
| SS J. Rutledge | MOD | A+ | 22 | 523 | 91 | 33 | 9 | 9 | 71 | 41 | 91 | 16-3 | .348/.414/.517 | .325 | .417 | 2.6 | -16.3 | 4.6 |
| SS T. Story | CAS | RK | 18 | 210 | 37 | 8 | 2 | 6 | 28 | 26 | 41 | 13-1 | .268/.364/.436 | .271 | .313 | 3.7 | -6.3 | 1.1 |
| C W. Swanner | CAS | RK | 19 | 182 | 33 | 14 | 1 | 10 | 24 | 20 | 60 | 1-2 | .264/.357/.553 | .294 | .360 | -1.5 | -1.5 | 1.1 |
| RF C. Thomore | CAS | RK | 18 | 177 | 25 | 8 | 0 | 3 | 25 | 18 | 52 | 4-1 | .192/.288/.301 | .209 | .267 | 2.3 | -11 | -1.4 |
| 2B R. Wilson | ASH | A | 22 | 236 | 40 | 5 | 4 | 3 | 15 | 35 | 82 | 15-2 | .228/.366/.342 | .276 | .380 | 4.1 | -0.8 | 1.3 |

**Cristhian Adames** is a defense-first shortstop who hit better than expected in his full-season debut as a 19-year-old in the South Atlantic League. ⌀ As a hitter, **Eliezer Alfonzo** lacks Adam Wainwright's power and Miguel Olivo's plate discipline. In September, Alfonzo received a 100-game suspension for a second positive test for PEDs, which boggles the mind on so many levels. ⌀ **Corey Dickerson** is a power-hitting outfielder who benefited from playing half his games in Asheville, where he hit 26 of his 32 home runs in 2011. ⌀ **Brad Emaus** possesses a keen batting eye, gap power, and the ability to play second or third base. There are worse places to be a Quad-A infielder than the Rockies organization. ⌀ **Thomas Field** can play either middle infield position, pop a few homers, and draw a few walks. His ceiling is that of a big-league utility infielder, which is more than most former 24th-round picks can claim. ⌀ Dominican teenager **Rosell Herrera** opened eyes in his North American debut. Scouts like Herrera's offensive potential, although it remains to be seen whether his future lies at shortstop or third base. ⌀ With just four major-league plate appearances in the past two years, **Jamie Hoffmann**'s career stalled out in the Dodger organization; the former NHL pick still gets high marks for his work ethic and defense, and perhaps he'll get a better shot with the Rockies. ⌀ **Joe Mather** is a corner outfielder approaching 30 who has barely cleared an 800 OPS in nearly 1,400 Triple-A plate appearances. ⌀ **Rafael Ortega** is a Venezuelan center fielder with gap power and speed who put up good numbers in his full-season debut, although enthusiasm must be tempered by his home park in Asheville, where his OPS was about 250 points higher than it was on the road. ⌀ Shortstop **Josh Rutledge** was old for the California League but hit a ton at Modesto in 2011 and was nearly unstoppable in the second half. ⌀ Supplemental first-round pick **Trevor Story** is a legitimate shortstop who displayed across-the-board offensive skills in his pro debut. ⌀ **Will Swanner** is a catcher whose offensive skills are way ahead of his defensive skills. He has power but will swing at anything. ⌀ Second-round pick **Carl Thomore**, who overcame a gruesome ankle injury in a 2010 high school showcase game, appeared overmatched in his pro debut at Casper. The power-hitting corner outfielder has a lot of work to do. ⌀ Athletic second baseman **Russell Wilson** played just 61 games at Asheville on account of his also being the starting quarterback at the University of Wisconsin.

## PITCHERS

| PLAYER | TEAM | LVL | AGE | W | L | SV | IP | H | HR | BB | SO | EqBB9 | EqSO9 | GB% | BABIP | WHIP | ERA | FIP | FRA | WARP |
|--------|------|-----|-----|---|---|----|----|---|----|----|----|-------|-------|-----|-------|------|-----|-----|-----|------|
| E. Cabrera | ASH | A | 23 | 4 | 1 | 0 | 86 | 71 | 9 | 17 | 101 | 1.9 | 11.5 | 46% | .316 | 1.10 | 3.14 | 3.27 | 3.93 | 2.2 |
| | MOD | A+ | 23 | 3 | 1 | 0 | 81 | 83 | 9 | 24 | 114 | 2.6 | 11.9 | 48% | .347 | 1.25 | 3.56 | 3.49 | 4.01 | 1.4 |
| A. Campos | ASH | A | 20 | 4 | 1 | 0 | 86² | 102 | 4 | 19 | 60 | 2.0 | 6.6 | 48% | .367 | 1.50 | 5.19 | 3.57 | 5.05 | 1.1 |
| M. Ekstrom | DUR | AAA | 27 | 6 | 4 | 5 | 68¹ | 77 | 5 | 29 | 65 | 3.8 | 8.6 | 48% | .360 | 1.52 | 4.35 | 3.60 | 5.15 | 0.6 |
| | TBA | MLB | 27 | 0 | 0 | 0 | 1 | 1 | 0 | 0 | 1 | 0.0 | 9.0 | 33% | .333 | 1.00 | 0.00 | 1.06 | 0.61 | 0.0 |
| E. Escalona | CSP | AAA | 24 | 2 | 0 | 1 | 39² | 35 | 4 | 11 | 40 | 2.5 | 9.1 | 34% | .304 | 1.16 | 3.18 | 4.09 | 4.54 | 0.8 |
| | COL | MLB | 24 | 0 | 0 | 0 | 25² | 17 | 3 | 7 | 14 | 2.5 | 4.9 | 38% | .189 | 0.94 | 1.75 | 4.24 | 4.40 | 0.2 |
| C. Mortensen | CSP | AAA | 26 | 2 | 6 | 0 | 64 | 104 | 13 | 29 | 54 | 4.1 | 7.6 | 41% | .417 | 2.08 | 9.42 | 6.14 | 6.48 | 0.7 |
| | COL | MLB | 26 | 2 | 4 | 0 | 58¹ | 55 | 9 | 24 | 30 | 3.7 | 4.6 | 54% | .263 | 1.35 | 3.86 | 5.31 | 6.02 | -0.5 |
| G. Reynolds | CSP | AAA | 26 | 5 | 3 | 0 | 109² | 160 | 10 | 32 | 65 | 2.6 | 5.3 | 47% | .378 | 1.75 | 6.81 | 4.67 | 5.33 | 1.5 |

strikeouts. ⟂ Big right-hander **Albert Campos** got hit hard in his full-season debut, although part of that is due to his home park in Asheville, where his ERA was nearly five runs higher than his road ERA. ⟂ **Mike Ekstrom** spent most of the past two seasons working in relief at Triple-A Durham in the Rays system, making occasional cameos with the big club. The right-hander also has experience starting and provides the Rockies with insurance in case they need a body at some point during the season. ⟂ After a nightmarish 2010, **Edgmer Escalona** improved his control in a return stint at Triple-A and was effective in a brief trial with the big club. Opponents are 1-for-26 against him away from Coors Field. ⟂ **Clayton Mortensen** posted some of the most brutal numbers you will ever see from a pitcher at Triple-A Colorado Springs last year, making his decent showing in limited time with the big club seem like a fluke. There is no upside here. ⟂ **Greg Reynolds**, taken one pick ahead of Evan Longoria in the 2006 draft, owns a career minor-league K/9 of 5.2 in 377 1/3 innings. Here's hoping he invested his signing bonus wisely. ⟂ **Cory Riordan** is a habitual strike thrower (2.0 BB/9, 3.8 K/BB in 714 minor-league innings) whose approach might be good enough to overcome a lack of stuff. ⟂ Although **Josh Roenicke** has posted nice strikeout numbers in the minors, his control wavers, and the rest of his game isn't good enough for him to get away with that at the big-league level. ⟂ A 2010 supplemental first-round pick, **Peter Tago** is more projection than production at this point. He draws praise for his fastball, clean delivery, and maturity, but struggled with command in his pro debut.

# MANAGER: JIM TRACY

| YEAR | TEAM | W-L | Pythag +/- | Avg PC | 100+ P | 120+ P | QS | BQS | REL | REL w Zero R | IBB | Subs | PH | PH Avg | PH HR | SB2 | CS2 | SB3 | CS3 | SAC Att | SAC % | POS SAC | Squeeze | Swing | In Play |
|------|------|-----|-----------|--------|--------|--------|----|-----|-----|--------------|-----|------|----|--------|-------|-----|-----|-----|-----|---------|-------|---------|---------|-------|---------|
| 2009 | COL | 73-42 | 1 | 95.9 | 55 | 5 | 66 | 7 | 347 | 225 | 39 | 50 | 182 | .281 | 3 | 9 | 2 | 0 | 2 | 85 | 64.7% | 30 | 3 | 102 | 75 |
| 2010 | COL | 83-79 | 1 | 191.8 | 161 | 155 | 107 | 4 | 513 | 407 | 108 | — | 512 | .236 | 12 | 10 | 6 | 1 | 0 | 166 | 77.1% | 64 | 4 | 349 | 110 |
| 2011 | COL | 73-89 | 0 | 94.0 | 56 | 0 | 71 | 3 | 517 | 410 | 47 | — | 251 | .221 | 4 | 11 | 3 | 1 | 1 | 109 | 76.1% | 38 | 1 | 423 | 145 |

Since taking over as manager of the Rockies at the end of May 2009 and leading them to the postseason that year, Tracy hasn't enjoyed much success in Colorado. That 2009 showing led to his being named National League Manager of the Year, but he followed with a lackluster 83-79 showing. Still, there was reason to be hopeful entering 2011, in a division devoid of any single dominant team. Much of the core of that 2009 club remained, but injuries to key players (Ubaldo Jimenez, Jorge De La Rosa) conspired to undermine the Rockies; beyond that, there were undercurrents of discontent within the ranks. Tracy's calm de-meanor in the face of mounting losses rubbed some people the wrong way. It is oversimplifying matters and perhaps too convenient to blame a team's struggles on the manager's personality, but at some point perception becomes a problem. When the skipper has to spend time fighting (or avoiding) public relations battles, he has less time to work on fixing whatever ails his team. Tracy is no stranger to such battles, as he saw even more explosive ones toward the end of his Dodgers tenure (Milton Bradley vs. Jeff Kent, anyone?). In addition, Tracy drew criticism for his handling of Ian Stewart, who in May was shipped to Triple-A so that veteran imports Ty Wigginton (who wasn't hitting at the time) and Jose Lopez (who won't ever hit) could get their plate appearances while a once-promising youngster drafted by the organization languished in Colorado Springs. Stewart's poor showing isn't Tracy's fault, but it would be interesting to know how the third baseman, traded to the Cubs in December, might have responded had he been given the opportunity to work through his difficulties at the big-league level.

# Detroit Tigers

Though his club fell six wins short of their first champion ship in a quarter-century, Tigers GM Dave Dombrowski must have found the 2011 season extremely satisfying on many levels. His team overcame a slow start (winning 18 of 36) to run away with the divi sion, taking over first place [...] the stretch but is more than a short-term rental, promising continued rewards in the future. His superstar players more than lived up to their billing, with Miguel Cabrera winning the batting title and Justin Verlander taking home both the Cy Young and Most Valuable Player awards, while one young supporting player had a breakout season. And, perhaps most importantly for their future, Detroit's division rivals struggled, as the rebuilding Royals and Indians showed they're not yet ready for prime time, while the traditionally competitive White Sox and Twins sank under the weight of bloated veteran contracts and bad health—a position the Tigers had found themselves in not so long ago.

Last year in these pages, we discussed how the trades of starter Edwin Jackson to the Diamondbacks and center fielder Curtis Granderson to the Yankees prior to the 2010 season had set the Tigers on a path to fiscal sanity and fu ture success. Both the Yankees, who last year benefited from Granderson's MVP-caliber breakthrough season, and the Diamondbacks, who were quickly able to spin Jackson into Daniel Hudson's golden future, should be happy, but with another season in the books, Dombrowski should be thrilled. At the time of the trade, the organization owed millions to injured and ineffective veterans like Magglio Ordonez, Jeremy Bonderman, and Carlos Guillen. Rather than sit tight and wait for those radioactive contracts to expire, Dombrowski took the bold step of trading away two young, mid-priced veterans for a handful of younger, cheaper alter natives: starter Max Scherzer, relievers Phil Coke and Daniel Schlereth, and center fielder Austin Jackson. The trade paid [...] years from free agency, provid ing Detroit with a heavy dose of baseball's most valuable commodity: cost-controlled talent (see Table 1).

Several of the players Detroit acquired in the trade were less productive last year than they had been in their first seasons in Comerica. A good chunk of Jackson's value disappeared in a cloud of BABIP regression, though his defense in the center pasture makes him an important fac tor in the team's success. Scherzer didn't pitch like the ace he impersonated in the second half of 2010, but was still a solid rotation cog. Schlereth has yet to work his way into a high-leverage bullpen job, while Coke washed out in his attempted conversion to a starter's workload. Taken together the four-some provided less total value than Granderson and Jackson in 2011, but keep in mind the Tigers used the savings they realized from the trade to sign free agent Victor Martinez to hit designatedly. With V-Mart's value added in, Detroit again earned more wins for millions less than last year; overall, the Tigers won 14 more games than the year before, while their total payroll dropped from $122 million to $105 million.

In the process, Detroit's salary structure has suddenly reached a level of elegant simplicity that would earn nods of approval from Steve Jobs and Dieter Rams. Their best play-ers, Cabrera and Verlander, are also their highest paid and are signed through their peak seasons—a situation that's

| | | |
|---|---|---|
| TAv | .281 | 4th |
| TAv-P | .263 | 17th |
| FIP | 3.99 | 17th |
| DER | .708 | 18th |
| DL | 548 | 5th |
| B-Age | 28.6 | 15th |
| P-Age | 27.4 | 8th |
| Salary | $107.0 | 12th |
| M$/MW | $2.02 | 13th |

**2011:** Come out on top with stars and scrubs strategy, where stars include... Alex Avila?

**2012:** A team with some holes may not need to win 95 games again to take the division

**Action Items:** Infielders, outfielders, pitchers, hitting prospects, and an MVP award for Cabrera

more rare than you might think. Cabrera has no big salary increases scheduled through the end of his contract in 2016, at which point he'll be nearly 33 years old and ripe enough to sign a 10-year deal with the Angels. Verlander reaches his maximum $20 million salary this season, a bump that's more than covered by the expiration of Guillen's contract; when his deal ends in 2015, Verlander will be nearing age 32. Martinez is the only other player slated to earn eight figures, but he should remain productive and will be off the books before he turns 36. A handful of supporting veterans earn seven figures on short deals, and the whole structure is supported by a plethora of low-cost youngsters in the rotation and filling out the lineup. There's very little dead money on the books, and that fiscal responsibility provides the Tigers with the flexibility they need to sign a veteran here and there to fill a lineup hole. Such flexibility primes them for a multi-year run of Central Division dominance during Verlander's and Cabrera's peaks—if they're bold enough to seize the opportunity.

How far the Tigers can press their current financial advantage will depend in large part on the continued development of their young starting staff. Despite Verlander's epic season, Detroit was in the middle of the pack in run prevention, but the Tigers have enough high-octane arms to make a great leap forward. Scherzer pitched better than his numbers would otherwise betray and has the stuff to be a solid second starter. Mid-season pickup Doug Fister was a beast down the stretch but profiles as more of a mid-rotation workhorse, a job he can currently perform for a pittance. Former teen heartthrob Rick Porcello is still only 23, has a three-year record of proven performance, and may still achieve the breakthrough some have long foretold. Top prospect Jacob Turner has a higher ceiling than any non-MVP-winning pitcher on the roster, and may very well earn a spot in the rotation before his 21st birthday. Their collection of low-cost starting talent is impressive on paper, but the kids will need to make more progress at converting their potential into production for the Tigers to become perennial playoff participants. If

they can get there, the prospect of facing Verlander multiple times in a short series makes Detroit a postseason foe no one will want to face.

The Tigers picked up Jose Valverde's option, so Papa Grande will return to entertain viewers, earn saves, and lead a bullpen whose lack of depth was exposed in Detroit's ALCS loss to the Rangers. Joaquin Benoit overcame a rough start to his new three-year deal to enforce his will in the eighth inning, and Coke is a perfectly serviceable lefty reliever, but the rest of the pen is either unproven or uninspiring. Rookie Al Alburquerque showcased an unhittable slider for much of the year but faded down the stretch and will miss half the season recovering from elbow surgery, while Schlereth and former Nats farmhand Collin Balester have yet to leverage their plus stuff into reliable production. Dombrowski added grizzled righty Octavio Dotel to the bullpen mix over the winter, hoping the same fastball/slider mix he once used to baffle Marc Antony during the Second Triumvirate can still get big outs in the American League—if so, the Tigers will have an enviable collection of late-inning weapons.

While there's good reason to think Detroit's pitching will improve, the offense will likely regress unless a few lineup holes are addressed. Cabrera is the heart of the order and will remain one of the most feared hitters in baseball, but V-Mart left his power bat in Boston and isn't likely to hit .330 again. Alex Avila's standout year at the plate is unlikely to be duplicated, though his patience, power, and defensive acumen will still rank him among the best catchers in the league. Likewise Jhonny Peralta, whose on-base percentage is certain to drop but whose power will remain an asset at shortstop. Options at the other infield positions are less inspiring, with the warmed-over remains of Brandon Inge seemingly headed for a third-base job-share with Jim Leyland's favorite toy, Don Kelly. The possibility of a Ryan Raburn/Ramon Santiago platoon looming at second base doesn't exactly inspire confidence. If that sounds to you like the same old trouble the Tigers have been having for years, you'd be right, but when the walls come tumbling down at midseason

## Table 1: And That's . . . One to Grow On

| Ex-Tigers | 2010 WARP | 2010 Salary ($M) | 2011 WARP | 2011 Salary ($M) | Total WARP | Total Salary ($M) | Controlled Seasons Remaining |
|---|---|---|---|---|---|---|---|
| Curtis Granderson | 3.4 | $5.50 | 5.3 | $8.25 | 8.7 | $13.75 | 2 |
| Edwin Jackson | 2.3 | $5.00 | 1.5 | $8.35 | 3.8 | $13.35 | 0 |
| Ex-Tiger Total | 5.7 | $10.50 | 6.8 | $16.60 | 12.5 | $27.10 | 2 |

| Current Tigers | 2010 WARP | 2010 Salary ($M) | 2011 WARP | 2011 Salary ($M) | Total WARP | Total Salary ($M) | Controlled Seasons Remaining |
|---|---|---|---|---|---|---|---|
| Max Scherzer | 2.5 | $1.00 | 1.0 | $0.60 | 3.7 | $1.60 | 3 |
| Daniel Schlereth | 0.0 | $0.40 | 0.2 | $0.42 | 0.2 | $0.82 | 5 |
| Phil Coke | 0.6 | $0.43 | 1.2 | $0.44 | 2.0 | $0.87 | 3 |
| Austin Jackson | 3.5 | $0.40 | 2.0 | $0.44 | 5.8 | $0.84 | 4 |
| Victor Martinez | — | — | 3.1 | $12.00 | 6.5 | $12.00 | 3 |
| Current Tiger Total | 6.9 | $2.23 | 7.5 | $13.90 | 18.2 | $16.13 | 18 |

Dombrowski should have the payroll flexibility to prop up at least one more infield position with an actual major league player worthy of playing every day.

The offensive outlook isn't much brighter in an outfield populated with flawed players suffering from acute OBP deficiency. Brennan Boesch will return from thumb surgery to take his place in right field, and if healthy could provide significant lefty power, but will need to demonstrate that his improved approach last season wasn't a small-sample mirage. Jackson is miscast as a leadoff man but might well develop more power lower in the order, but with no other obvious candidate for the top of the order he may be stuck in the role. More distressingly, the Tigers seem committed to

Since the Tigers are devoid of hitting prospects in the upper minors—their best young bat belongs to Nick Castellanos, a 20-year-old with a single season in the Midwest League under his belt—their lineup holes can only be filled via trade or free agency, but as of press time Detroit has yet to address their offensive needs. A second baseman or outfielder who can draw a few walks and bat at the top of the order—think David DeJesus—wouldn't cost much in blood or treasure, but would be a huge help to the Tigers. With the Twins and White Sox in some disarray, with the Royals and Indians building towards contention but not yet there, and with their two superstars under contract for a few more years, Detroit's window is open right now. If their young pitching stays healthy

### Alex Avila — C

Born: 1/29/1987 Age: 25
Bats: L Throws: R Height: 6' 0" Weight: 210
Breakout: 1% Improve: 24% Collapse: 5%
Attrition: 37% MLB: 79%

**Comparables:**
Ben Petrick, John Sullivan, Tom Tischinski

| YEAR | TEAM | LVL | AGE | PA | R | 2B | 3B | HR | RBI | BB | SO | SB | CS | AVG/OBP/SLG | TAv | BABIP | BRR | FRAA | WARP |
|------|------|-----|-----|-----|----|----|----|----|-----|----|-----|----|----|-------------|------|-------|------|-----------|------|
| 2009 | ERI | AA  | 22 | 387 | 52 | 23 | 1 | 12 | 55 | 52 | 77  | 2 | 1 | .264/.364/.450 | .291 | .309 | -2.4 | -0.2 | 2.6 |
| 2009 | DET | MLB | 22 | 72  | 9  | 4  | 0 | 5  | 14 | 10 | 18  | 0 | 0 | .279/.375/.590 | .333 | .308 | -0.8 | -0.2 | 0.8 |
| 2010 | DET | MLB | 23 | 333 | 28 | 12 | 0 | 7  | 31 | 36 | 71  | 2 | 2 | .228/.316/.340 | .231 | .278 | -2.7 | -2.3 | 0.0 |
| 2011 | DET | MLB | 24 | 551 | 63 | 33 | 4 | 19 | 82 | 73 | 131 | 3 | 1 | .295/.389/.506 | .317 | .366 | 2.8 | 1.2 | 6.5 |
| 2012 | DET | MLB | 25 | 474 | 60 | 22 | 2 | 15 | 57 | 55 | 106 | 2 | 1 | .263/.351/.439 | .282 | .315 | -0.1 | C -1, 3B -0 | 3.2 |

Avila's patience and power potential made him a breakout candidate last year, but few expected him to go off so fully that he would be ranked among the league leaders in WARP and earn MVP votes. There are no weaknesses in his game, as Avila's strong arm and solid receiving skills—particularly his outstanding ability to frame pitches and earn borderline strike calls—would make him a valuable commodity even without the offensive fireworks. Add his potent lefty bat, solid work ethic, and the fact he won't reach free agency until 2016, and Avila is an inexpensive building block who can give the Tigers a competitive advantage for years to come. He won't maintain a .366 BABIP, and he may never again put together a complete season quite like 2011, but even a significant drop in offensive value will leave him among the best all-around backstops in the league.

### Wilson Betemit — 3B

Born: 11/2/1981 Age: 30
Bats: B Throws: R Height: 6' 3" Weight: 155
Breakout: 3% Improve: 47% Collapse: 6%
Attrition: 23% MLB: 88%

**Comparables:**
Mike Coolbaugh, Howard Johnson, Bill Hall

| YEAR | TEAM | LVL | AGE | PA | R | 2B | 3B | HR | RBI | BB | SO | SB | CS | AVG/OBP/SLG | TAv | BABIP | BRR | FRAA | WARP |
|------|------|-----|-----|-----|----|----|----|----|-----|----|-----|----|----|-------------|------|-------|------|-----------|------|
| 2009 | CHR | AAA | 27 | 286 | 36 | 19 | 0 | 11 | 49 | 21 | 73 | 2 | 0 | .241/.298/.441 | .249 | .294 | 1 | 8.1 | 0.9 |
| 2009 | CHA | MLB | 27 | 50  | 2  | 5  | 0 | 0  | 3  | 5  | 13 | 0 | 0 | .200/.280/.311 | .199 | .281 | -0.4 | -0.3 | -0.3 |
| 2010 | OMA | AAA | 28 | 135 | 9  | 6  | 2 | 2  | 17 | 17 | 23 | 1 | 1 | .265/.364/.407 | .269 | .315 | -0.7 | -0.2 | 0.4 |
| 2010 | KCA | MLB | 28 | 315 | 36 | 20 | 0 | 13 | 43 | 36 | 74 | 0 | 0 | .297/.378/.511 | .311 | .361 | -2.1 | -4.4 | 1.7 |
| 2011 | DET | MLB | 29 | 133 | 11 | 7  | 3 | 5  | 19 | 11 | 47 | 1 | 0 | .292/.346/.525 | .314 | .429 | -0.9 | -0.2 | 1.0 |
| 2011 | KCA | MLB | 29 | 226 | 29 | 15 | 1 | 3  | 27 | 20 | 58 | 3 | 1 | .281/.341/.409 | .261 | .372 | -0.3 | 1.1 | 0.7 |
| 2012 | DET | MLB | 30 | 344 | 41 | 17 | 2 | 11 | 41 | 31 | 92 | 2 | 1 | .255/.323/.426 | .266 | .324 | -0.1 | 3B -0, 1B -0 | 1.9 |

A leather-deficient corner infielder and nominal switch-hitter, Betemit traditionally struggles against lefties but has posted a solid .292/.363/.486 line against right-handed pitching over the last three seasons. After acquiring him from the Royals last July, Detroit plugged him into its yawning third-base void and made the most of the incremental benefits his bat can provide, but a sore knee slowed Betemit down the stretch and he is not high on the Tigers' free agent wish list. His modest power and ability to at least masquerade as a third sacker make him a decent low-cost option for a contender spending money in other places, especially one with a strikeout-oriented pitching staff and a more defensively accomplished platoon partner. Funny, that sounds a lot like the Tigers.

**Brennan Boesch** RF

Born: 4/12/1985 Age: 27
Bats: L Throws: L Height: 6' 5" Weight: 235
Breakout: 2% Improve: 40% Collapse: 8%
Attrition: 17% MLB: 80%

**Comparables:**
Wes Covington, Joe Charboneau, Andy Barkett

| YEAR | TEAM | LVL | AGE | PA | R | 2B | 3B | HR | RBI | BB | SO | SB | CS | AVG/OBP/SLG | TAv | BABIP | BRR | FRAA | WARP |
|------|------|-----|-----|----|---|----|----|----|-----|----|----|----|----|------------|-----|-------|-----|------|------|
| 2009 | ERI | AA | 24 | 571 | 89 | 26 | 7 | 28 | 93 | 33 | 127 | 11 | 2 | .275/.321/.510 | .285 | .314 | 1.7 | -2.3 | 2.4 |
| 2010 | TOL | AAA | 25 | 66 | 6 | 3 | 1 | 3 | 17 | 4 | 17 | 2 | 1 | .379/.455/.621 | .345 | .500 | -1.4 | -0.6 | 0.5 |
| 2010 | DET | MLB | 25 | 512 | 49 | 26 | 3 | 14 | 67 | 40 | 99 | 7 | 1 | .256/.320/.416 | .264 | .297 | -2.8 | 1.5 | 1.1 |
| 2011 | DET | MLB | 26 | 472 | 75 | 25 | 1 | 16 | 54 | 35 | 83 | 5 | 3 | .283/.341/.458 | .285 | .315 | -1.1 | 2.6 | 2.2 |
| 2012 | DET | MLB | 27 | 451 | 55 | 20 | 3 | 15 | 58 | 30 | 89 | 6 | 2 | .268/.320/.445 | .271 | .304 | 0 | RF -1, LF 0 | 1.4 |

Boesch recovered from a historically atrocious 2010 second half to display continued power and a more selective plate approach in 2011, at least until his season was cut short by a thumb injury that resulted in September surgery. His newfound willingness to lay off pitches out of the zone certainly increases his offensive upside, but only time will tell if the approach sticks, and since he fields as if Comerica's outfield were made of tapioca pudding his career will be defined by his bat. A healthy Boesch could launch 20 bombs this year while earning peanuts, so the Tigers will pencil him in for the right field job and hope he avoids enough outs to provide value.

**Miguel Cabrera** 1B

Born: 4/18/1983 Age: 29
Bats: R Throws: R Height: 6' 3" Weight: 180
Breakout: 3% Improve: 45% Collapse: 2%
Attrition: 9% MLB: 87%

**Comparables:**
Eddie Murray, Mark Teixeira, Todd Helton

| YEAR | TEAM | LVL | AGE | PA | R | 2B | 3B | HR | RBI | BB | SO | SB | CS | AVG/OBP/SLG | TAv | BABIP | BRR | FRAA | WARP |
|------|------|-----|-----|----|---|----|----|----|-----|----|----|----|----|------------|-----|-------|-----|------|------|
| 2009 | DET | MLB | 26 | 685 | 96 | 34 | 0 | 34 | 103 | 68 | 107 | 6 | 2 | .324/.396/.547 | .320 | .348 | -2.9 | -4.7 | 4.3 |
| 2010 | DET | MLB | 27 | 648 | 111 | 45 | 1 | 38 | 126 | 89 | 95 | 3 | 3 | .328/.420/.622 | .351 | .336 | -1.4 | -4.4 | 6.4 |
| 2011 | DET | MLB | 28 | 688 | 111 | 48 | 0 | 30 | 105 | 108 | 89 | 2 | 1 | .344/.448/.586 | .354 | .365 | -2.7 | -11.9 | 6.5 |
| 2012 | DET | MLB | 29 | 638 | 97 | 35 | 2 | 31 | 102 | 73 | 101 | 3 | 1 | .314/.394/.553 | .329 | .334 | -0.2 | 1B -8 | 5.4 |

Another year, another alcohol-related incident, another top five finish in the MVP voting. It was business as usual for the AL's best pure hitter, as Cabrera brushed past his offseason DUI arrest to post baseball's highest batting average and OBP, lead the league in doubles, and set career bests in WARP, VORP, and True Average. He walked more and struck out less than ever before, and perhaps most encouraging for his future Cabrera seemed committed to the league-recommended sobriety program that can only help him both on and off the field. Cabrera will turn 29 this April and is under contract through 2015, at which point the Tigers will have benefited from the very best seasons of what has every chance of being a Hall of Fame career.

**Nick Castellanos** 3B

Born: 3/4/1992 Age: 20
Bats: R Throws: R Height: 6' 5" Weight: 195
Breakout: 1% Improve: 6% Collapse: 1%
Attrition: 5% MLB: 9%

**Comparables:**
Brian Mathews, Tyler Kolodny, Bobby Borchering

| YEAR | TEAM | LVL | AGE | PA | R | 2B | 3B | HR | RBI | BB | SO | SB | CS | AVG/OBP/SLG | TAv | BABIP | BRR | FRAA | WARP |
|------|------|-----|-----|----|---|----|----|----|-----|----|----|----|----|------------|-----|-------|-----|------|------|
| 2011 | WMI | A | 19 | 562 | 65 | 36 | 3 | 7 | 76 | 45 | 130 | 3 | 2 | .312/.367/.436 | .295 | .402 | -5.7 | -15.1 | 2.1 |
| 2012 | DET | MLB | 20 | 250 | 23 | 11 | 1 | 2 | 20 | 11 | 68 | 0 | 0 | .228/.262/.307 | .205 | .305 | 0 | 3B -9 | -0.8 |

Detroit's top hitting prospect by a country mile, Castellanos made his full-season debut and overcame a cold April to spray line drives all over the Midwest League, leading the circuit in hits as a 19-year-old. No one doubted he would hit, but Castellanos showed improved patience as the season went on and enough power potential in his swing to profile as a future middle-of-the-order force. Perhaps most importantly for his future, the former high school shortstop showed enough defensive chops at the hot corner to make scouts think he can stick at third, a position where his bat will play nicely. There's a long way to go, of course, but if Castellanos can continue to develop there will be All-Star games in his future.

**Tyler Collins** LF

Born: 6/6/1990 Age: 22
Bats: L Throws: L Height: 6' 0" Weight: 205
Breakout: 6% Improve: 17% Collapse: 4%
Attrition: 14% MLB: 27%

**Comparables:**
Angelo Songco, Rich Chiles, Chih-Hsien Chiang

| YEAR | TEAM | LVL | AGE | PA | R | 2B | 3B | HR | RBI | BB | SO | SB | CS | AVG/OBP/SLG | TAv | BABIP | BRR | FRAA | WARP |
|------|------|-----|-----|----|---|----|----|----|-----|----|----|----|----|------------|-----|-------|-----|------|------|
| 2011 | ONE | A- | 21 | 178 | 28 | 10 | 1 | 8 | 31 | 10 | 17 | 6 | 1 | .313/.360/.534 | .324 | .307 | 3 | 1.5 | 2.0 |
| 2012 | DET | MLB | 22 | 250 | 24 | 10 | 1 | 7 | 27 | 9 | 50 | 3 | 1 | .226/.257/.361 | .218 | .255 | 0 | LF -5, RF 0 | -1.0 |

A sixth-round pick out of Howard Junior College, Collins signed quickly last summer and grabbed the organization's attention with an impressive debut. A corner outfielder whose build is as angular as a file cabinet, Collins looks at home at the plate and shows the potential to hit for average and power, though his overly aggressive approach may become a millstone. His bat will have to carry him, as he lacks the range for center and his arm may limit him to left, but if he continues to hit in his full-season debut, Collins will be someone to keep an eye on. Is it too soon to suggest the nickname Ripper?

**Andy Dirks**  LF

Born: 1/24/1986 Age: 26
Bats: L Throws: L Height: 6' 1" Weight: 195
Breakout: 2% Improve: 58% Collapse: 6%
Attrition: 18% MLB: 92%

Comparables:
Jim Piersall, Paul Blair, Amos Otis

| YEAR | TEAM | LVL | AGE | PA | R | 2B | 3B | HR | RBI | BB | SO | SB | CS | AVG_OBP_SLG | TAv | BABIP | BRR | FRAA | WARP |
|------|------|-----|-----|----|---|----|----|----|-----|----|----|----|----|-------------|-----|-------|-----|------|------|
| 2009 | LAK | A+ | 23 | 117 | 11 | 5 | 0 | 0 | 18 | 13 | 11 | 10 | 2 | .330/.410/.379 | .275 | .370 | 1 | 0.6 | 0.6 |
| 2009 | ERI | AA | 23 | 408 | 46 | 14 | 1 | 6 | 44 | 36 | 61 | 11 | 5 | .255/.326/.349 | .241 | .291 | 2.5 | 3.8 | 0.4 |
| 2010 | ERI | AA | 24 | 434 | 64 | 20 | 2 | 11 | 46 | 35 | 59 | 19 | 4 | .278/.345/.425 | .277 | .304 | 1.4 | -4.2 | 1.9 |
| 2010 | TOL | AAA | 24 | 93 | 14 | 10 | 1 | 4 | 17 | 3 | 12 | 3 | 0 | .375/.402/.648 | .348 | .403 | 0.6 | 3.6 | 1.6 |
| 2011 | TOL | AAA | 25 | 172 | 30 | 8 | 1 | 7 | 24 | 12 | 28 | 12 | 2 | .325/.368/.522 | .279 | .355 | 0.5 | 4.4 | 1.3 |
| 2011 | DET | MLB | 25 | 235 | 34 | 13 | 0 | 7 | 28 | 11 | 36 | 5 | 2 | .251/.296/.406 | .245 | .273 | -0.4 | 2.3 | 0.2 |
| 2012 | DET | MLB | 26 | 261 | 30 | 12 | 1 | 6 | 29 | 15 | 43 | 9 | 2 | .263/.310/.399 | .253 | .292 | 0.2 | LF 2, CF -1 | 0.8 |

A prototypical fourth outfielder, Dirks is a defensive asset in a corner and won't hurt you in center field, but doesn't have quite enough bat or glove to start in either position. His first look at major league pitching last year didn't go well, as Dirks showed middling power but walked far less than he had during his minor league career—something he'll have to correct to move ahead of Brennan Boesch on the depth charts. As it is he'll likely compete for a roster spot with human multi-tools Don Kelly

Guillen limped to the end of his four-year, $48 million contract, as recovery from microfracture knee surgery kept him out of the lineup until July, while recurring wrist and calf issues limited him to 28 games. The final tally: a .266/.345/.421 line in 1188 plate appearances. Creditable rates for a middle infielder, but Guillen only managed 72 starts at second base and none at shortstop during his expensive years. It is easy to forget how valuable Guillen was during his first four seasons in Detroit, posting a .313/.377/.506 line and earning 18.4 WARP, but the Tigers gambled on his health and lost. He could regain some semblance of his old stroke, but he no longer has enough bat for a corner, and he's as likely to stay healthy at second base as he is to bend forks through telekinesis.

**Jerad Head**  LF

Born: 11/15/1982 Age: 29
Bats: R Throws: R Height: 6' 2" Weight: 205
Breakout: 3% Improve: 36% Collapse: 1%
Attrition: 17% MLB: 75%

Comparables:
Benny Ayala, Zeke Bella, Jeff McKnight

| YEAR | TEAM | LVL | AGE | PA | R | 2B | 3B | HR | RBI | BB | SO | SB | CS | AVG_OBP_SLG | TAv | BABIP | BRR | FRAA | WARP |
|------|------|-----|-----|----|---|----|----|----|-----|----|----|----|----|-------------|-----|-------|-----|------|------|
| 2009 | AKR | AA | 26 | 368 | 49 | 23 | 4 | 6 | 47 | 23 | 72 | 6 | 2 | .282/.347/.433 | .290 | .340 | 0.6 | -2.7 | 2.0 |
| 2010 | AKR | AA | 27 | 263 | 47 | 18 | 0 | 15 | 51 | 18 | 46 | 2 | 1 | .312/.369/.578 | .314 | .333 | 4.4 | -1.3 | 2.3 |
| 2010 | COH | AAA | 27 | 83 | 12 | 9 | 0 | 2 | 15 | 5 | 20 | 0 | 0 | .257/.329/.459 | .270 | .327 | 1.3 | 1.9 | 0.6 |
| 2011 | COH | AAA | 28 | 463 | 67 | 28 | 1 | 24 | 70 | 25 | 99 | 3 | 1 | .284/.338/.526 | .261 | .317 | 0.7 | -3.2 | 0.9 |
| 2011 | CLE | MLB | 28 | 25 | 2 | 1 | 0 | 0 | 1 | 0 | 5 | 1 | 0 | .125/.160/.167 | .185 | .158 | -0.4 | -0.1 | -0.2 |
| 2012 | DET | MLB | 29 | 250 | 30 | 13 | 1 | 9 | 33 | 12 | 55 | 1 | 1 | .256/.305/.439 | .263 | .295 | 0 | LF -3, RF -1 | 1.1 |

Quite the enigmatic player, Head didn't start his pro career until age 23 and just registered his first full season at Triple-A in 2011. While he has played every position on the field in the minors, he roamed the outfield almost exclusively in 2011. Now 29, there's little projection left for Head, but he might be good enough to fill the role of a fourth or fifth outfielder. He is a bit below average on defense but not enough to kill you. While he has posted great power numbers the past couple of seasons, he has a reputation as a guess hitter, which doesn't translate particularly well to the majors for anyone not named Alex Rodriguez.

**Brandon Inge**  3B

Born: 5/19/1977 Age: 35
Bats: R Throws: R Height: 6' 0" Weight: 185
Breakout: 2% Improve: 23% Collapse: 14%
Attrition: 22% MLB: 79%

Comparables:
Cody Ransom, Howard Johnson, Bob Elliott

| YEAR | TEAM | LVL | AGE | PA | R | 2B | 3B | HR | RBI | BB | SO | SB | CS | AVG_OBP_SLG | TAv | BABIP | BRR | FRAA | WARP |
|------|------|-----|-----|----|---|----|----|----|-----|----|----|----|----|-------------|-----|-------|-----|------|------|
| 2009 | DET | MLB | 32 | 637 | 71 | 16 | 1 | 27 | 84 | 54 | 170 | 2 | 5 | .230/.314/.406 | .261 | .277 | -1.7 | 4.2 | 2.5 |
| 2010 | DET | MLB | 33 | 580 | 47 | 28 | 5 | 13 | 70 | 54 | 134 | 4 | 3 | .247/.321/.397 | .258 | .305 | -4.1 | 9.3 | 2.0 |
| 2011 | TOL | AAA | 34 | 126 | 18 | 4 | 0 | 7 | 19 | 17 | 30 | 0 | 0 | .287/.389/.519 | .304 | .338 | -1 | 2.9 | 1.3 |
| 2011 | DET | MLB | 34 | 303 | 29 | 10 | 2 | 3 | 23 | 24 | 74 | 1 | 1 | .197/.265/.283 | .201 | .256 | 0.4 | 9.6 | 0.1 |
| 2012 | DET | MLB | 35 | 359 | 38 | 12 | 2 | 9 | 35 | 30 | 91 | 2 | 2 | .224/.300/.362 | .239 | .278 | -0.4 | 3B 9 | 0.8 |

Most men Dave Dombrowski's age have their own version of Brandon Inge stashed away somewhere—a tattered college rugby jersey that's now two sizes too small, or a threadbare work shirt that has helped re-shingle two roofs, brick a few patios, and wire the new rec room. These things are comforting to have around but should never be worn outside of the house, and in fact are no longer suitable for their former roles, no matter how much you wish they were. Inge is a clubhouse catalyst and can still pick it at third base, but his .223/.292/.346 three-year line against right-handed pitching makes him unplayable in anything but a platoon role. For that the Tigers are on the hook for $6 million next year, including his inevitable 2013 buyout. Sentimentality rarely comes cheap.

### Austin Jackson    CF

Born: 2/1/1987 Age: 25
Bats: R Throws: R Height: 6' 2" Weight: 185
Breakout: 3% Improve: 49% Collapse: 11%
Attrition: 31% MLB: 88%

**Comparables:**
Brian Anderson, Drew Stubbs, Dante Powell

| YEAR | TEAM | LVL | AGE | PA | R | 2B | 3B | HR | RBI | BB | SO | SB | CS | AVG/OBP/SLG | TAv | BABIP | BRR | FRAA | WARP |
|------|------|-----|-----|-----|-----|-----|-----|-----|-----|-----|-----|-----|-----|-------------|------|-------|------|----------|------|
| 2009 | SWB | AAA | 22 | 557 | 67 | 23 | 9 | 4 | 65 | 40 | 123 | 24 | 4 | .300/.358/.405 | .277 | .389 | 5.3 | -1.4 | 1.8 |
| 2010 | DET | MLB | 23 | 675 | 103 | 34 | 10 | 4 | 41 | 47 | 170 | 27 | 6 | .293/.345/.400 | .271 | .396 | 4.7 | 3 | 3.5 |
| 2011 | DET | MLB | 24 | 668 | 90 | 22 | 11 | 10 | 45 | 56 | 181 | 22 | 5 | .249/.317/.374 | .250 | .340 | 0.7 | 5.7 | 2.0 |
| 2012 | DET | MLB | 25 | 629 | 72 | 25 | 9 | 7 | 63 | 46 | 157 | 21 | 5 | .271/.328/.383 | .255 | .355 | 0.6 | CF -0, LF -0 | 1.7 |

The 2010 Rookie of the Year runner-up suffered through a season that casual observers might call a sophomore slump, but analysts would label an expected regression to his true talent level. A-Jax continues to strike out in more than a quarter of his plate appearances, so when his BABIP dropped from a league-leading .396 to a more realistic .340 alongside only moderate increases in isolated power and walk rate, his offensive value cratered. On the plus side, he plays terrific defense in center—a particularly valuable skill given Detroit's propensity to populate the corners with zombie outfielders—and continues to steal bases at a high success rate. Still only 25, he is unlikely to develop the on-base skills he'll need to remain in the lead-off spot, but might well develop more home run pop. The Tigers would be wise to drop him into the seven-hole and let him unleash his burgeoning power stroke.

### Don Kelly    3B

Born: 2/15/1980 Age: 32
Bats: L Throws: R Height: 6' 5" Weight: 190
Breakout: 1% Improve: 35% Collapse: 6%
Attrition: 17% MLB: 82%

**Comparables:**
Mike Lowell, Ray Knight, B.J. Surhoff

| YEAR | TEAM | LVL | AGE | PA | R | 2B | 3B | HR | RBI | BB | SO | SB | CS | AVG/OBP/SLG | TAv | BABIP | BRR | FRAA | WARP |
|------|------|-----|-----|-----|-----|-----|-----|-----|-----|-----|-----|-----|-----|-------------|------|-------|------|----------|------|
| 2009 | TOL | AAA | 29 | 420 | 57 | 20 | 6 | 6 | 40 | 43 | 51 | 27 | 4 | .331/.402/.465 | .295 | .369 | 0.4 | 1.8 | 2.8 |
| 2009 | DET | MLB | 29 | 62 | 8 | 3 | 1 | 0 | 3 | 4 | 10 | 1 | 0 | .250/.311/.339 | .243 | .304 | 0.2 | 0.7 | 0.2 |
| 2010 | DET | MLB | 30 | 251 | 30 | 4 | 0 | 9 | 27 | 8 | 42 | 3 | 0 | .244/.272/.374 | .238 | .259 | 0.3 | 3.7 | 0.5 |
| 2011 | DET | MLB | 31 | 281 | 35 | 8 | 3 | 7 | 28 | 14 | 32 | 2 | 1 | .245/.291/.381 | .245 | .256 | 0.1 | 3 | 0.7 |
| 2012 | DET | MLB | 32 | 258 | 29 | 9 | 2 | 5 | 26 | 16 | 37 | 6 | 1 | .261/.312/.379 | .249 | .286 | 0.2 | 3B 4, LF 0 | 1.0 |

Exhibit A in the landmark case *Leyland vs. American League Baseball*, Kelly's only real talent is his admirable willingness to wear a glove and stand anywhere on the field—including on the mound or behind the plate, should an emergency arise. Keeping a chameleon on the bench is a necessity in the double-switch league, but the only explanation for Kelly getting 250 plate appearances for the Tigers is a managerial fetish. Kelly's defense is above-average on the corners and he hits better against right-handed pitching, but when "better" means a career line of .246/.292/.380, he's not a major league hitter. The Tigers are considering a Kelly/Inge third base platoon, a plan that leaves them approximately 1.5 players short of a load and virtually ins another midseason trade to shore up the hot corner.

### Gerald Laird    C

Born: 11/13/1979 Age: 32
Bats: R Throws: R Height: 6' 3" Weight: 190
Breakout: 0% Improve: 24% Collapse: 14%
Attrition: 37% MLB: 82%

**Comparables:**
Yorvit Torrealba, Larry Cox, Jim Sundberg

| YEAR | TEAM | LVL | AGE | PA | R | 2B | 3B | HR | RBI | BB | SO | SB | CS | AVG/OBP/SLG | TAv | BABIP | BRR | FRAA | WARP |
|------|------|-----|-----|-----|-----|-----|-----|-----|-----|-----|-----|-----|-----|-------------|------|-------|------|----------|------|
| 2009 | DET | MLB | 29 | 477 | 49 | 23 | 2 | 4 | 33 | 40 | 68 | 5 | 0 | .225/.306/.320 | .229 | .258 | -0.2 | 0.3 | 1.0 |
| 2010 | DET | MLB | 30 | 299 | 22 | 11 | 0 | 5 | 25 | 18 | 57 | 3 | 1 | .207/.263/.304 | .201 | .243 | -0.3 | 2 | -0.1 |
| 2011 | SLN | MLB | 31 | 108 | 11 | 7 | 1 | 1 | 12 | 9 | 19 | 1 | 1 | .232/.302/.358 | .232 | .276 | -2 | 0.5 | -0.2 |
| 2012 | DET | MLB | 32 | 250 | 26 | 11 | 1 | 3 | 22 | 17 | 46 | 2 | 1 | .235/.295/.342 | .230 | .273 | -0.1 | C 1, 1B 0 | 0.7 |

Laird missed six weeks with a broken finger in late May, limiting him to just 108 plate appearances as Yadier Molina's backup. Despite his reputation as a strong defender, Laird threw out just 20 percent of runners trying to steal, but fulfilled his reputation as a weak hitter by posting a .229 TAv. The Tigers signed him in the offseason to back up Alex Avila, which means Detroit's lineup will feature yet another hole approximately once per week.

### Victor Martinez    C

Born: 12/23/1978 Age: 33
Bats: B Throws: R Height: 6' 3" Weight: 170
Breakout: 1% Improve: 28% Collapse: 4%
Attrition: 14% MLB: 90%

**Comparables:**
Hal McRae, Mike Sweeney, Nomar Garciaparra

| YEAR | TEAM | LVL | AGE | PA | R | 2B | 3B | HR | RBI | BB | SO | SB | CS | AVG/OBP/SLG | TAv | BABIP | BRR | FRAA | WARP |
|------|------|-----|-----|-----|-----|-----|-----|-----|-----|-----|-----|-----|-----|-------------|------|-------|------|----------|------|
| 2009 | BOS | MLB | 30 | 237 | 32 | 12 | 0 | 8 | 41 | 24 | 23 | 1 | 0 | .336/.405/.507 | .315 | .348 | -1.5 | -0.8 | 1.7 |
| 2009 | CLE | MLB | 30 | 435 | 56 | 21 | 1 | 15 | 67 | 51 | 51 | 0 | 0 | .284/.368/.464 | .290 | .291 | -1.4 | -2.8 | 1.8 |
| 2010 | BOS | MLB | 31 | 538 | 64 | 32 | 1 | 20 | 79 | 40 | 52 | 1 | 0 | .302/.351/.493 | .295 | .303 | -4.3 | 0.9 | 3.1 |
| 2011 | DET | MLB | 32 | 595 | 76 | 40 | 0 | 12 | 103 | 46 | 51 | 1 | 0 | .330/.380/.470 | .298 | .343 | -3.5 | -0.2 | 3.1 |
| 2012 | DET | MLB | 33 | 549 | 71 | 30 | 1 | 14 | 67 | 47 | 60 | 1 | 0 | .295/.357/.448 | .288 | .310 | 0 | C -1, 1B 0 | 3.1 |

Detroit's big offseason addition could hardly have worked out any better last year, as Martinez settled comfortably into his best defensive position—Designated Hitter—and provided enough offense from the five-hole to earn a few deeply misguided down-ballot MVP votes. V-Mart was productive from both sides of the plate but posted the lowest ISO of his career, a troubling power outage that was evident both at spacious Comerica and on the road. Combine that with a batting average that is sure to fall and Martinez is more likely to be less an elite bat and merely a solid one. Alas, just as this book was headed to the printer, Martinez tore his ACL and was feared lost for the season.

**Magglio Ordonez** RF

Born: 1/28/1974 Age: 38
Bats: R Throws: R Height: 6' 0" Weight: 170
Breakout: 0% Improve: 22% Collapse: 17%
Attrition: 22% MLB: 78%

Comparables:
Bernie Williams, Al Kaline, Carl Furillo

| YEAR | TEAM | LVL | AGE | PA | R | 2B | 3B | HR | RBI | BB | SO | SB | CS | AVG/OBP/SLG | TAv | BABIP | BRR | FRAA | WARP |
|------|------|-----|-----|-----|----|----|----|----|-----|----|----|----|----|-------------|------|-------|------|--------|------|
| 2009 | DET | MLB | 35 | 518 | 54 | 24 | 2 | 9 | 50 | 51 | 65 | 3 | 1 | .310/.376/.428 | .278 | .344 | -2.2 | -8.4 | 0.5 |
| 2010 | DET | MLB | 36 | 365 | 56 | 17 | 1 | 12 | 59 | 40 | 38 | 1 | 0 | .303/.378/.474 | .297 | .313 | 2.7 | -2.1 | 1.9 |
| 2011 | DET | MLB | 37 | 357 | 33 | 10 | 0 | 5 | 32 | 23 | 41 | 2 | 1 | .255/.303/.331 | .226 | .275 | -1.9 | -6 | -1.4 |
| 2012 | DET | MLB | 38 | 343 | 44 | 16 | 1 | 9 | 40 | 30 | 44 | 2 | 1 | .294/.356/.438 | .283 | .318 | -0.1 | RF -8 | 1.9 |

Bats: R Throws: R Height: 6' 2" Weight: 180
Breakout: 1% Improve: 39% Collapse: 3%
Attrition: 7% MLB: 83%

Comparables:
Juan Uribe, Derek Jeter, Michael Young

| YEAR | TEAM | LVL | AGE | PA | R | 2B | 3B | HR | RBI | BB | SO | SB | CS | AVG/OBP/SLG | TAv | BABIP | BRR | FRAA | WARP |
|------|------|-----|-----|-----|----|----|----|----|-----|----|-----|----|----|-------------|------|-------|------|----------|------|
| 2010 | CLE | MLB | 28 | 373 | 37 | 23 | 2 | 7 | 43 | 32 | 69 | 1 | 0 | .246/.308/.389 | .262 | .284 | -5.6 | 4.8 | 1.2 |
| 2010 | DET | MLB | 28 | 242 | 23 | 7 | 0 | 8 | 38 | 21 | 34 | 0 | 0 | .253/.314/.396 | .263 | .263 | -0.6 | 0.1 | 0.8 |
| 2011 | DET | MLB | 29 | 576 | 68 | 25 | 3 | 21 | 86 | 40 | 95 | 0 | 2 | .299/.345/.478 | .287 | .325 | -1.9 | 2 | 3.9 |
| 2012 | DET | MLB | 30 | 549 | 65 | 26 | 2 | 15 | 63 | 43 | 105 | 1 | 1 | .265/.324/.415 | .266 | .305 | -0.3 | SS -0, 3B 1 | 2.4 |

Last year in these pages we questioned Dombrowski's decision to re-up the left side of the Tigers infield with multi-year deals. As right as we were about Brandon Inge, that's how wrong we were about Peralta, who last year ranked among the top shortstops in the American League. Peralta made good on his promise of improved flexibility and conditioning to play above-average defense, offsetting his limited range with sure hands and an accurate arm, and hitting for both power and average. That last part won't continue so long as he gets under nearly two-thirds of his balls in play; odds are that more of those fly balls will settle into outfielders' mitts going forward. Even so, now that he has rediscovered his shortstop glove, he has a much lower offensive bar to clear, meaning he can survive a likely drop in OBP and still remain an asset.

**Ryan Raburn** LF

Born: 4/17/1981 Age: 31
Bats: R Throws: R Height: 6' 1" Weight: 180
Breakout: 0% Improve: 29% Collapse: 12%
Attrition: 21% MLB: 86%

Comparables:
Dan Uggla, Rod Booker, Bill Hall

| YEAR | TEAM | LVL | AGE | PA | R | 2B | 3B | HR | RBI | BB | SO | SB | CS | AVG/OBP/SLG | TAv | BABIP | BRR | FRAA | WARP |
|------|------|-----|-----|-----|----|----|----|----|-----|----|-----|----|----|-------------|------|-------|------|----------|------|
| 2009 | TOL | AAA | 28 | 56 | 11 | 3 | 0 | 5 | 9 | 7 | 13 | 2 | 1 | .255/.364/.638 | .317 | .241 | 0.4 | 0.4 | 0.6 |
| 2009 | DET | MLB | 28 | 291 | 44 | 11 | 2 | 16 | 45 | 26 | 60 | 5 | 4 | .291/.359/.533 | .305 | .323 | -0.3 | 4.4 | 2.4 |
| 2010 | DET | MLB | 29 | 410 | 54 | 25 | 1 | 15 | 62 | 27 | 92 | 2 | 2 | .280/.340/.474 | .284 | .333 | 1.7 | -0.4 | 2.0 |
| 2011 | DET | MLB | 30 | 418 | 53 | 22 | 2 | 14 | 49 | 21 | 114 | 1 | 1 | .256/.297/.432 | .261 | .324 | -0.1 | -0.8 | 1.3 |
| 2012 | DET | MLB | 31 | 395 | 49 | 19 | 3 | 14 | 52 | 29 | 92 | 4 | 2 | .267/.325/.454 | .274 | .317 | -0.4 | LF 3, 2B -3 | 1.8 |

Raburn began last season as Detroit's starting left fielder, ended it as an emergency second baseman, and in between reminded observers why he is best suited to a utility role. A certified lefty-killer, Raburn has posted a .305 TAv against portside pitching throughout his career, but his .246 career TAv against righties prevents him from being an everyday option. His subpar second base glove is something the Tigers would be wise to stow behind emergency glass, and his notoriously slow starts (a career .228/.287/.402 first-half line) have undermined the club's confidence in him. Still, his talent for punishing lefties gives him value, and at press time Detroit was mulling a Raburn/Santiago platoon at second base, a notion that would be fine if either player had a clue against right-handed pitching. Color us confused.

## Will Rhymes — 2B

Born: 4/1/1983 Age: 29
Bats: L Throws: R Height: 5' 10" Weight: 155
Breakout: 1% Improve: 35% Collapse: 4%
Attrition: 11% MLB: 80%

Comparables:
Joe Thurston, Dave Cash, Cookie Rojas

| YEAR | TEAM | LVL | AGE | PA | R | 2B | 3B | HR | RBI | BB | SO | SB | CS | AVG_OBP_SLG | TAv | BABIP | BRR | FRAA | WARP |
|---|---|---|---|---|---|---|---|---|---|---|---|---|---|---|---|---|---|---|---|
| 2009 | TOL | AAA | 26 | 455 | 48 | 17 | 6 | 3 | 41 | 36 | 58 | 20 | 8 | .260/.318/.354 | .241 | .289 | 0.4 | -3 | 0.2 |
| 2010 | TOL | AAA | 27 | 421 | 59 | 20 | 7 | 2 | 35 | 36 | 35 | 22 | 5 | .305/.362/.415 | .273 | .321 | 3.1 | -2.2 | 2.0 |
| 2010 | DET | MLB | 27 | 213 | 30 | 12 | 3 | 1 | 19 | 14 | 16 | 0 | 3 | .304/.350/.414 | .278 | .326 | -1.3 | 2.1 | 1.0 |
| 2011 | TOL | AAA | 28 | 464 | 57 | 17 | 4 | 3 | 24 | 46 | 46 | 13 | 8 | .306/.377/.390 | .257 | .337 | -2.8 | -3.8 | 0.5 |
| 2011 | DET | MLB | 28 | 99 | 13 | 3 | 0 | 0 | 2 | 11 | 12 | 1 | 0 | .235/.323/.271 | .228 | .274 | -0.3 | -1.1 | -0.2 |
| 2012 | DET | MLB | 29 | 250 | 28 | 10 | 2 | 1 | 22 | 20 | 30 | 6 | 3 | .269/.329/.358 | .247 | .297 | -0.6 | 2B -4, 3B 0 | 0.8 |

Last year, in one of the multitude of parallel universes theoretical physicists prattle on about, Rhymes took hold of the reins at second base and provided the Tigers with solid defense, the patient lefty bat they needed at the top of the order, and a name perfectly suited for marketing in Eminem's home town. In our universe, however, Rhymes spit the bit and sent the Tigers rifling through a series of bad options at second base. He was his normal self at Triple-A, a powerless grinder who works his way on base, but Detroit released him in December, meaning he'll need to unleash his inner Fernando Vina for some other organization if he wants a big league career.

## Ramon Santiago — SS

Born: 8/31/1979 Age: 32
Bats: B Throws: R Height: 6' 0" Weight: 150
Breakout: 2% Improve: 34% Collapse: 7%
Attrition: 16% MLB: 79%

Comparables:
Bobby Avila, Nelson Liriano, Joe Inglett

| YEAR | TEAM | LVL | AGE | PA | R | 2B | 3B | HR | RBI | BB | SO | SB | CS | AVG_OBP_SLG | TAv | BABIP | BRR | FRAA | WARP |
|---|---|---|---|---|---|---|---|---|---|---|---|---|---|---|---|---|---|---|---|
| 2009 | DET | MLB | 29 | 296 | 29 | 6 | 2 | 7 | 35 | 17 | 57 | 1 | 2 | .267/.318/.385 | .249 | .313 | -0.1 | 0 | 0.6 |
| 2010 | DET | MLB | 30 | 367 | 38 | 9 | 1 | 3 | 22 | 30 | 56 | 2 | 2 | .262/.337/.325 | .248 | .308 | 0.1 | 5.9 | 1.7 |
| 2011 | DET | MLB | 31 | 294 | 29 | 11 | 3 | 5 | 30 | 17 | 38 | 0 | 0 | .260/.311/.384 | .247 | .283 | 1.3 | 1.1 | 1.0 |
| 2012 | DET | MLB | 32 | 291 | 32 | 10 | 2 | 4 | 27 | 19 | 46 | 2 | 1 | .260/.320/.360 | .244 | .290 | -0.3 | SS 5, 2B -2 | 0.9 |

Santiago has spent his Motor City career essentially functioning as a donut tire, beginning each season in the trunk but ending it bolted into the lineup replacing that year's inevitable infield blowout. Santiago's minuscule offensive contributions keep him from being a long-term solution anywhere on the field, but his plus glove in the middle infield makes him a valuable utility player, and moderate skills against lefty pitching make him a possible platoon partner. Unable to find a starting gig on the free agent market, Santiago chose to re-up with the Tigers, where Jim Leyland is already familiar with his strengths and weaknesses and won't be tempted to drive him above his rated speed.

## Ryan Strieby — 1B

Born: 8/9/1985 Age: 26
Bats: R Throws: R Height: 6' 6" Weight: 235
Breakout: 5% Improve: 30% Collapse: 5%
Attrition: 19% MLB: 74%

Comparables:
Erubiel Durazo, Jonny Gomes, Brandon Sing

| YEAR | TEAM | LVL | AGE | PA | R | 2B | 3B | HR | RBI | BB | SO | SB | CS | AVG_OBP_SLG | TAv | BABIP | BRR | FRAA | WARP |
|---|---|---|---|---|---|---|---|---|---|---|---|---|---|---|---|---|---|---|---|
| 2009 | ERI | AA | 23 | 362 | 64 | 18 | 1 | 19 | 58 | 57 | 80 | 2 | 0 | .303/.428/.565 | .339 | .357 | -1 | 0.9 | 3.5 |
| 2010 | TOL | AAA | 24 | 325 | 29 | 15 | 0 | 10 | 49 | 33 | 85 | 1 | 1 | .245/.324/.400 | .249 | .313 | -2.9 | -5.6 | -0.6 |
| 2011 | TOL | AAA | 25 | 557 | 66 | 28 | 0 | 19 | 76 | 60 | 171 | 5 | 2 | .255/.341/.429 | .257 | .349 | -0.9 | -8.4 | -0.4 |
| 2012 | DET | MLB | 26 | 250 | 30 | 10 | 1 | 9 | 29 | 27 | 73 | 1 | 0 | .237/.324/.416 | .265 | .306 | 0 | 1B -9, LF -3 | 1.0 |

After battling wrist problems over the last few years, Strieby was finally able to stay healthy for a full season, but was unable to recover the power he'd shown in the past. Though the organization still feels his home run stroke will return as Strieby grows to believe he is not one big swing away from the DL, health isn't the only thing standing in his way. His strikeout rate is abysmal, he has already dropped to the bottom of the defensive spectrum, and he is a 26-year-old prospect for a club whose two main offensive stars are a first baseman and a DH/first baseman, both under contract for years to come. Good luck with that.

## Aaron Westlake — 1B

Born: 12/27/1988 Age: 23
Bats: L Throws: R Height: 6' 5" Weight: 235
Breakout: 2% Improve: 5% Collapse: 1%
Attrition: 3% MLB: 9%

Comparables:
Carmelo Martinez, Chris Nash, Mark Ori

| YEAR | TEAM | LVL | AGE | PA | R | 2B | 3B | HR | RBI | BB | SO | SB | CS | AVG_OBP_SLG | TAv | BABIP | BRR | FRAA | WARP |
|---|---|---|---|---|---|---|---|---|---|---|---|---|---|---|---|---|---|---|---|
| 2011 | ONE | A- | 22 | 117 | 14 | 4 | 1 | 2 | 15 | 10 | 23 | 1 | 0 | .264/.328/.377 | .266 | .321 | 1.4 | 0.5 | 0.4 |
| 2012 | DET | MLB | 23 | 250 | 21 | 8 | 1 | 4 | 20 | 12 | 67 | 1 | 0 | .197/.240/.288 | .190 | .254 | 0 | 1B -1 | -2.7 |

A third round pick from Vanderbilt, Westlake is a massive presence at the plate and in the field, with the kind of power stroke best described using the rumbling basso voice of a truck pull voiceover. He didn't show much in his short-season debut but no one doubts his raw power, and he doesn't project to be a defensive liability at first base. If Westlake can demonstrate a good batting eye he can be a prospect, though he's not particularly young and the Tigers already have a pretty decent first sacker.

## Danny Worth    3B

Born: 9/30/1985 Age: 26
Bats: R Throws: R Height: 6' 2'' Weight: 185
Breakout: 1% Improve: 20% Collapse: 11%
Attrition: 28% MLB: 55%

**Comparables:**
Don Wert, Eddie Williams, Adam Heether

| YEAR | TEAM | LVL | AGE | PA | R | 2B | 3B | HR | RBI | BB | SO | SB | CS | AVG_OBP_SLG | TAv | BABIP | BRR | FRAA | WARP |
|------|------|-----|-----|-----|----|----|----|----|-----|----|----|----|----|-------------|-----|-------|------|-----------|------|
| 2009 | ERI | AA | 23 | 318 | 33 | 17 | 3 | 0 | 24 | 26 | 74 | 4 | 5 | .239/.306/.319 | .239 | .318 | 0.3 | -3 | -0.2 |
| 2009 | TOL | AAA | 23 | 162 | 9 | 4 | 1 | 0 | 4 | 11 | 40 | 3 | 1 | .212/.265/.252 | .188 | .288 | -0.7 | -3.3 | -1.1 |
| 2010 | TOL | AAA | 24 | 177 | 18 | 5 | 0 | 2 | 18 | 10 | 29 | 12 | 2 | .287/.335/.354 | .243 | .338 | -0.7 | 0.5 | 0.3 |
| 2010 | DET | MLB | 24 | 115 | 10 | 5 | 0 | 2 | 8 | 6 | 13 | 1 | 2 | .255/.295/.358 | .246 | .275 | 1.2 | -1.6 | 0.0 |
| 2011 | TOL | AAA | 25 | 357 | 45 | 19 | 4 | 8 | 37 | 36 | 86 | 13 | 2 | .256/.338/.421 | .248 | .329 | 3.3 | 2.6 | 1.6 |
| 2011 | DET | MLB | 25 | 39 | 6 | 2 | 0 | 0 | 3 | 2 | 9 | 0 | 0 | .270/.308/.324 | .212 | .357 | -0.7 | -0.6 | -0.1 |
| 2012 | DET | MLB | 26 | 250 | 25 | 10 | 2 | 3 | 22 | 17 | 56 | 6 | 2 | .239/.293/.336 | .228 | .297 | -0.1 | 3B 2, 2B -2 | 0.3 |

This winter's roster machinations may let Worth, the heir-apparent to Santiago, finally strap on Detroit's utility belt. He provides the same mix of solid defense and suspect offense as Santiago, and has the advantages of youth, a smaller paycheck, and the wide-eyed belief that he can grow into something more. He won't, but with the dread specter of a Santiago/Raburn platoon at second base possibly in the offing, Worth may break camp as the final infield reserve.

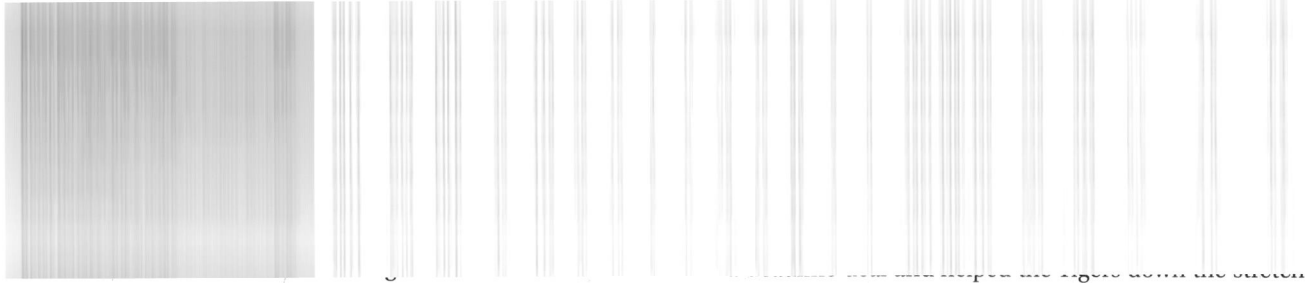

and in the playoffs, clubbing three home runs against the Yankees before missing the ALCS with a strained oblique. Detroit was one of the few clubs that could be "helped" by an iron-gloved left fielder with a sub-.300 OBP, however, and taken as a whole Young is hardly more than a replacement-level player. If you were to take Jeff Francoeur, remove some of his plate discipline, much of his power, and all of his defensive chops, you'd be left with Young, whose obvious hitting skills are completely undermined by his Will Rogers plate approach. The Tigers appear content to let him man left field for them again this year, and while some hold out hope that his power will grow and enough safeties will fall in to keep his OBP above water, you can color us skeptical.

# PITCHERS

## Al Alburquerque

Born: 6/10/1986 Age: 26
Bats: R Throws: R Height: 6' 1'' Weight: 195
Breakout: 27% Improve: 51% Collapse: 23%
Attrition: 11% MLB: 92%

**Comparables:**
Mike Schooler, Ken Howell, David Robertson

| YEAR | TEAM | LVL | AGE | W | L | SV | G | GS | IP | H | HR | BB | SO | EqBB9 | EqSO9 | GB% | BABIP | WHIP | ERA | FIP | FRA | WARP |
|------|------|-----|-----|---|---|----|----|----|-----|----|----|----|----|-------|-------|-----|-------|------|------|------|------|------|
| 2011 | DET | MLB | 25 | 6 | 1 | 0 | 41 | 0 | 43¹ | 21 | 0 | 29 | 67 | 6.0 | 13.9 | 58% | .256 | 1.15 | 1.87 | 2.12 | 3.11 | 1.0 |
| 2012 | DET | MLB | 26 | 1 | 1 | 0 | 26 | 0 | 31 | 28 | 3 | 16 | 34 | 4.7 | 9.8 | 50% | .312 | 1.43 | 3.93 | 3.82 | 4.28 | 0.3 |

The Tigers took a flyer on Alburquerque as a minor league free agent and were rewarded with one of the most surprisingly impressive relief performances of the year. Alburquerque has always been short on control but look at that strikeout rate! The slight Dominican can dial his heater up to the high-90s and his slider was virtually unhittable. No, really: he allowed only a single extra-base hit all year and his .149 opponent's slugging percentage was the lowest of the post-war era. The only player able to hit him was Robert Andino, whose batting practice liner accidentally drilled Alburquerque in the head and put him on the shelf for most of August. When he returned he was still effective but his velocity was down, an issue possibly related to the arm problems that surfaced during winter ball, culminating in offseason surgery to insert a screw in his elbow. He is scheduled to return by midseason, and with Benoit, Valverde, and Dotel on hand to work high-leverage situations, the Tigers can ease Alburquerque into the middle innings and see if he can recapture the magic.

### Collin Balester

Born: 6/6/1986 Age: 26
Bats: R Throws: R Height: 6' 6'' Weight: 194
Breakout: 25% Improve: 55% Collapse: 19%
Attrition: 20% MLB: 79%

**Comparables:**
Eddie Erautt, Frank Castillo, Carlos Almanzar

| YEAR | TEAM | LVL | AGE | W | L | SV | G | GS | IP | H | HR | BB | SO | EqBB9 | EqSO9 | GB% | BABIP | WHIP | ERA | FIP | FRA | WARP |
|---|---|---|---|---|---|---|---|---|---|---|---|---|---|---|---|---|---|---|---|---|---|---|
| 2009 | SYR | AAA | 23 | 7 | 10 | 0 | 20 | 20 | 107¹ | 129 | 5 | 37 | 71 | 3.1 | 6.0 | 48% | .352 | 1.55 | 4.45 | 3.63 | 4.88 | 0.7 |
| 2009 | WAS | MLB | 23 | 1 | 4 | 0 | 7 | 7 | 30¹ | 34 | 10 | 14 | 20 | 4.2 | 5.9 | 35% | .264 | 1.58 | 6.82 | 7.41 | 8.14 | -0.7 |
| 2010 | SYR | AAA | 24 | 3 | 3 | 0 | 35 | 5 | 69 | 53 | 7 | 17 | 32 | 4.2 | 6.8 | 54% | .317 | 1.54 | 5.87 | 4.79 | 6.29 | -0.1 |
| 2010 | WAS | MLB | 24 | 0 | 1 | 0 | 17 | 0 | 21 | 15 | 2 | 11 | 28 | 4.7 | 12.0 | 56% | .295 | 1.24 | 2.57 | 3.53 | 4.24 | 0.2 |
| 2011 | SYR | AAA | 25 | 2 | 0 | 1 | 28 | 0 | 39¹ | 45 | 2 | 15 | 44 | 3.4 | 10.5 | 49% | .410 | 1.58 | 4.35 | 2.88 | 4.19 | 0.6 |
| 2011 | WAS | MLB | 25 | 1 | 4 | 0 | 23 | 0 | 35² | 38 | 7 | 14 | 34 | 3.5 | 8.6 | 44% | .304 | 1.46 | 4.54 | 4.90 | 4.79 | -0.1 |
| 2012 | DET | MLB | 26 | 1 | 1 | 0 | 26 | 1 | 41¹ | 48 | 6 | 16 | 26 | 3.5 | 5.6 | 43% | .309 | 1.54 | 5.39 | 4.99 | 5.86 | -0.4 |

In a challenge trade of former top prospects, Balester came to Detroit this offseason in exchange for the similarly disappointing Ryan Perry. A former starter, Balester was moved to the bullpen in 2010 and looked promising, as his fastball improved a few ticks and his curveball showed more bite, but last season the wheels fell off. His strikeout rate dropped and he suffered a recurrence of the gopher-ball syndrome that has dogged him throughout his career, causing him to spend the year shuttling between the big club and Triple A. If he can learn to keep the ball in the yard he could become a reliable long man or even work the late innings, but time is not on his side.

### Duane Below

Born: 11/15/1985 Age: 26
Bats: L Throws: L Height: 6' 4'' Weight: 220
Breakout: 18% Improve: 48% Collapse: 18%
Attrition: 17% MLB: 89%

**Comparables:**
Bill Henry, Lynn McGlothen, Sterling Hitchcock

| YEAR | TEAM | LVL | AGE | W | L | SV | G | GS | IP | H | HR | BB | SO | EqBB9 | EqSO9 | GB% | BABIP | WHIP | ERA | FIP | FRA | WARP |
|---|---|---|---|---|---|---|---|---|---|---|---|---|---|---|---|---|---|---|---|---|---|---|
| 2009 | LAK | A+ | 23 | 1 | 4 | 0 | 6 | 6 | 28² | 22 | 4 | 14 | 38 | 4.4 | 11.9 | 47% | .269 | 1.25 | 3.14 | 3.83 | 4.41 | 0.6 |
| 2010 | ERI | AA | 24 | 7 | 11 | 0 | 28 | 28 | 126 | 95 | 12 | 22 | 70 | 2.6 | 7.4 | 44% | .325 | 1.38 | 4.93 | 4.29 | 4.85 | 1.2 |
| 2011 | TOL | AAA | 25 | 7 | 2 | 0 | 18 | 18 | 115 | 99 | 12 | 37 | 83 | 2.9 | 6.5 | 43% | .260 | 1.18 | 3.13 | 4.25 | 4.54 | 1.4 |
| 2011 | DET | MLB | 25 | 0 | 2 | 0 | 14 | 2 | 29 | 28 | 2 | 11 | 14 | 3.4 | 4.3 | 52% | .265 | 1.34 | 4.34 | 4.23 | 4.94 | 0.1 |
| 2012 | DET | MLB | 26 | 4 | 4 | 0 | 11 | 11 | 56 | 63 | 8 | 25 | 36 | 4.1 | 5.8 | 40% | .308 | 1.58 | 5.31 | 5.12 | 5.77 | -0.3 |

Two years removed from Tommy John surgery, Below has recovered nicely and last year toted his four-pitch repertoire to the Show, with mixed results. There's not a lot of swing-and-miss in his arsenal: a straight fastball that tops out in the low 90s, average breaking stuff, and a deceptive delivery. If that smells like a swingman to you, then you're an acute observer of the pitching condition. Below will be in the mix for the fifth starter job but will likely work in long relief, where his stuff might play better in shorter stints.

### Joaquin Benoit

Born: 7/26/1977 Age: 34
Bats: R Throws: R Height: 6' 4'' Weight: 205
Breakout: 12% Improve: 31% Collapse: 45%
Attrition: 4% MLB: 96%

**Comparables:**
Brendan Donnelly, J.J. Putz, Pedro Martinez

| YEAR | TEAM | LVL | AGE | W | L | SV | G | GS | IP | H | HR | BB | SO | EqBB9 | EqSO9 | GB% | BABIP | WHIP | ERA | FIP | FRA | WARP |
|---|---|---|---|---|---|---|---|---|---|---|---|---|---|---|---|---|---|---|---|---|---|---|
| 2010 | TBA | MLB | 32 | 1 | 2 | 1 | 63 | 0 | 60¹ | 30 | 6 | 11 | 75 | 1.6 | 11.2 | 39% | .192 | 0.68 | 1.34 | 2.40 | 2.76 | 1.4 |
| 2011 | DET | MLB | 33 | 4 | 3 | 2 | 66 | 0 | 61 | 47 | 5 | 17 | 63 | 2.5 | 9.3 | 40% | .275 | 1.05 | 2.95 | 3.00 | 4.06 | 0.7 |
| 2012 | DET | MLB | 34 | 3 | 1 | 1 | 53 | 0 | 50² | 42 | 5 | 18 | 53 | 3.2 | 9.5 | 38% | .288 | 1.19 | 3.05 | 3.46 | 3.32 | 1.0 |

The braying could be heard from Muskegon to Munising last year when Benoit and his shiny new contract—three years and $15.5 million of pure, unadulterated speculation—struggled in the early going. He righted the ship, however, unleashing his mid-90s fastball and one of the game's best changeups to hold hitters to a minuscule .169/.228/.272 line from June 1 on, and running roughshod over the Yankees and Rangers in the playoffs. Showering millions on a set-up man is often a bad idea, as their low innings totals and widely varying performances are rarely worth the cost. However, since his move to the pen Benoit has shown closer-level stuff when healthy, and he is a good bet to once again earn his pay as the opening act of Detroit's dynamic late-inning duo.

### Phil Coke

Born: 7/19/1982 Age: 29
Bats: L Throws: L Height: 6' 2'' Weight: 210
Breakout: 19% Improve: 44% Collapse: 29%
Attrition: 16% MLB: 93%

**Comparables:**
Doug Slaten, Jeff Fassero, Juan Pizarro

| YEAR | TEAM | LVL | AGE | W | L | SV | G | GS | IP | H | HR | BB | SO | EqBB9 | EqSO9 | GB% | BABIP | WHIP | ERA | FIP | FRA | WARP |
|---|---|---|---|---|---|---|---|---|---|---|---|---|---|---|---|---|---|---|---|---|---|---|
| 2009 | NYA | MLB | 26 | 4 | 3 | 2 | 72 | 0 | 60 | 44 | 10 | 20 | 49 | 3.0 | 7.3 | 39% | .217 | 1.07 | 4.50 | 4.73 | 5.29 | 0.3 |
| 2010 | DET | MLB | 27 | 7 | 5 | 2 | 74 | 1 | 64² | 67 | 2 | 26 | 53 | 3.6 | 7.4 | 38% | .339 | 1.44 | 3.76 | 3.20 | 4.30 | 0.6 |
| 2011 | DET | MLB | 28 | 3 | 9 | 1 | 48 | 14 | 108² | 118 | 5 | 40 | 69 | 3.3 | 5.7 | 45% | .321 | 1.45 | 4.47 | 3.60 | 4.26 | 1.2 |
| 2012 | DET | MLB | 29 | 6 | 3 | 1 | 62 | 8 | 90 | 94 | 8 | 32 | 64 | 3.2 | 6.4 | 46% | .310 | 1.40 | 4.12 | 4.00 | 4.48 | 0.7 |

Which would you rather receive from a given pitcher: 180 innings of mundane production, or 70 innings of above-average work? The correct answer depends on the alternatives, though the Tigers chose Option B by moving Coke out of the rotation last July, and they're pegging him for a relief role in 2012. As a starter he proved to be inconsistent, pitching with diminished velocity and suffering a significant drop in his strikeout rate. Though the results were still more than adequate for a fifth starter, Coke appeared uncomfortable in the role. When moved back to the pen, his K-rate climbed and he dominated same-side hitters. While he could certainly function at the back of the rotation and would provide more raw value there, the Tigers have starting options with more upside (paging Jacob Turner!) and will benefit from letting Coke thrive as their primary bullpen lefty.

### Casey Crosby

Born: 9/17/1988 Age: 23
Bats: R Throws: L Height: 6' 6'' Weight: 200
Breakout: 20% Improve: 54% Collapse: 20%
Attrition: 17% MLB: 87%

**Comparables:**
Mike Pelfrey, Lance McCullers, Ubaldo Jimenez

| YEAR | TEAM | LVL | AGE | W | L | SV | G | GS | IP | H | HR | BB | SO | EqBB9 | EqSO9 | GB% | BABIP | WHIP | ERA | FIP | FRA | WARP |
|------|------|-----|-----|---|---|----|---|----|----|---|----|----|----|-------|-------|-----|-------|------|-----|-----|-----|------|
| 2009 | WMI | A | 20 | 10 | 5 | 0 | 24 | 24 | 104² | 76 | 3 | 50 | 119 | 4.1 | 10.1 | 54% | .285 | 1.13 | 2.41 | 3.23 | 3.59 | 1.9 |
| 2011 | ERI | AA | 22 | 9 | 7 | 0 | 25 | 25 | 131² | 122 | 11 | 77 | 121 | 5.3 | 8.3 | 57% | .314 | 1.51 | 4.10 | 4.53 | 5.35 | 0.9 |
| 2012 | DET | MLB | 23 | 2 | 2 | 0 | 6 | 6 | 33¹ | 36 | 4 | 20 | 24 | 5.5 | 6.5 | 51% | .310 | 1.69 | 5.40 | 5.12 | 5.87 | -0.2 |

Crosby returned from recurring elbow problems and showed he was healthy enough to spend a full year in the rotation and could still miss bats, though his control remains a concern. A hard-throwing lefty with mid-90s heat and a big, looping curve, Crosby need only lower his walk rate to raise his ceiling as high as any pitcher in the system. That's far from guaranteed, however, and with his medical history the possibility of a move to the bullpen looms. If that's his final destination, he has the stuff to be

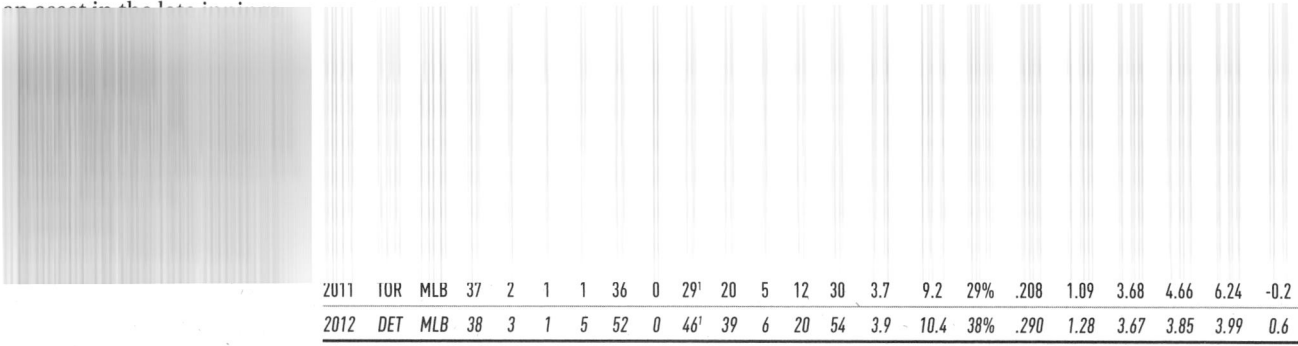

| | | | | | | | | | | | | | | | | | | | | | | |
|------|------|-----|-----|---|---|----|---|----|----|---|----|----|----|-------|-------|-----|-------|------|-----|-----|-----|------|
| 2011 | TOR | MLB | 37 | 2 | 1 | 1 | 36 | 0 | 29¹ | 20 | 5 | 12 | 30 | 3.7 | 9.2 | 29% | .208 | 1.09 | 3.68 | 4.66 | 6.24 | -0.2 |
| 2012 | DET | MLB | 38 | 3 | 1 | 5 | 52 | 0 | 46¹ | 39 | 6 | 20 | 54 | 3.9 | 10.4 | 38% | .290 | 1.28 | 3.67 | 3.85 | 3.99 | 0.6 |

Toiling away in the Toronto bullpen with a 4.66 FIP in late July, Dotel was transformed after being dealt to St. Louis. The right-hander with the Rally Squirrel hat threw 24 2/3 innings over the last two months, striking out 32 while allowing just five walks and one home run. Dotel can still unleash his slick fastball/slider combination to mow down same-side hitters but lefties give him fits, so his new employers in Detroit—his 13th major league city—had best spot him carefully. Still, he's a worthwhile low-cost pickup to work the seventh, and seems like a natural addition to a bullpen already sporting the similarly demonstrative Jose Valverde.

### Doug Fister

Born: 2/4/1984 Age: 28
Bats: L Throws: R Height: 6' 9'' Weight: 200
Breakout: 12% Improve: 40% Collapse: 22%
Attrition: 8% MLB: 80%

**Comparables:**
Mark Buehrle, Charles Nagy, Steve Howe

| YEAR | TEAM | LVL | AGE | W | L | SV | G | GS | IP | H | HR | BB | SO | EqBB9 | EqSO9 | GB% | BABIP | WHIP | ERA | FIP | FRA | WARP |
|------|------|-----|-----|---|----|----|----|----|------|-----|----|----|----|-------|-------|-----|-------|------|------|------|------|------|
| 2009 | TAC | AAA | 25 | 6 | 4 | 0 | 22 | 17 | 106¹ | 132 | 10 | 11 | 79 | 0.9 | 6.7 | 46% | .351 | 1.35 | 3.81 | 3.64 | 4.72 | 1.0 |
| 2009 | SEA | MLB | 25 | 3 | 4 | 0 | 11 | 10 | 61 | 63 | 11 | 15 | 36 | 2.2 | 5.3 | 41% | .271 | 1.28 | 4.13 | 5.14 | 5.77 | -0.2 |
| 2010 | SEA | MLB | 26 | 6 | 14 | 0 | 28 | 28 | 171 | 187 | 13 | 32 | 93 | 1.7 | 4.9 | 47% | .303 | 1.28 | 4.11 | 3.61 | 4.10 | 1.1 |
| 2011 | DET | MLB | 27 | 8 | 1 | 0 | 11 | 10 | 70¹ | 54 | 4 | 5 | 57 | 0.6 | 7.3 | 51% | .246 | 0.84 | 1.79 | 2.52 | 2.90 | 1.8 |
| 2011 | SEA | MLB | 27 | 3 | 12 | 0 | 21 | 21 | 146 | 139 | 7 | 32 | 89 | 2.0 | 5.5 | 47% | .286 | 1.17 | 3.33 | 3.31 | 4.01 | 1.5 |
| 2012 | DET | MLB | 28 | 12 | 8 | 0 | 27 | 27 | 175² | 188 | 16 | 34 | 104 | 1.7 | 5.3 | 46% | .301 | 1.26 | 3.84 | 3.78 | 4.18 | 1.9 |

The Tigers looked past Fister's 3-12 record last July, saw a good young pitcher, pried him loose from the Mariners, and were rewarded with one of the best hurlers in the American League down the stretch. Not only did Fister hack another chunk out of the already diminishing perception that the Pitcher Win statistic is meaningful, but the towering right hander posted peripherals that show his effectiveness wasn't a mirage. Fister pitched faster last year, cranking up his heater a few ticks. Taking advantage of the downward plane his height and over-the-top motion provides, he racked up more whiffs, while maintaining the control that leads to his minuscule walk rate. Combine that with the league's lowest rate of home runs per fly ball, and there's little wonder Fister's 3.02 FIP fit snugly between that of Justin Verlander and Felix Hernandez on AL leader boards. He is sure to regress somewhat this year as more of those fly balls become souvenirs, but Fister seems perfectly capable of being an excellent mid-rotation starter at a bargain price for years to come.

### Luis Marte
Born: 8/26/1986 Age: 25
Bats: R Throws: R Height: 6' 0" Weight: 170
Breakout: 37% Improve: 71% Collapse: 9%
Attrition: 13% MLB: 86%

**Comparables:**
Billy Loes, Kyle Davies, Mauro Zarate

| YEAR | TEAM | LVL | AGE | W | L | SV | G | GS | IP | H | HR | BB | SO | EqBB9 | EqSO9 | GB% | BABIP | WHIP | ERA | FIP | FRA | WARP |
|------|------|-----|-----|---|---|----|----|----|----|----|----|----|----|-------|-------|-----|-------|------|-----|-----|-----|------|
| 2009 | ERI | AA | 22 | 5 | 8 | 0 | 19 | 17 | 105¹ | 106 | 18 | 28 | 84 | 2.4 | 7.2 | 43% | .284 | 1.27 | 4.02 | 4.62 | 5.28 | 0.3 |
| 2010 | ERI | AA | 23 | 2 | 2 | 7 | 38 | 0 | 48 | 32 | 4 | 17 | 31 | 4.9 | 9.9 | 43% | .301 | 1.46 | 5.06 | 4.70 | 5.81 | -0.1 |
| 2011 | ERI | AA | 24 | 3 | 0 | 3 | 23 | 1 | 53 | 29 | 3 | 18 | 68 | 3.1 | 11.5 | 43% | .230 | 0.89 | 1.70 | 2.66 | 3.41 | 1.2 |
| 2011 | DET | MLB | 24 | 1 | 0 | 0 | 4 | 0 | 3² | 6 | 0 | 1 | 3 | 2.5 | 7.4 | 46% | .462 | 1.91 | 2.45 | 2.24 | 4.53 | 0.0 |
| *2012* | *DET* | *MLB* | *25* | *1* | *0* | *0* | *12* | *0* | *19¹* | *21* | *3* | *8* | *14* | *3.9* | *6.4* | *42%* | *.301* | *1.51* | *4.94* | *5.01* | *5.37* | *-0.1* |

A slight right hander whose development has been hampered by elbow and shoulder problems, Marte earned a September call-up after a productive year in Erie, and will get a long look this spring. Last year he showed good command of a fastball he can boost into the low 90s, changing speeds with aplomb and keeping hitters off balance with a slider, curve, and changeup. It's the sort of arsenal that bowls them over in Double-A but doesn't guarantee success in the Show, meaning he'll likely act as minor league insurance for the more pedigreed Daniel Schlereth and Collin Balester.

### Andrew Oliver
Born: 12/3/1987 Age: 24
Bats: L Throws: L Height: 6' 4" Weight: 209
Breakout: 35% Improve: 59% Collapse: 24%
Attrition: 13% MLB: 92%

**Comparables:**
Angel Miranda, Johan Santana, Gerry Arrigo

| YEAR | TEAM | LVL | AGE | W | L | SV | G | GS | IP | H | HR | BB | SO | EqBB9 | EqSO9 | GB% | BABIP | WHIP | ERA | FIP | FRA | WARP |
|------|------|-----|-----|---|---|----|----|----|----|----|----|----|----|-------|-------|-----|-------|------|-----|-----|-----|------|
| 2010 | ERI | AA | 22 | 5 | 4 | 0 | 14 | 14 | 77¹ | 39 | 4 | 17 | 50 | 2.9 | 8.2 | 40% | .259 | 1.28 | 3.61 | 3.63 | 4.26 | 1.0 |
| 2010 | TOL | AAA | 22 | 3 | 4 | 0 | 9 | 9 | 53 | 32 | 6 | 20 | 37 | 4.2 | 8.3 | 41% | .252 | 1.28 | 3.23 | 4.79 | 5.53 | 0.1 |
| 2010 | DET | MLB | 22 | 0 | 4 | 0 | 5 | 5 | 22 | 26 | 3 | 13 | 18 | 5.3 | 7.4 | 43% | .359 | 1.77 | 7.36 | 5.23 | 5.73 | -0.1 |
| 2011 | TOL | AAA | 23 | 6 | 6 | 0 | 26 | 26 | 147 | 145 | 15 | 78 | 137 | 4.9 | 8.8 | 39% | .339 | 1.56 | 4.71 | 4.37 | 5.39 | 0.7 |
| 2011 | DET | MLB | 23 | 0 | 1 | 0 | 2 | 2 | 9² | 11 | 3 | 8 | 5 | 7.4 | 4.7 | 27% | .258 | 1.97 | 6.52 | 9.16 | 9.52 | -0.3 |
| *2012* | *DET* | *MLB* | *24* | *4* | *3* | *0* | *10* | *10* | *56¹* | *60* | *7* | *28* | *44* | *4.4* | *7.0* | *40%* | *.309* | *1.55* | *5.03* | *4.75* | *5.47* | *-0.1* |

His mid-90s fastball, slider, and changeup equip him with the tools to craft a productive big league career, but too often Oliver pitches as if he were pounding in nails with a box-end wrench. As last season wore on, his command went farther and farther south, culminating in a wild Arizona Fall League stint featuring 16 walks in 17 innings and re-igniting whispers that he might be better off in the bullpen. The Tigers are rarely shy about letting youth be served, but Oliver had best spend the year learning to avoid ball four if he ever wants to win a job in a big league rotation.

### David Pauley
Born: 6/17/1983 Age: 29
Bats: R Throws: R Height: 6' 3" Weight: 185
Breakout: 26% Improve: 63% Collapse: 24%
Attrition: 14% MLB: 80%

**Comparables:**
Jorge Campillo, Rick Langford, Gary Majewski

| YEAR | TEAM | LVL | AGE | W | L | SV | G | GS | IP | H | HR | BB | SO | EqBB9 | EqSO9 | GB% | BABIP | WHIP | ERA | FIP | FRA | WARP |
|------|------|-----|-----|---|---|----|----|----|----|----|----|----|----|-------|-------|-----|-------|------|-----|-----|-----|------|
| 2009 | NOR | AAA | 26 | 9 | 12 | 0 | 27 | 26 | 152¹ | 171 | 15 | 45 | 108 | 2.7 | 6.4 | 49% | .323 | 1.42 | 4.37 | 4.19 | 4.94 | 0.7 |
| 2010 | TAC | AAA | 27 | 1 | 6 | 0 | 15 | 14 | 85² | 55 | 3 | 19 | 40 | 2.7 | 5.9 | 48% | .278 | 1.26 | 3.68 | 4.38 | 5.00 | 0.3 |
| 2010 | SEA | MLB | 27 | 4 | 9 | 0 | 19 | 15 | 90² | 89 | 13 | 30 | 51 | 3.0 | 5.1 | 50% | .262 | 1.31 | 4.07 | 4.91 | 5.02 | -0.1 |
| 2011 | DET | MLB | 28 | 0 | 2 | 0 | 14 | 0 | 19² | 26 | 4 | 6 | 10 | 2.7 | 4.6 | 49% | .328 | 1.63 | 5.95 | 5.76 | 7.45 | -0.5 |
| 2011 | SEA | MLB | 28 | 5 | 4 | 0 | 39 | 0 | 54¹ | 38 | 2 | 16 | 34 | 2.7 | 5.6 | 52% | .232 | 0.99 | 2.15 | 3.39 | 3.79 | 0.7 |
| *2012* | *DET* | *MLB* | *29* | *4* | *3* | *0* | *24* | *8* | *69²* | *75* | *9* | *22* | *40* | *2.9* | *5.2* | *51%* | *.292* | *1.39* | *4.53* | *4.68* | *4.93* | *0.2* |

Pauley came to the Tigers as part of the Doug Fister trade, and quickly proved that his productive half-season in Seattle's bullpen was an optical illusion produced by a rare intersection of defense, ballpark spaciousness, swamp gas, and ball lightning. His low-velo mix can fool some of the people some of the time, but few of those people are paid to hit in the American League, meaning Pauley's primary value to the Tigers will be as a walking, talking insurance policy stashed in the organization's Toledo filing cabinet.

### Brenny Paulino
Born: 2/21/1993 Age: 19
Bats: R Throws: R Height: 6' 5" Weight: 170
Breakout: 0% Improve: 64% Collapse: 36%
Attrition: 36% MLB: 63%

**Comparables:**
Rick Wise, Von McDaniel, Bob Miller

| YEAR | TEAM | LVL | AGE | W | L | SV | G | GS | IP | H | HR | BB | SO | EqBB9 | EqSO9 | GB% | BABIP | WHIP | ERA | FIP | FRA | WARP |
|------|------|-----|-----|---|---|----|----|----|----|----|----|----|----|-------|-------|-----|-------|------|-----|-----|-----|------|
| 2011 | TGR | RK | 18 | 4 | 3 | 0 | 11 | 8 | 45² | 34 | 1 | 18 | 45 | 3.5 | 8.9 | 47% | .270 | 1.14 | 2.36 | 3.17 | 4.62 | 0.7 |
| *2012* | *DET* | *MLB* | *19* | *0* | *0* | *0* | *4* | *1* | *12¹* | *15* | *2* | *8* | *7* | *5.9* | *5.3* | *46%* | *.317* | *1.85* | *6.33* | *6.12* | *6.88* | *-0.2* |

Hurricane Brenny blew through the Gulf Coast League last summer, hurling mid-90s thunderbolts and leaving a trail of strikeout victims in his wake. A long, lean Dominican, Paulino may add velocity as he grows into his frame, and his walk rate wasn't the eyesore one expects from a teenage fireballer. He's raw, of course, and his future will depend on his fastball command and the development of secondary stuff, but if everything comes together he could grow into a force of nature.

### Brad Penny

Born: 5/24/1978 Age: 34
Bats: R Throws: R Height: 6' 5" Weight: 200
Breakout: 10% Improve: 49% Collapse: 24%
Attrition: 9% MLB: 78%

**Comparables:**
Tim Burke, Jim Perry, Eddie Fisher

| YEAR | TEAM | LVL | AGE | W | L | SV | G | GS | IP | H | HR | BB | SO | EqBB9 | EqSO9 | GB% | BABIP | WHIP | ERA | FIP | FRA | WARP |
|------|------|-----|-----|---|---|----|----|----|------|-----|----|----|----|-------|-------|-----|-------|------|------|------|------|------|
| 2009 | SFN | MLB | 31 | 4 | 1 | 0 | 6 | 6 | 41² | 31 | 5 | 9 | 20 | 1.9 | 4.3 | 54% | .206 | 0.96 | 2.59 | 4.30 | 5.36 | 0.1 |
| 2009 | BOS | MLB | 31 | 7 | 8 | 0 | 24 | 24 | 131² | 160 | 17 | 42 | 89 | 2.9 | 6.1 | 42% | .327 | 1.53 | 5.61 | 4.54 | 5.30 | 1.0 |
| 2010 | SLN | MLB | 32 | 3 | 4 | 0 | 9 | 9 | 55² | 63 | 4 | 9 | 35 | 1.5 | 5.7 | 54% | .330 | 1.29 | 3.23 | 3.43 | 4.22 | 0.6 |
| 2011 | DET | MLB | 33 | 11 | 11 | 0 | 31 | 31 | 181² | 222 | 24 | 62 | 74 | 3.1 | 3.7 | 50% | .312 | 1.56 | 5.30 | 5.05 | 5.62 | -0.9 |
| *2012* | *DET* | *MLB* | *34* | *9* | *8* | *0* | *23* | *23* | *137²* | *162* | *15* | *43* | *70* | *2.8* | *4.6* | *49%* | *.315* | *1.49* | *4.87* | *4.54* | *5.29* | *-0.2* |

His year in Detroit wasn't quite a Penny Dreadful, as the big right hander was healthy enough to take 31 turns, win 11 games, and never once rampaged through the streets of Victorian London wearing a bloodied leather apron aboard an undead wolf. Nonetheless his starts grew increasingly stomach-churning as the season wore on, as Penny was pasted to the tune of .341/.394/.548 in 13 second half starts, a stretch in which he walked as many batters as he whiffed. After watching him post baseball's worst strikeout rate last season, the Tigers have no desire for a sequel, which means *The Revenge of the Innings-Eating Specie* will have to be marketed elsewhere. Don't expect it to be a good read.

the high expectations that have been pinned to him. He took a few more baby steps forward last year, inching his strikeout rate above five per nine innings, keeping his walk rate low, and generally pitching better than his 4.75 ERA shows. Porcello possesses an effective slider and changeup and can rear back for a mid-90s heater when necessary, but relies heavily on his two-seamer to get copious groundball outs—an approach that is more effective than electric, leaving observers wishing for more. Few still see him as a future ace, but Porcello suddenly seems undervalued, He may yet brew up the swing-and-miss elixir that vaults him into the upper ranks of AL hurlers.

### Max Scherzer

Born: 7/27/1984 Age: 27
Bats: R Throws: R Height: 6' 4" Weight: 215
Breakout: 22% Improve: 58% Collapse: 31%
Attrition: 13% MLB: 91%

**Comparables:**
Keith Foulke, Shawn Kelley, John Montefusco

| YEAR | TEAM | LVL | AGE | W | L | SV | G | GS | IP | H | HR | BB | SO | EqBB9 | EqSO9 | GB% | BABIP | WHIP | ERA | FIP | FRA | WARP |
|------|------|-----|-----|---|---|----|----|----|------|-----|----|----|-----|-------|-------|-----|-------|------|------|------|------|------|
| 2009 | ARI | MLB | 24 | 9 | 11 | 0 | 30 | 30 | 170¹ | 166 | 20 | 63 | 174 | 3.3 | 9.2 | 43% | .311 | 1.34 | 4.12 | 3.83 | 4.56 | 2.7 |
| 2010 | DET | MLB | 25 | 12 | 11 | 0 | 31 | 31 | 195² | 174 | 20 | 70 | 184 | 3.2 | 8.5 | 42% | .300 | 1.25 | 3.50 | 3.68 | 4.04 | 2.8 |
| 2011 | DET | MLB | 26 | 15 | 9 | 0 | 33 | 33 | 195 | 207 | 29 | 55 | 174 | 2.6 | 8.0 | 42% | .316 | 1.35 | 4.43 | 4.16 | 4.63 | 1.0 |
| *2012* | *DET* | *MLB* | *27* | *12* | *8* | *0* | *28* | *28* | *169¹* | *166* | *19* | *54* | *161* | *2.9* | *8.6* | *45%* | *.310* | *1.30* | *3.93* | *3.72* | *4.27* | *1.7* |

Last year Scherzer didn't dominate the way he had during the second half of 2010 and posted the worst numbers of his short career, but a quick look under the hood shows he is the same high-upside proposition he has always been. His walk and strikeout rates held steady, and though his ERA climbed almost a full run, his 3.70 xFIP (a fielding independent measure that assumes a normal number of home runs per fly ball allowed) was a virtual match for his career numbers. In other words, Scherzer was the same hurler he has always been except for a few extra souvenirs. Since that last bit tends to vary greatly from year to year, Scherzer is a great bet for a breakout this year. He still struggles against lefties and would benefit from an improved changeup, but if he can sort that out, his upper-90s fastball gives him ace potential.

### Daniel Schlereth

Born: 5/9/1986 Age: 26
Bats: L Throws: L Height: 6' 1" Weight: 210
Breakout: 34% Improve: 60% Collapse: 28%
Attrition: 9% MLB: 93%

**Comparables:**
Alex Hinshaw, Renyel Pinto, Dan Runzler

| YEAR | TEAM | LVL | AGE | W | L | SV | G | GS | IP | H | HR | BB | SO | EqBB9 | EqSO9 | GB% | BABIP | WHIP | ERA | FIP | FRA | WARP |
|------|------|-----|-----|---|---|----|----|----|-----|----|----|----|----|-------|-------|-----|-------|------|------|------|------|------|
| 2009 | ARI | MLB | 23 | 1 | 4 | 0 | 21 | 0 | 18¹ | 15 | 1 | 15 | 22 | 7.4 | 10.8 | 60% | .311 | 1.64 | 5.89 | 3.98 | 4.44 | 0.2 |
| 2010 | DET | MLB | 24 | 2 | 0 | 1 | 18 | 0 | 18² | 20 | 2 | 10 | 19 | 4.8 | 9.2 | 49% | .333 | 1.61 | 2.89 | 4.17 | 5.16 | 0.0 |
| 2011 | DET | MLB | 25 | 2 | 2 | 0 | 49 | 0 | 49 | 36 | 6 | 31 | 44 | 5.7 | 8.1 | 42% | .244 | 1.37 | 3.49 | 5.06 | 5.15 | 0.1 |
| *2012* | *DET* | *MLB* | *26* | *2* | *1* | *1* | *38* | *0* | *43²* | *38* | *4* | *24* | *46* | *5.0* | *9.4* | *48%* | *.297* | *1.43* | *3.83* | *3.94* | *4.17* | *0.4* |

Schlereth is a former first round pick with closer-level stuff that has yet to translate into big league dominance. He has good velocity for a southpaw, with a fastball that sits comfortably in the low-90s and a plus curve, but his control is often reminiscent of Raoul Duke on an ether bender. Rare indeed is the reliever who can thrive while walking nearly six men per nine innings, no matter how impressive their strikeout rate. Schlereth will break camp as the bullpen's second lefty behind Coke, but if he can develop any concept of the strike zone, he has the potential to move up the bullpen pecking order.

### Drew Smyly
Born: 6/13/1989 Age: 23
Bats: L Throws: L Height: 6' 4" Weight: 190
Breakout: 23% Improve: 47% Collapse: 26%
Attrition: 22% MLB: 95%

Comparables:
Steve Carlton, Curt Simmons, David Price

| YEAR | TEAM | LVL | AGE | W | L | SV | G | GS | IP | H | HR | BB | SO | EqBB9 | EqSO9 | GB% | BABIP | WHIP | ERA | FIP | FRA | WARP |
|------|------|-----|-----|---|---|----|---|----|----|---|----|----|----|-------|-------|-----|-------|------|-----|-----|-----|------|
| 2011 | LAK | A+ | 22 | 3 | 2 | 0 | 14 | 14 | 80¹ | 65 | 1 | 21 | 71 | 2.4 | 8.6 | 50% | .320 | 1.15 | 2.58 | 2.68 | 3.38 | 1.9 |
| 2011 | ERI | AA | 22 | 4 | 3 | 0 | 8 | 7 | 45² | 32 | 1 | 15 | 53 | 3.0 | 10.4 | 52% | .292 | 1.03 | 1.18 | 2.43 | 3.46 | 1.1 |
| 2012 | DET | MLB | 23 | 2 | 1 | 0 | 5 | 5 | 28² | 29 | 3 | 12 | 23 | 3.8 | 7.3 | 47% | .306 | 1.44 | 4.36 | 4.22 | 4.74 | 0.1 |

Smyly's first minor league season could hardly have gone better, as the former Arkansas starter pitched well and earned a promotion to Double-A, where he was surprisingly dominant down the stretch. Smyly has terrific command and knows how to pitch, mixing his upper-80s fastball and cutter with a wide array of off-speed offerings. He doesn't have the stuff or upside of fellow lefties Casey Crosby or Andrew Oliver, but he is a finished product and is more likely to reach his ceiling. If Smyly can continue to rack up the strikeouts at higher levels, he could quickly become a solid rotation contributor, though not a star.

### Jacob Turner
Born: 5/21/1991 Age: 21
Bats: R Throws: R Height: 6' 6" Weight: 210
Breakout: 22% Improve: 65% Collapse: 8%
Attrition: 2% MLB: 92%

Comparables:
Alex Fernandez, Dennys Reyes, Larry Dierker

| YEAR | TEAM | LVL | AGE | W | L | SV | G | GS | IP | H | HR | BB | SO | EqBB9 | EqSO9 | GB% | BABIP | WHIP | ERA | FIP | FRA | WARP |
|------|------|-----|-----|---|---|----|---|----|----|---|----|----|----|-------|-------|-----|-------|------|-----|-----|-----|------|
| 2010 | WMI | A | 19 | 2 | 3 | 0 | 11 | 10 | 54 | 49 | 3 | 8 | 50 | 1.5 | 8.5 | 44% | .293 | 1.15 | 3.67 | 3.17 | 4.34 | 0.6 |
| 2010 | LAK | A+ | 19 | 3 | 2 | 0 | 13 | 13 | 61¹ | 43 | 1 | 12 | 38 | 2.1 | 7.5 | 50% | .309 | 1.09 | 2.94 | 3.33 | 3.74 | 1.1 |
| 2011 | ERI | AA | 20 | 3 | 5 | 0 | 17 | 17 | 113² | 100 | 9 | 31 | 81 | 2.5 | 7.1 | 50% | .284 | 1.18 | 3.48 | 3.99 | 4.58 | 1.2 |
| 2011 | DET | MLB | 20 | 0 | 1 | 0 | 3 | 3 | 12² | 17 | 3 | 4 | 8 | 2.8 | 5.7 | 43% | .318 | 1.66 | 8.53 | 6.06 | 5.60 | 0.0 |
| 2012 | DET | MLB | 21 | 3 | 3 | 0 | 9 | 9 | 48 | 53 | 6 | 17 | 28 | 3.1 | 5.3 | 45% | .299 | 1.45 | 4.74 | 4.73 | 5.15 | 0.0 |

The future is now for Turner, Detroit's top pitching prospect. Never shy about challenging their young arms, the Tigers watched Turner more than hold his own last year as a 20-year-old in Double-A, and tapped him for three starts in the big leagues. He has smooth mechanics and a prototypical power pitcher's body and repertoire: a fastball that touches 95, a sharp curve he can throw for strikes, and a usable changeup that could be the key to his future. Turner's strikeout rate is a little lower than you'd expect from a young flamethrower, but so is his walk rate, which is likely a better harbinger of his future. He'll audition for the fifth starter position this spring, and if he stays healthy he can become Rick Porcello with more punchouts. That's even better than it sounds.

### Jose Valverde
Born: 3/24/1978 Age: 34
Bats: R Throws: R Height: 6' 5" Weight: 220
Breakout: 19% Improve: 35% Collapse: 41%
Attrition: 5% MLB: 97%

Comparables:
Brendan Donnelly, Akinori Otsuka, Scot Shields

| YEAR | TEAM | LVL | AGE | W | L | SV | G | GS | IP | H | HR | BB | SO | EqBB9 | EqSO9 | GB% | BABIP | WHIP | ERA | FIP | FRA | WARP |
|------|------|-----|-----|---|---|----|---|----|----|---|----|----|----|-------|-------|-----|-------|------|-----|-----|-----|------|
| 2009 | HOU | MLB | 31 | 4 | 2 | 25 | 52 | 0 | 54 | 40 | 5 | 21 | 56 | 3.5 | 9.3 | 41% | .261 | 1.13 | 2.33 | 3.46 | 3.75 | 0.9 |
| 2010 | DET | MLB | 32 | 2 | 4 | 26 | 60 | 0 | 63 | 41 | 5 | 32 | 63 | 4.6 | 9.0 | 54% | .231 | 1.16 | 3.00 | 3.75 | 4.98 | 0.2 |
| 2011 | DET | MLB | 33 | 2 | 4 | 49 | 75 | 0 | 72¹ | 52 | 5 | 34 | 69 | 4.2 | 8.6 | 44% | .250 | 1.19 | 2.24 | 3.59 | 4.13 | 0.7 |
| 2012 | DET | MLB | 34 | 3 | 1 | 29 | 61 | 0 | 61¹ | 51 | 6 | 24 | 63 | 3.5 | 9.2 | 42% | .280 | 1.22 | 3.20 | 3.60 | 3.48 | 1.1 |

The Big Potato is a walking homage to the tradition of quirky closers, bounding to the mound like a bespectacled Weeble and punctuating each appearance with fist pumps, screams, and skyward points. Despite the histrionics, he remains surprisingly productive, ruling the ninth with a mid-90s fastball and disappearing splitter while leading the league with a career high 49 saves. Like many great entertainers, Papa Grande thrived last year when the spotlight was brightest, holding batters to a .154/.251/219 line when the game was in doubt (compared to .280/.380/.398 in his 26 non-save appearances). His continued effectiveness, along with the stalled development of Schlereth and Perry, made it an easy decision for Detroit to pick up Valverde's 2012 option, making the end of Tigers games must-see TV for at least another year.

### Justin Verlander
Born: 2/20/1983 Age: 29
Bats: R Throws: R Height: 6' 6" Weight: 200
Breakout: 11% Improve: 35% Collapse: 37%
Attrition: 6% MLB: 97%

Comparables:
Chris Young, Jon Rauch, Jake Peavy

| YEAR | TEAM | LVL | AGE | W | L | SV | G | GS | IP | H | HR | BB | SO | EqBB9 | EqSO9 | GB% | BABIP | WHIP | ERA | FIP | FRA | WARP |
|------|------|-----|-----|---|---|----|---|----|----|---|----|----|----|-------|-------|-----|-------|------|-----|-----|-----|------|
| 2009 | DET | MLB | 26 | 19 | 9 | 0 | 35 | 35 | 240 | 219 | 20 | 63 | 269 | 2.4 | 10.1 | 38% | .323 | 1.17 | 3.45 | 2.85 | 3.29 | 6.1 |
| 2010 | DET | MLB | 27 | 18 | 9 | 0 | 33 | 33 | 224¹ | 190 | 14 | 71 | 219 | 2.8 | 8.8 | 42% | .289 | 1.16 | 3.37 | 2.94 | 3.33 | 5.2 |
| 2011 | DET | MLB | 28 | 24 | 5 | 0 | 34 | 34 | 251 | 174 | 24 | 57 | 250 | 2.0 | 9.0 | 42% | .237 | 0.92 | 2.40 | 3.03 | 3.18 | 5.8 |
| 2012 | DET | MLB | 29 | 15 | 7 | 0 | 29 | 29 | 202¹ | 181 | 18 | 56 | 191 | 2.5 | 8.5 | 41% | .292 | 1.17 | 3.05 | 3.30 | 3.31 | 4.2 |

Last season was probably (though not definitely) Verlander's magnum opus, as the Cy Young and MVP award winner tore through the American League like, well, Justin Verlander at his peak. We don't need to describe his power repertoire to you—you've seen it, so you know there's nothing our words can add to the majesty you've witnessed—or explain why only time and health are standing between Verlander and Hall of Fame votes. Last year he threw a career high 3,941 pitches, not counting the postseason, and has led the AL in that category three years running. It is tempting to point to those numbers and run shrieking with worry, but Verlander has proven his durability is as superlative as his stuff. For all we know, he might just get better. Enjoy.

**Brayan Villarreal**
Born: **5/10/1987** Age: **25**
Bats: **R** Throws: **R** Height: **6' 1''** Weight: **170**
Breakout: **36%** Improve: **67%** Collapse: **9%**
Attrition: **16%** MLB: **88%**

**Comparables:**
Bobby Parnell, Jose Capellan, Juan Rincon

| YEAR | TEAM | LVL | AGE | W | L | SV | G | GS | IP | H | HR | BB | SO | EqBB9 | EqSO9 | GB% | BABIP | WHIP | ERA | FIP | FRA | WARP |
|---|---|---|---|---|---|---|---|---|---|---|---|---|---|---|---|---|---|---|---|---|---|---|
| 2011 | TOL | AAA | 24 | 2 | 3 | 0 | 17 | 10 | 66 | 65 | 6 | 29 | 40 | 4.0 | 5.5 | 46% | .289 | 1.42 | 5.05 | 5.03 | 5.84 | 0.1 |
| 2011 | DET | MLB | 24 | 1 | 1 | 0 | 16 | 0 | 16 | 21 | 3 | 11 | 14 | 5.6 | 7.9 | 42% | .375 | 1.94 | 6.75 | 5.81 | 6.36 | -0.2 |
| 2012 | DET | MLB | 25 | 2 | 2 | 0 | 8 | 5 | 28² | 31 | 4 | 14 | 19 | 4.4 | 6.0 | 44% | .304 | 1.58 | 5.24 | 5.16 | 5.69 | -0.1 |

Villarreal started last season in the Detroit pen but pitched his way back to the bus leagues, where his strikeout and walk rates then took two giant steps in the wrong direction. The organization still believes his stuff can make him an asset in the bullpen, as his mid-90s fastball and

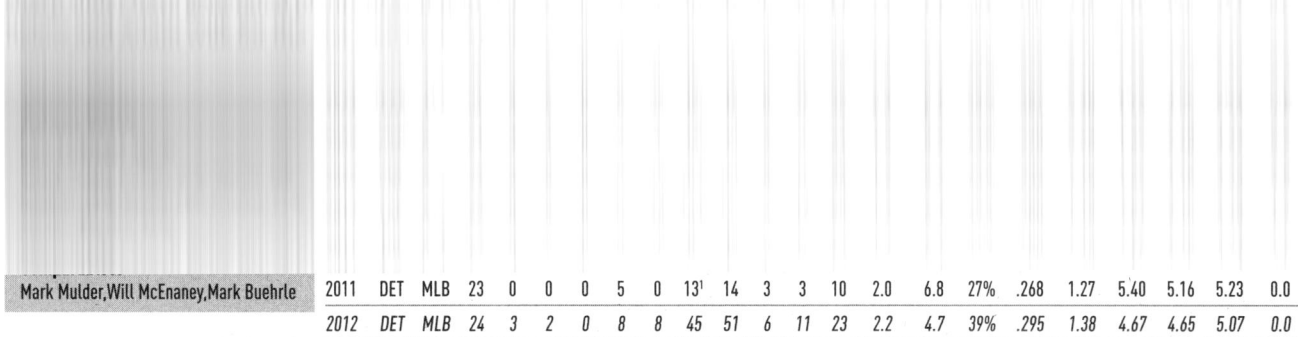

Mark Mulder, Will McEnaney, Mark Buehrle

| 2011 | DET | MLB | 23 | 0 | 0 | 0 | 5 | 0 | 13¹ | 14 | 3 | 3 | 10 | 2.0 | 6.8 | 27% | .268 | 1.27 | 5.40 | 5.16 | 5.23 | 0.0 |
| 2012 | DET | MLB | 24 | 3 | 2 | 0 | 8 | 8 | 45 | 51 | 6 | 11 | 23 | 2.2 | 4.7 | 39% | .295 | 1.38 | 4.67 | 4.65 | 5.07 | 0.0 |

A certifiable control freak, Wilk toted his bag of off-speed tricks to Comerica for a month of big-league meal money last summer. With a fastball that rarely breaks 90, his stuff is nothing special, but he doesn't give in to hitters, keeps his walks low, and isn't totally allergic to the punchout. He'll compete for a swingman role this spring, and in a system known for its power arms, Wilk is a refreshing change of pace.

## LINEOUTS

### HITTERS

| PLAYER | TEAM | LVL | AGE | PA | R | 2B | 3B | HR | RBI | BB | SO | SB-CS | AVG/OBP/SLG | TAv | BABIP | BRR | FRAA | WARP |
|---|---|---|---|---|---|---|---|---|---|---|---|---|---|---|---|---|---|---|
| CF D. Fields | LAK | A+ | 20 | 495 | 57 | 14 | 4 | 8 | 46 | 49 | 133 | 4-4 | .220/.308/.326 | .230 | .297 | -1.8 | -5.8 | -1.2 |
| RF A. Garcia | LAK | A+ | 20 | 515 | 53 | 16 | 6 | 11 | 56 | 18 | 132 | 14-5 | .264/.297/.389 | .241 | .339 | -2 | -4.3 | -0.6 |
| 3B W. Gaynor | LAK | A+ | 23 | 544 | 58 | 28 | 3 | 9 | 56 | 38 | 137 | 2-2 | .213/.287/.338 | .243 | .275 | -1.2 | 4.3 | 0.7 |
| RF B. Guez | ERI | AA | 24 | 146 | 18 | 4 | 5 | 4 | 24 | 13 | 22 | 2-6 | .299/.372/.504 | .288 | .330 | -0.3 | -4.3 | 0.2 |
|  | TOL | AAA | 24 | 348 | 41 | 27 | 3 | 3 | 32 | 21 | 72 | 10-9 | .278/.333/.411 | .253 | .350 | 1.2 | -1.2 | 0.5 |
| SS C. Iorg | ERI | AA | 25 | 90 | 8 | 1 | 0 | 2 | 6 | 4 | 28 | 2-1 | .167/.213/.250 | .169 | .222 | -0.3 | -1.4 | -0.9 |
|  | TOL | AAA | 25 | 339 | 33 | 18 | 1 | 5 | 21 | 15 | 79 | 12-7 | .208/.254/.321 | .199 | .260 | 0.2 | -3.9 | -1.1 |
| SS D. Machado | WMI | A | 19 | 491 | 47 | 1 | 2 | 0 | 28 | 46 | 77 | 25-5 | .235/.314/.247 | .229 | .285 | 6.4 | 12.4 | 1.9 |
| 2B H. Perez | WMI | A | 20 | 566 | 69 | 23 | 3 | 8 | 42 | 38 | 87 | 23-6 | .258/.314/.364 | .253 | .293 | 3.2 | -4.6 | 1.2 |
| C O. Santos | TOL | AAA | 30 | 163 | 12 | 5 | 0 | 2 | 16 | 3 | 29 | 0-0 | .245/.259/.318 | .204 | .285 | 0.7 | -0.6 | -0.3 |
|  | DET | MLB | 30 | 22 | 1 | 0 | 0 | 0 | 0 | 0 | 4 | 0-0 | .227/.227/.227 | .201 | .278 | -0.2 | -0.1 | -0.1 |
| RF D. Scram | ERI | AA | 27 | 258 | 40 | 12 | 4 | 7 | 39 | 39 | 68 | 3-1 | .258/.377/.451 | .292 | .343 | -1.5 | 2.2 | 1.6 |
|  | TOL | AAA | 27 | 58 | 4 | 5 | 0 | 1 | 4 | 13 | 10 | 0-0 | .267/.431/.444 | .299 | .324 | 0.7 | 1.9 | 0.7 |
| SS E. Suarez | ONE | A- | 19 | 229 | 37 | 11 | 5 | 5 | 24 | 18 | 43 | 9-5 | .250/.323/.426 | .293 | .295 | 0.7 | 0.9 | 2.1 |
| CF C. Thomas | TOL | AAA | 27 | 406 | 37 | 15 | 2 | 12 | 53 | 32 | 130 | 20-3 | .251/.314/.401 | .246 | .352 | 1.9 | 10.5 | 1.9 |
| RF D. Vasquez | TGR | RK | 17 | 224 | 25 | 8 | 1 | 2 | 30 | 7 | 34 | 3-2 | .272/.306/.350 | .239 | .314 | 0.2 | -6.1 | -0.8 |

Toolsy center fielder **Daniel Fields** regressed during his second spin through High-A; he was still young for the league, but if he continues to strike out in a quarter of his plate appearances he won't have a future. ⊘ Fellow Lakeland outfielder **Avisail Garcia** is similarly young, toolsy, and contact-deficient; his speed, strong arm, and power potential earned him a spot on the 40-man, but he'll have to start putting the ball in play or the organization will lose interest. ⊘ Yet another Lakeland player who spent the year fanning infielders with his bat, third baseman **Wade Gaynor** has always profiled as an offense-first prospect who may have to slide down the defensive spectrum, so flailing away helplessly in High-A at age 23 may have extinguished his already guttering prospect flame. ⊘ Corner outfielder **Ben Guez** has modest tools but raked at Erie and didn't sink in his first taste of Triple-A; in a system bereft of hitting prospects who can actually hit, he stands out among the tallest dwarfs. ⊘ Shortstop **Cale Iorg** has a premier glove and last year lowered his strikeout rate from disastrous to merely very bad, but it wasn't enough to keep him on the 40-man roster; he may yet see major league duty as a glove-first utility man. ⊘ Teenage shortstop **Dixon Machado** has a memorable name, a flashy glove, and draws a few walks, but with three extra base hits all year he has yet to show even Juan Pierre's power; his optimal future involves securing a position in the infield utility racket. ⊘ Young Venezuelan infielder **Hernan Perez** parlayed a Midwest League All-Star appearance and a successful AFL stint into a surprise spot on the 40-man roster; he is a plus defender at the keystone and playable at shortstop, but his bat is an open question. ⊘ Punchless receiver **Omir Santos** backed up starter Alex Avila down the stretch last year and will start the year as an insurance policy for new backup Gerald Laird; his offensive ceiling could function nicely as a mediocre prospect's floor. ⊘ Organizational soldier **Deik Scram** wielded a productive bat in Double-A but at 27 he darn well ought to, being old enough to spend the year bellowing Get out of my yard! at his youthful opponents. ⊘ Unlike many teenage short-stop prospects, **Eugenio Suarez** looks like he intends to do some damage at the plate; combine that with terrific hands and a strong arm and he is someone to keep an eye on. ⊘ Whiff-erific veteran **Clete Thomas** is set for another season awaiting his return to the big league roster, but with a bevy of similar fourth outfielder types blocking his way, he'll need to take the timeless advice of the Dread Pirate Roberts: get used to disappointment. ⊘ Venezuelan bonus baby **Danry Vasquez** has tools to dream on and didn't have the bat knocked out of his hands as a 17-year-old in the Gulf Coast League; if he grows into his lanky frame, develops some power, and learns to control the strike zone, he could become a solid corner outfielder.

## PITCHERS

| PLAYER | TEAM | LVL | AGE | W | L | SV | IP | H | HR | BB | SO | EqBB9 | EqSO9 | GB% | BABIP | WHIP | ERA | FIP | FRA | WARP |
|---|---|---|---|---|---|---|---|---|---|---|---|---|---|---|---|---|---|---|---|---|
| A. Burgos | WMI | A | 20 | 2 | 2 | 0 | 94² | 63 | 4 | 33 | 89 | 3.1 | 8.5 | 52% | .242 | 1.01 | 2.19 | 3.10 | 3.62 | 1.7 |
| B. Flynn | WMI | A | 21 | 2 | 0 | 0 | 67² | 58 | 3 | 23 | 57 | 3.1 | 7.6 | 45% | .288 | 1.20 | 3.46 | 3.45 | 4.31 | 0.9 |
| E. Gonzalez | TOL | AAA | 28 | 4 | 4 | 13 | 47² | 52 | 7 | 21 | 60 | 4.0 | 11.3 | 30% | .378 | 1.53 | 5.48 | 4.01 | 5.55 | 0.2 |
|  | DET | MLB | 28 | 0 | 0 | 0 | 9 | 12 | 1 | 7 | 3 | 7.0 | 3.0 | 29% | .333 | 2.11 | 10.00 | 6.17 | 5.49 | -0.1 |
| M. Hoffman | TOL | AAA | 22 | 1 | 3 | 0 | 62¹ | 60 | 3 | 23 | 46 | 3.3 | 6.6 | 57% | .302 | 1.33 | 3.18 | 3.69 | 5.39 | 0.2 |
| J. Ortega | TOL | AAA | 22 | 0 | 2 | 0 | 50 | 61 | 7 | 27 | 44 | 4.9 | 7.9 | 41% | .358 | 1.76 | 6.30 | 5.10 | 6.30 | -0.3 |
| B. Rondon | WMI | A | 20 | 2 | 2 | 19 | 40 | 22 | 0 | 34 | 61 | 7.7 | 13.7 | 52% | .293 | 1.40 | 2.03 | 3.23 | 4.41 | 0.4 |
| K. Ryan | WMI | A | 19 | 1 | 2 | 0 | 137 | 145 | 3 | 30 | 99 | 2.0 | 6.5 | 48% | .341 | 1.28 | 3.15 | 3.05 | 4.07 | 2.1 |
| T. Stohr | LAK | A+ | 24 | 1 | 0 | 0 | 31¹ | 22 | 2 | 8 | 22 | 2.3 | 6.6 | 52% | .238 | 1.02 | 3.45 | 3.78 | 4.94 | 0.2 |
|  | ERI | AA | 24 | 0 | 2 | 3 | 25² | 22 | 3 | 17 | 27 | 6.0 | 9.5 | 43% | .292 | 1.52 | 4.21 | 4.93 | 5.12 | 0.1 |
| B. Thomas | DET | MLB | 33 | 0 | 1 | 0 | 11 | 17 | 1 | 6 | 7 | 4.9 | 5.7 | 48% | .390 | 2.09 | 9.00 | 4.88 | 7.63 | -0.4 |
| J. Voss | LAK | A+ | 24 | 3 | 0 | 0 | 33² | 33 | 0 | 7 | 30 | 1.9 | 8.0 | 35% | .327 | 1.19 | 3.21 | 2.41 | 3.55 | 0.8 |
|  | ERI | AA | 24 | 9 | 7 | 0 | 115¹ | 96 | 11 | 37 | 101 | 2.9 | 7.9 | 39% | .272 | 1.15 | 3.67 | 3.94 | 4.12 | 2.0 |
| R. Weinhardt | ERI | AA | 25 | 1 | 1 | 1 | 26² | 29 | 3 | 11 | 23 | 3.7 | 7.8 | 51% | .347 | 1.50 | 4.05 | 4.50 | 4.95 | 0.2 |
|  | TOL | AAA | 25 | 1 | 4 | 1 | 34² | 36 | 3 | 14 | 31 | 3.6 | 8.0 | 50% | .308 | 1.44 | 6.49 | 4.39 | 5.54 | 0.0 |
|  | DET | MLB | 25 | 0 | 0 | 0 | 1² | 4 | 0 | 0 | 1 | 0.0 | 5.4 | 50% | .500 | 2.40 | 10.80 | 1.86 | 3.22 | 0.0 |

Low-velo lefty **Alex Burgos** knows how to pitch, as he used a solid cutter and an assortment of breaking balls to keep Midwest League hitters off-balance during an impressive full-season debut; if he can work the same magic against more advanced batsmen, he has a chance to see Comerica someday. ⊘ The Tigers acted on their power-lefty obsession by taking man-mountain **Brian Flynn** in last year's draft, and were rewarded with a minor league debut that featured impressive command of his mid-90s heat. ⊘ Squat reliever **Enrique Gonzalez** used a four-pitch arsenal to dominate the kids in Triple-A but once again struggled in Detroit; released at season's end, he is a good candidate for a low-profile role on a low-profile team to see if he can consistently retire big leaguers. ⊘ Hard-throwing lefty **Matt Hoffman** has seen his velocity jump since moving to the bullpen and has found a spot on the 40-man roster, but his secondary stuff is nothing special and he is most likely a LOOGY-in-waiting. ⊘ Relief suspect **Jose Ortega** throws hard but his fastball lacks wiggle and his control has taken a turn for the worse, making it hard to see him providing worthwhile innings for the big club. ⊘ Minor league closer **Bruce Rondon** wields a heavy mid-90s fastball and sharp slider, leading to mountains of punchouts and free passes; if he can iron out his mechanics, improve his control, and recover from the sore shoulder that cut his season short, he could become a bullpen asset. ⊘ Lefty strike-thrower **Kyle Ryan** survived an aggressive assignment to the Midwest League as a teenager, and if his cutter and changeup continue to improve he may someday reach his back-of-the-rotation ceiling. ⊘ Fastball/slider devotee **Tyler Stohr** returned from Tommy John surgery to work his way up to the Erie pen and onto the 40-man roster, though it's questionable whether his stuff can induce the world's best hitters to swing and miss. ⊘ Well-traveled Aussie **Brad Thomas** hurt his elbow after tossing a few nondescript innings in the Tigers pen, and is now on walkabout to find an organization looking for left-handed organizational depth. ⊘ Lefty **Jay Voss** was moved into the rotation for his second spin through Double-A and cut a wide swath, showing improved command of his fastball/slider combination; he's not young, but he could sneak up on us. ⊘ Ground-ball specialist **Robbie Weinhardt** keeps the ball in the park and gets a few strikeouts, but he lost his spot on

| YEAR | TEAM | W-L | +/- | PC | P | P | QS | BQS | REL | Zero R | IBB | Subs | PH | Avg | HR | SB2 | CS2 | SB3 | CS3 | Att | SAC % | SAC | Squeeze | Swing | In Play |
|---|---|---|---|---|---|---|---|---|---|---|---|---|---|---|---|---|---|---|---|---|---|---|---|---|---|
| 2009 | DET | 86-77 | 0 | 97.1 | 72 | 13 | 68 | 6 | 437 | 266 | 42 | 78 | 122 | .221 | 3 | 8 | 2 | 1 | 2 | 71 | 74.6% | 51 | 4 | 158 | 126 |
| 2010 | DET | 81-81 | 1 | 198.7 | 161 | 159 | 100 | 4 | 416 | 317 | 58 | — | 242 | .214 | 4 | 1 | 8 | 0 | 0 | 118 | 88.1% | 100 | 4 | 344 | 109 |
| 2011 | DET | 95-67 | 1 | 98.2 | 78 | 9 | 90 | 3 | 421 | 337 | 34 | — | 79 | .300 | 5 | 1 | 3 | 0 | 0 | 72 | 79.2% | 57 | 3 | 305 | 105 |

Leyland has always received high marks for that most important of all managerial traits: leadership. While there's no way we can definitively quantify such a thing, most observers notice that players seem to play hard for his teams, they take the field prepared, and few have left the Tigers, Marlins, or Pirates publicly grumbling about the way the old skipper handled them. He has also shown an admirable willingness over the years to adapt his tactics to the skills of the players he is given, bunting more last year when lineup disasters at second, third, and in the outfield made it less egregious to trade outs for bases, and ranking among the league leaders in both fast and slow hooks. While some questioned his stubbornness in keeping Peralta and Avila low in the order during their breakout seasons, given their track histories and the perpetual sabermetric drumbeat to ignore small sample sizes, isn't that something to celebrate? He has his fetishes, of course (we're looking at you, Don Kelly), but on the whole Leyland continues to rest comfortably in the upper tier of major league managers.

# Houston Astros

On December 14, the Astros traded closer Mark Melancon to the Red Sox for infielder Jed Lowrie and pitcher Kyle Weiland. As deals go, it was hardly a blockbuster, but as the opening salvo of new general manager Jeff Luhnow's regime, it was tough to miss the implications. In four years at the helm of the Astros, Luhnow's predecessor, Ed Wade, had gained notoriety for his willingness to sacrifice usable prospects and young players to obtain Proven Veterans (and particularly Proven Closers), and more generally for forestalling a much-needed rebuilding effort. With owner Drayton McLane clinging to memories of the bygone Killer B's era, Wade attempted to tinker with a core built around decreasingly effective superstars Roy Oswalt and Lance Berkman for one last-ditch attempt at contention, a "kamikaze run", as BP's Christina Kahrl termed it. Hired just a week earlier from the world champion Cardinals, where he served as vice president of scouting and player development, Luhnow's first trade was a solid attempt to reverse that trend by adding a potential lineup regular in exchange for a more fungible commodity.

Indeed, the times they are a-changin' for the Astros, who not only have a new GM but a new owner, and as of 2013 they'll have a new league and division. Luhnow was hired by new owner Jim Crane, a Houston freight executive who was approved unanimously by his fellow owners in late November after waiting more than six months for his $610 million purchase of the franchise, the lease on Minute Maid Park, and a stake in a new regional sports network to be finalized. McLane had been trying to unload the Astros for years. In fact, back in 2008, he had struck a deal with Crane, only to see the latter back out at the last minute. Since then, the franchise had existed in a sort of stasis, cutting payroll and eventually shedding Oswalt and Berkman, but slow to embrace the magnitude of the task ahead. "Rebuilding is not in my vocabulary," McLane famously said.

Rebuilding will have to be in Crane's vocabulary, but then, he must at least have some reserve of patience given how long he's waited to be in this position. His abortive 2008 run at the Astros was just one of his three unsuccessful attempts to buy a major-league franchise in recent years. In 2009, he bid on the Cubs, and in 2010, he attempted to buy the Rangers from Tom Hicks. In doing so, Crane had angered Bud Selig, first for jilting McLane, a close friend of the commissioner, and second for continuing to negotiate with Hicks to buy the Rangers despite an exclusive agreement between Hicks and the Chuck Greenberg-Nolan Ryan group after they won the bankruptcy auction.

After reaching agreement with McLane in May, Crane and his investment group were subjected to a great deal of scrutiny—and rightly so. As detailed by Baseball Prospectus contributor Maury Brown at Forbes.com, back in 1997, the Equal Employment Opportunity Commission issued a 104-page report detailing the practices of Crane's Eagle USA Airfreight company, which included paying female and minority employees less than white males doing similar work, failing to investigate employee allegations of sexual harassment, and destroying evidence pertaining to the investigation. In 2000, the *Houston Chronicle* reported that Crane told his subordinates not to hire blacks because "once you hire blacks, you can never fire them," and used various means of discouraging blacks and women from applying for jobs. The company's General Counsel corroborated those claims and was sued for violating attorney-client privilege. Ultimately, Eagle paid a $9 million settlement to plaintiffs for its discriminatory practices. Furthermore, another one of Crane's companies, Eagle Global Logistics, was sued four times by

## ASTROS PROSPECTUS
### 2011 W-L: 56-106, 6th in NL Central

| | | | |
|---|---|---|---|
| Pythag | .382 | 29th | **Ballpark:** Minute Maid Park (3-yr. PF: 103). New HD scoreboard makes the score harder to ignore |
| RS/G | 3.80 | 26th | |
| RA/G | 4.91 | 28th | |
| TAv | .244 | 27th | **2011:** Bad luck and bad players make them the first team mathematically eliminated |
| TAv-P | .271 | 25th | |
| FIP | 4.32 | 26th | |
| DER | .698 | 27th | **2012:** Their last year in the National League is going to involve a lot of losing |
| DL | 737 | 14th | |
| B-Age | 28.3 | 12th | **Action Items:** Patience, as it takes time for a new GM and owners to rebuild a broken system |
| P-Age | 27.4 | 11th | |
| Salary | $77.7 | 20th | |
| M$/MW | $8.74 | 30th | |

the Department of Justice over allegations of war profiteering, paying around $10 million in fines and civil suit settlements from 2006 to 2008.

Selig didn't prevent this charmer from joining the ranks of MLB owners, but then how could he keep such a distinguished gentleman out of a club that includes Fred Wilpon, Frank McCourt, Jeffrey Loria, and who knows how many other unsavory characters? Instead, Selig used his leverage with the other owners against Crane, telling him that the purchase would not be approved unless he consented to have the Astros move to the American League in order to create two 15-team leagues, six five-team divisions, and two more wild-card teams. For his troubles, Crane received a $70 mil-

DisAstros lost a franchise-record 106 games, nine more than in any of their 49 other seasons. They started the year 0-5, which had the benefit of helping to erase memories of the previous season's nightmarish 0-8 start. They had a two-month stretch when they went 11-39, a pace worse than that of the 1962 Mets. It's not like they were expected to do well, of course. PECOTA projected the Astros for an MLB-worst 68-94 record, and league lows in both scoring (636 runs) and on-base percentage (.304), with four regulars below .300. Those projections weren't too far off base: The team did have sub-.300 OBP sinkholes at three spots, but what was particularly odd was that while the offense tied for fourth in the league in batting average, it was 11th in OBP and 13th in slugging percentage. The Astros were second-to-last in isolated power (.116) and dead last in walk rate (6.5 percent), a combination that makes for an ironclad guarantee against scoring runs.

Some of that was bad luck. Twenty-four-year-old catcher Jason Castro, the team's first-round pick from 2008, tore his ACL in spring training and missed the entire season. While Castro had struggled to a .212 True Average as a rookie in 2010, the bar for improvement was low; this team hasn't had a catcher with a TAv above .240 since 2000, and it wasn't about to get one with Humberto Quintero, J.R. Towles, and Carlos Corporan splitting the duties. Second baseman Jeff Keppinger, one of the team's better hitters (a sad statement in its own right), needed foot surgery in January and didn't return until May 27; Bill Hall was so awful in his stead that he drew his release shortly afterwards. Shortstop Clint Barmes started the year on the DL as well due to a broken bone in his hand; he looked like Troy Tulowitzki compared to fill-in Angel Sanchez.

Some of it was bad design as well. First baseman Brett Wallace, a 2008 first-round pick who's already on his fourth organization, lacks the power for the position, as his .259/.334/.369 showing attests. Third baseman Chris Johnson, whose searing .308/.337/.481 line as a rookie was founded on an unsustainable .387 BABIP, crashed back to earth, partly because that last mark fell 71 points and mostly because pitchers figured him out. The outfield—Carlos Lee, Michael Bourn, and Hunter Pence—was actually productive, but it fell victim to the belated rebuilding imperative. Bourn and Pence were both traded away in late July, more on that momentarily. Lee, dreadful in 2010 (-1.9 WARP) and immobile both afield and on the balance sheet ($18.5 million

walks. Had they not been eighth in strikeouts, the damage might have been even worse given that their defense ranked second-to-last in converting batted balls into outs. Wandy Rodriguez (4.31 Fair Run Average, 1.7 WARP) and Bud Norris (4.54 FRA, 1.2 WARP) were the only pitchers worth more than one win above replacement, while Brett Myers and J.A. Happ—Wade's ex-Phillies—couldn't even manage that low standard. Top pitching prospect Jordan Lyles, the team's other 2008 first-round pick, took his lumps in a half-season of work. Closer Brandon Lyon suffered a torn labrum and threw just two innings after May 4, and the bullpen finished with the league's worst ERA (4.49) as well as the third-highest rate of allowing inherited runners to score (32 percent), with setup man Wilton Lopez and Rule 5 pick Aneury Rodriguez the only relievers worth more than 0.3 WARP.

Luhnow will have his hands full digging the team out of its current hole, but he brings an impressive set of credentials to town. An MBA from Northwestern with a background in business and consulting, he's a progressive 45-year-old executive who's not only well-versed in both the statistical analysis and scouting sides of things, but he has a proven ability to integrate them. Originally hired by the Cardinals in 2003 for his analytical acumen, he used his consulting background to assess the organization's strengths and weaknesses, not only creating an in-house analytical department but going on to reorganize the scouting department, encouraging numerous innovations on that side as well. Born and raised in Mexico City, his familiarity with Latin America and fluency in Spanish enabled him to oversee the Cardinals' opening of an academy in the Dominican Republic and to reestablish the franchise's operations in Venezuela.

In Luhnow's first three drafts as the Cardinals' scouting director, the team drafted an MLB-high 24 future major leaguers, including Jaime Garcia, John Jay, Allen Craig, Colby Rasmus, Chris Perez, and Luke Gregerson. During that same drafting timespan, the Astros produced an MLB-low four major leaguers. The unpopularity of Crane and the dire state of the team's system led many high-profile candidates to decline interviews for the GM job, including Rays GM Andrew Friedman, White Sox assistant GM Rick Hahn, Rangers assistant GM Thad Levine, and former Dodgers assistant GM Kim Ng. For the Astros to land Luhnow nonetheless appears to be an inspired move.

The hiring of George Postolos to be the team's president and CEO, a move that preceded the hiring of Luhnow, is another encouraging move. A 48-year-old Harvard Law School graduate, Postolos spent eight years in the front office of the Houston Rockets, four of them as team president and CEO, and he hired the analytically driven Daryl Morey to be the Rockets GM. Postolos was also involved in the launch of Comcast SportsNet Houston, the regional sports network formed in partnership between the Rockets and Astros. Between him and Luhnow, the Astros' culture change is well underway.

The hole they have to dig out of is a deep one, because the Astros have lagged behind in the draft for years. Wade did well to bring in Bobby Heck as scouting director; Castro and Lyles, from his inaugural draft, represent the first Astros first-rounders to reach the majors since 2001 pick Chris Burke. But even with better drafting under Heck, the Astros don't have much in the way of ready talent in the upper levels of their minor-league system yet, and as of last spring ranked 28th in BP's organizational rankings, 26th in those of *Baseball America*, up from a respective 28th and 30th the year before. The trade of Pence to the Phillies brought back four players, two of whom rank as the team's top hitting and pitching prospects, first baseman/outfielder Jonathan Singleton, a 2009 pick who spent 2011 in High-A, and pitcher Jared Cosart, a 2008 pick who debuted in Double-A after being acquired.

The trade of Bourn to Atlanta brought back four players, including lefty Brett Oberholtzer, an innings eater who spent all of 2011 at Double-A. The team's only other prospect who could be considered an equivalent talent is 2011 first-rounder George Springer, a 22-year-old center fielder with a power-speed combo whose pro experience consists of just eight games in Low-A. Of the team's 11 top prospects, according to Kevin Goldstein's list, Oberholtzer and righty Paul Clemens (who came over in the same deal) are the only ones likely to find themselves in the majors in 2012. Six of those 11 prospects came from outside the organization in the unloadings of Pence, Bourn, and Oswalt. The good news is that the team has the first pick of the 2012 draft, and should be able to add a player who instantly becomes their top prospect.

The core major-league roster Luhnow inherits isn't in great shape. Castro should get another shot at the catching job, but he doesn't have the upside the team once envisioned, and he's also coming off December surgery to remove the sesamoid bone in his foot, similar to what Keppinger went through in mid-January. Lee may be able to restore enough value at first base to entice another team into acquiring him if the Astros are willing to eat enough salary. Second baseman Jose Altuve may be a cult hero to listeners of the Prospectus Up and In podcast, but his lack of plate discipline was exposed during a 57-game big league trial in which he hit .276/.297/.357 and drew just five walks in 234 PA. Lowrie brings with him questions about his durability and his defensive prowess, not to mention his struggles against righties (.214/.293/.342 career). On the other hand, he hit .258/.332/.419 through his first 795 plate appearances, but just .221/.274/.345 over his last 125 following a seven-week stint on the DL due to a left-shoulder subluxation.

Neither Johnson nor Jimmy Paredes, who was obtained from the Yankees in the Berkman trade and who hit .286/.320/.393 in a 46-game trial, profiles as a long-term answer at the hot corner. Martinez, a 24-year-old 2009 pick, can hit but may lack the necessary power for a corner outfielder. Likewise for the 28-year-old Bogusevic, a converted pitcher who will be hard-pressed to match the .287/.348/.457 he hit in 182 PA as a rookie. Center fielder Jordan Schafer, obtained from the Braves in the Bourn deal, is a 25-year-old who has hit just .228/.311/.305 in 532 PA over the last three seasons; already dinged by a 2008 suspension for HGH use, he was arrested in October and charged with a felony count of marijuana possession. If there's good news, it's that five of those prospective starters are 25 or under, with Lee the only one over 28.

The rotation presents an opportunity for Luhnow to further improve the team, namely by trading Myers (owed $11 million for 2012, with a $3 million buyout of a $10 million club option for 2013) and Wandy Rodriguez (owed $23 million for 2012-13 , with a $13 million club option for 2014 that becomes a player option if he's traded) in a winter short of palatable free-agent pitching options. Rodriguez won't bring back the packages that Mat Latos or Gio Gonzalez did, but if the Astros eat a significant chunk of money, those returns suggest they stand to gain a couple of high-end prospects. Norris, Happ, and Lyles are all capable of improvement over their 2011 showings, but none profiles as more than mid-rotation material. Weiland and hard-throwing Henry Sosa, who made 10 starts for the Astros over the final two months, could round out the rotation if either of the front two are dealt, though both have long been thought better suited for relief roles. Aneury Rodriguez, who made eight starts, could be another option in that case as well, and then there's always the heap of free-agent leftovers from whom they can choose, hoping one can either provide bulk innings or reestablish his health enough to merit a late-season trade for a prospect. As for who takes over for Melancon at closer, Lopez and Sosa could both figure into the equation, as could Lyon if he's healthy enough. Don't expect Luhnow to toss and turn at night worrying about trading for the next Matt Lindstrom or Jose Valverde.

In the short term, the picture is grim enough that another 100-loss season is a strong possibility, but that's the long-overdue price for delaying what needed to be done, and if it means a second year in a row with the overall number-one pick in the draft, well, there are far worse outcomes than that. Crane, despite his considerable baggage, does bring some fresh blood to a franchise sorely in need of it, and the hirings of Postolos and Luhnow have gotten him off on the right foot. The new cable network and the 2013 league change further offer chances for the Astros to turn the page on the past few years, and reshape the franchise for a more prosperous future.

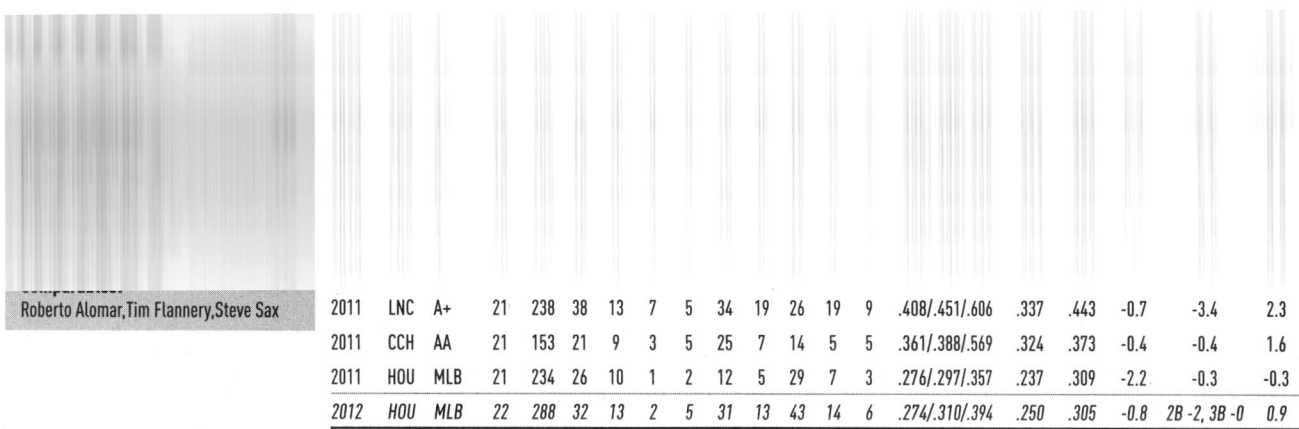

| | | | | | | | | | | | | | | | | | | | |
|---|---|---|---|---|---|---|---|---|---|---|---|---|---|---|---|---|---|---|---|
| 2011 | LNC | A+ | 21 | 238 | 38 | 13 | 7 | 5 | 34 | 19 | 26 | 19 | 9 | .408/.451/.606 | .337 | .443 | -0.7 | -3.4 | 2.3 |
| 2011 | CCH | AA | 21 | 153 | 21 | 9 | 3 | 5 | 25 | 7 | 14 | 5 | 5 | .361/.388/.569 | .324 | .373 | -0.4 | -0.4 | 1.6 |
| 2011 | HOU | MLB | 21 | 234 | 26 | 10 | 1 | 2 | 12 | 5 | 29 | 7 | 3 | .276/.297/.357 | .237 | .309 | -2.2 | -0.3 | -0.3 |
| *2012* | *HOU* | *MLB* | *22* | *288* | *32* | *13* | *2* | *5* | *31* | *13* | *43* | *14* | *6* | *.274/.310/.394* | *.250* | *.305* | *-0.8* | *2B -2, 3B -0* | *0.9* |

*Comparables:*
*Roberto Alomar, Tim Flannery, Steve Sax*

In 2010, the bantam Venezuelan infielder got his first taste of full-season baseball and smacked around Sally league pitching with a .310 TAv. That earned him an in-season promotion and he held his own in the California League. Proving that even his own organization can be guilty of "profiling," he was returned to the California League to start 2011, and 238 plate appearances later, the trauma ended for the league's pitchers as he took his .408/.451/.606 line to Double-A. Texas League hurlers weren't much happier to see him in his brief stop in that league. So, on July 20, he became the National League's youngest position player. Altuve is a slick fielder with the tiny strikeout rate one would expect from such impressive hand-eye coordination, and he has much better power than anyone would think possible from such a small player (82 extra-base hits in 952 full-season minor-league plate appearances). If Altuve was 70 inches tall instead of 65, the discussions would be centered around whether he or Dustin Ackley was the best up-and-coming second baseman. As it is, most are still not taking him seriously. Considering how thoroughly he has belittled minor-league pitching in ascending the ranks, such disrespect may be a huge mistake.

| **Brian Bogusevic** | **RF** | | YEAR | TEAM | LVL | AGE | PA | R | 2B | 3B | HR | RBI | BB | SO | SB | CS | AVG_OBP_SLG | TAv | BABIP | BRR | FRAA | WARP |
|---|---|---|---|---|---|---|---|---|---|---|---|---|---|---|---|---|---|---|---|---|---|---|
| Born: 2/18/1984 Age: 28 | | | 2009 | ROU | AAA | 25 | 581 | 68 | 25 | 3 | 6 | 53 | 53 | 118 | 22 | 3 | .271/.339/.365 | .249 | .337 | 1.6 | -2.7 | 0.7 |
| Bats: L Throws: L Height: 6' 4" Weight: 210 | | | 2010 | ROU | AAA | 26 | 575 | 91 | 26 | 2 | 13 | 57 | 67 | 108 | 23 | 1 | .277/.365/.414 | .276 | .330 | 5.7 | 0 | 3.0 |
| Breakout: 2% Improve: 16% Collapse: 13% | | | 2010 | HOU | MLB | 26 | 31 | 5 | 3 | 0 | 0 | 3 | 3 | 12 | 1 | 1 | .179/.258/.286 | .172 | .312 | 0.6 | 0.5 | -0.1 |
| Attrition: 27% MLB: 52% | | | 2011 | OKL | AAA | 27 | 254 | 27 | 11 | 5 | 3 | 35 | 30 | 49 | 20 | 3 | .261/.362/.399 | .245 | .323 | 0.8 | 1.8 | 0.4 |
| **Comparables:** | | | 2011 | HOU | MLB | 27 | 182 | 22 | 14 | 1 | 4 | 15 | 15 | 40 | 4 | 2 | .287/.348/.457 | .266 | .355 | -0.5 | 1.1 | 0.6 |
| Reid Gorecki, Caleb Stewart, Johnny Weekly | | | *2012* | *HOU* | *MLB* | *28* | *250* | *27* | *11* | *1* | *3* | *22* | *23* | *59* | *9* | *2* | *.241/.313/.347* | *.240* | *.308* | *0.4* | *RF 1, LF 0* | *0.1* |

Two of last year's top three most comparable players to Bogusevic were Cliff Floyd and Von Hayes. While this is stunning, inasmuch as both had very good careers compared to even the wildest dreams remaining for Bogusevic, it does hint at the five-tool talent and plate discipline Bogusevic has always been thought to have. It will be interesting to see how much of this talent can be converted into production, considering that four prime development years were lost while he pursued his other career, pitching. The biggest casualty appears to be his power, but that came and went even in college. His Triple-A stats—including in 2011—are those of a fourth (or even fifth) outfielder. But his surprisingly good MLB stats indicate that it's more than just a long shot now that he could turn into a player whose cannon arm and speed could serve a team well in center field. Fortunately for him, the Astros are the perfect setting for on-the-job training.

**Jason Bourgeois**  CF

Born: 1/4/1982 Age: 30
Bats: R Throws: R Height: 5' 10" Weight: 190
Breakout: 1% Improve: 48% Collapse: 7%
Attrition: 18% MLB: 87%

**Comparables:**
Darryl Hamilton, Rajai Davis, Matty Alou

| YEAR | TEAM | LVL | AGE | PA | R | 2B | 3B | HR | RBI | BB | SO | SB | CS | AVG_OBP_SLG | TAv | BABIP | BRR | FRAA | WARP |
|------|------|-----|-----|-----|----|----|----|----|-----|----|----|----|----|----------------|------|-------|------|-------------|------|
| 2009 | NAS | AAA | 27 | 454 | 61 | 18 | 6 | 2 | 41 | 22 | 40 | 36 | 7 | .316/.354/.401 | .271 | .344 | 6.6 | -5.4 | 1.8 |
| 2009 | MIL | MLB | 27 | 40 | 6 | 0 | 0 | 1 | 3 | 3 | 7 | 3 | 0 | .189/.250/.270 | .194 | .207 | 0.6 | 0.4 | -0.1 |
| 2010 | ROU | AAA | 28 | 261 | 37 | 10 | 3 | 5 | 28 | 21 | 28 | 18 | 6 | .345/.402/.477 | .300 | .373 | 0.5 | -5.5 | 1.3 |
| 2010 | HOU | MLB | 28 | 136 | 16 | 4 | 1 | 0 | 3 | 13 | 16 | 12 | 4 | .220/.294/.268 | .203 | .252 | -0.3 | 0.2 | -0.5 |
| 2011 | HOU | MLB | 29 | 252 | 30 | 8 | 2 | 1 | 16 | 10 | 24 | 31 | 6 | .294/.323/.357 | .247 | .324 | 2.3 | -1.9 | 0.6 |
| 2012 | HOU | MLB | 30 | 250 | 27 | 10 | 2 | 3 | 23 | 14 | 32 | 17 | 5 | .273/.318/.363 | .246 | .304 | 0.2 | CF -5, LF -1 | 0.7 |

At the end of July, Bourgeois was living large. He was hitting .354/.374/.449, had stolen 22 bases in just 132 plate appearances, and had just been handed the starting center-field job. But his success was illusory, with stats compiled mostly against left-handed pitching, which he's always hit well. The first three weeks of August became a seemingly endless blur of weak ground-ers and popups as Bourgeois wasn't even doing well against lefties en route to a .155/.210/.190 in the 14 games he started. Returned to a platoon role thereafter, he remained confused until back-to-back starts against Tom Milone and John Lannan on September 9-10, when he went a combined 6-for-10. As a platoon outfielder with great wheels who can play second base in a pinch, he could help even a good team.

**Travis Buck**  RF

Born: 11/18/1983 Age: 28
Bats: L Throws: R Height: 6' 3" Weight: 224
Breakout: 0% Improve: 25% Collapse: 11%
Attrition: 22% MLB: 62%

**Comparables:**
Bob Hazle, Bronson Sardinha, Johnny Weekly

| YEAR | TEAM | LVL | AGE | PA | R | 2B | 3B | HR | RBI | BB | SO | SB | CS | AVG_OBP_SLG | TAv | BABIP | BRR | FRAA | WARP |
|------|------|-----|-----|-----|----|----|----|----|-----|----|----|----|----|----------------|------|-------|------|-----------|------|
| 2009 | SAC | AAA | 25 | 266 | 37 | 13 | 3 | 5 | 29 | 23 | 44 | 3 | 1 | .272/.347/.418 | .284 | .314 | -1.9 | -1 | 0.9 |
| 2009 | OAK | MLB | 25 | 115 | 11 | 3 | 0 | 3 | 10 | 10 | 20 | 1 | 1 | .219/.287/.333 | .236 | .244 | 0 | 0.5 | -0.1 |
| 2010 | SAC | AAA | 26 | 141 | 22 | 7 | 2 | 3 | 17 | 11 | 28 | 3 | 2 | .298/.372/.463 | .284 | .363 | 1.4 | 2.1 | 1.0 |
| 2010 | OAK | MLB | 26 | 48 | 6 | 2 | 0 | 1 | 2 | 4 | 14 | 1 | 0 | .167/.255/.286 | .200 | .222 | -0.6 | -1 | -0.4 |
| 2011 | COH | AAA | 27 | 146 | 21 | 6 | 1 | 4 | 25 | 19 | 26 | 1 | 1 | .256/.366/.421 | .258 | .290 | -0.2 | -0.8 | 0.3 |
| 2011 | CLE | MLB | 27 | 160 | 18 | 11 | 0 | 2 | 18 | 8 | 30 | 1 | 1 | .228/.275/.342 | .234 | .271 | 2.8 | 1.1 | 0.2 |
| 2012 | HOU | MLB | 28 | 250 | 28 | 12 | 2 | 5 | 25 | 23 | 52 | 2 | 1 | .243/.321/.380 | .253 | .293 | -0.1 | RF 1, LF -2 | 0.5 |

After multiple injuries, poor performance, and public complaints, Buck left Oakland as a free agent last offseason and landed a job as a bench player for the Indians. Once the top prospect in the Athletics system, Buck hasn't lived up to scouts' projec-tions. This minor league doubles machine has failed to produce the average power many expected, even as recently as 2008. His .246 career batting average belies the reputation that his best tool coming up was contact hitting. While the chances of him being more than a hanger on at the MLB level are slim, he did hit .288/.377/.474 as a rookie in 2007, which is more than a lot of hitters can say.

**Delino DeShields**  2B

Born: 8/16/1992 Age: 19
Bats: R Throws: R Height: 5' 10" Weight: 188
Breakout: 0% Improve: 0% Collapse: 1%
Attrition: 3% MLB: 3%

**Comparables:**
Prilys Cuello, Anderson Feliz, Nino Leyja

| YEAR | TEAM | LVL | AGE | PA | R | 2B | 3B | HR | RBI | BB | SO | SB | CS | AVG_OBP_SLG | TAv | BABIP | BRR | FRAA | WARP |
|------|------|-----|-----|-----|----|----|----|----|----|-----|-----|----|----|----------------|------|-------|------|------------|------|
| 2010 | GRV | RK | 17 | 73 | 11 | 6 | 1 | 0 | 8 | 5 | 18 | 5 | 1 | .313/.361/.433 | .293 | .429 | 1 | -0.6 | 0.5 |
| 2011 | LEX | A | 18 | 541 | 73 | 17 | 2 | 9 | 48 | 52 | 118 | 30 | 11 | .220/.305/.322 | .238 | .271 | 4 | -7.3 | -0.3 |
| 2012 | HOU | MLB | 19 | 250 | 21 | 8 | 1 | 3 | 18 | 15 | 72 | 7 | 3 | .195/.248/.276 | .192 | .263 | -0.3 | 2B -3, CF -1 | -1.8 |

Deshields was one of only seven 18-year-olds in the SAL. And though he was making a lot of weak contact, his .271 BABIP was also partly due to bad luck. Okay, enough excuses. The Astros didn't use the number eight overall pick on this guy to see him hit like Luis Durango—he was expected to mature into a double-digit home run threat who also filled up box scores with doubles and triples. He is making good progress on the position switch to second base, and though he hasn't mastered it yet, the team expects he will.

**Matt Downs**  2B

Born: 3/19/1984 Age: 28
Bats: R Throws: R Height: 6' 3" Weight: 190
Breakout: 2% Improve: 31% Collapse: 3%
Attrition: 19% MLB: 85%

**Comparables:**
Ryne Sandberg, George Zeber, Brandon Phillips

| YEAR | TEAM | LVL | AGE | PA | R | 2B | 3B | HR | RBI | BB | SO | SB | CS | AVG_OBP_SLG | TAv | BABIP | BRR | FRAA | WARP |
|------|------|-----|-----|-----|----|----|----|----|----|-----|----|----|----|----------------|------|-------|------|-------------|------|
| 2009 | FRE | AAA | 25 | 467 | 68 | 33 | 3 | 14 | 74 | 25 | 58 | 8 | 2 | .300/.346/.491 | .292 | .317 | -0.7 | -6.8 | 2.1 |
| 2009 | SFN | MLB | 25 | 60 | 6 | 2 | 0 | 1 | 2 | 6 | 13 | 1 | 0 | .170/.250/.264 | .201 | .200 | 1.3 | 0.4 | 0.0 |
| 2010 | FRE | AAA | 26 | 228 | 37 | 9 | 1 | 7 | 28 | 25 | 35 | 3 | 4 | .254/.348/.416 | .269 | .276 | -0.5 | -1.6 | 0.8 |
| 2010 | SFN | MLB | 26 | 88 | 6 | 7 | 0 | 1 | 7 | 8 | 18 | 0 | 0 | .244/.318/.372 | .261 | .300 | -0.1 | 0.5 | 0.3 |
| 2010 | HOU | MLB | 26 | 21 | 2 | 0 | 0 | 0 | 0 | 1 | 2 | 0 | 0 | .105/.190/.105 | .166 | .118 | -0.2 | -0.2 | -0.2 |
| 2011 | HOU | MLB | 27 | 222 | 29 | 18 | 0 | 10 | 41 | 17 | 47 | 0 | 0 | .276/.347/.518 | .314 | .315 | 1.1 | -1.4 | 2.0 |
| 2012 | HOU | MLB | 28 | 250 | 30 | 15 | 1 | 8 | 31 | 17 | 48 | 2 | 1 | .260/.320/.432 | .269 | .294 | 0 | 2B -3, 3B -3 | 1.9 |

Downs has a long, slow swing. This is news only because he had a short, compact swing in 2010, but tinkered with it to add power. Broad-shouldered and tall for a middle infielder, Downs was killing mistakes, launching rockets and bombs to produce a slugging percentage better than anything he'd done in full-season ball—even topping his California League marks. So far, the price he's paid is a strikeout rate almost double the 11 percent he posted in the minors. Considering he had the second-leading VORP total among the surviving Astros batters while playing about one third of a full season, that's a pittance. Pitchers were caught by surprise by his power surge in 2011, and the book on him will change for 2012. Expect more strikeouts and a lower batting average, but as a player with multi-positional flexibility and the ability to play nearly average defense at the keystone, he's definitely a waiver wire success story.

**Chris Johnson** 3B

Born: 10/1/1984 Age: 27
Bats: R Throws: R Height: 6' 4" Weight: 220
Breakout: 3% Improve: 32% Collapse: 3%
Attrition: 15% MLB: 76%

Comparables:

| YEAR | TEAM | LVL | AGE | PA | R | 2B | 3B | HR | RBI | BB | SO | SB | CS | AVG_OBP_SLG | TAv | BABIP | BRR | FRAA | WARP |
|------|------|-----|-----|-----|----|----|----|----|-----|----|----|----|----|-------------|------|-------|------|-------|------|
| 2009 | ROU | AAA | 24 | 412 | 48 | 20 | 5 | 13 | 42 | 21 | 90 | 2 | 1 | .281/.325/.461 | .266 | .338 | -1.3 | -0.7 | 1.0 |
| 2009 | HOU | MLB | 24 | 23 | 1 | 0 | 0 | 0 | 1 | 1 | 6 | 0 | 0 | .091/.130/.091 | .088 | .125 | 0.1 | -0.5 | -0.4 |
| 2010 | ROU | AAA | 25 | 163 | 26 | 10 | 1 | 8 | 33 | 9 | 23 | 0 | 0 | .329/.371/.570 | .325 | .347 | -0.1 | -1.8 | 1.2 |
| 2010 | HOU | MLB | 25 | 362 | 40 | 22 | 2 | 11 | 52 | 15 | 91 | 3 | 0 | .308/.337/.481 | .285 | .387 | -0.7 | -11.5 | 0.9 |

sures that he'll get to keep working on those Triple-A batting stats for the foreseeable future.

**Carlos Lee** LF

Born: 6/20/1976 Age: 36
Bats: R Throws: R Height: 6' 3" Weight: 200
Breakout: 0% Improve: 30% Collapse: 5%
Attrition: 15% MLB: 77%

Comparables:
Luis Gonzalez, Raul Ibanez, Moises Alou

| YEAR | TEAM | LVL | AGE | PA | R | 2B | 3B | HR | RBI | BB | SO | SB | CS | AVG_OBP_SLG | TAv | BABIP | BRR | FRAA | WARP |
|------|------|-----|-----|-----|----|----|----|----|-----|----|----|----|----|-------------|------|-------|------|---------|------|
| 2009 | HOU | MLB | 33 | 662 | 65 | 35 | 1 | 26 | 102 | 41 | 51 | 5 | 3 | .300/.343/.489 | .282 | .290 | -5.3 | -18.7 | 0.6 |
| 2010 | HOU | MLB | 34 | 649 | 67 | 29 | 1 | 24 | 89 | 37 | 59 | 3 | 3 | .246/.291/.417 | .244 | .238 | -1.2 | -14.9 | -1.9 |
| 2011 | HOU | MLB | 35 | 653 | 66 | 38 | 4 | 18 | 94 | 59 | 60 | 4 | 3 | .275/.342/.446 | .292 | .279 | -3.9 | 0.3 | 3.3 |
| 2012 | HOU | MLB | 36 | 613 | 76 | 31 | 1 | 23 | 81 | 42 | 63 | 4 | 3 | .275/.327/.456 | .277 | .274 | -0.5 | LF -11, 1B 3 | 2.3 |

"El Caballo" hasn't had to worry about having playoff games interfere with his second career as a ranch owner since signing with the Astros in 2007. He seemed to be making a strong case for being put out to pasture himself in 2011, when his April batting line stood at .194/.237/.324. As a left fielder who'd racked up -33.6 FRAA over the previous two seasons, Lee was arguably the worst player in baseball at the time, and had done much to help sink yet another Astros season. Speaking of sinking, the $37 million the Astros would be paying him in 2011-12 was a sunk cost, so popular opinion was to cut Lee loose and let one of the colts from Triple-A run around the outfield instead. But he hit .294/.364/.474 from May 1 onward and handled a position switch to first base, posting a much-improved 0.1 FRAA between his two positions. Lee doesn't want to leave the Houston area, but with just one year remaining on his contract, the Astros may actually be able to find a team willing to take on some of his salary. Playing for a contract at age 35, hinting at some of the power/contact skills that made him a feared "RBI guy" for so long, and showing rediscovered defensive adequacy, Lee could prove to be an interesting trade target for a team with playoff aspirations and money.

**Jed Lowrie** SS

Born: 4/17/1984 Age: 28
Bats: B Throws: R Height: 6' 1" Weight: 180
Breakout: 4% Improve: 41% Collapse: 2%
Attrition: 13% MLB: 84%

Comparables:
Stephen Drew, Brendan Harris, John Valentin

| YEAR | TEAM | LVL | AGE | PA | R | 2B | 3B | HR | RBI | BB | SO | SB | CS | AVG_OBP_SLG | TAv | BABIP | BRR | FRAA | WARP |
|------|------|-----|-----|-----|----|----|----|----|-----|----|----|----|----|-------------|------|-------|------|----------|------|
| 2009 | PAW | AAA | 25 | 83 | 9 | 3 | 0 | 3 | 8 | 13 | 13 | 0 | 0 | .176/.317/.353 | .248 | .173 | 0 | -0.3 | 0.2 |
| 2009 | BOS | MLB | 25 | 76 | 5 | 2 | 0 | 2 | 11 | 6 | 20 | 0 | 0 | .147/.211/.265 | .185 | .167 | 0.2 | 0.1 | -0.3 |
| 2010 | BOS | MLB | 26 | 197 | 31 | 14 | 0 | 9 | 24 | 25 | 25 | 1 | 1 | .287/.381/.526 | .319 | .292 | 0.2 | -0.2 | 1.7 |
| 2011 | BOS | MLB | 27 | 341 | 40 | 14 | 4 | 6 | 36 | 23 | 60 | 1 | 1 | .252/.303/.382 | .254 | .289 | 1.9 | 1.6 | 1.1 |
| 2012 | HOU | MLB | 28 | 295 | 35 | 17 | 2 | 6 | 32 | 30 | 57 | 1 | 0 | .252/.332/.405 | .264 | .297 | -0.1 | SS -3, 3B 3 | 1.8 |

With the caveats that Lowrie is entering his age-28 season with a career batting line of .252/.324/.408, a three-year FRAA-per-inning rate at shortstop that's well below average (-.0140), an injury history that would shame Chipper Jones, and an awful weakness against right-handed pitching (.214/.293/.342 career) . . . trading a relief pitcher for this guy is the sort of move that should lead Astros fans to be thrilled about their new general manager. All his weaknesses showed themselves again in 2011, but he's expected to be able to shrug off the shoulder soreness, inflammation, tightness, and nerve injury that followed his collision with Carl Crawford. Staying healthy is a skill that Lowrie isn't likely to demonstrate, but when he is healthy, he's demonstrated enough run-producing skills that he's worth a chance.

### J.D. Martinez — LF

Born: 8/21/1987 Age: 24
Bats: R Throws: R Height: 6' 4" Weight: 200
Breakout: 1% Improve: 48% Collapse: 3%
Attrition: 18% MLB: 76%

Comparables:
Todd Frazier, Billy Williams, Adam Lind

| YEAR | TEAM | LVL | AGE | PA | R | 2B | 3B | HR | RBI | BB | SO | SB | CS | AVG_OBP_SLG | TAv | BABIP | BRR | FRAA | WARP |
|------|------|-----|-----|----|---|----|----|----|-----|----|----|----|----|-------------|-----|-------|-----|------|------|
| 2009 | TCV | A- | 21 | 208 | 25 | 15 | 2 | 7 | 33 | 15 | 30 | 1 | 0 | .326/.385/.540 | .323 | .360 | -1.8 | 3.1 | 1.9 |
| 2009 | GRV | RK | 21 | 83 | 17 | 9 | 1 | 5 | 23 | 5 | 14 | 0 | 0 | .403/.446/.740 | .391 | .448 | 1.1 | -0.1 | 1.3 |
| 2010 | LEX | A | 22 | 393 | 83 | 31 | 3 | 15 | 64 | 33 | 55 | 3 | 0 | .362/.434/.598 | .347 | .399 | -2.1 | 0.7 | 4.2 |
| 2010 | CCH | AA | 22 | 207 | 24 | 9 | 1 | 3 | 25 | 15 | 42 | 2 | 2 | .302/.359/.407 | .263 | .375 | -2.1 | -1.9 | 0.2 |
| 2011 | CCH | AA | 23 | 370 | 50 | 25 | 1 | 13 | 72 | 42 | 55 | 1 | 0 | .338/.414/.546 | .325 | .367 | -0.6 | -5.2 | 2.6 |
| 2011 | HOU | MLB | 23 | 226 | 29 | 13 | 0 | 6 | 35 | 13 | 48 | 0 | 1 | .274/.319/.423 | .259 | .325 | -2.4 | -0.4 | 0.2 |
| 2012 | HOU | MLB | 24 | 290 | 35 | 16 | 1 | 8 | 35 | 18 | 60 | 1 | 0 | .271/.324/.429 | .267 | .319 | 0 | LF -3, RF -2 | 1.2 |

Martinez can hit. He hasn't been highly regarded as a prospect due to an unconventional swing and a flat swing plane that's expected to limit his power, but he escaped the minors after just 1261 plate appearances and hit .342/.407/.551 combined in that time. He entered 2011 with an above-average defensive reputation, but that's been downgraded—by both scouting reports and metrics—to below-average. His 2011 TAv wasn't suggestive of the middle-of-the-order hitter he's expected to be, but Martinez hadn't played full-season ball until 2010, so more growth can be expected in 2012—and beyond—than from the typical 24-year-old second-year player. While Martinez sacrifices some power with his batting approach, he blasts line drives all around the diamond. He may swing and miss a lot early in the count, but his approach allows him to avoid striking out— expect his major-league strikeout rate to decline from over 20 percent to somewhere near his Double-A rate of 14.9.

### Telvin Nash — LF

Born: 2/20/1991 Age: 21
Bats: R Throws: R Height: 6' 2" Weight: 230
Breakout: 1% Improve: 12% Collapse: 2%
Attrition: 11% MLB: 24%

Comparables:
Greg Luzinski, Osvaldo Morales, Chris Parmelee

| YEAR | TEAM | LVL | AGE | PA | R | 2B | 3B | HR | RBI | BB | SO | SB | CS | AVG_OBP_SLG | TAv | BABIP | BRR | FRAA | WARP |
|------|------|-----|-----|----|---|----|----|----|-----|----|----|----|----|-------------|-----|-------|-----|------|------|
| 2009 | AST | RK | 18 | 157 | 15 | 10 | 1 | 1 | 20 | 12 | 45 | 1 | 2 | .218/.284/.324 | .220 | .312 | 0.9 | -1.6 | -0.8 |
| 2010 | GRV | RK | 19 | 227 | 30 | 12 | 1 | 12 | 39 | 25 | 64 | 1 | 1 | .265/.350/.515 | .302 | .331 | 1.6 | -6.2 | 0.9 |
| 2011 | LEX | A | 20 | 316 | 41 | 16 | 0 | 14 | 37 | 40 | 103 | 2 | 0 | .269/.373/.485 | .291 | .379 | -1.6 | -0.2 | 1.5 |
| 2012 | HOU | MLB | 21 | 250 | 24 | 8 | 0 | 8 | 25 | 20 | 90 | 0 | 0 | .196/.263/.345 | .218 | .275 | 0 | LF -8, 1B -2 | -1.3 |

Nash played high school ball with Tim Beckham, but scouts would have come to see his raw power anyway. He's the son of former pro football player Ray Nash, but chose baseball over football. While Michael Bourn is his mentor, his game is the opposite of Bourn's. Positionally, he'll end up stuck at first base eventually, though the Astros have tried him in the outfield in deference to Jonathan Singleton. Nash showed off his good power and patience in his full-season debut, and he can be expected to lay waste to the California League and get promoted to Double-A sometime in 2012. His current struggles at reacting to breaking pitches would likely prevent him from succeeding there, but he's making progress and every slight improvement in his approach will mean that much more of his power will show up in game situations.

### Ariel Ovando — RF

Born: 9/15/1993 Age: 18
Bats: L Throws: L Height: 6' 5" Weight: 190
Breakout: 1% Improve: 1% Collapse: 0%
Attrition: 1% MLB: 1%

Comparables:
Yorman Rodriguez, Alexander Diaz, Robert Rodriguez

| YEAR | TEAM | LVL | AGE | PA | R | 2B | 3B | HR | RBI | BB | SO | SB | CS | AVG_OBP_SLG | TAv | BABIP | BRR | FRAA | WARP |
|------|------|-----|-----|----|---|----|----|----|-----|----|----|----|----|-------------|-----|-------|-----|------|------|
| 2011 | GRV | RK | 17 | 184 | 16 | 10 | 3 | 2 | 30 | 12 | 51 | 0 | 0 | .235/.283/.365 | .237 | .319 | -1.1 | -4.5 | -0.5 |
| 2012 | HOU | MLB | 18 | 250 | 18 | 8 | 1 | 2 | 16 | 12 | 83 | 0 | 0 | .173/.214/.236 | .163 | .254 | 0 | RF -10 | -3.7 |

While "has all the tools" certainly applies to Ovando, the one that makes him special is the power. Huge for a teenager, he's expected to slow down and his defensive contributions will be limited mostly to his arm. For readers not used to looking at stat lines from 17-year-olds in U.S. professional leagues, the extra-base hits, strikeouts, and walks are all positives from Ovando's 2011 line, despite appearances, as most players his age have another year of high school to go.

### Jimmy Paredes — 3B

Born: 11/25/1988 Age: 23
Bats: B Throws: R Height: 6' 2" Weight: 200
Breakout: 8% Improve: 23% Collapse: 3%
Attrition: 8% MLB: 53%

Comparables:
Dave Hansen, Dave Roberts, Carlos Martinez

| YEAR | TEAM | LVL | AGE | PA | R | 2B | 3B | HR | RBI | BB | SO | SB | CS | AVG_OBP_SLG | TAv | BABIP | BRR | FRAA | WARP |
|------|------|-----|-----|----|---|----|----|----|-----|----|----|----|----|-------------|-----|-------|-----|------|------|
| 2009 | STA | A- | 20 | 221 | 36 | 8 | 4 | 2 | 17 | 10 | 30 | 23 | 9 | .302/.339/.410 | .291 | .345 | 1.9 | 4.5 | 2.0 |
| 2010 | CSC | A | 21 | 434 | 59 | 24 | 6 | 5 | 48 | 18 | 82 | 36 | 10 | .282/.312/.408 | .284 | .339 | 5.2 | -3.6 | 2.5 |
| 2010 | LEX | A | 21 | 154 | 24 | 10 | 1 | 3 | 17 | 7 | 25 | 14 | 1 | .299/.331/.442 | .280 | .345 | 3.7 | 2.5 | 1.3 |
| 2011 | CCH | AA | 22 | 407 | 69 | 22 | 4 | 10 | 41 | 15 | 84 | 29 | 12 | .270/.300/.426 | .250 | .322 | 6.2 | -1.4 | 0.9 |
| 2011 | HOU | MLB | 22 | 179 | 16 | 8 | 2 | 2 | 18 | 9 | 47 | 5 | 4 | .286/.320/.393 | .257 | .383 | 0.6 | -2.7 | 0.4 |
| 2012 | HOU | MLB | 23 | 250 | 25 | 11 | 2 | 3 | 25 | 7 | 60 | 16 | 6 | .246/.269/.351 | .220 | .309 | -0.4 | 3B -0, 2B -0 | -0.2 |

Paredes entered 2011 as a more highly regarded prospect than Jose Altuve at the same position. But with Altuve's Tour De Force and Chris Johnson's struggles, Paredes was moved to third base. He made a rash of errors initially at the new position (in Double-A), but mastered it well enough that the team thought his career would be best enhanced by exposure to the major leagues. Miraculously—one such miracle being a .383 BABIP—he held his own in Houston after posting just a .300 OBP in Corpus Christi. He's still very young, and has time to take the expected retrenchment before figuring everything out and taking strides toward becoming a decent third baseman. While stardom is far from expected, his great tools hint at some upside, and he could turn those strides forward into a running start if he remains healthy and coachable.

**Humberto Quintero** C

Born: 8/2/1979 Age: 32
Bats: R Throws: R Height: 5' 10" Weight: 215
Breakout: 4% Improve: 24% Collapse: 15%
Attrition: 57% MLB: 76%

| YEAR | TEAM | LVL | AGE | PA | R | 2B | 3B | HR | RBI | BB | SO | SB | CS | AVG_OBP_SLG | TAv | BABIP | BRR | FRAA | WARP |
|------|------|-----|-----|-----|----|----|----|----|-----|----|----|----|----|-------------|-----|-------|------|------|------|
| 2009 | HOU | MLB | 29 | 168 | 11 | 8 | 1 | 4 | 14 | 7 | 41 | 0 | 0 | .236/.286/.376 | .214 | .295 | -0.3 | 1 | -0.1 |
| 2010 | HOU | MLB | 30 | 276 | 13 | 10 | 0 | 4 | 20 | 8 | 59 | 0 | 0 | .234/.262/.317 | .202 | .287 | -0.7 | 1.3 | 0.0 |
| 2011 | HOU | MLB | 31 | 272 | 22 | 12 | 1 | 2 | 25 | 6 | 53 | 1 | 0 | .240/.258/.317 | .207 | .292 | 0.1 | 0.1 | -0.4 |

**Angel Sanchez** SS

Born: 9/20/1983 Age: 28
Bats: R Throws: R Height: 6' 3" Weight: 185
Breakout: 3% Improve: 24% Collapse: 11%
Attrition: 23% MLB: 76%

Comparables:
Chris De La Cruz, Tony Fernandez, Edgar Renteria

| YEAR | TEAM | LVL | AGE | PA | R | 2B | 3B | HR | RBI | BB | SO | SB | CS | AVG_OBP_SLG | TAv | BABIP | BRR | FRAA | WARP |
|------|------|-----|-----|-----|----|----|----|----|-----|----|----|----|----|-------------|-----|-------|------|------|------|
| 2009 | LVG | AAA | 25 | 506 | 67 | 29 | 4 | 6 | 60 | 39 | 67 | 1 | 2 | .305/.359/.428 | .268 | .339 | -0.3 | 11.3 | 3.4 |
| 2010 | PAW | AAA | 26 | 252 | 26 | 10 | 1 | 0 | 17 | 24 | 30 | 6 | 1 | .274/.347/.327 | .245 | .313 | 1.3 | -7.6 | 0.0 |
| 2010 | HOU | MLB | 26 | 269 | 30 | 9 | 4 | 0 | 25 | 11 | 45 | 0 | 1 | .280/.316/.348 | .229 | .341 | 0.7 | -8.1 | -0.6 |
| 2011 | HOU | MLB | 27 | 328 | 35 | 10 | 0 | 1 | 28 | 27 | 44 | 3 | 0 | .240/.305/.285 | .218 | .278 | 1.2 | 1.4 | 0.1 |
| 2012 | HOU | MLB | 28 | 327 | 34 | 14 | 2 | 2 | 27 | 23 | 51 | 2 | 1 | .258/.315/.339 | .235 | .298 | 0 | SS -2, 2B 1 | 0.6 |

Sanchez still hits like a backup shortstop, but at least the Astros received the benefit of the slick fielding he'd always shown prior to 2010. He didn't appear hurt in 2010, but wasn't getting to balls he was expected to get. In 2011, he showed many more of the athletic moves that got him to the majors in the first place. Nothing in his pedigree suggests he'll escape the "use only in case of emergency" label, but as long as he can keep his on-base percentage around .300 and bunt on demand, his glove should allow him to accrue service time for another couple of years.

**Domingo Santana** RF

Born: 8/5/1992 Age: 19
Bats: R Throws: R Height: 6' 6" Weight: 200
Breakout: 0% Improve: 2% Collapse: 0%
Attrition: 5% MLB: 8%

Comparables:
Travis Snider, Chris Parmelee, Michael Burgess

| YEAR | TEAM | LVL | AGE | PA | R | 2B | 3B | HR | RBI | BB | SO | SB | CS | AVG_OBP_SLG | TAv | BABIP | BRR | FRAA | WARP |
|------|------|-----|-----|-----|----|----|----|----|-----|----|-----|----|----|-------------|-----|-------|------|------|------|
| 2009 | PHL | RK | 16 | 139 | 17 | 6 | 1 | 6 | 28 | 15 | 44 | 3 | 1 | .288/.391/.508 | .313 | .412 | 0.5 | 2.6 | 1.1 |
| 2010 | LWD | A | 17 | 202 | 27 | 10 | 0 | 3 | 16 | 29 | 76 | 5 | 6 | .182/.325/.297 | .254 | .314 | -1.4 | -1.5 | -0.2 |
| 2010 | WPT | A- | 17 | 214 | 28 | 9 | 0 | 5 | 20 | 23 | 73 | 4 | 4 | .237/.336/.366 | .253 | .361 | -2.7 | 6.2 | 0.5 |
| 2011 | LEX | A | 18 | 76 | 13 | 4 | 0 | 5 | 21 | 6 | 15 | 1 | 0 | .382/.447/.662 | .371 | .438 | -1.1 | -1.8 | 0.8 |
| 2011 | LWD | A | 18 | 391 | 45 | 29 | 4 | 7 | 32 | 26 | 120 | 4 | 1 | .269/.345/.434 | .291 | .390 | -3 | -2.7 | 1.4 |
| 2012 | HOU | MLB | 19 | 250 | 22 | 9 | 1 | 5 | 20 | 15 | 93 | 1 | 0 | .193/.258/.304 | .206 | .296 | -0.1 | RF -5, LF -0 | -1.8 |

The Phillies really REALLY wanted Hunter Pence. That's why they were willing to include a guy who can pound the ball—teen sensation Santana—in the deal. A precocious 6-foot-5 at age 16 in 2009, when the Phillies signed him out of the Dominican Republic, Santana was showing some of his power at Lakewood before the trade. After the trade, he went nuts, and, perhaps most significantly, struck out less than 20 percent of the time while he was with Lexington. As with Nash, Santana's power makes for an enormous upside, limited only by his ability to make contact.

**Jordan Schafer** CF

Born: 9/4/1986 Age: 25
Bats: L Throws: L Height: 6' 2" Weight: 200
Breakout: 4% Improve: 29% Collapse: 7%
Attrition: 36% MLB: 73%

**Comparables:**
Javon Moran, Jim Eisenreich, Jerry Mumphrey

| YEAR | TEAM | LVL | AGE | PA | R | 2B | 3B | HR | RBI | BB | SO | SB | CS | AVG_OBP_SLG | TAv | BABIP | BRR | FRAA | WARP |
|------|------|-----|-----|-----|----|----|----|----|-----|----|----|----|----|-------------|------|-------|------|-----------|------|
| 2009 | ATL | MLB | 22 | 195 | 18 | 8 | 0 | 2 | 8 | 27 | 63 | 2 | 1 | .204/.313/.287 | .216 | .311 | 0.9 | 1.8 | -0.1 |
| 2010 | MIS | AA | 23 | 72 | 7 | 3 | 0 | 0 | 5 | 8 | 12 | 1 | 1 | .175/.268/.222 | .223 | .216 | 0.1 | 0 | 0.1 |
| 2010 | GWN | AAA | 23 | 209 | 16 | 5 | 1 | 1 | 8 | 14 | 47 | 9 | 8 | .201/.250/.254 | .192 | .253 | -2.3 | 4.7 | -0.7 |
| 2011 | GWN | AAA | 24 | 186 | 21 | 8 | 0 | 1 | 21 | 14 | 28 | 6 | 3 | .256/.309/.323 | .234 | .297 | 0 | 2.9 | 0.3 |
| 2011 | ATL | MLB | 24 | 219 | 32 | 6 | 3 | 1 | 7 | 18 | 42 | 15 | 4 | .240/.307/.316 | .237 | .301 | 1.4 | 0.2 | 0.2 |
| 2011 | HOU | MLB | 24 | 118 | 14 | 4 | 0 | 1 | 6 | 10 | 28 | 7 | 0 | .245/.314/.311 | .232 | .321 | 2.2 | 0.5 | 0.2 |
| 2012 | HOU | MLB | 25 | 316 | 32 | 12 | 1 | 3 | 25 | 28 | 74 | 16 | 7 | .237/.307/.320 | .227 | .303 | -0.7 | CF -1, LF -0 | -0.2 |

Time was, the mention of Schafer's name conjured up comparisons to players like Grady Sizemore. Posting a .300 TAv at Double-A at age 20 with a superior defensive reputation will lead to talk of this sort. Alas, while that was just 2008, it may well have been a lifetime ago. Schafer has lost weight since his HGH suspension in 2008, and posted an anemic .233 TAv at Triple-A Gwinnett and .237 in Atlanta before coming to the Astros in the Michael Bourn deal. Perhaps a result of being lighter on his feet, his defensive metrics have improved and now are in concurrence with his reputation. He also went 22-4 on stolen base attempts between Atlanta and Houston, making 2011 by far his most productive baserunning season. The natural talent is still there, and he's just 25, so he can't be counted out yet. But it's a long way to adequacy at the plate from where he's at, even as a slick-fielding center fielder.

**J.B. Shuck** LF

Born: 6/18/1987 Age: 25
Bats: L Throws: L Height: 6' 0" Weight: 195
Breakout: 1% Improve: 36% Collapse: 4%
Attrition: 21% MLB: 78%

**Comparables:**
Roy White, Shannon Stewart, Chris Stynes

| YEAR | TEAM | LVL | AGE | PA | R | 2B | 3B | HR | RBI | BB | SO | SB | CS | AVG_OBP_SLG | TAv | BABIP | BRR | FRAA | WARP |
|------|------|-----|-----|-----|----|----|----|----|-----|----|----|----|----|-------------|------|-------|------|-----------|------|
| 2009 | LNC | A+ | 22 | 628 | 98 | 30 | 11 | 1 | 36 | 64 | 55 | 18 | 9 | .315/.387/.414 | .289 | .345 | 3.2 | -7.2 | 2.7 |
| 2010 | CCH | AA | 23 | 435 | 52 | 14 | 2 | 2 | 28 | 46 | 56 | 9 | 9 | .298/.372/.360 | .277 | .344 | -1.6 | -9 | 0.9 |
| 2010 | ROU | AAA | 23 | 156 | 15 | 2 | 2 | 0 | 7 | 16 | 15 | 7 | 3 | .273/.346/.317 | .259 | .304 | -2.2 | -7.7 | -0.4 |
| 2011 | OKL | AAA | 24 | 419 | 60 | 11 | 7 | 0 | 30 | 56 | 30 | 20 | 11 | .297/.398/.367 | .275 | .323 | 4.4 | -2.4 | 1.9 |
| 2011 | HOU | MLB | 24 | 92 | 9 | 2 | 1 | 0 | 3 | 11 | 7 | 2 | 0 | .272/.359/.321 | .249 | .297 | -0.2 | 0.6 | 0.2 |
| 2012 | HOU | MLB | 25 | 250 | 27 | 9 | 2 | 1 | 20 | 23 | 31 | 6 | 3 | .270/.338/.339 | .248 | .308 | -0.6 | LF -5, CF -6 | 0.5 |

"The thing that will keep him on a major league bench as opposed to the starting lineup is a complete, total, absolute lack of power." —*Baseball Prospectus 2008* on Brett Gardner. Unfortunately for Shuck, even if his hitting matures as Gardner's has, he lacks the raw footspeed of the Yankees left fielder, which not only reduces his impact offensively, but limits him to the corner outfield positions except as a backup. He does have a decent arm, and shares the gritty, determined, stay-within-himself approach and—most importantly—the patience to draw walks, that have helped Gardner reach his potential. He also put in concerted effort this year on cutting down his swing to make better contact, and the result was a significant reduction in his strikeout rate that is likely to be repeated.

**Jonathan Singleton** 1B

Born: 9/18/1991 Age: 20
Bats: L Throws: L Height: 6' 3" Weight: 215
Breakout: 3% Improve: 12% Collapse: 4%
Attrition: 11% MLB: 25%

**Comparables:**
Anthony Rizzo, Logan Morrison, Ryan Westmoreland

| YEAR | TEAM | LVL | AGE | PA | R | 2B | 3B | HR | RBI | BB | SO | SB | CS | AVG_OBP_SLG | TAv | BABIP | BRR | FRAA | WARP |
|------|------|-----|-----|-----|----|----|----|----|-----|----|----|----|----|-------------|------|-------|------|-----------|------|
| 2009 | PHL | RK | 17 | 119 | 12 | 9 | 0 | 2 | 12 | 18 | 13 | 1 | 0 | .290/.398/.440 | .310 | .318 | -1.2 | 1.7 | 0.7 |
| 2010 | LWD | A | 18 | 450 | 64 | 25 | 2 | 14 | 77 | 62 | 74 | 9 | 7 | .290/.399/.479 | .323 | .330 | -1.4 | 6.2 | 4.0 |
| 2011 | CLR | A+ | 19 | 382 | 48 | 14 | 0 | 9 | 47 | 56 | 83 | 3 | 3 | .284/.387/.412 | .281 | .352 | -2 | 1.5 | 1.4 |
| 2011 | LNC | A+ | 19 | 148 | 20 | 9 | 1 | 4 | 16 | 14 | 40 | 0 | 0 | .333/.405/.512 | .314 | .448 | 0.8 | 0.6 | 1.2 |
| 2012 | HOU | MLB | 20 | 250 | 27 | 10 | 0 | 6 | 24 | 25 | 63 | 2 | 1 | .233/.312/.367 | .245 | .293 | -0.3 | 1B -8, LF -0 | -0.1 |

It could be said that Brett Wallace got shafted when the Astros traded for the hulking Singleton—not to be confused with Hollywood's John Singleton—from the Phillies, but it was poetic justice, as Wallace wasn't producing. The trade was the best thing to happen to Singleton, as his attempts to transition to the outfield weren't going well and he'd sometimes bring his defensive struggles to the plate. With great patience and a classic lefty power stroke, he has the potential to blast through the high minors and become the next Astros first baseman after Carlos Lee (whenever he departs). It could be said that he's too fast and too furious to let anyone stand in his way.

### Craig Tatum — C

Born: 3/18/1983 Age: **29**
Bats: **R** Throws: **R** Height: **6' 2"** Weight: **225**
Breakout: **1%** Improve: **26%** Collapse: **11%**
Attrition: **43%** MLB: **67%**

**Comparables:**
Scooter Tucker, Johnny Bucha, Dutch Dotterer

| YEAR | TEAM | LVL | AGE | PA | R | 2B | 3B | HR | RBI | BB | SO | SB | CS | AVG_OBP_SLG | TAv | BABIP | BRR | FRAA | WARP |
|------|------|-----|-----|-----|----|----|----|----|-----|----|----|----|----|---------------|------|-------|------|----------|------|
| 2009 | LOU | AAA | 26 | 233 | 22 | 12 | 0 | 3 | 21 | 17 | 55 | 0 | 0 | .239/.302/.338 | .232 | .310 | 1.2 | 1.1 | 0.3 |
| 2009 | CIN | MLB | 26 | 77 | 3 | 1 | 0 | 1 | 6 | 7 | 10 | 0 | 0 | .162/.250/.221 | .198 | .175 | 0.3 | 0.5 | -0.1 |
| 2010 | BAL | MLB | 27 | 126 | 11 | 4 | 0 | 0 | 9 | 12 | 21 | 1 | 0 | .281/.349/.316 | .231 | .344 | -1.3 | 1.3 | 0.0 |
| 2011 | NOR | AAA | 28 | 77 | 4 | 3 | 0 | 0 | 7 | 9 | 13 | 0 | 1 | .200/.289/.246 | .233 | .241 | 0.1 | 0.2 | 0.1 |
| 2011 | BAL | MLB | 28 | 96 | 7 | 3 | 0 | 0 | 7 | 6 | 21 | 1 | 0 | .195/.245/.230 | .167 | .254 | 1.7 | 0 | -0.3 |
| 2012 | HOU | MLB | 29 | 250 | 25 | 10 | 1 | 3 | 20 | 21 | 51 | 1 | 1 | .232/.299/.317 | .226 | .283 | -0.1 | C 1, 1B -0 | 0.5 |

Tatum assumed the backup catcher role in Baltimore in May after Jake Fox got off to a slow start, but with Matt Wieters healthy and averaging one day off per week, he only managed 27 starts. It's a good thing, too, because it's questionable whether Tatum even has a future as a backup catcher, much less as a guy who should be drawing multiple weekly starts. He has no bat whatsoever: no power, no speed, limited patience. The least a no-bat catcher can do is play solid defense, and Tatum did manage to catch attempted basestealers at a league average clip this year, but that was a small sample. They were successful on 93 per-

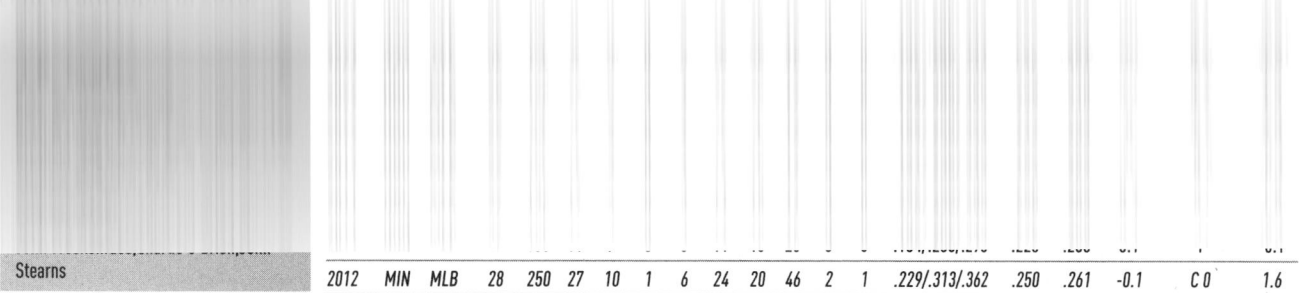

| | Stearns | | | | | | | | | | | | | | | | | | |
|---|---|---|---|---|---|---|---|---|---|---|---|---|---|---|---|---|---|---|---|
| 2012 | MIN | MLB | 28 | 250 | 27 | 10 | 1 | 6 | 24 | 20 | 46 | 2 | 1 | .229/.313/.362 | .250 | .261 | -0.1 | C 0 | 1.6 |

Any time now, the Astros could throw in the Towles in a trade. He'd decimated his prospect stock before the 2011 season, but the Castro injury gave him a golden second opportunity to prove that all those .300 TAv seasons he had in the minors weren't flukes. Instead, after a strong April that just started to whet the appetites of catching-starved Astros fans, the only .300 he was chasing was OPS, as he posted a .352 from May 6 until he was demoted on July 6 (102 plate appearances). While the holes in his swing account for some of his ineptitude, he also loses confidence in the majors and aids in his own demise. When he's aggressive and confident, he shows plenty of offensive skill that can combine with his average defense to produce a decent backup catcher. But with as many chances as Houston has given him, it may require a change of scenery for that to happen.

### Jonathan Villar — SS

Born: 5/2/1991 Age: **21**
Bats: **B** Throws: **R** Height: **6' 2"** Weight: **195**
Breakout: **1%** Improve: **18%** Collapse: **3%**
Attrition: **17%** MLB: **37%**

**Comparables:**
Jack Heidemann, Wil Cordero, Brent Brewer

| YEAR | TEAM | LVL | AGE | PA | R | 2B | 3B | HR | RBI | BB | SO | SB | CS | AVG_OBP_SLG | TAv | BABIP | BRR | FRAA | WARP |
|------|------|-----|-----|-----|----|----|----|----|-----|----|----|----|----|---------------|------|-------|------|--------|------|
| 2009 | PHL | RK | 18 | 111 | 14 | 7 | 1 | 0 | 14 | 13 | 24 | 11 | 2 | .277/.367/.372 | .261 | .366 | 0.6 | -2.1 | 0.1 |
| 2010 | LWD | A | 19 | 420 | 61 | 18 | 4 | 2 | 36 | 26 | 103 | 38 | 13 | .272/.323/.358 | .257 | .355 | 6.1 | 0 | 2.3 |
| 2010 | LNC | A+ | 19 | 143 | 18 | 6 | 2 | 3 | 19 | 12 | 50 | 7 | 2 | .225/.296/.372 | .224 | .342 | 0.1 | -1.6 | -0.2 |
| 2011 | LNC | A+ | 20 | 207 | 26 | 7 | 4 | 4 | 26 | 25 | 56 | 20 | 6 | .259/.353/.414 | .264 | .350 | -2.1 | -3.5 | 0.3 |
| 2011 | CCH | AA | 20 | 367 | 52 | 16 | 2 | 10 | 26 | 29 | 100 | 14 | 6 | .231/.301/.386 | .250 | .301 | 4.6 | -2.9 | 1.2 |
| 2012 | HOU | MLB | 21 | 250 | 22 | 9 | 1 | 3 | 20 | 15 | 79 | 13 | 4 | .207/.258/.302 | .202 | .290 | -0.1 | SS -2 | -0.9 |

Older than only Mike Trout among Texas League regulars in 2011, Villar made progress in three of the four areas where the Astros were hoping to see improvement: He cut his errors by 20 (that's the glass-half-full way of noting that he made 36 errors in 128 games at the expense of some range), he added walks, and he improved his power. That he's still striking out a lot makes him profile more like Jose Valentin than a top-flight shortstop, though his youth and tools make his upside sky high.

### Brett Wallace — 1B

Born: 8/26/1986 Age: **25**
Bats: **L** Throws: **R** Height: **6' 3"** Weight: **205**
Breakout: **6%** Improve: **31%** Collapse: **2%**
Attrition: **20%** MLB: **61%**

**Comparables:**
Bill White, Randy Bush, John Milner

| YEAR | TEAM | LVL | AGE | PA | R | 2B | 3B | HR | RBI | BB | SO | SB | CS | AVG_OBP_SLG | TAv | BABIP | BRR | FRAA | WARP |
|------|------|-----|-----|-----|----|----|----|----|-----|----|----|----|----|---------------|------|-------|------|------------|------|
| 2009 | SFD | AA | 22 | 154 | 22 | 5 | 0 | 5 | 16 | 18 | 34 | 0 | 0 | .281/.403/.438 | .273 | .348 | -1.9 | -0.2 | 0.4 |
| 2009 | MEM | AAA | 22 | 243 | 22 | 11 | 0 | 6 | 19 | 15 | 42 | 0 | 1 | .293/.349/.423 | .267 | .339 | -1.2 | 1 | 0.7 |
| 2009 | SAC | AAA | 22 | 203 | 32 | 10 | 0 | 9 | 28 | 14 | 40 | 1 | 1 | .302/.368/.505 | .302 | .346 | -0.6 | -5.2 | 0.9 |
| 2010 | LVG | AAA | 23 | 423 | 64 | 24 | 1 | 18 | 61 | 27 | 83 | 1 | 1 | .301/.361/.509 | .265 | .345 | -0.2 | -0.9 | 0.4 |
| 2010 | HOU | MLB | 23 | 159 | 14 | 6 | 1 | 2 | 13 | 8 | 50 | 0 | 0 | .222/.296/.319 | .236 | .326 | 0.2 | 1.7 | 0.3 |
| 2011 | OKL | AAA | 24 | 126 | 16 | 10 | 0 | 1 | 24 | 15 | 28 | 1 | 0 | .356/.437/.481 | .322 | .456 | -0.1 | 0.6 | 1.0 |
| 2011 | HOU | MLB | 24 | 378 | 37 | 22 | 0 | 5 | 29 | 36 | 91 | 1 | 0 | .259/.334/.369 | .249 | .339 | -3.9 | 7.8 | 0.2 |
| 2012 | HOU | MLB | 25 | 380 | 43 | 18 | 1 | 9 | 40 | 28 | 94 | 1 | 0 | .251/.319/.390 | .255 | .317 | -0.1 | 1B -2, 3B -1 | 0.5 |

Wallace hit .356/.437/.481 for Triple-A Oklahoma City in 2011, showing the sweet line-drive swing that's had him on prospect radars since high school. Unfortunately for Wallace, the naysayers were right all along, and he's firmly entrenched at first base defensively (i.e. no longer a third baseman), and was only playing for Oklahoma City because he failed to hold the major-league job despite the team's humble expectations for the 2011 season. The Astros still want him to claim first base, but with J.D. Martinez setting up camp in left field and Carlos Lee shifted to first, Wallace is going to have to have a white-hot spring training—akin to the .388/.458/.529 he hit in April—to avoid padding his Quadruple-A résumé at the start of the 2012 season.

**Chris Wallace** C

Born: **4/27/1988** Age: **24**
Bats: **R** Throws: **R** Height: **6' 1"** Weight: **205**
Breakout: **4%** Improve: **9%** Collapse: **2%**
Attrition: **32%** MLB: **57%**

**Comparables:**
Tom Nieto, Matt Spring, Raul Casanova

| YEAR | TEAM | LVL | AGE | PA | R | 2B | 3B | HR | RBI | BB | SO | SB | CS | AVG_OBP_SLG | TAv | BABIP | BRR | FRAA | WARP |
|---|---|---|---|---|---|---|---|---|---|---|---|---|---|---|---|---|---|---|---|
| 2010 | TCV | A- | 22 | 78 | 10 | 2 | 0 | 2 | 8 | 7 | 12 | 1 | 0 | .250/.321/.368 | .283 | .268 | 0 | 0.5 | 1.0 |
| 2010 | GRV | RK | 22 | 195 | 29 | 6 | 3 | 8 | 32 | 17 | 44 | 3 | 2 | .310/.392/.520 | .319 | .378 | -0.7 | -0.6 | 1.7 |
| 2011 | LEX | A | 23 | 275 | 37 | 16 | 3 | 14 | 49 | 17 | 52 | 0 | 3 | .285/.356/.550 | .313 | .306 | -2.3 | 0.3 | 2.1 |
| 2011 | CCH | AA | 23 | 136 | 17 | 4 | 0 | 6 | 29 | 12 | 41 | 1 | 0 | .244/.316/.423 | .252 | .316 | -1 | -0.6 | 0.2 |
| 2012 | HOU | MLB | 24 | 250 | 26 | 9 | 1 | 8 | 27 | 13 | 70 | 0 | 0 | .219/.270/.375 | .229 | .272 | 0 | C -1 | 0.1 |

Until 2011, the most newsworthy thing about Wallace was getting hit by a Barret Loux 95-mph fastball in 2009 while a junior at the University of Houston. The beaning caused an injury that now necessitates Wallace to play with four metal plates in his head. He returned for his senior year in 2010 and fell to the 16th round of the draft in part because of his gargantuan strikeout total (57 strikeouts in 179 AB his senior year). Wallace took on that weakness head-on and worked to improve his two-strike approach. The results of his adjustments were an OPS that would have been fourth in the SAL if he'd qualified and a very tolerable sub-20 percent strikeout rate, though with the caveat that he was a 23-year-old in Low-A. That he was allowed to skip a level and make the difficult jump to Double-A shows the confidence the organization has in him. The strikeouts found him again there, but otherwise he held his own, ensuring that he'll be making headlines for his prospect status now, not just for a painful experience he had in college.

**Austin Wates** CF

Born: **9/2/1988** Age: **23**
Bats: **R** Throws: **R** Height: **6' 2"** Weight: **179**
Breakout: **8%** Improve: **20%** Collapse: **6%**
Attrition: **22%** MLB: **45%**

**Comparables:**
Daniel Robertson, Charlie Blackmon, Jacoby Ellsbury

| YEAR | TEAM | LVL | AGE | PA | R | 2B | 3B | HR | RBI | BB | SO | SB | CS | AVG_OBP_SLG | TAv | BABIP | BRR | FRAA | WARP |
|---|---|---|---|---|---|---|---|---|---|---|---|---|---|---|---|---|---|---|---|
| 2011 | LNC | A+ | 22 | 592 | 85 | 23 | 9 | 6 | 75 | 47 | 86 | 26 | 7 | .300/.366/.413 | .275 | .345 | 3.7 | -12 | 1.6 |
| 2012 | HOU | MLB | 23 | 250 | 24 | 10 | 2 | 1 | 20 | 13 | 48 | 6 | 2 | .235/.281/.310 | .216 | .286 | 0 | CF -5, LF -7 | -0.9 |

The optimist sees that Wates makes good contact with advanced pitch recognition, has good speed, and hit .300 in his full-season debut. The pessimist sees nothing in his swing or statistical past to suggest the power to play a corner outfield or first base. Oh, and .300 at Lancaster doesn't really count.

# PITCHERS

**Fernando Abad**

Born: **12/17/1985** Age: **26**
Bats: **L** Throws: **L** Height: **6' 3"** Weight: **205**
Breakout: **15%** Improve: **33%** Collapse: **11%**
Attrition: **11%** MLB: **96%**

**Comparables:**
Johnny Podres, Scott Olsen, Eric Milton

| YEAR | TEAM | LVL | AGE | W | L | SV | G | GS | IP | H | HR | BB | SO | EqBB9 | EqSO9 | GB% | BABIP | WHIP | ERA | FIP | FRA | WARP |
|---|---|---|---|---|---|---|---|---|---|---|---|---|---|---|---|---|---|---|---|---|---|---|
| 2009 | LNC | A+ | 23 | 4 | 6 | 6 | 41 | 0 | 82² | 78 | 8 | 8 | 79 | 0.9 | 8.6 | 37% | .311 | 1.04 | 4.14 | 3.58 | 4.25 | 1.3 |
| 2010 | CCH | AA | 24 | 4 | 3 | 0 | 14 | 4 | 39² | 33 | 2 | 6 | 24 | 1.4 | 7.5 | 42% | .383 | 1.36 | 2.49 | 3.23 | 3.96 | 0.5 |
| 2010 | HOU | MLB | 24 | 0 | 1 | 0 | 22 | 0 | 19 | 14 | 3 | 5 | 12 | 2.4 | 5.7 | 32% | .196 | 1.00 | 2.84 | 4.69 | 4.24 | 0.2 |
| 2011 | OKL | AAA | 25 | 2 | 3 | 0 | 29 | 0 | 30 | 32 | 4 | 6 | 31 | 1.8 | 9.3 | 33% | .337 | 1.27 | 4.80 | 4.00 | 4.50 | 0.4 |
| 2011 | HOU | MLB | 25 | 1 | 4 | 0 | 29 | 0 | 19² | 28 | 5 | 9 | 15 | 4.1 | 6.9 | 39% | .338 | 1.88 | 7.32 | 6.30 | 7.23 | -0.5 |
| 2012 | HOU | MLB | 26 | 1 | 1 | 0 | 27 | 1 | 31¹ | 33 | 4 | 9 | 21 | 2.7 | 6.1 | 38% | .313 | 1.35 | 4.91 | 4.39 | 5.34 | -0.1 |

Astros fans probably thought that seeing "Abad, pitcher" in the lineup was redundant, but Fernando actually isn't all that bad against left-handed batters despite the bulky ERA (.236/.263/.361 against southpaws in his career). He works batters with a low-90s fastball, and though it appears he's trying to locate at the bottom of the strike zone most of the time, he gets a lot of balls up and gives up more than his share of fly balls. Against major-league right-handed batters, he's yet to discover anything that works and they've teed off on him relentlessly. He was shut down for most of July with shoulder tendinitis, but his velocity was fine both before and after, with no further complications expected.

### Juan Abreu

Born: 4/8/1985 Age: 27
Bats: R Throws: R Height: 6' 1" Weight: 180
Breakout: 35% Improve: 63% Collapse: 24%
Attrition: 19% MLB: 88%

**Comparables:**
Matt Mantei, Jack Meyer, Kerry Wood

| YEAR | TEAM | LVL | AGE | W | L | SV | G | GS | IP | H | HR | BB | SO | EqBB9 | EqSO9 | GB% | BABIP | WHIP | ERA | FIP | FRA | WARP |
|------|------|-----|-----|---|---|----|---|----|-----|----|----|----|----|-------|-------|-----|-------|------|------|------|------|------|
| 2009 | WIL | A+ | 24 | 3 | 2 | 12 | 20 | 0 | 21¹ | 8 | 1 | 14 | 28 | 5.9 | 11.8 | 35% | .171 | 1.03 | 1.69 | 3.30 | 4.31 | 0.1 |
| 2009 | NWA | AA | 24 | 2 | 2 | 4 | 16 | 0 | 20¹ | 20 | 3 | 25 | 25 | 9.8 | 11.1 | 40% | .327 | 2.02 | 5.76 | 6.54 | 7.11 | -0.3 |
| 2010 | MIS | AA | 25 | 4 | 2 | 11 | 39 | 0 | 44² | 34 | 1 | 14 | 32 | 4.4 | 9.5 | 30% | .367 | 1.41 | 3.02 | 3.35 | 4.64 | 0.2 |
| 2011 | GWN | AAA | 26 | 4 | 2 | 1 | 41 | 0 | 48 | 34 | 5 | 27 | 68 | 5.1 | 12.8 | 32% | .274 | 1.27 | 2.25 | 3.57 | 5.12 | 0.3 |
| 2011 | HOU | MLB | 26 | 0 | 0 | 0 | 7 | 0 | 6² | 6 | 1 | 3 | 12 | 4.1 | 16.2 | 36% | .385 | 1.35 | 2.70 | 4.94 | 4.93 | 0.0 |
| 2012 | HOU | MLB | 27 | 1 | 0 | 0 | 17 | 0 | 21¹ | 18 | 2 | 13 | 22 | 5.4 | 9.2 | 36% | .306 | 1.44 | 4.62 | 4.19 | 5.02 | 0.0 |

Abreu was part of the booty received for Michael Bourn, and he may have been a hidden gem—refined by the Braves farm system after they plucked him in minor-league free agency, where the Royals had left him after the 2009 season. Seeing one Abreu delivery tells almost the entire story of his game. He puts maximum effort into every pitch and relies on natural movement to give batters fits. Considering that even with his smallish frame, he generates consistent 96-97-mph heat, most batters are probably hoping he tries his nascent curve on them. Abreu will never have good control, but if he can keep the walks around

relief pitcher. He tops 95 mph on occasion and keeps things simple with a tried-and-true fastball-slider combination. He will have to reduce his OBP allowed from .372 to keep getting chances, but his minor-league WHIPs have been good, and considering Carpenter hadn't pitched in a full-season league until 2009, there's much more room for growth than most relievers his age.

### Jarred Cosart

Born: 5/25/1990 Age: 22
Bats: R Throws: R Height: 6' 4" Weight: 180
Breakout: 22% Improve: 56% Collapse: 19%
Attrition: 11% MLB: 80%

**Comparables:**
Jhoulys Chacin, Ryan Tucker, Nelson Briles

| YEAR | TEAM | LVL | AGE | W | L | SV | G | GS | IP | H | HR | BB | SO | EqBB9 | EqSO9 | GB% | BABIP | WHIP | ERA | FIP | FRA | WARP |
|------|------|-----|-----|---|---|----|----|----|------|----|----|----|----|-------|-------|-----|-------|------|------|------|------|------|
| 2009 | PHL | RK | 19 | 2 | 2 | 0 | 7 | 5 | 24¹ | 11 | 0 | 4 | 20 | 2.6 | 9.3 | 45% | .216 | 0.78 | 2.22 | 2.30 | 4.05 | 0.7 |
| 2010 | LWD | A | 20 | 7 | 3 | 0 | 14 | 14 | 71¹ | 53 | 2 | 16 | 71 | 2.0 | 9.7 | 61% | .283 | 1.07 | 3.79 | 2.92 | 4.27 | 0.6 |
| 2011 | CLR | A+ | 21 | 5 | 2 | 0 | 20 | 19 | 108 | 96 | 7 | 39 | 77 | 3.6 | 6.6 | 51% | .294 | 1.31 | 3.92 | 4.09 | 4.73 | 1.0 |
| 2011 | CCH | AA | 21 | 1 | 2 | 0 | 7 | 7 | 36¹ | 33 | 4 | 13 | 22 | 3.2 | 5.4 | 58% | .250 | 1.27 | 4.71 | 4.67 | 5.78 | 0.0 |
| 2012 | HOU | MLB | 22 | 2 | 4 | 0 | 8 | 8 | 41¹ | 43 | 5 | 18 | 24 | 4.0 | 5.2 | 50% | .304 | 1.48 | 5.25 | 4.92 | 5.70 | -0.1 |

Few have expressed any concern over Cosart's future despite the low strikeout rate. For now, he's the girl with the curl, because when he's good, he's very, very good. The Astros expect the times when he's very, very bad to get straightened out in time, and look forward to a rotation led by Cosart and Lyles for many years to come. Of course, most future ace pitchers show much loftier strikeout rates, so it's important that stats begin to catch up with scouting reports for Cosart in 2012.

### Enerio Del Rosario

Born: 10/16/1985 Age: 26
Bats: R Throws: R Height: 6' 3" Weight: 165
Breakout: 27% Improve: 51% Collapse: 28%
Attrition: 15% MLB: 91%

**Comparables:**
Scott Munter, John Farrell, Scott Erickson

| YEAR | TEAM | LVL | AGE | W | L | SV | G | GS | IP | H | HR | BB | SO | EqBB9 | EqSO9 | GB% | BABIP | WHIP | ERA | FIP | FRA | WARP |
|------|------|-----|-----|---|---|----|----|----|-----|----|----|----|----|-------|-------|-----|-------|------|-------|------|------|------|
| 2010 | HOU | MLB | 24 | 0 | 0 | 0 | 2 | 0 | 1¹ | 4 | 0 | 0 | 1 | 0.0 | 6.8 | 71% | .571 | 3.00 | 20.25 | 3.86 | 5.82 | 0.0 |
| 2010 | CIN | MLB | 24 | 1 | 1 | 0 | 9 | 0 | 8² | 13 | 0 | 4 | 3 | 4.2 | 3.1 | 57% | .406 | 1.96 | 2.08 | 3.80 | 6.90 | -0.2 |
| 2011 | HOU | MLB | 25 | 0 | 0 | 3 | 0 | 54 | 0 | 53 | 59 | 3 | 31 | 31 | 5.3 | 5.3 | 62% | .315 | 1.70 | 4.58 | 4.48 | 5.91 | -0.7 |
| 2012 | HOU | MLB | 26 | 2 | 1 | 1 | 43 | 0 | 48 | 53 | 5 | 20 | 20 | 3.8 | 3.8 | 52% | .308 | 1.53 | 5.52 | 4.98 | 6.00 | -0.5 |

Del Rosario was touted in last year's book as being good for double-play situations. While he does indeed have a power sinker, he brings his knee up to his chin during his stretch delivery, so anyone he walks who's faster than Prince Fielder has a good chance of stealing second, removing the chance of the double play. He's always shown fantastic control in the minors, and in 2011 he only had 13 walks through June (35 1/3 innings), so it's assumed that the shoulder strain that caused him to spend most of August on the DL was the cause of his control problems the rest of the year.

**Sergio Escalona**
Born: 8/3/1984 Age: 27
Bats: L Throws: L Height: 6' 1'' Weight: 210
Breakout: 27% Improve: 60% Collapse: 25%
Attrition: 20% MLB: 85%
Comparables:
Terry Forster,Kurt Birkins,Mike Magnante

| YEAR | TEAM | LVL | AGE | W | L | SV | G | GS | IP | H | HR | BB | SO | EqBB9 | EqSO9 | GB% | BABIP | WHIP | ERA | FIP | FRA | WARP |
|------|------|-----|-----|---|---|----|----|----|----|---|----|----|----|-------|-------|-----|-------|------|-----|-----|-----|------|
| 2009 | REA | AA | 24 | 2 | 1 | 12 | 32 | 0 | 40² | 31 | 1 | 14 | 38 | 3.1 | 8.4 | 57% | .273 | 1.11 | 1.77 | 2.84 | 3.85 | 0.6 |
| 2009 | PHI | MLB | 24 | 1 | 0 | 0 | 14 | 0 | 13² | 12 | 0 | 5 | 10 | 3.3 | 6.6 | 38% | .286 | 1.24 | 4.61 | 3.35 | 3.82 | 0.2 |
| 2010 | REA | AA | 25 | 2 | 8 | 10 | 50 | 0 | 54¹ | 34 | 4 | 12 | 36 | 3.6 | 8.8 | 55% | .309 | 1.25 | 3.81 | 3.89 | 5.37 | 0.0 |
| 2011 | HOU | MLB | 26 | 2 | 1 | 0 | 49 | 0 | 27² | 24 | 3 | 11 | 25 | 3.6 | 8.1 | 53% | .292 | 1.27 | 2.93 | 4.01 | 5.33 | -0.1 |
| 2012 | HOU | MLB | 27 | 1 | 0 | 0 | 27 | 0 | 23¹ | 23 | 3 | 10 | 17 | 3.9 | 6.7 | 50% | .314 | 1.43 | 4.94 | 4.70 | 5.37 | -0.1 |

Only on the Astros can a player be placed on the 60-day DL with a sprained ankle suffered when tripping over a glove in the outfield. The move was in September, and thus freed up a 40-man roster spot, but it was a humiliating end to an impressive season by the Astros' newest LOOGY. Escalona rotates his body during his windup, which hides the ball from lefties and makes his sweeping curve difficult to pick up. This resulted in a 483 OPS for left-handed batters in Reading (Phillies Double-A) in 2010, followed by a 590 OPS for Houston in 2011. Escalona appeared in 49 games in order to log just 27 2/3 innings, and he allowed a .333/.415/.444 batting line to right-handed batters. Manager Brad Mills accepts his limitations and has used him wisely.

**J.A. Happ**
Born: 10/19/1982 Age: 29
Bats: L Throws: L Height: 6' 7'' Weight: 200
Breakout: 22% Improve: 49% Collapse: 28%
Attrition: 11% MLB: 86%
Comparables:
Chris Narveson,Jeff Calhoun,Windy McCall

| YEAR | TEAM | LVL | AGE | W | L | SV | G | GS | IP | H | HR | BB | SO | EqBB9 | EqSO9 | GB% | BABIP | WHIP | ERA | FIP | FRA | WARP |
|------|------|-----|-----|---|---|----|----|----|----|---|----|----|----|-------|-------|-----|-------|------|-----|-----|-----|------|
| 2009 | PHI | MLB | 26 | 12 | 4 | 0 | 35 | 23 | 166 | 149 | 20 | 56 | 119 | 3.0 | 6.5 | 40% | .270 | 1.23 | 2.93 | 4.29 | 4.33 | 1.9 |
| 2010 | PHI | MLB | 27 | 1 | 0 | 0 | 3 | 3 | 15¹ | 13 | 1 | 12 | 9 | 7.0 | 5.3 | 37% | .255 | 1.63 | 1.76 | 5.13 | 4.42 | 0.1 |
| 2010 | HOU | MLB | 27 | 5 | 4 | 0 | 13 | 13 | 72 | 60 | 7 | 35 | 61 | 4.4 | 7.6 | 41% | .270 | 1.32 | 3.75 | 4.18 | 4.77 | 0.4 |
| 2011 | HOU | MLB | 28 | 6 | 15 | 0 | 28 | 28 | 156¹ | 157 | 21 | 83 | 134 | 4.8 | 7.7 | 35% | .306 | 1.54 | 5.35 | 4.66 | 4.88 | 0.6 |
| 2012 | HOU | MLB | 29 | 5 | 11 | 0 | 24 | 24 | 128² | 123 | 16 | 55 | 94 | 3.9 | 6.5 | 38% | .298 | 1.38 | 4.67 | 4.64 | 5.07 | 0.4 |

J.A. Happ is the one who started it all. Sure, J.R. Towles had debuted before Happ arrived, but he didn't stick as a full-time player until the next season. The next thing you know, there's a J.D. And a J.B. Who knows where it will end . . . J.Z.? The bill finally came due on Happ's charmed life and his ERA caught and surpassed his FIP, which also soared like the numerous moonshots he allowed. Facing more pressure situations, Happ pressed. He threw more fastballs, and while he actually showed slightly beter velocity than he had in the past, that wasn't a good thing. For J.A., less is more, and his best successes come when he's using the J.M., as in Jamie Moyer, playbook.

**Lucas Harrell**
Born: 6/3/1985 Age: 27
Bats: B Throws: R Height: 6' 3'' Weight: 200
Breakout: 14% Improve: 40% Collapse: 31%
Attrition: 10% MLB: 90%
Comparables:
Ruddy Lugo,Dan Petry,Bubba Church

| YEAR | TEAM | LVL | AGE | W | L | SV | G | GS | IP | H | HR | BB | SO | EqBB9 | EqSO9 | GB% | BABIP | WHIP | ERA | FIP | FRA | WARP |
|------|------|-----|-----|---|---|----|----|----|----|---|----|----|----|-------|-------|-----|-------|------|-----|-----|-----|------|
| 2009 | BIR | AA | 24 | 8 | 3 | 0 | 14 | 14 | 80¹ | 78 | 4 | 32 | 51 | 3.6 | 5.7 | 60% | .303 | 1.37 | 3.25 | 3.75 | 4.68 | 0.3 |
| 2009 | CHR | AAA | 24 | 4 | 1 | 0 | 11 | 11 | 65² | 58 | 3 | 37 | 42 | 5.1 | 5.8 | 58% | .286 | 1.45 | 3.29 | 4.29 | 5.72 | -0.1 |
| 2010 | CHR | AAA | 25 | 10 | 9 | 0 | 26 | 26 | 137² | 90 | 7 | 37 | 59 | 4.0 | 5.5 | 51% | .288 | 1.47 | 4.58 | 4.23 | 5.40 | 0.5 |
| 2010 | CHA | MLB | 25 | 1 | 0 | 0 | 8 | 3 | 24 | 34 | 2 | 17 | 15 | 6.4 | 5.6 | 53% | .381 | 2.12 | 4.88 | 5.01 | 5.73 | 0.0 |
| 2011 | OKL | AAA | 26 | 5 | 2 | 0 | 9 | 9 | 52¹ | 42 | 0 | 24 | 38 | 4.1 | 6.5 | 55% | .275 | 1.26 | 1.72 | 3.77 | 3.95 | 1.1 |
| 2011 | CHR | AAA | 26 | 4 | 0 | 0 | 13 | 12 | 74¹ | 61 | 5 | 25 | 51 | 3.1 | 6.8 | 56% | .279 | 1.25 | 3.27 | 3.79 | 4.61 | 1.0 |
| 2011 | CHA | MLB | 26 | 0 | 0 | 0 | 3 | 0 | 5 | 11 | 0 | 1 | 5 | 1.8 | 9.0 | 60% | .550 | 2.40 | 7.20 | 1.66 | 2.68 | 0.2 |
| 2011 | HOU | MLB | 26 | 0 | 2 | 0 | 6 | 2 | 13 | 12 | 0 | 7 | 10 | 4.8 | 6.9 | 55% | .293 | 1.46 | 3.46 | 3.30 | 5.18 | 0.0 |
| 2012 | HOU | MLB | 27 | 2 | 4 | 0 | 9 | 9 | 49 | 50 | 5 | 22 | 28 | 4.0 | 5.1 | 54% | .309 | 1.46 | 4.85 | 4.73 | 5.27 | 0.0 |

Signed off waivers from the White Sox in July, Harrell will likely serve as a useful swingman. His fastball touches 92 mph and he has the ability to induce ground ball after ground ball. He doesn't gain enough effectiveness as a reliever to warrant a larger role at the end of games, nor would he be the worst fifth starter in baseball, given a chance.

**Dallas Keuchel**
Born: 1/1/1988 Age: 24
Bats: L Throws: L Height: 6' 4'' Weight: 200
Breakout: 18% Improve: 54% Collapse: 27%
Attrition: 6% MLB: 95%
Comparables:
Bobby Livingston,Matt Harrison,Paul Quantrill

| YEAR | TEAM | LVL | AGE | W | L | SV | G | GS | IP | H | HR | BB | SO | EqBB9 | EqSO9 | GB% | BABIP | WHIP | ERA | FIP | FRA | WARP |
|------|------|-----|-----|---|---|----|----|----|----|---|----|----|----|-------|-------|-----|-------|------|-----|-----|-----|------|
| 2009 | TCV | A- | 21 | 2 | 3 | 0 | 11 | 10 | 56² | 52 | 2 | 9 | 44 | 1.4 | 7.0 | 57% | .292 | 1.08 | 2.70 | 2.81 | 4.43 | 0.6 |
| 2010 | LNC | A+ | 22 | 5 | 8 | 0 | 19 | 18 | 120² | 118 | 8 | 21 | 82 | 1.9 | 7.2 | 63% | .330 | 1.28 | 3.36 | 3.87 | 5.13 | 0.7 |
| 2010 | CCH | AA | 22 | 2 | 6 | 0 | 9 | 9 | 53² | 49 | 2 | 8 | 30 | 1.8 | 6.0 | 50% | .336 | 1.30 | 4.69 | 3.20 | 4.41 | 0.5 |
| 2011 | CCH | AA | 23 | 9 | 7 | 0 | 20 | 20 | 127² | 116 | 9 | 27 | 76 | 1.9 | 5.4 | 59% | .274 | 1.12 | 3.17 | 3.84 | 4.80 | 0.9 |
| 2011 | OKL | AAA | 23 | 1 | 1 | 0 | 7 | 7 | 36 | 52 | 5 | 12 | 15 | 3.0 | 3.8 | 58% | .359 | 1.78 | 7.50 | 5.71 | 6.38 | -0.4 |
| 2012 | HOU | MLB | 24 | 2 | 4 | 0 | 9 | 9 | 54¹ | 60 | 6 | 16 | 24 | 2.7 | 4.0 | 54% | .309 | 1.40 | 5.01 | 4.64 | 5.45 | -0.1 |

Assistant general manager Bobby Heck said that seventh-rounder Keuchel might have been the steal of the 2009 draft for the Astros. Orel Hershiser praised Keuchel during the 2009 College World Series for his poise and maturity. Fast forward two years, and Keuchel made the Texas League All-Star Game despite his puny strikeout rate. The lack of strikeouts stems from substandard velocity, but Keuchel works his sinker all across the bottom of the zone, seemingly inducing ground balls on demand. While more advanced hitters will hit him much harder, he'll benefit more than most from the better fielding and umpiring at the higher levels. There's no expectation of stardom, but he should keep out-performing his peripherals.

### Wilton Lopez

Born: **7/19/1983** Age: **28**
Bats: **R** Throws: **R** Height: **6' 1''** Weight: **200**
Breakout: **14%** Improve: **51%** Collapse: **24%**
Attrition: **8%** MLB: **91%**

**Comparables:**
Moose Haas, La Marr Hoyt, Ralph Terry

| YEAR | TEAM | LVL | AGE | W | L | SV | G | GS | IP | H | HR | BB | SO | EqBB9 | EqSO9 | GB% | BABIP | WHIP | ERA | FIP | FRA | WARP |
|---|---|---|---|---|---|---|---|---|---|---|---|---|---|---|---|---|---|---|---|---|---|---|
| 2009 | CCH | AA | 25 | 4 | 5 | 0 | 29 | 15 | 110¹ | 133 | 8 | 13 | 69 | 1.1 | 5.6 | 56% | .333 | 1.32 | 4.73 | 3.31 | 3.94 | 1.6 |
| 2009 | HOU | MLB | 25 | 0 | 2 | 0 | 8 | 2 | 19¹ | 32 | 4 | 8 | 9 | 3.7 | 4.2 | 59% | .389 | 2.07 | 8.38 | 6.21 | 7.71 | -0.5 |
| 2010 | HOU | MLB | 26 | 5 | 2 | 1 | 68 | 0 | 67 | 66 | 4 | 5 | 50 | 0.7 | 6.7 | 56% | .308 | 1.06 | 2.96 | 2.61 | 3.93 | 0.7 |
| 2011 | HOU | MLB | 27 | 2 | 6 | 0 | 73 | 0 | 71 | 72 | 6 | 18 | 56 | 2.3 | 7.1 | 57% | .313 | 1.27 | 2.79 | 3.40 | 4.18 | 0.5 |
| *2012* | *HOU* | *MLB* | *28* | *3* | *1* | *1* | *62* | *0* | *61²* | *68* | *7* | *13* | *36* | *1.9* | *5.2* | *56%* | *.326* | *1.32* | *4.63* | *4.14* | *5.04* | *0.1* |

Despite having ulnar nerve irritation, 2009 waiver-find Lopez turned in another very good sea-

Attrition: **2%** MLB: **90%**

**Comparables:**
Marcos Carvajal, Dennys Reyes, Don Drysdale

| YEAR | TEAM | LVL | AGE | W | L | SV | G | GS | IP | H | HR | BB | SO | EqBB9 | EqSO9 | GB% | BABIP | WHIP | ERA | FIP | FRA | WARP |
|---|---|---|---|---|---|---|---|---|---|---|---|---|---|---|---|---|---|---|---|---|---|---|
| 2011 | OKL | AAA | 20 | 3 | 3 | 0 | 12 | 10 | 62¹ | 57 | 4 | 15 | 41 | 2.5 | 6.1 | 40% | .310 | 1.30 | 3.61 | 4.22 | 4.64 | 0.6 |
| 2011 | HOU | MLB | 20 | 2 | 8 | 0 | 20 | 15 | 94 | 107 | 14 | 26 | 67 | 2.5 | 6.4 | 44% | .314 | 1.41 | 5.36 | 4.49 | 5.26 | 0.0 |
| *2012* | *HOU* | *MLB* | *21* | *4* | *8* | *0* | *16* | *16* | *92¹* | *96* | *11* | *31* | *63* | *3.0* | *6.1* | *41%* | *.316* | *1.37* | *4.91* | *4.40* | *5.34* | *-0.1* |

For the 102nd time in history, a pitcher 20 years old or younger (seasonal age) threw 94 or more innings. Lest Lyles get compared to Christy Mathewson, Bob Feller, Bert Blyleven, and Doc Gooden, however, it should be noted that his fastball averages only about 90 mph, and the rest of his four-pitch repertoire wasn't fooling anyone. The demotion he endured was to keep his innings down—certainly nothing Walter Johnson or Don Drysdale ever heard—and he was used in relief upon his return. On the bright side, he's expected to remain in the rotation, and he'll be about the same age as many college draftees next summer.

### Brandon Lyon

Born: **8/10/1979** Age: **32**
Bats: **R** Throws: **R** Height: **6' 2''** Weight: **175**
Breakout: **10%** Improve: **39%** Collapse: **37%**
Attrition: **15%** MLB: **95%**

**Comparables:**
Geoff Geary, Burt Hooton, Jeff Shaw

| YEAR | TEAM | LVL | AGE | W | L | SV | G | GS | IP | H | HR | BB | SO | EqBB9 | EqSO9 | GB% | BABIP | WHIP | ERA | FIP | FRA | WARP |
|---|---|---|---|---|---|---|---|---|---|---|---|---|---|---|---|---|---|---|---|---|---|---|
| 2009 | DET | MLB | 29 | 6 | 5 | 3 | 65 | 0 | 78² | 56 | 7 | 31 | 57 | 3.5 | 6.5 | 49% | .231 | 1.11 | 2.86 | 4.11 | 5.75 | 0.1 |
| 2010 | HOU | MLB | 30 | 6 | 6 | 20 | 79 | 0 | 78 | 68 | 2 | 31 | 54 | 3.6 | 6.2 | 42% | .276 | 1.27 | 3.12 | 3.36 | 3.52 | 1.2 |
| 2011 | HOU | MLB | 31 | 3 | 3 | 4 | 15 | 0 | 13¹ | 27 | 4 | 5 | 6 | 3.4 | 4.1 | 47% | .411 | 2.40 | 11.48 | 7.12 | 7.45 | -0.3 |
| *2012* | *HOU* | *MLB* | *32* | *1* | *1* | *4* | *27* | *0* | *26* | *25* | *2* | *8* | *16* | *2.7* | *5.6* | *44%* | *.295* | *1.26* | *3.93* | *3.90* | *4.27* | *0.3* |

Whatever criticisms people may have of Lyon—mostly about how overpaid he is—it would be difficult to question his toughness, as he tried to pitch through a torn labrum and detached biceps tendon in 2011. Based on FIP, he's had two seasons where he's pitched like a back-end bullpen guy so far in his career. It seems far-fetched to assume 2012 will be the third time, as it usually takes time for a pitcher to get back into the groove after major surgery.

### Brett Myers

Born: **8/17/1980** Age: **31**
Bats: **R** Throws: **R** Height: **6' 5''** Weight: **215**
Breakout: **19%** Improve: **56%** Collapse: **28%**
Attrition: **8%** MLB: **82%**

**Comparables:**
Dan Giese, John Habyan, Erik Hanson

| YEAR | TEAM | LVL | AGE | W | L | SV | G | GS | IP | H | HR | BB | SO | EqBB9 | EqSO9 | GB% | BABIP | WHIP | ERA | FIP | FRA | WARP |
|---|---|---|---|---|---|---|---|---|---|---|---|---|---|---|---|---|---|---|---|---|---|---|
| 2009 | PHI | MLB | 28 | 4 | 3 | 0 | 18 | 10 | 70² | 74 | 18 | 23 | 50 | 2.9 | 6.4 | 48% | .272 | 1.37 | 4.84 | 6.10 | 6.71 | -0.6 |
| 2010 | HOU | MLB | 29 | 14 | 8 | 0 | 33 | 33 | 223² | 212 | 20 | 66 | 180 | 2.7 | 7.2 | 50% | .292 | 1.24 | 3.14 | 3.58 | 4.16 | 3.0 |
| 2011 | HOU | MLB | 30 | 7 | 14 | 0 | 34 | 33 | 216 | 226 | 31 | 57 | 160 | 2.4 | 6.7 | 49% | .295 | 1.31 | 4.46 | 4.23 | 4.83 | 0.2 |
| *2012* | *HOU* | *MLB* | *31* | *8* | *13* | *0* | *28* | *28* | *185* | *182* | *25* | *52* | *133* | *2.5* | *6.5* | *48%* | *.300* | *1.26* | *4.43* | *4.37* | *4.82* | *0.7* |

Myers has learned a lot about pitching since coming up as a seemingly mindless fireballer. He now mixes two flavors of fastball and at least four different breaking pitches into a pile of slop, required because his fastball took yet another step backward in 2011. He was purportedly healthy, but the Astros are hoping that something was wrong and Myers rebounds in 2012 so they'll be able to trade him.

## Bud Norris

Born: 3/2/1985 Age: 27
Bats: R Throws: R Height: 6' 1" Weight: 225
Breakout: 26% Improve: 53% Collapse: 29%
Attrition: 22% MLB: 78%

**Comparables:**
Robb Nen, Stan Belinda, Matt Turner

| YEAR | TEAM | LVL | AGE | W | L | SV | G | GS | IP | H | HR | BB | SO | EqBB9 | EqSO9 | GB% | BABIP | WHIP | ERA | FIP | FRA | WARP |
|------|------|-----|-----|---|---|----|----|----|------|-----|----|----|-----|-------|-------|-----|-------|------|------|------|------|------|
| 2009 | ROU | AAA | 24 | 4 | 9 | 0 | 19 | 19 | 120 | 104 | 6 | 53 | 112 | 4.0 | 8.4 | 50% | .303 | 1.31 | 2.62 | 3.66 | 3.68 | 1.8 |
| 2009 | HOU | MLB | 24 | 6 | 3 | 0 | 11 | 10 | 55² | 59 | 9 | 25 | 54 | 4.0 | 8.7 | 41% | .318 | 1.51 | 4.53 | 4.73 | 4.56 | 0.7 |
| 2010 | HOU | MLB | 25 | 9 | 10 | 0 | 27 | 27 | 153² | 151 | 18 | 77 | 158 | 4.5 | 9.3 | 45% | .318 | 1.48 | 4.92 | 4.19 | 4.65 | 1.1 |
| 2011 | HOU | MLB | 26 | 6 | 11 | 0 | 31 | 31 | 186 | 177 | 24 | 70 | 176 | 3.4 | 8.5 | 42% | .299 | 1.33 | 3.77 | 3.99 | 4.54 | 1.4 |
| 2012 | HOU | MLB | 27 | 6 | 12 | 0 | 26 | 26 | 152 | 144 | 18 | 62 | 130 | 3.7 | 7.7 | 45% | .312 | 1.36 | 4.56 | 4.26 | 4.96 | 0.6 |

Norris throws a mid-90s fastball and a slider that's hell on right-handed batters. His changeup still isn't refined enough to use often, and lefties still tee off on him. The result is thoroughly average pitching, despite "Grade A" stuff. While not a workhorse, he's averaged almost 180 innings the past three seasons. As is, Norris helps a team. If he can figure out one trick to get lefties out, his effectiveness could increase greatly.

## Brett Oberholtzer

Born: 7/1/1989 Age: 22
Bats: L Throws: L Height: 6' 3" Weight: 230
Breakout: 27% Improve: 48% Collapse: 13%
Attrition: 9% MLB: 78%

**Comparables:**
Dana Eveland, Brad Havens, Leo Kiely

| YEAR | TEAM | LVL | AGE | W | L | SV | G | GS | IP | H | HR | BB | SO | EqBB9 | EqSO9 | GB% | BABIP | WHIP | ERA | FIP | FRA | WARP |
|------|------|-----|-----|---|---|----|----|----|------|-----|----|----|----|-------|-------|-----|-------|------|------|------|------|------|
| 2011 | CCH | AA | 22 | 2 | 3 | 0 | 6 | 6 | 27¹ | 28 | 3 | 10 | 28 | 3.3 | 9.2 | 45% | .338 | 1.39 | 5.27 | 3.97 | 5.07 | 0.1 |
| 2011 | MIS | AA | 22 | 9 | 9 | 0 | 21 | 21 | 127² | 119 | 6 | 42 | 93 | 3.0 | 6.6 | 43% | .293 | 1.26 | 3.74 | 3.46 | 4.11 | 1.4 |
| 2012 | HOU | MLB | 22 | 2 | 4 | 0 | 9 | 9 | 48² | 51 | 5 | 17 | 27 | 3.2 | 5.0 | 44% | .308 | 1.41 | 4.87 | 4.48 | 5.30 | 0.0 |

Oberholtzer came from Atlanta in the Michael Bourn deal, and could be mistaken for Joe Blanton viewed in a mirror. Oberholtzer is about major-league ready and he could potentially break camp in the rotation with a good spring. His fastball is often cited as a "plus" pitch, but that's a case of "pitchability" instead of raw velocity, as he usually works right around the 90-mph mark. His slider is also good, and his changeup is what makes the whole sequence work. Unlike Blanton's, his curve is just a "show me" pitch for now, though a little improvement in it would give him a good secondary offering on days when the slider isn't biting.

## Lance Pendleton

Born: 9/10/1983 Age: 28
Bats: L Throws: R Height: 6' 4" Weight: 195
Breakout: 26% Improve: 50% Collapse: 25%
Attrition: 17% MLB: 83%

**Comparables:**
Eude Brito, Ray King, Jeremy Affeldt

| YEAR | TEAM | LVL | AGE | W | L | SV | G | GS | IP | H | HR | BB | SO | EqBB9 | EqSO9 | GB% | BABIP | WHIP | ERA | FIP | FRA | WARP |
|------|------|-----|-----|---|---|----|----|----|-----|----|----|----|----|-------|-------|-----|-------|------|-------|-------|------|------|
| 2011 | SWB | AAA | 27 | 1 | 2 | 1 | 18 | 10 | 66² | 58 | 7 | 24 | 45 | 3.2 | 6.1 | 32% | .262 | 1.23 | 3.11 | 4.42 | 4.68 | 0.6 |
| 2011 | HOU | MLB | 27 | 0 | 0 | 0 | 4 | 0 | 4² | 10 | 4 | 1 | 5 | 1.9 | 9.6 | 26% | .400 | 2.36 | 17.36 | 13.92 | 9.79 | -0.3 |
| 2011 | NYA | MLB | 27 | 0 | 0 | 0 | 11 | 0 | 14 | 10 | 2 | 10 | 8 | 6.4 | 5.1 | 23% | .190 | 1.43 | 3.21 | 5.92 | 6.35 | -0.1 |
| 2012 | HOU | MLB | 28 | 2 | 3 | 0 | 11 | 7 | 42² | 43 | 5 | 19 | 26 | 4.0 | 5.5 | 40% | .305 | 1.46 | 5.03 | 4.84 | 5.47 | -0.1 |

Pendleton pitched three perfect innings against the Rangers in his major league debut. This was after he was claimed in the Rule 5 draft by the Astros and then returned to the Yankees in March when a deal couldn't be reached, only to be designated for assignment by New York and claimed again by the Astros. It was all downhill from there, however. His fastball is straight as a string and tops out at 91 mph on a good day, and he likes to work up in the strike zone. These traits combine to produce heaps of fly balls, and neither Yankee Stadium nor Minute Maid Park is ideal for that. The Astros outrighted Pendleton and he chose to become a free agent, so a team that plays in a more favorable park can pick him him, no strings attached.

## Aneury Rodriguez

Born: 12/13/1987 Age: 24
Bats: R Throws: R Height: 6' 5" Weight: 200
Breakout: 14% Improve: 38% Collapse: 21%
Attrition: 15% MLB: 94%

**Comparables:**
Bill Greif, Carlos Carrasco, Ray Burris

| YEAR | TEAM | LVL | AGE | W | L | SV | G | GS | IP | H | HR | BB | SO | EqBB9 | EqSO9 | GB% | BABIP | WHIP | ERA | FIP | FRA | WARP |
|------|------|-----|-----|---|---|----|----|----|-----|----|----|----|----|-------|-------|-----|-------|------|------|------|------|------|
| 2011 | HOU | MLB | 23 | 1 | 6 | 0 | 43 | 8 | 85¹ | 83 | 13 | 32 | 64 | 3.4 | 6.8 | 29% | .275 | 1.35 | 5.27 | 4.67 | 4.23 | 0.6 |
| 2012 | HOU | MLB | 24 | 2 | 4 | 0 | 23 | 9 | 68¹ | 70 | 9 | 28 | 44 | 3.7 | 5.8 | 37% | .304 | 1.43 | 5.20 | 4.86 | 5.65 | -0.2 |

Set free by the Rays and smartly grabbed by the pitching-hungry Astros, Rodriguez showed glimpses of why he was regarded as a prospect, utilizing his high leg kick (which is an open invitation to potential base thieves) to generate heat that reached 94 mph a few times during the season and showing—at times—a slider that gave right-handed batters fits. But the lack of an effective breaking pitch against lefties, combined with a fastball that's a bit flat and usually of pedestrian velocity, made a long season for Rodriguez, as fly ball after fly ball left opposing bats and only some stayed in the park. He was able to find another couple notches on his fastball when relieving and experienced much better success in that role, where he'll likely spend all of 2012.

## Fernando Rodriguez
Born: 6/18/1984 Age: 28
Bats: R Throws: R Height: 6' 4" Weight: 215
Breakout: 36% Improve: 61% Collapse: 17%
Attrition: 18% MLB: 79%

**Comparables:**
Brandon Backe, Dave Pagan, Jason Standridge

| YEAR | TEAM | LVL | AGE | W | L | SV | G | GS | IP | H | HR | BB | SO | EqBB9 | EqSO9 | GB% | BABIP | WHIP | ERA | FIP | FRA | WARP |
|------|------|-----|-----|---|---|----|----|----|------|----|----|----|----|-------|-------|-----|-------|------|------|------|------|------|
| 2009 | ANA | MLB | 25 | 0 | 0 | 0 | 1 | 0 | 0² | 1 | 1 | 2 | 1 | 27.0 | 13.5 | 33% | .000 | 4.50 | 27.00 | 28.64 | 24.50 | -0.1 |
| 2011 | OKL | AAA | 27 | 2 | 3 | 2 | 16 | 0 | 24 | 16 | 2 | 11 | 33 | 4.1 | 12.4 | 40% | .286 | 1.12 | 1.50 | 3.57 | 3.25 | 0.5 |
| 2011 | HOU | MLB | 27 | 2 | 3 | 0 | 47 | 0 | 52¹ | 51 | 6 | 30 | 57 | 5.2 | 9.8 | 38% | .346 | 1.55 | 3.96 | 4.20 | 5.11 | 0.1 |
| 2012 | HOU | MLB | 28 | 2 | 3 | 0 | 28 | 5 | 51² | 54 | 6 | 24 | 34 | 4.2 | 5.9 | 39% | .315 | 1.50 | 5.37 | 4.79 | 5.84 | -0.3 |

With his stature, his intimidating delivery, his mid-90s heat, and wicked big-breaking curve, Rodriguez looks like a closer when he's on the mound. He also looks like a closer when you examine his strikeout rates, which skyrocketed upon his move to the bullpen in 2009. He even looked like a closer as he went unscored-upon in 33 of his first 43 appearances in 2011, despite his high walk rate. But that 43rd game was an outing of 2 1/3 innings, his longest of the season, and while he didn't allow any runs in that one, he wasn't the same afterward. He allowed eight runs, all earned, in his final four outings (just three innings), while striking out just one. Though he did top 94 mph with 10 of his 90 pitches the rest of the way, far too many were up in the zone, and his curve didn't

Only 19 pitchers have tallied more WARP since 2007 than the 14.6 Rodriguez has amassed. While that's not too far out of line with the handsome salary he's collecting, none thought that the pitcher who came to the States under the assumed identity of Eny Cabreja would ever be this good, with many expecting almost nothing at all. When he was frequently getting hurt earlier in his career, any expectation that he'd both remain in the rotation and become durable seemed nothing more than wishful thinking. Cabreja, er, Rodriguez is a master of deception, epitomizing the "crafty lefty" monicker. He works a typical three-pitch repertoire of fastball, curve, changeup, though he'll do anything to get ahead—trying new pitches, changing sequencing, whatever it takes. That's the name of the game for an under-sized hurler like Rodriguez, who has been known to go entire games without topping 90 mph. The slight erosion in his stats last season doesn't reflect poorly on his future; he suffered a bout of shoulder tendinitis on March 13, and his first five starts were awful. After those, he posted a 3.13 ERA with correspondingly strong peripherals.

## Ross Seaton
Born: 9/18/1989 Age: 22
Bats: L Throws: R Height: 6' 5" Weight: 213
Breakout: 25% Improve: 51% Collapse: 11%
Attrition: 6% MLB: 82%

**Comparables:**
Ross Grimsley, Dick Ellsworth, Chris George

| YEAR | TEAM | LVL | AGE | W | L | SV | G | GS | IP | H | HR | BB | SO | EqBB9 | EqSO9 | GB% | BABIP | WHIP | ERA | FIP | FRA | WARP |
|------|------|-----|-----|---|---|----|----|----|------|-----|----|----|----|-------|-------|-----|-------|------|------|------|------|------|
| 2009 | LEX | A | 19 | 8 | 10 | 0 | 24 | 24 | 136² | 137 | 11 | 39 | 88 | 2.6 | 5.8 | 41% | .293 | 1.29 | 3.29 | 4.34 | 5.47 | -0.9 |
| 2010 | LNC | A+ | 20 | 6 | 13 | 0 | 28 | 28 | 146¹ | 164 | 18 | 42 | 73 | 2.8 | 5.2 | 45% | .330 | 1.66 | 6.64 | 5.45 | 6.09 | -0.7 |
| 2011 | CCH | AA | 21 | 4 | 9 | 0 | 28 | 28 | 155 | 168 | 19 | 47 | 97 | 2.7 | 5.6 | 39% | .302 | 1.39 | 5.23 | 4.77 | 5.11 | 1.5 |
| 2012 | HOU | MLB | 22 | 1 | 5 | 0 | 9 | 9 | 49² | 60 | 8 | 20 | 17 | 3.7 | 3.1 | 40% | .309 | 1.60 | 6.44 | 5.82 | 7.00 | -0.8 |

The Astros are hoping that 2008 third-round pick Seaton was just suffering from PTSD after his time pitching for the Lancaster JetHawks in 2010. The important thing is that he survived—it will get better in time (they hope). And he keeps pouring strikes into the strike zone, a skill he's always had. He was reported to have thrown 96 mph at least once in high school, has a perfect pitcher's frame, and has even been reported in the "mid-90s" recently. But he doesn't generate ground balls, and there's going to be more traumatic stress in his future if he doesn't make some adjustment.

## Henry Sosa
Born: 7/28/1985 Age: 26
Bats: R Throws: R Height: 6' 3" Weight: 205
Breakout: 30% Improve: 58% Collapse: 18%
Attrition: 12% MLB: 89%

**Comparables:**
John Maine, Don Bessent, Kevin Correia

| YEAR | TEAM | LVL | AGE | W | L | SV | G | GS | IP | H | HR | BB | SO | EqBB9 | EqSO9 | GB% | BABIP | WHIP | ERA | FIP | FRA | WARP |
|------|------|-----|-----|---|---|----|----|----|------|----|----|----|----|-------|-------|-----|-------|------|------|------|------|------|
| 2009 | NRW | AA | 23 | 6 | 0 | 0 | 14 | 14 | 72¹ | 61 | 4 | 25 | 44 | 3.1 | 5.5 | 33% | .258 | 1.19 | 2.37 | 3.72 | 4.62 | 0.2 |
| 2010 | FRE | AAA | 24 | 7 | 8 | 0 | 36 | 14 | 115 | 69 | 11 | 34 | 52 | 4.3 | 6.5 | 41% | .253 | 1.46 | 4.07 | 5.31 | 5.81 | -0.3 |
| 2011 | RIC | AA | 25 | 4 | 2 | 0 | 8 | 6 | 40¹ | 41 | 1 | 8 | 36 | 1.8 | 8.0 | 55% | .333 | 1.21 | 2.68 | 2.55 | 3.46 | 0.7 |
| 2011 | FRE | AAA | 25 | 3 | 0 | 0 | 17 | 0 | 23¹ | 39 | 3 | 17 | 21 | 6.6 | 8.1 | 38% | .439 | 2.40 | 10.41 | 6.44 | 7.25 | -0.4 |
| 2011 | HOU | MLB | 25 | 3 | 5 | 0 | 10 | 10 | 53¹ | 54 | 7 | 23 | 38 | 3.9 | 6.4 | 47% | .301 | 1.44 | 5.23 | 4.74 | 5.12 | 0.1 |
| 2012 | HOU | MLB | 26 | 2 | 4 | 0 | 17 | 8 | 60 | 60 | 7 | 25 | 39 | 3.8 | 5.9 | 40% | .307 | 1.43 | 4.97 | 4.67 | 5.40 | -0.1 |

Fireballing Sosa was included in the Jeff Keppinger trade and has a lively arm—topping 95 mph sometimes with a biting slider to accompany the heat. Unfortunately, he doesn't have a third pitch, and when he was used in relief, he produced that ugly Fresno line leading to his demotion and eventual trade as the Giants gave up on him. In his major-league time, he allowed a .300/.390/.500 batting line during the first 25 pitches of his starts before settling down somewhat, further reinforcing the idea that there won't be a seamless transition to the bullpen. If Sosa were 23 years old, there would be a lot of excitement over his pure stuff, but he's made alarmingly little progress during his six years of professional baseball.

**Kyle Weiland**
Born: 9/12/1986 Age: 25
Bats: L Throws: R Height: 6′ 5″ Weight: 195
Breakout: 24% Improve: 60% Collapse: 16%
Attrition: 9% MLB: 78%

Comparables:
Daryl Patterson, Doug Rau, Josh Outman

| YEAR | TEAM | LVL | AGE | W | L | SV | G | GS | IP | H | HR | BB | SO | EqBB9 | EqSO9 | GB% | BABIP | WHIP | ERA | FIP | FRA | WARP |
|------|------|-----|-----|---|---|----|----|----|-----|-----|----|----|-----|-------|-------|-----|-------|------|------|------|------|------|
| 2009 | SLM | A+ | 22 | 7 | 10 | 0 | 26 | 26 | 132² | 130 | 4 | 61 | 116 | 3.9 | 7.6 | 54% | .305 | 1.33 | 3.46 | 3.73 | 4.87 | 0.7 |
| 2010 | PME | AA | 23 | 5 | 9 | 0 | 25 | 25 | 128¹ | 78 | 9 | 31 | 80 | 3.4 | 8.4 | 45% | .304 | 1.25 | 4.42 | 4.22 | 4.54 | 1.8 |
| 2011 | PAW | AAA | 24 | 7 | 6 | 0 | 24 | 24 | 128¹ | 108 | 10 | 55 | 126 | 3.9 | 8.8 | 49% | .296 | 1.27 | 3.58 | 3.76 | 4.25 | 2.3 |
| 2011 | BOS | MLB | 24 | 0 | 3 | 0 | 7 | 5 | 24² | 29 | 5 | 12 | 13 | 4.4 | 4.7 | 43% | .286 | 1.66 | 7.66 | 6.59 | 7.24 | -0.4 |
| 2012 | HOU | MLB | 25 | 2 | 5 | 0 | 12 | 12 | 63 | 60 | 7 | 28 | 43 | 3.9 | 6.2 | 48% | .295 | 1.38 | 4.86 | 4.62 | 5.28 | 0.1 |

Weiland pitched well as a starter at Triple-A, and was given opportunities to start in the majors, but neither of those events mean his future is in a rotation. Weiland was starting for Pawtucket to give him ample practice at mastering his arsenal. With Boston's rotation in shambles and Felix Doubront unable to answer the call, Weiland's time to apply that practice came sooner than expected. He struggled in the bigs but his small-sample splits jibe with the story scouts have been telling about his stuff and where it belongs: in the bullpen. From pitches one through 25 in the majors, Weiland held opponents to .167/.231/.279, with strikeouts 21 percent of the time. From pitch 26 onward, opponents slugged .518, and he struck out just 9 percent of them. That screams reliever as much as anything, and if given the opportunity in that role, Weiland and his repertoire should excel.

**Wesley Wright**
Born: 1/28/1985 Age: 27
Bats: R Throws: L Height: 6′ 0″ Weight: 160
Breakout: 29% Improve: 45% Collapse: 40%
Attrition: 32% MLB: 79%

Comparables:
Dave Pagan, Cecilio Guante, Pedro Viola

| YEAR | TEAM | LVL | AGE | W | L | SV | G | GS | IP | H | HR | BB | SO | EqBB9 | EqSO9 | GB% | BABIP | WHIP | ERA | FIP | FRA | WARP |
|------|------|-----|-----|---|---|----|----|----|-----|----|----|----|----|-------|-------|-----|-------|------|------|------|------|------|
| 2009 | HOU | MLB | 24 | 3 | 4 | 0 | 49 | 0 | 44² | 53 | 9 | 25 | 47 | 5.0 | 9.5 | 44% | .358 | 1.75 | 5.44 | 5.25 | 5.44 | 0.1 |
| 2010 | ROU | AAA | 25 | 4 | 1 | 0 | 15 | 14 | 69² | 43 | 2 | 23 | 27 | 4.3 | 5.3 | 47% | .279 | 1.56 | 4.65 | 4.78 | 5.72 | 0.4 |
| 2010 | HOU | MLB | 25 | 1 | 2 | 0 | 14 | 4 | 33 | 37 | 6 | 13 | 29 | 3.5 | 7.9 | 45% | .326 | 1.52 | 5.73 | 5.17 | 6.06 | -0.4 |
| 2011 | OKL | AAA | 26 | 3 | 1 | 2 | 39 | 3 | 65¹ | 49 | 4 | 23 | 52 | 3.2 | 7.2 | 47% | .247 | 1.10 | 2.07 | 4.13 | 4.73 | 0.4 |
| 2011 | HOU | MLB | 26 | 0 | 0 | 0 | 21 | 0 | 12 | 6 | 1 | 5 | 11 | 3.8 | 8.2 | 57% | .185 | 0.92 | 1.50 | 3.49 | 4.36 | 0.0 |
| 2012 | HOU | MLB | 27 | 1 | 2 | 0 | 17 | 4 | 34 | 31 | 4 | 15 | 27 | 4.1 | 7.0 | 45% | .298 | 1.38 | 4.65 | 4.47 | 5.05 | 0.1 |

Dequam LaWesley Wright from Goshen, Alabama, should eventually be a major-league reliever. The Astros stretched him out as a starter in 2010, and the results were about what could be expected—reduced velocity, fewer strikeouts, biceps tendinitis, and . . . fewer walks! Having spent the time to tame his wild, deceptive delivery, he's produced his two best (minor-league) BB/9 rates these past two seasons. In his return to the bullpen in 2011, the walk rate he logged for Oklahoma City is less than 1/3 of his 2007 walk rate during his first exposure to Triple-A (9.7 BB/9). Wright has always been tougher on lefties, and his road may end at LOOGY-ville, but his 2011 minor-league splits kept hope alive that he can be a 2-way lefty; he held righties to an anemic .161/.222/.242 batting line.

# LINEOUTS

## HITTERS

| PLAYER | TEAM | LVL | AGE | PA | R | 2B | 3B | HR | RBI | BB | SO | SB-CS | AVG/OBP/SLG | TAv | BABIP | BRR | FRAA | WARP |
|--------|------|-----|-----|-----|----|----|----|----|-----|----|-----|-------|-------------|-----|-------|-----|------|------|
| CF J. Austin | LEX | A | 20 | 144 | 9 | 7 | 0 | 0 | 16 | 13 | 32 | 6-2 | .203/.301/.260 | .227 | .269 | -0.4 | 1.9 | 0.0 |
| | LNC | A+ | 20 | 350 | 47 | 17 | 4 | 3 | 37 | 29 | 73 | 17-11 | .257/.318/.365 | .244 | .321 | 1.9 | -3.5 | -0.4 |
| SS B. Bixler | SYR | AAA | 28 | 108 | 17 | 5 | 0 | 1 | 6 | 16 | 30 | 4-1 | .314/.439/.407 | .316 | .464 | 2.3 | -2.1 | 1.0 |
| | WAS | MLB | 28 | 94 | 9 | 1 | 2 | 0 | 2 | 7 | 19 | 4-3 | .205/.267/.265 | .202 | .266 | -1.4 | 0.5 | -0.4 |
| C R. Cancel | OKL | AAA | 35 | 358 | 37 | 19 | 0 | 4 | 51 | 37 | 59 | 10-3 | .299/.374/.396 | .262 | .355 | -2.3 | -0.8 | 1.2 |
| | HOU | MLB | 35 | 7 | 0 | 0 | 0 | 0 | 0 | 1 | 4 | 0-0 | .000/.143/.000 | .070 | .000 | 0.0 | 0 | -0.1 |
| 1B K. Clemens | OKL | AAA | 24 | 444 | 51 | 21 | 2 | 16 | 55 | 51 | 117 | 4-2 | .234/.331/.424 | .245 | .291 | -1.9 | 1.1 | -0.2 |
| SS J. Mier | LEX | A | 20 | 257 | 39 | 14 | 0 | 5 | 29 | 37 | 58 | 6-2 | .245/.354/.380 | .273 | .308 | 0.4 | 4.5 | 1.7 |
| | LNC | A+ | 20 | 248 | 35 | 7 | 1 | 2 | 23 | 29 | 54 | 5-3 | .233/.335/.306 | .236 | .301 | -1.7 | -2.1 | 0.0 |
| 3B S. Moore | IOW | AAA | 27 | 425 | 60 | 19 | 4 | 9 | 53 | 48 | 79 | 3-1 | .295/.380/.444 | .280 | .348 | 2.0 | -6.9 | 1.3 |
| RF B. Snyder | IOW | AAA | 29 | 407 | 48 | 27 | 3 | 11 | 57 | 27 | 109 | 6-1 | .290/.336/.465 | .276 | .380 | 1.0 | -7.7 | 1.0 |
| | CHN | MLB | 29 | 9 | 1 | 0 | 0 | 0 | 0 | 0 | 6 | 0-0 | .111/.111/.111 | .086 | .333 | 0.3 | 0 | -0.1 |
| 1B N. Stavinoha | MEM | AAA | 29 | 586 | 84 | 30 | 1 | 28 | 109 | 44 | 100 | 5-1 | .270/.329/.488 | .269 | .284 | 0.0 | -14.0 | -0.3 |
| 2B J. Thurston | NWO | AAA | 31 | 526 | 68 | 34 | 3 | 13 | 59 | 48 | 78 | 12-4 | .300/.388/.475 | .293 | .340 | -0.8 | 0.6 | 3.0 |
| 2B B. Wikoff | CCH | AA | 23 | 386 | 40 | 6 | 0 | 3 | 26 | 47 | 33 | 5-3 | .308/.398/.353 | .273 | .334 | 1.2 | 7.0 | 2.5 |

**Jay Austin**'s 2010 could look like a successful one with enough squinting, but the wheels came off in 2011, as he was taking pitches he should have driven and swinging at pitches he could barely hit. Now a longshot to get back on the prospect track. ⊘ Positional flexibility and a few good plate appearances at Syracuse mean it's not time to say **Brian Bixler**'s career stops here, but he's strictly filler and will bide his time at Triple-A again. ⊘ Astros catchers hit .211/.257/.293 as a group, and **Robinson Cancel** couldn't keep a roster spot. His 37 percent caught-stealing percentage and respectable batting stats in Triple-A mean there's some chance he'll see his 110th career plate appearance. ⊘ And back to third base he goes! Roger's kid **Koby Clemens** isn't much of a prospect, but he has some power, and the Astros' other options at third base are not so hot. Moving to catcher, left field, and first base in the minors has prepared him for his future as a utility player. ⊘ **Carlos Corporan** has always shown a strong arm in the minors and he's hit 19 home runs in 712 Triple-A plate appearances, but he threw out just 17 percent of would-be thieves and hit zero homers for Houston, so he'll again be lingering at Triple-A awaiting another opportunity to be a backup. ⊘ A cold-weather player, **Jake Goebbert** also missed time his senior year at Northwestern after running into an outfield wall and injuring his kidney. All indications are that his bat will be major-league quality, though being limited to left field by his lack of arm and range will probably prevent him from ever becoming a starter. ⊘ Take a good look at **Kody Hinze**'s stat line at age 23 at Lancaster—and keep it in mind when evaluating California League pitching stats. It's just that easy to hit there. ⊘ **Mike Kvasnicka** was drafted 33rd overall in 2010 as a catcher, but played just five games there before a hand injury forced a position switch to third base, where he's unlikely to hit enough to live up to his draft position. ⊘ The good news about **Jiovanni Mier** is that he's still showing the great shortstop range that made him a first-round selection. The bad new is everything else. ⊘ Despite showing some pop and patience in the minors and being nominally able to cover multiple positions—including second base—**Scott Moore** is running out of time to latch on as a 25th man. ⊘ **Brad Snyder** was twice a Top-100 *Baseball America* prospect whose robust slugging at Triple-A in 2009-10 put him in the queue for an emergency call-up, but his humdrum 2011 season moved him a lot closer to the back of the queue. ⊘ Outrighted off the Cardinals' 40-man roster after the 2010 season, **Nick Stavinoha** split his time in Memphis between first base and right field, then decided that Hiroshima would provide a better career path than Oklahoma City. Unlikely to be seen in the majors again.  ⊘  **Joe Thurston** made a cameo for the Marlins in September after yet another productive year at Triple-A, where he owns a career .297/.355/.438 line in nearly 5000 plate appearances since 2002. He should exceed his total of one game played from 2011, though not by much.  ⊘  Ironically, **Brandon Wikoff** is the only player to hit for the cycle in Fighting Illini history, yet has managed just 21 extra-base hits in 1110 professional plate appearances. If he had the arm for shortstop or any other offensive skill, his good bat control and on-base skills would be noteworthy.

## PITCHERS

| PLAYER | TEAM | LVL | AGE | W | L | SV | IP | H | HR | BB | SO | EqBB9 | EqSO9 | GB% | BABIP | WHIP | ERA | FIP | FRA | WARP |
|---|---|---|---|---|---|---|---|---|---|---|---|---|---|---|---|---|---|---|---|---|
| T. Bushue | LEX | A | 20 | 4 | 6 | 0 | 77¹ | 83 | 10 | 17 | 48 | 2.0 | 5.9 | 32% | .313 | 1.37 | 4.66 | 4.82 | 5.27 | 0.2 |
| P. Clemens | MIS | AA | 23 | 6 | 5 | 0 | 108² | 103 | 8 | 44 | 93 | 3.6 | 7.7 | 43% | .302 | 1.35 | 3.73 | 3.90 | 4.61 | 1.5 |
| J. De Leon | LEX | A | 23 | 6 | 2 | 16 | 55¹ | 47 | 5 | 13 | 50 | 2.1 | 8.3 | 47% | .271 | 1.10 | 3.42 | 3.65 | 4.63 | 0.4 |
| M. Foltynewicz | LEX | A | 19 | 5 | 9 | 0 | 134 | 149 | 10 | 51 | 88 | 3.4 | 5.9 | 45% | .329 | 1.49 | 4.97 | 4.48 | 5.15 | 0.7 |
| S. Gervacio | OKL | AAA | 26 | 4 | 0 | 1 | 33² | 24 | 5 | 10 | 26 | 2.7 | 7.0 | 45% | .207 | 1.01 | 4.01 | 5.19 | 6.13 | 0.0 |
| C. Hicks | LNC | A+ | 24 | 2 | 1 | 0 | 24² | 19 | 3 | 5 | 28 | 1.8 | 10.2 | 39% | .254 | 0.97 | 3.28 | 4.10 | 4.11 | 0.5 |
| A. Houser | AST | RK | 18 | 1 | 2 | 0 | 22¹ | 24 | 0 | 10 | 25 | 4.0 | 10.1 | 57% | .375 | 1.52 | 4.03 | 2.52 | 5.02 | 0.2 |
|  | GRV | RK | 18 | 1 | 2 | 0 | 25² | 25 | 1 | 15 | 19 | 5.3 | 6.7 | 51% | .308 | 1.56 | 4.56 | 4.57 | 5.54 | 0.2 |
| B. King | CCH | AA | 24 | 0 | 2 | 0 | 40² | 25 | 3 | 38 | 50 | 8.4 | 11.1 | 36% | .244 | 1.55 | 3.76 | 4.83 | 4.95 | 0.2 |
| D. Meszaros | CCH | AA | 25 | 0 | 4 | 5 | 35¹ | 38 | 4 | 15 | 44 | 3.8 | 11.2 | 36% | .366 | 1.50 | 5.09 | 3.72 | 4.25 | 0.5 |
|  | OKL | AAA | 25 | 1 | 1 | 0 | 25² | 34 | 6 | 14 | 27 | 4.9 | 9.5 | 41% | .373 | 1.87 | 4.56 | 6.31 | 5.76 | 0.1 |
| J. Stoffel | RIC | AA | 22 | 0 | 2 | 13 | 31² | 34 | 1 | 16 | 31 | 4.5 | 8.8 | 52% | .355 | 1.58 | 3.98 | 3.57 | 4.11 | 0.2 |
| N. Tropeano | TCV | A- | 20 | 3 | 2 | 0 | 53¹ | 42 | 1 | 21 | 63 | 3.5 | 10.6 | 55% | .304 | 1.18 | 2.36 | 2.49 | 3.53 | 1.3 |
| J. Valdez | OKL | AAA | 28 | 1 | 0 | 9 | 20² | 22 | 4 | 8 | 26 | 3.9 | 11.3 | 51% | .340 | 1.55 | 5.66 | 5.04 | 5.20 | 0.2 |
|  | HOU | MLB | 28 | 0 | 0 | 0 | 14 | 17 | 2 | 7 | 15 | 4.5 | 9.6 | 57% | .375 | 1.71 | 9.00 | 4.42 | 5.26 | -0.1 |

**Tanner Bushue** has good velocity and a power breaking pitch that is still far too inconsistent for prime time. Back issues in June led to a stint on the disabled list, but his stuff remained intact.  ⊘  **Paul Clemens** added 2-3 mph this year (depending on which scout you ask), making Houston's end of the Bourn deal a bit more palatable than it looked based on pre-2011 scouting reports.  ⊘  **Jorge De Leon** flailed away as a shortstop for four years, hitting .213/.283/.323 in the low minors, so a near-100 mph fastball made a shift to the mound a no-brainer.  ⊘  **Mike Foltynewicz** was clocked at 97 mph in high school, but didn't come anywhere near that for Lexington, raising a huge red flag for the 2010 19th overall pick.  ⊘  **Sammy Gervacio**'s mound theater—pre-pitch shenanigans, funky delivery, and strikeouts galore—was holding shows again in 2011 after recovery from shoulder inflmation in 2010, and should get another chance somewhere in the majors in 2012.  ⊘  Back from injuries and from his ill-fated conversion to starting, former Georgia Tech closer **Chris Hicks** is back in his comfort zone, and has a better shot at a career than most players his age with just 14 innings above A-ball.  ⊘  The Astros were happy that 2011 second-round pick **Adrian Houser** signed quickly—he has a pitcher's body, an advanced feel for pitching, and is young enough that his fastball could eventually sit higher than the 91 mph it's at now.  ⊘  With as little control as **Blake King** has, if he were co-editing *Baseball Prospectus* instead of King Kaufman, this comment could end up in the Royals section. Or the Mariners. Or the Phillies. He does have great stuff, though.  ⊘  **Daniel Meszaros** is a 48th-round success story from the 2008 draft, and it's only a matter of time before his upper-90s heat appears in the majors. His improving control is still holding him back, and the extent of the improvement will determine how long his career is.  ⊘  **Jason Stoffel**—acquired in the Jeff Keppinger trade—passed Mark Melancon to become the career leader in saves at the University of Arizona, but the mid-90s velocity he showed in college comes and goes now, and his chances of a career are dwindling.  ⊘  Fifth-round pick **Nick Tropeano** can barely throw 90 mph but is so deceptive that he projects as having a career.  ⊘  Since moving to the bullpen in 2007, **Jose Valdez** has shown promising strikeout rates in the minors, but he's been so riddled with injuries in his career he's rarely at his best. The Astros see the potential and kept him on the 40-man roster despite his age and struggles.

# MANAGER: BRAD MILLS

| YEAR | TEAM | W-L | Pythag +/- | Avg PC | 100+ P | 120+ P | QS | BQS | REL | REL w Zero R | IBB | Subs | PH | PH Avg | PH HR | SB2 | CS2 | SB3 | CS3 | SAC Att | SAC % | POS SAC | Squeeze | Swing | In Play |
|---|---|---|---|---|---|---|---|---|---|---|---|---|---|---|---|---|---|---|---|---|---|---|---|---|---|
| 2010 | HOU | 76-86 | 0 | 199.6 | 161 | 158 | 112 | 4 | 508 | 400 | 76 | — | 556 | .224 | 6 | 10 | 4 | 0 | 0 | 200 | 84.0% | 72 | 12 | 298 | 84 |
| 2011 | HOU | 56-106 | 0 | 100.3 | 88 | 3 | 80 | 8 | 503 | 378 | 59 | — | 278 | .263 | 6 | 20 | 1 | 0 | 2 | 112 | 73.2% | 48 | 2 | 318 | 87 |

Mills managed to survive the front-office purge, and he has the most important thing for the woeful Astros: the ability to see the glass as half full when it's 3/4 empty. Always expecting the best, and perhaps conditioned by six years as a bench coach watching Boston's stout starting rotations, Mills was one of just four managers who averaged more than 100 pitches from his starters. Yet, somewhat surprisingly—as Mills appeared to green-light a lot of runners—only the Padres and Mets had higher stolen-base percentages in 2011, suggesting that the optimism didn't result in recklessness. The team was about four wins

# Kansas City Royals

Trust the Process.

That has been the mantra coming from General Manager Dayton Moore and the Royals front office for the last several seasons. The Process being an increased focus on scouting, drafting, and player development in order to stock the major league team and return it to its former glory. There is no disputing that the minor league cupboard was bare when Moore took the helm of the Royals in June 2007. Years of budget-conscious drafts, cutting corners on scouting, and ignoring the international markets stripped the system to the bone. It was the lowest point of what had become a depressing cycle of losing baseball.

It has been said that Moore knew the years of neglect meant that his would be a Herculean task. It has also been said that although he knew things were bad, he was shocked at exactly how far behind the Royals had fallen.

There would be no quick fix to bring this once proud franchise back to respectability. In the five years since, Moore has devoted myriad resources to bring the Process to fruition. The Royals are now one of the top spending teams in the draft, cutting over $14 million in bonus checks last summer while going 249 percent over the commissioner's slot recommendations. The Royals have expanded their scouting department and redrawn territories so they could more efficiently search for talent. They rebuilt their academy in the Dominican Republic and overhauled their international efforts. And they hired some of the brightest scouting and development minds in the game in Mike Arbuckle, JJ Piccolo, Lonnie Goldberg, and Rene Francisco.

Slowly, the Process chugged along. The Royals, by dint of their record, were drafting high each year, but Moore was not going after budget picks. He was routinely chasing players who were regarded as difficult signs such as Scott Boras

clients Mike Moustakas and Eric Hosmer, and two-sport athletes such as Bubba Starling. He grabbed guys like Wil Myers who fell in the draft because of their signing demands. And he became uber-aggressive on the international market with the signing of Cuban defector Noel Argules. Those are just the high profile examples. The Royals have been going over slot for the last several years in their chase for young talent.

It's one thing to build a better minor league system, but there's still a major league team that takes the field. And the first few years of the Moore regime in Kansas City were lean ones. The Royals won 75 games in his first full season in charge in 2008, but fell back to 65 and 67 wins the next two years. This was when the Royals were filling their roster with the likes of Miguel Olivo, Jose Guillen, Mike Jacobs, and Jason Kendall. It wasn't that these teams were bad. (Though they were.) It's that they were utterly unlikable.

There was nothing remotely entertaining watching Jacobs offer at three straight sliders out of the strike zone with a runner on third with less than two outs or Guillen jogging to the corner after a ball down the line and turning a double into a sure-fire triple. Yes, there were pleasant distractions like Zack Greinke's Cy Young campaign of 2009 and the emergence of Joakim Soria as one of the best ninth-inning relievers in baseball, but these excellent individual performances were very much the exception, while mediocrity or worse was the rule.

To many the Process appeared to be about overpaying underachieving veterans. That was just a diversion. An unpleasant diversion, but a diversion nonetheless. The important work was being done out of sight of the playing field of Kauffman Stadium, in the scouting department and the minor leagues. Moore has never been shy about stating his belief that in order for the Royals to be competitive, they will

## ROYALS PROSPECTUS
### 2011 W-L: 71-91, 4th in AL Central

| | | |
|---|---|---|
| Pythag | .480 | 19th |
| RS/G | 4.51 | 10th |
| RA/G | 4.70 | 26th |
| TAv | .273 | 6th |
| TAv-P | .277 | 28th |
| FIP | 4.30 | 25th |
| DER | .701 | 24th |
| DL | 444 | 3rd |
| B-Age | 25.8 | 1st |
| P-Age | 26.6 | 3rd |
| Salary | $39.5 | 30th |
| M$/MW | $1.18 | 4th |

**Ballpark:** Kauffman Stadium (3-yr. PF: 99). Home to the 2012 All-Star Game. So there's that

**2011:** If a 71-win season can be a triumph, this one was, with the Royals of the future arriving

**2012:** The lineup is packed with home-grown thump, but a rejiggered rotation won't be enough

**Action Items:** Enough health and wins to keep players (and fans) optimistic

have to stock at least half of their roster with home-grown talent. On occasion, he has pushed that number as high as 60 or even 70 percent. Whatever number he settles on, he is ultimately looking for a majority of his players to advance through his system.

It has been a long, cold winter, but the Process finally began to bear fruit in 2011. The Royals served notice the future was on its way when they placed 10 players in our list of the Top 101 prospects in last year's annual and were anointed as having the top minor league system in the game. The evolution began in earnest in early May when top hitting prospect Eric Hosmer arrived after destroying Triple-A pitchers in just

made their major league debut wearing Royal blue in 2011. The Process, indeed.

Of course none of this would matter if the prospects weren't any good, but all signs point to this being a bumper crop of young hitters. Hosmer and Moustakas are building blocks at the corners. Perez has the tools to be the top defensive catcher in the game. By the time the dust settled on the year, no fewer than five of Kevin Goldstein's Top "11 in 2011" prospects entering the season were on the active Kansas City roster. Quite the graduation rate. At one point, the Royals 25 man roster featured 11 rookies. It was no surprise they were the youngest team in the league. With no regular position player over 30, the weighted average age of all Royal batters was 25.8 years. This collection of hitters was the youngest in team history and by far the youngest in baseball. (Pittsburgh checked in as the second youngest with an average age of 27.2 years.) Same for their arms. The average age of the Royals pitching staff was 26.4 years, tied with Cleveland for the youngest staff in baseball.

If these hitters continue to develop, that could be a very scary thing for the rest of the AL Central. Believe it or not, the Royals possessed one of the better offenses in the American League last summer. They averaged 4.5 runs a game, which was above league average. They also ranked in the top five in the league in batting average, on base percentage and even slugging. Their .270 TAv was the sixth best. And they were one of the top teams in the league at putting the bat on the ball, with a league-best contact rate of 82 percent. They put more balls in play than every team but the Rangers. Given the Royals' recent history of a "swing first, get on base later" approach at the plate, these numbers are nothing short of astonishing.

The real surprise would be the team slugging percentage of .415, which ranked fifth in the AL. The Royals have simply never been a power-hitting team. Part of that is a function of their ballpark (which has always played big) and part of that is the general lack of bombastic talent. (The Royals team record for most home runs in a season is 36. 36! Take a bow, Steve Balboni.) The Royals were able to elevate their slugging percentage by hitting a prodigious number of doubles. When Billy Butler hit his 40th double in the last week of the season, the Royals became the fourth team ever to have four players stroke at least 40 two-baggers. (The others were the '06 Rangers, the '32 Phillies, and the '28 Tigers.) At least par-

really paced the Royals offensively. The Royals outfield led all comers with 518 hits, 218 extra base hits and 944 total bases. Their collective 825 OPS was the third highest in baseball and tops in the AL. As good as they swung the bats, it was their strong arm tactics that really generated the buzz. The Royals recorded 51 outfield assists last summer, the most by any outfield since 1993. Of those 51 assists, a whopping 26 of them came at home plate. The Royals loved their outfield in 2011. Gordon picked up a Gold Glove for his exploits. And Jeff Francoeur, who was signed off the free agent scrap heap, was rewarded with a two year contract extension. (If the Royals' signing of Francoeur was the most predictable signing of the previous winter, the new deal bestowed upon the right fielder was the most predictable extension of this winter.)

The presence of depth in the system allowed Moore to open his offseason with, as has become habit, a flurry of activity. His first order of business was to sell high on center fielder Melky Cabrera, who enjoyed a career renaissance in Kansas City. Shipping the Melk-Man to the Giants netted erratic starting pitcher Jonathan Sanchez. He joins a rotation loaded with question marks, but the Royals are enticed by his high strikeout rate—he whiffed 9.1 batters per nine innings last year. As a team, the Royals punched out batters at a rate of 6.7 SO/9, which was a few clicks off the league average rate. But their team SO/BB ratio was a subpar 1.94, lowest in the league. Sanchez will move the strikeout needle in the correct direction, but the Royals have to be wary of his control.

More importantly, the Cabrera deal opened the door for Lorenzo Cain to take over in center. Cain, part of the package the Royals acquired in the Zack Greinke trade, will immediately be an upgrade over Cabrera defensively and with Alcides Escobar entrenched at short and Perez behind the plate, the Royals have significantly improved their defense up the middle from Opening Day 2011. The Royals ranked 24th in defensive efficiency last year, which was their best showing with the gloves since 2008. With Cain, aside from deciding upon a utility player who can give the left side of the infield an occasional breather, that settles the offensive portion of the 2012 *and 2013* rosters.

On the pitching side of the ledger, things aren't so rosy. The Royals' starting rotation in 2011 was by turns ineffective and abysmal. Their 4.64 FRA was worse than every team, save Baltimore. Royals hurlers also posted a 3.5 BB/9, which was the highest rate in the league. That happens when your rotation at some point includes guys like Kyle Davies, Sean O'Sullivan, and Vin Mazzaro. Nevertheless, there had to be a fall guy, so the Royals parted with long time pitching coach Bob McClure at the end of the season. His replacement is Dave Eiland, who gained a reputation of helping young arms as he worked his way up the Yankees chain. The Royals will count on him to nurture the next wave of pitching prospects that will arrive in Kansas City over the next couple of years.

As set as the lineup is for the Royals for the year ahead, the rotation is very much in flux. The Royals are hopeful Luke Hochevar can build on his second half success and they will count on Bruce Chen and newcomer Sanchez. Felipe Paulino and Duffy are in the mix, but they are far from locks. Aaron Crow and Everett Teaford will get some looks. If there's a reason for so much rotation uncertainty, it's because the Royals pitching prospects haven't developed at the same pace as the position players. Mike Montgomery and John Lamb were supposed to join Duffy in Kansas City at some point in 2011. Montgomery was derailed by control issues while Lamb was sidelined after undergoing Tommy John surgery. The second tier of pitching prospects seemed stunted in their development as well. Some will blame the organizational philosophy that mandates each player follow a strict team regimen for training, one that reportedly eschews the long-toss program that so many pitchers favor. Others will point to the the nature of the sport and how the game is littered with once-promising pitching prospects. It was a year where nearly every promising pitcher in the minors took a step backward. Whatever the reason for the setbacks, this is one area of the Process that the Royals need to get settled before they can make the jump to the next level.

Patience was the mantra in the early stages of the Process as the position players developed, and with the setbacks, it will again be preached for the young arms. For that reason, the Royals are loath to hit the free agent market for mediocre, over valued talent that could serve as a roadblock to the major league progress of some of their younger arms. It would seem the Royals would benefit from kicking the tires on a few free agent starters, but they want to give their prospects time.

Instead of a starter, Moore nabbed free agent reliever Jonathan Broxton in a surprise move just ahead of the Winter Meetings. The Royals' short-term strategy seems to be to cobble together a starting rotation of spare parts and upside and hope they can get a lead through six innings before handing things off to the bullpen for the final three. Crazier things have happened, but the Royals are banking on the health of two relievers who have had arm issues in the past: Broxton and closer Joakim Soria. The best case scenario is that the Broxton signing strengthens an already solid bullpen. The worst case is Moore bought himself some options down the road where he can flip one of his relievers at the deadline in a continuing effort to build depth. Or he can reposition one of his relievers to the rotation. Just the fact we're discussing options the team holds because of its depth shows how far the Royals have come.

Should they find themselves in the thick of the races, with the Royals committed to youth, they have the payroll flexibility to add pieces as needed. A wage bill of just under $75 million in 2010 was slashed in half for the 2011 season, down to $38 million. That wasn't the product of some edict from ownership that the fiscal belt needed tightening. It was simply the result of getting a few bad contracts off the ledger, going all-in with youth, and spending wisely on the free agent market to piece together a 25-man roster. The 2012 payroll looks to be close to $50 million, but ownership trusts Moore enough to give him the flexibility to add as he sees fit.

One order of business he will have to address is whether or not to extend Gordon. The left fielder finally came into his own in 2011 and was the Royals best—and most complete—player. The former Cornhusker has two more trips through the arbitration process, and the 28-year-old has stated his desire to remain in Kansas City long term. It would likely be in the Royals' best interest to buy out his remaining years of arbitration eligibility and a year or two of his free agency. That's something that would have been unthinkable just a year ago.

Step one of the Process was to build the best minor league system in baseball and begin funneling those prospects to the major league level. The 2011 season saw that step surmounted. Now Moore and the Royals move to step two, which is to give those prospects major league experience while surrounding them with a supporting cast. Step two will be a real challenge, especially if it entails stocking an entire starting rotation. But, there's real hope that the Royals can make this team competitive for the first time in over 25 years. If the Process works as imagined by its architect, they will move on to step three: remaining competitive for years to come.

# HITTERS

**Yuniesky Betancourt** SS
Born: 1/31/1982 Age: **30**
Bats: **R** Throws: **R** Height: **5' 11"** Weight: **190**
Breakout: **1%** Improve: **21%** Collapse: **8%**
Attrition: **17%** MLB: **75%**
**Comparables:**
Jesus Merchan, Neifi Perez, Alex Cintron

| YEAR | TEAM | LVL | AGE | PA | R | 2B | 3B | HR | RBI | BB | SO | SB | CS | AVG_OBP_SLG | TAv | BABIP | BRR | FRAA | WARP |
|------|------|-----|-----|----|----|----|----|----|-----|----|----|----|----|-------------|-----|-------|-----|------|------|
| 2009 | KCA | MLB | 27 | 263 | 25 | 10 | 5 | 4 | 27 | 11 | 26 | 0 | 2 | .240/.269/.370 | .220 | .251 | 0.2 | -4.2 | -0.6 |
| 2009 | SEA | MLB | 27 | 245 | 15 | 10 | 1 | 2 | 22 | 10 | 18 | 3 | 1 | .250/.278/.330 | .229 | .261 | -0.9 | -6.5 | -0.5 |
| 2010 | KCA | MLB | 28 | 588 | 60 | 29 | 2 | 16 | 78 | 23 | 64 | 2 | 3 | .259/.288/.405 | .244 | .267 | 2.3 | 6 | 1.9 |
| 2011 | MIL | MLB | 29 | 584 | 51 | 27 | 3 | 13 | 68 | 16 | 63 | 4 | 4 | .252/.271/.381 | .229 | .259 | 1.2 | 4.1 | 1.3 |
| 2012 | KCA | MLB | 30 | 549 | 59 | 28 | 4 | 8 | 59 | 19 | 54 | 4 | 3 | .265/.291/.382 | .238 | .278 | -0.8 | SS -3, 2B 0 | 1.0 |

Possibly baseball's worst regular in 2008-09, Betancourt posted a WARP total of -1.1 for those two seasons as he failed to refine the undisciplined swing of his youth and simultaneously posted dreadful fielding stats. Since then, he has remained an awful and undisciplined offensive player, though the home runs mask it a little. What has changed is that he's posting fielding stats that suggest he helped his teams in 2010–11. The error bars in fielding metrics are still extremely

Born: 4/18/1986 Age: **26**
Bats: **R** Throws: **R** Height: **6' 2"** Weight: **240**
Breakout: **3%** Improve: **40%** Collapse: **3%**
Attrition: **16%** MLB: **90%**
**Comparables:**
Sean Casey, Wally Joyner, Brian Giles

| YEAR | TEAM | LVL | AGE | PA | R | 2B | 3B | HR | RBI | BB | SO | SB | CS | AVG_OBP_SLG | TAv | BABIP | BRR | FRAA | WARP |
|------|------|-----|-----|----|----|----|----|----|-----|----|----|----|----|-------------|-----|-------|-----|------|------|
| 2010 | KCA | MLB | 24 | 678 | 77 | 45 | 0 | 15 | 78 | 69 | 78 | 0 | 0 | .318/.388/.469 | .297 | .341 | -4.6 | 0.3 | 2.7 |
| 2011 | KCA | MLB | 25 | 673 | 74 | 44 | 0 | 19 | 95 | 66 | 95 | 2 | 1 | .291/.361/.461 | .288 | .316 | -4.1 | -0.9 | 2.2 |
| 2012 | KCA | MLB | 26 | 633 | 83 | 39 | 3 | 15 | 78 | 58 | 84 | 1 | 0 | .299/.365/.455 | .290 | .327 | 0 | 1B -2 | 2.8 |

Billy Butler, Billy Butler. Doubles machine. Since 2009, Butler has pounded 140 two-baggers, the most in the majors. The gap power is nice, but the Royals continue to hope he can park some of those doubles over the wall. Those hopes may not be unfounded: historically, he's been a line drive and groundball hitter, but over the final three months of the season, he started generating more loft in his swing and became a line drive and fly ball hitter. Thirteen of his 19 home runs were hit in the season's second half. The arrival of Eric Hosmer means he can mothball the glove, which, given his defensive limitations, is a very good thing. Given the one dimension to his game, it's possible he's overvalued, as his TAv placed him between Jemile Weeks and Andre Ethier last year. If he can build on his second half power production, that won't be an issue. Plus, he's signed to a club-friendly contract through 2014, his age 28 season, making him one of the more affordable designated hitters in the game.

**Lorenzo Cain** CF
Born: 4/13/1986 Age: **26**
Bats: **R** Throws: **R** Height: **6' 3"** Weight: **200**
Breakout: **4%** Improve: **47%** Collapse: **8%**
Attrition: **29%** MLB: **85%**
**Comparables:**
Jordan Czarniecki, Angel Pagan, Rocco Baldelli

| YEAR | TEAM | LVL | AGE | PA | R | 2B | 3B | HR | RBI | BB | SO | SB | CS | AVG_OBP_SLG | TAv | BABIP | BRR | FRAA | WARP |
|------|------|-----|-----|----|----|----|----|----|-----|----|-----|----|----|-------------|-----|-------|-----|------|------|
| 2009 | WIS | A | 23 | 61 | 3 | 4 | 0 | 0 | 3 | 9 | 15 | 0 | 0 | .192/.311/.269 | .235 | .270 | -0.3 | 0.7 | 0.1 |
| 2009 | HUN | AA | 23 | 160 | 17 | 6 | 0 | 4 | 15 | 10 | 35 | 3 | 3 | .214/.277/.338 | .219 | .252 | 0.6 | 1.4 | -0.2 |
| 2010 | HUN | AA | 24 | 280 | 45 | 6 | 6 | 3 | 18 | 34 | 52 | 21 | 2 | .324/.407/.434 | .303 | .400 | 3.6 | 2.6 | 2.6 |
| 2010 | NAS | AAA | 24 | 100 | 13 | 5 | 3 | 0 | 9 | 11 | 17 | 5 | 1 | .299/.380/.425 | .255 | .366 | 1.3 | 2.4 | 0.6 |
| 2010 | MIL | MLB | 24 | 158 | 17 | 11 | 1 | 1 | 13 | 9 | 28 | 7 | 1 | .306/.348/.415 | .281 | .370 | 1.9 | 1.8 | 1.1 |
| 2011 | OMA | AAA | 25 | 549 | 84 | 28 | 7 | 16 | 81 | 40 | 102 | 16 | 6 | .312/.380/.497 | .307 | .366 | 0.9 | -3.9 | 4.7 |
| 2011 | KCA | MLB | 25 | 23 | 4 | 1 | 0 | 0 | 1 | 1 | 4 | 0 | 0 | .273/.304/.318 | .216 | .333 | 0.3 | -0.5 | 0.0 |
| 2012 | KCA | MLB | 26 | 250 | 27 | 11 | 2 | 4 | 26 | 14 | 54 | 5 | 2 | .257/.309/.377 | .247 | .315 | -0.2 | CF 0, RF -1 | 0.7 |

Conventional wisdom held that Melky Cabrera, acquired as a free agent just days before Cain arrived in the Zack Greinke trade, was simply a placeholder in center field and the team would recall Cain by midseason. It looked good on paper, but once the season started, Cain was left to toil in Triple-A. He's a strong defensive outfielder, but offensively he lost some of the plate discipline he found in 2010. The Royals worry his swing gets too long at times, making him susceptible to the strikeout.

### Christian Colon    SS

Born: 5/14/1989 Age: 23
Bats: R Throws: R Height: 6' 2" Weight: 180
Breakout: 4% Improve: 22% Collapse: 8%
Attrition: 22% MLB: 45%

Comparables:
Nate Samson, Jesus Lopez, Mark Hallberg

| YEAR | TEAM | LVL | AGE | PA | R | 2B | 3B | HR | RBI | BB | SO | SB | CS | AVG_OBP_SLG | TAv | BABIP | BRR | FRAA | WARP |
|------|------|-----|-----|-----|----|----|----|----|-----|----|----|----|----|-------------|------|-------|------|--------|------|
| 2010 | WIL | A+ | 21 | 271 | 38 | 12 | 2 | 3 | 30 | 13 | 33 | 2 | 4 | .278/.325/.380 | .240 | .305 | -0.6 | 4.4 | 0.9 |
| 2011 | NWA | AA | 22 | 568 | 69 | 14 | 2 | 8 | 61 | 46 | 51 | 17 | 7 | .257/.325/.342 | .221 | .271 | -1.9 | 13.5 | 1.2 |
| 2012 | KCA | MLB | 23 | 250 | 23 | 10 | 1 | 1 | 19 | 13 | 34 | 4 | 2 | .236/.282/.304 | .209 | .264 | -0.3 | SS 9, 2B 0 | -0.7 |

Considered a "safe" 2010 first round pick by the normally aggressive Royals, Colon is a solid contact hitter—nearly 83 percent of his plate appearances ended with the ball in play—but he has yet to develop any kind of a power stroke, collecting just 24 extra base hits. Last summer, he struggled against left-handed pitching with a line of .192/.296/.263. Colon has the hands and arm to stay at shortstop, but lacks the quick first step and range to flag down balls up the middle. Many feel his future lies on the other side of the bag, and he began the transition to second base last summer, making 15 appearances there for the Double-A Naturals.

### Cheslor Cuthbert    3B

Born: 11/16/1992 Age: 19
Bats: R Throws: R Height: 6' 2" Weight: 190
Breakout: 0% Improve: 2% Collapse: 2%
Attrition: 5% MLB: 7%

Comparables:
Matthew Sweeney, Aderlin Rodriguez, Jarek Cunningham

| YEAR | TEAM | LVL | AGE | PA | R | 2B | 3B | HR | RBI | BB | SO | SB | CS | AVG_OBP_SLG | TAv | BABIP | BRR | FRAA | WARP |
|------|------|-----|-----|-----|----|----|----|----|-----|----|----|----|----|-------------|------|-------|------|------|------|
| 2010 | IDA | RK | 17 | 64 | 10 | 4 | 1 | 2 | 10 | 3 | 16 | 1 | 0 | .233/.281/.433 | .250 | .286 | -0.1 | -2 | -0.1 |
| 2010 | ROY | RK | 17 | 76 | 14 | 3 | 2 | 1 | 5 | 6 | 19 | 1 | 1 | .265/.342/.412 | .264 | .354 | 1.7 | -2.8 | 0.1 |
| 2011 | KNC | A | 18 | 342 | 33 | 13 | 1 | 8 | 51 | 36 | 65 | 2 | 0 | .267/.345/.397 | .269 | .312 | -3.6 | -0.5 | 1.4 |
| 2012 | KCA | MLB | 19 | 250 | 22 | 9 | 1 | 3 | 20 | 14 | 65 | 0 | 0 | .211/.255/.299 | .199 | .275 | 0 | 3B -2 | -1.0 |

The youngest position player in the Midwest League, Cuthbert features lightning quick bat speed and has an advanced approach at the plate beyond his years. He wore down over the course of the season, but continues to possess tremendous upside. Defensively, he's adequate at third but there's some thought that as his body matures, he will end up across the diamond at first. With the first wave of position prospects arriving in Kansas City last summer, the Royals will be patient and move him methodically through the system.

### Jarrod Dyson    CF

Born: 8/15/1984 Age: 27
Bats: L Throws: R Height: 5' 10" Weight: 160
Breakout: 2% Improve: 31% Collapse: 4%
Attrition: 23% MLB: 73%

Comparables:
Mickey Rivers, Jamal Strong, Tom Goodwin

| YEAR | TEAM | LVL | AGE | PA | R | 2B | 3B | HR | RBI | BB | SO | SB | CS | AVG_OBP_SLG | TAv | BABIP | BRR | FRAA | WARP |
|------|------|-----|-----|-----|----|----|----|----|-----|----|----|----|----|-------------|------|-------|------|----------|------|
| 2009 | BUR | A | 24 | 75 | 14 | 2 | 1 | 0 | 5 | 5 | 14 | 9 | 4 | .343/.387/.403 | .298 | .418 | -0.3 | 1.6 | 0.6 |
| 2009 | NWA | AA | 24 | 283 | 38 | 7 | 4 | 0 | 14 | 27 | 54 | 37 | 6 | .258/.322/.319 | .246 | .317 | 3.4 | 0 | 0.7 |
| 2010 | WIL | A+ | 25 | 52 | 7 | 6 | 2 | 0 | 9 | 1 | 9 | 5 | 1 | .327/.340/.531 | .297 | .400 | 0.8 | 1.6 | 0.7 |
| 2010 | OMA | AAA | 25 | 219 | 33 | 10 | 1 | 1 | 19 | 16 | 32 | 13 | 3 | .272/.323/.349 | .254 | .311 | 0.1 | 7.3 | 1.4 |
| 2010 | KCA | MLB | 25 | 65 | 11 | 4 | 2 | 1 | 5 | 6 | 16 | 9 | 1 | .211/.286/.404 | .251 | .275 | 0 | 1.6 | 0.3 |
| 2011 | OMA | AAA | 26 | 369 | 69 | 10 | 3 | 3 | 26 | 35 | 47 | 38 | 2 | .279/.356/.357 | .252 | .320 | 5.7 | 1.3 | 1.8 |
| 2011 | KCA | MLB | 26 | 53 | 8 | 1 | 0 | 0 | 3 | 7 | 14 | 11 | 1 | .205/.308/.227 | .192 | .290 | 2.4 | 0.4 | 0.1 |
| 2012 | KCA | MLB | 27 | 250 | 24 | 9 | 2 | 1 | 18 | 18 | 50 | 20 | 4 | .236/.295/.304 | .217 | .291 | 1.1 | CF 4, RF -0 | -0.6 |

The second coming of Herb Washington, Dyson appeared in 26 games for the Royals, and in 12 of those he entered as a pinch runner. That's really the only way the Royals could get him on base as he's an out machine at the plate. You would think that would limit his ceiling, but the Royals are really keen on burners who can swipe a base and cover a lot of ground in the spacious Kauffman Stadium outfield. Dyson is the only player drafted in the 50th round of the 2006 draft to appear in the majors.

### Alcides Escobar    SS

Born: 12/16/1986 Age: 25
Bats: R Throws: R Height: 6' 2" Weight: 175
Breakout: 5% Improve: 57% Collapse: 3%
Attrition: 14% MLB: 86%

Comparables:
Chin-lung Hu, Julio Franco, Erick Aybar

| YEAR | TEAM | LVL | AGE | PA | R | 2B | 3B | HR | RBI | BB | SO | SB | CS | AVG_OBP_SLG | TAv | BABIP | BRR | FRAA | WARP |
|------|------|-----|-----|-----|----|----|----|----|-----|----|----|----|----|-------------|------|-------|------|----------|------|
| 2009 | NAS | AAA | 22 | 487 | 76 | 24 | 6 | 4 | 34 | 32 | 65 | 42 | 10 | .298/.340/.409 | .267 | .326 | 3.7 | 1.1 | 2.1 |
| 2009 | MIL | MLB | 22 | 134 | 20 | 3 | 1 | 1 | 11 | 4 | 18 | 4 | 2 | .304/.333/.368 | .244 | .346 | 1.5 | -0.6 | 0.4 |
| 2010 | MIL | MLB | 23 | 552 | 57 | 14 | 10 | 4 | 41 | 36 | 70 | 10 | 4 | .235/.288/.326 | .218 | .264 | 1 | -0.2 | -0.3 |
| 2011 | KCA | MLB | 24 | 598 | 69 | 21 | 8 | 4 | 46 | 25 | 73 | 26 | 9 | .254/.290/.343 | .239 | .285 | 0.7 | 0.9 | 1.0 |
| 2012 | KCA | MLB | 25 | 553 | 60 | 20 | 7 | 5 | 53 | 28 | 75 | 24 | 7 | .272/.313/.366 | .243 | .303 | 0 | SS 2, 2B -0 | 1.4 |

Acquired in the Greinke/Betancourt trade, Escobar was valued by the Royals for his stellar defense—which is a good thing, since his bat is all kinds of awful. Defensively, Escobar has superior range and a rocket of a right arm, and combines quick hands and excellent footwork around the bag in turning the double play. At the plate though, he's undisciplined, routinely going outside the strike zone in an effort to find a pitch to hit. He puts the bat on the ball often enough that he strikes out in just 12 percent of his plate appearances, a rate well below league average, but he all too often makes weak contact and pulls anemic groundball to the left side. Escobar finished ninth from the bottom among qualifiers in TAv, but that was still ahead of Betancourt.

**Jeff Francoeur** RF
Born: 1/8/1984 Age: 28
Bats: R Throws: R Height: 6' 5" Weight: 220
Breakout: 0% Improve: 36% Collapse: 5%
Attrition: 14% MLB: 70%
**Comparables:**
Bill McCarthy, Xavier Nady, Al Cowens

| YEAR | TEAM | LVL | AGE | PA | R | 2B | 3B | HR | RBI | BB | SO | SB | CS | AVG_OBP_SLG | TAv | BABIP | BRR | FRAA | WARP |
|---|---|---|---|---|---|---|---|---|---|---|---|---|---|---|---|---|---|---|---|
| 2009 | ATL | MLB | 25 | 324 | 32 | 12 | 2 | 5 | 35 | 12 | 46 | 5 | 1 | .250/.282/.352 | .221 | .276 | 0.8 | 2.1 | -0.5 |
| 2009 | NYN | MLB | 25 | 308 | 40 | 20 | 2 | 10 | 41 | 11 | 46 | 1 | 3 | .311/.338/.498 | .282 | .336 | -1.4 | -3.8 | 0.6 |
| 2010 | NYN | MLB | 26 | 447 | 43 | 16 | 2 | 11 | 54 | 29 | 76 | 8 | 2 | .237/.293/.369 | .247 | .259 | -2.2 | -7.3 | -0.1 |
| 2010 | TEX | MLB | 26 | 56 | 9 | 2 | 0 | 2 | 11 | 1 | 5 | 0 | 1 | .340/.357/.491 | .303 | .340 | 0 | -0.5 | 0.3 |
| 2011 | KCA | MLB | 27 | 656 | 77 | 47 | 4 | 20 | 87 | 37 | 123 | 22 | 10 | .285/.329/.476 | .282 | .323 | -2.7 | 6.9 | 4.1 |
| 2012 | KCA | MLB | 28 | 586 | 68 | 30 | 3 | 12 | 67 | 33 | 97 | 13 | 6 | .270/.318/.408 | .258 | .307 | -0.7 | RF 0, LF -0 | 0.9 |

Some things are meant to be together. Peanut butter and jelly. Bert and Ernie. And let's add Francoeur and the Dayton Moore-led Royals to the list. Picked up on a $2 million flyer last winter, Frenchy rewarded Moore's unwavering faith with perhaps his best season as a professional, posting full-season career highs in TAv, VORP, and WARP. A career .256/.296/.403 hitter against right-handed pitching, he hit .279/.318/.445 versus righties in 2011. That improvement was enough to fuel his boost in overall offensive performance. Defensively, he was as solid as ever, cutting down 16 base runners—eight at home. Moore reciprocated

Ted Sizemore, Cookie Rojas, Dave Cash

You could describe Getz as the obligatory "gritty" player who does "all the little things" and plays "mistake-free" baseball. That's a nice way of saying Getz is a slap-hitting out machine. He had an extra base hit in just 2.1 percent of his plate appearances, the lowest rate in the the majors among players with at least 300 trips to the plate. The Royals tried to sell fans on his defense, but he has a slow first step, limited range at second base, and an arm that won't play anywhere else on the infield. Despite the shortcomings, he's enough of a "gamer" the Royals can't help themselves. They'll try him as a utility infielder.

**Johnny Giavotella** 2B
Born: 7/10/1987 Age: 24
Bats: R Throws: R Height: 5' 9" Weight: 185
Breakout: 5% Improve: 25% Collapse: 6%
Attrition: 18% MLB: 68%
**Comparables:**
Garth Iorg, Mark Lemke, Keith Drumright

| YEAR | TEAM | LVL | AGE | PA | R | 2B | 3B | HR | RBI | BB | SO | SB | CS | AVG_OBP_SLG | TAv | BABIP | BRR | FRAA | WARP |
|---|---|---|---|---|---|---|---|---|---|---|---|---|---|---|---|---|---|---|---|
| 2009 | WIL | A+ | 21 | 561 | 84 | 24 | 8 | 6 | 52 | 66 | 54 | 26 | 9 | .258/.346/.380 | .280 | .274 | 4 | -6.7 | 2.5 |
| 2010 | NWA | AA | 22 | 597 | 92 | 35 | 5 | 9 | 65 | 61 | 67 | 13 | 7 | .322/.392/.460 | .292 | .351 | -1.8 | -0.4 | 3.8 |
| 2011 | OMA | AAA | 23 | 503 | 67 | 34 | 2 | 9 | 72 | 40 | 57 | 9 | 5 | .338/.390/.481 | .299 | .367 | -1.4 | -2.2 | 3.2 |
| 2011 | KCA | MLB | 23 | 187 | 20 | 9 | 4 | 2 | 21 | 6 | 32 | 5 | 2 | .247/.273/.376 | .231 | .288 | -0.6 | 0 | 0.0 |
| 2012 | KCA | MLB | 24 | 288 | 32 | 14 | 3 | 3 | 28 | 21 | 42 | 5 | 2 | .269/.324/.375 | .251 | .306 | -0.3 | 2B -1, LF -0 | 1.0 |

Giavotella has hit at every level of the minors, and when the Royals couldn't find a decent (or replacement level) solution for the second base position, they called him up from Omaha. Gio has plenty of bat speed and possesses gap power that translates well to the majors. He showed good plate discipline throughout his minor league career, but became way too aggressive when he made it to the big club, walking in just 3 percent of all plate appearances. The one thing that may hold him back is his defense. Lacking range up the middle and sporting an average arm for second base, he continues to be a work in progress with the glove. However, with his bat, he doesn't need to be spectacular defensively, merely adequate.

**Alex Gordon** LF
Born: 2/10/1984 Age: 28
Bats: L Throws: R Height: 6' 2" Weight: 220
Breakout: 0% Improve: 33% Collapse: 2%
Attrition: 18% MLB: 79%
**Comparables:**
Leon Wagner, David Cook, Jim Ray Hart

| YEAR | TEAM | LVL | AGE | PA | R | 2B | 3B | HR | RBI | BB | SO | SB | CS | AVG_OBP_SLG | TAv | BABIP | BRR | FRAA | WARP |
|---|---|---|---|---|---|---|---|---|---|---|---|---|---|---|---|---|---|---|---|
| 2009 | OMA | AAA | 25 | 85 | 17 | 4 | 1 | 2 | 10 | 13 | 16 | 0 | 0 | .313/.446/.493 | .335 | .388 | 1.2 | 1.7 | 1.1 |
| 2009 | KCA | MLB | 25 | 189 | 28 | 6 | 0 | 6 | 22 | 21 | 43 | 5 | 0 | .232/.324/.378 | .245 | .276 | 2.3 | 3 | 0.7 |
| 2010 | OMA | AAA | 26 | 321 | 59 | 20 | 3 | 14 | 44 | 51 | 72 | 7 | 2 | .315/.439/.577 | .338 | .386 | 0.4 | 2.4 | 3.9 |
| 2010 | KCA | MLB | 26 | 281 | 34 | 10 | 0 | 8 | 20 | 34 | 62 | 1 | 5 | .215/.315/.355 | .249 | .254 | -3.3 | 1.7 | 0.4 |
| 2011 | KCA | MLB | 27 | 688 | 101 | 45 | 4 | 23 | 87 | 67 | 139 | 17 | 8 | .303/.376/.502 | .313 | .358 | 3 | 9.8 | 7.2 |
| 2012 | KCA | MLB | 28 | 565 | 70 | 31 | 3 | 15 | 66 | 57 | 120 | 10 | 5 | .265/.347/.429 | .277 | .319 | -0.7 | LF 5, 3B 0 | 2.2 |

Following the 2010 season, a reporter approached Gordon and asked how he was going to perform in the 2011 season. "Dominate," was the one-word answer. Given Gordon's history of underperformance and injury, that seemed unlikely. But Gordon was prescient: He put up one of the best seasons by an outfielder in Kansas City history. He retooled his swing from scratch with hitting coach Kevin Seitzer. They did a battery of drills for a solid month that included taking only 10 full swings every 45 minutes. With his new swing Gordon found new life, jumping out to a scorching start and never letting up, finishing with career highs across the board. Converted from third base to the outfield, he has adapted surprisingly well defensively, leading the league with 20 assists and picking up a Gold Glove. He was the Royals' best all around player in 2011, but PECOTA sees a player who floundered until age 27, and sees a 50 point correction in BABIP leading to a year more like 2010 than 2011.

### Eric Hosmer 1B

Born: 10/24/1989 Age: 22
Bats: L Throws: L Height: 6' 5" Weight: 230
Breakout: 0% Improve: 37% Collapse: 4%
Attrition: 19% MLB: 81%

**Comparables:**
Mike Ivie, Logan Morrison, Billy Butler

| YEAR | TEAM | LVL | AGE | PA | R | 2B | 3B | HR | RBI | BB | SO | SB | CS | AVG_OBP_SLG | TAv | BABIP | BRR | FRAA | WARP |
|---|---|---|---|---|---|---|---|---|---|---|---|---|---|---|---|---|---|---|---|
| 2009 | BUR | A | 19 | 327 | 31 | 17 | 2 | 5 | 49 | 44 | 68 | 3 | 2 | .254/.355/.382 | .279 | .319 | -1.6 | 3.3 | 0.9 |
| 2009 | WIL | A+ | 19 | 107 | 9 | 2 | 2 | 1 | 10 | 9 | 22 | 0 | 0 | .206/.280/.299 | .216 | .257 | -0.8 | 1.1 | -0.5 |
| 2010 | WIL | A+ | 20 | 375 | 48 | 29 | 6 | 7 | 51 | 44 | 39 | 11 | 1 | .354/.434/.545 | .341 | .387 | -3.7 | -2.8 | 2.8 |
| 2010 | NWA | AA | 20 | 211 | 39 | 14 | 3 | 13 | 35 | 15 | 27 | 3 | 1 | .313/.365/.615 | .315 | .310 | 1 | 2.7 | 2.3 |
| 2011 | OMA | AAA | 21 | 118 | 21 | 5 | 0 | 3 | 15 | 19 | 16 | 3 | 0 | .439/.525/.582 | .370 | .500 | 0.1 | 0.8 | 1.6 |
| 2011 | KCA | MLB | 21 | 563 | 66 | 27 | 3 | 19 | 78 | 34 | 82 | 11 | 5 | .293/.334/.465 | .282 | .314 | 1 | -7.1 | 1.4 |
| 2012 | KCA | MLB | 22 | 507 | 64 | 25 | 4 | 14 | 64 | 38 | 82 | 6 | 2 | .287/.342/.450 | .279 | .321 | 0 | 1B -10 | 1.7 |

Hosmer has a way of messing with everyone's plans. He was slated to open the 2011 season in Double-A, but a torrid spring forced the Royals to accelerate his timetable and move him to Triple-A Omaha. Fine. Conventional wisdom would then suggest he spend most of the year in Triple-A. But in his first 26 games he absolutely terrorized opposing pitchers. And with Opening Day first baseman Kila Ka'aihue overmatched in the majors, Hosmer made his major league debut on May 6 (before the Super Two deadline, if you care about that kind of thing). Hosmer has a fluid swing that evokes comparisons to Will Clark, but with more power potential. If there's a flaw in his approach at the plate, it's that he will bite on the high heat. The defensive metrics didn't embrace him, but he plays a top-notch first base, with plus range, solid instincts, and what the Royals called "scoopability"—the skill of saving his infielders throwing errors by picking balls out of the dirt. It won't be long before he's the best all-around player on this team.

### Mitch Maier CF

Born: 6/30/1982 Age: 30
Bats: L Throws: R Height: 6' 3" Weight: 210
Breakout: 0% Improve: 38% Collapse: 8%
Attrition: 21% MLB: 68%

**Comparables:**
Bob Skinner, Hideki Matsui, Kevin Reese

| YEAR | TEAM | LVL | AGE | PA | R | 2B | 3B | HR | RBI | BB | SO | SB | CS | AVG_OBP_SLG | TAv | BABIP | BRR | FRAA | WARP |
|---|---|---|---|---|---|---|---|---|---|---|---|---|---|---|---|---|---|---|---|
| 2009 | OMA | AAA | 27 | 60 | 8 | 3 | 0 | 2 | 10 | 8 | 8 | 1 | 1 | .314/.407/.490 | .297 | .341 | -0.5 | 1 | 0.5 |
| 2009 | KCA | MLB | 27 | 397 | 42 | 15 | 3 | 3 | 31 | 43 | 76 | 9 | 2 | .243/.333/.331 | .240 | .303 | 0.8 | 4.3 | 0.9 |
| 2010 | KCA | MLB | 28 | 421 | 41 | 15 | 6 | 5 | 39 | 41 | 68 | 3 | 2 | .263/.333/.375 | .266 | .307 | -3.8 | 2 | 1.0 |
| 2011 | KCA | MLB | 29 | 113 | 19 | 4 | 3 | 0 | 7 | 16 | 32 | 1 | 0 | .232/.345/.337 | .249 | .344 | -0.7 | 1.8 | 0.2 |
| 2012 | KCA | MLB | 30 | 250 | 28 | 10 | 3 | 2 | 21 | 23 | 45 | 4 | 1 | .258/.331/.352 | .247 | .310 | -0.1 | CF 5, RF 1 | 0.6 |

Over the last several years, Maier carved out a nice little spot for himself as a fourth outfielder. His bat is replacement level, but his defense—and his willingness to accept his limited role—keeps him around. The risk the fourth outfielder runs is he can disappear for long stretches if the guys he's backing up are putting up quality numbers. With the Royals absolutely delighted with the production provided by the Gordon-Cabrera-Francoeur troika, it was nearly impossible for Maier to get himself a plate appearance. Never one to be perturbed by lack of playing time, with the Royals short on bullpen arms he did find himself on the mound at one point last summer, tossing a scoreless inning in a July contest against the Red Sox. According to PITCHf/x, Maier threw mostly change-ups and topped 80 mph once. His future is definitely as a fourth outfielder.

### Mike Moustakas 3B

Born: 9/11/1988 Age: 23
Bats: L Throws: R Height: 6' 0" Weight: 230
Breakout: 5% Improve: 30% Collapse: 6%
Attrition: 22% MLB: 68%

**Comparables:**
Eric Campbell, Neil Walker, Brandon Laird

| YEAR | TEAM | LVL | AGE | PA | R | 2B | 3B | HR | RBI | BB | SO | SB | CS | AVG_OBP_SLG | TAv | BABIP | BRR | FRAA | WARP |
|---|---|---|---|---|---|---|---|---|---|---|---|---|---|---|---|---|---|---|---|
| 2009 | WIL | A+ | 20 | 530 | 66 | 32 | 2 | 16 | 86 | 32 | 90 | 10 | 6 | .250/.298/.421 | .265 | .276 | 1.4 | 0 | 2.2 |
| 2010 | NWA | AA | 21 | 298 | 58 | 25 | 0 | 21 | 76 | 26 | 42 | 0 | 1 | .347/.421/.687 | .352 | .352 | -0.3 | 5 | 4.6 |
| 2010 | OMA | AAA | 21 | 236 | 36 | 16 | 0 | 15 | 48 | 8 | 25 | 2 | 0 | .293/.318/.564 | .295 | .276 | -0.3 | 1.1 | 2.0 |
| 2011 | OMA | AAA | 22 | 250 | 38 | 15 | 1 | 10 | 44 | 19 | 44 | 1 | 1 | .287/.347/.498 | .297 | .314 | -3.7 | 6.2 | 2.2 |
| 2011 | KCA | MLB | 22 | 365 | 26 | 18 | 1 | 5 | 30 | 22 | 51 | 2 | 0 | .263/.309/.367 | .251 | .296 | -1 | 1.2 | 1.0 |
| 2012 | KCA | MLB | 23 | 370 | 43 | 20 | 2 | 11 | 47 | 19 | 62 | 2 | 1 | .265/.306/.431 | .260 | .290 | -0.1 | 3B 5 | 1.8 |

Expected by many to be the first of the new wave of prospects who will launch Kansas City to contention in the AL Central, he was passed in the prospect pecking order by Hosmer. Moustakas's final line may not be much to look at, but that's on the back of a September where he hit .352/.380/.580. Slow starts have been the hallmark of his career at nearly every level, where he picks up steam once he adapts to his new environment. Credit to the Royals for sticking by him even when his line bottomed out at .182/.237/.227 just 53 games into his major league career. Equipped with outstanding bat speed, he can drive the ball to any area of the yard with power. That power arrived last summer once he learned to wait for his pitch instead of chasing pitches out of the zone and putting himself behind in the count. With a body type that can best be described as "bulky," he's a below average base runner, but does have a quick first step that serves him well at the hot corner.

**Wil Myers** RF
Born: **12/10/1990** Age: **21**
Bats: **R** Throws: **R** Height: **6' 4"** Weight: **205**
Breakout: **2%** Improve: **22%** Collapse: **8%**
Attrition: **19%** MLB: **54%**
**Comparables:**
Sixto Lezcano, Ron Fairly, Ken Henderson

| YEAR | TEAM | LVL | AGE | PA | R | 2B | 3B | HR | RBI | BB | SO | SB | CS | AVG_OBP_SLG | TAv | BABIP | BRR | FRAA | WARP |
|------|------|-----|-----|----|----|----|----|----|-----|----|----|----|----|-------------|-----|-------|-----|------|------|
| 2009 | IDA | RK | 18 | 80 | 18 | 7 | 1 | 4 | 14 | 9 | 15 | 2 | 0 | .426/.500/.735 | .412 | .510 | -0.5 | 0.3 | 1.6 |
| 2010 | BUR | A | 19 | 294 | 42 | 19 | 1 | 10 | 45 | 48 | 55 | 10 | 3 | .289/.411/.500 | .313 | .339 | -2.2 | 0.2 | 2.5 |
| 2010 | WIL | A+ | 19 | 247 | 28 | 18 | 2 | 4 | 38 | 37 | 39 | 2 | 3 | .346/.455/.512 | .344 | .414 | -0.1 | -0.2 | 2.7 |
| 2011 | NWA | AA | 20 | 416 | 50 | 23 | 1 | 8 | 49 | 52 | 87 | 9 | 2 | .254/.353/.393 | .253 | .312 | 2.2 | 1.6 | 0.9 |
| 2012 | KCA | MLB | 21 | 250 | 28 | 12 | 1 | 4 | 23 | 27 | 56 | 3 | 1 | .241/.328/.362 | .251 | .301 | 0 | RF 0, C -0 | 0.8 |

Myers was selected in the third round of the 2009 draft as a catcher, but his bat was so far ahead of his defense, the Royals decided to move him to the outfield to accelerate his arrival in the majors. Mother Nature had something to say about that. Myers fell and cut open his knee trying to run out of the rain and into his apartment. Two stitches and

Born: **11/1/1985** Age: **26**
Bats: **R** Throws: **R** Height: **6' 4"** Weight: **185**
Breakout: **6%** Improve: **27%** Collapse: **15%**
Attrition: **39%** MLB: **64%**
**Comparables:**
David Kelton, Onil Joseph, Chris Roberson

| YEAR | TEAM | LVL | AGE | PA | R | 2B | 3B | HR | RBI | BB | SO | SB | CS | AVG_OBP_SLG | TAv | BABIP | BRR | FRAA | WARP |
|------|------|-----|-----|----|----|----|----|----|-----|----|----|----|----|-------------|-----|-------|-----|------|------|
| 2010 | NWA | AA | 24 | 469 | 84 | 22 | 6 | 13 | 64 | 24 | 62 | 25 | 10 | .305/.365/.480 | .269 | .330 | 1 | 6.7 | 2.6 |
| 2011 | NWA | AA | 25 | 187 | 30 | 5 | 10 | 4 | 24 | 13 | 35 | 8 | 4 | .305/.362/.527 | .297 | .362 | 1.2 | 0.1 | 1.7 |
| 2011 | OMA | AAA | 25 | 205 | 24 | 10 | 2 | 1 | 27 | 11 | 30 | 6 | 3 | .235/.281/.326 | .198 | .276 | 0.7 | 1.8 | -0.7 |
| 2012 | KCA | MLB | 26 | 250 | 23 | 10 | 3 | 1 | 21 | 10 | 55 | 8 | 3 | .230/.265/.315 | .206 | .288 | -0.2 | RF 0, LF -1 | -1.5 |

Dayton Moore likes his outfielders fast and former track star Orlando certainly fits that bill. He developed a little power in Double-A, but struggled when promoted to Omaha. With his plus glove, he projects as a fourth outfielder.

**Brayan Pena** C
Born: **1/7/1982** Age: **30**
Bats: **B** Throws: **R** Height: **6' 0"** Weight: **210**
Breakout: **0%** Improve: **31%** Collapse: **14%**
Attrition: **28%** MLB: **82%**
**Comparables:**
Bob Boone, J.R. House, Brian Harper

| YEAR | TEAM | LVL | AGE | PA | R | 2B | 3B | HR | RBI | BB | SO | SB | CS | AVG_OBP_SLG | TAv | BABIP | BRR | FRAA | WARP |
|------|------|-----|-----|----|----|----|----|----|-----|----|----|----|----|-------------|-----|-------|-----|------|------|
| 2009 | OMA | AAA | 27 | 98 | 11 | 6 | 1 | 4 | 18 | 4 | 9 | 2 | 1 | .307/.351/.534 | .284 | .299 | -0.3 | -0.6 | 0.2 |
| 2009 | KCA | MLB | 27 | 183 | 17 | 10 | 0 | 6 | 18 | 12 | 18 | 0 | 0 | .273/.318/.442 | .263 | .273 | 0.5 | -0.2 | 0.6 |
| 2010 | KCA | MLB | 28 | 174 | 11 | 10 | 0 | 1 | 19 | 12 | 27 | 2 | 0 | .253/.306/.335 | .225 | .295 | -0.2 | 0.4 | 0.2 |
| 2011 | KCA | MLB | 29 | 240 | 17 | 11 | 0 | 3 | 24 | 12 | 24 | 0 | 0 | .248/.287/.338 | .225 | .261 | -1.8 | -1.6 | 0.0 |
| 2012 | KCA | MLB | 30 | 250 | 28 | 13 | 1 | 4 | 25 | 16 | 29 | 2 | 1 | .265/.317/.381 | .250 | .285 | -0.1 | C -2, LF -0 | 1.5 |

Pena's calling card throughout his minor league career was his ability to get on base. In over 1400 plate appearances, spread across a Triple-A career that spanned parts of five seasons, he flashed an outstanding ability to put the bat on the ball and complied a .358 OBP. Great potential, but his aggressive approach hasn't translated to the majors and his OBP cratered in 2011. Defensively, he threw out 35 percent of all would-be base stealers, the fifth best rate in the AL, but overall he is a poor receiver who has difficulty blocking pitches in the dirt. One could live with the defensive deficiencies if he were reaching base, but with a substandard OBP and no power, it is hard to justify carrying him as even a semi-regular. The good news is the arrival of Salvador Perez keeps him in a backup role.

**Salvador Perez** C
Born: **5/10/1990** Age: **22**
Bats: **R** Throws: **R** Height: **6' 4"** Weight: **230**
Breakout: **5%** Improve: **20%** Collapse: **12%**
Attrition: **26%** MLB: **51%**
**Comparables:**
Tim McCarver, Tony Cruz, Buck Martinez

| YEAR | TEAM | LVL | AGE | PA | R | 2B | 3B | HR | RBI | BB | SO | SB | CS | AVG_OBP_SLG | TAv | BABIP | BRR | FRAA | WARP |
|------|------|-----|-----|----|----|----|----|----|-----|----|----|----|----|-------------|-----|-------|-----|------|------|
| 2009 | BUR | A | 19 | 137 | 10 | 6 | 0 | 0 | 7 | 6 | 15 | 0 | 1 | .189/.228/.236 | .171 | .211 | -1.5 | 0.4 | -1.0 |
| 2009 | IDA | RK | 19 | 259 | 35 | 14 | 3 | 2 | 38 | 19 | 25 | 0 | 1 | .309/.362/.421 | .320 | .338 | 0.7 | 0.4 | 2.6 |
| 2010 | WIL | A+ | 20 | 396 | 35 | 21 | 1 | 7 | 53 | 18 | 38 | 1 | 1 | .290/.328/.411 | .269 | .308 | -3.2 | 0.8 | 1.9 |
| 2011 | NWA | AA | 21 | 309 | 35 | 14 | 0 | 9 | 43 | 16 | 30 | 0 | 1 | .283/.329/.427 | .254 | .290 | -1.3 | -1.2 | 1.1 |
| 2011 | KCA | MLB | 21 | 158 | 20 | 8 | 2 | 3 | 21 | 7 | 20 | 0 | 0 | .331/.361/.473 | .305 | .362 | -1.5 | -0.5 | 1.2 |
| 2012 | KCA | MLB | 22 | 250 | 26 | 12 | 1 | 3 | 24 | 9 | 35 | 0 | 0 | .261/.290/.358 | .235 | .292 | 0 | C -1 | 0.8 |

Perez entered the 2011 season as one of the top defensive catching prospects in the game. He only enhanced that reputation in his major league debut when he picked a runner off first, another off third, and very nearly gunned down another off second. By the end of the season, he had caught base-stealers only 21 percent of the time. The low success rate is more a product of him learning the Royals pitching staff and their inability to keep runners close than his throwing ability. His catch and release mechanics, footwork, and arm strength are outstanding: his caught stealing rate will only increase. While his defensive reputation rightly preceded him, there were questions about how his bat would hold up at the big league level. Perez answered that emphatically with an 89 percent contact rate and gap to gap power. The Royals have struggled to fill the backstop position for years, employing the likes of Brent Mayne, Jason Kendall, and Miguel Olivo. That problem has been solved.

### Manny Pina — C

Born: 6/5/1987 Age: 25
Bats: R Throws: R Height: 6' 1" Weight: 230
Breakout: 2% Improve: 27% Collapse: 10%
Attrition: 37% MLB: 73%

Comparables:
Jason Jaramillo, Joe Garagiola, Bobby Wilson

| YEAR | TEAM | LVL | AGE | PA | R | 2B | 3B | HR | RBI | BB | SO | SB | CS | AVG/OBP/SLG | TAv | BABIP | BRR | FRAA | WARP |
|------|------|-----|-----|-----|----|----|----|----|-----|----|----|----|----|-------------|------|-------|------|------|------|
| 2009 | FRI | AA | 22 | 355 | 36 | 17 | 1 | 8 | 42 | 19 | 58 | 1 | 0 | .259/.313/.393 | .257 | .291 | -3.1 | -0.6 | 0.8 |
| 2010 | NWA | AA | 23 | 302 | 39 | 16 | 0 | 7 | 44 | 24 | 37 | 0 | 0 | .259/.321/.398 | .230 | .274 | -1.4 | -1.2 | 0.3 |
| 2010 | OMA | AAA | 23 | 60 | 5 | 2 | 0 | 2 | 5 | 3 | 7 | 0 | 0 | .218/.271/.364 | .210 | .217 | -0.4 | -0.1 | -0.2 |
| 2011 | OMA | AAA | 24 | 259 | 34 | 13 | 0 | 5 | 25 | 34 | 37 | 0 | 0 | .238/.364/.371 | .280 | .266 | -1.8 | -1.2 | 2.0 |
| 2011 | KCA | MLB | 24 | 15 | 2 | 2 | 0 | 0 | 0 | 1 | 2 | 0 | 0 | .214/.267/.357 | .180 | .250 | -0.5 | -0.1 | -0.1 |
| 2012 | KCA | MLB | 25 | 250 | 26 | 12 | 1 | 5 | 24 | 17 | 45 | 0 | 0 | .231/.294/.352 | .232 | .264 | 0 | C -2 | 0.8 |

Pina is an excellent defensive catcher, but his bat will ultimately impede his opportunity to ply his trade at the major league level. Last summer was the first time in his minor league career he posted a respectable OBP, thanks to improved plate discipline. However, the improvement is relative. He still has a difficult time controlling the strike zone. When the Royals decide Brayan Pena is too expensive for their tastes, Pina will stick with the team as a backup to Salvador Perez.

### Clint Robinson — 1B

Born: 2/16/1985 Age: 27
Bats: L Throws: L Height: 6' 6" Weight: 235
Breakout: 1% Improve: 35% Collapse: 3%
Attrition: 13% MLB: 68%

Comparables:
Justin Morneau, Kent Hrbek, Glenn Davis

| YEAR | TEAM | LVL | AGE | PA | R | 2B | 3B | HR | RBI | BB | SO | SB | CS | AVG/OBP/SLG | TAv | BABIP | BRR | FRAA | WARP |
|------|------|-----|-----|-----|----|----|----|----|-----|----|----|----|----|-------------|------|-------|------|------|------|
| 2009 | WIL | A+ | 24 | 483 | 65 | 31 | 1 | 13 | 57 | 35 | 79 | 4 | 3 | .298/.360/.463 | .290 | .340 | -1.3 | -6.2 | 1.2 |
| 2010 | NWA | AA | 25 | 548 | 90 | 41 | 5 | 29 | 98 | 58 | 86 | 4 | 3 | .335/.413/.625 | .336 | .360 | -1.7 | 1.2 | 5.7 |
| 2011 | OMA | AAA | 26 | 572 | 86 | 35 | 0 | 23 | 100 | 58 | 88 | 2 | 1 | .326/.399/.533 | .310 | .356 | -1.2 | 0.2 | 4.1 |
| 2012 | KCA | MLB | 27 | 250 | 31 | 13 | 1 | 8 | 32 | 20 | 49 | 1 | 0 | .271/.333/.447 | .274 | .310 | 0 | 1B -8, LF -0 | 1.3 |

Robinson put his name on the map by winning the Texas League Triple Crown in 2010, and he adjusted well to his new home in the PCL, barely losing much power in the process. Still, he's seen as the classic Quad-A hitter, and with Hosmer and Butler ahead of him, there won't be opportunity to take his hacks in the majors.

### Derrick Robinson — CF

Born: 9/28/1987 Age: 24
Bats: B Throws: L Height: 6' 0" Weight: 170
Breakout: 3% Improve: 14% Collapse: 2%
Attrition: 19% MLB: 31%

Comparables:
Freddy Guzman, Emeel Salem, Leo Sutherland

| YEAR | TEAM | LVL | AGE | PA | R | 2B | 3B | HR | RBI | BB | SO | SB | CS | AVG/OBP/SLG | TAv | BABIP | BRR | FRAA | WARP |
|------|------|-----|-----|-----|----|----|----|----|-----|----|----|----|----|-------------|------|-------|------|------|------|
| 2009 | WIL | A+ | 21 | 571 | 72 | 19 | 5 | 5 | 47 | 35 | 90 | 69 | 23 | .239/.286/.324 | .224 | .275 | 1.2 | 7.2 | 0.1 |
| 2010 | NWA | AA | 22 | 570 | 74 | 26 | 8 | 2 | 48 | 45 | 86 | 50 | 17 | .286/.345/.380 | .253 | .336 | -0.7 | 8.6 | 1.9 |
| 2011 | NWA | AA | 23 | 483 | 56 | 6 | 2 | 1 | 25 | 46 | 87 | 55 | 15 | .251/.323/.282 | .220 | .311 | 6.3 | 9.8 | 0.6 |
| 2012 | KCA | MLB | 24 | 250 | 23 | 8 | 2 | 1 | 18 | 14 | 50 | 20 | 6 | .233/.277/.293 | .205 | .288 | 0.1 | CF 0, LF 0 | -1.1 |

Another outfielder with speed to burn and zero pop in his bat. He covers a ton of ground in center and generally plays an excellent defense, but needs to improve his contact rate and learn to mix in a few more walks before he can seriously be considered a future contributor.

## PITCHERS

### Jason Adam

Born: 8/4/1991 Age: 20
Bats: R Throws: R Height: 6' 5" Weight: 225
Breakout: 33% Improve: 59% Collapse: 30%
Attrition: 3% MLB: 72%

Comparables:
Catfish Hunter, Jim Waugh, Bob Miller

| YEAR | TEAM | LVL | AGE | W | L | SV | G | GS | IP | H | HR | BB | SO | EqBB9 | EqSO9 | GB% | BABIP | WHIP | ERA | FIP | FRA | WARP |
|------|------|-----|-----|---|---|----|---|----|-----|----|----|----|----|-------|-------|-----|-------|------|------|------|------|------|
| 2011 | KNC | A | 19 | 6 | 9 | 0 | 21 | 21 | 104¹ | 98 | 9 | 25 | 81 | 2.2 | 6.6 | 45% | .266 | 1.14 | 4.23 | 3.82 | 4.56 | 0.9 |
| 2012 | KCA | MLB | 20 | 1 | 2 | 0 | 5 | 5 | 25¹ | 32 | 3 | 12 | 11 | 4.2 | 3.7 | 44% | .309 | 1.71 | 6.04 | 5.30 | 6.57 | -0.3 |

The Royals needed to go over slot to convince this fifth-round pick in the 2010 draft to forgo a scholarship to the University of Missouri. In an effort to keep his innings under control in 2011, they held him in Arizona until mid-May before they assigned him to Class-A Kane County. Adam has a fastball that sits in the mid-90s and is refining his curve, which the Royals hope will develop into a nifty out pitch.

**Nathan Adcock**
Born: 2/25/1988 Age: 24
Bats: R Throws: R Height: 6' 6" Weight: 220
Breakout: 34% Improve: 63% Collapse: 19%
Attrition: 14% MLB: 84%

Comparables:
Bob Friend, Randy Moffitt, Livan Hernandez

| YEAR | TEAM | LVL | AGE | W | L | SV | G | GS | IP | H | HR | BB | SO | EqBB9 | EqSO9 | GB% | BABIP | WHIP | ERA | FIP | FRA | WARP |
|---|---|---|---|---|---|---|---|---|---|---|---|---|---|---|---|---|---|---|---|---|---|---|
| 2009 | LYN | A+ | 21 | 3 | 2 | 0 | 7 | 4 | 24 | 34 | 5 | 10 | 19 | 2.6 | 5.6 | 47% | .302 | 1.50 | 5.25 | 6.10 | 6.33 | -0.2 |
| 2009 | HDS | A+ | 21 | 5 | 7 | 0 | 21 | 19 | 102 | 103 | 10 | 54 | 71 | 4.8 | 6.3 | 51% | .299 | 1.54 | 5.29 | 5.41 | 6.16 | -0.2 |
| 2010 | BRD | A+ | 22 | 11 | 7 | 0 | 27 | 26 | 141$^1$ | 131 | 8 | 38 | 113 | 2.4 | 7.2 | — | .300 | 1.20 | 3.38 | 3.62 | — | 0.0 |
| 2011 | KCA | MLB | 23 | 1 | 1 | 1 | 24 | 3 | 60$^1$ | 63 | 5 | 26 | 36 | 3.9 | 5.4 | 56% | .302 | 1.48 | 4.62 | 4.39 | 5.67 | -0.1 |
| 2012 | KCA | MLB | 24 | 0 | 0 | 0 | 10 | 0 | 39$^2$ | 48 | 5 | 22 | 20 | 5.1 | 4.5 | 50% | .314 | 1.78 | 6.17 | 5.50 | 6.71 | -0.7 |

Adcock is a Rule 5 pick from the Pirates organization and the Royals liked him enough to keep him on the major league roster for the entire year. Liking him, though, is different than trusting him. He made only three appearances the entire month of June, and at one point in July went 20 days between trips to the mound. He never pitched above

Breakout: 33% Improve: 49% Collapse: 24%
Attrition: 10% MLB: 96%

Comparables:
Michael Gonzalez, Mark Wohlers, Francisco Rodriguez

| YEAR | TEAM | LVL | AGE | W | L | SV | G | GS | IP | H | HR | BB | SO | EqBB9 | EqSO9 | GB% | BABIP | WHIP | ERA | FIP | FRA | WARP |
|---|---|---|---|---|---|---|---|---|---|---|---|---|---|---|---|---|---|---|---|---|---|---|
| 2011 | LAN | MLB | 27 | 1 | 2 | 7 | 14 | 0 | 12$^2$ | 15 | 2 | 9 | 10 | 6.4 | 7.1 | 42% | .317 | 1.89 | 5.68 | 5.60 | 4.41 | 0.0 |
| 2012 | KCA | MLB | 28 | 1 | 1 | 7 | 23 | 0 | 21$^2$ | 18 | 1 | 8 | 27 | 3.2 | 11.3 | 48% | .312 | 1.17 | 2.60 | 2.42 | 2.83 | 0.6 |

Deposed from the Dodgers' closer role in August 2010, Broxton regained it in spring training, and notched three saves in the season's first four days despite allowing a pair of solo homers. Alas, by mid-April he was struggling again, and in early May he hit the disabled list with elbow soreness due to a bone spur. As it turns out, he'd been pitching through pain for who knows how long, not only concealing the injury but admitting that he planned to be no more forthcoming to the medical staff about any future woes. Not only did that stance suggest that Broxton is as dumb as he is big, it shed some light as to how he could go from an 0.83 ERA through his first 33 appearances in 2010 to a 7.58 mark in his final 31—the first of them that 48-pitch ordeal against the Yankees. In any event, Broxton tried to rehab before being shut down to undergo surgery to shave down the spur and remove loose bodies. The Royals signed him to a one-year, $4M deal, intending to have the 27-year-old set up for Joakim Soria.

**Bruce Chen**
Born: 6/19/1977 Age: 35
Bats: L Throws: L Height: 6' 3" Weight: 150
Breakout: 16% Improve: 42% Collapse: 33%
Attrition: 19% MLB: 83%

Comparables:
Rheal Cormier, Jamie Walker, Wilson Alvarez

| YEAR | TEAM | LVL | AGE | W | L | SV | G | GS | IP | H | HR | BB | SO | EqBB9 | EqSO9 | GB% | BABIP | WHIP | ERA | FIP | FRA | WARP |
|---|---|---|---|---|---|---|---|---|---|---|---|---|---|---|---|---|---|---|---|---|---|---|
| 2009 | OMA | AAA | 32 | 4 | 2 | 0 | 14 | 13 | 82 | 57 | 8 | 23 | 69 | 2.5 | 7.6 | 37% | .226 | 0.98 | 3.40 | 4.02 | 4.53 | 0.6 |
| 2009 | KCA | MLB | 32 | 1 | 6 | 0 | 17 | 9 | 62$^1$ | 74 | 12 | 25 | 45 | 3.6 | 6.5 | 32% | .325 | 1.59 | 5.78 | 5.60 | 6.10 | 0.1 |
| 2010 | KCA | MLB | 33 | 12 | 7 | 1 | 33 | 23 | 140$^1$ | 136 | 17 | 57 | 98 | 3.7 | 6.3 | 35% | .279 | 1.38 | 4.17 | 4.51 | 4.25 | 1.8 |
| 2011 | KCA | MLB | 34 | 12 | 8 | 0 | 25 | 25 | 155 | 152 | 18 | 50 | 97 | 2.9 | 5.6 | 37% | .280 | 1.30 | 3.77 | 4.42 | 4.56 | 1.7 |
| 2012 | KCA | MLB | 35 | 7 | 9 | 0 | 22 | 22 | 131$^2$ | 141 | 16 | 48 | 89 | 3.2 | 6.1 | 37% | .301 | 1.43 | 4.59 | 4.53 | 4.99 | 0.4 |

A marginal major league starter when signed by the Royals midway through 2010, Chen began experimenting with changing his arm slot. Normally, he throws with a delivery that comes over the top, but he began dropping to a three-quarters slot on occasion. The results are intriguing: he's throwing *fewer* strikes overall, but has been enticing hitters to chase out of the strike zone with greater frequency. More confounding is that while his ground-ball rate remains around 35 percent, he has been keeping the ball in the yard since joining the Royals, with a 1.05 HR/9. His ERA may be shiny, but his peripherals indicate he's living dangerously, allowing too many base runners to continue his modest run of success.

### Louis Coleman

Born: 4/4/1986 Age: 26
Bats: R Throws: R Height: 6′ 5″ Weight: 200
Breakout: 33% Improve: 50% Collapse: 19%
Attrition: 10% MLB: 93%

Comparables:
Al Hrabosky, Sergio Romo, Jonathan Papelbon

| YEAR | TEAM | LVL | AGE | W | L | SV | G | GS | IP | H | HR | BB | SO | EqBB9 | EqSO9 | GB% | BABIP | WHIP | ERA | FIP | FRA | WARP |
|------|------|-----|-----|---|---|----|----|----|-----|----|----|----|----|-------|-------|-----|-------|------|------|------|------|------|
| 2010 | NWA | AA | 24 | 2 | 1 | 6 | 21 | 1 | 51² | 21 | 5 | 10 | 47 | 2.4 | 9.6 | 38% | .205 | 0.87 | 2.09 | 3.40 | 3.54 | 1.1 |
| 2010 | OMA | AAA | 24 | 5 | 1 | 1 | 21 | 0 | 40¹ | 21 | 2 | 4 | 28 | 2.5 | 10.7 | 39% | .311 | 1.04 | 2.23 | 3.76 | 3.46 | 0.7 |
| 2011 | KCA | MLB | 25 | 1 | 4 | 1 | 48 | 0 | 59² | 44 | 9 | 26 | 64 | 3.9 | 9.7 | 32% | .248 | 1.17 | 2.87 | 4.34 | 4.49 | 0.5 |
| 2012 | KCA | MLB | 26 | 2 | 1 | 0 | 30 | 0 | 49¹ | 43 | 5 | 18 | 52 | 3.3 | 9.4 | 38% | .294 | 1.24 | 3.39 | 3.51 | 3.68 | 0.8 |

Coleman rocketed through the system in fewer than two years to emerge as one of the more effective relievers in the Royals Baby Bullpen in 2011. His fastball lives in the low 90s and his slider is close to a plus pitch. He features a crossfire delivery with a three quarter arm slot where he whips his pitches across his body. The arm action helps deceive right-handed hitters, who managed a feeble .180/.260/.360 line against him in 155 plate appearances. That deception disappears against left-handed batters who have ample time to get a read on his action. He just doesn't miss as many lefty bats. It's an issue he needs to solve if he's to have an important role in the Royals pen.

### Tim Collins

Born: 8/21/1989 Age: 22
Bats: L Throws: L Height: 5′ 8″ Weight: 170
Breakout: 36% Improve: 57% Collapse: 20%
Attrition: 7% MLB: 86%

Comparables:
Balor Moore, Clayton Kershaw, Scott Kazmir

| YEAR | TEAM | LVL | AGE | W | L | SV | G | GS | IP | H | HR | BB | SO | EqBB9 | EqSO9 | GB% | BABIP | WHIP | ERA | FIP | FRA | WARP |
|------|------|-----|-----|---|---|----|----|----|-----|----|----|----|----|-------|-------|-----|-------|------|------|------|------|------|
| 2009 | DUN | A+ | 19 | 7 | 4 | 3 | 40 | 0 | 64² | 47 | 2 | 28 | 99 | 3.9 | 13.8 | 44% | .331 | 1.16 | 2.36 | 1.98 | 2.68 | 2.0 |
| 2010 | NHP | AA | 20 | 1 | 0 | 9 | 35 | 0 | 43 | 18 | 3 | 13 | 41 | 3.3 | 15.3 | 33% | .306 | 1.00 | 2.51 | 3.50 | 3.77 | 0.8 |
| 2010 | OMA | AAA | 20 | 2 | 1 | 4 | 15 | 0 | 20¹ | 8 | 0 | 4 | 13 | 3.5 | 9.3 | 32% | .235 | 0.84 | 1.33 | 3.37 | 3.88 | 0.2 |
| 2011 | KCA | MLB | 21 | 4 | 4 | 0 | 68 | 0 | 67 | 52 | 5 | 48 | 60 | 6.4 | 8.1 | 42% | .266 | 1.49 | 3.63 | 4.48 | 4.73 | 0.4 |
| 2012 | KCA | MLB | 22 | 2 | 1 | 0 | 47 | 0 | 52¹ | 45 | 4 | 30 | 58 | 5.1 | 10.0 | 43% | .303 | 1.43 | 3.83 | 3.70 | 4.17 | 0.6 |

This diminutive left-hander uses a corkscrew delivery with a high leg kick to generate enough energy to bring heat in the low- to mid-90s. Against the odds, Collins proved himself at every level of the minors and opened the season as a set-up man in the Royals bullpen. Ned Yost likes to play favorites in his bullpen and Collins was the manager's pet early in the season, appearing in 28 of the Royals first 51 games. Yost backed off from June onward, but the heavy early workload appeared to exact a toll: Collins struggled with his control and finished with 24 walks over his final 37 innings of work. At times, he was the lone southpaw in the Royals bullpen, so he was miscast as a LOOGY, even though his splits versus lefties were worse. He finished with a 0.93 SO/BB ratio against said lefties. Collins can be a useful piece of the Royals bullpen puzzle, if they can figure out the best way to use him.

### Aaron Crow

Born: 11/10/1986 Age: 25
Bats: R Throws: R Height: 6′ 4″ Weight: 190
Breakout: 37% Improve: 67% Collapse: 10%
Attrition: 14% MLB: 88%

Comparables:
Bill Campbell, Randor Bierd, Brad Mills

| YEAR | TEAM | LVL | AGE | W | L | SV | G | GS | IP | H | HR | BB | SO | EqBB9 | EqSO9 | GB% | BABIP | WHIP | ERA | FIP | FRA | WARP |
|------|------|-----|-----|---|---|----|----|----|------|-----|----|----|----|-------|-------|-----|-------|------|------|------|------|------|
| 2010 | WIL | A+ | 23 | 2 | 3 | 0 | 7 | 7 | 44 | 42 | 4 | 5 | 45 | 1.2 | 10.8 | 55% | .392 | 1.30 | 5.93 | 3.00 | 4.50 | 0.4 |
| 2010 | NWA | AA | 23 | 7 | 7 | 0 | 22 | 22 | 119¹ | 103 | 11 | 46 | 65 | 4.5 | 6.8 | 60% | .345 | 1.58 | 5.66 | 4.69 | 6.15 | -0.5 |
| 2011 | KCA | MLB | 24 | 4 | 4 | 0 | 57 | 0 | 62 | 55 | 8 | 31 | 65 | 4.5 | 9.4 | 53% | .296 | 1.39 | 2.76 | 4.14 | 4.82 | 0.2 |
| 2012 | KCA | MLB | 25 | 3 | 3 | 0 | 21 | 7 | 54 | 58 | 7 | 25 | 44 | 4.1 | 7.3 | 52% | .315 | 1.53 | 4.87 | 4.65 | 5.29 | -0.0 |

After his first professional season (2010, Double-A), the Royals' top pick in the 2009 draft battled mechanical issues and was demoted to High-A. However, a strong spring meant Crow was a surprise addition to the Opening Day bullpen and he built an exceptional first half into a selection to the All-Star team as the Royals' lone representative. His fastball lives in the mid-90s and can approach 98 mph on occasion. His slider is a plus pitch with exceptional lateral movement. Shortly after the All-Star Game, it was revealed he had been dealing with a stiff shoulder and forearm tightness: he limped to the finish line with a 7.36 ERA over the final two months of the season. The poor finish doesn't discourage the Royals, who are going to give him a long look in the rotation this spring.

### Danny Duffy

Born: 12/21/1988 Age: 23
Bats: L Throws: L Height: 6′ 4″ Weight: 200
Breakout: 27% Improve: 50% Collapse: 27%
Attrition: 18% MLB: 96%

Comparables:
Dennis Bennett, Sparky Lyle, Scott Olsen

| YEAR | TEAM | LVL | AGE | W | L | SV | G | GS | IP | H | HR | BB | SO | EqBB9 | EqSO9 | GB% | BABIP | WHIP | ERA | FIP | FRA | WARP |
|------|------|-----|-----|---|---|----|----|----|------|-----|----|----|-----|-------|-------|-----|-------|------|------|------|------|------|
| 2009 | WIL | A+ | 20 | 9 | 4 | 0 | 24 | 24 | 126² | 111 | 6 | 43 | 132 | 2.9 | 8.9 | 46% | .297 | 1.18 | 2.98 | 2.92 | 4.29 | 1.3 |
| 2010 | NWA | AA | 21 | 6 | 2 | 0 | 7 | 7 | 39² | 41 | 3 | 9 | 38 | 2.0 | 9.3 | 48% | .365 | 1.18 | 2.95 | 3.15 | 3.73 | 1.3 |
| 2011 | OMA | AAA | 22 | 1 | 0 | 0 | 8 | 8 | 42 | 37 | 5 | 10 | 48 | 2.1 | 10.3 | 41% | .308 | 1.12 | 3.43 | 3.93 | 4.48 | 0.8 |
| 2011 | KCA | MLB | 22 | 4 | 8 | 0 | 20 | 20 | 105¹ | 119 | 15 | 51 | 87 | 4.4 | 7.4 | 40% | .331 | 1.61 | 5.64 | 4.86 | 4.85 | 0.5 |
| 2012 | KCA | MLB | 23 | 5 | 7 | 0 | 18 | 18 | 90 | 95 | 10 | 39 | 78 | 3.9 | 7.8 | 39% | .318 | 1.49 | 4.67 | 4.22 | 5.07 | 0.3 |

The first of what the Royals hope will be a wave of starting pitching prospects, Duffy arrived in Kansas City with much fanfare in mid-May when the club ran thin on viable starters. He certainly earned the call-up after punching out 48 hitters in 42 innings in Omaha. Once in the majors, Duffy at times exhibited brilliance, but far too often he nibbled and lost the ability to put hitters away once he jumped ahead in the count. He also developed an alarming habit of putting the ball right down the middle of the plate when he fell behind. Still, Duffy has good feel for a fastball that sits in the low- to mid-90s and favors a slow, sweeping curve as his top secondary pitch. He was shut down in September after approaching 150 innings between the majors and minors. Think of 2011 as his first step in the major league learning process. With his stuff, he is still more than capable of developing into a quality, front-line starter.

**Jeff Francis**
Born: **1/8/1981** Age: **31**
Bats: **L** Throws: **L** Height: **6' 6"** Weight: **200**
Breakout: **21%** Improve: **49%** Collapse: **22%**
Attrition: **13%** MLB: **81%**

**Comparables:**
Odalis Perez, Denny Neagle, Donnie Moore

| YEAR | TEAM | LVL | AGE | W | L | SV | G | GS | IP | H | HR | BB | SO | EqBB9 | EqSO9 | GB% | BABIP | WHIP | ERA | FIP | FRA | WARP |
|------|------|-----|-----|---|---|----|---|----|----|---|----|----|----|-------|-------|-----|-------|------|-----|-----|-----|------|
| 2010 | COL | MLB | 29 | 4 | 6 | 0 | 20 | 19 | 104[1] | 119 | 11 | 23 | 67 | 2.0 | 5.8 | 49% | .325 | 1.36 | 5.00 | 3.91 | 4.58 | 1.5 |
| 2011 | KCA | MLB | 30 | 6 | 16 | 0 | 31 | 31 | 183 | 224 | 19 | 39 | 91 | 1.9 | 4.5 | 49% | .319 | 1.44 | 4.82 | 4.14 | 4.90 | 0.6 |
| *2012* | *KCA* | *MLB* | *31* | *7* | *11* | *0* | *26* | *26* | *144[2]* | *179* | *17* | *38* | *83* | *2.3* | *5.2* | *46%* | *.328* | *1.49* | *5.05* | *4.37* | *5.49* | *-0.3* |

When the starting rotation resembles a moldy brick of Swiss cheese, you're forced to scour the bargain bin to fill the holes. For a team on a strict budget, a starter like Francis—moderately ef-

Born: **12/31/1989** Age: **22**
Bats: **R** Throws: **R** Height: **5' 11"** Weight: **162**
Breakout: **24%** Improve: **53%** Collapse: **22%**
Attrition: **12%** MLB: **89%**

**Comparables:**
Don Gullett, Troy Patton, Larry Dierker

| YEAR | TEAM | LVL | AGE | W | L | SV | G | GS | IP | H | HR | BB | SO | EqBB9 | EqSO9 | GB% | BABIP | WHIP | ERA | FIP | FRA | WARP |
|------|------|-----|-----|---|---|----|---|----|----|---|----|----|----|-------|-------|-----|-------|------|-----|-----|-----|------|
| 2011 | NWA | AA | 21 | 1 | 0 | 7 | 23 | 0 | 36 | 22 | 4 | 7 | 40 | 1.5 | 10.0 | 66% | .214 | 0.78 | 1.75 | 3.27 | 4.45 | 0.3 |
| 2011 | KCA | MLB | 21 | 0 | 1 | 0 | 2 | 0 | 2 | 2 | 1 | 0 | 0 | 0.0 | 0.0 | 38% | .167 | 1.00 | 13.50 | 11.06 | 12.84 | -0.1 |
| *2012* | *KCA* | *MLB* | *22* | *1* | *1* | *0* | *10* | *1* | *20[1]* | *22* | *2* | *8* | *13* | *3.6* | *5.9* | *52%* | *.302* | *1.49* | *4.79* | *4.38* | *5.21* | *-0.0* |

Herrera's checklist for the 2011 season: Breeze through High-A? Done. Dominate Double-A? Yep. Crush the spirits of Triple-A hitters? Complete. Earn a spot on the 40-man roster and a September call-up to Kansas City? Mission accomplished. After missing almost the entire 2009 season and most of 2010 with elbow issues, Herrera made a definite splash in 2011. Moved to the bullpen in an effort to protect his elbow, he fires a fastball in the upper 90s (touching triple digits at times), keeps the ball down, and flat misses bats. After moving so rapidly through the system, it's conceivable he could open the year in Triple-A for a dash more seasoning, but after his big year, the Royals are now counting on him to be a big part of the future bullpen in Kansas City.

**Luke Hochevar**
Born: **9/15/1983** Age: **28**
Bats: **R** Throws: **R** Height: **6' 6"** Weight: **205**
Breakout: **18%** Improve: **75%** Collapse: **13%**
Attrition: **9%** MLB: **83%**

**Comparables:**
T.J. Beam, Frank Sullivan, Mike Burns

| YEAR | TEAM | LVL | AGE | W | L | SV | G | GS | IP | H | HR | BB | SO | EqBB9 | EqSO9 | GB% | BABIP | WHIP | ERA | FIP | FRA | WARP |
|------|------|-----|-----|---|---|----|---|----|----|---|----|----|----|-------|-------|-----|-------|------|-----|-----|-----|------|
| 2009 | OMA | AAA | 25 | 5 | 1 | 0 | 8 | 8 | 48 | 41 | 2 | 12 | 36 | 2.2 | 6.8 | 63% | .287 | 1.10 | 1.50 | 3.24 | 4.26 | 0.5 |
| 2009 | KCA | MLB | 25 | 7 | 13 | 0 | 25 | 25 | 143 | 167 | 23 | 46 | 106 | 2.9 | 6.7 | 48% | .323 | 1.49 | 6.55 | 4.88 | 5.62 | 0.6 |
| 2010 | KCA | MLB | 26 | 6 | 6 | 0 | 18 | 17 | 103 | 110 | 9 | 37 | 76 | 3.2 | 6.6 | 46% | .314 | 1.43 | 4.81 | 3.90 | 4.64 | 0.8 |
| 2011 | KCA | MLB | 27 | 11 | 11 | 0 | 31 | 31 | 198 | 192 | 23 | 62 | 128 | 2.8 | 5.8 | 51% | .276 | 1.28 | 4.68 | 4.32 | 4.48 | 1.7 |
| *2012* | *KCA* | *MLB* | *28* | *8* | *11* | *0* | *25* | *25* | *152[2]* | *168* | *16* | *50* | *101* | *2.9* | *5.9* | *48%* | *.312* | *1.43* | *4.72* | *4.23* | *5.13* | *0.2* |

Often, it just takes a little time before things click and fall into place. For Hochevar, the epiphany came at the All-Star break when he decided to lean more on his best pitch—his slider—than before. At the same time, he adjusted the delivery of that pitch, slightly dropping his arm angle, which resulted in a tighter spin and a more effective pitch than previous incarnations. Now his slider release point mimics the release point of his sinker, making it difficult for opposing hitters to guess: will it dip or will it slide? Hochevar rode that deception to his finest stretch of starts as a professional, with a 3.52 ERA and 7.7 SO/9 over the season's second half. The Royals will count on the former number one overall draft pick to replicate that success over a full year.

### Greg Holland
Born: 11/20/1985 Age: 26
Bats: R Throws: R Height: 6' 0" Weight: 190
Breakout: 30% Improve: 54% Collapse: 19%
Attrition: 7% MLB: 84%
Comparables:
Pedro Martinez, Mark Worrell, Chris Ray

| YEAR | TEAM | LVL | AGE | W | L | SV | G | GS | IP | H | HR | BB | SO | EqBB9 | EqSO9 | GB% | BABIP | WHIP | ERA | FIP | FRA | WARP |
|------|------|-----|-----|---|---|----|---|----|----|---|----|----|----|-------|-------|-----|-------|------|-----|-----|-----|------|
| 2009 | NWA | AA | 23 | 3 | 2 | 8 | 29 | 0 | 45¹ | 46 | 2 | 19 | 49 | 3.8 | 9.7 | 48% | .355 | 1.43 | 3.18 | 2.91 | 3.59 | 0.8 |
| 2010 | OMA | AAA | 24 | 3 | 3 | 3 | 36 | 0 | 56² | 21 | 2 | 21 | 34 | 4.8 | 9.5 | 52% | .204 | 1.23 | 3.81 | 4.43 | 4.69 | 0.4 |
| 2010 | KCA | MLB | 24 | 0 | 1 | 0 | 15 | 0 | 18² | 23 | 3 | 8 | 23 | 3.9 | 11.1 | 36% | .385 | 1.66 | 6.75 | 3.96 | 5.01 | 0.0 |
| 2011 | OMA | AAA | 25 | 1 | 0 | 2 | 13 | 0 | 21² | 13 | 1 | 11 | 25 | 4.6 | 11.2 | 66% | .261 | 1.11 | 2.08 | 3.55 | 4.49 | 0.4 |
| 2011 | KCA | MLB | 25 | 5 | 1 | 4 | 46 | 0 | 60 | 37 | 3 | 19 | 74 | 2.8 | 11.1 | 45% | .252 | 0.93 | 1.80 | 2.24 | 3.45 | 1.1 |
| 2012 | KCA | MLB | 26 | 2 | 1 | 1 | 36 | 0 | 50² | 47 | 4 | 23 | 51 | 4.0 | 9.1 | 46% | .307 | 1.37 | 3.70 | 3.58 | 4.02 | 0.6 |

Had a cup of coffee in 2010, ran into a little bad luck, but his 11.1 SO/9 and swing and miss rate of 20 percent pointed to some upside. He opened the year in Omaha but was recalled in mid-May and quickly established himself as the most dependable reliever in the Royals bullpen. He again punched out hitters to a rate of 11.1 SO/9—this time with a 27 percent swing and miss rate—while he shaved a full walk off his BB/9 rate. Holland also didn't allow a home run over his final 27 innings of work. The combination of control and his ability to miss bats means he will begin the year as Kansas City's primary set-up man and could see a few save opportunities if Soria should experience another rough patch.

### Jeremy Jeffress
Born: 9/21/1987 Age: 24
Bats: R Throws: R Height: 6' 1" Weight: 195
Breakout: 29% Improve: 70% Collapse: 13%
Attrition: 7% MLB: 93%
Comparables:
Jeff Jones, Bobby Bolin, Rich Gossage

| YEAR | TEAM | LVL | AGE | W | L | SV | G | GS | IP | H | HR | BB | SO | EqBB9 | EqSO9 | GB% | BABIP | WHIP | ERA | FIP | FRA | WARP |
|------|------|-----|-----|---|---|----|---|----|----|---|----|----|----|-------|-------|-----|-------|------|-----|-----|-----|------|
| 2009 | BRV | A+ | 21 | 2 | 1 | 0 | 6 | 5 | 33 | 16 | 2 | 22 | 36 | 6.0 | 9.8 | 66% | .192 | 1.15 | 2.18 | 4.08 | 4.76 | 0.1 |
| 2009 | HUN | AA | 21 | 1 | 3 | 0 | 8 | 8 | 27¹ | 26 | 1 | 33 | 34 | 10.9 | 11.2 | 59% | .368 | 2.16 | 7.58 | 4.82 | 5.52 | 0.2 |
| 2010 | MIL | MLB | 22 | 1 | 0 | 0 | 10 | 0 | 10 | 8 | 0 | 6 | 8 | 5.4 | 7.2 | 57% | .286 | 1.40 | 2.70 | 3.31 | 2.96 | 0.2 |
| 2011 | NWA | AA | 23 | 1 | 1 | 0 | 9 | 8 | 31² | 38 | 3 | 25 | 23 | 6.3 | 5.7 | 61% | .315 | 1.71 | 4.26 | 5.72 | 6.15 | -0.1 |
| 2011 | OMA | AAA | 23 | 0 | 3 | 3 | 16 | 3 | 24 | 27 | 5 | 18 | 24 | 6.8 | 9.0 | 58% | .349 | 1.88 | 7.12 | 6.82 | 7.99 | -0.5 |
| 2011 | KCA | MLB | 23 | 1 | 1 | 1 | 14 | 0 | 15¹ | 12 | 1 | 11 | 13 | 6.5 | 7.6 | 58% | .275 | 1.50 | 4.70 | 4.37 | 6.18 | -0.1 |
| 2012 | KCA | MLB | 24 | 1 | 1 | 0 | 19 | 3 | 29¹ | 29 | 3 | 20 | 26 | 6.1 | 7.9 | 48% | .306 | 1.66 | 5.17 | 4.81 | 5.62 | -0.1 |

A key component of the deal that sent Zack Greinke to Milwaukee, Jeffress made the bullpen out of spring training as the obligatory "power arm" that could at times top 99 on the radar gun. Unfortunately, with that power comes a Nuke LaLoosh-style control problem. Shipped to Triple-A in May when his walk rate spiked at a gaudy 6.5 BB/9, he didn't fare any better against competition in the PCL. Finally, the Royals decided to move him to the rotation and demoted him again to build up arm strength and confidence. The control problems persisted against weaker competition. He will return to the bullpen and the Royals will be patient with Jeffress, but with a plethora of young arms moving up the minor league ranks, if he can't find a modicum of control, he will become some other organization's problem.

### John Lamb
Born: 7/10/1990 Age: 21
Bats: L Throws: L Height: 6' 5" Weight: 200
Breakout: 21% Improve: 46% Collapse: 12%
Attrition: 3% MLB: 93%
Comparables:
Ryan Feierabend, Chuck Stobbs, Billy Hoeft

| YEAR | TEAM | LVL | AGE | W | L | SV | G | GS | IP | H | HR | BB | SO | EqBB9 | EqSO9 | GB% | BABIP | WHIP | ERA | FIP | FRA | WARP |
|------|------|-----|-----|---|---|----|---|----|----|---|----|----|----|-------|-------|-----|-------|------|-----|-----|-----|------|
| 2009 | BNC | RK | 18 | 2 | 2 | 0 | 6 | 6 | 27¹ | 24 | 4 | 9 | 25 | 3.0 | 8.2 | 47% | .270 | 1.21 | 3.96 | 4.97 | 7.47 | -0.4 |
| 2009 | IDA | RK | 18 | 3 | 1 | 0 | 8 | 8 | 41¹ | 33 | 4 | 11 | 46 | 2.4 | 10.0 | 43% | .282 | 1.07 | 3.70 | 3.83 | 5.82 | 0.4 |
| 2010 | BUR | A | 19 | 2 | 3 | 0 | 8 | 8 | 40 | 23 | 2 | 17 | 42 | 3.8 | 9.7 | 41% | .241 | 1.08 | 1.58 | 3.77 | 3.49 | 0.9 |
| 2010 | WIL | A+ | 19 | 6 | 3 | 0 | 13 | 13 | 74² | 50 | 1 | 14 | 74 | 1.8 | 10.8 | 48% | .312 | 0.99 | 1.45 | 2.33 | 3.03 | 1.9 |
| 2010 | NWA | AA | 19 | 2 | 1 | 0 | 7 | 7 | 33 | 32 | 3 | 13 | 22 | 3.5 | 7.1 | 44% | .309 | 1.52 | 5.45 | 4.63 | 4.69 | 0.7 |
| 2011 | NWA | AA | 20 | 1 | 2 | 0 | 8 | 8 | 35 | 33 | 3 | 13 | 22 | 3.3 | 5.7 | 42% | .273 | 1.31 | 3.09 | 4.44 | 4.77 | 0.4 |
| 2012 | KCA | MLB | 21 | 1 | 1 | 0 | 4 | 4 | 18² | 20 | 2 | 9 | 14 | 4.3 | 6.6 | 43% | .310 | 1.56 | 5.04 | 4.54 | 5.48 | -0.0 |

He entered 2011 as the brightest pitching prospect in a loaded system. While Lamb typically throws in the mid-90s, his velocity was noticeably lower this spring, attributed to the residual effects of an oblique strain. Aside from one start, he didn't allow many hits, but his strikeout totals were way down. Then, he lasted just two pitches in a start in mid-May before exiting with elbow pain. The dreaded visit to Dr. Lewis Yocum followed, and Lamb had Tommy John surgery in early June. This isn't the first time he's missed large chunks of playing time to injury. He sat out his entire senior year of high school after fracturing his elbow in a car accident. The Royals will not be aggressive in Lamb's rehab, a la Stephen Strasburg, and are targeting a late 2012 return. There's even been talk he won't compete until the Instructional League convenes in September.

### Vin Mazzaro

Born: **9/27/1986** Age: **25**
Bats: **R** Throws: **R** Height: **6' 2"** Weight: **215**
Breakout: **28%** Improve: **52%** Collapse: **18%**
Attrition: **22%** MLB: **98%**

**Comparables:**
Jon Huber, Wayne Granger, Wes Littleton

| YEAR | TEAM | LVL | AGE | W | L | SV | G | GS | IP | H | HR | BB | SO | EqBB9 | EqSO9 | GB% | BABIP | WHIP | ERA | FIP | FRA | WARP |
|------|------|-----|-----|---|---|----|---|----|-----|-----|----|----|-----|-------|-------|-----|-------|------|------|------|------|------|
| 2009 | SAC | AAA | 22 | 2 | 2 | 0 | 10 | 9 | 56² | 42 | 2 | 17 | 44 | 2.7 | 7.0 | 59% | .250 | 1.04 | 2.38 | 3.57 | 3.46 | 0.9 |
| 2009 | OAK | MLB | 22 | 4 | 9 | 0 | 17 | 17 | 91¹ | 120 | 12 | 39 | 59 | 3.8 | 5.8 | 40% | .351 | 1.74 | 5.32 | 4.97 | 5.44 | 0.1 |
| 2010 | SAC | AAA | 23 | 4 | 1 | 0 | 7 | 6 | 37¹ | 24 | 2 | 11 | 32 | 4.1 | 9.2 | 42% | .297 | 1.39 | 3.14 | 3.92 | 4.33 | 0.4 |
| 2010 | OAK | MLB | 23 | 6 | 8 | 0 | 24 | 18 | 122¹ | 127 | 19 | 50 | 79 | 3.7 | 5.8 | 46% | .283 | 1.45 | 4.27 | 5.10 | 5.59 | -0.8 |
| 2011 | OMA | AAA | 24 | 2 | 0 | 0 | 22 | 22 | 123² | 150 | 11 | 65 | 115 | 4.4 | 7.8 | 52% | .339 | 1.62 | 4.29 | 4.80 | 5.13 | 0.5 |
| 2011 | KCA | MLB | 24 | 1 | 1 | 0 | 7 | 4 | 28¹ | 39 | 4 | 15 | 10 | 4.8 | 3.2 | 47% | .357 | 1.91 | 8.26 | 5.88 | 7.19 | -0.7 |
| 2012 | KCA | MLB | 25 | 4 | 6 | 0 | 14 | 14 | 78² | 85 | 8 | 33 | 51 | 3.7 | 5.8 | 49% | .306 | 1.50 | 4.65 | 4.49 | 5.05 | 0.2 |

Mazzaro is a sinkerball pitcher who can't keep the ball down, with predictable poor results. Time isn't on his side: the young arms in the system figure to blow by him on the organizational depth charts. Whatever happens, Royals fans will always have that outing in mid-May, when Yost brought Mazzaro on in relief against the Indians; then sat and watched him surrender 14 runs in 2.1 innings. He was the first relief pitcher to cough up 14 or more runs in an appearance since the immortal Les

Attrition: **7%** MLB: **83%**

**Comparables:**
Jake Westbrook, Jim Corsi, Kevin Brown

| YEAR | TEAM | LVL | AGE | W | L | SV | G | GS | IP | H | HR | BB | SO | EqBB9 | EqSO9 | GB% | BABIP | WHIP | ERA | FIP | FRA | WARP |
|------|------|-----|-----|---|---|----|---|----|-----|-----|----|----|-----|-------|-------|-----|-------|------|-------|-------|-------|------|
| 2010 | KCA | MLB | 26 | 0 | 1 | 0 | 4 | 0 | 4 | 10 | 4 | 3 | 1 | 6.8 | 2.2 | 38% | .353 | 3.25 | 22.50 | 17.80 | 18.02 | -0.6 |
| 2011 | OMA | AAA | 27 | 5 | 3 | 2 | 33 | 18 | 144¹ | 134 | 6 | 60 | 93 | 3.4 | 5.1 | 49% | .267 | 1.25 | 2.18 | 4.40 | 4.91 | 0.9 |
| 2011 | KCA | MLB | 27 | 2 | 0 | 0 | 2 | 2 | 14² | 11 | 0 | 5 | 7 | 3.1 | 4.3 | 46% | .239 | 1.09 | 1.23 | 3.54 | 3.28 | 0.3 |
| 2012 | KCA | MLB | 28 | 2 | 3 | 0 | 10 | 7 | 48¹ | 55 | 4 | 19 | 25 | 3.5 | 4.6 | 48% | .307 | 1.53 | 5.00 | 4.42 | 5.44 | -0.1 |

A funny thing happened on the way to Mendoza becoming a bona fide minor league journeyman. He put together an incredible season for Triple-A Omaha and was named the Pacific Coast League Pitcher of the Year. The odds of that happening were equal to Nancy Grace having a civil dinner with Casey Anthony. To confound the situation further, Mendoza made a pair of highly successful starts at the major league level to close out his season. That's just the kind of performance that will lead the Royals to think he can be a contributor to the rotation in 2012. That he struck out under five batters per nine innings for the season while posting an obscenely low BABIP and home run rate makes him an unlikely candidate to repeat his success.

### Jose Mijares

Born: **10/29/1984** Age: **27**
Bats: **L** Throws: **L** Height: **6' 1"** Weight: **230**
Breakout: **26%** Improve: **62%** Collapse: **18%**
Attrition: **17%** MLB: **87%**

**Comparables:**
J.A. Happ, Mark Lowe, Rudy May

| YEAR | TEAM | LVL | AGE | W | L | SV | G | GS | IP | H | HR | BB | SO | EqBB9 | EqSO9 | GB% | BABIP | WHIP | ERA | FIP | FRA | WARP |
|------|------|-----|-----|---|---|----|----|----|-----|----|----|----|----|-------|-------|-----|-------|------|------|------|------|------|
| 2009 | MIN | MLB | 24 | 2 | 2 | 0 | 71 | 0 | 61² | 50 | 7 | 23 | 55 | 3.4 | 8.0 | 39% | .262 | 1.18 | 2.34 | 4.05 | 4.30 | 0.9 |
| 2010 | MIN | MLB | 25 | 1 | 1 | 0 | 47 | 0 | 32² | 34 | 4 | 9 | 28 | 2.5 | 7.7 | 32% | .312 | 1.32 | 3.31 | 3.84 | 4.18 | 0.4 |
| 2011 | MIN | MLB | 26 | 0 | 2 | 0 | 58 | 0 | 49 | 53 | 4 | 30 | 30 | 5.5 | 5.5 | 33% | .304 | 1.69 | 4.59 | 4.92 | 5.44 | -0.2 |
| 2012 | KCA | MLB | 27 | 3 | 1 | 0 | 54 | 0 | 41² | 42 | 4 | 19 | 34 | 4.1 | 7.3 | 41% | .301 | 1.45 | 4.42 | 4.19 | 4.80 | 0.1 |

Mijares entered 2011 slated to be the Twins' top lefty reliever, but control problems greatly diminished his effectiveness, and he never recovered the dominant form that put him on the map in 2008–09. Through the season's first two months, he had a 7/12 K/BB ratio—a sore elbow that sidelined him in late May may have been a factor—and not until the final week of the season did he get back to an even ratio. Part of the problem was that 57 percent of his workload came against righties, who battered him (.292/.412/.462, 11/20 K/UIBB), while he tamed lefties (.253/.330/.368, 19/8 K/UIBB). His conditioning may have also been an issue; the plump portsider's fastball velocity is down a full 2 miles per hour from its peak. Because he's left-handed, he found a suitor in the Royals after the Twins non-tendered him.

### Mike Montgomery

Born: **7/1/1989** Age: **22**
Bats: **L** Throws: **L** Height: **6' 5"** Weight: **185**
Breakout: **27%** Improve: **49%** Collapse: **19%**
Attrition: **19%** MLB: **70%**

**Comparables:**
Whitey Ford, Jaime Garcia, Curt Simmons

| YEAR | TEAM | LVL | AGE | W | L | SV | G | GS | IP | H | HR | BB | SO | EqBB9 | EqSO9 | GB% | BABIP | WHIP | ERA | FIP | FRA | WARP |
|------|------|-----|-----|---|---|----|----|----|-----|-----|----|----|-----|-------|-------|-----|-------|------|------|------|------|------|
| 2011 | OMA | AAA | 22 | 2 | 2 | 0 | 28 | 27 | 150² | 160 | 16 | 74 | 135 | 4.1 | 7.7 | 50% | .324 | 1.50 | 5.32 | 4.92 | 5.26 | 0.6 |
| 2012 | KCA | MLB | 22 | 2 | 3 | 0 | 9 | 9 | 46² | 48 | 5 | 21 | 34 | 4.1 | 6.6 | 50% | .301 | 1.49 | 4.53 | 4.49 | 4.93 | 0.2 |

Montgomery was supposed to be at the head of the Royals pitching prospect class, but struggles in his first turn in Triple-A have delayed his progress. Command has been at the heart of his problems since he missed time with a strained forearm in 2010 and issued over four free passes per nine innings. He struggled to get ahead in the count, which led him to catch too much of the dish when he needed to throw strikes. Montgomery features three above-average pitches (fastball, curve, and change), so one bad season doesn't mean it's time to wave the white flag, but he will need to find his command and prove he can pitch at the highest level of the minors before the Royals give him a chance with the big league club.

**Sean O'Sullivan**
Born: 9/1/1987 Age: 24
Bats: R Throws: R Height: 6' 3" Weight: 230
Breakout: 20% Improve: 45% Collapse: 35%
Attrition: 22% MLB: 94%

Comparables:
Enrique Gonzalez, Jeff Karstens, Joe Kennedy

| YEAR | TEAM | LVL | AGE | W | L | SV | G | GS | IP | H | HR | BB | SO | EqBB9 | EqSO9 | GB% | BABIP | WHIP | ERA | FIP | FRA | WARP |
|------|------|-----|-----|---|---|----|---|----|-----|----|----|----|----|-------|-------|-----|-------|------|------|------|------|------|
| 2009 | ANA | MLB | 21 | 4 | 2 | 0 | 12 | 10 | 51² | 60 | 12 | 16 | 29 | 2.8 | 5.1 | 37% | .289 | 1.47 | 5.92 | 6.03 | 6.16 | -0.1 |
| 2010 | ANA | MLB | 22 | 1 | 0 | 0 | 5 | 1 | 13 | 7 | 1 | 4 | 6 | 2.8 | 4.2 | 44% | .158 | 0.85 | 2.08 | 4.05 | 3.97 | 0.1 |
| 2010 | KCA | MLB | 22 | 3 | 6 | 0 | 14 | 13 | 70² | 83 | 14 | 27 | 37 | 3.4 | 4.7 | 41% | .287 | 1.56 | 6.11 | 5.76 | 5.93 | -0.3 |
| 2011 | OMA | AAA | 23 | 4 | 1 | 0 | 14 | 14 | 74² | 87 | 7 | 17 | 62 | 1.9 | 6.6 | 42% | .309 | 1.35 | 4.22 | 4.14 | 4.43 | 0.8 |
| 2011 | KCA | MLB | 23 | 2 | 6 | 0 | 12 | 10 | 58¹ | 78 | 10 | 26 | 19 | 4.0 | 2.9 | 42% | .319 | 1.78 | 7.25 | 6.08 | 6.61 | -0.6 |
| 2012 | KCA | MLB | 24 | 4 | 6 | 0 | 14 | 14 | 76² | 90 | 10 | 27 | 38 | 3.1 | 4.4 | 46% | .301 | 1.52 | 5.16 | 4.97 | 5.61 | -0.2 |

How thin was the Royals starting rotation in 2011? Thin enough they gave O'Sullivan 10 starts. There's no mystery here. A 0.73 SO/BB ratio to go along with 10 home runs in 58 innings. He's destined for a career as Triple-A filler.

**Felipe Paulino**
Born: 10/5/1983 Age: 28
Bats: R Throws: R Height: 6' 3" Weight: 180
Breakout: 23% Improve: 49% Collapse: 25%
Attrition: 22% MLB: 85%

Comparables:
German Gonzalez, Carlos Diaz, Buddy Schultz

| YEAR | TEAM | LVL | AGE | W | L | SV | G | GS | IP | H | HR | BB | SO | EqBB9 | EqSO9 | GB% | BABIP | WHIP | ERA | FIP | FRA | WARP |
|------|------|-----|-----|---|---|----|---|----|-----|-----|----|----|-----|-------|-------|-----|-------|------|------|------|------|------|
| 2009 | ROU | AAA | 25 | 2 | 1 | 0 | 7 | 7 | 34² | 30 | 1 | 23 | 29 | 6.0 | 7.5 | 59% | .287 | 1.53 | 3.11 | 4.32 | 4.19 | 0.5 |
| 2009 | HOU | MLB | 25 | 3 | 11 | 0 | 23 | 17 | 97² | 126 | 20 | 37 | 93 | 3.4 | 8.6 | 45% | .371 | 1.67 | 6.27 | 5.07 | 5.51 | 0.1 |
| 2010 | HOU | MLB | 26 | 1 | 9 | 0 | 19 | 14 | 91² | 95 | 4 | 46 | 83 | 4.5 | 8.1 | 45% | .340 | 1.54 | 5.11 | 3.47 | 4.24 | 1.3 |
| 2011 | COL | MLB | 27 | 0 | 4 | 0 | 18 | 0 | 14² | 23 | 3 | 7 | 14 | 4.3 | 8.6 | 51% | .455 | 2.05 | 7.36 | 5.18 | 5.59 | -0.1 |
| 2011 | KCA | MLB | 27 | 4 | 6 | 0 | 21 | 20 | 124² | 123 | 10 | 48 | 119 | 3.5 | 8.6 | 46% | .331 | 1.37 | 4.11 | 3.54 | 4.21 | 1.3 |
| 2012 | KCA | MLB | 28 | 5 | 7 | 0 | 27 | 16 | 107² | 119 | 12 | 47 | 93 | 3.9 | 7.8 | 43% | .332 | 1.54 | 4.87 | 4.24 | 5.30 | -0.1 |

Proof that one man's trash is another man's treasure. Last winter, Paulino was shipped from Houston to Colorado (in exchange for Clint Barmes!) and lasted just 14 disastrous innings in the mountains before he was waived by the Rockies. Word was the Royals had long had their eye on Paulino, admiring his velocity (he averages 95 mph with his fastball) and his ability to keep the ball down, so once he was available, Dayton Moore snapped him up for cash considerations. He performed much as advertised for the Royals, riding his fastball to a career best strikeout rate and getting a groundball on 45 percent of all balls in play. The knock on Paulino has always been his spotty command, which reared its ugly head in a couple of starts where he issued at least five bases on balls. If he can find consistency around the strike zone, the Royals will have a bargain on their hands.

**Jonathan Sanchez**
Born: 11/19/1982 Age: 29
Bats: L Throws: L Height: 6' 3" Weight: 165
Breakout: 13% Improve: 28% Collapse: 49%
Attrition: 13% MLB: 97%

Comparables:
Mitch Stetter, Will Ohman, Randy Myers

| YEAR | TEAM | LVL | AGE | W | L | SV | G | GS | IP | H | HR | BB | SO | EqBB9 | EqSO9 | GB% | BABIP | WHIP | ERA | FIP | FRA | WARP |
|------|------|-----|-----|---|----|----|----|----|------|-----|----|----|-----|-------|-------|-----|-------|------|------|------|------|------|
| 2009 | SFN | MLB | 26 | 8 | 12 | 0 | 32 | 29 | 163¹ | 135 | 19 | 88 | 177 | 4.8 | 9.8 | 42% | .278 | 1.37 | 4.24 | 4.13 | 4.70 | 1.4 |
| 2010 | SFN | MLB | 27 | 13 | 9 | 0 | 34 | 33 | 193¹ | 142 | 21 | 96 | 205 | 4.5 | 9.5 | 41% | .255 | 1.23 | 3.07 | 4.03 | 4.04 | 2.3 |
| 2011 | SFN | MLB | 28 | 4 | 7 | 0 | 19 | 19 | 101¹ | 80 | 9 | 66 | 102 | 5.9 | 9.1 | 46% | .276 | 1.44 | 4.26 | 4.27 | 4.42 | 0.5 |
| 2012 | KCA | MLB | 29 | 5 | 6 | 0 | 17 | 17 | 97¹ | 88 | 10 | 50 | 97 | 4.6 | 9.0 | 43% | .297 | 1.41 | 4.06 | 4.09 | 4.42 | 0.9 |

It's never been easy to know what to do with Sanchez—he's always on the cusp of excellence, on the brink of collapse, less expensive than market-rate, and due for a raise. That was still true after 2011, arguably his worst season. His lifelong experimentation with bases on balls turned into walkaholism in 2011. His teammate Sergio Romo walked five batters all season; Sanchez walked six or more batters in four starts. Shoot, Sanchez walked four *pitchers*. It's possible that the Giants' World Series run caught up to him. Including the 2010 postseason, he threw 50 more innings than he had ever thrown. Consequently or coincidentally, he lost a mile off his fastball. He also struggled with his stamina, according to his manager, working just 5 1/3 innings per start and failing to complete the fifth inning in any of his final five outings. The Giants traded him to Kansas City early in the winter, so instead of having to earn a rotation spot in the spring, he'll be his staff's ace.

**Will Smith**

Born: 7/10/1989 Age: 22
Bats: R Throws: L Height: 6' 6" Weight: 235
Breakout: 28% Improve: 60% Collapse: 23%
Attrition: 13% MLB: 83%

**Comparables:**
Lary Sorensen, Jim Ollom, Tommy Hunter

| YEAR | TEAM | LVL | AGE | W | L | SV | G | GS | IP | H | HR | BB | SO | EqBB9 | EqSO9 | GB% | BABIP | WHIP | ERA | FIP | FRA | WARP |
|------|------|-----|-----|---|---|----|----|----|-----|-----|----|----|-----|-------|-------|-----|-------|------|------|------|------|------|
| 2009 | CDR | A | 19 | 10 | 6 | 0 | 20 | 19 | 115 | 117 | 12 | 30 | 111 | 1.9 | 7.4 | 48% | .283 | 1.16 | 3.76 | 3.90 | 5.17 | -0.2 |
| 2010 | RCU | A+ | 20 | 2 | 2 | 0 | 6 | 6 | 37¹ | 30 | 3 | 13 | 25 | 3.1 | 7.5 | 44% | .314 | 1.31 | 4.58 | 4.57 | 5.86 | -0.2 |
| 2010 | WIL | A+ | 20 | 4 | 1 | 0 | 8 | 8 | 54² | 45 | 5 | 4 | 47 | 0.7 | 8.4 | 52% | .288 | 0.95 | 2.80 | 3.15 | 3.79 | 0.9 |
| 2010 | SLC | AAA | 20 | 2 | 4 | 0 | 9 | 9 | 53 | 44 | 5 | 9 | 24 | 3.4 | 6.8 | 43% | .339 | 1.60 | 5.60 | 4.89 | 5.42 | 0.0 |
| 2011 | NWA | AA | 21 | 7 | 6 | 0 | 27 | 27 | 161¹ | 171 | 13 | 45 | 108 | 2.5 | 6.0 | 47% | .316 | 1.34 | 3.85 | 4.04 | 4.90 | 1.4 |
| 2012 | KCA | MLB | 22 | 2 | 4 | 0 | 8 | 8 | 51 | 63 | 7 | 19 | 27 | 3.4 | 4.7 | 44% | .320 | 1.61 | 5.52 | 5.05 | 6.00 | -0.4 |

Smith keeps his walk rate low, which is always a good thing. In his case, it's a really good thing, as he lacks a true strikeout pitch and is extremely hittable. In fact, he allows far too many base runners. The Royals will move him along to Triple-A, but he's a long shot to land on the major league staff.

**Joakim Soria**

| YEAR | TEAM | LVL | AGE | W | L | SV | G | GS | IP | H | HR | BB | SO | EqBB9 | EqSO9 | GB% | BABIP | WHIP | ERA | FIP | FRA | WARP |
|------|------|-----|-----|---|---|----|---|----|----|---|----|----|----|-------|-------|-----|-------|------|-----|-----|-----|------|

and a lower groundball rate. Too often, he fell behind in the count to batters early, then found himself in the difficult position of having to throw strikes on the hitter's terms. It's not a coincidence he posted a career high home run rate. For some reason, he's changed his approach since his dominant 2009 season, throwing more cutters and fewer changeups. Most troubling was his moving away from his devastating 12 to 6 curveball and turning to his not-as-effective slider. Once thought of as the heir apparent to Rivera, in 2012 Soria will just try to get back on track.

**Jeff Suppan**

Born: 1/2/1975 Age: 37
Bats: R Throws: R Height: 6' 2" Weight: 200
Breakout: 31% Improve: 53% Collapse: 26%
Attrition: 17% MLB: 64%

**Comparables:**
Mark Portugal, George Brunet, Wilbur Wood

| YEAR | TEAM | LVL | AGE | W | L | SV | G | GS | IP | H | HR | BB | SO | EqBB9 | EqSO9 | GB% | BABIP | WHIP | ERA | FIP | FRA | WARP |
|------|------|-----|-----|---|---|----|----|----|------|-----|----|----|----|-------|-------|-----|-------|------|------|------|------|------|
| 2009 | MIL | MLB | 34 | 7 | 12 | 0 | 30 | 30 | 161² | 200 | 25 | 74 | 80 | 4.1 | 4.5 | 51% | .320 | 1.69 | 5.29 | 5.65 | 6.35 | -0.6 |
| 2010 | MIL | MLB | 35 | 0 | 2 | 0 | 15 | 2 | 31 | 50 | 4 | 12 | 18 | 3.5 | 5.2 | 43% | .422 | 2.00 | 7.84 | 4.88 | 5.85 | -0.3 |
| 2010 | SLN | MLB | 35 | 3 | 6 | 0 | 15 | 13 | 70¹ | 80 | 9 | 25 | 33 | 3.2 | 4.2 | 44% | .307 | 1.49 | 3.84 | 4.94 | 5.06 | 0.2 |
| 2011 | OMA | AAA | 36 | 5 | 1 | 0 | 28 | 27 | 165² | 186 | 23 | 51 | 94 | 2.8 | 5.1 | 51% | .301 | 1.43 | 4.78 | 5.42 | 5.48 | 0.4 |
| 2012 | KCA | MLB | 37 | 2 | 4 | 0 | 12 | 9 | 56² | 70 | 8 | 22 | 27 | 3.5 | 4.3 | 48% | .320 | 1.64 | 5.77 | 5.25 | 6.27 | -0.6 |

Renowned for being an innings eater, Suppan dined all season at Triple-A. He's 37, so unless he's willing to spend another season riding the buses as organizational filler, it's likely he has bellied up to the buffet for the final time.

**Everett Teaford**

Born: 5/15/1984 Age: 28
Bats: L Throws: L Height: 6' 0" Weight: 155
Breakout: 21% Improve: 59% Collapse: 18%
Attrition: 16% MLB: 78%

**Comparables:**
John Tudor, Pete Schourek, Dick Donovan

| YEAR | TEAM | LVL | AGE | W | L | SV | G | GS | IP | H | HR | BB | SO | EqBB9 | EqSO9 | GB% | BABIP | WHIP | ERA | FIP | FRA | WARP |
|------|------|-----|-----|----|---|----|----|----|-----|----|----|----|----|-------|-------|-----|-------|------|------|------|------|------|
| 2009 | WIL | A+ | 25 | 7 | 1 | 0 | 11 | 11 | 64 | 51 | 7 | 12 | 49 | 1.7 | 6.9 | 44% | .246 | 0.98 | 2.39 | 3.85 | 5.11 | 0.0 |
| 2009 | NWA | AA | 25 | 3 | 7 | 0 | 16 | 16 | 81 | 91 | 12 | 36 | 46 | 3.8 | 4.7 | 41% | .277 | 1.48 | 5.11 | 5.47 | 6.37 | -0.6 |
| 2010 | NWA | AA | 26 | 15 | 3 | 0 | 27 | 12 | 99 | 80 | 5 | 30 | 95 | 2.9 | 10.3 | 43% | .336 | 1.24 | 3.36 | 3.06 | 4.08 | 2.5 |
| 2011 | OMA | AAA | 27 | 1 | 0 | 0 | 16 | 3 | 35 | 23 | 5 | 11 | 33 | 2.8 | 8.5 | 44% | .205 | 0.97 | 3.34 | 4.74 | 3.98 | 0.6 |
| 2011 | KCA | MLB | 27 | 2 | 1 | 1 | 26 | 3 | 44 | 36 | 8 | 14 | 28 | 2.9 | 5.7 | 46% | .228 | 1.14 | 3.27 | 5.18 | 5.78 | -0.2 |
| 2012 | KCA | MLB | 28 | 2 | 2 | 0 | 16 | 5 | 44 | 50 | 6 | 18 | 26 | 3.6 | 5.3 | 39% | .301 | 1.54 | 5.24 | 5.02 | 5.69 | -0.2 |

A 12th round pick in the 2006 draft, he was a starter until 2010 when a move to the bullpen accelerated his timeline to the majors. Teaford features a fastball in the low 90s, but changes speeds and locates well enough to keep hitters off balance. Did Yost not trust him with the lead? Teaford made 26 appearances for the Royals, but entered the game with his team ahead only three times all season. With the Royals thin on starting pitching heading to the 2012 season, Teaford is an option to be moved to the rotation and will be given a long look in spring training.

## Robinson Tejeda

Born: 3/24/1982 Age: 30
Bats: R Throws: R Height: 6' 4" Weight: 190
Breakout: 18% Improve: 47% Collapse: 26%
Attrition: 8% MLB: 89%

Comparables:
Hideo Nomo, Kelvim Escobar, Tug McGraw

| YEAR | TEAM | LVL | AGE | W | L | SV | G | GS | IP | H | HR | BB | SO | EqBB9 | EqSO9 | GB% | BABIP | WHIP | ERA | FIP | FRA | WARP |
|------|------|-----|-----|---|---|----|----|----|-----|----|----|----|----|-------|-------|-----|-------|------|------|------|------|------|
| 2009 | KCA | MLB | 27 | 4 | 2 | 0 | 35 | 6 | 73² | 43 | 4 | 50 | 87 | 6.1 | 10.6 | 36% | .234 | 1.26 | 3.54 | 3.65 | 4.46 | 1.1 |
| 2010 | KCA | MLB | 28 | 3 | 5 | 0 | 54 | 0 | 61 | 55 | 5 | 26 | 56 | 3.8 | 8.3 | 31% | .296 | 1.33 | 3.54 | 3.56 | 3.97 | 0.9 |
| 2011 | OMA | AAA | 29 | 0 | 1 | 1 | 31 | 0 | 45 | 42 | 8 | 16 | 45 | 3.0 | 8.6 | 30% | .270 | 1.22 | 3.80 | 5.38 | 4.83 | 0.2 |
| 2011 | KCA | MLB | 29 | 0 | 1 | 0 | 9 | 0 | 7¹ | 12 | 2 | 3 | 2 | 3.7 | 2.5 | 23% | .357 | 2.05 | 6.14 | 7.29 | 6.78 | -0.1 |
| 2012 | CLE | MLB | 30 | 1 | 0 | 1 | 22 | 0 | 27 | 25 | 3 | 14 | 25 | 4.7 | 8.4 | 35% | .290 | 1.43 | 4.15 | 4.35 | 4.51 | 0.1 |

Tejeda could be the poster boy for the volatility of the reliever. The Royals primary set-up man in the previous two seasons, he battled shoulder tendinitis, lost 3 mph off his fastball and his ability to miss bats, and ultimately found himself designated for assignment. He got healthy, pitched well enough in Omaha, and elected to become a free agent at the end of the year. Some team will take a chance.

## Blake Wood

Born: 8/8/1985 Age: 26
Bats: R Throws: R Height: 6' 6" Weight: 230
Breakout: 29% Improve: 56% Collapse: 18%
Attrition: 18% MLB: 92%

Comparables:
Ricky Romero, Freddy Garcia, Randy Messenger

| YEAR | TEAM | LVL | AGE | W | L | SV | G | GS | IP | H | HR | BB | SO | EqBB9 | EqSO9 | GB% | BABIP | WHIP | ERA | FIP | FRA | WARP |
|------|------|-----|-----|---|---|----|----|----|-----|----|----|----|----|-------|-------|-----|-------|------|------|------|------|------|
| 2009 | NWA | AA | 23 | 3 | 8 | 0 | 17 | 13 | 78² | 94 | 8 | 28 | 50 | 3.2 | 5.6 | 54% | .343 | 1.52 | 5.83 | 4.51 | 5.03 | 0.2 |
| 2010 | KCA | MLB | 24 | 1 | 3 | 0 | 51 | 0 | 49² | 54 | 6 | 22 | 31 | 4.0 | 5.6 | 51% | .304 | 1.53 | 5.07 | 4.76 | 5.84 | -0.3 |
| 2011 | KCA | MLB | 25 | 5 | 3 | 1 | 55 | 0 | 69² | 66 | 5 | 32 | 62 | 4.1 | 8.0 | 55% | .311 | 1.41 | 3.75 | 3.72 | 5.05 | 0.1 |
| 2012 | KCA | MLB | 26 | 2 | 1 | 1 | 50 | 0 | 58 | 63 | 6 | 25 | 42 | 3.8 | 6.5 | 46% | .313 | 1.51 | 4.73 | 4.39 | 5.14 | -0.0 |

Although Wood packs 95 mph heat, until 2011 he's never been much of a strikeout pitcher. In the past, he relied primarily on a fastball/slider combo, but last season added a fastball with a little more sinking action. That led to a huge increase in his strikeout rate and a modest uptick in groundballs, and made him a useful pitcher out of Kansas City's bullpen. He continues to walk enough batters to keep things "interesting" though.

# LINEOUTS

## HITTERS

| PLAYER | TEAM | LVL | AGE | PA | R | 2B | 3B | HR | RBI | BB | SO | SB-CS | AVG/OBP/SLG | TAv | BABIP | BRR | FRAA | WARP |
|--------|------|-----|-----|----|---|----|----|----|-----|----|----|-------|-------------|-----|-------|-----|------|------|
| CF B. Eibner | KNC | A | 22 | 324 | 46 | 13 | 2 | 12 | 31 | 48 | 90 | 2-3 | .213/.340/.408 | .277 | .271 | -0.7 | 0.9 | 1.8 |
| RF I. Falu | OMA | AAA | 28 | 437 | 50 | 10 | 9 | 2 | 47 | 35 | 47 | 21-11 | .301/.358/.390 | .253 | .335 | 0.0 | -2.8 | 0.7 |
| DH C. Gallagher | ROY | RK | 18 | 86 | 6 | 0 | 0 | 1 | 7 | 7 | 15 | 0-0 | .141/.209/.179 | .184 | .159 | -1.1 | -0.5 | -0.6 |
| CF G. Golson | SWB | AAA | 25 | 429 | 55 | 9 | 7 | 8 | 33 | 30 | 105 | 15-5 | .263/.330/.385 | .252 | .342 | 1.7 | 8.4 | 2.4 |
|  | NYA | MLB | 25 | 12 | 1 | 0 | 0 | 0 | 0 | 1 | 2 | 1-0 | .182/.250/.182 | .171 | .222 | -0.3 | -0.2 | -0.1 |
| 3B M. Lisson | NWA | AA | 27 | 328 | 58 | 21 | 0 | 15 | 45 | 31 | 81 | 15-2 | .293/.372/.527 | .286 | .362 | 0.4 | -6.5 | 1.8 |
| C M. Ramirez | FRE | AAA | 26 | 166 | 24 | 11 | 1 | 10 | 29 | 14 | 34 | 0-0 | .318/.388/.608 | .321 | .356 | -3.6 | 0.4 | 1.2 |
|  | OKL | AAA | 26 | 91 | 7 | 3 | 0 | 2 | 14 | 3 | 17 | 0-0 | .226/.253/.333 | .217 | .250 | 0.5 | -0.1 | 0.0 |
| 1B A. Seratelli | NWA | AA | 28 | 523 | 91 | 12 | 6 | 9 | 64 | 75 | 92 | 35-5 | .282/.392/.398 | .270 | .339 | 9.3 | 3.4 | 2.8 |

Drafted out of Arkansas, where he split time between the outfield and the mound, **Brett Eibner** gave the Royals a taste of his power potential by slamming a home run every 22 at bats in Single-A, his first season as strictly a position player. Still a bit raw with the bat, he should open the 2012 campaign in Double-A. ⊘ **Irving Falu** has played three full seasons at Triple-A, hitting a combined .280/.342/.352. It seems he's only an option to make the majors if several players ahead of him go down with injury. ⊘ The Royals second-round pick in the 2011 draft, **Cam Gallagher** is supposed to have plus power but he mustered only two extra base hits (both home runs) in 119 plate appearances. He struggled in every facet of his offensive game but had a particularly difficult time solving right-handed pitching. ⊘ When a team takes a tools player in the first round, it gambles that his obvious physical abilities will mature into advanced baseball skills. It never happened for **Greg Golson**. ⊘ The Royals once thought enough of **Mario Lisson** to place him on the 40-man roster. Injuries derailed his 2010 season, but he returned last year and mashed Texas League pitching. He could be a deep sleeper. ⊘ **Max Ramirez** is still at that stage where every fan wants his team to take a shot on him, and every team that tries regrets it. ⊘ Plucked from the Independent Leagues in 2007,

**Anthony Seratelli** brings plenty of value with his solid plate discipline and versatility. He finished with the fourth highest OBP in the Texas League last summer.

## PITCHERS

| PLAYER | TEAM | LVL | AGE | W | L | SV | IP | H | HR | BB | SO | EqBB9 | EqSO9 | GB% | BABIP | WHIP | ERA | FIP | FRA | WARP |
|--------|------|-----|-----|---|---|----|----|---|----|----|----|-------|-------|-----|-------|------|-----|-----|-----|------|
| G. Billo | KNC | A | 20 | 9 | 5 | 1 | 135 | 116 | 6 | 26 | 126 | 1.7 | 7.9 | 50% | .283 | 1.02 | 1.93 | 2.74 | 3.67 | 2.3 |
| C. Dwyer | NWA | AA | 23 | 6 | 6 | 0 | 141$^1$ | 126 | 14 | 81 | 133 | 5.0 | 8.0 | 44% | .281 | 1.43 | 5.60 | 4.63 | 5.08 | 1.0 |
| J. Gutierrez | ARI | MLB | 27 | 0 | 0 | 0 | 18$^1$ | 22 | 3 | 9 | 23 | 4.4 | 11.3 | 46% | .352 | 1.69 | 5.40 | 4.25 | 5.46 | -0.1 |
| T. Hottovy | PAW | AAA | 29 | 1 | 0 | 1 | 36 | 23 | 8 | 10 | 30 | 2.2 | 7.2 | 49% | .161 | 0.89 | 2.75 | 5.38 | 4.92 | 0.2 |
|  | BOS | MLB | 29 | 0 | 0 | 0 | 4 | 4 | 0 | 3 | 2 | 6.8 | 4.5 | 46% | .308 | 1.75 | 6.75 | 5.06 | 6.50 | -0.1 |
| K. Pucetas | OMA | AAA | 26 | 1 | 2 | 1 | 106$^2$ | 121 | 18 | 40 | 69 | 3.2 | 5.7 | 47% | .292 | 1.44 | 4.98 | 5.93 | 6.13 | -0.3 |

totals.  ⊘  Righty reliever **Juan Gutierrez** spent most of the season sidelined by arm issues that led to Tommy John surgery in September. He'll miss most or all of 2012.  ⊘  **Tommy Hottovy**, besides being the answer to the question, "What's a Tommy Hottovy?" is also left-handed. This has been another episode of "Tommy Hottovy And You." Join us next week when we tell you he is probably stuck in the minors forever.  ⊘  **Kevin Pucetas** pitched a little better when moved to the Omaha bullpen mid-season, but he had already set the bar extremely low as a starter.  ⊘  A groundball pitcher, **Brandon Sisk** enjoyed the best season of his minor league career with a 75 percent strand rate and a BABIP around .250.  ⊘  He's small in size, but **Yordano Ventura** throws a mighty fastball, touching triple digits at times. He also featured solid control in his first taste of full season minor league action. Struggles with the home run saw him demoted to Rookie ball in July and he did a much better job keeping the ball in the yard once he returned.

## MANAGER: NED YOST

| YEAR | TEAM | W-L | Pythag +/- | Avg PC | 100+ P | 120+ P | QS | BQS | REL | REL w Zero R | IBB | Subs | PH | PH Avg | PH HR | SB2 | CS2 | SB3 | CS3 | SAC Att | SAC % | POS SAC | Squeeze | Swing | In Play |
|------|------|-----|------------|--------|--------|--------|----|----|-----|--------------|-----|------|----|--------|-------|-----|-----|-----|-----|---------|-------|---------|---------|-------|---------|
| 2010 | KCA | 55-72 | 0 | 192.8 | 126 | 125 | 68 | 7 | 332 | 257 | 50 | — | 104 | .214 | 4 | 12 | 4 | 1 | 2 | 90 | 77.8% | 60 | 0 | 281 | 78 |
| 2011 | KCA | 71-91 | 0 | 96.9 | 74 | 0 | 75 | 5 | 420 | 339 | 42 | — | 36 | .152 | 1 | 23 | 8 | 0 | 2 | 75 | 84.0% | 58 | 2 | 399 | 113 |

While his predecessor filled out 141 different lineup cards in his final full season in charge, Yost kept things relatively simple, employing just 87 total batting orders. That, in a nutshell, is what Yost is all about. He believes in his players and he believes in their roles within the team. He may drop a guy a spot or two in the order if he's scuffling, but his ideal situation is one where he fills out his first lineup on Opening Day and never looks back. That extends to the bullpen as well, where everyone has a specific role. Relievers generally enjoy knowing how they're going to be used, but in Yost's case, it led him to severely lean on a couple of select, young bullpen arms early in the season. For example, Aaron Crow emerged from the pen 22 times in the Royals' first 52 games of the season, while Tim Collins appeared in 28 of the Royals' first 51 contests of 2011. No surprise both pitchers were less effective later in the season. The way Yost handles his bullpen and employs small ball tactics offensively, you would think he still believes he's managing in the National League. (Actually, both criticisms were leveled against him during his tenure in Milwaukee, too.) The Royals like to say they are aggressive on the bases. That's all well and good, except the data shows they haven't been aggressive—they've just been foolish. Kansas City baserunners attempted more steals than any team other than Tampa Bay, but their 73 percent success rate was barely above league average. They also ran into 64 outs on the bases, fourth highest tally in the AL, and their EqBRR was the fourth worst in the league. Bunt? We have bunts: Yost ordered more successful sacrifice attempts than any other skipper in the league. His time in Milwaukee proved he can handle a ballclub in transition and the growing pains that accompany young talent. However, his poor in-game management didn't translate well to the pressure of a pennant race in 2008, when Milwaukee fired him with just two weeks left in the season and his team clinging to first place. Three years removed from that, with similar complaints being lodged against his managerial style, the jury is still out on whether he will be able to handle the rigors that go with taking a team to the postseason. The Royals' young hitters seem to be jelling and if the Process is to be trusted, Kansas City could soon be in contention in the AL Central. If history is any guide, the Royals' may have to find themselves another skipper to take them to the promised land of October baseball.

# Los Angeles Angels of Anaheim

When Arte Moreno bought the Angels in 2003 and began the team's push to take a much larger share of the Southern California market than before, it changed the way the Angels could think of themselves. Big market teams don't punt seasons, so the reacted and traded for Vernon Wells. And big market teams can't be seen rebuilding.

The 2011 season was the Angels' stealthy rebuild. They entered the year knowing that as many as 10 of their players—Weaver, Kendrick, Hunter, Abreu, Santana, Izturis, Aybar, Takahashi, Kazmir and Mathis—would likely be free agents after the 2012 season. Those 10 combined to take 52 percent of the Angels' plate appearances in 2011, and pitch 37 percent of their innings, and produce nearly 60 percent of the team's WARP. The loaded farm system of the mid-2000s had created some great memories but no World Series win. On paper, the team was evidently behind Texas, pushing past a $140 million payroll, and reaching the end of its cycle.

The 2011 Angels managed to win 86 games and play meaningful contests in the final week of the season. Perhaps more significant than contention, though, they tested a new crop of young players, seamlessly recast their lead roles, and turned over most of the front office. The Angels will not play 2012 wondering whether their window in the AL West has closed.

The turnover actually began in the summer of 2010, when the Angels shifted Torii Hunter out of center field and called up Peter Bourjos. Bourjos's defensive value was obvious, but he often looked so lost at the plate—a .237 on-base percentage in 51 games that year—would they trust him with the full-time job? Manager Mike Scioscia made him the 2011 Opening Day center fielder and didn't flinch when Bourjos was hitting .224/.278/.367 after two weeks. He even moved him up to the top of the order occasionally. Bourjos had an 825 OPS in the second half, ing didn't just provide hope for the Angels' future, but kept the team in contention. Offseason gossip wanted to include him in a trade for David Wright, but Bourjos is a 3- to 5-WARP player worth building around.

He wasn't the only player with a key role and less than a year of service time. Mark Trumbo, a rookie first baseman, led the team in home runs and slugging percentage and slowly worked his way from seventh in the lineup to the cleanup spot. Hank Conger, a rookie catcher, actually dislodged Jeff Mathis as the Angels' most active catcher during May, before a prolonged offensive and defensive slump cost him playing time.

After Fernando Rodney blew his second save opportunity of the season, Scioscia didn't hesitate to replace him with Jordan Walden, a 23-year-old rookie whose poor performance in Double-A the previous year raised serious questions. Walden blew plenty of saves, but there are no longer questions about his future as a big league closer. When Scott Kazmir failed again, the Angels looked beyond the veterans on their Triple-A staff and called up Tyler Chatwood, who had been in High-A a year earlier and became the youngest player in the American League. When Joel Pineiro failed, they pulled Garrett Richards up from Double-A. There was a point mid-season when the median Angel was younger than the median Salt Lake Bee.

| | | |
|---|---|---|
| TAv | .268 | 9th |
| TAv-P | .264 | 20th |
| FIP | 3.93 | 14th |
| DER | .718 | 4th |
| DL | 547 | 4th |
| B-Age | 28.9 | 19th |
| P-Age | 28.4 | 18th |
| Salary | $145.4 | 4th |
| M$/MW | $3.54 | 21st |

**2011:** Despite falling 10 games short of catching the Rangers, the future looks bright

**2012:** This could now be the best rotation in the AL, and Pujols is still Pujols

**Action Items:** Some of these experiments—Mark Trumbo at third, Iannetta, Walden—need to work out

But the boldest move in the rebuilding plan came in July, when Bourjos strained his hamstring. Reggie Willits had been on the shuttle between Salt Lake and Anaheim for years in such situations, but the Angels instead called up Mike Trout. Trout struggled and was sent down when Bourjos returned, but after the Angels lost a series to Texas in August and desperation set in, Trout was called back. He hit .250/.318/.450 in 26 games after the second call-up. On August 20, the Angels fielded a lineup with Trout, Conger, Trumbo, and Bourjos—none of whom will be free agents until 2016 and 2017, making them quite a core of talent to build on.

The next day, they announced that Jered Weaver, too, would be with the team just as long. Quietly, agent Scott Boras and the Angels had been working out a five-year, $85 million deal that will keep Weaver in his native Southern California, playing in front of his family. "How much more money do you need?" Weaver said at a press conference. "I could have gotten more, who cares? I'm here, and that's all I care about."

The extension was good news for the Angels, but it will benefit Weaver just as much. Weaver has a career 2.70 ERA at Angel Stadium, where the air gets heavy at night; he has allowed a home run every 30 at bats on the road, but just one every 42 at bats at home. And the defense is constructed to support flyballers Weaver, Santana, and Dan Haren, all of whom benefited with BABIPs well below their career averages in 2011. Bourjos is among the game's best; Torii Hunter adjusted well to right field, where he can unleash a strong arm and his instincts make up for diminishing speed. Even Vernon Wells, one of the worst defensive center fielders, was above-average in a corner. Trout will be a plus defender in a corner when he takes over. The Angels' outfield saved 38 runs, according to the +/- defensive metric, the most in baseball in 2011.

With Weaver extended, the Angels now must decide which, if any, of their impending free agents to lock up next. The most difficult losses to absorb will be in the infield. Howie Kendrick, Erick Aybar, Maicer Izturis, and Alberto Callaspo shared three positions in 2011, and combined for 14.1 WARP. That's more than a theoretical infield of Robinson Cano, Troy Tulowitzki, and Ryan Zimmerman produced in 2011.

But it will be a new front office who will make that call. After missing the playoffs for a second consecutive year, owner Arte Moreno fired, demoted, or accepted the resignation of most of his team's masthead: General Manager Tony Reagins, director of player development Abe Flores, assistant GM Ken Forsch, special assistant Gary Sutherland, manager of baseball operations Tory Hernandez, and a handful of scouts. (Scouting director Eddie Bane was let go a year earlier.)

Jerry Dipoto, the Diamondbacks' senior vice president of scouting and player development, was named the new General Manager. Scott Servais was plucked from the Texas Rangers to lead scouting and player development, and 31-year-old Matt Klentak was hired from Baltimore to be an assistant GM. Justin Hollander, the Angels' in-house statistical analyst, was promoted to head of baseball operations. The moves, and the corresponding quotes from the new execs, point to a different brand of Angels baseball. Dipoto spoke of the importance of on-base percentage, "something that was never aggressively taught" in the Angels' system, he said. Asked in a TV interview whether he had created an analytics department yet, he said all of baseball operations is now an analytics department. "Each of the guys we've added have an analytic edge to what they do," he said. That he spoke publicly at all represents a cultural shift for the Angels, who were one of baseball's most impenetrable organizations during the Reagins years.

Dipoto backed up his talk, and ingratiated himself to Angels fans, with his first moves. In late November, he traded Tyler Chatwood for high-OBP catcher Chris Iannetta, a not-too-subtle acknowledgment that trading away the similarly skilled Mike Napoli had been a mistake. Days later, he thrust an *estoque* through the heart of sacred cow Jeff Mathis, trading him to the Blue Jays for soft-tossing lefty Brad Mills and his career 8.57 ERA.

All those smart front office guys, all those young players, all those extra years of Weaver starting Opening Day—and still Dipoto had a team that would be nobody's favorite in the AL West. The Angels haven't had a player receive even a single MVP vote in the past two years, a reflection of a lineup with balance but (until Trout emerges) no stars. Even the top-heavy pitching staff, which led the league in ERA in 2011, was vulnerable. Weaver and Haren gave the Angels an excellent start to a playoff rotation, but it's a definite drop-off to Ervin Santana and a treacherous one to Garrett Richards and the resurrected Jerome Williams. Williams was a great story, and he had a 1.00 ERA in six Venezuelan Winter League starts, but you'll never go wrong being skeptical of a great story.

The Angels went into the winter looking for answers, but Arte Moreno's soft payroll cap left only $15 million to $20 million to spend. Furthermore, the Angels had been awkward and unsuccessful on the free agent market the previous three seasons—complaining about the rising cost of free agents (particularly when they were narrowly outbid), nursing a grudge against Boras, and throwing out take-it-or-leave-it contract offers rather than negotiating with free agents. "It's crazy," Moreno said after whiffing on Crawford. "I paid $183 million for the team in 2003, and now we're talking $142 million for one player?"

But the Angels rebuild reached its ecstatic climax at the winter meetings, when they signed Albert Pujols and C.J. Wilson within minutes of each other. Even the pursuit of Pujols came as a surprise—the team's first contact with him had come just 36 hours earlier—and the signing of both was a bold statement that the Angels will act borderline irrationally if it makes enough sense.

Less than a year earlier, Tony Reagins had traded Mike Napoli and Juan Rivera for Vernon Wells and all but $5 million of Wells' contract. In 11 months, almost everything about the Angels of the past half-decade had changed. An era was over. In the five seasons from 2005 to 2009, the Angels won four division titles. Never did they have to fend off a team that won 90 or more games. The Angels, with a big budget and little competition, could waste money on long-term deals for aging relievers, as they did with Justin Speier and Scot Shields. They could outbid the rest of the

days are gone; the Rangers are a powerhouse, the Mariners could be contenders by 2013, and baseball's realignment will end the four-team division in the AL West. The Angels' arrogant refusal to acknowledge that fact earlier landed them Fernando Rodney, Scott Kazmir, and Vernon Wells—and the much smaller, $10,000 shares that go to players on second-place teams.

Ultimately, a more competitive AL West has done, and will do, the Angels good. As we saw in 2011, it's the unsuccessful seasons that lead to progress. The Angels are no longer a low-OBP organization. No longer a lousy offense without a star. No longer unable to lock up homegrown players to long-term contracts. No longer throwing way too much money at

| Bobby Abreu | RF |
|---|---|
| Born: 3/11/1974 Age: 38 | |
| Bats: L Throws: R Height: 6' 1'' Weight: 160 | |
| Breakout: 0% Improve: 18% Collapse: 16% | |
| Attrition: 20% MLB: 64% | |
| **Comparables:** | |
| Tommy Henrich, Tim Salmon, Harold Baines | |

| YEAR | TEAM | LVL | AGE | PA | R | 2B | 3B | HR | RBI | BB | SO | SB | CS | AVG_OBP_SLG | TAv | BABIP | BRR | FRAA | WARP |
|---|---|---|---|---|---|---|---|---|---|---|---|---|---|---|---|---|---|---|---|
| 2009 | ANA | MLB | 35 | 667 | 96 | 29 | 3 | 15 | 103 | 94 | 113 | 30 | 8 | .293/.390/.435 | .294 | .338 | -1.1 | -0.5 | 3.7 |
| 2010 | ANA | MLB | 36 | 667 | 88 | 41 | 1 | 20 | 78 | 87 | 132 | 24 | 10 | .255/.352/.435 | .295 | .296 | -6.1 | -1 | 1.8 |
| 2011 | ANA | MLB | 37 | 585 | 54 | 30 | 1 | 8 | 60 | 78 | 113 | 21 | 5 | .253/.353/.365 | .275 | .310 | 0 | -3.8 | 1.4 |
| 2012 | ANA | MLB | 38 | 566 | 65 | 26 | 2 | 10 | 53 | 67 | 109 | 20 | 7 | .251/.340/.373 | .268 | .302 | -0.3 | RF -2, LF -3 | 1.4 |

In 2011 the Angels finally cleared the designated hitter role for Abreu, immediately improving their run prevention by 20 or so just by getting him out of the outfield. But Abreu had trouble with the new job description, slugging 70 points lower than his previous worst. In his favor was the timeliness of his hits: six of his eight home runs tied the game or gave the Angels a lead, and his 3.66 Win Probability Added was the Angels' best by two wins. The Angels will pay him $9 million in 2012, so they'll have to choose between keeping Mike Trout in Triple-A or platooning $30 million of veteran lacklusterness at DH.

| Alexi Amarista | 2B |
|---|---|
| Born: 4/6/1989 Age: 23 | |
| Bats: L Throws: R Height: 5' 9'' Weight: 150 | |
| Breakout: 4% Improve: 21% Collapse: 4% | |
| Attrition: 17% MLB: 40% | |
| **Comparables:** | |
| Mike Richardt, Manny Lee, Jack Brohamer | |

| YEAR | TEAM | LVL | AGE | PA | R | 2B | 3B | HR | RBI | BB | SO | SB | CS | AVG_OBP_SLG | TAv | BABIP | BRR | FRAA | WARP |
|---|---|---|---|---|---|---|---|---|---|---|---|---|---|---|---|---|---|---|---|
| 2009 | CDR | A | 20 | 557 | 84 | 39 | 10 | 4 | 49 | 50 | 61 | 38 | 20 | .319/.380/.468 | .316 | .344 | -0.9 | 15.5 | 6.4 |
| 2010 | RCU | A+ | 21 | 323 | 39 | 19 | 6 | 4 | 39 | 19 | 42 | 17 | 10 | .303/.349/.448 | .301 | .340 | -3.2 | 8.6 | 3.0 |
| 2010 | ARK | AA | 21 | 213 | 25 | 2 | 1 | 1 | 20 | 13 | 15 | 4 | 1 | .288/.337/.325 | .259 | .305 | 1.2 | 0.2 | 0.7 |
| 2010 | SLC | AAA | 21 | 70 | 13 | 6 | 3 | 0 | 9 | 1 | 4 | 4 | 2 | .400/.406/.585 | .332 | .413 | 0.2 | -0.4 | 0.6 |
| 2011 | SLC | AAA | 22 | 396 | 49 | 24 | 5 | 4 | 50 | 22 | 56 | 15 | 8 | .292/.337/.419 | .245 | .333 | -1.6 | 3.3 | 0.4 |
| 2011 | ANA | MLB | 22 | 56 | 2 | 3 | 1 | 0 | 5 | 2 | 8 | 0 | 0 | .154/.182/.250 | .169 | .178 | -1.2 | -1 | -0.6 |
| 2012 | ANA | MLB | 23 | 250 | 24 | 12 | 2 | 1 | 22 | 10 | 40 | 8 | 4 | .249/.283/.329 | .228 | .290 | -0.7 | 2B 5, LF -0 | -0.1 |

The latest in the Angels' pursuit to field the shortest possible infield, Amarista may serve as the "You Must Be This Tall To Start In This Infield" sign for future Angels. The feeblest bat that the Angels sent to the plate in the majors this year is probably too nonthreatening to keep big league pitchers honest. He's a very good second baseman with enough arm to fill in on the left side, the cost of shipping him from city to city is remarkably low, and he's game for anything. He even started in left field for Mike Scioscia despite his most recent outfield experience coming back in Arizona Summer League in 2008. In his first game out there he made a twisting, leaping catch. If he blossoms he'll be a wonderful replacement utility guy when Maicer Izturis's contract runs out.

### Erick Aybar — SS

Born: 1/14/1984 Age: 28
Bats: B Throws: R Height: 5' 11" Weight: 170
Breakout: 1% Improve: 27% Collapse: 10%
Attrition: 23% MLB: 81%

**Comparables:**
Rafael Furcal, Jesus Merchan, Brendan Ryan

| YEAR | TEAM | LVL | AGE | PA | R | 2B | 3B | HR | RBI | BB | SO | SB | CS | AVG_OBP_SLG | TAv | BABIP | BRR | FRAA | WARP |
|------|------|-----|-----|----|----|----|----|----|-----|----|----|----|----|-------------|-----|-------|-----|------|------|
| 2009 | ANA | MLB | 25 | 556 | 70 | 23 | 9 | 5 | 58 | 30 | 54 | 14 | 7 | .312/.353/.423 | .272 | .338 | 2.3 | -6.2 | 2.9 |
| 2010 | ANA | MLB | 26 | 589 | 69 | 18 | 4 | 5 | 29 | 35 | 81 | 22 | 8 | .253/.306/.330 | .240 | .289 | 5.7 | -2.5 | 1.4 |
| 2011 | ANA | MLB | 27 | 605 | 71 | 33 | 8 | 10 | 59 | 31 | 68 | 30 | 6 | .279/.322/.421 | .275 | .301 | 4.4 | 3.3 | 4.1 |
| 2012 | ANA | MLB | 28 | 566 | 61 | 22 | 6 | 4 | 53 | 28 | 72 | 21 | 6 | .268/.311/.357 | .245 | .296 | -0.1 | SS -1 | 1.5 |

In last year's book, we patted ourselves on the back for foreseeing Aybar's steep decline from 2009. We weren't as prescient about 2011, when Aybar was one of the American League's best hitting shortstops, setting career highs in home runs, stolen bases, OPS+ and WARP. Advanced metrics don't love him as much as the trust-my-eyes crowd—the 3-6-2 double play he turned on July 30, in particular, is worth looking up in MLB.com's archives—but even the numbers make him a 4-win player if he keeps besting his PECOTA projections.

### Peter Bourjos — CF

Born: 3/31/1987 Age: 25
Bats: R Throws: R Height: 6' 2" Weight: 180
Breakout: 2% Improve: 35% Collapse: 6%
Attrition: 28% MLB: 73%

**Comparables:**
Felix Pie, Rocco Baldelli, Bobby Tolan

| YEAR | TEAM | LVL | AGE | PA | R | 2B | 3B | HR | RBI | BB | SO | SB | CS | AVG_OBP_SLG | TAv | BABIP | BRR | FRAA | WARP |
|------|------|-----|-----|----|----|----|----|----|-----|----|----|----|----|-------------|-----|-------|-----|------|------|
| 2009 | ARK | AA | 22 | 504 | 72 | 16 | 14 | 6 | 51 | 49 | 77 | 32 | 12 | .281/.351/.423 | .295 | .321 | 3.3 | 8.1 | 4.7 |
| 2010 | SLC | AAA | 23 | 455 | 85 | 13 | 12 | 13 | 52 | 24 | 78 | 27 | 5 | .314/.363/.498 | .294 | .358 | 7.2 | 4.1 | 4.2 |
| 2010 | ANA | MLB | 23 | 193 | 19 | 6 | 4 | 6 | 15 | 6 | 40 | 10 | 1 | .204/.237/.381 | .227 | .228 | 1.1 | 2 | 0.5 |
| 2011 | ANA | MLB | 24 | 552 | 72 | 26 | 11 | 12 | 43 | 32 | 124 | 22 | 9 | .271/.327/.438 | .282 | .338 | 5.6 | -7.3 | 2.9 |
| 2012 | ANA | MLB | 25 | 500 | 55 | 18 | 8 | 9 | 54 | 27 | 110 | 22 | 7 | .252/.301/.386 | .252 | .306 | -0.1 | CF -2, LF 0 | 1.2 |

Bourjos covered so much ground as a center fielder that it sometimes backfired early in the season. His corner outfielders, unaccustomed to flanking a player with such range, sometimes weren't giving way to Bourjos, while other times they flinched or backed away at his mere approach. The turf war ended around June, when Torii Hunter and Vernon Wells learned what we all learned: When Peter Bourjos is chasing a ball, it's more fun to just watch. He's an elite defender, well deserving of the Gold Gloves passed down through the organization from Pettis to White to Edmonds to Erstad to Hunter. The questions entering the season were all about his hitting, and he addressed those. He reached base on around half his bunt attempts, boosted his slugging percentage by taking unthinkable extra bases, and hit nine of those 12 home runs in the final two months. He can run, and he can trot, so now he just needs to learn to walk.

### Russell Branyan — 1B

Born: 12/19/1975 Age: 36
Bats: L Throws: R Height: 6' 4" Weight: 195
Breakout: 0% Improve: 23% Collapse: 10%
Attrition: 15% MLB: 78%

**Comparables:**
Jose Canseco, Dick Allen, Tony Clark

| YEAR | TEAM | LVL | AGE | PA | R | 2B | 3B | HR | RBI | BB | SO | SB | CS | AVG_OBP_SLG | TAv | BABIP | BRR | FRAA | WARP |
|------|------|-----|-----|----|----|----|----|----|-----|----|----|----|----|-------------|-----|-------|-----|------|------|
| 2009 | SEA | MLB | 33 | 505 | 64 | 21 | 1 | 31 | 76 | 58 | 149 | 2 | 0 | .251/.347/.520 | .310 | .300 | -2.2 | 2.2 | 3.0 |
| 2010 | CLE | MLB | 34 | 190 | 24 | 9 | 0 | 10 | 24 | 16 | 49 | 0 | 0 | .263/.328/.491 | .295 | .310 | -1 | 3 | 1.0 |
| 2010 | SEA | MLB | 34 | 238 | 23 | 10 | 0 | 15 | 33 | 30 | 82 | 1 | 0 | .215/.319/.483 | .287 | .266 | -1.4 | 0 | 0.8 |
| 2011 | ANA | MLB | 35 | 77 | 7 | 2 | 0 | 4 | 12 | 11 | 21 | 2 | 0 | .185/.299/.400 | .261 | .195 | -0.8 | 0.1 | 0.1 |
| 2011 | ARI | MLB | 35 | 69 | 4 | 5 | 0 | 1 | 2 | 7 | 20 | 0 | 0 | .210/.290/.339 | .228 | .293 | -0.3 | 0.3 | -0.2 |
| 2012 | ANA | MLB | 36 | 250 | 30 | 9 | 0 | 12 | 32 | 28 | 79 | 2 | 0 | .220/.312/.434 | .271 | .277 | 0.1 | 1B 2, 3B 0 | 1.2 |

The median length of time Branyan has stayed with a team is 51 major league games, a total he didn't quite reach with the Angels, the 16th club to iron his uniform. Signed to platoon with Mark Trumbo in the wake of Kendrys Morales' second surgery, Branyan arrived just in time to see Trumbo reverse his own platoon split, putting Branyan on the bench for weeks at a time. He started just five games after July 1, and despite a pinch-hit home run off Mariano Rivera and a couple more homers off the bench, he couldn't quite build a cult following in Southern California. He doesn't have much desire left to be a guy who starts five games in three months, so this could be it for the Grand Master of the Three True Outcomes. The longest hitting streak he ever put together in his career was 11 games; the longest striking-out streak was 22 games. That's our boy.

### Alberto Callaspo — 3B

Born: 4/19/1983 Age: 29
Bats: B Throws: R Height: 5' 11" Weight: 175
Breakout: 0% Improve: 33% Collapse: 7%
Attrition: 21% MLB: 85%

**Comparables:**
George Kell, Kevin Frandsen, Ken Oberkfell

| YEAR | TEAM | LVL | AGE | PA | R | 2B | 3B | HR | RBI | BB | SO | SB | CS | AVG_OBP_SLG | TAv | BABIP | BRR | FRAA | WARP |
|------|------|-----|-----|----|----|----|----|----|-----|----|----|----|----|-------------|-----|-------|-----|------|------|
| 2009 | KCA | MLB | 26 | 634 | 79 | 41 | 8 | 11 | 73 | 52 | 51 | 2 | 1 | .300/.356/.457 | .280 | .312 | 0.9 | -3.2 | 2.8 |
| 2010 | ANA | MLB | 27 | 228 | 21 | 8 | 0 | 2 | 13 | 12 | 13 | 2 | 2 | .249/.291/.315 | .221 | .256 | 1.8 | 5 | 0.4 |
| 2010 | KCA | MLB | 27 | 373 | 40 | 19 | 2 | 8 | 43 | 19 | 29 | 3 | 1 | .275/.308/.410 | .259 | .278 | -1.3 | -1.3 | 0.8 |
| 2011 | ANA | MLB | 28 | 536 | 54 | 23 | 0 | 6 | 46 | 58 | 48 | 8 | 1 | .288/.366/.375 | .273 | .310 | -1 | 14.7 | 4.0 |
| 2012 | ANA | MLB | 29 | 517 | 58 | 24 | 3 | 5 | 48 | 40 | 46 | 4 | 2 | .275/.331/.370 | .263 | .293 | -0.1 | 3B 8, 2B -1 | 2.2 |

The Angels have had unexpected success with switch-hitting middle infielders converted to the hot corner. Maicer Izturis, Chone Figgins, and Alberto Callaspo have combined for just 20 home runs in the five years they have been the Angels' primary third basemen, but all were very strong defenders with solid on-base skills. Noting that Callaspo led the Angels in on-base percentage in 2011 is both recognition of a very strong trade (and subsequent arbitration tender) made by Tony Reagins and an indictment of his overall team building.

**Hank Conger** C
Born: 1/29/1988 Age: 24
Bats: B Throws: R Height: 6' 2" Weight: 220
Breakout: 2% Improve: 19% Collapse: 13%
Attrition: 28% MLB: 73%
Comparables:
Kurt Suzuki, Don Slaught, Mark Wagner

| YEAR | TEAM | LVL | AGE | PA | R | 2B | 3B | HR | RBI | BB | SO | SB | CS | AVG_OBP_SLG | TAv | BABIP | BRR | FRAA | WARP |
|------|------|-----|-----|----|----|----|----|----|-----|----|----|----|----|-------------|-----|-------|-----|------|------|
| 2009 | ARK | AA | 21 | 524 | 61 | 20 | 3 | 11 | 68 | 55 | 68 | 4 | 2 | .295/.371/.424 | .296 | .325 | -0.9 | -2.1 | 3.1 |
| 2010 | SLC | AAA | 22 | 452 | 56 | 26 | 2 | 11 | 49 | 55 | 58 | 0 | 2 | .300/.384/.463 | .295 | .325 | -1.3 | -1.5 | 3.0 |
| 2010 | ANA | MLB | 22 | 34 | 2 | 1 | 1 | 0 | 5 | 5 | 9 | 0 | 0 | .172/.294/.276 | .221 | .250 | -0.1 | -0.1 | -0.1 |
| 2011 | SLC | AAA | 23 | 114 | 14 | 4 | 0 | 5 | 26 | 12 | 18 | 0 | 0 | .300/.375/.490 | .273 | .325 | -0.9 | 0.5 | 0.7 |
| 2011 | ANA | MLB | 23 | 197 | 14 | 8 | 0 | 6 | 19 | 17 | 37 | 0 | 0 | .209/.282/.356 | .242 | .231 | 0.3 | -0.5 | 0.3 |
| 2012 | ANA | MLB | 24 | 250 | 27 | 10 | 1 | 5 | 24 | 22 | 46 | 0 | 0 | .244/.314/.365 | .253 | .283 | 0 | C -2 | 1.5 |

The most predictable story of the year: Hank Conger losing Mike Scioscia's confidence and, consequently, losing playing time

**Kaleb Cowart** 3B
Born: 6/2/1992 Age: 20
Bats: B Throws: R Height: 6' 4" Weight: 190
Breakout: 1% Improve: 1% Collapse: 0%
Attrition: 1% MLB: 2%
Comparables:
Adam Coe, Garrison Lassiter, Julio Cedeno

| YEAR | TEAM | LVL | AGE | PA | R | 2B | 3B | HR | RBI | BB | SO | SB | CS | AVG_OBP_SLG | TAv | BABIP | BRR | FRAA | WARP |
|------|------|-----|-----|----|----|----|----|----|-----|----|----|----|----|-------------|-----|-------|-----|------|------|
| 2011 | ORM | RK | 19 | 319 | 49 | 12 | 3 | 7 | 40 | 25 | 81 | 11 | 4 | .283/.345/.420 | .279 | .363 | -0.4 | -7.5 | 1.0 |
| 2012 | ANA | MLB | 20 | 250 | 19 | 7 | 1 | 3 | 17 | 11 | 77 | 1 | 1 | .179/.218/.252 | .178 | .247 | -0.1 | 3B 3, 1B 0 | -2.1 |

There wasn't a fastball in the Pioneer League Cowart couldn't rake, and he was hitting .400 into July. After the league adjusted, though, Cowart struck out in 29 percent of his plate appearances and saw his OPS fall well below the league average. He has good bat speed from both sides, posting a strong line-drive rate and spraying balls from foul line to foul line. He made 17 errors in 68 games at third, but his arm is exceptional and his mobility good. He'll drop on the prospect lists, but the tools are there for a rebound at Cedar Rapids this year.

**C.J. Cron** —
Born: 1/5/1990 Age: 22
Bats: R Throws: R Height: 6' 7" Weight: 228
Breakout: 1% Improve: 20% Collapse: 4%
Attrition: 14% MLB: 40%
Comparables:
Cecil Fielder, Jerry Sands, Mike Ivie

| YEAR | TEAM | LVL | AGE | PA | R | 2B | 3B | HR | RBI | BB | SO | SB | CS | AVG_OBP_SLG | TAv | BABIP | BRR | FRAA | WARP |
|------|------|-----|-----|----|----|----|----|----|-----|----|----|----|----|-------------|-----|-------|-----|------|------|
| 2011 | ORM | RK | 21 | 159 | 30 | 5 | 1 | 13 | 41 | 10 | 34 | 0 | 0 | .308/.371/.629 | .328 | .320 | -1.9 | 0 | 1.2 |
| 2012 | ANA | MLB | 22 | 250 | 25 | 7 | 1 | 10 | 29 | 11 | 69 | 0 | 0 | .206/.246/.377 | .226 | .239 | 0 | — | -1.1 |

The Angels' first-round grab was an unusual Angels pick, though it set the tone for the rest of scouting director Ric Wilson's first draft: no toolsy outfielders, no risky high school arms, no tough signs in the first dozen rounds. Just a long string of college picks. Short-season ball shouldn't be much of a challenge for a polished college kid as strong as Cron, and it wasn't: he finished sixth in the Pioneer League in home runs—five of them going to right field—despite playing less than half the season. Five days after hitting three home runs in a game, he collapsed mid-AB with a dislocated knee. That required surgery, and it's probable that the labrum tear he suffered in college will, too.

**Torii Hunter** RF
Born: 7/18/1975 Age: 36
Bats: R Throws: R Height: 6' 3" Weight: 205
Breakout: 0% Improve: 20% Collapse: 7%
Attrition: 17% MLB: 75%
Comparables:
Paul O'Neill, Dave Winfield, Carl Furillo

| YEAR | TEAM | LVL | AGE | PA | R | 2B | 3B | HR | RBI | BB | SO | SB | CS | AVG_OBP_SLG | TAv | BABIP | BRR | FRAA | WARP |
|------|------|-----|-----|----|----|----|----|----|-----|----|----|----|----|-------------|-----|-------|-----|------|------|
| 2009 | ANA | MLB | 33 | 506 | 74 | 26 | 1 | 22 | 90 | 47 | 92 | 18 | 4 | .299/.366/.508 | .303 | .330 | -1 | 4.4 | 4.0 |
| 2010 | ANA | MLB | 34 | 646 | 76 | 36 | 0 | 23 | 90 | 61 | 106 | 9 | 12 | .281/.354/.464 | .298 | .307 | -4.9 | 3 | 4.2 |
| 2011 | ANA | MLB | 35 | 649 | 80 | 24 | 2 | 23 | 82 | 62 | 125 | 5 | 7 | .262/.336/.429 | .280 | .297 | -1 | 0.6 | 2.6 |
| 2012 | ANA | MLB | 36 | 609 | 72 | 28 | 1 | 19 | 71 | 48 | 117 | 11 | 7 | .259/.322/.417 | .273 | .295 | -1.4 | RF 2, CF 2 | 2.1 |

On his birthday in July, Hunter tweeted this: "I'm 36 years young and i don't need Viagra yet! LOL." LOL indeed except that Hunter was hitting .239/.310/.379 and if he couldn't get those rate stats (innuendo alert) up it was going to be a miserable final season and a half of his five-year $90 million contract. The next day he struck out three times but he homered the day after that and didn't slow down: .295/.373/.502 in 64 post-birthday games. Hunter has been worth 15 WARP in the four years of the contract, a cost of about $4.8 million per win. That's a respectable return on its own. Plus there are 24 guys in his locker room who are grateful that Hunter answers every obnoxious post-loss media question so they don't have to. As silly as the contract seemed when it was signed, there's nobody on the Angels or who cheers for the Angels who really regrets it. Hunter has to survive one more season—with or without a Viagra boost—to keep it that way.

### Chris Iannetta    C

Born: 4/8/1983 Age: 29
Bats: R Throws: R Height: 6' 0" Weight: 195
Breakout: 3% Improve: 40% Collapse: 7%
Attrition: 22% MLB: 91%

Comparables:
Tim Hosley, Dick Dietz, Gene Tenace

| YEAR | TEAM | LVL | AGE | PA | R | 2B | 3B | HR | RBI | BB | SO | SB | CS | AVG_OBP_SLG | TAv | BABIP | BRR | FRAA | WARP |
|------|------|-----|-----|----|---|----|----|----|----|----|----|----|----|-------------|-----|-------|-----|------|------|
| 2009 | COL | MLB | 26 | 350 | 41 | 15 | 2 | 16 | 52 | 43 | 75 | 0 | 1 | .228/.344/.460 | .265 | .245 | -0.2 | 2.6 | 1.7 |
| 2010 | CSP | AAA | 27 | 76 | 17 | 7 | 0 | 5 | 21 | 10 | 10 | 0 | 0 | .349/.453/.698 | .332 | .354 | 0.7 | 0 | 1.0 |
| 2010 | COL | MLB | 27 | 223 | 20 | 6 | 1 | 9 | 27 | 30 | 48 | 1 | 0 | .197/.318/.383 | .238 | .212 | -1.4 | 0.8 | 0.1 |
| 2011 | COL | MLB | 28 | 426 | 51 | 17 | 1 | 14 | 55 | 70 | 89 | 6 | 3 | .238/.370/.414 | .272 | .276 | -1 | -0.1 | 2.5 |
| 2012 | ANA | MLB | 29 | 360 | 45 | 14 | 2 | 13 | 41 | 48 | 78 | 2 | 1 | .237/.354/.426 | .288 | .274 | -0.1 | C 1, 1B 0 | 3.4 |

Since a 2008 campaign that hinted at Gene Tenace/Mickey Tettleton lite, Iannetta has drifted into a holding pattern at decidedly lower levels. He still draws walks and hits homers, which makes him somewhat useful, but his window of opportunity to develop into a cult hero is closing. Part of the problem is that he can't hit on the road. Iannetta batted .301/.419/.557 at Coors Field in 2011 but just .172/.321/.266 away from it, which is like Kirt Manwaring without the batting average. This isn't a one-year thing, either; the last time Iannetta did anything on the road was in that now-mythical 2008 season. The Angels must hope Iannetta feels at home at Angel Stadium. Iannetta, for his part, must hope Mike Scioscia is comfortable with his game-calling.

### Maicer Izturis    2B

Born: 9/12/1980 Age: 31
Bats: B Throws: R Height: 5' 9" Weight: 150
Breakout: 0% Improve: 32% Collapse: 6%
Attrition: 22% MLB: 91%

Comparables:
Skip Schumaker, Placido Polanco, Jose Vidro

| YEAR | TEAM | LVL | AGE | PA | R | 2B | 3B | HR | RBI | BB | SO | SB | CS | AVG_OBP_SLG | TAv | BABIP | BRR | FRAA | WARP |
|------|------|-----|-----|----|---|----|----|----|----|----|----|----|----|-------------|-----|-------|-----|------|------|
| 2009 | ANA | MLB | 28 | 437 | 74 | 22 | 3 | 8 | 65 | 35 | 41 | 13 | 5 | .300/.359/.434 | .289 | .313 | 0.9 | -3.1 | 2.3 |
| 2010 | ANA | MLB | 29 | 238 | 27 | 13 | 1 | 3 | 27 | 21 | 27 | 7 | 3 | .250/.321/.363 | .256 | .272 | -0.4 | -0.4 | 0.5 |
| 2011 | ANA | MLB | 30 | 494 | 51 | 35 | 0 | 5 | 38 | 33 | 65 | 9 | 6 | .276/.334/.388 | .266 | .311 | 1.2 | 1 | 2.4 |
| 2012 | ANA | MLB | 31 | 414 | 46 | 20 | 2 | 4 | 37 | 32 | 50 | 10 | 5 | .264/.325/.359 | .257 | .291 | -0.6 | 2B -2, 3B 0 | 1.4 |

In 1964, a 17-year-old San Diego high school student named Randy Gardner went nearly two weeks without sleep. It was an accomplishment of extraordinary endurance, intended solely to prove it could be done without causing harm. In 2011, Maicer Izturis started consecutive games for the Angels. This was not, objectively speaking, an act of extraordinary anything. But Izturis, too, wanted to prove that he wasn't a fragile part-timer. That reputation had cost him playing time in 2009 and 2010, as his manager always feared the groin strain around the turn. In 2011, though, Izturis set career highs in plate appearances and games, and other than a small heel problem that cost him a game or two, he avoided even nagging injuries.

### Howard Kendrick    2B

Born: 7/12/1983 Age: 28
Bats: R Throws: R Height: 5' 11" Weight: 195
Breakout: 1% Improve: 32% Collapse: 7%
Attrition: 17% MLB: 81%

Comparables:
Rod Carew, Ryne Sandberg, Luis Gonzalez

| YEAR | TEAM | LVL | AGE | PA | R | 2B | 3B | HR | RBI | BB | SO | SB | CS | AVG_OBP_SLG | TAv | BABIP | BRR | FRAA | WARP |
|------|------|-----|-----|----|---|----|----|----|----|----|----|----|----|-------------|-----|-------|-----|------|------|
| 2009 | SLC | AAA | 25 | 87 | 11 | 6 | 1 | 2 | 11 | 7 | 12 | 4 | 2 | .346/.414/.526 | .324 | .391 | 1.4 | 2.6 | 1.1 |
| 2009 | ANA | MLB | 25 | 400 | 61 | 21 | 3 | 10 | 61 | 20 | 71 | 11 | 4 | .291/.334/.444 | .282 | .338 | 1.1 | 3.4 | 2.3 |
| 2010 | ANA | MLB | 26 | 658 | 67 | 41 | 4 | 10 | 75 | 28 | 94 | 14 | 4 | .279/.313/.407 | .265 | .313 | -2.7 | -1.4 | 1.2 |
| 2011 | ANA | MLB | 27 | 583 | 86 | 30 | 6 | 18 | 63 | 33 | 119 | 14 | 6 | .285/.338/.464 | .284 | .338 | 0.9 | -2.3 | 2.7 |
| 2012 | ANA | MLB | 28 | 563 | 65 | 30 | 3 | 10 | 63 | 24 | 100 | 13 | 5 | .282/.320/.406 | .266 | .329 | -0.4 | 2B -1, 1B -0 | 2.0 |

Like those people who keep waiting for Radiohead to remake *The Bends*, there are those who wonder why Howie Kendrick never hits .300 anymore, or why he strikes out so much. But if Kendrick is barely recognizable as the batting-average phenom tabbed as our fifth best prospect in 2006, he has become perhaps the Angels' best everyday player. There's still mystery here, though. UZR and +/- say he was an elite defender, while FRAA says below average, if improved. Also, of his career-high 18 homers, two-thirds were to center or right fields, a rotten place to go deep at Angel Stadium. It's tempting, if perhaps statistically irresponsible, to hold out hope that his road numbers—.299/.356/.511, with 13 home runs—represent his true level.

**Taylor Lindsey**  2B

Born: 12/2/1991 Age: 20
Bats: L Throws: R Height: 6' 1" Weight: 195
Breakout: 0% Improve: 2% Collapse: 1%
Attrition: 1% MLB: 4%

Comparables:
Chih-Hsien Chiang,Adrian Cardenas,Nick Noonan

| YEAR | TEAM | LVL | AGE | PA | R | 2B | 3B | HR | RBI | BB | SO | SB | CS | AVG_OBP_SLG | TAv | BABIP | BRR | FRAA | WARP |
|------|------|-----|-----|-----|----|----|----|----|-----|----|----|----|----|-------------|-----|-------|-----|------|------|
| 2010 | ANG | RK | 18 | 211 | 26 | 12 | 6 | 0 | 18 | 12 | 33 | 8 | 3 | .284/.325/.407 | .270 | .337 | 1 | 2.9 | 1.2 |
| 2011 | ORM | RK | 19 | 307 | 64 | 28 | 6 | 9 | 46 | 13 | 46 | 10 | 4 | .362/.394/.593 | .327 | .407 | -1.4 | 0.6 | 3.4 |
| 2012 | ANA | MLB | 20 | 250 | 20 | 10 | 1 | 2 | 20 | 7 | 57 | 2 | 1 | .207/.231/.285 | .192 | .259 | -0.1 | 2B -1 | -1.7 |

On the way to being named Pioneer League MVP, Lindsey erased most of the concerns about him. He moved away from a pull-happy approach, knocking 10 doubles to left field and going the other way at a league-average rate. And he played a clean second base, committing just seven errors in 62 games and getting improved marks for his range. His strikeout rate dropped every month, and he slugged .586 against same-side pitchers. That leaves only the question of plate discipline, but who's going to tell the guy batting .360 to take more pitches? When that average inevitably drops in the less generous Midwest League, the Angels will have that talk with him.

and when he was drafted he had never seen an 85-mph fastball. He was so crude at 18 that it took him four years to get an idea at the plate. The tools are still exciting—he scored from first on a single in August and for the second year Moore held his own at a higher level. His plate discipline is terrible, even by the standards of the free-swinging Angels, and his stolen base success rate is disappointing, considering mentor Torii Hunter's claims that Moore is as fast as Mike Trout and Peter Bourjos. So he's raw. But he's no longer crude, and just a little bit of refinement could make him one of the more exciting fourth outfielders in the game.

**Efren Navarro**  1B

Born: 5/14/1986 Age: 26
Bats: L Throws: L Height: 6' 1" Weight: 200
Breakout: 4% Improve: 19% Collapse: 1%
Attrition: 10% MLB: 51%

Comparables:
Terry Francona,Stephen Vogt,Scott Bradley

| YEAR | TEAM | LVL | AGE | PA | R | 2B | 3B | HR | RBI | BB | SO | SB | CS | AVG_OBP_SLG | TAv | BABIP | BRR | FRAA | WARP |
|------|------|-----|-----|-----|----|----|----|----|-----|----|----|----|----|-------------|-----|-------|-----|------|------|
| 2009 | RCU | A+ | 23 | 540 | 64 | 32 | 3 | 5 | 61 | 53 | 72 | 3 | 2 | .287/.361/.397 | .277 | .328 | -1.3 | -2.6 | 1.1 |
| 2010 | ARK | AA | 24 | 494 | 46 | 24 | 2 | 6 | 50 | 31 | 47 | 6 | 4 | .267/.316/.369 | .267 | .285 | 0.9 | 0.6 | 0.9 |
| 2011 | SLC | AAA | 25 | 547 | 76 | 36 | 6 | 12 | 73 | 42 | 78 | 5 | 5 | .317/.368/.488 | .278 | .352 | 0.5 | 2.5 | 2.0 |
| 2011 | ANA | MLB | 25 | 12 | 1 | 1 | 0 | 0 | 0 | 1 | 1 | 0 | 0 | .200/.273/.300 | .182 | .222 | 0 | 0 | -0.1 |
| 2012 | ANA | MLB | 26 | 250 | 24 | 12 | 1 | 2 | 21 | 14 | 41 | 1 | 1 | .239/.282/.323 | .227 | .278 | -0.2 | 1B -10, RF 0 | -0.9 |

If Jamie Moyer is the comp-of-death for soft-tossing minor league lefties, Mark Grace is the hysterically optimistic comp for slick-fielding, powerless first basemen. Mike Scioscia evoked Grace when Navarro started hot in the Cactus League, and as far as his defense—he won the PCL's Gold Glove at the position—and contact skills, sure, one can sort of see it after a few beers. But few with that skill set ever hit enough to carry the position, and even Navarro's breakout season in Salt Lake was unimpressive in a league where entire teams were slugging .490. He's buried behind Kendrys Morales and Mark Trumbo on the depth chart, but a September call-up joined him with Buster Posey, David Murphy, and Anthony Chavez—0.93 ERA in 10 career innings—as the Angels' only 50th-round picks to qualify for a big-league pension.

**Albert Pujols**  1B

Born: 1/16/1980 Age: 32
Bats: R Throws: R Height: 6' 4" Weight: 210
Breakout: 1% Improve: 33% Collapse: 3%
Attrition: 7% MLB: 96%

Comparables:
Kent Hrbek,Lance Berkman,Todd Helton

| YEAR | TEAM | LVL | AGE | PA | R | 2B | 3B | HR | RBI | BB | SO | SB | CS | AVG_OBP_SLG | TAv | BABIP | BRR | FRAA | WARP |
|------|------|-----|-----|-----|-----|----|----|----|-----|-----|----|----|----|-------------|-----|-------|-----|------|------|
| 2009 | SLN | MLB | 29 | 700 | 124 | 45 | 1 | 47 | 135 | 115 | 64 | 16 | 4 | .327/.443/.658 | .361 | .299 | 1.4 | 26 | 11.5 |
| 2010 | SLN | MLB | 30 | 700 | 115 | 39 | 1 | 42 | 118 | 103 | 76 | 14 | 4 | .312/.414/.596 | .340 | .297 | 3.5 | 14.1 | 9.0 |
| 2011 | SLN | MLB | 31 | 651 | 105 | 29 | 0 | 37 | 99 | 61 | 58 | 9 | 1 | .299/.366/.541 | .315 | .277 | -0.9 | 13.5 | 6.1 |
| 2012 | ANA | MLB | 32 | 621 | 95 | 31 | 1 | 32 | 97 | 84 | 60 | 10 | 3 | .305/.402/.550 | .338 | .292 | 0 | 1B 15, 3B 0 | 5.9 |

Even after Pujols shut down all contract negotiations in spring training to avoid distractions, the specter of free agency loomed over him all season. A slow start didn't help matters as he tweaked a hamstring and hit just .211 on balls in play in April. A near-firestorm erupted in May when Pujols hugged it out with then-Cubs GM Jim Hendry at Wrigley, and Pujols was hitting a shockingly human .257/.326/.395 as late as May 29. Just as the Machine was finding his groove in June, he suffered a broken left wrist in a collision at first base. But after the All-Star break, he was his old dominant self, putting up a more typically Pujolsian .319/.375/.584 slash line and slugging near .700 in the postseason. That said, Pujols produced career lows in batting average, walk rate, and on-base and slugging percentage. He also hit more balls on the ground than ever before and led baseball by hitting into 29 double plays. Will any of those negatives matter in the short term for the Angels, who signed him for 10 years? If PECOTA is any indication, no, but the longer out we forecast, the greater the number of monsters here be. He is only 300 home runs short of the Angels' franchise record, an unlikely but reachable mark.

| Andrew Romine SS | | | | | | | | | | | | | | | | | |
|---|---|---|---|---|---|---|---|---|---|---|---|---|---|---|---|---|---|
| **YEAR** | **TEAM** | **LVL** | **AGE** | **PA** | **R** | **2B** | **3B** | **HR** | **RBI** | **BB** | **SO** | **SB** | **CS** | **AVG_OBP_SLG** | **TAv** | **BABIP** | **BRR** | **FRAA** | **WARP** |

Born: 12/24/1985 Age: 26
Bats: B Throws: R Height: 6' 2'' Weight: 190
Breakout: 2% Improve: 35% Collapse: 9%
Attrition: 30% MLB: 69%

**Comparables:**
Phil Linz, Brandon Chaves, Ted Kubiak

| YEAR | TEAM | LVL | AGE | PA | R | 2B | 3B | HR | RBI | BB | SO | SB | CS | AVG_OBP_SLG | TAv | BABIP | BRR | FRAA | WARP |
|---|---|---|---|---|---|---|---|---|---|---|---|---|---|---|---|---|---|---|---|
| 2009 | RCU | A+ | 23 | 555 | 68 | 13 | 9 | 1 | 36 | 51 | 83 | 26 | 11 | .278/.343/.349 | .277 | .321 | 5.1 | 6.4 | 4.7 |
| 2010 | ARK | AA | 24 | 453 | 55 | 15 | 4 | 3 | 34 | 50 | 66 | 21 | 9 | .282/.361/.366 | .275 | .321 | 6.2 | 11.3 | 4.4 |
| 2010 | ANA | MLB | 24 | 12 | 0 | 0 | 0 | 0 | 0 | 0 | 4 | 0 | 0 | .091/.091/.091 | .084 | .143 | 0.2 | 0 | -0.1 |
| 2011 | SLC | AAA | 25 | 438 | 67 | 9 | 2 | 4 | 35 | 45 | 87 | 23 | 6 | .281/.363/.346 | .243 | .355 | 2.1 | 3.5 | 2.0 |
| 2011 | ANA | MLB | 25 | 18 | 2 | 0 | 0 | 0 | 0 | 1 | 6 | 1 | 0 | .125/.176/.125 | .164 | .200 | 0.1 | 0.4 | -0.1 |
| 2012 | ANA | MLB | 26 | 250 | 23 | 6 | 2 | 0 | 16 | 18 | 54 | 8 | 3 | .226/.284/.275 | .214 | .287 | -0.1 | SS 6, 2B 0 | -0.4 |

Coming from a baseball family, Romine does a lot of little things—great hands at shortstop, draws walks, steals bases at a good clip, good bunter—but he has been prohibitively poor at one big thing: hitting. Slugging .346 in Salt Lake was the closing statement on his power, and the Angels—sensing Romine would never hit enough to start at shortstop on a $150 million team—began the process of making him useful as a utility player. With Amarista and Izturis ahead of him as utility options, the Angels' crowded infield might keep him riding buses for another season.

**Jean Segura 2B**

Born: 3/17/1990 Age: 22
Bats: R Throws: L Height: 6' 0'' Weight: 160
Breakout: 3% Improve: 16% Collapse: 10%
Attrition: 17% MLB: 36%

**Comparables:**
Eduardo Nunez, Erick Aybar, Robin Yount

| YEAR | TEAM | LVL | AGE | PA | R | 2B | 3B | HR | RBI | BB | SO | SB | CS | AVG_OBP_SLG | TAv | BABIP | BRR | FRAA | WARP |
|---|---|---|---|---|---|---|---|---|---|---|---|---|---|---|---|---|---|---|---|
| 2009 | ORM | RK | 19 | 177 | 33 | 10 | 4 | 3 | 21 | 11 | 11 | 11 | 3 | .346/.392/.512 | .352 | .356 | 3.6 | 8.3 | 3.3 |
| 2010 | CDR | A | 20 | 581 | 89 | 24 | 12 | 10 | 79 | 45 | 72 | 50 | 10 | .313/.363/.464 | .297 | .340 | 5.1 | 25 | 7.2 |
| 2011 | SBR | A+ | 21 | 202 | 26 | 9 | 4 | 3 | 21 | 15 | 26 | 18 | 6 | .281/.337/.422 | .280 | .312 | -0.4 | 2 | 1.5 |
| 2012 | ANA | MLB | 22 | 250 | 22 | 9 | 2 | 1 | 20 | 9 | 45 | 15 | 4 | .231/.260/.303 | .211 | .275 | 0.1 | 2B 11, SS 1 | -0.6 |

Segura was having a fine follow-up to his breakout 2010 campaign, his slash line at .364/.417/.545 after a two-homer game in late April. Shortly after, though, he injured his hamstring, returned too quickly, re-injured it, returned too quickly, re-injured it and missed two and a half months. It was the first time that Segura has had leg troubles since the Angels signed him, but the recovery time is certainly discouraging for a player whose speed makes him special.

**Mike Trout CF**

Born: 8/7/1991 Age: 20
Bats: R Throws: R Height: 6' 2'' Weight: 200
Breakout: 4% Improve: 19% Collapse: 6%
Attrition: 16% MLB: 43%

**Comparables:**
Ron Fairly, Juan Gonzalez, Ken Griffey

| YEAR | TEAM | LVL | AGE | PA | R | 2B | 3B | HR | RBI | BB | SO | SB | CS | AVG_OBP_SLG | TAv | BABIP | BRR | FRAA | WARP |
|---|---|---|---|---|---|---|---|---|---|---|---|---|---|---|---|---|---|---|---|
| 2009 | ANG | RK | 17 | 187 | 29 | 7 | 7 | 1 | 25 | 18 | 28 | 13 | 2 | .360/.416/.506 | .359 | .420 | 3.2 | 0.5 | 2.6 |
| 2010 | CDR | A | 18 | 368 | 76 | 19 | 7 | 6 | 39 | 46 | 52 | 45 | 9 | .362/.452/.526 | .346 | .418 | 7.2 | -2.1 | 5.3 |
| 2010 | RCU | A+ | 18 | 232 | 30 | 9 | 2 | 4 | 19 | 27 | 33 | 11 | 6 | .306/.384/.434 | .320 | .341 | 2.2 | -3.2 | 2.4 |
| 2011 | ARK | AA | 19 | 412 | 82 | 18 | 13 | 11 | 38 | 45 | 76 | 33 | 10 | .326/.414/.544 | .343 | .390 | 7.7 | -6.1 | 5.3 |
| 2011 | ANA | MLB | 19 | 135 | 20 | 6 | 0 | 5 | 16 | 9 | 30 | 4 | 0 | .220/.281/.390 | .261 | .247 | 0.8 | 1 | 0.4 |
| 2012 | ANA | MLB | 20 | 250 | 27 | 9 | 3 | 4 | 24 | 19 | 53 | 12 | 3 | .254/.317/.369 | .254 | .310 | 0.1 | CF -10, RF 0 | 1.1 |

Trout is the best prospect the Angels have ever had, a physical freak and a future star in most simulations of the universe. He's as fast down the line as anyone in baseball; he goes 420 feet the other way in batting practice. You know all this, so let's give a moment to consider where he failed in 2011. His arm is average at best, and while he was in Anaheim he had a habit of throwing to the wrong base. He's too passive at the plate—has been since the minors—and seems to take pitches just to take pitches, not because he's got such a dynamite eye. In 135 plate appearances, he swung at the first pitch just three times. He swung at only half of all pitches in the strike zone, the lowest rate in baseball (minimum 100 plate appearances). And his spray chart suggests he might have had trouble catching up to big league fastballs. Add all these concerns up, and you've still got a superstar—just one who wasn't quite ready to be one in his age 19 season.

**Mark Trumbo** 1B

Born: 1/16/1986 Age: 26
Bats: R Throws: R Height: 6' 5" Weight: 220
Breakout: 0% Improve: 26% Collapse: 3%
Attrition: 15% MLB: 57%

Comparables:
Joel Guzman, Brian R. Hunter, Joe Vitiello

| YEAR | TEAM | LVL | AGE | PA | R | 2B | 3B | HR | RBI | BB | SO | SB | CS | AVG_OBP_SLG | TAv | BABIP | BRR | FRAA | WARP |
|------|------|-----|-----|-----|-----|----|----|----|-----|----|-----|----|----|--------------|------|-------|------|-----------|------|
| 2009 | ARK | AA | 23 | 581 | 54 | 35 | 3 | 15 | 88 | 37 | 100 | 6 | 3 | .291/.337/.452 | .286 | .333 | -3.2 | -2.3 | 1.7 |
| 2010 | SLC | AAA | 24 | 595 | 103 | 29 | 5 | 36 | 122 | 58 | 126 | 3 | 4 | .301/.371/.577 | .313 | .335 | -2.9 | 3.7 | 4.1 |
| 2010 | ANA | MLB | 24 | 16 | 2 | 0 | 0 | 0 | 2 | 1 | 8 | 0 | 0 | .067/.125/.067 | .071 | .143 | 0.5 | 0.1 | -0.2 |
| 2011 | ANA | MLB | 25 | 573 | 65 | 31 | 1 | 29 | 87 | 25 | 120 | 9 | 4 | .254/.291/.477 | .278 | .274 | 1.3 | 1.9 | 2.3 |
| 2012 | ANA | MLB | 26 | 427 | 47 | 20 | 1 | 15 | 53 | 19 | 96 | 5 | 2 | .244/.282/.413 | .253 | .282 | -0.2 | 1B -9, RF 0 | 0.3 |

Trumbo swings at too many pitches but, in his defense, he can handle almost anything he can reach, viz: the Felix Hernandez two-seamer, six inches low and inside, that he hit 472 feet, the Brian Duensing fastball at the letters that he hit 457 feet, etc. But he acknowledges his lack of plate discipline is a challenge. "I don't think I was blessed with the greatest eye," he told a reporter earlier this year. "Some guys have a better sense. It's something I'm really having to work on but it's hard to do." If it is a skill that can be learned in one's late 20s Trumbo's upside starts to look like Paul Konerko but all PECOTA sees is Johnny Gomes. He's scary strong, a batting practice phenom with an all-fields approach and plenty of baseball

Comparables:
Daryl Spencer, Jim Davenport, Tom Foley

| YEAR | TEAM | LVL | AGE | PA | R | 2B | 3B | HR | RBI | BB | SO | SB | CS | AVG_OBP_SLG | TAv | BABIP | BRR | FRAA | WARP |
|------|------|-----|-----|-----|-----|----|----|----|-----|----|-----|----|----|--------------|------|-------|------|-----------|------|
| 2012 | ANA | MLB | 32 | 250 | 24 | 10 | 1 | 3 | 20 | 16 | 49 | 4 | 2 | .224/.278/.312 | .220 | .268 | -0.1 | SS 1, 2B -1 | -0.2 |

In 2011, the Pacific Coast League quit worrying about its figure and just let it all hang out. The league OPS was .807. There were more than 11 runs scored per game. The Reno Aces had a .381 OBP. The Colorado Sky Sox had a 6.41 ERA. Fifteen individual players had an OPS over 1.000. Cody Ransom slugged .629. Angel Berroa hit .320. Dogs and cats, living together, slugging .650. Anyway, Gil Velazquez entered the season with 4,070 minor league plate appearances and a .229/.288/.308 career line. In 494 plate appearances for Salt Lake, he hit .329/.399/.466. Nope, says Cody Ransom. No way, says Angel Berroa. Stupid silly, say the dog and the cat.

**Vernon Wells** CF

Born: 12/8/1978 Age: 33
Bats: R Throws: R Height: 6' 2" Weight: 195
Breakout: 1% Improve: 27% Collapse: 11%
Attrition: 13% MLB: 84%

Comparables:
Lee Lacy, Oscar Salazar, Eric Byrnes

| YEAR | TEAM | LVL | AGE | PA | R | 2B | 3B | HR | RBI | BB | SO | SB | CS | AVG_OBP_SLG | TAv | BABIP | BRR | FRAA | WARP |
|------|------|-----|-----|-----|-----|----|----|----|-----|----|-----|----|----|--------------|------|-------|------|-----------|------|
| 2009 | TOR | MLB | 30 | 684 | 84 | 37 | 3 | 15 | 66 | 48 | 86 | 17 | 4 | .260/.311/.400 | .253 | .279 | 1.6 | -13.3 | 0.4 |
| 2010 | TOR | MLB | 31 | 646 | 79 | 44 | 3 | 31 | 88 | 50 | 84 | 6 | 4 | .273/.331/.515 | .289 | .272 | -0.6 | -3.8 | 3.7 |
| 2011 | ANA | MLB | 32 | 529 | 60 | 15 | 4 | 25 | 66 | 20 | 86 | 9 | 4 | .218/.248/.412 | .247 | .214 | -1.4 | 8.2 | 1.1 |
| 2012 | ANA | MLB | 33 | 521 | 58 | 24 | 2 | 16 | 62 | 33 | 79 | 8 | 3 | .244/.293/.406 | .259 | .260 | -0.3 | CF -2, LF 3 | 1.4 |

Last year, we wrote in this space that Wells' "outrageous contract so colors every impression of him that it's become almost impossible to evaluate him as a player in isolation." Vernon Wells, hater of muddled narratives, took care of that problem: now we know he's simply bad. Only three players since the Deadball Era have had an OBP below .250 while qualifying for the batting title and none of them was a corner outfielder, none of them batted cleanup 50 times for a contending team, and none of them—we're back to this again—was paid $23 million to produce so many outs. Angels fans are stuck with his contract for three more years, so let's make the best of it and try to find some optimism. Swimming Scrooge McDuck style in a pool of money has not led to any obvious deterioration in Wells' athleticism. He did improve from one of the worst center fielders to an above-average left fielder. He slugged .455 after returning from the DL in June. His isolated power was in line with his career rates. No ringing endorsement but some echoes of the player who was at least good enough for a roster spot.

**Reggie Willits** LF

Born: 5/30/1981 Age: 31
Bats: B Throws: R Height: 6' 0" Weight: 185
Breakout: 0% Improve: 34% Collapse: 13%
Attrition: 39% MLB: 75%

Comparables:
Elliott Maddox, Richie Scheinblum, Danny Heep

| YEAR | TEAM | LVL | AGE | PA | R | 2B | 3B | HR | RBI | BB | SO | SB | CS | AVG_OBP_SLG | TAv | BABIP | BRR | FRAA | WARP |
|------|------|-----|-----|-----|-----|----|----|----|-----|----|-----|----|----|--------------|------|-------|------|-----------|------|
| 2009 | SLC | AAA | 28 | 280 | 40 | 10 | 1 | 1 | 27 | 34 | 44 | 11 | 4 | .261/.354/.325 | .236 | .311 | 4 | 2 | 0.4 |
| 2009 | ANA | MLB | 28 | 92 | 16 | 2 | 0 | 0 | 6 | 5 | 17 | 5 | 1 | .213/.256/.237 | .185 | .266 | 1.6 | -2.1 | -0.6 |
| 2010 | ANA | MLB | 29 | 182 | 23 | 7 | 0 | 0 | 8 | 19 | 26 | 2 | 4 | .258/.341/.302 | .249 | .308 | -0.6 | 0.5 | 0.4 |
| 2011 | SLC | AAA | 30 | 280 | 36 | 5 | 2 | 0 | 15 | 44 | 46 | 5 | 4 | .260/.385/.300 | .247 | .326 | -0.1 | 2 | 0.1 |
| 2011 | ANA | MLB | 30 | 28 | 0 | 0 | 0 | 0 | 0 | 7 | 0 | 0 | 0 | .045/.192/.091 | .142 | .067 | -0.6 | 0.4 | -0.3 |
| 2012 | ANA | MLB | 31 | 250 | 25 | 8 | 1 | 0 | 14 | 29 | 46 | 6 | 3 | .237/.330/.285 | .234 | .289 | -0.5 | LF 2, CF 2 | -0.1 |

Not only has Willits gone another year without hitting his first major league home run, but in the post-2008 Pitch/fx era he has still hit just one ball to the warning track and one ball over an outfielder's head. The fact that his career isolated power is .044, but his walk rate in that time was higher than those of Ryan Howard, Kevin Youkilis, and Gary Sheffield tells us more about pitching than we realize. The Angels dropped him from the 40-man roster late in the season.

**Bobby Wilson**   C

Born: 4/8/1983 Age: 29
Bats: R Throws: R Height: 6' 1" Weight: 220
Breakout: 0% Improve: 26% Collapse: 11%
Attrition: 31% MLB: 77%

Comparables:
Dave Sax, Josh Bard, Dave Valle

| YEAR | TEAM | LVL | AGE | PA | R | 2B | 3B | HR | RBI | BB | SO | SB | CS | AVG_OBP_SLG | TAv | BABIP | BRR | FRAA | WARP |
|------|------|-----|-----|-----|----|----|----|----|-----|----|----|----|----|-------------|------|-------|------|----------|------|
| 2009 | SLC | AAA | 26 | 381 | 38 | 19 | 1 | 8 | 55 | 22 | 56 | 0 | 0 | .271/.312/.398 | .234 | .299 | -1 | 4 | 0.7 |
| 2009 | ANA | MLB | 26 | 6 | 0 | 1 | 0 | 0 | 0 | 0 | 1 | 0 | 0 | .200/.200/.400 | .157 | .250 | 0 | 0 | -0.1 |
| 2010 | ANA | MLB | 27 | 106 | 12 | 6 | 0 | 4 | 15 | 8 | 23 | 0 | 0 | .229/.288/.417 | .249 | .261 | 0.7 | -0.4 | 0.4 |
| 2011 | ANA | MLB | 28 | 127 | 5 | 8 | 0 | 1 | 8 | 10 | 16 | 0 | 2 | .189/.252/.288 | .197 | .208 | -0.4 | 0.6 | -0.1 |
| 2012 | ANA | MLB | 29 | 250 | 26 | 12 | 1 | 5 | 24 | 18 | 46 | 1 | 0 | .241/.298/.361 | .243 | .277 | -0.1 | C 1, 1B -0 | 1.2 |

Call a no-hitter and some catchers are rewarded with a steak dinner; Bobby Wilson's prize was a whole lot of playing time. After starting 10 games all season, Wilson was behind the plate for Ervin Santana's no-hitter on July 27. Mike Scioscia was so impressed that he started Wilson 14 times in August and 10 in September, even as the former 48th-round draft pick hit .183/.224/.296 from the no-hitter on. He was the alternative to Mathis, so Angels fans briefly loved him, but he's in danger of becoming Mathis 2.0. He's got a massive platoon split in his career, and Conger has a sizable gap in the other direction, but the Angels opted not to gamble on a two-lousy-player platoon, adding Iannetta instead.

## PITCHERS

**Trevor Bell**

Born: 10/12/1986 Age: 25
Bats: L Throws: R Height: 6' 3" Weight: 180
Breakout: 24% Improve: 55% Collapse: 20%
Attrition: 11% MLB: 88%

Comparables:
Jimmy Gobble, John Smiley, Joe Sambito

| YEAR | TEAM | LVL | AGE | W | L | SV | G | GS | IP | H | HR | BB | SO | EqBB9 | EqSO9 | GB% | BABIP | WHIP | ERA | FIP | FRA | WARP |
|------|------|-----|-----|---|---|----|----|----|------|----|----|----|----|-------|-------|-----|-------|------|------|------|------|------|
| 2009 | ARK | AA | 22 | 4 | 3 | 0 | 11 | 11 | 68² | 54 | 1 | 20 | 51 | 2.6 | 6.7 | 52% | .260 | 1.08 | 2.23 | 2.90 | 3.89 | 0.6 |
| 2009 | SLC | AAA | 22 | 3 | 4 | 0 | 11 | 11 | 71¹ | 67 | 5 | 15 | 38 | 1.9 | 4.8 | 52% | .274 | 1.15 | 3.16 | 4.01 | 5.08 | 0.3 |
| 2009 | ANA | MLB | 22 | 1 | 2 | 0 | 8 | 4 | 20¹ | 40 | 3 | 11 | 14 | 4.9 | 6.2 | 39% | .451 | 2.51 | 9.74 | 5.31 | 4.79 | 0.2 |
| 2010 | SLC | AAA | 23 | 2 | 0 | 0 | 6 | 6 | 30 | 23 | 2 | 4 | 12 | 1.8 | 5.7 | 50% | .284 | 1.20 | 3.00 | 4.72 | 4.77 | 0.4 |
| 2010 | ANA | MLB | 23 | 2 | 5 | 0 | 25 | 7 | 61 | 77 | 2 | 21 | 45 | 3.1 | 6.6 | 45% | .373 | 1.61 | 4.72 | 3.08 | 3.87 | 0.7 |
| 2011 | SLC | AAA | 24 | 1 | 5 | 0 | 11 | 10 | 56 | 71 | 10 | 13 | 49 | 2.1 | 7.9 | 46% | .351 | 1.50 | 6.27 | 5.11 | 5.31 | 0.6 |
| 2011 | ANA | MLB | 24 | 1 | 1 | 0 | 19 | 0 | 34¹ | 39 | 2 | 10 | 17 | 2.6 | 4.5 | 56% | .319 | 1.43 | 3.41 | 3.79 | 4.86 | -0.1 |
| 2012 | ANA | MLB | 25 | 3 | 2 | 0 | 16 | 6 | 48¹ | 55 | 5 | 16 | 29 | 2.9 | 5.3 | 50% | .316 | 1.47 | 4.63 | 4.34 | 5.03 | -0.1 |

If Scott Kazmir had held on for just three or four starts before kabooming, it might have been Bell who took over his fifth spot in the rotation and earned a steady major league per diem. Instead, Kazmir lasted just one start, and while the Angels were surveying their options, Bell was still being stretched out in Triple-A after an injury-interrupted spring. Tyler Chatwood got the call, and Bell spent another season in swingman purgatory. He throws strikes and gets ground balls and would survive as a fifth starter, but he might never get a chance to show it.

**Bobby Cassevah**

Born: 9/11/1985 Age: 26
Bats: R Throws: R Height: 6' 4" Weight: 195
Breakout: 33% Improve: 59% Collapse: 17%
Attrition: 7% MLB: 94%

Comparables:
Danny Jackson, Ryan Drese, Al McBean

| YEAR | TEAM | LVL | AGE | W | L | SV | G | GS | IP | H | HR | BB | SO | EqBB9 | EqSO9 | GB% | BABIP | WHIP | ERA | FIP | FRA | WARP |
|------|------|-----|-----|---|---|----|----|----|------|----|----|----|----|-------|-------|-----|-------|------|------|------|------|------|
| 2009 | ARK | AA | 23 | 3 | 7 | 4 | 57 | 0 | 73¹ | 64 | 2 | 37 | 45 | 4.5 | 5.5 | 72% | .274 | 1.38 | 3.68 | 4.04 | 5.38 | -0.5 |
| 2010 | SLC | AAA | 24 | 3 | 4 | 5 | 45 | 0 | 59 | 51 | 2 | 20 | 24 | 3.8 | 5.8 | 74% | .371 | 1.59 | 4.27 | 4.85 | 6.93 | -0.8 |
| 2010 | ANA | MLB | 24 | 1 | 2 | 0 | 16 | 0 | 20 | 23 | 0 | 8 | 8 | 3.6 | 3.6 | 60% | .303 | 1.55 | 3.15 | 3.60 | 4.95 | -0.1 |
| 2011 | SLC | AAA | 25 | 1 | 3 | 0 | 18 | 0 | 21¹ | 23 | 2 | 10 | 12 | 4.2 | 5.1 | 60% | .288 | 1.55 | 4.64 | 5.24 | 5.48 | 0.0 |
| 2011 | ANA | MLB | 25 | 1 | 1 | 0 | 30 | 0 | 39² | 28 | 1 | 19 | 24 | 4.3 | 5.4 | 72% | .243 | 1.18 | 2.72 | 3.69 | 4.20 | 0.2 |
| 2012 | ANA | MLB | 26 | 2 | 1 | 0 | 30 | 0 | 39 | 40 | 3 | 19 | 22 | 4.3 | 5.0 | 58% | .289 | 1.49 | 4.44 | 4.54 | 4.82 | -0.1 |

Thrust into high-leverage roles by Mike Scioscia's unpredictable whims, Cassevah seemed to figure out a plan for dealing with troublesome lefties: he simply walked the bulk of them and hoped for a double play from the next guy. It worked in 2011: he got 10 double plays in 39 innings, the best rate in baseball. Only Jonny Venters and Brad Ziegler had higher groundball rates than Cassevah, whose two-seam fastball didn't miss bats but tended to find infielders. By September, Cassevah had the seventh inning to himself, and the Angels would have gotten away with it, too, if it weren't for those occasional groundballs sneaking through holes. He blew a lead in his penultimate appearance, then contributed to the epic September 25 bullpen meltdown against the A's, which effectively ended the Angels' playoff hopes.

### Scott Downs
Born: 3/17/1976 Age: 36
Bats: L Throws: L Height: 6' 3" Weight: 180
Breakout: 16% Improve: 34% Collapse: 41%
Attrition: 6% MLB: 89%

Comparables:
Andy Pettitte, David Cone, Whitey Ford

| YEAR | TEAM | LVL | AGE | W | L | SV | G | GS | IP | H | HR | BB | SO | EqBB9 | EqSO9 | GB% | BABIP | WHIP | ERA | FIP | FRA | WARP |
|------|------|-----|-----|---|---|----|----|----|------|----|----|----|----|-------|-------|-----|-------|------|------|------|------|------|
| 2009 | TOR | MLB | 33 | 1 | 3 | 9 | 48 | 0 | 46² | 46 | 4 | 13 | 43 | 2.5 | 8.3 | 57% | .304 | 1.26 | 3.09 | 3.38 | 3.61 | 1.1 |
| 2010 | TOR | MLB | 34 | 5 | 5 | 0 | 67 | 0 | 61¹ | 47 | 3 | 14 | 48 | 2.1 | 7.0 | 59% | .256 | 0.99 | 2.64 | 3.00 | 3.55 | 1.0 |
| 2011 | ANA | MLB | 35 | 6 | 3 | 1 | 60 | 0 | 53² | 39 | 3 | 15 | 35 | 2.5 | 5.9 | 64% | .225 | 1.01 | 1.34 | 3.32 | 4.95 | -0.1 |
| *2012* | *ANA* | *MLB* | *36* | *3* | *1* | *1* | *53* | *0* | *47²* | *41* | *3* | *15* | *40* | *2.8* | *7.5* | *60%* | *.278* | *1.16* | *2.86* | *3.29* | *3.10* | *0.9* |

It took about $70 million and five years of experimenting, but the Angels finally signed a reliever to a multi-year deal without it ending in release (Speier), trade (Fuentes), benching (Rodney), or awkward retirement (Shields). Downs' 1.34 ERA is the lowest in club history, with June the only month he allowed more than one earned run. He quit throwing a slider in 2011, and it showed in his strikeout rates: 5.9 Ks per 9 represents the worst rate of his career, low enough to be concerning for a late-inning reliever and perhaps a reason he never got any serious consideration for the ninth inning.

ity for four years and struggled to command his once-lethal splitter consistently, yet still led the league in strikeouts-to-walk ratio and posted the lowest FIP (fielding independent pitching) of his career. For that, he can thank the cutter, which he threw half the time in 2011, getting strikes on 71 percent of those throws. Jered Weaver got the Cy Young votes, but Haren's defense-independent stats and career-high innings totals made him the staff's co-ace, or better.

### LaTroy Hawkins
Born: 12/21/1972 Age: 39
Bats: R Throws: R Height: 6' 6" Weight: 195
Breakout: 22% Improve: 44% Collapse: 23%
Attrition: 5% MLB: 75%

Comparables:
Early Wynn, Kevin Brown, Darren Oliver

| YEAR | TEAM | LVL | AGE | W | L | SV | G | GS | IP | H | HR | BB | SO | EqBB9 | EqSO9 | GB% | BABIP | WHIP | ERA | FIP | FRA | WARP |
|------|------|-----|-----|---|---|----|----|----|------|----|----|----|----|-------|-------|-----|-------|------|------|------|------|------|
| 2009 | HOU | MLB | 36 | 1 | 4 | 11 | 65 | 0 | 63¹ | 60 | 7 | 16 | 45 | 2.3 | 6.4 | 47% | .283 | 1.20 | 2.13 | 3.92 | 4.30 | 0.6 |
| 2010 | MIL | MLB | 37 | 0 | 3 | 0 | 18 | 0 | 16 | 21 | 2 | 6 | 18 | 3.4 | 10.1 | 48% | .422 | 1.69 | 8.44 | 3.98 | 5.81 | -0.1 |
| 2011 | MIL | MLB | 38 | 3 | 1 | 0 | 52 | 0 | 48¹ | 50 | 1 | 11 | 28 | 1.9 | 5.2 | 63% | .299 | 1.24 | 2.42 | 2.79 | 3.92 | 0.6 |
| *2012* | *ANA* | *MLB* | *39* | *2* | *1* | *0* | *41* | *0* | *39¹* | *39* | *4* | *12* | *27* | *2.7* | *6.2* | *52%* | *.295* | *1.29* | *3.56* | *4.07* | *3.87* | *0.4* |

An exception that proves the rule, Hawkins has had a couple trials as a closer in his otherwise successful career as a setup man, and was found wanting each time—unlike the vast majority of pitchers, who pitch about the same in either role. Fully recovered from shoulder surgery, Hawkins was able to push the gun reading over 96 again, and interjects enough sliders and other breaking stuff to keep batters guessing. A scoreless postseason (four inning pitched) capped a nice bounceback season, and earned him $3 million and the Angels' half of the seventh inning.

### John Hellweg
Born: 10/29/1988 Age: 23
Bats: R Throws: R Height: 6' 10" Weight: 210
Breakout: 19% Improve: 52% Collapse: 25%
Attrition: 18% MLB: 87%

Comparables:
Dan Warthen, Jason Bere, John D'Acquisto

| YEAR | TEAM | LVL | AGE | W | L | SV | G | GS | IP | H | HR | BB | SO | EqBB9 | EqSO9 | GB% | BABIP | WHIP | ERA | FIP | FRA | WARP |
|------|------|-----|-----|---|---|----|----|----|------|----|----|----|-----|-------|-------|-----|-------|------|------|------|------|------|
| 2009 | ANG | RK | 20 | 1 | 1 | 6 | 18 | 0 | 24¹ | 14 | 0 | 6 | 22 | 3.0 | 9.3 | 50% | .280 | 0.99 | 2.96 | 3.81 | 4.35 | 0.7 |
| 2010 | CDR | A | 21 | 2 | 4 | 16 | 41 | 0 | 43² | 11 | 0 | 23 | 29 | 9.3 | 13.6 | 55% | .250 | 1.49 | 4.32 | 4.19 | 5.48 | -0.1 |
| 2011 | SBR | A+ | 22 | 6 | 4 | 0 | 28 | 14 | 89¹ | 76 | 3 | 60 | 119 | 5.9 | 11.4 | 62% | .330 | 1.50 | 3.73 | 4.29 | 4.81 | 0.6 |
| *2012* | *ANA* | *MLB* | *23* | *1* | *1* | *0* | *13* | *3* | *25¹* | *24* | *2* | *19* | *23* | *6.6* | *8.1* | *49%* | *.301* | *1.67* | *5.01* | *4.66* | *5.45* | *-0.2* |

The decision to move the 6-foot-9 Hellweg to Inland Empire's rotation was actually just a what-the-hell-else-can-we-try development tactic, not a long-term switch. Starting would give him a fixed time, on a fixed date, to work on his control, and it did need work. As a reliever, he had been unhittable—a dozen strikeouts per nine, the best groundball rate on his team—but he had walked more than a batter per inning three years in a row. Three months after the move, he started the first game of the California League playoffs, having made 14 starts with a 2.12 ERA, three Ks per walk, and five groundouts for every flyout. Hellweg used to be a triple-digits tease, then a sleeper. He's now an actual prospect.

**Kevin Jepsen**
Born: 7/26/1984 Age: 27
Bats: R Throws: R Height: 6' 4'' Weight: 215
Breakout: 29% Improve: 52% Collapse: 24%
Attrition: 7% MLB: 91%

Comparables:
Evan Meek, Darren Dreifort, Brandon Medders

| YEAR | TEAM | LVL | AGE | W | L | SV | G | GS | IP | H | HR | BB | SO | EqBB9 | EqSO9 | GB% | BABIP | WHIP | ERA | FIP | FRA | WARP |
|---|---|---|---|---|---|---|---|---|---|---|---|---|---|---|---|---|---|---|---|---|---|---|
| 2009 | ANA | MLB | 24 | 6 | 4 | 1 | 54 | 0 | 54² | 63 | 2 | 19 | 48 | 3.1 | 7.9 | 56% | .363 | 1.50 | 4.94 | 2.91 | 3.57 | 1.2 |
| 2010 | ANA | MLB | 25 | 2 | 4 | 0 | 68 | 0 | 59 | 54 | 2 | 29 | 61 | 4.4 | 9.3 | 56% | .335 | 1.41 | 3.97 | 3.00 | 4.83 | 0.0 |
| 2011 | SLC | AAA | 26 | 1 | 2 | 7 | 24 | 0 | 28¹ | 32 | 4 | 8 | 20 | 2.5 | 6.4 | 49% | .326 | 1.41 | 4.45 | 5.01 | 4.92 | 0.2 |
| 2011 | ANA | MLB | 26 | 1 | 2 | 0 | 16 | 0 | 13 | 21 | 2 | 9 | 6 | 6.2 | 4.2 | 56% | .388 | 2.31 | 7.62 | 6.45 | 6.99 | -0.4 |
| 2012 | ANA | MLB | 27 | 2 | 1 | 0 | 29 | 0 | 27¹ | 28 | 2 | 12 | 23 | 4.1 | 7.6 | 54% | .317 | 1.46 | 3.98 | 3.79 | 4.33 | 0.1 |

Jepsen's nightmare season turned especially surreal on May 11, when he lost a game in the 10th inning on an intentional ball that he sailed over his catcher's head. He had seemed, after 2010, to have defeated his minor league control problems, and entered the 2011 season as the Angels' eighth-inning right-hander. PECOTA didn't believe it, though, projecting Jepsen to walk nearly five batters per nine and allow a worse-than-average ERA. He did, and he did. Once tabbed as a future closer, Jepsen got to spend the year collecting saves in Triple-A.

**Scott Kazmir**
Born: 1/24/1984 Age: 28
Bats: L Throws: L Height: 6' 1'' Weight: 170
Breakout: 24% Improve: 56% Collapse: 25%
Attrition: 9% MLB: 87%

Comparables:
John Grabow, Sparky Lyle, C.J. Wilson

| YEAR | TEAM | LVL | AGE | W | L | SV | G | GS | IP | H | HR | BB | SO | EqBB9 | EqSO9 | GB% | BABIP | WHIP | ERA | FIP | FRA | WARP |
|---|---|---|---|---|---|---|---|---|---|---|---|---|---|---|---|---|---|---|---|---|---|---|
| 2009 | ANA | MLB | 25 | 2 | 2 | 0 | 6 | 6 | 36¹ | 28 | 1 | 10 | 26 | 2.5 | 6.4 | 27% | .257 | 1.05 | 1.73 | 2.98 | 2.51 | 1.2 |
| 2009 | TBA | MLB | 25 | 8 | 7 | 0 | 20 | 20 | 111 | 121 | 15 | 50 | 91 | 4.1 | 7.4 | 37% | .310 | 1.54 | 5.92 | 4.75 | 5.06 | 0.8 |
| 2010 | ANA | MLB | 26 | 9 | 15 | 0 | 28 | 28 | 150 | 158 | 25 | 79 | 93 | 4.7 | 5.6 | 40% | .283 | 1.58 | 5.94 | 5.79 | 5.65 | -0.5 |
| 2011 | ANA | MLB | 27 | 0 | 0 | 0 | 1 | 1 | 1² | 5 | 1 | 2 | 0 | 10.8 | 0.0 | 30% | .444 | 4.20 | 27.00 | 18.06 | 10.25 | -0.1 |
| 2012 | ANA | MLB | 28 | 2 | 2 | 0 | 7 | 7 | 33¹ | 31 | 4 | 14 | 31 | 3.8 | 8.3 | 39% | .297 | 1.37 | 4.08 | 4.16 | 4.43 | 0.2 |

Kazmir arrived in Salt Lake with 66 career big league wins, two All-Star appearances, and a strikeout title, but at 27 years old he was still a few months younger than his median teammate in Triple-A. Faced with the choice of releasing Kazmir or reinstating him on the major league roster, the Angels wished Kazmir safe travels and swallowed the $12 million or so they owed him. PECOTA's squinting real hard to see a Frank Viola mid-20s rough patch, but with a fastball down six mph from his prime, a suddenly dull slider, and no more command than he had as a rookie, Kazmir's odds of return are long.

**Michael Kohn**
Born: 6/26/1986 Age: 26
Bats: R Throws: R Height: 6' 1'' Weight: 200
Breakout: 27% Improve: 50% Collapse: 24%
Attrition: 11% MLB: 93%

Comparables:
Ken Howell, Brandon Morrow, David Robertson

| YEAR | TEAM | LVL | AGE | W | L | SV | G | GS | IP | H | HR | BB | SO | EqBB9 | EqSO9 | GB% | BABIP | WHIP | ERA | FIP | FRA | WARP |
|---|---|---|---|---|---|---|---|---|---|---|---|---|---|---|---|---|---|---|---|---|---|---|
| 2009 | CDR | A | 23 | 4 | 1 | 6 | 28 | 0 | 37 | 20 | 1 | 12 | 60 | 2.9 | 14.6 | 42% | .292 | 0.86 | 2.19 | 1.86 | 3.43 | 0.7 |
| 2009 | RCU | A+ | 23 | 3 | 0 | 3 | 22 | 0 | 28² | 16 | 0 | 16 | 50 | 4.4 | 13.5 | 34% | .276 | 0.94 | 0.94 | 1.95 | 1.85 | 1.2 |
| 2010 | SLC | AAA | 24 | 3 | 2 | 8 | 26 | 0 | 27² | 12 | 2 | 13 | 17 | 5.5 | 10.4 | 33% | .244 | 1.19 | 1.95 | 5.18 | 5.15 | 0.2 |
| 2010 | ANA | MLB | 24 | 2 | 0 | 1 | 24 | 0 | 21¹ | 17 | 0 | 16 | 20 | 6.8 | 8.4 | 44% | .309 | 1.55 | 2.11 | 3.42 | 4.79 | 0.0 |
| 2011 | SLC | AAA | 25 | 1 | 2 | 12 | 46 | 0 | 48¹ | 47 | 5 | 20 | 64 | 3.7 | 11.9 | 42% | .353 | 1.39 | 4.10 | 3.86 | 4.27 | 0.9 |
| 2011 | ANA | MLB | 25 | 0 | 1 | 1 | 14 | 0 | 12¹ | 14 | 6 | 9 | 9 | 6.6 | 6.6 | 24% | .229 | 1.86 | 7.30 | 10.36 | 10.10 | -0.7 |
| 2012 | ANA | MLB | 26 | 2 | 1 | 1 | 29 | 0 | 29² | 24 | 3 | 15 | 33 | 4.6 | 10.1 | 40% | .295 | 1.34 | 3.48 | 3.81 | 3.78 | 0.3 |

A late convert to pitching, Kohn entered the season with a 1.87 minor league ERA and 14 Ks per nine innings. But his walk rate jumped with each promotion, and the accumulation of all those free bases was too much to survive in the American League. After getting a sniff of high-leverage work in April—when Mike Scioscia is in full mix-and-match mode for his bullpen—Kohn was sent back to Triple-A, where he struck out a dozen per nine and had his lowest walk rate since the Midwest League. That was, surprisingly, not good enough to get him called up when rosters expanded in September. After allowing three home runs in his most recent major league appearance, it appears he'll have to do some more penance before his manager absolves him.

**Nick Maronde**
Born: 9/5/1989 Age: 22
Bats: S Throws: L Height: 6' 6'' Weight: 195
Breakout: 32% Improve: 52% Collapse: 22%
Attrition: 30% MLB: 85%

Comparables:
Ron Bryant, Edwin Jackson, Rob Gardner

| YEAR | TEAM | LVL | AGE | W | L | SV | G | GS | IP | H | HR | BB | SO | EqBB9 | EqSO9 | GB% | BABIP | WHIP | ERA | FIP | FRA | WARP |
|---|---|---|---|---|---|---|---|---|---|---|---|---|---|---|---|---|---|---|---|---|---|---|
| 2011 | ORM | RK | 21 | 5 | 0 | 0 | 11 | 11 | 46¹ | 41 | 5 | 19 | 56 | 2.9 | 9.7 | 50% | .286 | 1.10 | 2.14 | 4.60 | 3.54 | 1.4 |
| 2012 | ANA | MLB | 22 | 1 | 1 | 0 | 3 | 3 | 11¹ | 14 | 1 | 7 | 6 | 5.8 | 4.6 | 45% | .314 | 1.85 | 6.28 | 5.15 | 6.83 | -0.2 |

Maronde is a big lefty with a mid-90s fastball and above-average changeup, which was enough to mow down the Pioneer League even without a refined breaking pitch. Maronde was signed by Angels scout Tom Kotchman, an organizational elder who also managed Maronde at Orem. Kotchman picks almost always get high marks for demeanor, and Maronde already has a reputation in the organization as mature and confident on the mound. That reputation won't slow his ascent up the ladder.

### Brad Mills

Born: 3/5/1985 Age: 27
Bats: R Throws: L Height: 6' 0'' Weight: 185
Breakout: 32% Improve: 62% Collapse: 27%
Attrition: 20% MLB: 84%

Comparables:
Joe Coleman, Gaylord Perry, Gordie Richardson

| YEAR | TEAM | LVL | AGE | W | L | SV | G | GS | IP | H | HR | BB | SO | EqBB9 | EqSO9 | GB% | BABIP | WHIP | ERA | FIP | FRA | WARP |
|------|------|-----|-----|---|---|----|---|----|-----|-----|----|----|-----|-------|-------|-----|-------|------|------|------|------|------|
| 2009 | LVG | AAA | 24 | 2 | 8 | 0 | 14 | 14 | 84¹ | 83 | 6 | 35 | 72 | 3.7 | 7.7 | 46% | .321 | 1.40 | 4.06 | 4.06 | 5.37 | 0.3 |
| 2009 | TOR | MLB | 24 | 0 | 1 | 0 | 2 | 2 | 7² | 14 | 4 | 6 | 9 | 7.0 | 10.6 | 15% | .435 | 2.61 | 14.09 | 9.93 | 10.75 | -0.4 |
| 2010 | LVG | AAA | 25 | 8 | 6 | 0 | 20 | 20 | 112¹ | 72 | 9 | 29 | 58 | 3.4 | 8.0 | 44% | .286 | 1.43 | 4.97 | 4.87 | 5.74 | 0.4 |
| 2010 | TOR | MLB | 25 | 1 | 0 | 0 | 7 | 3 | 22¹ | 20 | 2 | 13 | 18 | 5.2 | 7.3 | 41% | .281 | 1.48 | 5.64 | 4.48 | 4.25 | 0.3 |
| 2011 | LVG | AAA | 26 | 10 | 5 | 0 | 24 | 24 | 157¹ | 154 | 20 | 38 | 127 | 2.2 | 7.8 | 43% | .311 | 1.27 | 4.00 | 4.59 | 4.58 | 2.5 |
| 2011 | TOR | MLB | 26 | 1 | 2 | 0 | 5 | 4 | 18¹ | 23 | 4 | 12 | 18 | 5.9 | 8.8 | 34% | .345 | 1.91 | 9.82 | 6.23 | 6.36 | -0.2 |
| 2012 | ANA | MLB | 27 | 4 | 3 | 0 | 11 | 11 | 64² | 65 | 8 | 25 | 52 | 3.5 | 7.3 | 42% | .303 | 1.40 | 4.34 | 4.36 | 4.71 | 0.1 |

Mills had a quietly good season at Triple-A that was an improvement over his 2010. That his brief major-league trial went disastrously doesn't mean Mills is further now from helping the club. His walk rate in Triple-A was the best of his minor league career, and that makes the 12 free passes he issued in 18 major-league innings all the more puzzling. He is left handed, durable, and throws a pretty good changeup, three qualities that the Angels probably weren't demanding in return for Jeff Mathis

over time. In 2009, under Duncan's guidance, Pineiro led the majors with a 60 percent ground-ball rate. In 2010, after leaving St. Louis, that rate dropped to 55 percent, and in 2010 it fell all the way to 47 percent—slightly lower, in fact, than the Cardinals as a staff. Pineiro's collapse—he says his sinker started sailing horizontally instead of downward—was devastating for an Angels staff that had little starting pitching depth and had already lost the faint hope of a Scott Kazmir bounceback. He lost his job as a starter in August and, out of necessity, was reinstated after two turns through the rotation. All of Pineiro's offerings rely on feel, so it's not inconceivable he's one adjustment from another good season. But his velocity sank after an oblique strain in late 2010, and there isn't a single peripheral trending in the right direction since departing Duncan.

### Garrett Richards

Born: 5/27/1988 Age: 24
Bats: R Throws: R Height: 6' 4'' Weight: 210
Breakout: 24% Improve: 54% Collapse: 26%
Attrition: 23% MLB: 94%

Comparables:
Noah Lowry, Alex Fernandez, Burt Hooton

| YEAR | TEAM | LVL | AGE | W | L | SV | G | GS | IP | H | HR | BB | SO | EqBB9 | EqSO9 | GB% | BABIP | WHIP | ERA | FIP | FRA | WARP |
|------|------|-----|-----|---|---|----|---|----|-----|-----|----|----|-----|-------|-------|-----|-------|------|------|------|------|------|
| 2009 | ORM | RK | 21 | 3 | 1 | 0 | 8 | 8 | 35¹ | 37 | 0 | 4 | 30 | 1.0 | 7.6 | 51% | .359 | 1.16 | 1.53 | 2.73 | 3.88 | 1.7 |
| 2010 | CDR | A | 22 | 8 | 4 | 0 | 19 | 19 | 108¹ | 81 | 5 | 26 | 89 | 2.8 | 9.0 | 59% | .308 | 1.16 | 3.41 | 3.56 | 4.45 | 1.1 |
| 2010 | RCU | A+ | 22 | 5 | 2 | 0 | 7 | 7 | 34² | 37 | 3 | 14 | 44 | 2.3 | 10.6 | 55% | .321 | 1.35 | 3.89 | 3.79 | 4.32 | 0.5 |
| 2011 | ARK | AA | 23 | 10 | 1 | 0 | 22 | 21 | 143 | 120 | 9 | 36 | 99 | 2.5 | 6.5 | 52% | .273 | 1.14 | 3.15 | 3.74 | 4.09 | 1.1 |
| 2011 | ANA | MLB | 23 | 0 | 2 | 0 | 7 | 3 | 14 | 16 | 4 | 7 | 9 | 4.5 | 5.8 | 43% | .286 | 1.64 | 5.79 | 6.99 | 5.72 | 0.0 |
| 2012 | ANA | MLB | 24 | 3 | 3 | 0 | 9 | 9 | 54 | 56 | 6 | 20 | 34 | 3.4 | 5.7 | 50% | .294 | 1.41 | 4.38 | 4.50 | 4.76 | 0.0 |

Richards threw strikes with impunity in the generous pitching environment of Arkansas' Dickey-Stephens Park, averaging just 13 pitches per inning and earning the start in the Texas League All-Star game. The Angels rewarded him by letting him skip the Pacific Coast League to make his big league debut, which is sort of like the DMV letting you skip parallel parking and giving you a license. Fate jumped in to mess with his head, first assigning him the Yankees in his first start, then making his groin go sproing in the first inning of his home debut. Both of his fastballs are plus pitches, all three off-speed pitches have improved steadily since he was drafted in 2009, and he's got excellent control for a young pitcher. He's ready to eat innings this year.

### Ervin Santana

Born: 1/10/1983 Age: 29
Bats: R Throws: R Height: 6' 3'' Weight: 160
Breakout: 19% Improve: 43% Collapse: 29%
Attrition: 8% MLB: 82%

Comparables:
Ed Halicki, Dave Veres, Jeff Gray

| YEAR | TEAM | LVL | AGE | W | L | SV | G | GS | IP | H | HR | BB | SO | EqBB9 | EqSO9 | GB% | BABIP | WHIP | ERA | FIP | FRA | WARP |
|------|------|-----|-----|----|----|----|----|----|------|-----|----|----|-----|-------|-------|-----|-------|------|------|------|------|------|
| 2009 | ANA | MLB | 26 | 8 | 8 | 0 | 24 | 23 | 139² | 159 | 24 | 47 | 107 | 3.0 | 6.9 | 40% | .319 | 1.47 | 5.03 | 5.07 | 5.11 | 0.7 |
| 2010 | ANA | MLB | 27 | 17 | 10 | 0 | 33 | 33 | 222² | 221 | 27 | 73 | 169 | 3.0 | 6.8 | 37% | .292 | 1.32 | 3.92 | 4.25 | 4.09 | 2.0 |
| 2011 | ANA | MLB | 28 | 11 | 12 | 0 | 33 | 33 | 228² | 207 | 26 | 72 | 178 | 2.8 | 7.0 | 45% | .274 | 1.22 | 3.38 | 4.03 | 4.48 | 0.8 |
| 2012 | ANA | MLB | 29 | 13 | 9 | 0 | 29 | 29 | 197² | 191 | 23 | 54 | 164 | 2.5 | 7.5 | 40% | .296 | 1.24 | 3.68 | 3.88 | 4.00 | 1.7 |

Santana was a big beneficiary of the rule of threes, as the sportswriter's desire for triplicates swept Santana into an imaginary Three Aces situation with Dan Haren and Jered Weaver.

Santana is no Dan Haren or Jered Weaver, and his ERA+ ended up identical to those of R.A. Dickey and Jeff Karstens. He improved his groundball rate as the Angels worked with him to get more downward movement on his fastball, apparently having given up hoping for the return of those two mph he lost after 2008. That two-seamer was never better than on July 27, when he got 13 groundouts, struck out 10 and didn't allow a hit. But he's still no ace.

### Matt Shoemaker

Born: 9/27/1986 Age: 25
Bats: R Throws: R Height: 6' 3'' Weight: 225
Breakout: 27% Improve: 59% Collapse: 12%
Attrition: 11% MLB: 92%

Comparables:
Dillon Gee, Brian Kingman, Cecil Upshaw

| YEAR | TEAM | LVL | AGE | W | L | SV | G | GS | IP | H | HR | BB | SO | EqBB9 | EqSO9 | GB% | BABIP | WHIP | ERA | FIP | FRA | WARP |
|------|------|-----|-----|---|---|----|----|----|-----|-----|----|----|-----|-------|-------|-----|-------|------|------|------|------|------|
| 2011 | ARK | AA | 24 | 6 | 4 | 0 | 23 | 23 | 156$^1$ | 138 | 17 | 38 | 146 | 2.0 | 7.4 | 41% | .260 | 1.07 | 2.48 | 3.83 | 3.76 | 2.1 |
| 2012 | ANA | MLB | 25 | 4 | 3 | 0 | 9 | 9 | 56$^2$ | 59 | 7 | 21 | 37 | 3.4 | 5.9 | 42% | .294 | 1.42 | 4.41 | 4.62 | 4.80 | -0.0 |

Shoemaker has gone from undrafted free agent to the Texas League Pitcher of the Year, but he'll always have to rely on performance to earn his next start. What has he got? A fastball that unexpectedly topped out at 94 mph this year, a go-to splitter, a 3.69 strikeout-to-walk ratio, bushy Frank Zappa facial hair, and Crazy Eyes. But when the Angels needed an emergency start, teammate Garrett Richards got the call instead.

### Hisanori Takahashi

Born: 4/2/1975 Age: 37
Bats: L Throws: L Height: 5' 11'' Weight: 170
Breakout: 14% Improve: 49% Collapse: 21%
Attrition: 9% MLB: 87%

Comparables:
Rudy May, Mike Stanton, Paul Assenmacher

| YEAR | TEAM | LVL | AGE | W | L | SV | G | GS | IP | H | HR | BB | SO | EqBB9 | EqSO9 | GB% | BABIP | WHIP | ERA | FIP | FRA | WARP |
|------|------|-----|-----|---|---|----|----|----|-----|-----|----|----|-----|-------|-------|-----|-------|------|------|------|------|------|
| 2010 | NYN | MLB | 35 | 10 | 6 | 8 | 53 | 12 | 122 | 116 | 13 | 43 | 114 | 3.2 | 8.4 | 40% | .307 | 1.30 | 3.61 | 3.68 | 4.42 | 1.0 |
| 2011 | ANA | MLB | 36 | 4 | 3 | 2 | 61 | 0 | 68 | 58 | 7 | 25 | 52 | 3.3 | 6.9 | 43% | .263 | 1.22 | 3.44 | 3.97 | 4.90 | 0.0 |
| 2012 | ANA | MLB | 37 | 3 | 2 | 2 | 40 | 4 | 66$^1$ | 62 | 6 | 22 | 56 | 3.0 | 7.5 | 42% | .290 | 1.27 | 3.41 | 3.69 | 3.71 | 0.8 |

GMs who sign relievers to multi-year deals always risk over-extrapolating from small samples. Signing Takahashi to a multi-year deal was especially fraught, as the relevant data in his favor comprised just 57 stateside innings with the Mets. The $8 million the Angels committed to him looked, at the time, to be a good investment in a versatile left-hander with a 2.04 ERA and strong supporting peripherals as a reliever. It looks wasteful now, as Takahashi was revealed to be little more than a low-leverage option who can go two innings with a minimal platoon split. As Tony Reagins' much-mocked huge splash, Hisa belly-flopped.

### Rich Thompson

Born: 7/1/1984 Age: 27
Bats: R Throws: R Height: 6' 2'' Weight: 180
Breakout: 19% Improve: 55% Collapse: 31%
Attrition: 10% MLB: 94%

Comparables:
Josh Beckett, Daisuke Matsuzaka, John Montefusco

| YEAR | TEAM | LVL | AGE | W | L | SV | G | GS | IP | H | HR | BB | SO | EqBB9 | EqSO9 | GB% | BABIP | WHIP | ERA | FIP | FRA | WARP |
|------|------|-----|-----|---|---|----|----|----|-----|----|----|----|----|-------|-------|-----|-------|------|------|------|------|------|
| 2009 | SLC | AAA | 25 | 3 | 1 | 0 | 29 | 0 | 43$^1$ | 41 | 7 | 11 | 51 | 2.3 | 10.6 | 35% | .306 | 1.20 | 3.12 | 4.10 | 3.92 | 0.9 |
| 2009 | ANA | MLB | 25 | 0 | 0 | 0 | 13 | 0 | 19$^1$ | 27 | 6 | 7 | 21 | 3.3 | 9.8 | 33% | .375 | 1.76 | 5.12 | 6.25 | 5.59 | 0.1 |
| 2010 | SLC | AAA | 26 | 1 | 1 | 2 | 19 | 0 | 29$^2$ | 13 | 0 | 7 | 20 | 3.0 | 9.1 | 43% | .283 | 0.91 | 0.61 | 3.42 | 3.81 | 0.5 |
| 2010 | ANA | MLB | 26 | 2 | 0 | 0 | 13 | 0 | 19$^2$ | 12 | 2 | 4 | 15 | 1.8 | 6.9 | 39% | .189 | 0.81 | 1.37 | 3.45 | 3.70 | 0.2 |
| 2011 | ANA | MLB | 27 | 1 | 3 | 0 | 44 | 0 | 54 | 46 | 5 | 20 | 56 | 3.3 | 9.3 | 41% | .281 | 1.22 | 3.00 | 3.30 | 4.41 | 0.2 |
| 2012 | ANA | MLB | 27 | 2 | 1 | 0 | 32 | 0 | 43$^2$ | 39 | 5 | 14 | 43 | 2.9 | 8.8 | 42% | .290 | 1.22 | 3.34 | 3.69 | 3.63 | 0.6 |

Over the past two seasons, in 103 innings split between Salt Lake and Anaheim, Thompson has allowed 2.1 runs per nine innings with nearly three Ks per walk. Yet he's never been more than a spare part in Scioscia's bullpen, with the sixth-highest leverage among Scioscia's seven regular relievers. He's a strike-thrower with a reliable cutter, but in 10 high-leverage outings he walked eight. Probably just bad timing, but the result was that whenever he was getting traction, he'd slip back. The Angels have had so much trouble filling the late innings over the past three seasons that, eventually, Thompson will put together a dozen good outings and wake up in the seventh inning, where he'll be just as good as Jason Bulger, Brandon Donnelly, Ben Weber and the rest of the unheralded relievers from whom Scioscia has squeezed value over the years.

### Jordan Walden

Born: 11/16/1987 Age: 24
Bats: R Throws: R Height: 6' 6'' Weight: 240
Breakout: 33% Improve: 54% Collapse: 25%
Attrition: 21% MLB: 95%

Comparables:
Wade Davis, Sean Gallagher, Blaine Boyer

| YEAR | TEAM | LVL | AGE | W | L | SV | G | GS | IP | H | HR | BB | SO | EqBB9 | EqSO9 | GB% | BABIP | WHIP | ERA | FIP | FRA | WARP |
|------|------|-----|-----|---|---|----|----|----|-----|----|----|----|----|-------|-------|-----|-------|------|------|------|------|------|
| 2009 | ARK | AA | 21 | 1 | 5 | 0 | 13 | 13 | 60 | 72 | 4 | 29 | 57 | 4.3 | 8.6 | 45% | .380 | 1.68 | 5.25 | 3.80 | 3.83 | 0.8 |
| 2010 | ARK | AA | 22 | 1 | 1 | 8 | 38 | 0 | 43 | 31 | 2 | 17 | 28 | 4.6 | 8.0 | 52% | .337 | 1.53 | 3.35 | 3.82 | 4.97 | -0.1 |
| 2010 | ANA | MLB | 22 | 0 | 1 | 1 | 16 | 0 | 15$^1$ | 13 | 1 | 7 | 23 | 4.1 | 13.5 | 63% | .353 | 1.30 | 2.35 | 2.26 | 2.63 | 0.4 |
| 2011 | ANA | MLB | 23 | 5 | 5 | 32 | 62 | 0 | 60$^1$ | 49 | 3 | 26 | 67 | 3.9 | 10.0 | 47% | .303 | 1.24 | 2.98 | 2.83 | 3.68 | 0.7 |
| 2012 | ANA | MLB | 24 | 2 | 1 | 18 | 46 | 0 | 47 | 46 | 4 | 22 | 40 | 4.2 | 7.6 | 52% | .302 | 1.44 | 4.03 | 4.01 | 4.38 | 0.2 |

Just as closers are overvalued for the saves they accumulate in good times, they are too harshly abused for the saves they blow. Walden's overall performance was good, but his 10 blown saves were the most in baseball, and his final opportunity—in which his own throwing error cost the Angels a three-run lead—all but ended the Angels' wild card pursuit. That error, and those blown saves, aren't the final word on his ability to pitch ninth innings. He threw the fastest average heater in the American League. To compliment an inconsistent slider, he has recovered the changeup he threw as a minor league starter. He threw that change just 31 times this year but got whiffs on a quarter of them. Overall, he struck out 27 percent of batters; with runners on, that number went up to 33 percent, and with a runner on third he struck out 40 percent, so he's got an extra gear. There's dominance in that arm.

**Jered Weaver**
Born: 10/4/1982 Age: 29
Bats: R Throws: R Height: 6' 8'' Weight: 205
Breakout: 10% Improve: 34% Collapse: 28%

| YEAR | TEAM | LVL | AGE | W | L | SV | G | GS | IP | H | HR | BB | SO | EqBB9 | EqSO9 | GB% | BABIP | WHIP | ERA | FIP | FRA | WARP |
|---|---|---|---|---|---|---|---|---|---|---|---|---|---|---|---|---|---|---|---|---|---|---|
| 2009 | ANA | MLB | 26 | 16 | 8 | 0 | 33 | 33 | 211 | 196 | 26 | 66 | 174 | 2.8 | 7.4 | 32% | .281 | 1.24 | 3.75 | 4.09 | 4.04 | 3.4 |
| 2010 | ANA | MLB | 27 | 13 | 12 | 0 | 34 | 34 | 224¹ | 187 | 23 | 54 | 233 | 2.2 | 9.3 | 38% | .277 | 1.07 | 3.01 | 3.02 | 3.17 | 4.8 |
| 2011 | ANA | MLB | 28 | 18 | 8 | 0 | 33 | 33 | 235² | 182 | 20 | 56 | 198 | 2.1 | 7.6 | 34% | .252 | 1.01 | 2.41 | 3.24 | 3.03 | 4.7 |

Bourjos and Trout converting outs behind him, until the next presidential campaign.

**Jerome Williams**
Born: 12/4/1981 Age: 30
Bats: R Throws: R Height: 6' 4'' Weight: 180
Breakout: 25% Improve: 52% Collapse: 28%
Attrition: 12% MLB: 76%

Comparables:
Sun-Woo Kim, Mike Smith, Dennis Tankersley

| YEAR | TEAM | LVL | AGE | W | L | SV | G | GS | IP | H | HR | BB | SO | EqBB9 | EqSO9 | GB% | BABIP | WHIP | ERA | FIP | FRA | WARP |
|---|---|---|---|---|---|---|---|---|---|---|---|---|---|---|---|---|---|---|---|---|---|---|
| 2009 | SAC | AAA | 27 | 6 | 7 | 0 | 27 | 14 | 101² | 131 | 15 | 44 | 63 | 3.6 | 4.6 | 45% | .319 | 1.54 | 5.58 | 5.69 | 6.15 | -1.1 |
| 2011 | SLC | AAA | 29 | 4 | 2 | 0 | 11 | 10 | 73² | 78 | 10 | 15 | 60 | 1.8 | 7.3 | 51% | .316 | 1.26 | 3.91 | 4.65 | 4.81 | 1.0 |
| 2011 | ANA | MLB | 29 | 4 | 0 | 0 | 10 | 6 | 44 | 45 | 6 | 15 | 28 | 3.1 | 5.7 | 51% | .291 | 1.36 | 3.68 | 4.65 | 5.66 | -0.4 |
| 2012 | ANA | MLB | 30 | 3 | 3 | 0 | 7 | 7 | 48 | 53 | 6 | 18 | 28 | 3.4 | 5.3 | 48% | .300 | 1.47 | 4.85 | 4.79 | 5.28 | -0.3 |

Williams is the rare dude who used to be a pitcher and now he's a thrower. When he came up as a Giant, he was unhealthily obsessed with mixing speeds and tricking batters: he wanted to be Greg Maddux. That got him sent to Triple-A, then Taiwan, where as an act of desperation he perfected a cutter—a slider grip that, he says, "I just throw the hell out of." He quit tinkering with his fastball velocity and he dropped his arm a bit to get more movement on his two-seamer and changeup. He started 2011 in independent ball and would have ended it in the Angels postseason rotation had the club made it. An optimist would note that his numbers were polluted by a couple awful relief outings and as a starter he had a 2.31 ERA and a 3.44 FIP. A pessimist would note that a spot in next year's rotation will distract him from running the Hawaiian BBQ joints he owns in Fresno and Crescent City.

**C.J. Wilson**
Born: 11/18/1980 Age: 31
Bats: L Throws: L Height: 6' 3'' Weight: 200
Breakout: 8% Improve: 58% Collapse: 29%
Attrition: 14% MLB: 93%

Comparables:
Jeff Fassero, John Grabow, Pedro Feliciano

| YEAR | TEAM | LVL | AGE | W | L | SV | G | GS | IP | H | HR | BB | SO | EqBB9 | EqSO9 | GB% | BABIP | WHIP | ERA | FIP | FRA | WARP |
|---|---|---|---|---|---|---|---|---|---|---|---|---|---|---|---|---|---|---|---|---|---|---|
| 2009 | TEX | MLB | 28 | 5 | 6 | 14 | 74 | 0 | 73² | 66 | 3 | 32 | 84 | 3.9 | 10.3 | 57% | .323 | 1.33 | 2.81 | 2.94 | 3.10 | 2.1 |
| 2010 | TEX | MLB | 29 | 15 | 8 | 0 | 33 | 33 | 204 | 161 | 10 | 93 | 170 | 4.1 | 7.5 | 50% | .267 | 1.25 | 3.35 | 3.53 | 4.01 | 3.3 |
| 2011 | TEX | MLB | 30 | 16 | 7 | 0 | 34 | 34 | 223¹ | 191 | 16 | 74 | 206 | 3.0 | 8.3 | 51% | .289 | 1.19 | 2.94 | 3.28 | 3.92 | 3.5 |
| 2012 | ANA | MLB | 31 | 13 | 8 | 0 | 30 | 30 | 188¹ | 162 | 14 | 74 | 168 | 3.5 | 8.0 | 50% | .290 | 1.25 | 3.33 | 3.57 | 3.62 | 2.6 |

After making the transition from the pen to the 2010 rotation with promising results, Wilson emerged as the staff ace in 2011, making 34 regular season starts, and becoming the Game One starter for a World Series team. Wilson lacks the traditional characteristics of a number one, as the raw stuff is very good but it's not in the same ballpark as the elite pitchers in the game. With limited mileage on the arm (relatively speaking), a competitive edge, and a deep arsenal, Wilson should give the Angels a quality second or third starter for several years. Of course, his 142 ERA+ over the past two years is right there with Jered Weaver's 144, so it's not inconceivable he'll keep pitching himself into Game One starts.

## LINEOUTS

### HITTERS

| PLAYER | TEAM | LVL | AGE | PA | R | 2B | 3B | HR | RBI | BB | SO | SB-CS | AVG/OBP/SLG | TAv | BABIP | BRR | FRAA | WARP |
|---|---|---|---|---|---|---|---|---|---|---|---|---|---|---|---|---|---|---|
| RF K. Calhoun | SBR | A+ | 23 | 594 | 94 | 36 | 6 | 22 | 99 | 73 | 96 | 20-10 | .324/.410/.547 | .341 | .362 | 2.8 | -3.3 | 6.3 |
| RF R. Grichuk | CDR | A | 19 | 131 | 12 | 7 | 4 | 2 | 13 | 6 | 29 | 0-1 | .230/.267/.402 | .242 | .280 | -1.2 | 1.8 | 0.0 |
|  | SBR | A+ | 19 | 57 | 13 | 4 | 2 | 1 | 6 | 0 | 13 | 0-0 | .283/.316/.491 | .261 | .350 | 1.8 | -1.7 | 0.2 |
| 3B L. Jimenez | ARK | AA | 23 | 541 | 62 | 40 | 1 | 18 | 94 | 27 | 72 | 15-6 | .290/.335/.486 | .293 | .303 | 1.5 | 2.8 | 4.7 |
| DH P. McAnulty | SLC | AAA | 30 | 495 | 67 | 41 | 0 | 19 | 79 | 42 | 92 | 5-3 | .311/.370/.532 | .292 | .352 | -2.6 | -2.7 | 1.8 |
| LF C. Pettit | ARK | AA | 26 | 289 | 40 | 13 | 1 | 7 | 34 | 29 | 74 | 15-2 | .195/.294/.341 | .232 | .243 | 2.7 | 0.9 | 0.1 |
|  | SLC | AAA | 26 | 243 | 23 | 8 | 2 | 3 | 33 | 23 | 51 | 3-4 | .167/.262/.268 | .198 | .203 | -1.2 | -4.5 | -1.7 |

Everybody hits at Orem, but only most people hit at Inland Empire, so after 2011 **Kole Calhoun** is in slightly rarer company. The eighth-round pick hit lefties almost as well as righties, stole 20 bases, and played 20 games in center field, quelling concerns that he won't be more than an immobile platoon player. ⊘ **Randal Grichuk** missed the first four months of the season with a knee injury, and for the first time since he was drafted, he didn't hit much upon his return. The guy drafted immediately after him, Mike Trout, is already a big leaguer, but Grichuk is only 20. There's still time. ⊘ The Texas League was the big test for power-hitting **Luis Jimenez,** who had spent most of his career in supercharged offensive environments. The third baseman passed, leading the league in doubles and finishing in the top 10 in OPS. ⊘ **Paul McAnulty** slugged minor league pitchers for the second year in a row. Unfortunately for him, the Angels didn't lose their starting first baseman to a walk-off-related injury for a second year in a row, so McAnulty never got the call. ⊘ Sometimes, 40-man roster spots seem so valuable. "Oh no, local sports team has to expose interesting prospect to the Rule V draft because there is no room on the 40-man," and so on. Other times, **Chris Pettit** spends the entire season on the roster even though he was a 26-year-old hitting under .200 in Double-A.

### PITCHERS

| PLAYER | TEAM | LVL | AGE | W | L | SV | IP | H | HR | BB | SO | EqBB9 | EqSO9 | GB% | BABIP | WHIP | ERA | FIP | FRA | WARP |
|---|---|---|---|---|---|---|---|---|---|---|---|---|---|---|---|---|---|---|---|---|
| D. Carpenter | SBR | A+ | 23 | 0 | 1 | 11 | 29 | 23 | 1 | 9 | 36 | 2.8 | 11.2 | 61% | .319 | 1.10 | 0.93 | 2.93 | 3.45 | 0.6 |
| S. Geltz | ARK | AA | 23 | 2 | 3 | 0 | 46² | 33 | 5 | 18 | 71 | 2.7 | 12.9 | 26% | .283 | 0.96 | 3.09 | 2.95 | 3.59 | 0.6 |
| B. Lawrence | SLC | AAA | 35 | 0 | 3 | 0 | 32¹ | 48 | 5 | 8 | 21 | 2.2 | 5.8 | 36% | .368 | 1.73 | 8.07 | 5.37 | 5.29 | 0.1 |
| A. Ortega | SLC | AAA | 25 | 1 | 2 | 0 | 35 | 54 | 9 | 15 | 28 | 3.9 | 7.2 | 55% | .413 | 1.97 | 8.23 | 6.85 | 7.05 | -0.2 |
| H. Ramirez | SLC | AAA | 31 | 3 | 2 | 6 | 52¹ | 52 | 8 | 15 | 21 | 2.6 | 3.6 | 50% | .267 | 1.28 | 3.96 | 5.84 | 6.40 | -0.2 |
|  | ANA | MLB | 31 | 1 | 0 | 0 | 9 | 16 | 1 | 2 | 4 | 2.0 | 4.0 | 65% | .455 | 2.00 | 6.00 | 4.28 | 5.05 | 0.0 |
| T. Reckling | ARK | AA | 22 | 3 | 4 | 0 | 99 | 104 | 11 | 35 | 63 | 3.2 | 5.7 | 44% | .301 | 1.40 | 3.73 | 4.77 | 5.49 | -0.5 |
| F. Rodriguez | ANA | MLB | 28 | 0 | 0 | 0 | 13² | 13 | 2 | 5 | 7 | 3.3 | 4.6 | 47% | .244 | 1.32 | 4.61 | 5.04 | 4.93 | 0.0 |
| C. Scholl | ARK | AA | 23 | 2 | 2 | 0 | 85¹ | 69 | 7 | 25 | 78 | 2.3 | 7.0 | 35% | .225 | 0.97 | 2.32 | 3.67 | 4.13 | 0.7 |
| L. Van Mil | ARK | AA | 26 | 3 | 4 | 0 | 66¹ | 59 | 4 | 28 | 53 | 3.1 | 6.2 | 51% | .243 | 1.15 | 2.04 | 4.15 | 4.43 | 0.3 |

**David Carpenter** didn't allow a run in his first 19 Double-A outings, until the ninth inning of the Texas League championships. That blown-save was unfortunate punctuation to another terrific year from the sinker/slider right-hander. ⊘ **Steven Geltz** has struck out 103 batters in 65 Double-A innings, primarily using a low-90s fastball with a ton of movement. Always root for undrafted free agents. ⊘ **Brian Lawrence** has now pitched for five of the PCL's 16 teams. It's a delicate balance required to stay in Triple-A forever, and giving up a run per inning is a little too much salt and not enough sugar. ⊘ **Anthony Ortega** was supposed to be the safe prospect—pitchability, no upside. Since 2009, though, he has an 8.22 ERA spread across four levels. No, it's not safe. It's very dangerous. Be careful. ⊘ "You're kidding me," Horacio Ramirez exclaimed when his agent told him the news. "I'm going back to the big leagues? Is there a strike? Am I a scab? Because I sure don't remember being as good as the regular players. They hit me so hard—so so hard. Oh I hope I'm a scab." ⊘ **Trevor Reckling** got his third crack at Double-A. He wasn't terrible—that's something—but the guy who was the Angels' top prospect in 2009 is just gone. He's only 22, but his middling peripherals look even worse now that he's in an age-appropriate league. ⊘ The Angels should call **Francisco Rodriguez** up and let him pitch the ninth inning, just once, so we can find out what the other Francisco Rodriguez does for a post-save celebration dance. Given how dissimilar to K-Rod this version is, he would probably tuck into the fetal position and wait for the stadium to empty.  ⊘  The Angels maintained as late as July that **Chris Scholl** was a reliever who was being developed as a reliever. But after Garrett Richards's promotion, Scholl joined the Arkansas rotation and allowed seven runs in five starts. Neither here nor there, but Scholl once threw 21 consecutive hitless innings in the Midwest League.  ⊘  Can't talk about **Loek van Mil** without mentioning his 7-foot-1 height. Because there's nothing else interesting about his performance in Double-A. He's seven feet, one inch tall.

## MANAGER: MIKE SCIOSCIA

| Pythag | Avg | 100+ | 120+ | | REL w | | PH | PH | | SAC | POS |

now missed the playoffs in back-to-back seasons, and cracks are showing. Does any of this matter on the field? The Angels, after all, did outperform their run differential for an eighth season in a row, though by the thinnest of margins. And they held on to playoff hopes until the final series of the year, despite never having playoff odds (according to our simulations) higher than 25 percent. Their position in the standings—long shots, but shots nonetheless—made Scioscia less risk-averse than he been since 2002. When he needed a fifth-starter, he called up a 21-year-old with just one outing above Double-A. Later in the year, he added Garrett Richards and Mike Trout straight from Double-A. He moved players to positions they had never played, with short notice. He made a rookie his closer, and—for the first time since 2007—he occasionally went to his closer in the eighth inning. To some degree, he even relinquished his security blanket, Mathis, late in the season. His skill at managing catchers remains one of the mysteries of his tenure. He should be the best manager a catcher could ask for, but touted prospect Hank Conger all but dissolved under his tutelage in 2011. Scioscia's 2012 evaluation, and the Angels' success this year, will largely hinge on how much production he gets from his catchers; how successfully he gets Trout into the lineup; how efficiently he can clear a seven-player pile-up at DH and the corners; and whether he extends that streak of beating Pythagoras.

# Los Angeles Dodgers

he end is nigh. After two seasons spent in the shadow of their owners' sordid divorce and its aftermath—two seasons that have turned the franchise into a punch line—the Dodgers will be freed from the clutches of Frank McCourt by April 30, 2012. That's the date by which McCourt must divest himself of the team and their stadium according to terms of a settlement with Major League Baseball filed in bankruptcy court on November 1, 2011. At this writing, initial bids are scheduled for acceptance by January 13. By the time this volume is in your hot little hands, a new owner will likely have been designated.

That the Dodgers wound up in bankruptcy court is a story unto itself, the fallout from heavily leveraged owner Frank and wife Jamie siphoning $189 million from the team to fund their extravagant lifestyle, breaking several MLB rules and alienating the team's fan base when its details—six-figure salaries for hairdressers, a Russian pseudoscientist, and two of the couple's sons were only the start—emerged during the surreal divorce proceedings that made so many headlines in 2010. Picking up the story where *BP2011* left off, in February commissioner Bud Selig turned down a proposal for Fox to loan a strapped McCourt $200 million using the team's cable television rights as collateral. Had McCourt defaulted, such a deal could have extended the team's contract with Fox by as many as four years beyond its current 2013 endpoint at a below-market annual rate of around $50 million, $30 million less than the Rangers' take via their new contract. This was no trivial hypothetical, either. In 2004, the McCourts put up a South Boston parking lot as collateral against a $145 million loan, and defaulted, with Fox taking ownership of the lot and selling it.

Desperate for cash, McCourt then negotiated a 17-year television contract with Fox reportedly valued at around

## DODGERS PROSPECTUS
### 2011 W-L: 82-79, 3rd in NL West

| | | |
|---|---|---|
| Pythag | .523 | 12th |
| RS/G | 4.00 | 20th |
| RA/G | 3.80 | 6th |
| TAv | .255 | 19th |
| TAv-P | .249 | 5th |
| FIP | 3.58 | 5th |
| DER | .715 | 9th |
| DL | 939 | 26th |
| B-Age | 29.9 | 25th |
| P-Age | 28.7 | 23rd |
| Salary | $108.4 | 11th |
| M$/MW | $2.81 | 18th |

**Ballpark:** Dodger Stadium (3-yr. PF: 97). Like many American homes, it has an underwater mortgage

**2011:** Divorce drama upstages a team that can't succeed despite two of the best players in baseball

**2012:** With a team of stars, stopgaps, and rookies, it matters how good those stopgaps turn out

**Action Items:** First base, third base, ownership that stays out of the headlines

$3 billion, which would have provided the Dodgers with $385 million in cash up-front. He presented it to Selig for approval in April. Given the opportunity to choke the life out of a regime that had become an embarrassment, Selig let McCourt twist in the wind while taking more than two months to consider the deal. Meanwhile, early-season attendance lagged, in part due to fallout from a horrific assault in the Dodger Stadium parking lot on Opening Day that left Giants fan Bryan Stow in critical condition with a traumatic brain injury. Stow would spend nearly six months in a coma and run up over $50 million in medical expenses, while his family would file suit against McCourt and the Dodgers in late May, contending that the team failed to provide adequate security.

With that bad publicity lingering and the TV deal not approved, McCourt was forced to take out a $30 million personal loan—to get around the need for MLB approval—from Fox to meet payroll for April and May. On April 20, after news of the loan broke, Selig announced that he would appoint a trustee to oversee the day-to-day operations of the franchise, effectively seizing control and giving MLB approval rights over every significant expenditure. Selig also launched an investigation into the operations and finances of the Dodgers and their related entities. Days later, Tom Schieffer, a former executive with the Texas Rangers during the '90s, was named trustee.

In June, Selig rejected the TV deal on the grounds that $173.5 million of that up-front payment was earmarked for the McCourts and their attorneys, and because MLB executives valued the deal closer to $1.7 billion, a valuation that arguably could have suppressed the future television deals of other teams. The rejection in turn nullified a divorce settlement between Frank and Jamie that hinged on its approval, and within a week forced the club into bankruptcy. At that point, McCourt had suited for the cycle, with legal battles going against Selig, his ex-wife (the divorce was said to have run up $35 million in legal fees), his former law firm (which had produced competing versions of the marital property agreement that had put ownership of the team in dispute), and the Stow family. In an ironic reminder of the decisions to defer significant portions of big contracts, Manny Ramirez ($21 million) and Andruw Jones ($11 million) were listed as the two largest creditors, with Juan Pierre ($3.05 million) further down the list.

To avoid borrowing from MLB, McCourt secured a $150 million loan from a hedge fund at 10 percent interest, 3 percent higher than the league was offering, to cover his bills.

other teams in order to show that the Dodgers' debts (said to be over $525 million) weren't out of line with those of other clubs) were refused.

In September, as the Dodgers completed a season in which their attendance declined by 18 percent—a drop said to cost $27 million, 9 percent of total 2009 revenue—MLB asked the bankruptcy court to force the sale of the franchise. Meanwhile, in an attempt to generate a higher franchise sale price, McCourt hatched a last-ditch plan to auction off the team's TV rights even before the expiration of an exclusive negotiating period with Fox, which of course filed suit to prevent that from happening. In October, after agreeing to pay Jamie $130 million to settle the divorce, Frank settled for an agreement with MLB allowing him some control over the sale process; he gets to pick the winning bid, not the league. In December, he won a ruling allowing him to sell the team's TV rights ahead of schedule in order to maximize the sale value, which could exceed $1 billion, though any buyer could still reject the TV deal and negotiate a new one. That's where we stand at this writing.

On the field, the Dodgers delivered considerably less drama. Despite a PECOTA forecast for 87 wins, largely based on the pitching staff being the league's stingiest, the team never came close to contending. They were 14-14 by the end of April, 4 1/2 games out, then went 27-37 to close the first half, falling to 11 games back. While fifth starter Jon Garland made just nine starts before needing shoulder surgery, and injuries to Jonathan Broxton, Hong-Chih Kuo, and Vicente Padilla turned the bullpen into a smoldering wreck early in the year, the offense was a much bigger problem. The Dodgers ranked 14th in first-half scoring at 3.70 runs per game.

General manager Ned Colletti's offseason plan had been downright brutal. Once again demonstrating a failure to understand the concept of positional scarcity, he had non-tendered catcher Russell Martin—admittedly banged up by injuries and overuse, but still an average-at-worst bat with an above-average glove at a key up-the-middle position—in December 2010 over his unwillingness to guarantee $5 million in base salary. At the same time, he retained first baseman James Loney, whose offense had been in continuous decline since 2007, at roughly the same cost. Already underpowered at that key offensive position, Colletti skimped on left field, hoping that a productive platoon would emerge from among lefties Tony Gwynn Jr., Jay Gibbons, and Trent

| Rafael Furcal | 3 | 2007-2011 | $30.0 | 7.9 | $3.62# |
| Hiroki Kuroda | 1 | 2011-2011 | $12.0 | 2.6 | $4.62 |
| Hiroki Kuroda | 3 | 2008-2010 | $35.5 | 5.8 | $6.12 |
| Manny Ramirez | 2 | 2009-2010 | $45.0 | 4.7 | $7.27# |
| Juan Pierre | 5 | 2007-2011 | $45.0 | 2.1 | $17.14# |
| Nomar Garciaparra | 2 | 2007-2008 | $18.5 | 1.0 | $18.50 |
| Jason Schmidt | 3 | 2007-2009 | $47.0 | 0.2 | $235.0 |
| Andruw Jones | 2 | 2008-2009 | $36.2 | -1.1 | -- |
| Juan Uribe | 3 | 2011-2013 | $21.0 | -1.0 | -- |
| Matt Guerrier | 3 | 2011-2013 | $12.0 | 0.0 | -- |

* Includes only 2011 salary and signing bonus
# Adjusted to exclude salaries paid by other teams or lost due to suspension

Meanwhile, the other three-quarters of the team's starting infield spent the bulk of the season on the disabled list. Second baseman Juan Uribe—last winter's big offseason signing at three years and $21 million—shortstop Rafael Furcal, and third baseman Casey Blake combined for just 177 games and a putrid .218/.293/.309 line while making seven trips to the DL totaling 226 days, not including Blake being shut down for all of September. The Uribe signing was lousy, and the loss of Carlos Santana to acquire Blake back in 2008 continues to carry ramifications, but Blake's subsequent free-agent deal and that of Furcal actually rank among the best of the GM's big-money transactions during his six-year tenure (see Table 1). Veteran utilityman Jamey Carroll did his slap-tastic best (.290/.359/.347) to offset the losses, but futility-man Aaron Miles (.275/.314/.346) was much less effective in about the same amount of playing time.

The offense was further hamstrung by a down season from Andre Ethier, who battled a knee problem that required off-season surgery and hit a comparatively light .292/.368/.421

with 11 homers. If nothing else, that left the spotlight to Matt Kemp, who rebounded from a season of squabbling with the team's coaching staff and hit .324/.399/.586 with 39 homers and 40 steals en route to a second-place finish in the MVP voting. Ethier filled the squabbling-with-staff void by accusing the team of forcing him to play through his knee injury.

Kemp's big season paired nicely with that of Clayton Kershaw, who won the pitchers' Triple Crown by leading the league in wins (21), strikeouts (248), and ERA (2.28) en route to the NL Cy Young award. Elsewhere, Hiroki Kuroda had a strong season but caused a stir just prior to the July 31 deadline when he declined to waive his no-trade clause. Ted Lilly pitched better than his 3.97 ERA despite gopher problems, but Chad Billingsley disappointed with a 4.21 mark and a 1.2 WARP season, less than half of what he averaged over his previous three years.

The myriad injuries afforded an opportunity to examine the fruits of a farm system that has grown lean due to years of talent drain via prospect-for-veteran trades and underspending on amateur talent, both in the draft and internationally. Shortstop and top hitting prospect Dee Gordon got a long look, hitting a thin .304/.325/.362 and showing rawness afield but swiping 24 bases in 56 games. Left fielder Jerry Sands (.253/.338/.389) struggled in his first stint but caught fire in his second. Heat-throwing Rubby De La Rosa posted a 3.71 ERA in 60 2/3 innings before needing Tommy John surgery. Nathan Eovaldi, Josh Lindblom, and 2004 first-round pick Scott Elbert also made positive showings in limited time.

Though nowhere near the bumper crop of Logan White picks that propelled the Dodgers to the playoffs four times in 2004-09, the rookies did help the club go a surprising 41-28 in the second half, the league's fourth-best record; the lineup produced a robust 4.41 runs per game. Rookie skipper Don Mattingly managed to keep his troops engaged long enough to push the overall record above .500, an impressive feat under the circumstances.

Even with that finish and the eventual sale, the Dodgers will have their work cut out to match those 82 wins. McCourt was loath to boost payroll for a team on the block, but that didn't stop Colletti from squandering his budget on quantity instead of quality, inking several players whose best years are behind them. Instead of re-signing Kuroda to a one-year deal for a modest increase above his $12 million 2011 salary, Colletti inked 2011 reclamation projects Chris Capuano (34 in August) and Aaron Harang (34 in May) to backloaded two-year deals for $10 million and $12 million, respectively. Instead of re-signing the 38-year-old Carroll, who went to the Twins for two years and $6.5 million, he signed second baseman Mark Ellis (35 in June) and utilityman Jerry Hairston Jr. (36 in May) to two-year deals for $8.75 million and $6 million, respectively. Instead of solving the left-field problem, he re-signed 33-year-old midseason acquisition

Juan Rivera—an adept lefty masher, but otherwise a liability both offensively and defensively—to a $4.5 million contract and brought back Gwynn with a two-year, $2 million deal. He tendered a contract to Loney, who had followed four terrible months with two good ones that may or may not have been the result of work with new hitting coach Dave Hansen.

Gordon and Sands will both have the opportunity to win starting jobs in the spring, as will catcher Tim Federowicz, obtained from the Red Sox in a three-way July 31 trade that the Dodgers had no business butting into. Concerned with the system's lack of catching depth—which he squandered by letting Martin walk and by trading Santana—the GM sent center-field prospect Trayvon Robinson to Seattle and received a catch-and-throw 2008 seventh-rounder and a pair of relief suspects. Federowicz, holdover A.J. Ellis, and journeyman Matt Treanor won't add much offensively, but they'll do an inspired job of keeping the ball from rolling to the backstop on every pitch.

The lineup sorely could have used a big bat acquired either via free agency or trade, a Prince Fielder or even a Carlos Beltran, but at least McCourt and Colletti took care of one pressing bit of business, signing the rejuvenated Kemp to an eight-year, $160 million extension; he could have been a free agent after 2012. On the other hand, Ethier, whose contract is up after the coming season, is a candidate to be dealt at some point rather than retained.

Colletti may not be long for the team either, as new owners generally tend to prefer new executives. Incoming Astros owner Jim Crane fired Ed Wade shortly after the sale was approved. Incoming owner Jeff Moorad fired Kevin Towers just a few months after taking over the Padres in 2009. Incoming Rays owner Stewart Sternberg fired Chuck Lamar after taking control in 2005. McCourt himself fired Dan Evans after taking over the Dodgers in 2004. On the other hand, the Cubs let Jim Hendry serve for a season and a half before axing him, and the Rangers retained Jon Daniels—but principal owner Nolan Ryan, who had served as team president, had already worked closely with him. Colletti's existing contract (whose length isn't publicly known) shouldn't be an impediment to finding a better GM than the unimaginative incumbent. One had to wince when in November, SI.com's Tom Verducci wrote an article declaring that Colletti had gone sabermetric, explaining that Rivera was re-signed because his quantitative analysis showed the Dodgers' lefthanded hitters posted a .566 OPS against lefthanded pitching, something anyone with 10 seconds and a browser open to Baseball-Reference. com could find.

The next owner is anybody's guess at this writing. One potential ownership group pairs former Dodger greats Orel Hershiser and Steve Garvey. Another involves Lakers great Magic Johnson and former Braves and Nationals president (and, importantly, Selig favorite) Stan Kasten, with Mark

Walter, chief executive of Guggenheim Partners, as the money man. Former Dodgers owner Peter O'Malley has expressed a willingness to run the team as part of another group. Former Dodgers GM Fred Claire is in another group, along with former A's president Andy Dolich and former Dodgers batboy Ben Hwang, now a biotechnology executive. Former agent and current White Sox special assistant Dennis Gilbert, who came up short in trying to buy the Rangers in 2010, is also said to be interested, and iconoclastic Dallas Mavericks owner Mark Cuban, who attempted to buy both the Rangers and the Cubs, may be as well. Eli Broad, Tom and Alec Gores, and Ron Burkle are among the other names that have been mentioned. McCourt will select the winning

of the owners. You can bet that Selig will stress that the new owner be better capitalized than McCourt was, to avoid similar shenanigans.

Change will not come instantly to this franchise. While the damage from two years of bad public relations and several more of developmental neglect won't heal overnight, a fresh start with an owner less despicable than McCourt and a GM more adept than Colletti should alleviate the Dodgers' attendance woes, and the coming television contract, which could approach $4 billion, will allow them to spend at a level befitting a franchise in the game's second-largest market. A new beginning is near.

| | | Born: 8/23/1973 Age: 38 |
| Bats: R Throws: R Height: 6' 3" Weight: 195 |
| Breakout: 0% Improve: 19% Collapse: 19% |
| Attrition: 26% MLB: 71% |
| Comparables: |
| Jose Hernandez, Graig Nettles, Ron Cey |

| YEAR | TEAM | LVL | AGE | PA | R | 2B | 3B | HR | RBI | BB | SO | SB | CS | AVG_OBP_SLG | TAv | BABIP | BRR | FRAA | WARP |
|------|------|-----|-----|----|----|----|----|----|-----|----|----|----|----|-------------|-----|-------|-----|------|------|
| 2007 | LAN | MLB | 39 | 585 | 64 | 29 | 0 | 18 | 77 | 63 | 110 | 3 | 4 | .288/.363/.400 | .270 | .327 | 1 | 4.0 | 4.3 |
| 2010 | LAN | MLB | 36 | 571 | 56 | 28 | 1 | 17 | 64 | 48 | 138 | 0 | 4 | .248/.320/.407 | .266 | .305 | 0.4 | -1.9 | 2.3 |
| 2011 | LAN | MLB | 37 | 239 | 32 | 10 | 1 | 4 | 26 | 26 | 50 | 1 | 2 | .252/.342/.371 | .254 | .311 | -0.4 | -3.2 | 0.3 |
| 2012 | COL | MLB | 38 | 294 | 35 | 14 | 2 | 8 | 34 | 26 | 64 | 2 | 1 | .256/.330/.417 | .256 | .305 | -0.4 | 3B -0, 1B -0 | 1.6 |

With or without his signature beard, Blake suffered through a miserable Dodger finale, serving three stints on the DL due to lower back inflammation, an infected bursa sac in his elbow, and arthritis in his neck. The elbow necessitated in-season surgery, the neck required postseason surgery to alleviate a pinched nerve; all in all, Blake shoulda stood in bed. The cumulative woes sapped Blake's power when he was available, and made declining his $6 million 2012 option automatic. He agreed to a non-guaranteed one-year deal with Colorado, where he'll be a candidate to keep third base warm for Arenado. The only downside is that he arrives just as Huston Street departs, depriving us all of a season's worth of tired Blake Street references.

| **Alex Castellanos** RF |
| Born: 8/4/1986 Age: 25 |
| Bats: R Throws: R Height: 6' 0" Weight: 180 |
| Breakout: 6% Improve: 28% Collapse: 5% |
| Attrition: 26% MLB: 83% |
| Comparables: |
| Dan Dobbek, Cody Ross, Felix Jose |

| YEAR | TEAM | LVL | AGE | PA | R | 2B | 3B | HR | RBI | BB | SO | SB | CS | AVG_OBP_SLG | TAv | BABIP | BRR | FRAA | WARP |
|------|------|-----|-----|----|----|----|----|----|-----|----|----|----|----|-------------|-----|-------|-----|------|------|
| 2009 | QUD | A | 22 | 346 | 51 | 21 | 4 | 5 | 34 | 20 | 89 | 21 | 4 | .270/.337/.412 | .279 | .362 | 1.7 | 5.3 | 1.6 |
| 2009 | PMB | A+ | 22 | 56 | 5 | 1 | 1 | 1 | 2 | 2 | 19 | 0 | 2 | .189/.232/.302 | .173 | .273 | -0.2 | 0.2 | -0.4 |
| 2010 | PMB | A+ | 23 | 517 | 62 | 35 | 7 | 13 | 58 | 38 | 112 | 19 | 9 | .270/.339/.462 | .292 | .328 | -0.1 | 0 | 2.3 |
| 2011 | CHT | AA | 24 | 143 | 30 | 14 | 4 | 4 | 23 | 15 | 24 | 4 | 1 | .322/.406/.603 | .316 | .365 | 0.6 | 1.5 | 1.4 |
| 2011 | SFD | AA | 24 | 391 | 72 | 21 | 4 | 19 | 62 | 24 | 94 | 10 | 1 | .319/.379/.562 | .306 | .387 | 1.2 | 0.1 | 3.4 |
| 2012 | LAN | MLB | 25 | 250 | 26 | 11 | 2 | 6 | 27 | 12 | 69 | 8 | 2 | .232/.284/.380 | .244 | .299 | 0.1 | RF -1, CF 0 | 0.2 |

Not the Republican political operative but a 2008 10th-round pick who arrived in the Rafael Furcal trade. Castellanos wasn't on anybody's radar as a prospect at the beginning of the season, and he was old for his level, but in tearing up Double-A pitching he won over a few scouting skeptics. Castellanos has real power, but he swings from the heels and has little plate discipline. He washed out as an infielder due to bad hands, and he's more likely to wind up a bench bat than an everyday player. An experiment to try first base in the Arizona Fall League was aborted by an oblique strain, but he should be fine for spring.

| **Brian Cavazos-Galvez** LF |
| Born: 5/17/1987 Age: 25 |
| Bats: R Throws: R Height: 6' 1" Weight: 215 |
| Breakout: 6% Improve: 28% Collapse: 3% |
| Attrition: 15% MLB: 45% |
| Comparables: |
| Mark Trumbo, Steve Garvey, Rebel Ridling |

| YEAR | TEAM | LVL | AGE | PA | R | 2B | 3B | HR | RBI | BB | SO | SB | CS | AVG_OBP_SLG | TAv | BABIP | BRR | FRAA | WARP |
|------|------|-----|-----|----|----|----|----|----|-----|----|----|----|----|-------------|-----|-------|-----|------|------|
| 2009 | OGD | RK | 22 | 323 | 59 | 29 | 3 | 18 | 63 | 10 | 43 | 17 | 8 | .322/.358/.618 | .348 | .329 | -5.1 | 1.1 | 2.8 |
| 2010 | GRL | A | 23 | 513 | 76 | 43 | 4 | 16 | 77 | 12 | 60 | 43 | 13 | .318/.345/.520 | .311 | .338 | -1 | 1.6 | 4.4 |
| 2011 | CHT | AA | 24 | 440 | 60 | 27 | 5 | 14 | 61 | 12 | 63 | 13 | 11 | .277/.311/.470 | .272 | .296 | 1.1 | -3.3 | 1.1 |
| 2012 | LAN | MLB | 25 | 250 | 25 | 13 | 1 | 7 | 28 | 3 | 51 | 10 | 5 | .232/.250/.374 | .228 | .264 | -0.7 | LF -3, 1B -1 | -0.7 |

This 2009 12th-round pick has a true blue pedigree: The son of former Dodger reliever Balvino Galvez, he played his college ball at the University of New Mexico, which shares a ballpark with the Albuquerque Isotopes. Age and a logjam of younger outfield prospects led the Dodgers to push Cavazos-Galvez to Double-A, where his long swing and overly aggressive approach caught up to him, particularly in the first half. As in 2010, he did adjust to the league in the second half (.291/.339/.539, 9 HR). Less flatteringly, he again showed a drastic park split and struggled mightily against righties. Despite his tremendous bat speed, ability to hit to all fields and strong arm, he needs to curb his hacktastic ways, particularly now that he's gravitating to the far left side of the defensive spectrum.

### Ivan De Jesus — 2B

Born: 5/1/1987 Age: 25
Bats: R Throws: R Height: 6' 0'' Weight: 200
Breakout: 0% Improve: 24% Collapse: 16%
Attrition: 33% MLB: 73%

**Comparables:**
Jim Lefebvre, Rich McKinney, Luis Valbuena

| YEAR | TEAM | LVL | AGE | PA | R | 2B | 3B | HR | RBI | BB | SO | SB | CS | AVG_OBP_SLG | TAv | BABIP | BRR | FRAA | WARP |
|---|---|---|---|---|---|---|---|---|---|---|---|---|---|---|---|---|---|---|---|
| 2010 | ABQ | AAA | 23 | 580 | 89 | 33 | 2 | 7 | 70 | 32 | 81 | 6 | 1 | .296/.334/.405 | .247 | .334 | 2.1 | -3.4 | 1.1 |
| 2011 | ABQ | AAA | 24 | 443 | 61 | 19 | 2 | 8 | 59 | 45 | 68 | 4 | 1 | .310/.389/.432 | .252 | .358 | 1.4 | -1.4 | 1.3 |
| 2011 | LAN | MLB | 24 | 35 | 2 | 0 | 0 | 0 | 1 | 2 | 11 | 0 | 0 | .188/.235/.188 | .154 | .286 | 0.4 | 0.5 | -0.2 |
| 2012 | LAN | MLB | 25 | 250 | 26 | 10 | 1 | 4 | 22 | 19 | 52 | 1 | 0 | .243/.308/.343 | .241 | .294 | 0 | 2B -2, SS -1 | 0.7 |

Prior to missing nearly all of 2009 with a broken tibia, DeJesus made for a nice little sleeper, with a patient, contact-oriented approach and excellent instincts. But the Dodgers yo-yoed him between Albuquerque and LA without ever giving him a real chance; Don Mattingly gave him seven starts in about five weeks of roster time. DeJesus did recover some of his lost plate discipline and power at Albuquerque, though the latter was mostly a park illusion. The signings of Mark Ellis and Jerry Hairston won't help his chances at a big league job, and likely doom him to an Albuquerque return.

### Mark Ellis — 2B

Born: 6/6/1977 Age: 35
Bats: R Throws: R Height: 6' 0'' Weight: 180
Breakout: 1% Improve: 18% Collapse: 11%
Attrition: 23% MLB: 75%

**Comparables:**
Kurt Bevacqua, Adam Kennedy, Tony Graffanino

| YEAR | TEAM | LVL | AGE | PA | R | 2B | 3B | HR | RBI | BB | SO | SB | CS | AVG_OBP_SLG | TAv | BABIP | BRR | FRAA | WARP |
|---|---|---|---|---|---|---|---|---|---|---|---|---|---|---|---|---|---|---|---|
| 2009 | OAK | MLB | 32 | 410 | 52 | 23 | 0 | 10 | 61 | 23 | 54 | 10 | 3 | .263/.305/.403 | .244 | .280 | -2.7 | 4.5 | 0.5 |
| 2010 | OAK | MLB | 33 | 492 | 45 | 24 | 0 | 5 | 49 | 40 | 56 | 7 | 6 | .291/.358/.381 | .281 | .321 | -1.1 | 3.4 | 2.5 |
| 2011 | COL | MLB | 34 | 286 | 34 | 13 | 0 | 6 | 25 | 14 | 43 | 7 | 3 | .274/.317/.392 | .240 | .307 | 2.4 | -0.2 | 0.1 |
| 2011 | OAK | MLB | 34 | 233 | 21 | 11 | 1 | 1 | 16 | 8 | 32 | 7 | 2 | .217/.253/.290 | .212 | .249 | 0.7 | 4.9 | 0.1 |
| 2012 | LAN | MLB | 35 | 485 | 50 | 20 | 1 | 7 | 43 | 34 | 71 | 14 | 6 | .244/.304/.344 | .242 | .272 | -0.5 | 2B 5, 1B 0 | 0.6 |

Traded from Oakland to Colorado in late June after Jonathan Herrera kept getting the bat knocked out of his hands, Ellis played a capable second base and helped stabilize the Rockies infield when it still looked like that might matter. Even so, his offensive and defensive values have fallen considerably since his Oakland heyday, as has his durability; he's averaged 34 days on the disabled list over the last four seasons. Why the Dodgers would opt to sign him for two years and $8.75 million when they could have retained the older but superior Jamey Carroll for less money is unclear; either Colletti thinks that signing a former Athletic equates to absorbing the lessons of *Moneyball*, or he just likes to catch falling knives.

### A.J. Ellis — C

Born: 4/9/1981 Age: 31
Bats: R Throws: R Height: 6' 4'' Weight: 230
Breakout: 2% Improve: 31% Collapse: 12%
Attrition: 33% MLB: 81%

**Comparables:**
Jim Essian, Ron Hassey, Glenn Borgmann

| YEAR | TEAM | LVL | AGE | PA | R | 2B | 3B | HR | RBI | BB | SO | SB | CS | AVG_OBP_SLG | TAv | BABIP | BRR | FRAA | WARP |
|---|---|---|---|---|---|---|---|---|---|---|---|---|---|---|---|---|---|---|---|
| 2009 | ABQ | AAA | 28 | 360 | 48 | 13 | 2 | 0 | 39 | 64 | 44 | 2 | 2 | .314/.441/.375 | .266 | .366 | 0.1 | 2.2 | 2.0 |
| 2009 | LAN | MLB | 28 | 10 | 0 | 0 | 0 | 0 | 1 | 0 | 1 | 0 | 0 | .100/.100/.100 | .072 | .111 | 0 | 0 | -0.2 |
| 2010 | ABQ | AAA | 29 | 76 | 11 | 5 | 1 | 0 | 7 | 13 | 12 | 1 | 0 | .262/.395/.377 | .250 | .320 | -0.6 | 0.7 | 0.3 |
| 2010 | LAN | MLB | 29 | 128 | 6 | 5 | 0 | 0 | 16 | 14 | 18 | 0 | 0 | .278/.363/.324 | .259 | .330 | -1.8 | -0.1 | 0.3 |
| 2011 | ABQ | AAA | 30 | 248 | 36 | 15 | 0 | 2 | 28 | 50 | 23 | 0 | 1 | .304/.467/.418 | .289 | .338 | -1.1 | -0.9 | 1.2 |
| 2011 | LAN | MLB | 30 | 103 | 8 | 1 | 1 | 2 | 11 | 14 | 16 | 0 | 1 | .271/.392/.376 | .288 | .313 | -1 | -0.3 | 0.6 |
| 2012 | LAN | MLB | 31 | 250 | 28 | 9 | 1 | 1 | 17 | 35 | 39 | 0 | 0 | .255/.371/.328 | .268 | .303 | -0.1 | C -0, 1B 0 | 2.4 |

Ellis renewed his membership in the International Brotherhood of Backup Catchers, but even with Russell Martin's non-tender and Dioner Navarro's injuries and ineffectiveness, he found playing time hard to come by. When he did play, he gave the Dodgers more of what they've come to expect, namely solid on-base skills that are less valuable when he bats eighth, a minimum of pop, zero speed, and sound defense (27 percent caught stealing, in all of 15 attempts). With Rod Barajas gone and Tim Federowicz quite underseasoned, the Dodgers appear ready to grant Ellis a larger share of playing time; he offers nothing fancy, but he won't be a detriment.

**Gorman Erickson** C
Born: 3/11/1988 Age: 24
Bats: B Throws: R Height: 6' 5" Weight: 220
Breakout: 3% Improve: 16% Collapse: 8%
Attrition: 25% MLB: 59%
**Comparables:**
Joel Collins, Todd Zeile, A.J. Pierzynski

| YEAR | TEAM | LVL | AGE | PA | R | 2B | 3B | HR | RBI | BB | SO | SB | CS | AVG_OBP_SLG | TAv | BABIP | BRR | FRAA | WARP |
|------|------|-----|-----|-----|----|----|----|----|-----|----|----|----|----|-------------|------|-------|------|------|------|
| 2009 | OGD | RK | 21 | 225 | 40 | 18 | 1 | 5 | 36 | 24 | 36 | 0 | 0 | .305/.383/.482 | .314 | .353 | -0.4 | 2.5 | 2.0 |
| 2010 | GRL | A | 22 | 299 | 32 | 13 | 3 | 2 | 27 | 34 | 45 | 3 | 0 | .215/.309/.310 | .234 | .251 | -1.2 | 0.8 | 0.3 |
| 2011 | RCU | A+ | 23 | 273 | 37 | 16 | 4 | 6 | 40 | 41 | 42 | 3 | 2 | .305/.408/.491 | .323 | .346 | 0.5 | -0.7 | 2.8 |
| 2011 | CHT | AA | 23 | 157 | 18 | 8 | 0 | 7 | 26 | 11 | 22 | 1 | 0 | .275/.329/.479 | .269 | .281 | 0.7 | -0.4 | 1.0 |
| 2012 | LAN | MLB | 24 | 250 | 24 | 10 | 1 | 4 | 21 | 20 | 54 | 1 | 0 | .216/.281/.322 | .226 | .262 | 0 | C -0 | 0.4 |

You can almost forgive Colletti for overlooking Erickson (nicknamed Griff) in his midsummer panic over the Dodgers' dearth of catching prospects. A 15th-round 2006 draft-and-follow Erickson took three years to clear rookie ball and struggled in Low-A but he enjoyed a breakout season at High-A last year. The Dodgers always liked his work behind the plate. He's an above-average receiver with good game-calling skills and a strong arm (career 30 percent caught stealing rate). At the plate he showed good discipline as well as some power though the discipline took a hit upon promotion to Double-A and he hit righties better than lefties. Erickson will likely return to Chattanooga to start 2012 but he could advance

Ethier started the season red-hot (.380/.440/.550 in April), but while he maintained a high batting average through the All-Star break, his power eroded considerably. After a horrific stretch from the break into late August, he suggested to *LA Times* columnist T.J. Simers that the Dodgers were pushing him to play through a right knee injury. An organizational Donny-brook followed, as the manager described himself as blindsided by the allegation and the GM took exception as well. Soon afterwards Ethier underwent surgery; the knee should heal fine but the relationship between player and team may be irreparably damaged as he approaches his walk year and it would shock nobody if he arrived at a new address sometime in 2012. The Gold Glove was worth a chuckle though most of the major systems suggest he was a shade above average after three years well below it.

**Tim Federowicz** C
Born: 8/5/1987 Age: 24
Bats: R Throws: R Height: 6' 0" Weight: 200
Breakout: 4% Improve: 13% Collapse: 6%
Attrition: 24% MLB: 52%
**Comparables:**
Wyatt Toregas, Stan Cliburn, Johnny Monell

| YEAR | TEAM | LVL | AGE | PA | R | 2B | 3B | HR | RBI | BB | SO | SB | CS | AVG_OBP_SLG | TAv | BABIP | BRR | FRAA | WARP |
|------|------|-----|-----|-----|----|----|----|----|-----|----|----|----|----|-------------|------|-------|------|------|------|
| 2009 | GRN | A | 21 | 247 | 34 | 19 | 0 | 10 | 34 | 15 | 42 | 1 | 0 | .345/.396/.562 | .352 | .391 | -2.5 | -0.7 | 2.9 |
| 2009 | SLM | A+ | 21 | 197 | 18 | 13 | 0 | 4 | 24 | 5 | 22 | 1 | 0 | .257/.278/.390 | .234 | .272 | -1.4 | -0.8 | 0.2 |
| 2010 | SLM | A+ | 22 | 457 | 47 | 34 | 1 | 4 | 61 | 43 | 86 | 1 | 1 | .253/.327/.371 | .252 | .312 | -1.5 | -0.8 | 0.7 |
| 2011 | PME | AA | 23 | 382 | 46 | 20 | 0 | 8 | 52 | 32 | 63 | 1 | 0 | .277/.338/.407 | .245 | .312 | -2.2 | 0.5 | 0.9 |
| 2011 | ABQ | AAA | 23 | 102 | 17 | 7 | 0 | 6 | 17 | 15 | 20 | 0 | 0 | .325/.431/.627 | .300 | .356 | -0.9 | 1.1 | 0.8 |
| 2011 | LAN | MLB | 23 | 16 | 0 | 0 | 0 | 0 | 1 | 2 | 4 | 0 | 0 | .154/.312/.154 | .211 | .222 | -0.1 | 0.1 | 0.0 |
| 2012 | LAN | MLB | 24 | 250 | 25 | 12 | 0 | 4 | 23 | 15 | 51 | 0 | 0 | .235/.285/.345 | .234 | .281 | 0 | C -0 | 0.5 |

Colletti's concern about the system's depth at catcher led him to surrender Trayvon Robinson in a three-way deadline deal for this seventh-round 2008 pick. The consensus was that he overreached, surrendering a top prospect who profiles as an everyday outfielder for a backstop who may be just backup material. Federowicz put a pretty face on the immediate aftermath of the deal because like all carbon-based life forms he hit at high-altitude Albuquerque en route to a brief taste of the majors. Colletti's stated intention to have him share the big-league job with A.J. Ellis in 2012 will provide a truer picture of what the Dodgers have. Federowicz is a catch-and-throw type who gets high marks for his intelligence, game-calling, and receiving ability. Offensively, he has gap power and will take the occasional walk. While not tremendously exciting, he could turn out to be a modest asset if he fulfills his potential.

**Dee Gordon** SS
Born: 4/22/1988 Age: 24
Bats: L Throws: R Height: 6' 0" Weight: 150
Breakout: 2% Improve: 30% Collapse: 7%
Attrition: 31% MLB: 82%
**Comparables:**
Luis Aparicio, Alvaro Espinoza, Jose Vizcaino

| YEAR | TEAM | LVL | AGE | PA | R | 2B | 3B | HR | RBI | BB | SO | SB | CS | AVG_OBP_SLG | TAv | BABIP | BRR | FRAA | WARP |
|------|------|-----|-----|-----|----|----|----|----|----|-----|----|----|----|----|-------------|------|-------|------|------|------|
| 2009 | GRL | A | 21 | 601 | 96 | 17 | 12 | 3 | 35 | 43 | 90 | 73 | 25 | .301/.360/.394 | .282 | .352 | 6.4 | -7.6 | 4.0 |
| 2010 | CHT | AA | 22 | 614 | 86 | 17 | 10 | 2 | 39 | 40 | 89 | 53 | 20 | .277/.329/.355 | .255 | .321 | 3.9 | -8 | 2.0 |
| 2011 | ABQ | AAA | 23 | 313 | 51 | 10 | 6 | 0 | 24 | 18 | 40 | 30 | 4 | .333/.373/.410 | .251 | .382 | 3.3 | 3.5 | 1.8 |
| 2011 | LAN | MLB | 23 | 233 | 34 | 9 | 2 | 0 | 11 | 7 | 27 | 24 | 7 | .304/.325/.362 | .253 | .345 | 3 | -2.4 | 0.9 |
| 2012 | LAN | MLB | 24 | 293 | 29 | 9 | 3 | 1 | 24 | 12 | 51 | 22 | 7 | .261/.297/.326 | .230 | .313 | 0 | SS -2 | 0.5 |

The Dodgers' top offensive prospect coming into 2011, Son of Flash had rocketed up the system in short order since being drafted in 2008. Even so, he didn't figure to see much time in the majors last year given his rawness. When Furcal went down in early June, the Dodgers took a peek at their pint-sized package, and the results were mixed. Gordon hit just .232/.250/.280 during his first four weeks, but he did show off his outstanding defensive range, strong arm, and electrifying speed—stealing second, third and home on one trip around the bases on July 1—before being sent back to Albuquerque. After a second stint was cut short due to a bruised shoulder, he returned in September; driven by an unsustainable .404 BABIP, he hit a sizzling .372/.398/.451 and swiped 12 bags. Gordon's lack of power, patience, and defensive fundamentals rate as concerns, but the Dodgers appear set on opening the 2012 season with him at short.

### Tony Gwynn — CF

Born: 10/4/1982 Age: 29
Bats: L Throws: R Height: 6' 1" Weight: 185
Breakout: 0% Improve: 25% Collapse: 6%
Attrition: 28% MLB: 61%

Comparables:
Whitey Lockman, Coby Smith, Rich Thompson

| YEAR | TEAM | LVL | AGE | PA | R | 2B | 3B | HR | RBI | BB | SO | SB | CS | AVG_OBP_SLG | TAv | BABIP | BRR | FRAA | WARP |
|------|------|-----|-----|-----|----|----|----|----|-----|----|----|----|----|-------------|------|-------|------|-----------|------|
| 2009 | NAS | AAA | 26 | 175 | 34 | 8 | 1 | 1 | 9 | 20 | 21 | 15 | 1 | .309/.385/.395 | .308 | .348 | 4.8 | -0.6 | 1.9 |
| 2009 | SDN | MLB | 26 | 451 | 59 | 11 | 6 | 2 | 21 | 48 | 65 | 11 | 7 | .270/.350/.344 | .259 | .316 | 1.5 | 10.5 | 2.2 |
| 2010 | SDN | MLB | 27 | 339 | 30 | 9 | 3 | 3 | 20 | 41 | 50 | 17 | 4 | .204/.304/.287 | .230 | .236 | 1.2 | -9 | -0.9 |
| 2011 | LAN | MLB | 28 | 340 | 37 | 12 | 6 | 2 | 22 | 23 | 61 | 22 | 6 | .256/.308/.353 | .253 | .311 | 2.9 | 2.2 | 1.1 |
| 2012 | LAN | MLB | 29 | 319 | 31 | 9 | 3 | 1 | 22 | 30 | 54 | 15 | 4 | .236/.310/.299 | .232 | .281 | 0.1 | CF 0, LF 1 | -0.1 |

As half of a center field platoon, this Phony Gwynn is playable so long as you don't have post-season aspirations; he was the definition of a Replacement-Level Killer in San Diego in 2010, so unproductive that he helped suck away a playoff berth. As the Dodgers' most frequent left fielder, he was hardly better. By any other name, he'd have settled somewhere along the fifth outfielder/Quad-A spectrum. He signed a two-year, $2 million deal to avoid arbitration.

### Jerry Hairston — 3B

Born: 5/29/1976 Age: 36
Bats: R Throws: R Height: 5' 11" Weight: 172
Breakout: 0% Improve: 22% Collapse: 13%
Attrition: 30% MLB: 74%

Comparables:
Joe Randa, Buddy Bell, Bill Madlock

| YEAR | TEAM | LVL | AGE | PA | R | 2B | 3B | HR | RBI | BB | SO | SB | CS | AVG_OBP_SLG | TAv | BABIP | BRR | FRAA | WARP |
|------|------|-----|-----|-----|----|----|----|----|-----|----|----|----|----|-------------|------|-------|------|-----------|------|
| 2009 | CIN | MLB | 33 | 340 | 47 | 18 | 1 | 8 | 27 | 21 | 46 | 7 | 3 | .254/.305/.397 | .254 | .273 | 2.2 | -2.7 | 0.6 |
| 2009 | NYA | MLB | 33 | 93 | 15 | 5 | 0 | 2 | 12 | 11 | 8 | 0 | 1 | .237/.352/.382 | .260 | .239 | 0 | 0.7 | 0.4 |
| 2010 | SDN | MLB | 34 | 476 | 53 | 13 | 2 | 10 | 50 | 31 | 54 | 9 | 6 | .244/.299/.353 | .248 | .255 | -0.3 | 1.9 | 1.0 |
| 2011 | MIL | MLB | 35 | 138 | 18 | 10 | 0 | 1 | 7 | 11 | 16 | 1 | 0 | .274/.348/.379 | .255 | .308 | 1.6 | 1.7 | 0.8 |
| 2011 | WAS | MLB | 35 | 238 | 25 | 11 | 1 | 4 | 24 | 22 | 30 | 2 | 2 | .268/.342/.385 | .262 | .296 | 1.2 | -3.1 | 0.4 |
| 2012 | LAN | MLB | 36 | 374 | 39 | 16 | 1 | 6 | 34 | 27 | 51 | 8 | 4 | .242/.306/.351 | .243 | .263 | -0.6 | 3B -3, 2B 0 | 1.0 |

More Two Buck Chuck than fine wine, Hairston nonetheless is getting better with age; his TAv was only .244 through age 31, and it's been .260 since, with 140 of his 146 career games at shortstop coming after age 31 as well. He did a solid job while starting at four different positions apiece for the Nationals and Brewers, with his real value coming as a replacement for the latter's Casey McGehee come October. Hairston BABIP'd his way to a 15-for-39 postseason, helping him net the first multi-year contract of his career, a two-year, $6 million pact. Bank on him being worth more than Juan Uribe at less than half the cost over that timespan.

### Matt Kemp — CF

Born: 9/23/1984 Age: 27
Bats: R Throws: R Height: 6' 3" Weight: 230
Breakout: 3% Improve: 45% Collapse: 4%
Attrition: 14% MLB: 86%

Comparables:
Larry Doby, Keith Miller, Josh Hamilton

| YEAR | TEAM | LVL | AGE | PA | R | 2B | 3B | HR | RBI | BB | SO | SB | CS | AVG_OBP_SLG | TAv | BABIP | BRR | FRAA | WARP |
|------|------|-----|-----|-----|-----|----|----|----|-----|----|-----|----|----|-------------|------|-------|------|-----------|------|
| 2009 | LAN | MLB | 24 | 667 | 97 | 25 | 7 | 26 | 101 | 52 | 139 | 34 | 8 | .297/.352/.490 | .297 | .345 | 2.2 | 6.8 | 5.4 |
| 2010 | LAN | MLB | 25 | 668 | 82 | 25 | 6 | 28 | 89 | 53 | 170 | 19 | 15 | .249/.310/.450 | .279 | .295 | -1.8 | -9 | 1.8 |
| 2011 | LAN | MLB | 26 | 689 | 115 | 33 | 4 | 39 | 126 | 74 | 159 | 40 | 11 | .324/.399/.586 | .355 | .380 | 4.6 | -8.6 | 9.2 |
| 2012 | LAN | MLB | 27 | 643 | 83 | 27 | 4 | 24 | 85 | 51 | 150 | 29 | 10 | .281/.340/.463 | .292 | .338 | -0.7 | CF -3, RF -0 | 4.2 |

Given squabbles with Joe Torre and staff over his failures to hustle, baserunning blunders, and general lack of intensity, no player stood to benefit more from a regime change than Kemp. He turned in an MVP-caliber season, leading the NL in homers and RBI, finishing third in batting average, fourth in on-base percentage, and second in slugging. He also led the league in WARP and runs scored, tied for second in steals, and took out the trash every day without being asked. He took home a Gold Glove, too, though our own defensive system wasn't much of a fan; the Total Zone system was alone in calling him significantly above average. Frank McCourt's major parting gesture was to secure Kemp's future in Dodger blue with an eight-year, $160 million deal, alleviating one pressing concern for the incoming regime.

**Adam Kennedy** 2B
Born: 1/10/1976 Age: 36
Bats: L Throws: R Height: 6' 2" Weight: 180
Breakout: 1% Improve: 23% Collapse: 16%
Attrition: 36% MLB: 67%

**Comparables:**
Cookie Rojas, Damion Easley, Howie Clark

| YEAR | TEAM | LVL | AGE | PA | R | 2B | 3B | HR | RBI | BB | SO | SB | CS | AVG_OBP_SLG | TAv | BABIP | BRR | FRAA | WARP |
|---|---|---|---|---|---|---|---|---|---|---|---|---|---|---|---|---|---|---|---|
| 2009 | DUR | AAA | 33 | 93 | 11 | 4 | 0 | 3 | 9 | 10 | 12 | 2 | 1 | .280/.366/.439 | .277 | .299 | -0.2 | -1.4 | 0.2 |
| 2009 | OAK | MLB | 33 | 586 | 65 | 29 | 1 | 11 | 63 | 45 | 86 | 20 | 6 | .289/.348/.410 | .276 | .326 | 0.7 | -1.4 | 2.8 |
| 2010 | WAS | MLB | 34 | 389 | 43 | 16 | 1 | 3 | 31 | 37 | 44 | 14 | 2 | .249/.327/.327 | .249 | .274 | -2.1 | 1.3 | 0.1 |
| 2011 | SEA | MLB | 35 | 409 | 36 | 23 | 1 | 7 | 38 | 22 | 67 | 8 | 2 | .234/.277/.355 | .232 | .266 | 0.4 | 2.8 | 0.2 |
| 2012 | LAN | MLB | 36 | 380 | 38 | 15 | 1 | 3 | 30 | 27 | 56 | 10 | 3 | .240/.298/.317 | .234 | .276 | 0.2 | 2B -1, 3B -1 | 0.2 |

On the last day of the 2006 season, Adam Kennedy walked into the clubhouse and saw he was batting cleanup. Mike Scioscia occasionally uses that spot in the lineup to reward players (he once let Chone Figgins hit fourth because he reached a stolen base milestone) and it was Kennedy's final game as an Angel. He had never batted cleanup before—not even high school or college—and didn't expect to again. Five years later, coming off a .327 slugging percentage, and one of the least utile utilitymen in the game, something unthinkable happened: Kennedy batted cleanup eight times for the 2011 Mariners, hitting a wretched-but-insignificant .167/.235/.233. More significantly, he hit .190/.218/.285 in the second

advanced quickly through the Dodgers' system, making the jump from rookie ball directly to High-A, then earning a promotion to Double-A by the end of his first year of full-season ball. Lemmerman is a heady, maximum-effort grinder with outstanding fundamentals and solid tools. He has a compact swing, a good approach and gap power. His lack of range at short has scouts convinced his future lies at second base, but he's likely to remain in his current position as he starts 2012 at Chattanooga.

**James Loney** 1B
Born: 5/7/1984 Age: 28
Bats: L Throws: L Height: 6' 4" Weight: 200
Breakout: 1% Improve: 31% Collapse: 3%
Attrition: 18% MLB: 79%

**Comparables:**
Pete O'Brien, Sean Casey, Wally Joyner

| YEAR | TEAM | LVL | AGE | PA | R | 2B | 3B | HR | RBI | BB | SO | SB | CS | AVG_OBP_SLG | TAv | BABIP | BRR | FRAA | WARP |
|---|---|---|---|---|---|---|---|---|---|---|---|---|---|---|---|---|---|---|---|
| 2009 | LAN | MLB | 25 | 651 | 73 | 25 | 2 | 13 | 90 | 70 | 68 | 7 | 3 | .281/.357/.399 | .268 | .299 | -3.1 | -4 | 0.3 |
| 2010 | LAN | MLB | 26 | 648 | 67 | 41 | 2 | 10 | 88 | 52 | 95 | 10 | 5 | .267/.329/.395 | .260 | .302 | 1.5 | -4 | 0.2 |
| 2011 | LAN | MLB | 27 | 582 | 56 | 30 | 1 | 12 | 65 | 42 | 67 | 4 | 0 | .288/.339/.416 | .274 | .309 | -1.4 | 3.1 | 2.0 |
| 2012 | LAN | MLB | 28 | 560 | 65 | 26 | 2 | 10 | 57 | 45 | 76 | 6 | 2 | .271/.331/.389 | .267 | .300 | -0.2 | 1B -2 | 1.2 |

Last December, Colletti demonstrated his fundamental misunderstanding of positional scarcity by nontendering Russell Martin, an above-average catcher, albeit one with injury concerns, because he was unwilling to guarantee $5 million in base salary, yet turning around to pay Loney, a below-average first baseman of alarming durability, nearly the same amount ($4.875 million). Loney, whose production had been declining since 2007, rewarded that bit of genius by helping to bury the Dodgers, hitting a craptastic .256/.301/.325 with four homers in 390 PA through the end of July. Loney, who did surge over the final two months (.357/.416/.608 with eight homers in 192 PA), has always been a streaky hitter who overpromised and underdelivered at the left end of the defensive spectrum. He was tendered another contract this offseason despite an arrest on suspicion of drunk driving stemming from a multi-car accident in November. Loney assured the team no drugs or alcohol were involved.

**Aaron Miles** 2B
Born: 12/15/1976 Age: 35
Bats: B Throws: R Height: 5' 9" Weight: 170
Breakout: 3% Improve: 28% Collapse: 11%
Attrition: 30% MLB: 71%

**Comparables:**
Tommy Helms, Lenny Harris, Cookie Rojas

| YEAR | TEAM | LVL | AGE | PA | R | 2B | 3B | HR | RBI | BB | SO | SB | CS | AVG_OBP_SLG | TAv | BABIP | BRR | FRAA | WARP |
|---|---|---|---|---|---|---|---|---|---|---|---|---|---|---|---|---|---|---|---|
| 2009 | IOW | AAA | 32 | 91 | 8 | 4 | 0 | 0 | 8 | 2 | 14 | 1 | 2 | .253/.267/.299 | .215 | .297 | 0.1 | 0.4 | -0.1 |
| 2009 | CHN | MLB | 32 | 170 | 17 | 7 | 1 | 0 | 5 | 8 | 21 | 3 | 0 | .185/.224/.242 | .161 | .213 | 0.7 | -1.8 | -1.6 |
| 2010 | SFD | AA | 33 | 71 | 11 | 4 | 0 | 0 | 13 | 7 | 8 | 0 | 1 | .279/.352/.344 | .260 | .309 | 0.3 | -1.5 | 0.2 |
| 2010 | SLN | MLB | 33 | 151 | 14 | 5 | 0 | 0 | 9 | 6 | 14 | 0 | 1 | .281/.311/.317 | .237 | .307 | 0.8 | 2.7 | 0.4 |
| 2011 | LAN | MLB | 34 | 490 | 49 | 17 | 3 | 3 | 45 | 25 | 49 | 4 | 3 | .275/.314/.346 | .248 | .300 | -1.1 | -5 | -0.1 |
| 2012 | LAN | MLB | 35 | 401 | 40 | 13 | 1 | 1 | 30 | 20 | 45 | 3 | 2 | .263/.301/.313 | .231 | .290 | -0.5 | 2B -2, 3B -4 | 0.2 |

Spots in the lineup don't get much more dead than when they're occupied by Miles, with whom Mattingly developed an unhealthy obsession amid the slew of injuries to the Dodgers infield. It was bad enough that Miles received more plate appearances than in any season since 2004, worse that more than 40 percent of them were in the lineup's top third, where he hit a crippling .262/.274/.318. Thanks to his below-average glovework, he rated as the eighth-least valuable player to receive at least 450 PA last year, outdone by some sudden collapses (Adam Dunn, Ichiro Suzuki, Casey McGehee, Kelly Johnson), ongoing boondoggles (Alex Rios, Alfonso Soriano), and old friend Ryan Theriot, with whom he essentially swapped places.

### Russell Mitchell    3B

Born: 2/15/1985 Age: 27
Bats: R Throws: R Height: 6' 0" Weight: 205
Breakout: 3% Improve: 38% Collapse: 4%
Attrition: 13% MLB: 75%

Comparables:
Chad Tracy, Andy Marte, Casey McGehee

| YEAR | TEAM | LVL | AGE | PA | R | 2B | 3B | HR | RBI | BB | SO | SB | CS | AVG_OBP_SLG | TAv | BABIP | BRR | FRAA | WARP |
|------|------|-----|-----|-----|----|----|----|----|-----|----|----|----|----|------------------|------|-------|------|-----------|------|
| 2009 | CHT | AA | 24 | 501 | 63 | 30 | 3 | 13 | 63 | 36 | 84 | 4 | 1 | .241/.297/.406 | .253 | .267 | -1.2 | 1 | 0.4 |
| 2010 | ABQ | AAA | 25 | 557 | 97 | 38 | 2 | 23 | 87 | 38 | 78 | 1 | 3 | .315/.365/.535 | .274 | .333 | -1.5 | 2.8 | 2.6 |
| 2010 | LAN | MLB | 25 | 43 | 3 | 0 | 0 | 2 | 4 | 0 | 8 | 0 | 0 | .143/.140/.286 | .150 | .121 | 0.4 | -0.2 | -0.3 |
| 2011 | ABQ | AAA | 26 | 392 | 66 | 22 | 2 | 16 | 69 | 46 | 62 | 1 | 1 | .283/.372/.503 | .279 | .300 | -0.6 | -0.8 | 1.4 |
| 2011 | LAN | MLB | 26 | 58 | 5 | 1 | 0 | 2 | 3 | 7 | 10 | 0 | 0 | .157/.259/.294 | .179 | .154 | 0.1 | 0.9 | -0.3 |
| 2012 | LAN | MLB | 27 | 250 | 27 | 11 | 1 | 8 | 28 | 18 | 50 | 1 | 0 | .235/.294/.393 | .253 | .266 | 0 | 3B 1, 1B -3 | 1.2 |

Once again, this former 15th-round 2003 pick bounced around the infield and outfield corners, showed a massive home/road split at Triple-A, and struggled during his brief stints in the majors. Called up in September, Mitchell caught bullpen sessions with an eye toward further work behind the plate in the Arizona Fall League, though offseason surgery on his left wrist shifted that plan to the Venezuelan Winter League. At the very least, the ability to serve as an emergency catcher could broaden his appeal in a bench role.

### Dioner Navarro    C

Born: 2/9/1984 Age: 28
Bats: B Throws: R Height: 5' 11" Weight: 190
Breakout: 4% Improve: 32% Collapse: 6%
Attrition: 57% MLB: 87%

Comparables:
Bill Heath, Dave Sax, Paul Lo Duca

| YEAR | TEAM | LVL | AGE | PA | R | 2B | 3B | HR | RBI | BB | SO | SB | CS | AVG_OBP_SLG | TAv | BABIP | BRR | FRAA | WARP |
|------|------|-----|-----|-----|----|----|----|----|-----|----|----|----|----|------------------|------|-------|------|-----------|------|
| 2009 | TBA | MLB | 25 | 410 | 38 | 15 | 0 | 8 | 32 | 18 | 51 | 5 | 2 | .218/.261/.322 | .206 | .231 | 0.9 | -2.8 | -0.6 |
| 2010 | DUR | AAA | 26 | 169 | 19 | 9 | 0 | 2 | 21 | 23 | 25 | 3 | 0 | .284/.389/.390 | .289 | .330 | 0.6 | -0.1 | 1.5 |
| 2010 | TBA | MLB | 26 | 142 | 11 | 5 | 0 | 1 | 7 | 12 | 20 | 0 | 1 | .194/.270/.258 | .200 | .223 | -4.9 | 0.7 | -0.6 |
| 2011 | LAN | MLB | 27 | 202 | 13 | 6 | 1 | 5 | 17 | 20 | 35 | 0 | 1 | .193/.276/.324 | .230 | .210 | -1.5 | 0 | 0.1 |
| 2012 | LAN | MLB | 28 | 250 | 26 | 10 | 0 | 4 | 22 | 19 | 36 | 2 | 1 | .235/.300/.342 | .241 | .258 | -0.1 | C -1, 1B -0 | 1.1 |

Elbowed out of town by Russell Martin's emergence in 2006, Navarro returned to LA after both catchers were non-tendered in December 2010, which was rather ironic. Alas, he was unable to recapture his youthful promise. After missing most of April with an oblique injury, he did little to arrest the impression that both his offense and his defense (25 percent caught stealing, below-average pitch framing, and an above-average rate of wild pitches and passed balls) have gone downhill, with a 2009 ulnar nerve injury in his non-throwing elbow one culprit. The Dodgers DFA'd him in late August due to philosophical differences borne more of his work ethic than his radical take on Nietzsche.

### Juan Rivera    LF

Born: 7/3/1978 Age: 33
Bats: R Throws: R Height: 6' 3" Weight: 170
Breakout: 3% Improve: 31% Collapse: 9%
Attrition: 13% MLB: 80%

Comparables:
Shannon Stewart, Eric Byrnes, Jay Payton

| YEAR | TEAM | LVL | AGE | PA | R | 2B | 3B | HR | RBI | BB | SO | SB | CS | AVG_OBP_SLG | TAv | BABIP | BRR | FRAA | WARP |
|------|------|-----|-----|-----|----|----|----|----|-----|----|----|----|----|------------------|------|-------|------|-----------|------|
| 2009 | ANA | MLB | 31 | 572 | 72 | 24 | 1 | 25 | 88 | 36 | 57 | 0 | 1 | .287/.332/.478 | .284 | .281 | -4.2 | -3.7 | 1.7 |
| 2010 | ANA | MLB | 32 | 455 | 53 | 20 | 0 | 15 | 52 | 33 | 58 | 2 | 2 | .252/.312/.409 | .266 | .261 | -1.5 | 4.5 | 1.6 |
| 2011 | LAN | MLB | 33 | 246 | 24 | 12 | 1 | 5 | 46 | 21 | 35 | 2 | 1 | .274/.333/.406 | .281 | .299 | -2 | -0.2 | 0.6 |
| 2011 | TOR | MLB | 33 | 275 | 22 | 11 | 0 | 6 | 28 | 22 | 41 | 3 | 2 | .243/.305/.360 | .235 | .265 | 0.8 | -1.8 | -0.3 |
| 2012 | LAN | MLB | 33 | 476 | 53 | 19 | 0 | 13 | 52 | 31 | 65 | 4 | 3 | .251/.303/.389 | .258 | .266 | -0.5 | LF -1, 1B -1 | 0.8 |

Traded from the Angels to the Blue Jays in the Vernon Wells swap, Rivera flatlined north of the border before being flipped to the Dodgers for a PTBNL or cash—found money as far as Alex Anthopoulos was concerned—during the All-Star break. His performance uptick in Dodger blue was ever so slight, but he basked in the reflected glory of the team's strong second-half showing long enough to convince Colletti that his return was a top priority. Predictably, the GM overpaid, inking Rivera to a $4.5 million one-year deal when comparably aged lefty-mashing fourth outfielders such as Marcus Thames and Reed Johnson earned $1 million or less in 2011.

### Kyle Russell    RF

Born: 6/27/1986 Age: 26
Bats: L Throws: L Height: 6' 6" Weight: 195
Breakout: 1% Improve: 39% Collapse: 3%
Attrition: 20% MLB: 86%

Comparables:
Jose Canseco, Bobby Bonds, Tim Salmon

| YEAR | TEAM | LVL | AGE | PA | R | 2B | 3B | HR | RBI | BB | SO | SB | CS | AVG_OBP_SLG | TAv | BABIP | BRR | FRAA | WARP |
|------|------|-----|-----|-----|----|----|----|----|-----|----|-----|----|----|------------------|------|-------|------|-----------|------|
| 2009 | GRL | A | 23 | 563 | 90 | 39 | 7 | 26 | 102 | 72 | 180 | 20 | 2 | .272/.374/.545 | .320 | .382 | 2.3 | 11.1 | 6.3 |
| 2010 | SBR | A+ | 24 | 239 | 42 | 11 | 4 | 16 | 53 | 32 | 64 | 8 | 3 | .354/.455/.692 | .398 | .458 | 0.4 | 1.8 | 4.0 |
| 2010 | CHT | AA | 24 | 308 | 36 | 23 | 3 | 10 | 28 | 29 | 113 | 3 | 2 | .245/.321/.462 | .269 | .377 | 0 | 0.2 | 1.3 |
| 2011 | CHT | AA | 25 | 447 | 61 | 29 | 4 | 19 | 69 | 45 | 144 | 5 | 1 | .259/.342/.497 | .286 | .356 | 0.7 | 2.9 | 2.6 |
| 2012 | LAN | MLB | 26 | 250 | 27 | 11 | 1 | 9 | 29 | 23 | 91 | 3 | 1 | .214/.289/.401 | .249 | .305 | 0 | RF 0, LF -1 | 0.4 |

Possessing 80 raw power, a long stroke, and a pull-conscious approach, this 2008 third-round pick from the University of Texas has been known as much for his strikeouts as anything. The Texas Wind Machine did make more contact last year—instead of finishing in the minors' top five in K's as he had in 2009 and 2010 he was merely 25th—but he has yet to adjust his approach still swinging for distant planets on 0-2. Additionally Russell continues to show a very pronounced platoon split. An outstanding arm athleticism and ability afield mark Russell as somebody with a big-league future.

**Jerry Sands** LF
Born: 9/28/1987 Age: 24
Bats: R Throws: R Height: 6' 5" Weight: 220
Breakout: 2% Improve: 36% Collapse: 0%
Attrition: 24% MLB: 73%
Comparables:
Ryan Klesko, Daniel Dorn, Al Ferrara

| YEAR | TEAM | LVL | AGE | PA | R | 2B | 3B | HR | RBI | BB | SO | SB | CS | AVG/OBP/SLG | TAv | BABIP | BRR | FRAA | WARP |
|------|------|-----|-----|-----|----|----|----|----|-----|----|----|----|----|-------------|-----|-------|-----|------|------|
| 2009 | GRL | A | 21 | 123 | 22 | 7 | 2 | 5 | 19 | 15 | 32 | 1 | 0 | .260/.361/.510 | .287 | .324 | 0.5 | -0.4 | 0.6 |
| 2009 | OGD | RK | 21 | 185 | 41 | 9 | 2 | 14 | 39 | 22 | 28 | 0 | 1 | .350/.427/.687 | .393 | .355 | 0.9 | 0.9 | 3.3 |
| 2010 | GRL | A | 22 | 287 | 48 | 16 | 3 | 18 | 46 | 40 | 61 | 14 | 2 | .333/.434/.646 | .368 | .384 | 1.6 | 6.5 | 5.0 |
| 2010 | CHT | AA | 22 | 303 | 54 | 12 | 2 | 17 | 47 | 33 | 62 | 4 | 0 | .270/.366/.529 | .304 | .294 | 3.6 | 0.2 | 2.6 |
| 2011 | ABQ | AAA | 23 | 418 | 78 | 21 | 3 | 29 | 88 | 38 | 86 | 3 | 1 | .278/.344/.586 | .266 | .282 | 2.7 | 2.2 | 1.7 |
| 2011 | LAN | MLB | 23 | 227 | 20 | 15 | 0 | 4 | 26 | 25 | 51 | 3 | 3 | .253/.338/.389 | .267 | .319 | 1.5 | 0.4 | 0.9 |

**Justin Sellers** SS
Born: 2/1/1986 Age: 26
Bats: R Throws: R Height: 5' 11" Weight: 160
Breakout: 6% Improve: 36% Collapse: 10%
Attrition: 31% MLB: 88%
Comparables:
John Valentin, Dick McAuliffe, Josh Wilson

| YEAR | TEAM | LVL | AGE | PA | R | 2B | 3B | HR | RBI | BB | SO | SB | CS | AVG/OBP/SLG | TAv | BABIP | BRR | FRAA | WARP |
|------|------|-----|-----|-----|----|----|----|----|-----|----|----|----|----|-------------|-----|-------|-----|-------------|------|
| 2009 | CHT | AA | 23 | 464 | 44 | 27 | 1 | 2 | 33 | 50 | 70 | 10 | 8 | .280/.370/.369 | .257 | .330 | -0.7 | -0.9 | 1.7 |
| 2010 | SBR | A+ | 24 | 109 | 15 | 7 | 0 | 0 | 12 | 9 | 16 | 2 | 0 | .260/.327/.333 | .264 | .309 | -1.3 | -2.6 | 0.2 |
| 2010 | ABQ | AAA | 24 | 344 | 51 | 17 | 1 | 14 | 56 | 40 | 49 | 5 | 3 | .285/.370/.497 | .271 | .293 | 0.9 | 2.7 | 2.2 |
| 2011 | ABQ | AAA | 25 | 322 | 57 | 17 | 2 | 14 | 49 | 41 | 57 | 3 | 3 | .304/.400/.537 | .277 | .335 | 2.5 | -1.9 | 1.6 |
| 2011 | LAN | MLB | 25 | 139 | 20 | 9 | 0 | 1 | 13 | 12 | 21 | 1 | 0 | .203/.283/.301 | .219 | .235 | 2 | -0.4 | 0.1 |
| 2012 | LAN | MLB | 26 | 250 | 28 | 12 | 1 | 5 | 25 | 23 | 47 | 3 | 2 | .243/.321/.376 | .256 | .281 | -0.3 | SS -0, 2B -1 | 1.6 |

A sixth-round 2005 pick by the A's, Sellers didn't look like more than organizational fodder by the time he wound up with the Dodgers by way of the Cubs in the spring of 2009. Augmenting strong defense and good on-base skills with an altitude-induced breakout at Albuquerque in 2010, he wound up on the big club's radar. Upon repeating the feat in 2011, he was called up in mid-August once Dee Gordon went on the disabled list. After filling in at shortstop for three weeks, he shared second base duties in September, but the more exposure he got, the worse he hit, particularly against righties (.172/.250/.269 in 105 PA). He could still carve out a career as a utilityman.

**Alfredo Silverio** CF
Born: 5/6/1987 Age: 25
Bats: R Throws: R Height: 6' 1" Weight: 205
Breakout: 4% Improve: 33% Collapse: 5%
Attrition: 29% MLB: 83%
Comparables:
Juan Encarnacion, Garry Maddox, Darrin Jackson

| YEAR | TEAM | LVL | AGE | PA | R | 2B | 3B | HR | RBI | BB | SO | SB | CS | AVG/OBP/SLG | TAv | BABIP | BRR | FRAA | WARP |
|------|------|-----|-----|-----|----|----|----|----|-----|----|-----|----|----|-------------|-----|-------|------|-------------|------|
| 2009 | GRL | A | 22 | 523 | 75 | 34 | 6 | 13 | 61 | 26 | 104 | 2 | 5 | .284/.322/.457 | .286 | .337 | -2.9 | -2 | 2.3 |
| 2010 | SBR | A+ | 23 | 417 | 66 | 27 | 6 | 12 | 43 | 18 | 63 | 17 | 7 | .292/.322/.486 | .307 | .318 | 0 | 0.3 | 3.2 |
| 2011 | CHT | AA | 24 | 572 | 90 | 42 | 18 | 16 | 85 | 30 | 91 | 11 | 12 | .306/.340/.542 | .297 | .340 | -5.1 | -1.4 | 3.8 |
| 2012 | LAN | MLB | 25 | 250 | 25 | 12 | 3 | 5 | 28 | 7 | 55 | 4 | 2 | .241/.263/.379 | .234 | .288 | -0.5 | CF -4, LF -3 | -0.1 |

This toolsy, athletic Dominican enjoyed a breakout year in Chattanooga, leading the league in triples and total bases while ranking fourth in slugging percentage. He turned heads in the Futures Game with a homer off Drew Pomeranz as well. Silverio's aggressive approach doesn't result in many walks, but he has good pitch-recognition skills and doesn't chase many bad pitches out of the strike zone. With 18 triples, he's obviously got the speed to steal bases, but his sub-50 percent success rate suggests he has much to learn about reading pitchers. Scouts are split on his ability to stick in center.

**Angelo Songco**    **LF**

Born: 9/9/1988 Age: 23
Bats: L Throws: R Height: 6' 1" Weight: 195
Breakout: 5% Improve: 22% Collapse: 4%
Attrition: 10% MLB: 35%

Comparables:
Mark Shorey, Jeremy Synan, Carl Yastrzemski

| YEAR | TEAM | LVL | AGE | PA | R | 2B | 3B | HR | RBI | BB | SO | SB | CS | AVG_OBP_SLG | TAv | BABIP | BRR | FRAA | WARP |
|------|------|-----|-----|-----|-----|-----|-----|-----|-----|-----|-----|-----|-----|----------------|------|-------|------|-----------|------|
| 2009 | GRL | A | 20 | 134 | 8 | 6 | 2 | 1 | 16 | 10 | 28 | 1 | 0 | .150/.226/.258 | .182 | .185 | 0.6 | -2.9 | -1.1 |
| 2009 | OGD | RK | 20 | 158 | 27 | 11 | 1 | 9 | 29 | 10 | 41 | 0 | 1 | .306/.363/.583 | .312 | .372 | 0.6 | -1.1 | 0.8 |
| 2010 | GRL | A | 21 | 570 | 87 | 30 | 6 | 15 | 71 | 51 | 91 | 6 | 1 | .274/.347/.446 | .288 | .308 | 3.9 | -7.4 | 2.5 |
| 2011 | RCU | A+ | 22 | 588 | 110 | 48 | 4 | 29 | 114 | 42 | 121 | 4 | 3 | .313/.367/.581 | .319 | .355 | -0.9 | -7 | 4.1 |
| 2012 | LAN | MLB | 23 | 250 | 25 | 12 | 1 | 7 | 27 | 11 | 63 | 0 | 0 | .222/.260/.367 | .228 | .268 | 0 | LF -13, 1B -1 | -0.7 |

Like many a corner outfielder in the Dodgers system, Songco was a bit old for his level, but he absolutely tore up the California League, leading the circuit in doubles and total bases while ranking second in homers and RBI. As imbalanced as his platoon split was (.337/.398/.623 vs. .255/.292/.478), the latter at least represented a marked power gain from 2010, when he slugged .346 against lefties. Unathletic, slow, and stiff, with an average arm, Songco's defensive limitations have led the Dodgers to decide that his future lies at first base, and he'll have to continue proving himself at upper levels to make it.

**Matt Treanor**    **C**

Born: 3/3/1976 Age: 36
Bats: R Throws: R Height: 6' 3" Weight: 220
Breakout: 1% Improve: 20% Collapse: 6%
Attrition: 35% MLB: 64%

Comparables:
Rick Dempsey, Dave Valle, Johnny Roseboro

| YEAR | TEAM | LVL | AGE | PA | R | 2B | 3B | HR | RBI | BB | SO | SB | CS | AVG_OBP_SLG | TAv | BABIP | BRR | FRAA | WARP |
|------|------|-----|-----|-----|-----|-----|-----|-----|-----|-----|-----|-----|-----|----------------|------|-------|------|------|------|
| 2009 | DET | MLB | 33 | 14 | 0 | 0 | 0 | 0 | 0 | 1 | 4 | 0 | 0 | .000/.071/.000 | .046 | .000 | 0 | 0 | -0.4 |
| 2010 | TEX | MLB | 34 | 272 | 22 | 6 | 1 | 5 | 27 | 22 | 43 | 1 | 2 | .211/.287/.308 | .221 | .233 | -1.8 | -1.2 | -0.1 |
| 2011 | KCA | MLB | 35 | 230 | 24 | 6 | 0 | 3 | 21 | 33 | 49 | 2 | 2 | .226/.351/.306 | .262 | .287 | -2.3 | -1.4 | 0.7 |
| 2011 | TEX | MLB | 35 | 12 | 0 | 0 | 0 | 0 | 0 | 1 | 1 | 4 | 0 | 0 | .000/.083/.000 | .084 | .000 | 0 | 0.1 | -0.2 |
| 2012 | LAN | MLB | 36 | 250 | 24 | 7 | 1 | 3 | 17 | 24 | 51 | 2 | 1 | .221/.310/.296 | .232 | .268 | -0.2 | C -1 | 0.8 |

Despite collecting extra-base hits at a rate around one every three weeks, Treanor drew enough walks to generate positive value with his bat. He threw out 25 percent of would-be base thieves and was about 17 runs below average in pitch framing, according to Mike Fast's study. After the Rangers reacquired him on August 31, he helped their title chances by not appearing in a single postseason game despite being on the roster. The lesson was apparently lost on Ned, who signed Treanor for $1 million to supplement his green catching corps. Expect too much playing time.

**Juan Uribe**    **3B**

Born: 7/22/1979 Age: 32
Bats: R Throws: R Height: 6' 0" Weight: 173
Breakout: 2% Improve: 25% Collapse: 6%
Attrition: 15% MLB: 73%

Comparables:
Andy Phillips, Greg Dobbs, Don LeJohn

| YEAR | TEAM | LVL | AGE | PA | R | 2B | 3B | HR | RBI | BB | SO | SB | CS | AVG_OBP_SLG | TAv | BABIP | BRR | FRAA | WARP |
|------|------|-----|-----|-----|-----|-----|-----|-----|-----|-----|-----|-----|-----|----------------|------|-------|------|-----------|------|
| 2009 | SFN | MLB | 29 | 432 | 50 | 26 | 4 | 16 | 55 | 25 | 82 | 3 | 1 | .289/.329/.495 | .288 | .325 | 1.3 | 1.5 | 3.0 |
| 2010 | SFN | MLB | 30 | 575 | 64 | 24 | 2 | 24 | 85 | 45 | 92 | 1 | 2 | .248/.310/.440 | .263 | .256 | -2.5 | -2.9 | 2.0 |
| 2011 | LAN | MLB | 31 | 295 | 21 | 12 | 0 | 4 | 28 | 17 | 60 | 2 | 0 | .204/.264/.293 | .205 | .245 | 0.5 | -1 | -0.9 |
| 2012 | LAN | MLB | 32 | 334 | 36 | 14 | 1 | 10 | 36 | 21 | 66 | 2 | 1 | .236/.290/.381 | .248 | .267 | -0.3 | 3B 2, SS -2 | 1.4 |

Even coming off two relatively strong seasons, this corpulent hacker looked like a dubious choice as the Dodgers' top free-agent expenditure last winter, but few envisioned that his performance would completely crater. In September, he underwent surgery to repair a sports hernia. His woes did provide dark comedy in the form of Emo Juan Uribe a Tumblr blog featuring pithy depressing assessments of his season (Teammates changed Juan Uribe's walkup song to crickets) set over a photo of him forlornly slumped against the wall in foul territory. He'll cheer up knowing that his salary jumps from $5 million to $8 million for both 2012 and 2013. Dodger fans not so much.

**Scott Van Slyke**    **RF**

Born: 7/24/1986 Age: 25
Bats: R Throws: R Height: 6' 6" Weight: 195
Breakout: 3% Improve: 32% Collapse: 2%
Attrition: 25% MLB: 76%

Comparables:
Leon Wagner, Chase Headley, Daniel Dorn

| YEAR | TEAM | LVL | AGE | PA | R | 2B | 3B | HR | RBI | BB | SO | SB | CS | AVG_OBP_SLG | TAv | BABIP | BRR | FRAA | WARP |
|------|------|-----|-----|-----|-----|-----|-----|-----|-----|-----|-----|-----|-----|----------------|------|-------|------|-----------|------|
| 2009 | SBR | A+ | 22 | 563 | 75 | 42 | 4 | 23 | 100 | 61 | 128 | 10 | 7 | .294/.375/.534 | .331 | .357 | 1.1 | 8 | 5.7 |
| 2010 | SBR | A+ | 23 | 209 | 34 | 12 | 2 | 9 | 35 | 17 | 39 | 3 | 1 | .307/.370/.534 | .314 | .348 | -0.1 | -2 | 1.3 |
| 2010 | CHT | AA | 23 | 241 | 28 | 7 | 3 | 4 | 29 | 18 | 37 | 4 | 2 | .235/.301/.350 | .223 | .266 | -0.8 | 0.5 | -0.4 |
| 2011 | CHT | AA | 24 | 529 | 81 | 45 | 4 | 20 | 92 | 65 | 100 | 6 | 5 | .348/.427/.595 | .343 | .406 | -1.1 | 5.1 | 6.1 |
| 2012 | LAN | MLB | 25 | 250 | 30 | 13 | 1 | 8 | 30 | 22 | 62 | 2 | 1 | .253/.320/.424 | .270 | .312 | -0.3 | RF -1, LF 1 | 1.3 |

The son of former major-league mainstay Andy Van Slyke absolutely tore up the Southern League in 2011, winning the batting title while ranking second in on-base and slugging percentages, earning the organization's Minor League Player of the Year award and making Baseball America's Double-A All-Star team. Caveats about advanced age and repeating a level certainly apply, and scouts are less sold on his tools than those numbers might suggest; he doesn't run well, and his power grades out at average. Still, on a team that has suffered an increasingly expensive and unproductive Loney at first base for half a decade, he may develop into an alternative yet.

# PITCHERS

### Chad Billingsley
Born: **7/29/1984** Age: **27**
Bats: **R** Throws: **R** Height: **6' 1"** Weight: **244**
Breakout: **21%** Improve: **57%** Collapse: **28%**
Attrition: **5%** MLB: **93%**

**Comparables:**
Darren O'Day, Dustin McGowan, Andrew Bailey

| YEAR | TEAM | LVL | AGE | W | L | SV | G | GS | IP | H | HR | BB | SO | EqBB9 | EqSO9 | GB% | BABIP | WHIP | ERA | FIP | FRA | WARP |
|------|------|-----|-----|---|---|----|---|----|----|---|----|----|----|-------|-------|-----|-------|------|-----|-----|-----|------|
| 2009 | LAN | MLB | 24 | 12 | 11 | 0 | 33 | 32 | 196¹ | 173 | 17 | 86 | 179 | 3.9 | 8.2 | 47% | .297 | 1.32 | 4.03 | 3.78 | 4.13 | 2.4 |
| 2010 | LAN | MLB | 25 | 12 | 11 | 0 | 31 | 31 | 191² | 176 | 8 | 69 | 171 | 3.2 | 8.0 | 51% | .304 | 1.28 | 3.57 | 3.10 | 3.55 | 3.0 |
| 2011 | LAN | MLB | 26 | 11 | 11 | 0 | 32 | 32 | 188 | 189 | 14 | 84 | 152 | 4.0 | 7.3 | 47% | .313 | 1.45 | 4.21 | 3.80 | 4.46 | 1.0 |
| *2012* | *LAN* | *MLB* | *27* | *10* | *9* | *0* | *28* | *28* | *169¹* | *145* | *11* | *62* | *141* | *3.3* | *7.5* | *47%* | *.301* | *1.22* | *3.47* | *3.48* | *3.77* | *2.3* |

While Clayton Kershaw was busy winning a Cy Young award, the Dodgers' former future ace took a step backwards with his worst season to date. As his swing-and-miss percentage declined for the second-straight year, his strikeout and walk rates were by far his worst since his rookie season, a problem compounded by a BABIP 17 points above league average. Batters teed off on him with men on base. What stands out in looking at his PITCHf/x data is the increased use of his changeup at the expense of his slider, despite [...]

Jamie Walker, Steve Carlton, Bruce Hurst

for the first time since 2006. While his strikeout and walk rates were impressive, his final numbers weren't much to write home about even with the considerable help of Citi Field. There's enough bad luck on balls in play and fly balls that his Fair Run Average came in well below his ERA, however, suggesting that he can be worth the backloaded two-year, $10 million deal to which the Dodgers signed him.

### Rubby De La Rosa
Born: **3/4/1989** Age: **23**
Bats: **R** Throws: **R** Height: **6' 2"** Weight: **185**
Breakout: **27%** Improve: **62%** Collapse: **20%**
Attrition: **22%** MLB: **93%**

**Comparables:**
Sean Gallagher, Ray Crone, Erv Palica

| YEAR | TEAM | LVL | AGE | W | L | SV | G | GS | IP | H | HR | BB | SO | EqBB9 | EqSO9 | GB% | BABIP | WHIP | ERA | FIP | FRA | WARP |
|------|------|-----|-----|---|---|----|---|----|----|---|----|----|----|-------|-------|-----|-------|------|-----|-----|-----|------|
| 2010 | GRL | A | 21 | 4 | 1 | 6 | 14 | 5 | 59¹ | 42 | 3 | 13 | 46 | 2.6 | 8.3 | 53% | .293 | 1.11 | 3.19 | 3.76 | 4.22 | 0.6 |
| 2010 | CHT | AA | 21 | 3 | 1 | 0 | 8 | 8 | 51 | 23 | 1 | 17 | 19 | 3.7 | 6.9 | 60% | .259 | 1.16 | 1.41 | 4.12 | 4.11 | 0.8 |
| 2011 | CHT | AA | 22 | 2 | 2 | 0 | 8 | 8 | 40 | 30 | 1 | 19 | 52 | 4.3 | 11.7 | 51% | .293 | 1.23 | 2.92 | 2.60 | 3.88 | 0.8 |
| 2011 | LAN | MLB | 22 | 4 | 5 | 0 | 13 | 10 | 60² | 54 | 6 | 31 | 60 | 4.6 | 8.9 | 49% | .310 | 1.40 | 3.71 | 3.83 | 4.81 | 0.1 |
| *2012* | *LAN* | *MLB* | *23* | *3* | *3* | *0* | *12* | *9* | *59¹* | *52* | *5* | *27* | *48* | *4.1* | *7.3* | *48%* | *.299* | *1.34* | *4.05* | *4.05* | *4.41* | *0.3* |

Even after a breakout 2010 campaign, De La Rosa didn't figure into the Dodgers' 2011 plans, but the combination of his dominance at Double-A and injuries to the big club's staff accelerated his timetable. He showed off mid-to-high-90s heat, touching triple digits on occasion, and while his changeup was good, his slider was less effective—a reminder that scouts are split on whether his future lies in the bullpen or the rotation. He underwent Tommy John surgery in early August, a timetable that could limit him to a late-2012 cameo at the big league level.

### Scott Elbert
Born: **8/13/1985** Age: **26**
Bats: **L** Throws: **L** Height: **6' 2"** Weight: **210**
Breakout: **37%** Improve: **60%** Collapse: **23%**
Attrition: **10%** MLB: **90%**

**Comparables:**
Hong-Chih Kuo, Taylor Tankersley, Bob Howry

| YEAR | TEAM | LVL | AGE | W | L | SV | G | GS | IP | H | HR | BB | SO | EqBB9 | EqSO9 | GB% | BABIP | WHIP | ERA | FIP | FRA | WARP |
|------|------|-----|-----|---|---|----|---|----|----|---|----|----|----|-------|-------|-----|-------|------|-----|-----|-----|------|
| 2009 | CHT | AA | 23 | 2 | 3 | 0 | 12 | 11 | 62¹ | 59 | 5 | 30 | 87 | 4.3 | 12.6 | 41% | .365 | 1.43 | 3.90 | 3.04 | 3.67 | 1.4 |
| 2009 | ABQ | AAA | 23 | 2 | 1 | 0 | 8 | 7 | 33² | 34 | 2 | 14 | 38 | 3.7 | 10.1 | 60% | .356 | 1.42 | 3.74 | 3.39 | 4.96 | 0.5 |
| 2009 | LAN | MLB | 23 | 2 | 0 | 0 | 19 | 0 | 19² | 19 | 4 | 7 | 21 | 3.2 | 9.6 | 47% | .300 | 1.32 | 5.03 | 4.63 | 5.07 | 0.0 |
| 2010 | ABQ | AAA | 24 | 1 | 1 | 0 | 9 | 9 | 43¹ | 36 | 2 | 23 | 35 | 7.1 | 9.4 | 49% | .378 | 1.85 | 4.99 | 4.70 | 6.08 | 0.3 |
| 2010 | LAN | MLB | 24 | 0 | 0 | 0 | 1 | 0 | 0² | 1 | 0 | 3 | 0 | 40.5 | 0.0 | % | .333 | 6.00 | 13.50 | 16.61 | 31.21 | -0.2 |
| 2011 | LAN | MLB | 25 | 0 | 1 | 2 | 47 | 0 | 33¹ | 27 | 1 | 14 | 34 | 3.8 | 9.2 | 43% | .292 | 1.23 | 2.43 | 2.69 | 3.56 | 0.4 |
| *2012* | *LAN* | *MLB* | *26* | *2* | *1* | *0* | *24* | *3* | *31²* | *27* | *3* | *15* | *30* | *4.2* | *8.6* | *41%* | *.306* | *1.32* | *3.99* | *3.96* | *4.33* | *0.2* |

High pitch counts and a lack of stamina prevented the Dodgers' 2004 first-round pick from living up to expectations as a starter, but he may have at least found a niche in the majors. After a 2010 that saw him go AWOL in midsummer due to unspecified personal difficulties, Elbert returned to the fold and accepted a future in the bullpen. Recalled from Albuquerque in mid-May, he stuck on the roster for the rest of the season thanks to the development of his slider as a major part of his arsenal and a reliable swing-and-miss pitch.

## Nathan Eovaldi

Born: 2/13/1990 Age: 22
Bats: R Throws: R Height: 6' 4" Weight: 195
Breakout: 20% Improve: 46% Collapse: 20%
Attrition: 12% MLB: 85%

Comparables:
Lloyd Allen, Richard Dotson, Jerome Williams

| YEAR | TEAM | LVL | AGE | W | L | SV | G | GS | IP | H | HR | BB | SO | EqBB9 | EqSO9 | GB% | BABIP | WHIP | ERA | FIP | FRA | WARP |
|------|------|-----|-----|---|---|----|----|----|------|-----|----|----|----|-------|-------|-----|-------|------|------|------|------|------|
| 2009 | GRL | A | 19 | 3 | 5 | 1 | 26 | 16 | 96¹ | 95 | 2 | 43 | 74 | 3.8 | .6.6 | 49% | .313 | 1.41 | 3.27 | 3.88 | 4.23 | 1.3 |
| 2010 | SBR | A+ | 20 | 3 | 5 | 0 | 16 | 14 | 85 | 81 | 3 | 25 | 51 | 3.5 | 6.1 | 48% | .364 | 1.55 | 4.45 | 4.07 | 4.49 | 0.5 |
| 2011 | CHT | AA | 21 | 6 | 5 | 0 | 20 | 19 | 103 | 76 | 3 | 46 | 99 | 4.0 | 8.7 | 52% | .264 | 1.18 | 2.62 | 3.15 | 4.35 | 2.2 |
| 2011 | LAN | MLB | 21 | 1 | 2 | 0 | 10 | 6 | 34² | 28 | 2 | 20 | 23 | 5.2 | 6.0 | 46% | .268 | 1.38 | 3.63 | 4.32 | 4.59 | 0.2 |
| 2012 | LAN | MLB | 22 | 3 | 4 | 0 | 10 | 10 | 55 | 54 | 5 | 28 | 31 | 4.6 | 5.1 | 48% | .302 | 1.49 | 4.88 | 4.79 | 5.30 | -0.2 |

Eovaldi's improved command of his 94-96 mph fastball and the rapid development of a new slider led to the best strikeout rate of his young career, not counting his 10 2/3 innings in rookie ball; just as importantly, he stayed healthy, and by the time he was recalled in early August, he had already thrown more innings than in any of his professional seasons. He delivered three quality starts out of six for the Dodgers, allowing more than two runs just once, before being effectively shut down due to innings concerns. Eovaldi's heavy fastball helps him keep the ball in the park, but he'll need to improve his secondary pitches and trim his walk rate significantly in order to have any staying power.

## Jon Garland

Born: 9/27/1979 Age: 32
Bats: R Throws: R Height: 6' 7" Weight: 205
Breakout: 17% Improve: 46% Collapse: 22%
Attrition: 12% MLB: 83%

Comparables:
Brian Lawrence, Danny Darwin, Steve Gromek

| YEAR | TEAM | LVL | AGE | W | L | SV | G | GS | IP | H | HR | BB | SO | EqBB9 | EqSO9 | GB% | BABIP | WHIP | ERA | FIP | FRA | WARP |
|------|------|-----|-----|---|----|----|----|----|------|-----|----|----|-----|-------|-------|-----|-------|------|------|------|------|------|
| 2009 | LAN | MLB | 29 | 3 | 2 | 0 | 6 | 6 | 36¹ | 37 | 4 | 9 | 26 | 2.2 | 6.4 | 49% | .292 | 1.27 | 2.72 | 3.80 | 3.46 | 0.6 |
| 2009 | ARI | MLB | 29 | 8 | 11 | 0 | 27 | 27 | 167² | 188 | 19 | 52 | 83 | 2.8 | 4.5 | 48% | .302 | 1.43 | 4.29 | 4.58 | 5.44 | 0.4 |
| 2010 | SDN | MLB | 30 | 14 | 12 | 0 | 33 | 33 | 200 | 176 | 20 | 87 | 136 | 3.9 | 6.1 | 53% | .268 | 1.32 | 3.46 | 4.44 | 4.60 | 1.8 |
| 2011 | LAN | MLB | 31 | 1 | 5 | 0 | 9 | 9 | 54 | 55 | 6 | 20 | 28 | 3.3 | 4.7 | 41% | .290 | 1.39 | 4.33 | 4.62 | 4.30 | 0.3 |
| 2012 | LAN | MLB | 32 | 4 | 4 | 0 | 12 | 12 | 70¹ | 69 | 7 | 21 | 35 | 2.7 | 4.5 | 47% | .293 | 1.29 | 4.24 | 4.40 | 4.61 | 0.2 |

The disabled list gets them all in the end. Garland had averaged 205 innings per year in 2002-10, never dropping below 191 2/3 and never hitting the DL in 11 big-league seasons. When bad medical reports regarding his shoulder prevented him from securing a multiyear deal last winter, the Dodgers signed him for a $5 million base salary and hoped for the best, but because Colletti built his 2011 roster atop an ancient Native American burial ground, Garland strained an oblique in March and started the year on the sidelines, missing half of April. He lasted just six weeks on the roster before shoulder inflammation forced him back to the sidelines, and underwent surgery to debride his labrum and rotator cuff in early July, shelving him for the season. Once healthy, he'll look for an incentive-laden deal.

## Garrett Gould

Born: 7/19/1991 Age: 20
Bats: R Throws: R Height: 6' 5" Weight: 190
Breakout: 26% Improve: 44% Collapse: 47%
Attrition: 2% MLB: 72%

Comparables:
Dick Brodowski, Jim Waugh, Bob Miller

| YEAR | TEAM | LVL | AGE | W | L | SV | G | GS | IP | H | HR | BB | SO | EqBB9 | EqSO9 | GB% | BABIP | WHIP | ERA | FIP | FRA | WARP |
|------|------|-----|-----|----|---|----|----|----|------|-----|---|----|-----|-------|-------|-----|-------|------|------|------|------|------|
| 2010 | OGD | RK | 18 | 1 | 4 | 0 | 13 | 13 | 57² | 63 | 4 | 20 | 52 | 3.1 | 8.1 | 51% | .358 | 1.53 | 4.06 | 4.37 | 6.00 | -0.4 |
| 2011 | GRL | A | 19 | 11 | 6 | 0 | 27 | 24 | 123² | 102 | 8 | 37 | 104 | 2.7 | 7.6 | 45% | .263 | 1.12 | 2.40 | 3.46 | 3.67 | 2.2 |
| 2012 | LAN | MLB | 20 | 2 | 3 | 0 | 8 | 8 | 35² | 38 | 4 | 18 | 17 | 4.5 | 4.2 | 45% | .303 | 1.57 | 5.62 | 5.22 | 6.11 | -0.4 |

A second-round 2009 pick from Maize, Kansas, Gould came into the year as a skinny hurler who oozed projection but offered little in the way of present performance, but he made great strides in 2011. Improved arm strength and cleaner mechanics helped him add a few ticks to his sinking fastball, pushing it into the low 90s while maintaining good control. He also showed off an excellent 12-to-6 curveball and an average changeup en route to the second-best ERA in the Midwest League. Having struggled in the hitter-friendly Pioneer League, he'll now face a similar challenge in the hitter-friendly California League, albeit with a much-improved arsenal.

## Javy Guerra

Born: 10/31/1985 Age: 26
Bats: R Throws: R Height: 6' 1" Weight: 205
Breakout: 20% Improve: 70% Collapse: 14%
Attrition: 20% MLB: 92%

Comparables:
Clem Labine, Robinson Tejeda, Darren Dreifort

| YEAR | TEAM | LVL | AGE | W | L | SV | G | GS | IP | H | HR | BB | SO | EqBB9 | EqSO9 | GB% | BABIP | WHIP | ERA | FIP | FRA | WARP |
|------|------|-----|-----|---|---|----|----|----|------|----|---|----|----|-------|-------|-----|-------|------|------|------|------|------|
| 2009 | GRL | A | 23 | 3 | 1 | 16 | 28 | 0 | 41 | 23 | 1 | 15 | 55 | 3.3 | 12.1 | 39% | .250 | 0.93 | 1.54 | 2.42 | 1.56 | 1.7 |
| 2009 | CHT | AA | 23 | 3 | 1 | 0 | 23 | 0 | 28¹ | 32 | 2 | 16 | 29 | 5.1 | 9.2 | 52% | .375 | 1.70 | 4.13 | 3.67 | 4.47 | 0.3 |
| 2010 | CHT | AA | 24 | 2 | 0 | 5 | 28 | 0 | 27 | 16 | 1 | 15 | 13 | 7.3 | 9.0 | 62% | .326 | 1.70 | 2.33 | 4.85 | 5.15 | 0.1 |
| 2011 | LAN | MLB | 25 | 2 | 2 | 21 | 47 | 0 | 46² | 37 | 2 | 18 | 38 | 3.5 | 7.3 | 44% | .267 | 1.18 | 2.31 | 3.27 | 4.63 | 0.2 |
| 2012 | LAN | MLB | 26 | 2 | 1 | 11 | 36 | 0 | 36² | 34 | 3 | 19 | 27 | 4.8 | 6.6 | 43% | .303 | 1.46 | 4.67 | 4.35 | 5.07 | -0.1 |

If you were to have bet on which Dodger organization pitcher would wind up leading the 2011 squad in saves, you'd have gotten odds longer than 1000-1 on Guerra. In his third go-round at Chattanooga, he cleaned up his delivery, enabling higher velocity and more strikes; with the Dodgers bullpen decimated by injuries in mid-May—Broxton, Kuo, Padilla and Hawksworth were on the DL, while Jansen was headed there—Guerra got the call. With his 94 mph fastball/slider combo, he pitched reasonably well amid a nine-week stretch where six Dodgers notched saves, took over as closer just before the All-Star break, and converted his first 10 opportunities and 21 of 23; notably, his strikeout rate rose from 6.1 before the break to 8.2 after. All in all, another data point for the closers are made not born camp. He'll likely enter 2012 in that role which hardly makes him the team's best reliever just the one with the most ninth-inning cookies.

**Matt Guerrier**
Born: 8/2/1978 Age: 33
Bats: R Throws: R Height: 6' 4" Weight: 180
Breakout: 14% Improve: 39% Collapse: 35%
Attrition: 12% MLB: 92%
Comparables:
Lee Gardner, Tim Burke, Ramon Hernandez

| YEAR | TEAM | LVL | AGE | W | L | SV | G | GS | IP | H | HR | BB | SO | EqBB9 | EqSO9 | GB% | BABIP | WHIP | ERA | FIP | FRA | WARP |
|------|------|-----|-----|---|---|----|---|----|-----|-----|----|----|----|-------|-------|-----|-------|------|------|------|------|------|
| 2009 | MIN | MLB | 30 | 5 | 1 | 1 | 79 | 0 | 76¹ | 58 | 10 | 16 | 47 | 1.9 | 5.5 | 44% | .214 | 0.97 | 2.36 | 4.40 | 4.88 | 0.6 |
| 2010 | MIN | MLB | 31 | 5 | 7 | 1 | 74 | 0 | 71 | 56 | 7 | 22 | 42 | 2.8 | 5.3 | 48% | .233 | 1.10 | 3.17 | 4.20 | 5.55 | -0.2 |
| 2011 | LAN | MLB | 32 | 4 | 3 | 1 | 70 | 0 | 66¹ | 59 | 4 | 25 | 50 | 3.4 | 6.8 | 41% | .275 | 1.27 | 4.07 | 3.40 | 4.68 | -0.1 |
| 2012 | LAN | MLB | 33 | 3 | 1 | 2 | 65 | 0 | 62¹ | 53 | 6 | 18 | 41 | 2.6 | 5.9 | 46% | .271 | 1.15 | 3.30 | 4.01 | 3.59 | 0.9 |

Signed to a three-year, $12 million deal at a time when the Dodgers could have better spent the money elsewhere—retaining Russell Martin, say, or sending James Loney on an interstellar voyage—Guerrier turned in a thoroughly unremarkable season. While his strikeout and homer rates were better than his

Comparables:
Jim Bunning, Bob Patterson, Jeff Reardon

| YEAR | TEAM | LVL | AGE | W | L | SV | G | GS | IP | H | HR | BB | SO | EqBB9 | EqSO9 | GB% | BABIP | WHIP | ERA | FIP | FRA | WARP |
|------|------|-----|-----|---|---|----|---|----|-----|-----|----|----|-----|-------|-------|-----|-------|------|------|------|------|------|
| 2012 | LAN | MLB | 34 | 8 | 9 | 0 | 24 | 24 | 139 | 138 | 19 | 37 | 101 | 2.4 | 6.5 | 40% | .305 | 1.26 | 4.34 | 4.33 | 4.72 | 0.3 |

Harang hasn't been the same since his 2008 forearm strain, but he joined a long line of down-on-their-luck veteran starters trying to rebuild value in Petco Park. Despite missing a few starts in June due to an injured right foot, the local product accomplished his mission by taking full advantage of the big ballpark. Batters hit .240/.304/.380 against him in Petco, .317/.374/.504 on the road, a red flag that didn't stop Colletti from signing him to a two-year, $12 million deal—$3 million in 2012, $7 million in 2013—with a vesting option for 2014 that can be bought out for $2 million. The next Dodger GM may as well cut that check as soon as Colletti cleans out his office.

**Blake Hawksworth**
Born: 3/1/1983 Age: 29
Bats: R Throws: R Height: 6' 4" Weight: 195
Breakout: 27% Improve: 57% Collapse: 24%
Attrition: 16% MLB: 86%
Comparables:
Willie Eyre, Rawly Eastwick, Sergio Mitre

| YEAR | TEAM | LVL | AGE | W | L | SV | G | GS | IP | H | HR | BB | SO | EqBB9 | EqSO9 | GB% | BABIP | WHIP | ERA | FIP | FRA | WARP |
|------|------|-----|-----|---|---|----|---|----|-----|-----|----|----|----|-------|-------|-----|-------|------|------|------|------|------|
| 2009 | SLN | MLB | 26 | 4 | 0 | 0 | 30 | 0 | 40 | 29 | 2 | 15 | 20 | 3.4 | 4.5 | 56% | .229 | 1.10 | 2.03 | 3.91 | 4.78 | 0.1 |
| 2010 | SLN | MLB | 27 | 4 | 8 | 0 | 45 | 8 | 90¹ | 113 | 15 | 35 | 61 | 3.5 | 6.1 | 52% | .336 | 1.64 | 4.98 | 5.14 | 5.50 | -0.6 |
| 2011 | LAN | MLB | 28 | 2 | 5 | 0 | 49 | 0 | 53 | 45 | 6 | 17 | 43 | 2.9 | 7.3 | 44% | .258 | 1.17 | 4.08 | 3.81 | 4.53 | 0.1 |
| 2012 | LAN | MLB | 29 | 3 | 2 | 0 | 36 | 4 | 53² | 51 | 6 | 17 | 33 | 2.9 | 5.5 | 47% | .290 | 1.28 | 4.17 | 4.38 | 4.53 | 0.3 |

In Hawksworth, the Dodgers managed to get something for almost nothing, flipping Ryan Theriot shortly before the 2010 nontender deadline and receiving this heat-throwing hurler in return. Used primarily in a low-leverage capacity, he showed much-improved command of his 93-96 mph sinker, curve, and changeup, enabling him to post by far the best strikeout and walk rates of his young career. If he can maintain his health and command, he merits a shot at a larger role.

**Kenley Jansen**
Born: 9/30/1987 Age: 24
Bats: B Throws: R Height: 6' 7" Weight: 220
Breakout: 32% Improve: 49% Collapse: 18%
Attrition: 6% MLB: 96%
Comparables:
Chris Perez, Jonathan Broxton, Francisco Rodriguez

| YEAR | TEAM | LVL | AGE | W | L | SV | G | GS | IP | H | HR | BB | SO | EqBB9 | EqSO9 | GB% | BABIP | WHIP | ERA | FIP | FRA | WARP |
|------|------|-----|-----|---|---|----|----|----|-----|----|----|----|----|-------|-------|-----|-------|------|------|------|------|------|
| 2010 | CHT | AA | 22 | 4 | 0 | 8 | 22 | 0 | 27 | 9 | 0 | 14 | 30 | 5.7 | 16.7 | 28% | .281 | 1.15 | 1.67 | 2.89 | 2.11 | 1.0 |
| 2010 | LAN | MLB | 22 | 1 | 0 | 4 | 25 | 0 | 27 | 12 | 0 | 15 | 41 | 5.0 | 13.7 | 36% | .235 | 1.00 | 0.67 | 1.85 | 2.27 | 0.9 |
| 2011 | LAN | MLB | 23 | 2 | 1 | 5 | 51 | 0 | 53² | 30 | 3 | 26 | 96 | 4.4 | 16.1 | 29% | .297 | 1.04 | 2.85 | 1.71 | 2.36 | 1.4 |
| 2012 | LAN | MLB | 24 | 2 | 1 | 2 | 41 | 0 | 47 | 27 | 3 | 20 | 68 | 3.8 | 13.0 | 37% | .293 | 1.00 | 1.90 | 2.42 | 2.07 | 1.6 |

The converted catcher from Curaçao's first full season in the majors was a rocky one, at least in the early going. Hit for three homers in his first 8 2/3 innings, he carried a hefty 6.43 ERA through late May, when he went on the disabled list with shoulder inflammation. Amid injury miseries, he honed his 92-95 mph cutter into one of the game's best, and posted a 1.20 ERA without allowing a homer over his final 45 innings, with a whopping 83 strikeouts and a 4.1 K/BB ratio. If that's not eye-popping enough, consider that from the point of his first return from the DL to the end of the season, he whiffed 61 of the 120 batters he faced, holding those hitters to a .094/.192/.104 line, and wound up setting a record for the highest K rate for any season with a 50-inning minimum, topping Carlos Marmol's 2010 rate of 16.0.

### Clayton Kershaw

Born: 3/19/1988 Age: 24
Bats: L Throws: L Height: 6' 4" Weight: 220
Breakout: 30% Improve: 58% Collapse: 17%
Attrition: 12% MLB: 97%

Comparables:
Tim Lincecum, Fernando Valenzuela, Rich Harden

| YEAR | TEAM | LVL | AGE | W | L | SV | G | GS | IP | H | HR | BB | SO | EqBB9 | EqSO9 | GB% | BABIP | WHIP | ERA | FIP | FRA | WARP |
|---|---|---|---|---|---|---|---|---|---|---|---|---|---|---|---|---|---|---|---|---|---|---|
| 2009 | LAN | MLB | 21 | 8 | 8 | 0 | 31 | 30 | 171 | 119 | 7 | 91 | 185 | 4.8 | 9.7 | 41% | .276 | 1.23 | 2.79 | 3.04 | 3.46 | 3.5 |
| 2010 | LAN | MLB | 22 | 13 | 10 | 0 | 32 | 32 | 204¹ | 160 | 13 | 81 | 212 | 3.6 | 9.3 | 42% | .279 | 1.18 | 2.91 | 3.15 | 3.38 | 3.6 |
| 2011 | LAN | MLB | 23 | 21 | 5 | 0 | 33 | 33 | 233¹ | 174 | 15 | 54 | 248 | 2.1 | 9.6 | 45% | .274 | 0.98 | 2.28 | 2.44 | 2.90 | 6.0 |
| 2012 | LAN | MLB | 24 | 12 | 9 | 0 | 28 | 28 | 190¹ | 144 | 12 | 68 | 180 | 3.2 | 8.5 | 45% | .285 | 1.11 | 2.71 | 3.20 | 2.95 | 4.5 |

At the ripe old age of 23, Kershaw put it all together, winning not only the Pitchers Triple Crown but the NL Cy Young award. The key—aside from the best offensive support of his career, a modest 4.5 runs per game—was the continued improvement of his slider. According to the PITCHf/x data at Texasleaguers.com, Kershaw's use of the pitch rose from 19.6 percent in 2010 to 24.6 percent in 2011, while the combined percentage of strikes on whiffs and fouls rose from 33.2 percent in 2010 to 40.8 percent in 2011, helping him get ahead of hitters more often and making them chase more pitches out of the zone. While there's certainly reason for the Dodgers to lock him up long term *à la* Matt Kemp, that's the next owner's job given that this past winter marked Kershaw's first year of arbitration eligibility.

### Hong-Chih Kuo

Born: 7/23/1981 Age: 30
Bats: L Throws: L Height: 6' 1" Weight: 200
Breakout: 30% Improve: 62% Collapse: 16%
Attrition: 9% MLB: 96%

Comparables:
George Sherrill, B.J. Ryan, Erik Bedard

| YEAR | TEAM | LVL | AGE | W | L | SV | G | GS | IP | H | HR | BB | SO | EqBB9 | EqSO9 | GB% | BABIP | WHIP | ERA | FIP | FRA | WARP |
|---|---|---|---|---|---|---|---|---|---|---|---|---|---|---|---|---|---|---|---|---|---|---|
| 2009 | LAN | MLB | 27 | 2 | 0 | 0 | 35 | 0 | 30 | 21 | 2 | 13 | 32 | 3.9 | 9.6 | 48% | .264 | 1.13 | 3.00 | 3.29 | 3.50 | 0.5 |
| 2010 | LAN | MLB | 28 | 3 | 2 | 12 | 56 | 0 | 60 | 29 | 1 | 18 | 73 | 2.7 | 10.9 | 38% | .207 | 0.78 | 1.20 | 1.84 | 2.36 | 1.7 |
| 2011 | LAN | MLB | 29 | 1 | 2 | 0 | 40 | 0 | 27 | 24 | 4 | 23 | 36 | 7.7 | 12.0 | 46% | .339 | 1.74 | 9.00 | 5.03 | 5.49 | -0.4 |
| 2012 | LAN | MLB | 30 | 2 | 1 | 2 | 38 | 0 | 34² | 25 | 2 | 12 | 38 | 3.1 | 9.8 | 43% | .287 | 1.07 | 2.59 | 2.80 | 2.81 | 0.8 |

Kuo emerged as one of the game's most dominant lefties from 2008-10, but even then he was unable to avoid the disabled list, serving 114 days over that three-year stretch due to elbow inflammation. Alas, Kuo hit rock bottom in 2011, missing time due to a lower back strain and, more debilitatingly, an anxiety disorder that caused him to lose his feel for his pitches. The results were hardly promising once he returned to the roster in late June; despite striking out 28 hitters in 22 1/3 innings, he walked 17 and yielded four homers en route to an 8.46 ERA through the end of the season. The Dodgers non-tendered him after he underwent his fifth elbow surgery in October. He's a special pitcher when he's healthy; here's hoping he can prove his resilience yet again.

### Hiroki Kuroda

Born: 2/10/1975 Age: 37
Bats: R Throws: R Height: 6' 2" Weight: 210
Breakout: 18% Improve: 38% Collapse: 36%
Attrition: 16% MLB: 88%

Comparables:
Early Wynn, Bob Gibson, LaTroy Hawkins

| YEAR | TEAM | LVL | AGE | W | L | SV | G | GS | IP | H | HR | BB | SO | EqBB9 | EqSO9 | GB% | BABIP | WHIP | ERA | FIP | FRA | WARP |
|---|---|---|---|---|---|---|---|---|---|---|---|---|---|---|---|---|---|---|---|---|---|---|
| 2009 | LAN | MLB | 34 | 8 | 7 | 0 | 21 | 20 | 117¹ | 110 | 12 | 24 | 87 | 1.8 | 6.7 | 53% | .277 | 1.14 | 3.76 | 3.54 | 4.27 | 1.1 |
| 2010 | LAN | MLB | 35 | 11 | 13 | 0 | 31 | 31 | 196¹ | 180 | 15 | 48 | 159 | 2.2 | 7.3 | 53% | .287 | 1.16 | 3.39 | 3.29 | 3.79 | 2.1 |
| 2011 | LAN | MLB | 36 | 13 | 16 | 0 | 32 | 32 | 202 | 196 | 24 | 49 | 161 | 2.2 | 7.2 | 46% | .290 | 1.21 | 3.07 | 3.75 | 3.69 | 2.6 |
| 2012 | LAN | MLB | 37 | 11 | 9 | 0 | 28 | 28 | 174² | 158 | 15 | 38 | 116 | 2.0 | 6.0 | 50% | .288 | 1.12 | 3.24 | 3.65 | 3.52 | 2.9 |

Kuroda put together another strong season, albeit one disguised by the worst run support of his career and featuring a bit of extra bad luck in the home runs per fly ball department. Otherwise, he was essentially the same pitcher he'd been the previous three years, a consistent control artist who misses plenty of bats. He did engender some frustration among the Dodger faithful by refusing to waive his no-trade clause at the July 31 deadline. His explanation serves to remind of the vast cultural differences between Japanese and American ballplayers. I recalled what I was feeling when I decided to re-sign here and pitch for this team this season he told the *LA Times*. Those feelings are important to me and I wanted them to remain important. I wanted to see this through until the end. A free agent as we went to press with a return to Japan a possibility.

### Zach Lee

Born: 9/13/1991 Age: 20
Bats: R Throws: R Height: 6' 5" Weight: 190
Breakout: 32% Improve: 58% Collapse: 33%
Attrition: 2% MLB: 71%

Comparables:
Catfish Hunter, Dick Brodowski, Bob Miller

| YEAR | TEAM | LVL | AGE | W | L | SV | G | GS | IP | H | HR | BB | SO | EqBB9 | EqSO9 | GB% | BABIP | WHIP | ERA | FIP | FRA | WARP |
|---|---|---|---|---|---|---|---|---|---|---|---|---|---|---|---|---|---|---|---|---|---|---|
| 2011 | GRL | A | 19 | 9 | 6 | 0 | 24 | 24 | 109 | 101 | 9 | 32 | 91 | 2.6 | 7.5 | 48% | .281 | 1.22 | 3.47 | 3.84 | 4.73 | 1.0 |
| 2012 | LAN | MLB | 20 | 1 | 2 | 0 | 6 | 6 | 28² | 31 | 4 | 13 | 14 | 4.1 | 4.4 | 45% | .302 | 1.52 | 5.51 | 5.40 | 5.99 | -0.3 |

The Dodgers haven't done much right in the draft over the past few years, but picking Lee 28th in 2010 and prying him away from a commitment to quarterback at LSU with a $5.25 million bonus looks like an excellent move—one that probably wouldn't happen under the new collective bargaining agreement. Focusing on baseball full-time for the first time, Lee made a strong professional debut, showing good command of a four-pitch mix that included an 89-94 mph fastball with natural sink, a solid curveball, and the makings of an above-average cutter and changeup; he also unveiled a new slider that helped him attack lefties. He impressed scouts with his polish and mound presence as well. He still has projection in his frame, so adding more velocity isn't out of the question.

### Ted Lilly

Born: 1/4/1976 Age: **36**
Bats: **L** Throws: **L** Height: **6' 2"** Weight: **180**
Breakout: **20%** Improve: **36%** Collapse: **40%**
Attrition: **3%** MLB: **89%**
Comparables:
Ron Guidry, David Wells, Mike Mussina

| YEAR | TEAM | LVL | AGE | W | L | SV | G | GS | IP | H | HR | BB | SO | EqBB9 | EqSO9 | GB% | BABIP | WHIP | ERA | FIP | FRA | WARP |
|------|------|-----|-----|---|---|----|---|----|----|---|----|----|----|-------|-------|-----|-------|------|-----|-----|-----|------|
| 2009 | CHN | MLB | 33 | 12 | 9 | 0 | 27 | 27 | 177 | 151 | 22 | 36 | 151 | 1.8 | 7.7 | 35% | .265 | 1.06 | 3.10 | 3.61 | 3.97 | 2.8 |
| 2010 | LAN | MLB | 34 | 7 | 4 | 0 | 12 | 12 | 76² | 61 | 13 | 15 | 77 | 1.8 | 9.0 | 33% | .251 | 0.99 | 3.52 | 4.01 | 3.75 | 0.9 |
| 2010 | CHN | MLB | 34 | 3 | 8 | 0 | 18 | 18 | 117 | 104 | 19 | 29 | 89 | 2.2 | 6.8 | 31% | .255 | 1.14 | 3.69 | 4.49 | 4.01 | 2.0 |
| 2011 | LAN | MLB | 35 | 12 | 14 | 0 | 33 | 33 | 192² | 172 | 28 | 51 | 158 | 2.4 | 7.4 | 35% | .266 | 1.16 | 3.97 | 4.18 | 3.74 | 1.8 |
| *2012* | *LAN* | *MLB* | *36* | *10* | *9* | *0* | *27* | *27* | *167* | *144* | *22* | *41* | *125* | *2.2* | *6.7* | *35%* | *.273* | *1.11* | *3.53* | *4.16* | *3.84* | *2.1* |

Born: 6/15/1987 Age: **25**
Bats: **R** Throws: **R** Height: **6' 6"** Weight: **240**
Breakout: **22%** Improve: **52%** Collapse: **11%**
Attrition: **9%** MLB: **93%**
Comparables:
James Shields, Jim Nash, Boof Bonser

| YEAR | TEAM | LVL | AGE | W | L | SV | G | GS | IP | H | HR | BB | SO | EqBB9 | EqSO9 | GB% | BABIP | WHIP | ERA | FIP | FRA | WARP |
|------|------|-----|-----|---|---|----|---|----|----|---|----|----|----|-------|-------|-----|-------|------|-----|-----|-----|------|
| 2009 | ABQ | AAA | 22 | 3 | 0 | 1 | 20 | 3 | 39 | 37 | 3 | 13 | 38 | 2.8 | 8.3 | 46% | .304 | 1.18 | 2.54 | 3.73 | 4.26 | 0.9 |
| 2010 | ABQ | AAA | 23 | 3 | 2 | 0 | 40 | 10 | 95 | 94 | 7 | 24 | 50 | 3.0 | 8.0 | 35% | .422 | 1.84 | 6.54 | 4.91 | 5.34 | 1.5 |
| 2011 | CHT | AA | 24 | 1 | 3 | 17 | 34 | 0 | 42¹ | 30 | 3 | 14 | 54 | 3.0 | 11.5 | 33% | .300 | 1.04 | 2.13 | 2.95 | 3.97 | 0.9 |
| 2011 | LAN | MLB | 24 | 1 | 0 | 0 | 27 | 0 | 29² | 21 | 0 | 10 | 28 | 3.0 | 8.5 | 34% | .284 | 1.04 | 2.73 | 2.32 | 3.31 | 0.4 |
| *2012* | *LAN* | *MLB* | *25* | *2* | *1* | *0* | *23* | *2* | *38* | *36* | *4* | *12* | *30* | *2.8* | *7.0* | *41%* | *.309* | *1.26* | *4.13* | *3.94* | *4.49* | *0.2* |

The Dodgers spent 2010 finding out that this 2008 second-rounder—a closer at Purdue—was a poor fit both for a rotation role and a high-altitude ballpark given his fly-ball nature, so they shrewdly sent Lindblom to the friendlier environs of Chattanooga to start the 2011 season. He dominated there, then impressed in what were primarily low-leverage opportunities in the big club's bullpen, demonstrating good command of a 91-93 mph fastball and slider, and smothering righties at a .153/.200/.194 line in 81 PA; obviously, small-sample caveats apply. He'll be in line for a bigger role in 2012.

### Mike MacDougal

Born: 3/5/1977 Age: **35**
Bats: **B** Throws: **R** Height: **6' 5"** Weight: **195**
Breakout: **26%** Improve: **54%** Collapse: **16%**
Attrition: **12%** MLB: **87%**
Comparables:
J.C. Romero, David Weathers, Hoyt Wilhelm

| YEAR | TEAM | LVL | AGE | W | L | SV | G | GS | IP | H | HR | BB | SO | EqBB9 | EqSO9 | GB% | BABIP | WHIP | ERA | FIP | FRA | WARP |
|------|------|-----|-----|---|---|----|---|----|----|---|----|----|----|-------|-------|-----|-------|------|-----|-----|-----|------|
| 2009 | CHA | MLB | 32 | 0 | 0 | 0 | 5 | 0 | 4¹ | 7 | 0 | 7 | 3 | 14.5 | 6.2 | 53% | .467 | 3.23 | 12.46 | 6.61 | 7.10 | -0.1 |
| 2009 | WAS | MLB | 32 | 1 | 1 | 20 | 52 | 0 | 50 | 45 | 3 | 31 | 31 | 5.6 | 5.6 | 65% | .278 | 1.52 | 3.60 | 4.64 | 5.87 | -0.3 |
| 2010 | SLN | MLB | 33 | 1 | 1 | 0 | 17 | 0 | 18² | 23 | 1 | 12 | 14 | 5.8 | 6.8 | 53% | .349 | 1.88 | 7.23 | 4.39 | 6.99 | -0.5 |
| 2011 | LAN | MLB | 34 | 3 | 1 | 1 | 69 | 0 | 57 | 54 | 3 | 29 | 41 | 4.6 | 6.5 | 64% | .304 | 1.46 | 2.05 | 3.92 | 5.92 | -1.0 |
| *2012* | *LAN* | *MLB* | *35* | *2* | *1* | *0* | *50* | *0* | *47* | *45* | *4* | *25* | *32* | *4.9* | *6.1* | *55%* | *.308* | *1.49* | *4.68* | *4.54* | *5.09* | *-0.2* |

Signed to a $500,000 minor league deal, MacDougal took advantage of a slew of injuries to other relievers, worked his way into medium-leverage duty, and wound up setting a career high for appearances while throwing more innings at the major league level than in any season since 2005, and with a lower walk rate than in any full season since then to boot. His control was typically shaky nonetheless, and while his groundball rate was fifth among pitchers with at least 50 innings, he still allowed more inherited runners to score (17) than all but five NL pitchers; his ERA far outstripped both his FIP and his FRA, suggesting that he'll be hard-pressed to pull off the feat again.

### Ethan Martin

Born: 6/6/1989 Age: **23**
Bats: **R** Throws: **R** Height: **6' 3"** Weight: **195**
Breakout: **17%** Improve: **48%** Collapse: **20%**
Attrition: **21%** MLB: **86%**
Comparables:
Ramon Monzant, Ray Culp, Chris Knapp

| YEAR | TEAM | LVL | AGE | W | L | SV | G | GS | IP | H | HR | BB | SO | EqBB9 | EqSO9 | GB% | BABIP | WHIP | ERA | FIP | FRA | WARP |
|------|------|-----|-----|---|---|----|---|----|----|---|----|----|----|-------|-------|-----|-------|------|-----|-----|-----|------|
| 2009 | GRL | A | 20 | 6 | 8 | 1 | 27 | 19 | 100 | 86 | 4 | 62 | 123 | 5.5 | 10.8 | 41% | .313 | 1.46 | 3.87 | 3.84 | 4.41 | 1.3 |
| 2010 | SBR | A+ | 21 | 9 | 14 | 0 | 25 | 22 | 113¹ | 101 | 9 | 69 | 90 | 6.4 | 8.3 | 43% | .330 | 1.77 | 6.35 | 5.25 | 5.44 | -0.2 |
| 2011 | RCU | A+ | 22 | 4 | 4 | 0 | 16 | 9 | 55 | 65 | 8 | 37 | 61 | 6.1 | 10.0 | 52% | .368 | 1.85 | 7.36 | 5.90 | 6.54 | -0.6 |
| 2011 | CHT | AA | 22 | 5 | 3 | 2 | 21 | 3 | 40¹ | 31 | 3 | 29 | 43 | 6.5 | 9.6 | 41% | .280 | 1.49 | 4.02 | 4.29 | 4.63 | 0.5 |
| *2012* | *LAN* | *MLB* | *23* | *1* | *2* | *0* | *10* | *6* | *35* | *34* | *4* | *24* | *26* | *6.1* | *6.6* | *41%* | *.308* | *1.64* | *5.58* | *5.26* | *6.07* | *-0.4* |

Martin has yet to live up to the promise that made him the first high school hurler chosen in the 2008 draft. Despite flashing electric stuff—a mid-90s fastball that can touch 98 and a big-breaking curve—and striking out more than one batter per inning during his pro career, he has struggled mightily with his mechanics, control, and stamina, leading to a whole lot of big innings. The Dodgers moved him to the bullpen in June, and promoted him to Chattanooga—a tougher level but a more pitcher-friendly environment—a month later. While his strikeout and walk percentages remained virtually unchanged across the transition, he wasn't hit nearly so hard thereafter, and shaved over three runs off his ERA, to the point where it was more in line with his FIP.

### Vicente Padilla

Born: 9/27/1977 Age: 34
Bats: R Throws: R Height: 6' 3'' Weight: 200
Breakout: 26% Improve: 47% Collapse: 36%
Attrition: 13% MLB: 80%

Comparables:
Mark Guthrie, Dave Giusti, Lindy McDaniel

| YEAR | TEAM | LVL | AGE | W | L | SV | G | GS | IP | H | HR | BB | SO | EqBB9 | EqSO9 | GB% | BABIP | WHIP | ERA | FIP | FRA | WARP |
|---|---|---|---|---|---|---|---|---|---|---|---|---|---|---|---|---|---|---|---|---|---|---|
| 2009 | LAN | MLB | 31 | 4 | 0 | 0 | 8 | 7 | 39¹ | 36 | 4 | 12 | 38 | 2.7 | 8.7 | 48% | .314 | 1.22 | 3.20 | 3.36 | 3.97 | 0.7 |
| 2009 | TEX | MLB | 31 | 8 | 6 | 0 | 18 | 18 | 108 | 120 | 12 | 42 | 59 | 3.5 | 4.9 | 49% | .308 | 1.50 | 4.92 | 4.88 | 5.82 | 0.0 |
| 2010 | LAN | MLB | 32 | 6 | 5 | 0 | 16 | 16 | 95 | 79 | 14 | 24 | 84 | 2.3 | 8.0 | 42% | .255 | 1.08 | 4.07 | 4.23 | 4.76 | 0.6 |
| 2011 | LAN | MLB | 33 | 0 | 0 | 3 | 9 | 0 | 8² | 7 | 0 | 5 | 9 | 5.2 | 9.3 | 68% | .318 | 1.38 | 4.15 | 2.65 | 3.96 | 0.1 |
| 2012 | LAN | MLB | 34 | 1 | 2 | 0 | 5 | 5 | 23¹ | 23 | 3 | 8 | 15 | 3.0 | 5.8 | 46% | .299 | 1.31 | 4.43 | 4.62 | 4.81 | 0.1 |

The minimal investment of re-signing Padilla to a $2 million base salary was a risk worth taking given his 2009-10 performance with the Dodgers as well as his injury concerns. Alas, the problems that cost him half of the latter season returned to haunt him in 2011. He underwent surgery to relieve an entrapped radial nerve shortly after pitchers and catchers reported, and lasted just four weeks on the big-league roster before needing a microdiscectomy to alleviate a herniated disc in his neck. Given that he's spent at least four weeks on the shelf in five straight years, his days as a rotation staple are probably over, but if he can recover the 92-93 mph fastball he's shown as a Dodger, he could find work as a reliever.

### Jon Michael Redding

Born: 11/16/1987 Age: 24
Bats: R Throws: R Height: 6' 2'' Weight: 195
Breakout: 16% Improve: 32% Collapse: 16%
Attrition: 12% MLB: 87%

Comparables:
Jeff Samardzija, Geremi Gonzalez, Jim Magnuson

| YEAR | TEAM | LVL | AGE | W | L | SV | G | GS | IP | H | HR | BB | SO | EqBB9 | EqSO9 | GB% | BABIP | WHIP | ERA | FIP | FRA | WARP |
|---|---|---|---|---|---|---|---|---|---|---|---|---|---|---|---|---|---|---|---|---|---|---|
| 2009 | GRL | A | 21 | 16 | 4 | 0 | 26 | 26 | 133 | 154 | 9 | 41 | 97 | 2.6 | 6.5 | 45% | .330 | 1.41 | 4.60 | 4.14 | 5.10 | 0.4 |
| 2010 | SBR | A+ | 22 | 4 | 10 | 0 | 27 | 23 | 144 | 151 | 10 | 48 | 74 | 3.3 | 5.4 | 51% | .350 | 1.60 | 5.56 | 4.99 | 5.26 | -0.5 |
| 2011 | RCU | A+ | 23 | 11 | 7 | 0 | 25 | 24 | 137² | 138 | 9 | 55 | 134 | 3.4 | 8.5 | 50% | .318 | 1.34 | 3.66 | 4.30 | 4.99 | 0.7 |
| 2012 | LAN | MLB | 24 | 2 | 4 | 0 | 9 | 9 | 48¹ | 53 | 5 | 22 | 21 | 4.1 | 4.0 | 45% | .310 | 1.55 | 5.65 | 5.05 | 6.14 | -0.6 |

This 2008 fifth-round pick from Florida Junior College struggled at High-A in 2010, but fared much better while repeating the level in 2011, boosting his strikeout rate considerably and getting much better defensive support. He did miss nearly three weeks in May and June to a suspension for violating team rules. Though Redding had four games in which he struck out nine or more hitters—topping out at 14—he isn't overpowering; he's a junkballer who relies on locating a sinking 88-91 mph fastball, a good slider, and a curve, leaving him little margin for error. He's bound for Chattanooga in 2012, and while his ceiling is probably that of a back-end starter; the world needs those, too.

### Shawn Tolleson

Born: 1/19/1988 Age: 24
Bats: R Throws: R Height: 6' 3'' Weight: 215
Breakout: 29% Improve: 49% Collapse: 23%
Attrition: 10% MLB: 93%

Comparables:
Ed Vande Berg, Joba Chamberlain, Jim York

| YEAR | TEAM | LVL | AGE | W | L | SV | G | GS | IP | H | HR | BB | SO | EqBB9 | EqSO9 | GB% | BABIP | WHIP | ERA | FIP | FRA | WARP |
|---|---|---|---|---|---|---|---|---|---|---|---|---|---|---|---|---|---|---|---|---|---|---|
| 2010 | OGD | RK | 22 | 1 | 1 | 17 | 26 | 0 | 28² | 16 | 1 | 5 | 29 | 1.6 | 12.2 | 63% | .268 | 0.77 | 0.63 | 3.18 | 4.17 | 1.5 |
| 2011 | CHT | AA | 23 | 4 | 2 | 12 | 38 | 0 | 44¹ | 42 | 2 | 12 | 57 | 2.2 | 11.2 | 41% | .360 | 1.20 | 1.62 | 2.26 | 3.81 | 0.8 |
| 2012 | LAN | MLB | 24 | 1 | 0 | 1 | 17 | 0 | 20² | 17 | 2 | 8 | 21 | 3.4 | 9.2 | 48% | .307 | 1.20 | 3.43 | 3.59 | 3.73 | 0.3 |

A Texas contemporary of Clayton Kershaw—the two pitched together on the 2005 USA Junior National Team—Tolleson sat out his first year at Baylor after Tommy John surgery and scared off scouts with his violent delivery. He was drafted in the 30th round in 2010. Since then, he's done nothing but dominate at four different stops, whiffing 13.3 per nine with a 6.3 K/BB ratio and a cumulative 1.01 ERA. Tolleson pounds the strike zone and misses bats with a nasty, major-league caliber cutter that runs 84-88 mph, making his 92-95 mph fastball seem like a reverse changeup. With continued success, he could see time in the Dodgers bullpen in 2012, but now that he's at a more age-appropriate level, the next steps will be the hardest.

**Ramon Troncoso**

Born: 2/16/1983 Age: **29**
Bats: **R** Throws: **R** Height: **6' 3"** Weight: **200**
Breakout: **25%** Improve: **52%** Collapse: **28%**
Attrition: **21%** MLB: **91%**

**Comparables:**
Blaine Boyer, Chad Bradford, Tony Pena

| YEAR | TEAM | LVL | AGE | W | L | SV | G | GS | IP | H | HR | BB | SO | EqBB9 | EqSO9 | GB% | BABIP | WHIP | ERA | FIP | FRA | WARP |
|------|------|-----|-----|---|---|----|----|----|------|----|----|----|----|-------|-------|-----|-------|------|------|------|------|------|
| 2009 | LAN | MLB | 26 | 5 | 4 | 6 | 73 | 0 | 82² | 83 | 3 | 34 | 55 | 3.7 | 6.0 | 57% | .314 | 1.42 | 2.72 | 3.54 | 4.25 | 0.7 |
| 2010 | ABQ | AAA | 27 | 0 | 2 | 1 | 15 | 0 | 22 | 14 | 1 | 5 | 12 | 4.5 | 7.8 | 61% | .302 | 1.55 | 5.73 | 4.24 | 7.40 | 0.0 |
| 2010 | LAN | MLB | 27 | 2 | 3 | 0 | 52 | 0 | 54 | 55 | 7 | 18 | 34 | 3.0 | 5.7 | 54% | .281 | 1.35 | 4.33 | 4.70 | 6.02 | -0.8 |
| 2011 | ABQ | AAA | 28 | 2 | 4 | 0 | 35 | 0 | 57 | 59 | 8 | 26 | 41 | 4.1 | 6.5 | 53% | .313 | 1.49 | 5.05 | 5.54 | 6.86 | -0.2 |
| 2011 | LAN | MLB | 28 | 0 | 0 | 0 | 18 | 0 | 22² | 38 | 5 | 4 | 14 | 1.6 | 5.6 | 53% | .418 | 1.85 | 6.75 | 5.16 | 6.86 | -0.5 |
| 2012 | LAN | MLB | 29 | 2 | 1 | 0 | 34 | 0 | 44¹ | 43 | 4 | 14 | 28 | 2.9 | 5.7 | 57% | .307 | 1.30 | 4.19 | 4.06 | 4.55 | 0.1 |

Though Troncoso can still generate groundballs with some frequency, he's become all too homer-prone, and while one can read that as bad luck on a HR/FB rate that's bound to regress, it's just as apparent that he's serving up more cookies than Mrs. Fields. He's just another fringe reliever at this point.

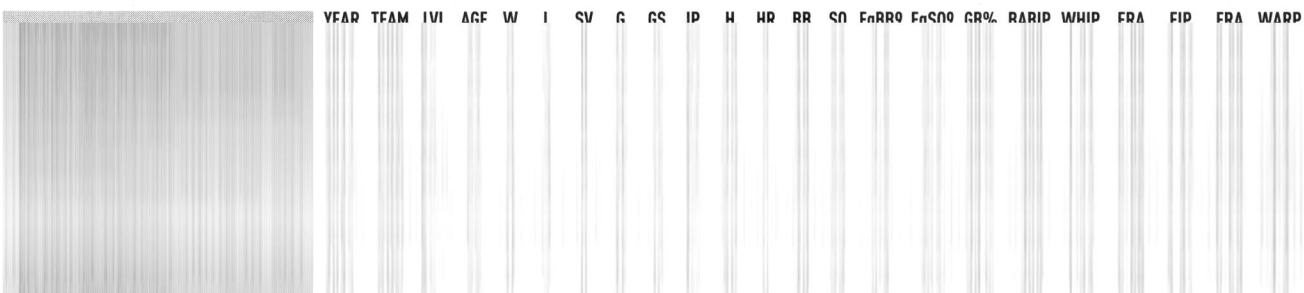

May. He carried a 3.40 Southern League ERA into early August, having climbed to number 48 on Kevin Goldstein's midseason top prospect list, but soon after throwing a 117-pitch shutout, he was clobbered for 20 runs over a three-start, 8 2/3-inning span; his ERA from August 3 onward was 9.47. Webster has an easy delivery and two plus pitches, a sinking low-90s fastball that can touch 95 and create plenty of groundballs, and a deceptive, sinking changeup, but his curveball and slider need work. Bound for a return to Chattanooga, he'll have to expand his arsenal and trim his walk rate to fulfill his potential as a mid-rotation starter.

**Chris Withrow**

Born: 4/1/1989 Age: **23**
Bats: **R** Throws: **R** Height: **6' 4"** Weight: **195**
Breakout: **35%** Improve: **57%** Collapse: **28%**
Attrition: **20%** MLB: **87%**

**Comparables:**
Eric Wilkins, Ken Cloude, Shawn Hillegas

| YEAR | TEAM | LVL | AGE | W | L | SV | G | GS | IP | H | HR | BB | SO | EqBB9 | EqSO9 | GB% | BABIP | WHIP | ERA | FIP | FRA | WARP |
|------|------|-----|-----|---|---|----|----|----|------|-----|----|----|-----|-------|-------|-----|-------|------|------|------|------|------|
| 2009 | SBR | A+ | 20 | 6 | 6 | 0 | 19 | 16 | 86¹ | 80 | 3 | 45 | 105 | 4.7 | 11.0 | 43% | .367 | 1.45 | 4.69 | 3.52 | 3.58 | 1.8 |
| 2009 | CHT | AA | 20 | 2 | 2 | 0 | 6 | 6 | 27¹ | 24 | 2 | 12 | 26 | 4.0 | 8.6 | 40% | .306 | 1.32 | 3.96 | 3.58 | 4.13 | 0.8 |
| 2010 | CHT | AA | 21 | 4 | 9 | 0 | 27 | 27 | 129² | 102 | 8 | 46 | 76 | 4.8 | 8.3 | 42% | .338 | 1.66 | 5.97 | 4.39 | 5.41 | 1.0 |
| 2011 | CHT | AA | 22 | 6 | 6 | 0 | 25 | 25 | 128² | 107 | 8 | 74 | 129 | 5.2 | 9.1 | 46% | .306 | 1.45 | 4.20 | 3.94 | 4.91 | 1.6 |
| 2012 | LAN | MLB | 23 | 2 | 3 | 0 | 8 | 8 | 41 | 39 | 4 | 23 | 32 | 5.0 | 6.9 | 42% | .311 | 1.50 | 5.11 | 4.59 | 5.56 | -0.2 |

A 2007 first-round pick out of a Midland, Texas, high school, Withrow has progressed slowly up the ladder due to injuries and control problems. In his second full season at Double-A, he cut his ERA significantly thanks to better defensive support and a lower home run rate, but his walk rate rose in direct proportion to his strikeout rate. Scouts are still high on Withrow's stuff—a mid-90s fastball that can touch 98 and a curve that has the makings of a plus offering—but he has difficulty repeating his delivery, causing his pitches to flatten out and forcing him into deep counts, where hitters can await his fastball. Not helping matters is that he tends to battle himself out of frustration and tinker mid-game. Some scouts feel as though he could be a force out of the bullpen, but the Dodgers have yet to conclude that's a better path for him.

## LINEOUTS

### HITTERS

| PLAYER | TEAM | LVL | AGE | PA | R | 2B | 3B | HR | RBI | BB | SO | SB-CS | AVG/OBP/SLG | TAv | BABIP | BRR | FRAA | WARP |
|---|---|---|---|---|---|---|---|---|---|---|---|---|---|---|---|---|---|---|
| 3B J. Baisley | SLC | AAA | 28 | 589 | 85 | 31 | 3 | 20 | 100 | 38 | 85 | 5-1 | .303/.355/.483 | .268 | .326 | -1.6 | 11 | 3.4 |
| CF J. Baldwin | OGD | RK | 19 | 227 | 47 | 9 | 3 | 10 | 39 | 18 | 74 | 22-5 | .250/.348/.480 | .264 | .345 | 6.8 | -0.3 | 1.5 |
| C J. Bard | TAC | AAA | 33 | 250 | 28 | 18 | 0 | 2 | 41 | 21 | 39 | 0-0 | .301/.359/.407 | .267 | .355 | -4.8 | -0.8 | 0.8 |
|  | SEA | MLB | 33 | 86 | 5 | 4 | 0 | 2 | 11 | 5 | 20 | 0-0 | .210/.256/.333 | .225 | .254 | -0.4 | -0.5 | 0.0 |
| 3B T. Delmonico | RCU | A+ | 24 | 484 | 66 | 22 | 2 | 12 | 63 | 57 | 99 | 1-2 | .268/.387/.424 | .297 | .324 | -0.9 | -4.9 | 2.3 |
| 1B O. Dickson | OGD | RK | 21 | 215 | 33 | 10 | 1 | 13 | 38 | 19 | 44 | 1-1 | .333/.402/.603 | .318 | .373 | -1.6 | -4.7 | 1.3 |
| RF J. Gibbons | ABQ | AAA | 34 | 310 | 38 | 12 | 1 | 9 | 46 | 44 | 44 | 1-0 | .300/.403/.456 | .277 | .332 | 0.7 | -6.2 | 0.6 |
|  | LAN | MLB | 34 | 62 | 5 | 2 | 0 | 1 | 5 | 5 | 14 | 0-0 | .255/.323/.345 | .259 | .317 | 0.3 | -0.8 | 0.1 |
| CF L. Landry | GRL | A | 21 | 552 | 59 | 21 | 11 | 4 | 41 | 37 | 67 | 28-12 | .250/.307/.360 | .253 | .281 | -2.2 | -7.4 | 0.1 |
| LF T. Oeltjen | ABQ | AAA | 28 | 212 | 33 | 14 | 3 | 8 | 34 | 25 | 50 | 7-4 | .339/.429/.583 | .309 | .431 | -1.1 | 2.7 | 1.2 |
|  | LAN | MLB | 28 | 91 | 10 | 1 | 1 | 2 | 6 | 13 | 30 | 6-0 | .197/.322/.324 | .259 | .293 | 0.3 | -0.1 | 0.2 |
| LF J. Pederson | GRL | A | 19 | 60 | 4 | 0 | 0 | 0 | 1 | 7 | 9 | 2-0 | .160/.288/.160 | .171 | .195 | 0 | 1.7 | -0.2 |
|  | OGD | RK | 19 | 310 | 54 | 20 | 2 | 11 | 64 | 36 | 54 | 24-5 | .353/.429/.568 | .325 | .403 | 0.1 | -5.3 | 2.5 |
| RF B. Smith | RCU | A+ | 23 | 329 | 59 | 24 | 0 | 16 | 63 | 32 | 83 | 3-2 | .294/.359/.539 | .310 | .354 | -1 | 10.4 | 3.4 |

A third baseman who got a cup of coffee in Oakland back in 2008, **Jeff Baisley** hit .400/.432/.718 in April for the Angels' Triple-A Salt Lake affiliate, but it didn't earn him a promotion, and his bat pouted the rest of the way. ⊘ A fourth-round 2010 pick whose father pitched in the majors for 11 seasons, **James Baldwin** is a 6-foot-3, switch-hitting center fielder with speed, power, and a strong arm; even so, he's very raw, with serious issues making contact, particularly against lefties (.183/.300/.367, 33 percent K rate). ⊘ In his twenties, **Josh Bard** hit a useful .275/.341/.415, but since turning 30, he's down at .217/.282/.332. A communications major in college, he might want to consider breaking out the audition tapes for a radio career. ⊘ Hand injuries and a disastrous attempt to convert from the middle infield to catcher have slowed the progress of 2008 sixth-round pick **Tony Delmonico**. He stayed healthy in 2011 and didn't embarrass himself in his move to third base, though he has a ways to go on both sides of the ball. ⊘ A wide-bodied 12th-round pick out of Sonoma State University, **O'Koyea Dickson** enjoyed the strongest pro debut of any of the Dodgers' 2011 picks; a pure hitter with good bat speed, he tore up the Pioneer League, but then that's what 21-year-olds are supposed to do. ⊘ After playing his way back from Mitchell Report/indie league oblivion in 2010, **Jay Gibbons** lost his shot at a share of the left-field job due to a bout of blurred vision in his left eye; he made the most of another summer in Albuquerque, but he'll never get an opportunity that good again. ⊘ Speedy, athletic center fielder **Leon Landry** made a splash in rookie ball but struggled in his full-season debut, though he did rebound in the second half while tying for the Midwest League lead in triples. ⊘ **Trent Oeltjen** lacks pop, but he's learned to take a walk, and isn't a liability afield; his future in this organization may hinge on his ability to pinch-hit, a role in which he's 5-for-31 with five walks. ⊘ **Joc Pederson** barrels up the ball consistently, and while his tools aren't star level, they're at least average across the board. ⊘ A sports hernia cost **Blake Smith** two months of his 2011, but when he played, he cut down his strikeouts significantly.

## PITCHERS

| PLAYER | TEAM | LVL | AGE | W | L | SV | IP | H | HR | BB | SO | EqBB9 | EqSO9 | GB% | BABIP | WHIP | ERA | FIP | FRA | WARP |
|---|---|---|---|---|---|---|---|---|---|---|---|---|---|---|---|---|---|---|---|---|
| S. Ames | CHT | AA | 23 | 2 | 2 | 5 | 32² | 33 | 3 | 11 | 43 | 3.0 | 11.3 | 52% | .353 | 1.32 | 2.48 | 2.87 | 4.36 | 0.5 |
| M. Antonini | CHT | AA | 25 | 10 | 9 | 0 | 148 | 164 | 19 | 42 | 132 | 2.6 | 8.0 | 32% | .315 | 1.39 | 4.01 | 4.22 | 4.42 | 2.5 |
| J. Ascanio | IND | AAA | 26 | 1 | 1 | 1 | 44 | 50 | 2 | 15 | 50 | 3.1 | 10.2 | 43% | .384 | 1.48 | 4.91 | 2.85 | 4.79 | 0.6 |
|  | PIT | MLB | 26 | 0 | 0 | 0 | 6¹ | 10 | 2 | 2 | 5 | 2.8 | 7.1 | 46% | .364 | 1.89 | 7.11 | 6.47 | 6.62 | -0.2 |
| A. Castillo | NOR | AAA | 36 | 0 | 2 | 1 | 33¹ | 24 | 1 | 8 | 26 | 2.2 | 7.0 | 47% | .264 | 0.96 | 1.89 | 3.06 | 4.32 | 0.4 |
|  | ARI | MLB | 36 | 1 | 0 | 0 | 11² | 10 | 0 | 7 | 6 | 5.4 | 4.6 | 44% | .278 | 1.46 | 2.31 | 4.02 | 4.07 | 0.1 |
| J. Ely | ABQ | AAA | 25 | 7 | 8 | 0 | 144¹ | 178 | 21 | 44 | 99 | 2.7 | 6.2 | 47% | .329 | 1.54 | 5.99 | 5.32 | 5.85 | 1.1 |
|  | LAN | MLB | 25 | 0 | 1 | 0 | 12² | 12 | 2 | 7 | 13 | 5.0 | 9.2 | 44% | .294 | 1.50 | 4.26 | 4.65 | 4.72 | -0.1 |
| S. Fife | CHT | AA | 24 | 3 | 0 | 0 | 33² | 44 | 3 | 16 | 29 | 4.0 | 6.7 | 56% | .342 | 1.51 | 4.01 | 4.25 | 5.50 | 0.0 |
|  | PME | AA | 24 | 11 | 4 | 0 | 103¹ | 107 | 7 | 37 | 70 | 3.2 | 6.1 | 50% | .309 | 1.39 | 3.66 | 4.19 | 5.11 | 1.0 |
| A. Sanchez | ORL | A | 21 | 0 | 4 | 0 | 77 | 72 | 5 | 37 | 64 | 3.5 | 7.0 | 50% | .242 | 1.12 | 2.02 | 3.02 | 4.00 | 0.7 |
| J. Wall | CHT | AA | 24 | 4 | 5 | 1 | 68² | 73 | 6 | 28 | 58 | 3.5 | 7.5 | 53% | .324 | 1.44 | 3.93 | 4.10 | 4.74 | 0.8 |

**Steve Ames** has put up eye-popping strikeout rates out of the bullpen at every level as he's risen through the Dodgers system. His stuff isn't as remarkable as the results. ⊘ **Michael Antonini** is not Michelangelo Antonioni, director of *Blow-Up* and *Zabriskie Point*, nor is he Michael Anthony, parachute-pants-wearing bassist for Van Halen. Instead he's a lefty with outstanding command of a high-80s fastball but a significant gopher problem. ⊘ Jose Ascanio has mid-90s heat, but he's been derailed by arm injuries—labrum surgery following the 2009 season, and an elbow strain last spring. He'll keep getting chances somewhere as long as he can throw hard. ⊘ Lefty reliever **Alberto Castillo** pitched well for two Triple-A affiliates, but didn't get a very long look in the majors. Big-league lefties have hit .296/.377/.519 against him in 123 PA over the course of his career, which helps explain why. ⊘ **John Ely** got a long look in 2010, but the magic he showed over his first two months wore off, his mediocre stuff exposed. ⊘ **Stephen Fife** was acquired from the Red Sox in the Trayvon Robinson debacle; alas, there was no drum to be named later. A third-round 2008 pick out of the University of Utah, he projects as a middle reliever, offering good command of an average-velocity fastball with a bit of sink and a solid curveball/change combo. ⊘ Living proof that being left-handed will always earn you another chance, **Wil Ledezma** has compiled a 5.40 ERA in 396 1/3 big-league innings for seven different clubs in 13 years. With just 31 1/3 innings over the past three seasons, it seems teams are catching onto his ruse, though. ⊘ Aussie strikeout king **Shane Lindsay** managed to avoid walking more than a man per inning this year, a feat you can file alongside conquering halitosis on the list of achievements for which there are no congratulatory greeting cards; the Sox were so impressed, they removed him from their 40-man roster, and he signed a minor-league deal with the Dodgers. ⊘ **Aaron Miller** has low-90s velocity with good command, but his secondary stuff is subpar. ⊘ Right-hander **Ariel Pena**, not to be confused with the Angels right-hander with the same name, was part of a touted quartet of Dominicans who came to the States in 2009. Each of the others has stalled in his own way, and Pena struggled in the Dominican Summer League last year. ⊘ Acquired in the Trayvon Robinson deal, **Juan Rodriguez** is a 6-foot-5 Dominican who didn't sign until age 19; among Latin prospects, he lags behind his age group. He can light up a radar gun with his 93-96 mph fastball, but his breaking ball is below average, as is his control. ⊘ Dominican **Angel Sanchez** made an impressive professional debut as a 21-year-old in the Midwest League, showing off a 95-97 mph fastball, curve, and changeup. ⊘ A 6-foot-6 Louisiana native who was chosen in the second round in 2005, **Josh Wall** pushed his fastball into the 96-99 mph range upon moving to the bullpen.

# MANAGER: DON MATTINGLY

| YEAR | TEAM | W-L | Pythag +/– | Avg PC P | 100+ P | 120+ | QS | BQS | REL | REL w Zero R | IBB | Subs | PH | PH Avg | PH HR | SB2 | CS2 | SB3 | CS3 | SAC Att | SAC % | POS SAC | Squeeze | Swing | In Play |
|---|---|---|---|---|---|---|---|---|---|---|---|---|---|---|---|---|---|---|---|---|---|---|---|---|---|
| 2011 | LAN | 82-79 | 1 | 97.8 | 66 | 3 | 94 | 4 | 461 | 369 | 48 | — | 229 | .199 | 4 | 17 | 9 | 1 | 0 | 101 | 80.2% | 46 | 2 | 360 | 118 |

It's easy to find fault with some of the rookie manager's decisions. Tactically, Mattingly fell into too many one-run traps for an offense-challenged ballclub. The Dodgers ranked fourth in the league in positional sacrifice bunts and fifth in hit-and-run plays. They did run the bases well (fifth in EqBRR), a testament to the influence of first-base coach Davey Lopes. Mattingly gave far too many at-bats to the low-wattage likes of Gwynn, Sellers, and Miles in the lineup's top two spots, and too much playing time to the aforementioned when he could have given Ivan DeJesus Jr. a shot. On the other hand, he strung together a reasonably effective bullpen despite the losses of Broxton, Kuo, and Padilla, and nursed outstanding partial seasons out of a host of green rookie pitchers. He kept a poorly designed team 10 games under .500 at the All-Star break invested enough to go 41-28 in the second half despite a sea of empty seats, a growing reaction to the maelstrom of McCourt misery that continuously threatened to overshadow the team. Most teams would have packed it in for a 95-loss season. This one didn't, and the credit for that has to land somewhere.

# Miami Marlins

Two years ago, nobody was asking whether the Marlins would be prepared to contend when their $634 million ballpark opened in 2012 because the club was already on the cusp after winning 87 games and edging Atlanta for second place in the NL East. That 2009 squad featured five players age

slipped into the division cellar. Last year, injuries to the team's top two players, rotation ace Josh Johnson and shortstop Hanley Ramirez, exposed the organization's lack of upper-level depth and overshadowed breakout seasons by right fielder Mike Stanton and starting pitcher Anibal Sanchez.

In mid-September, team president David Samson encouraged fans in South Florida to put their tumultuous two-decade relationship with the Florida Marlins in the past and embrace the new-look Miami Marlins. Samson echoed comments made by Marlins owner Jeffrey Loria that indicated the team was committed to spending what it took to field a winning team in the inaugural season of Marlins Ballpark and the rebranded Miami Marlins.

The organizational facelift began shortly after those comments were made, when Florida acquired disgruntled Chicago White Sox manager Ozzie Guillen. After Sox ownership declined his request for a contract extension, Guillen resigned with two games left in the season and another year remaining on his contract. The Marlins signed Guillen to a new four-year deal worth $16 million shortly after the White Sox accepted his resignation, and they sent shortstop Osvaldo Martinez and hard-throwing reliever Jhan Marinez to Chicago as compensation for Guillen's rights in 2012.

Guillen stabilizes baseball's most volatile managerial post, becoming the fifth man to serve as Marlins skipper since

| | | |
|---|---|---|
| TAv | .250 | 21st |
| TAv-P | .253 | 8th |
| FIP | 3.76 | 9th |
| DER | .708 | 17th |
| DL | 792 | 21st |
| B-Age | 27.4 | 3rd |
| P-Age | 27.9 | 13th |
| Salary | $57.7 | 24th |
| M$/MW | $1.91 | 11th |

**2011:** Blah blah Hanley blah blah last place blah blah, is that new stadium here yet?

**2012:** New stadium, new name, new stars, new expectations, new logo, new results?

**Action Items:** An extra 10,000 people to show up to every game

June 2010 (Table 1). To fully appreciate the degree of turmoil Miami has seen in recent years, consider that "stabilizes" was used in the preceding sentence in reference to Ozzie Guillen.

On December 3, days before the start of the annual Winter Meetings in Dallas, it was reported that the Securities and securities laws were violated when county commissioners, without reviewing the Marlins' financial records, were persuaded to agree to a stadium-funding arrangement that will cost taxpayers an estimated $2.4 billion over 40 years.

Loria brushed aside news of the federal inquiry, insisting that his organization would help the SEC "in any way possible" during its investigation. Days after the subpoenas were issued, Miami began a spending spree that pushed the government's concerns out of the minds of fans and invigorated a community anxious for tangible evidence of ownership's newfound commitment to winning.

### Table 1. Marlins Managers Since 2010

| Manager | First Yr | Last Yr | Games | Win Pct. |
|---|---|---|---|---|
| Jack McKeon | 2011 | 2011 | 90 | .444 |
| Brandon Hyde | 2011 | 2011 | 1 | .000 |
| Edwin Rodriguez | 2010 | 2011 | 163 | .479 |
| Fredi Gonzalez | 2007 | 2010 | 555 | .497 |

In five days, the Marlins handed out $191 million in guaranteed contracts to former Padres closer Heath Bell, ex-Mets shortstop Jose Reyes, and longtime White Sox ace Mark Buehrle. Miami remained the talk of the Winter Meetings for its aggressive, albeit ultimately unsuccessful, pursuit of the top two free agents on the board, first baseman Albert Pujols and starting pitcher C.J. Wilson, before both landed with the Angels on the meetings' final day.

Bell was the first player to sign, and his three-year, $27 million deal marked the largest free-agent commitment the Marlins had made since they signed Carlos Delgado for four years and $52 million in 2005. Reyes was persuaded to defect from the Marlins' division rivals in New York with six years and $106 million plus an option for a seventh year that could bring the contract's total value to $124 million. After a 12-year career spent entirely with the White Sox, Buehrle signed a four-year, $58 million deal to serve as Miami's number-two starter behind Johnson.

Signing Bell solidified the back of a bullpen that was not guaranteed to include Leo Nunez, the Marlins closer since 2009, after he was placed on the restricted list in September, suspected of falsifying his identity. As it turned out, Nunez's real name is Juan Carlos Oviedo and he's a year and a half older than he'd claimed. Given that, as well as his third-year arbitration eligibility, the Marlins' decision to tender Oviedo a contract in December came as a surprise.

But that was nothing compared to the shock of Miami acquiring Reyes, the first bombshell of the offseason, which quickly spawned a plethora of rumors involving the happiness and future whereabouts of the Marlins' incumbent All-Star shortstop, Ramirez.

Ramirez is expected to move from shortstop to third base to accommodate Reyes, though Ramirez was slow to publicly endorse the shift himself and reportedly was not asked about a potential move prior to the Marlins coming to terms with Reyes. Not that the team necessarily owed him an explanation or required his permission to bring Reyes to Miami. Ramirez is still a Marlins employee under contract, but the team's clumsy handling of the situation is a reminder that, no matter how badly it may want to distance itself from the past, leadership in Miami is still the same foot-in-mouth-prone band of miscreants it's been since 2002.

With Reyes taking over at shortstop and Ramirez presumably moving to third, Emilio Bonifacio enters spring training without an everyday role despite posting the Marlins' third-highest WARP (3.1) in 2011. Bonifacio spent time at six different positions last year, and settled in as the team's starter at shortstop while Ramirez missed time with injuries.

Bonifacio will compete with Chris Coghlan, Bryan Petersen, and Scott Cousins for the center field job, but could find himself bouncing around the diamond once again if injuries propagate throughout the lineup as in 2011.

Having Bonifacio around helped to ease the blow of losing Ramirez for extended parts of 2011, including the final two months of the season. Miami had no such luck when Johnson hit the disabled list after just nine starts with right shoulder inflammation, the Marlins having to call upon relief pitchers and unprepared minor leaguers to fill in for their ailing ace (Table 2).

Sean West, who made 20 starts for the Fish in 2009 and two more the following year, should have been the first in line to be called up once injuries hit the big-league rotation, but he never got on track in Triple-A. West lost several weeks in April and May to injuries and maintained an ERA over seven through his first 10 starts. He threw better down the stretch, but wasn't called up when rosters expanded in September.

The addition of Buehrle gives the Marlins some insurance at the top of the rotation in the event Johnson spends more time on the disabled list in 2012. Since 2001, Buehrle has made at least 30 starts and thrown more than 200 innings every single year, his ERA topping four only three times in those 11 seasons.

Buehrle's presence bumps Anibal Sanchez, Ricky Nolasco, and Chris Volstad down a peg each in the rotation. The Marlins' first-round pick in the 2005 draft, Volstad has made 102 major-league starts since 2008 but has yet to establish himself as much more than a slightly above average, back-of-the-rotation starter. For the first time since cracking the big leagues, Volstad enters spring training without a guaranteed spot in the rotation. His competition for the final slot is expected to be Alex Sanabia, who was injured for most of last year but returned for a pair of late-September starts; Wade LeBlanc, who was acquired from San Diego in an offseason trade; and fly ball-happy youngster Brad Hand.

Even before the team's offseason dalliance with free agency, there was reason to believe Miami could see a significant uptick in the win column in 2012. Bouncebacks from Ramirez and Johnson, as well as the continued development of young stars Stanton, Sanchez, and Logan Morrison, could have been enough to keep the Marlins in the wild-card hunt

## Table 2. Pitchers Used With Josh Johnson on the Disabled List

| Pitcher | Qualifications | Results |
| --- | --- | --- |
| Jay Buente | 5 starts in 189 minor-league games prior to 2011 | 0-1, 9.00 ERA, 0 HR 0.33 SO/BB in one start; designated for assignment two days after debut |
| Brian Sanches | 0 starts since 2005 | 0-0, 8.44 ERA, 2 HR, 2.33 SO/BB in two starts |
| Elih Villanueva | 4-5, 5.23 ERA, 16 HR in 13 Triple-A starts | 0-1, 24.00 ERA, 1 HR, 0.40 SO/BB in one start; immediately returned to Triple-A |
| Brad Hand | 1.63 SO/BB in 11 Double-A starts | 1-8, 4.20 ERA, 10 HR, 1.09 SO/BB in 12 starts |
| Clay Hensley | 40 starts from 2005-08, none since 2009 shoulder surgery | 2-4, 6.21 ERA, 7 HR, 1.44 SO/BB in nine starts |

throughout the summer (their ticket into the playoffs in both World Series-winning years). Instead, the Marlins are poised to challenge an injured and aging Phillies squad for NL East supremacy.

Between 1999 and 2011, the Florida Marlins ranked dead last among National League teams in attendance six times, next-to-last six more times, and 14th once. History has trained us to expect a sizable increase in attendance in a team's first year in a new facility, but the Marlins' relationship with the citizens of South Florida introduces a wrinkle for which recent history has no comparable. Ownership's years of lies, manipulation, and talent jettisoning have made it impossible to predict how the community will respond to the Miami Marlins and Marlins Ballpark.

As Yogi Berra might have said, if the people don't want to come to the ballpark, you can't stop them. If people don't come to Marlins Ballpark, it will be said that South Florida can't or won't support major league baseball, an unfair conclusion drawn from unfair circumstances that the victims never had an opportunity to oppose.

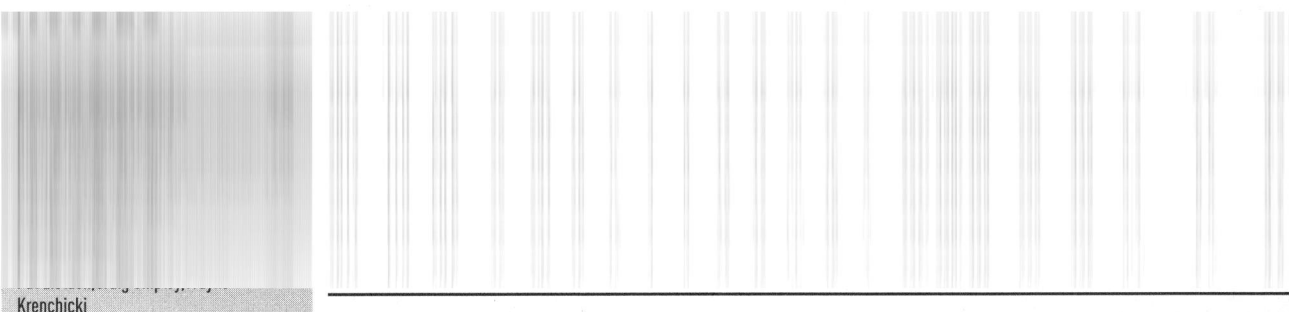

Krenchicki

Not projected as an everyday player entering the year, Bonifacio took advantage of opportunities created by others' injuries and ineffectiveness to collect 641 plate appearances, second behind Gaby Sanchez for the team lead and easily Bonifacio's career high. Though he posted one of the Marlins' worst FRAA totals, the majority of his negative defensive value was earned while playing shortstop, where his level of ineptitude actually marked an upgrade over what Hanley Ramirez offered in between stays on the disabled list. With Ramirez sliding over to third base to make room for Jose Reyes, Bonifacio once again enters the year without a clear path to regular at-bats.

**John Buck**    C
Born: 7/7/1980 Age: 31
Bats: R Throws: R Height: 6' 4'' Weight: 210
Breakout: 0% Improve: 21% Collapse: 27%
Attrition: 42% MLB: 88%

Comparables:
Ozzie Virgil, Matthew Lecroy, Don Pavletich

| YEAR | TEAM | LVL | AGE | PA | R | 2B | 3B | HR | RBI | BB | SO | SB | CS | AVG_OBP_SLG | TAv | BABIP | BRR | FRAA | WARP |
|------|------|-----|-----|-----|----|----|----|----|-----|----|-----|----|----|----------------|------|-------|------|------|------|
| 2009 | KCA | MLB | 29 | 202 | 16 | 12 | 4 | 8 | 36 | 13 | 55 | 1 | 1 | .247/.299/.484 | .262 | .306 | -1.5 | -0.6 | 0.4 |
| 2010 | TOR | MLB | 30 | 437 | 53 | 25 | 0 | 20 | 66 | 16 | 111 | 0 | 0 | .281/.314/.489 | .284 | .335 | 1 | -1.2 | 2.9 |
| 2011 | FLO | MLB | 31 | 530 | 41 | 15 | 1 | 16 | 57 | 54 | 115 | 0 | 1 | .227/.316/.367 | .241 | .268 | -0.3 | -2.1 | 0.9 |
| 2012 | FLO | MLB | 31 | 481 | 54 | 22 | 2 | 16 | 55 | 39 | 120 | 1 | 1 | .234/.306/.404 | .255 | .285 | -0.2 | C -2 | 1.9 |

Buck's signing of a three-year, $18 million contract to serve as the Marlins' starting catcher through 2013 brought stability to a position that had been a revolving door of mediocrity and roster filler since Miguel Olivo departed following the 2007 season. In his first year with the Fish, stability was about the only thing of value that Buck returned. Among major league catchers with at least 400 plate appearances at the position, Buck placed last in WARP, slugging average, and baserunner caught-stealing percentage, and second-to-last in OPS and FRAA. Research that measured the effectiveness of catchers at framing pitches and earning called strikes placed Buck in the bottom 20 percent in terms of runs saved (or, in Buck's case, cost) since 2007. All of that being said, he's reasonably secure as the starter in Miami, with top prospect Kyle Skipworth struggling in his first exposure to Double-A pitching and John Baker, Miami's 2010 starter, having been dealt to San Diego in November.

**Chris Coghlan**    LF
Born: 6/18/1985 Age: 27
Bats: L Throws: R Height: 6' 2'' Weight: 195
Breakout: 6% Improve: 49% Collapse: 3%
Attrition: 20% MLB: 84%

Comparables:
Bubba Bell, Jeff Salazar, Nate McLouth

| YEAR | TEAM | LVL | AGE | PA | R | 2B | 3B | HR | RBI | BB | SO | SB | CS | AVG_OBP_SLG | TAv | BABIP | BRR | FRAA | WARP |
|------|------|-----|-----|-----|----|----|----|----|-----|----|----|----|----|----------------|------|-------|------|----------|------|
| 2009 | NWO | AAA | 24 | 110 | 21 | 9 | 1 | 3 | 22 | 12 | 10 | 9 | 1 | .344/.422/.552 | .345 | .361 | 1.6 | -1.9 | 1.1 |
| 2009 | FLO | MLB | 24 | 565 | 84 | 31 | 6 | 9 | 47 | 53 | 77 | 8 | 5 | .321/.390/.460 | .293 | .365 | 1.4 | -3.8 | 2.9 |
| 2010 | FLO | MLB | 25 | 400 | 60 | 20 | 3 | 5 | 28 | 33 | 84 | 10 | 3 | .268/.335/.383 | .262 | .336 | 4.3 | -2.1 | 1.1 |
| 2011 | NWO | AAA | 26 | 68 | 11 | 4 | 0 | 1 | 7 | 8 | 5 | 3 | 1 | .245/.358/.377 | .253 | .240 | 1.4 | -0.8 | 0.3 |
| 2011 | FLO | MLB | 26 | 298 | 33 | 20 | 1 | 5 | 22 | 22 | 49 | 7 | 6 | .230/.296/.368 | .237 | .263 | -2.3 | 3.2 | 0.2 |
| 2012 | FLO | MLB | 27 | 320 | 38 | 17 | 2 | 5 | 33 | 29 | 56 | 8 | 4 | .273/.345/.400 | .270 | .321 | -0.5 | LF -2, CF -1 | 1.6 |

Injuries, mostly to his left knee, have cost Coghlan more than 120 games over the last two years, but it's what he's shown when healthy that causes concern. Since winning the National League Rookie of the Year award in 2009, Coghlan has hit a combined .252/.317/.376 in 156 games. The time he's lost has allowed Emilio Bonifacio and Bryan Petersen to emerge, and they and Scott Cousins will challenge Coghlan for playing time in 2012.

**Scott Cousins          CF**

Born: 1/22/1985 Age: 27
Bats: L Throws: L Height: 6' 2" Weight: 195
Breakout: 1% Improve: 27% Collapse: 9%
Attrition: 18% MLB: 61%

Comparables:
Michael Tucker, Mike Davis, Don Taussig

| YEAR | TEAM | LVL | AGE | PA | R | 2B | 3B | HR | RBI | BB | SO | SB | CS | AVG_OBP_SLG | TAv | BABIP | BRR | FRAA | WARP |
|------|------|-----|-----|----|----|----|----|----|-----|----|----|----|----|-------------|-----|-------|-----|------|------|
| 2009 | JAX | AA | 24 | 533 | 60 | 31 | 11 | 12 | 74 | 42 | 107 | 27 | 9 | .263/.326/.448 | .287 | .316 | -0.2 | -9.1 | 2.1 |
| 2010 | NWO | AAA | 25 | 451 | 74 | 20 | 5 | 14 | 49 | 32 | 78 | 12 | 4 | .285/.339/.461 | .285 | .323 | -2.8 | -0.9 | 2.1 |
| 2010 | FLO | MLB | 25 | 38 | 2 | 2 | 2 | 0 | 2 | 1 | 13 | 0 | 0 | .297/.316/.459 | .260 | .458 | -0.7 | 0.4 | 0.1 |
| 2011 | FLO | MLB | 26 | 58 | 5 | 1 | 0 | 1 | 4 | 6 | 21 | 1 | 1 | .135/.224/.212 | .181 | .200 | 0 | 0.3 | -0.2 |
| 2012 | FLO | MLB | 27 | 250 | 26 | 10 | 2 | 5 | 25 | 17 | 63 | 7 | 2 | .235/.287/.366 | .236 | .298 | -0.1 | CF -4, RF 1 | 0.1 |

Cousins received national attention for a hard hit at the plate that ended Giants catcher Buster Posey's season in late May. A few weeks later, Cousins himself landed on the disabled list with a bulging disc in his lower back that kept him out for the remainder of the year. When healthy, he has the speed and instincts to handle center field and just enough pop to get by if pushed to a corner.

**Greg Dobbs          3B**

Born: 7/2/1978 Age: 33
Bats: L Throws: R Height: 6' 2" Weight: 200
Breakout: 7% Improve: 32% Collapse: 14%
Attrition: 26% MLB: 84%

Comparables:
Tony Batista, Ken Caminiti, Herbert Perry

| YEAR | TEAM | LVL | AGE | PA | R | 2B | 3B | HR | RBI | BB | SO | SB | CS | AVG_OBP_SLG | TAv | BABIP | BRR | FRAA | WARP |
|------|------|-----|-----|----|----|----|----|----|-----|----|----|----|----|-------------|-----|-------|-----|------|------|
| 2009 | PHI | MLB | 31 | 169 | 15 | 6 | 0 | 5 | 20 | 11 | 29 | 1 | 0 | .247/.296/.383 | .246 | .268 | 0 | 0.5 | 0.1 |
| 2010 | LEH | AAA | 32 | 70 | 10 | 3 | 1 | 2 | 9 | 7 | 12 | 2 | 0 | .210/.290/.387 | .245 | .229 | -0.4 | 0 | 0.1 |
| 2010 | PHI | MLB | 32 | 176 | 13 | 7 | 0 | 5 | 15 | 12 | 39 | 1 | 1 | .196/.251/.331 | .204 | .227 | 0.3 | -3.9 | -0.9 |
| 2011 | FLO | MLB | 33 | 439 | 38 | 23 | 0 | 8 | 49 | 22 | 83 | 0 | 0 | .275/.311/.389 | .247 | .325 | -1.9 | -4.4 | -0.2 |
| 2012 | FLO | MLB | 33 | 368 | 40 | 17 | 1 | 9 | 40 | 24 | 74 | 2 | 0 | .251/.300/.388 | .247 | .294 | 0 | 3B -5, RF -0 | 1.1 |

Dobbs agreed to a minor-league deal with the Marlins just before the start of spring training, but by the second week of the season had emerged as the team's starting third baseman. His minimal contributions at the plate were offset by subpar defense at the hot corner, where he finished with a -4.4 FRAA in 755 innings. Dobbs may have added a few more years to his career, however, with a return to pinch-hitting prowess, batting .370 off the bench after combining for a .146 average in 103 pinch-hit at-bats the previous two years in Philadelphia.

**Matt Dominguez          3B**

Born: 8/28/1989 Age: 22
Bats: R Throws: R Height: 6' 2" Weight: 205
Breakout: 2% Improve: 19% Collapse: 7%
Attrition: 24% MLB: 57%

Comparables:
Lonnie Chisenhall, Taylor Green, Adrian Beltre

| YEAR | TEAM | LVL | AGE | PA | R | 2B | 3B | HR | RBI | BB | SO | SB | CS | AVG_OBP_SLG | TAv | BABIP | BRR | FRAA | WARP |
|------|------|-----|-----|----|----|----|----|----|-----|----|----|----|----|-------------|-----|-------|-----|------|------|
| 2009 | JUP | A+ | 19 | 429 | 49 | 25 | 1 | 11 | 53 | 38 | 68 | 1 | 0 | .262/.337/.420 | .275 | .295 | 0 | 8.4 | 2.5 |
| 2009 | JAX | AA | 19 | 114 | 10 | 7 | 0 | 2 | 9 | 14 | 24 | 0 | 0 | .186/.292/.320 | .220 | .222 | -1.2 | 0.2 | -0.3 |
| 2010 | JAX | AA | 20 | 577 | 61 | 34 | 2 | 14 | 81 | 56 | 96 | 0 | 2 | .252/.337/.411 | .286 | .286 | 0 | 5.7 | 4.2 |
| 2011 | NWO | AAA | 21 | 356 | 47 | 18 | 1 | 12 | 55 | 24 | 50 | 0 | 1 | .258/.312/.431 | .249 | .270 | -2.6 | 6.7 | 1.3 |
| 2011 | FLO | MLB | 21 | 48 | 2 | 4 | 0 | 2 | 2 | 2 | 8 | 0 | 0 | .244/.292/.333 | .203 | .297 | -1.6 | -0.4 | -0.3 |
| 2012 | FLO | MLB | 22 | 250 | 26 | 12 | 1 | 6 | 25 | 18 | 51 | 0 | 0 | .222/.284/.356 | .233 | .258 | 0 | 3B 4, 1B -0 | 0.5 |

There was some talk last winter that the slick-fielding Dominguez could win the Marlins third base job with an impressive showing in spring training, but a .190/.292/.357 performance punched his ticket to New Orleans for more seasoning. Days before the opening of the minor league season, Dominguez's left elbow was fractured when he was hit by a pitch in an exhibition game, delaying his start until mid-May. He remained in Triple-A until the Marlins called him up for the final three weeks of the season, where he started at third base in 13 of the team's final 21 games. It's hard to see where Dominguez made progress with the bat last year, but, as has been the case throughout his pro career, he was significantly younger than the majority of players in his league. The acquisition of Reyes, and subsequent shifting of Hanley Ramirez from shortstop to third base, all but guarantees that Dominguez's future is with another organization.

**Brett Hayes          C**

Born: 2/13/1984 Age: 28
Bats: R Throws: R Height: 6' 2" Weight: 200
Breakout: 5% Improve: 24% Collapse: 15%
Attrition: 47% MLB: 72%

Comparables:
John Boccabella, John Sullivan, Tim Hosley

| YEAR | TEAM | LVL | AGE | PA | R | 2B | 3B | HR | RBI | BB | SO | SB | CS | AVG_OBP_SLG | TAv | BABIP | BRR | FRAA | WARP |
|------|------|-----|-----|----|----|----|----|----|-----|----|----|----|----|-------------|-----|-------|-----|------|------|
| 2009 | NWO | AAA | 25 | 353 | 27 | 15 | 0 | 4 | 37 | 20 | 66 | 2 | 0 | .240/.283/.324 | .216 | .286 | 0 | -0.6 | 0.0 |
| 2009 | FLO | MLB | 25 | 12 | 5 | 1 | 0 | 1 | 2 | 0 | 4 | 0 | 0 | .273/.333/.636 | .315 | .333 | 0.3 | 0 | 0.1 |
| 2010 | NWO | AAA | 26 | 63 | 7 | 3 | 0 | 1 | 5 | 2 | 9 | 0 | 0 | .220/.258/.322 | .209 | .245 | 0.8 | 0.4 | 0.0 |
| 2010 | FLO | MLB | 26 | 83 | 6 | 6 | 1 | 2 | 6 | 6 | 26 | 0 | 0 | .208/.265/.390 | .219 | .286 | -0.8 | 0.4 | 0.0 |
| 2011 | FLO | MLB | 27 | 144 | 19 | 9 | 0 | 5 | 16 | 11 | 39 | 0 | 0 | .231/.291/.415 | .256 | .291 | -0.5 | 0.9 | 0.7 |
| 2012 | FLO | MLB | 28 | 250 | 25 | 12 | 1 | 6 | 25 | 17 | 65 | 0 | 0 | .225/.280/.357 | .229 | .284 | 0 | C 1, 1B -0 | 0.6 |

Hayes and John Buck combined to catch all but three innings of Marlins baseball in 2011, a stark contrast to the year before when six players made at least four appearances behind the dish. Like the majority of second-string backstops, Hayes earns his keep with defense, where he's thrown out 28 percent of runners attempting to steal for his career.

**Omar Infante** 2B
Born: 12/26/1981 Age: 30
Bats: R Throws: R Height: 6' 1" Weight: 150
Breakout: 2% Improve: 30% Collapse: 2%
Attrition: 11% MLB: 79%
Comparables:
Luis Maza, Clint Barmes, Freddy Sanchez

| YEAR | TEAM | LVL | AGE | PA | R | 2B | 3B | HR | RBI | BB | SO | SB | CS | AVG_OBP_SLG | TAv | BABIP | BRR | FRAA | WARP |
|------|------|-----|-----|-----|----|----|----|----|-----|----|----|----|----|-------------|-----|-------|------|------------|------|
| 2009 | ATL | MLB | 27 | 229 | 24 | 9 | 1 | 2 | 27 | 19 | 28 | 2 | 0 | .305/.361/.389 | .269 | .339 | 1 | 0.1 | 0.9 |
| 2010 | ATL | MLB | 28 | 506 | 65 | 15 | 3 | 8 | 47 | 29 | 62 | 7 | 6 | .321/.359/.416 | .270 | .355 | -0.9 | 4.8 | 2.3 |
| 2011 | FLO | MLB | 29 | 640 | 55 | 24 | 8 | 7 | 49 | 34 | 67 | 4 | 2 | .276/.315/.382 | .257 | .298 | -1.7 | 21.6 | 3.8 |
| 2012 | FLO | MLB | 30 | 575 | 66 | 24 | 5 | 6 | 57 | 37 | 75 | 5 | 3 | .286/.333/.384 | .260 | .317 | -0.4 | 2B 11, SS 1 | 1.8 |

The Marlins acquired America's favorite All-Star utility infielder along with lefty reliever Mike Dunn from Atlanta in exchange for second baseman Dan Uggla, with plans to strip Infante of the utility tag and install him as Uggla's replacement at the keystone in 2011. Predictably, Infante was unable to sustain his .355

Breakout: 2% Improve: 39% Collapse: 3%
Attrition: 11% MLB: 77%
Comparables:
Steve Kemp, Zach Daeges, Curt Blefary

| YEAR | TEAM | LVL | AGE | PA | R | 2B | 3B | HR | RBI | BB | SO | SB | CS | AVG_OBP_SLG | TAv | BABIP | BRR | FRAA | WARP |
|------|------|-----|-----|-----|----|----|----|----|-----|----|----|----|----|-------------|-----|-------|------|------------|------|
| 2010 | FLO | MLB | 22 | 287 | 43 | 20 | 7 | 2 | 18 | 41 | 51 | 0 | 1 | .283/.390/.447 | .295 | .351 | 1.8 | -1.9 | 1.9 |
| 2011 | FLO | MLB | 23 | 525 | 54 | 25 | 4 | 23 | 72 | 54 | 99 | 2 | 1 | .247/.330/.468 | .282 | .265 | -2.4 | -2.6 | 1.8 |
| 2012 | FLO | MLB | 24 | 452 | 57 | 23 | 4 | 13 | 53 | 56 | 87 | 3 | 2 | .258/.355/.437 | .287 | .299 | -0.2 | LF -2, 1B -3 | 2.2 |

Morrison responded to pitchers challenging him inside by yanking an uncharacteristic number of balls to right field, increasing his pull percentage by 10 percent at the expense of going the other way. The resulting power spike sent Morrison's trademark plate discipline on hiatus, and after the season he admitted that the aggressive approach wasn't his game. Part of the reason he couldn't get out of his funk was because hitting coach John Mallee, credited by Morrison for rebuilding his swing in the minors, was fired by the Marlins in early June. He was hitting .295/.382/.521 at the time of Mallee's dismissal, but slumped to .225/.304/.443 the rest of the way. Morrison criticized the firing and was subsequently demoted to Triple-A in a controversial move by the club. So which of Morrison's hitting personas will manifest itself in 2012? Marlins Ballpark will feature a very cozy, very tempting 335-foot right field porch that is sure to catch Morrison's attention. On the other hand, the thought of setting off the Las Vegas-inspired home run sculpture in center field could be all the motivation he needs to keep the loft in his swing to an absolute minimum.

**Donnie Murphy** SS
Born: 3/10/1983 Age: 29
Bats: R Throws: R Height: 5' 11" Weight: 180
Breakout: 2% Improve: 24% Collapse: 4%
Attrition: 17% MLB: 69%
Comparables:
Woodie Held, Ed Winceniak, Luis Aguayo

| YEAR | TEAM | LVL | AGE | PA | R | 2B | 3B | HR | RBI | BB | SO | SB | CS | AVG_OBP_SLG | TAv | BABIP | BRR | FRAA | WARP |
|------|------|-----|-----|-----|----|----|----|----|-----|----|----|----|----|-------------|-----|-------|------|------------|------|
| 2010 | NWO | AAA | 27 | 224 | 31 | 12 | 1 | 12 | 35 | 16 | 41 | 0 | 0 | .277/.335/.519 | .301 | .294 | 0.7 | 1.5 | 2.1 |
| 2010 | FLO | MLB | 27 | 47 | 9 | 6 | 1 | 3 | 16 | 2 | 19 | 0 | 0 | .318/.348/.705 | .342 | .500 | 0 | 0.1 | 0.5 |
| 2011 | FLO | MLB | 28 | 100 | 10 | 4 | 1 | 2 | 9 | 4 | 21 | 0 | 0 | .185/.240/.315 | .194 | .214 | 0.6 | 0.6 | -0.2 |
| 2012 | FLO | MLB | 29 | 250 | 28 | 12 | 1 | 9 | 29 | 18 | 70 | 1 | 0 | .225/.290/.402 | .248 | .281 | 0 | SS -1, 3B 1 | 1.1 |

Is it a coincidence that the Marlins were 15-3 in games Murphy participated in before a late-April wrist injury forced him to the disabled list? Probably. The injury cost Murphy four months of the season, but, more interestingly, it brought an end to Edwin Rodriguez's curious practice of regularly penciling Murphy's .103/.186/.128 bat into the lineup.

**Marcell Ozuna** RF
Born: 11/12/1990 Age: 21
Bats: R Throws: R Height: 6' 3" Weight: 190
Breakout: 1% Improve: 18% Collapse: 2%
Attrition: 14% MLB: 40%
Comparables:
Delmon Young, Angel Morales, Ken Henderson

| YEAR | TEAM | LVL | AGE | PA | R | 2B | 3B | HR | RBI | BB | SO | SB | CS | AVG_OBP_SLG | TAv | BABIP | BRR | FRAA | WARP |
|------|------|-----|-----|-----|----|----|----|----|-----|----|----|-----|----|-------------|-----|-------|------|------------|------|
| 2009 | MRL | RK | 18 | 244 | 32 | 22 | 0 | 5 | 39 | 22 | 52 | 4 | 2 | .313/.385/.486 | .333 | .395 | 0.6 | 3.1 | 2.3 |
| 2010 | JAM | A- | 19 | 293 | 53 | 11 | 2 | 21 | 60 | 17 | 94 | 3 | 1 | .267/.317/.556 | .292 | .329 | 1.5 | 5.3 | 2.2 |
| 2011 | GRB | A | 20 | 552 | 87 | 28 | 5 | 23 | 71 | 46 | 121 | 17 | 2 | .266/.330/.482 | .289 | .308 | 3.1 | 16 | 5.0 |
| 2012 | FLO | MLB | 21 | 250 | 25 | 10 | 1 | 8 | 28 | 14 | 72 | 2 | 0 | .219/.262/.374 | .225 | .274 | 0 | RF 3, CF -0 | -0.8 |

In his first real crack at full-season ball, Ozuna showcased five-tool ability and an improved approach at the plate as one of the Sally League's youngest everyday players. After a slow start led to a .663 OPS through the end of June, Ozuna batted .322/.376/.605 the rest of the way, adding nine steals in nine tries for good measure. Defensively, Ozuna's potent arm contributed to five double plays from right field, one shy of the league lead among outfielders. His raw power is already the best among Marlins farmhands, and his lean frame suggests more to come as he matures physically. In other words, no one at the Ozuna family reunion has to worry about confusing him with his cousin, former big-league infielder Pablo Ozuna.

### Bryan Petersen    CF

Born: 4/9/1986 Age: 26
Bats: L Throws: R Height: 6' 1" Weight: 205
Breakout: 3% Improve: 53% Collapse: 9%
Attrition: 30% MLB: 85%

**Comparables:**
Chris Denorfia, Nate McLouth, Jeff Fiorentino

| YEAR | TEAM | LVL | AGE | PA | R | 2B | 3B | HR | RBI | BB | SO | SB | CS | AVG_OBP_SLG | TAv | BABIP | BRR | FRAA | WARP |
|------|------|-----|-----|-----|----|----|----|----|-----|----|----|----|----|-------------|------|-------|------|---------|------|
| 2009 | JAX | AA | 23 | 494 | 64 | 15 | 7 | 7 | 49 | 50 | 66 | 13 | 12 | .297/.375/.413 | .295 | .338 | -1.9 | -7.2 | 2.2 |
| 2010 | NWO | AAA | 24 | 368 | 47 | 13 | 2 | 5 | 27 | 34 | 63 | 5 | 4 | .255/.332/.354 | .253 | .298 | 0.4 | 5.5 | 1.4 |
| 2010 | FLO | MLB | 24 | 25 | 1 | 0 | 0 | 0 | 2 | 1 | 6 | 0 | 0 | .083/.120/.083 | .095 | .111 | 0.2 | 0 | -0.4 |
| 2011 | NWO | AAA | 25 | 286 | 47 | 21 | 0 | 11 | 26 | 36 | 41 | 6 | 5 | .351/.434/.569 | .334 | .386 | 1 | -3.4 | 2.9 |
| 2011 | FLO | MLB | 25 | 241 | 18 | 13 | 3 | 2 | 10 | 26 | 49 | 7 | 1 | .265/.357/.387 | .271 | .333 | -1.3 | -3.1 | 0.9 |
| 2012 | FLO | MLB | 26 | 268 | 30 | 11 | 2 | 4 | 25 | 24 | 54 | 5 | 3 | .251/.324/.363 | .248 | .305 | -0.5 | CF -5, LF -3 | 0.6 |

Petersen received a quarter-season of regular at-bats in center field when injuries put Chris Coghlan and Scott Cousins on the disabled list in June. Playing every day exposed Petersen's lack of range in center, but his below-average bat isn't going to displace Mike Stanton or Logan Morrison in either of the corners any time soon. He's likely a fourth or fifth outfielder on a first-division roster, and he'll face stiff competition for playing time in 2012.

### Hanley Ramirez    SS

Born: 12/23/1983 Age: 28
Bats: R Throws: R Height: 6' 4" Weight: 195
Breakout: 1% Improve: 38% Collapse: 2%
Attrition: 11% MLB: 90%

**Comparables:**
Lee Tate, Nomar Garciaparra, Jim Smith

| YEAR | TEAM | LVL | AGE | PA | R | 2B | 3B | HR | RBI | BB | SO | SB | CS | AVG_OBP_SLG | TAv | BABIP | BRR | FRAA | WARP |
|------|------|-----|-----|-----|-----|----|----|----|-----|----|-----|----|----|-------------|------|-------|------|------|------|
| 2009 | FLO | MLB | 25 | 652 | 101 | 42 | 1 | 24 | 106 | 61 | 101 | 27 | 8 | .342/.410/.543 | .319 | .379 | 2.6 | -9.5 | 5.4 |
| 2010 | FLO | MLB | 26 | 619 | 92 | 28 | 2 | 21 | 76 | 64 | 93 | 32 | 10 | .300/.378/.475 | .298 | .327 | 1.2 | -9.3 | 3.8 |
| 2011 | FLO | MLB | 27 | 385 | 55 | 16 | 0 | 10 | 45 | 44 | 66 | 20 | 10 | .243/.333/.379 | .252 | .275 | 1.2 | -8.6 | 0.5 |
| 2012 | FLO | MLB | 28 | 412 | 58 | 22 | 2 | 15 | 56 | 44 | 70 | 20 | 7 | .302/.382/.494 | .311 | .338 | -0.4 | SS -8 | 4.3 |

Ramirez lost 69 games to various ailments and landed on the disabled list for the first time in his career. After a slow start to the season, he had started to pick things up on offense, hitting .293/.391/.505 in July before injuring his shoulder on a diving play in early August, missing the remainder of the year and undergoing surgery in September. Coupled with his "disappointing" 2010 campaign—fortunate is the player whose .300/.378/.475 performance is considered a disappointment—2011 can be seen as evidence that Ramirez's career is on the downturn. But consider that two of the more offense-minded shortstops of the last 30 years—Cal Ripken and Miguel Tejada— posted the worst WARP of their peak years at age 26 or 27 before earning MVP honors shortly thereafter. Aside from injury, there's no reason Ramirez can't follow in the footsteps of those two, rebounding from his recent slide to enjoy several wildly productive years for the remainder of his peak. The addition of Reyes means that Ramirez will shift from shortstop to third base in 2012, where his quickness and instincts should enable him to be an above-average defender.

### Jacob Realmuto    C

Born: 3/18/1991 Age: 21
Bats: R Throws: R Height: 6' 2" Weight: 190
Breakout: 1% Improve: 6% Collapse: 4%
Attrition: 8% MLB: 13%

**Comparables:**
Wilson Ramos, Chad Tracy, Juan Apodaca

| YEAR | TEAM | LVL | AGE | PA | R | 2B | 3B | HR | RBI | BB | SO | SB | CS | AVG_OBP_SLG | TAv | BABIP | BRR | FRAA | WARP |
|------|------|-----|-----|-----|----|----|----|----|-----|----|----|----|----|-------------|------|-------|------|---------|------|
| 2011 | GRB | A | 20 | 381 | 46 | 16 | 3 | 12 | 49 | 26 | 78 | 13 | 6 | .287/.347/.454 | .267 | .341 | 0.5 | 0.7 | 2.5 |
| 2012 | FLO | MLB | 21 | 250 | 23 | 9 | 1 | 5 | 24 | 11 | 67 | 3 | 1 | .213/.251/.329 | .208 | .270 | -0.2 | C -0, 3B 0 | -0.7 |

Considering he'd started the transition from high school shortstop to professional catcher less than eight months earlier, Realmuto's assignment to full-season Greensboro last April understandably raised a few eyebrows. Base coaches in the Sally League didn't miss the memo, sending their runners 100 times in Realmuto's 76 games behind the dish, but they may have skipped the postscript that mentioned his strong, accurate arm, which enabled him to gun down 42 percent of would-be thieves. Realmuto's bat heated up in the second half, as he slugged all 12 of his home runs, including one off of a rehabbing Stephen Strasburg, from July on.

### Jose Reyes    SS

Born: 6/11/1983 Age: 29
Bats: B Throws: R Height: 6' 1" Weight: 160
Breakout: 5% Improve: 28% Collapse: 9%
Attrition: 14% MLB: 92%

**Comparables:**
Jimmy Rollins, Bob Lillis, Barry Larkin

| YEAR | TEAM | LVL | AGE | PA | R | 2B | 3B | HR | RBI | BB | SO | SB | CS | AVG_OBP_SLG | TAv | BABIP | BRR | FRAA | WARP |
|------|------|-----|-----|-----|-----|----|----|----|-----|----|----|----|----|-------------|------|-------|------|------|------|
| 2009 | NYN | MLB | 26 | 166 | 18 | 7 | 2 | 2 | 15 | 18 | 19 | 11 | 2 | .279/.355/.395 | .267 | .307 | -0.3 | -0.6 | 0.7 |
| 2010 | NYN | MLB | 27 | 603 | 83 | 29 | 10 | 11 | 54 | 31 | 63 | 30 | 10 | .282/.321/.428 | .267 | .301 | 3.9 | -5.6 | 2.8 |
| 2011 | NYN | MLB | 28 | 586 | 101 | 31 | 16 | 7 | 44 | 43 | 41 | 39 | 7 | .337/.384/.493 | .314 | .353 | 4.6 | -1.4 | 6.1 |
| 2012 | FLO | MLB | 29 | 556 | 69 | 26 | 10 | 8 | 65 | 46 | 59 | 35 | 9 | .288/.348/.430 | .278 | .309 | 0.8 | SS -4 | 3.5 |

Here at BP, we have an injury database that shows the history for each player's maladies. Under Jose Reyes, the word "hamstring" appears 11 times, including two entries in 2011 that cost him more than a month's worth of games. He won the batting title last year—offending many by taking himself out of the last game of the season following a bunt single in the first inning—but this is still a player who has averaged just 98 games in the last three years, and the only way he stayed healthy in the second half of 2011 was to simply stop running. Before the All-Star break, Reyes had 15 triples and 30 stolen bases. After, he had just one and nine, respectively. The Marlins believed enough in Reyes' health to sign him for the next six years, bumping incumbent All-Star shortstop Ramirez to third base in the process.

### Aaron Rowand — CF

Born: 8/29/1977 Age: 34
Bats: R Throws: R Height: 6' 2" Weight: 200
Breakout: 0% Improve: 23% Collapse: 11%
Attrition: 24% MLB: 91%

| YEAR | TEAM | LVL | AGE | PA | R | 2B | 3B | HR | RBI | BB | SO | SB | CS | AVG/OBP/SLG | TAv | BABIP | BRR | FRAA | WARP |
|---|---|---|---|---|---|---|---|---|---|---|---|---|---|---|---|---|---|---|---|
| 2009 | SFN | MLB | 31 | 546 | 61 | 30 | 2 | 15 | 64 | 30 | 125 | 4 | 1 | .261/.319/.419 | .252 | .318 | 0.1 | -2.2 | 0.9 |
| 2010 | SFN | MLB | 32 | 357 | 42 | 12 | 2 | 11 | 34 | 16 | 74 | 5 | 3 | .230/.281/.378 | .232 | .263 | 0.5 | 1.4 | -0.1 |
| 2011 | SFN | MLB | 33 | 351 | 34 | 22 | 2 | 4 | 21 | 10 | 84 | 2 | 3 | .233/.274/.347 | .234 | .299 | 2.6 | 3.3 | 0.6 |
| 2012 | FLO | MLB | 34 | 331 | 37 | 17 | 1 | 8 | 36 | 19 | 74 | 3 | 2 | .254/.312/.391 | .256 | .310 | -0.4 | CF 4, LF -1 | 1.2 |

### Gaby Sanchez — 1B

Born: 9/2/1983 Age: 28
Bats: R Throws: R Height: 6' 3" Weight: 225
Breakout: 1% Improve: 36% Collapse: 3%
Attrition: 12% MLB: 83%

Comparables:
Don Baylor, Rafael Palmeiro, Ryan Garko

| YEAR | TEAM | LVL | AGE | PA | R | 2B | 3B | HR | RBI | BB | SO | SB | CS | AVG/OBP/SLG | TAv | BABIP | BRR | FRAA | WARP |
|---|---|---|---|---|---|---|---|---|---|---|---|---|---|---|---|---|---|---|---|
| 2009 | NWO | AAA | 25 | 370 | 55 | 11 | 0 | 16 | 56 | 41 | 44 | 5 | 0 | .289/.378/.475 | .300 | .293 | 2 | -6.1 | 1.7 |
| 2009 | FLO | MLB | 25 | 23 | 2 | 0 | 0 | 2 | 3 | 2 | 3 | 0 | 0 | .238/.304/.524 | .263 | .188 | -0.1 | 0 | 0.0 |
| 2010 | FLO | MLB | 26 | 643 | 72 | 37 | 3 | 19 | 85 | 57 | 101 | 5 | 0 | .273/.341/.448 | .273 | .299 | -1.4 | -5.1 | 1.0 |
| 2011 | FLO | MLB | 27 | 661 | 72 | 35 | 0 | 19 | 78 | 74 | 97 | 3 | 1 | .266/.352/.427 | .278 | .287 | -2.8 | 4.1 | 2.0 |
| 2012 | FLO | MLB | 28 | 617 | 77 | 33 | 1 | 18 | 73 | 63 | 103 | 5 | 1 | .266/.347/.432 | .280 | .296 | 0.1 | 1B -6, 3B -0 | 2.2 |

The Marlins believed enough in Sanchez's bat that they moved top first-base prospect Logan Morrison to left field in 2010. Sanchez has rewarded the Marlins' faith with two solid, strikingly similar seasons and improved defense at first base. Some of the subtle changes he made last year—better plate discipline and a tick up in his line drive rate—bode well for another step forward on offense. Defensively, Sanchez's 4.1 FRAA placed him sixth among NL first basemen with 250 plate appearances and was a 9.2-run improvement over 2010. He'll never be elite in the field, but having Omar Infante to his right instead of Dan Uggla decreases the amount of ground he needs to cover as well as opportunities for mistakes.

### Kyle Skipworth — C

Born: 3/1/1990 Age: 22
Bats: L Throws: R Height: 6' 5" Weight: 205
Breakout: 0% Improve: 8% Collapse: 1%
Attrition: 19% MLB: 25%

Comparables:
Michael Thomas, Alexander Soto, Dave Adlesh

| YEAR | TEAM | LVL | AGE | PA | R | 2B | 3B | HR | RBI | BB | SO | SB | CS | AVG/OBP/SLG | TAv | BABIP | BRR | FRAA | WARP |
|---|---|---|---|---|---|---|---|---|---|---|---|---|---|---|---|---|---|---|---|
| 2009 | GRB | A | 19 | 286 | 28 | 14 | 1 | 7 | 37 | 18 | 91 | 1 | 2 | .208/.263/.348 | .219 | .287 | -2.2 | 0.6 | -0.4 |
| 2010 | GRB | A | 20 | 436 | 55 | 17 | 1 | 17 | 59 | 32 | 132 | 1 | 2 | .249/.313/.426 | .258 | .331 | 1.7 | 1.7 | 1.8 |
| 2011 | JAX | AA | 21 | 434 | 35 | 12 | 2 | 11 | 49 | 34 | 143 | 0 | 4 | .207/.273/.331 | .213 | .292 | -4 | -1.6 | -1.4 |
| 2012 | FLO | MLB | 22 | 250 | 22 | 8 | 1 | 7 | 24 | 13 | 91 | 0 | 0 | .190/.235/.321 | .200 | .270 | -0.1 | C -1 | -1.0 |

It's difficult to make sense of the Marlins' decision to jump Skipworth two levels to Double-A Jacksonville, given his youth and ongoing struggles at the plate since turning pro as the sixth-overall pick in the 2008 draft. His batting average rarely crept above the Mendoza line in 2011, and it took a six-game hitting streak at the end of the season for him to hit his weight for the year. A logjam of catchers on the Triple-A and major league rosters could allow Skipworth to spend a second year in Double-A, where, at age 22, he'll still be one of the youngest players in the Southern League.

### Jake Smolinski — LF

Born: 2/9/1989 Age: 23
Bats: R Throws: R Height: 6' 0" Weight: 185
Breakout: 1% Improve: 10% Collapse: 20%
Attrition: 28% MLB: 53%

Comparables:
Alex Romero, Fred Lynn, Joe Keough

| YEAR | TEAM | LVL | AGE | PA | R | 2B | 3B | HR | RBI | BB | SO | SB | CS | AVG/OBP/SLG | TAv | BABIP | BRR | FRAA | WARP |
|---|---|---|---|---|---|---|---|---|---|---|---|---|---|---|---|---|---|---|---|
| 2009 | GRB | A | 20 | 322 | 50 | 25 | 0 | 7 | 31 | 38 | 45 | 2 | 5 | .283/.379/.448 | .288 | .317 | -0.8 | -4.5 | 1.1 |
| 2010 | JUP | A+ | 21 | 443 | 45 | 27 | 3 | 5 | 51 | 31 | 62 | 8 | 5 | .264/.321/.383 | .261 | .302 | 0.7 | -0.5 | 0.7 |
| 2011 | JAX | AA | 22 | 462 | 42 | 26 | 0 | 7 | 36 | 59 | 57 | 6 | 5 | .245/.342/.364 | .268 | .269 | -0.2 | -1.8 | 1.4 |
| 2012 | FLO | MLB | 23 | 250 | 25 | 12 | 1 | 4 | 22 | 20 | 45 | 2 | 1 | .229/.294/.338 | .233 | .267 | -0.3 | LF -4, 3B -1 | -0.1 |

A move out of the infield and to a less-demanding outfield corner did little to stimulate Smolinski's bat in his first taste of Double-A. Hope remains that some of his doubles will lead to average home-run power as he matures, but his .364 slugging average at Jacksonville set a new career low for the second consecutive year.

| Mike Stanton | RF |
| --- | --- |
| Born: 11/8/1989 Age: 22 |
| Bats: R Throws: R Height: 6' 6" Weight: 235 |
| Breakout: 2% Improve: 19% Collapse: 2% |
| Attrition: 22% MLB: 83% |
| **Comparables:** |
| Adam Dunn, Billy Jo Robidoux, Eric Anthony |

| YEAR | TEAM | LVL | AGE | PA | R | 2B | 3B | HR | RBI | BB | SO | SB | CS | AVG_OBP_SLG | TAv | BABIP | BRR | FRAA | WARP |
| --- | --- | --- | --- | --- | --- | --- | --- | --- | --- | --- | --- | --- | --- | --- | --- | --- | --- | --- | --- |
| 2009 | JUP | A+ | 19 | 210 | 27 | 9 | 3 | 12 | 39 | 28 | 45 | 2 | 2 | .294/.392/.578 | .331 | .333 | -0.9 | -1.2 | 1.7 |
| 2009 | JAX | AA | 19 | 341 | 49 | 15 | 2 | 16 | 53 | 31 | 99 | 1 | 1 | .231/.315/.455 | .276 | .288 | 0.8 | 10.8 | 2.5 |
| 2010 | JAX | AA | 20 | 240 | 42 | 13 | 4 | 21 | 52 | 44 | 53 | 1 | 0 | .312/.445/.729 | .393 | .331 | 0 | 3.5 | 4.3 |
| 2010 | FLO | MLB | 20 | 396 | 45 | 21 | 1 | 22 | 59 | 34 | 123 | 5 | 2 | .259/.326/.507 | .284 | .330 | -1.3 | 9.7 | 2.5 |
| 2011 | FLO | MLB | 21 | 601 | 79 | 30 | 5 | 34 | 87 | 70 | 166 | 5 | 5 | .262/.356/.537 | .303 | .314 | -2.5 | 11.7 | 4.9 |
| 2012 | FLO | MLB | 22 | 552 | 73 | 25 | 3 | 30 | 82 | 59 | 164 | 4 | 2 | .250/.336/.498 | .294 | .309 | -0.4 | RF 9, LF 0 | 3.0 |

It's no secret that PECOTA loves the precocious, and Stanton's projection (.256/.330/.527 in 580 PA) for last year was no exception. Sixteen players, including nine Hall of Famers and Junior Griffey, had achieved those numbers at or before the age of 21, and Stanton added himself to that group in 2011. In addition to his exploits with the bat, Stanton's defense was better than expected, placing him second in FRAA and tying for third in assists among NL outfielders. He improved in the second half, cutting his strikeout-to-walk ratio from 3.20 to 1.75 and raising his OPS by .120.

| Christian Yelich | LF |
| --- | --- |
| Born: 12/5/1991 Age: 20 |
| Bats: L Throws: R Height: 6' 5" Weight: 189 |
| Breakout: 4% Improve: 13% Collapse: 14% |
| Attrition: 21% MLB: 34% |
| **Comparables:** |
| Andrew Lambo, Brock Davis, Johnny Callison |

| YEAR | TEAM | LVL | AGE | PA | R | 2B | 3B | HR | RBI | BB | SO | SB | CS | AVG_OBP_SLG | TAv | BABIP | BRR | FRAA | WARP |
| --- | --- | --- | --- | --- | --- | --- | --- | --- | --- | --- | --- | --- | --- | --- | --- | --- | --- | --- | --- |
| 2011 | GRB | A | 19 | 521 | 73 | 32 | 1 | 15 | 77 | 55 | 102 | 32 | 5 | .312/.388/.484 | .298 | .373 | 0.8 | 2.1 | 3.9 |
| 2012 | FLO | MLB | 20 | 250 | 25 | 10 | 1 | 6 | 24 | 18 | 64 | 6 | 1 | .228/.284/.354 | .231 | .287 | 0.2 | LF -5, CF -1 | -0.3 |

Yelich worked quickly to justify the Marlins' use of the 23rd pick in the 2010 draft on him, earning the organization's Minor League Player of the Year award with a strong full-season debut in which he was the only teenager to rank among the top 10 in total bases in the South Atlantic League. Yelich displayed impressive consistency. Of his 122 games, 42 were multi-hit affairs and he went hitless just 32 times. He has the potential to hit for above-average power, which could make him a superstar if he slides from left to center field. That power isn't likely to manifest itself this year, however, as Yelich is slated to spend the bulk of his summer in the Florida State League.

# PITCHERS

| Heath Bell | |
| --- | --- |
| Born: 9/29/1977 Age: 34 |
| Bats: R Throws: R Height: 6' 4" Weight: 230 |
| Breakout: 15% Improve: 35% Collapse: 40% |
| Attrition: 5% MLB: 97% |
| **Comparables:** |
| Mariano Rivera, Bob Gibson, Rich Gossage |

| YEAR | TEAM | LVL | AGE | W | L | SV | G | GS | IP | H | HR | BB | SO | EqBB9 | EqSO9 | GB% | BABIP | WHIP | ERA | FIP | FRA | WARP |
| --- | --- | --- | --- | --- | --- | --- | --- | --- | --- | --- | --- | --- | --- | --- | --- | --- | --- | --- | --- | --- | --- | --- |
| 2009 | SDN | MLB | 31 | 6 | 4 | 42 | 68 | 0 | 69² | 54 | 3 | 24 | 79 | 3.1 | 10.2 | 47% | .297 | 1.12 | 2.71 | 2.38 | 2.83 | 1.6 |
| 2010 | SDN | MLB | 32 | 6 | 1 | 47 | 67 | 0 | 70 | 56 | 1 | 28 | 86 | 3.6 | 11.1 | 45% | .329 | 1.20 | 1.93 | 2.08 | 2.84 | 1.4 |
| 2011 | SDN | MLB | 33 | 3 | 4 | 43 | 64 | 0 | 62² | 51 | 4 | 21 | 51 | 3.0 | 7.3 | 45% | .269 | 1.15 | 2.44 | 3.20 | 3.77 | 0.3 |
| 2012 | FLO | MLB | 34 | 3 | 2 | 46 | 60 | 0 | 60¹ | 44 | 3 | 20 | 60 | 3.0 | 9.0 | 50% | .288 | 1.07 | 2.39 | 2.86 | 2.60 | 1.7 |

The two biggest news items about Bell in 2011 were that (A) his strikeout rate plummeted and (B) he wasn't traded at the deadline. That first one is a mystery, as he didn't lose any velocity. Still, when thirtysomething relievers other than Mariano Rivera experience a big drop in K/9, it sets off a few yellow flags. Regarding the second issue, Bell's contract status kept him from fetching as much as the younger and better Mike Adams, so the Padres moved the more marketable guy rather than accept less in return. Bell's days as an elite closer may be coming to an end, but the Marlins gambled on his rubber arm allowing him to succeed for a few more years when they signed him to a three-year, $27 million deal in December.

| Mark Buehrle | |
| --- | --- |
| Born: 3/23/1979 Age: 33 |
| Bats: L Throws: L Height: 6' 3" Weight: 195 |
| Breakout: 16% Improve: 50% Collapse: 17% |
| Attrition: 12% MLB: 93% |
| **Comparables:** |
| John Tudor, Zane Smith, Dick Donovan |

| YEAR | TEAM | LVL | AGE | W | L | SV | G | GS | IP | H | HR | BB | SO | EqBB9 | EqSO9 | GB% | BABIP | WHIP | ERA | FIP | FRA | WARP |
| --- | --- | --- | --- | --- | --- | --- | --- | --- | --- | --- | --- | --- | --- | --- | --- | --- | --- | --- | --- | --- | --- | --- |
| 2009 | CHA | MLB | 30 | 13 | 10 | 0 | 33 | 33 | 213¹ | 222 | 27 | 45 | 105 | 1.9 | 4.4 | 47% | .286 | 1.25 | 3.84 | 4.51 | 5.07 | 1.8 |
| 2010 | CHA | MLB | 31 | 13 | 13 | 0 | 33 | 33 | 210¹ | 246 | 17 | 49 | 99 | 2.1 | 4.2 | 47% | .316 | 1.40 | 4.28 | 3.87 | 4.36 | 2.7 |
| 2011 | CHA | MLB | 32 | 13 | 9 | 0 | 31 | 31 | 205¹ | 221 | 21 | 45 | 109 | 2.0 | 4.8 | 47% | .296 | 1.30 | 3.59 | 4.02 | 4.21 | 2.5 |
| 2012 | FLO | MLB | 33 | 12 | 10 | 0 | 29 | 29 | 191¹ | 195 | 20 | 43 | 100 | 2.0 | 4.7 | 47% | .301 | 1.24 | 4.17 | 4.19 | 4.53 | 1.2 |

In the 21st century, nothing is certain but death, taxes, and baseball analysts comparing Buehrle to death and taxes—but, you know, in a good way. For 11 straight seasons Buehrle has managed to negotiate his mid-80s fastball and collection of zone-tickling off-speed junk through 30-plus starts and 200-plus above-average innings per year, a level of consistency and durability that seemed to go out of style with whale-bone corsets and hairnets. Buehrle keeps his teammates interested with his rapid-fire tempo, superb fielding and ability to throttle the running game, and in return they convert the weak contact he induces into outs. Moving to the National League gives him a less-familiar audience to baffle, and Buehrle isn't too old to make good on his new four-year deal, but Marlins fans had best expect a mid-rotation workhorse, not an ace.

**Jose Ceda**
Born: 1/28/1987 Age: 25
Bats: R Throws: R Height: 6' 5" Weight: 275
Breakout: 29% Improve: 57% Collapse: 18%
Attrition: 13% MLB: 90%

| YEAR | TEAM | LVL | AGE | W | L | SV | G | GS | IP | H | HR | BB | SO | EqBB9 | EqSO9 | GB% | BABIP | WHIP | ERA | FIP | FRA | WARP |
|------|------|-----|-----|---|---|----|----|----|-----|---|----|----|----|-------|-------|-----|-------|------|------|------|------|------|
| 2010 | JAX | AA | 23 | 4 | 1 | 6 | 27 | 0 | 32¹ | 12 | 2 | 16 | 34 | 5.6 | 12.5 | 41% | .263 | 1.18 | 1.39 | 3.92 | 3.47 | 0.5 |
| 2010 | FLO | MLB | 23 | 0 | 0 | 0 | 8 | 0 | 8² | 8 | 1 | 11 | 9 | 11.4 | 9.3 | 29% | .304 | 2.19 | 5.19 | 6.68 | 5.32 | -0.1 |
| 2011 | NWO | AAA | 24 | 3 | 1 | 24 | 36 | 0 | 39² | 30 | 1 | 13 | 51 | 2.9 | 12.0 | 37% | .305 | 1.08 | 1.36 | 2.55 | 3.18 | 0.9 |
| 2011 | FLO | MLB | 24 | 0 | 1 | 0 | 17 | 0 | 20¹ | 16 | 1 | 12 | 21 | 5.3 | 9.3 | 40% | .278 | 1.38 | 4.43 | 3.34 | 3.71 | 0.3 |

tently hit the strike zone, hitters won't feel inclined to take the bat off of their shoulders unless it's a pitch they can drive, and Ceda won't be long for the big leagues.

**Randy Choate**
Born: 9/5/1975 Age: 36
Bats: L Throws: L Height: 6' 4" Weight: 180
Breakout: 16% Improve: 36% Collapse: 42%
Attrition: 9% MLB: 85%

Comparables:
Joey Eischen, Hisanori Takahashi, Scott Eyre

| YEAR | TEAM | LVL | AGE | W | L | SV | G | GS | IP | H | HR | BB | SO | EqBB9 | EqSO9 | GB% | BABIP | WHIP | ERA | FIP | FRA | WARP |
|------|------|-----|-----|---|---|----|----|----|-----|----|----|----|----|-------|-------|-----|-------|------|------|------|------|------|
| 2009 | TBA | MLB | 33 | 1 | 0 | 5 | 61 | 0 | 36¹ | 28 | 4 | 11 | 28 | 2.7 | 6.9 | 66% | .242 | 1.07 | 3.47 | 3.94 | 4.87 | 0.2 |
| 2010 | TBA | MLB | 34 | 4 | 3 | 0 | 85 | 0 | 44² | 41 | 3 | 17 | 40 | 3.4 | 8.1 | 61% | .311 | 1.30 | 4.23 | 3.47 | 4.50 | 0.2 |
| 2011 | FLO | MLB | 35 | 1 | 1 | 0 | 54 | 0 | 24² | 13 | 3 | 12 | 31 | 4.7 | 11.3 | 63% | .189 | 1.05 | 1.82 | 3.76 | 5.46 | -0.1 |
| 2012 | FLO | MLB | 36 | 3 | 1 | 1 | 51 | 0 | 25² | 22 | 2 | 10 | 21 | 3.4 | 7.4 | 59% | .301 | 1.25 | 3.77 | 3.75 | 4.10 | 0.3 |

In the first year of a two-year, $2.5 million contract that lured him from cross-state "natural rivals" Tampa Bay, Choate did for the Marlins what he has done for more than a decade: neutralize left-handed hitters. His 1.82 ERA and 11.3 strikeouts per nine innings were both career bests. Choate missed the final month and a half of the season with left elbow inflammation but should be ready to go for the start of the season.

**Steve Cishek**
Born: 6/18/1986 Age: 26
Bats: R Throws: R Height: 6' 7" Weight: 200
Breakout: 25% Improve: 59% Collapse: 15%
Attrition: 10% MLB: 92%

Comparables:
Ken Tatum, Chan Ho Park, Mel Rojas

| YEAR | TEAM | LVL | AGE | W | L | SV | G | GS | IP | H | HR | BB | SO | EqBB9 | EqSO9 | GB% | BABIP | WHIP | ERA | FIP | FRA | WARP |
|------|------|-----|-----|---|---|----|----|----|-----|----|----|----|----|-------|-------|-----|-------|------|------|------|------|------|
| 2009 | JUP | A+ | 23 | 3 | 4 | 2 | 37 | 0 | 57 | 36 | 2 | 16 | 45 | 2.5 | 7.1 | 59% | .224 | 0.91 | 2.84 | 3.39 | 4.46 | 0.3 |
| 2010 | JUP | A+ | 24 | 0 | 5 | 4 | 26 | 0 | 35 | 23 | 0 | 16 | 18 | 4.9 | 7.2 | 51% | .291 | 1.37 | 2.83 | 4.30 | 4.47 | 0.1 |
| 2010 | JAX | AA | 24 | 3 | 1 | 2 | 22 | 0 | 31¹ | 24 | 0 | 6 | 27 | 2.9 | 9.8 | 44% | .381 | 1.28 | 4.31 | 2.88 | 3.15 | 0.7 |
| 2010 | FLO | MLB | 24 | 0 | 0 | 0 | 3 | 0 | 4¹ | 1 | 0 | 1 | 3 | 2.1 | 6.2 | 45% | .091 | 0.46 | 0.00 | 2.41 | 3.53 | 0.1 |
| 2011 | NWO | AAA | 25 | 1 | 1 | 0 | 15 | 0 | 23 | 18 | 1 | 12 | 19 | 4.7 | 7.4 | 53% | .279 | 1.30 | 2.35 | 4.47 | 4.33 | 0.2 |
| 2011 | FLO | MLB | 25 | 2 | 1 | 3 | 45 | 0 | 54² | 45 | 1 | 19 | 55 | 3.1 | 9.1 | 57% | .297 | 1.17 | 2.63 | 2.43 | 3.66 | 0.6 |
| 2012 | FLO | MLB | 26 | 2 | 1 | 1 | 37 | 0 | 49² | 44 | 4 | 22 | 37 | 4.1 | 6.8 | 48% | .294 | 1.34 | 4.29 | 4.09 | 4.66 | 0.2 |

Cishek was called up when the Marlins designated Jay Buente for assignment in late May. He didn't allow a run over his first 11 1/3 innings of work and finished the season with another 11 1/3-inning scoreless stretch. In between, he emerged as one of Jack McKeon's most-trusted options to keep the Marlins close when trailing in the late innings. Like many tall pitchers, the 6-5 Cishek struggles at times to maintain a consistent release point, which led to a career 3.9 BB/9 in the minors. He has better stuff than his competitors for late-inning work out of the Marlins bullpen, complementing a low-90s fastball with a sweeping slider that reaches the mid-80s, and his effectiveness against batters of both handedness makes him a sleeper candidate for the occasional save opportunity.

### Michael Dunn

Born: 5/23/1985 Age: 27
Bats: L Throws: L Height: 6' 2" Weight: 185
Breakout: 25% Improve: 45% Collapse: 11%
Attrition: 40% MLB: 93%

Comparables:
Oliver Perez, Jack Harshman, Courtney Duncan

| YEAR | TEAM | LVL | AGE | W | L | SV | G | GS | IP | H | HR | BB | SO | EqBB9 | EqSO9 | GB% | BABIP | WHIP | ERA | FIP | FRA | WARP |
|------|------|-----|-----|---|---|----|----|----|------|----|----|----|----|-------|-------|-----|-------|------|------|------|------|------|
| 2009 | TRN | AA | 24 | 3 | 3 | 2 | 26 | 0 | 53¹ | 41 | 3 | 32 | 76 | 5.4 | 12.8 | 43% | .330 | 1.37 | 3.71 | 2.93 | 3.61 | 0.8 |
| 2009 | NYA | MLB | 24 | 0 | 0 | 0 | 4 | 0 | 4 | 3 | 1 | 5 | 5 | 11.2 | 11.2 | 40% | .222 | 2.00 | 6.75 | 7.64 | 6.50 | 0.0 |
| 2010 | GWN | AAA | 25 | 2 | 0 | 7 | 38 | 0 | 47¹ | 25 | 1 | 19 | 39 | 4.8 | 12.2 | 43% | .312 | 1.18 | 1.52 | 3.49 | 3.67 | 0.9 |
| 2010 | ATL | MLB | 25 | 2 | 0 | 0 | 25 | 0 | 19 | 15 | 1 | 17 | 27 | 8.1 | 12.8 | 32% | .326 | 1.68 | 1.89 | 3.63 | 4.88 | 0.2 |
| 2011 | FLO | MLB | 26 | 5 | 6 | 0 | 72 | 0 | 63 | 51 | 9 | 31 | 68 | 4.4 | 9.7 | 40% | .275 | 1.30 | 3.43 | 4.26 | 4.91 | -0.2 |
| 2012 | FLO | MLB | 27 | 2 | 1 | 1 | 50 | 0 | 48¹ | 44 | 5 | 26 | 43 | 4.8 | 8.0 | 38% | .312 | 1.44 | 4.68 | 4.38 | 5.08 | -0.0 |

Dunn partnered with Randy Choate to form something of a Jekyll and Hyde routine from the left side of the Marlins bullpen, with Choate sitting in the 70s and 80s with his slider and two-seam fastball and Dunn blowing hitters away with mid-90s heat and a slider that touched 87 mph. Pitching for his third team in three years after coming over from Atlanta as part of the bounty the Marlins received for Dan Uggla, Dunn improved steadily as the year progressed, lowering his ERA each month from May onward and cutting his walk rate by 60 percent in the second half.

### Brad Hand

Born: 3/20/1990 Age: 22
Bats: L Throws: L Height: 6' 4" Weight: 200
Breakout: 24% Improve: 47% Collapse: 14%
Attrition: 10% MLB: 77%

Comparables:
Buddy Carlyle, Odalis Perez, Cesar Jimenez

| YEAR | TEAM | LVL | AGE | W | L | SV | G | GS | IP | H | HR | BB | SO | EqBB9 | EqSO9 | GB% | BABIP | WHIP | ERA | FIP | FRA | WARP |
|------|------|-----|-----|---|---|----|----|----|------|-----|----|----|-----|-------|-------|-----|-------|------|------|------|------|------|
| 2009 | GRB | A | 19 | 7 | 13 | 0 | 26 | 26 | 127² | 130 | 12 | 66 | 122 | 4.7 | 8.6 | 52% | .326 | 1.53 | 4.86 | 4.49 | 5.72 | 0.2 |
| 2010 | JUP | A+ | 20 | 7 | 7 | 0 | 26 | 26 | 140² | 115 | 7 | 40 | 93 | 3.1 | 8.6 | 48% | .344 | 1.44 | 3.33 | 3.79 | 5.07 | 0.4 |
| 2011 | JAX | AA | 21 | 7 | 1 | 0 | 19 | 18 | 108² | 90 | 11 | 50 | 71 | 4.1 | 5.9 | 41% | .256 | 1.29 | 3.40 | 4.72 | 4.77 | 0.9 |
| 2011 | FLO | MLB | 21 | 1 | 8 | 0 | 12 | 12 | 60 | 53 | 10 | 35 | 38 | 5.2 | 5.7 | 30% | .246 | 1.47 | 4.20 | 5.69 | 5.81 | -0.4 |
| 2012 | FLO | MLB | 22 | 4 | 6 | 0 | 14 | 14 | 77¹ | 80 | 10 | 43 | 45 | 5.0 | 5.2 | 45% | .302 | 1.59 | 5.77 | 5.39 | 6.27 | -0.8 |

In his third full season since being drafted in the second round of the 2008 draft out of a Minnesota high school, Hand made 12 starts across four separate call-ups to the big leagues, pitching better than his 1-8 record indicates but not as well as the 4.20 ERA he posted. Hand averaged an even five innings per start, but struggled to keep the ball out of the air, posting an obscene 0.42 ground out-to-air out ratio that easily would have led the league had he thrown enough innings to qualify. He'll turn 22 in spring training and could use more seasoning, but the Marlins' Triple-A affiliate is in the Pacific Coast League, not known for its kindness to fly ball pitchers.

### Chris Hatcher

Born: 1/12/1985 Age: 27
Bats: B Throws: R Height: 6' 3" Weight: 205
Breakout: 10% Improve: 48% Collapse: 35%
Attrition: 16% MLB: 91%

Comparables:
Dennis Higgins, Len Barker, Josh Beckett

| YEAR | TEAM | LVL | AGE | W | L | SV | G | GS | IP | H | HR | BB | SO | EqBB9 | EqSO9 | GB% | BABIP | WHIP | ERA | FIP | FRA | WARP |
|------|------|-----|-----|---|---|----|----|----|------|----|----|----|----|-------|-------|-----|-------|------|------|------|------|------|
| 2011 | JAX | AA | 26 | 2 | 1 | 6 | 42 | 0 | 47¹ | 32 | 2 | 19 | 57 | 3.6 | 10.8 | 42% | .273 | 1.08 | 1.90 | 2.64 | 3.13 | 1.0 |
| 2011 | FLO | MLB | 26 | 0 | 0 | 0 | 11 | 0 | 10¹ | 14 | 2 | 4 | 8 | 3.5 | 7.0 | 53% | .353 | 1.74 | 6.97 | 5.12 | 7.62 | -0.4 |
| 2012 | FLO | MLB | 27 | 1 | 0 | 0 | 19 | 0 | 20² | 18 | 2 | 8 | 18 | 3.5 | 7.8 | 44% | .304 | 1.28 | 3.97 | 3.88 | 4.31 | 0.2 |

After making his major league debut in 2010 as a strong-armed, no-hit catcher, Hatcher returned to the big leagues last year as a relief pitcher, his prospects for a career much brighter because of the change. He was surprisingly effective in Double-A, striking out more than a batter per inning and minimizing hard contact. Hatcher's fastball/slider repertoire is similar to what Michael Dunn offers from the left side, and like Dunn, his command is a work in progress.

### Clay Hensley

Born: 8/31/1979 Age: 32
Bats: R Throws: R Height: 6' 0" Weight: 190
Breakout: 14% Improve: 39% Collapse: 31%
Attrition: 9% MLB: 83%

Comparables:
Tim Belcher, Bob Bruce, Tom Gordon

| YEAR | TEAM | LVL | AGE | W | L | SV | G | GS | IP | H | HR | BB | SO | EqBB9 | EqSO9 | GB% | BABIP | WHIP | ERA | FIP | FRA | WARP |
|------|------|-----|-----|---|---|----|----|----|------|-----|----|----|----|-------|-------|-----|-------|------|------|------|------|------|
| 2009 | NWO | AAA | 29 | 8 | 4 | 0 | 19 | 19 | 114 | 105 | 8 | 38 | 82 | 3.0 | 6.5 | 51% | .286 | 1.25 | 3.24 | 3.98 | 4.35 | 1.0 |
| 2010 | FLO | MLB | 30 | 3 | 4 | 7 | 68 | 0 | 75 | 54 | 3 | 29 | 77 | 3.5 | 9.2 | 55% | .267 | 1.11 | 2.16 | 2.89 | 3.51 | 1.4 |
| 2011 | FLO | MLB | 31 | 6 | 7 | 0 | 37 | 9 | 67² | 62 | 9 | 30 | 46 | 4.0 | 6.1 | 47% | .257 | 1.36 | 5.19 | 4.87 | 5.38 | -0.3 |
| 2012 | FLO | MLB | 32 | 3 | 2 | 1 | 44 | 4 | 63¹ | 59 | 6 | 28 | 43 | 3.9 | 6.1 | 50% | .295 | 1.37 | 4.49 | 4.40 | 4.88 | 0.2 |

The Marlins' lack of starting depth in the upper minors pushed Hensley into the rotation for nine starts last summer, and he gave up 29 earned runs in 42 innings before slipping back into the bullpen in September. Shoulder surgery in 2007 took a couple of ticks off of his average fastball, and roughly five miles per hour are now all that separate it from his low-80s changeup.

**Chad James**

Born: 1/23/1991 Age: 21
Bats: L Throws: L Height: 6' 4" Weight: 185
Breakout: 18% Improve: 37% Collapse: 39%
Attrition: 3% MLB: 89%

Comparables:
Chuck Stobbs, Joel Davis, Ryan Feierabend

| YEAR | TEAM | LVL | AGE | W | L | SV | G | GS | IP | H | HR | BB | SO | EqBB9 | EqSO9 | GB% | BABIP | WHIP | ERA | FIP | FRA | WARP |
|------|------|-----|-----|---|---|----|---|----|------|-----|----|----|-----|-------|-------|-----|-------|------|------|------|------|------|
| 2010 | GRB | A | 19 | 5 | 10 | 0 | 24 | 24 | 114¹ | 58 | 1 | 37 | 63 | 5.1 | 8.3 | 52% | .345 | 1.58 | 5.12 | 3.72 | 5.38 | 0.4 |
| 2011 | JUP | A+ | 20 | 3 | 9 | 0 | 27 | 27 | 149¹ | 173 | 12 | 51 | 124 | 3.1 | 7.5 | 43% | .354 | 1.50 | 3.80 | 3.84 | 4.88 | 0.4 |
| 2012 | FLO | MLB | 21 | 2 | 3 | 0 | 9 | 9 | 44 | 47 | 5 | 23 | 27 | 4.6 | 5.6 | 44% | .320 | 1.58 | 5.57 | 5.02 | 6.05 | -0.4 |

It takes more than a passing glance at his annual results to appreciate the progress James has made since the Marlins selected him with the 18th pick of the 2009 draft. Poor run support kept him winless through the first half, despite his posting a 3.16 ERA through 14 starts. He finally captured his first win in mid-July, and went 5-2 down the stretch. James rarely challenged hitters at Greensboro in 2010, despite the arsenal to do so, which led to a high number of walks but little hard contact. He threw more strikes last year, cutting his walk rate by nearly 40 percent, but received little help from his defense, evidenced by 173 hits and 14 unearned runs allowed. He'll join the Double-A Jacksonville rotation as a 21-year old, and could be a tempting option if the Marlins' rotation depth is once again challenged.

Jennings returned to Double-A Jacksonville after serving the final 11 games of the 50-game PED suspension that ended his 2010 season early. A mid-June promotion to New Orleans went poorly, with left-handers batting .349/.431/.558 against him as he struggled to throw strikes consistently, especially on the road. A strong year at New Orleans could put him in a position to take over for Choate in the Marlins bullpen when Choate's contract expires after the season.

**Josh Johnson**

Born: 1/31/1984 Age: 28
Bats: L Throws: R Height: 6' 8" Weight: 240
Breakout: 14% Improve: 37% Collapse: 35%
Attrition: 6% MLB: 93%

Comparables:
CC Sabathia, Don Mossi, Jon Matlack

| YEAR | TEAM | LVL | AGE | W | L | SV | G | GS | IP | H | HR | BB | SO | EqBB9 | EqSO9 | GB% | BABIP | WHIP | ERA | FIP | FRA | WARP |
|------|------|-----|-----|---|---|----|---|----|------|-----|----|----|-----|-------|-------|-----|-------|------|------|------|------|------|
| 2009 | FLO | MLB | 25 | 15 | 5 | 0 | 33 | 33 | 209 | 184 | 14 | 58 | 191 | 2.5 | 8.2 | 51% | .296 | 1.16 | 3.23 | 3.02 | 3.75 | 5.3 |
| 2010 | FLO | MLB | 26 | 11 | 6 | 0 | 28 | 28 | 183² | 155 | 7 | 48 | 186 | 2.4 | 9.1 | 47% | .301 | 1.11 | 2.30 | 2.44 | 2.96 | 4.6 |
| 2011 | FLO | MLB | 27 | 3 | 1 | 0 | 9 | 9 | 60¹ | 39 | 2 | 20 | 56 | 3.0 | 8.4 | 52% | .240 | 0.98 | 1.64 | 2.61 | 2.93 | 1.5 |
| 2012 | FLO | MLB | 28 | 5 | 3 | 0 | 10 | 10 | 68 | 59 | 4 | 20 | 62 | 2.6 | 8.2 | 49% | .314 | 1.16 | 3.18 | 3.03 | 3.45 | 1.3 |

When he's healthy, Johnson's plus fastball and hard slider make him the ace of the Marlins staff and one of the top handful of starting pitchers in the game. The problem is that he's missed the majority of three of the last five seasons with elbow, shoulder, and back injuries that have limited him to 88 starts since 2007. Last year, he was placed on the disabled list in mid-May with right shoulder inflammation, but wasn't officially shut down for the year until the end of July. Surgery has been ruled out for the time being, and the club expects Johnson to be available when the Marlins christen their new ballpark in April.

**Tom Koehler**

Born: 6/29/1986 Age: 26
Bats: R Throws: R Height: 6' 4" Weight: 225
Breakout: 30% Improve: 49% Collapse: 25%
Attrition: 10% MLB: 90%

Comparables:
Brett Tomko, Jerry Koosman, Ryan Drese

| YEAR | TEAM | LVL | AGE | W | L | SV | G | GS | IP | H | HR | BB | SO | EqBB9 | EqSO9 | GB% | BABIP | WHIP | ERA | FIP | FRA | WARP |
|------|------|-----|-----|---|---|----|---|----|------|-----|----|----|-----|-------|-------|-----|-------|------|------|------|------|------|
| 2009 | GRB | A | 23 | 5 | 5 | 0 | 18 | 18 | 98¹ | 88 | 9 | 39 | 82 | 3.6 | 7.5 | 49% | .282 | 1.29 | 3.20 | 4.51 | 4.86 | 1.0 |
| 2009 | JUP | A+ | 23 | 4 | 1 | 0 | 6 | 6 | 34² | 35 | 0 | 9 | 25 | 2.3 | 6.5 | 46% | .333 | 1.27 | 3.37 | 2.71 | 3.73 | 0.5 |
| 2010 | JAX | AA | 24 | 16 | 2 | 0 | 28 | 28 | 158² | 96 | 11 | 37 | 104 | 2.6 | 8.2 | 43% | .272 | 1.17 | 2.61 | 3.96 | 3.88 | 2.3 |
| 2011 | NWO | AAA | 25 | 12 | 7 | 0 | 28 | 28 | 150¹ | 144 | 18 | 79 | 116 | 4.7 | 6.9 | 42% | .286 | 1.48 | 4.97 | 5.43 | 5.80 | -0.3 |
| 2012 | FLO | MLB | 26 | 3 | 3 | 0 | 9 | 9 | 51 | 50 | 6 | 23 | 31 | 4.0 | 5.5 | 43% | .293 | 1.42 | 4.93 | 4.87 | 5.35 | -0.1 |

Koehler's first year at Triple-A began with three quality starts before a five-run, nine-hit outing at Albuquerque kicked off an 11-start, 6.43 ERA run that kept him out of the major leagues when the Marlins rotation was falling apart in mid-May. He didn't surrender an excessive number of hits, but the ones he did give up had a tendency to travel great distances, nearly 35 percent resulting in extra bases, and he finished second in the league in walks allowed, though he did show across-the-board improvement in the second half. Koehler lacks the pedigree and potential that will earn him multiple chances to find success, so he'll have to show marked improvement quickly if he wants to remain a candidate for a major-league career.

### Wade LeBlanc

Born: 8/7/1984 Age: 27
Bats: L Throws: L Height: 6' 4" Weight: 200
Breakout: 22% Improve: 62% Collapse: 24%
Attrition: 7% MLB: 88%

Comparables:
J.A. Happ, Fu-Te Ni, Mike Flanagan

| YEAR | TEAM | LVL | AGE | W | L | SV | G | GS | IP | H | HR | BB | SO | EqBB9 | EqSO9 | GB% | BABIP | WHIP | ERA | FIP | FRA | WARP |
|---|---|---|---|---|---|---|---|---|---|---|---|---|---|---|---|---|---|---|---|---|---|---|
| 2009 | POR | AAA | 24 | 4 | 9 | 0 | 24 | 20 | 121 | 109 | 15 | 31 | 95 | 2.3 | 7.1 | 45% | .268 | 1.16 | 3.87 | 4.31 | 5.14 | 0.0 |
| 2009 | SDN | MLB | 24 | 3 | 1 | 0 | 9 | 9 | 46$^1$ | 35 | 6 | 19 | 30 | 3.7 | 5.8 | 38% | .220 | 1.17 | 3.69 | 4.93 | 5.70 | -0.2 |
| 2010 | SDN | MLB | 25 | 8 | 12 | 0 | 26 | 25 | 146 | 157 | 24 | 51 | 110 | 3.1 | 6.8 | 36% | .309 | 1.42 | 4.25 | 4.83 | 4.42 | 1.5 |
| 2011 | SDN | MLB | 26 | 5 | 6 | 0 | 14 | 14 | 79$^2$ | 84 | 7 | 28 | 51 | 3.2 | 5.8 | 35% | .309 | 1.41 | 4.63 | 3.95 | 4.23 | 0.6 |
| 2012 | FLO | MLB | 27 | 7 | 6 | 0 | 18 | 18 | 105$^2$ | 97 | 12 | 36 | 77 | 3.1 | 6.6 | 39% | .291 | 1.26 | 4.07 | 4.25 | 4.42 | 0.9 |

Why is every finesse left-hander compared to Tom Glavine or Jamie Moyer? They were great pitchers, and it's unreasonable to place such expectations on kids who just happen to be short on stuff. Why do people forget about the Jeff Ballards and Jason Jacomes of the world, or the ones who never even made it that far? LeBlanc isn't Glavine or Moyer, but the changeup specialist from Louisiana has been marginally effective while plugging holes in the Padres rotation each of the past two seasons, although his minor-league ratios (8.3 K/9, 3.5 K/BB, 0.9 HR/9) haven't carried over to the big leagues (6.3 K/9, 1.8 K/BB, 1.4 HR/9). The difference between LeBlanc's career home (2.97 ERA, 1.0 HR/9) and road (6.16 ERA, 1.7 HR/9) numbers is illuminating. He'll compete with Brad Hand, Alex Sanabia, and Chris Volstad for the final slot in Miami's rotation this spring.

### Edward Mujica

Born: 5/10/1984 Age: 28
Bats: R Throws: R Height: 6' 3" Weight: 220
Breakout: 13% Improve: 40% Collapse: 22%
Attrition: 3% MLB: 96%

Comparables:
Shane Reynolds, Ben Sheets, James Shields

| YEAR | TEAM | LVL | AGE | W | L | SV | G | GS | IP | H | HR | BB | SO | EqBB9 | EqSO9 | GB% | BABIP | WHIP | ERA | FIP | FRA | WARP |
|---|---|---|---|---|---|---|---|---|---|---|---|---|---|---|---|---|---|---|---|---|---|---|
| 2009 | SDN | MLB | 25 | 3 | 5 | 2 | 67 | 4 | 93$^2$ | 101 | 14 | 19 | 76 | 1.8 | 7.3 | 40% | .307 | 1.28 | 3.94 | 3.99 | 4.13 | 1.0 |
| 2010 | SDN | MLB | 26 | 2 | 1 | 0 | 59 | 0 | 69$^2$ | 59 | 14 | 6 | 72 | 0.8 | 9.3 | 45% | .257 | 0.93 | 3.62 | 3.91 | 4.28 | 0.2 |
| 2011 | FLO | MLB | 27 | 9 | 6 | 0 | 67 | 0 | 76 | 64 | 7 | 14 | 63 | 1.7 | 7.5 | 51% | .277 | 1.03 | 2.96 | 3.17 | 3.95 | 0.9 |
| 2012 | FLO | MLB | 28 | 3 | 1 | 1 | 57 | 0 | 65$^1$ | 58 | 7 | 13 | 54 | 1.8 | 7.5 | 40% | .296 | 1.09 | 3.35 | 3.54 | 3.64 | 1.1 |

Mujica's career as a Marlin got off to a rough start when he allowed seven runs in April, but he recovered quickly, posting sub-three ERAs in each subsequent month, and ended the year as the bullpen leader in innings pitched, holds, WHIP, and on-base percentage allowed. Mujica's nine wins were the third-most earned by a Marlins pitcher last year, and the result of frequent use in high-leverage situations.

### Ricky Nolasco

Born: 12/13/1982 Age: 29
Bats: R Throws: R Height: 6' 3" Weight: 220
Breakout: 44% Improve: 63% Collapse: 14%
Attrition: 5% MLB: 91%

Comparables:
Lindy McDaniel, Shane Reynolds, James Shields

| YEAR | TEAM | LVL | AGE | W | L | SV | G | GS | IP | H | HR | BB | SO | EqBB9 | EqSO9 | GB% | BABIP | WHIP | ERA | FIP | FRA | WARP |
|---|---|---|---|---|---|---|---|---|---|---|---|---|---|---|---|---|---|---|---|---|---|---|
| 2009 | FLO | MLB | 26 | 13 | 9 | 0 | 31 | 31 | 185 | 188 | 23 | 44 | 195 | 2.1 | 9.5 | 40% | .322 | 1.25 | 5.06 | 3.31 | 4.46 | 2.3 |
| 2010 | FLO | MLB | 27 | 14 | 9 | 0 | 26 | 26 | 157$^2$ | 169 | 24 | 33 | 147 | 1.9 | 8.4 | 41% | .319 | 1.28 | 4.51 | 3.89 | 4.02 | 2.8 |
| 2011 | FLO | MLB | 28 | 10 | 12 | 0 | 33 | 33 | 206 | 244 | 20 | 44 | 148 | 1.9 | 6.5 | 47% | .337 | 1.40 | 4.67 | 3.50 | 4.37 | 1.1 |
| 2012 | FLO | MLB | 29 | 11 | 9 | 0 | 28 | 28 | 175 | 170 | 20 | 38 | 146 | 2.0 | 7.5 | 41% | .315 | 1.19 | 3.96 | 3.67 | 4.30 | 1.7 |

Of Nolasco's 33 starts, 18 of them were considered quality, but he earned wins in just nine of those outings and took the loss in four others. Compare that to the year before, when he posted a sexier won-lost record (14-9) but threw only 16 quality starts, quite fortunately collecting wins in 13 of them. The 1.17 difference between his 4.67 ERA and 3.50 FIP suggests that much of the bloat in the former can be attributed to bad luck. None of this is to imply that Nolasco was completely blameless for some of his poor results. Increased reliance upon his two-seam fastball and inconsistent slider led to a five percent increase in balls in play and an equal jump in line drives. His K/9 dropped for the second consecutive season. The upside of his changed approach was that he allowed fewer fly balls and, in turn, fewer home runs, averaging under one long ball per nine innings for the first time in his career.

### Juan Oviedo

Born: 8/14/1983 Age: 28
Bats: R Throws: R Height: 6' 2" Weight: 160
Breakout: 29% Improve: 55% Collapse: 14%
Attrition: 3% MLB: 93%

Comparables:
Roy Oswalt, Ted Higuera, Doug Corbett

| YEAR | TEAM | LVL | AGE | W | L | SV | G | GS | IP | H | HR | BB | SO | EqBB9 | EqSO9 | GB% | BABIP | WHIP | ERA | FIP | FRA | WARP |
|---|---|---|---|---|---|---|---|---|---|---|---|---|---|---|---|---|---|---|---|---|---|---|
| 2009 | FLO | MLB | 25 | 4 | 6 | 26 | 75 | 0 | 68$^2$ | 59 | 13 | 27 | 60 | 3.5 | 7.9 | 42% | .249 | 1.25 | 4.06 | 5.12 | 5.77 | -0.2 |
| 2010 | FLO | MLB | 26 | 4 | 3 | 30 | 68 | 0 | 65 | 62 | 5 | 21 | 71 | 2.9 | 9.8 | 54% | .331 | 1.28 | 3.46 | 2.89 | 3.58 | 1.2 |
| 2011 | FLO | MLB | 27 | 1 | 4 | 36 | 68 | 0 | 64$^1$ | 57 | 8 | 22 | 55 | 2.9 | 7.7 | 34% | .269 | 1.21 | 4.06 | 3.97 | 4.49 | 0.2 |
| 2012 | FLO | MLB | 28 | 3 | 1 | 29 | 62 | 0 | 59$^1$ | 52 | 6 | 18 | 49 | 2.7 | 7.5 | 42% | .291 | 1.18 | 3.61 | 3.78 | 3.92 | 0.8 |

The pitcher formerly known as Leo Nunez ran into trouble last September when questions about his identity forced him to return to his native Dominican Republic and prompted the Marlins to place him on the restricted list. An investigation revealed that Nunez's real name is Juan Carlos Oviedo and that he's 29, a year older than he had claimed. On the field, Nunez established a career high with 36 saves, tied for eighth-best in the NL, but wasn't as sharp as he was in 2010. Oviedo's K/9 fell from 9.8 to 7.7 and his ratio of groundballs to fly balls, a flukishly high 1.15 in 2010, fell to 0.50 last year, on the low end of his career norm. Miami inked former Padres closer Heath Bell to a three-year contract over the winter, so if Oviedo returns to the Marlins, it will be in a setup role.

## Rob Rasmussen
Born: 4/2/1989 Age: 23
Bats: R Throws: L Height: 5' 11" Weight: 155
Breakout: 12% Improve: 43% Collapse: 18%
Attrition: 15% MLB: 87%

**Comparables:**
Dave Giusti, Joe McIntosh, Gary Gentry

| YEAR | TEAM | LVL | AGE | W | L | SV | G | GS | IP | H | HR | BB | SO | EqBB9 | EqSO9 | GB% | BABIP | WHIP | ERA | FIP | FRA | WARP |
|------|------|-----|-----|---|---|----|----|----|-----|-----|----|----|-----|-------|-------|-----|-------|------|------|------|------|------|
| 2011 | JUP | A+ | 22 | 4 | 5 | 0 | 28 | 27 | 148[1] | 140 | 10 | 71 | 118 | 4.3 | 7.2 | 46% | .302 | 1.42 | 3.64 | 4.30 | 4.81 | 0.7 |
| 2012 | FLO | MLB | 23 | 2 | 3 | 0 | 7 | 7 | 39[1] | 40 | 4 | 21 | 23 | 4.7 | 5.2 | 44% | .306 | 1.55 | 5.42 | 4.96 | 5.89 | -0.3 |

Rasmussen put off what some consider an inevitable move to the bullpen with a solid, if not totally convincing, full-season debut at High-A Jupiter. Although he didn't give up a ton of hits, 71 walks contributed to a 1.42 WHIP. To his credit, after issuing five or more free passes in three of his first seven starts, Rasmussen walked as many as four just twice in his final 21 games. He finished the year strong, going 4-0, 0.82 with 33 strikeouts over his final six starts, and will make the jump to Double-A in 2012.

## Sandy Rosario
Born: 8/22/1985 Age: 26
Bats: R Throws: R Height: 6' 2" Weight: 170

| YEAR | TEAM | LVL | AGE | W | L | SV | G | GS | IP | H | HR | BB | SO | EqBB9 | EqSO9 | GB% | BABIP | WHIP | ERA | FIP | FRA | WARP |
|------|------|-----|-----|---|---|----|---|---|-----|----|----|----|----|-------|-------|-----|-------|------|------|------|------|------|
| 2009 | GRB | A | 23 | 3 | 2 | 0 | 7 | 7 | 40[1] | 57 | 4 | 6 | 36 | 1.3 | 8.0 | 46% | .387 | 1.56 | 5.14 | 3.49 | 4.69 | 0.6 |
| 2009 | JAM | A- | 23 | 4 | 2 | 0 | 9 | 9 | 42[1] | 48 | 1 | 8 | 41 | 1.7 | 8.7 | 50% | .359 | 1.32 | 1.70 | 2.61 | 3.71 | 0.8 |

but was used sparingly, averaging nearly a week between appearances. Rosario will likely start the season as the closer for Triple-A New Orleans, where he went 4-for-4 in save chances before his promotion to Miami last year.

## Alex Sanabia
Born: 9/8/1988 Age: 23
Bats: R Throws: R Height: 6' 2" Weight: 165
Breakout: 26% Improve: 53% Collapse: 23%
Attrition: 11% MLB: 82%

**Comparables:**
Joe Presko, Jesse Litsch, Bryan Augenstein

| YEAR | TEAM | LVL | AGE | W | L | SV | G | GS | IP | H | HR | BB | SO | EqBB9 | EqSO9 | GB% | BABIP | WHIP | ERA | FIP | FRA | WARP |
|------|------|-----|-----|---|---|----|----|----|-----|----|----|----|----|-------|-------|-----|-------|------|------|------|------|------|
| 2009 | JUP | A+ | 20 | 9 | 5 | 0 | 19 | 18 | 104[1] | 89 | 6 | 36 | 68 | 3.1 | 5.9 | 41% | .263 | 1.20 | 3.45 | 3.88 | 5.01 | 0.2 |
| 2010 | JAX | AA | 21 | 5 | 1 | 0 | 14 | 14 | 84[1] | 41 | 2 | 9 | 37 | 1.7 | 6.9 | 52% | .234 | 0.89 | 2.03 | 3.34 | 3.05 | 2.1 |
| 2010 | FLO | MLB | 21 | 5 | 3 | 0 | 15 | 12 | 72[1] | 74 | 6 | 16 | 47 | 2.0 | 5.8 | 39% | .293 | 1.24 | 3.73 | 3.67 | 3.85 | 1.1 |
| 2011 | FLO | MLB | 22 | 0 | 0 | 0 | 3 | 2 | 11 | 13 | 2 | 3 | 8 | 2.5 | 6.5 | 32% | .314 | 1.45 | 3.27 | 4.72 | 3.46 | 0.2 |
| 2012 | FLO | MLB | 23 | 2 | 2 | 0 | 7 | 7 | 36 | 38 | 4 | 12 | 19 | 3.0 | 4.7 | 43% | .301 | 1.38 | 4.95 | 4.59 | 5.38 | -0.1 |

Elbow soreness sidelined Sanabia for the first half of last year, but he made it back to the majors for a pair of starts at the end of September. Had he been healthy, Sanabia likely would have been called on to plug leaks that sprung in the Marlins rotation with Josh Johnson's shoulder injury and Javier Vazquez's early ineffectiveness. Still only 23, he'll enter spring training with plenty of competition for the fifth starter's job from Brad Hand, Wade LeBlanc, and Chris Volstad.

## Anibal Sanchez
Born: 2/27/1984 Age: 28
Bats: R Throws: R Height: 6' 1" Weight: 180
Breakout: 30% Improve: 56% Collapse: 17%
Attrition: 11% MLB: 88%

**Comparables:**
Carlos Muniz, Dave Smith, Jose Rijo

| YEAR | TEAM | LVL | AGE | W | L | SV | G | GS | IP | H | HR | BB | SO | EqBB9 | EqSO9 | GB% | BABIP | WHIP | ERA | FIP | FRA | WARP |
|------|------|-----|-----|----|----|----|----|----|-----|-----|----|----|-----|-------|-------|-----|-------|------|------|------|------|------|
| 2009 | FLO | MLB | 25 | 4 | 8 | 0 | 16 | 16 | 86 | 84 | 10 | 46 | 71 | 4.8 | 7.4 | 44% | .292 | 1.51 | 3.87 | 4.56 | 4.90 | 0.7 |
| 2010 | FLO | MLB | 26 | 13 | 12 | 0 | 32 | 32 | 195 | 192 | 10 | 70 | 157 | 3.2 | 7.2 | 47% | .312 | 1.34 | 3.55 | 3.35 | 3.76 | 3.6 |
| 2011 | FLO | MLB | 27 | 8 | 9 | 0 | 32 | 32 | 196[1] | 187 | 20 | 64 | 202 | 2.9 | 9.3 | 46% | .317 | 1.28 | 3.67 | 3.31 | 3.95 | 2.7 |
| 2012 | FLO | MLB | 28 | 10 | 9 | 0 | 27 | 27 | 166[1] | 155 | 14 | 63 | 138 | 3.4 | 7.5 | 45% | .313 | 1.31 | 4.12 | 3.78 | 4.48 | 1.2 |

Sanchez quietly developed into one of the National League's best starting pitchers in his second full season of health following 2007 shoulder surgery. He put less emphasis on his secondary offerings last year, opting to go with his two best pitches, a lively low-90s fastball and hard slider, nearly 60 percent of the time, and even more often against righties. The change led to the NL's fifth-best strikeout percentage (24 percent) and a 41 percent increase in Sanchez's SO/BB ratio. Miami's addition of Mark Buehrle pushes Sanchez into the number-three slot in the rotation, but don't be surprised if he out-pitches the former White Sox ace in 2012.

## Javier Vazquez
Born: 6/25/1976 Age: 36
Bats: R Throws: R Height: 6' 3" Weight: 180
Breakout: 20% Improve: 43% Collapse: 28%
Attrition: 12% MLB: 80%

**Comparables:**
Keith Foulke, Eddie Guardado, Tom Seaver

| YEAR | TEAM | LVL | AGE | W | L | SV | G | GS | IP | H | HR | BB | SO | EqBB9 | EqSO9 | GB% | BABIP | WHIP | ERA | FIP | FRA | WARP |
|------|------|-----|-----|----|----|----|----|----|-----|-----|----|----|-----|-------|-------|-----|-------|------|------|------|------|------|
| 2009 | ATL | MLB | 33 | 15 | 10 | 0 | 32 | 32 | 219[1] | 181 | 20 | 44 | 238 | 1.8 | 9.8 | 43% | .290 | 1.03 | 2.87 | 2.73 | 3.34 | 5.8 |
| 2010 | NYA | MLB | 34 | 10 | 10 | 0 | 31 | 26 | 157[1] | 155 | 32 | 65 | 121 | 3.7 | 6.9 | 36% | .270 | 1.40 | 5.32 | 5.53 | 5.52 | 0.6 |
| 2011 | FLO | MLB | 35 | 13 | 11 | 0 | 32 | 32 | 192[2] | 178 | 21 | 50 | 162 | 2.3 | 7.6 | 36% | .283 | 1.18 | 3.69 | 3.54 | 3.95 | 2.2 |
| 2012 | FLO | MLB | 36 | 11 | 8 | 0 | 28 | 28 | 163[2] | 145 | 20 | 44 | 144 | 2.4 | 7.9 | 40% | .296 | 1.16 | 3.67 | 3.84 | 3.99 | 2.3 |

Vazquez, owner of a 6.37 ERA through 15 starts, would have been released before the All-Star break had injuries not stretched the Marlins' rotation depth to its limits. Fortunately for Florida, they still had him around after he made mechanical and pitch selection adjustments that led to an 8-3, 2.15 record with 96 strikeouts in the second half, comparable to what the Marlins could have expected from their injured ace, Josh Johnson. Speculation is that Vazquez will retire before the start of 2012, but he'll find plenty of potential suitors if the itch to pitch returns.

### Elih Villanueva

Born: 7/27/1986 Age: 25
Bats: R Throws: R Height: 6' 3" Weight: 235
Breakout: 17% Improve: 48% Collapse: 15%
Attrition: 17% MLB: 91%

Comparables:
John Fulgham, Jeff D'Amico, Rick Rhoden

| YEAR | TEAM | LVL | AGE | W | L | SV | G | GS | IP | H | HR | BB | SO | EqBB9 | EqSO9 | GB% | BABIP | WHIP | ERA | FIP | FRA | WARP |
|------|------|-----|-----|---|---|----|----|----|------|-----|----|----|-----|-------|-------|-----|-------|------|-------|-------|-------|------|
| 2011 | NWO | AAA | 24 | 7 | 11 | 0 | 28 | 28 | 165 | 189 | 23 | 57 | 102 | 3.2 | 5.7 | 40% | .324 | 1.56 | 5.35 | 5.38 | 5.77 | -0.2 |
| 2011 | FLO | MLB | 24 | 0 | 1 | 0 | 1 | 1 | 3 | 5 | 1 | 5 | 2 | 15.0 | 6.0 | 31% | .364 | 3.33 | 24.00 | 11.99 | 13.53 | -0.3 |
| 2012 | FLO | MLB | 25 | 4 | 3 | 0 | 10 | 10 | 59¹ | 59 | 8 | 17 | 31 | 2.6 | 4.6 | 40% | .287 | 1.29 | 4.54 | 4.77 | 4.94 | 0.1 |

Like Koehler, Villanueva was roughed up in his first year at New Orleans after easily handling Double-A the year before. Villanueva's average stuff was exposed in Triple-A, where hitters were less likely to chase his breaking pitches out of the zone and get themselves out. The 59 walks Villanueva surrendered fell five short of his career total in 384 career innings prior to 2011, not surprising given how hard he was hit when he pitched around the zone (.499 SLG, 24 HR allowed). Villanueva found success in the lower minors by locating his fastball and coaxing immature hitters to swing at his breaking pitches out of the zone, tricks that rarely work in Triple-A. He isn't a soft-tosser, so there's a chance he could figure things out in his second trip around the Pacific Coast League.

### Chris Volstad

Born: 9/23/1986 Age: 25
Bats: R Throws: R Height: 6' 9" Weight: 225
Breakout: 29% Improve: 57% Collapse: 15%
Attrition: 15% MLB: 95%

Comparables:
Dave Bush, Doc Medich, Ryan Webb

| YEAR | TEAM | LVL | AGE | W | L | SV | G | GS | IP | H | HR | BB | SO | EqBB9 | EqSO9 | GB% | BABIP | WHIP | ERA | FIP | FRA | WARP |
|------|------|-----|-----|---|----|----|----|----|------|-----|----|----|-----|-------|-------|-----|-------|------|------|------|------|------|
| 2009 | FLO | MLB | 22 | 9 | 13 | 0 | 29 | 29 | 159 | 169 | 29 | 59 | 107 | 3.3 | 6.1 | 52% | .294 | 1.43 | 5.21 | 5.25 | 6.29 | -0.8 |
| 2010 | FLO | MLB | 23 | 12 | 9 | 0 | 30 | 30 | 175 | 187 | 17 | 60 | 102 | 3.1 | 5.2 | 49% | .302 | 1.41 | 4.58 | 4.37 | 4.66 | 1.5 |
| 2011 | FLO | MLB | 24 | 5 | 13 | 0 | 29 | 29 | 165² | 187 | 23 | 49 | 117 | 2.7 | 6.4 | 54% | .317 | 1.42 | 4.89 | 4.29 | 4.83 | 0.3 |
| 2012 | CHN | MLB | 25 | 8 | 10 | 0 | 25 | 25 | 146¹ | 159 | 17 | 48 | 85 | 2.9 | 5.3 | 53% | .317 | 1.41 | 5.02 | 4.54 | 5.45 | -0.1 |

Volstad has filled out since the Marlins drafted him in the first round of the 2005 draft, adding 35 pounds to his 6-9 frame. Unfortunately, better stuff hasn't accompanied his increased mass as many scouts thought it would when he was a skinny, projectable prep right-hander. At 25, Volstad looks more like a back-of-the-rotation starter than a potential number two. He has shown steady, if glacial, progress in lowering his walks allowed while increasing his strikeouts, and his 2.39 strikeout-to-walk ratio in 2011 was a career high. With Mark Buehrle in the rotation, Volstad enters the spring tentatively slated as Miami's fifth starter, a role for which he'll have plenty of competition.

### Ryan Webb

Born: 2/5/1986 Age: 26
Bats: R Throws: R Height: 6' 7" Weight: 215
Breakout: 31% Improve: 63% Collapse: 13%
Attrition: 14% MLB: 93%

Comparables:
Mike Adams, Gordie Richardson, Tony Pena

| YEAR | TEAM | LVL | AGE | W | L | SV | G | GS | IP | H | HR | BB | SO | EqBB9 | EqSO9 | GB% | BABIP | WHIP | ERA | FIP | FRA | WARP |
|------|------|-----|-----|---|---|----|----|----|-----|----|----|----|----|-------|-------|-----|-------|------|------|------|------|------|
| 2009 | SAC | AAA | 23 | 7 | 1 | 2 | 31 | 2 | 45² | 57 | 3 | 15 | 39 | 3.0 | 7.7 | 51% | .386 | 1.58 | 4.33 | 3.71 | 3.59 | 0.8 |
| 2009 | SDN | MLB | 23 | 2 | 1 | 0 | 28 | 0 | 25² | 27 | 3 | 11 | 19 | 3.9 | 6.7 | 58% | .296 | 1.48 | 3.86 | 4.50 | 4.62 | 0.1 |
| 2010 | POR | AAA | 24 | 1 | 0 | 1 | 17 | 0 | 20² | 10 | 1 | 0 | 18 | 2.2 | 10.0 | 65% | .281 | 0.82 | 0.87 | 2.95 | 3.30 | 0.3 |
| 2010 | SDN | MLB | 24 | 3 | 1 | 0 | 54 | 0 | 59 | 64 | 1 | 19 | 44 | 2.9 | 6.7 | 62% | .337 | 1.41 | 2.90 | 2.85 | 3.97 | 0.6 |
| 2011 | FLO | MLB | 25 | 2 | 4 | 0 | 53 | 0 | 50² | 48 | 2 | 20 | 31 | 3.6 | 5.5 | 62% | .295 | 1.34 | 3.20 | 3.59 | 5.05 | -0.2 |
| 2012 | FLO | MLB | 26 | 2 | 1 | 1 | 47 | 0 | 49¹ | 51 | 5 | 18 | 32 | 3.2 | 5.8 | 49% | .315 | 1.39 | 4.68 | 4.32 | 5.08 | -0.0 |

Webb was one of two relief pitchers the Marlins acquired when they shipped then-disappointing center fielder Cameron Maybin to the Padres after the 2010 season. Despite his huge frame and above-average fastball, Webb doesn't generate a lot of strikeouts, instead relying on the defense behind him to convert boatloads of ground balls into outs. Though he went 0-for-4 in save chances last year, his ability to limit hard contact makes him a dark horse candidate for stray saves when Heath Bell is unavailable.

### Sean West

Born: 6/15/1986 Age: 26
Bats: L Throws: L Height: 6' 9" Weight: 200
Breakout: 21% Improve: 40% Collapse: 29%
Attrition: 15% MLB: 91%

Comparables:
Paul Maholm, Matt Albers, Lenny DiNardo

| YEAR | TEAM | LVL | AGE | W | L | SV | G | GS | IP | H | HR | BB | SO | EqBB9 | EqSO9 | GB% | BABIP | WHIP | ERA | FIP | FRA | WARP |
|------|------|-----|-----|---|---|----|----|----|------|-----|----|----|----|-------|-------|-----|-------|------|------|------|------|------|
| 2009 | JAX | AA | 23 | 7 | 3 | 0 | 12 | 11 | 64 | 68 | 12 | 28 | 65 | 3.9 | 9.1 | 39% | .311 | 1.50 | 4.78 | 4.91 | 5.40 | 0.2 |
| 2009 | FLO | MLB | 23 | 8 | 6 | 0 | 20 | 20 | 103¹ | 115 | 11 | 44 | 70 | 3.8 | 6.1 | 42% | .311 | 1.54 | 4.79 | 4.45 | 5.10 | 0.5 |
| 2010 | NWO | AAA | 24 | 4 | 3 | 0 | 11 | 11 | 57² | 33 | 1 | 11 | 27 | 3.0 | 7.2 | 42% | .296 | 1.37 | 3.12 | 3.92 | 4.69 | 0.3 |
| 2010 | FLO | MLB | 24 | 0 | 2 | 0 | 2 | 2 | 9¹ | 15 | 2 | 4 | 8 | 3.9 | 7.7 | 46% | .433 | 2.04 | 7.71 | 5.46 | 5.80 | -0.1 |
| 2011 | NWO | AAA | 25 | 5 | 8 | 0 | 17 | 17 | 87 | 97 | 4 | 43 | 55 | 4.8 | 5.8 | 49% | .342 | 1.71 | 5.59 | 4.66 | 5.00 | 1.0 |
| 2012 | FLO | MLB | 26 | 2 | 2 | 0 | 5 | 5 | 28¹ | 28 | 3 | 12 | 19 | 3.9 | 6.0 | 45% | .309 | 1.44 | 4.92 | 4.51 | 5.35 | -0.0 |

Shoulder inflammation caused West to miss most of April and May, and ineffectiveness at Triple-A kept him out of the major leagues for the first time since 2008. The Marlins' decision to use relievers Clay Hensley and Brian Sanches in the rotation rather than call up West was a clear indication of their lack of confidence in his ability to get major-league hitters out, though his poor showing at New Orleans didn't inspire much confidence to begin with. He'll return to Triple-A for a third turn around the Pacific Coast League in 2012.

## LINEOUTS

### HITTERS

| PLAYER | TEAM | LVL | AGE | PA | R | 2B | 3B | HR | RBI | BB | SO | SB-CS | AVG/OBP/SLG | TAv | BABIP | BRR | FRAA | WARP |
|--------|------|-----|-----|----|----|----|----|----|-----|----|----|-------|-------------|-----|-------|-----|------|------|

**Chase Austin**'s bat wasn't the first to be deadened by the high humidity and spacious ballparks of the Florida State League, but a batting average on balls in play 18 percent below his career norm and 25 points lower than the next unluckiest hitter in the league suggests a likely rebound. ⊘ As a 22-year old drafted out of a major Division I program, **Mark Canha**'s success in the South Atlantic League last summer came as little surprise. The Marlins moved Canha, primarily an outfielder at Cal, to first base full time in 2011 and his polish, coupled with the organization's lack of upper-level depth, could put him on the fast track in 2012. ⊘ It took injuries to two catchers ahead of him and a 50-game suspension to a third for **Brad Davis** to make his major league debut in 2010, but the relative health of the major league corps of backstops last year relegated him to his second full tour of Triple-A. ⊘ The most encouraging number from **Isaac Galloway**'s 2011 season is the 445 plate appearances he accrued in his second year at Low-A Greensboro, finally healthy after two injury-truncated seasons. Forty-three extra-base hits and 17 stolen bases are evidence of the tools at his disposal, but a dismal on-base percentage and strikeout-to-walk ratio demonstrate how far those tools are from consistent utilization as skills. ⊘ **Kyle Jensen** led all Marlins farmhands with 27 home runs and 247 total bases between High-A Jupiter and Double-A Jacksonville, earning Florida State League player of the year accolades along the way. But he continued to pile up strikeouts, whiffing in more than a quarter of his plate appearances. Jensen's home run power is real and certainly won't be stifled as he tromps through the hitter-friendly environs of the upper minors, but his bulky frame and lack of athleticism make him a liability in the outfield and on the bases. ⊘ The Marlins took a 39th-round flyer in 2009 on Texas football recruit **Noah Perio** and wound up signing him away from the gridiron with a $150,000 bonus. He flashed unexpected pop in his full-season debut, collecting 39 extra-base hits in 488 at-bats at Greensboro.

## PITCHERS

| PLAYER | TEAM | LVL | AGE | W | L | SV | IP | H | HR | BB | SO | EqBB9 | EqSO9 | GB% | BABIP | WHIP | ERA | FIP | FRA | WARP |
|---|---|---|---|---|---|---|---|---|---|---|---|---|---|---|---|---|---|---|---|---|
| J. Allison | JAX | AA | 26 | 2 | 3 | 0 | 64² | 82 | 8 | 26 | 29 | 3.6 | 4.0 | 39% | .325 | 1.67 | 6.26 | 5.22 | 5.84 | -0.4 |
| J. Alvarez | JUP | A+ | 22 | 3 | 2 | 0 | 82 | 79 | 2 | 19 | 73 | 2.1 | 8.0 | 50% | .328 | 1.20 | 2.96 | 2.66 | 3.55 | 1.6 |
|  | JAX | AA | 22 | 1 | 2 | 0 | 65² | 80 | 9 | 22 | 45 | 3.0 | 6.2 | 40% | .338 | 1.55 | 5.35 | 4.76 | 5.47 | 0.1 |
| T. Doolittle | NWO | AAA | 28 | 3 | 2 | 0 | 52² | 52 | 6 | 19 | 56 | 3.2 | 9.6 | 50% | .319 | 1.35 | 3.08 | 4.34 | 5.15 | 0.0 |
| V. Garate | NWO | AAA | 26 | 3 | 3 | 2 | 56¹ | 44 | 5 | 33 | 56 | 5.4 | 9.4 | 39% | .275 | 1.38 | 2.72 | 4.98 | 4.96 | 0.0 |
| K. Harvey | JUP | A+ | 27 | 0 | 2 | 0 | 31² | 18 | 1 | 12 | 31 | 3.4 | 8.8 | 30% | .221 | 0.95 | 2.27 | 3.08 | 4.61 | 0.2 |
|  | JAX | AA | 27 | 1 | 1 | 0 | 32¹ | 37 | 6 | 15 | 23 | 4.2 | 6.4 | 38% | .304 | 1.61 | 6.68 | 5.96 | 7.01 | -0.6 |
| K. Kaminska | JUP | A+ | 22 | 1 | 0 | 0 | 77¹ | 69 | 5 | 16 | 69 | 1.9 | 8.0 | 51% | .292 | 1.10 | 2.33 | 3.15 | 3.85 | 1.0 |
| C. Madden | JAX | AA | 27 | 1 | 0 | 0 | 43 | 32 | 2 | 18 | 42 | 3.8 | 8.8 | 37% | .273 | 1.16 | 2.72 | 3.28 | 3.35 | 0.8 |
|  | NWO | AAA | 27 | 1 | 2 | 1 | 22¹ | 31 | 3 | 11 | 30 | 4.4 | 12.1 | 33% | .459 | 1.88 | 4.03 | 4.27 | 4.89 | 0.2 |
| J. Martin | SYR | AAA | 28 | 1 | 6 | 2 | 107² | 104 | 17 | 16 | 69 | 1.4 | 6.0 | 49% | .286 | 1.13 | 3.93 | 4.65 | 5.16 | 1.5 |
| M. Montgomery | JUP | A+ | 23 | 2 | 1 | 0 | 109 | 120 | 6 | 16 | 72 | 1.3 | 5.9 | 56% | .320 | 1.25 | 3.39 | 3.25 | 4.61 | 0.7 |
| J. O'Gara | JAX | AA | 23 | 4 | 4 | 0 | 158¹ | 181 | 11 | 45 | 72 | 2.6 | 4.1 | 51% | .312 | 1.43 | 4.55 | 4.41 | 5.49 | -0.1 |
| E. Olmos | JUP | A+ | 21 | 2 | 9 | 0 | 127² | 167 | 13 | 81 | 101 | 5.7 | 7.1 | 44% | .368 | 1.94 | 6.63 | 5.27 | 6.37 | -1.3 |
| O. Poveda | JAX | AA | 23 | 1 | 3 | 0 | 156¹ | 148 | 16 | 52 | 113 | 3.1 | 6.7 | 52% | .295 | 1.32 | 4.32 | 4.24 | 5.22 | 0.3 |
| J. Rosario | JUP | A+ | 25 | 0 | 2 | 2 | 70 | 62 | 2 | 21 | 74 | 2.7 | 9.5 | 36% | .319 | 1.19 | 2.31 | 2.59 | 3.61 | 1.2 |

A 6.26 ERA and 4.0 SO/9 in his second attempt at Double-A may spell the end of former first-round pick **Jeff Allison**'s disappointing career with the Marlins. ⊘ It's all about finding the silver lining, folks: Lefty **Jose Alvarez** was shelled in a dozen starts for Double-A Jacksonville, but righties (.815 OPS) and lefties (.903) feasted equally on his offerings, suggesting Alvarez's troubles extended beyond a simple platoon advantage held by hitters of a certain hand. ⊘ The Marlins signed slight right-hander **Todd Doolittle** as a non-drafted free agent out of Mississippi State in 2005. He reached Triple-A in 2010 and joined the New Orleans rotation for six starts last year before an elbow injury cost him the second half. ⊘ Left-handed reliever **Victor Garate** had better surface numbers in his second go-round at Triple-A, but he'll be challenged to get major league hitters out if he doesn't cut down on the 5.4 walks per nine innings he permitted in 2011. ⊘ Several teams preferred **Kris Harvey** as a pitcher coming out of Clemson in 2005, but the Marlins tried him in the outfield before finally taking the bat out of his hands after a .148/.228/.287 showing in Double-A in 2008. He's spent the last two years trying to get over the Double-A hump, but he could factor in the bullpen if he learns to keep the ball in the yard. ⊘ A move to the bullpen and the subsequent bump in his strikeout rate helped **Kyle Kaminska** reach Double-A in his fifth season. ⊘ **Corey Madden**'s ERA in his Triple-A debut would have been 1.33 had he not surrendered seven earned runs over two rough August outings. ⊘ **J.D. Martin** still throws just about everything as he tries to hang on as a utility pitcher; if he surfaces as your team's fifth starter, it's not a good sign. ⊘ **Matthew Montgomery** had quality starts in 12 of his first 15 appearances at High-A Jupiter before an injury shut him down for most of July. A polished product of UC-Riverside, Montgomery should begin the year in Jacksonville's rotation. ⊘ Tall, lanky right-hander **Joseph O'Gara** signed with the Marlins as the 938th-overall pick in the 2009 draft out of Indiana. Despite his less-than-overpowering arsenal, he's moved quickly, making it to Double-A in his second full season, and he could factor in the Marlins' back-of-the-rotation plans. ⊘ Lefty **Edgar Olmos** struggled to repeat his delivery, a common challenge for young, tall pitchers, and led the Florida State League in just about everything a pitcher doesn't want to lead a league in: losses, runs, earned runs, walks, WHIP. ⊘ **Omar Poveda** made 27 starts for Double-A Jacksonville in a healthy return from Tommy John surgery that cost him all of 2010. He finished the year strong, going 5-1 with a 3.87 ERA and .229 batting average allowed in the second half. More importantly, considering he's likely to draw an assignment to the PCL in 2012, Poveda decreased his hit rate by more than 25 percent and struck out an additional batter per inning over his final 13 starts. ⊘ **Jose Rosario** saw as much of the Southern U.S. as anyone in 2011, with nine separate stops at Jupiter, Jacksonville, and New Orleans between April and August. The cumulative results were positive, 88 strikeouts and just three home runs allowed in 83 innings, and he earned bonus points for resiliency.

# MANAGER: OZZIE GUILLEN

| YEAR | TEAM | W-L | Pythag +/- | Avg PC | 100+ P | 120+ P | QS | BQS | REL | REL w Zero R | IBB | Subs | PH | PH Avg | PH HR | SB2 | CS2 | SB3 | CS3 | SAC Att | SAC % | POS SAC | Squeeze | Swing | In Play |
|---|---|---|---|---|---|---|---|---|---|---|---|---|---|---|---|---|---|---|---|---|---|---|---|---|---|
| 2009 | CHA | 79-83 | 0 | 95.1 | 62 | 0 | 85 | 12 | 415 | 246 | 41 | 35 | 105 | .106 | 2 | 6 | 3 | 2 | 1 | 49 | 69.4% | 30 | 1 | 139 | 113 |
| 2010 | CHA | 88-74 | 1 | 197.4 | 158 | 155 | 101 | 10 | 407 | 331 | 82 | — | 132 | .271 | 6 | 24 | 4 | 2 | 2 | 136 | 86.8% | 114 | 6 | 457 | 145 |
| 2011 | CHA | 78-82 | 0 | 99.5 | 83 | 2 | 88 | 8 | 404 | 330 | 49 | — | 67 | .250 | 2 | 15 | 4 | 0 | 1 | 76 | 82.9% | 61 | 3 | 338 | 121 |

The Marlins traded shortstop Ozzie Martinez and reliever Jhan Marinez to the White Sox for the rights to Guillen, then signed him to a four-year contract, securing the skipper's services in the dugout for the start of the franchise's new era as the Miami Marlins. Guillen's game management was not dissimilar in 2011 to what he'd been doing in Chicago for years. His baserunners attempted fewer steals than previous clubs, slipping to the middle of the pack with only 134 tries. This, however, was prob-

Miami in the offseason, but don't be surprised if youngsters like Steve Cishek and Mike Dunn are given opportunities should Bell stumble.

# Milwaukee Brewers

The Prince Fielder window was open for six years. Now the Brewers are beyond it, defenestrated by the inevitable circumstance of the wealthy young slugger's reasonable expectation of even more fabulous wealth attained via free agency.

How well did Doug Melvin steer them through that six-year shot? Not too shabbily, at least by the standards of a franchise that had only made the postseason twice before. During the Prince-ipate, Melvin's Brewers doubled that total, winning the wild card in 2008 and the NL Central last season. They might have added a third bite at October glory in 2007, but a July-August tumble left it to the Cubs to win the division.

Any chance the Brewers had to expand on that success died with Melvin's missteps in selecting starting pitchers after he borrowed C.C. Sabathia for the 2008 stretch run. Sabathia's departure as a free agent was predictable, but Melvin's attempts to identify worthwhile free agents to round out the rotation proved disastrous, as first Jeff Suppan and then Braden Looper delivered expensive ineffectiveness. More forgivable was the investment of faith in homegrown product Manny Parra and trade acquisition Dave Bush, that they might provide Yovani Gallardo with company. Forgivable and well-intentioned, but ultimately fruitless.

As a result, those choices left the 2009 and '10 Brewers in the hopeless situation of trying to contend with rotations that finished 15th and 14th in quality starts. A Yo-and-go front five couldn't even profit from four days of rain, thanks to the pop-top lid on Miller Park. Melvin belatedly addressed the problem by adding Randy Wolf in 2010, but playing the market in free agency is expensive, and the upside among the collection of free agents who might elect to go to Milwaukee is understandably low. In a league where the super-rotations of the Phillies and Giants seemed to be the best guarantee for contention and pennants, the Brewers were as well-equipped to contend as if they'd shown up to a saber duel with a spork.

To Melvin's credit, he fashioned a multi-year solution to the problem of conjuring up a contender's rotation. Instead of resorting to a market he could ill afford to play in, he avoided it altogether by striking deals with the Royals and Blue Jays, acquiring Zack Greinke and Shaun Marcum in trades. Both came to the Brewers under club control through 2012.

As solutions go, it was creative, albeit expensive in currency other than cash. Instead of having to compete with money for talent as just one of 30 possible suitors for any single free agent, making a deal is a matter of pairing off, comparing goodies, and reaching some mutually satisfying bit of consummation. Instead of dollars, it takes a willingness to deal prospects at a time when prospect worship might be at an all-time high.

Admittedly, you can anticipate regret over the talent traded away, especially if Brett Lawrie or Alcides Escobar or Jake Odorizzi or any of the other players dealt become perennial All-Stars. But wailing over the cost in talent instead of treasure risks losing sight of something simple: Even as teams have an obligation to their future, they also have an obligation to try to win when they have a legitimate shot. Franchises cannot simply operate as holding tanks for talent, because however much affection and anticipation gets heaped on top of every pile of prospects, a well-run organization is going to be able to sustain that pool of talent. For a team with a win-now agenda and limited means, there really is no choice.

To achieve something in the last year of the Prince window, Melvin had to do something, and he did. Pulling the trigger on both deals made winning in 2011 possible, giving

## BREWERS PROSPECTUS
### 2011 W-L: 96-66, 1st in NL Central

| | | |
|---|---|---|
| Pythag | .556 | 6th |
| RS/G | 4.45 | 11th |
| RA/G | 3.94 | 8th |
| TAv | .260 | 14th |
| TAv-P | .243 | 4th |
| FIP | 3.56 | 4th |
| DER | .712 | 13th |
| DL | 760 | 17th |
| B-Age | 28.8 | 17th |
| P-Age | 29.2 | 24th |
| Salary | $84.3 | 17th |
| M$/MW | $1.50 | 7th |

**Ballpark:** Miller Park (3-yr. PF: 107). Has been hitter-friendly. Now hitter-loving

**2011:** Pitching acquisitions finally work out, propelling Brewers to first division win in decades

**2012:** Will try to homer their way to the top again, this time with Gamel instead of Fielder

**Action Items:** With no big offseason moves, hope for health and a few career seasons

the staff a front four capable of winning the six-month marathon of the regular season. The Brewers vaulted to third in the league in quality starts behind the Phillies and Giants, and cruised to the division title. Perhaps if Marcum hadn't suddenly lost all semblance of effectiveness down the stretch and into the playoffs, it might have resulted in a pennant and, beyond that, a shot at profiting from Ron Washington's latest postseason pratfall. That it didn't turn out that way can be taken as verification of the notion that every October is a crapshoot, however as an example of achieving tangible results, the 2011 Brewers and Doug Melvin's part in creating them deserve to be lauded. The team was a triumph of strategic and operational planning.

Weeks as he agreed to a multi-year extension through 2015 that ballooned out to eight-figure annual salaries starting in 2012. And even though Ryan Braun was already inked through 2015 via a multi-year deal he'd signed in 2008, he'll now be in Milwaukee for the next decade after he signed a $105 million extension for 2016-21.

As financial calculations go, Melvin could be said to have made another set of admirably rational transactions that any stathead could accept. Deciding that a fat first baseman is more easily replaced at considerably less cost than the team's other great slugging star or one of the best second basemen in baseball seems like an eminently sensible choice, even before getting into whether Mat Gamel's time is now. That kind of bloodless calculus might prove to be a form of thrifty solace to Brewers fans worried about their team's post-Fielder future, even if they don't make movies about it.

Unfortunately, offseason disaster has confounded postseason misfortune with the revelation that Braun is facing a 50-game suspension for testing positive for unnatural levels of testosterone (natural and synthetic). If the findings are validated and Braun winds up missing a third of the 2012 season, one of the league's better rotations might end up serving little purpose other than as a larder for other aspiring contenders who need starting pitchers. Greinke and Marcum will both be free agents, while the Brewers' 2013 club option on Wolf might mean that he's also in his last season in Milwaukee.

Having Braun's absence on top of Fielder's defection as an excuse for the Brewers' likely failure to defend their division title may be just as well, because they might serve as cover for some expensive choices this winter. As good as Melvin

did in putting his 2011 team together, he's had a considerably worse Hot Stove season this winter.

First, there was Melvin's entirely avoidable decision to offer Francisco Rodriguez arbitration. Although an inspired pickup for the stretch, K-Rod was exactly the sort of player to whom you *do not* offer arbitration. Between paydays over $12 million per year and an offseason market jam-packed with other top relievers, offering him arbitration was a virtual guarantee the Brewers would be spending eight figures on a set-up man. Even if they subsequently deal him in a face-saving gesture, as the Braves did following their similarly spectacular miscalculation with Rafael Soriano after the 2009 season, they're going to have to eat some portion of

be a problem if Gamel's already settling in there and earning his keep.

Signing Ramirez might notionally provide them with a Fielder substitute in the lineup, but even if Braun were available to play on Opening Day, it leaves them with a heavy rightward lean in the lineup. Gamel might correct that, but a career Triple-A line of .312/.374/.512 across parts of four separate seasons in Nashville suggests he'll do less at the major-league level. Paying the posting fee to get a shot at Japan's former "next Ichiro," Norichika Aoki, might provide Milwaukee with an additional left-handed bat, but like Nyjer Morgan, Aoki's a slappy plinker who won't be belting balls towards the gaps. As much as that might fit in nicely with Ron Roenicke's "Angels Way" willingness to bunt a bit and run with the players who can, it won't balance out losing Braun for 50 games or Fielder forever.

In the end, the Brewers' agony of the present is that, despite a few missteps along the way, they did a fairly reasonable job of getting their ducks in a row and taking their best shot at winning during Prince Fielder's presence on the roster. That they didn't win isn't cause to condemn Melvin's execution, any more than Fielder's departure is proof of any crippling financial limitations going forward. The real test will be how they handle the next several seasons. So far, Melvin's elective decisions in retooling his post-Fielder roster leave a lot to be desired. The Brewers may only fall as far as third place in the NL Central, but that's because it would be hard to climb down below the Pirates, Cubs, and Astros. But if Braun's gone and Melvin decides to cash in his rotation regulars before they reach free agency, don't be surprised if Milwaukee drops below 75 wins.

# HITTERS

### Erick Almonte    1B

Born: 2/1/1978 Age: 34
Bats: R Throws: R Height: 6' 3" Weight: 180
Breakout: 7% Improve: 37% Collapse: 19%
Attrition: 44% MLB: 72%

Comparables:
Tito Francona, Mickey Vernon, Tom McCraw

| YEAR | TEAM | LVL | AGE | PA | R | 2B | 3B | HR | RBI | BB | SO | SB | CS | AVG_OBP_SLG | TAv | BABIP | BRR | FRAA | WARP |
|------|------|-----|-----|----|----|----|----|----|-----|----|----|----|----|-------------|-----|-------|-----|------|------|
| 2009 | NAS | AAA | 31 | 277 | 29 | 11 | 0 | 2 | 31 | 27 | 53 | 4 | 0 | .291/.366/.360 | .250 | .365 | 1.1 | -3 | 0.0 |
| 2010 | NAS | AAA | 32 | 355 | 40 | 21 | 2 | 2 | 38 | 28 | 63 | 4 | 0 | .320/.377/.415 | .274 | .392 | -2.6 | -0.5 | 0.8 |
| 2011 | NAS | AAA | 33 | 276 | 43 | 15 | 1 | 6 | 42 | 31 | 46 | 2 | 1 | .303/.380/.447 | .280 | .352 | -2.4 | 0.7 | 0.9 |
| 2011 | MIL | MLB | 33 | 29 | 1 | 0 | 0 | 1 | 3 | 0 | 4 | 0 | 0 | .103/.103/.207 | .085 | .083 | 0 | -0.8 | -0.5 |
| 2012 | MIL | MLB | 34 | 250 | 25 | 10 | 1 | 3 | 20 | 20 | 57 | 1 | 0 | .238/.300/.321 | .225 | .303 | 0 | 1B -4, RF -2 | -0.9 |

Almonte earning a roster spot was a curious move by the Brewers this season, as he's a career minor-league utility man whose days of being able to play the infield have expired, and whose bat could barely have kept a good defensive shortstop in the bigs. Yet there he was, starting in right field and homering off of Travis Wood on April 2. Then, on April 26, he took his eyes off a throw from Craig Counsell during batting practice and the ball struck him in the face. Thus, he made baseball history as the first player to be put on the new seven-day disabled list for concussions. After April's excitement, things returned to normal for Almonte—he recovered from the blow and returned to the minors, likely never to be seen again in a major-league lineup.

### Ryan Braun    LF

Born: 11/17/1983 Age: 28
Bats: R Throws: R Height: 6' 3" Weight: 200
Breakout: 0% Improve: 30% Collapse: 1%
Attrition: 22% MLB: 85%

Comparables:
Frank Robinson, Albert Belle, Matt Holliday

| YEAR | TEAM | LVL | AGE | PA | R | 2B | 3B | HR | RBI | BB | SO | SB | CS | AVG_OBP_SLG | TAv | BABIP | BRR | FRAA | WARP |
|------|------|-----|-----|----|----|----|----|----|-----|----|----|----|----|-------------|-----|-------|-----|------|------|
| 2009 | MIL | MLB | 25 | 708 | 113 | 39 | 6 | 32 | 114 | 57 | 121 | 20 | 6 | .320/.386/.551 | .317 | .353 | 1.3 | -0.5 | 5.4 |
| 2010 | MIL | MLB | 26 | 684 | 101 | 45 | 1 | 25 | 103 | 56 | 105 | 14 | 3 | .304/.365/.501 | .298 | .331 | 5 | 4.2 | 4.6 |
| 2011 | MIL | MLB | 27 | 629 | 109 | 38 | 6 | 33 | 111 | 58 | 93 | 33 | 6 | .332/.397/.597 | .343 | .350 | 0.2 | 2.1 | 6.6 |
| 2012 | MIL | MLB | 28 | 602 | 89 | 34 | 4 | 32 | 102 | 50 | 109 | 19 | 5 | .306/.369/.562 | .326 | .331 | 0.4 | LF 1 | 5.6 |

The love affair between the Brewers and Braun should keep Bernie sliding for many years, as the team tied the knot with the elite slugger, giving him a contract that lasts until after the cows come home (that's 2020 for folks not living on a dairy farm). And why not? Braun has developed into a multi-faceted superstar who helps his team in every way. Despite still appearing awkward at times in the outfield, Braun's defense is better than par, and he led the league in slugging again in 2011—yes, the same league with Sir Albert of St. Louis—en route to winning the first MVP award for a Brewers player since 1989. While fans were hoping that Prince Fielder's last season would end with more glory, the playoff losses weren't Braun's fault, as he logged a cool .333/.385/.583 batting line against the Cards after dismantling the D-backs. It was also settled that the Hebrew Hammer will indeed play on Yom Kippur, a bonus for the playoff-hopeful Brew Crew. The "in sickness and in health" vow was already tested, as Braun missed nine games in July with leg issues. But he recovered fully and even swiped 14 bases in August and September.

### Craig Counsell    SS

Born: 8/21/1970 Age: 41
Bats: L Throws: R Height: 6' 1" Weight: 177
Breakout: 1% Improve: 13% Collapse: 3%
Attrition: 17% MLB: 47%

Comparables:
Wade Boggs, Omar Vizquel, Barry Larkin

| YEAR | TEAM | LVL | AGE | PA | R | 2B | 3B | HR | RBI | BB | SO | SB | CS | AVG_OBP_SLG | TAv | BABIP | BRR | FRAA | WARP |
|------|------|-----|-----|----|----|----|----|----|-----|----|----|----|----|-------------|-----|-------|-----|------|------|
| 2009 | MIL | MLB | 38 | 459 | 61 | 22 | 8 | 4 | 39 | 42 | 54 | 3 | 4 | .285/.357/.408 | .261 | .317 | 1.1 | 4.2 | 2.1 |
| 2010 | MIL | MLB | 39 | 230 | 16 | 8 | 0 | 2 | 21 | 21 | 29 | 1 | 1 | .250/.322/.319 | .240 | .282 | -0.7 | 0 | 0.3 |
| 2011 | MIL | MLB | 40 | 187 | 19 | 2 | 1 | 1 | 9 | 20 | 21 | 2 | 1 | .178/.280/.223 | .199 | .197 | 1.1 | -1.3 | -0.5 |
| 2012 | MIL | MLB | 41 | 250 | 26 | 9 | 2 | 2 | 18 | 27 | 37 | 2 | 1 | .230/.321/.318 | .231 | .262 | -0.2 | SS 0, 3B -0 | 0.2 |

Sometimes there's a single event that makes it clear to a player that it's time to hang up the cleats. In Counsell's case, there were 45 such events, as he had just raised his on-base percentage to .345 with a three-hit game on June 10 before embarking on a hitless streak the likes of which Joe Dimmagio couldn't even summon up nightmares. Counsell didn't get the message, however, and is planning to return to provide veteran leadership, backup infield play, and a walk or two. He has almost zero oomph on his batted balls anymore, but nobody deserves a .197 BABIP and a bit of a dead cat bounce can be expected from his batting average.

### Kentrail Davis    RF

Born: 6/29/1988 Age: 24
Bats: L Throws: R Height: 5' 10" Weight: 195
Breakout: 3% Improve: 9% Collapse: 2%
Attrition: 18% MLB: 44%

Comparables:
Joseph Batten, Gene Hiser, Carlos Quintana

| YEAR | TEAM | LVL | AGE | PA | R | 2B | 3B | HR | RBI | BB | SO | SB | CS | AVG_OBP_SLG | TAv | BABIP | BRR | FRAA | WARP |
|------|------|-----|-----|----|----|----|----|----|-----|----|----|----|----|-------------|-----|-------|-----|------|------|
| 2010 | WIS | A | 22 | 290 | 44 | 26 | 5 | 3 | 46 | 31 | 36 | 3 | 1 | .335/.428/.518 | .326 | .383 | -1.6 | 2.1 | 2.4 |
| 2010 | BRV | A+ | 22 | 150 | 20 | 2 | 5 | 0 | 17 | 17 | 28 | 8 | 2 | .244/.380/.341 | .257 | .316 | 0.5 | -1.5 | 0.4 |
| 2011 | BRV | A+ | 23 | 565 | 76 | 19 | 8 | 8 | 46 | 37 | 97 | 33 | 8 | .245/.317/.361 | .250 | .287 | 7 | 0.7 | 1.4 |
| 2012 | MIL | MLB | 24 | 250 | 23 | 8 | 2 | 3 | 20 | 15 | 56 | 9 | 2 | .211/.276/.310 | .213 | .262 | 0.1 | RF 0, CF -3 | -1.2 |

As a Golden Spikes semifinalist in college, Davis was impressing everyone, like Cinderella at the ball. He was compared to Kirby Puckett—despite batting left-handed—for his mad batting skills and athletic ability that overcame a bowling-ball physique. But if Kentrail was showing his inner Kirby for the Timber Rattlers in 2010, he lost it in 2011, becoming impatient at the plate and taking uncharacteristically bad swings at pitches he—unlike Puckett—couldn't handle. Now the narrative that he'd become a high-average hitter who developed power with time seems about as likely as a fairy tale, though both the Brewers and Kentrail are still hoping he'll get his golden shoe back.

**Eric Farris  2B**

Born: 3/3/1986 Age: 26
Bats: R Throws: R Height: 5' 10" Weight: 180
Breakout: 2% Improve: 14% Collapse: 7%
Attrition: 22% MLB: 50%

**Comparables:**
Marlon Anderson, Billy Moran, Mike

| YEAR | TEAM | LVL | AGE | PA | R | 2B | 3B | HR | RBI | BB | SO | SB | CS | AVG/OBP/SLG | TAv | BABIP | BRR | FRAA | WARP |
|------|------|-----|-----|-----|----|----|----|----|-----|----|----|----|----|-------------|------|-------|------|------------|------|
| 2009 | BRV | A+ | 23 | 534 | 68 | 18 | 1 | 7 | 49 | 29 | 46 | 70 | 6 | .298/.326/.385 | .273 | .300 | 2 | 13.6 | 3.8 |
| 2010 | NAS | AAA | 24 | 249 | 28 | 9 | 1 | 2 | 15 | 9 | 25 | 14 | 2 | .274/.306/.348 | .230 | .293 | 0.6 | 1.8 | 0.1 |
| 2011 | NAS | AAA | 25 | 594 | 70 | 26 | 5 | 6 | 55 | 32 | 70 | 21 | 7 | .271/.317/.372 | .243 | .300 | 2.2 | -2.8 | 0.6 |
| 2012 | MIL | MLB | 26 | 250 | 24 | 10 | 1 | 3 | 22 | 10 | 40 | 12 | 2 | .242/.277/.329 | .212 | .273 | 0.6 | 2B 4, SS 0 | -0.6 |

| YEAR | TEAM | LVL | AGE | PA | R | 2B | 3B | HR | RBI | BB | SO | SB | CS | AVG/OBP/SLG | TAv | BABIP | BRR | FRAA | WARP |
|------|------|-----|-----|-----|-----|----|----|----|-----|-----|-----|----|----|-------------|------|-------|------|------|------|
| 2011 | MIL | MLB | 27 | 692 | 95 | 36 | 1 | 38 | 120 | 107 | 106 | 1 | 1 | .299/.415/.566 | .329 | .306 | -3.3 | -0.8 | 5.3 |
| 2012 | MIL | MLB | 28 | 655 | 100 | 29 | 1 | 39 | 104 | 96 | 124 | 2 | 1 | .282/.398/.554 | .328 | .297 | -0.2 | 1B -3 | 5.5 |

Breakout: 3% Improve: 48% Collapse: 1%
Attrition: 11% MLB: 94%

**Comparables:**
Todd Helton, Norm Cash, Frank Thomas

The Milwaukee *Journal Sentinel* reports that Wisconsin has the highest rate of obesity among African-American adults, but didn't comment on how Fielder leaving via free-agency would impact this statistic. Whether Prince will be worth his new contract will depend on many things, such as his continued avoidance of injuries, the overall inflation rate of pay for top ballplayers, the percentage of his team's payroll, etc. But his "body type" has certainly received the most attention. Gone are the days of Babe Ruth, when large men who are dismissive of fitness concerns are taken in stride, as teams are constantly looking for every marginal edge they can get. Occluded by all that mass is the fact that Fielder's career TAv (.307) ranks 37th on the "through age 27" list among players who had 3000 or more plate appearances by that age (1969+). And while he won't sell as many jeans as Rickey Henderson or Dave Winfield (the guys closest to him on the list), he's done better through age 27 than John Olerud (.299 TAv), who went on to hit .296/.400/.461 in 5374 subsequent plate appearances. Fielder's obviously a much different type of hitter than Olerud was, but it seems clear he'd have gotten an even fatter contract if he had the same long and lean physique.

**Mat Gamel  3B**

Born: 7/26/1985 Age: 26
Bats: L Throws: R Height: 6' 1" Weight: 195
Breakout: 1% Improve: 20% Collapse: 1%
Attrition: 13% MLB: 47%

**Comparables:**
Daniel Dorn, Matthew Brown, Chris Smith

| YEAR | TEAM | LVL | AGE | PA | R | 2B | 3B | HR | RBI | BB | SO | SB | CS | AVG/OBP/SLG | TAv | BABIP | BRR | FRAA | WARP |
|------|------|-----|-----|-----|----|----|----|----|-----|----|----|----|----|-------------|------|-------|------|------------|------|
| 2009 | NAS | AAA | 23 | 320 | 42 | 18 | 1 | 11 | 48 | 38 | 89 | 1 | 0 | .278/.371/.473 | .293 | .374 | -0.2 | -3.9 | 1.8 |
| 2009 | MIL | MLB | 23 | 148 | 11 | 6 | 1 | 5 | 20 | 18 | 54 | 1 | 0 | .242/.338/.422 | .268 | .371 | 0.4 | -1 | 0.3 |
| 2010 | NAS | AAA | 24 | 359 | 54 | 24 | 0 | 13 | 67 | 38 | 64 | 3 | 1 | .309/.393/.511 | .303 | .355 | -3 | -8.3 | 2.1 |
| 2010 | MIL | MLB | 24 | 17 | 1 | 1 | 0 | 0 | 1 | 1 | 8 | 0 | 0 | .200/.294/.267 | .195 | .429 | 0.2 | -0.2 | -0.1 |
| 2011 | NAS | AAA | 25 | 545 | 90 | 29 | 0 | 28 | 96 | 46 | 84 | 2 | 0 | .310/.372/.540 | .314 | .326 | 1.9 | 1.4 | 4.2 |
| 2011 | MIL | MLB | 25 | 27 | 1 | 1 | 0 | 0 | 2 | 1 | 4 | 0 | 0 | .115/.148/.154 | .096 | .136 | 0 | -0.1 | -0.4 |
| 2012 | MIL | MLB | 26 | 250 | 30 | 11 | 1 | 9 | 31 | 21 | 66 | 1 | 0 | .254/.320/.433 | .265 | .314 | 0 | 3B -4, 1B -1 | 1.6 |

Gamel had seen his prospect stock drop over the past couple of seasons as his expected exile to first base took place, since his batting stats always projected as marginal for the easier position. The 2011 sweason brought tremendous news for both Mat and the Brewers, as slight adjustments to his swing led to both more frequent contact and more loft, resulting in more homers. One good Triple-A season does not an All-Star make, and Gamel's shown few signs of being start-worthy against left-handed pitching, but few would fault the Brewers for going with him as a low-cost option against righties.

### Scooter Gennett — 2B

Born: 5/1/1990 Age: 22
Bats: L Throws: R Height: 5' 10" Weight: 164
Breakout: 5% Improve: 20% Collapse: 2%
Attrition: 16% MLB: 55%

**Comparables:**
Tony Abreu, Bill Mazeroski, Rennie Stennett

| YEAR | TEAM | LVL | AGE | PA | R | 2B | 3B | HR | RBI | BB | SO | SB | CS | AVG_OBP_SLG | TAv | BABIP | BRR | FRAA | WARP |
|------|------|-----|-----|-----|----|----|----|----|-----|----|----|----|----|-------------|-----|-------|------|-----------|------|
| 2010 | WIS | A | 20 | 525 | 87 | 39 | 4 | 9 | 55 | 31 | 91 | 14 | 4 | .309/.355/.463 | .289 | .364 | -0.5 | 0.6 | 3.6 |
| 2011 | BRV | A+ | 21 | 601 | 74 | 20 | 6 | 9 | 51 | 27 | 69 | 11 | 10 | .300/.334/.406 | .275 | .326 | 0.1 | -9 | 1.7 |
| 2012 | MIL | MLB | 22 | 250 | 25 | 11 | 1 | 4 | 25 | 8 | 48 | 3 | 2 | .250/.277/.353 | .222 | .294 | -0.3 | 2B -5, SS 0 | -0.3 |

Gennett dropped to the 16th round in 2009 because he was expected to be difficult to sign away from Florida State. He's nicknamed "Scooter" and is an undersized gritty middle infielder for whom the game hasn't begun until his uniform is dirty. But until 2011 his approach was more that of a mid-order hitter waiting for a pitch he could drive and racking up the extra-base hits. Last year however he worked on being more aggressive with pitch selection while cutting down on his swing, leading to a much higher contact rate which will serve him well. His eruption in the AFL is a teaser that he may be able to tailor his stroke to the situation. If he can, he'll be on track to become an average second baseman despite unexceptional defensive skills and a lack of patience at the plate.

### Caleb Gindl — RF

Born: 8/31/1988 Age: 23
Bats: L Throws: L Height: 5' 10" Weight: 205
Breakout: 5% Improve: 46% Collapse: 4%
Attrition: 16% MLB: 70%

**Comparables:**
Lastings Milledge, Jeremy Hermida, Rene Tosoni

| YEAR | TEAM | LVL | AGE | PA | R | 2B | 3B | HR | RBI | BB | SO | SB | CS | AVG_OBP_SLG | TAv | BABIP | BRR | FRAA | WARP |
|------|------|-----|-----|-----|----|----|----|----|-----|----|----|----|----|-------------|-----|-------|------|-----------|------|
| 2009 | BRV | A+ | 20 | 462 | 61 | 15 | 3 | 17 | 71 | 57 | 92 | 18 | 4 | .277/.368/.459 | .299 | .321 | 0.7 | -2.7 | 2.7 |
| 2010 | HUN | AA | 21 | 534 | 61 | 33 | 1 | 9 | 60 | 55 | 78 | 10 | 5 | .272/.352/.406 | .279 | .306 | -3.5 | -7.6 | 1.3 |
| 2011 | NAS | AAA | 22 | 538 | 84 | 23 | 5 | 15 | 60 | 63 | 93 | 6 | 5 | .307/.390/.472 | .291 | .357 | 0.8 | -4.3 | 2.5 |
| 2012 | MIL | MLB | 23 | 250 | 28 | 10 | 1 | 7 | 26 | 23 | 54 | 3 | 1 | .246/.318/.391 | .252 | .292 | -0.2 | RF -6, CF -1 | 0.6 |

Between 2003 and '04, the Brewers got 0.8 batting WARP and 0.8 pitching WARP from Brooks Keischnick in limited playing time. With expanded bullpens these days, having a player who could function as both a fifth outfielder and a last resort in the bullpen would be useful. Though drafted as an outfielder/pitcher in 2007, Gindl isn't likely to become the next, but he has a good arm and a winning attitude, and his line-drive bat should play as a spare outfielder whenever he gets the call. Still, he'd help a team a lot more if he could soak up innings in blowouts as well.

### Carlos Gomez — CF

Born: 12/4/1985 Age: 26
Bats: R Throws: R Height: 6' 5" Weight: 195
Breakout: 4% Improve: 45% Collapse: 8%
Attrition: 28% MLB: 83%

**Comparables:**
Chris Duffy, Wayne Lydon, Russ Snyder

| YEAR | TEAM | LVL | AGE | PA | R | 2B | 3B | HR | RBI | BB | SO | SB | CS | AVG_OBP_SLG | TAv | BABIP | BRR | FRAA | WARP |
|------|------|-----|-----|-----|----|----|----|----|-----|----|----|----|----|-------------|-----|-------|------|-----------|------|
| 2009 | MIN | MLB | 23 | 349 | 51 | 15 | 5 | 3 | 28 | 22 | 72 | 14 | 7 | .229/.287/.337 | .222 | .286 | -0.1 | 12.8 | 0.9 |
| 2010 | MIL | MLB | 24 | 318 | 38 | 11 | 3 | 5 | 24 | 17 | 72 | 18 | 3 | .247/.298/.357 | .231 | .313 | 4.2 | -8.3 | -0.4 |
| 2011 | MIL | MLB | 25 | 258 | 37 | 11 | 3 | 8 | 24 | 15 | 64 | 16 | 2 | .225/.276/.403 | .245 | .273 | 0 | 7.3 | 1.4 |
| 2012 | MIL | MLB | 26 | 256 | 27 | 10 | 2 | 5 | 26 | 15 | 59 | 15 | 4 | .245/.296/.368 | .233 | .300 | 0.2 | CF 7, RF 0 | 0.2 |

Gomez has a terrible approach at the plate, but he has enough athletic ability that his "grip and rip" strategy resulted in a career-high ISO in 2011. That such a phenomenal defensive center fielder couldn't hold his job with a well-above-average rate of extra base hits is stark commentary on his inability to either make regular contact or draw walks. He's still young, though three organizations have yet to make progress with coaching his swing. The good news is that his approach lends itself to a fluky good season if he gets regular playing time, so he's a dark-horse candidate to have a surprisingly high WARP out of the blue.

### Alex Gonzalez — SS

Born: 2/15/1977 Age: 35
Bats: R Throws: R Height: 6' 1" Weight: 170
Breakout: 1% Improve: 18% Collapse: 10%
Attrition: 26% MLB: 71%

**Comparables:**
Dickie Thon, Dave Concepcion, Alex Gonzalez

| YEAR | TEAM | LVL | AGE | PA | R | 2B | 3B | HR | RBI | BB | SO | SB | CS | AVG_OBP_SLG | TAv | BABIP | BRR | FRAA | WARP |
|------|------|-----|-----|-----|----|----|----|----|-----|----|----|----|----|-------------|-----|-------|------|------|------|
| 2009 | BOS | MLB | 32 | 159 | 26 | 10 | 0 | 5 | 15 | 5 | 29 | 2 | 0 | .284/.316/.453 | .253 | .325 | 0.6 | -1.6 | 0.3 |
| 2009 | CIN | MLB | 32 | 270 | 16 | 12 | 0 | 3 | 26 | 15 | 36 | 0 | 1 | .210/.258/.296 | .201 | .231 | -0.5 | -3.9 | -1.1 |
| 2010 | ATL | MLB | 33 | 292 | 27 | 17 | 2 | 6 | 38 | 14 | 53 | 0 | 2 | .240/.291/.386 | .229 | .276 | -1.1 | 5.7 | 0.5 |
| 2010 | TOR | MLB | 33 | 348 | 47 | 25 | 1 | 17 | 50 | 17 | 65 | 1 | 0 | .259/.296/.497 | .275 | .274 | -0.6 | 10.7 | 3.4 |
| 2011 | ATL | MLB | 34 | 593 | 59 | 27 | 1 | 15 | 56 | 22 | 126 | 2 | 0 | .241/.270/.372 | .226 | .285 | -1.3 | 11 | 1.6 |
| 2012 | MIL | MLB | 35 | 566 | 61 | 29 | 1 | 17 | 66 | 27 | 112 | 3 | 2 | .241/.283/.397 | .239 | .272 | -0.3 | SS 8 | 1.1 |

Remember when Gonzalez hit 17 home runs for the Jays in half a season? Neither does his bat. In Atlanta, Gonzalez hit 21 homers in 885 plate appearances. No problem, since the Braves acquired him for his ferocious defense, yet let him leave without a clear replacement partly because he also helped opposing defenses—grounding into more double plays than any other shortstop. From the Brewers perspective, the fact that he's tallied 19.2 FRAA per 1440 innings at shortstop over the past three seasons—third-best rate among players with 6480 innings at the position—represents a huge upgrade over Yunieski Betancourt afield, and Roenicke's love of the sacrifice bunt should alleviate much of the GDP pain.

**Taylor Green**    3B

Born: 11/2/1986 Age: 25
Bats: L Throws: R Height: 6' 0" Weight: 198
Breakout: 2% Improve: 28% Collapse: 8%
Attrition: 54% MLB: 89%

Comparables:
Chris Arnold, Chris Brown, Brad Mills

| YEAR | TEAM | LVL | AGE | PA | R | 2B | 3B | HR | RBI | BB | SO | SB | CS | AVG_OBP_SLG | TAv | BABIP | BRR | FRAA | WARP |
|------|------|-----|-----|-----|----|----|----|----|-----|----|----|----|----|-------------|-----|-------|-----|-------------|------|
| 2009 | HUN | AA | 22 | 345 | 34 | 15 | 0 | 5 | 43 | 33 | 37 | 0 | 2 | .258/.334/.356 | .249 | .280 | 1.3 | -2.2 | 0.9 |
| 2010 | HUN | AA | 23 | 451 | 51 | 29 | 1 | 13 | 81 | 45 | 67 | 0 | 2 | .260/.341/.438 | .272 | .283 | 2 | 6.8 | 2.7 |
| 2011 | NAS | AAA | 24 | 487 | 74 | 36 | 1 | 22 | 88 | 55 | 72 | 1 | 0 | .336/.413/.583 | .324 | .360 | 0.1 | -7.8 | 4.8 |
| 2011 | MIL | MLB | 24 | 37 | 2 | 3 | 0 | 0 | 1 | 0 | 6 | 0 | 0 | .270/.270/.351 | .222 | .323 | 0.6 | 0.2 | 0.1 |
| 2012 | MIL | MLB | 25 | 250 | 30 | 13 | 1 | 7 | 29 | 20 | 45 | 0 | 0 | .260/.322/.419 | .260 | .290 | 0 | 3B -0, 2B -0 | 1.8 |

Wrist surgery following the 2008 season had enough of an impact on Green that he was on the verge of washing out as a prospect. But he had moved beyond those effects by 2011, and he hit .377 from June 1 through the end of Nashville's season. Certainly, he won't post .360 BABIPs in the majors as he did at Triple-A, but he's shown enough now that the organization expects him to hit if they need him, and views him as having the upside potential of a starting third baseman, though a utility role is still considered more likely.

not a contact hitter, but his height allows him to generate good power without a max-effort approach, and thus post a decent batting average. Much has been made of moving Hart to first base, where he'd presumably develop into the sort of defender who would prevent errant throws with his long wingspan. But the team would be best off if he returned to the outfield, where he's almost average defensively, since the lineup can use some balance and lefty bats are much more common at first base.

**Cesar Izturis**    SS

Born: 2/10/1980 Age: 32
Bats: B Throws: R Height: 5' 10" Weight: 175
Breakout: 4% Improve: 39% Collapse: 7%
Attrition: 33% MLB: 84%

Comparables:
Tim Foli, Rafael Bournigal, Luis Aparicio

| YEAR | TEAM | LVL | AGE | PA | R | 2B | 3B | HR | RBI | BB | SO | SB | CS | AVG_OBP_SLG | TAv | BABIP | BRR | FRAA | WARP |
|------|------|-----|-----|-----|----|----|----|----|-----|----|----|----|----|-------------|-----|-------|-----|-------------|------|
| 2009 | BAL | MLB | 29 | 412 | 34 | 14 | 4 | 2 | 30 | 18 | 38 | 12 | 4 | .256/.294/.328 | .213 | .280 | -4.3 | 9.9 | 0.0 |
| 2010 | BAL | MLB | 30 | 513 | 42 | 13 | 1 | 1 | 28 | 25 | 53 | 11 | 5 | .230/.277/.268 | .202 | .257 | 2 | -6.9 | -1.4 |
| 2011 | BAL | MLB | 31 | 33 | 4 | 0 | 0 | 0 | 1 | 2 | 10 | 0 | 0 | .200/.250/.200 | .169 | .300 | -0.5 | 1.6 | -0.1 |
| 2012 | MIL | MLB | 32 | 250 | 25 | 8 | 1 | 1 | 20 | 14 | 25 | 7 | 3 | .252/.299/.319 | .222 | .273 | -0.2 | SS 1, 2B -0 | 0.1 |

Last season was a lost one for Izturis, who scavenged just 33 plate appearances after elbow surgery and a groin injury. In those 33 plate appearances, Izturis managed to provide more value than when he was playing full time; he was only 0.1 wins below replacement level this year as opposed to -1.4 wins! He signed with the Brewers as a backup infielder on the strength of his admittedly serviceable defense and veteran leadership, but Milwaukee shouldn't expect much of the 32-year-old.

**George Kottaras**    C

Born: 5/16/1983 Age: 29
Bats: L Throws: R Height: 6' 1" Weight: 185
Breakout: 1% Improve: 20% Collapse: 9%
Attrition: 42% MLB: 83%

Comparables:
Miguel Ojeda, Ben Risinger, Tim Hosley

| YEAR | TEAM | LVL | AGE | PA | R | 2B | 3B | HR | RBI | BB | SO | SB | CS | AVG_OBP_SLG | TAv | BABIP | BRR | FRAA | WARP |
|------|------|-----|-----|-----|----|----|----|----|-----|----|----|----|----|-------------|-----|-------|-----|-----------|------|
| 2009 | BOS | MLB | 26 | 107 | 15 | 11 | 0 | 1 | 10 | 11 | 25 | 0 | 0 | .237/.308/.387 | .248 | .300 | 0.4 | -0.4 | 0.2 |
| 2010 | MIL | MLB | 27 | 250 | 24 | 12 | 1 | 9 | 26 | 33 | 44 | 2 | 0 | .203/.305/.396 | .261 | .209 | -4.6 | -1 | 0.2 |
| 2011 | NAS | AAA | 28 | 118 | 19 | 8 | 1 | 4 | 21 | 16 | 29 | 0 | 1 | .343/.432/.559 | .307 | .449 | -1.2 | 0.3 | 1.0 |
| 2011 | MIL | MLB | 28 | 123 | 15 | 6 | 1 | 5 | 17 | 10 | 26 | 0 | 1 | .252/.311/.459 | .266 | .284 | 0 | 0 | 0.6 |
| 2012 | MIL | MLB | 29 | 250 | 30 | 12 | 1 | 9 | 29 | 30 | 57 | 1 | 0 | .235/.329/.419 | .265 | .276 | -0.1 | C -1, 3B 0 | 2.3 |

Kottaras has hit 12 home runs in 368 plate appearances against right-handed pitching in his career, and slugged .500 against righties in 2011. He even walks enough to make up for the fact that his lack of foot speed drags down his batting average. If he could throw out anyone faster than Prince Fielder, he could provide some team the big half of a cheap catching platoon. As is, he can be spotted against tough right-handed starters on slow teams. But—despite the bat—he makes for a sub-optimal backup catcher, as there will always be the temptation to use the regular as a defensive replacement, or to—ugh—carry a third catcher.

### Felipe Lopez 2B

Born: 5/12/1980 Age: 32
Bats: B Throws: R Height: 6' 1" Weight: 175
Breakout: 2% Improve: 45% Collapse: 4%
Attrition: 18% MLB: 85%

Comparables:
Julio Franco, Nelson Liriano, Joe Inglett

| YEAR | TEAM | LVL | AGE | PA | R | 2B | 3B | HR | RBI | BB | SO | SB | CS | AVG/OBP/SLG | TAv | BABIP | BRR | FRAA | WARP |
|------|------|-----|-----|-----|----|----|----|----|-----|----|----|----|----|-------------|-----|-------|-----|------|------|
| 2009 | ARI | MLB | 29 | 383 | 44 | 18 | 1 | 6 | 25 | 34 | 59 | 6 | 3 | .301/.364/.412 | .267 | .348 | 1 | 5.7 | 1.8 |
| 2009 | MIL | MLB | 29 | 297 | 44 | 20 | 2 | 3 | 32 | 37 | 41 | 0 | 3 | .320/.407/.448 | .294 | .372 | -3.2 | -0.9 | 1.2 |
| 2010 | BOS | MLB | 30 | 16 | 2 | 0 | 0 | 1 | 1 | 1 | 4 | 0 | 0 | .267/.312/.467 | .273 | .300 | 0.2 | -0.1 | 0.0 |
| 2010 | SLN | MLB | 30 | 425 | 50 | 18 | 1 | 7 | 36 | 43 | 77 | 8 | 2 | .231/.310/.340 | .246 | .272 | 0 | -6.3 | 0.2 |
| 2011 | DUR | AAA | 31 | 207 | 25 | 11 | 0 | 7 | 37 | 14 | 41 | 1 | 0 | .305/.357/.474 | .282 | .357 | -2.5 | -1.8 | 0.5 |
| 2011 | MIL | MLB | 31 | 51 | 4 | 0 | 0 | 0 | 3 | 4 | 7 | 0 | 0 | .182/.245/.182 | .193 | .211 | 0.3 | 0.2 | -0.2 |
| 2011 | TBA | MLB | 31 | 102 | 8 | 4 | 0 | 2 | 8 | 4 | 28 | 1 | 1 | .216/.248/.320 | .204 | .284 | -0.4 | -0.6 | -0.4 |
| 2012 | MIL | MLB | 32 | 250 | 28 | 11 | 1 | 4 | 24 | 22 | 45 | 4 | 2 | .258/.326/.368 | .249 | .302 | -0.3 | 2B -1, 3B -2 | 1.0 |

Lopez was once tabbed by Tony La Russa to be an All-Star, but time has not been kind, and it's now difficult to believe he won't be 32 until May. When Rickie Weeks went down with an injury, picking up the one-time shortstop for cash from Tampa Bay seemed like a no-brainer. Of course, Lopez had been outrighted by the Rays because his plate appearances evoked images of a 3-year-old swinging at a piñata. He's never been much of a defender and complaints about him as a teammate have followed him as well. Though he stopped his flailing in Milwaukee, he made hard contact less often than Counsell, and Hairston quickly proved the better option at the keystone. A desperate team may give him another shot, but time is running out.

### Jonathan Lucroy C

Born: 6/13/1986 Age: 26
Bats: R Throws: R Height: 6' 1" Weight: 195
Breakout: 2% Improve: 28% Collapse: 13%
Attrition: 48% MLB: 88%

Comparables:
Ron Hassey, Don Pavletich, Keith Moreland

| YEAR | TEAM | LVL | AGE | PA | R | 2B | 3B | HR | RBI | BB | SO | SB | CS | AVG/OBP/SLG | TAv | BABIP | BRR | FRAA | WARP |
|------|------|-----|-----|-----|----|----|----|----|-----|----|----|----|----|-------------|-----|-------|-----|------|------|
| 2009 | HUN | AA | 23 | 506 | 61 | 32 | 2 | 9 | 66 | 78 | 66 | 1 | 1 | .267/.384/.418 | .288 | .299 | -2.7 | 1.5 | 3.9 |
| 2010 | NAS | AAA | 24 | 83 | 8 | 4 | 0 | 2 | 11 | 3 | 14 | 0 | 0 | .237/.265/.363 | .230 | .266 | 0.2 | -0.7 | 0.4 |
| 2010 | MIL | MLB | 24 | 297 | 24 | 9 | 0 | 4 | 26 | 18 | 44 | 4 | 2 | .253/.300/.329 | .218 | .287 | 1.5 | 1.1 | 0.3 |
| 2011 | MIL | MLB | 25 | 468 | 45 | 16 | 1 | 12 | 59 | 29 | 99 | 2 | 1 | .265/.312/.391 | .245 | .317 | 2.2 | -2.3 | 1.4 |
| 2012 | MIL | MLB | 26 | 423 | 49 | 18 | 1 | 11 | 45 | 35 | 78 | 2 | 1 | .260/.324/.395 | .255 | .299 | -0.1 | C -1 | 1.8 |

Lucroy had won many fans over by hitting .287 through August 24, when the Brewers already enjoyed a 10-game lead. Considering he was drafted as a bat-first catcher, the team has had high hopes for his offense. There are problems here, though. While his defense is improving—BP's Mike Fast's research shows that Lucroy's been among the best at getting borderline strike calls for his pitchers—his end-of-season slump exposed the fact that other than batting average, his offensive game is wanting. Without more development as a hitter, he's still a "will do" piece of the puzzle, and expectations for more aren't unfounded, as he's shown both patience and power in the minors—though never in the same season.

### Martin Maldonado C

Born: 8/16/1986 Age: 25
Bats: R Throws: R Height: 6' 2" Weight: 223
Breakout: 6% Improve: 33% Collapse: 5%
Attrition: 34% MLB: 61%

Comparables:
John Sullivan, Steven Lerud, Marc Hill

| YEAR | TEAM | LVL | AGE | PA | R | 2B | 3B | HR | RBI | BB | SO | SB | CS | AVG/OBP/SLG | TAv | BABIP | BRR | FRAA | WARP |
|------|------|-----|-----|-----|----|----|----|----|-----|----|----|----|----|-------------|-----|-------|-----|------|------|
| 2009 | BRV | A+ | 22 | 299 | 25 | 9 | 0 | 2 | 21 | 30 | 51 | 2 | 1 | .199/.293/.259 | .214 | .232 | -2.4 | -0.9 | 0.1 |
| 2010 | HUN | AA | 23 | 123 | 9 | 6 | 0 | 2 | 12 | 9 | 24 | 0 | 2 | .252/.347/.369 | .235 | .304 | -0.7 | -0.2 | 0.2 |
| 2010 | NAS | AAA | 23 | 201 | 19 | 9 | 0 | 7 | 26 | 14 | 45 | 0 | 1 | .253/.305/.425 | .254 | .287 | -4.7 | 1.9 | 0.5 |
| 2011 | HUN | AA | 24 | 241 | 24 | 13 | 0 | 3 | 34 | 19 | 56 | 2 | 1 | .264/.349/.370 | .251 | .344 | -0.7 | -0.3 | 1.0 |
| 2011 | NAS | AAA | 24 | 160 | 23 | 5 | 0 | 8 | 25 | 16 | 21 | 0 | 0 | .321/.410/.537 | .307 | .330 | -1.7 | -0.8 | 1.3 |
| 2012 | MIL | MLB | 25 | 250 | 25 | 9 | 0 | 5 | 22 | 19 | 59 | 1 | 0 | .220/.291/.333 | .223 | .269 | 0 | C -1 | 0.4 |

Maldonado's gaudy batting stats in Nashville aren't to be taken seriously, but he has grown quite a bit as an offensive player, a testament to his hard work and coachability, along with the Brewers' minor-league development staff. "Quite a bit" must be measured carefully in his case as he hit .221/.309/.288 in A-ball after three years of rookie ball to prepare him for the experience. He's a tremendous defender and with his newfound ability to impersonate a replacement-level hitter, he should be able to find work as a backup catcher as long as he can stand the abuse.

### Nyjer Morgan CF

Born: 7/2/1980 Age: 31
Bats: L Throws: L Height: 6' 1" Weight: 170
Breakout: 0% Improve: 35% Collapse: 3%
Attrition: 19% MLB: 74%

Comparables:
Steve Finley, Coco Crisp, Luis Matos

| YEAR | TEAM | LVL | AGE | PA | R | 2B | 3B | HR | RBI | BB | SO | SB | CS | AVG/OBP/SLG | TAv | BABIP | BRR | FRAA | WARP |
|------|------|-----|-----|-----|----|----|----|----|-----|----|----|----|----|-------------|-----|-------|-----|------|------|
| 2009 | WAS | MLB | 29 | 212 | 35 | 9 | 2 | 1 | 12 | 11 | 25 | 24 | 7 | .351/.396/.435 | .280 | .398 | 3.1 | 4.6 | 2.1 |
| 2009 | PIT | MLB | 29 | 321 | 39 | 6 | 5 | 2 | 27 | 29 | 49 | 18 | 10 | .277/.351/.356 | .259 | .325 | -0.2 | 6.3 | 1.6 |
| 2010 | WAS | MLB | 30 | 577 | 60 | 17 | 7 | 0 | 24 | 40 | 88 | 34 | 17 | .253/.319/.314 | .235 | .304 | 4.9 | 2.3 | 0.6 |
| 2011 | MIL | MLB | 31 | 429 | 61 | 20 | 6 | 4 | 37 | 19 | 70 | 13 | 4 | .304/.357/.421 | .269 | .362 | 4.4 | 5.5 | 2.8 |
| 2012 | MIL | MLB | 31 | 434 | 50 | 16 | 5 | 3 | 41 | 29 | 70 | 26 | 9 | .281/.341/.375 | .253 | .324 | -0.7 | CF 5, LF 1 | 1.0 |

Of all the characters in the game today, Morgan surprised nobody when he was the only one to say that he had a "Gentleman's Name"—Tony Plush—and that his Twitter account is "TheRealTPlush." The Nationals couldn't get rid of him quickly enough, despite his hitting .303/.353/.376 against right-handed pitchers while stealing 58 bases in 789 plate appearances over two seasons. His fumbling in the playoffs notwithstanding, Morgan still has above-average range in center field and the flexibility to play the corners when Gomez is in. Multiple leg injuries have tempered his speed, and he's made the concession of attempting fewer steals—a better outcome than leading the league in times caught stealing, as he did in 2010. He won't ever hit lefties (.201/.288/.270 in his career) and he's always a candidate to wear out his welcome, but so far, he's been a gentleman toward his teammates in Milwaukee.

### Aramis Ramirez 3B

Born: 6/25/1978 Age: 34
Bats: R Throws: R Height: 6' 2" Weight: 190
Breakout: 0% Improve: 35% Collapse: 7%
Attrition: 10% MLB: 93%

Comparables:
Mike Lowell, Chipper Jones, Scott Rolen

| YEAR | TEAM | LVL | AGE | PA | R | 2B | 3B | HR | RBI | BB | SO | SB | CS | AVG/OBP/SLG | TAv | BABIP | BRR | FRAA | WARP |
|---|---|---|---|---|---|---|---|---|---|---|---|---|---|---|---|---|---|---|---|
| 2009 | CHN | MLB | 31 | 342 | 46 | 14 | 1 | 15 | 65 | 28 | 43 | 2 | 1 | .317/.389/.516 | .302 | .331 | -0.1 | -2.7 | 2.0 |
| 2010 | CHN | MLB | 32 | 507 | 61 | 21 | 1 | 25 | 83 | 34 | 90 | 0 | 0 | .241/.294/.452 | .259 | .245 | -4 | -8 | 0.2 |
| 2011 | CHN | MLB | 33 | 626 | 80 | 35 | 1 | 26 | 93 | 43 | 69 | 1 | 1 | .306/.361/.510 | .302 | .308 | -5.3 | -15.1 | 2.6 |
| 2012 | MIL | MLB | 34 | 565 | 76 | 29 | 1 | 25 | 81 | 47 | 84 | 1 | 1 | .283/.350/.491 | .296 | .296 | -0.1 | 3B -9 | 4.3 |

in a three-year deal, and the team got a relative bargain, as free-agent prices go.

### Logan Schafer CF

Born: 9/8/1986 Age: 25
Bats: L Throws: L Height: 6' 2" Weight: 180
Breakout: 5% Improve: 45% Collapse: 5%
Attrition: 21% MLB: 84%

Comparables:
Mickey Stanley, Paul Molitor, Jose Ortiz

| YEAR | TEAM | LVL | AGE | PA | R | 2B | 3B | HR | RBI | BB | SO | SB | CS | AVG/OBP/SLG | TAv | BABIP | BRR | FRAA | WARP |
|---|---|---|---|---|---|---|---|---|---|---|---|---|---|---|---|---|---|---|---|
| 2009 | BRV | A+ | 22 | 505 | 76 | 31 | 6 | 6 | 58 | 38 | 53 | 16 | 8 | .313/.371/.446 | .299 | .343 | 2.4 | 0.3 | 3.8 |
| 2011 | HUN | AA | 24 | 211 | 31 | 9 | 4 | 0 | 19 | 17 | 25 | 10 | 5 | .302/.368/.392 | .266 | .348 | 0.2 | 5.1 | 1.2 |
| 2011 | NAS | AAA | 24 | 194 | 31 | 13 | 2 | 5 | 23 | 17 | 18 | 5 | 3 | .331/.401/.521 | .314 | .345 | 1.7 | -0.7 | 2.3 |
| 2012 | MIL | MLB | 25 | 250 | 28 | 12 | 2 | 4 | 25 | 17 | 40 | 6 | 3 | .263/.319/.378 | .246 | .301 | -0.4 | CF -2, RF -0 | 0.7 |

Schafer isn't the sort of prospect who gets scouts buzzing. He's not considered to have any standout tools, but he's made remarkable progress considering he was drafted in 2008 and missed almost all of 2010 with various injuries. He makes consistent hard contact and laces line drives all over the field against right-handed pitching, and he has enough speed to handle center field and not be a liability on the bases. He'll get to work on improving the .227/.269/.402 batting line he posted against left-handed pitching in Triple A, but he's already near the point of being able to replace Morgan's role as a platoon center fielder, if required.

### Rickie Weeks 2B

Born: 9/13/1982 Age: 29
Bats: R Throws: R Height: 6' 1" Weight: 195
Breakout: 2% Improve: 35% Collapse: 3%
Attrition: 15% MLB: 91%

Comparables:
Ben Zobrist, Rod Booker, Dan Uggla

| YEAR | TEAM | LVL | AGE | PA | R | 2B | 3B | HR | RBI | BB | SO | SB | CS | AVG/OBP/SLG | TAv | BABIP | BRR | FRAA | WARP |
|---|---|---|---|---|---|---|---|---|---|---|---|---|---|---|---|---|---|---|---|
| 2009 | MIL | MLB | 26 | 162 | 28 | 5 | 2 | 9 | 24 | 12 | 39 | 2 | 2 | .272/.340/.517 | .291 | .313 | -0.3 | 0.3 | 0.9 |
| 2010 | MIL | MLB | 27 | 754 | 112 | 32 | 4 | 29 | 83 | 76 | 184 | 11 | 4 | .269/.366/.464 | .289 | .332 | 5.5 | -3.3 | 3.9 |
| 2011 | MIL | MLB | 28 | 515 | 77 | 26 | 2 | 20 | 49 | 50 | 107 | 9 | 2 | .269/.350/.468 | .285 | .310 | 2.6 | 0.4 | 3.1 |
| 2012 | MIL | MLB | 29 | 531 | 69 | 22 | 4 | 20 | 66 | 61 | 123 | 11 | 3 | .256/.358/.454 | .289 | .305 | 0 | 2B -3 | 3.3 |

Third verse, same as the first. Weeks led the majors in plate appearances in 2010, but an ankle injury in 2011 reacquainted him with the disabled list. Weeks still doesn't look smooth afield, but he's been an average fielder for years now, and offensively, the song remains the same. His power has emerged in his prime years, and with his patient approach, he's always provided good on-base contributions. Since 2009, he's managed a .287 TAv with just a .269 batting average, and—health permitting—should keep bringing it for a few more years, making him one of the top second basemen in the game today.

# PITCHERS

### John Axford
Born: 4/1/1983 Age: 29
Bats: R Throws: R Height: 6' 6" Weight: 195
Breakout: 25% Improve: 46% Collapse: 30%
Attrition: 15% MLB: 85%

**Comparables:**
Duane Ward, Derrick Turnbow, David Aardsma

| YEAR | TEAM | LVL | AGE | W | L | SV | G | GS | IP | H | HR | BB | SO | EqBB9 | EqSO9 | GB% | BABIP | WHIP | ERA | FIP | FRA | WARP |
|------|------|-----|-----|---|---|----|----|----|-----|----|----|----|----|-------|-------|-----|-------|------|------|------|------|------|
| 2009 | BRV | A+ | 26 | 4 | 1 | 0 | 19 | 0 | 27² | 14 | 0 | 16 | 43 | 5.2 | 14.0 | 45% | .280 | 1.08 | 1.62 | 1.83 | 2.14 | 0.9 |
| 2009 | NAS | AAA | 26 | 5 | 0 | 0 | 22 | 0 | 33 | 23 | 2 | 19 | 37 | 5.2 | 10.1 | 54% | .266 | 1.27 | 3.55 | 3.72 | 4.58 | 0.4 |
| 2009 | MIL | MLB | 26 | 0 | 0 | 1 | 7 | 0 | 7² | 5 | 0 | 6 | 9 | 7.0 | 10.6 | 32% | .263 | 1.43 | 3.52 | 3.06 | 4.16 | 0.1 |
| 2010 | MIL | MLB | 27 | 8 | 2 | 24 | 50 | 0 | 58 | 42 | 1 | 27 | 76 | 4.2 | 11.8 | 50% | .313 | 1.19 | 2.48 | 2.16 | 2.88 | 1.5 |
| 2011 | MIL | MLB | 28 | 2 | 2 | 46 | 74 | 0 | 73² | 59 | 4 | 25 | 86 | 3.1 | 10.5 | 50% | .291 | 1.14 | 1.95 | 2.38 | 3.09 | 1.6 |
| 2012 | MIL | MLB | 29 | 3 | 1 | 29 | 60 | 0 | 63² | 52 | 6 | 33 | 65 | 4.7 | 9.1 | 44% | .307 | 1.34 | 3.99 | 3.94 | 4.34 | 0.6 |

Even though Axford was dominant as a closer down the stretch in 2010, there remained some concerns over his control entering 2011. With six walks in his first seven outings (6 1/3 IP) in 2011 contributing to his 8.53 ERA, the worst fears appeared to be coming true. But "Ax Man" sharpened his stuff after that, striking out 80 while walking just 19 the rest of the way. He rarely needs his good curve or slider, with his high heat having plenty of movement and velocity, but when either is working in a game he's as tough an assignment as anyone.

### Zach Braddock
Born: 8/23/1987 Age: 24
Bats: L Throws: L Height: 6' 3" Weight: 235
Breakout: 32% Improve: 64% Collapse: 20%
Attrition: 18% MLB: 98%

**Comparables:**
Sid Fernandez, Scott Elbert, Taylor Tankersley

| YEAR | TEAM | LVL | AGE | W | L | SV | G | GS | IP | H | HR | BB | SO | EqBB9 | EqSO9 | GB% | BABIP | WHIP | ERA | FIP | FRA | WARP |
|------|------|-----|-----|---|---|----|----|----|-----|----|----|----|----|-------|-------|-----|-------|------|------|------|------|------|
| 2009 | BRV | A+ | 21 | 1 | 1 | 0 | 14 | 0 | 24² | 12 | 2 | 4 | 40 | 1.5 | 14.6 | 37% | .238 | 0.65 | 1.09 | 1.74 | 2.28 | 0.8 |
| 2010 | MIL | MLB | 22 | 1 | 2 | 0 | 46 | 0 | 33² | 29 | 1 | 19 | 41 | 5.1 | 11.0 | 35% | .322 | 1.43 | 2.94 | 2.93 | 4.29 | 0.4 |
| 2011 | MIL | MLB | 23 | 0 | 1 | 0 | 25 | 0 | 17¹ | 16 | 2 | 11 | 18 | 5.7 | 9.3 | 33% | .286 | 1.56 | 7.27 | 4.67 | 4.45 | 0.1 |
| 2012 | MIL | MLB | 24 | 1 | 1 | 0 | 29 | 0 | 24 | 19 | 2 | 12 | 27 | 4.5 | 10.0 | 39% | .304 | 1.29 | 3.88 | 3.54 | 4.22 | 0.3 |

Braddock joins Johannes Brahms among famous people with a sleep disorder. He was working on moving beyond a Study For the Left Hand (aka "LOOGY") but his medical condition cost him some velocity on both fastball and slider. He's hoping it was just a Tragic Overture to a fine career as a setup man but there are many unknowns with the disease.

### Frankie De La Cruz
Born: 3/12/1984 Age: 28
Bats: R Throws: R Height: 6' 0" Weight: 175
Breakout: 27% Improve: 53% Collapse: 22%
Attrition: 19% MLB: 86%

**Comparables:**
Merkin Valdez, Shane Rawley, Manny Acosta

| YEAR | TEAM | LVL | AGE | W | L | SV | G | GS | IP | H | HR | BB | SO | EqBB9 | EqSO9 | GB% | BABIP | WHIP | ERA | FIP | FRA | WARP |
|------|------|-----|-----|---|---|----|----|----|-----|-----|----|----|-----|-------|-------|-----|-------|------|------|------|------|------|
| 2009 | POR | AAA | 25 | 2 | 6 | 9 | 48 | 4 | 69¹ | 52 | 2 | 44 | 59 | 5.7 | 7.7 | 54% | .263 | 1.39 | 3.12 | 4.03 | 4.07 | 0.6 |
| 2009 | SDN | MLB | 25 | 0 | 0 | 0 | 3 | 0 | 3¹ | 2 | 0 | 6 | 2 | 16.2 | 5.4 | 78% | .222 | 2.40 | 5.40 | 7.26 | 6.34 | -0.1 |
| 2011 | NAS | AAA | 27 | 2 | 2 | 0 | 25 | 23 | 137 | 130 | 14 | 63 | 126 | 4.1 | 8.3 | 54% | .301 | 1.41 | 3.88 | 4.69 | 5.02 | 0.8 |
| 2011 | MIL | MLB | 27 | 0 | 0 | 0 | 11 | 0 | 13 | 10 | 0 | 5 | 9 | 3.5 | 6.2 | 46% | .256 | 1.15 | 2.77 | 3.22 | 3.83 | 0.1 |
| 2012 | MIL | MLB | 28 | 2 | 3 | 0 | 11 | 7 | 45¹ | 43 | 5 | 21 | 32 | 4.2 | 6.2 | 55% | .298 | 1.41 | 4.69 | 4.62 | 5.10 | 0.1 |

De La Cruz was formerly a flamethrowing Tigers prospect whose struggles with control and finding a third pitch made it all but a foregone conclusion he'd end up in the bullpen. He's travelled far—including a stop in Japan—to again find himself a starting prospect. He still lacks a quality breaking ball, but has harnessed his control enough to suggest he'll have a career.

### Tim Dillard
Born: 7/19/1983 Age: 28
Bats: R Throws: R Height: 6' 5" Weight: 215
Breakout: 14% Improve: 46% Collapse: 33%
Attrition: 8% MLB: 80%

**Comparables:**
Terry Fox, Ben Hendrickson, Wayne Garland

| YEAR | TEAM | LVL | AGE | W | L | SV | G | GS | IP | H | HR | BB | SO | EqBB9 | EqSO9 | GB% | BABIP | WHIP | ERA | FIP | FRA | WARP |
|------|------|-----|-----|----|---|----|----|----|------|-----|----|----|----|-------|-------|-----|-------|------|-------|-------|-------|------|
| 2009 | NAS | AAA | 25 | 11 | 7 | 0 | 24 | 24 | 147² | 162 | 11 | 52 | 64 | 3.2 | 3.9 | 52% | .306 | 1.45 | 4.51 | 4.83 | 6.13 | -1.4 |
| 2009 | MIL | MLB | 25 | 0 | 1 | 0 | 2 | 0 | 4¹ | 7 | 1 | 5 | 1 | 10.4 | 2.1 | 53% | .375 | 2.77 | 12.46 | 9.06 | 11.74 | -0.3 |
| 2010 | NAS | AAA | 26 | 5 | 7 | 1 | 41 | 8 | 109¹ | 63 | 6 | 21 | 56 | 2.6 | 6.8 | 58% | .268 | 1.19 | 4.12 | 4.60 | 4.92 | 0.9 |
| 2011 | NAS | AAA | 27 | 1 | 1 | 1 | 17 | 0 | 37² | 31 | 3 | 13 | 28 | 3.1 | 7.2 | 58% | .286 | 1.17 | 3.58 | 4.48 | 5.28 | 0.1 |
| 2011 | MIL | MLB | 27 | 1 | 1 | 0 | 24 | 0 | 28² | 26 | 3 | 4 | 27 | 1.3 | 8.5 | 55% | .291 | 1.05 | 4.08 | 3.10 | 4.39 | 0.2 |
| 2012 | MIL | MLB | 28 | 1 | 1 | 0 | 13 | 1 | 28² | 29 | 3 | 10 | 14 | 3.2 | 4.5 | 53% | .297 | 1.38 | 4.95 | 4.63 | 5.38 | -0.0 |

There isn't much call for ROOGYs in the game today, but Dillard mixes his heavy sinking "fastball" and slider in a manner that causes right-handed batters to ground out hopelessly with great frequency. In a world with more than 25 roster slots he'd have a lot more job security.

### Marco Estrada

Born: 7/5/1983 Age: 28
Bats: R Throws: R Height: 6' 1" Weight: 180
Breakout: 19% Improve: 64% Collapse: 16%
Attrition: 33% MLB: 85%

**Comparables:**
Billy Loes, Joe Hesketh, Geraldo Guzman

| YEAR | TEAM | LVL | AGE | W | L | SV | G | GS | IP | H | HR | BB | SO | EqBB9 | EqSO9 | GB% | BABIP | WHIP | ERA | FIP | FRA | WARP |
|------|------|-----|-----|---|---|----|----|----|-----|-----|----|----|----|-------|-------|-----|-------|------|------|------|------|------|
| 2009 | SYR | AAA | 26 | 9 | 5 | 0 | 27 | 25 | 136[1] | 133 | 10 | 33 | 98 | 2.2 | 6.5 | 44% | .296 | 1.22 | 3.63 | 3.41 | 4.27 | 1.5 |
| 2009 | WAS | MLB | 26 | 0 | 1 | 0 | 4 | 1 | 7[1] | 6 | 1 | 4 | 9 | 4.9 | 11.0 | 35% | .278 | 1.36 | 6.14 | 4.01 | 6.35 | 0.0 |
| 2010 | NAS | AAA | 27 | 1 | 2 | 0 | 7 | 7 | 40 | 21 | 1 | 5 | 29 | 2.5 | 7.4 | 45% | .244 | 1.02 | 3.15 | 3.31 | 3.94 | 0.7 |
| 2010 | MIL | MLB | 27 | 0 | 0 | 0 | 7 | 1 | 11[1] | 14 | 3 | 6 | 13 | 4.8 | 10.3 | 32% | .324 | 1.76 | 9.53 | 6.11 | 6.94 | -0.2 |
| 2011 | MIL | MLB | 28 | 4 | 8 | 0 | 43 | 7 | 92[2] | 83 | 11 | 29 | 88 | 2.8 | 8.5 | 43% | .295 | 1.21 | 4.08 | 3.64 | 4.38 | 0.9 |
| 2012 | MIL | MLB | 28 | 3 | 3 | 0 | 26 | 7 | 65[1] | 67 | 9 | 24 | 47 | 3.3 | 6.5 | 45% | .313 | 1.39 | 4.99 | 4.66 | 5.42 | -0.1 |

With no warning, Estrada turned in an above-average season in the thankless swingman role. Minor-league hitters wouldn't be surprised, as he works a curve and changeup around his low-90s fastball and pounds the strike zone. In the past, too many hangers and flat fastballs have left major-league parks, but he tricked more batters into popping up in 2011, keeping the taters to a manageable level. His 2011 peripherals lend optimism that he could duplicate his effectiveness in 2012.

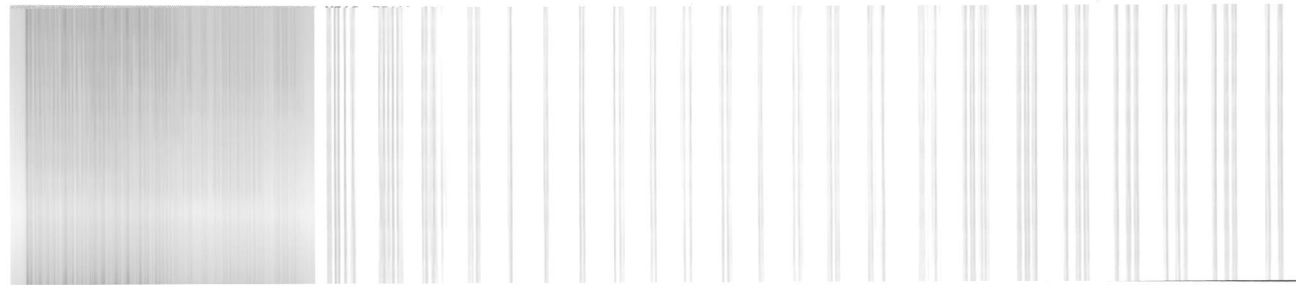

Last fall, roving pitching coordinator Lee Tunnell taught Fiers a cut fastball. With his exaggerated delivery and this new late-breaking movement, Fiers' sub-90 fastball constantly surprises hitters, with minor leaguers having no chance. The overall effect is unconventional enough that Fiers could prove to be Milwaukee's "secret weapon" in the second half of 2012, but whether there's a rotation slot in his future will depend on his ability to adapt and keep tricking hitters.

### Yovani Gallardo

Born: 2/27/1986 Age: 26
Bats: R Throws: R Height: 6' 2" Weight: 210
Breakout: 30% Improve: 50% Collapse: 17%
Attrition: 11% MLB: 97%

**Comparables:**
Fernando Salas, Victor Zambrano, Max Scherzer

| YEAR | TEAM | LVL | AGE | W | L | SV | G | GS | IP | H | HR | BB | SO | EqBB9 | EqSO9 | GB% | BABIP | WHIP | ERA | FIP | FRA | WARP |
|------|------|-----|-----|----|----|----|----|----|------|-----|----|----|-----|-------|-------|-----|-------|------|------|------|------|------|
| 2009 | MIL | MLB | 23 | 13 | 12 | 0 | 30 | 30 | 185[2] | 150 | 21 | 94 | 204 | 4.6 | 9.9 | 47% | .278 | 1.31 | 3.73 | 3.93 | 4.14 | 3.5 |
| 2010 | MIL | MLB | 24 | 14 | 7 | 0 | 31 | 31 | 185 | 178 | 12 | 75 | 200 | 3.6 | 9.7 | 45% | .331 | 1.37 | 3.84 | 3.05 | 3.66 | 5.1 |
| 2011 | MIL | MLB | 25 | 17 | 10 | 0 | 33 | 33 | 207[1] | 193 | 27 | 59 | 207 | 2.6 | 9.0 | 48% | .296 | 1.22 | 3.52 | 3.56 | 4.08 | 3.5 |
| 2012 | MIL | MLB | 26 | 11 | 9 | 0 | 28 | 28 | 174[2] | 152 | 19 | 62 | 169 | 3.2 | 8.7 | 44% | .307 | 1.23 | 3.84 | 3.75 | 4.18 | 2.3 |

Gallardo has been among the top eight starters in strikeouts per nine innings in each of his three full seasons, made possible by four high-quality pitches with the high heat as the centerpiece. Along the way, there's been tremendous growth, as Gallardo is now throwing his curve and slider for strikes along with both fastballs. With a little more command within the strike zone—entirely reasonable to expect him to grow into—he'll be among the top Cy Young candidates. The front office could improve his chances of winning the award by surrounding him with some better defenders.

### Zack Greinke

Born: 10/21/1983 Age: 28
Bats: R Throws: R Height: 6' 3" Weight: 190
Breakout: 27% Improve: 46% Collapse: 10%
Attrition: 2% MLB: 97%

**Comparables:**
Ben Sheets, Rod Beck, Rollie Fingers

| YEAR | TEAM | LVL | AGE | W | L | SV | G | GS | IP | H | HR | BB | SO | EqBB9 | EqSO9 | GB% | BABIP | WHIP | ERA | FIP | FRA | WARP |
|------|------|-----|-----|----|----|----|----|----|------|-----|----|----|-----|-------|-------|-----|-------|------|------|------|------|------|
| 2009 | KCA | MLB | 25 | 16 | 8 | 0 | 33 | 33 | 229[1] | 195 | 11 | 51 | 242 | 2.0 | 9.5 | 41% | .307 | 1.07 | 2.16 | 2.38 | 2.82 | 7.5 |
| 2010 | KCA | MLB | 26 | 10 | 14 | 0 | 33 | 33 | 220 | 219 | 18 | 55 | 181 | 2.2 | 7.4 | 47% | .309 | 1.25 | 4.17 | 3.31 | 4.14 | 2.9 |
| 2011 | MIL | MLB | 27 | 16 | 6 | 0 | 28 | 28 | 171[2] | 161 | 19 | 45 | 201 | 2.4 | 10.5 | 49% | .323 | 1.20 | 3.83 | 2.95 | 3.81 | 3.3 |
| 2012 | MIL | MLB | 28 | 10 | 8 | 0 | 26 | 26 | 162[2] | 147 | 15 | 39 | 149 | 2.2 | 8.2 | 42% | .315 | 1.15 | 3.58 | 3.29 | 3.89 | 2.7 |

While no Brewers fan is happy about the way Greinke hurled in the playoffs, neither are many wishing him back to Kansas City, though the first half of the season had many wondering how much worse of a smell Jake Odorizzi could have created. Zack didn't look himself while recovering from a broken rib (incurred playing pickup basketball), but he turned things around in the second half, destroying the eight-hitter lineups in the National League as the 2009 American League Cy Young Award winner would be expected to do. After the All-Star Break, he posted a 2.59 ERA, and ended the season ahead of all other major leaguers in strikeouts-per-nine. Barring setbacks, he and Gallardo will be vying for the number one designation on the team's staff all year and Cy Young ballots at year-end.

### Brandon Kintzler

Born: 8/1/1984 Age: 27
Bats: R Throws: R Height: 6' 2'' Weight: 185
Breakout: 19% Improve: 66% Collapse: 21%
Attrition: 12% MLB: 94%

Comparables:
Ron Davis, Carlos Villanueva, Brett Myers

| YEAR | TEAM | LVL | AGE | W | L | SV | G | GS | IP | H | HR | BB | SO | EqBB9 | EqSO9 | GB% | BABIP | WHIP | ERA | FIP | FRA | WARP |
|------|------|-----|-----|---|---|----|---|----|----|---|----|----|----|-------|-------|-----|-------|------|-----|-----|-----|------|
| 2009 | HUN | AA | 24 | 1 | 2 | 0 | 9 | 6 | 35² | 46 | 5 | 10 | 37 | 2.3 | 8.1 | 50% | .331 | 1.40 | 4.54 | 3.77 | 4.14 | 0.6 |
| 2010 | HUN | AA | 25 | 1 | 0 | 10 | 20 | 0 | 22¹ | 6 | 0 | 0 | 14 | 0.4 | 9.3 | 65% | .194 | 0.54 | 0.40 | 2.30 | 2.79 | 0.6 |
| 2010 | NAS | AAA | 25 | 3 | 0 | 6 | 22 | 0 | 26² | 11 | 1 | 3 | 12 | 2.0 | 7.1 | 67% | .204 | 0.94 | 2.36 | 3.98 | 4.24 | 0.3 |
| 2010 | MIL | MLB | 25 | 0 | 1 | 0 | 7 | 0 | 7¹ | 10 | 2 | 4 | 9 | 4.9 | 11.0 | 75% | .471 | 1.91 | 7.36 | 5.83 | 6.42 | -0.1 |
| 2011 | MIL | MLB | 26 | 1 | 1 | 0 | 9 | 0 | 14¹ | 14 | 3 | 3 | 15 | 1.8 | 9.2 | 60% | .275 | 1.16 | 3.68 | 4.22 | 4.34 | 0.1 |
| 2012 | MIL | MLB | 27 | 0 | 0 | 0 | 10 | 0 | 11² | 11 | 1 | 4 | 10 | 2.9 | 7.4 | 52% | .306 | 1.26 | 4.28 | 3.63 | 4.65 | 0.1 |

Nothing against Kintzler, but it's a telling commentary on organizational strength when a 27-year-old relief pitcher who was pitching in the Northern (Independent) League in 2008 makes the Arizona Fall League roster. He can throw 95 mph at times, appeared to be recovered from July forearm surgery in AFL action, and certainly won't be the worst pitcher in the bigs if he makes the team.

### Kameron Loe

Born: 9/10/1981 Age: 30
Bats: R Throws: R Height: 6' 9'' Weight: 220
Breakout: 13% Improve: 35% Collapse: 30%
Attrition: 16% MLB: 89%

Comparables:
Cha Seung Baek, Kevin Millwood, Mark Gubicza

| YEAR | TEAM | LVL | AGE | W | L | SV | G | GS | IP | H | HR | BB | SO | EqBB9 | EqSO9 | GB% | BABIP | WHIP | ERA | FIP | FRA | WARP |
|------|------|-----|-----|---|---|----|---|----|----|---|----|----|----|-------|-------|-----|-------|------|-----|-----|-----|------|
| 2010 | NAS | AAA | 28 | 4 | 3 | 0 | 10 | 10 | 62² | 39 | 4 | 12 | 27 | 2.7 | 5.6 | 61% | .257 | 1.21 | 3.16 | 4.79 | 5.13 | 0.2 |
| 2010 | MIL | MLB | 28 | 3 | 5 | 0 | 53 | 0 | 58¹ | 54 | 6 | 15 | 46 | 2.3 | 7.1 | 60% | .282 | 1.18 | 2.78 | 3.74 | 4.19 | 0.7 |
| 2011 | MIL | MLB | 29 | 4 | 7 | 1 | 72 | 0 | 72 | 65 | 4 | 16 | 61 | 2.0 | 7.6 | 64% | .296 | 1.12 | 3.50 | 2.77 | 4.32 | 0.4 |
| 2012 | MIL | MLB | 30 | 3 | 2 | 1 | 45 | 3 | 64² | 65 | 7 | 20 | 40 | 2.8 | 5.6 | 56% | .306 | 1.32 | 4.57 | 4.30 | 4.96 | 0.2 |

Most often, starter-turned-reliever success stories involve fireballers who can throw 100 percent and blow people away. Like a fastball-only pitcher, Loe really only has one above-average pitch, but it's his 90-mph sinker that breaks bats and leads to a 63 percent ground-ball rate. He was brought into games 10 times with a runner on first base and less than two outs, and as he further refines his command and enters games more often in GDP situations, he could have an even greater impact.

### Shaun Marcum

Born: 12/14/1981 Age: 30
Bats: R Throws: R Height: 6' 1'' Weight: 180
Breakout: 13% Improve: 55% Collapse: 17%
Attrition: 15% MLB: 93%

Comparables:
Dennis Leonard, Dick Hughes, Turk Farrell

| YEAR | TEAM | LVL | AGE | W | L | SV | G | GS | IP | H | HR | BB | SO | EqBB9 | EqSO9 | GB% | BABIP | WHIP | ERA | FIP | FRA | WARP |
|------|------|-----|-----|---|---|----|---|----|----|---|----|----|----|-------|-------|-----|-------|------|-----|-----|-----|------|
| 2010 | TOR | MLB | 28 | 13 | 8 | 0 | 31 | 31 | 195¹ | 181 | 24 | 43 | 165 | 2.0 | 7.6 | 39% | .280 | 1.15 | 3.64 | 3.71 | 3.96 | 3.3 |
| 2011 | MIL | MLB | 29 | 13 | 7 | 0 | 33 | 33 | 200² | 175 | 22 | 56 | 158 | 2.6 | 7.1 | 40% | .264 | 1.16 | 3.54 | 3.68 | 4.16 | 3.0 |
| 2012 | MIL | MLB | 30 | 11 | 9 | 0 | 28 | 28 | 172² | 150 | 23 | 46 | 135 | 2.4 | 7.0 | 41% | .279 | 1.14 | 3.75 | 4.17 | 4.08 | 2.5 |

Marcum is the change-of-pace for the two flamethrowers atop the rotation, barely breaking 90 mph on the gun. But he's also authored WHIPs among the top 21 starting pitchers in baseball each of the past two seasons, and he keeps hitters constantly off-balance by spotting six pitches (or more, if each of his several changeups is considered separately). His extra-low BABIP, weak second-half strikeout rate (5.8 K/9), and postseason ineptitude raise serious concerns about his ability to repeat in 2012. But he's a smart pitcher and used to adapting; the more serious concern—given his injury history—is that his late-season decline is due to a concealed health issue.

### Mike McClendon

Born: 4/3/1985 Age: 27
Bats: R Throws: R Height: 6' 6'' Weight: 215
Breakout: 34% Improve: 65% Collapse: 10%
Attrition: 8% MLB: 87%

Comparables:
Brian Lawrence, Nelson Briles, Brian Wolfe

| YEAR | TEAM | LVL | AGE | W | L | SV | G | GS | IP | H | HR | BB | SO | EqBB9 | EqSO9 | GB% | BABIP | WHIP | ERA | FIP | FRA | WARP |
|------|------|-----|-----|---|---|----|---|----|----|---|----|----|----|-------|-------|-----|-------|------|-----|-----|-----|------|
| 2010 | MIL | MLB | 25 | 2 | 0 | 0 | 17 | 0 | 21 | 15 | 2 | 7 | 21 | 3.0 | 9.0 | 46% | .241 | 1.05 | 3.00 | 3.34 | 3.87 | 0.4 |
| 2011 | NAS | AAA | 26 | 3 | 4 | 8 | 38 | 0 | 58² | 59 | 2 | 19 | 47 | 2.9 | 7.4 | 53% | .324 | 1.36 | 3.53 | 3.65 | 4.88 | 0.4 |
| 2011 | MIL | MLB | 26 | 3 | 0 | 0 | 9 | 0 | 13² | 15 | 1 | 3 | 10 | 2.0 | 6.6 | 49% | .318 | 1.32 | 2.63 | 3.36 | 4.51 | 0.1 |
| 2012 | MIL | MLB | 27 | 1 | 0 | 0 | 21 | 0 | 33² | 36 | 4 | 10 | 18 | 2.8 | 4.9 | 52% | .308 | 1.36 | 4.85 | 4.57 | 5.28 | -0.0 |

McClendon now has a sparkling 2.86 career ERA and 3.35 career FIP, but the eyeball test would suggest that the large righty will see these numbers inflate with time. He should remain effective at getting righties to beat his sinkers and sliders into the ground, but there's really little to explain his .200 career batting average against southpaws other than luck. As the .209 BABIP he's allowed to lefties normalizes, other four-letter words are likely to come to mind as he struggles to keep a roster spot.

**Daniel Meadows**

Born: **11/3/1987** Age: **24**
Bats: **L** Throws: **L** Height: **6' 7"** Weight: **223**
Breakout: **23%** Improve: **53%** Collapse: **26%**
Attrition: **15%** MLB: **90%**

**Comparables:**
Eric Milton, Jo-Jo Reyes, Andy Pettitte

| YEAR | TEAM | LVL | AGE | W | L | SV | G | GS | IP | H | HR | BB | SO | EqBB9 | EqSO9 | GB% | BABIP | WHIP | ERA | FIP | FRA | WARP |
|------|------|-----|-----|---|---|----|----|----|----|---|----|----|----|-------|-------|-----|-------|------|-----|-----|-----|------|
| 2009 | WIS | A | 21 | 13 | 6 | 2 | 33 | 11 | 116² | 122 | 8 | 32 | 108 | 2.5 | 8.3 | 38% | .339 | 1.32 | 4.01 | 3.58 | 4.11 | 1.1 |
| 2010 | BRV | A+ | 22 | 6 | 5 | 2 | 42 | 0 | 91¹ | 69 | 8 | 22 | 67 | 2.6 | 9.1 | 33% | .307 | 1.13 | 2.86 | 4.06 | 4.44 | 0.4 |
| 2011 | HUN | AA | 23 | 1 | 0 | 1 | 21 | 0 | 41² | 28 | 1 | 8 | 37 | 2.2 | 8.4 | 37% | .255 | 0.91 | 1.51 | 2.48 | 3.47 | 0.9 |
| 2011 | NAS | AAA | 23 | 0 | 1 | 1 | 20 | 1 | 35² | 33 | 4 | 13 | 35 | 3.3 | 8.8 | 37% | .305 | 1.29 | 4.04 | 4.41 | 4.61 | 0.3 |
| 2012 | MIL | MLB | 24 | 1 | 0 | 0 | 12 | 0 | 25 | 26 | 3 | 10 | 16 | 3.7 | 5.9 | 34% | .308 | 1.44 | 5.18 | 4.68 | 5.63 | -0.1 |

Meadows is a soft tosser found in the 49th round of the 2008 draft whose conversion to the bullpen added just enough velocity for his breaking stuff to become effective. He'll never be Billy Wagner, but minor-league righties have had every sort of problem with his changeup since the move. Arizona Fall League action made it clear that neither his control nor his stuff is quite ready yet, but left is right when it comes to carving out a fringe career.

**Chris Narveson**

| YEAR | TEAM | LVL | AGE | W | L | SV | G | GS | IP | H | HR | BB | SO | EqBB9 | EqSO9 | GB% | BABIP | WHIP | ERA | FIP | FRA | WARP |
|------|------|-----|-----|---|---|----|---|----|----|---|----|----|----|-------|-------|-----|-------|------|-----|-----|-----|------|

to knock half a run on his ERA in 2011 and enjoy results like a true rotation member. Considering his ERA (4.73) minus FIP (4.14) is the eighth-largest gap among pitchers with 324 or more innings over the past two seasons he enters 2012 as a strong candidate to improve his ERA yet again.

**Manny Parra**

Born: **10/30/1982** Age: **29**
Bats: **L** Throws: **L** Height: **6' 4"** Weight: **200**
Breakout: **27%** Improve: **45%** Collapse: **33%**
Attrition: **11%** MLB: **82%**

**Comparables:**
Steve Carlton, Ed Olwine, Casey Fossum

| YEAR | TEAM | LVL | AGE | W | L | SV | G | GS | IP | H | HR | BB | SO | EqBB9 | EqSO9 | GB% | BABIP | WHIP | ERA | FIP | FRA | WARP |
|------|------|-----|-----|---|---|----|----|----|----|-----|----|----|-----|-------|-------|-----|-------|------|-----|-----|-----|------|
| 2009 | MIL | MLB | 26 | 11 | 11 | 0 | 27 | 27 | 140 | 179 | 19 | 77 | 116 | 4.9 | 7.5 | 51% | .353 | 1.83 | 6.36 | 4.84 | 5.41 | 0.3 |
| 2010 | MIL | MLB | 27 | 3 | 10 | 0 | 42 | 16 | 122 | 135 | 18 | 63 | 129 | 4.6 | 9.5 | 48% | .343 | 1.62 | 5.02 | 4.53 | 4.92 | 1.0 |
| 2012 | MIL | MLB | 29 | 1 | 1 | 0 | 9 | 3 | 23 | 23 | 3 | 10 | 18 | 4.1 | 7.2 | 49% | .323 | 1.47 | 5.08 | 4.64 | 5.52 | -0.0 |

Parra went on the disabled list with a back injury before his season began, was later placed on the 60-day DL during his rehab assignment, and then had a bone spur removed in August, ending his season. It was disappointing timing on the setback, as his work in the pen in 2010 had indicated a victory of sorts over his control problems. With even average control, his 96-mph gas from the left side would make him a coveted setup man. The surgery was reported to be successful, so the Brewers are again optimistic.

**Wily Peralta**

Born: **5/8/1989** Age: **23**
Bats: **R** Throws: **R** Height: **6' 3"** Weight: **240**
Breakout: **29%** Improve: **60%** Collapse: **19%**
Attrition: **12%** MLB: **92%**

**Comparables:**
Waldis Joaquin, Mike Pelfrey, Jordan Walden

| YEAR | TEAM | LVL | AGE | W | L | SV | G | GS | IP | H | HR | BB | SO | EqBB9 | EqSO9 | GB% | BABIP | WHIP | ERA | FIP | FRA | WARP |
|------|------|-----|-----|---|---|----|----|----|------|-----|----|----|-----|-------|-------|-----|-------|------|-----|-----|-----|------|
| 2009 | WIS | A | 20 | 4 | 4 | 1 | 27 | 15 | 103² | 91 | 5 | 46 | 118 | 4.0 | 10.2 | 49% | .320 | 1.32 | 3.47 | 3.41 | 3.52 | 2.0 |
| 2010 | BRV | A+ | 21 | 6 | 3 | 0 | 19 | 17 | 105 | 82 | 2 | 34 | 63 | 3.4 | 6.4 | 55% | .309 | 1.35 | 3.86 | 3.63 | 4.93 | 0.0 |
| 2010 | HUN | AA | 21 | 2 | 3 | 0 | 8 | 8 | 42¹ | 25 | 3 | 17 | 17 | 5.1 | 6.2 | 53% | .239 | 1.58 | 3.62 | 5.09 | 5.87 | -0.1 |
| 2011 | HUN | AA | 22 | 4 | 2 | 0 | 21 | 21 | 119² | 106 | 9 | 48 | 117 | 3.6 | 8.8 | 57% | .308 | 1.29 | 3.46 | 3.63 | 4.34 | 1.7 |
| 2012 | MIL | MLB | 23 | 3 | 3 | 0 | 8 | 8 | 46² | 46 | 6 | 24 | 32 | 4.5 | 6.2 | 49% | .305 | 1.49 | 5.19 | 5.05 | 5.64 | -0.1 |

". . . yet to generate the strikeouts you'd like from a prospect" concluded the previous edition of this annual when discussing Peralta. Now that Tommy John surgery is another year behind him, the broad-shouldered Dominican put the concerns about missing bats to rest. His two-fastball (four-seam and two-seam offerings, both of which he can throw for strikes) and slider combination worked even better in the Pacific Coast League than it did at Double-A. He'll return to Triple-A again to fine-tune his changeup and wait his turn. His stuff isn't quite on a par with the two top dogs on the staff, but he's close to being a mid-rotation starter already.

### Francisco Rodriguez
Born: 1/7/1982 Age: 30
Bats: R Throws: R Height: 6' 1'' Weight: 165
Breakout: 24% Improve: 50% Collapse: 28%
Attrition: 7% MLB: 91%

**Comparables:**
Heath Bell, Juan Rincon, Duane Ward

| YEAR | TEAM | LVL | AGE | W | L | SV | G | GS | IP | H | HR | BB | SO | EqBB9 | EqSO9 | GB% | BABIP | WHIP | ERA | FIP | FRA | WARP |
|------|------|-----|-----|---|---|----|---|----|-----|----|----|----|----|-------|-------|-----|-------|------|------|------|------|------|
| 2009 | NYN | MLB | 27 | 3 | 6 | 35 | 70 | 0 | 68 | 51 | 7 | 38 | 73 | 5.0 | 9.7 | 38% | .256 | 1.31 | 3.71 | 3.97 | 4.19 | 0.9 |
| 2010 | NYN | MLB | 28 | 4 | 2 | 25 | 53 | 0 | 57¹ | 45 | 3 | 21 | 67 | 3.3 | 10.5 | 44% | .296 | 1.15 | 2.20 | 2.65 | 3.61 | 0.8 |
| 2011 | MIL | MLB | 29 | 4 | 0 | 0 | 31 | 0 | 29 | 23 | 1 | 10 | 33 | 3.1 | 10.2 | 52% | .289 | 1.14 | 1.86 | 2.20 | 3.21 | 0.6 |
| 2011 | NYN | MLB | 29 | 2 | 2 | 23 | 42 | 0 | 42² | 44 | 3 | 16 | 46 | 3.4 | 9.7 | 53% | .347 | 1.41 | 3.16 | 3.02 | 4.44 | 0.1 |
| *2012* | *MIL* | *MLB* | *30* | *3* | *1* | *20* | *63* | *0* | *64²* | *50* | *5* | *26* | *69* | *3.6* | *9.7* | *44%* | *.297* | *1.18* | *3.20* | *3.28* | *3.47* | *1.3* |

The tremendous slider that made "K-Rod" so feared in Anaheim gave Rodriguez the best years of his career. In return he gave his best years to the slider as his velocity has been on a steady decline since 2006. Even without a slider, his current mix of fastball-curve-change is still effective enough for late-inning work. While he longs to return to the glory of finishing games, he may find that he has to choose between more money as a setup man or a closer's role for a lower-payroll team.

### Mitch Stetter
Born: 1/16/1981 Age: 31
Bats: L Throws: L Height: 6' 5'' Weight: 195
Breakout: 17% Improve: 48% Collapse: 36%
Attrition: 15% MLB: 94%

**Comparables:**
Matt Thornton, Will Ohman, David Cone

| YEAR | TEAM | LVL | AGE | W | L | SV | G | GS | IP | H | HR | BB | SO | EqBB9 | EqSO9 | GB% | BABIP | WHIP | ERA | FIP | FRA | WARP |
|------|------|-----|-----|---|---|----|---|----|-----|----|----|----|----|-------|-------|-----|-------|------|------|------|------|------|
| 2009 | MIL | MLB | 28 | 4 | 1 | 1 | 71 | 0 | 45 | 37 | 4 | 27 | 44 | 5.4 | 8.8 | 36% | .268 | 1.42 | 3.60 | 4.39 | 4.24 | 0.7 |
| 2010 | NAS | AAA | 29 | 3 | 2 | 0 | 41 | 0 | 42 | 32 | 6 | 13 | 32 | 3.9 | 11.1 | 48% | .347 | 1.52 | 6.86 | 5.53 | 5.85 | -0.1 |
| 2010 | MIL | MLB | 29 | 0 | 0 | 0 | 9 | 0 | 3² | 7 | 1 | 3 | 3 | 7.4 | 7.4 | 47% | .429 | 2.73 | 14.73 | 8.29 | 8.66 | -0.2 |
| 2011 | MIL | MLB | 30 | 0 | 0 | 0 | 16 | 0 | 7 | 8 | 2 | 1 | 7 | 1.3 | 9.0 | 14% | .316 | 1.29 | 5.14 | 5.57 | 6.94 | -0.1 |
| *2012* | *MIL* | *MLB* | *31* | *1* | *0* | *0* | *10* | *0* | *8* | *7* | *1* | *4* | *8* | *4.2* | *8.6* | *44%* | *.293* | *1.29* | *4.07* | *4.33* | *4.43* | *0.1* |

The Stetter State Theory asserts that as the number of sliders expands, time on the disabled list destroys innings, keeping the season in balance. Though he leads all MLB pitchers in percentage of sliders thrown by a wide margin (according to PITCHf/x) since his debut in 2007, he's been moderately successful against right-handed batters, though his best fit for a good team is still that of a LOOGY.

### Tyler Thornburg
Born: 9/29/1988 Age: 23
Bats: R Throws: R Height: 6' 0'' Weight: 185
Breakout: 30% Improve: 58% Collapse: 19%
Attrition: 15% MLB: 86%

**Comparables:**
Tom Gordon, Gio Gonzalez, Emiliano Fruto

| YEAR | TEAM | LVL | AGE | W | L | SV | G | GS | IP | H | HR | BB | SO | EqBB9 | EqSO9 | GB% | BABIP | WHIP | ERA | FIP | FRA | WARP |
|------|------|-----|-----|---|---|----|---|----|-----|----|----|----|----|-------|-------|-----|-------|------|------|------|------|------|
| 2011 | WIS | A | 22 | 1 | 0 | 0 | 12 | 12 | 68² | 49 | 3 | 25 | 76 | 3.3 | 10.0 | 45% | .282 | 1.08 | 1.57 | 2.98 | 3.84 | 1.2 |
| 2011 | BRV | A+ | 22 | 3 | 6 | 0 | 12 | 12 | 68 | 45 | 5 | 33 | 84 | 4.4 | 11.1 | 35% | .261 | 1.15 | 3.57 | 3.51 | 3.98 | 1.0 |
| *2012* | *MIL* | *MLB* | *23* | *2* | *2* | *0* | *7* | *7* | *36²* | *33* | *4* | *20* | *33* | *4.8* | *8.2* | *41%* | *.305* | *1.43* | *4.62* | *4.46* | *5.02* | *0.2* |

Utilizing a similar delivery to Tim Lincecum, Thornburg put to rest most of the rumblings about a future as a reliever in 2011. Although he relieved in the Arizona Fall League, Thornburg added a killer changeup to go with his power curve and a fastball that can reach 94 mph. Comparing him to a two-time Cy Young Award winner because he uses a similar delivery to "The Freak" is premature, but he could already improve the rotations of some major-league teams. In this organization—with its glut of pitching talent—he'll have to prove himself against Double-A hitting to start the 2012 season. If he's not spectacular, his debut could come as late as mid-2013.

### Jose Veras
Born: 10/20/1980 Age: 31
Bats: R Throws: R Height: 6' 6'' Weight: 230
Breakout: 22% Improve: 51% Collapse: 23%
Attrition: 16% MLB: 90%

**Comparables:**
Jason Frasor, Scott Williamson, Jeff Nelson

| YEAR | TEAM | LVL | AGE | W | L | SV | G | GS | IP | H | HR | BB | SO | EqBB9 | EqSO9 | GB% | BABIP | WHIP | ERA | FIP | FRA | WARP |
|------|------|-----|-----|---|---|----|---|----|-----|----|----|----|----|-------|-------|-----|-------|------|------|------|------|------|
| 2009 | CLE | MLB | 28 | 1 | 2 | 0 | 22 | 0 | 24² | 19 | 3 | 14 | 22 | 5.1 | 8.0 | 42% | .250 | 1.34 | 4.38 | 4.89 | 5.98 | -0.1 |
| 2009 | NYA | MLB | 28 | 3 | 1 | 0 | 25 | 0 | 25² | 23 | 5 | 14 | 18 | 4.9 | 6.3 | 35% | .240 | 1.44 | 5.96 | 6.38 | 6.30 | -0.1 |
| 2010 | NWO | AAA | 29 | 1 | 1 | 2 | 24 | 0 | 29¹ | 21 | 1 | 10 | 22 | 4.6 | 11.4 | 49% | .357 | 1.67 | 4.61 | 4.02 | 4.61 | 0.1 |
| 2010 | FLO | MLB | 29 | 3 | 3 | 0 | 48 | 0 | 48 | 32 | 5 | 29 | 54 | 5.4 | 10.1 | 42% | .243 | 1.27 | 3.75 | 4.09 | 4.70 | 0.2 |
| 2011 | PIT | MLB | 30 | 2 | 4 | 1 | 79 | 0 | 71 | 54 | 6 | 34 | 79 | 4.3 | 10.0 | 39% | .267 | 1.24 | 3.80 | 3.47 | 4.61 | 0.1 |
| *2012* | *MIL* | *MLB* | *31* | *3* | *1* | *1* | *65* | *0* | *63¹* | *51* | *7* | *30* | *62* | *4.3* | *8.8* | *43%* | *.288* | *1.29* | *3.95* | *4.10* | *4.29* | *0.7* |

Another reliever in the mold the Pirates gravitate to—strong-armed, wild, and cheap—Veras is now 31 and his control problems are no longer the equivalent of a baby going through teething, but rather a middle-aged man dealing with strike-zone commitment issues. Mid-90s heat and a tantalizing curveball (a pitch that Veras threw at a career-high rate in 2011) have led to inspiring strikeout rates throughout his career and made his walk rates tolerable. Finding relievers similar to Veras is no tough task, but the Brewers weren't excited about hearing the arbitrator's decision on Casey McGehee (for whom Veras was traded) anyway, and Veras should be above-average and cheap.

**Randy Wolf**

Born: 8/22/1976 Age: 35
Bats: L Throws: L Height: 6' 1" Weight: 190
Breakout: 16% Improve: 43% Collapse: 30%
Attrition: 18% MLB: 82%

**Comparables:**
Todd Stottlemyre, Jamie Walker, Jarrod Washburn

| YEAR | TEAM | LVL | AGE | W | L | SV | G | GS | IP | H | HR | BB | SO | EqBB9 | EqSO9 | GB% | BABIP | WHIP | ERA | FIP | FRA | WARP |
|---|---|---|---|---|---|---|---|---|---|---|---|---|---|---|---|---|---|---|---|---|---|---|
| 2009 | LAN | MLB | 32 | 11 | 7 | 0 | 34 | 34 | 214$^1$ | 178 | 24 | 58 | 160 | 2.4 | 6.7 | 41% | .256 | 1.10 | 3.23 | 3.91 | 4.73 | 1.8 |
| 2010 | MIL | MLB | 33 | 13 | 12 | 0 | 34 | 34 | 215$^2$ | 213 | 29 | 87 | 142 | 3.6 | 5.9 | 41% | .279 | 1.39 | 4.17 | 4.87 | 4.67 | 3.2 |
| 2011 | MIL | MLB | 34 | 13 | 10 | 0 | 33 | 33 | 212$^1$ | 214 | 23 | 66 | 134 | 2.8 | 5.7 | 40% | .292 | 1.32 | 3.69 | 4.26 | 4.67 | 1.4 |
| 2012 | MIL | MLB | 35 | 11 | 10 | 0 | 28 | 28 | 181$^2$ | 173 | 23 | 62 | 121 | 3.1 | 6.0 | 41% | .292 | 1.29 | 4.49 | 4.54 | 4.88 | 0.9 |

Wolf is fifth on the lists of most games started over both the past three seasons and past four seasons. That he's turned into one of the most dependable—if average—starters in the game flies in the face of his past reputation as being injury-prone. He also has an FIP about half a run higher than his ERA over those periods, as he's proven to be the consummate crafty lefty, mixing two fastballs and four breaking pitches as needed. While his empirical data has earned him the expectation of outpitching his peripherals, a season where the theoretical model catches up to him wouldn't be a shocker.

| | TEAM | LVL | AGE | PA | R | 2B | 3B | HR | RBI | BB | SO | SB-CS | AVG/OBP/SLG | TAv | BABIP | BRR | FRAA | WARP |
|---|---|---|---|---|---|---|---|---|---|---|---|---|---|---|---|---|---|---|
| 1B J. Brown | CON | AAA | 27 | 65 | 10 | 5 | 1 | 5 | 13 | 11 | 15 | 0-0 | .278/.373/.472 | .275 | .315 | -0.5 | 0.5 | 0.2 |
| | NAS | AAA | 27 | 377 | 50 | 28 | 0 | 8 | 51 | 12 | 32 | 2-0 | .317/.340/.465 | .273 | .326 | 0 | 2 | 1.6 |
| LF K. Davis | BRV | A+ | 23 | 371 | 50 | 21 | 1 | 15 | 68 | 51 | 70 | 10-5 | .309/.415/.533 | .336 | .350 | -1.6 | 0.6 | 3.5 |
| | HUN | AA | 23 | 136 | 10 | 7 | 1 | 2 | 16 | 10 | 23 | 0-0 | .210/.272/.331 | .221 | .240 | 0 | 0.3 | -0.2 |
| 1B T. Ishikawa | FRE | AAA | 27 | 211 | 21 | 14 | 0 | 3 | 18 | 29 | 54 | 3-1 | .251/.368/.383 | .277 | .345 | 1.5 | 2.2 | 1.0 |
| DH B. Kjeldgaard | BRV | A+ | 25 | 268 | 39 | 9 | 2 | 18 | 49 | 26 | 75 | 13-2 | .268/.366/.558 | .319 | .317 | -1 | 0 | 1.8 |
| | HUN | AA | 25 | 229 | 18 | 9 | 2 | 6 | 27 | 17 | 66 | 2-1 | .271/.341/.424 | .271 | .366 | -0.5 | 4 | 1.0 |
| SS E. Maysonet | NAS | AAA | 29 | 436 | 57 | 24 | 2 | 3 | 39 | 27 | 70 | 2-1 | .290/.347/.386 | .253 | .345 | -0.4 | 5.1 | 1.8 |
| 2B S. Miranda | HUN | AA | 24 | 401 | 49 | 16 | 2 | 0 | 29 | 30 | 41 | 1-6 | .270/.332/.326 | .249 | .301 | 1.8 | -5.6 | -0.1 |
| 1B H. Morris | BRV | A+ | 22 | 531 | 75 | 28 | 5 | 19 | 67 | 18 | 84 | 7-3 | .271/.299/.461 | .282 | .289 | -1.9 | -11.8 | 0.5 |
| CF D. Richardson | BRV | A+ | 22 | 392 | 47 | 13 | 7 | 3 | 41 | 22 | 70 | 9-13 | .284/.327/.384 | .264 | .341 | 0.1 | 0.1 | 1.8 |
| C M. Rivera | NAS | AAA | 34 | 218 | 16 | 10 | 0 | 7 | 31 | 19 | 55 | 2-1 | .238/.315/.399 | .237 | .295 | -3.1 | 0.2 | 0.2 |
| | MIL | MLB | 34 | 6 | 0 | 0 | 0 | 0 | 0 | 0 | 1 | 0-0 | .333/.333/.333 | .237 | .400 | -0.1 | 0 | 0.0 |
| 3B Z. Wheeler | HUN | AA | 24 | 268 | 34 | 20 | 0 | 8 | 32 | 30 | 49 | 7-0 | .272/.377/.465 | .289 | .314 | -1.6 | 4.1 | 2.0 |
| | NAS | AAA | 24 | 61 | 7 | 3 | 1 | 1 | 6 | 9 | 8 | 0-0 | .275/.383/.431 | .257 | .310 | -1 | 0.8 | 0.2 |

**Jordan Brown** is stuck betwixt and between—he's battered Triple-A pitching around for years, but not quite enough to play a corner position, and he isn't quite rangy enough to start in center field. ⚾ The other "K. Davis"—**Khris**—doesn't have the tools of Kentrail, but showed up on the prospect radar by demonstrating his hitting prowess for the second year in a row. He'll stay there if he's able to rebound from his small sample size humiliation at Double-A. ⚾ **Travis Ishikawa** is a slick-fielding first baseman whose career stat line (.265/.327/.400) is quite comparable to Casey Kotchman's pre-2011 rate stats (.259/.326/.392). If only the Brewers had "The Extra 2%" they could expect a miracle, too. ⚾ **Brock Kjeldgaard** lived up to the "Double-A" with which he was born and is expected to have more developmental potential than the typical 25-year-old, having only been a position player in full-season ball since 2009. ⚾ Maysonet is an anagram for Team Sony, and **Edwin Maysonet** may have to settle for video games to participate in major league action again, but he'll be back in Nashville, available to man Thor's Post—er, shortstop—in Milwaukee in an emergency. ⚾ **Sergio Miranda** isn't exactly a prospect, but he made the Florida State League All-Star Game in 2010, plays slick defense at second base, and is willing to play anywhere, so anything's possible—just ask Erick Almonte. ⚾ Drafted in 2010, **Hunter Morris** saw his first Double-A action after just 845 minor-league plate appearances and has hit for more power than was expected, though his lack of patience is concerning and disappointing. ⚾ **D'Vontrey Richardson** cut his strikeouts by being more aggressive and focusing on making contact. The former Florida State quarterback still has fantastic tools and the power is expected to come. An early-season hip injury set back his growth as a basestealer. ⚾ **Mike Rivera** has hit 13 major-league home runs in 605 plate appearances; if he'd thrown out more than 25 percent of potential base thieves in his career, he'd have a better chance to collect number 14. ⊘ **Zelous Wheeler** plays with—you guessed it—zeal. And while he doesn't quite profile as a starter, his great attitude and on-base skills have him poised for a career as a useful reserve.

## PITCHERS

| PLAYER | TEAM | LVL | AGE | W | L | SV | IP | H | HR | BB | SO | EqBB9 | EqSO9 | GB% | BABIP | WHIP | ERA | FIP | FRA | WARP |
|--------|------|-----|-----|---|---|----|----|---|----|----|----|-------|-------|-----|-------|------|-----|-----|-----|------|
| E. Arnett | HEL | RK | 23 | 4 | 2 | 0 | 52 | 64 | 7 | 9 | 49 | 1.6 | 8.5 | 57% | .356 | 1.40 | 5.19 | 4.87 | 5.08 | 0.1 |
| N. Bucci | BRV | A+ | 20 | 8 | 11 | 0 | 150 | 143 | 12 | 51 | 119 | 3.1 | 7.1 | 45% | .289 | 1.29 | 3.84 | 4.07 | 4.94 | 0.9 |
| M. DiFelice | NAS | AAA | 34 | 2 | 1 | 6 | 29 | 25 | 3 | 6 | 30 | 1.9 | 9.6 | 29% | .297 | 1.07 | 2.17 | 3.74 | 4.71 | 0.3 |
| | MIL | MLB | 34 | 0 | 0 | 0 | 3 | 3 | 1 | 2 | 3 | 6.0 | 9.0 | 22% | .250 | 1.67 | 12.00 | 7.33 | 8.70 | -0.1 |
| D. Goforth | HEL | RK | 22 | 0 | 3 | 2 | $40^2$ | 44 | 5 | 10 | 42 | 2.2 | 9.3 | 44% | .348 | 1.33 | 4.43 | 4.60 | 4.56 | 0.4 |
| S. Green | NAS | AAA | 32 | 1 | 0 | 6 | 46 | 41 | 3 | 27 | 40 | 5.3 | 7.8 | 70% | .314 | 1.48 | 3.91 | 4.93 | 6.16 | -0.4 |
| | MIL | MLB | 32 | 0 | 1 | 0 | $11^2$ | 14 | 0 | 6 | 7 | 4.6 | 5.4 | 58% | .326 | 1.71 | 5.40 | 3.34 | 4.04 | 0.1 |
| K. Heckathorn | BRV | A+ | 23 | 5 | 6 | 0 | $79^2$ | 82 | 8 | 21 | 65 | 2.4 | 7.3 | 52% | .312 | 1.29 | 3.95 | 3.97 | 4.75 | 0.7 |
| | HUN | AA | 23 | 0 | 2 | 0 | $36^1$ | 45 | 7 | 17 | 24 | 4.2 | 5.9 | 44% | .314 | 1.71 | 7.18 | 6.05 | 5.99 | -0.3 |
| S. Manzanillo | BRV | A+ | 22 | 1 | 0 | 10 | $41^1$ | 31 | 2 | 14 | 43 | 3.0 | 9.4 | 41% | .259 | 1.09 | 1.52 | 3.03 | 3.93 | 0.6 |
| | HUN | AA | 22 | 0 | 1 | 7 | $20^1$ | 13 | 2 | 12 | 19 | 5.3 | 8.4 | 41% | .216 | 1.23 | 2.21 | 4.63 | 4.46 | 0.2 |
| J. Nelson | WIS | A | 22 | 2 | 3 | 0 | 146 | 146 | 9 | 65 | 120 | 4.0 | 7.4 | 55% | .322 | 1.45 | 4.38 | 3.97 | 4.79 | 1.0 |
| J. Perez | LEH | AAA | 32 | 0 | 5 | 4 | $36^1$ | 38 | 5 | 27 | 54 | 6.2 | 13.1 | 43% | .388 | 1.71 | 5.70 | 4.28 | 4.75 | 0.3 |
| | PHI | MLB | 32 | 1 | 0 | 0 | 5 | 1 | 0 | 5 | 8 | 9.0 | 14.4 | 38% | .125 | 1.20 | 3.60 | 2.79 | 4.63 | 0.0 |
| A. Rivas | NAS | AAA | 25 | 1 | 5 | 0 | $150^2$ | 148 | 14 | 81 | 106 | 4.8 | 6.5 | 42% | .302 | 1.54 | 4.72 | 5.19 | 5.24 | 0.7 |
| C. Scarpetta | HUN | AA | 22 | 4 | 2 | 0 | 117 | 100 | 8 | 61 | 98 | 4.7 | 7.5 | 40% | .283 | 1.38 | 3.85 | 4.21 | 4.93 | 1.0 |

If the rotator cuff injury that caused **Eric Arnett** to miss much of the beginning of 2011 was the root of his ineffectiveness these past two seasons, at least there's some hope that the former first-round pick will rebound with a return to health. ⊘ **Nick Bucci** regained the control for which he was known, but despite making the Florida State League All-Star team and having youth on his side, he's still a soft-tossing former 18th-round pick who posted a 4.06 FIP in a pitcher-friendly environment. Temper expectations. ⊘ **Mark DiFelice** was a nice feel-good story, a pitcher who got a late start on a career and proved effective, but he's probably done after the bad shoulder that kept him out of action in 2010 ended his 2011 in July. ⊘ **David Goforth** has a great name for headline writers and throws plenty hard enough to go forth into into full-season ball, but he could use more movement and a second pitch. ⊘ **Sean Green** is a sidearming righty with a career ground ball percentage of 63 who has always had trouble finding the strike zone. He's made obsolete by Tim Dillard, who does throw strikes. ⊘ **Kyle Heckathorn** is another 2009 first-rounder who's at least headed in the right direction, though few of his pitches were after his promotion to Double-A. ⊘ **Santo Manzanillo** throws hard enough that he could instantly appear as a major-league setup man whenever the team is convinced he can repeat his delivery. A right shoulder injury from a late November car wreck could sideline him through spring training. ⊘ **Jimmy Nelson** keeps the ball down well for someone so big, and can still occasionally show the mid-90s heat that got him drafted in the second round, but he lacks control and so far only his slider has shown promise among his attempts at adding breaking pitches. ⊘ **Juan Perez** is best known for being one of only 46 pitchers to ever strike out three batters on nine pitches, though he used up a month's quota of ball-free plate appearances in doing so. But, hey, Mitch Williams logged 192 saves. ⊘ The Pacific Coast League isn't an easy place to pitch, but **Amaury Rivas** saw every aspect of his game decay. With all the starters in the system, a move to the pen can be expected soon. ⊘ **Cody Scarpetta**'s last name means "small shoe"—ironic for a tall wide-bodied pitcher whose biggest concern is too many walks.

# MANAGER: RON ROENICKE

| YEAR | TEAM | W-L | Pythag +/– | Avg PC | 100+ P | 120+ P | QS | BQS | REL | REL w Zero R | IBB | Subs | PH | PH Avg | PH HR | SB2 | CS2 | SB3 | CS3 | SAC Att | SAC % | POS SAC | Squeeze | Swing | In Play |
|------|------|-----|-----------|--------|--------|--------|----|----|----|----|----|----|----|----|----|----|----|----|----|----|----|----|----|----|----|
| 2011 | MIL | 96-66 | 1 | 99.3 | 85 | 2 | 98 | 7 | 434 | 342 | 16 | — | 257 | .222 | 5 | 12 | 5 | 0 | 3 | 117 | 82.1% | 54 | 5 | 297 | 109 |

On the one hand, when a manager is handed a great starting rotation, a fearsome closer, two serious MVP candidates, and a couple of other guys who've made All-Star teams, he's only expected to be a caretaker for the regular season and then shine in the playoffs. On the other hand, the Brewers featured some players who had awful defensive reputations during rookie manager Roenicke's first year at the helm, putting his decision-making to the test. To the surprise of most, he waited until the playoffs to show any drastic reactions to perceived defensive shortcomings, benching Casey McGehee and even sending Nyjer Morgan to the penalty box (and starting Mark Kotsay in center field in the NLCS). Roenicke managed the team to five more

"Runnin' Ron" nickname—a relative reluctance to employ the stolen base (fifth-least stolen base attempts in the National League, with the sixth-best success rate).

# Minnesota Twins

Looking at them now, it's hard to believe that the Twins won 94 games just two years ago. Yes, injuries played a major role in their collapse last season, but in returning to his old job to pick up the pieces from that mighty fall, general manager Terry Ryan has taken over a team that looks more like Humpty Dumpty than a contender coming off a fluky down season.

Just to be clear, the Twins' injury plague in 2011 was catastrophic and the player capsules that follow this essay read like a set of hospital records. The Twins led the majors in Total Adjusted WARP Lost to the disabled list (TAWL). Altogether, 16 players combined for 26 disabled list stays and 1,042 days lost to injury including day-to-day absences (see Table 1). Fifteen players lost a month or more to injury. Seven lost two months or more, and among the five who lost a whopping three months or more were the team's two best players, Joe Mauer (90 days lost) and Justin Morneau (104).

According to our TAWL calculations, the net effect of all of those injuries was a loss of nearly 10 wins above replacement (9.85 to be exact), and one could argue that that number should be even higher, be it because of a shortcoming in our math (surely Morneau's 104 days lost cost the team more than our estimated one win above replacement), or because of the lingering effects those injuries had on the players in question even when they were able to play. Using Morneau again, he hit just .227/.285/.333 when "healthy." Mauer hit just .287/.360/.368, which resulted in the lowest True Average of his career (.272 against a career .306 TAv). Yet, even if you round the Twins' TAWL up to 15 wins, thereby increasing our estimate by more than 50 percent, adding that to the 63 games the Twins won in 2011 only gets them up to 78 wins and fourth place in the weak AL Central. That's using their actual wins. The Twins third-order record paints

an even bleaker picture, putting their baseline at 56.5-105.5. Add 15 wins to *that* and the Twins still lose 90 games.

Given that, it's difficult to see the Twins posting a winning record in the coming season, which is a damning comment on the four years that Bill Smith spent as the team's general manager in between Ryan's two tenures. Despite the Twins doubling their payroll from 2008 to 2011, Smith did little more than spin his wheels, doing at least as much harm as good and often finding a way to undermine the few good moves he did make (see Table 2).

In his first few months on the job, Smith was charged with getting maximum value for Johan Santana prior to the two-time Cy Young award winner's walk year. He botched the assignment badly, getting a weak package of leftovers from the Mets after playing hardball on better offers from other teams. Smith managed to salvage part of that return two years later by turning good-field/no-hit center fielder Carlos Gomez into shortstop J.J. Hardy, who represented a significant and badly needed upgrade in the middle infield for Minnesota, but then undermined that effort by ditching Hardy after one season so as not to have to pay arbitration prices for his services. The Orioles, who got Hardy for a pair of unspectacular minor league relievers, wound up paying Hardy $5.85 million for the 2011 season, while Smith spent $5.329 million just for the right to negotiate with Japanese shortstop Tsuyoshi Nishioka, who was a complete bust as Hardy's replacement last year and is still owed $6.25 million over the next two seasons.

Smith also did well cashing in another piece of the Santana package, righty starter Kevin Mulvey, for righty reliever Jon Rauch for the stretch run in 2009, a trade that proved particularly fortuitous as it gave the Twins a replacement closer when Joe Nathan was lost for the 2010 season following Tommy

## TWINS PROSPECTUS
### 2011 W-L: 63-99, 5th in AL Central

| | | |
|---|---|---|
| Pythag | .380 | 30th |
| RS/G | 3.82 | 25th |
| RA/G | 4.96 | 29th |
| TAv | .248 | 23rd |
| TAv-P | .285 | 29th |
| FIP | 4.34 | 28th |
| DER | .693 | 30th |
| DL | 785 | 20th |
| B-Age | 27.6 | 4th |
| P-Age | 28.6 | 21st |
| Salary | $113.2 | 9th |
| M$/MW | $6.96 | 29th |

**Ballpark:** Target Field (2-yr. PF: 97). Park factor doesn't include team-wide injury curse

**2011:** Players endure major injuries, and the team one of the worst seasons in memory

**2012:** Bad news: a possible last-place finish. Worse news: no help on the way

**Action Items:** High-paid players to stay productive, a DH, a second baseman, a better closer

John surgery. Yet, for some reason, Smith felt the need to re-place Rauch in that role at the 2010 trading deadline, trading catching prospect Wilson Ramos to the Nationals for Matt Capps. That move promptly came back to haunt the Twins the following year. Injuries to Mauer made Drew Butera their primary catcher in 2011 while the 23-year-old Ramos finished fourth in the National League Rookie of the Year voting with a .267/.334/.445 line, 15 home runs, and strong play behind the plate that combined to make him more valuable than all but two members of the 2011 Twins, according to WARP.

## Table 1: I Hate When That Happens: 2011 Twins Days Lost To Injury

| Player | | | | |
|---|---|---|---|---|
| Alexi Casilla | 1 | 62 | 2 | 64 |
| Scott Baker | 2 | 59 | 0 | 59 |
| Jim Thome | 2 | 45 | 7 | 52 |
| Jason Repko | 2 | 35 | 16 | 51 |
| Nick Blackburn | 1 | 38 | 7 | 45 |
| Francisco Liriano | 2 | 36 | 6 | 42 |
| Delmon Young | 2 | 39 | 0 | 39 |
| Joe Nathan | 1 | 31 | 0 | 31 |
| Glen Perkins | 1 | 25 | 6 | 31 |
| Michael Cuddyer | 0 | 0 | 24 | 24 |
| Jose Mijares | 1 | 15 | 3 | 18 |
| Matt Capps | 0 | 0 | 11 | 11 |
| Brian Duensing | 0 | 0 | 10 | 10 |
| Danny Valencia | 0 | 0 | 9 | 9 |
| Trevor Plouffe | 0 | 0 | 4 | 4 |
| Matt Tolbert | 0 | 0 | 3 | 3 |
| Ben Revere | 0 | 0 | 2 | 2 |
| Rene Tosoni | 0 | 0 | 1 | 1 |

One can't hold the Delmon Young/Matt Garza trade against Smith, as Young was considered the top prospect in baseball at the time, but that didn't work out either. Young was worth a total of 1.7 WARP in his three-plus seasons with the Twins while Garza and shortstop Jason Bartlett combined for 14.9 WARP in just three seasons with Tampa Bay, after which the Rays got a solid package of prospects from the Cubs for Garza's services. Smith did finally eradicate the plague of Nick Punto from Minnesota last winter, but only after being tricked by Punto's uncharacteristically valuable 2008 season into giving the scrappy infielder a two-year contract that December.

The only positive additions that Smith made at the major league level that he didn't undermine later were the trade for

and re-signing of Carl Pavano and the signing and re-signing of Jim Thome, and one could dispute the value of the Pavano singing as he has largely been a league-average innings eater for them (go figure) despite a hot stretch in mid 2010. Much as we love Jim Thome, and as valuable as he was to the Twins in 2010 (ranking fourth on the team in WARP and third among their hitters), signing a 39-year-old platoon des-ignated hitter isn't much to hang one's hat on.

## Table 2: Same Smith, Different Day: Major Transactions of Bill Smith's tenure (Oct. 1, 2007 to Nov. 7, 2011)

| Player(s) | How Acquired | Cost | Date |
|---|---|---|---|
| Kevin Mulvey, Deolis Guerra | | | |
| Joe Nathan | extended | $47M/4yrs | March 24, 2008 |
| Nick Punto | re-signed as FA | $8.5M/2yrs | Dec. 11, 2008 |
| Scott Baker | extended | $15.25M/4yrs | March 7, 2009 |
| Carl Pavano | trade | Yohan Piño | Aug. 7, 2009 |
| Jon Rauch | trade | Kevin Mulvey | Aug. 28, 2009 |
| J.J. Hardy | trade | Carlos Gomez | Nov. 6, 2009 |
| Jim Thome | signed as FA | $1.6M/1yr | Jan. 26, 2010 |
| Orlando Hudson | signed as FA | $5M/1yr | Feb. 5, 2010 |
| Nick Blackburn | extended | $14M/4yrs | March 7, 2010 |
| Denard Span | extended | $16.5M/5yrs | March 13, 2010 |
| Joe Mauer | extended | $184M/8yrs | March 22, 2010 |
| Matt Capps | trade | Wilson Ramos, Joe Testa | July 29, 2010 |
| Brian Fuentes | trade | Loek Van Mil | Sept. 1, 2010 |
| Jim Hoey, Brett Jacobson | trade | J.J. Hardy | Dec. 9, 2010 |
| Tsuyoshi Nishioka | purchase | $5.329M bid + $9.25M/3yrs | Dec. 16, 2010 |
| Jim Thome | re-signed as FA | $3M/1yr | Jan. 14, 2011 |
| Carl Pavano | re-signed as FA | $16.5M/2yrs | Jan. 19, 2011 |
| Lester Oliveros, Cole Nelson | trade | Delmon Young | Aug. 15, 2011 |

The Twins did hand out a lot of money to their own play-ers during Smith's four years on the job, signing Mauer, Morneau, Michael Cuddyer, Denard Span, Joe Nathan, Scott Baker, and Nick Blackburn to extensions totaling $380.75 million, but with the exception of the mega-deal given to Mauer, which accounts for nearly half of that $380.75 mil-lion, that was largely a continuation of the way the team did business during Ryan's first term, when Johan Santana and Torii Hunter were signed to four-year contracts that covered their later arbitration years and delayed their free agency. One could mock the Twins for committing to a pitcher as undistinguished as Blackburn, but his entire four-year deal was worth just $14 million, and while Morneau's contract looks problematic due to his struggles with post-concussion syndrome, locking up an American League MVP (however undeserving he may have been) for a maximum single-season salary of $14 million through his age-32 season is a solid move. It's even difficult to criticize the Twins for overspending on Mauer, the hometown golden boy who, prior to his injury-riddled 2011 season, was climbing up the list of the greatest catchers in major league history. After all, his contract will expire after his age-35 season, and while they failed to get a hometown discount, Mauer looked to all the world like a $23 million player prior to last season.

What makes those moves look bad now are the injuries. Morneau was on his way to earning his second MVP award in July 2010 when he slid into second base to break up a double play (which he did) and suffered a fluke concussion that has completely derailed his career. There was no way for the Twins to have seen that coming, nor Span's concussion in June of last year sustained in a collision at home plate, after which he played in just 15 games and hit .123/.167/.228. The uncertainty connected with those two players is a large part of the Twins' bleak outcome for the coming year. Concussions can end careers, as they did with former Twin Corey Koskie or new Cardinals manager Matt Matheny, and Morneau hasn't been right for more than a year and a half. To be fair, it was a herniated disc in his neck that cost Morneau the majority of his time last season, but after making a diving play at first base in late August, his concussion symptoms returned for the first time in months, which is extremely troubling.

That more recent play opened up the possibility of a full-time move to designated hitter for Morneau, though it's worth noting that both he and Span suffered their concussions running the bases, not in the field. A Morneau move to DH would in turn open up the possibility of significant playing time at first base for Mauer, who missed two months of the 2011 season with bilateral leg fatigue early in the year following offseason surgery in his left knee to alleviate irritation caused by the plica band. Mauer has had a history of problems with that left leg dating back to meniscus surgery in 2004 and a stress reaction (the precursor to a stress fracture that the team caught in time), as well as quad and hamstring strains in 2007. As a big-bodied catcher who will turn 30 next April, his days behind the plate may be numbered.

Of course, moving Mauer to first base undermines a great deal of his value, robbing the Twins not only of his excellent defense, but of the competitive advantage of having an elite bat at a typically weak offensive position. As a first-baseman, Mauer is problematically underpowered, particularly while playing his home games at the cavernous Target Field, where he has homered once in 457 career plate appearances (Morneau has just four home runs at the Twins'

new ballpark, all of them prior to his concussion). Moving Mauer would also make the pain of having traded Ramos all the more acute.

Ryan attempted to paper over that mistake by signing Ryan Doumit this offseason. It was an astute move as Doumit, signed to a one-year deal for just $3 million, gives the Twins needed depth both behind the plate and in the outfield corners while bringing a competent bat, but Doumit is a terrible defensive catcher (he led the National League in passed balls in 2008 and matched that number in 2010 while throwing out just 12 percent of opposing basestealers). He has also spent time on the disabled list in each of the last six seasons, including time lost to a concussion in 2010. If the Twins feel the need to give Mauer significant playing time somewhere other than catcher, they'll need someone other than Doumit to catch those games, and that player is not in their system.

In fact, for a team that prefers to build from within, there's not much help on the way from the Twins' farm system, period. They have one of the top prospects in baseball in slugging third baseman Miguel Sano, but Sano is a teenager who has yet to play above Rookie ball. Their top pitching prospect, Kyle Gibson, will miss the entire 2012 season following Tommy John surgery. Among their few prospects who have reached the upper levels, Chris Parmelee is an underpowered first baseman who would be stuck behind the Mauer/Morneau realignment, if that comes to pass. Liam Hendriks is yet another in the organization's seemingly endless line of low-ceiling, soft-tossing control artists. Claiming slick-fielding shortstop Pedro Florimon Jr. off waivers from the Orioles was a nice depth move, but the 25-year-old Dominican is a career .247/.322/.354 hitter in the minors, does not project as a viable major league starter, and was outrighted off the 40-man roster soon after his arrival.

That just leaves Joe Benson. A toolsy outfielder who made the jump from Double-A for a cup of coffee alongside Parmelee and Hendriks last September, Benson could play his way into a starting job in one of the pastures. He has speed, power, patience, and is viable in center, but he hasn't had a high rate of success on the bases, hasn't shown much power outside of Double-A, and has struggled to hit for average due to a high strikeout rate that has been consistently around one K per game.

Ryan picked up a couple of supplemental-round draft picks by offering Michael Cuddyer and Jason Kubel arbitration, then signing fellow outfielder Josh Willingham for $21 million over three years, effectively forcing Cuddyer and Kubel to sign elsewhere. But while Willingham will help keep up appearances, and the draft picks could prove valuable down the line, neither alter the Twins' bleak outlook for 2012.

Adding to that bleak outlook was Ryan's announcement upon returning to his old position that the Twins would scale back their payroll slightly from 2011, holding the line around $100 million for the 2012 season. That meant that the addition of Willingham's $7 million average annual salary was their "big" move. Elsewhere the team spun its wheels with small deals for the likes of Doumit, groundballer Jason Marquis ($3 million/1 year), Capps (inexplicably re-signed for $4.5 million plus an option for 2013), and 38-year-old utility-man-turned-shortstop Jamey Carroll ($6.5 million/2 years). Carroll has speed and patience, but no power whatsoever and is likely overextended as an everyday shortstop. He is thus unlikely to help the Twins improve their major league worst Park Adjusted Defensive Efficiency from a year ago.

The question facing the Twins right now isn't can they bounce back, but how long will they stay down. The answer depends heavily on Mauer and Morneau returning to health, productivity, and their original positions, and on Ryan avoiding the sort of blunders that had become all too common under Smith. The first two are not sure things, with Morneau's future looking particularly dubious, but even if they come through, they won't be enough to get the Twins back into contention without astute work from the general manager's chair, whether it's from Ryan, who returned on an interim basis, or his successor.

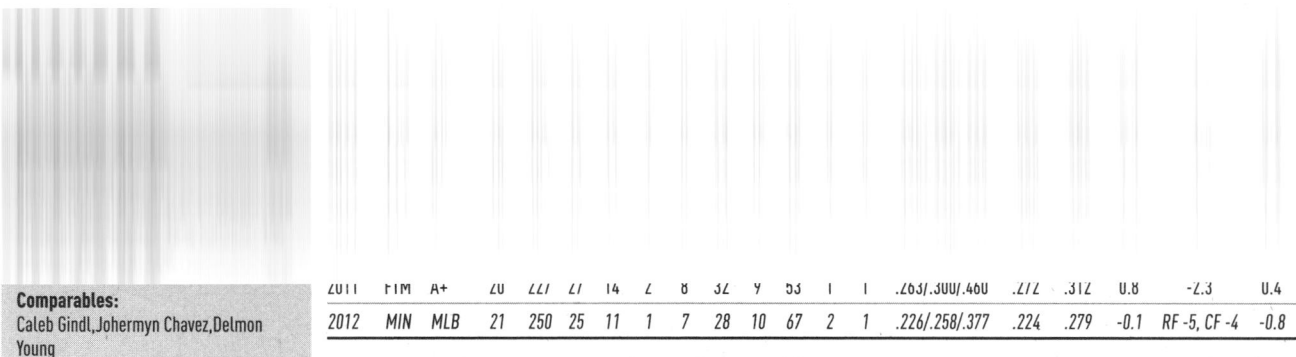

**Comparables:**
Caleb Gindl, Johermyn Chavez, Delmon Young

| YEAR | TEAM | LVL | AGE | PA | R | 2B | 3B | HR | RBI | BB | SO | SB | CS | AVG_OBP_SLG | TAv | BABIP | BRR | FRAA | WARP |
|---|---|---|---|---|---|---|---|---|---|---|---|---|---|---|---|---|---|---|---|
| 2011 | FTM | A+ | 20 | 227 | 27 | 14 | 2 | 8 | 32 | 9 | 53 | 1 | 1 | .263/.300/.460 | .272 | .312 | 0.8 | -2.3 | 0.4 |
| 2012 | MIN | MLB | 21 | 250 | 25 | 11 | 1 | 7 | 28 | 10 | 67 | 2 | 1 | .226/.258/.377 | .224 | .279 | -0.1 | RF -5, CF -4 | -0.8 |

An amateur free agent signed out of Venezuela in 2007, Arcia tore up the Appy League in 2010, and he continued his rampage during the 2011 season's first month at Beloit. Alas, surgery to remove bone chips in his elbow cost him two months, and a move to High-A exposed his aggressive approach. Arcia ranks among the system's best hitters, with good bat speed and above-average power to all fields, but he obviously needs to work on his plate discipline. He is stocky and not very athletic, with an average throwing arm. His future likely lies in left field, which sets the offensive bar high, but there's reason to believe the bat will play.

| **Joe Benson** | | **CF** | YEAR | TEAM | LVL | AGE | PA | R | 2B | 3B | HR | RBI | BB | SO | SB | CS | AVG_OBP_SLG | TAv | BABIP | BRR | FRAA | WARP |
|---|---|---|---|---|---|---|---|---|---|---|---|---|---|---|---|---|---|---|---|---|---|---|
| Born: **3/5/1988** Age: **24** | | | 2009 | FTM | A+ | 21 | 327 | 46 | 10 | 3 | 5 | 29 | 46 | 74 | 14 | 7 | .285/.412/.403 | .298 | .374 | -0.2 | 1.7 | 2.2 |
| Bats: **R** Throws: **R** Height: **6' 2"** Weight: **205** | | | 2010 | FTM | A+ | 22 | 96 | 16 | 11 | 1 | 4 | 13 | 8 | 21 | 5 | 0 | .294/.375/.588 | .340 | .350 | 0.9 | -0.4 | 1.1 |
| Breakout: **2%** Improve: **43%** Collapse: **3%** | | | 2010 | NBR | AA | 22 | 423 | 65 | 20 | 7 | 23 | 49 | 39 | 115 | 14 | 9 | .251/.336/.527 | .296 | .301 | 2.8 | -0.1 | 3.6 |
| Attrition: **17%** MLB: **87%** | | | 2011 | NBR | AA | 23 | 472 | 69 | 28 | 4 | 16 | 67 | 56 | 109 | 13 | 9 | .285/.388/.495 | .307 | .353 | 1.6 | 5.9 | 4.8 |
| **Comparables:** | | | 2011 | MIN | MLB | 23 | 74 | 3 | 6 | 1 | 0 | 2 | 3 | 21 | 2 | 2 | .239/.270/.352 | .229 | .340 | -1.5 | -0.1 | -0.2 |
| Grady Sizemore, Rick Monday, B.J. Upton | | | 2012 | MIN | MLB | 24 | 250 | 29 | 12 | 2 | 7 | 28 | 21 | 69 | 7 | 4 | .238/.317/.404 | .258 | .308 | -0.6 | CF -3, RF 0 | 1.1 |

A 2006 second-round pick who was recruited as a running back by Purdue, Benson always rated as a five-tool talent, but he finally broke out in 2010, showing off considerable power in addition to his above-average speed and arm. Repeating at Double-A, he demonstrated improved plate discipline and contact ability, and barely missed a beat despite surgery for a torn meniscus in his left knee that knocked him out all of June. His September cup of coffee was nothing to write home about; his numbers were dragged down by a .118/.167/.118 in 18 PA against lefties, something that shouldn't be a long-term problem. While his swing could still use further refinement—particularly when it comes to breaking balls and using the whole field—he will quickly be in the big-league mix. He is still more than playable in center field, though given the Twins' depth at that position, right field is likely where his destiny lies.

| **Drew Butera** | | **C** | YEAR | TEAM | LVL | AGE | PA | R | 2B | 3B | HR | RBI | BB | SO | SB | CS | AVG_OBP_SLG | TAv | BABIP | BRR | FRAA | WARP |
|---|---|---|---|---|---|---|---|---|---|---|---|---|---|---|---|---|---|---|---|---|---|---|
| Born: **8/9/1983** Age: **28** | | | 2009 | ROC | AAA | 25 | 333 | 23 | 16 | 1 | 2 | 25 | 22 | 49 | 0 | 1 | .211/.264/.292 | .204 | .239 | -0.7 | 0.5 | -0.3 |
| Bats: **R** Throws: **R** Height: **6' 2"** Weight: **205** | | | 2010 | MIN | MLB | 26 | 155 | 12 | 6 | 1 | 2 | 13 | 4 | 25 | 0 | 0 | .197/.237/.296 | .193 | .222 | -0.3 | 0.1 | -0.3 |
| Breakout: **2%** Improve: **35%** Collapse: **7%** | | | 2011 | MIN | MLB | 27 | 254 | 19 | 9 | 1 | 2 | 23 | 11 | 42 | 0 | 0 | .167/.210/.239 | .164 | .194 | -1.8 | 0.6 | -1.4 |
| Attrition: **28%** MLB: **69%** | | | 2012 | MIN | MLB | 28 | 250 | 23 | 11 | 1 | 2 | 20 | 12 | 42 | 0 | 0 | .218/.264/.308 | .207 | .251 | 0 | C 0 | -0.4 |
| **Comparables:** | | | | | | | | | | | | | | | | | | | | | |
| Ray Smith, Jose Yepez, Dick Bertell | | | | | | | | | | | | | | | | | | | | | |

Denial about the condition of Joe Mauer going into the regular season left the Twins ill-prepared when it came to catching depth in 2011, and Butera was as ill-equipped to pick up the slack as any catcher in the business. He started 75 games, and "hit" for a lower True Average than any batter with at least 250 plate appearances since at least 1950. He did throw out 31 percent of would-be base thieves but even with more or less average defense he was MLB's least valuable catcher in terms of WARP. Despite the signing of Ryan Doumit to back up Mauer, the Twins might find a way to hamstring themselves by squeezing Butera onto the roster as well.

**Jamey Carroll**    **SS**
Born: 2/18/1974 Age: 38
Bats: R Throws: R Height: 5' 11" Weight: 175
Breakout: 2% Improve: 22% Collapse: 13%
Attrition: 31% MLB: 64%
**Comparables:**
Cookie Rojas, Chris Gomez, Grady Hatton

| YEAR | TEAM | LVL | AGE | PA | R | 2B | 3B | HR | RBI | BB | SO | SB | CS | AVG_OBP_SLG | TAv | BABIP | BRR | FRAA | WARP |
|------|------|-----|-----|----|----|----|----|----|-----|----|----|----|----|-------------|-----|-------|-----|------|------|
| 2009 | CLE | MLB | 35 | 358 | 53 | 10 | 2 | 2 | 26 | 36 | 63 | 4 | 2 | .276/.355/.340 | .254 | .339 | 3.9 | -0.4 | 1.1 |
| 2010 | LAN | MLB | 36 | 414 | 48 | 15 | 1 | 0 | 23 | 51 | 64 | 12 | 4 | .291/.379/.339 | .284 | .349 | 2.9 | 8.4 | 3.3 |
| 2011 | LAN | MLB | 37 | 510 | 52 | 14 | 6 | 0 | 17 | 47 | 58 | 10 | 0 | .290/.359/.347 | .269 | .332 | 1.6 | -2.5 | 2.4 |
| 2012 | MIN | MLB | 38 | 460 | 49 | 14 | 3 | 0 | 31 | 43 | 73 | 8 | 2 | .265/.339/.316 | .243 | .313 | 0.1 | SS -1, 2B 2 | 0.8 |

The stakes were small—$3.85 million over two years—but the Dodgers got a fine return on this pint-sized utilityman, who for the second year in a row found himself more of an everyday player thanks to extensive DL-time for Rafael Furcal, Casey Blake, and Juan Uribe. Carroll's value rests in his ability to get on base, to run the bases well (+4.7 runs over the past two years) and to field multiple positions competently, but his lack of power is a bit of a drag on an offense. Thanks to his slaptastic nature and willingness to work a walk, he posted the lowest others batted in percentage (6.5) of any batting title qualifier since Luis Castillo in 2000 (6.2). Still, he is much handier to have around than Ryan Theriot or Aaron Freakin' Miles. The Twins signed him to a two-year, $6.5 million deal with a vesting option for 2014, intending to make him their starting shortstop; while he has handled the position reasonably well, not many shortstops succeed at 38, though at least he'll have utility both to the Twins and the contender to whom he's eventually traded.

**Alexi Casilla**    **2B**
Born: 7/20/1984 Age: 27
Bats: B Throws: R Height: 5' 10" Weight: 160
Breakout: 8% Improve: 45% Collapse: 5%
Attrition: 16% MLB: 83%
**Comparables:**
Chris Getz, Chris Stynes, Dave Cash

| YEAR | TEAM | LVL | AGE | PA | R | 2B | 3B | HR | RBI | BB | SO | SB | CS | AVG_OBP_SLG | TAv | BABIP | BRR | FRAA | WARP |
|------|------|-----|-----|----|----|----|----|----|-----|----|----|----|----|-------------|-----|-------|-----|------|------|
| 2009 | ROC | AAA | 24 | 171 | 21 | 3 | 4 | 2 | 17 | 11 | 23 | 9 | 6 | .340/.379/.449 | .292 | .383 | -1 | 0.4 | 0.9 |
| 2009 | MIN | MLB | 24 | 256 | 25 | 7 | 3 | 0 | 17 | 22 | 36 | 11 | 0 | .202/.280/.259 | .195 | .238 | 1.1 | -2.9 | -1.4 |
| 2010 | MIN | MLB | 25 | 170 | 26 | 7 | 4 | 1 | 20 | 13 | 17 | 6 | 1 | .276/.331/.395 | .255 | .304 | 1.5 | 1.6 | 0.8 |
| 2011 | MIN | MLB | 26 | 365 | 52 | 21 | 4 | 2 | 21 | 28 | 45 | 15 | 4 | .260/.322/.368 | .255 | .294 | 2.1 | 6.1 | 2.1 |
| 2012 | MIN | MLB | 27 | 311 | 33 | 12 | 3 | 2 | 27 | 23 | 40 | 12 | 4 | .262/.320/.347 | .241 | .292 | -0.1 | 2B -1, SS 1 | 0.8 |

The Twins spent spring training pondering whether Casilla or Tsuyoshi Nishioka would play shortstop, with the other one playing second, and they chose poorly. While Nishioka suffered a broken fibula in the season's seventh game due partly to his inexperience at the keystone, Casilla hit just .167/.227/.200 in April, struggled defensively, and lost his job. He didn't stay buried for long, as Trevor Plouffe disappointed on both sides of the ball. By mid-June, Casilla shifted back to second base to accommodate Nishioka's return. Alas, after a respectable .281/.344/.408 line from May through July, he strained his right hamstring on July 27, and re-injured it in his return 15 days later, shelving him for the season. The year where he holds onto a job may never come, and perhaps it shouldn't given his limitations, but the Twins appear ready to go into 2012 with him as their starting second baseman. Yippee.

**Brian Dinkelman**    **2B**
Born: 11/10/1983 Age: 28
Bats: L Throws: R Height: 6' 0" Weight: 195
Breakout: 3% Improve: 33% Collapse: 12%
Attrition: 32% MLB: 78%
**Comparables:**
Omar Quintanilla, Bernie Allen, Chris Burke

| YEAR | TEAM | LVL | AGE | PA | R | 2B | 3B | HR | RBI | BB | SO | SB | CS | AVG_OBP_SLG | TAv | BABIP | BRR | FRAA | WARP |
|------|------|-----|-----|----|----|----|----|----|-----|----|----|----|----|-------------|-----|-------|-----|------|------|
| 2009 | NBR | AA | 25 | 542 | 62 | 38 | 2 | 8 | 65 | 55 | 73 | 5 | 6 | .296/.380/.440 | .302 | .330 | 1.3 | -0.6 | 3.5 |
| 2010 | ROC | AAA | 26 | 592 | 58 | 32 | 2 | 8 | 54 | 52 | 99 | 9 | 4 | .265/.334/.379 | .254 | .309 | -0.6 | -7.4 | 0.3 |
| 2011 | ROC | AAA | 27 | 526 | 54 | 27 | 1 | 3 | 41 | 45 | 93 | 7 | 2 | .243/.316/.324 | .228 | .294 | 3.1 | 0.5 | -0.2 |
| 2011 | MIN | MLB | 27 | 78 | 5 | 1 | 0 | 0 | 4 | 4 | 14 | 2 | 0 | .301/.346/.315 | .243 | .373 | 0.5 | 0.2 | -0.1 |
| 2012 | MIN | MLB | 28 | 250 | 26 | 12 | 1 | 2 | 22 | 18 | 46 | 3 | 1 | .250/.313/.344 | .240 | .300 | -0.1 | 2B -1, LF -2 | 0.3 |

In last year's book, we predicted that Dinkelman's best hope for a taste of the majors would be an injury stack at the big league level. Sure enough, the prophecy came to pass. After plugging away in the minors for five seasons and change, the 2006 NAIA Player of the Year got the call in June, just after Jason Kubel and Jim Thome went on the DL, with Joe Mauer and Tsuyoshi Nishioka still serving extended stints. His moment quickly passed, but Dinkelman earned a September callup, and proceeded to hit just about the slappiest .301 that a man can hit. Dinkelman lacks the range or the hands to be a full-time infielder, the power to be an outfielder, or the utility to be a utilityman. Outrighted off the 40-man and re-signed to a minor league deal, he is organizational fodder in an organization that's all foddered up.

### Ryan Doumit — C

Born: 4/3/1981 Age: 31
Bats: B Throws: R Height: 6' 1" Weight: 200
Breakout: 0% Improve: 23% Collapse: 17%
Attrition: 32% MLB: 86%

**Comparables:**
Terry McGriff, Hector Ortiz, Michael Barrett

| YEAR | TEAM | LVL | AGE | PA | R | 2B | 3B | HR | RBI | BB | SO | SB | CS | AVG/OBP/SLG | TAv | BABIP | BRR | FRAA | WARP |
|------|------|-----|-----|-----|----|----|----|----|-----|----|----|----|----|-------------|------|-------|------|---------|------|
| 2009 | PIT | MLB | 28 | 304 | 31 | 16 | 0 | 10 | 38 | 20 | 49 | 4 | 0 | .250/.299/.414 | .238 | .268 | -0.1 | 1.6 | 0.8 |
| 2010 | PIT | MLB | 29 | 456 | 42 | 22 | 1 | 13 | 45 | 41 | 87 | 1 | 0 | .251/.331/.406 | .253 | .290 | -3.2 | 4.7 | 0.9 |
| 2011 | PIT | MLB | 30 | 236 | 17 | 12 | 1 | 8 | 30 | 16 | 35 | 0 | 1 | .303/.353/.477 | .288 | .331 | -2.6 | 0 | 1.3 |
| 2012 | MIN | MLB | 31 | 274 | 33 | 15 | 1 | 7 | 33 | 18 | 44 | 1 | 1 | .273/.327/.428 | .269 | .303 | -0.1 | C 1, RF -0 | 2.4 |

Doumit signed an extension with the Pirates in December 2008. In the three seasons since then, he has undergone wrist surgery, suffered a concussion, and fractured his ankle. He also hit 31 homers during that time, and the Pirates never lost hope they could swap him for prospects. Now that you know all that, you're an expert on Doumit. His whole career has been a race to see if his poor catching can cancel out his bat, and while the Pirates have let him stand at first and in the outfield, he still hits like a catcher. The Twins signed Doumit to a one-year, $3 million deal. With the move to the American League to spell Mauer and presumably DH a bit, he'll have a chance to show the world if he can be league average or just replacement level.

A 2009 eighth-round pick out of the University of Southern Mississippi, Dozier put himself on the map with a breakout 2011 season, tearing up the Florida State League in a slight return to Fort Myers, then continuing to roll through the Eastern League. Dozier has above-average bat speed and contact ability, as well as a polished approach at the plate. He's only got gap power, however, and doesn't profile to reach double digits in homers at the major league level. Scouts feel he lacks the athleticism and arm strength to play shortstop in the majors, so he's likely bound for second base. The Twins view Jamey Carroll as a bridge to Dozier, but it's not clear the latter has the range or arm to stick there for long either. In any event, the perpetual trainwreck in the Twins infield likely means Dozier will get a look sometime in 2012.

### Niko Goodrum — SS

Born: 2/28/1992 Age: 20
Bats: B Throws: R Height: 6' 4" Weight: 167
Breakout: 0% Improve: 1% Collapse: 1%
Attrition: 3% MLB: 3%

**Comparables:**
Pedro Florimon Jr., Deybis Benitez, Lifete Jose

| YEAR | TEAM | LVL | AGE | PA | R | 2B | 3B | HR | RBI | BB | SO | SB | CS | AVG/OBP/SLG | TAv | BABIP | BRR | FRAA | WARP |
|------|------|-----|-----|-----|----|----|----|----|-----|----|----|----|----|-------------|------|-------|------|---------|------|
| 2010 | TWI | RK | 18 | 128 | 10 | 4 | 0 | 0 | 5 | 9 | 34 | 4 | 2 | .161/.220/.195 | .167 | .226 | 1.2 | -1.6 | -0.4 |
| 2011 | ELZ | RK | 19 | 230 | 39 | 10 | 3 | 2 | 20 | 21 | 56 | 8 | 1 | .275/.352/.382 | .273 | .367 | -0.3 | -7.9 | 0.6 |
| 2012 | MIN | MLB | 20 | 250 | 17 | 8 | 1 | 0 | 13 | 12 | 82 | 1 | 0 | .171/.213/.214 | .159 | .255 | 0 | SS 1, 2B -0 | -2.9 |

A second-round 2010 pick out of a Georgia high school, Goodrum shook off a dismal professional debut and went on a late-season tear (.341/.438/.489 in August, compared to .224/.268/.276 prior) to finish with decent numbers at Elizabethton. Athletic but very raw, Goodrum has an outstanding arm, raw power, speed, and a whole lot of projection on his lean frame. Few think he'll stick at shortstop in the long run, but whether he winds up a third base, center field, or right field will depend upon how his skills and his body develop in the coming years.

### Aaron Hicks — CF

Born: 10/2/1989 Age: 22
Bats: B Throws: R Height: 6' 3" Weight: 185
Breakout: 3% Improve: 30% Collapse: 3%
Attrition: 20% MLB: 51%

**Comparables:**
Chad Hermansen, Clay Fuller, Roger Cedeno

| YEAR | TEAM | LVL | AGE | PA | R | 2B | 3B | HR | RBI | BB | SO | SB | CS | AVG/OBP/SLG | TAv | BABIP | BRR | FRAA | WARP |
|------|------|-----|-----|-----|----|----|----|----|-----|----|-----|----|----|-------------|------|-------|------|-----------|------|
| 2009 | BLT | A | 19 | 297 | 43 | 15 | 3 | 4 | 29 | 40 | 55 | 10 | 8 | .251/.354/.382 | .271 | .304 | 0.9 | 0.9 | 1.7 |
| 2010 | BLT | A | 20 | 518 | 86 | 27 | 6 | 8 | 49 | 88 | 112 | 21 | 11 | .279/.400/.428 | .309 | .358 | 5.5 | 7 | 5.7 |
| 2011 | FTM | A+ | 21 | 528 | 79 | 31 | 5 | 5 | 38 | 78 | 110 | 17 | 9 | .242/.354/.368 | .248 | .308 | -5.5 | 14.8 | 3.8 |
| 2012 | MIN | MLB | 22 | 250 | 24 | 11 | 1 | 2 | 18 | 27 | 64 | 6 | 4 | .211/.296/.302 | .220 | .281 | -0.6 | CF -2, RF 0 | -0.5 |

The 14th pick of the 2008 draft out of Long Beach, California, Hicks has the whole toolshed, with scouts drooling over his power (at least in batting practice), speed, and an arm that many consider among the minors' best. In fact, there were teams that considered him good enough to be a first-round pick as a pitcher, with a fastball that could reach 98 mph—so, *not* a Twins pitcher. While he is outstanding in center field and on the bases, through over 1500 plate appearances, Hicks has made little progress as a hitter, showing good pitch recognition but a passive approach at the plate—as in, "What was wrong with *that* pitch?"—and very little in-game power. As he makes the jump to Double-A he'll have to demonstrate the refinement of his tools by putting up some numbers.

**Luke Hughes    2B**
Born: 8/2/1984 Age: 27
Bats: R Throws: R Height: 6' 0" Weight: 205
Breakout: 2% Improve: 37% Collapse: 4%
Attrition: 25% MLB: 82%
**Comparables:**
Gil McDougald, Jim Finigan, Jayson Nix

| YEAR | TEAM | LVL | AGE | PA | R | 2B | 3B | HR | RBI | BB | SO | SB | CS | AVG/OBP/SLG | TAv | BABIP | BRR | FRAA | WARP |
|---|---|---|---|---|---|---|---|---|---|---|---|---|---|---|---|---|---|---|---|
| 2009 | NBR | AA | 24 | 229 | 22 | 15 | 3 | 6 | 36 | 19 | 38 | 1 | 1 | .250/.326/.445 | .281 | .280 | -1.7 | -2.5 | 1.0 |
| 2009 | ROC | AAA | 24 | 157 | 19 | 8 | 2 | 6 | 28 | 18 | 38 | 2 | 0 | .259/.351/.481 | .293 | .319 | -1.9 | 0.2 | 0.9 |
| 2010 | ROC | AAA | 25 | 81 | 12 | 8 | 0 | 1 | 7 | 5 | 18 | 2 | 0 | .257/.309/.405 | .241 | .321 | 0.8 | -0.1 | 0.1 |
| 2010 | MIN | MLB | 25 | 7 | 1 | 0 | 0 | 1 | 1 | 0 | 3 | 0 | 1 | .286/.286/.714 | .325 | .333 | 0 | 0 | 0.1 |
| 2011 | ROC | AAA | 26 | 129 | 16 | 6 | 1 | 4 | 11 | 10 | 18 | 2 | 0 | .231/.287/.402 | .236 | .237 | -1 | -0.7 | -0.1 |
| 2011 | MIN | MLB | 26 | 317 | 31 | 12 | 0 | 7 | 30 | 24 | 79 | 3 | 2 | .223/.289/.338 | .230 | .282 | 2.3 | -1.5 | -0.5 |
| *2012* | *MIN* | *MLB* | *27* | *255* | *28* | *11* | *1* | *6* | *27* | *19* | *58* | *2* | *1* | *.237/.300/.379* | *.244* | *.287* | *-0.1* | *2B -1, 3B -2* | *0.6* |

Apparently, Hughes is Australian for "futility infielder." Thanks to a slew of injuries, the Perth native started 34 games at second base 30 at first base and 12 at third base for the Twins and while he showed a modicum of pop he was done in by contact woes. He also missed a flight from Rochester to Minneapolis on August 18 by going to the wrong gate (9B instead of 9A, because apparently such sub-numbering is a Northern Hemisphere thing), leaving the Twins with just nine healthy position players, a situation that necessitated Mauer's debut in right field. Clearly out of place as a regular, Hughes's minor league track record shows enough power (.189 ISO at Double-A and Triple-A) to make him interesting. He'll have to do better than the 196/.282/.326 he hit against lefties (in 103 PA) to have a real major league career though.

**Joe Mauer    C**
Born: 4/19/1983 Age: 29
Bats: L Throws: R Height: 6' 5" Weight: 220
Breakout: 2% Improve: 51% Collapse: 7%
Attrition: 15% MLB: 94%
**Comparables:**
John Olerud, Victor Martinez, Ted Simmons

| YEAR | TEAM | LVL | AGE | PA | R | 2B | 3B | HR | RBI | BB | SO | SB | CS | AVG/OBP/SLG | TAv | BABIP | BRR | FRAA | WARP |
|---|---|---|---|---|---|---|---|---|---|---|---|---|---|---|---|---|---|---|---|
| 2009 | MIN | MLB | 26 | 606 | 94 | 30 | 1 | 28 | 96 | 76 | 63 | 4 | 1 | .365/.444/.587 | .349 | .373 | 1.6 | -2.9 | 8.0 |
| 2010 | MIN | MLB | 27 | 584 | 88 | 43 | 1 | 9 | 75 | 65 | 53 | 1 | 4 | .327/.402/.469 | .303 | .348 | 4.4 | -1.7 | 5.0 |
| 2011 | MIN | MLB | 28 | 333 | 38 | 15 | 0 | 3 | 30 | 32 | 38 | 0 | 0 | .287/.360/.368 | .266 | .319 | -1.4 | 2.2 | 1.5 |
| *2012* | *MIN* | *MLB* | *29* | *367* | *50* | *20* | *2* | *7* | *43* | *42* | *38* | *1* | *1* | *.315/.394/.454* | *.303* | *.338* | *-0.2* | *C -1, 1B 1* | *3.7* |

After a 2010 season spent battling shoulder, heel, and knee injuries, Mauer needed offseason surgery to alleviate irritation caused by the plica band, a fold of tissue in the lining of his left knee. Since he didn't go under the knife until mid-December, he wasn't fully recovered by the time camp opened, didn't catch his first Grapefruit League game until March 19, and was significantly below full strength as the season opened. After nine games, he landed on the disabled list with bilateral leg weakness exacerbated by a viral infection. Further slowed by shoulder issues—problems that were part of a cascade that Mauer believes began with his April 2010 heel woes—he didn't return until June 17, and showed very little power, not hitting his first homer until July 27. He played just 10 games in September (homering twice) before a bout of pneumonia ended his season on a fittingly dour note. Given his mess of a season and career-low in games played, the calls for Mauer to move from behind the plate are increasing in volume. While the Twins are understandably reluctant to do so, they're just one year into an eight-year, $184 million deal and can't afford to lose half seasons here and there.

**Justin Morneau    1B**
Born: 5/15/1981 Age: 31
Bats: L Throws: R Height: 6' 5" Weight: 200
Breakout: 1% Improve: 28% Collapse: 7%
Attrition: 13% MLB: 91%
**Comparables:**
Eddie Murray, Paul Konerko, Kent Hrbek

| YEAR | TEAM | LVL | AGE | PA | R | 2B | 3B | HR | RBI | BB | SO | SB | CS | AVG/OBP/SLG | TAv | BABIP | BRR | FRAA | WARP |
|---|---|---|---|---|---|---|---|---|---|---|---|---|---|---|---|---|---|---|---|
| 2009 | MIN | MLB | 28 | 590 | 85 | 31 | 1 | 30 | 100 | 72 | 86 | 0 | 0 | .274/.363/.516 | .304 | .273 | 0.1 | -2.7 | 3.2 |
| 2010 | MIN | MLB | 29 | 348 | 53 | 25 | 1 | 18 | 56 | 50 | 62 | 0 | 0 | .345/.437/.618 | .360 | .385 | -3.1 | -1.3 | 3.6 |
| 2011 | MIN | MLB | 30 | 288 | 19 | 16 | 0 | 4 | 30 | 19 | 44 | 0 | 0 | .227/.285/.333 | .220 | .257 | -1.7 | -5.2 | -1.7 |
| *2012* | *MIN* | *MLB* | *31* | *287* | *38* | *16* | *1* | *10* | *38* | *29* | *43* | *0* | *0* | *.277/.352/.471* | *.290* | *.296* | *0* | *1B -5* | *2.0* |

Bad enough that Morneau's MVP-pace 2010 campaign was shut down on July 7 of that year by a concussion. Worse was a 2011 season completely wrecked by myriad injuries and recurrence of concussion woes. Morneau struggled from the outset, and went on the disabled list on June 10 due to swelling in his left wrist, a problem related to a herniated disc in his neck. He underwent surgery in late June, didn't return until August 12, and played just 14 games before left shoulder soreness and lingering concussion symptoms—aggravated by a diving play at first base—sidelined him for the season. He underwent a trio of surgeries to remove a cyst in his left knee, a bone spur in his right foot, and to stabilize the left wrist. Despite the full-body overhaul, there's no way to know whether Morneau will still be haunted by his head injury. It could turn him into a very expensive shadow of the player he once was—he's owed $28 million through 2013— and affect his life far beyond the baseball field.

**Tsuyoshi Nishioka**  SS

Born: 7/27/1984 Age: 27
Bats: B Throws: R Height: 6' 2" Weight: 175
Breakout: 4% Improve: 37% Collapse: 21%
Attrition: 35% MLB: 81%

**Comparables:**
Phil Linz, Jason Bartlett, Al Pedrique

| YEAR | TEAM | LVL | AGE | PA | R | 2B | 3B | HR | RBI | BB | SO | SB | CS | AVG_OBP_SLG | TAv | BABIP | BRR | FRAA | WARP |
|------|------|-----|-----|----|----|----|----|----|-----|----|----|----|----|-------------|-----|-------|-----|------|------|
| 2011 | MIN | MLB | 26 | 240 | 14 | 5 | 0 | 0 | 19 | 15 | 43 | 2 | 4 | .226/.278/.249 | .209 | .281 | -1.6 | -1.7 | -0.9 |
| 2012 | MIN | MLB | 27 | 250 | 26 | 10 | 1 | 2 | 20 | 17 | 44 | 4 | 2 | .253/.309/.329 | .235 | .300 | -0.4 | SS -2, 2B -0 | 0.6 |

The Twins paid $5.3 million to win the posting rights to the 2010 NPB Pacific League batting champion, then signed him to a three-year, $9.25 million deal, but the unflattering comparisons to Kaz Matsui that followed Nishioka stateside foreshadowed disappointment. After juggling Nishioka and Alexi Casilla at the two middle infield spots during spring training, the Twins broke camp with their pricey import playing second base for the first time in his career. His inexperience quickly proved costly. Six games in, he straddled the bag too long on a potential double play, broke his fibula, and missed 10 weeks. He was below-average defensively after moving back to shortstop—our system didn't dislike him as much as Defensive Runs Saved (-10), Total Zone (-11) or Ultimate Zone Rating (-6)—and never demonstrated even a hint of power before his season mercifully ended three weeks early due to a trunk strain. The signing of Jamey Carroll to be the team's starting shortstop suggests

Fernandez

pick out of Puerto Rico began the 2011 season with a bang, hitting .377/.429/.788 with six homers through the end of April. Unfortunately, that was about the worst thing that could have happened to him, as it reinforced bad habits. Pitchers adjusted, and the holes in his swing soon revealed themselves; he hit just .237/.291/.383 the rest of the way, with a strikeout rate that jumped from 13 to 19 percent. Ortiz doesn't have a great deal going for him besides his bat; he's undersized, an average runner with an average arm, playable in center but already bound for a corner position in a system that has no shortage of center fielders.

**Chris Parmelee**  1B

Born: 2/24/1988 Age: 24
Bats: L Throws: L Height: 6' 2" Weight: 230
Breakout: 8% Improve: 41% Collapse: 0%
Attrition: 28% MLB: 58%

**Comparables:**
Mike Carp, Antone Williamson, Yonder Alonso

| YEAR | TEAM | LVL | AGE | PA | R | 2B | 3B | HR | RBI | BB | SO | SB | CS | AVG_OBP_SLG | TAv | BABIP | BRR | FRAA | WARP |
|------|------|-----|-----|----|----|----|----|----|-----|----|----|----|----|-------------|-----|-------|-----|------|------|
| 2009 | FTM | A+ | 21 | 501 | 61 | 27 | 1 | 16 | 73 | 65 | 109 | 2 | 2 | .258/.365/.441 | .284 | .313 | -1.6 | 1.6 | 1.8 |
| 2010 | FTM | A+ | 22 | 93 | 9 | 2 | 1 | 2 | 17 | 13 | 11 | 0 | 1 | .338/.430/.463 | .324 | .373 | -1.3 | 1.1 | 0.6 |
| 2010 | NBR | AA | 22 | 463 | 51 | 25 | 2 | 6 | 44 | 43 | 70 | 3 | 2 | .275/.346/.389 | .264 | .319 | -1.6 | 9.2 | 1.5 |
| 2011 | NBR | AA | 23 | 610 | 76 | 30 | 5 | 13 | 83 | 68 | 94 | 0 | 1 | .287/.366/.436 | .298 | .322 | 0.8 | 5.4 | 4.1 |
| 2011 | MIN | MLB | 23 | 88 | 8 | 6 | 0 | 4 | 14 | 12 | 13 | 0 | 0 | .355/.443/.592 | .360 | .390 | -0.3 | 1.6 | 1.1 |
| 2012 | MIN | MLB | 24 | 250 | 28 | 12 | 1 | 5 | 25 | 23 | 49 | 0 | 0 | .254/.324/.379 | .254 | .301 | 0 | 1B -3, RF -1 | 0.4 |

Parmelee blazed across the sky in September, but the annals of baseball history are filled with such tantalizing performances that proved unsustainable; look up Shane Spencer, Jeremy Reed, or Babe Ganzel sometime, or find Taylor Teagarden and Daric Barton elsewhere in this book. Parmelee was a 2006 first-round pick because of his sweet swing and his power potential, but he has plodded through the Twins system, not clearing A-ball until mid-2010. While he has decent plate discipline, his raw power hasn't translated to a single 20-homer season in part because the Twins had him focus on cutting down the strikeouts, bringing to mind David Ortiz's famous "you want me to hit like a little bitch" quote about his old org after he found success in Boston. Which isn't to say that Parmalee doesn't deserve a longer look, but he's not the second coming of Justin Morneau.

**Trevor Plouffe**  SS

Born: 6/15/1986 Age: 26
Bats: R Throws: R Height: 6' 3" Weight: 200
Breakout: 4% Improve: 33% Collapse: 1%
Attrition: 33% MLB: 85%

**Comparables:**
Ted Kubiak, Ramon Castro, Joe Millette

| YEAR | TEAM | LVL | AGE | PA | R | 2B | 3B | HR | RBI | BB | SO | SB | CS | AVG_OBP_SLG | TAv | BABIP | BRR | FRAA | WARP |
|------|------|-----|-----|----|----|----|----|----|-----|----|----|----|----|-------------|-----|-------|-----|------|------|
| 2009 | ROC | AAA | 23 | 477 | 53 | 23 | 5 | 10 | 60 | 34 | 68 | 3 | 6 | .260/.315/.407 | .254 | .287 | 0 | 2.9 | 2.1 |
| 2010 | ROC | AAA | 24 | 445 | 53 | 22 | 4 | 15 | 49 | 27 | 90 | 5 | 5 | .244/.296/.430 | .248 | .272 | 0.4 | -1.5 | 0.4 |
| 2010 | MIN | MLB | 24 | 44 | 7 | 1 | 0 | 2 | 6 | 0 | 14 | 0 | 0 | .146/.143/.317 | .172 | .154 | 0.3 | 0 | -0.3 |
| 2011 | ROC | AAA | 25 | 220 | 33 | 11 | 3 | 15 | 33 | 21 | 39 | 3 | 1 | .312/.384/.635 | .332 | .319 | -1.9 | 4.5 | 2.8 |
| 2011 | MIN | MLB | 25 | 320 | 47 | 18 | 1 | 8 | 31 | 25 | 71 | 3 | 3 | .238/.305/.392 | .260 | .286 | -0.7 | -7.8 | 0.4 |
| 2012 | MIN | MLB | 26 | 278 | 32 | 13 | 2 | 8 | 33 | 20 | 55 | 3 | 2 | .256/.312/.420 | .261 | .293 | -0.4 | SS -4, 2B -1 | 1.7 |

This 2004 first-round pick's first major league season of any substance didn't erase the notion that he's a bust, but in a year that saw Nishioka, Hughes, and Tolbert combine for 783 plate appearances of .213 True Average "hitting" and a collective

-2.9 WARP, Plouffe doesn't look so bad. Despite a fairly high strikeout rate and a modest BABIP, he showed enough pop that his isolated power ranked third behind Cuddyer and Kubel, his TAv fourth behind those two and Mauer. Of course, when a utility-man is your team's fourth-best hitter, plans have gone terribly awry. That's without getting into the nasty things that various systems say about his defense; suffice to say ours offers a relatively sunny take. Prior to his 51-game tear at Rochester, Plouffe had hit just .253/.303/.419 in nearly 1200 PA at Triple-A, so it's no given that he can maintain this level of production. The plan for him to focus on being a full-time corner outfielder only raises the offensive bar.

### Ben Revere    CF

Born: 5/3/1988 Age: 24
Bats: L Throws: R Height: 5' 10'' Weight: 175
Breakout: 2% Improve: 32% Collapse: 9%
Attrition: 29% MLB: 72%

Comparables:
Del Unser, J.B. Shuck, Rudy Law

| YEAR | TEAM | LVL | AGE | PA | R | 2B | 3B | HR | RBI | BB | SO | SB | CS | AVG_OBP_SLG | TAv | BABIP | BRR | FRAA | WARP |
|------|------|-----|-----|-----|----|----|----|----|-----|----|----|----|----|-------------|------|-------|------|--------|------|
| 2009 | FTM | A+ | 21 | 517 | 75 | 13 | 4 | 2 | 48 | 40 | 34 | 45 | 17 | .311/.374/.369 | .273 | .332 | 5.3 | 6.1 | 3.1 |
| 2010 | NBR | AA | 22 | 406 | 44 | 10 | 4 | 1 | 23 | 32 | 41 | 36 | 13 | .305/.372/.363 | .277 | .340 | 2.6 | 4.3 | 2.7 |
| 2010 | MIN | MLB | 22 | 30 | 1 | 0 | 0 | 0 | 2 | 2 | 5 | 0 | 1 | .179/.233/.179 | .146 | .217 | -0.2 | -0.1 | -0.4 |
| 2011 | ROC | AAA | 23 | 141 | 15 | 3 | 1 | 1 | 9 | 6 | 11 | 8 | 2 | .303/.338/.364 | .235 | .325 | -0.4 | 2.8 | 0.2 |
| 2011 | MIN | MLB | 23 | 481 | 56 | 9 | 5 | 0 | 30 | 26 | 41 | 34 | 9 | .267/.310/.309 | .230 | .293 | 8 | -2.1 | 0.1 |
| 2012 | MIN | MLB | 24 | 430 | 45 | 12 | 4 | 1 | 35 | 23 | 45 | 27 | 9 | .277/.320/.336 | .240 | .306 | -0.2 | CF -0, LF 0 | 0.4 |

Revere entered 2011 ranked number 62 on our Top 101 prospects list, but he appeared slated for another season in the minors to shore up holes in his game. Injuries accelerated his timetable and he debuted in early May, when both Delmon Young and Jason Repko were sidelined, and was up for good after Denard Span was concussed in early June. Revere didn't exactly tear up the league; aside from a .311/.342/.368 September, he was sub-replacement level. He finished with the majors' second-lowest isolated power among hitters with at least 400 PA, while his walk rate was in the bottom sixth of that group. Despite plenty of speed—he ranked fourth in EqBRR—and contact ability, the limitations of his slappy approach mean that he has to improve both his BABIP and his walk rate significantly in order to approximate the offensive contributions of a healthy Span. His arm is bad enough that it may not play in center either. He enters 2012 with serious question marks.

### Eddie Rosario    CF

Born: 9/28/1991 Age: 20
Bats: L Throws: R Height: 6' 1'' Weight: 170
Breakout: 4% Improve: 14% Collapse: 7%
Attrition: 25% MLB: 43%

Comparables:
Fernando Martinez, Ken Henderson, Juan Gonzalez

| YEAR | TEAM | LVL | AGE | PA | R | 2B | 3B | HR | RBI | BB | SO | SB | CS | AVG_OBP_SLG | TAv | BABIP | BRR | FRAA | WARP |
|------|------|-----|-----|-----|----|----|----|----|-----|----|----|----|----|-------------|------|-------|------|--------|------|
| 2010 | TWI | RK | 18 | 213 | 34 | 9 | 2 | 5 | 26 | 16 | 28 | 22 | 5 | .294/.348/.438 | .303 | .323 | 1.1 | 1.8 | 1.9 |
| 2011 | ELZ | RK | 19 | 298 | 71 | 9 | 9 | 21 | 60 | 27 | 60 | 17 | 6 | .337/.397/.670 | .363 | .370 | 2.8 | -1.7 | 4.7 |
| 2012 | MIN | MLB | 20 | 250 | 26 | 7 | 2 | 9 | 29 | 12 | 65 | 5 | 2 | .224/.263/.381 | .228 | .267 | -0.2 | CF -12, LF -0 | -0.1 |

This fourth-round 2010 pick out of a Puerto Rico high school made a monster showing at hitter-friendly Elizabethton, outdoing teammate Miguel Sano for the Appy League leads in homers, triples, and slugging percentage, and winning co-Player of the Year honors. Rosario is a true five-tool talent, though no single tool of his is star-level. He may have no outstanding strength, but has no obvious weaknesses either. His smaller frame may limit his power. He projects as more of a 20-homer, 20-steal player than a 30-30 one. Awash in center fielders, the Twins moved Rosario to second base during the fall instructional league, and will continue the experiment at Low-A Beloit in 2012.

### Miguel Sano    3B

Born: 5/11/1993 Age: 19
Bats: R Throws: R Height: 6' 4'' Weight: 195
Breakout: 0% Improve: 3% Collapse: 0%
Attrition: 6% MLB: 10%

Comparables:
Alex Rodriguez, Jharmidy De Jesus, Matt Dominguez

| YEAR | TEAM | LVL | AGE | PA | R | 2B | 3B | HR | RBI | BB | SO | SB | CS | AVG_OBP_SLG | TAv | BABIP | BRR | FRAA | WARP |
|------|------|-----|-----|-----|----|----|----|----|-----|----|----|----|----|-------------|------|-------|------|---------|------|
| 2010 | TWI | RK | 17 | 161 | 23 | 14 | 0 | 4 | 19 | 10 | 43 | 2 | 2 | .291/.338/.466 | .293 | .382 | -2.5 | -1.2 | 0.8 |
| 2011 | ELZ | RK | 18 | 293 | 58 | 18 | 7 | 20 | 59 | 23 | 77 | 5 | 4 | .292/.352/.637 | .329 | .339 | 3.5 | 11.3 | 5.0 |
| 2012 | MIN | MLB | 19 | 250 | 24 | 9 | 1 | 9 | 28 | 10 | 84 | 1 | 1 | .203/.237/.361 | .211 | .266 | -0.1 | 3B 10, SS 1 | -0.4 |

Signed to a $3.15 million bonus in 2009, this strapping Dominican put on an impressive show in the Appy League, ranking second only to teammate Eddie Rosario in both homers and slugging percentage. It wasn't some crazy home park thing, either, as he hit .308/.391/.654 with nine homers on the road, compared to .276/.310/.619 with 11 homers at home. At his young age, Sano already showcases rare 80 power to all fields under game conditions, and has the makings of a middle-of-the-lineup force. His pitch recognition and plate discipline could use some work, and while his arm is outstanding, his footwork is messy, so his defense at third base is fairly rough. He's growing rapidly—he's 30 pounds heavier than when signed—and will likely be moved off third, into right. He'll move slowly up the ladder but his steps will be worth watching.

### Denard Span — CF

Born: 2/27/1984 Age: 28
Bats: L Throws: L Height: 6' 1" Weight: 205
Breakout: 2% Improve: 46% Collapse: 11%
Attrition: 25% MLB: 88%

Comparables:
Kenny Lofton, Curt Flood, Johnny Damon

| YEAR | TEAM | LVL | AGE | PA | R | 2B | 3B | HR | RBI | BB | SO | SB | CS | AVG_OBP_SLG | TAv | BABIP | BRR | FRAA | WARP |
|---|---|---|---|---|---|---|---|---|---|---|---|---|---|---|---|---|---|---|---|
| 2009 | MIN | MLB | 25 | 676 | 97 | 16 | 10 | 8 | 68 | 70 | 89 | 23 | 10 | .311/.392/.415 | .288 | .353 | 0.7 | 3.4 | 3.9 |
| 2010 | MIN | MLB | 26 | 705 | 85 | 24 | 10 | 3 | 58 | 60 | 74 | 26 | 4 | .264/.331/.348 | .246 | .294 | 2.3 | 7.5 | 1.8 |
| 2011 | MIN | MLB | 27 | 311 | 37 | 11 | 5 | 2 | 16 | 27 | 36 | 6 | 1 | .264/.328/.359 | .257 | .297 | 2.2 | 7.8 | 1.7 |
| 2012 | MIN | MLB | 28 | 377 | 45 | 13 | 5 | 3 | 36 | 36 | 49 | 13 | 4 | .286/.359/.386 | .268 | .320 | 0 | CF 6, LF 1 | 1.8 |

It was a lost season for Span, who suffered a concussion and whiplash in a home plate collision with Kansas City's Brayan Pena on June 3. He was hitting .294/.361/.385 at the time, but hit just .132/.179/.245 in 56 plate appearances thereafter. After spending eight weeks on the disabled list due to headaches and dizziness, he played just nine games and went 2-for-35 before going back on the DL for another 39 days. He didn't reappear until the season's final week, but did close on a high note by collecting four extra-base hits in his final three games. When healthy, Span is a decent tablesetter and a plus defender in center field, better than newcomer Ben Revere. Despite heavy interest in trading for him, other teams—particularly the Nationals—were told he was off the market, so it would rate as a surprise if he

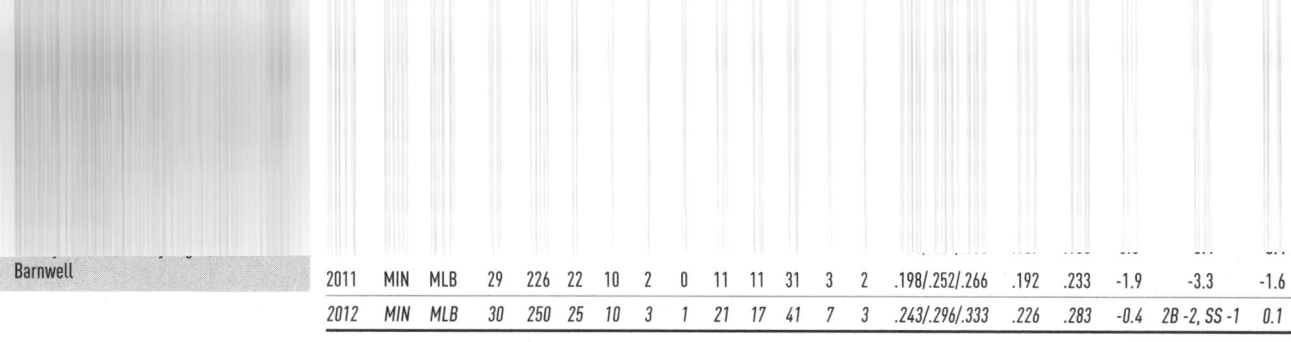

Barnwell

| YEAR | TEAM | LVL | AGE | PA | R | 2B | 3B | HR | RBI | BB | SO | SB | CS | AVG_OBP_SLG | TAv | BABIP | BRR | FRAA | WARP |
|---|---|---|---|---|---|---|---|---|---|---|---|---|---|---|---|---|---|---|---|
| 2011 | MIN | MLB | 29 | 226 | 22 | 10 | 2 | 0 | 11 | 11 | 31 | 3 | 2 | .198/.252/.266 | .192 | .233 | -1.9 | -3.3 | -1.6 |
| 2012 | MIN | MLB | 30 | 250 | 25 | 10 | 3 | 1 | 21 | 17 | 41 | 7 | 3 | .243/.296/.333 | .226 | .283 | -0.4 | 2B -2, SS -1 | 0.1 |

The Twins' insistence on settling for sub-mediocrity among their utilitymen led to another 200+ plate appearances wasted on Tolbert, whose best major league seasons have not coincidentally come when he has been limited to fewer than 125 PA. Tolbert simply doesn't offer a whole lot beyond the ability to pound his fist into his mitt enthusiastically at a variety of infield positions. Between his execrable hitting and sub-par defense, he did managed to be the majors' third least-valuable position player in terms of WARP, albeit with considerably less playing time than second-ranked Justin Morneau (who's got an excuse) and first-ranked Adam Dunn (who's got a big contract). So bravo, Ron Gardenhire and Bill Smith, well done.

### Rene Tosoni — RF

Born: 7/2/1986 Age: 25
Bats: L Throws: R Height: 6' 1" Weight: 195
Breakout: 2% Improve: 25% Collapse: 9%
Attrition: 29% MLB: 60%

Comparables:
Larry Whisenton, Doug Deeds, Troy O'Leary

| YEAR | TEAM | LVL | AGE | PA | R | 2B | 3B | HR | RBI | BB | SO | SB | CS | AVG_OBP_SLG | TAv | BABIP | BRR | FRAA | WARP |
|---|---|---|---|---|---|---|---|---|---|---|---|---|---|---|---|---|---|---|---|
| 2009 | NBR | AA | 23 | 490 | 64 | 25 | 4 | 15 | 71 | 45 | 98 | 8 | 8 | .271/.361/.454 | .287 | .319 | -0.3 | 0.9 | 2.4 |
| 2010 | NBR | AA | 24 | 219 | 22 | 8 | 4 | 4 | 24 | 25 | 52 | 3 | 1 | .270/.369/.422 | .284 | .351 | 0.4 | -0.2 | 1.0 |
| 2011 | ROC | AAA | 25 | 299 | 30 | 14 | 0 | 6 | 32 | 20 | 68 | 4 | 0 | .226/.283/.343 | .218 | .279 | 0.6 | -3.3 | -0.8 |
| 2011 | MIN | MLB | 25 | 189 | 20 | 7 | 1 | 5 | 22 | 14 | 42 | 0 | 2 | .203/.275/.343 | .232 | .240 | -1.6 | 0 | -0.6 |
| 2012 | MIN | MLB | 25 | 250 | 26 | 11 | 1 | 6 | 25 | 18 | 59 | 2 | 1 | .231/.296/.366 | .239 | .284 | -0.2 | RF -2, LF -0 | -0.1 |

Foot and shoulder injuries have cost this Toronto native, a 2005 draft-and-follow, considerable time in the minors. He lost most of his 2010 season to a torn labrum. Thanks to the Twins' injuries, Tosoni spent the 2011 season shuttling between Triple-A and the majors—two levels he had never experienced before—making it difficult for him to settle in for very long. As awful as his major league numbers were, they were boosted considerably by a season-ending nine-game hitting streak. Tosoni's pure swing, gap power, and ability to play center field had put him on many prospect lists prior to his shoulder injury. His destiny may only be fourth outfielder, but he's got enough tools to fulfill it.

### Danny Valencia — 3B

Born: 9/19/1984 Age: 27
Bats: R Throws: R Height: 6' 3" Weight: 210
Breakout: 2% Improve: 32% Collapse: 8%
Attrition: 16% MLB: 72%

Comparables:
Ken McMullen, James D'Antona, Ray Knight

| YEAR | TEAM | LVL | AGE | PA | R | 2B | 3B | HR | RBI | BB | SO | SB | CS | AVG_OBP_SLG | TAv | BABIP | BRR | FRAA | WARP |
|---|---|---|---|---|---|---|---|---|---|---|---|---|---|---|---|---|---|---|---|
| 2009 | NBR | AA | 24 | 252 | 44 | 14 | 4 | 7 | 29 | 31 | 40 | 0 | 2 | .284/.376/.482 | .308 | .322 | -0.1 | -1.2 | 2.1 |
| 2009 | ROC | AAA | 24 | 282 | 35 | 24 | 0 | 7 | 41 | 8 | 37 | 0 | 2 | .286/.309/.454 | .270 | .311 | 0 | -1.9 | 0.7 |
| 2010 | ROC | AAA | 25 | 202 | 22 | 15 | 0 | 0 | 24 | 14 | 34 | 2 | 0 | .292/.348/.373 | .249 | .358 | -1.2 | -1.5 | 0.1 |
| 2010 | MIN | MLB | 25 | 322 | 30 | 18 | 1 | 7 | 40 | 20 | 46 | 2 | 0 | .311/.351/.448 | .271 | .345 | -1.6 | 3.5 | 1.4 |
| 2011 | MIN | MLB | 26 | 608 | 63 | 28 | 2 | 15 | 72 | 40 | 102 | 2 | 6 | .246/.294/.383 | .246 | .275 | -1.4 | -6.6 | 0.0 |
| 2012 | MIN | MLB | 27 | 537 | 62 | 28 | 3 | 11 | 60 | 34 | 89 | 3 | 2 | .271/.317/.404 | .259 | .309 | -0.5 | 3B -1 | 2.0 |

Valencia's 2010 debut was a pleasant surprise, but his track record suggested that sustaining that high BABIP would be a stretch—and it was. The 70-point drop exposed his subpar walk rate and turned his bat into a liability, at least against righties; he hit .224/.274/.352 in 449 PA against them, compared to .309/.352/.470 in 159 PA against lefties. The story on defense wasn't any happier, even though our system thought more highly of him than either Defensive Runs Saved (-13) or Total Zone (-18). Ron Gardenhire was vocal in his criticism of Valencia's lack of focus afield, not the first time such a charge has been leveled against him. He may not be the Twins' long-term answer at third, but he's still young and inexpensive enough that a happy medium between his two seasons—his career .269/.314/.406 line—would have some value if he could stop the bleeding on defense.

### Josh Willingham   LF

Born: 2/17/1979 Age: 33
Bats: R Throws: R Height: 6' 2" Weight: 200
Breakout: 0% Improve: 28% Collapse: 2%
Attrition: 18% MLB: 91%

**Comparables:**
Eric Hinske, Carl Yastrzemski, Milton Bradley

| YEAR | TEAM | LVL | AGE | PA | R | 2B | 3B | HR | RBI | BB | SO | SB | CS | AVG_OBP_SLG | TAv | BABIP | BRR | FRAA | WARP |
|------|------|-----|-----|-----|----|----|----|----|-----|----|-----|----|----|-------------|------|-------|------|-----------|------|
| 2009 | WAS | MLB | 30 | 502 | 70 | 29 | 0 | 24 | 61 | 61 | 104 | 4 | 3 | .260/.367/.496 | .297 | .289 | -0.4 | 2.4 | 3.1 |
| 2010 | WAS | MLB | 31 | 450 | 54 | 19 | 2 | 16 | 56 | 67 | 85 | 8 | 0 | .268/.389/.459 | .298 | .304 | 1.4 | -9.1 | 2.0 |
| 2011 | OAK | MLB | 32 | 563 | 69 | 26 | 0 | 29 | 98 | 56 | 150 | 4 | 1 | .246/.332/.477 | .307 | .287 | -0.3 | -3 | 3.5 |
| 2012 | MIN | MLB | 33 | 507 | 65 | 23 | 2 | 19 | 62 | 57 | 113 | 5 | 1 | .251/.351/.443 | .286 | .295 | 0 | LF -6, RF 0 | 2.5 |

Traded to the A's in December 2010 for Corey Brown and Henry Rodriguez, Willingham had a fine year for the green and gold, ranking 14th in the league in True Average (right between Robinson Cano and Dustin Pedroia) and setting career highs in homers and RBI (the latter no small trick among a decrepit offense). Despite drops in batting average and on-base percentage, the notion that Willingham was hurt by the Mausoleum is incorrect. He hit .260/.350/.523 at home, but just .233/.315/.435 away, including—small sample size alert—.172/.269/.241 in 67 PA in AL Central ballparks. Signed by the Twins to a three-year, $21 million deal, he'll get plenty of chances to improve that line. He rates as a bargain relative to Jason Kubel and the departed Michael Cuddyer. He's been worth 9.0 WARP over the past three years, almost as much as the two of them put together, and he'll earn less than either through the life of the deal.

# PITCHERS

### Scott Baker

Born: 9/19/1981 Age: 30
Bats: R Throws: R Height: 6' 5" Weight: 215
Breakout: 12% Improve: 50% Collapse: 22%
Attrition: 12% MLB: 93%

**Comparables:**
Turk Farrell, Dan Haren, Dennis Leonard

| YEAR | TEAM | LVL | AGE | W | L | SV | G | GS | IP | H | HR | BB | SO | EqBB9 | EqSO9 | GB% | BABIP | WHIP | ERA | FIP | FRA | WARP |
|------|------|-----|-----|----|----|----|----|----|------|-----|----|----|-----|-------|-------|------|-------|------|------|------|------|------|
| 2009 | MIN | MLB | 27 | 15 | 9 | 0 | 33 | 33 | 200 | 190 | 28 | 48 | 162 | 2.2 | 7.3 | 35% | .277 | 1.19 | 4.36 | 4.12 | 4.35 | 3.2 |
| 2010 | MIN | MLB | 28 | 12 | 9 | 0 | 29 | 29 | 170¹ | 186 | 23 | 43 | 148 | 2.3 | 7.8 | 37% | .323 | 1.34 | 4.49 | 3.93 | 4.18 | 2.0 |
| 2011 | MIN | MLB | 29 | 8 | 6 | 0 | 23 | 21 | 134² | 126 | 15 | 32 | 123 | 2.1 | 8.2 | 35% | .298 | 1.17 | 3.14 | 3.48 | 3.78 | 2.1 |
| 2012 | MIN | MLB | 30 | 7 | 7 | 0 | 20 | 20 | 120² | 123 | 14 | 26 | 99 | 1.9 | 7.4 | 36% | .306 | 1.23 | 3.64 | 3.72 | 3.95 | 1.6 |

Despite being one of the team's few starters who can miss bats reliably, Baker was forced to battle Kevin Slowey for the 2011 rotation's final spot. That he wound up the team's most valuable pitcher is both some amount of vindication and an indicator that things didn't go as planned for the Twins. Relative to 2010, Baker nudged his strikeout and walk rates in the right direction while getting better luck on both balls in play and home runs per fly ball; he also sequenced better, dropping from a .262/.313/.421 showing with men in scoring position to .196/.240/.304. Unfortunately, he served time on the DL for the fourth straight season; a flexor strain sent him out in early July, then recurred after he returned too soon. He threw just 24 innings in the second half. On the heels of post-2010 arthroscopic surgery, this is not a good sign. It's fair to wonder if a move to the bullpen is the only way to keep him healthy.

### Nick Blackburn

Born: 2/24/1982 Age: 30
Bats: R Throws: R Height: 6' 5" Weight: 250
Breakout: 13% Improve: 41% Collapse: 19%
Attrition: 14% MLB: 93%

**Comparables:**
Moose Haas, Bill Wegman, Jon Garland

| YEAR | TEAM | LVL | AGE | W | L | SV | G | GS | IP | H | HR | BB | SO | EqBB9 | EqSO9 | GB% | BABIP | WHIP | ERA | FIP | FRA | WARP |
|------|------|-----|-----|----|----|----|----|----|------|-----|----|----|-----|-------|-------|------|-------|------|------|------|------|------|
| 2009 | MIN | MLB | 27 | 11 | 11 | 0 | 33 | 33 | 205² | 240 | 25 | 41 | 98 | 1.8 | 4.3 | 47% | .303 | 1.37 | 4.03 | 4.41 | 5.05 | 1.2 |
| 2010 | MIN | MLB | 28 | 10 | 12 | 0 | 28 | 26 | 161 | 194 | 25 | 40 | 68 | 2.2 | 3.8 | 52% | .306 | 1.45 | 5.42 | 5.04 | 5.33 | 0.3 |
| 2011 | MIN | MLB | 29 | 7 | 10 | 0 | 26 | 26 | 148¹ | 183 | 19 | 54 | 76 | 3.3 | 4.6 | 55% | .322 | 1.60 | 4.49 | 4.87 | 5.07 | 0.4 |
| 2012 | MIN | MLB | 30 | 7 | 9 | 0 | 23 | 23 | 137¹ | 165 | 16 | 30 | 64 | 2.0 | 4.2 | 49% | .314 | 1.42 | 4.70 | 4.44 | 5.11 | 0.1 |

Strikeouts are fine for coastal city slickers, but they're too flashy for Midwestern types who believe pitching to contact is a wholesome, honest way to make a living. That's the message the organization sent (yet again) when assembling their 2011 rotation, not only by re-signing Carl Pavano and hassling Francisco Liriano, but by anointing Blackburn a starter during the first week of March despite his awful 2010 numbers. Blackburn's brand of blandness was typically blah; he took the ball every fifth day until late August, and managed to provide sub-league average performances in all three defense-independent categories. Despite a high groundball rate, he can't keep the ball in the park. Surgery to alleviate a trapped radial nerve ended his season early. Unless doctors implanted an out pitch, expect more of the same.

### Alex Burnett
Born: 7/26/1987 Age: 24
Bats: R Throws: R Height: 6' 1" Weight: 210
Breakout: 21% Improve: 40% Collapse: 33%
Attrition: 27% MLB: 92%
Comparables:
Jake Westbrook, Troy Patton, Kip Young

| YEAR | TEAM | LVL | AGE | W | L | SV | G | GS | IP | H | HR | BB | SO | EqBB9 | EqSO9 | GB% | BABIP | WHIP | ERA | FIP | FRA | WARP |
|---|---|---|---|---|---|---|---|---|---|---|---|---|---|---|---|---|---|---|---|---|---|---|
| 2009 | FTM | A+ | 21 | 2 | 1 | 4 | 18 | 0 | 22² | 14 | 0 | 7 | 26 | 2.8 | 10.3 | 47% | .255 | 0.93 | 1.98 | 1.97 | 2.56 | 0.6 |
| 2009 | NBR | AA | 21 | 1 | 2 | 9 | 40 | 0 | 55¹ | 37 | 2 | 19 | 60 | 3.1 | 8.5 | 42% | .241 | 0.99 | 1.79 | 2.69 | 3.36 | 1.1 |
| 2010 | MIN | MLB | 22 | 2 | 2 | 0 | 41 | 0 | 47² | 52 | 6 | 23 | 37 | 4.3 | 7.0 | 48% | .331 | 1.57 | 5.29 | 4.70 | 5.02 | 0.1 |
| 2011 | MIN | MLB | 23 | 2 | 5 | 0 | 66 | 0 | 50² | 50 | 4 | 21 | 33 | 3.7 | 5.9 | 47% | .293 | 1.40 | 5.51 | 4.50 | 5.94 | -0.5 |
| 2012 | MIN | MLB | 24 | 2 | 1 | 0 | 47 | 0 | 45² | 52 | 5 | 18 | 26 | 3.5 | 5.2 | 44% | .307 | 1.53 | 5.00 | 4.67 | 5.43 | -0.2 |

While this hard-throwing 2005 12th round pick spent most of the year in the Twins bullpen, and ranked second on the team in appearances—32 of which were less than an inning—the results weren't pretty. Relying on a 92

Breakout: 25% Improve: 54% Collapse: 20%
Attrition: 4% MLB: 91%
Comparables:
Roy Halladay, Don Sutton, Burt Hooton

| | | | | | | | | | | | | | | | | | | | | | | |
|---|---|---|---|---|---|---|---|---|---|---|---|---|---|---|---|---|---|---|---|---|---|---|
| 2010 | WAS | MLB | 26 | 3 | 3 | 26 | 47 | 0 | 46 | 51 | 5 | 9 | 38 | 1.8 | 7.4 | 49% | .322 | 1.30 | 2.74 | 3.45 | 4.54 | 0.2 |
| 2011 | MIN | MLB | 27 | 4 | 7 | 15 | 69 | 0 | 65² | 66 | 10 | 13 | 34 | 1.8 | 4.7 | 43% | .265 | 1.20 | 4.25 | 4.78 | 5.53 | -0.3 |
| 2012 | MIN | MLB | 28 | 3 | 1 | 22 | 60 | 0 | 58¹ | 60 | 6 | 11 | 42 | 1.8 | 6.5 | 40% | .301 | 1.23 | 3.58 | 3.67 | 3.90 | 0.7 |

Re-signed by the Twins as a pricey insurance policy ($7.15 million) in case Joe Nathan faltered in his comeback from Tommy John surgery, Capps was pressed back into closer duty by mid-April. He was brutal, blowing 7-of-22 save opportunities through July 15 before Nathan mercifully reclaimed the job. Capps was typically stingy with the walks, but his strikeout rate crashed through the floor, and he struggled to keep the ball in the park. Among full or part-time closers, only Jon Rauch and Huston Street had higher homer rates. After the season, Capps revealed that he pitched through forearm pain. The Twins chose to pledge allegiance to the Proven Closer myth and to reward his grit—forgoing a compensatory draft pick in the process—by re-signing him. Even at the comparatively low price of $4.5 million with a $6 million option and $250,000 buyout for 2013, the move makes little sense for a team in cost-cutting mode. Meanwhile, Wilson Ramos is flourishing in Washington . . .

### Scott Diamond
Born: 7/30/1986 Age: 25
Bats: L Throws: L Height: 6' 4" Weight: 215
Breakout: 25% Improve: 57% Collapse: 13%
Attrition: 9% MLB: 89%
Comparables:
Paul Splittorff, Julian Tavarez, Dave Hamilton

| YEAR | TEAM | LVL | AGE | W | L | SV | G | GS | IP | H | HR | BB | SO | EqBB9 | EqSO9 | GB% | BABIP | WHIP | ERA | FIP | FRA | WARP |
|---|---|---|---|---|---|---|---|---|---|---|---|---|---|---|---|---|---|---|---|---|---|---|
| 2009 | MIS | AA | 22 | 5 | 10 | 0 | 23 | 23 | 131 | 152 | 5 | 53 | 111 | 3.6 | 7.6 | 54% | .362 | 1.56 | 3.50 | 3.16 | 3.86 | 1.8 |
| 2010 | MIS | AA | 23 | 4 | 6 | 0 | 17 | 17 | 102¹ | 83 | 1 | 33 | 55 | 3.4 | 7.9 | 57% | .396 | 1.49 | 3.52 | 3.63 | 4.37 | 0.8 |
| 2010 | GWN | AAA | 23 | 4 | 1 | 0 | 10 | 10 | 56¹ | 45 | 2 | 13 | 23 | 2.4 | 5.3 | 50% | .328 | 1.21 | 3.36 | 3.92 | 4.56 | 0.7 |
| 2011 | ROC | AAA | 24 | 4 | 8 | 0 | 23 | 23 | 123 | 158 | 11 | 36 | 90 | 2.6 | 6.6 | 53% | .356 | 1.58 | 5.56 | 3.84 | 5.01 | 1.6 |
| 2011 | MIN | MLB | 24 | 1 | 5 | 0 | 7 | 7 | 39 | 51 | 3 | 17 | 19 | 3.9 | 4.4 | 48% | .343 | 1.74 | 5.08 | 4.39 | 5.32 | -0.1 |
| 2012 | MIN | MLB | 25 | 3 | 5 | 0 | 12 | 12 | 70 | 88 | 7 | 27 | 40 | 3.5 | 5.1 | 51% | .333 | 1.64 | 5.42 | 4.52 | 5.89 | -0.5 |

The Twins thought they'd found themselves a, um, Diamond in the rough when they plucked this Canadian southpaw from the Braves in the 2010 Rule 5 draft. They shipped off 2009 second round pick Billy Bullock so they could stash their new treasure in the minors. Though he restored his strikeout rate, Diamond was doomed by a high BABIP in Triple-A. He nonetheless got a big league look, taking over Nick Blackburn's spot in the rotation in late August with shaky results. A pitch-to-contact groundballer, Diamond relies upon command of an 89 to 91-mph fastball, curveball, and changeup, none of which are knockout pitches. When his command is off, it's Goodnight Irene. Scouts feel he could wind up a LOOGY if nothing else, but that's not exactly aiming high.

## Terry Doyle

Born: 11/2/1985 Age: 26
Bats: R Throws: R Height: 6' 5" Weight: 225
Breakout: 28% Improve: 50% Collapse: 19%
Attrition: 16% MLB: 93%

Comparables:
John Burkett, Jimmy Key, Frank Lary

| YEAR | TEAM | LVL | AGE | W | L | SV | G | GS | IP | H | HR | BB | SO | EqBB9 | EqSO9 | GB% | BABIP | WHIP | ERA | FIP | FRA | WARP |
|---|---|---|---|---|---|---|---|---|---|---|---|---|---|---|---|---|---|---|---|---|---|---|
| 2009 | GRF | RK | 23 | 5 | 1 | 0 | 12 | 10 | 57¹ | 55 | 1 | 16 | 86 | 2.4 | 11.8 | 55% | .378 | 1.15 | 2.98 | 2.30 | 3.64 | 2.8 |
| 2010 | KAN | A | 24 | 4 | 2 | 0 | 7 | 7 | 47 | 31 | 2 | 12 | 58 | 2.3 | 11.1 | 59% | .276 | 0.91 | 0.96 | 2.51 | 3.56 | 1.0 |
| 2010 | WNS | A+ | 24 | 8 | 9 | 0 | 20 | 20 | 121¹ | 105 | 11 | 35 | 79 | 2.5 | 7.3 | 49% | .299 | 1.23 | 3.71 | 4.45 | 4.74 | 1.1 |
| 2011 | WNS | A+ | 25 | 1 | 5 | 0 | 11 | 11 | 73 | 66 | 3 | 10 | 41 | 1.4 | 6.0 | 56% | .284 | 1.12 | 2.84 | 3.12 | 4.36 | 1.0 |
| 2011 | BIR | AA | 25 | 6 | 3 | 0 | 15 | 15 | 100 | 98 | 8 | 24 | 79 | 2.0 | 6.6 | 47% | .283 | 1.13 | 3.24 | 3.63 | 4.20 | 1.0 |
| 2012 | MIN | MLB | 26 | 3 | 4 | 0 | 8 | 8 | 53² | 61 | 7 | 20 | 31 | 3.4 | 5.2 | 48% | .307 | 1.52 | 5.08 | 4.86 | 5.52 | -0.3 |

The pitching equivalent of Mike Tyson's voice, Doyle has a power pitcher's frame but a control artist's repertoire, with a fastball that touches 90, a serviceable cutter, a curve, and a change. Last year he capped a solid season in the White Sox system with an outstanding Arizona Fall League stint, drawing more of a spotlight than most 25-year-old hurlers who have yet to reach Triple-A ever see, and earning a move to the Twins in the Rule 5 draft. Doyle works fast, throws strikes, and has an undeniable talent for inducing young hitters to swing at his pitch, but he'll need to show he can pick on batters his own size to keep his spot as Minnesota's new long man.

## Brian Duensing

Born: 2/22/1983 Age: 29
Bats: L Throws: L Height: 6' 0" Weight: 195
Breakout: 14% Improve: 59% Collapse: 24%
Attrition: 15% MLB: 85%

Comparables:
Billy Traber, Dave Roberts, Doug Rau

| YEAR | TEAM | LVL | AGE | W | L | SV | G | GS | IP | H | HR | BB | SO | EqBB9 | EqSO9 | GB% | BABIP | WHIP | ERA | FIP | FRA | WARP |
|---|---|---|---|---|---|---|---|---|---|---|---|---|---|---|---|---|---|---|---|---|---|---|
| 2009 | ROC | AAA | 26 | 4 | 6 | 0 | 13 | 13 | 75¹ | 87 | 2 | 19 | 44 | 2.3 | 5.3 | 47% | .337 | 1.41 | 4.66 | 3.16 | 4.49 | 0.8 |
| 2009 | MIN | MLB | 26 | 5 | 2 | 0 | 24 | 9 | 84 | 84 | 7 | 31 | 53 | 3.3 | 5.7 | 47% | .294 | 1.37 | 3.64 | 4.18 | 4.37 | 1.2 |
| 2010 | MIN | MLB | 27 | 10 | 3 | 0 | 53 | 13 | 130² | 122 | 11 | 35 | 78 | 2.4 | 5.4 | 54% | .275 | 1.20 | 2.62 | 3.82 | 4.64 | 1.1 |
| 2011 | MIN | MLB | 28 | 9 | 14 | 0 | 32 | 28 | 161² | 193 | 21 | 52 | 115 | 2.9 | 6.4 | 46% | .334 | 1.52 | 5.23 | 4.31 | 4.66 | 0.9 |
| 2012 | MIN | MLB | 29 | 7 | 8 | 0 | 40 | 19 | 136¹ | 155 | 14 | 39 | 80 | 2.6 | 5.3 | 48% | .313 | 1.42 | 4.43 | 4.22 | 4.81 | 0.5 |

After shuttling between bullpen and rotation during his first two seasons, Duensing was anointed as a starter early in the spring of 2011. To that point, he had put up a sterling 2.93 ERA in 22 starts, with a .288 BABIP masking a not-so-sterling 3.96 FIP—a performance comparable to what he'd done in the bullpen. Alas, Duensing's 2011 was a nightmare, as his performance against righties collapsed from .277/.336/.411 in 2009–10 to .330/.387/.560, with both his BABIP and home run rate against them ballooning (from .294 to .357 on the former, and from 2.6 to 3.8 percent on the latter). Blame some on the Twins' substandard infield defense and bad luck on fly balls, but some is lack of stuff to take down righties. The Twins plan to move Duensing back to the bullpen, but with so many starters on thin ice, he could get another shot.

## Phil Dumatrait

Born: 7/12/1981 Age: 30
Bats: R Throws: L Height: 6' 3" Weight: 200
Breakout: 31% Improve: 53% Collapse: 22%
Attrition: 27% MLB: 78%

Comparables:
Jose Jimenez, John Frascatore, Richard Dotson

| YEAR | TEAM | LVL | AGE | W | L | SV | G | GS | IP | H | HR | BB | SO | EqBB9 | EqSO9 | GB% | BABIP | WHIP | ERA | FIP | FRA | WARP |
|---|---|---|---|---|---|---|---|---|---|---|---|---|---|---|---|---|---|---|---|---|---|---|
| 2009 | PIT | MLB | 27 | 0 | 2 | 0 | 15 | 0 | 13 | 13 | 4 | 11 | 7 | 7.6 | 4.8 | 46% | .214 | 1.85 | 6.92 | 8.52 | 10.75 | -0.7 |
| 2011 | MIN | MLB | 29 | 1 | 3 | 1 | 45 | 0 | 41¹ | 45 | 7 | 25 | 29 | 5.4 | 6.3 | 42% | .290 | 1.69 | 3.92 | 5.75 | 6.10 | -0.5 |
| 2012 | MIN | MLB | 30 | 2 | 2 | 0 | 25 | 3 | 37 | 44 | 5 | 18 | 17 | 4.5 | 4.3 | 44% | .306 | 1.69 | 5.81 | 5.50 | 6.31 | -0.5 |

Pummeled for a 7.06 ERA in 133 big-league innings in 2007–09, Dumatrait's time appeared to have come and gone, but he resurfaced with the Twins and survived in a relief role. A closer look shows that his underlying peripherals were no better than before, but his timing was; batters hit .231/.333/.308 via a .256 BABIP with runners in scoring position, compared to .325/.416/.597 with a .328 BABIP with the bases empty. When those splits even out, he'll be just another tomato can lefty.

## Kyle Gibson

Born: 10/23/1987 Age: 24
Bats: R Throws: R Height: 6' 7" Weight: 210
Breakout: 33% Improve: 65% Collapse: 19%
Attrition: 13% MLB: 91%

Comparables:
Juan Oviedo, Manuel Corpas, Brett Cecil

| YEAR | TEAM | LVL | AGE | W | L | SV | G | GS | IP | H | HR | BB | SO | EqBB9 | EqSO9 | GB% | BABIP | WHIP | ERA | FIP | FRA | WARP |
|---|---|---|---|---|---|---|---|---|---|---|---|---|---|---|---|---|---|---|---|---|---|---|
| 2010 | FTM | A+ | 22 | 4 | 0 | 0 | 7 | 7 | 43¹ | 23 | 0 | 9 | 30 | 2.5 | 8.3 | 72% | .245 | 1.04 | 1.87 | 2.91 | 4.00 | 0.6 |
| 2010 | NBR | AA | 22 | 7 | 5 | 0 | 16 | 16 | 93 | 57 | 3 | 13 | 48 | 2.1 | 7.5 | 54% | .300 | 1.22 | 3.68 | 3.43 | 4.06 | 1.1 |
| 2011 | ROC | AAA | 23 | 2 | 6 | 0 | 18 | 18 | 95¹ | 109 | 11 | 27 | 91 | 2.5 | 8.6 | 56% | .341 | 1.43 | 4.81 | 3.71 | 4.63 | 1.6 |
| 2012 | MIN | MLB | 24 | 2 | 2 | 0 | 6 | 6 | 35 | 38 | 4 | 11 | 24 | 2.8 | 6.2 | 53% | .312 | 1.41 | 4.46 | 4.26 | 4.84 | 0.1 |

This 2009 first-round pick out of the University of Missouri shot through the system and figured to make his major league debut in 2011. Alas, after a hot start (3.60 ERA, 59/11 K/BB ratio in 55 innings through May), he was knocked around in June, then diagnosed in July with both a strained flexor mass and a partially torn UCL. After a brief rehab attempt, he underwent Tommy John surgery on September 7, likely knocking him out for all of 2012. When healthy, Gibson is a command-and-control type who pounds the strike zone with an 88 to 92-mph fastball with outstanding sink, a swing-and-miss slider, a four-seamer, and a changeup. He's a third or fourth starter in the making, but the making is on hold.

**Jeff Gray**
Born: 11/19/1981 Age: 30
Bats: R Throws: R Height: 6' 3" Weight: 210
Breakout: 14% Improve: 46% Collapse: 22%
Attrition: 17% MLB: 93%
Comparables:
Dock Ellis, Jim Corsi, Gene Conley

| YEAR | TEAM | LVL | AGE | W | L | SV | G | GS | IP | H | HR | BB | SO | EqBB9 | EqSO9 | GB% | BABIP | WHIP | ERA | FIP | FRA | WARP |
|---|---|---|---|---|---|---|---|---|---|---|---|---|---|---|---|---|---|---|---|---|---|---|
| 2009 | SAC | AAA | 27 | 2 | 2 | 16 | 37 | 0 | 41 | 30 | 2 | 6 | 22 | 1.3 | 4.8 | 56% | .222 | 0.88 | 1.54 | 3.60 | 4.20 | 0.3 |
| 2009 | OAK | MLB | 27 | 0 | 1 | 0 | 24 | 0 | 26¹ | 30 | 3 | 4 | 19 | 1.4 | 6.5 | 58% | .314 | 1.29 | 3.76 | 3.87 | 4.28 | 0.3 |
| 2010 | IOW | AAA | 28 | 3 | 1 | 1 | 25 | 0 | 35 | 30 | 1 | 9 | 16 | 3.9 | 6.4 | 53% | .372 | 1.71 | 5.66 | 4.46 | 5.97 | -0.1 |
| 2010 | CHN | MLB | 28 | 1 | 0 | 0 | 7 | 0 | 9¹ | 12 | 1 | 5 | 4 | 4.8 | 3.9 | 66% | .333 | 1.82 | 6.75 | 5.57 | 6.44 | -0.1 |
| 2011 | CHA | MLB | 29 | 0 | 0 | 0 | 6 | 0 | 13¹ | 13 | 1 | 4 | 7 | 2.7 | 4.7 | 42% | .273 | 1.27 | 2.70 | 4.11 | 4.89 | 0.0 |
| 2011 | SEA | MLB | 29 | 0 | 1 | 1 | 24 | 0 | 35 | 39 | 3 | 17 | 16 | 4.4 | 4.1 | 54% | .298 | 1.60 | 4.89 | 4.72 | 6.52 | -0.7 |
| 2012 | MIN | MLB | 30 | 1 | 0 | 1 | 24 | 0 | 36² | 40 | 4 | 12 | 22 | 2.9 | 5.4 | 52% | .308 | 1.43 | 4.54 | 4.40 | 4.93 | 0.0 |

The Mariners claimed Gray off waivers on May 13, but for two months they treated him more like a civilian on a ride-along than a member of the force. In the entire month of June, he made one appearance, for an inning, down by seven. Gray has a 93 mph fastball that he doesn't locate well, and a slider that hitters have no problems with. At this point, he can either not get work while on a major league roster—with the waiver pickup by the Twins, he's onto his fifth organization in four seasons—or

The last hope for the Twins to salvage something of value from the Johan Santana trade, Guerra was once viewed as a potential number-two starter, and while he was knocked around particularly hard as he climbed up the system, a mid-2011 move to the bullpen appears to have taken. Strafed for a 9.00 ERA and 1.9 homers per nine in 43 innings as a starter, Guerra cut that to a 2.76 ERA and 0.3 homers per nine in 52 innings out of the bullpen. The move restored a bit of velocity to his low-90s fastball, which paired with a very good changeup to raise his strikeout rate as well. Still the youngest pitcher on the Twins' 40-man roster at this writing, he may well see time in the majors in 2012 if he can continue that effectiveness, and while he doesn't look like a late-game reliever, he's not a total write-off.

**Carlos Gutierrez**
Born: 9/22/1986 Age: 25
Bats: R Throws: R Height: 6' 4" Weight: 225
Breakout: 28% Improve: 58% Collapse: 26%
Attrition: 14% MLB: 93%
Comparables:
Luis Leal, Braden Looper, Carl Pavano

| YEAR | TEAM | LVL | AGE | W | L | SV | G | GS | IP | H | HR | BB | SO | EqBB9 | EqSO9 | GB% | BABIP | WHIP | ERA | FIP | FRA | WARP |
|---|---|---|---|---|---|---|---|---|---|---|---|---|---|---|---|---|---|---|---|---|---|---|
| 2011 | ROC | AAA | 24 | 1 | 0 | 0 | 43 | 0 | 62¹ | 60 | 2 | 31 | 57 | 4.5 | 8.2 | 63% | .312 | 1.46 | 4.62 | 3.46 | 5.58 | 0.3 |
| 2012 | MIN | MLB | 25 | 1 | 1 | 0 | 10 | 2 | 24² | 29 | 3 | 12 | 13 | 4.3 | 4.9 | 57% | .316 | 1.65 | 5.41 | 5.19 | 5.88 | -0.2 |

This 2008 first round pick out of the University of Miami underwent Tommy John surgery in 2007, and has had the kid-glove treatment since, never throwing more than 126 innings or making more than 16 starts in a season. His 92-mph sinker has been described as "a bowling ball" given batters' difficulty elevating the pitch, and his groundball rates have always been insanely high. Unfortunately, Gutierrez gets so much movement on the sinker that he sometimes tinkers with his release point and loses the strike zone. His other pitches (changeup and slider) are just average. His shift to the bullpen went reasonably well save for a higher walk rate; his strikeout rate jumped and his K/BB ratio was his best since his 2008 debut. Gardenhire sang his praises in spring training last year so it's not unreasonable to expect him to play a part in 2012.

**Liam Hendriks**
Born: 2/10/1989 Age: 23
Bats: R Throws: R Height: 6' 2" Weight: 190
Breakout: 30% Improve: 63% Collapse: 17%
Attrition: 8% MLB: 88%
Comparables:
Edward Mujica, Zack Greinke, Nino Espinosa

| YEAR | TEAM | LVL | AGE | W | L | SV | G | GS | IP | H | HR | BB | SO | EqBB9 | EqSO9 | GB% | BABIP | WHIP | ERA | FIP | FRA | WARP |
|---|---|---|---|---|---|---|---|---|---|---|---|---|---|---|---|---|---|---|---|---|---|---|
| 2009 | BLT | A | 20 | 3 | 5 | 0 | 11 | 11 | 66² | 73 | 3 | 15 | 62 | 2.0 | 8.4 | 60% | .352 | 1.32 | 3.51 | 3.11 | 4.10 | 0.8 |
| 2010 | BLT | A | 21 | 2 | 1 | 0 | 6 | 6 | 34 | 16 | 0 | 4 | 34 | 1.1 | 10.3 | 52% | .211 | 0.59 | 1.32 | 2.24 | 2.13 | 1.2 |
| 2010 | FTM | A+ | 21 | 5 | 3 | 0 | 13 | 12 | 74² | 49 | 2 | 7 | 57 | 1.0 | 8.0 | 53% | .273 | 0.95 | 1.93 | 2.67 | 3.40 | 1.4 |
| 2011 | NBR | AA | 22 | 7 | 1 | 0 | 16 | 15 | 90 | 85 | 5 | 18 | 81 | 1.8 | 8.1 | 44% | .310 | 1.14 | 2.70 | 3.04 | 3.86 | 1.7 |
| 2011 | ROC | AAA | 22 | 4 | 2 | 0 | 9 | 9 | 49¹ | 52 | 0 | 3 | 30 | 0.5 | 5.5 | 49% | .321 | 1.11 | 4.56 | 2.33 | 4.07 | 1.0 |
| 2011 | MIN | MLB | 22 | 0 | 2 | 0 | 4 | 4 | 23¹ | 29 | 3 | 6 | 16 | 2.3 | 6.2 | 47% | .347 | 1.50 | 6.17 | 4.13 | 4.85 | 0.1 |
| 2012 | MIN | MLB | 23 | 3 | 4 | 0 | 10 | 10 | 57 | 65 | 6 | 16 | 36 | 2.6 | 5.6 | 48% | .320 | 1.43 | 4.56 | 4.15 | 4.95 | 0.1 |

Renowned for his outstanding command, this Perth, Australia, native has put up impressive strikeout-to-walk ratios at virtually every stop since signing with the Twins in 2007, but he's a pitcher whose stats are ahead of his scouting reports. He's got an array of pitches—a fastball he throws anywhere from 88 to 93 miles per hour, curve, slider, changeup—but none of his pitches are to be feared. The combination plays up thanks to his ability to mix pitches and locate. In other words, he's a prototypical Twins pitching prospect. After climbing through Double-A and Triple-A—with a stop at the Futures Game—he got a look with the Twins at the end of the season, but was knocked around. A bit of misfortune on the balls in play and fly-ball fronts fluffed up his ERA.

### Francisco Liriano

Born: **10/26/1983** Age: **28**
Bats: **L** Throws: **L** Height: **6' 3"** Weight: **185**
Breakout: **21%** Improve: **52%** Collapse: **23%**
Attrition: **7%** MLB: **91%**

**Comparables:**
Steve Hamilton, Mitch Stetter, Rob Murphy

| YEAR | TEAM | LVL | AGE | W | L | SV | G | GS | IP | H | HR | BB | SO | EqBB9 | EqSO9 | GB% | BABIP | WHIP | ERA | FIP | FRA | WARP |
|------|------|-----|-----|---|---|----|----|----|------|-----|----|----|-----|-------|-------|-----|-------|------|------|------|------|------|
| 2009 | MIN | MLB | 25 | 5 | 13 | 0 | 29 | 24 | 136² | 147 | 21 | 65 | 122 | 4.3 | 8.0 | 43% | .323 | 1.55 | 5.80 | 4.91 | 5.41 | 0.6 |
| 2010 | MIN | MLB | 26 | 14 | 10 | 0 | 31 | 31 | 191² | 184 | 9 | 58 | 201 | 2.7 | 9.4 | 56% | .335 | 1.26 | 3.62 | 2.62 | 3.82 | 3.3 |
| 2011 | MIN | MLB | 27 | 9 | 10 | 0 | 26 | 24 | 134¹ | 125 | 14 | 75 | 112 | 5.0 | 7.5 | 49% | .290 | 1.49 | 5.09 | 4.58 | 5.03 | 0.4 |
| 2012 | MIN | MLB | 28 | 7 | 7 | 0 | 21 | 21 | 126¹ | 126 | 11 | 48 | 116 | 3.4 | 8.2 | 46% | .318 | 1.38 | 3.97 | 3.64 | 4.32 | 1.2 |

The Twins' ongoing battles with Liriano led them to float the possibility of trading him coming off his strong 2010. Now we see why, as the enigmatic lefty was maddeningly streaky in 2011. Torched for a 9.13 ERA in five April starts, he rebounded (sort of) with a six-walk no-hitter on May 3, kicking off a passable 19-start run (3.90 ERA, 11 quality starts) blemished by a 4.6 BB/9 and a 15-day stint on the DL due to shoulder inflammation. Alas, he left his August 25 start after two innings with continued shoulder woes, and threw just 2 1/3 additional innings, including a one-out, five-run sayonara on September 24. Unraveling the causality of his injury and ineffectiveness is well-nigh impossible given that the lines of communication between player and team have been muddled since before his need for Tommy John surgery in 2006. The chance to deal Liriano at peak value is gone, and the only question remaining is whether he'll get his change of scenery before or after his next date with the surgeon.

### Jeff Manship

Born: **1/16/1985** Age: **27**
Bats: **R** Throws: **R** Height: **6' 3"** Weight: **200**
Breakout: **35%** Improve: **60%** Collapse: **10%**
Attrition: **10%** MLB: **85%**

**Comparables:**
Ross Wolf, Jeff Gray, Sergio Mitre

| YEAR | TEAM | LVL | AGE | W | L | SV | G | GS | IP | H | HR | BB | SO | EqBB9 | EqSO9 | GB% | BABIP | WHIP | ERA | FIP | FRA | WARP |
|------|------|-----|-----|---|---|----|----|----|------|----|----|----|----|-------|-------|-----|-------|------|------|------|------|------|
| 2009 | NBR | AA | 24 | 6 | 4 | 0 | 13 | 13 | 75² | 72 | 2 | 20 | 45 | 2.4 | 5.4 | 54% | .287 | 1.22 | 4.28 | 3.16 | 4.48 | 0.5 |
| 2009 | ROC | AAA | 24 | 4 | 2 | 0 | 8 | 8 | 50¹ | 53 | 1 | 17 | 30 | 3.0 | 5.4 | 49% | .323 | 1.39 | 3.22 | 3.29 | 4.15 | 0.7 |
| 2009 | MIN | MLB | 24 | 1 | 1 | 0 | 11 | 5 | 31² | 39 | 4 | 15 | 21 | 4.3 | 6.0 | 45% | .337 | 1.71 | 5.68 | 4.98 | 5.05 | 0.3 |
| 2010 | ROC | AAA | 25 | 3 | 8 | 0 | 19 | 18 | 98¹ | 87 | 9 | 17 | 57 | 2.0 | 7.6 | 49% | .359 | 1.59 | 5.13 | 4.11 | 5.13 | 0.7 |
| 2010 | MIN | MLB | 25 | 2 | 1 | 0 | 13 | 1 | 29 | 34 | 3 | 6 | 21 | 1.9 | 6.5 | 47% | .333 | 1.38 | 5.28 | 3.56 | 4.28 | 0.3 |
| 2011 | ROC | AAA | 26 | 1 | 2 | 0 | 11 | 3 | 25 | 24 | 4 | 4 | 21 | 1.4 | 7.6 | 53% | .274 | 1.12 | 4.32 | 4.12 | 4.54 | 0.4 |
| 2011 | MIN | MLB | 26 | 0 | 0 | 0 | 5 | 0 | 3¹ | 5 | 0 | 4 | 2 | 10.8 | 5.4 | 23% | .385 | 2.70 | 8.10 | 5.46 | 5.96 | 0.0 |
| 2012 | MIN | MLB | 27 | 1 | 1 | 0 | 5 | 2 | 14² | 17 | 2 | 5 | 9 | 3.2 | 5.2 | 50% | .316 | 1.52 | 4.94 | 4.77 | 5.37 | -0.0 |

After dabbling with the Twins in each of the previous two seasons, Manship broke camp with the big club only to be manshipped out two weeks later in favor of Jim Hoey. A rotator cuff strain cost him six weeks, an oblique strain KO'd him in late July, and his year ended with surgery to remove a bone spur in his elbow: good morning, good afternoon, good night. Manship doesn't have dazzling stuff. He is a four-pitch pitcher whose fastball averages around 90 miles per hour, but while his minor league strikeout-to-walk ratios testify to good command, it hasn't always translated in the majors. Unless he discovers a swing-and-miss pitch, he's likely to remain a fringe proposition.

### Jason Marquis

Born: **8/21/1978** Age: **33**
Bats: **L** Throws: **R** Height: **6' 2"** Weight: **185**
Breakout: **18%** Improve: **45%** Collapse: **25%**
Attrition: **14%** MLB: **86%**

**Comparables:**
Kenny Rogers, Paul Lindblad, Brad Thomas

| YEAR | TEAM | LVL | AGE | W | L | SV | G | GS | IP | H | HR | BB | SO | EqBB9 | EqSO9 | GB% | BABIP | WHIP | ERA | FIP | FRA | WARP |
|------|------|-----|-----|----|----|----|----|----|------|-----|----|----|-----|-------|-------|-----|-------|------|------|------|------|------|
| 2009 | COL | MLB | 30 | 15 | 13 | 0 | 33 | 33 | 216 | 218 | 15 | 80 | 115 | 3.3 | 4.8 | 56% | .291 | 1.38 | 4.04 | 4.06 | 5.53 | 1.0 |
| 2010 | WAS | MLB | 31 | 2 | 9 | 0 | 13 | 13 | 58² | 76 | 9 | 24 | 31 | 3.7 | 4.8 | 55% | .333 | 1.70 | 6.60 | 5.68 | 5.87 | -0.3 |
| 2011 | ARI | MLB | 32 | 0 | 1 | 0 | 3 | 3 | 11¹ | 22 | 3 | 4 | 5 | 3.2 | 4.0 | 62% | .388 | 2.29 | 9.53 | 6.88 | 6.44 | -0.3 |
| 2011 | WAS | MLB | 32 | 8 | 5 | 0 | 20 | 20 | 120² | 132 | 8 | 39 | 71 | 2.9 | 5.3 | 55% | .316 | 1.42 | 3.95 | 3.75 | 4.44 | 0.3 |
| 2012 | MIN | MLB | 33 | 5 | 7 | 0 | 19 | 19 | 98 | 112 | 10 | 36 | 48 | 3.3 | 4.4 | 52% | .306 | 1.51 | 4.94 | 4.65 | 5.37 | -0.1 |

Mediocrity, thy name is Marquis. The righty slightly outpitched his career peripherals and produced his usual league-average ERA in just over 120 innings with the Nationals before being traded to Arizona for a High-A infielder on July 30. His arrival ended any uncertainty about the D-Backs being buyers, but they were left with little to show for their $2.5 million after an Angel Pagan liner broke Marquis's fibula in his third start for the team. (He faced five batters after the fracture, which suggests a pain threshold even higher than his groundball rate—in the top 10 among NL pitchers.) His stats aren't sexy, but Marquis has now pitched for playoff teams in 11 of his 12 seasons, which should give you some idea of the value of a league-average innings muncher. In December, he signed with Minnesota, where he'll feel right at home with a host of other contact-prone pitchers.

### Lester Oliveros

Born: 5/28/1988 Age: 24
Bats: R Throws: R Height: 6' 0'' Weight: 225
Breakout: 39% Improve: 60% Collapse: 21%
Attrition: 11% MLB: 87%

**Comparables:**
Jake Peavy, Cecilio Guante, Renie Martin

| YEAR | TEAM | LVL | AGE | W | L | SV | G | GS | IP | H | HR | BB | SO | EqBB9 | EqSO9 | GB% | BABIP | WHIP | ERA | FIP | FRA | WARP |
|------|------|-----|-----|---|---|----|----|----|-----|----|----|----|----|-------|-------|-----|-------|------|------|------|------|------|
| 2009 | LAK | A+ | 21 | 4 | 2 | 2 | 34 | 0 | 54 | 53 | 5 | 16 | 58 | 2.7 | 9.7 | 46% | .318 | 1.28 | 4.17 | 3.37 | 4.17 | 0.9 |
| 2010 | ERI | AA | 22 | 1 | 1 | 14 | 24 | 0 | 25¹ | 14 | 1 | 16 | 27 | 7.5 | 12.8 | 50% | .382 | 1.62 | 4.98 | 4.11 | 5.43 | 0.0 |
| 2011 | TOL | AAA | 23 | 1 | 3 | 5 | 22 | 0 | 28 | 37 | 7 | 17 | 26 | 5.5 | 8.4 | 52% | .357 | 1.93 | 6.43 | 6.45 | 7.22 | -0.5 |
| 2011 | DET | MLB | 23 | 0 | 0 | 0 | 9 | 0 | 8 | 8 | 0 | 4 | 4 | 4.5 | 4.5 | 63% | .296 | 1.50 | 5.62 | 3.56 | 4.02 | 0.1 |
| 2011 | MIN | MLB | 23 | 0 | 0 | 0 | 10 | 0 | 13¹ | 13 | 0 | 7 | 9 | 4.7 | 6.1 | 38% | .325 | 1.50 | 4.05 | 3.29 | 4.53 | 0.0 |
| 2012 | MIN | MLB | 24 | 1 | 0 | 0 | 23 | 0 | 26¹ | 28 | 3 | 12 | 21 | 4.1 | 7.3 | 43% | .316 | 1.53 | 4.78 | 4.46 | 5.20 | -0.1 |

A fireplug from Venezuela, Oliveros was one of two relievers acquired from the Tigers in the Delmon Young trade last August. His 93 to 95-mph heater gets high grades for its movement, but he is yet another reminder that man cannot live by fastball alone. Above Double-A, he hasn't been able to get batters to chase either his slider or his changeup, so he has been roughed up. If he can improve his secondary stuff and trim his walk rate, he has a chance to turn into a solid middle reliever.

durability—his 420.1 innings in 2009–10 ranked 19th in the majors—the Twins rewarded him with a two-year $16.5 million deal last winter and at the very least he continued to show up for work regularly. Problem was his strikeout rate dipped 15 percent from its already-low 2010 mark to the point where it was the majors' second lowest among ERA qualifiers; when backed by an inferior defense his BABIP shot up 25 points. Even given his pinpoint control he's a League Average Inning Muncher at a more or less breakeven price, which has its purposes on the roster of a contender, less so on a second-division club looking to cut payroll.

### Glen Perkins

Born: 3/2/1983 Age: 29
Bats: L Throws: L Height: 6' 0'' Weight: 200
Breakout: 19% Improve: 66% Collapse: 17%
Attrition: 10% MLB: 88%

**Comparables:**
Dick Donovan, John Smiley, Denny Neagle

| YEAR | TEAM | LVL | AGE | W | L | SV | G | GS | IP | H | HR | BB | SO | EqBB9 | EqSO9 | GB% | BABIP | WHIP | ERA | FIP | FRA | WARP |
|------|------|-----|-----|---|---|----|----|----|-----|-----|----|----|----|-------|-------|-----|-------|------|------|------|------|------|
| 2009 | MIN | MLB | 26 | 6 | 7 | 0 | 18 | 17 | 96¹ | 120 | 13 | 23 | 45 | 2.1 | 4.2 | 49% | .315 | 1.48 | 5.89 | 4.71 | 5.51 | 0.4 |
| 2010 | ROC | AAA | 27 | 3 | 9 | 0 | 26 | 24 | 124 | 119 | 11 | 24 | 71 | 2.6 | 7.1 | 48% | .367 | 1.58 | 5.81 | 4.19 | 5.24 | 0.8 |
| 2010 | MIN | MLB | 27 | 1 | 1 | 0 | 13 | 1 | 21² | 29 | 3 | 5 | 14 | 2.1 | 5.8 | 53% | .366 | 1.57 | 5.82 | 4.80 | 5.86 | -0.1 |
| 2011 | MIN | MLB | 28 | 4 | 4 | 0 | 65 | 0 | 61² | 55 | 2 | 21 | 65 | 3.1 | 9.5 | 52% | .333 | 1.23 | 2.48 | 2.45 | 3.86 | 0.8 |
| 2012 | MIN | MLB | 29 | 3 | 3 | 0 | 28 | 7 | 54² | 64 | 7 | 15 | 34 | 2.5 | 5.5 | 43% | .318 | 1.45 | 4.71 | 4.45 | 5.12 | 0.0 |

If you were going to bet that a Twins lefty reliever would whiff more than a hitter per inning in 2011, Perkins might have rated as the least likely choice. Yet once the team cut bait on the notion that this 2004 first-rounder should be in the rotation, lo and behold, Perkins blossomed as a full-time reliever. His average fastball velocity, which had lagged around 90 miles per hour as a starter and wasn't helped by various arm injuries, increased from 92 in 2010 to 94 in 2011, and his percentage of swinging strikes rose from 7.9 to 11.2 percent. Where he once struggled against same-siders, he handled lefties (.222/.300/.289) as well as righties (.259/.318/.363), and wound up with the eighth-best strikeout rate among southpaw relievers. The startling transformation rated as one of the few bright spots in the Twins' dark season, and set Perkins up to be one of the team's late-game relievers in 2012.

### Adrian Salcedo

Born: 4/24/1991 Age: 21
Bats: R Throws: R Height: 6' 5'' Weight: 175
Breakout: 30% Improve: 60% Collapse: 12%
Attrition: 7% MLB: 83%

**Comparables:**
Bob Friend, Rick Wise, Pedro Ramos

| YEAR | TEAM | LVL | AGE | W | L | SV | G | GS | IP | H | HR | BB | SO | EqBB9 | EqSO9 | GB% | BABIP | WHIP | ERA | FIP | FRA | WARP |
|------|------|-----|-----|---|---|----|----|----|-----|-----|----|----|----|-------|-------|-----|-------|------|------|------|------|------|
| 2009 | TWI | RK | 18 | 3 | 2 | 0 | 11 | 10 | 61² | 60 | 1 | 3 | 58 | 0.4 | 8.5 | 59% | .311 | 1.00 | 1.46 | 2.04 | 4.10 | 1.6 |
| 2010 | FTM | A+ | 19 | 0 | 3 | 0 | 6 | 6 | 27¹ | 33 | 3 | 5 | 12 | 2.6 | 5.3 | 44% | .441 | 1.83 | 6.26 | 4.85 | 5.90 | -0.2 |
| 2010 | ELZ | RK | 19 | 4 | 3 | 1 | 16 | 8 | 66 | 44 | 3 | 7 | 51 | 1.4 | 8.9 | 56% | .323 | 0.98 | 3.27 | 3.16 | 4.87 | 0.8 |
| 2011 | BLT | A | 20 | 6 | 6 | 0 | 29 | 20 | 135 | 131 | 4 | 28 | 92 | 1.8 | 6.1 | 54% | .298 | 1.17 | 2.93 | 3.20 | 4.29 | 1.5 |
| 2012 | MIN | MLB | 21 | 2 | 3 | 0 | 8 | 5 | 36 | 46 | 5 | 15 | 15 | 3.8 | 3.7 | 51% | .318 | 1.70 | 6.00 | 5.43 | 6.52 | -0.5 |

Overstretched as a teenage emergency starter in High-A in 2010, Salcedo put together a strong season at a more age-appropriate level in 2011, ranking third among Midwest League qualifiers in homer rate and sixth in walk rate. He's a long, lanky strike-thrower with a smooth delivery; his low-90s fastball plays up due to movement and command, but his changeup is average, his breaking ball below average, and he doesn't miss a ton of bats. Physically, he offers a good deal of projection, and could wind up a fourth starter. Expect him to fare better in his return to Fort Myers.

### Manuel Soliman

Born: **8/11/1989** Age: **22**
Bats: **R** Throws: **R** Height: **6' 3"** Weight: **185**
Breakout: **15%** Improve: **42%** Collapse: **38%**
Attrition: **20%** MLB: **79%**

**Comparables:**
Tony Cloninger, Moose Haas, George Lauzerique

| YEAR | TEAM | LVL | AGE | W | L | SV | G | GS | IP | H | HR | BB | SO | EqBB9 | EqSO9 | GB% | BABIP | WHIP | ERA | FIP | FRA | WARP |
|------|------|-----|-----|---|---|----|---|----|------|-----|----|----|-----|-------|-------|-----|-------|------|------|------|------|------|
| 2010 | ELZ | RK | 20 | 5 | 2 | 0 | 12 | 12 | 64² | 43 | 5 | 16 | 67 | 2.9 | 10.3 | 43% | .268 | 1.05 | 3.48 | 3.47 | 4.41 | 1.8 |
| 2011 | BLT | A | 21 | 7 | 11 | 0 | 28 | 25 | 136 | 128 | 17 | 49 | 118 | 3.3 | 7.9 | 44% | .293 | 1.31 | 3.97 | 4.53 | 4.71 | 1.1 |
| 2012 | MIN | MLB | 22 | 2 | 3 | 0 | 7 | 7 | 36² | 43 | 5 | 20 | 23 | 4.9 | 5.6 | 33% | .314 | 1.73 | 5.97 | 5.36 | 6.49 | -0.5 |

Soliman spent 2007 and 2008 playing shortstop in the Dominican Summer League and hitting a meager .199. He has fared better since converting to the mound, showing an ability to miss bats in his full-season debut, but struggling to keep the ball in the park. Soliman offers a low-to-mid-90s fastball and a hard slider that gives fits to hitters from both sides of the plate. He's still more thrower than pitcher, but if nothing else, his two-pitch combo could play up in a move to the bullpen. For the moment he'll remain as a starter and continue learning the craft.

### Anthony Swarzak

Born: **9/10/1985** Age: **26**
Bats: **R** Throws: **R** Height: **6' 5"** Weight: **225**
Breakout: **27%** Improve: **63%** Collapse: **15%**
Attrition: **19%** MLB: **86%**

**Comparables:**
Eric Rasmussen, Tim Stauffer, Jeff Karstens

| YEAR | TEAM | LVL | AGE | W | L | SV | G | GS | IP | H | HR | BB | SO | EqBB9 | EqSO9 | GB% | BABIP | WHIP | ERA | FIP | FRA | WARP |
|------|------|-----|-----|---|---|----|----|----|------|-----|----|----|----|-------|-------|-----|-------|------|------|------|------|------|
| 2009 | ROC | AAA | 23 | 4 | 5 | 0 | 13 | 13 | 79² | 79 | 4 | 21 | 45 | 2.4 | 5.1 | 42% | .293 | 1.25 | 3.27 | 3.57 | 4.54 | 0.9 |
| 2009 | MIN | MLB | 23 | 3 | 7 | 0 | 12 | 12 | 59 | 76 | 12 | 20 | 34 | 3.1 | 5.2 | 36% | .322 | 1.63 | 6.25 | 5.75 | 6.11 | -0.2 |
| 2010 | ROC | AAA | 24 | 5 | 12 | 0 | 22 | 22 | 111² | 95 | 8 | 25 | 50 | 3.1 | 5.6 | 36% | .337 | 1.62 | 6.20 | 4.32 | 5.72 | 0.3 |
| 2011 | ROC | AAA | 25 | 2 | 1 | 0 | 6 | 6 | 32¹ | 32 | 3 | 6 | 18 | 1.9 | 7.0 | 37% | .312 | 1.30 | 3.90 | 3.89 | 4.15 | 0.6 |
| 2011 | MIN | MLB | 25 | 4 | 7 | 0 | 27 | 11 | 102 | 111 | 9 | 26 | 55 | 2.3 | 4.9 | 40% | .297 | 1.34 | 4.32 | 4.07 | 4.58 | 0.7 |
| 2012 | MIN | MLB | 26 | 4 | 5 | 0 | 17 | 12 | 78 | 92 | 9 | 23 | 43 | 2.7 | 5.0 | 37% | .315 | 1.48 | 4.88 | 4.49 | 5.30 | -0.1 |

Swarzak once rated as a front-of-the-rotation candidate who could dial it up into the mid-90s—an anomaly in this organization—but he lost his way both on and off the field, most notably serving a 50-game suspension back in 2007 after testing positive for a "drug of abuse." Pummeled with the Twins in 2009 and at Triple-A in 2010, he pulled himself together at Rochester, and after bouncing between the minors and the majors, long relief and the occasional spot start, he replaced Francisco Liriano and made four quality starts out of six. Swarzak's stuff isn't what it used to be; his fastball averages 91.3 miles per hour and occasionally touches 94 with a slider, changeup, and curveball rounding out his arsenal. As his strikeout rate attests, he doesn't miss many bats anymore, making him a guy unlikely to meet with much success as a starter.

## LINEOUTS

### HITTERS

| PLAYER | TEAM | LVL | AGE | PA | R | 2B | 3B | HR | RBI | BB | SO | SB-CS | AVG/OBP/SLG | TAv | BABIP | BRR | FRAA | WARP |
|--------|------|-----|-----|-----|----|----|----|----|-----|----|-----|-------|-------------|------|-------|------|------|------|
| SS P. Florimon Jr. | BOW | AA | 24 | 520 | 53 | 27 | 4 | 8 | 60 | 51 | 114 | 15-12 | .267/.344/.396 | .262 | .336 | -2.5 | 11.1 | 3.3 |
|  | BAL | MLB | 24 | 10 | 1 | 1 | 0 | 0 | 2 | 1 | 6 | 0-0 | .125/.222/.250 | .234 | .500 | 0.1 | 0.1 | 0.1 |
| C S. Holm | ROC | AAA | 31 | 174 | 13 | 6 | 0 | 1 | 13 | 17 | 38 | 0-0 | .179/.267/.238 | .190 | .228 | -0.9 | -0.6 | -0.9 |
|  | MIN | MLB | 31 | 18 | 1 | 1 | 0 | 0 | 0 | 1 | 4 | 0-0 | .118/.167/.176 | .142 | .154 | -0.4 | -0.1 | -0.2 |
| LF M. Kepler | ELZ | RK | 18 | 221 | 29 | 11 | 3 | 1 | 24 | 23 | 54 | 1-1 | .262/.347/.366 | .264 | .355 | -0.7 | -7.2 | -0.3 |
| LF W. Ramirez | GWN | AAA | 25 | 313 | 40 | 16 | 3 | 11 | 36 | 17 | 70 | 19-6 | .267/.307/.458 | .251 | .314 | -0.3 | 2.4 | 0.2 |
|  | ATL | MLB | 25 | 30 | 5 | 2 | 0 | 0 | 2 | 4 | 11 | 0-2 | .231/.333/.308 | .240 | .400 | 0.4 | -0.4 | 0.0 |
| RF J. Repko | MIN | MLB | 30 | 144 | 21 | 2 | 0 | 2 | 11 | 6 | 38 | 7-2 | .226/.270/.286 | .205 | .301 | 2.4 | -1.3 | -0.4 |
| C R. Rivera | ROC | AAA | 27 | 166 | 15 | 12 | 0 | 5 | 24 | 11 | 27 | 0-0 | .268/.325/.450 | .245 | .297 | -3.6 | 1.5 | 0.4 |
|  | MIN | MLB | 27 | 114 | 9 | 3 | 0 | 1 | 5 | 8 | 32 | 0-0 | .144/.211/.202 | .171 | .194 | -1.4 | 0.5 | -0.6 |

**Pedro Florimon** got his first call to Baltimore in September, more a sip than a full cup of coffee. While he's come a long way since his days as a scrawny free-swinger at Single-A, he strikes out far too often for a middle infielder with little power—but then they can't all grow up to be Robert Andino. ⊘ Aside from kindling fond recollections of *Arrested Development*, **Steve Holm**—STEVE HOLM!—doesn't have a whole lot that distinguishes him from dozens of other backup catchers. Then again, replicating Drew Butera's season one level down takes some doing. ⊘ Signed to the biggest bonus ($800,000) of any European player, German **Max Kepler** put together a surprisingly solid season in the Appy League. He's extremely raw, but has above-average speed and arm strength, a fluid swing, and a projection for power once his frame fills out. ⊘ **Wilkin Ramirez** continues to waste his athleticism and tools. He turned 26 in October, and is past the point where potential is supposed to turn into results. ⊘ **Jason Repko** has spent a good portion of his major league career battling injuries; the 2011 season saw him make trips to the DL for quad and shoulder woes. A decent defender, he lacks the power or patience to merit even a fifth outfielder job at this point. ⊘ In **Rene Rivera**, the Twins found a catcher with even less offensive ability than Drew Butera, though he did at least throw out a team-high 40 percent of would-be base thieves.

## PITCHERS

| PLAYER | TEAM | LVL | AGE | W | L | SV | IP | H | HR | BB | SO | EqBB9 | EqSO9 | GB% | BABIP | WHIP | ERA | FIP | FRA | WARP |
|--------|------|-----|-----|---|---|----|----|----|----|----|----|-------|-------|-----|-------|------|-----|-----|-----|------|
| A. Slama | ROC | AAA | 27 | 1 | 2 | 1 | 37 | 27 | 4 | 16 | 42 | 3.9 | 10.2 | 40% | .261 | 1.16 | 2.92 | 3.91 | 4.03 | 0.7 |
|  | MIN | MLB | 27 | 0 | 0 | 0 | 2¹ | 0 | 0 | 2 | 3 | 7.7 | 11.6 | 25% | .000 | 0.86 | 0.00 | 3.06 | 2.68 | 0.1 |
| A. Thompson | ALT | AA | 24 | 1 | 5 | 0 | 83² | 100 | 6 | 20 | 51 | 2.2 | 5.5 | 43% | .344 | 1.43 | 5.16 | 3.92 | 5.11 | 0.0 |
|  | PIT | MLB | 24 | 0 | 0 | 0 | 7² | 13 | 2 | 6 | 1 | 7.0 | 1.2 | 38% | .355 | 2.48 | 7.04 | 8.47 | 8.72 | -0.3 |
| E. Vasquez | RNO | AAA | 27 | 2 | 2 | 0 | 27² | 29 | 4 | 22 | 27 | 6.8 | 8.5 | 23% | .291 | 1.70 | 6.18 | 6.37 | 6.35 | 0.0 |
|  | ARI | MLB | 27 | 1 | 1 | 0 | 30¹ | 27 | 2 | 13 | 20 | 3.9 | 5.9 | 36% | .269 | 1.32 | 4.15 | 4.21 | 5.55 | -0.3 |
| K. Waldrop | ROC | AAA | 25 | 4 | 5 | 3 | 79 | 84 | 7 | 18 | 44 | 2.1 | 5.0 | 66% | .303 | 1.29 | 3.87 | 4.11 | 5.88 | 0.1 |
|  | MIN | MLB | 25 | 1 | 0 | 0 | 11 | 10 | 1 | 6 | 5 | 4.9 | 4.1 | 77% | .243 | 1.45 | 5.73 | 4.97 | 4.31 | 0.1 |
| P. Walters | LVG | AAA | 26 | 1 | 1 | 0 | 29 | 44 | 4 | 16 | 26 | 5.0 | 8.1 | 38% | .408 | 2.07 | 8.38 | 5.70 | 5.96 | 0.2 |
|  | MEM | AAA | 26 | 7 | 4 | 0 | 103¹ | 99 | 9 | 40 | 82 | 3.7 | 7.6 | 45% | .311 | 1.42 | 4.27 | 4.73 | 4.95 | 0.3 |
|  | TOR | MLB | 26 | 0 | 0 | 0 | 1 | 0 | 0 | 1 | 1 | 9.0 | 9.0 | % | .000 | 1.00 | 0.00 | 4.06 | 3.23 | 0.0 |
|  | SLN | MLB | 26 | 0 | 0 | 0 | 4 | 3 | 1 | 2 | 3 | 4.5 | 6.8 | 39% | .167 | 1.25 | 9.00 | 6.24 | 9.86 | -0.2 |

Not the Grammy-nominated bluegrass musician, **David Bromberg** is a pitchability guy who led the Appy, Midwest, and Florida State Leagues in strikeouts, but whose performance has leveled off at upper levels. A line drive broke his ulna, requiring surgery and costing him three months of 2011. ⊘ In his first two outings of 2011, **Jason Bulger** came into extra-inning games as Mike Scioscia's last non-emergency option, and walked four batters both times. From there it was only a matter of time before he pitched his way out of the organization, live arm or no. ⊘ **Samuel Deduno** features a mid-90s fastball and solid curve but has battled control problems throughout his career. He's a Quadruple-A pitcher. ⊘ **Matt Maloney**'s attempts to move beyond the Quad-A label weren't helped by losing three and a half months to a sneeze-induced rib fracture. Moving to a bigger yard than Great American Ball Park can't hurt his chances to carve out a bullpen role. ⊘ A 19th-round 2008 pick out of Hillsborough Community College in Tampa, **Bruce Pugh** is an unheralded righty who can hit the mid-90s with his fastball and miss plenty of bats, but he has a hard time keeping the ball in the park. ⊘ A third-round pick back in 2006, **Tyler Robertson** couldn't find a second plus pitch to accompany his slider as a starter, but he fared pretty well upon converting to relief last year. The 6-foot-5 lefty did show a significant reverse platoon split, which could prevent him from getting pigeonholed as a LOOGY. ⊘ Despite strong numbers in the minors, and a plus slider, **Anthony Slama**'s ongoing efforts to crack the Twins' bullpen have been rather fruitless; he didn't pitch after July 1 due to a flexor pronator strain in his elbow, and was outrighted off the 40-man roster in October. ⊘ Pittsburgh removed **Aaron Thompson** from its 40-man roster in June before re-adding him in August for a spot start. His fastball sits in the high 80s and his change is nifty; however, his upside is limited to a lefty specialist, if that. ⊘ Plucked from the Diamondbacks off waivers just before the end of the season, **Esmerling Vasquez** can pump it in the mid-90s, but has been beset by control problems; the addition of an ineffective curveball did little to help, but maybe an organizational change will. ⊘ A 2004 first-rounder whose climb up the ladder was derailed by Tommy John surgery and an inability to miss bats, **Kyle Waldrop** finally reached the majors last September as a reliever. A sinkerballer who rarely cracks 90, his future is as a groundballin' machine.  ⊘  A big righty with big dreams, **P.J. Walters** was let go by the Blue Jays and signed as a minor league free agent with the Twins.

## MANAGER: RON GARDENHIRE _____

| YEAR | TEAM | W-L | Pythag +/- | Avg PC | 100+ P | 120+ P | QS | BQS | REL | REL w Zero R | IBB | Subs | PH | PH Avg | PH HR | SB2 | CS2 | SB3 | CS3 | SAC Att | SAC % | POS SAC | Squeeze | Swing | In Play |
|------|------|-----|------------|--------|--------|--------|----|-----|-----|--------------|-----|------|----|--------|-------|-----|-----|-----|-----|---------|-------|---------|---------|-------|---------|
| 2009 | MIN | 87-76 | 1 | 92.4 | 56 | 1 | 76 | 10 | 477 | 301 | 20 | 49 | 83 | .303 | 4 | 11 | 2 | 0 | 2 | 80 | 63.7% | 46 | 4 | 150 | 127 |
| 2010 | MIN | 94-68 | 1 | 187.1 | 157 | 155 | 105 | 6 | 465 | 377 | 38 | — | 150 | .156 | 4 | 8 | 5 | 0 | 0 | 100 | 86.0% | 76 | 2 | 272 | 101 |
| 2011 | MIN | 63-99 | 0 | 95.2 | 66 | 2 | 80 | 9 | 457 | 340 | 37 | — | 87 | .175 | 0 | 6 | 4 | 0 | 2 | 52 | 86.5% | 45 | 1 | 361 | 135 |

In his first nine seasons on the job, Gardy finished below .500 just once, had finished as low as third only twice, and had missed the playoffs a mere three times, an impressive run that may have owed more to the team's player development system—as well as the Johan Santana Rule 5 pick and the A.J. Pierzynski haul—than to his managerial acumen. For better or worse, he had never managed his way through a season where his team was buried so early, or dealt with so many catastrophic injuries. Though the team was hamstrung by bad planning (particularly regarding the rotation) and didn't have much effective help to offer from the minors, Gardenhire didn't cover himself in glory, either. While the Twins showed some life in June and July, going 33-22 after a 17-36 start, they limped home 13-41 over the final two months, 8 1/2 games worse than any other AL team, which didn't reflect well on Gardenhire's ability to keep his team motivated during bad times. (Compare: with a slightly worse record through July and plenty of structural problems with his own roster, Don Mattingly oversaw the Dodgers rallying to a .500+ finish.) As usual, Gardenhire was one of the game's most cautious managers in terms of starter pitch counts. After curbing his reliance upon smallball tactics at least somewhat in 2010—curious timing given the team's move to the lower-scoring environment Target Field—he went back to using the hit-and-run far more often than the average AL team. He did lay off the sacrifice bunting a bit, which is appropriate given how often the Twins fell behind. He has two years remaining on his contract. Even as strong as his track record has been, another subpar season could put him on the hot seat.

# New York Mets

No one said rebuilding the Mets was going to be easy. Between bloated contracts, a subpar collection of major-league talent, a near-barren farm system, an ownership group with financial and legal troubles, a poor organizational philosophy, and a fan base notoriously more rabid than a ra-

...might be unhappy with the early returns, those who are more thoughtful and even-keeled have to be pleased with the direction the franchise is headed.

Completely rebuilding in a market like New York would never fly with the fans, but Alderson has made it clear that the team's top priority is turning the club into a long-term contender: "What we need to do is continue to make good decisions in the best interests of the team long-term while recognizing the interests of fans, which incorporates more of the short term," he told *Newsday* in September.

| | | |
|---|---|---|
| TAv | .263 | 12th |
| TAv-P | .268 | 24th |
| FIP | 3.97 | 15th |
| DER | .701 | 23rd |
| DL | 862 | 24th |
| B-Age | 27.9 | 6th |
| P-Age | 29.7 | 27th |
| Salary | $142.8 | 5th |
| M$/MW | $4.57 | 27th |

**2011:** Citi Field disguises offensive talent, but they posted the NL's second-best True Average

**2012:** Impatient Mets fans won't like short-term results, but Alderson's turning things around

**Action Items:** Loss of deadweight payroll, fixed owners, restocked farm system

### Table 1. Clearing the Books

| Player | Expiring Salary |
|---|---|
| Carlos Beltran | $18.5M |
| Oliver Perez | $12M |
| Francisco Rodriguez | $11.5M |
| Jose Reyes | $11M |
| Luis Castillo | $6M |
| Total | $59M |

One of the biggest obstacles that Alderson and the Mets will face is the financial imposition the club's owners, Fred Wilpon and Saul Katz, have placed on the team. Facing a $1 billion lawsuit connected to allegedly negligent investments with Bernie Madoff, the Mets owners have already been loaned $25 million by Major League Baseball and another $40 million by Bank of America. Add in that the Mets lost $70 million this past season alone, according to Alderson, and they are in quite the bind. Predicting the outcome of this...

...and Katz could be forced to sell their majority shares of the team.

A big part of Alderson's commitment to the long-term is simply waiting, particularly through the 2011 season. One can't put a contender together overnight, and after years of former GM Omar Minaya simply trying to throw money at the team's problems, the team has wised up under Alderson, realizing that putting a competitive team on the field in today's game will require more than asking, "Waiter, what's the most expensive item on the menu?" Refusing to dole out anything more than a single-year contract last offseason, Alderson let $59 million worth of big contracts expire at the end of 2011. The Mets still have Johan Santana ($24M, $25.5M) and Jason Bay ($16M twice) signed to much-too-large contracts, but those only run for two more years, at which point the Mets will hope to be transitioning into contention. Alderson's moves from this point forward will likely be made with an eye toward 2014, by which time, the hope is, the team will have a firm handle on its financial predicament and, with any luck, some minor-league talent approaching major-league readiness.

Early in the offseason, reports were that the Mets were limiting their closer options to those who would accept two-year deals, and they wound up netting Frank Francisco for just that. In fact, as of press time, the team hadn't committed to any new players beyond 2013. Aside from Jose Reyes, there was little chance Mets brass would have gone beyond a two-year commitment to any free agent. Indeed, Alderson has stood fast to his vision this winter, exploring deals for long-term pieces, remaining resolute in retaining the cost-effective pieces he already has, and adding good-enough short-term chips like Francisco, Jon Rauch, Ramon Ramirez, and Andres Torres, who should at least give Mets fans a reason to come to the stadium.

While the Mets are a large-market team with the potential to have large amounts of cash to spend (at least they've had this luxury in the past and hope to again—they do play in New York, after all), it's imprudent for a team to rely solely upon its purse to build a playoff contender, as the team's fan base witnessed with Minaya. Developing young, cost-effective talent of its own is important for any club, and a team with the financial resources the Mets had under Minaya should have had an advantage over teams that can't afford to bring in the same quality of personnel. Despite this advantage, during Minaya's regime the Mets drafted and developed very few quality prospects, and the ones who did show promise either had their development hampered by being rushed to the majors, often to fill minor roles (Jenrry Mejia); or fizzled out, were dumped in trades, or both (Lastings Milledge, Eddie Kunz, Kevin Mulvey, Philip Humber). Sure, there have been some exceptions (Mike Pelfrey, Ike Davis), but as a whole, the system has been underwhelming.

This might be partially bad luck, but a lot of it can be attributed to poor organizational philosophy. Aside from asinine individual personnel decisions like putting promising starting pitcher Mejia in the bullpen (how difficult is it to find a capable reliever to pitch the kind of low-leverage innings—0.82 leverage index—Mejia did?), the general lack of value placed on draft picks and prospects, combined with Minaya's inability to maintain a competent major-league roster, has put the Mets' farm system in quite the bind. Twice the Mets forfeited their first-round pick to sign a free-agent closer (Billy Wagner and K-Rod), and when they did keep their picks, they were often misused as a result of Minaya's stubborn adherence to Bud Selig's slotting system, bypassing superior players in favor of ones who would be easier to sign.

When Alderson joined the team, he vowed to make changes, and it's become clear that he has—very much for the better. Alderson and his VP of player development and amateur scouting, Paul DePodesta, expressed their intent to be aggressive in the draft and their willingness to go over slot, and they did just that in 2011, selecting toolsy outfielder Brandon Nimmo in the first round and paying him 27 percent more than the number 13 pick called for. The team wound up signing 19 of its first 20 selections, going over slot where warranted.

The new collective bargaining agreement finalized this winter, however, penalizes teams that go over slot by a certain amount (not just in terms of money, but also by stripping them of future draft picks), which will unfortunately limit the Mets' aggressiveness in this area before they could really get it going. Still, Mets fans can be sure that Alderson and DePo will do the proper cost-benefit analysis that will lead to continued sound decisions, something that didn't happen when Minaya was in charge.

### Table 2. Mets Top 101 Prospects

| Prospect | Goldstein Rank |
| --- | --- |
| Matt Harvey | 25 |
| Zack Wheeler | 30 |
| Jeurys Familia | 89 |

Alderson's emphasis on rebuilding the farm was further exemplified in his midseason trade of Carlos Beltran, which put the Mets into a sort of quasi-rebuilding mode Minaya could never bring himself to commence. Beltran was dealt to the Giants along with a substantial amount of cash for top pitching prospect Zack Wheeler, a former first-round pick. Wheeler joins 2011 first-rounder Matt Harvey and former Dominican signee Jeurys Familia to give the Mets three "Top 101" MLB prospects and a trio of high-upside starters the likes of which the team hasn't seen since Bill Pulsipher, Jason Isringhausen, and Paul Wilson (with the hope that this new trio makes good on their promise).

In addition to philosophy, Alderson has made quite a few changes to the scouting department since taking over his post, letting some personnel go, shifting others into new roles, and bringing in an all-star cast of top scouting personnel that he, DePodesta, and special assistant J.P. Ricciardi have worked with in the past, along with others who are highly regarded in the industry. Additionally, he's reorganized the way the team approaches scouting, now assigning scouts to organizations instead of leagues. While this can create some logistical problems, it will give the Mets an internal authority on the farm system of every team in baseball, which will be beneficial when it comes to trade negotiations.

There's been very little to fault Alderson for since he took over. He's been patient when needed, aggressive when appropriate, and reasoned throughout. Perhaps more than anything else, though, he has a real plan. He's giving the organization direction as opposed to the blind-folded piñata-stick flailing that was Minaya's tenure.

Some have argued that Alderson missed an opportunity by failing to trade Reyes, that trading Beltran wasn't enough, but a lot of that is hindsight bias. Reyes was clearly going to be a rental player for the acquiring team, lowering his value off the bat, and when he didn't look to be 100 percent coming off the DL in July, his value was lowered further. Add in the potential backlash from fans (it's better from a business standpoint for fans to be mad at the player who chose money over loyalty than at the team that shipped him out of town), what was a real desire by the Mets to re-sign Reyes, and the at-the-time likelihood that they'd receive two draft picks if he signed elsewhere, and holding onto him through the end of the 2011 season becomes a very defensible decision.

Now that Reyes is gone, some will contend that David Wright should follow him out the door, that it's best to barrel ahead full steam into rebuilding mode. While that might sound good in principle, there are some compelling reasons to keep Wright around, at least for the time being. First, he's still just 29, reasonably priced, and could contribute to a

into rebuilding mode since they're not going to the playoffs in 2012, but part of rebuilding a franchise like the Mets means

not only acquiring young players but putting the team in the best possible position financially so that when it comes time to make that playoff push, it has money to spend on the necessary pieces. Selling tickets now generates money to spend later. There's a decent chance Wright is eventually dealt, but it makes much more sense to be patient and feel things out at the trade deadline or even wait until next offseason, when the acquiring team will get him for a full year. Wright has a reasonable team option for 2013, but it gets voided if he's traded this season.

All in all, even though impatient Mets fans hoping for an immediate turnaround are surely disappointed with Alderson's tenure thus far (and will be for at least another

Alderson was the right man for the job and that the Mets are finally, *finally* in capable hands.

## HITTERS

**Jason Bay** LF
Born: 9/20/1978 Age: 33
Bats: R Throws: R Height: 6' 3" Weight: 200
Breakout: 1% Improve: 27% Collapse: 6%
Attrition: 21% MLB: 88%
**Comparables:**
Mack Jones, Bob Nieman, Milton Bradley

| YEAR | TEAM | LVL | AGE | PA | R | 2B | 3B | HR | RBI | BB | SO | SB | CS | AVG/OBP/SLG | TAv | BABIP | BRR | FRAA | WARP |
|------|------|-----|-----|-----|-----|----|----|----|-----|----|-----|----|----|-------------|------|-------|------|--------|------|
| 2009 | BOS | MLB | 30 | 638 | 103 | 29 | 3 | 36 | 119 | 94 | 162 | 13 | 3 | .267/.384/.537 | .316 | .315 | 1 | 10.6 | 6.1 |
| 2010 | NYN | MLB | 31 | 401 | 48 | 20 | 6 | 6 | 47 | 44 | 91 | 10 | 0 | .259/.347/.402 | .277 | .329 | 1.9 | -8.6 | 0.9 |
| 2011 | NYN | MLB | 32 | 509 | 59 | 19 | 1 | 12 | 57 | 56 | 109 | 11 | 1 | .245/.329/.374 | .263 | .295 | 0.6 | -1.5 | 1.2 |
| 2012 | NYN | MLB | 33 | 459 | 58 | 20 | 2 | 15 | 54 | 51 | 104 | 9 | 1 | .261/.349/.435 | .284 | .315 | 0.7 | LF -2 | 2.3 |

Remember the cool Jason Bay? The guy every team wanted at the 2008 trade deadline and the guy who hit 36 home runs and drew 94 walks in 2009? That's the player the Mets paid for, but injuries have aged him before our very eyes. His bat has slowed down considerably and he's become a stiff, almost laughably bad defensive player. If you are expecting him to rebound to his old level, we have a bridge in the next borough over to sell you, and the Mets are on the hook for $32 million over the next two years for this guy, who clearly isn't Jason Bay anymore.

**Darrell Ceciliani** CF
Born: 6/22/1990 Age: 22
Bats: L Throws: L Height: 6' 2" Weight: 220
Breakout: 1% Improve: 5% Collapse: 1%
Attrition: 11% MLB: 17%
**Comparables:**
Chad Hermansen, Jason Denham, David Rubinstein

| YEAR | TEAM | LVL | AGE | PA | R | 2B | 3B | HR | RBI | BB | SO | SB | CS | AVG/OBP/SLG | TAv | BABIP | BRR | FRAA | WARP |
|------|------|-----|-----|-----|----|----|----|----|-----|----|----|----|----|-------------|------|-------|------|---------|------|
| 2009 | KNG | RK | 19 | 176 | 29 | 6 | 0 | 2 | 13 | 13 | 31 | 14 | 2 | .234/.312/.310 | .240 | .280 | 1.8 | 6.9 | 0.6 |
| 2010 | BRO | A- | 20 | 303 | 56 | 19 | 12 | 2 | 35 | 24 | 56 | 21 | 14 | .351/.407/.531 | .331 | .431 | 3.5 | 7.5 | 4.5 |
| 2011 | SAV | A | 21 | 488 | 62 | 23 | 4 | 4 | 40 | 52 | 96 | 25 | 8 | .259/.351/.361 | .286 | .327 | -1.6 | 3.1 | 3.0 |
| 2012 | NYN | MLB | 22 | 250 | 21 | 9 | 1 | 0 | 15 | 17 | 64 | 6 | 2 | .200/.261/.255 | .192 | .270 | -0.1 | CF -3, RF 0 | -1.9 |

After chasing the New York-Penn League batting title in 2010, Ceciliani earned some very poorly thought-out Jacoby Ellsbury comparisons, but his full-season debut showed there is still work to be done. He's fast and he has the approach one looks for in a potential leadoff hitter, but he rarely makes loud contact, with a disturbing number of weak outs keeping his batting average low. The tools to be something are here, but that something is probably just a nice fourth outfielder.

### Ike Davis 1B

Born: 3/22/1987 Age: 25
Bats: L Throws: L Height: 6' 5" Weight: 215
Breakout: 2% Improve: 36% Collapse: 2%
Attrition: 18% MLB: 84%

Comparables:
Kent Hrbek, Jeff Larish, Chuck Harrison

| YEAR | TEAM | LVL | AGE | PA | R | 2B | 3B | HR | RBI | BB | SO | SB | CS | AVG_OBP_SLG | TAv | BABIP | BRR | FRAA | WARP |
|------|------|-----|-----|-----|----|----|----|----|-----|----|-----|----|----|----------------|------|-------|------|--------------|------|
| 2009 | SLU | A+ | 22 | 255 | 28 | 17 | 3 | 7 | 28 | 31 | 52 | 0 | 2 | .288/.378/.486 | .306 | .350 | -1 | 5.3 | 1.9 |
| 2009 | BIN | AA | 22 | 233 | 30 | 14 | 0 | 13 | 43 | 26 | 60 | 0 | 0 | .309/.386/.565 | .329 | .381 | 0.6 | 4.3 | 2.4 |
| 2010 | NYN | MLB | 23 | 601 | 73 | 33 | 1 | 19 | 71 | 72 | 138 | 3 | 2 | .264/.351/.440 | .286 | .321 | 0.2 | 5.8 | 2.9 |
| 2011 | NYN | MLB | 24 | 149 | 20 | 8 | 1 | 7 | 25 | 17 | 31 | 0 | 0 | .302/.383/.543 | .321 | .344 | 1.7 | 1 | 1.5 |
| 2012 | NYN | MLB | 25 | 250 | 32 | 13 | 1 | 8 | 31 | 27 | 56 | 1 | 0 | .268/.349/.451 | .286 | .321 | -0.1 | 1B -1, RF -0 | 1.8 |

Following a promising rookie campaign in 2010, Davis seemed to be blossoming into a star until May 10, when he collided with David Wright as the two converged on a pop fly. What seemed like a standard ankle injury turned into a mystery for the ages, as every time it seemed like it was healing, Davis would report pain once again, and it got to the point where even a high-risk microfracture procedure was considered. In the end, rest seems to have finally healed Davis, who by November had resumed full workouts and reported no issues. If he can return to form in 2012, and improve against left-handers, he's the position player the Mets' future could hinge upon the most.

### Lucas Duda LF

Born: 2/3/1986 Age: 26
Bats: L Throws: R Height: 6' 6" Weight: 240
Breakout: 6% Improve: 39% Collapse: 7%
Attrition: 19% MLB: 83%

Comparables:
Roy Foster, Vic Wertz, Joe Mather

| YEAR | TEAM | LVL | AGE | PA | R | 2B | 3B | HR | RBI | BB | SO | SB | CS | AVG_OBP_SLG | TAv | BABIP | BRR | FRAA | WARP |
|------|------|-----|-----|-----|----|----|----|----|-----|----|----|----|----|----------------|------|-------|------|------------|------|
| 2009 | BIN | AA | 23 | 467 | 49 | 29 | 1 | 9 | 53 | 61 | 91 | 2 | 2 | .281/.383/.428 | .288 | .345 | -3.8 | 0.1 | 1.6 |
| 2010 | BIN | AA | 24 | 197 | 30 | 17 | 0 | 6 | 34 | 29 | 27 | 1 | 0 | .286/.413/.503 | .311 | .312 | 0.5 | 1.7 | 1.3 |
| 2010 | BUF | AAA | 24 | 298 | 44 | 23 | 2 | 17 | 53 | 31 | 57 | 0 | 0 | .314/.391/.610 | .321 | .347 | 0.6 | -4 | 2.0 |
| 2010 | NYN | MLB | 24 | 92 | 11 | 6 | 0 | 4 | 13 | 6 | 22 | 0 | 0 | .202/.261/.417 | .248 | .220 | 0.7 | -1.5 | -0.1 |
| 2011 | BUF | AAA | 25 | 157 | 22 | 8 | 0 | 10 | 24 | 23 | 27 | 0 | 0 | .302/.414/.597 | .335 | .309 | -1.1 | -2.9 | 1.3 |
| 2011 | NYN | MLB | 25 | 347 | 38 | 21 | 3 | 10 | 50 | 33 | 57 | 1 | 0 | .292/.370/.482 | .310 | .326 | -3.8 | -1.4 | 1.7 |
| 2012 | NYN | MLB | 26 | 357 | 46 | 21 | 1 | 12 | 45 | 35 | 68 | 0 | 0 | .270/.350/.455 | .286 | .307 | 0 | LF -4, 1B -2 | 2.1 |

Duda's athleticism, or lack thereof, is what dropped him to the seventh round of the 2007 draft. He's massive, and almost unbearably slow, so to make it in the big leagues as a bat-only player, he was going to have to *really* hit. That was the knock against him all along, but a funny thing happened over the last couple of years: While he was compiling a .310/.398/.606 line at Triple-A, scouts began to come over to his side. Why? Because he can *really* hit. While his power tends to disappear against left-handers, Duda has a surprisingly good contact rate for a huge man with a huge swing, and he's being handed the everyday right-field job in 2012. Don't be surprised one bit if he turns into one of the team's top offensive performers.

### Wilmer Flores SS

Born: 8/6/1991 Age: 20
Bats: R Throws: R Height: 6' 4" Weight: 175
Breakout: 1% Improve: 7% Collapse: 2%
Attrition: 4% MLB: 15%

Comparables:
Jose Flores, Robin Yount, Lonnie Chisenhall

| YEAR | TEAM | LVL | AGE | PA | R | 2B | 3B | HR | RBI | BB | SO | SB | CS | AVG_OBP_SLG | TAv | BABIP | BRR | FRAA | WARP |
|------|------|-----|-----|-----|----|----|----|----|-----|----|----|----|----|----------------|------|-------|------|------|------|
| 2009 | SAV | A | 17 | 528 | 44 | 20 | 2 | 3 | 36 | 22 | 72 | 3 | 3 | .264/.307/.332 | .248 | .303 | -3.1 | -6.8 | 0.8 |
| 2010 | SAV | A | 18 | 307 | 30 | 18 | 2 | 7 | 44 | 23 | 37 | 2 | 1 | .278/.344/.433 | .297 | .300 | -0.5 | -1.2 | 2.5 |
| 2010 | SLU | A+ | 18 | 290 | 32 | 18 | 1 | 4 | 40 | 9 | 40 | 2 | 4 | .300/.326/.415 | .253 | .339 | 0.4 | 0 | 1.1 |
| 2011 | SLU | A+ | 19 | 559 | 52 | 26 | 2 | 9 | 81 | 27 | 68 | 2 | 2 | .269/.309/.380 | .252 | .291 | -3.4 | 7.3 | 2.2 |
| 2012 | NYN | MLB | 20 | 250 | 23 | 11 | 1 | 2 | 22 | 6 | 44 | 0 | 0 | .236/.257/.319 | .208 | .275 | 0 | SS 4 | -0.5 |

Flores has gotten a lot of breaks as a prospect, as good seasons without power or walks were often given more praise than they deserved because Flores was consistently so young for his level. While he's still just 20, at some point you have to perform, and while Flores definitely has some hitting ability, he still undoes himself with an overly aggressive approach, and the power is still very much in the projection phase. Even more troubling is what he does in the field. He's growing, and there's been some significant thickening of his frame. There's no way he'll remain an up-the-middle player for long, and with first base or a corner outfield slot his most likely destination, it's time for the bat to start playing.

### Scott Hairston LF

Born: 5/25/1980 Age: 32
Bats: R Throws: R Height: 6' 1" Weight: 190
Breakout: 1% Improve: 24% Collapse: 6%
Attrition: 17% MLB: 77%

Comparables:
Jose Guillen, Ryan Church, Tim Tolman

| YEAR | TEAM | LVL | AGE | PA | R | 2B | 3B | HR | RBI | BB | SO | SB | CS | AVG_OBP_SLG | TAv | BABIP | BRR | FRAA | WARP |
|------|------|-----|-----|-----|----|----|----|----|-----|----|----|----|----|----------------|------|-------|------|-----------|------|
| 2009 | SDN | MLB | 29 | 216 | 26 | 14 | 1 | 10 | 29 | 17 | 45 | 8 | 1 | .299/.358/.533 | .309 | .345 | 0.3 | -3.1 | 1.3 |
| 2009 | OAK | MLB | 29 | 248 | 24 | 13 | 1 | 7 | 35 | 8 | 38 | 3 | 2 | .236/.262/.391 | .236 | .249 | -2.5 | 3.3 | 0.0 |
| 2010 | SDN | MLB | 30 | 336 | 34 | 10 | 1 | 10 | 36 | 31 | 69 | 6 | 1 | .210/.295/.346 | .253 | .236 | -0.7 | 0.3 | 0.3 |
| 2011 | NYN | MLB | 31 | 145 | 20 | 8 | 1 | 7 | 24 | 11 | 34 | 1 | 1 | .235/.303/.470 | .273 | .264 | -0.5 | -0.3 | 0.4 |
| 2012 | NYN | MLB | 32 | 250 | 28 | 11 | 1 | 8 | 29 | 19 | 53 | 5 | 2 | .239/.303/.407 | .254 | .274 | 0 | LF 1, CF -1 | 0.9 |

Signed for a bench role, Hairston did just that in 2011 before a season-ending oblique injury, backing up at all three outfield positions and being one of Terry Collins' most oft-used pinch-hitters while providing his usual offense, which consists of a low batting average combined with a bit of power. It's what he is, it's what he's been for years, and as he turns 32 in May, nothing is going to change. He was a free agent at press time.

| | | | | | | | | | | | | | | | | | | |
|---|---|---|---|---|---|---|---|---|---|---|---|---|---|---|---|---|---|---|
| **Willie Harris** | **LF** | YEAR | TEAM | LVL | AGE | PA | R | 2B | 3B | HR | RBI | BB | SO | SB | CS | AVG/OBP/SLG | TAv | BABIP | BRR | FRAA | WARP |

| YEAR | TEAM | LVL | AGE | PA | R | 2B | 3B | HR | RBI | BB | SO | SB | CS | AVG/OBP/SLG | TAv | BABIP | BRR | FRAA | WARP |
|---|---|---|---|---|---|---|---|---|---|---|---|---|---|---|---|---|---|---|---|
| 2009 | WAS | MLB | 31 | 393 | 47 | 18 | 6 | 7 | 27 | 57 | 62 | 11 | 4 | .235/.364/.393 | .267 | .271 | -1.3 | -1.5 | 1.1 |
| 2010 | WAS | MLB | 32 | 262 | 25 | 6 | 2 | 10 | 32 | 33 | 60 | 5 | 2 | .183/.291/.362 | .229 | .199 | 1.2 | 1 | -0.2 |
| 2011 | NYN | MLB | 33 | 283 | 36 | 11 | 0 | 2 | 23 | 36 | 62 | 5 | 4 | .246/.351/.317 | .252 | .320 | -0.9 | -0.7 | 0.3 |
| 2012 | NYN | MLB | 34 | 262 | 29 | 10 | 2 | 4 | 23 | 30 | 49 | 7 | 3 | .238/.334/.359 | .255 | .282 | -0.5 | LF -0, CF 1 | 0.9 |

**Willie Harris** LF
Born: 6/22/1978 Age: 34
Bats: L Throws: R Height: 5' 10" Weight: 175
Breakout: 2% Improve: 40% Collapse: 9%
Attrition: 30% MLB: 86%

**Comparables:**
Minnie Minoso, Roy White, Brian Downing

It's hard to believe that Harris has lasted 11 years in the big leagues. It's a tribute to two things: versatility, and the ability to take a walk. Harris played second, third, and all three outfield positions in 2011, and while he hit just .246, his .351 on-base percentage gave him some value at the plate. He's also reportedly one hell of a guy, and while we have no number to measure that kind of thing, it's certainly worth something.

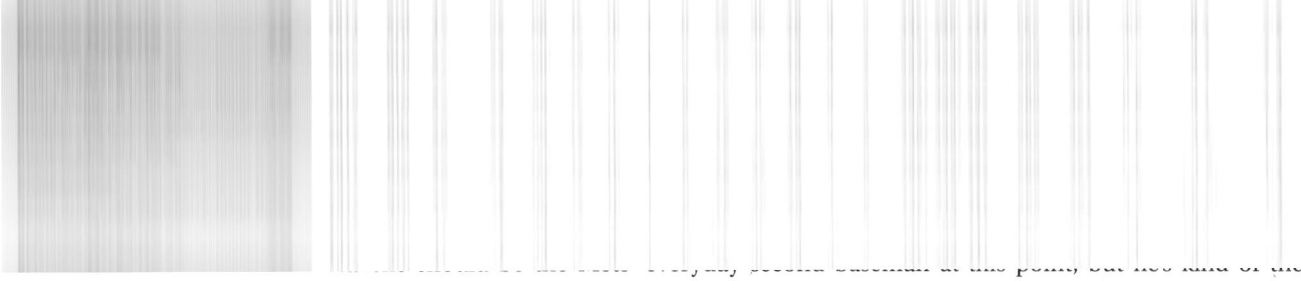

Fernando Martinez of infield prospects in the Mets system, playing a grand total of 190 games in his three full seasons, including just 61 in 2011 as he recovered from 2010 rib surgery and then some late-season back issues. The sad thing is, when he's healthy, he can do a lot of things with the bat, with patience at the plate and above-average power for the position. If he can ever stay healthy, he's got the potential to be the long-term answer at second, but every year he plays just 60 or so games, that becomes a bigger if.

**Rob Johnson** C
Born: 7/22/1983 Age: 28
Bats: R Throws: R Height: 6' 2" Weight: 200
Breakout: 8% Improve: 31% Collapse: 10%
Attrition: 43% MLB: 68%

**Comparables:**
Jake Gibbs, Charlie O'Brien, Chris Denove

| YEAR | TEAM | LVL | AGE | PA | R | 2B | 3B | HR | RBI | BB | SO | SB | CS | AVG/OBP/SLG | TAv | BABIP | BRR | FRAA | WARP |
|---|---|---|---|---|---|---|---|---|---|---|---|---|---|---|---|---|---|---|---|
| 2009 | SEA | MLB | 25 | 290 | 21 | 19 | 2 | 2 | 27 | 26 | 60 | 1 | 1 | .213/.289/.326 | .215 | .269 | -2 | -0.3 | -0.2 |
| 2010 | TAC | AAA | 26 | 77 | 9 | 7 | 0 | 1 | 8 | 10 | 12 | 0 | 0 | .297/.408/.453 | .288 | .353 | -0.6 | 0.5 | 0.6 |
| 2010 | SEA | MLB | 26 | 209 | 24 | 10 | 0 | 2 | 13 | 25 | 46 | 1 | 1 | .191/.293/.281 | .221 | .241 | -0.9 | -1.6 | 0.0 |
| 2011 | SDN | MLB | 27 | 199 | 9 | 6 | 1 | 3 | 16 | 14 | 58 | 3 | 0 | .190/.259/.285 | .199 | .261 | 0.1 | 2.8 | -0.1 |
| 2012 | NYN | MLB | 28 | 250 | 24 | 12 | 1 | 2 | 20 | 20 | 51 | 2 | 1 | .226/.292/.314 | .221 | .279 | -0.2 | C 1 | 0.2 |

Johnson is a dreadful hitter. On days when both he and Alberto Gonzalez were in the Padres lineup, a strong case could be made to bat the pitcher seventh. Johnson has neither plate discipline nor power. If there is a bright side, it's that his poor on-base skills keep him from clogging the basepaths. He doesn't throw particularly well, but pitchers like working with him. Johnson is better than Jeff Mathis but worse than Gary Bennett, which puts him in the sweet spot of catchers who hang around forever for no obvious reason. The Mets signed him as insurance in case intended backup Mike Nickeas just flat out doesn't hit.

**Juan Lagares** LF
Born: 3/17/1989 Age: 23
Bats: R Throws: R Height: 6' 2" Weight: 175
Breakout: 4% Improve: 15% Collapse: 6%
Attrition: 14% MLB: 31%

**Comparables:**
Derrell Griffith, Leo Sutherland, Jake Shaffer

| YEAR | TEAM | LVL | AGE | PA | R | 2B | 3B | HR | RBI | BB | SO | SB | CS | AVG/OBP/SLG | TAv | BABIP | BRR | FRAA | WARP |
|---|---|---|---|---|---|---|---|---|---|---|---|---|---|---|---|---|---|---|---|
| 2009 | SAV | A | 20 | 177 | 23 | 6 | 2 | 0 | 13 | 6 | 42 | 9 | 4 | .274/.307/.333 | .258 | .365 | 0.3 | 2.8 | 0.6 |
| 2010 | SAV | A | 21 | 307 | 42 | 13 | 9 | 5 | 39 | 7 | 44 | 18 | 2 | .300/.321/.459 | .308 | .337 | 3.9 | 3.8 | 3.5 |
| 2010 | SLU | A+ | 21 | 137 | 16 | 5 | 0 | 2 | 16 | 2 | 18 | 7 | 3 | .233/.250/.316 | .205 | .257 | 0.6 | 0.2 | 0.0 |
| 2011 | SLU | A+ | 22 | 335 | 51 | 15 | 6 | 7 | 49 | 21 | 47 | 5 | 6 | .338/.380/.494 | .301 | .379 | -0.2 | 0.2 | 2.3 |
| 2011 | BIN | AA | 22 | 170 | 21 | 11 | 3 | 2 | 22 | 5 | 29 | 10 | 2 | .370/.391/.512 | .302 | .439 | 0.7 | 4.7 | 1.7 |
| 2012 | NYN | MLB | 23 | 250 | 25 | 10 | 3 | 3 | 25 | 5 | 51 | 6 | 2 | .255/.270/.350 | .221 | .308 | -0.1 | LF -1, RF 1 | -0.8 |

Legares began his career as a shortstop, but his bat was always ahead of his glove. He ended up a corner outfielder with contact ability but a tendency to swing at everything, and we mean everything: In 444 plate appearances in 2010, he drew a grand total of nine walks. His 26 in 2011 still stinks, but it almost qualifies as a transformation for Legares, who, more importantly, by just becoming a bit more selective, turned into a dangerous hitter. He still needs to improve his secondary skills, but he's at least turned himself into a prospect.

| Adam Loewen RF | YEAR | TEAM | LVL | AGE | PA | R | 2B | 3B | HR | RBI | BB | SO | SB | CS | AVG_OBP_SLG | TAv | BABIP | BRR | FRAA | WARP |
|---|---|---|---|---|---|---|---|---|---|---|---|---|---|---|---|---|---|---|---|---|
| Born: 4/9/1984 Age: 28 | 2009 | DUN | A+ | 25 | 391 | 47 | 22 | 3 | 4 | 31 | 50 | 114 | 5 | 2 | .236/.342/.355 | .256 | .346 | -1.9 | 0.4 | 0.3 |
| Bats: L Throws: L Height: 6' 6" Weight: 235 | 2010 | NHP | AA | 26 | 537 | 70 | 31 | 3 | 13 | 70 | 66 | 142 | 17 | 6 | .246/.351/.412 | .258 | .328 | 1.7 | 0 | 0.8 |
| Breakout: 4% Improve: 35% Collapse: 13% | 2011 | LVG | AAA | 27 | 585 | 83 | 46 | 4 | 17 | 85 | 61 | 136 | 11 | 7 | .306/.377/.508 | .289 | .384 | 1.6 | -2.7 | 2.8 |
| Attrition: 31% MLB: 74% | 2011 | TOR | MLB | 27 | 37 | 4 | 1 | 0 | 1 | 4 | 3 | 13 | 0 | 0 | .188/.297/.312 | .227 | .278 | 0.1 | 0.4 | 0.1 |
| **Comparables:**<br>Al Ferrara, Will Venable, Willie Crawford | 2012 | NYN | MLB | 28 | 250 | 27 | 13 | 1 | 5 | 24 | 23 | 73 | 4 | 2 | .228/.305/.358 | .241 | .313 | -0.2 | RF -0, LF -1 | -0.1 |

Everybody loves pitching prospects turned hitting prospects, but the fact is they face more challenges than other players. They are older and have to relearn skills they haven't used in years. Chronic elbow injuries led to Loewen's conversion to right field. His arm is healthy enough that he had 11 outfield assists in 111 games in the outfield, but most of the improvement in his bat was due to the move to the PCL. That being said, Loewen made it back to the majors and recorded his first hit as a position player in September. His 67 extra-base hits should be enough to extend his comeback attempt another year.

| Fernando Martinez RF | YEAR | TEAM | LVL | AGE | PA | R | 2B | 3B | HR | RBI | BB | SO | SB | CS | AVG_OBP_SLG | TAv | BABIP | BRR | FRAA | WARP |
|---|---|---|---|---|---|---|---|---|---|---|---|---|---|---|---|---|---|---|---|---|
| Born: 10/10/1988 Age: 23 | 2009 | BUF | AAA | 20 | 190 | 24 | 16 | 2 | 8 | 28 | 11 | 33 | 2 | 1 | .290/.339/.540 | .299 | .319 | 0.2 | -1.2 | 0.9 |
| Bats: L Throws: R Height: 6' 2" Weight: 190 | 2009 | NYN | MLB | 20 | 100 | 11 | 6 | 0 | 1 | 8 | 5 | 14 | 2 | 0 | .176/.242/.275 | .212 | .197 | 0.3 | -0.8 | -0.4 |
| Breakout: 7% Improve: 49% Collapse: 3% | 2010 | BUF | AAA | 21 | 287 | 39 | 16 | 0 | 12 | 33 | 17 | 65 | 1 | 0 | .253/.316/.455 | .252 | .290 | -0.8 | 0.4 | 0.1 |
| Attrition: 14% MLB: 67% | 2010 | NYN | MLB | 21 | 22 | 1 | 0 | 0 | 0 | 2 | 1 | 5 | 0 | 1 | .167/.273/.167 | .198 | .214 | -0.2 | -0.1 | -0.2 |
| **Comparables:**<br>Kellen Kulbacki, Benny Distefano, Domonic Brown | 2011 | BUF | AAA | 22 | 250 | 29 | 11 | 0 | 8 | 30 | 18 | 60 | 0 | 0 | .260/.329/.417 | .242 | .318 | -2.9 | -0.5 | -0.5 |
| | 2011 | NYN | MLB | 22 | 23 | 3 | 2 | 0 | 1 | 2 | 1 | 7 | 0 | 0 | .227/.261/.455 | .260 | .286 | 0.4 | -0.1 | 0.1 |
| | 2012 | HOU | MLB | 23 | 250 | 28 | 13 | 1 | 7 | 29 | 15 | 53 | 1 | 1 | .247/.304/.405 | .255 | .287 | -0.1 | RF -1, LF -1 | 0.7 |

Another year, and more injuries for Martinez. How much has Martinez been injured? He's 23 years old and missed time in 2011 due to soreness in his arthritic knees. While never blazing, he simply can't run anymore, his swing has lost all fluidity, and he's just not much of a prospect any longer. He's really not on the radar of the Mets or anyone else. We're just left with tales of what could have been.

| Daniel Murphy 1B | YEAR | TEAM | LVL | AGE | PA | R | 2B | 3B | HR | RBI | BB | SO | SB | CS | AVG_OBP_SLG | TAv | BABIP | BRR | FRAA | WARP |
|---|---|---|---|---|---|---|---|---|---|---|---|---|---|---|---|---|---|---|---|---|
| Born: 4/1/1985 Age: 27 | 2009 | NYN | MLB | 24 | 556 | 60 | 38 | 4 | 12 | 63 | 38 | 69 | 4 | 2 | .266/.313/.427 | .255 | .284 | 3.8 | 5.7 | 1.1 |
| Bats: L Throws: R Height: 6' 4" Weight: 210 | 2011 | NYN | MLB | 26 | 423 | 49 | 28 | 2 | 6 | 49 | 24 | 42 | 5 | 5 | .320/.362/.448 | .282 | .345 | -3.3 | 0.4 | 1.6 |
| Breakout: 1% Improve: 37% Collapse: 4% | 2012 | NYN | MLB | 27 | 319 | 40 | 20 | 2 | 6 | 38 | 22 | 39 | 4 | 2 | .290/.340/.433 | .275 | .314 | -0.4 | 1B 1, 3B 1 | 1.7 |
| Attrition: 15% MLB: 83% | | | | | | | | | | | | | | | | | | | | |
| **Comparables:**<br>Wally Joyner, Rafael Palmeiro, James Loney | | | | | | | | | | | | | | | | | | | | |

After a lost 2010 season due to knee problems, Murphy was a long shot to make the team, but he ended up getting more than 400 plate appearances as a fill-in guy, whether for the injured Ike Davis and David Wright on the corners, or as one of the many who got an audition at second base. Even more remarkable is the fact that he hit .320, although it came without walks or power. Nobody thinks he'll do that again, not even the Mets, but he does have big-league value as a player who can play multiple positions and hit a bit, which will be his role once again in 2012.

| Mike Nickeas C | YEAR | TEAM | LVL | AGE | PA | R | 2B | 3B | HR | RBI | BB | SO | SB | CS | AVG_OBP_SLG | TAv | BABIP | BRR | FRAA | WARP |
|---|---|---|---|---|---|---|---|---|---|---|---|---|---|---|---|---|---|---|---|---|
| Born: 2/13/1983 Age: 29 | 2009 | BIN | AA | 26 | 67 | 3 | 1 | 0 | 0 | 7 | 9 | 9 | 0 | 0 | .182/.288/.200 | .199 | .208 | -0.2 | 0.6 | -0.1 |
| Bats: R Throws: R Height: 6' 1" Weight: 210 | 2010 | BIN | AA | 27 | 318 | 27 | 15 | 0 | 5 | 33 | 49 | 43 | 1 | 1 | .283/.403/.396 | .288 | .323 | -2.1 | 0.3 | 2.2 |
| Breakout: 2% Improve: 20% Collapse: 11% | 2010 | NYN | MLB | 27 | 10 | 0 | 0 | 0 | 0 | 0 | 0 | 5 | 0 | 0 | .200/.200/.200 | .119 | .400 | 0 | 0 | -0.1 |
| Attrition: 33% MLB: 67% | 2011 | BUF | AAA | 28 | 192 | 15 | 9 | 0 | 2 | 15 | 16 | 27 | 0 | 0 | .214/.286/.304 | .206 | .239 | 0.1 | 0.7 | -0.2 |
| **Comparables:**<br>Johnny Estrada, Marv Foley, Johnny Bucha | 2011 | NYN | MLB | 28 | 59 | 4 | 1 | 0 | 1 | 6 | 4 | 11 | 0 | 1 | .189/.246/.264 | .202 | .220 | 0.6 | -0.2 | 0.0 |
| | 2012 | NYN | MLB | 29 | 250 | 24 | 10 | 1 | 2 | 20 | 19 | 46 | 1 | 0 | .228/.289/.313 | .221 | .270 | -0.1 | C 0, 1B -0 | 0.2 |

Nickeas can't hit. Never has. In 527 career minor-league games, he has a batting line of .237/.329/.342, and it actually gets worse at every level. Still, he played 21 big-league games last year—not hitting, of course—and could end up competing for a backup job in the spring. How does this happen? Nickeas can catch. He's an excellent receiver with a good arm, pitchers love throwing to him, and if you made a list of current players most likely to turn into coaches and managers, he'd be one of the first considered. He might or might not remain in the major leagues, but he could be around baseball for a very long time.

**Kirk Nieuwenhuis** CF
Born: 8/7/1987 Age: 24
Bats: L Throws: R Height: 6' 4" Weight: 215
Breakout: 6% Improve: 44% Collapse: 0%
Attrition: 11% MLB: 86%
**Comparables:**
Joe Wallis, Steve Whitaker, Dave Henderson

| YEAR | TEAM | LVL | AGE | PA | R | 2B | 3B | HR | RBI | BB | SO | SB | CS | AVG_OBP_SLG | TAv | BABIP | BRR | FRAA | WARP |
|------|------|-----|-----|-----|----|----|----|----|-----|----|-----|----|----|-------------|-----|-------|------|-----------|------|
| 2009 | SLU | A+ | 21 | 547 | 91 | 35 | 5 | 16 | 71 | 53 | 118 | 16 | 4 | .274/.357/.467 | .279 | .332 | 1.3 | -3.3 | 2.3 |
| 2010 | BIN | AA | 22 | 433 | 81 | 35 | 2 | 16 | 60 | 30 | 93 | 13 | 7 | .289/.339/.510 | .295 | .340 | -0.2 | 15.2 | 4.2 |
| 2010 | BUF | AAA | 22 | 133 | 10 | 8 | 1 | 2 | 17 | 11 | 39 | 0 | 0 | .225/.293/.358 | .232 | .312 | 0.2 | -3.9 | -0.1 |
| 2011 | BUF | AAA | 23 | 221 | 33 | 17 | 2 | 6 | 14 | 32 | 59 | 5 | 2 | .298/.403/.505 | .299 | .407 | -0.2 | 0.3 | 1.6 |
| 2012 | NYN | MLB | 24 | 250 | 29 | 14 | 1 | 6 | 29 | 19 | 65 | 5 | 2 | .248/.309/.407 | .255 | .315 | -0.2 | CF -3, RF -0 | 1.1 |

His difficult last name has him more commonly referred to as Captain Kirk among the faithful, but unfortunately, Nieuwenhuis spent too much time in the sick bay with Dr. McCoy in 2011. A torn labrum required surgery early in the year, limiting him to just 53 games. The good news is that in those 53 games, Nieuwenhuis not only proved that

**Comparables:**
Jimmie Coker, Yorvit Torrealba, John Wathan

Paulino was the bottom part of the catching platoon in 2011, getting the majority of playing time against left-handers, not that he's especially deft against them. He's a tribute to a dearth of catching in baseball, as he's not especially good at anything, either at the plate or behind it, and he did himself no favors with his employers with his attitude. Teams need catchers, even bad ones, but when picking through the scrap heap, they're going to take the nice guy over the one who, at one point in a late-season game, almost refused to pinch-hit. Thus, the Mets cut ties with Paulino in December.

**Ruben Tejada** SS
Born: 10/27/1989 Age: 22
Bats: R Throws: R Height: 6' 0" Weight: 160
Breakout: 1% Improve: 24% Collapse: 6%
Attrition: 22% MLB: 62%
**Comparables:**
Bobby Valentine, Juan Beniquez, Milt Ramirez

| YEAR | TEAM | LVL | AGE | PA | R | 2B | 3B | HR | RBI | BB | SO | SB | CS | AVG_OBP_SLG | TAv | BABIP | BRR | FRAA | WARP |
|------|------|-----|-----|-----|----|----|----|----|-----|----|----|----|----|-------------|-----|-------|------|-----------|------|
| 2009 | BIN | AA | 19 | 553 | 59 | 24 | 3 | 5 | 46 | 37 | 59 | 19 | 3 | .289/.343/.381 | .256 | .310 | 0.7 | -8.6 | 1.2 |
| 2010 | BUF | AAA | 20 | 244 | 25 | 11 | 0 | 1 | 16 | 14 | 36 | 1 | 3 | .280/.322/.344 | .228 | .319 | 0.6 | 4 | 0.5 |
| 2010 | NYN | MLB | 20 | 255 | 28 | 12 | 0 | 1 | 15 | 22 | 38 | 2 | 2 | .213/.305/.282 | .220 | .250 | 2.2 | -0.1 | -0.1 |
| 2011 | BUF | AAA | 21 | 231 | 26 | 7 | 3 | 3 | 21 | 19 | 30 | 4 | 2 | .246/.314/.353 | .229 | .274 | 1.6 | -2.6 | -0.1 |
| 2011 | NYN | MLB | 21 | 376 | 31 | 15 | 1 | 0 | 36 | 35 | 50 | 5 | 1 | .284/.360/.335 | .271 | .331 | 1.8 | 0.2 | 2.1 |
| 2012 | NYN | MLB | 22 | 391 | 42 | 17 | 1 | 2 | 32 | 27 | 54 | 6 | 2 | .263/.324/.339 | .242 | .297 | -0.2 | SS -1, 2B 0 | 0.8 |

Tejada should assume shortstop duties in Queens with Jose Reyes gone to Miami, and on paper, he should be the cause for plenty of excitement. As a 21-year-old, he had a better season in the big leagues than Reyes did at the same age. Unfortunately, Tejada has always been a player whose polish far outweighs his tools. His offensive value comes from his ability to work the count and make contact, as he has no power and is merely an average runner. His defense is more notable for fundamentals than flashiness. The total package will keep him in the big leagues for a very long time, but always as a guy playing because his team can't find something better.

**Josh Thole** C
Born: 10/28/1986 Age: 25
Bats: L Throws: R Height: 6' 2" Weight: 205
Breakout: 4% Improve: 50% Collapse: 1%
Attrition: 30% MLB: 89%
**Comparables:**
Bob Barton, Bengie Molina, Biff Pocoroba

| YEAR | TEAM | LVL | AGE | PA | R | 2B | 3B | HR | RBI | BB | SO | SB | CS | AVG_OBP_SLG | TAv | BABIP | BRR | FRAA | WARP |
|------|------|-----|-----|-----|----|----|----|----|-----|----|----|----|----|-------------|-----|-------|------|---------|------|
| 2009 | BIN | AA | 22 | 442 | 48 | 29 | 2 | 1 | 46 | 42 | 34 | 8 | 4 | .328/.402/.422 | .287 | .357 | -1.8 | 1.3 | 3.1 |
| 2009 | NYN | MLB | 22 | 59 | 2 | 2 | 1 | 0 | 9 | 4 | 5 | 1 | 0 | .321/.356/.396 | .269 | .340 | -0.7 | -0.2 | 0.2 |
| 2010 | BUF | AAA | 23 | 191 | 20 | 19 | 1 | 2 | 17 | 22 | 25 | 0 | 0 | .267/.354/.430 | .267 | .302 | -1.3 | -1.3 | 0.7 |
| 2010 | NYN | MLB | 23 | 227 | 17 | 7 | 1 | 3 | 17 | 24 | 25 | 1 | 0 | .277/.357/.366 | .252 | .305 | 1.1 | 1.6 | 1.2 |
| 2011 | NYN | MLB | 24 | 386 | 22 | 17 | 0 | 3 | 40 | 38 | 47 | 0 | 2 | .268/.345/.344 | .255 | .300 | -3 | 1.9 | 1.2 |
| 2012 | NYN | MLB | 25 | 331 | 38 | 16 | 1 | 2 | 29 | 29 | 36 | 2 | 1 | .281/.348/.367 | .260 | .310 | -0.2 | C 1, 1B -0 | 2.0 |

With no other options, the Mets made Thole their primary catcher in 2011, but in platoon form only, as he was kept away from left-handed pitchers while delivering a performance that was perfectly Thole-esque. He draws a fair number of walks, rarely strikes out, and laces balls all over the park, but with power that can almost be described as nonexistent, he doesn't have offensive value unless he's hitting closer to .300 than .250. Throw in poor receiving skills and a below-average arm, and he's nothing more than filler, but the kind of filler who will likely stick around for another decade or so simply because he's willing to wear the tools of ignorance.

**Andres Torres**  CF

Born: 1/26/1978 Age: 34
Bats: B Throws: R Height: 5' 11" Weight: 175
Breakout: 1% Improve: 18% Collapse: 8%
Attrition: 17% MLB: 89%

**Comparables:**
Adam Hyzdu, Fred Lynn, Amos Otis

| YEAR | TEAM | LVL | AGE | PA | R | 2B | 3B | HR | RBI | BB | SO | SB | CS | AVG_OBP_SLG | TAv | BABIP | BRR | FRAA | WARP |
|------|------|-----|-----|-----|----|----|----|----|-----|----|-----|----|----|-------------|------|-------|-----|---------|------|
| 2009 | SFN | MLB | 31 | 170 | 30 | 6 | 8 | 6 | 23 | 16 | 45 | 6 | 1 | .270/.343/.533 | .295 | .347 | 1.1 | 3.2 | 1.5 |
| 2010 | SFN | MLB | 32 | 570 | 84 | 43 | 8 | 16 | 63 | 56 | 128 | 26 | 7 | .268/.343/.479 | .284 | .331 | 7.8 | 9 | 4.7 |
| 2011 | FRE | AAA | 33 | 62 | 10 | 2 | 2 | 4 | 11 | 6 | 13 | 1 | 0 | .273/.355/.600 | .301 | .289 | 1 | 0.8 | 0.6 |
| 2011 | SFN | MLB | 33 | 398 | 50 | 24 | 1 | 4 | 19 | 42 | 95 | 19 | 6 | .221/.312/.330 | .242 | .293 | 5.5 | 0.8 | 1.3 |
| 2012 | NYN | MLB | 34 | 417 | 47 | 22 | 5 | 8 | 44 | 38 | 103 | 17 | 5 | .240/.315/.390 | .251 | .306 | 0 | CF 5, RF 2 | 0.9 |

Torres's power deserted him in 2011—not just the lost home runs, which you can see, but an entire spray chart creeping in ominously. It's those lazy fly balls that make it impossible to brush aside his BABIP drop or put too much hope in a still-strong walk rate. His bat has slowed, especially from the right side, though the regression isn't for lack of effort. Torres is a workout fiend who worried the Giants coaching staff with how much pressure he put on himself during slumps. He had to take sleeping pills to get rest in 2011. As a leadoff hitter, he was a destructive part of the Giants' league-worst offense; as an excellent center fielder making just $2.2 million, he was still a bargain. After another arbitration raise, the Giants' trade for Melky Cabrera, and the impending ascension of Gary Brown, the Giants dealt him to the Mets, where his loss of power could become even more worrisome if the new dimensions don't lead to expected results.

**Justin Turner**  2B

Born: 11/23/1984 Age: 27
Bats: R Throws: R Height: 6' 0" Weight: 180
Breakout: 3% Improve: 32% Collapse: 17%
Attrition: 30% MLB: 87%

**Comparables:**
Eric Young, Craig Counsell, Jarrett Hoffpauir

| YEAR | TEAM | LVL | AGE | PA | R | 2B | 3B | HR | RBI | BB | SO | SB | CS | AVG_OBP_SLG | TAv | BABIP | BRR | FRAA | WARP |
|------|------|-----|-----|-----|----|----|----|----|-----|----|----|----|----|-------------|------|-------|-----|----------|------|
| 2009 | NOR | AAA | 24 | 441 | 54 | 28 | 0 | 2 | 43 | 34 | 37 | 9 | 4 | .300/.365/.388 | .267 | .324 | 1.7 | 1.4 | 1.8 |
| 2009 | BAL | MLB | 24 | 22 | 2 | 0 | 0 | 0 | 3 | 4 | 3 | 0 | 0 | .167/.318/.167 | .212 | .200 | 1 | 0 | 0.0 |
| 2010 | BUF | AAA | 25 | 348 | 58 | 22 | 1 | 11 | 35 | 24 | 38 | 5 | 3 | .333/.387/.516 | .301 | .348 | -0.5 | -5.3 | 2.1 |
| 2010 | NOR | AAA | 25 | 95 | 11 | 8 | 0 | 1 | 8 | 9 | 13 | 2 | 0 | .250/.319/.381 | .248 | .282 | -0.3 | 3.5 | 0.5 |
| 2010 | BAL | MLB | 25 | 9 | 0 | 0 | 0 | 0 | 0 | 0 | 3 | 0 | 0 | .000/.000/.000 | .006 | .000 | 0 | -0.1 | -0.2 |
| 2010 | NYN | MLB | 25 | 9 | 1 | 1 | 0 | 0 | 0 | 1 | 0 | 0 | 0 | .125/.222/.250 | .179 | .125 | 0 | -0.1 | 0.0 |
| 2011 | NYN | MLB | 26 | 487 | 49 | 30 | 0 | 4 | 51 | 39 | 59 | 7 | 2 | .260/.334/.356 | .253 | .292 | 0.9 | -0.4 | 1.0 |
| 2012 | NYN | MLB | 27 | 369 | 41 | 21 | 1 | 3 | 33 | 28 | 44 | 5 | 2 | .265/.332/.360 | .254 | .294 | -0.1 | 2B -1, 3B -2 | 1.3 |

The revolving door at second base for the Mets in 2011 finally stopped in late May with Turner, who held onto the job simply by being not awful. He's one of those college second baseman who played a big role at a big program (Cal State Fullerton) and is loved by teams for his grit and energy and love of the game and all that jazz. Those are wonderful qualities, but they can only get you so far, and Turner is low on tools. You're already looking at his upside, which means the Mets should already be looking for his replacement.

**Jordany Valdespin**  SS

Born: 12/23/1987 Age: 24
Bats: L Throws: R Height: 6' 1" Weight: 190
Breakout: 5% Improve: 24% Collapse: 8%
Attrition: 27% MLB: 77%

**Comparables:**
Alvaro Espinoza, Eddie Miksis, Angel Chavez

| YEAR | TEAM | LVL | AGE | PA | R | 2B | 3B | HR | RBI | BB | SO | SB | CS | AVG_OBP_SLG | TAv | BABIP | BRR | FRAA | WARP |
|------|------|-----|-----|-----|----|----|----|----|-----|----|----|----|----|-------------|------|-------|------|----------|------|
| 2009 | SAV | A | 21 | 164 | 30 | 9 | 3 | 3 | 18 | 11 | 32 | 7 | 2 | .322/.368/.480 | .318 | .393 | 4.2 | 1.2 | 2.2 |
| 2009 | BRO | A- | 21 | 76 | 10 | 3 | 1 | 1 | 5 | 5 | 16 | 4 | 3 | .279/.329/.397 | .271 | .340 | 0.8 | 2.3 | 0.8 |
| 2010 | SLU | A+ | 22 | 288 | 40 | 16 | 3 | 6 | 33 | 8 | 45 | 13 | 10 | .289/.321/.437 | .268 | .324 | 0.5 | 0 | 1.3 |
| 2010 | BIN | AA | 22 | 117 | 8 | 8 | 0 | 0 | 8 | 2 | 23 | 4 | 2 | .232/.241/.304 | .183 | .286 | 0.6 | -2 | -0.8 |
| 2011 | BIN | AA | 23 | 441 | 62 | 24 | 3 | 15 | 51 | 21 | 68 | 33 | 14 | .297/.341/.483 | .282 | .325 | 1.5 | -5.2 | 2.2 |
| 2011 | BUF | AAA | 23 | 113 | 7 | 8 | 0 | 2 | 9 | 4 | 25 | 4 | 4 | .280/.304/.411 | .242 | .346 | -1.6 | -0.5 | 0.0 |
| 2012 | NYN | MLB | 24 | 250 | 26 | 12 | 1 | 5 | 27 | 7 | 50 | 11 | 5 | .253/.278/.375 | .231 | .296 | -0.8 | SS -3, 2B 0 | 0.1 |

One of the more intriguing prospects in the system, Valdespin offers both power and speed from the middle of the diamond, but his game is best characterized as out of control. Along with the power comes a horrible approach, his 37 stolen bases in 2011 were offset by 18 caught stealing, and his defensive play still revolves more around his athleticism than fundamentals, leading to plenty of sloppy errors. He's a bit of a spectacular mess, but there is certainly potential here if he can just take a deep breath once in a while.

**David Wright**    3B
Born: 12/20/1982 Age: 29
Bats: R Throws: R Height: 6' 1'' Weight: 200
Breakout: 2% Improve: 38% Collapse: 2%
Attrition: 13% MLB: 94%

Comparables:
Hank Thompson, Rico Petrocelli, Jack Lohrke

| YEAR | TEAM | LVL | AGE | PA | R | 2B | 3B | HR | RBI | BB | SO | SB | CS | AVG_OBP_SLG | TAv | BABIP | BRR | FRAA | WARP |
|------|------|-----|-----|-----|----|----|----|----|-----|----|-----|----|----|-------------|-----|-------|-----|------|------|
| 2009 | NYN | MLB | 26 | 618 | 88 | 39 | 3 | 10 | 72 | 74 | 140 | 27 | 9 | .307/.390/.447 | .294 | .394 | 3 | -9.3 | 3.3 |
| 2010 | NYN | MLB | 27 | 670 | 87 | 36 | 3 | 29 | 103 | 69 | 161 | 19 | 11 | .283/.354/.503 | .302 | .335 | 0.1 | -0.9 | 5.0 |
| 2011 | NYN | MLB | 28 | 447 | 60 | 23 | 1 | 14 | 61 | 52 | 97 | 13 | 2 | .254/.345/.427 | .283 | .302 | -2.1 | -11.4 | 0.9 |
| 2012 | NYN | MLB | 29 | 468 | 63 | 25 | 2 | 16 | 60 | 54 | 92 | 15 | 5 | .287/.372/.472 | .302 | .335 | -0.2 | 3B -4, SS -0 | 3.9 |

The last three seasons have been the three worst of Wright's career, with 2011 tough for him not only on a performance level, but also as the first in which he dealt with a long-term injury. A stress fracture in his lower back cost him more than two months. The new park doesn't help him, and the Mets hope to address that by moving the fences in, but the general feeling on Wright seems to have gone from face of the franchise to potential trade chip come July if the new dimensions lead to a return to form.

Comparables:
Jeff Reardon, Mel Rojas, Tug McGraw

| YEAR | TEAM | LVL | AGE | W | L | SV | G | GS | IP | H | HR | BB | SO | EqBB9 | EqSO9 | GB% | BABIP | WHIP | ERA | FIP | FRA | WARP |
|------|------|-----|-----|---|---|----|----|----|----|----|----|----|----|-------|-------|-----|-------|------|-----|-----|-----|------|
| 2011 | BUF | AAA | 30 | 1 | 0 | 4 | 20 | 0 | 20¹ | 13 | 0 | 17 | 27 | 7.5 | 12.0 | 47% | .295 | 1.48 | 1.77 | 3.09 | 4.48 | 0.2 |
| 2011 | NYN | MLB | 30 | 4 | 1 | 4 | 44 | 0 | 47 | 50 | 6 | 15 | 46 | 2.9 | 8.8 | 38% | .326 | 1.38 | 3.45 | 3.78 | 4.04 | 0.5 |
| 2012 | NYN | MLB | 31 | 2 | 1 | 2 | 46 | 0 | 50 | 45 | 5 | 21 | 39 | 3.8 | 7.1 | 49% | .301 | 1.32 | 4.19 | 4.20 | 4.56 | 0.3 |

He's been released by the Yankees, waived by the Braves, yet he's turned into the kind of reliever who can pitch in the late innings for a second-division team, which is exactly what he did in 2011. With a 94-96 mph fastball, Acosta has a true plus big-league heater. His slider is solid and he generally throws strikes. There is no reason to think he's going to get much better, but he is certainly much better than your standard guy whom two teams have given up on.

**Miguel Batista**
Born: 2/19/1971 Age: 41
Bats: R Throws: R Height: 6' 1'' Weight: 160
Breakout: 12% Improve: 36% Collapse: 28%
Attrition: 18% MLB: 76%

Comparables:
Jose Mesa, Charlie Hough, Steve Reed

| YEAR | TEAM | LVL | AGE | W | L | SV | G | GS | IP | H | HR | BB | SO | EqBB9 | EqSO9 | GB% | BABIP | WHIP | ERA | FIP | FRA | WARP |
|------|------|-----|-----|---|---|----|----|----|----|----|----|----|----|-------|-------|-----|-------|------|-----|-----|-----|------|
| 2009 | SEA | MLB | 38 | 7 | 4 | 1 | 56 | 0 | 71¹ | 79 | 7 | 39 | 52 | 4.9 | 6.6 | 48% | .324 | 1.65 | 4.04 | 4.69 | 4.74 | 0.5 |
| 2010 | WAS | MLB | 39 | 1 | 2 | 2 | 58 | 1 | 82² | 71 | 9 | 39 | 55 | 4.2 | 6.0 | 50% | .257 | 1.33 | 3.70 | 4.79 | 5.79 | -0.5 |
| 2011 | BUF | AAA | 40 | 1 | 0 | 0 | 10 | 8 | 46² | 46 | 4 | 25 | 36 | 4.8 | 6.9 | 49% | .304 | 1.52 | 4.24 | 4.55 | 4.49 | 0.7 |
| 2011 | NYN | MLB | 40 | 2 | 0 | 0 | 9 | 4 | 30² | 22 | 0 | 14 | 15 | 4.1 | 4.4 | 54% | .239 | 1.17 | 2.64 | 3.58 | 3.97 | 0.3 |
| 2011 | SLN | MLB | 40 | 3 | 2 | 0 | 26 | 1 | 29¹ | 27 | 2 | 19 | 16 | 5.8 | 4.9 | 39% | .266 | 1.57 | 4.60 | 5.14 | 5.67 | -0.3 |
| 2012 | NYN | MLB | 41 | 3 | 3 | 0 | 37 | 5 | 67² | 68 | 6 | 32 | 37 | 4.3 | 5.0 | 46% | .303 | 1.48 | 5.12 | 4.68 | 5.57 | -0.3 |

Batista hooked on with the Cardinals in spring training, hooked on with the Mets when he was released, was pretty much a garbage-time arm for both teams, and then had the single most improbable line of the year, throwing a two-hit shutout against Cincinnati in the last game of the season as the Reds made vacation plans and reserved tee times. He'll turn 41 when pitchers and catchers report, but spent the winter pitching in the Dominican with the hope that he can hook on again.

**Pedro Beato**
Born: 10/27/1986 Age: 25
Bats: R Throws: R Height: 6' 5'' Weight: 220
Breakout: 11% Improve: 42% Collapse: 26%
Attrition: 19% MLB: 75%

Comparables:
Matt Wise, Rick Bauer, Carlos Monasterios

| YEAR | TEAM | LVL | AGE | W | L | SV | G | GS | IP | H | HR | BB | SO | EqBB9 | EqSO9 | GB% | BABIP | WHIP | ERA | FIP | FRA | WARP |
|------|------|-----|-----|---|---|----|----|----|----|----|----|----|----|-------|-------|-----|-------|------|-----|-----|-----|------|
| 2009 | FRD | A+ | 22 | 5 | 7 | 0 | 20 | 20 | 105¹ | 125 | 12 | 40 | 70 | 3.4 | 6.0 | 48% | .330 | 1.57 | 4.53 | 4.90 | 5.24 | 0.3 |
| 2009 | BOW | AA | 22 | 1 | 3 | 0 | 6 | 5 | 32 | 33 | 6 | 7 | 18 | 2.0 | 5.1 | 45% | .270 | 1.25 | 4.50 | 5.11 | 5.27 | -0.1 |
| 2010 | BOW | AA | 23 | 2 | 0 | 16 | 43 | 0 | 59² | 27 | 3 | 12 | 31 | 2.9 | 7.5 | 43% | .276 | 1.14 | 2.11 | 3.91 | 4.61 | 0.4 |
| 2011 | NYN | MLB | 24 | 2 | 1 | 0 | 60 | 0 | 67 | 59 | 5 | 27 | 39 | 3.6 | 5.2 | 50% | .262 | 1.28 | 4.30 | 4.19 | 4.98 | -0.1 |
| 2012 | NYN | MLB | 25 | 2 | 1 | 1 | 41 | 0 | 49² | 56 | 6 | 21 | 21 | 3.7 | 3.7 | 47% | .308 | 1.54 | 5.83 | 5.20 | 6.34 | -0.7 |

It took a long time for Beato to ultimately become a Met. The team drafted him in the 17th round of the 2005 draft, but had problems getting a well-above-slot bonus approved by MLB, and Beato ended up being the 32nd overall pick by Baltimore the following year. He didn't develop, was exposed in the Rule 5, and the Mets scooped him up last December, as he's always been a big guy with some arm strength. While on the surface, it looks like Beato held his own, he really wasn't very good. He started his big-league career with a 0.00 ERA after 12 games and 18 2/3 innings, but he has a 5.84 mark since. Beato's fastball sits in the low 90s, has sink, and can touch 95-96 mph, but it's also the sum of his abilities, as neither his curve nor his slider are good enough for the majors, and unless your name is Mariano Rivera, you need a second pitch. We've seen Mariano Rivera, and you, sir, are not Mariano Rivera.

### Taylor Buchholz

Born: 10/13/1981 Age: 30
Bats: R Throws: R Height: 6' 5" Weight: 220
Breakout: 9% Improve: 50% Collapse: 22%
Attrition: 16% MLB: 91%

Comparables:
Turk Farrell, Julio Mateo, Curt Schilling

| YEAR | TEAM | LVL | AGE | W | L | SV | G | GS | IP | H | HR | BB | SO | EqBB9 | EqSO9 | GB% | BABIP | WHIP | ERA | FIP | FRA | WARP |
|---|---|---|---|---|---|---|---|---|---|---|---|---|---|---|---|---|---|---|---|---|---|---|
| 2010 | TOR | MLB | 28 | 0 | 0 | 0 | 2 | 0 | 2 | 0 | 0 | 0 | 0 | 0.0 | 0.0 | 50% | .000 | 0.00 | 0.00 | 3.05 | 1.25 | 0.1 |
| 2010 | COL | MLB | 28 | 1 | 0 | 0 | 7 | 0 | 10 | 10 | 2 | 6 | 9 | 5.4 | 8.1 | 36% | .320 | 1.60 | 4.50 | 5.71 | 4.45 | 0.1 |
| 2011 | NYN | MLB | 29 | 1 | 1 | 0 | 23 | 0 | 26 | 22 | 5 | 7 | 26 | 2.4 | 9.0 | 42% | .258 | 1.12 | 3.12 | 4.42 | 5.07 | -0.2 |
| 2012 | NYN | MLB | 30 | 1 | 0 | 0 | 20 | 0 | 22² | 22 | 2 | 6 | 16 | 2.2 | 6.3 | 43% | .300 | 1.20 | 3.82 | 3.73 | 4.15 | 0.2 |

Once a top-flight starting prospect, Buchholz saw his career descend into journeyman status due to injuries and ineffectiveness. But in 2011 he had his first run of big-league success in three years with the Mets, though he was a bit of a roster luxury on a bad team as a right-hander who can only get out his fellow right-handers. Unfortunately, his season ended just two months in, and it was revealed that he's been struggling with anxiety and depression. The Mets were left with no choice but to release him, and nobody has a good feel if he'll pitch again. These are human beings, folks, and while we can look at numbers and try to make deductions about why something good or bad happened, sometimes it goes well beyond the stat sheet.

### Tim Byrdak

Born: 10/31/1973 Age: 38
Bats: L Throws: L Height: 6' 0" Weight: 170
Breakout: 13% Improve: 30% Collapse: 22%
Attrition: 6% MLB: 84%

Comparables:
Scott Eyre, Dennis Cook, David Cone

| YEAR | TEAM | LVL | AGE | W | L | SV | G | GS | IP | H | HR | BB | SO | EqBB9 | EqSO9 | GB% | BABIP | WHIP | ERA | FIP | FRA | WARP |
|---|---|---|---|---|---|---|---|---|---|---|---|---|---|---|---|---|---|---|---|---|---|---|
| 2009 | HOU | MLB | 35 | 1 | 2 | 0 | 76 | 0 | 61¹ | 39 | 10 | 36 | 58 | 5.3 | 8.5 | 43% | .188 | 1.22 | 3.23 | 5.19 | 6.02 | -0.3 |
| 2010 | HOU | MLB | 36 | 2 | 2 | 0 | 64 | 0 | 38² | 40 | 4 | 20 | 29 | 4.7 | 6.8 | 31% | .308 | 1.55 | 3.49 | 4.50 | 4.92 | 0.1 |
| 2011 | NYN | MLB | 37 | 2 | 1 | 1 | 72 | 0 | 37² | 34 | 3 | 19 | 47 | 4.5 | 11.2 | 42% | .330 | 1.41 | 3.82 | 3.13 | 4.32 | 0.2 |
| 2012 | NYN | MLB | 38 | 3 | 1 | 1 | 63 | 0 | 35² | 31 | 4 | 17 | 31 | 4.3 | 7.9 | 41% | .294 | 1.34 | 4.35 | 4.35 | 4.73 | 0.1 |

A tribute to commitment, Byrdak did not become an established reliever until he was 33, and with five straight solid seasons with the Tigers, the Astros, and now the Mets, he's become one of those rare commodities—the consistent reliever. His job is simply to get lefties out. He faced just one batter in more than a third of his appearances, and his slider gives them fits. He could do this into his 40s, and the Mets signed him to a $1 million contract before the 2011 season was over.

### D.J. Carrasco

Born: 4/12/1977 Age: 35
Bats: R Throws: R Height: 6' 2" Weight: 210
Breakout: 25% Improve: 46% Collapse: 27%
Attrition: 20% MLB: 83%

Comparables:
Frank Castillo, Bob Feller, Anthony Telford

| YEAR | TEAM | LVL | AGE | W | L | SV | G | GS | IP | H | HR | BB | SO | EqBB9 | EqSO9 | GB% | BABIP | WHIP | ERA | FIP | FRA | WARP |
|---|---|---|---|---|---|---|---|---|---|---|---|---|---|---|---|---|---|---|---|---|---|---|
| 2009 | CHA | MLB | 32 | 5 | 1 | 0 | 49 | 1 | 93¹ | 103 | 5 | 29 | 62 | 2.8 | 6.0 | 49% | .322 | 1.41 | 3.76 | 3.51 | 3.94 | 1.8 |
| 2010 | ARI | MLB | 33 | 1 | 0 | 0 | 18 | 0 | 22² | 18 | 1 | 12 | 20 | 4.8 | 7.9 | 51% | .266 | 1.32 | 3.18 | 3.64 | 3.93 | 0.3 |
| 2010 | PIT | MLB | 33 | 2 | 2 | 0 | 45 | 0 | 55² | 50 | 4 | 22 | 45 | 3.6 | 7.3 | 47% | .299 | 1.29 | 3.88 | 3.82 | 4.19 | 0.4 |
| 2011 | BUF | AAA | 34 | 1 | 1 | 0 | 9 | 8 | 46² | 46 | 4 | 17 | 37 | 3.3 | 7.1 | 40% | .309 | 1.35 | 3.47 | 4.12 | 4.77 | 0.5 |
| 2011 | NYN | MLB | 34 | 1 | 3 | 0 | 42 | 1 | 49¹ | 67 | 7 | 16 | 27 | 2.9 | 4.9 | 45% | .364 | 1.68 | 6.02 | 5.08 | 6.01 | -0.8 |
| 2012 | NYN | MLB | 35 | 2 | 2 | 0 | 39 | 3 | 60 | 64 | 5 | 21 | 35 | 3.2 | 5.2 | 48% | .322 | 1.42 | 4.96 | 4.17 | 5.39 | -0.2 |

While Carrasco was a mop-up guy in 2011, more often than not he left a bigger mess than when he entered. Lefties hit him hard, righties hit him hard. He actually pitched worse at Citi Field, and at no point was there ever really a run of effectiveness that made anyone feel he was figuring anything out, as he has decent velocity but everything he throws could be best described as flat. The Mets are stuck with him in 2012, but at $1.2 million, cutting bait isn't the most painful thing in the world.

### Robert Carson

Born: 1/23/1989 Age: 23
Bats: L Throws: L Height: 6' 4" Weight: 220
Breakout: 37% Improve: 71% Collapse: 16%
Attrition: 15% MLB: 88%

Comparables:
Jim Umbarger, Claude Osteen, Brian Bohanon

| YEAR | TEAM | LVL | AGE | W | L | SV | G | GS | IP | H | HR | BB | SO | EqBB9 | EqSO9 | GB% | BABIP | WHIP | ERA | FIP | FRA | WARP |
|---|---|---|---|---|---|---|---|---|---|---|---|---|---|---|---|---|---|---|---|---|---|---|
| 2009 | SAV | A | 20 | 8 | 10 | 0 | 25 | 25 | 131² | 139 | 4 | 45 | 90 | 3.1 | 6.2 | 57% | .317 | 1.40 | 3.21 | 3.63 | 5.39 | -0.8 |
| 2010 | SLU | A+ | 21 | 6 | 4 | 0 | 17 | 16 | 86¹ | 70 | 3 | 21 | 42 | 3.4 | 7.2 | 44% | .353 | 1.52 | 4.17 | 3.81 | 4.73 | 0.8 |
| 2010 | BIN | AA | 21 | 1 | 6 | 0 | 10 | 10 | 48² | 52 | 4 | 17 | 24 | 4.3 | 5.5 | 50% | .384 | 1.87 | 8.32 | 4.73 | 6.62 | -0.5 |
| 2011 | BIN | AA | 22 | 0 | 7 | 0 | 25 | 24 | 128¹ | 154 | 14 | 55 | 91 | 3.9 | 6.4 | 39% | .337 | 1.63 | 5.05 | 4.77 | 5.40 | 0.7 |
| 2012 | NYN | MLB | 23 | 1 | 4 | 0 | 8 | 8 | 42¹ | 52 | 5 | 21 | 16 | 4.5 | 3.4 | 50% | .326 | 1.73 | 6.71 | 5.47 | 7.29 | -0.8 |

Despite Carson putting up ERAs over five in each of the last two seasons, the Mets added him to the 40-man roster in the offseason. After all, big, physical left-handers who can throw 92-94 mph don't exactly grow on trees. Youth is still on Carson's side, but he's yet to develop pitches to compliment the fastball, and he's consistently struggled with his command. He's a frustrating type: He has the body and stamina to start, but his actual skill set could push him to the bullpen as early as this year.

**R.A. Dickey**
Born: 10/29/1974 Age: 37
Bats: R Throws: R Height: 6' 4" Weight: 205
Breakout: 19% Improve: 40% Collapse: 38%
Attrition: 21% MLB: 73%
Comparables:
Tom Candiotti,Dennis Lamp,Brian Sweeney

| YEAR | TEAM | LVL | AGE | W | L | SV | G | GS | IP | H | HR | BB | SO | EqBB9 | EqSO9 | GB% | BABIP | WHIP | ERA | FIP | FRA | WARP |
|------|------|-----|-----|---|---|----|---|----|----|----|----|----|----|-------|-------|-----|-------|------|-----|-----|-----|------|
| 2009 | MIN | MLB | 34 | 1 | 1 | 0 | 35 | 1 | 64¹ | 74 | 8 | 30 | 42 | 4.2 | 5.9 | 48% | .319 | 1.62 | 4.62 | 5.04 | 5.74 | 0.1 |
| 2010 | BUF | AAA | 35 | 4 | 2 | 0 | 8 | 8 | 60² | 32 | 2 | 1 | 23 | 1.2 | 5.5 | 56% | .240 | 1.04 | 2.22 | 3.35 | 3.77 | 1.5 |
| 2010 | NYN | MLB | 35 | 11 | 9 | 0 | 27 | 26 | 174¹ | 165 | 13 | 42 | 104 | 2.2 | 5.4 | 56% | .280 | 1.19 | 2.84 | 3.67 | 4.30 | 3.0 |
| 2011 | NYN | MLB | 36 | 8 | 13 | 0 | 33 | 32 | 208² | 202 | 18 | 54 | 134 | 2.3 | 5.8 | 53% | .285 | 1.23 | 3.28 | 3.74 | 4.29 | 2.5 |
| 2012 | NYN | MLB | 37 | 9 | 11 | 0 | 26 | 26 | 175² | 175 | 15 | 51 | 92 | 2.6 | 4.7 | 51% | .298 | 1.29 | 4.15 | 4.14 | 4.51 | 1.2 |

With Tim Wakefield sailing into the sunset, it's good to have a knuckleballer still around, especially one who seems to be in the prime of his craft. Dickey's impossible to scout and maybe to project, but unlike many who depend on the pitch (he throws it around 80 percent of the time), he rarely has those off days when he just gets hammered. He

Neil Allen,Reggie Harris,Pete Broberg

| YEAR | TEAM | LVL | AGE | W | L | SV | G | GS | IP | H | HR | BB | SO | EqBB9 | EqSO9 | GB% | BABIP | WHIP | ERA | FIP | FRA | WARP |
|------|------|-----|-----|---|---|----|---|----|----|----|----|----|----|-------|-------|-----|-------|------|-----|-----|-----|------|
| 2012 | NYN | MLB | 22 | 2 | 3 | 0 | 7 | 7 | 37 | 38 | 4 | 19 | 25 | 4.7 | 5.9 | 47% | .310 | 1.53 | 5.49 | 4.80 | 5.96 | -0.2 |

Familia has always had among the strongest arms in the system. He'll sit in the mid-90s, can touch triple digits, and had his best season as a pro in 2011 while reaching Double-A. If scouts were convinced he could remain a starter, he'd rank with any prospect in the system, but concern about his arm action was validated when he missed some time with a sore shoulder, and his secondary pitches are still works in progress. He's more likely to be the closer of the future than a rotation piece, and if the Mets move him to the bullpen now, he could be ready quickly.

**Frank Francisco**
Born: 9/11/1979 Age: 32
Bats: R Throws: R Height: 6' 3" Weight: 180
Breakout: 22% Improve: 39% Collapse: 26%
Attrition: 6% MLB: 92%
Comparables:
Kiko Calero,Skip Lockwood,John Hiller

| YEAR | TEAM | LVL | AGE | W | L | SV | G | GS | IP | H | HR | BB | SO | EqBB9 | EqSO9 | GB% | BABIP | WHIP | ERA | FIP | FRA | WARP |
|------|------|-----|-----|---|---|----|----|----|----|----|----|----|----|-------|-------|-----|-------|------|-----|-----|-----|------|
| 2009 | TEX | MLB | 29 | 2 | 3 | 25 | 51 | 0 | 49¹ | 40 | 6 | 15 | 57 | 2.7 | 10.4 | 30% | .274 | 1.11 | 3.83 | 3.39 | 3.81 | 1.0 |
| 2010 | TEX | MLB | 30 | 6 | 4 | 2 | 56 | 0 | 52² | 49 | 5 | 18 | 60 | 3.1 | 10.3 | 40% | .328 | 1.27 | 3.76 | 3.09 | 3.88 | 0.8 |
| 2011 | TOR | MLB | 31 | 1 | 4 | 17 | 54 | 0 | 50² | 49 | 7 | 18 | 53 | 3.2 | 9.4 | 40% | .302 | 1.32 | 3.55 | 3.83 | 3.79 | 0.8 |
| 2012 | NYN | MLB | 32 | 3 | 1 | 6 | 52 | 0 | 49¹ | 42 | 5 | 18 | 49 | 3.3 | 9.0 | 37% | .306 | 1.21 | 3.58 | 3.63 | 3.90 | 0.7 |

Here's the trouble projecting a guy like Francisco. Historically, he has been very consistent: Put him down for 50 innings of 1 WARP ball with just over a strikeout per inning in each of the last three years. Solid back-of-the-bullpen guy, right? But the reason it has been 50 innings instead of 60 or 70 is that injuries nip him for a few weeks each season. He has had three straight years with time lost to right shoulder injuries, and each time it is re-aggravated, the possibility of a more serious injury looms larger. That being said, he avoided the DL after his April return, so teams evaluating him as a free agent have five healthy months to rely on, which was enough for the Mets to give him a two-year deal for $12 million; a relative bargain compared to some of the closer contracts out there.

**Dillon Gee**
Born: 4/28/1986 Age: 26
Bats: R Throws: R Height: 6' 2" Weight: 200
Breakout: 27% Improve: 53% Collapse: 18%
Attrition: 17% MLB: 94%
Comparables:
Randy Messenger,Cal Eldred,Eddie Watt

| YEAR | TEAM | LVL | AGE | W | L | SV | G | GS | IP | H | HR | BB | SO | EqBB9 | EqSO9 | GB% | BABIP | WHIP | ERA | FIP | FRA | WARP |
|------|------|-----|-----|---|---|----|----|----|----|----|----|----|----|-------|-------|-----|-------|------|-----|-----|-----|------|
| 2009 | BUF | AAA | 23 | 1 | 3 | 0 | 9 | 9 | 48¹ | 47 | 5 | 16 | 42 | 3.0 | 7.8 | 39% | .298 | 1.30 | 4.10 | 4.06 | 4.05 | 0.7 |
| 2010 | BUF | AAA | 24 | 13 | 8 | 0 | 28 | 28 | 161¹ | 114 | 19 | 31 | 111 | 2.3 | 9.2 | 44% | .312 | 1.33 | 4.97 | 4.45 | 4.68 | 2.2 |
| 2010 | NYN | MLB | 24 | 2 | 2 | 0 | 5 | 5 | 33 | 25 | 2 | 15 | 17 | 4.1 | 4.6 | 49% | .232 | 1.21 | 2.18 | 4.23 | 4.17 | 0.3 |
| 2011 | NYN | MLB | 25 | 13 | 6 | 0 | 30 | 27 | 160² | 150 | 18 | 71 | 114 | 4.0 | 6.4 | 50% | .276 | 1.38 | 4.43 | 4.62 | 5.11 | 0.3 |
| 2012 | NYN | MLB | 26 | 6 | 10 | 0 | 23 | 23 | 133¹ | 131 | 14 | 43 | 83 | 2.9 | 5.6 | 43% | .300 | 1.31 | 4.54 | 4.29 | 4.93 | 0.4 |

Gee came up as one of those pitchers who had much better stats than scouting reports, but he was able to maintain good peripherals all the way up the ladder, which earned him a rotation job when Chris Young broke and resulted in a won-loss record that has the potential to give him far more future opportunities than he deserves. Gee is yet another Mets starter without a good breaking ball: His best pitch is a changeup, which compliments his ability to throw strikes with a fastball that averages right around 90 mph. The league began to catch up to him during the second half, as he put up a 5.25 ERA after the All-Star break, which combined with his 5.74 ERA away from Citi Field should tell you everything you need to know about his future.

### Darin Gorski

Born: 10/6/1987 Age: 24
Bats: L Throws: L Height: 6' 5" Weight: 210
Breakout: 22% Improve: 48% Collapse: 35%
Attrition: 25% MLB: 89%

**Comparables:**
Jason Vargas, Andy Pettitte, Jo-Jo Reyes

| YEAR | TEAM | LVL | AGE | W | L | SV | G | GS | IP | H | HR | BB | SO | EqBB9 | EqSO9 | GB% | BABIP | WHIP | ERA | FIP | FRA | WARP |
|------|------|-----|-----|---|---|----|----|----|-----|-----|----|----|-----|-------|-------|-----|-------|------|------|------|------|------|
| 2009 | BRO | A- | 21 | 3 | 4 | 0 | 13 | 11 | 62$^1$ | 51 | 6 | 26 | 50 | 3.8 | 7.2 | 43% | .251 | 1.24 | 4.91 | 4.37 | 5.34 | -0.3 |
| 2010 | SAV | A | 22 | 6 | 8 | 3 | 25 | 18 | 114 | 61 | 5 | 22 | 51 | 3.4 | 8.6 | 35% | .327 | 1.47 | 4.58 | 3.99 | 5.45 | -0.5 |
| 2011 | SLU | A+ | 23 | 5 | 1 | 1 | 27 | 21 | 138$^2$ | 125 | 11 | 31 | 147 | 1.9 | 9.1 | 41% | .279 | 1.00 | 2.08 | 3.13 | 3.73 | 3.6 |
| 2012 | NYN | MLB | 24 | 2 | 3 | 0 | 9 | 7 | 42$^2$ | 45 | 5 | 17 | 25 | 3.7 | 5.3 | 39% | .307 | 1.45 | 5.25 | 4.75 | 5.70 | -0.2 |

Gorski was the Mets' breakout pitcher in the system. After a mediocre showing in 2010, he was one of the Florida State League's top performers. Gorski gained significant velocity last year, and now sits at 89-91, which allows him to take even more advantage of his best pitch, an outstanding changeup with plenty of deception and movement. Still, he's more of a strike thrower than anything else, and at 24, he's well behind the standard age/level development curve. His prospect star is much brighter than it was 12 months ago, but only in the sense that he now has one.

### Matt Harvey

Born: 3/27/1989 Age: 23
Bats: R Throws: R Height: 6' 5" Weight: 210
Breakout: 25% Improve: 61% Collapse: 15%
Attrition: 12% MLB: 93%

**Comparables:**
Ramon Martinez, Matt Garza, Ray Crone

| YEAR | TEAM | LVL | AGE | W | L | SV | G | GS | IP | H | HR | BB | SO | EqBB9 | EqSO9 | GB% | BABIP | WHIP | ERA | FIP | FRA | WARP |
|------|------|-----|-----|---|---|----|----|----|-----|----|----|----|----|-------|-------|-----|-------|------|------|------|------|------|
| 2011 | SLU | A+ | 22 | 4 | 1 | 0 | 14 | 14 | 76 | 62 | 5 | 22 | 83 | 2.8 | 10.9 | 51% | .328 | 1.20 | 2.37 | 3.01 | 4.08 | 1.6 |
| 2011 | BIN | AA | 22 | 2 | 2 | 0 | 12 | 12 | 59$^2$ | 58 | 4 | 23 | 64 | 3.5 | 9.7 | 52% | .333 | 1.36 | 4.53 | 3.45 | 4.53 | 0.8 |
| 2012 | NYN | MLB | 23 | 2 | 3 | 0 | 7 | 7 | 34$^1$ | 33 | 3 | 14 | 28 | 3.6 | 7.2 | 48% | .314 | 1.36 | 4.44 | 3.93 | 4.82 | 0.2 |

Harvey was the seventh overall pick in the 2010 draft, but there certainly were some risks involved, as he did not live up to expectations in college until his junior year, and North Carolina worked him at a disturbing level. None of those factors came into play in his full-season debut. He stayed healthy, dominated the Florida State League, and was making adjustments at Double-A when the season came to an end. With a classic pitcher frame and two plus pitches in a 93-96 mph fastball and a devastating slider, Harvey, like so many other pitching prospects, needs to improve his command and pitch efficiency. If he fails in that regard he's still a solid starting pitcher in the big leagues. If he succeeds, he's a star.

### Daniel Herrera

Born: 10/21/1984 Age: 27
Bats: L Throws: L Height: 5' 7" Weight: 165
Breakout: 26% Improve: 54% Collapse: 27%
Attrition: 11% MLB: 91%

**Comparables:**
Dontrelle Willis, Phil Coke, Ryan Rowland-Smith

| YEAR | TEAM | LVL | AGE | W | L | SV | G | GS | IP | H | HR | BB | SO | EqBB9 | EqSO9 | GB% | BABIP | WHIP | ERA | FIP | FRA | WARP |
|------|------|-----|-----|---|---|----|----|----|-----|----|----|----|----|-------|-------|-----|-------|------|-------|-------|-------|------|
| 2009 | CIN | MLB | 24 | 4 | 4 | 0 | 70 | 0 | 61$^2$ | 63 | 5 | 24 | 44 | 3.5 | 6.4 | 52% | .315 | 1.41 | 3.06 | 3.95 | 4.76 | 0.5 |
| 2010 | LOU | AAA | 25 | 2 | 2 | 5 | 26 | 1 | 37$^2$ | 27 | 1 | 3 | 30 | 1.2 | 8.1 | 57% | .302 | 0.95 | 4.30 | 2.92 | 4.62 | 0.4 |
| 2010 | CIN | MLB | 25 | 1 | 3 | 0 | 36 | 0 | 23 | 31 | 2 | 6 | 14 | 2.3 | 5.5 | 42% | .354 | 1.61 | 3.91 | 3.80 | 5.25 | -0.1 |
| 2011 | NAS | AAA | 26 | 1 | 0 | 2 | 29 | 0 | 42$^2$ | 32 | 2 | 8 | 39 | 1.7 | 8.2 | 57% | .254 | 0.94 | 1.48 | 3.15 | 4.15 | 0.6 |
| 2011 | MIL | MLB | 26 | 0 | 0 | 0 | 2 | 0 | 1$^2$ | 6 | 1 | 1 | 0 | 5.4 | 0.0 | 50% | .556 | 4.20 | 21.60 | 12.59 | 12.75 | -0.2 |
| 2011 | NYN | MLB | 26 | 0 | 1 | 0 | 16 | 0 | 8 | 7 | 0 | 2 | 5 | 2.2 | 5.6 | 58% | .292 | 1.12 | 1.12 | 2.49 | 3.38 | 0.1 |
| 2012 | NYN | MLB | 27 | 2 | 1 | 0 | 30 | 0 | 31 | 30 | 3 | 9 | 21 | 2.5 | 6.2 | 51% | .308 | 1.24 | 3.94 | 3.98 | 4.28 | 0.3 |

The little engine that could, Herrera is a miniature left-on-left groundball machine who was the player to be named later in the K-Rod trade. He's fun because he's small, he's fun because he got to the big leagues as a 45th-round draft pick, and he's fun because he throws a screwball, but his value is solely as a LOOGY, and the Mets already have one in Byrdak. It's not that he struggles against right-handers, it's that he turns them into MVP-level players with a career mark of .364/.417/.543 against him. That will never change, but he does have a skill that is of big-league value.

### Jason Isringhausen

Born: 9/7/1972 Age: 39
Bats: R Throws: R Height: 6' 4" Weight: 195
Breakout: 15% Improve: 43% Collapse: 23%
Attrition: 12% MLB: 70%

**Comparables:**
Troy Percival, David Weathers, Hector Carrasco

| YEAR | TEAM | LVL | AGE | W | L | SV | G | GS | IP | H | HR | BB | SO | EqBB9 | EqSO9 | GB% | BABIP | WHIP | ERA | FIP | FRA | WARP |
|------|------|-----|-----|---|---|----|----|----|-----|----|----|----|----|-------|-------|-----|-------|------|------|------|------|------|
| 2009 | TBA | MLB | 36 | 0 | 1 | 0 | 9 | 0 | 8 | 6 | 0 | 5 | 6 | 5.6 | 6.8 | 33% | .250 | 1.38 | 2.25 | 4.27 | 4.66 | 0.1 |
| 2011 | NYN | MLB | 38 | 3 | 3 | 7 | 53 | 0 | 46$^2$ | 36 | 6 | 24 | 44 | 4.6 | 8.5 | 41% | .244 | 1.29 | 4.05 | 4.39 | 5.03 | -0.1 |
| 2012 | NYN | MLB | 39 | 2 | 1 | 4 | 40 | 0 | 35 | 32 | 3 | 15 | 26 | 3.9 | 6.6 | 46% | .292 | 1.34 | 4.24 | 4.12 | 4.61 | 0.2 |

The Mets didn't have a lot of feel-good stories in 2011, but Isringhausen is one of them. He considered retirement in the offseason and then said he would do so if he didn't break camp with his original team. He not only made the team, he pitched very well and moved into the closer role, earning his 300th career save after K-Rod was dealt to Milwaukee. His numbers look worse than he pitched, as he fell apart in the second half while trying to pitch through a back injury that ultimately cut his season short. His cut fastball and curve are still effective offerings.

**Jenrry Mejia**
Born: 10/11/1989 Age: 22
Bats: R Throws: R Height: 6' 1" Weight: 160
Breakout: 22% Improve: 51% Collapse: 19%
Attrition: 10% MLB: 89%
Comparables:
Sean Gallagher, Trevor Cahill, Jhoulys Chacin

| YEAR | TEAM | LVL | AGE | W | L | SV | G | GS | IP | H | HR | BB | SO | EqBB9 | EqSO9 | GB% | BABIP | WHIP | ERA | FIP | FRA | WARP |
|------|------|-----|-----|---|---|----|----|----|-----|----|----|----|----|-------|-------|-----|-------|------|------|------|------|------|
| 2009 | SLU | A+ | 19 | 4 | 1 | 0 | 9 | 9 | 50¹ | 41 | 0 | 16 | 44 | 2.9 | 7.9 | 68% | .283 | 1.13 | 1.97 | 2.52 | 3.97 | 0.7 |
| 2009 | BIN | AA | 19 | 0 | 5 | 0 | 10 | 10 | 44¹ | 44 | 2 | 23 | 47 | 4.7 | 9.5 | 64% | .353 | 1.51 | 4.47 | 3.43 | 4.38 | 0.9 |
| 2010 | BIN | AA | 20 | 2 | 0 | 0 | 6 | 6 | 27¹ | 12 | 0 | 12 | 18 | 4.6 | 8.6 | 66% | .250 | 1.21 | 1.32 | 3.60 | 3.66 | 0.6 |
| 2010 | NYN | MLB | 20 | 0 | 4 | 0 | 33 | 3 | 39 | 46 | 3 | 20 | 22 | 4.6 | 5.1 | 61% | .319 | 1.69 | 4.62 | 4.75 | 5.13 | 0.0 |
| 2012 | NYN | MLB | 22 | 1 | 1 | 0 | 7 | 2 | 15 | 15 | 1 | 7 | 9 | 4.1 | 5.5 | 57% | .305 | 1.46 | 4.89 | 4.27 | 5.31 | 0.0 |

The Mets rushed Mejia to the big leagues in 2010, but he was well on his way to getting back there legitimately in 2011 when his elbow went pop, leading to a lost season as he recovered from Tommy John surgery. That will also cost him spring training and the first month or two of the 2012 season. Lost develop-

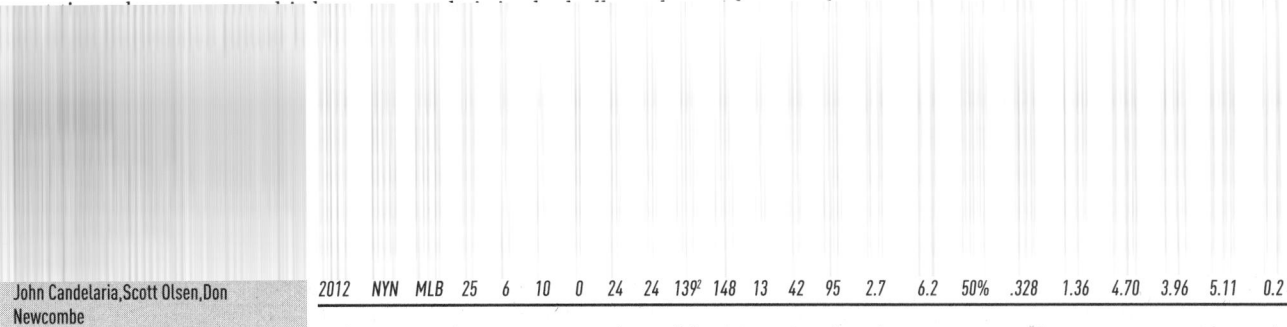

John Candelaria, Scott Olsen, Don Newcombe

| 2012 | NYN | MLB | 25 | 6 | 10 | 0 | 24 | 24 | 139² | 148 | 13 | 42 | 95 | 2.7 | 6.2 | 50% | .328 | 1.36 | 4.70 | 3.96 | 5.11 | 0.2 |

In his second year as a member of the Mets rotation, it was very much next verse, same as the first for Niese, who basically had the same year as 2010. That said, there was some progress, as his second half struggles were blamed on an intercostal strain that ultimately ended his season. Niese's best two pitches are a curveball and a low-90s fastball, and he throws enough strikes and keeps it in the ballpark to generally keep his team competitive. He's not a star, he's not ever going to be a star, but left-handers who can take the bump every five days and be competitive are a valuable commodity.

**Bobby Parnell**
Born: 9/8/1984 Age: 27
Bats: R Throws: R Height: 6' 5" Weight: 200
Breakout: 31% Improve: 53% Collapse: 22%
Attrition: 10% MLB: 89%
Comparables:
Kevin Gregg, Brandon Medders, Kelly Downs

| YEAR | TEAM | LVL | AGE | W | L | SV | G | GS | IP | H | HR | BB | SO | EqBB9 | EqSO9 | GB% | BABIP | WHIP | ERA | FIP | FRA | WARP |
|------|------|-----|-----|---|---|----|----|----|-----|-----|----|----|----|-------|-------|-----|-------|------|------|------|------|------|
| 2009 | NYN | MLB | 24 | 4 | 8 | 1 | 68 | 8 | 88¹ | 101 | 8 | 46 | 74 | 4.7 | 7.5 | 48% | .335 | 1.66 | 5.30 | 4.26 | 4.69 | 1.1 |
| 2010 | BUF | AAA | 25 | 1 | 1 | 4 | 24 | 0 | 41¹ | 29 | 3 | 11 | 19 | 3.7 | 9.2 | 63% | .347 | 1.28 | 4.14 | 4.43 | 5.70 | 0.0 |
| 2010 | NYN | MLB | 25 | 0 | 1 | 0 | 41 | 0 | 35 | 41 | 1 | 8 | 33 | 2.1 | 8.5 | 58% | .381 | 1.40 | 2.83 | 2.28 | 3.11 | 0.8 |
| 2011 | NYN | MLB | 26 | 4 | 6 | 6 | 60 | 0 | 59¹ | 60 | 4 | 27 | 64 | 4.1 | 9.7 | 55% | .339 | 1.47 | 3.64 | 3.18 | 4.10 | 0.4 |
| 2012 | NYN | MLB | 27 | 2 | 1 | 2 | 50 | 0 | 53² | 55 | 5 | 21 | 39 | 3.5 | 6.5 | 50% | .325 | 1.41 | 4.66 | 4.14 | 5.06 | 0.0 |

Everybody loves the radar gun, but Parnell is a lesson in how velocity isn't everything. Parnell's fastball averages more than 97 mph, and few pitchers in baseball are as likely to touch triple digits, yet 175 games into his pro career he's yet to establish himself as a reliable reliever in the late innings. He can miss a good share of bats based solely on his ability to throw hard, but the pitch is flat and straight, he doesn't command it well, and his slider is one in name only. He's going to get plenty of chances because of that ability to light up the third digit, but he's peaked unless he makes some major adjustments.

**Mike Pelfrey**
Born: 1/14/1984 Age: 28
Bats: R Throws: R Height: 6' 8" Weight: 190
Breakout: 12% Improve: 56% Collapse: 24%
Attrition: 10% MLB: 86%
Comparables:
Jake Westbrook, Terry Fox, Pedro Astacio

| YEAR | TEAM | LVL | AGE | W | L | SV | G | GS | IP | H | HR | BB | SO | EqBB9 | EqSO9 | GB% | BABIP | WHIP | ERA | FIP | FRA | WARP |
|------|------|-----|-----|----|----|----|----|----|------|-----|----|----|-----|-------|-------|-----|-------|------|------|------|------|------|
| 2009 | NYN | MLB | 25 | 10 | 12 | 0 | 31 | 31 | 184¹ | 213 | 18 | 66 | 107 | 3.2 | 5.2 | 52% | .316 | 1.51 | 5.03 | 4.35 | 5.01 | 1.2 |
| 2010 | NYN | MLB | 26 | 15 | 9 | 1 | 34 | 33 | 204 | 213 | 12 | 68 | 113 | 3.0 | 5.0 | 51% | .308 | 1.38 | 3.66 | 3.85 | 4.27 | 1.9 |
| 2011 | NYN | MLB | 27 | 7 | 13 | 0 | 34 | 33 | 193² | 220 | 21 | 65 | 105 | 3.0 | 4.9 | 48% | .305 | 1.47 | 4.74 | 4.43 | 4.65 | 0.5 |
| 2012 | NYN | MLB | 28 | 8 | 12 | 0 | 28 | 28 | 169² | 181 | 13 | 53 | 82 | 2.8 | 4.3 | 51% | .313 | 1.38 | 4.65 | 4.17 | 5.05 | 0.3 |

Now that he's been in the rotation for four years, it's pretty safe to say that Pelfrey is never going to turn into the pitcher the Mets envisioned when they selected him with the ninth overall pick in the 2005 draft. He doesn't throw a changeup, and his slider never developed, so he's basically reduced to throwing two- and four-seam fastballs, and he's lost at least 2 mph off the pitch since his early days, as what was once 92-96 is now more often parked at 90-94 mph. He's not bad as much as he's just treading water.

### Ramon Ramirez

Born: 8/31/1981 Age: 30
Bats: R Throws: R Height: 6' 0" Weight: 190
Breakout: 11% Improve: 35% Collapse: 36%
Attrition: 8% MLB: 97%

Comparables:
Aaron Heilman, A.J. Burnett, Mel Rojas

| YEAR | TEAM | LVL | AGE | W | L | SV | G | GS | IP | H | HR | BB | SO | EqBB9 | EqSO9 | GB% | BABIP | WHIP | ERA | FIP | FRA | WARP |
|------|------|-----|-----|---|---|----|---|----|-----|----|----|----|----|-------|-------|-----|-------|------|-----|-----|-----|------|
| 2009 | BOS | MLB | 27 | 7 | 4 | 0 | 70 | 0 | 69² | 61 | 7 | 32 | 52 | 4.1 | 6.7 | 37% | .266 | 1.33 | 2.84 | 4.51 | 4.14 | 1.2 |
| 2010 | SFN | MLB | 28 | 1 | 0 | 1 | 25 | 0 | 27 | 13 | 1 | 11 | 15 | 3.7 | 5.0 | 39% | .152 | 0.89 | 0.67 | 3.70 | 3.07 | 0.5 |
| 2010 | BOS | MLB | 28 | 0 | 3 | 2 | 44 | 0 | 42¹ | 39 | 6 | 16 | 31 | 3.4 | 6.6 | 36% | .268 | 1.30 | 4.46 | 4.56 | 5.42 | -0.1 |
| 2011 | SFN | MLB | 29 | 3 | 3 | 4 | 66 | 0 | 68² | 54 | 3 | 26 | 66 | 3.4 | 8.7 | 51% | .280 | 1.17 | 2.62 | 2.91 | 3.86 | 0.3 |
| 2012 | NYN | MLB | 30 | 3 | 1 | 1 | 58 | 0 | 59² | 51 | 4 | 22 | 47 | 3.3 | 7.1 | 44% | .290 | 1.22 | 3.54 | 3.61 | 3.85 | 0.8 |

Since the trade that sent him from Boston to San Francisco, Ramirez has leaned ever more heavily on his slider, and the benefits have shown up in both his groundball and strikeout rates. The former was the best of his career in 2011, with his GB/FB rate exactly doubling his 2010 mark. The latter was the result of a dramatic increase in his whiff rate, as Ramirez got swinging strikes more often than such flamethrowers as Jordan Walden, Aroldis Chapman, and Neftali Feliz. While much of the focus on the Mets-Giants trade was on Pagan and Torres, Ramirez could turn into the key piece.

### Jon Rauch

Born: 9/27/1978 Age: 33
Bats: R Throws: R Height: 6' 11" Weight: 230
Breakout: 18% Improve: 40% Collapse: 32%
Attrition: 17% MLB: 87%

Comparables:
John Smoltz, Don Sutton, Roy Oswalt

| YEAR | TEAM | LVL | AGE | W | L | SV | G | GS | IP | H | HR | BB | SO | EqBB9 | EqSO9 | GB% | BABIP | WHIP | ERA | FIP | FRA | WARP |
|------|------|-----|-----|---|---|----|---|----|-----|----|----|----|----|-------|-------|-----|-------|------|-----|-----|-----|------|
| 2009 | MIN | MLB | 30 | 5 | 1 | 0 | 17 | 0 | 15² | 13 | 1 | 6 | 14 | 3.4 | 8.0 | 35% | .300 | 1.21 | 1.72 | 3.53 | 4.09 | 0.3 |
| 2009 | ARI | MLB | 30 | 2 | 2 | 2 | 58 | 0 | 54¹ | 57 | 5 | 17 | 35 | 2.8 | 5.8 | 39% | .295 | 1.36 | 4.14 | 3.96 | 4.31 | 0.8 |
| 2010 | MIN | MLB | 31 | 3 | 1 | 21 | 59 | 0 | 57² | 61 | 3 | 14 | 46 | 2.2 | 7.2 | 38% | .322 | 1.30 | 3.12 | 2.91 | 3.12 | 1.3 |
| 2011 | TOR | MLB | 32 | 5 | 4 | 11 | 53 | 0 | 52 | 56 | 11 | 14 | 36 | 2.4 | 6.2 | 36% | .280 | 1.35 | 4.85 | 5.29 | 4.85 | 0.2 |
| 2012 | NYN | MLB | 33 | 3 | 1 | 11 | 52 | 0 | 51 | 48 | 5 | 12 | 36 | 2.0 | 6.4 | 37% | .300 | 1.17 | 3.65 | 3.77 | 3.96 | 0.7 |

Rauch pitched 320 1/3 innings from 2006 to 2009, meaning he averaged over 80 innings a year during that stretch. In 2010, he was generally healthy, but prior to the 2011 season, he underwent knee surgery. Then, during the year, he missed games with knee and back problems before ultimately requiring knee surgery again in September. Rauch is the tallest pitcher in major-league history. How much cartilage he has in his right knee and how healthy it can stay will determine his future. The Blue Jays declined his nearly $4 million option, and the Mets picked him up for $3.5 million on a relatively low-risk, make-good deal as part of their bullpen rebuild.

### Armando Rodriguez

Born: 1/28/1988 Age: 24
Bats: R Throws: R Height: 6' 4" Weight: 250
Breakout: 25% Improve: 51% Collapse: 26%
Attrition: 19% MLB: 90%

Comparables:
Gavin Floyd, Mike Warren, Randy Messenger

| YEAR | TEAM | LVL | AGE | W | L | SV | G | GS | IP | H | HR | BB | SO | EqBB9 | EqSO9 | GB% | BABIP | WHIP | ERA | FIP | FRA | WARP |
|------|------|-----|-----|---|---|----|---|----|-----|----|----|----|----|-------|-------|-----|-------|------|-----|-----|-----|------|
| 2011 | SLU | A+ | 23 | 2 | 1 | 0 | 16 | 16 | 75 | 63 | 11 | 31 | 76 | 3.5 | 8.9 | 34% | .252 | 1.19 | 3.96 | 4.71 | 4.51 | 1.3 |
| 2012 | NYN | MLB | 24 | 1 | 2 | 0 | 5 | 5 | 26² | 27 | 3 | 14 | 16 | 4.7 | 5.4 | 38% | .302 | 1.53 | 5.47 | 5.04 | 5.94 | -0.2 |

Rodriguez ended the 2010 season with a flourish, but an oblique problem delayed his 2011 start and limited his workload. The Mets protected him on the 40-man roster based on a low-90s fastball, improving slider, and the ability the throw strikes, and his 250-pound frame is built to eat up innings. But he'll need to be careful that he doesn't eat up too much of anything else, or conditioning could become an issue. A healthy, successful season at Double-A makes him a much more well-known name.

### Johan Santana

Born: 3/13/1979 Age: 33
Bats: L Throws: L Height: 6' 1" Weight: 195
Breakout: 13% Improve: 57% Collapse: 14%
Attrition: 13% MLB: 97%

Comparables:
Billy Pierce, Mike Cuellar, Willie Hernandez

| YEAR | TEAM | LVL | AGE | W | L | SV | G | GS | IP | H | HR | BB | SO | EqBB9 | EqSO9 | GB% | BABIP | WHIP | ERA | FIP | FRA | WARP |
|------|------|-----|-----|---|---|----|---|----|------|-----|----|----|-----|-------|-------|-----|-------|------|-----|-----|-----|------|
| 2009 | NYN | MLB | 30 | 13 | 9 | 0 | 25 | 25 | 166² | 156 | 20 | 46 | 146 | 2.5 | 7.9 | 38% | .285 | 1.21 | 3.13 | 3.75 | 3.47 | 4.5 |
| 2010 | NYN | MLB | 31 | 11 | 9 | 0 | 29 | 29 | 199 | 179 | 16 | 55 | 144 | 2.5 | 6.5 | 37% | .276 | 1.18 | 2.98 | 3.56 | 3.76 | 3.5 |
| 2012 | NYN | MLB | 33 | 2 | 2 | 0 | 5 | 5 | 33² | 29 | 3 | 8 | 26 | 2.0 | 6.9 | 41% | .285 | 1.10 | 3.24 | 3.53 | 3.52 | 0.7 |

By late December, GM Sandy Alderson was calling him a question mark for Opening Day. It's safe to say he'll never be the same pitcher, as few are after shoulder surgery, but with so much misinformation, we have no idea what the percentage of decline will be, or when we'll be able to figure it out. We wouldn't bet the future of a fantasy team on that projection, for instance.

### Chris Schwinden

Born: 9/22/1986 Age: 25
Bats: R Throws: R Height: 6' 4" Weight: 215
Breakout: 21% Improve: 66% Collapse: 10%
Attrition: 10% MLB: 94%

**Comparables:**
Taylor Buchholz, John Lackey, Eric Rasmussen

| YEAR | TEAM | LVL | AGE | W | L | SV | G | GS | IP | H | HR | BB | SO | EqBB9 | EqSO9 | GB% | BABIP | WHIP | ERA | FIP | FRA | WARP |
|------|------|-----|-----|---|---|----|---|----|----|---|----|----|----|-------|-------|-----|-------|------|-----|-----|-----|------|
| 2011 | BUF | AAA | 24 | 7 | 6 | 0 | 26 | 26 | 145² | 138 | 14 | 48 | 134 | 3.0 | 8.3 | 36% | .306 | 1.28 | 3.95 | 3.84 | 4.81 | 1.8 |
| 2011 | NYN | MLB | 24 | 0 | 2 | 0 | 4 | 4 | 21 | 23 | 1 | 6 | 17 | 2.6 | 7.3 | 41% | .324 | 1.38 | 4.71 | 2.99 | 3.50 | 0.3 |
| 2012 | NYN | MLB | 25 | 2 | 4 | 0 | 11 | 9 | 53² | 57 | 6 | 17 | 31 | 2.9 | 5.3 | 39% | .316 | 1.39 | 4.94 | 4.45 | 5.37 | -0.1 |

Schwinden can throw strikes. Not only that, he can throw good strikes. He can use both sides of the plate and paint the corners. That's the sum of what he can do with a fastball that rarely gets out of the 80s, but it allowed him to hold his own all the way up the Mets ladder, and when the Mets needed anybody who could throw a baseball at the end of the year, it allowed him to hold his own in a quartet of big-league starts. Hold his own is the most anyone can ever hope for out of Schwinden, and players with his profile can last for more than a decade, bouncing from team to team and applying their trade when emergency needs pop up. It beats working at Sears.

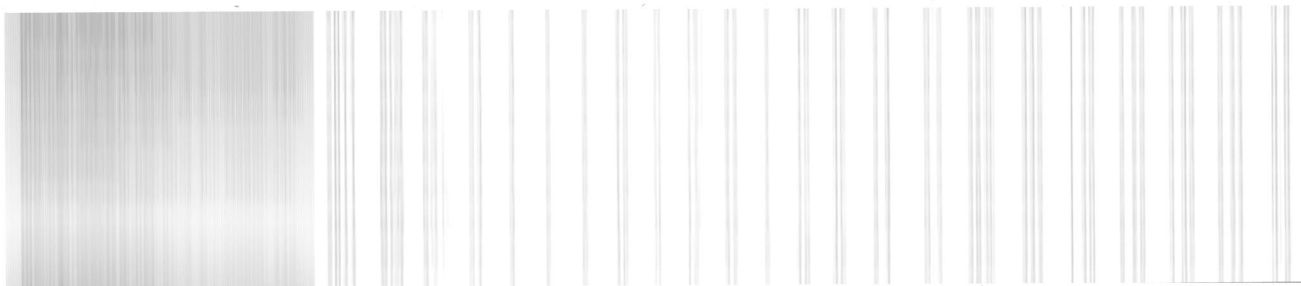

It was a strange 2011 campaign for Stinson, who was awful as a starter at Triple-A, found some success out of the bullpen following a demotion, and suddenly found himself in the majors by September. He's a classic fastball/slider type who sits in the low-90s and tends to keep the ball on the ground, but he's never figured out how to miss bats, with a career minor-league rate of just six per nine, with it dropping a bit at every level. He was certainly better as a starter than as a reliever, but it's probably not good enough.

### Zack Wheeler

Born: 5/30/1990 Age: 22
Bats: R Throws: R Height: 6' 4" Weight: 180
Breakout: 23% Improve: 47% Collapse: 28%
Attrition: 7% MLB: 92%

**Comparables:**
Chris Tillman, Chad Billingsley, Moe Drabowsky

| YEAR | TEAM | LVL | AGE | W | L | SV | G | GS | IP | H | HR | BB | SO | EqBB9 | EqSO9 | GB% | BABIP | WHIP | ERA | FIP | FRA | WARP |
|------|------|-----|-----|---|---|----|---|----|----|---|----|----|----|-------|-------|-----|-------|------|-----|-----|-----|------|
| 2010 | AUG | A | 20 | 3 | 3 | 0 | 21 | 13 | 58² | 23 | 0 | 17 | 35 | 5.8 | 10.7 | 59% | .343 | 1.45 | 3.99 | 3.44 | 4.15 | 0.7 |
| 2011 | SLU | A+ | 21 | 0 | 1 | 0 | 6 | 6 | 27 | 31 | 0 | 7 | 38 | 1.7 | 10.3 | 51% | .378 | 1.15 | 2.00 | 1.69 | 3.41 | 1.0 |
| 2011 | SJO | A+ | 21 | 7 | 5 | 0 | 16 | 16 | 88 | 74 | 7 | 47 | 98 | 4.8 | 10.0 | 51% | .295 | 1.38 | 3.99 | 4.48 | 4.53 | 0.8 |
| 2012 | NYN | MLB | 22 | 2 | 3 | 0 | 7 | 7 | 34¹ | 32 | 3 | 17 | 27 | 4.4 | 7.1 | 48% | .312 | 1.43 | 4.74 | 4.25 | 5.16 | 0.1 |

The Mets took an interesting tack last summer when they put Carlos Beltran on the market. Instead of focusing on quantity, they made their decision based on the best single talent they could find, and that turned out to be Wheeler. A first-round pick in 2009, Wheeler has front-of-the-rotation potential thanks to mid-90s heat and a fantastic slow curveball. Like many young pitchers, his changeup still needs plenty of development, and his control needs work, but the Mets found some success in the latter department when they tinkered with his mechanics. The Mets' system looks better than it has in years, and with Wheeler and Harvey, they have a pair of potential starters who could begin to pay dividends by 2013.

### Chris Young

Born: 5/25/1979 Age: 33
Bats: R Throws: R Height: 6' 11" Weight: 260
Breakout: 13% Improve: 30% Collapse: 42%
Attrition: 9% MLB: 92%

**Comparables:**
Guillermo Mota, Felix Rodriguez, Jason Schmidt

| YEAR | TEAM | LVL | AGE | W | L | SV | G | GS | IP | H | HR | BB | SO | EqBB9 | EqSO9 | GB% | BABIP | WHIP | ERA | FIP | FRA | WARP |
|------|------|-----|-----|---|---|----|---|----|----|---|----|----|----|-------|-------|-----|-------|------|-----|-----|-----|------|
| 2009 | SDN | MLB | 30 | 4 | 6 | 0 | 14 | 14 | 76 | 70 | 12 | 40 | 50 | 4.7 | 5.9 | 33% | .254 | 1.45 | 5.21 | 5.45 | 4.84 | 0.8 |
| 2010 | SDN | MLB | 31 | 2 | 0 | 0 | 4 | 4 | 20 | 10 | 1 | 11 | 15 | 4.9 | 6.8 | 32% | .167 | 1.05 | 0.90 | 3.91 | 2.95 | 0.4 |
| 2011 | NYN | MLB | 32 | 1 | 0 | 0 | 4 | 4 | 24 | 12 | 3 | 11 | 22 | 4.1 | 8.2 | 21% | .158 | 0.96 | 1.88 | 4.29 | 3.70 | 0.4 |
| 2012 | NYN | MLB | 33 | 1 | 1 | 0 | 4 | 4 | 19² | 16 | 2 | 8 | 15 | 3.8 | 7.0 | 30% | .264 | 1.22 | 3.47 | 4.22 | 3.77 | 0.4 |

The Mets signed Young to a $1.1 million dollar deal loaded with incentives, but that's all they had to pay him, as after just four starts, his right shoulder required season-ending surgery. He's always been an enigma, getting the job done, and more, with a mid-80s fastball because of the uniqueness of his arm angles and the shortening of the distance to the plate due to his NBA-center height. The Mets are interested in giving him a look this spring despite the surgery. If there has ever been a pitcher who has proven that he can do his job without much in the way of stuff, it's Young.

## LINEOUTS

### HITTERS

| PLAYER | TEAM | LVL | AGE | PA | R | 2B | 3B | HR | RBI | BB | SO | SB-CS | AVG/OBP/SLG | TAv | BABIP | BRR | FRAA | WARP |
|---|---|---|---|---|---|---|---|---|---|---|---|---|---|---|---|---|---|---|
| RF M. Baxter | BUF | AAA | 26 | 71 | 4 | 0 | 2 | 1 | 7 | 5 | 19 | 1-0 | .188/.257/.297 | .185 | .250 | 0.4 | -1 | -0.6 |
| | NYN | MLB | 26 | 40 | 6 | 2 | 1 | 1 | 4 | 5 | 9 | 0-0 | .235/.350/.441 | .282 | .292 | -0.3 | -1 | 0.2 |
| CF M. Den Dekker | SLU | A+ | 23 | 302 | 54 | 19 | 8 | 6 | 36 | 24 | 65 | 12-5 | .296/.362/.494 | .293 | .369 | 4.3 | -4.8 | 2.1 |
| | BIN | AA | 23 | 314 | 49 | 13 | 3 | 11 | 32 | 27 | 91 | 12-5 | .235/.312/.426 | .259 | .305 | 2.4 | -2.1 | 1.0 |
| 2B C. Hu | NYN | MLB | 27 | 23 | 2 | 0 | 0 | 0 | 1 | 1 | 11 | 1-0 | .050/.091/.050 | .118 | .100 | 0.3 | -0.1 | -0.3 |
| | MTS | RK | 27 | 57 | 8 | 0 | 0 | 0 | 1 | 8 | 7 | 2-1 | .184/.298/.184 | .202 | .214 | 1.4 | 5.3 | 0.6 |
| 3B Z. Lutz | BUF | AAA | 25 | 250 | 38 | 12 | 0 | 11 | 31 | 27 | 70 | 0-0 | .295/.380/.500 | .293 | .388 | 0 | 1 | 1.4 |
| 1B V. Pascucci | BUF | AAA | 32 | 523 | 58 | 29 | 1 | 21 | 91 | 76 | 149 | 1-2 | .264/.375/.476 | .278 | .350 | -7.1 | -3.8 | 0.7 |
| | NYN | MLB | 32 | 11 | 1 | 0 | 0 | 1 | 2 | 0 | 3 | 0-0 | .273/.273/.545 | .285 | .286 | 0 | 0 | 0.1 |
| RF C. Puello | SLU | A+ | 20 | 488 | 67 | 21 | 5 | 10 | 50 | 18 | 103 | 19-9 | .259/.313/.397 | .248 | .311 | 0.5 | -0.9 | 0.5 |
| 3B A. Rodriguez | SAV | A | 19 | 554 | 59 | 23 | 2 | 17 | 78 | 29 | 106 | 2-1 | .221/.265/.372 | .246 | .245 | 2.1 | -6 | 0.2 |
| LF V. Rottino | NWO | AAA | 31 | 524 | 81 | 31 | 2 | 10 | 59 | 50 | 62 | 17-9 | .304/.374/.443 | .278 | .333 | 0.2 | 4.4 | 3.1 |
| | FLO | MLB | 31 | 14 | 1 | 0 | 0 | 0 | 0 | 2 | 4 | 0-0 | .167/.286/.167 | .186 | .250 | 0.1 | -0.2 | -0.1 |
| 2B J. Satin | BIN | AA | 26 | 404 | 60 | 35 | 2 | 11 | 60 | 57 | 91 | 2-2 | .325/.423/.538 | .329 | .411 | 1.6 | -11.5 | 3.0 |
| | BUF | AAA | 26 | 160 | 17 | 8 | 0 | 1 | 16 | 14 | 33 | 1-2 | .317/.381/.393 | .261 | .405 | -1.6 | -0.3 | 0.2 |
| | NYN | MLB | 26 | 27 | 3 | 1 | 0 | 0 | 2 | 1 | 11 | 0-0 | .200/.259/.240 | .172 | .357 | -0.1 | 0.2 | -0.2 |
| RF C. Vaughn | SAV | A | 22 | 297 | 33 | 14 | 2 | 4 | 30 | 36 | 64 | 8-5 | .286/.405/.408 | .313 | .371 | 0.1 | -0.7 | 2.4 |
| | SLU | A+ | 22 | 241 | 29 | 8 | 1 | 9 | 29 | 23 | 53 | 2-3 | .219/.308/.395 | .242 | .247 | 0.5 | -7.3 | -0.4 |

Minor-league veteran **Mike Baxter** is one of those players with no defensive home and not enough bat for the few positions he can play. Even being from Queens wasn't enough for the Mets to keep him. ⊘ **Matt Den Dekker** is one of the better defensive outfielders in the game, but he might not ever hit enough for it to matter. ⊘ **Chin-Lung Hu** has regressed as a prospect and now he can't stay healthy. His window is nearly closed. ⊘ **Zach Lutz** is a bulky, slow third baseman who can hit a bit, but that's really his only tool. ⊘ **Val Pascucci** went seven years between big-league stints, and the Mets re-signed him to mash at Triple-A. It's what he does. ⊘ Outfielder **Cesar Puello** has great tools, and little to show for it on the stat sheet. ⊘ **Aderlin Rodriguez** has as much raw power as anyone in the system, and we're done saying good things about him. ⊘ A solid approach at the plate and the ability to throw out baserunners means that **Vinny Rottino** will keep getting chances, but he remains a below-average receiver. ⊘ Infielder **Josh Satin** has utility potential due to his bat and his ability to man first, second and third, although he's not especially good at any of them. ⊘ The son of Greg, **Cory Vaughn** has plenty of tools, but failed to build on his impressive 2010 debut, making 2012 an early make-or-break season in his career.

### PITCHERS

| PLAYER | TEAM | LVL | AGE | W | L | SV | IP | H | HR | BB | SO | EqBB9 | EqSO9 | GB% | BABIP | WHIP | ERA | FIP | FRA | WARP |
|---|---|---|---|---|---|---|---|---|---|---|---|---|---|---|---|---|---|---|---|---|
| C. James | ROC | AAA | 29 | 2 | 1 | 1 | 62² | 48 | 4 | 26 | 64 | 3.9 | 9.6 | 32% | .277 | 1.21 | 2.30 | 3.32 | 4.14 | 1.2 |
| | MIN | MLB | 29 | 0 | 0 | 0 | 10¹ | 12 | 1 | 4 | 8 | 3.5 | 7.0 | 23% | .333 | 1.55 | 6.10 | 3.93 | 4.87 | 0.0 |
| G. Olson | IND | AAA | 27 | 3 | 1 | 0 | 85² | 63 | 7 | 47 | 61 | 4.9 | 6.4 | 36% | .232 | 1.28 | 3.05 | 4.63 | 4.79 | 1.0 |
| | PIT | MLB | 27 | 1 | 1 | 0 | 4¹ | 2 | 0 | 3 | 4 | 6.2 | 8.3 | 50% | .154 | 1.15 | 2.08 | 3.22 | 4.59 | 0.0 |

Half a decade ago, **Chuck James** was a Braves prospect of note, renowned for his extreme fly-ball ways as well as his off-field antics. He once broke both wrists jumping off a roof. His brief midsummer stint with the Twins marked his first major-league action since 2008 rotator-cuff and labrum surgery. ⊘ The Mets signed former Orioles prospect **Garrett Olson** in the offseason, and scouts report that he is still left-handed.

## MANAGER: TERRY COLLINS

| YEAR | TEAM | W-L | Pythag +/- | Avg PC | 100+ P | 120+ P | QS | BQS | REL | REL w Zero R | IBB | Subs | PH | PH Avg | PH HR | SB2 | CS2 | SB3 | CS3 | SAC Att | SAC % | POS SAC | Squeeze | Swing | In Play |
|------|------|-----|-----------|--------|--------|--------|----|-----|-----|--------------|-----|------|-----|--------|-------|-----|-----|-----|-----|---------|-------|---------|---------|-------|---------|
| 2011 | NYN | 77-85 | 0 | 95.7 | 63 | 6 | 84 | 7 | 514 | 398 | 48 | — | 306 | .203 | 8 | 16 | 4 | 1 | 0 | 102 | 72.5% | 35 | 2 | 347 | 114 |

Collins served a nearly decade-long sentence for his previous stints as a manager, or rather mis-manager, in the 1990s, with his late-decade Angels tenure ending with a team revolt. Always a good baseball mind but more than a little bit intense, Collins stayed in baseball, working in the minor-league system of the Dodgers, managing in Japan, leading the China national team in the 2009 World Baseball Classic, and even taking an independent-league stint. What we've seen over the last two years is a kinder, gentler Collins. He's still tense, but hardly a hothead, and players seem to genuinely like playing for him. Back-to-back 77-win seasons don't look so bad considering the cards he's been dealt in terms of talent and injuries, and his option to man-

# New York Yankees

On October 28, 2007, during Game Four of the World Series between the Boston Red Sox and the Colorado Rockies, Alex Rodriguez chose to exercise his contractual right to opt out of the 10-year, $252 million agreement he had originally signed with the Texas Rangers in the Year 2000. The Yankees, desperate to retain the third baseman, gave him $275 million to keep him in the Bronx through the 2017 season. While Rodriguez was then one of baseball's premier talents, and would win a third MVP award shortly thereafter, such a mammoth contract would have to come back to bite the Yankees. Indeed, Rodriguez has missed time every season since, is now over 35 with declining power at a power position, and has an utterly immovable contract.

Teams can work around the occasional poor signing—the Phillies ended last season with the best record in baseball despite Ryan Howard's terrible contract extension, for example. But the Yankees have multiple instances of players who cannot possibly live up to the needs set by their huge paychecks. Besides Rodriguez, we have other egregious examples: Mark Teixeira (eight years, $180 million through 2016, his age-36 season), CC Sabathia (five years, $122 million through 2016, his age-35 season, along with a vesting option for 2017; this replaced a seven-year deal that would have ended in 2015), and A.J. Burnett (five years, $82.5 million through 2013, or age-36). In fact, all three of those players came in the same spending spree prior to the 2009 season. The short term result was a championship, but in the long term, will the team be paying for that excess for years to come? There are more recent examples that don't exactly speak of austerity measures, too, like the money and years given to Rafael Soriano (three years, $35 million) and Derek Jeter (three years, $51 million, including a likely buyout of the shortstop's age-40 season) before the 2011 season.

And yet, the most notable thing about this most recent off-season isn't what the Yankees have spent; it's what they haven't spent. The winter progressed with painful deliberateness for the Yankees. On October 29, they picked up Nick Swisher's option. On Halloween they re-signed Sabathia, apparently unwilling to gamble that he could not top the four years and $92 million remaining on his old deal on the open market, and gave him an extra year and $30 million. In December they re-signed Freddy Garcia. Having acted to ensure that the 2012 team would be a doppelganger for the 2011 edition, they rested, passing on such tantalizing but risky investments as Yu Darvish and C.J. Wilson.

The Yankees are so well-known for freely spending to get what they want that this financial restraint seems wholly out of character, as if the other Joseph McCarthy had suddenly decided that he quite liked Communists after all. And out-of-character behavior raises questions. One can argue that a business that exhibits restraint and spends wisely should be lauded, but if this hurts said business's ability to compete, is the practice to be praised?

Short of gaining access to their books, there is no way of knowing if the Yankees are being affected by Great Depression II: The Economy Strikes Back. Have the un-leased luxury boxes and empty Legends seats in the Stadium's lower dish caused them to pull back the ever-climbing payroll? Or is spending less part of an actual plan? No business is immune from the pitfalls of a bear economy, and the Yankees are a business. At a time of greater prosperity, we've seen them gamble money recklessly as they did in 2008-09 on Sabathia, Burnett, and Teixeira. Just a year ago they dropped $35 million (and forfeited a first-round draft choice in the process) on reliever Rafael Soriano just because he lingered on the market. But as early as winter 2008, Brian Cashman made

## YANKEES PROSPECTUS
### 2011 W-L: 97-65, 1st in AL East

| | | | |
|---|---|---|---|
| Pythag | .629 | 2nd | **Ballpark:** Yankee Stadium (3-yr. PF: 100). AL's most hitter-friendly park is only average overall |
| RS/G | 5.35 | 2nd | |
| RA/G | 4.06 | 10th | |
| TAv | .283 | 3rd | **2011:** Third-best offense plus fourth-best bullpen equals 97 wins, but an early playoff exit |
| TAv-P | .265 | 21st | |
| FIP | 3.90 | 13th | |
| DER | .703 | 21st | **2012:** Standing pat on the roster means only a best-case scenario will get them into October |
| DL | 1333 | 30th | |
| B-Age | 30.6 | 29th | |
| P-Age | 30.9 | 30th | **Action Items:** Starting pitching, big years from Teixeira and A-Rod, don't let Jeter or Mo age |
| Salary | $207.4 | 1st | |
| M$/MW | $4.02 | 25th | |

statements to the press corps about reducing payroll. In the case of the Yankees, "reducing" may have meant "holding steady without the huge jumps we're used to." After nearly doubling the payroll from 2000 to 2005, things have held relatively steady around $200 million. This December the team paid its lowest luxury tax bill since the inception of the tax, while the tax threshold and other teams' payrolls continue to rise.

## Yankees Payroll Year by Year[1]

| Year | Payroll | Luxury Tax (in millions) |
| --- | --- | --- |
| 2000 | $107.6 | N/A |
| 2009 | $201.5 | $25.7 |
| 2010 | $206.3 | $18.0 |
| 2011 | $202.6 | $13.9 |

Whether Cashman and the front office simply decided there was nothing worth getting on the market, or the Yankees found themselves unable to make a move for financial or other reasons, or if they are operating under a self-imposed cap, the fact remains that a major offseason move was not made as of Christmas. Some would count the re-signing of Sabathia and the re-upping of Cashman himself as the most important priorities, but the roster is nearly identical to last year's.

This offseason the Yankees passed on the risky C.J. Wilson and Yu Darvish, even though their biggest area of concern remains their starting rotation. The Yankees have potential homegrown solutions to their pitching woes, especially in top prospects Manny Banuelos and Dellin Betances, but neither pitcher has a major league season under his belt, and both have significant command issues that may delay the former and force the latter to the bullpen. Perhaps, had the Yankees not resisted starting Hector Noesi until the very end of the season, they might now have another experienced starter on hand, but at the time keeping A.J. Burnett in the starting rotation was deemed the greater priority.

The Yankees are in both a better and a worse situation when it comes to their offense. Unlike Banuelos and Betances, Jesus Montero is ready to take up his major league burden. Though judging a player by his September production is rarely accurate, there is still as of yet nothing to suggest he cannot hit at the highest level. But the declining Rodriguez and Jeter, along with a disappointing Teixeira—who has yet to turn in a hoped-for MVP-caliber season in New York—may leave a hole too big for just Montero's bat to fill.

At the start of 2011, many prognosticators, including this publication's authors, predicted the Yankees would be in for a rude awakening. While not necessarily a bad team, we said, the rotation was cobbled together after the club was spurned by Cliff Lee and would be unable to compete with fellow AL East stalwarts in Tampa and Boston. The ace that Cashman turned out to have tucked up his sleeve was not the debut of Montero (which didn't occur until September) or a trade for rotation help (the best pitching acquisition of the deadline, Doug Fister, went to Detroit). Instead, Cashman's surprises were all scrap-heap gems: Bartolo Colon, Russell Martin,

pitchers trying to establish themselves in the major leagues. He was hurt again last season, and in five major league seasons, Hughes has managed a full season as a starter just once, in 2010. His best season, arguably, was 2009, in which he spent most of the season in the bullpen, an instance of a very wrong decision having unintended beneficial consequences. The Yankees' ability to trade him on potential alone could very well be past, but the question of whether or not he will actually help the team remains.

Hughes, at least, remains inexpensive and potentially movable. The same cannot be said of Burnett. His five-year, $88 million contract would have made him about as transferable as William Howard Taft in his bathtub,[2] even if he had pitched well enough to be considered an ace. Burnett, however, has not pitched anywhere near that level: an ERA of 5.20 over the last two seasons. His heroic effort in last season's ALDS Game Four notwithstanding, his overall performance inspires little confidence that he will earn the last two seasons of his contract.

That contract is an albatross dragging him and the team down. With a contract of any lesser size, Burnett would have pitched himself out of the rotation long ago, but the Yankees can't afford to throw such an expensive player into the recycle bin. Even if he and Hughes are little more than bodies keeping the rotation warm, no one is ready to replace them. This may change as the season progresses, but it would be an act of undue optimism to count on top performances out of Betances, Banuelos, or any other untried pitcher right out of the box. The Yankees learned that lesson the hard way in 2008, the year that they relied too much on three rookie pitchers: Hughes, Ian Kennedy, and Joba Chamberlain.

In another division, maybe, or in a park friendlier to pitchers, the Yankees could get by on the backs of Sabathia, Freddy Garcia, and Ivan Nova alone. The AL East is not such a division. Even if Garcia repeats his success and Nova shows that his rookie season was not a one-hit wonder (see player capsule), it would be a tough task: Fenway Park, Camden Yards and Yankee Stadium are not known for being a pitcher's best friends.

Of course, the starting pitching is not the entire staff. Last season, Yankees starters had a FAIR RA of of 4.41, which ranked eighth in the American League. Conversely, their relief FAIR RA of 4.64 was fourth in the league, behind Chicago, Boston, and Oakland. Yankees relievers, particularly Mariano Rivera, David Robertson, and Cory Wade, were amazingly effective last year, but individual relievers and by extension bullpens as a whole are notoriously volatile. Normally, Rivera is an exception to that rule, but he is now the same age as his number (42) and no player can excel forever.

Could the offense carry the team in 2012? The Yankees are not the Mariners or the A's or the Giants; their offense remains the team's calling card. Still, that does not mean there are not concerns. As ranked by True Average, the Yankees had the third-best offense in the league in 2011, but continuity is not a sure thing. Jeter's season was a tale of two halves, which was one more good half than might have been expected after 2010; shortstops on the other side of 35 don't usually age gracefully and the Yankees are paying him now for past production. A healthy Rodriguez is still a weapon, but A) he hasn't been healthy for the majority of a season since 2008, and B) his power numbers declined significantly last season. His 16 home runs might be accounted for by the time and potency lost to injury, but his .461 SLG was his lowest since 1995. If Rodriguez played a defense-first position, the drop in power might be less concerning, but for good or ill, Rodriguez will remain on the roster through 2017.

The Yankees are less now the team of Jeter and Rodriguez than they are that of Robinson Cano and Curtis Granderson—the latter two putting up stellar numbers last season, Cano flirting with the batting title and Granderson with the MVP Award. Concerns about Cano increase the further he gets from his age-27 season—second basemen are not known for aging well due to the pounding that they take—but Cano has proven himself to be exceptionally durable. For the moment, as long as he is occasionally reminded that it is okay to take a pitch, he remains the Yankees' most valuable player.

The Yankees have one of the game's longest-tenured general managers in Cashman, who re-upped for three more years this offseason. (Few thought he would actually leave the organization he grew up in.) The farm system is in better shape now than it has been in decades, even if the brain trust has yet to figure out how to handle a prospect once he is actually ready to break into the majors. However, as in George Steinbrenner's day, the Yankees remain an organization of too many chefs, in which the baseball men can be overruled by some combination of the Steinbrenner scions and the former attorneys who run the organization. No GM operates with carte blanche; owners and designated proxies will intervene on any team if they deem it necessary to protect their investment. Still, the never-ending divisions within the Yankees executive suites means that they are incapable of fully exploiting their massive financial advantages. If only some would learn that the greatest market inefficiency is not shutting up and getting out of the way when you don't know what you're talking about.

A best-case scenario for 2012 would see Montero join the Yankees with as flawless a rookie season as Jeter had, increased production from Hughes, no sophomore slump from Nova, and more consistency from Swisher. Even supposing all of these things happen, and all else remains equal, it still might not be enough. The biggest movers and shakers in the offseason in the American League were the Rangers and the Angels; the Yankees can't assume that if they fail to win the AL East title, they will have the wild card as a fallback option.

Best-case scenarios rarely happen anywhere; they happen even less often in baseball. The Yankees were able to make the most out of their team last season, but the most likely scenario with that team would not have had them winning the AL East, much less making the playoffs at all. The Yankees, for whatever reason—be it the restraint they are employing or their own belief that what they have now is good enough—are rolling the dice going into 2012 with much the same team that they had in 2011, sans Colon and Jorge Posada. Barring a major acquisition subsequent to our going to press, the Yankees' theme for 2012 is "meet the new team, same as the old team."

The 2012 Yankees won't—or at least, shouldn't—be a bad team. With so many question marks, however, and either an unwillingness or inability to acquire outside players who could help the team win, the 2012 Yankees, while good, will not be good enough to win their 28th championship, the organization's avowed goal.

[1] Sources: Cot's Baseball Contracts, USATODAY Salaries Database

[2] Taft, the heaviest president, did a lot of emotional eating. He wasn't much into being president; Theodore Roosevelt pushed him there, and when Taft's policies diverged from his own, he broke with his old friend, leaving Taft to cry into ever more chocolate eclairs. Later in life, Taft got the job he truly wanted, Chief Justice of the Supreme court, and, truly happy for the first time, dropped an almost-literal ton of weight. Moral of the story: A.J. Burnett needs to be named to the Supreme Court.

# HITTERS

## Dante Bichette — 3B

Born: 9/26/1992 Age: 19
Bats: R Throws: R Height: 6' 2" Weight: 215
Breakout: 0% Improve: 2% Collapse: 2%
Attrition: 5% MLB: 7%

**Comparables:**
Matthew Sweeney, Jarek Cunningham, Edinson Rincon

| YEAR | TEAM | LVL | AGE | PA | R | 2B | 3B | HR | RBI | BB | SO | SB | CS | AVG_OBP_SLG | TAv | BABIP | BRR | FRAA | WARP |
|------|------|-----|-----|-----|----|----|----|----|-----|----|----|----|----|-------------|------|-------|------|-------|------|
| 2011 | YAN | RK | 18 | 240 | 33 | 17 | 3 | 3 | 47 | 30 | 41 | 3 | 3 | .342/.446/.505 | .339 | .410 | -0.3 | -11.2 | 2.0 |
| 2012 | NYA | MLB | 19 | 250 | 24 | 9 | 0 | 4 | 20 | 19 | 67 | 1 | 0 | .207/.278/.310 | .211 | .270 | -0.1 | 3B 2 | -0.6 |

The Yankees' pick in the supplemental phase of the June 2011 draft, and their first pick overall, Bichette is the namesake and offspring of the outfielder who hit .316/.352/.540 for the Rockies (and about half that for everyone else). Daddy never had a minor league season like his boy's pro debut, in which the latter won Gulf Coast League MVP honors. Considered something of an overdraft in June, Bichette was felt to be a decent hitting prospect but that was all—professional ball would see him moving from the hot corner to the outfield. The Yankees have said, "Whoa, not so fast. We like him just where he is." Scouts outside the organization concur that Bichette can be an average third baseman. If Bichette can stay

Chase Utley, Ian Kinsler, Brandon Phillips

The 2011 Yankees MVP as per WARP and one of the 10 most valuable players in baseball by that same stat, Cano had one of his most consistent seasons last year, largely eschewing the unsustainable highs and Slough-of-Despond lows of past seasons. Although Dustin Pedroia reclaimed the Gold Glove from him, he is also an excellent fielder. The Yankees will face a difficult decision following 2013, when Cano's contract is up. Though Cano has been highly durable for a middle infielder, by the time second basemen are in their early 30s the demands of the position have often greatly reduced their potency. Cano's lack of patience means that if his batting average ebbs, he will need to maintain his power and glove to be worth playing as he ages. He just might do it, but it's going to cost quite a bit of money to find out.

## Francisco Cervelli — C

Born: 3/6/1986 Age: 26
Bats: R Throws: R Height: 6' 2" Weight: 210
Breakout: 2% Improve: 32% Collapse: 14%
Attrition: 39% MLB: 84%

**Comparables:**
Hobie Landrith, Hardy Peterson, Thurman Munson

| YEAR | TEAM | LVL | AGE | PA | R | 2B | 3B | HR | RBI | BB | SO | SB | CS | AVG_OBP_SLG | TAv | BABIP | BRR | FRAA | WARP |
|------|------|-----|-----|-----|----|----|----|----|-----|----|----|----|----|-------------|------|-------|------|--------|------|
| 2009 | TRN | AA | 23 | 64 | 8 | 1 | 0 | 2 | 7 | 6 | 13 | 0 | 0 | .190/.266/.310 | .210 | .209 | 0.6 | 0.5 | 0.1 |
| 2009 | SWB | AAA | 23 | 75 | 7 | 5 | 0 | 1 | 7 | 3 | 13 | 0 | 2 | .275/.311/.391 | .274 | .321 | 0 | 0.1 | 0.5 |
| 2009 | NYA | MLB | 23 | 101 | 13 | 4 | 0 | 1 | 11 | 2 | 11 | 0 | 3 | .298/.309/.372 | .244 | .325 | -0.7 | -0.4 | 0.1 |
| 2010 | NYA | MLB | 24 | 317 | 27 | 11 | 3 | 0 | 38 | 33 | 42 | 1 | 1 | .271/.359/.335 | .252 | .316 | -2.5 | 1.1 | 0.7 |
| 2011 | NYA | MLB | 25 | 137 | 17 | 4 | 0 | 4 | 22 | 9 | 29 | 4 | 1 | .266/.324/.395 | .261 | .315 | 0.2 | 0 | 0.6 |
| 2012 | NYA | MLB | 26 | 250 | 28 | 10 | 1 | 4 | 23 | 20 | 44 | 2 | 1 | .263/.335/.372 | .252 | .305 | -0.3 | C 0, 3B -0 | 1.7 |

Cervelli's season was bookended by injuries. He fractured his foot in spring training, delaying his season debut until May 1. On September 8, a collision at home plate with Nick Markakis resulted in a concussion (reportedly the fourth or fifth of Cervelli's career) that erased the rest of his season and the playoffs. In between, "Cervie" was roughly the same player he was in 2010, though, adding a few home runs and subtracting a few walks. He's a singles-flicking catcher who doesn't throw well (14 percent caught stealing 2010-11), and has had enough concussion problems that worries over his future well-being are not unwarranted. During the offseason, Joe Girardi strongly suggested that Cervelli would be the first option to back up Russell Martin. Cervelli is likeable, but there isn't any particular reason he should have so strong a grip on his job.

## Brett Gardner — LF

Born: 8/24/1983 Age: 28
Bats: L Throws: L Height: 5' 11" Weight: 180
Breakout: 4% Improve: 35% Collapse: 7%
Attrition: 22% MLB: 85%

**Comparables:**
Minnie Minoso, Lew Ford, Roy White

| YEAR | TEAM | LVL | AGE | PA | R | 2B | 3B | HR | RBI | BB | SO | SB | CS | AVG_OBP_SLG | TAv | BABIP | BRR | FRAA | WARP |
|------|------|-----|-----|-----|----|----|----|----|-----|----|----|----|----|-------------|------|-------|------|---------|------|
| 2009 | NYA | MLB | 25 | 284 | 48 | 6 | 6 | 3 | 23 | 26 | 40 | 26 | 5 | .270/.345/.379 | .260 | .311 | 3.8 | 2.8 | 1.8 |
| 2010 | NYA | MLB | 26 | 569 | 97 | 20 | 7 | 5 | 47 | 79 | 101 | 47 | 9 | .277/.383/.379 | .280 | .340 | 8.7 | 6.1 | 4.4 |
| 2011 | NYA | MLB | 27 | 588 | 87 | 19 | 8 | 7 | 36 | 60 | 93 | 49 | 13 | .259/.345/.369 | .256 | .303 | 7.7 | 13.7 | 3.5 |
| 2012 | NYA | MLB | 28 | 549 | 67 | 18 | 7 | 8 | 51 | 66 | 96 | 45 | 10 | .268/.365/.385 | .268 | .316 | 1.4 | LF 7, CF 2 | 2.0 |

Gardner isn't the prototypical mashing left fielder, but the aggregate of his defense, baserunning, and hitting (such as it is) makes him a valuable player even in a corner. Very streaky, Gardner started off the season in a slump, batted .302/.380/.401 from May through July, then disappeared thereafter, hitting only .220/.320/.313 the rest of the way (he did hit well in the ALDS, going 7-for-17). Despite the subpar production, with speed that is overqualified for left (he was the AL's most productive defensive outfielder according to FRAA) and his league-leading 49 steals, he can add two or three wins with his legs instead of his bat. Gardner is not young, however, and is likely now at his peak. Eligible for arbitration for the first time this past winter, Gardner is about to reach the point when he can command high salaries and long-term contracts, neither of which is in the Yankees' best interest. A more traditional left fielder would be a safer investment.

### Curtis Granderson　CF

Born: 3/16/1981 Age: 31
Bats: L Throws: R Height: 6' 2" Weight: 180
Breakout: 0% Improve: 40% Collapse: 11%
Attrition: 16% MLB: 94%

**Comparables:**
Fred Lynn, Willie Mays, Andruw Jones

| YEAR | TEAM | LVL | AGE | PA | R | 2B | 3B | HR | RBI | BB | SO | SB | CS | AVG_OBP_SLG | TAv | BABIP | BRR | FRAA | WARP |
|------|------|-----|-----|-----|-----|----|----|----|-----|----|-----|----|----|-------------|------|-------|------|-------|------|
| 2009 | DET | MLB | 28 | 710 | 91 | 23 | 8 | 30 | 71 | 72 | 141 | 20 | 6 | .249/.327/.453 | .274 | .275 | 3.3 | -0.8 | 3.1 |
| 2010 | NYA | MLB | 29 | 528 | 76 | 17 | 7 | 24 | 67 | 53 | 116 | 12 | 2 | .247/.324/.468 | .284 | .277 | 3.2 | 1.8 | 3.4 |
| 2011 | NYA | MLB | 30 | 691 | 136 | 26 | 10 | 41 | 119 | 85 | 169 | 25 | 10 | .262/.364/.552 | .312 | .295 | 4.8 | -13.2 | 5.3 |
| 2012 | NYA | MLB | 31 | 619 | 83 | 23 | 9 | 28 | 89 | 65 | 137 | 18 | 6 | .262/.345/.491 | .290 | .298 | 0 | CF -1 | 3.9 |

After years of being dismissed as a strikeout-prone platoon player, Granderson came within an ice-cold September of being a serious candidate for the AL MVP award. The August 2010 reworking of his swing held, and by the end of May he had launched 17 home runs, including nine in 62 at-bats against his former nemeses, left-handers. Normally, when a 30-year-old has a season out of line with established norms, we'd be crying, "Regression off the starboard bow!" However, this is for all purposes a new Granderson, something PECOTA is incapable of knowing when it predicts that regression. Unless you're irrationally averse to strikeouts, the only knock on Granderson now is his defense, which the major metrics do not like. Unlike, say, Derek Jeter, the reasons for this are not obvious to the eye. Signed at reasonable prices through 2012 with a similarly friendly club option for 2013, Granderson should be a safe bet for the duration, and if the Yankees come up with a more glove-ly candidate for center field, his bat can carry left with aplomb.

### Derek Jeter　SS

Born: 6/26/1974 Age: 38
Bats: R Throws: R Height: 6' 4" Weight: 175
Breakout: 1% Improve: 25% Collapse: 17%
Attrition: 23% MLB: 68%

**Comparables:**
Pee Wee Reese, Alan Trammell, Tony Graffanino

| YEAR | TEAM | LVL | AGE | PA | R | 2B | 3B | HR | RBI | BB | SO | SB | CS | AVG_OBP_SLG | TAv | BABIP | BRR | FRAA | WARP |
|------|------|-----|-----|-----|-----|----|----|----|-----|----|-----|----|----|-------------|------|-------|------|-------|------|
| 2009 | NYA | MLB | 35 | 716 | 107 | 27 | 1 | 18 | 66 | 72 | 90 | 30 | 5 | .334/.406/.465 | .300 | .368 | -0.6 | -15.4 | 4.0 |
| 2010 | NYA | MLB | 36 | 739 | 111 | 30 | 3 | 10 | 67 | 63 | 106 | 18 | 5 | .270/.340/.370 | .248 | .307 | 2.6 | -13.6 | 0.8 |
| 2011 | NYA | MLB | 37 | 607 | 84 | 24 | 4 | 6 | 61 | 46 | 81 | 16 | 6 | .297/.355/.388 | .271 | .336 | -2.7 | -1.2 | 1.6 |
| 2012 | NYA | MLB | 38 | 597 | 73 | 23 | 2 | 10 | 60 | 50 | 90 | 16 | 5 | .290/.358/.398 | .272 | .330 | 0 | SS -13 | 3.2 |

Jeter's production collapsed in 2010, and 2011 was initially even worse; he was hitting a powerless .260/.324/.324 in 62 games when a strained right calf sent him to the disabled list for nearly three weeks. Shortly after returning, he reached 3,000 hits with a flourish, smacking a home run, and found the Fountain of Youth thereafter, stroking a classically Jeterian .331/.384/.447 over the remainder of the season. While baseball's most stubborn megastar finally made adjustments to his slowing hands that allowed him to hit with renewed authority, there are still limitations: over the last two seasons, the Captain has hit just .261/.321/.327 against right-handers (versus .332/.405/.499). Even in his post-3,000 surge, he slugged just .376 against same-side pitchers. Defense also remains the same problem it ever was. Still, the glass half-full interpretation of his comeback is that the old man might now give a good-for-a-shortstop offensive performance over the two guaranteed seasons remaining on his contract, and that would be a far more dignified ending to a great career than 2010 seemed to portend.

### Andruw Jones　RF

Born: 4/23/1977 Age: 35
Bats: R Throws: R Height: 6' 2" Weight: 170
Breakout: 3% Improve: 29% Collapse: 15%
Attrition: 29% MLB: 88%

**Comparables:**
Darren Daulton, Ron Gant, David Justice

| YEAR | TEAM | LVL | AGE | PA | R | 2B | 3B | HR | RBI | BB | SO | SB | CS | AVG_OBP_SLG | TAv | BABIP | BRR | FRAA | WARP |
|------|------|-----|-----|-----|-----|----|----|----|-----|----|-----|----|----|-------------|------|-------|------|-------|------|
| 2009 | TEX | MLB | 32 | 331 | 43 | 18 | 0 | 17 | 43 | 45 | 72 | 5 | 1 | .214/.323/.459 | .274 | .221 | -1.3 | -0.4 | 0.7 |
| 2010 | CHA | MLB | 33 | 328 | 41 | 12 | 1 | 19 | 48 | 45 | 73 | 9 | 2 | .230/.341/.486 | .281 | .239 | -0.9 | -2.7 | 0.8 |
| 2011 | NYA | MLB | 34 | 222 | 27 | 8 | 0 | 13 | 33 | 29 | 62 | 0 | 0 | .247/.356/.495 | .299 | .296 | -2.2 | 1.2 | 1.2 |
| 2012 | NYA | MLB | 35 | 250 | 29 | 9 | 0 | 11 | 29 | 30 | 62 | 3 | 1 | .220/.321/.416 | .264 | .255 | 0 | RF -1, LF 1 | 1.0 |

Jones's days as a star starter are gone, but over the last two seasons he has excelled as a lefty masher who can still play passable defense in a corner. He hit .274/.379/.547 against left-handed pitchers in that time, launching 16 home runs in 212 at-bats. He still shows power against right-handers as well (16 home runs in 256 at-bats), but the Yankees gave him so little playing time against them (just 76 plate appearances/64 at-bats) that it's impossible to accurately infer anything from how helpless he looked (.172 average, 23 strikeouts). He re-upped for one more year at $2 million, with another $1.45 million in incentive bonuses.

### Corban Joseph — 2B

Born: 10/28/1988 Age: 23
Bats: L Throws: R Height: 6' 1" Weight: 168
Breakout: 4% Improve: 17% Collapse: 3%
Attrition: 15% MLB: 33%

**Comparables:**
David Adams, Chris Coghlan, Chico Walker

| YEAR | TEAM | LVL | AGE | PA | R | 2B | 3B | HR | RBI | BB | SO | SB | CS | AVG_OBP_SLG | TAv | BABIP | BRR | FRAA | WARP |
|------|------|-----|-----|-----|----|----|----|----|-----|----|-----|----|----|----------------|------|-------|------|-----------|------|
| 2009 | CSC | A | 20 | 436 | 39 | 17 | 8 | 4 | 57 | 49 | 61 | 8 | 5 | .300/.384/.418 | .303 | .349 | 0 | -1 | 2.9 |
| 2010 | TAM | A+ | 21 | 437 | 52 | 27 | 3 | 6 | 52 | 43 | 74 | 5 | 8 | .302/.382/.436 | .292 | .361 | -2.7 | -6.4 | 1.5 |
| 2010 | TRN | AA | 21 | 130 | 11 | 6 | 4 | 0 | 13 | 15 | 33 | 1 | 0 | .216/.305/.342 | .259 | .300 | -1.1 | 2.2 | 0.0 |
| 2011 | TRN | AA | 22 | 564 | 75 | 38 | 8 | 5 | 58 | 59 | 104 | 4 | 3 | .277/.353/.415 | .282 | .339 | 1 | -3.9 | 2.7 |
| 2012 | NYA | MLB | 23 | 250 | 26 | 11 | 2 | 2 | 22 | 21 | 53 | 1 | 1 | .240/.307/.340 | .231 | .300 | -0.2 | 2B -7, 3B 2 | 0.1 |

"Corban Bleu's" 2011 rates don't seem impressive until you realize that the Eastern League as a whole hit only .259/.339/.395, that he was playing at Trenton (where he hit better than he did on the road), and that he was coming off wrist surgery. The Tennessean can hit a little bit, but he's not going to be challenging Robinson Cano on offense or (particularly) defense any time soon. Darwin Barney, on the other hand, could be feeling some pressure if Joseph ever breaks free.

baseball's great unanswered questions is if terminal impatience is a matter of skill, vision, or simple hubris. Is the strike zone something that can be taught, or does something in a ballplayer's genetic makeup foretell his having the persnickety forbearance of Ted Williams or the swing-at-anything generosity of Shawon Dunston? Does every Laird who refuses to take ball four do so because he really thinks he can hit the pitcher's pitch, or is he helpless to do otherwise? Whatever the answer, until Laird finds a way to make better than a .288 OBP at Triple-A he's doomed to wander the earth, a four-corner pariah whose ability to swat the occasional long ball won't ameliorate his inability to reach base.

### Russell Martin — C

Born: 2/15/1983 Age: 29
Bats: R Throws: R Height: 5' 11" Weight: 210
Breakout: 1% Improve: 47% Collapse: 7%
Attrition: 34% MLB: 88%

**Comparables:**
Joe Nolan, Sherm Lollar, Smoky Burgess

| YEAR | TEAM | LVL | AGE | PA | R | 2B | 3B | HR | RBI | BB | SO | SB | CS | AVG_OBP_SLG | TAv | BABIP | BRR | FRAA | WARP |
|------|------|-----|-----|-----|----|----|----|----|-----|----|----|----|----|----------------|------|-------|------|-----------|------|
| 2009 | LAN | MLB | 26 | 588 | 63 | 19 | 0 | 7 | 53 | 69 | 80 | 11 | 6 | .250/.352/.329 | .249 | .284 | 2.9 | 0 | 2.2 |
| 2010 | LAN | MLB | 27 | 387 | 45 | 13 | 0 | 5 | 26 | 48 | 61 | 6 | 2 | .248/.347/.332 | .257 | .287 | -0.2 | -0.9 | 1.5 |
| 2011 | NYA | MLB | 28 | 476 | 57 | 17 | 0 | 18 | 65 | 50 | 81 | 8 | 2 | .237/.324/.408 | .253 | .252 | -0.7 | -0.6 | 1.9 |
| 2012 | NYA | MLB | 29 | 429 | 52 | 16 | 0 | 10 | 42 | 51 | 67 | 9 | 3 | .261/.357/.391 | .269 | .292 | -0.2 | C -1, 3B 0 | 2.5 |

The Dodgers non-tendered Martin after the 2010 season rather than risk arbitration. McCourt's team was always penurious and rarely smart, but their decision was not entirely unreasonable given Martin's offensive stagnation and season-ending hairline pelvic fracture. Initially, the Yankees seemed to have made one of their all-time great moves when Martin, who proved to be better than advertised on defense, exploded out of the gates with a six-homer, .293 April. He had a similar period of torrid hitting in August, but otherwise proved to be a non-factor at the plate. Behind it, though, he threw well and according to research by BP's Mike Fast was among the best in the game at getting his pitchers extra strikes via adept framing. With the Canuck catcher in his final year of arbitration, it would not be surprising if the Yankees have signed him to a new contract by the time you read this.

### Jesus Montero — C

Born: 11/28/1989 Age: 22
Bats: R Throws: R Height: 6' 4" Weight: 235
Breakout: 2% Improve: 32% Collapse: 2%
Attrition: 23% MLB: 83%

**Comparables:**
Johnny Bench, Matt Nokes, Orlando Mercado

| YEAR | TEAM | LVL | AGE | PA | R | 2B | 3B | HR | RBI | BB | SO | SB | CS | AVG_OBP_SLG | TAv | BABIP | BRR | FRAA | WARP |
|------|------|-----|-----|-----|----|----|----|----|-----|----|----|----|----|----------------|------|-------|------|------|------|
| 2009 | TAM | A+ | 19 | 198 | 26 | 15 | 1 | 8 | 37 | 14 | 26 | 0 | 0 | .356/.406/.583 | .365 | .381 | -3.2 | -0.9 | 2.0 |
| 2009 | TRN | AA | 19 | 181 | 19 | 10 | 0 | 9 | 33 | 14 | 21 | 0 | 0 | .317/.370/.539 | .317 | .321 | -2.3 | -0.3 | 1.5 |
| 2010 | SWB | AAA | 20 | 504 | 66 | 34 | 3 | 21 | 75 | 46 | 91 | 0 | 0 | .289/.356/.517 | .295 | .323 | -4 | -1.7 | 3.4 |
| 2011 | SWB | AAA | 21 | 463 | 52 | 19 | 1 | 18 | 67 | 36 | 98 | 0 | 0 | .288/.348/.467 | .275 | .336 | -1.8 | -1.9 | 2.1 |
| 2011 | NYA | MLB | 21 | 69 | 9 | 4 | 0 | 4 | 12 | 7 | 17 | 0 | 0 | .328/.406/.590 | .333 | .400 | -2.1 | 0 | 0.4 |
| 2012 | NYA | MLB | 22 | 250 | 32 | 12 | 1 | 10 | 34 | 18 | 52 | 0 | 0 | .279/.334/.471 | .282 | .318 | 0 | C -2 | 2.7 |

To paraphrase Rogers and Hammerstein, how do you solve a problem like Montero? The answer is and has always been that you make him the DH and let him hit. Why the Yankees refused to do this last year, when

Montero had already shown he could hit Triple-A pitching in 2010 and Jorge Posada scuffled, is one of those examples of a perversely counterproductive policy that can damage not one but two seasons, as Posada hit but little more and was gone, while Montero remains unproven. Teams resist admitting a young player is so poor a defender that he can do little but DH, but sometimes you have to call something by its name and move on. This is especially true of the Yankees, where Mark Teixeira's everlasting gobstopper of a contract prevents Montero from pursuing the Carlos Delgado career path. The time for dreaming is past. Montero needs to show what he can do with the skills he *does* possess or be dealt for the best possible return—though Montero's defensive limitations mean he should be allowed to establish his value first, as the same factors that make him a difficult fit on the Yankees apply to every team. Thus we have come full circle to "just let him hit."

**JR Murphy                        C**
Born: 5/13/1991 Age: 21
Bats: B Throws: R Height: 6'1" Weight: 190
Breakout: 3% Improve: 4% Collapse: 1%
Attrition: 6% MLB: 6%
**Comparables:**
Angel Salome, Albert Cordero, Julio Rodriguez

| YEAR | TEAM | LVL | AGE | PA | R | 2B | 3B | HR | RBI | BB | SO | SB | CS | AVG_OBP_SLG | TAv | BABIP | BRR | FRAA | WARP |
|---|---|---|---|---|---|---|---|---|---|---|---|---|---|---|---|---|---|---|---|
| 2010 | CSC | A | 19 | 374 | 46 | 15 | 2 | 7 | 54 | 36 | 64 | 4 | 5 | .255/.331/.376 | .269 | .296 | -0.4 | 0.7 | 1.3 |
| 2011 | CSC | A | 20 | 277 | 31 | 23 | 0 | 6 | 32 | 19 | 38 | 2 | 0 | .297/.343/.457 | .293 | .327 | -4.3 | 1.1 | 1.4 |
| 2011 | TAM | A+ | 20 | 89 | 8 | 6 | 0 | 1 | 14 | 2 | 9 | 0 | 0 | .259/.270/.365 | .231 | .273 | 0.6 | 0.1 | 0.0 |
| 2012 | NYA | MLB | 21 | 250 | 22 | 12 | 0 | 3 | 22 | 8 | 54 | 1 | 1 | .221/.248/.311 | .196 | .268 | -0.1 | C 0, 3B 0 | -1.4 |

"Do cats eat bats," Alice wondered sleepily. "Do bats eat cats?" Is a catcher a third baseman? Is a third baseman a catcher? The Yankees are wondering. They have a huge inventory of tyro backstops and an aging third baseman in the majors (and, by extension, a rookie DH who will one day have to disappear so the old guy can have someplace to play), so Murphy is getting the chance to make the transition to the hot corner. The jury is still out on the success of that conversion, but Murphy enjoyed a nice breakthrough with the bat last year, and should he maintain his progress in a full season at High-A Tampa, we can talk about this 2009 second-round pick as a true prospect. Right now, as Lewis Carroll might have put it, he's neither raven nor writing desk.

**Eduardo Nuñez                        SS**
Born: 6/15/1987 Age: 25
Bats: R Throws: R Height: 6'1" Weight: 155
Breakout: 7% Improve: 59% Collapse: 3%
Attrition: 17% MLB: 90%
**Comparables:**
Erick Aybar, Chin-lung Hu, Jose Reyes

| YEAR | TEAM | LVL | AGE | PA | R | 2B | 3B | HR | RBI | BB | SO | SB | CS | AVG_OBP_SLG | TAv | BABIP | BRR | FRAA | WARP |
|---|---|---|---|---|---|---|---|---|---|---|---|---|---|---|---|---|---|---|---|
| 2009 | TRN | AA | 22 | 528 | 70 | 26 | 1 | 9 | 55 | 22 | 63 | 19 | 7 | .322/.349/.433 | .291 | .352 | 1.7 | -1.9 | 2.6 |
| 2010 | SWB | AAA | 23 | 506 | 55 | 25 | 3 | 4 | 50 | 32 | 60 | 23 | 5 | .289/.339/.381 | .251 | .323 | 1.3 | -6.9 | 1.1 |
| 2010 | NYA | MLB | 23 | 53 | 12 | 1 | 0 | 1 | 7 | 3 | 2 | 5 | 0 | .280/.321/.360 | .237 | .277 | 0.7 | -0.1 | 0.1 |
| 2011 | NYA | MLB | 24 | 338 | 38 | 18 | 2 | 5 | 30 | 22 | 37 | 22 | 6 | .265/.313/.385 | .246 | .287 | 0.5 | -4.4 | 0.4 |
| 2012 | NYA | MLB | 25 | 261 | 30 | 12 | 1 | 5 | 29 | 14 | 35 | 12 | 4 | .279/.320/.403 | .252 | .303 | 0.1 | SS -4, 3B -3 | 1.4 |

The Yankees like to tout Nuñez as a potential starter or multi-position sub. Nuñez's talent is flattered but declines the honor on account of the Yankees having confused it with someone else. Nuñez can run a bit, but is spectacularly prone to errors for a player whose main job is to play solid defense when called off the bench (Jeter made 12 errors in 1047.1 innings at short; Nunez made 14 in 386.1). As for his bat, barring some BABIP-related swelling, this is it. Starting potential: nil. Reserve potential: still TBD pending softer hands. The Yankees' position on both: disproportionately enthusiastic bordering on delusional.

**Jorge Posada                        C**
Born: 8/17/1971 Age: 40
Bats: B Throws: R Height: 6'3" Weight: 190
Breakout: 0% Improve: 16% Collapse: 13%
Attrition: 29% MLB: 70%
**Comparables:**
Matt Stairs, Ken Griffey, Frank Robinson

| YEAR | TEAM | LVL | AGE | PA | R | 2B | 3B | HR | RBI | BB | SO | SB | CS | AVG_OBP_SLG | TAv | BABIP | BRR | FRAA | WARP |
|---|---|---|---|---|---|---|---|---|---|---|---|---|---|---|---|---|---|---|---|
| 2009 | NYA | MLB | 37 | 438 | 55 | 25 | 0 | 22 | 81 | 48 | 101 | 1 | 0 | .285/.363/.522 | .296 | .328 | -4.5 | 0.4 | 2.9 |
| 2010 | NYA | MLB | 38 | 451 | 49 | 23 | 1 | 18 | 57 | 59 | 99 | 3 | 1 | .248/.357/.454 | .284 | .287 | -5.1 | -1.3 | 1.6 |
| 2011 | NYA | MLB | 39 | 387 | 34 | 14 | 0 | 14 | 44 | 39 | 76 | 0 | 2 | .235/.315/.398 | .251 | .262 | -3.5 | -1 | -0.3 |
| 2012 | NYA | MLB | 40 | 376 | 48 | 18 | 0 | 13 | 45 | 43 | 82 | 1 | 1 | .260/.350/.440 | .280 | .307 | -0.1 | C -0, 1B -0 | 2.1 |

Posada's final season in pinstripes was hardly the dignified send-off that one of the most important players in franchise history deserved, though he didn't help by refusing to play when Girardi dropped him to ninth in the order in mid-May. His outrage might have been more understandable had he been hitting at all, but despite a six-home run April, his batting average remained well under .200 into June. Though he then heated up, the old consistency eluded him, and the defrocked catcher batted .279/.336/.438 after May, about average production for a 2011 DH. Posada's right-handed swing, a career-long asset, flatlined, leaving him with with just six hits in 65 at-bats against portsiders. Posada's potency from the left side (.269/.348/.466) might make him useful as a reserve catcher/first baseman/DH, but his defense at his old position had become untenable even before a concussion inspired the Yankees to ban him from behind the plate. There are animals that have been extinct since the Cenozoic era that have greater mobility. It's been a great career, a near Hall-of-Fame career, but this really might be the end.

### Alex Rodriguez — 3B

Born: 7/27/1975 Age: 36
Bats: R Throws: R Height: 6' 4" Weight: 190
Breakout: 1% Improve: 29% Collapse: 8%
Attrition: 12% MLB: 87%

**Comparables:**
Manny Ramirez, Larry Walker, Chipper Jones

| YEAR | TEAM | LVL | AGE | PA | R | 2B | 3B | HR | RBI | BB | SO | SB | CS | AVG_OBP_SLG | TAv | BABIP | BRR | FRAA | WARP |
|------|------|-----|-----|-----|----|----|----|----|-----|----|----|----|----|-------------|-----|-------|-----|------|------|
| 2009 | NYA | MLB | 33 | 535 | 78 | 17 | 1 | 30 | 100 | 80 | 97 | 14 | 2 | .286/.402/.532 | .312 | .303 | 1.1 | 1.7 | 5.0 |
| 2010 | NYA | MLB | 34 | 595 | 74 | 29 | 2 | 30 | 125 | 59 | 98 | 4 | 3 | .270/.341/.506 | .299 | .274 | -0.5 | 5.6 | 5.0 |
| 2011 | NYA | MLB | 35 | 428 | 67 | 21 | 0 | 16 | 62 | 47 | 80 | 4 | 1 | .276/.362/.461 | .286 | .311 | 2 | 5.3 | 3.2 |
| 2012 | NYA | MLB | 36 | 437 | 63 | 18 | 0 | 24 | 66 | 52 | 85 | 7 | 2 | .279/.377/.525 | .314 | .299 | 0.1 | 3B 5 | 4.3 |

The fourth year of A-Rod's monster 10-year deal with the Yankees may have been the scariest yet: mid-season knee surgery and his worst power numbers in pinstripes (as said knee compromised the leverage in his swing) do not portend well for an immovable contract. A healthy Rodriguez still has plenty of value (indeed, he was having one of his best defensive seasons at third before the injuries set in), but any player on the wrong side of 35 is going to decline, and Rodriguez's decay, which may not be especially graceful, may have begun sooner than the Yankees expected. Rodriguez's bat may have at least one Elvis Comeback Special in it, but he has not played more than 140 games since 2007, so durability may be a problem from now until (choke) 2017. Moral of the story:

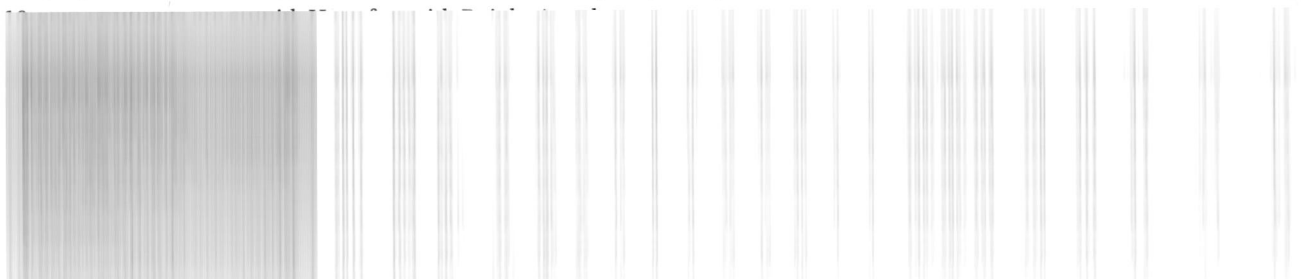

Romine made it to the majors when Cervelli's concussion required the Yankees to add another catcher. Blocked by Montero from moving up to Scranton (another negative consequence of the Village Posada Preservation Society movement), Romine repeated Double-A. Unlike many players, who explode offensively when repeating a level, Romine seemed to stagnate while acting in *Return to Trenton: More Tomato Pies, Please.* He hit .276/.336/.392 in the New Jersey capital. He also still needs to refine his defensive game; Romine lacks strong receiving skills and tends to stab at the ball, costing his pitchers strikes. The tough ballpark and injuries (back inflammation, concussion) weren't wholly to blame for his disappointing showing. Though still young enough to improve substantially, Romine now looks like a second-division starter or a contending team's reserve, albeit one with more pop than Cervelli.

### Gary Sanchez — C

Born: 12/2/1992 Age: 19
Bats: R Throws: R Height: 6' 3" Weight: 220
Breakout: 0% Improve: 2% Collapse: 0%
Attrition: 5% MLB: 8%

**Comparables:**
Michael Burgess, Tommy Joseph, Dave Duncan

| YEAR | TEAM | LVL | AGE | PA | R | 2B | 3B | HR | RBI | BB | SO | SB | CS | AVG_OBP_SLG | TAv | BABIP | BRR | FRAA | WARP |
|------|------|-----|-----|-----|----|----|----|----|-----|----|----|----|----|-------------|-----|-------|-----|------|------|
| 2010 | STA | A- | 17 | 60 | 8 | 2 | 0 | 2 | 7 | 3 | 16 | 1 | 1 | .278/.339/.426 | .306 | .361 | -0.1 | -0.4 | 0.5 |
| 2010 | YAN | RK | 17 | 136 | 25 | 11 | 0 | 6 | 36 | 11 | 28 | 1 | 1 | .353/.425/.597 | .365 | .424 | -0.9 | -0.1 | 1.6 |
| 2011 | CSC | A | 18 | 343 | 49 | 16 | 1 | 17 | 52 | 36 | 93 | 2 | 1 | .256/.335/.485 | .289 | .308 | 1.3 | 1.6 | 2.6 |
| 2012 | NYA | MLB | 19 | 250 | 25 | 9 | 0 | 9 | 28 | 16 | 79 | 0 | 0 | .214/.266/.376 | .226 | .276 | 0 | C 0 | 0.0 |

Sanchez hit like Mike Piazza's more robust older brother in the Gulf Coast League and continued to show excellent power in the Sally League, but disciplinary problems caused the Yankees to send him to the extended spring training gulag. He hit well after returning, particularly during a torrid August, before his season ended early due to a hand injury. Given his age, his season shouldn't be rated a disappointment—for any 18-year-old who had not done what Sanchez had done at 17, this level of production would be a triumph. As to his 26 passed balls in 60 games, is he so bad defensively he will ultimately have to be moved, or was he just sleepwalking on the job? Time will tell.

### Nick Swisher — RF

Born: 11/25/1980 Age: 31
Bats: B Throws: L Height: 6' 1" Weight: 190
Breakout: 2% Improve: 43% Collapse: 5%
Attrition: 10% MLB: 93%

**Comparables:**
Reggie Smith, Rocky Colavito, Roger Maris

| YEAR | TEAM | LVL | AGE | PA | R | 2B | 3B | HR | RBI | BB | SO | SB | CS | AVG_OBP_SLG | TAv | BABIP | BRR | FRAA | WARP |
|------|------|-----|-----|-----|----|----|----|----|-----|----|----|----|----|-------------|-----|-------|-----|-----------|------|
| 2009 | NYA | MLB | 28 | 607 | 84 | 35 | 1 | 29 | 82 | 97 | 126 | 0 | 0 | .249/.371/.498 | .295 | .272 | -1 | 2.5 | 3.3 |
| 2010 | NYA | MLB | 29 | 635 | 91 | 33 | 3 | 29 | 89 | 58 | 139 | 1 | 2 | .288/.359/.511 | .303 | .335 | -1 | 10.3 | 4.6 |
| 2011 | NYA | MLB | 30 | 635 | 81 | 30 | 0 | 23 | 85 | 95 | 125 | 2 | 2 | .260/.374/.449 | .289 | .295 | -0.3 | 2.8 | 3.5 |
| 2012 | NYA | MLB | 31 | 597 | 78 | 27 | 1 | 25 | 75 | 83 | 131 | 2 | 1 | .251/.361/.457 | .288 | .287 | -0.3 | RF 6, 1B -0 | 2.8 |

Swisher, whose undulating career is a never-ending source of soul-rippingly simultaneous elation and frustration, began 2011 in a deep and sustained slump, hitting .213/.335/.314 through the end of May. He homered on the first day of June and was off to the races for the next half-season, hitting .305/.418/.556 with

18 home runs in 79 games. Then September came, the bat fell off faster than the leaves left the trees, and Swisher sleepwalked right through the playoffs, where he now has a career record of .169/.295/.323 in nearly 150 PAs. That he is harder to pin down than the Higgs boson notwithstanding, Swisher's power, patience, and aesthetically unappealing but effective defense make him a valuable player. In his last season before free agency, it will be fascinating to see if the promise of an impending payday will cause Swisher to A) Bear down and focus or B) Totally crack. Knowing him, the answer is probably C) All of the above.

### Mark Teixeira    1B

Born: 4/11/1980 Age: 32
Bats: B Throws: R Height: 6' 4'' Weight: 220
Breakout: 0% Improve: 29% Collapse: 3%
Attrition: 7% MLB: 93%

Comparables:
Jason Giambi, Kevin Youkilis, Lance Berkman

| YEAR | TEAM | LVL | AGE | PA | R | 2B | 3B | HR | RBI | BB | SO | SB | CS | AVG_OBP_SLG | TAv | BABIP | BRR | FRAA | WARP |
|------|------|-----|-----|-----|-----|----|----|----|-----|----|-----|----|----|-------------|-----|-------|-----|------|------|
| 2009 | NYA | MLB | 29 | 707 | 103 | 43 | 3 | 39 | 122 | 81 | 114 | 2 | 0 | .292/.383/.565 | .322 | .302 | -3.8 | -6.8 | 4.3 |
| 2010 | NYA | MLB | 30 | 712 | 113 | 36 | 0 | 33 | 108 | 93 | 122 | 0 | 1 | .256/.365/.481 | .298 | .268 | -2.2 | 14 | 4.8 |
| 2011 | NYA | MLB | 31 | 684 | 90 | 26 | 1 | 39 | 111 | 76 | 110 | 4 | 1 | .248/.341/.494 | .296 | .239 | -3.3 | -1.3 | 2.2 |
| 2012 | NYA | MLB | 32 | 648 | 92 | 31 | 1 | 33 | 96 | 81 | 114 | 2 | 1 | .275/.376/.515 | .311 | .289 | 0 | 1B 2 | 4.3 |

Last season was Teixeira's worst since his rookie year, a fact that must be troubling to the Yankees given that they have him signed through 2016. Teixeira was a career .290/.378/.545 hitter through 2009, but over the last two seasons he has dropped to .252/.353/.487, and as impressive as his 2011 home run total was, on a per-at-bat level those dingers came at one of the lowest rates of his career. On the plus side, after years of somnambulant Aprils, Teixeira hit six home runs that month and had totaled 25 by the end of June. His pace slowed thereafter, and he never did put together a sustained run of all-around hitting. Of course, when a player's worst season includes 39 home runs and good defense you can only be so upset, but if Teixeira has taken a step back at 31, what is he going to be like at 36?

## PITCHERS

### Luis Ayala

Born: 1/12/1978 Age: 34
Bats: R Throws: R Height: 6' 3'' Weight: 170
Breakout: 14% Improve: 31% Collapse: 47%
Attrition: 12% MLB: 77%

Comparables:
Geoff Geary, Jim Brosnan, Doug Drabek

| YEAR | TEAM | LVL | AGE | W | L | SV | G | GS | IP | H | HR | BB | SO | EqBB9 | EqSO9 | GB% | BABIP | WHIP | ERA | FIP | FRA | WARP |
|------|------|-----|-----|---|---|----|---|----|----|----|----|----|----|-------|-------|-----|-------|------|-----|-----|-----|------|
| 2009 | FLO | MLB | 31 | 0 | 3 | 0 | 10 | 0 | 7² | 12 | 1 | 6 | 7 | 7.0 | 8.2 | 39% | .440 | 2.35 | 11.74 | 5.67 | 6.21 | -0.1 |
| 2009 | MIN | MLB | 31 | 1 | 2 | 0 | 28 | 0 | 32¹ | 38 | 4 | 8 | 21 | 2.2 | 5.8 | 41% | .337 | 1.42 | 4.18 | 4.47 | 4.55 | 0.3 |
| 2010 | RNO | AAA | 32 | 0 | 6 | 0 | 18 | 0 | 26¹ | 32 | 0 | 9 | 9 | 3.8 | 5.8 | 51% | .464 | 1.86 | 7.87 | 4.63 | 5.24 | 0.3 |
| 2011 | NYA | MLB | 33 | 2 | 2 | 0 | 52 | 0 | 56 | 51 | 5 | 20 | 39 | 3.2 | 6.3 | 52% | .289 | 1.27 | 2.09 | 4.22 | 5.91 | -0.4 |
| 2012 | NYA | MLB | 34 | 2 | 1 | 0 | 36 | 0 | 42² | 46 | 5 | 14 | 29 | 3.1 | 6.1 | 46% | .307 | 1.43 | 4.74 | 4.35 | 5.15 | 0.0 |

Journeyman Ayala was a decent middle-relief option for the Expos/Nats back before overuse caught up with him and forced Tommy John surgery. He then pitched his way out of memory by going 5-25 with a 5.90 ERA between the majors and minors from 2008 to 2010. The Yankees signed him to a minor-league deal despite that track record, and lo and behold, he won the final roster spot in spring training, because why give a tertiary relief job to a rookie for the major-league minimum when you can pay a 33-year-old $650,000? Ayala posted a good ERA in a low-leverage relief role, but that fails to convey the unearned runs, poor peripherals, and bequeathed runners stranded by subsequent relievers. In short, Ayala pitched about as well as his most recent seasons suggested he would, while another kid was stranded at Triple-A. Mission accomplished?

### Manny Banuelos

Born: 3/13/1991 Age: 21
Bats: L Throws: L Height: 6' 0'' Weight: 155
Breakout: 26% Improve: 54% Collapse: 13%
Attrition: 4% MLB: 90%

Comparables:
Billy Hoeft, Oliver Perez, Clayton Kershaw

| YEAR | TEAM | LVL | AGE | W | L | SV | G | GS | IP | H | HR | BB | SO | EqBB9 | EqSO9 | GB% | BABIP | WHIP | ERA | FIP | FRA | WARP |
|------|------|-----|-----|---|---|----|---|----|----|----|----|----|-----|-------|-------|-----|-------|------|-----|-----|-----|------|
| 2009 | CSC | A | 18 | 9 | 5 | 0 | 25 | 19 | 108 | 88 | 4 | 28 | 104 | 2.3 | 8.7 | 46% | .284 | 1.07 | 2.67 | 3.02 | 3.97 | 1.4 |
| 2010 | TAM | A+ | 19 | 0 | 2 | 0 | 10 | 10 | 44¹ | 29 | 1 | 11 | 43 | 2.8 | 12.6 | 47% | .354 | 1.17 | 2.23 | 2.69 | 3.51 | 0.9 |
| 2011 | TRN | AA | 20 | 4 | 5 | 0 | 20 | 20 | 95¹ | 94 | 7 | 52 | 94 | 4.9 | 8.9 | 51% | .333 | 1.53 | 3.59 | 4.22 | 4.53 | 1.2 |
| 2011 | SWB | AAA | 20 | 2 | 1 | 0 | 7 | 7 | 34¹ | 36 | 2 | 19 | 31 | 5.0 | 8.1 | 50% | .340 | 1.60 | 4.19 | 3.94 | 5.25 | 0.1 |
| 2012 | NYA | MLB | 21 | 3 | 2 | 0 | 8 | 8 | 37² | 39 | 5 | 20 | 30 | 4.9 | 7.2 | 45% | .311 | 1.59 | 5.05 | 4.93 | 5.49 | 0.0 |

Still spectacularly young, particularly by the standards of the New YAARP Yankees, Banuelos is nonetheless about to knock on the door to the majors. With a low-to-mid-90s fastball, curve, and changeup, he has a starter's full assortment, but the problem is that as his stuff has improved his command has diminished. His 2011 walk rate of 4.9 per nine innings bordered on untenable given that it was the third season in a row that rate had climbed. Despite a solid ERA at Trenton, there were some other troubling notes; though he continued to be stingy with the home run, right-handed hitters batted .285 against him between Double- and Triple-A, and Double-A hitters averaged .279/.376/.421 away from his cushy home ballpark. Given Man-Ban's age and stuff, none of this is particularly concerning. Rather, it should be taken as yet another cautionary note that not every pitcher bursts upon the major league scene fully formed; as good as he is, Banuelos will require patience, and perhaps more time than his biggest boosters would like to think.

**Dellin Betances**
Born: 3/23/1988 Age: 24
Bats: R Throws: R Height: 6' 9" Weight: 260
Breakout: 35% Improve: 65% Collapse: 14%
Attrition: 12% MLB: 85%
**Comparables:**
John Rocker, Jon Meloan, Emiliano Fruto

| YEAR | TEAM | LVL | AGE | W | L | SV | G | GS | IP | H | HR | BB | SO | EqBB9 | EqSO9 | GB% | BABIP | WHIP | ERA | FIP | FRA | WARP |
|---|---|---|---|---|---|---|---|---|---|---|---|---|---|---|---|---|---|---|---|---|---|---|
| 2009 | TAM | A+ | 21 | 2 | 5 | 0 | 11 | 11 | 44¹ | 48 | 2 | 27 | 44 | 5.5 | 8.9 | 52% | .357 | 1.69 | 5.49 | 3.76 | 4.21 | 0.8 |
| 2010 | TAM | A+ | 22 | 8 | 1 | 0 | 14 | 14 | 71 | 40 | 1 | 18 | 69 | 2.4 | 11.2 | 45% | .264 | 0.87 | 1.77 | 2.66 | 2.83 | 2.0 |
| 2011 | TRN | AA | 23 | 4 | 6 | 0 | 21 | 21 | 105¹ | 86 | 7 | 55 | 115 | 4.7 | 9.8 | 52% | .292 | 1.34 | 3.42 | 3.92 | 4.75 | 0.9 |
| 2011 | NYA | MLB | 23 | 0 | 0 | 0 | 2 | 1 | 2² | 1 | 0 | 6 | 2 | 20.2 | 6.8 | 14% | .143 | 2.62 | 6.75 | 9.44 | 9.64 | -0.1 |
| 2012 | NYA | MLB | 24 | 3 | 2 | 0 | 8 | 8 | 40 | 39 | 5 | 25 | 37 | 5.6 | 8.3 | 42% | .302 | 1.59 | 4.93 | 4.85 | 5.35 | 0.1 |

After being exposed to gamma rays in a freak accident, this mild-mannered scientist was transformed into a pitching behemoth! Look out, true believers! Here comes . . . the Rampaging Dellin! As with other giant mon-

Breakout: 20% Improve: 37% Collapse: 28%
Attrition: 11% MLB: 91%
**Comparables:**
Kyle Farnsworth, Barney Schultz, Dan Miceli

| YEAR | TEAM | LVL | AGE | W | L | SV | G | GS | IP | H | HR | BB | SO | EqBB9 | EqSO9 | GB% | BABIP | WHIP | ERA | FIP | FRA | WARP |
|---|---|---|---|---|---|---|---|---|---|---|---|---|---|---|---|---|---|---|---|---|---|---|
| 2011 | NYA | MLB | 34 | 11 | 11 | 0 | 33 | 32 | 190¹ | 190 | 31 | 83 | 173 | 3.9 | 8.2 | 51% | .296 | 1.43 | 5.15 | 4.81 | 5.22 | -0.1 |
| 2012 | NYA | MLB | 35 | 11 | 9 | 0 | 29 | 29 | 166 | 164 | 24 | 71 | 159 | 3.9 | 8.6 | 50% | .307 | 1.42 | 4.59 | 4.45 | 4.99 | 0.7 |

After an August start in Minnesota in which Burnett could not make it through the second inning, Yankees fans were treated to a peevish Girardi berating YES's Jack Curry after the latter dared ask, in so many words, if this trip was really necessary. The Yankees clearly thought it was, as Girardi vehemently argued. After the season, the manager suggested that Burnett had "only one bad month." Indeed, his August ERA of nearly 12.00 sticks out badly. Yet, Burnett was often thrashed all season long. His quality start percentage of 31 was last in the AL among qualified starters and was the lowest of *any* pitcher who was allowed to make more than 13 starts and about even with such luminaries as Jo-Jo Reyes and John Lackey. Since there is apparently nothing Burnett can do to get bounced from the rotation, sit back and enjoy another 60-odd erratic starts from now through the end of 2013, and think about how unfair the universe can be—if you did your job half as badly as Burnett does, you'd be out on your ass.

**Joba Chamberlain**
Born: 9/23/1985 Age: 26
Bats: R Throws: R Height: 6' 3" Weight: 230
Breakout: 30% Improve: 51% Collapse: 22%
Attrition: 11% MLB: 94%
**Comparables:**
Josh Beckett, Al Hrabosky, Bobby Jenks

| YEAR | TEAM | LVL | AGE | W | L | SV | G | GS | IP | H | HR | BB | SO | EqBB9 | EqSO9 | GB% | BABIP | WHIP | ERA | FIP | FRA | WARP |
|---|---|---|---|---|---|---|---|---|---|---|---|---|---|---|---|---|---|---|---|---|---|---|
| 2009 | NYA | MLB | 23 | 9 | 6 | 0 | 32 | 31 | 157¹ | 167 | 21 | 76 | 133 | 4.3 | 7.6 | 46% | .317 | 1.54 | 4.75 | 4.87 | 5.17 | 1.6 |
| 2010 | NYA | MLB | 24 | 3 | 4 | 3 | 73 | 0 | 71² | 71 | 6 | 22 | 77 | 2.8 | 9.7 | 46% | .327 | 1.30 | 4.40 | 2.95 | 4.30 | 0.8 |
| 2011 | NYA | MLB | 25 | 2 | 0 | 0 | 27 | 0 | 28² | 23 | 3 | 7 | 24 | 2.2 | 7.5 | 60% | .267 | 1.05 | 2.83 | 3.58 | 4.16 | 0.3 |
| 2012 | NYA | MLB | 26 | 2 | 1 | 1 | 30 | 0 | 29² | 28 | 3 | 12 | 31 | 3.5 | 9.5 | 49% | .314 | 1.34 | 3.83 | 3.64 | 4.16 | 0.4 |

Philip K. Dick wrote, 'there is no perfect defense. *There is no protection*. Being alive means being exposed; it's the nature of life to be hazardous. The Yankees spent years trying to deny this truth where Chamberlain is concerned, crafting one plan after another to keep him healthy. Instead, he underwent Tommy John surgery in June, and neither we nor the Yankees will ever know if their efforts delayed the inevitable, hastened it, or were (most likely) completely irrelevant. All we know for sure is that their machinations meant that they got less out of Chamberlain than they otherwise could have. As for what they will get now, we won't begin to know until midseason. Nowadays, pitchers often come back from the TJ procedure ready to pick up where they left off, but Chamberlain was moved around so much it's hard to identify exactly what that would mean in his case. He's just another sore-armed reliever now.

**Bartolo Colon**
Born: 5/24/1973 Age: 39
Bats: R Throws: R Height: 6' 1" Weight: 185
Breakout: 17% Improve: 36% Collapse: 37%
Attrition: 6% MLB: 57%

Comparables:
Jim Bunning, Rick Aguilera, Mickey Lolich

| YEAR | TEAM | LVL | AGE | W | L | SV | G | GS | IP | H | HR | BB | SO | EqBB9 | EqSO9 | GB% | BABIP | WHIP | ERA | FIP | FRA | WARP |
|---|---|---|---|---|---|---|---|---|---|---|---|---|---|---|---|---|---|---|---|---|---|---|
| 2009 | CHA | MLB | 36 | 3 | 6 | 0 | 12 | 12 | 62¹ | 69 | 13 | 21 | 38 | 3.0 | 5.5 | 48% | .283 | 1.44 | 4.19 | 5.74 | 6.00 | 0.0 |
| 2011 | NYA | MLB | 38 | 8 | 10 | 0 | 29 | 26 | 164¹ | 172 | 21 | 40 | 135 | 2.2 | 7.4 | 45% | .306 | 1.29 | 4.00 | 3.86 | 4.16 | 2.2 |
| 2012 | NYA | MLB | 39 | 8 | 6 | 0 | 19 | 19 | 112² | 128 | 17 | 33 | 81 | 2.7 | 6.4 | 45% | .312 | 1.43 | 4.87 | 4.61 | 5.30 | 0.1 |

Colon was supposed to be a swing-man or spot starter, but for the first half of the season a pitcher who hadn't appeared in the majors since 2009 ended up being the Yankees' most important pitcher not named Sabathia. Whether the cause was the stem cell procedure he underwent or just rest, his fastball was back, bringing with it terrific late movement. He used it almost exclusively, tossing in only the occasional offspeed pitch. That all changed following a hamstring-inspired trip to the DL. Colon's second-half drop off (4.96 ERA, and 6.8 K/9, down from 7.9 in the first half) was significant enough that he did not start a postseason game though A.J. Burnett did. We shouldn't be surprised: Colon hadn't pitched more than 150 innings in a major league season since 2005, is about to turn 39, and is so heavy that if this were the 19th century he could keep the Nantucket fleet in oil for a year. These factors make him a risk going forward, but the 2011 Yankees wouldn't have won without him.

**Freddy Garcia**
Born: 10/6/1976 Age: 35
Bats: R Throws: R Height: 6' 5" Weight: 235
Breakout: 22% Improve: 44% Collapse: 20%
Attrition: 6% MLB: 85%

Comparables:
Brett Tomko, Luis Tiant, Rick Wise

| YEAR | TEAM | LVL | AGE | W | L | SV | G | GS | IP | H | HR | BB | SO | EqBB9 | EqSO9 | GB% | BABIP | WHIP | ERA | FIP | FRA | WARP |
|---|---|---|---|---|---|---|---|---|---|---|---|---|---|---|---|---|---|---|---|---|---|---|
| 2009 | CHA | MLB | 34 | 3 | 4 | 0 | 9 | 9 | 56 | 56 | 4 | 12 | 37 | 1.9 | 5.9 | 46% | .295 | 1.21 | 4.34 | 3.39 | 3.89 | 1.1 |
| 2010 | CHA | MLB | 35 | 12 | 6 | 0 | 28 | 28 | 157 | 171 | 23 | 45 | 89 | 2.6 | 5.1 | 42% | .293 | 1.38 | 4.64 | 4.74 | 4.68 | 1.1 |
| 2011 | NYA | MLB | 36 | 12 | 8 | 0 | 26 | 25 | 146² | 152 | 16 | 45 | 96 | 2.8 | 5.9 | 39% | .294 | 1.34 | 3.62 | 4.15 | 4.33 | 1.9 |
| 2012 | NYA | MLB | 35 | 8 | 7 | 0 | 22 | 22 | 126² | 142 | 19 | 39 | 85 | 2.8 | 6.0 | 41% | .306 | 1.43 | 4.91 | 4.74 | 5.34 | 0.0 |

Another of Brian Cashman's fliers that paid off, Garcia signed a one-year, $1.5 million deal coming off of a five-year span in which he posted a 4.69 ERA and a crashing strikeout rate over just 84 starts—which is a bit like saying, "The food at that restaurant is terrible and the portions are too small." A fly-ball pitcher who had allowed home runs at a rate of 1.3 per nine innings over those difficult five years, Garcia allowed just nine in his first 122 1/3 innings (0.7 per nine, one of the lowest rates in the AL) through early August. Garcia then cut his right index finger in a kitchen accident, and either the trauma (which necessitated a 20-day DL stay) altered the way he gripped his split-fingered fastball or a phenomenon that had no good reason for happening in the first place chose to reverse itself. Over his last five starts, Garcia gave up seven home runs, or 2.6 per nine innings. Overall, Garcia was as good as he looked last year, but with his declining strikeout rate, home-run reversal, and injury history, the Yankees' decision to bring him back on another one-year ($4 million) deal looks risky.

**Phil Hughes**
Born: 6/24/1986 Age: 26
Bats: R Throws: R Height: 6' 6" Weight: 220
Breakout: 34% Improve: 60% Collapse: 15%
Attrition: 6% MLB: 95%

Comparables:
Jake Peavy, Luis Tiant, Jensen Lewis

| YEAR | TEAM | LVL | AGE | W | L | SV | G | GS | IP | H | HR | BB | SO | EqBB9 | EqSO9 | GB% | BABIP | WHIP | ERA | FIP | FRA | WARP |
|---|---|---|---|---|---|---|---|---|---|---|---|---|---|---|---|---|---|---|---|---|---|---|
| 2009 | NYA | MLB | 23 | 8 | 3 | 3 | 51 | 7 | 86 | 68 | 8 | 28 | 96 | 2.9 | 10.0 | 36% | .280 | 1.12 | 3.03 | 3.27 | 3.39 | 2.3 |
| 2010 | NYA | MLB | 24 | 18 | 8 | 0 | 31 | 29 | 176¹ | 162 | 25 | 58 | 146 | 3.0 | 7.5 | 36% | .275 | 1.25 | 4.19 | 4.22 | 4.67 | 1.6 |
| 2011 | NYA | MLB | 25 | 5 | 5 | 0 | 17 | 14 | 74² | 84 | 9 | 27 | 47 | 3.3 | 5.7 | 34% | .307 | 1.49 | 5.79 | 4.61 | 4.76 | 0.6 |
| 2012 | NYA | MLB | 26 | 6 | 4 | 0 | 15 | 15 | 86 | 83 | 11 | 31 | 77 | 3.2 | 8.0 | 39% | .295 | 1.32 | 3.98 | 4.16 | 4.33 | 1.0 |

It's getting late early out there for no-longer-so-young master Hughes. He was so bad in April 2011 (16 earned runs in 10 1/3 innings and noticeably diminished velocity) that he hit the 60-day disabled list with a disturbingly vague case of "shoulder inflammation" and "fatigue." He returned, supposedly healthy, 82 games later, but a 4.48 ERA and opponents' line of .261/.331/.406 thereafter does not provide much solace. Hughes is no longer a prospect, has an injury history much too long to be ignored, and might soon find himself fighting for a rotation spot among the next crop of homegrown Yankees arms. If Hughes is going to find "it," he needs to do it fast.

**George Kontos**
Born: 6/12/1985 Age: 27
Bats: R Throws: R Height: 6' 4" Weight: 215
Breakout: 30% Improve: 59% Collapse: 27%
Attrition: 21% MLB: 83%

Comparables:
Joe Coleman, Jose Capellan, Scott Sullivan

| YEAR | TEAM | LVL | AGE | W | L | SV | G | GS | IP | H | HR | BB | SO | EqBB9 | EqSO9 | GB% | BABIP | WHIP | ERA | FIP | FRA | WARP |
|---|---|---|---|---|---|---|---|---|---|---|---|---|---|---|---|---|---|---|---|---|---|---|
| 2009 | SWB | AAA | 24 | 3 | 4 | 0 | 9 | 9 | 51 | 44 | 6 | 21 | 39 | 3.7 | 6.9 | 45% | .257 | 1.27 | 3.35 | 4.50 | 4.70 | 0.4 |
| 2010 | TRN | AA | 25 | 0 | 2 | 0 | 17 | 0 | 32 | 25 | 1 | 9 | 18 | 3.1 | 7.9 | 42% | .364 | 1.28 | 3.38 | 3.72 | 4.28 | 0.2 |
| 2011 | SWB | AAA | 26 | 2 | 3 | 2 | 40 | 4 | 89¹ | 70 | 11 | 26 | 89 | 2.6 | 9.2 | 38% | .268 | 1.10 | 2.62 | 3.79 | 4.33 | 1.0 |
| 2011 | NYA | MLB | 26 | 0 | 0 | 0 | 7 | 0 | 6 | 4 | 1 | 3 | 6 | 4.5 | 9.0 | 20% | .214 | 1.17 | 3.00 | 4.73 | 4.36 | 0.0 |
| 2012 | NYA | MLB | 27 | 1 | 1 | 0 | 14 | 1 | 28 | 29 | 4 | 12 | 24 | 3.8 | 7.5 | 40% | .301 | 1.44 | 4.63 | 4.63 | 5.03 | 0.1 |

Tommy John survivor Kontos nearly escaped the ignominy of being a Yankees afterthought when he was Rule 5'd to the Padres in spring training. Unfortunately, he failed to make the team and headed back to Scranton.

Now an ex-starter, Kontos has shown good strikeout rates with his fastball-slider combination, but 13 home runs allowed in 95 1/3 innings split between the majors and minors is troubling, as are Triple-A left-handers slugging .460 against him. He held same-side hitters to .185/.243/.328, so perhaps there is something to be exploited here, albeit with care.

### Boone Logan

Born: 8/13/1984 Age: 27
Bats: R Throws: L Height: 6' 6" Weight: 200
Breakout: 23% Improve: 55% Collapse: 32%
Attrition: 16% MLB: 89%

Comparables:
Len Barker, Shawn Kelley, Carlos Villanueva

| YEAR | TEAM | LVL | AGE | W | L | SV | G | GS | IP | H | HR | BB | SO | EqBB9 | EqSO9 | GB% | BABIP | WHIP | ERA | FIP | FRA | WARP |
|------|------|-----|-----|---|---|----|---|----|----|---|----|----|----|-------|-------|-----|-------|------|-----|-----|-----|------|
| 2009 | GWN | AAA | 24 | 4 | 2 | 2 | 29 | 0 | 35² | 26 | 2 | 17 | 39 | 4.3 | 9.8 | 49% | .276 | 1.20 | 3.28 | 3.62 | 4.49 | 0.3 |
| 2009 | ATL | MLB | 24 | 1 | 1 | 0 | 20 | 0 | 17¹ | 21 | 1 | 9 | 10 | 4.7 | 5.2 | 63% | .328 | 1.73 | 5.19 | 4.38 | 5.11 | 0.0 |
| 2010 | SWB | AAA | 25 | 0 | 1 | 0 | 14 | 0 | 21¹ | 13 | 1 | 3 | 16 | 1.7 | 9.7 | 44% | .286 | 1.03 | 2.11 | 3.34 | 3.64 | 0.3 |
| 2010 | NYA | MLB | 25 | 2 | 0 | 0 | 51 | 0 | 40 | 34 | 3 | 20 | 38 | 4.5 | 8.6 | 48% | .290 | 1.35 | 2.92 | 3.70 | 4.56 | 0.3 |
| 2011 | NYA | MLB | 26 | 5 | 3 | 0 | 64 | 0 | 41² | 43 | 4 | 13 | 46 | 2.8 | 9.9 | 45% | .336 | 1.34 | 3.46 | 3.33 | 4.86 | 0.2 |
| 2012 | NYA | MLB | 27 | 2 | 1 | 1 | 45 | 0 | 36¹ | 37 | 5 | 15 | 33 | 3.6 | 8.2 | 47% | .313 | 1.42 | 4.49 | 4.42 | 4.88 | 0.1 |

Someday there will be a children's book called, "Logan, the Counterproductive LOOGY," in which our youngsters learn to

### D.J. Mitchell

Born: 5/13/1987 Age: 25
Bats: R Throws: R Height: 6' 1" Weight: 160
Breakout: 22% Improve: 63% Collapse: 15%
Attrition: 11% MLB: 98%

Comparables:
Dave Stieb, Kanekoa Texeira, Jim Bouton

| YEAR | TEAM | LVL | AGE | W | L | SV | G | GS | IP | H | HR | BB | SO | EqBB9 | EqSO9 | GB% | BABIP | WHIP | ERA | FIP | FRA | WARP |
|------|------|-----|-----|---|---|----|---|----|----|---|----|----|----|-------|-------|-----|-------|------|-----|-----|-----|------|
| 2009 | CSC | A | 22 | 4 | 1 | 0 | 6 | 6 | 37 | 31 | 1 | 6 | 42 | 1.5 | 10.2 | 62% | .323 | 1.00 | 1.95 | 2.11 | 3.80 | 0.5 |
| 2009 | TAM | A+ | 22 | 9 | 6 | 0 | 19 | 18 | 103¹ | 98 | 1 | 40 | 86 | 3.3 | 7.2 | 68% | .301 | 1.27 | 2.88 | 3.05 | 4.70 | 0.9 |
| 2010 | TRN | AA | 23 | 11 | 4 | 0 | 23 | 22 | 133 | 86 | 8 | 30 | 63 | 3.9 | 6.5 | 58% | .306 | 1.39 | 4.06 | 4.20 | 5.40 | -0.7 |
| 2011 | SWB | AAA | 24 | 11 | 7 | 0 | 28 | 24 | 161¹ | 155 | 10 | 63 | 112 | 3.5 | 6.2 | 48% | .298 | 1.35 | 3.18 | 3.99 | 4.86 | 1.2 |
| 2012 | NYA | MLB | 25 | 3 | 3 | 0 | 8 | 8 | 50² | 55 | 6 | 23 | 32 | 4.1 | 5.6 | 53% | .306 | 1.55 | 4.92 | 4.84 | 5.35 | -0.0 |

It was an odd year for this erstwhile groundball pitcher. His sinking fastball, which had heretofore provided him with a way to survive his low velocity and unpromising strikeout rates, didn't have the same bite as in previous seasons, so his ground-out to air-out ratio, which stood at 3.06 in 2009 and 2.08 in 2010, was down to 1.22 in 2011, still favorable but hardly in elite territory. He also failed to make major progress with his command, which is still a bit shaky for a pitcher who can't count on stranding batters at home plate. Another oddity of his season was that left-handed hitters, normally a problem for Mitchell, hit only .251/.307/.376 against him versus .261/.358/.319 for righties. He still remained difficult to hit for power and an ERA of 3.18 at Triple-A is nothing to scoff about, even if it's not reflected in the pitcher's peripherals. Mitchell still looks like a decent candidate for a middle-relief job, or perhaps a bit more if he can get his sinker working again.

### Hector Noesi

Born: 1/26/1987 Age: 25
Bats: R Throws: R Height: 6' 4" Weight: 200
Breakout: 27% Improve: 67% Collapse: 7%
Attrition: 9% MLB: 94%

Comparables:
James Baldwin, Charles Hudson, Taylor Buchholz

| YEAR | TEAM | LVL | AGE | W | L | SV | G | GS | IP | H | HR | BB | SO | EqBB9 | EqSO9 | GB% | BABIP | WHIP | ERA | FIP | FRA | WARP |
|------|------|-----|-----|---|---|----|---|----|----|---|----|----|----|-------|-------|-----|-------|------|-----|-----|-----|------|
| 2009 | CSC | A | 22 | 3 | 4 | 0 | 17 | 11 | 75² | 62 | 3 | 11 | 78 | 1.3 | 9.3 | 49% | .291 | 0.96 | 2.38 | 2.35 | 3.40 | 1.3 |
| 2009 | TAM | A+ | 22 | 4 | 0 | 0 | 9 | 9 | 41¹ | 43 | 3 | 5 | 48 | 0.9 | 8.7 | 36% | .303 | 0.92 | 3.92 | 2.26 | 4.20 | 0.7 |
| 2010 | TAM | A+ | 23 | 5 | 2 | 0 | 8 | 8 | 43 | 28 | 3 | 6 | 37 | 1.3 | 11.1 | 43% | .287 | 0.95 | 2.72 | 3.20 | 3.52 | 1.0 |
| 2010 | TRN | AA | 23 | 7 | 4 | 0 | 17 | 16 | 98² | 64 | 3 | 11 | 49 | 1.6 | 7.8 | 34% | .353 | 1.09 | 3.10 | 3.36 | 3.91 | 1.2 |
| 2011 | SWB | AAA | 24 | 0 | 1 | 0 | 6 | 5 | 24² | 28 | 0 | 9 | 17 | 3.3 | 6.2 | 41% | .337 | 1.50 | 3.28 | 3.20 | 4.11 | 0.5 |
| 2011 | NYA | MLB | 24 | 2 | 2 | 0 | 30 | 2 | 56¹ | 63 | 6 | 22 | 45 | 3.5 | 7.2 | 43% | .333 | 1.51 | 4.47 | 4.13 | 4.64 | 0.4 |
| 2012 | NYA | MLB | 25 | 3 | 2 | 0 | 12 | 7 | 45² | 52 | 6 | 18 | 33 | 3.5 | 6.5 | 39% | .316 | 1.53 | 5.11 | 4.65 | 5.56 | -0.1 |

It was something of a lost year for Noesi. The former starter was optioned four times beginning with spring training and largely worked in low-leverage relief when he was in the majors. Girardi took advantage of Noesi's recent time as a starter to give him seven relief appearances of three or more innings, though whenever the subject of his starting in place of Burnett was raised, the manager explained that the youngster wasn't sufficiently "stretched out," an ancient rule of pitcher-handling that the Yankees invented to justify keeping a failing vet in his place. Despite two bumpy late-season starts against the Rays, Noesi did nothing to show that he can't pitch in the big leagues.

### Ivan Nova
Born: 1/12/1987 Age: 25
Bats: R Throws: R Height: 6' 5" Weight: 210
Breakout: 22% Improve: 49% Collapse: 17%
Attrition: 15% MLB: 99%

Comparables:
Brad Thompson, Joe Blanton, Vicente Padilla

| YEAR | TEAM | LVL | AGE | W | L | SV | G | GS | IP | H | HR | BB | SO | EqBB9 | EqSO9 | GB% | BABIP | WHIP | ERA | FIP | FRA | WARP |
|------|------|-----|-----|---|---|----|----|----|-----|-----|----|----|----|-------|-------|-----|-------|------|------|------|------|------|
| 2009 | TRN | AA | 22 | 5 | 4 | 0 | 12 | 12 | 72¹ | 65 | 3 | 31 | 47 | 3.9 | 5.9 | 65% | .283 | 1.33 | 2.37 | 3.75 | 5.41 | -0.4 |
| 2009 | SWB | AAA | 22 | 2 | 4 | 0 | 12 | 12 | 67 | 81 | 4 | 31 | 53 | 3.8 | 5.8 | 49% | .304 | 1.49 | 5.10 | 3.86 | 4.54 | 0.4 |
| 2010 | SWB | AAA | 23 | 12 | 3 | 0 | 23 | 23 | 145 | 102 | 8 | 37 | 83 | 3.0 | 7.1 | 55% | .303 | 1.26 | 2.86 | 3.89 | 4.31 | 1.6 |
| 2010 | NYA | MLB | 23 | 1 | 2 | 0 | 10 | 7 | 42 | 44 | 4 | 17 | 26 | 3.6 | 5.6 | 51% | .296 | 1.45 | 4.50 | 4.33 | 4.73 | 0.4 |
| 2011 | NYA | MLB | 24 | 16 | 4 | 0 | 28 | 27 | 165¹ | 163 | 13 | 57 | 98 | 3.1 | 5.3 | 54% | .284 | 1.33 | 3.70 | 4.04 | 4.36 | 1.6 |
| 2012 | NYA | MLB | 25 | 9 | 7 | 0 | 22 | 22 | 132² | 147 | 16 | 53 | 79 | 3.6 | 5.4 | 50% | .305 | 1.50 | 4.78 | 4.78 | 5.20 | 0.2 |

On July 3, Nova was optioned to the minors despite an ERA of 3.42 in 13 starts going back to the end of April. Hughes was coming off the DL, room was needed, and Nova had hardly been dominant. In fact, given a strikeout rate just scraping 5.0 and a walk rate around 3.0, the Yankees must've had thoughts along the lines of, "Might as well demote the fellow; this is just a bit of the old Charles Hudson '87, wot?" However, the secret is simply that Nova showed himself to be a groundball pitcher, posting the seventh-highest groundball/fly-ball ratio in the AL (100 or more innings). Outside of Yankee Stadium, he gave up just three home runs in 80 innings, and he had the fourth-lowest neutral park isolated power allowed of any pitcher in baseball. Whether Nova is as good in 2012 as he was last year depends, given his style of pitching, on his infield defense and some lucky bounces.

### David Phelps
Born: 10/9/1986 Age: 25
Bats: R Throws: R Height: 6' 3" Weight: 185
Breakout: 13% Improve: 41% Collapse: 23%
Attrition: 24% MLB: 94%

Comparables:
Brian Kingman, Ray Crone, Justin Germano

| YEAR | TEAM | LVL | AGE | W | L | SV | G | GS | IP | H | HR | BB | SO | EqBB9 | EqSO9 | GB% | BABIP | WHIP | ERA | FIP | FRA | WARP |
|------|------|-----|-----|---|---|----|----|----|-----|-----|----|----|----|-------|-------|-----|-------|------|------|------|------|------|
| 2009 | CSC | A | 22 | 10 | 3 | 0 | 19 | 19 | 112² | 117 | 9 | 25 | 90 | 2.0 | 7.2 | 54% | .322 | 1.26 | 2.80 | 3.68 | 4.71 | 0.4 |
| 2009 | TAM | A+ | 22 | 4 | 2 | 0 | 7 | 7 | 38¹ | 45 | 1 | 8 | 37 | 1.4 | 7.5 | 60% | .312 | 1.04 | 1.17 | 2.23 | 3.81 | 0.9 |
| 2010 | TRN | AA | 23 | 6 | 0 | 0 | 14 | 14 | 88¹ | 40 | 2 | 14 | 59 | 2.3 | 8.6 | 49% | .257 | 0.97 | 2.04 | 3.10 | 3.13 | 1.9 |
| 2010 | SWB | AAA | 23 | 4 | 2 | 0 | 12 | 11 | 70¹ | 55 | 3 | 11 | 46 | 1.7 | 7.3 | 40% | .299 | 1.27 | 3.07 | 3.29 | 3.94 | 1.4 |
| 2011 | SWB | AAA | 24 | 5 | 5 | 0 | 18 | 18 | 107¹ | 109 | 10 | 24 | 89 | 2.2 | 7.5 | 39% | .336 | 1.31 | 3.19 | 3.55 | 4.28 | 1.1 |
| 2012 | NYA | MLB | 25 | 2 | 2 | 0 | 6 | 6 | 37¹ | 43 | 5 | 13 | 24 | 3.2 | 5.7 | 46% | .313 | 1.50 | 4.88 | 4.70 | 5.30 | 0.0 |

Phelps nearly made it to the big leagues last year when Colon got hurt, but the Yankees opted to sign 32-year-old Brian Gordon instead. Such is life as a Yankees farmhand. Shortly thereafter, shoulder discomfort sent Phelps to the DL and the opportunity was gone; however, he returned in August and pitched well in the Arizona Fall League. Phelps has a low-90s fastball, but lacks the offspeed pitches to be a top starter. That said, his minor league performances have earned him a look from the Yankees, one he will receive just as soon as the Yankees have exhausted every journeyman option on the planet.

### Mariano Rivera
Born: 11/29/1969 Age: 42
Bats: R Throws: R Height: 6' 5" Weight: 168
Breakout: 18% Improve: 28% Collapse: 56%
Attrition: 4% MLB: 82%

Comparables:
John Smoltz, Hoyt Wilhelm, Trevor Hoffman

| YEAR | TEAM | LVL | AGE | W | L | SV | G | GS | IP | H | HR | BB | SO | EqBB9 | EqSO9 | GB% | BABIP | WHIP | ERA | FIP | FRA | WARP |
|------|------|-----|-----|---|---|----|----|----|-----|----|----|----|----|-------|-------|-----|-------|------|------|------|------|------|
| 2009 | NYA | MLB | 39 | 3 | 3 | 44 | 66 | 0 | 66¹ | 48 | 7 | 12 | 72 | 1.6 | 9.8 | 54% | .248 | 0.90 | 1.76 | 2.93 | 3.21 | 2.1 |
| 2010 | NYA | MLB | 40 | 3 | 3 | 33 | 61 | 0 | 60 | 39 | 2 | 11 | 45 | 1.6 | 6.8 | 52% | .222 | 0.83 | 1.80 | 2.78 | 3.96 | 1.1 |
| 2011 | NYA | MLB | 41 | 1 | 2 | 44 | 64 | 0 | 61¹ | 47 | 3 | 8 | 60 | 1.2 | 8.8 | 48% | .278 | 0.90 | 1.91 | 2.23 | 3.21 | 1.4 |
| 2012 | NYA | MLB | 42 | 3 | 1 | 35 | 52 | 0 | 50¹ | 43 | 5 | 10 | 49 | 1.8 | 8.7 | 51% | .282 | 1.05 | 2.62 | 3.14 | 2.85 | 1.4 |

In *The Hitchhiker's Guide to the Galaxy*, Douglas Adams postulated that the answer to Life, the Universe and Everything is the number 42. Although Rivera might not be the answer to everything (and someone as devout as he is might indeed find the mere suggestion blasphemous), in terms of career goals he does seem to have achieved everything. With five championship rings and the all-time record for games saved, the only thing left to check off is a date with Cooperstown. He could stick around beyond this final year of his current contract and try to bury the saves record so deep that no one will ever find it, but no active pitcher is close. Not that there is an urgent need for him to stop; Rivera was as good as ever last year. The only possible knock on him is that his age and presumed fragility requires Girardi to restrict him to 60 innings a year. He can't go on forever, of course, and like Cary Grant retiring from the screen while he still had his looks, let's hope Rivera quits before his famous cut fastball does. The only thing worse than not having him would be seeing him fail.

**David Robertson**
Born: 4/9/1985 Age: 27
Bats: R Throws: R Height: 6' 0" Weight: 180
Breakout: 26% Improve: 40% Collapse: 34%
Attrition: 15% MLB: 99%

Comparables:
Bryan Harvey, Hideo Nomo, Francisco Rodriguez

| YEAR | TEAM | LVL | AGE | W | L | SV | G | GS | IP | H | HR | BB | SO | EqBB9 | EqSO9 | GB% | BABIP | WHIP | ERA | FIP | FRA | WARP |
|---|---|---|---|---|---|---|---|---|---|---|---|---|---|---|---|---|---|---|---|---|---|---|
| 2009 | NYA | MLB | 24 | 2 | 1 | 1 | 45 | 0 | 43² | 36 | 4 | 23 | 63 | 4.7 | 13.0 | 36% | .320 | 1.35 | 3.30 | 3.10 | 2.87 | 1.4 |
| 2010 | NYA | MLB | 25 | 4 | 5 | 1 | 64 | 0 | 61¹ | 59 | 5 | 33 | 71 | 4.8 | 10.4 | 43% | .346 | 1.50 | 3.82 | 3.55 | 4.72 | 0.4 |
| 2011 | NYA | MLB | 26 | 4 | 0 | 1 | 70 | 0 | 66² | 40 | 1 | 35 | 100 | 4.7 | 13.5 | 48% | .291 | 1.12 | 1.08 | 1.88 | 2.77 | 1.8 |
| 2012 | NYA | MLB | 27 | 3 | 1 | 1 | 58 | 0 | 55² | 44 | 5 | 28 | 72 | 4.5 | 11.7 | 49% | .307 | 1.29 | 3.13 | 3.29 | 3.41 | 1.1 |

With Chamberlain and Rafael Soriano ahead of him in the setup hierarchy, Robertson seemed doomed to a year of low-leverage work. Injuries soon shuffled the deck, and the right-hander again emerged as one of the most important relievers in the AL. He's also one of the most stress-inducing. Nicknamed "Houdini" because of his ability to pitch out of jams, he likes to pitch his way into them as well; give him an inherited baserunner and he'll walk two more to make things *really* interesting. He led the league in strikeouts per nine (50 or more innings), offsetting his wildness, but it's uncertain how long he can sustain this high-wire act. He held batters to just .053/.053/.105/ in 19 plate appearances with the bases loaded, and in 120 plate appearances in situations defined as high

Comparables:
Cliff Lee, Sparky Lyle, Willie Hernandez

| 2012 | NYA | MLB | 31 | 16 | 7 | 0 | 29 | 29 | 208 | 196 | 20 | 54 | 189 | 2.3 | 8.2 | 48% | .304 | 1.20 | 3.31 | 3.42 | 3.60 | 3.9 |

Every year, the same concern: will Sabathia's massive workload cause a breakdown? On the surface, Sabathia's 2011 was just one more good season, but take a closer look: from the start of the season through his July 26 start against the Mariners (where he flirted with a no-hitter and more), Sabathia was 17-6, 2.56, 156 strikeouts and 45 walks and opponents hitting .228/.283/.300 against him. Sabathia threw only 102 pitches against the Mariners in what would be a seven-inning 14-strikeout game, but the total is less important than the "how." Girardi put Sabathia back on the mound—shades of his 2006 handling of Josh Johnson—after a 30-minute rain delay. Coincidentally or not, Sabathia took a step backwards afterwards, with a 4.06 ERA and an opponents' slash line of .316/.356/.502. Perhaps most telling, of the 17 home runs Sabathia allowed in 2011, 11 of them came on August 1 or later. He pitched poorly in the ALDS as well. Sabathia signed an extension with the Yankees in the offseason that will keep him in pinstripes through at least 2016, so his employers will hope that the latter part of 2011 was a blip on the radar and not a portent of things to come.

**Rafael Soriano**
Born: 12/19/1979 Age: 32
Bats: R Throws: R Height: 6' 2" Weight: 175
Breakout: 17% Improve: 40% Collapse: 40%
Attrition: 6% MLB: 95%

Comparables:
Roberto Hernandez, Trevor Hoffman, Scott Linebrink

| YEAR | TEAM | LVL | AGE | W | L | SV | G | GS | IP | H | HR | BB | SO | EqBB9 | EqSO9 | GB% | BABIP | WHIP | ERA | FIP | FRA | WARP |
|---|---|---|---|---|---|---|---|---|---|---|---|---|---|---|---|---|---|---|---|---|---|---|
| 2009 | ATL | MLB | 29 | 1 | 6 | 27 | 77 | 0 | 75² | 53 | 6 | 27 | 102 | 3.2 | 12.1 | 33% | .281 | 1.06 | 2.97 | 2.50 | 2.79 | 2.2 |
| 2010 | TBA | MLB | 30 | 3 | 2 | 45 | 64 | 0 | 62¹ | 36 | 4 | 14 | 57 | 2.0 | 8.2 | 32% | .199 | 0.80 | 1.73 | 2.77 | 3.15 | 1.2 |
| 2011 | NYA | MLB | 31 | 2 | 3 | 2 | 42 | 0 | 39¹ | 33 | 4 | 18 | 36 | 4.1 | 8.2 | 36% | .279 | 1.30 | 4.12 | 4.00 | 4.83 | 0.2 |
| 2012 | NYA | MLB | 32 | 2 | 1 | 15 | 41 | 0 | 39 | 31 | 4 | 13 | 42 | 2.9 | 9.8 | 35% | .274 | 1.12 | 2.88 | 3.38 | 3.13 | 0.9 |

"Twenty-nine GMs would love to have their owners force Rafael Soriano down their throat," Brian Cashman said upon having had that exact experience. The Yankees vented $35 million (over three years, along with two team-unfriendly opt-outs) and a first-round pick (which the Rays spent on top outfield prospect Mikie Mathook). In return, they theoretically received an experienced, dominant closer as aged-Rivera insurance. Alas, Soriano spent almost half the season on the disabled list with elbow inflammation and wasn't particularly special when he did pitch. When healthy, Soriano has been an excellent pitcher, and you can argue that trading a wholly speculative draft pick for the All-Star reality of his record makes sense, but when you add in the money, the blackmail-inducing opt-outs, and that almost no reliever is so consistent as to be worth this kind of commitment, it was a foolish decision by whoever in the organization overruled the GM.

### Cory Wade

Born: 5/28/1983 Age: 29
Bats: R Throws: R Height: 6' 3" Weight: 185
Breakout: 10% Improve: 44% Collapse: 28%
Attrition: 8% MLB: 97%

Comparables:
Roy Oswalt, Curt Schilling, Alex Fernandez

| YEAR | TEAM | LVL | AGE | W | L | SV | G | GS | IP | H | HR | BB | SO | EqBB9 | EqSO9 | GB% | BABIP | WHIP | ERA | FIP | FRA | WARP |
|---|---|---|---|---|---|---|---|---|---|---|---|---|---|---|---|---|---|---|---|---|---|---|
| 2009 | ABQ | AAA | 26 | 1 | 1 | 1 | 18 | 0 | 22² | 22 | 5 | 7 | 19 | 2.8 | 7.5 | 41% | .266 | 1.19 | 6.74 | 5.70 | 7.71 | -0.3 |
| 2009 | LAN | MLB | 26 | 2 | 3 | 0 | 27 | 0 | 27² | 28 | 3 | 10 | 18 | 3.3 | 5.9 | 37% | .281 | 1.37 | 5.53 | 4.36 | 4.20 | 0.3 |
| 2010 | ABQ | AAA | 27 | 3 | 0 | 2 | 21 | 0 | 29¹ | 20 | 2 | 1 | 13 | 0.9 | 6.1 | 41% | .290 | 1.30 | 4.91 | 4.26 | 6.63 | -0.1 |
| 2011 | DUR | AAA | 28 | 2 | 1 | 0 | 21 | 0 | 36² | 34 | 4 | 6 | 34 | 1.5 | 8.3 | 27% | .303 | 1.09 | 1.23 | 3.37 | 3.97 | 0.7 |
| 2011 | NYA | MLB | 28 | 6 | 1 | 0 | 40 | 0 | 39² | 33 | 5 | 8 | 30 | 1.8 | 6.8 | 39% | .246 | 1.03 | 2.04 | 3.79 | 4.59 | 0.3 |
| 2012 | NYA | MLB | 29 | 2 | 1 | 0 | 30 | 0 | 38¹ | 37 | 5 | 11 | 29 | 2.5 | 6.8 | 39% | .284 | 1.26 | 3.88 | 4.25 | 4.22 | 0.4 |

Curveball "n" Command specialist Wade was the surprise of the Dodgers' 2008 pen, but after spending two seasons coping with shoulder problems and their surgical aftermath, he was non-tendered. The Rays gave him a minor-league deal, but when they didn't come calling despite some stellar pitching at Triple-A, Wade played the opt-out card to come to New York. He joined a bullpen depleted by Soriano's injury and pitched excellently, performing especially well with runners on base. Right-handed hitters have hit just .206 against Wade, and lefties haven't had it easy either (.236/.274/.368). Wade is the anti-Soriano, cheap and effective, and is an example of what a team can achieve at low cost when it trusts its GM to do his job.

### Adam Warren

Born: 8/25/1987 Age: 24
Bats: R Throws: R Height: 6' 3" Weight: 215
Breakout: 23% Improve: 53% Collapse: 21%
Attrition: 13% MLB: 96%

Comparables:
Jair Jurrjens, Joel Pineiro, Jeremy Accardo

| YEAR | TEAM | LVL | AGE | W | L | SV | G | GS | IP | H | HR | BB | SO | EqBB9 | EqSO9 | GB% | BABIP | WHIP | ERA | FIP | FRA | WARP |
|---|---|---|---|---|---|---|---|---|---|---|---|---|---|---|---|---|---|---|---|---|---|---|
| 2009 | STA | A- | 21 | 5 | 2 | 0 | 12 | 12 | 56² | 60 | 1 | 13 | 65 | 1.6 | 7.9 | 69% | .319 | 1.04 | 1.43 | 1.95 | 3.24 | 1.4 |
| 2010 | TAM | A+ | 22 | 7 | 4 | 0 | 15 | 15 | 81 | 59 | 2 | 13 | 51 | 1.9 | 7.4 | 61% | .297 | 1.10 | 2.22 | 3.26 | 3.75 | 1.4 |
| 2010 | TRN | AA | 22 | 4 | 3 | 0 | 10 | 10 | 54¹ | 43 | 3 | 11 | 55 | 2.7 | 9.8 | 49% | .310 | 1.20 | 3.15 | 3.06 | 3.46 | 1.0 |
| 2011 | SWB | AAA | 23 | 5 | 6 | 0 | 27 | 27 | 152¹ | 145 | 13 | 53 | 111 | 3.1 | 6.6 | 39% | .286 | 1.30 | 3.60 | 4.09 | 4.84 | 1.1 |
| 2012 | NYA | MLB | 24 | 3 | 3 | 0 | 9 | 9 | 48² | 51 | 6 | 18 | 34 | 3.4 | 6.3 | 48% | .301 | 1.42 | 4.41 | 4.52 | 4.80 | 0.3 |

If Dr. Seuss had written a book about Yankees prospects, it would have been titled, *Oh, the Places You Won't Go!* In late July, the Yankees faced a doubleheader and the possibility was raised that Warren would come up from Scranton to start it if Nova, who had recently injured his ankle, wasn't good to go. Nova made it; Warren stayed in Pennsylvania. Warren has the best fastball of the Yankees' various mid-range pitching prospects, but the offspeed stuff that would make him a front-of-rotation candidate is lacking, as evidenced by his low strikeout rate. Left-handed hitters hit .274/.349/.378 against him last year, hardly terrifying but an indicator that his changeup could use refinement. Still, as with Phelps, Warren is ready for an audition. With the 2011 rotation returning as a unit, he's going to have to wait for an injury to create an opening.

### Chase Whitley

Born: 6/14/1989 Age: 23
Bats: R Throws: R Height: 6' 5" Weight: 220
Breakout: 27% Improve: 63% Collapse: 17%
Attrition: 11% MLB: 88%

Comparables:
Frank Castillo, John Smoltz, Craig Hansen

| YEAR | TEAM | LVL | AGE | W | L | SV | G | GS | IP | H | HR | BB | SO | EqBB9 | EqSO9 | GB% | BABIP | WHIP | ERA | FIP | FRA | WARP |
|---|---|---|---|---|---|---|---|---|---|---|---|---|---|---|---|---|---|---|---|---|---|---|
| 2010 | STA | A- | 21 | 4 | 2 | 15 | 28 | 0 | 34¹ | 18 | 0 | 15 | 44 | 3.9 | 11.5 | — | .253 | 0.96 | 1.31 | 2.31 | 3.48 | 0.5 |
| 2011 | TAM | A+ | 22 | 0 | 1 | 6 | 23 | 0 | 48¹ | 38 | 2 | 10 | 38 | 1.9 | 7.4 | 58% | .281 | 1.06 | 1.68 | 3.16 | 3.82 | 0.7 |
| 2011 | TRN | AA | 22 | 3 | 4 | 1 | 19 | 1 | 42² | 46 | 6 | 19 | 37 | 4.0 | 7.8 | 43% | .323 | 1.52 | 3.38 | 4.84 | 5.39 | -0.1 |
| 2012 | NYA | MLB | 23 | 1 | 0 | 0 | 12 | 0 | 21² | 24 | 3 | 10 | 16 | 4.0 | 6.4 | 47% | .307 | 1.53 | 5.04 | 4.91 | 5.48 | -0.1 |

A 15th-round pick in the 2010 draft, Whitley and his changeup pitched their way up to Double-A Trenton in year two of his career, then continued to excel in the Arizona Fall League. Whitley is a big guy (6-foot-4) but doesn't throw hard, with a fastball that sits in the 89-91 range. The Yankees thought that if this two-way player in college were to focus solely on pitching, he might have starter potential. His 2011 strikeout rate of 7.6 per nine out of the pen does not seem to bode well for such a transformation. He was hard on right-handed hitters, at least at Tampa (.193 average). They hit .288 against him at Trenton, left-handers hitting .276. Clearly there is an adjustment to be made, relieving or not.

## LINEOUTS

### HITTERS

| PLAYER | TEAM | LVL | AGE | PA | R | 2B | 3B | HR | RBI | BB | SO | SB-CS | AVG/OBP/SLG | TAv | BABIP | BRR | FRAA | WARP |
|---|---|---|---|---|---|---|---|---|---|---|---|---|---|---|---|---|---|---|
| 2B D. Adams | TAM | A+ | 24 | 57 | 6 | 3 | 0 | 0 | 4 | 4 | 8 | 0-2 | .308/.368/.365 | .251 | .364 | -1.4 | -0.4 | -0.1 |
|  | YAN | RK | 24 | 64 | 13 | 9 | 0 | 1 | 11 | 5 | 10 | 2-1 | .429/.469/.643 | .380 | .489 | 0.6 | 3.9 | 1.5 |
| 3B E. Chavez | NYA | MLB | 33 | 175 | 16 | 7 | 1 | 2 | 26 | 14 | 34 | 0-0 | .262/.320/.356 | .241 | .320 | 0.3 | 0.1 | 0.3 |
| SS C. Culver | STA | A- | 18 | 312 | 40 | 14 | 2 | 2 | 33 | 30 | 57 | 10-0 | .250/.323/.337 | .260 | .305 | -0.2 | -1.7 | 0.1 |
| CF C. Dickerson | SWB | AAA | 29 | 247 | 33 | 10 | 1 | 2 | 16 | 30 | 63 | 18-4 | .241/.341/.325 | .258 | .331 | 0.1 | 1.2 | 1.1 |
|  | NYA | MLB | 29 | 55 | 9 | 2 | 0 | 1 | 7 | 2 | 17 | 4-0 | .260/.296/.360 | .260 | .364 | 0.5 | -0.1 | 0.2 |
| 2B A. Gumbs | STA | A- | 18 | 220 | 32 | 11 | 4 | 3 | 29 | 20 | 57 | 11-7 | .264/.332/.406 | .276 | .353 | -2.8 | -0.4 | 0.9 |
| CF S. Heathcott | CSC | A | 20 | 227 | 34 | 11 | 4 | 4 | 16 | 18 | 57 | 4-7 | .271/.342/.410 | .270 | .358 | 1.8 | 5.8 | 1.4 |
| CF R. Santana | YAN | RK | 19 | 185 | 43 | 11 | 3 | 9 | 29 | 17 | 40 | 10-3 | .296/.361/.568 | .308 | .336 | 2.4 | 5.6 | 2.3 |
| CF M. Williams | STA | A- | 19 | 298 | 42 | 11 | 6 | 3 | 31 | 20 | 41 | 28-12 | .349/.395/.468 | .317 | .399 | 2.4 | 4.6 | 3.8 |

**David Adams** spent the year trying to stay on the field after season-ending ankle surgery in 2010. Assuming full functionality, Adams is a good hitter for a second baseman and can field his position, but if he doesn't get back on track at 25, the parade will pass him by. ⌀ **Eric Chavez** left stardom behind many injuries ago; the question now is if he can even be a role player. Pop-free hitting and a 71-game DL stay suggest the answer is "no." ⌀ The Yankees' surprise first-round pick in 2010, **Cito Culver** received good reviews for the defensive skills he showed in short-season ball, but offense still remains a concept; he's still young enough to turn into almost anything from Honus Wagner to Honus Schwartz. The smart money is on the latter. ⌀ **Chris Dickerson** has now had about a season's-worth of big-league at-bats over the last four seasons and has hit .266/.351/.399 with nine home runs, 64 walks, and 24 steals in 30 attempts. This is not without value in an outfield reserve, but the Yankees lacked room for him in 2011 and probably will again in 2012. ⌀ Everything about **Angelo Gumbs** is a work in progress, particularly his defense (he was a shortstop and outfielder in high school), but he showed surprising advanced hitting skills to go with across-the-board tools. ⌀ After two separate shoulder surgeries, the Yankees 2009 first-rounder **Slade Heathcott** retains promise, but a consistent approach to the strike zone, power, and most of all durability await. ⌀ The Yankees traded for fourth outfielder **Justin Maxwell** just before spring training, but Tommy John surgery knocked him out before the power he showed at Scranton could help the parent club. ⌀ It is obligatory to say that **Gustavo "the Wrong" Molina** is unrelated to Bengie, Jose, or Yadier, but shares their defensive abilities, while his bat has less basis in reality than most episodes of *Star Trek*. ⌀ The lesser of the Nix brothers, excellent fielder **Jayson Nix** is a career .195/.268/.335 hitter against right-handed pitching (588 PAs) and the occasional home run represents the totality of his offensive game. ⌀ **Ramiro Pena** is the quintessential good-field/no-hit shortstop and in ye olden days he would have made a fine late-inning defensive replacement for the geriatric Jeter, but rosters swollen with relievers mean that bench players with such extremely limited applications have been permanently deselected in the Darwinian sense of the word. ⌀ **Ravel Santana** hit for power and showed a true center fielder's defensive ability in his stateside debut, but his season was cut short by a severe leg injury, so we'll have to see if his speed survived. ⌀ A 2010 fourth-rounder, **Mason Williams** is so fast he once made the Kessel run in less than 12 parsecs. Given speed and the ability to hit for average he should have a career despite subpar power, but he's still far from the Bronx.

## PITCHERS

| PLAYER | TEAM | LVL | AGE | W | L | SV | IP | H | HR | BB | SO | EqBB9 | EqSO9 | GB% | BABIP | WHIP | ERA | FIP | FRA | WARP |
|---|---|---|---|---|---|---|---|---|---|---|---|---|---|---|---|---|---|---|---|---|
| A. Brackman | SWB | AAA | 25 | 1 | 5 | 1 | 96 | 82 | 10 | 75 | 75 | 7.0 | 7.0 | 49% | .269 | 1.64 | 6.00 | 5.81 | 6.30 | -0.6 |
|  | NYA | MLB | 25 | 0 | 0 | 0 | $2^1$ | 1 | 0 | 3 | 0 | 11.6 | 0.0 | 50% | .100 | 1.71 | 0.00 | 6.92 | 5.59 | 0.0 |
| B. Carlyle | SWB | AAA | 33 | 2 | 1 | 1 | 43 | 35 | 5 | 16 | 31 | 3.3 | 6.5 | 40% | .248 | 1.19 | 3.98 | 4.49 | 5.25 | 0.1 |
|  | NYA | MLB | 33 | 0 | 1 | 0 | $7^2$ | 5 | 1 | 7 | 9 | 8.2 | 10.6 | 22% | .235 | 1.57 | 4.70 | 5.15 | 5.12 | 0.0 |
| M. Daley | COL | MLB | 29 | 0 | 0 | 0 | 6 | 8 | 1 | 2 | 7 | 3.0 | 10.5 | 22% | .412 | 1.67 | 10.50 | 3.83 | 5.87 | 0.0 |
| B. Gordon | LEH | AAA | 32 | 5 | 0 | 0 | $55^1$ | 39 | 4 | 7 | 56 | 1.1 | 9.1 | 41% | .252 | 0.83 | 1.14 | 2.59 | 3.15 | 1.9 |
|  | NYA | MLB | 32 | 0 | 1 | 0 | $10^1$ | 12 | 3 | 3 | 4 | 2.6 | 3.5 | 30% | .273 | 1.45 | 5.23 | 7.51 | 7.54 | -0.1 |
| T. Kahnle | CSC | A | 21 | 3 | 5 | 2 | 81 | 69 | 1 | 49 | 112 | 5.4 | 12.4 | 48% | .342 | 1.46 | 4.22 | 2.77 | 3.86 | 1.3 |
| S. Mitre | NYA | MLB | 30 | 0 | 0 | 0 | $5^1$ | 9 | 0 | 4 | 2 | 6.8 | 3.4 | 61% | .391 | 2.44 | 11.81 | 5.12 | 8.06 | -0.2 |
|  | MIL | MLB | 30 | 0 | 1 | 0 | 33 | 30 | 3 | 10 | 14 | 2.7 | 3.8 | 52% | .248 | 1.21 | 3.27 | 4.33 | 5.38 | -0.2 |
| M. Montgomery | CSC | A | 20 | 0 | 0 | 14 | $24^1$ | 17 | 0 | 11 | 41 | 4.1 | 15.2 | 52% | .327 | 1.15 | 1.85 | 1.64 | 3.52 | 0.5 |
| M. O'Connor | BUF | AAA | 30 | 5 | 3 | 0 | $60^1$ | 68 | 7 | 19 | 64 | 2.8 | 9.8 | 45% | .370 | 1.46 | 5.22 | 3.57 | 4.72 | 0.6 |
|  | NYN | MLB | 30 | 0 | 1 | 0 | $6^2$ | 5 | 0 | 3 | 8 | 4.1 | 10.8 | 29% | .294 | 1.20 | 2.70 | 2.39 | 3.80 | 0.1 |
| S. Proctor | NYA | MLB | 34 | 0 | 3 | 0 | 11 | 19 | 6 | 12 | 11 | 9.8 | 9.0 | 41% | .406 | 2.82 | 9.00 | 11.43 | 11.60 | -0.8 |
|  | ATL | MLB | 34 | 2 | 3 | 0 | $29^1$ | 31 | 5 | 19 | 18 | 5.8 | 5.5 | 33% | .289 | 1.70 | 6.44 | 6.03 | 6.66 | -0.7 |
| A. Sanit | NYA | MLB | 32 | 0 | 0 | 0 | 7 | 12 | 0 | 3 | 4 | 3.9 | 5.1 | 53% | .400 | 2.14 | 12.86 | 4.49 | 4.89 | 0.0 |
| G. Stoneburner | TRN | AA | 23 | 1 | 5 | 0 | $58^1$ | 72 | 3 | 20 | 36 | 3.1 | 5.6 | 54% | .350 | 1.58 | 4.17 | 4.03 | 5.83 | -0.2 |
| K. Whelan | SWB | AAA | 27 | 1 | 2 | 23 | $52^1$ | 38 | 5 | 14 | 54 | 2.4 | 9.3 | 42% | .252 | 0.99 | 2.75 | 3.28 | 5.15 | 0.2 |
|  | NYA | MLB | 27 | 0 | 0 | 0 | $1^2$ | 0 | 0 | 5 | 1 | 27.0 | 5.4 | 50% | .000 | 3.00 | 5.40 | 10.86 | 8.91 | 0.0 |

A college basketball player trying to pass himself off as a pitcher, former first-rounder **Andrew Brackman** became a free agent when the Yankees failed to pick up his option after an abysmal 2011. ⌀ The Yankees brought canonical journeyman **Buddy Carlyle** back from Japan and called him up not once but twice because Our Book of the Blessed Steinbrenner says that you should try every possible oldster option before turning to a kid. He was released in August. ⌀ **Matt Daley** attended Bucknell University, which also produced Hall of Famer Christy Mathewson, and the two alums have combined to win 374 big-league games, with Mathewson accounting for 373 of those. ⌀ When the Yankees needed a quick fill-in for the injured Bartolo Colon and calling up a pitcher would have caused uncomfortable contortions of the 40-man, the Yankees turned to **Brian Gordon**, then in the Phillies' system. The converted outfielder showed excellent command in the minors, but proved pedestrian in the majors, and the club exiled him to the Korean Professional League. *Ahn-nyong-hee gaseyo!* ⌀ Reliever **Tommy Kahnle** can get his fastball into the high 90s, leading to a career 12.7 strikeouts per nine innings and just one home run allowed in 97 innings, but his mechanics and command await refinement. ⌀ Whenever **Sergio Mitre** is unemployed, Joe Girardi puts him to work, but not even benefactor Girardi could protect Mitre from half a season on the DL due to rotator cuff tendinitis. Even when healthy, this groundball pitcher needs great defense and a whole lotta luck to get by. ⌀ **Mark Montgomery**'s advanced slider led to some sick strikeout rates; in his Sally League debut, he struck out *five* batters in one inning (with some help from Gary Sanchez's buttered glove). ⌀ Left-hander **Mike O'Connor** found himself in the big leagues for the first time last May with the Mets, but they didn't think highly enough of him to bring him back in September. ⌀ Watching **Scott Proctor** give up six home runs in 11 September innings was undoubtedly painful for everyone who took pleasure in seeing him emerge as Joe Torre's favorite reliever back in 2006. ⌀ If you know why the Yankees ever thought that **Amauri Sanit**, a thirtysomething Cuban import with a career ERA of 5.99 at Triple-A, was a major league pitcher, you're one up on us. ⌀ Neck and shoulder injuries kept **Graham Stoneburner** on the sidelines for three months, but when healthy, he throws a sinking fastball; establishing a second plus pitch remains on the to-do list. ⌀ The last survivor of the 2006 Gary Sheffield trade, **Kevin Whelan** has always struck out more than his share of batters but had zero command. He got the walks under control last year, but when his chance came to impress the Yankees—whoops!—he walked five in two appearances and that was that, probably for good.

## MANAGER: JOE GIRARDI

| YEAR | TEAM | W-L | Pythag +/- | Avg PC | 100+ P | 120+ P | QS | BQS | REL | REL w Zero R | IBB | Subs | PH | PH Avg | PH HR | SB2 | CS2 | SB3 | CS3 | SAC Att | SAC % | POS SAC | Squeeze | Swing | In Play |
|---|---|---|---|---|---|---|---|---|---|---|---|---|---|---|---|---|---|---|---|---|---|---|---|---|---|
| 2009 | NYA | 103-59 | 1 | 96.8 | 79 | 4 | 74 | 5 | 461 | 304 | 28 | 58 | 97 | .237 | 3 | 12 | 1 | 0 | 1 | 49 | 63.3% | 28 | 0 | 145 | 108 |
| 2010 | NYA | 95-67 | 1 | 194.2 | 160 | 157 | 105 | 3 | 431 | 349 | 74 | — | 190 | .167 | 4 | 9 | 4 | 1 | 0 | 96 | 93.8% | 78 | 0 | 362 | 110 |
| 2011 | NYA | 97-65 | 1 | 95.7 | 69 | 2 | 84 | 6 | 465 | 404 | 43 | — | 54 | .196 | 0 | 21 | 3 | 1 | 1 | 54 | 83.3% | 38 | 0 | 357 | 94 |

Joe Girardi is one of the most competent managers in baseball, but that's a double-edged compliment, for managing is a degraded profession. The problem is that rather than use the brain in his head, which is excellent, Girardi uses the one he keeps in his famous binder. That binder contains a sinister intelligence that overrides Girardi's better instincts and forces him to adopt a foolish rigidity that requires him to make moves by meaningless small samples, use pitchers inflexibly according to roles established in spring training regardless of whether they have pitched up to those roles, bat Derek Jeter leadoff prior

Guillen. That just might be the best the world of managers has to offer the modern game.

# Oakland Athletics

The venue has been a frustrating thing. I'd like to see the people who follow this team, myself, the people who work here, have at least a fighting chance, and until we get a new venue it's going to be an uphill climb, and we're slipping down that slope. —Billy Beane to Bob Costas on MLB Network's *Studio 42*

The A's home ballpark is a problem. As Table 1 shows, the A's revenues and payroll have largely stagnated in the last half-decade under owner Lew Wolff, who bought the team in April 2005. With the revenues climbing for Major League Baseball overall, that has led to the A's falling further and further behind. One large reason for the lack of revenue growth is the Oakland Coliseum. Dating back to the opening of SkyDome in Toronto in 1989, 23 of the 30 major league teams have moved into new ballparks. Two others, the Angels and Royals, have renovated their parks, and of the remaining five, three—the Red Sox, Cubs, and Dodgers—were among the four top earners during the 2010 season. Meanwhile, the A's are the only one of the 29 American teams that still shares its ballpark with a National Football League franchise, and it was the Raiders, not the A's, who were in charge of the most recent renovation to the Coliseum in 1996, the infamous addition of "Mount Davis," a massive new upper deck in center field that the A's ultimately decided to cover with a decorative tarp during their games.

The ballpark is a problem, but it is not the only problem. The Rays and Diamondbacks both made the playoffs last year with lower end-of-year payrolls than the A's $70.5 million, and the Brewers were a popular preseason pick that went all the way to the National League Championship Series despite opening the season with a salary less than $14 million higher than where the A's finished. In 2010, the difference between the A's Opening Day payroll and that of the division champion

Rangers, who were running away with the American League West even before they traded for Cliff Lee, was less than $4 million. Teams win with modest payrolls every year. Some of them, like the Rays and, until last year, the Twins, do so consistently. The A's used to be one of those teams. From 1999 to 2006, the A's made the playoffs five times, finished second every other year, and didn't post a single losing record despite not ranking above 24th in final-day payroll from 1999 to 2003. The ballpark hasn't changed since then, and for Beane to suddenly take the position that his team doesn't have a fighting chance because of where they play is selective reasoning at best.

The A's competitive decline was a popular topic in the wake of the September release of the movie *Moneyball*, which, like the book on which it was based, focused on the 2002 A's and Beane's efforts to compensate for his lack of financial might by making his organization smarter than the other 29. Beane's typical response to such inquiries was to say that, once teams with more spending power caught on to the sort of advanced thinking the A's were doing during that period, that competitive advantage was lost. That's not inaccurate, but, again, it is only part of the story. The Moneyball A's didn't win by Moneyball alone. It was the team's excellent player development (which produced, among others, the rotation trio of Tim Hudson, Mark Mulder, and Barry Zito, league MVPs Jason Giambi at first base and Miguel Tejada at shortstop, Gold Glove third baseman Eric Chavez, and All-Star catcher Ramon Hernandez) and Beane's astute wheeling and dealing (getting power-hitting right fielder Jermaine Dye from the Rockies for three nobodies, acquiring center fielder Johnny Damon, second baseman Mark Ellis, and starter Cory Lidle in a three-team deal for Rookie of the Year flame-outs Ben Grieve and Angel Berroa and backup catcher A.J. Hinch),

## ATHLETICS PROSPECTUS
### 2011 W-L: 74-88, 3rd in AL West

| | | |
|---|---|---|
| Pythag | .477 | 20th |
| RS/G | 3.98 | 21st |
| RA/G | 4.19 | 14th |
| TAv | .264 | 11th |
| TAv-P | .268 | 23rd |
| FIP | 3.84 | 11th |
| DER | .711 | 15th |
| DL | 693 | 13th |
| B-Age | 29.1 | 20th |
| P-Age | 26.9 | 4th |
| Salary | $67.4 | 23rd |
| M$/MW | $2.14 | 14th |

**Ballpark:** The Coliseum (3-yr. PF: 91). This extreme pitcher's park's days may be numbered

**2011:** The top two pitchers head for surgery, and the offense sputters on life support

**2012:** Stadiumball. Dismantle team, build San Jose park, up payroll, compete with big spenders

**Action Items:** Cheap veteran filler and the official shovel date on that new San Jose field that allowed the Moneyball advantage to make the marginal difference that put the A's over the top.

The adoption of a Moneyball-style approach to advanced analysis and market inefficiencies by some of baseball's wealthiest teams hasn't eroded the A's competitive edge nearly as much as their near-catastrophic list of player development busts over the last half decade. Among those disasters was shortstop Bobby Crosby, who won the AL Rookie of the Year in 2004, was better in 2005, then hit .229/.292/.341 after his 26th birthday and is now out of baseball. Right-hander Rich Harden posted a 114 ERA+ in 31 starts at age 22, also in 2004, but hasn't been healthy enough to qualify for an ERA title since. Outfielder Travis Buck hit .288/.377/.474

## Table 1: Standing Still: Oakland A's Revenues and Payrolls from 2003 to 2010

| Year | Revenue | MLB Rank | Payroll | MLB Rank |
|------|---------|----------|---------|----------|
| 2003 | $110 | 21 | $56.6 | 26 |
| 2004 | $116 | 22 | $60.3 | 18 |
| 2005 | $134 | 24 | $58.4 | 19 |
| 2006 | $146 | 23 | $71.0 | 19 |
| 2007 | $154 | 24 | $78.5 | 18 |
| 2008 | $160 | 26 | $55.2 | 27 |
| 2009 | $155 | 28 | $61.7 | 27 |
| 2010 | $161 | 26 | $61.8 | 26 |

All dollar amounts in millions. Revenue figures from Forbes. Payroll amounts are end-of-season figures from the Associated Press. Data from BizofBaseball.com. 2011 figures were not yet available at press time.

Looking at that list of disappointments, health is a common theme. Injury was a significant factor in the struggles of Crosby, Buck, Harden, and Herrera. Indeed, injuries have devastated the A's in recent years. Perhaps most significantly, the one player from their Moneyball heyday that the A's did decide to invest in, Chavez, developed shoulder and back problems almost immediately after signing his six-year, $66 million contract. As a result of those injuries and the numerous surgeries they required, Chavez managed to play in just 64 games and hit a mere .222/.265/.330 over the final three years of that deal, for which the A's paid him $34 million.

Finally free of Chavez's contract in 2011, the A's increased their payroll by almost $9 million, trading for outfielders Josh Willingham and David DeJesus, each of whom made $6 million in their final season before free agency, signing free-agent designated hitter Hideki Matsui for $4.25 million,

picking up center fielder Coco Crisp's $5.75 million option, and adding relievers Grant Balfour and Brian Fuentes on a pair of two-year contracts worth a total of $18.6 million. The hope was that, with the Rangers losing Lee to free agency, the A's might be able to field a legitimate contender by adding those upgrades to their strong young rotation of righty Trevor Cahill and lefties Brett Anderson, Gio Gonzalez, and Dallas Braden.

Then injury struck, again. Braden and Anderson combined to make just 16 starts in 2011. Braden made just three starts before a stiff pitching shoulder forced him to the disabled list. He had had surgery to repair a torn capsule in the shoulder in May. The oft-injured Anderson went under the

since, nor has Mark Prior, who had shoulder capsule tears in 2007 and 2008. Former Mets LOOGY Pedro Feliciano was diagnosed with a torn capsule soon after joining the Yankees in camp last March. He missed the entire season hoping in vain to avoid surgery but went under the knife in September. Exactly two calendar years elapsed between Chien-Ming Wang's July 2009 capsule repair and his return with the Nationals last year, and that counts as a success story for a pitcher with that injury.

Those injuries came just as fellow lefty Josh Outman was returning from the June 2009 Tommy John surgery that interrupted his promising rookie campaign, which itself came two months after relief prospect Joey Devine had the same surgery, which ultimately cost him the entirety of both the 2009 and 2010 seasons. The A's did get some unexpectedly strong work from one-time White Sox prospect Brandon McCarthy, who is still just 28 and was released by the Rangers after 2010, but McCarthy's right scapula, which he fractured in 2007, has become a chronic problem that has sent him to the disabled list every year since including a month-and-a-half-long stay last year.

Meanwhile, Cahill's big 2010 season (18-8, 2.97 ERA) was revealed to be the BABIP fluke we thought it was and he regressed to being a league-average starter, leaving Gonzalez, who led the majors in walks but also managed to recover an extra strikeout per inning, as the only A's starter able to build on his success from the year before. Realizing the jig was up, Beane flipped both pitchers for prospects this offseason, sending Cahill to the Diamondbacks for a three-player package built around right-handed pitching prospect Jarrod Parker, and Gonzalez to the Nationals for a four-player prospect package headed by catcher Derek Norris and right-ies A.J. Cole and Brad Peacock.

Beane did well in those deals, acquiring seven players, all with legitimate major league potential, five of them having already made their major league debuts, but all still with their rookie status intact and all six team-controlled seasons remaining. Peacock, strike-throwing lefty Tom Milone (the last player in the Gonzalez package), and Parker could all be in the A's rotation at some point this season. Parker and Cole, the latter of whom is just 20 and heading to High-A this year, have front-of-the-rotation potential. Peacock could be a number-three or better. Milone should be able to remain a starter at the major league level, albeit at the back end. Three-true-outcome backstop Norris could be Mickey Tettleton with actual catching ability, a nice upgrade on the stagnating Kurt Suzuki, and one who will arrive just in time to keep Suzuki's 2014 option from vesting (which it would with 113 starts in 2013). Collin Cowgill is more of a fourth outfielder, but could start by default in the wake of the free agent departures of Willingham and DeJesus, and righty reliever Ryan Cook could make the team as well. Those two, the other two-thirds of the Cahill package, could be the worst of the seven players Beane acquired in those two deals.

That's a hearty haul for two pitchers who could look very ordinary outside of the ballpark Beane ironically complains so much about. It also provides a much-needed re-infusion of young, high-upside, major league-ready talent for a team whose perceived opportunity to contend in 2011 proved to be little more than a cruel mirage. Of course, in order for those deals to pay off, the A's luck in player development will have to reverse itself.

When Kevin Goldstein compiled his list of the A's best players under the age of 25 prior to the 2011 season, Anderson, Gonzalez, and Cahill occupied three of the top four spots. Joining them was Daric Barton, an under-powered, on-base-machine of a first baseman who came over in the December 2004 deal that sent Mulder to the Cardinals. Barton appeared to finally break through in 2010 at age 24, leading the AL in walks and posting a .393 on-base percentage, but he hit just .212/.325/.267 through late June of last season before being shipped back to Triple-A, after which a labrum tear in his left shoulder prevented his return. Chris Carter, the slugging first baseman/left fielder who topped Goldstein's pre-season prospect list, had a similar dispiriting campaign, missing most of the first half due to a thumb injury and struggling in his brief major league looks. Now 24, Carter has hit just .167/.226/.254 in 124 career major league plate appearances.

Player development is a notoriously low-percentage endeavor, but the A's have had a brutal string of luck. Four-star center field prospect Grant Desme retired to join the priesthood in January 2010. Top pitching prospect Michael Ynoa had Tommy John surgery in August 2010. Left-handed rotation prospect Ian Krol, also rated four-stars by Goldstein, missed the first half of the 2011 season with an elbow injury, then, after just three rehab starts, was suspended for the remainder of the season for using an anti-gay slur on Twitter. Michael Taylor, the end result of sending Carlos Gonzalez to the Rockies, via Matt Holliday and Brett Wallace, hasn't looked like the same player since joining the A's organization two years ago. While he did rebound some in 2011 after a mysterious power-outage in 2010, he is now a 26-year-old with just 35 major league plate appearances to his credit. Some of those young men may still pan out, particularly Ynoa and Krol, the elder of whom is still just 20, but it's this string of player development disasters that is killing the A's, not their ballpark.

Where the ballpark comes in is in the A's inability to absorb those failures and injuries. The Angels can make a disastrous trade, add Vernon Wells' $23 million-a-year salary, and still go out the next year and commit over $300 million to Albert Pujols and C.J. Wilson. The Yankees, spending roughly $200 million a year on payroll, can spend $40 million for 26 below-average starts by Carl Pavano, then shell out $82.5 million for A.J. Burnett to be one of the worst starting pitchers in baseball while watching Wang, Phil Hughes, and Joba Chamberlain battle major arm injuries, and still make the playoffs in 16 of 17 seasons. But if the A's prospects don't pan out, they're in big trouble, and if you add a Chavez contract to that, they're shot.

The new collective bargaining agreement's restrictions on free agent compensation and spending on amateur talent won't help matters. The A's gave Dominican teenager Ynoa $4.25 million in 2008, and top prospects Grant Green and Michael Choice signed for a combined $4.75 million in 2009 and 2010. The new CBA will limit teams to a *total* of $2.9 million for international signees in the coming year, with that limit topping out at $5 million for teams with the worst record in subsequent years, and will place similar slotting restrictions on the draft.

As for the A's efforts to secure a new ballpark, Beane's Sisyphean metaphor is apt, and the organization's ballpark boulder has been higher on the hill in recent years than it is now. The only major development in the A's relocation efforts in the last year was a 10-1 vote in the San Jose City Council in November to approve giving the A's a three-year option on a steeply reduced price for 5 1/2 acres in downtown San Jose to be used only as the site of a new ballpark. The A's would be able to purchase the land for $6.98 million, less than a third of what the city paid for it, and roughly half what it was valued at in a September 2010 appraisal, but the A's haven't actually purchased it, and they haven't even purchased the option to buy it, priced at $50,000 for the first two years and $25,000 for the third. Even if they do purchase the option, the A's won't be able to finalize their purchase of the land until the matter goes to a public vote, which is no slam dunk to come out in the A's favor, as evidenced by the lawsuit filed against the city in early December by a local group claiming the environmental impact studies done by the city were insufficient and that the option should have been put to a vote as well.

It was local opposition that convinced the A's to abandon their plans to move to suburban Fremont in early 2009, a decision that came after the team had already purchased nearly 200 acres in the city less than two years earlier. The A's still own that land nearly five years later, which serves as an expensive reminder that they've reached this precipice before only to have their boulder roll back down the mountain. Now they're rolling that rock back up a similar incline, only this one leads right to the headwall that is the San Francisco Giants' territorial rights and the buttress that is the Giants' California League affiliate, which backed the aforementioned lawsuit.

All of which is to say, no matter how loudly the A's pine for a new ballpark, a move doesn't seem likely to happen any time soon. While blaming their ballpark for their troubles may be the message that is most important for them to get across to the commissioner and the other 29 teams, there are other, more significant reasons that they're not winning.

**Comparables:**
Brandon Sing, Boog Powell, Erubiel Durazo

| YEAR | TEAM | LVL | AGE | PA | R | 2B | 3B | HR | RBI | BB | SO | SB | CS | AVG_OBP_SLG | TAv | BABIP | BRR | FRAA | WARP |
|---|---|---|---|---|---|---|---|---|---|---|---|---|---|---|---|---|---|---|---|
| 2009 | ARI | MLB | 23 | 116 | 13 | 7 | 0 | 4 | 14 | 12 | 40 | 0 | 0 | .202/.284/.385 | .221 | .283 | 0 | -1.9 | -0.7 |
| 2010 | RNO | AAA | 24 | 469 | 72 | 18 | 3 | 25 | 86 | 83 | 95 | 14 | 4 | .261/.409/.528 | .306 | .287 | -0.7 | -3.8 | 2.2 |
| 2010 | ARI | MLB | 24 | 56 | 5 | 3 | 0 | 1 | 6 | 10 | 20 | 0 | 0 | .267/.393/.400 | .284 | .440 | 0 | 0.7 | 0.3 |
| 2011 | RNO | AAA | 25 | 377 | 75 | 21 | 4 | 18 | 66 | 64 | 90 | 7 | 4 | .306/.427/.579 | .308 | .373 | 2.6 | 1.8 | 2.5 |
| 2011 | ARI | MLB | 25 | 37 | 5 | 0 | 0 | 3 | 7 | 7 | 13 | 1 | 0 | .172/.351/.483 | .299 | .154 | 0.5 | 0.9 | 0.3 |
| 2011 | OAK | MLB | 25 | 158 | 18 | 9 | 2 | 3 | 11 | 11 | 55 | 2 | 0 | .205/.259/.356 | .234 | .303 | 0.7 | 2.2 | -0.1 |
| 2012 | OAK | MLB | 26 | 250 | 30 | 11 | 2 | 9 | 29 | 28 | 69 | 4 | 1 | .237/.324/.417 | .268 | .303 | 0 | 1B -8, LF -1 | 1.1 |

After being acquired from the Diamondbacks in exchange for Brad Ziegler at the trade deadline in 2011, Allen did his best impression of a very bad hitter. Allen is always going to strike out a ton, as his swing isn't exactly short nor his trigger quick. But his bat does have some thunder and when he barrels a ball it can go a long way. As a first baseman with a lot of raw power and an inability to recognize or make contact with a breaking ball, his future looks to be more Quad-A than consistent starter at the major league level. The bat just doesn't provide enough value for the position, and as a 26-year-old, he can't play the youth card for much longer.

**Daric Barton** 1B
Born: 8/16/1985 Age: 26
Bats: L Throws: R Height: 6' 1" Weight: 225
Breakout: 1% Improve: 39% Collapse: 3%
Attrition: 14% MLB: 82%
**Comparables:**
Gene Larkin, Dan Johnson, Ron Fairly

| YEAR | TEAM | LVL | AGE | PA | R | 2B | 3B | HR | RBI | BB | SO | SB | CS | AVG_OBP_SLG | TAv | BABIP | BRR | FRAA | WARP |
|---|---|---|---|---|---|---|---|---|---|---|---|---|---|---|---|---|---|---|---|
| 2009 | SAC | AAA | 23 | 313 | 48 | 21 | 1 | 9 | 48 | 45 | 43 | 1 | 0 | .261/.388/.458 | .299 | .281 | 0.2 | 2.6 | 1.9 |
| 2009 | OAK | MLB | 23 | 192 | 31 | 12 | 1 | 3 | 24 | 26 | 25 | 0 | 2 | .269/.372/.412 | .289 | .296 | -1.7 | 2.1 | 0.8 |
| 2010 | OAK | MLB | 24 | 686 | 79 | 33 | 5 | 10 | 57 | 110 | 102 | 7 | 3 | .273/.393/.405 | .299 | .316 | 2.1 | 3.7 | 4.1 |
| 2011 | SAC | AAA | 25 | 75 | 10 | 2 | 0 | 0 | 4 | 14 | 16 | 0 | 0 | .197/.347/.230 | .220 | .267 | 0.3 | 1.3 | 0.0 |
| 2011 | OAK | MLB | 25 | 280 | 27 | 13 | 0 | 0 | 21 | 39 | 47 | 2 | 1 | .212/.325/.267 | .237 | .260 | 1.6 | 2.2 | 0.0 |
| 2012 | OAK | MLB | 26 | 355 | 40 | 16 | 2 | 5 | 29 | 50 | 57 | 2 | 1 | .240/.351/.351 | .262 | .278 | -0.2 | 1B -1 | 0.7 |

Barton struggled all season with a shoulder injury, an injury that sapped his bat and required surgery in September. Because of the injury, Barton managed to play in only 67 games, showing the same approach that resulted in a league leading 110 walks in 2010, but slugged a beyond anemic .267, a number even the staff of *Baseball Prospectus* might be able to best if given the same number of at-bats. When healthy, Barton has the glove to be a good defensive first-baseman and the bat to provide value at the offense-heavy position, despite not being a big prototypical power threat. It remains to be seen how he will return from the labrum injury, but the queue of quality candidates doesn't exist in Oakland, so any value the 26-year-old can provide to the team will be appreciated.

### Chris Carter — 1B

Born: 12/18/1986 Age: 25
Bats: R Throws: R Height: 6' 6'' Weight: 230
Breakout: 1% Improve: 19% Collapse: 1%
Attrition: 45% MLB: 87%

Comparables:
Boog Powell, Chris Shelton, Eric Wedge

| YEAR | TEAM | LVL | AGE | PA | R | 2B | 3B | HR | RBI | BB | SO | SB | CS | AVG_OBP_SLG | TAv | BABIP | BRR | FRAA | WARP |
|------|------|-----|-----|----|----|----|----|----|-----|----|-----|----|----|-------------|------|-------|------|----------|------|
| 2009 | MID | AA | 22 | 593 | 108 | 41 | 2 | 24 | 101 | 82 | 119 | 13 | 5 | .337/.443/.576 | .335 | .406 | -1.9 | -1 | 4.0 |
| 2009 | SAC | AAA | 22 | 58 | 7 | 2 | 0 | 4 | 14 | 3 | 14 | 0 | 1 | .259/.298/.519 | .334 | .278 | -1.8 | -0.6 | 0.5 |
| 2010 | SAC | AAA | 23 | 551 | 92 | 29 | 2 | 31 | 94 | 73 | 138 | 1 | 1 | .258/.368/.529 | .301 | .301 | 0.2 | -6.5 | 2.3 |
| 2010 | OAK | MLB | 23 | 78 | 8 | 1 | 0 | 3 | 7 | 7 | 21 | 1 | 0 | .186/.256/.329 | .223 | .213 | -0.8 | -1.2 | -0.3 |
| 2011 | SAC | AAA | 24 | 344 | 55 | 18 | 2 | 18 | 72 | 42 | 85 | 5 | 1 | .274/.366/.530 | .300 | .321 | -1 | -5.8 | 1.1 |
| 2011 | OAK | MLB | 24 | 46 | 2 | 0 | 0 | 0 | 0 | 2 | 20 | 0 | 0 | .136/.174/.136 | .116 | .250 | -0.1 | -0.3 | -0.7 |
| 2012 | OAK | MLB | 25 | 250 | 30 | 10 | 1 | 10 | 30 | 27 | 68 | 3 | 1 | .241/.327/.430 | .274 | .298 | 0 | 1B -14, LF -1 | 1.4 |

For several years now, the talk has been that Carter will eventually become the middle-of-the-order power hitter that the A's so desperately need. The slugger has all the characteristics of a prototypical cleanup hitter: enormous power, on-base ability, and an intimidating presence in the box. So far in his career, Carter looks the part in the minors, but when called upon for major league action, the weaknesses in his game are easily exploited by experienced pitchers. The sample size at the highest level is small, so it's too early to label Carter as a Quad-A hitter, mashing in the minors then getting mashed in the majors. But his ability to make contact against superior pitching seems suspect, and the 25-year-old needs to take a step forward in 2012 or his status as a future Japanese import will be cemented.

### Michael Choice — CF

Born: 11/10/1989 Age: 22
Bats: R Throws: R Height: 6' 1'' Weight: 215
Breakout: 3% Improve: 32% Collapse: 1%
Attrition: 35% MLB: 86%

Comparables:
Billy Conigliaro, Mike Jorgensen, Chad Hermansen

| YEAR | TEAM | LVL | AGE | PA | R | 2B | 3B | HR | RBI | BB | SO | SB | CS | AVG_OBP_SLG | TAv | BABIP | BRR | FRAA | WARP |
|------|------|-----|-----|----|----|----|----|----|-----|----|-----|----|----|-------------|------|-------|------|----------|------|
| 2010 | VAN | A- | 20 | 121 | 20 | 10 | 2 | 7 | 26 | 15 | 43 | 6 | 1 | .284/.392/.627 | .356 | .423 | -1.7 | 0.2 | 1.4 |
| 2011 | STO | A+ | 21 | 542 | 79 | 28 | 1 | 30 | 82 | 61 | 134 | 9 | 5 | .285/.376/.542 | .317 | .336 | -0.3 | -3.3 | 4.7 |
| 2012 | OAK | MLB | 22 | 250 | 28 | 9 | 1 | 10 | 30 | 20 | 69 | 2 | 1 | .228/.294/.407 | .254 | .278 | -0.1 | CF -8, RF 0 | 1.0 |

Selected with the 10th overall pick in the 2010 draft, power-hitting outfielder Choice destroyed the California League in his first-full year of minor league action, showing the patience and the pop that made him such a highly coveted amateur. The 22-year-old Texas native has a big swing and will probably always feature high strikeout totals in his game. But he also draws a lot of walks, and when he does connect, his power grade rests near the top of the scouting scale, with some scouts going as far to throw 80-grades on his power potential. Choice will move to Double-A in 2012, a big test for any hitter, especially one with some exploitable aspects to his game.

### Collin Cowgill — CF

Born: 5/22/1986 Age: 26
Bats: R Throws: L Height: 5' 10'' Weight: 185
Breakout: 1% Improve: 58% Collapse: 5%
Attrition: 18% MLB: 86%

Comparables:
Amos Otis, Jayce Tingler, Nate McLouth

| YEAR | TEAM | LVL | AGE | PA | R | 2B | 3B | HR | RBI | BB | SO | SB | CS | AVG_OBP_SLG | TAv | BABIP | BRR | FRAA | WARP |
|------|------|-----|-----|----|----|----|----|----|-----|----|-----|----|----|-------------|------|-------|------|----------|------|
| 2009 | VIS | A+ | 23 | 260 | 39 | 9 | 5 | 6 | 36 | 29 | 49 | 11 | 4 | .277/.379/.445 | .298 | .333 | 0.8 | 1.6 | 1.8 |
| 2010 | MOB | AA | 24 | 577 | 89 | 34 | 4 | 16 | 83 | 57 | 73 | 25 | 9 | .285/.367/.464 | .288 | .308 | -3.1 | -1.9 | 2.8 |
| 2011 | RNO | AAA | 25 | 456 | 95 | 24 | 8 | 13 | 70 | 51 | 63 | 30 | 3 | .354/.430/.554 | .310 | .397 | 3.4 | 0.1 | 4.1 |
| 2011 | ARI | MLB | 25 | 100 | 8 | 3 | 0 | 1 | 9 | 8 | 28 | 4 | 2 | .239/.300/.304 | .232 | .333 | -1.3 | 1.9 | 0.0 |
| 2012 | OAK | MLB | 26 | 250 | 28 | 10 | 2 | 5 | 25 | 22 | 47 | 10 | 3 | .252/.321/.378 | .258 | .295 | 0.2 | CF -2, RF -1 | 1.1 |

After meriting only a lineout mention in *BP2011*, Cowgill upgraded himself to full-comment status—and more importantly, made the major leagues—with a torrid Triple-A season, though his numbers came with a serious caveat: Reno was an offensive paradise, and Cowgill's line lost well over 200 OPS points on the road. It's telling that the *second*-best OBP in the league belonged to teammate Ryan Langerhans, since the former fourth outfielder's career could offer a vision of Cowgill's future. He can play all three outfield positions passably and can pinch-run.

### Kila Ka'aihue — 1B

Born: 3/29/1984 Age: 28
Bats: L Throws: R Height: 6' 4'' Weight: 233
Breakout: 0% Improve: 35% Collapse: 2%
Attrition: 7% MLB: 70%

Comparables:
Mike Jorgensen, Alvin Davis, Nick Johnson

| YEAR | TEAM | LVL | AGE | PA | R | 2B | 3B | HR | RBI | BB | SO | SB | CS | AVG_OBP_SLG | TAv | BABIP | BRR | FRAA | WARP |
|------|------|-----|-----|----|----|----|----|----|-----|----|-----|----|----|-------------|------|-------|------|--------|------|
| 2009 | OMA | AAA | 25 | 555 | 83 | 27 | 1 | 17 | 57 | 102 | 85 | 0 | 1 | .252/.396/.433 | .299 | .276 | -2.2 | -5.8 | 2.3 |
| 2010 | OMA | AAA | 26 | 416 | 67 | 16 | 1 | 24 | 78 | 88 | 69 | 2 | 0 | .319/.465/.598 | .369 | .342 | 0.4 | 1 | 5.4 |
| 2010 | KCA | MLB | 26 | 206 | 22 | 6 | 1 | 8 | 25 | 24 | 39 | 0 | 1 | .217/.307/.394 | .243 | .231 | 0.3 | 0 | -0.3 |
| 2011 | OMA | AAA | 27 | 388 | 43 | 19 | 0 | 11 | 65 | 57 | 81 | 1 | 1 | .272/.379/.433 | .284 | .325 | -0.5 | -3.7 | 1.1 |
| 2011 | KCA | MLB | 27 | 96 | 6 | 4 | 0 | 2 | 6 | 12 | 26 | 0 | 0 | .195/.295/.317 | .235 | .255 | 0.7 | -0.8 | -0.1 |
| 2012 | OAK | MLB | 28 | 250 | 30 | 9 | 1 | 8 | 26 | 37 | 51 | 0 | 0 | .233/.349/.400 | .275 | .265 | 0 | 1B -11 | 1.3 |

Acquired from the Royals for the great Ethan Hollingsworth, Ka'aihue is not the answer to the A's offensive prayers. Known more for his name and his ability to hit Triple-A pitching than his major league success, the soon-to-be 28 year-old is a classic

Quad-A player who just might be able to show a little something at the highest level before he is exposed by more advanced pitching.

**Derek Norris** C
Born: 2/14/1989 Age: 23
Bats: R Throws: R Height: 6' 1" Weight: 210
Breakout: 2% Improve: 28% Collapse: 4%
Attrition: 22% MLB: 72%
Comparables:
Frank Thomas, Matt Wieters, Ben Petrick

| YEAR | TEAM | LVL | AGE | PA | R | 2B | 3B | HR | RBI | BB | SO | SB | CS | AVG_OBP_SLG | TAv | BABIP | BRR | FRAA | WARP |
|---|---|---|---|---|---|---|---|---|---|---|---|---|---|---|---|---|---|---|---|
| 2009 | HAG | A | 20 | 540 | 78 | 30 | 0 | 23 | 84 | 90 | 116 | 6 | 3 | .286/.417/.513 | .333 | .342 | 0.6 | -1.4 | 6.4 |
| 2010 | POT | A+ | 21 | 399 | 67 | 19 | 0 | 12 | 49 | 89 | 94 | 6 | 3 | .235/.423/.419 | .308 | .302 | -0.9 | 1.6 | 4.3 |
| 2011 | HAR | AA | 22 | 423 | 75 | 17 | 1 | 20 | 46 | 77 | 117 | 13 | 4 | .210/.367/.446 | .284 | .251 | 1.9 | 0.9 | 4.0 |
| 2012 | OAK | MLB | 23 | 250 | 29 | 9 | 0 | 9 | 24 | 41 | 70 | 2 | 1 | .208/.344/.383 | .268 | .264 | -0.1 | C -0 | 2.3 |

Acquired from the Nationals in the Gio Gonzalez trade, Norris represents the future behind the plate for the A's. Despite a peculiar statistical line in Double-A, Norris projects to be at least a second-division catcher at the major league level. His contact rates aren't pretty, as the 22-year-old has a lot of swing and miss in his game (117 K in 104 games last season). But he also draws a ton of walks and has legit plus power, showing the ability to

Bats: B Throws: R Height: 6' 0" Weight: 185
Breakout: 3% Improve: 30% Collapse: 7%
Attrition: 23% MLB: 76%
Comparables:
Casey Benjamin, Alan Trammell, Paul Janish

| YEAR | TEAM | LVL | AGE | PA | R | 2B | 3B | HR | RBI | BB | SO | SB | CS | AVG_OBP_SLG | TAv | BABIP | BRR | FRAA | WARP |
|---|---|---|---|---|---|---|---|---|---|---|---|---|---|---|---|---|---|---|---|
| 2009 | OAK | MLB | 25 | 229 | 27 | 11 | 3 | 4 | 21 | 19 | 46 | 7 | 5 | .279/.342/.418 | .266 | .342 | 0.6 | 0.3 | 1.1 |
| 2010 | OAK | MLB | 26 | 576 | 64 | 26 | 8 | 6 | 46 | 50 | 96 | 29 | 5 | .250/.319/.368 | .266 | .296 | 4.2 | 13.2 | 5.1 |
| 2011 | OAK | MLB | 27 | 570 | 57 | 26 | 2 | 8 | 58 | 42 | 104 | 14 | 9 | .264/.319/.369 | .258 | .314 | -1.3 | -11.9 | 1.0 |
| 2012 | OAK | MLB | 28 | 537 | 57 | 22 | 4 | 3 | 42 | 54 | 94 | 22 | 7 | .247/.325/.331 | .244 | .296 | 0 | SS 0, 2B -0 | 1.4 |

A first-round selection in the 2005 draft, Pennington has emerged as the starting shortstop the last two and a half seasons, but his production in 2011 was barely above replacement level. Normally seen as a glove-first type who has flashed some offensive prowess in the past, Pennington saw his defensive value sink after a very solid 2010 campaign, though his offensive production in 2011 was eerily similar to his previous season. Points for offensive consistency, but Pennington loses points for not providing much offensive production. His slash line would be acceptable if the glove were elite, but sadly, the glove is closer to good than great, and with more flash than fire, the bat isn't strong enough to carry the weight.

**Jason Pridie** CF
Born: 10/9/1983 Age: 28
Bats: L Throws: R Height: 6' 2" Weight: 200
Breakout: 5% Improve: 36% Collapse: 6%
Attrition: 20% MLB: 69%
Comparables:
Henri Stanley, James Shanks, Tommy Murphy

| YEAR | TEAM | LVL | AGE | PA | R | 2B | 3B | HR | RBI | BB | SO | SB | CS | AVG_OBP_SLG | TAv | BABIP | BRR | FRAA | WARP |
|---|---|---|---|---|---|---|---|---|---|---|---|---|---|---|---|---|---|---|---|
| 2009 | ROC | AAA | 25 | 546 | 69 | 23 | 5 | 9 | 53 | 19 | 85 | 25 | 7 | .265/.296/.382 | .239 | .301 | 5.5 | 13 | 1.9 |
| 2010 | BUF | AAA | 26 | 177 | 17 | 6 | 1 | 3 | 19 | 12 | 36 | 9 | 3 | .280/.328/.384 | .242 | .341 | 0.3 | 2.9 | 0.5 |
| 2011 | BUF | AAA | 27 | 62 | 8 | 1 | 0 | 3 | 6 | 3 | 12 | 1 | 0 | .186/.226/.356 | .212 | .182 | 0.6 | 0.6 | -0.1 |
| 2011 | NYN | MLB | 27 | 236 | 28 | 11 | 3 | 4 | 20 | 24 | 64 | 7 | 1 | .231/.309/.370 | .249 | .312 | 2.9 | -0.3 | 0.5 |
| 2012 | OAK | MLB | 28 | 250 | 26 | 9 | 3 | 4 | 25 | 15 | 58 | 9 | 3 | .240/.288/.357 | .236 | .298 | 0 | CF 3, LF 0 | 0.2 |

A second-round pick nearly 10 years ago, Pridie was once seen as a decent outfield prospect with the Rays, but he entered the 2011 season as a Met with a grand total of six major league plate appearances. The injury bug in the New York outfield led to a full-time job for him early in the season, until the Mets realized why he'd been stuck in Triple-A so long. A left-handed hitter who runs well and can play all three outfield positions, Pridie just never developed as a hitter at the upper levels, and if anything, he has regressed of late. He's becoming a bounce around guy, and his next stop is Oakland, which signed him to a minor league deal.

## Josh Reddick — RF

Born: 2/19/1987 Age: 25
Bats: L Throws: R Height: 6' 3" Weight: 180
Breakout: 6% Improve: 33% Collapse: 7%
Attrition: 34% MLB: 75%

Comparables:
Tim Corcoran, Robin Jennings, Billy Baldwin

| YEAR | TEAM | LVL | AGE | PA | R | 2B | 3B | HR | RBI | BB | SO | SB | CS | AVG_OBP_SLG | TAv | BABIP | BRR | FRAA | WARP |
|---|---|---|---|---|---|---|---|---|---|---|---|---|---|---|---|---|---|---|---|
| 2009 | PME | AA | 22 | 287 | 47 | 17 | 3 | 13 | 29 | 30 | 62 | 5 | 5 | .277/.353/.520 | .306 | .320 | 2.6 | -3.5 | 2.2 |
| 2009 | PAW | AAA | 22 | 79 | 1 | 0 | 2 | 0 | 6 | 6 | 13 | 0 | 1 | .127/.195/.183 | .155 | .155 | -0.9 | 1.8 | -0.5 |
| 2009 | BOS | MLB | 22 | 62 | 5 | 4 | 0 | 2 | 4 | 2 | 17 | 0 | 0 | .169/.210/.339 | .200 | .200 | -0.5 | 0.6 | -0.2 |
| 2010 | PAW | AAA | 23 | 481 | 59 | 28 | 4 | 18 | 65 | 25 | 73 | 4 | 7 | .266/.305/.466 | .269 | .283 | 0.3 | -1.6 | 2.0 |
| 2010 | BOS | MLB | 23 | 63 | 5 | 3 | 1 | 1 | 5 | 1 | 15 | 1 | 0 | .194/.206/.323 | .204 | .239 | 0.4 | 0.5 | -0.2 |
| 2011 | PAW | AAA | 24 | 231 | 37 | 9 | 1 | 14 | 36 | 33 | 39 | 4 | 1 | .230/.333/.508 | .289 | .207 | -0.5 | -1.8 | 1.2 |
| 2011 | BOS | MLB | 24 | 278 | 41 | 18 | 3 | 7 | 28 | 19 | 50 | 1 | 2 | .280/.327/.457 | .286 | .318 | 0.6 | 6.2 | 2.1 |
| 2012 | OAK | MLB | 25 | 310 | 35 | 15 | 2 | 9 | 37 | 23 | 61 | 3 | 2 | .243/.299/.409 | .258 | .276 | -0.6 | RF 2, CF -3 | 1.0 |

In his previous 125 plate appearances in the majors, all Reddick had done was prove why his free-swinging ways were going to be a problem. Something clicked for the 24-year-old in 2011, though: Reddick finally understands the *why* of plate discipline. In the big leagues, Reddick saw 3.8 pitches per plate appearance and walked 6.8 percent of the time while cutting down his strikeout rate. The difference isn't so much in pitches seen, but Reddick's new trick of waiting for a pitch he can do something with, and fighting the others off. A .290 TAv and above-average defense in a difficult right field corner was enough to interest the A's, who took Reddick in a deal with two other players for closer Andrew Bailey.

## Adam Rosales — 2B

Born: 5/20/1983 Age: 29
Bats: R Throws: R Height: 6' 2" Weight: 195
Breakout: 4% Improve: 29% Collapse: 15%
Attrition: 32% MLB: 81%

Comparables:
Bobby Crosby, Eric Bruntlett, Brendan Harris

| YEAR | TEAM | LVL | AGE | PA | R | 2B | 3B | HR | RBI | BB | SO | SB | CS | AVG_OBP_SLG | TAv | BABIP | BRR | FRAA | WARP |
|---|---|---|---|---|---|---|---|---|---|---|---|---|---|---|---|---|---|---|---|
| 2009 | LOU | AAA | 26 | 125 | 27 | 8 | 2 | 5 | 20 | 12 | 15 | 4 | 0 | .349/.418/.596 | .337 | .371 | 0.8 | 1 | 1.5 |
| 2009 | CIN | MLB | 26 | 266 | 23 | 10 | 1 | 4 | 19 | 26 | 46 | 1 | 2 | .213/.303/.317 | .225 | .246 | 0 | 0.7 | -0.2 |
| 2010 | OAK | MLB | 27 | 279 | 31 | 8 | 2 | 7 | 31 | 19 | 65 | 2 | 2 | .271/.321/.400 | .280 | .335 | 0 | -1.4 | 1.3 |
| 2011 | SAC | AAA | 28 | 164 | 23 | 5 | 1 | 3 | 22 | 13 | 32 | 1 | 1 | .265/.323/.374 | .285 | .313 | 0.6 | -0.8 | 1.1 |
| 2011 | OAK | MLB | 28 | 68 | 5 | 0 | 0 | 2 | 8 | 4 | 13 | 0 | 0 | .098/.162/.197 | .149 | .083 | 0.2 | -0.9 | -0.7 |
| 2012 | OAK | MLB | 29 | 250 | 26 | 9 | 2 | 5 | 23 | 19 | 50 | 2 | 1 | .238/.303/.354 | .245 | .282 | -0.1 | 2B -0, SS -0 | 0.9 |

Rosales is a classic utility player, capable of playing every position on the field. Unfortunately, Rosales doesn't play any one position at a high-level, but the 28-year-old does provide a valuable service to a 25-man roster. An ankle injury and subsequent surgery in 2010 limited his effectiveness in 2011, both in the field and at the plate. But when healthy, this versatile player has some contact ability and pop in his bat, and enough defensive chops to handle the left-side of the infield.

## Scott Sizemore — 3B

Born: 1/4/1985 Age: 27
Bats: R Throws: R Height: 6' 1" Weight: 185
Breakout: 4% Improve: 37% Collapse: 7%
Attrition: 9% MLB: 86%

Comparables:
Dave Hollins, Leo Gomez, Willie Greene

| YEAR | TEAM | LVL | AGE | PA | R | 2B | 3B | HR | RBI | BB | SO | SB | CS | AVG_OBP_SLG | TAv | BABIP | BRR | FRAA | WARP |
|---|---|---|---|---|---|---|---|---|---|---|---|---|---|---|---|---|---|---|---|
| 2009 | ERI | AA | 24 | 269 | 39 | 17 | 4 | 9 | 33 | 35 | 46 | 7 | 3 | .307/.399/.535 | .328 | .347 | -1.4 | -2.2 | 2.5 |
| 2009 | TOL | AAA | 24 | 330 | 49 | 22 | 1 | 8 | 33 | 29 | 49 | 14 | 1 | .308/.373/.473 | .282 | .342 | -1 | -2.6 | 1.1 |
| 2010 | TOL | AAA | 25 | 342 | 49 | 23 | 1 | 9 | 37 | 31 | 77 | 2 | 2 | .298/.379/.472 | .285 | .374 | -0.3 | -0.6 | 1.8 |
| 2010 | DET | MLB | 25 | 163 | 19 | 7 | 0 | 3 | 14 | 15 | 40 | 0 | 0 | .224/.296/.336 | .226 | .287 | 1.5 | -1.5 | -0.3 |
| 2011 | TOL | AAA | 26 | 92 | 17 | 7 | 1 | 2 | 15 | 12 | 19 | 3 | 1 | .408/.495/.605 | .363 | .518 | 0.4 | -2.4 | 1.0 |
| 2011 | DET | MLB | 26 | 74 | 8 | 1 | 0 | 0 | 4 | 10 | 19 | 1 | 1 | .222/.329/.238 | .241 | .318 | 0.3 | 1.4 | 0.2 |
| 2011 | OAK | MLB | 26 | 355 | 42 | 21 | 1 | 11 | 52 | 43 | 93 | 4 | 2 | .249/.345/.433 | .292 | .322 | 3.2 | -7.6 | 1.6 |
| 2012 | OAK | MLB | 27 | 409 | 49 | 20 | 2 | 9 | 42 | 46 | 95 | 8 | 3 | .253/.343/.395 | .270 | .315 | -0.2 | 3B -5, 2B -1 | 2.1 |

Acquired from the Tigers for David Purcey, Sizemore quickly became the A's starting third baseman, playing in 93 games and adding some much needed punch to the lifeless offense. Not a high-contact hitter, Sizemore's swing features a lot of miss, leading to 93 strikeouts to go along with those 93 games played. But his bat also features some legit pop, sending 11 bombs out of the yard and spraying 21 doubles. Not known for being a glove-man, Sizemore will cash his checks on the back of his offensive production, highlighted by decent power and patience. The 27-year-old is going to get an opportunity to play every day, either turning his offensive tools into a second-division career or proving that his offensive flash was merely a spark.

## Kurt Suzuki — C

Born: 10/4/1983 Age: 28
Bats: R Throws: R Height: 6' 1" Weight: 205
Breakout: 3% Improve: 38% Collapse: 6%
Attrition: 50% MLB: 92%

Comparables:
Smoky Burgess, Paul Lo Duca, Brayan Pena

| YEAR | TEAM | LVL | AGE | PA | R | 2B | 3B | HR | RBI | BB | SO | SB | CS | AVG_OBP_SLG | TAv | BABIP | BRR | FRAA | WARP |
|---|---|---|---|---|---|---|---|---|---|---|---|---|---|---|---|---|---|---|---|
| 2009 | OAK | MLB | 25 | 614 | 74 | 37 | 1 | 15 | 88 | 28 | 59 | 8 | 2 | .274/.313/.421 | .267 | .280 | 0.9 | 1.7 | 3.1 |
| 2010 | OAK | MLB | 26 | 544 | 55 | 18 | 2 | 13 | 71 | 33 | 49 | 3 | 2 | .242/.303/.366 | .243 | .245 | -3.5 | -3 | 0.5 |
| 2011 | OAK | MLB | 27 | 515 | 54 | 26 | 0 | 14 | 44 | 38 | 64 | 2 | 2 | .237/.301/.385 | .259 | .244 | -1.6 | -1.8 | 1.7 |
| 2012 | OAK | MLB | 28 | 491 | 53 | 21 | 1 | 8 | 45 | 36 | 59 | 3 | 2 | .249/.313/.357 | .251 | .269 | -0.3 | C -2 | 1.8 |

The catcher had another disappointing season, especially at the plate, where he failed to crack a 700 OPS for the second straight season. The former second-round selection isn't without some quality as a hitter, as the bat has some pop in it and he did deliver 40 extra-base hits from a premium defensive position. The problem is that although he doesn't strike out often, Suzuki doesn't make good contact, resulting in a low average. He doesn't reach base at a high-clip and gives pitchers a recipe for his own demise. Suzuki is good behind the plate, with some catch-and-throw skills and a reputation as a good game-caller, but despite being considered a solid catcher by many, he isn't considered a special catcher by any. The pressure of success still hinges on his ability to swing the stick. If the bat doesn't rebound and rebound soon, Suzuki's days as a starter are going to be over.

**Jemile Weeks**   **2B**
Born: 1/26/1987 Age: 25
Bats: B Throws: R Height: 5' 10" Weight: 160
Breakout: 0% Improve: 25% Collapse: 15%

| YEAR | TEAM | LVL | AGE | PA | R | 2B | 3B | HR | RBI | BB | SO | SB | CS | AVG_OBP_SLG | TAv | BABIP | BRR | FRAA | WARP |
|------|------|-----|-----|-----|-----|-----|-----|-----|-----|-----|-----|-----|-----|-------------|------|-------|------|------|------|
| 2009 | STO | A+ | 22 | 232 | 29 | 9 | 2 | 7 | 31 | 26 | 40 | 5 | 1 | .299/.385/.468 | .322 | .342 | -0.4 | -1.5 | 2.0 |
| 2009 | MID | AA | 22 | 123 | 10 | 5 | 0 | 2 | 13 | 10 | 16 | 4 | 0 | .238/.300/.343 | .258 | .253 | 1.3 | 1.7 | 0.6 |
| 2010 | MID | AA | 23 | 312 | 43 | 14 | 7 | 3 | 33 | 28 | 37 | 11 | 6 | .267/.340/.403 | .258 | .298 | 0.4 | 1.5 | 1.0 |

for average with pop to all fields. As he finds more comfort at the level and makes the necessary adjustments against quality pitching, Weeks will show a well-balanced offensive attack, with contact, power, and speed playing a big role in this overall game.

# PITCHERS

**Brett Anderson**
Born: 2/1/1988 Age: 24
Bats: L Throws: L Height: 6' 5" Weight: 215
Breakout: 22% Improve: 55% Collapse: 20%
Attrition: 7% MLB: 98%

**Comparables:**
Britt Burns, Fernando Valenzuela, Curt Simmons

| YEAR | TEAM | LVL | AGE | W | L | SV | G | GS | IP | H | HR | BB | SO | EqBB9 | EqSO9 | GB% | BABIP | WHIP | ERA | FIP | FRA | WARP |
|------|------|-----|-----|-----|-----|-----|-----|-----|------|-----|-----|-----|-----|-------|-------|-----|-------|------|------|------|------|------|
| 2009 | OAK | MLB | 21 | 11 | 11 | 0 | 30 | 30 | 175¹ | 180 | 20 | 45 | 150 | 2.3 | 7.7 | 52% | .312 | 1.28 | 4.06 | 3.74 | 4.80 | 1.9 |
| 2010 | OAK | MLB | 22 | 7 | 6 | 0 | 19 | 19 | 112¹ | 112 | 6 | 22 | 75 | 1.8 | 6.0 | 55% | .297 | 1.19 | 2.80 | 3.18 | 3.47 | 1.8 |
| 2011 | OAK | MLB | 23 | 3 | 6 | 0 | 13 | 13 | 83¹ | 86 | 8 | 25 | 61 | 2.7 | 6.6 | 59% | .311 | 1.33 | 4.00 | 4.00 | 5.10 | 0.2 |
| 2012 | OAK | MLB | 24 | 4 | 5 | 0 | 14 | 14 | 79² | 79 | 7 | 22 | 61 | 2.5 | 6.9 | 54% | .305 | 1.27 | 3.53 | 3.64 | 3.83 | 1.1 |

When healthy, Anderson's name deserves a spot on the list of talented young lefties in the game. His slider-heavy arsenal features a lively low-90s fastball he can spot in the zone to induce weak contact. But after a promising rookie campaign in 2009, injuries limited his overall effectiveness during his sophomore season, and thanks to a chance encounter between his elbow and Dr. James Andrews, the up-and-coming southpaw will be on the shelf for the foreseeable future. It's a big blow for the Athletics and for Anderson, as that talented arm isn't guaranteed to return to the field with the same sharp stuff that gave him the label in the first place.

**Grant Balfour**
Born: 12/30/1977 Age: 34
Bats: R Throws: R Height: 6' 3" Weight: 170
Breakout: 12% Improve: 31% Collapse: 41%
Attrition: 5% MLB: 97%

**Comparables:**
Joe Nelson, Brendan Donnelly, Pedro Martinez

| YEAR | TEAM | LVL | AGE | W | L | SV | G | GS | IP | H | HR | BB | SO | EqBB9 | EqSO9 | GB% | BABIP | WHIP | ERA | FIP | FRA | WARP |
|------|------|-----|-----|-----|-----|-----|-----|-----|------|-----|-----|-----|-----|-------|-------|-----|-------|------|------|------|------|------|
| 2009 | TBA | MLB | 31 | 5 | 4 | 4 | 73 | 0 | 67¹ | 59 | 6 | 33 | 69 | 4.4 | 9.2 | 37% | .298 | 1.37 | 4.81 | 3.81 | 4.63 | 0.9 |
| 2010 | TBA | MLB | 32 | 2 | 1 | 0 | 57 | 0 | 55¹ | 43 | 3 | 17 | 56 | 2.8 | 9.1 | 30% | .278 | 1.08 | 2.28 | 2.65 | 3.30 | 1.1 |
| 2011 | OAK | MLB | 33 | 5 | 2 | 2 | 62 | 0 | 62 | 44 | 8 | 20 | 59 | 2.9 | 8.6 | 39% | .234 | 1.03 | 2.47 | 3.80 | 4.12 | 0.5 |
| 2012 | OAK | MLB | 34 | 3 | 1 | 1 | 52 | 0 | 50² | 40 | 4 | 22 | 56 | 3.9 | 10.0 | 38% | .287 | 1.21 | 2.89 | 3.32 | 3.14 | 1.0 |

Signed as a free agent before the 2011 season, Balfour brought much needed stability to the A's bullpen, logging 62 innings of quality ball, mostly in a setup capacity. The 34-year-old Australian righty relies mostly on a plus fastball and hard slider with tilt to limit damage, and keeps inherited runners from scoring. His left/right splits have tightened up, making him equally effective against hitters from either side of the plate. Signed to a team-friendly deal for 2012 with a team-friendlier option for 2013, Balfour looks to continue to provide above-average relief for below-market price for the next two seasons.

**Jerry Blevins**
Born: 9/6/1983 Age: 28
Bats: L Throws: L Height: 6' 7" Weight: 180
Breakout: 24% Improve: 46% Collapse: 29%
Attrition: 6% MLB: 93%

Comparables:
Dan Plesac, Rob Murphy, Joe Thatcher

| YEAR | TEAM | LVL | AGE | W | L | SV | G | GS | IP | H | HR | BB | SO | EqBB9 | EqSO9 | GB% | BABIP | WHIP | ERA | FIP | FRA | WARP |
|------|------|-----|-----|---|---|----|----|----|-----|----|----|----|----|-------|-------|-----|-------|------|-----|-----|-----|------|
| 2009 | SAC | AAA | 25 | 5 | 3 | 2 | 45 | 0 | 63¹ | 65 | 5 | 18 | 62 | 2.6 | 8.8 | 44% | .345 | 1.31 | 3.84 | 3.56 | 3.80 | 1.0 |
| 2009 | OAK | MLB | 25 | 0 | 0 | 0 | 20 | 0 | 22¹ | 19 | 2 | 6 | 23 | 2.4 | 9.3 | 31% | .288 | 1.12 | 4.84 | 3.05 | 3.86 | 0.4 |
| 2010 | OAK | MLB | 26 | 2 | 1 | 1 | 63 | 0 | 48² | 54 | 7 | 18 | 46 | 3.3 | 8.5 | 39% | .324 | 1.48 | 3.70 | 4.20 | 4.69 | 0.1 |
| 2011 | SAC | AAA | 27 | 2 | 0 | 0 | 27 | 0 | 29² | 25 | 3 | 7 | 35 | 2.1 | 10.6 | 36% | .301 | 1.08 | 4.85 | 3.50 | 4.44 | 0.3 |
| 2011 | OAK | MLB | 27 | 0 | 0 | 0 | 26 | 0 | 28¹ | 24 | 2 | 14 | 26 | 4.4 | 8.3 | 41% | .286 | 1.34 | 2.86 | 3.73 | 4.61 | 0.1 |
| 2012 | OAK | MLB | 28 | 2 | 1 | 0 | 40 | 0 | 36² | 33 | 3 | 12 | 35 | 3.1 | 8.7 | 43% | .301 | 1.25 | 3.28 | 3.34 | 3.57 | 0.5 |

Despite not owning sexy radar gun readings on the fastball, the 6-foot-6 long-levered reliever delivers the ball so close to the plate that a fringy upper-80s heater appears to be much faster. With many pitches to choose from, featuring a slow curve, a cutter, and a fading changeup, Blevins is astute at sequence and situation, changing speeds, attacking hitters, and using all quadrants of the plate to force weak contact and miss bats. The 28-year-old lefty isn't arbitration eligible for another season, so he remains a cost-effective relief option in the middle innings. But he lacks the type of stuff to pitch in a late-inning capacity and will be replaceable when his sticker price increases during his arbitration years.

**Dallas Braden**
Born: 8/13/1983 Age: 28
Bats: L Throws: L Height: 6' 2" Weight: 185
Breakout: 12% Improve: 34% Collapse: 27%
Attrition: 5% MLB: 87%

Comparables:
Joe Saunders, Mark Mulder, Steve Howe

| YEAR | TEAM | LVL | AGE | W | L | SV | G | GS | IP | H | HR | BB | SO | EqBB9 | EqSO9 | GB% | BABIP | WHIP | ERA | FIP | FRA | WARP |
|------|------|-----|-----|----|----|----|----|----|------|-----|----|----|-----|-------|-------|-----|-------|------|-----|-----|-----|------|
| 2009 | OAK | MLB | 25 | 8 | 9 | 0 | 22 | 22 | 136² | 144 | 9 | 42 | 81 | 2.8 | 5.3 | 39% | .299 | 1.36 | 3.89 | 3.78 | 3.82 | 2.2 |
| 2010 | OAK | MLB | 26 | 11 | 14 | 0 | 30 | 30 | 192² | 180 | 17 | 43 | 113 | 2.0 | 5.3 | 42% | .273 | 1.16 | 3.50 | 3.77 | 4.04 | 1.9 |
| 2011 | OAK | MLB | 27 | 1 | 1 | 0 | 3 | 3 | 18 | 18 | 2 | 5 | 15 | 2.5 | 7.5 | 38% | .314 | 1.28 | 3.00 | 3.67 | 4.04 | 0.2 |
| 2012 | OAK | MLB | 28 | 2 | 3 | 0 | 7 | 7 | 42¹ | 42 | 3 | 12 | 28 | 2.6 | 6.1 | 41% | .292 | 1.27 | 3.47 | 3.65 | 3.77 | 0.6 |

After making his first three starts of the 2011 season, Braden was headed back to the 209 after shoulder surgery. When healthy, Braden made his bones on deception and location, getting ahead in counts with a mid-80s fastball (that could touch the upper-80s when he reached back for it!), then forcing awkward rollover swings on his well above-average changeup. His change plays well off the fastball with both velocity separation and late movement to the arm-side. Braden pitches with the confidence of a flamethrower, despite an arsenal with the intensity of a Disney movie. As a pitcher with a small margin of error to begin with, any residual effect from the shoulder surgery could spell curtains for his major league run.

**A.J. Cole**
Born: 1/5/1992 Age: 20
Bats: R Throws: R Height: 6' 5" Weight: 180
Breakout: 54% Improve: 68% Collapse: 6%
Attrition: 2% MLB: 90%

Comparables:
Jose Rijo, Edwin Nunez, Don Drysdale

| YEAR | TEAM | LVL | AGE | W | L | SV | G | GS | IP | H | HR | BB | SO | EqBB9 | EqSO9 | GB% | BABIP | WHIP | ERA | FIP | FRA | WARP |
|------|------|-----|-----|---|---|----|----|----|----|----|----|----|-----|-------|-------|-----|-------|------|-----|-----|-----|------|
| 2011 | HAG | A | 19 | 3 | 7 | 0 | 20 | 18 | 89 | 87 | 6 | 24 | 108 | 2.4 | 10.9 | 39% | .345 | 1.25 | 4.04 | 2.85 | 3.58 | 2.2 |
| 2012 | OAK | MLB | 20 | 1 | 2 | 0 | 5 | 4 | 22 | 23 | 2 | 11 | 18 | 4.4 | 7.3 | 41% | .313 | 1.53 | 4.77 | 4.25 | 5.18 | -0.0 |

The golden prize in the Gio Gonzalez trade, Cole joins Sonny Gray as the top pitching prospect in the A's system. With prototypical size and a projectable arsenal, Cole emerged as a legit blue-chipper in 2011, missing 108 Sally League bats in only 89 innings. Not bad for a 19-year-old pitching a full season for the first time. With a lively plus fastball and a plus potential curve that shows both depth and sharp vertical movement, Cole has the stuff that makes scouts excited about his ceiling. The command needs refinement as does the changeup, but the future is incredibly bright for the young right-hander.

**Ryan Cook**
Born: 6/30/1987 Age: 25
Bats: R Throws: R Height: 6' 4" Weight: 200
Breakout: 20% Improve: 51% Collapse: 30%
Attrition: 14% MLB: 91%

Comparables:
Dock Ellis, Charlie Haeger, Bret Prinz

| YEAR | TEAM | LVL | AGE | W | L | SV | G | GS | IP | H | HR | BB | SO | EqBB9 | EqSO9 | GB% | BABIP | WHIP | ERA | FIP | FRA | WARP |
|------|------|-----|-----|----|----|----|----|----|------|-----|----|----|-----|-------|-------|-----|-------|------|-----|-----|-----|------|
| 2009 | SBN | A | 22 | 11 | 11 | 0 | 25 | 25 | 142² | 143 | 6 | 46 | 109 | 2.8 | 6.5 | 48% | .310 | 1.29 | 3.66 | 3.81 | 4.61 | 0.9 |
| 2010 | VIS | A+ | 23 | 4 | 7 | 0 | 20 | 20 | 108¹ | 94 | 3 | 34 | 92 | 3.0 | 8.3 | 62% | .325 | 1.35 | 4.24 | 3.75 | 4.40 | 1.0 |
| 2011 | MOB | AA | 24 | 0 | 3 | 13 | 34 | 0 | 44 | 28 | 2 | 13 | 48 | 2.9 | 10.2 | 60% | .250 | 0.95 | 2.25 | 2.73 | 3.98 | 0.6 |
| 2011 | ARI | MLB | 24 | 0 | 1 | 0 | 12 | 0 | 7² | 11 | 0 | 8 | 7 | 9.4 | 8.2 | 46% | .423 | 2.48 | 7.04 | 4.30 | 4.18 | 0.0 |
| 2012 | OAK | MLB | 25 | 1 | 2 | 0 | 12 | 3 | 29 | 31 | 3 | 14 | 17 | 4.5 | 5.3 | 50% | .302 | 1.58 | 5.01 | 4.82 | 5.45 | -0.2 |

Cook picked up 19 saves across two minor-league levels last season, but those might be the last save situations he sees for a while. Arizona's 27th-round pick in 2008 exceeded expectations just by making the Show, but his fastball/slider combo probably won't take him all the way to the back of a major-league bullpen. In his brief big-league audition, Cook averaged 94 with his fastball but walked eight batters against seven strikeouts. In light of his record of acceptable, if hardly eye-catching, walk rates, we'll choose to be charitable and chalk that up to a case of rookie jitters. If his sophomore season produces improved control, he'll have his uses somewhere in the bullpen bucket line that leads to the ninth inning.

### Fautino De Los Santos

Born: 2/15/1986 Age: 26
Bats: R Throws: R Height: 6' 3'' Weight: 225
Breakout: 28% Improve: 47% Collapse: 22%
Attrition: 14% MLB: 94%

**Comparables:**
Ugueth Urbina,Brandon Morrow,Steve Bedrosian

| YEAR | TEAM | LVL | AGE | W | L | SV | G | GS | IP | H | HR | BB | SO | EqBB9 | EqSO9 | GB% | BABIP | WHIP | ERA | FIP | FRA | WARP |
|------|------|-----|-----|---|---|----|---|----|----|---|----|----|----|-------|-------|-----|-------|------|-----|-----|-----|------|
| 2011 | OAK | MLB | 25 | 3 | 2 | 0 | 34 | 0 | 33¹ | 27 | 4 | 17 | 43 | 4.6 | 11.6 | 40% | .299 | 1.32 | 4.32 | 3.57 | 5.16 | 0.0 |
| 2012 | OAK | MLB | 26 | 2 | 1 | 1 | 30 | 0 | 34² | 31 | 3 | 17 | 37 | 4.5 | 9.6 | 44% | .304 | 1.38 | 3.75 | 3.67 | 4.08 | 0.3 |

A flame-throwing righty with a plus-plus fastball and a tight slider with two-plane break, De Los Santos has the type of stuff to close games for the Athletics at some point in the near future. The ability to miss bats is there; in his debut season, De Los Santos struck out 43 major league hitters in only 33 innings of work. But his command isn't sharp, and his mechanical profile doesn't allow for plus command projection. If the 26-year-old pitcher can find more consistency with his strike-throwing, the stuff could be more than good enough to play in high-leverage relief situations.

### Joey Devine

Born: 9/19/1983 Age: 28

| YEAR | TEAM | LVL | AGE | W | L | SV | G | GS | IP | H | HR | BB | SO | EqBB9 | EqSO9 | GB% | BABIP | WHIP | ERA | FIP | FRA | WARP |
|------|------|-----|-----|---|---|----|---|----|----|---|----|----|----|-------|-------|-----|-------|------|-----|-----|-----|------|
| 2011 | SAC | AAA | 27 | 4 | 0 | 3 | 23 | 0 | 23¹ | 15 | 2 | 9 | 35 | 3.5 | 13.5 | 35% | .283 | 1.03 | 4.24 | 3.65 | 5.04 | 0.2 |

league bullpen. Asking for more isn't going to be met with promising results, unless, of course, Devine gets to face a plethora of right-handed hitters at home. If that's the case, he could provide well-above-average production.

### Brian Fuentes

Born: 8/9/1975 Age: 36
Bats: L Throws: L Height: 6' 5'' Weight: 220
Breakout: 14% Improve: 29% Collapse: 38%
Attrition: 6% MLB: 89%

**Comparables:**
Jim Brewer,Arthur Rhodes,David Cone

| YEAR | TEAM | LVL | AGE | W | L | SV | G | GS | IP | H | HR | BB | SO | EqBB9 | EqSO9 | GB% | BABIP | WHIP | ERA | FIP | FRA | WARP |
|------|------|-----|-----|---|---|----|---|----|----|---|----|----|----|-------|-------|-----|-------|------|-----|-----|-----|------|
| 2009 | ANA | MLB | 33 | 1 | 5 | 48 | 65 | 0 | 55 | 53 | 6 | 24 | 46 | 3.9 | 7.5 | 37% | .296 | 1.40 | 3.93 | 4.47 | 4.49 | 0.7 |
| 2010 | MIN | MLB | 34 | 0 | 0 | 1 | 9 | 0 | 9² | 3 | 0 | 2 | 8 | 1.9 | 7.4 | 25% | .125 | 0.52 | 0.00 | 2.32 | 1.07 | 0.4 |
| 2010 | ANA | MLB | 34 | 4 | 1 | 23 | 39 | 0 | 38¹ | 28 | 5 | 18 | 39 | 4.2 | 9.2 | 25% | .240 | 1.20 | 3.52 | 4.20 | 4.25 | 0.2 |
| 2011 | OAK | MLB | 35 | 2 | 8 | 12 | 67 | 0 | 58¹ | 52 | 6 | 20 | 42 | 3.1 | 6.5 | 39% | .264 | 1.23 | 3.70 | 4.19 | 4.39 | 0.3 |
| 2012 | OAK | MLB | 36 | 3 | 1 | 12 | 54 | 0 | 49² | 43 | 4 | 19 | 46 | 3.4 | 8.3 | 37% | .286 | 1.25 | 3.28 | 3.55 | 3.57 | 0.7 |

Fuentes used to be considered one of the better closers in the game, selected to four All-Star Games in a five-year window for the Rockies and later for the Angels. But his stuff has slowly declined, and despite solid (not spectacular) production for Oakland in 2011, the second-tier closer candidate didn't live up to his $5M price tag. That money could have been better allocated. With another $5M paycheck coming Fuentes's way in 2012, Oakland hopes he provides production better than just-slightly-better-than-replacement-level.

### Brandon McCarthy

Born: 7/7/1983 Age: 28
Bats: R Throws: R Height: 6' 8'' Weight: 190
Breakout: 23% Improve: 56% Collapse: 19%
Attrition: 10% MLB: 88%

**Comparables:**
Luis Ayala,Dave Schmidt,Chad Bradford

| YEAR | TEAM | LVL | AGE | W | L | SV | G | GS | IP | H | HR | BB | SO | EqBB9 | EqSO9 | GB% | BABIP | WHIP | ERA | FIP | FRA | WARP |
|------|------|-----|-----|---|---|----|---|----|----|---|----|----|----|-------|-------|-----|-------|------|-----|-----|-----|------|
| 2009 | TEX | MLB | 26 | 7 | 4 | 0 | 17 | 17 | 97¹ | 96 | 13 | 36 | 65 | 3.3 | 6.0 | 40% | .274 | 1.36 | 4.62 | 4.75 | 5.71 | 0.1 |
| 2010 | OKL | AAA | 27 | 4 | 3 | 0 | 11 | 9 | 56¹ | 26 | 3 | 9 | 29 | 1.8 | 7.0 | 55% | .205 | 1.10 | 3.36 | 4.25 | 4.38 | 0.9 |
| 2011 | OAK | MLB | 28 | 9 | 9 | 0 | 25 | 25 | 170² | 168 | 11 | 25 | 123 | 1.3 | 6.5 | 48% | .298 | 1.13 | 3.32 | 2.90 | 3.42 | 2.9 |
| 2012 | OAK | MLB | 28 | 6 | 8 | 0 | 19 | 19 | 124 | 122 | 10 | 36 | 84 | 2.6 | 6.1 | 42% | .290 | 1.27 | 3.60 | 3.77 | 3.91 | 1.4 |

After spending the majority of his career battling assorted injuries, McCarthy finally found his stability in Oakland, logging a career high 170 2/3 innings, and solidifying himself as a rotation mainstay. Armed with a so-so upper-80s/low-90s fastball, thrown with good angle on a steep plane, McCarthy used the fastball to set up his money pitch: a hard cutter thrown with similar velocity and excellent darting action. With well-above-average command and good overall feel for pitching, McCarthy kept hitters off-balance by mixing in an upper-70s curve to change the sightline and keep hitters off the harder stuff. If the once brittle starter can stay off the disabled list, the arb-eligible 28-year-old can look forward to the riches of free agency that await him in 2013.

### Jim Miller

Born: 4/28/1982 Age: 30
Bats: R Throws: R Height: 6' 2" Weight: 200
Breakout: 15% Improve: 66% Collapse: 19%
Attrition: 13% MLB: 85%

Comparables:
Hoyt Wilhelm,Todd Worrell,Don Elston

| YEAR | TEAM | LVL | AGE | W | L | SV | G | GS | IP | H | HR | BB | SO | EqBB9 | EqSO9 | GB% | BABIP | WHIP | ERA | FIP | FRA | WARP |
|------|------|-----|-----|---|---|----|---|----|-----|----|----|----|----|-------|-------|-----|-------|------|------|------|------|------|
| 2009 | NOR | AAA | 27 | 4 | 4 | 17 | 54 | 0 | 64² | 64 | 3 | 19 | 59 | 2.6 | 8.2 | 34% | .323 | 1.28 | 2.64 | 2.85 | 2.92 | 1.7 |
| 2010 | NOR | AAA | 28 | 1 | 0 | 0 | 33 | 0 | 57² | 38 | 6 | 12 | 36 | 2.8 | 8.3 | 34% | .291 | 1.35 | 4.84 | 4.26 | 5.80 | -0.1 |
| 2011 | CSP | AAA | 29 | 6 | 4 | 24 | 65 | 0 | 72 | 88 | 7 | 19 | 73 | 2.6 | 9.1 | 42% | .386 | 1.58 | 5.25 | 3.97 | 5.06 | 1.2 |
| 2011 | COL | MLB | 29 | 0 | 0 | 0 | 6 | 0 | 7 | 3 | 0 | 4 | 5 | 5.1 | 6.4 | 25% | .150 | 1.00 | 2.57 | 3.28 | 5.07 | 0.0 |
| 2012 | OAK | MLB | 30 | 1 | 0 | 0 | 21 | 0 | 27¹ | 27 | 3 | 12 | 24 | 3.8 | 7.8 | 38% | .311 | 1.42 | 4.20 | 4.19 | 4.57 | 0.1 |

Every once in a while there is a pitcher who enjoys a fair amount of success at the minor-league level but who doesn't get a shot in the big leagues until relatively late, if at all. Joel Peralta, Brad Ziegler, and Rafael Betancourt are current examples of guys who have succeeded despite being overlooked for too long. Miller might be another. His numbers aren't overwhelming, but he does own a 10.3 K/9 and a 3.1 K/BB in 403 minor-league appearances. This won't necessarily buy him a chance to prove that his performance isn't a fluke, but it should.

### Guillermo Moscoso

Born: 11/14/1983 Age: 28
Bats: R Throws: R Height: 6' 2" Weight: 165
Breakout: 19% Improve: 49% Collapse: 25%
Attrition: 14% MLB: 93%

Comparables:
Mike Witt,Geraldo Guzman,Jeremy Accardo

| YEAR | TEAM | LVL | AGE | W | L | SV | G | GS | IP | H | HR | BB | SO | EqBB9 | EqSO9 | GB% | BABIP | WHIP | ERA | FIP | FRA | WARP |
|------|------|-----|-----|---|---|----|---|----|------|-----|----|----|----|-------|-------|-----|-------|------|-------|-------|-------|------|
| 2009 | FRI | AA | 25 | 3 | 1 | 0 | 9 | 7 | 42¹ | 41 | 1 | 14 | 36 | 3.0 | 7.7 | 31% | .305 | 1.30 | 4.47 | 2.83 | 3.51 | 0.9 |
| 2009 | OKL | AAA | 25 | 5 | 4 | 0 | 12 | 11 | 70 | 56 | 2 | 15 | 60 | 1.9 | 7.7 | 38% | .274 | 1.01 | 2.31 | 2.88 | 3.09 | 1.6 |
| 2009 | TEX | MLB | 25 | 0 | 0 | 0 | 10 | 0 | 14 | 15 | 1 | 6 | 12 | 3.9 | 7.7 | 31% | .318 | 1.50 | 3.21 | 3.86 | 4.70 | 0.2 |
| 2010 | OKL | AAA | 26 | 7 | 8 | 0 | 23 | 22 | 123¹ | 105 | 13 | 32 | 72 | 3.6 | 7.8 | 34% | .359 | 1.55 | 5.18 | 5.11 | 5.50 | 0.5 |
| 2010 | TEX | MLB | 26 | 0 | 0 | 0 | 1 | 0 | 0² | 2 | 0 | 2 | 2 | 27.0 | 27.0 | % | .000 | 6.00 | 27.00 | 10.55 | 12.48 | -0.1 |
| 2011 | SAC | AAA | 27 | 3 | 3 | 0 | 9 | 8 | 46¹ | 41 | 3 | 16 | 52 | 3.1 | 10.1 | 32% | .309 | 1.23 | 3.88 | 3.37 | 3.20 | 1.1 |
| 2011 | OAK | MLB | 27 | 8 | 10 | 0 | 23 | 21 | 128 | 102 | 14 | 38 | 74 | 2.7 | 5.2 | 27% | .222 | 1.09 | 3.38 | 4.26 | 4.63 | 0.3 |
| 2012 | OAK | MLB | 28 | 5 | 7 | 0 | 18 | 18 | 101 | 95 | 9 | 34 | 75 | 3.0 | 6.7 | 33% | .284 | 1.27 | 3.53 | 3.89 | 3.83 | 1.4 |

He started 21 games for Oakland, logging 128 innings and offering respectable production despite a lack of overwhelming stuff. Moscoso, a 28-year-old acquired from the Texas Rangers for minor league reliever Ryan Kelly, features a ghost-fastball, a pitch that seems to disappear as it approaches the plate. Thrown with average velocity for a fastball, the pitch butters its bread with intense movement, and thanks to Moscoso's great extension, the ball appears to explode, then disappear as it approaches the plate. It's a wonder of nature. The rest of his pitches are so-so, and despite the ghost-ball and a minor-league strikeout rate of 8.8, Moscoso fails to miss a lot of big-league bats. His rotational success doesn't seem overly sustainable, but the ability to throw strikes and log innings could allow the Venezuelan to stick around the big leagues, perhaps even in the rotation if the competition for spots proves thin.

### Josh Outman

Born: 9/14/1984 Age: 27
Bats: L Throws: L Height: 6' 2" Weight: 185
Breakout: 36% Improve: 64% Collapse: 17%
Attrition: 10% MLB: 85%

Comparables:
Wil Ledezma,John Franco,Tom Gorzelanny

| YEAR | TEAM | LVL | AGE | W | L | SV | G | GS | IP | H | HR | BB | SO | EqBB9 | EqSO9 | GB% | BABIP | WHIP | ERA | FIP | FRA | WARP |
|------|------|-----|-----|---|---|----|---|----|------|----|----|----|----|-------|-------|-----|-------|------|------|------|------|------|
| 2009 | OAK | MLB | 24 | 4 | 1 | 0 | 14 | 12 | 67¹ | 53 | 9 | 25 | 53 | 3.3 | 7.1 | 39% | .234 | 1.16 | 3.48 | 4.42 | 5.12 | 0.1 |
| 2011 | SAC | AAA | 26 | 8 | 3 | 0 | 17 | 17 | 78¹ | 75 | 7 | 43 | 69 | 5.4 | 8.3 | 48% | .322 | 1.58 | 3.91 | 4.86 | 5.06 | 0.3 |
| 2011 | OAK | MLB | 26 | 3 | 5 | 0 | 13 | 9 | 58¹ | 62 | 4 | 23 | 35 | 3.5 | 5.4 | 42% | .309 | 1.46 | 3.70 | 3.94 | 4.17 | 0.4 |
| 2012 | OAK | MLB | 27 | 3 | 5 | 0 | 12 | 12 | 61 | 60 | 6 | 28 | 44 | 4.2 | 6.5 | 44% | .297 | 1.46 | 4.26 | 4.42 | 4.63 | 0.3 |

Another guy coming back from Tommy John surgery who shows exaggerated lefty/righty splits. Stop me if you've heard this before. Outman made his major league return after the aforementioned surgery put him on the shelf for the 2010 season. The stuff was slightly depressed from his pre-surgery form, with a fastball sitting in the low-90s and a two-plane slider that didn't quite have the snap or velocity of his 2009 offering. Command is usually the last component to return after surgery, and if Outman can sharpen his ability to throw strikes while increasing his ability to miss bats, he should be able to carve out a future in a major league rotation. If not, Outman could find a home as a short-burst reliever, where his best two pitches could play up with more intensity.

### Jarrod Parker

Born: 11/24/1988 Age: 23
Bats: R Throws: R Height: 6' 2" Weight: 195
Breakout: 21% Improve: 51% Collapse: 20%
Attrition: 14% MLB: 93%

Comparables:
Bobby Thigpen,Jose Ascanio,Kevin Millwood

| YEAR | TEAM | LVL | AGE | W | L | SV | G | GS | IP | H | HR | BB | SO | EqBB9 | EqSO9 | GB% | BABIP | WHIP | ERA | FIP | FRA | WARP |
|------|------|-----|-----|---|---|----|----|----|------|-----|----|----|-----|-------|-------|-----|-------|------|------|------|------|------|
| 2009 | MOB | AA | 20 | 4 | 6 | 0 | 16 | 16 | 78¹ | 82 | 2 | 34 | 74 | 3.9 | 8.5 | 56% | .352 | 1.48 | 3.68 | 3.11 | 3.57 | 2.2 |
| 2011 | MOB | AA | 22 | 7 | 1 | 0 | 26 | 26 | 130² | 121 | 8 | 58 | 124 | 3.8 | 7.7 | 56% | .291 | 1.28 | 3.79 | 3.78 | 4.60 | 2.2 |
| 2011 | ARI | MLB | 22 | 0 | 0 | 0 | 1 | 1 | 5² | 4 | 0 | 1 | 1 | 1.6 | 1.6 | 45% | .222 | 0.88 | 0.00 | 3.17 | 2.83 | 0.2 |
| 2012 | OAK | MLB | 23 | 1 | 3 | 0 | 7 | 7 | 36¹ | 38 | 4 | 17 | 25 | 4.2 | 6.1 | 47% | .307 | 1.52 | 4.74 | 4.66 | 5.16 | -0.0 |

Parker's comeback from October 2009 Tommy John surgery was so highly anticipated that he actually climbed three spots on *Baseball America*'s 2011 top prospects list despite not having thrown a pitch in 2010. He didn't disappoint, making 26 starts without suffering a setback and debuting for the Diamondbacks with a scoreless start in September. More whiffs would have been nice, but given that his workload was closely monitored and his stuff and command weren't all the way back, it wouldn't be fair to call fanning nearly eight batters per nine innings a discouraging result. Parker's breaking stuff was the slowest to return, so he largely eschewed his slider and curveball and leaned heavily on a well-disguised changeup in the low- to mid-80s. Acquired by the A's in the December 2011 trade that sent Trevor Cahill to Arizona, the potential ace should be at the height of his powers with all of his pitches at his disposal.

**Brad Peacock**
Born: 2/2/1988 Age: 24
Bats: R Throws: R Height: 6' 2" Weight: 175
Breakout: 25% Improve: 49% Collapse: 26%
Attrition: 21% MLB: 84%
Comparables:
Marcos Carvajal, Mark Guthrie, Don Aase

| YEAR | TEAM | LVL | AGE | W | L | SV | G | GS | IP | H | HR | BB | SO | EqBB9 | EqSO9 | GB% | BABIP | WHIP | ERA | FIP | FRA | WARP |
|------|------|-----|-----|---|---|----|---|----|-----|-----|----|----|-----|-------|-------|------|-------|------|------|------|------|------|
| 2009 | HAG | A | 21 | 5 | 8 | 0 | 19 | 17 | 100 | 104 | 10 | 32 | 77 | 2.9 | 6.9 | 53% | .316 | 1.36 | 4.05 | 4.42 | 5.62 | -0.2 |
| 2009 | POT | A+ | 21 | 3 | 3 | 0 | 8 | 7 | 47² | 46 | 4 | 10 | 27 | 1.9 | 5.1 | 49% | .276 | 1.17 | 4.34 | 4.12 | 5.04 | 0.1 |
| 2010 | POT | A+ | 22 | 4 | 9 | 0 | 19 | 18 | 103¹ | 85 | 11 | 18 | 95 | 2.2 | 10.3 | 49% | .333 | 1.30 | 4.44 | 3.64 | 3.89 | 1.9 |
| 2010 | HAR | AA | 22 | 2 | 2 | 0 | 7 | 7 | 38² | 19 | 5 | 13 | 17 | 5.1 | 7.0 | 45% | .197 | 1.42 | 4.65 | 5.40 | 5.05 | 0.4 |
| 2011 | HAR | AA | 23 | 7 | 2 | 0 | 16 | 14 | 98² | 62 | 4 | 24 | 129 | 2.1 | 11.8 | 41% | .269 | 0.86 | 2.01 | 2.12 | 2.63 | 2.8 |

no reason why Peacock can't have similar success in the rotation, although his ceiling is probably as a third or fourth starter.

**Tyson Ross**
Born: 4/22/1987 Age: 25
Bats: R Throws: R Height: 6' 7" Weight: 225
Breakout: 22% Improve: 52% Collapse: 18%
Attrition: 17% MLB: 93%
Comparables:
Noah Lowry, Mike Witt, Wade Davis

| YEAR | TEAM | LVL | AGE | W | L | SV | G | GS | IP | H | HR | BB | SO | EqBB9 | EqSO9 | GB% | BABIP | WHIP | ERA | FIP | FRA | WARP |
|------|------|-----|-----|---|---|----|----|----|-----|----|----|----|----|-------|-------|------|-------|------|------|------|------|------|
| 2009 | STO | A+ | 22 | 5 | 6 | 0 | 18 | 18 | 86¹ | 78 | 10 | 33 | 82 | 3.4 | 8.6 | 56% | .282 | 1.29 | 4.17 | 4.79 | 5.44 | -0.1 |
| 2009 | MID | AA | 22 | 6 | 4 | 0 | 9 | 9 | 50 | 47 | 3 | 23 | 50 | 3.6 | 5.6 | 62% | .257 | 1.20 | 3.96 | 3.46 | 5.25 | 0.6 |
| 2010 | SAC | AAA | 23 | 2 | 1 | 0 | 6 | 6 | 25¹ | 14 | 1 | 8 | 22 | 4.6 | 10.7 | 62% | .406 | 1.38 | 3.56 | 3.90 | 4.01 | 0.6 |
| 2010 | OAK | MLB | 23 | 1 | 4 | 1 | 26 | 2 | 39¹ | 39 | 4 | 20 | 32 | 4.6 | 7.3 | 55% | .312 | 1.50 | 5.49 | 4.27 | 5.31 | -0.2 |
| 2011 | SAC | AAA | 24 | 3 | 2 | 0 | 9 | 9 | 36² | 70 | 6 | 23 | 40 | 5.4 | 8.3 | 43% | .403 | 2.02 | 7.61 | 5.64 | 5.75 | 0.0 |
| 2011 | OAK | MLB | 24 | 3 | 3 | 0 | 9 | 6 | 36 | 33 | 1 | 13 | 24 | 3.2 | 6.0 | 49% | .302 | 1.28 | 2.75 | 3.17 | 3.65 | 0.5 |
| 2012 | OAK | MLB | 25 | 2 | 3 | 0 | 16 | 8 | 45² | 45 | 4 | 21 | 34 | 4.1 | 6.7 | 53% | .299 | 1.45 | 4.25 | 4.23 | 4.62 | 0.2 |

This long-levered righty has always had good stuff, throwing downhill with a lively low-90s fastball and a tight slider with velocity and bite, but the results just haven't gelled. Cutting down his walks in 2011 was a step in the right direction, but the 24-year-old also saw a decrease in his strikeout totals, clouding his already cloudy future. Some scouts see Ross as a better fit for the bullpen as a max-effort reliever, where the fastball/slider combo can play up. Others think the mechanical profile has improved enough to suggest a workhorse, innings-eating starter, especially if the changeup also takes developmental steps forward.

**Evan Scribner**
Born: 7/19/1985 Age: 26
Bats: R Throws: R Height: 6' 4" Weight: 190
Breakout: 33% Improve: 54% Collapse: 19%
Attrition: 12% MLB: 97%
Comparables:
Len Barker, Shawn Kelley, Don Drysdale

| YEAR | TEAM | LVL | AGE | W | L | SV | G | GS | IP | H | HR | BB | SO | EqBB9 | EqSO9 | GB% | BABIP | WHIP | ERA | FIP | FRA | WARP |
|------|------|-----|-----|---|---|----|----|----|-----|----|----|----|----|-------|-------|------|-------|------|------|------|------|------|
| 2009 | SAN | AA | 23 | 8 | 5 | 21 | 58 | 0 | 70¹ | 63 | 4 | 20 | 82 | 2.6 | 9.9 | 35% | .303 | 1.14 | 3.07 | 2.50 | 2.87 | 2.0 |
| 2010 | SAN | AA | 24 | 4 | 5 | 16 | 57 | 0 | 66 | 35 | 5 | 10 | 57 | 2.0 | 11.0 | 49% | .297 | 1.00 | 2.59 | 3.22 | 3.36 | 1.1 |
| 2011 | SDN | MLB | 25 | 0 | 0 | 0 | 10 | 0 | 14 | 18 | 1 | 4 | 10 | 2.6 | 6.4 | 42% | .347 | 1.57 | 7.07 | 3.35 | 5.92 | -0.2 |
| 2012 | OAK | MLB | 26 | 1 | 0 | 0 | 19 | 0 | 21² | 20 | 2 | 8 | 20 | 3.4 | 8.4 | 37% | .300 | 1.31 | 3.71 | 3.67 | 4.03 | 0.2 |

The Padres acquired Scribner at the 2008 trade deadline in exchange for 36 games of late-career Tony Clark. Scribner has escaped the attention of scouts due to a shortness of stuff and is best described as one of those guys who just gets people out. His career K/9 (10.9) and K/BB (4.6) are nice to look at but he didn't show much in his first (admittedly brief) big-league trial. He is likely a Quadruple-A pitcher but insurance is never a bad thing and the A's plucked him off waivers in October.

**Michael Wuertz**

Born: 12/15/1978 Age: 33
Bats: R Throws: R Height: 6' 4" Weight: 200
Breakout: 15% Improve: 39% Collapse: 44%
Attrition: 8% MLB: 94%

**Comparables:**
Jose Valverde, Kerry Wood, Norm Charlton

| YEAR | TEAM | LVL | AGE | W | L | SV | G | GS | IP | H | HR | BB | SO | EqBB9 | EqSO9 | GB% | BABIP | WHIP | ERA | FIP | FRA | WARP |
|------|------|-----|-----|---|---|----|----|----|-----|----|----|----|-----|-------|-------|-----|-------|------|------|------|------|------|
| 2009 | OAK | MLB | 30 | 6 | 1 | 4 | 74 | 0 | 78² | 52 | 6 | 23 | 102 | 2.6 | 11.7 | 47% | .269 | 0.95 | 2.63 | 2.42 | 2.61 | 2.4 |
| 2010 | OAK | MLB | 31 | 2 | 3 | 6 | 48 | 0 | 39² | 35 | 6 | 21 | 40 | 4.8 | 9.1 | 44% | .290 | 1.41 | 4.31 | 4.59 | 5.01 | 0.0 |
| 2011 | OAK | MLB | 32 | 0 | 0 | 0 | 39 | 0 | 33² | 37 | 5 | 26 | 32 | 7.0 | 8.6 | 47% | .337 | 1.87 | 6.68 | 5.50 | 5.89 | -0.2 |
| 2012 | OAK | MLB | 33 | 2 | 1 | 1 | 41 | 3 | 35² | 31 | 3 | 17 | 37 | 4.3 | 9.3 | 46% | .298 | 1.35 | 3.58 | 3.65 | 3.89 | 0.5 |

After a good start to the season, Wuertz got progressively worse, losing all feel for command and getting righteously punished by right-handed bats to the tune of .311/.420/.500. Seriously, that's rough. The 33 year-old righty lives and dies on his slider, a pitch that he throws over 60 percent of the time, but in 2011, the pitch killed him, as the angular offering was often flat and completely ineffective against opponents on his arm-side. Without the ability to throw his fastball for strikes or freeze righties with a sharp slider, Wuertz is dead-weight. The A's released Wuertz in October to make room for waiver wire pickups.

## LINEOUTS

### HITTERS

| PLAYER | TEAM | LVL | AGE | PA | R | 2B | 3B | HR | RBI | BB | SO | SB-CS | AVG/OBP/SLG | TAv | BABIP | BRR | FRAA | WARP |
|--------|------|-----|-----|-----|----|----|----|----|-----|----|-----|-------|-------------|------|-------|------|------|------|
| SS Y. Cabrera | BUR | A | 20 | 401 | 59 | 21 | 5 | 6 | 47 | 31 | 110 | 23-6 | .231/.297/.368 | .247 | .309 | 1.6 | -6.3 | 0.7 |
| LF A. Cardenas | SAC | AAA | 23 | 545 | 70 | 28 | 4 | 5 | 51 | 47 | 56 | 13-6 | .314/.374/.418 | .270 | .344 | -0.3 | -7 | 0.9 |
| RF B. Crocker | VER | A- | 21 | 129 | 19 | 5 | 0 | 3 | 15 | 8 | 22 | 6-1 | .322/.367/.441 | .314 | .372 | -0.4 | 1.8 | 1.4 |
| | ATH | RK | 21 | 95 | 14 | 4 | 3 | 0 | 4 | 5 | 22 | 2-2 | .261/.316/.375 | .294 | .348 | 0.3 | -0.6 | 0.5 |
| 2B C. Crumbliss | STO | A+ | 24 | 542 | 75 | 18 | 4 | 7 | 52 | 96 | 85 | 24-7 | .268/.404/.378 | .291 | .316 | 1.3 | 5.9 | 4.2 |
| C J. Donaldson | SAC | AAA | 25 | 503 | 79 | 28 | 0 | 17 | 70 | 51 | 100 | 13-4 | .261/.344/.439 | .277 | .301 | 2.3 | 0.7 | 3.5 |
| SS G. Green | MID | AA | 23 | 587 | 76 | 33 | 1 | 9 | 62 | 39 | 119 | 6-8 | .291/.343/.408 | .264 | .355 | -1.9 | -3.8 | 1.7 |
| 1B M. Head | GRN | A | 20 | 298 | 61 | 25 | 1 | 15 | 53 | 30 | 53 | 4-2 | .338/.409/.612 | .354 | .376 | -1.3 | 1.2 | 3.2 |
| | SLM | A+ | 20 | 259 | 27 | 12 | 1 | 7 | 29 | 20 | 56 | 0-2 | .254/.328/.405 | .247 | .306 | -4.8 | -2.3 | -0.6 |
| CF J. Miller | SAC | AAA | 26 | 475 | 81 | 24 | 4 | 32 | 88 | 54 | 179 | 16-0 | .276/.368/.588 | .312 | .401 | 2.3 | -3.8 | 3.6 |
| | OAK | MLB | 26 | 12 | 2 | 0 | 0 | 1 | 2 | 0 | 5 | 0-0 | .250/.250/.500 | .292 | .333 | 0.2 | -0.2 | 0.0 |
| CF J. Mitchell | MID | AA | 26 | 360 | 67 | 15 | 13 | 10 | 50 | 54 | 65 | 14-13 | .355/.453/.589 | .347 | .426 | 3.3 | -2.2 | 4.5 |
| | SAC | AAA | 26 | 275 | 48 | 14 | 3 | 5 | 28 | 39 | 47 | 13-5 | .302/.401/.453 | .286 | .359 | 5.1 | 6.9 | 2.7 |
| LF B. Moss | LEH | AAA | 27 | 506 | 66 | 31 | 1 | 23 | 80 | 62 | 127 | 4-6 | .275/.368/.509 | .311 | .334 | 2.7 | 3.5 | 5.2 |
| | PHI | MLB | 27 | 6 | 0 | 0 | 0 | 0 | 0 | 0 | 2 | 0-0 | .000/.000/.000 | .035 | .000 | 0 | 0.1 | -0.2 |
| 3B S. Parker | MID | AA | 23 | 576 | 72 | 30 | 2 | 10 | 74 | 69 | 107 | 1-1 | .286/.373/.413 | .274 | .345 | -1.6 | -1.6 | 2.8 |
| C L. Powell | SAC | AAA | 29 | 53 | 6 | 0 | 0 | 1 | 5 | 7 | 9 | 0-0 | .283/.377/.348 | .223 | .333 | -1.3 | -0.3 | -0.1 |
| | OAK | MLB | 29 | 122 | 10 | 3 | 0 | 1 | 4 | 11 | 32 | 0-0 | .171/.246/.225 | .180 | .231 | -1.9 | -0.4 | -0.8 |
| C A. Recker | SAC | AAA | 27 | 412 | 61 | 24 | 1 | 16 | 48 | 56 | 81 | 7-5 | .287/.388/.501 | .301 | .328 | -0.2 | 2.6 | 3.4 |
| | OAK | MLB | 27 | 21 | 3 | 1 | 0 | 0 | 4 | 0 | 7 | 0-0 | .176/.333/.235 | .243 | .300 | -0.3 | 0.1 | 0.0 |
| SS E. Sogard | SAC | AAA | 25 | 366 | 55 | 16 | 2 | 5 | 37 | 40 | 34 | 13-3 | .298/.381/.410 | .280 | .319 | 0.8 | -6.4 | 1.5 |
| | OAK | MLB | 25 | 74 | 7 | 3 | 0 | 2 | 4 | 4 | 13 | 0-0 | .200/.243/.329 | .197 | .218 | -0.9 | -0.2 | -0.3 |
| DH M. Stassi | STO | A+ | 20 | 139 | 22 | 6 | 0 | 2 | 19 | 16 | 22 | 1-1 | .231/.331/.331 | .258 | .268 | 1.1 | 0 | 0.2 |
| LF M. Taylor | SAC | AAA | 25 | 400 | 51 | 16 | 0 | 16 | 64 | 46 | 80 | 14-5 | .272/.360/.456 | .277 | .310 | 0.9 | 0.1 | 1.6 |
| | OAK | MLB | 25 | 35 | 4 | 0 | 0 | 1 | 1 | 5 | 11 | 0-0 | .200/.314/.300 | .271 | .278 | 0.1 | 0.6 | 0.1 |

A raw middle-of-the-diamond player with tools, former second-round pick **Yordy Cabrera** should make the jump to High-A in 2012. ⊘ Once the second baseman of the future, **Adrian Cardenas** is now a future utility option, having yet to escape the grasp of the minors. ⊘ A fourth-round pick in the 2011 draft, **Bobby Crocker** has the tools on both sides of the ball to play at the highest level . . . eventually. ⊘ With some versatility in the field and the best approach at the plate in the entire system, **Conner Crumbliss** just might walk his way into prospect status in 2012. ⊘ **Josh Donaldson** profiles as a backup catcher in the bigs, with good catch-and-throw skills, some on-base ability, and occasional power. ⊘ Selected in the first-round of the

2009 draft, shortstop **Grant Green** changed his name to center fielder Grant Green in 2011, giving the prospect more versatility and value as he climbs toward the majors. ⊘ First baseman **Miles Head** had never hit much before, but something woke the dragon, and he destroyed Greenville (41 extra-base hits in half a season) and earned a promotion to High-A, where his bat resumed its slumber. ⊘ A versatile outfielder who shows plenty of pop at the minor league level, 27-year-old **Jai Miller** hopes to bring some of that Triple-A power to the majors Real Soon Now . . . if only his extreme inability to make contact doesn't get in the way. ⊘ Another of the growing legion of versatile outfielders in their mid-twenties who have yet to taste major league success, **Jermaine Mitchell** might have the best skills for the next level, with a mature approach at the plate and some thump in the bat. ⊘ A recent free agent addition to the A's, **Brandon Moss** is looking to put his career back on track and earn a roster spot. ⊘ A fifth round selection in the 2009 draft, **Stephen Parker** spent the majority of the 2011 season at Double-A, showing some gap power, though his production might have been helped by a hitter-friendly home park. ⊘ A backup catcher the last three seasons, former first-round pick **Landon Powell** was recently removed from the 40-man roster after his offensive performance went from acceptable to bad to putrid. ⊘ **Anthony Recker** is a 28-year-old backup catcher drafted in the 18th round of the 2005 draft, and we're pretty sure that even A's fans have no idea who he is. ⊘ 25-year-old utility infielder **Eric**

| PLAYER | TEAM | LVL | AGE | W | L | SV | IP | H | HR | BB | SO | EqBB9 | EqSO9 | GB% | BABIP | WHIP | ERA | FIP | FRA | WARP |
|---|---|---|---|---|---|---|---|---|---|---|---|---|---|---|---|---|---|---|---|---|
| B. Billings | SAC | AAA | 25 | 1 | 0 | 0 | 26¹ | 26 | 1 | 15 | 29 | 4.4 | 8.5 | 45% | .301 | 1.33 | 4.44 | 3.85 | 4.40 | 0.3 |
| | CSP | AAA | 25 | 4 | 0 | 1 | 50¹ | 55 | 4 | 20 | 46 | 3.8 | 8.4 | 34% | .352 | 1.57 | 4.47 | 4.25 | 5.33 | 0.8 |
| | COL | MLB | 25 | 0 | 0 | 0 | 2 | 5 | 0 | 0 | 0 | 0.0 | 0.0 | 56% | .556 | 2.50 | 4.50 | 2.99 | 5.42 | 0.0 |
| | OAK | MLB | 25 | 0 | 0 | 0 | 5 | 8 | 1 | 6 | 7 | 10.8 | 12.6 | 44% | .467 | 2.80 | 12.60 | 6.46 | 12.28 | -0.3 |
| A. Carignan | OAK | MLB | 24 | 0 | 0 | 0 | 6¹ | 8 | 1 | 2 | 5 | 2.8 | 7.1 | 46% | .304 | 1.58 | 4.26 | 4.48 | 4.18 | 0.1 |
| B. Cramer | SAC | AAA | 31 | 0 | 0 | 0 | 22¹ | 22 | 3 | 12 | 26 | 4.8 | 10.5 | 56% | .328 | 1.52 | 4.03 | 5.17 | 5.07 | 0.2 |
| | OAK | MLB | 31 | 0 | 1 | 0 | 8¹ | 6 | 1 | 1 | 6 | 1.1 | 6.5 | 42% | .217 | 0.84 | 1.08 | 3.54 | 3.79 | 0.1 |
| G. Godfrey | SAC | AAA | 26 | 14 | 3 | 0 | 107¹ | 108 | 8 | 34 | 93 | 2.5 | 7.5 | 41% | .282 | 1.14 | 2.68 | 4.15 | 4.13 | 1.7 |
| | OAK | MLB | 26 | 1 | 2 | 0 | 25 | 32 | 3 | 5 | 13 | 1.8 | 4.7 | 46% | .326 | 1.48 | 3.96 | 4.30 | 4.68 | 0.1 |
| E. Gonzalez | DUR | AAA | 28 | 3 | 3 | 0 | 53¹ | 62 | 4 | 17 | 34 | 2.9 | 5.7 | 47% | .322 | 1.48 | 4.56 | 3.89 | 4.80 | 0.7 |
| | CSP | AAA | 28 | 5 | 3 | 0 | 80 | 93 | 9 | 24 | 53 | 2.7 | 6.0 | 43% | .322 | 1.46 | 5.29 | 4.92 | 5.39 | 1.1 |
| | COL | MLB | 28 | 0 | 0 | 0 | 2 | 5 | 0 | 1 | 1 | 4.5 | 4.5 | 56% | .556 | 3.00 | 9.00 | 3.49 | 4.28 | 0.0 |
| T. Milone | SYR | AAA | 24 | 7 | 5 | 0 | 148¹ | 137 | 9 | 16 | 155 | 1.0 | 9.4 | 40% | .316 | 1.03 | 3.22 | 2.28 | 3.28 | 4.5 |
| | WAS | MLB | 24 | 1 | 0 | 0 | 26 | 28 | 2 | 4 | 15 | 1.4 | 5.2 | 35% | .310 | 1.23 | 3.81 | 3.53 | 3.85 | 0.4 |
| J. Norberto | RNO | AAA | 24 | 6 | 2 | 1 | 48² | 46 | 1 | 26 | 54 | 4.8 | 10.0 | 55% | .344 | 1.48 | 4.25 | 3.57 | 5.53 | 0.2 |
| | OAK | MLB | 24 | 0 | 0 | 0 | 6² | 8 | 0 | 7 | 4 | 9.4 | 5.4 | 39% | .348 | 2.25 | 8.10 | 5.46 | 6.19 | -0.1 |

With a plus fastball and a hard slider with good tilt, reliever **Bruce Billings** needs to harness his command to have any shot at sticking around in the majors in 2012. ⊘ Promising two-pitch reliever **Andrew Carignan** has the stuff to miss bats (11.7 K/9 in 150 career minor-league innings) and force weak contact, relying heavily on the lively plus fastball he commands. ⊘ 32-year-old lefty specialist **Bobby Cramer**, who relies on pinpoint control (career 2.2 BB/9 in minors), logged over 500 innings at the minor league level before finally getting his shot with the A's in 2010 at the tender age of 30. ⊘ 27-year-old back-of-the-rotation pitcher, **Graham Godfrey** commands a deep arsenal of average offerings. ⊘ Boiler-plate reliever **Edgar Gonzalez** might be a fringy major league option for 2012, but his nearly 1000 minor-league innings serve as a testament to his perseverance. ⊘ Included in the Gio Gonzalez trade, **Tom Milone** might lack the ceiling of AJ Cole or even Brad Peacock, but he is ready to contribute to the big club in 2012, most likely as an innings-eating back-of-the-rotation starter. ⊘ Acquired in the Brad Ziegler trade, lefty reliever **Jordan Norberto** has a good arm and is capable of missing bats, but his well below-average control makes him a fringy option.

# MANAGER: BOB MELVIN

| YEAR | TEAM | W-L | Pythag +/- | Avg PC | 100+ P | 120+ P | QS | BQS | REL | REL w Zero R | IBB | Subs | PH | PH Avg | PH HR | SB2 | CS2 | SB3 | CS3 | SAC Att | SAC % | POS SAC | Squeeze | Swing | In Play |
|------|------|-----|-----|------|------|------|----|-----|-----|-------|-----|------|----|------|------|-----|-----|-----|-----|-----|-------|-----|---------|-------|---------|
| 2009 | ARI | 12-17 | 0 | 96.1 | 11 | 0 | 16 | 2 | 91 | 53 | 3 | 11 | 47 | .209 | 3 | 5 | 1 | 0 | 0 | 18 | 50.0% | 6 | 0 | 25 | 17 |
| 2011 | OAK | 47-52 | 0 | 100.4 | 51 | 1 | 55 | 3 | 282 | 220 | 9 | — | 30 | .276 | 2 | 19 | 2 | 0 | 0 | 38 | 78.9% | 28 | 0 | 229 | 63 |

After finishing his playing career with negative WARP, former catcher Bob Melvin has had a more successful career as a manager, one who gets to start another act with the Oakland Athletics. Known for his insider communication skills and player-friendly approach, Melvin will face a tough task as a full-time manager. Having taken over in an interim role partway through the season, he was awarded a three-year contract in September. For all his lauded communication skills, all the talk in the world might not be enough to convince the players under his leadership that they can compete, as the A's continue to sell off major league players in exchange for younger, more cost-controlled talent. Fans of the green-and-gold hope that being close to home will allow the native of Palo Alto and one-time Manager of the Year to channel some of his latent managerial magic, as it's going to take an act of sorcery to propel the Athletics beyond the dungeon of the American League West. But with strong character and conviction, Melvin is actually a very good choice for a ship in desperate need of new supplies; it's not easy to keep a team playing hard in the face of what very well could be several 100 loss seasons in the coming years. Situation aside, Melvin will get the most from his players, and when the talent proves to be a little thin and the ship starts to sink, Melvin will be the first one to suggest they are a team with a chance to win.

# Philadelphia Phillies

Imagine there are two different Ruben Amaro Jrs. One is a freewheeling spendthrift who gets an adrenaline rush from the thrill of the chase and the release of major roster transactions. The other is a careful and patient calculator who sets a target and moves doggedly to achieve it. How

Jonathan Papelbon. It reportedly came on the heels of a lucrative offer to Ryan Madson. What exactly happened in the Madson negotiations isn't clear, but there are a number of possibilities. One is that Amaro wanted to lock down the closer spot before making any other moves, since it was likely to be his biggest payroll outlay and would set his budget for the rest of the winter. The other is that Amaro—petulantly feeling spurned by Madson's refusal to accept the rumored $44 million he was offered—turned around and got his fix by catching an even bigger fish in Papelbon. Both of these stories would fit with the events as they unfolded in the public eye.

If this story sounds familiar, that's because it's vaguely reminiscent of the twin Roy Halladay/Cliff Lee deals prior to the 2010 season. The reports at the time suggested that contract extension talks between the Phillies and Lee had stalled, leading Amaro to react by trading Lee to the Mariners and acquiring Halladay from the Blue Jays. As with the Papelbon signing, there are two possible stories we could tell about these two trades. One is that Amaro was simply testing the limits of the market for starting pitchers. Once he realized that wins from Halladay were cheaper than wins from Lee, he made the necessary adjustment. Either way he would have achieved his goal of adding an ace for several years to

come. The other possible explanation is that—petulant over Lee's refusal to accept whatever contract extension was on the table at the time—Amaro struck back by shipping him to the rainy Northwest to toil in relative obscurity.

According to the Amaro-as-grasshopper theory, he

| | | |
|---|---|---|
| TAv | .258 | 17th |
| TAv-P | .234 | 1st |
| FIP | 3.21 | 1st |
| DER | .714 | 10th |
| DL | 639 | 8th |
| B-Age | 31.6 | 30th |
| P-Age | 29.4 | 25th |
| Salary | $166.0 | 2nd |
| M$/MW | $2.86 | 20th |

baseball, thanks to the rotation, if you don't count the postseason

**2012:** The key parts are coming back, locked in for years, and getting older all the time

**Action Items:** The only thing that would let the Braves pass them is too many injuries

away if need be. But this story doesn't fit the facts perfectly. For example, it fails to account for Amaro throwing $125 million at Ryan Howard a year before Howard was to become a free agent—and a year before Albert Pujols and Prince Fielder would be free agents as well. Here was a situation in which there were clear alternatives that could have provided better value, and yet Amaro pushed forward on a timetable that seemed more like Howard's than his own. His BATNA (waiting patiently for one of the many alternatives at first base, as fungible a position as you'll find) appeared never to have received serious consideration.

According to the Amaro-as-ant story, Amaro cares more about running up his cell phone bill, making headlines, smiling for the press, and signing on the dotted line than he does about building a franchise that will succeed in the long term. Burn $50 million on 60 innings a year? No problem. Pay a two-win player a five-win salary? Put it on the board. Average reliever coming off serious elbow injury? Two-year contracts for everyone! But this theory also overlooks critical facts. Just this past offseason, Amaro waited out Jimmy Rollins and every other team in the market for a shortstop. Would he have done so if he didn't think Freddy Galvis could survive 400 major-league plate appearances? Was he just waiting for Jimmy to get off the dime and come back home?

What kept him from swooping in as the "mystery team" in the Jose Reyes sweepstakes?

Second-guessing executive psychology is usually as worthwhile as recounting the hits of Billy Ray Cyrus: it's achy breaky heart and then you're done. But in the case of the Philadelphia front office, it's important to understand the Phillies' seemingly erratic movements both because they are so large in scale and because they range so widely from commendable to dumbfounding. If you want to know whether Cole Hamels will remain a Phillie beyond 2012 or what will happen when the core of talent hits the wrong side of 35, you have to understand the bizarre decision process that calls the shots.

What gives the fable of the ant and the grasshopper its analytic simplicity is that the ant and the grasshopper both have the same needs, and they both come to value the food they eat at exactly the same amount. And while an economist might say the grasshopper has a higher discount rate or that he pays more attention to the time value of money, there isn't any serious doubt that the ant is the one with the better strategy. But with Amaro and the Phillies, he might be every bit as plan-oriented and analytic as the ant and yet appear to those of us with spreadsheets and linear weights as a grasshopper. In other words, he might be that rare beast, hunted to the brink of the Endangered Species List, the traditional GM.

Imagine that he is every bit as patient as the ant, but he really thought he was getting a discount when he signed Howard to an extension one year early. Imagine that he pursues doggedly what he takes to be his goal, but that goal is a number that is wildly at odds with sabermetric wisdom. Imagine that he truly believes that Ryan Howard is a good substitute for Prince Fielder. Imagine his index cards with salary numbers for Papelbon in the range of $15 million. So while some of his decisions will break in such a way that many will hail them as successes (think of the Lee deal or the Halladay extension, or perhaps the Rollins contract), others won't even register on the sanity charts.

That assessment doesn't make the future any clearer. The Phillies had the oldest hitters in the league last year by more than 15 months. Swapping Raul Ibanez for some combination of Domonic Brown, John Mayberry, and Laynce Nix will just barely offset everyone else being a year older. Over a certain time horizon, the process of locking every core player up in a long-term deal is the equivalent of nailing down the deck chairs on the Titanic. Even if you could guarantee that Chase Utley would be a Phillie forever, could you stomach watching the poor, hipless guy run out to second base every day? The cumulative effect of the extensions doled out to guys like Howard and Rollins is that the team has remained largely the same, but older and more expensive.

This concern is compounded by Amaro's seeming willingness to mortgage the excellent farm system the Phillies have been good or lucky enough to rebuild several times over. Last year's golden boys, Jarred Cosart and Jonathan Singleton, got optioned to Triple-A Houston in the Hunter Pence deal. Anthony Gose, Kyle Drabek, and Travis d'Arnaud are all on the Blue Jays 40-man. The inflow of talent, both from trades and the draft, has yet to prove it can replace what the front office tosses overboard in a mad dash to win now. The result is a farm system that is badly depleted and an aging roster that will need replacements sooner than new guys are likely to develop.

Amid all this doubt about Amaro's ability to provide for the winter is the fact that he has crucial information that outside observers lack. First, and most importantly, Amaro knows how much money he has to spend. That the Phillies were a bidder for Lee was a secret kept close to his chest until the last possible moment in large measure because few believed the Phillies would be willing to spend the money it ended up taking to sign him. Second, only Amaro knows just how unpredictable he really is. He's not entirely different from a mad dictator with a nuclear weapon: Everyone doubts he's as crazy as he seems, but no one is willing to press his luck to find out for sure. The result is the ability to make irrational but credible threats, a valuable weapon in any negotiator's arsenal.

All those doubts to one side, Amaro has managed to keep the band together for at least one more year, and that means the Phillies are once again heavyweights in the National League. The remaining questions are minor ones. How sustainable was Vance Worley's breakout? (Mostly.) What to expect from Utley going forward? (130-game seasons played through injury.) How quickly will Howard return? (Two to three months into the season.) How will the team ever replace his production? (Two wins aren't that hard to find.) Will Howard ever learn to deal with the shift? (No.)

Make no mistake. This is basically the same team that won 102 games a year ago, but with full seasons of Hunter Pence and Papelbon, no starts from Roy Oswalt, and an injured Howard. That's a very good baseball team that still has three of the best half-dozen pitchers in the National League. The concerns with this team, and with Amaro, are long-term ones. As the season changes from autumn to winter, Amaro gets on the phone and pulls out his checkbook. It is looking less and less like he'll have any food left for the long winter. Here's guessing the rest of the league won't be willing to share when that time comes.

# HITTERS

**Domonic Brown** RF
Born: 9/3/1987 Age: 24
Bats: L Throws: L Height: 6' 6'' Weight: 200
Breakout: 1% Improve: 28% Collapse: 5%
Attrition: 23% MLB: 91%

**Comparables:**
Carlos Quintana, Dwight Evans, Jeremy Hermida

| YEAR | TEAM | LVL | AGE | PA | R | 2B | 3B | HR | RBI | BB | SO | SB | CS | AVG/OBP/SLG | TAv | BABIP | BRR | FRAA | WARP |
|---|---|---|---|---|---|---|---|---|---|---|---|---|---|---|---|---|---|---|---|
| 2009 | CLR | A+ | 21 | 280 | 41 | 12 | 3 | 11 | 44 | 34 | 48 | 15 | 8 | .303/.394/.517 | .319 | .341 | -0.2 | -1.3 | 2.2 |
| 2009 | REA | AA | 21 | 162 | 20 | 9 | 4 | 3 | 20 | 14 | 37 | 8 | 1 | .279/.346/.456 | .278 | .355 | 0.5 | -4.8 | 0.1 |
| 2010 | REA | AA | 22 | 271 | 50 | 16 | 3 | 15 | 47 | 29 | 51 | 12 | 6 | .318/.397/.602 | .333 | .353 | -1.8 | 4.1 | 3.1 |
| 2010 | LEH | AAA | 22 | 118 | 15 | 6 | 1 | 5 | 21 | 8 | 23 | 5 | 1 | .346/.397/.561 | .326 | .405 | 1.8 | -0.5 | 1.2 |
| 2010 | PHI | MLB | 22 | 70 | 8 | 3 | 0 | 2 | 13 | 5 | 24 | 2 | 1 | .210/.257/.355 | .239 | .282 | -0.1 | 0.8 | 0.1 |
| 2011 | LEH | AAA | 23 | 174 | 22 | 6 | 0 | 3 | 15 | 28 | 33 | 12 | 4 | .261/.391/.370 | .253 | .311 | -0.4 | -0.7 | 0.0 |
| 2011 | PHI | MLB | 23 | 210 | 28 | 10 | 1 | 5 | 19 | 25 | 35 | 3 | 1 | .245/.333/.391 | .270 | .276 | 2.8 | -4.3 | 0.2 |
| 2012 | PHI | MLB | 24 | 250 | 30 | 11 | 2 | 8 | 29 | 23 | 56 | 8 | 3 | .254/.326/.420 | .271 | .302 | -0.3 | RF -5, LF -1 | 1.4 |

When Brown fractured the hamate bone in his wrist during spring training, cries went up that his power would never be the

**Jack Cust** RF
Born: 1/16/1979 Age: 33
Bats: L Throws: R Height: 6' 3'' Weight: 200
Breakout: 1% Improve: 27% Collapse: 4%
Attrition: 9% MLB: 87%

**Comparables:**
Carlos Pena, Ken Phelps, Jack Clark

| YEAR | TEAM | LVL | AGE | PA | R | 2B | 3B | HR | RBI | BB | SO | SB | CS | AVG/OBP/SLG | TAv | BABIP | BRR | FRAA | WARP |
|---|---|---|---|---|---|---|---|---|---|---|---|---|---|---|---|---|---|---|---|
| 2009 | OAK | MLB | 30 | 612 | 88 | 16 | 0 | 25 | 70 | 93 | 185 | 4 | 1 | .240/.356/.417 | .286 | .319 | 0.2 | -8.5 | 1.6 |
| 2010 | SAC | AAA | 31 | 144 | 21 | 6 | 0 | 4 | 19 | 33 | 33 | 0 | 0 | .273/.444/.436 | .316 | .356 | -1.6 | 1.2 | 0.9 |
| 2010 | OAK | MLB | 31 | 425 | 50 | 19 | 0 | 13 | 52 | 68 | 127 | 2 | 2 | .272/.395/.438 | .313 | .387 | -2.1 | 0.3 | 2.7 |
| 2011 | SEA | MLB | 32 | 270 | 19 | 15 | 1 | 3 | 23 | 44 | 87 | 0 | 0 | .213/.344/.329 | .254 | .333 | -0.9 | 0 | 0.0 |
| 2012 | PHI | MLB | 33 | 305 | 37 | 10 | 0 | 11 | 31 | 51 | 99 | 1 | 0 | .222/.356/.398 | .278 | .314 | -0.1 | RF -1, LF -0 | 1.4 |

There wasn't a qualifying hitter on the Phillies with an on-base percentage in 2011 higher than Cust's career .374 mark (Carlos Ruiz, at .371 thanks to plenty of intentional walks, is closest). He may have been a bust as a part-time DH in Seattle, but given a friendlier home park and a chance to face mostly righties off the bench (he's got a career 35 point OBP split against righties), it isn't hard to imagine Cust recapturing his whiffarific aesthetic in Philadelphia. He'd get more chances with the Phillies if he hit righty, but then again, he'd get more chances elsewhere if he could play defense. But even if Jack Cust's defense and a few bucks can buy you a cup of coffee, he and Jim Thome buy Charlie Manuel twice as many chances to punish mediocre righty relievers late in games.

**Freddy Galvis** SS
Born: 11/14/1989 Age: 22
Bats: B Throws: R Height: 5' 11'' Weight: 170
Breakout: 3% Improve: 16% Collapse: 9%
Attrition: 16% MLB: 32%

**Comparables:**
Erick Aybar, Adeiny Hechavarria, Joaquin Arias

| YEAR | TEAM | LVL | AGE | PA | R | 2B | 3B | HR | RBI | BB | SO | SB | CS | AVG/OBP/SLG | TAv | BABIP | BRR | FRAA | WARP |
|---|---|---|---|---|---|---|---|---|---|---|---|---|---|---|---|---|---|---|---|
| 2009 | CLR | A+ | 19 | 272 | 29 | 8 | 2 | 1 | 15 | 10 | 43 | 6 | 3 | .247/.273/.307 | .216 | .284 | -0.4 | -2.1 | -0.5 |
| 2009 | REA | AA | 19 | 63 | 6 | 0 | 0 | 1 | 5 | 2 | 7 | 0 | 1 | .197/.222/.246 | .188 | .208 | -0.6 | -1 | -0.4 |
| 2010 | REA | AA | 20 | 545 | 58 | 16 | 4 | 5 | 48 | 30 | 89 | 15 | 4 | .233/.274/.311 | .216 | .269 | 5.3 | 8.3 | 0.8 |
| 2011 | REA | AA | 21 | 464 | 63 | 22 | 4 | 8 | 35 | 28 | 68 | 19 | 11 | .273/.326/.400 | .251 | .308 | 2.8 | 12.6 | 2.8 |
| 2011 | LEH | AAA | 21 | 126 | 15 | 6 | 1 | 0 | 8 | 3 | 18 | 4 | 2 | .298/.315/.364 | .240 | .350 | 1.6 | 0.7 | 0.6 |
| 2012 | PHI | MLB | 22 | 250 | 23 | 9 | 1 | 3 | 21 | 8 | 47 | 6 | 3 | .231/.257/.313 | .207 | .272 | -0.3 | SS 7, 3B -0 | -0.6 |

The re-signing of Jimmy Rollins spares Delaware Valley residents a season of watching a yet-unready Freddy Galvis hit every day. In the meantime, he'll give Lehigh Valley residents the pleasure of watching him field. He had a nice enough year in Double-A, but it was the first year he ever posted an OPS above 600. If he can prove the gains are real—most importantly in batting average and power—by repeating them at Triple-A, then it will be reasonable to start thinking about Galvis as an everyday player.

### Ross Gload    1B

Born: 4/5/1976 Age: 36
Bats: L Throws: L Height: 6' 3" Weight: 210
Breakout: 0% Improve: 25% Collapse: 12%
Attrition: 31% MLB: 69%

**Comparables:**
Denny Walling, Keith Moreland, Bill Buckner

| YEAR | TEAM | LVL | AGE | PA | R | 2B | 3B | HR | RBI | BB | SO | SB | CS | AVG_OBP_SLG | TAv | BABIP | BRR | FRAA | WARP |
|---|---|---|---|---|---|---|---|---|---|---|---|---|---|---|---|---|---|---|---|
| 2009 | FLO | MLB | 33 | 259 | 33 | 10 | 2 | 6 | 30 | 23 | 30 | 0 | 0 | .261/.329/.400 | .265 | .274 | 0.3 | 3.2 | 0.7 |
| 2010 | PHI | MLB | 34 | 138 | 16 | 8 | 0 | 6 | 22 | 8 | 15 | 1 | 0 | .281/.328/.484 | .282 | .280 | -0.6 | -0.4 | 0.4 |
| 2011 | PHI | MLB | 35 | 116 | 3 | 8 | 0 | 0 | 8 | 3 | 23 | 0 | 0 | .257/.276/.327 | .220 | .322 | -0.4 | -0.3 | -0.4 |
| 2012 | PHI | MLB | 36 | 250 | 27 | 12 | 1 | 4 | 25 | 14 | 34 | 1 | 1 | .259/.302/.368 | .247 | .287 | -0.1 | 1B -1, RF -0 | 0.4 |

Oh, how timing matters. In 2010-11, Gload posted a combined .270/.304/.411 line, which is a few singles and a couple of walks shy of his career slash line. When Ruben Amaro Jr. signed Gload to a two-year deal before the 2010 season, the second year seemed like a measure of overpayment for a guy who was a bench player at best. But with the benefit of hindsight, Gload would have been better off if he had become a free agent after 2010 solely because of the superficial bump given to him by the arbitrary endpoint of the end of the 2010 season. Now he hits the free agent market as an aging lefty pinch-hitter who struggles to draw a walk.

### Ryan Howard    1B

Born: 11/19/1979 Age: 32
Bats: L Throws: L Height: 6' 5" Weight: 230
Breakout: 1% Improve: 23% Collapse: 5%
Attrition: 9% MLB: 86%

**Comparables:**
Dick Allen, Mark McGwire, Carlos Pena

| YEAR | TEAM | LVL | AGE | PA | R | 2B | 3B | HR | RBI | BB | SO | SB | CS | AVG_OBP_SLG | TAv | BABIP | BRR | FRAA | WARP |
|---|---|---|---|---|---|---|---|---|---|---|---|---|---|---|---|---|---|---|---|
| 2009 | PHI | MLB | 29 | 703 | 105 | 37 | 4 | 45 | 141 | 75 | 186 | 8 | 1 | .279/.360/.571 | .307 | .325 | -6.2 | 11 | 4.0 |
| 2010 | PHI | MLB | 30 | 620 | 87 | 23 | 5 | 31 | 108 | 59 | 157 | 1 | 1 | .276/.353/.505 | .294 | .332 | -8.3 | -3 | 1.4 |
| 2011 | PHI | MLB | 31 | 644 | 81 | 30 | 1 | 33 | 116 | 75 | 172 | 1 | 0 | .253/.346/.488 | .296 | .303 | -9.4 | 0.4 | 1.6 |
| 2012 | PHI | MLB | 32 | 600 | 81 | 24 | 2 | 35 | 91 | 67 | 171 | 2 | 1 | .252/.341/.506 | .300 | .303 | 0 | 1B 1 | 3.3 |

Not even Aeschylus could have written it more poetically. But Howard's tragic end occurred not offstage but on national television. His left Achilles tendon was shot through not with an arrow but on a grounder to second, and now he is likely to miss several months of the 2012 season. This season also marks the beginning of the five-year, $125 million contract Howard signed in 2010. It is unrealistic to expect him to perform significantly better than his established sub-Olympic heights: average defense, a True Average in the range of .290 to .300, and explosive power. Howard's most outsized weakness is against the shift: Evidence from Acta Sports suggests he loses 100 points of batting average against it. Since he hasn't figured out how to adjust yet, there isn't much reason to think he'll learn to hit the other way before his contract ends after the 2016 season. Howard's lefty-righty splits were again extreme in 2011, so pinch-hitting for him late in games—when LOOGYs will prowl—is a better idea now than ever. That's a solution that Howard's pride, not to mention his contract, is likely to preclude.

### Raul Ibañez    LF

Born: 6/2/1972 Age: 40
Bats: L Throws: R Height: 6' 3" Weight: 200
Breakout: 1% Improve: 19% Collapse: 11%
Attrition: 27% MLB: 70%

**Comparables:**
Jose Cruz, Hank Sauer, Ken Griffey

| YEAR | TEAM | LVL | AGE | PA | R | 2B | 3B | HR | RBI | BB | SO | SB | CS | AVG_OBP_SLG | TAv | BABIP | BRR | FRAA | WARP |
|---|---|---|---|---|---|---|---|---|---|---|---|---|---|---|---|---|---|---|---|
| 2009 | PHI | MLB | 37 | 565 | 93 | 32 | 3 | 34 | 93 | 56 | 119 | 4 | 0 | .272/.347/.552 | .298 | .290 | -2.4 | -7.1 | 2.2 |
| 2010 | PHI | MLB | 38 | 636 | 75 | 37 | 5 | 16 | 83 | 68 | 108 | 4 | 3 | .275/.349/.444 | .276 | .311 | -0.2 | -17 | 0.6 |
| 2011 | PHI | MLB | 39 | 575 | 65 | 31 | 1 | 20 | 84 | 33 | 106 | 2 | 0 | .245/.289/.419 | .252 | .268 | -0.6 | -4.3 | 0.0 |
| 2012 | PHI | MLB | 40 | 552 | 64 | 28 | 3 | 17 | 65 | 43 | 108 | 3 | 1 | .251/.311/.416 | .264 | .287 | -0.1 | LF -8, 1B 0 | 1.5 |

This was the worst full season of Ibañez's career, not just in total offense but also in every triple-slash category. This is what being 39 looks like. Past consistency, once a friend to the steady Ibañez, becomes a purgatory of mediocrity that is harder and harder to break out of. Despite a career .282 True Average, Ibañez finds himself with just one All-Star appearance and no World Series rings. There aren't many years left in Ibañez's body, his defense hasn't been good in a decade, and his bat is barely good enough to fill a DH role.

### Michael Martinez    2B

Born: 9/16/1982 Age: 29
Bats: B Throws: R Height: 5' 10" Weight: 145
Breakout: 2% Improve: 33% Collapse: 5%
Attrition: 23% MLB: 64%

**Comparables:**
Jamey Carroll, David Bell, Ray Olmedo

| YEAR | TEAM | LVL | AGE | PA | R | 2B | 3B | HR | RBI | BB | SO | SB | CS | AVG_OBP_SLG | TAv | BABIP | BRR | FRAA | WARP |
|---|---|---|---|---|---|---|---|---|---|---|---|---|---|---|---|---|---|---|---|
| 2009 | POT | A+ | 26 | 218 | 40 | 14 | 5 | 4 | 29 | 16 | 31 | 10 | 6 | .293/.346/.475 | .289 | .327 | 2.7 | -0.3 | 1.6 |
| 2009 | HAR | AA | 26 | 219 | 22 | 7 | 2 | 1 | 8 | 20 | 34 | 0 | 3 | .223/.307/.298 | .231 | .259 | 0.7 | -0.5 | 0.3 |
| 2010 | HAR | AA | 27 | 387 | 41 | 14 | 6 | 8 | 37 | 20 | 54 | 15 | 9 | .253/.295/.393 | .256 | .276 | 2.6 | -0.7 | 1.2 |
| 2010 | SYR | AAA | 27 | 135 | 16 | 7 | 0 | 3 | 19 | 3 | 20 | 8 | 3 | .325/.351/.452 | .269 | .362 | 2.2 | -1.1 | 0.7 |
| 2011 | PHI | MLB | 28 | 234 | 25 | 5 | 2 | 3 | 24 | 18 | 35 | 3 | 0 | .196/.258/.282 | .219 | .220 | 1.7 | -0.6 | -0.3 |
| 2012 | PHI | MLB | 29 | 250 | 24 | 9 | 2 | 3 | 22 | 13 | 45 | 6 | 3 | .229/.275/.331 | .225 | .266 | -0.5 | 2B -0, 3B -1 | 0.0 |

Selected as a Rule 5 pick from the Nationals before the season, Martinez had to remain on the major-league roster or be offered back to Washington. So remain he did, despite being on the wrong side of every line Mario Mendoza could draw in the sand. His benefit was his versatility: he filled in in center while Shane Victorino was out, at third base while Placido Polanco was out, at second base while Chase Utley was out, and at shortstop while Jimmy Rollins was out. But considering how bad his bat is, Martinez is like the converse of the Woody Allen joke from Annie Hall. One old lady eating at a restaurant says, "My, what terrible food." And the other one replies, "Yes, but such big portions!"

**John Mayberry** RF

Born: 12/21/1983 Age: 28
Bats: R Throws: R Height: 6' 7" Weight: 230
Breakout: 1% Improve: 39% Collapse: 4%
Attrition: 11% MLB: 91%

Comparables:
Cody Ross, Curtis Granderson, Rick Ankiel

| YEAR | TEAM | LVL | AGE | PA | R | 2B | 3B | HR | RBI | BB | SO | SB | CS | AVG_OBP_SLG | TAv | BABIP | BRR | FRAA | WARP |
|---|---|---|---|---|---|---|---|---|---|---|---|---|---|---|---|---|---|---|---|
| 2009 | LEH | AAA | 25 | 358 | 44 | 20 | 2 | 13 | 43 | 34 | 94 | 6 | 2 | .256/.336/.456 | .281 | .325 | -0.7 | 1 | 1.6 |
| 2009 | PHI | MLB | 25 | 60 | 8 | 3 | 0 | 4 | 8 | 2 | 23 | 0 | 0 | .211/.250/.474 | .230 | .267 | 0.2 | 0.7 | 0.1 |
| 2010 | LEH | AAA | 26 | 547 | 75 | 25 | 1 | 15 | 65 | 39 | 111 | 20 | 3 | .267/.330/.412 | .263 | .316 | 0.8 | 7.1 | 1.9 |
| 2010 | PHI | MLB | 26 | 13 | 4 | 0 | 0 | 2 | 6 | 1 | 4 | 0 | 1 | .333/.385/.833 | .398 | .333 | -1.1 | -0.1 | 0.1 |
| 2011 | LEH | AAA | 27 | 122 | 16 | 8 | 0 | 4 | 15 | 5 | 23 | 2 | 0 | .265/.287/.442 | .262 | .289 | 0.9 | -1.1 | 0.3 |
| 2011 | PHI | MLB | 27 | 296 | 37 | 17 | 1 | 15 | 49 | 26 | 55 | 8 | 3 | .273/.341/.513 | .293 | .293 | -0.4 | 0.2 | 1.7 |
| 2012 | PHI | MLB | 28 | 250 | 30 | 12 | 1 | 11 | 34 | 19 | 62 | 4 | 2 | .249/.310/.451 | .273 | .292 | -0.1 | RF -1, LF 0 | 1.7 |

Now that's how you win a starting job. Mayberry was a better hitter last year than he has ever been in his career—and by quite

Bats: R Throws: R Height: 6' 3" Weight: 200
Breakout: 0% Improve: 26% Collapse: 6%
Attrition: 20% MLB: 73%

Comparables:
Rob Butler, Barry Bonnell, Tito Francona

| YEAR | TEAM | LVL | AGE | PA | R | 2B | 3B | HR | RBI | BB | SO | SB | CS | AVG_OBP_SLG | TAv | BABIP | BRR | FRAA | WARP |
|---|---|---|---|---|---|---|---|---|---|---|---|---|---|---|---|---|---|---|---|
| 2010 | NOR | AAA | 28 | 101 | 14 | 5 | 2 | 2 | 20 | 4 | 12 | 2 | 1 | .289/.317/.443 | .266 | .313 | -0.4 | 0.3 | 0.4 |
| 2010 | BAL | MLB | 28 | 58 | 2 | 0 | 0 | 0 | 3 | 1 | 9 | 1 | 0 | .140/.155/.140 | .099 | .167 | 0 | 0.2 | -0.8 |
| 2011 | IOW | AAA | 29 | 382 | 52 | 22 | 7 | 7 | 69 | 38 | 47 | 4 | 6 | .321/.396/.492 | .301 | .355 | 0.2 | 0.8 | 2.9 |
| 2011 | CHN | MLB | 29 | 57 | 6 | 4 | 0 | 1 | 9 | 2 | 9 | 0 | 1 | .222/.263/.352 | .212 | .250 | -0.9 | 0.1 | -0.2 |
| 2012 | PHI | MLB | 30 | 250 | 28 | 12 | 2 | 5 | 28 | 13 | 43 | 2 | 2 | .258/.304/.393 | .254 | .293 | -0.4 | LF -2, RF -1 | 0.7 |

The Cubs have contributed to the disappointment in number-three overall picks in recent years with Corey Patterson (1998), Montanez (2000), and maybe Josh Vitters (2007). Back with the Cubs after four years in the Baltimore organization, Montanez put up a good year in Triple-A, which has him back in the running for a career as a spare outfielder, though he's a far cry from the promising five-tool shortstop Chicago drafted all those years ago. He signed a minor-league deal with the Phillies that includes an invite to spring training.

**Laynce Nix** LF

Born: 10/30/1980 Age: 31
Bats: L Throws: L Height: 6' 1" Weight: 190
Breakout: 2% Improve: 48% Collapse: 6%
Attrition: 14% MLB: 93%

Comparables:
Willie Horton, Ben Oglivie, Mike Easler

| YEAR | TEAM | LVL | AGE | PA | R | 2B | 3B | HR | RBI | BB | SO | SB | CS | AVG_OBP_SLG | TAv | BABIP | BRR | FRAA | WARP |
|---|---|---|---|---|---|---|---|---|---|---|---|---|---|---|---|---|---|---|---|
| 2009 | CIN | MLB | 28 | 337 | 42 | 26 | 1 | 15 | 46 | 22 | 81 | 0 | 1 | .239/.291/.476 | .262 | .272 | 1.4 | -3.5 | 0.6 |
| 2010 | CIN | MLB | 29 | 182 | 16 | 11 | 2 | 4 | 18 | 15 | 39 | 0 | 1 | .291/.350/.455 | .275 | .361 | -0.1 | -0.8 | 0.9 |
| 2011 | WAS | MLB | 30 | 351 | 38 | 15 | 1 | 16 | 44 | 23 | 82 | 2 | 2 | .250/.299/.451 | .276 | .284 | -1.6 | -2.9 | 0.9 |
| 2012 | PHI | MLB | 31 | 296 | 34 | 14 | 1 | 12 | 38 | 20 | 75 | 1 | 1 | .239/.292/.432 | .260 | .281 | -0.2 | LF -4, RF -0 | 1.0 |

The good news is that Nix is another solid power bat off the bench. The bad is news is that he's just as left-handed as the Phillies' other lefty bench options, most notably Jim Thome and Jack Cust. Nix was able to hack it as a platoon starter on the second-division Nationals, but he and his .288 career on-base percentage leave a lot of outs in the middle of the lineup. The Phillies managed to be about league average in that department last year, but 300 plate appearances of Laynce Nix might hurt their chances for a repeat.

**Hunter Pence** RF

Born: 4/13/1983 Age: 29
Bats: R Throws: R Height: 6' 5" Weight: 210
Breakout: 1% Improve: 33% Collapse: 2%
Attrition: 19% MLB: 72%

Comparables:
Corey Hart, Tim Tolman, Jim Rushford

| YEAR | TEAM | LVL | AGE | PA | R | 2B | 3B | HR | RBI | BB | SO | SB | CS | AVG_OBP_SLG | TAv | BABIP | BRR | FRAA | WARP |
|---|---|---|---|---|---|---|---|---|---|---|---|---|---|---|---|---|---|---|---|
| 2009 | HOU | MLB | 26 | 647 | 76 | 26 | 5 | 25 | 72 | 58 | 109 | 14 | 11 | .282/.346/.472 | .266 | .308 | 3 | 6.9 | 2.6 |
| 2010 | HOU | MLB | 27 | 658 | 93 | 29 | 3 | 25 | 91 | 41 | 105 | 18 | 9 | .282/.325/.461 | .280 | .304 | 3.7 | 10 | 3.9 |
| 2011 | HOU | MLB | 28 | 432 | 49 | 26 | 3 | 11 | 62 | 30 | 86 | 7 | 1 | .308/.356/.471 | .302 | .368 | 1.4 | -1 | 2.8 |
| 2011 | PHI | MLB | 28 | 236 | 35 | 12 | 2 | 11 | 35 | 26 | 38 | 1 | 1 | .324/.394/.560 | .335 | .348 | 0.2 | -3.5 | 2.3 |
| 2012 | PHI | MLB | 29 | 626 | 80 | 31 | 5 | 22 | 85 | 43 | 117 | 12 | 6 | .284/.335/.469 | .290 | .322 | -1 | RF 4 | 3.0 |

In his second game with the Phillies, Pence scored the game-winning run in the bottom of the tenth. After the game, Sarge Matthews asked him what was going through his mind as he rounded third base.

Pence's reply: "Great game. Let's go eat." That he doesn't overthink things is what inures him to baseball's traditionalists. But don't let that sour you on him. Pence's age-28 season was the best of his career, and it got even better after he came to Philly. He upped his walk and power rates and showed off his impressive arm strength in right. It'll cost the Phillies that the Astros went to arbitration with Pence last year and lost (meaning he made $6.9 million instead of $5.15 million), but in all likelihood that just lowered the price the Phillies had to pay to acquire him. The Phillies will happily pay his escalating salary for two more years if he can produce like he did last year. Despite surgery on a sports hernia in the offseason, there are reasons to be optimistic about Pence, even if he can't produce at the high level he did for two months in Philadelphia.

### Placido Polanco — 3B

Born: 10/10/1975 Age: 36
Bats: R Throws: R Height: 5' 11" Weight: 168
Breakout: 0% Improve: 19% Collapse: 16%
Attrition: 27% MLB: 70%

**Comparables:**
Wade Boggs, Bill Madlock, Buddy Bell

| YEAR | TEAM | LVL | AGE | PA | R | 2B | 3B | HR | RBI | BB | SO | SB | CS | AVG_OBP_SLG | TAv | BABIP | BRR | FRAA | WARP |
|------|------|-----|-----|-----|----|----|----|----|-----|----|----|----|----|-------------|------|-------|------|----------|------|
| 2009 | DET | MLB | 33 | 675 | 82 | 31 | 4 | 10 | 72 | 36 | 46 | 7 | 2 | .285/.331/.396 | .258 | .293 | 0.8 | 3.4 | 2.3 |
| 2010 | PHI | MLB | 34 | 602 | 76 | 27 | 2 | 6 | 52 | 32 | 47 | 5 | 0 | .298/.339/.386 | .262 | .312 | 1.9 | 8.5 | 2.6 |
| 2011 | PHI | MLB | 35 | 523 | 46 | 14 | 0 | 5 | 50 | 42 | 44 | 3 | 0 | .277/.335/.339 | .245 | .292 | -2 | 13.3 | 2.1 |
| 2012 | PHI | MLB | 36 | 508 | 57 | 22 | 2 | 5 | 47 | 28 | 45 | 4 | 1 | .280/.327/.366 | .256 | .298 | 0.2 | 3B 9, 2B -0 | 1.8 |

Polly had a scorching April (.398/.447/.524), one that propelled him to the All-Star game and glory in Philadelphia. That he followed it with a .248/.289/.294 May and a .213/.279/.266 June demonstrates how fleeting April stats can be. Two trips to the disabled list (lower back and sports hernia) knocked Polanco out of the lineup during the summer. When he returned, he hit a more respectable .282/.350/.331. His defense remains strong, and like Pence he had surgery to repair the sports hernia in the offseason, so despite the declining bat, Polanco is a good bet to earn his $6.25 million salary in the last year of his contract.

### Matt Rizzotti — 1B

Born: 12/24/1985 Age: 26
Bats: L Throws: L Height: 6' 6" Weight: 265
Breakout: 5% Improve: 30% Collapse: 2%
Attrition: 18% MLB: 70%

**Comparables:**
Willie Aikens, Luis Antonio Jimenez, Travis Hafner

| YEAR | TEAM | LVL | AGE | PA | R | 2B | 3B | HR | RBI | BB | SO | SB | CS | AVG_OBP_SLG | TAv | BABIP | BRR | FRAA | WARP |
|------|------|-----|-----|-----|----|----|----|----|-----|----|-----|----|----|-------------|------|-------|------|------|------|
| 2009 | CLR | A+ | 23 | 404 | 44 | 26 | 1 | 13 | 58 | 48 | 91 | 0 | 0 | .263/.355/.454 | .282 | .321 | -2.2 | -0.9 | 0.8 |
| 2010 | CLR | A+ | 24 | 122 | 18 | 8 | 1 | 1 | 10 | 13 | 22 | 0 | 0 | .358/.426/.477 | .318 | .442 | 0.1 | -0.6 | 0.8 |
| 2010 | REA | AA | 24 | 310 | 48 | 25 | 0 | 16 | 62 | 40 | 56 | 1 | 1 | .361/.452/.635 | .363 | .412 | 1.8 | 0.1 | 3.7 |
| 2010 | LEH | AAA | 24 | 52 | 0 | 3 | 0 | 0 | 4 | 6 | 14 | 0 | 0 | .200/.308/.267 | .179 | .290 | 0 | -0.5 | -0.4 |
| 2011 | REA | AA | 25 | 587 | 73 | 34 | 1 | 24 | 84 | 79 | 125 | 4 | 1 | .295/.392/.511 | .301 | .346 | -6.1 | -2.2 | 2.5 |
| 2012 | PHI | MLB | 26 | 250 | 29 | 11 | 1 | 8 | 28 | 25 | 63 | 1 | 0 | .236/.315/.405 | .260 | .288 | 0 | 1B -8 | 0.6 |

Hitters, hitters everywhere, and not a one a righty. Rizzotti's return to Reading wasn't nearly as eye-catching as his first go-round, but he proved the breakout wasn't a complete fluke. The biggest puzzle here is why he wasn't promoted more aggressively given his age. As it was, Rizzotti treaded water at an age where that is no better than moving backward. He might be a good trade chip for a second-division team.

### Jimmy Rollins — SS

Born: 11/27/1978 Age: 33
Bats: B Throws: R Height: 5' 9" Weight: 160
Breakout: 2% Improve: 34% Collapse: 7%
Attrition: 13% MLB: 94%

**Comparables:**
Jerry Hairston, Cal Ripken Jr., Alan Trammell

| YEAR | TEAM | LVL | AGE | PA | R | 2B | 3B | HR | RBI | BB | SO | SB | CS | AVG_OBP_SLG | TAv | BABIP | BRR | FRAA | WARP |
|------|------|-----|-----|-----|-----|----|----|----|-----|----|----|----|----|-------------|------|-------|------|-------|------|
| 2009 | PHI | MLB | 30 | 725 | 100 | 43 | 5 | 21 | 77 | 44 | 70 | 31 | 8 | .250/.296/.423 | .246 | .251 | 1.2 | -13.4 | 0.2 |
| 2010 | PHI | MLB | 31 | 394 | 48 | 16 | 3 | 8 | 41 | 40 | 32 | 17 | 1 | .243/.320/.374 | .261 | .246 | 0.3 | -3.3 | 1.1 |
| 2011 | PHI | MLB | 32 | 631 | 87 | 22 | 2 | 16 | 63 | 58 | 59 | 30 | 8 | .268/.338/.399 | .272 | .275 | -0.1 | 1.1 | 3.6 |
| 2012 | PHI | MLB | 33 | 548 | 64 | 26 | 6 | 13 | 64 | 40 | 60 | 25 | 5 | .258/.316/.413 | .267 | .268 | 1.1 | SS -3 | 2.9 |

The last of the big pieces of the 2012 team to fall into place, Rollins and the Phillies were destined for each other. There were few options available in the free agent market that could produce the two or three wins the Phillies wanted at shortstop without costing more than the $12 million per year they had available to spend. Rafael Furcal was too risky, Jose Reyes too pricey, and internal option Freddy Galvis was a too lousy a hitter. Meanwhile, Rollins proved his worth by staying healthy, hitting better for average by avoiding looking for the long ball, and playing solid defense. His decline over the life of the deal should be gradual, but just hope he isn't still batting leadoff in three years.

### Carlos Ruiz — C

Born: 1/22/1979 Age: 33
Bats: R Throws: R Height: 6' 1" Weight: 170
Breakout: 1% Improve: 29% Collapse: 6%
Attrition: 28% MLB: 80%

**Comparables:**
Clint Courtney, Earl Battey, Tim McCarver

| YEAR | TEAM | LVL | AGE | PA | R | 2B | 3B | HR | RBI | BB | SO | SB | CS | AVG_OBP_SLG | TAv | BABIP | BRR | FRAA | WARP |
|------|------|-----|-----|-----|----|----|----|----|-----|----|----|----|----|-------------|------|-------|------|------|------|
| 2009 | PHI | MLB | 30 | 379 | 32 | 26 | 1 | 9 | 43 | 47 | 39 | 3 | 2 | .255/.355/.425 | .264 | .264 | -2.8 | 0.3 | 1.6 |
| 2010 | PHI | MLB | 31 | 433 | 43 | 28 | 1 | 8 | 53 | 55 | 54 | 0 | 1 | .302/.400/.447 | .295 | .335 | -4.6 | 0.9 | 3.1 |
| 2011 | PHI | MLB | 32 | 472 | 49 | 23 | 0 | 6 | 40 | 48 | 48 | 1 | 0 | .283/.371/.383 | .281 | .308 | -1.7 | 0.7 | 3.1 |
| 2012 | PHI | MLB | 33 | 437 | 50 | 23 | 1 | 6 | 40 | 46 | 54 | 2 | 1 | .256/.344/.371 | .265 | .280 | -0.1 | C 1 | 2.3 |

In True Average terms, Ruiz split the difference between his 2009 and his 2010, and the result was another very good season from the veteran backstop. He set a career high in games played, runs, and hits. And while he caught a career low 23% of base runners, he consistently ranks well among catchers in block percentage. The only knock on his defense comes from Mike Fast's research into pitch framing (in which Ruiz ranked in the bottom third of catchers), but good luck getting Roy Halladay to agree on that count.

### Brian Schneider    C

Born: 11/26/1976 Age: 35
Bats: L Throws: R Height: 6' 2" Weight: 200
Breakout: 0% Improve: 33% Collapse: 9%
Attrition: 31% MLB: 80%

Comparables:
Bob Boone, Ron Hassey, Tom Lampkin

| YEAR | TEAM | LVL | AGE | PA | R | 2B | 3B | HR | RBI | BB | SO | SB | CS | AVG_OBP_SLG | TAv | BABIP | BRR | FRAA | WARP |
|------|------|-----|-----|----|---|----|----|----|-----|----|----|----|----|-------------|-----|-------|-----|------|------|
| 2009 | NYN | MLB | 32 | 194 | 11 | 11 | 0 | 3 | 24 | 18 | 21 | 0 | 0 | .218/.292/.335 | .230 | .228 | -1.5 | 1.9 | 0.2 |
| 2010 | PHI | MLB | 33 | 147 | 17 | 4 | 1 | 4 | 15 | 19 | 25 | 0 | 0 | .240/.345/.384 | .251 | .271 | 1.3 | -0.6 | 0.5 |
| 2011 | PHI | MLB | 34 | 139 | 11 | 4 | 0 | 2 | 9 | 11 | 35 | 0 | 0 | .176/.246/.256 | .186 | .225 | -1.5 | -0.1 | -0.7 |
| 2012 | PHI | MLB | 35 | 250 | 25 | 9 | 1 | 4 | 19 | 25 | 40 | 0 | 0 | .223/.305/.318 | .232 | .253 | 0 | C -0 | 0.7 |

Just as backup catchers can have fluke good seasons because of the relatively small number of

Comparables:
Hank Aaron, Frank Robinson, Willie Stargell

| YEAR | TEAM | LVL | AGE | PA | R | 2B | 3B | HR | RBI | BB | SO | SB | CS | AVG_OBP_SLG | TAv | BABIP | BRR | FRAA | WARP |
|------|------|-----|-----|----|---|----|----|----|-----|----|----|----|----|-------------|-----|-------|-----|------|------|
| 2011 | MIN | MLB | 40 | 242 | 21 | 12 | 0 | 12 | 40 | 35 | 69 | 0 | 0 | .243/.351/.476 | .296 | .302 | -3.8 | 0 | 0.8 |
| 2011 | CLE | MLB | 40 | 82 | 11 | 4 | 0 | 3 | 10 | 11 | 23 | 0 | 0 | .296/.390/.479 | .314 | .400 | 0.3 | 0 | 0.6 |
| 2012 | PHI | MLB | 41 | 308 | 40 | 11 | 1 | 16 | 41 | 46 | 86 | 0 | 0 | .236/.352/.469 | .295 | .284 | 0 | — | 2.2 |

Last summer, Thome became the eighth member of baseball's 600 home-run club. In the second stop of his reunion tour, he returns to the town that watched him hit number 400. One of the most remarkable things about Thome's career is the way he has won over audiences in each of the towns he has played in. This despite his obvious deficiencies as a ballplayer: his plodding defense, his frequent strikeouts, and his increasingly frequent injuries. It's the same in Philly, where fans couldn't have been more eager to welcome back a slugger who only spent three years there—and one was equal parts injured and ineffective. But it's not just sentimentalism: Thome's bat has retained a remarkable amount of life and will provide a menacing threat at Manuel's disposal, both during Howard's absence and afterward.

### Chase Utley    2B

Born: 12/17/1978 Age: 33
Bats: L Throws: R Height: 6' 2" Weight: 170
Breakout: 0% Improve: 24% Collapse: 4%
Attrition: 9% MLB: 92%

Comparables:
Chipper Jones, Joe Morgan, George Brett

| YEAR | TEAM | LVL | AGE | PA | R | 2B | 3B | HR | RBI | BB | SO | SB | CS | AVG_OBP_SLG | TAv | BABIP | BRR | FRAA | WARP |
|------|------|-----|-----|----|---|----|----|----|-----|----|----|----|----|-------------|-----|-------|-----|------|------|
| 2009 | PHI | MLB | 30 | 687 | 112 | 28 | 4 | 31 | 93 | 88 | 110 | 23 | 0 | .282/.397/.508 | .311 | .300 | 2.2 | 7.7 | 6.4 |
| 2010 | PHI | MLB | 31 | 511 | 75 | 20 | 2 | 16 | 65 | 63 | 63 | 13 | 2 | .275/.387/.445 | .302 | .288 | 2 | 7.5 | 5.0 |
| 2011 | PHI | MLB | 32 | 454 | 54 | 21 | 6 | 11 | 44 | 39 | 47 | 14 | 0 | .259/.344/.425 | .278 | .269 | 0.9 | 8.6 | 2.9 |
| 2012 | PHI | MLB | 33 | 445 | 59 | 22 | 3 | 16 | 57 | 43 | 68 | 11 | 1 | .273/.366/.466 | .301 | .294 | 0.9 | 2B 3 | 3.5 |

Last season was the worst of Utley's career, the first time in five years he missed the All-Star game, and the shortest since his breakout as a regular. The last of those is thanks to knee inflammation that knocked him out for the first 45 games of the season. Utley is the type of player that wants to play through every injury, so there is no guarantee that the patellar tendinitis that forced him under the knife won't jump back up to nip him again. The Phillies owe him $30 million over the next two seasons, but even a pair of seasons like 2011 would be just about enough to make Utley worth it. But given the composition of the Phillies roster—clearly designed to win in the short term—the Phillies have to hope for more than this. Whether he's up to it is a secret held by Utley and his orthopedic surgeon.

### Wilson Valdez    SS

Born: 5/20/1978 Age: 34
Bats: R Throws: R Height: 6' 0" Weight: 160
Breakout: 2% Improve: 25% Collapse: 10%
Attrition: 36% MLB: 82%

Comparables:
Bobby Avila, Nelson Liriano, Aaron Miles

| YEAR | TEAM | LVL | AGE | PA | R | 2B | 3B | HR | RBI | BB | SO | SB | CS | AVG_OBP_SLG | TAv | BABIP | BRR | FRAA | WARP |
|------|------|-----|-----|----|---|----|----|----|-----|----|----|----|----|-------------|-----|-------|-----|------|------|
| 2009 | BUF | AAA | 31 | 126 | 13 | 4 | 0 | 0 | 6 | 7 | 10 | 1 | 1 | .298/.336/.333 | .248 | .318 | 2.2 | 0.9 | 0.7 |
| 2009 | COH | AAA | 31 | 137 | 17 | 1 | 0 | 0 | 6 | 10 | 19 | 5 | 1 | .198/.257/.207 | .184 | .226 | 2.6 | -1.2 | -0.6 |
| 2009 | NYN | MLB | 31 | 95 | 11 | 3 | 2 | 0 | 7 | 8 | 10 | 0 | 1 | .256/.326/.337 | .218 | .289 | 0.3 | -1.2 | -0.2 |
| 2010 | PHI | MLB | 32 | 363 | 37 | 16 | 3 | 4 | 35 | 21 | 43 | 7 | 0 | .258/.306/.360 | .226 | .287 | 2.9 | -2 | -0.1 |
| 2011 | PHI | MLB | 33 | 300 | 39 | 14 | 4 | 1 | 30 | 18 | 41 | 3 | 3 | .249/.294/.341 | .223 | .288 | 3.2 | -2 | -0.3 |
| 2012 | PHI | MLB | 34 | 298 | 30 | 12 | 2 | 1 | 24 | 19 | 42 | 5 | 2 | .255/.306/.328 | .234 | .291 | -0.3 | SS -2, 2B -0 | 0.4 |

If you're reading this book, you've probably had the experience of trying to explain the concept of "replacement level" to a friend or family member. They usually want to get a real-world comp for replacement level. Valdez is a good example, at least among shortstops. He's a good explanation of why we assume replacement-level players sport average defense: Valdez certainly plays passable short. He's a good example of the fact that, while replacement-level players are not free, they can be retained on a series of minor-league or near-minimum contracts. In small doses, he's good medicine. But if too many injuries stack on the roster, you end up with baseball's lowest common denominator.

**Sebastian Valle**  C

Born: 7/24/1990 Age: 21
Bats: R Throws: L Height: 6' 2" Weight: 170
Breakout: 1% Improve: 6% Collapse: 3%
Attrition: 6% MLB: 12%

Comparables:
Welington Castillo, Mark Thomas, Juan Apodaca

| YEAR | TEAM | LVL | AGE | PA | R | 2B | 3B | HR | RBI | BB | SO | SB | CS | AVG_OBP_SLG | TAv | BABIP | BRR | FRAA | WARP |
|------|------|-----|-----|-----|----|----|----|----|-----|----|-----|----|----|-------------|------|-------|------|------|------|
| 2009 | LWD | A | 18 | 179 | 16 | 12 | 1 | 1 | 15 | 16 | 37 | 1 | 2 | .223/.315/.331 | .265 | .286 | -0.6 | 0.7 | 0.2 |
| 2009 | WPT | A- | 18 | 206 | 25 | 15 | 5 | 6 | 40 | 10 | 41 | 0 | 0 | .307/.342/.531 | .316 | .366 | -0.3 | 1.5 | 2.0 |
| 2010 | LWD | A | 19 | 485 | 51 | 28 | 1 | 16 | 74 | 27 | 101 | 3 | 2 | .255/.301/.430 | .258 | .295 | -1.3 | 3.2 | 2.3 |
| 2011 | CLR | A+ | 20 | 365 | 34 | 19 | 2 | 5 | 40 | 13 | 84 | 0 | 0 | .284/.312/.394 | .243 | .360 | -0.5 | 0.1 | 1.1 |
| 2012 | PHI | MLB | 21 | 250 | 22 | 11 | 1 | 4 | 24 | 7 | 69 | 0 | 0 | .218/.242/.326 | .206 | .283 | 0 | C 1 | -0.6 |

Valle held his own as a twenty-year-old in the Florida State League, but more importantly he showed big improvements in his defensive abilities. Once considered a weak defender despite a strong arm, Valle's athletic build has allowed him to develop a more three-dimensional game. That's good, because the flaws in his approach at the plate are become increasingly obvious. Schooled at the Olivo–Barajas school of catcher batting philosophy (suggested motto: "You Can't Walk to Second Base!"), Valle had a walk rate of just 3.6%. He also lost the power he had shown in the previous two years. He is still young, though, and Carlos Ruiz is still a bargain, so Valle has time to develop.

**Shane Victorino**  CF

Born: 11/30/1980 Age: 31
Bats: B Throws: R Height: 5' 10" Weight: 160
Breakout: 0% Improve: 44% Collapse: 3%
Attrition: 11% MLB: 90%

Comparables:
Vernon Wells, Robin Yount, Jody Gerut

| YEAR | TEAM | LVL | AGE | PA | R | 2B | 3B | HR | RBI | BB | SO | SB | CS | AVG_OBP_SLG | TAv | BABIP | BRR | FRAA | WARP |
|------|------|-----|-----|-----|-----|----|----|----|-----|----|----|----|----|-------------|------|-------|------|-------|------|
| 2009 | PHI | MLB | 28 | 694 | 102 | 39 | 13 | 10 | 62 | 60 | 71 | 25 | 8 | .292/.358/.445 | .277 | .315 | 2.5 | -17.1 | 1.9 |
| 2010 | PHI | MLB | 29 | 648 | 84 | 26 | 10 | 18 | 69 | 53 | 79 | 34 | 6 | .259/.327/.429 | .266 | .273 | 5.8 | 4.9 | 3.6 |
| 2011 | PHI | MLB | 30 | 586 | 95 | 27 | 16 | 17 | 61 | 55 | 63 | 19 | 3 | .279/.355/.491 | .301 | .292 | 5.4 | 5.1 | 5.3 |
| 2012 | PHI | MLB | 31 | 567 | 69 | 26 | 8 | 13 | 67 | 44 | 70 | 24 | 6 | .271/.336/.428 | .277 | .290 | 0.5 | CF 1 | 2.9 |

Through the morning of September 1, Victorino's triple-slash line was .305/.382/.539. A much weaker September (.186/.258/.319) dropped him all the way to 13th in MVP voting, but a stronger finish might have put him in contention for greater consideration. He had the best slugging percentage and OPS on the team, and the second-best OBP on the team. His league-leading 16 triples helped him reach 60 extra-base hits, and despite a drop in stolen bases, his base running value was almost identical to what it was in 2010. He was twice knocked to the DL by a sprained thumb caused by a blooper-reel worthy groaner in center, but it's an injury that isn't chronic. Despite the injuries, this was the best season of Victorino's career. A totally healthy 2012 could prove even better, but it's more likely this season was the best we'll see from him.

**Ty Wigginton**  1B

Born: 10/11/1977 Age: 34
Bats: R Throws: R Height: 6' 1" Weight: 200
Breakout: 1% Improve: 31% Collapse: 9%
Attrition: 17% MLB: 85%

Comparables:
Ken Caminiti, Casey Blake, Michael Young

| YEAR | TEAM | LVL | AGE | PA | R | 2B | 3B | HR | RBI | BB | SO | SB | CS | AVG_OBP_SLG | TAv | BABIP | BRR | FRAA | WARP |
|------|------|-----|-----|-----|----|----|----|----|-----|----|-----|----|----|-------------|------|-------|------|-----------|------|
| 2009 | BAL | MLB | 31 | 436 | 44 | 19 | 0 | 11 | 41 | 23 | 57 | 1 | 2 | .273/.314/.400 | .239 | .294 | -1.8 | -8.7 | -1.1 |
| 2010 | BAL | MLB | 32 | 649 | 63 | 29 | 1 | 22 | 76 | 50 | 116 | 0 | 1 | .248/.312/.415 | .259 | .270 | -2 | 2.6 | 1.1 |
| 2011 | COL | MLB | 33 | 446 | 52 | 21 | 2 | 15 | 47 | 38 | 84 | 8 | 1 | .242/.315/.416 | .252 | .271 | 0.9 | -1.4 | -0.6 |
| 2012 | PHI | MLB | 34 | 461 | 54 | 21 | 1 | 15 | 55 | 31 | 85 | 4 | 2 | .253/.312/.417 | .266 | .283 | -0.4 | 1B -1, 3B -3 | 1.4 |

If you were asked to name active players with 1,000 hits and 150 home runs in their career, you would be excused for forgetting Wigginton. He crossed both thresholds in 2011 despite being less than useful at the plate (and even less useful than that in the field). Thanks to Ian Stewart's collapse, Wigginton logged 520 1/3 innings at third base, which is at least 520 more than he should have. Wigginton, who is sort of his generation's Ed Sprague, launched 13 homers by the All-Star break. For the second straight season, he faded down the stretch, hitting .230/.320/.329 with just two bombs in the second half. With his defensive deficiencies, that kind of production will push him out of baseball faster than you can say Kristen Babb. The Phillies picked him up for a PTBNL to fill in half of a possible first-base platoon while Ryan Howard is out.

# PITCHERS

**Phillippe Aumont**
Born: 1/7/1989 Age: 23
Bats: R Throws: R Height: 6' 8" Weight: 255
Breakout: 31% Improve: 55% Collapse: 25%
Attrition: 17% MLB: 89%
Comparables:
Neil Allen, Dennys Reyes, Ken Cloude

| YEAR | TEAM | LVL | AGE | W | L | SV | G | GS | IP | H | HR | BB | SO | EqBB9 | EqSO9 | GB% | BABIP | WHIP | ERA | FIP | FRA | WARP |
|---|---|---|---|---|---|---|---|---|---|---|---|---|---|---|---|---|---|---|---|---|---|---|
| 2009 | HDS | A+ | 20 | 1 | 2 | 12 | 29 | 0 | 33¹ | 24 | 3 | 12 | 35 | 3.2 | 9.5 | 53% | .247 | 1.08 | 3.24 | 4.09 | 4.94 | 0.3 |
| 2010 | CLR | A+ | 21 | 2 | 4 | 1 | 16 | 10 | 72¹ | 64 | 5 | 31 | 61 | 5.2 | 9.6 | 43% | .355 | 1.60 | 4.48 | 4.24 | 4.96 | 0.3 |
| 2010 | REA | AA | 21 | 0 | 5 | 0 | 11 | 11 | 49² | 38 | 2 | 23 | 23 | 6.9 | 6.9 | 49% | .324 | 1.87 | 7.42 | 4.94 | 6.06 | -0.1 |
| 2011 | REA | AA | 22 | 0 | 1 | 4 | 25 | 0 | 31 | 23 | 2 | 11 | 40 | 3.2 | 11.9 | 60% | .280 | 1.10 | 2.32 | 2.83 | 4.08 | 0.4 |
| 2011 | LEH | AAA | 22 | 1 | 0 | 3 | 18 | 0 | 22² | 25 | 0 | 18 | 45 | 5.6 | 14.7 | 50% | .417 | 1.54 | 3.18 | 1.92 | 4.11 | 0.5 |
| 2012 | PHI | MLB | 23 | 1 | 1 | 0 | 10 | 3 | 25 | 24 | 3 | 13 | 20 | 4.8 | 7.3 | 48% | .313 | 1.49 | 5.06 | 4.72 | 5.50 | -0.1 |

*Le rondelle roule pour lui!* The French-Canadian Aumont had a renaissance season as a late-inning fireman at Double- and Triple-A. The biggest improvement was in his strikeout rate, which jumped above where it had been in 2009, his last year in the Seattle system—the season that led to the Phillies' interest in the first place. While Aumont hasn't completely defeated

Comparables:
Chris Ray, Steve Bedrosian, Jeff Stevens

| YEAR | TEAM | LVL | AGE | W | L | SV | G | GS | IP | H | HR | BB | SO | EqBB9 | EqSO9 | GB% | BABIP | WHIP | ERA | FIP | FRA | WARP |
|---|---|---|---|---|---|---|---|---|---|---|---|---|---|---|---|---|---|---|---|---|---|---|
| 2011 | PHI | MLB | 25 | 6 | 1 | 8 | 64 | 0 | 58 | 28 | 6 | 26 | 70 | 4.0 | 10.9 | 27% | .182 | 0.93 | 2.64 | 3.27 | 3.33 | 0.9 |
| 2012 | PHI | MLB | 26 | 3 | 1 | 2 | 50 | 0 | 43¹ | 35 | 5 | 18 | 41 | 3.8 | 8.5 | 34% | .286 | 1.23 | 3.71 | 4.06 | 4.03 | 0.5 |

The wonders that former minor-league starters can work in the pen are why smart folks get upset when guys like Danys Baez get two-year deals. Bastardo was one of the better lefty specialists in the game last year. In fact, he was so good he was briefly thrust into the closer role while Ryan Madson was out. That's a role it's possible to imagine Bastardo one day filling, despite the fact that he faces New Jersey when he pitches. He's got roughly even splits, throws a decent changeup to go along with his wipeout slider, and has good mound presence. In the meantime, the Phillies have a nice eighth-inning guy they can leave in against the occasional righty, and they didn't even have to give him a multi-year contract.

**Jesse Biddle**
Born: 10/22/1991 Age: 20
Bats: L Throws: L Height: 6' 5" Weight: 225
Breakout: 20% Improve: 42% Collapse: 44%
Attrition: 27% MLB: 95%
Comparables:
Mike McCormick, Bruce Robbins, Chris Zachary

| YEAR | TEAM | LVL | AGE | W | L | SV | G | GS | IP | H | HR | BB | SO | EqBB9 | EqSO9 | GB% | BABIP | WHIP | ERA | FIP | FRA | WARP |
|---|---|---|---|---|---|---|---|---|---|---|---|---|---|---|---|---|---|---|---|---|---|---|
| 2010 | PHL | RK | 18 | 3 | 1 | 0 | 9 | 9 | 33¹ | 34 | 2 | 8 | 38 | 2.4 | 11.1 | 45% | .386 | 1.32 | 4.32 | 2.99 | 4.99 | 0.7 |
| 2011 | LWD | A | 19 | 4 | 6 | 0 | 25 | 24 | 133 | 104 | 5 | 66 | 124 | 4.5 | 8.4 | 43% | .284 | 1.28 | 2.98 | 3.71 | 3.97 | 1.3 |
| 2012 | PHI | MLB | 20 | 2 | 2 | 0 | 8 | 8 | 36 | 36 | 4 | 20 | 24 | 5.0 | 5.9 | 42% | .305 | 1.54 | 5.26 | 4.98 | 5.71 | -0.2 |

The Phillies' number-one pick in the 2010 draft, Biddle took big steps forward in his first full season. His good, sinking fastball lost some life from 2010, but it still let him get away with some nibbling in the Sally League, especially as the season wore on. After the All-Star break, Biddle had 64 strikeouts (against 30 walks) and just three home runs in 66 innings to go with a 1.91 ERA in 11 starts. The biggest reason for his strong finish was the development of his secondary offerings (curveball and change), but the Germantown Friends School grad still has a way to go before he becomes the next Biddle to make a name for himself in Philadelphia.

**Joe Blanton**
Born: 12/11/1980 Age: 31
Bats: R Throws: R Height: 6' 4" Weight: 225
Breakout: 14% Improve: 43% Collapse: 33%
Attrition: 6% MLB: 82%
Comparables:
Gil Heredia, Wilbur Wood, Dave Schmidt

| YEAR | TEAM | LVL | AGE | W | L | SV | G | GS | IP | H | HR | BB | SO | EqBB9 | EqSO9 | GB% | BABIP | WHIP | ERA | FIP | FRA | WARP |
|---|---|---|---|---|---|---|---|---|---|---|---|---|---|---|---|---|---|---|---|---|---|---|
| 2009 | PHI | MLB | 28 | 12 | 8 | 0 | 31 | 31 | 195¹ | 198 | 30 | 59 | 163 | 2.7 | 7.5 | 42% | .297 | 1.32 | 4.05 | 4.41 | 4.85 | 1.4 |
| 2010 | PHI | MLB | 29 | 9 | 6 | 0 | 29 | 28 | 175² | 206 | 27 | 43 | 134 | 2.2 | 6.9 | 42% | .324 | 1.42 | 4.82 | 4.36 | 4.79 | 0.8 |
| 2011 | PHI | MLB | 30 | 1 | 2 | 0 | 11 | 8 | 41¹ | 52 | 5 | 9 | 35 | 2.0 | 7.6 | 58% | .376 | 1.48 | 5.01 | 3.60 | 4.45 | 0.1 |
| 2012 | PHI | MLB | 31 | 4 | 3 | 0 | 11 | 11 | 59² | 60 | 7 | 13 | 37 | 2.0 | 5.6 | 46% | .302 | 1.23 | 4.11 | 4.14 | 4.46 | 0.4 |

Remember him? Blanton started the season as a sort of latter-day Pete Smith, forgotten-man type among the Phillies' four aces. After six middling starts, Blanton succumbed to an elbow injury in May and only returned in a relief role in September. He did look sharp in 11 innings there, and all indications are that he is now healthy. With the departure of Roy Oswalt and the emergence of Vance Worley, Blanton will once again slot in the back of the rotation for the last year of his three-year contract. Whether he'll be forgotten again depends on his ability to take the ball every fifth day.

### Brody Colvin

Born: 8/14/1990 Age: 21
Bats: R Throws: R Height: 6' 4" Weight: 195
Breakout: 28% Improve: 61% Collapse: 14%
Attrition: 7% MLB: 83%

**Comparables:**
Bob Miller, Dan Petry, Rick Wise

| YEAR | TEAM | LVL | AGE | W | L | SV | G | GS | IP | H | HR | BB | SO | EqBB9 | EqSO9 | GB% | BABIP | WHIP | ERA | FIP | FRA | WARP |
|---|---|---|---|---|---|---|---|---|---|---|---|---|---|---|---|---|---|---|---|---|---|---|
| 2010 | LWD | A | 19 | 6 | 8 | 0 | 27 | 27 | 138 | 78 | 7 | 30 | 77 | 2.7 | 7.8 | 51% | .282 | 1.30 | 3.39 | 4.01 | 4.56 | 1.0 |
| 2011 | CLR | A+ | 20 | 1 | 3 | 0 | 22 | 21 | 116² | 131 | 10 | 42 | 78 | 3.2 | 6.0 | 49% | .328 | 1.48 | 4.71 | 4.51 | 5.53 | 0.1 |
| 2012 | PHI | MLB | 21 | 2 | 2 | 0 | 7 | 7 | 38 | 41 | 5 | 17 | 19 | 4.1 | 4.4 | 46% | .304 | 1.53 | 5.66 | 5.26 | 6.15 | -0.4 |

Colvin was the biggest disappointment among the Phillies' top prospects, as his turn in the usually pitcher-friendly Florida State League alternated between injured and disappointing. Placed on the disabled list in April with a back injury, Colvin had lost his swing-and-miss ability when he returned. He still generated plenty of groundballs, some of which went for hits out of Colvin's control, but he never got into the groove many expected after a strong 2010. Enough of his season was beset by injury that significant upside remains, as evidenced by an eight-inning, nine-strikeout game in July in which he allowed just three hits. Nevertheless, his stock needs rehabilitation, and his star has been eclipsed by those of Biddle and Trevor May.

### Jose Contreras

Born: 12/6/1971 Age: 40
Bats: R Throws: R Height: 6' 5" Weight: 224
Breakout: 27% Improve: 53% Collapse: 19%
Attrition: 10% MLB: 71%

**Comparables:**
Marv Grissom, Ron Reed, Gene Garber

| YEAR | TEAM | LVL | AGE | W | L | SV | G | GS | IP | H | HR | BB | SO | EqBB9 | EqSO9 | GB% | BABIP | WHIP | ERA | FIP | FRA | WARP |
|---|---|---|---|---|---|---|---|---|---|---|---|---|---|---|---|---|---|---|---|---|---|---|
| 2009 | COL | MLB | 37 | 1 | 0 | 0 | 7 | 2 | 17 | 20 | 2 | 8 | 17 | 4.2 | 9.0 | 47% | .391 | 1.65 | 1.59 | 4.00 | 2.62 | 0.6 |
| 2009 | CHA | MLB | 37 | 5 | 13 | 0 | 21 | 21 | 114² | 121 | 11 | 45 | 89 | 3.5 | 7.0 | 50% | .310 | 1.45 | 5.42 | 4.17 | 5.03 | 0.9 |
| 2010 | PHI | MLB | 38 | 6 | 4 | 4 | 67 | 0 | 56² | 53 | 5 | 16 | 57 | 2.5 | 9.1 | 47% | .327 | 1.22 | 3.34 | 3.30 | 4.23 | 0.5 |
| 2011 | PHI | MLB | 39 | 0 | 0 | 5 | 17 | 0 | 14 | 11 | 0 | 8 | 13 | 5.1 | 8.4 | 47% | .297 | 1.36 | 3.86 | 3.07 | 2.58 | 0.3 |
| 2012 | PHI | MLB | 40 | 1 | 0 | 1 | 25 | 0 | 20² | 21 | 2 | 7 | 13 | 2.9 | 5.7 | 49% | .305 | 1.32 | 4.53 | 4.22 | 4.93 | 0.0 |

There! In the bullpen! It's an aging Cuban relief star! Give him a two-year deal! No, Contreras serves as yet another reminder why giving multi-year deals to older relievers is a mistake. Contreras got a guaranteed $5.5 million in the contract he signed after his fine 2010, but he didn't even make it to the All-Star break before he succumbed to elbow surgery. The Phillies hope to have him back on the mound in April, but there are no guarantees in his rehab process. When healthy, Contreras and his splitter are useful assets in the bullpen, but given his injuries he will have a hard time earning his salary.

### Justin De Fratus

Born: 10/21/1987 Age: 24
Bats: B Throws: R Height: 6' 5" Weight: 220
Breakout: 23% Improve: 54% Collapse: 18%
Attrition: 14% MLB: 90%

**Comparables:**
Noah Lowry, Chris Carpenter, John Verhoeven

| YEAR | TEAM | LVL | AGE | W | L | SV | G | GS | IP | H | HR | BB | SO | EqBB9 | EqSO9 | GB% | BABIP | WHIP | ERA | FIP | FRA | WARP |
|---|---|---|---|---|---|---|---|---|---|---|---|---|---|---|---|---|---|---|---|---|---|---|
| 2009 | LWD | A | 21 | 5 | 6 | 3 | 36 | 12 | 110 | 108 | 3 | 16 | 101 | 1.3 | 8.3 | 58% | .329 | 1.13 | 3.19 | 2.69 | 4.08 | 1.0 |
| 2010 | CLR | A+ | 22 | 2 | 0 | 15 | 29 | 0 | 40¹ | 26 | 1 | 11 | 32 | 2.5 | 9.6 | 55% | .287 | 1.04 | 1.79 | 3.08 | 3.86 | 0.6 |
| 2010 | REA | AA | 22 | 1 | 0 | 6 | 20 | 0 | 24² | 10 | 1 | 3 | 16 | 1.8 | 10.2 | 42% | .281 | 0.89 | 2.19 | 3.19 | 3.16 | 0.5 |
| 2011 | REA | AA | 23 | 1 | 0 | 8 | 23 | 0 | 34¹ | 25 | 1 | 13 | 42 | 3.7 | 11.3 | 65% | .308 | 1.22 | 2.10 | 2.74 | 3.53 | 0.6 |
| 2011 | LEH | AAA | 23 | 2 | 3 | 7 | 28 | 0 | 41 | 38 | 3 | 14 | 64 | 2.4 | 12.3 | 51% | .337 | 1.12 | 3.73 | 2.38 | 3.83 | 0.9 |
| 2011 | PHI | MLB | 23 | 1 | 0 | 0 | 5 | 0 | 4 | 1 | 0 | 3 | 3 | 6.8 | 6.8 | 50% | .111 | 1.00 | 2.25 | 4.49 | 3.49 | 0.0 |
| 2012 | PHI | MLB | 24 | 1 | 0 | 0 | 21 | 0 | 28¹ | 28 | 3 | 10 | 19 | 3.3 | 6.2 | 48% | .310 | 1.36 | 4.63 | 4.30 | 5.03 | -0.0 |

Two and a half years ago, De Fratus was a middling starting pitcher and former juco draftee in the Sally League. Like Bastardo, De Fratus demonstrates the benefit a roster of young starting prospects can have on a team's bullpen. Once converted to relief, De Fratus racked up 36 saves across two seasons and three levels. His repertoire includes a mid-90s fastball and an above-average slider, and he has shown improved command of the latter. His changeup is still a work in progress, but plenty of hard-throwing relievers have survived with just one off-speed pitch. De Fratus made his first appearance in the majors in 2011 as a late-season call-up, but fans can expect him to play a bigger role in 2012.

### Roy Halladay

Born: 5/14/1977 Age: 35
Bats: R Throws: R Height: 6' 7" Weight: 205
Breakout: 20% Improve: 40% Collapse: 35%
Attrition: 7% MLB: 88%

**Comparables:**
Roy Face, Doug Jones, Chris Carpenter

| YEAR | TEAM | LVL | AGE | W | L | SV | G | GS | IP | H | HR | BB | SO | EqBB9 | EqSO9 | GB% | BABIP | WHIP | ERA | FIP | FRA | WARP |
|---|---|---|---|---|---|---|---|---|---|---|---|---|---|---|---|---|---|---|---|---|---|---|
| 2009 | TOR | MLB | 32 | 17 | 10 | 0 | 32 | 32 | 239 | 234 | 22 | 35 | 208 | 1.3 | 7.8 | 51% | .306 | 1.13 | 2.79 | 3.10 | 3.65 | 4.6 |
| 2010 | PHI | MLB | 33 | 21 | 10 | 0 | 33 | 33 | 250² | 231 | 24 | 30 | 219 | 1.1 | 7.9 | 53% | .294 | 1.04 | 2.44 | 3.03 | 3.56 | 4.6 |
| 2011 | PHI | MLB | 34 | 19 | 6 | 0 | 32 | 32 | 233² | 208 | 10 | 35 | 220 | 1.3 | 8.5 | 53% | .305 | 1.04 | 2.35 | 2.17 | 3.23 | 3.8 |
| 2012 | PHI | MLB | 35 | 16 | 6 | 0 | 28 | 28 | 206² | 182 | 16 | 28 | 163 | 1.2 | 7.1 | 53% | .299 | 1.01 | 2.77 | 3.04 | 3.01 | 4.8 |

When the question is whether you'll have one more Cy Young award to list on your plaque in Cooperstown or put on your mantle, you're more willing to be generous. Halladay had better

RA, ERA, K/9, HR/9, and H/9 marks in 2011 than he did in 2010, but he graciously allowed Clayton Kershaw to take home the NL's highest pitching honor. His season ended with a performance every bit as gutsy as the no-hitter he threw in the 2010 playoffs: an eight-inning, one-run start that was surpassed only by—not sure if you heard this the first thousand times Tim McCarver and Joe Buck mentioned it!—his good friend Chris Carpenter's. His face gets red when he pitches, but that isn't anger; it's dedication. His $20 million salary will be surpassed by rotation-mate Cliff Lee's $21.5 million in 2012, but that doesn't bother Halladay; that's just the kind of guy he is. He won't mind if you don't watch him pitch, but you'll be doing yourself a disservice if you don't.

**Cole Hamels**
Born: 12/27/1983 Age: 28
Bats: L Throws: L Height: 6' 4'' Weight: 175
Breakout: 19% Improve: 42% Collapse: 24%
Attrition: 8% MLB: 93%

| YEAR | TEAM | LVL | AGE | W | L | SV | G | GS | IP | H | HR | BB | SO | EqBB9 | EqSO9 | GB% | BABIP | WHIP | ERA | FIP | FRA | WARP |
|------|------|-----|-----|---|---|----|----|----|------|-----|----|----|-----|-------|-------|-----|-------|------|------|------|------|------|
| 2009 | PHI | MLB | 25 | 10 | 11 | 0 | 32 | 32 | 193² | 206 | 24 | 43 | 168 | 2.0 | 7.8 | 44% | .321 | 1.29 | 4.32 | 3.68 | 3.96 | 3.8 |
| 2010 | PHI | MLB | 26 | 12 | 11 | 0 | 33 | 33 | 208² | 185 | 26 | 61 | 211 | 2.6 | 9.1 | 47% | .293 | 1.18 | 3.06 | 3.70 | 3.87 | 3.9 |
| 2011 | PHI | MLB | 27 | 14 | 9 | 0 | 32 | 31 | 216 | 169 | 19 | 44 | 194 | 1.8 | 8.1 | 55% | .259 | 0.99 | 2.79 | 3.02 | 3.49 | 3.1 |
| 2012 | PHI | MLB | 28 | 14 | 6 | 0 | 28 | 28 | 181² | 154 | 21 | 36 | 151 | 1.8 | 7.5 | 45% | .284 | 1.05 | 3.19 | 3.64 | 3.46 | 3.3 |

much more the team has to spend.

**David Herndon**
Born: 9/4/1985 Age: 26
Bats: R Throws: R Height: 6' 6'' Weight: 230
Breakout: 39% Improve: 57% Collapse: 24%
Attrition: 29% MLB: 79%
Comparables:
Kevin Kobel, Kyle Snyder, Gary Ryerson

| YEAR | TEAM | LVL | AGE | W | L | SV | G | GS | IP | H | HR | BB | SO | EqBB9 | EqSO9 | GB% | BABIP | WHIP | ERA | FIP | FRA | WARP |
|------|------|-----|-----|---|---|----|----|----|------|----|----|----|----|-------|-------|-----|-------|------|------|------|------|------|
| 2009 | ARK | AA | 23 | 5 | 6 | 11 | 50 | 0 | 65¹ | 70 | 9 | 14 | 35 | 1.9 | 4.8 | 62% | .299 | 1.29 | 3.03 | 4.69 | 6.14 | -1.0 |
| 2010 | PHI | MLB | 24 | 1 | 3 | 0 | 47 | 0 | 52¹ | 67 | 2 | 17 | 29 | 2.9 | 5.0 | 58% | .361 | 1.61 | 4.30 | 3.58 | 4.70 | 0.1 |
| 2011 | PHI | MLB | 25 | 1 | 4 | 1 | 45 | 0 | 57 | 54 | 9 | 24 | 39 | 3.8 | 6.2 | 57% | .278 | 1.37 | 3.32 | 5.05 | 5.66 | -0.4 |
| 2012 | PHI | MLB | 26 | 2 | 1 | 0 | 43 | 0 | 52² | 59 | 6 | 15 | 23 | 2.6 | 3.9 | 56% | .312 | 1.41 | 5.13 | 4.67 | 5.58 | -0.4 |

Herndon was asked to issue seven intention walks in 2011, which was tied for eighth most among relievers. He shouldn't feel too bad about it, since Ryan Madson was asked to walk eight, but it does say something about the way Herndon is used on the Phillies. Despite his full workload, he wasn't included on the postseason roster. He had the lowest leverage of any reliever on the team not named Baez, and the batters he faced had a lower OPS than those who faced any other full-time reliever on the team. In short, Charlie Manuel doesn't trust him, and neither should you.

**Kyle Kendrick**
Born: 8/26/1984 Age: 27
Bats: R Throws: R Height: 6' 4'' Weight: 185
Breakout: 28% Improve: 57% Collapse: 14%
Attrition: 7% MLB: 88%
Comparables:
Rod Nichols, Dick Drago, Bobby J. Jones

| YEAR | TEAM | LVL | AGE | W | L | SV | G | GS | IP | H | HR | BB | SO | EqBB9 | EqSO9 | GB% | BABIP | WHIP | ERA | FIP | FRA | WARP |
|------|------|-----|-----|---|---|----|----|----|------|-----|----|----|----|-------|-------|-----|-------|------|------|------|------|------|
| 2009 | LEH | AAA | 24 | 9 | 7 | 0 | 24 | 24 | 143 | 133 | 9 | 35 | 62 | 2.2 | 3.9 | 53% | .266 | 1.17 | 3.34 | 3.94 | 5.29 | 0.2 |
| 2009 | PHI | MLB | 24 | 3 | 1 | 0 | 9 | 2 | 26¹ | 27 | 1 | 9 | 15 | 3.1 | 5.1 | 57% | .306 | 1.37 | 3.42 | 3.55 | 4.97 | 0.1 |
| 2010 | PHI | MLB | 25 | 11 | 10 | 0 | 33 | 31 | 180² | 199 | 26 | 49 | 84 | 2.4 | 4.2 | 45% | .288 | 1.37 | 4.73 | 4.91 | 5.24 | 0.8 |
| 2011 | PHI | MLB | 26 | 8 | 6 | 0 | 34 | 15 | 114² | 110 | 14 | 31 | 59 | 2.4 | 4.6 | 46% | .265 | 1.22 | 3.22 | 4.55 | 4.94 | 0.2 |
| 2012 | PHI | MLB | 27 | 7 | 5 | 0 | 24 | 16 | 107¹ | 112 | 13 | 27 | 45 | 2.2 | 3.8 | 47% | .293 | 1.30 | 4.79 | 4.69 | 5.20 | -0.1 |

The last of the traditionalist holdouts for ERA might want to take notice of Kendrick's 2011 season. It was almost identical to his horrendous 2010 season. He struck out a batter on average once every two innings and gave up plenty of hits. The difference in his seasons is attributable to two stats. First, he had a friendly BABIP of .261, 25 points better than his career average. Second, nine of the runs he allowed (18 percent of the total) were counted as unearned, a benefit he "earns" because he's a groundball-type (if not groundball-effect) pitcher. He made $2.45 million in his first year of arbitration eligibility. We'll see what the Phillies do given the possibility that an arbitrator might very well look at Kendrick's ERA and conclude he's much more valuable than he is. He wasn't non-tendered this year, but he's a good bet to be a free agent after this season.

### Cliff Lee
Born: 8/30/1978 Age: 33
Bats: L Throws: L Height: 6' 4" Weight: 190
Breakout: 15% Improve: 47% Collapse: 22%
Attrition: 13% MLB: 96%
Comparables:
Carl Willis, Mike Mussina, Willie Hernandez

| YEAR | TEAM | LVL | AGE | W | L | SV | G | GS | IP | H | HR | BB | SO | EqBB9 | EqSO9 | GB% | BABIP | WHIP | ERA | FIP | FRA | WARP |
|---|---|---|---|---|---|---|---|---|---|---|---|---|---|---|---|---|---|---|---|---|---|---|
| 2009 | PHI | MLB | 30 | 7 | 4 | 0 | 12 | 12 | 79² | 80 | 7 | 10 | 74 | 1.1 | 8.4 | 40% | .319 | 1.13 | 3.39 | 2.79 | 3.89 | 1.6 |
| 2009 | CLE | MLB | 30 | 7 | 9 | 0 | 22 | 22 | 152 | 165 | 10 | 33 | 107 | 2.0 | 6.3 | 46% | .322 | 1.30 | 3.14 | 3.30 | 3.59 | 3.0 |
| 2010 | SEA | MLB | 31 | 8 | 3 | 0 | 13 | 13 | 103² | 92 | 5 | 6 | 89 | 0.5 | 7.7 | 41% | .283 | 0.95 | 2.34 | 2.13 | 2.71 | 2.0 |
| 2010 | TEX | MLB | 31 | 4 | 6 | 0 | 15 | 15 | 108² | 103 | 11 | 12 | 96 | 1.0 | 8.0 | 43% | .296 | 1.06 | 3.98 | 2.96 | 3.34 | 2.4 |
| 2011 | PHI | MLB | 32 | 17 | 8 | 0 | 32 | 32 | 232² | 197 | 18 | 42 | 238 | 1.6 | 9.2 | 49% | .293 | 1.03 | 2.40 | 2.57 | 3.12 | 5.2 |
| 2012 | PHI | MLB | 33 | 15 | 6 | 0 | 27 | 27 | 196 | 176 | 15 | 32 | 155 | 1.5 | 7.1 | 44% | .302 | 1.06 | 2.99 | 3.11 | 3.25 | 4.0 |

See, Ruben? *That's* how you spend $120 million. WARP suggests Lee was worth a full four wins more than Ryan Howard was last year. Even if Howard manages two or three WARP this season, Lee is a good bet to accumulate at least 10 more wins over the life of his contract than Howard does over the life of his. As for Lee, he looked better than ever last year. He set career highs in strikeouts (his first 200-plus season) and innings pitched, set a new career best in ERA, and racked up six shutouts (more than doubling his career total). His median Game Score was 66, just a notch better than Halladay's 65, and he did it all while making it look easy. As easy as spending $120 million can look, that is.

### Brad Lidge
Born: 12/23/1976 Age: 35
Bats: R Throws: R Height: 6' 6" Weight: 200
Breakout: 20% Improve: 42% Collapse: 30%
Attrition: 14% MLB: 89%
Comparables:
Lee Smith, Joe Nelson, John Hiller

| YEAR | TEAM | LVL | AGE | W | L | SV | G | GS | IP | H | HR | BB | SO | EqBB9 | EqSO9 | GB% | BABIP | WHIP | ERA | FIP | FRA | WARP |
|---|---|---|---|---|---|---|---|---|---|---|---|---|---|---|---|---|---|---|---|---|---|---|
| 2009 | PHI | MLB | 32 | 0 | 8 | 31 | 67 | 0 | 58² | 72 | 11 | 34 | 61 | 5.2 | 9.4 | 41% | .363 | 1.81 | 7.21 | 5.41 | 5.59 | -0.1 |
| 2010 | PHI | MLB | 33 | 1 | 1 | 27 | 50 | 0 | 45² | 32 | 5 | 24 | 52 | 4.7 | 10.2 | 40% | .250 | 1.23 | 2.96 | 3.89 | 4.58 | 0.3 |
| 2011 | PHI | MLB | 34 | 0 | 2 | 1 | 25 | 0 | 19¹ | 16 | 0 | 13 | 23 | 6.1 | 10.7 | 57% | .333 | 1.50 | 1.40 | 2.79 | 3.55 | 0.2 |
| 2012 | PHI | MLB | 35 | 2 | 1 | 8 | 29 | 0 | 25² | 20 | 2 | 11 | 28 | 3.9 | 9.8 | 45% | .301 | 1.22 | 3.58 | 3.32 | 3.89 | 0.3 |

It's incredible just how many of the Phillies' recent multi-year deals for free-agent relievers have blown up in their faces. In terms of dollars wasted, Lidge's contract was the worst. After his improbably bad 2009, he was only average when he was healthy in 2010 and 2011. Between injuries and a decline in performance, Lidge was a $5 million reliever getting paid $12 million a year, which meant his salary was costing the Phillies the equivalent of at least one more pitcher as good as he was. Once his fastball abandoned him, Lidge was left to live by his slider. It remains a good pitch, but few late-inning relievers get by throwing breaking pitches more than half the time. If the trend continues, he'll be out of baseball in a year or two. The Phillies declined his option, and he was a free agent as we went to press.

### Ryan Madson
Born: 8/28/1980 Age: 31
Bats: L Throws: R Height: 6' 7" Weight: 180
Breakout: 8% Improve: 49% Collapse: 26%
Attrition: 10% MLB: 91%
Comparables:
Johan Santana, Erik Bedard, Willie Hernandez

| YEAR | TEAM | LVL | AGE | W | L | SV | G | GS | IP | H | HR | BB | SO | EqBB9 | EqSO9 | GB% | BABIP | WHIP | ERA | FIP | FRA | WARP |
|---|---|---|---|---|---|---|---|---|---|---|---|---|---|---|---|---|---|---|---|---|---|---|
| 2009 | PHI | MLB | 28 | 5 | 5 | 10 | 79 | 0 | 77¹ | 73 | 7 | 22 | 78 | 2.6 | 9.1 | 48% | .319 | 1.23 | 3.26 | 3.19 | 3.46 | 1.6 |
| 2010 | PHI | MLB | 29 | 6 | 2 | 5 | 55 | 0 | 53 | 42 | 4 | 13 | 64 | 2.2 | 10.9 | 52% | .292 | 1.04 | 2.55 | 2.63 | 3.44 | 0.9 |
| 2011 | PHI | MLB | 30 | 4 | 2 | 32 | 62 | 0 | 60² | 54 | 2 | 16 | 62 | 2.4 | 9.2 | 52% | .327 | 1.15 | 2.37 | 2.22 | 3.31 | 1.0 |
| 2012 | PHI | MLB | 31 | 3 | 1 | 13 | 56 | 0 | 55¹ | 47 | 4 | 14 | 50 | 2.2 | 8.1 | 50% | .298 | 1.09 | 2.94 | 3.10 | 3.19 | 1.1 |

Last year was the year Madson finally learned to close. For years he bounced between the rotation and the bullpen. Then for more years he bounced between the set-up role and temporary stints in the closer role. Since finding his role as a reliever, he has been remarkably consistent. His changeup is one of the very best in the game, and he sets it up with a mid-90s fastball that has excellent late life. It's a superlative combination, and in 2010 Madson proved it was plenty to close—just in time to hit free agency. After narrowly missing on a deal to stay with the Phillies, Madson will head elsewhere and earn the first big payday of his career.

### Trevor May
Born: 9/23/1989 Age: 22
Bats: R Throws: R Height: 6' 6" Weight: 215
Breakout: 19% Improve: 40% Collapse: 42%
Attrition: 4% MLB: 91%
Comparables:
Vinegar Bend Mizell, Victor Cruz, Tom Griffin

| YEAR | TEAM | LVL | AGE | W | L | SV | G | GS | IP | H | HR | BB | SO | EqBB9 | EqSO9 | GB% | BABIP | WHIP | ERA | FIP | FRA | WARP |
|---|---|---|---|---|---|---|---|---|---|---|---|---|---|---|---|---|---|---|---|---|---|---|
| 2009 | LWD | A | 19 | 5 | 1 | 0 | 15 | 15 | 77¹ | 63 | 3 | 48 | 106 | 5.0 | 11.1 | 41% | .294 | 1.31 | 2.56 | 3.17 | 3.36 | 1.6 |
| 2010 | LWD | A | 20 | 8 | 4 | 0 | 11 | 11 | 65 | 11 | 1 | 5 | 12 | 2.8 | 12.7 | 43% | .370 | 1.09 | 2.91 | 3.77 | 2.95 | 2.1 |
| 2010 | CLR | A+ | 20 | 5 | 4 | 0 | 16 | 14 | 70 | 43 | 5 | 47 | 77 | 7.8 | 11.6 | 44% | .306 | 1.63 | 5.01 | 4.49 | 4.72 | 0.7 |
| 2011 | CLR | A+ | 21 | 4 | 4 | 0 | 27 | 27 | 151¹ | 121 | 8 | 67 | 208 | 4.0 | 12.4 | 36% | .334 | 1.24 | 3.63 | 2.76 | 3.58 | 3.6 |
| 2012 | PHI | MLB | 22 | 3 | 2 | 0 | 8 | 8 | 45 | 38 | 4 | 27 | 45 | 5.5 | 9.0 | 38% | .309 | 1.46 | 4.59 | 4.16 | 4.99 | 0.1 |

It's a wonder what a second go-round can do for a guy's confidence. After a brief hiccup early in the season, May established himself as the best pitching prospect in the Phillies system by pumping his power stuff past High-A hitters. He still needs to work on his control, but between his plus fastball and his sharp breaking ball, he has the stuff of a potential front-of-the-rotation pitcher. He will likely start out at Double-A, but if his success continues there, he will set his own timetable.

## Roy Oswalt

Born: 8/29/1977 Age: 34
Bats: R Throws: R Height: 6' 1" Weight: 170
Breakout: 15% Improve: 36% Collapse: 35%
Attrition: 9% MLB: 89%

**Comparables:**
Bobby Tiefenauer, Pascual Perez, LaTroy Hawkins

| YEAR | TEAM | LVL | AGE | W | L | SV | G | GS | IP | H | HR | BB | SO | EqBB9 | EqSO9 | GB% | BABIP | WHIP | ERA | FIP | FRA | WARP |
|------|------|-----|-----|---|---|----|----|----|-----|-----|----|----|-----|-------|-------|-----|-------|------|-----|-----|-----|------|
| 2009 | HOU | MLB | 31 | 8 | 6 | 0 | 30 | 30 | 181¹ | 183 | 19 | 42 | 138 | 2.1 | 6.8 | 47% | .305 | 1.24 | 4.12 | 3.72 | 4.26 | 2.8 |
| 2010 | PHI | MLB | 32 | 7 | 1 | 0 | 13 | 12 | 82² | 53 | 6 | 21 | 73 | 2.3 | 7.9 | 52% | .227 | 0.90 | 1.74 | 3.15 | 3.02 | 2.2 |
| 2010 | HOU | MLB | 32 | 6 | 12 | 0 | 20 | 20 | 129 | 109 | 13 | 34 | 120 | 2.4 | 8.4 | 45% | .276 | 1.11 | 3.42 | 3.39 | 3.51 | 2.7 |
| 2011 | PHI | MLB | 33 | 9 | 10 | 0 | 23 | 23 | 139 | 153 | 10 | 33 | 93 | 2.1 | 6.0 | 47% | .321 | 1.34 | 3.69 | 3.41 | 3.78 | 1.7 |
| 2012 | PHI | MLB | 34 | 10 | 5 | 0 | 22 | 22 | 137¹ | 127 | 13 | 30 | 94 | 2.0 | 6.2 | 50% | .294 | 1.14 | 3.59 | 3.72 | 3.90 | 1.8 |

Oswalt's back started to go several years ago. He was diagnosed with a herniated disc in 2008 that sent him to the disabled list for a short stay. The next year he was diagnosed with degenerative disc disease and missed a total of about a month with lower back injuries. Despite this history, Oswalt hadn't started fewer than 30 games since 2003 before last year. In 2010, he avoided the DL. So here was the mystery of Oswalt: Everyone knew he would break down eventually, but nobody had a clue when that would be. Even after he missed a quarter of the season with another bulging disc, Oswalt looked mostly recovered after his return. A free agent at press time, he is a good bet to give the

cumulative 300 IP with an ERA below 3.00 and a strikeout-to-walk ratio above 3.0: Mariano Rivera, Trevor Hoffman, Bryan Harvey, Billy Wagner, John Wetteland, Mike Adams, Rod Beck, and, after a spectacular year punctuated by a terrible finish, Papelbon. In fact, his K/BB (4.43) is the best on the list over those first seven seasons. Perhaps because of his outsized personality or his conspicuous habit of over-relying on his fastball, many do not realize that Papelbon has been on one of the best runs any modern closer has ever strung together. The Phillies offered him $50 million, and like all relief pitchers offered that much money, he accepted. Every four-year deal given to a reliever is an enormous risk, but Papelbon is one of the best relievers in baseball.

## Brian Sanches

Born: 8/8/1978 Age: 33
Bats: R Throws: R Height: 6' 1" Weight: 190
Breakout: 23% Improve: 45% Collapse: 35%
Attrition: 17% MLB: 86%

**Comparables:**
Tyler Walker, Bob Gibson, Jeff Brantley

| YEAR | TEAM | LVL | AGE | W | L | SV | G | GS | IP | H | HR | BB | SO | EqBB9 | EqSO9 | GB% | BABIP | WHIP | ERA | FIP | FRA | WARP |
|------|------|-----|-----|---|---|----|----|----|-----|----|----|----|----|-------|-------|-----|-------|------|-----|-----|-----|------|
| 2009 | FLO | MLB | 30 | 4 | 2 | 0 | 47 | 0 | 56¹ | 50 | 5 | 26 | 51 | 4.2 | 8.1 | 35% | .287 | 1.35 | 2.56 | 4.10 | 4.24 | 0.8 |
| 2010 | FLO | MLB | 31 | 2 | 2 | 0 | 61 | 0 | 63² | 43 | 7 | 27 | 54 | 3.8 | 7.6 | 34% | .220 | 1.10 | 2.26 | 4.16 | 4.59 | 0.5 |
| 2011 | FLO | MLB | 32 | 4 | 1 | 0 | 39 | 2 | 61² | 52 | 7 | 36 | 53 | 5.3 | 7.7 | 35% | .263 | 1.43 | 3.94 | 4.60 | 4.68 | 0.0 |
| 2012 | PHI | MLB | 33 | 2 | 1 | 0 | 46 | 0 | 56¹ | 48 | 6 | 23 | 48 | 3.6 | 7.7 | 36% | .291 | 1.27 | 3.97 | 4.11 | 4.32 | 0.4 |

An influx of talent combined with his own lackluster performance rendered Sanches relatively useless in the Marlins bullpen in 2011. His WHIP, walk rate, and strikeout-to-walk ratio were all worst among Florida relievers. Neither manager trusted him to get high-leverage outs, despite Sanches stranding 73 percent of inherited runners in 2010 and, as it turned out, all 17 inherited runners in 2011. He became a free agent after refusing an outright assignment in October, and signed a minor-league deal with the Phillies shortly thereafter.

## Joe Savery

Born: 11/4/1985 Age: 26
Bats: L Throws: L Height: 6' 4" Weight: 215
Breakout: 30% Improve: 61% Collapse: 18%
Attrition: 24% MLB: 89%

**Comparables:**
Scott Schoeneweis, John Dopson, Jason Marquis

| YEAR | TEAM | LVL | AGE | W | L | SV | G | GS | IP | H | HR | BB | SO | EqBB9 | EqSO9 | GB% | BABIP | WHIP | ERA | FIP | FRA | WARP |
|------|------|-----|-----|----|----|----|----|----|------|-----|----|----|----|-------|-------|-----|-------|------|-----|-----|-----|------|
| 2009 | REA | AA | 23 | 12 | 4 | 0 | 21 | 20 | 112¹ | 111 | 13 | 53 | 77 | 4.2 | 6.2 | 50% | .291 | 1.46 | 4.41 | 4.71 | 5.67 | -0.1 |
| 2009 | LEH | AAA | 23 | 4 | 2 | 0 | 7 | 7 | 39 | 42 | 0 | 24 | 19 | 5.5 | 4.4 | 44% | .318 | 1.69 | 4.38 | 4.10 | 5.93 | -0.3 |
| 2010 | LEH | AAA | 24 | 1 | 12 | 0 | 28 | 19 | 127¹ | 103 | 6 | 36 | 40 | 3.6 | 4.7 | 46% | .316 | 1.61 | 4.67 | 4.46 | 5.99 | -0.4 |
| 2011 | LEH | AAA | 25 | 4 | 0 | 2 | 18 | 0 | 25 | 25 | 0 | 8 | 27 | 2.2 | 9.4 | 65% | .338 | 1.16 | 1.80 | 2.04 | 4.11 | 0.5 |
| 2011 | PHI | MLB | 25 | 0 | 0 | 0 | 4 | 0 | 2² | 1 | 0 | 0 | 2 | 0.0 | 6.8 | 57% | .167 | 0.38 | 0.00 | 1.49 | 1.59 | 0.1 |
| 2012 | PHI | MLB | 26 | 1 | 0 | 0 | 4 | 1 | 10² | 12 | 1 | 5 | 6 | 4.2 | 4.7 | 48% | .313 | 1.56 | 5.60 | 4.70 | 6.09 | -0.1 |

Converted from relief to first base and allowed to hit full time to start the season, Savery went 14-for-18 in his first five games in the Florida State League. That's not a typo. The rest of the spring was the slow reemergence of statistical likelihood. By summer, Savery was back on the mound and looking much more like the first-rounder he was in 2007. He broke through for his major-league debut, so he could be in the mix for bullpen innings if another stint in Triple-A goes well and any of the more established options succumb to injury. At the very least, he has the potential to warm the hearts of the Brooks Kieschnick fans of the world.

**Michael Schwimer**
Born: 2/19/1986 Age: 26
Bats: R Throws: R Height: 6' 9" Weight: 240
Breakout: 29% Improve: 48% Collapse: 19%
Attrition: 14% MLB: 94%

Comparables:
Max Scherzer, John Wetteland, Ugueth Urbina

| YEAR | TEAM | LVL | AGE | W | L | SV | G | GS | IP | H | HR | BB | SO | EqBB9 | EqSO9 | GB% | BABIP | WHIP | ERA | FIP | FRA | WARP |
|---|---|---|---|---|---|---|---|---|---|---|---|---|---|---|---|---|---|---|---|---|---|---|
| 2009 | CLR | A+ | 23 | 2 | 1 | 20 | 48 | 0 | 60 | 44 | 2 | 19 | 82 | 2.8 | 12.3 | 47% | .316 | 1.05 | 2.85 | 1.95 | 2.82 | 1.6 |
| 2010 | REA | AA | 24 | 4 | 2 | 11 | 32 | 0 | 40 | 20 | 4 | 10 | 39 | 3.2 | 13.1 | 42% | .302 | 1.20 | 3.60 | 3.77 | 4.20 | 0.7 |
| 2011 | LEH | AAA | 25 | 9 | 1 | 10 | 47 | 0 | 68 | 51 | 4 | 22 | 86 | 2.9 | 11.4 | 38% | .290 | 1.07 | 1.85 | 2.49 | 3.80 | 1.3 |
| 2011 | PHI | MLB | 25 | 1 | 1 | 0 | 12 | 0 | 14¹ | 15 | 2 | 7 | 16 | 4.4 | 10.0 | 28% | .361 | 1.53 | 5.02 | 4.25 | 5.52 | -0.1 |
| 2012 | PHI | MLB | 26 | 1 | 1 | 1 | 26 | 0 | 34 | 28 | 3 | 13 | 35 | 3.4 | 9.2 | 45% | .306 | 1.20 | 3.51 | 3.44 | 3.82 | 0.4 |

Schwimer, a Brobdingnagian righty out of the University of Virginia, has an over-the-top delivery. Even though his fastball velocity isn't anything special, he is effective in large part because of how quickly it bears down on batters. He complements the fastball with a good slider and a decent splitter. He tore up Triple-A competition, so both his track record and his advanced age suggest he'll get an extended shot to make the major-league roster out of spring training.

**Michael Stutes**
Born: 9/4/1986 Age: 25
Bats: R Throws: R Height: 6' 2" Weight: 185
Breakout: 34% Improve: 66% Collapse: 12%
Attrition: 16% MLB: 89%

Comparables:
Ricky Romero, Randor Bierd, Homer Bailey

| YEAR | TEAM | LVL | AGE | W | L | SV | G | GS | IP | H | HR | BB | SO | EqBB9 | EqSO9 | GB% | BABIP | WHIP | ERA | FIP | FRA | WARP |
|---|---|---|---|---|---|---|---|---|---|---|---|---|---|---|---|---|---|---|---|---|---|---|
| 2009 | REA | AA | 22 | 8 | 9 | 0 | 27 | 27 | 145² | 156 | 16 | 59 | 114 | 3.6 | 6.7 | 41% | .308 | 1.41 | 4.26 | 4.38 | 4.39 | 1.5 |
| 2010 | REA | AA | 23 | 2 | 0 | 2 | 25 | 0 | 35² | 19 | 0 | 15 | 24 | 5.3 | 9.3 | 41% | .317 | 1.37 | 3.78 | 3.93 | 4.39 | 0.3 |
| 2010 | LEH | AAA | 23 | 4 | 1 | 1 | 28 | 0 | 40² | 19 | 2 | 16 | 31 | 5.1 | 9.3 | 39% | .239 | 1.28 | 3.10 | 3.90 | 5.24 | -0.1 |
| 2011 | PHI | MLB | 24 | 6 | 2 | 0 | 57 | 0 | 62 | 49 | 7 | 27 | 58 | 4.1 | 8.4 | 35% | .259 | 1.24 | 3.63 | 3.99 | 3.55 | 0.8 |
| 2012 | PHI | MLB | 25 | 2 | 1 | 0 | 36 | 0 | 46¹ | 43 | 5 | 20 | 34 | 3.8 | 6.7 | 43% | .293 | 1.35 | 4.52 | 4.43 | 4.91 | 0.0 |

Stutes found a place for himself on the roster over the course of the season largely by proving himself in low-leverage situations. By the end of the year, he was a go-to arm: In eight of his last 11 games, Stutes recorded either a hold or a decision. That was enough to win him a spot on the NLDS roster, and while his solitary appearance in that series was both poor and in a mop-up role, inclusion alone speaks to the confidence the team has in the Oregon State product. That faith might not be fully justified, since neither of Stutes' two main pitches—a low-90s fastball and a slider—is a true out pitch.

**Dontrelle Willis**
Born: 1/12/1982 Age: 30
Bats: L Throws: L Height: 6' 5" Weight: 200
Breakout: 29% Improve: 52% Collapse: 19%
Attrition: 13% MLB: 76%

Comparables:
Valerio De Los Santos, Jerry Don Gleaton, Tom House

| YEAR | TEAM | LVL | AGE | W | L | SV | G | GS | IP | H | HR | BB | SO | EqBB9 | EqSO9 | GB% | BABIP | WHIP | ERA | FIP | FRA | WARP |
|---|---|---|---|---|---|---|---|---|---|---|---|---|---|---|---|---|---|---|---|---|---|---|
| 2009 | DET | MLB | 27 | 1 | 4 | 0 | 7 | 7 | 33² | 37 | 4 | 28 | 17 | 7.5 | 4.5 | 54% | .306 | 1.93 | 7.49 | 6.26 | 8.29 | -0.4 |
| 2010 | ARI | MLB | 28 | 1 | 1 | 0 | 6 | 5 | 22¹ | 24 | 3 | 27 | 14 | 10.9 | 5.6 | 47% | .318 | 2.28 | 6.85 | 7.63 | 8.95 | -0.5 |
| 2010 | DET | MLB | 28 | 1 | 2 | 0 | 9 | 8 | 43¹ | 48 | 3 | 29 | 33 | 6.0 | 6.9 | 47% | .338 | 1.78 | 4.98 | 4.57 | 5.15 | 0.0 |
| 2011 | LOU | AAA | 29 | 5 | 1 | 0 | 13 | 13 | 75¹ | 71 | 5 | 20 | 67 | 2.4 | 8.0 | 55% | .308 | 1.21 | 2.63 | 3.16 | 3.56 | 1.7 |
| 2011 | CIN | MLB | 29 | 1 | 6 | 0 | 13 | 13 | 75² | 78 | 6 | 37 | 57 | 4.4 | 6.8 | 57% | .316 | 1.52 | 5.00 | 4.06 | 5.17 | 0.7 |
| 2012 | PHI | MLB | 30 | 5 | 5 | 0 | 15 | 15 | 82 | 85 | 9 | 41 | 52 | 4.5 | 5.7 | 49% | .315 | 1.54 | 5.47 | 4.86 | 5.95 | -0.7 |

There's an old Far Side comic that depicts a sparsely populated meeting of the "Didn't Like *Dances With Wolves* Society." And while Kevin Costner's directorial debut hasn't aged well, the classic Gary Larson comic is a good metaphor for how most fans feel about Dontrelle Willis. Since his salad days with the Marlins, Willis has walked through the twin valleys of knee surgery and anxiety disorder. He emerged throwing bullets in Louisville, where he began to resurrect the withered remains of his career. A call-up to the Reds didn't go nearly as well because his control once again eluded him much of the time. It was, however, enough to convince the Phillies to gamble a cool million on the D-Train, who they hope will be better than *Waterworld* or *The Postman*.

**Vance Worley**
Born: 9/25/1987 Age: 24
Bats: R Throws: R Height: 6' 3" Weight: 230
Breakout: 36% Improve: 62% Collapse: 18%
Attrition: 13% MLB: 93%

Comparables:
Larry Dierker, Justin Verlander, Don Gullett

| YEAR | TEAM | LVL | AGE | W | L | SV | G | GS | IP | H | HR | BB | SO | EqBB9 | EqSO9 | GB% | BABIP | WHIP | ERA | FIP | FRA | WARP |
|---|---|---|---|---|---|---|---|---|---|---|---|---|---|---|---|---|---|---|---|---|---|---|
| 2009 | REA | AA | 21 | 7 | 12 | 0 | 27 | 27 | 153¹ | 155 | 17 | 47 | 98 | 2.9 | 5.9 | 42% | .297 | 1.38 | 5.34 | 4.32 | 4.66 | 1.2 |
| 2010 | REA | AA | 22 | 7 | 4 | 0 | 19 | 19 | 112² | 76 | 7 | 20 | 53 | 2.9 | 6.6 | 46% | .325 | 1.33 | 3.19 | 4.05 | 4.40 | 1.2 |
| 2010 | LEH | AAA | 22 | 1 | 2 | 0 | 8 | 8 | 45¹ | 32 | 0 | 5 | 25 | 2.0 | 7.2 | 49% | .352 | 1.24 | 3.77 | 2.82 | 3.56 | 0.7 |
| 2010 | PHI | MLB | 22 | 1 | 1 | 0 | 5 | 2 | 13 | 8 | 1 | 4 | 12 | 2.8 | 8.3 | 51% | .219 | 0.92 | 1.38 | 3.18 | 3.23 | 0.3 |
| 2011 | LEH | AAA | 23 | 5 | 2 | 0 | 9 | 9 | 50² | 37 | 5 | 11 | 41 | 2.1 | 8.9 | 47% | .269 | 1.05 | 2.31 | 3.67 | 4.22 | 0.6 |
| 2011 | PHI | MLB | 23 | 11 | 3 | 0 | 25 | 21 | 131² | 116 | 10 | 46 | 119 | 3.1 | 8.1 | 42% | .290 | 1.23 | 3.01 | 3.29 | 4.06 | 1.4 |
| 2012 | PHI | MLB | 24 | 8 | 5 | 0 | 20 | 20 | 116 | 111 | 12 | 36 | 79 | 2.8 | 6.1 | 45% | .297 | 1.27 | 4.23 | 4.12 | 4.60 | 0.6 |

With an eminently pun-prone name and a pair of glasses that make you want to visit the optometrist, Worley was an immediate sensation. Given the ball when Blanton went down, Worley never gave it back. His unsustainable white-hot glare before the All-Star break (a 2.20 ERA despite a 1.85 K/BB ratio) gave way to a stable, warm glow in the second half (82/26 K/BB in 82.2 innings). His stuff—led by a 90-mph fastball and a good slider—is by no means overpowering, but it's just junky enough to work well with his solid command. While his ERA is in for a hit next season, Worley should be a more-than-serviceable fourth starter for the next few years.

## LINEOUTS

### HITTERS

| | | | AGE | | | | | | | | | | | AVG/OBP/SLG | | | | | WARP |
|---|---|---|---|---|---|---|---|---|---|---|---|---|---|---|---|---|---|---|---|
| C E. Kratz | LEH | AAA | 31 | 409 | 56 | 19 | 0 | 15 | 53 | 38 | 72 | 2-0 | .288/.372/.466 | .280 | .322 | 3.0 | 1.1 | 3.3 |
| | PHI | MLB | 31 | 6 | 0 | 1 | 0 | 0 | 0 | 0 | 1 | 0-0 | .333/.333/.500 | .292 | .400 | -0.1 | 0 | 0.1 |
| 3B P. Orr | LEH | AAA | 32 | 309 | 40 | 16 | 2 | 5 | 26 | 17 | 56 | 15-5 | .267/.324/.391 | .250 | .317 | 0.8 | 6.9 | 1.4 |
| | PHI | MLB | 32 | 104 | 7 | 3 | 0 | 0 | 4 | 6 | 19 | 3-0 | .219/.279/.250 | .199 | .273 | 0.1 | 0.3 | -0.3 |
| C D. Sardinha | LEH | AAA | 32 | 106 | 6 | 3 | 0 | 0 | 1 | 10 | 32 | 0-0 | .140/.238/.172 | .188 | .213 | -1.2 | -0.2 | -0.5 |
| | PHI | MLB | 32 | 43 | 8 | 1 | 0 | 0 | 1 | 10 | 13 | 0-0 | .219/.419/.250 | .281 | .368 | -0.6 | 0.1 | 0.2 |

With Ryan Howard out, this may be **John Bowker**'s best chance to get regular major-league plate appearances, but it'll take at least one more injury or a terrific spring for that to happen. ⊘ An 18-year-old Dominican first baseman, **Maikel Franco** has big upside but little in the way of results; the glove and arm lead the bat in development. ⊘ Toolsy and with a ways to go, **Jiwan James** might as well be the mold for Phillies draftees, but he mostly held serve last season. ⊘ A catcher with three straight 800 OPS seasons who still hasn't gotten a look-see in the majors, **Erik Kratz** is either the next Chris Coste or the next Dane Sardinha. ⊘ It was a competitive race, but **Pete Orr** came out on top. His .197 True Average took the cake for worst among hitters who received any serious number of plate appearances for the Phillies. He's an organizational body who can run the bases and play good defense. ⊘ Speaking of **Dane Sardinha**, he posted his eighth consecutive lousy Triple-A season—that's gotta be some kind of record.

### PITCHERS

| PLAYER | TEAM | LVL | AGE | W | L | SV | IP | H | HR | BB | SO | EqBB9 | EqSO9 | GB% | BABIP | WHIP | ERA | FIP | FRA | WARP |
|---|---|---|---|---|---|---|---|---|---|---|---|---|---|---|---|---|---|---|---|---|
| D. Baez | PHI | MLB | 33 | 2 | 4 | 0 | 36 | 43 | 5 | 13 | 18 | 3.2 | 4.5 | 52% | .306 | 1.56 | 6.25 | 5.13 | 6.10 | -0.6 |
| D. Bush | TEX | MLB | 31 | 0 | 1 | 0 | 37¹ | 47 | 6 | 9 | 23 | 2.2 | 5.5 | 48% | .333 | 1.50 | 5.79 | 4.88 | 5.35 | 0.1 |
| P. Misch | BUF | AAA | 29 | 5 | 6 | 0 | 141² | 142 | 18 | 41 | 94 | 2.6 | 6.0 | 50% | .282 | 1.29 | 4.00 | 4.60 | 5.28 | 0.9 |
| | NYN | MLB | 29 | 1 | 0 | 0 | 7 | 11 | 1 | 4 | 5 | 5.1 | 6.4 | 44% | .385 | 2.14 | 10.29 | 5.57 | 6.72 | -0.2 |
| J. Pettibone | CLR | A+ | 20 | 6 | 5 | 0 | 161 | 149 | 5 | 34 | 115 | 1.9 | 6.4 | 45% | .296 | 1.14 | 2.96 | 3.11 | 3.97 | 2.9 |
| D. Purcey | TOR | MLB | 29 | 0 | 0 | 0 | 2¹ | 3 | 0 | 4 | 3 | 15.4 | 11.6 | 43% | .429 | 3.00 | 11.57 | 5.63 | 5.51 | 0.0 |
| | OAK | MLB | 29 | 0 | 0 | 0 | 12² | 9 | 1 | 3 | 7 | 2.1 | 5.0 | 35% | .205 | 0.95 | 2.13 | 3.69 | 2.79 | 0.3 |
| | DET | MLB | 29 | 1 | 2 | 0 | 18² | 21 | 1 | 20 | 12 | 9.6 | 5.8 | 49% | .345 | 2.20 | 7.23 | 5.69 | 5.61 | -0.1 |
| J. Rodriguez | CLR | A+ | 20 | 6 | 2 | 0 | 156² | 102 | 13 | 56 | 168 | 3.2 | 9.7 | 30% | .240 | 1.01 | 2.76 | 3.65 | 4.23 | 2.2 |
| R. Valdes | MEM | AAA | 33 | 6 | 2 | 0 | 59 | 61 | 8 | 11 | 62 | 1.7 | 9.5 | 35% | .327 | 1.22 | 4.73 | 4.16 | 4.29 | 0.7 |
| | NYA | MLB | 33 | 0 | 0 | 0 | 6² | 8 | 1 | 2 | 8 | 2.7 | 10.8 | 28% | .412 | 1.50 | 2.70 | 3.51 | 4.20 | 0.0 |
| | SLN | MLB | 33 | 0 | 1 | 0 | 5¹ | 6 | 0 | 4 | 7 | 6.8 | 11.8 | 47% | .400 | 1.88 | 3.38 | 3.18 | 4.52 | 0.0 |

**Danys Baez** is why we can't have nice things. ⊘ **Dave Bush** is a journeyman without stuff, so he is only suited to emergency roles or roster filling. ⊘ The Mets grew increasingly impatient with **Pat Misch**, who hasn't thrown a 90-mph pitch in the major leagues since 2008, and the Phillies picked him up to pitch in Lehigh Valley. ⊘ **Jonathan Pettibone** is the rare young pitcher who survives based on command and control but is nevertheless a prospect; the usual caveats apply, but his groundball style masks his talent. ⊘ A former first-round pick, **David Purcey** bounced from the Jays to the A's to the Tigers last year before being designated for assignment and ultimately outrighted to Toledo. The big lefty throws hard but has long treated the strike zone like a DMZ, and last year walked more men than he whiffed. ⊘ Right-hander **Julio Rodriguez** continues to put up much better statistics than his stuff would suggest, and Double-A will be a big test for his deception-heavy ways. ⊘ **Raul Valdes** may not have defected from Cuba just to tour America's Triple-A ballparks, but that's how it has ended up. As a lefty with two decent years under his belt, he may yet get chances.

## MANAGER: CHARLIE MANUEL

| YEAR | TEAM | W-L | Pythag +/− | Avg PC | 100+ P | 120+ P | QS | BQS | REL | REL w Zero R | IBB | Subs | PH | PH Avg | PH HR | SB2 | CS2 | SB3 | CS3 | SAC Att | SAC % | POS SAC | Squeeze | Swing | In Play |
|------|------|-----|-----|------|-----|-----|----|-----|-----|------|-----|------|-----|------|-----|-----|-----|-----|-----|-----|-------|-----|---------|-------|---------|
| 2009 | PHI | 93-69 | 1 | 97.5 | 86 | 7 | 82 | 5 | 458 | 298 | 31 | 28 | 271 | .186 | 9 | 21 | 8 | 2 | 1 | 84 | 65.5% | 16 | 0 | 140 | 98 |
| 2010 | PHI | 97-65 | 1 | 196.7 | 159 | 157 | 106 | 9 | 452 | 362 | 84 | — | 538 | .188 | 16 | 20 | 3 | 0 | 2 | 140 | 68.6% | 38 | 2 | 279 | 101 |
| 2011 | PHI | 102-60 | 1 | 98.0 | 86 | 10 | 107 | 7 | 394 | 308 | 41 | — | 259 | .236 | 4 | 15 | 3 | 0 | 0 | 91 | 74.7% | 28 | 0 | 276 | 105 |

Charlie Manuel's Virginia drawl and Droopy Dog visage often give the impression that he isn't paying attention very closely. To a certain type of baseball fan, so too does his calling for the third-fewest intentional walks and the tied-for-fifth-fewest sacrifices in the league last year. From a traditionalist perspective, Manuel can look like a go-along-to-get-along player's manager who cannot make the tough decisions. Face facts: This is a guy who once thought it was a good idea to wear a football face mask at the plate to protect a broken jaw. But he's also a guy who coaxed a star turn from John Mayberry by pinch-hitting him liberally against lefties when he wasn't yet the starter. Even after the departure of former Phillies first-base coach Davey Lopes, Manuel led the Phillies to an 80 percent stolen-base percentage. In a season in which the closer role was like a lightning rod for injury, he built a coherent bullpen and doled out high-leverage appearances roughly in proportion to reliever quality. Charlie Manuel is quietly one of the brightest baseball men in the game whose theories of pure hitting are as detailed as the velvety tapestry of his prolonged vowels.

# Pittsburgh Pirates

The life of a Pirates fan: The future is always up, the present is always down.

Pittsburgh spent seven days in first place in 2011, the last of them in late July. It was an achievement noteworthy more for the team involved than the feat accomplished. It had been [...] Justin Bieber was 5 years old and Barack Obama was a state senator. The Devil Rays and Diamondbacks had yet to play a game. When the Pirates fell out of first place, the *New York Times* had still not begun to use color photographs on its front page.

The results are just as stunning if the same game is played for the Pirates' last playoff team, in 1992. Clint Hurdle, now the Pirates manager, entered that season managing above the Double-A level for the first time in his career. It took Hurdle a shorter time to graduate into a viable major-league managerial candidate in two different cities than it has for the Pirates to get back to the playoffs. Whatever factoid we use to show time, the conclusion remains the same: The Pirates have stunk for a while.

Changing a losing culture is no easy task. Doing so requires getting good players, removing bad players, and altering the perception. It is doable, but it requires time. Having a dollar and a dream would have been an upgrade over what Neal Huntington inherited in 2007. The major-league roster held precious few assets, the farm was mostly barren, and the ownership group did not have the best reputation. At least PNC Park had a pretty backdrop.

Likewise, the Pirates were pretty for a while in 2011. So comely that Huntington had to ponder sacrificing a future piece for some short-term help. Would the ends justify the means for the added goodwill? Huntington said no. Instead, he acquired Derrek Lee and Ryan Ludwick for lesser pieces. The conservative approach looked smart almost immediately. The Pirates, who had won 47 of their first 90 games, would lose 47 of their remaining 72 games.

| | | |
|---|---|---|
| TAv | .241 | 30th |
| TAv-P | .264 | 19th |
| FIP | 4.17 | 23rd |
| DER | .700 | 25th |
| DL | 1197 | 29th |
| B-Age | 27.1 | 2nd |
| P-Age | 28.0 | 16th |
| Salary | $44.5 | 28th |
| M$/MW | $1.35 | 5th |

**2011:** Buyers instead of sellers at the trade deadline, they still finished 18 games under .500

**2012:** Improving young stars plus some Band-Aids could conceivably, barely, add up to 81 wins

**Action Items:** Someone—anyone—besides McCutchen to put up a league-average season

allowed 10 or more runs on four occasions. Even the usually punch-free Padres averaged close to 12 runs per game during a three-game set.

Yinzers may wish the season had ended in July; however, they did have a special day after the season had gone down the drain. Draftee-signing deadline came in mid-August and caused great celebration in Pittsburgh. Not only did the Pirates sign the first-overall pick, collegiate ace Gerrit Cole, they also inked their second-round pick, high school third baseman Josh Bell. The latter spent the weeks leading into the draft sending letters to prospective teams advising them against selecting him, stating his desire to attend the University of Texas. Universally labeled an unlikely sign, Bell did indeed put his name next to an X when push came to shove, and he was a big part of the reason the Pirates spent the most money on the draft in the league—$10 million more than the league-average team. Pirates fans had little opportunity to flex their muscles after that faithful July day, but draftee-signing day belonged to them.

Spending money on the draft and in the international market is a new experience for the Pirates, who had to deal with a parsimonious reputation earlier in Huntington's regime. Now, however, baseball's new collective bargaining agreement could undercut future efforts. Under the new CBA, teams will have limits on their draft and international amateur free-agent spending. Teams that go over slot value for an individual pick or their total allotment will have to pay a tax, too far over and they'll lose draft picks. Thus, any hope the Pirates had of mimicking the Royals or Rangers as they try to build up the farm system is dashed.

It gets worse for the Pirates. Huntington did pursue major-league upgrades without yielding prospects or draft picks in exchange for the second straight season, but neither Rod Barajas nor Clint Barmes will be the player who steers the Pirates back into contention. Admittedly, both are honest-to-goodness major leaguers better than Pittsburgh's in-house alternatives. Barajas will ostensibly serve as a tutor for a young staff and Tony Sanchez alike. Barmes will help the pitching staff in another way, by picking anything hit near him, although his bat is a favor only to opposing hurlers.

The problem is that the Pirates are pushing toward mediocrity at the worst time. It does not pay to be a middle-of-the-road team with the new cap restrictions, which get tighter the better a team's record is.

How can the Pirates overcome these changes that seem to rob them of an avenue to success? The most obvious route is by developing the players they were able to draft and sign—often over slot—while operating under the old CBA. Everyone knows about Cole, Bell, Jameson Taillon, and Stetson Allie, but the Pirates have names like Luis Heredia, Colton Cain, Zach Von Rosenberg, Zack Dodson, and Robbie Grossman. Those players, most of them part of an over-slot strategy throughout the draft that led to the Pirates being leading spenders in recent years, are anonymous entities to the common baseball fan who could turn into difference makers for the Pirates if everything breaks right.

Over-slot deals may be headed for extinction, meaning the Pirates will have to settle for more mundane draft classes as they head toward the middle of the pack. And without paying over slot as an option, the Pirates will simply have to get better at developing the talent they have on hand.

Despite selecting within the top 15 picks in each draft since 2001, the Pirates have come away mostly empty-handed in cornerstone talent. Disasters like John Van Benschoten, Bryan Bullington, and Daniel Moskos have left fans annoyed, wondering what might have been if their organization had drafted a reasonable alternative in those spots instead. B.J. Upton, Clayton Kershaw, Tim Lincecum, and Matt Wieters were all available when the Pirates picked. Where would the Pirates be with some of those guys?

Where would the Pirates be if Brad Lincoln and Pedro Alvarez had worked out as they were supposed to? Where will the Pirates be if Cole continues to pitch woefully? Pessimism is a birthright in Pittsburgh.

Even so, the coldest Pirates observers have some traces of optimism in their hearts. If you squint you can see the makings of a playoff contender. The rotation still needs work, the lineup could use a little more tinkering, but Andrew McCutchen is a legitimate star on the rise. Neil Walker and Jose Tabata are nice complimentary players, with upside left to burn. Sanchez and Lincoln could still become major-league contributors yet. Moskos, too. Pittsburgh still has potential rotation stalwarts Charlie Morton and Jeff Locke from the Nate McLouth trade and James McDonald from the Octavio Dotel deal. Once the other pieces of the core, like Cole, Bell, Starling Marte, and Taillon, reach the majors, the Pirates could have something special cooking.

Huntington has done his best to put together an organization that can compete soon and later despite obvious limitations. The higher-ups within the organization were encouraged enough by the progress to extend his contract through the 2014 season, with a club option for 2015. Giving Huntington another three years to turn the impossible dream into a reality seems like a wise move.

One day, one glorious day, the Pirates will return to the postseason, driven by their talented youngsters and years of hard work. When will the curtain go up on the Pirates in October? Not likely in 2012 or '13, and while 2014 is far off, 2015 might be a more realistic target. Until then, the future is always up, the present is always down.

# HITTERS

**Pedro Alvarez**  3B

Born: 2/6/1987 Age: 25
Bats: L Throws: R Height: 6' 4" Weight: 225
Breakout: 3% Improve: 41% Collapse: 9%
Attrition: 22% MLB: 80%

Comparables:
Scott Rolen, Ian Stewart, Jim Thome

| YEAR | TEAM | LVL | AGE | PA | R | 2B | 3B | HR | RBI | BB | SO | SB | CS | AVG/OBP/SLG | TAv | BABIP | BRR | FRAA | WARP |
|------|------|-----|-----|-----|-----|-----|-----|-----|-----|-----|-----|-----|-----|-------------|-----|-------|-----|------|------|
| 2009 | LYN | A+ | 22 | 284 | 38 | 14 | 1 | 14 | 55 | 37 | 70 | 1 | 1 | .247/.346/.486 | .299 | .289 | 1.9 | 1.6 | 2.1 |
| 2009 | ALT | AA | 22 | 258 | 42 | 18 | 0 | 13 | 40 | 34 | 59 | 1 | 0 | .333/.422/.590 | .348 | .407 | -1.9 | 0.5 | 2.9 |
| 2010 | IND | AAA | 23 | 278 | 42 | 15 | 4 | 13 | 53 | 32 | 68 | 4 | 4 | .277/.366/.533 | .302 | .335 | -2.2 | 6.2 | 2.4 |
| 2010 | PIT | MLB | 23 | 386 | 42 | 21 | 1 | 16 | 64 | 37 | 119 | 0 | 0 | .256/.326/.461 | .269 | .341 | -1.3 | 0.6 | 1.4 |
| 2011 | IND | AAA | 24 | 148 | 16 | 5 | 1 | 5 | 19 | 22 | 42 | 0 | 1 | .256/.365/.432 | .260 | .342 | -0.6 | 2.5 | 0.6 |
| 2011 | PIT | MLB | 24 | 262 | 18 | 9 | 1 | 4 | 19 | 24 | 80 | 1 | 0 | .191/.272/.289 | .195 | .272 | -2 | 5.3 | -0.6 |
| 2012 | PIT | MLB | 25 | 329 | 39 | 15 | 1 | 12 | 40 | 32 | 90 | 1 | 1 | .244/.319/.424 | .265 | .307 | -0.1 | 3B 6 | 2.0 |

Strong finishes evoke an optimism rivaled only on report day during spring training. Alvarez hit .306/.355/.577 over the final month in 2010 and appeared primed to take the next step in 2011. He did take a step, just in the wrong direction. A meek start was compounded when Alvarez strained his thigh. He then failed to hit at any level during a rehab stint, return to the majors, and subsequent demotion to the minors. Alvarez resurfaced in September and cemented a poor season by hitting .171/.306/.317 in 49 plate appearances. The reality is that Alvarez might have ensured a poor season before spring training ever began. He skipped his offseason conditioning program, opting instead to focus on his wedding. There is nothing wrong with tying the knot. The Pirates just hope he spends this winter mending his relationship with the ballclub.

**Rod Barajas**   **C**
Born: **9/5/1975** Age: **36**
Bats: **R** Throws: **R** Height: **6' 3''** Weight: **220**
Breakout: **1%** Improve: **18%** Collapse: **13%**
Attrition: **29%** MLB: **65%**

| YEAR | TEAM | LVL | AGE | PA | R | 2B | 3B | HR | RBI | BB | SO | SB | CS | AVG_OBP_SLG | TAv | BABIP | BRR | FRAA | WARP |
|------|------|-----|-----|----|---|----|----|----|-----|----|----|----|----|-------------|-----|-------|-----|------|------|
| 2009 | TOR | MLB | 33 | 460 | 43 | 19 | 0 | 19 | 71 | 20 | 76 | 1 | 0 | .226/.258/.403 | .237 | .229 | 0.2 | -1.8 | 0.9 |
| 2010 | LAN | MLB | 34 | 72 | 9 | 3 | 0 | 5 | 13 | 5 | 15 | 0 | 0 | .297/.361/.578 | .350 | .311 | -0.7 | 0.1 | 0.9 |
| 2010 | NYN | MLB | 34 | 267 | 30 | 11 | 0 | 12 | 34 | 8 | 39 | 0 | 0 | .225/.263/.414 | .242 | .219 | -3 | -0.3 | 0.2 |
| 2011 | LAN | MLB | 35 | 334 | 29 | 13 | 0 | 16 | 47 | 22 | 71 | 0 | 0 | .230/.287/.430 | .259 | .244 | | 0.4 | 0.8 |

Pirates, with a $3.5 million option for 2013, a deal that makes more sense for a stopgap-type player than for an organization that's trying to turn the corner.

**Clint Barmes**   **SS**
Born: **3/6/1979** Age: **33**
Bats: **R** Throws: **R** Height: **6' 1''** Weight: **170**
Breakout: **2%** Improve: **37%** Collapse: **5%**
Attrition: **11%** MLB: **87%**

Comparables:
Rich Aurilia, Miguel Tejada, Alex Gonzalez

| YEAR | TEAM | LVL | AGE | PA | R | 2B | 3B | HR | RBI | BB | SO | SB | CS | AVG_OBP_SLG | TAv | BABIP | BRR | FRAA | WARP |
|------|------|-----|-----|----|---|----|----|----|-----|----|----|----|----|-------------|-----|-------|-----|------|------|
| 2009 | COL | MLB | 30 | 604 | 69 | 32 | 3 | 23 | 76 | 31 | 121 | 12 | 10 | .245/.294/.440 | .241 | .271 | -1.8 | 10.6 | 1.3 |
| 2010 | COL | MLB | 31 | 432 | 43 | 21 | 0 | 8 | 50 | 35 | 66 | 3 | 2 | .235/.305/.351 | .235 | .263 | 2.1 | 3.5 | 0.7 |
| 2011 | HOU | MLB | 32 | 495 | 47 | 27 | 0 | 12 | 39 | 38 | 88 | 3 | 1 | .244/.312/.386 | .250 | .279 | -2 | 5.5 | 2.0 |
| 2012 | PIT | MLB | 33 | 455 | 51 | 23 | 2 | 11 | 51 | 26 | 76 | 6 | 3 | .252/.304/.396 | .251 | .281 | -0.6 | SS 6, 2B 0 | 1.2 |

Over the past three seasons, Barmes has played just over 1500 innings at shortstop and has accumulated 36.3 Fielding Runs Above Average at the position. This rate is second to Brendan Ryan among players with 750 or more shortstop innings, on a FRAA-per-Inning basis. Barmes's historic platoon preference for left-handed pitching was reversed in 2011, but he should still be considered a sub-par offensive player against righties, even by shortstop standards. A gritty, team-player type who has shown true positional versatility, Barmes looks like the starting shortstop now that he's reunited with Hurdle, his Colorado manager, and the Pirates have declined Ronny Cedeno's 2012 option.

**Brandon Boggs**   **LF**
Born: **1/9/1983** Age: **29**
Bats: **B** Throws: **R** Height: **6' 0''** Weight: **205**
Breakout: **8%** Improve: **34%** Collapse: **7%**
Attrition: **20%** MLB: **68%**

Comparables:
Gary Redus, Mike Adams, Jon Nunnally

| YEAR | TEAM | LVL | AGE | PA | R | 2B | 3B | HR | RBI | BB | SO | SB | CS | AVG_OBP_SLG | TAv | BABIP | BRR | FRAA | WARP |
|------|------|-----|-----|----|---|----|----|----|-----|----|----|----|----|-------------|-----|-------|-----|------|------|
| 2009 | OKL | AAA | 26 | 398 | 45 | 15 | 2 | 8 | 47 | 59 | 98 | 9 | 2 | .268/.382/.398 | .287 | .357 | 0.4 | -6.7 | 1.0 |
| 2009 | TEX | MLB | 26 | 18 | 0 | 1 | 0 | 0 | 0 | 1 | 8 | 0 | 0 | .059/.111/.118 | .088 | .111 | -0.2 | 0.1 | -0.4 |
| 2010 | OKL | AAA | 27 | 439 | 72 | 25 | 5 | 10 | 50 | 72 | 93 | 3 | 6 | .290/.408/.470 | .301 | .365 | 2.9 | -1.1 | 3.2 |
| 2010 | TEX | MLB | 27 | 8 | 0 | 0 | 0 | 0 | 0 | 1 | 4 | 0 | 0 | .000/.125/.000 | .023 | .000 | 0 | 0.1 | -0.2 |
| 2011 | NAS | AAA | 28 | 333 | 45 | 19 | 1 | 9 | 38 | 53 | 82 | 3 | 5 | .241/.381/.419 | .279 | .313 | -0.8 | -0.3 | 1.0 |
| 2011 | MIL | MLB | 28 | 22 | 4 | 0 | 0 | 2 | 2 | 3 | 8 | 1 | 0 | .158/.273/.474 | .236 | .111 | 0.6 | -0.2 | 0.1 |
| 2012 | PIT | MLB | 29 | 250 | 27 | 10 | 2 | 5 | 22 | 31 | 70 | 3 | 2 | .218/.322/.349 | .246 | .293 | -0.3 | LF -4, RF 0 | 0.4 |

Boggs could potentially represent a new market inefficiency—a valuable bench player who doesn't hit for a lot of average or power and doesn't make a big impact on either defense or the basepaths. Still, he's posted a .389 combined on-base percentage at the Triple-A level, and as a pinch-rally-starter and backup leadoff hitter, he could make a viable spare outfielder, backing up at all three spots.

**Ronny Cedeno**    SS

Born: 2/2/1983 Age: 29
Bats: R Throws: R Height: 6' 1" Weight: 180
Breakout: 5% Improve: 36% Collapse: 7%
Attrition: 22% MLB: 81%

Comparables:
Dickie Thon, Dave Concepcion, Alvin Dark

| YEAR | TEAM | LVL | AGE | PA | R | 2B | 3B | HR | RBI | BB | SO | SB | CS | AVG/OBP/SLG | TAv | BABIP | BRR | FRAA | WARP |
|------|------|-----|-----|----|----|----|----|----|-----|----|----|----|----|-------------|-----|-------|-----|------|------|
| 2009 | PIT | MLB | 26 | 170 | 17 | 4 | 1 | 5 | 21 | 9 | 29 | 2 | 0 | .258/.307/.394 | .238 | .289 | 1.8 | 0.4 | 0.2 |
| 2009 | SEA | MLB | 26 | 206 | 15 | 4 | 2 | 5 | 17 | 10 | 50 | 3 | 2 | .167/.213/.290 | .179 | .198 | 1.9 | 2.4 | -0.6 |
| 2010 | PIT | MLB | 27 | 502 | 42 | 29 | 3 | 8 | 38 | 23 | 106 | 12 | 3 | .256/.293/.382 | .242 | .315 | 0.7 | -5.7 | 0.1 |
| 2011 | PIT | MLB | 28 | 454 | 43 | 25 | 3 | 2 | 32 | 30 | 93 | 2 | 5 | .249/.297/.339 | .229 | .313 | 1.7 | 9.3 | 1.6 |
| 2012 | NYN | MLB | 29 | 438 | 47 | 20 | 3 | 7 | 44 | 24 | 85 | 7 | 4 | .255/.299/.367 | .239 | .300 | -0.6 | SS 2, 2B -0 | 0.9 |

A rough April and Brandon Wood's acquisition clouded Cedeno's future, and if not for a solid May and a bizarre stretch during interleague play when he hit five doubles in 12 games, the Pirates could have bid Cedeno adieu without much fuss. Cedeno's bat makes him an easy scapegoat for the Pirates' woes, but he finished 2011 with a comparable True Average to those posted by Willie Bloomquist and Yuniesky Betancourt, and those two shortstops were playoff starters. Cedeno may still be the Pirates' best shortstop option, but the club declined his option, making him a free agent.

**Pedro Ciriaco**    SS

Born: 9/27/1985 Age: 26
Bats: R Throws: R Height: 6' 1" Weight: 160
Breakout: 5% Improve: 37% Collapse: 16%
Attrition: 28% MLB: 77%

Comparables:
Robbie Hudson, Chico Salmon, Cristian Guzman

| YEAR | TEAM | LVL | AGE | PA | R | 2B | 3B | HR | RBI | BB | SO | SB | CS | AVG/OBP/SLG | TAv | BABIP | BRR | FRAA | WARP |
|------|------|-----|-----|----|----|----|----|----|-----|----|----|----|----|-------------|-----|-------|-----|------|------|
| 2009 | MOB | AA | 23 | 497 | 56 | 15 | 3 | 4 | 54 | 16 | 71 | 38 | 10 | .296/.319/.367 | .248 | .338 | 1.6 | 0.1 | 1.4 |
| 2010 | IND | AAA | 24 | 126 | 19 | 9 | 1 | 0 | 6 | 2 | 21 | 5 | 1 | .281/.290/.372 | .234 | .337 | 1.5 | -1.6 | 0.3 |
| 2010 | RNO | AAA | 24 | 376 | 44 | 15 | 7 | 6 | 51 | 10 | 53 | 14 | 3 | .259/.277/.392 | .226 | .285 | 2.3 | 4.6 | 0.9 |
| 2010 | PIT | MLB | 24 | 6 | 3 | 1 | 1 | 0 | 1 | 0 | 3 | 0 | 0 | .500/.500/1.000 | .495 | .000 | -1 | 0 | 0.1 |
| 2011 | IND | AAA | 25 | 289 | 31 | 7 | 3 | 2 | 24 | 5 | 49 | 13 | 7 | .231/.243/.300 | .195 | .272 | 2.7 | -6.5 | -1.4 |
| 2011 | PIT | MLB | 25 | 34 | 4 | 2 | 1 | 0 | 6 | 1 | 6 | 2 | 1 | .303/.324/.424 | .267 | .370 | -1.1 | 0.7 | 0.2 |
| 2012 | BOS | MLB | 26 | 250 | 25 | 11 | 2 | 2 | 25 | 5 | 46 | 13 | 5 | .265/.281/.354 | .219 | .313 | -0.3 | SS -1, 2B -1 | -0.2 |

Hitting like Rey Ordonez in the majors is bad enough. Mimicking Ordonez as a 25-year-old at Triple-A is downright regrettable. Ciriaco has no desire to accept walks and does not hit for enough average or power to atone for his stubbornness. One positive from his 2011 season is an increased familiarity with third base and the outfield corners, adding to his résumé to assume the club's super utility player role. Ciriaco is without options and the Pirates will probably stash him on the bench until his hacking ways drive them to action.

**Chase d'Arnaud**    SS

Born: 1/21/1987 Age: 25
Bats: R Throws: R Height: 6' 2" Weight: 200
Breakout: 3% Improve: 39% Collapse: 8%
Attrition: 27% MLB: 79%

Comparables:
Larvell Blanks, Kurt Stillwell, Ricky Adams

| YEAR | TEAM | LVL | AGE | PA | R | 2B | 3B | HR | RBI | BB | SO | SB | CS | AVG/OBP/SLG | TAv | BABIP | BRR | FRAA | WARP |
|------|------|-----|-----|----|----|----|----|----|-----|----|----|----|----|-------------|-----|-------|-----|------|------|
| 2009 | WVA | A | 22 | 255 | 32 | 14 | 3 | 3 | 31 | 30 | 31 | 17 | 3 | .291/.397/.427 | .318 | .328 | 3.2 | 4.3 | 3.3 |
| 2009 | LYN | A+ | 22 | 253 | 45 | 19 | 4 | 4 | 26 | 30 | 41 | 14 | 5 | .295/.402/.481 | .307 | .347 | 1.4 | -2.6 | 2.0 |
| 2010 | ALT | AA | 23 | 607 | 91 | 33 | 9 | 6 | 48 | 56 | 102 | 33 | 7 | .247/.330/.377 | .283 | .293 | 7 | -7.1 | 4.2 |
| 2011 | IND | AAA | 24 | 321 | 43 | 12 | 6 | 4 | 37 | 23 | 53 | 20 | 4 | .264/.328/.389 | .237 | .310 | 2.5 | -0.2 | 0.6 |
| 2011 | PIT | MLB | 24 | 151 | 17 | 6 | 2 | 0 | 6 | 4 | 36 | 12 | 2 | .217/.242/.287 | .194 | .287 | 3.4 | -0.5 | -0.2 |
| 2012 | PIT | MLB | 25 | 250 | 26 | 11 | 2 | 2 | 22 | 16 | 46 | 12 | 3 | .240/.298/.341 | .233 | .284 | 0.3 | SS -3, 2B 1 | 0.5 |

Meet the closest thing the Pirates had to a homegrown shortstop last season. Nowhere near the prospect that his brother Travis is, Chase reached the show first and proceeded to lay an egg. Impressive baserunning aptitude aside, d'Arnaud underwhelmed during his major league stint. Pittsburgh elected to push d'Arnaud to Triple-A in 2011 despite meager output at Double-A the season before, and the results were about what you'd expect.

**Nick Evans**    1B

Born: 1/30/1986 Age: 26
Bats: R Throws: R Height: 6' 4" Weight: 210
Breakout: 0% Improve: 27% Collapse: 3%
Attrition: 13% MLB: 57%

Comparables:
Chris Smith, Francisco Melendez, Joe Vitiello

| YEAR | TEAM | LVL | AGE | PA | R | 2B | 3B | HR | RBI | BB | SO | SB | CS | AVG/OBP/SLG | TAv | BABIP | BRR | FRAA | WARP |
|------|------|-----|-----|----|----|----|----|----|-----|----|----|----|----|-------------|-----|-------|-----|------|------|
| 2009 | BIN | AA | 23 | 117 | 16 | 9 | 1 | 3 | 9 | 10 | 22 | 2 | 0 | .276/.350/.467 | .283 | .325 | 0.7 | -0.7 | 0.5 |
| 2009 | BUF | AAA | 23 | 261 | 27 | 12 | 3 | 10 | 30 | 23 | 55 | 0 | 0 | .211/.281/.414 | .243 | .233 | 0.3 | 0.1 | -0.1 |
| 2009 | NYN | MLB | 23 | 69 | 5 | 5 | 1 | 1 | 7 | 4 | 20 | 0 | 0 | .231/.275/.385 | .208 | .318 | -0.2 | -0.4 | -0.4 |
| 2010 | BIN | AA | 24 | 391 | 62 | 30 | 0 | 17 | 55 | 40 | 65 | 0 | 1 | .294/.369/.527 | .300 | .321 | -2 | 5.2 | 2.7 |
| 2010 | BUF | AAA | 24 | 157 | 26 | 14 | 1 | 6 | 25 | 15 | 23 | 0 | 0 | .314/.382/.557 | .316 | .339 | 1.2 | -0.8 | 1.3 |
| 2010 | NYN | MLB | 24 | 37 | 5 | 3 | 0 | 1 | 5 | 1 | 10 | 0 | 0 | .306/.324/.472 | .262 | .400 | 0.1 | 0 | 0.1 |
| 2011 | BUF | AAA | 25 | 277 | 31 | 13 | 0 | 8 | 32 | 26 | 50 | 3 | 0 | .313/.375/.462 | .268 | .363 | -3.2 | -0.7 | 0.4 |
| 2011 | NYN | MLB | 25 | 194 | 26 | 10 | 2 | 4 | 25 | 15 | 48 | 0 | 0 | .256/.314/.403 | .261 | .325 | 1.6 | 2.1 | 0.6 |
| 2012 | PIT | MLB | 26 | 250 | 29 | 13 | 2 | 7 | 30 | 17 | 54 | 1 | 0 | .259/.310/.419 | .262 | .307 | 0 | 1B -7, LF -1 | 0.9 |

Evans is a nice addition to the Pirates. Consider him the inverse of Garrett Jones, with the ability to play first base or the corner outfield and a bat that's useful against left-handed pitching. While Evans has hit .295/.360/.489 vs. southpaws, he struggles against righties. That means a heavy-handed platoon or pinch-hitting should be the extent of his playing time. Still, it took little to sign Evans, and he is a major-league quality bench player. The Pirates could—and have—played worse.

### Jake Fox — 1B

Born: 7/20/1982 Age: 29
Bats: R Throws: R Height: 6' 1" Weight: 210
Breakout: 3% Improve: 31% Collapse: 3%
Attrition: 19% MLB: 72%

Comparables:
Glenn Davis, Ossie Blanco, Micah Hoffpauir

| YEAR | TEAM | LVL | AGE | PA | R | 2B | 3B | HR | RBI | BB | SO | SB | CS | AVG_OBP_SLG | TAv | BABIP | BRR | FRAA | WARP |
|------|------|-----|-----|-----|----|----|----|----|-----|----|----|----|----|-------------|------|-------|------|---------------|------|
| 2009 | IOW | AAA | 26 | 194 | 44 | 14 | 3 | 17 | 53 | 21 | 31 | 2 | 1 | .409/.497/.841 | .411 | .431 | -1.3 | -0.1 | 3.1 |
| 2009 | CHN | MLB | 26 | 241 | 23 | 12 | 0 | 11 | 44 | 14 | 47 | 0 | 0 | .259/.311/.468 | .267 | .274 | -2.4 | 0.7 | 0.5 |
| 2010 | BAL | MLB | 27 | 105 | 10 | 5 | 1 | 5 | 10 | 3 | 23 | 0 | 0 | .220/.257/.440 | .267 | .236 | -1.1 | 0.4 | 0.2 |
| 2010 | OAK | MLB | 27 | 106 | 11 | 5 | 0 | 2 | 12 | 5 | 26 | 0 | 0 | .214/.264/.327 | .204 | .268 | -0.4 | -0.1 | -0.4 |
| 2011 | NOR | AAA | 28 | 299 | 38 | 19 | 1 | 12 | 58 | 22 | 52 | 0 | 0 | .275/.351/.491 | .289 | .300 | -1.8 | -2.8 | 1.2 |
| 2011 | BAL | MLB | 28 | 67 | 8 | 4 | 1 | 2 | 6 | 4 | 8 | 0 | 0 | .246/.313/.443 | .257 | .255 | -1.5 | -0.9 | -0.1 |
| 2012 | PIT | MLB | 29 | 250 | 31 | 13 | 1 | 11 | 35 | 13 | 48 | 1 | 0 | .261/.313/.465 | .276 | .283 | 0 | 1B -4, C -0 | 1.9 |

From sabermetrics cause célèbre to spring training home run king to non-entity just hoping for another shot. Fox can stand

Breakout: 16% Improve: 39% Collapse: 2%
Attrition: 28% MLB: 56%

Comparables:
Dwight Evans, Eric Anthony, Wladimir Balentien

| YEAR | TEAM | LVL | AGE | PA | R | 2B | 3B | HR | RBI | BB | SO | SB | CS | AVG_OBP_SLG | TAv | BABIP | BRR | FRAA | WARP |
|------|------|-----|-----|-----|-----|----|----|----|-----|-----|-----|----|----|-------------|------|-------|------|--------------|------|
| 2011 | BRD | A+ | 21 | 616 | 127 | 34 | 2 | 13 | 56 | 104 | 111 | 24 | 10 | .294/.418/.451 | .291 | .351 | 6.8 | -13.1 | 1.4 |
| 2012 | PIT | MLB | 22 | 250 | 26 | 10 | 1 | 4 | 20 | 31 | 68 | 7 | 3 | .228/.324/.332 | .243 | .306 | -0.3 | RF -6, CF -5 | 0.2 |

Athletic and now with a successful season under his belt, Grossman conquered Bradenton and continued to show an improvement in his strikeout and walk rates. He has to show last season is more than a transient success, and his stock will skyrocket if he does. It's worth noting that Grossman shifted to right field last season, and his arm is strong enough to work there.

### Josh Harrison — 3B

Born: 7/8/1987 Age: 24
Bats: R Throws: R Height: 5' 9" Weight: 185
Breakout: 2% Improve: 27% Collapse: 10%
Attrition: 32% MLB: 64%

Comparables:
Sergio Miranda, Michael Griffin, Barry Evans

| YEAR | TEAM | LVL | AGE | PA | R | 2B | 3B | HR | RBI | BB | SO | SB | CS | AVG_OBP_SLG | TAv | BABIP | BRR | FRAA | WARP |
|------|------|-----|-----|-----|----|----|----|----|-----|----|----|----|----|-------------|------|-------|------|------------|------|
| 2009 | PEO | A | 21 | 335 | 51 | 17 | 7 | 4 | 33 | 16 | 25 | 16 | 9 | .337/.369/.479 | .322 | .346 | -0.1 | -0.7 | 3.0 |
| 2009 | LYN | A+ | 21 | 155 | 15 | 8 | 1 | 1 | 13 | 1 | 19 | 4 | 1 | .270/.283/.362 | .223 | .291 | 0.1 | -0.6 | -0.5 |
| 2009 | DAY | A+ | 21 | 78 | 10 | 3 | 1 | 1 | 9 | 6 | 7 | 10 | 1 | .286/.346/.400 | .268 | .302 | -0.5 | -0.1 | 0.2 |
| 2010 | ALT | AA | 22 | 585 | 74 | 33 | 3 | 4 | 75 | 32 | 52 | 19 | 7 | .300/.343/.398 | .280 | .318 | 3.2 | 2.6 | 3.9 |
| 2011 | IND | AAA | 23 | 254 | 35 | 15 | 2 | 5 | 23 | 15 | 28 | 13 | 5 | .310/.365/.460 | .286 | .333 | -2.4 | 0.5 | 1.3 |
| 2011 | PIT | MLB | 23 | 204 | 21 | 13 | 2 | 1 | 16 | 3 | 24 | 4 | 1 | .272/.281/.374 | .233 | .304 | -0.7 | 4.2 | 0.5 |
| 2012 | PIT | MLB | 24 | 262 | 27 | 13 | 2 | 2 | 25 | 7 | 30 | 9 | 3 | .267/.291/.355 | .233 | .290 | -0.1 | 3B 2, 2B 2 | 0.5 |

Harrison is a puny utility infielder who has the thighs, bat, and glove of a normal-sized human being. He spent 2011 primarily at third base, but he freelanced at second and is passable at either position. At the plate, Harrison is all about putting the ball in play, although he has more power than you would expect from his 5-foot-8 frame. It's a shame Harrison has no interest in taking free passes, since he could be a useful player if his walk rate ever exceeded his height.

### Gorkys Hernandez — CF

Born: 9/7/1987 Age: 24
Bats: R Throws: R Height: 6' 1" Weight: 185
Breakout: 8% Improve: 41% Collapse: 3%
Attrition: 29% MLB: 65%

Comparables:
Shaun Cumberland, Brandon Guyer, Joshua Flores

| YEAR | TEAM | LVL | AGE | PA | R | 2B | 3B | HR | RBI | BB | SO | SB | CS | AVG_OBP_SLG | TAv | BABIP | BRR | FRAA | WARP |
|------|------|-----|-----|-----|----|----|----|----|-----|----|----|----|----|-------------|------|-------|------|-----------|------|
| 2009 | ALT | AA | 21 | 374 | 45 | 14 | 2 | 3 | 31 | 24 | 76 | 9 | 8 | .262/.312/.340 | .241 | .326 | 3.9 | 2.1 | 1.0 |
| 2009 | MIS | AA | 21 | 228 | 33 | 11 | 2 | 0 | 19 | 15 | 54 | 10 | 8 | .316/.360/.387 | .279 | .421 | 2.7 | 2.6 | 1.9 |
| 2010 | ALT | AA | 22 | 414 | 45 | 11 | 4 | 2 | 26 | 33 | 95 | 17 | 3 | .266/.330/.334 | .246 | .347 | 3.5 | -4.8 | 0.7 |
| 2011 | IND | AAA | 23 | 475 | 48 | 25 | 9 | 1 | 40 | 35 | 91 | 21 | 9 | .283/.348/.392 | .250 | .357 | 6.8 | -2.2 | 1.6 |
| 2012 | PIT | MLB | 24 | 250 | 25 | 11 | 2 | 1 | 21 | 13 | 53 | 11 | 6 | .255/.297/.332 | .229 | .321 | -1.3 | CF -1, RF 0 | -0.2 |

The Pirates had Hernandez repeat Double-A in 2010 and he made progress until breaking a finger. In 2011, they skipped him to Triple-A and he responded by posting his highest isolated power since 2008. Not only that, Hernandez maintained his walk rate and slashed his strikeout totals. The only area where Hernandez took a step back was on the basepaths, as his stolen base success rate dipped from 85 percent to 70 percent.

Now 23, the big questions are whether Hernandez's bat will work in the majors, and whether it can play in a corner, as he is unlikely to displace Andrew McCutchen with the Pirates. Otherwise, look for Pittsburgh to dangle him in a trade.

### Garrett Jones  RF

Born: 6/21/1981 Age: 31
Bats: L Throws: L Height: 6' 5" Weight: 225
Breakout: 6% Improve: 36% Collapse: 6%
Attrition: 20% MLB: 82%

Comparables:
Paul O'Neill, Jason Lane, Johnny Blanchard

| YEAR | TEAM | LVL | AGE | PA | R | 2B | 3B | HR | RBI | BB | SO | SB | CS | AVG_OBP_SLG | TAv | BABIP | BRR | FRAA | WARP |
|------|------|-----|-----|----|----|----|----|----|----|----|----|----|----|------|-----|------|-----|------|------|
| 2009 | IND | AAA | 28 | 299 | 44 | 18 | 0 | 12 | 50 | 18 | 47 | 14 | 4 | .307/.351/.502 | .292 | .335 | 2.9 | 3.3 | 2.2 |
| 2009 | PIT | MLB | 28 | 358 | 45 | 21 | 1 | 21 | 44 | 40 | 76 | 10 | 2 | .293/.372/.567 | .302 | .323 | -1.3 | -1.3 | 1.8 |
| 2010 | PIT | MLB | 29 | 654 | 64 | 34 | 1 | 21 | 86 | 53 | 123 | 7 | 3 | .247/.306/.414 | .252 | .274 | -3.1 | 1.5 | 0.0 |
| 2011 | PIT | MLB | 30 | 477 | 51 | 30 | 1 | 16 | 58 | 48 | 104 | 6 | 3 | .243/.321/.433 | .269 | .283 | -0.5 | -0.7 | 1.1 |
| 2012 | PIT | MLB | 31 | 483 | 58 | 26 | 1 | 17 | 61 | 39 | 92 | 8 | 3 | .257/.318/.436 | .268 | .287 | -0.2 | RF -0, 1B -1 | 1.2 |

Jones is a thoroughbred platoon player, one you can count on to hit 12-plus home runs against right-handed pitching in any given season. A hallmark of good managing is putting your players into situations where they can succeed. Whether Clint Hurdle is a good manager or not is up for debate, but he used Jones better than John Russell had, as Jones faced righties more often than at any other time in his Pirates career (85 percent in 2011—his previous Pittsburgh marks were 70 and 65 percent). Since good results are a rarity, limiting Jones's exposure to lefties is smart. Expect more of the same from Jones in 2012, meaning some time at first base, in right field, and off the bench as a pinch hitter.

### Derrek Lee  1B

Born: 9/6/1975 Age: 36
Bats: R Throws: R Height: 6' 6" Weight: 205
Breakout: 0% Improve: 21% Collapse: 13%
Attrition: 22% MLB: 81%

Comparables:
Roy Sievers, David Justice, Mike Piazza

| YEAR | TEAM | LVL | AGE | PA | R | 2B | 3B | HR | RBI | BB | SO | SB | CS | AVG_OBP_SLG | TAv | BABIP | BRR | FRAA | WARP |
|------|------|-----|-----|----|----|----|----|----|----|----|----|----|----|------|-----|------|-----|------|------|
| 2009 | CHN | MLB | 33 | 615 | 91 | 36 | 2 | 35 | 111 | 76 | 109 | 1 | 0 | .306/.393/.579 | .327 | .327 | -1.2 | 1.3 | 4.6 |
| 2010 | ATL | MLB | 34 | 151 | 17 | 14 | 0 | 3 | 24 | 21 | 33 | 0 | 0 | .287/.384/.465 | .283 | .362 | -1.3 | -3.5 | 0.0 |
| 2010 | CHN | MLB | 34 | 475 | 63 | 21 | 0 | 16 | 56 | 52 | 101 | 1 | 3 | .251/.335/.416 | .256 | .293 | 0.2 | 6.3 | 0.7 |
| 2011 | BAL | MLB | 35 | 364 | 39 | 15 | 1 | 12 | 41 | 25 | 83 | 2 | 1 | .246/.302/.404 | .244 | .290 | -1.3 | -6.2 | -1.1 |
| 2011 | PIT | MLB | 35 | 113 | 16 | 2 | 1 | 7 | 18 | 8 | 27 | 0 | 0 | .337/.398/.584 | .333 | .397 | -1.9 | -0.7 | 0.7 |
| 2012 | PIT | MLB | 36 | 478 | 62 | 25 | 1 | 16 | 60 | 47 | 91 | 3 | 2 | .279/.353/.454 | .290 | .319 | -0.3 | 1B -1 | 2.1 |

Added at the deadline to feign the appearance of a playoff push, Lee played his part by impersonating a big bat—even hitting two home runs in his Pirates debut. Lee came cheap and appeased those who urged the Pirates to make the most of their hot first half. An errant pitch from Carlos Marmol fractured Lee's wrist soon thereafter and the Pirates were out of the race by the time he returned. As such, the most value Lee will provide to a Pirates team in contention is going to come from the draft pick Pittsburgh gains from his Type B designation.

### Ryan Ludwick  RF

Born: 7/13/1978 Age: 33
Bats: R Throws: L Height: 6' 4" Weight: 203
Breakout: 1% Improve: 23% Collapse: 8%
Attrition: 18% MLB: 92%

Comparables:
Eric Hinske, Jerry Lynch, Cliff Floyd

| YEAR | TEAM | LVL | AGE | PA | R | 2B | 3B | HR | RBI | BB | SO | SB | CS | AVG_OBP_SLG | TAv | BABIP | BRR | FRAA | WARP |
|------|------|-----|-----|----|----|----|----|----|----|----|----|----|----|------|-----|------|-----|------|------|
| 2009 | SLN | MLB | 30 | 539 | 63 | 20 | 1 | 22 | 97 | 41 | 106 | 4 | 2 | .265/.329/.447 | .269 | .296 | 1.9 | -2.2 | 1.3 |
| 2010 | SDN | MLB | 31 | 239 | 19 | 7 | 0 | 6 | 26 | 24 | 57 | 0 | 1 | .211/.301/.330 | .234 | .257 | 0 | 3.1 | -0.1 |
| 2010 | SLN | MLB | 31 | 312 | 44 | 20 | 2 | 11 | 43 | 24 | 64 | 0 | 3 | .281/.343/.484 | .302 | .325 | -3 | 4.3 | 2.1 |
| 2011 | SDN | MLB | 32 | 420 | 42 | 18 | 0 | 11 | 64 | 32 | 87 | 1 | 1 | .238/.301/.373 | .249 | .277 | -2.2 | -6.4 | -0.6 |
| 2011 | PIT | MLB | 32 | 133 | 14 | 5 | 0 | 2 | 11 | 19 | 37 | 0 | 0 | .232/.341/.330 | .265 | .324 | -0.2 | -0.4 | 0.1 |
| 2012 | PIT | MLB | 33 | 523 | 63 | 24 | 1 | 18 | 63 | 43 | 111 | 2 | 2 | .254/.322/.428 | .269 | .292 | -0.5 | RF 3, LF -3 | 1.5 |

Since leaving the comforts of St. Louis, Ludwick has hit .254/.308/.353 while playing his home games in San Diego and Pittsburgh—two parks not built for right-handed batters. It is unsurprising that Ludwick has better numbers on the road since the trade that sent him to San Diego, although even those numbers pale in comparison to what he did for the Cardinals. He turns 34 in July and is three seasons removed from hitting 37 home runs.

### Starling Marte  CF

Born: 10/9/1988 Age: 23
Bats: R Throws: R Height: 6' 2" Weight: 170
Breakout: 4% Improve: 36% Collapse: 9%
Attrition: 22% MLB: 71%

Comparables:
Peter Bourjos, Rocco Baldelli, Ellis Burks

| YEAR | TEAM | LVL | AGE | PA | R | 2B | 3B | HR | RBI | BB | SO | SB | CS | AVG_OBP_SLG | TAv | BABIP | BRR | FRAA | WARP |
|------|------|-----|-----|----|----|----|----|----|----|----|----|----|----|------|-----|------|-----|------|------|
| 2009 | WVA | A | 20 | 247 | 41 | 9 | 5 | 3 | 34 | 12 | 55 | 24 | 7 | .312/.380/.439 | .282 | .405 | 1.8 | 0.8 | 1.4 |
| 2010 | BRD | A+ | 21 | 253 | 41 | 16 | 5 | 0 | 33 | 12 | 59 | 22 | 8 | .315/.386/.432 | .292 | .424 | 0 | 0 | 0.0 |
| 2011 | ALT | AA | 22 | 572 | 91 | 38 | 8 | 12 | 50 | 22 | 100 | 24 | 12 | .332/.370/.500 | .306 | .390 | 5.7 | 0.5 | 6.0 |
| 2012 | PIT | MLB | 23 | 250 | 27 | 12 | 2 | 4 | 27 | 6 | 50 | 11 | 4 | .267/.294/.385 | .241 | .319 | -0.4 | CF -6, RF 1 | 0.5 |

Marte's exit from an in-progress game in late July caused the internet to stir with curiosity. He hadn't been traded, just disciplined for violating a team rule. That incident was the only blemish on an otherwise strong campaign for Marte, who showed that he had no residual effects from a broken hamate bone. Marte's hand-eye coordination is top-notch and he hits for a high average because of it, but the blessing is a curse when he becomes too aggressive at the plate. Scouts think he can develop more power, and his defensive palette features a healthy mixture of outstanding tools and instincts. Marte even manages to atone for low walk rates by crowding the plate, and 60 pitches have struck him since 2007. He should start in Indianapolis and a major league promotion is likely.

**Andrew McCutchen CF**
Born: **10/10/1986** Age: **25**
Bats: **R** Throws: **R** Height: **6′ 0″** Weight: **175**
Breakout: **6%** Improve: **44%** Collapse: **5%**
Attrition: **20%** MLB: **94%**
**Comparables:**
Oscar Brown, Al Kaline, Tom Tresh

| YEAR | TEAM | LVL | AGE | PA | R | 2B | 3B | HR | RBI | BB | SO | SB | CS | AVG_OBP_SLG | TAv | BABIP | BRR | FRAA | WARP |
|------|------|-----|-----|-----|-----|-----|-----|-----|-----|-----|-----|-----|-----|-------------|------|-------|------|------|------|
| 2009 | IND | AAA | 22 | 219 | 41 | 10 | 8 | 4 | 20 | 17 | 24 | 10 | 2 | .303/.361/.493 | .296 | .329 | 1.5 | -2.7 | 1.4 |
| 2009 | PIT | MLB | 22 | 493 | 74 | 26 | 9 | 12 | 54 | 54 | 83 | 22 | 5 | .286/.365/.471 | .286 | .327 | 3.1 | -11.4 | 1.7 |
| 2010 | PIT | MLB | 23 | 653 | 94 | 35 | 5 | 16 | 56 | 70 | 89 | 33 | 10 | .286/.365/.449 | .292 | .311 | 4.1 | -12.3 | 3.1 |
| 2011 | PIT | MLB | 24 | 678 | 87 | 34 | 5 | 23 | 89 | 89 | 126 | 23 | 10 | .259/.364/.456 | .297 | .291 | -2.8 | 9.6 | 5.2 |
| 2012 | PIT | MLB | 25 | 632 | 83 | 33 | 6 | 17 | 79 | 68 | 90 | 26 | 9 | .282/.362/.456 | .294 | .307 | -0.3 | CF -2, LF -0 | 4.2 |

Meet the franchise player. McCutchen finally earned a trip to the Midsummer Classic thanks to the Pirates' hot start. He does it all. He hits for average and power alike, has an idea at the plate and steals bases when he

Born: **10/12/1982** Age: **27**
Bats: **R** Throws: **R** Height: **6′ 2″** Weight: **195**
Breakout: **2%** Improve: **49%** Collapse: **12%**
Attrition: **26%** MLB: **88%**
**Comparables:**
Chris Sabo, Joe Crede, Jorge Cantu

| YEAR | TEAM | LVL | AGE | PA | R | 2B | 3B | HR | RBI | BB | SO | SB | CS | AVG_OBP_SLG | TAv | BABIP | BRR | FRAA | WARP |
|------|------|-----|-----|-----|-----|-----|-----|-----|-----|-----|-----|-----|-----|-------------|------|-------|------|------|------|
| 2010 | MIL | MLB | 27 | 670 | 70 | 38 | 1 | 23 | 104 | 50 | 102 | 1 | 1 | .285/.337/.464 | .278 | .306 | -4.2 | -9.5 | 2.6 |
| 2011 | MIL | MLB | 28 | 600 | 46 | 24 | 2 | 13 | 67 | 45 | 104 | 0 | 3 | .223/.280/.346 | .223 | .249 | -5.2 | -1.5 | -0.9 |
| 2012 | PIT | MLB | 29 | 578 | 68 | 28 | 1 | 17 | 67 | 43 | 95 | 1 | 1 | .263/.317/.415 | .263 | .289 | -0.3 | 3B -2, 2B -0 | 2.4 |

McGehee is not as bad as his 2011 statistics suggest. So the Pirates hope. McGehee, normally a masher of left-handed pitching, stumbled into a .169/.228/.185 line against southpaws in 2011. Should he return to form (defined as his 2010 line of .316/.358/.589 against lefties), the Pirates would have some options to pore over. They could platoon McGehee with Alvarez at third base, demote Alvarez until his conditioning and performance meet their standards, relocate Alvarez to first base, or let McGehee become the everyday first baseman. Now, if McGehee will just do his part to precipitate any of those events.

**Michael McKenry C**
Born: **3/4/1985** Age: **27**
Bats: **R** Throws: **R** Height: **5′ 11″** Weight: **200**
Breakout: **9%** Improve: **30%** Collapse: **7%**
Attrition: **37%** MLB: **73%**
**Comparables:**
Jeff Mathis, Phil Lombardi, Nick Hundley

| YEAR | TEAM | LVL | AGE | PA | R | 2B | 3B | HR | RBI | BB | SO | SB | CS | AVG_OBP_SLG | TAv | BABIP | BRR | FRAA | WARP |
|------|------|-----|-----|-----|-----|-----|-----|-----|-----|-----|-----|-----|-----|-------------|------|-------|------|------|------|
| 2009 | TUL | AA | 24 | 417 | 52 | 25 | 1 | 12 | 50 | 54 | 69 | 2 | 2 | .279/.375/.455 | .288 | .315 | -2.3 | 0.2 | 2.7 |
| 2010 | CSP | AAA | 25 | 384 | 44 | 23 | 1 | 10 | 49 | 32 | 77 | 1 | 1 | .265/.331/.424 | .238 | .315 | -4 | 1.1 | 0.6 |
| 2010 | COL | MLB | 25 | 9 | 0 | 0 | 0 | 0 | 0 | 1 | 5 | 0 | 0 | .000/.111/.000 | .046 | .000 | -0.1 | 0 | -0.2 |
| 2011 | PAW | AAA | 26 | 111 | 10 | 5 | 0 | 3 | 12 | 14 | 24 | 1 | 0 | .274/.369/.421 | .279 | .333 | -1.7 | 0.2 | 0.5 |
| 2011 | PIT | MLB | 26 | 201 | 17 | 12 | 0 | 2 | 11 | 14 | 49 | 0 | 1 | .222/.276/.322 | .224 | .290 | -0.2 | -0.5 | -0.1 |
| 2012 | PIT | MLB | 27 | 250 | 27 | 13 | 0 | 5 | 24 | 21 | 56 | 1 | 0 | .239/.304/.365 | .242 | .291 | -0.1 | C -1, 3B -0 | 1.2 |

Acquired from Boston after injuries left Wyatt Toregas and Dusty Brown as the last catchers standing, McKenry profiles as a typical reserve catcher. A hitch in his swing limits his ability to make contact, so he relies on walks and the occasional extra-base hit. His defensive reputation is stellar, but he only threw out 25 percent of attempted thieves.

**Nate McLouth CF**
Born: **10/28/1981** Age: **30**
Bats: **L** Throws: **R** Height: **6′ 0″** Weight: **185**
Breakout: **2%** Improve: **38%** Collapse: **6%**
Attrition: **10%** MLB: **95%**
**Comparables:**
Cesar Cedeno, Amos Otis, Bernie Williams

| YEAR | TEAM | LVL | AGE | PA | R | 2B | 3B | HR | RBI | BB | SO | SB | CS | AVG_OBP_SLG | TAv | BABIP | BRR | FRAA | WARP |
|------|------|-----|-----|-----|-----|-----|-----|-----|-----|-----|-----|-----|-----|-------------|------|-------|------|------|------|
| 2009 | ATL | MLB | 27 | 396 | 59 | 20 | 1 | 11 | 36 | 47 | 70 | 12 | 6 | .257/.354/.419 | .270 | .292 | 1.1 | -2.4 | 1.4 |
| 2009 | PIT | MLB | 27 | 195 | 27 | 7 | 1 | 9 | 34 | 21 | 29 | 7 | 0 | .256/.349/.470 | .279 | .258 | 0.5 | -0.7 | 1.0 |
| 2010 | GWN | AAA | 28 | 151 | 18 | 1 | 0 | 6 | 18 | 19 | 21 | 7 | 0 | .234/.342/.383 | .266 | .238 | 0 | 2.9 | 0.8 |
| 2010 | ATL | MLB | 28 | 288 | 30 | 12 | 1 | 6 | 24 | 33 | 57 | 7 | 2 | .190/.298/.322 | .225 | .221 | 3.4 | -1.8 | -0.2 |
| 2011 | ATL | MLB | 29 | 321 | 35 | 12 | 2 | 4 | 16 | 44 | 52 | 4 | 2 | .228/.344/.333 | .251 | .270 | 2.6 | -1.8 | 0.5 |
| 2012 | PIT | MLB | 30 | 314 | 38 | 15 | 1 | 9 | 34 | 33 | 49 | 9 | 2 | .251/.341/.411 | .270 | .272 | 0.2 | CF -0, LF -1 | 1.9 |

Fewer things are sadder in baseball than injuries derailing a young player's career. McLouth had earned an All-Star bid, a Gold Glove, and a ticket to a contender when the injury bug gravitated to him. A concussion, strained oblique, and sports hernia limited him in 2010-11, and wore his power production to a shadow of its former self. The Braves had no choice but to decline McLouth's option—worth almost $11 million—and the Pirates decided to welcome their old flame back at a reduced cost. If McLouth can stay healthy, he could be an everyday player who supplies a little of everything. More realistically, the Pirates should be satisfied if he can serve in a timeshare with a righty.

**Yamaico Navarro    SS**

Born: 10/31/1987 Age: 24
Bats: R Throws: R Height: 6' 0'' Weight: 170
Breakout: 3% Improve: 21% Collapse: 8%
Attrition: 46% MLB: 84%

Comparables:
Greg Smith, Fausto Cruz, Mark Loretta

| YEAR | TEAM | LVL | AGE | PA | R | 2B | 3B | HR | RBI | BB | SO | SB | CS | AVG_OBP_SLG | TAv | BABIP | BRR | FRAA | WARP |
|------|------|-----|-----|-----|----|----|----|----|-----|----|----|----|----|-------------|------|-------|------|-----------|------|
| 2009 | SLM | A+ | 21 | 102 | 10 | 9 | 0 | 4 | 17 | 6 | 12 | 2 | 2 | .319/.373/.543 | .302 | .333 | -0.1 | -2.9 | 0.5 |
| 2009 | PME | AA | 21 | 152 | 16 | 6 | 2 | 2 | 11 | 14 | 28 | 5 | 1 | .185/.272/.304 | .204 | .219 | -0.3 | 0.6 | -0.4 |
| 2010 | PME | AA | 22 | 378 | 49 | 19 | 3 | 8 | 55 | 42 | 53 | 16 | 5 | .274/.360/.422 | .275 | .305 | 0.3 | -5.2 | 1.6 |
| 2010 | PAW | AAA | 22 | 59 | 8 | 4 | 0 | 3 | 6 | 5 | 6 | 2 | 1 | .283/.345/.528 | .308 | .273 | 1.1 | -1.2 | 0.6 |
| 2010 | BOS | MLB | 22 | 46 | 4 | 0 | 0 | 0 | 5 | 2 | 17 | 0 | 0 | .143/.174/.143 | .132 | .222 | 0.2 | -0.3 | -0.4 |
| 2011 | PAW | AAA | 23 | 149 | 25 | 8 | 2 | 5 | 13 | 17 | 25 | 3 | 2 | .258/.362/.469 | .281 | .286 | 0.5 | 0.8 | 0.8 |
| 2011 | OMA | AAA | 23 | 101 | 11 | 3 | 1 | 2 | 9 | 7 | 18 | 3 | 4 | .272/.317/.391 | .257 | .311 | -1.3 | -2.4 | -0.1 |
| 2011 | KCA | MLB | 23 | 26 | 2 | 1 | 0 | 0 | 6 | 2 | 5 | 0 | 0 | .304/.346/.348 | .295 | .368 | 0 | -0.3 | 0.2 |
| 2011 | BOS | MLB | 23 | 40 | 6 | 2 | 0 | 1 | 3 | 3 | 9 | 0 | 0 | .216/.275/.351 | .230 | .259 | 0.6 | -0.6 | 0.1 |
| 2012 | PIT | MLB | 24 | 250 | 26 | 11 | 1 | 5 | 24 | 18 | 47 | 7 | 4 | .239/.299/.362 | .240 | .279 | -0.9 | SS -6, 3B -1 | 0.6 |

Traded once at the deadline (from Boston to Kansas City) and then again not even six months later (from Kansas City to Boston), Navarro possesses quick hands and modest power aspirations at the plate. In the field, his athleticism plays up at a number of positions, making him a prime candidate to become a utility infielder. With Clint Barmes and Neil Walker entrenched at shortstop and second base, expect Navarro to spend quality time on the bench, and for Pittsburgh to benefit from his presence.

**Steve Pearce    1B**

Born: 4/13/1983 Age: 29
Bats: R Throws: R Height: 6' 0'' Weight: 200
Breakout: 2% Improve: 45% Collapse: 4%
Attrition: 20% MLB: 91%

Comparables:
Jim Ray Hart, Jack Lohrke, Eric Soderholm

| YEAR | TEAM | LVL | AGE | PA | R | 2B | 3B | HR | RBI | BB | SO | SB | CS | AVG_OBP_SLG | TAv | BABIP | BRR | FRAA | WARP |
|------|------|-----|-----|-----|----|----|----|----|-----|----|----|----|----|-------------|------|-------|------|-----------|------|
| 2009 | IND | AAA | 26 | 317 | 37 | 18 | 1 | 13 | 54 | 34 | 46 | 3 | 7 | .286/.376/.502 | .296 | .302 | -1.9 | 3.9 | 1.7 |
| 2009 | PIT | MLB | 26 | 186 | 19 | 13 | 1 | 4 | 16 | 21 | 43 | 1 | 0 | .206/.296/.370 | .224 | .254 | -0.4 | 2.2 | -0.4 |
| 2010 | IND | AAA | 27 | 158 | 25 | 14 | 2 | 3 | 15 | 24 | 27 | 7 | 2 | .326/.435/.535 | .319 | .394 | 0.4 | -0.2 | 1.4 |
| 2010 | PIT | MLB | 27 | 38 | 4 | 2 | 1 | 0 | 5 | 7 | 6 | 0 | 0 | .276/.395/.414 | .306 | .320 | 0.3 | 1 | 0.4 |
| 2011 | PIT | MLB | 28 | 105 | 8 | 2 | 0 | 1 | 10 | 7 | 21 | 0 | 0 | .202/.260/.255 | .189 | .243 | -0.4 | -0.5 | -0.7 |
| 2012 | MIN | MLB | 29 | 250 | 30 | 14 | 1 | 7 | 30 | 21 | 45 | 3 | 2 | .259/.326/.426 | .268 | .292 | -0.2 | 1B -4, 3B -0 | 1.2 |

Injuries and the worst managerial malady of them all—veteran obsession—killed Pearce's chance of having a meaningful career with the Pirates. Pearce made the team out of spring training and hit acceptably (.291/.339/.382 in 62 plate appearances) before suffering a partially torn calf muscle. When he returned, the only thing he accomplished was successfully torpedoing his seasonal line (.077/.143/.077 in 43 plate appearances). True to form, Pearce then missed the rest of the year when he broke a finger. Better suited for first base or right field than third base, Pearce has hit major league lefties and could be a useful bench piece should he ever stay healthy.

**Alex Presley    LF**

Born: 7/25/1985 Age: 26
Bats: L Throws: L Height: 5' 10'' Weight: 180
Breakout: 2% Improve: 36% Collapse: 10%
Attrition: 25% MLB: 75%

Comparables:
Lou Piniella, Billy Baldwin, Jonel Pacheco

| YEAR | TEAM | LVL | AGE | PA | R | 2B | 3B | HR | RBI | BB | SO | SB | CS | AVG_OBP_SLG | TAv | BABIP | BRR | FRAA | WARP |
|------|------|-----|-----|-----|----|----|----|----|-----|----|----|----|----|-------------|------|-------|------|-----------|------|
| 2009 | LYN | A+ | 23 | 456 | 51 | 17 | 11 | 4 | 37 | 30 | 87 | 9 | 5 | .257/.302/.379 | .252 | .309 | 0.1 | -1.7 | 0.2 |
| 2010 | ALT | AA | 24 | 269 | 42 | 13 | 7 | 6 | 47 | 19 | 33 | 5 | 1 | .350/.399/.533 | .332 | .385 | 1.1 | 1.3 | 2.9 |
| 2010 | IND | AAA | 24 | 296 | 44 | 15 | 6 | 6 | 38 | 22 | 42 | 8 | 7 | .294/.348/.460 | .269 | .329 | 2.7 | -0.7 | 1.4 |
| 2010 | PIT | MLB | 24 | 25 | 2 | 1 | 0 | 0 | 0 | 1 | 8 | 1 | 1 | .261/.292/.304 | .214 | .400 | -0.5 | -0.5 | -0.2 |
| 2011 | IND | AAA | 25 | 376 | 58 | 18 | 5 | 8 | 41 | 28 | 54 | 22 | 8 | .333/.388/.485 | .290 | .376 | 1.2 | 5.2 | 3.0 |
| 2011 | PIT | MLB | 25 | 231 | 27 | 12 | 6 | 4 | 20 | 13 | 40 | 9 | 3 | .298/.339/.465 | .279 | .349 | 0.8 | -4.1 | 0.6 |
| 2012 | PIT | MLB | 26 | 299 | 34 | 13 | 5 | 4 | 32 | 16 | 50 | 8 | 4 | .275/.316/.396 | .254 | .319 | -0.5 | LF -3, CF -2 | 0.8 |

Elvis puns, grit, and outs against left-handed pitching. What are three things Presley's career will offer in high doses? After shedding the non-entity label in 2010, Presley validated his newfound status as a future major leaguer and became the Pirates' everyday left fielder down the stretch while Jose Tabata recuperated from a broken hand. Presley was not without an injury of his own, as he damaged his thumb in late July and chose to alter his swing to compensate for the condition by the time he returned in late August. He hit .276/.297/.448 from his reinsertion point onward, which resembles a line he may produce when healthy.

## Tony Sanchez — C

Born: 5/20/1988 Age: 24
Bats: R Throws: R Height: 6' 1" Weight: 215
Breakout: 1% Improve: 13% Collapse: 7%
Attrition: 26% MLB: 51%

Comparables:
Jamie Nelson, Jason Castro, Rick Dempsey

| YEAR | TEAM | LVL | AGE | PA | R | 2B | 3B | HR | RBI | BB | SO | SB | CS | AVG/OBP/SLG | TAv | BABIP | BRR | FRAA | WARP |
|------|------|-----|-----|----|----|----|----|----|-----|----|----|----|----|-------------|-----|-------|-----|------|------|
| 2009 | WVA | A | 21 | 188 | 29 | 15 | 1 | 7 | 46 | 21 | 34 | 1 | 0 | .316/.424/.561 | .345 | .368 | -0.4 | -0.4 | 2.3 |
| 2010 | BRD | A+ | 22 | 250 | 31 | 17 | 0 | 4 | 35 | 28 | 41 | 2 | 1 | .314/.423/.454 | .315 | .377 | 0 | 0 | 0.0 |
| 2011 | ALT | AA | 23 | 469 | 46 | 14 | 1 | 5 | 44 | 47 | 76 | 5 | 5 | .241/.340/.318 | .251 | .285 | 1.5 | 0.9 | 1.2 |
| 2012 | PIT | MLB | 24 | 250 | 25 | 10 | 1 | 3 | 20 | 18 | 48 | 1 | 1 | .224/.294/.321 | .227 | .266 | -0.1 | C -0 | 0.4 |

Sanchez's offense is a point of consternation for fans and analysts alike, since his value is driven by his defense. Good glove or not, spending 2009's number-four pick on the next Mike Matheny is an undesirable outcome. Complicating matters is Sanchez's weak caught-stealing rates over the last two seasons. All scouting reports suggest Sanchez has a strong if sometimes inaccurate arm, receiving skills that make Hines Ward blush, and a plethora of intangibles, so it could be a mechanical issue more than a fatal flaw.

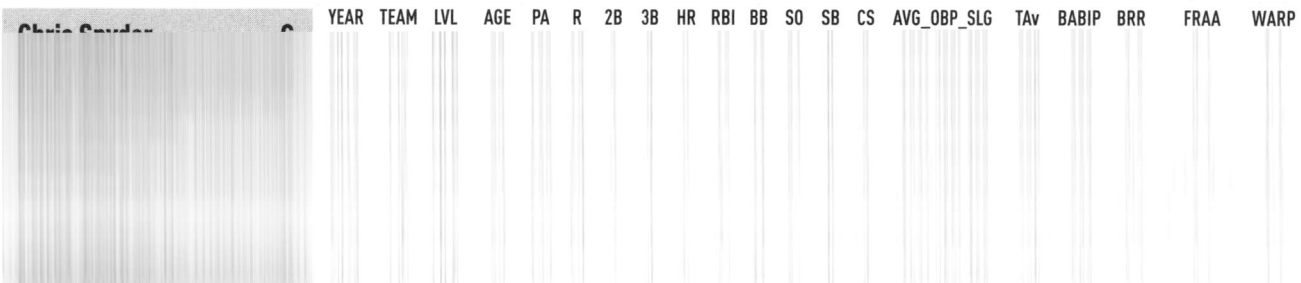

## Chris Snyder — C

| YEAR | TEAM | LVL | AGE | PA | R | 2B | 3B | HR | RBI | BB | SO | SB | CS | AVG/OBP/SLG | TAv | BABIP | BRR | FRAA | WARP |
|------|------|-----|-----|----|----|----|----|----|-----|----|----|----|----|-------------|-----|-------|-----|------|------|

way to a more walk-heavy approach. Pittsburgh elected to decline Snyder's $6.75 million club option in favor of paying him a $750,000 buyout. The book on Snyder has not changed for a few years now: When healthy, he hits more than most catchers while providing a solid target behind the dish.

## Jose Tabata — LF

Born: 8/12/1988 Age: 23
Bats: R Throws: R Height: 6' 0" Weight: 210
Breakout: 2% Improve: 31% Collapse: 7%
Attrition: 22% MLB: 79%

Comparables:
Jerry Turner, Roy White, Fred Lynn

| YEAR | TEAM | LVL | AGE | PA | R | 2B | 3B | HR | RBI | BB | SO | SB | CS | AVG/OBP/SLG | TAv | BABIP | BRR | FRAA | WARP |
|------|------|-----|-----|----|----|----|----|----|-----|----|----|----|----|-------------|-----|-------|-----|------|------|
| 2009 | ALT | AA | 20 | 254 | 31 | 15 | 1 | 2 | 25 | 20 | 25 | 7 | 6 | .303/.372/.404 | .287 | .333 | -0.4 | 0.2 | 1.2 |
| 2009 | IND | AAA | 20 | 148 | 21 | 7 | 1 | 3 | 10 | 10 | 18 | 4 | 2 | .276/.333/.410 | .263 | .298 | 1.1 | -1.5 | 0.3 |
| 2010 | IND | AAA | 21 | 252 | 42 | 13 | 2 | 3 | 19 | 23 | 35 | 25 | 6 | .308/.378/.424 | .280 | .355 | 2.6 | 0.4 | 1.4 |
| 2010 | PIT | MLB | 21 | 441 | 61 | 21 | 4 | 4 | 35 | 28 | 57 | 19 | 7 | .299/.346/.400 | .264 | .339 | 3.5 | 4.3 | 1.5 |
| 2011 | PIT | MLB | 22 | 382 | 53 | 18 | 1 | 4 | 21 | 40 | 61 | 16 | 7 | .266/.349/.362 | .249 | .312 | 3 | -0.4 | 0.5 |
| 2012 | PIT | MLB | 23 | 408 | 48 | 21 | 2 | 4 | 40 | 31 | 51 | 18 | 7 | .286/.344/.387 | .265 | .318 | -0.8 | LF 2, CF -1 | 1.2 |

Age- and injury-related questions continued to linger as the Pirates threw caution to the wind by re-signing Tabata to a six-year extension worth $15 million with three club options. Superstar aspirations are just a rumor now for this classic outfield tweener, but if Tabata is his listed age, then some added power as he matures is a possibility. Tabata's improved grasp of the strike zone is an encouraging sign, as the added walks should help to buoy an on-base percentage otherwise driven by batting average.

## Neil Walker — 2B

Born: 9/10/1985 Age: 26
Bats: B Throws: R Height: 6' 4" Weight: 215
Breakout: 7% Improve: 45% Collapse: 5%
Attrition: 34% MLB: 85%

Comparables:
Kevin Jordan, Danny Richar, Ian Kinsler

| YEAR | TEAM | LVL | AGE | PA | R | 2B | 3B | HR | RBI | BB | SO | SB | CS | AVG/OBP/SLG | TAv | BABIP | BRR | FRAA | WARP |
|------|------|-----|-----|----|----|----|----|----|-----|----|----|----|----|-------------|-----|-------|-----|------|------|
| 2009 | IND | AAA | 23 | 390 | 38 | 31 | 2 | 14 | 69 | 26 | 60 | 5 | 2 | .264/.315/.480 | .261 | .283 | 0.3 | -7.4 | 0.2 |
| 2009 | PIT | MLB | 23 | 40 | 5 | 1 | 0 | 0 | 0 | 4 | 11 | 1 | 0 | .194/.275/.222 | .179 | .280 | -0.4 | -0.5 | -0.4 |
| 2010 | IND | AAA | 24 | 189 | 25 | 18 | 2 | 6 | 26 | 19 | 31 | 10 | 1 | .321/.394/.560 | .307 | .366 | -0.6 | 3.2 | 1.7 |
| 2010 | PIT | MLB | 24 | 469 | 57 | 29 | 3 | 12 | 66 | 34 | 83 | 2 | 3 | .296/.349/.462 | .280 | .340 | -1.9 | -15.8 | 0.7 |
| 2011 | PIT | MLB | 25 | 662 | 76 | 36 | 4 | 12 | 83 | 54 | 112 | 9 | 6 | .273/.334/.408 | .262 | .315 | 1 | -5.8 | 1.5 |
| 2012 | PIT | MLB | 26 | 606 | 73 | 36 | 3 | 14 | 72 | 44 | 96 | 9 | 4 | .273/.328/.424 | .268 | .306 | -0.6 | 2B -9, 3B -0 | 2.4 |

Before the ink dried on Tabata's new deal, rumor had it that Walker would be the next up in the non-McCutchen extension line. It makes sense for qualitative (hometown kid, the club's first-round draft pick in 2004, fan favorite, etc.) and quantitative (pre-arb 25-year-old second baseman with offensive skills) purposes. Walker improved defensively in his second full season at the keystone, relocating on the spectrum from horrific to poor. As a switch-hitter, Walker shows better chops from the left side with more pop and tighter strike zone judgment, but his total walk and strikeout rates went the right way for the second straight season. PECOTA is bullish on Walker developing further in 2012. The Pirates might consider it worth the gamble to lock him up now in case he does.

**Brandon Wood** 3B

Born: 3/2/1985 Age: 27
Bats: R Throws: R Height: 6' 4" Weight: 185
Breakout: 3% Improve: 26% Collapse: 4%
Attrition: 14% MLB: 73%

**Comparables:**
Marty Brown, Travis Fryman, Tony Blanco

| YEAR | TEAM | LVL | AGE | PA | R | 2B | 3B | HR | RBI | BB | SO | SB | CS | AVG_OBP_SLG | TAv | BABIP | BRR | FRAA | WARP |
|------|------|-----|-----|-----|----|----|----|----|-----|----|----|----|----|-------------|-----|-------|-----|------|------|
| 2009 | SLC | AAA | 24 | 428 | 65 | 28 | 4 | 22 | 72 | 36 | 80 | 1 | 1 | .293/.356/.557 | .296 | .320 | -1.7 | -13.3 | 1.5 |
| 2009 | ANA | MLB | 24 | 46 | 5 | 1 | 0 | 1 | 3 | 3 | 19 | 0 | 0 | .195/.267/.293 | .195 | .333 | -1.3 | -0.6 | -0.5 |
| 2010 | SLC | AAA | 25 | 54 | 4 | 0 | 0 | 1 | 2 | 3 | 17 | 0 | 0 | .196/.241/.255 | .170 | .273 | 0.2 | -0.6 | -0.3 |
| 2010 | ANA | MLB | 25 | 243 | 20 | 2 | 0 | 4 | 14 | 6 | 71 | 1 | 0 | .146/.174/.208 | .156 | .191 | 1.8 | -2.8 | -2.1 |
| 2011 | PIT | MLB | 26 | 257 | 25 | 9 | 0 | 7 | 31 | 19 | 65 | 0 | 0 | .220/.277/.347 | .229 | .273 | 0.1 | -1.8 | -0.1 |
| 2011 | ANA | MLB | 26 | 15 | 1 | 1 | 0 | 0 | 0 | 0 | 8 | 0 | 0 | .143/.143/.214 | .141 | .333 | -0.1 | -0.4 | -0.2 |
| 2012 | COL | MLB | 27 | 256 | 29 | 10 | 1 | 10 | 32 | 16 | 66 | 1 | 0 | .241/.292/.422 | .243 | .288 | 0 | 3B -4, SS -4 | 1.1 |

Under normal circumstances, Wood finishing the season with a comparable TAv to Justin Morneau and better than Adam Dunn would have been grounds for celebration. Instead, Wood's career year served as another reminder that hitting prospects fail too. Pittsburgh roped Wood in after the Angels ditched him in April, then used him at third base during Alvarez's absence. For a brief moment, Wood reminded everyone what made him a desirable good before regressing into a melancholy puddle and spending most of September on the bench. He turns 27 in March. Don't be surprised if he winds up with another organization before hitting 28.

# PITCHERS

**Erik Bedard**

Born: 3/5/1979 Age: 33
Bats: L Throws: L Height: 6' 2" Weight: 180
Breakout: 25% Improve: 54% Collapse: 21%
Attrition: 10% MLB: 98%

**Comparables:**
Hideki Okajima, Matt Thornton, Arthur Rhodes

| YEAR | TEAM | LVL | AGE | W | L | SV | G | GS | IP | H | HR | BB | SO | EqBB9 | EqSO9 | GB% | BABIP | WHIP | ERA | FIP | FRA | WARP |
|------|------|-----|-----|---|---|----|---|----|-----|----|----|----|----|-------|-------|-----|-------|------|------|------|------|------|
| 2009 | SEA | MLB | 30 | 5 | 3 | 0 | 15 | 15 | 83 | 65 | 8 | 34 | 90 | 3.7 | 9.8 | 45% | .271 | 1.19 | 2.82 | 3.60 | 3.73 | 1.5 |
| 2011 | BOS | MLB | 32 | 1 | 2 | 0 | 8 | 8 | 38 | 41 | 3 | 18 | 38 | 4.3 | 9.0 | 43% | .349 | 1.55 | 4.03 | 3.51 | 4.65 | 0.4 |
| 2011 | SEA | MLB | 32 | 4 | 7 | 0 | 16 | 16 | 91¹ | 77 | 11 | 30 | 87 | 3.0 | 8.6 | 42% | .272 | 1.17 | 3.45 | 3.74 | 3.96 | 0.9 |
| 2012 | PIT | MLB | 33 | 7 | 5 | 0 | 19 | 19 | 99 | 80 | 9 | 33 | 92 | 3.0 | 8.4 | 45% | .291 | 1.14 | 3.21 | 3.53 | 3.49 | 2.1 |

Bedard's knee, not his shoulder, gave him trouble in 2011. He still mustered 129 innings—129 more than he did in 2010—and showed that his fastball-curveball combination can work, provided that he has his good command. The Pirates signed Bedard with the hope that he can be the legitimate strikeout artist lacking from their rotation since Oliver Perez. A move to the National League for the first time in his career should help. But this is Bedard, so like always, health will be the determinant.

**Kevin Correia**

Born: 8/24/1980 Age: 31
Bats: R Throws: R Height: 6' 4" Weight: 200
Breakout: 18% Improve: 51% Collapse: 25%
Attrition: 10% MLB: 87%

**Comparables:**
Geoff Geary, LaTroy Hawkins, Alex Fernandez

| YEAR | TEAM | LVL | AGE | W | L | SV | G | GS | IP | H | HR | BB | SO | EqBB9 | EqSO9 | GB% | BABIP | WHIP | ERA | FIP | FRA | WARP |
|------|------|-----|-----|----|----|----|----|----|-----|-----|----|----|-----|-------|-------|-----|-------|------|------|------|------|------|
| 2009 | SDN | MLB | 28 | 12 | 11 | 0 | 33 | 33 | 198 | 194 | 17 | 64 | 142 | 2.9 | 6.5 | 47% | .298 | 1.30 | 3.91 | 3.77 | 4.42 | 1.3 |
| 2010 | SDN | MLB | 29 | 10 | 10 | 0 | 28 | 26 | 145 | 152 | 20 | 64 | 115 | 4.0 | 7.1 | 50% | .306 | 1.49 | 5.40 | 4.74 | 5.00 | -0.5 |
| 2011 | PIT | MLB | 30 | 12 | 11 | 0 | 27 | 26 | 154 | 175 | 24 | 39 | 77 | 2.3 | 4.5 | 47% | .295 | 1.39 | 4.79 | 4.82 | 5.39 | -0.1 |
| 2012 | PIT | MLB | 31 | 8 | 8 | 0 | 23 | 23 | 132 | 131 | 14 | 42 | 76 | 2.9 | 5.2 | 45% | .296 | 1.31 | 4.33 | 4.39 | 4.70 | 0.8 |

Correia blew another good April to smithereens by pitching poorly after the calendar flipped to May. His earned-run average worsened in each sequential month and he forgot to pack his strikeouts when moving from San Diego, yet the community's attention focused on Correia's win-loss record and his questionable All-Star bid. The Pirates lineup did provide him with the most run support on staff, but he also managed a quality start in 11 of his 12 wins. Given a two-year deal, Correia can recover from an oblique injury that ended his season in August with the knowledge that his job is safe for now.

**Jason Grilli**

Born: 11/11/1976 Age: 35
Bats: R Throws: R Height: 6' 5" Weight: 185
Breakout: 15% Improve: 39% Collapse: 43%
Attrition: 23% MLB: 78%

**Comparables:**
Scot Shields, Sam Jones, Armando Benitez

| YEAR | TEAM | LVL | AGE | W | L | SV | G | GS | IP | H | HR | BB | SO | EqBB9 | EqSO9 | GB% | BABIP | WHIP | ERA | FIP | FRA | WARP |
|------|------|-----|-----|---|---|----|----|----|-----|----|----|----|----|-------|-------|-----|-------|------|------|------|------|------|
| 2009 | COL | MLB | 32 | 0 | 1 | 1 | 22 | 0 | 19¹ | 29 | 2 | 13 | 22 | 6.1 | 10.2 | 34% | .443 | 2.17 | 6.05 | 4.14 | 4.49 | 0.3 |
| 2009 | TEX | MLB | 32 | 2 | 2 | 0 | 30 | 0 | 26¹ | 21 | 2 | 14 | 27 | 4.8 | 9.2 | 39% | .279 | 1.33 | 4.78 | 3.79 | 3.83 | 0.5 |
| 2011 | LEH | AAA | 34 | 4 | 1 | 3 | 28 | 0 | 32² | 24 | 2 | 11 | 42 | 3.3 | 11.8 | 42% | .306 | 1.16 | 1.93 | 2.57 | 3.40 | 0.6 |
| 2011 | PIT | MLB | 34 | 2 | 1 | 1 | 28 | 0 | 32² | 24 | 2 | 15 | 37 | 4.1 | 10.2 | 49% | .272 | 1.19 | 2.48 | 3.27 | 4.37 | 0.3 |
| 2012 | PIT | MLB | 35 | 1 | 1 | 1 | 27 | 0 | 31² | 29 | 2 | 13 | 26 | 3.7 | 7.3 | 44% | .309 | 1.31 | 4.01 | 3.61 | 4.36 | 0.3 |

You have to live up to certain requirements to be a real journeyman reliever. You have to make up for an absentee season by signing a minor league deal and pitching well enough to earn a major league shot with another team after exercising your opt-out. You then have to bemuse onlookers by putting up an uncharacteristically strong season in order to generate additional human-interest stories. The last step in becoming an official journeyman reliever is the most difficult and vital. You have to qualify for arbitration after age 35. Everything checks out for you, Mr. Grilli. Congratulations. Your membership card is in the mail.

**Joel Hanrahan**
Born: 10/6/1981 Age: 30
Bats: R Throws: R Height: 6' 4" Weight: 215
Breakout: 27% Improve: 59% Collapse: 24%
Attrition: 7% MLB: 91%

Comparables:
Kevin Gregg, Michael Wuertz, Jason Frasor

| YEAR | TEAM | LVL | AGE | W | L | SV | G | GS | IP | H | HR | BB | SO | EqBB9 | EqSO9 | GB% | BABIP | WHIP | ERA | FIP | FRA | WARP |
|---|---|---|---|---|---|---|---|---|---|---|---|---|---|---|---|---|---|---|---|---|---|---|
| 2009 | PIT | MLB | 27 | 0 | 1 | 0 | 33 | 0 | 31¹ | 23 | 0 | 20 | 37 | 5.7 | 10.6 | 28% | .303 | 1.37 | 1.72 | 2.71 | 2.28 | 1.1 |
| 2009 | WAS | MLB | 27 | 1 | 3 | 5 | 34 | 0 | 32² | 50 | 3 | 14 | 35 | 3.9 | 9.6 | 46% | .431 | 1.96 | 7.71 | 3.58 | 4.12 | 0.6 |
| 2010 | PIT | MLB | 28 | 4 | 1 | 6 | 72 | 0 | 69² | 58 | 6 | 26 | 100 | 3.4 | 12.9 | 42% | .329 | 1.21 | 3.62 | 2.65 | 3.17 | 1.6 |
| 2011 | PIT | MLB | 29 | 1 | 4 | 40 | 70 | 0 | 68² | 56 | 1 | 16 | 61 | 2.1 | 8.0 | 54% | .284 | 1.05 | 1.83 | 2.15 | 3.59 | 0.9 |
| *2012* | *PIT* | *MLB* | *30* | *3* | *1* | *14* | *62* | *0* | *60* | *53* | *5* | *23* | *54* | *3.4* | *8.1* | *41%* | *.309* | *1.27* | *3.80* | *3.64* | *4.13* | *0.6* |

Nabbed from the Nationals when he was just a feral arm with a high-90s fastball, plus-slider,

Born: 7/4/1985 Age: 26
Bats: R Throws: R Height: 6' 8" Weight: 220
Breakout: 22% Improve: 53% Collapse: 22%
Attrition: 19% MLB: 85%

Comparables:
Bob Miller, Jake Westbrook, Mike Walters

| YEAR | TEAM | LVL | AGE | W | L | SV | G | GS | IP | H | HR | BB | SO | EqBB9 | EqSO9 | GB% | BABIP | WHIP | ERA | FIP | FRA | WARP |
|---|---|---|---|---|---|---|---|---|---|---|---|---|---|---|---|---|---|---|---|---|---|---|
| 2010 | ALT | AA | 25 | 8 | 7 | 0 | 30 | 23 | 150² | 102 | 9 | 29 | 92 | 2.4 | 7.2 | 58% | .313 | 1.37 | 4.42 | 3.93 | 4.58 | 1.2 |
| 2011 | ALT | AA | 26 | 2 | 2 | 0 | 13 | 11 | 61² | 62 | 2 | 18 | 31 | 2.6 | 4.8 | 55% | .294 | 1.30 | 4.09 | 4.09 | 5.69 | -0.5 |
| 2011 | IND | AAA | 26 | 3 | 1 | 0 | 35 | 0 | 42² | 35 | 1 | 18 | 45 | 3.8 | 9.5 | 73% | .318 | 1.24 | 2.11 | 2.91 | 4.63 | 0.5 |
| 2011 | PIT | MLB | 26 | 0 | 1 | 0 | 12 | 0 | 11 | 9 | 1 | 4 | 10 | 3.3 | 8.2 | 69% | .267 | 1.18 | 4.09 | 3.45 | 4.61 | 0.0 |
| *2012* | *PIT* | *MLB* | *26* | *2* | *2* | *0* | *11* | *4* | *33¹* | *38* | *4* | *14* | *12* | *3.9* | *3.2* | *54%* | *.313* | *1.58* | *5.86* | *5.30* | *6.37* | *-0.4* |

Big and bulky, Hughes generates copious groundball totals due to a mid-90s fastball with sink. His strikeout rates ascended once the organization moved him into the bullpen, possibly because he ditched his changeup and curveball, opting for a fastball-slider attack. Righties had issues hitting Hughes and his three-quarters delivery, reaching base just seven times in 28 plate appearances during his September promotion. In a perfect world, he turns into Kameron Loe.

**Ryota Igarashi**
Born: 5/28/1979 Age: 33
Bats: R Throws: R Height: 6' 0" Weight: 200
Breakout: 36% Improve: 53% Collapse: 32%
Attrition: 11% MLB: 94%

Comparables:
Jesse Orosco, Orlando Hernandez, Matt Miller

| YEAR | TEAM | LVL | AGE | W | L | SV | G | GS | IP | H | HR | BB | SO | EqBB9 | EqSO9 | GB% | BABIP | WHIP | ERA | FIP | FRA | WARP |
|---|---|---|---|---|---|---|---|---|---|---|---|---|---|---|---|---|---|---|---|---|---|---|
| 2009 | YKL | NPB | 30 | 3 | 2 | 3 | 56 | 0 | 53² | 42 | 3 | 20 | 44 | 3.4 | 7.4 | — | .265 | 1.15 | 3.18 | 3.09 | — | 0.0 |
| 2010 | NYN | MLB | 31 | 1 | 1 | 0 | 34 | 0 | 30¹ | 29 | 4 | 18 | 25 | 5.3 | 7.4 | 38% | .284 | 1.55 | 7.12 | 4.95 | 6.71 | -0.5 |
| 2011 | BUF | AAA | 32 | 0 | 1 | 5 | 21 | 0 | 31 | 15 | 2 | 8 | 32 | 2.6 | 9.9 | 46% | .194 | 0.77 | 0.87 | 2.79 | 3.74 | 0.5 |
| 2011 | NYN | MLB | 32 | 4 | 1 | 0 | 45 | 0 | 38² | 43 | 2 | 28 | 42 | 6.5 | 9.8 | 47% | .366 | 1.84 | 4.66 | 3.98 | 5.31 | -0.3 |
| *2012* | *PIT* | *MLB* | *33* | *2* | *1* | *0* | *45* | *0* | *46¹* | *42* | *4* | *21* | *37* | *4.1* | *7.1* | *43%* | *.303* | *1.37* | *4.40* | *4.09* | *4.79* | *0.1* |

The Mets designated Igarashi for assignment before the season, but nobody bit, so in the end they got 69 innings of pretty bad relief work for their $2 million investment. Like many Japanese pitchers, Igarashi has a deep arsenal, but none of his pitches are especially good on a big-league level, and his arm angle and lack of size caused most of his fastball variations (four-seam, two-seam, splitter) to flatten out. He signed with the Pirates, which makes a lot of sense if you think about it.

**Jeff Karstens**
Born: 9/24/1982 Age: 29
Bats: R Throws: R Height: 6' 4" Weight: 175
Breakout: 20% Improve: 51% Collapse: 26%
Attrition: 16% MLB: 85%

Comparables:
Brian Tollberg, Dave Rozema, Rusty Meacham

| YEAR | TEAM | LVL | AGE | W | L | SV | G | GS | IP | H | HR | BB | SO | EqBB9 | EqSO9 | GB% | BABIP | WHIP | ERA | FIP | FRA | WARP |
|---|---|---|---|---|---|---|---|---|---|---|---|---|---|---|---|---|---|---|---|---|---|---|
| 2009 | PIT | MLB | 26 | 4 | 6 | 0 | 39 | 13 | 108 | 115 | 12 | 45 | 52 | 3.8 | 4.3 | 41% | .291 | 1.48 | 5.42 | 4.84 | 5.52 | 0.0 |
| 2010 | PIT | MLB | 27 | 3 | 10 | 0 | 26 | 19 | 122² | 146 | 21 | 27 | 72 | 2.0 | 5.3 | 43% | .311 | 1.41 | 4.92 | 4.84 | 4.56 | 0.8 |
| 2011 | PIT | MLB | 28 | 9 | 9 | 0 | 30 | 26 | 162¹ | 163 | 22 | 33 | 96 | 1.8 | 5.3 | 48% | .278 | 1.21 | 3.38 | 4.26 | 4.25 | 0.9 |
| *2012* | *PIT* | *MLB* | *29* | *7* | *7* | *0* | *26* | *20* | *129* | *138* | *16* | *32* | *57* | *2.2* | *4.0* | *43%* | *.297* | *1.31* | *4.67* | *4.68* | *5.08* | *0.1* |

What looked like a career year became a career half, since Karstens' hit and walk rates increased after the All-Star break at a pace that a drop in home runs could not cancel. The Pirates shut him down in late August as he dealt with soreness in his throwing shoulder, and that provides a convenient excuse for his post-break decline. Credit Karstens' pitching intelligence, but IQ points are less valuable than fastball miles per hour on a baseball mound, and his brains have never outwitted the opposition's brawn except in the first half of last season.

### Chris Leroux

Born: 4/14/1984 Age: 28
Bats: L Throws: R Height: 6' 7" Weight: 210
Breakout: 23% Improve: 37% Collapse: 24%
Attrition: 14% MLB: 84%

Comparables:
Chris Narveson, Ron Flores, J.A. Happ

| YEAR | TEAM | LVL | AGE | W | L | SV | G | GS | IP | H | HR | BB | SO | EqBB9 | EqSO9 | GB% | BABIP | WHIP | ERA | FIP | FRA | WARP |
|------|------|-----|-----|---|---|----|---|----|----|---|----|----|----|-------|-------|-----|-------|------|-----|-----|-----|------|
| 2009 | JAX | AA | 25 | 5 | 3 | 2 | 46 | 0 | 60 | 58 | 0 | 20 | 55 | 2.5 | 8.2 | 53% | .326 | 1.27 | 2.70 | 2.32 | 3.16 | 1.2 |
| 2009 | FLO | MLB | 25 | 0 | 0 | 0 | 5 | 0 | 6² | 11 | 0 | 4 | 2 | 5.4 | 2.7 | 52% | .379 | 2.25 | 10.80 | 4.26 | 5.03 | 0.0 |
| 2010 | NWO | AAA | 26 | 0 | 3 | 1 | 21 | 0 | 22 | 14 | 2 | 5 | 13 | 2.9 | 8.2 | 46% | .364 | 1.50 | 6.95 | 4.88 | 4.72 | 0.2 |
| 2010 | PIT | MLB | 26 | 0 | 1 | 0 | 6 | 0 | 4² | 4 | 0 | 3 | 4 | 5.8 | 7.7 | 50% | .286 | 1.50 | 5.79 | 3.32 | 4.15 | 0.0 |
| 2010 | FLO | MLB | 26 | 0 | 0 | 0 | 17 | 0 | 18 | 24 | 1 | 11 | 18 | 5.5 | 9.0 | 53% | .426 | 1.94 | 7.00 | 3.66 | 5.28 | 0.0 |
| 2011 | IND | AAA | 27 | 6 | 2 | 1 | 32 | 0 | 61 | 47 | 1 | 21 | 57 | 3.1 | 8.4 | 53% | .286 | 1.13 | 2.80 | 2.91 | 4.12 | 0.9 |
| 2011 | PIT | MLB | 27 | 1 | 1 | 0 | 23 | 0 | 25 | 26 | 0 | 7 | 24 | 2.5 | 8.6 | 42% | .338 | 1.32 | 2.88 | 2.03 | 4.38 | 0.1 |
| 2012 | PIT | MLB | 28 | 1 | 1 | 1 | 30 | 0 | 40 | 40 | 3 | 15 | 27 | 3.5 | 6.2 | 47% | .315 | 1.39 | 4.58 | 3.95 | 4.97 | 0.0 |

Leroux is a tall Canadian the Pirates snagged off waivers from Florida in September 2010. Pittsburgh rewarded Leroux for mastering Triple-A by giving him an extended look in the major leagues, and he pitched well enough to create optimism. A mid-90s fastball and sharp slider resulted in poor swings, misses, and frustration for right-handed batters as they managed a total of 18 hits and walks in 70 plate appearances. Leroux is out of options, so expect the former collegiate backstop to open the 2012 season in the Pirates bullpen.

### Brad Lincoln

Born: 5/25/1985 Age: 27
Bats: L Throws: R Height: 6' 1" Weight: 210
Breakout: 19% Improve: 47% Collapse: 15%
Attrition: 9% MLB: 77%

Comparables:
Donovan Osborne, John Smiley, Tom Browning

| YEAR | TEAM | LVL | AGE | W | L | SV | G | GS | IP | H | HR | BB | SO | EqBB9 | EqSO9 | GB% | BABIP | WHIP | ERA | FIP | FRA | WARP |
|------|------|-----|-----|---|---|----|---|----|----|---|----|----|----|-------|-------|-----|-------|------|-----|-----|-----|------|
| 2009 | ALT | AA | 24 | 1 | 5 | 0 | 13 | 13 | 75 | 63 | 4 | 18 | 65 | 2.2 | 7.8 | 46% | .284 | 1.08 | 2.28 | 2.90 | 3.73 | 1.2 |
| 2009 | IND | AAA | 24 | 6 | 2 | 0 | 12 | 12 | 61¹ | 72 | 7 | 10 | 42 | 1.5 | 6.2 | 35% | .332 | 1.34 | 4.70 | 3.80 | 4.89 | 0.5 |
| 2010 | IND | AAA | 25 | 7 | 5 | 0 | 17 | 17 | 94 | 53 | 5 | 15 | 48 | 2.3 | 8.0 | 44% | .291 | 1.14 | 4.12 | 3.81 | 4.36 | 1.9 |
| 2010 | PIT | MLB | 25 | 1 | 4 | 0 | 11 | 9 | 52² | 66 | 9 | 15 | 25 | 2.6 | 4.3 | 39% | .311 | 1.54 | 6.66 | 5.52 | 5.93 | -0.2 |
| 2011 | IND | AAA | 26 | 5 | 5 | 0 | 19 | 19 | 111² | 115 | 6 | 21 | 94 | 1.7 | 7.6 | 44% | .329 | 1.22 | 4.19 | 3.06 | 4.36 | 1.8 |
| 2011 | PIT | MLB | 26 | 2 | 3 | 0 | 12 | 8 | 47² | 54 | 4 | 16 | 29 | 3.0 | 5.5 | 53% | .316 | 1.47 | 4.72 | 4.00 | 4.24 | 0.3 |
| 2012 | PIT | MLB | 27 | 4 | 5 | 0 | 13 | 13 | 71¹ | 79 | 8 | 18 | 32 | 2.3 | 4.1 | 44% | .310 | 1.37 | 5.00 | 4.52 | 5.44 | -0.2 |

Five years have passed since the Pirates selected Lincoln with the fourth-overall pick in the 2006 draft (ahead of Clayton Kershaw and Tim Lincecum), yet he is still trying to break into the major-league rotation. His best opportunity came during the spring, but a line drive to his pitching arm ensured a trip back to the farm. Lincoln still managed a 4.48 strikeout-to-walk ratio during his time at Indianapolis and has just one option remaining, so the Pirates owe it to themselves to give him more than a courtesy look during camp.

### Jeff Locke

Born: 11/20/1987 Age: 24
Bats: L Throws: L Height: 6' 3" Weight: 215
Breakout: 20% Improve: 55% Collapse: 30%
Attrition: 11% MLB: 93%

Comparables:
Chuck Stobbs, Neal Heaton, Jarrod Washburn

| YEAR | TEAM | LVL | AGE | W | L | SV | G | GS | IP | H | HR | BB | SO | EqBB9 | EqSO9 | GB% | BABIP | WHIP | ERA | FIP | FRA | WARP |
|------|------|-----|-----|---|---|----|---|----|----|---|----|----|----|-------|-------|-----|-------|------|-----|-----|-----|------|
| 2009 | MYR | A+ | 21 | 1 | 4 | 0 | 10 | 10 | 45² | 47 | 1 | 26 | 43 | 5.1 | 8.5 | 56% | .351 | 1.60 | 5.51 | 3.79 | 5.04 | 0.2 |
| 2009 | LYN | A+ | 21 | 4 | 4 | 0 | 17 | 17 | 81² | 107 | 4 | 22 | 63 | 2.0 | 6.2 | 49% | .361 | 1.42 | 4.08 | 3.32 | 4.90 | 0.4 |
| 2010 | BRD | A+ | 22 | 9 | 3 | 0 | 17 | 17 | 86¹ | 82 | 6 | 14 | 83 | 1.5 | 8.7 | — | .320 | 1.11 | 3.55 | 3.24 | — | 0.0 |
| 2010 | ALT | AA | 22 | 4 | 2 | 0 | 10 | 10 | 57² | 43 | 3 | 11 | 52 | 1.9 | 8.7 | 47% | .315 | 1.20 | 3.59 | 3.15 | 4.35 | 0.2 |
| 2011 | ALT | AA | 23 | 5 | 6 | 0 | 23 | 22 | 125 | 114 | 9 | 45 | 110 | 3.3 | 8.2 | 47% | .311 | 1.31 | 4.03 | 3.86 | 4.69 | 0.6 |
| 2011 | PIT | MLB | 23 | 0 | 3 | 0 | 4 | 4 | 16² | 21 | 3 | 10 | 5 | 5.4 | 2.7 | 39% | .310 | 1.86 | 6.48 | 6.71 | 6.96 | -0.3 |
| 2012 | PIT | MLB | 24 | 2 | 3 | 0 | 10 | 7 | 54¹ | 60 | 5 | 22 | 27 | 3.6 | 4.4 | 48% | .318 | 1.51 | 5.43 | 4.62 | 5.90 | -0.4 |

Locke is a gangly southpaw equipped with a plus low-90s sinker, a bender that sits in the mid-70s, and a developing changeup. Add in strong command and Locke is without a glaring weakness. At the same time, he lacks enough strengths to project him beyond a number-four or -five starter. Locke spent most of the season in Altoona with cameos in Indianapolis and Pittsburgh. The smart money is on a return to Indianapolis to open the season with a trip to Pittsburgh sometime during the summer.

### Paul Maholm

Born: 6/25/1982 Age: 30
Bats: L Throws: L Height: 6' 3" Weight: 225
Breakout: 29% Improve: 57% Collapse: 12%
Attrition: 17% MLB: 78%

Comparables:
Lenny DiNardo, Mark Mulder, Dave Roberts

| YEAR | TEAM | LVL | AGE | W | L | SV | G | GS | IP | H | HR | BB | SO | EqBB9 | EqSO9 | GB% | BABIP | WHIP | ERA | FIP | FRA | WARP |
|------|------|-----|-----|---|---|----|---|----|----|---|----|----|----|-------|-------|-----|-------|------|-----|-----|-----|------|
| 2009 | PIT | MLB | 27 | 8 | 9 | 0 | 31 | 31 | 194² | 221 | 14 | 60 | 119 | 2.8 | 5.5 | 54% | .329 | 1.44 | 4.44 | 3.79 | 4.30 | 2.9 |
| 2010 | PIT | MLB | 28 | 9 | 15 | 0 | 32 | 32 | 185¹ | 228 | 15 | 62 | 102 | 3.0 | 5.0 | 53% | .332 | 1.56 | 5.10 | 4.21 | 4.85 | 1.1 |
| 2011 | PIT | MLB | 29 | 6 | 14 | 0 | 26 | 26 | 162¹ | 160 | 11 | 50 | 97 | 2.8 | 5.4 | 52% | .290 | 1.29 | 3.66 | 3.75 | 4.17 | 1.6 |
| 2012 | CHN | MLB | 30 | 7 | 10 | 0 | 24 | 24 | 141¹ | 155 | 13 | 39 | 70 | 2.5 | 4.5 | 53% | .320 | 1.37 | 4.86 | 4.24 | 5.28 | 0.2 |

What kind of pitcher is Paul Maholm? Only five National League pitchers have given up more hits over the past three years, all in more innings: Derek Lowe, Mike Pelfrey, Livan Hernandez, Bronson Arroyo, and Chris Carpenter. It's an odd group, because you have to be good enough to pitch all those innings and bad enough to give up all those hits. It feels like just yesterday Maholm was often mentioned in a different group, the quartet of promising young pitchers named Perez, Snell, Duke, and Maholm that would lift the franchise back to respectability. Six years later, Pittsburgh chose to decline Maholm's club option, thus guaranteeing all four would be elsewhere when the Pirates finally enjoy their first winning season since 1992.

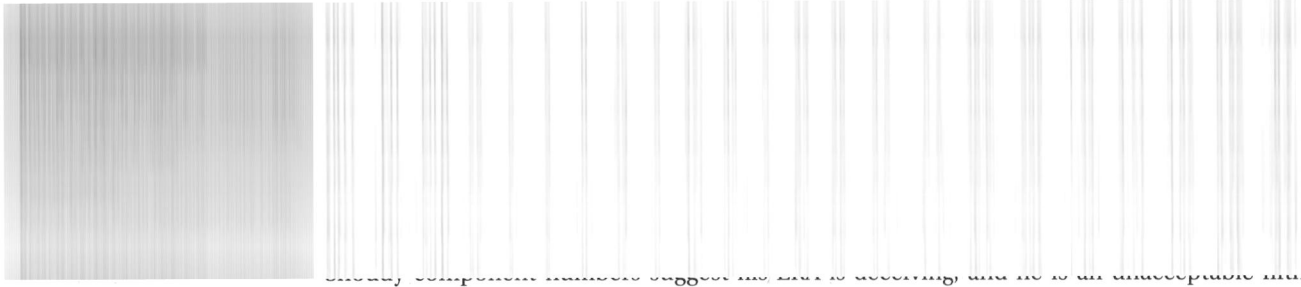

starter candidate, leaving him as nothing more than a long reliever. Mop-up types can walk a thin line between big-league employment and the minors, and McCutchen is no different since he features no standout skill.

### James McDonald

Born: 10/19/1984 Age: 27
Bats: L Throws: R Height: 6' 6" Weight: 195
Breakout: 27% Improve: 62% Collapse: 18%
Attrition: 12% MLB: 89%

Comparables:
Fu-Te Ni, Todd Jones, Tom Sturdivant

| YEAR | TEAM | LVL | AGE | W | L | SV | G | GS | IP | H | HR | BB | SO | EqBB9 | EqSO9 | GB% | BABIP | WHIP | ERA | FIP | FRA | WARP |
|------|------|-----|-----|---|---|----|---|----|----|---|----|----|----|-------|-------|-----|-------|------|-----|-----|-----|------|
| 2009 | ABQ | AAA | 24 | 1 | 0 | 0 | 6 | 6 | 30¹ | 21 | 2 | 14 | 40 | 4.2 | 11.9 | 27% | .288 | 1.16 | 3.27 | 3.05 | 3.88 | 0.6 |
| 2009 | LAN | MLB | 24 | 5 | 5 | 0 | 45 | 4 | 63 | 60 | 6 | 34 | 54 | 4.9 | 7.7 | 46% | .302 | 1.49 | 4.00 | 4.44 | 4.97 | 0.0 |
| 2010 | ABQ | AAA | 25 | 6 | 1 | 0 | 12 | 12 | 63¹ | 43 | 3 | 19 | 35 | 3.4 | 8.1 | 44% | .328 | 1.39 | 4.41 | 4.66 | 4.78 | 1.2 |
| 2010 | LAN | MLB | 25 | 0 | 1 | 0 | 4 | 1 | 7² | 11 | 1 | 5 | 7 | 5.9 | 8.2 | 27% | .400 | 2.09 | 8.22 | 4.93 | 5.27 | -0.1 |
| 2010 | PIT | MLB | 25 | 4 | 5 | 0 | 11 | 11 | 64 | 59 | 3 | 24 | 61 | 3.4 | 8.6 | 33% | .320 | 1.30 | 3.52 | 2.93 | 3.41 | 1.2 |
| 2011 | PIT | MLB | 26 | 9 | 9 | 0 | 31 | 31 | 171 | 176 | 24 | 78 | 142 | 4.1 | 7.5 | 40% | .306 | 1.49 | 4.21 | 4.65 | 5.08 | -0.2 |
| 2012 | PIT | MLB | 27 | 9 | 7 | 0 | 24 | 24 | 133² | 124 | 14 | 48 | 102 | 3.2 | 6.9 | 37% | .300 | 1.29 | 4.15 | 4.12 | 4.51 | 1.1 |

Despite missing time in camp with left trunk soreness, McDonald returned and made his designated April starts. In retrospect, letting him jump into the fire so quickly looks like a mistake. McDonald averaged fewer than five innings per start, gave up more than a hit per inning, walked one more batter than he struck out, and posted a 7.66 earned-run average in his five April starts. From May onward, he looked like the pitcher from 2010. In those final 26 starts, McDonald went nearly six innings per outing, struck out more than twice as many as he walked, and finished with a 3.63 ERA. He might be nothing more than a middle-of-the-rotation starter, but McDonald is better than what his 2011 numbers say.

### Kyle McPherson

Born: 11/11/1987 Age: 24
Bats: B Throws: R Height: 6' 4" Weight: 205
Breakout: 22% Improve: 48% Collapse: 26%
Attrition: 22% MLB: 92%

Comparables:
Collin Balester, John Thomson, Kirk Saarloos

| YEAR | TEAM | LVL | AGE | W | L | SV | G | GS | IP | H | HR | BB | SO | EqBB9 | EqSO9 | GB% | BABIP | WHIP | ERA | FIP | FRA | WARP |
|------|------|-----|-----|---|---|----|---|----|----|---|----|----|----|-------|-------|-----|-------|------|-----|-----|-----|------|
| 2011 | BRD | A+ | 23 | 4 | 1 | 0 | 12 | 12 | 71² | 58 | 4 | 6 | 57 | 0.8 | 7.5 | 41% | .283 | 0.95 | 2.89 | 3.07 | 3.83 | 1.3 |
| 2011 | ALT | AA | 23 | 3 | 4 | 0 | 16 | 16 | 89¹ | 75 | 7 | 21 | 82 | 2.1 | 8.3 | 37% | .275 | 1.07 | 3.02 | 3.37 | 3.86 | 1.3 |
| 2012 | PIT | MLB | 24 | 3 | 3 | 0 | 8 | 8 | 45¹ | 49 | 6 | 15 | 19 | 3.0 | 3.9 | 38% | .297 | 1.42 | 5.44 | 5.08 | 5.92 | -0.3 |

It took McPherson five seasons to reach Double-A, and he did not disappoint upon arrival. As a benefit of his turtle pace, he had time to work on crafting his pitches and smoothing his mechanics. His velocity crept upward last season (now touching 94-95 mph) and his changeup is considered plus. A zone-pounder through and through, McPherson has a 4.77 minor league career strikeout-to-walk ratio and a number four starter's ceiling—not bad for a mostly anonymous prospect.

## Evan Meek

Born: 5/12/1983 Age: 29
Bats: R Throws: R Height: 6' 1" Weight: 220
Breakout: 21% Improve: 42% Collapse: 24%
Attrition: 9% MLB: 97%

Comparables:
Danys Baez, Andy Messersmith, Tim Burke

| YEAR | TEAM | LVL | AGE | W | L | SV | G | GS | IP | H | HR | BB | SO | EqBB9 | EqSO9 | GB% | BABIP | WHIP | ERA | FIP | FRA | WARP |
|------|------|-----|-----|---|---|----|----|----|-----|----|----|----|----|-------|-------|-----|-------|------|-----|-----|-----|------|
| 2009 | PIT | MLB | 26 | 1 | 1 | 0 | 41 | 0 | 41 | 47 | 34 | 2 | 29 | 42 | 5.6 | 8.0 | 52% | .267 | 1.34 | 3.45 | 3.67 | 4.81 | 0.3 |
| 2010 | PIT | MLB | 27 | 5 | 4 | 4 | 70 | 0 | 70 | 80 | 53 | 5 | 31 | 70 | 3.5 | 7.9 | 57% | .226 | 1.05 | 2.14 | 3.48 | 4.19 | 1.0 |
| 2011 | PIT | MLB | 28 | 1 | 1 | 0 | 24 | 0 | 20² | 27 | 1 | 12 | 17 | 5.2 | 7.4 | 49% | .377 | 1.89 | 3.48 | 3.72 | 3.95 | 0.2 |
| 2012 | PIT | MLB | 29 | 2 | 1 | 1 | 30 | 0 | 32 | 28 | 2 | 13 | 22 | 3.8 | 6.3 | 53% | .290 | 1.31 | 3.95 | 3.86 | 4.30 | 0.3 |

Shoulder tightness and inflammation are an undefeated tag-team, and they beat the stuffing out of Meek's season. Limited to 24 appearances just a season removed from an All-Star bid, Meek's walk rates jitterbugged, but the stuff looked lively and PITCHf/x data had his fastball averaging the same velocity (92.6 miles per hour) that it did in 2009. Meek pumped up the velocity in 2010, perhaps overthrowing in order to achieve an average fastball near 95 mph, and look what it got him. On the bright side, he relieved in seven games in September, albeit none on back-to-back days, which suggests he will be ready to go when camp starts.

## Bryan Morris

Born: 3/28/1987 Age: 25
Bats: L Throws: R Height: 6' 4" Weight: 220
Breakout: 19% Improve: 52% Collapse: 18%
Attrition: 13% MLB: 80%

Comparables:
Neal Heaton, Ross Baumgarten, Rick Baldwin

| YEAR | TEAM | LVL | AGE | W | L | SV | G | GS | IP | H | HR | BB | SO | EqBB9 | EqSO9 | GB% | BABIP | WHIP | ERA | FIP | FRA | WARP |
|------|------|-----|-----|---|---|----|----|----|-----|----|----|----|----|-------|-------|-----|-------|------|-----|-----|-----|------|
| 2009 | LYN | A+ | 22 | 5 | 9 | 0 | 15 | 15 | 72² | 94 | 2 | 35 | 33 | 4.2 | 4.0 | 58% | .322 | 1.66 | 5.57 | 4.24 | 7.02 | -1.2 |
| 2010 | BRD | A+ | 23 | 3 | 0 | 0 | 8 | 8 | 44² | 37 | 0 | 7 | 40 | 1.4 | 8.1 | — | .300 | 0.98 | 0.60 | 2.34 | — | 0.0 |
| 2010 | ALT | AA | 23 | 5 | 5 | 0 | 19 | 16 | 89 | 55 | 4 | 26 | 57 | 3.1 | 8.5 | 55% | .354 | 1.33 | 4.25 | 3.94 | 4.99 | 0.3 |
| 2011 | ALT | AA | 24 | 1 | 4 | 3 | 35 | 6 | 78 | 68 | 1 | 28 | 61 | 3.8 | 7.4 | 62% | .318 | 1.35 | 3.35 | 3.13 | 4.41 | 1.0 |
| 2012 | PIT | MLB | 25 | 1 | 1 | 0 | 5 | 2 | 18 | 21 | 2 | 9 | 6 | 4.4 | 3.1 | 53% | .312 | 1.65 | 5.97 | 5.48 | 6.49 | -0.2 |

With Andy LaRoche, Craig Hansen, and Brandon Moss elsewhere, Morris is the last chance for romance from the Jason Bay return. He started 2011 in the Altoona rotation before suffering an oblique injury. It didn't take long once he came back for the Pirates to change course and move him into a relief role. Morris could become a late-inning reliever with a low-to-mid-90s fastball and two quality breaking pitches.

## Charlie Morton

Born: 11/12/1983 Age: 28
Bats: R Throws: R Height: 6' 5" Weight: 190
Breakout: 25% Improve: 54% Collapse: 19%
Attrition: 17% MLB: 79%

Comparables:
Dick Lines, Kelvin Jimenez, Ryan Speier

| YEAR | TEAM | LVL | AGE | W | L | SV | G | GS | IP | H | HR | BB | SO | EqBB9 | EqSO9 | GB% | BABIP | WHIP | ERA | FIP | FRA | WARP |
|------|------|-----|-----|----|----|----|----|----|------|-----|----|----|-----|-------|-------|-----|-------|------|------|------|------|------|
| 2009 | GWN | AAA | 25 | 7 | 2 | 0 | 10 | 10 | 64² | 52 | 3 | 16 | 55 | 2.2 | 7.7 | 45% | .277 | 1.05 | 2.50 | 2.89 | 3.21 | 1.3 |
| 2009 | PIT | MLB | 25 | 5 | 9 | 0 | 18 | 18 | 97 | 102 | 7 | 40 | 62 | 3.7 | 5.8 | 51% | .316 | 1.46 | 4.55 | 4.11 | 4.83 | 0.7 |
| 2010 | IND | AAA | 26 | 4 | 3 | 0 | 14 | 14 | 80 | 51 | 5 | 19 | 36 | 3.4 | 6.0 | 54% | .313 | 1.41 | 3.83 | 4.34 | 5.36 | 0.7 |
| 2010 | PIT | MLB | 26 | 2 | 12 | 0 | 17 | 17 | 79² | 112 | 15 | 26 | 59 | 2.9 | 6.7 | 48% | .361 | 1.73 | 7.57 | 5.32 | 6.39 | -1.1 |
| 2011 | PIT | MLB | 27 | 10 | 10 | 0 | 29 | 29 | 171² | 186 | 6 | 77 | 110 | 4.0 | 5.8 | 61% | .327 | 1.53 | 3.83 | 3.74 | 4.92 | 0.1 |
| 2012 | PIT | MLB | 28 | 8 | 9 | 0 | 24 | 24 | 133² | 145 | 11 | 50 | 72 | 3.4 | 4.8 | 52% | .320 | 1.45 | 5.04 | 4.32 | 5.47 | -0.3 |

You know how the old saying goes: If you want to pitch like Roy Halladay then just *pitch like* Roy Halladay. Morton took the idiom to heart and reconstructed his mechanics in the image of the pitching deity, from set-up to delivery. Lefties hit an Albert Pujols-like .364/.460/.500 against Morton, while righties hit a Luis Pujols-like .220/.289/.278. The difference is Morton's bread-and-butter pitch: his sinker. It runs arm-side and Morton loves to throw it regardless of the situation or count. His commitment to the down-and-in sinker worked on righties, but 60 percent of his walks came against lefties despite facing nearly 60 percent righties on the season. Maybe Morton can revisit Halladay's film and focus on copying his curveball. He'll have extra time to study with offseason hip surgery that could cost him spring training.

## Daniel Moskos

Born: 4/28/1986 Age: 26
Bats: R Throws: L Height: 6' 2" Weight: 210
Breakout: 26% Improve: 54% Collapse: 23%
Attrition: 19% MLB: 80%

Comparables:
Tom Candiotti, Howie Judson, Runelvys Hernandez

| YEAR | TEAM | LVL | AGE | W | L | SV | G | GS | IP | H | HR | BB | SO | EqBB9 | EqSO9 | GB% | BABIP | WHIP | ERA | FIP | FRA | WARP |
|------|------|-----|-----|----|----|----|----|----|------|-----|----|----|----|-------|-------|-----|-------|------|------|------|------|------|
| 2009 | ALT | AA | 23 | 11 | 10 | 0 | 27 | 25 | 149 | 159 | 11 | 58 | 77 | 3.5 | 4.7 | 58% | .306 | 1.46 | 3.74 | 4.35 | 5.72 | -0.7 |
| 2010 | ALT | AA | 24 | 2 | 1 | 21 | 37 | 0 | 41¹ | 19 | 0 | 15 | 31 | 3.5 | 9.4 | 62% | .271 | 1.02 | 1.53 | 3.26 | 4.00 | 0.4 |
| 2011 | IND | AAA | 25 | 1 | 1 | 3 | 30 | 0 | 42 | 39 | 2 | 10 | 27 | 2.4 | 6.2 | 56% | .298 | 1.21 | 3.43 | 3.36 | 4.56 | 0.5 |
| 2011 | PIT | MLB | 25 | 1 | 1 | 0 | 31 | 0 | 24¹ | 29 | 0 | 9 | 11 | 3.3 | 4.1 | 52% | .337 | 1.56 | 2.96 | 3.20 | 4.52 | 0.0 |
| 2012 | PIT | MLB | 26 | 1 | 0 | 0 | 30 | 0 | 32¹ | 36 | 3 | 14 | 13 | 3.8 | 3.6 | 52% | .312 | 1.55 | 5.56 | 4.91 | 6.04 | -0.4 |

Known in Pittsburgh as "Not Matt Wieters," who was taken with the next pick in the 2007 draft, Moskos is not going to fulfill the old regime's hope that he would become a fierce end-game reliever. With a low-to-mid-90s fastball and wipeout slider, Moskos is more likely to develop into a lefty specialist, despite reverse splits during his time in the majors last season. Should Moskos become a useful reliever, Pirates fans will have to curb their truculence by gracing him with a different nickname. Perhaps, Daily 'Kos?

### Ross Ohlendorf

Born: 8/8/1982 Age: 29
Bats: R Throws: R Height: 6' 5" Weight: 235
Breakout: 31% Improve: 61% Collapse: 14%
Attrition: 21% MLB: 76%

Comparables:
Dustin Moseley, Mike Moore, Greg Hansell

| YEAR | TEAM | LVL | AGE | W | L | SV | G | GS | IP | H | HR | BB | SO | EqBB9 | EqSO9 | GB% | BABIP | WHIP | ERA | FIP | FRA | WARP |
|------|------|-----|-----|---|---|----|----|----|------|-----|----|----|-----|-------|-------|-----|-------|------|------|------|------|------|
| 2009 | PIT | MLB | 26 | 11 | 10 | 0 | 29 | 29 | 176² | 165 | 25 | 53 | 109 | 2.7 | 5.6 | 43% | .269 | 1.23 | 3.92 | 4.68 | 5.34 | 0.1 |
| 2010 | PIT | MLB | 27 | 1 | 11 | 0 | 21 | 21 | 108¹ | 106 | 12 | 44 | 79 | 3.7 | 6.6 | 35% | .289 | 1.38 | 4.07 | 4.47 | 4.34 | 1.0 |
| 2011 | PIT | MLB | 28 | 1 | 3 | 0 | 9 | 9 | 38² | 60 | 9 | 15 | 27 | 3.5 | 6.3 | 42% | .386 | 1.94 | 8.15 | 6.25 | 6.59 | -0.5 |
| 2012 | PIT | MLB | 29 | 3 | 4 | 0 | 12 | 12 | 57¹ | 62 | 7 | 18 | 31 | 2.9 | 4.9 | 44% | .310 | 1.40 | 5.20 | 4.65 | 5.65 | -0.2 |

**Ross Ohlendorf** started nine games and registered the sixth-worst FRA in baseball (minimum 35 innings) before shoulder problems finished his season. The Pirates released him in December.

### Rudy Owens

Born: 12/18/1987 Age: 24
Bats: L Throws: L Height: 6' 4" Weight: 215
Breakout: 21% Improve: 53% Collapse: 23%
Attrition: 7% MLB: 95%

| YEAR | TEAM | LVL | AGE | W | L | SV | G | GS | IP | H | HR | BB | SO | EqBB9 | EqSO9 | GB% | BABIP | WHIP | ERA | FIP | FRA | WARP |
|------|------|-----|-----|---|---|----|----|----|------|----|----|----|----|-------|-------|-----|-------|------|------|------|------|------|
| 2009 | WVA | A | 21 | 10 | 1 | 0 | 19 | 19 | 100² | 71 | 8 | 15 | 91 | 1.3 | 8.1 | 42% | .240 | 0.85 | 1.70 | 3.40 | 4.09 | 1.5 |
| 2009 | LYN | A+ | 21 | 2 | 1 | 0 | 6 | 6 | 23¹ | 37 | 4 | 4 | 35 | 0.8 | 8.5 | 39% | .333 | 1.33 | 3.86 | 3.22 | 3.84 | 0.6 |
| 2010 | ALT | AA | 22 | 10 | 5 | 0 | 26 | 26 | 150 | 89 | 7 | 20 | 93 | 1.4 | 7.9 | 48% | .303 | 0.98 | 2.46 | 3.42 | 3.55 | 2.7 |

and 2010, he could make his major-league debut in 2012.

### Chris Resop

Born: 11/4/1982 Age: 29
Bats: R Throws: R Height: 6' 4" Weight: 220
Breakout: 18% Improve: 32% Collapse: 39%
Attrition: 9% MLB: 88%

Comparables:
Al Hrabosky, Tim Stoddard, Todd Worrell

| YEAR | TEAM | LVL | AGE | W | L | SV | G | GS | IP | H | HR | BB | SO | EqBB9 | EqSO9 | GB% | BABIP | WHIP | ERA | FIP | FRA | WARP |
|------|------|-----|-----|---|---|----|----|----|-----|----|----|----|----|-------|-------|-----|-------|------|-------|------|------|------|
| 2010 | GWN | AAA | 27 | 6 | 3 | 0 | 15 | 15 | 82 | 36 | 2 | 27 | 60 | 3.5 | 10.0 | 49% | .260 | 1.04 | 2.09 | 3.45 | 3.62 | 2.0 |
| 2010 | ATL | MLB | 27 | 0 | 0 | 0 | 1 | 0 | 2 | 5 | 0 | 3 | 2 | 13.5 | 9.0 | 22% | .556 | 4.00 | 22.50 | 5.61 | 7.41 | -0.1 |
| 2010 | PIT | MLB | 27 | 0 | 0 | 0 | 22 | 0 | 19 | 10 | 1 | 10 | 24 | 4.7 | 11.4 | 40% | .220 | 1.05 | 1.89 | 2.84 | 3.18 | 0.4 |
| 2011 | PIT | MLB | 28 | 5 | 4 | 1 | 76 | 0 | 69² | 73 | 8 | 30 | 79 | 3.9 | 10.2 | 37% | .344 | 1.48 | 4.39 | 3.64 | 5.17 | -0.3 |
| 2012 | PIT | MLB | 29 | 4 | 2 | 1 | 41 | 6 | 62² | 55 | 6 | 24 | 53 | 3.4 | 7.7 | 42% | .303 | 1.27 | 3.81 | 3.91 | 4.14 | 0.7 |

Meek's absence bollixed the Pirates bullpen hierarchy and left Jose Veras and Resop as the team's de facto set-up men. Resop's gaudy strikeout rate (he fanned more than a quarter of the batters he faced) aside, he showed why the Braves were content to let the former sabermetrics cause célèbre go without real compensation. A reliever can get by allowing too many hits, issuing too many free passes, or even having a home run-allowing binge every now and again as long as he excels at two of the other three areas, but Resop's season was a deadly sin cocktail. Need proof? He made consecutive appearances against the Astros early in the season and allowed five runs without recording an out. That counts as grounds for termination in most cities.

### Jameson Taillon

Born: 11/18/1991 Age: 20
Bats: R Throws: R Height: 6' 7" Weight: 225
Breakout: 68% Improve: 81% Collapse: 5%
Attrition: 1% MLB: 83%

Comparables:
Milt Pappas, Dick Brodowski, Don Drysdale

| YEAR | TEAM | LVL | AGE | W | L | SV | G | GS | IP | H | HR | BB | SO | EqBB9 | EqSO9 | GB% | BABIP | WHIP | ERA | FIP | FRA | WARP |
|------|------|-----|-----|---|---|----|----|----|------|----|----|----|----|-------|-------|-----|-------|------|------|------|------|------|
| 2011 | WVA | A | 19 | 2 | 2 | 0 | 23 | 23 | 92² | 89 | 9 | 22 | 97 | 2.1 | 9.4 | 46% | .315 | 1.20 | 3.98 | 3.70 | 4.57 | 1.1 |
| 2012 | PIT | MLB | 20 | 2 | 2 | 0 | 6 | 6 | 24² | 25 | 3 | 10 | 15 | 3.7 | 5.6 | 44% | .309 | 1.44 | 5.17 | 4.79 | 5.62 | -0.0 |

Prior to Cole's addition, Taillon was the undisputed best pitching prospect in the system, and for good reason. Labeled the best high school pitching prospect since Josh Beckett, Taillon throws a mid-90s fastball that can bounce into the upper-90s when needed, and that isn't the best offering in his repertoire as he throws an ethereal curveball that combines optimal movement and speed. He still has to work out the kinks on his changeup, along with some poor habits he picked up while dominating unworthy high school competition. Even with the sins, there are few better pitching prospects in baseball.

## Tony Watson

Born: 5/30/1985 Age: 27
Bats: L Throws: L Height: 6' 5" Weight: 223
Breakout: 39% Improve: 63% Collapse: 21%
Attrition: 10% MLB: 78%

**Comparables:**
Gustavo Chacin, Bill Scherrer, Jason Vargas

| YEAR | TEAM | LVL | AGE | W | L | SV | G | GS | IP | H | HR | BB | SO | EqBB9 | EqSO9 | GB% | BABIP | WHIP | ERA | FIP | FRA | WARP |
|------|------|-----|-----|---|---|----|---|----|----|---|----|----|----|-------|-------|-----|-------|------|-----|-----|-----|------|
| 2010 | ALT | AA | 25 | 6 | 3 | 2 | 34 | 9 | 111¹ | 56 | 10 | 16 | 78 | 1.9 | 8.5 | 35% | .214 | 0.95 | 2.67 | 3.85 | 3.79 | 1.5 |
| 2011 | IND | AAA | 26 | 3 | 2 | 0 | 26 | 1 | 34¹ | 24 | 2 | 9 | 34 | 2.9 | 9.2 | 40% | .256 | 1.02 | 2.36 | 2.98 | 4.97 | 0.2 |
| 2011 | PIT | MLB | 26 | 2 | 2 | 0 | 43 | 0 | 41 | 34 | 6 | 20 | 37 | 4.4 | 8.1 | 36% | .262 | 1.32 | 3.95 | 4.63 | 4.93 | -0.1 |
| 2012 | PIT | MLB | 27 | 2 | 1 | 0 | 24 | 3 | 46¹ | 46 | 6 | 15 | 27 | 3.0 | 5.3 | 33% | .292 | 1.32 | 4.61 | 4.69 | 5.01 | 0.1 |

Watson's pitching attitude is described as tough—like a bulldog—yet cunning—like a fox. The bullfox made his way to the majors in 2011 and looked like a future lefty specialist. He throws with a side-armed delivery and five of the six home runs he allowed came against righties, suggesting perhaps they get a better look at the ball. Watson also posted a better strikeout-to-walk ratio when facing same-handed batters. He goes after adversaries with a low-90s fastball, slider, and changeup.

## Justin Wilson

Born: 8/18/1987 Age: 24
Bats: L Throws: L Height: 6' 3" Weight: 233
Breakout: 25% Improve: 58% Collapse: 22%
Attrition: 8% MLB: 93%

**Comparables:**
Pat Combs, Sean Marshall, Paul Maholm

| YEAR | TEAM | LVL | AGE | W | L | SV | G | GS | IP | H | HR | BB | SO | EqBB9 | EqSO9 | GB% | BABIP | WHIP | ERA | FIP | FRA | WARP |
|------|------|-----|-----|---|---|----|---|----|----|---|----|----|----|-------|-------|-----|-------|------|-----|-----|-----|------|
| 2009 | LYN | A+ | 21 | 7 | 9 | 0 | 26 | 26 | 116 | 129 | 14 | 57 | 106 | 4.3 | 7.3 | 53% | .307 | 1.49 | 4.50 | 4.77 | 5.61 | -0.1 |
| 2010 | ALT | AA | 22 | 12 | 8 | 0 | 27 | 26 | 142² | 83 | 4 | 42 | 93 | 4.5 | 8.5 | 51% | .279 | 1.26 | 3.09 | 3.64 | 4.22 | 1.2 |
| 2011 | IND | AAA | 23 | 7 | 6 | 3 | 30 | 21 | 124¹ | 121 | 12 | 67 | 94 | 4.8 | 6.8 | 50% | .292 | 1.51 | 4.13 | 4.69 | 5.58 | 0.6 |
| 2012 | PIT | MLB | 24 | 3 | 3 | 0 | 8 | 8 | 44² | 44 | 4 | 22 | 25 | 4.4 | 5.0 | 48% | .296 | 1.47 | 4.95 | 4.73 | 5.39 | -0.1 |

Following two and a half seasons of wildness in the rotation, the left-handed Wilson was tossed into the bullpen in Indianapolis. During short spurts, Wilson's fastball can encroach the upper-90s and comes with impressive movement. Unfortunately, that velocity and movement cripple his ability to control the pitch. The Pirates have enough first-hand experience in soothing scattershotitis from strong arms in the bullpen that Wilson could progress into a nice relief arm if the Pirates choose to keep him in the pen.

## LINEOUTS

### HITTERS

| PLAYER | TEAM | LVL | AGE | PA | R | 2B | 3B | HR | RBI | BB | SO | SB-CS | AVG/OBP/SLG | TAv | BABIP | BRR | FRAA | WARP |
|--------|------|-----|-----|----|---|----|----|----|-----|----|----|-------|-------------|-----|-------|-----|------|------|
| CF E. Chambers | BRD | A+ | 22 | 525 | 57 | 24 | 2 | 11 | 55 | 70 | 131 | 20-12 | .234/.350/.374 | .261 | .303 | 2.2 | 14.5 | 3.1 |
| DH J. Clement | IND | AAA | 27 | 67 | 5 | 5 | 0 | 1 | 5 | 7 | 15 | 0-0 | .271/.358/.407 | .259 | .349 | 0 | 0.6 | 0.1 |
| C E. Fryer | ALT | AA | 25 | 134 | 24 | 4 | 2 | 5 | 16 | 16 | 21 | 1-0 | .345/.427/.549 | .345 | .386 | -0.8 | -1.4 | 1.1 |
|  | IND | AAA | 25 | 143 | 16 | 5 | 1 | 2 | 11 | 21 | 30 | 3-0 | .203/.333/.314 | .228 | .256 | -0.7 | 0.2 | 0.1 |
|  | PIT | MLB | 25 | 29 | 5 | 0 | 0 | 0 | 0 | 3 | 7 | 1-1 | .269/.345/.269 | .223 | .368 | 0.2 | 0 | 0.0 |
| 1B M. Hague | IND | AAA | 25 | 594 | 70 | 37 | 3 | 12 | 75 | 47 | 68 | 4-3 | .309/.372/.457 | .275 | .334 | -1.4 | 4.1 | 2.0 |
| 2B B. Holt | ALT | AA | 23 | 579 | 62 | 30 | 9 | 1 | 40 | 50 | 85 | 18-10 | .288/.356/.387 | .273 | .340 | 3.4 | -3.3 | 2.4 |
| C J. Jaramillo | IND | AAA | 28 | 155 | 13 | 7 | 0 | 2 | 23 | 17 | 22 | 1-1 | .276/.368/.373 | .246 | .315 | -0.2 | 0.3 | 0.6 |
|  | PIT | MLB | 28 | 45 | 1 | 3 | 0 | 0 | 6 | 2 | 12 | 1-0 | .326/.356/.395 | .253 | .452 | -1.8 | -0.2 | -0.1 |
| RF A. Lambo | ALT | AA | 22 | 286 | 35 | 17 | 0 | 8 | 41 | 26 | 59 | 4-3 | .274/.345/.437 | .283 | .324 | 1.1 | -5.4 | 1.0 |
|  | IND | AAA | 22 | 207 | 19 | 11 | 0 | 3 | 17 | 17 | 48 | 1-0 | .184/.257/.292 | .198 | .228 | -1.3 | 1.6 | -1.1 |
| LF Q. Latimore | ALT | AA | 22 | 509 | 52 | 32 | 1 | 15 | 59 | 33 | 140 | 7-8 | .239/.297/.411 | .261 | .304 | 0.9 | 6.1 | 2.2 |
| SS J. Mercer | ALT | AA | 24 | 301 | 40 | 17 | 1 | 13 | 48 | 23 | 35 | 6-3 | .268/.329/.487 | .305 | .260 | -2.3 | 7.2 | 3.3 |
|  | IND | AAA | 24 | 250 | 39 | 13 | 1 | 6 | 21 | 13 | 43 | 3-3 | .239/.304/.385 | .232 | .271 | 1.7 | -0.8 | 0.3 |
| C J. Morales | COL | MLB | 28 | 71 | 6 | 3 | 0 | 0 | 7 | 9 | 12 | 0-1 | .267/.352/.317 | .253 | .320 | -2.5 | -0.3 | 0.0 |
| SS G. Nunez | LAK | A+ | 23 | 294 | 46 | 10 | 7 | 3 | 18 | 25 | 40 | 14-10 | .304/.368/.431 | .284 | .349 | 1.3 | 1.2 | 2.5 |
|  | ERI | AA | 23 | 131 | 13 | 3 | 0 | 2 | 8 | 5 | 27 | 4-3 | .215/.252/.289 | .193 | .261 | -0.5 | -1.2 | -0.6 |
| 2B J. Rodriguez | ALT | AA | 26 | 246 | 24 | 3 | 0 | 5 | 19 | 18 | 41 | 3-1 | .267/.321/.347 | .256 | .304 | -1.7 | 6.2 | 1.2 |
|  | COH | AAA | 26 | 65 | 6 | 1 | 0 | 2 | 5 | 6 | 22 | 1-0 | .193/.270/.316 | .202 | .273 | 0 | 0 | -0.4 |
|  | PIT | MLB | 26 | 14 | 1 | 0 | 0 | 0 | 1 | 1 | 8 | 0-0 | .083/.214/.083 | .131 | .250 | 0.4 | -0.3 | -0.1 |

At his best, **Evan Chambers** has displayed a tantalizing speed and power combination. For now, he needs to work on his approach and cut down on the strikeouts. ⊘ Hard to say which part of **Jeff Clement**'s season was worse: missing time while rehabbing a knee injury or failing to hit when he did play. ⊘ Triple-A humbled **Eric Fryer**'s bat and the Pirates chose against a September promotion, suggesting he could be well down on a depth chart chock full of reserve and organizational soldier types. ⊘ **Matt Hague**'s best asset is his versatility, as he isn't good defensively, lacks speed, and does not pack the wallop necessary to be an everyday major league first baseman or corner outfielder. ⊘ **Brock Holt**'s stock dropped with a letdown season. His future is at second base and his grit is off the charts, but he has to hit for average and draw walks to make up for a lack of obvious tools. ⊘ Good catch-and-throw skills are the only things **Jason Jaramillo** has going for him, as his bat does nothing to distinguish him from the other defense-only backstops in the system. ⊘ Scouts were pessimistic about **Andrew Lambo**'s chances entering the season, and he did nothing to change their minds while struggling in his first exposure to Triple-A. ⊘ **Quincy Lattimore**'s athleticism is impressive, but his projection has to turn into results soon, and a poor plate approach is weighing him down. ⊘ A 6-foot-3 shortstop with power, **Jordy Mercer** lacks other offensive skills, but could sneak into the bottom of the Pirates lineup one day. ⊘ **Jose Morales** extended his string of consecutive seasons with exactly

## PITCHERS

| PLAYER | TEAM | LVL | AGE | W | L | SV | IP | H | HR | BB | SO | EqBB9 | EqSO9 | GB% | BABIP | WHIP | ERA | FIP | FRA | WARP |
|--------|------|-----|-----|---|---|----|----|----|----|----|----|-------|-------|-----|-------|------|-----|-----|-----|------|
| B. Burres | IND | AAA | 30 | 2 | 5 | 0 | 129¹ | 134 | 18 | 42 | 92 | 3.1 | 6.6 | 40% | .309 | 1.43 | 4.66 | 4.76 | 4.87 | 1.4 |
|  | PIT | MLB | 30 | 1 | 0 | 0 | 14 | 12 | 4 | 4 | 10 | 2.6 | 6.4 | 30% | .200 | 1.14 | 3.86 | 6.14 | 5.58 | -0.1 |
| C. Cain | WVA | A | 20 | 4 | 7 | 0 | 106¹ | 92 | 6 | 31 | 81 | 2.6 | 6.9 | 42% | .277 | 1.16 | 3.64 | 3.95 | 4.32 | 1.2 |
| K. Cofield | BIR | AA | 24 | 0 | 1 | 0 | 28 | 26 | 0 | 13 | 23 | 4.2 | 7.4 | 54% | .321 | 1.39 | 2.89 | 3.26 | 4.84 | 0.0 |
| M. Crotta | PIT | MLB | 26 | 0 | 1 | 0 | 10² | 20 | 2 | 5 | 7 | 4.2 | 5.9 | 61% | .429 | 2.34 | 9.28 | 5.53 | 6.54 | -0.3 |
| Z. Dodson | WVA | A | 20 | 4 | 3 | 0 | 66² | 61 | 3 | 15 | 46 | 2.0 | 6.2 | 55% | .290 | 1.14 | 2.57 | 3.59 | 4.00 | 0.9 |
| N. Kingham | SCO | A- | 19 | 6 | 2 | 0 | 71 | 63 | 5 | 15 | 47 | 1.9 | 6.0 | 45% | .272 | 1.10 | 2.15 | 3.68 | 3.96 | 1.3 |
| S. Martis | HAR | AA | 24 | 5 | 5 | 0 | 133 | 124 | 9 | 43 | 155 | 2.6 | 9.9 | 41% | .318 | 1.22 | 3.05 | 2.95 | 3.60 | 2.7 |
| Z. Von Rosenberg | WVA | A | 20 | 3 | 7 | 0 | 125² | 143 | 19 | 23 | 114 | 1.6 | 8.2 | 38% | .338 | 1.32 | 5.73 | 4.47 | 5.00 | 0.9 |

**Brian Burres** has a career 5.75 ERA, a fastball that rarely hits 90 mph, and 106 major league appearances—as if you needed more justification for teaching your kid how to throw lefty. ⊘ **Colton Cain** is a well-built southpaw from Texas who featured a power fastball out of high school but sat in the high 80s during 2011. His secondary pitches could develop into above-average offerings. ⊘ Injuries have reduced **Kyle Cofield** to an organizational arm. The once-promising sinkerballer will attempt to latch on in the Pirates bullpen. ⊘ **Michael Crotta** left a grim first impression in his big-league debut, allowing 20 hits and five walks in 10 2/3 innings and missing most of the season due to right elbow inflammation. ⊘ After returning from a broken hand and shaking the rust off, **Zach Dodson** pitched well. A lefty with a low-90s fastball and solid secondary stuff, he figures to be a back-of-the-rotation starter. ⊘ Another arm from the 2010 draft class, **Nicholas Kingham** has a fastball that can hit 94 mph. He should be done with short-season ball. ⊘ When you start moving down levels after several cracks at Triple-A and a couple of trips to the big club, as **Shairon Martis** did last year, you're eventually going to wind up pitching for Morris Buttermaker's Bears—bad news for you. ⊘ **Zack Von Rosenberg** received a $1.2 million bonus out of the sixth-round in 2009 and has plus secondary stuff that showed up in his strikeout rate, but he left too many pitches over the plate in his first voyage beyond short-season ball.

# MANAGER: CLINT HURDLE

| YEAR | TEAM | W-L | Pythag +/- | Avg PC | 100+ P | 120+ P | QS | BQS | REL | REL w Zero R | IBB | Subs | PH | PH Avg | PH HR | SB2 | CS2 | SB3 | CS3 | SAC Att | SAC % | POS SAC | Squeeze | Swing | In Play |
|------|------|-----|-----|------|------|------|----|-----|-----|------|-----|------|-----|------|------|-----|-----|-----|-----|-----|-------|-----|---------|-------|---------|
| 2009 | COL | 19-28 | 0 | 92.9 | 20 | 0 | 26 | 1 | 136 | 79 | 12 | 16 | 74 | .302 | 2 | 6 | 2 | 0 | 0 | 31 | 67.7% | 8 | 0 | 52 | 48 |
| 2011 | PIT | 72-90 | 0 | 89.5 | 26 | 0 | 78 | 2 | 549 | 452 | 65 | — | 275 | .201 | 1 | 13 | 3 | 0 | 2 | 110 | 76.4% | 45 | 1 | 384 | 114 |

Hurdle spent parts of eight seasons guiding the Rockies. Reaching the playoffs just once over six full seasons is grounds for termination, even if that berth did culminate in a pennant. After spending a season with the Rangers—thereby reaching the World Series again—Hurdle decided to re-enter the managerial game by taking on a historically tough gig in Pittsburgh. Thus, Hurdle became the seventh Pirates manager since their most recent winning season, back in 1992. Pittsburgh overachieved in the first half, flirting with—and seducing—first place into the summer months. During the unexpected run, Hurdle received the highest panegyric, with scribes crediting his ability to keep players loose and focused. Aside from the second-half melt-down, Hurdle shared more in common with former manager John Russell than many Yinzers would like to admit. One such similarity is a dependence on the bullpen. Like Russell the year before, Hurdle led the league in relievers used. It did not help Hurdle that he finished with fewer 100-plus pitch starts than fired managers like Bob Geren and Edwin Rodriguez, despite managing more than 90 additional games. A manager is only as good as the men he gets to manage, but Hurdle made some questionable decisions with the talent he was allowed. Start with the anecdotal—like having Andrew McCutchen bunt—then move on to the hard stuff—finishing second in the league in intentional walks issued. Blaming Hurdle for the Pirates' collapse is as silly as giving him full credit for their rise. Often the truth is found in the middle, and that seems to be the case with the job Hurdle did in 2011.

# St. Louis Cardinals

Last year may have been the most significant for the Cardinals since 1964. It was certainly the most eventful. The drama started all the way back in February, when pending free agent Albert Pujols cut off his unsuccessful contract negotiations with

April, they lost their highest-paid player, Matt Holliday, to an appendectomy. Holliday returned quickly, but Pujols got off to the slowest start of his career, hitting just .257/.326/.395 through May 29, then breaking his wrist in late June just after he had finally found his stroke.

Pujols, too, healed quickly and picked up where he'd left off, and despite Wainwright's absence and the team's early struggles, the Cardinals found themselves in first place on July 26. However, the division-rival Brewers and wild card-leading Braves took off in August, leaving St. Louis in the dust. After losing to the Pirates on August 27, the Redbirds were 10 games behind in the wild-card race and 10 1/2 games behind in the Central with 29 left to play, giving them roughly a 1 percent chance of reaching the postseason. The Cardinals then won 17 of their next 22 games, including a sweep of the Braves and five wins in six games against Milwaukee. They ended up going 21-8 over those final 29 games. The Braves, meanwhile, won just five of their last 18, allowing St. Louis to pull into a tie for the wild card on the season's penultimate day. The Cardinals claimed the final National League playoff spot on the final day when Chris Carpenter shut out the lowly Astros and Atlanta's Rookie of the Year closer, Craig Kimbrel, blew his most important save of the year, setting up a 13-inning loss to the Phillies that eliminated Atlanta.

Then came the Redbirds' rollercoaster ride through the playoffs. In a Division Series that will be remembered in part for a St. Louis squirrel dashing in front of home plate just after Roy Oswalt delivered a pitch to Skip Schumaker with the Phillies up two

in the National League Championship Series was relatively uneventful, though it did see six home runs hit and nine runs scored between the two teams in the first two and a half innings of the last game. Finally, the Cardinals met the Rangers in one of the most thrilling World Series in history.

After trading one-run victories in the first two games in St. Louis, the teams traveled to Texas, where the Cards burst forth with 16 runs in Game Three, keyed by Pujols, who turned in the greatest single-game hitting performance in postseason history, going 5-for-6 with three home runs. But St. Louis managed just two more runs in the next two games and headed home down 3-2. In Game Six, the Cardinals twice came within a strike of losing the World Series. In the bottom of the ninth inning, they were down 7-5 with two outs and two strikes on David Freese when he hit a triple off Rangers closer Neftali Feliz to tie the game. Down 9-7 in the bottom of the 10th following what looked like a Series-winning home run by Josh Hamilton in the top of the inning, they pushed across one but were still down 9-8 with two outs and two strikes on Lance Berkman. Big Puma, a widely criticized signing from the previous winter who proved to be the team's best hitter during the regular season, singled off Scott Feldman to again tie the game. Freese then led off the bottom of the 11th with a game-winning home run to tie

| | | |
|---|---|---|
| TAv | .271 | 7th |
| TAv-P | .257 | 14th |
| FIP | 3.71 | 8th |
| DER | .704 | 20th |
| DL | 754 | 16th |
| B-Age | 29.3 | 22nd |
| P-Age | 30.2 | 28th |
| Salary | $109.8 | 10th |
| M$/MW | $2.34 | 16th |

**2011:** Good bat, bad glove team can't win division; wins Series after being down to last strike

**2012:** So much resting on older hitters, pitcher rebounds, and untested rookies, it could go either way

**Action Items:** A new infield, a healthy Wainwright, an outlet store to sell all those Pujols jerseys

the series at three games apiece. The next day, the Cardinals erased an early 2-0 deficit to win Game Seven and their 11th world championship.

Three days later, Tony La Russa, the third-winningest manager in major-league history and the Cardinals skipper since 1996, retired. Less than two months after that, Pujols signed a 10-year, $254 million contract with the Los Angeles Angels of Anaheim, complete with a 10-year post-retirement personal-services contract that will keep him on the Angels payroll until at least 2031. In between those two franchise-altering departures, scouting director Jeff Luhnow left to become the new general manager of the Houston Astros. It was as if every dream and nightmare came true for the Cardinals over the course of 11 months.

The 2012 season seems likely to be remembered primarily as an epilogue to that sure to be often-told tale, but the Cardinals obviously hope it will be a prologue to another. That hope isn't entirely unfounded. Yes, Pujols and La Russa are gone, but Wainwright is returning, and the Cardinals should be right back in the thick of the NL Central race.

The bright side of losing Wainwright for the season, enduring Pujols' least productive year (which, admittedly, is like the least delicious forkful of steak), and still winning 90 games is that it makes it that much easier to repeat. From 2003 to 2010, Pujols averaged 9.1 Wins Above Replacement Player. Since 1954, only Willie Mays, Mickey Mantle, and Barry Bonds have had a higher average WARP over an eight-year span. In 2011, Pujols' value dropped to 5.7 WARP due both to his time missed and his slow start, which left him with the lowest True Average of his career (still .312, of course, not much gristle on that steak). Wainwright, who was throwing off a mound during the postseason and should be ready to go from Opening Day this year, was worth exactly 5.1 WARP in both 2009 and 2010. It would be too much to expect Wainwright to return to his former dominance right away, but he should be able to compensate for at least half, if not more, of the wins lost in Pujols' departure.

That puts the Cardinals just a couple of wins shy of 2011, a difference that could be made up in small ways, such as through a fortunate swing in performance variations. Holliday, for example, averaged 5.2 WARP in 2006-10, and PECOTA expects him to bounce back to being a five-win player after dropping below three wins in 2011, largely due to a series of minor, fluky injuries (most amusingly a moth flying into his ear in late August, though that only cost him a few innings). Healthy seasons from Wainwright and Holliday alone could make up for the loss of Pujols' 2011 production. The Cards could also benefit from Lance Berkman's move to first base as Pujols' short-term replacement, as that will allow them to put a qualified defender in right, which could add a win by itself.

The Cardinals also have upside plays on the left side of the infield in postseason hero David Freese (the MVP in both the NLCS and World Series) and veteran Rafael Furcal, the latter of whom was acquired from the Dodgers at the 2011 trading deadline for now-25-year-old minor league outfielder Alex Castellanos, then re-signed to a two-year, $14 million deal in the wake of Pujols' departure. Neither is a good bet to stay healthy. Furcal has played in 100 or more games just once in the last four years, while Freese has missed at least 50 games in each of the last three seasons, will be 29 at the end of April, and has never played in 100 games or hit more than 10 home runs in the majors in a single season. Still, Furcal replaces an essentially replacement-level Ryan Theriot, who was non-tendered shortly after Furcal re-signed, so he can break even with just two healthy months (replacing his performance after the trade), with anything more being pure upgrade. Freese, a career .303/.362/.538 hitter in Triple-A, has break-out potential, though PECOTA advises Redbird fans against getting their hopes up.

So there's plenty of opportunity for the Cardinals to compensate for Pujols' departure in the coming season without even getting into the man who will actually take over his at-bats, which will be Berkman's replacement in right field. The Cardinals' contingency plan for Pujols' departure, smartly put into place in late September with a one-year extension for Berkman, included a full season from 27-year-old Allen Craig in right field. That was disrupted just before Thanksgiving when Craig underwent surgery to repair the kneecap he fractured colliding with the outfield wall in Houston in early June. The recovery time for Craig was set at four to six months, which puts him in doubt for Opening Day and could keep him out for the entire first half of the season if he has any setbacks.

That injury prompted the addition of All-Star right fielder Carlos Beltran via a two-year, $26 million contract. Beltran is coming off a season in which he was worth 3.4 WARP, a figure that likely falls a bit short of his actual value due to a particularly harsh evaluation of his defense by our Fielding Runs system (Ultimate Zone Rating concurs, but Total Zone and plus/minus have him close to and even above average). Figure Beltran to be a four-win player, but even at three wins, he and Wainwright alone more than compensate for Pujols' 2011 production.

In that way, Craig's injury may have been fortuitous. PECOTA projected the 27-year-old's WARP to decrease in 2012 even with a significant increase in playing time, and with Colby Rasmus now in Toronto, standing pat in the outfield this offseason could have left the Cardinals short-handed. Now, they have a legitimate, heart-of-the-order switch-hitter in right field, and when the versatile Craig returns, he can help fill the various gaps created by age and injury at the four corners, as well as occasionally spotting for the barely above-replacement Skip Schumaker at second base.

With Wainwright back in the rotatoin and Beltran in right, the Cardinals are in excellent shape heading into 2012, particularly with the Brewers likely having lost Prince Fielder to free agency and possibly Ryan Braun to a 50-game drug suspension. Replacing Pujols over the long haul, particularly without Rasmus's remaining upside (who'd have thought both Rasmus *and* La Russa would be gone by now?), will be more difficult. Or rather, it will be impossible. No one can replace Albert Pujols. The Cardinals can only hope to com-

baseman for 2013, his age-24 season. Adams is no Pujols (who is?): He won't walk much, and he's not particularly mobile on the bases or in the field, but he'll hit for solid averages and lots of power and projects as a solid number-five hitter on a contending team. That's not a nine-win player, but could be a four-win player. The Cards also have one of the top pitching prospects in baseball in 21-year-old righty Shelby Miller, who successfully made the jump to Double-A in 2011 and could arrive alongside Adams in 2013, if not before.

The Cardinals don't have an especially deep or strong farm system at the moment, but they do have those two potential impact players in the upper levels and a roster that's

# HITTERS

### Matt Adams    1B

Born: 8/31/1988 Age: 23
Bats: L Throws: R Height: 6' 4" Weight: 230
Breakout: 4% Improve: 32% Collapse: 9%
Attrition: 20% MLB: 56%

**Comparables:**
Kent Hrbek, Jim Breazeale, Kendrys Morales

| YEAR | TEAM | LVL | AGE | PA | R | 2B | 3B | HR | RBI | BB | SO | SB | CS | AVG/OBP/SLG | TAv | BABIP | BRR | FRAA | WARP |
|------|------|-----|-----|----|----|----|----|----|-----|----|----|----|----|-------------|-----|-------|-----|------|------|
| 2009 | BAT | A- | 20 | 142 | 16 | 11 | 0 | 4 | 27 | 11 | 21 | 0 | 0 | .346/.397/.523 | .316 | .390 | -0.9 | -0.7 | 0.7 |
| 2009 | JCY | RK | 20 | 128 | 15 | 6 | 0 | 6 | 25 | 9 | 20 | 0 | 0 | .365/.416/.574 | .337 | .404 | -0.6 | 1.6 | 1.2 |
| 2010 | QUD | A | 21 | 510 | 71 | 41 | 0 | 22 | 88 | 33 | 78 | 5 | 1 | .310/.361/.541 | .315 | .335 | -1.7 | 2.1 | 3.2 |
| 2011 | SFD | AA | 22 | 513 | 80 | 23 | 2 | 32 | 101 | 40 | 90 | 0 | 1 | .300/.357/.566 | .311 | .308 | 0.6 | 6.4 | 3.9 |
| 2012 | SLN | MLB | 23 | 250 | 29 | 11 | 0 | 11 | 34 | 13 | 51 | 0 | 0 | .257/.296/.445 | .265 | .283 | 0 | 1B -9 | 0.8 |

The legend of Matt Adams continues to grow. The 23rd-rounder from Slippery Rock set a Springfield team record with 32 home runs, pounding Texas League pitching at a .300/.357/.566 clip en route to an MVP award. The performance won his short, powerful lefty stroke a trip to the Arizona Fall League, and he should be the Memphis first baseman in 2012. If he stays with St. Louis, Adams is destined for first base, because his size and body type make it unlikely he can patrol left field in the majors.

### Bryan Anderson    C

Born: 12/16/1986 Age: 25
Bats: L Throws: R Height: 6' 2" Weight: 200
Breakout: 8% Improve: 26% Collapse: 4%
Attrition: 37% MLB: 65%

**Comparables:**
Alan Ashby, Chris Turner, Jose Lobaton

| YEAR | TEAM | LVL | AGE | PA | R | 2B | 3B | HR | RBI | BB | SO | SB | CS | AVG/OBP/SLG | TAv | BABIP | BRR | FRAA | WARP |
|------|------|-----|-----|----|----|----|----|----|-----|----|----|----|----|-------------|-----|-------|-----|------|------|
| 2009 | MEM | AAA | 22 | 174 | 22 | 7 | 3 | 4 | 11 | 10 | 42 | 1 | 0 | .245/.293/.399 | .264 | .308 | -0.5 | -0.2 | 0.5 |
| 2010 | MEM | AAA | 23 | 302 | 39 | 12 | 0 | 12 | 42 | 27 | 54 | 0 | 0 | .270/.343/.448 | .259 | .299 | 0.6 | -0.1 | 1.4 |
| 2010 | SLN | MLB | 23 | 35 | 1 | 2 | 0 | 0 | 4 | 1 | 7 | 0 | 0 | .281/.314/.344 | .243 | .346 | 0 | -0.2 | 0.0 |
| 2011 | MEM | AAA | 24 | 378 | 39 | 19 | 0 | 8 | 37 | 36 | 76 | 1 | 1 | .281/.357/.409 | .255 | .340 | -4.5 | -3.3 | 0.7 |
| 2012 | SLN | MLB | 25 | 250 | 25 | 10 | 1 | 4 | 21 | 17 | 58 | 1 | 0 | .228/.288/.330 | .228 | .286 | 0 | C -2, 1B -0 | 0.5 |

Once one of the organization's top prospects, Anderson's progress has stalled. After a brief stint with the big club in 2010, he returned to Triple-A for a fourth season while Gerald Laird was brought in to serve as Yadier Molina's caddy. When opportunity knocked in May in the form of a broken finger for Laird, Anderson remained in Memphis, leapfrogged by Tony Cruz. Given a chance, Anderson's bat should play at the next level. But concern about his catch-and-throw skills remains, despite an endorsement from Mike Matheny, the former Gold Glove receiver who has worked with Anderson to improve his defense. Still on the 40-man roster, Anderson should be in the mix to battle for a backup spot. But with an option year remaining, he could find himself with the Memphis blues again.

### Carlos Beltran — RF

Born: 4/24/1977 Age: 35
Bats: B Throws: R Height: 6' 1" Weight: 175
Breakout: 1% Improve: 20% Collapse: 7%
Attrition: 10% MLB: 84%

Comparables:
Bobby Abreu, Magglio Ordonez, Moises Alou

| YEAR | TEAM | LVL | AGE | PA | R | 2B | 3B | HR | RBI | BB | SO | SB | CS | AVG/OBP/SLG | TAv | BABIP | BRR | FRAA | WARP |
|------|------|-----|-----|-----|----|----|----|----|-----|----|----|----|----|-------------|------|-------|------|--------------|------|
| 2009 | NYN | MLB | 32 | 357 | 50 | 22 | 1 | 10 | 48 | 47 | 43 | 11 | 1 | .325/.415/.500 | .318 | .352 | 0.6 | 1.7 | 3.5 |
| 2010 | SLU | A+ | 33 | 57 | 5 | 5 | 0 | 0 | 5 | 7 | 6 | 0 | 0 | .367/.446/.469 | .326 | .419 | 0.5 | 0.3 | 0.5 |
| 2010 | NYN | MLB | 33 | 255 | 21 | 11 | 3 | 7 | 27 | 30 | 39 | 3 | 1 | .255/.341/.427 | .278 | .275 | -2.7 | -1.4 | 0.8 |
| 2011 | NYN | MLB | 34 | 419 | 61 | 30 | 2 | 15 | 66 | 60 | 61 | 3 | 0 | .289/.391/.513 | .325 | .310 | -0.4 | -8.4 | 2.6 |
| 2011 | SFN | MLB | 34 | 179 | 17 | 9 | 4 | 7 | 18 | 11 | 27 | 1 | 2 | .323/.369/.551 | .312 | .353 | -0.1 | 0.1 | 1.2 |
| 2012 | SLN | MLB | 35 | 500 | 65 | 25 | 3 | 16 | 61 | 59 | 75 | 9 | 2 | .270/.356/.449 | .292 | .291 | 0.3 | RF -5, CF 0 | 2.9 |

The nine-figure contracts we remember are the ones that go horribly wrong, that remind us how fragile baseball careers are and how relentless the aging curve is. Beltran's, though, shows that baseball careers are often quite resilient, too. Over the course of his just-concluded seven-year, $119 million deal, Beltran had bad seasons, concussions, and surgeries, he was booed, he changed positions, he lost the ability to steal bases, and he turned into an old man. And yet, at the end of it, he produced the best OPS+ of his career and earned the Mets a pretty sterling pitching prospect to keep the value coming. After producing in San Francisco while the Giants collapsed around him, Beltran and his balky knees were lured to St. Louis with a more modest $26 million deal for two years. If he can stay healthy, he'll bring flexibility to the batting order and the outfield and provide the Cardinals with a healthy measure of consolation for Albert Pujols' decision to chase a nine-figure deal of his own in Anaheim.

### Lance Berkman — 1B

Born: 2/10/1976 Age: 36
Bats: B Throws: L Height: 6' 2" Weight: 205
Breakout: 2% Improve: 27% Collapse: 7%
Attrition: 12% MLB: 91%

Comparables:
Al Kaline, Gary Sheffield, Frank Robinson

| YEAR | TEAM | LVL | AGE | PA | R | 2B | 3B | HR | RBI | BB | SO | SB | CS | AVG/OBP/SLG | TAv | BABIP | BRR | FRAA | WARP |
|------|------|-----|-----|-----|----|----|----|----|-----|----|----|----|----|-------------|------|-------|------|-------------|------|
| 2009 | HOU | MLB | 33 | 562 | 73 | 31 | 1 | 25 | 80 | 97 | 98 | 7 | 4 | .274/.399/.509 | .304 | .296 | -1.1 | 9.1 | 3.9 |
| 2010 | HOU | MLB | 34 | 358 | 39 | 16 | 1 | 13 | 49 | 60 | 70 | 3 | 2 | .245/.372/.436 | .289 | .279 | -0.5 | 1.5 | 1.4 |
| 2010 | NYA | MLB | 34 | 123 | 9 | 7 | 0 | 1 | 9 | 17 | 15 | 0 | 0 | .255/.358/.349 | .242 | .289 | 0.4 | -0.8 | -0.2 |
| 2011 | SLN | MLB | 35 | 587 | 90 | 23 | 2 | 31 | 94 | 92 | 93 | 2 | 6 | .301/.412/.547 | .344 | .315 | -1.7 | -1.9 | 4.7 |
| 2012 | SLN | MLB | 36 | 532 | 73 | 23 | 1 | 22 | 67 | 80 | 93 | 6 | 4 | .267/.380/.469 | .305 | .292 | -0.8 | 1B 3, RF -5 | 3.3 |

The Cardinals' decision to make a free-agent splash by signing Berkman was met with snickers. First, there was the $8 million price tag, which seemed high for a 35-year-old who posted career lows in just about every statistical category in 2010. Then there was the plan to release the Big Puma in the Busch Stadium outfield, an area he had not roamed since 2007. Well, no one's laughing now. Berkman got in shape, stayed healthy and posted a monster .301/.412/.547 line. His defensive range remains a liability, and at this point, Allen Craig is a better option against left-handed pitching. But Berkman produced enough at the plate to command a one-year extension and a nice raise to $12 million.

### Matt Carpenter — 3B

Born: 11/26/1985 Age: 26
Bats: L Throws: R Height: 6' 4" Weight: 200
Breakout: 0% Improve: 33% Collapse: 4%
Attrition: 17% MLB: 86%

Comparables:
Robin Ventura, Steve Braun, Steve Ontiveros

| YEAR | TEAM | LVL | AGE | PA | R | 2B | 3B | HR | RBI | BB | SO | SB | CS | AVG/OBP/SLG | TAv | BABIP | BRR | FRAA | WARP |
|------|------|-----|-----|-----|----|----|----|----|-----|----|----|----|----|-------------|------|-------|------|--------------|------|
| 2009 | QUD | A | 23 | 126 | 11 | 6 | 2 | 0 | 10 | 17 | 13 | 2 | 0 | .295/.408/.390 | .288 | .337 | -0.3 | 2 | 0.9 |
| 2009 | PMB | A+ | 23 | 128 | 13 | 6 | 1 | 2 | 9 | 10 | 24 | 1 | 0 | .219/.283/.342 | .235 | .256 | -1.1 | 4.3 | 0.4 |
| 2010 | PMB | A+ | 24 | 128 | 17 | 5 | 2 | 1 | 16 | 26 | 14 | 0 | 1 | .283/.438/.404 | .316 | .318 | -0.8 | 0.7 | 0.9 |
| 2010 | SFD | AA | 24 | 472 | 76 | 26 | 3 | 12 | 53 | 41 | 88 | 11 | 2 | .316/.412/.487 | .310 | .377 | 3.2 | 15.4 | 6.4 |
| 2011 | MEM | AAA | 25 | 535 | 61 | 29 | 3 | 12 | 70 | 84 | 68 | 5 | 4 | .300/.417/.463 | .304 | .328 | -0.2 | 12.9 | 5.5 |
| 2011 | SLN | MLB | 25 | 19 | 0 | 1 | 0 | 0 | 0 | 4 | 4 | 0 | 0 | .067/.263/.133 | .157 | .091 | -0.2 | 0.2 | -0.2 |
| 2012 | SLN | MLB | 26 | 250 | 28 | 11 | 1 | 4 | 22 | 30 | 46 | 2 | 1 | .244/.341/.363 | .260 | .287 | -0.1 | 3B 12, 1B -0 | 1.8 |

A 2009 ninth-round pick, Carpenter got the call to the majors when Matt Holliday hit the disabled list in June. After doubling against Kerry Wood in his first game, he did not collect another hit before being optioned back to Memphis. Carpenter lacks the power you might like from a third baseman, but his advanced approach at the plate makes him an on-base machine. Seeing Triple-A pitching for the first time in 2011, he posted more walks (84) than strikeouts (68) and reached base more than 40 percent of the time. At 26, Carpenter is blocked by World Series MVP David Freese, with 2010 first-rounder Zack Cox looming behind him.

**Adron Chambers** CF

Born: 10/8/1986 Age: 25
Bats: L Throws: L Height: 5' 11" Weight: 185
Breakout: 5% Improve: 36% Collapse: 7%
Attrition: 45% MLB: 85%

Comparables:
Roger Bernadina, Ron Roenicke, Jim Eisenreich

| YEAR | TEAM | LVL | AGE | PA | R | 2B | 3B | HR | RBI | BB | SO | SB | CS | AVG/OBP/SLG | TAv | BABIP | BRR | FRAA | WARP |
|------|------|-----|-----|----|----|----|----|----|-----|----|----|----|----|-------------|-----|-------|-----|------|------|
| 2009 | PMB | A+ | 22 | 517 | 66 | 17 | 16 | 1 | 46 | 47 | 96 | 21 | 12 | .283/.369/.400 | .280 | .355 | 1.6 | -0.6 | 2.5 |
| 2010 | SFD | AA | 23 | 292 | 52 | 9 | 5 | 5 | 27 | 31 | 50 | 8 | 4 | .282/.373/.417 | .277 | .332 | 4.4 | -3.9 | 1.7 |
| 2010 | MEM | AAA | 23 | 83 | 11 | 0 | 1 | 1 | 8 | 9 | 18 | 6 | 1 | .290/.390/.362 | .278 | .373 | 0.9 | 0 | 0.4 |
| 2011 | MEM | AAA | 24 | 501 | 73 | 19 | 5 | 10 | 44 | 53 | 90 | 22 | 13 | .277/.368/.415 | .277 | .328 | -0.2 | -1.7 | 2.1 |
| 2011 | SLN | MLB | 24 | 8 | 2 | 0 | 1 | 0 | 4 | 0 | 1 | 0 | 0 | .375/.375/.625 | .350 | .429 | -0.1 | 0.1 | 0.1 |
| 2012 | SLN | MLB | 25 | 250 | 25 | 8 | 3 | 2 | 20 | 20 | 54 | 7 | 4 | .230/.306/.324 | .235 | .288 | -0.6 | CF -4, LF -1 | 0.1 |

Called up in September, Chambers became a hero when his first major league hit drove in the go-ahead run in the 11th inning of a crucial game in Philadelphia. Still somewhat raw defensively and on the bases, the former college quarterback could battle for a reserve spot in 2012. But a crowd in the St. Louis outfield likely means a return to Memphis.

93 games, and questions remain about both his defensive range and his power potential. Signed to a major league contract worth $3.2 million, Cox could qualify for a fourth option year in the unlikely event he does not reach St. Louis sometime before 2014. He's likely to begin 2012 in Springfield, but a mid-season call to Memphis is a possibility.

**Allen Craig** LF

Born: 7/18/1984 Age: 27
Bats: R Throws: R Height: 6' 3" Weight: 210
Breakout: 4% Improve: 28% Collapse: 8%
Attrition: 14% MLB: 63%

Comparables:
Johnny Weekly, Joe Charboneau, Andy Barkett

| YEAR | TEAM | LVL | AGE | PA | R | 2B | 3B | HR | RBI | BB | SO | SB | CS | AVG/OBP/SLG | TAv | BABIP | BRR | FRAA | WARP |
|------|------|-----|-----|----|----|----|----|----|-----|----|----|----|----|-------------|-----|-------|-----|------|------|
| 2009 | MEM | AAA | 24 | 521 | 78 | 26 | 1 | 26 | 83 | 37 | 95 | 3 | 0 | .322/.379/.547 | .313 | .359 | -4 | -2 | 3.4 |
| 2010 | MEM | AAA | 25 | 350 | 57 | 24 | 2 | 14 | 81 | 34 | 59 | 1 | 0 | .320/.395/.549 | .315 | .361 | -1.2 | -0.1 | 2.6 |
| 2010 | SLN | MLB | 25 | 124 | 12 | 7 | 0 | 4 | 18 | 9 | 26 | 0 | 1 | .246/.298/.412 | .260 | .282 | -0.7 | -1.3 | 0.1 |
| 2011 | SLN | MLB | 26 | 219 | 33 | 15 | 0 | 11 | 40 | 15 | 40 | 5 | 0 | .315/.362/.555 | .324 | .344 | 1.6 | -0.2 | 2.3 |
| 2012 | SLN | MLB | 27 | 250 | 31 | 12 | 1 | 10 | 33 | 19 | 49 | 1 | 0 | .267/.326/.452 | .279 | .299 | 0 | LF -3, RF -1 | 1.8 |

After winning a reserve spot on the Opening Day roster, Craig missed two months in June when he broke his kneecap sliding into the right-field wall in Houston. He returned to an expanded role after the trade of Colby Rasmus and ended up posting a gaudy .313/.343/.657 line against lefties. Tony La Russa took full advantage of Craig's versatility, playing him at first, second, and third base as well as all three outfield spots. Craig's late-season heroics (.327/.364/.692 in September and .243/.391/.622 in the postseason) put him in position for duty as the regular right fielder in 2012, but the Lance Berkman extension short-circuited those hopes. Nevertheless, his play impressed enough that John Mozeliak spoke with Craig in September to assure him he remains in the club's plans in the wake of the Berkman deal. He'll again serve as a fourth outfielder and the top right-handed bat off the bench.

**Tony Cruz** C

Born: 8/18/1986 Age: 25
Bats: R Throws: R Height: 6' 0" Weight: 205
Breakout: 8% Improve: 25% Collapse: 8%
Attrition: 34% MLB: 69%

Comparables:
Del Crandall, Bill Nahorodny, Brian Schneider

| YEAR | TEAM | LVL | AGE | PA | R | 2B | 3B | HR | RBI | BB | SO | SB | CS | AVG/OBP/SLG | TAv | BABIP | BRR | FRAA | WARP |
|------|------|-----|-----|----|----|----|----|----|-----|----|----|----|----|-------------|-----|-------|-----|------|------|
| 2009 | SFD | AA | 22 | 444 | 44 | 25 | 2 | 10 | 48 | 34 | 85 | 1 | 0 | .220/.281/.366 | .233 | .254 | 0.8 | 0 | 1.0 |
| 2010 | PMB | A+ | 23 | 202 | 21 | 16 | 1 | 1 | 25 | 19 | 33 | 0 | 2 | .282/.348/.398 | .282 | .338 | -2.8 | 0.7 | 1.4 |
| 2010 | SFD | AA | 23 | 169 | 26 | 10 | 0 | 6 | 20 | 17 | 30 | 0 | 0 | .289/.363/.477 | .283 | .325 | -1.5 | 0.1 | 1.3 |
| 2011 | MEM | AAA | 24 | 164 | 13 | 5 | 1 | 4 | 25 | 11 | 31 | 0 | 1 | .262/.315/.389 | .238 | .304 | -0.4 | -0.7 | 0.2 |
| 2011 | SLN | MLB | 24 | 72 | 8 | 5 | 0 | 0 | 6 | 6 | 13 | 0 | 1 | .262/.333/.338 | .257 | .327 | 0 | 0 | 0.2 |
| 2012 | SLN | MLB | 25 | 250 | 25 | 12 | 1 | 4 | 23 | 16 | 54 | 0 | 0 | .225/.278/.339 | .228 | .270 | -0.1 | C -1, 3B 0 | 0.4 |

Cruz, a converted third baseman, turned heads with his strong arm in spring training and outlasted long-heralded prospect Bryan Anderson as the final catcher cut before the Cardinals headed north. Promoted to St. Louis when Gerald Laird broke a finger, Cruz threw out two of four base-stealers and held his own at the plate. Cruz could battle for the backup job in the spring, and he's the in-house favorite if free agent Laird does not return.

**Daniel Descalso   3B**
Born: 10/19/1986 Age: 25
Bats: L Throws: R Height: 5' 11" Weight: 190
Breakout: 4% Improve: 36% Collapse: 10%
Attrition: 34% MLB: 75%
Comparables:
Junior Moore, Edgardo Alfonzo, Brad Mills

| YEAR | TEAM | LVL | AGE | PA | R | 2B | 3B | HR | RBI | BB | SO | SB | CS | AVG_OBP_SLG | TAv | BABIP | BRR | FRAA | WARP |
|------|------|-----|-----|-----|-----|-----|-----|-----|-----|-----|-----|-----|-----|-------------|------|-------|------|------|------|
| 2009 | SFD | AA | 22 | 324 | 46 | 26 | 5 | 8 | 51 | 31 | 41 | 0 | 1 | .323/.395/.531 | .313 | .354 | 0 | 4.5 | 3.3 |
| 2009 | MEM | AAA | 22 | 172 | 23 | 4 | 0 | 2 | 17 | 16 | 21 | 3 | 0 | .253/.322/.320 | .239 | .275 | 1.1 | 1.6 | 0.2 |
| 2010 | MEM | AAA | 23 | 531 | 86 | 32 | 3 | 9 | 71 | 47 | 48 | 8 | 4 | .282/.350/.421 | .273 | .296 | 5 | -1.2 | 2.4 |
| 2010 | SLN | MLB | 23 | 37 | 6 | 2 | 0 | 0 | 4 | 2 | 6 | 1 | 0 | .265/.324/.324 | .272 | .321 | 0.7 | 0.1 | 0.2 |
| 2011 | SLN | MLB | 24 | 375 | 35 | 20 | 3 | 1 | 28 | 33 | 65 | 2 | 2 | .264/.334/.353 | .265 | .323 | -0.3 | -9.2 | 0.5 |
| 2012 | SLN | MLB | 25 | 351 | 38 | 17 | 2 | 4 | 32 | 28 | 53 | 3 | 1 | .253/.320/.355 | .251 | .288 | -0.2 | 3B -5, 2B 1 | 1.3 |

Pegged in the role of late-inning defensive replacement at third base, Descalso filled in admirably as a starter early in the season while David Freese battled injury. With 24 extra-base hits in part-time duty, Descalso's short, lefty swing brings gap pop. "Dirty Dan" also logged time at shortstop and second base, where he could battle for more regular playing time as a younger, less expensive alternative to Skip Schumaker and pending free agents Ryan Theriot and Nick Punto.

**David Freese   3B**
Born: 4/28/1983 Age: 29
Bats: R Throws: R Height: 6' 3" Weight: 220
Breakout: 4% Improve: 44% Collapse: 4%
Attrition: 26% MLB: 86%
Comparables:
Doug Decinces, Jim Ray Hart, Mark Teahen

| YEAR | TEAM | LVL | AGE | PA | R | 2B | 3B | HR | RBI | BB | SO | SB | CS | AVG_OBP_SLG | TAv | BABIP | BRR | FRAA | WARP |
|------|------|-----|-----|-----|-----|-----|-----|-----|-----|-----|-----|-----|-----|-------------|------|-------|------|------|------|
| 2009 | MEM | AAA | 26 | 225 | 34 | 15 | 0 | 10 | 37 | 22 | 51 | 1 | 0 | .300/.372/.525 | .310 | .360 | -3.4 | -4.1 | 1.3 |
| 2009 | SLN | MLB | 26 | 34 | 3 | 2 | 0 | 1 | 7 | 2 | 7 | 0 | 0 | .323/.353/.484 | .291 | .375 | 0.2 | -0.4 | 0.2 |
| 2010 | SLN | MLB | 27 | 270 | 28 | 12 | 1 | 4 | 36 | 21 | 59 | 1 | 1 | .296/.361/.404 | .275 | .376 | 1.6 | 1.5 | 1.4 |
| 2011 | SLN | MLB | 28 | 363 | 41 | 16 | 1 | 10 | 55 | 24 | 75 | 1 | 1 | .297/.350/.441 | .278 | .356 | -3.3 | 0.3 | 1.6 |
| 2012 | SLN | MLB | 29 | 325 | 38 | 14 | 0 | 8 | 35 | 25 | 68 | 1 | 0 | .270/.332/.404 | .267 | .322 | 0 | 3B -0, 1B -0 | 2.2 |

Never again will Freese be known simply as the Cardinals' return in the trade of Jim Edmonds. A World Series MVP will have that effect. But the road to becoming a hometown hero was not smooth. A career-long battle with injuries has limited his speed and his range in the field. The bad luck continued this spring when he was struck by a Scott Linebrink fastball, causing him to miss most of May and June with a broken hamate bone in his left hand. Freese managed to put together a productive second half, despite a bad hamstring and a beaning from Clay Hensley. Then, in October, he caught fire, grinding out one at-bat after another en route to a Pujols-like postseason slash line of .397/.465/.794. PECOTA is not optimistic Freese can continue his October surge, and he'll be nearly 30 years old when he becomes eligible for arbitration after the 2012 season. But his postseason hardware gives him a little more leverage than the typical arbitration rookie.

**Rafael Furcal   SS**
Born: 10/24/1977 Age: 34
Bats: B Throws: R Height: 5' 11" Weight: 150
Breakout: 0% Improve: 20% Collapse: 11%
Attrition: 19% MLB: 90%
Comparables:
Marco Scutaro, Edgar Renteria, Julio Lugo

| YEAR | TEAM | LVL | AGE | PA | R | 2B | 3B | HR | RBI | BB | SO | SB | CS | AVG_OBP_SLG | TAv | BABIP | BRR | FRAA | WARP |
|------|------|-----|-----|-----|-----|-----|-----|-----|-----|-----|-----|-----|-----|-------------|------|-------|------|------|------|
| 2009 | LAN | MLB | 31 | 680 | 92 | 28 | 5 | 9 | 47 | 61 | 89 | 12 | 6 | .269/.335/.375 | .255 | .302 | 5 | 10 | 3.6 |
| 2010 | LAN | MLB | 32 | 428 | 66 | 23 | 7 | 8 | 43 | 40 | 60 | 22 | 4 | .300/.366/.460 | .303 | .338 | 3.2 | 6.9 | 4.4 |
| 2011 | LAN | MLB | 33 | 152 | 15 | 4 | 0 | 1 | 12 | 11 | 21 | 5 | 3 | .197/.272/.248 | .218 | .226 | 0.4 | 0.7 | -0.1 |
| 2011 | SLN | MLB | 33 | 217 | 29 | 11 | 0 | 7 | 16 | 17 | 18 | 4 | 2 | .255/.316/.418 | .265 | .250 | 2 | 2.7 | 1.6 |
| 2012 | SLN | MLB | 34 | 366 | 40 | 14 | 2 | 4 | 32 | 32 | 46 | 11 | 4 | .259/.326/.355 | .254 | .286 | -0.1 | SS 6 | 1.6 |

Furcal's tenure as the Dodgers' free-agent answer at shortstop was a six-year catalog of soreness, tightness, fractures, and strains. Still battling to overcome the effects of an oblique strain and a broken thumb in July, he was hitting just .197/.272/.248 when St. Louis acquired him for little more than the promise to pay $1.4 million of his remaining salary. Furcal provided an upgrade over incumbant Ryan Theriot at short, much to the delight of the Cardinals pitching staff, and he finally began to hit in September, delivering a .275/.347/.473 line over the season's final month. But his injury history—if not his 15-for-77 postseason performance—should serve as a red flag to any club with designs on paying for the privilege of penciling Furcal into the lineup every day.

**Tyler Greene   SS**
Born: 8/17/1983 Age: 28
Bats: R Throws: R Height: 6' 3" Weight: 180
Breakout: 2% Improve: 25% Collapse: 7%
Attrition: 21% MLB: 74%
Comparables:
Derek Jeter, Lee Tate, Jim Smith

| YEAR | TEAM | LVL | AGE | PA | R | 2B | 3B | HR | RBI | BB | SO | SB | CS | AVG_OBP_SLG | TAv | BABIP | BRR | FRAA | WARP |
|------|------|-----|-----|-----|-----|-----|-----|-----|-----|-----|-----|-----|-----|-------------|------|-------|------|------|------|
| 2009 | MEM | AAA | 25 | 388 | 70 | 10 | 5 | 15 | 42 | 38 | 86 | 31 | 3 | .291/.368/.482 | .296 | .347 | 7 | 7.1 | 4.4 |
| 2009 | SLN | MLB | 25 | 116 | 9 | 5 | 0 | 2 | 7 | 4 | 32 | 3 | 0 | .222/.270/.324 | .219 | .297 | 1 | 0.1 | 0.1 |
| 2010 | MEM | AAA | 26 | 385 | 67 | 21 | 5 | 9 | 34 | 32 | 89 | 12 | 5 | .284/.349/.456 | .284 | .351 | 0.9 | 0.7 | 2.6 |
| 2010 | SLN | MLB | 26 | 122 | 14 | 3 | 1 | 2 | 10 | 13 | 24 | 2 | 0 | .221/.328/.327 | .255 | .266 | 1.6 | -0.8 | 0.5 |
| 2011 | MEM | AAA | 27 | 303 | 53 | 19 | 2 | 14 | 43 | 37 | 75 | 19 | 2 | .323/.422/.579 | .326 | .407 | 3.8 | -2 | 3.4 |
| 2011 | SLN | MLB | 27 | 121 | 22 | 5 | 0 | 1 | 11 | 13 | 31 | 11 | 0 | .212/.322/.288 | .240 | .292 | 1.7 | -0.7 | 0.5 |
| 2012 | SLN | MLB | 28 | 250 | 28 | 9 | 1 | 6 | 25 | 22 | 61 | 12 | 2 | .241/.323/.381 | .259 | .301 | 0.9 | SS 2, 2B -2 | 1.8 |

For the third year in a row, Greene spent the season shuttling between Triple-A and the big leagues, solidifying the suspicion that at 27, what you see with him is what you get. He's a passable reserve at second base and shortstop who can even play the outfield in a pinch. But his offensive skills have never translated to the majors, and the former first-rounder appears destined for a career in a utility role.

**Matt Holliday** LF
Born: 1/15/1980 Age: 32
Bats: R Throws: R Height: 6' 5" Weight: 230
Breakout: 0% Improve: 30% Collapse: 5%
Attrition: 11% MLB: 92%
Comparables:
Billy Williams, Dave Winfield, Andy Pafko

| YEAR | TEAM | LVL | AGE | PA | R | 2B | 3B | HR | RBI | BB | SO | SB | CS | AVG/OBP/SLG | TAv | BABIP | BRR | FRAA | WARP |
|------|------|-----|-----|-----|----|----|----|----|-----|----|----|----|----|---------------|------|-------|------|-------|------|
| 2009 | OAK | MLB | 29 | 400 | 52 | 23 | 1 | 11 | 54 | 46 | 58 | 12 | 3 | .286/.377/.454 | .300 | .315 | 1.4 | 3.4 | 3.0 |
| 2009 | SLN | MLB | 29 | 270 | 42 | 16 | 2 | 13 | 55 | 26 | 43 | 2 | 4 | .353/.419/.604 | .353 | .380 | 2.3 | -7.3 | 2.6 |
| 2010 | SLN | MLB | 30 | 675 | 95 | 45 | 1 | 28 | 103 | 69 | 93 | 9 | 5 | .312/.390/.532 | .323 | .331 | -0.7 | -2.5 | 5.4 |
| 2011 | SLN | MLB | 31 | 516 | 83 | 36 | 0 | 22 | 75 | 60 | 93 | 2 | 1 | .296/.388/.525 | .318 | .330 | 0 | -8.1 | 3.1 |
| 2012 | SLN | MLB | 32 | 516 | 74 | 30 | 1 | 20 | 73 | 54 | 81 | 11 | 4 | .303/.383/.505 | .318 | .332 | -0.3 | LF -5 | 4.2 |

When we last saw Matt Holliday, he was returning to the dugout, hand injured, after being

**Jon Jay** CF
Born: 3/15/1985 Age: 27
Bats: L Throws: L Height: 6' 0" Weight: 200
Breakout: 2% Improve: 38% Collapse: 6%
Attrition: 22% MLB: 81%
Comparables:
Coco Crisp, Lynn Jones, Mickey Stanley

| YEAR | TEAM | LVL | AGE | PA | R | 2B | 3B | HR | RBI | BB | SO | SB | CS | AVG/OBP/SLG | TAv | BABIP | BRR | FRAA | WARP |
|------|------|-----|-----|-----|----|----|----|----|-----|----|----|----|----|---------------|------|-------|------|----------|------|
| 2009 | MEM | AAA | 24 | 564 | 72 | 23 | 2 | 10 | 54 | 34 | 64 | 20 | 8 | .281/.336/.394 | .259 | .301 | 4.3 | -1.2 | 1.6 |
| 2010 | MEM | AAA | 25 | 191 | 31 | 16 | 0 | 4 | 32 | 17 | 22 | 13 | 0 | .321/.392/.491 | .298 | .345 | 4.2 | 3.3 | 2.1 |
| 2010 | SLN | MLB | 25 | 323 | 47 | 19 | 2 | 4 | 27 | 24 | 50 | 2 | 4 | .300/.359/.422 | .283 | .350 | 1.3 | -3 | 1.4 |
| 2011 | SLN | MLB | 26 | 503 | 56 | 24 | 2 | 10 | 37 | 28 | 81 | 6 | 7 | .297/.344/.424 | .274 | .340 | 0.3 | 4.3 | 2.1 |
| 2012 | SLN | MLB | 27 | 437 | 49 | 20 | 1 | 7 | 43 | 28 | 64 | 7 | 5 | .270/.326/.379 | .256 | .300 | -1.1 | CF 2, RF -0 | 0.9 |

Jay's solid first-half production (.304/.352/.438) gave the Cardinals the confidence of knowing center field would be adequately covered without Colby Rasmus, allowing the club to make the much-dissected eight-player trade with Toronto that revamped the St. Louis bullpen and kick-started a title run. But after struggling with the bat much of the postseason, Jay was replaced in center for the final three games of the World Series by Skip Schumaker, an inferior defender. Jay's lofty .340 average on balls in play suggests a regression could come in 2012, and PECOTA shares the suspicion. But the Miami product is the favorite to be the Opening Day center fielder.

**Yadier Molina** C
Born: 7/13/1982 Age: 29
Bats: R Throws: R Height: 6' 0" Weight: 185
Breakout: 1% Improve: 41% Collapse: 9%
Attrition: 25% MLB: 92%
Comparables:
Dave Rader, Ryan Hanigan, Tim McCarver

| YEAR | TEAM | LVL | AGE | PA | R | 2B | 3B | HR | RBI | BB | SO | SB | CS | AVG/OBP/SLG | TAv | BABIP | BRR | FRAA | WARP |
|------|------|-----|-----|-----|----|----|----|----|-----|----|----|----|----|---------------|------|-------|------|---------|------|
| 2009 | SLN | MLB | 26 | 544 | 45 | 23 | 1 | 6 | 54 | 50 | 39 | 9 | 3 | .293/.366/.383 | .255 | .309 | -1.4 | 1.4 | 2.1 |
| 2010 | SLN | MLB | 27 | 521 | 34 | 19 | 0 | 6 | 62 | 42 | 51 | 8 | 4 | .262/.329/.342 | .243 | .281 | -3.8 | 1.5 | 1.7 |
| 2011 | SLN | MLB | 28 | 518 | 55 | 32 | 1 | 14 | 65 | 33 | 44 | 4 | 5 | .305/.349/.465 | .285 | .311 | -4.8 | 0.1 | 3.1 |
| 2012 | SLN | MLB | 29 | 487 | 55 | 20 | 0 | 6 | 45 | 38 | 37 | 5 | 3 | .277/.337/.368 | .260 | .286 | -0.6 | C 0, 1B 0 | 2.2 |

Molina enjoyed the finest season of his career in 2011, setting career highs in almost every offensive category while delivering his usual stellar defense behind the plate. Workload remains a concern, however. Molina played 139 games last season and no one in baseball has caught more innings (3,464 2/3) over the last three years. The Cardinals made the easy choice of picking up their $7 million option on Molina's contract, but absent an extension, he figures to be in demand on the free-agent market for 2013.

**Skip Schumaker** 2B
Born: 2/3/1980 Age: 32
Bats: L Throws: R Height: 5' 11" Weight: 175
Breakout: 3% Improve: 33% Collapse: 8%
Attrition: 19% MLB: 85%
Comparables:
John Donaldson, Alex Cora, Red Schoendienst

| YEAR | TEAM | LVL | AGE | PA | R | 2B | 3B | HR | RBI | BB | SO | SB | CS | AVG/OBP/SLG | TAv | BABIP | BRR | FRAA | WARP |
|------|------|-----|-----|-----|----|----|----|----|-----|----|----|----|----|---------------|------|-------|------|----------|------|
| 2009 | SLN | MLB | 29 | 586 | 85 | 34 | 1 | 4 | 35 | 52 | 69 | 2 | 2 | .303/.364/.393 | .272 | .341 | 1.1 | -8 | 1.5 |
| 2010 | SLN | MLB | 30 | 529 | 66 | 18 | 1 | 5 | 42 | 43 | 64 | 5 | 3 | .265/.328/.338 | .246 | .294 | -0.4 | 2.8 | 1.0 |
| 2011 | SLN | MLB | 31 | 400 | 34 | 19 | 0 | 2 | 38 | 27 | 50 | 0 | 2 | .283/.333/.351 | .253 | .321 | -1.2 | 1.4 | 0.7 |
| 2012 | SLN | MLB | 32 | 401 | 44 | 17 | 1 | 3 | 34 | 31 | 45 | 3 | 2 | .275/.332/.347 | .254 | .304 | -0.3 | 2B -2, RF 0 | 1.1 |

With Nick Punto and Ryan Theriot, Schumaker serves as the left-handed bat in the Cardinals' collection of the most interesting super-utilitymen in the world. Actually, Schu started 89 games at second base, though he was often replaced for defensive purposes. At the plate, he fights through each at-bat, as evidenced by his 10-pitch struggle with Roy Halladay early in the final game of the NLDS, a battle that ended with Schumaker driving in the game's only run with a double. Still a year away from free agency, Schumaker figures to be in the mix at second base and in the outfield at least one more season.

### Oscar Taveras    RF

Born: 6/19/1992 Age: 20
Bats: L Throws: L Height: 6' 3" Weight: 180
Breakout: 9% Improve: 18% Collapse: 5%
Attrition: 13% MLB: 33%

**Comparables:**
Vada Pinson, Caleb Gindl, Danny Murphy

| YEAR | TEAM | LVL | AGE | PA | R | 2B | 3B | HR | RBI | BB | SO | SB | CS | AVG/OBP/SLG | TAv | BABIP | BRR | FRAA | WARP |
|------|------|-----|-----|-----|----|----|----|----|-----|----|----|----|----|-------------|-----|-------|------|--------|------|
| 2010 | JCY | RK | 18 | 229 | 39 | 13 | 3 | 8 | 43 | 12 | 41 | 8 | 5 | .322/.367/.526 | .324 | .370 | 0.2 | 2 | 2.5 |
| 2011 | QUD | A | 19 | 347 | 52 | 27 | 5 | 8 | 62 | 32 | 52 | 1 | 4 | .386/.444/.584 | .349 | .440 | -4.2 | 3.9 | 4.5 |
| 2012 | SLN | MLB | 20 | 250 | 26 | 11 | 1 | 5 | 25 | 14 | 55 | 0 | 0 | .243/.288/.363 | .237 | .294 | 0 | RF 2, CF -2 | 0.0 |

Dispatched to Low-A Quad Cities at just 19 for his full-season debut, Taveras started fast (26 hits in his first 52 at-bats), then spent much of the spring battling a hamstring injury. But the left-handed hitter sparkled upon his return, leading the Midwest League in batting average, on-base percentage, and slugging despite being the youngest player on the Quad Cities roster. Signed in late 2008 for just $145,000, Taveras could push his way to Double-A Springfield for 2012 with a successful stint in the Arizona Fall League.

### Ryan Theriot    SS

Born: 12/7/1979 Age: 32
Bats: R Throws: R Height: 6' 0" Weight: 175
Breakout: 1% Improve: 36% Collapse: 9%
Attrition: 24% MLB: 86%

**Comparables:**
Alex Arias, Jack Wilson, Oscar Robles

| YEAR | TEAM | LVL | AGE | PA | R | 2B | 3B | HR | RBI | BB | SO | SB | CS | AVG/OBP/SLG | TAv | BABIP | BRR | FRAA | WARP |
|------|------|-----|-----|-----|----|----|----|----|-----|----|----|----|----|-------------|-----|-------|------|-----------|------|
| 2009 | CHN | MLB | 29 | 677 | 81 | 20 | 5 | 7 | 54 | 51 | 93 | 21 | 10 | .284/.343/.369 | .240 | .323 | 0.5 | 4.2 | 1.8 |
| 2010 | CHN | MLB | 30 | 412 | 45 | 10 | 2 | 1 | 21 | 19 | 46 | 16 | 6 | .284/.320/.327 | .235 | .319 | 0.1 | -0.6 | 0.3 |
| 2010 | LAN | MLB | 30 | 228 | 27 | 5 | 0 | 1 | 8 | 22 | 28 | 4 | 3 | .242/.323/.283 | .240 | .276 | 0.2 | 0 | 0.2 |
| 2011 | SLN | MLB | 31 | 483 | 46 | 26 | 1 | 1 | 47 | 29 | 41 | 4 | 6 | .271/.321/.342 | .239 | .296 | -1.6 | -5.3 | 0.3 |
| 2012 | SLN | MLB | 32 | 485 | 52 | 17 | 2 | 1 | 36 | 38 | 50 | 13 | 7 | .272/.333/.327 | .248 | .297 | -1.1 | SS -3, 2B -0 | 1.1 |

John Mozeliak acquired Theriot from the Dodgers in a November 2010 trade for reliever Blake Hawksworth. The St. Louis starting shortstop on Opening Day, Theriot took a back seat after the July 31 trade deadline, when the Cardinals acquired another Dodger, Rafael Furcal, to provide a much-needed defensive boost. After earning $3.1 million in 2011, Theriot has reached the point where his price tag exceeds his production.

### Kolten Wong    2B

Born: 10/10/1990 Age: 21
Bats: L Throws: R Height: 5' 10" Weight: 180
Breakout: 6% Improve: 31% Collapse: 1%
Attrition: 9% MLB: 47%

**Comparables:**
Jose Altuve, Johnny Giavotella, Glenn Hubbard

| YEAR | TEAM | LVL | AGE | PA | R | 2B | 3B | HR | RBI | BB | SO | SB | CS | AVG/OBP/SLG | TAv | BABIP | BRR | FRAA | WARP |
|------|------|-----|-----|-----|----|----|----|----|-----|----|----|----|----|-------------|-----|-------|------|-------|------|
| 2011 | QUD | A | 20 | 222 | 39 | 15 | 2 | 5 | 25 | 21 | 24 | 9 | 5 | .335/.401/.510 | .316 | .355 | 2.3 | 2.4 | 2.4 |
| 2012 | SLN | MLB | 21 | 250 | 25 | 11 | 1 | 3 | 22 | 16 | 46 | 4 | 2 | .235/.286/.335 | .229 | .275 | -0.3 | 2B 5 | 0.0 |

Wong took the rare step of signing 10 days after the Cardinals selected him 22nd overall in the 2011 draft, receiving a $1.3 million signing bonus, $30,000 more than the recommended amount for his slot. The decision allowed him to start his pro career in June at Low-A Quad Cities, where he won praise for his advanced approach and excellent instincts for the game. The Hawaiian is ticketed for High-A Palm Beach to start the season and could reach Double-A by the summer. With the potential to hit .280-.300 with on-base skills and double-digit power, the sky is the limit.

# PITCHERS

### Seth Blair

Born: 3/3/1989 Age: 23
Bats: R Throws: R Height: 6' 3" Weight: 185
Breakout: 36% Improve: 62% Collapse: 25%
Attrition: 12% MLB: 73%

**Comparables:**
Ryan Dempster, Jim Nelson, Whammy Douglas

| YEAR | TEAM | LVL | AGE | W | L | SV | G | GS | IP | H | HR | BB | SO | EqBB9 | EqSO9 | GB% | BABIP | WHIP | ERA | FIP | FRA | WARP |
|------|------|-----|-----|---|---|----|----|----|-----|----|----|----|----|-------|-------|-----|-------|------|------|------|------|------|
| 2011 | QUD | A | 22 | 6 | 3 | 0 | 21 | 21 | 81² | 79 | 9 | 62 | 70 | 6.8 | 7.7 | 53% | .303 | 1.73 | 5.29 | 5.87 | 6.52 | -0.5 |
| 2012 | SLN | MLB | 23 | 1 | 2 | 0 | 6 | 6 | 22² | 24 | 3 | 15 | 11 | 6.0 | 4.4 | 48% | .306 | 1.75 | 6.51 | 5.94 | 7.08 | -0.4 |

The Cardinals selected Blair out of Arizona State with the 46th pick of the 2010 draft, which they received as compensation when Mark DeRosa left St. Louis to join the Giants after the 2009 season. The right-hander's repertoire includes a heavy 91-95 mph fastball and plus curveball, but his changeup needs work. Signed too late to make his pro debut in 2010, Blair was inconsistent in 21 starts at Low-A Quad Cities, allowing 155 baserunners while striking out 70 in 82 2/3 innings. After a stint on the disabled list in August, he was left off the Quad Cities postseason roster for an unspecified violation of organizational policy.

## Mitchell Boggs

Born: 2/15/1984 Age: 28
Bats: R Throws: R Height: 6' 5" Weight: 215
Breakout: 39% Improve: 62% Collapse: 22%
Attrition: 21% MLB: 85%

Comparables:
Bob Kuzava, Steven Jackson, Ryan Speier

| YEAR | TEAM | LVL | AGE | W | L | SV | G | GS | IP | H | HR | BB | SO | EqBB9 | EqSO9 | GB% | BABIP | WHIP | ERA | FIP | FRA | WARP |
|---|---|---|---|---|---|---|---|---|---|---|---|---|---|---|---|---|---|---|---|---|---|---|
| 2009 | MEM | AAA | 25 | 6 | 4 | 0 | 14 | 14 | 76¹ | 90 | 8 | 32 | 58 | 3.8 | 6.8 | 45% | .340 | 1.60 | 4.84 | 4.71 | 4.81 | 0.5 |
| 2009 | SLN | MLB | 25 | 2 | 3 | 0 | 16 | 9 | 58 | 71 | 3 | 33 | 46 | 5.1 | 7.1 | 55% | .376 | 1.79 | 4.19 | 4.06 | 4.46 | 0.4 |
| 2010 | SLN | MLB | 26 | 2 | 3 | 0 | 61 | 0 | 67¹ | 60 | 5 | 27 | 52 | 3.6 | 7.0 | 55% | .285 | 1.29 | 3.61 | 3.91 | 4.67 | 0.0 |
| 2011 | SLN | MLB | 27 | 2 | 3 | 4 | 51 | 0 | 60² | 62 | 4 | 21 | 48 | 3.1 | 7.1 | 53% | .317 | 1.37 | 3.56 | 3.41 | 4.09 | 0.3 |
| 2012 | SLN | MLB | 28 | 3 | 1 | 1 | 47 | 2 | 58¹ | 57 | 5 | 24 | 33 | 3.7 | 5.1 | 50% | .302 | 1.39 | 4.72 | 4.42 | 5.13 | -0.1 |

Next in line for save opportunities after Opening Day closer Ryan Franklin imploded, Boggs started May by allowing seven hits and five earned runs in five innings, then found himself optioned to Triple-A. In Memphis, Boggs moved to the rotation to get an opportunity to work on his secondary pitches. Recalled to the majors in mid-June, he reclaimed a spot in the bullpen before hitting a rough patch in August, when he was diagnosed with a bulging disc after fighting recurring back pain for about a year. Armed with a set of exercises to target the problem, Boggs should again be part of the bullpen mix.

year started slowly, as he was the victim of poor run support, a shaky bullpen, and his own hand, allowing more hits per nine innings than he did in any season since 2002. By mid-June, Carp carried an unsightly 1–7 record and a 4.47 ERA. But he delivered a second half on par with his 2005 Cy Young performance, walking just 24 while striking out 95 in 108 1/3 innings over 15 starts. Along the way, he helped spark the Cards' improbable wild-card run with an August team meeting. Then, for good measure, he won two winner-take-all games in the postseason. PECOTA suggests that his age and heavy 2011 workload do not bode well for the future. But it's hard not to think the Cardinals got a bargain in September when Carpenter signed a two-year, $21 million extension.

## Maikel Cleto

Born: 5/1/1989 Age: 23
Bats: R Throws: R Height: 6' 4" Weight: 220
Breakout: 11% Improve: 43% Collapse: 18%
Attrition: 12% MLB: 85%

Comparables:
Carlos Castillo, Chris Carpenter, Brett Myers

| YEAR | TEAM | LVL | AGE | W | L | SV | G | GS | IP | H | HR | BB | SO | EqBB9 | EqSO9 | GB% | BABIP | WHIP | ERA | FIP | FRA | WARP |
|---|---|---|---|---|---|---|---|---|---|---|---|---|---|---|---|---|---|---|---|---|---|---|
| 2009 | CLN | A | 20 | 0 | 3 | 0 | 8 | 8 | 25¹ | 35 | 4 | 10 | 24 | 3.9 | 8.5 | 51% | .378 | 1.82 | 5.34 | 5.20 | 5.18 | 0.2 |
| 2010 | HDS | A+ | 21 | 4 | 9 | 0 | 23 | 21 | 102¹ | 109 | 9 | 39 | 74 | 3.9 | 7.3 | 50% | .361 | 1.65 | 6.16 | 4.84 | 5.99 | 0.3 |
| 2011 | SFD | AA | 22 | 2 | 2 | 0 | 7 | 6 | 34¹ | 40 | 2 | 12 | 36 | 3.1 | 9.4 | 52% | .396 | 1.51 | 3.93 | 3.53 | 5.25 | 0.1 |
| 2011 | MEM | AAA | 22 | 5 | 3 | 0 | 13 | 13 | 71¹ | 57 | 6 | 43 | 66 | 5.4 | 8.3 | 46% | .267 | 1.40 | 4.29 | 4.91 | 4.69 | 0.4 |
| 2011 | SLN | MLB | 22 | 0 | 0 | 0 | 3 | 0 | 4¹ | 7 | 2 | 4 | 6 | 8.3 | 12.5 | 47% | .385 | 2.54 | 12.46 | 8.99 | 9.77 | -0.3 |
| 2012 | SLN | MLB | 23 | 2 | 4 | 0 | 9 | 9 | 46 | 49 | 5 | 23 | 23 | 4.5 | 4.5 | 48% | .306 | 1.57 | 5.72 | 5.12 | 6.21 | -0.5 |

A product of the Mets system who came to St. Louis from Seattle in the Brendan Ryan trade, Cleto made a brief major-league debut in June, flashing an electric fastball and shaky command. The Dominican held opposing hitters to a .218 batting average in 13 starts at Memphis, but issued more than five walks per nine innings. His control and command of his secondary stuff will have to improve before he gets another call to the majors.

## Jaime Garcia

Born: 7/8/1986 Age: 25
Bats: L Throws: L Height: 6' 3" Weight: 200
Breakout: 23% Improve: 51% Collapse: 17%
Attrition: 5% MLB: 97%

Comparables:
Johnny Antonelli, Eric O'Flaherty, Steve Carlton

| YEAR | TEAM | LVL | AGE | W | L | SV | G | GS | IP | H | HR | BB | SO | EqBB9 | EqSO9 | GB% | BABIP | WHIP | ERA | FIP | FRA | WARP |
|---|---|---|---|---|---|---|---|---|---|---|---|---|---|---|---|---|---|---|---|---|---|---|
| 2010 | SLN | MLB | 23 | 13 | 8 | 0 | 28 | 28 | 163¹ | 151 | 9 | 64 | 132 | 3.5 | 7.3 | 57% | .293 | 1.32 | 2.70 | 3.44 | 3.95 | 2.5 |
| 2011 | SLN | MLB | 24 | 13 | 7 | 0 | 32 | 32 | 194² | 207 | 15 | 50 | 156 | 2.3 | 7.2 | 55% | .324 | 1.32 | 3.56 | 3.19 | 4.46 | 0.7 |
| 2012 | SLN | MLB | 25 | 10 | 10 | 0 | 28 | 28 | 165¹ | 151 | 13 | 52 | 109 | 2.8 | 5.9 | 56% | .296 | 1.23 | 3.74 | 3.85 | 4.06 | 1.9 |

The youngster in the St. Louis rotation at just 25, Garcia built on his breakout 2010 with another solid season. The sinkerballing lefty stepped into the second slot in the rotation left vacant when Adam Wainwright had surgery in the spring. Garcia continues to do his best work at Busch Stadium, where he limits opposing hitters to a .230/.280/.320 line. But on the road, opponents rake him at an unsettling .313/.353/.463 clip. Signed to a club-friendly contract extension in July, Garcia should be a mainstay of the Cardinals pitching staff until at least 2015.

### John Gast

Born: 2/16/1989 Age: 23
Bats: L Throws: L Height: 6' 2" Weight: 195
Breakout: 29% Improve: 64% Collapse: 15%
Attrition: 18% MLB: 86%

**Comparables:**
Jason Jennings, Tom Gorzelanny, Bud Smith

| YEAR | TEAM | LVL | AGE | W | L | SV | G | GS | IP | H | HR | BB | SO | EqBB9 | EqSO9 | GB% | BABIP | WHIP | ERA | FIP | FRA | WARP |
|------|------|-----|-----|---|---|----|---|----|-----|----|----|----|----|-------|-------|-----|-------|------|------|------|------|------|
| 2010 | BAT | A- | 21 | 6 | 0 | 0 | 8 | 6 | 35 | 27 | 1 | 8 | 36 | 2.1 | 9.3 | — | .292 | 1.00 | 1.54 | 2.56 | 4.41 | 0.5 |
| 2011 | PMB | A+ | 22 | 5 | 4 | 0 | 13 | 12 | 82 | 81 | 7 | 27 | 56 | 3.1 | 6.5 | 51% | .319 | 1.38 | 3.95 | 4.42 | 5.62 | -0.1 |
| 2011 | SFD | AA | 22 | 4 | 4 | 0 | 13 | 13 | 79¹ | 80 | 9 | 33 | 54 | 3.7 | 6.1 | 49% | .295 | 1.42 | 4.08 | 4.89 | 5.33 | 0.4 |
| 2012 | SLN | MLB | 23 | 2 | 3 | 0 | 7 | 7 | 41¹ | 44 | 5 | 18 | 20 | 3.9 | 4.3 | 47% | .300 | 1.49 | 5.44 | 5.12 | 5.91 | -0.4 |

Signed for $140,000 after being selected out of Florida State in the sixth round of the 2010 draft, Gast moved fast in 2011. After he made an impressive showing in big-league camp in the spring, the Cardinals jumped him a level to Palm Beach, leapfrogging Quad Cities. By June, he had earned a promotion to Double-A Springfield. Gast works with a low-90s fastball, a hard curveball, and a changeup, but he'll have to reverse his increasing walk rate to continue moving up.

### Edwin Jackson

Born: 9/9/1983 Age: 28
Bats: R Throws: R Height: 6' 4" Weight: 190
Breakout: 28% Improve: 67% Collapse: 13%
Attrition: 13% MLB: 91%

**Comparables:**
Geraldo Guzman, Gavin Floyd, Dan Wheeler

| YEAR | TEAM | LVL | AGE | W | L | SV | G | GS | IP | H | HR | BB | SO | EqBB9 | EqSO9 | GB% | BABIP | WHIP | ERA | FIP | FRA | WARP |
|------|------|-----|-----|----|----|----|----|----|------|-----|----|----|-----|-------|-------|-----|-------|------|------|------|------|------|
| 2009 | DET | MLB | 25 | 13 | 9 | 0 | 33 | 33 | 214 | 200 | 27 | 70 | 161 | 2.9 | 6.8 | 41% | .278 | 1.26 | 3.62 | 4.33 | 4.60 | 1.9 |
| 2010 | CHA | MLB | 26 | 4 | 2 | 0 | 11 | 11 | 75 | 73 | 8 | 18 | 77 | 2.2 | 9.2 | 48% | .308 | 1.21 | 3.24 | 3.14 | 3.62 | 1.4 |
| 2010 | ARI | MLB | 26 | 6 | 10 | 0 | 21 | 21 | 134¹ | 141 | 13 | 60 | 104 | 4.0 | 7.0 | 52% | .321 | 1.50 | 5.16 | 4.27 | 4.69 | 0.9 |
| 2011 | CHA | MLB | 27 | 7 | 7 | 0 | 19 | 19 | 121² | 134 | 8 | 39 | 97 | 2.7 | 5.9 | 49% | .339 | 1.42 | 3.92 | 3.28 | 4.12 | 1.4 |
| 2011 | SLN | MLB | 27 | 5 | 2 | 0 | 13 | 12 | 78 | 91 | 8 | 23 | 51 | 2.9 | 7.2 | 42% | .337 | 1.46 | 3.58 | 3.98 | 4.81 | 0.1 |
| 2012 | SLN | MLB | 28 | 10 | 11 | 0 | 28 | 28 | 181 | 176 | 18 | 62 | 121 | 3.1 | 6.0 | 44% | .306 | 1.32 | 4.32 | 4.19 | 4.69 | 0.6 |

Jackson's excellent adventure touring the pitching mounds of North America made two more stops in 2011 as he hopped from Chicago to St. Louis, with a brief layover north of the border. That's five trades and six teams for Jackson in just six full seasons, and he continues teasing front offices and pitching coaches with his athleticism, mid-90s fastball, and plus slider. But somehow, he's consistently less than the sum of his parts, occasionally struggling with his command, his changeup and his confidence. In between packing and unpacking, EJax made 30-plus starts for the fifth year in a row, though his strikeout rate dropped and he continued to allow an unhealthy number of baserunners. One of the more reliable free agent starters on the market at just 28 years old, he'll get to decide for himself where he pitches next. Three words, Edwin: No-trade clause.

### Tyrell Jenkins

Born: 7/20/1992 Age: 19
Bats: R Throws: R Height: 6' 5" Weight: 180
Breakout: 0% Improve: 76% Collapse: 24%
Attrition: 24% MLB: 40%

**Comparables:**
Jim Bethke, Bob Miller, Rick Wise

| YEAR | TEAM | LVL | AGE | W | L | SV | G | GS | IP | H | HR | BB | SO | EqBB9 | EqSO9 | GB% | BABIP | WHIP | ERA | FIP | FRA | WARP |
|------|------|-----|-----|---|---|----|----|----|----|----|----|----|----|-------|-------|-----|-------|------|------|------|------|------|
| 2011 | JCY | RK | 18 | 4 | 1 | 0 | 11 | 11 | 56 | 70 | 3 | 13 | 57 | 2.1 | 8.8 | 59% | .376 | 1.36 | 3.86 | 3.30 | 4.47 | 1.1 |
| 2012 | SLN | MLB | 19 | 1 | 2 | 0 | 3 | 3 | 15 | 18 | 2 | 9 | 5 | 5.2 | 3.2 | 49% | .317 | 1.76 | 6.61 | 6.07 | 7.19 | -0.3 |

The Cardinals wooed Jenkins away from a scholarship offer to play football at Baylor with a $1.3 million signing bonus, nearly double the recommended amount for his slot. Selected with the compensation pick St. Louis received when Joel Piñeiro signed with the Angels, the athletic Texan works in the 91-94 mph range with both a curve and slider. Still raw, he should get the innings and development time he needs in his full-season debut in 2012.

### Kyle Lohse

Born: 10/4/1978 Age: 33
Bats: R Throws: R Height: 6' 3" Weight: 190
Breakout: 19% Improve: 35% Collapse: 43%
Attrition: 27% MLB: 82%

**Comparables:**
Brad Penny, Steve Gromek, Matt Morris

| YEAR | TEAM | LVL | AGE | W | L | SV | G | GS | IP | H | HR | BB | SO | EqBB9 | EqSO9 | GB% | BABIP | WHIP | ERA | FIP | FRA | WARP |
|------|------|-----|-----|----|----|----|----|----|------|-----|----|----|-----|-------|-------|-----|-------|------|------|------|------|------|
| 2009 | SLN | MLB | 30 | 6 | 10 | 0 | 23 | 22 | 117² | 125 | 16 | 36 | 77 | 2.8 | 5.9 | 46% | .289 | 1.37 | 4.74 | 4.51 | 5.58 | 0.1 |
| 2010 | SLN | MLB | 31 | 4 | 8 | 0 | 18 | 18 | 92 | 129 | 9 | 35 | 54 | 3.4 | 5.3 | 44% | .369 | 1.78 | 6.55 | 4.44 | 4.99 | 0.4 |
| 2011 | SLN | MLB | 32 | 14 | 8 | 0 | 30 | 30 | 188¹ | 178 | 16 | 42 | 111 | 2.0 | 5.3 | 43% | .272 | 1.17 | 3.39 | 3.64 | 4.14 | 1.7 |
| 2012 | SLN | MLB | 33 | 8 | 9 | 0 | 25 | 25 | 145¹ | 148 | 14 | 38 | 69 | 2.3 | 4.3 | 43% | .297 | 1.28 | 4.34 | 4.29 | 4.72 | 0.6 |

Healthy for a full season for the first time since 2008, Lohse finally delivered on the $41 million extension he signed late that season, giving the Cardinals 16 quality starts in his 30 outings. The righty kept his middling strikeout rate constant but managed to reduce his walk and home-run rates. He was nasty down the stretch, limiting opposing hitters to a .245/.282/.284 line in four September starts, including a crucial game in Philadelphia when he boosted the Cardinals' wild-card chances by outdueling Roy Halladay. With one year left on his contract, Lohse projects to be the highest-paid pitcher on the St. Louis staff at $12.875 million.

### Lance Lynn

Born: 5/12/1987 Age: 25
Bats: R Throws: R Height: 6' 6" Weight: 250
Breakout: 17% Improve: 42% Collapse: 17%
Attrition: 12% MLB: 95%

**Comparables:**
Robbie Weinhardt,Jose Arredondo,Mark Melancon

| YEAR | TEAM | LVL | AGE | W | L | SV | G | GS | IP | H | HR | BB | SO | EqBB9 | EqSO9 | GB% | BABIP | WHIP | ERA | FIP | FRA | WARP |
|------|------|-----|-----|---|---|----|----|----|-----|-----|----|----|-----|-------|-------|-----|-------|------|------|------|------|------|
| 2009 | SFD | AA | 22 | 11 | 4 | 0 | 22 | 22 | 126¹ | 123 | 7 | 55 | 103 | 3.6 | 7.0 | 49% | .304 | 1.33 | 2.92 | 3.75 | 4.04 | 1.8 |
| 2010 | MEM | AAA | 23 | 14 | 10 | 0 | 29 | 29 | 164 | 116 | 11 | 36 | 99 | 3.4 | 7.7 | 45% | .309 | 1.38 | 4.77 | 4.49 | 4.80 | 1.3 |
| 2011 | MEM | AAA | 24 | 7 | 3 | 0 | 12 | 12 | 75 | 79 | 2 | 25 | 64 | 3.0 | 7.7 | 46% | .350 | 1.39 | 3.84 | 3.46 | 4.26 | 0.9 |
| 2011 | SLN | MLB | 24 | 1 | 1 | 1 | 18 | 2 | 34² | 25 | 3 | 11 | 40 | 2.9 | 10.4 | 58% | .275 | 1.04 | 3.12 | 2.85 | 3.79 | 0.3 |
| 2012 | SLN | MLB | 25 | 3 | 3 | 0 | 10 | 10 | 56 | 49 | 5 | 20 | 42 | 3.3 | 6.8 | 45% | .291 | 1.24 | 3.81 | 3.94 | 4.14 | 0.6 |

Lynn established himself as one of the Cardinals' primary setup relievers after being promoted from the Memphis starting rotation in June. After making starts in his first two appearances, the hulking right-hander excelled in the bullpen, where he struck out 32 and walked just eight in 24 1/3 innings. A strained oblique in early August appeared to end his season, but he returned for some postseason work out of the bullpen. Given his big frame and good command of a low-90s fastball and a variety of breaking pitches, he could be a fit at the back of a starting rotation.

office revealed doubts about his identity and resulted in a one-year suspension. His velocity soared in the ensuing 12 months, and Martinez signed with the Cardinals for $1.5 million the following June. In his full-season debut at Quad Cities in 2011, he made eight dominant starts before being promoted to Palm Beach, where he struggled. He'll return there to start 2012, with an eye toward refining his upper-90s fastball, his low-80s curve, and his changeup.

### Kyle McClellan

Born: 6/12/1984 Age: 28
Bats: R Throws: R Height: 6' 5" Weight: 205
Breakout: 18% Improve: 46% Collapse: 27%
Attrition: 18% MLB: 92%

**Comparables:**
Geraldo Guzman,Matt Morris,Steve Rogers

| YEAR | TEAM | LVL | AGE | W | L | SV | G | GS | IP | H | HR | BB | SO | EqBB9 | EqSO9 | GB% | BABIP | WHIP | ERA | FIP | FRA | WARP |
|------|------|-----|-----|---|---|----|----|----|------|-----|----|----|----|-------|-------|-----|-------|------|------|------|------|------|
| 2009 | SLN | MLB | 25 | 4 | 4 | 3 | 66 | 0 | 66² | 56 | 4 | 34 | 51 | 4.6 | 6.9 | 51% | .271 | 1.35 | 3.38 | 3.93 | 4.23 | 0.6 |
| 2010 | SLN | MLB | 26 | 1 | 4 | 2 | 68 | 0 | 75¹ | 58 | 9 | 23 | 60 | 2.7 | 7.2 | 52% | .236 | 1.08 | 2.27 | 4.10 | 4.26 | 0.5 |
| 2011 | SLN | MLB | 27 | 12 | 7 | 0 | 43 | 17 | 141² | 143 | 21 | 43 | 76 | 2.7 | 4.8 | 52% | .268 | 1.31 | 4.19 | 4.89 | 5.34 | -1.2 |
| 2012 | SLN | MLB | 28 | 6 | 4 | 1 | 59 | 9 | 116¹ | 102 | 11 | 35 | 69 | 2.7 | 5.4 | 50% | .275 | 1.18 | 3.62 | 4.15 | 3.94 | 1.4 |

An often overlooked key to the Cards' 2011 success, McClellan provided a boost by filling the void left in the starting rotation when Adam Wainwright was lost for the season in spring training. McClellan—whose last professional start had come in 2007 for High-A Palm Beach—gave Tony La Russa and Dave Duncan 17 starts and 141.2 innings, nearly double his workload in any one of the past five seasons. Returned to the bullpen after the acquisition of Edwin Jackson, McClellan predictably battled fatigue in September, walking six and allowing five home runs in 11 2/3 innings. His changeup remains an effective weapon against lefties, however, and he's ticketed for the bullpen again in 2012.

### Shelby Miller

Born: 10/10/1990 Age: 21
Bats: R Throws: R Height: 6' 4" Weight: 195
Breakout: 26% Improve: 52% Collapse: 17%
Attrition: 3% MLB: 91%

**Comparables:**
Gary Nolan,Jose Rijo,Felix Hernandez

| YEAR | TEAM | LVL | AGE | W | L | SV | G | GS | IP | H | HR | BB | SO | EqBB9 | EqSO9 | GB% | BABIP | WHIP | ERA | FIP | FRA | WARP |
|------|------|-----|-----|---|---|----|----|----|------|----|----|----|----|-------|-------|-----|-------|------|------|------|------|------|
| 2010 | QUD | A | 19 | 8 | 5 | 0 | 24 | 24 | 104¹ | 48 | 3 | 17 | 69 | 2.8 | 12.1 | 45% | .352 | 1.25 | 3.62 | 3.40 | 3.67 | 2.4 |
| 2011 | PMB | A+ | 20 | 2 | 3 | 0 | 9 | 9 | 53 | 36 | 2 | 19 | 72 | 3.4 | 13.8 | 33% | .327 | 1.13 | 2.89 | 2.30 | 2.71 | 1.5 |
| 2011 | SFD | AA | 20 | 9 | 3 | 0 | 16 | 16 | 86² | 72 | 2 | 33 | 89 | 3.4 | 9.2 | 45% | .312 | 1.21 | 2.70 | 2.91 | 3.39 | 2.1 |
| 2012 | SLN | MLB | 21 | 2 | 3 | 0 | 8 | 8 | 39 | 34 | 3 | 17 | 35 | 3.9 | 8.0 | 41% | .303 | 1.30 | 4.00 | 3.72 | 4.35 | 0.4 |

The Cardinals bucked their recent trend by selecting Miller, a Texas high schooler, with the 19th overall pick in the 2009 draft. But they have not been disappointed. The hard-throwing right-hander followed up a solid first full season with an impressive 2011 performance. After dominating Florida State League hitters in eight starts at Palm Beach, he moved to Double-A Springfield, where he whiffed 89 and allowed just two home runs in 86 2/3 innings. However, Miller, 20, was suspended in August for violating team policy in the wake of an altercation involving alcohol at a Springfield apartment complex. A strong spring could earn him a spot in the Triple-A Memphis rotation.

### Jason Motte
Born: 6/22/1982 Age: 30
Bats: R Throws: R Height: 6' 1" Weight: 195
Breakout: 35% Improve: 57% Collapse: 23%
Attrition: 5% MLB: 96%

**Comparables:**
Jeff Montgomery, Juan Rincon, Robb Nen

| YEAR | TEAM | LVL | AGE | W | L | SV | G | GS | IP | H | HR | BB | SO | EqBB9 | EqSO9 | GB% | BABIP | WHIP | ERA | FIP | FRA | WARP |
|------|------|-----|-----|---|---|----|----|----|------|----|----|----|----|-------|-------|-----|-------|------|------|------|------|------|
| 2009 | SLN | MLB | 27 | 4 | 4 | 0 | 69 | 0 | 56² | 57 | 10 | 23 | 54 | 3.7 | 8.6 | 39% | .303 | 1.41 | 4.76 | 4.77 | 4.78 | 0.5 |
| 2010 | SLN | MLB | 28 | 4 | 2 | 2 | 56 | 0 | 52¹ | 41 | 5 | 18 | 54 | 3.1 | 9.3 | 40% | .277 | 1.13 | 2.24 | 3.32 | 4.34 | 0.2 |
| 2011 | SLN | MLB | 29 | 5 | 2 | 9 | 78 | 0 | 68 | 49 | 2 | 16 | 63 | 2.1 | 8.3 | 46% | .260 | 0.96 | 2.25 | 2.45 | 4.14 | 0.6 |
| 2012 | SLN | MLB | 30 | 3 | 1 | 3 | 63 | 0 | 57 | 46 | 5 | 19 | 53 | 2.9 | 8.3 | 41% | .293 | 1.13 | 3.17 | 3.49 | 3.45 | 1.0 |

The latest in a long line of quirky bearded relievers, Motte took the closer baton from Fernando Salas in late August and sprinted all the way to Game 7 of the World Series. The converted catcher's mid-90s fastball and much-improved secondary offerings were brutal on right-handed hitters, who hit just .162/.220/.234 against him. Lefties, however, remain another story, as they drummed him to the tune of .270/.333/.404. Scheduled to make his first trip through arbitration for 2012, Motte should be first in line to close games on Opening Day.

### Adam Reifer
Born: 6/3/1986 Age: 26
Bats: R Throws: R Height: 6' 3" Weight: 195
Breakout: 21% Improve: 63% Collapse: 18%
Attrition: 21% MLB: 86%

**Comparables:**
Brian Slocum, Kelvim Escobar, Ron Piche

| YEAR | TEAM | LVL | AGE | W | L | SV | G | GS | IP | H | HR | BB | SO | EqBB9 | EqSO9 | GB% | BABIP | WHIP | ERA | FIP | FRA | WARP |
|------|------|-----|-----|---|---|----|----|----|------|----|----|----|----|-------|-------|-----|-------|------|------|------|------|------|
| 2009 | PMB | A+ | 23 | 4 | 7 | 21 | 54 | 0 | 48¹ | 51 | 2 | 24 | 50 | 4.5 | 9.3 | 44% | .348 | 1.55 | 4.47 | 3.53 | 4.40 | 0.3 |
| 2010 | SFD | AA | 24 | 3 | 1 | 17 | 51 | 0 | 54 | 39 | 2 | 11 | 41 | 2.5 | 8.7 | 53% | .363 | 1.26 | 3.00 | 3.01 | 4.02 | 0.9 |
| 2012 | SLN | MLB | 26 | 0 | 0 | 0 | 5 | 0 | 5¹ | 5 | 1 | 2 | 4 | 4.0 | 6.2 | 47% | .303 | 1.40 | 4.77 | 5.27 | 5.18 | -0.0 |

The Cards' 2011 magic did not extend to Reifer. Optioned to Triple-A to put his power arm to work as the Memphis closer, Reifer slipped on a wet mound in Des Moines in mid-April and blew out his knee, ending his season. He'll get his mid-90s fastball and plus slider cranked up again in the Memphis bullpen, with an eye toward eventually winning a relief role in the majors.

### Arthur Rhodes
Born: 10/24/1969 Age: 42
Bats: L Throws: L Height: 6' 3" Weight: 190
Breakout: 10% Improve: 27% Collapse: 18%
Attrition: 41% MLB: 79%

**Comparables:**
Jamie Moyer, Dan Plesac, Doug Brocail

| YEAR | TEAM | LVL | AGE | W | L | SV | G | GS | IP | H | HR | BB | SO | EqBB9 | EqSO9 | GB% | BABIP | WHIP | ERA | FIP | FRA | WARP |
|------|------|-----|-----|---|---|----|----|----|------|----|----|----|----|-------|-------|-----|-------|------|------|------|------|------|
| 2009 | CIN | MLB | 39 | 1 | 1 | 0 | 66 | 0 | 53¹ | 37 | 3 | 20 | 48 | 3.4 | 8.1 | 44% | .246 | 1.07 | 2.53 | 3.17 | 3.84 | 0.7 |
| 2010 | CIN | MLB | 40 | 4 | 4 | 0 | 69 | 0 | 55 | 38 | 4 | 18 | 50 | 2.9 | 8.2 | 39% | .239 | 1.02 | 2.29 | 3.27 | 3.71 | 0.8 |
| 2011 | TEX | MLB | 41 | 3 | 3 | 1 | 32 | 0 | 24¹ | 28 | 6 | 8 | 15 | 3.1 | 6.2 | 33% | .289 | 1.48 | 4.81 | 6.02 | 6.25 | -0.2 |
| 2011 | SLN | MLB | 41 | 0 | 1 | 0 | 19 | 0 | 8² | 6 | 2 | 3 | 6 | 3.0 | 5.5 | 48% | .182 | 1.04 | 4.15 | 5.65 | 7.86 | -0.3 |
| 2012 | SLN | MLB | 42 | 2 | 1 | 1 | 46 | 0 | 34 | 28 | 3 | 12 | 26 | 3.2 | 7.0 | 39% | .279 | 1.19 | 3.42 | 3.88 | 3.72 | 0.5 |

Life after 40 has been good to Rhodes. A first-time All-Star in 2010 at 40, the lefty specialist collected a World Series ring with St. Louis at 41. Released by the Rangers in early August, Rhodes was snapped up by the Cardinals four days later for slightly more than $100,000, the minimum salary for the remainder of the year. Over eight postseason appearances, he allowed no hits and only one walk in 2 2/3 innings. Rhodes says he would like to play one more season, but his .245/.344/.528 line against lefties in 2011 is not encouraging.

### Marc Rzepczynski
Born: 8/29/1985 Age: 26
Bats: L Throws: L Height: 6' 4" Weight: 205
Breakout: 35% Improve: 55% Collapse: 25%
Attrition: 13% MLB: 93%

**Comparables:**
Jose Mijares, Rich Hill, Bob Howry

| YEAR | TEAM | LVL | AGE | W | L | SV | G | GS | IP | H | HR | BB | SO | EqBB9 | EqSO9 | GB% | BABIP | WHIP | ERA | FIP | FRA | WARP |
|------|------|-----|-----|---|---|----|----|----|------|----|----|----|----|-------|-------|-----|-------|------|------|------|------|------|
| 2009 | TOR | MLB | 23 | 2 | 4 | 0 | 11 | 11 | 61¹ | 51 | 7 | 30 | 60 | 4.4 | 8.8 | 52% | .273 | 1.32 | 3.67 | 4.19 | 4.78 | 0.6 |
| 2010 | TOR | MLB | 24 | 4 | 4 | 0 | 14 | 12 | 63² | 72 | 8 | 30 | 57 | 4.2 | 8.1 | 53% | .344 | 1.60 | 4.95 | 4.54 | 5.19 | 0.2 |
| 2011 | TOR | MLB | 25 | 2 | 3 | 0 | 43 | 0 | 39¹ | 28 | 2 | 15 | 33 | 4.4 | 11.1 | 65% | .250 | 1.09 | 2.97 | 3.42 | 4.11 | 0.5 |
| 2011 | SLN | MLB | 25 | 0 | 3 | 0 | 28 | 0 | 22² | 22 | 1 | 11 | 28 | 3.4 | 7.6 | 64% | .375 | 1.46 | 3.97 | 2.69 | 3.58 | 0.3 |
| 2012 | SLN | MLB | 26 | 3 | 3 | 1 | 31 | 8 | 61² | 56 | 6 | 26 | 50 | 3.8 | 7.3 | 58% | .310 | 1.33 | 4.35 | 4.11 | 4.73 | 0.2 |

Part of John Mozeliak's trade-deadline bullpen makeover, Rzepczynski wields a heavy sinker and still harbors thoughts of working in the starting rotation. Given the crowd in the St. Louis rotation and Scrabble's success against left-handed hitters—they managed to hit just .163/.256/.221 against him in Toronto and St. Louis in 2011—he'll probably have to be satisfied with a return to a relief role and the honor of one of the best nicknames in baseball.

### Fernando Salas
Born: 5/30/1985 Age: 27
Bats: R Throws: R Height: 6' 3" Weight: 200
Breakout: 18% Improve: 55% Collapse: 29%
Attrition: 7% MLB: 94%

**Comparables:**
Rollie Fingers, Pedro Martinez, John Montefusco

| YEAR | TEAM | LVL | AGE | W | L | SV | G | GS | IP | H | HR | BB | SO | EqBB9 | EqSO9 | GB% | BABIP | WHIP | ERA | FIP | FRA | WARP |
|------|------|-----|-----|---|---|----|----|----|------|----|----|----|----|-------|-------|-----|-------|------|------|------|------|------|
| 2009 | MEM | AAA | 24 | 3 | 2 | 0 | 24 | 0 | 27 | 24 | 4 | 10 | 27 | 3.3 | 8.0 | 30% | .256 | 1.19 | 3.67 | 4.60 | 4.93 | 0.2 |
| 2010 | MEM | AAA | 25 | 1 | 0 | 19 | 34 | 0 | 35² | 22 | 2 | 7 | 33 | 2.3 | 11.1 | 33% | .385 | 0.98 | 3.78 | 3.61 | 3.43 | 0.6 |
| 2010 | SLN | MLB | 25 | 0 | 0 | 0 | 27 | 0 | 30² | 28 | 4 | 15 | 29 | 4.4 | 8.5 | 36% | .286 | 1.40 | 3.52 | 4.38 | 4.54 | 0.1 |
| 2011 | SLN | MLB | 26 | 5 | 6 | 24 | 68 | 0 | 75 | 50 | 7 | 21 | 75 | 2.5 | 9.0 | 36% | .230 | 0.95 | 2.28 | 3.13 | 3.82 | 0.8 |
| 2012 | SLN | MLB | 27 | 3 | 1 | 10 | 58 | 0 | 63 | 51 | 7 | 19 | 55 | 2.7 | 7.8 | 36% | .279 | 1.11 | 3.27 | 3.81 | 3.56 | 1.0 |

Salas, a Mexican League veteran, assumed the Cardinals' closer job by default in May and racked up 24 saves in 30 opportunities before yielding to Jason Motte down the stretch. Nevertheless, Salas was an important contributor in the Cards' volatile bullpen, striking out a batter per inning while reducing his walk and home-run rates. PECOTA envisions a slight regression, however, as Salas held opposing hitters to an unusually low BABIP of .230.

### Eduardo Sanchez
Born: 2/16/1989 Age: 23
Bats: R Throws: R Height: 6' 0'' Weight: 170
Breakout: 32% Improve: 60% Collapse: 21%
Attrition: 9% MLB: 92%
**Comparables:**
Ryan Perry, Brandon Morrow, Ian Kennedy

| YEAR | TEAM | LVL | AGE | W | L | SV | G | GS | IP | H | HR | BB | SO | EqBB9 | EqSO9 | GB% | BABIP | WHIP | ERA | FIP | FRA | WARP |
|------|------|-----|-----|---|---|----|---|----|----|---|----|----|----|-------|-------|-----|-------|------|-----|-----|-----|------|
| 2009 | PMB | A+ | 20 | 0 | 1 | 3 | 19 | 0 | 25 | 12 | 2 | 5 | 26 | 1.8 | 9.4 | 53% | .182 | 0.68 | 1.44 | 3.12 | 3.97 | 0.2 |
| 2009 | SFD | AA | 20 | 2 | 0 | 10 | 41 | 0 | 50 | 35 | 5 | 20 | 56 | 3.6 | 10.1 | 52% | .256 | 1.04 | 2.70 | 3.74 | 3.82 | 0.8 |
| 2010 | SFD | AA | 21 | 1 | 1 | 11 | 24 | 0 | 26 | 15 | 1 | 5 | 16 | 2.8 | 9.3 | 64% | .333 | 1.15 | 3.12 | 3.29 | 4.80 | 0.2 |
| 2010 | MEM | AAA | 21 | 0 | 1 | 3 | 26 | 0 | 27 | 18 | 2 | 9 | 20 | 4.0 | 10.3 | 48% | .333 | 1.15 | 1.67 | 4.76 | 4.04 | 0.4 |
| 2011 | SLN | MLB | 22 | 3 | 1 | 5 | 26 | 0 | 30 | 14 | 1 | 16 | 35 | 4.8 | 10.5 | 34% | .206 | 1.00 | 1.80 | 2.99 | 3.64 | 0.3 |
| 2012 | SLN | MLB | 23 | 1 | 0 | 3 | 20 | 0 | 23 | 18 | 2 | 11 | 20 | 4.2 | 7.9 | 47% | .282 | 1.26 | 3.81 | 4.03 | 4.14 | 0.2 |

Bats: B Throws: R Height: 6' 3'' Weight: 175
Breakout: 26% Improve: 54% Collapse: 20%
Attrition: 10% MLB: 92%
**Comparables:**
Mat Latos, Larry Dierker, Trevor Cahill

| YEAR | TEAM | LVL | AGE | W | L | SV | G | GS | IP | H | HR | BB | SO | EqBB9 | EqSO9 | GB% | BABIP | WHIP | ERA | FIP | FRA | WARP |
|------|------|-----|-----|---|---|----|---|----|-----|----|----|----|----|-------|-------|-----|-------|------|-----|-----|-----|------|
| 2012 | SLN | MLB | 22 | 1 | 1 | 0 | 9 | 3 | 23[1] | 22 | 2 | 9 | 15 | 3.6 | 5.9 | 49% | .296 | 1.34 | 4.39 | 4.19 | 4.77 | 0.1 |

Swagerty, a second-rounder selected from Arizona State in 2010, started the season in the Quad Cities rotation to give him an opportunity to work on all of his pitches. By the end of the season, he had rocketed through High-A Palm Beach and up to Double-A Springfield. Moved to the back of the bullpen at midseason to limit his workload, the former college closer has good command of a low-90s fastball, a plus power curveball, and an occasional splitter. He could push himself into the mix in the St. Louis bullpen soon.

### Adam Wainwright
Born: 8/30/1981 Age: 30
Bats: R Throws: R Height: 6' 8'' Weight: 205
Breakout: 8% Improve: 27% Collapse: 17%
Attrition: 8% MLB: 98%
**Comparables:**
Mariano Rivera, Roy Halladay, Don Drysdale

| YEAR | TEAM | LVL | AGE | W | L | SV | G | GS | IP | H | HR | BB | SO | EqBB9 | EqSO9 | GB% | BABIP | WHIP | ERA | FIP | FRA | WARP |
|------|------|-----|-----|----|----|----|----|----|------|-----|----|----|-----|-------|-------|-----|-------|------|-----|-----|-----|------|
| 2009 | SLN | MLB | 27 | 19 | 8 | 0 | 34 | 34 | 233 | 216 | 17 | 66 | 212 | 2.5 | 8.2 | 52% | .301 | 1.21 | 2.63 | 3.07 | 3.55 | 5.1 |
| 2010 | SLN | MLB | 28 | 20 | 11 | 0 | 33 | 33 | 230[1] | 186 | 15 | 56 | 213 | 2.2 | 8.3 | 54% | .281 | 1.05 | 2.42 | 2.88 | 3.45 | 4.6 |
| 2012 | SLN | MLB | 30 | 2 | 2 | 0 | 5 | 5 | 35 | 31 | 2 | 9 | 24 | 2.3 | 6.2 | 50% | .292 | 1.14 | 3.23 | 3.35 | 3.51 | 0.6 |

The highlight of Wainwright's year came in a ceremonial role, as he joined Cardinals legends Bob Gibson and Bruce Sutter in throwing out first pitches before Game 1 of the World Series. The big right-hander had reconstructive elbow surgery in March and was throwing twice a week by late summer. By October, he was lobbying for a spot on the postseason roster, a request the club quickly dismissed. St. Louis picked up its two-year option on Wainwright's contract (worth $9 million in 2012 and $12 million in 2013), and he's expected to be ready for spring training, though as with most Tommy John survivors, his control is likely to lag behind by several months.

### Jake Westbrook
Born: 9/29/1977 Age: 34
Bats: R Throws: R Height: 6' 4'' Weight: 190
Breakout: 7% Improve: 36% Collapse: 41%
Attrition: 13% MLB: 86%
**Comparables:**
Burt Hooton, Karl Drews, Salomon Torres

| YEAR | TEAM | LVL | AGE | W | L | SV | G | GS | IP | H | HR | BB | SO | EqBB9 | EqSO9 | GB% | BABIP | WHIP | ERA | FIP | FRA | WARP |
|------|------|-----|-----|----|----|----|----|----|------|-----|----|----|-----|-------|-------|-----|-------|------|-----|-----|-----|------|
| 2010 | SLN | MLB | 32 | 4 | 4 | 0 | 12 | 12 | 75 | 70 | 5 | 24 | 55 | 2.9 | 6.6 | 65% | .284 | 1.25 | 3.48 | 3.55 | 3.56 | 1.7 |
| 2010 | CLE | MLB | 32 | 6 | 7 | 0 | 21 | 21 | 127[2] | 133 | 15 | 44 | 73 | 3.1 | 5.1 | 54% | .294 | 1.39 | 4.65 | 4.61 | 5.40 | 0.0 |
| 2011 | SLN | MLB | 33 | 12 | 9 | 0 | 33 | 33 | 183[1] | 208 | 16 | 73 | 104 | 3.6 | 5.1 | 60% | .318 | 1.53 | 4.66 | 4.22 | 4.57 | 1.3 |
| 2012 | SLN | MLB | 34 | 9 | 11 | 0 | 28 | 28 | 165 | 166 | 15 | 56 | 80 | 3.1 | 4.4 | 56% | .300 | 1.35 | 4.48 | 4.43 | 4.87 | 0.4 |

Sometimes, it's funny how things work out. After not making an appearance in the Division Series, the Cards' fourth starter was left off the roster in favor of an extra reliever for the NLCS. But by the end of the World Series, Westbrook and his turbo sinker had made two appearances, earning the victory in one of the wildest finishes in postseason history with a scoreless 11th inning in Game 6. Westbrook lasted beyond the sixth inning in just eight of his 33 starts, but he's locked in at the back of the St. Louis rotation for at least one more season at a cost of $8.5 million.

# LINEOUTS

## HITTERS

| PLAYER | TEAM | LVL | AGE | PA | R | 2B | 3B | HR | RBI | BB | SO | SB-CS | AVG/OBP/SLG | TAv | BABIP | BRR | FRAA | WARP |
|---|---|---|---|---|---|---|---|---|---|---|---|---|---|---|---|---|---|---|
| 1B M. Hamilton | MEM | AAA | 26 | 303 | 46 | 26 | 0 | 2 | 39 | 42 | 44 | 0-0 | .345/.439/.472 | .304 | .403 | 0.7 | -4.6 | 1.5 |
|  | SLN | MLB | 26 | 51 | 5 | 3 | 0 | 0 | 4 | 4 | 16 | 0-0 | .213/.275/.277 | .219 | .323 | -0.2 | -0.3 | -0.2 |
| SS R. Jackson | SFD | AA | 23 | 599 | 65 | 34 | 3 | 11 | 73 | 44 | 91 | 2-0 | .278/.334/.415 | .253 | .314 | -2.2 | -4.9 | 1.1 |
| SS P. Kozma | MEM | AAA | 23 | 448 | 48 | 17 | 2 | 3 | 47 | 36 | 91 | 2-2 | .214/.280/.289 | .203 | .265 | 2.3 | 10.4 | 0.3 |
|  | SLN | MLB | 23 | 22 | 2 | 1 | 0 | 0 | 1 | 4 | 4 | 0-0 | .176/.333/.235 | .215 | .231 | -0.4 | -0.3 | -0.1 |
| LF C. Patterson | TOR | MLB | 31 | 341 | 44 | 16 | 3 | 6 | 33 | 15 | 65 | 13-8 | .252/.287/.379 | .236 | .298 | -1.4 | 0.5 | -0.2 |
|  | SLN | MLB | 31 | 56 | 5 | 4 | 0 | 0 | 3 | 2 | 12 | 0-1 | .157/.189/.235 | .179 | .205 | -0.3 | 0.5 | -0.4 |
| LF S. Robinson | MEM | AAA | 26 | 193 | 35 | 8 | 3 | 4 | 23 | 19 | 16 | 9-1 | .299/.366/.455 | .260 | .305 | 3.3 | 1.4 | 0.9 |
|  | SLN | MLB | 26 | 8 | 0 | 0 | 0 | 0 | 0 | 1 | 2 | 0-0 | .000/.125/.000 | .028 | .000 | 0 | -0.2 | -0.2 |
| 2B E. Velez | ABQ | AAA | 29 | 235 | 33 | 15 | 3 | 2 | 31 | 11 | 36 | 6-6 | .339/.371/.463 | .262 | .396 | 2.3 | 2.1 | 0.9 |
|  | LAN | MLB | 29 | 40 | 5 | 0 | 0 | 0 | 1 | 2 | 11 | 1-0 | .000/.075/.000 | .040 | .000 | 0 | 0.2 | -0.8 |

After an early-season stint as a reserve in St. Louis, lefty first baseman **Mark Hamilton** put together a productive season in Memphis. But his loss of power was a red flag. Hamilton hit just two home runs after clubbing 20 in 2010. For a 27-year-old with precious few tools beyond his bat, that's not encouraging. ⊘ A glove-first shortstop drafted from the University of Miami in 2009, **Ryan Jackson** impressed with his bat at Springfield, logging career highs in hits, home runs and slugging percentage. A mid- and postseason Texas League All-Star, he could supplant Pete Kozma as the shortstop of the future with a strong performance at Triple-A Memphis. ⊘ **Pete Kozma** collected just three hits during a pair of early-season cameos spelling Nick Punto in St. Louis, and his first full season at Triple-A wasn't exactly a wild success either. He's still just 24, but the 2007 first-rounder will have to improve his contact rate and get on base more often to approach even Punto status. ⊘ Acquired in the blockbuster eight-player deadline deal with Toronto, **Corey Patterson** made just three plate appearances after dropping a fly ball in the ninth inning of a crucial September game in Philadelphia. Now well into his mid-30s, Patterson will shop the free-agent market for a minor-league deal with an invitation to major league camp. ⊘ **Shane Robinson** missed most of the first half of the season after a scary outfield collision with teammate Andrew Brown left him with a broken orbital bone in his face. The fracture—a less severe version of the horrible injury that ended the career of former Cardinal Juan Encarnacion—required surgery. But Robinson returned, posted an impressive .314/.385/.505 line in August, then received a September promotion to St. Louis. ⊘ No position player has come to bat more times in a season without logging a single hit than **Eugenio Velez**, who broke Hal Finney's 0-for-35 record from 1936, but why he was given the opportunity to approach that mark by the Dodgers is a mystery. Justin Sellers could have done better, and for that matter, so could Peter Sellers, even with the handicap of being dead for 31 years.

## PITCHERS

| PLAYER | TEAM | LVL | AGE | W | L | SV | IP | H | HR | BB | SO | EqBB9 | EqSO9 | GB% | BABIP | WHIP | ERA | FIP | FRA | WARP |
|---|---|---|---|---|---|---|---|---|---|---|---|---|---|---|---|---|---|---|---|---|
| B. Augenstein | MEM | AAA | 24 | 3 | 0 | 0 | $35^2$ | 36 | 5 | 12 | 35 | 3.0 | 8.8 | 40% | .295 | 1.35 | 4.04 | 4.69 | 4.77 | 0.3 |
| | SLN | MLB | 24 | 0 | 1 | 0 | $5^2$ | 11 | 1 | 3 | 6 | 4.8 | 9.5 | 38% | .500 | 2.47 | 9.53 | 5.29 | 5.01 | 0.0 |
| B. Boyer | NYN | MLB | 29 | 0 | 2 | 1 | $6^2$ | 13 | 2 | 1 | 1 | 1.4 | 1.4 | 60% | .407 | 2.10 | 10.80 | 7.49 | 8.01 | -0.3 |
| B. Broderick | MEM | AAA | 24 | 7 | 7 | 0 | 91 | 121 | 11 | 21 | 45 | 2.1 | 4.5 | 49% | .340 | 1.56 | 5.04 | 5.11 | 5.93 | -0.3 |
| | WAS | MLB | 24 | 0 | 1 | 0 | $12^1$ | 16 | 0 | 3 | 4 | 2.2 | 2.9 | 62% | .340 | 1.54 | 6.57 | 3.56 | 5.46 | -0.1 |
| B. Dickson | MEM | AAA | 26 | 8 | 9 | 0 | $157^1$ | 169 | 22 | 32 | 124 | 1.8 | 7.1 | 55% | .313 | 1.28 | 3.95 | 4.66 | 4.67 | 1.9 |
| | SLN | MLB | 26 | 0 | 0 | 0 | $8^1$ | 9 | 2 | 3 | 7 | 3.2 | 7.6 | 62% | .318 | 1.44 | 3.24 | 5.51 | 5.54 | 0.1 |
| R. Franklin | SLN | MLB | 38 | 1 | 4 | 1 | $27^2$ | 44 | 9 | 7 | 17 | 2.3 | 5.5 | 43% | .368 | 1.84 | 8.46 | 6.86 | 5.83 | -0.4 |
| J. Kelly | PMB | A+ | 23 | 5 | 2 | 0 | $72^2$ | 56 | 1 | 34 | 62 | 4.2 | 7.7 | 62% | .278 | 1.24 | 2.60 | 3.60 | 4.69 | 0.3 |

**Bryan Augenstein** made five nondescript relief appearances, spent two months on the disabled list with a groin injury, then was outrighted to the minors, where he finished the year in the Memphis bullpen. ⊘ Signed to a minor-league contract in July after being dropped by the Mets, **Blaine Boyer** was not a hit in Memphis, allowing 26 runs in just four starts before being released in August. ⊘ Plucked from the St. Louis system by Washington in the Rule 5 draft, tall right-hander **Brian Broderick** made just 11 relief appearances before the Nationals returned him to the Cardinals. He worked out of the Memphis bullpen before moving back to the starting rotation in June. ⊘ Signed as an undrafted free agent in 2006, **Brandon Dickson** has been the most reliable Memphis starter for the last two seasons. Lacking overwhelming stuff, he succeeds by throwing strikes and inducing ground balls. He's a good bet to start 2012 in the Redbirds rotation again. ⊘ **Ryan Franklin** enjoyed a productive two and a half-year stint as the Cardinals closer, but the run ended unceremoniously in April as he blew four of five save opportunities. Released in late June, he's leaning toward retirement. ⊘ With a slight frame and an electric fastball that reaches the upper 90s, **Joe Kelly** fits the closer profile. But the Cardinals have him starting in the minors to work on his secondary pitches. He still lacks command but showed enough to earn a promotion to Double-A in July. Kelly generates impressive ground-ball rates and could move fast if he can harness his stuff. ⊘ **David Kopp** began the season on the disabled list in Double-A, lost his spot on the 40-man roster in June, then was moved to the bullpen, where he thrived, allowing just five runs in 18 innings. That earned the Clemson product a promotion to Memphis in August and a spot in the Arizona Fall League. ⊘ In need of Triple-A relief help in April, the Cardinals purchased **Victor Marte** from the Royals, who had removed him from their 40-man roster after a disastrous 2010. The change worked wonders as Marte reduced his walks, increased his strikeout rate, and settled in as the Memphis closer, converting 31 of 38 save opportunities. ⊘ **J.C. Romero** has always had trouble throwing strikes but remains tough against lefties, which keeps him in the big leagues. If you're trying to hang onto a career with one skill, that isn't a bad one to have. ⊘ Righty **Trevor Rosenthal**, a 21st-rounder, skipped a level to start the season at Quad Cities, where he struck out 133 in 120 1/3 innings and was selected to the All-Star team. He also made two postseason starts, opening the Midwest League playoffs with a nine-inning shutout before striking out nine in six innings in the clincher. ⊘ Claimed off waivers from the Yankees in May, **Jess Todd** returned to the organization that drafted him in 2007, then shipped him to Cleveland in the 2009 Mark DeRosa trade. The Cardinals dropped him from the 40-man roster in June, and he did little in Memphis to warrant a promotion back to the big leagues.

# MANAGER: MIKE MATHENY

This space was to be a dispassionate, reasoned analysis of Game 5 of the 2011 World Series, a managerial quagmire of such breadth and depth that it might never be fully explained or understood. That plan changed somewhat after the Cardinals rallied to win the final two games of the Series and the championship, La Russa's second title in St. Louis and the third of his career. And that plan changed again, more dramatically, when La Russa announced his retirement the day after the Cardinals celebrated their 11th title with a parade through downtown St. Louis.

La Russa's legacy is unquestioned, starting with his rank of third on the all-time list of managerial victories. Former Cards catcher Mike Matheny, who has never managed at any level, faces a daunting task in living up to his predecessor.

# San Diego Padres

On the heels of a surprising 2010 campaign that saw the Padres eliminated from contention on the season's final day, expectations were higher than perhaps they should have been entering 2011. This was, after all, a team that had lost 99 and 87 games the pre-vious two seasons. San Diego [...]

[...]ing streak at the end of August, fans might not have been as jolted by the 91-loss season that followed.

If it wasn't obvious at the time, it is now: 2010 was a fluke.

Going back further, the Padres have failed to capitalize on the initial surge in popular-ity that coincided with their move to Petco Park in 2004. Part of this is due to the econ-omy, but it's easy to use tough times as an excuse for many things, including the lack of trust in various ownership/management groups that have headed the franchise since its inception in 1969.

Attendance has rebounded somewhat over the past two seasons after plummeting in each of the previous two. Still, the average per game in 2011 was lower after a 90-win sea-son in a beautiful, relatively new baseball-only facility than it had been a decade earlier after a 76-win season in a cavern-ous old football stadium.

Some of this is explained by the fact that the Padres op-erate in a smallish media market. But as teams such as Cleveland and Milwaukee can attest, this doesn't need to be a death sentence. However, it does present certain challenges.

In direct contrast to the even smaller-market Brewers, who parlayed a new ballpark into more ticket sales, the Padres have struggled to gain traction in a city whose denizens aren't engaged with its ballclub. Still, if Milwaukee can make it work, San Diego should be able to do so as well.

If only it were that easy.

As always, many factors are at play. A bad television con-tract that limited viewership to San Diegans who have cable [...]

| | | |
|---|---|---|
| TAv | .241 | 29th |
| TAv-P | .252 | 7th |
| FIP | 3.70 | 7th |
| DER | .717 | 5th |
| DL | 806 | 22nd |
| B-Age | 28.0 | 7th |
| P-Age | 27.8 | 12th |
| Salary | $45.9 | 27th |
| M$/MW | $1.47 | 6th |

**2011:** After shedding costly players, they get promising performances from younger, cheaper hitters

**2012:** Fans are sick of "rebuilding," but this is going to be another year of it

**Action Items:** A slugger to keep them from finishing last in HR again, even in away games

That contract is now, after 15 years, a thing of the past. What takes its place remains to be seen, although it's hard to imagine anything worse than the previous arrangement.

There is also the matter of geography. Locals may tire of hearing about it, but San Diego remains bounded by Los Angeles and its two teams to the north, vast stretches of desert to the east, a country whose economy is in even worse shape than that of the United States not 20 minutes to the south of Petco Park, and the planet's largest body of water to the west. There is zero growth potential.

Add the fact that the Padres play their weeknight home games after most of the country has gone to bed, in a time zone that wields minimal advertising clout (only 15 percent of the U.S. population lives in the Pacific Time Zone) and offers little chance for national exposure even when things are going well, and it becomes clear that the Padres must de-velop and retain fans from within. In a city filled with trans-plants from other parts of the country (due in large part to the city's strong military presence) who retain loyalties to their old teams, this is no easy feat.

Beyond geographical considerations, the constant on-field turnover of players detracts from a sense of identity that fans crave. The Padres are the brand, but customers associate with the brand's people. When a team is unable or unwilling to retain its best and most visible talent, this sends a message to customers who are being asked to pay for a product that they may perceive as being inferior due to such actions.

The concept of rebuilding isn't a bad one. However, when you've been through this exercise before, under various regimes that never finished the job, it becomes tiresome. Folks around town spit the word "prospect" the way John Lydon spat "God Save the Queen" circa 1977. They've come to believe that the Padres have no future.

Whether young talent develops or not, according to the whims of such things, the current organization boasts a stronger farm system now than it has in several years. Trading Adrian Gonzalez helped, although moving him sooner might have netted the Padres more—but then 2010 wouldn't have happened, although in light of the fact that they fell short, this may not have mattered. Trading Mike Adams at the deadline also helped (some may lament that Heath Bell wasn't the one traded, but he wouldn't have fetched anywhere near what Adams did), as did a strong 2011 draft that impressed many observers, and the December trade that sent Mat Latos to Cincinnati for, among others, top prospects Yonder Alonso and Yasmani Grandal.

The Padres, under GM Jed Hoyer, assistant GM Jason McLeod, and scouting director Jaron Madison, had extra picks thanks to the defections of Jon Garland, Yorvit Torrealba, and Kevin Correia (as well as compensation for failure to sign 2010 first-rounder Karsten Whitson). The team used those picks on high-upside players who might not have been targeted under Grady Fuson, who oversaw the draft from 2006 to 2009 and who employed a more risk-averse strategy akin to the approach he'd taken with the A's as chronicled in *Moneyball*.

More importantly, ownership coughed up big money to sign those players, stealing Joe Ross, Michael Kelly, and Austin Hedges away from strong college commitments. For a team that once let expensive high school kids such as Todd Helton and Troy Glaus slip away (not to mention Whitson), this is a novel and welcome twist.

The Padres spent a club-record $11 million, ranking them eighth among teams in money allocated toward signing 2011 draft picks. It is uncertain whether these prospects have a future, but for a fan base that often bemoans the real or imagined cheapness of the folks doling out cash, there can be no questioning the team's intent. The player-development people need to make sure these investments provide significant return, but at least they have been given something to work with for a change.

The downside is that under the new CBA, such extravagant investment in amateur talent may not be possible. Although it is good that the Padres hopped on the spend now, save later train, they may have arrived too late for it to do them as much good as it might have a few years ago. On the bright side, smart people find ways around such obstacles, and the San Diego front office—despite a few notable offseason defections—is populated with smart people.

The most prominent departure was that of Hoyer, who followed former boss Theo Epstein to Chicago's North Side in an attempt to resurrect the Cubs. In a strange dance initiated by Boston's historic collapse at the end of 2011, Epstein moved to the Midwest and put as much of the band back together as possible. He pried Hoyer and McLeod from Padres owner Jeff Moorad, who allowed them to leave due to the presence of Josh Byrnes, Moorad's GM in Arizona.

Epstein reportedly also sought Byrnes, who worked alongside Hoyer under Epstein in Boston, but Moorad wouldn't let him go. Hoyer, for his part, indicated that he wouldn't have left San Diego for anyone other than Epstein. It was a perfect storm that saw the Padres lose two of the current rebuilding project's primary architects before the job had been completed.

Although his reputation might not reflect it, Byrnes did a capable job as GM for the Diamondbacks. Yes, he signed Eric Byrnes (no relation) to a terrible contract extension and gave away Carlos Quentin just before Quentin emerged as a big-league slugger, but he also engineered several trades that helped Arizona in its surprising run of 2011. Much like former Padres staffer Paul DePodesta, who briefly served as GM of the Dodgers, Byrnes is not as well remembered for his efforts as the facts of his tenure merit.

The names may change—along with Hoyer and McLeod, scouting department mainstay Chris Gwynn left to become the Seattle Mariners' director of player development—but the vision remains the same. Byrnes, Madison, A.J. Hinch, and newcomer Chad MacDonald (who comes from the Mets, where he worked alongside DePodesta to oversee amateur scouting and the draft) all face challenges that existed under the previous regime: bring the Padres back to respectability, build from within, make the occasional shrewd trade (e.g., two generic middle relievers for Cameron Maybin or, as in Byrnes' first big splash, one young player who can help now and into the future for several who can do the same), and get the club at least to where it was when Petco Park first opened in 2004.

One other aspect of Hoyer's departure bears mentioning. On the final day of the 2011 season, the Cubs lost to the Padres, giving the two teams identical 71-91 records. Tiebreakers are determined by the previous year's standings, so because the Padres won 90 games in 2010 and the Cubs won only 75, Hoyer's new team picks one slot ahead of his old one throughout the draft. The potential for delivering a few blows to a team that desperately needs to make a killing in the draft is very real.

That notwithstanding, the new regime's task remains the same—and as difficult—as the old regime's: identify, procure, develop, and retain talent. If the Padres build a sustainable model, then maybe they can win games and put fannies in the seats for more than two or three years at a time.

Identifying (Matt Bush), procuring (Whitson), developing (Sean Burroughs), and retaining (Gonzalez) haven't always worked. On the bright side, the club's last few drafts have helped restock a barren shelf, and not just with "safe," low-upside talent.

Most of these kids haven't reached Double-A, but there are some decent prospects—many acquired via trade—at

kets (despite the Padres having been burned twice in the past year by age/identity falsification, someone like Rymer Liriano could be special and make the risk worthwhile), the team must lock up its core players. Stealing Maybin from the Marlins was a good first step; keeping him in San Diego through his prime is next.

Guys like Chase Headley and Nick Hundley (the December acquisition of talented but untested Yasmani Grandal notwithstanding) are also good candidates for long-term deals. Although they lack Maybin's star potential, Headley and Hundley came up through the system and proved that they can thrive at the big-league level. They can provide some sense of continuity for a fan base desperate to see familiar names and faces.

After seeing payroll jump from $38 million in 2010 to $46 million in 2011, the Padres expect another significant increase this year (Byrnes' reacquisition of Quentin, who figures to receive between $6 million and $7 million

after arbitration, will help in that regard). Moorad said in September that payroll would be between $53 and $55 million in 2012, and while more money doesn't always translate into more wins, unless you're Peter Angelos, it seldom hurts.

The payroll should continue to rise in the future, as transfer of ownership from John Moores to Moorad becomes complete (the deadline is March 2014). That and a new television deal won't be a panacea, but they will help. The Padres never will compete with large-market teams in terms of throwing money at players, but in a few years, they should be back where they were in 2005-06.

More importantly, if the front office and development

a positive message to fans that need one. Spending it wisely reinforces that message with something tangible. Of course, if this were as easy as those last two sentences make it sound, everyone would be doing it.

Bottom line: The Padres are poised for a return to respectability. They had it from 2004 to 2007, slipped, caught a glimpse in 2010, and now are looking to make their next move. These next few years are critical for the franchise. Despite San Diego's geographical disadvantages, if the Padres string together some winning seasons (a deep playoff run would help), they could do what the Brewers have done in Milwaukee.

That is a big "if" and it's a long way from here to there, but as the 2010 team demonstrated, anything is possible once you put a bunch of guys on the field. Shoot for .500 in 2012, integrate more young talent into the everyday lineup, and keep your fingers crossed.

# HITTERS

### Yonder Alonso — 1B

Born: 4/8/1987 Age: 25
Bats: L Throws: R Height: 6' 3" Weight: 210
Breakout: 6% Improve: 35% Collapse: 5%
Attrition: 24% MLB: 78%

**Comparables:**
Carmelo Martinez, Fernando Valenzuela Jr., Pete O'Brien

| YEAR | TEAM | LVL | AGE | PA | R | 2B | 3B | HR | RBI | BB | SO | SB | CS | AVG_OBP_SLG | TAv | BABIP | BRR | FRAA | WARP |
|------|------|-----|-----|----|----|----|----|----|----|----|----|----|----|-------------|-----|-------|-----|------|------|
| 2009 | SAR | A+ | 22 | 201 | 21 | 13 | 0 | 7 | 38 | 24 | 30 | 0 | 1 | .303/.387/.497 | .306 | .333 | -0.8 | 0.8 | 1.3 |
| 2009 | CAR | AA | 22 | 121 | 12 | 11 | 0 | 2 | 14 | 14 | 15 | 1 | 0 | .295/.378/.457 | .302 | .330 | 0.8 | 2.2 | 1.0 |
| 2010 | CAR | AA | 23 | 121 | 19 | 5 | 0 | 3 | 13 | 19 | 16 | 4 | 2 | .267/.388/.406 | .271 | .293 | -1 | -0.8 | 0.3 |
| 2010 | LOU | AAA | 23 | 445 | 50 | 31 | 2 | 12 | 56 | 37 | 76 | 9 | 1 | .296/.356/.470 | .279 | .340 | -4.3 | -1.7 | 1.0 |
| 2010 | CIN | MLB | 23 | 29 | 2 | 2 | 0 | 0 | 3 | 0 | 10 | 0 | 0 | .207/.207/.276 | .166 | .316 | -0.3 | 0.7 | -0.1 |
| 2011 | LOU | AAA | 24 | 409 | 46 | 24 | 4 | 12 | 56 | 46 | 60 | 6 | 5 | .296/.374/.486 | .279 | .324 | -2.2 | -6.7 | 0.8 |
| 2011 | CIN | MLB | 24 | 98 | 9 | 4 | 0 | 5 | 15 | 10 | 21 | 0 | 0 | .330/.398/.545 | .308 | .387 | 0.9 | -0.5 | 0.6 |
| 2012 | SDN | MLB | 25 | 250 | 29 | 12 | 1 | 7 | 28 | 23 | 47 | 3 | 1 | .252/.322/.404 | .269 | .289 | -0.2 | 1B -4, LF -7 | 1.3 |

Alonso, selected seventh overall by the Reds in the 2008 draft, is increasingly being stalked by the specter of adequacy as a producer at a key power position. He is headed into his age-25 season with good-not-great numbers at Triple-A and has seen his prospect status slip every year. The Reds gave him some looks in left field in the hope of getting his and Joey Votto's bat into the lineup at the same time, but Alonso's lack of speed and mobility suggests that his future lies at first base. Coming to San Diego as part of the haul for Mat Latos, the University of Miami product now gets to contend with Petco Park, which is not kind to left-handed power hitters. Although his ceiling is lower than it was three years ago, he is closer to contributing at the big-league level than Anthony Rizzo, whose tenure as the Padres first baseman of the future may have ended by the time this book reaches the shelves.

### Jason Bartlett — SS

Born: 10/30/1979 Age: 32
Bats: R Throws: R Height: 6' 1" Weight: 170
Breakout: 1% Improve: 39% Collapse: 5%
Attrition: 16% MLB: 89%

**Comparables:**
Julio Lugo, Edgar Renteria, Marco Scutaro

| YEAR | TEAM | LVL | AGE | PA | R | 2B | 3B | HR | RBI | BB | SO | SB | CS | AVG_OBP_SLG | TAv | BABIP | BRR | FRAA | WARP |
|------|------|-----|-----|----|----|----|----|----|----|----|----|----|----|-------------|-----|-------|-----|------|------|
| 2009 | TBA | MLB | 29 | 567 | 90 | 29 | 7 | 14 | 66 | 54 | 89 | 30 | 7 | .320/.389/.490 | .310 | .364 | 3.5 | -0.6 | 5.4 |
| 2010 | TBA | MLB | 30 | 532 | 71 | 27 | 3 | 4 | 47 | 45 | 83 | 11 | 6 | .254/.324/.350 | .256 | .299 | -1 | 3.4 | 2.5 |
| 2011 | SDN | MLB | 31 | 618 | 61 | 22 | 3 | 2 | 40 | 48 | 98 | 23 | 10 | .245/.308/.307 | .228 | .291 | 3 | 2.4 | 1.3 |
| 2012 | SDN | MLB | 32 | 564 | 59 | 22 | 5 | 4 | 46 | 46 | 93 | 19 | 7 | .249/.318/.335 | .248 | .292 | -0.5 | SS 1 | 1.7 |

Bartlett, originally drafted by the Padres, returned to his first organization and suffered through his worst full big-league season. That he led the team in games played and hits says more about the Padres than about Bartlett. He hit .224/.292/.281 at Petco Park and accumulated 90 percent of his plate appearances in the two hole, where he did a devastating Juan Bonilla impersonation. The Padres signed Bartlett to an extension through 2012 with a club option for 2013, so he and his outs will call San Diego home a little longer.

### Vincent Belnome — 3B

Born: 3/11/1988 Age: 24
Bats: R Throws: L Height: 6' 0" Weight: 205
Breakout: 1% Improve: 12% Collapse: 4%
Attrition: 63% MLB: 82%

**Comparables:**
Sean Rodriguez, Reese Havens, Felipe Crespo

| YEAR | TEAM | LVL | AGE | PA | R | 2B | 3B | HR | RBI | BB | SO | SB | CS | AVG_OBP_SLG | TAv | BABIP | BRR | FRAA | WARP |
|------|------|-----|-----|----|----|----|----|----|----|----|----|----|----|-------------|-----|-------|-----|------|------|
| 2009 | EUG | A- | 21 | 295 | 53 | 16 | 1 | 10 | 44 | 52 | 55 | 0 | 0 | .297/.433/.500 | .346 | .351 | 0.7 | -2.7 | 2.9 |
| 2010 | LEL | A+ | 22 | 606 | 81 | 31 | 1 | 16 | 84 | 102 | 136 | 4 | 1 | .273/.398/.436 | .311 | .346 | -6.2 | -0.8 | 4.9 |
| 2011 | SAN | AA | 23 | 318 | 56 | 19 | 1 | 17 | 62 | 47 | 59 | 0 | 5 | .333/.432/.603 | .347 | .373 | -3.8 | 4 | 4.4 |
| 2012 | SDN | MLB | 24 | 250 | 28 | 10 | 1 | 6 | 22 | 34 | 63 | 0 | 0 | .224/.330/.355 | .260 | .285 | -0.1 | 3B 1, 2B 1 | 1.6 |

Belnome went from error-prone third baseman with on-base skills in a hitter-friendly High-A league to sure-handed second baseman with across-the-board offensive skills in a challenging environment at Double-A. San Antonio's Wolff Stadium proved no match for Belnome, whose OPS approached 1000 at home. The only thing that could stop him was an abdominal strain, which forced him to miss most of July and August. As a former 28th-round pick, Belnome will need to prove himself every step of the way. If he stays healthy and shows that last season's gains are real, the Padres could have themselves a Tony Phillips-type super utility infielder. Who doesn't want one of those?

### Kyle Blanks — LF

Born: 9/11/1986 Age: 25
Bats: R Throws: R Height: 6' 7" Weight: 285
Breakout: 1% Improve: 26% Collapse: 5%
Attrition: 24% MLB: 78%

**Comparables:**
Mark Teixeira, Chris Shelton, Eric Wedge

| YEAR | TEAM | LVL | AGE | PA | R | 2B | 3B | HR | RBI | BB | SO | SB | CS | AVG_OBP_SLG | TAv | BABIP | BRR | FRAA | WARP |
|------|------|-----|-----|----|----|----|----|----|----|----|----|----|----|-------------|-----|-------|-----|------|------|
| 2009 | POR | AAA | 22 | 280 | 35 | 9 | 1 | 12 | 38 | 39 | 63 | 0 | 0 | .283/.397/.485 | .336 | .342 | -1.5 | 3.4 | 2.8 |
| 2009 | SDN | MLB | 22 | 172 | 24 | 9 | 0 | 10 | 22 | 18 | 55 | 1 | 1 | .250/.355/.514 | .296 | .325 | -0.4 | -2 | 0.6 |
| 2010 | SDN | MLB | 23 | 120 | 14 | 6 | 1 | 3 | 15 | 15 | 46 | 1 | 0 | .157/.283/.324 | .238 | .245 | 1.7 | -0.7 | -0.1 |
| 2011 | SAN | AA | 24 | 201 | 33 | 16 | 3 | 4 | 27 | 17 | 41 | 3 | 0 | .282/.353/.475 | .308 | .341 | 1.2 | 1.6 | 1.4 |
| 2011 | SDN | MLB | 24 | 190 | 21 | 7 | 1 | 7 | 26 | 16 | 51 | 2 | 0 | .229/.300/.406 | .271 | .281 | 0.5 | -0.3 | 0.8 |
| 2012 | SDN | MLB | 25 | 250 | 29 | 10 | 1 | 9 | 28 | 26 | 73 | 2 | 0 | .226/.317/.408 | .270 | .291 | 0 | LF -2, 1B -3 | 1.3 |

The mountain-sized Blanks has trouble staying healthy and making consistent contact, but his power will play anywhere (his career numbers are slightly better at Petco Park than away from it). He is a gifted athlete who runs better than you might imagine from someone with his build, and who plays a capable left field, although concerns about the physical pounding his body takes out there persist. He battled foot problems toward the end of 2009 and began last season on the disabled list while recovering from August 2010 Tommy John surgery. Blanks's main goal now is to remain healthy so that he can get enough reps against big-league pitching to plug those holes in his swing.

**James Darnell**    3B
Born: 1/19/1987 Age: 25
Bats: R Throws: R Height: 6' 3" Weight: 195
Breakout: 2% Improve: 44% Collapse: 12%
Attrition: 32% MLB: 89%
Comparables:

| YEAR | TEAM | LVL | AGE | PA | R | 2B | 3B | HR | RBI | BB | SO | SB | CS | AVG_OBP_SLG | TAv | BABIP | BRR | FRAA | WARP |
|------|------|-----|-----|-----|----|----|----|----|-----|----|----|----|----|----------------|------|-------|------|-------|------|
| 2009 | FTW | A | 22 | 283 | 40 | 17 | 2 | 7 | 38 | 57 | 51 | 5 | 5 | .329/.468/.518 | .351 | .400 | -3 | -6.5 | 2.7 |
| 2009 | LEL | A+ | 22 | 269 | 40 | 18 | 2 | 13 | 43 | 30 | 38 | 3 | 1 | .294/.377/.553 | .342 | .303 | -0.9 | 0 | 3.0 |
| 2010 | SAN | AA | 23 | 426 | 46 | 21 | 1 | 10 | 50 | 44 | 64 | 2 | 0 | .265/.350/.408 | .289 | .297 | -3.1 | -7.2 | 1.5 |
| 2011 | SAN | AA | 24 | 346 | 62 | 25 | 1 | 17 | 62 | 52 | 48 | 2 | 1 | .333/.434/.604 | .372 | .348 | -2.3 | -11.4 | 4.0 |

pected to be ready for spring training, although the position and level at which he will play remain unclear. If healthy, Darnell could hit 20-25 homers over a full season, even with half his games at Petco Park.

**Jaff Decker**    LF
Born: 2/23/1990 Age: 22
Bats: L Throws: L Height: 5' 11" Weight: 190
Breakout: 3% Improve: 24% Collapse: 0%
Attrition: 17% MLB: 54%
Comparables:
Reid Fronk, Billy Jo Robidoux, Nick Weglarz

| YEAR | TEAM | LVL | AGE | PA | R | 2B | 3B | HR | RBI | BB | SO | SB | CS | AVG_OBP_SLG | TAv | BABIP | BRR | FRAA | WARP |
|------|------|-----|-----|-----|----|----|----|----|-----|-----|-----|----|----|----------------|------|-------|------|-----------|------|
| 2009 | FTW | A | 19 | 455 | 78 | 25 | 2 | 16 | 64 | 85 | 92 | 10 | 6 | .299/.445/.514 | .340 | .364 | -0.9 | -2.9 | 4.5 |
| 2010 | LEL | A+ | 20 | 348 | 53 | 14 | 2 | 17 | 58 | 47 | 80 | 5 | 4 | .262/.378/.500 | .320 | .306 | -0.4 | 4.9 | 3.3 |
| 2011 | SAN | AA | 21 | 613 | 90 | 29 | 2 | 19 | 92 | 103 | 145 | 15 | 5 | .236/.373/.417 | .297 | .291 | -1.4 | -0.6 | 3.9 |
| 2012 | SDN | MLB | 22 | 250 | 27 | 9 | 1 | 7 | 23 | 35 | 67 | 3 | 1 | .205/.325/.358 | .257 | .258 | -0.1 | LF -7, RF -0 | 0.9 |

There have been concerns about Decker's physique and conditioning since the Padres drafted him in 2008. Those concerns were validated in 2010 when injuries limited him to 79 games at Lake Elsinore. Decker came to camp last year looking trimmer and sleeker, and he started strong at San Antonio, posting an OPS north of 1200 in April. He knocked eight of his 19 home runs that month but faded before righting himself somewhat in August and September. Decker has legitimate power and a terrific batting eye, although some wonder if he might be *too* patient. He is a better athlete than he gets credit for and plays a respectable left field (even making a few starts in center in 2011). Decker will begin the season at Triple-A Tucson, where he could put up silly numbers and force a promotion after the All-Star break.

**Chris Denorfia**    RF
Born: 7/15/1980 Age: 31
Bats: R Throws: R Height: 6' 1" Weight: 195
Breakout: 1% Improve: 38% Collapse: 8%
Attrition: 38% MLB: 80%
Comparables:
Tito Francona, Carl Furillo, Alex Ochoa

| YEAR | TEAM | LVL | AGE | PA | R | 2B | 3B | HR | RBI | BB | SO | SB | CS | AVG_OBP_SLG | TAv | BABIP | BRR | FRAA | WARP |
|------|------|-----|-----|-----|----|----|----|----|-----|----|----|----|----|----------------|------|-------|------|----------|------|
| 2009 | SAC | AAA | 28 | 474 | 62 | 18 | 5 | 9 | 49 | 31 | 52 | 15 | 6 | .271/.318/.398 | .263 | .288 | 0.8 | 4.6 | 1.5 |
| 2010 | POR | AAA | 29 | 134 | 17 | 10 | 4 | 2 | 12 | 12 | 18 | 7 | 1 | .306/.366/.504 | .322 | .343 | 0.4 | 0.6 | 1.5 |
| 2010 | SDN | MLB | 29 | 317 | 41 | 15 | 2 | 9 | 36 | 27 | 51 | 8 | 4 | .271/.335/.433 | .287 | .300 | 1.9 | 2.1 | 2.3 |
| 2011 | SDN | MLB | 30 | 340 | 38 | 13 | 2 | 5 | 19 | 28 | 49 | 11 | 6 | .277/.337/.381 | .260 | .314 | 0.7 | 2.5 | 0.8 |
| 2012 | SDN | MLB | 31 | 335 | 35 | 12 | 2 | 5 | 30 | 27 | 57 | 9 | 4 | .244/.306/.348 | .248 | .281 | -0.5 | RF 3, CF 1 | 0.5 |

At the turn of the millennium, the Padres had an outfielder named Eric Owens. He lacked overwhelming tools but played all out, all the time, which made him a fan favorite in San Diego. Denorfia is like that. He makes solid contact and occasionally knocks one out of the park despite his severe ground-ball tendencies. He is a good defender in either corner outfield spot and can play center in a pinch, although his limitations are exposed if he is left out there too long. Denorfia killed lefties in 2011 (.328/.391/.496), a tendency he hadn't displayed in previous years. Stretched as an everyday player, Denorfia has a good enough tool set to succeed as part of the supporting cast. For someone whose career was in serious jeopardy a few years ago due to injuries, that ain't bad.

**Logan Forsythe**  2B

Born: 1/14/1987 Age: 25
Bats: R Throws: R Height: 6' 2" Weight: 205
Breakout: 0% Improve: 22% Collapse: 10%
Attrition: 28% MLB: 65%

Comparables:
Gary Kolb, Delino DeShields, Danny Garcia

| YEAR | TEAM | LVL | AGE | PA | R | 2B | 3B | HR | RBI | BB | SO | SB | CS | AVG_OBP_SLG | TAv | BABIP | BRR | FRAA | WARP |
|------|------|-----|-----|-----|----|----|----|----|-----|----|----|----|----|-------------|-----|-------|-----|------|------|
| 2009 | LEL | A+ | 22 | 305 | 46 | 13 | 3 | 8 | 30 | 61 | 48 | 6 | 2 | .322/.474/.504 | .370 | .378 | -1 | 0 | 4.2 |
| 2009 | SAN | AA | 22 | 290 | 37 | 9 | 3 | 3 | 31 | 41 | 63 | 5 | 0 | .279/.385/.377 | .287 | .363 | 0.8 | -1.7 | 1.8 |
| 2010 | SAN | AA | 23 | 472 | 66 | 22 | 1 | 3 | 38 | 75 | 95 | 17 | 5 | .253/.378/.337 | .282 | .327 | 1.3 | -2.3 | 2.3 |
| 2011 | SDN | MLB | 24 | 169 | 12 | 9 | 1 | 0 | 12 | 12 | 33 | 3 | 1 | .213/.281/.287 | .219 | .269 | 0.7 | -0.8 | -0.3 |
| 2012 | SDN | MLB | 25 | 250 | 26 | 9 | 1 | 2 | 17 | 31 | 58 | 4 | 1 | .224/.329/.312 | .250 | .292 | 0 | 2B -4, 3B 0 | 1.1 |

In an organization deep with third basemen, Forsythe shifted to second base in 2010 to expedite his path to the big leagues and help the Padres where they need it most. Although he won't be mistaken for Bill Mazeroski, Forsythe isn't a complete zero with the glove. The key to his success will be defensive utility and on-base skills (non-existent in his first big-league exposure, but he owns a career .414 OBP in the minors). Before he resumes his quest to become a big-league utility player, Forsythe must recover from September 2010 surgery to repair a torn meniscus in his left knee.

**Reymond Fuentes**  CF

Born: 2/12/1991 Age: 21
Bats: L Throws: L Height: 6' 1" Weight: 160
Breakout: 0% Improve: 7% Collapse: 0%
Attrition: 6% MLB: 10%

Comparables:
Derrick Robinson, Peter Bourjos, Eury Perez

| YEAR | TEAM | LVL | AGE | PA | R | 2B | 3B | HR | RBI | BB | SO | SB | CS | AVG_OBP_SLG | TAv | BABIP | BRR | FRAA | WARP |
|------|------|-----|-----|-----|----|----|----|----|-----|----|-----|----|----|-------------|-----|-------|-----|------|------|
| 2009 | RSX | RK | 18 | 159 | 16 | 6 | 2 | 1 | 14 | 7 | 24 | 9 | 5 | .290/.331/.379 | .265 | .336 | -1 | -0.5 | 0.1 |
| 2010 | GRN | A | 19 | 414 | 59 | 15 | 5 | 5 | 41 | 25 | 87 | 42 | 5 | .270/.325/.377 | .247 | .334 | 1.3 | 1.1 | 0.6 |
| 2011 | LEL | A+ | 20 | 573 | 84 | 15 | 9 | 5 | 45 | 44 | 117 | 41 | 14 | .275/.342/.369 | .266 | .347 | 2.1 | -8 | 1.5 |
| 2012 | SDN | MLB | 21 | 250 | 20 | 7 | 2 | 1 | 17 | 11 | 64 | 13 | 4 | .206/.247/.265 | .194 | .272 | 0.1 | CF -12, LF -0 | -1.7 |

Fuentes, Boston's 2009 first-round pick, came to the Padres in the Adrian Gonzalez deal. An athletic center fielder whose primary selling points as a prospect are speed and the fact that he is Carlos Beltran's cousin, Fuentes hasn't produced at any level. He did raise his walk rate to a still-paltry 7.7 in 2011, but with no appreciable power, this is the Tom Goodwin skill set. Unless he improves in other areas, Fuentes must hit .300 to have value.

**Yasmani Grandal**  C

Born: 11/8/1988 Age: 23
Bats: B Throws: R Height: 6' 3" Weight: 205
Breakout: 5% Improve: 24% Collapse: 4%
Attrition: 28% MLB: 60%

Comparables:
Koby Clemens, Ben Petrick, Alex Avila

| YEAR | TEAM | LVL | AGE | PA | R | 2B | 3B | HR | RBI | BB | SO | SB | CS | AVG_OBP_SLG | TAv | BABIP | BRR | FRAA | WARP |
|------|------|-----|-----|-----|----|----|----|----|-----|----|----|----|----|-------------|-----|-------|-----|------|------|
| 2011 | BAK | A+ | 22 | 251 | 47 | 14 | 0 | 10 | 40 | 41 | 57 | 0 | 0 | .296/.410/.510 | .323 | .359 | 0 | -0.4 | 3.0 |
| 2011 | CAR | AA | 22 | 172 | 20 | 15 | 0 | 4 | 26 | 13 | 39 | 0 | 1 | .301/.360/.474 | .280 | .377 | -2.3 | -0.8 | 1.2 |
| 2012 | SDN | MLB | 23 | 250 | 26 | 10 | 1 | 6 | 23 | 24 | 63 | 0 | 0 | .222/.301/.352 | .246 | .280 | 0 | C -2 | 1.2 |

The Reds took Grandal with the 12th overall pick in 2010, and the switch-hitting catcher out of the University of Miami ended his first full season in Triple-A. Such rapid advancement placed him at number 30 on Kevin Goldstein's midseason Top 50 prospects list. Stuck behind Devin Mesoraco in Cincinnati, Grandal was the key piece in the Latos trade. He gives the Padres options in case Nick Hundley's 2011 turns out to have been a fluke or Austin Hedges doesn't develop as anticipated. Grandal ranked among organizational leaders in doubles in 2011, and the hope is that some of those will translate into homers as he matures. He also exhibited strong plate discipline in the California League, although that slipped considerably on promotion to Double-A, which is likely where he will spend most of his first season with the Padres tightening up an already promising defensive game.

**Jesus Guzman**  1B

Born: 6/14/1984 Age: 28
Bats: R Throws: R Height: 6' 2" Weight: 215
Breakout: 2% Improve: 29% Collapse: 5%
Attrition: 23% MLB: 81%

Comparables:
Tim Talton, Jorge Cantu, Hal Morris

| YEAR | TEAM | LVL | AGE | PA | R | 2B | 3B | HR | RBI | BB | SO | SB | CS | AVG_OBP_SLG | TAv | BABIP | BRR | FRAA | WARP |
|------|------|-----|-----|-----|----|----|----|----|-----|----|----|----|----|-------------|-----|-------|-----|------|------|
| 2009 | FRE | AAA | 25 | 500 | 75 | 26 | 5 | 16 | 71 | 37 | 82 | 0 | 2 | .321/.380/.507 | .302 | .363 | -0.9 | 2.3 | 2.5 |
| 2009 | SFN | MLB | 25 | 20 | 0 | 0 | 0 | 0 | 0 | 0 | 3 | 0 | 0 | .250/.250/.250 | .146 | .294 | -0.5 | 0.1 | -0.3 |
| 2010 | FRE | AAA | 26 | 492 | 66 | 28 | 1 | 18 | 72 | 38 | 68 | 6 | 4 | .321/.376/.510 | .298 | .345 | -0.8 | -6.5 | 2.3 |
| 2011 | SDN | MLB | 27 | 271 | 33 | 22 | 2 | 5 | 44 | 22 | 43 | 9 | 2 | .312/.369/.478 | .316 | .360 | 2.2 | 1.7 | 2.2 |
| 2012 | SDN | MLB | 28 | 300 | 36 | 15 | 2 | 7 | 34 | 23 | 55 | 3 | 1 | .265/.326/.414 | .274 | .305 | -0.2 | 1B -3, 3B -2 | 1.6 |

The Padres inked Guzman, who had been in the Giants system, to a minor-league deal in November 2010. He proceeded to destroy the PCL for 2 1/2 months before being recalled to a Padres team in desperate need of offense. Guzman's success, which depends more on his ability to hit line drives than on lofting the ball into trade winds that don't exist in San Diego, continued in the big leagues and he ended up being the club's most productive hitter. He even hit .346/.412/.551 at Petco Park. Guzman's FRAA suggests that he plays acceptable defense. Of course, FRAA doesn't have to watch him field a position; he is a liability anywhere.

**Jedd Gyorko**    **3B**

Born: 9/23/1988 Age: 23
Bats: R Throws: R Height: 5' 11" Weight: 195
Breakout: 2% Improve: 29% Collapse: 3%
Attrition: 22% MLB: 65%

**Comparables:**
Eric Campbell, Andy Marte, Andy Carey

| YEAR | TEAM | LVL | AGE | PA | R | 2B | 3B | HR | RBI | BB | SO | SB | CS | AVG_OBP_SLG | TAv | BABIP | BRR | FRAA | WARP |
|------|------|-----|-----|----|----|----|----|----|-----|----|----|----|----|-------------|-----|-------|-----|------|------|
| 2010 | FTW | A | 21 | 183 | 19 | 11 | 0 | 2 | 23 | 19 | 31 | 1 | 0 | .284/.366/.389 | .273 | .341 | -1.1 | 1 | 0.5 |
| 2010 | EUG | A- | 21 | 115 | 16 | 6 | 0 | 5 | 18 | 9 | 26 | 1 | 1 | .330/.383/.528 | .355 | .400 | -0.8 | -1.2 | 1.4 |
| 2011 | LEL | A+ | 22 | 382 | 78 | 35 | 2 | 18 | 74 | 38 | 64 | 11 | 3 | .365/.429/.638 | .362 | .408 | -0.3 | 2.3 | 5.7 |
| 2011 | SAN | AA | 22 | 265 | 41 | 12 | 0 | 7 | 40 | 26 | 50 | 1 | 0 | .288/.358/.428 | .267 | .337 | 1.8 | 4.9 | 2.1 |
| 2012 | SDN | MLB | 23 | 250 | 26 | 11 | 1 | 6 | 25 | 18 | 55 | 2 | 1 | .234/.292/.366 | .245 | .282 | 0 | 3B 6, 2B -0 | 0.9 |

Selected in the second round of the 2010 draft, Gyorko has done nothing but hit as a professional. He posted ridiculous numbers at Lake Elsinore (California League, but his OPS topped 1000 at home, which is a neutral park), where he split time between third base and designated hitter not because of any defensive deficiencies but to accommodate fellow prospect Edinson Rincon. Gyorko's performance at San Antonio was more subdued but still impressive. He is a strong kid with thick legs and a quick bat that generates line drives from the right side a la Jeff Cirillo. Gyorko added power to his game in 2011, although 25 homers might be pushing the limits of his ability. The Padres have a logjam at the hot corner

Signed to stand near first base and buy time for Anthony Rizzo, Hawpe showed no bat speed during spring training. When the season started, he had trouble even fouling off good fastballs and began his Padres career in a 5-for-51 funk, striking out in 40 percent of his plate appearances. Hawpe's bat eventually woke up a bit, and he hit .278/.354/.424 in his next 44 games before blowing out his elbow and undergoing season-ending Tommy John surgery. Hawpe's walk rate reached an all-time low, while his strikeout rate reached an all-time high. He never looked comfortable at first base, a position he hadn't played regularly since 2002 in the Carolina League. PECOTA likes his chances to rebound, but it won't happen in San Diego.

**Chase Headley**    **3B**

Born: 5/9/1984 Age: 28
Bats: B Throws: R Height: 6' 3" Weight: 195
Breakout: 1% Improve: 39% Collapse: 3%
Attrition: 17% MLB: 78%

**Comparables:**
Jack Lohrke, Adam Heether, Bob Bailey

| YEAR | TEAM | LVL | AGE | PA | R | 2B | 3B | HR | RBI | BB | SO | SB | CS | AVG_OBP_SLG | TAv | BABIP | BRR | FRAA | WARP |
|------|------|-----|-----|----|----|----|----|----|-----|----|----|----|----|-------------|-----|-------|-----|------|------|
| 2009 | SDN | MLB | 25 | 612 | 62 | 31 | 2 | 12 | 64 | 62 | 133 | 10 | 2 | .262/.342/.392 | .263 | .325 | -0.2 | -8.2 | 0.2 |
| 2010 | SDN | MLB | 26 | 674 | 77 | 29 | 3 | 11 | 58 | 56 | 139 | 17 | 5 | .264/.327/.375 | .265 | .323 | 3.5 | -0.1 | 3.1 |
| 2011 | SDN | MLB | 27 | 439 | 43 | 28 | 1 | 4 | 44 | 52 | 92 | 13 | 2 | .289/.374/.399 | .290 | .368 | 0.3 | -9.4 | 1.8 |
| 2012 | SDN | MLB | 28 | 459 | 51 | 20 | 2 | 8 | 42 | 48 | 109 | 8 | 2 | .242/.327/.364 | .261 | .309 | 0.2 | 3B -4, LF -1 | 1.9 |

After years of struggling to produce at Petco Park, Headley stopped trying to hit home runs and focused instead on reaching base. The change didn't improve his results at home, but he hit .330/.399/.465 on the road, making his overall numbers resemble those of vintage Bill Mueller, a classic number two hitter. The switch-hitting Headley, who bats lower in the Padres' offensively challenged order, finally solved lefties, raising his OPS against them by 300 points from 2010 to 2011. He missed much of the final two months due to a broken left pinky and was ineffective when he returned in late September. Headley plays capable defense at third base, runs well, and is a smart player. As long as he calls San Diego home (career .229/.319/.336 there versus .303/.364/.441 on the road), the best he can hope for is to duplicate 2011's success. PECOTA doesn't like his chances to do that, but if Headley sticks with last year's approach, he should beat the projection.

**Jeremy Hermida** RF
Born: 1/30/1984 Age: 28
Bats: L Throws: R Height: 6' 5" Weight: 200
Breakout: 2% Improve: 58% Collapse: 5%
Attrition: 18% MLB: 88%
Comparables:
Ken Harrelson, Gary Matthews, Richard Hidalgo

| YEAR | TEAM | LVL | AGE | PA | R | 2B | 3B | HR | RBI | BB | SO | SB | CS | AVG_OBP_SLG | TAv | BABIP | BRR | FRAA | WARP |
|---|---|---|---|---|---|---|---|---|---|---|---|---|---|---|---|---|---|---|---|
| 2009 | FLO | MLB | 25 | 491 | 48 | 14 | 2 | 13 | 47 | 56 | 101 | 5 | 2 | .259/.348/.392 | .261 | .309 | 1.5 | -1.5 | 0.9 |
| 2010 | PAW | AAA | 26 | 73 | 7 | 1 | 0 | 2 | 12 | 4 | 16 | 0 | 0 | .288/.338/.394 | .249 | .354 | -0.3 | 0.7 | 0.0 |
| 2010 | BOS | MLB | 26 | 171 | 14 | 8 | 0 | 5 | 27 | 12 | 45 | 1 | 0 | .203/.257/.348 | .227 | .248 | -0.5 | 2.2 | -0.1 |
| 2010 | OAK | MLB | 26 | 68 | 5 | 4 | 0 | 1 | 2 | 4 | 13 | 0 | 0 | .250/.294/.359 | .220 | .300 | -0.4 | -0.9 | -0.3 |
| 2011 | LOU | AAA | 27 | 450 | 67 | 28 | 1 | 17 | 55 | 46 | 97 | 3 | 0 | .319/.400/.524 | .311 | .387 | -3.3 | 4 | 3.4 |
| 2011 | CIN | MLB | 27 | 18 | 2 | 0 | 0 | 1 | 3 | 0 | 7 | 0 | 0 | .111/.111/.278 | .140 | .100 | 0 | 0 | -0.2 |
| 2011 | SDN | MLB | 27 | 48 | 3 | 2 | 1 | 1 | 6 | 7 | 19 | 0 | 0 | .225/.354/.400 | .285 | .400 | 0.2 | 0.6 | 0.4 |
| 2012 | SDN | MLB | 28 | 250 | 29 | 10 | 1 | 7 | 27 | 24 | 60 | 1 | 0 | .245/.324/.397 | .269 | .302 | 0 | RF 1, LF -1 | 1.3 |

Hermida now has about the same number of plate appearances in the big leagues as in the minors, and although the power portion of his game has translated well enough, the on-base skills that ignited dreams of Erubiel Durazo or Hee Seop Choi have fizzled. Hermida's walk rate in the minors was 13.9 percent but is 9.5 in the big leagues, which is the difference between Willie McCovey and Willie Tasby. Who is Tasby? Exactly. Hermida showed signs of life in September with the Padres, who took a flier on him because teams with nothing left to lose will do that sort of thing. Maybe this is the beginning of Hermida 2.0. Or maybe he is just one of those guys that peaks at age 23.

**Orlando Hudson** 2B
Born: 12/12/1977 Age: 34
Bats: B Throws: R Height: 6' 1" Weight: 175
Breakout: 1% Improve: 34% Collapse: 9%
Attrition: 20% MLB: 84%
Comparables:
Lou Whitaker, Mark Ellis, Ray Durham

| YEAR | TEAM | LVL | AGE | PA | R | 2B | 3B | HR | RBI | BB | SO | SB | CS | AVG_OBP_SLG | TAv | BABIP | BRR | FRAA | WARP |
|---|---|---|---|---|---|---|---|---|---|---|---|---|---|---|---|---|---|---|---|
| 2009 | LAN | MLB | 31 | 631 | 74 | 35 | 6 | 9 | 62 | 62 | 99 | 8 | 1 | .283/.357/.417 | .269 | .328 | 0.2 | 5.6 | 2.7 |
| 2010 | MIN | MLB | 32 | 559 | 80 | 24 | 5 | 6 | 37 | 50 | 87 | 10 | 3 | .268/.338/.372 | .254 | .312 | 2.4 | 6.6 | 1.6 |
| 2011 | SDN | MLB | 33 | 454 | 54 | 15 | 3 | 7 | 43 | 49 | 84 | 19 | 3 | .246/.329/.352 | .257 | .293 | 2.7 | 1.1 | 1.2 |
| 2012 | SDN | MLB | 34 | 450 | 50 | 18 | 4 | 5 | 39 | 45 | 76 | 10 | 2 | .251/.329/.355 | .258 | .295 | 0.3 | 2B 1 | 1.4 |

Signed as a free agent to replace David Eckstein and provide veteran leadership on a young team, Hudson disappointed on many levels. His mental gaffes in the field and public comments didn't endear him to anyone. Only a torrid August, during which he hit .292/.349/.500, kept Hudson's overall performance from looking as bad as it was (he hit .232/.323/.305 the rest of the year). Hudson did set a career high in stolen bases. In a damning indictment of San Diego's offense, Hudson batted fifth 42 times in 2011 despite having started in that slot just once over his first nine seasons.

**Nick Hundley** C
Born: 9/8/1983 Age: 28
Bats: R Throws: R Height: 6' 2" Weight: 210
Breakout: 8% Improve: 28% Collapse: 16%
Attrition: 40% MLB: 78%
Comparables:
Charlie O'Brien, John Sullivan, Creighton Gubanich

| YEAR | TEAM | LVL | AGE | PA | R | 2B | 3B | HR | RBI | BB | SO | SB | CS | AVG_OBP_SLG | TAv | BABIP | BRR | FRAA | WARP |
|---|---|---|---|---|---|---|---|---|---|---|---|---|---|---|---|---|---|---|---|
| 2009 | SDN | MLB | 25 | 289 | 23 | 15 | 2 | 8 | 30 | 28 | 76 | 5 | 1 | .238/.312/.406 | .256 | .303 | -1.4 | 0.9 | 0.7 |
| 2010 | SDN | MLB | 26 | 307 | 33 | 18 | 2 | 8 | 43 | 25 | 66 | 0 | 5 | .249/.308/.418 | .273 | .293 | -5.6 | -1.1 | 1.1 |
| 2011 | SDN | MLB | 27 | 308 | 34 | 16 | 5 | 9 | 29 | 22 | 74 | 1 | 1 | .288/.347/.477 | .307 | .362 | -0.1 | -0.1 | 3.2 |
| 2012 | SDN | MLB | 28 | 295 | 31 | 12 | 2 | 8 | 30 | 25 | 72 | 2 | 1 | .225/.295/.371 | .249 | .277 | -0.3 | C -1 | 1.5 |

Hundley quietly enjoyed a breakout season. He carried a strong Cactus League showing into April, then got hurt (oblique) and came back too soon. After hitting just .159/.247/.147 from May through July, Hundley finally returned to the lineup healthy and abused pitchers at a .367/.404/.656 clip over the season's final two months. On defense, he improved his footwork and throwing, nailing a career high 36 percent of would-be basestealers. Hundley isn't intimidated by Petco Park, hitting .271/.340/.478 at home for his career, with 21 of his 30 home runs coming there. If he stays healthy, he could enjoy a nice run in the big leagues, even if 2011 was over his head.

**Mark Kotsay** 1B
Born: 12/2/1975 Age: 36
Bats: L Throws: L Height: 6' 1" Weight: 180
Breakout: 0% Improve: 20% Collapse: 10%
Attrition: 34% MLB: 66%
Comparables:
Al Spangler, Timo Perez, Tommy Holmes

| YEAR | TEAM | LVL | AGE | PA | R | 2B | 3B | HR | RBI | BB | SO | SB | CS | AVG_OBP_SLG | TAv | BABIP | BRR | FRAA | WARP |
|---|---|---|---|---|---|---|---|---|---|---|---|---|---|---|---|---|---|---|---|
| 2009 | BOS | MLB | 33 | 79 | 4 | 2 | 0 | 1 | 5 | 4 | 12 | 2 | 1 | .257/.291/.324 | .225 | .290 | -0.5 | 0 | -0.2 |
| 2009 | CHA | MLB | 33 | 127 | 12 | 7 | 0 | 3 | 18 | 11 | 9 | 1 | 1 | .292/.349/.434 | .281 | .291 | 0.8 | -1 | 0.4 |
| 2010 | CHA | MLB | 34 | 359 | 30 | 17 | 2 | 8 | 31 | 32 | 36 | 1 | 3 | .239/.306/.376 | .238 | .247 | -4.1 | -1.6 | -1.0 |
| 2011 | MIL | MLB | 35 | 255 | 18 | 13 | 1 | 3 | 31 | 21 | 27 | 3 | 0 | .270/.329/.373 | .258 | .294 | -0.8 | -3.5 | 0.0 |
| 2012 | SDN | MLB | 36 | 260 | 26 | 11 | 1 | 3 | 22 | 21 | 31 | 2 | 2 | .236/.298/.332 | .242 | .258 | -0.3 | 1B -1, RF -2 | 0.0 |

Many moons ago, when the Padres still called Qualcomm Stadium home, Kotsay was a valuable player. In his twenties, he was a better version of Randy Winn—some power, some speed, good glove in center field. In his thirties, Kotsay has become Geoff Blum with less pop and less defensive utility. As veteran "clubhouse presence" signings go, a team could do worse than spend $1.25 million for a guy who presumably is being counted on to show the kids how to conduct themselves. Kotsay once employed Jeff Moorad as his agent and was a fan favorite during his first stint with the Padres from 2001 to 2003. This isn't much of an endorsement but it beats: "Not young, not good."

**Rymer Liriano** RF
Born: 6/20/1991 Age: 21
Bats: R Throws: R Height: 6' 1" Weight: 211
Breakout: 0% Improve: 13% Collapse: 1%
Attrition: 7% MLB: 31%

Comparables:
Reid Fronk, Luis Sumoza, Lloyd Moseby

| YEAR | TEAM | LVL | AGE | PA | R | 2B | 3B | HR | RBI | BB | SO | SB | CS | AVG/OBP/SLG | TAv | BABIP | BRR | FRAA | WARP |
|------|------|-----|-----|----|---|----|----|----|-----|----|----|----|----|-------------|-----|-------|-----|------|------|
| 2009 | PDR | RK | 18 | 216 | 44 | 8 | 1 | 8 | 44 | 15 | 52 | 14 | 5 | .350/.402/.523 | .328 | .445 | 0.6 | 0.3 | 1.8 |
| 2010 | FTW | A | 19 | 201 | 21 | 11 | 1 | 2 | 20 | 10 | 54 | 11 | 6 | .191/.236/.293 | .201 | .258 | 0.2 | 1 | -0.5 |
| 2010 | EUG | A- | 19 | 225 | 35 | 13 | 6 | 0 | 12 | 17 | 53 | 17 | 7 | .271/.335/.394 | .280 | .364 | 0.6 | 0.7 | 1.4 |
| 2010 | LEL | A+ | 19 | 55 | 3 | 2 | 0 | 1 | 6 | 5 | 12 | 3 | 0 | .220/.291/.320 | .255 | .270 | 0.1 | -0.2 | 0.0 |
| 2011 | FTW | A | 20 | 519 | 81 | 30 | 8 | 12 | 62 | 47 | 95 | 65 | 20 | .319/.383/.499 | .316 | .373 | 0 | -6.7 | 3.5 |
| 2011 | LEL | A+ | 20 | 61 | 8 | 1 | 1 | 0 | 6 | 6 | 13 | 1 | 1 | .127/.213/.182 | .166 | .167 | 1 | 0.5 | -0.3 |
| 2012 | SDN | MLB | 21 | 250 | 23 | 9 | 2 | 4 | 22 | 13 | 67 | 13 | 5 | .217/.259/.319 | .218 | .282 | -0.4 | RF -7, CF -1 | -1.0 |

Bats: R Throws: R Height: 6' 5" Weight: 205
Breakout: 2% Improve: 39% Collapse: 6%
Attrition: 29% MLB: 85%

Comparables:
Jim Eisenreich, Ellis Burks, Brian Barton

| YEAR | TEAM | LVL | AGE | PA | R | 2B | 3B | HR | RBI | BB | SO | SB | CS | AVG/OBP/SLG | TAv | BABIP | BRR | FRAA | WARP |
|------|------|-----|-----|----|---|----|----|----|-----|----|----|----|----|-------------|-----|-------|-----|------|------|
| 2009 | FLO | MLB | 22 | 199 | 30 | 12 | 2 | 4 | 13 | 17 | 51 | 1 | 3 | .250/.318/.409 | .260 | .328 | 0.2 | 2.3 | 0.7 |
| 2010 | NWO | AAA | 23 | 147 | 21 | 6 | 2 | 4 | 23 | 13 | 24 | 5 | 1 | .338/.401/.508 | .304 | .385 | 2.4 | 3 | 1.6 |
| 2010 | FLO | MLB | 23 | 322 | 46 | 7 | 3 | 8 | 28 | 24 | 92 | 9 | 2 | .234/.302/.361 | .240 | .312 | 2.9 | 7.5 | 1.3 |
| 2011 | SDN | MLB | 24 | 568 | 82 | 24 | 8 | 9 | 40 | 44 | 125 | 40 | 8 | .264/.323/.393 | .267 | .331 | 7.2 | 7.6 | 3.4 |
| 2012 | SDN | MLB | 25 | 486 | 54 | 18 | 6 | 9 | 48 | 44 | 126 | 20 | 5 | .243/.316/.374 | .258 | .316 | 0.5 | CF 8, LF 0 | 1.5 |

One advantage of calling Petco Park home is that it makes decent arms look great. If you're lucky, you can turn the occasional Edward Mujica and Ryan Webb into a young, toolsy center fielder who hasn't yet put it all together. Maybin doesn't hit many home runs or get on base as often as you'd like to see from a guy being groomed for the top of the order, but he has line-drive power to all fields, excellent speed (PECOTA underestimates his base-stealing ability), and an above-average glove. After three years of bouncing between Triple-A and the big leagues in the Marlins organization, Maybin shined in his first season with the Padres. His game remains raw in spots (notably, he will expand the strike zone at times), but his physical gifts are undeniable and he has a reputation for working hard to improve himself. The Padres are looking to lock him up long-term, as well they should be.

**Andy Parrino** SS
Born: 10/31/1985 Age: 26
Bats: B Throws: R Height: 6' 1" Weight: 180
Breakout: 2% Improve: 33% Collapse: 17%
Attrition: 33% MLB: 76%

Comparables:
Ron Hansen, Don Buddin, Tug Hulett

| YEAR | TEAM | LVL | AGE | PA | R | 2B | 3B | HR | RBI | BB | SO | SB | CS | AVG/OBP/SLG | TAv | BABIP | BRR | FRAA | WARP |
|------|------|-----|-----|----|---|----|----|----|-----|----|----|----|----|-------------|-----|-------|-----|------|------|
| 2009 | LEL | A+ | 23 | 371 | 52 | 16 | 1 | 2 | 29 | 51 | 85 | 8 | 2 | .235/.349/.312 | .267 | .316 | 1.6 | -1.2 | 1.3 |
| 2010 | SAN | AA | 24 | 492 | 70 | 28 | 4 | 11 | 49 | 68 | 115 | 4 | 2 | .246/.361/.415 | .287 | .312 | 1.7 | -4.1 | 2.8 |
| 2011 | SAN | AA | 25 | 179 | 28 | 7 | 1 | 9 | 32 | 22 | 40 | 3 | 1 | .303/.388/.539 | .347 | .349 | -0.1 | -1.8 | 2.2 |
| 2011 | SDN | MLB | 25 | 55 | 3 | 1 | 0 | 0 | 4 | 9 | 17 | 1 | 0 | .182/.327/.205 | .253 | .286 | -0.1 | 1.1 | 0.2 |
| 2012 | SDN | MLB | 26 | 250 | 24 | 10 | 1 | 3 | 18 | 28 | 64 | 2 | 1 | .207/.302/.305 | .234 | .273 | 0 | SS -2, 2B 3 | 0.3 |

The versatile Parrino has played everywhere but catcher in five professional seasons. Primarily a middle infielder, he walks a little and hits a few doubles but struggles to make consistent contact. Parrino, who joined the big club toward the end of August when Logan Forsythe was lost to injury, didn't do much with the bat but made an impression in the field. The former 26th-round pick out of Le Moyne College saw action at five positions in 24 games and made a couple of dazzling plays at shortstop in a memorable (well, for Padres fans who were still watching) game against the Cubs in the season's final week. There is something to be said for a hungry kid who gives his best effort in the face of futility.

**Carlos Quentin    RF**
Born: 8/28/1982 Age: 29
Bats: R Throws: R Height: 6' 2" Weight: 225
Breakout: 4% Improve: 43% Collapse: 2%
Attrition: 5% MLB: 94%

**Comparables:**
Billy Williams, Al Kaline, Vladimir Guerrero

| YEAR | TEAM | LVL | AGE | PA | R | 2B | 3B | HR | RBI | BB | SO | SB | CS | AVG_OBP_SLG | TAv | BABIP | BRR | FRAA | WARP |
|------|------|-----|-----|----|----|----|----|----|-----|----|----|----|----|-------------|-----|-------|-----|------|------|
| 2009 | CHA | MLB | 26 | 399 | 47 | 14 | 0 | 21 | 56 | 31 | 52 | 3 | 0 | .236/.323/.456 | .265 | .221 | -2.1 | -1.8 | 0.6 |
| 2010 | CHA | MLB | 27 | 527 | 73 | 25 | 2 | 26 | 87 | 50 | 83 | 2 | 2 | .243/.342/.479 | .284 | .241 | 0.8 | -9.2 | 0.9 |
| 2011 | CHA | MLB | 28 | 483 | 53 | 31 | 0 | 24 | 77 | 34 | 84 | 1 | 1 | .254/.340/.499 | .301 | .261 | -0.7 | -4.5 | 1.9 |
| 2012 | SDN | MLB | 29 | 463 | 59 | 20 | 2 | 22 | 61 | 43 | 76 | 2 | 1 | .242/.340/.463 | .298 | .246 | -0.2 | RF -4, LF -0 | 2.7 |

Since Quentin has never again risen to the heights of his 2008 breakout, it's become fashionable to focus on the things he can't do (like stay healthy, draw walks, or play a passable right field) to the exclusion of what he can. A more even-handed assessment would note that Quentin is a quality power bat, miscast as a franchise savior and cleanup hitter but perfectly suited for a complementary role—think Corey Hart or Nick Swisher. Reunited in his hometown with Josh Byrnes, who traded him out of the NL West four years earlier, Quentin will shift to left field, take at-bats away from Blanks and Guzman, and be expected to bear more of the offensive burden than he would have in Chicago.

**Anthony Rizzo    1B**
Born: 8/8/1989 Age: 22
Bats: L Throws: L Height: 6' 4" Weight: 220
Breakout: 2% Improve: 23% Collapse: 4%
Attrition: 16% MLB: 52%

**Comparables:**
Cecil Fielder, Jerry Sands, Phillip Hawke

| YEAR | TEAM | LVL | AGE | PA | R | 2B | 3B | HR | RBI | BB | SO | SB | CS | AVG_OBP_SLG | TAv | BABIP | BRR | FRAA | WARP |
|------|------|-----|-----|----|----|----|----|----|-----|----|----|----|----|-------------|-----|-------|-----|------|------|
| 2009 | GRN | A | 19 | 274 | 40 | 21 | 0 | 9 | 42 | 25 | 60 | 2 | 1 | .298/.368/.494 | .319 | .364 | -1.6 | 1.5 | 2.0 |
| 2009 | SLM | A+ | 19 | 229 | 23 | 16 | 0 | 3 | 24 | 25 | 39 | 2 | 0 | .295/.376/.420 | .282 | .354 | -1.9 | 1.4 | 0.7 |
| 2010 | SLM | A+ | 20 | 135 | 26 | 12 | 0 | 5 | 20 | 16 | 32 | 3 | 0 | .248/.338/.479 | .280 | .300 | 1.7 | -0.3 | 0.7 |
| 2010 | PME | AA | 20 | 467 | 66 | 30 | 0 | 20 | 80 | 45 | 100 | 4 | 1 | .263/.338/.481 | .285 | .303 | -2.2 | 7.9 | 2.5 |
| 2011 | SDN | MLB | 21 | 153 | 9 | 8 | 1 | 1 | 9 | 21 | 46 | 2 | 1 | .141/.281/.242 | .221 | .210 | -2.3 | -2.3 | -1.0 |
| 2012 | CHN | MLB | 22 | 250 | 29 | 14 | 1 | 8 | 30 | 21 | 64 | 2 | 0 | .246/.315/.422 | .260 | .303 | 0 | 1B -8 | 0.6 |

The problem with having your Triple-A club play in a bandbox while your big-leaguers play in baseball's most unfavorable hitting environment is that it creates unreasonable expectations. Rizzo, part of the haul for hometown hero Adrian Gonzalez, got off to a blistering start at Tucson. That and Brad Hawpe's struggles forced the Padres to recall Rizzo after just 52 games at Triple-A, where he'd been hitting .365/.444/.715 with 16 home runs. Rizzo tripled in his Petco Park debut, crushing a ball that would have left any other ballpark. He spent the rest of June and July flailing at everything before being shipped back to Tucson, where he worked on shortening his stroke. Rizzo returned in September for a cameo but didn't do much. He is young, his power is real, and he plays a good first base. Rizzo has overcome worse obstacles than scuffling against big-league pitching (namely, Hodgkin's lymphoma). Once he makes the necessary adjustments and gains experience, he will develop into the Adam LaRoche clone he was meant to be.

**Cory Spangenberg    2B**
Born: 3/16/1991 Age: 21
Bats: L Throws: R Height: 6' 1" Weight: 185
Breakout: 6% Improve: 22% Collapse: 0%
Attrition: 8% MLB: 27%

**Comparables:**
Steve Lombardozzi, LJ Hoes, Wally Backman

| YEAR | TEAM | LVL | AGE | PA | R | 2B | 3B | HR | RBI | BB | SO | SB | CS | AVG_OBP_SLG | TAv | BABIP | BRR | FRAA | WARP |
|------|------|-----|-----|----|----|----|----|----|-----|----|----|----|----|-------------|-----|-------|-----|------|------|
| 2011 | FTW | A | 20 | 209 | 35 | 7 | 1 | 2 | 24 | 14 | 42 | 15 | 4 | .286/.345/.365 | .278 | .359 | 2.8 | 2.1 | 1.6 |
| 2011 | EUG | A- | 20 | 121 | 20 | 10 | 0 | 1 | 20 | 31 | 15 | 10 | 4 | .384/.545/.535 | .400 | .444 | -0.6 | -0.6 | 2.0 |
| 2012 | SDN | MLB | 21 | 250 | 23 | 9 | 1 | 1 | 16 | 21 | 60 | 8 | 3 | .213/.285/.281 | .219 | .279 | -0.3 | 2B 5 | -0.5 |

Spangenberg signed a deal within days of being selected 10th overall in the 2011 draft and tore up the Northwest League for 25 games before being challenged in the Midwest League. Spangenberg, who was drafted out of junior college, got off to a terrible start after his promotion, but finished strong. He hits, gets on base, runs well, and plays a passable second base. There is little power potential here, but he could develop into a useful table setter.

**Blake Tekotte    CF**
Born: 5/24/1987 Age: 25
Bats: L Throws: R Height: 6' 0" Weight: 175
Breakout: 7% Improve: 48% Collapse: 5%
Attrition: 26% MLB: 87%

**Comparables:**
Ron Roenicke, Jim Eisenreich, Gary Geiger

| YEAR | TEAM | LVL | AGE | PA | R | 2B | 3B | HR | RBI | BB | SO | SB | CS | AVG_OBP_SLG | TAv | BABIP | BRR | FRAA | WARP |
|------|------|-----|-----|----|----|----|----|----|-----|----|----|----|----|-------------|-----|-------|-----|------|------|
| 2009 | FTW | A | 22 | 610 | 83 | 24 | 5 | 13 | 56 | 68 | 97 | 30 | 12 | .258/.345/.396 | .276 | .292 | -1.2 | 14.8 | 4.2 |
| 2010 | LEL | A+ | 23 | 241 | 41 | 17 | 1 | 8 | 27 | 36 | 46 | 22 | 8 | .310/.419/.522 | .342 | .369 | -0.6 | -8.6 | 1.8 |
| 2010 | SAN | AA | 23 | 301 | 44 | 8 | 7 | 10 | 37 | 26 | 63 | 6 | 9 | .250/.323/.444 | .280 | .289 | 1.4 | 0.9 | 2.0 |
| 2011 | SAN | AA | 24 | 498 | 77 | 27 | 2 | 19 | 67 | 67 | 108 | 36 | 12 | .285/.393/.498 | .327 | .343 | 1.6 | -1.1 | 4.8 |
| 2011 | SDN | MLB | 24 | 40 | 1 | 1 | 1 | 0 | 1 | 4 | 21 | 2 | 1 | .176/.263/.265 | .200 | .462 | -0.1 | -0.8 | -0.2 |
| 2012 | SDN | MLB | 25 | 250 | 26 | 9 | 2 | 5 | 22 | 25 | 63 | 10 | 4 | .214/.298/.343 | .241 | .268 | -0.4 | CF -10, LF -0 | 0.5 |

Tekotte possesses a broad base of skills but doesn't do any one thing exceptionally well. He has gap power, draws a few walks, steals bases with some success, and plays a solid center field. Tekotte has always been old for his league (he's only a few weeks younger than Cameron Maybin) and doesn't have the strongest arm. Tekotte elicits comparisons to Mark Kotsay and David

DeJesus, the downside of which is. . . Jeremy Reed? There isn't much growth potential for Tekotte, but he could be a decent fourth outfielder.

### Jeudy Valdez — SS

Born: 5/5/1989 Age: 23
Bats: R Throws: R Height: 6' 0'' Weight: 155
Breakout: 7% Improve: 18% Collapse: 8%
Attrition: 24% MLB: 53%

Comparables:
Adolfo Gonzalez, Felix Mantilla, Casey Frawley

| YEAR | TEAM | LVL | AGE | PA | R | 2B | 3B | HR | RBI | BB | SO | SB | CS | AVG/OBP/SLG | TAv | BABIP | BRR | FRAA | WARP |
|------|------|-----|-----|----|----|----|----|----|-----|----|----|----|----|-------------|-----|-------|-----|------|------|
| 2009 | FTW | A | 20 | 215 | 25 | 11 | 2 | 1 | 14 | 17 | 51 | 11 | 3 | .212/.279/.306 | .230 | .278 | -0.7 | -0.1 | -0.4 |
| 2010 | FTW | A | 21 | 590 | 81 | 34 | 3 | 10 | 76 | 43 | 115 | 34 | 14 | .247/.306/.380 | .250 | .296 | 3.3 | -3.7 | 0.7 |
| 2011 | LEL | A+ | 22 | 560 | 93 | 37 | 7 | 15 | 92 | 31 | 108 | 34 | 11 | .295/.339/.481 | .288 | .346 | -2.3 | -12.1 | 2.8 |
| 2012 | SDN | MLB | 23 | 250 | 21 | 10 | 2 | 2 | 20 | 10 | 64 | 9 | 3 | .205/.238/.291 | .199 | .265 | -0.1 | SS -2, 2B -1 | -1.2 |

Valdez is an athletic but erratic infielder from the Dominican Republic who has power, speed, and trouble controlling the strike zone. Valdez was old for his level in 2011 and has been slow to advance since joining the organization in 2006. His arm may not be strong enough for shortstop, but if he patches the holes in his game, he could be something. That said, he hasn't reached Double-A and those

Venable is one of the Padres' most exhilarating and exasperating players. He can drive the ball to left-center with backspin and make Petco Park, which destroys left-handed hitters, look small. He can play all three outfield spots and run the bases like Dave Winfield. But Venable focused more on basketball at Princeton, and years later, it shows. He still expands his strike zone too often and is clueless against southpaws (.212/.289/.261 for his career). Venable is a fantastic athlete who sometimes appears to be feeling his way around the diamond in a manner that calls to mind, say, Al Martin. There are very few things that Venable cannot do on the ball field. There are fewer still that he can do with any degree of consistency.

## PITCHERS

### Anthony Bass

Born: 11/1/1987 Age: 24
Bats: R Throws: R Height: 6' 3'' Weight: 190
Breakout: 15% Improve: 36% Collapse: 30%
Attrition: 13% MLB: 93%

Comparables:
Brad Penny, Don Dennis, Jake Westbrook

| YEAR | TEAM | LVL | AGE | W | L | SV | G | GS | IP | H | HR | BB | SO | EqBB9 | EqSO9 | GB% | BABIP | WHIP | ERA | FIP | FRA | WARP |
|------|------|-----|-----|---|---|----|---|----|-----|----|----|----|----|-------|-------|-----|-------|------|------|------|------|------|
| 2009 | FTW | A | 21 | 9 | 3 | 0 | 18 | 18 | 90¹ | 79 | 5 | 25 | 69 | 2.5 | 6.9 | 48% | .281 | 1.15 | 2.19 | 3.74 | 4.43 | 1.0 |
| 2009 | LEL | A+ | 21 | 3 | 0 | 0 | 10 | 8 | 33¹ | 40 | 4 | 16 | 24 | 3.8 | 5.4 | 54% | .303 | 1.41 | 3.51 | 5.50 | 5.53 | 0.0 |
| 2010 | LEL | A+ | 22 | 8 | 7 | 0 | 27 | 27 | 132¹ | 105 | 7 | 16 | 91 | 1.4 | 7.4 | 54% | .316 | 1.09 | 3.13 | 3.52 | 4.21 | 1.5 |
| 2011 | SAN | AA | 23 | 3 | 3 | 0 | 13 | 13 | 69² | 62 | 6 | 21 | 62 | 2.7 | 8.0 | 49% | .293 | 1.19 | 3.75 | 3.63 | 4.34 | 0.8 |
| 2011 | SDN | MLB | 23 | 2 | 0 | 0 | 27 | 3 | 48¹ | 41 | 3 | 21 | 24 | 3.9 | 4.5 | 47% | .259 | 1.28 | 1.68 | 4.17 | 4.45 | 0.2 |
| 2012 | SDN | MLB | 24 | 3 | 4 | 0 | 17 | 11 | 62² | 58 | 6 | 25 | 33 | 3.5 | 4.8 | 47% | .280 | 1.32 | 4.24 | 4.59 | 4.61 | 0.2 |

Bass features an unusual delivery that elicits comparisons to that of San Francisco's Tim Lincecum. Bass, as do most mortals, lacks Lincecum's stuff and command but has a good feel for pitching. After starting the season in the San Antonio rotation, he was brought up midsummer and worked mostly out of the bullpen, where he added a few ticks to his fastball. When the Padres shut down Tim Stauffer at season's end, Bass took his spot in the rotation and pitched well in limited starting opportunities, although his command could have been better. Bass will compete for a spot at the back end of the Padres rotation in 2012 and could be effective in that role or as a swingman.

### Brad Boxberger

Born: 5/27/1988 Age: 24
Bats: R Throws: R Height: 6' 3'' Weight: 200
Breakout: 31% Improve: 47% Collapse: 33%
Attrition: 8% MLB: 89%

Comparables:
Ambiorix Burgos, Gio Gonzalez, Jim York

| YEAR | TEAM | LVL | AGE | W | L | SV | G | GS | IP | H | HR | BB | SO | EqBB9 | EqSO9 | GB% | BABIP | WHIP | ERA | FIP | FRA | WARP |
|------|------|-----|-----|---|---|----|----|----|-----|----|----|----|----|-------|-------|-----|-------|------|------|------|------|------|
| 2011 | CAR | AA | 23 | 1 | 2 | 4 | 30 | 0 | 34¹ | 15 | 2 | 11 | 53 | 3.4 | 14.9 | 51% | .245 | 0.84 | 1.31 | 1.93 | 2.70 | 1.0 |
| 2011 | LOU | AAA | 23 | 1 | 1 | 7 | 25 | 0 | 27² | 16 | 2 | 15 | 36 | 4.9 | 11.7 | 48% | .237 | 1.12 | 2.93 | 3.20 | 4.38 | 0.3 |
| 2012 | SDN | MLB | 24 | 1 | 1 | 1 | 13 | 2 | 22² | 18 | 2 | 10 | 23 | 4.1 | 9.1 | 47% | .294 | 1.24 | 3.62 | 3.65 | 3.93 | 0.2 |

A supplemental first-round pick of the Reds in 2009, right-hander Brad Boxberger has racked up big strikeout numbers throughout his minor-league career but sometimes forgets where home plate is. Acquired in the Latos deal, he'll vie for a spot in the Padres bullpen.

### Brad Brach

Born: 4/12/1986 Age: 26
Bats: R Throws: R Height: 6' 7'' Weight: 210
Breakout: 35% Improve: 52% Collapse: 20%
Attrition: 7% MLB: 95%

Comparables:
Sergio Romo, Al Hrabosky, Jonathan Papelbon

| YEAR | TEAM | LVL | AGE | W | L | SV | G | GS | IP | H | HR | BB | SO | EqBB9 | EqSO9 | GB% | BABIP | WHIP | ERA | FIP | FRA | WARP |
|------|------|-----|-----|---|---|----|----|----|-----|----|----|----|----|-------|-------|-----|-------|------|------|------|------|------|
| 2009 | FTW | A | 23 | 4 | 3 | 33 | 60 | 0 | 63² | 42 | 2 | 11 | 95 | 1.6 | 11.6 | 36% | .261 | 0.74 | 1.27 | 1.75 | 2.78 | 1.8 |
| 2010 | LEL | A+ | 24 | 5 | 3 | 41 | 62 | 0 | 65² | 41 | 6 | 10 | 67 | 1.5 | 10.1 | 46% | .271 | 0.93 | 2.47 | 3.42 | 4.26 | 0.4 |
| 2011 | SAN | AA | 25 | 2 | 2 | 23 | 42 | 0 | 44 | 32 | 3 | 5 | 64 | 1.0 | 13.1 | 31% | .305 | 0.84 | 2.25 | 1.84 | 2.39 | 1.4 |
| 2011 | SDN | MLB | 25 | 0 | 2 | 0 | 9 | 0 | 7 | 9 | 0 | 7 | 11 | 9.0 | 14.1 | 26% | .474 | 2.29 | 5.14 | 3.28 | 4.80 | -0.1 |
| 2012 | SDN | MLB | 26 | 2 | 1 | 0 | 29 | 0 | 30² | 24 | 3 | 10 | 29 | 3.1 | 8.7 | 40% | .294 | 1.14 | 3.10 | 3.56 | 3.37 | 0.5 |

The Padres have had good fortune with their 42nd-round picks in recent years, with Kyle Blanks in 2004 and Brach in 2008. Brach is a big right-hander with a funky delivery who has racked up strikeouts (11.4 K/9, 7.3 K/BB) in 206 minor-league appearances despite average stuff. He works around the plate, and his fly-ball tendencies won't hurt him at Petco Park. Brach could soak up middle relief innings in 2012 or become trade bait for a team that miscalculates park effects and/or the fungibility of relievers.

### Robert Erlin

Born: 10/8/1990 Age: 21
Bats: L Throws: L Height: 6' 1'' Weight: 175
Breakout: 26% Improve: 53% Collapse: 11%
Attrition: 6% MLB: 93%

Comparables:
Billy Hoeft, Clayton Kershaw, Frank Tanana

| YEAR | TEAM | LVL | AGE | W | L | SV | G | GS | IP | H | HR | BB | SO | EqBB9 | EqSO9 | GB% | BABIP | WHIP | ERA | FIP | FRA | WARP |
|------|------|-----|-----|---|---|----|----|----|-----|----|----|----|----|-------|-------|-----|-------|------|------|------|------|------|
| 2010 | HIC | A | 19 | 6 | 3 | 1 | 28 | 17 | 114² | 44 | 2 | 12 | 69 | 1.3 | 9.8 | 40% | .251 | 0.92 | 2.12 | 3.10 | 3.51 | 2.7 |
| 2011 | MYR | A+ | 20 | 3 | 0 | 0 | 9 | 9 | 54² | 25 | 7 | 5 | 62 | 0.8 | 10.2 | 34% | .149 | 0.55 | 2.14 | 3.05 | 3.07 | 1.6 |
| 2011 | SAN | AA | 20 | 1 | 0 | 0 | 6 | 6 | 26 | 35 | 2 | 4 | 36 | 1.4 | 10.7 | 42% | .388 | 1.15 | 1.38 | 2.07 | 4.05 | 0.6 |
| 2011 | FRI | AA | 20 | 3 | 1 | 0 | 11 | 10 | 66² | 73 | 9 | 7 | 61 | 0.9 | 8.2 | 40% | .333 | 1.20 | 4.32 | 3.71 | 4.00 | 1.0 |
| 2012 | SDN | MLB | 21 | 2 | 3 | 0 | 9 | 7 | 44² | 39 | 5 | 12 | 34 | 2.5 | 6.9 | 39% | .286 | 1.15 | 3.58 | 3.94 | 3.89 | 0.5 |

Erlin, who came over from Texas as part of the package for Mike Adams, is a polished left-hander with a clean delivery who works with a fastball that tops out in the low 90s. His secondary pitches aren't great, but he throws them all for strikes (8.5 K/BB for his career in the minors) in any count. He is a fly-ball pitcher, which won't matter in San Diego as much as it would have in Arlington. Erlin will start 2012 at Tucson, which is another story. He is young and the Padres have other options, but it wouldn't be surprising to see him up at some point during the season if only to extract him from the PCL for his own good.

### Ernesto Frieri

Born: 7/19/1985 Age: 26
Bats: R Throws: R Height: 6' 3'' Weight: 200
Breakout: 35% Improve: 55% Collapse: 18%
Attrition: 16% MLB: 95%

Comparables:
Jeff Reardon, Scott Strickland, Tyler Clippard

| YEAR | TEAM | LVL | AGE | W | L | SV | G | GS | IP | H | HR | BB | SO | EqBB9 | EqSO9 | GB% | BABIP | WHIP | ERA | FIP | FRA | WARP |
|------|------|-----|-----|----|---|----|----|----|------|-----|----|----|-----|-------|-------|-----|-------|------|------|------|------|------|
| 2009 | SAN | AA | 23 | 10 | 9 | 0 | 27 | 26 | 140¹ | 127 | 13 | 63 | 124 | 4.0 | 7.6 | 35% | .273 | 1.33 | 3.59 | 4.11 | 4.73 | 0.9 |
| 2009 | SDN | MLB | 23 | 0 | 0 | 0 | 2 | 0 | 2 | 0 | 0 | 1 | 2 | 4.5 | 9.0 | % | .000 | 0.50 | 0.00 | 2.56 | 3.36 | 0.0 |
| 2010 | POR | AAA | 24 | 3 | 1 | 17 | 34 | 0 | 37² | 7 | 0 | 15 | 31 | 4.3 | 11.7 | 20% | .146 | 0.85 | 1.43 | 3.77 | 3.44 | 0.6 |
| 2010 | SDN | MLB | 24 | 1 | 1 | 0 | 33 | 0 | 31² | 18 | 2 | 17 | 41 | 4.8 | 11.7 | 24% | .235 | 1.11 | 1.71 | 2.95 | 3.29 | 0.5 |
| 2011 | SDN | MLB | 25 | 1 | 2 | 0 | 59 | 0 | 63 | 51 | 3 | 34 | 76 | 4.9 | 10.9 | 25% | .314 | 1.35 | 2.71 | 3.25 | 3.73 | 0.5 |
| 2012 | SDN | MLB | 26 | 3 | 1 | 0 | 51 | 0 | 53¹ | 43 | 5 | 25 | 45 | 4.1 | 7.6 | 30% | .280 | 1.27 | 3.91 | 4.14 | 4.24 | 0.3 |

After a couple of decent but not great seasons as a starter, Frieri returned to his original bullpen role in 2010 and became a different pitcher. His fastball sits in the low-to-mid 90s, but a deceptive delivery makes it difficult to pick up out of his hand. The Colombian right-hander, who is the longest-tenured player in the Padres organization, is aggressive with the fastball and a sharp-breaking slider. Frieri's two main weaknesses are extreme fly-ball tendencies and occasional lapses in control, neither of which (stop me if you've heard this one before) will hurt him as much at Petco Park as they would elsewhere. PECOTA has doubts, but he is a solid setup man who could close if needed.

### Luke Gregerson

Born: 5/14/1984 Age: 28
Bats: L Throws: R Height: 6' 4'' Weight: 200
Breakout: 15% Improve: 34% Collapse: 38%
Attrition: 5% MLB: 93%

Comparables:
Rich Harden, Craig Breslow, Dave Righetti

| YEAR | TEAM | LVL | AGE | W | L | SV | G | GS | IP | H | HR | BB | SO | EqBB9 | EqSO9 | GB% | BABIP | WHIP | ERA | FIP | FRA | WARP |
|------|------|-----|-----|---|---|----|----|----|-----|----|----|----|----|-------|-------|-----|-------|------|------|------|------|------|
| 2009 | SDN | MLB | 25 | 2 | 4 | 1 | 72 | 0 | 75 | 62 | 3 | 31 | 93 | 3.7 | 11.2 | 47% | .319 | 1.24 | 3.24 | 2.46 | 2.91 | 1.8 |
| 2010 | SDN | MLB | 26 | 4 | 7 | 2 | 80 | 0 | 78¹ | 47 | 8 | 18 | 89 | 2.1 | 10.2 | 48% | .217 | 0.83 | 3.22 | 2.89 | 3.80 | 0.8 |
| 2011 | SDN | MLB | 27 | 3 | 3 | 0 | 61 | 0 | 55² | 57 | 2 | 19 | 34 | 3.1 | 5.5 | 52% | .307 | 1.37 | 2.75 | 3.37 | 4.92 | -0.4 |
| 2012 | SDN | MLB | 28 | 3 | 2 | 1 | 61 | 0 | 57¹ | 41 | 4 | 19 | 54 | 3.0 | 8.4 | 52% | .272 | 1.06 | 2.54 | 3.22 | 2.77 | 1.3 |

Gregerson's slider of death disappeared in 2011. After posting a 10.7 K/9 and 3.7 K/BB over his first two big-league seasons, he saw those numbers slip to 5.5 and 1.8, respectively, last year.

Like Cla Meredith, another Padres reliever who relied on a gimmick and was worked hard, Gregerson runs the risk of having a short career. Don't let the shiny ERA fool you; he needs to rediscover the tilt on his slider if he is to continue much longer.

### Casey Kelly

Born: 10/4/1989 Age: 22
Bats: R Throws: R Height: 6' 4" Weight: 195
Breakout: 17% Improve: 52% Collapse: 28%
Attrition: 13% MLB: 81%

Comparables:
Jim Ollom, Don Kaiser, Johnny Kucks

| YEAR | TEAM | LVL | AGE | W | L | SV | G | GS | IP | H | HR | BB | SO | EqBB9 | EqSO9 | GB% | BABIP | WHIP | ERA | FIP | FRA | WARP |
|---|---|---|---|---|---|---|---|---|---|---|---|---|---|---|---|---|---|---|---|---|---|---|
| 2009 | GRN | A | 19 | 6 | 1 | 0 | 9 | 9 | 48¹ | 32 | 0 | 9 | 39 | 1.7 | 7.3 | 54% | .237 | 0.85 | 1.12 | 2.41 | 3.26 | 1.3 |
| 2009 | SLM | A+ | 19 | 1 | 4 | 0 | 8 | 8 | 46² | 33 | 4 | 7 | 35 | 1.3 | 6.7 | 53% | .225 | 0.86 | 3.08 | 3.48 | 4.83 | 0.4 |
| 2010 | PME | AA | 20 | 3 | 5 | 0 | 21 | 21 | 95 | 81 | 7 | 26 | 60 | 3.3 | 7.7 | 47% | .370 | 1.61 | 5.31 | 4.11 | 4.97 | 0.8 |
| 2011 | SAN | AA | 21 | 4 | 2 | 0 | 27 | 27 | 142¹ | 159 | 8 | 50 | 107 | 2.9 | 6.6 | 56% | .327 | 1.40 | 3.98 | 3.83 | 4.68 | 1.9 |
| 2012 | SDN | MLB | 22 | 2 | 4 | 0 | 9 | 9 | 47 | 47 | 5 | 18 | 26 | 3.4 | 4.9 | 50% | .300 | 1.39 | 4.76 | 4.63 | 5.17 | -0.1 |

Although Kelly was trumpeted as the centerpiece of the Adrian Gonzalez trade, the numbers have never justified the hype. The former shortstop hasn't been pitching full time for very long, but even given his age and relative lack of experience, a 6.6 K/9 in the Texas League doesn't translate into a front-line starter, which is what Padres fans

Breakout: 15% Improve: 48% Collapse: 27%
Attrition: 16% MLB: 89%

Comparables:
Joe Gibbon, Tim Crabtree, Dennis Leonard

| YEAR | TEAM | LVL | AGE | W | L | SV | G | GS | IP | H | HR | BB | SO | EqBB9 | EqSO9 | GB% | BABIP | WHIP | ERA | FIP | FRA | WARP |
|---|---|---|---|---|---|---|---|---|---|---|---|---|---|---|---|---|---|---|---|---|---|---|
| 2010 | SAN | AA | 25 | 5 | 1 | 0 | 10 | 8 | 56¹ | 34 | 2 | 9 | 28 | 1.9 | 7.0 | 44% | .271 | 0.94 | 2.40 | 3.33 | 3.51 | 0.7 |
| 2010 | POR | AAA | 25 | 5 | 0 | 0 | 9 | 9 | 57² | 26 | 4 | 11 | 27 | 2.7 | 6.9 | 41% | .234 | 1.02 | 2.96 | 4.60 | 4.38 | 0.8 |
| 2010 | SDN | MLB | 25 | 1 | 1 | 0 | 4 | 3 | 17² | 17 | 3 | 6 | 18 | 3.1 | 9.2 | 47% | .292 | 1.30 | 4.08 | 4.46 | 4.91 | 0.0 |
| 2011 | SDN | MLB | 26 | 6 | 10 | 0 | 46 | 17 | 139² | 105 | 12 | 44 | 154 | 2.8 | 9.9 | 41% | .274 | 1.07 | 3.29 | 2.89 | 3.25 | 2.8 |
| 2012 | SDN | MLB | 27 | 4 | 5 | 0 | 24 | 13 | 95² | 83 | 10 | 33 | 72 | 3.1 | 6.8 | 45% | .286 | 1.21 | 3.75 | 4.09 | 4.08 | 0.7 |

Luebke, a 2007 supplemental first-round pick out of Ohio State, made the Padres out of spring training thanks to an injury to lefty reliever Joe Thatcher. Despite having made just 10 relief appearances in four minor-league seasons, he warmed to his new role. He posted a 3.23 ERA and held opponents to a .183/.267/.244 line in 29 appearances. After injuries to Dustin Moseley and Clayton Richard, the Padres moved Luebke back to his more familiar starting role and he didn't miss a beat. Luebke works with a low-90s fastball and sharp-breaking slider. He is aggressive with both pitches, although his command sometimes deserts him for stretches, forcing high pitch counts. Luebke figures to be a solid mid-rotation option for the Padres into the future.

### Dustin Moseley

Born: 12/26/1981 Age: 30
Bats: R Throws: R Height: 6' 5" Weight: 190
Breakout: 10% Improve: 48% Collapse: 26%
Attrition: 15% MLB: 86%

Comparables:
Dave Borkowski, Cory Lidle, Ryan Franklin

| YEAR | TEAM | LVL | AGE | W | L | SV | G | GS | IP | H | HR | BB | SO | EqBB9 | EqSO9 | GB% | BABIP | WHIP | ERA | FIP | FRA | WARP |
|---|---|---|---|---|---|---|---|---|---|---|---|---|---|---|---|---|---|---|---|---|---|---|
| 2009 | ANA | MLB | 27 | 1 | 0 | 0 | 3 | 3 | 14² | 20 | 3 | 3 | 8 | 1.8 | 4.9 | 41% | .333 | 1.57 | 4.30 | 5.33 | 4.90 | 0.1 |
| 2010 | SWB | AAA | 28 | 4 | 4 | 0 | 12 | 12 | 72² | 53 | 5 | 14 | 46 | 2.2 | 6.8 | 60% | .327 | 1.39 | 4.21 | 3.90 | 4.62 | 0.6 |
| 2010 | NYA | MLB | 28 | 4 | 4 | 0 | 16 | 9 | 65¹ | 66 | 13 | 27 | 33 | 3.7 | 4.5 | 51% | .261 | 1.42 | 4.96 | 5.96 | 6.00 | -0.2 |
| 2011 | SDN | MLB | 29 | 3 | 10 | 0 | 20 | 20 | 120 | 117 | 10 | 36 | 64 | 2.7 | 4.8 | 51% | .276 | 1.27 | 3.30 | 3.96 | 4.04 | 0.7 |
| 2012 | SDN | MLB | 30 | 5 | 7 | 0 | 17 | 17 | 99¹ | 98 | 11 | 31 | 54 | 2.8 | 4.9 | 49% | .292 | 1.30 | 4.41 | 4.49 | 4.79 | -0.0 |

The Padres signed Moseley, who worked under Bud Black when Black was the pitching coach in Anaheim, to a one-year, $900,000 deal. A reliever for most of his career, Moseley came to San Diego in part because he would be given a shot at the rotation. Despite pedestrian stuff, he pitched surprisingly well in that role and put together a career year before seeing his season end in July due to a dislocated left (non-throwing) shoulder incurred while swinging a bat. Moseley required surgery and is expected to be ready for spring training, although which team's uniform he will be wearing remains an open question.

### Chad Qualls

Born: 8/17/1978 Age: 33
Bats: R Throws: R Height: 6' 6" Weight: 220
Breakout: 22% Improve: 40% Collapse: 33%
Attrition: 18% MLB: 92%

Comparables:
Kevin Millwood, Alejandro Pena, Mark Eichhorn

| YEAR | TEAM | LVL | AGE | W | L | SV | G | GS | IP | H | HR | BB | SO | EqBB9 | EqSO9 | GB% | BABIP | WHIP | ERA | FIP | FRA | WARP |
|---|---|---|---|---|---|---|---|---|---|---|---|---|---|---|---|---|---|---|---|---|---|---|
| 2009 | ARI | MLB | 30 | 2 | 2 | 24 | 51 | 0 | 52 | 53 | 5 | 7 | 45 | 1.2 | 7.8 | 59% | .306 | 1.15 | 3.63 | 3.09 | 4.39 | 0.6 |
| 2010 | TBA | MLB | 31 | 2 | 0 | 0 | 27 | 0 | 21 | 24 | 2 | 6 | 15 | 2.6 | 6.4 | 55% | .328 | 1.43 | 5.57 | 3.86 | 6.25 | -0.2 |
| 2010 | ARI | MLB | 31 | 1 | 4 | 12 | 43 | 0 | 38 | 61 | 5 | 15 | 34 | 3.6 | 8.1 | 57% | .427 | 2.00 | 8.29 | 4.29 | 5.14 | 0.0 |
| 2011 | SDN | MLB | 32 | 6 | 8 | 0 | 77 | 0 | 74¹ | 73 | 7 | 20 | 43 | 2.4 | 5.2 | 60% | .288 | 1.25 | 3.51 | 3.87 | 5.00 | -0.4 |
| 2012 | SDN | MLB | 33 | 4 | 2 | 5 | 75 | 0 | 67² | 61 | 6 | 17 | 51 | 2.3 | 6.8 | 56% | .298 | 1.15 | 3.45 | 3.60 | 3.75 | 0.7 |

The Padres signed Qualls to a one-year deal with a club option for 2012 to help fill the void left by Edward Mujica and Ryan Webb. Like his predecessors, Qualls ate low-leverage innings for much of the year. He later inherited Mike Adams' eighth-inning role, where things didn't go as well. Qualls' ERA in the eighth was more than twice as high as it had been in the seventh, in a similar number of innings. The periodic implosions that occurred when he couldn't locate his sinker made him somewhat less than easy to watch.

### Clayton Richard

Born: 9/12/1983 Age: 28
Bats: L Throws: L Height: 6' 6" Weight: 240
Breakout: 10% Improve: 31% Collapse: 18%
Attrition: 9% MLB: 93%

Comparables:
Lenny DiNardo, Curt Simmons, Andy Pettitte

| YEAR | TEAM | LVL | AGE | W | L | SV | G | GS | IP | H | HR | BB | SO | EqBB9 | EqSO9 | GB% | BABIP | WHIP | ERA | FIP | FRA | WARP |
|------|------|-----|-----|---|---|----|----|----|-----|-----|----|----|-----|-------|-------|-----|-------|------|------|------|------|------|
| 2009 | SDN | MLB | 25 | 5 | 2 | 0 | 12 | 12 | 64 | 60 | 7 | 34 | 48 | 4.8 | 6.8 | 53% | .291 | 1.47 | 4.08 | 4.57 | 5.43 | -0.2 |
| 2009 | CHA | MLB | 25 | 4 | 3 | 0 | 26 | 14 | 89 | 94 | 10 | 37 | 66 | 3.7 | 6.7 | 49% | .313 | 1.47 | 4.65 | 4.47 | 5.40 | 0.4 |
| 2010 | SDN | MLB | 26 | 14 | 9 | 0 | 33 | 33 | 201² | 206 | 16 | 78 | 153 | 3.5 | 6.8 | 47% | .315 | 1.41 | 3.75 | 3.84 | 4.40 | 1.4 |
| 2011 | SDN | MLB | 27 | 5 | 9 | 0 | 18 | 18 | 99² | 104 | 8 | 38 | 53 | 3.4 | 4.8 | 52% | .298 | 1.42 | 3.88 | 4.18 | 4.30 | 0.4 |
| 2012 | SDN | MLB | 28 | 5 | 7 | 0 | 17 | 17 | 102² | 95 | 9 | 38 | 59 | 3.4 | 5.2 | 51% | .289 | 1.30 | 4.02 | 4.30 | 4.37 | 0.5 |

After a surprising first full season in San Diego, Richard backslid in his encore. Many of his qualitative numbers look similar in 2010 and 2011, but the drop from 6.8 K/9 to 4.8 K/9 is disconcerting. One of Richard's problems is that, as a former college quarterback, he sometimes has trouble with the slower pace of baseball. He is an extremely quick worker, which is great when he is hitting his spots but leads to trouble when he isn't. Richard is one of those pitchers, like Adam Eaton during his stay in San Diego, who can cruise along for innings at a time and then unravel in an instant. Richard underwent season-ending left shoulder surgery at the end of July but expects to be ready for spring training. When healthy, he is a dependable workhorse at the back end of the rotation.

### Keyvius Sampson

Born: 1/6/1991 Age: 21
Bats: R Throws: R Height: 6' 1" Weight: 185
Breakout: 28% Improve: 57% Collapse: 19%
Attrition: 6% MLB: 88%

Comparables:
Dick Drott, Marcos Carvajal, Matt Cain

| YEAR | TEAM | LVL | AGE | W | L | SV | G | GS | IP | H | HR | BB | SO | EqBB9 | EqSO9 | GB% | BABIP | WHIP | ERA | FIP | FRA | WARP |
|------|------|-----|-----|---|---|----|----|----|-----|----|----|----|-----|-------|-------|-----|-------|------|------|------|------|------|
| 2010 | EUG | A- | 19 | 3 | 3 | 0 | 10 | 10 | 43 | 35 | 4 | 17 | 58 | 3.6 | 12.1 | — | .327 | 1.21 | 3.56 | 3.32 | 4.24 | 0.4 |
| 2011 | FTW | A | 20 | 4 | 1 | 0 | 24 | 24 | 118 | 87 | 8 | 51 | 137 | 3.7 | 10.9 | 39% | .280 | 1.10 | 2.90 | 3.37 | 4.19 | 2.0 |
| 2012 | SDN | MLB | 21 | 1 | 3 | 0 | 6 | 6 | 30² | 27 | 3 | 16 | 23 | 4.7 | 6.9 | 41% | .294 | 1.42 | 4.66 | 4.54 | 5.06 | -0.0 |

Sampson started his 2011 with a bang, retiring all 18 batters he faced on Opening Day in his full-season debut. He struck out 10 in that game en route to 143 on the season, third best in the Midwest League. Sampson features a mid-90s fastball but is smallish and, considering he's had shoulder problems in the past, there are concerns about how he will handle heavier workloads. The good news is that he survived the season without any major incidents. Beyond staying healthy, Sampson must continue to improve his command and secondary offerings. With the sudden organizational depth in pitching, he will advance one level at a time and should arrive in San Diego by the second half of 2014. There is plenty of upside here, but patience and health are keys to his development.

### Josh Spence

Born: 1/22/1988 Age: 24
Bats: L Throws: L Height: 6' 2" Weight: 170
Breakout: 38% Improve: 63% Collapse: 16%
Attrition: 12% MLB: 98%

Comparables:
Barry Zito, Josh Johnson, Tim Lincecum

| YEAR | TEAM | LVL | AGE | W | L | SV | G | GS | IP | H | HR | BB | SO | EqBB9 | EqSO9 | GB% | BABIP | WHIP | ERA | FIP | FRA | WARP |
|------|------|-----|-----|---|---|----|----|----|-----|----|----|----|----|-------|-------|-----|-------|------|------|------|------|------|
| 2011 | SAN | AA | 23 | 1 | 1 | 0 | 35 | 0 | 47¹ | 29 | 4 | 11 | 42 | 2.1 | 8.0 | 36% | .217 | 0.85 | 1.71 | 3.47 | 3.51 | 0.8 |
| 2011 | SDN | MLB | 23 | 0 | 2 | 0 | 40 | 0 | 29² | 14 | 2 | 19 | 31 | 5.8 | 9.4 | 38% | .176 | 1.11 | 2.73 | 3.90 | 4.06 | 0.1 |
| 2012 | SDN | MLB | 24 | 2 | 1 | 0 | 29 | 2 | 33² | 25 | 3 | 14 | 30 | 3.7 | 8.0 | 41% | .271 | 1.17 | 3.18 | 3.83 | 3.45 | 0.5 |

A 2010 ninth-round pick out of Arizona State, Australian left-hander Spence wasted no time, arriving in San Diego after just 71 1/3 minor-league innings. He works with a low-80s fastball and a slider that dips out of the zone. His game is deception, moving the ball around and changing speeds. That approach paid immediate dividends upon reaching the big leagues as Spence had a 0.45 ERA in his first 23 appearances, with opponents batting a ridiculous .106/.192/.182 against him. Then hitters realized that they don't have to swing at his stuff, and he issued 13 walks in his final 17 appearances, spanning 9 2/3 innings. Spence has zero margin for error. If he can fool hitters into swinging at bad pitches, he will succeed. If not, they will wait him out and hope he makes a mistake, or they'll take the freebie.

### Tim Stauffer

Born: 6/2/1982 Age: 30
Bats: R Throws: R Height: 6' 3" Weight: 205
Breakout: 12% Improve: 47% Collapse: 26%
Attrition: 10% MLB: 94%

Comparables:
Bob Rush, Mark Gubicza, Bob Welch

| YEAR | TEAM | LVL | AGE | W | L | SV | G | GS | IP | H | HR | BB | SO | EqBB9 | EqSO9 | GB% | BABIP | WHIP | ERA | FIP | FRA | WARP |
|------|------|-----|-----|---|---|----|----|----|-----|-----|----|----|-----|-------|-------|-----|-------|------|------|------|------|------|
| 2009 | SDN | MLB | 27 | 4 | 7 | 0 | 14 | 14 | 73 | 71 | 8 | 34 | 53 | 4.2 | 6.5 | 46% | .294 | 1.44 | 3.58 | 4.63 | 5.52 | -0.3 |
| 2010 | SDN | MLB | 28 | 6 | 5 | 0 | 32 | 7 | 82² | 65 | 3 | 24 | 61 | 2.6 | 6.6 | 56% | .266 | 1.08 | 1.85 | 3.05 | 3.07 | 1.6 |
| 2011 | SDN | MLB | 29 | 9 | 12 | 0 | 31 | 31 | 185² | 180 | 20 | 53 | 128 | 2.6 | 6.2 | 54% | .289 | 1.25 | 3.73 | 4.00 | 4.54 | 1.1 |
| 2012 | SDN | MLB | 30 | 7 | 8 | 0 | 35 | 22 | 143² | 125 | 13 | 44 | 91 | 2.8 | 5.7 | 48% | .276 | 1.18 | 3.57 | 4.03 | 3.88 | 1.6 |

Stauffer, the former first-round pick who has battled through all kinds of arm problems to become a useful big-league starter, enjoyed another fine season . . . well, part of one. After his August 3 outing against the Dodgers, Stauffer owned a 2.96 ERA in 23 starts and opponents were hitting .258/.316/.376 against him with eight home runs. From that point on, in his final eight starts, he sported a 6.33 ERA with opponents batting .258/.318/.534 including 12 homers. Stauffer's demise was not surprising given his recent workloads. The last time he'd pitched more than 140 innings (which is when he began to lose effectiveness) was in 2006, on the other side of shoulder surgery. It's easy to lodge complaints after the fact, but someone should have seen this coming.

**Huston Street**
Born: 8/2/1983 Age: 28
Bats: R Throws: R Height: 6' 1" Weight: 190
Breakout: 29% Improve: 52% Collapse: 12%
Attrition: 4% MLB: 96%

| YEAR | TEAM | LVL | AGE | W | L | SV | G | GS | IP | H | HR | BB | SO | EqBB9 | EqSO9 | GB% | BABIP | WHIP | ERA | FIP | FRA | WARP |
|------|------|-----|-----|---|---|----|---|----|-----|----|----|----|----|-------|-------|-----|-------|------|------|------|------|------|
| 2009 | COL | MLB | 25 | 4 | 1 | 35 | 64 | 0 | 61² | 43 | 7 | 13 | 70 | 1.9 | 10.2 | 41% | .245 | 0.91 | 3.06 | 2.89 | 3.75 | 1.2 |
| 2010 | COL | MLB | 26 | 4 | 4 | 20 | 44 | 0 | 47¹ | 39 | 5 | 11 | 45 | 2.1 | 8.6 | 38% | .274 | 1.06 | 3.61 | 3.40 | 3.91 | 0.8 |
| 2011 | COL | MLB | 27 | 1 | 4 | 29 | 62 | 0 | 58¹ | 62 | 10 | 9 | 55 | 1.4 | 8.5 | 38% | .323 | 1.22 | 3.86 | 3.85 | 4.23 | 0.9 |
| 2012 | SDN | MLB | 28 | 3 | 1 | 24 | 55 | 0 | 54² | 42 | 5 | 13 | 52 | 2.1 | 8.6 | 41% | .280 | 1.01 | 2.61 | 3.20 | 2.84 | 1.2 |

**Joe Thatcher**
Born: 10/4/1981 Age: 30
Bats: L Throws: L Height: 6' 3" Weight: 230
Breakout: 30% Improve: 65% Collapse: 13%
Attrition: 7% MLB: 95%

**Comparables:**
Sparky Lyle, Erik Bedard, CC Sabathia

| YEAR | TEAM | LVL | AGE | W | L | SV | G | GS | IP | H | HR | BB | SO | EqBB9 | EqSO9 | GB% | BABIP | WHIP | ERA | FIP | FRA | WARP |
|------|------|-----|-----|---|---|----|----|----|-----|----|----|----|----|-------|-------|-----|-------|------|------|------|------|------|
| 2009 | SDN | MLB | 27 | 1 | 0 | 0 | 52 | 0 | 45 | 37 | 2 | 18 | 55 | 3.6 | 11.0 | 44% | .324 | 1.22 | 2.80 | 2.66 | 2.66 | 1.1 |
| 2010 | SDN | MLB | 28 | 1 | 0 | 0 | 65 | 0 | 35 | 23 | 1 | 7 | 45 | 1.8 | 11.6 | 44% | .275 | 0.86 | 1.29 | 1.59 | 3.24 | 0.5 |
| 2011 | SDN | MLB | 29 | 0 | 0 | 0 | 18 | 0 | 10 | 8 | 1 | 7 | 9 | 6.3 | 8.1 | 43% | .259 | 1.50 | 4.50 | 4.59 | 5.25 | -0.1 |
| 2012 | SDN | MLB | 30 | 1 | 1 | 0 | 27 | 0 | 16¹ | 12 | 1 | 5 | 16 | 3.0 | 8.8 | 49% | .289 | 1.09 | 2.73 | 2.96 | 2.96 | 0.3 |

After being an integral part of Bud Black's bullpen each of the previous two seasons, Thatcher developed soreness in the back of his left shoulder during spring training and required surgery in May. The sidewinding southpaw, who began 2010 on the disabled list due to a strain in the same area of his shoulder, didn't make his 2011 debut until August. When healthy, Thatcher's deceptive delivery is difficult on left-handed hitters, although he handled righties just as well in 2010. Because of his funky pitching motion, Thatcher experiences occasional lapses in control, as he did last year after returning from surgery. With the benefit of rest and a full spring training, he should regain his status as a late-inning option for the Padres.

**Edinson Volquez**
Born: 7/3/1983 Age: 28
Bats: R Throws: R Height: 6' 2" Weight: 187
Breakout: 26% Improve: 48% Collapse: 32%
Attrition: 19% MLB: 82%

**Comparables:**
Antonio Osuna, Eric Hull, Jorge Julio

| YEAR | TEAM | LVL | AGE | W | L | SV | G | GS | IP | H | HR | BB | SO | EqBB9 | EqSO9 | GB% | BABIP | WHIP | ERA | FIP | FRA | WARP |
|------|------|-----|-----|---|---|----|----|----|------|-----|----|----|-----|-------|-------|-----|-------|------|------|------|------|------|
| 2009 | CIN | MLB | 26 | 4 | 2 | 0 | 9 | 9 | 49² | 34 | 6 | 32 | 47 | 5.8 | 8.5 | 47% | .222 | 1.33 | 4.35 | 4.97 | 5.68 | 0.0 |
| 2010 | CIN | MLB | 27 | 4 | 3 | 0 | 12 | 12 | 62² | 59 | 6 | 35 | 67 | 5.0 | 9.6 | 57% | .329 | 1.50 | 4.31 | 4.03 | 4.75 | 1.0 |
| 2011 | LOU | AAA | 28 | 4 | 2 | 0 | 13 | 13 | 87¹ | 72 | 5 | 29 | 83 | 3.0 | 8.6 | 52% | .284 | 1.16 | 2.37 | 3.22 | 3.70 | 1.5 |
| 2011 | CIN | MLB | 28 | 5 | 7 | 0 | 20 | 20 | 108² | 106 | 19 | 65 | 104 | 5.4 | 8.6 | 55% | .298 | 1.57 | 5.71 | 5.26 | 5.65 | -1.0 |
| 2012 | SDN | MLB | 28 | 6 | 8 | 0 | 20 | 20 | 116¹ | 91 | 11 | 54 | 106 | 4.1 | 8.2 | 47% | .280 | 1.24 | 3.76 | 4.00 | 4.08 | 1.0 |

Part of the trade that sent Latos to Cincinnati, Volquez hasn't been the same pitcher since August 2009 Tommy John surgery (and even a little before then). After enjoying a breakout campaign a year earlier, he has made 41 starts over the past three seasons, posting a 5.01 ERA in 221 IP. Although he still puts the ball past hitters (8.9 K/9 in 2009-11), his command is lacking (1.7 K/BB). One problem in 2011 was susceptibility to the long ball (he owned the second worst HR/9 among NL pitchers with at least 100 IP), which shouldn't be an issue at spacious Petco Park. No longer the front-line starter he appeared to be blossoming into prior to surgery and a subsequent PED-related suspension, Volquez is expected to fill the more modest role previously occupied by Kevin Correia, Jon Garland, and Aaron Harang. To do that, Volquez will need to stay healthy enough to make a full season's worth of starts, something he hasn't done since 2008.

**Joseph Wieland**

Born: 1/21/1990 Age: 22
Bats: R Throws: R Height: 6' 4" Weight: 175
Breakout: 19% Improve: 46% Collapse: 33%
Attrition: 11% MLB: 92%

**Comparables:**
Zack Greinke, Manny Sarmiento, Gary Serum

| YEAR | TEAM | LVL | AGE | W | L | SV | G | GS | IP | H | HR | BB | SO | EqBB9 | EqSO9 | GB% | BABIP | WHIP | ERA | FIP | FRA | WARP |
|------|------|-----|-----|---|---|----|----|-----|-----|-----|----|----|----|-------|-------|-----|-------|------|------|------|------|------|
| 2009 | HIC | A | 19 | 4 | 6 | 0 | 19 | 18 | 83 | 102 | 7 | 24 | 73 | 2.6 | 7.9 | 48% | .356 | 1.52 | 5.31 | 3.85 | 5.02 | 0.4 |
| 2010 | HIC | A | 20 | 7 | 4 | 0 | 15 | 15 | 89 | 82 | 4 | 13 | 65 | 1.5 | 7.2 | 51% | .305 | 1.11 | 3.34 | 3.32 | 4.19 | 1.3 |
| 2010 | BAK | A+ | 20 | 4 | 3 | 0 | 11 | 10 | 59 | 47 | 5 | 9 | 52 | 1.5 | 9.5 | 41% | .323 | 1.31 | 5.19 | 3.72 | 3.83 | 0.9 |
| 2011 | MYR | A+ | 21 | 5 | 3 | 0 | 14 | 13 | 85² | 78 | 7 | 4 | 96 | 0.4 | 10.1 | 44% | .320 | 0.96 | 2.10 | 2.24 | 3.27 | 2.1 |
| 2011 | FRI | AA | 21 | 2 | 0 | 0 | 7 | 7 | 44 | 35 | 2 | 11 | 36 | 2.2 | 7.4 | 44% | .266 | 1.05 | 1.23 | 3.09 | 3.63 | 0.9 |
| 2012 | SDN | MLB | 22 | 2 | 4 | 0 | 9 | 9 | 53¹ | 52 | 6 | 18 | 32 | 3.0 | 5.4 | 43% | .297 | 1.31 | 4.42 | 4.48 | 4.80 | -0.0 |

Wieland came to San Diego in the Mike Adams deal. Like Robbie Erlin, who also was part of the package, Wieland is an obsessive strike thrower. He boasts a 5.1 K/BB in 430 1/3 career minor-league innings. His stuff isn't overpowering but he has a clean delivery and strong command of a low-90s fastball, backed up by a plus curveball. His changeup remains a work in progress. Wieland is yet another fly-ball pitcher, which could be problematic in Tucson but which ultimately won't keep him from settling in at the back of the Padres rotation sometime in 2013.

## LINEOUTS

### HITTERS

| PLAYER | TEAM | LVL | AGE | PA | R | 2B | 3B | HR | RBI | BB | SO | SB-CS | AVG/OBP/SLG | TAv | BABIP | BRR | FRAA | WARP |
|--------|------|-----|-----|-----|----|----|----|----|-----|----|-----|-------|-------------|-----|-------|-----|------|------|
| C J. Baker | FLO | MLB | 30 | 16 | 0 | 0 | 0 | 0 | 1 | 2 | 3 | 0-0 | .154/.267/.154 | .174 | .200 | 0 | 0 | -0.1 |
| SS E. Cabrera | SDN | MLB | 24 | 9 | 1 | 0 | 0 | 0 | 0 | 1 | 3 | 2-0 | .125/.222/.125 | .312 | .200 | 0.2 | 0 | 0.1 |
| LF L. Domoromo | FTW | A | 19 | 486 | 66 | 20 | 3 | 9 | 68 | 36 | 83 | 7-7 | .283/.335/.405 | .261 | .322 | 0.3 | -3.6 | 0.8 |
| 2B J. Galvez | LEL | A+ | 20 | 545 | 84 | 36 | 5 | 13 | 86 | 41 | 123 | 37-9 | .291/.355/.465 | .296 | .361 | -1.1 | -1 | 3.6 |
| C J. Hagerty | LEL | A+ | 23 | 293 | 53 | 25 | 2 | 8 | 47 | 26 | 62 | 3-2 | .311/.386/.518 | .327 | .379 | -0.8 | 0.2 | 3.1 |
| | SAN | AA | 23 | 150 | 15 | 6 | 1 | 1 | 18 | 14 | 40 | 0-1 | .231/.318/.315 | .219 | .322 | 0.8 | -0.5 | 0.1 |
| 2B E. Patterson | SDN | MLB | 28 | 103 | 8 | 2 | 1 | 2 | 8 | 12 | 22 | 8-2 | .180/.272/.292 | .227 | .209 | -0.1 | 0.1 | -0.1 |
| C K. Phillips | SAN | AA | 27 | 82 | 10 | 4 | 0 | 2 | 15 | 4 | 1 | 0-0 | .316/.341/.447 | .287 | .293 | -0.3 | 0.2 | 0.6 |
| | SDN | MLB | 27 | 85 | 9 | 3 | 0 | 2 | 10 | 8 | 19 | 0-0 | .171/.259/.289 | .198 | .200 | 1.8 | -0.2 | -0.1 |
| 3B E. Rincon | LEL | A+ | 20 | 340 | 54 | 24 | 1 | 8 | 50 | 32 | 59 | 1-1 | .329/.394/.497 | .321 | .380 | -1.8 | -2.9 | 3.0 |
| CF D. Tate | EUG | A- | 20 | 155 | 24 | 8 | 4 | 0 | 20 | 25 | 32 | 17-5 | .283/.406/.409 | .291 | .375 | 1.2 | 0 | 1.0 |

**John Baker** began 2010 as the Marlins' starting catcher, but elbow soreness landed him on the disabled list in early May. After rehabilitation failed to ease the discomfort, he underwent offseason Tommy John surgery and spent the majority of 2011 on the 60-day DL. With John Buck signed through 2013, the Marlins shipped Baker to San Diego in exchange for left-handed starter Wade LeBlanc. ⊘ **Everth Cabrera** jumped from Low-A ball after being taken from Colorado in the 2008 Rule 5 draft and showed initial flashes of Rafael Furcal brilliance but since has slipped to the brink of Mike Caruso obscurity. ⊘ One of the players signed in San Diego's big 2008 international push, **Luis Domoromo** made his full-season debut and posted decent numbers in the Midwest League at age 19, although he did little damage after June. ⊘ While shifting from shortstop to second base, the free-swinging **Jonathan Galvez** displayed a blend of power and speed as one of the California League's youngest everyday players. ⊘ A switch-hitting catcher with dubious defensive skills, **Jason Hagerty** did some damage at Lake Elsinore but struggled on moving to the more age-appropriate Double-A level. He looks suspiciously like the new Mitch Canham. ⊘ Like his older brother Corey, **Eric Patterson** is fast but short on usable baseball skills. ⊘ **Kyle Phillips** is a poor man's Robert Fick, a left-handed batter who can drive the ball once in a while but who is miscast as a catcher. ⊘ **Edinson Rincon** is a right-handed hitter with power potential who is a complete disaster at third base and who missed two months in 2011 due to a left wrist injury before returning in September. ⊘ Taken with the third pick overall in 2009 (after Stephen Strasburg and Dustin Ackley), toolsy center fielder **Donavan Tate** continues to frustrate with his inability to stay healthy and, most recently, was suspended for 50 games due to a positive recreational drug test.

## PITCHERS

| PLAYER | TEAM | LVL | AGE | W | L | SV | IP | H | HR | BB | SO | EqBB9 | EqSO9 | GB% | BABIP | WHIP | ERA | FIP | FRA | WARP |
|--------|------|-----|-----|---|---|----|-----|-----|-----|-----|-----|-------|-------|-----|-------|------|-----|-----|-----|------|
| J. Barbato | EUG | A- | 18 | 1 | 3 | 0 | 57 | 52 | 4 | 31 | 50 | 4.9 | 7.9 | 48% | .293 | 1.46 | 4.89 | 4.65 | 5.12 | 0.2 |
| C. Burns | AKR | AA | 23 | 1 | 3 | 35 | 59² | 46 | 3 | 15 | 67 | 2.3 | 10.6 | 48% | .305 | 1.04 | 2.11 | 2.58 | 3.70 | 1.0 |
| Z. Cates | FTW | A | 21 | 0 | 6 | 0 | 118 | 109 | 4 | 58 | 115 | 4.0 | 8.5 | 47% | .310 | 1.36 | 4.73 | 3.45 | 4.20 | 2.0 |
| E. Hamren | SAN | AA | 24 | 2 | 0 | 0 | 49 | 34 | 0 | 12 | 48 | 2.2 | 8.8 | 66% | .279 | 0.94 | 0.92 | 2.52 | 3.56 | 1.0 |
|  | SDN | MLB | 24 | 1 | 0 | 0 | 12¹ | 10 | 2 | 9 | 10 | 6.6 | 7.3 | 32% | .267 | 1.54 | 4.38 | 6.16 | 7.68 | -0.4 |
| C. Hebner | EUG | A- | 20 | 3 | 2 | 0 | 37² | 30 | 1 | 17 | 45 | 3.6 | 9.3 | 55% | .266 | 1.14 | 3.35 | 2.91 | 3.16 | 0.9 |
| M. Lollis | LEL | A+ | 20 | 4 | 8 | 1 | 119¹ | 134 | 11 | 44 | 111 | 3.4 | 8.6 | 47% | .350 | 1.51 | 5.35 | 4.70 | 5.38 | 0.2 |
| P. Neshek | SDN | MLB | 30 | 1 | 1 | 0 | 24² | 19 | 4 | 22 | 20 | 8.0 | 7.3 | 30% | .234 | 1.66 | 4.01 | 6.28 | 6.69 | -0.6 |
| J. Oramas | SAN | AA | 21 | 5 | 1 | 0 | 104² | 105 | 11 | 30 | 108 | 2.4 | 8.8 | 37% | .311 | 1.21 | 3.10 | 3.66 | 3.94 | 2.2 |
| M. Palmer | SLC | AAA | 32 | 6 | 5 | 0 | 137 | 170 | 14 | 65 | 109 | 4.3 | 7.2 | 56% | .363 | 1.72 | 6.44 | 5.25 | 6.52 | -0.3 |

ated an 11.5 K/9 and 5.4 K/BB in 130 career minor-league relief appearances. With multiple openings in San Diego, the former eighth-round pick out of the University of Arizona could find himself in the late-inning mix with the big club sooner rather than later. ⊘ Right-hander **Zach Cates**, a third-round pick in 2010, throws hard but was erratic in his professional debut at Fort Wayne. ⊘ **Erik Hamren**, signed as a minor-league free agent, tore through High-A and Double-A before stumbling in a brief trial with the big club. He is the 11th or 12th man on a staff at best. ⊘ Diminutive right-hander **Cody Hebner**, taken in the fourth round of the 2011 draft, features a low-90s fastball and draws praise for his athleticism. ⊘ **Matt Lollis**, a 6'9" right-hander taken in the 15th round of the 2009 draft generated some buzz in spring training but his power arsenal didn't translate into results at Lake Elsinore. ⊘ The Padres signed **Pat Neshek** to a minor-league contract in the hope that he might be ready to contribute following a slow road back from 2008 Tommy John surgery. Poor velocity and poor command conspired to dash those hopes, and he was released after the season. ⊘ **Juan Oramas** is a short, squat left-hander whose advanced feel for pitching and good command allow him to rack up strikeouts despite a lack of overpowering stuff. ⊘ **Matt Palmer**, an older, less accomplished version of Dustin Moseley, enjoyed marginal success with the Angels in 2009 but served primarily as a Triple-A insurance policy over the past two seasons, a role he will continue to fill for the Padres in 2012. ⊘ Signed in 2008 out of Venezuela, **Adys Portillo** is a lithe right-hander whose stuff is ahead of his command. He throws hard (mid-90s), but his secondary pitches need work. Don't expect him in San Diego soon. ⊘ Originally signed by the Padres in 2002, **Dale Thayer** has gotten brief cups of coffee in each of the past three seasons with the Rays and Mets. Back with his original organization, the strike-throwing right-hander resumes his quest for 200 minor-league saves.

# MANAGER: BUD BLACK

| YEAR | TEAM | W-L | Pythag +/- | Avg PC | 100+ P | 120+ P | QS | BQS | REL | REL w Zero R | IBB | Subs | PH | PH Avg | PH HR | SB2 | CS2 | SB3 | CS3 | SAC Att | SAC % | POS SAC | Squeeze | Swing | In Play |
|------|------|-----|-----------|--------|--------|--------|-----|-----|-----|--------------|-----|------|-----|--------|-------|-----|-----|-----|-----|---------|-------|---------|---------|-------|---------|
| 2009 | SDN | 75-87 | 0 | 91.0 | 47 | 1 | 73 | 5 | 527 | 349 | 58 | 43 | 263 | .248 | 9 | 10 | 5 | 0 | 1 | 116 | 63.8% | 38 | 2 | 123 | 90 |
| 2010 | SDN | 90-72 | 1 | 189.6 | 162 | 160 | 116 | 2 | 499 | 431 | 102 | — | 556 | .206 | 18 | 10 | 1 | 0 | 2 | 222 | 80.2% | 108 | 2 | 359 | 97 |
| 2011 | SDN | 71-91 | 0 | 96.7 | 65 | 1 | 91 | 4 | 489 | 416 | 56 | — | 283 | .160 | 2 | 21 | 2 | 2 | 0 | 86 | 72.1% | 30 | 4 | 391 | 88 |

Bud Black is a methodical, process-oriented manager who will not be rushed in anything. Black attended San Diego State and understands the Southern California culture. His laid-back personality makes him a natural fit for the Padres. One of Black's strengths is his ability to listen and discuss. Watching him  argue with umpires is fascinating. There are no histrionics; he just strolls out of the dugout and chats with them as one might chat with old friends over tea and miniature cucumber sandwiches. He shows similar patience working with young players, whether it be sticking with Kevin Kouzmanoff through his early-season struggles in 2007, or giving Cameron Maybin a full complement of plate appearances despite periodic slumps. Black even kept running Anthony Rizzo out to first base long after it had become evident that more minor-league seasoning was needed, which is a downside of such patience. As a former pitching coach, Black is attuned to the needs of his moundsmen and tends to have a quick hook with his starters. Like most managers of his era, Black's usage of relievers borders on mechanical, and he seldom deviates from the established order of things. Pitchers are given a defined role and left there, although he has adopted the Earl Weaver strategy of breaking in young arms out of the bullpen, with Tim Stauffer, Cory Luebke, and Anthony Bass being three recent examples. Black's lineup construction sometimes lacks imagination; then again with the options at his disposal in 2011, all the imagination in the world wouldn't have helped.

# San Francisco Giants

On July 28, Tim Lincecum pitched six shutout innings, Pablo Sandoval homered, the Giants took the deciding game in a three-game series against the Phillies in Philadelphia, and the Diamondbacks lost to San Diego. At the end of that day, the Giants were four games ahead of Arizona and, by our odds, 97.9 percent

| | | |
|---|---|---|
| TAv | .243 | 28th |
| TAv-P | .242 | 28th |
| FIP | 3.30 | 2nd |
| DER | .717 | 6th |
| DL | 903 | 25th |
| B-Age | 30.2 | 28th |
| P-Age | 28.2 | 17th |
| Salary | $118.2 | 8th |
| M$/MW | $2.81 | 17th |

**2011:** Defending champs contend with good pitching, but can't score enough runs

**2012:** Ex-champs contend with good pitching, but can they score enough runs?

**Action Items:** A right fielder and shortstop, and Belt, Posey, and Panda to make their projections

had lost that game against the Phillies in particularly heartbreaking fashion, or if Lincecum had left the game with a sprained ligament in his elbow, we would identify July 28 as a turning point, and our narrative would write itself. But what actually happened on July 28 was the Giants traded for Carlos Beltran, vastly improving a team that was prepared to defend its title in October. Narratives don't always write themselves.

Over the past three decades, teams that were defending a World Series title have slightly underperformed the teams they defeated. It's not a big difference—on average, the World Series losers claim about an extra win and a half the following season—but the 2011 Giants show the trap of success.

**Agent:** Come on, Brian. My guy wants to play for a winner. He'll take a discount. He's really good, way better than Aubrey Huff.

**Brian Sabean:** {ponders}

**Brian Sabean:** {distracted by something shiny}

**Brian Sabean:** {sees big ol' ring on his finger}

**Brian Sabean:** Nice try! But Huff is a Proven Winner.

Sabean brought back 23 of the 25 players on the Giants' World Series roster. By contrast, the World-Series-losing Rangers went into the offseason looking to improve; they turned over six roster spots and added Adrian Beltre and Mike Napoli. Juan Uribe bolted for a three-year deal with the Dodgers, and Sabean replaced him with the most similar player available, Miguel Tejada. Edgar Renteria, calling the Giants' $1 million contract offer "total disrespect," signed for $2 million in Cincinnati, and a temporarily healthy Mark DeRosa took his spot.

getting costly in arbitration. If any team should have been wary of Sanchez repeating his season, considering he has never been able to repeat even his delivery, it was the long-suffering co-dependents to his performance swings. Sanchez battled injuries and wildness in 2011 and Sabean traded him, a year late, at his lowest value.

2. Re-signing Aubrey Huff for two years, $22 million. Huff's oscillations made him either a bargain or an albatross, nothing in between; Sabean went all in on the hope he would repeat, at age 34, his career-best season. The move not only partially blocked his best prospect, Brandon Belt, but absorbed most of Sabean's walking-around money for the 2011 offseason.

3. Signing Tejada to replicate Uribe's season. Counting on a replacement-level 34-year-old shortstop was particularly dangerous considering the Giants' lack of depth at the position. For the second time in four years, Sabean was forced to call up a shortstop from High-A as an emergency measure; the Crawford Protocol wasn't much more successful than the Bocock Fail-Safe had been.

All three of these moves have a theme: Sabean didn't upgrade the offense. True, he had proven that a team could win a World Series with a lousy lineup. But a smart warrior doesn't learn just from his mistakes; he also learns from his successes, and it is notable that the 2010 Giants had won because they got better-than-expected offense. They entered 2011 a year older at every position and due for regression.

Regression, man. Regression is just so reliable. The 2011 Giants finished last in the National League in runs, nearly one per game lower than 2010. Only one San Francisco squad—the 100-loss 1985 team—has ever scored fewer. Their shortstops hit .210/.265/.299, by far the worst line in the National League. Their center fielders hit .228/.299/.347, league worst. Their first basemen ranked 13th in the league in OPS, as did their left fielders. Their catchers, with a cumulative line of .224/.298/.330, were 15th.

Ah, yes, the catchers. At this stage, we must remember that Brian Sabean built a team that was, in the second half of the season, 98 percent likely to make the postseason, a team that could easily have won a second consecutive World Series and changed the text of this chapter into 2,000 words of frothing. We must remember there are segments of this team that reflect a bit of brilliant team building. Sure, some of the 2011 Giants' doom is on Sabean, but an awful lot of it was nothing but bad luck. On May 25, bad luck tagged up at third base, raced home on a fly ball to shallow right-center field, and smashed into Buster Posey.

This, of course, is the point when—in a rational sport—the Giants' season would have pivoted to disaster. It was a brutal loss, in a narrow sense—the Scott Cousins-Buster Posey collision meant a 12th-inning defeat, nullifying the Giants' four-run comeback in the ninth inning—and, obviously, in the broader picture. Posey's arrival in 2010 had been logged by history as the catalyst for the team's World Series run, and now, a year to the week later, he had been stolen from them. Few teams were less prepared for the loss of any one player. Posey was at the top of a terribly shallow depth chart at the position; Eli Whiteside and Chris Stewart are the 150th and 184th best-hitting catchers alive, if you believe our PECOTA projections. And he was the cleanup hitter on a team that would be forced to count on Huff, Nate Schierholtz, and Cody Ross, among others, in that spot.

Would the Giants have won the World Series if Cousins had tried a hook slide? Who knows, really. Maybe a healthy Buster Posey would have torn a knee ligament running out a double the next day. Maybe he would have slumped. Maybe a single flap of Buster's wings would have caused famine in China and led to a shortage of rice flour, ruining Dim Sum throughout San Francisco's Chinatown. But if we average the three most common measures of player value, we find that Posey was worth 1.3 wins over the first two months, perfectly consistent with PECOTA's projected value for him. If he'd been 2.6 wins better than replacement the rest of the way—well, it still wouldn't have closed the four-game gap between the Giants and the wild card-winning Cardinals. But you never know.

It wasn't just Posey. Back in August, Grant Brisbee of *McCovey Chronicles* tweeted: "Posey/Burrell/Sanchez/Keppinger/Schierholtz/Torres/Beltran would be a sweet start to a lineup." That sweet start to a lineup was the list of Giants who were injured, not at some point in the season but on that very day. This was a team that was so beaten down by injuries in the second half that it traded for Orlando Cabrera—and let him lead off. A team so unfortunate that it let Aaron Rowand play 108 games, even as it prepared to designate him (and the final year and a half of his contract) for assignment. There were games in the second half when Tejada was batting fifth, games when DeRosa was batting cleanup. Surely, these things couldn't have been anticipated.

And Sabean deserves credit for very nearly surviving them. Yes, Sabean gets all the obvious moves wrong—when he signs expensive veterans, they're not just overpaid, but downright unrosterable. Rowand, Huff, DeRosa, Tejada, and Barry Zito earned $53 million in 2011; they produced a combined 1.0 WARP. Oh, Sabes. You're the worst! But bad free-agent signings happen to almost every team, and it's often the GMs who compensate in other areas who are praised. Sabean does two things brilliantly.

1. Brian Sabean finds free talent. Here's the headline in the San Jose *Mercury News* on January 14, the day the Giants signed Ryan Vogelsong: "Giants extend non-roster invitations to 22 players for Spring Training." Can't you just feel the impact of the move in every letter of that announcement? Vogelsong was an All-Star for the Giants this year. The Andres Torres invitation in 2009 didn't even get a headline, yet adding Torres turned out to be one of the best moves any GM has made in the past three years, producing 7.2 WARP for a few bucks more than the major-league minimum. Pat Burrell, picked up as a waiver claim, gave the Giants a 127 OPS+ in 560 plate appearances over two seasons. Santiago Casilla, signed for the minimum, has the third-best ERA in baseball in two years with the Giants. Even Huff, before becoming dead weight, was a spectacular success, found before 2010 for just $3 million.

2. Brian Sabean makes the most of his first-round picks. Since 2002, Sabean has had a remarkable run of success with his top picks. That year, it was Matt Cain. In 2003, he took David Aardsma first. He forfeited his top picks to sign free agents in 2004 and 2005, then took Lincecum first in 2006, Madison Bumgarner in 2007, and Posey in 2008. In 2009 he drafted Zack Wheeler, swapped for Beltran in the aggressive 2011 playoff push. And in 2010 he got Gary Brown, whose breakout in 2011 puts him on track to take over center field in 2013.

This is what we hope general managers do: draft and develop high-upside talent, build young and cost-controlled cores, scour the junk heaps for free talent, and turn to trades and free agency only to fill in the final holes on competitive teams.

Four Giants starters ranked in the National League's top 10 ERAs. The Giants bullpen had the second-best ERA in the league, a hundredth of a run worse than the Braves. They should get full seasons from Posey and Belt in 2012 without losing a single significant part of a team that was 98 percent likely to make the playoffs in late July. They also have Zito, Huff and the ghost of Rowand adding a thousand-dollar surcharge to every transaction. Their future is bright; their future is doomed. Such is baseball—conflicting narratives that produce just one outcome. In 2009, that outcome was failure. In 2010, it was a parade. In 2011, failure. Yet the Giants' win totals never fluctuated by more than six wins in that period, and they're likely to win between 86 and 92 once more in 2012.

# HITTERS

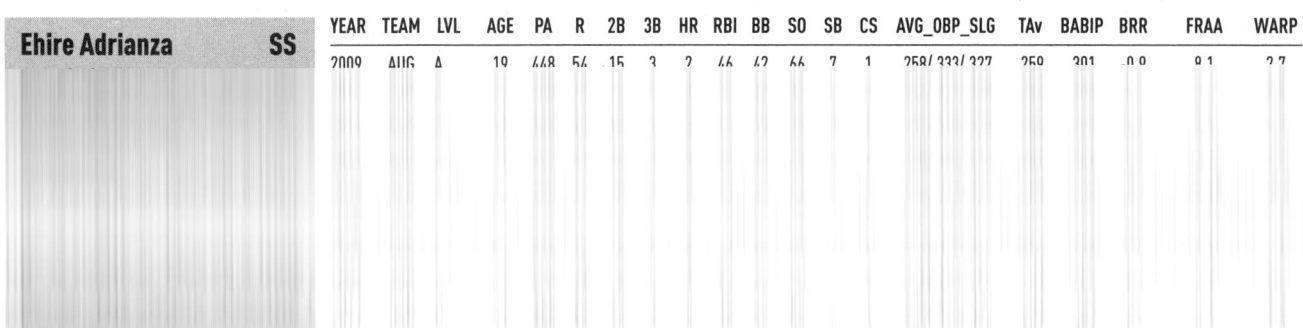

| YEAR | TEAM | LVL | AGE | PA | R | 2B | 3B | HR | RBI | BB | SO | SB | CS | AVG/OBP/SLG | TAv | BABIP | BRR | FRAA | WARP |
|------|------|-----|-----|-----|-----|-----|-----|-----|-----|-----|-----|-----|-----|-------------|-----|-------|-----|------|------|
| 2009 | AUG | A | 19 | 448 | 54 | 15 | 3 | 2 | 46 | 42 | 66 | 7 | 1 | .258/.333/.327 | .259 | .301 | -0.0 | 9.1 | 2.7 |

**Ehire Adrianza**   SS

walks, he hits line drives, and as his thin frame began to fill out in 2011, he added a dash of power. Still it was a lost year of development which likely costs him a shot at cracking the Giants' weak depth chart in 2012.

**Brandon Belt**   1B
Born: 4/20/1988 Age: 24
Bats: L Throws: L Height: 6' 6" Weight: 220
Breakout: 4% Improve: 39% Collapse: 2%
Attrition: 18% MLB: 77%

Comparables:
Al Ferrara, Boog Powell, Barry Bonds

| YEAR | TEAM | LVL | AGE | PA | R | 2B | 3B | HR | RBI | BB | SO | SB | CS | AVG/OBP/SLG | TAv | BABIP | BRR | FRAA | WARP |
|------|------|-----|-----|-----|-----|-----|-----|-----|-----|-----|-----|-----|-----|-------------|-----|-------|-----|------|------|
| 2010 | SJO | A+ | 22 | 333 | 62 | 28 | 4 | 10 | 62 | 58 | 50 | 18 | 7 | .383/.497/.628 | .387 | .445 | -2.1 | 4.2 | 5.3 |
| 2010 | RIC | AA | 22 | 201 | 26 | 11 | 6 | 9 | 40 | 22 | 34 | 2 | 1 | .337/.417/.623 | .367 | .379 | -1.8 | 1.6 | 2.3 |
| 2010 | FRE | AAA | 22 | 61 | 11 | 4 | 0 | 4 | 10 | 13 | 15 | 2 | 0 | .229/.393/.562 | .319 | .241 | -0.7 | -0.5 | 0.4 |
| 2011 | FRE | AAA | 23 | 212 | 32 | 12 | 0 | 8 | 32 | 42 | 47 | 4 | 4 | .309/.448/.527 | .326 | .381 | 0.8 | -0.1 | 2.0 |
| 2011 | SFN | MLB | 23 | 209 | 21 | 6 | 1 | 9 | 18 | 20 | 57 | 3 | 2 | .225/.306/.412 | .260 | .273 | 0.1 | 0.2 | 0.4 |
| 2012 | SFN | MLB | 24 | 259 | 32 | 11 | 1 | 8 | 29 | 32 | 62 | 5 | 2 | .248/.345/.417 | .281 | .306 | -0.3 | 1B -5, LF -1 | 1.8 |

Prospects fail because their skills fail, not because of how they were handled. That said: Free Brandon Belt! The Giants seemed to think every small major league sample was the final word on Belt, who had the third-best OBP in the Pacific Coast League, though he didn't have enough PAs to qualify for the title. After a strong spring, he broke camp as the starting first baseman; after 13 games, he lost the starting job, and a week later was sent back to Fresno. In all, he would spend four different stretches in the majors. Does this matter to his development? It might. In his first stint in the majors, he swung at 42 percent of pitches. In his second, he swung at 50 percent. The same trend shows up in his Fresno numbers, as he swung at 35 percent of pitches in 2010, before the shuttle began, and 40 percent in 2011. It's understandable that a young player, eager to impress, would swing more, but Belt's control of the strike zone was part of what made him so exceptional.

**Gary Brown**   CF
Born: 9/28/1988 Age: 23
Bats: R Throws: R Height: 6' 1" Weight: 170
Breakout: 4% Improve: 27% Collapse: 8%
Attrition: 21% MLB: 67%

Comparables:
Miguel Dilone, Paul Blair, Jim Qualls

| YEAR | TEAM | LVL | AGE | PA | R | 2B | 3B | HR | RBI | BB | SO | SB | CS | AVG/OBP/SLG | TAv | BABIP | BRR | FRAA | WARP |
|------|------|-----|-----|-----|-----|-----|-----|-----|-----|-----|-----|-----|-----|-------------|-----|-------|-----|------|------|
| 2011 | SJO | A+ | 22 | 638 | 115 | 34 | 13 | 14 | 80 | 46 | 77 | 53 | 19 | .336/.407/.519 | .332 | .369 | 4.1 | -0.5 | 8.0 |
| 2012 | SFN | MLB | 23 | 250 | 25 | 11 | 2 | 2 | 22 | 11 | 43 | 13 | 5 | .245/.292/.337 | .237 | .287 | -0.3 | CF -6 | 0.2 |

Brown was coming back from a broken hand in 2010, when he hit .159 in his pro debut. Healthy in 2011, he torched the California League and quieted concerns about his non-stathead-approved plate approach by drawing 46 walks—five more than he took in his entire college career. He's as fast as anybody in the minors, but no one-tool sensation, with everything but his arm projecting as above average. The walk rate slowed as the season progressed, and his stolen base success rate—hampered, reportedly, by a hitch in his sliding technique—is a pale reflection of his speed. Still, it was surprising that the Giants didn't promote him to Double-A in the second half, and he's now unlikely to make the majors until late 2012. He spent the Arizona Fall League in the same outfield as Bryce Harper and Mike Trout. Brown is a tier below those two, but a tier ahead of most of his 2010 draft contemporaries.

### Emmanuel Burriss    2B

Born: 1/17/1985 Age: 27
Bats: B Throws: R Height: 6' 1" Weight: 190
Breakout: 6% Improve: 41% Collapse: 6%
Attrition: 13% MLB: 80%

Comparables:
Steve Sax, Rey Sanchez, Juan Bonilla

| YEAR | TEAM | LVL | AGE | PA | R | 2B | 3B | HR | RBI | BB | SO | SB | CS | AVG_OBP_SLG | TAv | BABIP | BRR | FRAA | WARP |
|------|------|-----|-----|-----|----|----|----|----|-----|----|----|----|----|-------------|------|-------|------|------------|------|
| 2009 | FRE | AAA | 24 | 77 | 9 | 2 | 1 | 1 | 7 | 3 | 4 | 6 | 2 | .268/.316/.366 | .222 | .273 | 0.3 | 0.7 | 0.0 |
| 2009 | SFN | MLB | 24 | 220 | 18 | 6 | 0 | 0 | 13 | 14 | 34 | 11 | 4 | .238/.292/.267 | .208 | .284 | 2.1 | -2.4 | -0.7 |
| 2010 | FRE | AAA | 25 | 305 | 32 | 11 | 2 | 0 | 22 | 19 | 29 | 11 | 5 | .282/.326/.337 | .236 | .304 | 1 | -1.9 | 0.2 |
| 2011 | FRE | AAA | 26 | 206 | 31 | 8 | 1 | 2 | 10 | 22 | 19 | 24 | 5 | .297/.386/.389 | .268 | .323 | 2.4 | -3.2 | 0.8 |
| 2011 | SFN | MLB | 26 | 152 | 14 | 1 | 0 | 0 | 4 | 6 | 17 | 11 | 3 | .204/.253/.212 | .196 | .233 | 0.6 | 1 | -0.6 |
| 2012 | SFN | MLB | 27 | 250 | 24 | 8 | 1 | 1 | 17 | 16 | 33 | 14 | 5 | .244/.301/.297 | .228 | .276 | -0.2 | 2B -2, SS -1 | 0.1 |

Between Fresno and San Francisco, Burriss played seven positions in 2011 as the Giants scrambled for injury replacements and Burriss scrambled for a chance to be something more than a pinch-runner. Burriss switch-hits, rarely strikes out, has good speed, and learned to take ball four while he was in Fresno this year, which, in theory, puts him about 10 home runs shy of being a perfect super-utility player. Alas, those 10 home runs aren't coming. He hasn't hit a ball over an outfielder's head in the majors since May 2009.

### Orlando Cabrera    SS

Born: 11/2/1974 Age: 37
Bats: R Throws: R Height: 6' 0" Weight: 165
Breakout: 0% Improve: 22% Collapse: 5%
Attrition: 32% MLB: 64%

Comparables:
Keith Lockhart, Tony Fernandez, Cookie Rojas

| YEAR | TEAM | LVL | AGE | PA | R | 2B | 3B | HR | RBI | BB | SO | SB | CS | AVG_OBP_SLG | TAv | BABIP | BRR | FRAA | WARP |
|------|------|-----|-----|-----|----|----|----|----|-----|----|----|----|----|-------------|------|-------|------|------------|------|
| 2009 | MIN | MLB | 34 | 260 | 42 | 13 | 3 | 5 | 36 | 11 | 32 | 2 | 0 | .289/.313/.430 | .258 | .308 | 3.6 | -0.4 | 1.1 |
| 2009 | OAK | MLB | 34 | 448 | 41 | 23 | 0 | 4 | 41 | 25 | 39 | 11 | 4 | .280/.318/.365 | .244 | .299 | 1.7 | -9.8 | 0.1 |
| 2010 | CIN | MLB | 35 | 537 | 64 | 33 | 0 | 4 | 42 | 28 | 53 | 11 | 4 | .263/.303/.354 | .235 | .284 | 1.2 | -6.5 | 0.2 |
| 2011 | CLE | MLB | 36 | 344 | 35 | 13 | 0 | 4 | 38 | 13 | 40 | 6 | 2 | .244/.277/.321 | .215 | .265 | -0.7 | -1 | -1.0 |
| 2011 | SFN | MLB | 36 | 133 | 4 | 3 | 0 | 1 | 13 | 4 | 17 | 2 | 2 | .222/.241/.270 | .208 | .243 | -0.1 | 0.8 | 0.0 |
| 2012 | SFN | MLB | 37 | 460 | 45 | 21 | 1 | 3 | 38 | 25 | 56 | 11 | 4 | .251/.293/.322 | .234 | .279 | -0.3 | SS -3, 2B -0 | 0.5 |

Signs that a player is nearing the end: career-low walk rate, career-high strikeout rate, career-low isolated power, nearly career-low BABIP, career-low WARP, career-low on-base and slugging percentages, career-low stolen bases, negative defensive value by the major advanced metrics, and, most significantly, career-high interest by Brian Sabean, who has been known to overestimate the dead and dying from time to time.

### Melky Cabrera    CF

Born: 8/11/1984 Age: 27
Bats: B Throws: L Height: 6' 0" Weight: 170
Breakout: 5% Improve: 41% Collapse: 4%
Attrition: 23% MLB: 83%

Comparables:
Mark Kotsay, Curt Flood, Angel Bravo

| YEAR | TEAM | LVL | AGE | PA | R | 2B | 3B | HR | RBI | BB | SO | SB | CS | AVG_OBP_SLG | TAv | BABIP | BRR | FRAA | WARP |
|------|------|-----|-----|-----|-----|----|----|----|-----|----|----|----|----|-------------|------|-------|------|------------|------|
| 2009 | NYA | MLB | 24 | 540 | 66 | 28 | 1 | 13 | 68 | 43 | 59 | 10 | 2 | .274/.336/.416 | .259 | .288 | 0.1 | -2 | 1.1 |
| 2010 | ATL | MLB | 25 | 509 | 50 | 27 | 3 | 4 | 42 | 42 | 64 | 7 | 1 | .255/.317/.354 | .241 | .288 | -2.4 | -2.8 | -0.2 |
| 2011 | KCA | MLB | 26 | 706 | 102 | 44 | 5 | 18 | 87 | 35 | 94 | 20 | 10 | .305/.339/.470 | .287 | .332 | 4.2 | -18 | 2.7 |
| 2012 | SFN | MLB | 27 | 624 | 71 | 29 | 4 | 10 | 64 | 44 | 80 | 13 | 5 | .271/.324/.388 | .264 | .296 | -0.5 | CF -5, LF -1 | 2.0 |

Cabrera's 2011 was a renaissance after he'd been cast adrift by the Braves. The Royals, desperately retooling their outfield, signed a slimmed-down Melky, who produced career bests in slugging, TAv, and WARP. Not a bad piece of business by Dayton Moore. Cabrera's batted ball rates were in line with his career output and his walk rate bottomed out at 5 percent, meaning his improvement was the byproduct of an increase in BABIP. Owning a career .290 BABIP entering 2011, he finished at a career best .332. He's miscast as a center fielder, lacking the range to patrol that much ground. Whether the Giants ever intended to let him cover their massive center-field gaps is academic; the trade of Andres Torres for Angel Pagan shifts Cabrera to a corner, where he belongs.

### Justin Christian    LF

Born: 4/3/1980 Age: 32
Bats: R Throws: R Height: 6' 2" Weight: 190
Breakout: 5% Improve: 29% Collapse: 7%
Attrition: 37% MLB: 85%

Comparables:
Ted Uhlaender, Manny Mota, Scott Podsednik

| YEAR | TEAM | LVL | AGE | PA | R | 2B | 3B | HR | RBI | BB | SO | SB | CS | AVG_OBP_SLG | TAv | BABIP | BRR | FRAA | WARP |
|------|------|-----|-----|-----|----|----|----|----|----|-----|----|----|----|----|-------------|------|-------|------|-----------|------|
| 2009 | NOR | AAA | 29 | 386 | 54 | 18 | 5 | 3 | 25 | 20 | 51 | 26 | 3 | .270/.308/.374 | .239 | .303 | 2.8 | 7.2 | 1.2 |
| 2010 | TRN | AA | 30 | 394 | 65 | 21 | 6 | 9 | 51 | 40 | 47 | 20 | 5 | .297/.378/.472 | .305 | .323 | 2.2 | 5.3 | 3.3 |
| 2010 | SWB | AAA | 30 | 74 | 9 | 0 | 0 | 0 | 4 | 8 | 9 | 2 | 0 | .242/.324/.242 | .250 | .281 | -0.5 | 0.3 | 0.2 |
| 2011 | RIC | AA | 31 | 309 | 46 | 12 | 2 | 4 | 32 | 23 | 31 | 18 | 2 | .256/.328/.359 | .259 | .275 | 5.5 | 2.6 | 1.3 |
| 2011 | FRE | AAA | 31 | 280 | 57 | 20 | 3 | 10 | 41 | 35 | 31 | 36 | 3 | .338/.428/.574 | .341 | .354 | 3.4 | 0.6 | 3.4 |
| 2011 | SFN | MLB | 31 | 51 | 6 | 5 | 0 | 0 | 4 | 2 | 8 | 3 | 2 | .255/.286/.362 | .265 | .308 | 0.4 | -0.4 | 0.1 |
| 2012 | SFN | MLB | 32 | 250 | 26 | 12 | 1 | 3 | 22 | 16 | 39 | 16 | 6 | .245/.300/.345 | .242 | .280 | 1 | LF 1, CF 0 | 0.3 |

Christian was a two-sport athlete in high school, but he chose baseball over football for its longevity—less likely to get hurt, he figured. Oh, irony, you're a cad. Christian has been hurt constantly—six surgeries and counting—but he's still going a decade and a half later, catching the Giants' attention with a strong performance in the Mexican Winter League in 2010. Even at 31, he struggled against Double-A pitching before taking off in the Pacific Coast League's generous air. That earned a September call-up for the Bay Area native. This is as famous as he's likely to get, but he is a remarkably efficient basestealer: After swiping 54 bags in 59 tries in 2011, he now has an 87 percent success rate in nine minor league seasons.

**Brandon Crawford** SS
Born: 1/21/1987 Age: 25
Bats: L Throws: R Height: 6' 3" Weight: 215
Breakout: 4% Improve: 38% Collapse: 9%
Attrition: 35% MLB: 81%
Comparables:
Brent Lillibridge, Tim Naehring, Jim Fregosi

| YEAR | TEAM | LVL | AGE | PA | R | 2B | 3B | HR | RBI | BB | SO | SB | CS | AVG_OBP_SLG | TAv | BABIP | BRR | FRAA | WARP |
|------|------|-----|-----|-----|----|----|----|----|-----|----|-----|----|----|----------------|------|-------|------|----------|------|
| 2009 | SJO | A+ | 22 | 119 | 21 | 2 | 2 | 6 | 17 | 10 | 32 | 2 | 4 | .371/.445/.600 | .372 | .493 | 0.1 | -0.2 | 1.9 |
| 2009 | NRW | AA | 22 | 423 | 38 | 26 | 2 | 4 | 31 | 20 | 100 | 11 | 7 | .258/.290/.365 | .239 | .328 | -2.8 | 2.7 | 0.8 |
| 2010 | RIC | AA | 23 | 342 | 43 | 12 | 3 | 7 | 22 | 39 | 77 | 4 | 1 | .241/.341/.375 | .267 | .303 | 1.9 | 16.3 | 3.5 |
| 2011 | SJO | A+ | 24 | 69 | 14 | 5 | 1 | 3 | 15 | 9 | 13 | 0 | 0 | .322/.412/.593 | .343 | .372 | 0.2 | 1.5 | 1.1 |
| 2011 | FRE | AAA | 24 | 118 | 13 | 5 | 1 | 1 | 9 | 9 | 20 | 5 | 2 | .234/.291/.327 | .215 | .276 | -0.2 | 0.9 | 0.1 |
| 2011 | SFN | MLB | 24 | 220 | 22 | 5 | 2 | 3 | 21 | 23 | 31 | 1 | 3 | .204/.288/.296 | .212 | .228 | 0.4 | 0.4 | -0.1 |
| 2012 | SFN | MLB | 25 | 250 | 24 | 9 | 2 | 3 | 21 | 18 | 57 | 3 | 2 | .224/.284/.321 | .227 | .280 | -0.4 | SS 7, 3B -0 | 0.3 |

The question has always been whether Crawford would hit enough to play in the majors, but we won't really have a conclusive

**Mike Fontenot** 2B
Born: 6/9/1980 Age: 32
Bats: L Throws: R Height: 5' 9" Weight: 165
Breakout: 2% Improve: 45% Collapse: 1%
Attrition: 11% MLB: 87%
Comparables:
Michael Young, Alan Trammell, Miguel Tejada

| YEAR | TEAM | LVL | AGE | PA | R | 2B | 3B | HR | RBI | BB | SO | SB | CS | AVG_OBP_SLG | TAv | BABIP | BRR | FRAA | WARP |
|------|------|-----|-----|-----|----|----|----|----|-----|----|----|----|----|----------------|------|-------|------|-----------|------|
| 2009 | CHN | MLB | 29 | 419 | 38 | 22 | 2 | 9 | 43 | 35 | 83 | 4 | 1 | .236/.301/.377 | .239 | .276 | -3.2 | 1.2 | -0.1 |
| 2010 | CHN | MLB | 30 | 185 | 14 | 11 | 3 | 1 | 20 | 10 | 28 | 1 | 2 | .284/.332/.402 | .256 | .331 | -0.3 | -1.1 | 0.1 |
| 2010 | SFN | MLB | 30 | 76 | 10 | 2 | 0 | 0 | 5 | 5 | 13 | 0 | 2 | .282/.329/.310 | .242 | .345 | 0.5 | 0.3 | 0.2 |
| 2011 | SFN | MLB | 31 | 252 | 22 | 15 | 3 | 4 | 21 | 25 | 48 | 5 | 1 | .227/.304/.377 | .248 | .267 | 2.2 | -0.8 | 0.6 |
| 2012 | SFN | MLB | 32 | 250 | 28 | 13 | 2 | 4 | 24 | 21 | 48 | 3 | 1 | .248/.315/.371 | .256 | .296 | -0.2 | 2B -2, SS -2 | 1.5 |

In an odd twist, Fontenot's 2011 line was propped up by success against left-handers, against whom he is almost never allowed to bat. In an odder twist, Fontenot was actually the Giants' best hitter at shortstop. Neither of these facts should encourage the Giants—or any team—to make him a full-time player. The first fact reflects nothing more than a bunch of groundballs slipping past infielders, barely offsetting a career-worst performance against right-handers. The second fact reflects nothing more than the Giants' futile group of too-young and too-old alternatives.

**Conor Gillaspie** 3B
Born: 7/18/1987 Age: 24
Bats: L Throws: R Height: 6' 2" Weight: 200
Breakout: 2% Improve: 11% Collapse: 8%
Attrition: 39% MLB: 61%
Comparables:
Taylor Green, Jorge Jimenez, Brad Mills

| YEAR | TEAM | LVL | AGE | PA | R | 2B | 3B | HR | RBI | BB | SO | SB | CS | AVG_OBP_SLG | TAv | BABIP | BRR | FRAA | WARP |
|------|------|-----|-----|-----|----|----|----|----|-----|----|----|----|----|----------------|------|-------|------|----------|------|
| 2009 | SJO | A+ | 21 | 530 | 62 | 31 | 2 | 4 | 67 | 55 | 68 | 2 | 3 | .286/.363/.386 | .290 | .326 | -3.9 | -6.4 | 2.1 |
| 2010 | RIC | AA | 22 | 540 | 57 | 25 | 8 | 8 | 67 | 37 | 67 | 0 | 4 | .287/.338/.420 | .285 | .318 | 0.1 | -3.2 | 3.0 |
| 2011 | FRE | AAA | 23 | 503 | 63 | 22 | 6 | 11 | 61 | 66 | 79 | 9 | 9 | .297/.389/.453 | .292 | .339 | -2.9 | 6.1 | 3.5 |
| 2011 | SFN | MLB | 23 | 21 | 2 | 0 | 0 | 1 | 2 | 2 | 1 | 0 | 0 | .263/.333/.421 | .283 | .235 | 0 | -0.2 | 0.1 |
| 2012 | SFN | MLB | 24 | 250 | 25 | 10 | 2 | 2 | 20 | 19 | 45 | 1 | 1 | .237/.296/.321 | .233 | .283 | -0.4 | 3B -1, 1B 0 | 0.5 |

As a condition of his first pro contract, Gillaspie got to briefly join the Giants in late 2008. He finally earned a more deserved call-up in 2011 after recovering his splendid walk rate and cleaning up his defense at third base. He doesn't have the power to project as a starter, but his plate discipline and bat control, along with lopsided platoon splits and positional value, should earn him service time as a pinch-hitter.

**Aubrey Huff** 1B
Born: 12/20/1976 Age: 35
Bats: L Throws: R Height: 6' 5" Weight: 220
Breakout: 1% Improve: 29% Collapse: 2%
Attrition: 22% MLB: 77%
Comparables:
Rico Carty, Mike Sweeney, Hal McRae

| YEAR | TEAM | LVL | AGE | PA | R | 2B | 3B | HR | RBI | BB | SO | SB | CS | AVG_OBP_SLG | TAv | BABIP | BRR | FRAA | WARP |
|------|------|-----|-----|-----|-----|----|----|----|-----|----|----|----|----|----------------|------|-------|------|----------|------|
| 2009 | BAL | MLB | 32 | 480 | 51 | 24 | 1 | 13 | 72 | 41 | 74 | 0 | 6 | .253/.321/.405 | .250 | .276 | -2.4 | -5.3 | -0.8 |
| 2009 | DET | MLB | 32 | 117 | 8 | 6 | 0 | 2 | 13 | 10 | 13 | 0 | 0 | .189/.265/.302 | .202 | .198 | -0.9 | 0 | -0.7 |
| 2010 | SFN | MLB | 33 | 668 | 100 | 35 | 5 | 26 | 86 | 83 | 91 | 7 | 0 | .290/.385/.506 | .313 | .303 | 2.7 | 10.3 | 5.7 |
| 2011 | SFN | MLB | 34 | 579 | 45 | 27 | 1 | 12 | 59 | 47 | 90 | 5 | 3 | .246/.306/.370 | .257 | .271 | -4.7 | 6.7 | 0.2 |
| 2012 | SFN | MLB | 35 | 562 | 65 | 28 | 2 | 15 | 63 | 49 | 90 | 4 | 2 | .253/.321/.406 | .270 | .280 | -0.3 | 1B 3, RF -1 | 1.4 |

Like a later season of *24*, Huff has become nothing but a series of increasingly unrealistic twists. For the third year in a row, his VORP swung by at least 40 runs, this time dropping him below replacement level in the first year of a two-year, $22 million deal. His slash line when he was ahead in the count was nearly on par with his 2010 and career numbers. But when the count was even or the pitcher was ahead, Huff hit .217/.219/.301 with four home runs; in the same counts in 2010, he hit .282/.287/.510 with 21 home runs. Bruce Bochy admitted in September that Huff hadn't worked out enough in the offseason and had fallen out of shape. "Aubrey knows as we're coming into 2012 it's going to be a little bit different," Bochy said.

**Tommy Joseph      C**

Born: 7/16/1991 Age: 20
Bats: R Throws: R Height: 6' 2" Weight: 220
Breakout: 2% Improve: 7% Collapse: 3%
Attrition: 7% MLB: 15%

Comparables:
Sebastian Valle, Wilson Ramos, Hank Conger

| YEAR | TEAM | LVL | AGE | PA | R | 2B | 3B | HR | RBI | BB | SO | SB | CS | AVG_OBP_SLG | TAv | BABIP | BRR | FRAA | WARP |
|------|------|-----|-----|-----|----|----|----|----|-----|----|-----|----|----|-------------|------|-------|------|-----------|------|
| 2010 | AUG | A | 18 | 473 | 46 | 22 | 1 | 16 | 68 | 26 | 116 | 0 | 0 | .236/.291/.401 | .247 | .286 | -3.8 | -0.5 | 0.3 |
| 2011 | SJO | A+ | 19 | 560 | 80 | 33 | 2 | 22 | 95 | 29 | 102 | 1 | 0 | .270/.317/.471 | .284 | .295 | -4.8 | 1.4 | 3.9 |
| 2012 | SFN | MLB | 20 | 250 | 23 | 10 | 1 | 6 | 25 | 7 | 63 | 0 | 0 | .209/.236/.338 | .215 | .252 | 0 | C -1, 1B -0 | -0.6 |

Joseph was the second-youngest player to qualify for the batting title in the California League in 2011. Through May, he was badly overmatched, but he improved each month afterward and hit .301/.346/.574 in the second half. Joseph doesn't take many pitches, but a better contact rate in 2011 took some of the lopsidedness out of his strikeout-to-walk numbers. He's not an athletic defender—he's not an athletic anything, really—but he did cut his passed ball rate by half and threw out 37 percent of baserunners. A promotion to Double-A will keep him ahead of his peers, but advanced pitching won't suit his free swinging.

**Jeff Keppinger      2B**

Born: 4/21/1980 Age: 32
Bats: R Throws: R Height: 6' 1" Weight: 180
Breakout: 1% Improve: 27% Collapse: 8%
Attrition: 16% MLB: 89%

Comparables:
Dave Cash, Eric Young, Placido Polanco

| YEAR | TEAM | LVL | AGE | PA | R | 2B | 3B | HR | RBI | BB | SO | SB | CS | AVG_OBP_SLG | TAv | BABIP | BRR | FRAA | WARP |
|------|------|-----|-----|-----|----|----|----|----|-----|----|----|----|----|-------------|------|-------|------|-----------|------|
| 2009 | HOU | MLB | 29 | 344 | 35 | 13 | 3 | 7 | 29 | 27 | 33 | 0 | 2 | .256/.320/.387 | .240 | .266 | -1.8 | -2.4 | -0.3 |
| 2010 | HOU | MLB | 30 | 575 | 62 | 34 | 1 | 6 | 59 | 51 | 36 | 4 | 1 | .288/.351/.393 | .264 | .298 | -1.7 | 9.5 | 2.6 |
| 2011 | HOU | MLB | 31 | 169 | 22 | 9 | 0 | 4 | 20 | 4 | 7 | 0 | 1 | .307/.320/.436 | .262 | .299 | 0.3 | 1.3 | 0.8 |
| 2011 | SFN | MLB | 31 | 230 | 17 | 11 | 0 | 2 | 15 | 8 | 17 | 0 | 0 | .255/.285/.333 | .223 | .266 | -1.5 | -2.5 | -0.8 |
| 2012 | SFN | MLB | 32 | 418 | 46 | 20 | 1 | 4 | 39 | 28 | 33 | 2 | 1 | .269/.321/.361 | .254 | .280 | -0.2 | 2B 3, 3B -0 | 1.3 |

Few players whiff as rarely as Keppinger—in 2011, only Juan Pierre struck out more rarely, minimum 350 PA—but this skill comes with a catch. On pitches out of the zone, batters are sometimes better off missing completely and living to swing again rather than making weak contact and ending the at-bat. Keppinger makes contact on 90 percent of his swings at pitches outside the strike zone, and in 2011 he swung at more wayward offerings than he ever had. Keppinger's sub-replacement play in San Francisco made an arbitration tender questionable, as he has just one season above zero in the past four, and is now more a second baseman than a super utility guy.

**Angel Pagan      CF**

Born: 7/2/1981 Age: 30
Bats: B Throws: R Height: 6' 2" Weight: 180
Breakout: 0% Improve: 40% Collapse: 6%
Attrition: 13% MLB: 89%

Comparables:
Marquis Grissom, Chris Denorfia, Coco Crisp

| YEAR | TEAM | LVL | AGE | PA | R | 2B | 3B | HR | RBI | BB | SO | SB | CS | AVG_OBP_SLG | TAv | BABIP | BRR | FRAA | WARP |
|------|------|-----|-----|-----|----|----|----|----|-----|----|----|----|----|-------------|------|-------|------|----------|------|
| 2009 | NYN | MLB | 28 | 376 | 54 | 22 | 11 | 6 | 32 | 25 | 56 | 14 | 7 | .306/.350/.487 | .291 | .349 | 2.3 | -3.8 | 2.1 |
| 2010 | NYN | MLB | 29 | 633 | 80 | 31 | 7 | 11 | 69 | 44 | 97 | 37 | 9 | .290/.340/.425 | .275 | .331 | 9.3 | 10.2 | 5.2 |
| 2011 | NYN | MLB | 30 | 532 | 68 | 24 | 4 | 7 | 56 | 44 | 62 | 32 | 7 | .262/.322/.372 | .260 | .285 | 4 | 1.1 | 2.1 |
| 2012 | SFN | MLB | 30 | 525 | 59 | 25 | 6 | 6 | 54 | 39 | 82 | 26 | 7 | .264/.319/.383 | .260 | .302 | 0.2 | CF 3, LF 1 | 1.6 |

After spending much of his career as an up-and-down player, Pagan has somehow in his late 20s turned into an everyday outfielder, but neither 2010 (he's not that good) nor 2011 (he's not that bad) represents his true abilities. He can play center, but he's not especially good at it, and he's an average hitter with some extra-base ability, some walks, and good speed. More a guy without weaknesses than one with strengths, he doesn't hurt, doesn't help, and just kind of hangs around. In other words, there are 30 starting center fielders in baseball, and he's one of them.

**Joe Panik      SS**

Born: 10/30/1990 Age: 21
Bats: L Throws: R Height: 6' 2" Weight: 193
Breakout: 3% Improve: 26% Collapse: 1%
Attrition: 8% MLB: 41%

Comparables:
Robin Yount, Bobby Murcer, Omar Infante

| YEAR | TEAM | LVL | AGE | PA | R | 2B | 3B | HR | RBI | BB | SO | SB | CS | AVG_OBP_SLG | TAv | BABIP | BRR | FRAA | WARP |
|------|------|-----|-----|-----|----|----|----|----|-----|----|----|----|----|-------------|------|-------|------|------|------|
| 2011 | SLO | A- | 20 | 304 | 49 | 10 | 3 | 6 | 54 | 28 | 25 | 13 | 5 | .341/.401/.467 | .307 | .354 | 2 | 1.4 | 3.0 |
| 2012 | SFN | MLB | 21 | 250 | 24 | 9 | 1 | 3 | 21 | 14 | 47 | 4 | 2 | .227/.270/.319 | .221 | .267 | -0.2 | SS 4 | 0.1 |

The Giants' 2011 first-round pick took the first step toward proving everybody wrong with a strong debut in the Northwest League. Considering scouts' low regard for his tools and athleticism, Panik's promotions will always be tied to approach, fundamentals, and performance. He had more walks than strikeouts for Salem-Kaizer, just as he did in college, and was unspectacular but steady at shortstop. He kept a similar slash line going in the Arizona Fall League. Expect his gap power and mature approach to play especially well in the California League in 2012.

**Francisco Peguero** RF

Born: 6/1/1988 Age: 24
Bats: R Throws: R Height: 6' 1'' Weight: 195
Breakout: 7% Improve: 31% Collapse: 2%
Attrition: 18% MLB: 49%

**Comparables:**
Roberto Clemente, Chico Salmon, Jose Guillen

| YEAR | TEAM | LVL | AGE | PA | R | 2B | 3B | HR | RBI | BB | SO | SB | CS | AVG_OBP_SLG | TAv | BABIP | BRR | FRAA | WARP |
|------|------|-----|-----|----|----|----|----|----|-----|----|----|----|----|-------------|-----|-------|-----|------|------|
| 2009 | AUG | A | 21 | 252 | 28 | 12 | 4 | 1 | 34 | 5 | 39 | 15 | 5 | .340/.363/.437 | .297 | .402 | 1 | 3.6 | 2.4 |
| 2009 | SLO | A- | 21 | 76 | 14 | 3 | 1 | 0 | 12 | 3 | 9 | 7 | 0 | .394/.427/.465 | .320 | .452 | 1.6 | 1.9 | 1.0 |
| 2010 | SJO | A+ | 22 | 538 | 78 | 19 | 16 | 10 | 77 | 18 | 88 | 40 | 22 | .329/.358/.488 | .302 | .382 | 0.9 | -7.7 | 3.4 |
| 2011 | SJO | A+ | 23 | 76 | 12 | 2 | 0 | 2 | 9 | 7 | 8 | 4 | 0 | .324/.387/.441 | .302 | .345 | 0.4 | -0.1 | 0.5 |
| 2011 | RIC | AA | 23 | 296 | 34 | 12 | 6 | 5 | 37 | 5 | 45 | 8 | 1 | .309/.318/.446 | .279 | .346 | 0.4 | 1 | 1.2 |
| 2012 | SFN | MLB | 24 | 250 | 25 | 9 | 3 | 2 | 24 | 4 | 50 | 8 | 3 | .260/.274/.341 | .230 | .317 | -0.3 | RF -3, CF -2 | -0.4 |

Peguero's speed has driven his gaudy minor league batting averages, which have propped up an otherwise empty offensive game. Preseason knee surgery slowed him, though, and there were ripples throughout his game. The Giants moved him off center field to a corner in 2011, and his stolen bases dipped from 40 to 12. More troubling for one of the most extreme ground-ball hitters in the minors, his BABIP dropped by 50 points. By the end of the year, he was once again a plus runner, so there's no short-term worry. But he's fairly heavy for a gazelle, and if his speed goes, the Giants have a preview of the player he'll be.

Pill's been hitting doubles in the minors for years, but in 2011 his home run total jumped, boosting his isolated power above .200 for the first time. That's an exciting threshold for a second baseman, but Pill is not exciting. (*"Hey not fair!"—Brett Pill.*) For one thing he's not a second baseman. He's a first baseman who played second in Fresno because Brandon Belt was blocking him and he played it with all the range you would expect from somebody with Pill's size and inexperience. For another he's 27 and his on-base percentage was worse than the PCL average. So he's not exciting (*"Stop saying that!"—Brett Pill*) but he should be useful as a right-handed utility guy playing his peak years for the major league minimum.

**Buster Posey** C

Born: 3/27/1987 Age: 25
Bats: R Throws: R Height: 6' 2'' Weight: 205
Breakout: 0% Improve: 40% Collapse: 2%
Attrition: 33% MLB: 92%

**Comparables:**
Brian McCann, Bob Barton, Hobie Landrith

| YEAR | TEAM | LVL | AGE | PA | R | 2B | 3B | HR | RBI | BB | SO | SB | CS | AVG_OBP_SLG | TAv | BABIP | BRR | FRAA | WARP |
|------|------|-----|-----|----|----|----|----|----|-----|----|----|----|----|-------------|-----|-------|-----|------|------|
| 2009 | SJO | A+ | 22 | 346 | 63 | 23 | 0 | 13 | 58 | 45 | 45 | 6 | 0 | .326/.430/.540 | .357 | .352 | -1.4 | 0.8 | 5.3 |
| 2009 | FRE | AAA | 22 | 151 | 21 | 8 | 1 | 5 | 22 | 17 | 23 | 0 | 1 | .321/.399/.511 | .310 | .359 | -1.1 | -0.6 | 1.3 |
| 2009 | SFN | MLB | 22 | 17 | 1 | 0 | 0 | 0 | 0 | 0 | 4 | 0 | 0 | .118/.118/.118 | .192 | .154 | 0 | 0.1 | 0.0 |
| 2010 | FRE | AAA | 23 | 208 | 31 | 13 | 2 | 6 | 32 | 28 | 30 | 1 | 1 | .349/.451/.552 | .338 | .397 | -2.5 | 2 | 2.5 |
| 2010 | SFN | MLB | 23 | 443 | 58 | 23 | 2 | 18 | 67 | 30 | 55 | 0 | 2 | .305/.357/.505 | .299 | .315 | -1.6 | -0.3 | 3.5 |
| 2011 | SFN | MLB | 24 | 185 | 17 | 5 | 0 | 4 | 21 | 18 | 30 | 3 | 0 | .284/.368/.389 | .267 | .326 | -1 | -0.2 | 0.9 |
| 2012 | SFN | MLB | 25 | 250 | 32 | 12 | 1 | 7 | 30 | 21 | 39 | 1 | 0 | .280/.348/.438 | .289 | .309 | 0 | C -0, 1B -0 | 3.2 |

In 1936, 25-year-old Hank Greenberg broke his wrist in a collision at first base and missed the rest of the season. The next year, he drove in 183 runs. In 1968, 24-year-old Joe Morgan tore the ligaments in his knee and missed all but 10 games of his age 24 season. He credits the time on the bench, studying pitchers, with teaching him how to steal bases. And in 1974, Carlton Fisk tore knee ligaments in a home plate collision; they said he would never play again, but 16 months later he hit his Game 6 home run, and about 100 years after that he was still playing. Injuries aren't just a part of baseball, but a part of most Hall of Fame careers. Until we see Posey on the field, it's fair to worry about him, but his recovery from a broken fibula and torn ankle ligaments was ahead of schedule as the season ended. He was catching bullpen sessions by October and challenging reporters to wind sprints in November. The Giants are confident enough that they ruled out a position change. At this point, all seems ready for him to be the Giants catcher in 2012, which puts him on track to start for the National League on July 10.

**Cody Ross** CF

Born: 12/23/1980 Age: 31
Bats: R Throws: L Height: 6' 0'' Weight: 180
Breakout: 2% Improve: 42% Collapse: 7%
Attrition: 18% MLB: 91%

**Comparables:**
Hoot Evers, Mike Easler, Gary Matthews

| YEAR | TEAM | LVL | AGE | PA | R | 2B | 3B | HR | RBI | BB | SO | SB | CS | AVG_OBP_SLG | TAv | BABIP | BRR | FRAA | WARP |
|------|------|-----|-----|----|----|----|----|----|-----|----|----|----|----|-------------|-----|-------|-----|------|------|
| 2009 | FLO | MLB | 28 | 604 | 73 | 37 | 1 | 24 | 90 | 34 | 122 | 5 | 2 | .270/.321/.469 | .262 | .306 | -1.4 | 1.5 | 1.5 |
| 2010 | FLO | MLB | 29 | 487 | 60 | 24 | 3 | 11 | 58 | 30 | 100 | 9 | 1 | .265/.316/.405 | .258 | .319 | 1.9 | -2.4 | 0.8 |
| 2010 | SFN | MLB | 29 | 82 | 11 | 4 | 0 | 3 | 7 | 7 | 21 | 0 | 1 | .288/.354/.466 | .277 | .360 | -0.8 | -1.6 | 0.2 |
| 2011 | SFN | MLB | 30 | 461 | 54 | 25 | 0 | 14 | 52 | 49 | 96 | 5 | 2 | .240/.325/.405 | .266 | .279 | -0.3 | -0.7 | 1.1 |
| 2012 | SFN | MLB | 31 | 456 | 53 | 24 | 2 | 14 | 55 | 34 | 104 | 5 | 2 | .252/.314/.421 | .270 | .302 | 0 | CF -2, RF 1 | 1.7 |

Ross will always have those six amazing games in October 2010, when he hit .350/.435/.950 in the NLCS. He'll also have those six games in May and June of 2011, when he hit .458/.500/.875. And the six games in August and September 2011, when he hit .368/.478/.842. And the four other six-game stretches in 2011 in which his OPS was better than 1.000. If Ross was considered a disappointment in his first full season as a Giant, it was our problem, faulty wiring in the human brain, not anything he did wrong. His OPS+ was 105, the same as his career OPS+. He should be a league-average outfielder again in 2012, with a few heroic weeks quietly sprinkled in, mostly unnoticed.

**Freddy Sanchez    2B**

Born: 12/21/1977 Age: 34
Bats: R Throws: R Height: 6' 0" Weight: 185
Breakout: 0% Improve: 28% Collapse: 10%
Attrition: 27% MLB: 77%

Comparables:
Mark Ellis, Ronnie Belliard, Rich Aurilia

| YEAR | TEAM | LVL | AGE | PA | R | 2B | 3B | HR | RBI | BB | SO | SB | CS | AVG_OBP_SLG | TAv | BABIP | BRR | FRAA | WARP |
|------|------|-----|-----|-----|----|----|----|----|-----|----|----|----|----|-------------|-----|-------|------|-------|------|
| 2009 | PIT | MLB | 31 | 382 | 45 | 28 | 3 | 6 | 34 | 20 | 60 | 5 | 1 | .296/.334/.442 | .266 | .339 | -1.2 | -8.1 | 0.0 |
| 2009 | SFN | MLB | 31 | 107 | 11 | 1 | 0 | 1 | 7 | 2 | 16 | 0 | 0 | .284/.295/.324 | .215 | .326 | 0.8 | 2.1 | -0.2 |
| 2010 | SFN | MLB | 32 | 479 | 55 | 22 | 1 | 7 | 47 | 32 | 68 | 3 | 1 | .292/.342/.397 | .268 | .330 | -2.1 | 1.3 | 1.8 |
| 2011 | SFN | MLB | 33 | 261 | 21 | 15 | 1 | 3 | 24 | 13 | 35 | 0 | 1 | .289/.332/.397 | .264 | .327 | 0.5 | -6.4 | 0.2 |
| 2012 | SFN | MLB | 34 | 292 | 32 | 15 | 1 | 3 | 28 | 14 | 41 | 1 | 1 | .273/.310/.364 | .252 | .307 | -0.1 | 2B -7 | 1.1 |

That WARP figure up there says 0.0, but in real life, replacement is a moving target. After Sanchez busted his right shoulder diving for a grounder up the middle, the Giants tried to find patches internally, on the free-talent heap, and via trade, but couldn't replicate even Sanchez's modest contributions. That experience validates Brian Sabean's decision to extend Sanchez to 2012 before the 2011 season began, as this winter's free agent market and the Giants minor league system were both light on second basemen. The $6 million deal is not without risk—our injury database has nine entries since 2009 for Sanchez's shoulders alone—but when he plays, Sanchez has been remarkably consistent. The same can't be said for Replacement Player.

**Hector Sanchez    C**

Born: 11/17/1989 Age: 22
Bats: B Throws: R Height: 6' 1" Weight: 185
Breakout: 2% Improve: 6% Collapse: 8%
Attrition: 29% MLB: 36%

Comparables:
Orlando Mercado, Travis d'Arnaud, Matt Nokes

| YEAR | TEAM | LVL | AGE | PA | R | 2B | 3B | HR | RBI | BB | SO | SB | CS | AVG_OBP_SLG | TAv | BABIP | BRR | FRAA | WARP |
|------|------|-----|-----|-----|----|----|----|----|-----|----|----|----|----|-------------|-----|-------|------|-------|------|
| 2009 | GIA | RK | 19 | 139 | 13 | 8 | 1 | 1 | 22 | 16 | 21 | 0 | 0 | .299/.406/.410 | .332 | .358 | -0.5 | -0.6 | 1.5 |
| 2010 | AUG | A | 20 | 341 | 29 | 20 | 1 | 5 | 31 | 28 | 50 | 0 | 2 | .274/.334/.394 | .268 | .311 | -1.7 | 1.5 | 1.7 |
| 2011 | SJO | A+ | 21 | 228 | 31 | 14 | 1 | 11 | 58 | 11 | 49 | 0 | 1 | .302/.338/.533 | .306 | .342 | -1 | -0.3 | 1.8 |
| 2011 | FRE | AAA | 21 | 168 | 15 | 9 | 0 | 1 | 26 | 13 | 22 | 0 | 1 | .261/.315/.340 | .216 | .295 | 0.2 | 0.6 | 0.1 |
| 2011 | SFN | MLB | 21 | 34 | 0 | 2 | 0 | 0 | 1 | 3 | 6 | 0 | 0 | .258/.324/.323 | .224 | .320 | 0.1 | 0 | 0.0 |
| 2012 | SFN | MLB | 22 | 250 | 23 | 11 | 1 | 3 | 22 | 13 | 55 | 0 | 0 | .223/.267/.320 | .221 | .274 | 0 | C -0, 1B -0 | -0.1 |

Buster Posey's injury accelerated Sanchez's rise through the system, as the Giants pushed him from High-A San Jose (where he had played just 52 games) to Triple-A Fresno so they could see whether he was ready for the majors. He hit .305/.370/.366 and got good reviews from Fresno manager and ex-catcher Steve Decker in his month there, so the Giants promoted him again. He evokes a young Pablo Sandoval in a lot of ways: very heavy, but athletic for his size, with inconsistent plate discipline and the ability to square up anything close. "Evokes" doesn't equal "comp" though, and Sandoval represents a best-case scenario that only the most optimistic fanboys would expect. The return of Posey in 2012 will let the Giants take the foot off the accelerator, allowing Sanchez a full year in the high minors to hone his plate discipline, pitch blocking, and catching mechanics.

**Pablo Sandoval    3B**

Born: 8/11/1986 Age: 25
Bats: B Throws: R Height: 6' 0" Weight: 245
Breakout: 3% Improve: 45% Collapse: 6%
Attrition: 26% MLB: 92%

Comparables:
Ron Santo, Ryan Zimmerman, Brad Mills

| YEAR | TEAM | LVL | AGE | PA | R | 2B | 3B | HR | RBI | BB | SO | SB | CS | AVG_OBP_SLG | TAv | BABIP | BRR | FRAA | WARP |
|------|------|-----|-----|-----|----|----|----|----|-----|----|----|----|----|-------------|-----|-------|------|-------|------|
| 2009 | SFN | MLB | 22 | 633 | 79 | 44 | 5 | 25 | 90 | 52 | 83 | 5 | 5 | .330/.387/.556 | .322 | .350 | -3.8 | -3.1 | 4.9 |
| 2010 | SFN | MLB | 23 | 616 | 61 | 34 | 3 | 13 | 63 | 47 | 81 | 3 | 2 | .268/.323/.409 | .260 | .291 | -1.4 | -6 | 1.4 |
| 2011 | SFN | MLB | 24 | 466 | 55 | 26 | 3 | 23 | 70 | 32 | 63 | 2 | 4 | .315/.357/.552 | .318 | .320 | -1.7 | 8.2 | 5.2 |
| 2012 | SFN | MLB | 25 | 471 | 61 | 27 | 3 | 14 | 63 | 32 | 66 | 3 | 2 | .293/.341/.466 | .295 | .316 | -0.5 | 3B 1, 1B -1 | 3.5 |

If one metric tells you Sandoval is the best defensive third baseman in the National League, you laugh it off. But when all the advanced metrics agree . . . you still laugh it off. But then you chastise yourself for being closed-minded, especially after seeing Sandoval play. He may not actually be the league's best—one year of defensive data is limited, whether you're looking at one metric or a half-dozen—but he is dramatically better than he was in 2010. He has always been better when he has had a chance to set his feet before a throw, and his improved range to both sides gets him to more grounders and puts him in better position to throw once he has the ball. His 2010 collapse and 2011 recovery both coincided with weight fluctuations, so Panda's waistline will be an area of interest for the rest of his career. He spent the winter with the same trainers who helped him lose 38 pounds before the 2011 season.

### Nate Schierholtz    RF

Born: 2/15/1984 Age: 28
Bats: L Throws: R Height: 6' 3" Weight: 215
Breakout: 1% Improve: 38% Collapse: 5%
Attrition: 14% MLB: 71%

Comparables:
Felipe Alou, Roberto Clemente, Ruben Sierra

| YEAR | TEAM | LVL | AGE | PA | R | 2B | 3B | HR | RBI | BB | SO | SB | CS | AVG_OBP_SLG | TAv | BABIP | BRR | FRAA | WARP |
|------|------|-----|-----|-----|----|----|----|----|-----|----|----|----|----|----------------|------|-------|------|-----------|------|
| 2009 | SFN | MLB | 25 | 308 | 33 | 19 | 2 | 5 | 29 | 16 | 58 | 3 | 1 | .267/.302/.400 | .249 | .311 | 0 | 2.6 | 0.3 |
| 2010 | SFN | MLB | 26 | 252 | 34 | 13 | 3 | 3 | 17 | 20 | 38 | 4 | 5 | .242/.311/.366 | .245 | .278 | 1.1 | 1.6 | 0.5 |
| 2011 | SFN | MLB | 27 | 362 | 42 | 22 | 1 | 9 | 41 | 21 | 61 | 7 | 4 | .278/.326/.430 | .276 | .315 | 1.5 | -0.8 | 1.4 |
| 2012 | SFN | MLB | 28 | 318 | 36 | 17 | 3 | 6 | 36 | 17 | 55 | 5 | 3 | .263/.307/.404 | .261 | .303 | -0.5 | RF 0, LF 0 | 0.9 |

Score one for PECOTA. Schierholtz's projection for 2011 was .278/.325/.447— his actual .278/.326/.430 line was just six total bases away from being a direct hit. PECOTA also projected him to be one run worse than average on defense, which, according to FRAA, he was. While it's nice that Schierholtz has finally provided some value to the Giants, it took an age-27 season to get there, and he still has only minimal power and plate discipline. The Giants were sitting on an underpaid league-average player; now they're sitting on an arbitration-eligible league average player, which is fine.

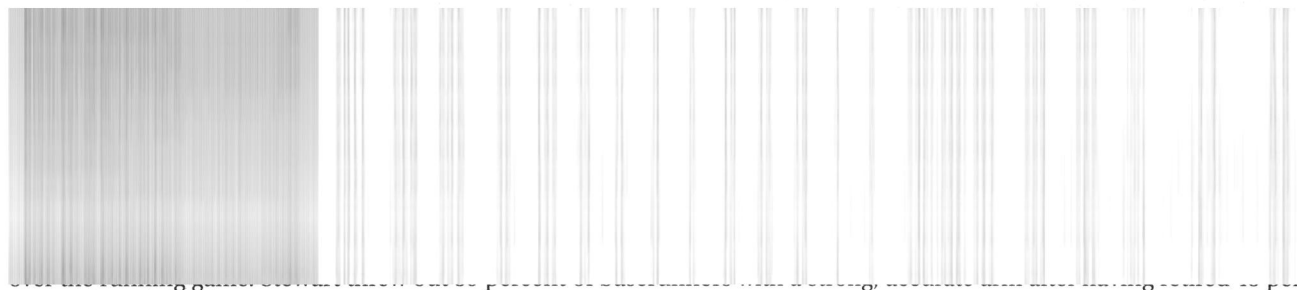

cent of attempted basestealers in his long and otherwise undistinguished minor-league career. Stewart didn't hit any worse than Eli Whiteside, and he had the decisive defensive edge.

### Miguel Tejada    SS

Born: 5/25/1974 Age: 38
Bats: R Throws: R Height: 5' 11" Weight: 170
Breakout: 1% Improve: 26% Collapse: 16%
Attrition: 27% MLB: 72%

Comparables:
Tony Fernandez, Cal Ripken Jr., Melvin Mora

| YEAR | TEAM | LVL | AGE | PA | R | 2B | 3B | HR | RBI | BB | SO | SB | CS | AVG_OBP_SLG | TAv | BABIP | BRR | FRAA | WARP |
|------|------|-----|-----|-----|----|----|----|----|-----|----|----|----|----|----------------|------|-------|------|-----------|------|
| 2009 | HOU | MLB | 35 | 673 | 83 | 46 | 1 | 14 | 86 | 19 | 48 | 5 | 2 | .313/.340/.455 | .265 | .318 | 0 | 1.9 | 3.4 |
| 2010 | BAL | MLB | 36 | 428 | 40 | 16 | 0 | 7 | 39 | 15 | 39 | 0 | 0 | .269/.308/.362 | .230 | .282 | -1.1 | 3.9 | 0.3 |
| 2010 | SDN | MLB | 36 | 253 | 31 | 10 | 0 | 8 | 32 | 15 | 28 | 2 | 0 | .268/.317/.413 | .264 | .276 | -1.6 | 0 | 1.2 |
| 2011 | SFN | MLB | 37 | 343 | 28 | 16 | 0 | 4 | 26 | 12 | 35 | 4 | 4 | .239/.270/.326 | .223 | .254 | -0.4 | 7.5 | 0.8 |
| 2012 | SFN | MLB | 38 | 390 | 41 | 18 | 1 | 6 | 38 | 16 | 45 | 3 | 2 | .260/.297/.361 | .246 | .280 | -0.3 | SS -0, 3B 5 | 1.0 |

One benefit of Brian Sabean's veteran fetish is that the older set will often sign one-year contracts, so the Giants' exposure to season-crippling awfulness is minimal. Tejada was season-cripplingly awful, but now he's gone; in contrast, the Dodgers are still going to be paying Juan Uribe long after the world ends (in 2012, obviously). As you know, PECOTA projects each player out 10 years. Before the season, it projected Tejada to hit .232/.284/.310 in 2018, when he will be 44. That he matched that line in 2011, at age 37, is obviously not encouraging for his future or present.

### Eli Whiteside    C

Born: 10/22/1979 Age: 32
Bats: R Throws: R Height: 6' 3" Weight: 210
Breakout: 4% Improve: 29% Collapse: 12%
Attrition: 46% MLB: 82%

Comparables:
Paul Hoover, Darrell Johnson, Adam Melhuse

| YEAR | TEAM | LVL | AGE | PA | R | 2B | 3B | HR | RBI | BB | SO | SB | CS | AVG_OBP_SLG | TAv | BABIP | BRR | FRAA | WARP |
|------|------|-----|-----|-----|----|----|----|----|-----|----|----|----|----|----------------|------|-------|------|------|------|
| 2009 | FRE | AAA | 29 | 126 | 16 | 7 | 1 | 6 | 24 | 8 | 40 | 0 | 0 | .241/.286/.474 | .239 | .306 | -0.4 | 0.1 | 0.3 |
| 2009 | SFN | MLB | 29 | 134 | 15 | 1 | 2 | 2 | 13 | 4 | 30 | 0 | 0 | .228/.269/.339 | .200 | .284 | 0.9 | 0.4 | -0.1 |
| 2010 | SFN | MLB | 30 | 140 | 19 | 6 | 1 | 4 | 10 | 8 | 35 | 1 | 2 | .238/.299/.397 | .252 | .299 | -0.9 | -0.2 | 0.5 |
| 2011 | SFN | MLB | 31 | 236 | 14 | 8 | 2 | 4 | 17 | 18 | 59 | 2 | 1 | .197/.264/.310 | .209 | .250 | 0.6 | -0.7 | -0.2 |
| 2012 | SFN | MLB | 32 | 250 | 24 | 10 | 2 | 5 | 23 | 15 | 67 | 2 | 1 | .214/.270/.332 | .223 | .276 | -0.2 | C -0 | 0.4 |

Sixty-four starts from Whiteside is just too many starts, for a team and for a Whiteside. After Buster Posey's injury, the gray-haired backup stepped in for his first full-time job; it took two months before he was gassed, and in the final two months he hit .150/.179/.213. The Giants don't want to overtax Posey as he returns in 2012, so they'll aim to enter the season with a better-than-average backup.

# PITCHERS

### Jeremy Affeldt

Born: 6/6/1979 Age: 33
Bats: L Throws: L Height: 6' 5" Weight: 185
Breakout: 23% Improve: 56% Collapse: 12%
Attrition: 20% MLB: 95%

Comparables:
David Cone, Scott Downs, Pedro Feliciano

| YEAR | TEAM | LVL | AGE | W | L | SV | G | GS | IP | H | HR | BB | SO | EqBB9 | EqSO9 | GB% | BABIP | WHIP | ERA | FIP | FRA | WARP |
|------|------|-----|-----|---|---|----|---|----|----|---|----|----|----|-------|-------|-----|-------|------|-----|-----|-----|------|
| 2009 | SFN | MLB | 30 | 2 | 2 | 0 | 74 | 0 | 62¹ | 42 | 3 | 31 | 55 | 4.5 | 7.9 | 65% | .250 | 1.17 | 1.73 | 3.55 | 3.93 | 0.9 |
| 2010 | SFN | MLB | 31 | 4 | 3 | 4 | 53 | 0 | 50 | 56 | 4 | 24 | 44 | 4.3 | 7.9 | 60% | .356 | 1.60 | 4.14 | 4.01 | 4.78 | 0.0 |
| 2011 | SFN | MLB | 32 | 3 | 2 | 3 | 67 | 0 | 61² | 47 | 5 | 24 | 54 | 3.5 | 7.9 | 63% | .250 | 1.15 | 2.63 | 3.66 | 4.35 | 0.1 |
| 2012 | SFN | MLB | 33 | 3 | 1 | 3 | 60 | 0 | 55² | 45 | 4 | 21 | 46 | 3.4 | 7.5 | 56% | .290 | 1.20 | 3.44 | 3.62 | 3.74 | 0.7 |

If you want to make God laugh, show him your projections for a reliever. Affeldt was once again excellent for the Giants in 2011, after being terrible in 2010, after being elite in 2009. Or was he? Affeldt's core stats stayed steady from year to year, as did his velocity and strike percentages. The most recent year was a touch more encouraging, as he consolidated 2009's superior groundball rate with 2010's improved control. But those are just a few extra outs on the margins. If you had spent the past 1,000 days staring at his FIP you would have reached a state of pure enlightenment regarding Affeldt: good arm, pretty consistent.

### Madison Bumgarner

Born: 8/1/1989 Age: 22
Bats: R Throws: L Height: 6' 5" Weight: 215
Breakout: 16% Improve: 52% Collapse: 21%
Attrition: 8% MLB: 99%

Comparables:
Don Robinson, Dean Chance, Storm Davis

| YEAR | TEAM | LVL | AGE | W | L | SV | G | GS | IP | H | HR | BB | SO | EqBB9 | EqSO9 | GB% | BABIP | WHIP | ERA | FIP | FRA | WARP |
|------|------|-----|-----|---|---|----|---|----|----|---|----|----|----|-------|-------|-----|-------|------|-----|-----|-----|------|
| 2009 | SFN | MLB | 19 | 0 | 0 | 0 | 4 | 1 | 10 | 8 | 2 | 3 | 10 | 2.7 | 9.0 | 59% | .250 | 1.10 | 1.80 | 4.56 | 4.62 | 0.0 |
| 2010 | SFN | MLB | 20 | 7 | 6 | 0 | 18 | 18 | 111 | 119 | 11 | 26 | 86 | 2.1 | 7.0 | 46% | .314 | 1.31 | 3.00 | 3.68 | 3.92 | 1.8 |
| 2011 | SFN | MLB | 21 | 13 | 13 | 0 | 33 | 33 | 204² | 202 | 12 | 46 | 191 | 2.0 | 8.4 | 48% | .329 | 1.21 | 3.21 | 2.64 | 3.35 | 3.3 |
| 2012 | SFN | MLB | 22 | 11 | 8 | 0 | 27 | 27 | 167² | 151 | 12 | 40 | 123 | 2.2 | 6.6 | 43% | .299 | 1.14 | 3.25 | 3.38 | 3.53 | 2.7 |

Eight times in history a pitcher has thrown at least 162 innings with a FIP below 2.65 while 21 or younger: Dwight Gooden and Bert Blyleven twice each, Fernando Valenzuela, Vida Blue, Don Sutton, and the Bummer. The lefty doesn't overpower hitters like Gooden, and no single pitch he throws compares to Blyleven's curve. He's more like a left-handed Jered Weaver, throwing from an extreme angle and getting a tremendous strike rate on off-speed pitches, especially his slider. The lone blemish on his season—a 1/3-inning disaster start against Minnesota—is easily brushed aside as a BABIP-induced hallucination, as he allowed five consecutive singles on ground balls before the start really got away from him. Take away that start and his ERA is 2.86, more in line with his FIP.

### Matt Cain

Born: 10/1/1984 Age: 27
Bats: R Throws: R Height: 6' 4" Weight: 230
Breakout: 16% Improve: 54% Collapse: 27%
Attrition: 5% MLB: 92%

Comparables:
Darren O'Day, Kyle McClellan, Adam Wainwright

| YEAR | TEAM | LVL | AGE | W | L | SV | G | GS | IP | H | HR | BB | SO | EqBB9 | EqSO9 | GB% | BABIP | WHIP | ERA | FIP | FRA | WARP |
|------|------|-----|-----|---|---|----|---|----|----|---|----|----|----|-------|-------|-----|-------|------|-----|-----|-----|------|
| 2009 | SFN | MLB | 24 | 14 | 8 | 0 | 33 | 33 | 217² | 184 | 22 | 73 | 171 | 3.0 | 7.1 | 41% | .267 | 1.18 | 2.89 | 3.85 | 4.25 | 2.5 |
| 2010 | SFN | MLB | 25 | 13 | 11 | 0 | 33 | 33 | 223¹ | 181 | 22 | 61 | 177 | 2.5 | 7.1 | 37% | .254 | 1.08 | 3.14 | 3.67 | 3.82 | 3.0 |
| 2011 | SFN | MLB | 26 | 12 | 11 | 0 | 33 | 33 | 221² | 177 | 9 | 63 | 179 | 2.6 | 7.3 | 44% | .265 | 1.08 | 2.88 | 2.88 | 3.44 | 3.1 |
| 2012 | SFN | MLB | 27 | 12 | 8 | 0 | 28 | 28 | 189² | 152 | 14 | 56 | 143 | 2.7 | 6.8 | 39% | .275 | 1.10 | 2.92 | 3.40 | 3.18 | 3.8 |

Thesis: Matt Cain is a cyborg sent from the future to destroy pitcher wins by demonstrating beyond doubt the absolute absurdity of them. Antithesis: Actually, that sounds pretty reasonable. Go with that. Cain now has a career ERA+ of 125, the highest ever for a starting pitcher with a losing record in at least 100 decisions. He had the league's eighth-best ERA and fifth-best FIP in 2011, but the Giants rewarded him with a 12-11 record. In 10 no-decisions, he had a 2.36 ERA and 0.83 WHIP, which is basically Justin Verlander's season. Don't even stress about a low BABIP regressing; Cain now has more than 1,300 innings as a big leaguer and the lowest career BABIP of any 21st century pitcher. Only the stubbornest DIPS theorist would deny his hit-suppressing ability at this point.

### Santiago Casilla

Born: 6/25/1980 Age: 32
Bats: R Throws: R Height: 6' 1" Weight: 165
Breakout: 18% Improve: 39% Collapse: 41%
Attrition: 10% MLB: 91%

Comparables:
Felix Rodriguez, Guillermo Mota, Jason Schmidt

| YEAR | TEAM | LVL | AGE | W | L | SV | G | GS | IP | H | HR | BB | SO | EqBB9 | EqSO9 | GB% | BABIP | WHIP | ERA | FIP | FRA | WARP |
|------|------|-----|-----|---|---|----|---|----|----|---|----|----|----|-------|-------|-----|-------|------|-----|-----|-----|------|
| 2009 | OAK | MLB | 29 | 1 | 2 | 0 | 46 | 0 | 48¹ | 61 | 6 | 25 | 35 | 4.7 | 6.5 | 51% | .337 | 1.78 | 5.96 | 5.05 | 5.67 | 0.0 |
| 2010 | SFN | MLB | 30 | 7 | 2 | 2 | 52 | 0 | 55¹ | 40 | 2 | 26 | 56 | 4.2 | 9.1 | 51% | .281 | 1.19 | 1.95 | 3.18 | 4.29 | 0.3 |
| 2011 | SFN | MLB | 31 | 2 | 2 | 6 | 49 | 0 | 51² | 33 | 1 | 25 | 45 | 4.4 | 7.8 | 54% | .239 | 1.12 | 1.74 | 3.07 | 3.10 | 0.8 |
| 2012 | SFN | MLB | 32 | 2 | 1 | 1 | 45 | 0 | 48 | 40 | 3 | 20 | 41 | 3.7 | 7.6 | 45% | .295 | 1.24 | 3.58 | 3.56 | 3.89 | 0.5 |

Casilla's season began with right elbow inflammation and a fastball 3 mph slower than it had been in 2010. Fortunately for him, the velocity turned out to be less important to his success than the development of a low-80s curveball to complement his power slider. A second effective season finally convinced Bruce Bochy that Casilla was for real, and he got the save opportunities with Sergio Romo and Brian Wilson injured in the final month. Over the past two seasons, only two relievers in baseball have a better ERA than

Casilla. He's done so with an unspectacular strikeout rate, too many walks and more wild pitches per inning than anybody in baseball, but all those outs—which cost the Giants less than $2 million—counted just the same.

**Steve Edlefsen**
Born: 6/27/1985 Age: 27
Bats: B Throws: R Height: 6' 3" Weight: 180
Breakout: 16% Improve: 56% Collapse: 17%
Attrition: 11% MLB: 91%

Comparables:
Matt DeSalvo, Shawn Estes, Shane Rawley

| YEAR | TEAM | LVL | AGE | W | L | SV | G | GS | IP | H | HR | BB | SO | EqBB9 | EqSO9 | GB% | BABIP | WHIP | ERA | FIP | FRA | WARP |
|------|------|-----|-----|---|---|----|---|----|----|----|----|----|----|-------|-------|-----|-------|------|-----|-----|-----|------|
| 2009 | SJO | A+ | 24 | 1 | 1 | 7 | 20 | 0 | 28 | 15 | 1 | 13 | 40 | 4.2 | 12.9 | 64% | .233 | 1.00 | 0.96 | 2.76 | 2.56 | 0.8 |
| 2009 | FRE | AAA | 24 | 5 | 0 | 2 | 22 | 0 | 30 | 23 | 2 | 16 | 24 | 4.8 | 7.2 | 56% | .250 | 1.30 | 2.40 | 4.62 | 5.95 | -0.2 |
| 2010 | FRE | AAA | 25 | 7 | 2 | 6 | 49 | 0 | 64¹ | 39 | 3 | 26 | 40 | 4.8 | 7.0 | 66% | .295 | 1.38 | 2.38 | 4.68 | 5.33 | 0.1 |
| 2011 | FRE | AAA | 26 | 0 | 4 | 1 | 32 | 0 | 41¹ | 49 | 2 | 19 | 29 | 4.1 | 6.3 | 60% | .373 | 1.67 | 5.66 | 4.49 | 6.23 | 0.0 |
| 2011 | SFN | MLB | 26 | 0 | 0 | 0 | 13 | 0 | 11¹ | 17 | 2 | 10 | 6 | 7.9 | 4.8 | 58% | .366 | 2.38 | 9.53 | 7.14 | 6.71 | -0.4 |
| *2012* | *SFN* | *MLB* | *27* | *1* | *0* | *0* | *18* | *0* | *22* | *21* | *2* | *12* | *15* | *4.9* | *5.9* | *56%* | *.298* | *1.47* | *4.83* | *4.66* | *5.25* | *-0.1* |

On September 15, Edlefsen was called upon to get Ryan Vogelsong out of a sixth-inning jam. Edlefsen got the grounder, which is what Edlefsen does, and the double play ended the inning and gave him a 3.00 ERA in the majors. It was a nice time to be

Born: 1/13/1989 Age: 23
Bats: R Throws: R Height: 6' 5" Weight: 210
Breakout: 29% Improve: 61% Collapse: 20%
Attrition: 11% MLB: 95%

Comparables:
Ryan Perry, Gio Gonzalez, Tommy Hanson

| YEAR | TEAM | LVL | AGE | W | L | SV | G | GS | IP | H | HR | BB | SO | EqBB9 | EqSO9 | GB% | BABIP | WHIP | ERA | FIP | FRA | WARP |
|------|------|-----|-----|---|---|----|---|----|----|----|----|----|----|-------|-------|-----|-------|------|-----|-----|-----|------|
| 2011 | SJO | A+ | 22 | 0 | 0 | 21 | 26 | 0 | 24² | 16 | 1 | 12 | 44 | 4.4 | 16.1 | 34% | .349 | 1.14 | 0.73 | 2.47 | 3.68 | 0.4 |
| 2011 | RIC | AA | 22 | 2 | 0 | 17 | 28 | 0 | 28² | 23 | 2 | 17 | 35 | 4.1 | 10.7 | 34% | .262 | 1.15 | 2.83 | 3.66 | 4.95 | 0.1 |
| *2012* | *SFN* | *MLB* | *23* | *1* | *0* | *1* | *16* | *0* | *16* | *13* | *1* | *7* | *16* | *4.1* | *8.9* | *41%* | *.302* | *1.26* | *3.63* | *3.33* | *3.95* | *0.2* |

Heath Hembree was born in a city called Cowpens, so of course he's a reliever. Not just any reliever, though. He's the best in the Giants system, a tall right-hander who pitches in the high 90s and has struck out 14 batters per nine innings. His walk rate isn't improving, but holding it steady as he moves up the system is an accomplishment.

**Marc Kroon**
Born: 4/2/1973 Age: 39
Bats: R Throws: R Height: 6' 3" Weight: 195
Breakout: 16% Improve: 44% Collapse: 28%
Attrition: 18% MLB: 68%

Comparables:
Troy Percival, Tim Wakefield, Lee Smith

| YEAR | TEAM | LVL | AGE | W | L | SV | G | GS | IP | H | HR | BB | SO | EqBB9 | EqSO9 | GB% | BABIP | WHIP | ERA | FIP | FRA | WARP |
|------|------|-----|-----|---|---|----|---|----|----|----|----|----|----|-------|-------|-----|-------|------|-----|-----|-----|------|
| 2009 | YOM | NPB | 36 | 1 | 3 | 27 | 46 | 0 | 50 | 36 | 1 | 19 | 57 | 3.4 | 10.3 | — | .293 | 1.10 | 1.26 | 1.96 | — | 0.0 |
| 2010 | YOM | NPB | 37 | 4 | 3 | 25 | 52 | 0 | 50² | 35 | 5 | 29 | 73 | 5.1 | 13.0 | — | .299 | 1.26 | 4.26 | 3.11 | — | 0.0 |
| 2011 | FRE | AAA | 38 | 1 | 5 | 20 | 49 | 0 | 49¹ | 48 | 8 | 33 | 52 | 6.0 | 9.5 | 44% | .305 | 1.64 | 5.11 | 5.86 | 6.34 | -0.3 |
| *2012* | *SFN* | *MLB* | *39* | *1* | *0* | *1* | *14* | *0* | *14²* | *13* | *1* | *7* | *12* | *4.2* | *7.3* | *44%* | *.297* | *1.35* | *4.31* | *3.89* | *4.69* | *0.0* |

When Kroon made his major league debut for San Diego, Bruce Bochy was his skipper. That was Bochy's first year as a manager, 16 years ago, and since then Kroon has pitched just 25 innings in the big leagues, spent six years in Japan, pitched for seven teams' minor league systems, and turned 38. Alas, in the year of the unlikely comeback, Kroon didn't quite push his way back to the big leagues, despite an excellent spring training, a strikeout per inning in the Pacific Coast League, and a featured spot in the Showtime series "The Franchise." That spot focused on his strained relationship with his mostly absent father and now Kroon says he'll focus on being around for his own kids. "i think I'm done" he tweeted in October but you never know.

**Tim Lincecum**
Born: 6/15/1984 Age: 28
Bats: L Throws: R Height: 6' 0" Weight: 160
Breakout: 16% Improve: 33% Collapse: 43%
Attrition: 6% MLB: 94%

Comparables:
Hong-Chih Kuo, Johan Santana, Rich Harden

| YEAR | TEAM | LVL | AGE | W | L | SV | G | GS | IP | H | HR | BB | SO | EqBB9 | EqSO9 | GB% | BABIP | WHIP | ERA | FIP | FRA | WARP |
|------|------|-----|-----|---|---|----|---|----|----|----|----|----|----|-------|-------|-----|-------|------|-----|-----|-----|------|
| 2009 | SFN | MLB | 25 | 15 | 7 | 0 | 32 | 32 | 225¹ | 168 | 10 | 68 | 261 | 2.7 | 10.4 | 49% | .288 | 1.05 | 2.48 | 2.30 | 3.23 | 5.5 |
| 2010 | SFN | MLB | 26 | 16 | 10 | 0 | 33 | 33 | 212¹ | 194 | 18 | 76 | 231 | 3.2 | 9.8 | 50% | .315 | 1.27 | 3.43 | 3.18 | 4.06 | 2.2 |
| 2011 | SFN | MLB | 27 | 13 | 14 | 0 | 33 | 33 | 217 | 176 | 15 | 86 | 220 | 3.6 | 9.1 | 49% | .287 | 1.21 | 2.74 | 3.14 | 3.80 | 1.9 |
| *2012* | *SFN* | *MLB* | *28* | *13* | *8* | *0* | *29* | *29* | *189¹* | *143* | *10* | *61* | *194* | *2.9* | *9.2* | *47%* | *.295* | *1.08* | *2.54* | *2.81* | *2.76* | *4.9* |

For the third year in a row, Lincecum's strikeout rate dropped and he lost a bit of velocity down the stretch. His walks were a career high and his strikeouts a career low. And still he was one of the best pitchers in the National League, which shows how gentle his decline has been. As he does every year, Lincecum tinkered a bit, leaning heavily on a slider while moving away from his traditional curveball; the slider got more strikes, and swinging strikes, than the curve ever did. After just four full seasons, Lincecum has already produced the most WARP by a Giants pitcher since Juan Marichal.

### Javier Lopez

Born: **7/11/1977** Age: **34**
Bats: **L** Throws: **L** Height: **6' 5"** Weight: **200**
Breakout: **20%** Improve: **47%** Collapse: **17%**
Attrition: **7%** MLB: **95%**

**Comparables:**
Scott Eyre, Rudy May, Bob Lemon

| YEAR | TEAM | LVL | AGE | W | L | SV | G | GS | IP | H | HR | BB | SO | EqBB9 | EqSO9 | GB% | BABIP | WHIP | ERA | FIP | FRA | WARP |
|------|------|-----|-----|---|---|----|----|----|-----|----|----|----|----|-------|-------|-----|-------|------|------|------|------|------|
| 2009 | PAW | AAA | 31 | 1 | 1 | 0 | 38 | 0 | 39² | 35 | 2 | 13 | 23 | 2.9 | 5.2 | 62% | .277 | 1.21 | 3.17 | 3.70 | 5.11 | 0.0 |
| 2009 | BOS | MLB | 31 | 0 | 2 | 0 | 14 | 0 | 11² | 20 | 1 | 9 | 5 | 6.9 | 3.9 | 50% | .413 | 2.49 | 9.26 | 6.23 | 6.54 | -0.1 |
| 2010 | SFN | MLB | 32 | 2 | 0 | 0 | 27 | 0 | 19 | 11 | 0 | 2 | 16 | 0.9 | 7.6 | 67% | .216 | 0.68 | 1.42 | 1.74 | 2.66 | 0.5 |
| 2010 | PIT | MLB | 32 | 2 | 2 | 0 | 50 | 0 | 38² | 39 | 2 | 18 | 22 | 4.2 | 5.1 | 60% | .306 | 1.47 | 2.79 | 4.19 | 5.19 | 0.1 |
| 2011 | SFN | MLB | 33 | 5 | 2 | 1 | 70 | 0 | 53 | 42 | 0 | 26 | 40 | 4.4 | 6.8 | 64% | .280 | 1.28 | 2.72 | 3.13 | 4.71 | 0.1 |
| 2012 | SFN | MLB | 34 | 3 | 1 | 2 | 64 | 0 | 48¹ | 44 | 3 | 20 | 30 | 3.7 | 5.6 | 57% | .295 | 1.31 | 3.97 | 4.01 | 4.31 | 0.3 |

On August 29, with the Cubs up by six, Blake DeWitt ripped a hanging Javier Lopez slider into right field for a triple. That would be the only extra-base hit Lopez would allow to a left-handed hitter in 2011, in more than 100 plate appearances. As far as the LOOGY portion of his mandate, 2011 was Lopez's best season, as lefties batted just .163/.245/.185 against him. Alas, all that success earned him added responsibility, and right-handers—who aren't nearly so impressed—were 53 percent of his opponents, the biggest share he has ever faced in a full season. When he gets two strikes against same-siders, he likes to drop down, using an extreme arm angle for both the slider and the fastball. He has done it for years, but since joining the Giants has exaggerated the motion ever further, his release point falling off the PITCHf/x maps completely. That angle makes him deadly with two strikes—his whiff rate on 0-2 is better than those of Justin Verlander and Carlos Marmol—and one of the least comfortable LOOGY at-bats in the game. One day into the offseason, the Giants extended him for two years and $8.5 million.

### Guillermo Mota

Born: **7/25/1973** Age: **38**
Bats: **R** Throws: **R** Height: **6' 7"** Weight: **200**
Breakout: **24%** Improve: **41%** Collapse: **25%**
Attrition: **13%** MLB: **75%**

**Comparables:**
Hector Carrasco, David Weathers, Early Wynn

| YEAR | TEAM | LVL | AGE | W | L | SV | G | GS | IP | H | HR | BB | SO | EqBB9 | EqSO9 | GB% | BABIP | WHIP | ERA | FIP | FRA | WARP |
|------|------|-----|-----|---|---|----|----|----|-----|----|----|----|----|-------|-------|-----|-------|------|------|------|------|------|
| 2009 | LAN | MLB | 35 | 3 | 4 | 0 | 61 | 0 | 65¹ | 53 | 6 | 24 | 39 | 3.3 | 5.4 | 39% | .240 | 1.18 | 3.44 | 4.39 | 5.23 | 0.1 |
| 2010 | SFN | MLB | 36 | 1 | 3 | 1 | 56 | 0 | 54 | 49 | 4 | 22 | 38 | 3.7 | 6.3 | 39% | .274 | 1.31 | 4.33 | 3.88 | 4.46 | 0.2 |
| 2011 | SFN | MLB | 37 | 2 | 2 | 1 | 52 | 0 | 80¹ | 71 | 10 | 30 | 77 | 3.4 | 8.6 | 43% | .289 | 1.26 | 3.81 | 3.89 | 4.56 | 0.0 |
| 2012 | SFN | MLB | 38 | 3 | 1 | 1 | 52 | 0 | 64² | 56 | 6 | 23 | 47 | 3.2 | 6.6 | 44% | .285 | 1.23 | 3.67 | 4.02 | 3.99 | 0.6 |

Mota pitched in the lowest average leverage of his career in 2011, but that disguises how important he was as the Giants' designated rubber arm. Thrice he was asked to throw more than 50 pitches in a game; seven times he went at least three innings, with a 1.46 ERA in those outings. There's a vast difference between being a team's mop-up man, as Mota had been at a series of stops since Paul DePodesta traded him away from the Dodgers in 2004, and being a team's long-man. He has now thrown more innings without a start than any active pitcher; only Mariano Rivera and Arthur Rhodes have thrown more relief innings.

### Sergio Romo

Born: **3/4/1983** Age: **29**
Bats: **R** Throws: **R** Height: **6' 0"** Weight: **190**
Breakout: **11%** Improve: **41%** Collapse: **38%**
Attrition: **7%** MLB: **99%**

**Comparables:**
John Wetteland, Sandy Koufax, Jonathan Papelbon

| YEAR | TEAM | LVL | AGE | W | L | SV | G | GS | IP | H | HR | BB | SO | EqBB9 | EqSO9 | GB% | BABIP | WHIP | ERA | FIP | FRA | WARP |
|------|------|-----|-----|---|---|----|----|----|----|----|----|----|----|-------|-------|-----|-------|------|------|------|------|------|
| 2009 | SFN | MLB | 26 | 5 | 2 | 2 | 45 | 0 | 34 | 30 | 1 | 11 | 41 | 2.9 | 10.9 | 32% | .333 | 1.21 | 3.97 | 2.09 | 2.61 | 1.1 |
| 2010 | SFN | MLB | 27 | 5 | 3 | 0 | 68 | 0 | 62 | 46 | 6 | 14 | 70 | 2.0 | 10.2 | 37% | .265 | 0.97 | 2.18 | 2.98 | 3.93 | 0.6 |
| 2011 | SFN | MLB | 28 | 3 | 1 | 1 | 65 | 0 | 48 | 29 | 2 | 5 | 70 | 0.9 | 13.1 | 36% | .281 | 0.71 | 1.50 | 0.93 | 2.42 | 1.1 |
| 2012 | SFN | MLB | 29 | 3 | 2 | 2 | 54 | 0 | 45 | 31 | 3 | 10 | 51 | 2.0 | 10.2 | 35% | .282 | 0.90 | 1.91 | 2.47 | 2.08 | 1.5 |

The Giants bullpen follows the blueprint of most great rock bands: Brian Wilson is the lead singer, radiating charisma and soaking up fame. But Sergio Romo is the lead guitarist and the real genius, a virtuoso who woodshedded his slider until it turned into something transcendent. Romo's strikeout-to-walk rate in 2011 was the third-best in history, minimum 25 strikeouts, behind a couple of vintage Eckersley seasons, and his 0.93 FIP was one for the ages. Romo was underutilized in 2011 in the interest of protecting him from lefties, as half his appearances were less than an inning and 72 percent of batters he faced were right-handed. That rate of same-side opponents is just insanely high—even Chad Bradford only topped it once—and it was unnecessary, as Romo has had no platoon disadvantage in his career. Someday, Wilson will leave for a solo project, and Romo will get the ninth inning to himself.

**Dan Runzler**
Born: 3/30/1985 Age: 27
Bats: L Throws: L Height: 6' 5'' Weight: 230
Breakout: 36% Improve: 56% Collapse: 19%
Attrition: 28% MLB: 87%

Comparables:
Royce Ring, Courtney Duncan, Renyel Pinto

| YEAR | TEAM | LVL | AGE | W | L | SV | G | GS | IP | H | HR | BB | SO | EqBB9 | EqSO9 | GB% | BABIP | WHIP | ERA | FIP | FRA | WARP |
|------|------|-----|-----|---|---|----|---|----|----|---|----|----|----|-------|-------|-----|-------|------|-----|-----|-----|------|
| 2009 | AUG | A | 24 | 1 | 1 | 11 | 19 | 0 | 26¹ | 8 | 0 | 13 | 45 | 4.4 | 15.4 | 78% | .195 | 0.80 | 0.68 | 1.98 | 2.40 | 0.8 |
| 2009 | SJO | A+ | 24 | 1 | 0 | 5 | 19 | 0 | 21¹ | 8 | 1 | 4 | 26 | 1.7 | 11.0 | 59% | .140 | 0.56 | 0.85 | 2.49 | 2.07 | 0.7 |
| 2009 | SFN | MLB | 24 | 0 | 0 | 0 | 11 | 0 | 8² | 6 | 1 | 5 | 11 | 5.2 | 11.4 | 48% | .250 | 1.27 | 1.04 | 4.09 | 3.41 | 0.1 |
| 2010 | SFN | MLB | 25 | 3 | 0 | 0 | 41 | 0 | 32² | 29 | 1 | 20 | 37 | 5.5 | 10.2 | 57% | .346 | 1.50 | 3.03 | 3.17 | 4.16 | 0.2 |
| 2011 | FRE | AAA | 26 | 2 | 2 | 0 | 17 | 10 | 52 | 47 | 2 | 32 | 59 | 5.5 | 10.2 | 55% | .324 | 1.52 | 3.98 | 3.99 | 4.86 | 0.4 |
| 2011 | SFN | MLB | 26 | 1 | 2 | 0 | 31 | 1 | 27¹ | 29 | 0 | 16 | 25 | 5.3 | 8.2 | 49% | .367 | 1.65 | 6.26 | 2.92 | 4.05 | 0.3 |
| 2012 | SFN | MLB | 27 | 2 | 2 | 0 | 33 | 4 | 41¹ | 33 | 3 | 21 | 40 | 4.6 | 8.6 | 56% | .301 | 1.32 | 3.75 | 3.74 | 4.08 | 0.4 |

Super-small-sample-size caveats, but Runzler was again excellent against lefties, which is all he would be asked to do in a perfectly efficient system. The Giants have an excellent LOOGY in Javier Lopez, though, so they had to go looking for ways to use Runzler. He started 10 games for Fresno and got one start in the majors, against a lefty-free Astros lineup. Though he maintained his 95 mph velocity, he was otherwise terrible in that start, got sent back to the bullpen, and allowed no runz in September.

Rzepczynski

Finesse lefties who barely crack 90 mph don't generally excite baseball men, but after four years of Jonathan Sanchez's boom/bust routine, the low-beta Surkamp might be just what Bruce Bochy's ulcer needs. Surkamp has two well-developed off-speed pitches and a long, low arm motion that's hard to pick up. Despite the underwhelming fastball, he's never had a problem getting strikeouts, with 10.6 per nine innings in three minor league seasons. The statistical profile evokes Ted Lilly, another high-80s lefthander with a trunkful of pitchability-induced strikeouts.

**Ryan Vogelsong**
Born: 7/22/1977 Age: 34
Bats: R Throws: R Height: 6' 4'' Weight: 195
Breakout: 13% Improve: 41% Collapse: 33%
Attrition: 9% MLB: 91%

Comparables:
Mike Marshall, Bob Wickman, Gary Lavelle

| YEAR | TEAM | LVL | AGE | W | L | SV | G | GS | IP | H | HR | BB | SO | EqBB9 | EqSO9 | GB% | BABIP | WHIP | ERA | FIP | FRA | WARP |
|------|------|-----|-----|---|---|----|---|----|----|---|----|----|----|-------|-------|-----|-------|------|-----|-----|-----|------|
| 2011 | SFN | MLB | 33 | 13 | 7 | 0 | 30 | 28 | 179² | 164 | 15 | 61 | 139 | 3.1 | 7.0 | 48% | .285 | 1.25 | 2.71 | 3.63 | 4.03 | 1.7 |
| 2012 | SFN | MLB | 34 | 8 | 7 | 0 | 30 | 20 | 132² | 118 | 11 | 51 | 102 | 3.4 | 6.9 | 45% | .297 | 1.27 | 3.86 | 3.90 | 4.20 | 1.0 |

Vogelsong wins the award for best player unmentioned in the 2011 BP Annual. Indeed, we hadn't included him in a book since 2008. Back when we did care about Vogelsong, in 2001, we wrote, "He has the stuff to be a front-of-the-rotation starter but that's not enough. He needs a year in Triple-A perhaps two." Or perhaps three. And perhaps another three in Japan. Vogelson's comeback wasn't a steady climb; even in 2010 he walked six batters per nine in Triple-A and was set free by two organizations. The question then is how much is fluke—and surely some of it must be—and how much is sustainable. The fluke shows itself in Vogelsong's strand rate, the fourth best in baseball. The sustainable part is this: His peripheral stats were credible. He cut his walk rate by 30 percent and he has excellent command of two pitches—curve and sinker—that allow him to work below the knees, away from any danger zones. He has middle-of-the-rotation stuff and middle-of-the-rotation command and he'll serve the Giants another year in the middle of the rotation.

**Brian Wilson**
Born: 3/16/1982 Age: 30
Bats: R Throws: R Height: 6' 2'' Weight: 205
Breakout: 18% Improve: 42% Collapse: 28%
Attrition: 11% MLB: 93%

Comparables:
Heath Bell, Juan Rincon, Jesse Orosco

| YEAR | TEAM | LVL | AGE | W | L | SV | G | GS | IP | H | HR | BB | SO | EqBB9 | EqSO9 | GB% | BABIP | WHIP | ERA | FIP | FRA | WARP |
|------|------|-----|-----|---|---|----|---|----|----|---|----|----|----|-------|-------|-----|-------|------|-----|-----|-----|------|
| 2009 | SFN | MLB | 27 | 5 | 6 | 38 | 68 | 0 | 72¹ | 60 | 3 | 27 | 83 | 3.4 | 10.3 | 49% | .308 | 1.20 | 2.74 | 2.46 | 3.41 | 1.4 |
| 2010 | SFN | MLB | 28 | 3 | 3 | 48 | 70 | 0 | 74² | 62 | 3 | 26 | 93 | 3.1 | 11.2 | 49% | .317 | 1.18 | 1.81 | 2.22 | 3.00 | 1.3 |
| 2011 | SFN | MLB | 29 | 6 | 4 | 36 | 57 | 0 | 55 | 50 | 2 | 31 | 54 | 5.1 | 8.8 | 55% | .314 | 1.47 | 3.11 | 3.30 | 4.03 | 0.2 |
| 2012 | SFN | MLB | 30 | 3 | 1 | 40 | 56 | 0 | 56² | 44 | 3 | 21 | 58 | 3.3 | 9.1 | 49% | .298 | 1.13 | 2.75 | 2.96 | 2.99 | 1.2 |

Boy, that Brian Wilson character, isn't he wild! Like, wild, man. No, really, he's wild—he walked five batters per nine, giving Giants fans more heartburn than, say, a XXL Chalupa. Wilson dealt with an oblique injury in spring training and never did pitch with full velocity, his four-seam fastball coming in a mile-and-a-half slower than in 2010, his swinging strike rate dropping to Chad Durbin levels. He compensated by leaning ever more heavily on his slider—nearly half the pitches he threw had a wrinkle—and toying with a two-seamer. His public act has worn thin on some baseball fans; his performance has him walking a thin line with the San Francisco faithful, too.

**Barry Zito**
Born: 5/13/1978 Age: 34
Bats: L Throws: L Height: 6' 5" Weight: 205
Breakout: 32% Improve: 57% Collapse: 18%
Attrition: 8% MLB: 94%
**Comparables:**
Matt Herges, Scott Schoeneweis, Rudy May

| YEAR | TEAM | LVL | AGE | W | L | SV | G | GS | IP | H | HR | BB | SO | EqBB9 | EqSO9 | GB% | BABIP | WHIP | ERA | FIP | FRA | WARP |
|------|------|-----|-----|---|---|----|----|----|-----|-----|----|----|-----|-------|-------|-----|-------|------|------|------|------|------|
| 2009 | SFN | MLB | 31 | 10 | 13 | 0 | 33 | 33 | 192 | 179 | 21 | 81 | 154 | 3.8 | 7.2 | 40% | .291 | 1.35 | 4.03 | 4.26 | 4.73 | 1.5 |
| 2010 | SFN | MLB | 32 | 9 | 14 | 0 | 34 | 33 | 199¹ | 184 | 20 | 84 | 150 | 3.8 | 6.8 | 38% | .286 | 1.34 | 4.15 | 4.28 | 4.24 | 1.9 |
| 2011 | SFN | MLB | 33 | 3 | 4 | 0 | 13 | 9 | 53² | 51 | 10 | 24 | 32 | 4.0 | 5.4 | 41% | .258 | 1.40 | 5.87 | 5.57 | 5.72 | -0.5 |
| 2012 | SFN | MLB | 34 | 5 | 5 | 0 | 13 | 13 | 77¹ | 69 | 7 | 31 | 49 | 3.7 | 5.7 | 40% | .282 | 1.30 | 4.07 | 4.32 | 4.43 | 0.4 |

For the first four years of Zito's contract, he at least kept ticking, starting 131 games as an over-priced, league-average pitcher. But 2011 was the year he started to smell like rot. The strikeout rate was a career low; for those with at least 50 innings, his 10 homers in 53 innings were the seventh-worst rate in baseball and his FIP was the sixth-worst. For the first time as a Giant, he also dealt with stints on the DL—at least one of them looked like a phantom injury, but the ankle injury in August was legit. He asked for, and got, a shot in the bullpen late in the season, but he doesn't do any one thing well enough to be worth a roster spot as a reliever. Remember that disastrous contract the Dodgers gave Juan Pierre a few years ago? The Giants still owe Zito more than that—$46 million over the next two years.

# LINEOUTS

## HITTERS

| PLAYER | TEAM | LVL | AGE | PA | R | 2B | 3B | HR | RBI | BB | SO | SB-CS | AVG/OBP/SLG | TAv | BABIP | BRR | FRAA | WARP |
|--------|------|-----|-----|-----|----|----|----|----|-----|----|-----|-------|-------------|-----|-------|-----|------|------|
| 2B R. Cavan | SJO | A+ | 24 | 588 | 86 | 38 | 5 | 12 | 90 | 64 | 92 | 10-4 | .270/.352/.435 | .285 | .302 | 3 | 10.3 | 4.7 |
| 2B C. Culberson | RIC | AA | 22 | 587 | 69 | 34 | 2 | 10 | 56 | 22 | 129 | 14-4 | .259/.293/.382 | .245 | .320 | 2.3 | 0.3 | 1.3 |
| 3B C. Dominguez | SJO | A+ | 24 | 279 | 40 | 10 | 1 | 11 | 40 | 18 | 73 | 8-2 | .291/.337/.465 | .280 | .364 | 0.6 | 1.2 | 1.7 |
| | RIC | AA | 24 | 313 | 35 | 22 | 2 | 7 | 45 | 9 | 78 | 1-5 | .244/.272/.403 | .242 | .302 | -1.8 | -5.9 | -0.3 |
| RF B. Eldred | FRE | AAA | 30 | 413 | 61 | 23 | 2 | 23 | 57 | 34 | 94 | 9-4 | .278/.351/.536 | .284 | .315 | -1.3 | -6.5 | 0.9 |
| SS E. Gonzalez | FRE | AAA | 33 | 564 | 69 | 30 | 0 | 14 | 82 | 51 | 73 | 14-6 | .315/.378/.457 | .289 | .343 | 2.8 | 2.3 | 3.9 |
| 2B B. Hall | FRE | AAA | 31 | 125 | 17 | 9 | 0 | 7 | 20 | 9 | 36 | 0-0 | .274/.328/.540 | .284 | .333 | -0.4 | -1.1 | 0.7 |
| | HOU | MLB | 31 | 158 | 18 | 7 | 2 | 2 | 13 | 8 | 55 | 1-1 | .224/.272/.340 | .215 | .341 | -0.8 | -6.3 | -1.0 |
| | SFN | MLB | 31 | 41 | 6 | 2 | 0 | 0 | 1 | 3 | 8 | 2-1 | .158/.220/.211 | .145 | .200 | 0.2 | -0.8 | -0.5 |
| RF J. Parker | SJO | A+ | 22 | 571 | 81 | 25 | 3 | 13 | 61 | 74 | 144 | 20-5 | .253/.360/.397 | .284 | .333 | 3.6 | 0.5 | 3.0 |

**Ryan Cavan**'s slugging percentages would be a lot more encouraging from a second baseman who wasn't playing a league behind his peers and who didn't have the benefit of the California League's magical powers. ⊘ Since the Giants drafted **Charlie Culberson** as a sandwich pick in 2007, he has hit well in the California League, hit well in the Arizona Fall League, and struggled everywhere else. In his favor, he has cleaned up his defense since moving to second base. ⊘ **Chris Dominguez** has 80 power that hasn't shown up in games, and one of the worst hitting approaches in the system. He's been old for every level yet still unable to put up a decent slash line, while committing 60 errors in the past two seasons. ⊘ **Brad Eldred** has now spent seven years in Triple-A, slugging .535 over the past four. "That's what I love about these Triple-A pitchers man. I get older, they stay the same age," he probably says to his teammates who don't get it because they were 4 years old when that movie came out. ⊘ There's a tendency to view 33-year-olds in Triple-A like the guys trying to outrun a police pursuit. You're not going to make it, dude. Just give it up before somebody gets hurt! But it's obviously not like that, and appreciating **Edgar Gonzalez** is a big part of appreciating just how special baseball is. ⊘ **Bill Hall** is the oldest 31 in the sport. He did get to cross one thing off his bucket list, as he crushed Triple-A pitching for the first time in his career, but major league opponents weren't so accommodating. ⊘ Entering the season, **Jarrett Parker** was a good body with a bad swing. He shortened the swing but kept striking out, and the Giants are still waiting for his power to show up.

## PITCHERS

| PLAYER | TEAM | LVL | AGE | W | L | SV | IP | H | HR | BB | SO | EqBB9 | EqSO9 | GB% | BABIP | WHIP | ERA | FIP | FRA | WARP |
|---|---|---|---|---|---|---|---|---|---|---|---|---|---|---|---|---|---|---|---|---|
| C. Blackburn | GIA | RK | 18 | 2 | 1 | 0 | 33$^1$ | 23 | 2 | 3 | 35 | 0.8 | 8.1 | 66% | .208 | 0.57 | 1.08 | 3.67 | 3.37 | 0.9 |
| J. Dunnington | AUG | A | 20 | 2 | 3 | 1 | 43 | 29 | 1 | 29 | 52 | 6.7 | 11.1 | 45% | .304 | 1.42 | 3.77 | 3.57 | 4.58 | 0.1 |
|  | SJO | A+ | 20 | 2 | 1 | 1 | 22$^1$ | 13 | 1 | 10 | 31 | 4.0 | 12.5 | 29% | .255 | 1.03 | 2.82 | 3.22 | 3.44 | 0.4 |
| M. Kickham | AUG | A | 22 | 3 | 7 | 0 | 111$^2$ | 116 | 9 | 38 | 107 | 3.0 | 8.3 | 50% | .316 | 1.33 | 4.11 | 3.76 | 4.72 | 0.8 |
| S. Loux | FRE | AAA | 31 | 5 | 6 | 0 | 179$^1$ | 202 | 19 | 41 | 84 | 2.1 | 4.2 | 53% | .304 | 1.36 | 4.67 | 5.10 | 5.71 | 0.5 |
| M. Main | SJO | A+ | 22 | 2 | 4 | 0 | 52$^2$ | 64 | 11 | 37 | 46 | 6.2 | 7.9 | 39% | .333 | 1.86 | 6.84 | 7.35 | 6.96 | -0.6 |
| K. Marte | SJO | A+ | 23 | 12 | 6 | 0 | 147$^2$ | 165 | 11 | 47 | 84 | 2.9 | 5.1 | 55% | .324 | 1.39 | 3.47 | 4.84 | 5.48 | -0.1 |
| L. Mendoza | SLO | A- | 19 | 5 | 5 | 0 | 73 | 77 | 5 | 16 | 68 | 2.0 | 8.4 | 45% | .330 | 1.27 | 4.19 | 3.32 | 4.40 | 1.1 |

came on third strikes. ⊘ **Michael Main** spent his third consecutive year in the California League, but neither repetition nor a midseason switch to the bullpen could solve his control problems. The Rangers seem to have known what they were doing when they sent him to the Giants for Bengie Molina. ⊘ **Kelvin Marte**'s best chance will probably come as a LOOGY, so his line against lefties—26 Ks, six free passes, two home runs, and an above-average groundball rate—is encouraging. Nothing else is. ⊘ **Lorenzo Mendoza** has added three strikeouts per nine innings over the past two years, and he's still a teenager. The strike thrower will be tested as one of the younger pitchers in the South Atlantic League this year.

## MANAGER: BRUCE BOCHY

| YEAR | TEAM | W-L | Pythag +/- | Avg PC | 100+ P | 120+ P | QS | BQS | REL | REL w Zero R | IBB | Subs | PH | PH Avg | PH HR | SB2 | CS2 | SB3 | CS3 | SAC Att | SAC % | POS SAC | Squeeze | Swing | In Play |
|---|---|---|---|---|---|---|---|---|---|---|---|---|---|---|---|---|---|---|---|---|---|---|---|---|---|
| 2009 | SFN | 88-74 | 1 | 97.6 | 74 | 5 | 81 | 6 | 457 | 292 | 49 | 76 | 231 | .250 | 2 | 8 | 0 | 1 | 1 | 101 | 66.3% | 18 | 0 | 118 | 99 |
| 2010 | SFN | 92-70 | 1 | 198.8 | 161 | 161 | 119 | 4 | 476 | 402 | 116 | — | 438 | .262 | 12 | 6 | 3 | 0 | 1 | 212 | 77.4% | 58 | 0 | 264 | 85 |
| 2011 | SFN | 86-76 | 0 | 99.8 | 90 | 7 | 103 | 3 | 480 | 411 | 46 | — | 244 | .212 | 4 | 7 | 6 | 2 | 3 | 86 | 79.1% | 35 | 2 | 395 | 118 |

The most important thing a manager can do is make sure his players' shirts are tucked in when he takes them to meet the president. Bruce Bochy totally did that, because Bochy is a World Series-winning manager. The next most important thing a manager can do is hard to say. If it's avoiding outs by resisting the urge to smallball every strategy, Bochy did pretty well—his Giants were below the league average in sacrifice bunts, after going bunt crazy in 2010. If it's managing a bullpen, Bochy did pretty well. He got the best work of Ramon Ramirez and Santiago Casilla's careers, and when his first two choices to close were injured in August and September, his Giants still had calm ninth innings. He didn't do perfectly, too often leaving Javier Lopez in to face righties and pulling Sergio Romo at the threat of a lefty, but pretty well. If it's finding the right balance between youth and veterans, Bochy continues to struggle, most notably in the case of Aubrey Huff vs. Brandon Belt. Huff showed up to camp out of shape, Bochy said later. He slugged .335 through the first two months and never did have an OPS over .800 in any month. Yet Bochy, with a credible prospect as leverage, never did give up on Huff, who led the team in games played by 29. Belt, meanwhile, was called up in July and started just half the Giants' games until the final week of the season. But veterans have served Bochy well in his career, and it's unlikely one bad experience at first base will change him now.

# Seattle Mariners

On July 5, the Seattle Mariners won their third consecutive game to improve to 43-43. This is not an achievement that historians will bother to recall, because the 2011 Seattle Mariners were an awful team that lost 95 games and finished 29 games out of first place. Finishing .500 isn't a particularly glorious achievement, but merely touching .500 and holding onto it for 18 hours before crushing it into an unrecognizable mash is noteworthy to a negative extreme. The Mariners were at .500 for a day. They lost the next game, then the next, and the next . . . They lost 17 games in a row. They were awful.

The 17-game losing streak came three crucial weeks into the team's shift from "not now" to "maybe soon." Just 18 months earlier, the Mariners had made a bold push to compete for the American League West. Far from contending, though, the Mariners have remained the division's worst team, with the worst offense in franchise history and merely average run suppression. But over the course of 17 losing days in July, the Mariners began to consolidate, and discovered that, actually, the next good Mariners team might—might—not be that far away.

Consider the first loss in the streak. Chone Figgins started at third base. He had already been dropped from the second spot in the lineup and was batting ninth, but he was playing. He was only a year-and-a-half into a four-year deal; not just a waste of money but a waste of a roster spot, the backwash that polluted what should have been a future-focused team. He went 0 for 2 in the shutout loss, dropping his average to a season-low .183. He popped out to shortstop twice—his pop-up rate in 2011 was three times what it had been in 2010—and he made an error.

He wouldn't play again for a week, as the Mariners finally conceded that Figgins's cost was sunk. Seattle called up 23-year-old Kyle Seager the following day. Seager made his major league debut just two years after being drafted, having been promoted aggressively: no short-season ball, quick promotions past Double-A and Triple-A. He is naturally a second baseman, but the Mariners moved him to third base, partly to dislodge Figgins and partly because he was blocked at second by Dustin Ackley.

Ackley, like Seager, had been drafted two years earlier. Not only was he in the majors already, but for the third game of the losing streak, Eric Wedge put him in the third spot in the batting order. In the Mariners' previous 15 games, their number three hitters had been Adam Kennedy 14 times and Franklin Gutierrez once. But Ackley would hit third for the Mariners in all but three of the team's remaining games. The striking thing wasn't that the Mariners would, in the midst of a rebuilding effort, have a pretty good collection of young talent, headed by Ackley. The striking thing was how close to the majors most of that young talent was, and how immediately good Ackley was.

Besides Ackley and Seager, there was Michael Pineda, who started game four of the losing streak. Pineda was hit hard in his outing—two homers and seven runs allowed in five innings, the worst start of his career at that point—but still left the game with an ERA just a shade over three. He struck out seven in the start, got 13 swinging strikes, and on his final pitch of the night he whiffed Howie Kendrick on a filthy 3-2 slider. Pineda was 22. The next pitch he threw was in the All-Star Game, where he was the youngest player on either roster. He struck out two of the three batters he faced, and got three swinging strikes in 10 total pitches.

Top 2011 pick Danny Hultzen is considered so advanced that by the time you read this the Mariners will be giving him a chance to make the rotation in spring training. Same goes for 2010 pick James Paxton, after he dominated Double-A in his second pro season.

## MARINERS PROSPECTUS
### 2011 W-L: 67-95, 4th in AL West

| | | | |
|---|---|---|---|
| Pythag | .414 | 27th | **Ballpark:** Safeco Field (3-yr. PF: 90). Yes, the worst offense plays in the worst offensive park |
| RS/G | 3.43 | 30th | |
| RA/G | 4.17 | 12th | |
| TAv | .248 | 24th | **2011:** Reigning Cy Young winner Hernandez and Pineda can't overcome support from paltriest of offenses |
| TAv-P | .270 | 22nd | |
| FIP | 3.88 | 12th | |
| DER | .715 | 7th | **2012:** With the offense destined to be below average, 70 wins is a reasonable goal |
| DL | 769 | 19th | |
| B-Age | 29.4 | 23rd | |
| P-Age | 26.5 | 2nd | **Action Items:** Anyone who can hit 25 doubles, 20 home runs, or over .280 |
| Salary | $93.6 | 14th | |
| M$/MW | $4.38 | 26th | |

The losing streak made easy the decision to sell off a trio of useful parts. There, again, the Mariners didn't just get young players; they got young players who are immediately useful to a major league roster. Erik Bedard brought back Trayvon Robinson, a speedy line-drive hitter whose .374 on-base percentage in the upper minors offers some hope he can lead off when the Mariners finally concede Ichiro Suzuki is old. Doug Fister and David Pauley brought back a major league-ready starting pitcher (Charlie Furbush), a major-league-ready outfielder (Casper Wells) and a major-league-ready reliever (Chance Ruffin, who made his debut in the big leagues less than a year after signing). None of this trio has much upside—a fourth player in the deal, third baseman and whose designated hitters went .225/.316/.352.

In the two months between early June and early August, the Mariners turned over half their lineup to competent, under-25 replacements. On Opening Day, the average age of the Mariners' starting lineup was 32 years. On September 1, it was 27 years, and only two of the nine were older than 30.

This is a particularly optimistic take on a 17-game losing streak. Teams don't lose 17 games in a row without some serious flaws. The Mariners' main flaw was lack of offense. They scored 3.4 runs per game during the streak. Only three teams have scored fewer than 600 runs since 2000, and two of those are the Mariners of 2010 and 2011.

In game seven of the streak, Ichiro went 0 for 4, popping out in the infield twice, flying out to right field, and grounding out weakly. It was the third consecutive hitless game for Suzuki, and already the third time in 2011 he had gone hitless three days in a row. Before 2011, he hadn't gone hitless in three consecutive games since May 2007. Only the White Sox got less from the leadoff spot than the Mariners did in 2011. For years, Suzuki defied the typical aging curve, but the bubble popped last year, and Ichiro led an extraordinarily punchless group of Seattle veterans. Ten players in their thirties batted for the Mariners in 2011, and none—including Ichiro—came close to a league-average OPS. Of the 10, only Ichiro and Miguel Olivo are likely to play a significant role on this year's roster, and Ichiro's collapse makes it doubtful that even he will play a significant role on the next Mariners' playoff roster.

In game 11 of the streak, Justin Smoak went 0-for-5 with three strikeouts. After a fast start to his season, Smoak ran into a three-month slump that coincided, in part, with hand injuries. Smoak started 16 of 17 losses and batted .138/.190/.172, finally going on the disabled list a week after the losing streak ended. He was the above-the-fold prize of the Cliff Lee trade in 2010, but a 714 OPS in 153 post-trade games raises questions about his future.

And their problems aren't limited to offense. In 2009, the Mariners' defense was the best in baseball, according to Ultimate Zone Rating and the +/- system. They signed Figgins, re-signed Jack Wilson, and signed Brendan Ryan, all of whom had strong defensive reputations at premium infield positions. This was supposed to be a run-suppression team, surviving a lousy lineup by smothering opponents' lineups. The plan failed, largely because the Mariners' out the stretch surely contributed.

Since a 116-win season in 2001, the Mariners have continually been fooled by pyrite. They unexpectedly won 88 games in 2007, and thought they were close, so they traded for Erik Bedard and signed Carlos Silva. A negative run differential in 2007, though, hinted at the collapse to come, and they lost 101 games in 2008. Then, in 2009, they again were outscored by plenty but won 85 games, leading to Jack Zduriencik's big push before 2010. That effort has clearly failed, and an organization that expected to compete has instead lost 196 games over two seasons.

Zduriencik nonetheless had his contract extended in August, and he will soon have to decide whether the Mariners are any closer than they were after 2007 or 2009. These Mariners, unlike those teams, are young and cost-controlled. They have one of baseball's best 25-and-under cores, so there are no windows closing on them, at least until Felix Hernandez's contract expires in 2014. They have a bullpen packed with young and inexpensive arms that improved by 50 runs in 2011, and have added veteran left-hander George Sherrill to that mix. Zduriencik will once more get a chance to pick up the final pieces, but this time he can afford to be patient.

There are teams that lose 95 games and are absolutely funless to watch. There are also teams that lose 95 games but aren't—teams that point to something better to come. The 2010 Mariners were the first kind of bad team. The 2011 Mariners, even in the midst of a 17-game losing streak, even with the worst offense in the league and a startlingly depressing Ichiro Suzuki, point to something better.

# HITTERS

### Dustin Ackley — 2B

Born: 2/26/1988 Age: 24
Bats: L Throws: R Height: 6' 2" Weight: 185
Breakout: 5% Improve: 23% Collapse: 10%
Attrition: 19% MLB: 72%

Comparables:
Phil Gagliano, Dave Rosello, Alex Cintron

| YEAR | TEAM | LVL | AGE | PA | R | 2B | 3B | HR | RBI | BB | SO | SB | CS | AVG_OBP_SLG | TAv | BABIP | BRR | FRAA | WARP |
|------|------|-----|-----|----|----|----|----|----|-----|----|----|----|----|-------------|-----|-------|-----|------|------|
| 2010 | WTN | AA | 22 | 350 | 42 | 21 | 4 | 2 | 28 | 55 | 41 | 8 | 2 | .263/.390/.384 | .284 | .301 | 1.2 | -5.9 | 1.4 |
| 2010 | TAC | AAA | 22 | 237 | 37 | 12 | 4 | 5 | 23 | 20 | 38 | 2 | 1 | .274/.342/.439 | .290 | .314 | 1.6 | -1.4 | 0.7 |
| 2011 | TAC | AAA | 23 | 331 | 57 | 17 | 3 | 9 | 35 | 55 | 38 | 7 | 3 | .303/.421/.487 | .294 | .324 | -1.3 | -4.4 | 1.4 |
| 2011 | SEA | MLB | 23 | 376 | 39 | 16 | 7 | 6 | 36 | 40 | 79 | 6 | 0 | .273/.348/.417 | .296 | .339 | -0.5 | -1.7 | 2.5 |
| 2012 | SEA | MLB | 24 | 401 | 45 | 17 | 3 | 6 | 36 | 43 | 78 | 5 | 2 | .247/.330/.361 | .260 | .299 | 0 | 2B -8, 1B -0 | 1.5 |

They say you're never as good as you look when you're going well, or as bad as you look in a slump. During Ackley's first two months in Seattle, he hit like Chase Utley: loads of walks, few strikeouts, power to all fields, and a .245 isolated power boosting his overall line to .315/.377/.559 on July 3. Then came the adjustment period and a .242/.327/.311 line the rest of the way. Baseball is, after all, just a bunch of good at bats and a bunch of bad at bats, averaging out to a career. Ackley's overall season line is a good guess for what the next 16 years will hold, but he'll top that line if he continues to develop power. Ackley keeps his weight back better than he did when he was drafted as a front-foot hitter, and his power numbers had improved at every stop before his summer slump in Seattle.

### Mike Carp — 1B

Born: 6/30/1986 Age: 26
Bats: L Throws: R Height: 6' 3" Weight: 215
Breakout: 4% Improve: 36% Collapse: 6%
Attrition: 28% MLB: 78%

Comparables:
Marty Cordova, Tony Alvarez, Joe Charboneau

| YEAR | TEAM | LVL | AGE | PA | R | 2B | 3B | HR | RBI | BB | SO | SB | CS | AVG_OBP_SLG | TAv | BABIP | BRR | FRAA | WARP |
|------|------|-----|-----|----|----|----|----|----|-----|----|----|----|----|-------------|-----|-------|-----|------|------|
| 2009 | TAC | AAA | 23 | 490 | 66 | 25 | 1 | 15 | 64 | 58 | 99 | 0 | 1 | .271/.376/.446 | .287 | .323 | -2.6 | 7.4 | 1.9 |
| 2009 | SEA | MLB | 23 | 65 | 7 | 3 | 1 | 1 | 5 | 8 | 10 | 0 | 0 | .315/.415/.463 | .332 | .364 | 0.9 | 1.3 | 0.8 |
| 2010 | TAC | AAA | 24 | 463 | 67 | 17 | 1 | 29 | 76 | 41 | 93 | 1 | 2 | .257/.333/.516 | .296 | .265 | -2.2 | 4.5 | 2.9 |
| 2010 | SEA | MLB | 24 | 41 | 1 | 2 | 0 | 0 | 4 | 8 | 0 | 0 | 0 | .189/.268/.243 | .230 | .241 | -0.7 | -0.1 | -0.1 |
| 2011 | TAC | AAA | 25 | 286 | 55 | 14 | 0 | 21 | 64 | 28 | 50 | 6 | 2 | .343/.411/.649 | .348 | .355 | 0.2 | 1 | 3.2 |
| 2011 | SEA | MLB | 25 | 313 | 27 | 17 | 1 | 12 | 46 | 19 | 81 | 0 | 2 | .276/.326/.466 | .280 | .343 | -2.1 | -0.9 | 0.8 |
| 2012 | SEA | MLB | 26 | 341 | 40 | 13 | 1 | 13 | 41 | 27 | 84 | 1 | 1 | .242/.311/.418 | .270 | .288 | -0.2 | 1B -5, LF -1 | 1.3 |

Ladies and gentleman, the best hitter on the 2011 Seattle Mariners, Doug Fister (.333/.333/.500 in seven plate appearances) excluded. Carp was called up in early June and put into the eighth spot; by the end of July, he was the Mariners' cleanup hitter. His success in that role masks some moderately troubling trends. He is drawing fewer walks and hitting more grounders than he ever has. It's a waste of resources from a slugger who can hit the ball forever—all 12 of his homers went at least 385 feet, and nine cleared 400—but who offers nothing but a bat. A strong season against left-handed pitching, in Tacoma and Seattle, gives hope that he won't need to be platooned.

### Johermyn Chavez — RF

Born: 1/26/1989 Age: 23
Bats: R Throws: R Height: 6' 4" Weight: 220
Breakout: 1% Improve: 53% Collapse: 1%
Attrition: 5% MLB: 77%

Comparables:
Mike Marshall, Larry Walker, Jesse Barfield

| YEAR | TEAM | LVL | AGE | PA | R | 2B | 3B | HR | RBI | BB | SO | SB | CS | AVG_OBP_SLG | TAv | BABIP | BRR | FRAA | WARP |
|------|------|-----|-----|----|----|----|----|----|-----|----|----|----|----|-------------|-----|-------|-----|------|------|
| 2009 | LNS | A | 20 | 569 | 87 | 22 | 6 | 21 | 89 | 40 | 137 | 10 | 6 | .283/.351/.474 | .290 | .351 | 0.7 | -14.1 | 1.6 |
| 2010 | HDS | A+ | 21 | 605 | 109 | 30 | 7 | 32 | 96 | 52 | 131 | 6 | 9 | .315/.387/.577 | .308 | .364 | -3.5 | 7.6 | 5.0 |
| 2011 | WTN | AA | 22 | 510 | 47 | 16 | 4 | 13 | 50 | 49 | 124 | 6 | 9 | .216/.312/.360 | .239 | .268 | -6.6 | 6.2 | -0.4 |
| 2012 | SEA | MLB | 23 | 250 | 26 | 8 | 1 | 9 | 28 | 15 | 71 | 2 | 2 | .222/.279/.382 | .244 | .278 | -0.4 | RF -3, CF -0 | 0.1 |

Like a drunk college student jumping out of the hot tub and into a cold pool, Chavez must have shrieked with shock when he landed in the Southern League after a massive 2010 season in High Desert. If you squint a little, you could possibly see his control of the strike zone improved as the season went on, and he did manage to hold his own against the league's right-handed pitchers. But the Venezuelan with a big arm (18 assists in 2011) and big power is now, after his A-Ball breakout, back to being just a bag of tools. The good news is that, even if he has to repeat Double-A, he's only a hot month or two away from a promotion to the Pacific Coast League, a new hot tub to splash around in.

### Chone Figgins — 3B

Born: 1/22/1978 Age: 34
Bats: B Throws: R Height: 5' 9" Weight: 155
Breakout: 2% Improve: 26% Collapse: 13%
Attrition: 30% MLB: 74%

Comparables:
Billy Goodman, Bill Spiers, Buddy Bell

| YEAR | TEAM | LVL | AGE | PA | R | 2B | 3B | HR | RBI | BB | SO | SB | CS | AVG_OBP_SLG | TAv | BABIP | BRR | FRAA | WARP |
|------|------|-----|-----|----|----|----|----|----|-----|----|----|----|----|-------------|-----|-------|-----|------|------|
| 2009 | ANA | MLB | 31 | 729 | 114 | 30 | 7 | 5 | 54 | 101 | 114 | 42 | 17 | .298/.395/.393 | .292 | .356 | 3.4 | 17 | 6.9 |
| 2010 | SEA | MLB | 32 | 702 | 62 | 21 | 2 | 1 | 35 | 74 | 114 | 42 | 15 | .259/.340/.306 | .245 | .314 | 2.2 | -17.1 | -0.6 |
| 2011 | SEA | MLB | 33 | 313 | 24 | 11 | 1 | 1 | 15 | 21 | 42 | 11 | 6 | .188/.241/.243 | .199 | .215 | 0.1 | 0.5 | -0.8 |
| 2012 | SEA | MLB | 34 | 372 | 39 | 12 | 2 | 1 | 24 | 39 | 66 | 20 | 8 | .255/.335/.306 | .246 | .311 | -0.7 | 3B 3, 2B -5 | 1.0 |

"I'm going to be great again," Figgins said in September. "The best part is I'm not worried about it." In other words, the best part of hitting .188 with no power and almost shockingly deteriorated baserunning is that Chone Figgins ain't bumming. The rest of the Seattle organization, though, is. Should the Mariners pay Figgins $17 million to play the next two seasons or pay Figgins $17 million to sit at home and scroll through the Netflix Instant offerings? The best argument for the former is that Figgins has been bad before for stretches of hundreds of at bats and bounced back to play at near-MVP levels. The best argument for the latter is that the above statement aside, he has reportedly been testy with one manager and the media and he is a boo magnet for Seattle's paying customers. His age makes a bounceback less likely than ever and his tools—speed, defense, and power—are crumbling.

**Darren Ford** CF

Born: 10/1/1985 Age: 26
Bats: R Throws: R Height: 5' 10" Weight: 195
Breakout: 4% Improve: 39% Collapse: 8%

| YEAR | TEAM | LVL | AGE | PA | R | 2B | 3B | HR | RBI | BB | SO | SB | CS | AVG_OBP_SLG | TAv | BABIP | BRR | FRAA | WARP |
|---|---|---|---|---|---|---|---|---|---|---|---|---|---|---|---|---|---|---|---|
| 2009 | SJO | A+ | 23 | 441 | 81 | 17 | 9 | 9 | 50 | 49 | 97 | 35 | 12 | .300/.386/.463 | .314 | .379 | 1.5 | 2.8 | 4.5 |
| 2010 | RIC | AA | 24 | 516 | 64 | 20 | 9 | 5 | 40 | 39 | 106 | 37 | 15 | .251/.311/.365 | .258 | .308 | 2.4 | 1.1 | 1.4 |
| 2011 | RIC | AA | 25 | 97 | 11 | 3 | 0 | 0 | 3 | 9 | 24 | 6 | 3 | .279/.347/.314 | .227 | .287 | 0.0 | 1.7 | 0.1 |

**Nick Franklin** SS

Born: 3/2/1991 Age: 21
Bats: B Throws: R Height: 6' 2" Weight: 170
Breakout: 1% Improve: 19% Collapse: 5%
Attrition: 21% MLB: 49%

Comparables:
Alfredo Griffin, Omar Infante, Yamaico Navarro

| YEAR | TEAM | LVL | AGE | PA | R | 2B | 3B | HR | RBI | BB | SO | SB | CS | AVG_OBP_SLG | TAv | BABIP | BRR | FRAA | WARP |
|---|---|---|---|---|---|---|---|---|---|---|---|---|---|---|---|---|---|---|---|
| 2010 | CLN | A | 19 | 574 | 89 | 22 | 7 | 23 | 65 | 50 | 123 | 25 | 10 | .281/.351/.485 | .292 | .328 | 3.1 | -9.7 | 3.4 |
| 2011 | HDS | A+ | 20 | 297 | 50 | 10 | 5 | 5 | 20 | 31 | 56 | 13 | 1 | .275/.356/.411 | .250 | .333 | 4.3 | -4.4 | 0.9 |
| 2011 | WTN | AA | 20 | 92 | 13 | 3 | 2 | 2 | 6 | 6 | 18 | 5 | 3 | .325/.371/.482 | .291 | .397 | -0.5 | 0.7 | 0.7 |
| 2012 | SEA | MLB | 21 | 250 | 24 | 8 | 2 | 5 | 25 | 12 | 63 | 8 | 3 | .227/.267/.348 | .226 | .281 | -0.1 | SS -4, 2B 0 | 0.1 |

This week on *House*: A young athlete is struck by a series of freak injuries, as he is first hit in the face by a teammate's batting practice swing, then comes down with food poisoning, and is finally felled by mononucleosis. Are these ailments the result of a curse stripping the young man of his strength? Or is there some logic to be found in a patient who, in 2010, hit 23 home runs as a teenager in the Midwest League, then abruptly lost all power in the hitter's paradise of High Desert? The truth could be somewhere in between, as demonstrated by an impressive, but not shocking, performance as a 20-year-old in Double-A, and by steady improvement in both defense and plate discipline. Tune in this year for answers.

**Chris Gimenez** C

Born: 12/27/1982 Age: 29
Bats: R Throws: R Height: 6' 3" Weight: 200
Breakout: 2% Improve: 27% Collapse: 24%
Attrition: 49% MLB: 80%

Comparables:
Ben Risinger, Dusty Brown, Johnny Roseboro

| YEAR | TEAM | LVL | AGE | PA | R | 2B | 3B | HR | RBI | BB | SO | SB | CS | AVG_OBP_SLG | TAv | BABIP | BRR | FRAA | WARP |
|---|---|---|---|---|---|---|---|---|---|---|---|---|---|---|---|---|---|---|---|
| 2009 | COH | AAA | 26 | 157 | 20 | 8 | 0 | 6 | 15 | 15 | 40 | 0 | 0 | .235/.321/.426 | .247 | .283 | -1 | -1.8 | 0.0 |
| 2009 | CLE | MLB | 26 | 130 | 12 | 2 | 0 | 3 | 7 | 17 | 36 | 1 | 1 | .144/.256/.243 | .184 | .178 | -0.5 | -0.1 | -1.0 |
| 2010 | COH | AAA | 27 | 219 | 32 | 10 | 0 | 9 | 32 | 20 | 38 | 1 | 1 | .276/.339/.464 | .263 | .298 | -1.4 | -1.2 | 0.4 |
| 2010 | CLE | MLB | 27 | 67 | 6 | 5 | 0 | 1 | 8 | 8 | 22 | 0 | 0 | .190/.288/.328 | .223 | .286 | -0.4 | 0.1 | 0.0 |
| 2011 | TAC | AAA | 28 | 56 | 8 | 1 | 0 | 1 | 4 | 7 | 13 | 0 | 1 | .265/.357/.347 | .242 | .343 | -0.3 | 0 | 0.1 |
| 2011 | SEA | MLB | 28 | 70 | 6 | 1 | 0 | 1 | 6 | 10 | 13 | 0 | 1 | .203/.314/.271 | .234 | .239 | 0.3 | -0.6 | 0.1 |
| 2012 | SEA | MLB | 29 | 250 | 25 | 9 | 0 | 5 | 20 | 28 | 69 | 1 | 1 | .205/.296/.323 | .235 | .268 | -0.2 | C -0, RF -1 | 0.4 |

Gimenez says he carries six different gloves in his equipment bag. Other than catcher, he can play first base, third base, and the outfield. That versatility got him called up to replace Adam Moore as the Mariners' backup in early April, but a variety of Gimenezes is more attractive in principle than in practice. His bat, after all, is flimsy even for a backup catcher. Besides his weekly start behind the plate, the Mariners let him play outfield just once and first base twice. Ultimately, he got loads of starts for Tacoma after a June demotion. His career .268/.376/.461 minor league line (generally in leagues for which he was a year too old) made him a better backup bet than the various Josh Bards available to teams like Seattle, but chances of a payout now that he's pushing 30 are extremely long.

### Franklin Gutierrez CF

Born: 2/21/1983 Age: 29
Bats: R Throws: R Height: 6' 3" Weight: 180
Breakout: 3% Improve: 39% Collapse: 8%
Attrition: 28% MLB: 86%

**Comparables:**
Jacob Brumfield, Tommy Murphy, Jackie Brandt

| YEAR | TEAM | LVL | AGE | PA | R | 2B | 3B | HR | RBI | BB | SO | SB | CS | AVG/OBP/SLG | TAv | BABIP | BRR | FRAA | WARP |
|------|------|-----|-----|-----|----|----|----|----|-----|----|-----|----|----|------------------|------|-------|------|------|------|
| 2009 | SEA | MLB | 26 | 629 | 85 | 24 | 1 | 18 | 70 | 46 | 122 | 16 | 5 | .283/.339/.425 | .282 | .333 | 4.4 | 10.7 | 5.0 |
| 2010 | SEA | MLB | 27 | 629 | 61 | 25 | 3 | 12 | 64 | 50 | 137 | 25 | 3 | .245/.303/.363 | .256 | .297 | -0.7 | 1.9 | 1.4 |
| 2011 | SEA | MLB | 28 | 344 | 26 | 13 | 0 | 1 | 19 | 16 | 56 | 13 | 2 | .224/.261/.273 | .200 | .266 | 0.9 | 4.8 | -0.2 |
| 2012 | SEA | MLB | 29 | 387 | 40 | 15 | 1 | 7 | 36 | 26 | 85 | 12 | 3 | .244/.297/.353 | .244 | .296 | 0.4 | CF 6 | 0.7 |

Skeptics tend to dismiss modern defensive metrics because they fluctuate wildly from year to year. But Gutierrez's otherworldly ratings on UZR and +/- have stayed pretty steady over the last four years, while his OPS and other offensive numbers have ranged from average to Mathis. That doesn't make offensive stats irrelevant, of course. It does make Gutierrez almost irrelevant, as even his good glove only gets him to the general vicinity of replacement level. The Mariners can hope the drop in his walk rate and cratering of his power numbers was caused by the irritable bowel syndrome that sidelined him for six weeks to start the season. Gutierrez claimed to be 100 percent in late May, but his impotent bat syndrome persisted until an oblique strain in early September.

### John Jaso C

Born: 9/19/1983 Age: 28
Bats: L Throws: R Height: 6' 3" Weight: 205
Breakout: 1% Improve: 35% Collapse: 5%
Attrition: 38% MLB: 96%

**Comparables:**
Tim McCarver, Russell Martin, Ryan Hanigan

| YEAR | TEAM | LVL | AGE | PA | R | 2B | 3B | HR | RBI | BB | SO | SB | CS | AVG/OBP/SLG | TAv | BABIP | BRR | FRAA | WARP |
|------|------|-----|-----|-----|----|----|----|----|-----|----|----|----|----|------------------|------|-------|------|---------|------|
| 2009 | DUR | AAA | 25 | 387 | 42 | 14 | 2 | 5 | 30 | 46 | 49 | 1 | 0 | .266/.366/.366 | .261 | .300 | -2.5 | 1.7 | 1.4 |
| 2010 | TBA | MLB | 26 | 404 | 57 | 18 | 3 | 5 | 44 | 59 | 39 | 4 | 0 | .263/.372/.378 | .277 | .282 | -0.7 | -2 | 2.0 |
| 2011 | TBA | MLB | 27 | 273 | 26 | 15 | 1 | 5 | 27 | 25 | 36 | 1 | 2 | .224/.298/.354 | .231 | .244 | 0.7 | -1 | 0.1 |
| 2012 | SEA | MLB | 28 | 286 | 32 | 12 | 1 | 4 | 24 | 34 | 40 | 1 | 1 | .240/.336/.351 | .262 | .268 | -0.1 | C -1, 1B -0 | 2.1 |

There were high hopes for Jaso in 2011 coming off his breakthrough 2010 season that saw him post a slash line of .263/.372/.378 and even saw him hit out of the leadoff position more than any other hitter on the club in 2010. He had his flaws: he was a poor hitter against left-handed pitching and he was a bit rough behind the plate. The thought was that he and Kelly Shoppach could be an effective platoon. Unfortunately, those flaws were even more glaring in 2011 and his slash line dropped to .224/.298/.354 in 273 plate appearances. He hit just .161/.316/.258 against left-handed pitching in 38 plate appearances and his ability to block pitches and throw runners out remained a work in progress. His on base percentage fell 74 points from 2010 to 2011 as his strike zone expanded and his walk rate fell five percentage points while his strikeout rate went up nearly four. He and new platoon partner Miguel Olivo are so radically different that they must be stored in separate containers, for safety.

### Alex Liddi 3B

Born: 8/14/1988 Age: 23
Bats: R Throws: R Height: 6' 5" Weight: 230
Breakout: 3% Improve: 43% Collapse: 1%
Attrition: 19% MLB: 85%

**Comparables:**
Alex Gordon, Eddie Williams, Pedro Alvarez

| YEAR | TEAM | LVL | AGE | PA | R | 2B | 3B | HR | RBI | BB | SO | SB | CS | AVG/OBP/SLG | TAv | BABIP | BRR | FRAA | WARP |
|------|------|-----|-----|-----|-----|----|----|----|-----|----|-----|----|----|------------------|------|-------|------|-----------|------|
| 2009 | HDS | A+ | 20 | 565 | 97 | 44 | 5 | 23 | 104 | 53 | 122 | 10 | 6 | .345/.415/.594 | .321 | .419 | -1.3 | -2.9 | 5.4 |
| 2010 | WTN | AA | 21 | 565 | 78 | 37 | 8 | 15 | 92 | 50 | 145 | 5 | 7 | .281/.352/.476 | .281 | .364 | -1.7 | 5.6 | 3.3 |
| 2011 | TAC | AAA | 22 | 637 | 121 | 32 | 3 | 30 | 104 | 61 | 170 | 5 | 1 | .259/.332/.488 | .275 | .312 | 4 | -4.6 | 2.9 |
| 2011 | SEA | MLB | 22 | 44 | 7 | 3 | 0 | 3 | 6 | 3 | 17 | 1 | 0 | .225/.295/.525 | .285 | .300 | 0.8 | 0 | 0.3 |
| 2012 | SEA | MLB | 23 | 250 | 28 | 11 | 1 | 9 | 31 | 18 | 74 | 2 | 1 | .236/.294/.416 | .261 | .299 | -0.1 | 3B -0, SS -0 | 1.8 |

Liddi has added 50 pounds to his frame since the Mariners signed him in 2005, and his power has grown in concert. That's important if he is to stick in the Mariners lineup, as his strikeouts—170 in Triple-A—limit what else he'll be able to do as a major league hitter. His hands and footwork at third improved in 2011, though the couple dozen games he started at shortstop in Tacoma will give you more false optimism than any indication of his future. Still, getting experience at shortstop is a lot better development than being moved to first base—a move that would erase most of Liddi's value, but a move that no longer looks necessary. His unusual background offers hope he'll continue to refine the rest of his game as he gets more exposure to top competition.

### Adam Moore C

Born: 5/8/1984 Age: 28
Bats: R Throws: R Height: 6' 4" Weight: 220
Breakout: 1% Improve: 19% Collapse: 21%
Attrition: 54% MLB: 76%

**Comparables:**
John Sullivan, John Boccabella, Barry Lyons

| YEAR | TEAM | LVL | AGE | PA | R | 2B | 3B | HR | RBI | BB | SO | SB | CS | AVG/OBP/SLG | TAv | BABIP | BRR | FRAA | WARP |
|------|------|-----|-----|-----|----|----|----|----|----|-----|----|----|----|----|------------------|------|-------|------|------|------|
| 2009 | WTN | AA | 25 | 116 | 14 | 5 | 0 | 3 | 13 | 16 | 21 | 0 | 0 | .263/.381/.411 | .279 | .310 | 0.1 | -0.5 | 0.7 |
| 2009 | TAC | AAA | 25 | 368 | 41 | 19 | 0 | 9 | 43 | 26 | 51 | 1 | 1 | .294/.345/.429 | .267 | .324 | -1.5 | -1.4 | 1.8 |
| 2009 | SEA | MLB | 25 | 24 | 4 | 1 | 0 | 1 | 2 | 0 | 7 | 1 | 0 | .217/.250/.391 | .211 | .267 | -0.3 | -0.1 | -0.1 |
| 2010 | TAC | AAA | 26 | 142 | 18 | 8 | 1 | 3 | 15 | 7 | 24 | 1 | 0 | .321/.359/.463 | .293 | .374 | 0 | -0.1 | 1.0 |
| 2010 | SEA | MLB | 26 | 218 | 12 | 6 | 0 | 4 | 15 | 8 | 63 | 0 | 1 | .195/.230/.283 | .190 | .257 | -0.9 | -0.7 | -1.0 |
| 2011 | SEA | MLB | 27 | 6 | 0 | 1 | 0 | 0 | 0 | 0 | 2 | 0 | 0 | .167/.167/.333 | .159 | .250 | 0 | 0 | -0.1 |
| 2012 | SEA | MLB | 28 | 250 | 24 | 10 | 0 | 5 | 23 | 14 | 62 | 1 | 0 | .227/.276/.336 | .229 | .283 | 0 | C -2 | 0.6 |

... and then one day you wake up and your age 27 season is just gone. You go to bed earlier, but you're always still tired. There's nothing left to feel ambitious about. What did you even accomplish this year? Nothing. Not a thing. A week of playing time, a torn medial meniscus, surgery, a bunch of rehab, another year gone. The biggest thing, though, is nobody treats you like you're special anymore. And, as much as it hurts to admit it, you're not special. You're just a guy, a guy trying to hit just one ball a week like you did when you were 22. If you could just do that, the rest of the grind would be tolerable.

### Miguel Olivo    C

Born: 7/15/1978 Age: 33
Bats: R Throws: R Height: 6' 2" Weight: 215
Breakout: 3% Improve: 20% Collapse: 11%
Attrition: 31% MLB: 74%

Comparables:
Lance Parrish, Bruce Bochy, Les Fusselman

| YEAR | TEAM | LVL | AGE | PA | R | 2B | 3B | HR | RBI | BB | SO | SB | CS | AVG/OBP/SLG | TAv | BABIP | BRR | FRAA | WARP |
|------|------|-----|-----|-----|----|----|----|----|-----|----|-----|----|----|----------------|------|-------|------|------|------|
| 2009 | KCA | MLB | 30 | 416 | 51 | 15 | 5 | 23 | 65 | 19 | 126 | 5 | 2 | .249/.292/.490 | .261 | .306 | 0.4 | -2.4 | 1.6 |
| 2010 | COL | MLB | 31 | 427 | 55 | 17 | 6 | 14 | 58 | 27 | 117 | 7 | 4 | .269/.315/.449 | .253 | .346 | 2.6 | -0.2 | 2.2 |
| 2011 | SEA | MLB | 32 | 507 | 54 | 19 | 1 | 19 | 62 | 20 | 140 | 6 | 5 | .224/.253/.388 | .241 | .270 | -0.3 | 1.7 | 1.1 |
| 2012 | SEA | MLB | 33 | 460 | 48 | 18 | 3 | 15 | 54 | 18 | 135 | 6 | 3 | .231/.264/.390 | .238 | .295 | -0.5 | C -0 | 1.0 |

The Great Man theory would posit Miguel Olivo accomplished something historical in 2011:

### Carlos Peguero    LF

Born: 2/22/1987 Age: 25
Bats: L Throws: L Height: 6' 6" Weight: 210
Breakout: 1% Improve: 24% Collapse: 3%
Attrition: 37% MLB: 93%

Comparables:
Brad Wilkerson, Hawk Taylor, Jim Beauchamp

| YEAR | TEAM | LVL | AGE | PA | R | 2B | 3B | HR | RBI | BB | SO | SB | CS | AVG/OBP/SLG | TAv | BABIP | BRR | FRAA | WARP |
|------|------|-----|-----|-----|----|----|----|----|-----|----|-----|----|----|----------------|------|-------|------|----------|------|
| 2009 | HDS | A+ | 22 | 544 | 92 | 21 | 14 | 31 | 98 | 42 | 172 | 3 | 4 | .271/.336/.560 | .287 | .353 | 1.3 | 11.3 | 3.5 |
| 2010 | WTN | AA | 23 | 553 | 86 | 23 | 5 | 23 | 73 | 56 | 178 | 7 | 9 | .254/.341/.463 | .277 | .352 | 0.8 | 5.9 | 3.1 |
| 2011 | TAC | AAA | 24 | 258 | 44 | 15 | 2 | 13 | 47 | 15 | 82 | 8 | 0 | .317/.364/.558 | .297 | .434 | 2.3 | -4.7 | 1.5 |
| 2011 | SEA | MLB | 24 | 155 | 14 | 3 | 2 | 6 | 19 | 8 | 54 | 0 | 1 | .196/.252/.371 | .228 | .262 | -0.4 | 2.1 | 0.1 |
| 2012 | SEA | MLB | 25 | 250 | 27 | 8 | 2 | 11 | 31 | 13 | 89 | 2 | 1 | .220/.267/.410 | .247 | .300 | -0.1 | LF -1, RF 1 | 0.3 |

As countless teenagers have learned in back seats, sometimes we're just not as ready as we thought we were. The Mariners made the strange decision to call up Peguero in April, and let him play regularly, despite a Wily Mo Pena-esque skill set that just shrieks for more development. His home runs, admittedly, can make a fan giddy. His first homer was the second-longest by a Mariner all year; two others he hit were, at a peak elevation of 39 feet each, the lowest home runs hit by any major leaguer in 2011. But Peguero has struck out every three at bats in the minors, a terribly negative indicator of his overall abilities. It's not too late for the Mariners to slow things down and let Peguero grow up a little bit.

### Trayvon Robinson    CF

Born: 9/1/1987 Age: 24
Bats: B Throws: R Height: 5' 11" Weight: 200
Breakout: 3% Improve: 29% Collapse: 3%
Attrition: 27% MLB: 61%

Comparables:
Willie Horton, Mel Hall, Benny Ayala

| YEAR | TEAM | LVL | AGE | PA | R | 2B | 3B | HR | RBI | BB | SO | SB | CS | AVG/OBP/SLG | TAv | BABIP | BRR | FRAA | WARP |
|------|------|-----|-----|-----|----|----|----|----|----|----|-----|----|----|----------------|------|-------|------|-----------|------|
| 2009 | SBR | A+ | 21 | 529 | 82 | 28 | 9 | 15 | 54 | 50 | 125 | 43 | 18 | .306/.377/.500 | .321 | .390 | -1 | 1.5 | 4.8 |
| 2009 | CHT | AA | 21 | 70 | 8 | 1 | 2 | 2 | 10 | 10 | 18 | 4 | 2 | .246/.343/.439 | .284 | .300 | 0.3 | -1.5 | 0.3 |
| 2010 | CHT | AA | 22 | 523 | 80 | 23 | 5 | 9 | 57 | 73 | 125 | 38 | 15 | .300/.400/.438 | .305 | .393 | 2.3 | -9.3 | 3.6 |
| 2011 | ABQ | AAA | 23 | 416 | 70 | 9 | 6 | 26 | 71 | 45 | 122 | 8 | 6 | .293/.375/.562 | .290 | .373 | 0.1 | 7.7 | 3.1 |
| 2011 | SEA | MLB | 23 | 155 | 12 | 12 | 0 | 2 | 14 | 8 | 61 | 1 | 0 | .210/.250/.336 | .227 | .346 | -0.8 | -1.4 | -0.6 |
| 2012 | SEA | MLB | 24 | 250 | 27 | 9 | 2 | 7 | 26 | 21 | 78 | 9 | 4 | .236/.303/.381 | .255 | .324 | -0.4 | CF -6, LF 2 | 1.0 |

The Dodgers were reportedly unhappy with Robinson's attitude, and the Mariners, continuing a theme in their player acquisitions, were happy to relieve them of it. Robinson has made great strides in his plate discipline since he was drafted, which is important. If he walks in 10 percent of his plate appearances, he'll be a good major league leadoff hitter, and the Mariners badly need one. More importantly, Robinson is really, really bad when he expands the strike zone. He had the majors' lowest contact rate, by a lot, on pitches outside the strike zone; if he can quit swinging at so many, his strikeout rate should find a good level. Even if he does keep whiffing, he may still hit enough line drives to prop up his batting average, so the Mariners are the only team likely to get anything out of the three-team Erik Bedard deal.

**Luis Rodriguez**                SS

Born: 6/27/1980 Age: 32
Bats: B Throws: R Height: 5' 10'' Weight: 180
Breakout: 2% Improve: 38% Collapse: 6%
Attrition: 23% MLB: 83%

**Comparables:**
Spike Owen,Orlando Cabrera,Oscar Robles

| YEAR | TEAM | LVL | AGE | PA | R | 2B | 3B | HR | RBI | BB | SO | SB | CS | AVG_OBP_SLG | TAv | BABIP | BRR | FRAA | WARP |
|------|------|-----|-----|-----|----|----|----|----|-----|----|----|----|----|-------------|------|-------|------|------------|------|
| 2009 | SDN | MLB | 29 | 251 | 18 | 6 | 0 | 2 | 16 | 37 | 23 | 1 | 0 | .202/.319/.260 | .215 | .215 | -0.8 | -0.6 | -0.4 |
| 2010 | CHR | AAA | 30 | 400 | 50 | 17 | 2 | 16 | 56 | 42 | 35 | 3 | 5 | .293/.367/.493 | .301 | .285 | -3.6 | 2.8 | 2.9 |
| 2011 | SEA | MLB | 31 | 139 | 10 | 10 | 0 | 2 | 14 | 16 | 21 | 1 | 2 | .197/.299/.333 | .251 | .219 | -1 | -1.8 | 0.4 |
| 2012 | SEA | MLB | 32 | 250 | 26 | 9 | 1 | 3 | 20 | 24 | 30 | 2 | 2 | .235/.309/.325 | .240 | .253 | -0.4 | SS -2, 2B -1 | 0.7 |

Students studying Spanish in high school know the trickiest words are the ones that sound like one English word but mean something else. Sopa, for instance, doesn't mean soap, and darned if anybody can remember that. Or the word Franchiso. Sounds like it would mean franchise, but Luis Rodriguez's nickname is "El Franchiso," so obviously it means something else, like "utility infielder hoping for a non-roster invitation, slow and squat backup shortstop, patient hitter who draws walks despite hitting like Glass Joe, persistent old guy in Triple-A, hard player to hate."

**Brendan Ryan**                SS

Born: 3/26/1982 Age: 30
Bats: R Throws: R Height: 6' 3'' Weight: 195
Breakout: 2% Improve: 23% Collapse: 6%
Attrition: 19% MLB: 83%

**Comparables:**
Bob Lillis,Don Kessinger,Greg Pryor

| YEAR | TEAM | LVL | AGE | PA | R | 2B | 3B | HR | RBI | BB | SO | SB | CS | AVG_OBP_SLG | TAv | BABIP | BRR | FRAA | WARP |
|------|------|-----|-----|-----|----|----|----|----|-----|----|----|----|----|-------------|------|-------|------|-----------|------|
| 2009 | SLN | MLB | 27 | 429 | 55 | 19 | 7 | 3 | 37 | 24 | 56 | 14 | 7 | .292/.340/.400 | .265 | .332 | -2 | 25.1 | 4.2 |
| 2010 | SLN | MLB | 28 | 486 | 50 | 19 | 3 | 2 | 36 | 33 | 60 | 11 | 4 | .223/.279/.294 | .218 | .253 | 1.8 | 8.7 | 0.8 |
| 2011 | SEA | MLB | 29 | 494 | 51 | 19 | 3 | 3 | 39 | 34 | 87 | 13 | 3 | .248/.313/.326 | .248 | .299 | 2.5 | 13.3 | 3.5 |
| 2012 | SEA | MLB | 30 | 463 | 45 | 17 | 2 | 3 | 35 | 29 | 72 | 12 | 4 | .243/.298/.313 | .232 | .281 | -0.2 | SS 12, 2B -0 | 0.6 |

The Mariners moved incumbent Jack Wilson off shortstop to make way for Ryan. It was a nod to Ryan's long-term role with the team and the impending arrival of Dustin Ackley to play second base. It was also acknowledgement that Ryan is really, really good at catching baseballs. By John Dewan's +/- system, Ryan has led all major league shortstops in runs saved over the past two seasons—by a bunch—and he is second according to UZR. Ryan's frenetic personality never played well in Tony La Russa's clubhouse. The jury was still out in Seattle until his infield triple in August, which made him something of a cult hero. Ryan's BABIP-driven offensive production of 2009 probably isn't coming back, but if there's any team that can appreciate great defense with no bat, it's Seattle.

**Michael Saunders**                CF

Born: 11/19/1986 Age: 25
Bats: L Throws: R Height: 6' 5'' Weight: 210
Breakout: 3% Improve: 42% Collapse: 13%
Attrition: 33% MLB: 79%

**Comparables:**
Drew Stubbs,Dante Powell,Brian Anderson

| YEAR | TEAM | LVL | AGE | PA | R | 2B | 3B | HR | RBI | BB | SO | SB | CS | AVG_OBP_SLG | TAv | BABIP | BRR | FRAA | WARP |
|------|------|-----|-----|-----|----|----|----|----|-----|----|----|----|----|-------------|------|-------|------|-----------|------|
| 2009 | TAC | AAA | 22 | 282 | 58 | 15 | 2 | 13 | 32 | 25 | 48 | 6 | 3 | .310/.375/.544 | .313 | .335 | 2.8 | 4.1 | 2.7 |
| 2009 | SEA | MLB | 22 | 129 | 13 | 1 | 3 | 0 | 4 | 6 | 40 | 4 | 1 | .221/.258/.279 | .196 | .329 | -0.1 | 3.5 | -0.3 |
| 2010 | TAC | AAA | 23 | 93 | 6 | 1 | 0 | 0 | 5 | 11 | 17 | 4 | 0 | .200/.293/.213 | .215 | .250 | 0.9 | 0.2 | 0.0 |
| 2010 | SEA | MLB | 23 | 327 | 29 | 11 | 2 | 10 | 33 | 35 | 84 | 6 | 3 | .211/.295/.367 | .250 | .260 | -1 | 4.9 | 0.8 |
| 2011 | TAC | AAA | 24 | 291 | 51 | 11 | 3 | 7 | 38 | 50 | 71 | 10 | 3 | .288/.415/.449 | .286 | .384 | 2.6 | 8.8 | 2.4 |
| 2011 | SEA | MLB | 24 | 179 | 16 | 5 | 0 | 2 | 8 | 12 | 56 | 1 | 2 | .149/.207/.217 | .163 | .212 | 0.8 | 3.3 | -0.9 |
| 2012 | SEA | MLB | 25 | 252 | 25 | 8 | 1 | 5 | 22 | 23 | 70 | 6 | 2 | .216/.290/.332 | .233 | .283 | -0.1 | CF 4, LF 3 | 0.0 |

The Mariners tried to fix Saunders's quirky swing in spring training. The swing is improved, the swinger, far from it. Saunders still can't hit anything on the outer half of the plate, he still has no off-field approach, and he still swings at the wrong pitches given these limitations. In an otherwise lost season, Saunders did show better patience in Tacoma, but a brutal September call-up—he went 1 for 24, improbably lowering an already minuscule OPS—means a winter of hard introspection (and Venezuelan food) for the fading former prospect.

**Kyle Seager**                2B

Born: 11/3/1987 Age: 24
Bats: L Throws: R Height: 5' 11'' Weight: 175
Breakout: 4% Improve: 16% Collapse: 7%
Attrition: 19% MLB: 55%

**Comparables:**
Luis Valbuena,Garth Iorg,Keith Drumright

| YEAR | TEAM | LVL | AGE | PA | R | 2B | 3B | HR | RBI | BB | SO | SB | CS | AVG_OBP_SLG | TAv | BABIP | BRR | FRAA | WARP |
|------|------|-----|-----|-----|-----|----|----|----|-----|----|----|----|----|-------------|------|-------|------|-----------|------|
| 2009 | CLN | A | 21 | 178 | 17 | 8 | 0 | 1 | 22 | 22 | 20 | 4 | 2 | .275/.366/.346 | .290 | .311 | -1.2 | -3.2 | 0.5 |
| 2010 | HDS | A+ | 22 | 643 | 126 | 40 | 3 | 14 | 74 | 71 | 94 | 13 | 12 | .345/.421/.503 | .319 | .394 | 3.6 | 0.8 | 6.6 |
| 2011 | WTN | AA | 23 | 299 | 33 | 25 | 1 | 4 | 37 | 26 | 38 | 8 | 5 | .312/.381/.459 | .300 | .350 | 2.2 | -0.5 | 2.2 |
| 2011 | TAC | AAA | 23 | 117 | 24 | 8 | 2 | 3 | 17 | 11 | 12 | 3 | 1 | .387/.444/.585 | .332 | .418 | 0.4 | -0.5 | 1.5 |
| 2011 | SEA | MLB | 23 | 201 | 22 | 13 | 0 | 3 | 13 | 13 | 36 | 3 | 1 | .258/.312/.379 | .266 | .303 | -1.1 | 1.8 | 0.7 |
| 2012 | SEA | MLB | 24 | 287 | 32 | 14 | 1 | 4 | 27 | 21 | 53 | 4 | 2 | .263/.320/.367 | .260 | .313 | -0.4 | 2B -1, 3B 3 | 1.6 |

Even by the standards of the Pacific Coast League, Seager's .387/.444/.585 line was impressive, especially from a 23-year-old who played all three infield positions and committed just one error in 24 games. He didn't hit .387 in the majors, because it turns out that the majors are hard, but it was a promising debut: a .121 isolated power, supported by 13 doubles and an extremely high line-drive rate. He's not particularly rangy, but his hands are quick, so he'll fit nicely at third base, with Dustin Ackley presumably monopolizing second base for the next six years.

**Justin Smoak**   **1B**

Born: **12/5/1986** Age: **25**
Bats: **B** Throws: **L** Height: **6' 5"** Weight: **220**
Breakout: **7%** Improve: **39%** Collapse: **1%**
Attrition: **16%** MLB: **73%**

**Comparables:**
Ed Bouchee, Mike Carp, Nick Johnson

| YEAR | TEAM | LVL | AGE | PA | R | 2B | 3B | HR | RBI | BB | SO | SB | CS | AVG_OBP_SLG | TAv | BABIP | BRR | FRAA | WARP |
|------|------|-----|-----|-----|-----|-----|-----|-----|-----|-----|-----|-----|-----|-------------|------|-------|------|------|------|
| 2009 | FRI | AA | 22 | 227 | 30 | 10 | 0 | 6 | 29 | 39 | 35 | 0 | 0 | .328/.453/.481 | .343 | .380 | -3.3 | 0.1 | 1.9 |
| 2009 | OKL | AAA | 22 | 237 | 25 | 11 | 0 | 4 | 23 | 35 | 45 | 0 | 0 | .244/.366/.360 | .252 | .297 | -1.5 | 0.1 | -0.1 |
| 2010 | OKL | AAA | 23 | 66 | 10 | 6 | 0 | 2 | 5 | 16 | 8 | 0 | 0 | .300/.470/.540 | .340 | .325 | -0.2 | 0.3 | 0.6 |
| 2010 | TAC | AAA | 23 | 159 | 23 | 7 | 0 | 7 | 25 | 23 | 32 | 0 | 0 | .271/.382/.481 | .320 | .309 | -1.1 | -1.2 | 1.1 |
| 2010 | SEA | MLB | 23 | 122 | 11 | 4 | 0 | 5 | 14 | 8 | 34 | 0 | 0 | .239/.287/.407 | .244 | .293 | -0.3 | -0.9 | -0.3 |
| 2010 | TEX | MLB | 23 | 275 | 29 | 10 | 0 | 8 | 34 | 38 | 57 | 1 | 0 | .209/.316/.353 | .240 | .238 | 0.4 | 4.3 | 0.0 |
| 2011 | SEA | MLB | 24 | 489 | 38 | 24 | 0 | 15 | 55 | 55 | 105 | 0 | 0 | .234/.323/.396 | .272 | .273 | -3.1 | -6.3 | 0.3 |
| 2012 | SEA | MLB | 25 | 474 | 53 | 18 | 0 | 13 | 45 | 58 | 109 | 0 | 0 | .229/.326/.367 | .261 | .277 | 0 | 1B -7 | 0.7 |

**Ichiro Suzuki**   **RF**

Born: **10/22/1973** Age: **38**
Bats: **L** Throws: **R** Height: **5' 10"** Weight: **160**
Breakout: **1%** Improve: **25%** Collapse: **16%**
Attrition: **29%** MLB: **69%**

**Comparables:**
Rick Miller, Frank Baumholtz, Jim Eisenreich

| YEAR | TEAM | LVL | AGE | PA | R | 2B | 3B | HR | RBI | BB | SO | SB | CS | AVG_OBP_SLG | TAv | BABIP | BRR | FRAA | WARP |
|------|------|-----|-----|-----|-----|-----|-----|-----|-----|-----|-----|-----|-----|-------------|------|-------|------|------|------|
| 2009 | SEA | MLB | 35 | 678 | 88 | 31 | 4 | 11 | 46 | 32 | 71 | 26 | 9 | .352/.386/.465 | .313 | .384 | 1.5 | 0.5 | 4.9 |
| 2010 | SEA | MLB | 36 | 732 | 74 | 30 | 3 | 6 | 43 | 45 | 86 | 42 | 9 | .315/.359/.394 | .285 | .353 | 2.2 | -0.9 | 3.2 |
| 2011 | SEA | MLB | 37 | 721 | 80 | 22 | 3 | 5 | 47 | 39 | 69 | 40 | 7 | .272/.310/.335 | .242 | .295 | 8.9 | -18.2 | -0.7 |
| 2012 | SEA | MLB | 38 | 680 | 74 | 21 | 3 | 2 | 55 | 36 | 89 | 34 | 7 | .290/.330/.340 | .251 | .331 | 1.3 | RF -6 | 0.8 |

For a few weeks in August and September, a flurry of singles got Ichiro within range of his 11th consecutive 200-hit season. It was probably good for his legacy that he failed. Had he collected 16 extra singles to get to 200, he would have had a .295/.332/.363 season line, the 22nd-best performance out of 23 qualifying right fielders. If that's all it takes to get to 200, what good is 200? Instead, Ichiro came up short, and we can remember the first decade of his career in the best possible light. The question, after a negative-WARP season, is whether this is it for the Ichiro we used to love. He struck out just as infrequently as ever, hit just as many line drives, and stole just as many bases, at the same high success rate, as ever. His offensive collapse, then, comes to a 100-point BABIP drop on line drives (luck) and a 40-point BABIP drop on grounders (age?). Ichiro has tormented PECOTA by defying BABIP expectations, in a positive way, for years. Ironically, his career now depends on BABIP treating him as it does every other player, and regressing to his career norms.

**Casper Wells**   **CF**

Born: **11/23/1984** Age: **27**
Bats: **R** Throws: **R** Height: **6' 3"** Weight: **210**
Breakout: **6%** Improve: **35%** Collapse: **2%**
Attrition: **14%** MLB: **72%**

**Comparables:**
Jeff Burroughs, Justin Ruggiano, Marcus Thames

| YEAR | TEAM | LVL | AGE | PA | R | 2B | 3B | HR | RBI | BB | SO | SB | CS | AVG_OBP_SLG | TAv | BABIP | BRR | FRAA | WARP |
|------|------|-----|-----|-----|-----|-----|-----|-----|-----|-----|-----|-----|-----|-------------|------|-------|------|------|------|
| 2009 | ERI | AA | 24 | 367 | 52 | 18 | 4 | 15 | 41 | 43 | 103 | 8 | 8 | .260/.369/.489 | .294 | .340 | 1.1 | -0.3 | 2.3 |
| 2010 | TOL | AAA | 25 | 430 | 56 | 22 | 6 | 21 | 46 | 34 | 111 | 7 | 8 | .233/.309/.483 | .261 | .271 | -0.6 | 0.2 | 1.3 |
| 2010 | DET | MLB | 25 | 99 | 14 | 6 | 1 | 4 | 17 | 6 | 19 | 0 | 1 | .323/.364/.538 | .324 | .371 | 0.6 | -2.1 | 0.8 |
| 2011 | SEA | MLB | 26 | 116 | 14 | 1 | 0 | 7 | 15 | 9 | 42 | 2 | 2 | .216/.310/.431 | .285 | .283 | -0.4 | 1.5 | 0.7 |
| 2011 | DET | MLB | 26 | 125 | 16 | 10 | 0 | 4 | 12 | 9 | 29 | 1 | 0 | .257/.323/.451 | .278 | .312 | -0.3 | 0.8 | 0.8 |
| 2012 | SEA | MLB | 27 | 253 | 29 | 10 | 2 | 10 | 31 | 20 | 75 | 4 | 3 | .233/.305/.426 | .269 | .296 | -0.7 | CF -1, RF -1 | 1.5 |

Brandon Morrow's average fastball is 94 mph, but on August 17, in the sixth inning, he reached back and threw his first pitch to Casper Wells at 97. The pitch hit Wells in the face. Wells somehow escaped injury and was back in the lineup the next day. That pitch, though, is the pivot point to Wells's season, as either the cause or a symptom of a problem that may not be resolved. After the pitch, he batted just .125/.222/.250. He admitted he was uncomfortable in the batter's box after the pitch, that it was "something I've got to work on, keeping my head in there." But it gets more complicated. When Morrow threw the pitch Wells was dealing with equilibrium and vision problems later diagnosed as vertigo, and he says it caused him to react slowly to Morrow's pitch and affected his hitting afterward. Wells was eventually shut down in mid-September. One way or another his final month was excusable, but the uncertainty surrounding head injuries isn't exactly reassuring.

# PITCHERS

### David Aardsma

Born: **12/27/1981** Age: **30**
Bats: **R** Throws: **R** Height: **6' 6''** Weight: **200**
Breakout: **28%** Improve: **57%** Collapse: **28%**
Attrition: **8%** MLB: **91%**

**Comparables:**
Michael Wuertz, Hideo Nomo, Mike Jackson

| YEAR | TEAM | LVL | AGE | W | L | SV | G | GS | IP | H | HR | BB | SO | EqBB9 | EqSO9 | GB% | BABIP | WHIP | ERA | FIP | FRA | WARP |
|------|------|-----|-----|---|---|----|----|----|-----|----|----|----|----|-------|-------|-----|-------|------|------|------|------|------|
| 2009 | SEA | MLB | 27 | 3 | 6 | 38 | 73 | 0 | 71¹ | 49 | 4 | 34 | 80 | 4.3 | 10.1 | 27% | .257 | 1.16 | 2.52 | 3.06 | 3.33 | 1.6 |
| 2010 | SEA | MLB | 28 | 0 | 6 | 31 | 53 | 0 | 49² | 33 | 5 | 25 | 49 | 4.5 | 8.9 | 41% | .246 | 1.17 | 3.44 | 4.01 | 4.56 | 0.1 |
| 2012 | SEA | MLB | 30 | 1 | 0 | 6 | 10 | 0 | 9 | 7 | 1 | 4 | 10 | 4.3 | 9.8 | 38% | .293 | 1.32 | 3.38 | 3.76 | 3.67 | 0.1 |

Aardsma recovered from offseason hip surgery and was rehabbing in Tacoma when his forearm started aching. Doc Yocum diagnosed it as a sprained ulnar collateral ligament but recommended rest, not Tommy John surgery. That recommendation complicates 2012, as Aardsma eventually did get shut down for the surgery in July; a second half return would be the earliest possible. The bummer for most injured closers is that most organizations have some undermarketed option who can do the job, and the incumbent's proven-closer sheen rubs off without him blowing a single save. Rather than non-tender Aardsma, the Mariners simply waived him after the World Series, giving him a few extra weeks to find a deal as a free agent.

### Blake Beavan

Born: **1/17/1989** Age: **23**
Bats: **R** Throws: **R** Height: **6' 8''** Weight: **240**
Breakout: **28%** Improve: **57%** Collapse: **17%**
Attrition: **11%** MLB: **86%**

**Comparables:**
Andy Rincon, Tommy Hunter, Dave Rozema

| YEAR | TEAM | LVL | AGE | W | L | SV | G | GS | IP | H | HR | BB | SO | EqBB9 | EqSO9 | GB% | BABIP | WHIP | ERA | FIP | FRA | WARP |
|------|------|-----|-----|----|---|----|----|----|------|-----|----|----|----|-------|-------|-----|-------|------|------|------|------|------|
| 2009 | BAK | A+ | 20 | 5 | 4 | 0 | 12 | 12 | 73¹ | 75 | 6 | 16 | 51 | 2.0 | 6.3 | 54% | .299 | 1.24 | 4.30 | 4.29 | 5.32 | 0.0 |
| 2009 | FRI | AA | 20 | 4 | 4 | 0 | 15 | 15 | 89² | 113 | 4 | 12 | 34 | 1.3 | 3.4 | 46% | .325 | 1.40 | 4.01 | 3.49 | 4.49 | 0.6 |
| 2010 | FRI | AA | 21 | 10 | 5 | 0 | 17 | 17 | 110 | 72 | 5 | 10 | 56 | 1.0 | 5.6 | 49% | .278 | 1.02 | 2.78 | 3.20 | 3.57 | 1.9 |
| 2010 | TAC | AAA | 21 | 3 | 2 | 0 | 7 | 7 | 40¹ | 47 | 3 | 8 | 25 | 1.8 | 4.9 | 43% | .370 | 1.59 | 6.48 | 4.45 | 5.20 | 0.1 |
| 2011 | TAC | AAA | 22 | 4 | 2 | 0 | 16 | 16 | 93 | 118 | 10 | 20 | 62 | 1.9 | 6.2 | 41% | .345 | 1.48 | 4.45 | 4.48 | 4.81 | 0.6 |
| 2011 | SEA | MLB | 22 | 5 | 6 | 0 | 15 | 15 | 97 | 106 | 13 | 15 | 42 | 1.4 | 3.9 | 39% | .281 | 1.25 | 4.27 | 4.49 | 4.54 | 0.3 |
| 2012 | SEA | MLB | 23 | 5 | 7 | 0 | 17 | 17 | 105² | 119 | 12 | 22 | 51 | 1.8 | 4.4 | 44% | .297 | 1.33 | 4.26 | 4.34 | 4.63 | 0.1 |

The Rangers drafted a high school pitcher with a 98 mph fastball and two strikeouts per inning, and ended up with a low-upside strike thrower edging his way through the system with a high-80s fastball. But the Mariners traded for a control pitcher who would trust his defense and eat innings in a spacious ballpark, and got it. Happiness is all about expectations. Beavan's 11 percent swinging-strike percentage is a negative indicator, but not a death sentence; it was the same as those of Mark Buehrle, Brett Anderson, Jason Marquis, Doug Fister, and Jake Westbrook, all of whom have had some measure of success. Those guys may be the 11-percenter exceptions, not the rule, but Beavan is only 22 and precociously in control of his pitches. League average is closer than you'd think.

### Dan Cortes

Born: **3/4/1987** Age: **25**
Bats: **R** Throws: **R** Height: **6' 7''** Weight: **230**
Breakout: **23%** Improve: **59%** Collapse: **19%**
Attrition: **14%** MLB: **87%**

**Comparables:**
Eddy Rodriguez, Aaron Sele, Danys Baez

| YEAR | TEAM | LVL | AGE | W | L | SV | G | GS | IP | H | HR | BB | SO | EqBB9 | EqSO9 | GB% | BABIP | WHIP | ERA | FIP | FRA | WARP |
|------|------|-----|-----|---|---|----|----|----|-----|----|----|----|----|-------|-------|-----|-------|------|------|------|------|------|
| 2009 | WTN | AA | 22 | 1 | 5 | 0 | 10 | 10 | 54² | 51 | 4 | 35 | 55 | 5.8 | 9.0 | 44% | .315 | 1.57 | 4.94 | 4.01 | 5.12 | 0.2 |
| 2009 | NWA | AA | 22 | 6 | 6 | 0 | 16 | 15 | 80¹ | 77 | 3 | 50 | 57 | 5.6 | 6.4 | 48% | .303 | 1.58 | 3.92 | 4.32 | 4.54 | 0.7 |
| 2010 | WTN | AA | 23 | 6 | 4 | 1 | 25 | 16 | 83² | 45 | 2 | 35 | 58 | 5.7 | 9.1 | 53% | .256 | 1.55 | 5.27 | 3.80 | 5.03 | 0.6 |
| 2010 | SEA | MLB | 23 | 0 | 1 | 0 | 4 | 0 | 5¹ | 3 | 0 | 3 | 6 | 5.1 | 10.1 | 21% | .214 | 1.12 | 3.38 | 2.48 | 4.78 | 0.0 |
| 2011 | TAC | AAA | 24 | 0 | 1 | 3 | 32 | 0 | 39 | 42 | 3 | 28 | 44 | 6.7 | 10.6 | 44% | .402 | 1.85 | 5.08 | 4.71 | 5.19 | 0.1 |
| 2011 | SEA | MLB | 24 | 0 | 2 | 0 | 10 | 0 | 10² | 13 | 1 | 6 | 3 | 5.1 | 2.5 | 42% | .308 | 1.78 | 5.91 | 5.69 | 4.78 | -0.1 |
| 2012 | WAS | MLB | 25 | 1 | 1 | 0 | 11 | 2 | 20¹ | 19 | 2 | 10 | 14 | 4.6 | 6.3 | 40% | .301 | 1.47 | 4.94 | 4.58 | 5.37 | -0.0 |

The great Nate Silver last decade found that the starting pitchers who most benefit from a move to the bullpen are the dangerously wild ones—the good stuff, bad control guys. Cortes fits the profile, but his first full season as a reliever didn't go well. His walk rate actually spiked to a career high in Tacoma, offsetting the benefits of a moderate strikeout increase. So he's still wild, but he's also still dangerous, hitting 95 mph with a long, muscular frame. His season ended with a hand broken in what the

Mariners called an off-field incident, a suspicious injury note for a player whose past includes a bowling alley brawl and an arrest for public urination.

**Steve Delabar**
Born: 7/17/1983 Age: 28
Bats: R Throws: R Height: 6' 6" Weight: 220
Breakout: 29% Improve: 64% Collapse: 19%
Attrition: 12% MLB: 93%

Comparables:
Mike Ignasiak, Scott Sauerbeck, Larry Sherry

| YEAR | TEAM | LVL | AGE | W | L | SV | G | GS | IP | H | HR | BB | SO | EqBB9 | EqSO9 | GB% | BABIP | WHIP | ERA | FIP | FRA | WARP |
|---|---|---|---|---|---|---|---|---|---|---|---|---|---|---|---|---|---|---|---|---|---|---|
| 2011 | WTN | AA | 27 | 1 | 3 | 12 | 23 | 0 | 30² | 23 | 0 | 26 | 30 | 7.6 | 8.8 | 50% | .287 | 1.60 | 2.05 | 3.98 | 5.70 | 0.0 |
| 2011 | SEA | MLB | 27 | 1 | 1 | 0 | 6 | 0 | 7 | 5 | 1 | 4 | 7 | 5.1 | 9.0 | 31% | .267 | 1.29 | 2.57 | 5.06 | 3.81 | 0.1 |
| 2012 | SEA | MLB | 28 | 1 | 0 | 0 | 14 | 0 | 18² | 19 | 2 | 12 | 14 | 5.8 | 6.9 | 42% | .303 | 1.68 | 5.29 | 5.03 | 5.75 | -0.2 |

How do you project a guy like this? It's impossible, so here are the facts as we know them: Delabar washed out of baseball in 2009 without ever reaching Double-A, with a steel plate in his arm and a janky elbow. He worked as a substitute teacher and assistant for a high school team. While testing a velocity improvement program for the students at John Hardin High, his fastball grew back into the mid-90s. Then he threw for a Mariners scout, signed a minor league contract and pitched at five

Bats: L Throws: L Height: 6' 6" Weight: 215
Breakout: 33% Improve: 59% Collapse: 16%
Attrition: 18% MLB: 94%

Comparables:
Matt Maloney, Johnny Podres, Scott Olsen

| YEAR | TEAM | LVL | AGE | W | L | SV | G | GS | IP | H | HR | BB | SO | EqBB9 | EqSO9 | GB% | BABIP | WHIP | ERA | FIP | FRA | WARP |
|---|---|---|---|---|---|---|---|---|---|---|---|---|---|---|---|---|---|---|---|---|---|---|
| 2010 | LAK | A+ | 24 | 4 | 5 | 0 | 13 | 13 | 77 | 55 | 5 | 9 | 86 | 1.6 | 12.7 | 43% | .325 | 1.06 | 3.39 | 2.57 | 3.55 | 1.5 |
| 2010 | TOL | AAA | 24 | 3 | 4 | 0 | 9 | 9 | 48² | 45 | 8 | 7 | 32 | 3.0 | 6.8 | 41% | .330 | 1.54 | 6.28 | 4.78 | 5.97 | 0.0 |
| 2011 | TOL | AAA | 25 | 4 | 3 | 0 | 10 | 9 | 54 | 35 | 7 | 16 | 61 | 2.7 | 10.2 | 39% | .222 | 0.94 | 3.17 | 3.61 | 4.33 | 1.0 |
| 2011 | SEA | MLB | 25 | 3 | 7 | 0 | 11 | 10 | 53 | 61 | 11 | 16 | 41 | 2.7 | 7.0 | 43% | .309 | 1.45 | 6.62 | 5.29 | 5.34 | -0.2 |
| 2011 | DET | MLB | 25 | 1 | 3 | 0 | 17 | 2 | 32¹ | 36 | 5 | 14 | 26 | 3.9 | 7.2 | 45% | .348 | 1.55 | 3.62 | 5.04 | 5.86 | -0.1 |
| 2012 | SEA | MLB | 26 | 4 | 6 | 0 | 15 | 15 | 84² | 89 | 12 | 30 | 72 | 3.2 | 7.6 | 43% | .307 | 1.40 | 4.48 | 4.41 | 4.87 | -0.1 |

The Mariners cashed in on Doug Fister's career year by trading for his younger mirror image. Furbush, a tall lefty, has the same low-90s velocity as Fister, the same broad repertoire, the same general pitch selection, the same precise command, slightly better strikeout rate, slightly worse walk and groundball rates, and the same musical taste, political leanings, and secret family chili recipe. Of course, Fister has spun his fourth-starter stuff into number-two results; Furbush won't necessarily make the same leap. He is especially vulnerable to home runs, a problem that followed him even to Safeco's forgiving boundaries.

**Felix Hernandez**
Born: 4/8/1986 Age: 26
Bats: R Throws: R Height: 6' 4" Weight: 225
Breakout: 23% Improve: 48% Collapse: 27%
Attrition: 13% MLB: 96%

Comparables:
Chad Cordero, Bryan Harvey, Tom Niedenfuer

| YEAR | TEAM | LVL | AGE | W | L | SV | G | GS | IP | H | HR | BB | SO | EqBB9 | EqSO9 | GB% | BABIP | WHIP | ERA | FIP | FRA | WARP |
|---|---|---|---|---|---|---|---|---|---|---|---|---|---|---|---|---|---|---|---|---|---|---|
| 2009 | SEA | MLB | 23 | 19 | 5 | 0 | 34 | 34 | 238² | 200 | 15 | 71 | 217 | 2.7 | 8.2 | 54% | .280 | 1.14 | 2.49 | 3.14 | 3.98 | 3.2 |
| 2010 | SEA | MLB | 24 | 13 | 12 | 0 | 34 | 34 | 249² | 194 | 17 | 70 | 232 | 2.5 | 8.4 | 55% | .265 | 1.06 | 2.27 | 3.01 | 3.75 | 3.3 |
| 2011 | SEA | MLB | 25 | 14 | 14 | 0 | 33 | 33 | 233² | 218 | 19 | 67 | 222 | 2.6 | 8.6 | 52% | .308 | 1.22 | 3.47 | 3.17 | 3.95 | 2.2 |
| 2012 | SEA | MLB | 26 | 12 | 11 | 0 | 29 | 29 | 209¹ | 180 | 14 | 56 | 200 | 2.4 | 8.6 | 54% | .294 | 1.12 | 2.61 | 2.97 | 2.84 | 4.8 |

Many a lazy analysis begins and ends with BABIP! BABIP BABIP check out this guy's BABIP! But Hernandez's season is the sort of year for which DIPS was discovered. Despite only a minor bump in line drives allowed, a 46-point BABIP spike ruined his ERA. Every other performance measure including his FIP held steady with his Cy Young-winning 2010 season. Hitters got more aggressive early in the count against Hernandez and did most of their damage on the first pitch. Opponents' OPS on Hernandez's first pitch was 400 points higher than it had been in 2010. But after the first pitch hitters hit just .216/.287/.284 against him; in 2010 after the first pitch they hit .215/.283/.319. This is either a useful bit of information that Hernandez can use to adjust—and he already has, throwing more off-speed pitches to start at bats—or the sort of misleading small sample that makes baseball analysis maddening. BABIP!

## Cesar Jimenez

Born: 11/12/1984 Age: 27
Bats: L Throws: L Height: 6' 0" Weight: 180
Breakout: 22% Improve: 69% Collapse: 14%
Attrition: 9% MLB: 94%

Comparables:
J.P. Howell, Tom Sturdivant, Jon Lester

| YEAR | TEAM | LVL | AGE | W | L | SV | G | GS | IP | H | HR | BB | SO | EqBB9 | EqSO9 | GB% | BABIP | WHIP | ERA | FIP | FRA | WARP |
|------|------|-----|-----|---|---|----|---|----|-----|-----|----|----|----|-------|-------|-----|-------|------|------|------|------|------|
| 2011 | TAC | AAA | 26 | 4 | 2 | 1 | 43 | 0 | 71 | 71 | 3 | 35 | 81 | 4.4 | 10.3 | 39% | .358 | 1.49 | 4.06 | 3.48 | 4.05 | 1.1 |
| 2011 | SEA | MLB | 26 | 1 | 0 | 0 | 8 | 0 | 6² | 6 | 0 | 3 | 7 | 4.1 | 9.4 | 48% | .300 | 1.35 | 5.40 | 2.31 | 3.53 | 0.1 |
| 2012 | SEA | MLB | 27 | 1 | 0 | 0 | 17 | 0 | 25 | 23 | 2 | 9 | 23 | 3.4 | 8.5 | 41% | .306 | 1.32 | 3.61 | 3.48 | 3.93 | 0.2 |

Like a comet that nobody bothers to name or notice, Cesar Jimenez circles back around to the big league club every few years. Then he goes right back to Triple-A, where, at 26 years old, he has already spent parts of six seasons. A torn labrum cost him most of 2010, but he returned with the same velocity in 2011 that he had before the injury, and his work for Tacoma—10 Ks per nine, just three homers allowed in the crazybananas PCL—was reassuring. Out of options and now certified healthy, he probably won't clear waivers again in 2012, forcing the Mariners to move him up for good or let him fly to somebody else's solar system.

## Shawn Kelley

Born: 4/26/1984 Age: 28
Bats: R Throws: R Height: 6' 3" Weight: 215
Breakout: 26% Improve: 54% Collapse: 20%
Attrition: 10% MLB: 92%

Comparables:
Chris Ray, Todd Worrell, John Montefusco

| YEAR | TEAM | LVL | AGE | W | L | SV | G | GS | IP | H | HR | BB | SO | EqBB9 | EqSO9 | GB% | BABIP | WHIP | ERA | FIP | FRA | WARP |
|------|------|-----|-----|---|---|----|---|----|-----|-----|----|----|----|-------|-------|-----|-------|------|------|------|------|------|
| 2009 | SEA | MLB | 25 | 5 | 4 | 0 | 41 | 0 | 46 | 45 | 9 | 9 | 41 | 1.8 | 8.0 | 33% | .283 | 1.17 | 4.50 | 4.69 | 5.20 | 0.1 |
| 2010 | SEA | MLB | 26 | 3 | 1 | 0 | 22 | 0 | 25 | 26 | 5 | 12 | 26 | 4.3 | 9.4 | 26% | .313 | 1.52 | 3.96 | 5.13 | 6.18 | -0.4 |
| 2011 | SEA | MLB | 27 | 0 | 0 | 0 | 10 | 0 | 12² | 7 | 0 | 3 | 10 | 2.1 | 7.1 | 40% | .206 | 0.79 | 0.00 | 2.19 | 2.98 | 0.2 |
| 2012 | SEA | MLB | 28 | 1 | 0 | 0 | 14 | 0 | 17 | 16 | 2 | 6 | 16 | 2.9 | 8.4 | 42% | .297 | 1.26 | 3.53 | 3.91 | 3.84 | 0.2 |

Kelley spent most of 2011 working his way back from elbow surgery, after having his frayed ligament reattached, rather than replaced, by Dr. Lewis Yocum in September 2010. None of his assignments were long enough to draw any conclusions, but as a whole they were encouraging. He allowed earned runs in just two of his 25 appearances, struck out 28, and walked just nine in 30 total innings. He did leave about two miles per hour on the operating table, which is a bit troubling for a control pitcher who was already short on stuff.

## Brandon League

Born: 3/16/1983 Age: 29
Bats: R Throws: R Height: 6' 3" Weight: 180
Breakout: 21% Improve: 49% Collapse: 26%
Attrition: 12% MLB: 98%

Comparables:
Dean Chance, Peter Moylan, Brandon Webb

| YEAR | TEAM | LVL | AGE | W | L | SV | G | GS | IP | H | HR | BB | SO | EqBB9 | EqSO9 | GB% | BABIP | WHIP | ERA | FIP | FRA | WARP |
|------|------|-----|-----|---|---|----|---|----|-----|-----|----|----|----|-------|-------|-----|-------|------|------|------|------|------|
| 2009 | TOR | MLB | 26 | 3 | 6 | 0 | 67 | 0 | 74² | 72 | 8 | 21 | 76 | 2.5 | 9.2 | 56% | .327 | 1.25 | 4.58 | 3.63 | 4.98 | 0.5 |
| 2010 | SEA | MLB | 27 | 9 | 7 | 6 | 70 | 0 | 79 | 67 | 7 | 27 | 56 | 3.1 | 6.4 | 63% | .261 | 1.19 | 3.42 | 3.88 | 5.66 | -0.7 |
| 2011 | SEA | MLB | 28 | 1 | 5 | 37 | 65 | 0 | 61¹ | 56 | 3 | 10 | 45 | 1.5 | 6.6 | 59% | .285 | 1.08 | 2.79 | 2.82 | 3.84 | 0.7 |
| 2012 | SEA | MLB | 29 | 3 | 1 | 13 | 54 | 0 | 56 | 51 | 5 | 17 | 47 | 2.7 | 7.5 | 60% | .293 | 1.21 | 3.29 | 3.60 | 3.57 | 0.7 |

There was a four-game stretch in May when League had a 30.00 ERA, took the loss in all four games, and gave up 12 hits in three innings. Predators picked up the scent of non-proven closer (*hawkins latroyus*) and closed in. "League, isn't a closer," one local columnist wrote. "Closers are a different breed, as much about attitude as stuff." From that point on, League threw 45 innings with a 1.12 ERA, saved 28 of his 30 opportunities, and started walking around town with Samuel L. Jackson's wallet from *Pulp Fiction*. He's an unconventional closer who—despite a 95 mph fastball—had the third-lowest strikeout rate among pitchers with at least 20 saves. Career-best walk and home run rates, though, make him far less stressful to watch than many of his contemporaries.

## Yoervis Medina

Born: 7/27/1988 Age: 23
Bats: R Throws: R Height: 6' 4" Weight: 250
Breakout: 30% Improve: 57% Collapse: 13%
Attrition: 8% MLB: 85%

Comparables:
Ramon Garcia, Dick Pole, Brian Rose

| YEAR | TEAM | LVL | AGE | W | L | SV | G | GS | IP | H | HR | BB | SO | EqBB9 | EqSO9 | GB% | BABIP | WHIP | ERA | FIP | FRA | WARP |
|------|------|-----|-----|---|---|----|---|----|-----|-----|----|----|----|-------|-------|-----|-------|------|------|------|------|------|
| 2010 | CLN | A | 21 | 6 | 1 | 0 | 6 | 6 | 36 | 30 | 3 | 12 | 42 | 3.0 | 10.5 | — | .311 | 1.17 | 2.50 | 3.71 | 4.47 | 0.4 |
| 2010 | EVE | A- | 21 | 3 | 2 | 0 | 8 | 8 | 40² | 49 | 4 | 15 | 48 | 3.3 | 10.6 | — | .401 | 1.57 | 4.20 | 3.66 | 5.15 | 0.2 |
| 2011 | HDS | A+ | 22 | 1 | 13 | 0 | 20 | 19 | 101 | 134 | 19 | 36 | 69 | 3.4 | 6.5 | 49% | .363 | 1.75 | 6.50 | 6.23 | 6.97 | -0.5 |
| 2012 | SEA | MLB | 23 | 1 | 3 | 0 | 6 | 6 | 33 | 40 | 5 | 14 | 17 | 3.9 | 4.6 | 47% | .310 | 1.65 | 5.78 | 5.42 | 6.28 | -0.5 |

The Mariners kept Medina in Venezuela for four years, so now he's moving quickly through the system . . . mostly for worse. He started the season in High-A after making just six starts in the Midwest League last year. His new home, High Desert, is just the rottenest place in the world to pitch, but that doesn't entirely excuse his huge drop in strikeouts, or the 19 home runs he allowed in 105 innings. He was rescued by a social promotion to Double-A, but the home runs followed him. Medina is a thick body who throws hard, has good breaking stuff, and doesn't walk many, but it might do him good to get settled in and repeat a level.

**James Paxton**

Born: **11/6/1988** Age: **23**
Bats: **L** Throws: **L** Height: **6' 5"** Weight: **220**
Breakout: **18%** Improve: **51%** Collapse: **33%**
Attrition: **12%** MLB: **96%**

**Comparables:**
Sid Fernandez, Zach Braddock, Scott Kazmir

| YEAR | TEAM | LVL | AGE | W | L | SV | G | GS | IP | H | HR | BB | SO | EqBB9 | EqSO9 | GB% | BABIP | WHIP | ERA | FIP | FRA | WARP |
|---|---|---|---|---|---|---|---|---|---|---|---|---|---|---|---|---|---|---|---|---|---|---|
| 2011 | CLN | A | 22 | 3 | 3 | 0 | 10 | 10 | 56 | 45 | 1 | 30 | 80 | 4.8 | 12.9 | 51% | .367 | 1.34 | 2.73 | 2.39 | 3.26 | 1.4 |
| 2011 | WTN | AA | 22 | 3 | 0 | 0 | 7 | 7 | 39 | 28 | 2 | 13 | 51 | 3.0 | 11.8 | 56% | .302 | 1.05 | 1.85 | 2.43 | 3.08 | 1.1 |
| 2012 | SEA | MLB | 23 | 1 | 2 | 0 | 4 | 4 | 23¹ | 21 | 2 | 12 | 26 | 4.5 | 9.8 | 48% | .309 | 1.38 | 3.79 | 3.63 | 4.12 | 0.2 |

Not only did Paxton, a fourth-round pick in 2010, have no problems with a level-skipping promotion to Double-A, he actually improved. In his final three starts for Jackson he struck out 28, walked two, and allowed two runs in 20 innings. His fastball velocity, which had dipped in 2010, returned to the mid-90s after the Mariners drafted him. He throws a very good curve that he can spin in different ways at different speeds. Because he spent a year in independent ball after the Blue Jays drafted but didn't sign him, Paxton is old enough to contend for a spot in the rotation now: older than Blake Beavan, Michael Pineda, and Danny Hultzen, who will also have a shot to start in the majors in 2012. None of those four pitchers was alive when Kirk Gibson hit his home run off Dennis Eckersley. That's how promising the Mariners' young rotation is, and that's how old you are.

Only five players since 2000 have had a better strikeout rate in an age-22-or-younger season than Pineda. Of course, three of the five are Oliver Perez, Mark Prior, and Rick Ankiel, which is worth bringing up to illustrate the fragility of young pitchers and to irritate Mariners fans. Really, though, it was a wonderful rookie year, as Pineda pounded batters with strikes (ninth-best rate in baseball) and survived (fifth-lowest opponents' batting average). Opposing teams loaded their lineups with left-handed batters against Pineda, whose lack of a changeup was supposed to make him vulnerable to such tactics. It didn't work. He held left-handers to a .237/.296/.357 line; by comparison, Cliff Lee has allowed a .260/.296/.392 line against lefties in his career. The Mariners treated him gently, shutting him down at 170 innings and never asking him to throw more than 106 pitches. That's obviously no guarantee of long-term health, and all those sliders may eventually get him.

**Chance Ruffin**

Born: **9/8/1988** Age: **23**
Bats: **R** Throws: **R** Height: **6' 1"** Weight: **185**
Breakout: **26%** Improve: **63%** Collapse: **18%**
Attrition: **11%** MLB: **96%**

**Comparables:**
Ryan Perry, Gio Gonzalez, Tommy Hanson

| YEAR | TEAM | LVL | AGE | W | L | SV | G | GS | IP | H | HR | BB | SO | EqBB9 | EqSO9 | GB% | BABIP | WHIP | ERA | FIP | FRA | WARP |
|---|---|---|---|---|---|---|---|---|---|---|---|---|---|---|---|---|---|---|---|---|---|---|
| 2011 | ERI | AA | 22 | 3 | 3 | 10 | 31 | 0 | 34 | 23 | 2 | 16 | 43 | 4.2 | 11.4 | 34% | .288 | 1.15 | 2.12 | 3.15 | 3.43 | 0.7 |
| 2011 | DET | MLB | 22 | 0 | 0 | 0 | 2 | 0 | 3² | 5 | 2 | 0 | 3 | 0.0 | 7.4 | 23% | .273 | 1.36 | 4.91 | 8.52 | 7.17 | -0.1 |
| 2011 | SEA | MLB | 22 | 1 | 0 | 0 | 13 | 0 | 14 | 13 | 2 | 9 | 15 | 5.8 | 9.6 | 37% | .306 | 1.57 | 3.86 | 4.70 | 5.98 | -0.1 |
| 2012 | SEA | MLB | 23 | 1 | 0 | 0 | 22 | 0 | 25¹ | 23 | 3 | 11 | 26 | 3.8 | 9.1 | 40% | .298 | 1.32 | 3.60 | 3.99 | 3.92 | 0.2 |

Ruffin's first professional season couldn't have gone much better, his 2.03 ERA between Double- and Triple-A earning him a promotion to the Show less than a year after the Tigers signed him. He sits at 93 mph with a plus slider and a low arm angle that makes him an uncomfortable at-bat for righties. Lefties, alas, get a correspondingly good look at that arm angle, so he'll have to prove he can get them out or he'll find himself limited to situational work.

**George Sherrill**

Born: **4/19/1977** Age: **35**
Bats: **L** Throws: **L** Height: **6' 1"** Weight: **210**
Breakout: **15%** Improve: **43%** Collapse: **36%**
Attrition: **15%** MLB: **94%**

**Comparables:**
Scott Eyre, Arthur Rhodes, Brian Fuentes

| YEAR | TEAM | LVL | AGE | W | L | SV | G | GS | IP | H | HR | BB | SO | EqBB9 | EqSO9 | GB% | BABIP | WHIP | ERA | FIP | FRA | WARP |
|---|---|---|---|---|---|---|---|---|---|---|---|---|---|---|---|---|---|---|---|---|---|---|
| 2009 | LAN | MLB | 32 | 1 | 0 | 1 | 30 | 0 | 27² | 19 | 1 | 11 | 22 | 3.6 | 7.2 | 45% | .237 | 1.08 | 0.65 | 3.13 | 3.08 | 0.6 |
| 2009 | BAL | MLB | 32 | 0 | 1 | 20 | 42 | 0 | 41¹ | 34 | 3 | 13 | 39 | 2.8 | 8.5 | 34% | .272 | 1.14 | 2.40 | 3.29 | 3.17 | 1.0 |
| 2010 | LAN | MLB | 33 | 2 | 2 | 0 | 65 | 0 | 36¹ | 46 | 4 | 24 | 25 | 5.9 | 6.2 | 43% | .347 | 1.93 | 6.69 | 5.23 | 6.94 | -1.2 |
| 2011 | ATL | MLB | 34 | 3 | 1 | 0 | 51 | 0 | 36 | 36 | 3 | 12 | 38 | 3.0 | 9.5 | 48% | .323 | 1.25 | 3.00 | 3.05 | 4.11 | 0.2 |
| 2012 | SEA | MLB | 35 | 3 | 1 | 1 | 49 | 0 | 31 | 28 | 3 | 13 | 30 | 3.7 | 8.9 | 38% | .294 | 1.30 | 3.37 | 3.78 | 3.66 | 0.4 |

A late bloomer, Sherrill did not make his major league debut until age 27. From there, he spent a few successful seasons in Seattle and Baltimore before struggling in 2010 in Los Angeles and settling for a minor league deal with the Braves. He rebounded in 2011 and earned 51 appearances by showing flashes of what made him a Mariners fan favorite. Sherrill is most effective against left-handed batters, holding them to a .256/.275/.333 line while striking out 32 batters and walking just one in 2011. He'll be returning to Seattle now, after signing a one-year $1.1 million deal with the Mariners.

### Jason Vargas

Born: 2/2/1983 Age: 29
Bats: L Throws: L Height: 6' 1" Weight: 215
Breakout: 15% Improve: 57% Collapse: 22%
Attrition: 14% MLB: 91%

Comparables:
Doug Rau, Charles Nagy, Mark Buehrle

| YEAR | TEAM | LVL | AGE | W | L | SV | G | GS | IP | H | HR | BB | SO | EqBB9 | EqSO9 | GB% | BABIP | WHIP | ERA | FIP | FRA | WARP |
|------|------|-----|-----|---|---|----|---|----|-----|-----|----|----|-----|-------|-------|-----|-------|------|------|------|------|------|
| 2009 | TAC | AAA | 26 | 4 | 3 | 0 | 9 | 9 | 51² | 48 | 3 | 15 | 46 | 2.6 | 8.0 | 30% | .321 | 1.22 | 3.13 | 3.30 | 3.52 | 1.0 |
| 2009 | SEA | MLB | 26 | 3 | 6 | 0 | 23 | 14 | 91² | 98 | 16 | 24 | 54 | 2.4 | 5.3 | 39% | .288 | 1.33 | 4.91 | 5.12 | 5.70 | 0.1 |
| 2010 | SEA | MLB | 27 | 9 | 12 | 0 | 31 | 31 | 192² | 187 | 18 | 54 | 116 | 2.5 | 5.4 | 37% | .274 | 1.25 | 3.78 | 3.91 | 3.79 | 2.2 |
| 2011 | SEA | MLB | 28 | 10 | 13 | 0 | 32 | 32 | 201 | 205 | 22 | 59 | 131 | 2.6 | 5.9 | 39% | .287 | 1.31 | 4.25 | 4.12 | 3.97 | 2.3 |
| 2012 | SEA | MLB | 29 | 9 | 11 | 0 | 28 | 28 | 176 | 174 | 18 | 47 | 121 | 2.4 | 6.2 | 37% | .288 | 1.26 | 3.57 | 3.96 | 3.88 | 1.8 |

You don't hope for, or expect, any surprises from a guy like Vargas. But in September, Felix Hernandez suggested he tweak his motion, and wouldn't you know Vargas had the best month of his career. Before the change—a little extra torso twist on his leg kick—Vargas's fastball averaged 87.1 mph; after, it was 88.2. The effects cascaded. He began to throw his changeup half as often. Consequently, when he did throw the changeup, his whiff rate went way up, and his overall strike rate also improved. Yes, sample size issues. We want to be responsible here. But the numbers are just too pretty not to publish: 23 strikeouts, five walks, and a 2.03 ERA in 27 innings. Surprise!

### Anthony Vasquez

Born: 9/19/1986 Age: 25
Bats: L Throws: L Height: 6' 1" Weight: 175
Breakout: 23% Improve: 62% Collapse: 23%
Attrition: 9% MLB: 88%

Comparables:
Allan Anderson, Jason Dickson, Brad Halsey

| YEAR | TEAM | LVL | AGE | W | L | SV | G | GS | IP | H | HR | BB | SO | EqBB9 | EqSO9 | GB% | BABIP | WHIP | ERA | FIP | FRA | WARP |
|------|------|-----|-----|---|---|----|----|----|------|-----|----|----|----|-------|-------|-----|-------|------|------|------|------|------|
| 2009 | CLN | A | 22 | 3 | 3 | 0 | 7 | 7 | 35 | 47 | 2 | 8 | 24 | 2.1 | 6.2 | 51% | .385 | 1.57 | 5.66 | 3.93 | 4.69 | 0.2 |
| 2009 | PUL | RK | 22 | 2 | 1 | 2 | 8 | 2 | 23² | 20 | 2 | 8 | 27 | 3.0 | 10.3 | 61% | .290 | 1.18 | 3.80 | 3.64 | 5.62 | 0.5 |
| 2010 | CLN | A | 23 | 2 | 2 | 0 | 8 | 8 | 48² | 30 | 2 | 6 | 42 | 1.3 | 8.3 | 56% | .264 | 0.78 | 1.29 | 3.10 | 3.38 | 0.9 |
| 2010 | HDS | A+ | 23 | 7 | 4 | 0 | 13 | 11 | 85 | 69 | 6 | 10 | 48 | 1.3 | 5.6 | 50% | .292 | 1.16 | 3.07 | 4.03 | 4.72 | 1.1 |
| 2010 | WTN | AA | 23 | 2 | 4 | 0 | 7 | 6 | 38 | 37 | 4 | 2 | 24 | 1.2 | 6.4 | 53% | .351 | 1.29 | 2.61 | 4.29 | 4.37 | 0.5 |
| 2011 | WTN | AA | 24 | 5 | 7 | 0 | 16 | 16 | 100¹ | 116 | 5 | 17 | 56 | 1.7 | 5.3 | 49% | .348 | 1.44 | 3.77 | 3.55 | 4.39 | 1.4 |
| 2011 | TAC | AAA | 24 | 2 | 2 | 0 | 8 | 8 | 53¹ | 51 | 6 | 18 | 32 | 3.0 | 5.4 | 43% | .276 | 1.29 | 3.21 | 5.01 | 4.96 | 0.5 |
| 2011 | SEA | MLB | 24 | 1 | 6 | 0 | 7 | 7 | 29¹ | 46 | 13 | 10 | 13 | 3.1 | 4.0 | 38% | .311 | 1.91 | 8.90 | 9.27 | 8.34 | -0.9 |
| 2012 | SEA | MLB | 25 | 3 | 6 | 0 | 12 | 12 | 72¹ | 85 | 10 | 21 | 38 | 2.6 | 4.7 | 47% | .305 | 1.46 | 5.00 | 4.82 | 5.44 | -0.6 |

In 1961, Roger Maris homered every 11.4 times he batted. To commemorate the 50th anniversary of that season, Anthony Vasquez allowed a home run to every 11.2 batters he faced in 2011. Apparently Vasquez loves history, and there's no way around it. The Mariners, somewhat curiously, stuck with Vasquez through the final five weeks of the season, and his woefulness ended up influencing the pennant race. In back-to-back starts against the Angels, he gave up 15 total runs. Perhaps in the interest of fairness, Seattle allowed him to make consecutive starts against Texas later in the month; he allowed 10 runs in 6 1/3 total innings. His upside is awfully low, but soft-tossing lefties who throw strikes have made millions in Safeco before. If you can't name one, you're either reading this book out of sequence or your short-term memory is atrocious.

### Taijuan Walker

Born: 8/13/1992 Age: 19
Bats: R Throws: R Height: 6' 5" Weight: 195
Breakout: 0% Improve: 60% Collapse: 40%
Attrition: 40% MLB: 86%

Comparables:
Bob Miller, Larry Dierker, Von McDaniel

| YEAR | TEAM | LVL | AGE | W | L | SV | G | GS | IP | H | HR | BB | SO | EqBB9 | EqSO9 | GB% | BABIP | WHIP | ERA | FIP | FRA | WARP |
|------|------|-----|-----|---|---|----|----|----|-----|----|----|----|-----|-------|-------|-----|-------|------|------|------|------|------|
| 2011 | CLN | A | 18 | 6 | 5 | 0 | 18 | 18 | 96² | 69 | 4 | 39 | 113 | 3.6 | 10.5 | 54% | .289 | 1.12 | 2.89 | 2.86 | 3.53 | 2.1 |
| 2012 | SEA | MLB | 19 | 1 | 2 | 0 | 4 | 4 | 23 | 22 | 2 | 12 | 21 | 4.8 | 8.1 | 49% | .305 | 1.49 | 4.36 | 4.07 | 4.74 | 0.0 |

Walker was the third-youngest pitcher in the Midwest League, and his ERA was a run better than the league average, so consider yourself alerted, keeper league managers. The 2010 supplemental draft pick has added velocity, with a sinker that hits 95 mph. His curveball went from below-average in the spring to plus by July. The control problems you would expect from an inexperienced teenager were minimal. And the inexperience that was a concern—he was focused on basketball for most of his teen years—now looks like an advantage, as he has a relatively unabused arm. Just so much good here.

**Tom Wilhelmsen**
Born: **12/16/1983** Age: **28**
Bats: **R** Throws: **R** Height: **6' 7"** Weight: **230**
Breakout: **30%** Improve: **62%** Collapse: **16%**
Attrition: **11%** MLB: **87%**

**Comparables:**
Kevin Correia, John Smoltz, Bob Locker

| YEAR | TEAM | LVL | AGE | W | L | SV | G | GS | IP | H | HR | BB | SO | EqBB9 | EqSO9 | GB% | BABIP | WHIP | ERA | FIP | FRA | WARP |
|---|---|---|---|---|---|---|---|---|---|---|---|---|---|---|---|---|---|---|---|---|---|---|
| 2011 | WTN | AA | 27 | 4 | 5 | 0 | 14 | 12 | 60² | 66 | 8 | 26 | 40 | 3.9 | 5.9 | 44% | .305 | 1.52 | 5.49 | 5.33 | 6.03 | 0.0 |
| 2011 | SEA | MLB | 27 | 2 | 0 | 0 | 25 | 0 | 32² | 25 | 2 | 13 | 30 | 3.6 | 8.3 | 35% | .258 | 1.16 | 3.31 | 3.40 | 4.65 | 0.0 |
| 2012 | SEA | MLB | 28 | 2 | 2 | 0 | 12 | 6 | 39 | 39 | 4 | 16 | 30 | 3.6 | 6.8 | 43% | .296 | 1.40 | 4.26 | 4.23 | 4.63 | 0.1 |

After testing positive for weed a couple times during his first pro season, Wilhelmsen essentially dropped out, quitting baseball to backpack and tend bar. That was 2004, and his world tour lasted about six years, until Wilhelmsen called the Mariners in 2010, asked for a tryout, impressed Jack Zduriencik, blew away batters in the low minors and made the 2011 big league team. As far as character arcs go, that's a good one, and his performance arc in 2011 was just as intriguing. Wilhelmsen struggled in April, unable to complement a 94 mph fastball with any breaking pitches he could throw for strikes. He was sent to Double-A, where, as a starter, his badness continued. The Mariners called him back up anyway, and this time he was tremendous. His post-promotion fastball sat at 96 mph, and he had a 2.35 ERA, 22 Ks, and just four walks in the final two months of the season. The Mariners were im-

At this point in a career, it's about small accomplishments. Wright earned his first save, so that's a game ball to put on the mantle. He pitched the eighth inning 33 times, a career high that reflected Seattle's trust in him. He pitched in his 500th major league game, and he passed Bob Tewksbury in career innings pitched. That's what it means to be Jamey Wright: obscure achievements, interspersed with humbling trips to Triple-A. The Mariners will hope not to need much from Wright next season, with a crop of young Seattle relievers gunning for late-inning roles. Every team, in fact, will hope not to need much from Wright next season, but some team will, and Wright will be ready.

# LINEOUTS

## HITTERS

| PLAYER | TEAM | LVL | AGE | PA | R | 2B | 3B | HR | RBI | BB | SO | SB-CS | AVG/OBP/SLG | TAv | BABIP | BRR | FRAA | WARP |
|---|---|---|---|---|---|---|---|---|---|---|---|---|---|---|---|---|---|---|
| RF J. Blash | CLN | A | 22 | 162 | 13 | 5 | 1 | 3 | 13 | 38 | 43 | 5-2 | .218/.401/.347 | .275 | .308 | -1.0 | 0.7 | 0.5 |
| | EVE | A- | 22 | 229 | 26 | 16 | 3 | 11 | 43 | 28 | 65 | 10-3 | .292/.393/.574 | .348 | .383 | -1.1 | -1.7 | 2.4 |
| SS L. Bonilla | HDS | A+ | 26 | 138 | 26 | 5 | 1 | 6 | 21 | 4 | 27 | 2-3 | .326/.351/.519 | .278 | .375 | 0.1 | -0.2 | 0.6 |
| | WTN | AA | 26 | 85 | 16 | 0 | 3 | 0 | 5 | 10 | 15 | 2-4 | .247/.333/.329 | .241 | .305 | -0.5 | 0.9 | 0.1 |
| | TAC | AAA | 26 | 77 | 7 | 0 | 0 | 0 | 5 | 2 | 14 | 2-0 | .205/.227/.205 | .154 | .254 | 0.4 | 0.4 | -0.6 |
| LF D. Carroll | HDS | A+ | 22 | 594 | 117 | 20 | 6 | 18 | 57 | 88 | 157 | 62-14 | .299/.418/.477 | .304 | .405 | 6.4 | 3.4 | 5.9 |
| 3B V. Catricala | HDS | A+ | 22 | 324 | 56 | 19 | 1 | 14 | 61 | 33 | 45 | 8-3 | .351/.421/.574 | .316 | .374 | 1.7 | 1.6 | 3.2 |
| | WTN | AA | 22 | 276 | 45 | 29 | 3 | 11 | 45 | 24 | 47 | 9-1 | .347/.420/.632 | .358 | .389 | 1.0 | 1.8 | 4.1 |
| RF C. Chiang | PME | AA | 23 | 358 | 68 | 37 | 4 | 18 | 76 | 25 | 61 | 6-2 | .340/.402/.648 | .331 | .373 | 0 | -1.6 | 3.4 |
| | WTN | AA | 23 | 141 | 11 | 7 | 0 | 0 | 10 | 6 | 30 | 1-2 | .208/.255/.262 | .196 | .265 | -1.1 | -0.6 | -0.9 |
| 3B J. Extrano | CLN | A | 22 | 80 | 8 | 2 | 2 | 1 | 2 | 7 | 19 | 2-0 | .176/.291/.309 | .229 | .229 | 0.4 | -1.8 | -0.2 |
| | EVE | A- | 22 | 84 | 11 | 3 | 2 | 1 | 8 | 7 | 14 | 2-2 | .192/.286/.329 | .271 | .220 | 0.5 | -1.3 | 0.2 |
| SS S. Kazmar | TAC | AAA | 26 | 519 | 50 | 29 | 3 | 3 | 45 | 36 | 68 | 7-6 | .253/.311/.348 | .235 | .286 | -3.7 | -5.3 | -0.6 |
| SS M. Littlewood | CLN | A | 19 | 106 | 7 | 0 | 1 | 1 | 6 | 10 | 23 | 0-1 | .158/.236/.211 | .162 | .194 | 0.2 | -2.4 | -0.8 |
| | EVE | A- | 19 | 279 | 45 | 13 | 1 | 8 | 30 | 45 | 81 | 3-3 | .206/.337/.373 | .261 | .278 | -0.7 | -4.9 | 0.4 |
| 3B F. Martinez | ERI | AA | 20 | 372 | 63 | 14 | 4 | 7 | 46 | 19 | 80 | 7-8 | .282/.319/.405 | .249 | .346 | 5.7 | 9.3 | 2.3 |
| | WTN | AA | 20 | 137 | 20 | 7 | 3 | 3 | 23 | 4 | 24 | 3-2 | .310/.326/.481 | .267 | .356 | 0.2 | 0.7 | 0.6 |
| DH E. Martinez-Esteve | WTN | AA | 27 | 62 | 8 | 4 | 1 | 0 | 5 | 8 | 14 | 0-0 | .269/.377/.385 | .261 | .368 | -1.6 | -0.1 | -0.1 |
| SS B. Miller | CLN | A | 21 | 59 | 9 | 4 | 1 | 0 | 7 | 4 | 9 | 1-0 | .415/.458/.528 | .338 | .489 | -0.9 | -2.5 | 0.6 |
| 1B D. Raben | HDS | A+ | 23 | 347 | 61 | 23 | 3 | 18 | 75 | 28 | 76 | 2-1 | .330/.387/.599 | .311 | .382 | 0.1 | -3 | 1.7 |
| SS C. Triunfel | WTN | AA | 21 | 433 | 45 | 22 | 2 | 6 | 35 | 25 | 71 | 5-7 | .281/.340/.392 | .261 | .330 | 1.7 | -0.4 | 1.8 |
| | TAC | AAA | 21 | 117 | 7 | 6 | 1 | 0 | 10 | 2 | 17 | 1-0 | .279/.302/.351 | .228 | .326 | -1.6 | 1.9 | 0.1 |
| RF M. Wilson | TAC | AAA | 28 | 388 | 73 | 27 | 0 | 16 | 49 | 45 | 86 | 5-2 | .331/.418/.555 | .325 | .404 | 2.2 | 1.6 | 4.0 |
| | SEA | MLB | 28 | 28 | 0 | 1 | 0 | 0 | 3 | 1 | 7 | 0-0 | .148/.179/.185 | .171 | .200 | -0.7 | -0.2 | -0.3 |

**Jabari Blash**'s combination of athleticism, plate discipline, size, and name will make him your favorite non-star player in 2015 or 2016. He rarely swings at a ball, which is great, but he'll need to learn to leverage those hitters counts into extra-base hits, not just bushels of walks. ⊘ **Leury Bonilla** played every position but first base and pitcher, and he has played each of those before too, which makes him a superutility player, if not a super utility player. In four different stints over the past three years, he still hasn't hit anywhere higher than the California League. ⊘ **Daniel Carroll** led the Cal League in steals, was second in walks, and (partly due to his skill at being hit by pitches) eighth in OBP. Excitement about his breakout season is tempered by the Mariners' decision to move him off center field to a corner. ⊘ **Vincent Catricala** had a big half-season at High Desert, but nobody pays any attention to what hitters do in High Desert. Then he had an even bigger half-season in Jackson, but his path to the majors gets bumpier when the Mariners move his poor glove to first base permanently. ⊘ **Chih-Hsien Chiang** broke out in his second year at Double-A, giving credit to an improved diet after years of struggling to manage his Type-1 diabetes. As far as ex-post-facto explanations go, this might not be quite on the level of Kevin Mench changing shoe sizes, but it is a bit flimsy, and Chiang came undone like a worn-out flip-flop after going to the Mariners in the Erik Bedard trade. ⊘ **Jetsy Extrano** has been hit by 39 pitches in 900 minor league at bats, which demonstrates his willingness to . . . awwww who are we kidding, we just wanted to say Jetsy Extrano. ⊘ **Sean Kazmar** is a throwback player, if by throwback you mean hits like he's playing in the Deadball Era, fields like the ball is lopsided, and doesn't play baseball in Seattle. He made 23 errors in a half-season at shortstop. ⊘ **Marcus Littlewood**, a second-round pick in 2010, has been an offensive disappointment, even by shortstop standards. The Mariners decided to convert him to catcher, where the requirements are even lower, so that's what he worked on this winter. If that doesn't work, expect to see him training for LOOGY work next. ⊘ **Francisco Martinez** is the upside piece of the Doug Fister trade, a Venezuelan third baseman who has been among his league's youngest players since the Tigers signed him in 2007. Because of his youth, he has never put up eye-popping numbers, but had a fine month with Jackson after the trade. ⊘ **Eddy Martinez-Esteve** put up a good on-base percentage in Double-A, made four errors in six games at first base, then got injured and missed the rest of the season. He was awarded the Eddy Martinez-Esteve Award for having the most

Eddy Martinez-Esteve season. ⊘ Second-round shortstop **Brad Miller** hit .415 in his professional debut. It was only 59 plate appearances in the Midwest League, but he also won the ACC batting title, so he spent just about all of 2011 batting over .400. Small sample sizes giveth, and small sample sizes taketh away: he committed four errors in 14 games as a pro. ⊘ An injury once again slowed **Dennis Raben**'s climb through the system, as knee surgery ended his season in June. In 116 Cal League games over two seasons, Raben has slugged .626 and hit 30 home runs, though 22 of those bombs and a disproportionate share of his rate stats have come at home. ⊘ **Carlos Triunfel** was a bit young for the Southern League, even as he repeated the level, and he put up a close approximation of the league's .263/.339/.400 slash line. That's moderately encouraging, but a ton of errors on top of poor range make it as obvious as ever that he's not a shortstop. ⊘ **Mike Wilson** made his big league debut, at age 28, as a pinch-hitter. He popped out to first base, but the Mariners rallied to send the game into extra-innings and Wilson ended up getting four plate appearances. In the 13th inning, he got his first big league hit to drive in the go-ahead run. And then the Mariners lost anyway, because nothing truly great ever happens to Mike Wilson.

|  |  |  |  |  |  |  |  |  |  |  |  |  |  |  |  |  |  |  |  |
|---|---|---|---|---|---|---|---|---|---|---|---|---|---|---|---|---|---|---|---|
|  | NYA | MLB | 26 | 0 | 0 | 0 | 4 | 5 | 0 | 0 | 2 | 0.0 | 4.5 | 44% | .312 | 1.25 | 2.25 | 2.06 | 4.19 | 0.1 |
| S. Patterson | WTN | AA | 32 | 1 | 1 | 10 | 21¹ | 18 | 1 | 1 | 24 | 0.4 | 10.1 | 38% | .321 | 0.89 | 2.53 | 1.94 | 3.02 | 0.5 |
|  | TAC | AAA | 32 | 2 | 2 | 9 | 47¹ | 47 | 4 | 6 | 53 | 1.1 | 10.1 | 27% | .328 | 1.12 | 3.99 | 2.98 | 3.43 | 1.1 |
| C. Ray | SEA | MLB | 29 | 3 | 2 | 0 | 32² | 33 | 2 | 12 | 22 | 3.3 | 6.1 | 49% | .307 | 1.38 | 4.68 | 3.61 | 4.84 | -0.1 |
| N. Robertson | TAC | AAA | 33 | 5 | 4 | 0 | 93¹ | 133 | 14 | 38 | 55 | 3.7 | 5.3 | 42% | .361 | 1.85 | 7.14 | 5.86 | 6.17 | 0.0 |

The last time **Steve Garrison** pitched in the Pacific Northwest, he put up an 8.87 ERA in Portland. As if 200-plus cloudy days per year weren't depressing enough. ⊘ Slider-iffic reliever **Josh Kinney** struggled on the South Side and was outrighted; he's never been the same since his 2007 Tommy John surgery, and is rapidly running out of chances. ⊘ Four good innings for the Yankees in June spared **Jeff Marquez** the indignity of having to carry around an 18.00 ERA for the rest of his life. The Mariners signed him to a minor league deal. ⊘ Thirty-two-year-old **Scott Patterson** (77 Ks, seven walks between Double- and Triple-A) wishes he could play Little League now. He'd be way better than before. ⊘ This is what's known as the **Nate Robertson** Infinity Loop: Step 1. Gives up 10 runs in the PCL on August 26. "Well, I'm certainly not going to end my career on that." Step 2. Throws eight innings, allows no earned runs on August 31. "Woohoo I've still got it!" Step 1. Allows nine earned runs on September 5. "Well, I'm certainly not going to end my career on that". Forever.

# MANAGER: ERIC WEDGE

| YEAR | TEAM | W-L | Pythag +/- | Avg PC | 100+ P | 120+ P | QS | BQS | REL | REL w Zero R | IBB | Subs | PH | PH Avg | PH HR | SB2 | CS2 | SB3 | CS3 | SAC Att | SAC % | POS SAC | Squeeze | Swing | In Play |
|---|---|---|---|---|---|---|---|---|---|---|---|---|---|---|---|---|---|---|---|---|---|---|---|---|---|
| 2009 | CLE | 65-97 | 0 | 94.5 | 65 | 2 | 70 | 10 | 444 | 256 | 31 | 19 | 63 | .231 | 0 | 13 | 2 | 0 | 0 | 54 | 72.2% | 35 | 0 | 138 | 107 |
| 2011 | SEA | 67-95 | 0 | 99.7 | 83 | 6 | 94 | 10 | 351 | 272 | 27 | — | 49 | .209 | 1 | 18 | 3 | 0 | 0 | 49 | 91.8% | 44 | 2 | 322 | 90 |

There are odd things Eric Wedge did this year that would matter . . . if they had mattered. If the Mariners were competing for something and Adam Kennedy were still batting cleanup, or Carlos Peguero were still playing every day, or Ichiro were still locked into the leadoff spot, Wedge would have had to explain himself. But Wedge didn't sweat the details in his first year, focusing instead on evaluating a roster that is in a state of almost total turnover. That position led to some unusual playing-time decisions, and 152 different batting orders—he used only one lineup more than twice—but it also gave him extended looks at every upper level prospect in the system. Wedge is more the leader-of-men type than a creative strategist, and little stands out about his game management. His Mariners tallied exactly the league average number of sacrifice bunts and issued one fewer intentional pass than league average. Seattle has been willing to take on a lot of bad-makeup guys lately, yet 2011 was a relatively drama-free season, even during a 17-game losing streak in July. Wedge deserves credit for that and for maintaining a disciplined clubhouse that may pay long-term dividends as prospects matriculate. But the attitude demands he puts on his players—"It takes men to win championships," he said in a September radio interview—will really pay off or backfire when the Mariners are playing games that matter.

# Tampa Bay Rays

**B**leeding talent is an unfortunate situation for any organization, no matter the industry: publishing, finance, or baseball. Too often, top talent leaves because of budget cuts to meet a bottom line, but the moves may have immediate negative impact on a group of free agents that compiled 152.3 runs over replacement for the Rays in 2010, when the entire team's value was 361.8 runs.

Columnist John Romano wrote the following in the *St. Pete Times* prior to the 2011 Winter Meetings in Orlando:

"If it looks like their best deal is to strip down and go longer-term, the Rays should not hesitate to put themselves in position to contend in 2012 or '13. Even if it means taking a couple of steps backward in 2011 to do it.

"For what the Rays should not do is waste either time or money. And history says they are too smart for that. Because, for a team of limited resources, it makes absolutely no sense to play to the middle."

And 2011 looked like it was going to be a season lost to mediocrity. PECOTA had Tampa Bay's playoff odds at the start of the season at just 19 percent and projected the team to go 83-79. Since the implementation of the wild-card format, no team had ever clinched the wild card in the American League with fewer than 94 wins. Just to meet that criterion, the Rays would have needed to exceed their projections by 12 percent and hope that Boston or New York would *not* meet their preseason projections of 94 and 91 wins respectively. *Baseball Prospectus* alumnus Jonah Keri wrote about how the Rays found *The Extra 2%*, but no book has yet been written on how to find an additional 12 percent.

The tone of last offseason changed from despair to hope for Rays fans when the team announced the dual-signing of Johnny Damon and Manny Ramirez. While their combined projected WARP was a full two wins less than Crawford's, the name recognition greatly

| | | |
|---|---|---|
| TAv-P | .256 | 11th |
| FIP | 4.07 | 19th |
| DER | .735 | 1st |
| DL | 313 | 1st |
| B-Age | 28.2 | 9th |
| P-Age | 27.1 | 7th |
| Salary | $43.2 | 29th |
| M$/MW | $.712 | 1st |

team with the AL's best defense wins the wild card, but another ALDS loss

**2012:** A few quiet, smart moves, and this team wins another wild card (then loses to Texas again)

**Action Items:** Cheap but effective first baseman and DH, perhaps in a trade for some of their pitching depth

tive twist. Seventy-eight-win projections by local media personalities became 85-win projections overnight. Even a few of the ESPN baseball personalities picked the Rays to reach the postseason in a late spring survey, something that would have been considered laughable earlier in the offseason.

In the end that offseason boost was Ramirez's only positive contribution, as he chose retirement over serving a 100-game suspension for a second violation of MLB's policy against use of performance enhancing drugs. The 2011 season got off to an ominous start when the team was not only swept by Baltimore but also dropped all five games of the opening homestand. The mood darkened when the club learned during the first road trip of the season about Manny's failed test. The player projected to hit in the middle of the lineup, for a team everyone expected to struggle to produce runs, was gone for the season. The Rays' answer to replacing Ramirez in the lineup was to promote Kotchman, who went on to surprise everyone with a career best .299 TAv and a 2.1 WARP in what became known as "The Magic of Kotch," and that narrative was just one of many that evolved during the season. The defensive excellence and pitching that were expected to carry the club blossomed.

The Legend of Sam Fuld helped drag the team out of its early April doldrums, Month of May (MOM) Matt Joyce helped carry that into May, and the team defense led by Evan Longoria and Ben Zobrist, with a completely rebuilt bullpen, kept the team competitive while the offense went through peaks and valleys depending on the schedule. You see, Tropicana Field did not take kindly to the new stadium talk after the 2008 season and has slowly been forcing stronger park factors onto to the Rays to the point their home/road splits are now rather drastic. All the while, James Shields seemingly completed every game he started while picking off each runner that reached first base. Shields' 2011 turnaround was extra special given the 2010 season ended with some questioning his presence on the postseason roster and many wondering why he was allowed to start Game Two against Texas. Last season saw a refined Shields, with a cleaner delivery and command of all of his pitches, with less predictability than in the past. That included his move to first base, which became a lethal weapon in keeping baserunners anchored to the bag. Shields posted a career best 3.45 FIP and a 3.8 WARP.

By the end of the season, the team overcame a 9 1/2-game deficit. With a little help from cheap beer and bad fried chicken, the Rays made the postseason at 91-71. The question going into 2012, though, is: can can they do it again? Can they depend on some role-players overacheiving and their competitors underachieving? No. But the young core the Rays are built on remains: Shields, Longoria, Zobrist, David Price, and others.

Most teams worry when their ace pitcher comes off a career year because it means either a big payday through arbitration or free agency, but neither is an issue with "Big Game" James. Shields remains under team control thanks to a team-friendly extension signed in 2008 that allowed the Rays to exercise an option for 2012 at the cost of just $7 million. That, and the controlled costs associated with the contracts of Wade Davis, Zobrist, and the uniquely team-friendly Longoria deal allow the Rays to stay within their budgetary constraints. They aren't all bargains, however. Price made the Super Two cutoff after the season and his salary will escalate. B.J. Upton will likely return for a final season in the bay area and be the team's highest-paid player, making slightly more than Shields in 2012. Nonetheless, projected payroll should still be below $50 million this year: one of the lowest payrolls in all of baseball. There is little hope of that changing any time soon.

The stadium situation has remained unchanged since the club shelved plans to open a waterfront stadium in downtown St. Petersburg in 2009. Since then, the economic outlook in the greater Tampa Bay area has worsened. Tourism and construction are key industries in the area and do not flourish in down economic times; unemployment is two percentage points above the national average. Add an extremely high rate of home foreclosures in the region and it is no wonder that despite the team's on-field successes, attendance is in a three-year decline. The empty seats continue to inspire national scorn. The season ended with principal owner Stuart Sternberg airing his frustrations with the "untenable" situation: "I am frustrated this year. We've replicated last year [on the field] and our attendance numbers were down 15 percent and our ratings were down. The rubber has got to meet the road at some point here. When you go through the season, you control your own destiny, if you win out. We're getting to the point where we don't control our own destiny. This is untenable as a model going forward.

"When you're sitting here at this point and you lost by a run, you know another X dollars might have changed things. Three or five million wouldn't have changed things necessarily but 15 to 30 might have. That's where we were. And for the foreseeable future that's what we've got . . . Whatever you want to say, there are 29 other teams passing us like we're going in reverse right now. Except on the field. And at some point that changes."

The names on the jerseys may continue to change for the Rays, but the economic woes appear as constant as the 95 degree temperatures and afternoon thunderstorms in the summer. Playing in a depressed home market, in an antiquated stadium that does not attract the type of corporate support the team's competitors enjoy, leaves the team at a competitive disadvantage. Yet, over the past four seasons, the team has been able to cast aside those burdens and win two division titles in the toughest division in the league, make the postseason three times, and make it to the World Series once.

This season remains tough to project because the Rays let the market play out before jumping into the fray. While other teams push large stacks of chips into the center of the table at the Winter Meetings, signing the big name free agents to contracts that rarely return the investment, the Rays wait for things too cool off and for the supply of players to be larger than the demand for their services. That is how they were able to get Damon and Ramirez below market value and how they were able to get Pat Burrell at a perceived discount when that contract was written. At press time, the only three moves the Rays had made were the controversial acquisition of Josh Lueke and the signings of Jose Molina and Burke Badenhop. But it could be argued that retaining Friedman and signing Matt Moore to his new extension are two of the best moves of the offseason. The first base and designated hitter situation are still unfilled, making it difficult to project how different the team will look from the one that posted the sixth-best team VORP in all of baseball. (Unfortunately, that was only good enough for fifth-best in the American League.)

The process the Rays have in place has proven to be successful on the field, but Sternberg is not the only one doubting its sustainability in the coming years. A record haul of draft picks in the most recent amateur draft (before the new collective bargaining agreement changed the terms of the game) provided more talent to an already rich farm system well stocked with starting pitching talent, but the value of those prospects is all in potential at this time. None of them will be in a position to help the Rays win, either on the field or as trading chips, for some time yet. The Rays' process requires constant internal talent development to get players to the major leagues and sign them to pre-agency deals.

Zobrist, Davis, Shields, and most recently Moore were signed in order to avoid the toxic process of paying free agents for past performance rather than future results. How the process adapts against a changing landscape will determine the sustainability of the franchise for the coming years. This season remains a murky picture, and the years beyond even more so. If the economic situation or the stadium news brightens, so will the entire picture. Until then, the product on the field will have to speak for itself.

The former top overall pick turned his career around and hit .271/.328/.408 between Double-A and Triple-A. A 736 OPS and "turned his career around" should never be used in the same sentence for a former top overall draft pick but there is no way to sugarcoat the disappointing career that Beckham has had to date. He will return to Durham, where he took his last 111 plate appearances in 2011 while walking just three times and striking out 29 times. Ideally, Beckham would be competing for the Rays' starting shortstop position after the team suffered through the terribly unproductive trio of Brignac, Johnson, and Rodriguez last season, but he is not there. He will likely never be Buster Posey, but at least now Beckham's career has a pulse again, and he is only 22.

**Ryan Brett**    **2B**
Born: **10/9/1991** Age: **20**
Bats: **B** Throws: **R** Height: **5' 10''** Weight: **180**
Breakout: **0%** Improve: **1%** Collapse: **0%**
Attrition: **0%** MLB: **1%**

Comparables:
LJ Hoes, Logan Watkins, Cesar Hernandez

| YEAR | TEAM | LVL | AGE | PA | R | 2B | 3B | HR | RBI | BB | SO | SB | CS | AVG_OBP_SLG | TAv | BABIP | BRR | FRAA | WARP |
|------|------|-----|-----|----|---|----|----|----|-----|----|----|----|----|-------------|-----|-------|-----|------|------|
| 2010 | RAY | RK | 18 | 99 | 8 | 5 | 2 | 0 | 9 | 8 | 17 | 12 | 3 | .303/.367/.404 | .297 | .375 | 0.7 | 1.9 | 1.0 |
| 2011 | PRI | RK | 19 | 270 | 42 | 22 | 5 | 3 | 24 | 26 | 24 | 21 | 3 | .300/.370/.471 | .315 | .321 | 1.7 | 5.9 | 2.9 |
| 2012 | TBA | MLB | 20 | 250 | 19 | 9 | 1 | 0 | 15 | 13 | 56 | 7 | 2 | .192/.237/.248 | .189 | .247 | 0.1 | 2B 1 | -1.9 |

The offensive-minded sparkplug hit .300/.370/.471 for Princeton in 270 plate appearances, showcasing some of the desired skills for leadoff hitters. He walked more often than he struck out and was once again very efficient in stealing bases: caught just three times in 24 attempts. Brett has the speed and athleticism to move to center field if the middle infield gets crowded. He switch-hits but is more effective from the left side of the plate (just seven extra base hits in 76 plate appearances from the right side). For a guy with his speed, it would behoove him to raise his 40 percent groundball rate while cutting down on his 40 percent fly-ball rate.

**Reid Brignac**    **SS**
Born: **1/16/1986** Age: **26**
Bats: **L** Throws: **R** Height: **6' 4''** Weight: **180**
Breakout: **2%** Improve: **40%** Collapse: **4%**
Attrition: **22%** MLB: **71%**

Comparables:
Robert Andino, Dale Berra, Julio Lugo

| YEAR | TEAM | LVL | AGE | PA | R | 2B | 3B | HR | RBI | BB | SO | SB | CS | AVG_OBP_SLG | TAv | BABIP | BRR | FRAA | WARP |
|------|------|-----|-----|----|---|----|----|----|-----|----|----|----|----|-------------|-----|-------|-----|------|------|
| 2009 | DUR | AAA | 23 | 453 | 51 | 28 | 2 | 8 | 44 | 27 | 69 | 5 | 5 | .282/.328/.417 | .251 | .320 | 0.5 | -0.1 | 1.3 |
| 2009 | TBA | MLB | 23 | 93 | 10 | 8 | 2 | 1 | 6 | 3 | 20 | 2 | 2 | .278/.301/.444 | .253 | .348 | 0.3 | -0.2 | 0.3 |
| 2010 | TBA | MLB | 24 | 326 | 39 | 13 | 1 | 8 | 45 | 20 | 77 | 3 | 3 | .256/.307/.385 | .253 | .317 | 1.9 | 3.5 | 1.4 |
| 2011 | TBA | MLB | 25 | 264 | 18 | 4 | 0 | 1 | 15 | 10 | 63 | 3 | 1 | .193/.227/.221 | .172 | .254 | 0.1 | 5.6 | -0.6 |
| 2012 | TBA | MLB | 26 | 268 | 26 | 11 | 1 | 5 | 25 | 15 | 62 | 3 | 2 | .226/.274/.341 | .229 | .278 | -0.4 | SS 3, 2B 0 | 0.3 |

One of eight players in baseball who hit under .200 while seeing at least 250 plate appearances in 2011. Only Drew Butera managed that many plate appearances and had a lower True Average in 2011 than Brignac. He managed just five extra-base hits, though his sole home run was off Jered Weaver. Despite Brignac's struggles at the plate, he remained one of the better defensive shortstops in baseball; his FRAA was sixth best in baseball at 5.6, and his glovework up the middle was a big reason the pitching staff posted a league-best BABIP for a second consecutive season. That glove is his best big-league feature, but his bat will continue to limit his playing time unless he makes some positive changes to a swing with a pronounced uppercut. Out of options, Brignac figures to open the season on a major league roster. Which one is the question.

| Russ Canzler | 3B |
|---|---|
| Born: 4/11/1986 Age: 26 | |
| Bats: R Throws: R Height: 6' 3" Weight: 220 | |
| Breakout: 3% Improve: 34% Collapse: 5% | |
| Attrition: 17% MLB: 91% | |
| **Comparables:** | |
| Dwight Evans, Jeff Burroughs, Joe Hague | |

| YEAR | TEAM | LVL | AGE | PA | R | 2B | 3B | HR | RBI | BB | SO | SB | CS | AVG_OBP_SLG | TAv | BABIP | BRR | FRAA | WARP |
|---|---|---|---|---|---|---|---|---|---|---|---|---|---|---|---|---|---|---|---|
| 2009 | DAY | A+ | 23 | 108 | 14 | 8 | 1 | 2 | 14 | 7 | 24 | 2 | 0 | .270/.318/.430 | .258 | .338 | 1.2 | 2.4 | 0.4 |
| 2009 | TEN | AA | 23 | 267 | 27 | 15 | 0 | 6 | 35 | 31 | 41 | 2 | 5 | .258/.346/.399 | .269 | .289 | -2.4 | -2.7 | 0.1 |
| 2010 | TEN | AA | 24 | 411 | 68 | 28 | 4 | 21 | 66 | 46 | 95 | 5 | 4 | .287/.377/.566 | .317 | .339 | -0.5 | -3.9 | 3.0 |
| 2011 | DUR | AAA | 25 | 549 | 78 | 40 | 4 | 18 | 83 | 67 | 129 | 5 | 2 | .314/.401/.530 | .298 | .396 | 1.5 | -1.6 | 3.4 |
| 2012 | TBA | MLB | 26 | 250 | 30 | 12 | 1 | 8 | 30 | 23 | 62 | 2 | 1 | .249/.319/.425 | .274 | .306 | -0.2 | 3B -1, 1B -4 | 2.0 |

As with Dan Johnson's addition, an under-the-radar minor league acquisition paid off in spades for the Durham Bulls as Canzler won the International League MVP honors (just as Johnson had). He produced a .315/.399/.531 slash line on the season with 62 extra base hits, but there are some strikes against him. He doesn't hit with enough power to play the corners on an everyday basis and bats on the wrong side of a platoon. Like Johnson before him, Canzler has earned his chance to take his hacks against major league pitching. It should not surprise anyone if the two players' stories continue to mirror one another.

| Robinson Chirinos | C |
|---|---|
| Born: 6/5/1984 Age: 28 | |
| Bats: R Throws: R Height: 6' 2" Weight: 195 | |
| Breakout: 4% Improve: 23% Collapse: 8% | |
| Attrition: 40% MLB: 94% | |
| **Comparables:** | |
| Johnny Romano, Don Pavletich, Charlie O'Brien | |

| YEAR | TEAM | LVL | AGE | PA | R | 2B | 3B | HR | RBI | BB | SO | SB | CS | AVG_OBP_SLG | TAv | BABIP | BRR | FRAA | WARP |
|---|---|---|---|---|---|---|---|---|---|---|---|---|---|---|---|---|---|---|---|
| 2009 | DAY | A+ | 25 | 270 | 40 | 13 | 5 | 11 | 47 | 35 | 40 | 2 | 2 | .300/.404/.546 | .328 | .324 | -0.9 | 0.5 | 2.9 |
| 2010 | TEN | AA | 26 | 318 | 53 | 24 | 0 | 15 | 64 | 42 | 35 | 1 | 5 | .318/.421/.580 | .339 | .322 | -1.5 | 0.5 | 4.1 |
| 2010 | IOW | AAA | 26 | 62 | 10 | 4 | 0 | 3 | 10 | 2 | 8 | 0 | 0 | .364/.435/.600 | .334 | .386 | 0.2 | 0.3 | 0.8 |
| 2011 | DUR | AAA | 27 | 319 | 24 | 13 | 1 | 6 | 24 | 29 | 69 | 1 | 1 | .259/.343/.376 | .243 | .324 | -2 | 0 | 0.5 |
| 2011 | TBA | MLB | 27 | 60 | 4 | 2 | 0 | 1 | 7 | 5 | 13 | 0 | 0 | .218/.283/.309 | .242 | .268 | -1 | -0.1 | -0.1 |
| 2012 | TBA | MLB | 28 | 250 | 29 | 11 | 1 | 8 | 28 | 23 | 50 | 1 | 1 | .247/.326/.410 | .273 | .283 | -0.2 | C -0, 1B -0 | 2.5 |

Part of the haul the Rays got in return for sending Matt Garza to the Cubs, Chirinos had received praise for his defense and an improving bat in Chicago, but only one of those attributes came with him. He continued to hit lefties well (.312/.369/.468) in Durham but his defense received mixed reviews. Chirinos was called up just after the break when both John Jaso and Jose Lobaton went on the disabled list. Chirinos looked overmatched both at the plate and behind it, as his developing footwork and release allowed baserunners to steal at will. A broken wrist in winter ball probably hampers his arrival in the bigs as well.

| Johnny Damon | LF |
|---|---|
| Born: 11/5/1973 Age: 38 | |
| Bats: L Throws: L Height: 6' 1" Weight: 175 | |
| Breakout: 0% Improve: 20% Collapse: 16% | |
| Attrition: 16% MLB: 66% | |
| **Comparables:** | |
| Tommy Henrich, Harold Baines, Paul Molitor | |

| YEAR | TEAM | LVL | AGE | PA | R | 2B | 3B | HR | RBI | BB | SO | SB | CS | AVG_OBP_SLG | TAv | BABIP | BRR | FRAA | WARP |
|---|---|---|---|---|---|---|---|---|---|---|---|---|---|---|---|---|---|---|---|
| 2009 | NYA | MLB | 35 | 626 | 107 | 36 | 3 | 24 | 82 | 71 | 98 | 12 | 0 | .282/.365/.489 | .296 | .305 | 3.1 | -5.6 | 3.2 |
| 2010 | DET | MLB | 36 | 613 | 81 | 36 | 5 | 8 | 51 | 69 | 90 | 11 | 1 | .271/.355/.401 | .276 | .312 | 2.2 | -0.8 | 2.0 |
| 2011 | TBA | MLB | 37 | 647 | 79 | 29 | 7 | 16 | 73 | 51 | 92 | 19 | 6 | .261/.326/.418 | .284 | .284 | -3.1 | 0.3 | 2.1 |
| 2012 | TBA | MLB | 38 | 601 | 69 | 25 | 4 | 12 | 60 | 59 | 96 | 16 | 3 | .254/.329/.384 | .269 | .286 | 0.5 | LF -0, CF -0 | 1.5 |

At last, the local kid returned. The Rays efforts to claim Damon on waivers the season beforehand were negated by Boston's own claim, but they signed him as a free agent for 2011. Damon did not disappoint, as his 2.4 Wins Above Replacement Player were more than the Rays received from the position over the previous three seasons combined. He endeared himself to the fan base with several key hits during the team's 21-7 streak that turned the season around after an abysmal start. Damon showed power and speed, belying his 37 years as he tried to join Gary Sheffield and Paul O'Neill as the only players to pull off a 20/20 season at age 37 or older. Both of those players did that at age 38. Damon can stake claim to being the only player to go 20/20 multiple times after age 37 should he do it again.

| Sam Fuld | LF |
|---|---|
| Born: 11/20/1981 Age: 30 | |
| Bats: L Throws: L Height: 5' 11" Weight: 185 | |
| Breakout: 1% Improve: 37% Collapse: 8% | |
| Attrition: 24% MLB: 87% | |
| **Comparables:** | |
| Tom Poquette, Bob Molinaro, Brady Clark | |

| YEAR | TEAM | LVL | AGE | PA | R | 2B | 3B | HR | RBI | BB | SO | SB | CS | AVG_OBP_SLG | TAv | BABIP | BRR | FRAA | WARP |
|---|---|---|---|---|---|---|---|---|---|---|---|---|---|---|---|---|---|---|---|
| 2009 | IOW | AAA | 27 | 370 | 62 | 17 | 10 | 2 | 33 | 38 | 24 | 23 | 5 | .284/.359/.415 | .274 | .300 | 4.1 | 2.3 | 2.2 |
| 2009 | CHN | MLB | 27 | 115 | 17 | 6 | 1 | 1 | 2 | 17 | 10 | 2 | 1 | .299/.409/.412 | .296 | .326 | 0.7 | 0.2 | 0.8 |
| 2010 | IOW | AAA | 28 | 440 | 69 | 15 | 9 | 4 | 27 | 66 | 37 | 21 | 9 | .272/.384/.394 | .282 | .293 | 0 | 13.1 | 4.4 |
| 2010 | CHN | MLB | 28 | 31 | 3 | 1 | 0 | 0 | 3 | 3 | 5 | 0 | 0 | .143/.226/.179 | .135 | .174 | -0.1 | 1 | -0.2 |
| 2011 | TBA | MLB | 29 | 346 | 41 | 18 | 5 | 3 | 27 | 32 | 49 | 20 | 8 | .240/.313/.360 | .256 | .276 | 0.5 | 8.2 | 1.9 |
| 2012 | TBA | MLB | 30 | 262 | 27 | 11 | 3 | 2 | 21 | 26 | 35 | 12 | 4 | .239/.317/.333 | .249 | .270 | -0.1 | LF 6, CF 2 | 0.7 |

It was a legendary season for the diminutive Stanford grad for many reasons. After a special April that featured numerous high-light reel grabs and a near-cycle, Fuld became perhaps the first player to earn his own Twitter hashtag (#LegendofSamFuld). That legendary status faded when the Rays were forced to play him every day due to a lack of options. Fuld hit .218/.292/.327 over the final five months of the season and gave way to Desmond Jennings in left field in July. Pitchers challenged him within the strike zone due to his lack of power. Fuld's defensive and baserunning abilities make him a worthy bench player. Expect him to receive fewer plate appearances and *New Yorker* features than he did last season.

**Brandon Guyer** RF

Born: 1/28/1986 Age: 26
Bats: R Throws: R Height: 6' 2" Weight: 210
Breakout: 2% Improve: 41% Collapse: 10%
Attrition: 25% MLB: 88%

**Comparables:**
Franklin Gutierrez, Nate Schierholtz, Chris

| YEAR | TEAM | LVL | AGE | PA | R | 2B | 3B | HR | RBI | BB | SO | SB | CS | AVG_OBP_SLG | TAv | BABIP | BRR | FRAA | WARP |
|---|---|---|---|---|---|---|---|---|---|---|---|---|---|---|---|---|---|---|---|
| 2009 | DAY | A+ | 23 | 305 | 40 | 16 | 3 | 2 | 32 | 24 | 34 | 23 | 2 | .347/.418/.453 | .318 | .393 | 0.1 | -4 | 2.1 |
| 2009 | TEN | AA | 23 | 205 | 22 | 12 | 2 | 1 | 14 | 10 | 33 | 7 | 5 | .190/.236/.291 | .218 | .223 | -3 | -3.5 | -1.0 |
| 2010 | TEN | AA | 24 | 410 | 76 | 39 | 6 | 13 | 58 | 27 | 51 | 30 | 3 | .344/.395/.588 | .330 | .368 | -0.7 | 10.2 | 5.9 |
| 2011 | DUR | AAA | 25 | 443 | 78 | 29 | 5 | 14 | 61 | 35 | 79 | 16 | 6 | .312/.384/.521 | .294 | .360 | 1.3 | 7.2 | 3.7 |
| 2011 | TBA | MLB | 25 | 43 | 7 | 1 | 0 | 2 | 3 | 1 | 9 | 0 | 0 | .195/.214/.366 | .220 | .200 | 0.4 | 0 | 0.0 |

**Jake Hager** SS

Born: 3/4/1993 Age: 19
Bats: R Throws: R Height: 6' 2" Weight: 170
Breakout: 0% Improve: 1% Collapse: 0%
Attrition: 0% MLB: 1%

**Comparables:**
Jesus Lopez, Ydwin Villegas, Edwin Garcia

| YEAR | TEAM | LVL | AGE | PA | R | 2B | 3B | HR | RBI | BB | SO | SB | CS | AVG_OBP_SLG | TAv | BABIP | BRR | FRAA | WARP |
|---|---|---|---|---|---|---|---|---|---|---|---|---|---|---|---|---|---|---|---|
| 2011 | PRI | RK | 18 | 204 | 29 | 11 | 1 | 4 | 17 | 9 | 26 | 5 | 7 | .269/.305/.399 | .237 | .294 | -0.1 | -9.8 | -0.6 |
| 2012 | TBA | MLB | 19 | 250 | 17 | 8 | 1 | 1 | 16 | 7 | 61 | 3 | 2 | .180/.205/.237 | .168 | .232 | -0.6 | SS -1 | -2.5 |

He was a bit of a surprise as the 32nd overall pick in the 2011 draft but the prep star from Vegas garners a lot of "gamer" praise. The $963,000 Tampa Bay offered Hager was just a bit over slot but enough to convince him to drop his commitment to Arizona State and quickly report to Princeton, where the 18-year-old hit .269/.305/.399 as the eighth youngest player in the Appalachian League. Hager earned praise for his actions and play belying his age, which helps frame his selection as one made on merit and projection rather than the popular initial surmise of a signing made on signability.

**Desmond Jennings** CF

Born: 10/30/1986 Age: 25
Bats: R Throws: R Height: 6' 3" Weight: 200
Breakout: 4% Improve: 42% Collapse: 8%
Attrition: 24% MLB: 90%

**Comparables:**
Dexter Fowler, Jim Eisenreich, Tom Tresh

| YEAR | TEAM | LVL | AGE | PA | R | 2B | 3B | HR | RBI | BB | SO | SB | CS | AVG_OBP_SLG | TAv | BABIP | BRR | FRAA | WARP |
|---|---|---|---|---|---|---|---|---|---|---|---|---|---|---|---|---|---|---|---|
| 2009 | MNT | AA | 22 | 440 | 69 | 25 | 8 | 8 | 45 | 48 | 52 | 37 | 5 | .316/.399/.486 | .325 | .350 | 9.9 | 9.3 | 6.5 |
| 2009 | DUR | AAA | 22 | 137 | 23 | 6 | 2 | 3 | 17 | 19 | 15 | 15 | 2 | .325/.422/.491 | .287 | .351 | 1.8 | -0.5 | 1.1 |
| 2010 | DUR | AAA | 23 | 458 | 82 | 25 | 6 | 3 | 36 | 47 | 67 | 37 | 4 | .278/.359/.393 | .267 | .323 | 6.3 | 6.1 | 3.1 |
| 2010 | TBA | MLB | 23 | 24 | 5 | 1 | 1 | 0 | 2 | 2 | 4 | 2 | 2 | .190/.292/.333 | .230 | .235 | 0 | 0.3 | 0.0 |
| 2011 | DUR | AAA | 24 | 397 | 68 | 19 | 3 | 12 | 39 | 45 | 78 | 17 | 1 | .275/.374/.456 | .277 | .325 | 5.9 | 4.1 | 2.8 |
| 2011 | TBA | MLB | 24 | 287 | 44 | 9 | 4 | 10 | 25 | 31 | 59 | 20 | 6 | .259/.356/.449 | .297 | .303 | 1.4 | -0.9 | 1.6 |
| 2012 | TBA | MLB | 25 | 276 | 33 | 10 | 3 | 7 | 30 | 27 | 54 | 15 | 3 | .254/.338/.409 | .276 | .295 | 0.6 | CF 3, LF -0 | 2.1 |

At age 25, Jennings is finally trading in his prospect badge for a spot in a major league lineup. He is carrying high expectations on a frame that has had trouble staying healthy throughout his minor league career. Once the Manny Ramirez debacle unfolded, all eyes shifted to Durham as everyone wondered when the Rays would call-up their top hitting prospect. Partly due to an untimely wrist injury, Jennings stayed in Durham longer than expected and fell eight plate appearances short of reaching 1000 at Triple-A. Once called up, he showcased his talents in spurts. He hit .337 with a 1056 OPS in his first 23 games. But over his final 40 contests, pitchers got him to first expand his zone upward and then off the plate, resulting in just a .215 average with a 664 OPS.

## Dan Johnson    1B

Born: 8/10/1979 Age: 32
Bats: L Throws: R Height: 6' 3" Weight: 220
Breakout: 1% Improve: 26% Collapse: 5%
Attrition: 11% MLB: 81%

Comparables:
Kent Hrbek, Eddie Murray, Norm Cash

| YEAR | TEAM | LVL | AGE | PA | R | 2B | 3B | HR | RBI | BB | SO | SB | CS | AVG/OBP/SLG | TAv | BABIP | BRR | FRAA | WARP |
|------|------|-----|-----|-----|----|----|----|----|-----|----|----|----|----|-------------|------|-------|------|-----------|------|
| 2010 | DUR | AAA | 30 | 426 | 66 | 19 | 0 | 30 | 95 | 75 | 71 | 0 | 0 | .303/.436/.624 | .335 | .305 | -3.5 | 0.8 | 3.9 |
| 2010 | TBA | MLB | 30 | 140 | 15 | 3 | 0 | 7 | 23 | 25 | 27 | 1 | 0 | .198/.343/.414 | .280 | .188 | 0.1 | -0.9 | 0.3 |
| 2011 | DUR | AAA | 31 | 395 | 52 | 23 | 0 | 13 | 52 | 58 | 65 | 0 | 1 | .273/.382/.459 | .283 | .304 | -0.9 | 3.9 | 2.0 |
| 2011 | TBA | MLB | 31 | 91 | 7 | 1 | 0 | 2 | 4 | 6 | 18 | 0 | 0 | .119/.187/.202 | .141 | .125 | 0.2 | 1.3 | -0.9 |
| 2012 | TBA | MLB | 32 | 250 | 31 | 9 | 0 | 10 | 29 | 36 | 47 | 0 | 0 | .230/.344/.423 | .285 | .245 | 0 | 1B -1, 3B 0 | 2.0 |

Johnson employed the Teddy Roosevelt strategy of speaking softly and carrying a big stick. Unfortunately for Johnson, that big stick only showed up twice all season, but fortunately for the Rays, it showed up at two very big moments. His first home run came on a cold, wet night in Chicago against Matt Thornton to snap the Rays' season-opening losing streak at six. Then, going into the final day of the season, Johnson had been just 1-for-45 all season with two strikes. In the bottom of the ninth, facing Cory Wade with two outs and a 2-2 count, Johnson hit his second dinger of the year. That home run saved the Rays from going home, but even that was not enough to save Johnson's status in the organization. He was outrighted off the 40-man roster after the season and elected free agency. The Great Pumpkin will have to rise somewhere else in 2012.

## Elliot Johnson    SS

Born: 3/9/1984 Age: 28
Bats: B Throws: R Height: 6' 1" Weight: 185
Breakout: 2% Improve: 27% Collapse: 7%
Attrition: 14% MLB: 73%

Comparables:
Jeff Blauser, Jim Smith, Lee Tate

| YEAR | TEAM | LVL | AGE | PA | R | 2B | 3B | HR | RBI | BB | SO | SB | CS | AVG/OBP/SLG | TAv | BABIP | BRR | FRAA | WARP |
|------|------|-----|-----|-----|----|----|----|----|-----|----|----|----|----|-------------|------|-------|------|-----------|------|
| 2009 | DUR | AAA | 25 | 260 | 31 | 9 | 1 | 11 | 35 | 17 | 56 | 7 | 2 | .262/.313/.451 | .263 | .291 | 1.3 | -1.1 | 0.9 |
| 2010 | DUR | AAA | 26 | 481 | 72 | 24 | 5 | 11 | 56 | 37 | 92 | 30 | 6 | .319/.367/.475 | .277 | .372 | 4.1 | -1 | 3.1 |
| 2011 | TBA | MLB | 27 | 181 | 20 | 7 | 2 | 4 | 17 | 14 | 53 | 6 | 7 | .194/.257/.338 | .224 | .260 | -1.7 | 0.5 | -0.3 |
| 2012 | TBA | MLB | 28 | 250 | 26 | 10 | 2 | 6 | 25 | 18 | 63 | 8 | 3 | .235/.292/.368 | .244 | .293 | -0.2 | SS -2, 2B -0 | 0.9 |

After collecting over 1700 plate appearances in Triple-A, Johnson finally played a full season in the major leagues, mainly because he was out of options. His defensive versatility was helpful at times, but his bat was nearly as awful as Brignac's and he was just 6-for-13 in stolen base attempts. The undrafted free agent has been in the organization since 2002, but his skill set is fungible and easily replaced. It is improbable that the Rays carry two offensively challenged shortstops again in 2012.

## Matt Joyce    RF

Born: 8/3/1984 Age: 27
Bats: L Throws: R Height: 6' 3" Weight: 185
Breakout: 3% Improve: 43% Collapse: 7%
Attrition: 13% MLB: 87%

Comparables:
Roger Maris, Manny Ramirez, Vic Wertz

| YEAR | TEAM | LVL | AGE | PA | R | 2B | 3B | HR | RBI | BB | SO | SB | CS | AVG/OBP/SLG | TAv | BABIP | BRR | FRAA | WARP |
|------|------|-----|-----|-----|----|----|----|----|-----|----|----|----|----|-------------|------|-------|------|-----------|------|
| 2009 | DUR | AAA | 24 | 493 | 73 | 35 | 2 | 16 | 66 | 67 | 98 | 14 | 5 | .273/.378/.482 | .294 | .323 | -2 | 4.5 | 3.1 |
| 2009 | TBA | MLB | 24 | 37 | 3 | 1 | 0 | 3 | 7 | 3 | 7 | 1 | 0 | .188/.270/.500 | .294 | .130 | -0.6 | -0.2 | 0.1 |
| 2010 | DUR | AAA | 25 | 115 | 18 | 8 | 0 | 3 | 12 | 22 | 21 | 1 | 3 | .293/.435/.478 | .314 | .353 | 0.4 | 0.3 | 0.9 |
| 2010 | TBA | MLB | 25 | 261 | 30 | 15 | 3 | 10 | 40 | 40 | 55 | 2 | 2 | .241/.360/.477 | .299 | .273 | -2.2 | 3.6 | 1.9 |
| 2011 | TBA | MLB | 26 | 522 | 69 | 32 | 2 | 19 | 75 | 49 | 106 | 13 | 1 | .277/.347/.478 | .301 | .317 | -0.3 | -4 | 2.7 |
| 2012 | TBA | MLB | 27 | 438 | 55 | 22 | 3 | 16 | 55 | 50 | 100 | 7 | 2 | .244/.334/.444 | .285 | .285 | -0.1 | RF 1, LF 0 | 2.1 |

Joyce sat against left-handed pitching until late in the season but still had a career year and made the All-Star team. Joyce's isolated power against right-handed pitching in 2011 was higher than that of Ian Kinsler, Aramis Ramirez, Jay Bruce, Alex Gordon, or Nick Swisher. His All-Star selection hinged in large part on the run from late April to early June when he hit .409/.464/.782 in 125 plate appearances, and during which he hit 10 of his 19 home runs. An old shoulder issue flared up in early June, lingered for the rest of the summer, and he hit .225/.302/.381 the rest of the way. Defensively, his numbers took a hit in right field in 2011 and a few analysts within the Rays blogosphere have made a case for Joyce to move to first base. The idea has traction given the organization's outfield depth and the void at first.

## Casey Kotchman    1B

Born: 2/22/1983 Age: 29
Bats: L Throws: L Height: 6' 4" Weight: 210
Breakout: 1% Improve: 45% Collapse: 13%
Attrition: 19% MLB: 85%

Comparables:
Gregg Jefferies, Gail Hopkins, Mark Grace

| YEAR | TEAM | LVL | AGE | PA | R | 2B | 3B | HR | RBI | BB | SO | SB | CS | AVG/OBP/SLG | TAv | BABIP | BRR | FRAA | WARP |
|------|------|-----|-----|-----|----|----|----|----|-----|----|----|----|----|-------------|------|-------|------|--------|------|
| 2009 | ATL | MLB | 26 | 336 | 28 | 20 | 0 | 6 | 41 | 32 | 28 | 0 | 0 | .282/.354/.409 | .268 | .292 | -1 | -0.3 | 0.5 |
| 2009 | BOS | MLB | 26 | 95 | 9 | 3 | 0 | 1 | 7 | 7 | 14 | 1 | 0 | .218/.284/.287 | .219 | .250 | -0.3 | 1.8 | -0.2 |
| 2010 | SEA | MLB | 27 | 457 | 37 | 20 | 1 | 9 | 51 | 35 | 57 | 0 | 0 | .217/.280/.336 | .221 | .229 | -3.7 | -3 | -2.2 |
| 2011 | TBA | MLB | 28 | 563 | 44 | 24 | 2 | 10 | 48 | 48 | 66 | 2 | 2 | .306/.378/.422 | .297 | .335 | -4.4 | -2.4 | 1.9 |
| 2012 | TBA | MLB | 29 | 509 | 57 | 24 | 2 | 9 | 50 | 42 | 56 | 2 | 1 | .257/.325/.377 | .266 | .273 | -0.2 | 1B -2 | 1.0 |

One of the biggest surprises in baseball, Kotchman revived his comatose career to start for a playoff team. Kotchman had been playing with an eye infection that was "like looking through a dirty windshield." Offseason surgery corrected the issue and looking through a clean windshield can't have hurt given that he hit over .300 for the first time in his career. At a pure skill level, Kotchman was the same player he has always been but the results were better. His walk and strikeout rates and batted ball outcomes were all identical to previous years, except for one puzzling developement: an increase in infield hits. Kotchman possesses grade-20 foot speed only because there is not a grade lower, yet he had a higher percentage of infield hits than Shane Victorino, Dexter Fowler, or Jimmy Rollins. Kotchman was viewed as one of the worst players in baseball just a year ago. Unlike, say, Jose Bautista, this does not feel like a legitimate change in true talent level.

**Hak-Ju Lee** SS

Born: 11/4/1990 Age: 21
Bats: L Throws: R Height: 6' 3" Weight: 170
Breakout: 2% Improve: 27% Collapse: 1%
Attrition: 14% MLB: 47%

**Comparables:**
Elvis Andrus, Alfredo Griffin, Omar Infante

| YEAR | TEAM | LVL | AGE | PA | R | 2B | 3B | HR | RBI | BB | SO | SB | CS | AVG_OBP_SLG | TAv | BABIP | BRR | FRAA | WARP |
|------|------|-----|-----|-----|----|----|----|----|-----|----|----|----|----|-------------|------|-------|------|------|------|
| 2009 | BOI | A- | 18 | 304 | 56 | 14 | 2 | 2 | 33 | 31 | 50 | 25 | 8 | .330/.394/.420 | .304 | .390 | 2.2 | 11.9 | 4.0 |
| 2010 | PEO | A | 19 | 551 | 85 | 22 | 4 | 1 | 40 | 49 | 86 | 32 | 7 | .282/.347/.351 | .265 | .333 | 6.5 | 8.2 | 4.1 |
| 2011 | PCH | A+ | 20 | 454 | 82 | 16 | 11 | 4 | 23 | 42 | 72 | 28 | 14 | .317/.389/.442 | .287 | .380 | 1.5 | 3 | 3.7 |
| 2011 | MNT | AA | 20 | 114 | 16 | 1 | 4 | 1 | 7 | 11 | 22 | 5 | 2 | .190/.272/.310 | .227 | .228 | -0.2 | 0.2 | 0.2 |
| 2012 | TBA | MLB | 21 | 250 | 23 | 8 | 2 | 1 | 19 | 15 | 55 | 11 | 4 | .226/.275/.296 | .214 | .284 | -0.3 | SS 9 | -0.3 |

Born: 10/21/1984 Age: 27
Bats: B Throws: R Height: 6' 1" Weight: 195
Breakout: 7% Improve: 33% Collapse: 4%
Attrition: 26% MLB: 71%

**Comparables:**
George Kottaras, Logan Johnson, Luke Montz

| YEAR | TEAM | LVL | AGE | PA | R | 2B | 3B | HR | RBI | BB | SO | SB | CS | AVG_OBP_SLG | TAv | BABIP | BRR | FRAA | WARP |
|------|------|-----|-----|-----|----|----|----|----|-----|----|----|----|----|-------------|------|-------|------|------|------|
| 2009 | MNT | AA | 24 | 102 | 13 | 7 | 0 | 3 | 11 | 15 | 19 | 0 | 0 | .262/.376/.452 | .294 | .302 | 0 | -0.5 | 0.7 |
| 2009 | POR | AAA | 24 | 148 | 14 | 6 | 0 | 3 | 8 | 10 | 35 | 0 | 0 | .241/.286/.353 | .249 | .293 | -0.9 | -0.5 | 0.5 |
| 2009 | SDN | MLB | 24 | 17 | 0 | 0 | 0 | 0 | 0 | 0 | 5 | 0 | 0 | .176/.176/.176 | .083 | .250 | -0.4 | 0 | -0.4 |
| 2010 | DUR | AAA | 25 | 271 | 26 | 11 | 0 | 7 | 33 | 27 | 52 | 1 | 0 | .261/.337/.394 | .250 | .306 | -2.1 | -0.5 | 0.6 |
| 2011 | DUR | AAA | 26 | 224 | 24 | 10 | 1 | 8 | 31 | 37 | 50 | 0 | 0 | .293/.410/.489 | .301 | .362 | -4.3 | 0.7 | 1.7 |
| 2011 | TBA | MLB | 26 | 39 | 2 | 1 | 0 | 0 | 0 | 4 | 8 | 0 | 0 | .118/.231/.147 | .138 | .154 | 0 | 0 | -0.3 |
| 2012 | TBA | MLB | 27 | 250 | 26 | 9 | 1 | 6 | 23 | 25 | 62 | 0 | 0 | .222/.305/.349 | .245 | .277 | 0 | C -1 | 1.1 |

Lobaton was an afterthought of a pickup during the 2010 season who blossomed in 2011 at Triple-A. He hit .293/.411/.486 for the Bulls in 221 plate appearances while playing alongside Robinson Chirinos. Lobaton's defense and strong throwing arm were what had merited him a slot on the 40-man roster, so the offensive numbers breed optimism. After little exposure or success against left-handed pitching as a switch-hitter in the Padres system, Lobaton has hit .333/.396/.486 against left-handers in 155 plate appearances in the Rays' organization. Out of options, Lobaton could be the odds-on favorite to caddy Jose Molina.

**Evan Longoria** 3B

Born: 10/7/1985 Age: 26
Bats: R Throws: R Height: 6' 3" Weight: 210
Breakout: 0% Improve: 31% Collapse: 3%
Attrition: 22% MLB: 91%

**Comparables:**
Jim Ray Hart, Ron Santo, David Wright

| YEAR | TEAM | LVL | AGE | PA | R | 2B | 3B | HR | RBI | BB | SO | SB | CS | AVG_OBP_SLG | TAv | BABIP | BRR | FRAA | WARP |
|------|------|-----|-----|-----|-----|----|----|----|-----|----|-----|----|----|-------------|------|-------|------|------|------|
| 2009 | TBA | MLB | 23 | 671 | 100 | 44 | 0 | 33 | 113 | 72 | 140 | 9 | 0 | .281/.364/.526 | .297 | .313 | 3.1 | 15.6 | 6.6 |
| 2010 | TBA | MLB | 24 | 661 | 96 | 46 | 5 | 22 | 104 | 72 | 124 | 15 | 5 | .294/.372/.507 | .314 | .336 | 3.4 | 8 | 6.9 |
| 2011 | TBA | MLB | 25 | 574 | 78 | 26 | 1 | 31 | 99 | 80 | 93 | 3 | 2 | .244/.355/.495 | .314 | .239 | -2.1 | 9.7 | 6.3 |
| 2012 | TBA | MLB | 26 | 559 | 74 | 29 | 3 | 25 | 77 | 61 | 115 | 7 | 2 | .257/.345/.479 | .300 | .287 | 0 | 3B 11 | 4.5 |

Playing 26 of the first 28 games without their franchise player may explain some of the Rays' rough start to 2011. Longoria strained an oblique muscle in the second game of the season and did not return until early May. If not for the injury and his slow recovery, he could have had a career year at the plate. He nearly had career high home run and RBI totals despite 100 fewer plate appearances than his previous low. Longoria also battled a nerve problem in his left foot in the second half that did not hurt him in the field as much as it did on the basepaths, as he became more of a station-to-station player than ever before. He, and his extremely team-friendly contract, continue to be the most vital pieces to the team's overall success.

### Juan Miranda    1B

Born: 4/25/1983 Age: 29
Bats: L Throws: L Height: 6' 1" Weight: 220
Breakout: 7% Improve: 34% Collapse: 9%
Attrition: 21% MLB: 73%

**Comparables:**
Jim Breazeale, Willie Aikens, Ron Johnson

| YEAR | TEAM | LVL | AGE | PA | R | 2B | 3B | HR | RBI | BB | SO | SB | CS | AVG_OBP_SLG | TAv | BABIP | BRR | FRAA | WARP |
|------|------|-----|-----|----|----|----|----|----|-----|----|----|----|----|-------------|-----|-------|-----|------|------|
| 2009 | SWB | AAA | 26 | 502 | 74 | 30 | 2 | 19 | 82 | 55 | 101 | 1 | 0 | .290/.373/.498 | .303 | .340 | -0.5 | 10.3 | 3.5 |
| 2009 | NYA | MLB | 26 | 9 | 2 | 0 | 0 | 1 | 3 | 0 | 4 | 0 | 0 | .333/.333/.667 | .358 | .500 | -0.1 | -0.1 | 0.1 |
| 2010 | SWB | AAA | 27 | 340 | 52 | 15 | 1 | 15 | 43 | 33 | 71 | 1 | 0 | .285/.374/.495 | .279 | .330 | 0.1 | 1.7 | 1.2 |
| 2010 | NYA | MLB | 27 | 71 | 7 | 2 | 1 | 3 | 10 | 7 | 12 | 0 | 0 | .219/.296/.422 | .245 | .224 | -0.3 | 0.3 | 0.0 |
| 2011 | RNO | AAA | 28 | 126 | 17 | 4 | 1 | 5 | 24 | 20 | 36 | 0 | 1 | .229/.357/.429 | .251 | .297 | -0.1 | -3.5 | -0.3 |
| 2011 | ARI | MLB | 28 | 202 | 18 | 8 | 2 | 7 | 23 | 23 | 48 | 0 | 1 | .213/.315/.402 | .259 | .252 | -2.8 | -1.2 | -0.1 |
| 2012 | TBA | MLB | 29 | 250 | 29 | 10 | 1 | 8 | 27 | 27 | 59 | 0 | 0 | .232/.322/.402 | .268 | .276 | 0 | 1B -9 | 1.0 |

First base often seems so stacked with sluggers that it's hard to see how the average TAv at the position ends up at .284 instead of something more in line with the lofty .300-plus figures recorded by the Cabreras, Fielders, and Vottos of the world. We'll let you in on a little secret: it's Miranda's doing. Granted, he had some accomplices—a few of whom also played first for Arizona last season—but the left-handed hitter was one of the least productive first basemen to get 200 plate appearances. Not surprisingly, he didn't make it much past 200 before being busted back to Triple-A, where his bat barely picked up, despite the advantages of his home park. This Cuban import of a certain age (it's hard to be more specific) also lacks the reputation for good glovework. His hold on a roster spot will be tenuous at best.

### Jose Molina    C

Born: 6/3/1975 Age: 37
Bats: R Throws: R Height: 6' 2" Weight: 195
Breakout: 3% Improve: 24% Collapse: 11%
Attrition: 37% MLB: 59%

**Comparables:**
Jerry McNertney, Sandy Martinez, Bob Scheffing

| YEAR | TEAM | LVL | AGE | PA | R | 2B | 3B | HR | RBI | BB | SO | SB | CS | AVG_OBP_SLG | TAv | BABIP | BRR | FRAA | WARP |
|------|------|-----|-----|----|----|----|----|----|-----|----|----|----|----|-------------|-----|-------|-----|------|------|
| 2009 | NYA | MLB | 34 | 155 | 15 | 4 | 0 | 1 | 11 | 14 | 28 | 0 | 0 | .217/.292/.268 | .202 | .264 | -0.5 | 0.5 | -0.5 |
| 2010 | TOR | MLB | 35 | 183 | 13 | 4 | 0 | 6 | 12 | 9 | 36 | 1 | 0 | .246/.304/.377 | .236 | .280 | -2.2 | -0.5 | 0.2 |
| 2011 | TOR | MLB | 36 | 191 | 19 | 12 | 1 | 3 | 15 | 15 | 44 | 2 | 1 | .281/.342/.415 | .278 | .363 | -1 | -1.4 | 1.0 |
| 2012 | TBA | MLB | 37 | 250 | 24 | 10 | 1 | 3 | 21 | 14 | 54 | 1 | 0 | .224/.276/.317 | .223 | .271 | 0 | C -2, 1B 0 | 0.3 |

The increased power Molina showed in 2010 stuck around (but with more doubles and fewer home runs), and he added 80 points of BABIP. The result was his best season at the plate and the first year he has gotten on base at a league-average rate. The Blue Jays have a surplus of young catchers, though, so even a career year for Molina didn't keep him in Toronto. The Rays will be the fifth major-league organization to benefit from Molina's gaudy defense.

### Manny Ramirez    LF

Born: 5/30/1972 Age: 40
Bats: R Throws: R Height: 6' 1" Weight: 190
Breakout: 1% Improve: 19% Collapse: 9%
Attrition: 25% MLB: 74%

**Comparables:**
Frank Thomas, Edgar Martinez, Jason Giambi

| YEAR | TEAM | LVL | AGE | PA | R | 2B | 3B | HR | RBI | BB | SO | SB | CS | AVG_OBP_SLG | TAv | BABIP | BRR | FRAA | WARP |
|------|------|-----|-----|----|----|----|----|----|-----|----|----|----|----|-------------|-----|-------|-----|------|------|
| 2009 | LAN | MLB | 37 | 431 | 62 | 24 | 2 | 19 | 63 | 71 | 81 | 0 | 1 | .290/.418/.531 | .322 | .328 | -2.3 | -4.2 | 2.8 |
| 2010 | CHA | MLB | 38 | 88 | 6 | 1 | 0 | 1 | 2 | 14 | 23 | 0 | 0 | .261/.420/.319 | .270 | .378 | -0.3 | 0 | 0.1 |
| 2010 | LAN | MLB | 38 | 232 | 32 | 15 | 0 | 8 | 40 | 32 | 38 | 1 | 1 | .311/.405/.510 | .327 | .346 | -2.2 | 0.8 | 1.9 |
| 2011 | TBA | MLB | 39 | 17 | 0 | 0 | 0 | 0 | 1 | 0 | 4 | 0 | 0 | .059/.059/.059 | .081 | .077 | 0.2 | 0 | -0.3 |
| 2012 | TBA | MLB | 40 | 250 | 33 | 11 | 1 | 9 | 30 | 32 | 51 | 1 | 0 | .265/.368/.450 | .299 | .308 | -0.1 | LF -3 | 2.7 |

Everyone's favorite idiot showed a new level of stupidity by violating baseball's performance-enhancing drug policy for the second time. Manny's bay area retreat lasted only slightly longer than the Bay of Pigs invasion in Cuba as Ramirez retired rather than sit out 100 games. We would have written a goodbye to Manny in this slot, except that MLB reinstated Ramirez from the voluntary retirement list in December, and reduced his suspension to 50 games in the sports equivalent of "time served." Will a PED-free 39-year-old Manny with a 50-game suspension yet to serve be tempting to any big-league GM?

### Sean Rodriguez    2B

Born: 4/26/1985 Age: 27
Bats: R Throws: R Height: 6' 2" Weight: 215
Breakout: 3% Improve: 32% Collapse: 9%
Attrition: 22% MLB: 85%

**Comparables:**
Jeff Blauser, Luis Aguayo, Jhonny Peralta

| YEAR | TEAM | LVL | AGE | PA | R | 2B | 3B | HR | RBI | BB | SO | SB | CS | AVG_OBP_SLG | TAv | BABIP | BRR | FRAA | WARP |
|------|------|-----|-----|----|----|----|----|----|-----|----|----|----|----|-------------|-----|-------|-----|------|------|
| 2009 | SLC | AAA | 24 | 435 | 81 | 17 | 6 | 29 | 93 | 51 | 119 | 9 | 2 | .299/.400/.616 | .327 | .364 | 4.6 | 18.1 | 6.3 |
| 2009 | ANA | MLB | 24 | 29 | 4 | 0 | 0 | 2 | 4 | 3 | 7 | 0 | 0 | .200/.276/.440 | .242 | .176 | -0.1 | -0.8 | -0.1 |
| 2010 | TBA | MLB | 25 | 378 | 53 | 19 | 2 | 9 | 40 | 21 | 97 | 13 | 3 | .251/.308/.397 | .254 | .324 | 0.1 | 3.9 | 1.0 |
| 2011 | TBA | MLB | 26 | 436 | 45 | 20 | 3 | 8 | 36 | 38 | 87 | 11 | 7 | .223/.323/.357 | .252 | .268 | 1.6 | 1.3 | 1.2 |
| 2012 | TBA | MLB | 27 | 398 | 45 | 16 | 2 | 13 | 44 | 33 | 100 | 10 | 4 | .228/.312/.398 | .263 | .276 | -0.2 | 2B 3, SS -1 | 1.8 |

Rodriguez became the new Ben Zobrist while playing five positions in 2011, including all four spots on the infield. Despite showing improved plate discipline, resulting in increased walk and contact rates, Rodriguez's numbers declined in 2011 thanks to his continued inability to handle right-handed pitching. In 242 plate appearances in 2010, he hit .229 with a 642 OPS, but those numbers fell to .192 and 567 in 269 plate appearances last season. He has a very good chance to nab primary shortstop responsibilities in 2012 given Brignac's extreme struggles, but if his numbers against righties do not improve, it will be tough to swallow seeing him get more than 450 plate appearances.

| | | | | | | | | | | | | | | | | | | | |
|---|---|---|---|---|---|---|---|---|---|---|---|---|---|---|---|---|---|---|---|
| **Justin Ruggiano** LF | YEAR | TEAM | LVL | AGE | PA | R | 2B | 3B | HR | RBI | BB | SO | SB | CS | AVG_OBP_SLG | TAv | BABIP | BRR | FRAA | WARP |
| Born: 4/12/1982 Age: 30 | 2009 | DUR | AAA | 27 | 532 | 71 | 28 | 1 | 15 | 72 | 51 | 147 | 23 | 4 | .253/.331/.412 | .254 | .335 | -0.9 | 1.3 | 1.0 |
| Bats: R Throws: R Height: 6' 3" Weight: 205 | 2010 | DUR | AAA | 28 | 507 | 77 | 31 | 0 | 15 | 70 | 42 | 129 | 24 | 6 | .287/.357/.453 | .264 | .371 | -2.8 | 7.5 | 2.0 |
| Breakout: 2% Improve: 29% Collapse: 9% | 2011 | DUR | AAA | 29 | 190 | 29 | 13 | 1 | 7 | 34 | 20 | 42 | 12 | 2 | .304/.378/.518 | .282 | .370 | 0.3 | 0.5 | 1.1 |
| Attrition: 25% MLB: 91% | 2011 | TBA | MLB | 29 | 111 | 11 | 4 | 0 | 4 | 13 | 4 | 26 | 1 | 1 | .248/.273/.400 | .256 | .289 | -1.7 | 1.5 | 0.2 |
| **Comparables:** Billy McMillon, Brant Alyea, Harry Bright | 2012 | TBA | MLB | 30 | 250 | 28 | 11 | 1 | 8 | 28 | 19 | 74 | 9 | 2 | .240/.304/.401 | .260 | .316 | 0.2 | LF 2, RF 1 | 1.1 |

This organizational soldier has been in the Rays' system since a mid-2006 season trade from the Dodgers. He has racked up 2064 plate appearances with the Durham Bulls over the past five seasons and he has polished the Quad-A patch on his uniform quite well. Ruggiano has the flexibility to man all three outfield positions and shows occa-

Hyun-wook Choi, Kyeong Kang, Brandon Short

hindered by a wrist issue. That slash line belies a player drafted for his power potential, but the young lefty did show some positives in small sample sizes. He had an 810 OPS against left-handed pitching compared to just a 599 OPS against righties. Sale signed on the dotted line just minutes before the 2010 signing deadline and thus missed a chance at getting games under his belt before 2011. Travis Snider is a comparison often made to Sale; both are bat-first types who fall short in other aspects of the game.

| | | | | | | | | | | | | | | | | | | | |
|---|---|---|---|---|---|---|---|---|---|---|---|---|---|---|---|---|---|---|---|
| **B.J. Upton** CF | YEAR | TEAM | LVL | AGE | PA | R | 2B | 3B | HR | RBI | BB | SO | SB | CS | AVG_OBP_SLG | TAv | BABIP | BRR | FRAA | WARP |
| Born: 8/21/1984 Age: 27 | 2009 | TBA | MLB | 24 | 626 | 79 | 33 | 4 | 11 | 55 | 57 | 152 | 42 | 14 | .241/.313/.373 | .248 | .310 | 0.7 | -2.1 | 1.0 |
| Bats: R Throws: R Height: 6' 4" Weight: 180 | 2010 | TBA | MLB | 25 | 610 | 89 | 38 | 4 | 18 | 62 | 67 | 164 | 42 | 9 | .237/.322/.424 | .270 | .304 | 4.6 | 4.6 | 3.7 |
| Breakout: 5% Improve: 43% Collapse: 4% | 2011 | TBA | MLB | 26 | 640 | 82 | 27 | 4 | 23 | 81 | 71 | 161 | 36 | 12 | .243/.331/.429 | .275 | .298 | 2.3 | 1.6 | 3.4 |
| Attrition: 14% MLB: 82% | 2012 | TBA | MLB | 27 | 595 | 70 | 27 | 3 | 16 | 63 | 68 | 153 | 37 | 12 | .241/.331/.398 | .271 | .308 | -0.2 | CF 4 | 2.6 |
| **Comparables:** Justin Maxwell, Chris Dickerson, Chet Lemon | | | | | | | | | | | | | | | | | | | | |

As polarizing a player as exists in any major league market, Upton has displayed questionable baseball IQ at times. Those moments have caused two distinct parties to form: the haters and the apologists. The haters see a player who loses focus, is picked off by pitchers or thrown out by catchers far too often, and who strikes out looking even more frequently. The apologists see a very talented player entering his prime who has shown flashes of brilliance, such as his power display during the Rays' 2008 postseason run or down the stretch last season. The real Upton lies somewhere in between. A change to his swing in late August resulted in a strong end to the season in which he had 16 extra base hits and a .333/.432/.606 slash line along with nine stolen bases. Perhaps that was a harbinger for 2012. This is his final year before free agency so expect the trade rumors to intensify.

| | | | | | | | | | | | | | | | | | | | |
|---|---|---|---|---|---|---|---|---|---|---|---|---|---|---|---|---|---|---|---|
| **Drew Vettleson** RF | YEAR | TEAM | LVL | AGE | PA | R | 2B | 3B | HR | RBI | BB | SO | SB | CS | AVG_OBP_SLG | TAv | BABIP | BRR | FRAA | WARP |
| Born: 7/19/1991 Age: 20 | 2011 | PRI | RK | 19 | 267 | 33 | 13 | 4 | 7 | 40 | 27 | 53 | 20 | 6 | .282/.357/.462 | .296 | .333 | 0.1 | 14.9 | 3.1 |
| Bats: L Throws: R Height: 6' 1" Weight: 185 | 2012 | TBA | MLB | 20 | 250 | 19 | 7 | 1 | 3 | 17 | 15 | 71 | 7 | 3 | .179/.229/.259 | .186 | .238 | -0.2 | RF 0 | -2.7 |
| Breakout: 1% Improve: 1% Collapse: 0% | | | | | | | | | | | | | | | | | | | | |
| Attrition: 1% MLB: 4% | | | | | | | | | | | | | | | | | | | | |
| **Comparables:** Luis Soto, Leonardo Reyes, Eric Fry | | | | | | | | | | | | | | | | | | | | |

Of the three 2010 first-rounders the Rays sent to Princeton, Vettleson easily had the best year of the trio. He hit righties with authority at a .296/.372/.505 clip through 223 plate appearances but showed no ability to hit with power against lefties, with just one extra base hit in 44 plate appearances against them. He played center field in high school but projects more as a right fielder. Playing right in 2011, he tied for the team lead in outfield assists with six. The organization voted him as the team's player of the year, a choice echoed by the fan vote, and Vettleson was the team's nominee for the prestigious Erik Walker Award.

(The award's namesake died in a tragic 2006 accident and recognizes a player who "exemplifies teamwork, sportsmanship, and community involvement.")

### Ben Zobrist — 2B

Born: 5/26/1981 Age: 31
Bats: B Throws: R Height: 6' 4" Weight: 200
Breakout: 0% Improve: 31% Collapse: 2%
Attrition: 16% MLB: 90%

Comparables:
Dick McAuliffe, Rod Booker, Felix Mantilla

| YEAR | TEAM | LVL | AGE | PA | R | 2B | 3B | HR | RBI | BB | SO | SB | CS | AVG_OBP_SLG | TAv | BABIP | BRR | FRAA | WARP |
|------|------|-----|-----|-----|----|----|----|----|-----|----|-----|----|----|-------------|------|-------|-----|-----------|------|
| 2009 | TBA | MLB | 28 | 599 | 91 | 28 | 7 | 27 | 91 | 91 | 104 | 17 | 6 | .297/.405/.543 | .331 | .326 | 2 | 7.9 | 7.0 |
| 2010 | TBA | MLB | 29 | 655 | 77 | 28 | 2 | 10 | 75 | 92 | 107 | 24 | 3 | .238/.346/.353 | .268 | .273 | 1 | 1.8 | 2.8 |
| 2011 | TBA | MLB | 30 | 674 | 99 | 46 | 6 | 20 | 91 | 77 | 128 | 19 | 6 | .269/.353/.469 | .302 | .310 | 5 | -5.7 | 4.1 |
| 2012 | TBA | MLB | 31 | 629 | 76 | 27 | 4 | 18 | 68 | 80 | 119 | 18 | 5 | .243/.342/.409 | .279 | .277 | 0.3 | 2B -2, RF 2 | 3.1 |

Zobrist answered the concerns that 2009 was a fluke at the plate by going out and posting the 15th best BVORP in baseball last season at 51.0, while continuing to play premium defense at two positions. Joe Maddon went out of his way during one pregame chat to say that as good as Zobrist was at second base, he was even better in right field. While the defensive metrics may or may not agree, it shows how comfortable Maddon is with Zobrist in right. Zobrist's slash line did not match his career year of 2009, but he did come within a stolen base of joining the 20/20 club, and was a run and a stolen base from joining the likes of Ryan Braun, Jacoby Ellsbury, Curtis Granderson, Matt Kemp, Ian Kinsler, Dustin Pedroia, and Justin Upton as the only players to go 20/20 while scoring 100 or more runs. His 4.5 WARP trailed only Longoria's value on the team, as did his .310 TAv. There are bigger stars and bigger names on the Rays roster, but Zobrist has played a huge part in the team's success these past few seasons.

## PITCHERS

### Christopher Archer

Born: 9/26/1988 Age: 23
Bats: R Throws: R Height: 6' 4" Weight: 185
Breakout: 15% Improve: 42% Collapse: 26%
Attrition: 16% MLB: 89%

Comparables:
Barry Latman, Dan Warthen, Moe Drabowsky

| YEAR | TEAM | LVL | AGE | W | L | SV | G | GS | IP | H | HR | BB | SO | EqBB9 | EqSO9 | GB% | BABIP | WHIP | ERA | FIP | FRA | WARP |
|------|------|-----|-----|---|---|----|----|----|------|-----|----|----|-----|-------|-------|-----|-------|------|------|------|------|------|
| 2009 | PEO | A | 20 | 6 | 4 | 0 | 27 | 26 | 109 | 78 | 0 | 66 | 119 | 5.4 | 9.8 | 56% | .290 | 1.32 | 2.81 | 3.44 | 4.03 | 1.7 |
| 2010 | DAY | A+ | 21 | 7 | 1 | 0 | 15 | 14 | 72¹ | 44 | 1 | 23 | 63 | 3.2 | 10.2 | 48% | .301 | 1.11 | 2.86 | 3.00 | 3.42 | 1.6 |
| 2010 | TEN | AA | 21 | 9 | 3 | 0 | 13 | 13 | 70 | 35 | 3 | 28 | 46 | 5.0 | 8.6 | 58% | .237 | 1.24 | 1.80 | 4.08 | 4.30 | 1.3 |
| 2011 | MNT | AA | 22 | 8 | 7 | 0 | 25 | 25 | 134¹ | 136 | 11 | 80 | 118 | 5.4 | 7.9 | 47% | .324 | 1.61 | 4.42 | 4.62 | 5.13 | 0.5 |
| 2012 | TBA | MLB | 23 | 3 | 4 | 0 | 9 | 9 | 48² | 48 | 6 | 32 | 38 | 5.9 | 7.0 | 48% | .291 | 1.63 | 4.95 | 5.22 | 5.38 | -0.3 |

The highest-rated prospect to come over in the Garza deal saw his season scarred by continual problems throwing strikes as he walked 80 batters in just 134 innings. Archer is in his third organization despite never throwing a pitch at the major league level and while his power arsenal is very enticing, it is still unclear whether his future is garnering wins in a rotation or saves out of the bullpen. Only by the strictest legal definition does he throw a changeup, but the lack of an effective off-speed pitch as well as the inconsistency with his control is pointing him toward the bullpen. The organizational pitching depth will permit him the time in the minors to help the club finalize on that decision.

### Burke Badenhop

Born: 2/8/1983 Age: 29
Bats: R Throws: R Height: 6' 6" Weight: 220
Breakout: 23% Improve: 56% Collapse: 30%
Attrition: 26% MLB: 90%

Comparables:
Mark Gubicza, Dock Ellis, Blaine Boyer

| YEAR | TEAM | LVL | AGE | W | L | SV | G | GS | IP | H | HR | BB | SO | EqBB9 | EqSO9 | GB% | BABIP | WHIP | ERA | FIP | FRA | WARP |
|------|------|-----|-----|---|---|----|----|----|------|----|----|----|----|-------|-------|-----|-------|------|------|------|------|------|
| 2009 | FLO | MLB | 26 | 7 | 4 | 0 | 35 | 2 | 72 | 71 | 5 | 24 | 57 | 3.0 | 7.1 | 56% | .310 | 1.32 | 3.75 | 3.42 | 4.71 | 0.6 |
| 2010 | FLO | MLB | 27 | 2 | 5 | 1 | 53 | 0 | 67² | 62 | 5 | 21 | 47 | 2.8 | 6.3 | 59% | .284 | 1.23 | 3.99 | 3.70 | 5.21 | 0.4 |
| 2011 | FLO | MLB | 28 | 2 | 3 | 1 | 50 | 0 | 63² | 65 | 1 | 24 | 51 | 3.4 | 7.2 | 61% | .328 | 1.40 | 4.10 | 2.92 | 3.90 | 0.8 |
| 2012 | TBA | MLB | 29 | 2 | 1 | 1 | 46 | 0 | 58² | 60 | 5 | 20 | 38 | 3.1 | 5.8 | 55% | .297 | 1.37 | 4.04 | 4.04 | 4.39 | 0.2 |

As the Rays are wont to do each offseason, they take others' castoffs in hopes of turning them into treasures. As luck would have it, the Marlins were planning on non-tendering Badenhop. The Rays sent them minor league catcher Jake Jefferies so that the team could tender Badenhop and put him into the annual bullpen rebuilding project. Maddon loves his toys in the bullpen and Badenhop's career 56 percent groundball rate could find its way into the role Chad Bradford once filled for this team. Badenhop is best served as a ROOGY; he struggles to command the strike zone against lefties. He also fills the vacancy left by Dirk Hayhurst as the writer in the organization: the *magna cum laude* graduate from Bowling Green State University has dabbled in both movie scripts and financial planning books with friends.

### Matt Bush
Born: **2/8/1986** Age: **26**
Bats: **R** Throws: **R** Height: **5' 10"** Weight: **180**
Breakout: **28%** Improve: **47%** Collapse: **26%**
Attrition: **12%** MLB: **92%**

**Comparables:**
John Wetteland, Fernando Cabrera, Ken Howell

| YEAR | TEAM | LVL | AGE | W | L | SV | G | GS | IP | H | HR | BB | SO | EqBB9 | EqSO9 | GB% | BABIP | WHIP | ERA | FIP | FRA | WARP |
|---|---|---|---|---|---|---|---|---|---|---|---|---|---|---|---|---|---|---|---|---|---|---|
| 2011 | MNT | AA | 25 | 5 | 3 | 5 | 36 | 0 | 50¹ | 47 | 5 | 23 | 76 | 4.3 | 13.8 | 45% | .393 | 1.43 | 4.83 | 3.06 | 4.06 | 0.8 |
| 2012 | TBA | MLB | 26 | 1 | 0 | 0 | 10 | 0 | 13¹ | 11 | 1 | 6 | 15 | 3.9 | 10.4 | 45% | .301 | 1.28 | 3.36 | 3.28 | 3.65 | 0.2 |

One of the former top five overall draft picks on the 40-man roster, the former shortstop is now a power reliever with a live arm and improving command. In just 50 innings of work (36 outings) in Double-A, he struck out 77 batters while walking 24. He has yet to pitch in Triple-A, but he could very well be on the Durham-St.Pete shuttle a time or three in 2012.

### Alex Cobb
Born: **10/7/1987** Age: **24**
Bats: **R** Throws: **R** Height: **6' 3"** Weight: **195**
Breakout: **22%** Improve: **55%** Collapse: **20%**
Attrition: **17%** MLB: **91%**

| YEAR | TEAM | LVL | AGE | W | L | SV | G | GS | IP | H | HR | BB | SO | EqBB9 | EqSO9 | GB% | BABIP | WHIP | ERA | FIP | FRA | WARP |
|---|---|---|---|---|---|---|---|---|---|---|---|---|---|---|---|---|---|---|---|---|---|---|
| 2009 | PCH | A+ | 21 | 9 | 6 | 0 | 24 | 23 | 124² | 126 | 6 | 36 | 115 | 2.2 | 7.7 | 55% | .306 | 1.18 | 3.03 | 3.06 | 4.06 | 1.9 |
| 2010 | MNT | AA | 22 | 7 | 5 | 0 | 23 | 22 | 119² | 92 | 6 | 26 | 91 | 2.6 | 9.6 | 54% | .360 | 1.29 | 2.71 | 3.44 | 3.77 | 2.2 |
| 2011 | DUR | AAA | 23 | 5 | 1 | 0 | 12 | 12 | 67¹ | 61 | 4 | 16 | 70 | 2.1 | 9.4 | 58% | .335 | 1.14 | 1.87 | 2.73 | 3.88 | 1.5 |

### Alexander Colome
Born: **12/31/1988** Age: **23**
Bats: **R** Throws: **R** Height: **6' 3"** Weight: **184**
Breakout: **13%** Improve: **47%** Collapse: **19%**
Attrition: **16%** MLB: **89%**

**Comparables:**
Charlie Haeger, Gary Gentry, Lance McCullers

| YEAR | TEAM | LVL | AGE | W | L | SV | G | GS | IP | H | HR | BB | SO | EqBB9 | EqSO9 | GB% | BABIP | WHIP | ERA | FIP | FRA | WARP |
|---|---|---|---|---|---|---|---|---|---|---|---|---|---|---|---|---|---|---|---|---|---|---|
| 2009 | HUD | A- | 20 | 7 | 4 | 0 | 15 | 15 | 76 | 46 | 0 | 32 | 94 | 3.8 | 11.1 | 56% | .267 | 1.03 | 1.66 | 2.27 | 3.67 | 1.0 |
| 2010 | BGR | A | 21 | 6 | 6 | 0 | 22 | 22 | 114 | 67 | 10 | 33 | 86 | 3.6 | 9.3 | 50% | .253 | 1.25 | 3.95 | 4.38 | 4.41 | 1.3 |
| 2011 | PCH | A+ | 22 | 9 | 5 | 0 | 19 | 19 | 105² | 73 | 7 | 39 | 91 | 3.7 | 7.8 | 44% | .252 | 1.15 | 3.66 | 3.81 | 4.30 | 1.2 |
| 2011 | MNT | AA | 22 | 3 | 4 | 0 | 9 | 9 | 52 | 41 | 5 | 28 | 31 | 4.8 | 5.4 | 43% | .237 | 1.33 | 4.15 | 5.32 | 5.10 | 0.3 |
| 2012 | TBA | MLB | 23 | 2 | 3 | 0 | 8 | 8 | 43 | 42 | 5 | 24 | 30 | 5.0 | 6.2 | 44% | .279 | 1.53 | 4.79 | 4.99 | 5.21 | -0.2 |

There are many jokes made about middle-child syndrome as the parental units focus on the oldest and youngest while neglecting the child in the middle. Colome could be one of the best arms in many of the organizations in baseball, but with the Rays, he has to fight for attention with 10 or more siblings who are all trying to impress the minor league operations staff as well as Andrew Friedman. Colome split time between High A and Double-A but struggled with his control as he walked 72 batters in just under 158 innings of work. He held lefties to a 603 OPS while righties were 100 points higher on the season, but with all of the talent in front of him, the Rays can afford to be patient with his arm and his potential.

### Juan Cruz
Born: **10/15/1978** Age: **33**
Bats: **R** Throws: **R** Height: **6' 3"** Weight: **155**
Breakout: **20%** Improve: **44%** Collapse: **31%**
Attrition: **10%** MLB: **91%**

**Comparables:**
Sam Jones, Jeff Nelson, Troy Percival

| YEAR | TEAM | LVL | AGE | W | L | SV | G | GS | IP | H | HR | BB | SO | EqBB9 | EqSO9 | GB% | BABIP | WHIP | ERA | FIP | FRA | WARP |
|---|---|---|---|---|---|---|---|---|---|---|---|---|---|---|---|---|---|---|---|---|---|---|
| 2009 | KCA | MLB | 30 | 3 | 4 | 2 | 46 | 0 | 50¹ | 46 | 6 | 29 | 38 | 5.2 | 6.8 | 27% | .278 | 1.49 | 5.72 | 4.97 | 6.01 | -0.2 |
| 2010 | KCA | MLB | 31 | 0 | 0 | 0 | 5 | 0 | 5¹ | 9 | 0 | 4 | 7 | 6.8 | 11.8 | 35% | .562 | 2.44 | 3.38 | 2.67 | 6.06 | 0.0 |
| 2011 | TBA | MLB | 32 | 5 | 0 | 0 | 56 | 0 | 48² | 36 | 5 | 28 | 46 | 5.2 | 8.5 | 36% | .256 | 1.32 | 3.88 | 4.23 | 4.37 | 0.1 |
| 2012 | TBA | MLB | 33 | 2 | 1 | 0 | 39 | 0 | 34² | 28 | 3 | 18 | 38 | 4.6 | 9.9 | 35% | .288 | 1.33 | 3.49 | 3.69 | 3.80 | 0.4 |

Cruz was yet another one of the Rays Reclamation specials as the team rebuilt a nearly completely vacated bullpen from 2010. Cruz was used in every role except closer and bounced back from missing nearly all of 2010 to put up numbers in line with his past successes. His command is still not good enough to work effectively in high-leverage situations but he continues to do very well in medium and low leverage situations, mainly on the strength of his swing and miss stuff. He is no longer the same strikeout machine he was in his prime, but for a reclamation project, count him as a Rays success.

## Wade Davis

Born: 9/7/1985 Age: 26
Bats: R Throws: R Height: 6' 6" Weight: 220
Breakout: 29% Improve: 59% Collapse: 12%
Attrition: 14% MLB: 92%

Comparables:
Tony Pena, Darren O'Day, Noah Lowry

| YEAR | TEAM | LVL | AGE | W | L | SV | G | GS | IP | H | HR | BB | SO | EqBB9 | EqSO9 | GB% | BABIP | WHIP | ERA | FIP | FRA | WARP |
|------|------|-----|-----|---|---|----|---|----|------|-----|----|----|-----|-------|-------|-----|-------|------|------|------|------|------|
| 2009 | DUR | AAA | 23 | 10 | 8 | 0 | 28 | 28 | 158² | 139 | 14 | 60 | 140 | 3.4 | 7.9 | 41% | .277 | 1.25 | 3.40 | 3.78 | 4.09 | 2.6 |
| 2009 | TBA | MLB | 23 | 2 | 2 | 0 | 6 | 6 | 36¹ | 33 | 2 | 13 | 36 | 3.2 | 8.9 | 40% | .316 | 1.27 | 3.72 | 2.95 | 3.47 | 0.9 |
| 2010 | TBA | MLB | 24 | 12 | 10 | 0 | 29 | 29 | 168 | 165 | 24 | 62 | 113 | 3.3 | 6.1 | 40% | .274 | 1.35 | 4.07 | 4.76 | 4.73 | 0.7 |
| 2011 | TBA | MLB | 25 | 11 | 10 | 0 | 29 | 29 | 184 | 190 | 23 | 63 | 105 | 3.1 | 5.1 | 38% | .283 | 1.38 | 4.45 | 4.70 | 4.41 | 0.7 |
| 2012 | TBA | MLB | 26 | 10 | 9 | 0 | 26 | 26 | 159² | 150 | 18 | 59 | 116 | 3.3 | 6.5 | 43% | .276 | 1.31 | 3.81 | 4.33 | 4.14 | 1.1 |

It was a tale of two seasons for Davis. He started the 2011 season with an apparent mindset of pitching to contact: his strikeout rate plummeted like most of our 401-K plans. His delivery looked forced as he fell off to the first base side, and his lack of an effective off-speed pitch led to high pitch counts and low inning totals. Then forearm tightness lessened the effectiveness of his slider and eventually landed him on the disabled list. He returned with his slider intact and a cleaner delivery. Staying more upright over the mound restored the fastball velocity that was missing in the first half of the season. The offspeed pitch still does not exist, but the team made a long-term commitment to him with a pre-arbitration deal. The package includes team options to control his future costs. The Rays made an interesting move with Davis for the postseason by taking him out of the rotation and putting him into the bullpen. Whether that is a harbinger of things to come in the future remains to be seen.

## Dane De La Rosa

Born: 2/1/1983 Age: 29
Bats: R Throws: R Height: 6' 7" Weight: 220
Breakout: 20% Improve: 37% Collapse: 34%
Attrition: 8% MLB: 88%

Comparables:
Mike Schooler, Todd Worrell, Mike Hartley

| YEAR | TEAM | LVL | AGE | W | L | SV | G | GS | IP | H | HR | BB | SO | EqBB9 | EqSO9 | GB% | BABIP | WHIP | ERA | FIP | FRA | WARP |
|------|------|-----|-----|---|---|----|----|----|-----|----|----|----|----|-------|-------|-----|-------|------|------|------|------|------|
| 2010 | MNT | AA | 27 | 9 | 3 | 4 | 47 | 0 | 73 | 48 | 3 | 16 | 54 | 3.2 | 9.2 | 54% | .338 | 1.26 | 1.97 | 3.27 | 3.84 | 1.0 |
| 2011 | DUR | AAA | 28 | 6 | 5 | 6 | 52 | 0 | 70¹ | 66 | 8 | 26 | 83 | 3.3 | 10.6 | 49% | .328 | 1.27 | 3.20 | 3.64 | 4.80 | 0.8 |
| 2011 | TBA | MLB | 28 | 0 | 0 | 0 | 7 | 0 | 7¹ | 10 | 1 | 3 | 8 | 3.7 | 9.8 | 52% | .409 | 1.77 | 9.82 | 3.88 | 5.00 | 0.0 |
| 2012 | TBA | MLB | 29 | 1 | 0 | 0 | 17 | 0 | 24² | 23 | 3 | 9 | 24 | 3.3 | 8.6 | 48% | .298 | 1.29 | 3.61 | 3.93 | 3.92 | 0.2 |

Not too long ago, De La Rosa was trying to sell real estate in a down market. Now, he is trying to live on the positive side of the ledger as a major league reliever. De La Rosa only logged a handful of innings at the major league level, but was quite successful in Durham, finishing with one of the better FIPs in the league and performing above to well-above league average in several key metrics: strikeout rate, swinging strike rate, and opponents' isolated power. Maddon has a preference for a 12-man pitching staff and with only three spots locked up for Farnsworth, Peralta, and McGee, De La Rosa has a chance to be the Rays' next gaudy return on investment.

## Rob Delaney

Born: 9/8/1984 Age: 27
Bats: L Throws: R Height: 6' 4" Weight: 230
Breakout: 28% Improve: 58% Collapse: 24%
Attrition: 10% MLB: 93%

Comparables:
Mike Flanagan, Tom Sturdivant, Fu-Te Ni

| YEAR | TEAM | LVL | AGE | W | L | SV | G | GS | IP | H | HR | BB | SO | EqBB9 | EqSO9 | GB% | BABIP | WHIP | ERA | FIP | FRA | WARP |
|------|------|-----|-----|---|---|----|----|----|-----|----|----|----|----|-------|-------|-----|-------|------|-------|-------|-------|------|
| 2009 | NBR | AA | 24 | 1 | 1 | 0 | 26 | 0 | 36 | 32 | 1 | 6 | 40 | 1.5 | 10.0 | 45% | .337 | 1.06 | 2.00 | 1.86 | 2.35 | 1.1 |
| 2009 | ROC | AAA | 24 | 7 | 3 | 7 | 36 | 0 | 47² | 43 | 5 | 15 | 38 | 2.8 | 7.2 | 31% | .273 | 1.22 | 4.53 | 3.86 | 5.23 | 0.2 |
| 2010 | ROC | AAA | 25 | 7 | 9 | 4 | 61 | 0 | 80 | 60 | 11 | 15 | 62 | 2.6 | 10.4 | 38% | .353 | 1.31 | 4.72 | 4.33 | 5.55 | 0.1 |
| 2010 | MIN | MLB | 25 | 0 | 0 | 0 | 1 | 0 | 1 | 2 | 1 | 1 | 0 | 9.0 | 0.0 | 75% | .333 | 3.00 | 9.00 | 19.05 | 18.54 | -0.1 |
| 2011 | DUR | AAA | 26 | 4 | 2 | 13 | 51 | 0 | 67² | 49 | 3 | 17 | 55 | 2.3 | 7.6 | 41% | .256 | 1.00 | 1.86 | 2.94 | 4.13 | 1.1 |
| 2011 | TBA | MLB | 26 | 0 | 0 | 0 | 4 | 0 | 5 | 4 | 0 | 7 | 3 | 12.6 | 5.4 | 13% | .267 | 2.20 | 10.80 | 6.06 | 7.47 | -0.2 |
| 2012 | FLO | MLB | 27 | 1 | 0 | 0 | 21 | 0 | 27² | 25 | 3 | 9 | 23 | 3.0 | 7.4 | 37% | .301 | 1.24 | 3.86 | 3.93 | 4.19 | 0.3 |

"Big Daddy" Delaney is trying to escape the Quad-A label but hasn't been given a chance. Despite effective numbers at Triple-A for the Twins, they designated him for assignment. The Rays quickly snatched him up and bounced him back and forth between Durham and Tampa Bay in 2011. Delaney's usually solid control betrayed him during his time in the majors and the Rays removed him from the 40-man roster after the season. Whatever hopes he has of shedding the Quad-A label might have to come with another organization.

## Kyle Farnsworth

Born: 4/14/1976 Age: 36
Bats: R Throws: R Height: 6' 5" Weight: 205
Breakout: 22% Improve: 36% Collapse: 27%
Attrition: 10% MLB: 61%

Comparables:
Tug McGraw, Jerry Koosman, Justin Speier

| YEAR | TEAM | LVL | AGE | W | L | SV | G | GS | IP | H | HR | BB | SO | EqBB9 | EqSO9 | GB% | BABIP | WHIP | ERA | FIP | FRA | WARP |
|------|------|-----|-----|---|---|----|----|----|-----|----|----|----|----|-------|-------|-----|-------|------|------|------|------|------|
| 2009 | KCA | MLB | 33 | 1 | 5 | 0 | 41 | 0 | 37¹ | 43 | 3 | 14 | 42 | 3.4 | 10.1 | 49% | .374 | 1.53 | 4.58 | 3.14 | 3.56 | 0.9 |
| 2010 | ATL | MLB | 34 | 0 | 2 | 0 | 23 | 0 | 20 | 15 | 2 | 7 | 25 | 3.2 | 11.2 | 42% | .283 | 1.10 | 5.40 | 2.96 | 3.28 | 0.4 |
| 2010 | KCA | MLB | 34 | 3 | 0 | 0 | 37 | 0 | 44² | 40 | 2 | 12 | 36 | 2.4 | 7.3 | 44% | .292 | 1.16 | 2.42 | 3.09 | 3.93 | 0.6 |
| 2011 | TBA | MLB | 35 | 5 | 1 | 25 | 63 | 0 | 57² | 45 | 5 | 12 | 51 | 1.9 | 8.0 | 51% | .252 | 0.99 | 2.18 | 3.20 | 3.59 | 0.7 |
| 2012 | TBA | MLB | 36 | 3 | 1 | 6 | 49 | 0 | 48² | 46 | 6 | 16 | 45 | 2.9 | 8.2 | 40% | .294 | 1.27 | 3.62 | 3.94 | 3.93 | 0.4 |

Yankees fans may have laughed first when the Rays trotted Farnsworth out as their closer, but the Rays and Farnsworth ended up with the last laugh as he led the team in saves and was extremely effective in his "unofficial" closer role all season (Maddon refused to slap that label on any of the relievers). What many overlooked while Farnsworth was pitching in Kansas City was his addition of an effective cut fastball. Said cutter and inproved command made Farnsworth a pitcher rather than the thrower who flamed out in Chicago and New York. He did break down late in the season with elbow soreness, but the Rays' medical staff felt comfortable enough with the tests to recommend the Rays pick up the $3.3 million team option for 2012.

### Brandon Gomes

Born: **7/15/1984** Age: **27**
Bats: **R** Throws: **R** Height: **6' 0''** Weight: **175**
Breakout: **19%** Improve: **46%** Collapse: **37%**
Attrition: **14%** MLB: **90%**

Comparables:
Josh Beckett, Len Barker, Josh Roenicke

| YEAR | TEAM | LVL | AGE | W | L | SV | G | GS | IP | H | HR | BB | SO | EqBB9 | EqSO9 | GB% | BABIP | WHIP | ERA | FIP | FRA | WARP |
|------|------|-----|-----|---|---|----|---|----|----|---|----|----|----|-------|-------|-----|-------|------|-----|-----|-----|------|
| 2009 | SAN | AA | 24 | 4 | 1 | 3 | 65 | 0 | 72 | 56 | 4 | 29 | 103 | 3.5 | 12.5 | 48% | .308 | 1.14 | 2.62 | 2.39 | 2.70 | 2.3 |
| 2010 | SAN | AA | 25 | 7 | 2 | 1 | 51 | 0 | 72$^1$ | 37 | 2 | 22 | 68 | 3.1 | 11.6 | 46% | .292 | 1.07 | 1.87 | 2.72 | 3.25 | 1.3 |
| 2011 | DUR | AAA | 26 | 0 | 1 | 7 | 20 | 0 | 25$^1$ | 17 | 1 | 7 | 40 | 2.5 | 14.2 | 34% | .333 | 0.95 | 1.07 | 1.54 | 2.59 | 0.8 |
| 2011 | TBA | MLB | 26 | 2 | 1 | 0 | 40 | 0 | 37 | 34 | 3 | 16 | 32 | 3.9 | 7.8 | 33% | .292 | 1.35 | 2.92 | 3.76 | 4.30 | 0.3 |
| 2012 | TBA | MLB | 27 | 2 | 1 | 0 | 31 | 0 | 37$^2$ | 35 | 4 | 15 | 35 | 3.6 | 8.4 | 42% | .298 | 1.32 | 3.67 | 3.92 | 3.99 | 0.3 |

### Jeremy Hellickson

Born: **4/8/1987** Age: **25**
Bats: **R** Throws: **R** Height: **6' 2''** Weight: **185**
Breakout: **15%** Improve: **40%** Collapse: **16%**
Attrition: **11%** MLB: **96%**

Comparables:
Jeremy Accardo, Tom Seaver, Justin Verlander

| YEAR | TEAM | LVL | AGE | W | L | SV | G | GS | IP | H | HR | BB | SO | EqBB9 | EqSO9 | GB% | BABIP | WHIP | ERA | FIP | FRA | WARP |
|------|------|-----|-----|---|---|----|---|----|----|---|----|----|----|-------|-------|-----|-------|------|-----|-----|-----|------|
| 2010 | TBA | MLB | 23 | 4 | 0 | 0 | 10 | 4 | 36$^1$ | 32 | 5 | 8 | 33 | 2.0 | 8.2 | 38% | .267 | 1.10 | 3.47 | 3.85 | 3.48 | 0.6 |
| 2011 | TBA | MLB | 24 | 13 | 10 | 0 | 29 | 29 | 189 | 146 | 21 | 72 | 117 | 3.4 | 5.6 | 36% | .224 | 1.15 | 2.95 | 4.47 | 4.20 | 1.2 |
| 2012 | TBA | MLB | 25 | 9 | 7 | 0 | 23 | 23 | 140$^1$ | 118 | 17 | 44 | 111 | 2.8 | 7.1 | 39% | .257 | 1.16 | 3.17 | 4.14 | 3.45 | 2.2 |

The Rays cleared the rotation spot for him by trading away Matt Garza, and Hellickson did not disappoint, parlaying solid surface stats into the American League Rookie of the Year award. Despite a stellar ERA, his skills were a bit of a disappointment: his walk rate was 3.4 (per nine innings) and his strikeout rate was below 6.0. Hellickson had a significant gap between his ERA and FIP (1.52 runs) in part due to two factors. Normally, doom is forecast for any pitcher with a low strikeout rate, high fly-ball rate, and fortunate BABIP. But 25 percent of Hellickson's fly balls never left the infield, and the Rays' team BABIP against was .265 in 2011, leading all of baseball for the third time in four seasons. Hellickson's chances of repeating this level of success with his current skills are slim, and he must improve against left-handed batters, but keep an eye on whether his infield flies are a legitimate skill or a one-time wonder.

### J.P. Howell

Born: **4/25/1983** Age: **29**
Bats: **L** Throws: **L** Height: **6' 1''** Weight: **175**
Breakout: **14%** Improve: **34%** Collapse: **49%**
Attrition: **10%** MLB: **97%**

Comparables:
Damaso Marte, Ricardo Rincon, Mark Davis

| YEAR | TEAM | LVL | AGE | W | L | SV | G | GS | IP | H | HR | BB | SO | EqBB9 | EqSO9 | GB% | BABIP | WHIP | ERA | FIP | FRA | WARP |
|------|------|-----|-----|---|---|----|---|----|----|---|----|----|----|-------|-------|-----|-------|------|-----|-----|-----|------|
| 2009 | TBA | MLB | 26 | 7 | 5 | 17 | 69 | 0 | 66$^2$ | 47 | 7 | 33 | 79 | 4.5 | 10.7 | 49% | .260 | 1.20 | 2.84 | 3.76 | 3.68 | 1.3 |
| 2011 | TBA | MLB | 28 | 2 | 3 | 1 | 46 | 0 | 30$^2$ | 30 | 5 | 18 | 26 | 5.3 | 7.6 | 54% | .291 | 1.57 | 6.16 | 5.44 | 6.11 | -0.4 |
| 2012 | TBA | MLB | 29 | 2 | 1 | 1 | 37 | 0 | 25 | 21 | 3 | 10 | 26 | 3.6 | 9.2 | 52% | .285 | 1.25 | 3.45 | 3.88 | 3.75 | 0.3 |

After missing 2010 with a shoulder injury, Howell came back in 2011 in spirit, but in body he was far from the same pitcher. The new Howell came with a cleaner delivery that did not have him falling into the opposition's dugout after every pitch, but his stuff was clearly a downgrade post-surgery. His swings and misses fell off the table while his walk rate was too high for the critical relief role he filled. By season's end, McGee was seeing most of the high leverage work against lefties and Howell was relegated to limited duty. The Rays tendered Howell a contract, and he could battle with Ramos to become the team's lefty specialist.

### Josh Lueke

Born: **12/5/1984** Age: **27**
Bats: **R** Throws: **R** Height: **6' 6''** Weight: **235**
Breakout: **17%** Improve: **46%** Collapse: **37%**
Attrition: **9%** MLB: **96%**

Comparables:
Dwight Gooden, Len Barker, Blaine Boyer

| YEAR | TEAM | LVL | AGE | W | L | SV | G | GS | IP | H | HR | BB | SO | EqBB9 | EqSO9 | GB% | BABIP | WHIP | ERA | FIP | FRA | WARP |
|------|------|-----|-----|---|---|----|---|----|----|---|----|----|----|-------|-------|-----|-------|------|-----|-----|-----|------|
| 2011 | TAC | AAA | 26 | 1 | 1 | 11 | 30 | 0 | 42$^1$ | 33 | 1 | 12 | 35 | 2.6 | 7.4 | 50% | .264 | 1.09 | 2.76 | 3.59 | 4.30 | 0.4 |
| 2011 | SEA | MLB | 26 | 1 | 1 | 0 | 25 | 0 | 32$^2$ | 34 | 2 | 13 | 29 | 3.6 | 8.0 | 44% | .333 | 1.44 | 6.06 | 3.28 | 4.39 | 0.1 |
| 2012 | TBA | MLB | 27 | 2 | 1 | 0 | 30 | 0 | 39$^2$ | 36 | 4 | 14 | 37 | 3.1 | 8.3 | 45% | .295 | 1.26 | 3.46 | 3.71 | 3.76 | 0.4 |

PECOTA loves Lueke, projecting him to have the lowest ERA among his former Seattle bullpen mates. This is fitting; Lueke is a lot easier to root for in a binomial world stripped of emotion.

Computers don't get hung up on his criminal history. Lueke has plenty of stuff to take on a closer or other high-leverage role, with a fastball that can dart into the mid-and-upper-90s and worthwhile secondary offerings. His ERA reflects a terrible strand rate, and an opponents' OPS 500 points higher with runners on than without. Stranding runners is, obviously, a crucial skill for a late-inning reliever, but at this point it's more likely a fluke of sequencing than anything suggestive about Lueke. The Rays are gambling that the PR hit is worth buying low on what could become a vital arm in their bullpen.

### Jake McGee

Born: 8/6/1986 Age: 25
Bats: L Throws: L Height: 6' 4" Weight: 190
Breakout: 40% Improve: 60% Collapse: 16%
Attrition: 4% MLB: 92%

Comparables:
Dave LaRoche, Johan Santana, J.P. Howell

| YEAR | TEAM | LVL | AGE | W | L | SV | G | GS | IP | H | HR | BB | SO | EqBB9 | EqSO9 | GB% | BABIP | WHIP | ERA | FIP | FRA | WARP |
|------|------|-----|-----|---|---|----|----|----|-----|----|----|----|----|-------|-------|-----|-------|------|------|------|------|------|
| 2009 | PCH | A+ | 22 | 0 | 3 | 0 | 11 | 11 | 22¹ | 28 | 2 | 10 | 29 | 3.6 | 10.5 | 48% | .406 | 1.57 | 6.46 | 3.11 | 4.35 | 0.7 |
| 2010 | MNT | AA | 23 | 3 | 7 | 0 | 19 | 19 | 88¹ | 62 | 2 | 22 | 68 | 3.4 | 10.2 | 45% | .343 | 1.29 | 3.57 | 3.09 | 3.89 | 1.6 |
| 2010 | TBA | MLB | 23 | 0 | 0 | 0 | 8 | 0 | 5 | 2 | 0 | 3 | 6 | 5.4 | 10.8 | 55% | .182 | 1.00 | 1.80 | 2.45 | 4.35 | 0.0 |
| 2011 | DUR | AAA | 24 | 4 | 2 | 9 | 24 | 0 | 33¹ | 30 | 4 | 8 | 38 | 2.2 | 10.3 | 52% | .306 | 1.14 | 2.70 | 3.33 | 4.80 | 0.3 |
| 2011 | TBA | MLB | 24 | 5 | 2 | 0 | 37 | 0 | 28 | 30 | 5 | 12 | 27 | 3.9 | 8.7 | 33% | .316 | 1.50 | 4.50 | 4.74 | 5.45 | -0.2 |
| 2012 | TBA | MLB | 25 | 2 | 1 | 0 | 17 | 3 | 29² | 28 | 4 | 13 | 27 | 3.9 | 8.3 | 42% | .294 | 1.37 | 3.96 | 4.45 | 4.31 | 0.2 |

Clockhands McGee split time between St. Pete and Durham before settling down near season's end to be the kind of reliever the team thought he would be to start the season with his mid-90s heat and power slider. At one point, McGee and Wade Davis were coming up the organizational ladder side by side as starters, but Tommy John surgery derailed that story, and McGee's mechanics and inability to pick up a changeup put him on the reliever path. He was very effective as a LOOGY in limited usage, holding lefties to a .164 average with just a 510 OPS on the season, but had no answer for righties, who hit .400 against him with an 1143 OPS.

### Matt Moore

Born: 6/18/1989 Age: 23
Bats: L Throws: L Height: 6' 3" Weight: 205
Breakout: 20% Improve: 46% Collapse: 39%
Attrition: 10% MLB: 95%

Comparables:
Clay Buchholz, Scott Kazmir, Zach Braddock

| YEAR | TEAM | LVL | AGE | W | L | SV | G | GS | IP | H | HR | BB | SO | EqBB9 | EqSO9 | GB% | BABIP | WHIP | ERA | FIP | FRA | WARP |
|------|------|-----|-----|---|---|----|----|----|------|----|----|----|-----|-------|-------|-----|-------|------|------|------|------|------|
| 2009 | BGR | A | 20 | 8 | 5 | 0 | 26 | 26 | 123 | 86 | 6 | 70 | 176 | 5.1 | 12.9 | 48% | .308 | 1.27 | 3.15 | 3.09 | 3.73 | 1.9 |
| 2010 | PCH | A+ | 21 | 5 | 10 | 0 | 26 | 26 | 144² | 88 | 5 | 45 | 166 | 3.8 | 12.9 | 45% | .324 | 1.17 | 3.36 | 2.72 | 3.72 | 3.1 |
| 2011 | MNT | AA | 22 | 8 | 3 | 0 | 18 | 18 | 102¹ | 66 | 8 | 28 | 124 | 2.5 | 11.5 | 47% | .269 | 0.94 | 2.20 | 2.80 | 3.59 | 2.1 |
| 2011 | DUR | AAA | 22 | 4 | 0 | 0 | 9 | 9 | 52² | 42 | 4 | 19 | 82 | 3.1 | 13.5 | 40% | .302 | 0.97 | 1.37 | 2.25 | 3.19 | 1.7 |
| 2011 | TBA | MLB | 22 | 1 | 0 | 0 | 3 | 1 | 9¹ | 9 | 1 | 3 | 15 | 2.9 | 14.5 | 45% | .381 | 1.29 | 2.89 | 2.20 | 3.91 | 0.2 |
| 2012 | TBA | MLB | 23 | 3 | 3 | 0 | 10 | 10 | 54 | 44 | 5 | 27 | 62 | 4.5 | 10.4 | 45% | .293 | 1.31 | 3.44 | 3.61 | 3.74 | 0.7 |

All Moore did last year was win Minor League Pitcher of the Year and shut out the American League champions in his first ever playoff start. Moore dominated the minor leagues, going 12-3 with a 1.92 ERA between Double-A and Triple-A while posting a strikeout rate over 12 for the fifth consecutive season. He also reduced his walk rate for a third consecutive season. His career numbers at the minor league level look almost too incredible to be real: 700 strikeouts and just 338 hits in 497 1/3 innings. His hit batsmen total (26) is higher than his home runs allowed (25). The Rays called Moore up and in his only start, he struck out 11 Yankees in Yankee Stadium. Like Hellickson before him, he has announced his presence with authority. Moore signed a team-friendly extension in the offseason; expect to see him in the major league rotation.

### Jeff Niemann

Born: 2/28/1983 Age: 29
Bats: R Throws: R Height: 6' 10" Weight: 280
Breakout: 21% Improve: 42% Collapse: 30%
Attrition: 12% MLB: 89%

Comparables:
Bob Welch, Bill Singer, Gaylord Perry

| YEAR | TEAM | LVL | AGE | W | L | SV | G | GS | IP | H | HR | BB | SO | EqBB9 | EqSO9 | GB% | BABIP | WHIP | ERA | FIP | FRA | WARP |
|------|------|-----|-----|----|----|----|----|----|------|-----|----|----|-----|-------|-------|-----|-------|------|------|------|------|------|
| 2009 | TBA | MLB | 26 | 13 | 6 | 0 | 31 | 30 | 180² | 185 | 17 | 59 | 125 | 2.9 | 6.2 | 42% | .302 | 1.35 | 3.94 | 4.11 | 4.47 | 1.9 |
| 2010 | TBA | MLB | 27 | 12 | 8 | 0 | 30 | 29 | 174¹ | 159 | 25 | 61 | 131 | 3.1 | 6.8 | 45% | .266 | 1.26 | 4.39 | 4.58 | 4.49 | 0.7 |
| 2011 | TBA | MLB | 28 | 11 | 7 | 0 | 23 | 23 | 135¹ | 131 | 18 | 37 | 105 | 2.5 | 7.0 | 47% | .279 | 1.24 | 4.06 | 4.17 | 4.04 | 1.5 |
| 2012 | TBA | MLB | 29 | 8 | 7 | 0 | 22 | 22 | 127² | 119 | 15 | 42 | 98 | 3.0 | 6.9 | 44% | .280 | 1.26 | 3.63 | 4.18 | 3.94 | 1.3 |

There were concerns about Niemann's durability coming out of Rice that proved valid in the minors. Those concerns might be creeping into the picture again, as for a third straight season Niemann's innings total declined. He made only 23 starts in 2011 as he missed six weeks with a strained muscle in his back. Upon return, he was very effective: 9-3 with a 2.57 ERA before running out of gas in September. That script was a re-run of 2010, when a hot summer gave way to a pitcher who crawled to the finish line, even as his team was racing toward the post-season. Niemann has the body type and stuff of a prototypical innings eater but he has yet to eat more than 177 in a single season. The former top five draft pick has turned into a back half of the rotation starter with durability issues and a lack of ability to control the running game.

### Joel Peralta

Born: **3/23/1976** Age: **36**
Bats: **R** Throws: **R** Height: **6' 0"** Weight: **160**
Breakout: **22%** Improve: **44%** Collapse: **33%**
Attrition: **10%** MLB: **82%**

Comparables:
Rich Gossage, Tom Seaver, Tug McGraw

| YEAR | TEAM | LVL | AGE | W | L | SV | G | GS | IP | H | HR | BB | SO | EqBB9 | EqSO9 | GB% | BABIP | WHIP | ERA | FIP | FRA | WARP |
|---|---|---|---|---|---|---|---|---|---|---|---|---|---|---|---|---|---|---|---|---|---|---|
| 2009 | CSP | AAA | 33 | 6 | 0 | 4 | 31 | 0 | 36² | 31 | 3 | 11 | 32 | 2.7 | 7.8 | 37% | .267 | 1.14 | 2.45 | 3.67 | 3.78 | 0.8 |
| 2009 | COL | MLB | 33 | 0 | 3 | 0 | 27 | 0 | 24² | 27 | 3 | 12 | 22 | 4.4 | 8.0 | 28% | .329 | 1.58 | 6.20 | 4.68 | 5.58 | -0.1 |
| 2010 | SYR | AAA | 34 | 2 | 0 | 20 | 28 | 0 | 33¹ | 14 | 0 | 5 | 27 | 1.9 | 10.3 | 43% | .241 | 0.93 | 1.08 | 2.45 | 3.08 | 0.8 |
| 2010 | WAS | MLB | 34 | 1 | 0 | 0 | 39 | 0 | 49 | 30 | 5 | 9 | 49 | 1.7 | 9.0 | 29% | .203 | 0.80 | 2.02 | 3.05 | 3.17 | 0.9 |
| 2011 | TBA | MLB | 35 | 3 | 4 | 6 | 71 | 0 | 67² | 44 | 7 | 18 | 61 | 2.4 | 8.1 | 28% | .220 | 0.92 | 2.93 | 3.40 | 3.63 | 0.9 |
| 2012 | TBA | MLB | 36 | 3 | 1 | 2 | 50 | 0 | 54 | 48 | 6 | 15 | 45 | 2.4 | 7.5 | 36% | .274 | 1.16 | 3.28 | 3.82 | 3.56 | 0.7 |

An undrafted free agent originally signed by Oakland in 1996, Peralta has pitched for five organizations and has found his niche as an effective high leverage reliever at the tender age of 36. He was another imported piece into the recycled bullpen and was able to exceed his career year in 2010. Peralta was seemingly brought in as the replacement for Dan Wheeler since he showed strong numbers against right-handed batters the previous two seasons. He was able to fill that role and much more as he quickly earned Maddon's trust. Maddon turned to him in any situation in the later innings, including filling in

Attrition: **4%** MLB: **70%**

Comparables:
Clay Buchholz, Jon Lester, Josh Johnson

| YEAR | TEAM | LVL | AGE | W | L | SV | G | GS | IP | H | HR | BB | SO | EqBB9 | EqSO9 | GB% | BABIP | WHIP | ERA | FIP | FRA | WARP |
|---|---|---|---|---|---|---|---|---|---|---|---|---|---|---|---|---|---|---|---|---|---|---|
| 2011 | TBA | MLB | 25 | 12 | 13 | 0 | 34 | 34 | 224¹ | 192 | 22 | 63 | 218 | 2.5 | 8.7 | 45% | .282 | 1.14 | 3.49 | 3.36 | 3.62 | 3.3 |
| 2012 | TBA | MLB | 26 | 12 | 9 | 0 | 29 | 29 | 191² | 160 | 18 | 64 | 177 | 3.0 | 8.3 | 47% | .274 | 1.17 | 2.94 | 3.58 | 3.20 | 3.6 |

Price posted a higher FIP than he did in 2010, a higher WARP than he did in 2010, and was rewarded with some of the worst run support in baseball. The result? A 12-13 season. In 11 of those 13 losses, the Rays provided Price with two runs or less of support, and were shut out in three of those contests. Only the miraculous comeback in the season's final game stopped him from earning a 14th no-run-support loss. Price's strikeout rate and walk rate both improved from 2010 but a spike in home runs slowed his overall gains a bit. He continues to dominate left-handed batters, holding them to a 508 OPS last season while allowing just 12 extra base hits in 230 at bats. The further development of his changeup will help against righties, who again slugged over .400 against him. Price got in just ahead of the Super Two cutoff, making him arbitration-eligible a season earlier than the organization would have liked.

### Cesar Ramos

Born: **6/22/1984** Age: **28**
Bats: **L** Throws: **L** Height: **6' 3"** Weight: **205**
Breakout: **16%** Improve: **48%** Collapse: **21%**
Attrition: **14%** MLB: **82%**

Comparables:
Eric DuBose, Lenny DiNardo, Dooley Womack

| YEAR | TEAM | LVL | AGE | W | L | SV | G | GS | IP | H | HR | BB | SO | EqBB9 | EqSO9 | GB% | BABIP | WHIP | ERA | FIP | FRA | WARP |
|---|---|---|---|---|---|---|---|---|---|---|---|---|---|---|---|---|---|---|---|---|---|---|
| 2009 | POR | AAA | 25 | 5 | 6 | 0 | 15 | 15 | 76² | 84 | 7 | 31 | 45 | 3.6 | 5.3 | 56% | .301 | 1.50 | 3.99 | 4.68 | 5.74 | -0.4 |
| 2009 | SDN | MLB | 25 | 0 | 1 | 0 | 5 | 2 | 14² | 19 | 0 | 4 | 10 | 2.5 | 6.1 | 47% | .396 | 1.57 | 3.07 | 2.51 | 2.99 | 0.2 |
| 2010 | POR | AAA | 26 | 6 | 7 | 0 | 30 | 15 | 96 | 62 | 4 | 32 | 44 | 4.0 | 5.9 | 48% | .319 | 1.39 | 3.28 | 4.71 | 5.06 | 0.4 |
| 2010 | SDN | MLB | 26 | 0 | 1 | 0 | 14 | 0 | 8¹ | 18 | 1 | 4 | 9 | 4.3 | 9.7 | 41% | .515 | 2.64 | 11.88 | 3.95 | 4.91 | -0.1 |
| 2011 | TBA | MLB | 27 | 0 | 1 | 0 | 59 | 0 | 43² | 36 | 4 | 25 | 31 | 5.2 | 6.4 | 50% | .250 | 1.40 | 3.92 | 4.76 | 5.40 | -0.3 |
| 2012 | TBA | MLB | 28 | 2 | 2 | 0 | 28 | 4 | 40¹ | 43 | 4 | 17 | 23 | 3.7 | 5.0 | 45% | .292 | 1.47 | 4.50 | 4.62 | 4.89 | -0.1 |

One of the two former first round draft picks the Padres sent the Rays for Jason Bartlett, Ramos was the only one who displayed any value during the season. He ended up replacing Howell as the LOOGY on the team until McGee stepped up to fill the role. Ramos struck out 20 percent of the left-handed batters he faced while limiting them to a 639 OPS in 100 plate appearances. In all, he gave up just eight extra base hits in 192 plate appearances, but his sweeping breaking ball is more effective against lefties. With Ramos's stuff it would behoove him to be sly on the mound, yet he shows an aggressive and combative streak.

### Fernando Rodney

Born: **3/18/1977** Age: **35**
Bats: **R** Throws: **R** Height: **6' 0"** Weight: **170**
Breakout: **22%** Improve: **48%** Collapse: **27%**
Attrition: **15%** MLB: **81%**

Comparables:
Jim Gott, Al Reyes, Mike DeJean

| YEAR | TEAM | LVL | AGE | W | L | SV | G | GS | IP | H | HR | BB | SO | EqBB9 | EqSO9 | GB% | BABIP | WHIP | ERA | FIP | FRA | WARP |
|---|---|---|---|---|---|---|---|---|---|---|---|---|---|---|---|---|---|---|---|---|---|---|
| 2009 | DET | MLB | 32 | 2 | 5 | 37 | 73 | 0 | 75² | 70 | 8 | 41 | 61 | 4.9 | 7.3 | 58% | .290 | 1.47 | 4.40 | 4.61 | 5.09 | 0.4 |
| 2010 | ANA | MLB | 33 | 4 | 3 | 14 | 72 | 0 | 68 | 70 | 4 | 35 | 53 | 4.6 | 7.0 | 51% | .316 | 1.54 | 4.24 | 4.02 | 4.75 | 0.0 |
| 2011 | ANA | MLB | 34 | 3 | 5 | 3 | 39 | 0 | 32 | 26 | 1 | 28 | 26 | 7.9 | 7.3 | 59% | .281 | 1.69 | 4.50 | 4.75 | 5.68 | -0.3 |
| 2012 | TBA | MLB | 35 | 2 | 1 | 4 | 40 | 0 | 36 | 32 | 3 | 19 | 32 | 4.8 | 8.0 | 49% | .290 | 1.44 | 4.02 | 4.09 | 4.37 | 0.1 |

When the Angels signed Rodney, they got a reliever who had a 4.48 ERA in his previous three seasons. His ERA in two seasons as an Angel: 4.32. Considering his consistency, it is almost understandable that Rodney got his hat bent out of shape when Mike Scioscia abruptly quit giving him innings late in the 2011 season. Signing Rodney for two years and $11 million was a clear failure by deposed GM Tony Reagins, to be sure, but the Angels didn't seem to realize their mistake until the final two months of the deal. Over the past two seasons, only 17 relievers pitched in higher leverage than Rodney (minimum 80 innings); 119 had better ERAs than Rodney.

### Wilking Rodriguez

Born: 3/2/1990 Age: 22
Bats: R Throws: R Height: 6' 2'' Weight: 160
Breakout: 20% Improve: 47% Collapse: 32%
Attrition: 23% MLB: 78%

Comparables:
Joe Moeller, Don Schulze, Mike Johnson

| YEAR | TEAM | LVL | AGE | W | L | SV | G | GS | IP | H | HR | BB | SO | EqBB9 | EqSO9 | GB% | BABIP | WHIP | ERA | FIP | FRA | WARP |
|---|---|---|---|---|---|---|---|---|---|---|---|---|---|---|---|---|---|---|---|---|---|---|
| 2011 | BGR | A | 21 | 0 | 3 | 0 | 9 | 9 | 36² | 38 | 3 | 14 | 34 | 3.4 | 8.3 | 33% | .330 | 1.42 | 4.66 | 3.96 | 4.96 | 0.4 |
| 2012 | TBA | MLB | 22 | 1 | 1 | 0 | 4 | 4 | 17 | 20 | 2 | 8 | 9 | 4.4 | 5.0 | 43% | .304 | 1.64 | 5.59 | 5.09 | 6.08 | -0.2 |

Rodriguez has thrown fewer than 160 innings over the past two seasons due to shoulder woes, but the Rays thought enough of him to protect him on the 40-man roster this offseason. Rodriguez was 10th in Kevin Goldstein's organizational rankings last season with this caveat: "He just needed innings to refine his game." Unfortunately, shoulder problems limited him to just 45 innings of work at two levels. The mid-90s velocity is still there but the fact that at age 22 he hasn't thrown a single pitch at an advanced level of the minor leagues is somewhat concerning.

### Enny Romero

Born: 1/24/1991 Age: 21
Bats: L Throws: L Height: 6' 4'' Weight: 165
Breakout: 32% Improve: 58% Collapse: 9%
Attrition: 4% MLB: 70%

Comparables:
Oliver Perez, Juan Pizarro, Mark Davis

| YEAR | TEAM | LVL | AGE | W | L | SV | G | GS | IP | H | HR | BB | SO | EqBB9 | EqSO9 | GB% | BABIP | WHIP | ERA | FIP | FRA | WARP |
|---|---|---|---|---|---|---|---|---|---|---|---|---|---|---|---|---|---|---|---|---|---|---|
| 2009 | RAY | RK | 18 | 2 | 4 | 0 | 11 | 4 | 39 | 38 | 2 | 21 | 33 | 4.8 | 7.4 | 46% | .313 | 1.51 | 4.85 | 4.15 | 5.95 | -0.4 |
| 2010 | PRI | RK | 19 | 4 | 1 | 0 | 13 | 13 | 69¹ | 41 | 2 | 8 | 62 | 1.8 | 9.4 | 61% | .273 | 0.94 | 1.95 | 2.72 | 4.41 | 2.1 |
| 2011 | BGR | A | 20 | 2 | 0 | 0 | 26 | 26 | 114 | 103 | 9 | 67 | 132 | 5.4 | 11.1 | 54% | .346 | 1.51 | 4.26 | 3.94 | 5.00 | 1.2 |
| 2012 | TBA | MLB | 21 | 2 | 3 | 0 | 6 | 6 | 30¹ | 32 | 4 | 20 | 23 | 5.9 | 6.8 | 51% | .308 | 1.72 | 5.45 | 5.38 | 5.92 | -0.3 |

After taking a strong step forward with his overall command of his stuff, Romero took a step backwards at Bowling Green, issuing walks to 14 percent of the batters he faced. On the plus side, Romero struck out double that—28 percent—and more than half of his balls in play were of the groundball variety. In fact, after allowing five home runs in the first 19 innings of the season, Romero allowed only four more over the final 95 innings. As he makes the jump to the Florida State League, Romero will need to find a happy medium between dominance and location. He has the stuff to garner attention, but how he locates it will determine if that attention is deserved.

### James Shields

Born: 12/20/1981 Age: 30
Bats: R Throws: R Height: 6' 5'' Weight: 214
Breakout: 18% Improve: 54% Collapse: 18%
Attrition: 6% MLB: 95%

Comparables:
Larry Jansen, Erik Hanson, Shane Reynolds

| YEAR | TEAM | LVL | AGE | W | L | SV | G | GS | IP | H | HR | BB | SO | EqBB9 | EqSO9 | GB% | BABIP | WHIP | ERA | FIP | FRA | WARP |
|---|---|---|---|---|---|---|---|---|---|---|---|---|---|---|---|---|---|---|---|---|---|---|
| 2009 | TBA | MLB | 27 | 11 | 12 | 0 | 33 | 33 | 219² | 239 | 29 | 52 | 167 | 2.1 | 6.8 | 43% | .311 | 1.32 | 4.14 | 4.06 | 4.43 | 2.7 |
| 2010 | TBA | MLB | 28 | 13 | 15 | 0 | 34 | 33 | 203¹ | 246 | 34 | 51 | 187 | 2.3 | 8.3 | 42% | .344 | 1.46 | 5.18 | 4.21 | 4.72 | 0.9 |
| 2011 | TBA | MLB | 29 | 16 | 12 | 0 | 33 | 33 | 249¹ | 195 | 26 | 65 | 225 | 2.3 | 8.1 | 47% | .260 | 1.04 | 2.82 | 3.45 | 3.63 | 3.2 |
| 2012 | TBA | MLB | 30 | 13 | 10 | 0 | 30 | 30 | 206 | 193 | 25 | 43 | 174 | 1.9 | 7.6 | 45% | .288 | 1.15 | 3.30 | 3.72 | 3.59 | 2.7 |

There was nowhere to go but up for him after his disastrous 2010 season and up Shields went. He bounced back to put up career numbers across the board as the bedrock of the Rays rotation. He spent the offseason tightening up his delivery and working on all of his pitches to become less predictable than he was in previous seasons. He emerged from the offseason cocoon as a pitcher who could throw all of his pitches for strikes on any count and could work so deep into games that he ended up more than doubling his career total for complete games, finishing 11 of his starts. Over the past four seasons, he has the seventh-highest innings total of all pitchers, but just the 13th highest pitch count in that same time frame. To properly frame that, consider that A.J. Burnett has thrown 66 more pitches than Shields over the past four seasons despite throwing 82 fewer innings. Despite the career numbers, the organization still has him at a comfortable price, He is under a $7 million option for 2012 with two more team options to come. This is a pitcher at the peak of his game with confidence in his stuff.

### Alexander Torres

Born: 12/8/1987 Age: 24
Bats: L Throws: L Height: 5' 11'' Weight: 175
Breakout: 33% Improve: 55% Collapse: 24%
Attrition: 12% MLB: 96%

Comparables:
Andrew Miller, Jonathan Sanchez, Adam Loewen

| YEAR | TEAM | LVL | AGE | W | L | SV | G | GS | IP | H | HR | BB | SO | EqBB9 | EqSO9 | GB% | BABIP | WHIP | ERA | FIP | FRA | WARP |
|---|---|---|---|---|---|---|---|---|---|---|---|---|---|---|---|---|---|---|---|---|---|---|
| 2009 | RCU | A+ | 21 | 10 | 3 | 0 | 21 | 19 | 121¹ | 93 | 4 | 63 | 124 | 4.7 | 9.2 | 64% | .294 | 1.29 | 2.75 | 3.85 | 4.78 | 0.5 |
| 2010 | MNT | AA | 22 | 11 | 6 | 0 | 27 | 27 | 142² | 93 | 5 | 46 | 101 | 4.4 | 9.5 | 54% | .327 | 1.44 | 3.47 | 3.64 | 4.50 | 1.4 |
| 2011 | DUR | AAA | 23 | 9 | 7 | 0 | 27 | 27 | 146¹ | 141 | 7 | 87 | 161 | 5.1 | 9.6 | 48% | .337 | 1.48 | 3.08 | 3.57 | 5.07 | 1.6 |
| 2011 | TBA | MLB | 23 | 1 | 1 | 0 | 4 | 0 | 8 | 8 | 0 | 7 | 9 | 7.9 | 10.1 | 59% | .364 | 1.88 | 3.38 | 3.81 | 4.87 | 0.0 |
| 2012 | TBA | MLB | 24 | 3 | 3 | 0 | 8 | 8 | 45 | 42 | 4 | 27 | 40 | 5.4 | 7.9 | 52% | .298 | 1.53 | 4.35 | 4.38 | 4.73 | 0.1 |

Torres had but four big league appearances in 2011, but his first and his last outings were memorable. The first came in a crucial series against the Yankees just after the All-Star break. Torres was called on for the ninth, but threw 44 pitches and blew the save. His last outing came in relief of Niemann, who was pulled after one inning due to ineffectiveness. Torres scattered three hits across five scoreless innings in a must-win against Toronto in the last week of the season. This came on the heels of a season with Durham in which he struck out 156 batters in 146 innings, walked 83, and was taken deep only seven times. He could likely hop into the fifth spot of any rotation in baseball except this one, which is the most crowded of any team. His stature and wildness could land him in the bullpen, or on another team.

## LINEOUTS

| | | | | | | | | | | | | | | | | | | |
|---|---|---|---|---|---|---|---|---|---|---|---|---|---|---|---|---|---|---|
| 1B J. Malm | HUD | A- | 20 | 301 | 36 | 15 | 0 | 12 | 47 | 38 | 65 | 3-2 | .257/.382/.462 | .309 | .301 | 0.4 | -1.1 | 1.9 |
| 1B M. Mangini | TAC | AAA | 25 | 259 | 34 | 9 | 1 | 2 | 41 | 24 | 45 | 3-1 | .336/.399/.409 | .281 | .409 | 0.2 | -1.4 | 0.7 |
| C S. Vogt | MNT | AA | 26 | 427 | 52 | 21 | 6 | 13 | 85 | 30 | 51 | 4-2 | .301/.344/.487 | .292 | .310 | 1.3 | -4.8 | 2.7 |
| | DUR | AAA | 26 | 131 | 15 | 14 | 1 | 4 | 20 | 4 | 29 | 0-0 | .290/.305/.516 | .276 | .340 | -1.9 | 0.4 | 0.5 |

**Leslie Anderson** came to the Rays via Cuba and once earned the praise of Michael Lewis, but lacks the plate discipline necessary to make it in the majors. ⊘ **Yoel Araujo** is the organization's largest international investment to date but remains international, as he has yet to play a game on U.S. soil. The 18-year-old had just 15 extra base hits while striking out in one-third of his 212 Dominican Summer League plate appearances. ⊘ One of four catchers on the 40-man roster, **Nevin Ashley** is known more for his defense than his bat and is already 27 years old without a single plate appearance in the majors. ⊘ He was old at age 22 to be in Low-A, but **Derek Dietrich** made the most of it, posting a top 20 OPS and a top eight ISO. Plate discipline continues to be an issue as he has a .29 BB/K ratio through his first two seasons, but he does make excellent contact when he does get his bat on the ball. ⊘ **Jeff Malm** had the eighth-best OPS in the New York-Penn League last season, quite the step up from his first two seasons of subpar statistical production. ⊘ After the Mariners cut ties with 2007 supplemental pick **Matt Mangini**, who left baseball for undisclosed personal reasons in August, the Rays signed him to a minor league deal with an invite to spring training. ⊘ **Stephen Vogt** played at two levels and five positions in search of a position last season, but the Rays must believe in the 27-year-old's bat, as they protected him from the Rule 5 draft.

## PITCHERS

| PLAYER | TEAM | LVL | AGE | W | L | SV | IP | H | HR | BB | SO | EqBB9 | EqSO9 | GB% | BABIP | WHIP | ERA | FIP | FRA | WARP |
|---|---|---|---|---|---|---|---|---|---|---|---|---|---|---|---|---|---|---|---|---|
| J. Buente | NWO | AAA | 27 | 3 | 0 | 0 | $41^2$ | 23 | 1 | 9 | 41 | 2.2 | 9.5 | 51% | .229 | 0.79 | 1.94 | 2.80 | 3.25 | 0.9 |
| | DUR | AAA | 27 | 1 | 3 | 1 | $42^2$ | 50 | 4 | 17 | 43 | 3.6 | 9.1 | 44% | .362 | 1.52 | 5.70 | 3.92 | 5.10 | 0.4 |
| | FLO | MLB | 27 | 0 | 1 | 0 | 3 | 5 | 0 | 3 | 1 | 9.0 | 3.0 | 54% | .385 | 2.67 | 9.00 | 6.33 | 6.35 | -0.1 |
| | TBA | MLB | 27 | 0 | 0 | 0 | 2 | 2 | 0 | 2 | 1 | 9.0 | 4.5 | 57% | .286 | 2.00 | 9.00 | 5.06 | 5.56 | 0.0 |
| L. Cormier | DUR | AAA | 30 | 4 | 3 | 0 | $47^1$ | 62 | 8 | 18 | 25 | 3.4 | 4.8 | 58% | .331 | 1.69 | 5.51 | 5.52 | 6.11 | 0.0 |
| | LAN | MLB | 30 | 0 | 1 | 0 | $13^2$ | 22 | 4 | 5 | 7 | 3.3 | 4.6 | 64% | .333 | 1.98 | 9.88 | 6.87 | 8.25 | -0.7 |
| M. Fleming | MNT | AA | 24 | 5 | 4 | 4 | $80^1$ | 57 | 5 | 43 | 100 | 4.7 | 11.7 | 47% | .304 | 1.23 | 3.59 | 3.37 | 3.95 | 1.2 |
| J. Nunez | CHR | AAA | 25 | 1 | 1 | 0 | $47^1$ | 43 | 7 | 18 | 50 | 3.4 | 9.5 | 38% | .308 | 1.29 | 4.75 | 4.38 | 5.18 | 0.6 |

**Jay Buente** has put up moderately successful numbers in Triple-A but his limited major league experience has involved far too many free passes and not enough missed bats. ⊘ **Lance Cormier** was the equivalent of a low-leverage reliever for the Rays until he was jettisoned and claimed by the Dodgers. ⊘ **Marquis Fleming** has piled up impressive strikeout totals as a reliever, striking out 307 batters in 255 innings on the strength of a Bugs Bunny changeup that makes his rather average fastball look better than it is. Triple-A will be a big test for his stuff in 2012. ⊘ Despite an impressive fastball/slider arsenal, reliever **Jhonny Nunez** has always been too easy to hit, which is why he had no future with the White Sox and probably has no future in Tampa Bay either.

# MANAGER: JOE MADDON

| YEAR | TEAM | W-L | Pythag +/- | Avg PC | 100+ P | 120+ P | QS | BQS | REL | REL w Zero R | IBB | Subs | PH | PH Avg | PH HR | SB2 | CS2 | SB3 | CS3 | SAC Att | SAC % | POS SAC | Squeeze | Swing | In Play |
|------|------|-----|-----------|--------|--------|--------|----|-----|-----|-------------|-----|------|-----|--------|-------|-----|-----|-----|-----|---------|-------|---------|---------|-------|---------|
| 2009 | TBA | 84-78 | 1 | 99.4 | 81 | 1 | 72 | 8 | 508 | 323 | 21 | 48 | 138 | .160 | 7 | 26 | 11 | 1 | 1 | 45 | 55.6% | 24 | 9 | 141 | 101 |
| 2010 | TBA | 96-66 | 1 | 197.9 | 159 | 159 | 114 | 5 | 491 | 412 | 68 | — | 308 | .242 | 6 | 25 | 7 | 0 | 1 | 134 | 88.1% | 116 | 12 | 404 | 120 |
| 2011 | TBA | 91-71 | 1 | 102.1 | 98 | 5 | 99 | 10 | 438 | 355 | 38 | — | 129 | .252 | 1 | 20 | 8 | 1 | 0 | 63 | 77.8% | 47 | 5 | 441 | 138 |

Maddon continues to keep fans and experts alike on their toes. He hit 10 different hitters in the leadoff spot in 2011, including a catcher five times and even Evan Longoria for three games at the end of May. In all, he used 130 different batting orders, wore a football helmet to a postgame media session, and ejected the entire umpiring crew in an early April game in Chicago that was reminiscent of Scarface's restaurant scene in the movie *Half-Baked*. He works closely with the front office staff behind the scenes to comb through the data available to see where the team can make up the gaps. He also comes to them with things he picks up while observing the game from the dugout or reading up on his iPad. Baseball Info Solutions tells us the Rays had more defensive shifts employed during outs made on the field than any team in baseball in 2011 by a considerable margin. The data on where to place the fielders come from the spray charts and other data the back office group shares with Maddon. This relationship originally began when Maddon employed the Danks Theory at the behest of the guys behind the curtain. They had noted how much Danks struggled with left-handed hitters; his change-up on the outside corner that so effectively neutralized right-handed hitters was useless on lefties. Maddon mixes together advanced data and scouting into a perfect mix of what he often refers to as "the information at hand" to put a winning product on the field. *Sports Illustrated* published a players' poll this season that had 291 responses from players; Maddon was selected as the Most Popular Manager by the group. When you see how he openly encourages aggressive mistakes, how he sets up road trip dress themes for the team, and how he runs a self-described "Republican-style running game," it is easy to see why players enjoy playing for him. Merlot Joe, as he is known in the area, loves his wines but you will never hear him whine about what the Rays do not have on the roster. He takes what he is given. With the tools at hand he has guided the Rays to the postseason in three of the last four seasons and to the third-highest win total over the past four seasons behind only the huge payrolls in New York, Philadelphia, and Boston.

# Texas Rangers

Exceptionalism Made Easy

It's an easy (and often fun) exercise for fans to comically assume that members of their favorite team's front office are a bunch of fools, making decisions that you either know to be foolish or assume will, when looked into, foolish in question. The converse might also be comical if you blindly assume that the front office of your favorite team is filled with intellectually superior beings, those blessed with not only brains but also balls, to put it rather crudely. Baseball, like any other business, has its stars and its slouches, and the reality of that construct does in fact allow for some teams to be run by fools while other teams are in fact run by people who are very smart and very astute in their chosen vocation. While it's not pleasant to be made aware that your favorite team happens to be run by people who aren't that exceptional, it is quite refreshing to be told that your favorite team is under the leadership of people who do possess exceptional qualities. For fans of the Texas Rangers, allow us to offer that form of refreshment, as the front office for your team is in the top tier in the game. Let's take a closer look at what makes it exceptional and separates it from the fools on the other end of the spectrum.

Everything starts with the man with the biggest voice, and no, I'm not talking about Nolan Ryan; whereas Ryan is a walking legend of Texas baseball and a major player in not only the business, but also the operational side of the organization, the booming voice of the Texas Rangers comes from a man who speaks with a controlled inflection at a sensible volume: Jon Daniels.

| | | |
|---|---|---|
| TAv | .290 | 2nd |
| TAv-P | .254 | 9th |
| FIP | 4.01 | 18th |
| DER | .722 | 2nd |
| DL | 1018 | 28th |
| B-Age | 29.2 | 21st |
| P-Age | 28.5 | 19th |
| Salary | $93.9 | 13th |
| M$/MW | $1.71 | 8th |

**2011:** Relying on core lineup of sluggers, they win two more games in Series than last season

**2012:** The division will be a cakewalk as long as the Angels don't make any big ... aw, crap

**Action Items:** Sign Darvish, more offense from first, leverage deep farm system for midseason upgrades

Much is known about Daniels, the youngest general manager in baseball history upon his arrival, and still the youngest general manager in the game as we head into the 2012 season. As the man in the big chair for one of baseball's up-and-coming elite teams, defined as exceptional, rather than looked upon as a fool, a distinction he almost failed to dodge after taking over the reins in late 2005.

As a 28-year-old general manager taking control of an unremarkable franchise located in the heart of Dallas Cowboys country, Daniels was starting from a disadvantage, and thanks to a series of questionable trades right out of the chute, the disadvantage looked like a disaster. The fans of the team started to pencil the young general manager in as a fool, Ivy-League pedigree be damned, after he traded away Alfonso Soriano for Brad Wilkerson's personal stench and sent future All-Star first-baseman Adrian Gonzalez and pitcher Chris Young to San Diego for Adam Eaton's stench and a reliever. The following off-season, Daniels gave the fan base a permanent marker for which to write him off as a fool, sending top-prospect and Texas native John Danks to the White Sox for Brandon McCarthy's medical bills. Daniels had only been at the wheel for a calendar year, yet his future looked as shaky as the roster he had compiled. The team finished under .500 and the exit sign over his office door was starting to be installed.

So what happened? How did Daniels go from perceived chump to champ in such a short window of time? Unlike several people in this industry, Daniels saw his mistakes as stepping-stones to success, learning the nuances of failure in order to avoid repeating the process. Not to point fingers, but you would probably be shocked to learn how often the same mistakes are made over and over by baseball front offices; some are fortunate enough to get bailed out by the talent on the field, while others just rinse and repeat as if the consequences of their failures were insignificant. These recidivists of failure usually find a way to stick around in highly important roles despite being grossly incompetent, hoping that their luck will change if they continue to make foolish decisions based on foolish approaches. Daniels started to separate himself from the pack of fools by learning and adjusting his game to suit the market he found himself in. In other words, Daniels proved that intelligence isn't defined by your diploma; rather, he proved that in order to become exceptional, you have to not only surround yourself with exceptional people, you have to learn from the failures of the past in order to find success in the present.

With a cloudy future and the failures of year one tattooed on his forehead, Daniels and his inner-circle rebounded in a major way in 2007, making the astute decision to build a solid foundation rather than construct something that was aesthetically appealing yet narrow in scope and space. The Rangers had a plan in place and the plan was to start the process of acquiring high-ceiling talent at premium positions in order to find cost-controlled and sustainable success at the major league level. To execute this plan, Daniels threw more trust and responsibility into his player development and scouting departments, with two men leading the charge in what would become a reservoir of talent for the Rangers: the Latin American market.

The two men in question were Don Welke, a veteran scout and former confidant to the great Pat Gillick, the architect of three World Series winning teams, and AJ Preller, former college chum of Daniels who had quickly risen through the ranks of baseball and was now director of international scouting for the Rangers. With Welke and Preller, Daniels had two people (among others) he trusted in the field of talent evaluation; two men who would spearhead the Rangers' interests in the Latin American market, setting up academies, casting wider nets in wider markets, and changing the future of the Rangers in the process. It was the push behind these endeavors that led to a franchise-altering deal for Daniels and company in the summer of 2007, when former free agent targets Neftali Feliz and Elvis Andrus were acquired from the Braves for marquee first-baseman Mark Teixeira, along with young lefty prospect Matt Harrison and catcher Jarrod Saltalamacchia.

This trade could have been disastrous for the Daniels regime, as it's never easy to sell a rebuild, especially when you sell off your best player for a package of young unproven prospects most people had either never heard of or didn't pay much attention to if they had. You always have to consider that it was only a year and a half prior that Daniels had sold off another talented first-baseman in Gonzalez, for a return that was neither youthful nor successful. The Rangers couldn't afford to make the same mistake again; with a losing team at the major league level the need to acquire hope for the future was paramount. Thankfully for the Rangers, the people in place did their due diligence with the Teixeira trade, having a strong familiarity with both Andrus and Feliz from their amateur days, and numerous eyes on the other prizes included in the deal. The trade changed the landscape of the organization, as three players the Rangers received from Atlanta would play major roles in the future success, with Andrus becoming a big-league starter as a 20 year-old, Feliz developing into a tantalizing talent, and Harrison, after a few bumps in the road, putting the pieces together in 2011 and establishing himself as a viable third or fourth starter at the major league level. Add to this haul a 2007 draft class that included players later used to acquire Cliff Lee and Bengie Molina, two important cogs in the 2010 postseason push, starting first-baseman Mitch Moreland, and blue-chip prospect Neil Ramirez, who is now knocking on the door of the majors.

As the Rangers worked hard to acquire high-ceiling talent via trades and the Rule 4 draft, the aforementioned duo of Welke and Preller, as well as talented up-and-coming scouting minds like Mike Daly, the Rangers' footprint in the Latin American free agent market continued to grow, starting with a wave of talent in 2006 and growing each subsequent year, with the likes of Wilmer Font, Martin Perez, Jurickson Profar, Luis Sardinas, Jorge Alfaro, Nomar Mazara, and Ronald Guzman, just to name a few who have been signed as amateurs in the market. Because of the nature of the market itself, the Rangers positioned themselves as major players, allocating funds to acquire and develop high-ceiling amateur talent rather than purchase expensive retreads at the major league level. The focus was sharp and dangerous, as the payoff could be extreme but the letdown equally so, and after the building blocks started to form a foundation, it was time for Daniels to up the intensity by staying true to the process while also collecting pieces that could help the major league team change the culture of winning in Arlington.

Daniels and his team continued to move forward, using their established approach to acquire amateur talent while starting to simultaneously look for pieces ready to contribute at the major league level. It would have been easier to just rebuild at the lower levels and hope for the best, or stop the process halfway and put all available resources into the major league squad in order to appease the fan base and gain job security through a more appealing won-loss record. But the Daniels posse worked equally hard on both fronts, spending big in the draft while looking to arbitrage under-valued talents at the major league level, as was best exemplified when pitching prospect Edinson Volquez was traded to the Reds for Josh Hamilton, a player who had only 90 major league games under his belt and a history of drug abuse and injury that would scare off even the most confident of teams. Four All-Star Games, a Most Valuable Player award, and two trips to the World Series later, the move looks as brilliant as one of Hamilton's own moonshots. It was a gamble, but the organization didn't just jump into the water and hope for the best. It was a calculated gamble, one that keen talent evaluator Don Welke felt would pay off in a major way. The Rangers once again followed their own script of

those of equal mental capacity, regardless of their background or specific focus. He encourages discussion and debate, and if you have a case to make, he has the desire to hear it. Fools are those who think their own voice is more important because of the title on their door or the elegance of the business card. Daniels isn't one to get caught up in titles or stature, or even pomp; rather, he is the first to give credit to his infrastructure, the ones he trusts to scout and develop the talent he signs off on. He is not a one-man army or even a general of said army. Daniels is a master facilitator, making the machine work with efficiency rather than being the one tasked with making the machine itself. Therein lies his real brilliance, and the central reason he and his team are considered exceptional. This isn't the Jon Daniels show. It's the Texas Rangers organization.

Despite the rocky start, and several imposing hurdles along the way, Daniels and his staff stand among baseball's elite, both in terms of talent on the field, in the field, and in the office. They understand the evolution of the game and will be among the first teams that take advantage of market

trends or scouting trends that others are either scared of, unfamiliar with, or in opposition to. Staying ahead of this curve requires a little luck, but mostly it requires a form of baseball exceptionalism; the ability to read the recipe of the game and not only adjust accordingly, but proceed with a cunning intelligence that will offer rewards in the approach. If you are reading this and you are a fan of the Texas Rangers, you should feel very confident in the abilities of your front office. New CBA got you down and you think the Rangers' Latin American presence will suffer as a result? The Rangers spent over $15M on bonuses alone in 2011. Looking nervously at the Angels and wondering who will take CJ Wilson's place

by a healthy Julio Borbon and 23-year-old Cuban defector Leonys Martin. The vast majority of the Rangers' starting position players are in their prime, and the club is beginning to talk extensions with breakout catcher Mike Napoli and second baseman Ian Kinsler. As always, one of the primary keys will be keeping slugging outfielders Josh Hamilton and Nelson Cruz away from their oft-nagging injuries and off the disabled list.

With an elite nucleus of players at the major league level and one of baseball's strongest farm systems, the Rangers are in position to compete for the long haul. Having an aggressive and intelligent front office will give the Rangers every advantage in their pursuit. Add financial luxury to the mix and you are served with a potent cocktail for sustainable success. As fans of the team, you can rest assured that the Rangers' front office is aware of the curves in the road and will adjust its game to exploit and manipulate the market as it presents itself. If you find yourself supporting another team and think they are fools for lacking such exceptionalism —well, you might just be right.

# HITTERS

**Elvis Andrus**    SS

Born: **8/26/1988** Age: **23**
Bats: **R** Throws: **R** Height: **6' 1''** Weight: **185**
Breakout: **3%** Improve: **30%** Collapse: **7%**
Attrition: **25%** MLB: **76%**

**Comparables:**
Dustin Pedroia, Placido Polanco, Jerry Kenney

| YEAR | TEAM | LVL | AGE | PA | R | 2B | 3B | HR | RBI | BB | SO | SB | CS | AVG_OBP_SLG | TAv | BABIP | BRR | FRAA | WARP |
|------|------|-----|-----|-----|----|----|----|----|-----|----|----|----|----|-------------|-----|-------|-----|------|------|
| 2009 | TEX | MLB | 20 | 541 | 72 | 17 | 8 | 6 | 40 | 40 | 77 | 33 | 6 | .267/.329/.373 | .246 | .305 | 3.7 | 0.9 | 2.2 |
| 2010 | TEX | MLB | 21 | 674 | 88 | 15 | 3 | 0 | 35 | 64 | 96 | 32 | 15 | .265/.342/.301 | .242 | .317 | 4.9 | 2.8 | 2.5 |
| 2011 | TEX | MLB | 22 | 665 | 96 | 27 | 3 | 5 | 60 | 56 | 74 | 37 | 12 | .279/.347/.361 | .261 | .312 | 7.1 | 2.6 | 3.7 |
| 2012 | TEX | MLB | 23 | 627 | 75 | 22 | 5 | 8 | 61 | 54 | 77 | 33 | 11 | .282/.351/.387 | .258 | .304 | -0.5 | SS 5 | 2.5 |

In 2011, Andrus showed the same impressive chops in the field that earned him the "slick" distinction to begin with, but his progress at the plate provided hope that his glove won't stand alone in the glory. Although he will never be a legitimate power threat, Elvis is starting to show more strength in his swing without sacrificing bat speed. The 23-year-old Venezuelan should see his gap approach yield more doubles and perhaps more home runs in the future. Both advanced in 2011, almost doubling the extra-base-hits from his previous campaign. In combination with his plus speed and his defensive wizardry, Andrus has all the physical tools necessary to develop into a first-division player on both sides of the ball. He is just going to keep getting better.

**Adrian Beltre** 3B

Born: 4/7/1979 Age: 33
Bats: R Throws: R Height: 6' 0" Weight: 200
Breakout: 2% Improve: 19% Collapse: 6%
Attrition: 11% MLB: 88%

**Comparables:**
Vinny Castilla,Chris Sabo,Michael Young

| YEAR | TEAM | LVL | AGE | PA | R | 2B | 3B | HR | RBI | BB | SO | SB | CS | AVG_OBP_SLG | TAv | BABIP | BRR | FRAA | WARP |
|------|------|-----|-----|-----|----|----|----|----|-----|----|----|----|----|-------------|------|-------|-----|------|------|
| 2009 | SEA | MLB | 30 | 477 | 54 | 27 | 0 | 8 | 44 | 19 | 74 | 13 | 2 | .265/.304/.379 | .246 | .301 | 3.2 | 8.1 | 1.8 |
| 2010 | BOS | MLB | 31 | 641 | 84 | 49 | 2 | 28 | 102 | 40 | 82 | 2 | 1 | .321/.365/.553 | .311 | .331 | 2 | 15.7 | 7.6 |
| 2011 | TEX | MLB | 32 | 525 | 82 | 33 | 0 | 32 | 105 | 25 | 53 | 1 | 1 | .296/.331/.561 | .316 | .273 | 1 | 3 | 5.3 |
| 2012 | TEX | MLB | 33 | 518 | 67 | 29 | 2 | 22 | 75 | 31 | 75 | 5 | 1 | .281/.328/.484 | .278 | .293 | 0 | 3B 8 | 3.0 |

After signing a massive five-year, $80M free agent contract in the 2010 offseason, Beltre arrived in Arlington as the so-called "consolation prize" for losing out on Cliff Lee. After he won over the fans with his Gold Glove work at third and his 65 extra-base-hits at the plate (including 32 homers), the signs that filled Rangers Ballpark in Arlington pondering, "Cliff Lee Who?" weren't of the ironic variety. In year one of his deal, the 32-year-old Dominican more than lived up to the hype. He plays the game with an infectious and precocious style that makes it feel like his presence was missing all along. As an added bonus, his teammates quickly learned of the hidden joys that can erupt when they unexpectedly touched the top of his head. Cue the reaction.

**Engel Beltre** CF

Born: 11/1/1989 Age: 22
Bats: L Throws: L Height: 6' 3" Weight: 180
Breakout: 2% Improve: 8% Collapse: 0%
Attrition: 9% MLB: 17%

**Comparables:**
Jarvis Tatum,Jose Valdez,Charlie Blackmon

| YEAR | TEAM | LVL | AGE | PA | R | 2B | 3B | HR | RBI | BB | SO | SB | CS | AVG_OBP_SLG | TAv | BABIP | BRR | FRAA | WARP |
|------|------|-----|-----|-----|----|----|----|----|-----|----|----|----|----|-------------|------|-------|------|--------|------|
| 2009 | BAK | A+ | 19 | 389 | 44 | 13 | 5 | 3 | 23 | 17 | 77 | 17 | 7 | .227/.278/.317 | .204 | .277 | 4.4 | 1 | -0.3 |
| 2010 | BAK | A+ | 20 | 290 | 38 | 11 | 4 | 5 | 35 | 11 | 34 | 10 | 7 | .331/.376/.460 | .299 | .361 | -1.4 | 3.4 | 2.2 |
| 2010 | FRI | AA | 20 | 198 | 14 | 4 | 4 | 1 | 14 | 10 | 24 | 8 | 2 | .254/.301/.337 | .235 | .285 | -1.6 | 7.4 | 0.8 |
| 2011 | FRI | AA | 21 | 482 | 64 | 15 | 6 | 1 | 28 | 28 | 103 | 16 | 6 | .231/.285/.300 | .207 | .299 | 3.1 | 7.5 | -0.3 |
| 2012 | TEX | MLB | 22 | 250 | 22 | 9 | 2 | 2 | 21 | 7 | 52 | 6 | 2 | .220/.252/.307 | .193 | .267 | -0.2 | CF -1, RF 0 | -1.7 |

A highly gifted athlete, Engel Beltre remains one of the toolsiest prospects in the Rangers system despite production that suggests otherwise. Aside from the makeup issues that are a natural by-product of his on-the-field indiscretions, Beltre's biggest developmental hindrance is his approach at the plate. The 22-year-old Dominican looks to swing early in the count. In fact, his untreated addiction to swinging early in the count often becomes a monkey on his back, forcing lunges, poor contact, and easy outs. Until he works to refine this aspect of his game, Beltre will remain a prospect capable of boom while living in the reality of a bust.

**Julio Borbon** CF

Born: 2/20/1986 Age: 26
Bats: L Throws: L Height: 6' 2" Weight: 180
Breakout: 1% Improve: 45% Collapse: 7%
Attrition: 19% MLB: 74%

**Comparables:**
Rajai Davis,Rudy Law,Bake McBride

| YEAR | TEAM | LVL | AGE | PA | R | 2B | 3B | HR | RBI | BB | SO | SB | CS | AVG_OBP_SLG | TAv | BABIP | BRR | FRAA | WARP |
|------|------|-----|-----|-----|----|----|----|----|-----|----|----|----|----|-------------|------|-------|------|----------|------|
| 2009 | OKL | AAA | 23 | 457 | 71 | 12 | 7 | 2 | 34 | 33 | 40 | 25 | 7 | .307/.363/.386 | .268 | .330 | 6.3 | 1.7 | 2.2 |
| 2009 | TEX | MLB | 23 | 179 | 30 | 4 | 0 | 4 | 20 | 15 | 28 | 19 | 4 | .312/.376/.414 | .280 | .360 | 0.2 | 0.6 | 0.6 |
| 2010 | TEX | MLB | 24 | 468 | 60 | 11 | 4 | 3 | 42 | 19 | 59 | 15 | 7 | .276/.309/.340 | .233 | .313 | 2.3 | 3.7 | 0.4 |
| 2011 | ROU | AAA | 25 | 153 | 27 | 10 | 4 | 0 | 14 | 14 | 22 | 16 | 4 | .298/.376/.435 | .262 | .355 | 1 | 2.8 | 0.9 |
| 2011 | TEX | MLB | 25 | 98 | 10 | 1 | 3 | 0 | 11 | 3 | 9 | 6 | 2 | .270/.305/.348 | .253 | .296 | 0.6 | 0.4 | 0.4 |
| 2012 | TEX | MLB | 26 | 250 | 29 | 8 | 3 | 3 | 25 | 15 | 31 | 14 | 4 | .283/.332/.388 | .250 | .308 | -0.1 | CF 3, LF 0 | 0.9 |

A catalytic player who has been anything but catalytic so far in his brief career, Borbon's injury-plagued 2011 campaign has put his future with the team in doubt. Borbon looked to be the center fielder of the future, showing plus-plus speed, a good glove, and enough stick to hit for average and put pressure on opposing defenses. The reality is that Borbon's approach at the plate has limited his function with the bat, and despite being a true 70 runner, Borbon's speed on both sides of the ball hasn't been enough to overcome other shortcomings in his skill set. With center fielder Leonys Martin already in the fold and other options at the position being explored, Borbon's name might be on the back of another team's jersey in the not-so-distant future.

**Nelson Cruz** RF

Born: 7/1/1980 Age: 31
Bats: R Throws: R Height: 6' 4" Weight: 175
Breakout: 1% Improve: 39% Collapse: 4%
Attrition: 12% MLB: 91%

**Comparables:**
Juan Gonzalez,Larry Walker,Matias Carrillo

| YEAR | TEAM | LVL | AGE | PA | R | 2B | 3B | HR | RBI | BB | SO | SB | CS | AVG_OBP_SLG | TAv | BABIP | BRR | FRAA | WARP |
|------|------|-----|-----|-----|----|----|----|----|----|-----|----|-----|----|----|-------------|------|-------|------|----------|------|
| 2009 | TEX | MLB | 29 | 515 | 75 | 21 | 1 | 33 | 76 | 49 | 118 | 20 | 4 | .260/.332/.524 | .283 | .278 | -0.2 | 17.7 | 3.5 |
| 2010 | TEX | MLB | 30 | 445 | 60 | 31 | 3 | 22 | 78 | 38 | 81 | 17 | 4 | .318/.374/.576 | .320 | .348 | 1.4 | 13.8 | 5.1 |
| 2011 | TEX | MLB | 31 | 513 | 64 | 28 | 1 | 29 | 87 | 33 | 116 | 9 | 5 | .263/.312/.509 | .286 | .288 | -2.4 | 9 | 2.7 |
| 2012 | TEX | MLB | 31 | 476 | 66 | 23 | 2 | 27 | 77 | 41 | 103 | 14 | 5 | .278/.343/.531 | .296 | .304 | -0.2 | RF 9, LF 1 | 2.7 |

What can be said about Nelson Cruz's hamstring that hasn't already been said about James Patterson's prose or the *Star Wars* prequels? After three trips to the disabled list in 2010 with hamstring-related injuries, Cruz once again found himself back in the training room in 2011, limited to 124 games and inconsistent results. The 31-year-old Dominican has elite power and gave the world a prolonged taste of his talents during a remarkable postseason power barrage. But the injury issues cloud Cruz's future and severely restrict the potential of his offensive prowess. When healthy, Cruz could hit in the middle of any lineup in baseball. The key words being "when" and "could."

**Craig Gentry** CF
Born: 11/29/1983 Age: 28
Bats: R Throws: R Height: 6' 3" Weight: 190
Breakout: 1% Improve: 39% Collapse: 12%
Attrition: 23% MLB: 78%
Comparables:

| YEAR | TEAM | LVL | AGE | PA | R | 2B | 3B | HR | RBI | BB | SO | SB | CS | AVG/OBP/SLG | TAv | BABIP | BRR | FRAA | WARP |
|------|------|-----|-----|----|---|----|----|----|-----|----|----|----|----|-------------|-----|-------|-----|------|------|
| 2009 | FRI | AA | 25 | 588 | 100 | 21 | 7 | 8 | 53 | 49 | 64 | 49 | 6 | .303/.377/.418 | .296 | .330 | 7.3 | -7.3 | 4.2 |
| 2009 | TEX | MLB | 25 | 19 | 4 | 1 | 0 | 0 | 1 | 2 | 5 | 0 | 0 | .118/.211/.176 | .179 | .167 | 0.4 | -0.2 | -0.1 |
| 2010 | OKL | AAA | 26 | 301 | 43 | 7 | 4 | 4 | 35 | 29 | 47 | 12 | 5 | .309/.391/.413 | .285 | .360 | 1.5 | 5.8 | 2.6 |
| 2010 | TEX | MLB | 26 | 35 | 4 | 0 | 0 | 0 | 3 | 1 | 11 | 1 | 0 | .212/.229/.212 | .163 | .304 | 0.5 | -0.5 | -0.2 |

**Alberto Gonzalez** 2B
Born: 4/18/1983 Age: 29
Bats: R Throws: R Height: 6' 0" Weight: 165
Breakout: 1% Improve: 27% Collapse: 5%
Attrition: 12% MLB: 65%
Comparables:
Rennie Stennett, Fernando Cortez, Melvin Dorta

| YEAR | TEAM | LVL | AGE | PA | R | 2B | 3B | HR | RBI | BB | SO | SB | CS | AVG/OBP/SLG | TAv | BABIP | BRR | FRAA | WARP |
|------|------|-----|-----|----|---|----|----|----|-----|----|----|----|----|-------------|-----|-------|-----|------|------|
| 2009 | SYR | AAA | 26 | 92 | 5 | 3 | 1 | 0 | 8 | 1 | 8 | 1 | 0 | .311/.315/.367 | .225 | .337 | 0.1 | -1.4 | 0.0 |
| 2009 | WAS | MLB | 26 | 316 | 31 | 16 | 3 | 1 | 33 | 14 | 27 | 1 | 1 | .265/.299/.351 | .231 | .283 | -2 | -3.8 | -0.6 |
| 2010 | WAS | MLB | 27 | 198 | 19 | 8 | 1 | 0 | 5 | 7 | 30 | 0 | 0 | .247/.277/.301 | .201 | .293 | -1.7 | 3 | -0.6 |
| 2011 | SDN | MLB | 28 | 267 | 18 | 10 | 2 | 1 | 32 | 13 | 37 | 1 | 2 | .215/.256/.283 | .213 | .244 | 0.6 | -3.3 | -0.5 |
| *2012* | *TEX* | *MLB* | *29* | *250* | *26* | *12* | *2* | *3* | *24* | *12* | *30* | *2* | *1* | *.251/.293/.353* | *.224* | *.273* | *-0.3* | *2B -4, SS -1* | *0.0* |

To appreciate how bad the Padres offense was in 2011, consider that Gonzalez finished third (behind Will Venable and team leader Orlando Hudson) in RBIs with two out and runners in scoring position. Defensively, Gonzalez has the range, hands, and arm to play anywhere on the infield. That said, Ron Washington would be well advised to avoid a repeat of a September 23 contest against the Dodgers, in which Bud Black started Gonzalez at first base.

**Josh Hamilton** LF
Born: 5/21/1981 Age: 31
Bats: L Throws: L Height: 6' 5" Weight: 235
Breakout: 1% Improve: 43% Collapse: 3%
Attrition: 8% MLB: 90%
Comparables:
Dave Winfield, Albert Belle, Matt Holliday

| YEAR | TEAM | LVL | AGE | PA | R | 2B | 3B | HR | RBI | BB | SO | SB | CS | AVG/OBP/SLG | TAv | BABIP | BRR | FRAA | WARP |
|------|------|-----|-----|----|---|----|----|----|-----|----|----|----|----|-------------|-----|-------|-----|------|------|
| 2009 | TEX | MLB | 28 | 365 | 43 | 19 | 2 | 10 | 54 | 24 | 79 | 8 | 3 | .268/.315/.426 | .259 | .319 | 1.1 | -2.1 | 0.9 |
| 2010 | TEX | MLB | 29 | 571 | 95 | 40 | 3 | 32 | 100 | 43 | 95 | 8 | 1 | .359/.411/.633 | .351 | .390 | 0.9 | 2.3 | 7.7 |
| 2011 | TEX | MLB | 30 | 538 | 80 | 31 | 5 | 25 | 94 | 39 | 93 | 8 | 1 | .298/.346/.536 | .310 | .317 | -2 | 3.4 | 4.4 |
| *2012* | *TEX* | *MLB* | *31* | *515* | *74* | *27* | *4* | *26* | *83* | *42* | *94* | *8* | *2* | *.301/.362/.541* | *.308* | *.327* | *0.2* | *LF 2, CF -2* | *3.9* |

After a 2010 campaign that saw the storybook star put up storybook numbers and win the American League Most Valuable Player award (among others), Hamilton's 2011 faced a tall task to live up to the tall tale. Thanks to breaking his arm during a much-discussed collision at home plate in late May, plus other injuries, Hamilton failed to play a full-season's worth of games for the fourth time in his brief five-year career. Despite offering above-average on-the-field production when healthy, Hamilton's season will be viewed as a disappointment when compared with the heroic feats of the previous season. With free agency looming after 2012, the Rangers must soon decide whether or not to hitch the middle of their lineup to Hamilton's fragile yet incandescent talent.

**Ian Kinsler** 2B
Born: 6/22/1982 Age: 30
Bats: R Throws: R Height: 6' 1" Weight: 200
Breakout: 2% Improve: 40% Collapse: 5%
Attrition: 12% MLB: 95%
Comparables:
Roberto Alomar, Jose Vidro, Luis Ordaz

| YEAR | TEAM | LVL | AGE | PA | R | 2B | 3B | HR | RBI | BB | SO | SB | CS | AVG/OBP/SLG | TAv | BABIP | BRR | FRAA | WARP |
|------|------|-----|-----|----|---|----|----|----|-----|----|----|----|----|-------------|-----|-------|-----|------|------|
| 2009 | TEX | MLB | 27 | 640 | 101 | 32 | 4 | 31 | 86 | 59 | 77 | 31 | 5 | .253/.327/.488 | .278 | .241 | 4.9 | 13.3 | 5.0 |
| 2010 | TEX | MLB | 28 | 460 | 73 | 20 | 1 | 9 | 45 | 56 | 57 | 15 | 5 | .286/.382/.412 | .287 | .313 | 1.6 | 5.7 | 3.2 |
| 2011 | TEX | MLB | 29 | 723 | 121 | 34 | 4 | 32 | 77 | 89 | 71 | 30 | 4 | .255/.355/.477 | .292 | .243 | 11.6 | 8.7 | 6.8 |
| *2012* | *TEX* | *MLB* | *30* | *629* | *86* | *30* | *4* | *26* | *87* | *67* | *74* | *26* | *5* | *.278/.362/.489* | *.294* | *.277* | *1.3* | *2B 6* | *4.4* |

Playing in a career high 155 games, the Rangers' most valuable player was dynamic on both sides of the ball, showing leather and range in the field, and pop, patience, and speed at the plate. Kinsler sacrificed some contact for power, but didn't sell out his approach for the same, drawing more walks than strikeouts for the first time in his six-year career. When healthy, Kinsler is one of the best all-around second baseman in the game, and if he can stay on the field, his production should remain in-line with the output from 2011.

**Leonys Martin** CF

Born: 3/6/1988 Age: 24
Bats: L Throws: R Height: 6' 2" Weight: 180
Breakout: 3% Improve: 29% Collapse: 20%
Attrition: 33% MLB: 79%

Comparables:
Jim Dwyer, McKay Christensen, Tom Umphlett

| YEAR | TEAM | LVL | AGE | PA | R | 2B | 3B | HR | RBI | BB | SO | SB | CS | AVG_OBP_SLG | TAv | BABIP | BRR | FRAA | WARP |
|------|------|-----|-----|-----|----|----|----|----|-----|----|----|----|----|----------------|------|-------|------|-----------|------|
| 2011 | FRI | AA | 23 | 135 | 24 | 9 | 2 | 4 | 24 | 15 | 8 | 10 | 8 | .348/.435/.571 | .365 | .347 | 1.9 | -0.7 | 2.3 |
| 2011 | ROU | AAA | 23 | 192 | 27 | 7 | 1 | 0 | 17 | 11 | 24 | 9 | 2 | .263/.316/.314 | .220 | .303 | 1.1 | 1.1 | 0.0 |
| 2011 | TEX | MLB | 23 | 8 | 2 | 1 | 0 | 0 | 0 | 0 | 1 | 0 | 0 | .375/.375/.500 | .371 | .429 | -0.1 | 0.2 | 0.1 |
| 2012 | TEX | MLB | 24 | 250 | 28 | 11 | 2 | 4 | 26 | 15 | 37 | 11 | 5 | .263/.315/.385 | .243 | .290 | -0.9 | CF -1, RF -0 | 0.5 |

After defecting from Cuba and signing a five year/$15.5M major league deal, Martin hit the ground running in the Texas League, showing all five tools and looking like the international steal of the year. A promotion to Triple-A tempered the excitement; the 23-year-old center fielder struggled in all phases of his game, with fatigue very much a part of the equation. At his best, Martin could be a solid-average to plus defensive center fielder, with a plus arm and glove, and enough speed and quickness for at least average range. At the plate, Leonys has the hands and the strength to generate bat speed and make contact, with a good approach and some pop. A gamer with all five tools (though not all the tools are above-average), Martin has the potential to be a first-division player. The Rangers hope that potential defects to the major leagues at some point in 2012.

**Luis Martinez** C

Born: 4/3/1985 Age: 27
Bats: R Throws: R Height: 6' 1" Weight: 210
Breakout: 1% Improve: 25% Collapse: 12%
Attrition: 46% MLB: 65%

Comparables:
Bill Fahey, Buck Martinez, Chris Bando

| YEAR | TEAM | LVL | AGE | PA | R | 2B | 3B | HR | RBI | BB | SO | SB | CS | AVG_OBP_SLG | TAv | BABIP | BRR | FRAA | WARP |
|------|------|-----|-----|-----|----|----|----|----|-----|----|----|----|----|----------------|------|-------|------|----------|------|
| 2009 | LEL | A+ | 24 | 321 | 39 | 20 | 0 | 4 | 41 | 34 | 58 | 2 | 1 | .300/.389/.414 | .287 | .367 | -2 | -0.9 | 2.6 |
| 2010 | SAN | AA | 25 | 410 | 48 | 16 | 1 | 2 | 31 | 49 | 59 | 3 | 2 | .282/.370/.349 | .284 | .333 | -1.2 | 0.9 | 3.2 |
| 2011 | SDN | MLB | 26 | 68 | 7 | 1 | 1 | 1 | 10 | 8 | 14 | 1 | 0 | .203/.309/.305 | .233 | .250 | 1.2 | 0 | 0.2 |
| 2012 | TEX | MLB | 27 | 250 | 26 | 11 | 1 | 2 | 20 | 21 | 50 | 1 | 0 | .241/.310/.326 | .226 | .297 | 0 | C -1, LF -0 | 0.4 |

Martinez is a catch-and-throw guy with marginal on-base ability and zero power. The Padres liked the way he works with pitchers, which is useful for someone who may or may not represent an upgrade offensively at the plate. Martinez has a decent arm, having nabbed 33 percent of runners who have tried to steal against him in five minor-league seasons. His skill set is that of a career backup catcher and the Rangers, who carried three catchers on their World Series roster, acquired him for depth at the position. He has options so could be moved back and forth between the big club and Triple-A.

**Mitch Moreland** 1B

Born: 9/6/1985 Age: 26
Bats: L Throws: L Height: 6' 3" Weight: 230
Breakout: 4% Improve: 31% Collapse: 3%
Attrition: 18% MLB: 80%

Comparables:
Mike Squires, Matt LaPorta, Sean Casey

| YEAR | TEAM | LVL | AGE | PA | R | 2B | 3B | HR | RBI | BB | SO | SB | CS | AVG_OBP_SLG | TAv | BABIP | BRR | FRAA | WARP |
|------|------|-----|-----|-----|----|----|----|----|-----|----|----|----|----|----------------|------|-------|------|-----------|------|
| 2009 | BAK | A+ | 23 | 197 | 34 | 19 | 0 | 8 | 26 | 21 | 26 | 1 | 0 | .341/.426/.594 | .348 | .368 | 0 | 0.4 | 2.0 |
| 2009 | FRI | AA | 23 | 327 | 51 | 19 | 3 | 8 | 59 | 23 | 42 | 1 | 1 | .326/.375/.488 | .297 | .359 | -3.5 | -5.6 | 1.0 |
| 2010 | OKL | AAA | 24 | 412 | 52 | 29 | 2 | 12 | 65 | 47 | 63 | 2 | 1 | .289/.375/.484 | .290 | .321 | -0.2 | 3.5 | 2.4 |
| 2010 | TEX | MLB | 24 | 173 | 20 | 4 | 0 | 9 | 25 | 25 | 36 | 3 | 1 | .255/.364/.469 | .297 | .275 | -0.1 | -3.4 | 0.6 |
| 2011 | TEX | MLB | 25 | 512 | 60 | 22 | 1 | 16 | 51 | 39 | 92 | 2 | 2 | .259/.320/.414 | .263 | .290 | 0.2 | -1.8 | 0.7 |
| 2012 | TEX | MLB | 26 | 462 | 58 | 22 | 2 | 17 | 59 | 41 | 82 | 2 | 1 | .270/.339/.453 | .274 | .297 | -0.1 | 1B -4, RF -1 | 1.4 |

Ever since he was drafted in the 17th round in the 2007 draft, Mitch Moreland has defied expectations and played above the level suggested by his physical tools. In 2011, the realities of his skills finally settled in, as the husky slugger failed to slug his way into long-term job security. First base in the American League demands that the bat stand in the spotlight, but unfortunately for Moreland, the lefty's bat wasn't ready for the bright lights. His second half collapse left his season line looking more like an average second-division platoon player than someone capable of providing value at the position.

**David Murphy** LF

Born: 10/18/1981 Age: 30
Bats: L Throws: L Height: 6' 5" Weight: 192
Breakout: 1% Improve: 42% Collapse: 4%
Attrition: 15% MLB: 87%

Comparables:
Rob Butler, Carlos Lee, Ryan Spilborghs

| YEAR | TEAM | LVL | AGE | PA | R | 2B | 3B | HR | RBI | BB | SO | SB | CS | AVG_OBP_SLG | TAv | BABIP | BRR | FRAA | WARP |
|------|------|-----|-----|-----|----|----|----|----|-----|----|----|----|----|----------------|------|-------|------|-----------|------|
| 2009 | TEX | MLB | 27 | 493 | 61 | 24 | 1 | 17 | 57 | 49 | 106 | 9 | 4 | .269/.338/.447 | .280 | .311 | 0.9 | 0.7 | 2.3 |
| 2010 | TEX | MLB | 28 | 467 | 54 | 26 | 2 | 12 | 65 | 45 | 71 | 14 | 2 | .291/.358/.449 | .291 | .324 | -2.8 | -2.2 | 1.8 |
| 2011 | TEX | MLB | 29 | 440 | 46 | 14 | 2 | 11 | 46 | 33 | 61 | 11 | 6 | .275/.328/.401 | .259 | .299 | -2 | 2 | 0.8 |
| 2012 | TEX | MLB | 30 | 419 | 53 | 21 | 3 | 13 | 54 | 36 | 69 | 9 | 3 | .279/.341/.455 | .276 | .308 | -0.2 | LF 0, RF -0 | 1.7 |

Fans like David Murphy because he is a Texas native, plays with the requisite grit and hustle of someone without top-shelf physical gifts, and has the good face. Some like David Murphy so much that they champion his name as a starter, a player with enough all-around skill to play every day at the major league level. The reality is that David Murphy is a platoon left-fielder with a good (not great) stick against right-handed pitching, a well below-average stick against left-handed pitching, and a defensive skill set that no longer has utility outside of left-field. As he gets deeper into arbitration and deeper into age, Murphy is losing his luster as a cheap fourth outfielder, moving into the category of luxury despite not possessing luxury performance.

**Mike Napoli**    C

Born: 10/31/1981 Age: 30
Bats: R Throws: R Height: 6' 1" Weight: 205
Breakout: 0% Improve: 27% Collapse: 3%
Attrition: 21% MLB: 86%

Comparables:
Raul Chavez, B.J. Waszgis, Roy Campanella

| YEAR | TEAM | LVL | AGE | PA | R | 2B | 3B | HR | RBI | BB | SO | SB | CS | AVG/OBP/SLG | TAv | BABIP | BRR | FRAA | WARP |
|------|------|-----|-----|-----|----|----|----|----|-----|----|-----|----|----|-------------|------|-------|------|----------|------|
| 2009 | ANA | MLB | 27 | 432 | 60 | 22 | 1 | 20 | 56 | 40 | 103 | 3 | 3 | .272/.350/.492 | .299 | .321 | 0 | -0.5 | 3.1 |
| 2010 | ANA | MLB | 28 | 510 | 60 | 24 | 1 | 26 | 68 | 42 | 137 | 4 | 2 | .238/.316/.468 | .282 | .279 | 0.5 | 3.3 | 3.2 |
| 2011 | TEX | MLB | 29 | 432 | 72 | 25 | 0 | 30 | 75 | 58 | 85 | 4 | 2 | .320/.414/.631 | .366 | .344 | -1.8 | -0.9 | 5.8 |
| 2012 | TEX | MLB | 30 | 424 | 59 | 19 | 1 | 24 | 66 | 45 | 100 | 4 | 2 | .269/.356/.523 | .303 | .303 | -0.3 | C -0, 1B 0 | 3.4 |

**Mike Olt**    3B

Born: 8/27/1988 Age: 23
Bats: R Throws: R Height: 6' 3" Weight: 210
Breakout: 3% Improve: 40% Collapse: 3%
Attrition: 21% MLB: 74%

Comparables:
Andy Van Slyke, Alex Gordon, Scott Rolen

| YEAR | TEAM | LVL | AGE | PA | R | 2B | 3B | HR | RBI | BB | SO | SB | CS | AVG/OBP/SLG | TAv | BABIP | BRR | FRAA | WARP |
|------|------|-----|-----|-----|----|----|----|----|-----|----|----|----|----|-------------|------|-------|------|-------|------|
| 2010 | SPO | A- | 21 | 310 | 57 | 16 | 1 | 9 | 43 | 40 | 77 | 6 | 0 | .293/.394/.464 | .313 | .384 | 0.3 | -3.7 | 1.9 |
| 2011 | MYR | A+ | 22 | 292 | 39 | 15 | 0 | 14 | 42 | 48 | 70 | 0 | 1 | .267/.387/.504 | .319 | .314 | -1.6 | 8.8 | 3.8 |
| 2012 | TEX | MLB | 23 | 250 | 29 | 9 | 1 | 10 | 29 | 28 | 67 | 0 | 0 | .229/.317/.409 | .254 | .277 | 0 | 3B 11 | 1.5 |

A supplemental first-round draft selection in 2010, Olt had a breakout year in 2011 until a breakout injury (broken collarbone) cut a wedge in his season. As a mature collegiate talent, Olt jumped to the High-A level to start 2011, after getting his feet wet in the short-season Northwest League the previous year. In 69 games in the pitcher-friendly Carolina League, Olt showed the skills that give him first-division major league projection: patience and pop at the plate, slick actions and a strong arm at the hot corner. Some question how much contact Olt will make at the higher levels and if that will squelch his power, but his swing mechanics are sound, his approach is mature, and his makeup allows for adjustment. He profiles as a 50/55-grade hitter, with plus power potential and plus defense at third. That's a very valuable player, but the Rangers already have a similar player locked up for the foreseeable future. If Olt is to stay with the team that drafted him, a position switch will be in order. If not, Olt could be a nice chip on the trade market.

**Jurickson Profar**    SS

Born: 2/20/1993 Age: 19
Bats: B Throws: R Height: 6' 0" Weight: 165
Breakout: 0% Improve: 5% Collapse: 1%
Attrition: 4% MLB: 8%

Comparables:
Jonathan Galvez, Jiovanni Mier, Tony La Russa

| YEAR | TEAM | LVL | AGE | PA | R | 2B | 3B | HR | RBI | BB | SO | SB | CS | AVG/OBP/SLG | TAv | BABIP | BRR | FRAA | WARP |
|------|------|-----|-----|-----|----|----|----|----|-----|----|----|----|----|-------------|------|-------|------|-------|------|
| 2010 | SPO | A- | 17 | 288 | 42 | 19 | 0 | 4 | 23 | 28 | 46 | 8 | 3 | .250/.318/.373 | .256 | .284 | -1.3 | 14.6 | 2.7 |
| 2011 | HIC | A | 18 | 516 | 86 | 37 | 8 | 12 | 65 | 65 | 63 | 23 | 9 | .286/.390/.493 | .306 | .309 | 4.7 | -2.4 | 5.1 |
| 2012 | TEX | MLB | 19 | 250 | 27 | 11 | 2 | 5 | 24 | 21 | 46 | 6 | 2 | .234/.305/.361 | .232 | .269 | -0.3 | SS 8 | 0.6 |

One of the top prospects in the minor leagues, shortstop Jurickson Profar profiles as a first-division player at the highest level. The 18-year-old native of Curacao shows all five-tools in game action, with a remarkable combination of polish and projection for his age. At the plate, Profar has well-above average hands, showing contact and pop from both sides. His power projection is a subject of debate, with some envisioning 20-25 home runs at his peak, while others only see 10-15 at maturity. In the field, Profar has the tools to not only stick at shortstop as he climbs the professional ladder, but to excel at the highest level at the position; his hands are soft, his actions are smooth, his range is above-average, his arm is a plus-plus tool and his instincts are off the chart. The total package comes together thanks to a mature approach to the game itself, making Profar an elite prospect at an elite position.

### Yorvit Torrealba — C

Born: 7/19/1978 Age: 33
Bats: R Throws: R Height: 6' 0" Weight: 190
Breakout: 4% Improve: 27% Collapse: 11%
Attrition: 31% MLB: 70%

Comparables:
Milt May, Raul Casanova, Robby Hammock

| YEAR | TEAM | LVL | AGE | PA | R | 2B | 3B | HR | RBI | BB | SO | SB | CS | AVG_OBP_SLG | TAv | BABIP | BRR | FRAA | WARP |
|------|------|-----|-----|-----|----|----|----|----|-----|----|----|----|----|-------------|-----|-------|-----|------|------|
| 2009 | COL | MLB | 30 | 242 | 27 | 11 | 1 | 2 | 31 | 21 | 42 | 1 | 1 | .291/.351/.380 | .253 | .347 | 0.1 | 0.3 | 0.9 |
| 2010 | SDN | MLB | 31 | 363 | 31 | 14 | 0 | 7 | 37 | 33 | 67 | 7 | 5 | .271/.343/.378 | .268 | .321 | 1.6 | -0.7 | 2.1 |
| 2011 | TEX | MLB | 32 | 419 | 40 | 27 | 1 | 7 | 37 | 20 | 65 | 0 | 2 | .273/.306/.399 | .246 | .310 | -4.8 | 0.1 | 0.7 |
| 2012 | TEX | MLB | 33 | 382 | 44 | 18 | 1 | 8 | 41 | 27 | 64 | 3 | 2 | .266/.323/.394 | .249 | .300 | -0.6 | C -0, 1B 0 | 1.4 |

Signed as a free agent in the fall of 2010, Torrealba was brought in to become the de facto starter behind the plate, a field general for a team looking to go forward with a young staff of arms. The 33-year-old Venezuelan provided just that, remaining steady when called upon to wear the mask and solid with the stick, except for one horrid month at the plate (May) that saw Torrealba produce a woeful 346 OPS. With the emergence of Napoli and aging skills that offer more value with the intangible than the tangible, Torrealba looks to have a decreased role on the field in 2012, although he will remain a presence in the clubhouse.

### Michael Young — 3B

Born: 10/19/1976 Age: 35
Bats: R Throws: R Height: 6' 1" Weight: 175
Breakout: 0% Improve: 25% Collapse: 4%
Attrition: 31% MLB: 81%

Comparables:
Al Oliver, David Segui, Paul Molitor

| YEAR | TEAM | LVL | AGE | PA | R | 2B | 3B | HR | RBI | BB | SO | SB | CS | AVG_OBP_SLG | TAv | BABIP | BRR | FRAA | WARP |
|------|------|-----|-----|-----|----|----|----|----|-----|----|-----|----|----|-------------|-----|-------|-----|------|------|
| 2009 | TEX | MLB | 32 | 593 | 76 | 36 | 2 | 22 | 68 | 47 | 90 | 8 | 3 | .322/.374/.518 | .302 | .351 | -2.6 | -17.5 | 2.7 |
| 2010 | TEX | MLB | 33 | 718 | 99 | 36 | 3 | 21 | 91 | 50 | 115 | 4 | 2 | .284/.330/.444 | .267 | .311 | 2.7 | -8.9 | 1.9 |
| 2011 | TEX | MLB | 34 | 689 | 88 | 41 | 6 | 11 | 106 | 47 | 78 | 6 | 2 | .338/.380/.474 | .299 | .367 | 0.7 | -5.5 | 3.5 |
| 2012 | TEX | MLB | 35 | 653 | 84 | 33 | 4 | 16 | 81 | 47 | 98 | 6 | 2 | .299/.351/.448 | .278 | .333 | 0 | 3B -6, 1B -2 | 3.3 |

Michael Young is 35 years old? When did he get that old? Anyway, after yet another positional demotion (or reassignment) and its subsequent backlash, Young made the most of what appeared to be a very tumultuous situation by bringing his bat back to life, hitting a career high .338 in 2011. While predominantly a designated hitter, Young did make over 90 appearances at various infield positions, playing like a man who is predominantly a designated hitter. Defensive value aside, Young's offensive contribution was a needed boost to the offense, and with two more years remaining on his present contract, one that will pay him $16M per, the bat will continue to bear the brunt of those 32 million remaining expectations.

## PITCHERS

### Mike Adams

Born: 7/29/1978 Age: 33
Bats: R Throws: R Height: 6' 6" Weight: 190
Breakout: 14% Improve: 35% Collapse: 37%
Attrition: 9% MLB: 91%

Comparables:
Joe Nathan, Robb Nen, Heath Bell

| YEAR | TEAM | LVL | AGE | W | L | SV | G | GS | IP | H | HR | BB | SO | EqBB9 | EqSO9 | GB% | BABIP | WHIP | ERA | FIP | FRA | WARP |
|------|------|-----|-----|---|---|----|----|----|-----|----|----|----|----|-------|-------|-----|-------|------|------|------|------|------|
| 2009 | SDN | MLB | 30 | 0 | 0 | 0 | 37 | 0 | 37 | 14 | 1 | 8 | 45 | 1.9 | 10.9 | 53% | .162 | 0.59 | 0.73 | 1.62 | 2.81 | 0.8 |
| 2010 | SDN | MLB | 31 | 4 | 1 | 0 | 70 | 0 | 66² | 48 | 2 | 23 | 73 | 3.1 | 9.9 | 41% | .271 | 1.07 | 1.75 | 2.34 | 2.69 | 1.5 |
| 2011 | TEX | MLB | 32 | 2 | 3 | 1 | 27 | 0 | 25² | 18 | 3 | 5 | 25 | 1.8 | 8.8 | 46% | .234 | 0.90 | 2.10 | 3.22 | 3.68 | 0.4 |
| 2011 | SDN | MLB | 32 | 3 | 1 | 1 | 48 | 0 | 48 | 26 | 2 | 9 | 49 | 1.7 | 9.2 | 45% | .203 | 0.73 | 1.12 | 2.06 | 2.38 | 1.1 |
| 2012 | TEX | MLB | 33 | 3 | 2 | 1 | 62 | 0 | 60 | 47 | 6 | 18 | 64 | 2.7 | 9.6 | 45% | .273 | 1.08 | 2.51 | 3.27 | 2.72 | 1.8 |

Acquired at the 2011 trade deadline from San Diego for minor league command/control wizards Robbie Erlin and Joe Wieland, Adams quickly helped to stabilize the back end of the Rangers' bullpen, becoming the main setup man for closer Neftali Feliz. With Feliz moving into the rotation and newcomer Joe Nathan tasked with pitching the ninth, the Rangers will once again look to the 33-year-old righty to provide stability in a late-innings role. With a filthy cutter, thrown with deception and angle thanks to his 6-foot-5 body and long arms, Adams has the necessary nastiness to slide into the spotlight role of closer, should the situation warrant his services.

### Jacob Brigham

Born: 2/10/1988 Age: 24
Bats: R Throws: R Height: 6' 4" Weight: 210
Breakout: 24% Improve: 48% Collapse: 23%
Attrition: 13% MLB: 91%

Comparables:
Andy Ashby, Jeff Sellers, Rich Yett

| YEAR | TEAM | LVL | AGE | W | L | SV | G | GS | IP | H | HR | BB | SO | EqBB9 | EqSO9 | GB% | BABIP | WHIP | ERA | FIP | FRA | WARP |
|------|------|-----|-----|---|---|----|----|----|------|-----|----|----|-----|-------|-------|-----|-------|------|------|------|------|------|
| 2009 | HIC | A | 21 | 2 | 11 | 1 | 25 | 17 | 89² | 104 | 10 | 38 | 81 | 3.8 | 8.1 | 45% | .349 | 1.58 | 5.52 | 4.75 | 5.14 | 0.6 |
| 2010 | HIC | A | 22 | 6 | 6 | 0 | 14 | 13 | 83 | 7 | 0 | 4 | 6 | 2.6 | 7.3 | 67% | .212 | 1.08 | 3.36 | 3.70 | 4.44 | 0.9 |
| 2010 | BAK | A+ | 22 | 1 | 5 | 0 | 11 | 10 | 49¹ | 63 | 5 | 24 | 34 | 4.7 | 7.1 | 38% | .392 | 1.89 | 6.94 | 5.40 | 5.69 | -0.1 |
| 2011 | FRI | AA | 23 | 1 | 5 | 0 | 35 | 14 | 114¹ | 109 | 13 | 56 | 116 | 4.3 | 9.0 | 50% | .300 | 1.42 | 4.49 | 4.40 | 4.74 | 0.9 |
| 2012 | TEX | MLB | 24 | 2 | 2 | 0 | 8 | 5 | 32² | 39 | 6 | 19 | 19 | 5.2 | 5.3 | 44% | .310 | 1.77 | 6.51 | 6.17 | 7.08 | -0.5 |

A minor league starter who finally hit his power stride after a move to the pen during the 2011 season, Brigham was added to the 40-man roster and has a chance to contribute to the major league club at some point during the 2012 season. Armed with a low-to-mid-90s fastball (that can touch higher in bursts) thrown with some movement, Brigham also mixes in a power slider and a hard curve. Brigham profiles as a seventh-inning reliever, although his career arc will depend on his ability to harness his plus stuff against plus competition.

**Fabio Castillo**

Born: 2/19/1989 Age: 23
Bats: R Throws: R Height: 6' 2" Weight: 235
Breakout: 24% Improve: 41% Collapse: 24%
Attrition: 11% MLB: 77%

Comparables:
Tommie Sisk, Kevin Correia, Joe Grahe

| YEAR | TEAM | LVL | AGE | W | L | SV | G | GS | IP | H | HR | BB | SO | EqBB9 | EqSO9 | GB% | BABIP | WHIP | ERA | FIP | FRA | WARP |
|------|------|-----|-----|---|---|----|---|----|-----|----|----|----|----|-------|-------|------|-------|------|------|------|------|------|
| 2009 | HIC | A | 20 | 3 | 5 | 2 | 40 | 2 | 80 | 87 | 5 | 25 | 67 | 2.8 | 7.5 | 58% | .324 | 1.40 | 4.05 | 3.69 | 4.38 | 0.8 |
| 2010 | BAK | A+ | 21 | 1 | 3 | 6 | 36 | 0 | 51² | 35 | 2 | 21 | 58 | 4.5 | 11.3 | 52% | .330 | 1.30 | 1.91 | 3.41 | 4.13 | 0.6 |
| 2011 | FRI | AA | 22 | 2 | 2 | 9 | 42 | 0 | 52¹ | 61 | 7 | 26 | 38 | 4.0 | 6.4 | 54% | .314 | 1.55 | 6.36 | 5.44 | 6.42 | -0.7 |
| 2012 | TEX | MLB | 23 | 1 | 0 | 0 | 13 | 0 | 17¹ | 21 | 3 | 10 | 9 | 5.5 | 4.6 | 47% | .312 | 1.85 | 6.67 | 6.15 | 7.25 | -0.3 |

An injury-plagued 2011 season didn't paint an accurate picture of reliever Fabio Castillo; a broken bone in his foot turned his power arsenal into a powerless arsenal. When healthy, Castillo has the stuff to pitch at the major league level, with a plus (to plus-plus) fastball and a sharp slider thrown with velocity and tilt.

Sid Fernandez, Al Leiter, Zach Braddock

Owner of the best changeup in the Rangers system—a screwball-like twister pitch thrown brilliantly off the fastball, offering up deception and movement—De Los Santos is a subject of debate over his future. With a solid-average fastball and a fringy curveball that has flashed promise, the 23-year-old Dominican southpaw might have the necessary arsenal to find success in the rotation. But his command isn't sharp and that curveball flashes fringe more than it flashes first-class, making De Los Santos a more realistic option in the bullpen. At the very least, his fastball/changeup combo will make him a lefty specialist at the major league level, but his extreme bat-missing ability gives him a higher ceiling if only he can grasp command.

**Cody Eppley**

Born: 10/8/1985 Age: 26
Bats: R Throws: R Height: 6' 6" Weight: 205
Breakout: 24% Improve: 56% Collapse: 18%
Attrition: 21% MLB: 93%

Comparables:
Roberto Novoa, Boone Logan, Warner Madrigal

| YEAR | TEAM | LVL | AGE | W | L | SV | G | GS | IP | H | HR | BB | SO | EqBB9 | EqSO9 | GB% | BABIP | WHIP | ERA | FIP | FRA | WARP |
|------|------|-----|-----|---|---|----|---|----|-----|----|----|----|----|-------|-------|------|-------|------|------|------|------|------|
| 2009 | HIC | A | 23 | 1 | 3 | 6 | 37 | 0 | 67² | 65 | 4 | 6 | 76 | 0.8 | 10.1 | 60% | .324 | 1.05 | 2.92 | 2.39 | 3.57 | 1.4 |
| 2010 | FRI | AA | 24 | 1 | 1 | 9 | 19 | 0 | 22² | 10 | 0 | 7 | 18 | 3.6 | 10.7 | 76% | .244 | 0.93 | 1.19 | 2.67 | 3.83 | 0.4 |
| 2010 | OKL | AAA | 24 | 2 | 1 | 1 | 18 | 0 | 28² | 24 | 2 | 10 | 20 | 4.1 | 9.7 | 56% | .431 | 1.57 | 4.08 | 4.62 | 5.55 | 0.1 |
| 2011 | ROU | AAA | 25 | 4 | 2 | 10 | 43 | 0 | 55¹ | 55 | 3 | 35 | 56 | 5.5 | 8.9 | 60% | .313 | 1.54 | 3.90 | 4.37 | 6.31 | -0.3 |
| 2011 | TEX | MLB | 25 | 1 | 1 | 0 | 10 | 0 | 9 | 11 | 3 | 5 | 6 | 5.0 | 6.0 | 55% | .296 | 1.78 | 8.00 | 8.06 | 8.74 | -0.2 |
| 2012 | TEX | MLB | 26 | 1 | 0 | 1 | 21 | 0 | 27 | 28 | 4 | 12 | 22 | 3.8 | 7.4 | 54% | .306 | 1.47 | 4.69 | 4.83 | 5.10 | 0.1 |

At the major league level, deception specialists like Eppley have a small margin of error and a short shelf-life in general, so maximizing their window of opportunity is paramount. Drafted in the 43rd round of the 2008 draft, this side-arming reliever already defied all the odds to reach the bigs in 2011, and he will have to continue to defy those odds in order to find sustainable success at that level in 2012. With long arms, a highly deceptive release, and a good feel for command, Eppley can function as a righty specialist, using his upper-80s fastball and sweeping slider to tie-up hitters and coerce weak contact.

**Scott Feldman**

Born: 2/7/1983 Age: 29
Bats: L Throws: R Height: 6' 7" Weight: 210
Breakout: 13% Improve: 46% Collapse: 25%
Attrition: 13% MLB: 84%

Comparables:
Mark Hendrickson, Jason Marquis, Jarrod Washburn

| YEAR | TEAM | LVL | AGE | W | L | SV | G | GS | IP | H | HR | BB | SO | EqBB9 | EqSO9 | GB% | BABIP | WHIP | ERA | FIP | FRA | WARP |
|------|------|-----|-----|----|----|----|----|----|------|-----|----|----|-----|-------|-------|------|-------|------|------|------|------|------|
| 2009 | TEX | MLB | 26 | 17 | 8 | 0 | 34 | 31 | 189² | 178 | 18 | 65 | 113 | 3.1 | 5.4 | 48% | .274 | 1.28 | 4.08 | 4.36 | 4.74 | 2.3 |
| 2010 | TEX | MLB | 27 | 7 | 11 | 0 | 29 | 22 | 141¹ | 181 | 18 | 45 | 75 | 2.9 | 4.8 | 43% | .331 | 1.60 | 5.48 | 4.70 | 4.97 | 0.9 |
| 2011 | ROU | AAA | 28 | 2 | 1 | 0 | 8 | 8 | 40² | 48 | 5 | 9 | 24 | 2.0 | 5.3 | 55% | .323 | 1.40 | 4.43 | 4.89 | 5.31 | 0.4 |
| 2011 | TEX | MLB | 28 | 2 | 1 | 0 | 11 | 2 | 32 | 25 | 3 | 10 | 22 | 2.8 | 6.2 | 63% | .239 | 1.09 | 3.94 | 4.03 | 4.48 | 0.3 |
| 2012 | TEX | MLB | 29 | 3 | 3 | 0 | 13 | 8 | 56¹ | 63 | 8 | 20 | 30 | 3.2 | 4.7 | 48% | .297 | 1.48 | 5.14 | 5.05 | 5.59 | 0.0 |

Feldman is not Amish, but his personal appearance didn't get the memo; his beard can raise a barn or churn butter on its own merits. After a down year in 2010 and microfracture knee surgery in the offseason, Feldman didn't make his 2011 major league debut until the second half of the season. Upon return, it was evident that the Scott Feldman of old was back on the hill, as all his pitches were sharper. His sinker/cutter/curve offerings were tough for hitters to square up. Feldman pitched well enough, mostly in relief, to spark debate over his role for 2012. His value in long relief can't measure up to the potential value he could bring to the rotation. Spots are limited and the competition is fierce, but if Feldman's arsenal can maintain the edge it showed in the fall of 2011, he should be in the mix for a rotational opportunity.

**Neftali Feliz**
Born: 5/2/1988 Age: 24
Bats: R Throws: R Height: 6' 4" Weight: 190
Breakout: 23% Improve: 48% Collapse: 20%
Attrition: 7% MLB: 99%

Comparables:
Chad Cordero, Al Downing, Andy Messersmith

| YEAR | TEAM | LVL | AGE | W | L | SV | G | GS | IP | H | HR | BB | SO | EqBB9 | EqSO9 | GB% | BABIP | WHIP | ERA | FIP | FRA | WARP |
|------|------|-----|-----|---|---|----|----|----|-----|----|----|----|----|-------|-------|-----|-------|------|-----|-----|-----|------|
| 2009 | OKL | AAA | 21 | 4 | 6 | 0 | 25 | 13 | 77¹ | 68 | 2 | 30 | 75 | 3.5 | 8.7 | 46% | .314 | 1.28 | 3.49 | 3.13 | 3.37 | 1.6 |
| 2009 | TEX | MLB | 21 | 1 | 0 | 2 | 20 | 0 | 31 | 13 | 2 | 8 | 39 | 2.3 | 11.3 | 40% | .172 | 0.68 | 1.74 | 2.53 | 3.01 | 0.8 |
| 2010 | TEX | MLB | 22 | 4 | 3 | 40 | 70 | 0 | 69¹ | 43 | 5 | 18 | 71 | 2.3 | 9.2 | 36% | .225 | 0.88 | 2.73 | 2.93 | 3.74 | 1.2 |
| 2011 | TEX | MLB | 23 | 2 | 3 | 32 | 64 | 0 | 62¹ | 42 | 4 | 30 | 54 | 4.3 | 7.8 | 38% | .236 | 1.16 | 2.74 | 3.61 | 4.36 | 0.7 |
| 2012 | TEX | MLB | 24 | 3 | 1 | 27 | 54 | 0 | 53 | 44 | 5 | 22 | 51 | 3.8 | 8.7 | 43% | .281 | 1.26 | 3.48 | 3.75 | 3.78 | 1.0 |

After two years in the closer's chair, flame-throwing righty Neftali Feliz is moving (back) into the rotation in 2012. Heard that before? This time it's actually going forward, with Joe Nathan brought in to secure the ninth. Having lived on the back of an 80-grade fastball in the pen, Feliz will need to rediscover his pace in the rotation, re-learning the nuances of velocity manipulation and pitch sequence. Feliz's secondary arsenal has stagnated somewhat, but his slider and changeup both have qualities that will play nicely in a rotational role. The total package might take some developmental dips before we see some positive production, but the patience will be well worth it, given Feliz's ultimate ceiling as a starter.

**Mark Hamburger**
Born: 2/5/1987 Age: 25
Bats: R Throws: R Height: 6' 5" Weight: 195
Breakout: 34% Improve: 68% Collapse: 7%
Attrition: 28% MLB: 93%

Comparables:
Zach Miner, Fred Holdsworth, Clayton Mortensen

| YEAR | TEAM | LVL | AGE | W | L | SV | G | GS | IP | H | HR | BB | SO | EqBB9 | EqSO9 | GB% | BABIP | WHIP | ERA | FIP | FRA | WARP |
|------|------|-----|-----|---|---|----|----|----|-----|----|----|----|----|-------|-------|-----|-------|------|-----|-----|-----|------|
| 2011 | ROU | AAA | 24 | 7 | 4 | 0 | 31 | 4 | 62² | 54 | 5 | 20 | 48 | 2.9 | 6.9 | 43% | .272 | 1.18 | 3.88 | 4.34 | 4.37 | 0.9 |
| 2011 | TEX | MLB | 24 | 1 | 0 | 0 | 5 | 0 | 8 | 5 | 0 | 3 | 6 | 3.4 | 6.8 | 23% | .227 | 1.00 | 4.50 | 2.69 | 3.21 | 0.1 |
| 2012 | TEX | MLB | 25 | 1 | 0 | 0 | 17 | 1 | 28¹ | 32 | 4 | 13 | 18 | 4.2 | 5.6 | 45% | .302 | 1.58 | 5.35 | 5.15 | 5.82 | -0.1 |

Culinary jokes aside, Mark Hamburger is a classic success story, plucked from obscurity by the Twins at an open tryout, then traded to the Rangers in 2008 with a subsequent taste of major league action out of the pen in 2011. An up-and-down middle reliever at best, Hamburger has a chance to stick on the menu if his two-seamer, curve, and change can catch up to the quality of his fastball.

**Matt Harrison**
Born: 8/16/1985 Age: 26
Bats: L Throws: L Height: 6' 5" Weight: 225
Breakout: 23% Improve: 49% Collapse: 23%
Attrition: 17% MLB: 82%

Comparables:
Steve Avery, Jose Rosado, Clayton Richard

| YEAR | TEAM | LVL | AGE | W | L | SV | G | GS | IP | H | HR | BB | SO | EqBB9 | EqSO9 | GB% | BABIP | WHIP | ERA | FIP | FRA | WARP |
|------|------|-----|-----|----|---|----|----|----|------|-----|----|----|-----|-------|-------|-----|-------|------|-----|-----|-----|------|
| 2009 | TEX | MLB | 23 | 4 | 5 | 0 | 11 | 11 | 63¹ | 81 | 9 | 23 | 34 | 3.3 | 4.8 | 48% | .336 | 1.64 | 6.11 | 5.10 | 5.84 | 0.3 |
| 2010 | TEX | MLB | 24 | 3 | 2 | 2 | 37 | 6 | 78¹ | 80 | 10 | 39 | 46 | 4.5 | 5.3 | 48% | .272 | 1.52 | 4.71 | 5.10 | 5.86 | -0.6 |
| 2011 | TEX | MLB | 25 | 14 | 9 | 0 | 31 | 30 | 185² | 180 | 13 | 57 | 126 | 2.8 | 6.1 | 50% | .295 | 1.28 | 3.39 | 3.55 | 4.05 | 3.1 |
| 2012 | TEX | MLB | 26 | 8 | 7 | 1 | 36 | 19 | 137¹ | 157 | 18 | 49 | 76 | 3.2 | 5.0 | 47% | .307 | 1.50 | 5.12 | 4.87 | 5.56 | -0.0 |

Developmental patience paid off for the Rangers and for Harrison in 2011, as the promise finally translated to production on the big stage. With a deep arsenal and a feel for pitching, what Harrison lacked was the approach; more often than not, Harrison failed to trust his own ability, becoming a command/control nibbler instead of a pitcher capable of attacking the opposition with legit stuff. The 6-foot-4, 240-pound. lefty started the season as a rotational maybe and ended the reason as rotational most definitely pitching his way into the future plans for the Rangers.

**Derek Holland**
Born: 10/9/1986 Age: 25
Bats: B Throws: L Height: 6' 3" Weight: 185
Breakout: 21% Improve: 57% Collapse: 10%
Attrition: 11% MLB: 94%

Comparables:
Mark Guthrie, Erik Hanson, Jordan Zimmermann

| YEAR | TEAM | LVL | AGE | W | L | SV | G | GS | IP | H | HR | BB | SO | EqBB9 | EqSO9 | GB% | BABIP | WHIP | ERA | FIP | FRA | WARP |
|------|------|-----|-----|----|----|----|----|----|------|-----|----|----|-----|-------|-------|-----|-------|------|-----|-----|-----|------|
| 2009 | TEX | MLB | 22 | 8 | 13 | 0 | 33 | 21 | 138¹ | 160 | 26 | 47 | 107 | 3.1 | 7.0 | 42% | .315 | 1.50 | 6.12 | 5.15 | 5.98 | 0.0 |
| 2010 | OKL | AAA | 23 | 6 | 2 | 0 | 11 | 11 | 62² | 30 | 4 | 13 | 34 | 2.6 | 7.3 | 48% | .210 | 1.08 | 1.87 | 4.52 | 3.97 | 1.1 |
| 2010 | TEX | MLB | 23 | 3 | 4 | 0 | 14 | 10 | 57¹ | 55 | 6 | 24 | 54 | 3.8 | 8.5 | 42% | .297 | 1.38 | 4.08 | 3.99 | 4.47 | 0.6 |
| 2011 | TEX | MLB | 24 | 16 | 5 | 0 | 32 | 32 | 198 | 201 | 22 | 67 | 162 | 3.0 | 7.4 | 48% | .306 | 1.35 | 3.95 | 3.98 | 4.47 | 2.2 |
| 2012 | TEX | MLB | 25 | 10 | 8 | 0 | 26 | 26 | 152 | 159 | 22 | 53 | 120 | 3.2 | 7.1 | 44% | .301 | 1.40 | 4.66 | 4.55 | 5.07 | 0.9 |

Adolescent mustache jokes aside, Holland really grew up in 2011, taking a huge developmental step forward and emerging as one of the best young lefties in the American League.

The 25 year-old southpaw has a lively plus-plus fastball, a pitch that works in the 93-95 range with some arm-side movement, a slider with tilt that still has room for improvement, a change-of-pace curve, and a true changeup that he is still trying to command. As he refined his stuff and grew more comfortable with the big-league stage, Holland became a candidate for dominance with each start; Holland was particularly sharp in the second-half of the season, with an increased strikeout rate to go along with decreased walk and hit rates. Holland's star is on the rise, and if he manages another developmental step in the right direction in 2012, the ceiling he owns will join hands with his floor.

**Colby Lewis**
Born: 8/2/1979 Age: 32
Bats: R Throws: R Height: 6' 5" Weight: 215
Breakout: 20% Improve: 37% Collapse: 36%
Attrition: 10% MLB: 92%
Comparables:
Joel Peralta, Mark DiFelice, Rick Aguilera

| YEAR | TEAM | LVL | AGE | W | L | SV | G | GS | IP | H | HR | BB | SO | EqBB9 | EqSO9 | GB% | BABIP | WHIP | ERA | FIP | FRA | WARP |
|---|---|---|---|---|---|---|---|---|---|---|---|---|---|---|---|---|---|---|---|---|---|---|
| 2009 | HRO | NPB | 29 | 11 | 9 | 0 | 29 | 28 | 176[1] | 156 | 13 | 19 | 186 | 1.0 | 9.5 | — | .314 | 0.99 | 2.96 | 2.13 | — | 0.0 |
| 2010 | TEX | MLB | 30 | 12 | 13 | 0 | 32 | 32 | 201 | 174 | 21 | 65 | 196 | 2.9 | 8.8 | 39% | .277 | 1.19 | 3.72 | 3.51 | 3.82 | 3.2 |
| 2011 | TEX | MLB | 31 | 14 | 10 | 0 | 32 | 32 | 200[1] | 187 | 35 | 56 | 169 | 2.5 | 7.6 | 35% | .268 | 1.21 | 4.40 | 4.57 | 4.61 | 1.9 |
| 2012 | TEX | MLB | 32 | 12 | 8 | 0 | 27 | 27 | 172 | 166 | 26 | 52 | 145 | 2.7 | 7.6 | 41% | .284 | 1.27 | 4.08 | 4.39 | 4.44 | 2.0 |

**Mark Lowe**
Born: 6/7/1983 Age: 29
Bats: L Throws: R Height: 6' 5" Weight: 180
Breakout: 23% Improve: 42% Collapse: 27%
Attrition: 11% MLB: 93%
Comparables:
Steve Hamilton, Sparky Lyle, Don Heinkel

| YEAR | TEAM | LVL | AGE | W | L | SV | G | GS | IP | H | HR | BB | SO | EqBB9 | EqSO9 | GB% | BABIP | WHIP | ERA | FIP | FRA | WARP |
|---|---|---|---|---|---|---|---|---|---|---|---|---|---|---|---|---|---|---|---|---|---|---|
| 2009 | SEA | MLB | 26 | 2 | 7 | 3 | 75 | 0 | 80 | 71 | 7 | 29 | 69 | 3.3 | 7.8 | 41% | .274 | 1.25 | 3.26 | 3.64 | 4.40 | 0.8 |
| 2010 | TEX | MLB | 27 | 0 | 0 | 0 | 3 | 0 | 3 | 7 | 1 | 1 | 5 | 3.0 | 15.0 | 30% | .667 | 2.67 | 12.00 | 5.05 | 5.26 | 0.0 |
| 2010 | SEA | MLB | 27 | 1 | 3 | 0 | 11 | 0 | 10[1] | 11 | 1 | 5 | 7 | 4.4 | 6.1 | 27% | .312 | 1.55 | 3.48 | 4.40 | 3.86 | 0.1 |
| 2011 | TEX | MLB | 28 | 2 | 3 | 1 | 52 | 0 | 45 | 46 | 6 | 19 | 42 | 3.8 | 8.4 | 50% | .312 | 1.44 | 3.80 | 4.19 | 4.89 | 0.3 |
| 2012 | TEX | MLB | 29 | 2 | 1 | 0 | 39 | 0 | 36[2] | 38 | 4 | 15 | 31 | 3.7 | 7.6 | 43% | .308 | 1.45 | 4.60 | 4.16 | 5.00 | 0.2 |

Acquired along with Cliff Lee in the summer of 2010, Lowe finally made an impact in 2011, appearing in 52 games and showing the type of stuff that can find a home in the back of any major league bullpen. Despite owning well above-average stuff, most notably a 96-97 mph fastball and a nasty hard slider, Lowe doesn't have the numbers to back up the nastiness; he misses bats but he doesn't overwhelm hitters. He struggles with control, which makes him hittable and prone to the free pass, and he lacks consistency, pitching well for a few weeks before losing his release point and pitching poorly for a few weeks. His stuff will keep Lowe employed, but the inconsistency will keep fans and management frustrated.

**Roman Mendez**
Born: 7/25/1990 Age: 21
Bats: R Throws: R Height: 6' 3" Weight: 180
Breakout: 30% Improve: 58% Collapse: 19%
Attrition: 7% MLB: 86%
Comparables:
Mark Grant, Vern Law, Hayden Penn

| YEAR | TEAM | LVL | AGE | W | L | SV | G | GS | IP | H | HR | BB | SO | EqBB9 | EqSO9 | GB% | BABIP | WHIP | ERA | FIP | FRA | WARP |
|---|---|---|---|---|---|---|---|---|---|---|---|---|---|---|---|---|---|---|---|---|---|---|
| 2009 | RSX | RK | 18 | 2 | 3 | 0 | 12 | 10 | 49[2] | 33 | 1 | 8 | 47 | 1.4 | 8.5 | 39% | .244 | 0.82 | 1.99 | 2.42 | 4.27 | 1.5 |
| 2010 | LOW | A- | 19 | 2 | 3 | 0 | 8 | 8 | 33 | 31 | 5 | 19 | 35 | 5.2 | 9.5 | — | .308 | 1.52 | 4.36 | 5.14 | 5.35 | 0.0 |
| 2011 | HIC | A | 20 | 9 | 1 | 1 | 26 | 20 | 117 | 115 | 7 | 44 | 125 | 3.5 | 10.0 | 38% | .347 | 1.38 | 3.31 | 3.42 | 4.13 | 1.8 |
| 2012 | TEX | MLB | 21 | 2 | 2 | 0 | 6 | 6 | 29 | 34 | 4 | 16 | 20 | 5.0 | 6.2 | 38% | .317 | 1.73 | 6.05 | 5.27 | 6.57 | -0.2 |

Yet another power arm developing in the Rangers system, Mendez has the raw strength to emerge as one of the best. Acquired from Boston in the Jarrod Salta-Ralph Macchio trade, the 21-year-old righty has one of the easiest fastballs in the minors, sitting in the mid-90s and touching near triple digits with the casualness of a front yard pitch-and-catch. His secondary arsenal is still a work in progress and his command can come and go, which leads some to believe Mendez's future role is as a flame-thrower in the pen. Regardless, the recent 40-man addition's future rides on the back of his near-elite fastball, a pitch that can make a career if he develops and deploys it properly.

**Joe Nathan**
Born: 11/22/1974 Age: 37
Bats: R Throws: R Height: 6' 5" Weight: 195
Breakout: 15% Improve: 33% Collapse: 40%
Attrition: 8% MLB: 91%
Comparables:
Trevor Hoffman, Al Reyes, Tom Gordon

| YEAR | TEAM | LVL | AGE | W | L | SV | G | GS | IP | H | HR | BB | SO | EqBB9 | EqSO9 | GB% | BABIP | WHIP | ERA | FIP | FRA | WARP |
|---|---|---|---|---|---|---|---|---|---|---|---|---|---|---|---|---|---|---|---|---|---|---|
| 2009 | MIN | MLB | 34 | 2 | 2 | 47 | 70 | 0 | 68[2] | 42 | 7 | 22 | 89 | 2.9 | 11.7 | 42% | .233 | 0.93 | 2.10 | 2.93 | 2.66 | 2.2 |
| 2011 | MIN | MLB | 36 | 2 | 1 | 14 | 48 | 0 | 44[2] | 38 | 7 | 14 | 43 | 2.8 | 8.7 | 37% | .252 | 1.16 | 4.84 | 4.32 | 4.45 | 0.4 |
| 2012 | TEX | MLB | 37 | 2 | 1 | 7 | 37 | 0 | 34 | 28 | 4 | 10 | 37 | 2.7 | 9.7 | 44% | .282 | 1.12 | 2.92 | 3.44 | 3.18 | 0.9 |

After missing all of the 2010 season following Tommy John surgery, Nathan struggled mightily at the start of 2011, blowing two of his first five save opportunities, handing the closer's job back to Matt Capps, and finishing April with a 10.00 ERA. He was still carrying a 7.63 ERA when he went on the DL in late May due to forearm inflammation, but the difference was night and day once he returned: 3.38 ERA, 28/5 K/BB ratio in 29 1/3 innings, 11 saves in 12 opportunities. After the season, he acknowledged that he had come back from the surgery too quickly, not an uncommon occurrence. Even if he's in tip-top shape, the move to hitter-friendly Arlington and its sweltering summers will present a challenge for the 37-year-old.

### Alexi Ogando

Born: 10/5/1983 Age: 28
Bats: R Throws: R Height: 6' 5'' Weight: 185
Breakout: 25% Improve: 56% Collapse: 22%
Attrition: 10% MLB: 95%

Comparables:
Darren O'Day, Adam Wainwright, Don Drysdale

| YEAR | TEAM | LVL | AGE | W | L | SV | G | GS | IP | H | HR | BB | SO | EqBB9 | EqSO9 | GB% | BABIP | WHIP | ERA | FIP | FRA | WARP |
|------|------|-----|-----|---|---|----|----|----|------|-----|----|----|-----|-------|-------|-----|-------|------|------|------|------|------|
| 2010 | TEX | MLB | 26 | 4 | 1 | 0 | 44 | 0 | 41² | 31 | 2 | 16 | 39 | 3.5 | 8.4 | 45% | .264 | 1.13 | 1.30 | 3.02 | 3.98 | 0.5 |
| 2011 | TEX | MLB | 27 | 13 | 8 | 0 | 31 | 29 | 169 | 149 | 16 | 43 | 126 | 2.3 | 6.7 | 38% | .267 | 1.14 | 3.51 | 3.69 | 4.08 | 2.7 |
| 2012 | TEX | MLB | 28 | 8 | 5 | 0 | 49 | 17 | 126 | 119 | 15 | 37 | 100 | 2.6 | 7.1 | 41% | .285 | 1.24 | 3.69 | 4.05 | 4.01 | 2.2 |

An underappreciated story of the 2011 season, outfielder-turned-reliever-turned-starter Ogando continued his magical journey, transforming into one of the better young arms (as far as mileage goes) in a division stacked with quality arms. A failed outfielder in the A's system, Ogando's elite arm-strength enticed the Rangers to nab him in the Rule 5 draft and convert him to pitching. Before that move could bear fruit, Ogando was caught in a marriage-for-visa scandal, was denied entry to the United States, and left to toil in the Dominican Summer League for five years. The long nightmare ended in 2010, when Ogando and Omar Beltre (one of the other ballplayers caught in the trafficking scandal) were granted visas. Ogando pitched well in the minors and eventually logged 40 innings of late-innings work for the big club. In 2011, Ogando took another step forward, taking his high-octane, short-burst heat and turning it into high-octane, long-burst heat, making 29 starts and pitching well until the increased workload started to affect his stuff. Going forward, Ogando should stick around in a major league rotation, but if his changeup fails to develop or his mechanical profile suggests a move to the pen is necessary, that transition should be an easy one.

### Martin Perez

Born: 4/4/1991 Age: 21
Bats: L Throws: L Height: 6' 1'' Weight: 178
Breakout: 27% Improve: 53% Collapse: 15%
Attrition: 5% MLB: 90%

Comparables:
Juan Pizarro, Billy Hoeft, Ryan Feierabend

| YEAR | TEAM | LVL | AGE | W | L | SV | G | GS | IP | H | HR | BB | SO | EqBB9 | EqSO9 | GB% | BABIP | WHIP | ERA | FIP | FRA | WARP |
|------|------|-----|-----|---|---|----|----|----|------|-----|----|----|-----|-------|-------|-----|-------|------|------|------|------|------|
| 2009 | HIC | A | 18 | 5 | 5 | 1 | 22 | 14 | 93² | 82 | 3 | 33 | 105 | 3.2 | 10.1 | 53% | .324 | 1.23 | 2.31 | 2.73 | 3.95 | 1.5 |
| 2010 | FRI | AA | 19 | 6 | 8 | 0 | 24 | 23 | 99² | 92 | 9 | 38 | 82 | 4.5 | 9.1 | 51% | .349 | 1.68 | 5.96 | 4.00 | 5.09 | 0.5 |
| 2011 | FRI | AA | 20 | 4 | 0 | 0 | 17 | 16 | 88¹ | 75 | 6 | 34 | 80 | 3.7 | 8.5 | 52% | .301 | 1.31 | 3.16 | 3.64 | 4.04 | 1.4 |
| 2011 | ROU | AAA | 20 | 4 | 4 | 0 | 10 | 10 | 49 | 77 | 4 | 23 | 42 | 3.7 | 6.8 | 55% | .390 | 1.88 | 6.43 | 4.49 | 5.81 | 0.1 |
| 2012 | TEX | MLB | 21 | 3 | 3 | 0 | 9 | 9 | 42² | 50 | 6 | 20 | 30 | 4.3 | 6.3 | 48% | .321 | 1.64 | 5.61 | 5.03 | 6.10 | -0.1 |

A fixture on the national prospect scene since 2008, Venezuelan southpaw Martin Perez scuffled a bit in 2011, but the developmental hurdles at the present will lead to developmental progress going forward. With a fluid and repeatable delivery, Perez brings an above-average pitch assortment to the mound, including a 91-96 mph fastball with some arm-side run, a knee-buckling spike curve, and a changeup that some project to be a 70 grade pitch at maturity. Only 20, Perez is still years ahead of the curve, so allowing him time to fail and adjust at Triple-A will be worth the extra patience. At the top of his developmental arc, Perez profiles as number-two starter on a championship level team. He should get a taste of the major leagues at some point in 2012.

### Neil Ramirez

Born: 5/25/1989 Age: 23
Bats: R Throws: R Height: 6' 4'' Weight: 185
Breakout: 31% Improve: 56% Collapse: 23%
Attrition: 20% MLB: 86%

Comparables:
Tyler Clippard, Don Demola, Ken Cloude

| YEAR | TEAM | LVL | AGE | W | L | SV | G | GS | IP | H | HR | BB | SO | EqBB9 | EqSO9 | GB% | BABIP | WHIP | ERA | FIP | FRA | WARP |
|------|------|-----|-----|---|---|----|----|----|------|-----|----|----|-----|-------|-------|-----|-------|------|------|------|------|------|
| 2009 | HIC | A | 20 | 3 | 6 | 0 | 18 | 14 | 66¹ | 58 | 8 | 41 | 56 | 5.6 | 7.6 | 33% | .272 | 1.49 | 4.75 | 5.83 | 5.04 | 0.4 |
| 2010 | HIC | A | 21 | 10 | 9 | 0 | 28 | 26 | 140¹ | 96 | 12 | 23 | 75 | 2.4 | 9.1 | 37% | .349 | 1.33 | 4.43 | 4.43 | 4.43 | 2.0 |
| 2011 | ROU | AAA | 22 | 4 | 3 | 0 | 18 | 18 | 74¹ | 65 | 6 | 37 | 91 | 4.2 | 10.4 | 35% | .301 | 1.32 | 3.63 | 4.07 | 4.37 | 1.4 |
| 2012 | TEX | MLB | 23 | 2 | 2 | 0 | 6 | 6 | 29¹ | 31 | 5 | 16 | 23 | 5.0 | 7.1 | 35% | .300 | 1.61 | 5.55 | 5.49 | 6.04 | -0.1 |

One of the hardest-working players in the system (if not the entire minors), Ramirez transformed himself from a boom-or-bust first round pick (2007) into one of the premium right-handed starting pitchers in the minors. With a potent three-pitch mix, including a 92-96 mph fastball, a hard hammer curve, and a vastly improved changeup, Ramirez profiles as a quality second or third starter at the major league level. His command needs refinement and he needs more innings in the upper minors before making the next step onto the biggest stage, but Ramirez is on the cusp of major league contribution. Look for him either in the rotation or as a late-season call-up out of the pen. His future is very bright.

### Yoshinori Tateyama

Born: 12/26/1975 Age: 36
Bats: R Throws: R Height: 5' 11" Weight: 165
Breakout: 23% Improve: 40% Collapse: 34%
Attrition: 13% MLB: 80%

**Comparables:**
Justin Speier, Tug McGraw, Eddie Guardado

| YEAR | TEAM | LVL | AGE | W | L | SV | G | GS | IP | H | HR | BB | SO | EqBB9 | EqSO9 | GB% | BABIP | WHIP | ERA | FIP | FRA | WARP |
|------|------|-----|-----|---|---|----|----|----|-----|----|----|----|----|-------|-------|-----|-------|------|------|------|------|------|
| 2009 | NIP | NPB | 33 | 5 | 7 | 0 | 46 | 0 | 47² | 53 | 3 | 15 | 43 | 2.8 | 8.1 | — | .352 | 1.43 | 3.77 | 3.03 | — | 0.0 |
| 2010 | NIP | NPB | 34 | 1 | 2 | 4 | 58 | 0 | 55 | 43 | 3 | 11 | 59 | 1.8 | 9.7 | — | .293 | 0.98 | 1.80 | 2.42 | — | 0.0 |
| 2011 | ROU | AAA | 35 | 1 | 0 | 1 | 14 | 0 | 21 | 17 | 1 | 4 | 26 | 1.7 | 11.1 | 33% | .308 | 1.00 | 2.14 | 2.88 | 3.36 | 0.5 |
| 2011 | TEX | MLB | 35 | 2 | 0 | 1 | 39 | 0 | 44 | 37 | 8 | 11 | 43 | 2.2 | 8.8 | 40% | .248 | 1.09 | 4.50 | 4.36 | 6.06 | -0.1 |
| 2012 | TEX | MLB | 36 | 1 | 1 | 0 | 29 | 0 | 35² | 35 | 5 | 10 | 33 | 2.6 | 8.2 | 42% | .298 | 1.26 | 3.93 | 4.02 | 4.27 | 0.5 |

With a deceptive side-arm release and pitches that move all over the place, Tateyama might just have a future as a bullpen specialist. His heavy mid-80s fastball, sweeping slider, and screwball-like changeup make the 36-year-old Japanese veteran murder on right-handed hitters, but situational relievers who rely on deception and command over raw stuff have small windows for success and small margins for error. Spotty command or bad matchups could prove disastrous.

Davis, Uehara appeared in 22 regular season games for the Rangers, but failed to impact the postseason bullpen with his presence. More than just a situational reliever, Uehara is effective against both lefties and righties, showing pinpoint command of an upper-80s fastball and a nasty off-speed arsenal, including a trapdoor splitter that misses a ton of bats.

## LINEOUTS

### HITTERS

| PLAYER | TEAM | LVL | AGE | PA | R | 2B | 3B | HR | RBI | BB | SO | SB-CS | AVG/OBP/SLG | TAv | BABIP | BRR | FRAA | WARP |
|--------|------|-----|-----|-----|----|----|----|----|-----|----|-----|-------|----------------|------|-------|------|------|------|
| CF J. Akins | RNG | RK | 19 | 190 | 37 | 12 | 4 | 2 | 31 | 6 | 42 | 13-2 | .283/.312/.428 | .256 | .358 | 1.3 | -4.8 | 0.1 |
| C J. Alfaro | SPO | A- | 18 | 171 | 18 | 9 | 1 | 6 | 23 | 4 | 54 | 1-0 | .300/.345/.481 | .284 | .420 | -0.9 | 0.7 | 0.8 |
| C D. Brown | IND | AAA | 29 | 199 | 18 | 17 | 0 | 7 | 28 | 22 | 35 | 0-2 | .285/.367/.506 | .285 | .316 | -2.1 | 0.4 | 1.4 |
|  | PIT | MLB | 29 | 30 | 2 | 0 | 0 | 0 | 0 | 0 | 10 | 1-0 | .107/.138/.107 | .090 | .167 | 0.2 | 0 | -0.4 |
| RF J. Butler | FRI | AA | 25 | 55 | 11 | 1 | 0 | 2 | 4 | 7 | 16 | 2-1 | .227/.382/.386 | .260 | .308 | 0.7 | -0.1 | 0.0 |
|  | ROU | AAA | 25 | 474 | 73 | 27 | 5 | 12 | 57 | 43 | 138 | 13-4 | .322/.388/.493 | .304 | .451 | 1.3 | -7.1 | 2.9 |
| SS L. Garcia | MYR | A+ | 20 | 482 | 65 | 19 | 5 | 3 | 38 | 28 | 100 | 30-12 | .256/.306/.342 | .234 | .324 | 7.8 | 5.9 | 1.9 |
| 3B T. Mendonca | FRI | AA | 23 | 556 | 75 | 27 | 3 | 25 | 87 | 35 | 160 | 0-1 | .278/.335/.492 | .277 | .355 | -2.5 | -5.6 | 2.4 |
| 2B R. Odor | SPO | A- | 17 | 258 | 33 | 9 | 3 | 2 | 29 | 13 | 37 | 10-4 | .262/.323/.352 | .253 | .301 | 0 | -0.1 | 0.4 |
| CF J. Skole | HIC | A | 19 | 501 | 76 | 14 | 6 | 9 | 62 | 65 | 138 | 21-14 | .264/.366/.389 | .269 | .365 | 1.7 | 3.7 | 2.1 |
| 3B C. Villanueva | HIC | A | 20 | 529 | 78 | 30 | 3 | 17 | 84 | 37 | 86 | 32-6 | .278/.338/.465 | .280 | .300 | 4.6 | 16.6 | 5.5 |

One of the toolsiest prospects in baseball, Division I football recruit-turned-center-fielder **Jordan Akins** is still in the process of learning how to turn his raw physical gifts into baseball skills. With average-to-plus (even plus-plus) tool projections across the board, Akins is your prototypical boom or bust prospect. ⊘ One of the top prospects in the system with one of the highest tool-based ceilings, 18-year-old Colombian catcher **Jorge Alfaro** has an 80-grade arm and 70-grade power potential. ⊘ Signed to a minor league deal, **Dusty Brown** is a catcher with one of the most apropos baseball names ever. If the name sounds familiar, it's more likely you remember him for pitching a major-league inning as a position player for the Red Sox last year than for his catching prowess. ⊘ An organizational player for most of his most of his career, 25 year-old outfielder **Joey Butler** exploded in 2011, hitting .322/.388/.493 in a full-season at the Triple-A level. Seen by most as a Four-A type rather than a legit major league option, Butler will keep trying to earn that shot at the bigs. ⊘ Another super-toolsy player in the system, little **Leury Garcia** shows plus-plus attributes in the field and with his legs, prompting some to compare him to an even smaller Rafael Furcal. ⊘ Forgotten in the prospect world after a disappointing 2010 season, former second-round pick (2009) **Tommy Mendonca** rebounded in 2011, playing the entire year at Double-A, showing legit major league pop and a glove that can stick at third base at the next level. ⊘ As a player who more than held his own in the Northwest league as a 17-year old, Venezuelan second baseman **Rougned Odor** has the combination of polish and promise to make him one of the top infield prospects in the system. ⊘ **Jacob Skole** made his full-season debut in 2011, struggling at times but also flashing some of the physical gifts that made him the 15th overall selection in the 2010 draft. ⊘ Slick-fielding third baseman **Christian Villanueva** put his name on the prospect map in 2011, showing power, a plus defensive skill-set at the hot corner, and polish beyond his 20 years.

## PITCHERS

| PLAYER | TEAM | LVL | AGE | W | L | SV | IP | H | HR | BB | SO | EqBB9 | EqSO9 | GB% | BABIP | WHIP | ERA | FIP | FRA | WARP |
|---|---|---|---|---|---|---|---|---|---|---|---|---|---|---|---|---|---|---|---|---|
| C. Buckel | HIC | A | 19 | 7 | 2 | 0 | 96² | 85 | 7 | 28 | 125 | 2.5 | 11.2 | 49% | .310 | 1.14 | 2.61 | 2.78 | 3.66 | 2.3 |
| L. Jackson | HIC | A | 19 | 4 | 4 | 0 | 75 | 83 | 9 | 48 | 78 | 5.8 | 9.4 | 41% | .338 | 1.75 | 5.64 | 5.09 | 5.64 | 0.1 |
| M. Kirkman | ROU | AAA | 24 | 3 | 3 | 1 | 73 | 79 | 4 | 36 | 85 | 4.6 | 10.4 | 47% | .371 | 1.70 | 5.05 | 3.76 | 4.48 | 1.1 |
|  | TEX | MLB | 24 | 1 | 1 | 0 | 27¹ | 26 | 5 | 12 | 21 | 4.0 | 6.9 | 37% | .262 | 1.39 | 6.59 | 5.55 | 5.32 | 0.1 |
| J. Miller | FRI | AA | 24 | 5 | 1 | 13 | 69² | 46 | 2 | 26 | 76 | 3.1 | 9.9 | 37% | .262 | 1.00 | 1.81 | 2.86 | 3.71 | 1.1 |
| D. Perez | SPO | A- | 18 | 1 | 2 | 0 | 30¹ | 25 | 2 | 29 | 43 | 8.6 | 12.8 | 45% | .329 | 1.78 | 8.60 | 5.28 | 6.55 | -0.1 |
| R. Ross | MYR | A+ | 22 | 7 | 3 | 0 | 123¹ | 102 | 1 | 28 | 96 | 2.0 | 7.2 | 57% | .288 | 1.05 | 2.26 | 2.59 | 3.88 | 2.1 |
|  | FRI | AA | 22 | 1 | 1 | 0 | 38 | 34 | 5 | 9 | 48 | 1.2 | 8.5 | 49% | .261 | 1.00 | 2.61 | 3.28 | 3.51 | 0.9 |
| T. Scheppers | FRI | AA | 24 | 1 | 1 | 0 | 23 | 18 | 1 | 9 | 24 | 3.5 | 9.4 | 43% | .279 | 1.17 | 3.13 | 3.16 | 3.73 | 0.4 |
|  | ROU | AAA | 24 | 2 | 0 | 2 | 20² | 28 | 1 | 13 | 22 | 5.2 | 8.7 | 52% | .386 | 1.69 | 4.35 | 4.41 | 5.74 | 0.0 |
| J. Yan | MYR | A+ | 22 | 3 | 2 | 10 | 41¹ | 33 | 2 | 13 | 48 | 2.8 | 10.5 | 77% | .298 | 1.11 | 1.52 | 2.68 | 5.14 | 0.2 |
|  | FRI | AA | 22 | 0 | 0 | 2 | 26² | 20 | 0 | 9 | 21 | 3.0 | 6.1 | 66% | .241 | 1.01 | 0.34 | 3.04 | 4.96 | 0.1 |

A second-round selection from the 2010 draft, righty **Cody Buckel** might lack elite projection, but he has a deep arsenal, an excellent feel for pitching, and a high baseball IQ. ⊘ A supplemental first-round selection in 2010, power righty **Luke Jackson** already shows a promising three-pitch mix, with a plus fastball, a plus potential curve, and a developing changeup. ⊘ With the stuff to pitch in a late-inning capacity and the command to shuttle between the majors and the minors, hard-throwing lefty **Michael Kirkman** is only a small developmental step away from solidifying a role on the 25-man roster. ⊘ Added to the 40-man roster in the offseason, righty reliever **Justin Miller** can dial up a plus fastball in the mid-90s and mix in a good, hard slider with some late tilt. ⊘ A top 10 prospect in the Rangers farm system, projectable starter **David Perez** is a raw dream at the present, but he has the tools to develop into one of the premier starters in the minors. Armed with a low-90s fastball that can touch much higher, the 6-foot-5 righty's arsenal also features a promising curve and an underdeveloped changeup. ⊘ Former second-round pick **Robbie Ross** continues to make developmental progress, advancing to Double-A and more than holding his own in the rotation. As a diminutive southpaw with two above-average pitches and a good feel for throwing strikes, Ross might end up being a better fit for the bullpen than a major league rotation. ⊘ An up-and-down 2011 season, thanks to injury and inconsistency, has pushed hard-throwing reliever **Tanner Scheppers** down the prospect food chain, but with two 70-grade pitches at his fingertips, a late-inning future is still very possible. ⊘ A former position player turned side-arming reliever, **Johan Yan** uses a heavy mid-to-upper-80s fastball and a sweeping slider thrown from a deceptive release to induce weak contact.

# MANAGER: RON WASHINGTON

| YEAR | TEAM | W-L | Pythag +/− | Avg PC | 100+ P | 120+ P | QS | BQS | REL | REL w Zero R | IBB | Subs | PH | PH Avg | PH HR | SB2 | CS2 | SB3 | CS3 | SAC Att | SAC % | POS SAC | Squeeze | Swing | In Play |
|------|------|------|------------|--------|--------|--------|-----|-----|-----|------|-----|------|-----|------|----|-----|-----|-----|-----|-----|-------|-----|---------|-------|---------|
| 2009 | TEX | 87-75 | 1 | 96.7 | 67 | 5 | 66 | 12 | 436 | 283 | 14 | 12 | 48 | .119 | 0 | 32 | 3 | 0 | 2 | 55 | 72.7% | 35 | 4 | 128 | 96 |
| 2010 | TEX | 90-72 | 1 | 196.1 | 159 | 158 | 105 | 10 | 482 | 397 | 48 | — | 164 | .229 | 2 | 16 | 6 | 2 | 0 | 164 | 81.7% | 128 | 6 | 325 | 107 |
| 2011 | TEX | 96-66 | 1 | 99.2 | 103 | 3 | 99 | 5 | 417 | 335 | 21 | — | 59 | .204 | 1 | 18 | 4 | 2 | 2 | 63 | 73.0% | 45 | 3 | 374 | 117 |

As outside observers, it is difficult for us to quantify the value a manager provides for a team. Success on the field is the obvious measure of good or bad, reductive as it might be, but the talent on the field is the overwhelming deciding factor in that equation. Perhaps we might consider, then, that getting the most from that talent is the manager's most crucial role. Successful managers are sagacious psychologists, scientists of the minds of men, and what Ron Washington might lack in articulate

# Toronto Blue Jays

Consider a world in which the Blue Jays would not have to play any meaningful games against teams in the American League East. In this alternate universe, all those games are played but are not reflected in the standings. How would the Blue Jays have fared in this bizarro world? They would have been a winning team in each of the last five seasons. Last year, their record would have pegged them as equals of the Angels or the Giants—not quite a playoff team, but certainly not a fourth-place team either. In the 2009 season, in which the actual Blue Jays were 75-87, the bizarro-Jays would have held a .544 winning percentage. As Table 1 demonstrates, the bizarro-Jays would have, on average, significantly outperformed the actual Blue Jays.

The trouble with the Blue Jays is that they are not on the cusp of becoming a good team; they have been a good team for quite some time. The problem is that in order to be competitive, they are forced by circumstances largely beyond their control not only to be a very good team but an excellent one. If you're thinking that under the new CBA, the second wild card slot in the American League is tailor-made for the Jays, think again. If history is any guide, that slot will still go to whichever of the Yankees, Red Sox, or Rays would have been playing early golf under the old system.

## BLUE JAYS PROSPECTUS
### 2011 W-L: 81-81, 4th in AL East

| | | |
|---|---|---|
| Pythag | .489 | 15th |
| RS/G | 4.59 | 6th |
| RA/G | 4.70 | 25th |
| TAv | .270 | 8th |
| TAv-P | .275 | 27th |
| FIP | 4.32 | 27th |
| DER | .710 | 16th |
| DL | 680 | 12th |
| B-Age | 28.3 | 11th |
| P-Age | 27.0 | 6th |
| Salary | $70.3 | 21st |
| M$/MW | $1.77 | 10th |

**Ballpark:** Rogers Centre (3-yr. PF: 98). Hosted the first stadium UFC event. Cage match versus the Red Sox next

**2011:** Continuing to make progress in competing in the tough AL East, but still come up short

**2012:** Won't make the playoffs (again), but Joey Bats is still the most fun story in baseball

**Action Items:** Center field, DH, first base, and three league-average starting pitchers

Indeed, there is very little that would help the Blue Jays short of placing them in a different division, because what harms them is not just that they are forced to get in line behind the three powerhouses, but rather that they have to play each of those teams 18 times per season. As far as the Blue Jays are concerned, the only benefit they get from those additional games is their players get the bona fides of an AL East veteran, which might raise their trade value by some incremental amount.

That's not much of a consolation.

Given the stacked deck that the Blue Jays face every year, watching the organization react to its circumstances is a real joy for the analytically minded fan. Watching the constellation of smart people in the front office in Toronto—starting with Alex Anthopoulos but including decision makers all the way down the chain of hierarchy—confront this interesting and complex problem filled with uncertainty is a sport unto itself. How have A.A. and the team responded to five straight seasons of not-good-enough?

The main thing they have *not* done is sign free agents. The only player Toronto signed to a major-league free agent deal was on the roster at the end of last season: Kelly Johnson. And even Johnson only got a contract because he accepted arbitration. While the Blue Jays were undoubtedly willing to deal with the risk he might accept their offer, they were much more motivated by the fact that he was a ("modified") Type-A free agent. If Johnson had signed somewhere else, in other words, the Blue Jays would have gotten a prime draft pick in return. Instead, they will most likely get a fine second baseman on a one-year deal.

Other than Johnson, the Blue Jays have focused entirely on internal player development and the acquisition of cost-effective players via the trade market. This offseason they

### Table 1

| Year | Actual Win Pct. | Non-division Win Pct. | Difference |
|------|-----------------|------------------------|------------|
| 2011 | 0.500 | 0.533 | 0.033 |
| 2010 | 0.525 | 0.511 | -0.014 |
| 2009 | 0.463 | 0.544 | 0.081 |
| 2008 | 0.531 | 0.544 | 0.013 |
| 2007 | 0.512 | 0.522 | 0.010 |

acquired Sergio Santos from the White Sox and Ben Francisco from the Phillies. These versatile players give John Farrell considerable flexibility in managing late in ballgames. They claimed Jim Hoey—a pitcher who needs only a modicum of control to become a useful player—off waivers from the Twins. Last summer, the Blue Jays sent prospect Zach Stewart and reliever Jason Frasor to Chicago for Edwin Jackson. Then they turned around and packaged Jackson with Octavio Dotel and some valuable Words With Friends tiles to bring Colby Rasmus north of the border from St. Louis. It was the kind of high-wire act you'd only work extremely hard to pull off if you thought acquiring pre-arbitration players was the only pos-

course of events has vindicated the Blue Jays' decisions at least three times over.

In fact, Bautista's 2011 season was quite likely the best ever by a Blue Jays hitter. Other than John Olerud's 1993 (.363/.473/.599) and perhaps Jesse Barfield's 1986 (.289/.368/.559 with 40 home runs and some great defense), it is hard even to come up with plausible competition. All of Carlos Delgado's seasons (2000 and 2003 are the best) have to get dinged by the turbo-charged offensive environment. Vernon Wells had a great 2006 (.303/.357/.542 playing CF), but Bautista had 90 points of OBP on him. Even if we add pitchers to the equation, only the elite seasons from Clemens, Halladay, Stieb, and Hentgen enter the discussion.

And the truly ridiculous part of it all is that the Blue Jays paid Bautista $8 million in 2011, but he was probably worth about $40 million to them in baseball terms. In other words, the Blue Jays made back more than 60 percent of their contractual obligation to Bautista in the first year of the contract. Of course, that isn't quite accurate, since Bautista's 2011 would have been, in the absence of an extension, his last year of arbitration. Can you imagine the money he would have earned as a free agent after his 2011? Suffice to say it would be more than four years and $56 million, and it's safe to assume that Bautista has established a level of performance that will make him worth more than the $14 million he'll be paid each year between now and 2015. Did we mention there's a team option for 2016?

The sign-'em-while-they're-young strategy isn't always so historically successful. It went badly with Adam Lind, whom the Blue Jays signed to a four-year, $17.4 million deal that bought out all of his arbitration years. Lind wouldn't have made that much if the team had gone year-to-year with

him. And if he had won a costly arbitration victory, the team would have retained the option of non-tendering him.

Plus there is no guarantee the pre-arbitration players the Blue Jays have stockpiled will pan out. In their first tastes of Canadian baseball, Kyle Drabek and Rasmus have both faltered. There is still plenty of reason to think these two high-upside types will reach much of their potential, but we were saying the same things about Lind and Travis Snider two years ago. Brett Lawrie was almost too good to believe last year, and injury-prone to boot. Can all of these pieces really break Toronto's way in a big enough fashion to help them make the playoffs? In the AL East?

different relationship—Toronto is a big-market powerhouse.

There's reason to think the Blue Jays could return to the top tier of baseball's markets. The team's attendance heyday was the golden period from 1991–93, in which the team regularly attracted 4 million fans per season. After the strike, attendance never recovered—it has hovered around 2 million for over a decade. But the Rogers Centre (nee SkyDome) holds only about 1250 fewer fans for baseball now than it did back in the 1990s, meaning the Blue Jays are selling half or fewer of their available tickets each season. But we know that attendance is at least somewhat correlated to winning, particularly to playoff appearances.

Here's a possible plan. Every time you identify a young player with some significant value, attempt to sign him to a long-term deal to buy out his arbitration years, and include team options for his first few years of free agency if possible. Be aggressive about this goal and do not regret the occasional bust like Lind. While you are doing this, be prepared to enter stage two if you accumulate three or four such contracts. Stage two consists of an aggressive push on the free agent market to purchase wins—financed by the surplus you will reap from the successful bargain contracts—sufficient to secure a good shot at the playoffs. Engage in aggressive ticket promotions during this critical period and attempt to create a virtuous circle like the one ignited in 2007 in Philadelphia.

If this plan is plausible, what seems like stagnation in the face of an impossible task—evidenced by low payrolls and poor attendance—is just stage one of a larger plan. The necessary conditions for stage two have not yet coalesced, but they are coming. Rest assured that Toronto is in talks with Lawrie for a deal similar to the one given to Lind after his excellent 2009 season—only maybe this one will work out.

That would give the Blue Jays two banner contracts, and there moderate bargains elsewhere on the roster. Most notably, the Ricky Romero contract bought out the right-hander's arbitration years plus one year of free agency and added a team option for the second year of free agency. Similarly, Yunel Escobar is signed for two more years plus two more team options at $5 million per year. One or two more extensions like that, and the Blue Jays can engage in aggressive spending for 2014, 2015, and 2016.

If it works, the Blue Jays could challenge the AL East hegemony and really make things tough on the Orioles.

# HITTERS

**J.P. Arencibia**    C

Born: 1/5/1986 Age: 26
Bats: R Throws: R Height: 6' 2" Weight: 210
Breakout: 3% Improve: 16% Collapse: 11%
Attrition: 46% MLB: 80%

Comparables:
Doug Camilli, Chris Widger, Mike O'Berry

| YEAR | TEAM | LVL | AGE | PA | R | 2B | 3B | HR | RBI | BB | SO | SB | CS | AVG/OBP/SLG | TAv | BABIP | BRR | FRAA | WARP |
|------|------|-----|-----|-----|----|----|----|----|-----|----|-----|----|----|----------------|------|-------|------|--------|------|
| 2009 | LVG | AAA | 23 | 500 | 67 | 32 | 1 | 21 | 75 | 26 | 114 | 0 | 1 | .236/.285/.444 | .246 | .269 | -0.4 | -1 | 1.0 |
| 2010 | LVG | AAA | 24 | 459 | 76 | 36 | 1 | 32 | 85 | 38 | 85 | 0 | 0 | .301/.364/.626 | .312 | .312 | -3.5 | -2.8 | 3.8 |
| 2010 | TOR | MLB | 24 | 37 | 3 | 1 | 0 | 2 | 4 | 2 | 11 | 0 | 0 | .143/.189/.343 | .185 | .136 | -1.1 | -0.1 | -0.3 |
| 2011 | TOR | MLB | 25 | 486 | 47 | 20 | 4 | 23 | 78 | 36 | 133 | 1 | 1 | .219/.282/.438 | .261 | .255 | -2.3 | 1.4 | 2.2 |
| 2012 | TOR | MLB | 26 | 367 | 42 | 17 | 2 | 16 | 49 | 24 | 99 | 1 | 0 | .229/.285/.435 | .253 | .271 | -0.1 | C -1 | 1.7 |

It's easy enough to focus on what Arencibia can't do (hit for average) or on who his competition might be by midseason (Travis d'Arnaud). But what Arencibia can do is drive the ball to left field. His isolated power would have landed him at about the 75th percentile of all major league hitters had he qualified for the batting title. His 23 home runs were second among all rookies and trailed only Angels first baseman Mark Trumbo's 29. Be careful of overstating Arencibia's platoon tendency—he was much better against lefties this year—since he actually had a reverse split in Triple-A in 2010. If d'Arnaud takes the job away from Arencibia, it'll be because of d'Arnaud's defense and ability to get on base.

**Jose Bautista**    RF

Born: 10/19/1980 Age: 31
Bats: R Throws: R Height: 6' 1" Weight: 195
Breakout: 1% Improve: 42% Collapse: 2%
Attrition: 5% MLB: 95%

Comparables:
Reggie Smith, Frank Robinson, Roger Maris

| YEAR | TEAM | LVL | AGE | PA | R | 2B | 3B | HR | RBI | BB | SO | SB | CS | AVG/OBP/SLG | TAv | BABIP | BRR | FRAA | WARP |
|------|------|-----|-----|-----|-----|----|----|----|-----|-----|-----|----|----|----------------|------|-------|------|----------|------|
| 2009 | TOR | MLB | 28 | 404 | 54 | 13 | 3 | 13 | 40 | 56 | 85 | 4 | 0 | .235/.349/.408 | .268 | .275 | 3.9 | -2.9 | 1.4 |
| 2010 | TOR | MLB | 29 | 683 | 109 | 35 | 3 | 54 | 124 | 100 | 116 | 9 | 2 | .260/.378/.617 | .341 | .233 | -1.6 | -12.4 | 6.5 |
| 2011 | TOR | MLB | 30 | 655 | 105 | 24 | 2 | 43 | 103 | 132 | 111 | 9 | 5 | .302/.447/.608 | .370 | .309 | 1.4 | 10.3 | 10.3 |
| 2012 | TOR | MLB | 31 | 621 | 87 | 28 | 2 | 31 | 89 | 87 | 118 | 7 | 3 | .259/.370/.501 | .304 | .275 | -0.2 | RF -2, 3B 2 | 4.2 |

One of the cons pulled by "Fast" Eddie Felson, Paul Newman's poolshark protagonist of *The Hustler*, is to sink an impossible rail shot while stumblingly inebriated. When his partner challenges him to repeat the trick, Felson misses badly. To the rest of the pool hall, Fast Eddie looks too hardheaded and harddrinking to realize when he's been lucky. But when the bet is laid down for the second time, it's to the unsuspecting onlooker's surprise (and significant pecuniary disadvantage) that Fast Eddie straightens up and nails the shot. Joey Bats took what looked like the hardest shot on the table—following up a season in which he quadrupled his career high in home runs—straightened his tie, squared his hips, and drilled one in the corner pocket. Never mind the decrease in home runs (he still led the majors), Bautista increased his walk rate and decreased his strikeout rate for an unbelievable fourth season in a row. Part of the increase in walks was due to the league figuring out that, like Fast Eddie, Bautista was no fluke: his 24 intentional walks led the league. But even if you take away the IBBs, Bautista still took more walks this year than last. In other words: pay up, fellas.

**David Cooper**    1B

Born: 2/12/1987 Age: 25
Bats: L Throws: L Height: 6' 1" Weight: 200
Breakout: 2% Improve: 41% Collapse: 2%
Attrition: 16% MLB: 68%

Comparables:
Chris Carter, Paul Konerko, Daniel Murphy

| YEAR | TEAM | LVL | AGE | PA | R | 2B | 3B | HR | RBI | BB | SO | SB | CS | AVG/OBP/SLG | TAv | BABIP | BRR | FRAA | WARP |
|------|------|-----|-----|-----|----|----|----|----|-----|----|----|----|----|----------------|------|-------|------|--------|------|
| 2009 | NHP | AA | 22 | 538 | 62 | 32 | 0 | 10 | 66 | 59 | 92 | 0 | 0 | .258/.343/.389 | .263 | .302 | -3 | 1.2 | 0.4 |
| 2010 | NHP | AA | 23 | 553 | 59 | 30 | 1 | 20 | 78 | 52 | 74 | 0 | 0 | .257/.328/.442 | .269 | .267 | -3.8 | 6.6 | 1.1 |
| 2011 | LVG | AAA | 24 | 545 | 77 | 51 | 1 | 9 | 96 | 67 | 43 | 1 | 3 | .364/.439/.535 | .307 | .380 | -4.2 | -8 | 1.8 |
| 2011 | TOR | MLB | 24 | 81 | 9 | 7 | 0 | 2 | 12 | 7 | 14 | 0 | 0 | .211/.284/.394 | .252 | .228 | 0 | -0.2 | 0.0 |
| 2012 | TOR | MLB | 25 | 250 | 29 | 16 | 0 | 6 | 28 | 22 | 41 | 0 | 0 | .259/.326/.406 | .258 | .292 | 0 | 1B -11 | 0.5 |

Doubles are a fine outcome in a baseball game. But that's not why you like that a prospect hits a lot of doubles. No, you like a prospect's doubles because you can imagine them becoming home runs. When a 24-year-old first baseman puts up 51 doubles in Las Vegas and only nine home runs, it's only natural to focus more on the paucity of home runs than on the high batting average. Guys like Cooper occasionally put it all together this late in their careers, but it becomes less likely as time goes on. Right now, Cooper looks like a career pinch hitter of the Ross Gload variety.

**Travis d'Arnaud**   C

Born: 2/10/1989 Age: 23
Bats: R Throws: R Height: 6' 3" Weight: 195
Breakout: 6% Improve: 19% Collapse: 4%
Attrition: 21% MLB: 58%

Comparables:
Matt Nokes, Bill Freehan, Josh Donaldson

| YEAR | TEAM | LVL | AGE | PA | R | 2B | 3B | HR | RBI | BB | SO | SB | CS | AVG_OBP_SLG | TAv | BABIP | BRR | FRAA | WARP |
|---|---|---|---|---|---|---|---|---|---|---|---|---|---|---|---|---|---|---|---|
| 2009 | LWD | A | 20 | 540 | 71 | 38 | 1 | 13 | 71 | 41 | 75 | 8 | 4 | .255/.324/.419 | .289 | .279 | -2.5 | -1 | 3.2 |
| 2010 | DUN | A+ | 21 | 292 | 36 | 20 | 1 | 6 | 38 | 20 | 63 | 3 | 1 | .259/.321/.411 | .261 | .320 | -2.3 | -1.1 | 0.9 |
| 2011 | NHP | AA | 22 | 466 | 72 | 33 | 1 | 21 | 78 | 33 | 100 | 4 | 2 | .311/.371/.542 | .309 | .365 | -1.7 | -0.4 | 4.4 |
| 2012 | TOR | MLB | 23 | 250 | 28 | 14 | 1 | 7 | 29 | 15 | 54 | 1 | 0 | .243/.296/.406 | .247 | .284 | -0.1 | C -1 | 1.3 |

It looked like d'Arnaud was having the healthy, productive season that would catapult him to the top of prospect lists. He demonstrated that his is the complete package: he is athletic, moves well behind the plate, hits for both average and power, and has a fine throwing arm. But his season ended after he tore up the ligaments in his thumb while playing for Team USA in the World Baseball Classic. It's the second season that has ended with surgery for d'Arnaud, and health is the only remaining knock on his prospect profile. Give d'Arnaud one more good year (look out, Pacific Coast League!), and J.P. Arencibia won't be much of an obstacle.

and he wound up with a strained hamstring that caused him to lose the final six weeks of the season. That leaves his future value in doubt. It would be wrong to attribute any change to his new ballpark, as Davis had an OPS more than 200 points higher at home than on the road. To return to the form that made him a useful outfielder three years ago, Davis will need to avoid re-injuring his hamstring and rediscover his line-drive swing, the loss of which contributed to a .292 BABIP, 30 points below his career average.

**Edwin Encarnacion**   3B

Born: 1/7/1983 Age: 29
Bats: R Throws: R Height: 6' 2" Weight: 195
Breakout: 12% Improve: 50% Collapse: 6%
Attrition: 14% MLB: 82%

Comparables:
Kent Hrbek, Justin Morneau, Rafael Palmeiro

| YEAR | TEAM | LVL | AGE | PA | R | 2B | 3B | HR | RBI | BB | SO | SB | CS | AVG_OBP_SLG | TAv | BABIP | BRR | FRAA | WARP |
|---|---|---|---|---|---|---|---|---|---|---|---|---|---|---|---|---|---|---|---|
| 2009 | CIN | MLB | 26 | 165 | 10 | 6 | 1 | 5 | 16 | 24 | 38 | 1 | 1 | .209/.333/.374 | .235 | .250 | -1.5 | -1.3 | -0.2 |
| 2009 | TOR | MLB | 26 | 173 | 25 | 5 | 1 | 8 | 23 | 13 | 29 | 1 | 0 | .240/.306/.442 | .265 | .242 | 0.6 | -1.8 | 0.5 |
| 2010 | TOR | MLB | 27 | 367 | 47 | 16 | 0 | 21 | 51 | 29 | 60 | 1 | 0 | .244/.305/.482 | .272 | .235 | 1.7 | -3.3 | 1.5 |
| 2011 | TOR | MLB | 28 | 530 | 70 | 36 | 0 | 17 | 55 | 43 | 77 | 8 | 2 | .272/.334/.453 | .279 | .292 | -3.6 | -4.6 | 1.1 |
| 2012 | TOR | MLB | 29 | 471 | 60 | 24 | 1 | 20 | 63 | 42 | 80 | 4 | 1 | .262/.336/.463 | .283 | .280 | 0 | 3B -4, 1B -1 | 2.6 |

No longer able to play a convincing third base, Encarnacion spent most of his time DHing for the Blue Jays. There, he cut his strikeout rate to 15 percent, the lowest of his career, and his BABIP and batting average both rose in the deal. The result was less power than in 2010 but a more productive offensive campaign. The home runs he hit tended to clear the wall in left field by a wide margin: eight of them went more than 400 feet. That augurs well for his production.

**Yunel Escobar**   SS

Born: 11/2/1982 Age: 29
Bats: R Throws: R Height: 6' 3" Weight: 200
Breakout: 3% Improve: 26% Collapse: 10%
Attrition: 17% MLB: 92%

Comparables:
Barry Larkin, Cal Ripken Jr., Ryan Theriot

| YEAR | TEAM | LVL | AGE | PA | R | 2B | 3B | HR | RBI | BB | SO | SB | CS | AVG_OBP_SLG | TAv | BABIP | BRR | FRAA | WARP |
|---|---|---|---|---|---|---|---|---|---|---|---|---|---|---|---|---|---|---|---|
| 2009 | ATL | MLB | 26 | 604 | 89 | 26 | 2 | 14 | 76 | 57 | 62 | 5 | 4 | .299/.377/.436 | .278 | .317 | 1.7 | 14.6 | 5.1 |
| 2010 | ATL | MLB | 27 | 301 | 28 | 12 | 0 | 0 | 19 | 37 | 31 | 5 | 1 | .238/.334/.284 | .230 | .270 | -0.7 | 10.6 | 1.2 |
| 2010 | TOR | MLB | 27 | 266 | 32 | 7 | 0 | 4 | 16 | 19 | 26 | 1 | 1 | .275/.340/.356 | .247 | .296 | 0.4 | -5.2 | 0.1 |
| 2011 | TOR | MLB | 28 | 590 | 77 | 24 | 3 | 11 | 48 | 61 | 70 | 3 | 3 | .290/.369/.413 | .288 | .316 | 0.3 | -3.9 | 3.7 |
| 2012 | TOR | MLB | 29 | 550 | 69 | 25 | 2 | 10 | 57 | 53 | 64 | 6 | 3 | .288/.365/.409 | .277 | .309 | -0.6 | SS 4 | 3.3 |

Forget everything else. There are only two things that matter when evaluating Escobar. He has a career .366 OBP and he plays shortstop. In his first full season after being swapped (with a few other players) for Alex Gonzalez, Escobar came out ahead in True Average by a margin of .289 to .226. Escobar has rejoined the four-win path he was originally on in Atlanta, only now he's doing it in Toronto and for just $5 million a year. Deals like the one that brought Escobar to Toronto are the kind that make other GMs eventually stop taking your calls. The only bump in the road came when Escobar was hit on the elbow by a pitch in early September and missed the final weeks of the season. In 2015, after the Blue Jays have exercised the second of their two $5 million club options on Escobar's contract extension, it's a good bet that Alex Gonzalez won't even be in the majors.

**Ben Francisco** RF
Born: 10/23/1981 Age: 30
Bats: R Throws: R Height: 6' 2" Weight: 190
Breakout: 2% Improve: 40% Collapse: 2%
Attrition: 13% MLB: 84%
Comparables:
Kevin Millar, Prentice Redman, Michael Cuddyer

| YEAR | TEAM | LVL | AGE | PA | R | 2B | 3B | HR | RBI | BB | SO | SB | CS | AVG_OBP_SLG | TAv | BABIP | BRR | FRAA | WARP |
|------|------|-----|-----|-----|----|----|----|----|-----|----|----|----|----|-------------|------|-------|------|-------------|------|
| 2009 | CLE | MLB | 27 | 355 | 48 | 21 | 1 | 10 | 33 | 33 | 59 | 13 | 3 | .250/.336/.422 | .274 | .278 | 2.5 | -1.5 | 1.4 |
| 2009 | PHI | MLB | 27 | 104 | 10 | 9 | 0 | 5 | 13 | 5 | 24 | 1 | 4 | .278/.317/.526 | .297 | .319 | -1.2 | 0.9 | 0.6 |
| 2010 | PHI | MLB | 28 | 197 | 24 | 13 | 0 | 6 | 28 | 14 | 35 | 8 | 0 | .268/.327/.441 | .259 | .302 | -0.5 | 0.7 | 0.2 |
| 2011 | PHI | MLB | 29 | 293 | 24 | 10 | 1 | 6 | 34 | 33 | 42 | 4 | 4 | .244/.340/.364 | .261 | .268 | -1.4 | -2.2 | 0.2 |
| 2012 | TOR | MLB | 30 | 256 | 31 | 15 | 1 | 7 | 31 | 22 | 47 | 8 | 3 | .263/.334/.431 | .271 | .297 | -0.4 | RF -1, LF 1 | 1.5 |

An injury to Domonic Brown forced Francisco into an everyday role in Philadelphia. An increase in his walk rate helped him offset a sizable drop in power. He is a good bet to be just about average in every triple-slash category, which has to be worth something—especially off the bench. He was sent to Toronto for a minor-league reliever, and he'll have a chance to fill in before an even more frustrating, late-arriving set of young hitters shows up.

**Anthony Gose** CF
Born: 8/10/1990 Age: 21
Bats: L Throws: L Height: 6' 2" Weight: 190
Breakout: 2% Improve: 21% Collapse: 3%
Attrition: 15% MLB: 41%
Comparables:
Brett Jackson, Thad Bosley, Starling Marte

| YEAR | TEAM | LVL | AGE | PA | R | 2B | 3B | HR | RBI | BB | SO | SB | CS | AVG_OBP_SLG | TAv | BABIP | BRR | FRAA | WARP |
|------|------|-----|-----|-----|----|----|----|----|-----|----|-----|----|----|-------------|------|-------|------|-------------|------|
| 2009 | LWD | A | 18 | 572 | 72 | 24 | 9 | 2 | 52 | 35 | 110 | 76 | 20 | .259/.320/.353 | .269 | .319 | 3.1 | -5.7 | 2.1 |
| 2010 | CLR | A+ | 19 | 461 | 67 | 17 | 11 | 4 | 21 | 32 | 103 | 36 | 27 | .263/.321/.385 | .260 | .335 | -0.8 | 0 | 1.8 |
| 2010 | DUN | A+ | 19 | 113 | 21 | 3 | 2 | 3 | 6 | 13 | 29 | 9 | 5 | .255/.357/.426 | .275 | .328 | 1.1 | 1.1 | 0.7 |
| 2011 | NHP | AA | 20 | 587 | 87 | 20 | 7 | 16 | 59 | 62 | 154 | 70 | 15 | .253/.349/.415 | .268 | .332 | 6.8 | -4 | 3.4 |
| 2012 | TOR | MLB | 21 | 250 | 25 | 9 | 3 | 3 | 23 | 16 | 68 | 19 | 6 | .224/.286/.341 | .224 | .296 | -0.3 | CF -6, LF -0 | -0.3 |

Most prospects don't immediately realize their potential in one week, one month, or one year. More usually, they improve individual aspects of their game as they climb the ladder one stop at a time. That's why young prospects with excellent tools are so desirable: if they can just follow a normal development path, they'll be All-Stars by their 25th birthdays. In 2011, Gose improved his walk rate, his power numbers, and his base running. That leaves only one major tool left to develop: his contact rate. His strikeouts remain high, and his free-swinging ways and difficulty with off-speed stuff mean the last step of the developmental path will be the hardest. It's worth wondering whether the high-offense environment at Triple-A Las Vegas will curb or encourage Gose's bad habits.

**Adeiny Hechavarria** SS
Born: 4/15/1989 Age: 23
Bats: R Throws: R Height: 6' 0" Weight: 180
Breakout: 7% Improve: 24% Collapse: 12%
Attrition: 39% MLB: 62%
Comparables:
Tito Fuentes, Robin Yount, Dickie Thon

| YEAR | TEAM | LVL | AGE | PA | R | 2B | 3B | HR | RBI | BB | SO | SB | CS | AVG_OBP_SLG | TAv | BABIP | BRR | FRAA | WARP |
|------|------|-----|-----|-----|----|----|----|----|-----|----|----|----|----|-------------|------|-------|------|------|------|
| 2011 | NHP | AA | 22 | 502 | 58 | 22 | 6 | 6 | 46 | 25 | 78 | 19 | 13 | .235/.275/.347 | .223 | .267 | 1.7 | -5.4 | -0.3 |
| 2011 | LVG | AAA | 22 | 116 | 16 | 6 | 2 | 2 | 11 | 8 | 21 | 1 | 2 | .389/.431/.537 | .313 | .471 | 1.5 | -2.7 | 1.1 |
| 2012 | TOR | MLB | 23 | 250 | 24 | 11 | 2 | 3 | 23 | 9 | 47 | 7 | 4 | .234/.264/.330 | .211 | .278 | -0.8 | SS 0 | -0.4 |

The glove will play: he plays slick defense up the middle. The contract will play: he has three years left on the major league contract he signed when he came stateside. The question is whether the bat will play. His walk rates have been increasing, as have his power numbers. There were enough bursts of offense from Hechavarria in 2011—most notably his stint in Triple-A—to think he will eventually find a home on a major league roster. With Escobar locked up at short and the development of Hechavarria's bat uncertain, it's hard to imagine him taking over the starting job in Toronto any time soon. That means either something has to give or Hechavarria won't play. When he does get in the game, though, expect plenty of defensive showmanship.

**Brian Jeroloman** C
Born: 5/10/1985 Age: 27
Bats: L Throws: R Height: 6' 1" Weight: 200
Breakout: 5% Improve: 24% Collapse: 4%
Attrition: 27% MLB: 58%
Comparables:
Lou Berberet, Chad Kreuter, Mark Bailey

| YEAR | TEAM | LVL | AGE | PA | R | 2B | 3B | HR | RBI | BB | SO | SB | CS | AVG_OBP_SLG | TAv | BABIP | BRR | FRAA | WARP |
|------|------|-----|-----|-----|----|----|----|----|-----|----|-----|----|----|-------------|------|-------|------|------|------|
| 2009 | NHP | AA | 24 | 432 | 32 | 16 | 1 | 6 | 32 | 62 | 120 | 1 | 0 | .217/.331/.316 | .240 | .304 | -1.1 | -1.4 | 1.1 |
| 2010 | NHP | AA | 25 | 319 | 37 | 16 | 0 | 7 | 33 | 69 | 91 | 0 | 1 | .261/.431/.412 | .308 | .388 | -5.7 | 0.6 | 2.7 |
| 2011 | LVG | AAA | 26 | 318 | 30 | 9 | 0 | 2 | 26 | 38 | 72 | 3 | 3 | .240/.335/.295 | .211 | .317 | -0.4 | -2.9 | -1.0 |
| 2012 | TOR | MLB | 27 | 250 | 25 | 9 | 0 | 4 | 18 | 33 | 74 | 1 | 1 | .207/.317/.308 | .229 | .293 | -0.1 | C -2 | 0.7 |

The most noteworthy thing about Jeroloman is that he bats lefty. The only such catchers to play 100 games in the last two seasons are Joe Mauer, John Jaso, Brian McCann, Miguel Montero, and Alex Avila. Jeroloman isn't nearly as good a hitter as any of those players. He had a 631 OPS playing in one of the most offense-friendly environments in baseball: Triple-A Las Vegas. In his minor-league career, he has hit a home run once every 78 plate appearances. His walk rate and strong defense have always been his strengths, but it's looking increasingly unlikely those will be enough to carry him as a major-league backup.

**Kelly Johnson 2B**
Born: 2/22/1982 Age: 30
Bats: L Throws: R Height: 6' 2" Weight: 205
Breakout: 4% Improve: 27% Collapse: 4%
Attrition: 16% MLB: 69%
**Comparables:**
Sibby Sisti, Dick McAuliffe, Jack Lohrke

| YEAR | TEAM | LVL | AGE | PA | R | 2B | 3B | HR | RBI | BB | SO | SB | CS | AVG_OBP_SLG | TAv | BABIP | BRR | FRAA | WARP |
|---|---|---|---|---|---|---|---|---|---|---|---|---|---|---|---|---|---|---|---|
| 2009 | GWN | AAA | 27 | 59 | 9 | 2 | 2 | 3 | 16 | 4 | 8 | 1 | 0 | .308/.357/.596 | .335 | .317 | -0.6 | 0.6 | 0.6 |
| 2009 | ATL | MLB | 27 | 346 | 47 | 20 | 3 | 8 | 29 | 32 | 54 | 7 | 2 | .224/.303/.389 | .243 | .247 | 1.2 | 2.2 | 0.3 |
| 2010 | ARI | MLB | 28 | 671 | 93 | 36 | 5 | 26 | 71 | 79 | 148 | 13 | 7 | .284/.370/.496 | .298 | .339 | -1.5 | -5.3 | 4.0 |
| 2011 | ARI | MLB | 29 | 481 | 59 | 23 | 5 | 18 | 49 | 44 | 132 | 13 | 3 | .209/.287/.412 | .243 | .257 | 1.1 | -11.7 | -0.9 |
| 2011 | TOR | MLB | 29 | 132 | 16 | 4 | 2 | 3 | 9 | 16 | 31 | 3 | 3 | .270/.364/.417 | .290 | .346 | -0.9 | -1.4 | 0.7 |
| 2012 | TOR | MLB | 30 | 587 | 73 | 30 | 6 | 17 | 72 | 61 | 126 | 18 | 7 | .258/.339/.442 | .274 | .305 | -0.8 | 2B -7 | 2.6 |

Johnson's 2011 woes began with his strikeouts. He whiffed over 27 percent of the time while in Arizona, compared to just 22 percent the year before. When he was shipped to Toronto for his brother in the fraternity of beleaguered keystone guys, Aaron Hill, Johnson's strikeout rate fell back to 22 percent. As if on cue, his batting average and on-base percentage rose more than

Attrition: 22% MLB: 83%
**Comparables:**
David Wright, Travis Fryman, Ryan Zimmerman

| YEAR | TEAM | LVL | AGE | PA | R | 2B | 3B | HR | RBI | BB | SO | SB | CS | AVG_OBP_SLG | TAv | BABIP | BRR | FRAA | WARP |
|---|---|---|---|---|---|---|---|---|---|---|---|---|---|---|---|---|---|---|---|
| 2010 | HUN | AA | 20 | 609 | 90 | 36 | 10 | 8 | 63 | 47 | 118 | 30 | 13 | .285/.345/.451 | .274 | .349 | 2.4 | 8.7 | 3.5 |
| 2011 | LVG | AAA | 21 | 329 | 64 | 24 | 6 | 18 | 61 | 26 | 53 | 13 | 2 | .353/.415/.661 | .337 | .383 | -0.8 | 3.1 | 4.1 |
| 2011 | TOR | MLB | 21 | 171 | 26 | 8 | 4 | 9 | 25 | 16 | 31 | 7 | 1 | .293/.373/.580 | .338 | .318 | 0.2 | 9.8 | 3.3 |
| 2012 | TOR | MLB | 22 | 250 | 31 | 12 | 3 | 8 | 33 | 16 | 54 | 8 | 3 | .264/.318/.452 | .269 | .309 | -0.2 | 3B 9, 2B 1 | 2.1 |

The first of the bats has arrived. After years of disappointment from top hitting prospects, the Jays finally found one who'll play. Never mind that they acquired him from the Brewers after much of his development was completed; it wasn't until he got to the Blue Jays organization that he put it all together. The worry with Lawrie used to be that he didn't have a definitive defensive home, and so it wasn't clear if his plus bat would carry him. A shift to third base and 3.3 WARP in 43 major-league games later, that isn't the worry anymore. He's got an excellent swing that covers the entire plate, and his wrists generate a tremendous amount of bat speed. The only knock on Lawrie's remarkable breakout was his health: he spent two stints on the DL with injuries to bones in each of his hands. PECOTA is pessimistic he'll repeat, but still looks for positive contributions from the 22-year-old.

**Adam Lind 1B**
Born: 7/17/1983 Age: 28
Bats: L Throws: L Height: 6' 3" Weight: 195
Breakout: 2% Improve: 30% Collapse: 2%
Attrition: 28% MLB: 79%
**Comparables:**
Mike Jacobs, John Poff, Adam LaRoche

| YEAR | TEAM | LVL | AGE | PA | R | 2B | 3B | HR | RBI | BB | SO | SB | CS | AVG_OBP_SLG | TAv | BABIP | BRR | FRAA | WARP |
|---|---|---|---|---|---|---|---|---|---|---|---|---|---|---|---|---|---|---|---|
| 2009 | TOR | MLB | 25 | 654 | 93 | 46 | 0 | 35 | 114 | 58 | 110 | 1 | 1 | .305/.370/.562 | .316 | .323 | 0.6 | -6.2 | 4.0 |
| 2010 | TOR | MLB | 26 | 613 | 57 | 32 | 3 | 23 | 72 | 38 | 144 | 0 | 0 | .237/.287/.425 | .247 | .277 | -2.6 | -0.2 | -0.7 |
| 2011 | TOR | MLB | 27 | 542 | 56 | 16 | 0 | 26 | 87 | 32 | 107 | 1 | 1 | .251/.295/.439 | .267 | .265 | 2 | -4.8 | 0.5 |
| 2012 | TOR | MLB | 28 | 525 | 65 | 28 | 2 | 22 | 73 | 35 | 109 | 1 | 1 | .264/.316/.467 | .273 | .296 | -0.1 | 1B -2, LF -1 | 1.5 |

The chief virtue of Lind's campaign was that it was better than his 2010. The chief vice of Lind's campaign was that it was only slightly so. Only through the magic of arbitrary endpoints is the similarity of his two seasons obscured. It looked, during a first half in which he hit .300/.349/.515, that perhaps the Adam Lind that made a four-year, $17 million contract look like a steal was back. By the All-Star break, it seemed like he was picking up where he left off after a stronger (.267/.309/.498) second half in 2010. He did suffer a back injury that sidelined him for several weeks in the first half, but he came back before the All-Star break and went on a small tear. That isn't decisive, but it suggests the back injury was not to blame for his moribund second half (.197/.233/.356). There is no longer much reason to think that Lind will wind up any better than a league-average hitter.

### Jake Marisnick    CF

Born: 3/30/1991 Age: 21
Bats: R Throws: R Height: 6' 5'' Weight: 200
Breakout: 2% Improve: 24% Collapse: 4%
Attrition: 14% MLB: 53%

**Comparables:**
Jack Clark, Thad Bosley, Willie Davis

| YEAR | TEAM | LVL | AGE | PA | R | 2B | 3B | HR | RBI | BB | SO | SB | CS | AVG_OBP_SLG | TAv | BABIP | BRR | FRAA | WARP |
|------|------|-----|-----|----|---|----|----|----|-----|----|----|----|----|-------------|-----|-------|-----|------|------|
| 2010 | LNS | A | 19 | 143 | 16 | 8 | 2 | 1 | 12 | 9 | 37 | 9 | 2 | .220/.294/.339 | .221 | .297 | 1.8 | 5.1 | 0.4 |
| 2010 | BLJ | RK | 19 | 142 | 17 | 12 | 0 | 3 | 14 | 13 | 18 | 14 | 1 | .287/.379/.459 | .310 | .317 | 0.1 | 1 | 1.5 |
| 2011 | LNS | A | 20 | 523 | 68 | 27 | 6 | 14 | 77 | 43 | 91 | 37 | 8 | .320/.392/.496 | .313 | .371 | -0.5 | -1.6 | 4.6 |
| 2012 | TOR | MLB | 21 | 250 | 26 | 11 | 1 | 5 | 25 | 13 | 58 | 8 | 2 | .240/.288/.364 | .232 | .295 | 0.1 | CF -6, LF 0 | 0.1 |

Cue the montage of grainy clips from old Frankenstein movies—it's alive! Or imagine spending hours stringing elaborate exterior Christmas lights—you're uncertain if they'll actually come on or not, but boy, if and when they do, the neighbors sure will be jealous. The Jays can't wait for Marisnick to come on. He is huge, fast, and strong, and it appears he can also play baseball. After a year in the Midwest League, he finished second in batting, fourth in on-base percentage, and eighth in slugging. He was also seventh in steals. He did all that while he was more than a year younger than the average Midwest League player. There isn't anything he can't do well, and it isn't hard to imagine him starting in right field (or perhaps even center) in 2013.

### Darin Mastroianni    CF

Born: 8/26/1985 Age: 26
Bats: R Throws: R Height: 6' 0'' Weight: 190
Breakout: 1% Improve: 47% Collapse: 7%
Attrition: 26% MLB: 75%

**Comparables:**
Freddy Guzman, Kenny Lofton, Rick Peters

| YEAR | TEAM | LVL | AGE | PA | R | 2B | 3B | HR | RBI | BB | SO | SB | CS | AVG_OBP_SLG | TAv | BABIP | BRR | FRAA | WARP |
|------|------|-----|-----|----|---|----|----|----|-----|----|----|----|----|-------------|-----|-------|-----|------|------|
| 2009 | DUN | A+ | 23 | 274 | 55 | 11 | 2 | 0 | 26 | 37 | 38 | 32 | 7 | .325/.423/.390 | .295 | .385 | 4.2 | 1.8 | 2.5 |
| 2009 | NHP | AA | 23 | 292 | 39 | 10 | 2 | 1 | 25 | 39 | 45 | 38 | 8 | .271/.368/.340 | .275 | .322 | 3.7 | -1.9 | 1.5 |
| 2010 | NHP | AA | 24 | 617 | 101 | 25 | 7 | 4 | 46 | 77 | 96 | 46 | 10 | .301/.389/.398 | .285 | .356 | 4.9 | -1.9 | 4.3 |
| 2011 | NHP | AA | 25 | 198 | 29 | 8 | 3 | 1 | 13 | 22 | 24 | 14 | 3 | .254/.342/.355 | .260 | .286 | 2.7 | 6 | 1.2 |
| 2011 | LVG | AAA | 25 | 364 | 63 | 18 | 6 | 2 | 23 | 40 | 54 | 20 | 7 | .276/.358/.389 | .246 | .327 | 2.7 | 2.6 | 1.3 |
| 2012 | TOR | MLB | 26 | 250 | 27 | 10 | 2 | 1 | 20 | 25 | 46 | 16 | 4 | .252/.329/.335 | .241 | .307 | 0.5 | CF -2, LF 1 | 0.5 |

Mastroianni is too old to be a real prospect and does not hit well enough to be intriguing otherwise. He plays acceptable defense in center, so he may yet find a role as a fourth outfielder, particularly given his skills on the basepaths and potential as a pinch runner (note his nine triples). The key question is whether he can maintain his plate discipline and walk rate against pitchers who are not afraid to throw strikes against him. His lack of power suggests he may not.

### Jeff Mathis    C

Born: 3/31/1983 Age: 29
Bats: R Throws: R Height: 6' 1'' Weight: 180
Breakout: 1% Improve: 15% Collapse: 17%
Attrition: 48% MLB: 70%

**Comparables:**
Choo-Choo Coleman, Jimmie Schaffer, Darrell Johnson

| YEAR | TEAM | LVL | AGE | PA | R | 2B | 3B | HR | RBI | BB | SO | SB | CS | AVG_OBP_SLG | TAv | BABIP | BRR | FRAA | WARP |
|------|------|-----|-----|----|---|----|----|----|-----|----|----|----|----|-------------|-----|-------|-----|------|------|
| 2009 | ANA | MLB | 26 | 272 | 26 | 8 | 0 | 5 | 28 | 22 | 73 | 2 | 3 | .211/.288/.308 | .214 | .281 | -1.9 | 1.9 | -0.1 |
| 2010 | ANA | MLB | 27 | 218 | 19 | 6 | 1 | 3 | 18 | 6 | 59 | 3 | 0 | .195/.219/.278 | .193 | .253 | 0.8 | 1.2 | -0.4 |
| 2011 | ANA | MLB | 28 | 281 | 18 | 12 | 0 | 3 | 22 | 15 | 75 | 1 | 2 | .174/.225/.259 | .191 | .233 | -0.8 | 0.3 | -0.8 |
| 2012 | TOR | MLB | 29 | 256 | 24 | 10 | 1 | 5 | 22 | 17 | 68 | 2 | 1 | .208/.267/.318 | .208 | .262 | -0.2 | C 1 | -0.4 |

The Arizona Diamondbacks' pitching staff hit .186/.230/.250 in 2011, with four home runs in 312 at bats. The Jeff Mathis Catcher ERA Traveling Circus hit .174/.225/.259 in 2011, with three home runs in 247 at bats. The Diamondbacks pitchers played in the easier league and had the ballpark advantage, but oh my gosh are we really resorting to park factors to decide who is the better hitter between Jeff Mathis and Barry Enright? Mathis' historical ineptitude at the plate was so bad that, even without a Napoli-strength alternative, Mike Scioscia gave up on him in August, giving Bobby Wilson the bulk of the starts down the stretch. Mathis did improve his throwing in 2011, at least to the extent that he quit throwing so many balls into center field. Mathis would be one more Jeff Mathis season away from dropping below Tom Egan as the worst OPS+ in Angels' history, but the move to Toronto won't allow him that chance.

### Mike McCoy    SS

Born: 4/2/1981 Age: 31
Bats: R Throws: R Height: 5' 10'' Weight: 171
Breakout: 1% Improve: 31% Collapse: 12%
Attrition: 23% MLB: 84%

**Comparables:**
Roy McMillan, Andy Cannizaro, Craig Grebeck

| YEAR | TEAM | LVL | AGE | PA | R | 2B | 3B | HR | RBI | BB | SO | SB | CS | AVG_OBP_SLG | TAv | BABIP | BRR | FRAA | WARP |
|------|------|-----|-----|----|---|----|----|----|-----|----|----|----|----|-------------|-----|-------|-----|------|------|
| 2009 | CSP | AAA | 28 | 572 | 102 | 27 | 5 | 2 | 52 | 80 | 70 | 40 | 6 | .307/.401/.400 | .280 | .345 | 10.1 | 12.7 | 5.2 |
| 2009 | COL | MLB | 28 | 6 | 1 | 0 | 0 | 0 | 0 | 0 | 2 | 2 | 0 | .000/.000/.000 | .040 | .000 | 0.1 | 0 | -0.1 |
| 2010 | LVG | AAA | 29 | 259 | 48 | 14 | 1 | 6 | 26 | 37 | 31 | 17 | 2 | .310/.405/.469 | .286 | .330 | 3.7 | 9.6 | 3.0 |
| 2010 | TOR | MLB | 29 | 90 | 9 | 4 | 0 | 3 | 8 | 8 | 20 | 5 | 1 | .195/.267/.244 | .199 | .258 | 1.7 | 2 | -0.1 |
| 2011 | LVG | AAA | 30 | 186 | 33 | 6 | 0 | 2 | 20 | 33 | 23 | 14 | 5 | .311/.440/.392 | .287 | .358 | 0.8 | 0.4 | 1.4 |
| 2011 | TOR | MLB | 30 | 228 | 26 | 8 | 0 | 2 | 10 | 25 | 41 | 12 | 2 | .198/.291/.269 | .227 | .240 | 2 | 2.4 | 0.4 |
| 2012 | TOR | MLB | 31 | 250 | 28 | 11 | 1 | 2 | 20 | 30 | 44 | 13 | 3 | .249/.343/.344 | .250 | .295 | 0.4 | SS 6, CF 1 | 1.2 |

In 2010, McCoy played every position except first base and catcher. In 2011, he didn't play left field either, but he did pitch one (perfect) inning. On offense, though, he's a total liability. His only saving grace is his ability to draw a walk, but it doesn't do much for his OBP when he's approaching a full season's worth of major league at bats on the wrong side of the Mendoza Line. But he is a manager's dream because of his versatility: he was brought in after the beginning of the game in nearly half of his appearances. In that role, he's best able to provide a defensive upgrade when the team has a lead. As a result, there will always be one guy in the clubhouse who wants him to be the 25th man on the roster.

**Colby Rasmus** CF

Born: 8/11/1986 Age: 25
Bats: L Throws: L Height: 6' 3" Weight: 195
Breakout: 6% Improve: 37% Collapse: 1%
Attrition: 30% MLB: 92%

**Comparables:**
Carl Yastrzemski, Reggie Smith, Jim Eisenreich

| YEAR | TEAM | LVL | AGE | PA | R | 2B | 3B | HR | RBI | BB | SO | SB | CS | AVG/OBP/SLG | TAv | BABIP | BRR | FRAA | WARP |
|------|------|-----|-----|-----|----|----|----|----|-----|----|-----|----|----|-------------|------|-------|------|-----------|------|
| 2009 | SLN | MLB | 22 | 520 | 72 | 22 | 2 | 16 | 52 | 36 | 95 | 3 | 1 | .251/.307/.407 | .248 | .282 | 2.4 | 4.3 | 1.4 |
| 2010 | SLN | MLB | 23 | 534 | 85 | 28 | 3 | 23 | 66 | 63 | 148 | 12 | 8 | .276/.361/.498 | .303 | .354 | 2.4 | -18.8 | 2.3 |
| 2011 | SLN | MLB | 24 | 386 | 61 | 14 | 6 | 11 | 40 | 45 | 77 | 5 | 2 | .246/.332/.420 | .267 | .286 | 0.4 | -3.1 | 1.2 |
| 2011 | TOR | MLB | 24 | 140 | 14 | 10 | 0 | 3 | 13 | 5 | 39 | 0 | 0 | .173/.201/.316 | .188 | .217 | -0.3 | -0.6 | -0.8 |
| 2012 | TOR | MLB | 25 | 498 | 60 | 24 | 3 | 17 | 61 | 46 | 111 | 9 | 4 | .251/.322/.431 | .265 | .294 | -0.6 | CF -4, RF -0 | 1.8 |

It took a series of well-planned trades to bring Rasmus to Toronto, so it would be premature to sour on the plan after only two months. A jammed wrist landed him on the DL for a stint in

Born: 7/24/1988 Age: 23
Bats: R Throws: R Height: 6' 1" Weight: 225
Breakout: 3% Improve: 36% Collapse: 7%
Attrition: 18% MLB: 55%

**Comparables:**
Nate Schierholtz, Benny Distefano, Gus Bell

| | | | | | | | | | | | | | | | | | | | |
|------|------|-----|-----|-----|----|----|----|----|-----|----|-----|----|----|-------------|------|-------|------|-----------|------|
| 2011 | NHP | AA | 22 | 551 | 81 | 19 | 3 | 18 | 67 | 39 | 93 | 16 | 14 | .277/.342/.436 | .269 | .307 | 1.8 | 0.1 | 1.9 |
| 2012 | TOR | MLB | 23 | 250 | 27 | 11 | 1 | 6 | 26 | 13 | 50 | 4 | 3 | .246/.299/.381 | .242 | .287 | -0.5 | RF -6, CF -0 | -0.1 |

Developers of baseball video games face a constant problem. On the one hand, they want to provide the most realistic rosters possible. On the other hand, they want players to be able to play "season mode" many seasons into the future. The most common solution is to make up players and give them names made from combinations of other players' names. These fictional players, with names like "Ruben Alou," are usually pretty middling by the time they are called up. The typical one is a corner outfielder who slugs .436 in his age-22 season. If you're lucky, a guy like that might turn into a useful trade chip or a utility player. But his best function is to fill out an organizational roster for years to come.

**Travis Snider** LF

Born: 2/2/1988 Age: 24
Bats: L Throws: L Height: 6' 0" Weight: 245
Breakout: 2% Improve: 42% Collapse: 2%
Attrition: 23% MLB: 73%

**Comparables:**
Benny Ayala, Al Ferrara, Willie Horton

| YEAR | TEAM | LVL | AGE | PA | R | 2B | 3B | HR | RBI | BB | SO | SB | CS | AVG/OBP/SLG | TAv | BABIP | BRR | FRAA | WARP |
|------|------|-----|-----|-----|----|----|----|----|-----|----|----|----|----|-------------|------|-------|------|-----------|------|
| 2009 | LVG | AAA | 21 | 204 | 32 | 13 | 1 | 14 | 40 | 28 | 47 | 2 | 3 | .337/.431/.663 | .371 | .395 | -2.7 | -5.9 | 1.8 |
| 2009 | TOR | MLB | 21 | 276 | 34 | 14 | 1 | 9 | 29 | 29 | 78 | 1 | 1 | .241/.328/.419 | .267 | .316 | -1 | -2.6 | 0.3 |
| 2010 | NHP | AA | 22 | 85 | 14 | 5 | 0 | 5 | 17 | 2 | 21 | 3 | 1 | .296/.313/.543 | .273 | .345 | -0.6 | -0.3 | 0.1 |
| 2010 | TOR | MLB | 22 | 319 | 36 | 20 | 0 | 14 | 32 | 21 | 79 | 6 | 3 | .255/.304/.463 | .267 | .302 | -3.9 | -1.4 | 0.0 |
| 2011 | LVG | AAA | 23 | 277 | 47 | 22 | 2 | 4 | 42 | 25 | 44 | 12 | 1 | .327/.394/.480 | .265 | .383 | -1.3 | -0.2 | 0.4 |
| 2011 | TOR | MLB | 23 | 202 | 23 | 14 | 0 | 3 | 30 | 11 | 56 | 9 | 3 | .225/.269/.348 | .221 | .300 | 1.5 | -0.6 | -0.2 |
| 2012 | TOR | MLB | 24 | 266 | 32 | 15 | 1 | 9 | 34 | 21 | 72 | 5 | 2 | .254/.317/.440 | .266 | .320 | -0.1 | LF -4, RF -2 | 1.2 |

Snider has been tracking somewhere below the 10th percentile of performance expectations for several years running. Snider's career batting average in the majors is now 75 points below his career batting average in Triple-A. The difference is 100 points in on-base percentage and 125 in slugging percentage. There have been plenty of excuses, the latest of which is a case of wrist inflammation that kept Snider from being a September call-up. What there hasn't been, in nearly 900 major-league plate appearances, is a sustained demonstration of above average hitting ability. Manager John Farrell stated in September that Snider's problems were tied up in his timing. There is still potential here, but it's not long before Snider becomes a reminder of two great axioms of player development and tourism marketing. First, potential often goes unfulfilled. Second, what happens in Vegas, stays in Vegas.

## Mark Teahen — 3B

Born: 9/6/1981 Age: 30
Bats: L Throws: R Height: 6' 4" Weight: 210
Breakout: 1% Improve: 37% Collapse: 7%
Attrition: 15% MLB: 85%

Comparables:
Ken McMullen, Scott Brosius, Yurendell de Caster

| YEAR | TEAM | LVL | AGE | PA | R | 2B | 3B | HR | RBI | BB | SO | SB | CS | AVG_OBP_SLG | TAv | BABIP | BRR | FRAA | WARP |
|------|------|-----|-----|-----|----|----|----|----|-----|----|-----|----|----|-------------|-----|-------|------|-----------|------|
| 2009 | KCA | MLB | 27 | 571 | 69 | 34 | 1 | 12 | 50 | 37 | 123 | 8 | 1 | .271/.325/.408 | .254 | .332 | 0.8 | -8.2 | 0.0 |
| 2010 | CHA | MLB | 28 | 262 | 31 | 13 | 2 | 4 | 25 | 25 | 61 | 3 | 5 | .258/.327/.382 | .246 | .329 | -1.5 | -0.8 | -0.4 |
| 2011 | TOR | MLB | 29 | 47 | 3 | 1 | 0 | 1 | 3 | 4 | 17 | 0 | 0 | .190/.261/.286 | .230 | .292 | 0.3 | 0.4 | 0.0 |
| 2011 | CHA | MLB | 29 | 130 | 11 | 3 | 0 | 3 | 11 | 12 | 28 | 0 | 1 | .203/.277/.305 | .217 | .241 | -0.1 | 0.3 | -0.3 |
| 2012 | TOR | MLB | 30 | 250 | 28 | 13 | 2 | 5 | 26 | 21 | 56 | 2 | 1 | .255/.320/.388 | .252 | .317 | -0.3 | 3B -0, RF -0 | 1.2 |

A fun game to play with both very good and very bad seasons is to see which counting stats—ones that are usually very disparate—are close to equal. For example, in 2004, Barry Bonds had more intentional walks than RBI. Well, in 2011, Mark Teahen had approximately as many total bases as he had strikeouts (in fact, five more in his short stint with Toronto). The Blue Jays mostly took on his contract as a way to get Edwin Jackson, who in turn was a way to get Colby Rasmus. (The branch on the tree and the tree in the bog and the bog down in the valley-o!) They'll pay him $5.5 million next year whether they cut him or not, but on the plus side, his dog has over 16,000 Twitter followers.

## Eric Thames — LF

Born: 11/10/1986 Age: 25
Bats: L Throws: R Height: 6' 2" Weight: 205
Breakout: 4% Improve: 30% Collapse: 2%
Attrition: 27% MLB: 71%

Comparables:
Leon Wagner, Fernando Valenzuela Jr., Daniel Dorn

| YEAR | TEAM | LVL | AGE | PA | R | 2B | 3B | HR | RBI | BB | SO | SB | CS | AVG_OBP_SLG | TAv | BABIP | BRR | FRAA | WARP |
|------|------|-----|-----|-----|----|----|----|----|-----|----|-----|----|----|-------------|-----|-------|------|-----------|------|
| 2009 | DUN | A+ | 22 | 220 | 33 | 15 | 5 | 3 | 38 | 21 | 40 | 1 | 1 | .313/.388/.487 | .305 | .382 | -1.1 | -3.7 | 0.9 |
| 2010 | NHP | AA | 23 | 573 | 95 | 25 | 6 | 27 | 104 | 50 | 121 | 8 | 5 | .288/.373/.526 | .308 | .331 | 0 | 2.4 | 4.2 |
| 2011 | LVG | AAA | 24 | 241 | 38 | 25 | 4 | 7 | 45 | 23 | 41 | 5 | 2 | .352/.423/.610 | .321 | .406 | 0.8 | -1.7 | 1.8 |
| 2011 | TOR | MLB | 24 | 394 | 58 | 24 | 5 | 12 | 37 | 23 | 88 | 2 | 1 | .262/.313/.456 | .271 | .313 | 4.5 | 0 | 1.5 |
| 2012 | TOR | MLB | 25 | 395 | 49 | 22 | 4 | 13 | 52 | 27 | 92 | 3 | 2 | .259/.321/.451 | .270 | .311 | -0.2 | LF -4, RF -0 | 1.4 |

Thames broke out in a big way in 2011. After shellacking Triple-A pitching in the first half (save a brief, two-week stint in Toronto), Thames was called up for good on June 24 and took over in left. He has good power and middling discipline, which is par for the Blue Jays in Rogers Centre. Most importantly, Thames went from being a 24-year-old in Triple-A to a contributing young member of a solid major-league ballclub. He has a quick, powerful swing that lets him drive the ball with ease, but he will occasionally struggle against lefties. If he can hold off Travis Snider in the spring, the left field job will be his to lose this year. Thames is the anti-Snider: he's already realized his potential, but his ceiling remains lower.

## Luis Valbuena — 2B

Born: 11/30/1985 Age: 26
Bats: L Throws: R Height: 5' 11" Weight: 200
Breakout: 3% Improve: 33% Collapse: 8%
Attrition: 27% MLB: 76%

Comparables:
Joe Millette, Ted Kubiak, Ramon Castro

| YEAR | TEAM | LVL | AGE | PA | R | 2B | 3B | HR | RBI | BB | SO | SB | CS | AVG_OBP_SLG | TAv | BABIP | BRR | FRAA | WARP |
|------|------|-----|-----|-----|----|----|----|----|-----|----|-----|----|----|-------------|-----|-------|------|-----------|------|
| 2009 | COH | AAA | 23 | 95 | 15 | 4 | 2 | 3 | 13 | 16 | 13 | 3 | 3 | .321/.432/.538 | .327 | .349 | -1.8 | -1 | 0.6 |
| 2009 | CLE | MLB | 23 | 398 | 52 | 25 | 3 | 10 | 31 | 26 | 83 | 2 | 3 | .250/.298/.416 | .253 | .296 | 0.7 | 0.9 | 0.9 |
| 2010 | COH | AAA | 24 | 119 | 23 | 8 | 1 | 6 | 20 | 19 | 21 | 2 | 0 | .312/.424/.604 | .331 | .338 | 0.6 | -0.7 | 1.3 |
| 2010 | CLE | MLB | 24 | 310 | 22 | 12 | 0 | 2 | 24 | 28 | 61 | 1 | 2 | .193/.273/.258 | .203 | .238 | -1.4 | 2.3 | -0.8 |
| 2011 | COH | AAA | 25 | 472 | 64 | 22 | 0 | 17 | 75 | 46 | 96 | 6 | 3 | .302/.372/.476 | .269 | .355 | -2.2 | -6.8 | 1.4 |
| 2011 | CLE | MLB | 25 | 44 | 4 | 0 | 0 | 1 | 1 | 1 | 9 | 1 | 0 | .209/.227/.279 | .182 | .242 | 0.4 | -0.9 | -0.3 |
| 2012 | TOR | MLB | 26 | 250 | 28 | 12 | 1 | 5 | 26 | 21 | 50 | 3 | 2 | .250/.315/.385 | .249 | .295 | -0.3 | 2B -1, SS -2 | 1.1 |

Best friends with Asdrubal Cabrera in the minors, Valbuena has followed a vastly different career path. While the stocky infielder has the potential to be a major league regular and has more than proven himself at Triple-A, he has been abysmal every time he has gotten the call to the bigs. The Indians didn't believe he was overmatched against major league pitching, but the Blue Jays believe he can be a quality hitter. The poor performance could just be a matter of pressing or the lack of consistent at-bats.

## Dewayne Wise — CF

Born: 2/24/1978 Age: 34
Bats: L Throws: L Height: 6' 2" Weight: 180
Breakout: 3% Improve: 29% Collapse: 10%
Attrition: 22% MLB: 88%

Comparables:
Roberto Kelly, Devon White, Claudell Washington

| YEAR | TEAM | LVL | AGE | PA | R | 2B | 3B | HR | RBI | BB | SO | SB | CS | AVG_OBP_SLG | TAv | BABIP | BRR | FRAA | WARP |
|------|------|-----|-----|-----|----|----|----|----|-----|----|-----|----|----|-------------|-----|-------|------|-----------|------|
| 2009 | CHA | MLB | 31 | 153 | 17 | 8 | 3 | 2 | 11 | 3 | 27 | 4 | 5 | .225/.262/.366 | .220 | .265 | 0.7 | 0.9 | 0.0 |
| 2010 | LEH | AAA | 32 | 146 | 17 | 11 | 5 | 4 | 13 | 8 | 27 | 2 | 2 | .270/.315/.511 | .272 | .311 | -1 | 1.4 | 0.8 |
| 2010 | TOR | MLB | 32 | 118 | 20 | 3 | 2 | 3 | 14 | 4 | 29 | 4 | 0 | .250/.282/.393 | .225 | .312 | 1.3 | 0.6 | 0.4 |
| 2011 | LVG | AAA | 33 | 144 | 28 | 10 | 3 | 4 | 19 | 6 | 21 | 8 | 3 | .338/.382/.549 | .299 | .376 | 0.7 | 1.2 | 1.3 |
| 2011 | FLO | MLB | 33 | 72 | 6 | 2 | 0 | 0 | 5 | 3 | 21 | 4 | 2 | .239/.278/.269 | .214 | .340 | -0.2 | 1.8 | 0.0 |
| 2011 | TOR | MLB | 33 | 32 | 4 | 0 | 1 | 2 | 2 | 0 | 15 | 2 | 0 | .125/.125/.375 | .173 | .133 | 0.3 | 0.4 | 0.0 |
| 2012 | NYA | MLB | 34 | 250 | 27 | 11 | 3 | 7 | 29 | 12 | 59 | 10 | 4 | .241/.287/.401 | .240 | .289 | -0.3 | CF 7, RF -1 | 0.2 |

As you read this chapter, you may notice references to the hitter-friendly environment at Triple-A Las Vegas. You may wonder if the extreme skepticism that environment engenders is warranted. Well, consider this: when the Blue Jays re-signed Wise, they sent him to Las Vegas. In 31 games, he had a .338/.382/.549 line with 17 extra base hits. That performance got him cut, and then he caught on with the Marlins, for whom he posted a .217 TAv. His value to the Blue Jays was mostly as a pinch runner and late game defensive replacement. But his value to you is as a human park factor.

**Chris Woodward** SS
Born: 6/27/1976 Age: 36
Bats: R Throws: R Height: 6' 1" Weight: 160
Breakout: 7% Improve: 23% Collapse: 10%
Attrition: 32% MLB: 71%

Comparables:
Dave Concepcion, Chris Speier, Mike Bordick

| YEAR | TEAM | LVL | AGE | PA | R | 2B | 3B | HR | RBI | BB | SO | SB | CS | AVG_OBP_SLG | TAv | BABIP | BRR | FRAA | WARP |
|------|------|-----|-----|-----|----|----|----|----|-----|----|----|----|----|----------------|------|-------|------|------|------|
| 2009 | TAC | AAA | 33 | 197 | 24 | 12 | 1 | 1 | 15 | 19 | 30 | 4 | 0 | .299/.367/.397 | .271 | .352 | 2.2 | 7.6 | 1.6 |
| 2009 | BOS | MLB | 33 | 16 | 0 | 0 | 0 | 0 | 0 | 2 | 4 | 0 | 0 | .083/.312/.083 | .226 | .125 | -0.2 | -0.1 | 0.0 |
| 2009 | SEA | MLB | 33 | 74 | 7 | 1 | 0 | 0 | 5 | 5 | 15 | 1 | 0 | .239/.288/.254 | .218 | .302 | 0.7 | 1.6 | 0.2 |
| 2010 | TAC | AAA | 34 | 453 | 49 | 17 | 2 | 6 | 35 | 40 | 73 | 4 | 1 | .232/.300/.329 | .233 | .264 | 0.8 | -0.3 | 0.4 |
| 2010 | SEA | MLB | 34 | 22 | 0 | 1 | 0 | 0 | 0 | 3 | 9 | 0 | 0 | .158/.273/.211 | .185 | .300 | -0.5 | -0.9 | -0.2 |
| 2011 | LVG | AAA | 35 | 469 | 67 | 32 | 2 | 13 | 65 | 39 | 70 | 4 | 2 | .296/.353/.474 | .272 | .325 | -1.2 | -4.4 | 1.4 |
| 2011 | TOR | MLB | 35 | 10 | 3 | 0 | 0 | 0 | 0 | 0 | 4 | 0 | 0 | .000/.000/.000 | .008 | .000 | 0 | 0 | -0.2 |
| 2012 | TOR | MLB | 36 | 250 | 23 | 11 | 1 | 2 | 19 | 18 | 53 | 2 | 1 | .218/.277/.304 | .210 | .249 | 0 | 55.0 2B | -0.7 |

# PITCHERS

**Henderson Alvarez**
Born: 4/18/1990 Age: 22
Bats: R Throws: R Height: 6' 2" Weight: 195
Breakout: 26% Improve: 60% Collapse: 21%
Attrition: 14% MLB: 88%

Comparables:
Sidney Ponson, Sean O'Sullivan, Tommy Hunter

| YEAR | TEAM | LVL | AGE | W | L | SV | G | GS | IP | H | HR | BB | SO | EqBB9 | EqSO9 | GB% | BABIP | WHIP | ERA | FIP | FRA | WARP |
|------|------|-----|-----|---|---|----|----|----|------|-----|----|----|----|-------|-------|-----|-------|------|------|------|------|------|
| 2009 | LNS | A | 19 | 9 | 6 | 0 | 23 | 23 | 124¹ | 121 | 1 | 19 | 92 | 1.4 | 6.7 | 53% | .305 | 1.13 | 3.48 | 2.84 | 3.92 | 2.0 |
| 2010 | DUN | A+ | 20 | 8 | 6 | 0 | 23 | 21 | 112¹ | 114 | 7 | 23 | 62 | 2.2 | 6.3 | 52% | .336 | 1.46 | 4.33 | 4.01 | 5.47 | 0.1 |
| 2011 | NHP | AA | 21 | 8 | 4 | 0 | 15 | 14 | 88 | 81 | 7 | 17 | 66 | 1.7 | 6.8 | 54% | .286 | 1.11 | 2.86 | 3.66 | 4.28 | 1.1 |
| 2011 | TOR | MLB | 21 | 1 | 3 | 0 | 10 | 10 | 63² | 64 | 8 | 8 | 40 | 1.1 | 5.7 | 55% | .283 | 1.13 | 3.53 | 4.00 | 4.34 | 0.6 |
| 2012 | TOR | MLB | 22 | 4 | 5 | 0 | 13 | 13 | 72 | 87 | 10 | 22 | 36 | 2.7 | 4.5 | 50% | .312 | 1.52 | 5.47 | 4.93 | 5.95 | -0.5 |

The Venezuelan righty was probably the biggest gainer in an impressive year for the Blue Jays farm system. Seen prior to the season as a live arm with little to show for it, he went from High-A to the majors in less than 100 innings—even after he lost a month to injury. Alvarez sits in the mid-90s with his fastball (which has electric late movement), generates plenty of ground balls, and has an advanced changeup. His best start of the season was a 97-pitch, eight-inning outing against the Orioles. He allowed just three hits and no walks while recording five strikeouts and 18 ground balls. He'll be slotted into the back end of the rotation next year, but his ceiling is considerably higher than that.

**Chad Beck**
Born: 1/17/1985 Age: 27
Bats: R Throws: R Height: 6' 5" Weight: 245
Breakout: 28% Improve: 53% Collapse: 23%
Attrition: 32% MLB: 73%

Comparables:
Dick Tidrow, Beltran Perez, Bryan Eversgerd

| YEAR | TEAM | LVL | AGE | W | L | SV | G | GS | IP | H | HR | BB | SO | EqBB9 | EqSO9 | GB% | BABIP | WHIP | ERA | FIP | FRA | WARP |
|------|------|-----|-----|---|---|----|----|----|------|-----|----|----|----|-------|-------|-----|-------|------|------|------|------|------|
| 2009 | LNS | A | 24 | 6 | 8 | 0 | 20 | 20 | 110² | 135 | 10 | 29 | 85 | 2.4 | 6.9 | 38% | .343 | 1.48 | 5.93 | 4.28 | 4.31 | 1.7 |
| 2010 | DUN | A+ | 25 | 3 | 6 | 0 | 41 | 11 | 101¹ | 77 | 4 | 23 | 58 | 2.7 | 7.0 | 48% | .293 | 1.26 | 3.72 | 3.58 | 4.37 | 1.2 |
| 2011 | NHP | AA | 26 | 7 | 4 | 0 | 22 | 14 | 95 | 92 | 7 | 28 | 70 | 2.7 | 6.6 | 43% | .299 | 1.26 | 3.69 | 3.88 | 3.93 | 1.5 |
| 2011 | LVG | AAA | 26 | 0 | 3 | 0 | 8 | 8 | 41² | 61 | 7 | 26 | 23 | 5.6 | 5.0 | 35% | .358 | 2.09 | 6.70 | 6.83 | 6.38 | -0.1 |
| 2011 | TOR | MLB | 26 | 0 | 0 | 0 | 3 | 0 | 2¹ | 1 | 0 | 0 | 3 | 0.0 | 11.6 | 40% | .200 | 0.43 | 0.00 | 0.49 | 0.50 | 0.1 |
| 2012 | TOR | MLB | 27 | 2 | 2 | 0 | 11 | 5 | 36¹ | 44 | 5 | 16 | 20 | 4.1 | 5.0 | 40% | .312 | 1.66 | 5.94 | 5.21 | 6.46 | -0.4 |

Beck spent most of the year in Double-A, where he mostly benefited from the pitcher-friendly home run park factor in New Hampshire. Yes, he still needs polish. He is big and throws hard but doesn't strike many batters out. More important, though, is his price tag. He can be a cheap bullpen arm. He came to Toronto in a deal that sent David Eckstein packing. In his second major league appearance, Beck struck out Vernon Wells looking. To put it a slightly different way: Beck represents the new way of doing things in Toronto.

**Shawn Camp**

Born: 11/18/1975 Age: 36
Bats: R Throws: R Height: 6' 2" Weight: 200
Breakout: 27% Improve: 48% Collapse: 33%
Attrition: 12% MLB: 81%

Comparables:
Larry Andersen, Jeff Montgomery, Joe Hoerner

| YEAR | TEAM | LVL | AGE | W | L | SV | G | GS | IP | H | HR | BB | SO | EqBB9 | EqSO9 | GB% | BABIP | WHIP | ERA | FIP | FRA | WARP |
|------|------|-----|-----|---|---|----|----|----|------|----|----|----|----|-------|-------|-----|-------|------|------|------|------|------|
| 2009 | TOR | MLB | 33 | 2 | 6 | 1 | 59 | 0 | 79² | 73 | 7 | 29 | 58 | 3.3 | 6.6 | 56% | .282 | 1.28 | 3.50 | 4.07 | 5.36 | 0.2 |
| 2010 | TOR | MLB | 34 | 4 | 3 | 2 | 70 | 0 | 72¹ | 71 | 8 | 18 | 46 | 2.2 | 5.7 | 52% | .284 | 1.23 | 2.99 | 4.13 | 4.94 | 0.0 |
| 2011 | TOR | MLB | 35 | 6 | 3 | 1 | 67 | 0 | 66¹ | 79 | 3 | 22 | 32 | 3.0 | 4.3 | 55% | .335 | 1.52 | 4.21 | 3.95 | 5.25 | 0.0 |
| 2012 | TOR | MLB | 36 | 3 | 1 | 1 | 58 | 0 | 59¹ | 64 | 7 | 19 | 42 | 2.9 | 6.5 | 53% | .315 | 1.40 | 4.59 | 4.28 | 4.99 | 0.1 |

Imagine you set out on an eight-year major-league career in which your primary goal was to be the most forgettable player possible. First, you'd want to play for multiple teams, none of them with especially high national visibility—let's say the Royals, the antepennant Devil Rays, and the Blue Jays. Of course, you'd be a reliever whose fastball tops out in the high-80s and who relies heavily on off-speed stuff. You'd want to suffer a drop off in performance, mostly due to fewer strikeouts, just before your first shot at free agency. The resilience of the market for soft-tossing righties never ceases to amaze, and you could soldier on with another flyover team. The Astros, perhaps, or the Pirates?

**Joel Carreno**

Born: 3/7/1987 Age: 25
Bats: R Throws: R Height: 6' 1" Weight: 190
Breakout: 37% Improve: 64% Collapse: 12%
Attrition: 11% MLB: 90%

Comparables:
Brad Mills, Pete Cimino, Jason Bergmann

| YEAR | TEAM | LVL | AGE | W | L | SV | G | GS | IP | H | HR | BB | SO | EqBB9 | EqSO9 | GB% | BABIP | WHIP | ERA | FIP | FRA | WARP |
|------|------|-----|-----|---|---|----|----|----|------|-----|----|----|-----|-------|-------|-----|-------|------|------|------|------|------|
| 2009 | LNS | A | 22 | 2 | 4 | 0 | 14 | 14 | 79² | 76 | 5 | 29 | 62 | 3.3 | 7.0 | 44% | .302 | 1.32 | 3.61 | 4.01 | 4.92 | 0.4 |
| 2010 | DUN | A+ | 23 | 9 | 7 | 0 | 27 | 25 | 137² | 126 | 6 | 23 | 149 | 2.0 | 11.3 | 42% | .395 | 1.29 | 3.73 | 2.63 | 3.55 | 3.2 |
| 2011 | NHP | AA | 24 | 7 | 9 | 0 | 24 | 23 | 134² | 99 | 12 | 67 | 150 | 4.5 | 10.2 | 37% | .279 | 1.25 | 3.41 | 4.08 | 4.38 | 1.6 |
| 2011 | TOR | MLB | 24 | 1 | 0 | 0 | 11 | 0 | 15² | 11 | 1 | 4 | 14 | 2.3 | 8.0 | 54% | .250 | 0.96 | 1.15 | 2.87 | 3.43 | 0.3 |
| 2012 | TOR | MLB | 25 | 3 | 3 | 0 | 9 | 9 | 50² | 54 | 7 | 24 | 42 | 4.3 | 7.5 | 40% | .314 | 1.55 | 5.13 | 4.76 | 5.58 | -0.1 |

He is old for his level and he walks too many batters. He doesn't get much recognition on top prospect lists. But wait until you see the breaking ball. It's a late-breaker that clocks in at about 80 mph and tails away from left-ies. With an off-speed option like his, you can hardly blame Carreno for throwing it too often. But his breaking ball, like most, requires a fastball to set it up as an out pitch, and Carreno's fastball is not a finished product. He's on the bubble between the bullpen and the rotation, but he should be a useful piece of the staff in 2012.

**Brett Cecil**

Born: 7/2/1986 Age: 25
Bats: R Throws: L Height: 6' 3" Weight: 225
Breakout: 24% Improve: 66% Collapse: 8%
Attrition: 8% MLB: 95%

Comparables:
Scott Baker, Johnny Cueto, Reggie Cleveland

| YEAR | TEAM | LVL | AGE | W | L | SV | G | GS | IP | H | HR | BB | SO | EqBB9 | EqSO9 | GB% | BABIP | WHIP | ERA | FIP | FRA | WARP |
|------|------|-----|-----|----|----|----|----|----|------|-----|----|----|-----|-------|-------|-----|-------|------|------|------|------|------|
| 2009 | LVG | AAA | 23 | 1 | 5 | 0 | 9 | 9 | 49 | 53 | 2 | 19 | 32 | 3.5 | 5.9 | 61% | .317 | 1.47 | 5.69 | 4.02 | 5.45 | 0.1 |
| 2009 | TOR | MLB | 23 | 7 | 4 | 0 | 18 | 17 | 93¹ | 116 | 17 | 38 | 69 | 3.7 | 6.7 | 43% | .338 | 1.65 | 5.30 | 5.42 | 5.51 | 0.4 |
| 2010 | TOR | MLB | 24 | 15 | 7 | 0 | 28 | 28 | 172² | 175 | 18 | 54 | 117 | 2.8 | 6.1 | 44% | .293 | 1.33 | 4.22 | 4.00 | 4.60 | 1.3 |
| 2011 | LVG | AAA | 25 | 5 | 2 | 0 | 12 | 12 | 78² | 89 | 15 | 24 | 63 | 2.7 | 7.2 | 43% | .310 | 1.44 | 5.26 | 5.53 | 5.88 | 0.6 |
| 2011 | TOR | MLB | 25 | 4 | 11 | 0 | 20 | 20 | 123² | 122 | 22 | 42 | 87 | 3.1 | 6.3 | 40% | .269 | 1.33 | 4.73 | 5.13 | 5.14 | 0.2 |
| 2012 | TOR | MLB | 25 | 8 | 8 | 0 | 22 | 22 | 136² | 144 | 19 | 46 | 102 | 3.0 | 6.8 | 50% | .303 | 1.39 | 4.57 | 4.53 | 4.97 | 0.4 |

After almost 400 innings from a guy who is now 25, you start to wonder if this is it: ERA just a notch above league average and middling peripherals. At least Cecil is left-handed. He had a strange reverse split in 2011 that can be chalked up to noise. But more worrisome is the fact that his groundball and home-run rates took a turn for the worse. He also lost velocity from his fastball and his best offering, a slider. Last year, Cecil had a handful of starts in which the fastball didn't even crack 90. That didn't happen once in 2010. He's still a worthwhile starter, but he is looking more like a back-of-the-rotation type than a go-to guy.

**Jesse Chavez**

Born: 8/21/1983 Age: 28
Bats: R Throws: R Height: 6' 3" Weight: 175
Breakout: 13% Improve: 68% Collapse: 16%
Attrition: 17% MLB: 84%

Comparables:
Dave Bush, Jason Hammel, Jeremy Bonderman

| YEAR | TEAM | LVL | AGE | W | L | SV | G | GS | IP | H | HR | BB | SO | EqBB9 | EqSO9 | GB% | BABIP | WHIP | ERA | FIP | FRA | WARP |
|------|------|-----|-----|---|---|----|----|----|------|----|----|----|----|-------|-------|-----|-------|------|-------|------|-------|------|
| 2009 | PIT | MLB | 25 | 1 | 4 | 0 | 73 | 0 | 67¹ | 69 | 11 | 22 | 47 | 2.9 | 6.3 | 39% | .284 | 1.35 | 4.01 | 4.81 | 5.79 | -0.4 |
| 2010 | KCA | MLB | 26 | 2 | 3 | 0 | 23 | 0 | 26 | 29 | 5 | 11 | 16 | 3.8 | 5.5 | 41% | .286 | 1.54 | 5.88 | 5.59 | 5.12 | 0.0 |
| 2010 | ATL | MLB | 26 | 3 | 2 | 0 | 28 | 0 | 36² | 40 | 6 | 12 | 29 | 2.9 | 7.1 | 31% | .306 | 1.42 | 5.89 | 4.72 | 4.51 | 0.2 |
| 2011 | OMA | AAA | 27 | 2 | 2 | 16 | 45 | 0 | 57² | 63 | 6 | 16 | 54 | 2.5 | 8.4 | 52% | .341 | 1.37 | 3.75 | 4.05 | 4.99 | 0.3 |
| 2011 | KCA | MLB | 27 | 0 | 0 | 0 | 4 | 0 | 7² | 12 | 3 | 5 | 8 | 5.9 | 9.4 | 58% | .391 | 2.22 | 10.57 | 8.02 | 10.23 | -0.4 |
| 2012 | TOR | MLB | 28 | 1 | 0 | 0 | 24 | 0 | 31 | 34 | 4 | 10 | 23 | 2.9 | 6.8 | 41% | .306 | 1.41 | 4.58 | 4.37 | 4.98 | 0.1 |

Chavez tagged along in the deal that netted the Royals Tim Collins in exchange for Kyle Farnsworth and Rick Ankiel at the 2010 trade deadline. The Royals have this habit of stashing fringe pitchers in Triple-A; the guys pitch moderately well there, then crash and burn when promoted to the big club. Chavez appeared in just four games for the Royals, but the carnage that ensued convinced the KC decision-makers not to try that again. They put him on the waiver wire and his sixth organization, the Blue Jays, snagged him. In December he was outrighted to Triple-A.

### Kyle Davies

Born: 9/9/1983 Age: 28
Bats: R Throws: R Height: 6' 3" Weight: 205
Breakout: 19% Improve: 51% Collapse: 27%
Attrition: 23% MLB: 83%

Comparables:
Chad Reineke, Ken Forsch, Frank Smith

| YEAR | TEAM | LVL | AGE | W | L | SV | G | GS | IP | H | HR | BB | SO | EqBB9 | EqSO9 | GB% | BABIP | WHIP | ERA | FIP | FRA | WARP |
|---|---|---|---|---|---|---|---|---|---|---|---|---|---|---|---|---|---|---|---|---|---|---|
| 2009 | OMA | AAA | 25 | 4 | 2 | 0 | 8 | 8 | 46¹ | 47 | 3 | 14 | 44 | 2.7 | 8.6 | 45% | .331 | 1.32 | 2.14 | 3.30 | 3.59 | 0.8 |
| 2009 | KCA | MLB | 25 | 8 | 9 | 0 | 22 | 22 | 123 | 122 | 18 | 66 | 86 | 4.8 | 6.3 | 44% | .288 | 1.53 | 5.27 | 5.35 | 5.99 | -0.1 |
| 2010 | KCA | MLB | 26 | 8 | 12 | 0 | 32 | 32 | 183² | 206 | 20 | 80 | 126 | 3.9 | 6.2 | 41% | .317 | 1.56 | 5.34 | 4.43 | 4.56 | 1.8 |
| 2011 | KCA | MLB | 27 | 1 | 9 | 0 | 13 | 13 | 61¹ | 84 | 7 | 26 | 50 | 3.8 | 7.3 | 41% | .381 | 1.79 | 6.75 | 4.43 | 4.92 | 0.5 |
| 2012 | TOR | MLB | 28 | 5 | 5 | 0 | 15 | 15 | 82¹ | 91 | 10 | 35 | 58 | 3.8 | 6.4 | 42% | .314 | 1.53 | 4.97 | 4.65 | 5.40 | -0.0 |

Kyle Davies is probably not the worst starting pitcher of the last four years. But he is close. Of the 152 starting pitchers with at least 300 innings pitched over that period, he had the 6th worst ERA, 10th worst K/BB, 16th worst strikeout rate, and 26th worst hit rate. Two of the pitchers with worse ERAs, however, are his former teammates Brian Bannister and Luke Hochevar. Just goes to show the importance of the company you keep.

### Kyle Drabek

| YEAR | TEAM | LVL | AGE | W | L | SV | G | GS | IP | H | HR | BB | SO | EqBB9 | EqSO9 | GB% | BABIP | WHIP | ERA | FIP | FRA | WARP |
|---|---|---|---|---|---|---|---|---|---|---|---|---|---|---|---|---|---|---|---|---|---|---|

It's not that there is no such thing as a pitching prospect. There is, and Drabek was one of them. It's that the twin specters of health risk and performance uncertainty hover over them like vultures in the Las Vegas desert. It's that pitching prospects usually don't turn into great pitchers, and even the ones who do often suffer years of bumpy performance along the way. Drabek was beset by poor performance and minor injuries all season and the result was an unmitigated disaster. The crucible of big league hitters will always expose the straight fastball of the unprepared, and Drabek's low strikeout rates foretold trouble. With expectations reduced and an offseason to recover his groove, Drabek has a shot to regain his composure and his control.

### Alan Farina

Born: 8/9/1986 Age: 25
Bats: R Throws: R Height: 6' 0" Weight: 190
Breakout: 33% Improve: 50% Collapse: 26%
Attrition: 23% MLB: 88%

Comparables:
Wayne Twitchell, Pete Cimino, Dave Boswell

| YEAR | TEAM | LVL | AGE | W | L | SV | G | GS | IP | H | HR | BB | SO | EqBB9 | EqSO9 | GB% | BABIP | WHIP | ERA | FIP | FRA | WARP |
|---|---|---|---|---|---|---|---|---|---|---|---|---|---|---|---|---|---|---|---|---|---|---|
| 2009 | DUN | A+ | 22 | 1 | 3 | 5 | 27 | 2 | 37¹ | 47 | 4 | 24 | 34 | 5.8 | 8.2 | 38% | .374 | 1.90 | 6.51 | 4.78 | 5.92 | -0.1 |
| 2010 | DUN | A+ | 23 | 2 | 1 | 2 | 32 | 0 | 36¹ | 17 | 0 | 8 | 38 | 2.7 | 11.4 | 54% | .288 | 0.83 | 1.24 | 2.10 | 3.54 | 0.6 |
| 2012 | TOR | MLB | 25 | 0 | 0 | 0 | 7 | 0 | 7¹ | 7 | 1 | 4 | 7 | 5.2 | 8.0 | 40% | .309 | 1.58 | 4.98 | 4.70 | 5.41 | -0.0 |

A 5-11 juco/Clemson reliever who racks up strikeouts, Farina went on the DL in late May and never came back. He had Tommy John surgery in July and is unlikely to appear in a game before May. That's a shame because, before going down, he was excellent closing in Double-A: he stranded all but one of his base runners and posted another microscopic ERA. If he can stay healthy, he can be a useful part of the bullpen picture. If not, he'll be another datapoint in the raging battle about the effectiveness of shorter pitchers who throw hard.

### Danny Farquhar

Born: 2/17/1987 Age: 25
Bats: R Throws: R Height: 6' 0" Weight: 180
Breakout: 26% Improve: 60% Collapse: 15%
Attrition: 10% MLB: 91%

Comparables:
Steve Bedrosian, Chan Ho Park, Al Downing

| YEAR | TEAM | LVL | AGE | W | L | SV | G | GS | IP | H | HR | BB | SO | EqBB9 | EqSO9 | GB% | BABIP | WHIP | ERA | FIP | FRA | WARP |
|---|---|---|---|---|---|---|---|---|---|---|---|---|---|---|---|---|---|---|---|---|---|---|
| 2009 | NHP | AA | 22 | 1 | 3 | 15 | 37 | 0 | 45² | 31 | 1 | 30 | 51 | 5.9 | 10.0 | 51% | .270 | 1.33 | 2.36 | 3.49 | 3.49 | 0.8 |
| 2010 | NHP | AA | 23 | 4 | 3 | 17 | 53 | 0 | 76² | 38 | 5 | 28 | 47 | 4.9 | 9.3 | 45% | .254 | 1.20 | 3.52 | 4.55 | 4.94 | 0.3 |
| 2011 | LVG | AAA | 24 | 1 | 2 | 14 | 50 | 0 | 51² | 63 | 4 | 18 | 43 | 3.1 | 7.5 | 52% | .360 | 1.57 | 4.70 | 4.36 | 5.16 | 0.6 |
| 2011 | TOR | MLB | 24 | 0 | 0 | 0 | 3 | 0 | 2. | 4 | 0 | 2 | 1 | 9.0 | 4.5 | 25% | .500 | 3.00 | 13.50 | 5.06 | 9.41 | -0.1 |
| 2012 | TOR | MLB | 25 | 1 | 0 | 0 | 18 | 0 | 23 | 22 | 2 | 12 | 20 | 4.7 | 7.9 | 51% | .299 | 1.48 | 4.52 | 4.16 | 4.92 | 0.1 |

"Lord" Farquhar was traded back and forth between Toronto and Oakland twice in six months. In November 2010, he went to Oakland in the Rajai Davis deal. By mid-April, he was back in Toronto in return for David Purcey. His first taste of Triple-A exposed some of his weaknesses as a future closer candidate: he doesn't overpower hitters despite his mid-90s velocity, and his control has been his biggest professional hurdle. Like Chad Beck, he's a viable bullpen candidate and a graduate of the University of Louisiana-Lafayette (go Ragin' Cajuns!). Farquhar has the edge in velocity but not size, but he uses three arm angles (including a true sidearm) to confuse batters.

### Jason Frasor

Born: 8/9/1977 Age: 34
Bats: R Throws: R Height: 5' 11" Weight: 170
Breakout: 12% Improve: 27% Collapse: 46%
Attrition: 6% MLB: 97%

Comparables:
Armando Benitez, Brendan Donnelly, Mike Jackson

| YEAR | TEAM | LVL | AGE | W | L | SV | G | GS | IP | H | HR | BB | SO | EqBB9 | EqSO9 | GB% | BABIP | WHIP | ERA | FIP | FRA | WARP |
|---|---|---|---|---|---|---|---|---|---|---|---|---|---|---|---|---|---|---|---|---|---|---|
| 2009 | TOR | MLB | 31 | 7 | 3 | 11 | 61 | 0 | 57² | 43 | 4 | 16 | 56 | 2.5 | 8.7 | 39% | .264 | 1.02 | 2.50 | 3.04 | 3.79 | 1.1 |
| 2010 | TOR | MLB | 32 | 3 | 4 | 4 | 69 | 0 | 63² | 61 | 4 | 27 | 65 | 3.8 | 9.2 | 47% | .320 | 1.38 | 3.68 | 3.28 | 3.99 | 0.9 |
| 2011 | CHA | MLB | 33 | 1 | 2 | 0 | 20 | 0 | 17² | 20 | 3 | 11 | 20 | 5.6 | 10.2 | 35% | .354 | 1.75 | 5.09 | 5.04 | 4.58 | 0.1 |
| 2011 | TOR | MLB | 33 | 2 | 1 | 0 | 44 | 0 | 42¹ | 38 | 4 | 15 | 37 | 3.2 | 7.9 | 41% | .288 | 1.25 | 2.98 | 3.75 | 5.17 | 0.1 |
| 2012 | TOR | MLB | 34 | 3 | 1 | 1 | 58 | 0 | 53² | 49 | 5 | 22 | 53 | 3.7 | 8.9 | 43% | .296 | 1.32 | 3.75 | 3.67 | 4.08 | 0.7 |

A perfectly serviceable middle reliever whose career has been most notable for several desultory and unsatisfying flings with the Toronto closer job, Frasor was packaged off to Chicago in the Edwin Jackson trade. The White Sox wanted him to bring stability and depth to the pen, but after a nondescript second half he was shipped back to the Blue Jays for two minor leaguers. Frasor can dominate right-handed hitters. He whips surprising heat out of his slight frame, while mixing in a slider and a fosh, the unique changeup he learned in an attempt to have something else to show lefties after determining his hand was too small for a standard split-finger grip. That trick didn't last, however, as lefties have reached base against Frasor at a .356 clip over the last three seasons, undermining his chances to be much more than a low-leverage sponge and occasional ROOGY.

### Jim Hoey

Born: 12/30/1982 Age: 29
Bats: R Throws: R Height: 6' 7" Weight: 200
Breakout: 35% Improve: 52% Collapse: 20%
Attrition: 22% MLB: 74%

Comparables:
Rocky Cherry, Jim Mecir, Tyler Yates

| YEAR | TEAM | LVL | AGE | W | L | SV | G | GS | IP | H | HR | BB | SO | EqBB9 | EqSO9 | GB% | BABIP | WHIP | ERA | FIP | FRA | WARP |
|---|---|---|---|---|---|---|---|---|---|---|---|---|---|---|---|---|---|---|---|---|---|---|
| 2009 | BOW | AA | 26 | 2 | 6 | 0 | 36 | 0 | 48 | 48 | 4 | 32 | 47 | 6.0 | 8.8 | 35% | .344 | 1.67 | 4.50 | 4.33 | 4.77 | 0.1 |
| 2010 | BOW | AA | 27 | 2 | 0 | 0 | 24 | 0 | 31¹ | 16 | 1 | 13 | 25 | 4.9 | 10.9 | 43% | .294 | 1.37 | 3.16 | 3.66 | 3.69 | 0.5 |
| 2010 | NOR | AAA | 27 | 4 | 0 | 0 | 18 | 0 | 21¹ | 7 | 0 | 12 | 23 | 7.2 | 13.5 | 43% | .233 | 1.31 | 3.38 | 3.48 | 4.50 | 0.2 |
| 2011 | ROC | AAA | 28 | 0 | 2 | 9 | 33 | 0 | 42¹ | 32 | 6 | 21 | 38 | 4.5 | 8.1 | 55% | .241 | 1.25 | 3.83 | 4.84 | 5.69 | 0.1 |
| 2011 | MIN | MLB | 28 | 1 | 2 | 0 | 26 | 0 | 24² | 34 | 4 | 13 | 14 | 4.7 | 5.1 | 45% | .345 | 1.91 | 5.47 | 5.62 | 7.63 | -0.7 |
| 2012 | TOR | MLB | 29 | 1 | 0 | 0 | 25 | 0 | 29 | 30 | 4 | 15 | 24 | 4.7 | 7.5 | 44% | .306 | 1.54 | 4.82 | 4.89 | 5.24 | -0.0 |

In the annals of Things That Left Egg on the 2011 Twins' Collective Face, the trade that sent J.J Hardy, Brendan Harris, and $500,000 to Baltimore for Hoey and Brett Jacobson rates as a novelty-sized omelet. Hardy had a strong 4.4-WARP season for the Orioles while the Twins got sub-replacement level performances both from their shortstops and from Hoey. While he showed off high-90s heat in his first major league appearances since 2007, his control was subpar and he had a hard time keeping the ball in the park. So, for dumping less than $6 million salary, the Twins got pure organizational fodder, a guy who ranked as one of the International League's less dominating closers, and a guy who was claimed on waivers by the Blue Jays in mid-December.

### Drew Hutchison

Born: 8/22/1990 Age: 21
Bats: L Throws: R Height: 6' 3" Weight: 165
Breakout: 30% Improve: 56% Collapse: 14%
Attrition: 7% MLB: 93%

Comparables:
Frank Tanana, Rick Ankiel, Clayton Kershaw

| YEAR | TEAM | LVL | AGE | W | L | SV | G | GS | IP | H | HR | BB | SO | EqBB9 | EqSO9 | GB% | BABIP | WHIP | ERA | FIP | FRA | WARP |
|---|---|---|---|---|---|---|---|---|---|---|---|---|---|---|---|---|---|---|---|---|---|---|
| 2011 | LNS | A | 20 | 6 | 2 | 0 | 14 | 14 | 72 | 68 | 1 | 19 | 84 | 2.4 | 10.5 | 52% | .345 | 1.21 | 2.62 | 2.12 | 3.62 | 1.7 |
| 2011 | DUN | A+ | 20 | 2 | 2 | 0 | 11 | 10 | 62¹ | 42 | 3 | 14 | 66 | 2.0 | 9.5 | 54% | .260 | 0.90 | 2.74 | 2.77 | 3.43 | 1.5 |
| 2012 | TOR | MLB | 21 | 2 | 2 | 0 | 7 | 7 | 37¹ | 37 | 4 | 15 | 33 | 3.6 | 7.9 | 47% | .309 | 1.39 | 4.27 | 4.03 | 4.64 | 0.3 |

A strong commitment to Stetson earned Hutchison an over-slot signing in the 15th round of the 2009 draft. The Jays gave him the equivalent of the major league minimum salary—$400,000—to sign, and their investment has only begun to pay off. Another starting pitcher who climbed the system rapidly in 2011, Hutchison dominated across three levels thanks to an effective fastball-changeup combination. In part because he lacks a solid feel for his slider, he isn't all the way to where he might end up, which is most likely as a solid number three. Hutchison is a good example of the kind of signing that teams like the Blue Jays won't be able to swing under the new collective bargaining agreement.

### Casey Janssen

Born: 9/17/1981 Age: 30
Bats: R Throws: R Height: 6' 5" Weight: 205
Breakout: 17% Improve: 47% Collapse: 22%
Attrition: 15% MLB: 94%

Comparables:
Matt Guerrier, Chad Qualls, Dean Chance

| YEAR | TEAM | LVL | AGE | W | L | SV | G | GS | IP | H | HR | BB | SO | EqBB9 | EqSO9 | GB% | BABIP | WHIP | ERA | FIP | FRA | WARP |
|---|---|---|---|---|---|---|---|---|---|---|---|---|---|---|---|---|---|---|---|---|---|---|
| 2009 | TOR | MLB | 27 | 2 | 4 | 1 | 21 | 5 | 40 | 59 | 5 | 14 | 24 | 3.2 | 5.4 | 50% | .370 | 1.83 | 5.85 | 4.77 | 5.26 | 0.2 |
| 2010 | TOR | MLB | 28 | 5 | 2 | 0 | 56 | 0 | 68² | 74 | 8 | 21 | 63 | 2.8 | 8.3 | 47% | .327 | 1.38 | 3.67 | 3.82 | 4.75 | 0.3 |
| 2011 | TOR | MLB | 29 | 6 | 0 | 2 | 55 | 0 | 55² | 47 | 2 | 14 | 53 | 2.3 | 8.6 | 49% | .298 | 1.10 | 2.26 | 2.49 | 3.54 | 1.1 |
| 2012 | TOR | MLB | 30 | 2 | 1 | 0 | 45 | 0 | 50 | 51 | 5 | 15 | 39 | 2.6 | 7.1 | 49% | .306 | 1.31 | 3.98 | 3.84 | 4.32 | 0.5 |

As improbable as Janssen's success in 2010 seemed, his follow-up campaign was an improvement across the board. The only knock on his year was a month lost to a forearm strain. But despite his strong peripherals and 2.26 ERA, Janssen was used primarily in low-leverage situations. With the departure of both Jon Rauch and Frank Francisco, Janssen could become a more important part of the bullpen this season. He added yet another tick to his fastball and has grown to rely more on his cutter, which gives him a weapon against lefties that he once lacked.

### Jesse Litsch
Born: 3/9/1985 Age: 27
Bats: R Throws: R Height: 6' 2" Weight: 205
Breakout: 32% Improve: 52% Collapse: 12%
Attrition: 6% MLB: 89%
Comparables:
J.D. Martin,Daniel McCutchen,Chad Bradford

| YEAR | TEAM | LVL | AGE | W | L | SV | G | GS | IP | H | HR | BB | SO | EqBB9 | EqSO9 | GB% | BABIP | WHIP | ERA | FIP | FRA | WARP |
|------|------|-----|-----|---|---|----|---|----|----|---|----|----|----|-------|-------|-----|-------|------|-----|-----|-----|------|
| 2009 | TOR | MLB | 24 | 0 | 1 | 0 | 2 | 2 | 9 | 14 | 4 | 1 | 8 | 1.0 | 8.0 | 38% | .357 | 1.67 | 9.00 | 7.81 | 8.07 | -0.2 |
| 2010 | TOR | MLB | 25 | 1 | 5 | 0 | 9 | 9 | 46² | 53 | 7 | 15 | 16 | 2.9 | 3.1 | 45% | .284 | 1.46 | 5.79 | 5.40 | 5.19 | 0.3 |
| 2011 | LVG | AAA | 26 | 1 | 1 | 0 | 6 | 6 | 28² | 41 | 5 | 11 | 27 | 3.5 | 8.5 | 49% | .396 | 1.81 | 8.16 | 5.58 | 5.90 | 0.3 |
| 2011 | TOR | MLB | 26 | 6 | 3 | 1 | 28 | 8 | 75 | 69 | 10 | 28 | 66 | 3.4 | 7.9 | 45% | .284 | 1.29 | 4.44 | 4.27 | 5.14 | 0.2 |
| 2012 | TOR | MLB | 27 | 4 | 4 | 0 | 19 | 12 | 72 | 75 | 10 | 20 | 45 | 2.4 | 5.7 | 50% | .291 | 1.32 | 4.41 | 4.59 | 4.79 | 0.4 |

The Blue Jays' surfeit of live arms has led them to give new life to the swingman role. Litsch and his five-pitch repertoire demonstrate this flexibility as well as anybody. In eight starts at the beginning of the season, Litsch was 4-3 with a 4.66 ERA and a K/BB ratio of exactly two. In other words, serviceable as a fourth or fifth starter. In 20 appearances out of the bullpen, Litsch had a 4.08 ERA with a K/BB ratio of exactly three. In other words, pretty good for a long reliever. Eight of those appearances were longer than an inning, and six were two innings or more. Treated properly, most starters can become good relievers, and many relievers can start as well. Keep enough guys like Litsch

September starts last year. In one of those starts, he touched 96, walked five batters in three innings, and did not record a strikeout. Two starts later, he struck out eight in five innings without walking a batter. What we know is that the velocity and stuff are back. If he can stay healthy, there's plenty of reason to think the results will follow.

### Deck McGuire
Born: 6/23/1989 Age: 23
Bats: R Throws: R Height: 6' 7" Weight: 220
Breakout: 34% Improve: 62% Collapse: 15%
Attrition: 12% MLB: 86%
Comparables:
Don Demola,Ray Burris,Chris Tillman

| YEAR | TEAM | LVL | AGE | W | L | SV | G | GS | IP | H | HR | BB | SO | EqBB9 | EqSO9 | GB% | BABIP | WHIP | ERA | FIP | FRA | WARP |
|------|------|-----|-----|---|---|----|---|----|----|---|----|----|----|-------|-------|-----|-------|------|-----|-----|-----|------|
| 2011 | DUN | A+ | 22 | 4 | 2 | 0 | 19 | 18 | 104² | 86 | 9 | 37 | 97 | 3.3 | 8.8 | 42% | .283 | 1.21 | 2.75 | 3.86 | 4.15 | 1.9 |
| 2012 | TOR | MLB | 23 | 2 | 2 | 0 | 5 | 5 | 30² | 32 | 4 | 15 | 24 | 4.3 | 7.0 | 43% | .307 | 1.54 | 5.09 | 4.80 | 5.54 | -0.1 |

Picked 11th overall in the 2010 draft out of Georgia Tech, Deck McGuire was seen as a safe, polished selection. His first taste of professional action was successful; McGuire's ability suggests he will move quickly through the system. He has a four-pitch arsenal (fastball, slider, curve, and changeup) that allows him to gain a strategic edge against most minor-league hitters. The real test begins this season with extended looks in Double-A and Triple-A, where the hitters are more advanced.

### Brandon Morrow
Born: 7/26/1984 Age: 27
Bats: R Throws: R Height: 6' 4" Weight: 190
Breakout: 29% Improve: 49% Collapse: 28%
Attrition: 21% MLB: 92%
Comparables:
Anthony Slama,Daisuke Matsuzaka,Steve Bedrosian

| YEAR | TEAM | LVL | AGE | W | L | SV | G | GS | IP | H | HR | BB | SO | EqBB9 | EqSO9 | GB% | BABIP | WHIP | ERA | FIP | FRA | WARP |
|------|------|-----|-----|---|---|----|---|----|----|---|----|----|----|-------|-------|-----|-------|------|-----|-----|-----|------|
| 2009 | TAC | AAA | 24 | 5 | 3 | 0 | 10 | 10 | 55 | 50 | 2 | 23 | 40 | 3.8 | 6.5 | 41% | .287 | 1.33 | 3.60 | 3.78 | 3.89 | 1.0 |
| 2009 | SEA | MLB | 24 | 2 | 4 | 6 | 26 | 10 | 69² | 66 | 10 | 44 | 63 | 5.7 | 8.1 | 36% | .287 | 1.58 | 4.39 | 5.10 | 5.07 | 0.6 |
| 2010 | TOR | MLB | 25 | 10 | 7 | 0 | 26 | 26 | 146¹ | 136 | 11 | 66 | 178 | 4.1 | 10.9 | 40% | .344 | 1.38 | 4.49 | 3.13 | 4.12 | 2.4 |
| 2011 | TOR | MLB | 26 | 11 | 11 | 0 | 30 | 30 | 179¹ | 162 | 21 | 69 | 203 | 3.5 | 10.2 | 37% | .301 | 1.29 | 4.72 | 3.67 | 4.04 | 2.8 |
| 2012 | TOR | MLB | 27 | 10 | 8 | 0 | 27 | 27 | 152 | 135 | 16 | 71 | 170 | 4.2 | 10.0 | 38% | .303 | 1.35 | 3.89 | 3.74 | 4.23 | 1.9 |

In 325 2/3 innings with the Jays, Morrow has an ERA of 4.62, but a strikeout-to-walk ratio of 2.8. The calls for a breakout season in 2011 were a dime a dozen last March, and perhaps they will be again this year. Morrow led the league in strikeouts per inning—a mark aided in part by his healthy walk rate—and nearly every sophisticated statistical estimator of pitching performance, including FRA and FIP, suggests he was above average. His splits with runners in scoring position are ugly (705 OPS against all batters, 888 with RISP) and they get worse when you add two outs (977). Neither of those facts was true of his 2010, when he suffered a brutal .344 BABIP, and that bad BABIP was seemingly cured in 2011 (.301). Put simply, in 2010 he had bad outcomes on balls in play; in 2011 he had unfortunate sequencing of his strikeouts, walks, and balls in play. If he can exorcise both demons in 2012, he'll be every bit the fireballer he so frequently seems capable of becoming.

### Darren Oliver

Born: 10/6/1970 Age: 41
Bats: R Throws: L Height: 6' 1" Weight: 170
Breakout: 30% Improve: 49% Collapse: 35%
Attrition: 25% MLB: 81%

Comparables:
Hoyt Wilhelm, Doug Jones, John Smoltz

| YEAR | TEAM | LVL | AGE | W | L | SV | G | GS | IP | H | HR | BB | SO | EqBB9 | EqSO9 | GB% | BABIP | WHIP | ERA | FIP | FRA | WARP |
|------|------|-----|-----|---|---|----|----|----|----|----|----|----|----|-------|-------|-----|-------|------|-----|-----|-----|------|
| 2009 | ANA | MLB | 38 | 5 | 1 | 0 | 63 | 1 | 73 | 61 | 5 | 22 | 65 | 2.7 | 8.0 | 46% | .292 | 1.14 | 2.71 | 3.36 | 4.12 | 1.1 |
| 2010 | TEX | MLB | 39 | 1 | 2 | 1 | 64 | 0 | 61² | 53 | 4 | 15 | 65 | 2.2 | 9.5 | 49% | .320 | 1.10 | 2.48 | 2.61 | 3.87 | 0.9 |
| 2011 | TEX | MLB | 40 | 5 | 5 | 2 | 61 | 0 | 51 | 47 | 3 | 11 | 44 | 1.9 | 7.8 | 43% | .289 | 1.14 | 2.29 | 2.81 | 3.87 | 0.9 |
| 2012 | TOR | MLB | 41 | 3 | 1 | 1 | 51 | 0 | 45² | 44 | 4 | 13 | 38 | 2.6 | 7.4 | 47% | .296 | 1.25 | 3.54 | 3.53 | 3.84 | 0.7 |

Oliver signed a one-year deal with a club option for 2013, which would mean he could be pitching for the Jays until he is 43 years old. Currently 41, he has been defying age for a while, giving up fewer home runs and walking fewer men per nine as he ages. The move from the hitter-friendly Rangers Ballpark in Arlington to pitcher-friendly Rogers Centre will only make him look better. There's no reason to believe he can't repeat his 2011 performance, getting out both lefties and righties in high-leverage situations.

### Luis Perez

Born: 1/20/1985 Age: 27
Bats: L Throws: L Height: 6' 1" Weight: 160
Breakout: 16% Improve: 42% Collapse: 36%
Attrition: 14% MLB: 90%

Comparables:
Pedro Feliciano, Dave Hamilton, Eude Brito

| YEAR | TEAM | LVL | AGE | W | L | SV | G | GS | IP | H | HR | BB | SO | EqBB9 | EqSO9 | GB% | BABIP | WHIP | ERA | FIP | FRA | WARP |
|------|------|-----|-----|---|----|----|----|----|------|-----|----|----|-----|-------|-------|-----|-------|------|------|------|------|------|
| 2009 | NHP | AA | 24 | 9 | 11 | 0 | 28 | 27 | 162¹ | 145 | 11 | 67 | 112 | 3.7 | 6.2 | 59% | .275 | 1.31 | 3.55 | 4.12 | 5.72 | -1.1 |
| 2010 | NHP | AA | 25 | 5 | 6 | 0 | 13 | 12 | 73¹ | 42 | 4 | 24 | 33 | 4.5 | 6.0 | 57% | .317 | 1.42 | 4.54 | 4.51 | 5.50 | 0.0 |
| 2010 | LVG | AAA | 25 | 5 | 5 | 0 | 15 | 15 | 86² | 72 | 3 | 25 | 43 | 4.9 | 5.8 | 61% | .342 | 1.78 | 6.12 | 4.59 | 6.86 | -0.6 |
| 2011 | LVG | AAA | 26 | 1 | 1 | 0 | 8 | 8 | 45 | 37 | 5 | 22 | 43 | 4.6 | 8.6 | 63% | .283 | 1.33 | 4.60 | 4.94 | 5.98 | 0.3 |
| 2011 | TOR | MLB | 26 | 3 | 3 | 0 | 37 | 4 | 65 | 74 | 9 | 27 | 54 | 3.7 | 7.5 | 61% | .328 | 1.55 | 5.12 | 4.68 | 6.11 | -0.5 |
| 2012 | TOR | MLB | 27 | 3 | 4 | 0 | 18 | 10 | 68 | 76 | 8 | 35 | 45 | 4.6 | 5.9 | 56% | .311 | 1.62 | 5.51 | 4.95 | 5.99 | -0.5 |

During an uninspiring second go-round as a starter at Triple-A, Perez was called up to provide help in the bullpen. He had a short stint with the club in April, then was called up more or less for good in late May. As a reliever, he wasn't so bad: the Dominican lefty posted a 4.27 ERA and a 2.44 strikeout-to-walk ratio. However, when called on to make four starts in the wake of Brad Mills's demotion, Perez fared hardly better than Mills and allowed 15 runs in 18 2/3 innings. Perez is a lefty with a decent fastball-slider combination, and the Blue Jays have plenty of fringy starters, so why get fancy? Perez's future is in the bullpen.

### Ricky Romero

Born: 11/6/1984 Age: 27
Bats: R Throws: L Height: 6' 1" Weight: 215
Breakout: 21% Improve: 46% Collapse: 28%
Attrition: 10% MLB: 87%

Comparables:
John Maine, Tim Crabtree, Eric Show

| YEAR | TEAM | LVL | AGE | W | L | SV | G | GS | IP | H | HR | BB | SO | EqBB9 | EqSO9 | GB% | BABIP | WHIP | ERA | FIP | FRA | WARP |
|------|------|-----|-----|----|----|----|----|----|-----|-----|----|----|-----|-------|-------|-----|-------|------|------|------|------|------|
| 2009 | TOR | MLB | 24 | 13 | 9 | 0 | 29 | 29 | 178 | 192 | 18 | 79 | 141 | 4.0 | 7.1 | 55% | .335 | 1.52 | 4.30 | 4.37 | 4.62 | 1.9 |
| 2010 | TOR | MLB | 25 | 14 | 9 | 0 | 32 | 32 | 210 | 189 | 15 | 82 | 174 | 3.5 | 7.5 | 56% | .293 | 1.29 | 3.73 | 3.60 | 4.67 | 2.0 |
| 2011 | TOR | MLB | 26 | 15 | 11 | 0 | 32 | 32 | 225 | 176 | 26 | 80 | 178 | 3.2 | 7.1 | 56% | .245 | 1.14 | 2.92 | 4.23 | 4.61 | 1.9 |
| 2012 | TOR | MLB | 27 | 11 | 10 | 0 | 27 | 27 | 184 | 181 | 20 | 75 | 148 | 3.6 | 7.2 | 52% | .301 | 1.39 | 4.30 | 4.23 | 4.68 | 1.0 |

Consider Romero's season on two levels. Superficially, it was as good a season as the Blue Jays could have expected when they handed him $30 million and the keys to the front of the rotation. He set career bests in ERA, wins, strikeouts, complete games, innings pitched, and hits allowed. His velocity was up across the board and he made his first All-Star team. On another level, though, Romero continues to be somewhat of a mystery. His peripherals are good but not spectacular: a decline in his strikeout rate and a jump in his home run rate were masked by a low BABIP. Could it be that Romero's jack-of-all-skills, master-of-none act means that the whole of his outcomes is greater than the sum of his peripherals?

### Sergio Santos

Born: 7/4/1983 Age: 28
Bats: R Throws: R Height: 6' 4" Weight: 240
Breakout: 33% Improve: 45% Collapse: 36%
Attrition: 17% MLB: 94%

Comparables:
Bryan Harvey, Mark Wohlers, Jose Valverde

| YEAR | TEAM | LVL | AGE | W | L | SV | G | GS | IP | H | HR | BB | SO | EqBB9 | EqSO9 | GB% | BABIP | WHIP | ERA | FIP | FRA | WARP |
|------|------|-----|-----|---|---|----|----|----|-----|----|----|----|----|-------|-------|-----|-------|------|------|------|------|------|
| 2010 | CHA | MLB | 27 | 2 | 2 | 1 | 56 | 0 | 51² | 53 | 2 | 26 | 56 | 4.5 | 9.8 | 45% | .349 | 1.53 | 2.96 | 3.07 | 4.42 | 0.5 |
| 2011 | CHA | MLB | 28 | 4 | 5 | 30 | 63 | 0 | 63¹ | 41 | 6 | 29 | 92 | 4.1 | 13.1 | 43% | .271 | 1.11 | 3.55 | 2.90 | 3.06 | 1.5 |
| 2012 | TOR | MLB | 28 | 3 | 1 | 9 | 54 | 0 | 52 | 44 | 5 | 24 | 62 | 4.1 | 10.7 | 42% | .310 | 1.31 | 3.50 | 3.45 | 3.80 | 0.8 |

Who among us can forget that moment when we learned that Santos had broken Mariano Rivera's record? For most it was over morning coffee, perusing the crumb-sprinkled game notes from the Sox-Orioles tilt on August 11; for Santos himself, it was in the postgame clubhouse, when the White Sox media department announced he had set a new standard for scoreless road appearances to begin the season. Now closing in Toronto after an offseason trade for prospect Nestor Molina, Santos can set his sights on some of Mo's more impressive achievements, as a new long-term deal will allow him to continue to uncork his mid-90s heat and ridiculous slider in save situations for years to come. Like Carlos Marmol, Santos has come a long way from his days as a failed position prospect; unlike Marmol, he can consistently throw his fastball for strikes. AL hitters are going to need a bigger boat.

**Carlos Villanueva**
Born: 11/28/1983 Age: 28
Bats: R Throws: R Height: 6' 3" Weight: 190
Breakout: 23% Improve: 57% Collapse: 20%
Attrition: 11% MLB: 90%
**Comparables:**
Heath Bell, Dan Wheeler, Dwight Gooden

| YEAR | TEAM | LVL | AGE | W | L | SV | G | GS | IP | H | HR | BB | SO | EqBB9 | EqSO9 | GB% | BABIP | WHIP | ERA | FIP | FRA | WARP |
|------|------|-----|-----|---|---|----|----|----|-----|-----|----|----|----|-------|-------|-----|-------|------|------|------|------|------|
| 2009 | MIL | MLB | 25 | 4 | 10 | 3 | 64 | 6 | 96 | 102 | 13 | 35 | 83 | 3.3 | 7.8 | 43% | .312 | 1.43 | 5.34 | 4.24 | 4.70 | 1.1 |
| 2010 | MIL | MLB | 26 | 2 | 0 | 1 | 50 | 0 | 52² | 48 | 7 | 22 | 67 | 3.8 | 11.4 | 36% | .313 | 1.33 | 4.61 | 3.77 | 4.32 | 0.5 |
| 2011 | TOR | MLB | 27 | 6 | 4 | 0 | 33 | 13 | 107 | 103 | 11 | 32 | 68 | 2.7 | 5.7 | 37% | .272 | 1.26 | 4.04 | 4.14 | 4.77 | 0.6 |
| 2012 | TOR | MLB | 28 | 4 | 3 | 1 | 46 | 7 | 84² | 83 | 12 | 29 | 72 | 3.1 | 7.6 | 42% | .293 | 1.32 | 4.15 | 4.37 | 4.51 | 0.7 |

People say there's no such thing as too much starting pitching. From the looks of things, the Blue Jays have put the aphorism to the test. Count one for conventional wisdom. Toronto acquired Villanueva from Milwaukee for cash and slotted him into the bullpen. When Jesse Litsch hit the DL, Villanueva stepped in as a replacement and notched five quality starts in his first nine tries. After he was knocked from the rotation by a string of bad starts most likely caused by strained forearm, Villanueva eventually settled back into the bullpen. His season shows the value of live arms that can start, but it doesn't explain what happened to his strikeouts. He lost some sparkle from his stuff, which meant hitters did not swing and miss at his curveball nearly as much as they had in 2010.

| | | | AGE | PA | R | 2B | 3B | HR | RBI | BB | SO | SB-CS | AVG/OBP/SLG | TAv | BABIP | BRR | FRAA | WARP |
|---|---|---|-----|-----|----|----|----|----|-----|----|----|-------|-------------|-----|-------|-----|------|------|
| 1B M. McDade | NHP | AA | 22 | 524 | 71 | 37 | 0 | 16 | 74 | 28 | 104 | 0-1 | .281/.328/.457 | .269 | .326 | -3.9 | -2.6 | 0.5 |
| C C. Perez | LNS | A | 20 | 429 | 58 | 17 | 6 | 3 | 41 | 37 | 74 | 6-2 | .256/.320/.355 | .261 | .304 | -1.8 | -0.4 | 1.2 |
| SS D. Thon | BLJ | RK | 19 | 151 | 23 | 3 | 0 | 3 | 15 | 23 | 44 | 6-2 | .223/.369/.322 | .273 | .324 | 2.1 | -3.9 | 0.7 |

In a system without many big-time power prospects, **Mike McDade** is a poor-man's pinch hitter. ⊘ Last year was a big step backward for **Carlos Perez**, who saw his offensive numbers drop across the board. ⊘ A toolsy son of the longtime Astros shortstop, **Dickie Joe Thon** has a projectable bat and showed flashes of excellence in his debut.

## PITCHERS

| PLAYER | TEAM | LVL | AGE | W | L | SV | IP | H | HR | BB | SO | EqBB9 | EqSO9 | GB% | BABIP | WHIP | ERA | FIP | FRA | WARP |
|--------|------|-----|-----|---|---|----|----|----|----|----|----|-------|-------|-----|-------|------|------|------|------|------|
| A. Carpenter | LEH | AAA | 26 | 5 | 1 | 0 | 60¹ | 48 | 2 | 11 | 65 | 1.6 | 9.7 | 50% | .289 | 0.98 | 1.79 | 2.06 | 3.13 | 1.4 |
| | PHI | MLB | 26 | 0 | 0 | 0 | 9¹ | 13 | 2 | 4 | 10 | 3.9 | 9.6 | 29% | .407 | 1.82 | 7.71 | 4.92 | 5.17 | -0.1 |
| | SDN | MLB | 26 | 0 | 0 | 0 | 5¹ | 6 | 1 | 3 | 6 | 5.1 | 10.1 | 67% | .385 | 1.69 | 8.44 | 4.87 | 7.89 | -0.2 |
| R. Coello | IOW | AAA | 26 | 2 | 2 | 1 | 95 | 85 | 11 | 41 | 94 | 3.9 | 8.9 | 36% | .295 | 1.33 | 4.45 | 4.65 | 4.81 | 1.2 |
| C. Gaudin | LVG | AAA | 28 | 2 | 2 | 0 | 29¹ | 37 | 2 | 9 | 13 | 2.8 | 4.0 | 48% | .347 | 1.57 | 6.14 | 5.07 | 4.73 | 0.4 |
| | WAS | MLB | 28 | 1 | 1 | 0 | 8¹ | 12 | 1 | 8 | 10 | 8.6 | 10.8 | 33% | .440 | 2.40 | 6.48 | 5.03 | 5.39 | -0.1 |
| C. Jenkins | DUN | A+ | 23 | 2 | 2 | 0 | 67¹ | 71 | 3 | 14 | 44 | 1.9 | 5.9 | 57% | .306 | 1.26 | 3.07 | 3.29 | 4.64 | 0.9 |
| | NHP | AA | 23 | 5 | 7 | 0 | 100¹ | 106 | 9 | 30 | 87 | 2.4 | 6.6 | 51% | .297 | 1.20 | 4.13 | 3.80 | 4.28 | 1.4 |
| A. Laffey | NYA | MLB | 26 | 2 | 1 | 0 | 10² | 13 | 0 | 5 | 6 | 4.2 | 5.1 | 38% | .351 | 1.69 | 3.38 | 3.91 | 5.44 | 0.0 |
| | SEA | MLB | 26 | 1 | 1 | 0 | 42² | 54 | 7 | 16 | 24 | 3.4 | 5.1 | 54% | .320 | 1.64 | 4.01 | 5.26 | 5.79 | -0.5 |
| R. Lewis | LVG | AAA | 28 | 3 | 2 | 4 | 58² | 71 | 10 | 29 | 50 | 4.4 | 7.7 | 52% | .335 | 1.70 | 6.60 | 5.73 | 6.28 | 0.1 |
| | TOR | MLB | 28 | 0 | 0 | 0 | 5 | 12 | 1 | 2 | 5 | 3.6 | 9.0 | 35% | .524 | 2.80 | 9.00 | 6.06 | 8.33 | -0.2 |
| T. Magnuson | SAC | AAA | 26 | 4 | 2 | 5 | 45¹ | 34 | 4 | 19 | 46 | 3.8 | 9.1 | 41% | .263 | 1.17 | 2.98 | 4.24 | 4.46 | 0.5 |
| | OAK | MLB | 26 | 0 | 0 | 0 | 14² | 15 | 3 | 5 | 11 | 3.1 | 6.8 | 33% | .261 | 1.36 | 6.14 | 5.24 | 5.81 | -0.2 |
| S. Richmond | LVG | AAA | 31 | 6 | 6 | 0 | 113 | 149 | 24 | 56 | 87 | 4.5 | 6.9 | 42% | .346 | 1.81 | 7.33 | 6.52 | 6.60 | 0.0 |
| | TOR | MLB | 31 | 0 | 0 | 0 | 0¹ | 0 | 0 | 0 | 0 | 0.0 | 0.0 | % | .000 | 0.00 | 0.00 | 3.06 | 8.66 | 0.0 |
| A. Sanchez | BLU | RK | 19 | 2 | 2 | 1 | 42² | 45 | 4 | 18 | 43 | 3.8 | 9.1 | 48% | .339 | 1.48 | 5.48 | 4.32 | 6.30 | 0.2 |
| N. Syndergaard | BLU | RK | 18 | 2 | 0 | 0 | 32 | 23 | 1 | 11 | 37 | 3.1 | 10.4 | 53% | .278 | 1.06 | 1.41 | 2.91 | 3.14 | 1.0 |
| B. Tallet | TOR | MLB | 33 | 0 | 1 | 0 | 0¹ | 2 | 0 | 2 | 1 | 54.0 | 27.0 | 33% | .000 | 12.00 | 54.00 | 15.06 | 11.46 | -0.1 |
| | SLN | MLB | 33 | 0 | 1 | 0 | 13 | 20 | 4 | 5 | 9 | 3.5 | 6.2 | 50% | .340 | 1.92 | 8.31 | 7.22 | 7.79 | -0.5 |
| A. Wojciechowski | DUN | A+ | 22 | 5 | 3 | 0 | 130¹ | 161 | 15 | 31 | 99 | 2.1 | 6.6 | 43% | .331 | 1.43 | 4.70 | 4.17 | 5.14 | 1.3 |

Claimed on waivers from Philadelphia in September, former second-round pick **Drew Carpenter** didn't impress in a cameo with the Padres and remains a fringe right-hander with good control but little else. ⊘ Preseason trade acquisition **Robert Coello** survived a designation for assignment in late May and went on to attract some attention by posting a 1.01 ERA in relief (with 47 K in 35 2/3 IP) at Iowa after failing as a starter. ⊘ Nothing gets you in the spotlight faster than two stints with the Yankees, and nothing gets you out of it faster than a year in the Nationals and Blue Jays organizations, as **Chad Gaudin** learned the hard way. ⊘ A 2009 first rounder, **Chad Jenkins** has power stuff but finesse results. He could still end up as a decent extra arm. ⊘ It's a given that lefties get a million chances, but **Aaron Laffey's** fastball sits at 87-88 mph and he lacks a specialist's dominance over same-side hitters, so what's the point? ⊘ Maybe **Rommie Lewis** should have just stayed on the DL, since he posted a second straight season with an ERA above 6.00 at Las Vegas. ⊘ Purchased from the Athletics for cash considerations, **Trystan Magnuson** is nothing to write home about, in a system full of promising young pitchers, all of whom could become relievers if need be. ⊘ All hail the terrible beast Lasvegas, to whom we feed all our quadrupliest-A pitchers! Feast on **Scott Richmond**, Lasvegas, and be nourished! ⊘ **Aaron Sanchez** has electric stuff but struggled with his command in his second pro season. He still has impact potential. ⊘ The first thing you notice about **Noah Syndergaard** is how tall he is (6-foot-5). The second thing you notice about him is his big, Texan fastball. ⊘ It was the classic "boy sneezes, boy strains right intercostal muscle, boy learns he has polycystic kidney disease" story for **Brian Tallet**. He was a throw-in in the Colby Rasmus trade, and the Blue Jays released him in September. ⊘ **Asher Wojciechowski** relies heavily on his fastball, so opinions are split over whether he'll end up as a starter or a reliever.

## MANAGER: JOHN FARRELL

| YEAR | TEAM | W-L | Pythag +/- | Avg PC | 100+ P | 120+ P | QS | BQS | REL | REL w Zero R | IBB | Subs | PH | PH Avg | PH HR | SB2 | CS2 | SB3 | CS3 | SAC Att | SAC % | POS SAC | Squeeze | Swing | In Play |
|---|---|---|---|---|---|---|---|---|---|---|---|---|---|---|---|---|---|---|---|---|---|---|---|---|---|
| 2011 | TOR | 81-81 | 0 | 97.7 | 81 | 4 | 81 | 3 | 474 | 383 | 28 | — | 58 | .185 | 0 | 32 | 6 | 1 | 3 | 54 | 81.5% | 44 | 2 | 372 | 103 |

John Farrell gets it. Perhaps because of his five-year stint as Director of Player Development with the Indians under Mark Shapiro, or his time as the pitching coach of the Boston Red Sox, Farrell issued the third fewest intentional walks and called for the fourth fewest sacrifices in the American League in 2011. In an interview at the Winter Meetings this offseason, when asked about newly acquired closer Sergio Santos, Farrell repeatedly emphasized his strikeout rates and downplayed his relative inexperience. Farrell understands so well how to implement a complex analytic plan for a team that when the Red Sox asked the Blue Jays for permission to interview Farrell for their vacant manager job, the Blue Jays reportedly demanded Clay Buchholz in return. The only real knock on him is his relative lack of managing experience, but that's the kind of deficiency that time is uniquely qualified to remedy. He finessed a rough and injured bullpen until they cohered into a solid unit, balancing closers Frank Francisco and Jon Rauch and deploying other late inning options like Marc Rzepczynski (before his departure) and Jason Frasor so they had their best possible seasons. His use of his bench accurately reflected the fact that, for most of the season, the bench wasn't very good. If given the right weapons, John Farrell will use them judiciously, and that's all a team can ask for.

# Washington Nationals

Imagine you're a team that in the broad strokes does all the right things, only to see them blow up in your face.

You get a brand-new park from a pliant metropolis, but stadium cognoscenti immediately deem it bland. You haven't drawn as many fans in [...]

pitcher who hasn't been on the DL in a decade? *He* gets hurt. You spend $16 million on a power-hitting first baseman who's averaged 30 homers per season for five years; he gives you three before he suffers his own season-ending injury. You invest $126 million on a free-agent outfielder, and his OPS drops by 200 points in the first year of the contract.

You're in the middle of making your first run at topping .500 since the franchise came to the nation's capital . . . and your manager decides he'd rather walk away.

Looking at all of that, you might think that the Nats have a unique ability to take great opportunities or major investments and screw them up. But if you get too hung up on the season-to-season setbacks, you risk losing sight of the Nationals' burgeoning upside as a team primed to explode on the rest of the league.

Thanks to the slow reform of the player-development program and the demonstrated willingness to spend top dollar on top talent, the Nationals are the team perhaps best prepared to challenge and ultimately replace the Phillies as the NL East's power club. The question is whether they can do that in 2012. While the Phillies' aging offense already seems likely to bring them back toward the pack, the Braves aren't just going away, and the Marlins' noisy offseason activities

| | | |
|---|---|---|
| TAv | .247 | 25th |
| TAv-P | .251 | 6th |
| FIP | 3.80 | 10th |
| DER | .713 | 12th |
| DL | 1003 | 27th |
| B-Age | 28.4 | 13th |
| P-Age | 28.0 | 14th |
| Salary | $68.0 | 22nd |
| M$/MW | $1.72 | 9th |

**2011:** A third-place finish is kind of progress, but they still failed to win more than they lost

**2012:** Strasburg's back, Harper's on the way, and something big is building in Anacostia

**Action Items:** Someone to play center, Gio Gonzalez living up to his price tag

will make them a popular choice for contention. But the Nats aren't counting themselves out of even that crowded field.

This season represents the first legitimate chance they've had to promote the club for something more than the initial novelty of major-league base- [...] way toward the Snow.

The anticipation that Strasburg and Harper already command might top that of any pair of prospects on one team since the last power duo manager Davey Johnson was associated with almost 30 years ago: Doc Gooden and Darryl Strawberry. If you're looking for a couple of very good reasons why Johnson came back to the dugout after a decade away, you can probably start with those two.

Even if Harper's arrival winds up being delayed until later on during the season, the lineup should already enjoy the benefit of a healthy Adam LaRoche back at first base and a full season from Ryan Zimmerman at third. Add that to Michael Morse, Jayson Werth, Wilson Ramos, and Danny Espinosa, and you've got a lineup with tons of power from top to bottom, though Ramos is something of a question mark in the wake of a two-day kidnapping ordeal in his native Venezuela. Ramos was rescued unhurt, but he struggled badly at the plate in that country's winter league, and one has to wonder if the experience left a lingering psychological impact.

Still, there's a lot of lumber in that batting order. Even so, the Nats have a trio of problems that time or patience will not heal. They're correctable and the Nats are aware of them, but the question is whether they can fix them in 2012.

First, there's assembling a rotation that can compete with the standard set by the Phillies, Giants, or even the Cardinals with Adam Wainwright's return. Between the six-month slog of the regular season or needing to have somebody capable of winning a 1-0 game in October against Cliff Lee, an aspiring contender really has to have a couple of starters capable of cranking out quality starts two out of every three or three out of every four turns.

Solid mid-rotation innings eaters might get very rich making 30 starts while providing a quality start half the time, but it's extremely difficult to win in a season or a series with just those guys. Call him Jason Marquis or Livan Hernandez or even John Lannan; those guys are valuable. What you lack in postseason series wins you'll make up for with dowdy respectability.

You can't just conjure up front-end starting pitchers, but the Nats have already invested time and effort to develop a couple. Simply assuming that Strasburg will be an ace worthy of the label might give them one of those guys; Jordan Zimmermann might develop into a second. So far, so good—less Livan large is a sign of progress.

However, general manager Mike Rizzo didn't settle for that sort of wishcasting, which suggests that the timetable for the Nats' bid for relevance is set for sooner, not later. Initially, Rizzo appeared to make a priority of landing one of the premium lefties on the market, but after Mark Buehrle spurned Washington's entreaties and went to Miami, Rizzo reached beyond the market's limited options and shipped off four prospects to Oakland for four years of Gio Gonzalez.

As major exchanges go, it might turn out well enough if you focus on Gonzalez's potential success in the weaker league and less on the steep price paid in talent to get him. A front three of Strasburg, Gonzalez, and Zimmermann is certainly young, and not a bad threesome to bank on, but shipping off that much horseflesh makes it clear that Rizzo's compunction is to make something happen. Now.

Which brings us to the Nats' second problem, which is the one they haven't done anything about yet, and for which there may not be an easy answer. However much power the Nats may have, the lineup nevertheless suffers from one obvious dysfunction: the utter absence of any legitimate table-setters.

Taking this from the top, Nationals leadoff men produced a .285 OBP, while the gents stocking the second slot did even worse with a .283 OBP. The two lineup positions drew just 101 unintentional walks combined, and their combined .284 OBP was the lowest of any one-two punch in the league. That clip of getting aboard—or not, in this case—represents an OBP shortfall that was almost 40 points lower than the NL *average* for those two slots. That's before we get into suggesting that maybe the Nats might want to employ someone up front who might be, you know, better than average. Good, even.

This isn't a shortcut to saying that Johnson or his predecessor, Jim Riggleman, has no idea what he's doing. But it isn't like the Nationals managers had an obvious high-OBP choice lying around on their roster. There just weren't a lot of alternatives to the players they used most often—Ian Desmond, Rick Ankiel, Roger Bernadina, and Espinosa. At season's end, Johnson was using Desmond as his primary leadoff man, but much like Chris Marrero's month-long spin at first base, that wasn't really about creating a lasting opportunity for a home-grown kid.

This is really Rizzo's problem to fix, but so far, a solution hasn't been actively pursued. Part of the problem is that there are only two places in the lineup where the Nats might look at upgrades, and they're both skill positions. It's hard enough to find affordable talent at shortstop or center field, let alone high-end ballplayers.

The Nats' inaction is in itself suggestive. Moving Morse back to the outfield during Marrero's dead-end "audition" might have appeared to erect a veteran stumbling block in front of Harper in the outfield. However, between Werth's starting more than half of the last month's games in center field and talk that Harper might have the athleticism to play the middle pasture, Rizzo might not be in the market for a solution for this winter's third open question: Who's the Nationals' center fielder?

The answers to that question and to their top o' the order issue may already be in-house, and either way it won't involve another extended dose of Bernadina. If Harper's power gets added as soon as Opening Day to a lineup already more than a little slugly, tomorrow's leadoff man might be yesterday's free-agent disappointment: Jayson Werth.

Werth's career walk rate is north of 12 percent and he's a net positive on the bases; he's already going to be a target for what he isn't, but placed in a role where he creates scoring opportunities for the rest of the lineup could help redeem an otherwise answer-less proposition on who leads off for the Nationals.

Coming up with ideal answers to these three problems would have put the Nats on the short list for intriguing wild-card contenders *before* the addition of a fifth playoff team from each league. Because of the Gonzalez trade, not landing Buehrle to front the rotation might have proven hideously expensive in terms of talent instead of cash. But even after that deal they're nevertheless in the happy position of having a young core of top talent in its mid-20s almost entirely under club control for the next several seasons.

As a result, even in the increasingly dynamic NL East, the Nationals should be able to manage an above-.500 finish. Perhaps the money saved on the market this winter might get applied toward an extension for Ryan Zimmerman beyond 2013. By that point, playing on the same team as Stephen Strasburg and Bryce Harper might be the sort of opportunity you can't put a price on.

# HITTERS

### Rick Ankiel — CF

Born: 7/19/1979 Age: **32**
Bats: **L** Throws: **L** Height: **6' 2"** Weight: **210**
Breakout: **4%** Improve: **31%** Collapse: **2%**
Attrition: **16%** MLB: **87%**

Comparables:
Dave Henderson, Jim Northrup, Andy Van Slyke

| YEAR | TEAM | LVL | AGE | PA | R | 2B | 3B | HR | RBI | BB | SO | SB | CS | AVG_OBP_SLG | TAv | BABIP | BRR | FRAA | WARP |
|---|---|---|---|---|---|---|---|---|---|---|---|---|---|---|---|---|---|---|---|
| 2009 | SLN | MLB | 29 | 404 | 50 | 21 | 2 | 11 | 38 | 26 | 99 | 4 | 3 | .231/.285/.387 | .237 | .283 | 1.2 | 2.9 | 0.4 |
| 2010 | OMA | AAA | 30 | 68 | 8 | 6 | 0 | 4 | 9 | 1 | 19 | 0 | 0 | .254/.265/.522 | .269 | .295 | -0.6 | -0.8 | 0.1 |
| 2010 | ATL | MLB | 30 | 139 | 17 | 6 | 1 | 2 | 9 | 19 | 42 | 2 | 1 | .210/.324/.328 | .230 | .307 | 0.4 | -2.3 | -0.1 |
| 2010 | KCA | MLB | 30 | 101 | 14 | 7 | 0 | 4 | 15 | 7 | 29 | 1 | 0 | .261/.317/.467 | .273 | .333 | -0.3 | 0.1 | 0.3 |
| 2011 | WAS | MLB | 31 | 415 | 46 | 20 | 0 | 9 | 37 | 29 | 96 | 10 | 3 | .239/.296/.363 | .241 | .297 | 0.6 | -0.3 | 0.8 |
| 2012 | WAS | MLB | 32 | 365 | 42 | 16 | 1 | 14 | 45 | 25 | 85 | 6 | 2 | .243/.299/.421 | .254 | .283 | -0.2 | CF -2, RF -1 | 1.1 |

Now 32, Ankiel has enough left to be a platoon outfielder for a few more years. He plays all three positions well enough to hold a job, but has a hard time controlling the strike zone well enough to get good pitches to hit. In the right circumstances, such as a team looking for a left-handed fourth outfielder, he could help a club as the pinch-hitter

Comparables:
Eric Byrnes, Angel Pagan, Mitch Webster

| YEAR | TEAM | LVL | AGE | PA | R | 2B | 3B | HR | RBI | BB | SO | SB | CS | AVG_OBP_SLG | TAv | BABIP | BRR | FRAA | WARP |
|---|---|---|---|---|---|---|---|---|---|---|---|---|---|---|---|---|---|---|---|
| 2012 | WAS | MLB | 28 | 377 | 43 | 14 | 3 | 8 | 40 | 28 | 74 | 19 | 5 | .260/.320/.390 | .255 | .304 | 0.4 | CF -6, LF 0 | 1.0 |

The Nats have, at the time of writing, dialed back their attempts to acquire another outfielder in a deal, and have decided to see how things go with Bernadina. The strange thing about that decision is that there's not a lot of mystery in Bernadina's career. He's a solid basestealer, middling defender, and all-around generic surplus outfielder. Even if you do catch lightning in a bottle, shouldn't you have at least tried it with someone with more upside?

### Corey Brown — CF

Born: 11/26/1985 Age: **26**
Bats: **L** Throws: **L** Height: **6' 2"** Weight: **205**
Breakout: **4%** Improve: **39%** Collapse: **6%**
Attrition: **26%** MLB: **89%**

Comparables:
Curtis Granderson, Bill Wilson, Brad Wilkerson

| YEAR | TEAM | LVL | AGE | PA | R | 2B | 3B | HR | RBI | BB | SO | SB | CS | AVG_OBP_SLG | TAv | BABIP | BRR | FRAA | WARP |
|---|---|---|---|---|---|---|---|---|---|---|---|---|---|---|---|---|---|---|---|
| 2009 | MID | AA | 23 | 281 | 46 | 20 | 4 | 9 | 43 | 27 | 69 | 5 | 2 | .268/.349/.488 | .277 | .337 | -1 | 4.1 | 1.5 |
| 2010 | MID | AA | 24 | 386 | 63 | 14 | 8 | 10 | 49 | 52 | 93 | 19 | 1 | .320/.416/.502 | .318 | .421 | 2.8 | -1.9 | 3.4 |
| 2010 | SAC | AAA | 24 | 148 | 21 | 4 | 3 | 5 | 20 | 11 | 36 | 3 | 1 | .193/.250/.378 | .211 | .219 | 2 | 3 | 0.0 |
| 2011 | SYR | AAA | 25 | 462 | 50 | 18 | 3 | 14 | 39 | 47 | 134 | 4 | 7 | .235/.326/.402 | .248 | .317 | -1.5 | 6.2 | 1.0 |
| 2012 | WAS | MLB | 26 | 250 | 27 | 10 | 2 | 7 | 27 | 22 | 71 | 4 | 2 | .230/.303/.384 | .244 | .299 | -0.1 | CF -1, LF 0 | 0.6 |

We'd like to say Brown's a higher risk/higher upside guy than Bernadina just to make the story simpler, but he's not higher risk. He's not on the 40-man roster, so he'll probably start the season at Triple-A, but Brown hits and fields at least as well as Bernadina, and has demonstrated the ability to draw a few more walks. A good example of a guy you can take a flyer on who's out there to be had in a cheap deal, rather than spending a few million bucks on a guy who you know is going to be a mediocrity.

### Mike Cameron — CF

Born: 1/8/1973 Age: **39**
Bats: **R** Throws: **R** Height: **6' 2"** Weight: **170**
Breakout: **0%** Improve: **16%** Collapse: **7%**
Attrition: **25%** MLB: **59%**

Comparables:
Steve Finley, Willie Mays, Jim Edmonds

| YEAR | TEAM | LVL | AGE | PA | R | 2B | 3B | HR | RBI | BB | SO | SB | CS | AVG_OBP_SLG | TAv | BABIP | BRR | FRAA | WARP |
|---|---|---|---|---|---|---|---|---|---|---|---|---|---|---|---|---|---|---|---|
| 2009 | MIL | MLB | 36 | 628 | 78 | 32 | 3 | 24 | 70 | 75 | 156 | 7 | 3 | .250/.342/.452 | .268 | .304 | 0.1 | 10.1 | 3.1 |
| 2010 | BOS | MLB | 37 | 180 | 24 | 11 | 0 | 4 | 15 | 14 | 44 | 0 | 1 | .259/.328/.401 | .266 | .330 | 0 | -0.1 | 0.8 |
| 2011 | FLO | MLB | 38 | 164 | 18 | 8 | 0 | 6 | 18 | 20 | 34 | 1 | 0 | .238/.331/.420 | .261 | .272 | 1.2 | 1.3 | 0.7 |
| 2011 | BOS | MLB | 38 | 105 | 9 | 2 | 0 | 3 | 9 | 8 | 25 | 0 | 0 | .149/.212/.266 | .176 | .162 | 0.2 | 1.2 | -0.6 |
| 2012 | WAS | MLB | 39 | 250 | 28 | 11 | 1 | 8 | 28 | 25 | 65 | 3 | 1 | .228/.310/.398 | .254 | .280 | -0.1 | CF 3, RF 1 | 1.1 |

The end of the line may have come for the 17-year veteran, who drew his release from the Marlins in mid-September following an altercation with a flight attendant on a team charter. Cameron's season totals weren't pretty, but he did pick things up offensively after the Marlins acquired him from Boston on July 5. If 2011 was his swan song, Cameron would walk away as one of the most productive and under-acknowledged players of the last decade and a half, registering the third-highest FRAA and 13th-best WARP among outfielders since 1997. But he signed a minor-league deal with the Nationals and will try to win a job in the spring.

## Alex Cora — 2B

Born: 10/18/1975 Age: 36
Bats: L Throws: R Height: 6' 1" Weight: 180
Breakout: 0% Improve: 16% Collapse: 18%
Attrition: 36% MLB: 69%

Comparables:
Carney Lansford, Lenny Harris, Buddy Bell

| YEAR | TEAM | LVL | AGE | PA | R | 2B | 3B | HR | RBI | BB | SO | SB | CS | AVG_OBP_SLG | TAv | BABIP | BRR | FRAA | WARP |
|---|---|---|---|---|---|---|---|---|---|---|---|---|---|---|---|---|---|---|---|
| 2009 | NYN | MLB | 33 | 308 | 31 | 11 | 1 | 1 | 18 | 25 | 28 | 8 | 3 | .251/.320/.310 | .229 | .276 | -0.7 | -3.5 | -0.3 |
| 2010 | NYN | MLB | 34 | 187 | 14 | 6 | 3 | 0 | 20 | 10 | 16 | 4 | 1 | .207/.265/.278 | .207 | .226 | -0.6 | -6.4 | -1.2 |
| 2010 | TEX | MLB | 34 | 7 | 0 | 0 | 0 | 0 | 0 | 0 | 0 | 0 | 0 | .286/.286/.286 | .210 | .286 | -0.5 | -0.2 | -0.1 |
| 2011 | WAS | MLB | 35 | 172 | 12 | 6 | 1 | 0 | 6 | 12 | 23 | 2 | 0 | .224/.287/.276 | .207 | .261 | -0.2 | 0.9 | -0.5 |
| 2012 | WAS | MLB | 36 | 250 | 25 | 10 | 2 | 1 | 20 | 15 | 25 | 5 | 1 | .240/.302/.320 | .226 | .258 | 0 | 2B -5, SS -1 | 0.2 |

Think carefully: Do you *really* want to be an agent? Imagine you're making that phone call on Cora's behalf. . .

## Mark DeRosa — 3B

Born: 2/26/1975 Age: 37
Bats: R Throws: R Height: 6' 2" Weight: 185
Breakout: 0% Improve: 11% Collapse: 17%
Attrition: 28% MLB: 71%

Comparables:
Jay Bell, Richie Hebner, Ken Boyer

| YEAR | TEAM | LVL | AGE | PA | R | 2B | 3B | HR | RBI | BB | SO | SB | CS | AVG_OBP_SLG | TAv | BABIP | BRR | FRAA | WARP |
|---|---|---|---|---|---|---|---|---|---|---|---|---|---|---|---|---|---|---|---|
| 2009 | CLE | MLB | 34 | 314 | 47 | 13 | 0 | 13 | 50 | 29 | 63 | 1 | 1 | .270/.342/.457 | .281 | .302 | -0.9 | -4.2 | 1.0 |
| 2009 | SLN | MLB | 34 | 262 | 31 | 10 | 1 | 10 | 28 | 18 | 58 | 2 | 1 | .228/.291/.405 | .245 | .257 | 1.4 | -5.5 | 0.0 |
| 2010 | SFN | MLB | 35 | 104 | 9 | 3 | 0 | 1 | 10 | 9 | 16 | 0 | 2 | .194/.279/.258 | .194 | .224 | -1.4 | 0.3 | -0.6 |
| 2011 | SFN | MLB | 36 | 97 | 9 | 2 | 0 | 0 | 12 | 8 | 18 | 1 | 1 | .279/.351/.302 | .260 | .348 | 1.6 | -1.1 | 0.4 |
| 2012 | WAS | MLB | 37 | 250 | 29 | 10 | 1 | 6 | 26 | 22 | 47 | 2 | 1 | .258/.333/.392 | .263 | .298 | -0.2 | 3B -4, LF -1 | 1.8 |

Over the course of a two-year, $12 million contract with the Giants, Mark DeRosa had more stays on the 60-day disabled list (two) than home runs. The wrist injury that shelved him for most of 2010 returned on a check-swing a month into 2011, sending him back to the DL and affecting him even after he rejoined the team in August. Playing with a torn wrist tendon after his return, he managed a .367 average in 57 plate appearances, but 17 of his 18 hits were singles, and just two of his batted balls reached left field. At 37, he doesn't appear to have much left, but the Nats gave him a guaranteed contract to fill a utility role.

## Ian Desmond — SS

Born: 9/20/1985 Age: 26
Bats: R Throws: R Height: 6' 3" Weight: 210
Breakout: 3% Improve: 39% Collapse: 7%
Attrition: 31% MLB: 88%

Comparables:
Joe Millette, Derek Jeter, Jim Fregosi

| YEAR | TEAM | LVL | AGE | PA | R | 2B | 3B | HR | RBI | BB | SO | SB | CS | AVG_OBP_SLG | TAv | BABIP | BRR | FRAA | WARP |
|---|---|---|---|---|---|---|---|---|---|---|---|---|---|---|---|---|---|---|---|
| 2009 | HAR | AA | 23 | 189 | 29 | 12 | 1 | 6 | 18 | 16 | 40 | 13 | 4 | .306/.370/.494 | .302 | .368 | -0.9 | 0.4 | 1.6 |
| 2009 | SYR | AAA | 23 | 205 | 25 | 12 | 2 | 1 | 14 | 20 | 31 | 8 | 1 | .354/.420/.461 | .314 | .413 | 1.6 | -1.9 | 2.1 |
| 2009 | WAS | MLB | 23 | 89 | 9 | 7 | 2 | 4 | 12 | 5 | 14 | 1 | 0 | .280/.318/.561 | .286 | .292 | -0.2 | -1.3 | 0.4 |
| 2010 | WAS | MLB | 24 | 574 | 59 | 27 | 4 | 10 | 65 | 28 | 109 | 17 | 5 | .269/.308/.392 | .251 | .317 | 1.6 | -7.9 | 1.0 |
| 2011 | WAS | MLB | 25 | 639 | 65 | 27 | 5 | 8 | 49 | 35 | 139 | 25 | 10 | .253/.298/.358 | .241 | .317 | 4.8 | -3.9 | 1.4 |
| 2012 | WAS | MLB | 26 | 587 | 67 | 28 | 4 | 12 | 65 | 31 | 110 | 20 | 7 | .270/.313/.400 | .254 | .313 | -0.2 | SS -4, 2B -0 | 2.1 |

Desmond is kind of a known quantity at this point. He's a hacking shortstop with a little bit of pop, won't kill you with the glove, enough speed to steal a few bases. Played a little better down the stretch, but not well enough to preempt challenges to his position on the depth chart. The Nats will be running a constant audition for his replacement throughout his career with them, in all likelihood.

## Danny Espinosa — 2B

Born: 4/25/1987 Age: 25
Bats: B Throws: R Height: 6' 1" Weight: 190
Breakout: 3% Improve: 25% Collapse: 11%
Attrition: 38% MLB: 83%

Comparables:
Craig Stansberry, Jason Hardtke, Sean Rodriguez

| YEAR | TEAM | LVL | AGE | PA | R | 2B | 3B | HR | RBI | BB | SO | SB | CS | AVG_OBP_SLG | TAv | BABIP | BRR | FRAA | WARP |
|---|---|---|---|---|---|---|---|---|---|---|---|---|---|---|---|---|---|---|---|
| 2009 | POT | A+ | 22 | 576 | 90 | 31 | 4 | 18 | 72 | 74 | 129 | 29 | 11 | .264/.371/.460 | .280 | .318 | 0.8 | 8.7 | 4.3 |
| 2010 | HAR | AA | 23 | 434 | 66 | 16 | 4 | 18 | 54 | 33 | 94 | 20 | 8 | .262/.333/.464 | .283 | .300 | 0.7 | -0.5 | 3.2 |
| 2010 | SYR | AAA | 23 | 108 | 14 | 2 | 1 | 4 | 15 | 8 | 22 | 5 | 3 | .295/.349/.463 | .271 | .338 | 0.5 | -1.2 | 0.5 |
| 2010 | WAS | MLB | 23 | 112 | 16 | 4 | 1 | 6 | 15 | 9 | 30 | 0 | 2 | .214/.277/.447 | .251 | .239 | 1.6 | 0.4 | 0.4 |
| 2011 | WAS | MLB | 24 | 658 | 72 | 29 | 5 | 21 | 66 | 57 | 166 | 17 | 6 | .236/.323/.414 | .261 | .292 | 2.7 | 11.7 | 3.2 |
| 2012 | WAS | MLB | 25 | 573 | 67 | 23 | 3 | 21 | 68 | 45 | 139 | 17 | 7 | .238/.312/.416 | .257 | .281 | -0.7 | 2B 6, SS 1 | 1.8 |

There are reasons not to play Espinosa at shortstop, but Desmond isn't really one of them. Espinosa played a full season at second and held up remarkably well, putting together a nice stretch of offense in September. His power's prodigious, and he'll be able to move comfortably on the defensive spectrum whether he ends up at shortstop or not. He's definitely got the arm to play third base should that need eventually arise, but that's awfully far down the road; he's got the hands and feet to play not just an acceptable second, but a very good one.

**Jesus Flores**    C

Born: **10/26/1984** Age: **27**
Bats: **R** Throws: **R** Height: **6' 2"** Weight: **180**
Breakout: **3%** Improve: **22%** Collapse: **10%**
Attrition: **47%** MLB: **74%**

Comparables:
John Sullivan, Jose Molina, Shawn Riggans

| YEAR | TEAM | LVL | AGE | PA | R | 2B | 3B | HR | RBI | BB | SO | SB | CS | AVG_OBP_SLG | TAv | BABIP | BRR | FRAA | WARP |
|------|------|-----|-----|-----|----|----|----|----|-----|----|----|----|----|-------------|------|-------|------|------|------|
| 2009 | WAS | MLB | 24 | 106 | 13 | 3 | 2 | 4 | 15 | 11 | 26 | 0 | 0 | .301/.371/.505 | .298 | .375 | -1.1 | -0.4 | 0.7 |
| 2011 | SYR | AAA | 26 | 218 | 17 | 15 | 0 | 5 | 30 | 5 | 54 | 0 | 0 | .234/.252/.378 | .204 | .288 | -1.7 | -0.1 | -0.4 |
| 2011 | WAS | MLB | 26 | 91 | 5 | 6 | 0 | 1 | 2 | 5 | 27 | 0 | 0 | .209/.253/.314 | .203 | .293 | -1.5 | -0.5 | -0.4 |
| 2012 | WAS | MLB | 27 | 250 | 27 | 12 | 1 | 6 | 26 | 14 | 60 | 0 | 0 | .244/.292/.377 | .238 | .301 | 0 | C -2 | 0.9 |

BP's resident dermatologist, Rany Jazayerli, had a theory about backup catchers that he called The Junior Ortiz Axiom if memory serves. The concept is that if a backup catcher hangs around long enough he will eventually hit .300 no matter his skill level. Since Flores has already done this (in 2009) does it make sense to let him go because he's fired the arrows in his quiver? Flores is the epitome of backup catcherdom and should have been allowed to move along once he began costing more than the league minimum.

**Jonny Gomes**    LF

| YEAR | TEAM | LVL | AGE | PA | R | 2B | 3B | HR | RBI | BB | SO | SB | CS | AVG_OBP_SLG | TAv | BABIP | BRR | FRAA | WARP |
|------|------|-----|-----|-----|----|----|----|----|-----|----|----|----|----|-------------|------|-------|------|------|------|

career to lose that dimension. Gomes is a better hitter than he showed in 2011—balls just didn't drop in for him. He's always at risk to drop into a platoon or reduced role because he can struggle against righties and isn't a plus defensive outfielder. He'll catch on somewhere and is young enough to have a Marcus Thames-like stretch for a few years. He can help out a club that needs a solid bat and he won't tarpit the team's season if its cleanup hitter misses two months.

**Bryce Harper**    RF

Born: **10/16/1992** Age: **19**
Bats: **L** Throws: **R** Height: **6' 4"** Weight: **205**
Breakout: **0%** Improve: **5%** Collapse: **0%**
Attrition: **9%** MLB: **13%**

Comparables:
Travis Snider, Michael Burgess, Danny Murphy

| YEAR | TEAM | LVL | AGE | PA | R | 2B | 3B | HR | RBI | BB | SO | SB | CS | AVG_OBP_SLG | TAv | BABIP | BRR | FRAA | WARP |
|------|------|-----|-----|-----|----|----|----|----|-----|----|----|----|----|-------------|------|-------|------|------|------|
| 2011 | HAG | A | 18 | 305 | 49 | 17 | 1 | 14 | 46 | 44 | 61 | 19 | 5 | .318/.423/.554 | .334 | .372 | 1.5 | -1 | 3.7 |
| 2011 | HAR | AA | 18 | 147 | 14 | 7 | 1 | 3 | 12 | 15 | 26 | 7 | 2 | .256/.329/.395 | .253 | .294 | 2.9 | -1.4 | 0.5 |
| 2012 | WAS | MLB | 19 | 250 | 27 | 10 | 1 | 7 | 26 | 21 | 58 | 8 | 3 | .239/.304/.383 | .245 | .286 | 0 | RF 0, LF -2 | 0.3 |

We blame House for this. Somewhere along the line jerks across America decided that they were just like the misanthropic physician—their brilliance and otherworldly excellence at work both created and somehow permitted their being a complete psychopathic tool. No. It might be true for a fictional character but that guy at your office is really just a gaper. For Harper that side of it is overblown. He gets attention for showing up an opponent who instigated it earlier in the game. He gets attention for buying eyeblack in bulk at Sam's Club and smearing it all over himself. But mostly what he gets attention for is hitting the snot out of the ball. And he's going to do that in spades. For a very long time. Think of it as if A.J. Pierzynski had the talent that he thinks he has. Pro scouts have Harper's power at 80 and he covers a surprising and increasing amount of ground in the outfield. He's going to be a beast and he'll have a chance to break camp with the big club. Believe the hype.

**Jarrett Hoffpauir**    2B

Born: **6/18/1983** Age: **29**
Bats: **R** Throws: **R** Height: **5' 10"** Weight: **190**
Breakout: **5%** Improve: **38%** Collapse: **5%**
Attrition: **17%** MLB: **82%**

Comparables:
Bobby Avila, Todd Haney, Brian Roberts

| YEAR | TEAM | LVL | AGE | PA | R | 2B | 3B | HR | RBI | BB | SO | SB | CS | AVG_OBP_SLG | TAv | BABIP | BRR | FRAA | WARP |
|------|------|-----|-----|-----|----|----|----|----|-----|----|----|----|----|-------------|------|-------|------|------|------|
| 2009 | MEM | AAA | 26 | 402 | 53 | 22 | 3 | 14 | 53 | 35 | 28 | 4 | 1 | .291/.355/.486 | .301 | .281 | -1.4 | -0.2 | 2.7 |
| 2009 | SLN | MLB | 26 | 16 | 1 | 2 | 0 | 0 | 2 | 4 | 2 | 0 | 0 | .250/.438/.417 | .289 | .300 | -0.2 | 0.2 | 0.1 |
| 2010 | LVG | AAA | 27 | 500 | 73 | 26 | 6 | 16 | 73 | 58 | 34 | 8 | 3 | .295/.379/.494 | .285 | .289 | 1.6 | 3.4 | 3.3 |
| 2010 | TOR | MLB | 27 | 37 | 1 | 1 | 0 | 0 | 0 | 2 | 5 | 0 | 0 | .206/.250/.235 | .175 | .241 | 0.5 | 0.8 | -0.1 |
| 2012 | WAS | MLB | 29 | 250 | 28 | 13 | 1 | 5 | 26 | 19 | 31 | 1 | 0 | .253/.315/.382 | .251 | .269 | 0 | 2B -2, 3B -1 | 1.1 |

Nice little pickup. If life were a meritocracy, Hoffpauir would get at least a crack at the shortstop job, and would be the favorite for a utility role where he could get 350 PA and help solve the Nats' leadoff conundrum. He's a good contact hitter, has some pop, will draw a few walks, and plays credible defense pretty much anywhere you put him. At least 50-75 guys with MLB jobs should be displaced by Hoffpauir, but incumbency and inertia matter. He should probably be encouraged that the Nats went and got him—maybe Rizzo and Johnson see the value here, and he'll end up in that sweet spot on the roster that gives him a career and gives the Nationals a couple more wins.

### Adam LaRoche — 1B

Born: 11/6/1979 Age: 32
Bats: L Throws: L Height: 6' 4" Weight: 180
Breakout: 1% Improve: 25% Collapse: 8%
Attrition: 19% MLB: 75%

Comparables:
Vic Wertz, Glenn Davis, Kevin Barker

| YEAR | TEAM | LVL | AGE | PA | R | 2B | 3B | HR | RBI | BB | SO | SB | CS | AVG_OBP_SLG | TAv | BABIP | BRR | FRAA | WARP |
|---|---|---|---|---|---|---|---|---|---|---|---|---|---|---|---|---|---|---|---|
| 2009 | ATL | MLB | 29 | 242 | 30 | 11 | 1 | 12 | 40 | 28 | 59 | 0 | 0 | .325/.401/.557 | .339 | .399 | -2 | 0.9 | 2.2 |
| 2009 | BOS | MLB | 29 | 19 | 2 | 2 | 0 | 1 | 3 | 0 | 2 | 0 | 0 | .263/.263/.526 | .247 | .250 | -0.2 | 0.2 | 0.0 |
| 2009 | PIT | MLB | 29 | 368 | 46 | 25 | 1 | 12 | 40 | 41 | 81 | 2 | 2 | .247/.329/.441 | .258 | .291 | -1 | 5.7 | 0.7 |
| 2010 | ARI | MLB | 30 | 615 | 75 | 37 | 2 | 25 | 100 | 48 | 172 | 0 | 1 | .261/.320/.468 | .271 | .330 | -2.4 | 10 | 1.9 |
| 2011 | WAS | MLB | 31 | 177 | 15 | 4 | 0 | 3 | 15 | 25 | 37 | 1 | 0 | .172/.288/.258 | .205 | .205 | 1.7 | 3 | -0.5 |
| 2012 | WAS | MLB | 32 | 254 | 31 | 13 | 0 | 9 | 32 | 23 | 58 | 1 | 0 | .256/.326/.439 | .270 | .303 | -0.1 | 1B 5 | 1.1 |

LaRoche had about as rotten a 2011 as you can have—hard shots at defenders, nagging injury that ends up lingering and eventually requires season-ending surgery. Probably even had his luggage lost at some point. He's a gamble that the Nationals have no choice but to take—he's under contract for $8 million, coming off an injury that can really sap production, and getting to an age when players can just drop off a cliff.

### Steve Lombardozzi — 2B

Born: 9/20/1988 Age: 23
Bats: B Throws: R Height: 6' 1" Weight: 170
Breakout: 4% Improve: 33% Collapse: 5%
Attrition: 23% MLB: 61%

Comparables:
Adrian Cardenas, Mark Lemke, Ken Boswell

| YEAR | TEAM | LVL | AGE | PA | R | 2B | 3B | HR | RBI | BB | SO | SB | CS | AVG_OBP_SLG | TAv | BABIP | BRR | FRAA | WARP |
|---|---|---|---|---|---|---|---|---|---|---|---|---|---|---|---|---|---|---|---|
| 2009 | HAG | A | 20 | 576 | 90 | 26 | 7 | 3 | 58 | 62 | 80 | 16 | 7 | .296/.376/.395 | .296 | .344 | 3.2 | 7.9 | 4.7 |
| 2010 | POT | A+ | 21 | 507 | 71 | 30 | 9 | 1 | 38 | 49 | 60 | 20 | 10 | .293/.364/.409 | .280 | .329 | 2.2 | -1.7 | 1.5 |
| 2010 | HAR | AA | 21 | 118 | 19 | 5 | 2 | 5 | 11 | 12 | 15 | 4 | 2 | .295/.373/.524 | .315 | .306 | 0.1 | -2.6 | 1.0 |
| 2011 | HAR | AA | 22 | 291 | 40 | 12 | 7 | 4 | 23 | 18 | 38 | 16 | 3 | .309/.366/.454 | .293 | .348 | 4.8 | -5 | 1.6 |
| 2011 | SYR | AAA | 22 | 325 | 46 | 13 | 2 | 4 | 29 | 21 | 40 | 14 | 5 | .310/.354/.408 | .250 | .344 | -0.4 | 2.4 | 0.7 |
| 2011 | WAS | MLB | 22 | 32 | 3 | 1 | 0 | 0 | 1 | 1 | 4 | 0 | 0 | .194/.219/.226 | .165 | .222 | -0.7 | 0.2 | -0.3 |
| 2012 | WAS | MLB | 23 | 250 | 27 | 10 | 2 | 2 | 23 | 16 | 38 | 6 | 2 | .260/.310/.355 | .239 | .297 | -0.2 | 2B -5, SS -0 | 0.5 |

If one of the things a prospect brings to the table is versatility, he's generally not much of a prospect. Lombardozzi's fast, and pro scouts believe he'll be able to play all over the field, but he's not a great player at any one position, nor is he likely to be. Davey will have the options to cobble together some sort of arrangement with Desmond, but neither should take playing time away from Espinosa.

### Chris Marrero — 1B

Born: 7/2/1988 Age: 23
Bats: R Throws: R Height: 6' 4" Weight: 210
Breakout: 8% Improve: 18% Collapse: 7%
Attrition: 25% MLB: 44%

Comparables:
Jim Breazeale, Nelson Simmons, Nick Evans

| YEAR | TEAM | LVL | AGE | PA | R | 2B | 3B | HR | RBI | BB | SO | SB | CS | AVG_OBP_SLG | TAv | BABIP | BRR | FRAA | WARP |
|---|---|---|---|---|---|---|---|---|---|---|---|---|---|---|---|---|---|---|---|
| 2009 | POT | A+ | 21 | 469 | 58 | 21 | 2 | 16 | 65 | 42 | 97 | 2 | 3 | .287/.364/.464 | .288 | .342 | -2.4 | -1.9 | 1.3 |
| 2009 | HAR | AA | 21 | 84 | 9 | 6 | 0 | 1 | 11 | 8 | 18 | 0 | 1 | .267/.345/.387 | .251 | .339 | -0.7 | -2 | -0.4 |
| 2010 | HAR | AA | 22 | 577 | 73 | 28 | 0 | 18 | 82 | 43 | 102 | 1 | 3 | .294/.353/.450 | .279 | .337 | -3.3 | 1.2 | 1.3 |
| 2011 | SYR | AAA | 23 | 546 | 59 | 30 | 0 | 14 | 69 | 58 | 97 | 3 | 2 | .300/.375/.449 | .277 | .349 | 1.8 | 1 | 1.9 |
| 2011 | WAS | MLB | 23 | 117 | 6 | 5 | 0 | 0 | 10 | 4 | 27 | 0 | 0 | .248/.274/.294 | .214 | .318 | -0.7 | -0.1 | -0.7 |
| 2012 | WAS | MLB | 23 | 250 | 28 | 11 | 0 | 6 | 27 | 16 | 52 | 0 | 0 | .261/.312/.392 | .253 | .310 | -0.1 | 1B -11 | 0.3 |

Marrero looked good at Syracuse, and thanks to the LaRoche situation and the prescient farewell to Adam Dunn, a little window of opportunity opened up for him in Washington. Unfortunately, he suffered a severe hamstring injury playing winter ball. The extent of the injury isn't so bad that Marrero expects to miss the 2012 season, but it's unlikely he'll be ready at full speed for the start of it.

### Jason Michaels — LF

Born: 5/4/1976 Age: 36
Bats: R Throws: R Height: 6' 1" Weight: 205
Breakout: 0% Improve: 25% Collapse: 6%
Attrition: 17% MLB: 57%

Comparables:
Leon Wagner, Jay Johnstone, Jerry Mumphrey

| YEAR | TEAM | LVL | AGE | PA | R | 2B | 3B | HR | RBI | BB | SO | SB | CS | AVG_OBP_SLG | TAv | BABIP | BRR | FRAA | WARP |
|---|---|---|---|---|---|---|---|---|---|---|---|---|---|---|---|---|---|---|---|
| 2009 | HOU | MLB | 33 | 152 | 17 | 12 | 1 | 4 | 16 | 16 | 38 | 1 | 2 | .237/.322/.430 | .254 | .301 | -0.9 | 0.4 | 0.2 |
| 2010 | HOU | MLB | 34 | 203 | 23 | 14 | 1 | 8 | 26 | 12 | 29 | 0 | 0 | .253/.310/.468 | .272 | .260 | 0.6 | -2.8 | 0.3 |
| 2011 | HOU | MLB | 35 | 169 | 10 | 9 | 0 | 2 | 10 | 11 | 31 | 1 | 0 | .199/.256/.295 | .192 | .236 | 0.1 | 0.4 | -0.8 |
| 2012 | WAS | MLB | 36 | 250 | 26 | 12 | 1 | 6 | 25 | 18 | 47 | 2 | 1 | .234/.295/.369 | .238 | .268 | -0.2 | LF -1, RF 1 | 0.1 |

A cautionary tale for Reed Johnson fans: Entering 2011, Michaels was the same age as Johnson is now, with an almost identical career stat line, and Michaels was coming off a decent 2010 season. Yet, how quickly things change. The end is near for Michaels as he's no longer able to fake it in center field, and he's never hit well enough to play full time at a corner. He's reached base 35 percent of the time against left-handed pitching in his career, been a willing pinch-hitter, and has generally shown the sort of good attitude that's required of a fourth outfielder. His season ended with a broken hand in September, but that should be fully healed by spring training. The Nationals signed him to a minor-league deal in December.

### Tyler Moore 1B

Born: 1/30/1987 Age: 25
Bats: R Throws: R Height: 6' 3" Weight: 185
Breakout: 1% Improve: 31% Collapse: 6%
Attrition: 20% MLB: 68%

**Comparables:**
Glenn Davis, Rico Brogna, Ossie Blanco

| YEAR | TEAM | LVL | AGE | PA | R | 2B | 3B | HR | RBI | BB | SO | SB | CS | AVG_OBP_SLG | TAv | BABIP | BRR | FRAA | WARP |
|------|------|-----|-----|-----|----|----|----|----|-----|----|-----|----|----|-------------|-----|-------|------|---------|------|
| 2009 | HAG | A | 22 | 477 | 38 | 30 | 3 | 9 | 87 | 40 | 111 | 2 | 2 | .297/.369/.447 | .301 | .385 | -3.4 | -0.2 | 2.1 |
| 2010 | POT | A+ | 23 | 553 | 78 | 43 | 3 | 31 | 111 | 40 | 125 | 0 | 0 | .269/.324/.552 | .307 | .299 | -2 | 11.7 | 4.5 |
| 2011 | HAR | AA | 24 | 561 | 70 | 35 | 4 | 31 | 90 | 30 | 139 | 2 | 0 | .270/.314/.532 | .287 | .307 | -2.1 | 4.5 | 2.8 |
| 2012 | WAS | MLB | 25 | 250 | 28 | 12 | 1 | 10 | 33 | 12 | 66 | 0 | 0 | .240/.278/.434 | .249 | .284 | 0 | 1B -7 | 0.1 |

Moore's ridden the age train in the minors. He lit up the scoreboard in the second half of 2010, but with a pretty lackluster control of the strike zone and a batting average that paid the price for it. He had a similar year in Double-A in 2011, again popping 31 home runs, but also bearing a BB:K ratio that doesn't bode well for future development. He did tighten his swing up somewhat, but that effort doesn't seem to have borne fruit in the batter's box just yet. For a bomber, walking 30 times in Double-A (including intentionals) while fanning 139 times means there's still a lot of work to do, and the trend is going the other way. Moore's future will depend very heavily on his next 300 PA. Right now, he looks like a .220 hitter with few walks and a few bombs in the majors.

| YEAR | TEAM | LVL | AGE | PA | R | 2B | 3B | HR | RBI | BB | SO | SB | CS | AVG_OBP_SLG | TAv | BABIP | BRR | FRAA | WARP |
|------|------|-----|-----|-----|----|----|----|----|-----|----|-----|----|----|-------------|-----|-------|------|------------|------|
| 2012 | WAS | MLB | 30 | 491 | 65 | 25 | 1 | 21 | 70 | 32 | 100 | 2 | 1 | .283/.340/.485 | .291 | .319 | -0.3 | 1B -1, LF -1 | 2.5 |

Nicely done. When LaRoche's shoulder took him out, Morse stepped up and performed exceptionally well for the Nats, playing a championship-caliber first base. There's some significant downside risk, as Morse turns 30 before the season starts and has always had troublesome strike zone control, but he's a serviceable defender, can hit the ball out of the park, and is on a single-year contract. Good circumstance for all involved.

### Xavier Paul RF

Born: 2/25/1985 Age: 27
Bats: L Throws: R Height: 6' 1" Weight: 195
Breakout: 2% Improve: 26% Collapse: 9%
Attrition: 27% MLB: 62%

**Comparables:**
Mark Ryal, Don Taussig, Gene Green

| YEAR | TEAM | LVL | AGE | PA | R | 2B | 3B | HR | RBI | BB | SO | SB | CS | AVG_OBP_SLG | TAv | BABIP | BRR | FRAA | WARP |
|------|------|-----|-----|-----|----|----|----|----|-----|----|----|----|----|-------------|-----|-------|------|------------|------|
| 2009 | ABQ | AAA | 24 | 129 | 13 | 10 | 2 | 2 | 16 | 10 | 22 | 8 | 2 | .328/.375/.500 | .267 | .383 | -0.7 | -4.3 | 0.1 |
| 2009 | LAN | MLB | 24 | 16 | 3 | 1 | 0 | 1 | 1 | 2 | 4 | 0 | 1 | .214/.312/.500 | .305 | .222 | 0.1 | -0.1 | 0.1 |
| 2010 | ABQ | AAA | 25 | 250 | 46 | 20 | 1 | 12 | 38 | 18 | 41 | 7 | 3 | .325/.384/.579 | .287 | .354 | 2.2 | 0.8 | 1.5 |
| 2010 | LAN | MLB | 25 | 133 | 16 | 8 | 1 | 0 | 11 | 8 | 24 | 3 | 1 | .231/.277/.314 | .222 | .286 | 1.2 | -0.8 | -0.2 |
| 2011 | LAN | MLB | 26 | 11 | 0 | 0 | 0 | 0 | 0 | 0 | 5 | 0 | 0 | .273/.273/.273 | .193 | .500 | 0.1 | 0 | 0.0 |
| 2011 | PIT | MLB | 26 | 251 | 30 | 6 | 5 | 2 | 20 | 13 | 57 | 16 | 6 | .254/.293/.349 | .245 | .328 | -0.5 | -3 | -0.1 |
| 2012 | WAS | MLB | 27 | 250 | 27 | 11 | 2 | 3 | 25 | 14 | 51 | 12 | 4 | .257/.301/.367 | .238 | .307 | -0.3 | RF -2, LF -1 | 0.0 |

Walk around PNC Park for more than an hour and you are bound to run into a former Dodgers prospect, an outfield tweener, or a combination thereof—like Paul. Besides a proficiency for making outs against lefties (he reached base four times in 29 plate appearances), Paul did not show much in 2011 after the Pirates grabbed him off waivers. He'll try to catch on as outfield depth for the Nationals.

### Eury Perez CF

Born: 5/30/1990 Age: 22
Bats: R Throws: R Height: 6' 1" Weight: 180
Breakout: 2% Improve: 13% Collapse: 2%
Attrition: 11% MLB: 24%

**Comparables:**
Peter Bourjos, Francisco Peguero, Adrian Ortiz

| YEAR | TEAM | LVL | AGE | PA | R | 2B | 3B | HR | RBI | BB | SO | SB | CS | AVG_OBP_SLG | TAv | BABIP | BRR | FRAA | WARP |
|------|------|-----|-----|-----|----|----|----|----|----|-----|----|----|----|----|-------------|-----|-------|------|-----------|------|
| 2009 | NAT | RK | 19 | 205 | 38 | 3 | 5 | 3 | 24 | 15 | 20 | 16 | 8 | .381/.434/.503 | .338 | .407 | 1.4 | 2.8 | 2.6 |
| 2010 | HAG | A | 20 | 491 | 88 | 17 | 5 | 3 | 42 | 23 | 74 | 64 | 13 | .299/.331/.381 | .283 | .335 | 14.1 | 6.2 | 5.1 |
| 2011 | POT | A+ | 21 | 465 | 54 | 9 | 2 | 1 | 41 | 22 | 63 | 45 | 15 | .283/.319/.321 | .237 | .326 | 2.4 | 1.1 | 0.7 |
| 2012 | WAS | MLB | 22 | 250 | 23 | 7 | 1 | 1 | 20 | 6 | 47 | 19 | 6 | .248/.268/.307 | .204 | .294 | 0 | CF -6, RF -0 | -1.2 |

Do any of these guys ever actually get better? Perez is a waterbug, as Whitey Herzog occasionally put it. He runs well. He can't hit. He won't hit. He doesn't control the strike zone. He doesn't hit the ball with enough authority to keep the outfielders even close to honest. Since Rookie ball, he's drawn 45 walks in about 900 PA. There's no reason not to just throw him BP fastballs. If everything breaks his way, Eury could have a 20 percent chance to be Endy Chavez lite. One more reason rotisserie baseball is vile is that it causes the occasional baseball fan to think that someone like Perez is a valuable player. Uh-uh.

### Wilson Ramos    C

Born: 8/10/1987 Age: 24
Bats: R Throws: R Height: 6' 1" Weight: 220
Breakout: 3% Improve: 21% Collapse: 9%
Attrition: 32% MLB: 76%

Comparables:
Don Slaught, Angel Salome, Joe Torre

| YEAR | TEAM | LVL | AGE | PA | R | 2B | 3B | HR | RBI | BB | SO | SB | CS | AVG_OBP_SLG | TAv | BABIP | BRR | FRAA | WARP |
|---|---|---|---|---|---|---|---|---|---|---|---|---|---|---|---|---|---|---|---|
| 2009 | NBR | AA | 21 | 214 | 31 | 16 | 0 | 4 | 29 | 6 | 23 | 0 | 0 | .317/.343/.454 | .302 | .343 | -0.2 | 1.5 | 2.2 |
| 2010 | ROC | AAA | 22 | 295 | 25 | 14 | 0 | 5 | 30 | 12 | 49 | 1 | 2 | .241/.278/.345 | .217 | .274 | -0.5 | -1 | 0.0 |
| 2010 | SYR | AAA | 22 | 82 | 14 | 3 | 1 | 3 | 8 | 3 | 12 | 0 | 0 | .316/.341/.494 | .281 | .344 | 0.7 | 0.5 | 0.9 |
| 2010 | MIN | MLB | 22 | 28 | 2 | 3 | 0 | 0 | 1 | 0 | 3 | 0 | 0 | .296/.321/.407 | .258 | .333 | 0 | -0.1 | 0.1 |
| 2010 | WAS | MLB | 22 | 54 | 3 | 4 | 0 | 1 | 4 | 2 | 9 | 0 | 0 | .269/.296/.404 | .237 | .310 | -1.2 | 0.2 | 0.1 |
| 2011 | WAS | MLB | 23 | 435 | 48 | 22 | 1 | 15 | 52 | 38 | 76 | 0 | 2 | .267/.334/.445 | .264 | .297 | 0.7 | -1.4 | 2.2 |
| 2012 | WAS | MLB | 24 | 382 | 45 | 19 | 1 | 11 | 47 | 20 | 60 | 1 | 1 | .271/.313/.425 | .261 | .296 | -0.1 | C -1 | 2.1 |

So, how was *your* offseason? Ramos' misfortune as a kidnapping victim in Venezuela—he was rescued unharmed after two days—illustrates in the starkest possible terms that vulnerability is a fate shared by all of us. Ramos' youth and success at the plate were key drivers in the Nationals front office deciding it needed to dramatically undervalue Derek Norris, because as everyone knows, surpluses are fatal. Ramos hit considerably better at home than on the road, which should even out somewhat over time. He's a young catcher who's got a broad offensive skill set and can handle the position defensively. On the potential downside, he makes outs on the ground, often two at a time, and runs about as fast as devotees of *The Secret* do arithmetic.

### Carlos Rivero    3B

Born: 5/20/1988 Age: 24
Bats: R Throws: R Height: 6' 4" Weight: 220
Breakout: 2% Improve: 17% Collapse: 5%
Attrition: 21% MLB: 57%

Comparables:
Ivanon Coffie, Casey McGehee, Andy Carey

| YEAR | TEAM | LVL | AGE | PA | R | 2B | 3B | HR | RBI | BB | SO | SB | CS | AVG_OBP_SLG | TAv | BABIP | BRR | FRAA | WARP |
|---|---|---|---|---|---|---|---|---|---|---|---|---|---|---|---|---|---|---|---|
| 2009 | AKR | AA | 21 | 546 | 50 | 24 | 2 | 7 | 58 | 50 | 73 | 1 | 0 | .242/.312/.344 | .235 | .269 | -5 | -6.3 | -0.6 |
| 2010 | AKR | AA | 22 | 444 | 39 | 16 | 2 | 6 | 43 | 28 | 81 | 0 | 3 | .232/.281/.325 | .225 | .274 | -3.2 | 9.6 | 0.7 |
| 2011 | REA | AA | 23 | 538 | 70 | 36 | 0 | 15 | 66 | 38 | 106 | 5 | 3 | .275/.331/.440 | .261 | .321 | 0.8 | -1.1 | 0.7 |
| 2012 | WAS | MLB | 24 | 250 | 26 | 11 | 1 | 5 | 25 | 15 | 47 | 1 | 0 | .237/.284/.358 | .230 | .271 | -0.1 | 3B -3, SS 1 | 0.6 |

Rivero was jettisoned by the Phillies and snagged by Team Rizzo in December. He's not the worst prospect in the world, but there's a reason he was available on waivers. He's a decent defender at third base, but his bat needs to develop, and quickly. He'll probably start the year at Triple-A, but it's not clear that he's ready for it. In his third year at Double-A, he hit .275/.331/.440, and that was by far his best season. Improvement is good, but that's not enough improvement to make him a lock for the next level up. He's organizational filler at this point, until he shows people there's some reason to view him more favorably.

### Ivan Rodriguez    C

Born: 11/27/1971 Age: 40
Bats: R Throws: R Height: 5' 10" Weight: 165
Breakout: 2% Improve: 17% Collapse: 10%
Attrition: 33% MLB: 54%

Comparables:
Birdie Tebbetts, Benito Santiago, Ray Mueller

| YEAR | TEAM | LVL | AGE | PA | R | 2B | 3B | HR | RBI | BB | SO | SB | CS | AVG_OBP_SLG | TAv | BABIP | BRR | FRAA | WARP |
|---|---|---|---|---|---|---|---|---|---|---|---|---|---|---|---|---|---|---|---|
| 2009 | HOU | MLB | 37 | 344 | 41 | 15 | 2 | 8 | 34 | 13 | 74 | 0 | 2 | .251/.280/.382 | .220 | .300 | 2 | 3.5 | 0.7 |
| 2009 | TEX | MLB | 37 | 104 | 14 | 8 | 0 | 2 | 13 | 5 | 18 | 1 | 0 | .245/.279/.388 | .228 | .278 | 0.7 | 0.8 | 0.2 |
| 2010 | WAS | MLB | 38 | 421 | 32 | 18 | 1 | 4 | 49 | 16 | 66 | 2 | 3 | .266/.294/.347 | .221 | .307 | -5.1 | 3.2 | 0.4 |
| 2011 | WAS | MLB | 39 | 137 | 14 | 7 | 0 | 2 | 19 | 10 | 28 | 0 | 0 | .218/.281/.323 | .213 | .266 | 0.4 | 0 | 0.3 |
| 2012 | WAS | MLB | 40 | 250 | 25 | 11 | 1 | 4 | 24 | 8 | 46 | 2 | 1 | .248/.275/.350 | .224 | .291 | -0.2 | C 2 | 0.4 |

I-Rod hadn't caught on as a free agent at the time of this writing in late December. No matter whether he makes 3,000 hits or some other arbitrary milestone based on the fact that we have 10 fingers, he was an exceptionally exciting player to watch throughout a long and distinguished career. We at BP salute anyone who can put on the pads and catch one game in Arlington in August, much less 140 games a year for the better part of two decades. Thanks for putting in the hard work to make it look easy, Ivan. It was fun to watch your progression in the eyes of the media from rebellious talented kid to mentoring elder statesman.

### Matt Stairs    LF

Born: 2/27/1968 Age: 44
Bats: L Throws: R Height: 5' 10" Weight: 175
Breakout: 0% Improve: 7% Collapse: 0%
Attrition: 19% MLB: 34%

Comparables:
Dave Winfield, Tony Perez, Luke Appling

| YEAR | TEAM | LVL | AGE | PA | R | 2B | 3B | HR | RBI | BB | SO | SB | CS | AVG_OBP_SLG | TAv | BABIP | BRR | FRAA | WARP |
|---|---|---|---|---|---|---|---|---|---|---|---|---|---|---|---|---|---|---|---|
| 2009 | PHI | MLB | 41 | 129 | 15 | 4 | 0 | 5 | 17 | 23 | 30 | 0 | 0 | .194/.357/.379 | .270 | .221 | -0.2 | 0.2 | 0.5 |
| 2010 | SDN | MLB | 42 | 111 | 14 | 6 | 0 | 6 | 16 | 11 | 32 | 2 | 0 | .232/.306/.475 | .275 | .274 | 0.7 | 0 | 0.5 |
| 2011 | WAS | MLB | 43 | 74 | 4 | 1 | 0 | 0 | 2 | 9 | 23 | 0 | 0 | .154/.257/.169 | .177 | .238 | 0.4 | -0.1 | -0.4 |
| 2012 | WAS | MLB | 44 | 250 | 29 | 10 | 0 | 9 | 27 | 27 | 59 | 1 | 1 | .230/.318/.397 | .257 | .273 | 0 | LF -0, 1B -0 | 1.0 |

Bravo! The hitter who sort of ushered in the era of baseball analysis in front offices has called it a career. Stairs has spent most of the last decade as either a pinch-hitter or professional hitter swinging from the heels and occasionally just pounding the bejesus out of a ball. Stairs will never have to buy a drink in Philadelphia and wraps up his career with 12 different teams on his résumé along with 265 HRs second most among MLBers from Canada. MLB has lost one of its great everymen and it's safe to say that the Rob Deer Hall of Fame has gained its second inductee.

**Jayson Werth** RF
Born: 5/20/1979 Age: 33
Bats: R Throws: R Height: 6' 6" Weight: 215
Breakout: 0% Improve: 32% Collapse: 3%
Attrition: 10% MLB: 87%
Comparables:
Reggie Smith, Jeromy Burnitz, Dwight Evans

| YEAR | TEAM | LVL | AGE | PA | R | 2B | 3B | HR | RBI | BB | SO | SB | CS | AVG_OBP_SLG | TAv | BABIP | BRR | FRAA | WARP |
|------|------|-----|-----|-----|-----|----|----|----|-----|----|-----|----|----|-------------|------|-------|------|---------|------|
| 2009 | PHI | MLB | 30 | 676 | 98 | 26 | 1 | 36 | 99 | 91 | 156 | 20 | 3 | .268/.373/.506 | .299 | .304 | 4.1 | 12.3 | 5.8 |
| 2010 | PHI | MLB | 31 | 652 | 106 | 46 | 2 | 27 | 85 | 82 | 147 | 13 | 3 | .296/.388/.532 | .321 | .352 | -0.3 | -1.8 | 5.5 |
| 2011 | WAS | MLB | 32 | 649 | 69 | 26 | 1 | 20 | 58 | 74 | 160 | 19 | 3 | .232/.330/.389 | .259 | .286 | 2.1 | 5.1 | 2.3 |
| 2012 | WAS | MLB | 33 | 610 | 80 | 25 | 2 | 25 | 78 | 71 | 143 | 16 | 3 | .263/.356/.460 | .291 | .313 | 0.8 | RF 4, CF 1 | 3.3 |

Definitely the Washington National who looks most like he should be in a Southern Progressive Metal Band. In 2011, Werth gave a lot of ammunition to fans who enjoy sharing contract agony with the front office, slipping to a pedestrian .232/.330/.389, fueled principally by a 64-point drop in BABIP and a series of nagging injuries to his calf, knee, and elbow. One of those phenomena is likely to abate; the other correlates well with increasing

David Wright, Hank Blalock, Edwin Encarnacion

Season stat lines are really misleading. In a great many cases, they don't really tell you anything interesting or accurate at all. There was almost no time during the season when Zimmerman was really a .289/.355/.443 hitter, but that's probably what we'd all use as a baseline to figure out things like future performance, modeling, valuation, or deciding on future actions. Zimmerman's BABIP was 70 points higher in the second half, when he was playing full time, than it was in the first half. Considering that he underwent surgery to fix up a sports hernia, rehabbed and recovered well, and turns 28 at the end of the upcoming season, this could be the place to look for a surprise MVP.

# PITCHERS

**Sean Burnett**
Born: 9/17/1982 Age: 29
Bats: L Throws: L Height: 6' 2" Weight: 170
Breakout: 24% Improve: 49% Collapse: 23%
Attrition: 9% MLB: 94%
Comparables:
John Franco, Juan Pizarro, Johnny Antonelli

| YEAR | TEAM | LVL | AGE | W | L | SV | G | GS | IP | H | HR | BB | SO | EqBB9 | EqSO9 | GB% | BABIP | WHIP | ERA | FIP | FRA | WARP |
|------|------|-----|-----|---|---|----|----|----|------|----|----|----|----|-------|-------|-----|-------|------|------|------|------|------|
| 2009 | WAS | MLB | 26 | 1 | 1 | 0 | 33 | 0 | 25¹ | 14 | 3 | 13 | 20 | 4.6 | 7.1 | 59% | .167 | 1.07 | 3.20 | 4.56 | 4.62 | 0.3 |
| 2009 | PIT | MLB | 26 | 1 | 2 | 1 | 38 | 0 | 32¹ | 22 | 3 | 15 | 23 | 4.2 | 6.4 | 46% | .224 | 1.14 | 3.06 | 4.51 | 5.78 | -0.2 |
| 2010 | WAS | MLB | 27 | 1 | 7 | 3 | 73 | 0 | 63 | 52 | 3 | 20 | 62 | 2.9 | 8.9 | 56% | .287 | 1.14 | 2.14 | 2.76 | 3.60 | 1.0 |
| 2011 | WAS | MLB | 28 | 5 | 5 | 4 | 69 | 0 | 56² | 54 | 6 | 21 | 33 | 3.3 | 5.2 | 56% | .273 | 1.32 | 3.81 | 4.48 | 5.20 | 0.1 |
| 2012 | WAS | MLB | 29 | 3 | 1 | 3 | 62 | 0 | 52² | 48 | 5 | 20 | 32 | 3.4 | 5.5 | 51% | .284 | 1.30 | 4.10 | 4.36 | 4.46 | 0.4 |

For a reliever, particularly a semi-junkballer who works down in the zone and induces groundballs like ramen induces acne, an inch here or there with your landing foot, or 1 degree in an arm slot, can make a big difference in your ERA. (ERA's a dumb single vector to evaluate relievers, but people use it.) Burnett's K rate and G/F ratio both dropped from his 2010 campaign, which was an outlier anyway. He's a serviceable bullpen guy to bring in to kill some worms and try for the double play. He'll continue that role in a pen that needs some shoring up.

**Tyler Clippard**
Born: 2/14/1985 Age: 27
Bats: R Throws: R Height: 6' 5" Weight: 170
Breakout: 23% Improve: 54% Collapse: 26%
Attrition: 17% MLB: 86%
Comparables:
Steve Bedrosian, Daisuke Matsuzaka, Jeff Reardon

| YEAR | TEAM | LVL | AGE | W | L | SV | G | GS | IP | H | HR | BB | SO | EqBB9 | EqSO9 | GB% | BABIP | WHIP | ERA | FIP | FRA | WARP |
|------|------|-----|-----|----|---|----|----|----|------|----|----|----|-----|-------|-------|-----|-------|------|------|------|------|------|
| 2009 | SYR | AAA | 24 | 4 | 1 | 1 | 24 | 0 | 39 | 20 | 2 | 15 | 42 | 3.5 | 9.7 | 45% | .200 | 0.90 | 0.92 | 2.81 | 3.73 | 0.6 |
| 2009 | WAS | MLB | 24 | 4 | 2 | 0 | 41 | 0 | 60¹ | 36 | 9 | 32 | 67 | 4.8 | 10.0 | 32% | .201 | 1.13 | 2.69 | 4.42 | 4.82 | 0.3 |
| 2010 | WAS | MLB | 25 | 11 | 8 | 1 | 78 | 0 | 91 | 69 | 8 | 41 | 112 | 4.1 | 11.1 | 29% | .288 | 1.21 | 3.07 | 3.21 | 4.44 | 0.6 |
| 2011 | WAS | MLB | 26 | 3 | 0 | 0 | 72 | 0 | 88¹ | 48 | 11 | 26 | 104 | 2.6 | 10.6 | 24% | .201 | 0.84 | 1.83 | 3.14 | 3.42 | 1.4 |
| 2012 | WAS | MLB | 27 | 3 | 1 | 2 | 63 | 0 | 74² | 60 | 9 | 30 | 67 | 3.6 | 8.0 | 34% | .277 | 1.20 | 3.65 | 4.18 | 3.97 | 1.0 |

In 239 2/3 innings in 2009-11, Clippard allowed 155 hits and struck out 283. And with a fastball that's nice, but not otherworldly, he was fifth in baseball in inducing swings and misses on fastballs. Fun to watch, and crucial for the Nats' chances in 2012.

**Todd Coffey**
Born: 9/9/1980 Age: 31
Bats: R Throws: R Height: 6' 6" Weight: 230
Breakout: 19% Improve: 54% Collapse: 25%
Attrition: 7% MLB: 79%

Comparables:
Erik Hanson, Wandy Rodriguez, Dean Chance

| YEAR | TEAM | LVL | AGE | W | L | SV | G | GS | IP | H | HR | BB | SO | EqBB9 | EqSO9 | GB% | BABIP | WHIP | ERA | FIP | FRA | WARP |
|------|------|-----|-----|---|---|----|----|----|-----|----|----|----|----|-------|-------|-----|-------|------|-----|-----|-----|------|
| 2009 | MIL | MLB | 28 | 4 | 4 | 2 | 78 | 0 | 83² | 76 | 8 | 21 | 65 | 2.3 | 7.0 | 53% | .287 | 1.16 | 2.90 | 3.61 | 4.37 | 0.7 |
| 2010 | MIL | MLB | 29 | 2 | 4 | 0 | 69 | 0 | 62¹ | 65 | 8 | 23 | 56 | 3.3 | 8.1 | 49% | .313 | 1.41 | 4.76 | 4.23 | 5.46 | -0.1 |
| 2011 | WAS | MLB | 30 | 5 | 1 | 0 | 69 | 0 | 59² | 55 | 4 | 20 | 46 | 3.0 | 6.9 | 44% | .287 | 1.26 | 3.62 | 3.38 | 3.59 | 0.8 |
| 2012 | WAS | MLB | 31 | 3 | 1 | 1 | 62 | 0 | 55 | 54 | 7 | 15 | 38 | 2.5 | 6.3 | 52% | .305 | 1.25 | 4.19 | 4.30 | 4.55 | 0.4 |

The Nationals claim to have liked Coffey more in a usage pattern where he went more often, but for fewer batters. They apparently didn't discover this until somewhat later in the season. Coffey's slider is tough for righties to track. He's a big guy, and pretty much the definition of bullpen filler. He'll catch on somewhere as either a guy to fill out the back end of the right-handed stable or, well, or nothing. That'll be what happens.

**Ross Detwiler**
Born: 3/6/1986 Age: 26
Bats: R Throws: L Height: 6' 6" Weight: 185
Breakout: 30% Improve: 54% Collapse: 18%
Attrition: 22% MLB: 88%

Comparables:
Ben Hendrickson, Luis Mendoza, Mike Caldwell

| YEAR | TEAM | LVL | AGE | W | L | SV | G | GS | IP | H | HR | BB | SO | EqBB9 | EqSO9 | GB% | BABIP | WHIP | ERA | FIP | FRA | WARP |
|------|------|-----|-----|---|---|----|----|----|-----|----|----|----|----|-------|-------|-----|-------|------|-----|-----|-----|------|
| 2009 | HAR | AA | 23 | 0 | 3 | 0 | 6 | 6 | 27¹ | 28 | 2 | 10 | 28 | 3.3 | 9.2 | 49% | .325 | 1.39 | 2.97 | 3.25 | 4.36 | 0.4 |
| 2009 | SYR | AAA | 23 | 4 | 2 | 0 | 10 | 10 | 49¹ | 56 | 2 | 20 | 42 | 3.7 | 7.7 | 51% | .346 | 1.54 | 3.10 | 3.19 | 4.05 | 1.1 |
| 2009 | WAS | MLB | 23 | 1 | 6 | 0 | 15 | 14 | 75² | 87 | 3 | 33 | 43 | 3.9 | 5.1 | 45% | .328 | 1.59 | 5.00 | 3.82 | 4.13 | 1.2 |
| 2010 | HAR | AA | 24 | 2 | 2 | 0 | 7 | 7 | 32² | 25 | 0 | 6 | 24 | 1.9 | 8.5 | 45% | .379 | 1.38 | 2.48 | 2.86 | 3.86 | 0.9 |
| 2010 | WAS | MLB | 24 | 1 | 3 | 0 | 8 | 5 | 29² | 34 | 5 | 14 | 17 | 4.2 | 5.2 | 44% | .302 | 1.62 | 4.25 | 5.67 | 6.23 | -0.2 |
| 2011 | SYR | AAA | 25 | 6 | 4 | 0 | 16 | 16 | 87¹ | 94 | 4 | 31 | 55 | 3.3 | 6.5 | 53% | .340 | 1.49 | 4.53 | 3.67 | 4.84 | 1.1 |
| 2011 | WAS | MLB | 25 | 4 | 5 | 0 | 15 | 10 | 66 | 63 | 7 | 20 | 41 | 2.7 | 5.6 | 46% | .281 | 1.26 | 3.00 | 4.18 | 4.67 | 0.2 |
| 2012 | WAS | MLB | 26 | 4 | 5 | 0 | 14 | 14 | 72² | 81 | 8 | 26 | 37 | 3.2 | 4.6 | 49% | .318 | 1.47 | 5.22 | 4.69 | 5.67 | -0.2 |

Detwiler took a step forward in terms of his health and performance, particularly late in the year, when he did what he's supposed to against some junior varsity squads and held them down. His injury history is worrisome, but that's true for a huge proportion of pitchers. If he can retain the velocity boost and somehow keep hitters off balance to the tune of a .275 BABIP or so, he can be effective. Both of those outcomes are long shots.

**Gio Gonzalez**
Born: 9/19/1985 Age: 26
Bats: R Throws: L Height: 6' 0" Weight: 185
Breakout: 28% Improve: 57% Collapse: 20%
Attrition: 8% MLB: 87%

Comparables:
Byung-Hyun Kim, Manny Delcarmen, Joel Zumaya

| YEAR | TEAM | LVL | AGE | W | L | SV | G | GS | IP | H | HR | BB | SO | EqBB9 | EqSO9 | GB% | BABIP | WHIP | ERA | FIP | FRA | WARP |
|------|------|-----|-----|---|---|----|----|----|------|-----|----|----|-----|-------|-------|-----|-------|------|-----|-----|-----|------|
| 2009 | SAC | AAA | 23 | 4 | 1 | 0 | 12 | 12 | 61 | 42 | 5 | 34 | 71 | 5.0 | 10.5 | 45% | .262 | 1.25 | 2.51 | 4.01 | 4.21 | 0.7 |
| 2009 | OAK | MLB | 23 | 6 | 7 | 0 | 20 | 17 | 98² | 113 | 14 | 56 | 109 | 5.1 | 9.9 | 47% | .363 | 1.71 | 5.75 | 4.51 | 4.99 | 1.2 |
| 2010 | OAK | MLB | 24 | 15 | 9 | 0 | 33 | 33 | 200² | 171 | 15 | 92 | 171 | 4.1 | 7.7 | 51% | .277 | 1.31 | 3.23 | 3.75 | 4.19 | 2.3 |
| 2011 | OAK | MLB | 25 | 16 | 12 | 0 | 32 | 32 | 202 | 175 | 17 | 91 | 197 | 4.1 | 8.8 | 48% | .288 | 1.32 | 3.12 | 3.68 | 4.08 | 2.2 |
| 2012 | WAS | MLB | 26 | 12 | 10 | 0 | 30 | 30 | 188¹ | 158 | 17 | 79 | 164 | 3.8 | 7.8 | 47% | .295 | 1.26 | 3.70 | 3.89 | 4.02 | 2.6 |

Gonzalez has plenty of warning signs, like his 2.70 ERA at the friendly O.co Coliseum (and concomitant exposure on the road) and his ERA climb in the second half. We won't even mention the rain-erased debacle start of seven runs in three innings against Texas. A lot of the blemishes will be erased by staying in a pitcher's park in a sissy league where they let pitchers hit and if Gonzalez shines in that situation fans will quickly forget how high a price Rizzo paid. A.J. Cole, Brad Peacock, Tom Milone, and Derek Norris? This is like paying retail price for jewelry at a mall. No matter how much Gonzalez looks like Ray Romano do you really need him that badly? Is it clear that straight up Milone won't outperform him even just in 2012? How about Peacock? Is it even 50-50 that Gonzalez will pitch better than both of them in 2012? And that's before considering Norris. Even if the deal were a net plus for the Nats (and it won't be) it was a move reminscent of an overmatched newbie in a fantasy league. Either Rizzo got rolled like a sucker in a David Mamet movie or he didn't stand up to ownership.

**Tom Gorzelanny**
Born: 7/12/1982 Age: 29
Bats: L Throws: L Height: 6' 3" Weight: 205
Breakout: 22% Improve: 53% Collapse: 26%
Attrition: 19% MLB: 81%

Comparables:
Don Heinkel, Bob Ojeda, Jeff Calhoun

| YEAR | TEAM | LVL | AGE | W | L | SV | G | GS | IP | H | HR | BB | SO | EqBB9 | EqSO9 | GB% | BABIP | WHIP | ERA | FIP | FRA | WARP |
|------|------|-----|-----|---|---|----|----|----|------|-----|----|----|-----|-------|-------|-----|-------|------|-----|-----|-----|------|
| 2009 | PIT | MLB | 26 | 3 | 1 | 0 | 9 | 0 | 8² | 6 | 0 | 4 | 7 | 4.2 | 7.3 | 48% | .250 | 1.15 | 5.19 | 2.83 | 3.04 | 0.2 |
| 2009 | CHN | MLB | 26 | 4 | 2 | 0 | 13 | 7 | 38¹ | 39 | 6 | 13 | 40 | 3.1 | 9.4 | 41% | .311 | 1.36 | 5.63 | 4.10 | 4.87 | 0.5 |
| 2010 | CHN | MLB | 27 | 7 | 9 | 1 | 29 | 23 | 136¹ | 136 | 11 | 68 | 119 | 4.5 | 7.9 | 43% | .312 | 1.50 | 4.09 | 3.95 | 4.42 | 1.5 |
| 2011 | WAS | MLB | 28 | 4 | 6 | 0 | 30 | 15 | 105 | 102 | 15 | 33 | 95 | 2.8 | 8.1 | 38% | .300 | 1.29 | 4.03 | 4.16 | 4.42 | 0.5 |
| 2012 | WAS | MLB | 29 | 5 | 6 | 0 | 23 | 15 | 96 | 96 | 11 | 34 | 63 | 3.2 | 5.9 | 42% | .306 | 1.35 | 4.61 | 4.44 | 5.01 | 0.3 |

One (1) ACME back-of-the-rotation starter/swingman. Left-handed model. This model includes a set multiplier of walk rate and HR rate, fueled by a fastball that's deadly to the ERA if left in the strike zone. Changes speed well and frustrates batters by pounding the mystery corner until the umpire realizes he's not going to stop and eventually starts calling them strikes. May eventually undergo Tony Fossas/Jesse Orosco brainwashing and get sent to Tony La Russa Re-Education camp to join the Khmer Sinister. Don't pay any attention to the nagging injuries as an excuse for performance; Gorzelanny's career path as a starter is very limited and likely contains some truly gruesome pitching lines. He's protected by the league and park as much as he can be.

**Livan Hernandez**
Born: 2/20/1975 Age: 37
Bats: R Throws: R Height: 6' 3" Weight: 220
Breakout: 17% Improve: 40% Collapse: 32%
Attrition: 23% MLB: 74%

| YEAR | TEAM | LVL | AGE | W | L | SV | G | GS | IP | H | HR | BB | SO | EqBB9 | EqSO9 | GB% | BABIP | WHIP | ERA | FIP | FRA | WARP |
|------|------|-----|-----|---|---|----|---|----|----|---|----|----|----|-------|-------|-----|-------|------|-----|-----|-----|------|
| 2009 | WAS | MLB | 34 | 2 | 4 | 0 | 8 | 8 | 48² | 56 | 3 | 16 | 27 | 3.0 | 5.0 | 47% | .327 | 1.48 | 5.36 | 3.73 | 4.39 | 0.5 |
| 2009 | NYN | MLB | 34 | 7 | 8 | 0 | 23 | 23 | 135 | 164 | 16 | 51 | 75 | 3.4 | 5.0 | 42% | .335 | 1.59 | 5.47 | 4.64 | 4.80 | 1.3 |
| 2010 | WAS | MLB | 35 | 10 | 12 | 0 | 33 | 33 | 211² | 216 | 16 | 64 | 114 | 2.7 | 4.8 | 40% | .294 | 1.32 | 3.66 | 3.98 | 4.23 | 3.0 |
| 2011 | WAS | MLB | 36 | 8 | 13 | 0 | 29 | 29 | 175¹ | 199 | 16 | 46 | 99 | 2.4 | 5.1 | 44% | .318 | 1.40 | 4.47 | 3.92 | 4.30 | 2.2 |

pinch-hitter available if he ends up in Milwaukee. (Couldn't resist.)

**Cole Kimball**
Born: 8/1/1985 Age: 26
Bats: R Throws: R Height: 6' 4" Weight: 225
Breakout: 33% Improve: 65% Collapse: 18%
Attrition: 15% MLB: 94%
Comparables:
Al Osuna, Jason Bere, Tom Phoebus

| YEAR | TEAM | LVL | AGE | W | L | SV | G | GS | IP | H | HR | BB | SO | EqBB9 | EqSO9 | GB% | BABIP | WHIP | ERA | FIP | FRA | WARP |
|------|------|-----|-----|---|---|----|---|----|----|---|----|----|----|-------|-------|-----|-------|------|-----|-----|-----|------|
| 2009 | POT | A+ | 23 | 4 | 5 | 9 | 39 | 0 | 46² | 49 | 4 | 28 | 52 | 5.4 | 10.0 | 42% | .346 | 1.65 | 6.36 | 4.16 | 4.85 | 0.4 |
| 2010 | POT | A+ | 24 | 3 | 0 | 6 | 19 | 0 | 24² | 14 | 0 | 4 | 22 | 2.9 | 9.8 | 42% | .286 | 1.01 | 1.82 | 2.40 | 3.58 | 0.4 |
| 2010 | HAR | AA | 24 | 5 | 1 | 12 | 38 | 0 | 54 | 19 | 2 | 18 | 53 | 5.2 | 12.3 | 48% | .213 | 1.19 | 2.33 | 3.28 | 4.00 | 0.9 |
| 2011 | WAS | MLB | 25 | 1 | 0 | 0 | 12 | 0 | 14 | 8 | 0 | 11 | 11 | 7.1 | 7.1 | 31% | .222 | 1.36 | 1.93 | 3.99 | 3.98 | 0.1 |
| 2012 | WAS | MLB | 26 | 1 | 0 | 0 | 14 | 0 | 18 | 17 | 2 | 11 | 13 | 5.8 | 6.6 | 38% | .302 | 1.58 | 5.38 | 5.04 | 5.85 | -0.1 |

Kimball spent the winter being claimed by the Blue Jays, then reclaimed by the Nats. He's rehabbing from rotator cuff surgery and is expected back sometime around the All-Star break. As with any pitcher trying to regain his health, his future depends on how his rehab goes, but unless he comes back walking a lot fewer hitters, his MLB future isn't bright.

**John Lannan**
Born: 9/27/1984 Age: 27
Bats: L Throws: L Height: 6' 6" Weight: 200
Breakout: 20% Improve: 55% Collapse: 23%
Attrition: 8% MLB: 86%
Comparables:
Ray Fontenot, Claude Osteen, Jim Abbott

| YEAR | TEAM | LVL | AGE | W | L | SV | G | GS | IP | H | HR | BB | SO | EqBB9 | EqSO9 | GB% | BABIP | WHIP | ERA | FIP | FRA | WARP |
|------|------|-----|-----|---|---|----|---|----|----|---|----|----|----|-------|-------|-----|-------|------|-----|-----|-----|------|
| 2009 | WAS | MLB | 24 | 9 | 13 | 0 | 33 | 33 | 206¹ | 210 | 22 | 68 | 89 | 3.0 | 3.9 | 54% | .277 | 1.35 | 3.88 | 4.66 | 5.62 | -0.3 |
| 2010 | HAR | AA | 25 | 1 | 3 | 0 | 7 | 7 | 40² | 34 | 3 | 7 | 14 | 2.2 | 6.2 | 49% | .392 | 1.45 | 4.20 | 4.60 | 4.57 | 0.5 |
| 2010 | WAS | MLB | 25 | 8 | 8 | 0 | 25 | 25 | 143¹ | 175 | 14 | 49 | 71 | 3.1 | 4.5 | 52% | .322 | 1.56 | 4.65 | 4.49 | 5.00 | 0.7 |
| 2011 | WAS | MLB | 26 | 10 | 13 | 0 | 33 | 33 | 184² | 194 | 15 | 76 | 106 | 3.7 | 5.2 | 57% | .301 | 1.46 | 3.70 | 4.25 | 4.96 | 0.1 |
| 2012 | WAS | MLB | 27 | 9 | 10 | 0 | 27 | 27 | 155¹ | 160 | 16 | 49 | 63 | 2.9 | 3.6 | 54% | .294 | 1.35 | 4.72 | 4.68 | 5.13 | 0.3 |

Atypical junkballing lefty groundball starter. Atypical because he's held onto a starting job and not been horrific despite having only a show fastball. Lannan will start the season in the rotation, and he'll live on the edge, using everything in his arsenal to keep his infielders busy and trying to limit the free passes to those hitters who can routinely go deep. He has demonstrated the ability to take the mound and get guys out. If there's a clear path to improvement for him, it might be in the direction of an even more extreme groundball tendency.

**Ryan Mattheus**
Born: 11/10/1983 Age: 28
Bats: R Throws: R Height: 6' 4" Weight: 215
Breakout: 21% Improve: 45% Collapse: 27%
Attrition: 21% MLB: 77%
Comparables:
Ron Herbel, Kelvin Jimenez, Mike Schultz

| YEAR | TEAM | LVL | AGE | W | L | SV | G | GS | IP | H | HR | BB | SO | EqBB9 | EqSO9 | GB% | BABIP | WHIP | ERA | FIP | FRA | WARP |
|------|------|-----|-----|---|---|----|---|----|----|---|----|----|----|-------|-------|-----|-------|------|-----|-----|-----|------|
| 2011 | WAS | MLB | 27 | 2 | 2 | 0 | 35 | 0 | 32 | 26 | 1 | 15 | 12 | 4.2 | 3.4 | 53% | .245 | 1.28 | 2.81 | 4.24 | 5.50 | -0.2 |
| 2012 | WAS | MLB | 28 | 1 | 0 | 0 | 28 | 0 | 28 | 29 | 3 | 11 | 14 | 3.5 | 4.5 | 53% | .300 | 1.43 | 5.08 | 4.78 | 5.53 | -0.1 |

Mattheus has pitched well enough at several stops to warrant at least a sustained look in the bigs. He finally got that in 2011, mostly in a mop-up role, and he struggled through pretty well, fighting through some shoulder pain in the process. He's had a history of tendinitis, so there's always going to be some risk associated with him, but he's hardly the only pitcher for which that's true. When healthy, he's got a plus fastball that burrows in to the bats of left-handed hitters. There is some low-hanging fruit here; the velocity is a good start, and Mattheus has shown flashes of dominance in various stops before.

### Yunesky Maya

Born: 8/28/1981 Age: 30
Bats: R Throws: R Height: 6' 0'' Weight: 170
Breakout: 9% Improve: 48% Collapse: 20%
Attrition: 8% MLB: 91%

Comparables:
Sergio Mitre, Mike Caldwell, John Burkett

| YEAR | TEAM | LVL | AGE | W | L | SV | G | GS | IP | H | HR | BB | SO | EqBB9 | EqSO9 | GB% | BABIP | WHIP | ERA | FIP | FRA | WARP |
|------|------|-----|-----|---|---|----|---|----|----|---|----|----|----|-------|-------|-----|-------|------|-----|-----|-----|------|
| 2010 | WAS | MLB | 28 | 0 | 3 | 0 | 5 | 5 | 26 | 30 | 3 | 11 | 12 | 3.8 | 4.2 | 34% | .307 | 1.58 | 5.88 | 5.18 | 5.79 | -0.1 |
| 2011 | SYR | AAA | 29 | 3 | 7 | 0 | 22 | 22 | 129² | 125 | 13 | 26 | 96 | 1.9 | 6.8 | 47% | .300 | 1.24 | 5.00 | 3.76 | 4.49 | 2.1 |
| 2011 | WAS | MLB | 29 | 1 | 1 | 0 | 10 | 5 | 32² | 40 | 3 | 10 | 15 | 2.8 | 4.1 | 45% | .346 | 1.53 | 5.23 | 4.37 | 4.47 | 0.0 |
| 2012 | WAS | MLB | 30 | 3 | 4 | 0 | 11 | 11 | 59¹ | 64 | 7 | 15 | 27 | 2.3 | 4.0 | 46% | .302 | 1.33 | 4.71 | 4.59 | 5.12 | 0.1 |

Branding works. People actually enjoy the product more, or perceive it as better, if they've been prepped with branding—the brain acts differently, so you'll like Coke more if you *know* it's Coke when you drink it. Apparently, the same thing's true for baseball players. He's a *Cuban* bad pitcher! You don't get this kind of quality from a guy from Indiana who specializes in thigh-high BP fastballs! No way. You need a guy from off the Florida coast for that. So going into 2012, he's 30 years old, with a track record that demonstrates no success anywhere outside of Rookie Ball at age 28 for about 2/3 of a game, sporting a fastball that wouldn't impress Tim Wakefield. Maybe it's the first name that dictates a player's likely value.

### Ryan Perry

Born: 2/13/1987 Age: 25
Bats: R Throws: R Height: 6' 5'' Weight: 200
Breakout: 21% Improve: 56% Collapse: 16%
Attrition: 11% MLB: 95%

Comparables:
Mark Melancon, Joe Smith, Tim Hudson

| YEAR | TEAM | LVL | AGE | W | L | SV | G | GS | IP | H | HR | BB | SO | EqBB9 | EqSO9 | GB% | BABIP | WHIP | ERA | FIP | FRA | WARP |
|------|------|-----|-----|---|---|----|---|----|----|---|----|----|----|-------|-------|-----|-------|------|-----|-----|-----|------|
| 2009 | DET | MLB | 22 | 0 | 1 | 0 | 53 | 0 | 61² | 56 | 7 | 38 | 60 | 5.5 | 8.8 | 43% | .299 | 1.52 | 3.79 | 4.57 | 4.78 | 0.5 |
| 2010 | DET | MLB | 23 | 3 | 5 | 2 | 60 | 0 | 62² | 55 | 6 | 23 | 45 | 3.3 | 6.5 | 46% | .275 | 1.24 | 3.59 | 4.20 | 4.97 | 0.2 |
| 2011 | TOL | AAA | 24 | 2 | 0 | 7 | 20 | 0 | 32² | 24 | 1 | 9 | 30 | 2.5 | 8.3 | 45% | .267 | 1.01 | 3.03 | 2.72 | 3.75 | 0.5 |
| 2011 | DET | MLB | 24 | 2 | 0 | 0 | 36 | 0 | 37 | 39 | 1 | 21 | 24 | 5.1 | 5.8 | 38% | .319 | 1.62 | 5.35 | 3.98 | 5.40 | -0.1 |
| 2012 | WAS | MLB | 25 | 2 | 1 | 1 | 42 | 0 | 48 | 44 | 4 | 19 | 35 | 3.6 | 6.6 | 45% | .298 | 1.32 | 4.15 | 4.02 | 4.51 | 0.3 |

Once considered Detroit's closer-in-waiting, Perry struggled through a subpar 2011 that saw him spend significant time in the minors trying to regain his late-inning mojo. After working on his mechanics in Toledo, Perry returned to post better run-prevention numbers down the stretch and earn his way onto the playoff roster, though his peripherals belied any real improvement. Perry throws hard but his fastball lacks movement and he struggles to command his slider, and last year his walk and strikeout rates tried hard to intersect. Perry's stuff should lead to better results, but the Tigers grew tired of waiting and shipped him to Washington for the similarly disappointing Collin Balester. Perry's appeal to the Nationals lies mostly in his minor-league options, something Balester lacks, so Perry had best learn to enjoy the journey from Anacostia to Syracuse and back.

### Robbie Ray

Born: 10/1/1991 Age: 20
Bats: L Throws: L Height: 6' 3'' Weight: 170
Breakout: 27% Improve: 40% Collapse: 46%
Attrition: 40% MLB: 96%

Comparables:
Bruce Robbins, Terry Forster, Chris Zachary

| YEAR | TEAM | LVL | AGE | W | L | SV | G | GS | IP | H | HR | BB | SO | EqBB9 | EqSO9 | GB% | BABIP | WHIP | ERA | FIP | FRA | WARP |
|------|------|-----|-----|---|---|----|---|----|----|---|----|----|----|-------|-------|-----|-------|------|-----|-----|-----|------|
| 2011 | HAG | A | 19 | 2 | 2 | 0 | 20 | 20 | 89 | 71 | 3 | 38 | 95 | 3.8 | 9.6 | 41% | .304 | 1.22 | 3.13 | 3.52 | 4.14 | 1.5 |
| 2012 | WAS | MLB | 20 | 1 | 2 | 0 | 5 | 5 | 23 | 23 | 3 | 12 | 16 | 4.5 | 6.2 | 42% | .308 | 1.49 | 5.23 | 5.07 | 5.69 | -0.0 |

Ray's exceptionally polished for a high school product, and not in a "Gee we really like the way you spot your 87 mph fastball" way. He's got quality pitches and uses a remarkably consistent delivery to spot them all over the strike zone even using offspeed pitches off the plate inside effectively—something you don't see in most 19-year-olds. Another instance where the Nationals were willing to spend the money on a kid with "signability issues" and he's part of a nice portfolio that should more than justify the incremental expense. He'll likely start the season at High-A and should start climbing prospect lists sooner rather than later.

### Henry Rodriguez

Born: 2/25/1987 Age: 25
Bats: R Throws: R Height: 6' 1'' Weight: 210
Breakout: 22% Improve: 44% Collapse: 19%
Attrition: 12% MLB: 91%

Comparables:
Joel Zumaya, Michael Kohn, Mark Clear

| YEAR | TEAM | LVL | AGE | W | L | SV | G | GS | IP | H | HR | BB | SO | EqBB9 | EqSO9 | GB% | BABIP | WHIP | ERA | FIP | FRA | WARP |
|------|------|-----|-----|---|---|----|---|----|----|---|----|----|----|-------|-------|-----|-------|------|-----|-----|-----|------|
| 2009 | OAK | MLB | 22 | 0 | 0 | 0 | 3 | 0 | 4 | 4 | 0 | 2 | 4 | 4.5 | 9.0 | 54% | .308 | 1.50 | 2.25 | 3.39 | 3.63 | 0.1 |
| 2010 | OAK | MLB | 23 | 1 | 0 | 0 | 29 | 0 | 27² | 25 | 2 | 13 | 33 | 4.2 | 10.7 | 41% | .329 | 1.37 | 4.55 | 3.12 | 4.15 | 0.3 |
| 2011 | WAS | MLB | 24 | 3 | 3 | 2 | 59 | 0 | 65² | 54 | 1 | 45 | 70 | 6.2 | 9.6 | 47% | .301 | 1.51 | 3.56 | 3.21 | 4.23 | 0.4 |
| 2012 | WAS | MLB | 25 | 3 | 1 | 1 | 53 | 0 | 57² | 49 | 5 | 35 | 56 | 5.4 | 8.8 | 47% | .309 | 1.45 | 4.33 | 4.21 | 4.71 | 0.3 |

At some point, Rodriguez is going to find 5 percent more control, and he'll be the toughest guy in the league to face. Of course, that league might be in Italy or something, but it might be MLB.

He just throws goddamned hard. Often, the ball travels in the direction of the strike zone. Well, towards home plate, anyway. Rodriguez managed to be somewhat effective in 2011 despite walking 45 batters in just 65 2/3 innings. This was an improvement from some of his memorable minor-league campaign, when he'd walk over a batter per inning as well as actually issuing free passes to vendors, reporters, and the occasional fan. He's a great gamble, though, because some season, he might put it all together, and you end up with a bullpen that causes opposing managers to score Ambien on the street just to keep functioning in society.

**Atahualpa Severino**
Born: **11/6/1984** Age: **27**
Bats: **L** Throws: **L** Height: **5' 10"** Weight: **170**
Breakout: **18%** Improve: **59%** Collapse: **19%**
Attrition: **14%** MLB: **84%**
**Comparables:**
Bill Murphy, Felix Heredia, Bill Simas

| YEAR | TEAM | LVL | AGE | W | L | SV | G | GS | IP | H | HR | BB | SO | EqBB9 | EqSO9 | GB% | BABIP | WHIP | ERA | FIP | FRA | WARP |
|------|------|-----|-----|---|---|----|----|----|----|---|----|----|----|-------|-------|-----|-------|------|-----|-----|-----|------|
| 2009 | POT | A+ | 24 | 4 | 0 | 13 | 29 | 0 | 46 | 35 | 4 | 14 | 39 | 2.7 | 7.6 | 59% | .252 | 1.07 | 2.54 | 3.89 | 4.60 | 0.4 |
| 2009 | HAR | AA | 24 | 6 | 0 | 2 | 15 | 0 | 22² | 19 | 1 | 14 | 27 | 5.6 | 10.7 | 47% | .340 | 1.45 | 2.78 | 3.58 | 3.02 | 0.5 |
| 2010 | SYR | AAA | 25 | 6 | 3 | 1 | 54 | 0 | 67¹ | 43 | 4 | 21 | 37 | 3.9 | 6.2 | 51% | .285 | 1.32 | 3.34 | 4.27 | 5.77 | -0.1 |
| 2011 | SYR | AAA | 26 | 1 | 0 | 1 | 35 | 0 | 32 | 37 | 2 | 23 | 38 | 6.5 | 10.7 | 47% | .376 | 1.88 | 4.50 | 4.02 | 5.89 | 0.1 |
| 2011 | WAS | MLB | 26 | 1 | 0 | 0 | 6 | 0 | 4² | 5 | 1 | 1 | 7 | 1.9 | 13.5 | 27% | .400 | 1.29 | 3.86 | 3.42 | 5.25 | 0.0 |

Bats: **R** Throws: **L** Height: **6' 6"** Weight: **230**
Breakout: **32%** Improve: **66%** Collapse: **10%**
Attrition: **11%** MLB: **85%**
**Comparables:**
Daryl Thompson, Rafael Soriano, Ron Robinson

| YEAR | TEAM | LVL | AGE | W | L | SV | G | GS | IP | H | HR | BB | SO | EqBB9 | EqSO9 | GB% | BABIP | WHIP | ERA | FIP | FRA | WARP |
|------|------|-----|-----|---|---|----|----|----|----|---|----|----|----|-------|-------|-----|-------|------|-----|-----|-----|------|
| 2011 | POT | A+ | 22 | 6 | 0 | 0 | 10 | 10 | 56¹ | 66 | 5 | 12 | 60 | 1.8 | 8.5 | 51% | .351 | 1.28 | 2.72 | 2.98 | 3.76 | 1.3 |
| 2012 | WAS | MLB | 23 | 1 | 2 | 0 | 5 | 5 | 26² | 28 | 3 | 10 | 16 | 3.3 | 5.4 | 48% | .314 | 1.43 | 5.11 | 4.59 | 5.56 | -0.1 |

Solis's initial development was somewhat slowed by a groin injury at the start of the 2011 season. After healing up and returning to Hagerstown, where he'd thrown four innings in his 2010 debut, he pitched pretty well, not showing any signs of deteriorating delivery. He struck out about a batter per inning, his fastball velocity remained solid, if not overwhelming, and he got guys to hit the ball on the ground. By midseason, he might be the fourth- or fifth-best option for the Nationals rotation. It doesn't mean he'll get one of those jobs, but the option will likely be available to Johnson and crew.

**Craig Stammen**
Born: **3/9/1984** Age: **28**
Bats: **R** Throws: **R** Height: **6' 4"** Weight: **210**
Breakout: **29%** Improve: **62%** Collapse: **22%**
Attrition: **17%** MLB: **88%**
**Comparables:**
Bob Moose, Reggie Cleveland, Ron Reed

| YEAR | TEAM | LVL | AGE | W | L | SV | G | GS | IP | H | HR | BB | SO | EqBB9 | EqSO9 | GB% | BABIP | WHIP | ERA | FIP | FRA | WARP |
|------|------|-----|-----|---|---|----|----|----|----|---|----|----|----|-------|-------|-----|-------|------|-----|-----|-----|------|
| 2009 | SYR | AAA | 25 | 4 | 2 | 0 | 7 | 7 | 40 | 33 | 4 | 8 | 14 | 1.8 | 3.2 | 61% | .221 | 1.02 | 1.80 | 4.35 | 5.42 | 0.0 |
| 2009 | WAS | MLB | 25 | 4 | 7 | 0 | 19 | 19 | 105² | 112 | 14 | 24 | 48 | 2.0 | 4.1 | 47% | .276 | 1.29 | 5.11 | 4.64 | 5.74 | 0.0 |
| 2010 | WAS | MLB | 26 | 4 | 4 | 0 | 35 | 19 | 128 | 151 | 13 | 41 | 85 | 2.9 | 6.0 | 52% | .331 | 1.50 | 5.13 | 4.08 | 4.59 | 1.5 |
| 2011 | SYR | AAA | 27 | 9 | 4 | 0 | 25 | 24 | 142 | 163 | 18 | 40 | 127 | 2.5 | 8.0 | 55% | .341 | 1.43 | 4.75 | 3.96 | 4.95 | 1.3 |
| 2011 | WAS | MLB | 27 | 1 | 1 | 0 | 7 | 0 | 10¹ | 3 | 0 | 4 | 12 | 3.5 | 10.5 | 52% | .136 | 0.68 | 0.87 | 1.83 | 3.28 | 0.2 |
| 2012 | WAS | MLB | 28 | 3 | 4 | 0 | 15 | 10 | 64¹ | 70 | 8 | 18 | 32 | 2.6 | 4.4 | 52% | .308 | 1.38 | 5.08 | 4.67 | 5.52 | -0.2 |

Stammen is a righty sinker/slider pitcher with a slightly below-average fastball. He induces lots of ground balls, and will likely spend the rest of his career trying to catch on in a major-league bullpen so he can have one great season that he can turn into a big contract. With the arrival of Perry and a number of other competitors for roster space, he'll have to have a lights-out spring in order to guarantee a spot on the roster, then he'll have to get hot in order to move out of a mop-up role.

**Drew Storen**
Born: **8/11/1987** Age: **24**
Bats: **B** Throws: **R** Height: **6' 3"** Weight: **180**
Breakout: **22%** Improve: **47%** Collapse: **34%**
Attrition: **6%** MLB: **99%**
**Comparables:**
Phil Hughes, Brian Fisher, Vida Blue

| YEAR | TEAM | LVL | AGE | W | L | SV | G | GS | IP | H | HR | BB | SO | EqBB9 | EqSO9 | GB% | BABIP | WHIP | ERA | FIP | FRA | WARP |
|------|------|-----|-----|---|---|----|----|----|----|---|----|----|----|-------|-------|-----|-------|------|-----|-----|-----|------|
| 2010 | WAS | MLB | 22 | 4 | 4 | 5 | 54 | 0 | 55¹ | 48 | 3 | 22 | 52 | 3.6 | 8.5 | 41% | .308 | 1.27 | 3.58 | 3.29 | 3.92 | 0.7 |
| 2011 | WAS | MLB | 23 | 6 | 3 | 43 | 73 | 0 | 75¹ | 57 | 8 | 20 | 74 | 2.4 | 8.8 | 48% | .247 | 1.02 | 2.75 | 3.29 | 3.61 | 1.0 |
| 2012 | WAS | MLB | 24 | 3 | 1 | 18 | 63 | 0 | 66² | 56 | 6 | 18 | 57 | 2.4 | 7.7 | 43% | .289 | 1.10 | 3.12 | 3.47 | 3.40 | 1.3 |

A number of baseball analysts really detest the idea of a closer. We love dominant relievers; we just hate the idea of wasting the best guy in circumstances where you could probably get away with using a guy who's not as good and still win the game. But the game is what it is, and if you're going to have a closer, you might as well have an excellent one. That's Storen. Mid-90s fastball, slider that incapacitates right-handed hitters like a blowdart that's been frogrubbed, and location that allows his manager to exhale. Storen's a championship-caliber closer, and the incremental gain of using him in slightly higher leverage situations is dwarfed by the club harmony you get by having him in a defined role. He's a badass, and there's no reason to expect that to change.

### Stephen Strasburg

Born: **7/20/1988** Age: **23**
Bats: **R** Throws: **R** Height: **6' 5"** Weight: **220**
Breakout: **21%** Improve: **49%** Collapse: **21%**
Attrition: **5%** MLB: **98%**

**Comparables:**
Vida Blue,Felix Hernandez,Dwight Gooden

| YEAR | TEAM | LVL | AGE | W | L | SV | G | GS | IP | H | HR | BB | SO | EqBB9 | EqSO9 | GB% | BABIP | WHIP | ERA | FIP | FRA | WARP |
|------|------|-----|-----|---|---|----|----|----|-----|----|----|----|----|-------|-------|-----|-------|------|------|------|------|------|
| 2010 | WAS | MLB | 21 | 5 | 3 | 0 | 12 | 12 | 68 | 56 | 5 | 17 | 92 | 2.2 | 12.2 | 47% | .323 | 1.07 | 2.91 | 2.11 | 3.05 | 1.5 |
| 2011 | WAS | MLB | 22 | 1 | 1 | 0 | 5 | 5 | 24 | 15 | 0 | 2 | 24 | 0.8 | 9.0 | 42% | .246 | 0.71 | 1.50 | 1.24 | 2.25 | 0.9 |
| 2012 | WAS | MLB | 23 | 3 | 2 | 0 | 7 | 7 | 35$^2$ | 28 | 3 | 8 | 36 | 2.0 | 9.0 | 49% | .296 | 1.01 | 2.59 | 2.95 | 2.82 | 1.1 |

Should Tommy John get 1 percent of all the money pitchers earn after his namesake surgery? The top 40 percent of the Nats rotation will be a combined 50 years old, throw bloody hard, and likely be a source of most of the best batter-pitcher confrontations in baseball. Strasburg might struggle a little, but let's face it, he's always been more than just a pretty fastball. There's still no established ceiling for his performance, and if Johnson's smart, he'll shift a few of the pitcher abuse points from Strasburg to the bullpen. The only real questions regarding Strasburg are how much of a workload cap the Nationals will place on him and when his teammates will sit him down for a much-needed intervention about his facial hair.

### Chien-Ming Wang

Born: **3/31/1980** Age: **32**
Bats: **R** Throws: **R** Height: **6' 4"** Weight: **200**
Breakout: **14%** Improve: **36%** Collapse: **42%**
Attrition: **9%** MLB: **94%**

**Comparables:**
Chris Bosio,Ken Forsch,Charlie Leibrandt

| YEAR | TEAM | LVL | AGE | W | L | SV | G | GS | IP | H | HR | BB | SO | EqBB9 | EqSO9 | GB% | BABIP | WHIP | ERA | FIP | FRA | WARP |
|------|------|-----|-----|---|---|----|----|----|-----|----|----|----|----|-------|-------|-----|-------|------|------|------|------|------|
| 2009 | NYA | MLB | 29 | 1 | 6 | 0 | 12 | 9 | 42 | 66 | 7 | 19 | 29 | 4.1 | 6.2 | 56% | .404 | 2.02 | 9.64 | 5.43 | 6.00 | 0.0 |
| 2011 | WAS | MLB | 31 | 4 | 3 | 0 | 11 | 11 | 62$^1$ | 67 | 8 | 13 | 25 | 1.9 | 3.6 | 54% | .274 | 1.28 | 4.04 | 4.53 | 5.12 | -0.2 |
| 2012 | WAS | MLB | 32 | 3 | 3 | 0 | 9 | 9 | 50$^2$ | 53 | 5 | 14 | 22 | 2.5 | 3.9 | 55% | .300 | 1.32 | 4.44 | 4.45 | 4.83 | 0.3 |

Coming back from a bad shoulder, Wang showed decent form (less a little bit of velocity) for the Nats, particularly late in the season. He's re-upped for 2012, and he'll be in the mix for the tail two slots in the rotation. People underestimate how much effort and tenacity it takes to come back from one discrete injury, much less a clusterf--k of injuries, form degradation, surgeries, interrupted practice and training regimens, etc. Wang's still got that hard sinking pitch that he occasionally leaves up, but it's lost a little nastiness. He's a reasonable bet to pitch well, but without a lot of upside. If he can get another mph back on his stuff, he could be a quality rotation guy, even without the gaudy K rates usually necessary to do that.

### Jordan Zimmermann

Born: **5/23/1986** Age: **26**
Bats: **R** Throws: **R** Height: **6' 3"** Weight: **200**
Breakout: **21%** Improve: **56%** Collapse: **19%**
Attrition: **10%** MLB: **98%**

**Comparables:**
Edward Mujica,Frank Funk,Jeremy Bonderman

| YEAR | TEAM | LVL | AGE | W | L | SV | G | GS | IP | H | HR | BB | SO | EqBB9 | EqSO9 | GB% | BABIP | WHIP | ERA | FIP | FRA | WARP |
|------|------|-----|-----|---|----|----|----|----|------|-----|----|----|-----|-------|-------|-----|-------|------|------|------|------|------|
| 2009 | WAS | MLB | 23 | 3 | 5 | 0 | 16 | 16 | 91$^1$ | 95 | 10 | 29 | 92 | 2.9 | 9.1 | 46% | .339 | 1.36 | 4.63 | 3.55 | 4.33 | 1.4 |
| 2010 | WAS | MLB | 24 | 1 | 2 | 0 | 7 | 7 | 31 | 31 | 8 | 10 | 27 | 2.9 | 7.8 | 49% | .264 | 1.32 | 4.94 | 5.88 | 6.11 | -0.1 |
| 2011 | WAS | MLB | 25 | 8 | 11 | 0 | 26 | 26 | 161$^1$ | 154 | 12 | 31 | 124 | 1.7 | 6.9 | 41% | .296 | 1.15 | 3.18 | 3.13 | 3.49 | 2.9 |
| 2012 | WAS | MLB | 26 | 7 | 7 | 0 | 22 | 22 | 118 | 113 | 13 | 29 | 84 | 2.2 | 6.4 | 45% | .300 | 1.20 | 4.02 | 3.95 | 4.37 | 1.3 |

The Nationals only need like three more punch-holes in their Frequent TJ Surgery card before they get a free one. Zimmerman recovered well from his foray onto the table and looked very good with his form, velocity, and command. No reason to think that he and Strasburg won't be the highest-upside 1-2 tandem in baseball, possibly along with Tampa Bay's top two. Zimmerman has exceptional command of a plus fastball, works all over the plate well, and by all accounts has a great work ethic and learns quickly. If he can stay away from hanging the occasional bender, his ceiling isn't that far from his more heralded rotationmate.

# LINEOUTS

## HITTERS

| PLAYER | TEAM | LVL | AGE | PA | R | 2B | 3B | HR | RBI | BB | SO | SB-CS | AVG/OBP/SLG | TAv | BABIP | BRR | FRAA | WARP |
|--------|------|-----|-----|-----|----|-----|----|----|-----|----|-----|-------|-------------|-----|-------|-----|------|------|
| CF B. Carroll | NAS | AAA | 28 | 381 | 66 | 14 | 2 | 15 | 51 | 34 | 73 | 9-3 | .281/.356/.469 | .276 | .316 | -0.3 | -0.8 | 2.4 |
|  | PAW | AAA | 28 | 94 | 10 | 6 | 1 | 1 | 12 | 8 | 20 | 2-0 | .229/.298/.361 | .225 | .281 | 0.5 | -1.7 | -0.3 |
| C D. Freitas | HAG | A | 22 | 516 | 67 | 30 | 0 | 13 | 73 | 82 | 87 | 2-1 | .288/.409/.450 | .306 | .335 | -3.7 | -1.1 | 3.7 |
| RF K. Keyes | HAG | A | 22 | 342 | 49 | 22 | 1 | 17 | 65 | 32 | 80 | 6-0 | .263/.336/.510 | .299 | .300 | -2.1 | -1.3 | 1.6 |
| SS J. Martinson | HAG | A | 22 | 522 | 64 | 22 | 3 | 19 | 64 | 66 | 144 | 26-6 | .252/.360/.448 | .291 | .327 | -0.2 | -1.1 | 3.3 |
| LF R. Oduber | HAG | A | 22 | 238 | 31 | 6 | 1 | 5 | 26 | 15 | 64 | 22-2 | .301/.361/.407 | .267 | .405 | 3.3 | -1.6 | 0.9 |
| RF W. Ramos | NAT | RK | 21 | 172 | 32 | 12 | 1 | 12 | 37 | 19 | 45 | 7-4 | .313/.401/.653 | .345 | .370 | -1.7 | -5.4 | 1.4 |

plate make him noteworthy. ✐ Raw can be both compliment and complaint about **Kevin Keyes** referring to his defense and his power but he got a shot at everyday play once Harper was promoted and hit .281/.355/.528 with 13 homers in the second half. ✐ Texas State product **Jason Martinson** was a fifth-round pick for his athleticism, but poor defense in his full-season debut figures to move him off short, potentially condemning him to a utilityman's career path. ✐ Aruban **Randolph Oduber** looked like he was breaking through before a torn hamstring cost him nearly half the season; he still needs to work on hitting breaking stuff. ✐ Dominican **Wander Ramos** went nuts at the plate in the GCL, earning a spot on its All-Star team, but it was a repeat assignment; watch to see where it gets him promoted to this spring. ✐ Hackmaster **Adrian Sanchez** landed at the infield position he can best handle (second base), but being the Damaso Garcia of the Sally League isn't really a compliment, not even at 20. ✐ **Jhonatan Solano** is an organizational soldier with a good defensive rep. See also: Every other catch and throw guy. ✐ Former shortstop **Michael Taylor** was moved to the outfield for his first full season, and broke out for an 848 second-half OPS.

## PITCHERS

| PLAYER | TEAM | LVL | AGE | W | L | SV | IP | H | HR | BB | SO | EqBB9 | EqSO9 | GB% | BABIP | WHIP | ERA | FIP | FRA | WARP |
|--------|------|-----|-----|---|---|----|-----|----|----|----|----|-------|-------|-----|-------|------|------|-----|-----|------|
| J. Fulchino | SDN | MLB | 31 | 0 | 0 | 0 | 1² | 3 | 0 | 4 | 2 | 21.6 | 10.8 | 50% | .500 | 4.20 | 16.20 | 7.79 | 7.20 | -0.1 |
|  | HOU | MLB | 31 | 1 | 4 | 0 | 33 | 34 | 5 | 18 | 31 | 4.9 | 8.5 | 39% | .309 | 1.58 | 5.18 | 4.72 | 5.18 | -0.2 |
| W. Joaquin | FRE | AAA | 24 | 1 | 0 | 1 | 49² | 53 | 5 | 23 | 27 | 4.2 | 4.9 | 53% | .302 | 1.53 | 3.44 | 5.59 | 6.61 | -0.5 |
|  | SFN | MLB | 24 | 1 | 0 | 0 | 6¹ | 6 | 0 | 3 | 3 | 4.3 | 4.3 | 62% | .286 | 1.42 | 4.26 | 3.47 | 6.47 | -0.1 |
| P. Lehman | HAR | AA | 24 | 0 | 3 | 6 | 34 | 25 | 2 | 5 | 35 | 1.1 | 9.0 | 57% | .264 | 0.76 | 3.71 | 2.74 | 4.27 | 0.4 |
| O. Perez | HAR | AA | 29 | 2 | 1 | 0 | 75² | 80 | 10 | 27 | 58 | 3.2 | 6.9 | 36% | .306 | 1.39 | 3.09 | 4.83 | 4.68 | 1.0 |
| D. Rosenbaum | POT | A+ | 23 | 5 | 3 | 0 | 132 | 113 | 4 | 41 | 108 | 2.8 | 7.4 | 56% | .291 | 1.17 | 2.59 | 3.06 | 4.50 | 1.5 |
|  | HAR | AA | 23 | 1 | 0 | 0 | 39¹ | 27 | 0 | 11 | 27 | 2.5 | 6.2 | 58% | .233 | 0.97 | 2.29 | 3.03 | 3.82 | 0.7 |
| D. Slaten | WAS | MLB | 31 | 0 | 2 | 0 | 16¹ | 26 | 3 | 9 | 13 | 5.0 | 7.2 | 46% | .404 | 2.14 | 4.41 | 5.63 | 6.95 | -0.5 |
| J. Smoker | POT | A+ | 22 | 3 | 0 | 2 | 50² | 32 | 4 | 38 | 56 | 6.6 | 9.9 | 43% | .233 | 1.36 | 2.31 | 4.46 | 6.19 | -0.3 |
| C. VanAllen | HAR | AA | 26 | 2 | 4 | 0 | 57² | 52 | 6 | 22 | 74 | 3.4 | 11.1 | 48% | .336 | 1.23 | 2.50 | 3.34 | 3.91 | 0.9 |

**Jeff Fulchino** is a right-hander built like Charlie Kerfeld whom the Padres claimed off waivers from the Astros in September. As career moves go, waived by the Astros doesn't look good on the ol' résumé. ✐ **Waldis Joaquin** rejected the White Sox' waiver claim, re-signed with the Giants and ended up back in the big leagues, but his strikeouts have deserted him, and San Francisco cut him loose in November. ✐ The Nats grab a few local products to fill out the ranks of organizational soldiery; **Pat Lehman**'s one of the latest, a strike-throwing changeup fiend out of GWU. ⊘ Signing with the Nats after getting released by the Mets in March might have seemed like a good idea for **Oliver Perez**, but an attempt at a mechanical makeover was hampered by a midseason lat injury. ⊘ While **Daniel Rosenbaum** won't be mistaken for a top prospect, he mixes sinkers, cutters, and sliders with a plus change to induce DP grounders. He's on the Lannan path, where his performance, not his stuff, will determine how seriously he'll be taken. ⊘ **Doug Slaten** was reminded that situational specialists need good work and good health to get job security; he had neither, earning his non-tender. ⊘ Finally healthy again and converted to relief, **Josh Smoker** had his best season yet, throwing with the velocity that helped make him the 31st overall selection of the 2007 draft. ⊘ With a good move to first and lefty-killing stuff, **Cory VanAllen** might show up as somebody's second southpaw in the pen.

## MANAGER: DAVEY JOHNSON

| YEAR | TEAM | W-L | Pythag +/- | Avg PC | 100+ P | 120+ P | QS | BQS | REL | REL w Zero R | IBB | Subs | PH | PH Avg | PH HR | SB2 | CS2 | SB3 | CS3 | SAC Att | SAC % | POS SAC | Squeeze | Swing | In Play |
|---|---|---|---|---|---|---|---|---|---|---|---|---|---|---|---|---|---|---|---|---|---|---|---|---|---|
| 2011 | WAS | 40-43 | 0 | 84.0 | 12 | 0 | 33 | 3 | 271 | 218 | 19 | — | 137 | .179 | 1 | 11 | 3 | 0 | 0 | 58 | 74.1% | 19 | 1 | 170 | 51 |

It's hard to draw too many conclusions about Davey Johnson's comeback so far. It isn't like he came down from stathead heaven and did things that much tactically different from Jim Riggleman. He'll order a position player to bunt about as often as Dusty Baker, and put someone on first base as often as Ron Gardenhire, which is neither smart nor dumb. Remember, he inherited this team, he didn't design it. On offense, the biggest difference was his late-season willingness to move Morse to an outfield corner and explore using Werth in center to get another bat in the lineup; that bodes well for Harper's arriving in the majors sooner rather than later, and Johnson *really* likes Harper, in the same way that he likes putting together a high-powered offense, something that will be hard to initiate without a solution to the team's leadoff problem. Another notable distinction was his aggressiveness in bringing in relievers early and often; only Jim Tracy used more pen men per 162 games. While that was also a function of the talent on hand (a good pen and weak starters), his rotation will again feature a number of guys with workloads to watch, and even with all those innings, his relievers did pick up a full strikeout in the second half.

# The Baseball Prospectus Top 101 Prospects

*Kevin Goldstein*

### 1. Matt Moore, LHP, Rays

Moore was number 10 on this list last year and the highest-ranked left-handed starter, yet somehow, he got better. And not just a little bit better, but significantly so. He gained both velocity and command on what was already a plus-plus fast-ball, tightened his breaking balls into a distinct curve and

One could argue that Harper entered the year as the most hyped prospect in the history of the game, yet somehow he managed to live up to, if not exceed, expectations. His power is not only tremendous, but already shows up in games, and concerns about his violent swing leading to huge strike-out totals turned out to be unfounded. While his attitude rubs plenty of people the wrong way, nobody questions his work ethic, which showed in the problem-free transition to the outfield, where his top-of-the-line arm turned into a weapon. While Moore is the most likely to win a Cy Young award, Harper is the most likely to win an MVP award, and will likely hit the majors as a teenager.

### 3. Mike Trout, OF, Angels

His big-league batting line actually looks quite good when you consider that we're talking about a 19-year-old not getting consistent playing time for the first time in his ca-reer. Every skill is there, from hitting to defense to power to speed, and while Peter Bourjos was one of the more pleas-ant surprises for the Angels in 2011, it could be in their best interest to deal him now at his maximum value to make room for Trout, who still could develop into either a 20/40 player or a 30/30 type, depending on how the power comes or the speed remains.

### 4. Jurickson Profar, SS, Rangers

Most teams preferred this former Little League World Series hero as a pitcher. The Rangers were one of the few that wanted him as a shortstop, and they certainly made the right call. His great year on a statistical level is one thing, but scouts rave about how mature his game is. His defen-sive fundamentals are advanced, he had more walks than

strikeouts; he already recognizes pitches to drive; and he was the clear leader of his team as an 18-year-old. There are no weaknesses in his game, but no huge tools either. A 20/20 shortstop with outstanding defense will be a nice thing to have in Texas when Elvis Andrus is a free agent in three years.

nobody is perfect. What Teheran needs to do is continue to refine his breaking ball and adjust his location after learn-ing which upper-level locations that worked in the minors turned into home runs in the big leagues. The Braves want to go young in the rotation, and Teheran will lead the way.

### 6. Manny Machado, SS, Orioles

Machado would rank ahead of Profar if the world were con-vinced that he'd stay at shortstop. He offers more offensive potential, with the possibility of one day hitting in the middle of a big-league batter order. It's not that he's a bad shortstop as much as he's big and getting bigger, and an average run-ner at best, with the expectation that he'll slow down. The difference between third base and shortstop is dramatic, but Machado looks like a star either way.

### 7. Jesus Montero, C, Yankees

Should we really keep throwing that C next to his name and pretending he's going to catch in the big leagues? During an offseason press conference, Joe Girardi told anyone who would listen that Francisco Cervelli would be on the roster, and that the only scenarios in which Montero would catch involved nuclear winter. He can't catch, but he sure can hit, and nearly 20 years after Bill James insisted that some play-ers should just be turned into designated hitters, the Yankees are finally heeding the call.

### 8. Dylan Bundy, RHP, Orioles

Some think he's the best high school right-hander since Josh Beckett, and if he were 6-foot-4 instead of 6-foot-1, scouts might have been going further back in history. There have been plenty of high school arms who can get into the upper 90s, but Bundy does things most of them do not, such as adding a breaking ball and having a highly advanced changeup for his age and the ability to throw not only strikes, but good ones. He has the ability to move quickly and help make up for the first-round mistake of Matt Hobgood a couple years back.

## 9. Gerrit Cole, RHP, Pirates

If the stats matched the stuff, Cole would be in the top five. Until then, we're left wondering why he doesn't dominate every time out when he can throw in the upper 90s, touching 100, and has a slider and changeup that are both well above average. On a pure stuff level, Cole matches up with Stephen Strasburg, but he's far from harnessing it the way the future Nationals ace can. His ceiling is as high as any pitcher's in baseball, but he comes with risk, and has equal potential to pitch in the big leagues by August or get stuck in Double-A for a while.

## 10. Shelby Miller, RHP, Cardinals

In 2010, Miller was one of the best, if not *the* best pitcher in the Midwest League. In 2011, he upped the ante by being perhaps the best pitcher in both the Florida State and Texas leagues. He's on pace to be a permanent part of the Cardinals rotation in 2013, but should get a September look after starting this year at Triple-A. He's similar to Matt Cain but with a bit more velocity, and with a few refinements on his secondary pitches, he'll be a star.

## 11. Trevor Bauer, RHP, Diamondbacks

Bauer was a lightning rod in the scouting community this spring. While his stuff came nowhere close to UCLA teammate Gerrit Cole, he far outstripped Cole in performance, striking out 203 batters over 136 2/3 innings while allowing just 73 hits. He's hardly a finesse arm, sitting at 93–96 mph with his fastball and throwing three quality secondary pitches, and he's advanced enough to compete for an Opening Day rotation spot. Don't be surprised if he earns it.

## 12. Miguel Sano, 3B, Twins

What we learned in 2011 is that Sano is not a shortstop, nor is he a third baseman, as he's simply not built for the infield. Whether right field or first base is his final destination, it's not going to matter because his power ceiling sits with anyone on this list other than Harper. It's rare to find a player so young who has already translated his raw power to in-game results. His Low-A debut will be among the most anticipated of 2012.

## 13. Jameson Taillon, RHP, Pirates

We just didn't learn much about Taillon in 2011. While I'm all for being cautious with young arms, the Pirates went a bit overboard with Taillon, rarely allowing him to throw more than four innings and taking away pitches from his arsenal. At some point, such behavior is bad for a player's development, and one hopes a looser leash will allow Taillon to shine in 2012, as he clearly has front-of-the-rotation potential.

## 14. Taijuan Walker, RHP, Mariners

We enter every season with a handful of teenage pitchers who are loaded with athleticism and ceiling and the ability to explode up prospect lists if everything comes together. Every year, we're lucky if just one of them does, and in 2011, it was Walker. It wasn't just the upper-90s fastball that made Walker shine. He showed one of the Midwest League's best breaking balls as well, and while he struck out 113 in 96 2/3 innings, many feel he's just scratched the surface of his potential.

## 15. Jacob Turner, RHP, Tigers

The Tigers are notorious for pushing their prospects, so while Turner's minor-league numbers are good but well short of amazing, he's already proven himself in the upper levels and held his own in the big leagues before his 21st birthday. He'll spend more time in the big leagues this year, but he's also somewhere between five and seven years away from peaking, while already showing well-above-average stuff and location.

## 16. Travis D'Arnaud, C, Blue Jays

D'Arnaud has always tantalized scouts with his tools and impressive athleticism for a catcher, and 2011 was the year in which he stayed healthy and put it all together while earning Eastern League MVP honors. He's merely an average (but getting better) defender, but his kind of hitting ability makes him the rare backstop who projects to hit in the middle of a big-league lineup. The Blue Jays got 23 home runs from a rookie catcher in 2011, yet his grip on the job long term is in doubt because of D'Arnaud.

## 17. Francisco Lindor, SS, Indians

Lindor's pre-draft private workouts nearly made him the number-two overall pick in the 2011 draft, and based on those reports as well as those from instructs, many are thinking that Seattle should have taken the risk. It's hard to find a shortstop in the draft who can actually stay at the position, and beyond the potential plus defense, there is a smooth swing from both sides of the plate with the potential for average power. Between promotions and trades, the Indians system took a big hit in 2011, but Lindor helps to make up for it.

## 18. Gary Brown, OF, Giants

There was a loud group of people who just didn't like Gary Brown because he didn't walk in college. That said, it's hard to tell a guy hitting well over .400 that he should work the count better. His walk rate was only on the slightly low scale in 2011, and Brown's .336/.407/.519 line was actually brought down by a one-month slump. One of the fastest players in the game, Brown has the potential to hit 20 home runs in the big leagues while stealing 50 bases, and he's an outstanding center fielder as well.

### 19. Wil Myers, OF, Royals

Myers didn't put up big numbers as a 20-year-old in Double-A, but worry over the performance was mitigated by a knee laceration that ended up infected and bothered him for much of the year. Scouts still loved the approach and swing, and his showing in the Arizona Fall League returned

[text obscured]

numbers put up by Rockies prospects need to be taken with a grain of salt since they play in friendly hitting environments at every level. With that out of the way, scouts think Arenado is the real deal, as he has the enviable combination of extreme contact ability and plus power. He took even greater strides defensively, transforming his body and going from a player most thought would have to move off the hot corner to one who is a plus defender. He'll start 2012 in Double-A and could reach Colorado quickly.

### 21. Tyler Skaggs, LHP, Diamondbacks

The big prize in the deal that sent Dan Haren to the Angels, Skaggs was always seen as the picture of a projectable arm, and in 2011, that projection began to turn into reality as he gained a couple of ticks on his fastball, turned his curveball from a pitch that flashes plus to one that is consistently there, and just learned to pitch. He struck out 73 Double-A batters over 57 2/3 innings as a 20-year-old. He could still get better and rank even higher next year.

### 22. Billy Hamilton, SS, Reds

The 103 stolen bases don't really tell the story of just how fast Hamilton is. He went from first to third on singles to left, he scored from second on sacrifice flies, he stole second base on pick offs. If there is any player with impact speed, it's Hamilton, who also made plenty of adjustments at the plate, hitting .318/.382/.387 after the All-Star break. He's probably not a shortstop, but it's probably not going to matter.

### 23. Oscar Taveras, OF, Cardinals

Taveras is not exceptionally toolsy, but the one thing he can do is hit. It's remarkable to see a hitter with such a violent

swing yet so much control of it, and he flirted with .400 for much of his full-season debut while dealing with constant hamstring issues. Sent to the Arizona Fall League to get more at-bats as a teenager, he handled far more advanced pitching, and the Cardinals are talking about pushing him to Double-A in 2012.

### 24. Devin Mesoraco, C, Reds

Mesoraco was big-league ready for most of 2011, and now that Ramon Hernandez is out of the way, he'll get his shot, although Dusty Baker's penchant for veterans could lead to more of a shared catching situation with Ryan Hanigan. Mesoraco is clearly the superior talent, with the potential to

[text obscured]

also abused, including one complete game in which he threw 157 pitches. He showed no ill effects in his full-season debut, maintaining his mid-90s fastball throughout the season and reaching Double-A. The Mets don't have much in their system in terms of hitters, but there are a number of exciting young arms getting close to Queens, led by Harvey.

### 26. Anthony Rendon, 3B, Nationals

Rendon was expected to be the first pick in the 2011 draft, but an injured shoulder limited him at Rice, and numbers that fell well below expectations dropped him to Washington at number six overall. He was an on-base machine in college, drawing 145 walks over 126 games in his final two seasons, and when healthy he showed the ability to hit for both average and power along with fine defense at third. The Nationals already have a fine third baseman in Ryan Zimmerman, but Rendon could be ready to step in when the incumbent becomes a free agent after the 2013 season.

### 27. Bubba Starling, OF, Royals

On a tools level, everything is there. He's 6-foot-4, with plus-plus raw power and speed, a combination rarely seen in baseball. It took $7.5 million to steer him away from becoming the next great option quarterback at Nebraska. Now, we just have to figure out if he can play baseball, as it's never been his focus, and his exposure to top-flight competition is minimal. If going by pure ceiling, he'd rank in the single digits, and he could be there next year. Or he could be nearly off the list after striking out 185 times. This is a hedge.

## 28. Jake Marisnick, OF, Blue Jays

A quick lesson on why tools matter. Marisnick looked lost in the Midwest League in 2010, batting just .220/.298/.339 in a late-season look, but then, as teams hope will happen with any prospect more athlete than baseball player, things just started to click, leading to a .320/.392/.496 breakthrough campaign. While his power ceiling is likely in the 18–20 home run range, he does everything else, including hit, run, and play an outstanding center field.

## 29. Manny Banuelos, LHP, Yankees

Banuelos was the victim of the New York hype machine after ending the 2010 season on a strong note and making an impressive showing during spring training. He didn't disappoint in 2011 as much as he just showed people that he was only 20 years old and there's still some work to be done. His fastball is plus, his changeup is even better, and his curveball is good enough. He's only some command tweaks away from being ready for the big leagues.

## 30. Zack Wheeler, RHP, Mets

The Mets added another high-ceiling arm to a system already packed with them when they traded Carlos Beltran for Wheeler. They altered his delivery upon arrival, or rather returned him to his form from high school, and he began throwing strikes while not losing any of his mid-90s velocity. He'll begin the year at Double-A, and based solely on the growth we saw last August, he has a shot at seeing Citi Field by September.

## 31. Carlos Martinez, RHP, Cardinals

Martinez created plenty of hype before he arrived in the United States, thanks to a $1.5 million bonus and an 0.76 ERA in the Dominican League. His stateside debut did not disappoint other than some hiccups in the Florida State League, but scouts vary in their projection of him. His arm is remarkable, as it seems nearly impossible for a skinny 6-foot-tall pitcher to touch 100 mph, but that's part of his potential problem. Between his size and the effort in his delivery, it won't be a shock if he ends up a dominant big leaguer, but as a closer.

## 32. Xander Bogaerts, SS, Red Sox

Bogaerts was so impressive in extended spring training that the Red Sox threw him to the dogs in a full-season league, and he responded with 16 home runs in 265 at-bats. When teenagers show that kind of in-game power, it's a special thing. He's not especially athletic, and he's still growing, so he's not going to be a shortstop in the end. He also strikes out too much and needs to stop chasing breaking balls in the dirt, but with this kind of power, nobody cares.

## 33. Christian Yelich, OF, Marlins

Nobody was especially surprised that Yelich, the Marlins' first-round pick in 2010, hit .312/.388/.484 in his full-season debut, but he pulled off the rare feat of proving to be more athletic than he was in high school. Drafted for his bat, he suddenly added a genuine speed element to his game, stealing 32 bases and playing a solid center field. The ability to stay up the middle boosts any prospect's status significantly, and Yelich could do just that.

## 34. Drew Pomeranz, LHP, Rockies

Pomeranz was on his way to the big leagues when he was the key component to the trade that sent Ubaldo Jimenez to Cleveland. An emergency appendectomy hampered his brief time with Colorado, but he'll get a shot at the Rockies rotation this spring. A classic power pitcher made all the more impressive due to his left-handedness, Pomeranz's low-90s fastball and monster curve dominated minor-league hitters, and the development of his curve will define just how well he ends up doing in the big leagues.

## 35. Danny Hultzen, LHP, Mariners

Hultzen put up incredible numbers at the University of Virginia, was the second overall pick in the draft, and had a 1.40 ERA in limited Arizona Fall League innings against advanced hitters. That sounds like a player who should rank in the Top 10, yet scouts see more pitchability than stuff, because while Hultzen throws strikes and features a deep arsenal of pitches, he doesn't have the kind of monster stuff one generally finds in a front-line starter. He'll get to Seattle quickly, but could end up more of a good, consistent pitcher than a star.

## 36. Martin Perez, LHP, Rangers

He's left-handed, throws in the low-90s with a downright pretty delivery, and has an excellent curveball. He reached the upper levels as a teenager and is on the verge of the big leagues. All that is wonderful, but this is the last chance Perez gets to be an elite prospect, as he's either established in the big leagues by the end of the year or his inconsistency has gotten to the point where it's time to wonder just how good he can be.

## 37. Archie Bradley, RHP, Diamondbacks

The seventh overall pick in last year's draft, Bradley has everything scouts look for in a high school pitcher. He's big, can touch the mid-to-upper 90s with his fastball, and already has an impressive breaking ball. All he needs are innings and a changeup, but that's the case with so many million-dollar arms. The attrition rate for talents like this is still a concern, but you can either take a chance on them or end up never reaping the potential benefits.

## 38. Yasmani Grandal, C, Padres

Blocked in Cincinnati by Devin Mesoraco, Grandal was the primary piece in the deal that netted potential ace Mat Latos from San Diego. His timetable is more 2013 than '12, but he projects as a solid receiver with both patience and a bit of power at the plate. San Diego will reduce him to more of a doubles hitter with on-base skills, but in today's game, any offensive production from a catcher is valuable.

## 39. Michael Choice, OF, Athletics

Oakland's first-round pick in 2010, Choice has classic right-field tools, and they were all on display in his first full season. He has plenty of power, outstanding plate discipline, and a

Sanchez somehow got labeled as a disappointment after hitting .256/.335/.485 in Low-A, which in reality is a remarkable line for an 18-year-old at that level. He has tremendous power and is a potential above-average hitter, but he unfortunately has the potential to be the next Jesus Montero as well—a player with a bat, but no position to play. Don't worry about his numbers in 2012, as good numbers in the Florida State League are rare. Just pay attention to the defensive reports.

## 41. Randall Delgado, RHP, Braves

Delgado seems to get lost at times among all of the young Braves arms. He doesn't have the explosive stuff of Julio Teheran or Arodys Vizcaino, nor the polish of Mike Minor, yet he reached the majors just four months after his 21st birthday, and he was more prepared for the rigors of pitching in the big leagues than other options, including Teheran. His stuff is that of a good mid-rotation starter, but he has enough command to exceed that ceiling, and he's nearly ready for a full-time shot.

## 42. Luis Heredia, LHP, Pirates

Heredia has the potential to be a true number one as he's touched the mid-90s as a 16-year-old, but for all of the promise, there are still all sorts of things that need to break right. His changeup is well ahead of most at his age, but he's just learning how to spin a breaking ball, as well as simply figuring out how to pitch to professional hitters as opposed to just rearing back and trying to blow everyone away. There is no bigger lottery ticket on this list, but the potential payoff is tremendous.

## 43. Josh Bell, OF, Pirates

The last symbol of the Pirates' free-spending ways as part of their rebuilding process, Bell's $5 million bonus as a second-round pick will be all but impossible to dole out under the new CBA. But Bell immediately became the top position prospect in the system, and was the high school hitter in the 2011 draft deemed most likely to hit third in a big-league-level lineup. A switch-hitter with power from both sides and an arm for right field, Bell carries a heavy load on his back, because at some point, you have to stop rebuilding and start winning.

## 44. Brett Jackson, OF, Cubs

live with, but with power, speed, and walks, Jackson more than makes up for them.

## 45. Mike Olt, 3B, Rangers

Olt was having a breakout full-season debut before breaking his clavicle in a home-plate collision that cost him most of the second half. With a fantastic sense of the strike zone and plus power, Olt has a traditional profile for the position at the plate, and he's one of the better defensive third baseman in the minors, with outstanding instincts and a plus arm. With Adrian Beltre signed for the long term, it's hard to envision his future in Texas. Moving him to first base would take away a significant source of his value.

## 46. Brandon Jacobs, OF, Red Sox

Prior to the new collective bargaining agreement, the Red Sox made a habit of using later picks on high-ceiling, risky talent with high bonus demands. Jacobs was that player in 2009, earning $750,000 as a 10th-round pick to steer him clear of a football career, and the progress he made in turning his athleticism into baseball skills during the 2011 season was nothing short of shocking. A compact athlete with power and speed, like many raw players Jacobs needs to develop a better approach, but his pure ability tops any position prospect in the system.

## 47. Jake Odorizzi, RHP, Royals

While Odorizzi was among the least-known players heading to the Royals in last winter's Zack Greinke deal, he has the potential to be the best. One of the most athletic pitchers in the minors, Odorizzi has an excellent delivery, and while none of his pitches are plus-plus, his fastball, curve, and changeup are all above average and play up on his ability to locate them. Having entered 2011 behind a flurry of left-handers, he's lined up for a shot at a rotation job in 2013.

## 48. Jarred Cosart, RHP, Astros

In a 2011 Futures Game loaded with elite arms, Cosart's stuff outstripped every other right-hander in the game. He can sit in the mid-90s, touch 97–98 consistently, and make hitters look foolish with a power curveball with heavy late movement. His ceiling is as a potential ace, which is why the Astros got him from the Phillies in the Hunter Pence deal, but at the same time, the results rarely match the ability, as he has trouble repeating his delivery and can have issues throwing strikes. He could go in many directions from here.

## 49. George Springer, OF, Astros

Springer is the kind of pure athlete that's rare to find among college players. He has well-above-average power, runs well, and has a solid chance to stick in center field if he can improve his instincts. The issue is will his hit tool develop, but he made huge strides in his final year at Connecticut when it came to making more contact and trusting his swing as opposed to muscling up. Between trades and the draft, the Astros are finally turning around their system, and Springer is the prize among position players.

## 50. Jarred Parker, RHP, Athletics

Parker was the top pitching prospect in the Arizona system since being a first-round pick in the 2007 draft, but more recent pitching picks, pick-ups via trade, and Parker's Tommy John surgery made him expendable, and he became the A's top pitching prospect as soon as the Trevor Cahill deal was concluded. While his stuff isn't all the way back from pre-surgery days, the most important fact is that he stayed healthy in 2011, and year two back from the procedure will give Oakland a much better feel for whether he's a future number two or number three.

## 51. Trevor May, RHP, Phillies

The Phillies had always been intrigued by May's upside, much of it based on his 6-foot-5 frame, but that was also his biggest problem, as his long levers led to control issues and he struggled to maintain his delivery and release point. Everything came together in 2011: May struck out 208 over 151 1/3 innings, and a repeat of that at Double-A in 2012 could move him into elite status.

## 52. Rymer Liriano, OF, Padres

For the first two weeks of the season, Liriano didn't look worthy of a Top 1000 list, as he hit .127 in 15 California League games. Sent down to the Midwest League, Liriano, still just 19, ended up an unlikely MVP, hitting .319/.383/.499 with 12 home runs and 65 stolen bases. In a system filled with good players, Liriano is more of a toolsy guy who is starting to mature his game with the potential for 20–homer power to go with his impressive speed and approach.

## 53. Robbie Erlin, RHP, Padres

If you want command and control, few in all of baseball can match Erlin, who in 266 minor-league innings has struck out 288 and walked 34. While he's not a power pitcher, his stuff is well above that pure finesse classification, and if anything, he throws too many strikes, allowing batters to prepare to swing at every pitch. That will require some adjustments, but while his ceiling is a bit lacking, his floor is as high as nearly anyone's.

## 54. Daniel Norris, LHP, Blue Jays

Ignore the fact that Norris was the 74th pick in the 2011 draft. He was the best high school left-hander in the country, and ultimately signed for a $2 million bonus. Athletic and projectable, Norris can already get into the mid-90s at times, and his breaking ball and changeup both show signs of developing into above-average offerings. No team has as much high-ceiling young pitching talent as Toronto, and Norris leads the pack.

## 55. Will Middlebrooks, 3B, Red Sox

Middlebrooks has always been an excellent defensive third baseman, and after showing signs of life at the plate in 2010, he put even more together offensively, nearly doubling his home run total from the previous year with 23 while hitting over .300 at Double-A Portland. A constant subject of trade rumors in the offseason, Middlebrooks projects as an above-average big-league third baseman, and could force some difficult decisions for Boston by 2013.

## 56. Starling Marte, OF, Pirates

A broken hand in 2010 left scouts wondering about Marte's power ceiling, but the healthy version not only hit .332 at Double-A in 2011, but added 38 doubles, eight triples and 12 home runs. A true center fielder with above-average speed, Marte is a dynamic talent, but still one who plays a bit out of control. He makes plenty of outs on the basepaths and rarely draws walks.

## 57. Jedd Gyorko, 3B, Padres

He's just 5-foot-10, he's a bit bow-legged, and nothing he does looks pretty, but at the same time, he just can flat out hit. In 208 pro games, Gyorko's batting line now sits at .323/.392/.518. A doubles machine with a good approach, Gyorko's most significant achievement in 2011 was his growth at the hot corner, where most scouts now believe he can stay.

## 58. Cory Spangenberg, 2B, Padres

The 10th overall pick in the 2011 draft, Spangenberg combines the fastest bat in the system with a true leadoff man's approach and speed. While power will never be a big part of his game, he projects as a solid second baseman who can put up .400 on-base percentages and steal 30–40 bases a year in an igniter role. He has the potential to put up massive numbers in the California League in 2012.

## 59. James Paxton, LHP, Mariners

After not signing with Toronto as a 2009 first-round pick, Paxton finally got his career going and quickly made up for lost time by reaching Double-A in his full-season debut, put-

Gonzalez, Cole offers the most risk, based on his age and experience alone, but also the most potential. Just 19, tall and skinny, Cole touched 97–98 mph in his full-season debut while comfortably parked at 92–95. While his curve and changeup both only show flashes, there is enough potential in him to give Cole a top-of-the-rotation ceiling.

## 61. Wilin Rosario, C, Rockies

Rosario's 2010 breakout campaign was cut short by knee surgery, which hampered him in 2011 as well. Still, he's a catcher with above-average power and one of the best arms in the minors. The Rockies signed Ramon Hernandez to a two-year deal in the offseason, meaning Rosario will likely get one more year in the minors, and then one year in the big leagues learning from a wily veteran.

## 62. Arodys Vizcaino, RHP, Braves

The biggest question concerning Vizcaino now is his future role. He's been plenty effective as a starter with mid-90s heat and a nasty power breaking ball, but that combination also got him to the big leagues as a reliever before his 21st birthday. As a starter he's had some bouts with arm soreness that present the question of whether he can handle a 200-inning workload. Combined with the flurry of Braves pitching prospects, he's likely to make the Braves bullpen even nastier, but the tease of starting will be there for a while.

## 63. Dellin Betances, RHP, Yankees

He's a massive individual with equally massive stuff, but his 2011 season left many questions about his future. He has a long history of arm troubles, is a highly inefficient pitcher,

and has inconsistencies with his command and secondary offerings. More and more scouts think it would be best to just turn him into a closer, where he could dominate.

## 64. Brad Peacock, RHP, Athletics

Another part of the Gio haul from Washington, Peacock is the most big-league ready talent going to Oakland, and he'll likely be a part of the A's rotation on Opening Day. With a low-90s fastball and outstanding location, Peacock's key to success is his plus velocity and command, and he adds an above-average curveball to the mix as well. His ceiling is a number-three starter, but he's also arguably that right now, and should be for years.

some walks, and 20–30 stolen bases.

## 66. Javier Baez, SS, Cubs

He's listed as a shortstop for now, but the ninth-overall pick in the 2011 draft earned that slot and a bonus north of $2.6 million for his bat. For some, no player in the draft could match his pure bat speed, and he should develop at least average power and maybe more if he fills out. He'll never stay at shortstop, as he's just not that kind of an athlete, but he has the potential to be a middle-of-the-order presence at either second or third base.

## 67. Jean Segura, SS, Angels

The bad news is that Segura missed the majority of the 2011 season with hamstring issues. The good news is that he's moved from second base to shortstop, and scouts found the transition to be a rare success. A speed-based player who can also hit and provide gap power, Segura is a dynamic talent with the ability to move up this list in a big way with a healthy season at Double-A.

## 68. Anthony Gose, OF, Blue Jays

The tools are insane. He's a plus-plus runner who stole 70 bases in 2011, and his raw power finally began to manifest in games as he hit 16 home runs. He's a fantastic center fielder with a plus-plus arm that touched the upper 90s when he pitched in high school. The question is just how much he'll hit. He has a career .258 batting average in the minors with 408 strikeouts in 409 games. At minimum, he could be like Drew Stubbs, but there's the potential for so much more.

### 69. Matt Adams, 1B, Cardinals

As a 2009 23rd-round pick out of the baseball hotbed that is Slippery Rock University, Adams has had to fight through a lack of pedigree, but all he does is hit, hit for power, and show a nearly shocking amount of contact ability for a man of his size and power. At 6-foot-3 and somewhere north of 250 pounds, depending on the day, Adams is the very definition of a bat-only player, but the reigning Texas League MVP could be ready to fill the giant hole left by the departure of Albert Pujols by 2013.

### 70. Zach Lee, RHP, Dodgers

Some seemed almost disappointed by Lee's full-season debut, in which he had a 3.47 ERA with 91 strikeouts in 109 innings. Just because a player doesn't break out immediately doesn't mean he's not a prospect. Lee's ceiling hasn't changed one bit from where it was 12 months ago. All we've learned is he's just a little bit further from it than we'd thought.

### 71. Nick Castellanos, 3B, Tigers

One of the few glimmers of hope when it comes to position players in the Tigers system, Castellanos' .312/.367/.436 line is impressive enough for the pitcher-friendly Midwest League, but he also got better throughout the year, showing the potential to be a player who hits for average and power while playing a solid third base. The Florida State League will continue to depress his numbers in 2012, but the talent should still shine through.

### 72. Sonny Gray, RHP, Athletics

It was shocking to watch Gray fall to the number-18 overall pick in the 2011 draft, but the A's are happy to benefit from it. His 5-foot-11 height worked against him, but after he allowed just one run in 20 Double-A innings, teams are wondering why they passed on him as his 92–95 mph fastball is good and his overhand curveball is even better.

### 73. Jonathan Singleton, 1B, Astros

Another player who came to Houston in the Hunter Pence deal, Singleton in some ways is still living off his tremendous start to the 2010 season. Since then, he's been more good than great, as his raw power remains just that, although he can hit for average and get on base with plenty of walks. Still, any chink in the armor of a first-base prospect is significant, and Singleton still has plenty to prove before fulfilling his promise.

### 74. Joe Wieland, RHP, Padres

When Wieland went to the Padres along with Erlin in the Matt Adams deal, it was hard to tell the difference between the two. Both are extreme strike throwers with solid stuff, and both are without question going to be solid big-league starters, barring injuries. Wieland is more impressive physically, but his secondary pitchers are not in the same class as Erlin's, thus the slightly lower ranking.

### 75. Anthony Rizzo, 1B, Padres

Rizzo hit .331/.404/.652 in the high-octane environment of Triple-A Tucson, and in some ways, it was the worst thing that could have happened, as it led to some poor habits. His swing got loopy and his approach became power conscious. That led to disturbing troubles in the big leagues.

### 76. Robbie Grossman, OF, Pirates

Grossman became a favorite of the stats kids with a .294/.418/.451 line that included a minor league-leading 104 walks, but there are plenty of dings in his game as well, as he was repeating High-A and proved that he's not a center fielder long term. While he lacks the power normally associated with a corner outfielder, he's similar to Rusty Greer, who was an awfully productive player.

### 77. Neil Ramirez, RHP, Rangers

Ramirez was barely on the radar entering the year, despite signing for $1 million in 2007, but everything suddenly came together as he reached Triple-A while showcasing mid-90s heat and a plus curve in one of the most sudden transformations of the year. If not for some shoulder issues, he'd rank higher, and he could hit the majors at some point in 2012 if the shoulder turns out not to be a long-term issue.

### 78. Casey Kelly, RHP, Padres

Kelly was the big prize when the Padres dealt Adrian Gonzalez to Boston, but he's still a frustrating talent who has yet to have the season scouts expect based on his athleticism and stuff. He throws hard with location and movement and shows a plus curve, but he's rarely dominant, and his consistent rate of six-to-seven strikeouts per nine is almost baffling. Nobody thinks he's a future number two anymore, but despite the numbers, he still looks like a good future number three.

### 79. Chad Bettis, RHP, Rockies

The Rockies made Bettis a second-round pick in 2011 based almost solely on his arm strength, but he proved to be a much more complete pitcher in 2011, falling just short of winning the pitching triple crown in the California League. While he sits consistently in the mid-90s, his fastball is even better based on his command, and he made enough progress on his slider and changeup to leave scouts believing in his ability to remain a starter after a college career in the bullpen.

### 80. Jose Fernandez, RHP, Marlins

A Cuban émigré who escaped the island just four years ago, Fernandez turned into one of the best high school right-handers in the 2011 draft. With a big, strong build, Fernandez already has low-to-mid-90s heat and the ability to spin a ball, as well as more feel for a changeup than your average teenager. The Marlins' pipeline of young talent has dried up, but the last two drafts have the potential of providing another wave.

### 81. Addison Reed, RHP, White Sox

Reed made me look good in 2011. I was lucky enough to have a scout tell me in April, after he'd seen Reed in Low-A, that Reed could pitch in the big leagues by the end of the year. That proved to be prophetic, as with 94–98 mph heat and a wipeout slider, Reed is not just big-league ready, he's poten-

for returning from the procedure has grown exponentially over the past decade. The bad news is he still had Tommy John surgery. Lamb could turn into a left-handed version of Jeremy Hellickson, but we can't be sure until he returns midseason.

### 83. Cheslor Cuthbert, 3B, Royals

Cuthbert would rank higher had he not slumped significantly during the second half of the season. Even taken as a whole, it was an impressive performance from an 18-year-old in a full-season league, and scouts were impressed with how mature his game was, from his approach to his defensive fundamentals. He doesn't have the kind of tools normally associated with high-ranking teenagers, but he's quite the ballplayer.

### 84. Jessie Biddle, LHP, Phillies

A first-round pick in 2011, Biddle got better as the season wore on, including a 1.91 ERA after the All-Star break. His fastball velocity varies wildly, from 88–94 mph, but he features two plus secondary pitches in his curveball and changeup. At 6-foot-4 and 225 pounds, his physique certainly suggests more consistent plus velocity in the future, which would lead to a higher ranking next year.

### 85. Jonathan Schoop, INF, Orioles

Schoop began to garner attention in the New York-Penn League in 2010, and his full-season debut did not disappoint. He has an impressive bat and the potential for power, but in deference to the much more talented Manny Machado and his own lack of speed, he's been moved around the infield in search of a defensive home. He'll need more power to be

a good third baseman, but as an offensive-oriented second baseman, he could be a star.

### 86. Yonder Alonso, 1B, Padres

It was confusing to see Alonso as one of the primary prospects heading to San Diego in the Mat Latos trade, primarily because of the presence of Anthony Rizzo on the Padres depth chart at the time. Like Rizzo, Alonso is an impressive hitter, but it's easy to find flaws, including power that has yet to fully show up in games and some struggles against left-handers.

### 87. Eddie Rosario, OF/2B, Twins

where early returns were encouraging.

### 88. Kolten Wong, 2B, Cardinals

If Wong were 6-foot-1 instead of 5-foot-9, he would have gone much higher than the 22nd-overall pick in the 2011 draft. Even though he's small, he can really play. His professional career consists of a .335/.401/.510 line in 47 Low-A games, but in that short time, he showed scouts hitting ability, gap power, a good approach, surprisingly solid defensive abilities, and the potential to move quickly through the system.

### 89. Jeurys Familia, RHP, Mets

Familia has always had one of the best arms in the Mets system, and it started to come together for him in 2011. He reached Double-A and averaged well over a strikeout per inning, thanks mostly to a dominating fastball that consistently gets into the upper 90s. The knock against him is a changeup that is still a work in progress and a delivery that is far from pretty. That could lead to a future in the back of a bullpen, and with that a distinct possibility, it's hard to rank him higher.

### 90. Joe Benson, OF, Twins

Benson doesn't get much attention for a player with his tools. His power, speed, and arm are all at least above average, but the hit tool is the one that trumps all, and there is still a significant amount of swing and miss in his game. Josh Willingham blocks him for now, but Benson has the ability to convince the Twins that the speed combination of Revere and Span might not be the best solution.

## 91. Matt Purke, LHP, Nationals

Purke entered the spring with a shot at being the top pick in the draft and a single-digit fit on this list, but he struggled with shoulder issues throughout the year, and his bonus demands dropped him to the third round, where the Nats met his high price tag. His showing in the Arizona Fall League showed that he's nowhere near back to the 2010 version of Purke, a lefty with mid-80s heat and a killer slider, but if rest proves to be the solution, this ranking is way too low. He's here because we haven't seen that pitcher for more than a year.

## 92. Wily Peralta, RHP, Brewers

After failing to put a player on last year's list, the Brewers squeak onto this one thanks to Peralta finally beginning to live up to his potential by harnessing what has always been evident. He's always had mid-90s heat, but his slider, changeup, and overall command improved throughout the year, and he's suddenly on pace for a look in the rotation as early as mid-2012.

## 93. Noah Syndergaard, RHP, Blue Jays

The Blue Jays have drafted and signed countless high-ceiling arms over the past two years, and while many of them have already performed, Syndergaard stood out the most thanks to the fact that he touched 100 mph in one start while consistently sitting in the mid-90s. He generally throws strikes, but his secondary pitches will have to improve for him to become elite.

## 94. Austin Hedges, C, Padres

According to some scouts, he's the best defensive catcher to come out of high school in a decade or more. He's a fantastic receiver and his arm earns the rare top-of-the-scale 80 score. There is plenty of debate over just how much he is going to hit, but even if he develops into a player who can play every day and bat seventh in the lineup, his defense alone will make him one of the better catchers in the game.

## 95. Joe Ross, RHP, Padres

Ross was a wild card in the 2011 draft, as he was rumored to go as high as number 10 overall before he went 25th due to bonus demands, not talent. It took $2.75 million to get him away from UCLA, and while his pro career consists of one inning right now, he's athletic, gets up to 96 mph, and has enough feel for spinning a breaking ball and throwing a changeup to be projected as a front-line starter. But it's going to take a while.

## 96. Derek Norris, C, Athletics

It's awfully hard to make a Top 101 list when you hit .210, but Norris has such amazing plate discipline and enough power to make a .210 average look good by showing enough secondary skills to finish the year with an 813 OPS. The most important part of his season was the great strides he made defensively, and he suddenly looks like he could become like Mickey Tettleton, but with defensive chops.

## 97. Tim Wheeler, OF, Rockies

Wheeler's tools are average to slightly above across the board. After seeing his prospect star dim with an ugly full-season debut, he exploded in the Texas League with 33 home runs and 21 stolen bases. Questions about his ability to play center long term hurt his value, and his high strikeout rate leaves plenty of questions about how much of an average he'll put up as well. Still, 20/20 outfielders are rare.

## 98. Ryan Lavarnway, C, Red Sox

Lavarnway exploded offensively in 2011, with 32 home runs and a .612 slugging percentage at Triple-A. And with two big-league home runs, he's already tied with Ron Darling for the all-time lead among players drafted out of Yale. The bad news is that he's a well-below-average catcher, and in the mind of some scouts, kind of the poor man's (very poor) version of Jesus Montero, only four years older.

## 99. Mason Williams, OF, Yankees

The Yankees gave Williams a seven-figure bonus as a sixth-round pick in 2010 based solely on his athleticism, and he made progress on the field in 2011 that is nothing less than shocking. Beyond batting .349/.395/.468 in the New York-Penn League, Williams showed hitting skills, plus-plus wheels and the potential to be a well-above-average center fielder. He's at least three years away from the big leagues, but it's been a long time since the Yankees developed an up-the-middle talent.

## 100. Grant Green, OF, Athletics

While Green was unable to match last year's big numbers in the California League, he hit .300 after an ugly April, remained a doubles machine, and made an almost shockingly impressive transition from shortstop, where he was error prone, to center field. He's Triple-A ready both offensively and defensively, and his path to Oakland couldn't be more wide open.

## 101. Jorge Alfaro, C, Rangers

A high-ceiling catcher, Alfaro hit .300/.345/.481 as an 18-year-old in the college-heavy Northwest League, and he's still far from a finished product. He's only starting to tap into his raw power, and he needs to improve his receiving skills and turn his impressive arm strength into an in-game weapon. There will be plenty of bumps in the road during his development, but catchers who can hit and throw are rare commodities.

# Team Name Codes

| CODE | TEAM | LEAGUE | AFFILIATION | NAME | | CODE | TEAM | LEAGUE | AFFILIATION | NAME |
|------|------|--------|-------------|------|---|------|------|--------|-------------|------|
| ABE | Aberdeen | NYP | Orioles | IronBirds | | COL | Colorado | NL | Rockies | Rockies |
| ABQ | Albuquerque | PCL | Dodgers | Isotopes | | CSC | Charleston | SAL | Yankees | RiverDogs |
| AKR | Akron | EAS | Indians | Aeros | | CSP | Colorado Springs | PCL | Rockies | Sky Sox |
| ALT | Altoona | EAS | Pirates | Curve | | CUB | AZL Cubs | AZL | Cubs | AZL Cubs |
| ANA | Los Angeles | AL | Angels | Angels | | DAY | Daytona | FSL | Cubs | Cubs |
| AUG | Augusta | SAL | Giants | GreenJackets | | DUR | Durham | INT | Rays | Bulls |
| BAK | Bakersfield | CAL | Reds | Blaze | | DYT | Dayton | MID | Reds | Dragons |
| BAL | Baltimore | AL | Orioles | Orioles | | ELZ | Elizabethton | APL | Twins | Twins |
| BAT | Batavia | NYP | Cardinals | Muckdogs | | ERI | Erie | EAS | Tigers | SeaWolves |
| BGR | Bowling Green | MID | Rays | Hot Rods | | EUG | Eugene | NWN | Padres | Emeralds |
| BIL | Billings | PIO | Reds | Mustangs | | EVE | Everett | NWN | Mariners | AquaSox |
| BIN | Binghamton | EAS | Mets | Mets | | FKU | Fukuoka Softbank | NPB | - | Hawks |
| BIR | Birmingham | SOU | White Sox | Barons | | FLO | Florida | NL | Marlins | Marlins |
| BLJ | GCL Blue Jays | GCL | Blue Jays | GCL Blue Jays | | FRD | Frederick | CAR | Orioles | Keys |
| BLT | Beloit | MID | Twins | Snappers | | FRE | Fresno | PCL | Giants | Grizzlies |
| BLU | Bluefield | APL | Blue Jays | Blue Jays | | FRI | Frisco | TEX | Rangers | RoughRiders |
| BNC | Burlington | APL | Royals | Royals | | FTM | Fort Myers | FSL | Twins | Miracle |
| BOI | Boise | NWN | Cubs | Hawks | | FTW | Fort Wayne | MID | Padres | TinCaps |
| BOS | Boston | AL | Red Sox | Red Sox | | GIA | AZL Giants | AZL | Giants | AZL Giants |
| BOW | Bowie | EAS | Orioles | Baysox | | GRB | Greensboro | SAL | Marlins | Grasshoppers |
| BRA | GCL Braves | GCL | Braves | GCL Braves | | GRF | Great Falls | PIO | White Sox | Voyagers |
| BRD | Bradenton | FSL | Pirates | Marauders | | GRL | Great Lakes | MID | Dodgers | Loons |
| BRI | Bristol | APL | White Sox | White Sox | | GRN | Greenville | SAL | Red Sox | Drive |
| BRO | Brooklyn | NYP | Mets | Cyclones | | GRV | Greeneville | APL | Astros | Astros |
| BRV | Brevard County | FSL | Brewers | Manatees | | GWN | Gwinnett | INT | Braves | Braves |
| BUF | Buffalo | INT | Mets | Bisons | | HAG | Hagerstown | SAL | Nationals | Suns |
| BUR | Burlington | MID | Athletics | Bees | | HAR | Harrisburg | EAS | Nationals | Senators |
| CAR | Carolina | SOU | Reds | Mudcats | | HDS | High Desert | CAL | Mariners | Mavericks |
| CAS | Casper | PIO | Rockies | Ghosts | | HEL | Helena | PIO | Brewers | Brewers |
| CCH | Corpus Christi | TEX | Astros | Hooks | | HIC | Hickory | SAL | Rangers | Crawdads |
| CDR | Cedar Rapids | MID | Angels | Kernels | | HNS | Hanshin | NPB | - | Tigers |
| CHA | Chicago | AL | White Sox | White Sox | | HOL | Holguin | CUB | - | Sabuesos |
| CHN | Chicago | NL | Cubs | Cubs | | HOU | Houston | NL | Astros | Astros |
| CHR | Charlotte | INT | White Sox | Knights | | HRO | Hiroshima | NPB | - | Carp |
| CHT | Chattanooga | SOU | Dodgers | Lookouts | | HUD | Hudson Valley | NYP | Rays | Renegades |
| CIN | Cincinnati | NL | Reds | Reds | | HUN | Huntsville | SOU | Brewers | Stars |
| CLE | Cleveland | AL | Indians | Indians | | IDA | Idaho Falls | PIO | Royals | Chukars |
| CLN | Clinton | MID | Mariners | LumberKings | | IND | AZL Indians | AZL | Indians | AZL Indians |
| CLR | Clearwater | FSL | Phillies | Threshers | | IND | Indianapolis | INT | Pirates | Indians |
| COH | Columbus | INT | Indians | Clippers | | | | | | |

| CODE | TEAM | LEAGUE | AFFILIATION | NAME | CODE | TEAM | LEAGUE | AFFILIATION | NAME |
|------|------|--------|-------------|------|------|------|--------|-------------|------|
| IOW | Iowa | PCL | Cubs | Cubs | ORI | GCL Orioles | GCL | Orioles | GCL Orioles |
| JAM | Jamestown | NYP | Marlins | Jammers | ORI | Caribes | VWL | - | Caribes |
| JAX | Jacksonville | SOU | Marlins | Suns | ORM | Orem | PIO | Angels | Owlz |
| JCY | Johnson City | APL | Cardinals | Cardinals | PAW | Pawtucket | INT | Red Sox | Red Sox |
| JUP | Jupiter | FSL | Marlins | Hammerheads | PCH | Charlotte | FSL | Rays | Stone Crabs |
| KAN | Kannapolis | SAL | White Sox | Intimidators | PDR | AZL Padres | AZL | Padres | AZL Padres |
| KCA | Kansas City | AL | Royals | Royals | PEO | Peoria | MID | Cubs | Chiefs |
| KIN | Kinston | CAR | Indians | Indians | PHI | Philadelphia | NL | Phillies | Phillies |
| KNC | Kane County | MID | Royals | Cougars | PHL | GCL Phillies | GCL | Phillies | GCL Phillies |
| KNG | Kingsport | APL | Mets | Mets | PIR | GCL Pirates | GCL | Pirates | GCL Pirates |
| LAK | Lakeland | FSL | Tigers | Flying Tigers | PIT | Pittsburgh | NL | Pirates | Pirates |
| LAN | Los Angeles | NL | Dodgers | Dodgers | PMB | Palm Beach | FSL | Cardinals | Cardinals |
| LEH | Lehigh Valley | INT | Phillies | IronPigs | PME | Portland | EAS | Red Sox | Sea Dogs |
| LEL | Lake Elsinore | CAL | Padres | Storm | POR | Portland | PCL | Padres | Beavers |
| LEX | Lexington | SAL | Astros | Legends | POT | Potomac | CAR | Nationals | Nationals |
| LKC | Lake County | MID | Indians | Captains | PRI | Princeton | APL | Rays | Rays |
| LNC | Lancaster | CAL | Astros | JetHawks | PUL | Pulaski | APL | Mariners | Mariners |
| LNS | Lansing | MID | Blue Jays | Lugnuts | PZA | Minatitlan | MEX | - | Petroleros |
| LOU | Louisville | INT | Reds | Bats | QUD | Quad Cities | MID | Cardinals | River Bandits |
| LOW | Lowell | NYP | Red Sox | Spinners | RAY | GCL Rays | GCL | Rays | GCL Rays |
| LVG | Las Vegas | PCL | Blue Jays | 51s | RCU | Rancho Cucamonga | CAL | Dodgers | Quakes |
| LWD | Lakewood | SAL | Phillies | BlueClaws | RDS | GCL Reds | GCL | Reds | GCL Reds |
| LYN | Lynchburg | CAR | Braves | Hillcats | REA | Reading | EAS | Phillies | Phillies |
| MCD | Mexico | MEX | - | Diablos Rojos | RED | AZL Reds | AZL | Reds | AZL Reds |
| MCT | Quintana Roo | MEX | - | Tigres | RIC | Richmond | EAS | Giants | Flying Squirrels |
| MEM | Memphis | PCL | Cardinals | Redbirds | RNG | AZL Rangers | AZL | Rangers | AZL Rangers |
| MHV | Mahoning Valley | NYP | Indians | Scrappers | RNO | Reno | PCL | Diamondbacks | Aces |
| MID | Midland | TEX | Athletics | RockHounds | ROC | Rochester | INT | Twins | Red Wings |
| MIL | Milwaukee | NL | Brewers | Brewers | ROM | Rome | SAL | Braves | Braves |
| MIN | Minnesota | AL | Twins | Twins | ROU | Round Rock | PCL | Rangers | Express |
| MIS | Mississippi | SOU | Braves | Braves | ROY | AZL Royals | AZL | Royals | AZL Royals |
| MNT | Montgomery | SOU | Rays | Biscuits | RSX | GCL Red Sox | GCL | Red Sox | GCL Red Sox |
| MOB | Mobile | SOU | Diamondbacks | BayBears | SAC | Sacramento | PCL | Athletics | River Cats |
| MOD | Modesto | CAL | Rockies | Nuts | SAN | San Antonio | TEX | Padres | Missions |
| MRL | GCL Marlins | GCL | Marlins | GCL Marlins | SAR | Sarasota | FSL | Reds | Reds |
| MRN | AZL Mariners | AZL | Mariners | AZL Mariners | SAV | Savannah | SAL | Mets | Sand Gnats |
| MSO | Missoula | PIO | D-backs | Osprey | SBN | South Bend | MID | Diamondbacks | Silver Hawks |
| MTS | GCL Mets | GCL | Mets | GCL Mets | SBR | Inland Empire | CAL | Angels | 66ers |
| MYR | Myrtle Beach | CAR | Rangers | Pelicans | SCO | State College | NYP | Pirates | Spikes |
| NAS | Nashville | PCL | Brewers | Sounds | SDN | San Diego | NL | Padres | Padres |
| NAT | GCL Nationals | GCL | Nationals | GCL Nationals | SEA | Seattle | AL | Mariners | Mariners |
| NBR | New Britain | EAS | Twins | Rock Cats | SFD | Springfield | TEX | Cardinals | Cardinals |
| NHP | New Hampshire | EAS | Blue Jays | Fisher Cats | SFN | San Francisco | NL | Giants | Giants |
| NIP | Nippon Ham | NPB | - | Fighters | SJO | San Jose | CAL | Giants | Giants |
| NRW | Connecticut | EAS | Giants | Defenders | SLC | Salt Lake | PCL | Angels | Bees |
| NWA | NW Arkansas | TEX | Royals | Naturals | SLM | Salem | CAR | Red Sox | Red Sox |
| NWN | Norfolk | INT | Orioles | Tides | SLN | St. Louis | NL | Cardinals | Cardinals |
| NWO | New Orleans | PCL | Marlins | Zephyrs | SLO | Salem-Keizer | NWN | Giants | Volcanoes |
| NYA | New York | AL | Yankees | Yankees | SLU | St. Lucie | FSL | Mets | Mets |
| NYN | New York | NL | Mets | Mets | SPO | Spokane | NWN | Rangers | Indians |
| OAK | Oakland | AL | Athletics | Athletics | STA | Staten Island | NYP | Yankees | Yankees |
| OGD | Ogden | PIO | Dodgers | Raptors | STO | Stockton | CAL | Athletics | Ports |
| OKL | Oklahoma City | PCL | Astros | RedHawks | SWB | Scranton/WB | INT | Yankees | Yankees |
| OMA | Omaha | PCL | Royals | Storm Chasers | SYR | Syracuse | INT | Nationals | Chiefs |
| ONE | Connecticut | NYP | Tigers | Tigers | TAC | Tacoma | PCL | Mariners | Rainiers |

| CODE | TEAM | LEAGUE | AFFILIATION | NAME |
|------|------|--------|-------------|------|
| TAM | Tampa | FSL | Yankees | Yankees |
| TBA | Tampa Bay | AL | Rays | Rays |
| TCV | Tri-City | NYP | Astros | ValleyCats |
| TEN | Tennessee | SOU | Cubs | Smokies |
| TEX | Texas | AL | Rangers | Rangers |
| TGR | GCL Tigers | GCL | Tigers | GCL Tigers |
| TOL | Toledo | INT | Tigers | Mud Hens |
| TOR | Toronto | AL | Blue Jays | Blue Jays |
| TRI | Tri-City | NWN | Rockies | Dust Devils |
| TRN | Trenton | EAS | Yankees | Thunder |
| TUL | Tulsa | TEX | Rockies | Drillers |
| TWI | GCL Twins | GCL | Twins | GCL Twins |
| VAN | Vancouver | NWN | Athletics | Canadians |
| WTN | Jackson | SOU | Mariners | Generals |
| WVA | West Virginia | SAL | Pirates | Power |
| YAK | Yakima | NWN | D-backs | Bears |
| YAN | GCL Yankees | GCL | Yankees | GCL Yankees |
| YKL | Yakult | NPB | - | Swallows |
| YOM | Yomiuri | NPB | - | Giants |

# PECOTA Leaderboards

## BATTERS

### Home Runs

| RANK | NAME | TEAM | HR |
|---|---|---|---|
| 1 | Prince Fielder | MIL | 39 |
| 2 | Ryan Howard | PHI | 35 |
| 3 | Mark Teixeira | NYA | 33 |
| 3 | Joey Votto | CIN | 33 |
| 5 | Albert Pujols | ANA | 32 |
| 5 | Ryan Braun | MIL | 32 |
| 5 | Jay Bruce | CIN | 32 |
| 8 | Miguel Cabrera | DET | 31 |
| 8 | Jose Bautista | TOR | 31 |
| 8 | Mark Reynolds | BAL | 31 |
| 11 | Carlos Pena | CHN | 30 |
| 11 | Mike Stanton | FLO | 30 |
| 13 | Paul Konerko | CHA | 29 |
| 13 | Adrian Gonzalez | BOS | 29 |
| 13 | Dan Uggla | ATL | 29 |
| 16 | Curtis Granderson | NYA | 28 |
| 17 | Nelson Cruz | TEX | 27 |
| 18 | Adam Dunn | CHA | 26 |
| 18 | Josh Hamilton | TEX | 26 |
| 18 | Ian Kinsler | TEX | 26 |

### Runs Batted In

| RANK | NAME | TEAM | RBI |
|---|---|---|---|
| 1 | Prince Fielder | MIL | 104 |
| 2 | Joey Votto | CIN | 103 |
| 3 | Miguel Cabrera | DET | 102 |
| 3 | Ryan Braun | MIL | 102 |
| 5 | Albert Pujols | ANA | 97 |
| 6 | Mark Teixeira | NYA | 96 |
| 7 | Adrian Gonzalez | BOS | 94 |
| 7 | Robinson Cano | NYA | 94 |
| 9 | Ryan Howard | PHI | 91 |
| 10 | Troy Tulowitzki | COL | 90 |
| 11 | Jose Bautista | TOR | 89 |
| 11 | Curtis Granderson | NYA | 89 |
| 11 | Jay Bruce | CIN | 89 |
| 14 | Justin Upton | ARI | 88 |
| 15 | Ian Kinsler | TEX | 87 |
| 16 | Carlos Gonzalez | COL | 86 |
| 17 | Brandon Phillips | CIN | 85 |
| 17 | Matt Kemp | LAN | 85 |
| 17 | Hunter Pence | PHI | 85 |
| 20 | David Ortiz | BOS | 83 |

## Runs Scored

| RANK | NAME | TEAM | R |
|---|---|---|---|
| 1 | Prince Fielder | MIL | 100 |
| 1 | Joey Votto | CIN | 100 |
| 3 | Miguel Cabrera | DET | 97 |
| 4 | Albert Pujols | ANA | 95 |
| 5 | Adrian Gonzalez | BOS | 94 |
| 6 | Mark Teixeira | NYA | 92 |
| 7 | Ryan Braun | MIL | 89 |
| 8 | Robinson Cano | NYA | 87 |
| 8 | Jose Bautista | TOR | 87 |
| 8 | Nick Markakis | BAL | 87 |
| 11 | Ian Kinsler | TEX | 86 |
| 12 | Dustin Pedroia | BOS | 85 |
| 13 | Michael Young | TEX | 84 |
| 14 | Curtis Granderson | NYA | 83 |
| 14 | Billy Butler | KCA | 83 |
| 14 | Matt Kemp | LAN | 83 |
| 14 | Andrew McCutchen | PIT | 83 |
| 14 | Justin Upton | ARI | 83 |
| 19 | Troy Tulowitzki | COL | 82 |
| 20 | David Ortiz | BOS | 81 |

## Stolen Bases

| RANK | NAME | TEAM | SB |
|---|---|---|---|
| 1 | Michael Bourn | ATL | 55 |
| 2 | Brett Gardner | NYA | 45 |
| 3 | Juan Pierre | CHA | 44 |
| 4 | Jacoby Ellsbury | BOS | 40 |
| 5 | Coco Crisp | OAK | 37 |
| 5 | B.J. Upton | TBA | 37 |
| 7 | Drew Stubbs | CIN | 36 |
| 8 | Jose Reyes | FLO | 35 |
| 9 | Ichiro Suzuki | SEA | 34 |
| 9 | Rajai Davis | TOR | 34 |
| 11 | Elvis Andrus | TEX | 33 |
| 12 | Carl Crawford | BOS | 32 |
| 13 | Matt Kemp | LAN | 29 |
| 14 | Emilio Bonifacio | FLO | 28 |
| 15 | Ben Revere | MIN | 27 |
| 16 | Angel Pagan | SFN | 26 |
| 16 | Ian Kinsler | TEX | 26 |
| 16 | Andrew McCutchen | PIT | 26 |
| 16 | Nyjer Morgan | MIL | 26 |
| 20 | Jimmy Rollins | PHI | 25 |

## Batting Average

| RANK | NAME | TEAM | AVG |
|---|---|---|---|
| 1 | Joe Mauer | MIN | .315 |
| 1 | Dustin Pedroia | BOS | .315 |
| 3 | Miguel Cabrera | DET | .314 |
| 4 | Troy Tulowitzki | COL | .310 |
| 5 | Jacoby Ellsbury | BOS | .308 |
| 6 | Ryan Braun | MIL | .306 |
| 7 | Albert Pujols | ANA | .305 |
| 7 | Joey Votto | CIN | .305 |
| 7 | Carlos Gonzalez | COL | .305 |
| 10 | Starlin Castro | CHN | .304 |
| 11 | Matt Holliday | SLN | .303 |

## On Base Percentage

| RANK | NAME | TEAM | OBP |
|---|---|---|---|
| 1 | Albert Pujols | ANA | .402 |
| 2 | Prince Fielder | MIL | .398 |
| 3 | Todd Helton | COL | .394 |
| 3 | Miguel Cabrera | DET | .394 |
| 3 | Joe Mauer | MIN | .394 |
| 3 | Joey Votto | CIN | .394 |
| 7 | Kevin Youkilis | BOS | .391 |
| 8 | Dustin Pedroia | BOS | .385 |
| 9 | Nick Johnson | CLE | .383 |
| 9 | Matt Holliday | SLN | .383 |
| 11 | Hanley Ramirez | FLO | .382 |
| 12 | Lance Berkman | SLN | .380 |
| 12 | Troy Tulowitzki | COL | .380 |
| 14 | Chipper Jones | ATL | .379 |
| 15 | Alex Rodriguez | NYA | .377 |
| 15 | Adrian Gonzalez | BOS | .377 |
| 17 | David Ortiz | BOS | .376 |
| 17 | Mark Teixeira | NYA | .376 |
| 19 | David Wright | NYN | .372 |
| 20 | A.J. Ellis | LAN | .371 |

## Isolated Slugging

| RANK | NAME | TEAM | ISO |
|---|---|---|---|
| 1 | Prince Fielder | MIL | .272 |
| 2 | Ryan Braun | MIL | .256 |
| 3 | Mike Napoli | TEX | .254 |
| 3 | Ryan Howard | PHI | .254 |
| 5 | Nelson Cruz | TEX | .253 |
| 6 | Mike Stanton | FLO | .248 |
| 7 | Carlos Pena | CHN | .247 |
| 8 | Alex Rodriguez | NYA | .246 |

| 9 | Albert Pujols | ANA | .245 |
| 10 | Troy Tulowitzki | COL | .242 |
| 10 | Jose Bautista | TOR | .242 |
| 12 | Joey Votto | CIN | .241 |
| 12 | Mark Reynolds | BAL | .241 |
| 14 | Josh Hamilton | TEX | .240 |
| 14 | Mark Teixeira | NYA | .240 |
| 16 | Miguel Cabrera | DET | .239 |
| 16 | Carlos Gonzalez | COL | .239 |
| 18 | Adam Dunn | CHA | .237 |
| 19 | David Ortiz | BOS | .235 |
| 20 | Jim Thome | PHI | .233 |

## True Average

| 7 | Troy Tulowitzki | COL | .314 |
|---|---|---|---|
| 9 | Kevin Youkilis | BOS | .313 |
| 10 | Mark Teixeira | NYA | .311 |
| 10 | Hanley Ramirez | FLO | .311 |
| 12 | Josh Hamilton | TEX | .308 |
| 13 | David Ortiz | BOS | .306 |
| 14 | Lance Berkman | SLN | .305 |
| 15 | Jose Bautista | TOR | .304 |
| 16 | Mike Napoli | TEX | .303 |
| 16 | Joe Mauer | MIN | .303 |
| 16 | Carlos Gonzalez | COL | .303 |
| 19 | Adrian Gonzalez | BOS | .302 |
| 19 | David Wright | NYN | .302 |

## Wins Above Replacement Player, American League

| RANK | NAME | TEAM | WARP |
|---|---|---|---|
| 1 | Albert Pujols | ANA | 5.9 |
| 2 | Miguel Cabrera | DET | 5.4 |
| 3 | Dustin Pedroia | BOS | 4.7 |
| 4 | Evan Longoria | TBA | 4.5 |
| 5 | Robinson Cano | NYA | 4.4 |
| 5 | Ian Kinsler | TEX | 4.4 |
| 7 | Alex Rodriguez | NYA | 4.3 |
| 7 | Mark Teixeira | NYA | 4.3 |
| 9 | Jose Bautista | TOR | 4.2 |
| 10 | Kevin Youkilis | BOS | 4.1 |

## Wins Above Replacement Player, National League

| RANK | NAME | TEAM | WARP |
|---|---|---|---|
| 1 | Ryan Braun | MIL | 5.6 |
| 2 | Prince Fielder | MIL | 5.5 |
| 3 | Joey Votto | CIN | 5.4 |
| 3 | Troy Tulowitzki | COL | 5.4 |
| 5 | Aramis Ramirez | MIL | 4.3 |

| | | | |
|---|---|---|---|
| 5 | Hanley Ramirez | FLO | 4.3 |
| 7 | Matt Holliday | SLN | 4.2 |
| 7 | Matt Kemp | LAN | 4.2 |
| 7 | Andrew McCutchen | PIT | 4.2 |
| 10 | Brian McCann | ATL | 4.0 |

## Wins Above Replacement Player, Catcher

| RANK | NAME | TEAM | WARP |
|---|---|---|---|
| 1 | Carlos Santana | CLE | 4.1 |
| 2 | Brian McCann | ATL | 4.0 |
| 3 | Joe Mauer | MIN | 3.7 |
| 4 | Geovany Soto | CHN | 3.6 |
| 5 | Mike Napoli | TEX | 3.4 |
| 5 | Chris Iannetta | ANA | 3.4 |
| 7 | Buster Posey | SFN | 3.2 |
| 7 | Alex Avila | DET | 3.2 |
| 9 | Miguel Montero | ARI | 3.1 |
| 9 | Victor Martinez | DET | 3.1 |

## Wins Above Replacement Player, First Base

| RANK | NAME | TEAM | WARP |
|---|---|---|---|
| 1 | Albert Pujols | ANA | 5.9 |
| 2 | Prince Fielder | MIL | 5.5 |
| 3 | Miguel Cabrera | DET | 5.4 |
| 3 | Joey Votto | CIN | 5.4 |
| 5 | Mark Teixeira | NYA | 4.3 |
| 6 | Adrian Gonzalez | BOS | 3.8 |
| 7 | David Ortiz | BOS | 3.5 |
| 8 | Ryan Howard | PHI | 3.3 |
| 8 | Lance Berkman | SLN | 3.3 |
| 10 | Paul Konerko | CHA | 3.1 |

## Wins Above Replacement Player, Second Base

| RANK | NAME | TEAM | WARP |
|---|---|---|---|
| 1 | Dustin Pedroia | BOS | 4.7 |
| 2 | Robinson Cano | NYA | 4.4 |
| 2 | Ian Kinsler | TEX | 4.4 |
| 4 | Dan Uggla | ATL | 3.6 |
| 5 | Chase Utley | PHI | 3.5 |
| 6 | Rickie Weeks | MIL | 3.3 |
| 7 | Ben Zobrist | TBA | 3.1 |
| 8 | Brandon Phillips | CIN | 2.9 |
| 9 | Kelly Johnson | TOR | 2.6 |
| 10 | Neil Walker | PIT | 2.4 |

## Wins Above Replacement Player, Third Base

| RANK | NAME | TEAM | WARP |
|---|---|---|---|
| 1 | Evan Longoria | TBA | 4.5 |
| 2 | Alex Rodriguez | NYA | 4.3 |
| 2 | Aramis Ramirez | MIL | 4.3 |
| 4 | Kevin Youkilis | BOS | 4.1 |
| 5 | David Wright | NYN | 3.9 |
| 6 | Chipper Jones | ATL | 3.6 |
| 7 | Pablo Sandoval | SFN | 3.5 |
| 7 | Mark Reynolds | BAL | 3.5 |

| | | | |
|---|---|---|---|
| 9 | Ryan Zimmerman | WAS | 3.4 |
| 10 | Michael Young | TEX | 3.3 |

## Wins Above Replacement Player, Shortstop

| RANK | NAME | TEAM | WARP |
|---|---|---|---|
| 1 | Troy Tulowitzki | COL | 5.4 |
| 2 | Hanley Ramirez | FLO | 4.3 |
| 3 | Jose Reyes | FLO | 3.5 |
| 4 | Starlin Castro | CHN | 3.4 |
| 5 | Yunel Escobar | TOR | 3.3 |
| 6 | Derek Jeter | NYA | 3.2 |
| 7 | Jimmy Rollins | PHI | 2.9 |
| 7 | Alexei Ramirez | CHA | 2.9 |
| 9 | Asdrubal Cabrera | CLE | 2.8 |
| 10 | J.J. Hardy | BAL | 2.6 |

## Wins Above Replacement Player, Left Field

| RANK | NAME | TEAM | WARP |
|---|---|---|---|
| 1 | Ryan Braun | MIL | 5.6 |
| 2 | Matt Holliday | SLN | 4.2 |
| 3 | Josh Hamilton | TEX | 3.9 |
| 4 | Carlos Gonzalez | COL | 3.7 |
| 5 | Manny Ramirez | TBA | 2.7 |
| 6 | Josh Willingham | MIN | 2.5 |
| 7 | Martin Prado | ATL | 2.4 |
| 8 | Jason Bay | NYN | 2.3 |
| 8 | Carlos Lee | HOU | 2.3 |
| 10 | Alex Gordon | KCA | 2.2 |

## Wins Above Replacement Player, Center Field

| RANK | NAME | TEAM | WARP |
|---|---|---|---|
| 1 | Matt Kemp | LAN | 4.2 |
| 1 | Andrew McCutchen | PIT | 4.2 |
| 3 | Curtis Granderson | NYA | 3.9 |
| 4 | Jacoby Ellsbury | BOS | 3.4 |
| 5 | Shane Victorino | PHI | 2.9 |
| 6 | Adam Jones | BAL | 2.7 |
| 7 | B.J. Upton | TBA | 2.6 |
| 7 | Chris Young | ARI | 2.6 |
| 9 | Dexter Fowler | COL | 2.5 |
| 10 | Marlon Byrd | CHN | 2.3 |

## Wins Above Replacement Player, Right Field

| RANK | NAME | TEAM | WARP |
|---|---|---|---|
| 1 | Jose Bautista | TOR | 4.2 |
| 2 | Nick Markakis | BAL | 3.4 |
| 2 | Justin Upton | ARI | 3.4 |
| 4 | Jayson Werth | WAS | 3.3 |
| 5 | Hunter Pence | PHI | 3.0 |
| 5 | Mike Stanton | FLO | 3.0 |
| 7 | Carlos Beltran | SLN | 2.9 |
| 8 | Nick Swisher | NYA | 2.8 |
| 8 | Jay Bruce | CIN | 2.8 |
| 10 | Nelson Cruz | TEX | 2.7 |

## Wins Above Replacement Player, Rookies

| RANK | NAME | TEAM | WARP |
|------|------|------|------|
| 1 | Jesus Montero | NYA | 2.7 |
| 2 | Robinson Chirinos | TBA | 2.5 |
| 3 | Ryan Lavarnway | BOS | 2.3 |
| 4 | James Darnell | SDN | 2.1 |
| 4 | Devin Mesoraco | CIN | 2.1 |
| 6 | Russ Canzler | TBA | 2.0 |
| 7 | Todd Frazier | CIN | 1.8 |
| 7 | Taylor Green | MIL | 1.8 |
| 7 | Alex Liddi | SEA | 1.8 |
| 7 | Erik Kratz | PHI | 1.8 |

## Wins Above Replacement Player, Top Risers

| | | | | | |
|------|------|------|------|------|------|
| 7 | Ryan Spilborghs | COL | -1.4 | 1.7 | 3.1 |
| 8 | David Wright | NYN | 0.9 | 3.9 | 3 |
| 8 | Manny Ramirez | TBA | -0.3 | 2.7 | 3 |
| 10 | Dan Johnson | TBA | -0.9 | 2 | 2.9 |

## Wins Above Replacement Player, Greatest Declines

| RANK | NAME | TEAM | 2011 WARP | 2012 WARP | DIFF WARP |
|------|------|------|-----------|-----------|-----------|
| 1 | Jose Bautista | TOR | 10.3 | 4.2 | -6.1 |
| 2 | Jacoby Ellsbury | BOS | 8.6 | 3.4 | -5.2 |
| 3 | Alex Gordon | KCA | 7.2 | 2.2 | -5.0 |
| 3 | Matt Kemp | LAN | 9.2 | 4.2 | -5.0 |
| 5 | Alex Avila | DET | 6.5 | 3.2 | -3.3 |
| 6 | Jeff Francoeur | KCA | 4.1 | 0.9 | -3.2 |
| 7 | Brendan Ryan | SEA | 3.5 | 0.6 | -2.9 |
| 8 | Jose Reyes | FLO | 6.1 | 3.5 | -2.6 |
| 8 | Erick Aybar | ANA | 4.1 | 1.5 | -2.6 |
| 10 | Shane Victorino | PHI | 5.3 | 2.9 | -2.4 |

# PITCHERS

## Wins

| RANK | NAME | TEAM | W |
|------|------|------|---|
| 1 | Roy Halladay | PHI | 16 |
| 1 | CC Sabathia | NYA | 16 |
| 3 | Cliff Lee | PHI | 15 |
| 3 | Dan Haren | ANA | 15 |
| 3 | Justin Verlander | DET | 15 |
| 6 | Cole Hamels | PHI | 14 |
| 6 | Jered Weaver | ANA | 14 |
| 8 | Chris Carpenter | SLN | 13 |

| 8 | Ervin Santana | ANA | 13 |
|------|------|------|-----|
| 8 | C.J. Wilson | ANA | 13 |
| 8 | James Shields | TBA | 13 |
| 8 | Jon Lester | BOS | 13 |
| 8 | Tim Lincecum | SFN | 13 |
| 14 | Josh Beckett | BOS | 12 |
| 14 | John Lackey | BOS | 12 |
| 14 | Tim Hudson | ATL | 12 |
| 14 | Colby Lewis | TEX | 12 |
| 14 | Mark Buehrle | FLO | 12 |
| 14 | Matt Cain | SFN | 12 |
| 14 | Gio Gonzalez | WAS | 12 |

## Strikeouts

| 8 | James Shields | TBA | 174 |
|------|------|------|-----|
| 9 | Jered Weaver | ANA | 171 |
| 10 | Brandon Morrow | TOR | 170 |
| 11 | Yovani Gallardo | MIL | 169 |
| 12 | C.J. Wilson | ANA | 168 |
| 13 | Ervin Santana | ANA | 164 |
| 13 | Gio Gonzalez | WAS | 164 |
| 15 | Roy Halladay | PHI | 163 |
| 16 | Max Scherzer | DET | 161 |
| 17 | Jon Lester | BOS | 160 |
| 18 | A.J. Burnett | NYA | 159 |
| 19 | Cliff Lee | PHI | 155 |
| 20 | Cole Hamels | PHI | 151 |

## Earned Run Average (min. 125 IP)

| RANK | NAME | TEAM | ERA |
|------|------|------|------|
| 1 | Tim Lincecum | SFN | 2.54 |
| 2 | Felix Hernandez | SEA | 2.61 |
| 3 | Clayton Kershaw | LAN | 2.71 |
| 4 | Roy Halladay | PHI | 2.77 |
| 5 | Dan Haren | ANA | 2.87 |
| 6 | Jered Weaver | ANA | 2.88 |
| 7 | Matt Cain | SFN | 2.92 |
| 8 | David Price | TBA | 2.94 |
| 9 | Michael Pineda | SEA | 2.97 |
| 10 | Cliff Lee | PHI | 2.99 |
| 11 | Justin Verlander | DET | 3.05 |
| 12 | Jeremy Hellickson | TBA | 3.17 |
| 13 | Chris Carpenter | SLN | 3.18 |
| 14 | Cole Hamels | PHI | 3.19 |
| 15 | Mat Latos | CIN | 3.20 |
| 16 | Hiroki Kuroda | LAN | 3.24 |
| 17 | Madison Bumgarner | SFN | 3.25 |
| 18 | James Shields | TBA | 3.30 |

| | | | |
|---|---|---|---|
| 19 | CC Sabathia | NYA | 3.31 |
| 20 | C.J. Wilson | ANA | 3.33 |

## Walks plus Hits per Innings Pitched (min. 125 IP)

| RANK | NAME | TEAM | WHIP |
|---|---|---|---|
| 1 | Roy Halladay | PHI | 1.01 |
| 2 | Cole Hamels | PHI | 1.05 |
| 3 | Cliff Lee | PHI | 1.06 |
| 4 | Tim Lincecum | SFN | 1.08 |
| 5 | Dan Haren | ANA | 1.09 |
| 6 | Matt Cain | SFN | 1.10 |
| 7 | Ted Lilly | LAN | 1.11 |
| 7 | Clayton Kershaw | LAN | 1.11 |
| 9 | Hiroki Kuroda | LAN | 1.12 |
| 9 | Chris Carpenter | SLN | 1.12 |
| 9 | Felix Hernandez | SEA | 1.12 |
| 12 | Daniel Hudson | ARI | 1.13 |
| 12 | Mat Latos | CIN | 1.13 |
| 14 | Jered Weaver | ANA | 1.14 |
| 14 | Roy Oswalt | PHI | 1.14 |
| 14 | Madison Bumgarner | SFN | 1.14 |
| 14 | Shaun Marcum | MIL | 1.14 |
| 18 | Zack Greinke | MIL | 1.15 |
| 18 | James Shields | TBA | 1.15 |
| 20 | Michael Pineda | SEA | 1.16 |

## Saves

| RANK | NAME | TEAM | SV |
|---|---|---|---|
| 1 | Heath Bell | FLO | 46 |
| 2 | Brian Wilson | SFN | 40 |
| 3 | Mariano Rivera | NYA | 35 |
| 4 | Francisco Cordero | CIN | 34 |
| 4 | Carlos Marmol | CHN | 34 |
| 6 | Jonathan Papelbon | PHI | 32 |
| 7 | Joakim Soria | KCA | 31 |
| 8 | Jose Valverde | DET | 29 |
| 8 | John Axford | MIL | 29 |
| 10 | Neftali Feliz | TEX | 27 |
| 10 | Craig Kimbrel | ATL | 27 |
| 12 | Kevin Gregg | BAL | 26 |
| 13 | Huston Street | SDN | 24 |
| 14 | Matt Capps | MIN | 22 |
| 15 | Chris Perez | CLE | 21 |
| 16 | Francisco Rodriguez | MIL | 20 |
| 17 | J.J. Putz | ARI | 19 |
| 18 | Andrew Bailey | BOS | 18 |
| 18 | Jordan Walden | ANA | 18 |
| 18 | Drew Storen | WAS | 18 |

## Strikeouts per Nine Innings (min. 125 IP)

| RANK | NAME | TEAM | SO9 |
|---|---|---|---|
| 1 | Brandon Morrow | TOR | 10.1 |
| 2 | Tim Lincecum | SFN | 9.2 |
| 3 | Michael Pineda | SEA | 8.8 |
| 4 | Yovani Gallardo | MIL | 8.7 |
| 4 | Jon Lester | BOS | 8.7 |

| | | | |
|---|---|---|---|
| 6 | A.J. Burnett | NYA | 8.6 |
| 6 | Felix Hernandez | SEA | 8.6 |
| 6 | Max Scherzer | DET | 8.6 |
| 9 | Clayton Kershaw | LAN | 8.5 |
| 9 | Justin Verlander | DET | 8.5 |
| 9 | Josh Beckett | BOS | 8.5 |
| 12 | David Price | TBA | 8.3 |
| 12 | Francisco Liriano | MIN | 8.3 |
| 14 | Zack Greinke | MIL | 8.2 |
| 14 | CC Sabathia | NYA | 8.2 |
| 16 | C.J. Wilson | ANA | 8.0 |
| 16 | Ubaldo Jimenez | CLE | 8.0 |
| 18 | Javier Vazquez | FLO | 7.9 |
| 18 | Jered Weaver | ANA | 7.9 |
| 20 | Dan Haren | ANA | 7.8 |

## Wins Above Replacement Player

| RANK | NAME | TEAM | WARP |
|---|---|---|---|
| 1 | Tim Lincecum | SFN | 4.9 |
| 2 | Felix Hernandez | SEA | 4.8 |
| 2 | Roy Halladay | PHI | 4.8 |
| 4 | Clayton Kershaw | LAN | 4.5 |
| 5 | Justin Verlander | DET | 4.2 |
| 6 | Dan Haren | ANA | 4.1 |
| 7 | Cliff Lee | PHI | 4.0 |
| 8 | CC Sabathia | NYA | 3.9 |
| 8 | Jered Weaver | ANA | 3.9 |
| 10 | Chris Carpenter | SLN | 3.8 |
| 10 | Matt Cain | SFN | 3.8 |
| 12 | Mat Latos | CIN | 3.7 |
| 13 | David Price | TBA | 3.6 |
| 14 | Cole Hamels | PHI | 3.3 |
| 15 | Daniel Hudson | ARI | 2.9 |
| 15 | Hiroki Kuroda | LAN | 2.9 |
| 17 | Tim Hudson | ATL | 2.8 |
| 18 | Ian Kennedy | ARI | 2.7 |
| 18 | James Shields | TBA | 2.7 |
| 18 | Madison Bumgarner | SFN | 2.7 |

## Wins Above Replacement Player, Rookies

| RANK | NAME | TEAM | WARP |
|---|---|---|---|
| 1 | Michael Pineda | SEA | 2.5 |
| 2 | Jeremy Hellickson | TBA | 2.2 |
| 2 | Alexi Ogando | TEX | 2.2 |
| 4 | Brandon Beachy | ATL | 1.8 |
| 4 | Craig Kimbrel | ATL | 1.8 |
| 5 | Kenley Jansen | LAN | 1.6 |
| 6 | Guillermo Moscoso | OAK | 1.4 |
| 7 | Chris Sale | CHA | 1.2 |
| 8 | Fernando Salas | SLN | 1.0 |
| 8 | Aroldis Chapman | CIN | 1.0 |

# Contributors

*The BP Team*

**R.J. Anderson** lives in Florida and joined Prospectus in 2011. In the past, Anderson's work has appeared on ESPN.com, SLAM, and Wired, as well as in the *Wall Street Journal* and *USA Today*. His nightmares include an endless loop of Hank Blalock playing third base.

**Tommy Bennett** is a law student in New York. He has written various columns for Baseball Prospectus and was formerly editor of Beyond the Box Score. He believes the best way to judge a baseball city is by the number of people who keep score at the games. His interests include statutes, administrative law, and Mickey Morandini's unassisted triple play.

**Craig Brown** has provided fantasy content at Baseball Prospectus for the last two seasons. Craig is a co-founder of RoyalsAuthority.com and has edited and published two annuals dedicated to the exploits of the Royals. He has contributed to ESPN.com, The Hardball Times, and Baseball Digest Daily and his work has also appeared in Rotoman's *Fantasy Baseball* magazine, *Heater Magazine*, and *The Graphical Player*. He lives in Kansas City with his wife and two daughters, who tolerate his baseball obsession.

**Derek Carty** joined BP in 2011 as fantasy manager after holding the post with The Hardball Times since 2007. He's also had his work published by ESPN Insider, SportsIllustrated. com, NBC's Rotoworld, FOXSports.com, and *USA Today* and maintains a personal website (DerekCarty.com) to aggregate his work. He is the COO of Fantasy Squared, a market-style game in which users "buy" and "sell" shares of events that transpire in an underlying fantasy league (either private or expert)—which team will win, who got the better end of a trade, etc. In 2009, he became the youngest champion in the history of LABR—the longest-running fantasy baseball expert league in existence—and graduated from the MLB Scouting Bureau's Scout Development Program (aka Scout School), the only active fantasy writer to have graduated from the program.

**Jason Collette** has been writing about baseball since 1999 for a variety of websites and publications. Since 2008, he has been a featured writer and now managing editor at the powerhouse Rays site DRaysBay.com, that has seen 11 million visits since its inception in 2005. During the season, Jason is also one of the featured writers on the Baseball Prospectus *Yankee Stadium Memories*, and he edited Howard Bryant's *Juicing the Game* and Brad Snyder's *Well-Paid Slave*, among others. A stay-at-home dad during regular business hours, he lives in northern New Jersey with a wife, daughter, and dog, all of whom he's pretty sure are out of his league.

**Jeff Euston** writes the Contractual Matters column at Baseball Prospectus and maintains BP's Compensation Pages, an extensive online database of contracts and salaries dating back to 2000. In 2005, he founded Cot's Baseball Contracts, a website tracking players, agents, salaries, and payrolls for each of the 30 major-league clubs. He lives near Kansas City, where he practices commercial real estate law and fixes his own speeding tickets.

**Ken Funck** has contributed his "Changing Speeds" column to Baseball Prospectus, focusing on issues both absurd and sublime, and written for the Baseball Prospectus Annual each year since winning the inaugural Prospectus Idol competition in 2009. Ken spends his days designing Business Intelligence systems and lives outside Madison, Wisconsin (America's greatest small city), with his ever-supportive wife, Stephanie, their children, Max and Abby, two cats, two dogs, and a half-complete shrine to Rick Reuschel and the 1977 Cubs.

**Rebecca Glass** is a writer and assistant editor for Baseball Prospectus. A 2008 graduate of Syracuse University, she is one of the co-founders of the You Can't Predict Baseball blog, and has also worked for ESPN's Stats and Info Group. She lives in the Northeast and in her spare time, when not going to baseball games at all levels, she enjoys collecting swords and all manner of medieval and renaissance history.

**Steven Goldman** is the Editor-in-Chief of Baseball Prospectus. In addition to writing numerous columns for BP's website, including the current "BP Broadside," he has edited the BP-authored books *Mind Game* and *It Ain't Over 'Til It's Over* and contributed to *Baseball Between the Numbers*. Steven is also the author of the biography *Forging Genius: The Making of Casey Stengel*. He has contributed to the BP annual since 2005 and was editor or co-editor of the 2006 through 2011 editions. He is the creator of the long-running Pinstriped Bible (Pinstripedbible.com) for the YES Network, cited by *Sports Illustrated* as "an essential online baseball destination," and has appeared on several of the network's television programs. He was a baseball columnist for the *New York Sun* from 2004 to 2008, and his work has appeared in *Yankees Magazine*, *The Village Voice*, *Commentary*, *American Heritage*, and other publications. In his spare time, he publishes original songs at casualobserver.music.net. Steven lives in New Jersey with his wife and two children.

**Kevin Goldstein** is a national writer on scouting and player development for Baseball Prospectus. He speaks with people throughout the industry on a daily basis, talking, texting, and messaging with everyone from scouts to general managers to find the next big thing, and following the trends in acquiring talent. When he's not writing, he's talking, be it for Sirius/XM radio or one of the most popular sports podcasts, *Up and In*, which he hosts with BP-mate Jason Parks. Kevin lives in DeKalb, Illinois, with his girlfriend Margaret, minors Xander and Cameron, a pit bull named Otto, and three cats (Pickles, Underpants, and Neko-Chan). Because of this, many things in his house are covered with hair.

**Gary Huckabay** is the Founder of Baseball Prospectus. He has served in a consulting capacity for several MLB clubs and player representation firms. His areas of focus are performance forecasting and valuation. Mr. Huckabay currently works in small business lending for a large financial services firm, and serves on the Board of Directors of the Epilepsy Foundation of Northern California. He lives in the NorCal East Bay with his wife Kathryn and son Charlie. Gary is a frequent speaker at universities, charitable fundraisers, and corporate events.

**Jay Jaffe** is the founder of the 11-year-old Futility Infielder website (www.futilityinfielder.com), one of the oldest baseball blogs. He's been a part of Baseball Prospectus since 2004, writing the Prospectus Hit and Run column, covering the annual Hall of Fame balloting, contributing to seven BP annuals as well as *It Ain't Over 'Til It's Over* and *Mind Game*. Elsewhere, he has written regularly for Fantasy Baseball Index and the YES Network's Pinstriped Bible. He has placed third in the famous Milwaukee Brewers sausage race, dropped an f-bomb in the *Wall Street Journal*, and been voted into the Baseball Writers Association of America.

**Christina Kahrl** is one of the five founders of Baseball Prospectus. Like many of her colleagues, that led to an unexpected career in sports, sparing her from a life spent studying 19th century Europe and trying to come up with witty jokes about *junkers*. She has participated as a contributor or editor of every edition of the Baseball Prospectus Annual as well as *Mind Game* and *It Ain't Over 'Til It's Over*. She has contributed columns to *Playboy*, *Salon*, *Slate*, the *New York Sun*, SportsIllustrated.com, and ESPN.com, and is also an associate editor of *The ESPN Pro Football Encyclopedia*. She is now a member of BBWAA and an editor at ESPN.com, and lives in Chicago with her partner, dog, cat, fish, and an everlasting sense of curiosity.

**King Kaufman** is a writer and editor who lives in San Francisco. He is the manager of the Writer Program at Bleacher Report. He previously wrote and edited for *Salon* and the *San Francisco Examiner*, among others. He might not be the world's preeminent fan of Neifi Perez, but he's in the photo.

**Ben Lindbergh** is an author and editor of Baseball Prospectus. This is his third year contributing to the BP Annual. He has also contributed to ESPN Insider and *Yankees Magazine*, and he served as assistant editor of *BP2011* and editor of the two-volume *Best of Baseball Prospectus* collection. He daylights as a baseball analyst for Bloomberg Sports, has interned for multiple MLB teams, and was inducted into the Baseball Writers' Association of America (BBWAA) in December. A recent graduate of Georgetown University, Ben makes his home on the western shore of his native Manhattan, where he fancies himself the first line of defense against New Jersey.

**Sam Miller** writes about baseball for the *Orange County Register*. He covered local government, education, and autism before moving to the sports section in 2009. He joined the Baseball Prospectus staff in 2011. He lives in Long Beach with his wife and young daughter.

SABR member **Rob McQuown** is a lifelong Cubs fan who was inspired by a Bill James Abstract to join STATS, Inc., where he was first published in *The Scouting Report*, 1993. Since then, neither starting up multiple dot-coms nor years in big corporate life could pull him convincingly away from his first love, baseball. Getting restarted in the industry in 2006 with Baseball Daily Digest, he was welcomed to the Baseball Prospectus team as a programmer and writer when BDD became a subsidiary of BP. He has contributed extensive web content with both words and programs for numerous sites, as well as writing sections of *Graphical Player*, 2010 and 2011 editions.

**Marc Normandin** wrote the "Fantasy Beat" and "Player Profile" columns at Baseball Prospectus and spent over five years and many hundreds of thousands of words with the website. Presently, Marc writes about the Red Sox at OvertheMonster.com and fantasy baseball at RotoHardball. com, and likes to juggle serious baseball news and Photoshops at Baseball Nation (mlb.sbnation.com). He is formerly the video game editor of BlastMagazine.com, as well as the founder of SB Nation's BeyondtheBoxScore.com.

Arlington (BBTIA), while also moonlighting as a pro scout in Mexico and the New York Penn League. In addition to his regular writing duties, you can listen to Jason on the ever popular *Up and In: The Baseball Prospectus Podcast,* that he co-hosts with Kevin Goldstein. A native Texan, Jason now calls Brooklyn his home, living in the Bushwick neighborhood with his lovely wife Arden, their three cats, and his three personalities.

**Cecilia Tan** is the founder of Why I Like Baseball, the oldest baseball blog on the Internet. She is the editor of the *Baseball Research Journal* for SABR (Society for American Baseball Research) and is the longtime editor of the *Maple Street Press Yankees Annual*. Her baseball writing has appeared in *Yankees Magazine, Gotham Baseball*, and elsewhere, and she is the author of *The 50 Greatest Yankees Games*, and co-author with Bill Nowlin of *The 50 Greatest Red Sox Games*. She lives in the Boston area with her partner and three cats, who enjoy sleeping across her laptop while the Yankees games are livestreaming.

**Colin Wyers** is the Director of Statistical Operations for

**Geoff Young** is the founder of Ducksnorts, which covered the Padres from 1997 to 2011. He also wrote and published three books under that title. His work has appeared in many places on the web, including The Hardball Times (2006–2011) and ESPN.com. Geoff has been a regular contributor to Baseball Prospectus since 2009 and lives in San Diego with his patient wife, Sandra.

# Acknowledgments

**Bradley Ankrom:** Juan Rodriguez, Brian Chattin, Marc Lippman, Joe Capozzi, James Bailey, Marteese Robinson, Chris Kline, and Conor Glassey.

**Tommy Bennett:** Jeff Zimmerman, Zach Kolodin, Caleb Ward, Jason Horwitz, Brian Levy, Dave Metz, Jonah Keri, Ben Kabak, Joel Wertheimer, Sara Sargent.

**Craig Brown:** Joe Hamrahi, Rany Jazayerli, Cecilia Tan, Clark Fosler, Nick Scott, Greg Schaum, Marc Normandin, Derek Carty, Mike Fast, David Schoenfield, Evan Brunell, Rob Blackstien, Jin Wong, Dayton Moore and Megan, Bridget and Amelia Brown.

**Derek Carty:** R.J. Anderson, Bradley Ankrom, Kevin Goldstein, Joe Hamrahi, King Kaufman, Eric Simon, Cecilia Tan, Patty and Mark Carty, and multiple anonymous baseball insiders.

**Jason Collette:** Tommy Rancel, Steve Slowinski, JB Long, Maury Brown, Jonah Keri, R.J. Anderson, Harry Pavlidis, Mike Fast, Marc Topkin, Roger Mooney, Bill Chastain, Mike Ferrin, Bob Rittner, William Fodadero, Cory Schwartz, Mike Siano, Matthew Leach, Bob Kohm, Byron Cox.

**Cliff Corcoran:** Alex Belth, Larry Burke, Paul Fichtenbaum, Steven Goldman, Ted Keith, the entire staff at SI.com, Rebecca Lorig, Amelia Corcoran, Nancy Boyajy, Gordon and Linda Lorig, John and Sue Corcoran.

**Jeff Euston:** Maureen and Michael Euston, Nancy and Brian Harrity, Brian Euston.

**Ken Funck:** Robert and Beverly Funck, Doug Ross, Chris Anderson, Gary Atkins, Frank Berta, Jon Bourdon, Randy Cross, Don Egan, Larry Hirt, John Kostyo, Mike Martin, Kraig Rowe, Bill Severn, Mike Payne, Geno Spain, Matt Schwei, The Founding Five, Baseball Prospectus Commenters.

**Kevin Goldstein:** Mark Newman, James Click, Chaim Bloom, Mike Hazen, Ben Cherrington, Ned Rice, John Mirabelli, Rick Hahn, J.J. Piccolo, Jon Daniels, Josh Boyd, Scott Engler, Billy Beane, David Forst, Eric Kubota, Sam Geaney, Billy Owens, Keith Lieppman, John Coppolellea, Adam Fisher, Mike Girsch, Joe Bohringer, John Sanders, Will Sharp, Scott Boras, Steve Canter, Peter Abraham, Mark Gonzales, Robert Ford, Anthony Andro, Susan Slusser, Andy McCullough, Juan Rodriguez, Jim Breen, Matt Leach, Derrick Goold, Rocco DeMaro, Dave Kaplan, Laurence Holmes, Mike Ferrin, Grant Paulsen, Zachary Levine, Dylan Hernandez, Jorge Arangure, Carlos Lugo, Kevin Cabral, Steve Albini, Brad Shoemaker, Corey Schwartz, Lincoln Mitchell, Aaron Tassano, Adam Rubin, Kendall Rogers, Mike Curto, Jim Callis, Juan Villareal, Will Kimmey, Rocco Baldelli, Buster Olney, Dan Evans, Matthew Leach, Phil Rogers, Rafael Rojas, Jeff Passan, Mike Plugh.

**Steven Goldman:** Andrew Baharlias; Rich Faber; Rebecca Glass; Alice Goldman; Reuven and Eliane Goldman; Stefanie, Sarah, and Clemens Goldman; Christina Kahrl; Sydelle Kramer; Keith Law; John McGraw; Dr. Richard Mohring; and all the writers and editors who patiently worked with me through so many previous editions of this book.

**Gary Huckaby:** Billy Beane, Tod Johnson, and the late Greg Spira.

**Jay Jaffe:** Emma Span, Bryan Jaffe, Nick Stone, Issa Clubb, Norm Wamer, Brian Kenny, Duke Castiglione, Steve Kaplowitz, Rex Snider, Thyrl Nelson, Ryan Chell, Alex Belth, Marc Carig, Zachary Levine, Pete Abraham, Keith Law.

**Christina Kahrl:** Sean Ahmed, Stephani Bee, Bob Beghtol, Brian Borawski, Jim Bowden, Eileen Canepari, Jason Carr, Peter Chase, John Dewan, Ray Garcia, Gary Gillette, Ozzie Guillen, Thomas Harding, Dani Holmes-Kirk, Gary Huckabay, David Kull, David Laurila, Stephanie Liscio, Dorothy Seymour Mills, Claudia Perry, Susan Petrone, Mike Quade, David Schoenfield, Susan Slusser, Ken Spindler, Gordon Wittenmyer, Wee Beastie & the Dingo, John Zajc.

**King Kaufman:** Jane Paris and Buster and Daisy for their patience. The entire BP staff for welcoming me.

**Sam Miller:** Bradley Ankrom, Grant Brisbee, Dave Cameron, Ryan Ghan, Kevin Goldstein, Daniel Mahan, Ian Miller, Mark Miller, Jeff Sullivan, Abe Flores, Betty Chin.

**Marc Normandin:** Neil deMause, Patrick Sullivan, Ben Lindbergh, R.J. Anderson, Dan Scotto, Mike Fast, Colin Wyers, Bradley Ankrom, Rob McQuown, Grant Brisbee, Al Yellon, Adam Morris, Jeff Sullivan, Jason Wojciechowski, Greg Rybarczyk, Jack Moore, Craig Brown, Sky Kalkman, Eric Simon, Mike Petriello, Chad Finn, Brian MacPherson, Owen Good, Jorge Arangure, Rob Bradford, Alex Speier, Tim Britton, Peter Gammons, Dave Brown, Tyler Bleszinski, Rob Neyer, Ben Buchanan, Matthew Kory, Dan Szymborski, Steven Goldman, Jay Jaffe, Kevin Goldstein.

**Jason Parks:** Christopher Hitchens.

**Cecilia Tan:** Gary Gillette, Steven Goldman, Joe Hamrahi, David Pease, for help and support, and all the writers for making this the most fun I've ever had in an offseason.

**Colin Wyers:** Jim & Astrid Wyers, Tessa Wyers, Samantha Trei.

**Geoff Young:** Sandy Alderson, Jim Armstrong, Ed Barnes, Jeff Barton, Steph Bee, Corey Brock, Logan Burdine, John Conniff, Paul DePodesta, Andrew Fisher, Sean Forman, Peter Friberg, Tom Garfinkel, Joe Hamrahi, Dan Hayes, Christina Kahrl, Tom Krasovic, Alex Lifeson, Howard Lynch, Rob Neyer, Jeff Nold, Marc Normandin, Dave Pease, Steve Poltz, Troy Renck, David Schoenfield, John Sickels, Dave Studenmund, Paul Swydan, Didi Tanadjadja, Derek Togerson, Sandra Tokashiki, Matt Vasgersian, Brandon Warne, Dan Watson, Dan Young, and countless others inadvertently missed.

# Index

Visit the product page for Baseball Prospectus 2012 at

# http://bbp.cx/bp2012

# The Best Baseball Analysis Anywhere
# Still only $4.95/mo or $34.95/yr*

Since 1996, Baseball Prospectus has been synonymous with cutting edge baseball commentary. The coverage you've enjoyed in this book continues in real-time at baseballprospectus.com. Get instant access to

* minor-league expert Kevin Goldstein and our team of prospect analysts
* Colin Wyers' brand-new statistical framework and updated PECOTA projections
* Steven Goldman, Ben Lindbergh, John Perrotto, Jay Jaffe, Jason Parks and Maury Brown on what's hot in baseball
* Fantasy advice and analysis from Derek Carty and his staff of experts

You get all that and more--and best of all, with hundreds of exclusive articles per year, your cost is just pennies per article.

* reflects $5 discount for renewals
** monthly accounts are recurring-- simply cancel in the first month and you will pay nothing